ARTHUR COHN studied at the Combs Conservatory of Music, the University of Pennsylvania, and the Juilliard Graduate School. For 18 years he was Director of the famed Edwin A. Fleisher Music Collection of the Free Library of Philadelphia. After serving as Executive Director of that city's Settlement Music School, he became Head of Symphonic and Foreign Music for Mills Music, later holding a similar position with MCA Music, Inc.

Winner of many grants, awards, and commissions, Cohn has composed 52 major-sized works. He has lectured and conducted widely, from the Philadelphia Orchestra Children's Concerts to guest performances with the National Orchestra of Mexico. He is presently conductor of the Haddonfield (N.J.) Symphony Orchestra. Former critic for the *American Record Guide*, he has also written program and liner notes and four books, including *The Collector's Haydn* and *Twentieth Century Music in the Western Hemisphere*. Arthur Cohn is currently Director of Serious Music for Carl Fischer, Inc., in New York, where he lives with his wife, daughter, and a collection of 20,000 classical recordings.

RECORDED CLASSICAL MUSIC

RECORDED CLASSICAL MUSIC

A CRITICAL GUIDE TO
COMPOSITIONS AND
PERFORMANCES

Arthur Cohn

SCHIRMER BOOKS
A Division of Macmillan Publishing Co., Inc.
NEW YORK

Collier Macmillan Publishers
LONDON

Schirmer Books
A Division of Macmillan Publishing Co., Inc.
866 Third Avenue, New York, N.Y. 10022

Collier Macmillan Canada, Ltd.

Library of Congress Catalog Card Number: 80-5224

Printed in the United States of America

printing number

1 2 3 4 5 6 7 8 9 10

Library of Congress Cataloging in Publication Data

Cohn, Arthur
    Recorded classical music.

    Includes index.
    1. Sound recordings—Reviews. 2. Music—Discography.
I. Title.
ML156.9.C63   789.9′131   80-5224
ISBN 0-02-870640-4   AACR2

For my daughter, *Leslie*
and my dearest friends, *Verna Fine* and *Carol Schwartz*

(and to Ginger, who was *always*
there between letters K and L)

PREFACE

Anyone who has considered buying recordings of classical music knows the marketplace is a jungle of confusion, with tens of thousands of discs available from close to a thousand record companies. How can one make informed consumer decisions? There are no listening booths in record stores (as there were in the pre-LP days) to allow sampling 20 versions of a Beethoven symphony or to compare various recorded performances of the Tchaikovsky Violin Concerto. How does one evaluate the lesser-known but still worthy compositions?

The need for a comprehensive and total assessment of classical music performances on records has become crucial. This guide, the most exhaustive coverage of classical recordings ever published, proposes to meet that need. It will aid the neophyte collector of recordings and stimulate new considerations by those already owning a good number of discs.*

How long will this guide maintain its validity? The choices in this book were made from recordings that have already stood the tests of time and marketplace. New sound techniques applied to recordings have neither supplanted the best of past performances nor have they provided better ones. There will be very few discs in the coming years that will surpass the artistry of the performances endorsed in this guide. Some good duplications may appear but superior duplicated releases will be the exception.

The music covered in this compendium ranges from the pre-Baroque to the twentieth-century avant-garde: from Bach to Beethoven to Bartók, from Machaut to Chopin to John Cage, from Dunstable to Dvořák to Stockhausen. The selections embrace all possible performing media, from the standard instrumental and vocal combinations to such exotica as music for piano, five hands; toy piano; a sextet for ondes Martenot; and a composition for 60 trombones.

As will be seen from the subtitle, this book considers the compositions as well as the recorded performances. Much of the compositional information appears here in print for the first time. Novices, seasoned listeners, and avid collectors of recordings should all find their interest deepened by judicious browsing.

Finally, a word on the selections and comments herein. The ''rightness'' of any critic is an elusive matter. The opinions expressed in this guide were formed during years of experience as a professional music critic, music publisher, and music librarian. It is hoped that these critical decisions will stimulate the reader to discover new continents of music and countless hours of listening pleasure.

Arthur Cohn

* Cassettes and tapes are not included in this book. The reader should refer to catalogues or dealers for information on the availability on cassettes or tapes of the recordings listed herein.

ACKNOWLEDGMENTS

No study of the scope of the present one would have been possible without the assistance of executives in the recording industry. For their unstinting cooperation in furnishing review copies of recordings I wish to thank the following: Earle Brown (Mainstream); Peter Christ (Crystal); Roger Commagere (Genesis); Giveon Cornfield (Orion); Jack Firestone (Louisville); Peter Fritsch (Lyrichord); Tom Frost (Columbia); T. C. Fry (Musical Heritage Society); Clark Galehouse (Golden Crest); Richard Gilbert (Grenadilla); A. A. Goldstein (Pandora); Leon Golovner (Desto); Carter Harman (Composers Recordings); Amelia S. Haygood (Delos); Harvey Neil Hunt (HNH); John Hurd (London); Paul Kapp (Serenus); M. Scott Lampe (Philips); Marshall Lewis (Desmar); John McKellen (MCA); George Mendelssohn (Vox); Ilhan Mimaroğlu (Finnadar); R. Peter Munves (Quintessence); Andrew Raeburn (New World); Lester Remsen (Avant); William Schmidt (Wim); Thomas Shephard (RCA); Seymour Solomon (Vanguard); George Sponhaltz (Angel); Tracy Sterne (Nonesuch); and Michael Stillman (Monitor).

Other personnel of these and other recording firms were also most helpful in tending to my requests and queries. My thanks is therefore extended to Terry Blackburn, Ira Bloom, Wayne Brachman, Steven Epstein, Thomas Fenn, Verna Fine, Janie Ganz, Laura A. Kloss, Tina McCarthy, Grace E. Patti, Daniel Pollock, James Ringo, and Peter Tracton.

For assistance of various kinds I am grateful to a number of specialists in various fields. These include Bailey Bird, David Drew, Horace Grennell, Margaret Jory, Karen Kieser, Charles R. Krigbaum, Ronald R. Napier, J. Theodore Procházka, John Russo, the late Tibor Serly, Nicolas Slonimsky, and Diana Steiner.

Above all, my particular thanks to my editors, Ken Stuart and Abbie Meyer. Their constant encouragement and help, belief in my work, as well as their understanding patience, place me in their debt.

For copy-editing perceptivity and responsivity it would be difficult to match the skills of Amy Litt and Deirdre Brady as they coped with my seven-foot high typescript. Their praises should be (and are) sung *triple forte*.

Most importantly, a special acknowledgment to my wife, Lois, who bore patiently with my totally antisocial work habits throughout the years this book was being created. She not only has my love but my admiration, gratitude, and truly inexpressible thanks.

INTRODUCTION

As a rule, each entry in this guide deals with one composition only, whether that composition lasts 30 seconds, occupies several record sides, or is included in a collection with numerous other titles. The choice of a work was in no way influenced by any of its companions on a disc, as in the case of shorter pieces issued with one or more other compositions. However, one commentary may serve for a series of compositions recorded by the same performer(s) on the same disc, but only when the performances of all the works are deemed the best. Nor have record prices had a bearing on this survey, despite the obvious attraction of budget-priced discs to the collector faced with the option of buying a complete recording for the sake of one splendidly performed short piece.

Composers (with their dates) are, of course, listed alphabetically. The title of the composition (with opus number or year of composition, when obtainable) is preceded by a marginal identification of its medium and is followed by the name or names of the performers and the record label and number. All recordings are stereophonic unless specifically identified as a monaural recording. Recordings ''electronically reproduced for stereo'' are listed (as in *Schwann*) with an ''E'' following the catalogue number, as well as with the monaural identification. No matter how one argues the point, such productions cannot be classified as authentic, made-at-the-source stereo discs.

Each composer's output is separated into specific categories and presented in the following order. (The title sequence in each category or subcategory is alphabetical.)

Orchestra (including Chamber Orchestra and multiple orchestral combinations)
String Orchestra
Band
Wind and Brass Ensemble
Brass Ensemble
Percussion (both solo and ensemble)
Solo Instrument(s) and Orchestra (or Band or other types of large ensemble—*contains alphabetically arranged subcategories*)
Instrumental (unaccompanied and with accompaniment—*contains alphabetically arranged subcategories*)
Chamber Music (sectionally divided as to the number of players utilized)
Vocal (divided into Voice Alone; Voice with Accompaniment; Voice and Instrumental Ensemble; Voice and Orchestra)
Choral (divided into Chorus Alone; Chorus with Accompaniment; Chorus and Instrumental Ensemble; Chorus and Orchestra)
Cantata and Oratorio (including Masses)
Opera and Dramatic Music
Ballet (complete versions—ballet suites are included in the Orchestra category)

Film Music (complete versions—film music suites are included in the Orchestra category)

Electronic Music

The following miscellaneous points, listed alphabetically, will further help the reader use this guide.

Chamber Music: This medium is divided by the total of performers involved, ranging from duos to dectets, with the compositions in each section discussed alphabetically. The sectional place of discussion strictly depends on the number of players and not on the number of instruments they are often required to use—the latter often found in twentieth-century chamber music. Each section is separated by a short marginal line.

Collections: If an individual recording is also available in an album with other compositions, mention of this is made in the commentary.

Compilations: Album captions like "Songs from Shakespeare" and "Gilels at Carnegie Hall" have been ignored. Each composition chosen from such a miscellaneous collection is treated separately, as are all the other works. The data provided are complete as to performer, record label, and catalogue number, but such album captions are omitted from the data.

Couplings: When more than one composition on a record is discussed, each is listed separately. To determine which of several works on a given record is included in this survey, consult the index—arranged alphabetically by record company, and numerically, within each label's listing, by catalogue number.

Deletions: Even though deleted from a record company's catalogue, some such records may still be available in record stores. Such discs often reappear on a cheaper label issued by the parent company, or they may be reissued by another company. Deleted recordings can also be supplied by shops specializing in record searches and by record libraries.

Integral Sets: In the case of a recorded collection (e.g., the Beethoven symphonies), the entire unit is discussed first followed by evaluations of the best issues of the individual compositions.

Performance Choice: When a composition is represented by several recordings, the listings are in order of preference. The commentary will discuss all choices.

Performers' Names: First names are supplied only when two or more performers have similar surnames.

Singles: When a recording that is part of a collection of two or more records is available as a single disc, that fact will be indicated in the commentary.

10-inch Recordings: A few of these (in the Donemus Audio-Visual Series) are included and are identified as such.

Title Arrangement: Titles are listed alphabetically, except when (as in a set of Haydn string quartets, for example), the series of opus numbers is followed.

Titles: Translations of titles are indicated when these are commonly used.

Transcriptions: Transcriptions have been limited to those that are a part of the standard repertoire, and a few such works that have been unjustly neglected. Transcriptions are listed alphabetically according to the transcriber's name, following the composer's body of work; e.g., Bach's transcribers follow the complete discussion of Bach recordings. (In the design of this book, a slash separates composer from transcriber.)

A

Evaristo Felice dall'Abaco   (1675-1742)

Concerto da chiesa in B minor for Four String Instruments, Op. 2, No. 8

String Orchestra

☐ V. L. Ciampi Instrumental Ensemble of Piacenza / Zanaboni (conductor) / Everest 3173

At this remove it is fairly easy to separate the ordinary from the extraordinary examples that fill the huge catalogue of baroque music. Dall'Abaco's three-movement opus deserves a place among the chosen key works by Corelli, Telemann, Vivaldi, and some others. It has presence and expressivity in the slow movement; the situations in the fast-tempi corner divisions are invigorating and avoid repetitive flat figurations.

The Ciampi group plays solidly and is consistently responsive to all the moods of the work. Everest provides sound that is positive, though not of gleaming transparency.

Sonata in F major for Two Violins and Continuo, Op. 3, No. 2

Chamber Music

☐ Instrumentalists of the Società Cameristica di Lugano / Nonesuch 73008

Forceful but fitting playing in the pair of polyphonic movements, nice tonal nourishment in the pair of slow movements. There are twelve Sonatas in dall'Abaco's Opus 3, and the second of the set is one of the most interesting.

Robert Abramson   (1928-)

Dance Variations for Piano and Orchestra (1965)

Solo Instrument and Orchestra

☐ Orchestra Sinfonica di Roma / Abramson (piano) / Flagello (conductor) / Serenus 12014

Piano

Though there is some contemporary fizz in the Dance Variations (and the slightest jazz flavoring), most of the juice in this concoction is updated romanticism. Good tunes and good rhythms, a good show. A gingery-alive performance.

Jean Absil   (1893-1974)

Suite from Rumanian Folklore for Saxophone Quartet, Op. 90

Chamber Music

☐ Marcel Mule Saxophone Quartet / Musical Heritage Society MHS-817

1

Colorful data is twined into the five movements of this quartet for soprano, alto, tenor, and baritone saxophones. There's a *Doina* in movement 1, a Christmas-carol type in movement 2, and, elsewhere, material from various Rumanian regions. Movement 3 is tempoed *scherzo leggiero*. Although the scherzo principle is observed (whimsy, rhythmic, pert), the pulse is anything but settled in this jazzy affair. The final section is just as rhythmic, but with less thin-skinned sensitivity to pulsatile palpitation. Its pulsed dance is somewhat of Bartókian order.

Performance? Brilliant and dynamic and with gorgeous sound qualities, as balanced as the best of string quartet teams. (Another performance, by the Nova Saxophone Quartet, is quite good, but second in choice. It's on Crystal S–153.)

Choral

Chorus Alone

Le Bestiaire, Op. 56

☐ Grenoble University Choir / Giroud (conductor) / Musical Heritage Society MHS–1078

Five little pieces dealing with Apollinaire texts; their titles include *The Crayfish, The Carp,* and *The Cat.* A colorful achievement by this Belgian composer, minus any folly of being cute. Intimate choral music, originally for mixed vocal quartet but sung here and sung delectably by multiple voices.

Joseph Achron   (1886-1943)

Instrumental

Violin

Hebrew Dance, Op. 35, No. 1

☐ Heifetz (violin); Isidor Achron (piano) / RCA ARM4–0942 (monaural)

Achron's music expresses the rhapsody and religious agitation that the Chassidic Jews manifest in their celebrations. Heifetz recorded the piece more than a half-century ago. It still enchants the ear and warms the blood.

Hebrew Lullaby, Op. 35, No. 2

☐ Heifetz (violin); Chotzinoff (piano) / RCA ARM4–0942 (monaural)

A Hebraic idealization marked by the yearning augmented interval. (One of the very early Heifetz recordings, made in 1922.)

Hebrew Melody, Op. 33

☐ Ricci (violin); Lush (piano) / London STS–15049

Based on a theme Achron recalled hearing in a synagogue when he was a young boy. It translates the expiatory fervor of the religious Jew when he prays to his God. Ricci's portrayal of this gorgeous melody and its developmental curves is of luminous intensity, never once even slightly sentimental. It is the mark of high artistry.

Stimmung, Op. 32, No. 1

☐ Heifetz (violin); Isidor Achron (piano) / RCA ARM4–0942 (monaural)

Stimmung means "mood," and the mood of this piece is nostalgic, somewhat poignant. The composer's expressive simplicity is fulfilled by absolutely liquescent playing. (The recording is a re-release of a very old acoustic disc, one of the many Heifetz made between 1917 and 1924.)

Adolphe-Charles Adam   *(1803-1856)*

Overture to *Giralda*   *Orchestra*

Overture to *La Poupée de Nuremberg*

☐ New Philharmonia Orchestra / Bonynge (conductor) / London 6643

Engaging and delectable performances of overtures to a pair of comic operas. No one can fault the way these are played. No one can fault the tuney stuff with which they are filled. (London's fine liner notes fail to mention that *Giralda* has an alternate title: "La Nouvelle Psyché.")

Overture to *Si j'étais Roi*

☐ Paris Conservatoire Orchestra / Wolff (conductor) / London STS-15021

The "If I Were King" overture bathes the ear with old-fashioned but sterling tunes. Wolff's performance, in an album called *Overture Encores,* is a total joy. Beautiful sound; the glockenspiel is captured exactly in proper proportions.

Suite from the Ballet *Giselle*

☐ Vienna Philharmonic Orchestra / von Karajan (conductor) / London 6251

One doesn't think of von Karajan giving much attention to music of this type. But this recording is an exception, and it's done with high intelligence as far as style is concerned and with full commitment. It is directed with knowledge and grace, a bountifully beautiful result.

Giselle   *Ballet*

☐ L'Orchestre National de l'Opéra de Monte Carlo / Bonynge (conductor) / London 2226

The only recordings worth considering of this perennial ballet score are the one noted above and Mercury's edition (2-77003), with Fistoulari conducting the London Symphony Orchestra. The playing is expert in both instances. However, the version Fistoulari presents, noted as "complete," is the opposite. It contains not only the standard deletions but a great number of others. Bonynge really covers it completely. His running time is three minutes over two hours; Fistoulari's version is heard in one hour and twenty-two minutes. It is utterly impossible to dismiss those forty-one minutes.

Not only does Bonynge play *all* of *Giselle,* but he makes all the required repeats. The orchestration is as Adam set it, and the performance includes the Burgmüller additions, which have become an authentic part of this classic.

Would that ballet orchestras could sound as good as this one! But the aural agonies derived from the pit bands that support stage action will have to be borne, since there is no doubt that as long as the art of the ballet exists *Giselle* will be produced.

Still, Bonynge's recorded edition can heal scarred ears. It is bright and rhythmically neat, vigorous where it should be, showing finesse in its treatment of details where that applies. In short, his is *the* recording of *Giselle* to own.

Le Diable à quatre

☐ London Symphony Orchestra / Bonynge (conductor) / London 6454

In what can be defined as the ultimate in soft-sell verbiage, L. A. Yeats, the program annotator for London's release, warns those who require either the "melodic vigour and abundance of Tchaikovsky'' or the ''cerebral astringencies [?-!]'' of Stravinsky that they ''will find little to engage them here.'' Such a stiff opinion is really a selling short of Adam's ballet score. Tchaikovsky himself did not downgrade Adam's music in this manner. Though the tunes in *Le Diable* indulge mostly in neutrality rather than specific individuality they are far from trite, and one can fully enjoy their simple and hummable qualities. This is especially so in Bonynge's recording, which does them full justice.

Claus Adam (1917-   )

Solo Instrument and Orchestra

Cello

Concerto for Cello and Orchestra (1973)

☐ Louisville Orchestra / Kates (cello) / Mester (conductor) / Louisville S–745

Adam's music has the decisive stamp of brooding introspection. It is powered by superb scoring and a knowledge of how to write tellingly for the solo instrument (Adam was the cellist of the Juilliard Quartet for almost twenty years). An emotive intensity seethes through the music, emphasized in the middle movement (an *Adagio lamentoso*, dedicated to the memory of Stefan Wolpe, one of the composer's teachers) but present also in the pyrotechnically detailed finale.

This is a peerless performance by both Stephen Kates and the Louisville Orchestra, directed by Jorge Mester. Kates perfectly conveys both the inner emotion of the piece (its total meaning) and the outer structural shape (its total syntax). He is, without doubt, one of the greatest of the new generation of cellists.

Murray Adaskin (1906-   )

Instrumental

Violin

Canzona and Rondo for Violin and Piano (1949)

☐ Hidy (violin); Duncan (piano) / RCA CC/CCS–1015

The name of the creative game here is viable neoclassicism. In the Canzona the music flows with *la grande ligne,* and the Rondo balances it with more extroverted rhythmic audibility.

Chamber Music

Rondino for Nine Instruments (1961)

☐ Chamber Ensemble of the Winnipeg Symphony Orchestra / Feldbrill (conductor) / RCA CC/CCS–1009

Classical structure and syntax peppered with contemporary joie de vivre. Delightful for the ear and delightfully played. (The nonet comprises wind and string quartets plus a horn.)

Richard Addinsell (1904-   )

Solo Instrument and Orchestra

Piano

Warsaw Concerto

☐ Boston Pops Orchestra / Litwin (piano) / Fiedler (conductor) / RCA LSC–2810

Even the longhairs will own up to knowing this popular item, a sugary key piece in the score for the movie *Dangerous Moonlight* that became an overnight success. Of course, for such an outcome a composer must tread a familiar path and Addinsell did so, affectionately gathering on his way Tchaikovsky and Rachmaninoff clovers. They turned out to be the four-leafed type.

Leo Litwin plays with appropriate appreciation of how this music should be styled, and Arthur Fiedler sees that the Pops personnel does likewise. No one could do it better. The piece is also in another Fiedler collection on RCA LSC-2380.

John Addison   (1920-   )

Concerto for Trumpet, Strings, and Percussion (1949)

Solo Instrument and Orchestra

☐ Louisville Orchestra / Rapier (trumpet) / Mester (conductor) / Louisville S-695

Trumpet

Addison is a spokesman for a Frenchified Prokofiev in his bright, slightly brash, somewhat saucy, always tuneful, altogether appealing work. And, importantly, Addison shows himself a master of trumpet-writing operations. This piece is *for* the trumpet. (How many works are turned out for a specific solo instrument but lack the unduplicatable personality of the solo voice! And one does not mean, in this connection, the use of technically stereotyped patterns that, depending on the instrument involved, are described as "violinistic" or "pianistic," et cetera.)

Leon Rapier performs with poise and incisiveness. He also has a tonal quality totally free of the edginess which in all too many cases is not totally absent, be the trumpeter a soloist in front of the orchestra or sitting in it.

Samuel Adler   (1928-   )

Recitative

Instrumental

☐ Noehren (organ) / Lyrichord 7191

Organ

A quiet emotional quality, subtly interwoven with rhythmic restlessness, permeates Adler's short work. Noehren's playing registers both nicely.

Xenia: **A Dialogue for Organ and Percussion**

☐ Craighead (organ); Stout (percussion) / Crystal S-858

As Adler explains, *Xenia* "is a term of Greek origin denoting a series of short incisive poems." His structural arrangements therefore follow suit in this fascinating combination of organ and percussion (a fast-growing fashionable medium today), by use of sectional depiction. But there's no overargumentation in Adler's tight, decisively dissonant prose. Pithy ideas are developed, with no semblance of making static mountains from musical molehills. Each portion is positive, and though sharply contrastive they link neatly. Adler's points are well made, absolutely incisive, and performed in complementary fashion.

Canto VIII for Piano Solo

Piano

☐ Gowen (piano) / Mark MM-1117

Split-personality music, both quiet and violent. Split-coloration as well, using the keyboard and direct contact on the strings of the instrument. Bradford Gowen, for whom the work was written and to whom it is dedicated, presents a bracing performance.

Mark has incorrectly designated the piece as "Canto VII." Since the correctly titled Canto VII, which is for unaccompanied tuba, is one of the companion pieces on the recording, this leads to annoying confusion. See under *tuba* (Canto VII for Tuba Solo).

Capriccio (1954)

☐ Helps (piano) / Composers Recordings S-288

A miniature gem. Thin in texture, nervous in pulse. It shows that Adler knows how to turn out a pithy piece with directness and no clutter. Indeed, a gem.

Trumpet

Canto I for Trumpet Solo

☐ Vizzutti (trumpet) / Mark MM-1117

This four-part piece is a humdinger for the trumpet: glides and curves, flutters and growls, trills and taps on the instrument's bell, dips and rips. The use of the range is total, the trumpet is treated like a fiddle in full swing. Extra color is supplied in the two middle sections, by contrasting types of mutes.

Trampoline-trumpet technique is demanded. This chap Allen Vizzutti is simply amazing. He drives through the work with enthusiasm, spitfire playing, and magnificent control. The listener will not be bored with this recording.

Tuba

Canto VII for Tuba Solo

☐ Beauregard (tuba) / Mark MM-1117

The tuba has been governed too long by reticence on the part of composers. Adler will have none of it. In this four-part set the tuba huffs and puffs nicely, but it also moves and bounces vigorously. Part 2 has some percussion effects, transacted by the tuba player himself. Beauregard's address to this work is expert.

Chamber Music

Four Dialogues for Euphonium and Marimba (1974)

☐ Bowman (euphonium); Stout (marimba) / Crystal S-393

Here is a unique combination. It probably is a debut in the chamber-music medium. (Even separately these instruments don't pop up in the bible that covers chamber-music literature: *Cobbett's Cyclopedic Survey of Chamber Music.*)

The timbre originality is matched by contemporary parlance in the best sense of the word. Individual moods are manifested and yet avoid any technical extravagances. Adler's music is superbly performed and recorded.

Fourth String Quartet (1963)

☐ Pro Arte Quartet / Lyrichord 7203

Free contrapuntalism is paramount in Adler's fine piece, ruled by practical form. In movement 4 an aleatoric system is followed, but the results are lyrical.

The Pro Arte group plays professionally. However, the liner note calling this team "the oldest musical organization of its kind in the world" must be corrected. That pertains to the name only. Certainly there is no other connection whatsoever between Messrs. Paulu, Moore, Blum, and Creitz and the great Franco-Belgian foursome that performed worldwide in the 1920s and 1930s.

Contrasts   **Five Choral Pictures**   *Choral*
Five American Folk Songs   **Five Choral Poems**

Chorus Alone

☐ North Texas State University A Cappella Choir / McKinley (conductor) / Mark MM–1117

There are succinct characterizations of the texts in these choral cycles. The Choral Poems and the *Contrasts* are basically conceived in madrigal style. In the latter, a pertinent rhythmic effect backs up the second of the set, *Drum* (to a text by Langston Hughes). Five regions are represented in the folk settings.

Satisfactory performances throughout, but if you want to read the texts as well as listen to them you'll have to provide your own, since they don't come with the recording.

Adler / *Louis Moreau Gottschalk.* See *Gottschalk* / Adler.

John Adson   *(?-?1640)*

Two Ayres for Cornetts and Sagbutts

Chamber Music

☐ Eastern Brass Quintet / Klavier KS–536

A pair of fine, jaunty examples of this composer's work. The music is from Adson's volume *Courtly Masquing Ayres*. Warmly timbred playing, including some discreet and fitting ornamentation.

Johan Joachim Agrell   *(1701-1765)*

Sonata

Instrumental

No. 1 in B flat major / No. 5 in D major

Harpsichord

☐ Nordenfelt (harpsichord) / Orion 74157

Eva Nordenfelt deserves praise for making these rewarding Sonatas available on disc. Her playing is sensitively phrased, knowledgeably ornamented, and in general several cuts above the average harpsichordal product. The reproduction is clear and faithful. Nordenfelt also supplies adequate notes, only erring in giving Agrell's dates as 1701–1752.

The Sonatas, in preclassical style, are from a set, *Sei sonate per il cembalo solo.* The first one consists of six movements, completed by a pair of minuets. A *Tempo di menuetto* is also used to finish the other Sonata—a five-movement affair.

Julián Aguirre   *(1868-1924)*

Triste (Elegy) No. 4, *Córdoba*

Instrumental

☐ Calligaris (piano) / Orion 7286

Piano

A gentle, romantic short piece that takes some folkloric turns. Sensitively played. (Orion lists this composer as "Juan B." Incorrect.)

Johann Rudolf Ahle (1625-1673)

Cantata and Oratorio

Merk auf mein Herz

☐ Instrumentalists and Freiburg Student Choir / Graf (soprano); Brinkmann (alto); Schmidt (tenor); Pommerien (bass) / Knall (conductor) / Vanguard C-10045

When music such as this affecting Christmas cantata is brought to light, one is reminded that other composers besides Bach helped feed the stockpile of great baroque music.

Ahle's six-sectioned "Take Heed, My Heart" (structured on a single chorale tune) calls for four vocal soloists, a four-part choir, two violins, and continuo. The performance is outstanding in all respects, matching the crystal-clear personality of the music itself.

Hugh Aitken (1924-   )

Instrumental

Bassoon

Montages for Solo Bassoon

☐ Grossman (bassoon) / Crystal 351

Registral differences propose the dialogue in this monologue. Still, there are natural shapes to the lines as well as to the phrases of thesis-antithesis in the piece.

Arthur Grossman's playing brings out the sense of unstated description in Aitken's essay. It isn't easy to hold the interest with an unaccompanied work for a homophonic instrument, unless it pours out a great deal of sonorous and rhythmic urgency. Aitken's Montages is principally lyrical and doesn't provide any pyrotechnical crutch for the performer. The more credit, therefore, for Grossman's refined statement.

Piano

Piano Fantasy (1967)

☐ Gary Kirkpatrick (piano) / Composers Recordings SD-365

Contemporary in mood, language, and demeanor, totally adhering to the fantasy objective, yet possessing formal solidity. In this sense Aitken follows a philosophical convention, since he swings far away from the rummaging commentary of ever-changing facets that mark so many present-day pieces set in fantasy formations. All to the better. And, let it be noted, no irrelevant gossip and chatter in the writing; the structure is tight, regardless of its almost seventeen-minute length.

Not for any but a pianist who can make the big gesture. Gary Kirkpatrick fills the bill, and also portrays a force in the less demonic sections.

Cantata and Oratorio

Cantata No. 1 on Elizabethan Texts (1958)

☐ Bressler (tenor); Kaplan (oboe); Kwalwasser (violin); Lynch (viola); Arico (cello) / Composers Recordings SD-365

Tuneful in the clearest manner, which brings the texts of this six-part work into high relief. The tonality plans are refreshing. And so is the fine voice of Charles Bressler. Add to that spittingly clear diction. This is super-high quality music matched by its performance.

Cantata No. 3, *From This White Island,* on Poems by Willis Barnstone (1960)

☐ Bressler (tenor); Kaplan (oboe); Lynch (viola) / Composers Recordings SD-365

The highlight of Aitken's haunting, modally sensitive six-part work is the third piece, *There*, with its scherzo-like patter for voice and viola. Superb contrast follows in the quiet, declarative *Now* for voice and oboe. Such differing coloration is basic to the cycle, with unaccompanied voice used for the first and fifth parts. *Only an Island* (part 2) and *Atlantic Coast: Afterward* (part 6) are for the total trio.

Immaculate clarity in the writing is matched by the exquisite singing of Bressler and the sensitive playing of Kaplan and Lynch.

Cantata No. 4 on Poems by Antonio Machado (1961)

☐ Hakes (soprano); Kraber (flute); Kaplan (oboe); Arico (cello); Levine (bass) / Composers Recordings SD–365

The pungent Spanish texts are defined by a mix of instrumental color, vocalism, and narration. A good balance is attained.

Robert Aitken *(1939 -   )*

Noësis (1963)

Electronic Music

☐ Folkways 33436

Formal balance (four sections in the piece) obtained from simple electronic items. Clearly detailed, with *musique concrète* (ordinary sounds from daily life) used a bit for coloristic intensity.

Yasushi Akutagawa *(1925 -   )*

Music for Symphony Orchestra (1950)

Orchestra

☐ Tokyo Symphony Orchestra / Mori (conductor) / Angel S–36577

Contemporary Japanese music rarely is tonal—herewith an exception. And boy, oh boy, a Japanese parallel to Khachaturian! (Are you listening, pops concert conductors?) Made to order for ballet, made to order for easy listening, and made to order for popularity in light-fare concerts.

No apologies needed for the Tokyo Orchestra's brilliant delivery of this music.

Triptique for String Orchestra (1953)

String Orchestra

☐ Tokyo Symphony Orchestra / Mori (conductor) / Angel S–36577

The three-panel altar painting alluded to in the title is analogously portrayed by surrounding a slow movement with two fast ones. The tempo does not absolutely conform to this concept, however, since in the last of the speedy movements there are two slow-paced sections. The music of the opening ricochets as if from a slingshot. It has a panting excitement—a type of urbanistic glorification. Indeed, Akutagawa's "pictures" differ. The second one is romantically heated; the finale indicates that Shostakovich is known to the composer.

All credit is due to a work that, even if eclectic, has imagery. All credit, likewise, to Tadashi Mori and his musicians. They produce topflight playing.

Jehan Alain   *(1911-1940)*

Instrumental	**Cistercian Chorale** **Litanies**
	Dorian Chorale **Phrygian Chorale**
Organ	**Intermezzo**

☐ Marie-Claire Alain (organ) / Musical Heritage Society MHS–868

Litanies is the key work in this group, having achieved the greatest success among Alain's organ compositions. Rhythm is the circuit that feeds the dynamic excitement directly or alternately to its musical lines. The chorales are freed of rigorous form, each actually a single movement of experience that has its balance because it is formed as a complete unit.

As can be expected, the deceased composer's sister plays with the fullest understanding. All the performances are fully stylish and sure-fingered. There is an impressive clarity given each piece, and carefully distinguished registration. The instrument used is a Härpfer-Ermann organ, located at the Château-Salins (Moselle), France.

Première Suite

☐ Isoir (organ) / Vox SVBX–5315

Intense polyphony is characteristic of all the three movements: *Prélude*, Scherzo, and *Choral*. There's packed action in the Scherzo, which is generally a lean form in order to move briskly. The slabs of spired sound in Alain's music may look unpleasantly crowded on the printed page, but in André Isoir's presentation all properties are fluently controlled, neat, and in place.

Second Fantasy

Three Dances

☐ Marie-Claire Alain (organ) / Musical Heritage Society MHS–868

A cogent mannerism in Alain's music is the rhythmic assortment used for plasticizing the melodic content. This excites the fantasy proportions. In the Three Dances—*Joies* ("Joy"); *Deuils* ("Grief"), subtitled "Funeral Dance in Honor of a Heroic Memory"; and *Luttes* ("Struggles")—some cyclic situations apply, but not of the blatant type characteristic of César Franck.

Outstanding organ playing, though a tendency for the use of darker colors is to be noted.

Chamber	### Trois Mouvements for Organ and Flute
Music	

☐ Rampal (flute); Marie-Claire Alain (organ) / Musical Heritage Society MHS-1277

Originally for "piano and flute," this was transcribed by Alain's sister and can therefore be considered an "official" translation. The *Trois Mouvements* is without doubt the best of the small amount of music Alain had time to produce before he was killed at age twenty-nine in the Second World War. The duo reveals lyrical grace and concise form. Each piece states its thesis and maintains it.

Movement 1 is like a song without words. In the second movement there is full duet decision, flowing in a quid pro quo setting. The most striking piece is the last one: toccata-like music with forty-two measures of the organ before the flute begins its articulations.

A striking performance.

Isaac Albéniz   (1860-1909)

Concerto No. 1 for Piano and Orchestra, Op. 78

☐ Torino Orchestra / Blumental (piano) / Zedda (conductor) / Turnabout 34372

Not Albéniz of Spain but Albéniz of Lisztian-romantic territory. That there is no commitment to the former does not mean outlinear pedanticism in terms of the latter. The opus rings pretty true, especially the verve of the first part and the logic and continuity of the second: *Reverie e scherzo.*

Although the orchestra is only fair, the solo part is nicely personalized by Felicja Blumental. She avoids both sentimentality and tawdry styling that wearies the ear.

Cantos de España, Op. 232
Iberia

☐ de Larrocha (piano) / London 2235

The dozen numbers in *Iberia* represent Albéniz' masterwork. However, the *Cantos de España* sing their nationalism with fervent depth and come a very close second.

These are exquisitely colored conceptions. Still, de Larrocha depicts the music without exaggerating or overemphasizing what is directly within it—instead providing all the meanings by superb pedaling and the finesse of *rubati.* Most important is her remarkable sense of continuity, so that a seamlessness pervades the music; the contrasts are built in by the composer rather than stressed by the performer. All the minute details are provided and all are in perfect balance. Truly, one cannot quibble about a single note in these works as conveyed by this superb artist.

Mallorca: Barcarola, Op. 202

☐ Kyriakou (piano) / Vox SVBX–5403

A charming, nostalgic, salonistic bit. Rena Kyriakou plays it with equal charm, and with proper fluency.

Navarra

☐ de Larrocha (piano) / London 2235

Navarra was one of Albéniz' final pieces, and twenty-six measures of completion were required after his death. Déodat de Séverac did what was necessary and in a completely Albénizian manner.

The piece is played with full tonal resource and an exuberance befitting its thematic format of a dance called the *Jota.*

Pavana-Capricho, Op. 12
Recuerdos de viaje, Op. 71
Rêves, Op. 201

☐ Kyriakou (piano) / Vox SVBX–5403

Opus 12 is so pat and nakedly naive that it can serve as nothing more than documentation of Albéniz' early period of work. However, it must be said that Kyriakou colors the music-box effects of the piece quite nicely.

The Opus 71 ''Recollections of a Journey'' is a few cuts above the Opus 12. A large,

Solo Instrument and Orchestra

Piano

Instrumental

Piano

seven-movement suite, it has nationalistic imprints: the *Alborada* of movement 3, a Bolero in movement 5, and *Malagueñas* in the sixth section. Other, less noticeable Hispanic reflections are to be observed throughout. *Iberia* or *Cantos de España* it isn't, but it has a certain passion that even in its restraint (as Kyriakou translates it) shows worth.

Rêves ("Dreams") consists of a Berceuse, a Scherzino, and a *Chant d'amour* ("Love Song").

Rumores de la caleta (Malagueñas)

☐ Beatriz Klien (piano) / Turnabout S–34327

Turnabout's miscellaneous *Spanish Piano Music* album (fourteen pieces by Falla, Granados, and Mompou, as well as Albéniz) blandly titles this piece "Malagueña." The correct heading is noted above, the *Rumores de la caleta* ("Echoes from the Bay") being the sixth piece in the seven-part *Recuerdos de viaje*, Op. 71 (*see above*, under *Pavana-Capricho*, Op. 12).

Klien does excellently with this small item, with crisp rhythmic delivery that suits the music perfectly.

Siete estudios en los tonos naturales mayores, Op. 65

Sonata No. 3, Op. 68

☐ Kyriakou (piano) / Vox SVBX–5403

Rather imposing titles, but even the Sonata with its three movements is to be catalogued in the light-music category. The melodies roll off unpretentiously. Albéniz is most dynamic in the finale of the Opus 68, but there is more momentum than there is importance of statement. Both compositions are minor chips from the composer's workbench.

Let it be said that Kyriakou makes as much intrinsic music from both works as possible. For that she deserves plaudits.

Suite española No. 1 (movements 3 and 4), Op. 47

Tango

☐ Beatriz Klien (piano) / Turnabout S–34327

From Opus 47, the *Sevilla (Sevillanas)* and *Cádiz (Canción)* movements are represented. The latter was first titled "Serenata española" and bore the opus number 181! Klien's performances are properly styled and sensitively colored.

Albéniz' Tango (often termed Tango in D) is widely known in transcribed form for a solo instrument with piano accompaniment as well as in orchestral arrangement. The original—the second of the six movements in *España*, Op. 165—is rarely heard, let alone the entire suite. It is typical Albéniz. Played minus subtlety in this instance.

Albéniz / Enrique Fernández Arbós (1863-1939)

Orchestra

Iberia Suite

☐ French National Radio Orchestra / Munch (conductor) / Nonesuch 71189

Five of the dozen piano originals, dressed stylishly and in perfect taste: *Evocación, Fête-Dieu à Séville, Triana, El Puerto,* and *El Albaicín.* Arbós made his translations between 1908 and 1919 (the fourth part of the suite in 1908, the first and second the year following, and *Triana* in 1916; the final piece was completed in 1919). For the original and complete solo piano work, see *Albéniz: Instrumental: piano* (under *Cantos de España*).

Record collectors should have both the orchestral and piano versions. The Arbós settings are not only true to the soul of the originals but are coloristic poems that have profound beauty in their own right. Munch's presentation is an inspired one, truly one of his very best in the recorded catalogue. It deserved being awarded the French *Grand Prix du Disque*.

Navarra

☐ Chicago Symphony Orchestra / Reiner (conductor) / RCA LSC–2230

Three hands are concerned with this piece: Arbós has transcribed the work of Albéniz and de Séverac—see *Albéniz: Instrumental: piano (Navarra)*. But this is no thirdhand product! Arbós's instrumentation is a lesson in impeccable coloristic expansion, just as Reiner's documentation is a lesson in orchestral interpretation of the music.

Mateo Albéniz   *(?-1831)*

Sonata in D major   *Instrumental*

☐ List (piano) / Musical Heritage Society MHS–733   *Piano*

Scarlatti trips along in this dance piece that has fanfarade contours. It's named a "Sonata" but only consists of a *Presto e gaio* that runs a few seconds over two and one-half minutes. List runs through the music with scintillating effect.

Eugène d'Albert   *(1864-1932)*

Concerto No. 2 in E major for Piano and Orchestra, Op. 12   *Solo Instrument and Orchestra*

☐ Orchestra of Radio Luxembourg / Ponti (piano) / Cao (conductor) / Candide 31078

A nice spitting image of Liszt in its four linked movements, the expressive Adagio section and the lively Scherzo being the highlights. Such music is made to order for Michael Ponti, and he provides a fine realization, consistently in good taste.   *Piano*

Henricus Albicastro   *(?-1738)*

Concerto Grosso, Op. 7, No. 6   *String Orchestra*

☐ Academy of St. Martin-in-the-Fields / Marriner (conductor) / Oiseau-Lyre 60045

Last I checked you won't find Albicastro in *Schwann*. This Swiss musician deserves hearing. His real name, according to Nicolas Slonimsky (and he ought to know!), was Heinrich Weissenburg. In *Grove's Dictionary of Music and Musicians* he is listed as "Enrico (del Biswang) Albicastro." Elsewhere the first name is spelled "Henrico." What is important, however, is the real worthiness of his work.

Tomaso Albinoni   (1671-1750)

**String
Orchestra**

Concerto a cinque

In C major / In E minor, Op. 5, No. 9 / In C major, Op. 5, No. 12

☐ Sinfonia Instrumental Ensemble / Lamacque (violin); Gouarne (harpsichord and organ) / Witold (conductor) / Nonesuch 71005

The formats of all three concerti are practically the same: fast-paced music in the initial and concluding movements, and in between them an Adagio (in the Opus 5 pair this is expanded to a tripartite design, with a faster section in the movement's center). As to content, Albinoni supplies the usual sprightly melodic lines and bouncing figurations, with simple yet emotive slow music.

These are all fine readings. The playing has cogent reasoning, the sound is firm and full, the tempi are well chosen. Artistic realizations, indeed.

Sonata a cinque

In A major, Op. 2, No. 3 / In G minor, Op. 2, No. 6

☐ English Chamber Orchestra / Leppard (conductor) / Klavier 518

In style this music is close to Vivaldi. You'll hear finely crafted playing, particularly in the fast movements, which have balletic lightness and fine rhythmic *esprit*.

**Solo
Instrument
and
Orchestra**

Oboe

Concerto in B flat major for Oboe and Strings, Op. 7, No. 3

☐ Chamber Orchestra of the Vienna State Opera / Lardrot (oboe); Nordberg (cembalo) / Prohaska (conductor) / Vanguard 2036

A skillful and engaging performance of a fine work with lusty, initial and concluding fast-paced movements, in which André Lardrot displays an infectious staccato style. The slow movement serves as an excellent foil, and is served well by the soloist and orchestra.

Concerto in C major for Oboe and Orchestra, Op. 9, No. 4

☐ Deutsche Bachsolisten / Winschermann (oboe) / Winschermann (conductor) / Nonesuch 71148

If Helmut Winschermann's conducting technique is as pointed as his oboe playing, the performing musicians must have been very pleased to make this recording. His tone is rounder in the slow movement than in the pair of outer movements, but that's the way most German-trained oboists play the instrument.

This recording is worth having just for the lyrical A minor slow movement. The fast-tempoed terminal portions have the patently traditional figurations needed to move the material along.

Concerto in D minor for Oboe and Strings, Op. 9, No. 2

☐ Wiener Solisten / Lardrot (oboe) / Böttcher (conductor) / Vanguard 2138

Crisp playing, everything conceived of as intimate chamber music. The slow movement, a meditative conception, is long-phrased, and the perspective of the music is ideally presented.

Concerto in B flat major for Trumpet

☐ Wiener Solisten / André (trumpet) / RCA CRL2-7002

Though the expected figurations of musical chitchat fill the two fast movements, the slow-paced pair gives the opus worthy stature. André's playing of the work (originally for oboe) is crisp in the former and gives indisputable shape to the latter.

Concerto in C major for Trumpet

☐ Schwarz (trumpet); Roseman, Weiner, and Virginia Brewer (oboes); MacCourt (bassoon); Edward Brewer (harpsichord) / Desto 6438

Two important points relate to this work. First, the accompaniment (though this expands until it almost reaches equality with the solo brass instrument) is for three oboes, bassoon, and continuo. Second, the virtuosic display element is rather restricted, especially after the opening movement of the three. In any case, everyone in the Desto production should receive heavy underlined credits.

Concerto for Violin, Strings, and Continuo

In B flat major, Op. 10, No. 1 / In G minor, Op. 10, No. 2 / In C major, Op. 10, No. 3 / In G major, Op. 10, No. 4 / In A major, Op. 10, No. 5 / In D major, Op. 10, No. 6 / In F major, Op. 10, No. 7 / In G minor, Op. 10, No. 8 / In C major, Op. 10, No. 9 / In F major, Op. 10, No. 10 / In C minor, Op. 10, No. 11 / In B flat major, Op. 10, No. 12

☐ I Musici / Michelucci (violin); Garatti (harpsichord) / Philips SC71-AX-308

Superb music heard in absolutely marvelous performances. The polished quality of this team in style, musicianship, and technique is perfection itself. To imagine better playing by any string group is an impossibility.

Sonata in A minor for Flute and Harpsichord, Op. 6, No. 6

☐ Rampal (flute); Gilbert (harpsichord) / Orion 7149

This is the sixth work in Albinoni's *Trattenimenti armonici per camera divisi in dodici sonate.* It was originally for violin, but the use of the flute is a liberty appropriate for music written in the days when instrumental substitution was in flower.

Rampal and Gilbert join in a stylish performance that is totally convincing. The sound is not as convincing in the same performance released by Everest (3194), in which the mastering has somewhat compressed the sonority. (Everest's album comprises seven discs highlighting Rampal's playing.)

Sonata

In D major / In F major

☐ André (trumpet); Alain (organ) / RCA CRL2-7001

No matter that these works were not originally for trumpet and organ (we are not told what instruments were indicated initially). The free instrumentation practices of the period involved make the change honest.

The playing is entirely refreshing. Maurice André's articulation is razor sharp, and his phrasing genuine for the music. Marie-Claire Alain's registration choices are ideal and her playing is neatly turned.

Johann Georg Albrechtsberger   (1736-1809)

**Solo
Instrument
and
Orchestra**

Harp

Concerto in C major for Harp

☐ Paul Kuentz Chamber Orchestra / Zabaleta (harp) / Kuentz (conductor) / Deutsche Grammophon 139304

Some baroque qualities are contained in this music, although it is fundamentally in Viennese classical style. It all runs logically, and Zabaleta tosses it off with his expected perception—meaning a flawlessly bright performance.

Harpsichord

Concerto in B flat major for Harpsichord

☐ Hungarian Chamber Orchestra / Sebestyen (harpsichord) / Tatrai (conductor) / Turnabout 34325

Tuneful and shaped with a slow movement of melodic continuity that is longer than the two fast divisions that frame it. The playing is elegant in the Adagio, warm and immediate in the other sections.

Organ

Concerto in B flat major for Organ and Strings

☐ German Bach Soloists / Chorzempa (organ) / Winschermann (conductor) / Philips 6700052

A standard but pleasing first movement, which includes a fitting cadenza by the soloist. The sweet-toned sound of the Bergkirche organ beautifies the simplicity of the Adagio; the Finale has the expected infectious gaiety.

There is some reverberation from the organ (built in the latter part of the eighteenth century and restored in 1951), but this flavors the piece's performance. Further enjoyment is obtained from the flawless Philips disc surface.

William Albright   (1944-   )

Instrumental

Organ

Juba (1965)

Organbook (1967)

☐ Albright (organ) / Composers Recordings S-277

More evidence of the contemporary resurgence of contemporary-styled organ music. It was a long time a-comin', and for the breakthrough all the thanks goes to Olivier Messiaen. Indeed, a long time existed between the output of Max Reger and the input of Messiaen. Since then the stockpile has grown and there are many fine additions to the catalogue, none of which have the slightest resemblance to the cherished delights organists find in the music of such men as Rheinberger, Dupré, and Karg-Elert.

It is understandable, then, why Messiaen is the seminal godfather for many composers, William Albright included. In *Juba* the splashes of sound combinations, the fantasy, and the perspective have been transferred from the Frenchman's studio to America. There's even a bit of mysticism if you look for it. But this is a high level of musical meaning and one doesn't care if it is the result of outer creative influences.

Organbook consists of four parts, each exploiting a different aspect of the instrument's capabilities. In *Benediction* it is soft coloration, in *Melisma* a unitary line, that is manipulated. Hell breaks loose in the toccata-like *Fanfare*, while in *Recessional* the composer's description is "atmospheric with a distorted perspective."

This is vividly fresh and alive music. Definitive playing, of course, making it possible to place Albright's name on the special list of virtuoso organists who have been composers as well.

Organbook II (1971)

☐ Albright (organ) / Nonesuch 71260

A continuation of the idea animating Albright's *Organbook* (see above). The behavior for this creative occasion is more profane, resulting in a *concordia discors* that rivets attention. No moon rays light up *Night Procession*, there is musical scorch and scourge in *Toccata satanique,* and in *Last Rites* the sound lumps are aided by electronic tape.

This is the kind of music that old silent-movie organists dreamed of playing but never did. If the few capable of doing so had tried it, they would have been fired on the spot.

Pneuma (1966)

☐ Mason (organ) / Composers Recordings S-277

Sound sequences that contrast in their textural and dynamic totality. These provide the inner force of the piece as well as its potent structural point of view. The blockbuster inserts of sonic power offer strong propaganda for Albright's piece and are a stimulating (if blatant) way of charming the ear.

Marilyn Mason is a superb organist, and contemporary music is one of her specialities. She proves it again in this instance.

Grand Sonata in Rag (1968)

Piano

☐ Mandel (piano) / Grenadilla GS-1020

Main titling notwithstanding, Albright's work is one in which suite ends justify the sonata means. No iffy question as to the rag content, since the subtitles of the three parts confirm it: *Scott Joplin's Victory, Ragtime Turtledove,* and *Behemoth Two-Step.* Catchy stuff, mild non-rock material, of course, that doesn't jar the ears and that Alan Mandel tosses off with beautiful style and proper panache.

(The liner note, written by Albright, neither gives him an author's credit nor places his remarks in quotes. Only the use of the first-person singular finally provides the clue that Albright is the writer.)

Pianoagogo

☐ Sanders (piano) / Trilogy CTS-1003

In this essay in fragments with some explosive footnotes, an emotional line of thought is maintained even though it's segmented.

Albright's profluvia require a contemporary-music virtuoso who realizes that pianistic percussion is not musically impolite or impolitic. Sanders understands. Sanders delivers.

Albright and William Bolcom (1938-   )

Brass Knuckles (1969)

Instrumental

☐ Bolcom (piano) / Nonesuch 71257

Piano

A joint effort which produced a rag that zings as well as swings. Bolcom wrote the first two tunes, Albright furnished the balance.

John Alcock, the Elder (1715-1806)

Instrumental

Trumpet

Voluntary in D

☐ Sautter (trumpet); Sherman (organ) / Crystal S-700

Well-formationed. The music begins with a minor-keyed organ section, followed by the trumpet's entrance in the opposite tonal mode. Then follows duo equality obtained by imitative passages. Good presentation.

Josef Alexander (1907-   )

Orchestra

Three Pieces for Eight (1965)

☐ New York Philomusica Chamber Ensemble / Johnson (conductor) / Serenus 12038

Dynamic contemporary tonalism, peppered by salty astringencies and jazz inflections, both stabilized and invigorated by constant color play—these phrases describe Alexander's hedonistic music. The mini-orchestra scoring covers winds (flute [alternating with piccolo] and clarinet), brass (trumpet), keyboard (piano), strings (violin, cello, and double bass), and percussion (nine instruments: timpani, snare drum, tenor drum, small bass drum, cymbals, triangle, wood block, maracas, and xylophone).

Johnson presents a bright performance of this brightly virtuosic music.

Instrumental

Piano

Incantation

☐ Helps (piano) / Composers Recordings S-288

Structured by quartal-insistent sounds, *Incantation* is carried to a stunning climax. The expressive intensity is given full effect by Helps's playing.

Trumpet

Burlesque and Fugue (1970)

☐ Ware (trumpet); Bernstein (piano) / Serenus 12038

An unbuttoned mood characterizes the Burlesque, and its unabashed use of melodic curves makes fine twentieth-century sense. There are no academic artificialities in the Fugue, which provides a fully independent consideration of its polyphonic design and shows top expertise.

Sensitive playing—with gusto when needed—marks the performance.

Vocal

Voice and Instrumental Ensemble

Songs for Eve (1958)

☐ Mandac (soprano); Sackson (violin); Bialkin (cello); Brenner (English horn); Chertok (harp) / Serenus 12038

Alexander's large vocal cycle (in fifteen parts, of which thirteen are here recorded) is set to poems by Archibald MacLeish. The pan-tonal freedom of the style matches the wide range of emotion of the songs, expertly interwoven with the selective instrumental quartet colors (a choice combination that enhances the textures). There is no mistaking the romantic urgency that underlies this contemporary composer's statements.

The surefooted individuality of Alexander's writing and the atmospheres of the various songs are effectively realized in this fine performance.

Javier Alfonso (1905-)

Cadenza

Instrumental

Harp

☐ Robles (harp) / Argo ZRG-5457

An extract from a Concerto, changed slightly so that it can stand alone. Nice little encore item.

(The composer is also known as Jean Alfonso.)

Hugo Alfvén (1872-1960)

Midsommarvaka (Swedish Rhapsody No. 1) (1904)

Orchestra

☐ Philadelphia Orchestra / Ormandy (conductor) / Columbia MS-6196

Alfvén's "Midsummer Vigil" is his best-known work. Crammed with luscious tunes, folk songs, and dance melodies, it is made to order for this virtuoso orchestra with golden sound. And they deliver, and how! (Also obtainable on Columbia MS-7674.)

Richard Alison (16th or 17th cent.)

Shall I Abide This Jesting?

Choral

Chorus Alone

☐ Purcell Consort of Voices / Burgess (conductor) / Turnabout 34202

A five-part madrigal from this sixteenth- or seventeenth-century English composer's two-volume collection of part-songs entitled *An Howres Recreation in Musicke*. Appealing only in an average way, but most appealingly sung by this fine vocal group.

Charles-Henri Valentin Alkan (1813-1888)

Allegro barbaro from Twelve *Etudes dans les tons majeurs*, Op. 35

Barcarolle (No. 6) from Six Chants, Op. 65

Capriccio alla soldatesca, Op. 50, No. 1

Capriccio: Le Tambour bat aux champs, Op. 50, No. 2

Fa (No. 2) from Twelve Chants, Op. 38

Forty-eight *Esquisses*, Op. 63, Nos. 4, 10, 21, 29, 41, 46, and 48

Instrumental

Piano

☐ Smith (piano) / CMS/Oryx 1803

Plentiful confirmation of Alkan's programmatic habits is to be heard in this program. Examples: in the Opus 63 excerpts, the insistence in *Morituri te Salutant*, the teasing in *Le Premier Billet-doux*, the tolling sounds in *Les Cloches*, the clever dynamic blows of *Increpatio*.

There are other sides to Alkan's creative personality. A Mendelssohnian relationship is heard in *Barcarolle*, a Mahlerian one in *Le Tambour*.

Pianos made in 1851 and 1855 were used for the recording. They are not as robust-sounding or as responsive as one might wish, but they're acceptable.

Symphony from Twelve *Etudes dans les tons mineurs*, Op. 39, Nos. 4, 5, 6, and 7

☐ Ponti (piano) / Candide 31045

Never pedantic and always colorful—Alkan always sang his own type of song—Alkan's Symphony is, of course, a formal sonata for the piano, but its title represents more. There is an orchestral mounting to the piano writing. The quality of orchestrational voicing and timbre is simulated, hence the symphonic designation. The same pertains to Alkan's Concerto, a three-movement work that is also for piano alone. There one can recognize the responses of the solo voice to the imitations of the eliminated orchestral tutti.

Twelve *Etudes dans les tons mineurs*, Op. 39, Nos. 1, 2, 3, and 12

☐ Ponti (piano) / Candide 31045

Even when Alkan didn't want to promulgate full-scaled programmatic intent, his music wasn't very far from the descriptive category. Notwithstanding the formal title, "Studies," pictorial intent is hinted at here by the *comme le vent–prestissimamente* designation of the first piece, the *en rhythme molossique–risoluto* instruction for the second, and the *scherzo diabolico–prestissimo* indication for the third. Both the music and Ponti's performance fully convey these characterizations.

The last piece is a magnificent set of twenty-five variations entitled *Le Festin d'Esope*. Such a heading further proves Alkan's penchant for picture painting regardless of formal framework. The theme is never smothered or fancifully disintegrated beyond recognition, but receives splendid variational handling, and the imagery of the capering of Aesop's animals is excellent. This piece needs a powerful pianist and Ponti has what it takes, including all the thrilling virtuosity.

Twenty-Five Preludes for Piano or Organ, Op. 31, Nos. 8, 11, 12, 13, 15, and 16

☐ Smith (piano) / CMS/Oryx 1803

All clearly detailed vignettes. The harmonic basis is relatively simple, but this does not negate excellent sound symbolism, as in No. 8, *The Song of the Madwoman on the Shore*.

Chamber Music

Piano Trio in G minor, Op. 30

☐ Mirecourt Trio / Genesis 1058/9

Though Alkan's fondness for matters programmatic does not surface in his four-movement trio, graphic formal considerations do. Initially contrasted themes are eventually combined in movement 1; coloristic opposition of pizzicati and lyricism is found in movement 2; and there is a persistent dialogue between staid strings and bravura piano in the slow movement.

The playing is clear and nicely focused.

Juan Allende-Blin *(1928-   )*

Instrumental

Organ

Sons brisés: In Memory of Lothar Schreyer (1967)

☐ Zacher (organ) / Wergo 60033

Devoted, in great part, to the shift of pitches produced by increasing and decreasing the pressure in the wind box of the organ. The sliding quality of intonation is probably meant to emphasize the music's threnodic intent. This work is not for those who are only comfortable with Virgil Fox's repertoire.

(Exact titling is not furnished. The album cover states "In memoriam." The liner copy and record label read "In memory of.")

Claude Almand (1915-1957)

John Gilbert: **A Steamboat Overture**   *Orchestra*

☐ Louisville Orchestra / Whitney (conductor) / Louisville 605 (monaural)

Title explanation: *John Gilbert* is the name of a tune that was sung by the roustabouts who loaded freight on the steamboat with the same name. There are full-heated substances in Almand's piece, which is played in a full-steam-ahead manner.

Johann Ernst Altenburg (1734-1801)

Concerto a 7 Clarini con Timpani   *Solo Instrument and Orchestra*

☐ Consortium Musicum / Tarr (trumpet) / Lehan (conductor) / Nonesuch 71217

Bright baroque trumpet music. The composition calls for a *clarino concertato*, played ideally by Edward H. Tarr, supported by a *Coro* I and II, each consisting of a "principal" and two other players. The timpani, as expected, lends the simplest support.

Trumpet

Well recorded in all respects.

William Alwyn (1905-   )

Four Elizabethan Dances (1957)   *Orchestra*

☐ London Philharmonic Orchestra / Alwyn (conductor) / Musical Heritage Society MHS-1672

The title will not be found in Alwyn's official catalogue or that of his publisher. The recording reviewed here is two-thirds of the total work titled Elizabethan Dances; Alwyn has opted for producing a sequence of Nos. 1, 2, 5, and 4 from the six-part total. Contrasted styles ("ancient and modern") are used, with the scoring for the fifth dance calling only for two flutes, two clarinets, harp, and muted strings.

A great performance. Alwyn should know, but one disagrees with his interpretation of his own score indication of *pochissimo meno mosso* in the first dance. He takes this rather "molto meno mosso." Be that as it may, the playing throughout is tops, and in the second dance it is of mouthwatering lushness.

Alfredo d'Ambrosio (1871-1914)

Serenade, Op. 4   *Instrumental*

☐ Heifetz (violin); Chotzinoff (piano) / RCA ARM4-0942 (monaural)

Violin

Sure it's a musical bonbon, not as large as a lollipop, but for double-sugary sweetmeats in the diet don't look to the three B's to supply them. A lot of fiddlers have played this piece and I wouldn't doubt that they still do—in the secrecy of their studios. Be that as it may, here is an old performance by Heifetz, made before the days of electrical recording. Who can flip a harmonic and inch into a *rubato* the way he can and does? Enjoy!

Leroy Anderson   *(1908-1975)*

Orchestra   **Belle of the Ball**

Blue Tango (1952)

☐ Boston Pops Orchestra / Fiedler (conductor) / RCA LSC–2638

Fiedler specialities. The hybrid Blue Tango is still in the recording record book, having achieved some two and a half decades ago a sale in a single year of over 2 million copies. You can't argue with such success.

Bugler's Holiday

☐ Eastman-Rochester "Pops" Orchestra / Fennell (conductor) / Mercury 75013

Frederick Fennell comes the closest to Arthur Fiedler in knowing the way to project an Anderson tune. F. F. produces full evidence in this case.

Chicken Reel

Classical Juke Box

Fiddle-Faddle

☐ Boston Pops Orchestra / Fiedler (conductor) / RCA LSC–2638

More by the Leroy Anderson conductorial expert. Fiedler, in this respect, is the best in the business. The spoofery accorded the melodic potpourri in *Classical Juke Box* is simply marvelous; *Fiddle-Faddle* moves with tempi truth, and the *Chicken Reel* snaps and zips in proper cornfed style.

Forgotten Dreams

☐ Eastman-Rochester "Pops" Orchestra / Fennell (conductor) / Mercury 75013

Pristine clarity minus the oft-heard *rubati* stuff that's nonsensical for a simple mood piece.

Irish Suite

☐ Eastman-Rochester "Pops" Orchestra / Gniewek (violin) / Fennell (conductor) / Mercury 75013
☐ Boston Pops Orchestra / Krips (violin) / Fiedler (conductor) / RCA LSC–2946

Fennell's group plays these distinctive, ting-a-ling arrangements of *The Irish Washerwoman, The Minstrel Boy,* and four others beautifully, cleanly, and without stirring up the sentimentality that can easily be brought to the surface. On the other hand, Fiedler socks them home with more guts but warmer string sounds. Krips is not as good as Gniewek in *The Last Rose of Summer.* And, if you choose Fiedler, you'll have to take applause after each movement; the suite was recorded live at Symphony Hall in Boston, during "Irish Night at the 'Pops'."

Penny-Whistle Song

Sandpaper Ballet

☐ Eastman-Rochester "Pops" Orchestra / Fennell (conductor) / Mercury 75013

The "penny" piece is doled out with ideal pace and refreshing sonority. The other item is an orchestral soft-shoe dance. Fennell's precision is masterful.

Saraband

Serenata

Sleigh Ride **(1950)**

☐ Boston Pops Orchestra / Fiedler (conductor) / RCA LSC-2638

Fiedler's identification with this music results in ideal performances.

Song of the Bells

☐ Utah Symphony Orchestra / Abravanel (conductor) / Vanguard C-10016

An Anderson waltz and Abravanel swings it very nicely, thank you.

The Syncopated Clock **(1950)**

☐ Boston Pops Orchestra / Fiedler (conductor) / RCA LSC-2638

Because of its use on TV as the musical theme for "The Late Show," *The Syncopated Clock* achieved special recognition far beyond any other Leroy Anderson piece. It also achieved a tremendous amount of ASCAP income for the composer. A great tune, this one, and played in a polished manner impossible to surpass.

Trumpeter's Lullaby

☐ Eastman-Rochester "Pops" Orchestra / Mear (trumpet) / Fennell (conductor) / Mercury 75013

Sensitive and appealing; nicely contrasted in tempi, nicely colored without exaggeration in regard to the special trumpet part.

The Typewriter

☐ Utah Symphony Orchestra / Abravanel (conductor) / Vanguard C-10016

The feature here is the typist, but he (or she) hasn't been given any credit. Too bad—the typing's good, and so are Abravanel and his musicians.

The Waltzing Cat

☐ Boston Pops Orchestra / Fiedler (conductor) / RCA LSC-2638

Proportions, tempi, and color all add up to a vital performance—the kind one expects (and receives) from this seasoned conductor of the pops music world.

Jazz Legato

Jazz Pizzicato

Plink, Plank, Plunk!

☐ Boston Pops Orchestra / Fiedler (conductor) / RCA LSC-2638

String Orchestra

The second piece came first. It introduced Anderson, formerly an arranger for the Fiedler group, to the Boston Pops audience as a composer in his own right. What followed is light-music history. There's no one who can outdo Fiedler in the first two pieces listed here. Flawless is the word.

The last title consists of plucked patter that bears out the alliterative title. Some swishes of sound add color. Fiedler's is the best performance obtainable of this short delight.

T. J. Anderson   (1928-   )

Vocal

Voice and Instrumental Ensemble

Variations on a Theme by M. B. Tolson (1969)

☐ Contemporary Chamber Ensemble / DeGaetani (mezzo-soprano) / Weisberg (conductor) / Nonesuch 71303

Slight jazz-flicked breezes add warmth to the twelve-tone climate that pervades Anderson's piece. The text consists of excerpts from the work of the black poet M. B. Tolson, and much of it is narrated. The instrumentation is for a sextet of alto saxophone, trumpet, trombone, violin, cello, and piano.

Hideously difficult for the voice—i.e., for all but a handful of singers, in which Jan DeGaetani is included. Anderson's music is worth listening to if only for her virtuosic rendition.

(The composer prefers to be called "T. J." These initials, for the curious, stand for "Thomas Jefferson.")

Hendrik Andriessen   (1892-   )

Orchestra

Symphony No. 1 (1930)

☐ Radio Philharmonic Orchestra / Hupperts (conductor) / Donemus Audio-Visual Series 6804 (monaural)

One-movement construction, but defined by separative tempi that match classical design proportions. Rich harmony and counterpoint that relate to romantic language. The orchestration is solid, bypassing any adventurous artifices (the scoring is average, there is no tuba, and only timpani represent the percussion). Lucidity is the central argument, and it is proved.

Some of the Donemus recordings, since they are made live, have minus factors in regard to sound and balance. This one does not, and the performance, checked against the score, is first class.

Instrumental

Organ

Due studi per organo (1953)

Sonata da chiesa (1927)

☐ de Klerk (organ) / Donemus Audio-Visual Series DAVS–6304 (monaural: 10-inch disc)

Traditional but worthy fare. No positing of new musical axioms. The *Sonata* has a D minor theme (which is a cross between a sarabande and a hymn tune), five variations, and a finale. As it progresses on its right-of-way it picks up chromatic steam.

The *Due studi* is considered a piece in its own right, though it is drawn (parts 3 and 2, respectively) from Andriessen's *Quattro studi per organo.* The first of the pair is a polyphonic item, rigidly maintained in three voices; the other is toccata-like. Albert de Klerk's playing is passable, his registration strictly devoted to neutral conditions.

Miroir de peine (1923)

Vocal

*Voice
and Orchestra*

☐ Concertgebouw Orchestra / Kolassi (soprano) / van Beinum (conductor) / Donemus Audio-Visual Series DAVS-6604 (monaural)

Five short poems by Henri Ghéon—*Agonie au jardin, Flagellation, Couronnement d'épines, Portement de croix,* and *Crucifixion*—serve as the textual basis for this composition, for soprano and string orchestra.

The piece was originally scored for voice and organ, and a carry-over in the second version is recognized by the pedal formations that knit the score. Sobriety defines the fundamental religious impulse of the work, but it is shot through with golden tonal amalgams.

Irma Kolassi is, of course, the star of the Donemus live recording. She proves herself to be an artist of the highest distinction. No better choice could have been made to present what is certainly the most telling and expressive of all of Andriessen's compositions.

Omaggio a Marenzio (1965)

Choral

Chorus Alone

☐ Netherlands Chamber Choir / de Nobel (conductor) / Donemus Audio-Visual Series 6903

A madrigal to words of Fazio degli Uberti of the fourteenth century. The setting is basically for the usual four-part chorus of sopranos, altos, tenors, and basses, though this spreads by *divisi* into as many as seven parts.

Clear a cappella singing.

Jurriaan Andriessen *(1925-   )*

Movimenti (1965)

*Solo
Instrument
and
Orchestra*

*Horn, Trumpet,
and Trombone*

☐ Limburg Symphony Orchestra / Rieu (conductor) / Donemus Audio-Visual Series DAVS-6602 (monaural)

No-nonsense music—its rhythmic profile sharp, its metrical patterns dynamically nervous, with an exciting dissonant text, validated by four note-rows, which, however, are not twelve-tone (one group covers eight pitches and the other three eleven each). Repetitions within the note-row sounds provide a total of fourteen pitches for each of three of the rows and a total of sixteen for the other one.

There are nine movements. The scoring is for horn, trumpet, and trombone with strings and timpani, so distributed as to obtain contrastive authority and to formulate a precise instrumentational balance. Thus, the first three and the final three movements are for the entire orchestral forces; movement 4 is for the horn with soli cello and bass, plus cello and bass tutti; movement 5 combines trumpet with timpani and both solo and tutti violas, while movement 6 utilizes the trombone with *divisi* violins 1 and 2.

The performance is vigorous, and where required has a natural degree of violence. One shortcoming: the Donemus label is termed "audio-visual," since scores come with all of its recordings. According to the score, there is a constant use of a high E on the timpani. This special pitch requires an extremely small timpano that the Limburg organization eliminated out of hand. Its special pitch coloration is thereby lost, and the result negates extremely effective octavial placement. It is also odd that Donemus fails to give credit to the three brass soloists, most deserving of such notice for their fine artistic performance.

Chamber Music

Sonata da camera for Flute, Viola, and Guitar (Trio No. 5) (1959)

☐ Barwahser (flute); Boon (viola); Goudswaard (guitar) / Donemus Audio-Visual Series DAVS-6302 (monaural: 10-inch disc)

The associated norms of neoclassicism prevail in Jurriaan Andriessen's work. Four movements form the structure: a *Preludio* and a concluding *Epilogo,* with a Cavatina and *Alla tedesca* in between.

A highly enjoyable presentation. The clarity of the recording helps the appeal of the trio.

Giovanni Francesco Anerio (ca. 1567-1630)

Cantata and Oratorio

La conversione di S. Paolo

☐ Instrumentalists and Choir of the Kirchenmusikschule, Münster-Westfalen / Speiser (soprano); Altmeyer and Jochims (tenors); Wenk (bass) / Ewerhart (conductor) / Turnabout 34172

Never fanciful, of course; not emotionally portentous, but refreshing in its intimate stability. *La conversione* represents oratorio writing in which dynamic push plays little part.

The eight-part choir writing is heard eight places in the work. Throughout, Ewerhart's choral group shows an integrated blend of singing with clear and clean articulation. Theo Altmeyer as Saul sings with refined command. The other vocalists provide proper sensitivity for Anerio's musical content.

Vivean Felici (The Story of Adam and Eve)

☐ Instrumentalists and Choir of the Kirchenmusikschule, Münster-Westfalen / Speiser and Friesenhausen (sopranos); Altmeyer (tenor); Wenk (bass) / Ewerhart (conductor) / Turnabout 34172

Anerio's *Vivean Felici,* which is a depiction of the Adam and Eve tale, is a short, seven-part oratorio for four solo voices, six-part choir, and basso continuo. Both this work and *La conversione di S. Paulo* (mentioned above) are from Anerio's *Teatro armonico spirituale,* a collection of oratorios, madrigals, and *lauda* settings. The music has a *declamando* quality and a healthy enthusiasm, which is reflected in the recording. There is splendid choral work and a fine tenor soloist taking the role of the Serpent.

John Antes (1740-1811)

Chamber Music

Trio for Two Violins and Cello

In E flat major, Op. 3, No. 1 / In D minor, Op. 3, No. 2 / In C major, Op. 3, No. 3

☐ Members of the Fine Arts Quartet / Columbia Special Products AMS-6741

According to Donald M. McCorkle, Antes "considered his works to be the efforts of a dilettante, i.e., an amateur, not as finished creations of a professional composer." Anyone listening to the string trios (superbly played by Leonard Sorkin, Abram Loft, and George Sopkin) would rightfully term this diagnosis as incorrect modesty. The quality is professional, the spontaneity and formal resolve apparent throughout. Music of such classical perceptivity deserves as much attention as that produced by the holy trinity of Haydn, Mozart, and Beethoven.

Loveliest Immanuel

Vocal

□ Moravian Festival Orchestra / Kombrinck (soprano) / Johnson (conductor) / Odyssey 32160340

Voice and Orchestra

An example of the traditional sacred song. Kombrinck's oratorio-styled delivery is fitting.

How Beautiful upon the Mountains

Choral

□ Gregg Smith Singers / Smith (conductor) / Vox SVBX–5350

Chorus Alone

A large-sized anthem with an instrumental prelude, interludes, and a postlude. Music worthy of Bach. Cogently presented, despite the difficulties of the high range for the sopranos.

Go, Congregation, Go! and Surely He Has Borne Our Griefs

Chorus and Orchestra

□ Moravian Festival Chorus and Orchestra / Kombrinck (soprano) / Johnson (conductor) / Odyssey 32160340

A soprano aria with orchestra partnered with an anthem for chorus and orchestra. The liner note indicates that "it is evident from existing manuscripts that the two works were intended to be performed as a unit."

George Antheil   (1900-1959)

Symphony No. 4: 1942

Orchestra

□ London Symphony Orchestra / Goossens (conductor) / Everest 3013

Everest's recording offers the opportunity of hearing a major Antheil work under the most propitious circumstances. This music is far different from his early period of work, when Antheil composed in a vigorous, experimental manner. Still, this kind of super-eclecticism is not hard to take. All composers retain a fondness for their individual gods and the dicta they preach. Antheil's symphony is warmed with Shostakovichian gospel, but the melodic lines are smoother than the Russian's verbiage. Nothing is subtle, either formally or harmonically. Goossens serves up an excellent presentation, with impact-producing directness.

Serenade No. 1 for Strings (1948)

String Orchestra

□ Oslo Philharmonic Orchestra / Antonini (conductor) / Composers Recordings 103 (monaural)

In this divertimento-like setting Antheil tunes along tonally, no more the "Bad Boy of Music." Rather, he is (in movements 1 and 3) the "Good Friend of Shostakovich." Indeed, one can imagine a Soviet writer describing the work as "socialistically realistic, cast in a melodious and harmonious idiom." Still, it falls on the ears with interest, which doesn't always follow if sophisticated crudities are chosen.

The performance is reliable.

Chamber Music

Sonata No. 1 for Violin and Piano

☐ Erickson (violin); Schwartz (piano) / Orion 73119

Primary primitivism. Six and one-quarter minutes of strong music, minus exposition, development, and thematic unification. But there's plenty of recapitulation—if by that you mean motoric ostinati and incessant repetitions of minute units—and there are also dozens of keyboard glissandi. Bartók's *Allegro barbaro,* written a dozen years prior to Antheil's Sonata, is father and mother to this wild duo. Add a few credits for Stravinsky of the pre-neoclassic days. In short, this is slightly mad music that captures the ear even though one recognizes all the sources.

Sonata No. 2 for Violin and Piano (Alternating Drums)

☐ Erickson (violin); Schwartz (piano); Amirkhanian (drums) / Orion 73119

The lyrical portion is "low-down," the rhythmic action delineates the hubbub of the old dance-hall dive. Also, there are plenty of noises and determined discord (far different from artful dissonance). Indeed, the listener is taken on a wild and woolly ride, furnishing a deluxe amusement as there passes in review a tabloid sound picture of what went on in the mind of an American composer living in Paris in 1923.

Mixed in are a motley of tunes, whipped by vertical supports and rebuttals. *The Old Oaken Bucket* is played a bit off pitch; a "hootchy-kootchy" dance tune is delivered sweetly in soured double stops; the nostalgic weeping of *Darling, I Am Growing Old* is heard, etc., etc. No attempt is made to obtain thematic savoir-faire.

The latter part of the Sonata deserves description. After a type of reprise going back to the beginning, the instruments part company. The piano delivers chunky chords with tight, rhythmic snaps (a forty-nine-measure solo bit), and the violin takes over the spotlight to the accompaniment of drums, jigging around the same phrase with assorted changes. The curtain is then lowered quickly on a two-beat percussion blackout.

This is the "famous" Sonata consistently listed *incorrectly* as being for "violin, piano, and drum." Presumably, the three instruments would require three performers. However, Antheil's Sonata calls for violin and piano plus *two* drums (tenor and bass), with the pianist playing the very simple paired drum parts. (There is no scurrying from keyboard instrument to the drums.) Accordingly, Antheil's opus is a duo sonata utilizing four instruments. However, in this recording, the percussion part is played by a third instrumentalist.

Sonata No. 3 for Violin and Piano
Sonatina for Violin and Piano

☐ Erickson (violin); Schwartz (piano) / Orion 73119

The Sonata No. 3 shadowboxes with and leans heavily on Igor Stravinsky. Flitting in and out, and occasionally for a fair amount of continuous time, are the shapes and levels of *The Rite of Spring* and *The Firebird,* as well as plenty of ostinati. This type of keen creative transfer is so bald and bold that it registers solidly and one doesn't mind the imitation. It takes a clever composer to bring it off, and in 1924 George Antheil was clever.

More imitation is found in the Sonatina. In movement 1 it is Shostakovich, and in movement 3 the images are Ivesian, with thematic outlines tracing a Beethoven *Contredanse, Hail Columbia,* and Bizet's *Carmen.* By the inclusion of a theme from movement 1 the work falls in the cyclic class. Plenty of rough edges in the design, but proper for Antheil's rough-and-ready conception of chamber music.

John Henry Antill   (1904-   )

Corroboree: Suite from the Ballet (1946)   *Orchestra*

☐ London Symphony Orchestra / Goossens (conductor) / Everest 3003

Antill's conception of Australian aboriginal life reminds one of Stravinsky's *Sacre du printemps.* Rhythm is the substance that is paramount. Goossens presents the score with authority and makes certain that none of its rewards are lost.

Jiří Antonín. *See Georg Anton Benda.*

Edward Applebaum   (1937-   )

Piano Sonata (1965)   *Instrumental*

☐ Bunger (piano) / Avant 1010   *Piano*

Two movements: *Mirrors* and *Gestures.* Their passionate eloquence reminds one of Stockhausen's piano music, with a tincture here and there of a lyrical curve.

The liner notes (?) on Avant's release (an all-Applebaum program of five works) are absolutely the most annoying this writer has ever encountered. They consist only of a poem (by Stuart M. Erwin) that hints, now and then, at saying something about the music and promptly makes certain to avoid doing so. The best information (?) to be found about the Piano Sonata reads: "And music gave a form to silence,/movements subtitled *Mirrors* and *Gestures.*" Make of that what you wish!

Foci (1971)   *Chamber Music*

☐ Mark (viola); Musgrave (piano) / Avant 1010

Applebaum focuses principally on the string instrument, with the piano interjecting. Interweaving is mainly avoided, so that although the piano is supportive there is a special independence between the two instruments in this mosaic excursion.

Peter Mark plays the extremely difficult viola part with great flair. The pianist is the well-known composer Thea Musgrave. She performs with full understanding.

Shantih (1969)

☐ Worthington (cello); Stevens (piano) / Avant 1010

Includes a great deal of avant-garde-fashioned antiphony that emphasizes declamatory rhetoric. (No explanation is given in the liner notes for the title.)

Montages (1968)

☐ Montagnana Trio / Avant 1010

Styled romantically atonal, *Montages* is firmed up by the development of the secundal intervallic condition. Freely formed, motivally motivated, the tangible balance of the structure is obtained by textural contrast (open-heavier-thin, in turn), paralleled by rhythmic differences (covering both metered and unmetered plans). The exact plotting of diversity gives compelling order and logic to Applebaum's trio for clarinet, cello, and piano.

The Montagnana Trio performance is also included in an Everest release (3262).

Piano Trio (*Reflections*) (1972)

☐ Fine Arts Trio / Avant 1010

Fragmented fantasy, the gestures contrasted between a violent disjunctiveness and a calmer, constantly recolored pitch containment. Applebaum's trio is in one movement. Its logic is derived from the post-Webern school.

Jean Baptiste Arban (1825-1889)

Instrumental	***Fantaisie* and Variations on *The Carnival of Venice***
Cornet	☐ Schwarz (cornet); Bolcom (piano) / Nonesuch 71298

Don't miss it! It may be good form to belittle this old-fashioned music, but within its genre it is well-nigh perfect. Listeners of today who have no snobbish pretensions will delight in it over and over again.

How Gerard Schwarz plays that horn! And the proper one, at that—no trumpet, but the mellower, rounder-toned cornet. He styles the work's bravura permutations with an artistic soundness of judgment that is simply marvelous. To repeat: Don't miss it!

Enrique Fernández Arbós / *Isaac Albéniz.* See *Albéniz* / Arbós.

Jacob Arcadelt (ca. 1505-1568) / **Franz Liszt (1811-1886)**

Instrumental	*Ave Maria*
Organ	☐ Sebestyen (organ) / Vox SVBX–5329

A sensitively beautiful example of one of Liszt's huge number of transcriptions, arrangements, paraphrases, and fantasies. For the organ some of the composers represented in this genre are Bach, Chopin, Lassus, Nicolai, and Wagner.

The haunting *Chanson* of the Flemish composer is fully respected stylistically as Liszt recolors it over a seven-minute period. It is a small gem.

Bülent Arel (1919-   )

For Violin and Piano (1967)

☐ Raimondi (violin); Miller (piano) / Composers Recordings S-264

Chamber Music

Serial music without academic reecho. Loosened by elimination of metrical control (paced only by metronomic indication in relation to accepted note valuations), the music develops with kaleidoscopic mannerisms. Toward the end there is an improvisational section. This specific extemporization blends with the preceding and succeeding portions, which have improvisational equivalence.

The performers are of major-league caliber, both specializing in the newest music. Their presentation provides special stimulus value to Arel's opus.

Stereo Electronic Music No. 1 (1961)

☐ Columbia MS-6566

Electronic Music

Arel's piece avoids repetition and adopts patchwork to achieve its ten and one-half minutes' length. It also is an example of the parallels that exist between engineered new music and composed old music. The piece contains a certain amount of humor.

Stereo Electronic Music No. 2 (1970)

☐ Finnadar 9010

Mostly heavy and dark consistencies mark Arel's work. Its general plan (described in the unsigned liner notes) is "based on the idea of a very smooth curve reaching two main climactic sections." The developments within the three-part structure are expressively evocative.

Arel's work is also available in the CRI album (268) titled *Columbia-Princeton Electronic Music Center Tenth Anniversary Celebration.*

Anton Arensky (1861-1906)

Variations on a Theme by Tchaikovsky, Op. 35a

☐ English Chamber Orchestra / Somary (conductor) / Vanguard C-10099

String Orchestra

This is the second movement of Arensky's second string quartet in string orchestra enlargement (merely adding double basses without changing the original scoring). Its seven variations and coda total one of the standards in the string orchestra medium.

The trick in playing this work is not to press too hard for dynamism. The styles of each variation are distinctly separated and easily identified. Pressure conducting would deflate the charm of the piece, and fortunately Somary does not attempt to provide it. Barbirolli (on Angel S-36269) does, and the result is much less effective.

Concerto for Piano with Orchestra, Op. 2

☐ Berlin Symphony Orchestra / Littauer (piano) / Faerber (conductor) / Candide 31029

Solo Instrument and Orchestra

Piano

A Chopinesque personality rules for the first two-thirds of the work but with a lesser total of chromatics. The last part is the most Russian. Maria Littauer's playing is sympathetic and comprehensive.

Violin

Violin Concerto in A minor, Op. 54

☐ Orchestra of Radio Luxembourg / Rosand (violin) / de Froment (conductor) / Turnabout 34629

Persuasive Russianisms, minus the attenuation found so often in the pre-Soviet school of composers. While Arensky's opus does not represent momentous music it nicely develops, quasi-symphonically, in its four-in-one movement format, including an engaging waltz portion.

Rosand's is the only recording, and it is beautiful. The richness of tone and scrupulous playing are maintained throughout, and there are no dubious *rubati* and other tainted tricks that our fiddle virtuosi are often prone to offer as ill-advised sources of excitement.

Instrumental

Piano

Barcarolle, Op. 36, No. 11
Impromptu, Op. 25, No. 1

☐ Tarnowsky (piano) / Genesis 1004

Lyricism with a tinge of nationalism. The Impromptu has as much a *barcarolle* contour as the *Barcarolle* itself, whereas the *Barcarolle* tends to shy away from its formal identity and sounds as casually originated as the Impromptu.

Chamber Music

Trio in D minor for Piano, Violin, and Cello, Op. 32

☐ Heifetz (violin); Piatigorsky (cello); Pennario (piano) / RCA LSC–2867

In this trio, the factor of simplicity is more meaningful than the complexities with which composers strive so often and then fail to make contact. The work is highlighted by the slow movement. The somberness that one finds in the Russian swig of *Weltschmerz* is reflected in Arensky's *Elegia,* a tenderly stated, haunting movement.

This performance is strong and incisive. Fortunately, the mournful "Elegy" is presented without any slobbery sentimentality; the string players avoid any undue portamento. That glide-link is absent in Piatigorsky's playing throughout; Heifetz tends to stress it where required, especially in the first movement. Nevertheless, the competition (Littauer-Terebesi-Michel on Candide 31029) is firmly in second place. Terebesi cannot come close to Heifetz's tonal ripeness, let alone match his phrasing. Further, RCA's sound is deeper and fuller than Candide's.

Dominick Argento   *(1927-   )*

Vocal

Voice with Accompaniment

Letters from Composers (1968)

☐ Sutton (tenor); Van (guitar) / Composers Recordings SD–291

Critics have lamented the musical poverty of the English-language vocal repertory, but the poverty has often been due to a carryover from the weak textual material elected or, conversely, the inability of the music to match the pervading strength of the words. No faint soul, Argento has chosen the extremely difficult matter of the musical translation of seven letters. Four of these (by Chopin, Schubert, Puccini, and Debussy) were written to friends; the Mozart text is a communication to his father; Schumann's is a letter to his wife-to-be; and Bach's was written to the Town Council of Leipzig. Certainly it is a tough chore to shape a vocal line for such texts as "Whereas the said fees make up the greater part of our emoluments, a perquisite of this position, and no one has hitherto endeavoured to withhold from us our lawful share." But Argento's project is successful.

The songs are developed with precision and care and provide a restrained virtuosity in their handling. The choice of a guitar rather than a piano was creative strategy at its best, since the selected instrumental thinness permits vocal amplitude.

The performers' expertise never falters in the nearly half-hour length of the cycle. Vern Sutton's diction is splendid. For once every word really registers instead of being smothered in a blend of undifferentiation. Jeffrey Van's guitar back-up shows keen understanding of Argento's score. This is noteworthy music, and just as noteworthy a recording.

To Be Sung upon the Water

☐ Stewart (tenor); Russo (clarinet and bass clarinet); Hassard (piano) / Desto 6443

Voice and Instrumental Ensemble

Argento's eight-part work, set to poems by William Wordsworth, is subtitled: Barcarolles and Nocturnes for High Voice, Piano, and Clarinet (also Bass Clarinet). This represents a rich neo-romantic score in all terms of harmony, meter, rhythm, phrasing, and dynamics. There is more, since the vocal line does not wander through the text. It finds its proper balance and contrast in each song, with recognizable firmly shaped phrases but without any square-cut, stilted construction.

To Be Sung represents one of the most beautiful (and thereby important) song cycles ever produced in America. Those who do not know this composer need not proceed with any caution, since music of such sensitive imagination is rare. The performance is genuine, expressive, and of the highest artistic degree.

Postcard from Morocco

☐ Center Opera of Minnesota / Brandt and Roche (sopranos); Hardy (mezzo-soprano); Marshall and Sutton (tenors); Busse (baritone); Foreman (bass) / Brunelle (conductor) / Desto 7137/8

Opera and Dramatic Music

Given the admitted resistance of our opera companies to mounting new operas, to write one is to live dangerously. Even if a commission is concerned, as in this case, the odds for survival (meaning that the work will be scheduled by other opera houses) are loaded against the composer. Writing in tonal style may appease the audience, but more than that kind of aesthetic courtesy is required to bring success for an opera. The mix of an ingenious conception with dramatic virtuosity must be available. It is offered in Argento's stage work, a divertissement of splendid tunes, smart orchestration, and discriminating humor, set to a masterly text.

The opera describes the revelations of a group of travelers, outlining their fears, dreams, and desires. The climax occurs when each of the characters refuses what the liner notes describe as "the ultimate symbolic self-revelation—the opening of their respective suitcases." Argento's tonalism is never an eclectic jargon, though many listeners will recognize a Kurt Weill element that filters through a section for orchestra alone. This section is a gem of spectacular snideness, including a number of swipes at Wagner by fractured quotation.

Postcard from Morocco was commissioned by The Center Opera Association, with the help of the National Opera Institute, for the Center Opera of Minnesota. The last-named repays the composer with a top-flight performance. The singing is always sensitive and expressive; the orchestra (in total a nonet of clarinet doubling on bass clarinet, saxophone, trombone, piano, percussion, violin, viola, double bass, and guitar) shares dramatic honors and is never a mere backdrop for the vocal action. Yes, one is positive that Argento's captivating conception will enjoy a long life.

Thomas Arne   (1710-1788)

Orchestra

Overture

No. 1 in E minor / No. 2 in A major / No. 3 in G major / No. 4 in F major / No. 5 in D major / No. 6 in B flat major / No. 7 in D major / No. 8 in G minor

☐ Academy of Ancient Music / Hogwood (harpsichord) / Hogwood (conductor) / Oiseau-Lyre DSLO–503

Hogwood and his colleagues provide a harvest of musical goodwill. Three of the overtures (Nos. 3, 7, and 8) were also used as the introductions to stage works. The playing is authentic and is accomplished on authentic instruments. There is a fine-honed, pressed-in suavity that defines the music and argues for its beauties.

Overture No. 4 in F major

☐ English Chamber Orchestra / Hurwitz (conductor) / London STS–15013

A warmly bright performance. The highlight is the joyous Fugue in the second of the three movements.

Solo Instrument and Orchestra

Concerto No. 5 in G minor for Harpsichord and Orchestra

☐ Academy of St. Martin-in-the-Fields / Malcolm (harpsichord) / Marriner (conductor) / Argo ZRG–577

Harpsichord

Fantasia-shaped music. It is played convincingly and with impeccable ensemble effect.

Instrumental

Sonata for Harpsichord

Harpsichord

No. 1 in F major / No. 2 in E minor / No. 3 in G major / No. 4 in D minor / No. 5 in B flat major / No. 6 in G minor / No. 7 in A major / No. 8 in G major

☐ Hogwood (harpsichord) / Oiseau-Lyre DSLO–502

Some clichés but in the majority of instances no weak, stereotyped structuring. Hogwood sensitively explores most of this music. The most memorable are his depictions of the third, fourth, fifth, and final works of the group.

Two types of harpsichord are used. For Nos. 1, 2, 5, and 6 a single-manual instrument is utilized, and a larger-focused instrument covers Nos. 3, 4, 7, and 8. (*Schwann* errs in its indication that only the four odd-numbered Sonatas are included in the release.)

Sonata No. 3 in G major for Harpsichord

☐ Kipnis (harpsichord) / Angel S–3816

If only one of Arne's Sonatas (or "Lessons," as he also called them) will suffice, here is the serving in a brilliant performance. Kipnis plays with incisiveness and makes boldly clear all of Arne's facts and ideas.

Malcolm Arnold   (1921-   )

Orchestra

Four Scottish Dances, Op. 59

☐ London Philharmonic Orchestra / Arnold (conductor) / Everest 3021

Having scored a huge success with his two sets of English Dances, Arnold tried again, this time with a set of Scottish Dances. These have likewise achieved a healthy performance record, and in a version for band (made by John Paynter) have become one of the most popular pieces in the repertory.

Correspondence to native dances is maintained in Arnold's simulations, including the Scotch snap rhythm and the terpsichorean catalogue of strathspey, reel, and fling. An expert performance with excellent sonics.

Symphony No. 3, Op. 63

☐ London Philharmonic Orchestra / Arnold (conductor) / Everest 3021

In terms of layout, Arnold's symphony follows routine intentions. The first movement is a sonata design; then a Scherzo follows, succeeded by Variations and a Rondo derived from three themes. The orchestration is not routine, however. Arnold knows the orchestra, and his scores always exude a vitality that is most stimulating. The only criticism is the use of sequence as the gimmick for attenuation.

A first-rate performance by the Londoners under the composer's direction. (Arnold once played trumpet in the same orchestra.)

Guitar Concerto, Op. 67

☐ Melos Ensemble / Bream (guitar) / Arnold (conductor) / RCA LSC–2487

Solo Instrument and Orchestra

Guitar

Themes for this instrument are generally focused on rhythm, quite often of Spanish cast. Arnold's music is otherwise. He considers the guitar without such creative insularity. The core of the Concerto is the elegiac second movement; its music is detailed by glides and blues substances. While the outer divisions consist of material that does not belie the basic character of guitar language, mere rhythmic patterns and other time-marking methods are absent. Arnold's Guitar Concerto is conservative contemporary music, with a blending of tunes and harmonies that satisfies the ear.

The performance is excellent, covering the neat thematic grace and rhythmic delights of the piece. It is also available in a collection, *Concertos for Guitar and Lute* (RCA CRL3–0997).

Concerto for Two Violins and String Orchestra, Op. 77

Two Violins

☐ Louisville Orchestra / Kling and McHugh (violins) / Mester (conductor) / Louisville 731

Quite serious Arnold, identifiable with his sparkling, sometimes spiky style. A kind of angst hangs over the music. This is even present in the short, final Vivace. However, artistic validity is evident, even if one prefers the joviality and extrovert let-go that marks the methodology by which Malcolm Arnold has made his reputation.

Sonatina for Clarinet and Piano

Chamber Music

☐ Campbell (clarinet); York (piano) / Crystal S–333

The kind of music some call slick, others term jazzy, while this writer considers it to be in the serious lowbrow category. Perky details are found in the first movement, with real humor displayed at its conclusion. There is a strong reminder of cartoon-chase music in the finale. A contrastive dark-pigmented slow movement separates the pair. Good show! And jolly good playing.

Piano Trio in D minor, Op. 54

☐ Lyric Trio / Concert-Disc 234

Motival tactics here. There's a great deal of propulsiveness but all linked by segmented hunks. A carryover of the sectionalism found in film scores (Arnold has written the music for over eighty motion pictures) is reflected in this case.

Quintet for Brass, Op. 73

☐ Berlin Brass Quintet / Crystal S-201

This has become one of the few contemporary classics in the brass chamber music category. Since it's by Arnold it's exuberant and melodic, exhibiting hedonistic toe-tapping style in the outer movements. The first part is hornpipey and peppered with polyphony, and in that portion plus the Finale Arnold treats the brass with the same zip and go used by Ibert and Françaix in their woodwind quintet music. The inner movement—a Chaconne—provides the needed contrastive balance.

Of the two recordings on the market, the Berliners are much smoother in their playing (or have been recorded that way) than the Philip Jones Brass Ensemble on Argo (ZRG-655). There is this to point out, however: The London-based group follows the instrumentation exactly (two trumpets, horn, trombone, and tuba). The Berliners do so four-fifths of the way, utilizing a bass trumpet in place of the horn.

Three Shanties for Wind Quintet (1952)

☐ London Wind Quintet / Argo 5326

A triple serving of good, clean spoofing, as animated as champagne bubbles, as titillating as a striptease. Arnold's clever avoidance of fully quoting any phrase of a sailor's tune is akin to brilliant dabs of conversation heard on the fly.

In the first shanty, after skirting around the contours of *What Will We Do with the Drunken Sailor?*, the use of habanera rhythm is artistic frivolity at its very best. The second piece is hinged on *Blow the Man Down* in a kind of slow motion. A montage of frisky melodic snippets forms the finale. The concluding cadence is perfect for this chamber-music skit.

The Londoners provide a genuineness of re-creation. Fresh-as-a-daisy sound.

Juan Crisóstomo Arriaga (1806-1826)

Chamber Music

String Quartet No. 1 in D minor

String Quartet No. 2 in A major

String Quartet No. 3 in E flat major

Theme and Variations

☐ Phoenix String Quartet / Golden Crest S-4061

Mozartian naturalism with a technical clarity that is always sure. The music deserves attention, but Arriaga does not appear on concert programs, though one recalls that two of the quartets were released by the old Concert Hall Society organization.

The playing here is short of ideal—call it only passable. So is the sound. The labeling is confused.

Claude Arrieu (1903-   )

Chamber Music

Quintet in C

☐ Soni Ventorum Wind Quintet / Crystal S-253

The pert and lighter side of neoclassicism conveyed perfectly in a five-part work. Delightful all the way, especially the swift movements, which have Haydnish bounce and verve.

The playing is also a delight, elegant where it should be, spirited where that temper applies. Splendid sound.

Alexander Arutiunian (1920-)

Concerto in A flat for Trumpet and Orchestra (1950)

☐ Bolshoi Theater Orchestra / Dokschitser (trumpet) / Rozhdestvensky (conductor) / Melodiya/Angel S-40149

Solo Instrument and Orchestra

The enticing, exuberant melodic turns laced with dancelike rhythms that mark Khachaturian's music have their analogue here. Arutiunian's Concerto is advancing into popularity, especially because there are so few trumpet concerti on the market that can find viability in the concert hall.

Trumpet

Arutiunian's composition is cast in one movement, with a large tripartite framework holding it in balance. It includes a cadenza, withheld until just before the conclusion.

The word "brilliant" describes Dokschitser's playing and tone, as well as the recording itself.

Alden Ashforth (1933-)

The Unquiet Heart

☐ UCLA Chamber Ensemble / Beardslee (soprano) / Dare (conductor) / Composers Recordings S-243

Vocal

Voice and Instrumental Ensemble

Ashforth's angular, disjunctively intervaled music has its edges smoothed and dusted with impressionistic instrumentation. Familiarity with the vocal style employed does not dull a full response to his fine invention. The text is by Kenneth Rexroth, taken from his *One Hundred Poems from the Japanese.*

Bethany Beardslee's singing is exceedingly communicative, as is the performance of the instrumental group.

Robert Ashley (1930-)

She Was a Visitor (1967)

☐ Brandeis University Chamber Chorus / Lucier (conductor) / Odyssey 32160156

Choral

Chorus Alone

Ostinato as it has never been practiced. Over the incessant repetition of the words "she was a visitor" by a solo voice (for close to six minutes), Ashley slowly spreads a thick blanket of sound. A unique vocal experience and deliciously accomplished.

Purposeful Lady Slow Afternoon (1968)

☐ Liddell (speaker); Ashley, Lloyd, and Lucier (singers) / Mainstream 5010

Opera and Dramatic Music

What Ashley terms a "solo song" turns out to be a solo narrative of an oral sexual experience. It is delivered with telling traumatic quality by Cynthia Liddell. The narration is punctuated by bell sounds and an electronically manipulated backup group of girls' voices.

Pierre Attaignant   (?-1552)

Instrumental

Lute

Chanson: Destre amoureux

Chanson: Tant que vivray

Dances

☐ Gerwig (lute) / RCA VICS-1362

There are eight dances, all with imaginative subtitles, such as *Pavane: La Rote de rode, Basse danse: "La Roque,"* and *Tordion.* All of the items have the charm and refinement of Renaissance music and Gerwig plays them with quietly elegant gentility. So does Schäffer, in his album *French Lute Music* (Turnabout 34137). However, his selection is smaller: the second *Chanson* listed above and five dances.

Daniel-François-Esprit Auber   (1782-1871)

Orchestra

Overture to *Fra Diavolo*

☐ L'Orchestre de la Suisse Romande / Ansermet (conductor) / London STS-15217

All the ingredients: rhythmic vivacity, a nicely portioned amount of sentiment, and tempo felicity. One can't do more than that for an Auber overture.

Overture to *La Neige*

☐ London Symphony Orchestra / Bonynge (conductor) / London 6744

A totally unfamiliar overture and probably the first time it has enjoyed a recording. Bonynge's exposure of this music adds to his credits for offbeat repertoire, and further credit applies to a fine execution under his direction.

Overture to *Le Domino noir*

☐ Paris Conservatoire Orchestra / Wolff (conductor) / London STS-15021

A rendition that is perfectly adjusted to the stylistic ambience of Auber's dance-framed piece. Wolff knows how to pace music of this type, and proper tempo is three quarters of the way to success. The remaining one quarter is also achieved.

Overture to *Lestocq*

Overture to *Marco Spada*

☐ New Philharmonia Orchestra / Bonynge (conductor) / London 6643

Neither of these pieces are nearly as well known as the overtures to *Crown Diamonds* and *Masaniello,* for example (although, paradoxically, there are no recordings of the latter two in print). But no matter. The *Lestocq* and *Marco Spada* overtures are just as good, as witty, as elegant, and as delightfully orchestrated. Bonynge's account of both is full of verve and precision. His contrastive tempi are exemplary.

Concerto No. 1 in A minor

Solo Instrument and Orchestra

Cello

☐ L'Orchestre de la Suisse Romande / Silberstein (cello) / Bonynge (conductor) / London 6750

Auber never orchestrated this work, the first of a set of four cello concerti. It has been done by Douglas Gamley, who deserves special credit for stylistic adherence in his scoring. The same applies to the rich and understanding projection of the solo part by Jascha Silberstein.

The standard romantic gestures cover the three movements. Conventional perhaps, but the vigor of the romantic tradition is exemplified in Auber's work. As such it offers a worthy aural supply.

Marco Spada

Ballet

☐ London Symphony Orchestra / Bonynge (conductor) / London 6923

A ballet that has long gone from the scene and a ballet that brings no discovery. Still, for rescue of the music and permanent placement on disc one must be grateful to that constant seeker for such material, Richard Bonynge, who provides a clearly direct documentation of the score. The score, not incidentally, is a weave of many of Auber's tunes: an aria from *Fra Diavolo*, a chorus from *La Fiancée*, and bits and pieces from other pieces.

Joseph Anton Auffmann (mid-18th cent.)

Organ Concerto in G major

Solo Instrument and Orchestra

Organ

☐ Stuttgart Soloists / Lehrndorfer (organ) / Turnabout 34244

Decidedly not run-of-the-mill, and a conception of more than ordinary interest. Auffmann's Concerto is pithy, with a *Largo biccato* and an *Allegro moderato* covered in just six minutes. It is the chromaticism focused in the piece that animates the material and strategically powers key points (listen to the final cadence!). Lehrndorfer is to be thanked for uncovering this gem.

Georges Auric (1899-   )

Trio (1938)

Chamber Music

☐ Adelstein (oboe); Listokin (clarinet); Popkin (bassoon) / Golden Crest S-4076

Music typical of the composer—smart but not arrogant, whimsical but not flippant. Always a melodist, Auric remains one in this wind trio. It is performed with elegance as well as exuberance where needed by the three members of the Clarion Wind Quintet.

Five French Chansons

Choral

Chorus Alone

☐ Grenoble University Choir / Giroud (conductor) / Musical Heritage Society MHS-1078

Auric is represented in his *Chansons* with a slightly twentieth-century mirroring of old madrigal style. It turns out to be a bittersweet recognition, linked to the use of fifteenth-century texts. The singing is fairly communicative.

Larry Austin   (1930-   )

Instrumental

Piano

Piano Set in Open Style (1964)

Piano Variations (1960)

☐ Floyd (piano) / Advance S–10

The Variations are free of formal display, there being no thematic tool with which the permutations are carved. But Austin's diffusions are interesting as abstracts.

Contemporary left-wing rhapsodicism means a kind of gun-'em-down writing that is characteristic of the Piano Set. This piece is wide-open music, indeed. Floyd has what it takes to play Austin's difficult works.

Charles Avison   (1709-1770)

String Orchestra

Concerto

In G minor, Op. 6, No. 1 / In B flat major, Op. 6, No. 2 / In D major, Op. 6, No. 6 / In E minor, Op. 6, No. 8 / In D major, Op. 6, No. 9 / In A major, Op. 6, No. 12

☐ Hurwitz Chamber Ensemble / Spinks (harpsichord) / Hurwitz (conductor) / Oiseau-Lyre S–318

A half dozen of the twenty-six concerti Avison produced. Handelian quality. The playing is authoritative, as close to the originals as a reproduction can be today. Modern instruments are used, of course, but there is no doubt as to the documentation or its artistic enforcement.

Concerto No. 13 in D major

☐ English Chamber Orchestra / Hurwitz (conductor) / London STS–15013

A representative example of Avison's orchestral output. Hurwitz paces the work efficiently and with stylistic spirit. The Fugue of the second movement is briskly delightful.

Tzvi Avni   (1927-   )

Electronic Music

Vocalise **(1964)**

☐ Pnina Avni (soprano) / Turnabout 34004

The voice is echoed and overlaid, creating the effect of a small chorus out of a solo line. Otherwise, the ripping and spitting sounds (technical terms would be confusing) equate metrical markers for the content. Avni's background as a free-tonal composer carries over in his quasi-diatonic choices and in the use of ostinato patterns.

Jacob Avshalomov   (1919-   )

Orchestra

Phases of the Great Land **(1958)**

☐ Portland Junior Symphony / Avshalomov (conductor) / Composers Recordings SD–194 (monaural)

The mix in Avshalomov's *Phases* places its creative faith in programmatic planning. It is divided into two parts, each of which covers two sections. The work opens with *The Long Night,* which has impressionistic scanning, while the following *Klondike Fever* touches bases with Ivesian methods, including such defined tunes as *Sweet Betsy from Pike* and *After the Ball Is Over.* The major second portion covers *The Summer Days* (with a sunny harmonic climate) and *Anchorage Aloft* (with majestic, somewhat Coplandesque attractivity).

This is a fine work and unfortunately seems to be heard only in its recorded form. It is worth conductors' attention. The playing of the Portland young people is professionally toned, and with the composer directing, the essay is definitive. Only the recorded sound is a bit below par.

The Taking of T'ung Kuan (1948)

☐ Oslo Philharmonic Orchestra / Buketoff (conductor) / Composers Recordings 117 (monaural)

The title refers to the fall of T'ung Kuan Pass in the year 755, during the An-lu-shan Rebellion in China. Instrumental vitality is the paramount feature in the piece, and its orchestrational resourcefulness is well worth a listener's attention. As a composer, Avshalomov has benefited from his long and successful career as a conductor. This has given him a special insight into the intricacies of orchestral scoring. The proof of this is the virtuosic perceptiveness of *The Taking of T'ung Kuan.* In his conducting, Buketoff follows suit.

Prophecy

Choral

Chorus with Accompaniment

☐ Mid-America Chorale / Matheson (tenor); Maher (soprano); Smith (organ) / Dexter (conductor) / Composers Recordings 191 (monaural)

Prophecy is for chorus, cantor, and organ. The inclusion of a cantor was the result of the original version, composed in 1948, for the Park Avenue Synagogue in New York. Avshalomov revised the work in 1952, which is the edition heard in this fervently recorded performance. The text is from the eleventh and twelfth chapters of Isaiah.

B

Kees van Baaren   (1906-1970)

Variazioni per orchestra (1959)   *Orchestra*

☐ Utrecht Philharmonic Orchestra / Hupperts (conductor) / Donemus Audio-Visual Series DAVS-6101 (monaural: 10-inch disc)

Dodecaphonic order in a miniature encyclopedic survey. Shades of Schoenberg, Webern, Bartók, Blacher, and Stockhausen appear. This musical journey oddly, crazily *works*. It shouldn't, but it does. And one doesn't mind the borrowing and the razzle-dazzle of techniques. It is quite stimulating and enjoyable, this eight and a half minutes of a serial travelogue.

Milton Babbitt   (1916-   )

All Set, for Jazz Ensemble (1957)   *Orchestra*

☐ Contemporary Chamber Ensemble / Weisberg (conductor) / Nonesuch 71303

The instrumentation is certainly jazz-standard: alto and tenor saxophones, trumpet, trombone, bull fiddle, piano, vibes, and percussion. The jazz, however, is implied by rhythmic bounce and swerve, push and shove, and not by precisely recognized patterns. And it's all serial to the last, twelfth tone, and it all works, with charm, with spirit, with delight—remaining vital and stimulating almost twenty-five years after it was composed.

Partitions (1957)   *Instrumental*

☐ Helps (piano) / Composers Recordings S-288   *Piano*

From the rigorous world of serialism. Special attention and coloration applies to the use of registration. (The piece is dedicated to the performer.)

Post-Partitions (1966)

☐ Miller (piano) / New World Records NW-209

A sequel to *Partitions* (see above), which can be performed immediately after the earlier work or by itself. The same twelve-tone row is used in both pieces, but the development processes totally differ. However, *Post-Partitions* likewise deals with registral structuring.

With Robert Miller a definitive performance is assured.

Reflections for Piano and Synthesized Tape (1974)

☐ Miller (piano) / New World Records NW-209

Babbitt's use of tape, whether alone or combined with voice or instruments, is always a model of textural clarity, though cold and abstract from an expressive point of view. This may not provide the warm conclusiveness many may demand, but there is no arguing the intellectual attractiveness of the creative product. Music of this kind bypasses the past but is not dead for the future.

Chamber Music

Composition for Viola and Piano (1950)

☐ Trampler (viola); Bauman (piano) / Composers Recordings 138 (monaural)

Superstrict serial language that covers a music of tensility. The architectural detail, rhythmic plotting, and sonoric structuring all are derived from the basic pitch series.

Sextets for Violin and Piano (1966)

☐ Zukofsky (violin); Kalish (piano) / Desto 6435/37

Sextets inhabits the world of total serialism. This explicit technique covers instrumental use, timbre variances in each of the instruments, registers, articulations, dynamics, and combinations, making a total that clarifies the title. No doubts exist as to the formal virtuosity of this composer. Neither are there any doubts as to the performance virtuosity of Zukofsky and Kalish. For both there is admiration. Whether love will follow, only time will tell.

Composition for Four Instruments (1948)

☐ Wummer (flute); Drucker (clarinet); Marsh (violin); McCall (cello) / Composers Recordings 138 (monaural)

The fundament in Composition is the combination of timbre with texture. This gives expression, overall form, and pitch contour, working hand in hand with the realities of the strict serial musical prosody. The four instruments are used to give weight and density, texture and sonority, color, light, and shade within the fifteen divisions of the whole. This total of fifteen equals the mathematical instrumentational possibilities existent in a work for four different instruments. Each of these possibilities—four solos, six duets, four trios, and one quartet—is singly utilized as a section of the piece, thereby presenting a changing coloristic canvas for the dissemination of the musical text.

To clarify the structural interrelations of a conception as complex as this demands superfine cohesion and equally superfine, sensitive, and understanding musicians. The all-star cast provided by CRI meets all the demands.

String Quartet No. 2 (1952)

☐ Composers Quartet / Nonesuch 71280

Thoroughly developed serial competence is expected in the music of Milton Babbitt. But the lack of fussiness in detailing the operations—the directness, clarity, and textural openness—makes his second quartet a special, highly civilized, creative transaction. It is this totality that is totally convincing. A flow of sound, quite often of high sparkle, makes this quartet not only serially significant but serially beautiful.

For this achievement the performance must be given a great deal of credit. Only the full involvement of the players could realize the transparent textures and musicality inherent in Babbitt's piece (the usual rendition is a cold struggle to keep beats together and play disjunctive pitches in tune). Lumpy, junky performances of advanced music have done more harm to proper understanding than is generally realized. The Composers Quartet has given full justice to Babbitt's creation. They are an outstandingly talented team, and exceedingly few can match them in the playing of music by such composers as Babbitt, Wuorinen, Carter, and others.

String Quartet No. 3 (1970)

☐ Fine Arts Quartet / Turnabout 34515

Like his style or not, there can be no denial of the technical clarity (and honesty), the passionate pursuit of absolute musical creativity minus the slightest resort to sonorous gimcracks, in Babbitt's work. The third quartet, in a single movement, but with flux in pace (derived from inner handling, not specific tempi change) is structured from pitch material that undergoes change but maintains continuity and integrality via inversion, retrograde motion, and retrograde inversion. Simple colorations, such as muted versus unmuted timbre or bowed versus plucked tone, help mark sections.

Indeed, there's a passion at work here that may seem almost ascetic but is as intense as the heated messages or dramatic perorations of certain other composers. For, in Babbitt's case, the logic is similarly heated in its polyphonic concentration, and its dramatic effect is produced by the fully successful working out of its message.

The quartet was commissioned for the Fine Arts team, who gave its premiere in 1970. They have made the work their own, and theirs is an evaluation of the clearest understanding. The artistic merit of the playing cannot be denied.

Phonemena for Soprano and Piano (1970)

Vocal

☐ Webber (soprano); Kuderna (piano) / New World Records NW-209

Voice with Accompaniment

The text consists entirely of the smallest sound units of speech: consonants and vowels. Such a fresh kind of parlando is especially effective, concentrated as it is in a work of five-minute length.

A second version (though actually a half-minute shorter in exact performance span) substitutes a musically identical synthesized tape for the piano part. *See below,* (Phonemena for Soprano and Tape).

Phonemena for Soprano and Tape (1974)

☐ Webber (soprano) / New World Records NW-209

A second version of Phonemena for Soprano and Piano (*see above*), using synthesized tape in place of a piano.

Vision and Prayer (1961)

☐ Beardslee (soprano) / Composers Recordings 268

The text for Babbitt's work for soprano and synthesized accompaniment is by Dylan Thomas. It consists of twelve stanzas, each of the first six beginning with a one-syllable line, followed by the addition of one syllable per line until a maximum of nine is reached;

the reverse then follows until the stanza is completed with a one-syllable line. The second set of six stanzas totally reverses the procedure. There are nine syllables in line 1, eight in line 2, and so on until a one-syllable line is reached; the additive process is then resumed, with each stanza completed by a nine-syllable line. This plan produces diamond shapes for the first six stanzas and pyramidal ones for the second six. Since CRI has included an exact duplication of the text, Thomas's picturization is made clear and is of special aid in hearing the work.

Babbitt has based his structure on Dylan's formation, in terms of speeds, durations, and phrase contours. The technicalia concerned is, indeed, complex but superbly crafted. The voice part begins with speech, progresses into *Sprechstimme* ("speech voice"—speech that is tinged with a singing quality), and is followed by defined singing. The reverse process of the texts is followed in the voice part by concluding the work with *Sprechstimme* and speech. Complete comprehensibility marks the text; it is not fractured, reorganized, or permutated in any way.

The Babbitt-Thomas facts cohere into a fascinating document. Though every particle of the music (and the words, as noted) is rigidly structured, the composition goes beyond its technical ingenuity and has a vivid, dramatic impact.

Electronic Music

Composition for Synthesizer (1963)

☐ Columbia MS-6566

Babbitt is unconcerned here with the discovery of new sonorities. His Composition has been described as "the control and specification of linear and total rhythms, loudness rhythms and relationships, and flexibility of pitch succession." It begins with a very clear "electro-row" (if I may be permitted such coinage), with fairly clear, recognizable permutations.

(Electronic music seems to me to be best heard via recordings in the home, rather than sitting in an auditorium and facing a stage populated only by loudspeakers.)

Ensembles for Synthesizer (1964)

☐ Finnadar 9010

A "classic" in the electronic medium. So much so that it is represented in the recorded catalogue in a duplicate version. This is available on Columbia MS-7051. Of course, thanks to the permanently fixed state of electronic music, no comparison is necessary!

Though the material differs in terms of quality, rhythmic shape, intensity, temporal arrangement, and registral placement, the main effect (not form!) places Ensembles in the world of the scherzo.

Salvador Bacarisse   *(1898-1963)*

Solo Instrument and Orchestra

Guitar

Concerto for Guitar and Orchestra, Op. 72

☐ Orquesta Sinfonica of Spanish Radio–TV / Yepes (guitar) / Alonso (conductor) / Deutsche Grammophon 2530326

There's a touch of nationalism here but the piece is mainly a neoclassic conception. Bacarisse does not seek great luminosity in his work, so the music is rather neutrally colored. Yepes does what he can with the score and provides fine guitar soloism.

Grażyna Bacewicz *(1909-1969)*

Second Sonata for Piano (1953)

Instrumental

Piano

☐ Fierro (piano) / Avant 1012

For the closing Toccata the word is "aggressiveness," but it is tempered with honorable harmoniousness, since Bacewicz followed neoclassic precepts in most of her work. These are aptly displayed in the sonata layout of the opening, the *largo* of the central movement, and the propulsiveness of the closing part. There is no preoccupation with style at the expense of real creativity in this piece. That it has not entered the standard contemporary repertoire shows only that performers' passionate loyalties need total reexamination. A hearing of this piece (well played on this recording) will substantiate that viewpoint.

String Quartet No. 7 (1965)

Chamber Music

☐ Bulgarian Quartet / Musical Heritage Society MHS-1889

Bacewicz completely casts aside her usual neoclassic politenesses in this three-movement work, which is violent and aggressive in tone. The diction is percussive, the instruments snarl, the lines are corrugated. Despite the variety, however, there is structural unity processed from the rolls, snaps, glides, and frictions of the composition.

The Bulgarian team plays this angry music with conviction and total verification.

Musical Heritage Society's release is a remastering of the recording originally released by Harmonia Mundi. It reprints the liner note by Geneviève Darras. Not good. There are four paragraphs of general data concerning contemporary Polish music, one paragraph of extremely flimsy background regarding Bacewicz, and not a single word about the quartet recorded. Even the indication of Bacewicz's birthdate is incorrect.

Carl Philipp Emanuel Bach *(1714-1788)*

Orchestral Symphony

Orchestra

In D major, W. 183, No. 1 / In E flat major, W. 183, No. 2 / In F major, W. 183, No. 3 / In G major, W. 183, No. 4

☐ Little Orchestra of London / Lester (harpsichord) / Jones (conductor) / Nonesuch 71180

Impressive, exciting and colorful music, with contrastive and strategic use of tutti and soli portions. There is a virtuosic conviction to the compositions, and it is fruitfully supplied in these masterful executions. Jones truly gets inside Bach's symphonies, and it will be difficult to rival his marvelously vivid performances.

Bach indicated that his symphonies were "for twelve obbligato parts." This calls for two flutes, two oboes, bassoon, two horns, and the usual five-part string section. Jones's orchestra consists of six each of the violins, four violas, three cellos, and two basses, with harpsichord continuo. A perfect total for these readings, which will be, one is certain, the standard for a long time to come.

Sinfonia No. 2 in B flat major

String Orchestra

☐ Academy of St. Martin-in-the-Fields / Marriner (conductor) / Argo ZRG-577

Vigorous music that avoids squared construction. The playing matches it with its full-scale style.

Wind Ensemble

March

In D major, W. 185, No. 1 / In C major, W. 185, No. 2 / In F major, W. 185, No. 3 / In G major, W. 185, No. 4 / In E flat major, W. 185, No. 5 / In D major, W. 185, No. 6 / In F major, W. 187, No. 1 / In D major, W. 187, No. 2

☐ Netherlands Wind Ensemble / Philips 6599172

No brass or percussion in this small band. Delightful bits, each and every one, played with the sensitivity of a topflight chamber music team.

Solo Instrument and Orchestra

Cello

Concerto in A major for Cello and String Orchestra, W. 172

☐ Paris Opera Orchestra / Bex (cello); Dreyfus (harpsichord) / Boulez (conductor) / CMS/Oryx 23

Though there is a tendency to want to get on with it in the finale, Bex and Boulez are otherwise in phase with C. P. E. Bach's Concerto. The slow movement holds the greatest interest and is played with solid registration of all its elements.

Flute

Concerto in D minor for Flute and Strings, W. 22

☐ Paris Opera Orchestra / Rampal (flute); Dreyfus (harpsichord) / Boulez (conductor) / CMS/Oryx 23

☐ Stuttgart Chamber Orchestra / Nicolet (flute) / Münchinger (conductor) / London 6739

Two performances as different as might be imagined. Neither is *totally* acceptable, though the Boulez is preferable. He plays the work with classic crispness; Münchinger romanticizes. Boulez is a shade too fast in the opening, storms the *presto* gates in the finale; Münchinger is several points too slow in the opening, much closer to acceptable tempo in the concluding part. The vote must be cast, however, and the primary choice is Boulez, whose vigor and stylistic address in the opening cannot be denied, despite the runaway pace of the conclusion. Both conductors shape the slow movement beautifully. Those listeners who can should own both discs.

Rampal has a velvetier tone than Nicolet. Still, Nicolet (who plays a slightly longer cadenza in the slow movement) is his equal in musicianship.

Harpsichord

Concerto in C minor for Harpsichord and Orchestra

☐ Academy of St. Martin-in-the-Fields / Malcolm (harpsichord) / Marriner (conductor) / Argo ZRG–577

No pat formal procedure exists in this case. Recapitulation, for example, is delayed to permit contrastive movements to be presented first, and some cyclic transfer is also utilized.

The balances between solo and accompaniment are perfect, and Malcolm's playing is of marvelous clarity.

Concerto in D minor for Harpsichord and Orchestra, W. 23

☐ Bath Festival Orchestra / Malcolm (harpsichord) / Menuhin (conductor) / Angel S–36336

Excellent playing, with a spirit that shows how much the performers enjoy this music. Malcolm is at his best, and that signifies top-of-the-class harpsichord playing.

Concerto for Oboe, Strings, and Continuo
In B flat major, W. 164 / In E flat major, W. 165

Oboe

☐ English Chamber Orchestra / Holliger (oboe) / Leppard (conductor) / Philips 6500830

The heart of each Concerto lies in the *Largo e mesto* of the B flat work and the *Adagio ma non troppo* of the E flat composition. Both these slow movements are set in a minor key and are displayed in a compelling manner by a master oboist. This does not downgrade the fast-paced music that surrounds the slow movements; it is also projected with style and feeling.

Sonata in G major, W. 139

Instrumental

Harp

☐ Jamet (harp) / Nonesuch 71098

Very cheerful music given a sure-handed and sensitively defined performance, especially in terms of dynamic coloration in the last of the three movements.

Variations on *Folies d'Espagne*

Harpsichord

☐ Malcolm (harpsichord) / Argo ZRG–577

A dozen variations are made here on the well-known tune. Though Corelli's *La folia* set is the most famous, C. P. E. Bach's variational account deserves equal rank, particularly because of his harmonic adventurousness.
George Malcolm's playing is both expert and beautiful.

Sonata for Flute and Harpsichord
No. 1 in B flat major, W. 125 / No. 2 in D major, W. 126 / No. 3 in G major, W. 127 / No. 4 in D major, W. 129 / No. 5 in B flat major, W. 130 / No. 6 in G major, W. 134

Chamber Music

☐ Rampal (flute); Veyron-Lacroix (harpsichord) / Nonesuch 71034

Though not displaying special ingenuity, these sonatas (all in one of three major keys) have a melodic vitality. All are three-movement affairs. All are produced with interpretative sympathy and clarity.

Sonata in E major for Flute and Harpsichord

☐ Wilson (flute); Fuller (harpsichord) / Orion 7283

Different in structure from the six noted above, each of which begins with an Adagio or Largo movement (always the longest part of the work) and ends with a pair of fast-paced movements. In the E major sonata the longest movement is again the initial one, but this time it is an Allegretto, followed by slow and fast divisions. Oddly, however, the time of the E major opus (thirteen minutes) far exceeds that of any of the six Rampal and Veyron-Lacroix play, which average seven minutes in length.

The difference also carries over to tone quality. Wilson's is sweeter and has slightly more body. Fuller's harpsichord is brighter than Veyron-Lacroix's. However, since no recorded competition exists for these compositions, both sides of the creative and interpretative coin are valid.

C. P. E. Bach / Raymond Leppard (1927 -)

Solo Instrument and Orchestra

Four Harpsichords

Concerto in F major for Four Harpsichords and Strings

☐ English Chamber Orchestra / Malcolm, Aveling, Parsons, and Preston (harpsichords) / Leppard (conductor) / London STS–15075

No, C. P. E. Bach did not write any four-harpsichord concertos. This is actually a work for two harpsichords which Leppard adapted and arranged for twice the number of solo instruments. A logical setting it turns out to be. It is given a vivid account by these very choice soloists. A fairly nice recorded balance considering that four harpsichords can certainly produce a tangle of sonority.

Johann Christian Bach   (1735 - 1782)

Orchestra

Overture to *Catone in Utica*

☐ New Philharmonia Orchestra / Leppard (conductor) / Philips 802901

"Overture," yes, but akin to a miniature symphony. Bach's rewarding preface to his second opera contains three movements, the second for strings alone.
The performance is a well-balanced, engaging one.

Sinfonia in D major for Double Orchestra, Op. 18, No. 3

☐ Little Orchestra of London / Jones (conductor) / Nonesuch 71165

Eighteenth-century anticipatory stereo treatment. The first orchestra has two oboes, two horns, one bassoon, and strings; the second orchestra calls for two flutes and strings. The contrast of the groups and echo phrases plus warmth of melody make a work of strong constructional impulse with a resourceful use of color. Jones and his musicians respond nicely.

Sinfonia in E flat major, Op. 9, No. 2

☐ English Chamber Orchestra / Bonynge (conductor) / London 6621

A fantastic neatness of ensemble and dynamic contrast defines the appealing middle movement, marked *Andante con sordini.* This C minor movement is one of the most sensitively shaped of all of Johann Christian Bach's music and the performance is worthy just for it alone. Not to be overlooked, of course, are the other pair of movements, especially the healthy manner in which the finale, marked *Tempo di menuetto,* is portrayed.

Sinfonia in E flat major for Double Orchestra, Op. 18, No. 1

☐ English Chamber Orchestra / Davis (conductor) / Oiseau-Lyre S–317

This is the first of the six symphonies that are included in the Opus 18 total. Of these, there is an exact split of three for orchestra and three for double orchestra. (The other two in the latter category are discussed elsewhere in this section.)
It would be expected that concerto grosso methods are emphasized in the scoring and it is just that principle that is paramount, even at the expense of integral development. No loss, especially with the presence of engaging melodic ideas and their striking interlacements.

The performance is ideal. Not a single detail falls by the wayside, and where energy is demanded it is supplied minus any heavy-textured handicaps. That can't be said for the competing edition (Columbia MS–6180), conducted by Ormandy.

Sinfonia in E major for Double Orchestra, Op. 18, No. 5

☐ English Chamber Orchestra / Hurwitz (conductor) / London STS–15013

The same setup as Bach's Sinfonia in D major, Op. 18, No. 3 (*see above*). Jones has recorded both works with the Little Orchestra of London. However, his pace in the E major Sinfonia is too leisurely, especially in the first movement, which is too much *moderato* and not enough *allegro,* and the same applies to the other two movements. Hurwitz moves along with matters and plays the work two minutes faster. It is certainly preferable.

Sinfonia in G minor, Op. 6, No. 6

☐ Saint Paul Chamber Orchestra / Davies (conductor) / Nonesuch 71323

Logical tempi, balanced chamber playing with all the proper strengths. A delight to the ears.

Concerto in E flat major for Bassoon and Orchestra

Solo Instrument and Orchestra

Bassoon

☐ Württemberg Chamber Orchestra, Heilbronn / Zukerman (bassoon) / Faerber (conductor) / Turnabout 34278

Soloistic realism is present in the first movement, with fast conjunct detail and athletic disjunct data, trills, and keyboardlike activity. Zukerman commands a brilliant technique and breath control and thus produces a most exhilarating event. But come on, Turnabout, who wrote that lengthy cadenza? Probably Zukerman. Its range and style are far removed from J. C. Bach. Although pleasant to hear, its confidences anticipate music written a century later. To a slightly lesser degree these remarks apply to the cadenza of the slow movement.

Sinfonia Concertante in C major for Flute, Oboe, Violin, Cello, and Orchestra

Flute, Oboe, Violin, and Cello

☐ Little Orchestra of London / Galway (flute); Wickens (oboe); Armon (violin); Norman Jones (cello) / Leslie Jones (conductor) / Nonesuch 71165

A beautiful match for Haydn's B flat Sinfonia Concertante, with almost the same soli group (Haydn uses a bassoon instead of a flute). The pliancy of the solo players is of telling finesse. No lesser credit is due the orchestra, which plays with rich tone and impeccable clarity.

Concerto in A major for Harpsichord and String Orchestra

Harpsichord

☐ Academy of St. Martin-in-the-Fields / Malcolm (harpsichord) / Marriner (conductor) / London STS–15172

The scalic urgency of the first movement (for which George Malcolm provides a fitting cadenza) has irresistible appeal. Bach's antiphonally designed figurations and chordal patterns in the finale are just as compelling. The performance is never less than one hundred percent perfect in style, dynamic relationship, tempo, and complete clarity.

Concerto in E flat major for Harpsichord, Two Violins, and Cello, Op. 7, No. 5

☐ Silver (harpsichord); Williams and Keenlyside (violins); Gauntlett (cello) / Nonesuch 71004

The central movement, a melancholic Andante set in the related minor tonality of the home key, is the highlight of this nicely fashioned Concerto. Bach's finale bubbles along and gives the harpsichord full spotlighting.

The playing has fine bravura, and genuine feeling in the slow movement. The performers are four of the five members who comprise the London Harpsichord Ensemble.

Oboe

Concerto in F major for Oboe and Orchestra

☐ English Chamber Orchestra / Holliger (oboe); Pearson (harpsichord) / Leppard (conductor) / Philips 839756

Wind-instrument lyricism is paramount in this exquisitely turned three-part Concerto. Though there are plentiful figurations in the *Rondeau* finale (splendidly made consequential by Heinz Holliger's liquescent playing), the scale of this work is oboistically vocal.

Holliger has provided cadenzas for each movement. Those in the first two are styled right up to par; the last one, short as it is, seems to be overreaching stylistic boundaries. An enchanting rapport exists between soloist and conductor; Leppard handles the orchestral accompaniment with fine range and fluid rhythm.

Chamber Music

Quartet in C major for Two Flutes, Violin, and Cello

☐ Rampal and Eugenia Zukerman (flutes); Pinchas Zukerman (violin); Tunnell (cello) / Columbia M-33310

Playing of the most polished elegance. In the third movement the oft-met tendency to toss off finale tunes that are carefree and uncomplicated at a dizzy pace is avoided. This team plays it as it should: *allegro* and no faster. For this, especially, bravo!

Quartet in D major for Two Flutes, Viola, and Cello

☐ Rampal and Eugenia Zukerman (flutes); Pinchas Zukerman (viola); Tunnell (cello) / Columbia M-33310

Set forth in superb, impeccably clear fashion. The color contrast of paired lower-ranged string instruments with the doubled soprano wind representatives caresses the ear.

Quintet for Flute, Oboe, Violin, Viola, and Cello

In C major, Op. 11, No. 1 / In G major, Op. 11, No. 2 / In F major, Op. 11, No. 3 / In E flat major, Op. 11, No. 4 / In A major, Op. 11, No. 5 / In D major, Op. 11, No. 6

☐ French String Trio / Rampal (flute); Pierlot (oboe) / Musical Heritage Society MHS-706

Magnificently chiseled presentations of these masterly examples of J. C. Bach's work. Every detail is placed in focus, and the balances are ideal. Inspired playing.

Symphony for Winds

No. 1 in E flat major / No. 2 in B flat major / No. 3 in E flat major / No. 4 in B flat major / No. 5 in E flat major / No. 6 in B flat major

☐ London Wind Soloists / Brymer (conductor) / London STS-15079

Not ''symphonies'' in the true sense of the word, since all six works are sextets for two clarinets, two bassoons, and two horns. All are in four movements, with a March replacing the *Menuetto* in half of the pieces. Movement 4 of No. 4 ends with a surprising Cotillion. The playing is delightful and most stylish.

Johann Christoph Friedrich Bach   *(1732-1795)*

Symphony   *Orchestra*

No. 1 in F major / No. 2 in B flat major / No. 3 in D minor / No. 4 in E major / No. 6 in C major / No. 10 in E flat major / No. 20 in B flat major

☐ Cologne Chamber Orchestra / Müller-Brühl (conductor) / Nonesuch 73027

The influence of Italian style permeates all of the music. With the exception of Symphony No. 20 all are in three movements. The latter embraces four movements, the first Allegro having a prefatory Largo. The vigor and rich color of this final symphony make it stand out above all the others.

All the performances are excellent. The Cologne organization has eighteen instrumentalists, a finely balanced total for this type of orchestral fare.

Johann Sebastian Bach   *(1685-1750)*

The Art of Fugue, S. 1080   *Orchestra*

☐ Stuttgart Chamber Orchestra / Münchinger (conductor) / London 2215

The treasure house of Bach's mighty final composition has been an open door to transcribers because he *carefully* did not denote any instrumentation, writing the gigantic opus in open score. Whether the work was to be played or merely studied is immaterial. To deprive ourselves of these polyphonic beauties would be artistic masochism. Accordingly, there have been innumerable versions: for organ, harpsichord, one and two pianos, orchestra, and string quartet (Roy Harris had a hand in this one and this writer recalls with nostalgia the 78-r.p.m. version that the Roth Quartet made). Current recordings even include a setting for saxophone quartet!

From the ten editions considered, three have been chosen in addition to Münchinger's orchestral setting. Two are discussed under *Instrumental: harpsichord* and *Instrumental: organ*, and one under *Bach/Baron: Chamber Music* (p. 80).

It is beyond argument that Bach's *Die Kunst der Fuge* is arranger-proof. Unless it is transcribed by a rank amateur, little harm can be done to it. The validity of the translation depends on how one likes the music served: plain without seasoning or piping hot with curried colors. However, flexibility is damned important, in order fully to project Bach's wonder-working polyphonic apprehensions.

Münchinger's reading is well-proportioned, ideally paced (some conductors slow the tempo to a point of no return: Ristenpart, for example, in his Nonesuch recording). The Stuttgart orchestra consists of five first violins, four second violins, four violas, three cellos, one double bass, and two harpsichordists, plus flute, English horn, and bassoon. Most of the work is assigned to the string section—the winds and solo strings being reserved for the Canons and portions of the Mirror Fugues. The sequence of the twenty-two sections follows the one made by Wolfgang Graeser, who prepared the first orchestral version of Bach's masterpiece.

Brandenburg Concerto

No. 1 in F major, S. 1046 / No. 2 in F major, S. 1047 / No. 3 in G major, S. 1048 / No. 4 in G major, S. 1049 / No. 5 in D major, S. 1050 / No. 6 in B flat major, S. 1051

☐ Jean-François Paillard Chamber Orchestra / Paillard (conductor) / RCA CRL2-5801
☐ English Chamber Orchestra / Somary (conductor) / Vanguard VSD-71208/9

If budgets permit, the most justifiable choices to be made from the many *Brandenburg* Concerti sets available are two: one (as in the RCA edition) using modern instruments except for a harpsichord, and the other (the Vanguard release) using the violino piccolo in the first work, recorders in the fourth concerto, a harpsichord in the penultimate concerto, and a violone and two violas da gamba in the final work.

The playing is magnificent in both instances and even a mite cleaner and more eloquent in the Somary setting. (The same applies to the engineering.) Paillard has some name soloists in his group: Maurice André plays the trumpet in the second concerto and Jean-Pierre Rampal is one of the flutists in the G major (No. 4) composition. For that matter Somary doesn't lack name performers: John Wilbraham is the trumpet soloist and one of the recordists is David Munrow. No matter—the performances given of these six masterful works speak eloquently.

A more conservative viewpoint, but still an excellent conception, is on London 2301, with Karl Münchinger conducting the Stuttgart Chamber Orchestra. Modern instruments are used throughout.

Sinfonia from Cantata No. 12: *Weinen, klagen, sorgen, zagen*

☐ Orchestre de la Suisse Romande / Reversy (oboe) / Ansermet (conductor) / London 6243

Hidden in the many Bach cantatas are exquisite pieces, hardly heard at all except if a whole cantata is performed, and many cantatas aren't. Hearing this beautiful short Sinfonia is evidence of what we miss and also evidence of skillful playing and beautifully phrased oboe sound.

Sonata from Cantata No. 31: *Der Himmel lacht, die Erde jubiliert*

☐ Orchestre de la Suisse Romande / Ansermet (conductor) / London 6243

Ansermet shows how alive contemporary-styled playing of Bach can be. This means vigorous and direct sounds, using a full string section and with no thinning of the content.

Suite

No. 1 in C major, S. 1066 / No. 2 in B minor, S. 1067 / No. 3 in D major, S. 1068 / No. 4 in D major, S. 1069

☐ Academy of St. Martin-in-the-Fields / Bennett (flute) / Marriner (conductor) / Argo ZRG-687/8
☐ Vienna Concentus Musicus / Harnoncourt (conductor) / Telefunken 2635046

Editorial overfastidiousness (yes, it can be thus) has neutralized certain music of past eras. There are editings in both cases but the Thurston Dart hand on the Bach Suites played by the Academy of St. Martin-in-the-Fields organization is a calm and knowing one. The result is practical and sound. The playing is marvelous, controlled yet colorful, with full baroque panache. Bennett does beautifully with the solo flute part in the B minor opus.

The Concentus Musicus edition has been included since it uses authentic original instruments. There is a caveat here. It is one thing to be concerned with honesty, quite another to accept music performed taciturnly. The techniques in Bach's days were not as advanced as those of today, but one thing is certain: the tempi used in the past were not as pace-bound as some (just some, gratefully) of those heard in this recording. Otherwise, no problem. So, if the listener prefers an edition using period instruments, the Harnoncourt disc is the one to obtain.

Suite No. 3 in D major, S. 1068

☐ Orchestre de la Suisse Romande / Ansermet (conductor) / London 6243

Minus *rubati* (Ansermet wouldn't be expected to indulge in *that*) but not minus a light, romantic sound quality. Fine consideration is unmistakably stamped on each of the five movements. The famous Air is in this suite, but, naturally, played as Bach wrote it, and not "on the G string."

Suite No. 2 in B minor, S. 1067

☐ Orchestre de la Suisse Romande / Pépin (flute) / Ansermet (conductor) / London 6243

Music that all flutists worship and then play. Richly textured here, with a finely detailed solo flute performance. André Pépin does not have a Rampal or Galway reputation but he deserves being placed in their class.

Concerto in A minor for Flute, Violin, and Harpsichord, S. 1044

☐ London Strings / Linde (flute); Marriner (violin); Kipnis (harpsichord); Tilney (continuo harpsichord) / Marriner (conductor) / Columbia M4–30540

A superb edition, with a full eloquence to the slow movement and one that doesn't need (as some contend) period instruments to make its fullest effect. The duple swing of the finale is not triggered into an uncomfortable speed. It has breadth and thereby Bach moves with firm security. Kipnis's harpsichord sound is ideal (just listen to his playing in the finale).

Concerto for Harpsichord and Orchestra
No. 1 in D minor, S. 1052 / No. 2 in E major, S. 1053 / No. 3 in D major, S. 1054 / No. 4 in A major, S. 1055 / No. 5 in F minor, S. 1056 / No. 6 in F major, S. 1057 / No. 7 in G minor, S. 1058 / "No. 8" in D minor, S. 1059

☐ London Strings / Kipnis (harpsichord); Tilney (continuo harpsichord) / Marriner (conductor) / Columbia M4–30540

Control of color and nuance, select registration, and a communicative totality make this set the choice of the several integral editions available. Above all, Kipnis's command of structure and detail is a musical power that never falters.

The London Strings is merely another name for the Academy of St. Martin-in-the-Fields. As to the eighth concerto, the quotation marks signify the special matter of a reconstruction made by Kipnis. Beginning with a fragment of only nine measures (the beginning of an adaptation of the first sinfonia from Bach's Cantata No. 35), Kipnis completed the work using two other movements from the same cantata.

Solo Instrument and Orchestra

Flute

Flute, Violin, and Harpsichord

Harpsichord

Concerto No. 1 in D minor for Harpsichord and Orchestra, S. 1052

☐ London Symphony Orchestra / Ashkenazy (piano) / Zinman (conductor) / London 6440

The only version for piano of any of the seven Bach harpsichord concerti that has taste and distinction. It also has the distinct point of view that a piano is a piano and not capable of imitating a harpsichord. So, full-scaled it is and fully appreciated for that viewpoint.

Two Harpsichords

Concerto for Two Harpsichords and Orchestra
No. 1 in C minor, S. 1060 / No. 2 in C major, S. 1061

☐ Collegium Musicum of Paris / Gerlin and Dreyfus (harpsichords) / Douatte (conductor) / Nonesuch 73001

Performances using pianos are not uncommon but the edge is honed down; the contrasts are more favorably and acutely exposed by use of harpsichords. Examples of the former are on disc by the Casadesus team on Odyssey 32160382. Their essays are excellent.

Fine control of Bachian reasoning is conveyed in the Nonesuch release. There is an occasional bass overload in the C major piece, none in the other (which is probably identical with a lost concerto for violin and oboe). However, the general fine quality of the performances makes this slight shortcoming irrelevant.

Concerto No. 3 in C minor for Two Harpsichords and Orchestra, S. 1062

☐ Collegium Musicum of Paris / Gerlin and Verlet (harpsichords) / Douatte (conductor) / Nonesuch 73001

This is Bach's transcription of his famous two-violin concerto, fleshed out a bit and transposed tonally from D minor. The acute investigation of the linear details and the harmonic plans produces music that is not only clean and clear but freshly alive in its pulse.

Three Harpsichords

Concerto for Three Harpsichords and Orchestra
No. 1 in D minor, S. 1063 / No. 2 in C major, S. 1064

☐ Chamber Orchestra of the Sarre / Neumeyer, Berger, and Burr (harpsichords) / Ristenpart (conductor) / Nonesuch 71019
☐ Munich Bach Orchestra / Richter, Pütterer, and Bilgram (harpsichords) / Richter (conductor) / Deutsche Grammophon ARC-2533171

Although performances of these Concertos have been recorded with pianos, both the loss of special timbre and the inflation of line negate acceptance when excellent depictions are available with Bach's exact instrumental color.

No richer Bach playing can be found than in the Nonesuch edition. The beauty, depth, and dignity of the conceptions are significant. The other team plays the pair of Concertos with less color, but their preciseness is ideal. In both issues the engineering is excellent, with total elimination of harpsichordish jingle-jangle.

Four Harpsichords

Concerto in A minor for Four Harpsichords and Orchestra, S. 1065

☐ Chamber Orchestra of the Sarre / Neumeyer, Berger, Burr, and Urbuteit (harpsichords) / Ristenpart (conductor) / Nonesuch 71019

☐ Mainz Chamber Orchestra / Galling, Bilgram, Lehrnodorfer, and Stolze (harpsichords) / Kehr (conductor) / Turnabout 34106

Bach's magnificent translation of a Vivaldi four-violin concerto marks his single work for four harpsichords. Using the mnemonics of 3–2–1, and 2–3–4, one can recall that Bach produced three two-harpsichord concertos, two three-harpsichord concertos, and one four-harpsichord concerto.

The Ristenpart-directed performance is an inspired one. It has sweeping expressive power and dynamic chordal thrust; the music is surcharged with emotion. Of the competitive editions (and there are a good number) the Kehr-conducted essay is most impressive. Nothing is arbitrary and nothing is overloaded in this distinguished edition. Turnabout has also released the performance in a jumbo Bach package under No. 34290/4.

Concerto in D minor for Oboe, Violin, Strings, and Continuo, S. 1060

Oboe and Violin

☐ New Philharmonia Orchestra / Grumiaux (violin); Holliger (oboe); Ledger (harpsichord) / De Waart (conductor) / Philips 6500119

The fraternity of purists will blackball this entry, a reconstruction (as though Bach had so conceived the concerto in the first place) of the C minor double concerto for harpsichords S. 1060 (see under *two harpsichords*). (The key *is* D minor, though *Schwann* in its main heading indicates the C minor tonality in order to stress the original setting.)

But if the purists can't accept arrangements (except those that Bach made himself!) they certainly should accept the sensitive and stylish playing of these soloists, equaled by Edo De Waart's orchestral group. The reconstruction in this case is by one Franz Giegling. Another excellent one was made by Christopher Hogwood, and its recorded performance (on Argo ZRG–820) closely rivals the Philips edition. Though the soloists are little known—Carmel Kaine (violin) and Tess Miller (oboe)—the orchestra is the famous and splendid Academy of St. Martin-in-the-Fields, conducted by Neville Marriner.

Concerto for Violin and Orchestra

Violin

No. 1 in A minor, S. 1041 / No. 2 in E major, S. 1042

☐ English Chamber Orchestra / Zukerman (violin) / Barenboim (conductor) / Columbia M–31072

Without the gush and lush sound of the Russian school of violin playing and its heavy-laden vibrato, these performances follow the current practice that sees Bach through clear, not orange- or crimson-tinted glasses. The sound is candidly clean, with a total apprehension of spaciousness. The orchestra deserves its share of applause.

Concerto in D minor for Two Violins, S. 1043

Two Violins

☐ English Chamber Orchestra / Perlman and Zukerman (violins) / Barenboim (conductor) / Angel S–36841
☐ Royal Philharmonic Orchestra / David and Igor Oistrakh (violins) / Goossens (conductor) / Deutsche Grammophon 138820

Extraordinary teamwork from Perlman, Zukerman, and Barenboim, all three being far more than professional colleagues. It shows in the performance rapport. The nuances are splendid; the give-and-take by the violinists is well-nigh perfect.

With the Oistrakhs there is an even closer relationship, naturally, and again it pays off in the playing, though there is greater difference in timbre coloration. But that's good since the recordings I've heard of overdubbing by one violinist, resulting in no difference in the two parts, makes the work dull and repetitive. The D.G. 138820 album includes other Bach music. On Deutsche Grammophon 138714 the Bach "double" concerto is coupled with music by Beethoven and Vivaldi.

Three Violins

Concerto in D major for Three Violins and Orchestra

☐ Chamber Orchestra of the Sarre / Hendel, Schlupp, and Bünte (violins) / Ristenpart (conductor) / Nonesuch 71057

Don't try to research this one. It does not officially belong to Bach literature but is a reconstruction by Rudolf Baumgartner of a lost Bach work, which he based on Bach's three-harpsichord concerto in C (see under *three harpsichords*). Baumgartner has produced a conceptual beauty and for that reason it's worth having, authentic or not. The playing is also beautiful, and that's another reason to own this disc.

Instrumental

Suite for Unaccompanied Cello

Cello

No. 1 in G major, S. 1007 / No. 2 in D minor, S. 1008 / No. 3 in C major, S. 1009 / No. 4 in E flat major, S. 1010 / No. 5 in C minor, S. 1011 / No. 6 in D major, S. 1012

☐ Starker (cello) / Mercury 77002

Bach is here considered as music to be played with expressiveness and formal positiveness rather than dissected in the name (an unholy one!) of "correct" Bach style (which is?). Warm tone and a sensitive use of vibrato to stimulate a slightly higher temperature are applied; the rhythmic plan is not fussed with nor is it academically straight-laced. There is no romanticizing, however, in the sense that phrases become distorted, rubatoed, and discolored (which has to do with disregard for a composer's individual style—something quite different from the arguments about what is correct Bach style).

Clavichord

French Suite

No. 1 in D minor, S. 812 / No. 2 in C minor, S. 813 / No. 3 in B minor, S. 814 / No. 4 in E flat major, S. 815 / No. 5 in G major, S. 816 / No. 6 in E major, S. 817

☐ Dart (clavichord) / Oiseau-Lyre 60039

A learned survey but far from dull. Dart has probed this music and it shows in superior playing that has personality in its pacing, interlining of the material, and phrasing. No repeats are taken, so the issue fits on one disc.

A close competitor is Leonhardt's harpsichord edition on ABC (AX-67036/2). Absolutely no competition comes from Gould's piano edition (the first four suites on Columbia M-32347, the last pair on Columbia M-32853). He displays personality, but of the kind that a listener needs commendable courage to accept. Truly this performance is so mannered that it amounts to a Bach-Gould "special edition." For absolutely correct Bach, Dreyfus is available (Deutsche Grammophon ARC-2533138/9), but certainly there is more joy in the Allemandes, Courantes, Gavottes, and Minuets contained in these works than is revealed by the coldly proper way in which she presents them.

Flute

Partita in A minor, S. 1013

☐ Rampal (flute) / RCA CRL3-5820

All four movements—an Allemande, a Courante, a *Sarabande*, and a *Bourrée anglaise*—are dances. The breath control that Rampal displays makes the first movement miraculously seamless. Such virtuosic success pertains to the other parts of the work in terms of the registral changes in the second movement and the articulative responsibilities of the finale. There's robust flute sound as well.

Fugue in A minor, S. 1000   *Guitar*

Prelude, Fugue, and Allegro in E flat major, S. 998

Prelude in C minor, S. 999

Suite No. 1 in E minor, S. 996

Suite No. 2 in C minor, S. 997

Suite No. 3 in A minor, S. 995

Suite No. 4 in E major, S. 1006a

☐ Williams (guitar) / Columbia M2–33510

Compare these titles with Gerwig's lute music program (see under *lute*), since one of these works is duplicated there and two are partially duplicated by excerpting.

Williams's playing, as usual with this artist, is coloristically detailed and musically shaped.

The Art of Fugue, S. 1080   *Harpsichord*

☐ Leonhardt (harpsichord) / Vanguard HM–18/19E (monaural)

(For a discussion of this work, see under *Orchestra*.)

Although the intensity of the music is subdued when performed on the harpsichord, Leonhardt's fluid playing is extremely fitting. There are some doublings that can be argued, but not the performance style.

Long note-lengths are, of course, out of the question on the harpsichord and this does interfere slightly with a totally meticulous edition, but no matter—this is stunning playing and the monaural recording has little effect on the sound quality.

Chromatic Fantasy and Fugue in D minor, S. 903

☐ Kipnis (harpsichord) / Angel S–36055

Kipnis's playing is superfine, styled to perfection, of golden sound, of instant response to every phrase and nuance. No harpsichordish twang and overcharge, simply healthy proper timbre. A matchless harpsichord recording. If piano is preferred there is Richter's solid performance, on Deutsche Grammophon 2530035.

English Suite

No. 1 in A major, S. 806 / No. 2 in A minor, S. 807 / No. 3 in G minor, S. 808 / No. 4 in F major, S. 809 / No. 5 in E minor, S. 810 / No. 6 in D minor, S. 811

☐ Galling (harpsichord) / Vox SVBX–5438

A nice quality pertains to Martin Galling's conceptions. One would have looked forward to Kipnis's performances of the entire set, since his playing of the second suite (on Columbia M–30231) is exceptional. For the time being we must be satisfied with a single such example.

Goldberg Variations, S. 988

☐ Malcolm (harpsichord) / Oiseau-Lyre S–261/2

A bountiful amount of color is found in Malcolm's performance of this subtly colorful set of thirty variations. This may mean a little more subjectivity than found in Galling's edition (Turnabout 34015), but it does not flaw Bach's fantastically varied structures. It certainly is miles ahead of the stolid viewpoint of Leonhardt (Telefunken 641198)—which is absolutely dead-on but absolutely deadly.

(For a piano version, see under *piano*.)

Italian Concerto in F major, S. 971

☐ Kipnis (harpsichord) / Columbia M–30231

Kipnis takes advantage of instrumental coloring but with musicianly and artistic taste. There is splendid effect from his interpretative insight. Indeed, this is great Bach playing. (For an edition of this work on piano; see under *piano*.)

Partita

No. 2 in C minor, S. 826 / No. 6 in E minor, S. 830

☐ Fuller (harpsichord) / Nonesuch 71176

Punchy when it should be (the Toccata in No. 6), solid and intense when it is demanded (the Sinfonia in No. 2), and so it goes for all the phrases, nuances, and objectives of these works. Fuller's command and confidence are in the superior category.

Six Concertos After Vivaldi

☐ Sebestyen (harpsichord) / Turnabout 34287

Bach's second look at original works by Vivaldi, Telemann, Marcello, one Duke Johann Ernst von Sachsen-Weimar, and others resulted in some sixteen concerti for solo clavier. Such evaluation and creative reconsideration resulted in bold and imaginative writing, with a conceptual viewpoint that is stimulating.

The six concerti based on Vivaldi materials are certainly the best. (A few others are available in responsible performances by Kenneth Gilbert on Orion 7156.) Janos Sebestyen's playing is clear and sound, neatly conceived in dynamic strengths.

Two-Part Inventions, S. 772–S. 786

No. 1 in C major / No. 2 in C minor / No. 3 in D major / No. 4 in D minor / No. 5 in E flat major / No. 6 in E major / No. 7 in E minor / No. 8 in F major / No. 9 in F minor / No. 10 in G major / No. 11 in G minor / No. 12 in A major / No. 13 in A minor / No. 14 in B flat major / No. 15 in B minor

Three-Part Inventions, S. 787–S. 801
(*Same total and key sequence as above*)

☐ Malcolm (harpsichord) / Nonesuch 71144

Malcolm takes a firm yet light approach to these famous sets and refuses to be didactically overserious. This registers splendidly.

If you wish piano versions by Gould they are available on Columbia MS-6622, and with the Partitas on Columbia D3S-754. I prefer in all ways the positiveness of Malcolm, coloristically and interpretively.

The Well-Tempered Clavier (Books I and II), S. 846-S. 893

☐ Landowska (harpsichord) / RCA VCM-6203/4 (monaural)

Although Bach's famous "48" needs no technical explanation, it would be difficult to find another work that would match the number of interpretative explanations that have been offered on its behalf. These include making Bach sound like a dull, pedantic bore; overzealousness in regard to the choice of stops and couplings on the part of harpsichordists; manifold matters of ornamentation, and the proper defining of trills.

The most outstanding and substantial performance remains Landowska's. She has provided a standard that is yet to be surpassed. (The closest is Ralph Kirkpatrick's recording of the first twenty-four preludes and fugues on Deutsche Grammophon 2707015.) Landowska's phrasing reveals every linear point of the music; her rhythmic scanning is never sticky or metronomic, always moving within the pulse—the music sings out and has a flowing naturalness. And her ornamentational response cannot be questioned.

There is no piano version that is not flawed. Gould (Columbia D3S-733 for Book I and Columbia D3M-31525 for Book II) is eccentric, turning in a masterful performance of one piece and proceeding to be unduly grim and ponderous in the next one. Richter's playing (on Melodiya/Angel S-4119 for Book I and Melodiya/Angel S-4120 for Book II) suffers from unordered balances and exceedingly odd ideas as to ornamentation. If you want the "48," choose Landowska and you will obtain performances as close to definitive as you will probably ever hear.

Allemande and Bourrée from Suite in E minor, S. 996   *Lute*
Fugue in G minor, S. 1000
Loure, Gavotte, *Menuett* I and II, and Gigue from Suite in E major, S. 1006a
Prelude in C minor, S. 999
Suite in A major, S. 1007

☐ Gerwig (lute) / Nonesuch 71137

Recordings of Bach "lute" music have been made using a lute in some cases and a guitar in others (see under *guitar*). The matter of Bach's lute music is completely confused and the instrumental authenticity of much of the material recorded for the lute or transcribed for the guitar can be argued.

Thus the Fugue is a lute version of a movement from the G minor violin sonata, and the *Loure*, etc., is a lute setting of material from one of the solo violin partitas. Only the Suite is acknowledged to be a direct transcription. It was made from one of the cello suites by the soloist.

In any event, Bach may actually have intended some of this music to be played on the lute. Regardless, it is here for those who wish to enjoy excellent performances by Walter Gerwig.

The Art of Fugue, S. 1080   *Organ*

☐ Walcha (organ) / Deutsche Grammophon ARC-2708002

(For a discussion of this work, see under *Orchestra*.)

Bach's work comes through very nicely on organ; the linear disposition is very clear in this instance and the presentation is musically intelligent. The last is due to an absence of registrational fancies that would mar the polyphonic document.

Canonic Variations on *Vom Himmel hoch,* S. 769

☐ Rogg (organ) / CMS/Oryx 1003

More clarity of texture and material are shown in Rogg's playing than in the other editions that were reviewed. In variations characterized by imitative processes the matter is crucial.

Concerto

In A minor (After Vivaldi), S. 593 / In C major, S. 595 / In D minor (After Vivaldi), S. 596 / In G major, S. 592

☐ Kraft (organ) / Vox SVBX–5443

Performances of tight discourse. The structural details become much more clearly outlined when the dynamic plane is not sent on a zig-zag course, as so often occurs with organists when they play Bach. The neutrality of Kraft's performance is not an artistic truce between musical virtue and vice, but is clearly the mark of a musician who trusts Bach.

The other two concerti Bach wrote for the organ are split in various recorded editions: one here, two there, etc. Those noted here are the best and the most representative, particularly the pair of Vivaldi transfers. Great sound.

Fantasia and Fugue in G minor, S. 542

☐ Richter (organ) / London 6173

A thoroughly sound success, with lucid articulation, clear pedaling, and admirable phrasing. The imagery in the Fantasia is splendid. The organ used is that of Geneva's Victoria Hall.

Orgelbüchlein: Chorale Preludes Nos. 1-23, S. 599-S. 621

☐ Heiller (organ) / Vanguard C–10026

Bach's forty-six chorale settings (forty-five chorales are used, the thirty-fifth of the set existing in two versions: *see below*) embrace the various aspects of the church year: Advent (Nos. 1–4), Christmas (Nos. 5–14), Easter (Nos. 27–32), Trinity Sunday (Nos. 34–35), and so on.

The imagery of these works is splendidly portrayed. Anton Heiller's supreme expertise and musicianship make this an authoritative and admirable release.

Orgelbüchlein: Chorale Preludes Nos. 24-45, S. 622-S. 644

☐ Heiller (organ) / Vanguard C–10027

(See above for commentary.)

Passacaglia and Fugue in C minor, S. 582

☐ Fox (organ) / RCA ARL1-0477

Don't be misled by Virgil Fox. Yes, he's a super showman and the organist fraternity frowns deeply on his hamming, but it wows them all the time. He can play the organ with the best of them. Here is proof. This is a vivid, spectacular, yet fully natural artistic performance. It's the way one should hear this masterpiece in its original state.

Pastorale in F major, S. 590

☐ Rogg (organ) / CMS/Oryx 1002

Finely crafted playing and finely selected registration make this a choice performance.

Prelude and Fugue (*St. Anne*) in E flat major, S. 552

☐ Biggs (organ) / Columbia MS-6748

Warmly incisive playing, defined by rich contrasts. Biggs's rendition is also available on Columbia D3M-33724.

Prelude and Fugue in E minor, S. 548

☐ Richter (organ) / London 6173

A strong and possessing performance. The fugue is the one known as the *Wedge*, due to its subject consisting of alternate sounds in a rocking style which then expand step by step. (It is also known as the *Scissors* Fugue.)

Six *Schübler* Chorale Settings, S. 645-S. 650

☐ Kraft (organ) / Vox SVBX-5445

These were published by J. G. Schübler in 1746, hence the title. Five are transcriptions Bach made from his cantatas.

Nothing heavy here; the intertwinements, overlays, and inlays relating to the chorales are always defined with faultless clarity; the registration is modest and fitting. Kraft shows imaginative playing in this set of pieces.

Toccata, Adagio, and Fugue in C major, S. 564

Toccata and Fugue in D minor, S. 565

Toccata and Fugue (*Dorian*) in D minor, S. 538

Toccata and Fugue in F major, S. 540

☐ Biggs (organ) / Columbia M-32933

One never forgets the greatness of the Toccata and Fugue in D minor, S. 565, or the C major opus. However, it is easy, between hearings, to forget the greatness of the other two pieces listed. The clarity of thought, tenacity of musical purpose, and symmetry of form are inspirational.

Biggs's accuracy with these works goes beyond the notes and color registration. The music is played with dramatic flexibility and with re-creative inspiration that adds to Bach's initial inspiration.

Plenty of other Columbia packagings include these performances. The F major piece is also on MS-6748; the *Dorian* opus is found on M2S-697 and MG-31207. The first title is repeated in two other albums: MS-6261 and D3M-33724. As for the D minor piece, the following albums contain Biggs's performance: MS-6261, M-31840, D3M-33724, MS-7269, MGP-13, KM-30648, and MG-31207.

(For those interested, Biggs has recorded this D minor opus on the harpsichord. It is in a Bach program, on Columbia MS-6804.)

Trio Sonata

No. 1 in E flat major, S. 525 / No. 2 in C minor, S. 526 / No. 3 in D minor, S. 527 / No. 4 in E minor, S. 528 / No. 5 in C major, S. 529 / No. 6 in G major, S. 530

☐ Chapuis (organ) / Telefunken 2635076

There are several performance versions of this work, in addition to the one on the organ. E. Power Biggs has recorded the set on the pedal harpsichord (see under *pedal harpsichord*), and there are versions for lute and harpsichord as well as for viola and harpsichord. Complete sets as well as a considerable number of excerpts are available; e.g., Biggs (on the organ this time) has done Nos. 1 and 5 (on Columbia M–32791).

Fine registration is provided by Chapuis, even though some may find it somewhat restricted. But no matter, the treatment is always imaginative.

Pedal Harpsichord

Trio Sonata

No. 1 in E flat major, S. 525 / No. 2 in C minor, S. 526 / No. 3 in D minor, S. 527 / No. 4 in E minor, S. 528 / No. 5 in C major, S. 529 / No. 6 in G major, S. 530

☐ Biggs (pedal harpsichord) / Columbia M2S–764

Since Bach's manuscript indicated "Sonatas for Two Keyboards and Pedal," the music is certified by performance on either organ (see under *organ*) or pedal harpsichord—a choice which offers the contrast of thinner tone widths versus organlike bass sonority.

In this particular recording, all the necessities are met with commendable musicianship. Biggs was always a decorous organist, and these readings provide clear documentation even if the colors are somewhat subdued.

Piano

Fantasia in C minor, S. 906

☐ de Larrocha (piano) / London 6748

This is doubtless the favorite among the several Fantasias Bach wrote. The clarity of Alicia de Larrocha's rendition is only one part of the total fidelity that she brings to the letter and spirit of the score. The transfer to the piano of Bach's harpsichord writing doesn't bother this critic, but if it does others then they should opt for Valenti's version on Columbia MS–6516.

Goldberg Variations, S. 988

☐ Peter Serkin (piano) / RCA LSC–2851

Less refinement for this work is found when played on the piano, but if one wishes that timbre this is a key performance, one that is totally sensitive, beautifully shaped and polished in every measure of the score. (For the harpsichord version see under *harpsichord*.)

Italian Concerto in F major, S. 971

☐ de Larrocha (piano) / London 6748

Alicia de Larrocha's playing is cohesive and sensitively balanced. She has the sense to play the Concerto as music for the piano and does not attempt to imitate a harpsichord. (For a recording of this work on the harpsichord, see under *harpsichord*.)

Toccata

In D major, S. 912 / In D minor, S. 913 / In F sharp minor, S. 910

☐ Gould (piano) / Columbia M–35144

Good, straightforward performances, with special attention to linear detail, touch, and accent. Certainly worthwhile.

Partita No. 2 in D minor for Solo Violin, S. 1004
Sonata No. 3 in C major for Solo Violin, S. 1006

Violin

☐ Chung (violin) / London 6940

Beautiful presentations, even if there is one caveat to mention—some unnecessarily romantic treatment—but in all such instances the objectives in view are very clear. Chung portrays the musical sense in every particular and it is this remarkable lucidity that makes her performances quite special. However, to repeat: only to be considered if a listener doesn't mind fiddlistic straying from Bachian straight-going.

Sonata for Solo Violin
No. 1 in G minor, S. 1001 / No. 2 in A minor, S. 1003 / No. 3 in C major, S. 1006
Partita for Solo Violin
No. 1 in B minor, S. 1002 / No. 2 in D minor, S. 1004 / No. 3 in E major, S. 1005

☐ Szeryng (violin) / Deutsche Grammophon 2709028
☐ Milstein (violin) / Deutsche Grammophon 2709047

There is a great variety of Bachian behavior in the recorded editions of these six monumental conceptions. Though performance diversity is common to all musical works, in the Bach *Sonaten und Partiten* such artistic advantages must be controlled and measure up to certain criteria. Romantic *rubato* disturbs the perfect structures of these compositions; undue speeds are a threat to harmonic clarity rather than a promise of success; and the polyphony depicted by the single violin must be rigidly controlled without impeding the linear flow.

One cannot fault either Szeryng or Milstein in regard to any of these particulars. There is profound musicality and great violin playing on the part of both. There are differences, naturally. Szeryng is warmer and displays more inner passion; Milstein's dynamism is more elegant. Both engage the ear with Bachian soundness and perfect stresses and phrasings. Many of the agogic accents within the lines Szeryng obtains by finger accentuation on the string, while Milstein tends to reflect these by direct bowing coloration.

(Szeryng previously recorded the entire set in monaural form, on Odyssey 32360013.)

Sonata No. 1 in G minor for Solo Violin, S. 1001

☐ Steinhardt (violin) / Sheffield S–7

Steinhardt recorded this two years after he had organized the Guarnieri String Quartet. He plays with profound insight and musicianship. Cohesiveness and fine tone mark his performance.

Sonata for Flute and Harpsichord
In A major, S. 1032 / In B minor, S. 1030 / In E flat major, S. 1031 / In G minor, S. 1020

Chamber Music

☐ Rampal (flute); Veyron-Lacroix (harpsichord) / RCA CRL3–5820

Rampal and his colleague show the way to play these Bach works: pointed articulation, which makes for eloquent pitch movement; the most relevant phrasing, which provides persuasive structuring; and firm and forthright ensemble. The ear is beguiled.

Sonata for Viola da Gamba and Harpsichord
No. 1 in G major, S. 1027 / No. 2 in D major, S. 1028 / No. 3 in G minor, S. 1029

☐ Heinitz (viola da gamba); Hamilton (harpsichord) / Delos 15341

Rarely heard in the concert hall in the original instrumental color but rather on the cello (various recordings are available with such substitution).

Bachian sense is in first place in these performances. And this means that the playing is pointed toward exposing the music with clarity, minus any mannerisms, minus any tricky conceptions of tempo, spiked phrases, overcolored dynamics, and the like. Thus the ingress of contrapuntalism is succinct.

Sonata for Violin and Harpsichord
No. 1 in B minor, S. 1014 / No. 2 in A major, S. 1015 / No. 3 in E major, S.1016 / No. 4 in C minor, S. 1017 / No. 5 in F minor, S. 1018 / No. 6 in G major, S. 1019

☐ Buswell IV (violin); Valenti (harpsichord) / Vanguard C–10080/1
☐ Melkus (violin); Dreyfus (harpsichord) / Deutsche Grammophon ARC–2708032

Either set will provide sensitive and penetrating Bach interpretations of the highest order. Neither violinist pushes his tone, withal retaining full power in the instrument's total homophonic role (except in two isolated instances within the total twenty-five movements). The harpsichordists display a sensitivity in phrasing and an articulative clarity that is a joy, especially in comparison to the pedantic coverage found in some of the other sets that are on the market.

In both releases the resonance is perfectly adjusted and details a splendid balance between the instruments. This negates a further fault to be heard in other editions—that of dry acoustics that deaden the aliveness of Bach's music.

Partita in C minor for Flute and Continuo, S. 987
Sonata in C major for Flute and Continuo, S. 1033
Sonata in E major for Flute and Continuo, S. 1035
Sonata in E minor for Flute and Continuo, S. 1034

☐ Rampal (flute); Veyron-Lacroix (harpsichord); Savall (viola da gamba) / RCA CRL3–5820

All the merits described for the performances of the Sonatas for Flute and Harpsichord (*see above*) are maintained in the case of these four works. The continuo is precise yet flexible. Warm sound.

Sonata in G major for Flute, Violin, and Continuo, S. 1038

☐ Rampal (flute); Gendre (violin); Veyron-Lacroix (harpsichord); Savall (viola da gamba) / RCA CRL3–5820

This Sonata is mainly enticing for its finale, a *Fugue alla breve* (in presto speed) that has an extremely concentrated subject of three pitches: G down a half step to F sharp and back again to G. But the linear workout is, of course, sharply focused and provides a vivid polyphonic traversal.

Rampal and his colleagues offer a finely disciplined presentation. There are no overbearing mannerisms—the music goes forward clearly, though the flute is slightly favored in terms of balance.

Since *Schwann* lists this work as two different compositions (as titled above and as the third of four Trio Sonatas) it is important to discuss the duplicated edition. It is performed by the London Harpsichord Ensemble on Nonesuch 71004, with slightly different instrumentation—a cello supports the harpsichord as the continuo. The Londoners execute the *Fugue alla breve* neatly. In the preceding Largo-Vivace-Adagio sequence they do not reach any particular high point. Soundwise, the RCA publication is far superior.

Sonata in G major for Two Flutes and Continuo, S. 1039

☐ Rampal and Marion (flutes); Veyron-Lacroix (harpsichord); Savall (viola da gamba) / RCA CRL3–5820

RCA's liner-note writer, Carl de Nys, rightly indicates that this composition exists in two other versions (one of these is for viola da gamba and harpsichord, the other is for a keyboard instrument with pedals). However, he terms the setting under review as "rather primitive." I cannot agree in any way with this description. Each of the four movements (in a slow-fast-slow-fast sequence) is a Bachian delight. The third one, in *adagio e piano*, concentrates in its eighteen measures a polyphonic intimacy which provides an aural thrill, while the concluding *presto* presents hale and hearty music in fugal style. If this be primitive, let's have more of it.

All of this is heard with fine-grained and elegant playing, impeccably balanced. The recorded quality is rich and alive, matching the beauty of the performance.

The Notebook for Anna Magdalena (excerpts)

☐ Tölzer Boys' Choir / Ameling (soprano); Linde (baritone); Leonhardt (harpsichord); Koch (viola da gamba); May (cello); Ewerhart (positive organ) / RCA VICS–1317

Some of the delights from the musical notebook that Bach compiled for the pleasure of his family. Included are dances, songs, a chorale prelude, and so on—even a Couperin piece. All nineteen of the excerpts are simply and beautifully presented in this sampler.

Motet: *Ich lasse Dich nicht, Du segnest mich denn,* S. Anh. 159

☐ Regensburg Cathedral Choir and Capella Academica of Vienna / Schneidt (conductor) / Deutsche Grammophon ARC–2708031

There has been some question as to the authenticity of this pleasing motet for double chorus. Worthy of credit, however, to J. S. B.

Sacred Part Songs from Schemelli's *Musikalisches Gesangbuch*

Breath of God, Life Giving
God Liveth Still
It Is Finished
Jesus Is This Dark World's Light
Lord, Pour Not Thy Vengeance on Me
Now Is the Mournful Time
O Jesu So Meek, O Jesu So Kind

☐ Choir of King's College, Cambridge / Willcocks (conductor) / Argo 5234

A seven-set group of lovely hymnodic choral pieces from the sixty-nine numbers Bach

Vocal

Voice and Instrumental Ensemble

Choral

Chorus Alone

helped prepare for Georg Christian Schemelli's *Gesangbuch.* Since similarity is rather constant, one record side is a sufficient sampling from the collection. The songs are sung with devotional artistry.

Chorus with Accompaniment

Motet: *Fürchte dich nicht, Ich bin bei dir,* S. 228

☐ Louis Halsey Singers / Lumsden (organ) / Halsey (conductor) / Oiseau-Lyre SOL–340/1

The Halsey group sings this work for two antiphonal four-part choirs with a fully articulated projection as well as a textural clarity that meets all requirements. The use of the organ is a great aid in regard to the latter.

Motet: *Lobet den Herrn, alle Heiden,* S. 230

☐ Louis Halsey Singers / Lumsden (organ) / Halsey (conductor) / Oiseau-Lyre SOL–340/1

A four-part choral work that *Grove's Dictionary of Music and Musicians* lists as a psalm, because the text is Psalm 117. A motet it is, however.

The performance is fine; the final section is especially effective.

Motet: *Sei Lob und Preis mit Ehren,* S. 231

Motet: *Singet dem Herrn ein neues Lied,* S. 225

☐ Louis Halsey Singers / Lumsden (organ) / Halsey (conductor) / Oiseau-Lyre SOL–340/1

Sei Lob und Preis appears as a chorale with a different text in Bach's twenty-eighth cantata. The high-pitched inner voices are special to the work and covered nicely by Halsey's singers.

The brilliant writing in the other motet produces a majestic conception that is fulfilled in the performance. With the aid of the organ continuo the intonation is never less than ideal, something otherwise quite difficult to achieve considering Bach's complex polyphonic writing.

Chorus and Instrumental Ensemble

Motet: *Der Geist hilft unsrer Schwachheit auf,* S. 226

☐ Norddeutscher Singkreis / Koch and Beckedorf (cellos); Lippert (contrabass); Siedel (positive organ) / Wolters (conductor) / Nonesuch 71060

It is now generally agreed that Bach's a cappella compositions were performed in his own church with instrumental support. The variety that has been used in the available recordings includes the string-organ combination of this reading, organ continuo in many instances, strings and woodwinds in a Deutsche Grammophon release (ARC–198401), etcetera.

The effectiveness of this superb performance cannot be overstressed. It has a richness and a keen balance that none of the competitive editions can match.

Motet: *Jesu, meine Freude,* S. 227

☐ Norddeutscher Singkreis / Koch (cello); Lippert (contrabass); Zacher (positive organ) / Wolters (conductor) / Nonesuch 71060

There are as many as six other editions of this intimately expressive eleven-part masterpiece—two as single Bach motet releases and four contained in collections of the motets. None is as clear, as well focused, and as balanced as the Wolters version. The closest competition would be that given by the Louis Halsey Singers with organ continuo (on Oiseau-Lyre SOL 340/1).

Bach's piece has a pair of three-part choruses; four sections are for four-part choir; and the remaining five are also for a soprano-alto-tenor-bass distribution, with the sopranos divided into two parts. Yes, that's the famed virtuoso of avant-garde organ music, Gerd Zacher, on the continuo team.

Motet: *Komm, Jesu, komm*, S. 229

☐ Norddeutscher Singkreis / Koch and Beckedorf (cellos); Lippert (contrabass); Siedel (positive organ) / Wolters (conductor) / Nonesuch 71060

Integration of the vocal forces as well as antiphony between them is utilized in Bach's motet. The prime example of these methods is in the initial chorus of the work. The flexibility, especially, of the performance makes it the ideal choice among the total of five editions currently available.

Motet: *O Jesu Christ, mein's Lebens Licht*, S. 118

☐ Aeolian Singers / Smith and Hunt (oboes); Gillard and Deakin (violins); Engelbrecht (viola); van Kampen (cello); Neary (organ) / Forbes (conductor) / London STS–15187

A single four-part movement with independent instrumental parts (Forbes has substituted oboes for the original litui, which are waldhorn-like instruments). The piece was considered by Bach as a motet (he used it thus at the funeral of the governor of Leipzig, von Flemming, in 1740), but the manner in which the instrumental parts are handled defines the work as a cantata, and it is usually known as Cantata No. 118.

Certainly a stylish performance, given by a well-disciplined group.

Cantata No. 4: *Christ lag in Todesbanden*

☐ German Bach Soloists and Westphalian Singers / Wehrung (soprano); Haasemann (alto); Hoefflin (tenor); Pommerein (bass) / Ehmann (conductor) / Vanguard S–225

Cantata and Oratorio

Bach's fourth cantata was composed for Easter Day. It is a powerful and moving work, dominated by the idea of death rather than the resurrection. The performance is strong and firm, the choral sound splendid.

Cantata No. 10: *Meine Seel' erhebt den Herrn*

☐ Stuttgart Chamber Orchestra and Wiener Akademiechor / Ameling (soprano); Watts (contralto); Krenn (tenor); Rintzler (bass) / Münchinger (conductor) / London 26103

This cantata begins with a large-scale chorus, and this sets the tone for the entire presentation. Tempi are bright; the voices, collectively and in solo, are perfectly proportioned and projected. Beautifully recorded.

Cantata No. 12: *Weinen, klagen, sorgen, zagen*

☐ Vienna State Opera Orchestra and Vienna Chamber Choir / Rössl-Majdan (alto); Dermota (tenor); Berry (bass) / Woldike (conductor) / Bach Guild 5036

The eloquence of this cantata is maintained in a superlative production with beautiful singing, bringing out all of the music's intensity. The fine oboist (he is featured with the alto in the searching aria *Kreuz und Krone*) deserves individual credit.

Cantata No. 29: *Wir danken Dir, Gott*

☐ Vienna State Opera Orchestra and Vienna Chamber Choir / Davrath (soprano); Rössl-Majdan (alto); Dermota (tenor); Berry (bass) / Woldike (conductor) / Bach Guild 5036

Don't think you've uncovered a mislabeling when you begin listening to this recording. The opening *presto*-tempoed Sinfonia for trumpets, oboes, violins, violas, timpani, organ, and continuo is Bach's version of the Prelude from the Partita in E major for Solo Violin.

The performance is of exceptional artistry. "Exceptional" also describes the tenor, who sings with admirable art and impeccable enunciation.

Cantata No. 33: *Allein zu Dir, Herr Jesu Christ*

☐ Bach Orchestra and Cathedral Choir of Bremen / Bornemann (alto); Jelden (tenor); Kunz (bass) / Heintze (conductor) / Vanguard S-243

Bach's thirty-third cantata opens with a tremendous chorale Fantasia, no less than 153 measures in length. It is sung not only with strength but with a clarity of the individual parts of the texture to make this one of the high spots in all of the recorded Bach cantatas. No less glorious is the third part of the work, an aria for the alto (*Fearful falter my steps*), which Eva Bornemann sings with lovely voice.

Fine meshing between instrumentalists and voices throughout.

Cantata No. 35: *Geist und Seele wird verwirret*

☐ Vienna Radio Orchestra / Forrester (contralto); Tachez (organ) / Scherchen (conductor) / Westminster Gold 8303

Maureen Forrester has never been in better voice and the very important organ part is beautifully served by Herbert Tachez. No musicological mustiness in Scherchen's reading.

Cantata No. 36: *Schwingt freudig euch empor*

☐ Instrumentalists and Westphalian Choir / Friesenhausen (soprano); von Ramm (alto); Feyerabend (tenor); Ochs (bass) / Ehmann (conductor) / Vanguard S-251

Borrowing from oneself is nothing new in a composer's output. In this case the transfer marks Bach's third use of the same material. Parts of this work were taken from a secular cantata written for a teacher's birthday and later were used in music composed for a princess's birthday. Furthermore, the famous Lutheran hymn *Nun komm, der Heiden Heiland* is utilized as the basis for three of the eight parts of the work. Indeed, the music for "Lift Yourself Up with Joy" lives up to its title.

The singing is well stated, the pace relaxed but not loose. Wilhelm Ehmann frames the singing with care; the orchestra consists of a pair of oboes d'amore, bassoon, and strings.

Cantata No. 42: *Am Abend aber desselbigen Sabbats*

☐ Vienna Radio Orchestra and Academy Chamber Choir / Stich-Randall (soprano); Forrester (contralto); Young (tenor); Boyden (baritone); Tachez (organ) / Scherchen (conductor) / Westminster Gold 8303

Bach's cantata is for the first Sunday after Easter. It includes a warmly beautiful Sinfonia and has superb solo sections, especially the arias for contralto and bass in Nos. 3 and 6, respectively. "Rich" and "full" describe the performance.

Cantata No. 46: *Schauet doch und sehet*

☐ Chamber Orchestra and Barmen Singers / Wolf-Matthäus (alto); Jelden (tenor); Stämpfli (bass) / Kahlhöfer (conductor) / Vanguard S-226

This cantata for the Tenth Sunday after Trinity requires, in addition to three vocal soloists and a four-part chorus, two recorders, two oboes da caccia, strings, and continuo. It has one of the most striking moments in all of Bach's cantatas in the opening chorus: a dissonant interweave of the recorders (sensitively adjusted in their balance) with the vocal polyphony. The twentieth-century effect is amazing.

The stars are the male singers, though Lotte Wolf-Matthäus does very well with the quite-difficult aria *Doch Jesus*. The entire performance is undeniably top-drawer Bach.

Cantata No. 47: *Wer sich selbst erhöhet, der soll erniedriget werden*

☐ English Chamber Orchestra and London Bach Society / Le Sage (soprano); Howlett (bass) / Steinitz (conductor) / Lyrichord 7175

Nicely detailed, especially in regard to the fine work of the chorus and the orchestra. The performance matches the optimistic tone of Bach's piece.

Cantata No. 50: *Nun ist das Heil und die Kraft*

☐ Orchestra and Choir of the Vienna State Opera / Prohaska (conductor) / Vanguard HM-22

A short cantata in one movement, calling for double chorus and an orchestra consisting of three oboes, three trumpets, timpani, and strings. The music's strength and command are conclusively detailed in this performance.

Cantata No. 51: *Jauchzet Gott in allen Landen*

☐ Concerto Amsterdam / Giebel (soprano); André (trumpet) / Schröder (conductor) / Telefunken 641077

Coloratura brilliance is required in the voice and almost the same for the trumpet. Dash and assurance are obtained in full from the vocalist, and no better candidate could be named in regard to negotiating the trumpet part. This is a notable release.

Cantata No. 53: *Schlage doch gewünschte Stunde*

Cantata No. 54: *Widerstehe doch der Sünde*

☐ I Solisti di Zagreb / Forrester (contralto); Anton Heiller (harpsichord and organ); Erna Heiller (harpsichord) / Janigro (conductor) / Bach Guild 70670

A field day for a contralto. Cantata No. 53 consists of a single aria; Cantata No. 54 has two arias surrounding a recitative. Rich and expressive singing, firmly balanced throughout the entire range.

Cantata No. 57: *Selig ist der Mann*

☐ Chamber Orchestra of the Sarre and Chorus of the Sarrebruck Conservatory / Buckel (soprano); Stämpfli (bass) / Ristenpart (conductor) / Nonesuch 71029

Bach covers a dialogue between Jesus and a believer in this cantata. A musical gem, and interpreted with the necessary Bachian glow. The orchestra does significant work.

Cantata No. 58: *Ach Gott, wie manches Herzeleid*

☐ Concentus Musicus Wien and Tölzer Knabenchor / Jelosits and Kronwitter (boy sopranos); van der Meer (bass) / Harnoncourt (conductor) / Telefunken 2635305

Real stylistic authenticity, including the use of original instrumental types for the three oboes, strings, and continuo. A substantial presentation.

Cantata No. 59: *Wer Mich liebet, der wird Mein Wort halten*

☐ Concentus Musicus Wien and Tölzer Knabenchor / Jelosits (boy soprano); van der Meer (bass) / Harnoncourt (conductor) / Telefunken 2635305

With Nikolaus Harnoncourt everything is precise and every minute point is covered. Though style and the use of old instruments denote the utmost authenticity, a slight revision is made in the total design. Originally the Cantata had four sections, the third being a Chorale. Harnoncourt amplifies the work slightly by repeating the Chorale after part 4 (a bass aria) to obtain a stronger conclusion. Such a solution really does not harm matters, since everything is so well drawn in this recorded performance.

Cantata No. 60: *O Ewigkeit, du Donnerwort*

☐ Concentus Musicus Wien and Tölzer Knabenchor / Esswood (alto); Equiluz (tenor); van der Meer (bass) / Harnoncourt (conductor) / Telefunken 2635305

Telefunken's edition of this dialogue cantata (between the alto, representing "fear," and the tenor, representing "hope"), with an orchestra of two oboes d'amore, horn, strings, and continuo, represents a fascinating flexibility. It is from this Cantata that Alban Berg chose the chorale *Est ist Genug* for use in his Violin Concerto.

The vocal quality is ideal and most sensitive. A total success.

Cantata No. 61: *Nun komm, der Heiden Heiland*

☐ Concentus Musicus Wien and Tölzer Knabenchor / Jelosits and Kronwitter (boy sopranos); Equiluz (tenor); van der Meer (bass) / Harnoncourt (conductor) / Telefunken 2635306

All the soloists have polish and display excellent stylistic craft. There are some minor questions of tempo, none in regard to the vocal artistry of Seppi Kronwitter.

Cantata No. 62: *Nun komm, der Heiden Heiland*
Cantata No. 63: *Christen ätzet diesen Tag*

☐ Concentus Musicus Wien and Tölzer Knabenchor / Jelosits (boy soprano); Esswood (alto); Equiluz (tenor); van der Meer (bass) / Harnoncourt (conductor) / Telefunken 2635305

Cantata No. 62 has the same title as No. 61—this one being a chorale cantata. It also has larger scope and different instrumentation. No. 61 has three solo voices; No. 62 has four. Only a bassoon plus strings and continuo are used in No. 61; No. 62 is scored for two oboes and a horn in addition to strings and continuo. Heard here is a definitive and prime performance with soloistic excellence, particularly in the cases of the tenor and bass.

Bach pulls out all the stops in his Christmas Day cantata (No. 63). The large (for Bach) orchestra consists of three oboes, one bassoon, four trumpets, and timpani, plus strings and continuo.

Harnoncourt provides splendid support for the soloists. The duet for alto and tenor

(*Praise the Lord with song and dancing*) is a pure delight. The duet for boy soprano and bass offers another one and again proves that all concord is born of contraries.

Cantata No. 64: *Sehet, welch eine Liebe*

☐ Instrumentalists and Westphalian Choir / Friesenhausen (soprano); Bornemann (alto); Ochs (bass) / Ehmann (conductor) / Vanguard S-251

A fine edition. The instrumental group includes oboe d'amore, zinke (a type of cornett—an ancient woodwind instrument sounded by a cup mouthpiece), baroque trombones, and strings. The principal solo credit belongs to Maria Friesenhausen, who negotiates the high range of her part beautifully.

Cantata No. 65: *Sie werden aus Saba alle kommen*

☐ Chamber Orchestra and Barmen Singers / Jelden (tenor); Stämpfli (bass) / Kahlhöfer (conductor) / Vanguard S-226

Bach's scoring for this Cantata calls for two horns (a coloring aid for the festive splendor that is basic to the work), two recorders, two oboes da caccia, strings, and continuo.

The music is presented with a balance of warmth and vitality. Stämpfli's delivery of his aria *Gold of Ophir is but dross* makes one pick up the needle, replace it in the proper groove, and listen to the aria immediately again. Above all, Kahlhöfer paces the score with impeccable taste, and in other respects as well he proves that he is one of the best Bach conductors on the scene.

Cantata No. 67: *Halt' im Gedächtnis Jesum Christ*

☐ L'Orchestre de la Suisse Romande and Choeur Pro Arte de Lausanne / Watts (contralto); Krenn (tenor); Krause (bass) / Ansermet (conductor) / London 26098

Poised mastery throughout. Everyone agrees that the highlight of this cantata is the penultimate aria, for bass with chorus, *Friede sei mit euch!* John Parry indicates in his fine notes that it is "one of the most remarkable numbers from all Bach's cantatas." Indeed, it is the high point of the work, and Tom Krause does full justice to it.

Cantata No. 70: *Wachet, betet, seid bereit allezeit*

☐ Instrumental Ensemble of Heilbronn and Heinrich Schütz Choir / Graf (soprano); Scherler (alto); Huber (tenor); Stämpfli (bass) / Werner (conductor) / Musical Heritage Society MHS-1119

Superb Bach and certainly one of his cantata masterpieces. Each of the soloists is assigned an aria, though the four recitatives are solely for the male voices.

A most convincing portrayal by all the soloists, with fine choral work. The trumpet playing in the instrumental group is deserving of special mention. Small wonder—it turns out to be Maurice André doing the playing!

Cantata No. 79: *Gott, der Herr, ist Sonn' und Schild*

☐ Consortium Musicum and South German Madrigal Choir / Ameling (soprano); Baker (alto); Sotin (bass) / Gönnenwein (conductor) / Seraphim S-60248

Gott, der Herr was composed for a Reformation festival. It has a stunning duo-aria for the soprano and bass, sung here with depth and personality. The cantata includes a marvelous opening chorus and two fine chorales, the closing one being very short. All are executed with excellent vocalism.

Seraphim's release is banded, and each band is carefully identified in the album copy. However, don't look for band 9—there isn't any. The material indicated in that place is joined to the preceding section; i.e., everything is on band 8.

Cantata No. 80: *Ein' feste Burg ist unser Gott*

☐ Orchestra of the Amsterdam Philharmonic Society and Bach Chorus / Giebel (soprano); Matthès (alto); Lewis (tenor); Rehfuss (bass) / Vandernoot (conductor) / Vanguard S-219

This performance has some of the best choral singing of any Bach cantata in the recorded catalogue. The chorus produces an enthusiastic communication that lifts the spirits. The soloists are fine and portray the dramaticism that binds Bach's great composition.

Cantata No. 93: *Wer nur den lieben Gott lasst walten*

☐ Frankfurt Cantata Orchestra and Göttingen City Chorus / Reichelt (soprano); Wolf-Mätthaus (alto); Feyerabend (tenor); Hudemann (bass) / Doormann (conductor) / Vanguard S-241

A thoroughly sound performance. All the soloists (there are single arias for soprano and tenor, an aria-duet for the two female vocalists, and substantial recitatives for the tenor and bass) sing attractively and with fine verbal inflection.

Cantata No. 95: *Christus, der ist mein Leben*

☐ Bach Orchestra and Cathedral Choir of Bremen / Bernat-Klein (soprano); Jelden (tenor); Kunz (bass) / Heintze (conductor) / Vanguard S-243

Bach's Cantata No. 95 is somewhat austere, colored by use of oboe and oboe d'amore and including no fewer than four chorales in its nine sections, one sung by the soprano.

Outstanding work by the tenor Georg Jelden and the oboe–oboe d'amore performers, Alfons Czaja and Wolfgang Hoth.

Cantata No. 104: *Du Hirte Israel, höre*

☐ Orchestra of the Amsterdam Philharmonic Society and Bach Chorus / Lewis (tenor); Rehfuss (bass) / Vandernoot (conductor) / Vanguard S-219

Bach's Cantata for the second Sunday after Easter is played and sung with a lyricism that is telling and compelling. Richard Lewis's singing is both fresh and eloquent, and his diction is a joy to hear. His recitative and aria (parts 2 and 3 of the total six) are matched by the same arrangement for the bass in parts 4 and 5. Heinz Rehfuss has a pleasant if not strong vocal instrument. Expert orchestra and a fine chorus round out this performance.

Cantata No. 117: *Sei Lob und Ehr' dem höchsten Gut*

☐ Frankfurt Cantata Orchestra and Göttingen City Chorus / Wolf-Mätthaus (alto); Feyerabend (tenor); Hudemann (bass) / Doormann (conductor) / Vanguard S-241

The work of the soloists is excellent, that of the chorus a shade too light in some places. Good and alive orchestral playing, consisting of two flutes, two each of oboes and oboes d'amore, strings, and continuo. Interpretative orthodoxy is maintained.

Cantata No. 118: *O Jesu Christ, mein's Lebens Licht.* See under *Choral: chorus and instrumental ensemble* (Motet: *O Jesu Christ, mein's Lebens Licht).*

Cantata No. 130: *Herr Gott, dich loben alle Wir*

☐ L'Orchestre de la Suisse Romande and Choeur Pro Arte de Lausanne / Ameling (soprano); Watts (contralto); Krenn (tenor); Krause (bass) / Ansermet (conductor) / London 26098

Dramatic and accordingly furnished with stirring music. Clean and fully polished singing throughout. Don't miss the magnificence of the bass aria placed against an unusual background of three trumpets, timpani, and continuo. Krause scores a great success with his dynamic delivery and Ansermet gives fine support.

Cantata No. 140: *Wachet auf ruft uns die Stimme*

☐ Chamber Orchestra of the Sarre and Chorus of the Sarrebruck Conservatory / Buckel (soprano); Stämpfli (bass) / Ristenpart (conductor) / Nonesuch 71029

Doubtless the best known of all the Bach cantatas. It is neatly and decisively designed, with a three-time use of the chorale, preceded in each case by a recitative (first by the soprano, later by the bass) and followed by a duet. The first of these duos is with violin obbligato and is exceptionally well done. (The string instrument heard meant editing of its part in the score, since Bach indicates the use of a violino piccolo. Still, the modern substitution will be fully acceptable except to the diehards.)

Cantata No. 151: *Süsser Trost, mein Jesus kommt*

☐ Vienna State Opera Orchestra and Chorus / Stich-Randall (soprano); Casei (mezzo-soprano); Equiluz (tenor); Schramm (bass) / Böttcher (conductor) / Nonesuch 71182

Rather different in view of the extremely minimal use of the chorus, which is heard only in the last forty-odd seconds of the nineteen-minute work. There is a substantial aria for the soprano and a shorter one for the mezzo. The male voices have only recitatives.
Illuminating singing on the part of the cantata's star, Teresa Stich-Randall.

Cantata No. 159: *Sehet, wir geh'n hinauf gen Jerusalem*

☐ Academy of St. Martin-in-the-Fields and St. Anthony Singers / Baker (contralto); Tear (tenor); Shirley-Quirk (bass); Ledger (harpsichord); Lord (oboe) / Marriner (conductor) / Oiseau-Lyre S-295

The solo voices are exemplary, the stylistic comprehension superb. Totally an eloquent performance, for which Neville Marriner must be given as much credit as the performers.

Cantata No. 169: *Gott soll allein mein Herze haben*

☐ I Solisti di Zagreb and Vienna Chamber Choir / Forrester (contralto); Anton Heiller (harpsichord and organ); Erna Heiller (harpsichord) / Janigro (conductor) / Bach Guild 70670

The solo voice commands five of the sections, preceded by a striking Sinfonia and followed by a Chorale. Forrester's voice has a natural luminosity that makes her rendition of the highest expressivity. This is a distinguished presentation deserving of a special place among all the Bach cantatas that have been recorded.

Cantata No. 170: *Vergnügte Ruh', beliebte Seelenlust*

☐ Academy of St. Martin-in-the-Fields / Baker (contralto); Lord (oboe d'amore); Ledger (organ) / Marriner (conductor) / Oiseau-Lyre S-295

Written for the sixth Sunday after Trinity, Bach's cantata requires only a single voice with orchestra and organ obbligato. There are three arias and a couple of recitatives. Janet Baker deals superbly with every note she has to sing; Marriner's group does no less. An illuminating performance.

Cantata No. 180: *Schmücke dich, O liebe Seele*

☐ Instrumental Ensemble of Heilbronn and Heinrich Schütz Choir / Graf (soprano); Scherler (alto); Huber (tenor); Stämpfli (bass) / Werner (conductor) / Musical Heritage Society MHS–1119

A beautifully molded performance, with fine soloists and an excellent chorus. The instrumentation is especially interesting calling for two recorders, flute, oboe, oboe da caccia (the part played here on an English horn), violoncello piccolo, strings, and continuo.

Cantata No. 182: *Himmelskönig, sei willkommen*

☐ German Bach Soloists and Westphalian Singers / Wehrung (soprano); Haasemann (alto); Hoefflin (tenor); Pommerien (bass) / Ehmann (conductor) / Vanguard S–225

This Cantata was written for Palm Sunday. The performance is a beautiful one, the phrases are molded with care, the tempi are fine, and the soloists are very good.

Cantata No. 199: *Mein Herze schwimmt im Blut*

☐ German Bach Soloists / Ameling (soprano); Schmalfuss (oboe); Kussmaul (viola); Bauer (cello); Meuter (double bass); Troog (bassoon); Bach (organ and harpsichord) / Winschermann (conductor) / Philips 6500014

There are some rough spots for the soprano in Bach's writing, but no eyebrows will be raised questioningly by Elly Ameling's singing. Her poised performance is matched by fine oboe and viola assistance.

Cantata No. 200: *Bekennen will ich seinen Namen*

☐ Philomusica of London / Watts (contralto) / Dart (conductor) / Oiseau-Lyre 60003

Only this aria survives from a lost cantata. Sung with eloquence.

Cantata No. 201: *Der Streit zwischen Phoebus und Pan*

☐ Bach-Collegium, Stuttgart and Chorus of the Gedächtniskirche / Mathis (soprano); Russ (contralto); Jochims and Schreier (tenors); Wenk and Stämpfli (basses) / Rilling (conductor) / Nonesuch 71166

Bach's "Phoebus and Pan" (fully translated as "The Contest Between Phoebus and Pan") is a *dramma per musica* depicting a contest between Phoebus (representing serious music) and Pan (who stands for lighter music). The winner is obvious. The music exemplifies Bach in a rather unbent mood. As Jason Farrow puts it, it "sparkles with wit, charm, and even a light-hearted transparency not always characteristic of the composer."

The splendid soloists demonstrate a marked understanding of Bach's objective and are exceptionally responsive. Rilling provides a positive sense of contrast and pace.

Cantata No. 202: *Weichet nur, betrübte Schatten (Wedding Cantata)*

☐ Württemberg Chamber Orchestra / Buckel (soprano); Keltsch (violin); Schnell (oboe); Galling (harpsichord); Buck (cello) / Ewerhart (conductor) / Turnabout 34042

This Cantata is a tender document, its intimacy akin to chamber music. Its alternation of arias and recitatives is presented by the soprano soloist in a singularly appealing way. Though some better-known singers are represented on competitive editions, there is a quality here that is preferable, especially thanks to the conceptual simplicity.

Cantata No. 204: *Ich bin in mir vergnügt*

☐ Württemberg Chamber Orchestra, Heilbronn / Speiser (soprano); Lautenbacher (violin); Steinkraus (flute); Schnell and Keller (oboes) / Ewerhart (conductor) / Turnabout 34127

A soprano solo affair with four recitatives, as many arias, and one arioso. Fine singing, excellent projection, and clarity throughout. The obbligato instrumental voices are especially worth mention.

Cantata No. 208: *Was mir behagt*

☐ Chamber Ensemble of the Bach-Collegium (Stuttgart) and Chorus of the Gedächtniskirche / Donath and Speiser (sopranos); Jochims (tenor); Stämpfli (bass) / Rilling (conductor) / Nonesuch 71147

This is Bach's earliest surviving secular cantata. It is a lively work and breeds good cheer throughout. One of the arias is the popular beauty *Sheep May Safely Graze*.

The singing is skillful in all respects, including fine work by the choral forces. Helmuth Rilling paces the music with apt consideration and obtains fine balances throughout.

Cantata No. 209: *Non sà che sia dolore*

☐ Collegium Aureum / Ameling (soprano); Linde (flute) / RCA VICS–1275

Beginning with a substantial Sinfonia, Bach's Italian Cantata includes alternate recitatives and arias. It is sung with excellent style by Elly Ameling, with fine vocal bravura and motility in the final part. This edition is not only better vocally than the other versions available but has the best sound. (It is duplicated on the BASF 20330 release.)

Cantata No. 210: *O holder Tag, erwünschte Zeit*

☐ Mitzelfelt Orchestra / Stevenson (soprano) / Mitzelfelt (conductor) / Crystal S–951

Bach's lyrical secular Cantata (composed for a wedding) is in ten sections, with five arias and five recitatives. The singing of Delcina Stevenson is a bit strained in the highest part of the tessitura, and in the recitatives she has been recorded rather distantly. The pickup orchestra of California musicians (nine strings, flute, oboe d'amore, and harpsichord) plays rather colorlessly. Because it is almost at the same pace throughout, the Cantata seems to have offered difficulties for the conductor. Mitzelfelt does fairly well, but a sense of dryness cannot be dismissed.

Cantata No. 211: *Schweigt stille, plaudert nicht* (*Coffee* Cantata)

☐ Vienna Concentus Musicus / Hansmann (soprano); Equiluz (tenor); van Egmond (bass) / Harnoncourt (conductor) / Telefunken 641079

The best approach to this lighter aspect of Bach (it concerns a young girl's addiction to coffee and her father's attempt to have her kick the habit) is to sing it as if it were truly solemn. This group gets the point and produces a triumph.

Cantata No. 212: *Mer hahn en neue Oberkeet* (*Peasant* Cantata)

☐ Vienna Concentus Musicus / Hansmann (soprano); van Egmond (bass) / Harnoncourt (conductor) / Telefunken 641079

Light, almost to the point of being an operetta. Styled to catch the bubbly content, sung with consummate artistry.

Cantata No. 213: *Lasst uns sorgen, lasst uns wachen*

☐ Bach Collegium, Stuttgart, and Chorus of the Gedächtniskirche / Armstrong (soprano); Töpper (alto); Altmeyer (tenor); Stämpfli (bass) / Rilling (conductor) / Nonesuch 71226

Bach's secular Cantata has the alternate titles *Die Wahl des Herkules* or *Herkules auf dem Scheidewege*. Some sections will be recognized as having been transferred to the Christmas Oratorio, but familiarity will bring no disrespect for this work, which preceded the oratorio.

The cantata is given a more or less straight-faced reading, but the voices are all good and attractive.

Christmas Oratorio, S. 248

☐ Munich Bach Orchestra and Munich Bach Choir / Janowitz (soprano); Ludwig (mezzo-soprano); Wunderlich (tenor); Crass (bass) / Richter (conductor) / Deutsche Grammophon ARC–2710004

There have been many insights into this Bach work, but whatever said, this interpretation has great understanding and results in a superb presentation. The soloists are all stars and prove it. Fritz Wunderlich's vocal delivery has never been more lyrical; Christa Ludwig's contributions are smooth and pure, perhaps, at times, placed in the neutral dynamic zone, but this is a minor quibble. Both Gundula Janowitz and Franz Crass (the top and bottom of the vocal quartet) have voices that are perfect for Bachian delivery.

Brilliance of execution is contained here, but it is fully viable since it provides decided clarity. In other performances "special" authenticity can be mentioned (using a boy soprano and a countertenor in place of the soprano and mezzo, on Telefunken's SKH–25T release). However, full, female voices are to be preferred, especially when they display the high sense of artistry they do in this case.

Easter Oratorio, S. 249

☐ Stuttgart Chamber Orchestra and Wiener Akademiechor / Ameling (soprano); Watts (contralto); Krenn (tenor); Krause (bass) / Münchinger (conductor) / London 26100

Only raves can be designated for this outstanding recording. Bach's *Oratorium: Festo Paschali* has the soloists designated as characters: Mary (soprano), Mary Magdalene (contralto), St. Peter (tenor), and St. John (bass). In each case the singers portray their roles with a rich vitality within the shifting relationships. There isn't one moment in the eleven parts of the work that is blunted by less than the fullest command. Ameling's delivery of *Oh my soul, thy drugs* (No. 5) is extremely moving, Krenn's singing of *Easy shall my death pangs be* (No. 7) is not only sensitive but has a lightly applied intensity that is perfect, and these are only two examples.

Münchinger is superb in his direction. The tempi are not only firm and confident, they are set for the greatest clarity of detail without minimizing the inner excitement of Bach's masterwork. Great sound, the best possible engineering, and a set of fine notes by Charles Cudworth round out a five-star release.

Magnificat in D, S. 243

☐ Orchestra and Choir of the Vienna State Opera / Coertse and Sjosted (sopranos); Rössl-Majdan (alto); Dermota (tenor); Guthrie (bass) / Prohaska (conductor) / Vanguard HM–22

There is no nullification of the musical breadth inherent in Bach's conception, despite a favoring of fast tempi on the part of Prohaska. But why not? Especially since a rhythmic snap and interpretive pertinence are exhibited that are most devoted to the musical meaning. There's an excess of gray-bearded Bach in the recorded catalogues, and when possible it is best to avoid getting aurally tangled in such heavy sonorous and linear growth.

Fine contributions by the soloists and excellent cohesion and definition from the orchestra.

Mass in B minor, S. 232

☐ English Chamber Orchestra and Amor Artis Chorale / Palmer (soprano); Watts (alto); Tear (tenor); Rippon (bass) / Somary (conductor) / Vanguard 71190/2

Listening to this recording brings to mind the story that Otto Klemperer, having directed a performance of the B minor Mass, restudied the work for thirty-five years before conducting it again. Johannes Somary need not. His grasp of Bach's composition is superb architecturally and dramatically. A strong sense of continuity and intrinsic totality pervades the music. At the same time there is an essential penetration into its spiritual meaning that makes this performance a superbly eloquent one.

The soloists are fine, the instrumental details minutely detailed, the continuo above criticism. This is a B minor Mass that ranks as an outstanding release.

St. John Passion, S. 245

☐ Munich Bach Orchestra and Munich Bach Choir / Lear (soprano); Töpper (mezzo-soprano); Haefliger (tenor); Prey (baritone); Engen (bass) / Richter (conductor) / Deutsche Grammophon ARC–2710002

More than Bachian scholarship is required in directing a work of this stature. And there must be more than fine voices. The first can be deadly academic and thereby affect the second. What one wishes is to have the dramaticism stressed and thereby produce the potent passion that is contained in Bach's Passion. Karl Richter provides this element in full and his edition is the clear-cut winner among the productions available. The emotional build of the work is thrilling, and there isn't a moment where slackness (or marking of time) takes place, which often occurs, for instance, in the chorales. These, of course, bring contrast, but in this recording there is never the feeling of action-stopping in those sections. There, the dignity and warmth of the singing provide a strong continuity of interest.

At no time do the vocalists merely sing and let it go at that. They understand the vivid drama in Bach's work (their vocalism is superbly conditioned, one is sure, by Richter's controls), so that the dialogues between Jesus (Hermann Prey) and Pilate (Kieth Engen), for example, provide the proper quotient of excitement. Ernst Haefliger is superfine as the Evangelist. The female soloists are fine; though Hertha Töpper has a light voice it is heard without strain.

The performance is given in German. Should English be preferred, London (on 13104) offers a good performance, with Peter Pears providing a superdramatic realization.

St. Matthew Passion, S. 244

☐ Philharmonia Orchestra and Philharmonia Choir and Boys of the Hampstead Parish

Church Choir / Schwarzkopf (soprano); Ludwig and Baker (mezzo-sopranos); Watts (alto); Pears and Gedda (tenors); Fischer-Dieskau, Case, and Evans (baritones); Berry (bass); Kraus and Brown (vocalists); Downes (organ) / Klemperer (conductor) / Angel S-3599

Unfailing depth that is magnificently ordered, poetic and imaginative to the ultimate degree—these phrases describe one of Otto Klemperer's greatest recorded achievements. Above all the performance is faithful to J. S. Bach and not to the man on the podium (which is to be noted in regard to the extremely mannered Karajan performance on Deutsche Grammophon 2711012). Every part of this inspired work is given its proper poised proportions.

There is an inner intensity that burns throughout Klemperer's rendition. Dietrich Fischer-Dieskau is exceptional as Jesus, and Peter Pears has never sounded better than in his role as the Evangelist. A re-creative document of the highest order.

J. S. Bach / Samuel Baron (1925-　　　　)

Chamber Music

The Art of Fugue, S. 1080

☐ Fine Arts Quartet and New York Woodwind Quintet / Everest 3335

A fine-colored transcription of Bach's score made by Samuel Baron. The nonet combination may bother some because of the use of the clarinet and a contemporary horn sound, but if we are to accept any setting of Bach's "unset" score there is no reason to bar Baron's.

This is an honest consideration, without recourse to undue weightings by pudgy doublings, and is colored in assorted ways without any fancy-Dan flippancies. Textural matters are nicely contrasted. For example, part 1 is for string quartet, the next for two low strings and English horn with bassoon; the third *Contrapunctus* is for the five winds, succeeded by part 4 for the nine-ply group. As the sections follow, the colors applied detail the design of Bach's work aptly. Purists may furrow their brows, of course—otherwise one accepts such matters as pizzicati pointing and muted string tone. I find it all an artistic conception and quite alive.

The performance is very good, though somewhat un-Bachian in its romantic sense of phrasing and style. However, the moment one accepts a transcription one is committed to a change of style from the original, and it's just as valid in this case as in Webern's fractionalized orchestration of the *Ricercare* from Bach's Musical Offering, or Schoenberg's post-Wagnerian scorings of his organ pieces.

J. S. Bach / Ferruccio Busoni (1866-1924)

Instrumental

Piano

Organ Toccata in C major, S. 564

☐ Horowitz (piano) / Columbia M2S-728

Purists notwithstanding and what does it matter anyway, this is a fantastic weapon for a pianist who can manage it and convince the listener. Horowitz just smacks a home run with the bases loaded in this performance, recorded live. He makes the piano sound like an organ and he makes Busoni's version an absolute success. A blockbuster.

J. S. Bach / Karl Münchinger (1915-)

The Musical Offering, S. 1079   *Orchestra*

Ricercare a 3
Canon Perpetuus
Canon a 2 Violini in Unisono
Canon a 2 per Motum Contrarium
Canon a 2 Augmentationem, Contrario Motu
Canon a 2 per Tonos
Canon a 2
Canon a 2 Quaerendo Invenietis (with inversion)
Canon Perpetuus
Canon a 4
Fuga Canonica
Trio Sonata
Ricercare a 6

☐ Stuttgart Chamber Orchestra / Krotzinger (violin); Strauss (viola); Barchet (cello); Glas (flute); Weber (oboe and English horn); Lechner (harpsichord) / Münchinger (conductor) / London STS-15063

Since Bach indicated the instrumentation for only three of the thirteen sections of his Musical Offering (a masterful offering it is!), a goodly number of instrumental and orchestral settings have been produced of the work, both in its entirety and for selected sections.

The transcription solution of this music can include richness providing it is not unorthodox. What is needed is plastic orthodoxy. Münchinger is not the first to try his hand at this work. Even old Czerny had a go at some of the canons. But Münchinger certainly is the best, making his choice of resources and scoring inventiveness matters of admiration. He restricts himself to chamber music scale. There are no pudgy doublings and triplings; the lines are not overcompounded. The result is a powerful conception of Bach's gigantic opus, matched by a performance worthy of everyone's attention.

J. S. Bach / Max Reger (1873-1916)

Brandenburg **Concerto**   *Instrumental*

No. 1 in F major, S. 1046 / **No. 2 in F major, S. 1047** / **No. 3 in G major, S.**   *Piano,*
1048 / **No. 4 in G major, S. 1049** / **No. 5 in D major, S. 1050** / **No. 6 in B flat**   *Four Hands*
major, S. 1051

☐ Berkofsky and Hagan (piano) / Musical Heritage Society MHS-3522/3

Don't sneer—these are fine artistic translations. They are done with care and impeccable attention to making the scores' data fit keyboard requirements. The playing of the Berkofsky and Hagan team is at a high level.

J. S. Bach / Leopold Stokowski (1882-1977)

Orchestra

Chorale Preludes

Ich ruf' zu dir
Nun komm der Heiden Heiland
Wir glauben all' an einen Gott

☐ Philadelphia Orchestra / Stokowski (conductor) / Odyssey Y-33228

Like what Stokowski does or not in the role of a transcriber, the *sound* of these versions is a thrilling experience. That doesn't apply to the other work on this release (first issued on the Columbia label), namely, the fifth *Brandenburg* Concerto. It is puffed out of shape, and the execution misrepresents the work. To paraphrase Shaw: to Stokowski the weapon, to Bach not the victory.

Passacaglia and Fugue in C minor, S. 582

☐ Czech Philharmonic Orchestra / Stokowski (conductor) / London 21096

Those who would prefer a rather staid and classically styled arrangement of this organ work will have to await a recording of the one produced by Alexander Goedicke. All the others that have been made use big forces. Respighi's, for example, calls for sixteen winds, fourteen brasses, timpani, strings, *and* organ. But this is small potatoes! Stokowski doesn't need an organ since he requires eighteen winds, seventeen brasses, timpani, and strings.

His version, regardless of the huge orchestral forces, is sensitive to the Bach original, making certain that every pitch, relationship, and nuance is heard. The mighty quality of Bach's organ work therefore becomes an orchestral blockbuster in Stokowski's hands. Fine playing is displayed here, with state-of-the-art sound.

Sheep May Safely Graze from Cantata No. 208

☐ Leopold Stokowski and His Orchestra / Stokowski (conductor) / Vanguard 701/2

This is one of the many Stokowski transcriptions of Bach music and one of the most successful in reflecting the original in different colors. Stokowski's work shows top artistry. No one can match him in playing his Bach translations. When he conducted the Philadelphia Orchestra, a number of the Bach settings were programmed every season in response to popular demand.

(The above-listed performance is also on Vanguard 707/8 and on a Bach Guild program [70696].)

Toccata and Fugue in D minor, S. 565

☐ Czech Philharmonic Orchestra / Stokowski (conductor) / London 21096

This is still another jumbo orchestration in the Stokowski catalogue. In addition to four each of the woodwinds there are fourteen brass instruments, timpani, and strings, plus two celestas and two harps. But it is crafted beautifully and is certainly the best of the many transcriptions of Bach's mighty work—turned out by Lucien Cailliet, Sir Henry J. Wood (under the pseudonym of Klenovsky), René Leibowitz (his arrangement is for double orchestra), Leon Leonardi, Alois Melichar, Eugene Ormandy, Fabien Sevitzky, and Stanislaw Skrowaczewski.

It will be noted that the great majority of these names represent conductors. This is not unexpected, since the Toccata and Fugue in D minor offers music that is made to order for powerhouse effect, be it played on the organ or spelled out by a large orchestra. It supplies the conductor with a built-in success, and for many, many years it was an annual triumph at Stokowski's concerts with the Philadelphia Orchestra and served as his visiting card for guest appearances elsewhere and in recording studios.

This performance provides a further smash hit. The imaginative and vivid realization of Stokowski's Bach transcription is displayed in full; the playing is magnificent and the result is of the greatest excitement.

J. S. Bach / Igor Stravinsky (1882-1971)

Chorale Variations on *Vom Himmel hoch*   *Orchestra*

☐ CBC Symphony Orchestra and Festival Singers of Toronto / Stravinsky (conductor) / Columbia M-31124

Despite the polyphony, which grows more and more involved as the work progresses, the Chorale Variations on the German Christmas carol "I Come to You from Heaven Above" are basically lyrical. The work begins with a chorale for the six brass instruments (this is not in the original organ work, Stravinsky having used Bach's setting in the Christmas Oratorio for preludial purposes). Five variations follow, each concerned with canon, plus a magnificent climax in stretto. A typical Stravinskian selectivity of instrumentation is applied: double winds plus English horn and double bassoon, but minus clarinets; three trumpets and three trombones, harp, and only violas and double basses from the string family, plus mixed chorus.

Stravinsky's Bach reconsideration is not a mere translation for instruments with subtle registration. Transposition of key is one point involved; more important is the acute elaboration including syncopations, cross-rhythms, and the addition of lines onto Bach's lines. The juxtaposition is magical. It is Stravinsky devoted to Bach and Stravinsky derived from Bach. The performance is beautifully shaped and phrased; the instrumental balances are a joy to hear.

J. S. Bach / William Walton (1902-   )

The Wise Virgins, Ballet Suite   *Ballet*

☐ Cleveland Orchestra / Lane (conductor) / Columbia M-31241

Bach made harpsichord settings of some sixteen concerti (most were for the violin) by such composers as Marcello and Vivaldi. In turn, his own music has been transcribed more than that of any other great composer. Walton chose his score from five cantatas and a chorale prelude of Bach. The fourth movement of Walton's compilation, *Sheep May Safely Graze*, is the most familiar. It includes the introductory recitative, rarely used in other versions, which adds tremendously to the effect.

Musical taste is sensitively illustrated in Walton's orchestration. It stands as a model of Bachian reworking; the performance is likewise tasteful.

J. S. Bach / Anton Webern (1883-1945)

Orchestra

Fuga (Ricercata) a 6 Voci, No. 2 from *Das Musikalische Opfer,* S. 1079

☐ London Symphony Orchestra / Boulez (conductor) / Columbia M4–35193

Webern's orchestration of the six-part ricercar from "The Musical Offering" is dipped into a bath of *Klangfarben.* It emerges with ruddy complexion and in full health. The classical text is broken up into units as Webern italicizes the motival coherence of the fascinating polyphony.

Some may shriek that Bach has been led astray and mocked, but Webern's ultrasensitive recasting of this magnificent fugue through a disciplined radiation of single timbres makes perfect artistic sense. The transcription is the equivalent of an acute aural analysis of the score.

Boulez obtains perfect smoothness and a chamber-music quality from his personnel. Each and every note in the score is delineated, not one sound being of secondary importance in a superfine performance of remarkable music.

Wilhelm Friedemann Bach   (1710-1784)

Chamber Music

Duet in F major for Two Flutes

☐ Rampal and Eugenia Zukerman (flutes) / Columbia M–33310

The highlight is the middle movement, a *Lamentabile* that embraces a tragic dialogue, undoubtedly one of the greatest pieces ever turned out for a pair of unaccompanied flutes. Bach's masterpiece is performed with noteworthy character. The seductive tone of this team especially marks the initial and terminal fast-paced movements.

Sonata for Two Violas

In G major / In G minor / In C major

☐ Phillips and Trampler (violas) / Musical Heritage Society OR–398

Each in three movements, with the central part of each work given a slightly picturesque heading—*Lamento* in the first, *Amoroso* in the second, and Scherzo in the last. The *Amoroso,* in canonic form, is followed by a Fugue as the final part of the duo. A further relationship exists in the set in that the Scherzo is a reworking of the *Amoroso.* These are totally two-voice works, with not a chord to be heard.

Clear playing by Walter Trampler and his former wife, Karen Phillips.

Trio in D major for Two Flutes and Cembalo

☐ Rampal and Duschenes (flutes); Gilbert (harpsichord) / Orion 7149

Lyrical warmth and playful imitative style mark this spirited piece, of joyful demeanor even in its slow-paced initial movement. The playing is just as perfect as might be wished.

The performance is duplicated on a seven-record Everest release (3194), and again by Everest on its 3299, a single disc which features Rampal and eliminates all credits for the other musicians involved. There are no liner notes offered by Everest.

Wilhelm Friedrich Ernst Bach   (1759-1845)

Trio in G major for Two Flutes and Viola

Chamber Music

☐ Rampal and Eugenia Zukerman (flutes); Pinchas Zukerman (viola) / Columbia M–33310

Light and downy music—to be expected, since the lowest possible sound is only one octave below middle C. Perhaps run-of-the-mill formal procedures to some, but there are plenty of delightful moments in this piece, especially the final Presto. The performance is attentive, gracious, and warm; it couldn't be bettered.

Agathe Backer-Grøndahl   (1847-1907)

Etude de concert **in A major, Op. 11, No. 6**

Instrumental

Etude de concert **in A minor, Op. 57, No. 1**

Piano

Etude de concert **in B flat minor, Op. 11, No. 1**

Etude de concert **in D flat major, Op. 11, No. 2**

Four *Skizzer,* **Op. 19**

Humoreske, **Op. 15, No. 3**

Paa Ballet, **Op. 15, No. 2**

Serenade, Op. 15, No. 1

☐ Pines (piano) / Genesis 1024

Spontaneously idiomatic romantic music. The most important works are the four *Etudes,* chips from the Chopin workbench but finished off into strong constructions. The set of *Skizzer,* which means "Scherzos," has viability without being vested with vitality. The remainder comprise vignettes identified with the salon. (*Paa Ballet* is self-descriptive in its translation, "At the Ball.")

Credit Doris Pines with delving into literature that no one else knows about, or at least gives any consideration to. The most pertinent quality of her performances is her ability to engender a consistently beautiful sound. She is also a pianist who understands style and how to convey it in tasteful performances.

Ernst Bacon   (1898-   )

The Enchanted Island **(1954)**

Orchestra

☐ Louisville Orchestra / Whitney (conductor) / Louisville 545–11 (monaural)

Program music requires an articulate aesthetic, and Ernst Bacon, writing from a traditionally neo-romantic position, fulfills this requirement aptly in *The Enchanted Island.* There are nine movements in this music drawn from material originally written for a production of Shakespeare's *Tempest.* Not academic accuracy but consistent coloration is the touchstone for the delineation of such characters as Ariel and Miranda, and for such events as *Repears and Nymphs* and *Prospero's Farewell.*

There is fine orchestration (Bacon has always been superexcellent in that department), including better than fair attention to the piano as an orchestral voice. Whitney's interpretative illustrations are quite good, and so are the balances.

Ford's Theatre (1943)

☐ Vienna Symphony Orchestra / Schoenherr (conductor) / Desto 6415E (monaural)

Bacon's suite (twelve movements), subtitled *A Few Glimpses of Easter Week, 1865,* was drawn from material composed as background for Paul Horgan's play *Yours, A. Lincoln.* Sensitive, inventive, and always interesting, Bacon's pieces can be termed "American Pictures at an Exhibition," containing intensive coloration similar to that of Mussorgsky's set.

Fortunately, each portion is of particular color and scoring, since Desto's disc is not banded. Fairly identifiable, therefore, are such items as *The Telegraph Fugue* (for strings and timpani), the balletic *The Theatre,* and *Premonition,* the last containing a singular ostinato laced with bell touches. The positive programmatic projection of Bacon's music survives the uncommunicative liner note regarding the music—that is, if one can call a single sentence of seven words a "liner note"!

Instrumental

Piano

The Pig Town Fling

☐ Helps (piano) / Composers Recordings SD–288

Rural Americana. The bass line is squared to the square-dance concept and rides under a cute melody. Obvious reasoning, but that doesn't detract from the attractiveness of the music.

Chamber Music

Sonata for Cello and Piano (1948)

☐ Greenhouse (cello); Pressler (piano) / Composers Recordings 201 (monaural)

Communicable logic in formal terms here: a slow introduction linked to a fast movement, a folksy song-and-dance second part, a slow division, and a fugally textured finale. However, this is but the overlay of Bacon's Sonata. The inlay is hinted at by the score's inscription: "with homage to Walt Whitman." With some nine different lines from Whitman's poems indicated throughout the four movements, the objective is clearly nailed down: implied program writing, though only in the most subtle manner. Nevertheless, the work is dissociated from extramusical implications—take or leave the lines that spurred or dictated the writing. And it is to Bacon's credit that he has maintained his belief in postromantic conservatism. There are sufficient boldnesses in this work.

The performers are chamber-music masters, and they prove their status in their performance. Balances between cello and piano, often hard to come by, are perfect in this recording.

Henk Badings   (1907-   )

Orchestra

The Louisville Symphony (No. 7) (1954)

☐ Louisville Orchestra / Whitney (conductor) / Louisville 56-6 (monaural)

A completely successful example of symphonic form that does not abandon traditional structural concepts. A dramatic introduction is linked to a passionate fast movement, and then follow a Scherzo-Presto, a slow movement, and a Finale in *Allegro vivace* tempo. The fast music is muscular and motoric, the slow music has pith as well. But Badings's orchestral virility never sets forth to delineate athletic gestures; rather, it brings into high relief the strong themes and counterpoints. The structural ingenuity is convincing. And so is the recorded performance.

Symphony No. 8 (1956)

☐ Utrecht Philharmonic Orchestra / Hupperts (conductor) / Donemus Audio-Visual Series DAVS-6303 (monaural: 10-inch disc)

Panchromaticism with the odd addition (in the first movement) of orchestration that reflects electronic-music qualities. The second movement, an *Adagietto* of thirty-three measures, is for strings alone. Scherzo drive marks the Finale.

Symphony No. 9 (1959)

String Orchestra

☐ Netherlands Chamber Orchestra / Zinman (conductor) / Donemus Audio-Visual Series DAVS-6602 (monaural)

Virtuosity is the creative truth of Badings's three-movement string symphony. This is paramount in the terminal fast movements—the opening one barbaric, the other a perpetual-motion Toccata that sprays sixteenth-note patterns in most of the measures.

David Zinman directs a rendition of structural and interpretative positivism. He especially makes razor-edge clear the pulsatile arrangement of fundamental quadruple beats combined with the division of the fourfold total into $\frac{3}{8}\frac{3}{8}\frac{2}{8}$ that is used in a majority of the measures. Because of the rhythmic conflict this could easily be smudged, even with precise playing of the patterns. Throughout, Badings's virtuosity is matched by the Netherlanders'.

Armageddon (1968)

Band

☐ American Wind Symphony Orchestra / Farley (soprano) / Boudreau (conductor) / Point Park College KP-101

A three-ply construction. In addition to the wind orchestra, there are prerecorded tape materials and a soprano voice. The tape functions both alone and with the instrumental body; the voice both is wordless and uses excerpts from the text of the Dies Irae. These assorted ingredients are applied to a heavy and dark music.

The Boudreau forces are young professionals but play like topflight veterans.

Concerto for Harp and Small Symphony Orchestra (1967)

Solo Instrument and Orchestra

☐ Radio Philharmonic Orchestra / Berghout (harp) / van Otterloo (conductor) / Donemus Audio-Visual Series DAVS-6902

Harp

One of the best harp concerti that has appeared in the twentieth century, because of its intrinsic artistry as a whole and the acute propitiousness of the harp writing. Without the use of any specific effects the potential of the instrument is fully utilized. That Badings is no harpist makes one's regard for his accomplishment stronger.

There is plenty of solo work, but it is all integral to the Concerto's three movements. The middle *grave*-tempoed movement is funereal in mood and is scored for the harp with only percussion and celesta. A ripsnorting finale is its antithesis.

The soloist, Phia Berghout, is the former solo harpist of the Concertgebouw Orchestra. Her command of the work deserves the highest praise.

Instrumental	**Sonata No. 2 for Violoncello Solo (1951)**
Cello	☐ Bijlsma (cello) / Donemus Audio-Visual Series DAVS–6102 (monaural: 10-inch disc)

In a medium that has not drawn many winners Badings's piece has the technical scope to keep one's attention every measure of the way, especially in a compelling *grave* that proposes and disposes keenly a tricolored timbre association that is clever and of consequence. This is managed by left-hand pizzicato pedal rhythm, melodic passages mainly in sixths, and a *col legno* retort. The music is tonal, though relatively unleashed.

Good playing by Anner Bijlsma.

Flute	**Cavatina (1952)**
	☐ Pellerite (flute); Webb (piano) / Coronet S–1713

A short romantic essay, somewhat on the dark side. It is rendered interesting by the elegance of its vocal-like line. Pellerite exhibits a beautiful tone.

Organ	**Passacaglia for Timpani and Organ (1958)**
	☐ Piehler (organ); Edson (timpani) / Lyrichord 7721

Since Badings wrote this work, in 1958, the literature for organ with percussion has been growing steadily. Without doubt, Badings's Passacaglia is one of the strongest that has been produced. It is freely serial and covers seven metrically involved variations on the basic subject. The organ-timpani combination is excellent, the percussion instrument being exploited to frame, punctuate, and timbre-counterpoint the massivity of the organ.

Lyrichord's recording was made at a live performance, and at times the timpani is overthrusted so that the keyboard instrument (the Woolsey Hall organ at Yale University) is unclear. Two notes: First, it takes considerable search to find the name of the timpanist, hidden in small type among the liner notes. Second, the composer's name is misspelled on the label copy. There he turns into "Hank Bodings."

Chamber Music	**Octet, Op. 67**
	☐ Vienna Octet / London STS–15243

As well structured as the instrumentation, which balances a string quintet (the usual quartet plus a double bass) with clarinet, bassoon, and horn. The neoclassic cohesion follows suit. Good performance, good recording all the way.

Edward Bairstow (1874 - 1946)

Choral	*Let All Mortal Flesh Keep Silence*
Chorus Alone	☐ Choir of St. John's College, Cambridge / Guest (conductor) / Argo ZRG–5340

An expressive example of this composer's work, styled in the traditional conventions of Anglican church music.

David Baker (1931-)

Orchestra	*Le Chat qui pêche,* **for Orchestra, Soprano, and Jazz Quartet**
	☐ Louisville Orchestra / Anderson (soprano); Aebersold (alto and tenor saxophones);

Haerle (piano and electric piano); Clayton (bass and electric bass); Craig (drums) / Mester (conductor) / Louisville LS–751

Baker "loosely" classifies his five-movement *Chat qui pêche* as "Thirdstream," but its melorhythms, colors, and beat are hardcore jazz—in various aspects. Most of the impetus comes from the instrumental quartet, aided by a fantastic soprano in the person of Linda Anderson. Still, there is nothing wrong with such wide-ranging jazz eclecticism.

The sound is volatile. A listener would swear he was in the audience in a New York Soho rock-music loft.

Sonata for Cello and Piano

Chamber Music

☐ Starker (cello); Planès (piano) / Columbia M–33432

The Blues movement is the highlight of this three-movement piece. It is music that intimately states rather than boldly describes, by use of the old-hat blues type of harmony. The outer movements are more showy, with the motility somewhat committed to jazz twists and turns.

With Starker and his fine partner, Alain Planès, all the music's resources are exposed clearly and in the most musical manner.

Sonata for Tuba and String Quartet (1971)

☐ Composers String Quartet / Phillips (tuba) / Golden Crest 4122

A medium that wouldn't be expected to be successful, but fully is successful in Baker's hands. The Sonata is no bag of tuba trivialities backed up with some string shenanigans. The syntax and speech are fully contemporary—jazzy here, succinctly dissonant there, and always theatrical. The last quality is especially dominant in the second movement, where Baker shows a unique gift for grotesquerie. It certainly will be admitted that it takes courage merely to attempt a full-scale quintet for tuba, paired violins, viola, and cello. However, there is more than an illustration of creative guts in this instance. The result is a fine artistic achievement.

This triumph is matched by a performance that can only be given extravagant praise. Harvey Phillips is one of the greatest of all tuba virtuosi, and the Composers String Quartet (Raimondi, Ajemian, Dupouy, and Rudiakov) is a superb team. The partnership is a magnificent one.

Larry Baker (1948-   )

Before Assemblages III

Orchestra

☐ Members of the Indiana Chamber Orchestra / Briccetti (conductor) / Crystal S–532

Development, not of theme but of bare sound, with use of echoes and reverberations. Thus the release (and realization) of the potential existing in the initial solo material of the work. From this developmental reaction an interaction is formed; the separate sonorous qualities are thus to be understood and enjoyed *as* particular and specific qualities. The instruments include a wind quartet, trumpet, piano, harp, percussion, and two strings—viola and double bass.

Thomas Briccetti is a fine conductor. One can be certain the rendition is above average.

Robert Baker and Lejaren Hiller. See Hiller and Baker.

Leonardo Balada   (1933-   )

Orchestra

Guernica (1966)

☐ Louisville Orchestra / Mester (conductor) / Louisville S–686

As would be expected, *Guernica* is fierce music. The horror found in Picasso's famous painting could not be expressed otherwise. So there are no tunes, but diffusive paragraphs and parenthetical statements that sonorously smash through the orchestra. In the sense of arranged disorder, avoiding formal strictures in its progress, actual meaning is made very clear. Balada's protest music rings true. So does the Louisville representation.

Homage to Sarasate (1976)

☐ Louisville Orchestra / Mester (conductor) / Louisville LS–765

Balada honors the famous Spanish violin virtuoso by utilizing the *Zapateado* dance rhythm as the basis for his work, including a quotation from Sarasate's own *Zapateado* for violin and piano. But there is much more, as the triple-beat rhythm is overlaid and interwoven with nippy harmonies and high-gloss orchestral colors. No stylistic confusion here at all—Balada has simply but vividly outlined the way a popular Spanish dance should be written in the late twentieth century.

Mester has the proper feeling for this type of music and even permits a bit of roughness from his orchestra. That is certainly no sign of disrespect for the score; rather, it helps define the general spirit of the music.

Band

Cumbres: A Short Symphony for Band

☐ Carnegie-Mellon University Symphony Band / Strange (conductor) / Serenus 12036

Just piles of dissonance, sensitively designed in swatch form, confirmed by ostinato stitching. Some of it sounds like the static sonority masses found in the music of the avant-garde Hungarian composer György Ligeti; all of it sounds convincing and compelling.

Balada makes certain there is no monotony as his wind-brass-percussion pigments change. The performance is ideal—supple and resonant. This is a superfine band.

Instrumental

Piano

Música en cuatro tiempos para piano (1959)

☐ Marshall (piano) / Serenus 12064

Four moods that contrast textures as well as speed rates. A further contrast is effected by expressionistic detail and lean linear activity. Everything is explicit, but the piano writing has the improvisation-like, virtuosic approach that marks so much of Liszt's music for the keyboard instrument.

Elizabeth Marshall's playing proves she has all the necessary capabilities for an innate understanding of Balada's score. Serenus's recording matches the performance in its excellence.

Sonata for Violin and Piano (1960)

☐ Harth (violin); Franklin (piano) / Serenus 12036

Balada practices formal democracy in his early composition that has simmerings of his confirmed style. The elements of sonata design are depicted in each of the four movements. Movement 1 presents three themes. The second theme is developed in movement 2, and the third is covered in movement 3. The first idea is germinated in the finale, and the work is then tied up with a condensed recapitulation of the previous material.

A crusty type of neoclassic syntax is utilized. It provides a textural bulk which the performers balance with expertise. There's a lot of movement in Balada's sonata house, but Harth and Franklin keep things in order.

Cuatris (1969)

☐ Conjunto Cameristico de Barcelona / Balada (conductor) / Serenus 12036

Alternative instrumentation for four players is involved here: flute or violin, clarinet or viola, bassoon or cello or even trombone, and a keyboard instrument such as piano or harpsichord or prepared piano. The version used for the recording is that for strings with what sounds like a prepared piano. (The instrument's timbre sometimes could well be that of a harpsichord, but that's one of the resultant values of ''orchestrating'' the piano. The liner notes give no clue in this case.)

The five concentrated movements are full of coloristic concourse and conflux. Thematic objectives are not Balada's concern; effects are—and good ones, let it be said. Most interesting is the ploy used in the second piece, where only one pitch is heard: sustained, rhythmicized, rhythmically counterpointed, registrally juggled and bounced. It's very effective, and is a sharp reminder of the Argentinian Jaime Pahissa's *Monodía*, composed forty-four years before Balada's work, which consists solely of various-pitched unisons and octaves, structured and sustained by registral change, rhythms, and orchestral color. Imitative or not, Balada's work is more successful, since it is concentrated on a single pitch and says what it has to say in a minute and a half, whereas Pahissa's essay is of nine-minute length.

Mosáico (1970)

☐ American Brass Quintet / Serenus 12041

Free-formed but paradoxically tightly styled. Most of Balada's detail consists of chromatic conflict, with disjunctive opposition or static polyrhythmic congress. The piece progresses in blocks akin to a series of vignettes that cohere through the secundal talons of the percussive line writing.

Balada treats the brass group (two trumpets, horn, tenor and bass trombones) as though they were woodwinds. The performance demands are fantastically difficult. However, the American Brass players master the situation perfectly. Quite a feat.

Geometrías No. 1 (1966)

☐ Conjunto Cameristico de Barcelona / Balada (conductor) / Serenus 12036
☐ Francis Chagrin Ensemble / Farberman (conductor) / Serenus 12028

A work of sophisticated primitivism that more than once reminds one of Silvestre Revueltas's music spiked with atonal flavoring. The scoring calls for an instrumental sextet of flute (doubling on piccolo), oboe (alternating with English horn), clarinet (doubling on bass clarinet), bassoon, trumpet, and percussion. This combination presents an abstract compilation of timbred dabs and dots, tight dissonances, and piquant clusters. Additionally, though Balada's music is acutely blocked in its textures, relationships between these and linear-detailed sections are utilized.

Both issues exhibit expert performances, with sensitive attention to proper balances and instrumental highlighting. However, the timing difference in the executions is acute. Farberman takes 10:35 in his version, Balada covers the ground in 8:35. On this basis the composer's consideration receives the highest vote.

Inexplicably, Serenus has chosen to bewilder (and lead astray) the record buyer with this pair of releases. Making no mention of duplicate performances of the identical composition, Serenus eliminates the important "No. 1" identification from the first-listed recording while indicating it for the other one. Further, *Schwann* follows suit, and to compound the problem assigns two different composition dates for the same work. And still further irritation is caused by the liner notes: both are practically identical.

Cantata and Oratorio

María Sabina **(1969)**

☐ Louisville Orchestra and University of Louisville Chorus / Dunham, Hardy, Helguera, and Cortés (narrators) / Mester (conductor) / Louisville S–726

Defined here as an oratorio, Balada's hefty, power-laden work, principally because of its stabbing text, is a hybrid—a mini-opera and an oratorio. His term for the opus is *Tragifonía (A Symphonic Tragedy)*. Its María Sabina is high priestess of a hallucinatory-mushroom cult in a Mexican village.

Though there are orchestral interludes and backgrounds of scalding-hot and frighteningly cold pigmentation, the emphasis is on the role of María Sabina and also on the chorus. Much of the writing for the latter emphasizes a Carl Orff *modus operandi* that is updated and is more contemporaneous in its sound structuring.

Burwell Hardy as the Town Crier has a sizable introductory part consisting of thirty-two lines. Guillermo Helgura as the Constable and Hector Cortés as the Executioner have extremely minor roles, with three lines each. The virtuoso and number one in the cast is América Dunham in the title part. She narrates nine sections. The first one covers an extraordinary total of seventy-three lines; another portion is also of considerable length, comprising forty-three lines. Her diction is marvelous. The only drawback is the use of Spanish rather than the fine English translation supplied in the program booklet. Only in English can the sting and fervidity of such lines as "I am a woman with three rows of teeth/ I am a woman who has teeth growing in her palate/ I am a woman who eats dirt/ I am a woman who cures her wounds with dirt/ . . . I am a woman without nipples/ I am a woman with six teats like bitches/ . . . I am a woman who drinks her father's semen in the flower of the mandrake/ I am a woman who smokes aromatic herbs in a pipe made of vertebrae from a blood-drained martyr" be fully appreciated. However, Dunham's performance is a fully appreciated triumph.

Mily Balakirev   *(1837-1910)*

Orchestra

Islamey (Oriental Fantasy)

☐ Philadelphia Orchestra / Ormandy (conductor) / Columbia MS–6875

Islamey is extremely exciting when one hears a pianist conquer its difficulties (see under *Instrumental: piano*). But if large orchestral sounds give you greater thrills, then listen to Ormandy and his musicians.

Tamara: **Symphonic Poem**

☐ L'Orchestre de la Suisse Romande / Ansermet (conductor) / London STS-15066

The lyrical and ebullient facts in *Tamara* (London's issue uses the spelling "Thamar") are all conveyed in Ansermet's reading. Balakirev's tale of a beautiful but murderous female has all the usual Russian melodic and coloristic ingredients. It also has, very oddly, certain rhythms and the outline of the solo violin passages that Rimsky-Korsakov used seven years later in his *Scheherazade*.

Islamey

☐ Katchen (piano) / London STS-15086

For this pianistic blockbuster, subtitled *Oriental Fantasia* or *Oriental Fantasy* (see under *Orchestra*), get Katchen. He scoops the field with an aliveness and a cleanness that are very stimulating. Brendel on Turnabout (34258) plays it all, but the sound is a tin pan and crackles horribly.

Nocturne in B flat minor

☐ Pleshakov (piano) / Orion 73111

The score reads 100 for Chopin and 0 for Balakirev. No belittling whatsoever. Chopin would have been proud to call this his own. A real beauty, masterfully played.

Polka in F sharp minor

☐ Tarnowsky (piano) / Genesis 1004

Playful and witty as any polka should be, but this one has a special character because of the minor-key tonality.

Instrumental

Piano

Balakirev / *Mikhail Glinka.* See *Glinka* / Balakirev.

Claude Balbastre [*Balbâtre*] (1727-1799)

Burgundian Noël

☐ Hamilton (organ) / Orion 73133

Variations on a Christmas tune, *Grand Dei, ribon ribeine.* No extraneous detail is included to disguise the simplicity of the compositional objective. Nothing else is needed for this charming type of music. Hamilton presents natural but strong playing. Fine timbre variance.

Noël **with Variations**

☐ Biggs (organ) / Columbia MS-7438

Instrumental

Organ

Another example of Balbastre's writing "in praise of Christmas." Biggs's playing is a triumph that signifies all of the charm in the figurations and ornamentations. His emphatic use of a variety of flute stops adds color points and increases listening enjoyment for this set of variations on *Joseph est bien marié*.

Swiss Noël

☐ Hamilton (organ) / Orion 73133

A brightly decorated set of variations on *Il est un petit ange*. An excellent account by this fine organist.

Matthias Bamert   (1942-   )

Orchestra

Mantrajana (1971)

☐ Louisville Orchestra / Bamert (conductor) / Louisville LS–741

Extreme color suffuses *Mantrajana* ("a Buddhist belief which seeks redemption through the repetition of sacred formulas [*mantras*]"). For this four gongs become excited in various ways by various beaters and are soloistic in that they are in front of the orchestra. Individuality of timbres, with extensive manipulation of each quality, surrounds the motival and intervallic development of the piece. The orchestral methods applied to the sonorous contents sharply remind the listener of electronic music in reverse. *Mantrajana* is always dynamic and rarely placid.

It is rare for the Louisville Orchestra to have a guest conductor. That by itself is worthy of note. And certainly Bamert the visiting conductor does well by Bamert the colorful composer.

Septuria Lunaris

☐ Louisville Orchestra / Mester (conductor) / Louisville S–725

The space age brings its own type of program music. Bamert's orchestral translation of seven of the moon's geographical areas is a catalogue of tone clusters, tremolos, glissandi, fractured fragments, aleatoricism, percussion from percussion, percussion on string instruments, etc. It represents music emancipated from thematic structure and development. One cannot escape the fact that Bamert's sonic bath water has been used by Penderecki, Xenakis, Stockhausen, Ligeti, and Nono. No matter, it's still fairly fresh.

**Chamber
Music**

Five Aphorisms for Flute and Harp

☐ Baron (flute); Maayani (harp) / Desto 7134

Colorful color dabs floating in a sea of fragmentation. The two vividly contrasted timbres receive and give in an endless and engrossing interchange. Excellent communication by the soloists.

Adriano Banchieri   (1568-1634)

**Brass
Ensemble**

Four *Fantasie overo canzoni alla francese*

☐ Brass Ensemble / Masson (conductor) / Nonesuch 71111

The four pieces are indicated *a 4 voci per sonar,* and sound they do with keen chamber-music quality by the groups of trumpets and trombones. The titling is interesting. The second *Fantasia* of the set is *in eco movendo un registro;* the third one is *in dialogo.* Fine playing indeed.

Joseph Edouard Barat   *(1882-?1950)*

Introduction and Dance

☐ Bobo (tuba); Grierson (piano) / Crystal S-125

Instrumental

Tuba

A smaller than usual tuba is utilized for Barat's piece, originally for bass saxhorn or saxtuba. This is lightweight but worthy music. It represents the typical *concours* item (music specifically composed as a test piece for use at the competitive examinations held at French music schools). Would that all *concours* entrants played with the mastery of this chap!

George Barati   *(1913-   )*

Chamber Concerto (1952)

☐ Members of the Philadelphia Orchestra / Ormandy (conductor) / Columbia Special Products AMS-6379

Orchestra

Barati's Concerto is played by "members of the Philadelphia Orchestra" because it calls only for four winds and strings. It is music for those who relish the school of severe chromaticism and don't want to bandy about with handy diatonic lines. The four movements are tight with cross-counterpoint, nervous rhythms, asymmetrics, and clash. The music is exciting not merely in its motoric resiliency but in its constant action.

Ormandy directs the piece mindful of its sting and friction. It is a triumph, with virtuosic playing that makes the mouth water and the heart race.

Concerto for Cello and Orchestra (1953)

☐ London Philharmonic Orchestra / Michelin (cello) / Barati (conductor) / Composers Recordings 184 (monaural)

Solo Instrument and Orchestra

Cello

A tidy tie-in of romantic syntax with rhapsodic paragraphing marks Barati's Concerto. The three movements have the basic carefully arranged tempo distinctions—*andante espansive* (of course with this tempo indication Carl Nielsen's *Sinfonia espansiva* comes to mind, but the resemblance is only in the verbiage), *scherzando,* and a combined slow movement leading into a fast-paced Finale—but such traditionalism is given full contemporary revision.

Bright playing by soloist and orchestra, the latter no mere accompanimental body.

Harpsichord Quartet (1964)

☐ Baroque Chamber Players of Indiana / Composers Recordings S-226

Chamber Music

The baroque element is in the use of the harpsichord, the other instruments being flute, oboe (doubling on English horn), and a cello (doubling on bass). Without rigidity the music verges on dodecaphonic speech, with most of the color shifts applied to the central movement of the three.

Samuel Barber   *(1910-   )*

Orchestra

Capricorn Concerto (1944)

☐ Eastman-Rochester Symphony Orchestra / Hanson (conductor) / Mercury 75049

A chamber-orchestra work calling for flute, oboe, trumpet, and strings. It has Barberesque charm with a Stravinskian beat. (The title is derived from the name of Barber's house in Mount Kisco, New York.)

Die Natali: **Chorale Preludes for Christmas, Op. 37**

☐ Louisville Orchestra / Mester (conductor) / Louisville S-745

Barber's ''Christmastide'' score is an orchestral mintage devoted to a montage of Christmas carols. But familiarity with the tunes does not breed any contempt for his richly contrapuntalized setting.

This work is far afield (in technique, meaning, creative objective, and stylistic stability) from the many Christmas-carol settings that have appeared—simple and straight, rhapsodic mix, collective suite. Barber's choice of eight carols forms a large fantasy tapestry utilizing canon, theme-and-variations, and cyclic techniques. The orchestration and metrical interplay are further assets in this, one of the composer's best pieces.

The Louisville performance is beautifully shaped and is further proof of the high rank of this organization.

Essay for Orchestra No. 2, Op. 17

☐ New York Philharmonic / Schippers (conductor) / Odyssey Y-33230

In his Opus 17 Barber's lyricism is darker and more impetuous than in most of his other works. Schippers realizes it better than Golschmann in his competitive performance directing the Symphony of the Air on Vanguard 2083.

Intermezzo from Act IV of *Vanessa*

☐ New York Philharmonic / Kostelanetz (conductor) / Columbia Special Products 91A02007 (monaural)

This is the only recorded remainder of Barber's four-act opera. The complete opera was once available on RCA Victor (LSC-6138) together with a separate, abridged version (on RCA Victor LSC-6062). The Intermezzo is an eloquent bit which Kostelanetz plays most effectively.

Medea: **Ballet Suite, Op. 23**

☐ Eastman-Rochester Orchestra / Hanson (conductor) / Mercury 75012E (monaural)
☐ New Symphony Orchestra of London / Barber (conductor) / Everest 3282E (monaural)

Music of archaic and contemporary contrasts, displaying Barber in his most dynamic stance. More than once in this seven-movement piece (originally conceived as a ballet score for Martha Graham with the title *Cave of the Heart,* then orchestrally amplified a year later and initially performed by Ormandy and the Philadelphia Orchestra), the harmonies take on a polytonal tang.

Hanson's vividly shaded execution is the first choice. However, the Barber-led entry has pertinent value. It represents the reissue of a disc first released in 1950 by London. The "electronically re-recorded to simulate stereo" method turns out fairly good to the ears. However, Everest should update its purchases before remarketing them. The liner note remains as it appeared originally, so one reads that Barber's "most recent works" do not go beyond 1947!

On a recording, Barber shows he is quite capable of conducting his own music. As a conductor in public, Barber remains totally unknown.

Medea: **Medea's Meditation and Dance of Vengeance, Op. 23a**

☐ Boston Symphony Orchestra / Munch (conductor) / RCA VICS-1391

The portion of the Ballet Suite (*see above*) that is fast becoming a modern perennial. Its performance is worthy of the Bostonians' reputation and is better projected than Schippers's conception with the New York Philharmonic, issued on Odyssey Y-33230.

Music for a Scene from Shelley, Op. 7

☐ Symphony of the Air / Golschmann (conductor) / Vanguard 2083

The scene Barber chose is the fifth in the second act of *Prometheus Bound*. Orchestral richness is given its full head in the music, and it is easy to identify the romantic territory we are in. But there are no clichés.

The defunct Symphony of the Air shows how competent an aggregation it was in this reading; the strings sound especially warm.

Overture to *The School for Scandal*, Op. 5

☐ New York Philharmonic / Schippers (conductor) / Odyssey Y-33230

Do not be misled by the early opus designation. Although this was Barber's graduation piece at the Curtis Institute in Philadelphia, it is far from pedantic.

Schippers neatly depicts the general light mood of Barber's subject. The conductor's conception of the elegant and sensitive second theme is especially compelling.

Symphony No. 1 (in One Movement), Op. 9

☐ Eastman-Rochester Orchestra / Hanson (conductor) / Mercury 75012E (monaural)

Though Barber's Symphony combines classical ideology with a romantic enlargement of harmony, it also has some latter-day touches—the orchestration contains Sibelian colors and the lusty drive of many a passage is kin to the music of Shostakovich.

Hanson performs Barber's opus with care for each of the separate divisions as well as for their integration. Strickland's mono release on CRI has considerably less merit; the same is true of the pair of stereo releases available (Measham conducting the London Symphony and Schermerhorn directing the Milwaukee Symphony).

Symphony No. 2, Op. 19

☐ New Symphony Orchestra / Barber (conductor) / Everest 3282E (monaural)

The only recording available—an old one, originally on London (LL-1328). Although the performance is acceptable, the sound is not as spacious as one desires these days.

Set forms contain Barber's work; yet some unorthodox handling of the designs makes the piece much more direct and personal than Barber's other compositions. The lines sing but have sting, and forceful harmony heightens the drama.

String Orchestra

Adagio for Strings, Op. 11

☐ Philadelphia Orchestra / Ormandy (conductor) / Columbia MS-6224

Currently, five conductors of this work are represented on seven releases. Some of the collections are quite a mixed bag. (No arguments from this end, except to state that it seems unsound merchandising to companion Barber's Adagio with Ives's *Fourth of July*, as Columbia has done on its MG-31155.)

Ormandy's emotional affinity for Barber's rich music (it has achieved a popularity that parallels the once ever-performed Prelude in C sharp minor by Rachmaninoff) makes his the prime recording. And where are there better string players than those in the Philadelphia aggregation? The Adagio is also in another Ormandy release, on Columbia M-30066.

Serenade for String Orchestra, Op. 1

☐ Symphony of the Air / Golschmann (conductor) / Vanguard 2083

An Opus 1 is sometimes a spilling of unnecessary creative blood, believed in by the creator but fraught with mishaps and miscalculations. Barber's Opus 1 is well ordered and is in no way pedantic. Especially, the contrapuntalistic opening movement deserves admiration.

The Serenade was written for either string quartet or string orchestra. In the latter setting Barber's restrained, semiaristocratic type of romanticism of course speaks with a fuller voice, but this only emphasizes the lyrical outpour. Golschmann directs a fitting portrayal and obtains a fine sound from his musicians.

Band

Commando March (1943)

☐ Cornell Wind Ensemble / Stith (conductor) / Cornell University 6

Composed during Barber's term of service in the army during World War II. A band march written by a leading contemporary composer is an extraordinary incident in any case, but unless one has the particular talents of a Sousa, the incident is a waste of musical powder and shot. In this writer's opinion, *Gebrauchsmusik* is not for this composer. Others may have a contrary opinion.

Solo Instrument and Orchestra

Organ

Toccata Festiva, Op. 36

☐ Philadelphia Orchestra / Biggs (organ) / Ormandy (conductor) / Columbia MS-6398

Set an organ with an orchestra and the monumental style appears. Thus the Barber work, a first-class essay of full-blown romantic music.

Biggs plays with authority, including the cadenza for the pedals alone. Nice cohesion with the orchestra.

Piano

Piano Concerto, Op. 38

☐ Cleveland Orchestra / Browning (piano) / Szell (conductor) / Columbia MS-6638

Doubtless the most performed piano concerto by a contemporary American composer,

Barber's work was further honored by winning the 1963 Pulitzer Prize.

One can understand its acceptance. Pianistic to the hilt, it contains no-nonsense tonal romanticism, dramatic tossing between solo voice and piano in the first movement, natural melody in the Canzona, and a Finale of touch-and-go character, with its meter excited by quintuple arrangement.

Barber wrote the work specifically for John Browning, and he is master of the piece (and has achieved most of his reputation because of it). This is a great performance, and that includes George Szell and the master orchestra he conducted.

Concerto for Violin and Orchestra, Op. 14

Violin

☐ New York Philharmonic / Stern (violin) / Bernstein (conductor) / Columbia MS-6713

A preface is required regarding this work. Though the tale has been, more or less, told elsewhere, the names of those involved have not. Now, after all, Samuel Barber has reached the three-score-and-ten mark, and it's time to indicate all the facts of a work he wrote forty years ago.

The Concerto was commissioned by the wealthy soap manufacturer Samuel Fels for his musical protégé Iso Briselli. On the arrival of the first two movements Briselli complained of the lack of brilliance for the solo instrument. Barber promised there would be plenty of opportunities in the finale. When that was delivered, our young violinist said it was too difficult. End of connection of Briselli and the Barber concerto. The premiere was then arranged and given by Albert Spalding. The odd point is that the finale, a *Presto in moto perpetuo,* needs a blaze of fiddling but that Briselli underestimated himself and was fully equipped to deliver the goods. This finale consists of an ostinato of triplet figures in all but 3 of the first 172 measures; parallel attention to sixteenth-note figuration is given in the 16-measure coda.

Well, time passes, and no one today is frightened away by that finale, least of all Isaac Stern. He plays the pants off the movement and is lyrically superlative in the assuasive quality of the first two-thirds of the piece.

Wondrous Love: Variations on a Shape-Note Theme, Op. 34

Instrumental

☐ Harmon (organ) / Orion 76255

Organ

The contrapuntal encounters of the four Variations show Barberesque fluency. The final one is the least conventional of the set. There is variational music aplenty in the world, much of it without a real note of music in it as it travels over the bar lines. This is never true of Barber's handling of variation technique, which is always beautifully turned in its tonal enthusiasm.

A sincere performance, well phrased and directed, and very decently recorded. The instrument Harmon uses is the Schoenberg Hall organ at UCLA.

Excursions, Op. 20

Piano

☐ Shaulis (piano) / Composers Recordings S-295

Barber's set of investigations are American in spirit, with a desire to express dance color, dance design, dance freedom. And they do this well. The feet will jig along with the square-dancey beat of the concluding piece in the group of four. Zola Shaulis serves up the concoction with splendid pulsion. She understands the affinity that lies in this music for quasi-nationalistic and free romantic impulses.

Nocturne (*Homage to John Field*)

☐ Johannesen (piano) / Golden Crest S-4065

Barber in Chopinesque disguise. However, his contemporary profile is recognized in the harmonic adornments. Grant Johannesen plays with sensuous tonal beauty and emphasizes the melancholy that pervades the music.

Sonata for Piano, Op. 26

☐ Cliburn (piano) / RCA LSC-3229
☐ Browning (piano) / Desto 7120

Traditional forms, but containing controlled twentieth-century temper. There is a key center (E flat minor), but aesthetic freedom allows Barber to dip into twelve-tone waters, a bit in the dramatic and energetic opening movement and much more in the emotive and dark-toned *Adagio mesto*. The Scherzo is snide and seems to be program music without a program. A virtuosic Fugue completes the work, a polyphonic product that Poulenc indicated ''knocks you out [*vous met knock-out*] in some five minutes.''

There is much to credit in both of the recorded entries. Cliburn is heavier in coloring the opening movement; Browning is more pointed in the Scherzo, though timewise both cover the ground practically in a dead heat. In the Fugue, Cliburn has greater blaze, while Browning is a bit more careful in describing the action of the polyphonic congress.

RCA certainly provides better sound. It also offers three band separations for the four movements. Desto offers none.

Chamber Music

Sonata for Cello and Piano, Op. 6

☐ Greco (cello); Zeyen (piano) / Orion 7297

An important part of this Sonata's design is the telescoping of the inner slow and Scherzo movements into one. The two outer movements are in set forms; the first is in sonata arrangement, with lines that sing in a traditional manner and neat romantic harmony, the last consists of a series of connected variations on a theme, though it is not so titled. But this movement's construction is exceedingly tight-knit. Its sections unfold with no recapitulated material.

If you can find the deleted RCA mono album LM-2013, then you can obtain the best recorded edition ever issued of Barber's piece. Piatigorsky and Ralph Berkowitz, pianist, are the artists. It is just this type of romantically constructed music that suited this team. Orion's musicians do well but are no match for them.

String Quartet, Op. 11

☐ Cleveland Quartet / RCA ARL1-1599

Styled with excellence of design and avoiding any rigid and complex technical system, Barber's quartet exemplifies his fine training and conservative outlook.

The Clevelanders perform with romantic regard for the score, and the sonics RCA supplies are luscious. The famed Adagio is heard here in its pristine four-stringed state. It is played beautifully and with a certain finesse that cannot be produced in the expanded string-orchestra version.

Summer Music for Woodwind Quintet, Op. 31

☐ New York Woodwind Quintet / Concert-Disc 216

If diplomatically written music is one's taste, then this quasi-impressionistic one-movement Quintet will certainly please. It shows Barber retaining his leading role as one of America's elect eclectics.

It is played by the Baron-Roth-Glazer-Barrows-Weisberg team beautifully. (If one can find the deleted Columbia Special Products AMS-6114 disc, its performance with greater tonal intensity by the Philadelphia Woodwind Quintet is worth obtaining.)

Beware of Concert-Disc's labeling error. In place of side 1 data, the label information for side 2 is repeated. The number of bands involved provides the solution. Side 1 has two bands; the first one covers a work by Ingolf Dahl (Allegro and Arioso), the other covers Barber's Summer Music. Side 2 consists of four bands, and these totally represent a Quintet for Winds by Alvin Etler.

Bessie Bobtail, Op. 2, No. 3   ***Nocturne*, Op. 13, No. 4**
I Hear an Army, Op. 10, No. 3   ***Sure on This Shining Night*, Op. 13, No. 3**

☐ Hanks (tenor); Friedberg (piano) / Duke University Press DWRM-7501 (monaural)

Barber's rich romantic craft is exhibited here, especially in the *Nocturne*. Barber is an expert contrapuntalist, and his textures are always alive because of this ability, illustrated by the canonic framework of *Sure on This Shining Night*. This first song has been described as having Mussorgskian strength; it is woven around a trenchant rhythmic figure. The second song of the group is the most frequently performed of Barber's vocal output.

If one prefers a soprano voice, *Sure on This Shining Night* is available on New World Records NW-243, with Bethany Beardslee as the very adequate vocalist and Robert Helps at the keyboard.

Hermit Songs, Op. 29

☐ Price (soprano); Barber (piano) / Columbia Special Products CML-4988 (monaural)

A set of ten Songs set to texts by anonymous Irish monks and scholars living between the years 700 and 1300. The music is sung exquisitely; the words, however, are not very clear.

Nuvoletta, Op. 25

☐ Steber (soprano); Biltcliffe (piano) / Desto 6411/2

An unusual choice of text here: a passage from James Joyce's *Finnegans Wake*. Nevertheless, Barber conquers the chosen problem with great flair and resourceful writing for the piano that simulates orchestral qualities. He also resorts to some sound parallels with the prose, but his use of musical literalness does not mean he is an active member of the programmatic-music party. Thus *Tristan* is quoted for "born to bride with Tristis Tristior Tristissimus"; a Gregorian-chant contour accompanies "From Vallee Maraia to Grasyaplaina, dormimust echo!"; and both intervallic size and rhythmic totality equal the counting in "the tears of night began to fall, first by ones and twos, then by threes and fours, at last by fives and sixes of sevens."

Be sure to follow the printed text. While Steber passes muster with her voice, the same does not apply to her diction. And even if it did, Joycean words ("spunn of sisteen," "sfumastelliacinous") need eye contact for the fullest appreciation.

Dover Beach, Op. 3

☐ Juilliard Quartet / Fischer-Dieskau (baritone) / Columbia Special Products AKS-7131

Full-blown romantic temper to fulfill the spirit of Matthew Arnold's poem. The piece was written at the early age of twenty-one, but is a work to be admired on its own merits. Fischer-Dieskau interprets this music with becoming intensity.

Voice and Orchestra

Knoxville: Summer of 1915, Op. 24

☐ New Philharmonia Orchestra / Price (soprano) / Schippers (conductor) / RCA LSC-3062

Barber in his most lyrical vein, with music magnificently designed for the voice. In some respects Barber's romanticism has never been so substantial and so subtly passionate.

There is superb certification of the music in this recording. *Knoxville* was commissioned by Eleanor Steber, who recorded it with William Strickland conducting. This version is still in print (a mono disc), on Odyssey 32160230. Very much worthwhile.

Two Scenes from *Antony and Cleopatra* (1966)

☐ New Philharmonia Orchestra / Price (soprano) / Schippers (conductor) / RCA LSC-3062

Since the possibility of seeing this opera is rather remote (Barber has not had many defeats in his career, but the reception of this work was a total disaster), herewith a couple of samplings.

As experts these are found to be rich, and they have been recorded with sumptuousness. Leontyne Price gives a magnificent rendition. It is truly an inspired performance.

Choral

Chorus Alone

Three Reincarnations, Op. 16

☐ Gregg Smith Singers / Smith (conductor) / Everest 3129

Mixed-voice settings of poems by James Stephens, mainly concerned with neo-Renaissance contrapuntalistic style.

A tasteful projection of Barber's music. Note, however, that Everest titles this work incorrectly as "Reincarnation," and even avoids the opus designation.

Chorus and Orchestra

A Stopwatch and an Ordnance Map, Op. 15

☐ Symphony of the Air and Robert DeCormier Chorale / Golschmann (conductor) / Vanguard 2083

Music inspired by the Spanish Civil War, set to a poem by Stephen Spender, describing the death of a soldier in the battle against Fascism. Impressive and direct, with the voices supported by brass and timpani; the latter provides a special punctuative color that adds to the tragic contour of the piece.

The performers have extracted all the sonorous testimony detailed by Barber. It is a vivid portrayal.

Opera and Dramatic Music

A Hand of Bridge, Op. 35

☐ Symphony of the Air / Neway (soprano); Alberts (contralto); Lewis (tenor); Maero (baritone) / Golschmann (conductor) / Vanguard 2083

Barber deals this music with finesse. This is an extremely concentrated chamber opera; the interweave of outward vocal conversation with sung inner monologues is extremely realistic and simultaneously carries forward a viable plot.

Some of the diction is hazy, but with the entire text by Menotti printed on the inside of the record jacket, this problem is easily solved. The performance can't be termed a grand slam, but it certainly is a small slam.

Souvenirs, Op. 28   *Ballet*

☐ London Symphony Orchestra / Serebrier (conductor) / Desto 6433

Well-shaped, alive, lighter Barber. The kind of music that reminds one of Shostakovich's ballets (minus Russian dressing) and Khachaturian's (minus the Caucasian melos and Oriental turns). No hits here, no runs therefore—but, for what is proposed, no errors either.

There are six bands on the disc, but no label identification as to subtitles; nor is there any on the album headings. If one reads the lengthy (excellent, however) liner note by the late James Lyons, one will discover the movements are Waltz, Schottische, *Pas de deux,* Two-Step, Hesitation-Tango, and *Galop.*

Elaine Barkin   *(1932-   )*

String Quartet (1969)   *Chamber Music*

☐ American String Quartet / Composers Recordings S–338

Movement 1 is heavier and fuller in its action than the intensely wrought, tighter fragments that comprise the Variations of movement 2. No simplistic permutational definition in this case—we are dealing with an unfolding musical structure and not a partitional one; the transformation of Barkin's panchromatic music is continuous.

The American Quartet's grasp of this highly involved music seems absolute. There can be no denial that if the music is heard sufficiently, a similar grasp will be achieved by an unbiased listener.

Samuel Barlow   *(1892-   )*

Circus Overture (1960)   *Orchestra*
Cortège from *Ballo Sardo* (1950)
Mon Ami Pierrot: Overture (1934)

☐ Lamoureux Orchestra / Cornman (conductor) / Composers Recordings 178 (monaural)

Tonally respectable eclectic gentility is heard here. Barlow knows how to shape a tune, as heard in the middle section of the *Mon Ami Pierrot* Overture. The melodic idea in the *Cortège* is the best part of a piece that is a minting of unassertive formalism. The circus piece follows safe and sane procedures.

Wayne Barlow   *(1912-   )*

Night Song (1957)   *Orchestra*

☐ Eastman-Rochester Orchestra / Hanson (conductor) / Eastman-Rochester Archives ERA-1011

An attractive and representative nocturnal essay. Not profound, but no apologies are necessary.

Solo Instrument and Orchestra

The Winter's Past: **Rhapsody for Oboe and Strings (1938)**

☐ Eastman-Rochester Symphony Orchestra / Sprenkle (oboe) / Hanson (conductor) / Eastman-Rochester Archives ERA–1001

Oboe

Five minutes of heart-warming, gorgeous modality, based on a pair of Carolina folk tunes. The unlisted solo violinist deserves credit in this sensitive recording.

Ernst Gottlieb Baron *(1696-1760)*

Instrumental

Le Drôle **and Trio from Suite in A major**

Lute

☐ Satoh (lute) / Klavier 528

A fairly quick dance piece, shaped in the manner of a gavotte. The trio presents not only contrast but expressive rhythmic strength. A clear and attractive performance.

Chamber Music

Concerto for Lute Obbligato, Violin, and Bass

☐ Tryssesoone (baroque violin); Podolski (lute); Terby (bass viol) / Orion 7032

Simple patterns are contained in the three movements. Baron is at his best in the fast-tempoed sections.

Samuel Baron / *J. S. Bach.* See *J. S. Bach* / Baron.

Jean Barrière *(?-1751)*

Chamber Music

Sonata IV in G major, Book V

☐ Members of the Oberlin Baroque Ensemble / Vox SVBX–5142

A Corelli-like opus with an Adagio-Allegro-Adagio-Aria sequence. It is presented by use of a quinton (the baroque violin), with harpsichord supported by a bass viol. Fully artistic realization and most satisfying, especially in reference to tonal smoothness.

Agustín Barrios *(1885-1944)*

Instrumental

El último canto

Guitar

Vals **No. 3**

Vals **No. 4, Op. 8**

☐ Benítez (guitar) / Nonesuch 71349

"The Last Song" is framed by tremolandi, emphasizing the nostalgic feeling of the piece. Neither of the other pieces (''Waltzes'') make any unexpected moves. Benítez's expertise places these works in full perspective. They certainly couldn't be played better.

Francesco Barsanti   *(ca. 1690-1772)*

Sonata in C major for Flute and Harpsichord   *Chamber*
                                                                   Music
☐ Zuppiger (flute); Sgrizzi (harpsichord) / Nonesuch 73008

   Barsanti's Sonata (four movements: Adagio, Allegro, Largo, and Presto) was originally for the recorder. It has been so recorded (on Telefunken), but this setting, which does no harm to the work, and which actually gives it not only textural strength but depth, is much better, much more assured.

Rudolf Barshai. *See Prokofiev* / Barshai; *Shostakovich* / Barshai.

John Bartlet   *(?-?1600)*

Whither Runneth My Sweetheart?   *Vocal*

☐ Poulter (soprano); Brown (tenor); Channon (lute) / Nonesuch 73010   *Voice*
                                                                   and
   Lightly sexy and lightly pattered. As a contrastive change, Bartlet uses some imitation.   *Accompaniment*
Sung with delightful style and clear diction.

Béla Bartók   *(1881-1945)*

Concerto for Orchestra (1943)   *Orchestra*

☐ New York Philharmonic / Boulez (conductor) / Columbia M-32132
☐ Boston Symphony Orchestra / Kubelik (conductor) / Deutsche Grammophon 2530479
☐ Chicago Symphony Orchestra / Reiner (conductor) / RCA VICS-1110

   Bartók never repeated himself. While this indicated a personality recast over the years, it did not mean a lessening of technical depth. Because of the popularity of the orchestral Concerto, some have accused Bartók of ''writing down.'' The fact is that his style had simply resolved into refinement.

   Boulez sometimes cools the fires that burn in this suite-like affair, but the intensity and the sharpness of detail bring emotional chills. He provides a volatile perpetual motion of sound without seams in the Finale, where Bartók's fugal technique is supremely evidenced. The Kubelik statement is full-blooded, quite elemental. It is impossible not to include Reiner's performance. In its lucidity, dramatic authority, and virtuosity on behalf of the music his is an unqualified triumph.

   A few remarks about some recorded performances not selected. The superb Cleveland aggregation under Szell (Columbia MS-6815) plays with a neoclassically cool demeanor.

The Concerto for Orchestra requires more gutsy impulsiveness. Stokowski and the Houston Symphony Orchestra (Everest 3069) do not provide sufficient solo virtuosity and suppleness. As for Bernstein (with the New York Philharmonic on Columbia MS–6140), there's too much personal display in his ideas and Bartók lands in second place. The disconnective phrases in the piece must be denoted fluidically, not rhapsodically.

Dance Suite (1923)

☐ London Philharmonic Orchestra / Ferencsik (conductor) / Everest 3022

Indigenous content and spirit characterized Bartók's creative doctrine, whether internalized and blended within the formal design or comprising the cardinal compositional element. The combined Hungarian, Slovak, and Rumanian folk resource became coalesced into his musical language. He thereby represented the artistic voice of his countrymen.

This union is exemplified in the stylistic personality of the Dance Suite. The thematic material is totally Bartók's, yet the focus is native song and dance. A Bartók scholar has called this work an example of "imaginary folk music." No better example of such artistic alliance exists.

Proper depiction of this score demands robustness and expressivity as equal ingredients. The best offering comes from the L.P.O. led by the Budapest-born Janos Ferencsik.

Deux Images, Op. 10

☐ New Symphony Orchestra of London / Serly (conductor) / Bartók 307 (monaural)

The stamp of Hungarian and French (impressionistic) qualities is on the first piece. Though the latter style is unique for this composer, it is explained by the early date of the composition—1910. More typical Bartókian dialect is heard in the kinetic, shifting-tempoed *Village Dance.*

It is not surprising to find this is the only listing in the current *Schwann.* It is just as rare to hear these orchestral representations on concert programs, probably because of the hip-pocket repertoire of most conductors, which contains only flashy, fashionable and/or conservative standard music. Serly does nicely, probing the poetry of the first of these *Images* and underlining the hedonism of the other.

Hungarian Sketches (1931)

☐ Chicago Symphony Orchestra / Reiner (conductor) / RCA VICS–1620

Bartók transcribes Bartók in this instance. So much of this composer's keyboard music lends itself to orchestral arrangement that it is surprising he did not indulge in the practice more often.

Reiner's interpretations are vivid—exceptionally so in the very pointedness of *Slightly Tipsy* (from the Three Burlesques) and the savagery brought to the Bear Dance (from Ten Easy Pieces). The remaining items are *An Evening in the Village* (also from Ten Easy Pieces), Melody (from Four Dirges), and Swineherd's Dance (from the second volume of *For Children*). See under *Instrumental: piano* (Four Dirges; Fifteen Hungarian Peasant Songs; Ten Easy Pieces).

The Miraculous Mandarin: **Suite from the Ballet, Op. 19**

☐ London Symphony Orchestra / Solti (conductor) / London 6783

The Suite, covering about half the total ballet (or pantomime, as the score heading indicates it), is one of Bartók's most breathtaking pieces (see also under *Ballet*). The stage tale concerns a prostitute and three male confederates who rob and beat a pair of victims. Their next intended prey is a mandarin. He is robbed, but all attempts to dispose of him by smothering, stabbing, and hanging are unsuccessful. His longing for the woman unsatisfied, he refuses to die from the brutal treatment. It is only when she shows pity and embraces him that his desire is appeased, his wounds bleed, and he dies.

No choreographic association is necessary to appreciate the manner in which Solti handles the scores's rhythmic proliferation, concluding with a real "chase" sequence in frenetic fugal fashion. Even in its relaxed moments the music is a triply powered orchestral *Allegro barbaro*, with pulsatile muscle and blood supply amply administered by Sir George. The violence, reiterative patterns, and glaring glissandi (chillingly set forth in the performance), display Bartók's primitivistic style.

Music for Strings, Percussion, and Celesta (1936)

☐ New York Philharmonic / Bernstein (conductor) / Columbia MS-6956
☐ BBC Symphony Orchestra / Boulez (conductor) / Columbia MS-7206
☐ Chicago Symphony Orchestra / Reiner (conductor) / RCA VICS-1620

Bernstein's dramatic, expressive and also fiery reading of this work is truly exciting. No one catches the depiction of the brave, new contrapuntal world of the opening Fugue the way he does. There's high scholarship in the Boulez performance, but it doesn't interfere with authentic and dynamic conclusions. As with Bernstein, the magnetic rhythmic discourse of Bartók's masterwork is revealed to its fullest. The oldest recording of these three is that made by Fritz Reiner. It is meticulous but does not deny the power of the score. Like Bernstein and Boulez, Reiner understands the impressionistic quality of the third movement, but realizes that its darkness and mystery are as distant from French style as can be imagined.

Rumanian Folk Dances (1917)

☐ L'Orchestre de la Suisse Romande / Ansermet (conductor) / London 6407

No heavy make-up was applied to these Dances, originally for piano. Their sensitive beauty projects a warming immediacy totally conveyed in this performance. Ansermet does not overargue these miniatures. His steadiness is a welcome relief from the fidgets that mark so many interpretations.

Two Portraits, Op. 5

☐ L'Orchestre de la Suisse Romande / Fenyves (violin) / Ansermet (conductor) / London 6407

Despite Bartók's "for orchestra" indication in his classification of this work, there is no arguing the principal role of the violin in the opening portion. Further, this part duplicates the opening movement of an earlier Concerto for Violin and Orchestra (No. 1), which was thought lost until rediscovered in 1958 (see under *Solo Instrument and Orchestra: violin*). The second movement also exemplifies self-borrowing, being an orchestration of the last of the Fourteen Bagatelles for piano (see under *Instrumental: piano*, Four Dirges).

There's no uncertainty regarding Bartók's musical drawings. The imagery is sharp and severely contrasted in length and type. The first of the pair of *Portraits* is lyrically contrapuntal (it is identified as *Idealistic*); the other (*Distorted*) is a surly *presto* waltz.

Fine interpretative behavior is displayed by the soloist. Ansermet is a sensitive partner in part 1, a bit more refined than need be in part 2.

The Wooden Prince: Suite from the Ballet, Op. 13

☐ Southwest German Radio Symphony Orchestra / Reinhardt (conductor) / Turnabout 34086

A good portion of the complete score. Reinhardt's outfit plays in a rather neutral fashion; the exoticisms that are sprinkled throughout could certainly be presented more colorfully. (The recording was first issued by Vox—12040.)
(See also under *Ballet*.)

String Orchestra

Divertimento for Strings (1939)

☐ Academy of St. Martin-in-the-Fields / Marriner (conductor) / Argo ZRG–657
☐ Moscow Chamber Orchestra / Barshai (conductor) / London STS–15364

This work is the equivalent of a thesaurus of string-orchestra techniques, but Bartók's instrumentation is not merely machinery to move the Divertimento. It punctuates, highlights, places the material in proper perspective, and is an organic part of its totality.

The title of the composition is deceiving. Bartók's Divertimento is no airy amusement. It has plentiful cheer, but balances this with throbbing emotionalism plus introspective intensity. It has concerto grosso particulars and a goodly portion of contrapuntal engagement (canons and a fugue in the finale). These are decorated with the fanciful embroideries of a fiddle cadenza of quasi-Gypsy turn and a short, high-energy polka in pizzicato color.

Mind you, there is power and this power is needed in the playing. However, the use of a large string section is not propitious, and in any event, though he did not completely rule out a full body of strings, Bartók *preferred* twenty-two players—six each of first and second violins, four each of violas and cellos, and two double basses. In that way the drama, rhythmic pungency, and meaning are clarified. Ormandy (on Columbia M–32874) goes all out and truly loses the compactness of enlarged chamber music which is at the heart of the work.

Thus the smaller groups are where the choice lies, and of these the Marriner performance contains all the strengths necessary and subtle mutations to match. Barshai's ensemble plays with a richly romantic style, providing lyricism that almost eliminates the enunciative law and order of Bartók's score. But it has a natural flow-and-let-go which is most appealing, and the discipline is magnificent, as is the sound that London has furnished.

Solo Instrument and Orchestra

Piano

Concerto No. 1 for Piano and Orchestra (1926)

☐ Columbia Symphony Orchestra / Rudolf Serkin (piano) / Szell (conductor) / Columbia MS–6405

A miracle of coloristic creation, especially the middle movement, which is for the most part a remarkable duologue for piano and percussion. The entire work shows an industrious affection for rhythm. Bartók indicated that his Concerto reflected a study he had made of pre-Bach music. Scarlattian clarity is abundantly present, but though the opus may have been born of classical parents, it seeks unclassical, pulsatile paths.

Recorded performances of this work show clearly the old boys are better than the young ones. Rudolf Serkin is not merely content to reset the notes into keyboard sound; a fresh spirit that translates the printed score sweeps through his performance. One need only listen to the Bartók to realize the presence of a genuine artist. Sándor does beautifully (Turnabout 34065), but he is not given good support by the orchestra with which he works. Both Barenboim (Angel S–36605) and Peter Serkin (RCA LSC–2929) seemingly do not understand that the total design of the Concerto is validated by the rhythmic designs. In their hands these are colorful stuff, not structural substances. And they both tend to sentimentalize the unsentimental nationalism Bartók preached in this work.

Concerto No. 2 for Piano and Orchestra (1931)

☐ Berlin Radio Symphony Orchestra / Anda (piano) / Fricsay (conductor) / Deutsche Grammophon 138111

Formal classical apparel is fabricated with native cloth in Bartók's second piano concerto. The designs are neat, enhanced and embroidered with engaging color. The allocation of thematic material to both protagonists is rooted in the systems of the eighteenth century; the structural development, rhythmic thrust, instrumentational vitality, and percussive pressures are strictly twentieth century. The total is a brilliant blend.

It is the secure balance of these properties that makes Géza Anda's discourse practically perfect. Others tend to stress either the color contrasts or the basal flavor. Fine but not enough. Anda's forthright conception also provides a lesson in the difference between a forceful realization of the score's contents and mere forceful piano playing.

Concerto No. 3 for Piano and Orchestra (1945)

☐ Chicago Symphony Orchestra / Peter Serkin (piano) / Ozawa (conductor) / RCA LSC–2929

Relaxed, almost quiet music, but far from laconic. It is a conception that places poetry above drama, with a recital that is devoted more to repose than to strife.

Young Serkin recognizes the almost El Greco order of Bartók's Concerto. He describes the nobility and crystalline quality of the music. In particular, the climate of the slow movement is beautifully presented.

Rhapsody for Piano and Orchestra, Op. 1

☐ Southwest German Radio Symphony Orchestra / Sándor (piano) / Reinhardt (conductor) / Turnabout 34130

Comparing this production, composed in 1904, with Bartók's later work reminds one of Haydn's remark after he had completed his first three dozen string quartets. Now, he explained, his music would be in an "entirely new special style" (*Ganz neue besondere Art*). In contrast to the belly-whopping vigor and gusty individuality of his subsequent output, Bartók's first opus (first only in numerical designation—there were earlier pieces) breathes the simplicity and poetically assorted airs of romanticism; the climate is that of mild nationalism.

The earlier realization of the composition, for piano only, lacks the cheerful orchestrational fires that warm the ear and lend needed contrast. Bartók was wise in amplifying his Rhapsody not only texturally but also in terms of length.

Sándor's playing is well contoured and projects fully a sustained utterance that benefits the music. The recording was first released on the Vox label. For those who would want the solo piano version, a mono recording is available on which the piece is aptly played with finesse by Leonid Hambro—Bartók 313.

Two Pianos

Concerto for Two Pianos, Percussion, and Orchestra (1940)

☐ New York Philharmonic / Gold and Fizdale (pianos); Goodman (timpani); Rosenberger, Bailey, and Lang (percussion) / Bernstein (conductor) / Columbia MS–6956

Three years after writing his Sonata for Two Pianos and Percussion (see under *Instrumental: two pianos*), Bartók made this version of the composition. For some reason the enlarged-instrumentation version has never hit paydirt and its performance record is painfully small. Aside from the special values of the timbre concentration in the initial conception, it is impossible to pigeonhole the reason for the transcription's neglect. After all, everything remains the same and there is the bonus of more color.

This is the only recording available presently. The Mercury 90515 edition rests in the deleted category. No harm, since it cannot compare, in any way, with the juiciness of Columbia's production, which displays a mastery of pianistic soloism, percussion artistry, and conductorial consequence. Columbia heads its package with the statement "A Percussion Spectacular" (the Concerto is coupled with Music for Strings, Percussion, and Celesta). Agreed, in part. It *is* "spectacular," but more than just "percussion." It is really a "total performance spectacular."

Viola

Concerto for Viola and Orchestra (1945)

☐ New Philharmonia Orchestra / Menuhin (viola) / Dorati (conductor) / Angel S–36438

Death from leukemia prevented Bartók from finishing the viola concerto. It was left as a rough draft of fifteen unnumbered pages without any logical sequence. It was up to composer-violist Tibor Serly (a pupil and very close friend of Bartók's) to unravel the tangled hieroglyphics of the composer's musical shorthand. Serly spent some two years in his task of reconstruction. Naturally, it will be forever unknown how much of the Concerto is as Bartók would have had it.

It may be hindsight, but the viola concerto persistently indicates autobiographical overtones. Bartók knew he was dying as he sketched the piece, and this fact entwines itself within the lines, not in black-striped emotion, but in a certain despondency within the *Adagio religioso* movement and a somewhat ironic concept that jars the Hungarian cast of the finale. The confusing mood of the opening (spliced with Magyar elements) is weak; the music is patchy. This does not carry over to the deeply expressive slow movement.-In this movement the pathos is a foil for the defiance found in the following movement. Was this Bartók's final show of strength in his swan song?

Menuhin the violinist is as good as he has ever been, truly even better than ever, in his playing of the viola in this Concerto. He is persuasive throughout—intense in the first part, flexible and fervent in proper degree in the striking slow movement, firmly decided in the dancelike portions. He has virtuosic impact within the stylistic frame of the work. This is far better than the more restrained and intimate quality Raphael Hillyer supplies on Nonesuch 71239. In this instance, Hillyer's long chamber-music life tells in his performance. It is clean, but a little less interpretative refinement is needed. Further, in certain places his orchestral partner is less dynamic than should be the case. That criticism does not apply to Dorati's musicians.

Mention should be made of Primrose's version, a mono setting on Bartók 309. If the pocketbook permits, this version is to be considered as well. There is command in Primrose's playing and a noble refinement to his tone. However, be warned that each side of the disc is half empty.

Concerto for Violin and Orchestra (No. 1), Op. Posth.

☐ New Philharmonia Orchestra / Menuhin (violin) / Dorati (conductor) / Angel S-36438

Composed in 1908 for Stefi Geyer, a Hungarian violinist, this Concerto was believed lost until after her death. Geyer had kept the score hidden for fifty years and willed it to the conductor Paul Sacher.

The first movement of the pair comprising the composition is a duplicate of the initial piece in the later *Two Portraits* (see under *Orchestra*). This could mean that Bartók was dissatisfied with the Concerto and simply retained what he wished of the opus under a different title. The opening (slow) movement, built on a single, generating theme, does display finer craftsmanship than the second. However, the second movement has interest beyond mere historical reference. It is rhapsodic but not Hungarian, of concerto size yet formally loose. In totality, the formation proposes a fantasy constructed around a number of themes, with abrupt changes of mood.

As yet the Concerto, in contrast to the other Concerto for Violin and Orchestra (No. 2) (*see below*), has been resisted by the main concert-making fraternity. To have a recording is in the nature of a blessed event.

Concerto for Violin and Orchestra (No. 2) (1938)

☐ London Symphony Orchestra / Perlman (violin) / Previn (conductor) / Angel S-37014

The published music for this Concerto, composed in 1937–38, does not bear a number. For a long time it was thought to be the only concerto Bartók had written for the violin and thus to have no need of chronological identification. However, a two-movement Concerto for violin and orchestra had been completed thirty years earlier (*see above*). To avoid confusion, the habit of speaking of "the Bartók Violin Concerto" must be abandoned.

The Concerto is music first: a fusion of subtle (read mellowed) nationalism with drama that lacks bombast. Its technical bravado feeds artistic demands, accounting for its unusual early success. It is one of the few violin concerti that have been taken into the repertoire since the mighty examples by Bach, Mozart, Beethoven, Brahms, Mendelssohn, Tchaikovsky, and Sibelius.

The Perlman-Previn disc does full justice to the tremendous art of the composer. These musicians do not blemish the work by overconsidering its percussive cast as do Stern and Bernstein. There isn't an ounce of undue force in Perlman's playing, and yet there is all the required dynamism. No other violinist comes close to his lyrical, almost sensuous conclusions. They place the Concerto in a new light and lend a particularly beautiful glow to the music. Previn is no mere accompanist in this presentation; he is a full partner. The collaboration is a striking and marvelous artistic accomplishment.

Rhapsody No. 1 for Violin and Orchestra (1928)

☐ New York Philharmonic / Stern (violin); Koves (cimbalom) / Bernstein (conductor) / Columbia MS-6373

Bartók spins an honest musical tale of Hungarian rural society in place of the pseudo-café-society yarns of the Gypsies in this two-movement piece (the Rhapsody No. 2 is similarly structured : *see below*). The capriciousness of the style characterizes total artistic nationalism. Bartók's touch is light and entertaining in this piece; his mood mostly gay, though probing. In the initial movement (*Lassú*) there is a free flow of *rubati*, the music's measures marking a fluctuating improvisational type of *Lassú* lassitude. The second movement, a fresh *Friss,* is directly opposite in content.

Gutsy and earthy playing by Stern and opulent sound by the New Yorkers. The cimbalom timbre adds a striking touch to it all.

The Rhapsody No. 1 is also available on records in its original form—for violin and piano (see under *Instrumental: violin*).

Rhapsody No. 2 for Violin and Orchestra (1928)

☐ New York Philharmonic / Stern (violin) / Bernstein (conductor) / Columbia MS-6373

As in the Rhapsody No. 1 (*see above*), the pair of sections forming this work consist of restyled Hungarian folk melodies. Though a solo work that contrasts rhapsodic phrases with block-busting propositions, the music is dedicated to a full artistic objective and not designed for the adulation of a featured performer.

The presentation is richly colored. Required listening for those who seek the bare facts of real Hungarian music.

Two Portraits, **Op. 5.** See under *Orchestra.*

Instrumental

Piano

Allegro barbaro (1911)

☐ Kalichstein (piano) / Vanguard C-10048

Intense, with pugnacious pulsatile drive, and as tight as a drum, this concentrated savage piece is a key to Bartók's percussive, steely rhythmic style. Once termed the work of a composer traveling down a blind alley, it constitutes one of the most important contributions to contemporary piano literature. Bartók's music thunder-strikes the ear; it haunts the memory.

But unfortunately Bartók's small gem does not glow in any of the recorded editions. Most are fairly *allegro,* none are *barbaro.* The most nourishment will be found in Joseph Kalichstein's essay. Bartók's own interpretation on a monaural Bartók disc—903—should not be overlooked; the sound of his recording is heavy going for today's ears, however.

Dance Suite (1923)

☐ Silverman (piano) / Orion 74152

A very little known piano transcription that Bartók made of his orchestral composition (see under *Orchestra*). It remains on the shelves, though as the liner-note writer, John Downey, states, it does project "the vital and percussive aspects of the work."

Silverman's playing is most communicative.

Fifteen Hungarian Peasant Songs (1917)

For Children, Vol. 1 (Based on Hungarian Folk Tunes) (1945)

For Children, Vol. 2 (Based on Slovakian Folk Tunes) (1945)

☐ Sándor (piano) / Vox SVBX-5426

The overall pattern of Bartók's Fifteen Hungarian Peasant Songs derives from the folklore research that he carried on. The structural plan divides the composition into four sections, with the outer portions' tunes and dance melodies balancing the inner parts, designed in turn as a scherzo and variations on a ballade theme. Sándor's phrasing and sensitive range of dynamics for this set are models for performers of this Bartók score.

Though the two sets of *For Children* were designed for pedagogic purposes at the lower grade levels, the pieces are not bound by the confines of the teaching studio and have fully established artistic power. Forty-eight of the total seventy-nine pieces (originally there were eighty-five when Bartók completed the work in 1909—six of these were eliminated in the revised edition made in 1945) are spotlighted by succinct descriptive titles. In his statements Sándor considers refinement first, but there is sufficient dynamism in his playing.

Four Dirges, Op. 9a

Fourteen Bagatelles, Op. 6

Improvisations, Op. 20

☐ Sándor (piano) / Vox SVBX–5427

Recitative qualities predominate in the Four Dirges. Some see a kinship with Debussy in the style of these funeral chants. There are color splashes and chordal blocks, yet the intensity (truthfully realized by Sándor) is far removed from the Frenchman's world. Bartók's phrases are longer than Debussy's—the music *sings* more.

Twelve of the Bagatelles are right out of Bartók's inventory—for example, the polymelodic routine of the first piece and the motoric ostinato surrounding the harmonic frictions of the second. A pair are defined as folk songs; they have been tinted and festooned by the composer. Only the final two bear titles: *She Is Dead* and *Valse—My Darling Is Dancing*. The last of these forms the second of the *Two Portraits* for orchestra (see under *Orchestra*). Its melodic and harmonic acridity is just as fascinating in the restricted palette of the keyboard instrument.

There are subtleties in Sándor's pianism that are not found in Silverman's performances on Orion 74152. Still, the latter's fluidic conception is extremely worthy.

Opus 20 is a suite of eight pieces (the seventh in memory of Debussy) sometimes titled ''Improvisations on Hungarian Peasant Songs.'' Folk melodies are the starting point for independent originality. Plenty of gritty sand rubs against the strands of these simple tunes. Unburdened of any romantic thought, the Improvisations are concerned only with a supersophisticated formula that has special fascinations. The effect of Bartók's sharp vertical and horizontal shapes is like knives dug into sound. A neutral demeanor would be horrible in playing these pieces. No problem here with Sándor, who makes his performance match the music's fantasy.

Mikrokosmos (1935)

☐ Sándor (piano) / Vox SVBX–5425

Bartók's compositional catechism is traced through the 153 pieces that comprise the six volumes of *Mikrokosmos*. These range from the most elementary to the virtuoso level, the reasoning process embracing an amazing number of musical facets. Strict concentration on a pertinent problem is the objective of numbers devoted to legato, staccato, dynamics, and the like; others concern modes, some cover dance constructions. Programmatic forms, folkloric identification, and many more ideas are included; the scope of the pieces ranges from a tidbit to a work of fair length. It would be difficult indeed to find any fundamental resource lacking—even such subjects as wrestling and the buzzing of a fly are to be found in the descriptive pieces.

Planned as a pianistic course of initiation into the essences of contemporary techniques, the *Mikrokosmos* is totally free of the doctrinaire impulse. It is pure music that Bartók is preaching, not the gospel that merely produces an instrumentalist. These are art pieces from first to last.

Sándor's survey of the complete work is most revealing. He gives each piece—even the smallest and simplest—particular meaning. Having studied with the composer, he has a unique and authoritative advantage. It is definitely displayed in this three-record release.

Mikrokosmos, Vol. 6 (1935)

☐ Bishop (piano) / Philips 6500013

Those who only wish a sampling of Bartók's huge assortment will find Bishop's portrayal totally one of artistic integrity. The sixth volume contains fourteen numbers and is highlighted by the third piece, *From the Diary of a Fly,* and by the last half-dozen, titled Six Dances in Bulgarian Rhythm. It is especially in these that Bishop strikingly demonstrates his stature as an important pianist.

Nine Little Pieces (1926)

☐ Sándor (piano) / Vox SVBX-5427

Concentrated polyphony, contemporaneous formality, satire, and nationalism are contained here. Bachian influence is apparent in the first four *Dialogues,* where classical two-voiced counterpoint becomes translated into Bartók's language.

The music is finely defined by the soloist. In the polyphonic portions Sándor plays with a crispness that is especially effective.

Out of Doors (1926)

☐ Bishop (piano) / Philips 6500013

A descriptive précis need not accompany certain music to identify it as programmatic. In three of the five parts of this suite the forcible directness of Bartók's speech is a sufficient guide—the militaristic and ceremonial tone of *With Drums and Pipes,* the assorted sonic susurrations of *The Night's Music,* and the triggered action of *The Chase.* Each projects a vivid wordless scenario.

Comparisons of recorded editions by Bishop, Lee, and Sándor show that Bishop's interpretative camera is the sharpest of all three. A truly amazing control of color and the deepest scrutiny mark his playing.

Petite Suite (1936)
Rumanian Christmas Carols (1915)
Rumanian Folk Dances (1915)

☐ Sándor (piano) / Vox SVBX-5426

The *Petite Suite* consists of adaptations of six of Bartók's forty-four violin duets. Further evidence of Bartók's intensive folklore investigations is presented in the Rumanian Christmas Carols (*Colindes*). These interesting twenty tunes are drawn from a compendium of no less than 484 melodies and slightly elaborated for the piano.

The Dances (seven in all) are catchy tunes that occupy one of the top rungs of Bartókian popularity. The setting for piano was the original version. This music has been transcribed for strings, violin and piano, and other instruments—even the somewhat ridiculous combination of mouth organ and accordion! Regardless, the pieces wear well.

The performances are finely negotiated in all instances. The strength and delicacy heard in the Dances provide a distinguished presentation. (The cover of the Vox album incorrectly calls the Carols "Chorales.")

Seven Sketches, Op. 9

☐ Sándor (piano) / Vox SVBX-5427

If these *Sketches* are meant to be brief accounts, the use of sprawling form becomes questionable. Further, there is a blend of the introspective quality that marks expressionism with some indigenous melodic material. The stylistic merger is far from successful. However, Sándor does the best he can with the material.

Sonata (1926)

☐ Kalichstein (piano) / Vanguard S-10048
☐ Chodos (piano) / Orion 73122

Primitivism stalks through Bartók's largest work for the solo piano. It is tumultuous in the opening, thrice so in the finale, and tense in the central movement. There is no compromise with dissonance; the harmonic language employed bypasses the triadic in favor of the secundal smash, the barbaric vociferousness of sevenths and ninths, the simulation of bass and snare drums depicted by tone clusters. The effect is magnificently orchestral, a concord of sweet percusiveness. The artistic rawness of the piece makes it one of the most powerful of all contemporary piano sonatas.

The strategy in playing this work is not to try to overpower the already powerful score. Permitting the musical prose to register as though it were hurling obscenities is sufficient; there is no need to italicize them. For that reason Kalichstein's performance is both ripe and most idiomatic. The sounds he produces are tight, not splashed. One appreciates Kalichstein's stunningly frank *musical* realization, which is a mark of artistic dedication. Chodos's is a strong essay simply because he sings Bartók's lines and harmonies. Here too the percussive demands are permitted to sound out from their inner strength and are not overstressed by fricative keyboard action.

Sonatina (1915)

☐ Bishop (piano) / Philips 6500013

The Sonatina is diminutive, its contents a minuscule three-part suite. The first two sections are descriptive (*Bagpipers* and *Bear Dance*), the last a bit coolly identified as *Finale*. Actually it is a string of dance tunes from the region of Transylvania.

Bishop does not assume more than the music depicts. He plays it neat and clear—honest musical baldness, as it were. His performance is a charmer and thereby it is impressive.

Suite, Op. 14

☐ Lee (piano) / Nonesuch 71175

Bartók described the Suite in his own words on a recording that he made. He indicated that it has "no folk tunes, it is based entirely on original themes of my own invention." His objective was quite special: a "refining of piano technique into a more transparent style . . . of bone and muscle."

The opening has all the turns, accents, and playfulness of peasant musical language; the imitative style is as rich as any authentic, earthy dance tune. No adornments are hung on the Scherzo, and the wild homophonically packed third movement is similarly lean. Bartók's "bone and muscle" purposes are fully verified. The final slow and sustained portion parallels the close of the String Quartet No. 2, composed during the same period.

Noël Lee's performance is beautifully conceived, representing the fullest comprehension of the composer's ideas. It is worth comparing with Bartók's own rendition—contained in a "must" album for the collector titled *Béla Bartók at the Piano* (in addition to his own music, Bartók plays Liszt's *Sursum Corda,* and four Sonatas by Domenico Scarlatti). This album is monaural, of course; and as it should be, it is issued by Bartók Records (founded and directed by the composer's son, Peter, a highly skilled recording engineer). The catalogue number is 903.

Ten Easy Pieces (1908)
Three Burlesques, Op. 8c

☐ Sándor (piano) / Vox SVBX-5427

"Easy" is not precisely the case. In a few instances the technical scope is several cuts above the elementary. Also, though the pieces are wedded to simplicity, they have an engaging depth of meaning—even the one devoted to fingering problems.

Two of the pieces are orchestrally represented in *Hungarian Sketches* (see under *Orchestra*): *Evening in Transylvania* (renamed *An Evening in the Village* in the instrumentally amplified version) and the exciting *Bear Dance.*

Opus 8c proves Bartók's wizardry at musical description. No stories are detailed to the last comma in this threefold depiction, yet each sketch is patently clear. The first depicts a quarrel, the second a slightly drunk person, the last a capricious individual. In his musical processes Bartók does not demand a story-following listener. If one wishes, the imagination can float along with these pungently harmonized lampoons.

Sándor's version of the Ten Easy Pieces is beautifully played and intelligently artistic. The other work is given a solid, musicianly depiction.

Three Etudes, Op. 18

☐ Jacobs (piano) / Nonesuch 71334

Paul Jacobs presents these pieces with flair and understanding. The first, a headlong toccata, is played full of *brio.* The second of the group deals with impressionistically conceived material. However, Jacobs emphasizes the sharp edges in the music. The finale is an essay in rhythmic and agogic unrest. Jacobs plays it swift and sure, smooth as a billiard table. Thereby the subtle touches in the score register much more than in a performance opting for a place in the show-off category.

Three Hungarian Folk Songs (1907)
Three Hungarian Folk Tunes (1917)

☐ Sándor (piano) / Vox SVBX-5427

The Folk Songs consist of one vivacious and two quiet settings of melodies originating in the Csik district of eastern Transylvania. No capriciousness on Sándor's part. The utmost simplicity rules, and the music makes its point thereby.

In the other set the harmonies are exceedingly reticent, as though they did not want to intrude on the *parlando-rubato* quality of the tunes, all in moderate speeds. The music registers well under Sándor's direction, who again doesn't indulge in any fancy-Dan fantasies.

Three Rondos on Folk Tunes (1927)

☐ Kalichstein (piano) / Vanguard C-10048

The first of the Rondos, composed in the period 1916 to 1927, is charming and lightweight music, trimmed with modality. This is in direct contrast to the remainder, written eleven years later, which have greater depth and leaner textures.

The difference in performing difficulty is just as marked, and care must be taken not to overemphasize the contrasts and thereby tear the continuity. Kalichstein's reading is tasteful, with all details brought to light, making everything eminently clear.

Two Elegies, Op. 8b

Two Rumanian Dances, Op. 8a

☐ Sándor (piano) / Vox SVBX-5427

"A return to the old romantic afflatus" is the way Bartók described his Two Elegies. Such discursive, quasi-Lisztian writing is perhaps a delight for some pianists, though it offers minimal returns to the listener. The inflated substances are neither elegaic nor stamped with the Bartókian insignia of creative authenticity. But in any event, this kind of music is a pianist's meat and potatoes, so Sándor gobbles it up.

Opus 8a is not to be confused with the Rumanian Folk Dances. This is completely Bartók's product. Bravura is the axiom that guides the Dances. No gentle and swaying *graziosos* relax the rhythmic dynamo that powers every measure. The vehemence and restless violence are like Rumanian relatives of the *Sacre du printemps*. Sándor plays this dazzling music to the hilt.

Sonata for Two Pianos and Percussion (1937)

Two Pianos

☐ Brendel and Zelka (pianos); Schuster, Berger, Minarich, and Zimmermann (percussion) / Turnabout 34465

Bartók's Sonata is a tour of a fascinating new timbre world. Always emphasizing the percussive qualities of the piano, Bartók employs it as part of a complex that calls for pitched and nonpitched wooden, membraneous, and metal pulsatile instruments. These include small drums with and without snares, plus bass drum, thereby affording graduated relative pitch. The same ratio of high-, middle-, and low-range sounds exists among the suspended and clash cymbals, the sopranino triangle, and the bass-zoned tam-tam. Further melodic interaction is realized between the wooden accented response of the xylophone and the string accentuation of the piano.

The integration of the instrumentation continues into a considerable application of massed formations of sound, either by chordal counterpoint or by two-dimensional harmony. This magnificent array of tonal power is not employed for mock experimentation. Though the designs of the three movements (sonata allegro, ternary, and rondo) are standard, they are given a complete new look by the color properties employed.

Though there are some blurred sonorities, for the greater part this is a very alive and stylish recorded conception. It was first issued by Vox (9600).

The work was later expanded into the Concerto for Two Pianos, Percussion, and Orchestra (see under *Solo Instrument and Orchestra: two pianos*).

Suite for Two Pianos, Op. 4b

☐ Richard and John Contiguglia (pianos) / Connoisseur Society S-2033

Bartók's redraft of his Suite No. 2 for Orchestra. In no sense is this the usual keyboard reduction, but a fresh approach to the composition itself as well as a voicing and texturing of the material to fulfill the requirements of the two-piano medium. A thoroughly balanced performance.

Violin

Rhapsody No. 1 for Violin and Piano (1928)

☐ Szigeti (violin); Bartók (piano) / Vanguard 304/5E (monaural)

Bartók wrote a pair of rhapsodies for violin and piano in 1928. He later set both of them for violin and orchestra (and he also arranged the first one for cello and piano). In no way does the orchestral format replace the keyboard-instrument setting. Neither does the transcription process deny the value of the initial version. It merely gives us two different coloristic conceptions of the same subject: one is achromatic, and the other, the orchestral one, is made from vivid instrumental dyestuffs.

Only the first Rhapsody in the violin-piano form is available on records at present. The choice is clearly that noted above, even with the sound a bit below par. Of course the decision may be to bypass this two-instrument setting in favor of the violin-orchestra transliteration. If so, see under *Solo Instrument and Orchestra: violin.*

In *Schwann* the work Szigeti and Bartók play is incorrectly indicated as the "Rhapsody No. 2." Another error: should one decide on the stereo performance on Klavier 535 (with Zsigmondy, violin, and Nissen, piano), be warned that the label information on the disc has been reversed.

Sonata for Solo Violin (1944)

☐ Ricci (violin) / London STS-15153

Bartók's Sonata for violin alone is music for a virtuoso. It requires virtuosic listening as well; its demanding scope extends to the auditor. However, despite the limits of the medium, the Sonata's formal organization is beautifully exposed.

Ricci has competition, but he leaves it behind with his stunning coverage. In the *Tempo di ciaccona* he underlines the Magyar contours. The difficult three-part Fugue is conquered, and in the kinetic concluding movement he emphasizes the darting insectlike sounds and the choreographic frenzy. Considering its huge emotional and technical range, Bartók's work is the equivalent of a symphony for a single violin. Ricci orchestrates it with documentation of punctilious, punctuated, amazing virtuosity. No note is left unturned or untuned—as though an X-ray had been turned on the music.

Chamber Music

Forty-four Duos for Two Violins (1931)

☐ Fenyves and Martin (violins) / Musical Heritage Society MHS-1722

Far from ordinary duets, these are among the most original compositions in the entire literature for two violins. Pithy and concentrated, almost raw, the Duos serve a double purpose—as important chamber music in their own right and as a succinct index of the composer's artistic philosophy and technical style, paralleling the huge *Mikrokosmos* for piano. In the Duos' tender and strong images (replete with color but free of trick effects) one again perceives Bartók's imposing individuality.

Fenyves and Martin play with poise and pay careful attention to all the details. Actually, a mite more sensitivity in the more difficult pieces (from No. 30 onward) is depicted in the recording by Victor Aitay and Michael Kuttner (on Bartók 907). However, it is an old mono disc (a re-release of Period's two-disc album [SPLP-506]), and the sound is not the best.

Sonata for Violin and Piano
No. 1 (1921) / No. 2 (1922)

☐ Stern (violin); Zakin (piano) / Columbia M-30944

The Sonata No. 1 was composed in 1921, at a time when Bartók was moving toward a synthesis of the native material he had gathered during his investigations and was casting off, at the same time, the type of euphony that can be termed semiromantic nationalism. It was a period of sinewy and dogmatic aggressiveness. No warm breezes were permitted to enter the music's territory. The Sonata storms, is violent, but is fortified with new conventions. The creative decree reads: free harmony, chord combinations joined by sharp spikes, vehement rhythm, almost a ravishing of the body of the sonority. This is not music for shy ears.

In the Sonata No. 2 a dazzling panorama is revealed replete with unconditional fantasy. Emotional impact emerges from the sheer independence of the design. The music's mercurial stride is not of mere velocity, but has an evolutionary objective as it gathers all portions into two related functions of muralistic dimension. The first one is depicted in brooding melismatic style designed with figurated typically Magyar improvisation—a musical statement with its complexity sharpened and given varied qualities by vibrant rhythm plus sonorous light and shade. The second function is an abstraction of Hungarian melos with the reality of folk-music translucence—the real thing, not something given fake romantic polish.

Now, Bartók does not play to the gallery in his Sonatas; he is not an exhibitionist. In the hands of some performers the temptation to overdramatize the exceedingly difficult problems of both scores has resulted in interpretative overkill. It is to Stern's and Zakin's credit that they respect this music as true musicians and do not act as virtuosi out to make a showy success. Zakin provides a radiant combination of colors in his playing, from flutelike swaying cascades to sharply enunciated brassy-brash percussions. Stern does not overemphasize what is already texturally tight. He fashions with Zakin a unifying force of balance while his instrument sings or scintillates with abandon.

One point to be noted: the violin has been recorded close up, and this sometimes interferes with the proportionate strength of the two instruments. (The independence of the two voices is a notable feature of the Sonatas.)

For a package release of the two works this album is given the highest recommendation. In addition, two single issues are available (*see below*), and both offer something very special.

Sonata No. 1 for Violin and Piano (1921)

☐ Mann (violin); Hambro (piano) / Bartók 922 (monaural)

Truly, one of the most superb performances ever recorded of any of the Bartók violin and piano sonatas. Probably *the* most superb. It is rich with marvelous sound, perfect balance, and minute knowledge of every note. It offers an exciting experience to the listener. Far better than the Stern-Zakin recording (*see above*) if one merely wishes this work and not both violin sonatas. The mono setting is no drawback whatsoever, but the fact that the work is spread over two sides results in a large number of empty record grooves for which the buyer pays.

Sonata No. 2 for Violin and Piano (1922)

☐ Szigeti (violin); Bartók (piano) / Vanguard 304/5E (monaural)

The reason for obtaining this recording is to be found in the name of the pianist, though Joseph Szigeti need not take a distant second place. The sound is not one to draw raves (the Sonata was recorded live at a Library of Congress concert held on April 13, 1940, then preserved on acetate discs from which this recording was made). However, the historic feature demands full attention, despite the fact that Vanguard's recording cannot sonically compete with Columbia's fully up-to-date release (*see above*). It's worth owning both Stern-Zakin and Szigeti-Bartók.

Contrasts for Violin, Clarinet, and Piano (1938)

☐ Mann (violin); Drucker (clarinet); Hambro (piano) / Bartók 916 (monaural)

Contrasts was composed specifically for the combined talents of Joseph Szigeti, the erudite violinist, and Benny Goodman, who has bridged the gap between dance hall and concert auditorium by appearing as a soloist in both. This team, together with Bartók fortunately, recorded the trio, and (like the chosen disc, Bartók 916) their record is monaural. However, it exemplifies important musical history, and it can be secured on the Odyssey label (32160220E).

The version listed above presents vital playing far better than the single stereophonic edition available (on Turnabout 34480, played by Lemser, Lautenbacher, and Kontarsky). It also has keener musical intelligence.

String Quartet
No. 1, Op. 7 / No. 2, Op. 17 / No. 3 (1927) / No. 4 (1928) / No. 5 (1934) / No. 6 (1939)

☐ Juilliard Quartet / Columbia D3S–717

Bartók's six String Quartets furnish an index to his creative career. Romantic elements are present in the first of the set, but checked by special use of rhythm. Tonality is only somewhat confirmed; Bartók merely hints at the folk tales brought back from his travels. Quartet No. 2 shows the hand of a more subtle artist, without a definite changing of style. The folk element is not distinct, but ingrained in contemporary harmonic forms.

In the next pair of Quartets, No. 3 and No. 4, all previous techniques are reshaped; the formal procedures are new, the writing for the instruments of amazing individuality. The pizzicato and glissando ideas and the fashioning of the texture itself give evidence of integral creation, not merely superficial invention. Romanticism has been cast off; the period of elaboration has arrived.

Assimilation begins in Quartet No. 4. This work is just past the boundaries of Quartet No. 3 and not quite into the territory of the final works in the medium. With the composition of the last two Quartets Bartók arrives at his final period of work. All elements—technical and aesthetic—have been solidified. The product represents mature reflection.

The Juilliard Quartet's performances are old standbys, and their Bartók conceptions are truly aged in the wood. No other group can really challenge their status as *the* spokesmen for the Bartók String Quartets. While the Végh foursome (Musical Heritage Society MHS–1501/3) form an excellent team, one expects greater passion and excitement than they express, as well as a more intense diagnosis of Bartók's fabulous scores. Security and verve mark the performances of the Fine Arts team of Quartets No. 3 and No. 4 on Concert-Disc 208. Unfortunately, the galvanism these players produce is not sufficiently strong here, nor do they probe the profound meanings of the music. But theirs is an honest re-creation if not a learned one. This cannot be said for the Ramor presentation of all six works (Vox SVBX–519). This team refuses to follow Bartók's minute score directions. *Crescendi, decrescendi,* and sudden dynamic thrusts are glossed over, and the electrical juice is short-circuited.

Worth tracking down is a long-out-of-print performance of Quartet No. 3 by the defunct New Music Quartet, issued by the Bartók firm (no. 901). The disc also includes five *Mikrokosmos* transcriptions and Stravinsky's Three Pieces for String Quartet. The playing of the Bartók is a triumph of understanding.

Eight Hungarian Folk Songs (1907-1917)

Vocal

Voice with Accompaniment

☐ Chabay (tenor); Kozma (piano) / Bartók 904 (monaural)

Bartók fashioned settings of a considerable number of folk songs for solo voice with piano. Four Songs constituted the initial group, produced in 1904, followed by Twenty Hungarian Folk Songs, in association with Zoltán Kodály (*see below*), issued in 1906. The eight under discussion were arranged by Bartók between 1907 and 1917, and he completed a collection of twenty more in 1929. (Excerpts from the last group have been recorded and issued in two separate releases and are also discussed below.)

The vitality of the Eight Songs (like Bartók's others) is fascinating, each Song containing unequal phrases, quartal and pentatonic contours, and intriguing rhythmic *rubati*. In their own special way these minuscule conceptions have as much depth as many large symphonic documents.

The recording has superior interpretation and extremely fine sound. Full texts in English translation are furnished.

Five Songs, Op. 15

☐ Magda (soprano); Hambro (piano) / Bartók 927 (monaural)

This opus had never been performed anywhere until it appeared in recorded form as noted above. The curtain of silence that covered the cycle after its composition was drawn by the composer, who refused to divulge the author of the texts he used and therefore could not obtain publication. It has been suggested that one of the reasons for this secrecy was that the poems border on erotica. This is far-fetched, since not even the prissy-minded could consider the anonymous love strains of bluish tinge. Neither is there any *al fresco* nationalism in these almost grim, tightly sparse songs. They are like arias without colorful cadences or extrovert effects.

László Magda has a beautiful voice. It is not large, but she uses it with sensitivity. She presents the songs with a quiet emotivity that is entrancing.

Five Songs, Op. 16

☐ Hamari (mezzo-soprano); Richter (piano) / Deutsche Grammophon 2530405

Ballad-type compositions, minus folkloric reflection—a special brand of Bartókian creation. The introspective dark-tinged atmosphere of these songs, set to texts by Endre Ady, defines them as belonging to the expressionistic school. The performance is but fair, a lack of shading being noticeable.

Twenty Hungarian Folk Songs (Excerpts) (1929)

☐ Chabay (tenor); Kozma (piano) / Bartók 904 (monaural)

Bartók called the native tunes his countrymen heard in public surroundings the work of "domestic folk-song factories." Comparing these with the truly indigenous melodies Bartók culled on his travels accentuates the artistic difference that exists between manufactured popularisms and the simon-pure product. The squared regularity of the former is obvious and controlled, the latter is alive with pronounced differences of line, rhythm, and formation.

Four Songs are presented by Leslie Chabay, two of which have specific titles: *In the*

Jailhouse and *Fugitive's Song.* He sings with sensitivity and is accompanied by as sensitive a pianist. Both men being Hungarian, authenticity is total. A set of nine from the collection is also available, performed by the same team (*see below*).

Twenty Hungarian Folk Songs (Excerpts) (1929)

☐ Chabay (tenor); Kozma (piano) / Bartók 914 (monaural)

A set of nine from the collection. Four others are also available, performed by the same team (*see above*).

Two Songs from Twenty Hungarian Folk Songs (in collaboration with Zoltán Kodály) (1906). See also *Kodály: Vocal: voice with accompaniment* (Two Songs from Twenty Hungarian Folk Songs).

☐ Chabay (tenor); Kozma (piano) / Bartók 904 (monaural)

Between Franz Liszt and the great school founded by Béla Bartók and Zoltán Kodály there is a tremendous hiatus in Hungarian musical history. Likewise, between Liszt (who absorbed cosmopolitan tenets by spending more time in Paris, Vienna, and Rome than in Budapest) and Bartók there is a huge aesthetic gap.

Liszt's so-called Hungarian music does not have the natural national speech which was the fruitful result of the research carried out by Bartók and Kodály as a team. An absolute, authentic summary of folk music is presented in this twentyfold collection. In addition to stylistic truth, there is more warmth, depth, and flavorsome enjoyment to be found within these melodies than in all of the Liszt rhapsodies. The pair cogently sung here give full evidence (*see also below*).

Bartók, and Kodály too, published other songs separately (*see above* [Eight Hungarian Folk Songs]).

Two Songs from Twenty Hungarian Folk Songs (in collaboration with Zoltán Kodály) (1906). See also *Kodály: Vocal: voice with accompaniment* (Two Songs from Twenty Hungarian Folk Songs).

☐ Chabay (tenor); Kozma (piano) / Bartók 914 (monaural)

Two additional examples from the collection. For details, *see above.*

Village Scenes (1924)

☐ Hamari (mezzo-soprano); Richter (piano) / Deutsche Grammophon 2530405

Village Scenes depicts a Slovak marriage. Seemingly, Bartók has utilized actual folk music within the five songs. Not so. The essential melodies are firmly rooted in native (here Slovakian) culture but are all Bartók-made, first note to last.

Julia Harmari proceeds rather neutrally in her rendition. However, Konrad Richter is fine in his playing of Bartók's stunningly conceived piano support for the set of songs.

Choral

Chorus Alone

Four Slovak Songs (1917)

☐ Concert Choir / Hillis (conductor) / Bartók 312 (monaural)

Here is rugged vitality containing a full measure of the composer's personality. Bartók shows how to present folk song without harmonic cliché in a group consisting of a wedding song, a *Song of the Harvesters,* and a pair of dancing melodies from two different localities (Medzibrod and Poniky). The setting for mixed voices can be performed with or without accompaniment. Either way the spontaneity of these native tunes is refreshing.

An updated recording is needed badly. The Concert Choir's singing is not clear and its diction is blurred. Notwithstanding, it's worth trying to get past these problems and at least hear some good Bartók.

Twenty-seven Choruses (Excerpts) (1935)

☐ Concert Choir / Hillis (conductor) / Bartók 312 (monaural)

Authentic, native material is at the core of this striking assortment for two- and three-part singing. (The score is for either women's or children's voices with ad libitum accompaniment.) Bartók's music is of gentle dynamic order with subtle chordal intensities, the result of a blend of the traditional and the sophisticated. In this composite it is impossible to know where indigenous tunes leave off and Béla Bartók steps in.

The Concert Choir's presentation of eight of the Choruses is superb. (The recording's label incorrectly gives the total as nine. *Schwann* once listed this as "Twelve A Cappella Choruses," which is also misleading. This was the result of combining the eight excerpts with the Four Slovak Songs [*see above*].)

Twenty-seven Choruses (Excerpts) (1935)

☐ Budapest Madrigal Ensemble / Szekeres (conductor) / Monitor MCS-2054

Monitor's fascinating release called *Madrigals and Motets* (twenty-two pieces by fifteen composers) includes three Bartók Choruses. The first and second of these are not represented elsewhere; the third (*Ne Hagyi Itt!*) is a duplicate of the seventh Chorus on the Bartók Records release. A word of caution, however: the Bartók firm translates this title as "Only Tell Me," whereas Monitor renders it as "Do Not Leave Me!" The problem is that practically the same title ("Don't Leave Me") is used for the *first* of the excerpts on the Bartók release. This is an entirely different portion and should not be confused with the third of the Monitor excerpts.

The Hungarian ensemble displays superlative vocalism and musicianship throughout. The entire recording deserves the highest possible rating.

Three Village Scenes (1926)

Chorus and Orchestra

☐ Budapest Radio Orchestra and Budapest Radio Choir / Lehel (conductor) / Westminster Gold 8210

The *Three Village Scenes* are parts 3, 4, and 5 of *Village Scenes* for voice and piano (see under *Vocal: voice with accompaniment*), reset for a small group of women's voices and chamber orchestra. This is a score bright with virtuosity of plan. The *Scenes*, which are based on Slovakian folk songs, concern a wedding, a lullaby, and a dance; instrumentational delights pepper the vocal lines. The double dimension of this suite is an extraordinary accomplishment that combines tartness with sugar—a fusion of harmonic percussiveness and instrumental sharpness with female vocal suavity, a purposeful contrariness of anti-romantic sonorities linked with folksy tunes.

There is no paradox in this combination of the vocal portion's emotionalism and the cold objectivity of the orchestra's procedures. This conflict is obsessive and forms its own style.

The chorus gives a fine account, and the orchestra is in excellent form. The only version on the books, but perfectly O.K.

Cantata Profana (1930)

Cantata and Oratorio

☐ New Symphony Orchestra of London and New Symphony Chorus / Lewis (tenor); Rothmuller (baritone) / Susskind (conductor) / Bartók 312 (monaural)

Based on an old Rumanian folk ballad. Despite naïve subject matter the music is powerful. It is like a symphonic poem enriched with voices, containing a commentarial use of the orchestra and an instrumentalized treatment of the chorus.

At one time there were versions conducted by Rozhoktvensky (on Period) and by Hollreiser (on Vox). Now only this monaural issue is in the catalogue. Not such a bad situation, considering that Susskind directs a beautifully clear performance, one that has proper vigor and intensity as well.

Opera and Dramatic Music

Bluebeard's Castle, Op. 11

☐ London Symphony Orchestra / Ludwig (mezzo-soprano); Berry (bass) / Kertész (conductor) / London 1158

Why Bartók's only opera (in one act) has not become part of the international repertory is difficult to understand. Encased with rich melody and color, dealing with the fascinating subject of the psychological barriers between man and woman, and provocative in its suggested sadism, it has all the elements for success. (Also, with only two singers required, the matter of economy should be appealing.)

This is music not for the *Traviata* multitude, but for the *Pelléas* and *Wozzeck* class. There are no set pieces, arias, or duets, but almost constant musical dialogue. This is an opera that has acute instrumental discourse. Underlining, paneling, and channeling the action, the orchestra is the third member of the cast.

Currently, there are three editions in the catalogue. They have been compared with the four that have been deleted—conducted by Dorati, Ormandy, Fricsay, and Haefner. Among these, specially important is the Ormandy performance, which presented the work in an excellent English translation. But none match the treatment given by Kertész. It has polish and beautiful color, and he has penetrated the soul of Bartók's masterpiece. You can't ask for better singing, with depth blended with sensuosity on Christa Ludwig's part and a dramatic imposing realization by Walter Berry. The intensity of the score is underlined by the use of the original Hungarian, the marriage of text and music by Bartók being superb. (A full translation is included in London's packaging.)

Of the other two editions on the market, the old Bartók version (310/311) does have the spoken Prologue; London eliminates this on its recording but provides the full text (in English) in the program book that accompanies the release. The Westminster production (8219) I find poor and dull. It is sung in Russian, which doesn't fit Bartók's opera at all.

Ballet

The Miraculous Mandarin (1919)

☐ New York Philharmonic and Schola Cantorum / Boulez (conductor) / Columbia M–31368

The entire pantomime in one act (Bartók's score heading). A précis is presented in the comment on the orchestral suite (see under *Orchestra*). Every bit of the dramatic detail and all the colliding colors are vivid in this sonorous adventure directed by Pierre Boulez. There is no underplaying, fortunately, of the boldness of the writing.

The Wooden Prince, Op. 13

☐ New Symphony Orchestra of London / Susskind (conductor) / Bartók 308 (monaural)

The complete score of a ballet may be authentic, but quite often it lacks the tight construction that is necessary for music separated from stage action. The most interesting sections in this opus, marked by eruptive rhythms and abrasive harmonies, are contained in the orchestral suite, discussed above (see under *Orchestra*). However, here is the entire documentation, played and sounding well, for those who want it all.

An excellent booklet comes with the recording, giving a bit-by-bit description of the action with no less than thirty-seven musical illustrations. The release covers two discs, but side 4 is blank.

Bartók / Tibor Serly (1900-1978)

Mikrokosmos Suite   *Orchestra*

☐ New Symphony Orchestra of London / Serly (conductor) / Bartók 303 (monaural)

Those who know the eight items chosen for orchestration (the first of the set is *not* from *Mikrokosmos,* but the third of a group of piano pieces Bartók contributed to a memorial album in homage to Paderewski) will appreciate the way Serly brings new elements to light in this second look.

All the colorings are a delight. Included are such images as an updated Bourrée, a flip and explicit scherzo called *Jack-in-the-Box,* and one of the most brilliantly successful examples of musical onomatopoeia in the orchestral literature, *From the Diary of a Fly.* Close your eyes when listening and you're likely to reach for the swatter.

Bartók / Zoltán Székely (1903-   )

Rumanian Folk Dances   *Instrumental*

☐ Zsigmondy (violin); Nissen (piano) / Klavier 503   *Violin*

For reasons of wide range of timbre and singing lines these attractive pieces—discussed both under their original medium (see *Instrumental: piano, Petite Suite*) and under *Orchestra*—are beautifully apt for the fiddle. Székely's edition is tasteful and nicely colored; the harmonics utilized in the third Dance are especially delightful.

The playing passes muster, the sound raises some questions. Also, there have been some queer doings by Klavier. The performance is duplicated in Klavier 535. There, for some unexplainable reason, the work is titled "Two Rumanian Dances," though there are actually seven, the types of which (such as *Jocul cu Bâta, Pe Loc,* and *Măruntel*) are as colorful as the names identifying the five areas of origin (such as *Mezöszabad, Egres,* and *Nyágra*). The liner notes offer no help and also maintain the title error. Finally, this release suffers from reverse labeling.

Bruno Bartolozzi   (1911-   )

Variazioni for Violin Solo (1963)   *Instrumental*

☐ Gross (violin) / Orion 73107   *Violin*

Despite the use of free serialism, Bartolozzi's set of six variations is conceived without technical esoterica. The offspring is clearly related to the thematic parent. An excellent representation of the unaccompanied string-instrument medium.

Except for a couple of harmonics all goes well with Robert Gross's conception.

Robert Basart   (1926-   )

Chamber   **Fantasy for Flute and Piano (1963)**
Music
☐ Ketchum (flute); Schwartz (piano) / Composers Recordings SD–371

There is no acute balance of design in Basart's Fantasy. The axiom followed here, and well proved, is that unity exists in variety. However, there is no stylistic randomness. Formally exposed like an improvisation, the continuity is maintained by adherence to total chromaticism. A special factor is the supple textural play, covering all possibilities: solo flute, solo piano, concentrated two-voice use (flute and one voice in the piano), and assorted combinations of the two instruments.

This work is not easy to play by any means and requires sensitive control of the musical prose so that it doesn't sound fractured. Janet Ketchum and Nathan Schwartz fulfill all demands.

Leslie Bassett   (1923-   )

Orchestra   **Variations for Orchestra (1963)**

☐ Radio Zurich Symphony Orchestra / Sternberg (conductor) / Composers Recordings S–203

Music that flirts with but does not succumb to serialism. Tonal polarities hold the balance of power even though they shift constantly; thus a sense of panchromaticism hangs over the piece. It is strong music, variationally constructed without the usual primary thematic textual source from which permutations are drawn. Motivic material is the engendering device.

A granitic composition but an extremely learned and powerful one (it was awarded the Pulitzer Prize in Music in 1966). Sternberg conducts a strong reading.

Chamber   **Music for Saxophone and Piano (1969)**
Music
☐ Sinta (saxophone); Weckler (piano) / New World Records NW–209

A four-part work of eloquence in panchromatic style. Eric Salzman (erudite writer on matters contemporary as well as an excellent composer) calls the music close to "abstract expressionism" but I must disagree. This is romanticism as it was creatively observed in the year 1968. The chromatics are clean, not muddy, and their clarity and depiction are seen, as it were, through a magnifying glass.

Sinta is terrific. He's got technical nimbleness and virtuosic dexterity, but he also has musical perceptivity through which he shows how this instrument ought to be played.

Music for Violoncello and Piano (1966)

☐ Jelinek (cello); Gurt (piano) / Composers Recordings S–311

A compact work, tonally embraced, but expanded and freed of rigidity, with clear logic. There are four movements: *Origin, Invention, Variation,* and *Conclusion.* Included are some Bartókian reflections but no tricky, cheap ear-tickling moves. This is well-pointed chamber-music oratory, similarly presented by these fine performers.

Sounds Remembered (1971)

☐ Treger (violin); Sanders (piano) / Desto 7142

The sounds Bassett recalls are from the music of one of his teachers, Roberto Gerhard. Nothing really quoted per se—just a chord here, a short line, an individually colored isolated sound there. There is no possible function of imitation, therefore, as will be realized by those who intimately know Gerhard's music, but these sound shadows serve as a springboard for Bassett's rhapsodic registration. However, the rhapsody is not just bits and pieces strung together; the total effect is one of a shifting recitative that has a dark-colored emotional impact. This is cogently realized and depicted in the recorded performance.

Trio for Clarinet, Viola, and Piano (1953)

☐ Russo (clarinet); Trampler (viola); Nordli (piano) / Composers Recordings 148 (monaural)

Chromatic flexibility is paramount here. This adds a warm drive to the two fast movements and intensifies the lyrical qualities of the pair of Adagios. A particular piquancy of rhythm gives a divertimento stance to the former.

An attractive performance, executed with musical intelligence. That some spots could use more polish is in the too-late-to-apologize category.

Sextet for Piano and Strings (1972)

☐ Concord String Quartet / Graham (viola); Kalish (piano) / Composers Recordings SD-323

This music is charged and overcharged with percussiveness, blocked chords, nervously disposed rhythmic entrances, splitting of the sextet into differing fulcrums, pithy ostinati, clustered curves, and sharpened tensilities.

Bassett's four-movement opus was commissioned by the Koussevitzky Music Foundation and had its premiere performance in 1972. This recording was made possible by a Naumburg Award and fully deserves the honor. It is performed with dramatic drive and possesses an inner nervousness that richly portrays Bassett's exciting creation.

Thomas Bateson   (ca. 1570-1630)

Sister, Awake

Choral

☐ Purcell Consort of Voices / Burgess (conductor) / Turnabout 34202

Chorus Alone

This five-part madrigal example is one of the best in Bateson's output.

Hubert Bath   (1883-1945)

Cornish Rhapsody

Solo Instrument and Orchestra

☐ Boston Pops Orchestra / Litwin (piano) / Fiedler (conductor) / RCA LSC-3297

This ordered, lucid, and light music, which parallels the pops music of the Warsaw Concerto and the like, is the kind of stuff that Fiedler did best.

Piano

Philip Batstone (1933-   )

Vocal

**Voice
and
Instrumental
Ensemble**

A Mother Goose Primer

☐ U. C. L. A. Chamber Ensemble / Beardslee and Bond (sopranos) / Dare (conductor) / Composers Recordings S–243

More than straightforward vocal creation is considered here. There are psychological meanings laced into Batstone's mini-drama, with an echo voice and some participation by the instrumentalists. According to the liner note, the technique used is strictly serial "with regard to both pitches and rhythms."

The disjunctive world of twelve-tone music is, naturally, present and provides the usual difficulties for the voice. Bethany Beardslee probes every pitch with ease and effect.

Marion Bauer (1887-1955)

**String
Orchestra**

Suite for String Orchestra (1940)

☐ Vienna Orchestra / Adler (conductor) / Composers Recordings 101 (monaural)

Lucid and expressive, severe, middle-of-the-road music. The movements are a Prelude, an Interlude, and a Fugue. The players are bound to the notes, resulting in an academic rendition.

**Solo
Instrument
and
Orchestra**

Flute

Prelude and Fugue for Flute and Strings (1948)

☐ Vienna Orchestra / Adler (conductor) / Composers Recordings 101 (monaural)

Although outwardly a neoclassic work, there are plenty of romantic paragraphs. Bauer's sentiments are stated with expressivity and elegance.

This is one of the very early CRI records, so the sound is only average. Production is extremely poor: not a word about the work (or the companion Bauer work on the disc, Suite for String Orchestra [see under *String Orchestra*]), and the flutist is not identified.

Jürg Baur (1918-   )

Orchestra

Romeo and Juliet, Visions for Orchestra (1963)

☐ Symphony Orchestra of the Süddeutscher Rundfunk, Stuttgart / Müller-Kray (conductor) / Wergo WER–70001

Another orchestral view of the famous tale, this time a totally different one, in twelve-tone style with no big blasts or intense love music. Baur's four movements are each prefaced with a line from Shakespeare and followed by an explanatory sentence. The last of the four parts holds the deepest range in its death music.

Such approach has an individuality that is most striking when compared to Tchaikovsky's and Prokofiev's extroverted conceptions. Baur's creative disciplines provide an especially fine means for considering the story with material that is *verhalten und innig*.

The playing of the orchestra exemplifies superb musicianship and a tonal quality that is proper for the score. No extra juice is added. For this avoidance of a totally false ingredient one must thank the conductor, Hans Müller-Kray.

Heptameron, Sieben Stücke für Klavier (1964)

☐ Kaul (piano) / Wergo WER-70001

Baur's seven pieces, decked out with a colorful title, are etude born and borne. Accordingly, tremolo figures in the first item, emphasis on secundal combinations in the second piece, oppositional registral differences in quintal meter arrangement in number six, and so forth. Confirmed playing. Nothing is violated in Alexander Kaul's response to the music.

Divertimento: *Drei Fantasien für Cembalo und Schlagzeug* (1962)

☐ Goebels (cembalo); Caskel (percussion) / Wergo WER-70001

An almost classical chasteness embraces Baur's freely dodecaphonic Divertimento. The duo instruments being already so opposite, no new or unharnessed timbral effects are used; the percussion is "normal," with three each of different-sized tom-toms and cymbals, plus triangle, vibraphone, and xylophone. The outer movements have toccata personalities; the central one is aloof, is padded in sound, and treads slowly. Short quasi-cadenzas are integrated.

The playing is sensitive. In the person of the well-known virtuoso Christoph Caskel, the percussion could not be in better hands. The instrumental placement, however, favors his role in the proceedings.

Quintetto sereno (1958)

☐ Wind Quintet of the Südwestfunk, Baden-Baden / Wergo WER-70001

Serial style with a full concern in each of the six movements for clear and expressive communication. The moods are most positive in the sharply contrasting *Spiegel und Krebs* (stabilized use of the row for mirror and retrograde projection) and the *In Memoriam* (written to honor a war comrade). Superb playing and superb sound throughout.

John Bavicchi *(1922-   )*

Short Sonata for Violin and Harpsichord, Op. 39

☐ Brink (violin); Pinkham (harpsichord) / Composers Recordings 138 (monaural)

No stale sonic sensations are produced by this contemporary piece for violin and harpsichord. Such colorful timbre partnership is further emphasized here in the opening, free-fantasy formation. Additional evidence is found in the kineticism of the *Precipitato* finale.

Trio No. 4 for Violin, Clarinet, and Harp, Op. 33

☐ Glazer (clarinet); Raimondi (violin); Dell'Aquila (harp) / Composers Recordings 138 (monaural)

Sharpness of detail matches the intoxicant of oppositional timbre in Bavicchi's trio. Chromaticism and pungent polyphonic writing dominate the material. These effectuations are well-supported by the formal plans.

Arnold Bax   (1883-1953)

Orchestra   **Coronation March 1953**

☐ London Symphony Orchestra / Sargent (conductor) / Everest 3277E (monaural)

Another march written for the Coronation of Queen Elizabeth II in 1953 (see also *Walton: Orchestra* [Orb and Sceptre]). Bax's contribution is much more subdued than one expects from a march. Within this style he succeeds beautifully. The ending is pomp and circumstance in Baxian scoring with full orchestra, organ, fanfares, and bells. Of course, the performance is ideal.

The Garden of Fand (1916)

Mediterranean (1921)

Northern Ballad No. 1 (1933)

☐ London Philharmonic Orchestra / Boult (conductor) / Musical Heritage Society MHS-1769

The sea, the south, and the north are the areas covered in these three works.

The Garden of Fand, "entirely enveloped in the atmosphere of the calm Atlantic," according to Bax, is explicit program music. However, Bax's seascape has no aural flaw if heard minus the Irish legend of an enchanted garden ruled by a beautiful woman. Indeed, Debussy floats on the waters of Bax's score, but the latter is not harmed by such eclectic steering.

Bax says that his Ballad is a "general impression of the fiery romantic life of the Highlands of Scotland before the opening of the country subsequent to '45." For a note on *Mediterranean,* see under *Instrumental: piano.*

Interpretative details are splendid. So is the sound of this original Lyrita Recorded Edition (England), re-pressed here by the Musical Heritage Society firm.

November Woods (1917)

☐ London Philharmonic Orchestra / Boult (conductor) / Musical Heritage Society MHS-1229

A mood evocation of somber beauty. Bax's tone poem (one of his most important and most successful compositions) has a golden brown, rotogravure-like orchestration.

Boult directs a powerful delineation of music that can be described as a depiction of autumnal atmosphere with its winds driving leaves, its burnt colors, its cold and husky restlessness.

Symphony No. 1 in E flat (1922)

☐ London Philharmonic Orchestra / Fredman (conductor) / Musical Heritage Society MHS-1586

No reticent guff marks Bax's first symphony. This covers his orchestrational attitude as well; the instrumentation calls for a large orchestra including a heckelphone and a sarrusophone. Both of the end movements are dynamically direct, fiery, and forceful; the first of the pair adds bitterness to the emotively impassioned total statement. Music of elegiac property gives central balance to the total structure.

Myer Fredman is a new name to this writer. On the basis of this recording a fine conductorial talent is to be credited.

Symphony No. 2 (1925)

☐ London Philharmonic Orchestra / Fredman (conductor) / Musical Heritage Society MHS-1632

The unleashed power of the first symphony is not braked in the second, but is in fact of greater magnitude. The volatility is conclusive and brooks no counterevidence. No phlegmatic Englishman, this Bax! Both the first and the last movements ride in this sea of vehemence; the latter climaxing with the entrance of the organ that propels the auditor out of his listening place. (The organ use is no mere color trick but is germane to the sonorous climax required by the symphony.) The slow middle movement is mystically enveloped but has a straining undertone that relates to the music that precedes and succeeds it. A magnificent symphonic document.

The recording truly represents an inspiring, thrilling performance.

The album cover has a big boo-boo. The picture occupying half of the space is of Gustav Holst, not Arnold Bax. Also, no key designation is noted on the recording. The publishers, however, list the symphony as "in E minor and C."

Symphony No. 5 in C sharp minor (1932)

☐ London Philharmonic Orchestra / Leppard (conductor) / Musical Heritage Society MHS-1652

Bax's favorite system in his symphonies consists of three movements: two fast-tempoed ones surrounding a slow-paced division and the entire work ending with a epilogue. The C sharp minor opus follows suit.

The vehemence of Bax's fast movements continues here, except that this pair is less dark-colored than those in the earlier symphonies. The slow movement is a contemplative essay.

Symphony No. 6 in C major (1934)

☐ New Philharmonia Orchestra / Del Mar (conductor) / Musical Heritage Society MHS-1198

Again, three movements and once more an epilogue to conclude a Bax symphony. However, a new formal device marks the finale, which begins with an introduction and moves into a brutal, brilliant *scherzo,* one of the most powerful sections in all of Bax's output. Ecstatic tranquillity marks the epilogue. Julian Herbage describes this as a tour de force "that even Bax himself has rarely surpassed." It sinks into the marrow, this section, with its horn timbre as the prime voice.

Del Mar leads a truly magnificent performance. The wonderful range of the sonorities and colors in the work are displayed with rare musicality.

Tintagel (1917)

☐ London Symphony Orchestra / Barbirolli (conductor) / Angel S-36415

Bax indicated his piece as being program music "only in the broadest sense." However, by stating he was offering "a tonal impression of the castle-crowned cliff of Tintagel, and more especially of the long distances of the Atlantic, as seen from the cliffs of Cornwall on a sunny, but not windless, summer day," Bax nullifies consideration of the music in the absolute sense. The composition itself bears out the program and is a Britisher's *La Mer.* Indeed, it is such stuff as impressionism is made of.

Barbirolli paints it as it should be. All the instrumentational simulations of the scene are underlined and most effectively so. His is a masterful translation of Bax's image-rich score.

Instrumental

Cello

Folk Tale (1918)

☐ Hooton (cello); Parry (piano) / Musical Heritage Society MHS–7016 (monaural)

Introspectiveness and a folk quality (nonquotable type) combine in a work that is of fantasy detail, though a ternary plan is readily discernible.

Piano

Burlesque (1920)

☐ Loveridge (piano) / Musical Heritage Society MHS–7014 (monaural)

Harriet Cohen, the chief exponent of Arnold Bax's piano music, has described this succinctly as a "knockabout" piece. Verily so, as the skittish tune is kicked all over the keyboard range.

Ceremonial Dance (1920)
Country Tune (1920)

☐ Loveridge (piano) / Musical Heritage Society MHS–7011 (monaural)

The Country Tune is as much a dance as the Ceremonial item. It starts slowly and builds. Bax's ritualistic dance turns out to be a stately minuet, but far from three-squared in its contours. It was originally a part of a ballet with the odd title *The Truth About Russian Dancers.*

Dream in Exile (Intermezzo) (1916)

☐ Loveridge (piano) / Musical Heritage Society MHS–7012 (monaural)

A poetic fantasy, though the format is a ternary division. The atmospheric flow of the music bears out Bax's description of himself as "a brazen romantic," though *Dream* is never loud, showy, or gaudy. Bax's descriptive adjective should be read as "intense."

Iris Loveridge's performances of Bax's piano music contained on a number of Musical Heritage discs (originally recorded for Lyrita in England) are all of artistic sagacity. Especial mention must be made of the sensitive coloration she applies to this early Bax work, published in 1918.

A Hill Tune (1920)

☐ Loveridge (piano) / Musical Heritage Society MHS–7011 (monaural)

An al fresco evocation in three-part design. The principal tune has a rather Irish flavor, though most commentators have classified it as English. In any case, A Hill Tune is a fresh and delightful piano miniature.

In a Vodka Shop (1915)
Lullaby (1920)
The Maiden with the Daffodil (1915)

☐ Loveridge (piano) / Musical Heritage Society MHS–7013 (monaural)

Versatile variety. The first piece is a Russian dance with some lyrical contrast. Bax's Lullaby has a simple melody which he treats with harmonic variation. It is structured like a song in three verses, each followed by a refrain, also changed on each appearance.

Bax's *Maiden* (written in 1915) is akin to Debussy's *The Girl with Flaxen Hair,* composed five years earlier. The Britisher's lass has a more affable personality.

Mediterranean (1920)

☐ Loveridge (piano) / Musical Heritage Society MHS-7011 (monaural)

An Englishman's consideration of Spain, outlining the languid personality and light-hearted exuberance of its people. Bax was fond of the piece and made an orchestral setting (see under *Orchestra*). Jascha Heifetz also liked what he heard in *Mediterranean,* including its implicit sensuousness, and fashioned a transcription for violin and piano.

O Dame Get Up and Bake Your Pies (Variations on a North Country Christmas Carol)

☐ Loveridge (piano) / Musical Heritage Society MHS-7013 (monaural)

A delightful set of seven variations derived from the theme. The reason for the choice of the tune itself and its generic type are immediately recognized in the dedication: "To Anna and Julian Herbage in acknowledgment of pies baked and enjoyed 'on Christmas Day in the morning' 1945."

Loveridge is truly compelling in her playing of this gem. It was Bax's last piano piece, composed just before his death.

Paean (Passacaglia) (1927)

☐ Loveridge (piano) / Musical Heritage Society MHS-7012 (monaural)

A five-note generator powers this mighty conception from first to last. Seventy-three times it is heard in succession, a perpetual ostinato that frames, binds, and rides herd on the variances that surround or are combined with it. The result is a plethoric (but beautiful) texture that cries for orchestral treatment. Bax realized this by his orchestration of *Paean* in 1938, eleven years after he had written his potent Passacaglia.

A Romance (1918)

☐ Loveridge (piano) / Musical Heritage Society MHS-7014 (monaural)

Writing right out of the romantic era, its moods sustained and very slightly contrasted, but always quiet and almost remote, introspective.

Serpent Dance (1920)

☐ Loveridge (piano) / Musical Heritage Society MHS-7011 (monaural)

Mostly slow; mostly, to quote Peter J. Pirie, "a half humorous piece of oriental tushery, complete with wailing pipe and swaying snake."

Sleepy-Head (1915)

☐ Loveridge (piano) / Musical Heritage Society MHS-7014 (monaural)

Bax in a very relaxed mood. A simple tune with accompaniment.

Sonata No. 1 in F sharp minor (1919)

☐ Loveridge (piano) / Musical Heritage Society MHS-7011 (monaural)

A one-movement piece in the epic-romantic manner. Thematically full and with involved development, Bax's sonata with structural looseness is actually a huge fantasy. What it contains is more important and meaningful than adhering to strict formal procedures.

Sonata No. 2 in G major (1919)

☐ Loveridge (piano) / Musical Heritage Society MHS-7012 (monaural)

Like the first piano sonata, Bax's second is in one continuous movement. A sense of tragedy is contained in the work, and mostly it is dark-colored and heavily textured. Rhapsody becomes Bax here. Five principal themes are used in the structure.

Sonata No. 3 in G sharp minor (1925)

☐ Loveridge (piano) / Musical Heritage Society MHS-7013 (monaural)

This is a romantic conception, its adventurousness contained within a three-movement structure: a central Lento flanked by two fast-tempoed movements. The affinity of the Lento to Celtic folk song is strong, but no quotation—it's all Bax-built. To secure his construction Bax cyclically recalls the initial theme at the conclusion of the third part of the work, a music of toccata pilotage, its perpetual action dramatically dark-toned.

To clarify the epic character of the first part, a knowledgeable performer is required. Further, the complicated writing in the middle movement and the virtuosic documentation of the finale require a superb pianist. Iris Loveridge meets all demands and achieves a stunning success.

Sonata No. 4 in G major (1932)
Two Russian Tone Pictures (No. 1: *May Night in the Ukraine*; No. 2: *Gopak*) (1911)

☐ Loveridge (piano) / Musical Heritage Society MHS-7014 (monaural)

The Sonata has a fascinating middle division. Built on a pedal tone that shifts only at the conclusion of the movement, it provides a tension to the Ravelian, dreamlike music that surrounds the repetitive pitch sound. This *allegretto*-tempoed portion is one of the most beautiful of all Bax's conceptions.

Classical procedures, with some romantic amplifications, are followed in the outer movements. The initial one is sonata-based, its fanfare-like subject spiked with neat dissonant prongs. The finale is a rondo that flourishes with brilliance. The fourth sonata represents a major contribution to the literature for the piano.

Bax visited Russia in 1910. Impressions made upon him during his stay resulted in three piano pieces: the pair here listed and *In a Vodka Shop* (see above). *May Night* is, as expected, a nocturne. Its elaborate figuration heats the usual demeanor of the night-music form. The contrastive national dance, *Gopak*, shows Bax as much as it shows his creative native disguise. Strong rhythmic conditions, of course.

Water Music (1920)

☐ Loveridge (piano) / Musical Heritage Society MHS-7011 (monaural)

Music of clear, limpid grace. Liquidity is present in the melodic line, fluidity in the harmonies. Another of Bax's miniature treasures. Played with stylistic sincerity that deserves a four-star accolade.

What the Minstrel Told Us (Ballad) (1919)

☐ Loveridge (piano) / Musical Heritage Society MHS-7012 (monaural)

Quasi-program music (but without a stated *précis*). It epitomizes Bax's fondness for depicting legends in his music. This one is of heroic summary.

Winter Waters (1915)

☐ Loveridge (piano) / Musical Heritage Society MHS–7013 (monaural)

A miniature tone poem for the keyboard instrument. The landscape it portrays is haunting, of forbidding power. Structured as a passacaglia, the form is strengthened by Bax's sensitive ear for textural arrangement. A compelling opus.

Legend for Viola and Piano (1929)

Viola

☐ Forbes (viola); Cassini (piano) / Dover 7260

This piece is marked by Bax's usual dark lyricism, devoted to a type of elegiac rhapsody. The music is restrained, retrospective in its three-sectioned design. (An alternate version replacing the piano by a harp was indicated by Bax.)

Fantasy Sonata for Harp and Viola (1928)

Chamber Music

☐ Ross (harp); Vardi (viola) / Musical Heritage Society MHS–3613

There is sensuous enchantment and enjoyment in this work signifying Bax's view of impressionism. A touch of Celtic musical extraction clings to every note. There are no folk tunes in the sonata, but the sounds are those one might well hear on the Isle of Manx.

Bax's music is integrated and transfigured by the glow intrinsically available in the haunting combination of silvery plucked tone with mellow, bowed string sound. It is, indeed, an eloquent conception played eloquently by these fine musicians.

Legend Sonata (1945)

☐ Hooton (cello); Parry (piano) / Musical Heritage Society MHS–7015 (monaural)

Bax's fondness for musical chronicle appears often. It is not explained in this instance. The "Legend" indication notwithstanding, formal command striking perfect balances regulates his expressive romantic piece. It is especially apparent in the ruggedness of the soulful stringed instrument in the lyrical slow (second) movement.

Sonata in E flat minor for Cello and Piano (1923)

☐ Hooton (cello); Parry (piano) / Musical Heritage Society MHS–7016 (monaural)

The first movement relates two themes, but unity also stems from thematic transformation—the cut is different, but the thematic cloth is of the same weave. There are barcarole contours to the middle movement, and a placid (though rhythmically alive) rondo style in the last.

Sonata in G major for Viola and Piano (1921)

☐ Vardi (viola); Bogin (piano) / Musical Heritage Society MHS–3613

The mellow viola is, more than any other, the proper instrument for this composer's brooding lyricism. In this work, he fuses the elements of superbly singing lines with dark quasi-orientalisms (not harmonic but evocative) that find root in the tenor ruggedness of this soulful string instrument.

Bax's Sonata is bound together by referring to the opening theme at the end portion of the declamatory final movement. The second movement is an exhibition of various energetic and less taut moods. In the former state, quartal harmony persists; in the latter, its more tertial opposite. The movement's theme is entirely subjected, however, to cellular development.

Emanuel Vardi is one of the best viola players around. His performance is superb and Abba Bogin's is no less so. Their coloring is as minutely sensitive as is their ensemble.

Sonatina in D major (1933)

☐ Hooton (cello); Parry (piano) / Musical Heritage Society MHS-7015 (monaural)

Most pieces written in the diminutive sonata form tend generally toward the lighter side. Bax's three-movement opus, by its serious stance, shows the other side of the formal coin. Concentrated sonata form in movement 1, a three-part slow movement, and a set of variations are the structural blueprint.

Elegiac Trio for Flute, Viola, and Harp (1916)

☐ Robles Trio / Argo ZRG-574

Bax's Elegiac Trio stays at one main tempo level, its threnodic character restrained, not bitter, but rather retrospective. It is rhapsodic but shaped in a three-sectional design.

The playing of this team is respectful of Bax's score, and there are no critical question marks.

Quintet in G major for Oboe and Strings (1923)

☐ Manhattan String Quartet / Lucarelli (oboe) / Musical Heritage Society MHS-3521

The oboe has the featured role and Bert Lucarelli responds with immaculate artistry. Only a player of his ability can cope with the part, since the instrument is taken from its lowest B flat to practically its ultimate soprano tessitura limit.

A pastoral tinge is contrasted with fast-paced music in the first movement. The vernal music has rhapsodic foliage, however. The poetical slow movement is mainly in septuple meter. The theme is stated in the strings alone, and only in its restatement is the oboe permitted to sing its sensitive lines. A flashy jig concludes the quintet, brightly contrasting with the preceding atmosphere. Bax's Quintet is actually a series of three moods, a suite in the quintet medium.

An excellent release in all respects.

Oscar Bazän   (1936-   )

Instrumental

Two Pianos

Sonogramas (1963)

☐ Mainstream MS-5017

Divided into seven short movements played continuously (by two pianists, apparently, but no performer credits are given). The music is sternly dedicated to working out its Boulezian (as in *Structures*) and Stockhausian destiny.

Irwin Bazelon   (1922-   )

Orchestra

Chamber Concerto No. 2 (*Churchill Downs*) (1970)

☐ Ensemble / Bazelon (conductor) / Composers Recordings S-287

Not music for most of the horsy set (Bazelon's concert music is contemporaneously dead-centered and needs active listening participation). Catchy title notwithstanding, the piece is not programmatic, though it has a philosophical relationship to racetrack ambience. Thus, the composer: "I hoped to catch in my music the pulse and rhythmic beat of this mass audience spectator sport."

The music's weight has considerable jazz poundage, sometimes implied, sometimes stressed, by the use of an electronic group of guitar, Fender bass, organ, and piano-harpsichord. The remaining colors are a brass sextet (horn, three trumpets, and two trombones), triple percussion, and a woodwind voice that alternates between flute, clarinet, and alto saxophone.

Bright, brash colors match a bright, vigorous style in this case. The unrestrained dogma that relates to Bazelon's piece is as exciting as the performance he directs.

Short Symphony (*Testament to a Big City*) (1962)

☐ Louisville Orchestra / Whitney (conductor) / Louisville S-664

The subtitle implies programmatic pictorialism but nothing pertinent is defined. The outer, fast movements are nervous in disposition, the inner, slow division (indicated "plaintively") has similar compact drama. The fact that there is no detailed narrative does not negate effectiveness. All the tensions are realized in the Louisville performance.

Symphony No. 5 (1967)

☐ Indianapolis Symphony Orchestra / Solomon (conductor) / Composers Recordings S-287

Standard four-movement plan but no standard situations pertain here. Bazelon's Symphony is a combination of freely approached serial conditions, judicially laced with jazzy material and rhythms. It produces a symphonic reality of stylistic co-ordination.

It is good to have Izler Solomon represented on a recording, his career having been cut down by a stroke. Solomon's talents, especially with contemporary music, are proven in this case. He provides Bazelon's composition with a sharply defined and sensitively balanced performance.

Propulsions (1974)

Percussion

☐ DesRoches, Fitz, Gottlieb, Harris, Lang, Rosenberger, and Walcott (percussion) / Bazelon (conductor) / Composers Recordings S-327

No hard-sell tactics are required when a sizable (eighteen-minute) percussion work (Bazelon speaks of it as a Concerto) includes such timbre infusions as log, friction, and African "talking" drums, shell and wood chimes, cricket-clickers, a bass slide whistle, and so forth. No limits are placed on influences on the sounds in Bazelon's *Propulsions*, which calls for a variety of performance techniques.

This is a fascinating percussion publication, skillfully constructed and performed.

Duo for Viola and Piano (1963)

Chamber Music

☐ Phillips (viola); Jacobson (piano) / Composers Recordings S-342

Music that has drive and propulsive rhythms but is not oblivious of inherited coloristic and jazzy conventions that give subtle contrasts. The performance is musicianly to the last fractional pitch length, intense in feeling, and brilliant in execution.

CRI pulls a gaffe by listing the work, in the liner copy and on the record label, as

"Duo (for Violin and Piano)." If the use of parentheses implies that it was originally for violin and piano but is played in transcription for viola and piano, there is no mention anywhere of such a fact. Further, Bazelon's analytical note begins thus: "My duo for Viola and Piano. . . ."

Brass Quintet (1963)

☐ American Brass Quintet / Composers Recordings S–327

Brass quintet scoring is not as confirmed as that applying to the wind quintet. However, Bazelon's work follows fairly general practice, calling for horn, two trumpets, and two trombones (tenor and bass). Colors are paramount in the piece, structured so that the corner movements hold the fast-actioned music and the pair of inner movements move at moderate and slow pace.

This is an impressive brass composition, contemporaneously fleshed, but not rigidly tied to a specific system. It receives a performance of puissance by the American Brass team.

Antonio Bazzini   *(1818 - 1897)*

Instrumental

Violin

La Ronde des lutins, Op. 25

☐ Ricci (violin); Lush (piano) / London STS–15049

The word for this performance of "The Dance of the Goblins" is "formidable." One must be a violinistic wizard to cope with Bazzini's music. Ruggiero Ricci is that wizard. He knocks off everything required (and what requirements!): consecutive tenths, string changes equating the same pitch, harmonics, and flying sets of left-hand pizzicati that jump out of the record grooves like firecrackers. A technical feast for the ear, this.

Mrs. H. H. A. Beach   *(1867 - 1944)*

*Solo
Instrument
and
Orchestra*

Piano

Concerto in C sharp minor for Piano and Orchestra, Op. 45

☐ Westphalian Symphony Orchestra, Recklinghausen / Boehm (piano) / Landau (conductor) / Turnabout 34665

That this rich, romantic score lay untouched from 1917 (performed with the composer as soloist with the Boston Symphony Orchestra), until 1976, when it was heard in New York with the present soloist and Morton Gould conducting the American Symphony Orchestra, is merely another performance record that makes no sense.

The structure is ideal, the piano writing perfect for any soloist, with its suffusion of hearty melodies, cadenza sections, and plenty of musically oriented technical divisions. Nicely orchestrated and not a trace of sentimentality anywhere. (Some Kreisler reminders of *Liebesleid* and *Liebesfreud* in the full romantic release of the finale, but what came first is immaterial and the resemblance may only be in the ears of this listener.)

Heartily recommended music to listeners and pianists. A heartily recommended performance as well. Mary Louise Boehm deserves special plaudits for her rediscovery of this fine concerto.

Ballad, Op. 6

Five Improvisations for Piano, Op. 148 (Nos. 1, 2, and 4)

Four Sketches, **Op. 15**

Hermit Thrush at Eve, **Op. 92, No. 1**

Hermit Thrush at Morn, **Op. 92, No. 2**

Nocturne, Op. 107

Prelude and Fugue, Op. 81

Trois Morceaux caractéristiques, **Op. 28**

Valse-Caprice, **Op. 6**

☐ Eskin (piano) / Genesis 1054

Mrs. Beach's is an honored name in American musical history. The craft is admirable. One cannot dismiss Beach's music because it is less than fancy-coursed and of a more gilded period than the present. The warm elucidations are firmly drawn in the romantic language, with Chopinesque and light Brahmsian accents. None of the picturesque pieces (such as the *Danse des fleurs* in the *Morceaux* or the pair of *Hermit Thrush* delineations) are drawing-room baubles, but simply drawn differently from the more formally designed ones. There are plenty of changes of pace in Eskin's recital choices. A prime example is the modal flavor in the fourth of the Improvisations.

Virginia Eskin's strong belief in Mrs. Beach's music shows in her engaging playing. It is always plausible, always flexible, always controlled.

Sonata in A minor for Violin and Piano, Op. 34

☐ Silverstein (violin); Kalish (piano) / New World Records NW–268

Mrs. Beach's four-movement opus follows formal conventions (outer fast movements, a Scherzo and slow movement in between) but academic rites are avoided by the boldly effective writing for the instruments, the cohesion of the duo concept, and the thematic content. Nice long lines are to be heard in comparison with the banter and bounce of the Scherzo. The piece exudes both charm and strength and is far beyond the results of a historical musical dig.

Silverstein makes every note alive and flourishing. Kalish is a masterful pianist. Together they perform with distinction.

Piano Quintet in F sharp minor, Op. 67

☐ Boehm (piano); Kooper and Rogers (violins); Maximoff (viola); Sherry (cello) / Turnabout 34556

Beach's three-movement quintet sings throughout its standard proportions. Sometimes its emotions are slightly sentimental, but they are never gushy. Though some may term the music academic, the word is incorrect. It is extremely well-wrought, which means altogether something else again. That it is Brahmsian is no disgrace and needs no apology, for Beach's quintet has creative honesty, even if it is imitative.

The five musicians blend well and present a first-rate performance.

The Year's at the Spring, **Op. 44, No. 1**

☐ Gadski (soprano) / New World Records NW–247 (monaural)

Text (by Browning) and music blend in Mrs. Beach's gay morning song. The recorded performance, made in 1908 (for Victor), has grainy sound, of course, but the value of hear-

Instrumental

Piano

Chamber Music

Vocal

Voice with Accompaniment

ing Johanna Gadski's voice cannot be overlooked. (The accompanist was not identified on the original disc.)

Gustavo Becerra Schmidt   (1925-   )

Orchestra

Symphony No. 1 (1957)

☐ Louisville Orchestra / Mester (conductor) / Louisville LS–714

This is dark-paneled music, its progress based on the characteristics of classical form, thereby making identification easier. Tonality escapes in various directions but the concentrated mood holds the material in balance. A strong performance.

Chamber Music

String Quartet No. 4 (1959)

☐ Philadelphia String Quartet / Olympic OLY–102

Becerra Schmidt (or Becerra, as he is better known) practices motival procedures in his Quartet, applying to them serialized data of transposition, inversion, and the like. He also practices the meaningful coloristic devices developed in the quartets of Bartók, Berg, and Webern. The two go together nicely; especially the sonority choices emphasize the clear rhythms and astringent harmonies of the work.

The Philadelphians (formerly all of the Philadelphia Orchestra) perform with dash and style, and are completely convincing. Since this recording was made, the personnel of the quartet has changed. Here the group consists of Veda Reynolds and Irwin Eisenberg, violins; Alan Iglitzin, viola; and Charles Brennand, cello.

John J. Becker   (1886-1961)

Orchestra

Symphonia Brevis (Symphony No. 3) (1929)

☐ Louisville Orchestra / Mester (conductor) / Louisville S–721

Becker wrote on the flyleaf of his score (in 1929) that his Symphony "was written with an outraged spirit," as a "protest against intolerance, prejudice, pretense and sham." Further, he protests against pseudo-humanitarians and "against a world civilization which starves millions in peacetime and murders those same millions in wartime."

This credo is represented in music of barbed-wire strength, brusquely sculptured, carrying out the titles of the two movements: *A Scherzo in the Spirit of Mockery* and *Memories of War: Sorrow–Struggle–A Protest!* Becker's symphony uses the mediation of contiguous intervals to form his harmonic and contrapuntal plans. Frictions are the backbone, to be regarded as the tonic post of the fencework for the various lines. The primal factor of dissonance is constant and forms the overall background.

Becker's music of protest is an important sonorous document. That the conductorial world has totally neglected him only emphasizes the aesthetic insularism of its repertoire. That Jorge Mester has chosen to record his *Symphonia Brevis* is an important exception, and a beautiful one. The special credit he deserves carries over to this immaculate and understanding recorded performance.

Concerto Arabesque (1930)

☐ Members of the Oslo Philharmonic Orchestra / Kayser (piano) / Strickland (conductor) / Composers Recordings 177 (monaural)

Actually a "concertette," being only nine minutes in length. It is sufficient to exemplify Becker's lean and laconic style. The euphony of his harmony is the reverse of the usual combination of mellifluous thirds and sixths. In place there are the more active and abrasive seconds, sevenths, diminished octaves, and the like. Against this framework are placed broad lines and pert declarations. The harmonic constituents, therefore, pin themselves on the melodic breadths rather than embrace them, causing a greater textural contrast. The blithe bravado of Becker's dissonances is a refreshing no-nonsense attitude. The only available recorded performance is an assured one.

*Solo
Instrument
and
Orchestra*

Piano

David Bedford (1937-   )

Spillihpnerak

☐ Phillips (viola) / Finnadar 9007

A cornucopia of effects, with an abundance of glissandi: in slow motion and plucked, especially. Pizzicati and harmonics are sprinkled throughout this extroverted exhibition. Fun to listen to. Played in a manner that shows Karen Phillips must have had just as much fun doing so. That title is her name spelled backward.

Instrumental

Viola

Come in Here, Child

☐ Manning (soprano); Tilbury (piano) / Mainstream 5001

Both voice and piano become orchestralized by the use of reverberation for the former and a variety of piano amplifications. The ending consists of rustling sounds, forming a suspended prolongation of the magical mood that surrounds the piece.

Jane Manning's voice is intense and committed. It is ideal for this exquisite, fully contemporary piece.

Vocal

*Voice
with
Accompaniment*

Tentacles of the Dark Nebula (1969)

☐ London Sinfonietta / Pears (tenor) / Bedford (conductor) / London HEAD-3

An unusual text, taken from a science-fiction short story by Arthur C. Clarke, which covers the story of mankind "from the beginning to the end," as seen from one point (a beach). Bedford employs nonthematic color devices such as pitch snips, microtones, glissandi, and muted timbre that frame the vocal line, most of which is related to recitative. The neo-programmaticism is treated with restraint and thereby its effect increases.

Bedford's somber imaginings are portrayed vocally in an able manner by Peter Pears. His diction is less satisfactory. The printed text must be followed.

*Voice
and Orchestra*

Thomas Beecham / Frederick Delius. See Delius / Beecham.

Burton Beerman   (1943-   )

Instrumental

Clarinet

Sensations for Clarinet and Tape (1969)

☐ Rehfeldt (clarinet) / Advance 15

The sensational point in Sensations is the mild, fully fitting use of the tape as a counterbalance, in terms of form, contrast, and almost sonic gentility, to the clarinet. Unique as well are the electronic qualities in the clarinet sounds and vice versa. This is far from sensational music, but it makes for an extremely creative opus.

Jack Beeson   (1921-   )

Orchestra

Symphony No. 1 in A (1959)

☐ Polish National Radio Orchestra / Strickland (conductor) / Composers Recordings S-196

Beeson's operatic successes have caused his instrumental and orchestral music to be overlooked. The Symphony shows that Beeson's symphonic craft is of the best, regardless of the modicum of eclectic significance that creeps in. Two techniques are major strengths: the expert orchestration and the polyphony. Beeson's counterpoint *sounds* rather than being the oft-met receptacle for holding academic waste.

Strickland maintains a sober viewpoint of the score. This fits the piece even when its gestures are not restrained.

Vocal

Voice with Accompaniment

Calvinistic Evensong

☐ Gramm (baritone); Cumming (piano) / Desto 6411/2

No sing-song for Vespers is to be expected here. Beeson, one of the most successful of American opera composers, deals with a stark set of lines. Accordingly, this is a compelling song presented with just the right amount of intensity.

Choral

Chorus Alone

Three Rounds

☐ Gregg Smith Singers / Smith (conductor) / Composers Recordings S-241.

Deft and coloristic handling of voices in these settings of anonymous texts. In the first, *Give the Poor Singer a Penny,* a pitter-patter style evolves into full-blown polyphony and a dynamic plan of softness to powerful sonority and back to softness is developed. The division of the female and male voices in the last piece, *Boys and Girls Together,* is another example of Beeson's unusual scoring skill in the choral field.

The Gregg Smith Singers—a baker's dozen voices here—are excellent.

Opera and Dramatic Music

Hello Out There (1953)

☐ Columbia Chamber Orchestra / Gabriele (soprano); Worden (tenor); Reardon (baritone) / Waldman (conductor) / Desto 6451

In Beeson's one-act chamber opera, the text by William Saroyan has been "transposed, telescoped, or extended in accordance with the needs of musical, that is to say, operatic timing." The story line is pointed: a man in jail accused of rape, his flirtation with a lonesome girl, and the shooting of the man by the husband of the woman supposedly raped.

Saroyan has best described Beeson's work. He terms it "sombre, dramatic, and true." To which one can add that it is mostly shaped by highly sensitive and extremely natural vocal lines.

It is beautifully sung with a clarity that fully defines the text. The orchestral support is firm. Desto's edition is a transfer from the original Columbia release ML-5265.

Lizzie Borden (1965)

☐ New York City Opera / Faull and Elgar (sopranos); Lewis (mezzo-soprano); Krause (tenor); Fredricks (baritone); Beatty (bass baritone) / Coppola (conductor) / Desto 6455/7

Beeson's "family portrait in three acts" is based on the famous case of the 1890s concerning Lizzie Borden, the New England spinster accused of murdering her father and her step-mother. It is a hefty and excellent subject for operatic treatment interlocked as it is with psychological complexities. For this Kenward Elmslie has supplied a clear libretto (included with the album) and Jack Beeson has written a vivid score, braced by atonically implied terrors.

Herbert Beatty provides a stunning characterization as the father. Brenda Lewis as Lizzie is dynamic. The entire production is first-class.

The Sweet Bye and Bye (1956)

☐ Kansas City Lyric Theater Orchestra and Chorus / Rogers, Anthony, Seibel, and Green (sopranos); James (mezzo-soprano); Jones and Claffy (tenors); Latimer (baritone); Howell (bass-baritone); Hook (bass) / Patterson (conductor) / Desto 7179/80

Evangelism is the subject of Beeson's two-act, five-scene opera, its fictional libretto carefully skirting biographical presentation of the once-famous revivalist, Aimée Mac-Pherson, by creating the character of Sister Rose Ora Easter. Kenward Elmslie's libretto is excellent, depicting the hypocrisy, sexual repression, and shake-and-bake of commercial religion, and Beeson's score makes it work and makes it believable.

The three leading roles are given accomplished performances by Noel Rogers as Sister Rose, Robert Owen Jones as her man, and Carolyn James as Mother Rainey. The other characters, orchestra, and chorus match these. There's no doubt about the permanence of this opera.

Ludwig van Beethoven (1770-1827)

Eleven Vienna (Mödlinger) Dances, WoO 17 *Orchestra*

☐ Vienna Mozart Ensemble / Boskovsky (conductor) / London 6656

Some are Waltzes, some are Minuets, and two of the set are *Ländler*. Of course, since the latter is really the true original of the waltz, only a bit slower in pace, this means that all the music of these dances is contained in triple-beat measures. And of course, with Willi Boskovsky playing and directing matters with his fiddle à la Johann Strauss, the results could not be more profitable.

German Dances (Nos. 2, 3, and 8), G. 140 (WoO 8)

☐ Vienna Mozart Ensemble / Boskovsky (conductor) / London 6656

These are three of the set of twelve German Dances that Beethoven wrote. Three more are available (*see below*). Rendered in the usual persuasive Willi Boskovsky manner.

German Dances (Nos. 5, 10, and 12), G. 140 (WoO 8)

☐ Consortium Musicum / Lehan (conductor) / Seraphim S-60180

Performances of Nos. 3 and 8 are also included, but Boskovsky is the choice for whatever one can obtain (*see above*).

Grand Overture in C major (*Namensfeier*), Op. 115

☐ Berlin Philharmonic Orchestra / von Karajan (conductor) / Deutsche Grammophon 2707046

The *Namensfeier* remains a curiosity. Though not in the same league as Beethoven's other overtures, it has a reasonable amount of interest within it. At least, the rendition in this case makes that possible.

Leonore Overture No. 1, Op. 138
Leonore Overture No. 2, Op. 72a
Leonore Overture No. 3, Op. 72b

☐ Cleveland Orchestra / Szell (conductor) / Columbia MS-7068

''Outstanding'' is a mild word to describe this release. The detail is so magnificently presented that every structural relationship is apparent. The dynamic contrasts are so perfect that they seem to have been controlled by a computer. The quadruple *pianissimo* Szell obtains, and one that has true body strength, is a performance miracle.

These presentations could well be claimed to be the finest on disc. Truly, for the three *Leonore* Overtures Szell's editions are in the area of compulsory listening. (The companion piece to this group, also recorded by Szell, is of course the *Fidelio* Overture. *See below*.)

The second of the *Leonore* Overtures is also on another record: Columbia MS-6966.

Overture: *The Consecration of the House*, Op. 124
Overture to *Coriolan*, Op. 62
Overture to *The Creatures of Prometheus*, Op. 43
Overture to *Egmont*, Op. 84

☐ Berlin Philharmonic Orchestra / von Karajan (conductor) / Deutsche Grammophon 2707046

All the listings of Beethoven's Overtures take up ninety-seven lines in *Schwann*. Mind you, only eleven works are concerned. The coverage is not evenly divided, naturally. However, the disproportion is quite acute. For eighteen conductors who have recorded *Egmont*, only four have given any attention to *King Stephen* (see below) and only one has recorded the *Namensfeier* (see above).

The attention von Karajan has given to all but one of the eleven Overtures is to be noted in the five different D.G. releases containing them, with, of course, certain duplications. (In addition to the chosen issue noted above, the catalogue numbers of these releases are 139001, 139015, 2530414, and 2720011.)

The readings on D.G. 2707046 are truly strong and the playing is superlative; in the case of Opus 124 there is such a fresh interpretative viewpoint as to make one revise one's opinion about the work, most often considered as extremely low grade Beethoven. This is due to the pedantic manner in which conductors usually treat the score. In von Karajan's hands the music comes completely alive; the important polyphony within it scintillates, rather than dragging its feet.

The *Coriolan* Overture is also in three other D.G. packages: 139001, 139015, and 2530414. The last catalogue number also includes a duplicate von Karajan performance of the *Egmont* Overture.

Overture to *The Creatures of Prometheus,* Op. 43

☐ Vienna Philharmonic Orchestra / Böhm (conductor) / Deutsche Grammophon 2530448

Just a smidgen lighter in tone than von Karajan's consideration (*see above*), but excellent and fitting for the material.

Overture to *Egmont,* Op. 84

☐ Los Angeles Philharmonic Orchestra / Mehta (conductor) / London 6870

Mehta's rendition is extremely effective, especially in his handling of the pair of tempi changes. Brilliant sound.

Overture to *Fidelio,* Op. 72c

☐ Cleveland Orchestra / Szell (conductor) / Columbia MS-7068

The dimensions of this conception match those of the companion works, the three *Leonore* Overtures (*see above*). The scope of color and contrast is further testimony to the greatness of the Cleveland Orchestra and its late conductor. A better *Fidelio* Overture cannot be found in the recorded catalogue. The extraordinary shaping of the music and the relationships of the inner details are unforgettable.

Overture to *King Stephen,* Op. 117

Overture to *The Ruins of Athens,* Op. 113

☐ Berlin Philharmonic Orchestra / von Karajan (conductor) / Deutsche Grammophon 2707046

Small beer though *King Stephen* may be, in this reading it is given an interpretative injection that brightens its personality considerably. Extremely well-controlled playing in Opus 113, which is also included in von Karajan's Beethoven overture assortment on Deutsche Grammophon 2530414.

Symphony
No. 1 in C major, Op. 21 / No. 2 in D major, Op. 36 / No. 3 (*Eroica*) in E flat major, Op. 55 / No. 4 in B flat major, Op. 60 / No. 5 in C minor, Op. 67 / No. 6 (*Pastoral*) in F major, Op. 68 / No. 7 in A major, Op. 92 / No. 8 in F major, Op. 93 / No. 9 (*Choral*) in D minor, Op. 125 (discussed on p. 147).

☐ Chicago Symphony Orchestra / Solti (conductor) / London CSP-9

Everyone tries his hand at the Beethoven "nine." They all score points and demerits. Quite simply, it's not a simple matter to choose among the integral sets available, but no one can afford to own them all (except a reviewer-critic, a few libraries, or some collectors). The choice here of Sir George Solti with the Chicago organization is founded on two principles: the magnificence of the *sound* of the Chicago players and the great flexibility (within style boundaries) obtained by their conductor. The caveat is that there is more than one way of looking at a blackbird and the same goes for listening to the immortal nine symphonies Beethoven produced. Noted below are individual choices for each of the symphonies. Except for No. 7, these choices are limited to only one each, in view of the selection of the above for the integral edition.

Symphony No. 1 in C major, Op. 21

☐ Academy of St. Martin-in-the-Fields / Marriner (conductor) / Philips 6500113

Especially special because Marriner keeps down the size of the orchestra with no loss to the musical content. The result is most revealing, with a consistent clarity, a sonorous warmth, and a sensitive sweep. It deserves an ear-catching endorsement.

Symphony No. 2 in D major, Op. 36

☐ Concertgebouw Orchestra / Jochum (conductor) / Philips 6500088

Bold playing but within Beethovian creative property rights. Anyway, such dynamic emphasis belongs properly and firmly to the final pair of movements. The slow movement has breadth and its distinguished values are sung beautifully.

Symphony No. 3 (*Eroica*) in E flat major, Op. 55

☐ Philharmonia Orchestra / Klemperer (conductor) / Angel S–35853

Everyone speaks of Klemperer's slow tempi but fails to mention that when pace gives breadth and/or stresses the majestic element then slowness isn't slow at all. The first movement here is a case in point. It is a tremendously dramatic consideration of the music, and that statement covers the orchestral balance as well. The Funeral March has a scale of emotion which realizes its potential to the fullest.

Symphony No. 4 in B flat major, Op. 60

☐ Vienna Philharmonic Orchestra / Schmidt-Isserstedt (conductor) / London 6512

The poetical stress of this performance gives it an extremely high rating. The V.P.O.'s playing is crisp yet well rounded; the finale does not ride on a conductorial racehorse, which so often is the case, even though today's players can manage it easily. But that in no way sweetens the stylistic error that results. In a Beethoven symphonic finale, tempo overdrive blurs required structural clarity. So extra credits to Schmidt-Isserstedt for his healthy and telling tempo decision.

Symphony No. 5 in C minor, Op. 67

☐ Vienna Philharmonic Orchestra / Carlos Kleiber (conductor) / Deutsche Grammophon 2530516

Rarely, and one emphasizes the word, has there been such critical unanimity about this performance. It is a classic interpretation, a dynamic one, and with no strictures against emphasizing dramaticism—but never at the expense of line, order, style, and balance.

If you can, obtain the mono disc with Toscanini conducting the NBC Symphony (RCA VICS-1648E) and compare greatness with greatness for this great symphony.

Symphony No. 6 (*Pastoral*) in F major, Op. 68

☐ Vienna Philharmonic Orchestra / Böhm (conductor) / Deutsche Grammophon 2530142

The "Sixth" has always been a toughie, simply because of the languors that conductors are prone to provide and for which Beethoven is partially responsible. It takes finesse and sensitive strategy to retain freshness in the Brook sequence and it also takes good stagemanship to make the Storm move out of its metrical measurement. Böhm fills the bill on all counts. His reading is clear and beautifully atmospheric. (He makes the expositional repeat in the first movement, which is rather rarely done, considering the symphony's conceptual breadth.)

Symphony No. 7 in A major, Op. 92

☐ Vienna Philharmonic Orchestra / Schmidt-Isserstedt (conductor) / London 6668
☐ Philadelphia Orchestra / Muti (conductor) / Angel S–37538
☐ New York Philharmonic / Toscanini (conductor) / RCA VIC–1502 (monaural)

Vivid differences, and yet each edition can be heartily recommended. Toscanini's admirable attention to detail is clearly exposed, but his is not simply a sonically analytical dissection—it is a total conception of unique realization. His interpretation has tremendous rhythmic thrust and the necessary contrastive coupling of lyrical warmth. Such pulsed impetus is manifested in Muti's version (one of the most recent recordings of the work), particularly in the gutsy finale. No one can improve on the scherzo, which Muti moves at an exciting speed. It is the voicing in Toscanini's performance that disproves the arguments that have been recently surfacing that he was overacademic. Such balances can be achieved only by a probing exploration of every line of the score in relation to all the others. If that is overacademicism, this writer hopes others will imitate the process.

Not that meticulous care for detail is overlooked in the other presentations. Certainly every point is made crystal-clear by both Muti and Schmidt-Isserstedt. The latter makes his presence felt in a most impressive handling of the introduction, and in the momentum he achieves in the first movement proper. The scherzo is lithe and magnificently controlled. Everything in the symphony is balanced so that Beethoven's masterpiece is neither heavy-handed nor too frenetic.

The sound of Muti's disc is golden, that of the London edition of total vivid ambience. True enough, the Toscanini recording is number three in regard to sound qualities, but still is not to be faulted. Any one of these three recordings will certainly stand the test of time.

Symphony No. 8 in F major, Op. 93

☐ Vienna Philharmonic Orchestra / Böhm (conductor) / Deutsche Grammophon 2707073

Impressive and superbly articulated, this account is significantly shaped. The essential spontaneity that Böhm brings to this symphony is a strong point.

Symphony No. 9 (*Choral*) in D minor, Op. 125

☐ Chicago Symphony Orchestra and Chorus / Lorengar (soprano); Minton (mezzo-soprano); Burrows (tenor); Talvela (bass) / Solti (conductor) / London CSP–9
☐ New Philharmonia Orchestra and Ambrosian Singers / Napier (soprano); Reynolds (contralto); Brilioth (tenor); Ridderbusch (bass) / Ozawa (conductor) / Philips 6747119

London's edition forms part of its issue of the complete Beethoven Symphonies. (For comments concerning Symphonies Nos. 1–8 performed by Solti and the Chicago Symphony *see above*. Symphony No. 9 is listed separately since it calls for a different total group of performers.) It remains to add that in the "Ninth" Solti's interpretation is magnificent. His conception of the finale is unchallenged in its emotional impact and placement of climax. There are no reservations whatsoever about the playing and singing in this conception.

Ozawa's performance is also quite an achievement and in most respects his greatest recorded contribution to date. The slow movement, which is the supreme test, is an artistic celebration of depth and devotional beauty, with shadings that are remarkable in their minute yet confirmed differences. Distinguished singing in the finale, presented with unique splendor and power. Ozawa is to be given the fullest credit. This is a superb recorded performance.

Twelve *Contretänze*, G. 141 (WoO 14)

☐ Vienna Mozart Ensemble / Boskovsky (conductor) / London 6656

Some short, some longer with trio sections, all are aurally appetizing. Beethoven is lucidly light, Boskovsky lucidly delightful.

Wellington's Victory, Op. 91

☐ Philadelphia Orchestra / Ormandy (conductor) / RCA LSC–3204

One of the other two releases containing this work is an album called *Showpieces*. Right on! This has everything you wanted and never got in hearing Beethoven's hoked-up piece of hokum. To Ormandy's credit he plays it straight—that is, straight with electronic cannon and other blasts. Show and tell, and Ormandy tells and shows 'em.

The other packages that include *Wellington* are RCA ARL1–0107 and RCA CRL3–0984 (the latter is a three-disc job that includes Mussorgsky's *Pictures at an Exhibition*, Ravel's *Bolero*, Tchaikovsky's *1812* Overture—of course!—and Rimsky-Korsakov's *Scheherazade*. This is the *Showpieces* collection referred to above).

String Orchestra

Grosse Fuge in B flat major, Op. 133

☐ Berlin Philharmonic Orchestra / von Karajan (conductor) / Deutsche Grammophon 2530066

Not even purists can deny the right to play this work with multiple strings. The scope of Beethoven's music presses out of the confines of its original string quartet framework, and use of an orchestral totality is absolutely valid. This was recognized by Felix Weingartner, who made the string orchestra edition, powerfully presented here.

The string quartet version is noted below (see under *Chamber Music*, p. 165). Having both settings is the best way to understand one of music's greatest documents.

String Quartet in F major, Op. 135 (Adagio and Scherzo)

☐ NBC Symphony Orchestra / Toscanini (conductor) / RCA VIC–8000 (monaural)

This amplification for string orchestra was a Toscanini favorite. As to being a propitious undertaking, the vote is affirmative, particularly because of the beauty of playing Toscanini draws out from the Adagio.

Band

March No. 1 in F major for Military Band, G. 145
March No. 2 in F major for Military Band, G. 145
Zapfenstreich: March in C major for Military Band

☐ Netherlands Wind Ensemble / Philips 6599172

These are somewhat known in an edited compilation made by Lukas Foss. The original versions are a delight to hear, especially in these perspicacious presentations.

Concerto in D major for Piano and Orchestra (arranged from the Violin Concerto), Op. 61a

☐ New Philharmonia Orchestra / Peter Serkin (piano) / Ozawa (conductor) / RCA LSC-3152

There are some who regard Beethoven's Opus 61a as a freak. This is doubtless because they hold the violin composition as sacred. But creative insult is only risked when transcription is done by someone other than the composer, and then only when the original is violated. Beethoven knew what he was doing with his translation, and did it well. The orchestral part remained intact; the solo voice was given certain available opportunities to expand, all within artistic reason. Finally, the cadenzas are Beethoven's, which is not the case for the Violin Concerto. In that work fiddlers offer cadenzas by such well-known names as Joachim, Kreisler, and Wilhelmj, sometimes choosing those by Auer and Vieuxtemps. Busoni put his hand to the cadenza matter but it is never heard. Neither are those written by Besekirsky and Singer.

In the younger Serkin's performance, though curiosity as to Beethoven's redraft remains throughout, it soon takes second place to appreciation of Serkin's searching conception. By far, his is the best available. It is better shaped than Barenboim's presentation on Deutsche Grammophon (2530457), which is, in turn, leagues ahead of Felicia Blumental's edition on Orion (7017). The last additionally suffers from an inferior orchestra and tinny sound. In Serkin's playing, the music flows and sings beautifully.

Concerto in E flat major for Piano and Orchestra

☐ Brno Philharmonic Orchestra / Blumental (piano) / Waldhans (conductor) / Orion 7016

This is a reconstruction made from a Beethoven manuscript which included the solo part together with only a piano reduction of the full score; the latter is lost. Willy Hess, a Beethoven scholar, did the remake, basing his work on the knowledge of the scoring (two flutes, two horns, and strings) and the available thematic material.

This is early Beethoven, of course; and to have such evidence, even though it required completion by proxy hands, is of value.

Concerto for Piano and Orchestra

No. 1 in C major, Op. 15 / No. 2 in B flat major, Op. 19 / No. 3 in C minor, Op. 37 / No. 4 in G major, Op. 58 / No. 5 (*Emperor*) in E flat major, Op. 73

☐ London Philharmonic Orchestra / Brendel (piano) / Haitink (conductor) / Philips 6767002

These Beethoven concerto performances rank as the most successful of the integral editions available. Brendel's playing is always sensitive, and stylistic presence is acutely determined. This is beautifully adjusted to make the second concerto lighter in its weight than the third work in the set (heard with extraordinary clarity), and, in turn, to provide the *Emperor* with requisite robustness. On the other hand the romantic colors that streak through the fourth concerto are admirably defined without negating the classical frame that surrounds it. The conception of the slow-movement dialogue of this work exemplifies exquisite musicianship.

There are no quirky solo moments at any time, and the orchestral support is superlative. Always the musical sense and structural definition are positively translated by these musicians, who make the meanings clear and direct.

Concerto No. 1 in C major for Piano and Orchestra, Op. 15

☐ Concertgebouw Orchestra / Arrau (piano) / Haitink (conductor) / Philips 839749

There may be more fiery performances of this Concerto, but I do not know of any that are cleaner. The classical controls are marvelous, and the perceptivity and analytical translation are splendid.

Concerto No. 2 in B flat major for Piano and Orchestra, Op. 19

☐ Philadelphia Orchestra / Rudolf Serkin (piano) / Ormandy (conductor) / Columbia MS-6839

A special sense of continuity makes this a special performance in the Beethoven concerto league. The scope of the playing (both solo and orchestra) goes far beyond the partnership of a marvelous pianist and a magnificent conductor. It illustrates performing scholarship.

Concerto No. 3 in C minor for Piano and Orchestra, Op. 37

☐ BBC Symphony Orchestra / Bishop-Kovacevich (piano) / Davis (conductor) / Philips 6500315

Beautifully proportioned and keenly defined. The finale is not rushed and turns out to be more decisive that way. The cleanliness of articulation is perfect, and there is none of the punctuative brittleness that often comes with the pronunciations in this movement. The lyrical warmth in the slow movement is laced with intensity, and the enchantment is twofold.

Concerto No. 4 in G major for Piano and Orchestra, Op. 58

☐ Philharmonia Orchestra / Gilels (piano) / Ludwig (conductor) / Angel S-35511

I read a review of this performance that termed it "exalted." If that means the music is heard with satisfying flexibility, the term is accepted. The imagery is superb, bearing in mind that of all the Beethoven piano concertos this one is the most lyrical. There is tremendous sensitivity in the detailing of the slow movement.

Concerto No. 5 (*Emperor*) in E flat major for Piano and Orchestra, Op. 73

☐ Chicago Symphony Orchestra / Ashkenazy (piano) / Solti (conductor) / London 6857

You name it—this performance has it: grandeur and authority, energy and tonal beauty, all brought together to the finest point of excitement yet consistently true to Beethoven style. The tonal weight and the resultant assurance in the slow movement are captivating, and the finale is exultant. Solti's manner in the proceedings is not only alert, it is as magnificent in its way as Ashkenazy is in his.

Romanza cantabile for Piano and Orchestra

☐ Prague Chamber Orchestra / Blumental (piano) / Zedda (conductor) / Orion 7016

Another splinter from Beethoven's workshop, turned into a solid chunk following a bit of reconstruction by Willy Hess, the Beethoven expert. Hess accomplished his project from an incomplete set of orchestral parts. Posthumous pickin's are not always as interesting as this one.

Rondo in B flat major for Piano and Orchestra, G. 151
Tempo di concerto in D major for Piano and Orchestra

☐ Brno Philharmonic Orchestra / Blumental (piano) / Waldhans (conductor) / Orion 7016

More Beethoven findings. The D major item, however, might be spurious, since a score by the Czech composer Rössler has been found containing this same movement. The Rondo is thought to be a rejected movement for the Opus 19 concerto. It needed completion, and that task was accomplished by Czerny.

Rondo in B flat major for Piano and Orchestra, G. 151

☐ London Symphony Orchestra / Katchen (piano) / Gamba (conductor) / London STS-15111

This very attractive posthumous piece hardly surfaces in the concert hall. Katchen is very, very good here. There is not a weakness, not an uncertainty in his top-drawer performance.

Fantasia in C minor for Piano, Chorus, and Orchestra, Op. 80

Piano and Chorus

☐ New Philharmonia Orchestra and Chorus / Barenboim (piano) / Klemperer (conductor) / Angel S-3752

There is no doubt that Klemperer is the commanding force in this interpretation, since it is paced in a manner that exemplifies his thinking regarding intensification (and clarity) via breadth of line. One cannot perceive the much younger musician dictating such tempo-shaping matters. This doesn't remove any credit from Barenboim's playing, which matches Klemperer's orchestra in its clarity, depth, and strength.

Some remarks concerning the other editions available: Rudolf Serkin with Bernstein is too loose a performance because of the speed chosen; Demus plays boldly and Brendel plays even better, but both suffer from the low-grade orchestral backup provided. Forget Barenboim's earlier recording on Westminster Gold. He's not bad, but the orchestra is.

Concerto in C major for Piano, Violin, Cello, and Orchestra, Op. 56

Piano, Violin, and Cello

☐ New Philharmonia Orchestra / Arrau (piano); Szeryng (violin); Starker (cello) / Inbal (conductor) / Philips 6500129

An instrumental combination that has escaped those few composers who have attempted to add to the single important example by Beethoven in the repertoire. (Double concerti have fared a bit better, however.)

Of course the recording companies have, for the greater part, assembled all-star casts for this work. It doesn't always work, however. Someone is always riding high in the saddle and it is quite noticeable. For example, Rostropovich dominates in the performance with Richter and Oistrakh (Angel S-36727) and Stern does likewise in his partnership with Rose and Istomin (Columbia D2S-720). This doesn't occur in the Serkin-Laredo-Parnas combine (Columbia MS-6564), but the stolidity portrayed in the finale rates a minus sign as compared with the Arrau-Szeryng-Starker conception, which has an authority that sings out in every one of the measures of the three movements. The Starker tone is pure classical cream, Szeryng's is just as rich without moving once into any segmentary romanticism, and Arrau's sound style is absolutely balanced with that of the two others. Because they avoid coercive individuality yet realize definite soloistic voicing, this team, with excellent support from Inbal, are the positive recorded choice for this work.

Violin

Concerto in D major for Violin and Orchestra, Op. 61

☐ Boston Symphony Orchestra / Heifetz (violin) / Munch (conductor) / RCA LSC-3317

☐ Concertgebouw Orchestra / Szeryng (violin) / Haitink (conductor) / Philips 6500531

What should one expect from a performance of a masterpiece? It must obey not so much tradition as recognized style (the two are sometimes not rightfully partnered). There have been many performances of the Beethoven Concerto, yet quite a few fail to understand the Beethoven dialect and grammar. This is music of classical shape; creasing it with *rubati* (an incorrect *Gemütlichkeit*), pushing the lines in zigzag fashion rather than firmly and straightforwardly, and applying romanticism are all wrong. Beethoven needs no help from specialized virtuosi—let him be. Also, let him be sung.

Heifetz and Szeryng (and some others, to be sure, but space can't permit all to be mentioned) have made their study of Beethoven and have scanned him well, extremely well. The voices sing, the playing is artistically intelligent, the structure is firm and balanced, and the phrasing is magnificently realized.

Szeryng's tone is nubbier than Heifetz's, but just as pure. In the slow movement Heifetz probes spiritually whereas Szeryng digs deeply. Neither way is contrary to the Beethoven voice.

There are three other issues that contain the Heifetz production—all RCA: the violin concerto alone on LSC-1992; with the *Emperor* piano concerto on VCS-7087; and in a jumbo six-record set on CRL6-0720.

Romance for Violin and Orchestra
No. 1 in G major, Op. 40 / No. 2 in F major, Op. 50

☐ London Philharmonic Orchestra / Zukerman (violin) / Barenboim (conductor) / Deutsche Grammophon 2530552

Broad concepts pay off in playing this pair of pieces. Zukerman's infatuation with the music is apparent. These are rich performances, even a bit romantic, but that's all to the good.

Instrumental

Piano

Andante favori in F major, G. 170

☐ Kempff (piano) / Deutsche Grammophon 138934

This rendition is intelligently scaled in all its points: dynamics, phrasing, touch, and style. The tempo chosen is choice.

Bagatelles

Eleven Bagatelles, Op. 119
Seven Bagatelles, Op. 33
Six Bagatelles, Op. 126

☐ Bishop (piano) / Philips 6500930

Of the complete sets on the market, Bishop (or Bishop-Kovacevich, as he is sometimes identified) turns in the most intelligent and natural conceptions. The concentrated focus of Beethoven's Bagatelles does not negate their solidity. This important point does not escape Bishop's attention. (See also *below:* Six Bagatelles.)

Fantasy in G minor, Op. 77

☐ Brendel (piano) / Turnabout 34402

Beethoven's Fantasy floats formally as though the pianist performing the work were improvising on the spot. The modulations are many; the ideas follow suit (one writer terms them ''a succession of entirely unrelated paragraphs''), then settle into a set of nine variations, and conclude with a short Adagio postscript.

It takes an Alfred Brendel to put it all together and make it work. He plays with a suppleness and a shaping of the phrases that are both beautiful and meaningful. Above all, Brendel has a sense of timing in his playing that solidifies the music to an extent that makes his the most representative of the issues available. In this Turnabout edition the Fantasy is coupled with the fifth piano concerto. Elsewhere it is part of a five-disc all-Beethoven set on Turnabout 34205/9, and it also can be heard in a five-disc all-Beethoven release on Vox VSPS-17.

Piano Sonata

No. 1 in F minor, Op. 2, No. 1 / No. 2 in A major, Op. 2, No. 2 / No. 3 in C major, Op. 2, No. 3 / No. 4 in E flat major, Op. 7 / No. 5 in C minor, Op. 10, No. 1 / No. 6 in F major, Op. 10, No. 2 / No. 7 in D major, Op. 10, No. 3 / No. 8 (Pathétique) in C minor, Op. 13 / No. 9 in E minor, Op. 14, No. 1 / No. 10 in G major, Op. 14, No. 2 / No. 11 in B flat major, Op. 22 / No. 12 (Funeral March) in A flat major, Op. 26 / No. 13 in E flat major, Op. 27, No. 1 / No. 14 (Moonlight) in C sharp minor, Op. 27, No. 2 / No. 15 (Pastoral) in D major, Op. 28 / No. 16 in G major, Op. 31, No. 1 / No. 17 (Tempest) in D minor, Op. 31, No. 2 / No. 18 in E flat major, Op. 31, No. 3 / No. 19 in G minor, Op. 49, No. 1 / No. 20 in G major, Op. 49, No. 2 / No. 21 (Waldstein) in C major, Op. 53 / No. 22 in F major, Op. 54 / No. 23 (Appassionata) in F minor, Op. 57 / No. 24 in F sharp major, Op. 78 / No. 25 in G major, Op. 79 / No. 26 (Les Adieux) in E flat major, Op. 81a / No. 27 in E minor, Op. 90 / No. 28 in A major, Op. 101 / No. 29 (Hammerklavier) in B flat major, Op. 106 / No. 30 in E major, Op. 109 / No. 31 in A flat major, Op. 110 / No. 32 in C minor, Op. 111

☐ Backhaus (piano) / London CSP-2

There is no lack, of course, of Beethoven piano sonata recordings. Three full columns in *Schwann* are devoted to the thirty-two compositions. Two editions of the complete sonatas stand out, bypassing differences of interpretative opinion that are to be expected in certain places within the totality.

Backhaus's playing is of force and authority and gives positive proof of deep musical intelligence. There isn't a single instance of any eccentric tempo choice in his essays, and there are no phrase irregularities or intrusive decisions that are indifferent to Beethoven's specific score blueprint.

The London set has ten discs. Separate recordings of fifteen of the sonatas are available on seven discs. In two instances one of the sonatas is coupled with a Beethoven piano concerto. Although the total set has been recorded in exact chronological order, the excerpted sonatas are of hit-and-miss choice. For example, on London 6535 the sonatas represented are Nos. 4, 25, and 31; on London 6247, the fifteenth and twenty-sixth of the thirty-two sonatas are included.

Artur Schnabel's performances of the complete set (on Seraphim 6063/6) are legendary. But there is considerably more than mere historic value in this case. Seraphim's monaural edition represents fundamental documentation and stands as a permanent reference source in regard to all of the Beethoven piano sonatas.

Piano Sonata No. 1 in F minor, Op. 2, No. 1

☐ Richter (piano) / Angel S-37266

Splendid Beethoven playing, but no conventional (workaday) tempo selections because of (academic) tradition. None of these choices need an apology. In this recorded edition every point of the work is fully revealed, due to Richter's superb insight.

Piano Sonata
No. 4 in E flat major, Op. 7 / No. 5 in C minor, Op. 10, No. 1

☐ Hungerford (piano) / Vanguard 10085

The freshly alive impact of these performances gladdens the ear. Hungerford brings out the strengths of this pair of early piano sonatas beautifully. Proof of this structural matter and its depiction are the orchestral-like weights to be found in the Opus 7 Sonata, which is most significantly detailed, minus any bang or bluster. Indeed, distinguished pianism.

Piano Sonata No. 7 in D major, Op. 10, No. 3

☐ Richter (piano) / Angel S-37266

Re-creative courage that must be applauded and is worthy of acceptance. The Minuet is slowed down a bit and such control certainly enhances the music. It doesn't need courage to dispatch the Finale at Richter's tempo, but if this movement is to be realized meaningfully, his flawless virtuosity and fully musical ability are necessary. A great performance of this sonata.

Piano Sonata No. 8 (*Pathétique*) in C minor, Op. 13

☐ Barenboim (piano) / Angel S-36424

All the necessary grandeur of this magnificent sonata is displayed. Barenboim knows he is playing musical detail of rock strength, not of pebble weight, and performs accordingly. One of the very best entries of the many in the recorded catalogue.

Piano Sonata No. 14 (*Moonlight*) in C sharp minor, Op. 27, No. 2

☐ Rudolf Serkin (piano) / Columbia M-31811

Curse the nickname of this work, for it bears heavily on a small part of the work and pulls attention away from the remainder. Pianists are certainly attracted to this opus, with some two dozen represented at this time of writing. Many are fine, others are good, Serkin is special. The beautiful rhythm in the second movement and the maintenance of a magnificent *cantabile* touch in the first movement (that's the "moonlight" atmosphere) represent cool, clear, cogent, and refined playing. A beautiful essay. (Other Columbia albums that contain Serkin's performance are: MS-6481, M2X-788, and M4X-821.)

Piano Sonata No. 15 (*Pastoral*) in D major, Op. 28

☐ Moravec (piano) / Connoisseur Society S-2021

Beautiful depiction of lines without bypassing detail, withal retaining the general mood of the title of this sonata. This is a radiant performance, never denatured by overstressing particulars at the expense of the totality.

Piano Sonata No. 18 in E flat major, Op. 31, No. 3

☐ Berman (piano) / Columbia M-34218

Piano playing that follows a dynamic rule. No fuss or unsuitable, overexpressive romanticism flaws the performance. The whole structure is clarified by directness, without superficial bypasses. The sound is bright, but it fits.

Piano Sonata

No. 19 in G minor, Op. 49, No. 1 / No. 20 in G major, Op. 49, No. 2

☐ Entremont (piano) / Columbia MG–33202

These sonatas offer no problems for the technique of a young student, so they have become perennials in the teaching studio. Accordingly, overweighting in the playing of these sonatina-like items (both in two movements) is inappropriate for their contents. Entremont presents them with admirable fastidiousness and with the tiniest and most effective *rubati*. Reversing the chronological order on the disc was a wise move, since the G major work has simpler material (and is easier to play, incidentally) and is an excellent foil for the G minor opus.

Piano Sonata No. 21 (*Waldstein*) in C major, Op. 53

☐ Horowitz (piano) / Columbia M–31371

No ordinary pianist need apply. The *Waldstein* demands a performer of powerful and brilliant technique. It also requires a musician who has knowledge of structure, for this is no ordinary depiction of form from an overused blueprint. Horowitz is your man. A similar kind of spontaneity, though a smidgen more reflective, is heard in Graffman's playing on Columbia M–30078.

Piano Sonata No. 23 (*Appassionata*) in F minor, Op. 57

☐ Richter (piano) / RCA VICS–1427

A great recording. *Variety* would term it a "smash hit." The sense of structural cohesion Richter obtains produces music that is signified not by its component sections but as a totality. This is profound pianism that provides a Beethoven document of unmatched eloquence.

Piano Sonata No. 24 in F sharp major, Op.78

☐ Brendel (piano) / Philips 6500139

A rare tonality, but it fits the unique sensitive quality of the piece. There is a gracious flow within the playing that provides the proper setting for the work without negating its spirit.

Piano Sonata No. 26 (*Les Adieux*) in E flat major, Op. 81a

☐ Barenboim (piano) / Angel S–36424

This is not only clean and concentrated piano playing but offers a rather thought-provoking consideration of the first movement. The drama there is measured, precise, and most effective.

Piano Sonata

No. 28 in A major, Op. 101 / No. 29 (*Hammerklavier*) in B flat major, Op. 106 / No. 30 in E major, Op. 109 / No. 31 in A flat major, Op. 110 / No. 32 in C minor, Op. 111

☐ Pollini (piano) / Deutsche Grammophon 709072

Meaningful statements of Beethoven's various piano sonatas are not uncommon, but meaningful continuity through the series of the last five of the total is certainly rare. Movement by movement through Pollini's rendition of these five works the dynamic musical effect in all of its varieties is magnificent. The stylistic temperature is perfect and remains that way. Pollini is truly a pianistic genius in this program.

His is one of the greatest of all portrayals of the *Hammerklavier,* from the opening through the tremendous fugal finale. Here is not only correctness but communication of artistic depth. It produces a double virtuosity—of technique and of musicianship. The particularly fascinating insight that Pollini brings to this sonata is equaled in his playing of the others.

Piano Sonata No. 30 in E major, Op. 109

☐ Hungerford (piano) / Vanguard 71172

No blow-by-blow report is necessary to verify Hungerford's brilliant performance, one that responds to every note and nuance in the score. This is playing one must cheer.

Piano Sonata No. 32 in C minor, Op. 111

☐ Hungerford (piano) / Vanguard 71172

A triumph. Tempo particulars that display the designs are perfect. The variations in the second movement have a spontaneity in their statement that provide structural power as well as nobility. Further, the music of the great Arietta flows naturally rather than being halted by the extremely slow speed that most pianists have adopted. Truly, a performance triumph.

Six Bagatelles, Op. 126

☐ Kempff (piano) / Deutsche Grammophon 138934

Firmly grasped performances of these miniatures. Kempff portrays their concentrated depth to the fullest extent. (See also *above:* Bagatelles.)

Six Variations on an Original Theme in F major, Op. 34

☐ Arrau (piano) / Philips 839743

Unsentimental as it should be, but with the variational sentiments clearly disposed—which is also as it should be. The method of individually shaping each section by specific color and dynamics is set forth in an exceptional manner. Paradoxically, these secondary contrasts (the variations themselves being the basic ones) supply an inner continuity that would be lacking by squarely stating each variation—the word ''academic'' would then apply to the performance.

Thirty-Two Variations on an Original Theme in C minor, G. 191

☐ Arrau (piano) / Philips 839743

A performance of fine temperamental temperature in which individual elements and the total structure are each delineated. In that manner the utmost in balance is realized. Arrau is a master of unsectioning variations and providing a musical fabric that is all of a piece. For this alone, and it is of prime importance, he is hardly to be surpassed.

Variations and Fugue (*Eroica*) in E flat, Op. 35

☐ Curzon (piano) / London 6727

The amplitude of Beethoven's set of variations (the title is also known as Fifteen Variations and Fugue on a Theme from *Prometheus*) is substantiated in this fine performance. Curzon is sensitive to the related coherences in the Variations and projects the Fugue with strong lines and staying power.

Variations on a Theme by Diabelli, Op. 120

☐ Brendel (piano) / Turnabout 34139

A brilliant, forceful, and totally musical conception. There are sections not according to the exact letter of the rule book (faster pacing without such indication in the score), but the totality, continuity, and virtuosity are there. To achieve that is what counts. (Brendel's recording is duplicated in a Vox Box, SVBX-5421.)

Three Marches for Piano Four-Hands, Op. 45

Piano, Four Hands

☐ Menuhin and Ryce (piano) / Everest 3112

Minor-league Beethoven but worth anyone's listening time. Especially enjoyable are the first and last Marches in C and D major; the central March is in E flat. A recommended performance.

Adagio in E flat major, WoO 43, No. 2
Andante and Variations in D major, WoO 44, No. 2

Chamber Music

☐ Scivittaro (mandolin); Veyron-Lacroix (harpsichord) / Nonesuch 71227

The first work has the precautionary tempo indication *ma non troppo*. It would seem that the performance selected here, which is a half-minute slower than that heard on Turnabout 34110 (by Kunschak and Hinterleitner), would therefore be less pertinent in carrying out the meaning of "*Adagio,* but not too much so." However, there is a flow that negates the total slower pace and an inner vitality that are significant. These qualities—plus sharper detail, better tonal quality, and substantial realization of the differing instrumental weights—make Nonesuch's version of the Variations the best of the two issues now available. (The Turnabout edition is also included in a five-record set, numbered 34195/9.)

Allegro and Minuet in G major for Two Flutes

☐ Rampal and Marion (flutes) / Vox SVBX-577

Early Beethoven, composed at the age of twenty-two.

Duet for Viola and Cello with Two Obbligato Eyeglasses, WoO 32

☐ Primrose (viola); Feuermann (cello) / RCA VIC-1476 (monaural)

The "eyeglasses" (*Augengläser*) are merely a flippancy in reference to the duet's title (the music is not flippant), explained by the fact that the work was written for two gentlemen (probably amateurs) who both needed aids to correct defective vision of some sort. The two players in question remain without identity. The duet was found in a volume of sketches in the possession of the British Museum.

As for the music, it is a one-movement Allegro in E flat major, set in sonata form, with one slight measure's worth of *adagio*. The parts are written equally, neatly managed in gay fashion.

As for the recorded performance decision, unbelievably there are three editions in the catalogue. This RCA disc, which presents two master musicians, is the best, and there's no quality loss in the monaural setting. The version by members of the Trio Bell' Arte (Vox SVBX–599) is quite satisfactory, and so is the one on Coronet 1715.

Rondo in G major, G. 155
Six Allemandes, G. 171

☐ Rosand (violin); Flissler (piano) / Vox SVBX–518

Lesser Beethoven, but valuable to have and stimulating to hear. The playing catches the moods of the music, which is enhanced by appropriate, clean, and direct depiction without fussy imagery.

The Rondo is gay and unproblematic. The ''German Dances'' (Allemandes) brightly (and properly) stay in the major-key orbit (two each in F and D, one each in A and G). When, oh when, will teachers use this type of music rather than feeding their pupils the ''educational'' junk that gluts the market?

Serenade in D major for Flute and Piano, Op. 41
Six Very Easy Themes Varied for Flute and Piano, Op. 105
Sonata in B flat major for Flute and Piano
Ten National Themes with Variations for Flute and Piano, Op. 107

☐ Rampal (flute); Veyron-Lacroix (piano) / Vox SVBX–577

The first-listed work is a transcription of the Serenade in D major for Flute, Violin, and Viola (see p. 163). It was not arranged by Beethoven, but he did revise and improve the transfer. Its charm remains, even though the original is more colorfully timbred.

Authenticity has not been established for the Sonata. If the work is not by Beethoven, proper composer's credit is certainly due to someone other than ''Anon.,'' because it is a very creditable example of early Beethoven style.

In the Opus 105 the tunes selected for variation are of Welsh, Scotch, Irish, and Austrian origin. In the larger Opus 107, five thematic categories are covered: Tyrolian, Scotch, Russian, Welsh, and Irish. The latter is represented by the fairly well-known *St. Patrick's Day*. The variations do not expound; they merely travel along new avenues of approach. Nice for occasional listening, just as nice for background music; if attention wanders there is no loss.

These performances are of absolute perfection. Whatever can be done with the music Rampal and his associate do thoroughly. The engineering is just as impeccable.

Seven Variations on *Bei Männern welche Liebe fühlen* from Mozart's *The Magic Flute*, WoO 46

☐ du Pré (cello); Barenboim (piano) / Angel S–3823

A clear and clean portrayal, without being too deadly serious, which is as it should be.

Sonata for Horn and Piano, Op. 17

☐ Baumann (horn); Hoogland (piano) / Telefunken 641251

All too often this work is performed with the substituted alternate of cello. (It is so recorded by Casals and Horszowski on Turnabout 34490.) Even though there is some timbre alliance between the two, the virtue of horn tone quality is lost on the cello, especially in the short but musically telling slow movement. Further, the introductory fanfare passages are innate to the horn—on the cello they are prosaic and even Casals can't make anything of them. No, choose the edition for horn and piano and use this authentic presentation.

Sonata for Violin and Piano

In D major, Op. 12, No. 1 / In A major, Op. 12, No. 2 / In E flat major, Op. 12, No. 3 / In A minor, Op. 23 / (*Spring*) in F major, Op. 24 / In A major, Op. 30, No. 1 / (*Eroica*) in C minor, Op. 30, No. 2 / In G major, Op. 30, No. 3 / (*Kreutzer*) in A major, Op. 47 / In G major, Op. 96

☐ Szigeti (violin); Arrau (piano) / Vanguard 300/3E (monaural)

We rarely have the opportunity of experiencing on discs the veracious live performance, the commitment to the "now-or-never" that takes place in public, the excitement of it all. There's nothing wrong, of course, with the bookkeeping that takes place in the recording studio—the balancing of balances, the removal of red-inked wrong notes, the auditing of every diacritical portion of the score. Something creeps into a live performance, however, that beats all the arrived-at perfection of tape takes. The truthful live performances here made available (from recordings of concerts given by Szigeti and Arrau at the Library of Congress in 1944) offer priceless advantages. These are doubled when one hears superb communication of a composer's conceptions.

Of course, there are faults if one measures each and every note with a computerlike slide rule (it is the minute divergences that make these readings so appealing and exciting). Thus there is a bass-line unclarity in parts of Opus 96, a tendency to overvibrate in sections of Opus 24, the failure for a sound here and there to speak from Szigeti's bow with exactness. But these are fully canceled by the overall beautiful realization of what Beethoven poured into these ten masterpieces. It proves again what a great musician Szigeti was in his prime; it also defines Arrau's insight into the colliquations of chamber music. Who cares that some audience coughs cross the grooves?

Sonata in A major for Violin and Piano, Op. 12, No. 2

☐ Perlman (violin); Ashkenazy (piano) / London 6845

A realization of strength and of immaculate playing. In the hands of these two superb musicians every note in Beethoven's work has its fullest meaning.

Sonata in A minor for Violin and Piano, Op. 23

☐ Menuhin (violin); Kempff (piano) / Deutsche Grammophon 2530458

Movement 1 emerges vividly with a fast-bitten quality. In the playing of the middle movement the effect is that of a Scherzo because of the music's syncopative dress. Still, a more relaxed attitude on the part of the players overcomes any of the more formalized particulars. In the finale Menuhin and Kempff splendidly understand that the music's intensity is stronger if depicted by deemphasized dynamic speech.

Sonata (*Spring*) in F major for Violin and Piano, Op. 24

☐ Szeryng (violin); Rubinstein (piano) / RCA LSC-2377

A superlative team playing in a superlative manner. They do not mislead by arbitrary readings. Their performance confirms Beethoven in every measure, while its fresh dewy-bright quality offers an exhilarating experience. It is performed without the oft-heard Germanic style that does not do justice to the Sonata's intercurrents.

Sonata in A major for Violin and Piano, Op. 30, No. 1

☐ Menuhin (violin); Kempff (piano) / Deutsche Grammophon 2530458

The highest standards of classical-styled playing are represented. Menuhin and Kempff prove their right to be called Beethoven experts. One example: these musicians understand the matter of pace, the difference between an allegro that gives flow, as in the first movement, and one that should have demand and excitement. •

Sonata (*Eroica*) in C minor for Violin and Piano, Op. 30, No. 2

☐ Menuhin (violin); Kempff (piano) / Deutsche Grammophon 2530346

An intrinsic reading that portrays the broad and intense sense of the work. Its cognomen *Eroica* (matching the orchestral counterpart in the related major tonality) is well chosen. In no small way, the playing supports the premise that this work is duo-symphonicism—Beethoven's *Appassionata* for violin and piano. (The cognomen might be changed therefore.)

Sonata (*Kreutzer*) in A major for Violin and Piano, Op. 47

☐ Perlman (violin); Ashkenazy (piano) / London 6845

A full understanding is proven here that the symphonicism that pertains to the opening of the *Kreutzer* nevertheless must be performed in chamber-music style. Too many violinists and pianists mistake this music for mere sound, and an opportunity for sonorous exaggeration. Perlman and Ashkenazy do not deny Beethoven his rights; they play the music in stormy trust, enriching the quality with correct turmoil. The other movements are realizations that make them the wondrous things they should be. The variations (in F major) are displayed with a purity of style and yet with coloristic detail that does not overlook a single special nuance in the music. Energy without roughness provides a dazzling display in the Presto A major conclusion.

Beethoven indicated that his sonata was *quasi, come d'un concerto*. However, these performers go beyond mere virtuosity of performance or sound projection. Their collaboration provides beautifully unforced playing with vitality in generous amount. It is a perfect match for Beethoven's special stylistic blend. London's issue deserves a five-star rating.

Sonata in G major for Violin and Piano, Op. 96

☐ Menuhin (violin); Kempff (piano) / Deutsche Grammophon 2530346

This music has a serenity that almost can be pictured as fitting in its formal shell with snug contentment. However, the last movement, which can be termed a set of variations, denotes a desire to change this mood. The players understand Beethoven's views and they understand each other. The result is positive.

Sonata

No. 1 in F major, Op. 5, No. 1 / No. 2 in G minor, Op. 5, No. 2 / No. 3 in A major, Op. 69 / No. 4 in C major, Op. 102, No. 1 / No. 5 in D major, Op. 102, No. 2

☐ Rostropovich (cello); Richter (piano) / Philips 835182/3

What magnificent musicianship is to be heard here! It is not only balanced language that these artists achieve in their performances of the complete Beethoven cello and piano sonatas but also a total realization of every Beethoven syllable. Each work is presented in masterful detail and with understanding. Indeed, the matched authority of these players is something to cherish.

Sonata
No. 3 in A major, Op. 69 / No. 5 in D major, Op. 102, No. 2

☐ du Pré (cello); Bishop (piano) / Angel S–36384

These two older recorded performances in which du Pré participated are exemplary. They should not be confused with the later Angel release (S–3823) of the complete Beethoven cello-piano sonatas in which she teamed with Barenboim. There is no comparison—the latter presentation is second-rate at best.

In the A major work the proportions are neatly conveyed; quiet volatility marks the Scherzo, with its sting of syncopation and pertness of grace notes. The performance given the later sonata is just as confirmed.

Sonatina in C major, WoO 44, No. 1

☐ Scivittaro (mandolin); Veyron-Lacroix (harpsichord) / Nonesuch 71227

Played crisp, fast, and zippy. A perfect conception of this concentrated rondo-like piece of 108 measures. The above duo covers the music in two and one-quarter minutes. Turnabout's team on 34110 (and duplicated in a five-disc set on 34195/9) runs the course in a bit over three minutes. That's a drag. Worse still is the CMS/Oryx 40 entry.

Sonatina in C minor, WoO 43, No. 1

☐ Thomas (mandolin); Krieger (harpsichord) / CMS/Oryx 40

This is a surprise performance. Thomas and Krieger play the same four Beethoven works for mandolin and harpsichord that are also available on Nonesuch (71227) and Turnabout (34110 and duplicated in a five-record set on 34195/9). However, while their tempi drag and their conceptions are painfully pedantic in the other three instances, in the Sonatina in C minor all the elements fall into place. The interpretation is fluent, the result most persuasive.

Three Duets for Clarinet and Bassoon, G. 147

☐ Zukovsky (clarinet); Breidenthal (bassoon) / Avant 1011

These three very charming works are often performed for the analogous combination of a violin and cello, though such a version was not made by Beethoven (*see below* for the string setting).

It is a pleasure to hear these lighthearted works, written in perfect harmony—both stylistically and in terms of each line's importance—for the two players. It is also a pleasure to hear this deft, perfectly balanced rendition.

Three Duets for Violin and Cello, G. 147

☐ Ricci (violin); Virizlay (cello) / Orion 7295

Published for paired stringed instruments after-the-Beethoven-fact of clarinet and bassoon instrumentation (*see above:* Three Duets for Clarinet and Bassoon). It does work well, though it is a whit less intimate in sound.

Obtaining the rich personality of Ruggiero Ricci was certainly a coup for Orion.

Twelve Variations on *Ein Mädchen oder Weibchen* **from Mozart's** *The Magic Flute,* **Op. 66**

Twelve Variations on *See, the conquering hero comes* **from Handel's** *Judas Maccabaeus,* **WoO 45**

☐ Rostropovich (cello); Devetzi (piano) / Angel S–37086

Handsome variations, and certainly not mechanically set forth despite their secondary importance in the Beethoven catalogue. The comprehension of the performers, who do not overestimate the content of these pieces, produces a joy for the listener. The impeccable ensemble and gorgeous sound enlarge the joyous quotient.

Twelve Variations on *Se vuol ballare, Signor Contino* **from Mozart's** *Marriage of Figaro,* **WoO 40**

☐ Rosand (violin); Flissler (piano) / Vox SVBX–518

No cut-and-dried variational mechanics. Though there are no special developmental excursions, the originality of thought is clearly observed within the traditional formal basis.

In a set of twelve variations for paired instruments an auditor might well expect one, at least, to be for a solo voice. Check! One of the variations is for piano alone. What is not expected is the thematic statement scored for violin pizzicato, doubled by the piano, or the quiet conclusion.

Fourteen Variations on an Original Theme (Piano Trio No. 10 in E flat major), Op. 44

Piano Trio No. 1 in E flat major, Op. 1, No. 1

Piano Trio No. 2 in G major, Op. 1, No. 2

Piano Trio No. 3 in C minor, Op. 1, No. 3

Piano Trio No. 4 in B flat major, Op. 11

Piano Trio No. 5 (*Ghost*) in D major, Op. 70, No. 1

Piano Trio No. 6 in E flat major, Op. 70, No. 2

Piano Trio No. 7 (*Archduke*) in B flat major, Op. 97

Piano Trio No. 8 in B flat major, Op. Posth.

Piano Trio No. 9 in E flat major, Op. Posth.

Ten Variations on *Ich bin der Schneider Kakadu* **(Piano Trio No. 11 in G major), Op. 121a**

☐ Beaux Arts Trio / Philips 6747142

High-level performances of these chamber-music works for violin, piano, and cello (the recordings were made when Daniel Guilet was the violinist of this team) that have the closest connection between Beethoven's ideas and images and the interpretative mode of thought. The ensemble is perfect; the sonorities are always those of marvelously voiced chamber music and never become shifted into nubby mini-symphonicism. That goes for the entire eleven works.

The Opus 11 is performed with the alternative violin in place of the clarinet. No matter. The fact that Beethoven made possible such a substitute shows unmistakably that his concern was less for clarinet color than for a soprano voice to fill out the trio need. The two posthumous trios are both slight Beethoven, especially the light and engaging music of the B flat opus. What makes the other posthumous opus worthy of performance is the early use of the scherzo form (the trio was written when the composer was twenty-two), not to mention the freedom in handling the instruments. The same age marks the time of composition of the set of fourteen variations. However, the other group of ten variations is a better offering. Through sheer instrumental manipulation (divisions for solo piano, violin and piano, cello and piano, violin and cello, and full trio) it stands up as a genuine trio contribution despite its conventional variational style.

Piano Trio No. 7 (*Archduke*) in B flat major for Violin, Piano, and Cello, Op. 97

☐ Casals (cello); Végh (violin); Horszowski (piano) / Turnabout 34411

Partly for Casals's participation and partly for its musical values, this live performance is worth having. Yes, tuning and applause are bonuses. The sound isn't.

Serenade in D major for Flute, Violin, and Viola, Op. 25

☐ Silverstein (violin); Fine (viola); Dwyer (flute) / RCA LSC-6167

Beethoven's Opus 25 is a gem of a work, too little known, too seldom performed. The clue to the entire composition lies in the latter part of the last movement's tempo, *disinvolto* ("free, easy, and graceful"). To this could be added "elfin and light as a bubble." But let it not be thought this trio is merely a musical bonbon; there is a solid covering to the creamy mellifluousness.

For this Beethoven work, one of the highlights in the chamber-music use of the flute, the members of the Boston Symphony Chamber Players hit the jackpot with their sing-and-dance interpretation.

Serenade in D major for Violin, Viola, and Cello, Op. 8

☐ Grumiaux Trio / Philips 6500167

Reputation-wise, Georges Janzer is not the equal of William Primrose, and certainly the same pertains to Eva Czako in comparison to Gregor Piatigorsky. However, these lesser known musicians combine with Arthur Grumiaux in a performance of this divertimento-like work that is far superior to the competitive edition (on RCA LSC-2550) made by Heifetz-Primrose-Piatigorsky.

Two principal reasons make the Grumiaux Trio's performance better: a blend and ensemble that has perfection in the togetherness of the voices, as well as giving light and shade to the material, and a stylishness that recognizes the formal variety contained in Beethoven's score. Unbelievably, the Heifetz-Primrose-Piatigorsky group displays some pitch blemishes, which are especially prevalent in the opening *Marcia*. Yes, it is the Grumiaux-Janzer-Czako team (the last two are husband and wife) that takes the laurels, playing with urgency without breathlessness, refinement, and eloquence all the way.

String Trio in C minor, Op. 9, No. 3

☐ Trio Bell' Arte / Vox SVBX-599

Ideal playing. This represents true chamber music, with every measure defined with sensitive consideration; each movement is proportioned with Beethoven's major premise in mind. The Bell 'Arte team probes the slow movement with keen relationships of accentuations and contrast of dynamic planes. The finale may remind one of the beginning of the last movement of the String Quartet in F major, Op. 18, No. 1. But the gay swing of that work is not here—merely its melodic shape.

(*See below* for the other works in Opus 9.)

String Trio in D major, Op. 9, No. 2

☐ Heifetz (violin); Primrose (viola); Piatigorsky (cello) / RCA LSC-2563

The lightest work in the set of the three Opus 9 string trios. The opening movement is stitched with sequence and in fairly square-cut construction. Here, the playing does not do more than follow suit. The best performance viewpoint lies in the last three movements, especially fine being the solo voices in the slow movement. There, the violin theme is given more individual contour by dainty cello pizzicato plus motioned accompaniment in the viola. The process is then reversed, the top voice has plucked timbre decoration, the cello now sings Beethoven's song. The finale is played a bit faster than is appropriate, but it is not too harmful. When Heifetz is involved in chamber music, it seems that all finales are stepped up metronomically.

String Trio

In E flat major, Op. 3 / In G major, Op. 9, No. 1

☐ Trio Bell'Arte / Vox SVBX-599

Beethoven's three string trios, Opus 9, were composed before he had written his first composition in symphonic form. They show how his exclusive concentration on pure string writing made possible absolute surety. Not that Beethoven had to worry about orchestration; even his first symphony is sure-fire in that respect. But these string trios, written before the first six string quartets (Opus 18), are musically and artistically well-wrought.

The playing of this team (the name hides the fact that it consists of well-known personalities: Susanne Lautenbacher, violin; Ulrich Koch, viola; and Thomas Blees, cello), exemplifies how ensemble can result from sharing artistic profits.

(*See above* for the other two works in the Opus 9 set.)

Trio Concertante in G major for Flute, Bassoon, and Piano

☐ Rampal (flute); Hongne (bassoon); Veyron-Lacroix (piano) / Vox SVBX-577

This work is written in Haydn style. Though an early composition, it is an attractive work; most interesting are the third-movement variations.

Trio in B flat major for Piano, Clarinet, and Cello, Op. 11

☐ David Glazer (clarinet); Soyer (cello); Frank Glazer (piano) / Vox SVBX-580

A fine statement of the basic setting of Beethoven's Opus 11. The alternative use of the violin in place of the clarinet also enjoys a superb rendition in the performance of the integral piano trios, made by the Beaux Arts Trio (*see above* under Fourteen Variations on an Original Theme [Piano Trio No. 10 in E flat major], Op. 44).

Trio in C major for Two Oboes and English Horn, Op. 87

Variations on *La ci darem la mano* from Mozart's *Don Giovanni*, WoO 28

☐ Schnell and Rast (oboes); Keller (English horn) / Vox SVBX-580

Despite the concentration on severity of color (ultrareedy, almost to a fault) both works are of lightness and joy, expressed with expert three-part writing. The instruments are treated as equals; the playing is exquisitely balanced and the nasal oboe response is totally absent. The listening rewards are special here.

There are eight variations in the *La ci darem la mano* piece. Four movements comprise the Opus 87 trio. The Minuet verges on the volatility of the scherzo form, with the trio entirely strung from syncopations. The Rondo that frames the last movement is a lineage of Beethoven out of Haydn.

Trio in G major for Three Flutes

☐ Rampal, Larde, and Marion (flutes) / Vox SVBX–577

Not listed in either *Grove's Dictionary of Music and Musicians* or *Cobbett's Cyclopedic Survey of Chamber Music*. Light as a feather both in timbre and in subject.

Grosse Fuge in B flat major for String Quartet, Op. 133

☐ Yale Quartet / Vanguard 10097

There are no reservations in regard to the playing of this symphonic essay for four stringed instruments that Beethoven composed in fugal style. Opus 133 uses all types of fugal techniques, but paradoxically achieves no semblance of ordinary fugal form. The formal disembodiment of this gigantic work, of counterpoint ruthlessly shaken out of its shell, has struck many a quartet team as insurmountable. Not in this case. The Yale Quartet possesses the work thoroughly and completely.

(The *Grosse Fuge* is also contained in the Yale Quartet's performances of the late Beethoven quartets [see p. 166], on Vanguard 10101/4. For a version in string orchestra form see under *String Orchestra.)*

Quartet in E flat major for Piano, Violin, Viola, and Cello, Op. 16

☐ Members of the Budapest String Quartet / Horszowski (piano) / Columbia MS–6473

A second setting of the quintet for piano and winds (see p. 167), with three string instruments replacing the four winds. (Both versions appeared in the same year, 1796.) Since string-instrument performers have bows to sustain the music, they are given more to do in this case than the winds in the parallel work, where breathing and lip-relaxation spaces are mandatory.

No reticence and no stylistic license in this rendition. It is certainly the only worthy one in the catalogue.

String Quartet in F major (arranged from the Sonata for Piano in E major, Op. 14, No. 1)

☐ New Music Quartet / Bartók 909 (monaural)

Proof of what a great composer can do when he puts his hand to refashioning his own creation. Beethoven's "second look" is a lesson in perfection for all transcribers. Indeed, it is one of the best resettings ever made and in the process became a splendid and original-sounding quartet.

The New Music Quartet deserves posthumous congratulations for the revival of this Beethoven specialty. Their recording is amazingly clear, resonant, and stylish. It is a marvelous contribution.

String Quartet

In F major, Op. 18, No. 1 / In G major, Op. 18, No. 2 / In D major, Op. 18, No. 3 / In C minor, Op. 18, No. 4 / In A major, Op. 18, No. 5 / In B flat major, Op. 18, No. 6

☐ Végh Quartet / Telefunken 3635042

There is no mistaking the excellence of these performances. All of the substances are incisively understood: the motival identification in the opening movement of the Op. 18, No. 1 quartet is flawless; the light-fantastic turns in the G major opus are of the fullest rhythmic generosity; the steamy script that starts and concludes the C minor work is exciting but never overbearing, etcetera.

What makes these readings so persuasive is that they are remarkably free of "early-period" interpretative influence. The Végh foursome does not mistake Opus 18 Beethoven for Opus 76 Haydn as some quartet teams do.

String Quartet

In F major, Op. 59, No. 1 / In E minor, Op. 59, No. 2 / In C major, Op. 59, No. 3 / (*Harp*) in E flat major, Op. 74 / (*Serioso*) in F minor, Op. 95

☐ Végh Quartet / Telefunken 3635041

Sensitive and musicianly playing, with never a single idea that might be termed eccentric or might have been included for showmanship purposes. There is meticulous attention to Beethoven's score details (acutely so in the dynamic area) and a seriousness that places the performances in the highest class.

A complete list of interpretative credits would be lengthy. A few follow. In the great scherzo of the first of the *Rasoumovsky* quartets, the various moods of tenderness, teasing, and tempestuousness are magnificently detailed. Movement 2 in the E minor opus is played "with great sentiment" but it is accomplished with finesse. The fugal tour de force of Op. 59, No. 3, is determined by an intoxicating tempo, but not one that has incessant motor drive. (Excessive speed for this movement is musical vulgarism.) In the *Harp* Quartet the quasi-variational arguments of the second movement are splendidly organized and stated. The contrastive tension that develops in the slow movement of the Opus 95 quartet is of unique re-creativity.

String Quartet (*Serioso*) in F minor, Op. 95

☐ Quartetto Italiano / Philips 6500180

Distinguished playing, clarifying the pithy motival basis of the opening, the semi-violence of the scherzo, the contrastive tensions of the slow movement, and the variety of the finale. Beautifully toned textures.

String Quartet

In E flat major, Op. 127 / In B flat major, Op. 130 / In C sharp minor, Op. 131 / In A minor, Op. 132 / In F major, Op. 135
Grosse Fuge **in B flat major, Op. 133**

☐ Yale Quartet / Vanguard 10101/4

Comparisons are not odious, for after considering seven sets covering these masterpieces first place is given to the Yale Quartet. Not that this team doesn't get burnt several times. But one must respect the problems presented by Beethoven's late quartets. Compared to them, even the most pyrotechnical display is like a toy. A thousand subtleties are found in the works, and performers are faced with psychological media in the voice leadings, tempo shifts, and completely new use of so-called "textual sonata form."

The performance of Opus 127 is magnificent; the four voices move constantly, and music is made without apparent use of technique. In Opus 130 and 131 there is superfine definition between the minutely stated dynamics. Aside from a slight unsettlement of tempi in the second movement of Opus 135 (it interferes with the pillow-fighting horseplay of the music) the Yale team plays this last quartet and Opus 132 with undistorted cognition. The realization of the knotty problems found in the *Grosse Fuge* results in an overwhelming performance success.

Broadus Erle (since deceased) is the first violinist; Aldo Parisot, the cellist. Syoko Aki, as second violinist, plays all the quartets except the Opus 127; in that work the performer is Yoko Matsuda. Personnel change also applies to the viola post. David Schwartz held that chair in the recording of the Opus 127, Opus 131, and Opus 132 Quartets. For the Opus 130 and Opus 135 Quartets, Walter Trampler substituted.

All five quartets are available as single discs. Opus 127 is on Vanguard C-10054, Opus 130 is covered by Vanguard 10096, Opus 131 is catalogued as Vanguard C-10062, and Opus 132 can be secured on Vanguard C-10005. The sixteenth quartet, paired with the *Grosse Fuge*, is listed as Vanguard 10097 (see p. 165).

String Quartet in A minor, Op. 132

☐ Quartetto Italiano / Philips 802806

If only for the elegiac third movement, this is a recording to treasure. This Beethoven movement holds terrible dangers for performers because of its sense of suspended motion. Given any but an exceptional quartet organization, it can breed a horrible monotony. The Italian team is poised and presents this inspirational music with a compelling serenity that is absolutely masterful and breathtaking.

A similar mastery characterizes the other movements. The balance of the voices in this performance is sustained throughout the work and so is an acutely differentiated scale of dynamics.

Quintet in E flat major for Piano, Oboe, Clarinet, Horn, and Bassoon, Op. 16

☐ London Wind Soloists / Ashkenazy (piano) / London 6494

Opus 16 exists in two versions, both appearing simultaneously and so published. The work consists of a gay, almost transparent first movement, with dancelike overtones; a beautiful slow movement; and a final, light Rondo in which most reliance is placed on the piano.

Produced in its quartet form, for piano with three strings (see p. 165), the work loses the color of the assorted wind instruments, which gives a less felicitous result. The comparison will be evident after listening to this most effective and warmly projected performance by Ashkenazy and the London Wind Soloists.

Quintet (*Storm*) in C major for Two Violins, Two Violas, and Cello, Op. 29

☐ Budapest Quartet / Trampler (viola) / Columbia MS-6952

Early Beethoven that has as much to offer as the all-important six Opus 18 string quartets. The Opus 29 two-viola quintet is in four movements, but Beethoven provides a type of extra movement by twice interjecting a slower thematic section in the last movement. This concluding division is a volatile Presto, and in its tumultuous magnificence one almost senses a preparatory scheme for a fully scaled symphonic essay. Shooting figures backed by firm tremolo-like ingredients create such effects that the work has been dubbed the *Storm* Quintet.

The performance lives up to every requirement: the tempi are well judged, the contrasts stated with proper weight and tone, and the interpretation stylish.

Septet in E flat major for Strings and Winds, Op. 20

☐ Melos Ensemble / Oiseau-Lyre 60015

Throughout the work, temperamental aspects of aesthetics clash. There is brilliance and virtuosity, restraint and intimacy. The first two are colorful currents that stir the air in the more formal preciseness of the opus. The listener has himself a double feast. Thus the Adagio is a stately introduction in serenade style; the following Allegro, generated by a four-note subject, is a sonata movement fully non-divertimento in concept and purpose. Similarly, the last movement, introduced in march style, leads to a rondo form, which in turn contains a chorale entwined with neat pizzicati, and is then followed by a brilliant violin cadenza.

A keen performance by this group. There is full warmth and considerable vim in the playing. All of it is fully idiomatic and avoids the solemnity that has marked recorded performances now deleted.

Octet in E flat major for Winds, Op. 103

☐ Paris Wind Ensemble / Nonesuch 71054

Don't mind the opus designation. This is an early work, published after Beethoven's death and assigned a high opus number. Later, it was arranged for string quintet (published as Opus 4), and for piano trio (as Opus 63). It is frankly music written for unconcentrated entertainment, and, appropriately, is tossed off neatly in this performance.

Rondino in E flat major for Wind Octet, G. 146

☐ New York Wind Ensemble / Baron (conductor) / Counterpoint/Esoteric 5559

A one-movement work—scored for two oboes, two clarinets, two bassoons, and two horns—written for utilitarian purposes and of considerable interest for its instrumental color. The form is simplicity itself. The playing is perfect.

Vocal

*Voice
with
Accompaniment*

Ah, Perfido!, Op. 65

☐ Farrell (soprano) / Odyssey Y-31739

Approved, but if you can, get this concert aria in a deleted Deutsche Grammophon disc 2538098.

An die ferne Geliebte, Op. 98

☐ Shirley-Quirk (baritone); Isepp (piano) / Argo ZRG-664

Satisfactory is the report for the singing of this song cycle.

An die Hoffnung, Op. 32
Ich liebe dich, G. 235

☐ Tourel (mezzo-soprano); Levine (piano) / Desto 7118/9

Tourel was never known as a Beethoven specialist, but her singing of this pair of songs, recorded live, should revise matters.

Six Songs to Poems by Gellert, Op. 48

☐ Shirley-Quirk (baritone); Isepp (piano) / Argo ZRG-664

Rare material if not top-drawer Beethoven.

Scottish and Irish Songs

☐ Dyer-Bennet (tenor); Natasha Magg (piano); Rossi (violin); Fritz Magg (cello) / Dyer-Bennet S-7000

Voice and Instrumental Ensemble

Hack-work projects providing a way of making money resulted in a number of volumes of Scotch, Irish, and Welsh songs being arranged by Beethoven. But professional expertise always went beyond the utilitarian aspect. These examples (six of each type) are enjoyable. Sample a few at a time. They are in a style that fits Richard Dyer-Bennet perfectly.

Opferlied, Op. 121b

☐ London Symphony Orchestra and Ambrosian Opera Chorus / Haywood (soprano) / Thomas (conductor) / Columbia M-33509

Voice and Orchestra

This setting—for soprano solo, chorus, and an orchestra of two each of clarinets, bassoons, and horns, plus strings—is preferable to the setting that Beethoven wrote simultaneously calling for soprano, alto, and tenor solo voices, chorus, and a very odd instrumental combination of two clarinets, horns, violas, cellos, and bass. The former provides a sharper and more cogent distinction between the single vocal timbre and the chorus; the orchestral body is more balanced as well.

Lorna Haywood's singing may not be outstanding but it certainly is good, and her interpretation has ample dignity. The chorus does excellent work and Thomas is in full control of the somewhat threnodic tone of the piece.

Bundeslied, Op. 122

☐ London Symphony Orchestra and Ambrosian Opera Chorus / Thomas (conductor) / Columbia M-33509

Choral

Chorus with Orchestra

Nothing special, but clean straightforward writing is offered here. This is no potboiler, as some critics have contended.

Interwoven within the chorus writing are two solo parts for soprano and alto (not that important to warrant credits on the recording). The "orchestra" must be revised really to read "wind sextet," since it consists only of two clarinets, two bassoons, and two horns. Thomas keeps things moving nicely by means of his direction.

Elegiac Song, Op. 118

☐ Strings of the London Symphony Orchestra and Ambrosian Opera Chorus / Thomas (conductor) / Columbia M-33509

A "sleeper" in the Beethoven catalogue as far as this writer is concerned. Michael Tilson Thomas's constant search for offbeat but completely valuable material pays off once again in his providing the initial recording of the work.

The first word of the text, *Sanft* ("Gently"), totally describes the hushed eloquence of Beethoven's piece. Though written for solo voices (soprano, alto, tenor, and bass) the use of multiple voices does no harm; the orchestral back-up is for strings only, without double basses. A four-star recording.

Cantata on the Death of the Emperor Joseph II, G. 196

☐ Vienna Symphony Orchestra and Vienna Akademie Chorus / Steingruber (soprano); Poell (baritone) / Krauss (conductor) / Turnabout 34399E (monaural)

Cantata and Oratorio

Beethoven composed this Cantata at the age of twenty, and it is certainly an impressive product considering this fact. The pertinent criticism is the length of certain sections—there are seven in all. Still, for the beauty of such music as the aria *Da stiegen die Menschen* one must bear with the length. (Some of the material found its way into *Fidelio*, which Beethoven began to compose thirteen years later.)

This is an oldie (originally released on Vox PL-6820). But the sound is good and the two vocal soloists are in top form. Though Beethoven had written for a bass, Poell negotiates his part with prime results. Clemens Krauss is in full command; the orchestra and chorus are responsive.

Christ on the Mount of Olives, Op. 85

☐ Orchestra of the Beethovenhalle, Bonn, and Bonn Theatre Chorus and Philharmonic Chorus / Deutekom (soprano); Gedda (tenor); Sotin (bass) / Wangenheim (conductor) / Angel S-36696

This work, intense with poetry and sacred dramaticism, needs above all a tenor who is of the operatic rather than the oratorio type. Nicolai Gedda, as Jesus, fulfills this requirement as no one else in the recorded catalogue. His is an absolutely thrilling conception, and he is ably partnered by Cristina Deutekom as a Seraph. Hans Sotin, as Peter, has a small part (he is not heard until the sixth and final part of the oratorio). What he offers is well-conceived. Vocally, this is Gedda's "work" and he is in full command. One only has to hear the opening *Recitativo* and Aria to realize the incandescence of his interpretation.

Mass in C major, Op. 86

☐ New Philharmonia Orchestra and Chorus / Ameling (soprano); Baker (mezzo-soprano); Altmeyer (tenor); Rintzler (bass) / Giulini (conductor) / Angel S-36775

The concert hall's loss is emphasized by the gain obtained through this recording. Beethoven's C major mass gives way slightly to the great *Missa Solemnis*, but that shouldn't mean it should be relegated to extremely rare hearings. That said, the glowing performance Giulini conjures up is all the evidence one needs for substantiation.

Throughout there is freshness. Nowhere is there slackness. Always there is superior solo singing, artistic choral work, and a fine orchestra. But, above all things, there is Carlo Maria Giulini. This is what distinguished conducting is all about.

Meeresstille und glückliche Fahrt, Op. 112

☐ London Symphony Orchestra and Ambrosian Opera Chorus / Thomas (conductor) / Columbia M-33509

"Calm Sea and Prosperous Voyage" is set to a pair of texts by Goethe. While there is some slight turbulence in the more agitated part of the second section of the work it is, indeed, a mini-storm at best. Most of the benefits and colors of Beethoven's short (eight and a half minutes) cantata are derived from the generally optimistic tone of the writing.

Thomas directs a well-defined reading. The solid singing he obtains is just a shade better than what Boulez provides in his recording on Columbia M-30085.

Missa Solemnis, Op. 123

☐ London Philharmonic Orchestra and New Philharmonia Chorus / Harper (soprano); Baker (mezzo-soprano); Tear (tenor); Sotin (bass) / Giulini (conductor) / Angel SB-3836

A profoundly spiritual quality pervades Giulini's performance. There is strength aplenty, obtained by unfolding the lines smoothly and without too brisk a speed (one is immediately reminded of how opposite were the tempi that Toscanini chose for this work, imparting an uneasy tautness to the score). The sense of uninterrupted cadential motion is a direct cause of the energy and life of the music, a power obtained without harshness. The manner in which statements, expansions, and resolutions are interpreted makes this recorded edition of special quality.

Beautiful color from the orchestra, and an equally fine contribution from the vocalists.

Egmont: Incidental Music, Op. 84

Opera and Dramatic Music

☐ Vienna Philharmonic Orchestra / Lorengar (soprano); Lehmayer (oboe); Wussow (speaker) / Szell (conductor) / London 6675

The complete incidental music for Goethe's *Egmont:* from the Overture to the concluding *Siegessymphonie,* including two songs, four entr'actes, the *Klärchens Tod* portion, and the penultimate *Melodrama.* The link between the ten sections is made by using a text of the nineteenth-century Austrian poet Franz Grillparzer, together with some of the original words from Goethe's tragic drama.

From first to last and from conductor to soloists and orchestra the music is characterized superbly. The Overture receives one of the greatest performances on disc, with a tempo that may seem slower than that used by many conductors but here sounds exactly perfect.

Fidelio, Op. 72

☐ Vienna Philharmonic Orchestra and Chorus of the Vienna State Opera / Nilsson and Sciutti (sopranos); McCracken, Grobe, and Equiluz (tenors); Krause and Adam (baritones); Böhme and Prey (basses) / Maazel (conductor) / London 1259

This rendition is particularly impressive due to a pace that carries the music forward so that its full vibrancy produces a stimulating stylistic spirit. There have been broader performances (most are, and in fact all other stereo recorded editions available take three discs while Maazel covers the score in two), but Maazel's tempi do not interfere with the heroic realization provided by Beethoven's heroic subject. It is an exciting production.

The cast is tops. Nilsson is superbly expressive, her phrasing outstanding. McCracken provides dramatic conviction in a role that requires careful control in order not to sound mannered or forced. The remainder of the cast is excellent, with special credit to Tom Krause for a penetrating characterization as the Governor of the Prison.

Those that might prefer a more spiritual performance should turn to Klemperer's on Angel (S-3625).

King Stephen: Incidental Music, Op. 117

☐ London Symphony Orchestra and Ambrosian Opera Chorus / Thomas (conductor) / Columbia M-33509

Aside from the Overture (see under *Orchestra* [Overture to *King Stephen*])—and even that is not on top of the concert-performance charts—this music is hardly known, rarely if ever performed. No one will insist this is great Beethoven, but the quality of most of the score does not deserve the put-down it has received over the years. That Michael Tilson Thomas has chosen to record the *King Stephen* materials is to his credit and a listener's gain.

The music consists of the Overture, a pair of men's choruses, a Victory March for orchestra alone, two choruses for women's voices, some music that is the background for spoken melodramas (the narrations eliminated), a Priestly March with chorus, and a final section for the full forces. It is a fairly substantial amount of music, running over twenty-three minutes.

Only a bit of the music for the melodramas has been omitted, preventing Columbia's edition from being termed "complete." But this is not criticism—the essentiality of this example of Beethoven's theater music will do very well, thank you, especially in the superbly crafted manner that Michael Tilson Thomas provides. In any event there is more here (notewise and interpretative-wise) than is to be heard in the competitive edition on Turnabout 34368, with Schönzeler conducting.

Ballet

The Creatures of Prometheus, Ballet (Excerpts), Op. 43

☐ Utah Symphony Orchestra / Abravanel (conductor) / Vanguard 71124

Beethoven's music for *Die Geschöpfe des Prometheus* includes the well-known overture, an introduction, and a total of sixteen numbers. Abravanel gives a generous helping. In addition to the overture and introduction, all three pieces in the first act are presented, and seven of the thirteen in the second act (Nos. 4, 5, 9, 10, 14, 15, and 16).

The score represents reasonably adequate Beethoven. The performance shows expert directorial exploration.

Musik zu einem Ritterballett, WoO 1

☐ Westphalian Symphony Orchestra / Reichert (conductor) / Turnabout 34409

This ballet music was composed when Beethoven was twenty. There are eight numbers, including a German Song, a Hunting Song, and a German Waltz. A *Ritornello* connects the pieces. The scoring is compact: piccolo; two each of clarinets, horns, and trumpets; timpani and strings. An average performance.

Beethoven / Franz Liszt (1811-1886)

Instrumental

Two Pianos

Symphony No. 9 in D minor, Op. 125

☐ Richard and John Contiguglia (pianos) / Connoisseur Society CSQ-2052

Reducing Beethoven's "Ninth" to the keys of two pianos is splendid for *Hausmusik* use. With concert performances and more than two dozen editions on disc there's no need these days for such educational-promotional devices. However, the existence of Liszt's textural condensation stimulates curiosity, and this recorded issue will fully satisfy it. Nevertheless, the Lisztian resemblance to Beethoven's orchestral-choral-vocal masterpiece is like the TV studio tricks of spraying glycerine on props to make them appear wet or adding dry ice to coffee to make it appear to steam.

Jack Behrens   (1935-   )

Instrumental

Piano

The Feast of Life (1975)

☐ Behrens (piano) / Opus One 13

Behrens mixes large clusters, heavy sonorities, and Chopinesque arpeggios. No mistake in formal identity since each element is clear, though an unstated program seems to be basic to the music because of the fantasy interchange.

David Behrman

(1937-   )

Runthrough (1967)

Electronic Music

☐ Mainstream 5010

Runthrough is chance electronic music. Thus, the composer states, after describing the equipment to be used, "no special skills or training are helpful . . . so whatever music can emerge from the equipment is as available to non-musicians as to musicians."

As an example of this party-game music-making the recording will pass muster. A *real* musical experience it ain't.

Vincenzo Bellini

(1801-1835)

Concerto in E flat for Oboe and Orchestra

Solo Instrument and Orchestra

Oboe

☐ Bamberg Symphony Orchestra / Holliger (oboe) / Maag (conductor) / Deutsche Grammophon 139152

A minuscule introduction, a slow movement, and a finale—these are so concentrated as to make this a "concertino." The rich tone and pinpointed articulation of Heinz Holliger project the ultimate lucidity of this score.

Beatrice di Tenda

Opera and Dramatic Music

☐ London Symphony Orchestra and Ambrosian Opera Chorus / Sutherland (soprano); Veasey (mezzo-soprano); Pavarotti (tenor); Ward and Opthof (vocalists) / Bonynge (conductor) / London 1384

Though the libretto has a truly silly plot (unrequited love on a round-robin basis, with the heroine falsely accused of infidelity, placed on trial, judged guilty and sent to the scaffold), the music (for the greater part) saves this opera, Bellini's penultimate stage work.

The star role is Joan Sutherland's, but because of her uneven work the plaudits go to Luciano Pavarotti, who steals the show even though he doesn't have a single solo aria. Fine conducting by Richard Bonynge, due to his full understanding of the Bellinian style.

I Puritani (1835)

☐ London Symphony Orchestra and Chorus of the Royal Opera House, Covent Garden / Sutherland (soprano); Caminada (mezzo-soprano); Pavarotti and Cazzaniga (tenors); Cappuccilli (baritone); Ghiaurov and Luccardi (basses) / Bonynge (conductor) / London 13111

Though not easy at all for the singers to perform (and in all the performances on this disc pitch problems prevail), they do so in the service of a typical asinine operatic plot. Still, there is individual melodicism in Bellini's final operatic score and a certain type of refinement that makes *I Puritani* an interesting piece.

The juciest part is the tenor's, and Pavarotti as Arturo delivers beautifully, if lacking some light and shade in his phrasing. This is the second time around for Sutherland (the earlier recording is on London 1373), and there is no doubt that she is deeper into the role. So is Bonynge deeper into the score (after his first recorded essay on the same London release, 1373). The rest of the cast provide wise and sensible characterizations and good singing for the most part.

La sonnambula (1831)

☐ Orchestra and Chorus of the Maggio Musicale Fiorentino / Sutherland and Stahlman (sopranos); Elkins (mezzo-soprano); Monti and Mercuriali (tenors); Foiani (baritone); Corena (bass) / Bonynge (conductor) / London 1365

Nothing is calculated in Sutherland's singing on this recording. Her naturalness is brilliant, as is her vocalism. She offers infinite variations in her projection of the part of Amina. Nicola Monti is cast perfectly in the role of Elvino; he sings well. There are some rough spots in Fernando Corena's conception of Alessio, a young peasant, but it fits most aptly.

Richard Bonynge is in complete charge. He defines the score with a consistent inner rhythm and fine proportions.

Norma (1831)

☐ London Symphony Orchestra and Chorus / Sutherland and Minton (sopranos); Horne (mezzo-soprano); Alexander and Ward (tenors); Cross (bass) / Bonynge (conductor) / London 1394

In this London production there is no single star reigning over subsidiary voices. Pairing Joan Sutherland with Marilyn Horne as Norma and Adalgisa is a one-two punch that provides a real winner. There are places in this recording where Horne shows a striking musicality which is hard to find duplicated in her other recorded performances. Such musical soundness, infused with dramaticism, is fully provided by Sutherland. Indeed, word clarity does get lost in the process, but is that anything new in the operatic world?

The other singers are fine; the conducting of Richard Bonynge is superb. There are many places in Bellini's score that are given a focus rarely heard emanating from an opera house pit. This is especially the case with rhythmic patterns.

London's engineering provides great sound.

Frank Bencriscutto   (1928-   )

Percussion

Rondeau

☐ University of Michigan Percussion Ensemble / Owen (conductor) / Golden Crest CRS-4145

Almost equal division between pitched instruments (piano, vibraphone, bells, marimba, and timpani) and unpitched instruments (bongos, timbales, snare drums, cymbals, tambourines, and cow bell) is involved. The use of the former makes easier the clarification of the rondo design. The latter is the principal supply of rhythmic energy.

Georg Anton Benda [Jiří Antonín]   (1722-1795)

Solo Instrument and Orchestra

Harpsichord

Concerto in F minor for Harpsichord and Orchestra

☐ Württemberg Chamber Orchestra, Heilbronn / Wallfisch (harpsichord) / Faerber (conductor) / Turnabout 34305

As to be expected, a similar method is followed in all three movements, with the orchestra of strings defining the exposition before the harpsichord enters. But the thematic differences show that while formal innovations did not interest Benda, thematic invention did. Thus, both Allegro movements have dramatic impetus, yet are totally opposite in shape.

The playing is extremely fine-honed. Lory Wallfisch is so recorded that her fine silvery tone is to the fore when it should be, and when it is part of the tutti texture it is not buried. It is fortunate that this fascinating work is available on disc, since it represents still another unreasonably neglected composition in the concert halls.

Sonata No. 9 in A minor

☐ Firkusny (piano) / Candide 31086

The matter of determining this composition's values becomes very easy after assessing Firkusny's reading. Under his direction Benda's music is anything but routine. It is graceful and sparkling, and a total joy to hear.

Instrumental

Piano

Sonata in D major for Flute and Harpsichord

☐ Linde (flute); Ruf (harpsichord) / RCA VICS-1503

The Sonata offers pleasant and far from provincially conventional music. A standard of comparison brings to mind the work of C. P. E. Bach.

Chamber Music

Paul Ben-Haim   (1897-   )

To the Chief Musician: Metamorphoses for Orchestra (1958)

☐ Louisville Orchestra / Whitney (conductor) / Louisville 601 (monaural)

Here is variation treatment freely considered on top of the freedom already present in variation form. Sometimes only a part of the theme is varied, or only a motive drawn from it; or, a variation is developed on a preceding one. Sometimes Eastern melos are present, but always with colorful instrumentation, and always interesting.

Good playing, especially from the solo desks in the wind section.

Orchestra

Pastorale variée for Clarinet Solo, Harp, and String Orchestra, Op. 31, No. 6

☐ Louisville Orchestra / Livingston (clarinet) / Whitney (conductor) / Louisville 626 (monaural)

Tonal commitment and Near-Eastern feeling pervade this quiet and beautiful essay. The touch is folkloric, although no actual existing folk melody is used.

The intimately shadowed performance is as potent in effect as one of sheer exuberance. Superb playing by James Livingston, the soloist.

Solo Instrument and Orchestra

Clarinet

Berceuse Sfaradite

☐ Perlman (violin); Sanders (piano) / Angel S-37003

The *Berceuse Sfaradite* is off-beat repertoire for the virtuoso violinist who performs it. Perlman deserves congratulations for its inclusion in a miscellaneous program and for the supreme suavity of his playing.

Instrumental

Violin

Arthur Benjamin   *(1893-1960)*

Orchestra

Jamaican Rhumba (1938)

☐ Morton Gould and His Orchestra / Gould (conductor) / Quintessence PMC-7018

This peppery bit has achieved great popularity at "pops" and children's concerts and has often been served up as encore fare.

Benjamin originally wrote the piece for two pianos and later transcribed it for orchestra: other arrangements have been made as well. Benjamin considered the Rhumba as forming the second of his Two Jamaican Pieces; the first is titled Jamaican Song.

Overture to an Italian Comedy (1937)

☐ Royal Philharmonic Orchestra / Fredman (conductor) / Musical Heritage Society MHS-1750

Witty and sparkling, the music of Benjamin's Overture lives up to the title of his work, since tuneful and rhythmic Italian flavor is sprinkled all over it. There is lilt and lift in the performance.

Solo
Instrument
and
Orchestra

Piano

Concertino for Piano and Orchestra (1928)

Concerto quasi una fantasia for Piano and Orchestra (1950)

☐ London Symphony Orchestra / Crowson (piano) / Benjamin (conductor) / Everest 3020

The second work listed is an elaborate conception requiring a large orchestra and plenty of percussion. There are five sections in the single movement, including a Passacaglia with nine variations. Lamar Crowson (who had studied with Benjamin) plays with great flair and, where needed, with delicacy.

He does satisfactorily with the Concertino, music in which Benjamin speaks with a jazzy accent.

Violin
and Viola

Romantic Fantasy for Violin, Viola, and Orchestra (1935)

☐ RCA Victor Orchestra / Heifetz (violin); Primrose (viola); Eger (horn) / Solomon (conductor) / RCA LSC-2767

Free flow conveys the title aptly, but without insistence that the writing remain placid. A meditative mood is primary, with sufficiently strong currents. The formal plan covers three movements—a Nocturne, Scherzino, and Sonata—merged as a unit.

The ensemble of two of the greatest exponents of their respective instruments is a delight. Eger's credit is a nice gesture, though the horn is far below obbligato strength.

Instrumental

Piano

Etudes improvisées

Pastorale, Arioso, and Finale (1936)

Scherzino (1936)

Siciliana (1936)

☐ Crowson (piano) / Musical Heritage Society MHS-7003 (monaural)

As a concert pianist (his career began at the age of seven!) Benjamin transferred such expert knowledge and understanding to his writing for the instrument. Thus the interesting rhetoric in the Finale section of the Pastorale, Arioso, and Finale; the fittingly beautiful light staccati format of the Scherzino, and the details covered in the eight *Etudes*. These include three simply headed by a tempo indication and the rest with such titles as Arietta, *Miroir,* and *Valse volante.*

Lamar Crowson was a pupil of Benjamin's. He knows this music thoroughly and he proves it, playing with convincing knowledge and style. These are very illuminating performances.

The MHS disc is a remastering of the original Lyrita edition, issued in 1964. It is available only in monaural but is totally satisfactory soundwise. (The label on side 2 fails to indicate that the *Siciliana* occupies band 2.)

Jamaican Rhumba (1938)

Two Pianos

☐ Judith and Doris Lang (pianos) / Golden Crest S-4070

The original version of Benjamin's smash hit; it was later arranged for innumerable combinations of instruments. *See above,* under Orchestra, for the orchestral setting.

The performance is passable, but turn down your volume control: the piece has been recorded exceedingly close up.

From San Domingo (1945)

Violin

☐ Elman (violin); Seiger (piano) / Vanguard 71173

Perhaps because this is one of Benjamin's most successful short pieces, the composer later made versions for orchestra and two pianos. The folkloric overtones of the work, bound with a rhythmic ritornello, are presented here with gorgeous tone and freshness.

Benjamin / *Domenico Cimarosa.* *See Cimarosa* / Benjamin.

John Bennet (ca. 1570-1625)

All Creatures Now Are Merry-Minded

Choral

☐ Purcell Consort of Voices / Burgess (conductor) / Turnabout 34202

Chorus Alone

In this infectious madrigal by this early seventeenth-century English composer the cross-voicing is a delight and so is the singing.

Richard Rodney Bennett (1936-   )

Calendar, for Chamber Ensemble (1960)

Orchestra

☐ Melos Ensemble / Carewe (conductor) / Argo ZRG-758

Bennett wrote a strong-armed hunk of instrumental combine. The lines of the three movements are alive with motility; the contrapuntalism is very determinative, the serialism open-hearted. There is a certain amount of sectionalism, but it takes the form of extended *outward* development, rather than the integrated, specific, classically partnered type. The heavy scoring is aided by the elimination of the piano and percussion in the central movement (the instrumentation consists of three winds, two brass, two percussion, piano, and three solo strings).

*Solo
Instrument
and
Orchestra*

Guitar

Concerto for Guitar and Chamber Ensemble (1970)

☐ Melos Ensemble / Bream (guitar) / Atherton (conductor) / RCA ARL1-0049

Usual guitar diatonicism notwithstanding, Bennett is scrupulous to safeguard his right to write chromatically, and thereby to avoid the many pattern clichés found even in contemporary guitar music. His Concerto is quiet and intimate, though it does loosen up rhythmically and has some widespread, wide-eyed action in its finale.

As expected, Julian Bream copes with all the difficulties that Bennett has thrust upon the soloist. The orchestral data, particularly the sensitive percussion coloration, is expertly controlled to be either forthright or subsidiary. (The instrumentation is for flute, oboe alternating with English horn, bass clarinet, horn, trumpet, percussion, celesta, and string trio.

The performance of Bennett's work is also included in a three-record set issued by RCA (catalogue number CRL3-0997). It covers four other concertos for the guitar by Villa-Lobos, Arnold, Rodrigo, and Giuliani, one for lute by Vivaldi, and a work by Britten for lute and five other instruments.

Instrumental

Piano

Five Studies for Piano (1964)

☐ Bennett (piano) / Argo ZRG-704

These Five Studies are a little unconventional in layout. The Presto (the second study) is a phantom-imaged piece for the right hand alone. This study is balanced by the fourth study, a recitative-spurred invention for the left hand alone. The moods of the other pieces in the set are, respectively, quietly rhapsodic, agitated, and nervously prospected.

Bennett plays Bennett with care, concentration, and control.

*Piano,
Four Hands*

Capriccio for Piano Duet (1968)

☐ Bennett and Musgrave (pianos) / Argo ZRG-704

A large rondo design is used in music that combines fastidious lyrical curves with expressionistic intensity. These knit well and provide a neat musical garment. The performance is neat as well, with Bennett in charge (of course) and companioned by another composer.

Robert Russell Bennett (1894-   )

Band

Symphonic Songs for Band (1958)

☐ Northwestern University Symphonic Wind Ensemble / Paynter (conductor) / New World Records NW-211

Publishers of rich and penetrating junk for bands would do well to give a listen to this light and lucid, gay and gingerly music. The titles of the Songs—Serenade, Spiritual, and *Celebration*—are self-explanatory as to their musical content. Bennett's disquisitions are further proof of his devout attention to a merge of Broadwayish snap with standard detail. Comfortable listening, and if your mind wanders a bit here and there, you don't lose anything.

Instrumental

Trumpet

Rose Variations

☐ Hickman (trumpet); Soderholm (piano) / Crystal S-363

The gimmick here is a set of "rose" melodies. They are, in order: *The Garden Gate,*

Carolina (wild) Rose, Dorothy Perkins (rambler) Rose, Fran Karl Druschki (white) Rose, plus two others. "Pops"-type music with good opportunities for the trumpeter.

Song Sonata

☐ Heifetz (violin); Smith (piano) / RCA LM-2382 (monaural)

While the three movements (*Belligerent, Slow and Lonely,* and *Madly Dancing*) of the Song Sonata are not jazz music per se, there is such matter in their sonorous overtones. The wisecrack, the letting down of the musical hair of this compact sonata is part and parcel of jazz delivery. Not in the hot or rock category, but in a seamlessly suave style.

The playing is right in the groove. RCA's production is not totally so. The composer is simply listed as "Bennett." There are at least two other Bennetts of importance: Richard Rodney Bennett and William Sterndale Bennett. How does RCA expect the average record buyer to know which one of the three is the composer? And why no liner notes on the piece?

Bennett / *George Gershwin.* See Gershwin / Bennett.

William Sterndale Bennett **(1816-1875)**

Sonata No. 1 in F minor, Op. 13

☐ Sykes (piano) / Orion 75182

Granting the Mendelssohnian and Schumannesque distillations that characterize the four movements of Bennett's work (movement 2 is a Scherzo; movement 3 is a *Serenata*), it reads and sounds beautifully. It fully justifies establishment in the repertory.

James Sykes is a fine pianist and a sensitively intelligent one. He deploys the material of this Sonata with certainty of effect, realizes the climaxes, and provides a statement that has top rewards for the listener. Indeed, this is masterly playing.

Warren Benson **(1924-   )**

The Leaves Are Falling (1964)
The Solitary Dancer (1966)
Transylvania Fanfare (1953)

☐ Indiana University Symphonic Band / Ebbs (conductor) / Coronet 2736

Benson's works for band are among the most communicative in the literature. Never does he use bombast: never does he merely retain fat textures for the sake of a "band sound." His approach is totally symphonic, with the same scoring perceptivity of the great orchestrators, never massing and substituting for the missing string instruments. It is a lesson for all composers of band music.

The Solitary Dancer is motival, set in a free fantasy that pervades the work. Toward the end there is a Spanish temper to the introspective character of the music. This example of contemporary romanticism is magnificently set forth by the young musicians. All of

Benson's fluent melodic invention and carefully unburdened textures are perfectly portrayed.

There is no Rumanian aspect in *Transylvania Fanfare,* in spite of the title. Transylvania was simply the name of the music camp that commissioned Benson's opus. Though there are fanfares fore and aft in the piece, the form is that of a concert march.

The Leaves Are Falling was inspired by the poem *Herbst* from Rilke's *Buch der Lieder.* The same introverted emotionalism of *The Solitary Dancer* is found in this music. It is much more brooding, is colored by much darker instrumentation, and has threnodic overtones. Again, one realizes that Warren Benson completely rejects facile methods in composing for the band. It is refreshing for the ear. More importantly, it captivates the ear. The splendid performance, directed by Frederick Ebbs, is a commanding contribution to the work's success.

Percussion

Trio for Percussion (1957)

☐ Price, Colgrass, and Smith (percussion) / Orion 7276

As a former top-flight percussionist, Benson knows his way around the "kitchen." He also knows his way around the pages of a percussion score. Shifting metrical dynamism is important here, but the recognition of the subtle power possibilities of fricative sonorities is the paramount point. The performers are Kreislers in the percussion field. They prove it.

Solo Instrument and Band

Oboe Doubling on English Horn

Recuerdo

☐ Interlochen's National Music Camp High School Symphonic Band / Jaeger (oboe and English horn) / Wilson (conductor) / Golden Crest 403

In his three-movement *Recuerdo* ("Souvenir"), Benson has created a fascinating score, utilizing the woodwind, brass, and percussion divisions of the band as though they comprised a chamber-music medium. Picking and choosing, and never opting for sonorous, corpulent credentials, he has produced a joy for the ear. For "bandstrators," the score would serve well as a guideline for serious consideration, for it represents band writing (even though here in an accompanimental reference) at a superb inventive level.

Movement 1, a *Sarabande,* is for the solo oboe with brass choir and marimba; movement 2 calls for the soloist to change to English horn, supported by percussion. In the finale (*Canción de las posadas*), the solo voice is again the oboe, this time backgrounded with woodwinds, trumpet, and marimba. (It will be noted that all three band families are represented.) A *Canción* is a Mexican folk hymn sung during a Nativity procession (*posadas*). It is presented here in theme-and-variation form.

(Jaeger, a fine musician, has also recorded the last movement in a secondary version, with piano, on Mark 25726.)

Saxophone

Star-Edge

☐ Ithaca High School Band / Sinta (saxophone) / Battisti (conductor) / Golden Crest S–6001

Outer-space reflections come to mind in Benson's colorful score. It proceeds mainly in slow-paced portions based on antiphonal gestures between the solo instrument and the band. The latter is handled for the greater part in large, chamber-music proportions.

Tuba

Helix (1966)

☐ Indiana University Symphonic Band / Turk (tuba) / Ebbs (conductor) / Coronet 2736

Helix has become a classic in the repertoire for the tuba, not because the total literature for the tuba is so poverty-stricken that anything resembling even half-decent music would be welcomed, but because *Helix* is an artistic entity that completely exhibits the brass instrument's potentials. They are here in abundance, meaning: virtuosity, rhythmic strength, and lyrical capabilities.

Helix is in two parts: *Dancing* and *Singing*. The band that frames the solo voice is employed in a very colorful fashion, with numerous percussion devices, including suspended flower pots (the equivalent of primitive clay bells). The music is rhapsodically nervous, but emerges as a coherent whole. Within its objective, it is a masterwork.

Benson wrote *Helix* at the request of the tuba virtuoso Harvey Phillips. Phillips has recorded the work twice: with Interlochen's National Music Camp High School Symphonic Band and with the Ithaca High School Band, both on Golden Crest, but neither recording can be recommended. Unfortunately, most band music in any form is rarely recorded other than by high school, college, and university groups. Exceedingly few such performances pass muster, and most are produced in a hit-and-miss manner that results in a miserable ''home tape recorder'' sound. An exception is the release noted above. Turk's playing is almost on a par with Phillips's, and the supporting forces are far better than those that accompany Phillips's playing.

Aeolian Song (1953)

Instrumental

Farewell (1964)

Saxophone

☐ Hemke (saxophone); Granger (piano) / Brewster 1203 (monaural)

Aeolian Song is a haunting conception. The climax of the seamless continuity of the piece is delayed, making it more powerful when it does occur. The playing of Frederick Hemke is truly beautiful.

Farewell is a nocturnal aria. It is pegged at a low voltage level but is extremely effective, thanks to Hemke's sensitivity.

Prologue

Trumpet

☐ Robert Levy (trumpet); Amy Lou Levy (piano) / Golden Crest RE–7045

In just a bit over two minutes, the warm, dark-colored lyricism of *Prologue* effectively registers its objective.

Marche: Encore for Woodwind Quintet (1924)

Chamber Music

☐ American Woodwind Quintet / Golden Crest S–4075

Marche is short, which is of course proper for encores, and it is snide, which type of musical cuteness is also apt for encore material. The tempo (''with comic dignity'') gives it all away.

The Beaded Leaf

Vocal

☐ Western Illinois University Wind Ensemble / Crawford (bass) / Benson (conductor) / Mark MC–5405

Voice and Instrumental Ensemble

The Beaded Leaf is a setting of Anthony Hecht's poem *Adam* and it uses the very uncommon combination of bass voice and wind ensemble (tripled winds, brass, harp, percussion, and string bass). The general tone is dark, the syntax panchromatic.

Niels Viggo Bentzon   (1919-   )

Orchestra   **Pezzi sinfonici, Op. 109**

☐ Louisville Orchestra / Whitney (conductor) / Louisville 58–6 (monaural)

Bentzon's music is always forthright in manner and forthright in its use of metamorphosis technique. Here, an initial four-pitch motive is the generator for the fast music, its diatonic shape contrasting with a slightly chromatic slow-moving idea. This is music that has contemporary fangs but never forgets to sing while grasping the textures.

One of Whitney's best performances, he conducts an orchestra showing a power that is excellent. The sound is both very good and well centered in its balances.

Nicolai Berezowsky   (1900-1953)

Orchestra   **Christmas Festival Overture, Op. 30, No. 2**

☐ Oslo Philharmonic Orchestra / Lipkin (conductor) / Composers Recordings S–209

Berezowsky spins his light-faceted opus on an axis of modality with some dissonance, the latter quite contrary to the childlike simplicity of the thematic material. (Berezowsky is another composer who is poorly represented in the recorded literature.) Lipkin was not a first-rate conductor, but he is to be commended for recording music off the beaten track.

Instrumental   **Fantasy for Two Pianos, Op. 9**

Two Pianos   ☐ Yarbrough and Cowan (pianos) / Composers Recordings S–279

Hearty, full-scale neo-romantic gestures are contained in Berezowsky's Fantasy. A second version was made for two pianos and orchestra—understandable, since the material of the first setting sounds as though the pianists were playing a reduction of a work for large orchestra, thoroughly detailed to include all textural concerns.

Yarbrough and Cowan overcome the problems of density and offer a clearly contoured reading of the piece. No blurring of the high-decibeled dynamics either.

Alban Berg   (1885-1935)

Orchestra   **Lulu Suite**

☐ Vienna Philharmonic Orchestra / Silja (soprano) / Dohnányi (conductor) / London 26397

During his work on the opera *Lulu*, Berg designed a set of five *Symphonische Stücke* from the composition-in-progress for concert performance. Publishing them as the *Lulu* Suite (also known as the *Lulu* Symphony), Berg hoped thereby to stimulate interest in the entire opus. This was good strategy, since the five pieces vividly delineate the nightmarish and fatalistic quality and the technical mode of the opera.

Most operatic music defies separation from the stage, especially when the listener has had the experience of knowing the opera, but the dramatic force of the *Lulu* excerpts is incontestable. The same applies to this cogently balanced and strongly colored performance.

Three Orchestral Pieces, Op. 6

☐ BBC Symphony Orchestra / Boulez (conductor) / Columbia MS-7179

In the opinion of Willi Reich, a friend of Berg's and his most important biographer, Opus 6 is one of Berg's greatest works. Conceived for a huge orchestra, the music has delicate textures as well as emotional heat, and it bristles with technical difficulties. Heavy chromaticism rams its way into the composition but does not take full possession.

Berg's titles—Prelude, Round Dance, and March—are mere springboards in terms of considering the music. Some of the sound combinations will seem to have been created for sheer musical sensationalism, but this is simply a full exhibition of the orchestration. The pieces have magnificent shock appeal.

Boulez's recording is nothing less than sensational. This conductor is a master of presenting the most torturous, complicated scores. He neither overlooks nor misjudges the minutest intricacy.

Three Movements from the Lyric Suite

String Orchestra

☐ Berlin Philharmonic Orchestra / von Karajan (conductor) / Deutsche Grammophon 2711014

Movements 2, 3, and 4 of the Lyric Suite for String Quartet (see p. 185) were instrumentally enlarged by the composer. The result has proven to be successful at concerts, and, indeed, is beautifully polished in this recorded edition, but there is greater truth in the same three parts of the original quartet version. Berg notwithstanding, the Lyric Suite is certainly not music for an instrumental crowd. But if you disagree, you won't disagree with the way the Berliners go at it.

Chamber Concerto for Piano and Violin with Thirteen Wind Instruments (1925)

Solo Instrument and Orchestra

Piano and Violin

☐ BBC Symphony Orchestra / Barenboim (piano); Gawriloff (violin) / Boulez (conductor) / Columbia MS-7179

Vivid contrasting colors of the winds pitted against the individually timbred solo instruments characterize the Concerto. Moreover, musical acrostics are woven into it. In the three movements the total chromaticized spectrum is aglow with fresh sonorities presented in a special manner: the violin is silent in the initial section, the piano is not used in the slow movement; both join with the winds in the final part after a dramatically arabesqued double cadenza.

The Concerto is full of relationships and permutations, such as mirror forms, inversion, retrograde inversion, and so on. The final part draws on a combination of the previous pair of movements, as though proving their validity by way of a powerful summation. Yet, schematic as the work may be, Berg understands that theoretical sport alone is as artistically cogent as the game of blind man's buff. The venture must be expressive, relate a range of sensitivity and vision. Berg's Chamber Concerto is a remarkable demonstration of this ability to be emotionally perceptive as well as technically astute. It has heart as well as brain.

The musicians led by Boulez are magical virtuosi, from the soloists to the double bassoonist. The balances are perfect, and the leading voices (Berg's score is meticulous in its marking of primary and subordinate parts) are exposed perfectly. Boulez's depiction of this score is as perfectly crafted as Berg's magnificent creation.

Mention should be made of a monaural version available on Lyrichord 94. The playing is expert and tasteful, especially Ivry Gitlis's soaring violin tone. Harold Byrns is the conductor, and Charlotte Zelka the pianist. Lyrichord's edition constitutes a reissue of a Vox

(8660) deletion. For some unknown reason, when Lyrichord put the disc on the market, what Vox had listed as the Pro Musica Wind Instrument Group was changed to the Viennese Wind Ensemble! No mention was made of the identificational switch. They're the same players, so who's kidding whom?

Violin

Violin Concerto (1935)

☐ Concertgebouw Orchestra / Grumiaux (violin) / Markevitch (conductor) / Philips 802785

☐ New York Philharmonic / Stern (violin) / Bernstein (conductor) / Columbia MS-6373

Berg's Concerto, a twentieth-century masterpiece, bristles with enough thorny formations to satisfy any virtuoso, but the piece places these formations in a richly poetic frame of reference. It is the revelation of that special character that intensifies Grumiaux's playing. It has a darker color than that of Stern, who gives in just a bit to the brighter romantic temptations that lie within the Concerto but are only of parenthetical reference in this violin and orchestra requiem.

There is no doubt that Stern and Bernstein have produced a splendid reading. Both soloist and conductor join in an individual conception without perjuring the music or being presumptive. It is simply that Grumiaux (with Markevitch) considers Berg's score in a more naked fashion. That way, it is extremely moving.

Instrumental

Piano

Piano Sonata, Op. 1

☐ Kuerti (piano) / Monitor S-2134

Written in extremely chromatic style, Berg's Opus 1 simmers with the flavors of his mature work. Vacillating harmonic and contrapuntal ingredients hold full sway in a pithy one-movement discourse that is restless from the unquiet of the tonal zigzag. Emanating from a period somewhat unfashionable in the jet age, the Sonata pianistically represents the pantheistic symphonicism of the Mahlerian world.

A pianist can get caught in the clutches of multitudinous chromatics and relax his way through them. No go! (Biret does this on her Finnadar 9008 release.) On the other hand, too extrovert an approach piles outward restlessness on top of inner restlessness (Colburn on Orion 7298). Webster (on the Dover label) is fine, but Kuerti is best of them all. His conception is ideal: the music is executed with the greatest clarity. In this work, Kuerti presents a perfect illustration of post-romantic piano playing style.

Chamber Music

Four Pieces for Clarinet and Piano, Op. 5

☐ Stoltzman (clarinet); Peter Serkin (piano) / Orion 73125

Berg's unique set of short pieces (respectively 12, $9\frac{1}{4}$, $18\frac{1}{6}$, and 20 measures in length) was composed in 1913. It represents romanticism in its ultimate, super-charged state. No work for clarinet and piano has ever had the intense syntax used in these pieces.

The fluid persuasion of these musicians is remarkable. Their ability to mark dynamic levels as minutely different as *pianissimo, triple piano,* and *quadruple piano* is top artistic virtuosity. Stoltzman's low *tremolandi* are dark and frightening. Serkin's touch is hypersensitive in all respects.

The closest approach to this team's perceptive penetration of Berg's music is Gervase de Peyer's clarinet playing on Oiseau-Lyre S-282. However, Lamar Crowson, in this instance, offers no competition to Peter Serkin.

Lyric Suite for String Quartet (1926)

☐ LaSalle Quartet / Deutsche Grammophon 2530283

One of the most important musical examples of the twentieth century, the Lyric Suite not only codifies both the ultimate goal of romanticism and twelve-tone technique but also combines them.

The Lyric Suite has delicate features as well as emotional heat, but like most of Berg's music, it gives softer explanations than Schoenberg's. Though chromatic restlessness is present, Berg's craftsmanship guides the accidentalized sounds so that they are not permitted too free a range. In combining twelve-tone technique (about half the quartet is in that style) with extended romanticism, a balance of technical power is maintained; accordingly, no belligerently free chromaticism runs riot. The composer's aesthetic is ingrained to such an extent that the fusion does not result in shifts between styles.

The Lyric Suite is the equivalent of a dramatic tragedy set in a chamber-music medium—one of the most thrilling combinations of sound to be found in any work. Its proper place is with the great last set of string quartets by Beethoven.

The LaSalle four give a supreme presentation. Theirs is truly one of the performance masterpieces in the entire recorded catalogue. Of course this means that the word "definitive" should be added. The tone color differentiations, the amazing scale of dynamic relationships, and meanings of every measure are perfect. One assumes (and strongly suggests) that this recording should be the reference point for all other organizations who wish to play Berg's masterwork.

(The Lyric Suite is also included in a jumbo Deutsche Grammophon release [2720029] which includes the complete string quartets of Schoenberg and Webern, plus Berg's Quartet, Opus 3.)

String Quartet, Op. 3

☐ New Music Quartet / Bartók 906 (monaural)
☐ LaSalle Quartet / Deutsche Grammophon 2530283

The Quartet, Op. 3, which marks the last work Berg composed under the supervision of Schoenberg, is intense to the point of incredibility. The emotion of the piece is of driven force from start to finish. There are no bald spots in the composition. The peaks are constant; when there is descent, it is slight. The music never drops into relaxation or weakness. This is an early work, so it is not surprising that some Wagnerian harmonies come forth, but none are of the sweet-tooth variety. Berg's tonal curves and ecstatic pronouncements are of a world unknown to Wagner.

Disregarding the sound of the Bartók Records disc—which is good but not as good as Deutsche Grammophon's—the performance of the New Music Quartet can in no way be bypassed. The synthesis and deep drive that they bring to this performance are memorable. It remains a permanent testament to the ability of this organization, which had become one of the greatest of quartet teams before its disbandment owing to financial demands.

The LaSalle performance is of great luminosity and intensity. To perform this work requires a group who must not only honor the music but believe in every one of its sounds. Both these quartet organizations hold the faith seriously and toss off Berg's finger-breaking passages with ease.

(The LaSalle performance is also available on Deutsche Grammophon 2720029. That five-disc release covers the string quartets of Schoenberg, Berg, and Webern.)

Vocal

*Voice
and Orchestra*

Altenberg Lieder, **Op. 4**

☐ BBC Symphony Orchestra / Lukomska (soprano) / Boulez (conductor) / Columbia MS-7179

Berg wrote his "Five Orchestral Songs to Picture Postcard Texts by Peter Altenberg" (to give the complete and precise English title) in 1912. When first performed, they created a riot, and the police intervened before they could be completed. When there's a riot, one can be sure a masterwork has been unveiled. There is plentiful proof, including the first hearing of Stravinsky's *Sacre du printemps.*

Almost seventy years later we find excitement and highly colored post-romanticism in the music that scared the Viennese: music born of Wagner and Mahler, yet subtle chamber music (though scored for a very large instrumental apparatus). In these songs Alban Berg is a German impressionist (no pictorial landscaping, however). The music is free-willed but fantastically appointed. Attention to the most minute scale of instrumental dynamism is equivalent to the careful chiseling, polishing, and sandpapering a sculptor makes on the stone on which he works. It is music of impressionism without exterior effects.

The excellent and expressive singing by Lukomska is totally controlled to elucidate Berg's minute timbre tracings. Boulez's role is that of an equal in this work, the orchestra not being an accompanimental assistant. And he is an equal as a superb musician. Once again we have a demonstration of his eminence as a conductor of twentieth-century music, especially that of the Second Viennese School represented by Schoenberg, Berg, and Webern.

Seven Early Songs for High Voice and Orchestra (1905-1908)

☐ BBC Symphony Orchestra / Harper (soprano) / Boulez (conductor) / Columbia M-32162

This was originally composed between the years 1905 and 1908; Berg made his orchestration of the supporting piano part twenty years later. The instrumental afterthought underlines the varied moods. Berg did not tamper with his youthful music, but his mastery of orchestral resource added compelling interest to the songs without impinging on their initial style.

Absolutely gorgeous singing by Heather Harper and positively superb orchestral backgrounds and foregrounds by Boulez.

*Opera
and Dramatic
Music*

Lulu (1934)

☐ Berlin German Opera Orchestra / Lear and Johnson (sopranos); Grobe (tenor); Fischer-Dieskau and Driscoll (baritones); Greindl (bass) / Böhm (conductor) / Deutsche Grammophon 2709029

Lulu is a study in depth of female carnality played against a Krafft-Ebing décor. Berg's potent music drama has enough grisly perversions to warrant a study by the Kinsey plus the Masters and Johnson staffs. The shock element is apparent from the story line: Lulu, who has a long history of sordid affairs and tragic marriages, murders her husband and flees with his son. Involved in a life of degradation, she becomes a whore, and is eventually murdered by a character calling to mind Jack the Ripper.

Each character is assigned a definite musical form that persists throughout the opera; for example, a scene between Lulu and one of her husbands is cast as a sonata movement, including full development and recapitulation. Despite such rigid use of classically oriented controls, Berg does not merely prove his point of technique but cannily employs it for dramatic purpose. The cohesiveness is confirmed by the use of a single tone row from which all themes and motives are drawn. In Berg's hands the twelve-tone ordering produces music that propels a plot of such lurid literalism that, in comparison, the sexual pathology in Strauss's famous *Salome* and *Elektra* becomes a fit subject for presentation to Sunday school audiences.

The production is exemplary in the singing and in the singers' understanding of the music. It takes many hearings to uncover the dozens of subtle allusions that move *Lulu* to its conclusion. Nonetheless, the overall expressivity becomes more and more fascinating as the work moves on.

Berg did not live to complete his opera in every detail. However, more data was available for the incomplete third act than was officially acknowledged by his widow and publisher. In an almost cloak-and-dagger atmosphere, the final act was realized and completed from Berg's manuscript material over many years of secret work by the composer-conductor Friedrich Cerha. The "new" première was given on February 24, 1979, at the Paris Opéra, with Pierre Boulez conducting. One assumes that a recording of this, now the "definite" version, will be made in the not-too-distant future. Until then, this edition by Deutsche Grammophon is the only one available (the older Columbia 121 version, conducted by Häfner, having been deleted). It is first-rate.

Wozzeck, Op. 7

☐ Paris Opera Orchestra and Chorus / Strauss (soprano); Uhl and van Vrooman (tenors); Weikenmeier and Berry (baritones); Dönch (bass-baritone) / Boulez (conductor) / Columbia M2-30852

A great work is often greeted with sneers and closed ears, except by the cognoscenti, and public recognition comes only posthumously. Thus did Berg's gigantic opus join the operatic list.

Seven years in the making, the opera is a creation of sweeping revolution, one in which musical design and dramatic content merge with uncanny unity. The music is cast in the form of old dances, a passacaglia, a complete five-movement symphony, sets of inventions and variations, and a fugue. To plan this to meet the concurrent needs of a fifteen-scene drama might be considered a frenzied desire for novelty. But Berg's brilliant intellectual vision materialized, and *Wozzeck* turns out to be one of the profound achievements of the century.

The opera traces the tragedy of the soldier Wozzeck, ridiculed by his fellows. His inamorata, Marie, has borne him a child, but she is unfaithful and Wozzeck kills her. He in turn drowns when he attempts to find the murder weapon. Within the composition, every minuscule point of sound has a relationship to other points and to the whole conception, and yet a tremendous variety of means is utilized: speaking, half-sung and half-spoken passages, full-voice delivery, offstage instruments, parodies, even an out-of-tune barrelhouse piano.

Iain Hamilton has pointed out that Berg's opera emphasizes "ferment, decay, and death." It is truly a work that transcends the fate of its characters as it bares the psychotic phobias and diseased morality of contemporary times.

No operatic record collection is complete without Berg's *Wozzeck,* a landmark in the medium. First there was the Mitropoulos-directed edition—on Columbia 118, then relabeled Odyssey Y2-33126, in monaural of course, and still available. This was followed by a production by Boulez (Columbia M2-30852) and one by Böhm (Deutsche Grammophon 2707023). Both editions provide excellent voices and polished orchestral playing, but their climates differ. Boulez goes for the jugular in his consideration of the score and in the way his singers consider their roles. Wozzeck, as sung by Fischer-Dieskau, is merely a tragic figure under Böhm's direction.

In this Columbia issue, Walter Berry delineates Wozzeck as an awkward person, sometimes a "nebbish"—a "sad sack" with some (but not much) guts. Isabel Strauss is excellent as the shallow Marie; the supporting cast is excellent in every respect. Boulez's sharp-edged direction makes *Wozzeck* the harsh tragedy it is. His refusal to beautify the particulars is a reflection of total Bergian truth.

Arthur Berger   *(1912-   )*

Orchestra

Serenade Concertante (1951)

☐ Brandeis Festival Orchestra / Solomon (conductor) / Composers Recordings 143 (monaural)

Carl Sigmon's note on Berger's work describes it as "rhythmic, asymmetric, and buoyant," which is readily accepted. However, to be added to this analysis is some Stravinsky-of-the-neoclassic-days laced with some Coplandesque curves. The result is no hit-or-miss-or-mess, but a decidedly fine mix that shows creative authority, especially in its closely concentrated handling of the instruments.

The recording offers a forthright performance. Though subtlety is not to be heard here, rhythmic presence is.

Instrumental

Piano

Two Episodes (1933)

☐ Helps (piano) / Composers Recordings S–288

An early example of Berger's twelve-tone music, the *Episodes* are much more outgoing than his later compositions. Dynamic playing for this pair of short pieces.

Two Pianos

Three Pieces for Two Pianos (1962)

☐ Jacobs and Kalish (pianos) / Composers Recordings S–290

Berger has created sharp and spiky bits and pieces that fit together in an abstract design. The relationship to Webern's aphoristic style is apparent, but Berger's chunks have more meat wrapped around them. Some prepared piano sounds enlarge the instrumentation.

Chamber Music

Duo for Cello and Piano (1951)

☐ Greenhouse (cello); Makas (piano) / Columbia Special Products AML–4846 (monaural)

There is neoclassic persuasion in both the movements, which are arranged with tempo contrasts. The rhythmic plasticity is a delight. Fresh and clear equality for the performers makes for an absolute duo. It is played accordingly and significantly.

Duo No. 2 for Violin and Piano (1950)

☐ Zukofsky (violin); Kalish (piano) / Desto 6435/37

Pastoral and balletic moods are in contrast in Berger's sensitive neoclassic work. Integration also applies, since the piano part of the first section has the rhythmic personality of the other division of the work. This adds a light tension to the lyrical, line-drawing flow of the violin.

Zukofsky plays his part with a poetry that exemplifies high artistry. Kalish partners him beautifully. There is no gap in their conception of Berger's duet—it is perfect duo playing.

Quartet in C major for Woodwinds (1941)

☐ Members of the Dorian Quintet / Vox SVBX-5307

Berger's quartet for the principal members (flute, oboe, clarinet, and bassoon) of the woodwind family is of twentieth-century simplicity, interlarded, however, with an acute intellect that is most rewarding. Though warmed by the Stravinskian neoclassic gospel, the quartet indicates a reaching toward romantic feeling. This sentient cast places a subjective jacket on Berger's musical book, which has the flow of classicism on every page.

This kind of music is made to order for the chit-chatty chirp of woodwind instrument conversation. However, wind teams often turn this into chirky sounds, overlooking the basic fact that music is not all hard consonants. It is to the credit of the Dorian's members that the rhythmic jets that pepper the piece are firm and clear, that beauty of sound is maintained throughout, and that grace is not overlooked. Everything is meaningful and musical.

String Quartet (1958)

☐ Lenox String Quartet / Composers Recordings 161E (monaural)

A virtuoso piece, the Quartet has the symbology of twelve-tone writing. Twelve-tone it is, but it is not a strict serial piece in the Schoenbergian manner. Tough tensions (the music is always unrelaxed), whiplashed rhythms (less precise in movements 4, 5, and 6, which constitute the major second part), and strongly marked phrase depictions describe Berger's chamber piece. What stimulates the listener in the Quartet is that mechanical application of the technical style is absent. Meaning is persistent and consistent. This is music not easy to whistle but easy to admire and respect.

The Lenox team (Marsh and Hersh, violins; Mantz, viola; and McCall, cello) produces a highly imaginative reading. This issue represents minutely disciplined quartet playing.

Chamber Music for 13 Players (1956)

☐ Columbia Chamber Ensemble / Schuller (conductor) / Composers Recordings S-290

Berger has used serial technique but with artistic meaning riding over row statistics. The seven variations of the first movement clearly propose and prove their objective, covering such designs as antiphonal chords, canons, canzona, et al. The diversity (acutely defined in a first-rate performance) holds one's interest.

Jean Berger (1909-   )

Short Overture for Strings

String Orchestra

☐ Orchestra da Camera di Roma / Flagello (conductor) / Peters International PLE-071

Berger's short piece (four and one quarter minutes in length) is a tonal delight—a real charmer. Despite the fact that the composer designed the music so that it would not tax the abilities of an amateur group, it could well grace the program of any major league professional outfit. Indeed, no apologies would be necessary—neither are any necessary in regard to this deft performance.

Choral	***I Lift Up My Eyes (Psalm 121) (1961)***
Chorus Alone	☐ Mormon Tabernacle Choir / Ottley (conductor) / Columbia M–34134

This is one of the best examples of this composer's fervent, yet controlled, romantic style, which has established him as one of the best of the middle-of-the-road choral composers in America.

In a Time of Pestilence

☐ Concordia Choir / Solum (vocalist) / Christiansen (conductor) / Concordia S–1

An example that shows why Jean Berger is one of the most successful American composers in the choral field. The commitment to harmonic clarity and a superior sense of vocal color, without resorting to gimmicks, makes *In a Time of Pestilence* produce creative profits.

Ludwig Berger   *(1777-1839)*

Instrumental	**Grand Sonata, Op. 7**
Piano	☐ Marvin (piano) / Genesis 1061

The point of view displayed in Berger's three-movement Sonata is a complete simulation of Beethoven. The model is clear: the Sonata No. 8 (*Pathétique*) in C minor, Op. 13. Nonetheless, Berger's work is far from a cheap imitation. There are creative responses that show excellent statements of individuality, which is quite different from sheer mimicking of distant tinklings. If this be too much of a protest in favor of Berger, so be it.

Marvin properly approaches the music and plays it as a Beethoven parallel. Such insight produces a fine reproduction of the score.

William Bergsma   *(1921-   )*

Orchestra	***A Carol on Twelfth Night (1953)***
	☐ Louisville Orchestra / Whitney (conductor) / Louisville 545–10 (monaural)

Bergsma's *Carol* is composed of variations on, in, and around the traditional English carol *The Twelve Days of Christmas* ("On the first day of Christmas my true love sent to me...."). Fair game for a composer, and Bergsma's game is mosaically successful.

Chameleon Variations (1960)

☐ Portland Junior Symphony / Avshalomov (conductor) / Composers Recordings 140 (monaural)

The Variations are so registered as to outline the movements of a symphony. Thus: fast tempo for the first three variants and a slow pace for the next pair, while parts 6 and 7 typify a scherzo, and then, as Bergsma describes it, "the Finale is a finale." A fairly good representation by this orchestra of young personnel.

Music on a Quiet Theme (1943)

☐ Japan Philharmonic Symphony Orchestra / Strickland (conductor) / Composers Recordings 131E (monaural)

Freshly tonal and freshly diatonic, Music on a Quiet Theme is illustrative of the neo-traditional school of composition, within which there is nary a false step. The vitality and robustness of the work are paralleled in the recording. The companion pieces by Roger Sessions and Russell Smith (see under *Sessions: Orchestra* [Symphony No. 1]; *Smith: Orchestra* [*Tetrameron*]) make this an exciting release.

The Fortunate Islands (1956)

☐ Orchestra of the Accademia Nazionale di Santa Cecilia, Rome / Antonini (conductor) / Composers Recordings 112 (monaural)

Music that celebrates the imagined discovery of the "Fortunate Isles," or the "Isles of the Blest." It combines lyricism with energy, plus a sense of mystery. (Bergsma describes the last as "elements of ritual or terror": they are contained in the "slashing" Passacaglia.) Optimum coloration is in the score, including some cogent two-dimensional dynamic textural layering. That Coplandesque sections are to be recognized does not decrease the value of Bergsma's music.

String Orchestra

Violin Concerto (1966)

☐ Polish Radio and Television Orchestra / Statkiewicz (violin) / Szostak (conductor) / Turnabout 34428

Bergsma's concerto begins with three merciless percussive pronouncements. The violin enters and takes up this dramatic motivation in fierce, creased-romantic outpourings, sprinkled, salted, and spiced by orchestrational blends. The middle division is much more quietly lyrical, but underneath there simmers a similar kind of musical anger. The finale has the same type of grip, pulsation, and frenzy. This is full-scale concerto writing—contemporaneously styled, using sharp twentieth-century language.

Supremely secure solo playing and good work by the orchestra. Why this concerto has not been picked up by our virtuosi is a good question. "No demand," would probably be the response. How can there be a demand when music is unplayed, hence, unfamiliar?

Solo Instrument and Orchestra

Violin

String Quartet No. 2 (1944)

☐ Walden String Quartet / Desto 6425

The constructive points are sensitive here. There are interlocked relationships between paired movements. In movement 1 the lines are wide: in movement 3 these lines are transferred with almost cyclic inference. Movement 2 (an Interlude with a scherzo demeanor) is made more demanding by use of mutes, providing a special timbre excitement. There is little *fortissimo* in this part of Bergsma's quartet, whereas the last movement bathes in it.

The Waldens play this music as if they wrote it collectively. A stunning performance all the way.

Chamber Music

Suite for Brass Quartet (1940)

☐ Members of the American Brass Quintet / Desto 6474/7

Bergsma's three-movement work opens with a Scherzo in shifting rhythm. A chorale-type second movement, titled *Song,* colors matters with quadruple muting. The finale, *Showpiece,* is in the stimulant of a toccata frame, with the first trumpet predominating—somewhat like the first violin in Haydn's early string quartets.

The first trumpet of the American Brass Quintet is the famed Gerard Schwarz. In the concluding (third) movement he trumpets as fast as a hockey puck sent flying from one end of the rink to the other.

Third Quartet (1953)

☐ Juilliard String Quartet / Columbia Special Products AML-5476 (monaural)

Bergsma's composition displays the shadow of Bartók in the second of the three sections comprising the work. The *ruvido* contour is, however, bathed in chromatic waters; this lends an effect that underplays the Bartókian effect. The keynote of the outer movements is contrapuntalism. Bergsma has genuine craftsmanship, and this splendid recording of his work is most profitable.

When it made this disc over fifteen years ago, the membership of the Juilliard group consisted of Mann and Koff, violins; Hillyer, viola; and Adam, cello. Only Mann remains in the present concertizing group.)

Concerto for Wind Quintet (1958)

☐ Clarion Wind Quintet / Golden Crest S-4076

The virtuosity expected from the title makes its appearance in the finale—a fiery-paced tarantella-like movement featuring, in turn, horn, bassoon, clarinet, oboe, and flute. Exciting stuff and tossed off by the Clarion group (Dunigan, Adelstein, Listokin, Bergstone, and Popkin) with brilliance and brio. The middle movement, based on a septuple-metered theme, is nocturnal in mood. Bergsma's creative virtuosity in this quiet fancy is just as impressive. It is also handsomely executed by the Clarion team.

Vocal

*Voice
with
Accompaniment*

Lullee, Lullay

☐ Steber (soprano); Biltcliffe (piano) / Desto 6411/2

An example of Bergsma's lyrical talent. The voice part is expressively set against a simple harmonic piano background.

Ballet

Gold and the Señor Commandante (1942)

☐ Eastman-Rochester Orchestra / Hanson (conductor) / Eastman-Rochester Archives ERA-1004

Bergsma indicates that the story line of his ballet is "distantly based" on Bret Harte's *The Right Eye of the Commander.* It mixes specific dance types: "elegant," "furious," "sinister," "Chinese," "tender," and "happy," as well as a *Siesta,* a *Parade,* and Chase Music. All of it is spun out healthily and organically in a contemporaneously tonal manner. Performance: stimulating.

Luciano Berio   (1925-   )

Orchestra

Allelujah II (1958)

☐ BBC Symphony Orchestra / Berio and Boulez (conductors) / RCA ARL1-1674

An investigation into spatialism, this work has the orchestra split into five groups of instruments placed in different locations; hence the need for more than a single conductor. The effect in a concert hall would doubtless be successful: on the recording, the five-group partition blends into a collectivity. However, this space-shrinking does not nullify a musical work of demanding strength and color.

Nones (1954)

☐ London Symphony Orchestra / Berio (conductor) / RCA ARL1-1674

Nones ("The Ninth Hour") was inspired by a poem by Auden. From that point on, Berio went on his own, minus any program, writing a music bound and balanced beautifully by serial procedures. These include permutations not only of pitches but of rhythmic values, dynamics, and modes of attack. Textures and densities play an important role in *Nones,* the contrasts within these formulating the design. The result is an orchestral work completely convincing and exceedingly expressive in its dodecaphonic dress.

Sinfonia (1969)

☐ New York Philharmonic and the Swingle Singers / Berio (conductor) / Columbia MS-7268

The symphony has been the freest of forms and yet the most fettered. Consider, then, the treatment given it by Berio in a creation that is truly a masterpiece. Stravinsky said that music could only express itself. Wrong—he hadn't heard Berio's Sinfonia.

There are four movements (termed "sections"). Short fragments from a book by an anthropologist constitute section 1. A tribute to Martin Luther King constitutes section 2 (this is known separately as *O King* and has been recorded separately as well. See under *Vocal: voice and instrumental ensemble*). In section 3 the climax is reached with a tremendous collage of quotes from composers mixed into the solidity of the third movement of Mahler's Symphony No. 2, and mashed with a collage of Joyce, Beckett, slogans, wall graffiti, etc. Section 4 is a type of epilogue.

The principal point is that nothing is compact: everything is mashed and smashed; the guts fly about and the sound body (words as well as music) is triply fractured. It is as if everything were permeated by huge seismic tremors. Indeed, the symphony is the most free of all forms: it has now become musical theatre.

Berio's Sinfonia is raw gorgeousness, a tract on the horrors of life that we face. Composed in 1969, it is still timely as we turn into the 1980s. (Things haven't changed.) This stunning recording tells us this is so.

Serenade I for Flute and 14 Instruments (1957)

☐ Soloists of the Rome Symphony Orchestra / Gazzelloni (flute) / Maderna (conductor) / RCA VICS-1313

Berio's piece dances and prances. Indeed, it "smiles a bit," as Berio explains, despite the mistaken idea that serial music can only indulge in *Weltschmerz* and pessimism.

The pillow-fighting rhythmic dispersions that mark the music are especially enjoyable. Gazzelloni plays in a devoted, dazzling, dramatic, and at times downright diabolical manner.

Concerto for Two Pianos and Orchestra (1973)

☐ London Symphony Orchestra / Canino and Ballista (pianos) / Berio (conductor) / RCA ARL1-1674

Solo Instrument and Orchestra

Flute

Two Pianos

Berio's double piano concerto was the result of a New York Philharmonic commission. It received its baptism on March 15, 1973—in New York, of course.

In a listing of Berio's works in one encyclopedia distinctions are made among serially styled pieces, electronic compositions, aleatoric music, eclectic types, and "other" (a catch-all). The Concerto for Two Pianos doesn't fit into any of these categories. Simply stated, its music mixes atonal and tonal materials with some coloristically free sounds. The musical action is always direct, comprehensive, and strongly contrasted, and is performed in a thoroughly handsome manner.

Viola

Chemins II (1967)

☐ Juilliard Ensemble / Trampler (viola) / Berio (conductor) / RCA LSC-3168

To realize fully the sense of *Chemins II*, one should first hear Berio's *Sequenza VI* for unaccompanied viola (discussed under *Instrumental: viola*), since it became the basis for *Chemins II*, which in turn became the basis for *Chemins III* (see below). Berio did not merely amplify by using the viola and scoring for an ensemble of nine instruments, thereby creating an "arrangement." Neither is *Chemins II* a paste-on of an "accompaniment" or a partner to the viola solo. It is created from the renewed use of *Sequenza VI* material and its further free development. Musically, therefore, it is a different-sized fraternal twin of delayed birth. (*Sequenza VI* was composed in 1967 and is twelve and a half minutes long in performance; *Chemins II* emerged in 1967 and totals ten and a quarter minutes.)

Chemins III (1967)

☐ Juilliard Ensemble and London Symphony Orchestra / Trampler (viola) / Berio (conductor) / RCA LSC-3168

Chemins III is a blood relative of *Chemins II*, which was fathered by *Sequenza VI*. Therefore, for the most complete realization of Berio's methods and objectives, these works should be heard in sequence: first, *Sequenza VI* (discussed under *Instrumental: viola*), then *Chemins II* (see above), followed by *Chemins III*.

As the substances of *Sequenza VI* were applied and bound in with the developments of *Chemins II*, so the latter's patterns and concepts were built and further structured into *Chemins III*. Berio describes it cogently: "the three pieces relate to each other something like the layers of an onion: distinct, separate, yet intimately contoured on each other." Jacques M. Poissenot characterizes it another way, stating that Berio's method here "can be likened to human memory in its ability to enlarge on an immediate fact of life."

Chemins II requires larger forces (solo instrument and chamber ensemble) than its single-instrument "feed," *Sequenza VI*, and yet it is shorter. Interestingly, the case of *Chemins III* is exactly the opposite. Calling for the largest number of performers (solo instrument, chamber ensemble, and orchestra), it matches this totality with the longest time span (fourteen and a quarter minutes) of the three compositions.

Instrumental

Flute

Sequenza I for Flute Solo (1958)

☐ Gazzelloni (flute) / Mainstream 5014

Much contemporary unaccompanied flute music is full of fussy and fustian shifts. Not this great example, which has become (together with Debussy's *Syrinx*) a classic for the instrument. Berio's piece is motivally engendered, decidedly permutative in its gestures. It has the new flute sounds (including a two-pitch chord toward the conclusion), but there is never a striving for effect or an attempt to obtain aural twitch. In its own way, Berio's flute *Sequenza* is a masterpiece.

Despite its much older issue, the Gazzelloni performance is brighter and more dynamic than the more recent one by Harvey Sollberger (on Nonesuch 73028). A kinship with chamber-music intimacy is reflected in the latter's interpretation; more soloistic conduct is projected in the former's playing. This in no way denigrates Sollberger's artistry, which is of such magnificence as to term him the American Gazzelloni.

Sequenza II for Harp (1963)

☐ DeCray (harp) / Coronet 2508

Harp

The clarity and facility of segmented phrases, though always of peripatetic action, are accompanied and additionally sonorized by percussion in Berio's fantastic piece. The detonations are harp-made, produced by hitting the sounding board of the instrument, by pedal shifts while sounds are in action, by *secco* staccati, *sons étouffés* effects, string smashes, and the like. After *Sequenza II*, harp music will never be the same.

Most harpists shy away from such hideously difficult, athletic music whereby finger bleeding and scraped knuckles can easily result. Marcella DeCray performs this work with a flair that is irresistible. Her performance will make anyone a believer in Berio's totally new brand of harp music.

Sequenza VII for Oboe (1969)

☐ Holliger (oboe) / Philips 6500202

Oboe

Imaginative invention that is aurally intoxicating. Over a constant pedal pitch, pithy variations on and around it occur, with disjunctive parentheses of tight ideas, etcetera. These always return to the pitch, which acts like a grapnel for the design. The refractions of the single pitch itself add color brushwork to the music: microtones and multiphonics are further suppliers. All of it produces the paradox of coloristic madness signifying a very clear structural premise.

Only a Heinz Holliger could be capable of successfully coping with the technical saturation of Berio's piece. Berio states that he had Holliger in mind when he composed the *Sequenza*. Indeed, Holliger was the perfect inspiration for this marvel of truly contemporary oboe music.

(This work is also included in an all-Berio program on Philips 6500631.)

Cinque variazioni for Piano (1952)

☐ Burge (piano) / Candide 31027

Piano

For his subject Berio has a tone row, a sufficient "theme" of departure for a series of variations. Although sections can be identified, the macromutations form a totally strong structure.

It is this transferred tightness of concept that carries David Burge's performance. There are more heavily purple (romantically related) considerations in Marie-Françoise Bucquet's playing of the piece on Philips 6500101. These do not add to the music's momentum but actually block it. The sound on her disc, however, is better.

Sequenza IV for Piano (1966)

☐ Bucquet (piano) / Philips 6500101

The primary element in *Sequenza IV* is a second dimension of sound quality, obtained by use of the third pedal, which isolates and prolongs pitches and chords after they have been produced. These create a fluctuating state of vibrational overhang that is in textural opposition to the articulated sounds—a non-imitative antiphony, therefore, since reflective harmonic change results.

Such sonorous imagery provides the best of two differing sound worlds. Marie-Françoise Bucquet executes accordingly, and in good form. There is great sound on this Philips disc—mandatory if Berio's piece is to be heard correctly and its full meaning understood.

Viola

Sequenza VI for Viola (1967)

☐ Trampler (viola) / RCA LSC–3168

The virtuosity of *Sequenza VI* avoids any resemblance to its traditional ambience of scalic, arpeggiated, chromatically unzippered, and mecurially disjunct passages. Most of *Sequenza VI* is a laying on of the bow on percussive static pitch combinations. It is akin to a synoptic picturing of a Varèse-like textured score reduced to a single four-stringed instrument.

The ritual is Paganiniesque. Only a great violist like Walter Trampler can bring it off and drive it home technically and musically. (Almost the same can be said for his ex-wife, Karen Phillips, who performs the piece on Finnadar 9007.)

(See *Chemins II* and *Chemins III*, under *Solo Instrument and Orchestra: viola,* for a discussion of the interrelationship between these two compositions and *Sequenza VI*.)

Chamber Music

Due pezzi for Violin and Piano (1951)

☐ Tecco (violin); Davies (piano) / Philips 6500631

Berio's serial-styled duo has lyrical substances in its first part, with balletic jocularity in the antithetical movement. It is played meaningfully and musically. The pianist is the excellent conductor Dennis Russell Davies.

Sincronie for String Quartet (1964)

☐ Lenox String Quartet / Desto 7129

Relentlessly *Sincronie* jolts and punches. Percussive pronouncements and a number of glides are constant; sustained sounds act as pivots (cadential points for nonharmonic music). In this case, the word "quartet" can only be used in the sense of a mathematical total. Quartet writing in the linear, four-voice sense is eliminated: no themes are developed, no counterpoint discussed. Berio's opus is a total integrated construction based on blocked-in frictions and clusters, out of which come resettings and redecorations, but always in the hermetic sense.

Sincronie has screaming virtuosity, and the Lenox four supply it. They have no opportunity of displaying timbre finesse, but they seize the opportunity of displaying their expertise in Cubist quartet-sound engineering.

Children's Play for Wind Quintet, *Opus Number Zoo* (1951)

☐ Dorian Quintet / Vox SVBX–5307

The title should be expanded to read "and Narrators." Each member of the quintet recites lines of texts concerning Tom cats, a horse, a grey mouse, and a barn dance, as well as playing his instrument. Light, jiggly Berio; indeed, quite a different Berio than one is accustomed to hearing. There is not too much mickey-mousing, though, so it's better than the usual "Meet the Orchestra, Kiddies" or "Clarissa and Her Clarinet" approach fed to the dubiously receptive ears at children's concerts, and it is worthy of finding a place at such affairs. However, it provides just as worthy encore fare for formal chamber music situations.

The Dorians have always been top-line performers. They display the same qualifications in the diction department.

Différences for Five Instruments and Magnetic Tape (1959)

☐ Bextresser (flute); Blackwell (clarinet); Phillips (viola); Sherry (cello); Bride (harp) / Berio (conductor) / Philips 6500631

Though actual resource differences obtain here, the coloration of the live quintet timbres closely approximates those on the tape. This meeting of the twain, therefore, gives subtle contrast and still permits a unification of the material. Berio's piece is nervous, asymmetric, and of checker-boarded action. It may lack warmth but it certainly doesn't lack interest. The playing is of split-hair positiveness.

(*Différences* is sometimes listed as calling for "Five Instruments and Stereophonic Tape." This makes no difference whatsoever in the music.)

Sequenza III for Female Voice (1966)

☐ Berberian (soprano) / Philips 6500631

Every variety of vocal production is put in action in *Sequenza III*. In addition to singing, there are babbling, laughter, muttering, screams, sighs, humming, declamation, and so forth. Such communication has never appeared in a vocalise. The solo singing role becomes mini-orchestral in its format.

Possibly three or four singers exist who can cope with this music. But even so, no one could match Cathy Berberian's extraordinary exhibition.

Chamber Music for Female Voice, Clarinet, Cello, and Harp (1952)

☐ Berberian (soprano); Blackwell (clarinet); Sherry (cello); Bride (harp) / Berio (conductor) / Philips 6500631

The Joyce text and the super-fastidious use of serial arrangement might invite the term impressionistic dodecaphonicism. Berio's intimate style fulfills the music's title, including a section of mono-pitch delivery by the voice and another of spoken text.

Chamber Music is one of the several works that Berio wrote specifically for Cathy Berberian (his former wife). She is in full command and sings with the most refined delivery. The instrumental trio plays with finesse.

Circles (1960)

☐ Berberian (soprano); Pierre (harp); Drouet and de Vinogradov (percussion) / Mainstream 5005

The text is a poem by E. E. Cummings. Thus, Berio demands and Berberian delivers perfectly: words of one syllable split into syllables, hard consonants pronounced with the quality of soft vowels. What it amounts to is that the Cummings text is made to sound as graphically as it appears on the printed page. Normal musical object-shapes are transformed into sonic cubism.

In live performance, *Circles* requires the vocalist to conduct the harp and percussion, give cues, and perform histrionics. Only the visual aspect is lacking on the recording. All of the theatricalism jumps out of the record grooves. A stunning, stimulating recording.

Vocal

Voice Alone

Voice and Instrumental Ensemble

El mar la mar

☐ London Sinfonietta / Ross and Thomas (sopranos) / Berio (conductor) / RCA ARL1-0037

A haunting evocation that seems to verge on folk music turns, but with Berio's sheen of fantasy there is never such patly squared stylization. The dramatic situation is apparent but is underplayed with keen creative strategy.

The voices are well matched, one being a mezzo-soprano (RCA lists both as sopranos). The instrumental background is for a septet of piccolo, two clarinets, harp, cello, bass, and accordion.

Folk Songs

☐ Juilliard Ensemble / Berberian (soprano) / Berio (conductor) / RCA LSC–3189

These are unique versions of eleven songs. Through Berio's inventions, a rich bounty is made available by his clever combine of contemporaneous innoculation of folk color. The product is never over-styled or out-styled.

The set begins with Black Is the Color of My True Love's Hair, followed by I Wonder As I Wander. The next three are from Armenia, France, and Sicily. Nos. 6 and 7 are songs in folk style by Berio; No. 8 is from Sardinia. The set is completed by a pair drawn from Joseph Canteloube's famous Chants d'Auvergne and an Azerbaijan Love Song.

Cathy Berberian simply scores a grand slam with her vocalism. She is fascinating. She is impressive. She is great. She gives one hell of a performance.

O King (1970)

☐ London Sinfonietta / Ross (soprano) / Berio (conductor) / RCA ARL1-0037

An unusual, but thoroughly compelling, threnodic tribute to Martin Luther King. Berio uses only the vowel sounds within his name, the voice functioning as an instrumentalized part of the whole ensemble of flute, clarinet, violin, cello, and piano.

The meticulous reading given is quite vivid in spite of the constancy of its extremely soft dynamic level. Another rendition of this work is on Delos 25406. It is almost as good. However, Berio brings more telling emphasis to the keyboard punctuations that collide against the pianissimo line as equivalents of the "K" in King's name.

Voice and Orchestra

Epifanie (1965)

☐ BBC Symphony Orchestra / Berberian (soprano) / Berio (conductor) / RCA LSC–3189

Epifanie is free-formed from two cycles, one of seven orchestral pieces and the other of five vocal pieces. Ten different sequential arrangements of these dozen items are offered. Even performances of the orchestral music alone are possible in this multiple-choice situation, with five varied possibilities existent.

So much for total structure. Pitches, rhythms, dynamics, etc., are absolutes defined by Berio. These pertain to a huge orchestra of sixteen woodwind players using nineteen instruments, fifteen brass instrumentalists using sixteen types, plus glockenspiel, celesta, two harps, a vibraphonist doubling on xylophone, a marimbaphone, three percussionists concerned with sixty-five different instruments, and forty-six string players (divided into violins A, B, and C, as well as violas, cellos, and double basses).

Berio's piece fuses pointillistic dabs with punctuative blocks, sharp color frames with pigmented blobs—all for orchestral effect or enhancement of the spoken texts and the vocal line. The sonorous materials swirl and are constantly excited but are always coherent in their free motility. This multiplicity of form, content, and scoring carries over to the texts (which are each by a different author, including Proust, Brecht, Machado, Joyce, and Simon) and still further to the mix of the voice part in which straight singing, *Sprech-stimme,* and narration are present.

The entire score is a block-buster affair for a virtuoso orchestra and a double virtuoso singer. In that respect, the BBC, with Berio handling the conductorial traffic, produces a fine result. The voice part is made-to-order for the amazing versatility of Cathy Berberian. To listen to her realization is to be present at the execution of vocal miracles.

Laborintus II (1965)

☐ Ensemble Musique Vivante / Berio (conductor) / RCA LSC-3267

Opera and Dramatic Music

Regardless of the style chosen—and this composer has touched base with every contemporary type—Berio's ability to master the style selected is a matter that many composers envy. Here the creative adventure can be classified as taking place in eclectic territory.

Laborintus, written to acknowledge the seventh centenary of Dante's birth, is a huge blend of poetry, cries, fractured words, interjections, laughing, shouting, and numerous other theatrical gestures. The music for voices, instruments, reciter, and tape throbs its way and thrusts in various directions. It is certainly "eclectic," with its glissandi sweeps, cluster poundage, jazzy phrases, and even madrigal reminders. Serial procedures will be found and so will self-quotation.

On a sound recording the composition fights a restricted ambiance. It's interesting to hear but would doubtless be far more effective if it would somehow be staged. How this could be accomplished one leaves to Berio.

Opera (Excerpts)

Agnus	*E Vó*
Air	*Melodrama*

☐ London Sinfonietta / Ross, Thomas, and Salvetta (sopranos); English (tenor) / Berio (conductor) / RCA ARL1-0037

Hardly opera as opera is known, since this work is a collection of scenes heavy on parody with similarly strong emphasis on the use of the voice to produce sounds *as sounds* in place of text definition. Instrumental coloration is acute: sustained organ clusters, special clarinet *tremolandi,* quarter-tone inflections on a viola, cancellation of solid sound surfaces stated in continuity.

The *Melodrama,* which is acted, sung, spoke, whispered, declaimed, and hummed by Gerald English, has a sort of black humor based on a heavily alliterative text by Berio. It runs for fifteen and a quarter minutes. Such length, tied in with the word parallels, is presumably part and parcel of Berio's bold parodic principle.

Visage (1961)

☐ Berberian (soprano) / Turnabout 34046

Electronic Music

A good many sexual sounds are simulated here, despite Berio's neutral statement that *Visage* is a "sound track for a 'drama' that was never written." Berio does allow listeners to make up their own minds when he makes the general remark that *Visage* describes "discourse mainly at the onomatopoeic level." Well, now! That can mean many things to many people. To this reviewer the suggestions are sultry events, as orgasmic undulations merge from human sound into electronic explanation. (This enlargement process is a reminder of the motion picture technique in which, for example, a person shrieks and the film cuts immediately into a train roaring through a tunnel.)

Visage is thoroughly, artistically, and beautifully dramatic. It is also sensitively striking. Berberian's delivery has a virtuosity that deserves a vocal Pulitzer Prize plus a recording Oscar. It encompasses an encyclopedia of emotions: crying, laughing, pain, joy, fear, and ecstasy, all of this while electronic counterpoints whizz by and about. But, above all, those literal sexy sounds! Perhaps this is not an example of musical bedroom hedonism. It matters not. Whatever the listener reads into Berio's work, it is an extraordinary conception, a smash success in the medium of electronic music.

Lennox Berkeley *(1903-   )*

Orchestra	***Mont Juic.** See Benjamin Britten and Lennox Berkeley: Orchestra.*

Symphony No. 3 (1969)

☐ London Philharmonic Orchestra / Berkeley (conductor) / Musical Heritage Society MHS-1672

Berkeley is, at heart, a classicist, his syntax drawing on considerable contemporary synonyms which color the contents. In this symphony the premise is expanded to a through-composed method, motivally engendered, defining a music of quenchless vitality that moves liberally and freely as though it were in a constant shuttle of development. Terming the composition a "symphonic fantasia" might not be agreeable to the composer, but the broadminded and generous continuity of scale fits that designation.

The recording is beautifully conceived. Berkeley well serves his own music.

Solo Instrument and Orchestra *Guitar*	**Guitar Concerto (1974)**

☐ Monteverdi Orchestra / Bream (guitar) / Gardiner (conductor) / RCA ARL1-1181

Behind any good art there must be the primum mobile. Berkeley's sources are to be found in pandiatonic technique, but his Concerto remains individual in type and taste and makes a clear, fresh-sounding, productive contribution to guitar literature.

Bream plays it precise and neatly, with immaculate candor and guitarish radiance. Nice support from the small orchestra of single winds, paired horns, and strings.

Instrumental *Guitar*	**Sonatina, Op. 51**

☐ Bream (guitar) / RCA LSC-2448

The clear textures of Berkeley's music lead to calling him an English Fauré. The guitar Sonatina is prime evidence of this designation. One writer has said Berkeley is "happiest with dance rhythms and serenade idiom." That description fits this opus, which includes some deft colorations such as muted chords, muffled sounds, and minuscule-timbred harmonics.

The Sonatina was written specifically for Julian Bream. His beautifully disciplined performance repays the composer in full.

Chamber Music	**Trio for Violin, Horn, and Piano, Op. 44**

☐ Parikian (violin); Brain (horn); Horsley (piano) / Seraphim 60073 (monaural)

An example of a cosmopolitan composer with clearly disposed musical ideas and the ability to convey them. The medium used is extremely rare. It does permit, as in this instance, a work that imparts precise musical values and sufficient dramatic messages in clear sonata, ternary, and variation forms. It is played with sensitiveness, and notice that the great Dennis Brain is a member of the ensemble.

Concertino for Recorder, Violin, Violoncello, and Harpsichord, Op. 48

☐ Dolmetsch-Schoenfeld Ensemble / Orion 73104

Divertimento aspects cover the four movements, neatly described in neoclassic terms. In place of a slow movement there are two short pieces titled Aria I and Aria II. These are set as duets, the first for recorder and cello, the other for violin and harpsichord. Total balance thereby of tempi (the corner movements are fast-paced) and textural color.

Clean playing but exceedingly neutral regard for dynamic flux and comparison.

Four Ronsard Sonnets for Tenor and Orchestra (1953)

☐ London Sinfonietta / Pears (tenor) / Berkeley (conductor) / London HEAD-3

Vocal

Voice and Orchestra

Both texts and music blend almost formal classical chasteness with romantically elegant lyricism. Berkeley's love poems balance in their quaternity. The first is joyful and forthright, the second is sweetly contemplative, then part three which is brashly passionate, followed by the serenity of the finale.

The same work is available on Louisville 662, with William Whitesides as the tenor soloist. However, though he has a stronger voice than Pears, the finely shaped delivery and the more subtle response of the latter soloist give him first place. Whitesides *sings*, Pears provides musical depth.

Herman Berlinski   *(1910-   )*

Symphonic Visions (1949)

Orchestra

☐ Ashai Orchestra of Tokyo / Korn (conductor) / Composers Recordings 115 (monaural)

Music of individual profile. The composition shows a composer aware of germinal development and the required rapport of style and finish. The four movements have the sense of huge recitative. A good performance.

Kol Nidre

Choral

Chorus Alone

☐ David Tilman Choir / Lam (baritone) / Serenus 12039

Quite different from the well-known portrayal by Max Bruch of the famous plaintive prayer that ushers in the all-important Jewish High Holy Day, *Yom Kippur*. Berlinski opts for a more pungent harmonic content, making a very touching and thrilling conception. So is the performance. (Serenus does not give the organist who assists any credit.)

Hector Berlioz   *(1803-1869)*

King Lear, Overture, Op. 4
Le Corsaire, Overture, Op. 21

Orchestra

☐ London Symphony Orchestra / Davis (conductor) / Philips 835367

What places Davis's readings far above the average is that he draws a big sound but it is never blatant, pugnacious, or overdrawn. The orchestra doesn't shout, and so often in Berlioz it is exactly that quality that conductors permit. Not in this case: for *Le Corsaire* this is the best there is—you couldn't do better. Ditto for *King Lear*. Its profound opening section is beautifully personified.

Les Francs-Juges, Overture, Op. 3

☐ London Symphony Orchestra / Davis (conductor) / Philips 835367

Dramatic when it should be—the smashing chords that spit out throughout the Overture have never been so forceful. But, importantly, there is substance within them and they do not register as merely loud punctuations. Knowing how to balance and adjust such formulations is a warranty of a superb and sensitive conducting ear. The opposite effect, and just as telling, is the supremely certain fluidity that marks the swingy tune of the Overture.

Marche funèbre pour la dernière scene d'Hamlet, Op. 18, No. 3

☐ London Symphony Orchestra and John Alldis Choir / Davis (conductor) / Philips 802913

Stark music framed by rhythmic consistency and filled with the expressive specialties of Berlioz's orchestration. Colin Davis's vivid re-creation of "The Funeral March for the Last Scene of Hamlet" makes one wonder why such powerfully tragic music is absent from concert programs.

Overture to Béatrice et Bénédict (1862)
Overture to Benvenuto Cellini, Op. 23

☐ New York Philharmonic / Boulez (conductor) / Columbia M–31799

Berlioz by way of Boulez? By all means, for the primary reason that with all the exuberances in Berlioz they register best when controlled on point and that's just what mastery Boulez possesses in this case. And pinpointed rhythm also. Just hear what he does with the syncopated melodic lines in the *Béatrice* Overture!

Prelude to Les Troyens à Carthage (1863)

☐ London Symphony Orchestra / Davis (conductor) / Philips 802913

Once related, but no longer, to the opera *Les Troyens*. In terms of the opera this Prelude can only be considered a special historic appendix, since it is not included (and has no pertinence) within the five acts (totaling nine tableaux embracing fifty-two sections) of the complete work. Berlioz wrote the piece when forced reluctantly to accept a truncated initial production omitting the first two acts, which became titled *La Prise de Troie* ("The Capture of Troy"), and presenting only the last three acts as *Les Troyens à Carthage* ("The Trojans at Carthage"). To preface the split-off, and only for that purpose, Berlioz conceived his Prelude as moderate declamatory-like music to define the background of the deleted two acts.

The Prelude should not be shelved (as it has been) because of its original utilitarian purpose. It deserves concert performances in its own right. Colin Davis's impressive recorded conception provides sufficient proof for this statement.

Rob Roy, Overture (1832)

☐ Philharmonic Promenade Orchestra / Boult (conductor) / Westminster Gold 8304 (monaural)

No stereo competition. One cannot term this an inspired performance, but for that matter there are no ecstatic conditions spread throughout the score.

Roman Carnival, Overture, Op. 9

☐ London Symphony Orchestra / Previn (conductor) / Angel S-37170

Of course this Overture can be battered and ravaged by overdoing the *rubati* effects that tempt the conductor (and in his version on Philips 83567 Colin Davis especially succumbs), and by force-feeding the brass. Proper panache is what the *Roman Carnival* needs, but without any panic that the message won't carry. Previn adjusts beautifully and his enthusiastic reading scores a great success.

Royal Hunt and Storm from *Les Troyens* (1859)

☐ Boston Symphony Orchestra / Munch (conductor) / RCA AGL1-1277

No attempt is made by Munch to tear the textures to tatters in the Storm (which appears in the second act of the opera), whereas there is an almost vaudevillian sonorous overobviousness in Boulez's reading (Columbia M-31799). The initial and final parts of the score are also better detailed (more poetry) in Munch's reading. Meaningful Berlioz by this Berliozian expert.

Symphonie fantastique, Op. 14

☐ Concertgebouw Orchestra / Davis (conductor) / Philips 6500774
☐ Berlin Philharmonic Orchestra / von Karajan (conductor) / Deutsche Grammophon 2530597
☐ New Philharmonia Orchestra / Stokowski (conductor) / London 21031

Davis's version has the freedom and flexibility of Berlioz's language. It also has its splendor and energy. Von Karajan's is dynamically rich and certain, with atmosphere and color twinned in an exciting presentation. One excision, the repeat in the opening movement, is a structural error on his part, but otherwise the representation is splendid. (Von Karajan's earlier edition, with the same orchestra, is pallid and even erratic in comparison. Proof can be obtained on Deutsche Grammophon 138964.)

The last is almost first, but Stoky being Stoky, that's the way it is. His is a magnetic reading, and the strings have never sounded better than in this case. However, he does tamper with expansion of tempi in certain sections, recomposes some dynamics, and inserts some fervent accents. Still, this is Berlioz and such re-creative necessity (if one wishes to call it that) cannot disturb the general evaluation. After all, overacademicism with Berlioz is exhausting.

There are many competitive editions. Some come very close to achieving a top success but spoil it by (1) lack of consistent intensity (Ozawa, with the B.S.O. on Deutsche Grammophon 2530358 and with the Toronto Symphony on Odyssey Y-31923), and (2) insistence on everything but the drama that courses through the score (Boulez, with the London Symphony Orchestra on Columbia M-30587).

Waverly, Overture, Op. 1b

☐ London Symphony Orchestra / Davis (conductor) / Philips 83567

A performance that rejuvenates this less-important Overture. Controlled dash and a fine lyrical climate warm the piece.

Philips makes confusion by listing *Waverly* as Opus 1 on its label copy. Opus 1 applies to a cantata, *Huit Scènes de Faust*. The dates of composition may have caused this. The overture was actually written (in 1827–1828) before the cantata, which was composed in 1829. Regardless, one must follow the opus designations as they stand.

Band

Symphonie funèbre et triomphale, Op. 15

☐ London Symphony Orchestra and John Alldis Choir / Wick (trombone) / Davis (conductor) / Philips 802913

Placing Berlioz's work in the band category is no error, since it calls for winds, brass, and percussion, with stringed instruments and chorus optional. Originally called "Military Symphony," the music carries out the descriptive adjective. It opens with an attenuated *Marche funèbre* ("Funeral March"), continues with an *Oraison funèbre* ("Funeral Oration"), and is completed by an *Apothéose* ("Apotheosis"). In the middle movement the trombone is featured in recitative-aria format.

The general plan and scoring fit the medium: rhythmic directness and healthy blocked sonorities. Colin Davis's reading is full-voiced, powerfully generous, but never bombastic. Denis Wick does well with his special part in the second movement's proceedings.

Solo Instrument and Orchestra

Viola

Harold in Italy, Op. 16

☐ London Symphony Orchestra / Imai (viola) / Davis (conductor) / Philips 9500026

Regardless of whether one visualizes pictorial action in Berlioz's work or considers it simply as a symphony in four movements with an obbligato solo viola is immaterial. Either alternative requires dramatic power to be expressed in the performance. There's plenty of opportunity for poetic production, but it is the theatrical extent of information that is most important.

Nobuko Imai and Colin Davis join in a production that projects the music in its fullest aspects.

Violin

Reverie and Caprice, Op. 8

☐ Southwest German Radio Orchestra / Rosand (violin) / Reinhardt (conductor) / Turnabout 34466

One of the fringe benefits in the Berlioz discography. The *Reverie and Caprice* never seems to find a place on concert programs since the solo fiddle fraternity has avoided it. No blame pertains. It is written in a conventional non-Berliozian way without special personality or identification.

Rosand's playing is warmly fitting, and he gets inside the music to the fullest extent. This is far better than the superficial manner that Grumiaux exhibits in the competitive edition available (on Philips 6580047), not to overlook his excessive vibrato.

Vocal

Voice and Orchestra

La Belle Voyageuse, Op. 2, No. 4

Zaïde, Op. 19, No. 1

☐ London Symphony Orchestra / Armstrong (soprano) / Davis (conductor) / Philips 6500009

Opposites that are both attractive. *La Belle* has salonistic turns; the other song has been neatly described as a "racy Bolero," though it doesn't always race. A fine performance.

La Captive, Op. 12

☐ London Symphony Orchestra / Veasey (contralto) / Davis (conductor) / Philips 6500009

Originally for voice and piano with cello obbligato. Much later Berlioz made the orchestral setting. Attractively sung.

Le Chasseur danois, Op. 19, No. 6

☐ London Symphony Orchestra / Shirley-Quirk (baritone) / Davis (conductor) / Philips 6500009

A lusty conception and provided with lusty singing. The latter gives the type of involvement required.

Le Jeune Pâtre breton, Op. 13, No. 4

☐ London Symphony Orchestra / Patterson (tenor) / Davis (conductor) / Philips 6500009

Berlioz's song is a sensitive, plaintive item. It features horn coloration (beautifully played). Only the slight vibrato in Frank Patterson's voice prevents high marks for his performance.

Les Nuits d'été, Op. 7

☐ New Philharmonia Orchestra / Baker (mezzo-soprano) / Barbirolli (conductor) / Angel S-36505

Certainly this is one of the most beautiful of all voice-with-orchestra cycles. And certainly the performances bear out that statement, with one exception. Janet Baker's rendition is totally exquisite, ideally conveyed in all six of the songs. It is brilliantly poised singing. Régine Crespin's version with Ansermet conducting (London 25821) is even stronger in vocal quality but weaker in subtlety—so it is placed second. Last is Leontyne Price supported by Fritz Reiner (on RCA LSC-2695). She sings beautifully, for the greater part, but with too much care, as though the pitches on the score page were being proofread.

The one version to discount totally is the Philips 6500009 edition. There four different singers participate in a division of the cycle so that a soprano and a tenor each sing a pair of songs and a mezzo and a bass sing one each. Rather ridiculous, and splitting the cycle is like dividing a three-movement violin concerto among violin, viola, and cello.

Roméo et Juliette, Op. 17

☐ Vienna Philharmonic Orchestra, Vienna State Opera Chorus, and Les Soloistes des Choeurs de l'ORTF / Ludwig (mezzo-soprano); Sénéchal (tenor); Ghiaurov (bass) / Maazel (conductor) / London 12102

Choral

Chorus and Orchestra

Not easy to categorize this work. Berlioz's opus joins symphonic procedures with total drama, and with program music. With solo voices, chorus, and full orchestra combined it can be termed symphonic opera. But all that is simply statistical. This is music of great sweep and color, of prodigious creativity and coloristic life, no matter how it is classified.

Maazel's is a performance of passion and tension that depicts Berlioz's inspired work to the utmost. The love scene is golden-toned, conveyed with fine pace; the Queen Mab Scherzo that follows moves with finesse. Superior singing from soloists and massed voices. A runner-up in the available editions would be Munch's on RCA VICS-6042.

L'Enfance du Christ, Op. 25

☐ Orchestra and Chorus of the French National Radio / Berbié (mezzo-soprano); Andreozzi and Vanzo (tenors); Calès and Brossmann (baritones); Soyer and Soumagnas (basses) / Martinon (conductor) / Nonesuch 73022

There is as much dramatic impact in this oratorio as one expects to find in the non-sacred field of opera. The production is transcendently impressive, its spirit is authoritative, and, gratefully, it is presented minus any cuts. One recalls the old Columbia issue, which played games with the many specific instructions Berlioz entered into his score. Martinon will have none of this. There can be a temptation to sweet-tooth this music, but Martinon will have none of that, either. A revealing presentation.

The full text in French and English is included in Nonesuch's production, and there is a splendid essay on the work by David Hamilton.

Requiem, Op. 5

☐ Boston Symphony Orchestra and New England Conservatory Chorus / Simoneau (tenor) / Munch (conductor) / RCA VICS–6043

Great Berlioz creation matched by great Munch re-creation. Munch recorded the *Grande Messe des morts* again, the repeat being with the Bavarian Radio Orchestra and Chorus (with Peter Schreier as the tenor soloist) on Deutsche Grammophon 2707032; but as good as that edition is, the earlier RCA text is better.

The perspective of each of the various parts of the work is acute. The sense of grandeur in the music is never lessened. No conductor represented on disc has achieved the intensity Munch brings to the opening movement, and to the way the *Lacrymosa* is led, by its tempo choice, to a superb climax. The brasses are intense and powerful but always convincingly musical. This recording, RCA emphasizes to the purchaser, was winner of the *Grand Prix du disque*. A perceptive jury, indeed.

Te Deum, Op. 22

☐ London Symphony Orchestra and Chorus and Wandsworth School Boys' Choir / Tagliavini (tenor); Kynaston (organ) / Davis (conductor) / Philips 839790

A score blown up with romantic accommodation. However, virtue goes with size in this case. Berlioz's work calls for three choirs (he wanted two of these to be of one hundred singers each and the third to have six hundred boys), orchestra, and organ. While Colin Davis's forces are considerably less, they are sufficient to produce the tonal volume and brilliance required, without negating the austerity and varying densities that color the music.

There is plenty of opportunity for a conductor to employ the smack-them-right-between-the-eyes method in directing this work. Not such for Mr. Davis. He is always artistically true in his Berlioz readings. Here he is magnificent—much more so than Barenboim is on Columbia; the latter doesn't exude a confidence in his sense of direction in a number of places.

There is a monaural version available on Odyssey (32160206E), conducted by Beecham. It's fine, but the diction of the singers is rather poor and the tenor soloist has been overmiked. Still, it's better than the Barenboim entry.

Béatrice et Bénédict (1862)

☐ London Symphony Orchestra and John Alldis Choir / Eda-Pierre (soprano); Baker (mezzo-soprano); Watts (alto); Tear (tenor); Allen (baritone); Bastin and Lloyd (basses); Van Allan (speaker) / Davis (conductor) / Philips 6700121

This is the second time Colin Davis has recorded Berlioz's comic opera, an adaptation of Shakespeare's *Much Ado About Nothing* made by Berlioz. The first release is still available, on Oiseau-Lyre S-256/7. It has less to offer, with musical cuts and no dialogue. (Incidentally, carryover from the earlier recording is Helen Watts.)

Berlioz and Davis make an attractive partnership, and this is a bright performance that the latter directs. There are some minor criticisms: Janet Baker as Béatrice is not as imposing as one would wish and Christiane Eda-Pierre as Héro roughens lines at times, but otherwise there is an attractive spark to the singing. Chorus and orchestra are first rate.

Benvenuto Cellini, Op. 23

☐ B.B.C. Symphony Orchestra and Chorus of the Royal Opera House, Covent Garden / Eda-Pierre (soprano); Berbié (mezzo-soprano); Gedda, Blackwell, and Cuenod (tenors); Massard and Herincx (baritones); Bastin, Soyer, and Lloyd (basses); Reiss (speaking role) / Davis (conductor) / Philips 6707019

A huge spectacle, *Benvenuto Cellini* poses difficulties to stage, especially because of the special role of the chorus, which is no mere minor supplement to the individual characters. But on discs (four of them in Philips's sumptuous release) there is magnificent responsiveness to one of Berlioz's great works.

The star is, of course, Cellini. Gedda's heroic characterization of the role is thrilling and in all respects his voice is magnificent. All of the other singers are above average; the ensembles are beautifully structured; the sound of the orchestra and chorus is rich, firm, and subtly nuanced. In all, a dynamically successful presentation of a difficult work, for which Colin Davis deserves overwhelming applause.

La Damnation de Faust, Op. 24

☐ London Symphony Orchestra and Chorus, Ambrosian Singers, and Wandsworth School Boys' Choir / Veasey and Knight (mezzo-sopranos); Gedda (tenor); Bastin and Van Allan (basses); Taylor (viola); Browne (English horn) / Davis (conductor) / Philips 6703042

Complete and unabridged and clearly one of the greatest of Colin Davis's recordings. The portrayal shows remarkable authority and stylistic discipline that never get in the way of Berlioz's great score. Neither does Davis mess about and around, but strongly details every measure and obtains a vigor, sensitivity, and fervor that are notable.

Jules Bastin as Méphistophélès is impressively debonair and Nicolai Gedda covers his part with breadth. The others in the cast are all very good, but the controlling force of this "concert opera" (Berlioz's term) comes from the star of the show, Colin Davis.

Lélio, ou Le Retour à la vie, Op. 14b

☐ London Symphony Orchestra and Chorus / Mitchinson (tenor); Shirley-Quirk (baritone); Barrault (speaker) / Boulez (conductor) / Columbia M-30588

Berlioz's monodrama, with plenty of monologue, is represented by two editions at present. However, it is the delivery of Jean-Louis Barrault on the Columbia disc that carries the day in comparison to Jean Topard on Angel 37139 (the performance conducted by Martinon). Barrault's histrionic style fits much better than the rather placid delivery of Topard. Further, the subtle staging simulation carried out on Columbia's recording adds a reality lacking on Angel's disc. Both conductors cover the six musical numbers equally well.

Les Troyens (1859)

☐ Orchestra and Chorus of the Royal Opera House, Covent Garden, and the Wandsworth School Boys' Choir / Lindholm (soprano); Veasey, Howells, and Bainbridge (mezzo-sopranos); Begg (contralto); Vickers, Partridge, Davies, and Lennox (tenors); Glossop (baritone); Soyer, Raffell, Thau, Herincx, and Wicks (basses); Hert (clarinet) / Davis (conductor) / Philips 6709002

The epic dimensions of this work (first concerned with the fall of Troy and then with the tragic Dido and Aeneas tale) cover both size and scope. Its incandescence and technical complexity demand virtuoso performances on the part of every singer and orchestral player as well as the conductor. Berlioz the individual creator must be paralleled by highly skilled re-creative musicians.

The demand is met in this sumptuous, superb production. No matter what future recordings may be made of this opera the Colin Davis performance will be the source for comparison. His command is thorough, the singing of dramatic decisiveness, the orchestral detail fully achieved. That Berit Lindholm sometimes microtones her pitch by slight instability and that Jon Vickers forces his voice occasionally does not negate the intense dramaticism of this portrayal. Berlioz is totally fulfilled in this recording.

Robert Bernat (1931-   )

Orchestra

In Memoriam: John F. Kennedy (Passacaglia for Orchestra) (1966)

☐ Louisville Orchestra / Mester (conductor) / Louisville S–692

Reading Bernat's analysis of his composition one expects technical fixations. But the document turns out to be an extremely moving piece of music, one of the best of the many that were composed after Kennedy's death. The featured interlacement is William Billings's *When Jesus Wept*. It saturates the structuralism of the seventeen variations that comprise the work.

Leonard Bernstein (1918-   )

Orchestra

Ballet Music from On the Town (1944)

☐ New York Philharmonic / Bernstein (conductor) / Columbia MG–32174

Fascinating at two levels: a heated set of dances for a Broadway musical that clinches a jazz and symphonic partnership and a performance that has gusto and yet includes a sensitivity not to overdo and thereby overkill.

Two other editions of the Bernstein version should be noted, both on Columbia: MS–6677 and M–30304. Forget what else is listed in *Schwann*.

Facsimile—A Choreographic Essay (1947)

☐ New York Philharmonic / Bernstein (conductor) / Columbia MS–6792

Facsimile is represented here as a concert piece, though most of it (except the final section) is a transplant from the original ballet. The subject: two guys and a gal in a somewhat Freudian give and mostly take. That little matters or interferes in considering the work in the absolute-music category. However, like title, like style. *Facsimile*'s eclectic tone is of minor total from Copland, but of major total from Stravinsky. But the music is scored with rich characteristics that are mostly Bernstein's own.

Little recorded competition, and that (on the Seraphim label S–60197) can't come close to Bernstein conducting Bernstein. The performance is also available in a two-disc package of all-Bernstein music on Columbia MG–32174.

Jeremiah Symphony (Symphony No. 1) (1943)

☐ Israel Philharmonic Orchestra / Ludwig (mezzo-soprano) / Bernstein (conductor) / Deutsche Grammophon 2530968

No mistaking the objective of Bernstein's initial symphony in three movements. The semi-proclamatory *Prophecy* is followed by a *con brio*–styled *Profanation*, dedicated to continual asymmetric detail. While note counting and the like is a game that can be played by anyone, nonetheless, the metrical statistics for this movement are worth noting. In a total of 349 measures there are 248 different time signatures! In the finale (*Lamentation*), the voice enters singing some Hebrew sacred verses.

There is no doubt that this spirited and polished performance replaces the old one, as good as it is, with Jennie Tourel as the vocal soloist and the New York Philharmonic, with Bernstein at the helm. However, it's still in the catalogue if it is wanted and will be found on Columbia MS–6303. Does anyone remember the RCA Camden item, on CAL–196, with Bernstein doing a first-rate presentation with the Schuyler Symphony Orchestra (whatever important group hid under that name) and Nan Merriam as the vocal soloist?

(Deutsche Grammophon includes the *Jeremiah* with the other two Bernstein symphonies, plus the *Chichester Psalms,* in a three-record package on 2709077.)

Overture to *Candide* (1956)

☐ New York Philharmonic / Bernstein (conductor) / Columbia D3S–818

You can second-guess some composer-conductors conducting their own compositions, but not Lenny. Abravanel, Fiedler, Previn, and Rogers have recorded this outgoing overture. They do very well; Lenny does better and best, especially because he is father to the pace the work should take and most cognizant of its fluid contrast 'twixt song and stir.

It's available in no fewer than seven packagings. Some are all-Bernstein affairs. The one listed here is a three-record set covering eighteen overtures by everyone from Bizet to Wolf-Ferrari.

Symphonic Dances from *West Side Story* (1957)

☐ San Francisco Symphony Orchestra / Ozawa (conductor) / Deutsche Grammophon 2530309

Not only dances, including a Mambo and a Cha-cha, but a Fugue and gang battle music are included in the nine connected sections of the piece. Bernstein's stage musical has nobility and sharp characterization. On the strength of its individuality, *West Side Story* can well be considered his finest achievement in a creative catalogue that has an extremely wide range.

Of course Bernstein has recorded the work (on Columbia MS–6251 and in a two-record set, MG–32174). However, the dazzle and vitality in Ozawa's conception produce a deeper effect in this counterpart of the *Romeo and Juliet* tale set in New York in the 1950s.

Symphonic Suite from *On the Waterfront* (1955)

☐ New York Philharmonic / Bernstein (conductor) / Columbia MS–6251

Nineteen and a half minutes' worth taken from the finely taut and lyrical score Bernstein wrote for the film that starred Marlon Brando. It holds together nicely and though tinged with eclectic research it works nicely, thank you.

Hidden away in very small print on the liner copy is the statement that the music was "orchestrated by Sid Ramin and Irwin Kostal under the supervision of Leonard Bernstein." Give the gentlemen full credit for a vivid job of scoring. Give the New York Philharmonic full credit for a vivid performance.

Solo Instrument and Orchestra

Clarinet

Prelude, Fugue, and Riffs (1950)

☐ Columbia Jazz Combo / Goodman (clarinet) / Bernstein (conductor) / Columbia MS-6805

Jazz jive as only Lenny Bernstein can turn it out, as perfect a combine (and as satisfactory a dish) as steak and potatoes. There's more than Goodman here as the star (he really doesn't have special solo status at all). The unnamed members of this Jazz Combo are all top artists, and with Bernstein swinging it with his colleagues this is a boldly colored, penetrating rhythmic evocation that titillates.

Bernstein's work can also be obtained on Columbia MS-6677; in that case it is companioned with three other of his works. On the 6805 disc the other three pieces (by Copland, Gould, and Stravinsky) all feature Benny Goodman as soloist.

Piano

Age of Anxiety (Symphony No. 2 for Piano and Orchestra) (1949)

☐ Israel Philharmonic Orchestra / Foss (piano) / Bernstein (conductor) / Deutsche Grammophon 2530969

Parallels exist here with Bernstein's Serenade (see under *violin*). It is made to order for ballet and has so been used. It highlights a solo instrument and is also inspired by a literary work (in this case, Auden's poem).

Part 1 of the piece consists of a prologue (very evocative of loneliness by the use of minimal means—a pair of clarinets) and two sets of variations (fourteen in all). The variants are not piecemeal refurbishings or reworkings of the same theme, but a development of one idea in a variation as the impetus for the variation of the next. Dramatic pronunciation and conceptual specialness are found in the second part of the work. This has a poetic dirge and a jazz division that only a Leonard Bernstein could produce. It's hot and cool, a hybrid of Broadway and Carnegie Hall, with the proper degree of nostalgic warmth. The finale has a tinge of pomposity, but has the necessary substances for properly concluding the piece.

D.G.'s recording presents a performance of lithe strength, and, of course, with Bernstein at the controls one is certain of authentic interpretations on the part of all concerned. Lukas Foss, in the solo role, is masterly in every respect—a reminder, again, of the prodigious pianism he possesses but rarely (these days) displays.

The earlier edition on Columbia (MS-6885) is quite good, with Entremont as the pianist. However, there is one fault in the engineering. In the last part of *The Masque* (the jazz section mentioned above) a pianino in the orchestra picks up where the solo piano leaves off. Here, the smaller keyboard instrument is undefined and quite hazy. The brilliant effect of scoring—a coloristic counterpunch—is thereby lost.

(This work, plus the *Chichester Psalms* and Bernstein's two other symphonies, is also available as a three-disc package. The call number for this larger Deutsche Grammophon entry is 2709077.)

Serenade for Solo Violin, String Orchestra, Harp, and Percussion (after Plato's *Symposium*) (1954)

☐ New York Philharmonic / Francescatti (violin) / Bernstein (conductor) / Columbia MS-7058

The more one listens to the Serenade the more one becomes convinced of its intense balletic thrust (like Bernstein's *Age of Anxiety* it was choreographed by Jerome Robbins). This does not lessen its value as a solo violin work with restrained partnership (itself displaying a scoring with as much color and strength as would pertain to a full ensemble of winds and brass, as well as percussion and strings). It isn't that rhythm predominates, even within the slowly presented, widely spanned melodic spinnings. It is the intensity of inner action that proposes the choreographic category, together with the total theatricality of the score.

There is a great deal of Stravinsky in the work, but any damn fool can recognize that. Eclectic, yes, but choice eclecticism. The Serenade is a superb piece, beautifully crafted, with a proper percentage of boldness. It is worth everyone's listening time, and in this case is convincingly played by the soloist, with rich backing by the New Yorkers.

Fanfare for Bima

☐ Cambridge Brass Quintet / Crystal S-204

Music guaranteed to make the listener smile. In three-quarters of a minute Bernstein uses for his theme the motif that summoned Koussevitzky's pet dog (which explains the title), throws in a take-off on a Bach subject, contrapuntalizes, and ends with the four-note opening of the Beethoven "Fifth." Fun in this brass game.

Songfest

☐ National Symphony Orchestra / Dale (soprano); Elias and Williams (mezzo-sopranos); Rosenshein (tenor); Reardon (baritone); Gramm (bass-baritone) / Bernstein (conductor) / Deutsche Grammophon 2531044

Songfest, subtitled (after passing through a whole slew of other titles while it was being composed) *A Cycle of American Poems for Six Singers and Orchestra,* has received sharply divided reactions from both public and reviewers. No surprise, since here are various creative profiles: the Bernstein of Broadway, of Madison Avenue, and of 57th at Seventh. This amalgam consists of thirteen songs by as many poets (including the biggies such as Walt Whitman, Langston Hughes, Gertrude Stein, E. E. Cummings, Conrad Aiken, Edgar Allan Poe, and Edna St. Vincent Millay) and apportioned into solo, duet, trio, and sextet frames.

The dedication to the creative idea is apparent, but it may be the miscellaneous exposition that has caused the split in the voting as it has come in from the critical precincts. This writer splits his ballot. But not about the performances, which are splendid. Don't let the ambivalence about Bernstein's work deter you from casting your own vote.

Chichester Psalms (1965)

☐ Israel Philharmonic Orchestra and Vienna Jeunesse Choir / Bernstein (conductor) / Deutsche Grammophon 2530968

Three complete psalms (Nos. 100, 23, and 131, in that order) and three in part (Nos. 108, verse 2; 2, verses 1–4; and 133, verse 1, in that order), all using the Hebrew text and some using unpsalmodic (but fitting) bouncy jazz rhythms.

A definitive performance by all means, with the scoring of three trumpets, three trombones, two harps, percussion, and strings. The version on Angel (S-37119) is just as incisive and propelled, but in the lesser-pigmented original scoring for organ, percussion, and harp. The young soloist used in this recording, as well as Bogart, the boy alto, in Columbia's release of the work (MS-6792), both provide a much better vocal timbre for the Psalm 23 section than Philip Ledger's choice of a countertenor in the Angel edition he conducts.

The *Psalms* are coupled with the *Jeremiah* Symphony. The opus can also be secured with Bernstein's three symphonies in a three-disc offering on Deutsche Grammophon 2709077.

Kaddish (Symphony No. 3) (1963)

☐ Israel Philharmonic Orchestra, Vienna Jeunesse Choir, and Vienna Choir Boys / Wager (speaker); Caballé (soprano) / Bernstein (conductor) / Deutsche Grammophon 2530970

The Hebraic Kaddish, a prayer in memory of the dead, forms a part of every synagogue service, as well as funeral service. Bernstein's *Kaddish* has little kinship with its sober connotations. The prose setting in Bernstein's case is royal purple, pertinently descriptive and philosophical, a mating of secularistic thought with sacred dogma—the former surrounds and overpowers the traditional words. It makes a plea (almost a demand) that God should put not only man's house in order but his own as well; if man is to praise and believe in God, then God must be worthy.

Many Jews have been bitter in their reactions to Bernstein's work, indicating that it falsifies the prayer's meaning. True, only in that Bernstein's *Kaddish* tears away from associational, traditional ties. Such a link is not mandatory. There is room for a Kaddish that avoids parochialism.

The sense of excitement within the work cannot be missed. It has the zeal of the believer even if its Hebraicness refuses to deal with musical archaeology.

Kaddish was premiered in Israel, under Bernstein's direction. Charles Munch gave the initial American performance; Bernstein followed with the first New York hearing and then recorded the work with the same forces. Since then he has revised the symphony as it is heard here. Bernstein's wife was the speaker in the original recording. The use of a male for that part in this later edition is a distinct plus in timbre definition. With the composer in charge, an overworked word still holds good. This recording is "definitive." It is, indeed, a notable achievement and a most vital addition to the recorded catalogue.

(D.G. has also released the *Kaddish* with Bernstein's two other symphonies, plus the *Chichester Psalms*, in 2709077.)

Opera and Dramatic Music

Mass (1971)

☐ Orchestra, Norman Scribner Choir, and Berkshire Boys' Choir / Titus (baritone) / Bernstein (conductor) / Columbia M2-31008

Bernstein's Mass, which he describes as "A Theatre Piece for Singers, Players and Dancers," celebrates the form in an unusual manner. The text is a hybrid from the liturgy of the Roman Mass with additional texts (by the composer and Stephen Schwartz) that often have the pungencies of the pop world. And the score is likewise. The musical game being played here is gamey and high-seasoned, and many will consider the result more profane than sacred. The critical reaction after the world premiere ranged from "fashionable *kitsch*" and "cheap and vulgar" to "a shattering experience that signally honors its creator." Whatever the findings there is no doubt that Bernstein has composed one of the most unusual masses ever written, with plenty of shock. Examples: lines such as "Go genuflect, but don't expect guarantees," "And it was good, Yeah!/And it was god-dam good!" plus the smashing of the holy sacraments by the celebrant.

There is no question as to the exciting theatricality of the work, and in this definitive recording the Bernstein allurement registers vividly. Alan Titus as the celebrant is brilliant; all of the singers are wonderfully incisive and move with remarkable ease within the music's shifting styles.

Two of the three Meditations in the work have been issued separately, as part of an all-Bernstein album, on Columbia MG–32174. Oddly enough, a set of highlights was released in England (CBS 73541) but not here. The CBS issue offers an excellent sampling, but to consider Bernstein's Mass properly, the entire production should be heard.

Trouble in Tahiti (1952)

☐ Columbia Wind Ensemble / Butler (soprano); Williams (mezzo-soprano); Clarke (tenor); Patrick and Browne (baritones) / Bernstein (conductor) / Columbia KM–32597

Husband-wife trouble in suburbia conveyed with a jazzy beat, plus some moments that can be tracked down to Copland and Stravinsky. Such eclectic touches don't interfere with the earnest-jest totality of Bernstein's one-act piece.

Certainly done well, even though some of the lines are less clear than one wishes.

The Dybbuk (1974)

Ballet

☐ New York City Ballet Orchestra / Johnson (baritone); Ostendorf (bass) / Bernstein (conductor) / Columbia M–33082

An off-shoot conception of the Jewish folktale that triggered the famous Ansky play. However, the play is not the subject of the ballet, which, rather, consists of dances conveying the general magico-religious spirit of the drama.

Some Hebraic touches are knitted into the score, which has the usual Bernstein verve and high-toned orchestration. The performance has verve to match.

Fancy Free (1944)

☐ New York Philharmonic / Bernstein (conductor) / Columbia MG–32174

True-blue Bernstein music, with Broadway zip and zest. The orchestration is glossy and brilliant, and the use of the piano is especially delightful.

Columbia has packaged this ballet three different ways, in each case totally consisting of music by Bernstein. That listed above is in a two-record album. Another is covered by the catalogue number MS–6677. This one-disc release is matched by M–30304, companioned by bits from *West Side Story* and a section from *On the Waterfront*. There is a fourth representation (Columbia MS–6871), but it includes only three of the total seven sections of the ballet. In any case Bernstein's consideration of his own music far outclasses Eric Rogers on London (21048) and Robert Irving on Seraphim (S–60197).

Wallace Berry (1928-   )

Canto Lirico for Viola and Piano

Chamber Music

☐ Bernard Zaslav (viola); Naomi Zaslav (piano) / Composers Recordings S–282

No gay lightness in this "Lyrical Song." Berry's piece is gorgeous in a very sober way, with a dignity that is extremely telling within its full introspectiveness. Alban Berg comes to mind, but in no sense of imitation—simply an intensity that is highly emotional without need for arrival at hot climaxes.

Duo for Flute and Piano

☐ Bryan (flute); Keys (piano) / Composers Recordings S-282

A mood of interpenetration and restlessness hangs over Berry's piece. The fantastic images these form do not fall within the Schoenberg atonal school of reference. Berry's language pertains to panchromatic tonality.

Trio for Piano, Violin, and Cello

☐ Pignotti (violin); Moores (cello); Mehta (piano) / Composers Recordings SD-371

Berry's piano trio (in six movements) stretches its panchromatic explanations almost to the point of tonality extinction. Action is paramount: in the harmonies, the counterpoints, and the rhythms. The music is nervous, always serious (even in the scherzo atmosphere of the second part, the whimsicality has a slight frown accompanying it). The scoring procedure forsakes piano trio formations for an equalized trialogue of the instruments.

String Quartet No. 2

☐ Composers String Quartet / Composers Recordings S-282

Each of the five parts of Berry's one-movement quartet is distinctly defined by tempo, dynamics, texture, and/or color. Earlier parts are spliced in as the work progresses, codifying the totality, as a type of formal cross-reference.

Berry's quartet is difficult, but simply for its final portion (a violent, frightening *Allegro precipitoso*) only the most virtuosic of virtuosi can qualify. That describes the team of Raimondi, Ajemian, Dupouy, and Rudiakov who have the corporate name of the Composers String Quartet.

This fully contemporaneous music has a magnificent, cogent effect. It is a prime contribution to string-quartet literature.

Pierre-Montan Berton   *(1727-1780)*

Orchestra **Chaconne for Orchestra**

☐ Caen Chamber Orchestra / Dautel (conductor) / Turnabout 34101

Though nothing terribly memorable concerns this example it does not deserve desuetude. Dautel's sympathetic portrayal proves it.

Franz Berwald   *(1796-1868)*

Orchestra *Bajadärfesten*

Elfenspiel

Erinnerung an die Norwegischen Alpen

Overture to *Drottningen av Golconda* (1864)

Overture to *Estrella de Soria* **(1841)**

Polonaise from *Estrella de Soria* **(1841)**

☐ Orchestra of the Swedish Radio / Ehrling (conductor) / Nonesuch 71218

A fine sampler of Berwald's music. The overtures have vim and dramatic flavor, the one prefacing the opera *Estrella de Soria* ending quietly. The third title, "Memories of the Norwegian Alps," has fine inner vitality with imaginative orchestration. So does the *Elfenspiel* ("Elves' Play"). However, the statement by Berwald's wife that it is "one of the most brilliant works ever written" must be edited. Rather, expect music that is lively in a Mendelssohnian manner. Like the other items on the disc it is played in a clean and appealing manner and has grateful sound.

Sinfonie Capricieuse

☐ Stockholm Philharmonic Orchestra / Dorati (conductor) / RCA VICS–1319

Not as dynamic as the other Berwald symphonies but with a sufficient quota of worthy material. The clear view of Berwald's romantic world is described in this neat performance, with a special refinement to the playing that is very pleasing.

(The numbering of Berwald's symphonies is rather confusing, and so as not to make matters more confusing no number is assigned in the above title heading.)

Symphony

No. 1 (*Sérieuse*) in G minor / No. 2 (*Singulière*) in C major

☐ Stockholm Philharmonic Orchestra / Schmidt-Isserstedt (conductor) / Nonesuch 71087

There are some Berliozian touches in Berwald's Schubertian music, but these performances tend to emphasize the latter. (Some commentators also perceive reminders of Dvořák and Tchaikovsky—a point that escapes the ears of this writer.) However, full agreement with those who have stressed that Berwald is an unjustly neglected composer.

Well-crafted playing throughout, especially compelling in the warmth of the tuttis and the grace of the *Scherzi* (in the G minor work this form is titled *Stretto*).

String Quartet No. 2 in A minor

☐ Copenhagen String Quartet / Turnabout 34091

Mostly the flow and climate that surrounds the work relate to Mendelssohn, though sharp gestures are made that are otherwise. But the last are of minor total. Fine-styled playing with energetic definition in the fast movements.

Piano Quintet

No. 1 in C minor / No. 2 in A major

☐ Benthien Quartet / Riefling (piano) / Nonesuch 71113

Two important points: first, the piano is favored in these two works—a problem of instrumentational balance which Berwald did not conquer anymore than the large number of other composers who have tried their hands in the medium. Second, similar to the partial subjective touch of romanticism which, at times, colored the concepts of the great classic composers, classicism is not entirely absent in these works.

Berwald's quintets (especially the C minor opus) have the logistics of the classic school merged with the song expressiveness that is the highlight of the romantic. They are certainly worthy of recording permanence.

Chamber Music

The performances are sufficiently perceptive, setting the music in a proper frame and with excellent phrasing. The sound is good and with just the proper resonance for chamber music.

Jean-Baptiste Besard   (1567-1625)

Instrumental

Two Guitars

Five *Branles de Village*

Saltus

☐ Duo Company-Paolini / Turnabout 34341

There is contrastive discourse between the lighter *Branles de Villages* ("Village Dances") and the more serious *Saltus*, also a dance piece. Expert ensemble playing is provided by this guitar team.

Lute

Music for Lute

☐ Gerwig (lute) / RCA VICS–1362

A compilation of eight pieces, including a *Prélude de 6 Bocquet* and three examples of the *branle*, a sixteenth-century group dance. True, simple, and sincere music of the Renaissance period.

Thomas Beversdorf   (1924-   )

Chamber Music

Sonata for Violin and Piano (1964)

☐ Israelievitch (violin); Upper (piano) / Orion 75170

The commentary is fantasy-driven in the first movement (thrice the size of the other movement), derived from intransigent sectionalism. Kineticism is the faith followed in the second movement of the work.

Carl Heinrich Biber   (?-?1750)

Orchestra

Sonata for Two Choirs

☐ New York Trumpet Ensemble / Schwarz (conductor) / Nonesuch 71301

Each choir has four trumpets and timpani, with two violins, harpsichord, cello, and bassoon operating as another group. Antiphony is the use made of this fifteen-piece instrumental body.

The liner notes state that the Sonata "was probably written for performance from the facing balconies of Salzburg Cathedral." It is, naturally, made to order for stereo reproduction.

Sonata in C

☐ Mansfield and Ravinah (violins); Schwarz, Dean, Soper, and Mase (trumpets); Kohloff (timpani); Zlotkin (cello); Hindell (bassoon); Cooper (harpsichord) / Nonesuch 71301

The interesting point of this work for two violins, four trumpets, timpani, and continuo is instrumental contrast in terms of color, style, and weight applied in a thesis-antithesis manner. The strings and continuo are soft, pliable, and lyrical; the brass and timpani are the roughage in the total diet. The outer movements apply these concepts in an antiphonal textural manner; the middle (slow) movement eliminates the brass.

Good reasoning here leads to right conclusions. And, the performance is a gem.

Heinrich Ignaz Franz von Biber . (1644 - 1704)

Battalia

☐ Angelicum Orchestra of Milan / Jenkins (conductor) / Nonesuch 71146

String Orchestra

The work is a charmer. Nice tunes and gentle harmonies—fair enough, but it's the added attractions of this semi-programmatic piece that get the points: striking the instruments with the bows in part 1 and anticipatory Ivesian tactics in movement 2 where eight different folk songs are plunged into a thoroughly dissonant polyphonic bath, and more. In the march, *Der Mars,* anticipatory Cowellian methods are applied, with a solo double bass played with a piece of paper covering the strings to imitate a small drum while a single violin simulates a fife, and in the battle, *Die Schlacht,* low-pitched pizzicati depict (if naïvely) cannon shots. Yes, a charmer.

Sonatae Tam Aris Quam Aulis Servientes

Sonata V a 6 in E minor / Sonata XI a 5 in A major

☐ Sinfonia of London String Ensemble / Rifkin (conductor) / Nonesuch 71172

The fifth Sonata calls for two violins, four violas, and continuo; the eleventh Sonata is the same except for one less viola. Both sonatas are played in exemplary fashion.

This refreshing music would remain silent if it were not for recordings. The opportunity should not be overlooked. (Four more Sonatas in this group of twelve works, whose Latin title is translated as "Sonatas Suitable for Use in Both Chapel and Court," are discussed under *Solo Instrument and Orchestra: trumpet* and *two trumpets.*)

Concerto in C major for Trumpet, Strings, and Basso Continuo

☐ Württemberg Chamber Orchestra, Heilbronn / Zickler (trumpet) / Faerber (conductor) / Turnabout 34090

Solo Instrument and Orchestra

Trumpet

A fine level of performance is achieved here. If you like the music of this high baroque composer you'll certainly like the clear writing heard in this five-and-a-fraction minute piece. (The piece is also included in a five-record anthology on Turnabout 34295/9.)

Sonatae Tam Aris Quam Aulis Servientes

Sonata IV a 5 in C major / Sonata X a 5 in G minor

☐ Sinfonia of London String Ensemble / Jones (trumpet) / Rifkin (conductor) / Nonesuch 71172

These two Sonatas are among the dozen works in Biber's set (four other Sonatas are discussed under *String Orchestra* and under *Solo Instrument and Orchestra: two trumpets*). In both cases the string body supporting the trumpet consists of one violin, three violas, and continuo.

Virtuosity is restrained in these Biber compositions but not in the performances. The balanced response is full and controlled, the trumpet playing full-breathed, the directing without blemish.

Two Trumpets

Sonatae Tam Aris Quam Aulis Servientes

Sonata I a 8 in C major / Sonata XII a 8 in C major

☐ Sinfonia of London String Ensemble / Rifkin (conductor) / Nonesuch 71172

In addition to the two trumpets, both works call for two violins, four violas, and continuo. The playing of this baroque music is of the highest stylistic understanding. The zest and expertise are truly magnificent. (Other Sonatas in the set are discussed under *String Orchestra* and under *Solo Instrument and Orchestra: trumpet.*)

Instrumental

Sonata a 7 for Six Trumpets, Timpani, and Continuo

☐ Schwarz, Ranger, Dean, Gould, Soper, and Mase (trumpets); Kohloff (timpani); Hindell (bassoon); Cooper (harpsichord) / Nonesuch 71301

In this ceremonious music, the brilliant scarlet timbre (by emphasis on the upper register of the trumpets) is contrasted to echo passages in soft-weighted dynamics. The playing is marvelous.

Violin

Passacaglia in G minor

☐ Lautenbacher (violin) / Vox SVBX-552

Biber's unaccompanied violin work, subtitled *Sonata of the Guardian Angel*, not only parallel's J. S. Bach's great unaccompanied violin chaconne in style but is a close match to its greatness.

Lautenbacher's seamless playing does not interfere with clear depiction of the many variations. It is an example of great re-creation.

Chamber Music

Rosenkranz: Sonaten über die 15 Mysterien aus dem Marienleben

☐ Lautenbacher (violin); Koch (viola da gamba); Ewerhart (positiv, harpsichord, and regal) / Vox SVBX-552

Biber's "Rosary Sonatas on the Fifteen Mysteries in the Life of the Virgin Mary" not only constitute deeply felt music without defining programmatic aspects, but magnificently display the total religio-dramatic potential of the subjects. There is important novelty in the use of *scordatura* (altered string tuning of an instrument). In this case only the first Sonata utilizes the normal G–D–A–E tuning. Otherwise each work employs the device for reasons of timbre, chordal settings not available in the normal tuning, and textural subtleties. Examples are: Sonata No. 3, in which every string is changed (three higher, one lower) to B–F♯–B–D, and Sonata No. 8, in which the changed setting has the G string raised to D, the "regular" D to F, the A string pitched a half-step higher to B flat, and the E string lowered a whole step to D.

The fifteen works are each titled and divided into three large sections: e.g., *The Mysteries of Joy,* including *The Annuaciation of the Birth of Christ; The Mysteries of Sorrow,* covering among its parts *The Crowning with Thorns* and *The Climbing of Calvary;* and *The Mysteries of Glory,* containing *The Resurrection* and *The Crowning of the Blessed Virgin Mary.*

There is great breadth and insight in these performances, with phrase definition and outlines beautifully depicted. Style is fully served, but not at the expense of the music or to manifest a cold musicological attitude (practically no embellishments are made). The continuo is sensitively carried out, and the warm sound is churchly and rich, with depth in all respects. A marvelous release for which all concerned should be congratulated.

Partita No. 7 for Two Violas d'Amore and Basso Continuo

☐ Phillips and Trampler (violas d'amore); Wilson (harpsichord); McCracken (cello) / Musical Heritage Society OR-398

This Partita is included in Biber's *Harmonia Artificiosa–Ariosa Diversimode Accordata.* To explain the last two words, both of the violas d'amore are retuned (*scordatura*) from the usual D major setting.

A delightful musical event, this six-part suite. Listen to the part 4 Gigue first—it's a great appetizer for the other dances and variations.

There is full representation of style and manner in this genuine presentation. Not only does one hear superb playing by Karen Phillips and Walter Trampler, but by Glen Wilson, who displays a good sense of harpsichord integration and, in the opening of the last movement (*Arietta variata e presto*), a fine solo personality.

Sonata

No. 3 in D minor / No. 6 in A minor

☐ Leonhardt Consort / Leonhardt (conductor) / Telefunken 641118

Both of these works are from Biber's *Fidicinium Sacro-Profanum,* a set of twelve sonatas in four and five parts. They are exceptionally well played.

Suite

No. 3 in A major / No. 3 in A minor

☐ Leonhardt Consort / Leonhardt (conductor) / Telefunken 641118

The first Suite is from the collection entitled *Harmonia Artificiosa–Ariosa Diversimode Accordata;* the other Suite is from the *Mensa Sonora* set. Special repertoire material and worthy, it is beautifully played on this release.

Serenade for Strings, Continuo, and Bass Solo

Vocal

☐ Mainz Chamber Orchestra / Malaguti (bass) / Kehr (conductor) / Turnabout 34324

Voice and Instrumental Ensemble

Known as the *Night Watchman Serenade,* this work is a delight, especially two of its six parts. There are antiphonal exchanges between bowed and plucked sounds in the Gavotte and a single, special use of the low voice in another movement.

It is in these places that the most subtlety occurs. Otherwise, the performance is a disciplined one, straight on the mark, which is all that is actually required for this crystal-clear composition.

William Billings   *(1746-1800)*

An Anthem, for Thanksgiving: *O Praise the Lord of Heaven* (Psalm 148)

Choral

☐ Western Wind Vocal Ensemble / Lesnick (mezzo-soprano); Murcell (bass-baritone) / Nonesuch 71276

Chorus Alone

One of Billings's six Thanksgiving anthems, it is gently and warmly sung by the Western Wind group (two sopranos, countertenor, two tenors, and baritone), plus two assisting voices.

As the Hart Panteth

☐ Gregg Smith Singers / Smith (conductor) / Vox SVBX-5350

An anthem of imposing strength and vitality, it is compellingly sung by this magnificent group.

A Virgin Unspotted (Judea)

When Jesus Wept (Fuging Tune)

☐ Gregg Smith Singers / Smith (conductor) / Columbia MS-7277

These two pieces are among the twenty performed in a complete all-Billings program. The cost of the recording is worth every penny solely for *When Jesus Wept*. It is memorable and moving. It is, unquestionably, Billings's greatest inspiration.

Be Glad Then, America (An Anthem for Fast Day)

The Bird

Boston (Christmas Anthem)

Chester

Cobham

Connection

Consonance

Creation

David's Lamentation

Hopkinton

☐ Gregg Smith Singers / Smith (conductor) / Columbia MS-7277

The magnificence of Billings magnificently sung. Though the spirited *Chester* melody and the initially exalted, later exulting, *Be Glad Then, America*, plus *David's Lamentation* are well known, the other pieces represented have much to offer. There is much variety, especially those wonderful "fuging tunes."

I Am Come into My Garden

I Am the Rose of Sharon

I Charge You

☐ Western Wind Vocal Ensemble / Nonesuch 71276

These three anthems are based on texts from *The Song of Songs*. Billings does not bypass rhythmic reinforcement, especially in *I Charge You* and even more positively in the dance swing found in I Am the Rose of Sharon. (The last is also included in the Gregg Smith Singers' all-Billings album, issued by Columbia on MS-7277.)

The Western Wind Ensemble (two female voices and four male voices) has outstanding musicianship and supports it with a creamy vocal sound.

Jargon

Kittery

The Lord Is Risen (Easter Anthem)

Modern Music

Morpheus

The Shepherd's Carol

Swift as an Indian Arrow Flies

☐ Gregg Smith Singers / Smith (conductor) / Columbia MS-7277

    (See commentary for *Be Glad Then, America*.)

Thus Saith the High, the Lofty One

☐ Gregg Smith Singers / Smith (conductor) / Vox SVBX-5350

It has been emphasized that Billings had little formal music training. Perhaps that's the way to accomplish canonic writing of the type illustrated here: a four-part sacred canon. It is an inspired bit and sung dynamically.

Gordon Binkerd (1916-   )

Symphony No. 2 (1960)

Orchestra

☐ Oslo Philharmonic Orchestra / Barati (conductor) / Composers Recordings 139 (monaural)

Counterpoint is the word for the first half of Binkerd's symphony. In the second movement, lyrical impulses prevail, as do the resources of chamber situations applied to the full orchestra. The development processes are constant, and only small reminders of thematic material are interjected. Nice astringencies keep the musical skin of the work properly toned. A music of individual freshness. To the credit of composer, conductor, and orchestra, it is extremely well played.

Sonata for Piano (1955)

Instrumental

Piano

☐ Fletcher (piano) / Composers Recordings 201 (monaural)

Binkerd's Sonata is a clear presentation of tonal fluidity; it can swim freely. Vertical and horizontal data give strengths and make certain that order prevails. Musical creeds have their relationships, but every age has its own writ. This work represents a sophistication of tonality as viewed in terms of the mid-twentieth century. The forms are solid, paralleling the traditional tonalism that Binkerd develops for his own purposes.

Sonata for Cello and Piano (1952)

Chamber Music

☐ Drinkall (cello); Corbett (piano); Composers Recordings S-289

A fine three-movement plan that adheres to sturdy forms. While these are not strictly orthodox, there is a solid affinity with traditional designs, minus any academicism, however. The style is derived from Schoenbergian technique without displaying any yearning passion for the rigid application of tone rows.

The performance is apt and direct, warm and expressive. The CRI release is to be criticized only in regard to information. Binkerd offers a fifty-four-line liner note and manages to say not a word about his Sonata. While some composers overdo the analytical process, he overdoes the reverse and CRI accepts it. Too bad.

Sonata for Violin and Piano

☐ Laredo (violin); Schein (piano) / Desto 6439

Structural complexity rates a fat zero unless it results in musical meaning. Retrograde technique is not necessarily a complex operation, per se, but to originate material that will work forward and backward with artistic sense is a severe (albeit, self-made) creative burden. Binkerd's success with retrogradation enhances his Sonata, whereby movement 3 is "roughly" (but sufficiently) a reverse run of movement 1. This gives, naturally, the most acute balance possible: they surround, and are pivotal to, the larger centralized scherzo movement.

Jaime Laredo has not bypassed contemporary music, as have so many other concert violinists. For that, he is to be given emphatic credit. A second, fat credit pertains to his first-class performance of Binkerd's duo Sonata, in which Ann Schein's playing deserves equal credit billing.

Choral

Chorus Alone

Ad Te Levavi **(1959)**

☐ Mid-America Chorale / Dexter (conductor) / Composers Recordings 191 (monaural)

"Unto the Father" has sacred simplicity with romantic strength. The text is the Latin version of Psalm 25. It is given a fine performance by this excellent organization.

Arthur Bird   (1856-1923)

Orchestra

Carnival Scene

☐ Louisville Orchestra / Mester (conductor) / Louisville LS-754

For the most part the piece is articulated with vigor. For the most part, it is extremely old-fashioned and perhaps worth exposure occasionally at pops concerts. Still, there is nothing messy in the harmony, tunes, or the way it is put together.

Harrison Birtwistle   (1934-   )

Orchestra

Tragoedia **(1965)**

☐ Melos Ensemble / Foster (conductor) / Argo ZRG-759

Tough and stark music written for wind quintet, harp, and string quartet, *Tragoedia* derives from the ritualistic and formalistic aspects of Greek tragedy. But the drama is posed solely by the action of the design, thereby attempting to bridge the gap between absolute and theatrical music.

Birtwistle's patterns are abstract by themselves. When compared and set off against each other (and each is minutely discriminative and sensitively selected), the results are vivid, pungent, uncompromising, and severely striking. One realizes this is creativity by an individual voice—a composer of aggressive personality.

The Triumph of Time (1970)

☐ BBC Symphony Orchestra / Boulez (conductor) / Argo ZRG-790

A fascinating piece of Mahlerian *angst* and Varèsian sound torsos that is a musical transmutation of an engraving by Bruegel. (A reproduction is printed on the inside of the record jacket; Argo is to be congratulated on a wise production move that is of decided benefit to the listener of the recording.)

As time slowly but surely destroys everything, so Birtwistle's concept of tempo for his piece. The music pulls back on its pulse which is more deliberate than a funeral procession. Time's persistency is delineated by metamorphoic technique and with emphasis on special colors: a soprano saxophone, an English horn, pitched percussion. Bruegel's piece is darkened by horror; Birtwistle's orchestration is blacker than black, quietly brutal.

This is a magnificent score and a triumph for the composer. The performance is a triumph for Boulez. No one could do it better since the music demands acute control, dried of any romanticizing or the slightest overstatement. In such dissection and statement of findings he is master to none for a contemporary score.

Ring a Dumb Carillon (1965)

☐ Thomas (soprano); Hacker (clarinet); Quinn (percussion) / Mainstream 5001

An imposing, dramatic work of fifteen-minute length (superbly tensed in the singing of Mary Thomas, which is exactly as it should be). The vocal line is angular and yet never obscures the projection of the words (a poem by Christopher Logue), many of which are imaged in the music. This is percussively emphasized by the use of wood-blocks, claves, maraca, cymbals, and so on. The underlying fundament (like a *cantus firmus*) is the clarinet part, against and from which the vocal line becomes focused.

The unity of Birtwistle's piece is gripping in terms of mood, feeling, and meaning. This is a music that flexes its muscles and compels respect.

Vocal

Voice and Instrumental Ensemble

Chronometer

☐ Argo ZRG-790

Chronometer is an essay devoted to clock and bell sounds that drift in and out. Some are immediately identifiable, others have been altered, but not in a way to yank the piece into subject variety. *Chronometer* can be described as a montage of ostinati. Its sounds are developed (*explored* might be a better word) for structural purposes. But, no matter how this is done, the passionate emphasis and concentration are the sounds of clock mechanisms: Big Ben, clock strikings, clock chiming.

Chronometer is certainly one of the most fascinating tape pieces that has been produced.

Electronic Music

Jacques Bittner (fl. 1682)

Pièces de lut

☐ Gerwig (lute) / RCA VICS-1362
☐ Schäffer (lute) / Turnabout 34137

No main title is given on the Turnabout record; the RCA disc identifies it as a Suite in G minor. It comprises five items: *Prélude, Allemande, Sarabande, Courante,* and *Passacaille.*

Instrumental

Lute

223

The performance viewpoint ends in a trade-off. Gerwig's tone is bright, yet with a mild percussive-edged border; Schäffer's sound is intimately restrained, but tends to be monochromatic. There's more to hear on the former's recording (almost two-and-a-half minutes worth). But this has nothing to do with tempo differences; Gerwig has simply extended the *Sarabande* by playing a *double* (melodic embellishment with ornamentation). No decision. Obviously, the instruction *Caveat emptor* is proper.

(Schäffer's rendition is also included in an anthology of lute, guitar, and mandolin compositions Turnabout has released on its No. 34195/9.)

Georges Bizet   *(1838-1875)*

Orchestra

Carmen Suite (1875)

☐ L'Orchestre de la Suisse Romande / Ansermet (conductor) / London STS-15052
☐ Detroit Symphony Orchestra / Paray (conductor) / Mercury 75060

Despite the standard (long established) pair of suites (*see below*), assorted compilations have been made. These two are illustrative. Ansermet touches all the opera's bases, beginning with the Prelude, moving on to the *Argonaise* in Act IV, then to the Intermezzo in Act III, and so on, totaling eight selections.

Paray duplicates five of these in his edition and adds one, *Les Toréadors,* that Ansermet didn't include. Further, and expectedly, the order of the numbers duplicated is dissimilar. Example: the *Argonaise* is the fifth piece in Paray's suite make-up, while it is the second piece in Ansermet's.

Pick 'em as you want 'em. They're both good and so are some of the others in the catalogue.

Carmen: Suites Nos. 1 and 2 (1875)

☐ New York Philharmonic / Bernstein (conductor) / Columbia M-31800

Lenny plays these as they're published, while others (*see above*) pick, choose, and arrange the order as they wish. But the best is in these two suites, and the sequences have built-in balance and audience success. So will this performance.

Entr'acte to Act II of Don Procopio (1858)

☐ London Symphony Orchestra / Bonynge (conductor) / London 6744

An interesting bit from Bizet's early-period two-act *opera buffa.* There is some question as to whether the Entr'acte was inserted by Charles Malherbe when editing the vocal score for publication. If so, it's an excellent imitation of Bizet's style.

Jeux d'enfants, Op. 22

☐ Paris Conservatoire Orchestra / Martinon (conductor) / London STS-15093
☐ French National Radio Orchestra / Munch (conductor) / Nonesuch 71183

Five (Nos. 6, 3, 2, 11, and 12) of the twelve pieces in this Little Suite for Orchestra were originally written for piano duet (discussed under *Instrumental: piano, four hands*). They emphasize the picturizations of *Trumpet and Drum; The Doll; The Top; Little Husband, Little Wife;* and *The Ball* with vivid, fitting, never overdrawn orchestration. Bizet chose and scored wisely.

Of the many versions obtainable, the most stimulating and fruitful is the sharply detailed Martinon reading. Munch's is only placed second because he opts for more moderated tempi and one prefers the extra pinch of zest that Martinon provides. Still, every part of the Munch recording is of top-quality definition and is subtly drawn coloristically.

Giulini comes close but is rather subdued and just a bit too serious (released on Seraphim S-60022, originally Angel 35462). Ansermet, who generally can be expected to be at least involved with the score he is conducting, is exceedingly matter-of-fact and pedestrian in his conception.

La Jolie Fille de Perth: **Suite (1866)**

☐ L'Orchestre de la Suisse Romande / Ansermet (conductor) / London 6208

Four parts from the opera make up this Suite: *Prélude, Sérénade, Marche,* and *Danse bohémienne.* Best known is the catchy melody and beat of the last, and there's where Ansermet does his best work. The *March* deserves more audience consideration than it has been given.

L'Arlésienne
Suite No. 1 (1872) / Suite No. 2 (1872)

☐ Philadelphia Orchestra / Ormandy (conductor) / Columbia M–31848
☐ Chicago Symphony Orchestra / Martinon (conductor) / RCA VICS–1593

Flawless, richly vivid characterizations in both cases, a bit more silky-toned in the case of Martinon. These conceptions are minus any interpretive hokum and are tops in the large list available. (Ormandy's edition is also on Columbia MS-6546.)

The reasons for placing the others in lower slots are many. A few examples: shockingly slow tempi by Cluytens (Seraphim S-60064), over-styling by von Karajan (Deutsche Grammophon 2530128), so-so sound by Paray (Mercury 75060), and depersonalized playing under Ansermet's direction (London STS-15052).

Patrie **Overture, Op. 19**

☐ French National Radio Orchestra / Munch (conductor) / Nonesuch 71183

It is easy to overplay this work, with its big tunes. Munch opts to let the music sing out but has matters under control. Nice sonorities for a nice, if not terribly important, Bizet piece.

Roma (Suite de concert **No. 3) (1868)**

☐ City of Birmingham Symphony Orchestra / Frémaux (conductor) / Klavier 546

Although this is little known and doesn't have the measure of creative ownership of the Symphony No. 1 in C, there is no relinquishment of Bizet's engaging melodicism. First the movements were titled ''Rome,'' ''Venice,'' ''Florence,'' and ''Naples'' (the work was to be called a ''symphony''). Eventually these designations were changed to *Hunt in the Ostian Forest,* Scherzo, *Procession,* and *Carnaval.*

Frémaux directs clean, musicianly playing from ''England's City of Birmingham Symphony Orchestra.'' The special identification certainly compliments the Birmingham, Alabama, orchestra indirectly, though the Alabamians have yet to make their initial recording.

Symphony in C major (1855)

☐ Royal Philharmonic Orchestra / Munch (conductor) / Quintessence PMC-7048

Superlatives are in order for this interpretation. The opening *Allegro vivo* sparkles; the final pair of movements (both *Allegro vivace*) have scintillating pace and yet, despite their similar tempo indication, are permitted the proper speed-rate difference to provide contrast. The secondary subject in the finale is not, as some conductors insist, allowed to slacken. Above all, the Adagio is masterful, with the most subtle *rubati* within phrases and at cadential points. Munch is masterful and so is his orchestra.

(A little less elegant, but still one of the prime examples of Munch's conductorial art is heard in his version with the French National Radio Orchestra, released on Nonesuch 71183.)

Instrumental	**Premier Nocturne (1868)**
Piano	**Variations chromatiques (1868)**

☐ Gould (piano) / Columbia M-32040

Bizet does not relinquish the delight of Chopinesque detail with some light Lisztian distillation in the *Nocturne*. The set of variations is a find, and Gould's discovery is a listener's benefit, for he presents the music with the highest artistic dispatch.

(For an orchestral transcription of *Variations chromatiques* by Felix Weingartner, see *Bizet/Weingartner: Orchestra* [*Variations chromatiques*].)

Piano,
Four Hands

Jeux d'enfants, Op. 22

☐ Klien and Kyriakou (piano) / Turnabout 34241

This set of twelve pieces for two pianists at one keyboard (in publishers' catalogues this is officially known as "Music for One Piano–Four Hands") portrays various aspects of childhood. "Children's Games" is an aural joy including such pieces as *La Toupie* ("The Top"), an impromptu; *La Poupée* ("The Doll"), a berceuse; *Les Bulles de savon* ("Soap Bubbles"), in rondino form; *Saute-Mouton* ("Leap-Frog"), a caprice; and *Le Bal* ("The Ball"), a *galop*. Five of the dozen conceptions were orchestrated by Bizet (see under *Orchestra*).

This piano team defines the lightness and humor found in the music. Not only is there perfect ensemble cohesion, but a fine matching of weights in terms of staccati and legati. In music of this classification there is no place for highlighting individuality. Klien and Kyriakou merge as one, blending the *primo* and *secondo* parts. This is further proof of discerning musicianship. A hearty "bravo" for this one.

Opera
and Dramatic
Music

Carmen (1875)

☐ Metropolitan Opera Orchestra, Manhattan Opera Chorus, and Metropolitan Opera Children's Chorus / Maliponte and Boky (sopranos); Horne and Baldwin (mezzo-sopranos); McCracken and Velis (tenors); Krause, Christopher, and Gibbs (baritones); Gramm (bass) / Bernstein (conductor) / Deutsche Grammophon 2709043

☐ Vienna Philharmonic Orchestra, Vienna State Opera Chorus, and Vienna Boys Choir / Price, Freni, and Linval (sopranos); Macaux (mezzo-soprano); Corelli and Besançon (tenors); Merrill, Benoît, and Demigny (baritones); Schooten (bass) / von Karajan (conductor) / RCA LSC-6199

The beauty of Bernstein's recording is the special attention he gives to tempi and rhythmic detailing, both of which carry forward the dramatic impact of this great opera. Rarely has the Met orchestra played as well. Rarely has Horne been so vital an operatic personality, displaying full sexuality and the tough temperament that pervades the Carmen role. McCracken as Don José sings well, though his French is certainly not of top level definition. (For that matter, neither is Franco Corelli's in the RCA release.) All the other parts are well covered, especially Adriana Maliponte's Micaëla.

Von Karajan also scores with his choice of tempi. Some are not the usual ones, but they fit and fit well. Leontyne Price conveys a compelling sultriness with her dark voice. Her Carmen is a heated depiction, and it is completely captivating. (The use of chest voice is strategically special to her conception of the role.) The rest of the cast project their parts sensitively and musically. There is superb choral work here as well.

Bizet / **Rodion Shchedrin (1932-   )**

The *Carmen* Ballet (1968)   *Ballet*

☐ Bolshoi Theatre Orchestra / Rozhdestvensky (conductor) / Melodiya/Angel S-40067

Everyone will recognize the tunes, but the treatment and the scoring will be an ear opener. Indeed, Rodion Shchedrin has concocted a tasty and very unusual Bizet sound package using the ingredients of strings and four dozen percussion instruments! And how this Soviet Morton Gould (in terms of instrumental know-how) scores! Examples: the Changing of the Guard section, with the melody colored by cow bells and woodblocks; mixing vibraphone, finger cymbals, and the rubbing of a steel rod into the Habanera. In addition, two Bizet items that are not from *Carmen* are included.

Only snobs can object. So can purists. But it's simply a unique idea of recoloring and there is no satire or vulgarity. There are no vices to be found in Shchedrin's admirable project. This writer applauds the artistic mating which was the objective that led to this transcriptional mating. The important fact is that Shchedrin wrote The *Carmen* Ballet for his wife, the well-known Soviet ballerina Maya Plisetskaya.

The performance is not as good as the peppier one Arthur Fiedler made with the Boston Pops Orchestra, unfortunately deleted. If a copy can be found (RCA LSC-3129), grab it. If not, the Soviet presentation is certainly acceptable.

Bizet / **Felix Weingartner (1863-1942)**

Variations chromatiques   *Orchestra*

☐ Louisville Orchestra / Mester (conductor) / Louisville 734

Bizet's *Variations chromatiques* for piano are hardly known (see under *Bizet: Instrumental: piano* [*Premier Nocturne*]). For that matter the same pertains to Felix Weingartner's orchestral transcription. Fourteen variations are covered in the essay. There are, understandably, some operatic touches, including a short violin cadenza, and a short but powerful conclusion.

Boris Blacher   *(1903-1975)*

Orchestral Fantasy (1956)   *Orchestra*

☐ Louisville Orchestra / Whitney (conductor) / Louisville S-671

Blacher passed through a variety of technical stages: tonal, pantonal, jazz infiltrations, and systemized metrical arrangement. The Orchestral Fantasy represents a further phase of operations: fully serial composition. It is colorfully drenched with glissandi, ponticello, and other orchestral pigments. It is also fully concerned with motival arrangement. This holds the mosaic panorama of the music in place. Impressively executed by the Louisville forces.

Orchestra Ornament, Op. 44

☐ Louisville Orchestra / Mester (conductor) / Louisville S-685

Opus 44 (embracing a single movement that contains four major tempi divisions) has the type of tonal base that is at the root of Hindemithian methodology. Pandiatonicism is utilized with vestiges of fringed tonal combines. Blacher's metrical bookkeeping (writing to a rigid scale of numerical sequences, forming thereby expanding and contracting phrase temporalities) does not interfere with the romantic flavor of the music. Expertly played.

Instrumental

Violin

Four Ornaments (1969)

Sonata for Violin Solo, Op. 40

☐ Edinger (violin) / Orion 75171

In the *Ornaments* there are no changes in average formal protocol; moderate-speeded movements alternate with very fast ones. Color emphasizes the separate divisions, with total pizzicati in part 2, harmonics in part 3, and the rush of perpetual action, which gives its own pigmentation, in the finale.

In both the *Ornaments* and the Sonata the music is lean, related to Hindemithian practice, but individually detailed by pliable rhythms, conditioned by a system of variable meters that form a parallel to tone-row procedures. Such metrical changes intensify the formal progress.

The prosperity of the performance is distinct. Edinger's tone is especially immaculate. In the playing of a nude, unaccompanied violin composition the slightest blemish shows. None here. Enjoy!

Vocal

Voice with Accompaniment

Francesca da Rimini for Voice and Violin, Op. 47

☐ Catherine Malfitano (soprano); Joseph Malfitano (violin) / Musical Heritage Society MHS-1976

Francesca da Rimini is an aria with accompaniment. The music has chromatic, post-romantic urge. If there is any triumph, it is in the warm, declamatory singing. No information on the work is given, except that it was written in the mid-1950s. No text data is indicated; neither is any text provided, and Malfitano's unclear German diction offers no clue. If this is meant to be a vocal sketch of the ill-fated Francesca, the musical sentiments are fully appropriate, but only in a general fashion.

Easley Blackwood   *(1933-)*

Orchestra

Chamber Symphony for Fourteen Wind Instruments, Op. 2

☐ Contemporary Chamber Ensemble / Weisberg (conductor) / Composers Recordings 144 (monaural)

Hard-crusted, severe neoclassicism is evidenced here. Blackwood's early work (he was only twenty years old when it was written) has a mature viewpoint in its bold and vigorous thematic resources, resolute linear and vertical data, plus tight rhythmic drive (the last especially in the final Toccata, the third movement).

Weisberg's superb organization is extremely positive in its attention to the manifold details of the score. The instrumentation of this group changes, of course, in terms of the requirements of the work. In this instance, the Contemporary Chamber Ensemble consists of two flutes, one doubling on piccolo; paired oboes, clarinets, and bassoons; bass clarinet; double bassoon; and a quartet of horns.

Concerto for Violin and Orchestra, Op. 21

Solo Instrument and Orchestra

Violin

☐ Louisville Orchestra / Kling (violin) / Mester (conductor) / Louisville S–694

Three movements in total are expressionistic in content and very tellingly related in that style. Blackwood's harmonies group themselves around, and are guided by pan-chromatic controls; the orchestration is very reserved.

With music in this style one does not immediately realize its virtuosity—not the top-surface kind that when broken down is naught more than a fiddlistic assortment of fit-for-the-instrument formulae. The peak of the work is the slow movement. It contains music that does not compromise and speaks with a freshness that also represents virtuosity, but of a different order.

It is difficult to believe that this work was written for Yehudi Menuhin. It doesn't seem to be the sort of stringed-instrument tea he would enjoy. Paul Kling does, though, and proves it in his playing.

Emile Blanchet (1877-1943)

Au Jardin du vieux serail

Instrumental

Piano

☐ Nyiregyházi (piano) / Columbia M–35125

An impressionistic sketch that exemplifies Blanchet's general style. As far as can be ascertained, this represents the initial recording of "The Garden of the Old Harem."

Allan Blank (1925-   )

Rotation: A Study for Piano (1960)

Instrumental

Piano

☐ Kalish (piano) / Composers Recordings S–329

Directional development and unfolding is obtained by contrasting decisiveness with more relaxed data. *Rotation* is an apt title. A binary formal schedule is stated and then presented in retrograde.

Music for Solo Violin (1972)

Violin

☐ Hoffman (violin) / Orion 75169

It is apparent that Blank approaches writing for unaccompanied violin with the thorough knowledge of one who is an accomplished performer on the instrument. To state that his "Music" is extremely "violinistic" does not belittle the product, nullify its sophistication, or indulge in technical disparagement. It is truly a big plus, making it possible to pack a maximum of sense into the confines of a four-stringed instrument.

The commentary is forceful, brilliant, and in the case of the second movement, *Pizzicato ostinato,* a most informative and fascinating exploration of plucked sound. For once, the use of pizzicato behind the bridge is an integrated part of the design, with full meaning rather than just timbre speckles.

Stanley Hoffman's playing is musical, displaying a fully-honed technique that is fully directed toward expounding the musical argument.

Vocal

Voice with Accompaniment

Two Songs for Voice and Bassoon (1964)

☐ DeGaetani (mezzo-soprano); Weisberg (bassoon) / Composers Recordings SD–370

Expressionism but minus restless mannerisms. According to the CRI liner note, Blank's chamber music (it is that!) makes "no special approach to the setting of the words other than the desire to both capture and project the changing moods and extend them into the bassoon writing." There would have been greater gain if a text were furnished with the recording made by these two super-artists.

Voice and Instrumental Ensemble

Poem (1963)

☐ Lavanne (soprano); Sussman (clarinet); Goberman (cello); Jolles (harp) / Gerber (conductor) / Composers Recordings S–250

Partial serial procedures knit, but do not interfere, with the nocturnal quality of Blank's piece. Performed with a confidence that shows indisputable musical intelligence on the part of Antonia Lavanne.

Thirteen Ways of Looking at a Blackbird (1965)

☐ Contemporary Chamber Ensemble / Lamoree (soprano) / Weisberg (conductor) / Composers Recordings S–250

Interlocking of detail plus serial thinking make for an eminently well-made song cycle, with an instrumentation of eight colors playable (via doubling) by a quintet. Steadfastness of texture and a generality of mood mark the thirteen sections.

Two Parables by Franz Kafka (1964)

☐ Lamoree (soprano); Raimondi (violin); Dengel (viola) / Blank (conductor) / Composers Recordings S–250

Here, there is no hardheadedness in which pitch logic comes before word meaning. Everything is predicated to project the moods and meanings of the two texts. *Die Sirenen* ("The Sirens") is music of mythification; *Kuriere* ("Couriers") is hop-skip-and-jump music. Within these poetical fancies Blank does not concede to any loss of formal identity and balance.

Considerable virtuosity is demanded in performing Blank's two-part work for voice and two stringed instruments. (It is to be noted that he conducts the recorded presentation.) Beautifully registered in both instances and fully depicting the atmospheres involved.

Cantata and Oratorio

Esther's Monologue (1970)

☐ Sabo (soprano); Colburn (oboe); Stanick (viola); Peepo (cello) / Orion 75169

Blank's text (written by his wife) concerns the biblical character Esther defining what she must do to foil Haman, who planned to destroy all the Persian Jews. The dark instrumental coloration aids the dramaticism of the piece.

The recorded performance sustains the excellent quality of Blank's music, communicating it with clear distinctions.

Michel Blavet   (1700-1768)

Menuet, *l'inconu* in E minor with Four Variations and *Rondeau*

☐ Wilson (flute) / Orion 7289

Instrumental

Flute

The mostly technical commentary on the theme is brilliantly achieved. The sound is rather enlarged for a single flute, but it does no real harm.

Sonata in B minor for Flute and Continuo

☐ Murray (baroque flute); Goldstein (harpsichord) / Pandora 103

Chamber Music

The interest grows from movement to movement, climaxing with a brilliant set of variations. The performance is well-accomplished, the players using a flute made in the latter part of the eighteenth century and a harpsichord dating from 1600.

Sonata in B minor, Op. 3, No. 2

☐ Rampal (flute); Alain (organ) / Musical Heritage Society MHS-1277

No matter where Rampal ventures he succeeds. Blavet's Sonata is one of three *pour la flûte traversière avec la basse*. Generally, of course, the basso continuo is played by a harpsichord with a cello or viola da gamba as support. Not that use of the organ is prohibited, but it is chosen much less—combined with a flute it is even more rare. Still, the results are extremely profitable.

Arthur Bliss   (1891-1975)

Discourse for Orchestra

☐ Louisville Orchestra / Whitney (conductor) / Louisville 592 (monaural)

Orchestra

The Discourse is a set of continual and partially recapitulated variations described as moods: gay, contemplative, and so on. It displays the composer's romantic aplomb.

When this was recorded, the Louisville group did not have a large string body. This is a drawback in music of solid-banked orchestration; otherwise, it is a fine performance.

Hymn to Apollo (1926)

☐ London Symphony Orchestra / Bliss (conductor) / Musical Heritage Society MHS-3096

The patterns of *Hymn* are derived from late romantic sources. The work has a fantasy design, molded like a mosaic.

Bliss directs a top-quality performance, structurally clear in every respect and sensitively balanced.

Introduction and Allegro (1925)

☐ Leicestershire Schools Symphony Orchestra / Bliss (conductor) / Argo ZRG–685

Though Bliss is a romantic, he is not the usual post-romantic type. His music is more athletic than the work of those contemporaries who basked in the post-Wagnerian light. Only in his penchant for weighty textures is there a modicum of relationship to the Wagnerian style. The move-and-go of this piece keeps the music in balance; it is terse and contemporary in its energetic excitement and rhythmic inquisitiveness.

"Good show" is the response to the recording.

Meditations on a Theme by John Blow

☐ City of Birmingham Symphony Orchestra / Rignold (conductor) / Musical Heritage Society MHS–1251

An Introduction, five Meditations, an Interlude, and a Finale comprise Bliss's piece. Though some of the sections are reflective and quiet, others are not. The technical span, regardless of the quasi-programmatic situation, covers a set of free variations. Each is prefaced with a motto—for the second Meditation, "Thy rod and staff comfort me"; for the fifth one, "In green pastures"; for the Finale, "In the house of the Lord."

Rignold has an excellent orchestra that plays the Bliss music most persuasively.

Mêlée fantasque (1920)

☐ London Symphony Orchestra / Bliss (conductor) / Musical Heritage Society MHS–1919

The *Mêlée* is early Bliss, but not in the style of his anti-romantic works such as *Madame Noy* and *Rout*. The sensations are fervent modalism and equally fervent lyricism. Plenty of big splash but not for the ending, which is an inspired mysterious conclusion and makes as much effect as the big splash. Fine playing by the London Symphony Orchestra.

Suite from *Adam Zero* (1946)

☐ London Philharmonic Orchestra / Bliss (conductor) / Musical Heritage Society MHS–1750

Actually, this consists of excerpts from the suite Bliss drew from his eight-movement ballet score, specifically movements 3, 4, and 5. Pleasant romantic ruminations concern the *Dance of Spring, Bridal Ceremony,* and *Dance of Summer.* Everything is clearly drawn, though no special creative insight is disclosed. One assumes from the two-in-one situation that the conductor obtains what the composer wishes.

Suite from the Film *Things to Come* (1935)

Welcome to the Queen (1954)

☐ London Symphony Orchestra / Bliss (conductor) / London STS–15112

The assortment drawn from the complete score for the motion picture covers such styles as à la light Delibes (*Ballet*), pseudo-modern (*Pestilence*), and four other sections.

Welcome to the Queen is the pomp and circumstance of ritually majestic England according to Arthur Bliss. It was composed in 1954 as a "song of welcome" for the homecoming of Queen Elizabeth II from her Commonwealth tour. This is English music, though not as English as Elgar's *Pomp and Circumstance* marches.

This recording was first issued by RCA Victor (2257), then deleted and reissued by London. The pieces are warmly played and totally satisfactory.

Music for Strings (1935)

☐ City of Birmingham Symphony Orchestra / Rignold (conductor) / Musical Heritage Society MHS–1251

One of Bliss's finest pieces, Music for Strings is lusty, British in its airiness, and romantic, but not a potboiler of sliding harmonies. Its spirit is daring, its materials consciously related, yet not labored. It is astringent, but polyphonically flavorsome and full of verve. The composer exemplifies the theorem that one of the most satisfactory of all instrumental media is the string body, in this case of tender sound and volatile brilliance.

An extremely well-proportioned performance, far better than the deleted Angel (35136) release in which Bliss conducted the strings of the Philharmonia Orchestra.

Conversations

No. 1: *The Committee Meeting* (1919)
No. 5: *In the Tube at Oxford Circus* (1919)

☐ Melos Ensemble of London / RCA LM–6092 (monaural)

These two numbers are the most illustrative of the five movements that constitute the *Conversations.* Bliss's *Committee Meeting* is a gem of musical humor. Thus, the violin represents a chairman who doggedly tries to keep to his point of order, while the committee members (the flute, oboe, viola, and cello) altercate and break all the rules of an orderly meeting. The chairman monotonously insists six times on his very dry point. Apparently he wins, as the final D major chord snaps Bliss's musical meeting to a close.

At the beginning of the *Oxford Circus* sketch the conversation in the London subway is very animated, and the cello imitates the rumbling of the underground. No trains are heard, however, in the middle of the movement.

These excerpts will prime one's appetite for a complete updated-in-sound recording. It is long overdue.

Quintet for Clarinet and Strings (1931)

☐ Melos Ensemble of London / Everest 3135

The Quintet is one of Bliss's most important chamber music achievements. He has always been stimulated by the entrance of an opposite type of instrument into the habitat of the strings, and accordingly transmits his ideas with the greatest clarity. The Quintet indicates a sensitive approach to formal demands and an avoidance of ordinary ideas. The opening movement is most illustrative. What sounds like a three-voiced fugue is only an interesting method of introducing a movement in free sonata form, refreshed and dulcified by the clarinet's beautiful timbre. This initial movement can well rank with the greatest examples in the medium produced by Mozart and Brahms. An authoritative performances in the medium produced by Mozart and Brahms. An authoritative performance (Bliss attended all the recording sessions) enhances the work.

Quintet for Oboe and Strings (1927)

☐ Melos Ensemble of London / Everest 3135

The only exception to true chamber-music style is found in a few places in the final movement, specifically, in its final measures, where there is a complete bowing of the strings to their woodwind fellow. The entire work is warm-hearted with a rich romantic tang, but without purple patches.

Excellent presentation by this top-flight group. Some listeners may find the tone of the oboe (played by Peter Graeme) somewhat hard and pinched, but the balance between the wind instrument and the strings is very good.

Vocal

Voice and Orchestra

Rout, for Soprano and Orchestra (1920)

☐ London Symphony Orchestra / Woodland (soprano) / Bliss (conductor) / Musical Heritage Society MHS–3096

Once considered a shocker, *Rout* today hasn't lost any of its special appeal. Bliss's polished and joyous consonance make it difficult to understand why a half-century ago *Rout* was insultingly termed a "riot."

It pits a soprano within and on top of the orchestra, becoming an "instrumental" timbre by singing meaningless but phonetically useful syllables.

Splendid performance here. It's a delight to have *Rout* on disc.

Serenade for Baritone and Orchestra (1929)

☐ London Symphony Orchestra / Shirley-Quirk (baritone) / Priestman (conductor) / Musical Heritage Society MHS–3096

Hidden away in this work is a splendid, swashbuckling overture (*The Serenader*) that one never hears. It is worth being performed separately. It is followed by a setting of a sonnet by Spenser, an orchestral *Idyll*, and another movement for voice and orchestra.

Neither exciting nor challenging in the technical sense, it is music romantically formed and gracefully sprayed with light dissonance.

Priestman here proves his ability as a conductor in solo position as well as a sensitive accompanist.

Choral

Chorus Alone

A Prayer to the Infant Jesus for Women's Voices (1968)

☐ Ambrosian Singers / Ledger (conductor) / Musical Heritage Society MHS–3096

The *Prayer* exhibits Bliss-full hymnody using pure unaccompanied voices and the chaste essences of romantic style. Subtly interfused, the rendition is a beautifully judged account.

Cantata and Oratorio

The World Is Charged with the Grandeur of God (1969)

☐ London Symphony Orchestra Wind and Brass Ensemble and Ambrosian Singers / Ledger (conductor) / Musical Heritage Society MHS–3096

A three-part cantata using poems by Gerard Manley Hopkins. Parts 1 and 3 combine three trumpets and four trombones with the mixed chorus; part 2 is sharply contrasted, set for women's voices and two flutes.

Marc Blitzstein   *(1905-1964)*

Cantata and Oratorio

The Airborne Symphony

☐ New York Philharmonic and Choral Art Society / Welles (narrator); Velis (tenor); Watson (baritone) / Bernstein (conductor) / Columbia M–34136

In twelve sections, the Airborne Symphony covers the history of human flight from Icarus through World War II. After the *Kittyhawk* portion (part 3) the text and music air matters pertaining to the war, covering such subjects as *The Enemy, Ballad of Hurry-Up, Ballad of the Bombardier,* and so on.

Blitzstein's oratorio passes muster only if it is heard as a documentary period piece. It is filled with agit-prop stuff and words—a *March of Time* movie music reminder. It is styled to fit: Hitler gets snide and crusty music, the young American receives collegiate snap in the melodic formation, barber shop style serves for motherly instructions to the air force, Fred Waring chorus format pops up all over the score, and Mickey-Mouse orchestration envelops the moods of the piece.

But history is sometimes rather quaint and curious. Blitzstein's Airborne Symphony (presented in an all-out performance, with Orson Welles and Leonard Bernstein repeating the roles they had in the 1946 concert premiere) reflects that statement.

The Cradle Will Rock (1937)

☐ Kingsley (piano); Bryant, Buckley, Andrews, Bova, Clarke, Cleary, David, Dittmann, Grant, Grimes, Gardner, Orbach, Peters, Meersman, Scott, Tucker, and Warfield (voices) / Composers Recordings S–266

Opera and Dramatic Music

Here we have an opportunity to hear Blitzstein's historic two-act proletarian opera dealing with capitalism and its battle with the workers attempting to organize a union. Everything is black and white in Blitzstein's story and music; there are no deep philosophies to consider or study.

This performance is a reissue from the old MGM release. No text is provided, but the diction of the cast negates the need of words to follow any more than one needs a text while attending a play on Broadway. Do not expect great voices, but be certain of professionals of top calibre, all with the ability to put across a song.

Ernest Bloch   (1880-1959)

America: An Epic Rhapsody (1926)

☐ Symphony of the Air and American Concert Choir / Stokowski (conductor) / Vanguard S–346

Orchestra

Bloch's work (awarded the *Musical America* prize in the competition it held in the 1927–1928 season) had the most auspicious baptism any orchestral composition has ever received. In addition to the $3,000 award (no mean sum in those days) it was given five premieres in two days: the first by the New York Philharmonic Orchestra on December 20, 1928, and on the following day by the Boston, Chicago, Philadelphia, and San Francisco Symphony Orchestras!

The work is in three sections: *... 1620 (The Soil–The Indians–England–The Mayflower–The Landing of the Pilgrims); ... 1861–1865 (Hours of Joy–Hours of Sorrow); ... 1926 (The Present–The Future ...).* The muralistic conception embraces a huge number of ideas in its continuity (forty-eight are indicated in Bloch's score, with such labels as *Struggles and Hardships, Building up a Nation, The Battle Call, Speed, Noise,* and *The Fulfillment,* including lines taken from Walt Whitman). Expectably, the musical tale is of length, covering fifty minutes. Bloch integrated all types of indigenous material (Indian, Negro, folk, popular, and patriotic) to flesh out and certify the American coloristic objective of his work. Examples: *Old Hundred, Old Folks at Home, Pop Goes the*

Weasel, Hail Columbia, Dixie, Yankee Doodle, a Chippewa mourning song, and the Negro song *Row on Row.* As a whole, the epic is masterfully constructed and blended in a continuity that is not dismembered by constant changes.

The performance of this musicorama is well made and gives its age away by the name of the now-defunct orchestra. However, it requires no apologies and can be termed a most convincing presentation. (An added bonus is Bloch speaking at the start of the recording about his work. The two-and-one-quarter minutes involved is, indeed, not only historic documentation, but is very impressive.)

Israel Symphony (1916)

☐ Utah Symphony Orchestra / Christensen and Fraenkel (sopranos); Politis and Heder (altos); Watts (bass) / Abravanel (conductor) / Vanguard C–10007

One half of this work is symphonic; the other includes voices used with almost symphonic effect. Describing the Jewish people's most sacred day, Yom Kippur, and its antithesis, the feast of Succoth, Bloch displays a multiple personality: he prays and declaims; he is tender and barbaric; and he is rhapsodic. But above all he is preaching the faith.

This extremely moving work is given a well-directed performance, with carefully regulated sound that balances the large forces of orchestra and five solo voices.

Sinfonia Breve (1953)

☐ Minneapolis Symphony Orchestra / Dorati (conductor) / Composers Recordings S–248

As in all his music, Bloch uses a rhetorical style here, including forceful rhythms as well as rhapsodic linear material. Nevertheless, these qualities are contained in a set of strong constructions: a vigorous initial part, a somber slow movement followed by a savage Scherzo, and a decisive finale. Though Hebraic pigmentation stains the fabric, it is simply Bloch's ethnic brush being used; the *Sinfonia Breve* is not part of his "Jewish Cycle."

Dorati understands this music. The brutality and the breast-beating (similar to Bloch's String Quartet No. 1) are defined acutely in the opening movement, and proper frenzy is applied to the third part of the work. First-rate in all respects.

This recording was originally released by Mercury, where it was paired with Wayne Peterson's Free Variations for Orchestra. While the latter has, unfortunately, disappeared from the catalogue, one is grateful that CRI obtained the re-release rights for the former, thereby saving a work overlooked by the conducting fraternity—concert-wise as well as recording-wise. Yes, the cellists play *Schelomo* and the fiddlers the *Nigun* from *Baal Shem,* but Bloch's orchestral works remain in oblivion.

Suite symphonique (1944)

☐ Portland Junior Symphony / Avshalomov (conductor) / Composers Recordings S-351

Bloch's knowledge and love of the music of Bach are found in the structural stability of this three-movement composition. It is emphasized in the central Passacaglia, comprising twenty-five variations, and in the Finale, which Bloch defined as "a grotesque sardonic fugue"—an apt description, since it has a recurrent use of the "Dies Irae."

The Portland Junior Symphony puts many of our minor-league organizations to shame the way they play in major-league style.

Trois Poèmes Juifs (1913)

☐ Vienna Symphony Orchestra / Hendl (conductor) / Desto 6409E (monaural)

The "Three Jewish Poems" (*Danse, Rite,* and *Cortège funèbre*) do not belie their title, but there are no downright and outright Hebraicisms in the modalistic opening part. However, a Kaddish-like correspondence is to be heard in the *Rite*. The most potent music and that which is closer to the emotional glow and agitation of the Jewish race is to be found in the final movement. *Schelomo* was written three years after the *Poèmes*, and the *Cortège* is shot through with what were originally anticipations but are now reminders of Bloch's great cello and orchestra piece.

A better-polished rendition and top-drawer sound are needed for this piece, but until they are available Desto's disc will have to suffice. One should not overlook Bloch's work because of this criticism. It has too many exquisite subtleties and colorful orchestration to be passed by. Neither is it impossible to pass by Desto's careless liner note, with names of instruments misspelled and incorrect accent marks.

Concerto Grosso No. 1 for String Orchestra and Piano Obbligato (1925)

String Orchestra

☐ Chicago Symphony Orchestra / Schick (piano) / Kubelik (conductor) / Mercury 75036E (monaural)

This music is a magnificent treatment in the classic style, displaying a fervent voice through the sophisticated musical sounds of this century. Although his four-movement work is rooted in designs of an earlier time, Bloch writes with a fresh viewpoint of neoclassic technique. Mass chordal writing marks the opening; the Dirge is searching, beautiful music. Swiss recollections are basic to the third movement, and the Concerto is completed by an exciting Fugue, employing all the manifold techniques of the form.

The most fully developed performance is noted above. A later entry by Hanson and the Eastman-Rochester Symphony fails in its passionate thrust. Full urgency is present with the Chicago players. They are directed so that the music displays its guts as well as verve.

Concerto Grosso No. 2 for Strings (1952)

☐ Eastman-Rochester Symphony / Hanson (conductor) / Mercury 75017

Similar to the first Concerto Grosso (*see above*), in that the basic string body is supplemented—in this case by a string quartet. Further similarity concerns the contemporary intertexture fashioned from classic models for the style. The gentle climaxes are not the Bloch of Jewish inspiration, but there are Hebraic qualities within the composition.

Though the climate of performance is somewhat temperate it will pass muster. The sound is truly beautiful.

Schelomo: Hebraic Rhapsody for Cello and Orchestra (1915)

Solo Instrument and Orchestra

Cello

☐ Philadelphia Orchestra / Rose (cello) / Ormandy (conductor) / Columbia MS-6253

Schelomo is probably Bloch's most important and communicative work and doubtless his lasting testament. The heart and sincerity of the man were never so potently expressed. The music of this rhapsodic proclamation-declamation has the full cry, the self-revelatory insistence, and the sumptuousness of the Jewish race within it. Few Jews fail to be filled with emotion on hearing this work of secular-sacred incandescence; few non-Jews do not react similarly.

Any recording of this work must be measured against the blazing performance recorded by Feuermann and the Stokowski-led Philadelphia Orchestra, in the very old wide-groove days. Somehow or other this treasure must be reissued, even by the "electronically processed for stereo" method.

The number one choice among currently available performances on disc must go to Leonard Rose. He plays with dignity, sensitivity, gorgeous tone, and poetic phrasing. There is exultation when needed and there is also heard a cellistic Solomon of passion. It's Rose and Ormandy for the magnificence obtainable from this score.

Voice in the Wilderness: **Symphonic Poem with Cello Obbligato (1936)**

☐ Israel Philharmonic Orchestra / Starker (cello) / Mehta (conductor) / London 6661
☐ London Philharmonic Orchestra / Nelsova (cello) / Ansermet (conductor) / Everest 3284E (monaural)

In a sense, this is a sequel to *Schelomo* (see above), but far more introverted in spirit, with visionary meditations in place of glowing splendors. Cellists seem to shy away from this work, for they must accept the secondary role of an instrumental commentator.

Bloch's rhapsodic shapes are placed properly in perspective by Zara Nelsova. In certain respects, she delivers a more intense realization than does Janos Starker. However, the Everest disc, a transfer from London (LL-1232), which was released in England on Decca, cannot match the sound qualities of the newer London stereo presentation.

Flute

Suite modale **(1957)**

☐ Philadelphia Orchestra / Panitz (flute) / Ormandy (conductor) / Columbia MS-6977

The *Suite modale* is modal, of course, but more importantly it is an introspective essay. Bloch, not unexpectedly, has a Hebraic patina on his music.

The deep loveliness of Murray Panitz's tone, the grace of his phrasing, the seamlessness of his projection of the principal line, are qualities rarely encountered. The man is a consummate artist, a lord and master of his instrument.

(*Suite modale* is listed by Columbia as written "for flute and orchestra." This is incorrect. Bloch's piece is for flute and string orchestra.)

Trombone

Symphony for Trombone and Orchestra (1954)

☐ Portland Junior Symphony / Prince (trombone) / Avshalomov (conductor) / Composers Recordings S-351

The Symphony may be described as *Schelomo* with his beard slightly trimmed, but not one whit less potent. The tempi designations (*maestoso, agitato,* and *allegro deciso*) are preparatory clues as to the content. Bloch's fanfare-like, declarative, exclamatory, and incantational style all firm up this splendid work, stunningly framed and excited by purplescent and ocherous orchestration.

All involved in this recording, with special credits to Howard Prince, the soloist, collaborate in an authentic depiction of Bloch's score. There is no doubt that the major-sized Symphony is the most important work ever composed for the extremely limited trombone and orchestra medium.

Trumpet

Proclamation for Trumpet and Orchestra (1955)

☐ Louisville Orchestra / Raper (trumpet) / Whitney (conductor) / Louisville S-636

Bloch's short piece adds considerable prestige to the limited repertoire existent for trumpet and orchestra. It is a peephole look at *Schelomo:* thus, the solo sweep up to an anguished chordal orchestral cry, the tender idea compared to the barbaric, formal rhapsody without pastiche, exciting melodic leaps, and augmented intervallic movement. Also present is the Blochian habit of resignation, the drawing inward after turbulence, that marks the majority of his endings.

One word describes Raper's soloism: sublimity. A triple-starred performance in which conductor and orchestra share.

Suite for Viola and Orchestra (1919) *Viola*

☐ Seattle Symphony Orchestra / Katims (viola) / Siegl (conductor) / Turnabout TV-S-34622

The winning of a $1,000 award for this work (in its initial setting for viola and piano) in the Berkshire Chamber Music Festival Competition of 1919 did more to bring Bloch's music to the attention of the world than any of his other compositions. Very shortly thereafter the orchestral scoring was completed (Bloch had the two versions in mind from the start). A third rendering for cello and piano was made by Alexander Barjansky, the Russian cellist; it was approved by Bloch, but it remained in manuscript. There is, however, another translation of the score, made jointly by the pianist Adolph Baller and the cellist Gabor Rejto; it can be heard on Orion 6904. It is well-defined, though (Bloch notwithstanding) one does miss the umber-colored timbre special to the viola and central to Bloch's line of musical reasoning.

Without musical scene-painting or programmaticism of any kind, Bloch's Suite is a composite of Oriental sounds suggesting Java, India, and China. That a Swiss Jew could produce such music is not odd at all, however, since Hebraic expression is cognate with Eastern music.

Though Katims had long been the conductor of the orchestra that partners him in his solo performance, his ability as a violist has not diminished in any way. (Siegl, the conductor in this recording, is the orchestra's concert-master.) Katims's playing has meaning and dramatic sweep, and he defines the assorted colors of the viola with minute sensitivity. The depth of his conception is a strong parallel to Primrose's long-deleted monophonic release (in the viola-piano edition) on the Capitol label (P-8355), and it is more vivid than Wallfisch's conception on the Musical Heritage Society label (MHS-1486), also in the viola-piano medium.

Violin Concerto (1938) *Violin*

☐ Paris Conservatoire Orchestra / Szigeti (violin) / Munch (conductor) / Turnabout THS-65007 (monaural)
☐ Philharmonia Orchestra / Menuhin (violin) / Kletzki (conductor) / Angel S-36192

The Bloch Violin Concerto "belonged" to Szigeti from the day in December 1938 when he gave the world premiere. His commitment to the work remains a permanent challenge to the fiddle fraternity. Not many have taken it up and there is still resistance to the Concerto. (We are in need of music repertoire lobbyists!)

The evidence of the musical capacity of Bloch's entrancing work is the great recorded performance that Szigeti made with Munch in 1939, when both men were in their mid-forties and at the peak of their careers. It is this EMI recording that Turnabout has issued in a two-channel re-recording from the original monaural tapes. It is a gem and of definitive imprint.

The Menuhin entry is communicative and compelling. Its dynamic and full-toned approach fits the Concerto, which is handsomely recorded.

Instrumental	*Méditation hébraïque*
Cello	**Three Pieces: *From Jewish Life* (1924)**

☐ Goodman (cello); Bogin (piano) / Orion 75181

The *Méditation* might easily have been included in Bloch's *Schelomo,* expressing as it does the same emotional, proclamative-declamative intensity.

The Three Pieces—*Prayer, Supplication,* and *Jewish Song*—are parallel musical petitions. There may be considerable similarities in all of Bloch's Hebraic or Jewish music, but subtle differences apply. One is reminded of the Talmud, which contains, among many things, conclusions on law, ethics, and traditions, and then commentaries on these conclusions, and further discussions on the commentaries.

Piano   **Sonata for Piano (1935)**

☐ Shaulis (piano) / Composers Recordings S-295

Bloch is in a stormy mood, despite a more relaxed central (Pastorale) section. The music is conceived on an orchestral scale and demands much from the performer. He must clarify the various masses of sound, which quite often are heard contrapuntally. However, Bloch's plan of composition makes everything as clear as a gigantic Gothic structure.

This performance is a clean one and presented without fuss. One wishes, however, a more red-blooded depiction. But the major-league virtuosi bypass Bloch, and that includes his piano output additional to the Sonata. The prospects for another (better) recording seem very remote.

Visions and Prophecies (1936)

☐ Chodos (piano) / Orion 73122

The five declamatory sections of *Visions and Prophecies* are mostly Bloch's *Voice in the Wilderness* revoiced for piano. Chodos provides all the rhapsodic and mystic details most effectively, though the piano sounds only fair.

Viola   ***Meditation and Processional (1951)***

Suite hébraïque (1951)

☐ Ernst Wallfisch (viola); Lory Wallfisch (piano) / Musical Heritage Society MHS-1486

Composers' short pieces sometimes tend to be set in a different, somewhat lighter frame, but this is not true of Bloch. The *Meditation* is as Blochian as are his large works. The *Processional* is in some degree an impressionistic piece. However, Bloch's impressionism is more earthbound than Debussy's. The Jewish characteristic is not paramount; neither is it absent.

The *Suite hébraïque,* Bloch's second suite for viola and piano, was composed in 1951. However, unlike his initial work in the medium, the stringed instrument is here in the spotlight; the piano is principally a background voice. (For that reason, it is discussed here, under *Instrumental,* rather than under *Chamber Music.*)

In this "Hebraic Suite" (with three parts: *Rhapsody, Processional,* and *Affirmation*), Bloch's Jewish musical thoughts are mingled with medieval modes and contemporary mannerisms. None of the latter are utilized haphazardly; in every case they are expressive.

These are beautiful performances in which Ernst Wallfisch demonstrates the highest type of stringed-instrument art. The availability of Bloch's viola-piano pieces is especially welcome, since the only other recording made (now in the deleted category) was a monaural edition, on Capitol (P-8355). (It consists of stunning performances by William Primrose, with David Stimer as the piano accompanist.)

Suite for Solo Viola (1958)

☐ Wallfisch (viola) / Musical Heritage Society MHS-1486

As the Suite was Bloch's final work, its fourth movement was left incomplete. It is rounded off by a partial reprise of the opening in Wallfisch's forthright reading. While it is good to have a recording of this unaccompanied music, don't expect a Blochian profile. Neutrality covers the formality of his conception.

Abodah (a Yom Kippur Melody) (1929)

Violin

☐ Bress (violin); Reiner (piano) / Folkways 3357 (monaural)

Bloch heard with his full Hebraic heart and voice. *Abodah* (meaning "God's Worship") was especially written for Yehudi Menuhin, and dedicated to the violinist when he was only seven years old.

Baal Shem: Three Pictures of Chassidic Life (1923)

☐ Stern (violin); Zakin (piano) / Columbia Special Products AMS-6717

Shofar-like calls and intervallic spans taken from the Hebrew ritual abound in this suite. Despite the Jewish melos, the augmented (crying) intervals, the heavy melancholy and despair which seep through the music's tissues, the sounds this Blochian Jewish credo makes have much in common with the music of other Semitic peoples. Bloch's music is, however, the first and most important example of modern secular Hebraic music. But this is not to limit its significance. *Baal Shem* is a nationalistic work, but its Hebraic dialect is only one aspect of the international musical speech it employs.

It is simply unbelievable that not one complete performance of *Baal Shem* with orchestral accompaniment is available. Only the favored *Nigun* ("Improvisation") can be heard (Zukerman and the Royal Philharmonic Orchestra, with Foster conducting, on Columbia M-30644) and even then it is a rather sober realization of the music's sacred passions. There are several *Nigun* performances with piano. On monaural settings, one can hear Bezrodni (on Monitor 2028) and Bress (on Folkways 3354). In stereo, Heifetz is available on Columbia M2-33444. The only complete performance either way—for violin and piano or violin and orchestra—is Stern's. Fortunately, it is a beauty. Stern's playing is acute, with technical power subordinated to the musical objective. The kaleidoscopic colors and free rhapsodizing of the Bloch suite are beautifully framed in his presentation.

Fantaisie (1897)

☐ Bress (violin); Reiner (piano) / Folkways 3357 (monaural)

A very early work, written in 1897 and unpublished, *Fantaisie* is one of the *Oeuvres de jeunesse* manuscripts deposited in the Library of Congress. Not merely of historical value, the *Fantaisie* is still worthy of being heard.

Suite No. 1 for Solo Violin (1958)

☐ Bress (violin) / Folkways 3357 (monaural)

The Suite is a classical discourse, smoothly conceived for the violin (it was Bloch's first instrument). Fine performance commitment by the soloist.

Chamber Music

Sonata No. 1 for Violin and Piano (1920)

☐ Stern (violin); Zakin (piano) / Columbia Special Products AMS-6717

The keynote of the work is its emotional barbarism, evident immediately in the opening *fortissimo* declaration. The same elemental savagery is called on in the final (third) movement. There is a prophetic bitterness that bespeaks the Biblical robes worn by this composer. There are moments when the violin and piano function like tribal instruments, giving evidence of Bloch's ethnic characteristics, which include that of dogged perseverance.

If Stern and Zakin seem to be striving for more than they are capable of, they are simply playing Bloch's music as it is written. Theirs is an engaging recording, fully displaying the architectural strength of the Sonata, with hearty, correct sound. A better version is hard to imagine. There is Bress on Folkways 3357 (in monaural) but in this case he's not in the same league with Isaac Stern. And the other available release, by Heifetz (also on monaural) is tame and doesn't have the blood and guts that Stern displays and the music requires. Even in the quiet middle movement Heifetz is far too restrained. (If you're interested, he's on RCA ARM4-0947.)

Sonata No. 2 (*Poème mystique*) for Violin and Piano (1924)

☐ Heifetz (violin); Smith (piano) / RCA ARM4-0947 (monaural)

The relationship between the first and second violin and piano Sonatas is similar to that between the pair of works for cello and orchestra, *Schelomo* and *Voice in the Wilderness*. In both instances, the later work is cooler and more serene than the earlier one. The second Sonata also differs formally from the first, its material being designed in one extended movement.

Heifetz does well with this work. It is styled beautifully and contains the proper quotient of intensity, whereas the companion Sonata (*see above*) tends to have an incorrect proportion of force. Smith does his share with proper understanding.

Three Nocturnes (1924)

☐ Western Arts Trio / Laurel LR-104

Bloch's impressionism is more restricted than Debussy's, though somewhat similarly pastoral; but Bloch is too motivally concerned to be a spiritual successor to the Frenchman. Even with the same disavowal of polyphonicism, these short pieces are more classic in orientation than the similarly titled orchestral pieces by Debussy. Actually, the vernal exposures of the first two of these pieces are less nocturnal, more matutinal. Bloch's Nocturnes should be considered as *aubades*.

The performers (in residence at the University of Wyoming) play at a high level and with rich tone.

String Quartet No. 3 (1951)

☐ Edinburgh Quartet / Monitor S-2123

The third Quartet begins with raw rhythms (meaning considerable block writing), continues with a slow division that has the usual Blochian nocturnal nosegay, goes on to a rather strictly designed Scherzo, and is completed by the most polyphonic section of all, one that begins with a passacaglia and moves into a fugue.

The single recording on the market is only fair. Not much cultivation of the subtle power of color is made. Such rigidity (especially in the first movement) dams and damns the music. The playing, overall, is ultra-conservative. It would be welcome news if London reissued the Griller String Quartet's impressive performance of this work.

String Quartet No. 5 (1956)

☐ Fine Arts Quartet / Concert-Disc 225

Though in classically styled format, including his favored use of cyclic restatement, Bloch's final String Quartet simmers with the juices found in the first Quartet, composed exactly forty years earlier. These are represented by lines that have perorative intervallic spans and motoric pulsations. However, there is less rhapsody and a weighted consideration of texture, with the usual Blochian use of sequence to knit these together. One also notes a twelve-tone theme (but not developed in twelve-tone fashion) in the finale.

The Fine Arts Quartet plays the music capably but downgrades some of its ecstatic data by a serious, perhaps even stolid, demeanor. The Presto is thereby checked somewhat. A brighter recording ambience would have been desirable. Still, this is the only recording of the work and one would not want to pass by Bloch's beautifully structured creation because of these views. The piece is coupled here with Hindemith's third Quartet. Bloch's Quartet is also available on the Everest label (3328), with his Concerto Grosso No. 1 as the companion work.

Quintet for Piano and Strings (1923)

☐ Fine Arts Quartet / Glazer (piano) / Concert-Disc 252

One of Bloch's best (and most important) works. The lean ruggedness of the score has all of the Blochian mannerisms, except that the Hebraic points of speech are of minor total—Afro-Indian elements predominate. A great deal of transmutative technique is utilized. The opening theme is slowed in speed and slightly reshaped for the slow movement. Contrasting material in that slow division is likewise taken from accompanimental backgrounds of the initial movement. In the last movement, the generic theme is compressed. The overall effectuation of the finale is barbaric, pulsatile, percussively bittered. The performance of this part of the Quintet is properly pugnacious, intensely detailed, carefully symphonicized.

This recording is most welcome. The only previous recording was made years ago by the Walden String Quartet with Johana Harris on MGM, and was only worth an A-minus for effort. The performance was too relaxed, the harmonic frictions too subdued, the sound rather negative. Concert-Disc's release has all the necessary properties: intensity, ruggedness in proper amount, keen balance, and excellent sonics. In short, all the grains of the music's wood show as they should. Absolutely a rich addition to recorded literature, with re-creative cogency, spontaneity, and perfect styling.

Sacred Service (Avodath Hakodesh) (1933)

☐ New York Philharmonic and Choirs of the Metropolitan Synagogue and Community Church of New York / Cahn (narrator); Merrill (baritone) / Bernstein (conductor) / Columbia MS–6221

Cantata and Oratorio

Music in the ancient synagogue consisted of abundant traditional melodies and cantillations handed down almost by rote. The organized synagogue musical service is a fairly recent development, sparked principally by the Reform movement within the Jewish community, who encouraged and also commissioned original synagogue music. Joseph Achron, David Diamond, Lukas Foss, Isadore Freed, Frederick Jacobi, Lazare Saminsky, Robert Starer, Lazar Weiner, and others composed such works. Among those considered to be the most important are the creations of Ernest Bloch and Darius Milhaud. (The latter is recorded. See under *Milhaud: Cantata and Oratorio* [*Sabbath Morning Service*].)

Bloch's work is unique in that it discards the set orientation of Eastern decorative ("old style") music in favor of a more neutral method. It is Hebraic at its roots, but completely universal in its appeal. It is music that combines the dignity and quietude necessary for worship with the drama and power that aid in its projection from the concert platform. Spiritually, it is Bloch's counterpart to Bach's great Mass in B minor.

Bernstein's performance is magnificent. The singing of Robert Merrill is of stirring vividness and keen personality. The performance is in Hebrew. If you want Bloch's work in English you'll have to probe the out-of-print sources for a London (5006) disc. It's worth acquiring, with Bloch himself conducting the London Philharmonic Orchestra and Choir and Marko Rothmuller as the principal solo voice.

Karl-Birger Blomdahl (1916-1968)

Orchestra

Sisyfos: Choreographic Suite No. 1 (1954)

☐ Stockholm Philharmonic Orchestra / Dorati (conductor) / RCA VICS-1319

Rather a mixed bag of styles. Included in Blomdahl's creative sampler are jazz and serial shapes. Dorati does splendidly and really juices it up.

It is interesting to note that Blomdahl's choreographic conception for orchestra (first performed in Stockholm on October 20, 1954) actually reached ballet realization (first presented in Stockholm on April 18, 1957).

Cantata and Oratorio

In the Hall of Mirrors (1952)

☐ Stockholm Philharmonic Orchestra and Swedish Radio Chorus / Hallin (soprano); Ericson (alto); Vikström (tenor); Näslund (baritone and narrator); Rundgren (bass) / Ehrling (conductor) / Caprice CAP-1006 (monaural)

In the Hall of Mirrors ("I speglarnas sal") is a documenting of the violence, brutality, and debasement of humanity during World War II. It is set to nine vivid sonnets by Erik Lindegren, including recitative, homophonic choral writing, choral speech, and narration. Within the twelve-tone writing there is a grotesque Scherzo, a twisted Boogie-woogie, and a Nocturne. A raw elucidation pervades the music, tied to the text in a very compelling manner.

The consistence of the performance can only be termed extraordinary. This is a monaural recording (though made in 1966!) but as excellent in all of its responses as one might wish. The production is excellent, with complete texts in Swedish, English, and German, plus first-rate annotations and related data.

John Blow (1649-1708)

Choral

Coronation Anthems

Chorus and Orchestra

God Spake Sometimes in Visions
I Was Glad

Symphony Anthems

Blessed Is the Man
Cry Aloud, and Spare Not
O Sing Unto the Lord

☐ Academy of St. Martin-in-the-Fields and Choir of King's College, Cambridge / Brett (countertenor); Langridge (tenor); Lancelot (organ); Heath (cello) / Willcocks (conductor) / Argo ZRG-767

These Restoration anthems are given reliable performances by chorus and soloists mainly concentrated in the middle and upper registers. When depth is required it is supplied, but it is in the minority. The accompaniment, especially the brassy splendor that enters here and there in the form of a pair of trumpets, is most impressive.

Luigi Boccherini (1743-1805)

Symphonies, Op. 35

Orchestra

No. 1 in D major / No. 2 in E flat major / No. 3 in A major / No. 4 in F major / No. 5 in E flat major / No. 6 in B flat major

☐ I Filarmonici di Bologna / Ephrikian (conductor) / Telefunken 3635021

Nicely stated material, though not much dramatic conflict is to be noticed in these works all in major tonalities. It's not the sort of music that requires other performances to bring greater force or pointedness to the narratives. What there is to say is said satisfactorily in this recorded edition, which offers rhythmic vitality and a nicely bright sound.

Concerto in B flat major for Cello and Orchestra

Solo Instrument and Orchestra

☐ English Chamber Orchestra / du Pré (cello) / Barenboim (conductor) / Angel S-36439

Cello

Most cellists opt to use the version that was adapted and edited by Friedrich Grützmacher, but only purists can object. Certainly they might also object to the richly warm playing of Jacqueline du Pré, since it isn't classically styled. But, with the vocalism of Boccherini's lines, the combination of romanticism and elegance in her portrayal is just irresistible.

(Angel also makes the performance available in a two-record release which additionally embraces a Beethoven piano sonata, a Brahms cello and piano sonata, and a Mozart piano concerto. Thus husband and wife each have solo concerto opportunities, join in sonata partnership, and the former has an individual spot. An interesting salesmanship mix and found on S-3749.)

Concerto in D major for Flute and Strings, Op. 27

Flute

☐ I Musici / Gazzelloni (flute) / Philips 6500611

A pair of finely poised movements (in *allegro moderato* tempo and an *allegretto*-paced Rondeau) frame a limpid Adagio in one of the best of Boccherini's concerti. It is all presented in a peerless manner, including worthy cadenzas by the soloist for all three movements.

The only competitive edition is on the Musical Heritage Society label with Graf as soloist and the Zurich Chamber Orchestra conducted by Tschupp (MHS-1366). Good, but not reaching the maximum effect obtained in the Gazzelloni-I Musici partnership.

Sonatas for Flute and Harpsichord, Op. 5

No. 1 in B flat major / No. 2 in C major / No. 3 in B flat major / No. 4 in D major / No. 5 in G minor / No. 6 in E flat major

☐ Stokes (flute); Karp (harpsichord) / Orion 75173

No patterned formal thinking is to be found in this set. Each design varies even when the movement total is similar. When three movements with terminal fast divisions are utilized (Nos. 1 and 5) the middle one differs in tempo and thereby in its formal (especially rhythmic) details. In the paired-movement Sonatas, one starts with a slow-fast tempo combination and is completed with a Rondo; another splits the work into Moderato and Allegro concepts, etc. But there are always spun melodies and expressive treatment, though the major emphasis is on the wind instrument.

One cannot fault this performance. Stokes's tonal warmth and sensitive phrasing are the major contribution.

Chamber
Music

Sonata in A major for Cello and Harpsichord

☐ Roveda (cello); Sgrizzi (piano) / Nonesuch 73008

Despite the fact that the tessitura practically avoids the lowest string of the instrument there is never a forced note in Egidio Roveda's playing. And in some spots the cello moves up into the stratosphere. Clean playing of the most unusual merit is delivered. These points bring the strongest recommendation for this recording.

Sonata in A major for Two Cellos

☐ Gabor and Peter Rejto (cellos) / Orion 7282

Most of Boccherini's duo emphasizes the importance of the first cello. This is in accordance with the heading *per violoncello col basso* ("for cello with bass"), the main objective of which is to feature a principal (higher) voice with a subsidiary (lower) one. However, the liner notes state that "in light of recent research" this means paired cellos. While the opus has Boccherini's usual felicitous themes and simplistic consideration of designs, one argues that such scoring tends to blend what should be contrastive. But no argument exists in regard to the excellence of the playing on Orion's release.

Sonata in D major

☐ Heifetz (violin); Piatigorsky (cello) / RCA LSC–3009

It's nice to have these two masters combine in the playing of a string duet. However (because it was recorded live), one must tolerate hearing a slightly ragged ending to the first movement and certainly not one hundred percent agreement between the two virtuosi on pitch. Then, too, there are some sounds of fixing music on the stands and very light tapping on strings for tuning purposes.

You can't fault RCA for wanting on disc a performance of Heifetz and Piatigorsky. Neither can you fault the self-assured and lusty way in which the music is played. Also, this is the only edition in the recorded catalogue. Take it, warts and all.

Trio

In G major, Op. 38, No. 2 / In G minor, Op. 9, No. 5

☐ Members of the Carmirelli Quartet / Turnabout 34550

The Trio in G minor was originally scored for two violins and cello. In this recording the second violin has been replaced by a viola. No harm. The violin-viola-cello formation thus matches the scoring Boccherini used for the G major opus. Urbane playing by the three musicians. It is sufficient.

La tiranna, Op. 44, No. 4

☐ Carmirelli Quartet / Turnabout 34550

This is a *quartettino*, consisting of only a pair of movements: Presto and *Tempo di minuetto*. No explanation is available for the subtitle of the first movement (*La tiranna*), which consists of lighthearted, optimistic music.

A routine work given a routine performance. (Another *quartettino* is discussed *below*.)

Quartettino in D major, Op. 40, No. 3

☐ Sinnhoffer String Quartet / Orion 7035

Half an average quartet in size, it has only a pair of movements, an *Andantino* and a *Menuetto and trio*. Running time: 9:26. There is no emotional rhetoric, just melody and harmony. The best point is the minor-keyed *trio* section. A professional presentation is provided by the Sinnhoffer group.

String Quartet

In D major, Op. 6, No. 1 / In E flat major, Op. 6, No. 3 / In E flat major, Op. 58, No. 2

☐ Quartetto Italiano / Philips 9500305

Little of Boccherini's vast string quartet output has ever found its way onto records, and that includes those in the deleted disc category. Boccherini cultivated the quartet form as assiduously as did Haydn. Authorities have never been able to ascertain, with the usual exactness of musicological research, how many quartets were in the vast amount of music he produced. The minimum seems to be 91, and the maximum may even be the staggering total of 102.

These three examples show what we have been missing. In the Opus 6 pair, there is an emphasis on vocalistic grace, with a lesser inclination to formal developmental directness. The later opus has a more substantial design, but this does not deny the beauties of the earlier pair of quartets.

The playing has a presence that deserves the highest praise. The Italiano foursome is not only minutely precise but aurally subtle in its playing. This release is very warmly recommended.

String Quartet in A major, Op. 39, No. 8

☐ Carmirelli Quartet / Turnabout 34550

A swinging rhythmic movement begins this fine work. Much more serious music follows, with half-lit moods in the *Andantino lentarello* and the *Minuetto con moto*. The gloves are taken off in the spirited finale. The playing is clear and sharply focused.

Quintet in D major for Guitar and Strings, Op. 50, No. 4

☐ Vienna Konzerthaus Quartet / Scheit (guitar) / Vanguard S-295E (monaural)

Credit Boccherini with not considering the guitar as set apart, quasi-soloistically, from the string group. This instrumentally unified Quintet is no ordinary opus—it is music of deep thought and substantial meaning. The final *Fandango*, utilizing a coloristic semi-glissando, is special to the work.

The performers are all excellent, but Scheit's role in the ensemble must be stressed. His playing is classically styled and the annoying habit of scooping in legati passages that so many guitarists have is totally avoided.

Quintet in E minor for Guitar and Strings, Op. 50, No. 3

☐ Cremona String Quartet / Bream (guitar) / RCA LSC–3027

Taking care of the integrated sense of Boccherini's quintet by maintaining a fully balanced disposition makes this a meaningful performance. Tempi are intelligently chosen. The transparency of the slow movement exemplifies great art.

In the competitive edition on Turnabout 34195/9 the dynamic level is far too strong, the playing approaching a roughness that is totally out of style. The reasons for the superiority of the RCA disc are clear: RCA's string team *is* a team; Turnabout's is a pick-up ensemble, and the playing is thereby prisoner to the individual notes, even with the great Siegfried Palm as the cellist of the foursome.

Quintet in E minor for Guitar and Strings, Op. 50, No. 7

☐ Melos Quartet of Stuttgart / Yepes (guitar) / Deutsche Grammophon 2530069

An elegant and enchanting performance notwithstanding, the Quintet is not as interesting as others in the set that have been recorded (*see above* and *below*), but the joy of listening to the ensemble playing of five excellent musicians has its own special rewards.

Quintet (*La ritirata di Madrid*) in C major for Guitar and Strings, Op. 50, No. 9

☐ Diaz (guitar); Schneider and Galimir (violins); Tree (viola); Soyer (cello) / Vanguard S–291

Self-borrowing is practiced here by Boccherini, who drew his guitar quintet from a set of twelve piano quintets he had composed. The principal interest is found in the finale, which presents twelve variations of the *Ritirata di Madrid* ("Madrid Retreat") theme. The flag-lowering-ceremony tune and its permutative handling were a favorite of the composer, who used them first in a string quintet, then as the concluding movement in one of the piano quintets, and once again as the finale of the second Op. 50 guitar quintet. Boccherini duplicated wisely: the movement's delightful unsophistication, with its militaristic imitations, is peripheral program music. The Schneider-led group delivers its message to the fullest extent.

String Quintet in A minor for Two Violins, Two Violas, and Cello, Op. 47, No. 1

☐ Kehr and Bartels (violins); Sichermann and Kirchner (violas); Braunholz (cello) / Turnabout 34094

The general classical concept of tonic-dominant relationship is not followed in the first movement. Keys emerge suddenly, and the lightness of the dynamic, contrasted with shifts to heavier sonority planes, makes these modulations more effective. Key contrasts also mark the *Minuetto*. A *Largo cantabile* (which this group plays rather fast) leads immediately (rather, it should, but not in this performance) into the finale. The former is filigreed; the latter a fillip in rondo style.

There is rather good playing on this release. The players are observant of the score's style and requirements, except for the tempi of the slow movement and the editing out of the *attacca* that binds the last two movements.

String Quintet in C major, Op. 37, No. 7

☐ Members of the Academy of St. Martin-in-the-Fields / Argo ZRG–569

A liner note that states this work "needs no introduction" must be responded to. Because of the huge number of string quintets with two cellos that Boccherini produced (between 113 and 125!), and because of their manifold key duplications, some specific identification is a help. Therefore this one has been termed the quintet with the "well-known finale." This relates to the bumpkin quality of the rhythmic tune that primes that movement in a highly individual manner.

This work is generally performed (often minus opus number) from the edition used here, wherein movements of various quintets have been combined by an editor (Pleyel). Much as such practice is not to be condoned, nonetheless the quintet sounds perfectly in order in its *zusammengesetzt* version.

In four movements that follow the usual classical plan, the gracefulness of the work favors the first cello without shame. The first movement is ornamentalized slow music, which keeps the pace moving by the use of pitch embroideries. In the *Menuett* the constant *Alberti bass* of the cello provides a drone ostinato that gives additional flavor to the central section of the movement, further emphasized by the use of a minor tonality in contrast to the principal major mode. Again it is the cello that is spotlighted as it introduces the material for the slow movement. It consists of one of the most expressive statements in all of Boccherini's chamber music. The finale is intertwined with sequences, its folk style a good example of "earthy" music.

The performance is outstanding and extremely well balanced. The more to regret, therefore, that the exact personnel of the Academy group is not specified.

String Quintet in E major for Two Violins, Viola, and Two Cellos, Op. 13, No. 5

☐ Schneider and Galimir (violins); Tree (viola); Soyer and Harrell (cellos) / Vanguard S–291

One of the most beautiful minuets is heard here (movement 3) in its original setting. Its muted tenderness makes for one of the outstanding small pieces in music literature and shows how much has been lost in the manifold transcriptions that have been produced.

Boccherini's quintet has interesting formal arguments. The first movement is marked *andantino mosso (amoroso),* reversing the usual speed order; the fast "opening" (*allegro con spirito*) is found here in second place. Further, the initial movement is totally muted, so in terms of color one-half of the movements are in muffled resonance. This forms an exact inner balance, since movements 1 and 3 are muted and movements 2 and 4 (the latter nicely described by the liner annotator, Jack Diether, as a "hearty, swinging rondo") are the opposite.

Boccherini / Gaspar Cassadó (1897-1966)

Concerto in E major for Guitar and Orchestra

☐ Symphony of the Air / Segovia (guitar); Galimir and Bergen (violins); Granick (viola); Bernstein (cello) / Jordá (conductor) / MCA 2525

Solo Instrument and Orchestra

Guitar

The rarity of a cellist making a transcription for another instrument and using for that purpose one of the compositions in his own repertoire should not be overlooked. Cassadó has made a good choice, especially in the middle (slow) movement. There the featured accompaniment is the string quartet concertino, though it does appear in places within the outer movements.

Cassadó's lucid and informative transcription works very well. It is given an attractive rendition and Segovia's playing offers a checklist of technical artistry on the guitar, including difficult cross-string work and trills. (The MCA disc is a transfer from the original Decca release [DL–710043].)

John Boda   (1922-   )

Orchestra

Sinfonia (1960)

☐ Knoxville Symphony Orchestra / Van Vactor (conductor) / Composers Recordings 155 (monaural)

There is tonal lucidity in every phrase of the Sinfonia, with plenty of warmth, especially the dramatic temperature in the finale. A straightforward view of form finds the three movements in the traditional (but not academic) orbit: sonata, ternary, and rondo. At first hearing, the objectives are perceived without trouble on the part of the auditor.

Instrumental

Euphonium

Sonatina for Euphonium and Synthesizer

☐ Bowman (euphonium) / Crystal S–393

It's a pleasure to hear a synthesizer treated musically rather than gimmicky. Its combination with the brass instrument is colorful, sets forth jazzy material in the outer movements, with quiet resource heard in the central slow-paced division. To convey this, Boda expertly avails himself of standard contemporary musical language.

Bowman's playing has spontaneity and freshness. This is a recording worthy of high recommendation.

Sebastian Bodinus   (fl. 1718-1756)

Chamber Music

Sonata in E major for Two Flutes

☐ Rampal and Duschenes (flutes) / Orion 7149

Bodinus was a little-known eighteenth-century German composer. On the basis of this piece that fact indicates poor judgement has taken place. The Sonata in E forms part of Bodinus's *Musikalischen Divertissements*. The slow portions have luscious spongy harmonic clashes (of course they resolve!) and the fast portions have real zip and go. A fine piece.

The same performance has been issued on the Everest label—twice, actually. On Everest 3194 it appears in a seven-disc set that features Rampal. On Everest 3229 it again features Rampal at the expense of Duschenes, who is nowhere given credit as the second member of the performing team.

Trio in E flat major

☐ Camerata Musicale / Nonesuch 71085

Bodinus's composition is contained in his collection titled *Musikalischen Divertissements*. However, Bodinus's four-part work for four-part instrumentation (flute, oboe, and a cello-harpsichord continuo) is in straight light-and-lovely late Baroque style; divertissement miscellany is not present. The third movement (*Siciliana*) deserves top billing. Its nice inflections contain generous melody pointed with a pizzicati underpinning. Everything is well managed by the Berlin ensemble.

Léon Boëllmann (1862-1897)

Suite gothique

Instrumental

☐ Raynaud (organ) / Vox SVBX-5314

Organ

A standard in the organ repertory, the *Suite gothique* is comprised of four movements: *Choral, Menuet gothique, Prière à Notre-Dame,* and Toccata.

Jean-Claude Raynaud plays with sensible registration so that the articulations in the Toccata are clear, the *Menuet* is not too heavy, and so on. There is some reverb but not too much to spoil a fine performance.

Alexandre Pierre François Boëly (1785-1858)

Suite (Five *Versets sur le Kyrie*)

Instrumental

☐ Darasse (organ) / Vox SVBX-5314

Organ

An excellent example of French traditional eighteenth-century music combined with Germanic romanticism. The playing of Xavier Darasse has fine imagery. The coloring of the sections is marked with decided differences that make graphic Boëly's work.

Georg Böhm (1661-1733)

Chorale Partita, *Ach wie nichtig, Ach wie flüchtig*

Instrumental

Prelude and Fugue in D minor

Organ

☐ Gilbert (organ) / Orion 74155

Gilbert provides a translation of Baroque style that is as true as can be accomplished and with a technical assurance that is of totally controlled authority. Both pieces are fine examples; above all the Prelude and Fugue. Gilbert's playing supplies a masterly architectural sense to the Fugue and is no less in command in the Partita.

According to the album cover, *The American Organist* termed Gilbert's program (other composers included are Buxtehude and Walther, each represented, as with Böhm, with a pair of compositions) "one of the finest recordings of Baroque organ music yet released." This writer is in full agreement.

Theobald Böhm (1794-1881)

Introduction and Variations on *Nel cor più*, Op. 4

Instrumental

☐ Robison (flute); Sanders (piano) / Vanguard 71207

Flute

Five of the six variations are presented. The composer's objective is simple and clear; though obvious, it is enjoyable. Paula Robison brings out whatever there is, sustaining interest to the very conclusion.

Variations brillantes sur un air allemand

☐ Shostac (flute); Swearengin (piano) / Crystal S–314

Show time for the flutist. Better yet, show-off time. There are technical twirls for the wind instrument, with trills, double-tonguing, octave leaps, and other pitch embroidery on the tune (*Du! Du! Liegst Mir am Herzen*), while the piano marks harmonic time. A listener may or may not be amused by this polite parlor music, but he won't be betrayed, since he'll know what to expect.

François-Adrien Boieldieu   (1775 - 1834)

Orchestra

Overture to *La Dame blanche* (1825)

☐ London Symphony Orchestra / Bonynge (conductor) / London 6744

The language of Boieldieu's operatic overture, composed in 1825, can only seem dated to those who must be served a totally serious diet. The delightful musical qualities of the piece will be apparent to the unbiased. It is given a splendid reading here.

Overture to *Le Calife de Bagdad*

☐ New Philharmonia Orchestra / Bonynge (conductor) / London 6643

One of the two remainders from the more than three dozen operatic works Boieldieu produced. (The other is *La Dame blanche*.) The remainders are reminders of musical viability and vitality. Bonynge's excellent presentation is valid evidence.

Overture to *Zoraïme et Zulnar*

☐ English Chamber Orchestra / Bonynge (conductor) / London 6735

The Overture is nicely contrasted between light and heavy qualities. The Overture also has telling dramatic shifts. It certainly deserves having been selected for recording purposes.

Solo Instrument and Orchestra

Harp

Concerto in C major for Harp and Orchestra

☐ Berlin Radio Symphony Orchestra / Zabaleta (harp) / Märzendorfer (conductor) / Deutsche Grammophon 138118

This is a charmer, a lightweight; it is almost obvious in its clinging to the tonic-subdominant-dominant vine. Who cares? It is clear that Boieldieu's three-movement opus could sound just as well on the piano; the harp's language is uttered in strict arpeggios, elementary bass lines, a good quota of *Alberti bass*, plus trills that lack the sparkle that can be obtained from the keyboard instrument. The color is severely black-white with question-answer dynamic planes (effectively defined in Zabaleta's performance).

The only exception to the above are the harmonics that are employed here and there. This leads one to believe that the version utilized is that published by Ricordi in 1940, which is titled *Concerto in tre tempi* and was "elaborated by Carlo Steuber." The liner notes give no clue, but one is fairly certain Zabaleta does not play the initial edition published by Le Duc, *ca.* 1800. A hint that bears out the abovementioned reasons for believing the Ricordi edition has been used is given by the subtitle on the record label (it appears nowhere else): *Concerto in 3 tempi per arpa ed orchestra.*

So much for conjectures. Whatever the version, the report is that Zabaleta plays with ravishing refinement and a stylistic perfection plus musicianship that makes more of the work than it actually contains.

Concerto in F major for Piano and Orchestra

Piano

☐ Innsbruck Symphony Orchestra / Galling (piano) / Wagner (conductor) / Turnabout 34148

Smoothly conceived, its best feature is its set of variations. Whatever need be accomplished has been done in this attractive presentation.

Joseph Bodin de Boismortier   (1689-1755)

Concerto in D major for Bassoon, Op. 26

Solo Instrument and Orchestra

☐ Chamber Orchestra of Versailles / Allard (bassoon) / Wahl (conductor) / Nonesuch 71080

Bassoon

The Concerto in D major is from the composer's Opus 26, which consists of five sonatas "for the Violoncello, Viola, or Bassoon with Figured Bass" plus a "Concerto" calling for "One of the Other of These Instruments."

Boismortier's Concerto is actually a *concertette,* since each of its three movements lasts only two and one-half minutes. But they are enjoyable ones, even with their sequences and noodled figures.

Concerto in D major for Bassoon, String Orchestra, and Continuo

☐ Württemberg Chamber Orchestra, Heilbronn / Zukerman (bassoon) / Faerber (conductor) / Turnabout 34304

Boismortier's Concerto provides music that is in the usual early-eighteenth-century creative orbit. *Allegro–largo–allegro* spell out the speeds, with the bland telling of the facts enlivened, as it would be expected, by nicely turned figurations for the solo instrument. All of it is respectable music with a low profile, but with a guaranteed surety of falling gently and easily on the ears. Zukerman turns in a professional job, and the orchestra keeps the beats and harmonies straight.

Concerto in A minor for Five Flutes without Bass, Op. 15, No. 2

Five Flutes

☐ Rampal (flute) / Everest 3180

What a feat! The use of sound-on-sound techniques has produced recorded "self-duets" and "self-trios," but I cannot recall a "self-quintet." Furthermore, the production has been made so that there are dynamic contrasts and proper balances between the quintuple voices. Bravo, Rampal, indeed!

The composition is in the standard three-movement format: an Allegro in quadruple meter, a Largo in triple-pulse definition, and a concluding Allegro in the form of a gigue, in $\frac{6}{8}$ meter.

(Since only one performer is involved in this recorded setting, the composition has been placed here in the *Solo Instrument* category. Two other of the six works in Boismortier's Opus 15 have been recorded—they are discussed under *Chamber Music,* p. 254.)

Instrumental	**Suite No. 3 in E major, Op. 59**
Harpsichord	☐ Kipnis (harpsichord) / Columbia M3X-31521

This delightful five-part item is carried out with lively fancy. Each part bears a title, the most noteworthy being *La Puce* ("The Flea"). Even if the title matter is stretched considerably, such as in *La Belliqueuse* ("The Belligerent Person"), which trots along at a friendly and happy gait, the rococo sophistication is undeniable. Kipnis's all-embracing sweep and know-how of this music's style cannot be refuted; it's validated in every measure.

Chamber Music	**Sonata in G major for Flute and Clavecin, Op. 91**
	☐ Members of the Oberlin Baroque Ensemble / Vox SVBX-5142

The performance is an exquisite attestation of the values to be found in playing music of this composer's era on authentic period instruments. Robert Willoughby of the Oberlin group uses a one-key flute made in London about 1790. Its woody-wind sound is produced with impeccable intonation and phrasing and is supported by sensitive harpsichord playing by Lisa Goode Crawford. The rococo sparkle of Boismortier's Sonata refreshes the ears.

Concertos for Five Flutes, Op. 15

No. 1 in B minor / No. 3 in E minor

☐ Jean-Pierre and Joseph Rampal, Larrieu, Marion, and Beuf (flutes) / Musical Heritage Society MHS-876

Both Concertos follow the sequence of an Adagio followed by a pair of Allegros. Both follow the plan of sections of solo statement with tutti contrast. Included are flute-fat unison measures (a special timbre results).

No polemic is being made that these are musical masterpieces, but better performing quality would be impossible.

Cantata and Oratorio	**Cantata, *Diane et Actéon***
	☐ New York Chamber Soloists / Bressler (tenor) / Nonesuch 71159

Boismortier's cantata consists of folk-like airs (one *Gai*, another *Vif*, and the last *Tendre*) with a recitative prefacing each aria. Interpretative intelligence is shown by the lighter spirit that marks this rendition. The instrumental group consists of violin, cello, and harpsichord.

Arrigo Boito   *(1842 - 1918)*

Opera and Dramatic Music	***Mefistofele***
	☐ Orchestra and Chorus of the Accademia di Santa Cecilia / Tebaldi and Cavalli (sopranos); Danieli (contralto); del Monaco and di Palma (tenors); Siepi (bass) / Serafin (conductor) / London 1307
	☐ London Symphony Orchestra, Ambrosian Opera Chorus, and Wandsworth School Boys' Choir / Caballé and Ligi (sopranos); Begg and Wallis (mezzo-sopranos); Domingo and Fyson (tenors); Allen (baritone); Treigle (bass) / Rudel (conductor) / Angel 3806

There are profits and losses in both editions. In the title role, one would expect Norman Treigle to duplicate the success he scored in the New York City Opera production given in the 1969 season. Without stage action, however, his projection of *Mefistofele* is exceedingly flat in comparison to the vividness of Cesare Siepi's in the London recording. As Faust, Placido Domingo does not dig into the characterization. However, his singing is far superior to the stolid, unfluid vocalism of Mario del Monaco. Tebaldi's Margherita is richly portrayed, while Caballé is mostly fine except when she has to provide emotional depth.

The stand-off in the casts ceases in terms of the conducting. Tullio Serafin directs with sustained musicianship and undoubtedly does more with this uneven score than any other conductor. Rudel is academic in comparison. Although the London production is much older than the Angel edition, the sound of the former is truly imposing.

César Bolaños   (20th cent.)

Divertimento III (1967)

Chamber Music

☐ New Sound Composers-Performers Group / Lanza (conductor) / Mainstream MS–5017

Epigrammatic diversity drawn from the way-far-out timbre catalogue: percussion inserts, flute flutters, inside the piano percussion, seismographic guidance of single pitches, and so on. Added to these are mouth sounds, mutterings, and some speech fragments that fluctuate dynamically due to placement of the speaker. No longer revolutionary in concept, nonetheless Bolaños's piece is quite revelatory in its colorful structuring.

William Bolcom   (1938-   )

Commedia, for (almost) 18th-Century Orchestra (1971)

Orchestra

☐ Saint Paul Chamber Orchestra / Davies (conductor) / Nonesuch 71324

Evocative data constantly reminds the listener that it's all been heard before (Rossini, by God!) but with a special kind of constructive dovetailing. This is no pastiche. *Commedia* (the composer was influenced by the *commedia dell'arte* style) is good-humored, crystal-clear, and with some serious moments. It is imitative and yet original and the paradox is explained by the clever way Bolcom has used past sources. A ten-minute gem and played with enthusiastic deftness and gorgeous sound.

Black Host, for Organ, Percussion, and Tape

Instrumental

Organ

☐ Albright (organ); Hodkinson (percussion) / Nonesuch 71260

Black Host provides a rich combination of sacred and profane material, tonal and atonal, chorale and clusters, bells, and tape sounds, some flip-flop insert of vocal gibberish, and a segment of pure, open-hearted ragtime. Title or not, it seems clear what Bolcom is defining is the attitude of the defrocked related to the devout.

William Albright states in his liner note that if Bolcom's piece "is *about* anything, it would be fear." Accept that as you wish. The music has such impulse and pigmentation that it needs no other responsibility and can be heard in an absolute sense. Whatever, don't avoid it.

Piano

Graceful Ghost (1970)

Sea Biscuits (1967)

☐ Bolcom (piano) / Nonesuch 71257

Showing that piano rags still live, these are just as good as Scott Joplin's and sound that way.

Twelve Etudes (1966)

☐ Bolcom (piano) / Advance S-14

Bolcom traverses the hard and craggy ground that marks modern sonorous territory. He does so with rhythmic courage and harmonic daring. Each study projects a central problem. Some examples: No. 1, touch and dynamics; No. 5, quintal against quartal rhythms; number 11, line versus staccato. The results not only solve the inquiry, but satisfy the ear.

The piece is best heard in portions taken from the division of the opus into three "books," and not necessarily in their chronological order. This, despite the composer's note that the finale, an *Apotheosis—slow, with majesty (in memoriam Béla Bartók)*, uses "bits of practically every texture in the other eleven etudes."

Vocal

Voice and Orchestra

Open House (1975)

☐ Saint Paul Chamber Orchestra / Sperry (tenor) / Davies (conductor) / Nonesuch 71324

Bolcom's song cycle is set to seven poems by Theodore Roethke. It has variety, and in this respect eclectic styles can be recognized and tabbed by the learned. However, vaunted creative virtuosity is required to make a large work hang together, especially when it invokes "styles that range from Bach to Gershwin," as well as expressionism. Regardless, the cycle is telling and the recording is worth obtaining if only for the intimacy and deeply touching quality found in the last song, *The Right Thing*.

Bolcom and William Albright. *See Albright and William Bolcom.*

Claude Bolling   *(1930-   )*

Instrumental

Guitar and Piano

Concerto for Classic Guitar and Jazz Piano

☐ Bolling (piano); Lagoya (guitar); Gaudry (bass); Sabiani (drums) / RCA FRL1-0149

With Jean-Pierre Rampal, Bolling has recorded (on Columbia M-33233) a Suite for Flute and Jazz Piano. On the weekly list of "Best Selling Classical LPs" issued by *Billboard* it held its place for close to four years! Another parallel recording, a Suite for Violin and Jazz Piano, with Zukerman, Bolling, and two other musicians (as in the work listed above), was also a commercial success. It is also a Columbia issue, number M-35128.

The Concerto for Classic Guitar and Jazz Piano is Bolling's most representative work. It is an international mix of baroque-ish data with jazz, performed by an international mix of musicians. Interesting and innovative certainly, but whether it will intrigue and involve a listener is another matter. After all, such a hybrid is not especially unique.

Willem Frederik Bon (1940-)

Symphony No. 2 (*Les Prédictions*), Op. 38

Orchestra

☐ Radio Philharmonic Orchestra / Bon (conductor) / Donemus Audio-Visual Series 7374/1

Bon's symphony is based on a specific four-pitched chord. The possibilities within this element are described by the subtitle. Static sets of patterns are major to the music which is color frictioned and rhythmically slightly nervous. A well-stated public performance, led by the composer (on December 22, 1972), was used for producing the recording.

Jacques Bondon (1927-)

Kaleidoscope

Orchestra

☐ Chamber Orchestra for Contemporary Music / Loriod (ondes Martenot) / Bondon (conductor) / Musical Heritage Society MHS–988

In the 1930s this type of music would have accompanied a film like *The Phantom of the Opera*. Nowadays it is recognizable as the kind of score that would back up films dealing with outer space, extra-terrestrial worlds, and the science fiction genre. Not to downgrade Bondon's opus, but it has such musical mnemonics as it portrays seven scenes such as *The Phosphorescent Grotto, The Magic Moon*, and *The Monster*.

The electronic musical instrument that Jeanne Loriod uses fits in perfectly with this objective. The playing by Bondon's group is relevant.

Giovanni Bononcini (1670-1747)

Sinfonia No. 10

Orchestra

☐ Academy of St. Martin-in-the-Fields / Smithers and Laird (trumpets); Dupré (chitarrone); Preston (organ) / Marriner (conductor) / Philips 6500110

The Sinfonia here is one of a group of Sinfonie written by Bononcini at the age of fifteen. A variety of moods replaces the square-cut framework of three-part design. Further, the trumpets are not withheld from the slow-paced music, which makes for a fine symphonic totality. The performance is brilliant and strong.

Francesco Antonio Bonporti (1672-1748)

Invenzione **in G minor for Violin and Continuo, Op. 10, No. 4**

Chamber Music

☐ Gay des Combes (violin); Sgrizzi (harpsichord) / Nonesuch 73008

Bonporti's origination rarely falls into the formalized monotony of so many works of the period in which he worked. Two movements are devoted to dances, each preceded by a slow-paced division. The plan is conventional in totality, but there is an inquisitive conception throughout. Fluidly performed.

Charles Boone   (1939-   )

Instrumental

Flute

A Cool Glow of Radiation, for Flute and Tape

☐ Bernhard (flute) / Desto 7166

Boone's piece is both representative of fantasy and a rhapsody with tape sound corrugations. It is not serial but totally pitch-freed. In short, it is a contemporary-mannered statement that has the clichés of the post-Webern school but manages not to be smothered by them.

One assumes Barbara Bernhard is the flutist. Desto does not give any performer credit, merely a list of the names of the eight musicians who participate somehow in the three works covering the total release. Neither is the instrumentation for Boone's work indicated. Digging in the composer's note on the liner copy produces that important information.

Eugene Bordeau   (20th cent.)

Instrumental

Bassoon

Premier Solo for Bassoon and Piano

☐ Weiss (bassoon); Carno (piano) / Crystal S–354

Soloistic enlightenment, composed for contest purposes in connection with the Paris Conservatory. The French are great at this sort of thing. No great music is generally produced but good stuff for the player to show what he can do. Abraham Weiss can do.

David Borden   (1938-   )

Chamber Music

Six Dialogues for Trombone and Trumpet

☐ Sauer (trombone); Stevens (trumpet) / Crystal S–384

Six of the total fifteen Dialogues are offered here. Presentable counterpoint is heard in a clearly balanced performance.

Elliot Borishansky   (1930-   )

Instrumental

Clarinet

Two Pieces for Unaccompanied Clarinet (1964)

☐ Rehfeldt (clarinet) / Advance 15

Twelve-tone but handled freely so that technical formula does not crush expressive needs. Contrast here is in terms of pitch choices rather than mood.

Alexander Borodin   (1833-1887)

Orchestra

In the Steppes of Central Asia (1880)

☐ Philadelphia Orchestra / Ormandy (conductor) / Columbia MS-6875

Borodin has written a calm portrayal with no overstress that thereby bypasses atmosphere for vivid but blunt declaration. Less by Ormandy gives much more in this instance.

The Borodin piece is contained in an all-Russian program. It is also included in another all-Russian presentation on Columbia MS-6073.

Overture to *Prince Igor*

☐ London Symphony Orchestra / Dorati (conductor) / Mercury 75016

This is decidedly a top presentation of Borodin's work, which mostly is neglected in concert programs in favor of the Polovtzian Dances (*see below*). Dorati opts for a far less demanding tempo than most conductors choose. The music thereby sings and the more dramatic sections benefit accordingly.

(Borodin never completed his opera *Prince Igor*. It was planned to cover four acts, and Borodin began composing the work in 1869. Posthumous completion was accomplished by Rimsky-Korsakov and Glazunov, and the opera was given its premiere three years after Borodin's death.)

Polovtzian Dances from *Prince Igor*

☐ London Symphony Orchestra and Chorus / Solti (conductor) / London 6730
☐ London Festival Orchestra and Chorus / Black (conductor) / London 21003
☐ Philadelphia Orchestra / Ormandy (conductor) / Columbia MS-6958

Some problems present themselves here. Some performances are with chorus, others are not; *Schwann*, with its haphazard editing, doesn't always tell you. (One example: Ormandy on RCA CRL3-0985) has the Mendelssohn Club of Philadelphia supporting, but it's listed exactly as his Columbia performance, which is totally orchestral.) And there's the usual multiplicity of releases with different program combinations for merchandising purposes (four editions for Bernstein, four for Ormandy on two different labels, two for Szell, etc.). Finally, there is the truncated item, such as Bernstein (on Columbia M3X-31068), who gives a snippet (no indication in the liner notes!) of three and a half minutes compared to the average performance time of the conceptions for chorus and orchestra, or orchestra alone, of around twelve and a half minutes. In such a case, *Schwann* cannot be held responsible for listing an excerpt. If *Schwann* had been properly informed, one is certain it would have been eliminated from their catalogue.

The Solti reading (also on London 6785) is exciting and rhythmically supple. The natural delivery of Borodin's music provides all the required vitality in Black's edition. Ormandy's conception is an earthy, rightly gutsy one. No interpretive eccentricities to grab the gallery. It is also included on Columbia MS-6073 and in a two-record set that Columbia has issued (MG-30947).

Symphony No. 1 in E flat major (1867)

☐ Moscow Radio Symphony Orchestra / Rozhdestvensky (conductor) / Melodiya/Angel S-40182

As in the case of the *Prince Igor* Overture, inattention can do a disservice to a fine composition. There is no bombast in the Symphony, which has a superb sparkling Scherzo with a Trio that sings of old Russia as does the romantically evocative slow movement.

An excellent performance, containing the proper vigor where needed, and played so that the long lines are permitted to breathe properly. The pace taken in the pair of Allegro movements benefits the music.

Symphony No. 2 in B minor (1876)

☐ Vienna Philharmonic / Kubelik (conductor) / Seraphim S–60106

The general conductorial reaction to the first movement of Borodin's Symphony is to attack and plunge. But the music will not survive in such an atmosphere; a calmer exposure brings benefits. Kubelik may sound somewhat tame in comparison to other conductors' portrayals, but have faith: in the long run one will be fully satisfied. The same applies to the Scherzo, a fast (*prestissimo*) one-click-to-the-beat music. Kubelik drops the speed a few notches and the outlines become exceedingly sharp, and with a full quota of excitement. The rest of the work is just as affectionately (read: knowingly) viewed. All this provides a freshness to the score and makes for a compellingly powerful documentation. It is an interpretation that this writer wholeheartedly defends.

Symphony No. 3 (*Unfinished*) in A minor

☐ L'Orchestre de la Suisse Romande / Ansermet (conductor) / London STS–15149

Borodin had only sketched two movements of this Symphony in 1886; these were completed and orchestrated by Glazunov. Movement 1, charmingly played, is a moderately paced, poetic, somewhat motival conception. Movement 2 is a Scherzo, quintuply sprung in its meter. No complexities, merely neutral nationalistic character that Ansermet regards and plays respectfully.

Instrumental

At the Convent from *Petite Suite* (1885)

Piano

Serenade from *Petite Suite* (1885)

☐ Tarnowsky (piano) / Genesis 1004

The first piece offers Borodin as Borodin is, with some bell simulation and full Russian-flavored minor-key modality. Borodin has a neutral voice in the Serenade, which is properly propped with a guitar-like accompaniment to the melody.

Some explanations: these are the first and sixth pieces, respectively, from the piano suite Borodin composed in 1885. (There are no liner notes whatsoever on the music, simply a few lines of rather inane biographical generalities.) Glazunov made an orchestral transcription of the entire suite in 1889. Further, the Genesis listing credits the Serenade as an excerpt from the *Petite Suite*, but omits the extracted identification for *At the Convent*.

Chamber Music

String Quartet No. 1 in A major (1879)

☐ Borodin Quartet / Odyssey/Melodiya Y–33827

This rarely played quartet certainly deserves performance, if only as a change of musical diet from Borodin's overplayed String Quartet No. 2. The first Quartet was dedicated to Rimsky-Korsakov's wife, and in parallel fashion Borodin kept wives in mind, and in personal harmony, by dedicating the second Quartet to his own.

String Quartet No. 1 is *angeregt durch ein Thema von Beethoven*—i.e., "offshooted" from a Beethoven theme, that of the viola in the sixth (final) movement of Beethoven's Quartet No. 13 in B flat major, Op. 130. The resemblance is most apparent in the main theme of the Allegro proper of Borodin's first movement, which is preceded by a Moderato introduction. There are snatches of the original in several other places, but they are extremely fleeting.

There is an incorrect view on the part of many that Borodin was a writer only of long and lush themes, that he could not develop his material—that, in short, he was not a constructivist, but rather a pure melodist. While melody pervades every moment of this work, the critical generality of opinion is not borne out by this quartet. There is counterpoint aplenty—a fugato in movement 1, combination of themes in the same part of the work; the slow movement begins contrapuntally and also includes another fugato (this one in chromatic form); furthermore, the Scherzo, in trinal pulse, is motivally generated.

In terms of color Borodin has not been criticized. An example of his aptness takes place at the conclusion of the first movement, where the final cadence is constructed entirely from string harmonics, with their light-textured quality. Again, it is color, by way of sparkling harmonics, that makes a filmy Trio section (as refined as anything by Mendelssohn) in the third movement. The finale exhibits the Tartar-like, barbaric personality that permeated most of Borodin's vivid sections.

This is the first recording since the old monaural release of a performance by the Vienna Konzerthaus Quartet. Nicely played as that one was, this rendition is twice as good, and of course has sonic advantages that the deleted Westminster recording did not have. The ensemble is top-notch; the interpretation is first-class.

String Quartet No. 2 in D major (1887)

☐ Borodin Quartet / London STS-15046

The Borodiners style Borodin with ease, freedom, warmth, and (fortunately) lack of schmaltz. They take liberties—plenty of them—but they are fitting. Perhaps a hesitant type of *ritard,* rather than one scaled equally, can be criticized, but this is a minor point in a performance that oozes with lightness, cheerfulness, and full Slavic flavor.

The penumbral reiterations in the Nocturne (which, on Broadway, became "Kismetized") are beautifully portrayed. In the second movement the Borodin group plays with correct swing in place of the usual, incorrect pulsed bounce. And in the finale the simulation of organ and accordion sounds is the essence of Russian color.

Quintet in C minor for Two Violins, Viola, Cello, and Piano (1862)

☐ Panhoffer (piano); Fietz and Hübner (violins); Breitenbach (viola); Mihaly (cello) / London 6636

An odd coincidence marks this work. It took fifty-three years between the time it was composed (1862) and the time it was discovered (1915) in the materials left by the famous Russian music patron and publisher Mitrofan Belaiev. And it took the same time span of fifty-three years before it was published in the Soviet Union in 1968.

The Quintet has freshness in its three movements, even if it lacks a Borodinesque profile. More than once, however, a Russian tang flavors the music.

The members of the Vienna Octet present a well-integrated production. The symphonic thrust that sometimes bruises the playing of piano quintets is, fortunately, absent.

Borodin / **Malcolm Sargent (1895 - 1967)**

Nocturne (from String Quartet No. 2) for String Orchestra

Orchestra

☐ Philadelphia Orchestra / Ormandy (conductor) / Columbia MS-6224

Borodin's expressive melody, enriched by canonic treatment thereby doubling one's pleasure, was turned into one of the hit tunes in the musical *Kismet*. Ormandy presents it in a lovely manner, the voicing full but not sentimentally lush. Other packages also contain his performance (Columbia MS-6575 and M-30066).

Felix Borowski   (1872-1956)

Orchestra   **The Mirror (1954)**

☐ Louisville Orchestra / Whitney (conductor) / Louisville 56–2 (monaural)

Quite different from the old favorite, *Adoration,* which until World War II was played by every fiddle student and restaurant trio. *The Mirror* is described in the liner notes as "a reflection of the soul of the beholder who, looking into the glass, sees something which moves him to emotions that are vivid and perturbing."

Whitney and his musicians play this romantically tissued work with full zeal.

Sergei Bortkiewicz   (1877-1952)

Instrumental   **Etude, Op. 15, No. 8**

Piano   ☐ Rosenthal (piano) / Klavier 108

The Etude is like a Puccini aria, with dramatic *brio,* orchestral-like use of the piano, and romantic passion. It is played passionately by this brilliant virtuoso.

Travel Pictures

☐ Nyiregyházi (piano) / Columbia M–35125

The set of three *Travel Pictures* covers Poland, Venice, and Spain. Bortkiewicz's style is a mix of Germanic romanticism with Russian melos.

Giovanni Bottesini   (1821-1889)

Solo
Instrument
and
Orchestra   **Grand Duo Concertante for Violin, Double Bass, and Strings**

☐ I Musici / Vicari (violin); Buccarella (double bass) / Philips 6500245

Violin
and Double
Bass   Most of the eight movements in this concerted duet consist of unabashed Italian operaticisms, strictly of the tune and accompaniment category. Sincere in its own way, of course, it charms the ear that wants to relax from intellectualism. It will be considered a campish commodity by some, but it truly is not trite and therefore offers light refreshment.

The performance is splendidly articulate and beautifully disciplined without being heavily serious. Marvelous sound.

André Boucourechliev   (1925-   )

Instrumental   **Archipel IV (1970)**

Piano   ☐ Collard (piano) / Philips 6504112

An open-form work that combines defined notation with improvisation by the performer. (The first of the series, *Archipel I,* calls for two pianists and two percussionists; *Archipel II* is for string quartet; *Archipel III* is for piano and six percussionists.)

The Bulgarian composer does not spare the sonorous horses in his work, some of the passages equating an orchestral torrent of sound. These are in sharp contrast to a huge variety of pianistic colors. The piece is highly difficult, but Catherine Collard conquers it. She also must be given top creative credits for her share in shaping the work.

Archipel II (1968)

Chamber Music

☐ Parrenin Quartet / Musical Heritage Society MHS–1228

Bulgarian-born Boucourechliev (a French citizen since 1956) has written a number of *Archipels* ("Archipelagoes") for various media. Usually, because these are open-form, mobile works, more than a single realization is heard in public performance. But only one is presented in this strikingly recorded essay, which covers almost twenty-two and one-half minutes.

Unlimited fantasy is made available by providing two different scores for each player—one of material more framed, contained, and static; the other uncovering timbre research that percusses, slides, wails, and shivers (among other things). Serialized statistical distribution is like salonistic music in comparison. The abstract imagery made possible fascinates the ear. So does this performance, in which one is certain of the Parrenin Quartet's complete involvement.

Lili Boulanger

(1893-1918)

Cortège

Instrumental

D'un Vieux Jardin

Piano

☐ Fierro (piano) / Avant 1012

A light-hearted rather than a stately procession is delineated in the first of the pair noted above. An impressionistic luminosity describes the second piece.

Cortège

Nocturne in F

Violin

☐ Heifetz (violin); Achron (piano) / RCA ARM4–0942 (monaural)

The *Cortège* reminds one of early Debussy, while the Nocturne in F illustrates a female Fauré. Nonetheless, they are charming examples in the miniature class.

The recordings are very old (made in 1924). As far as this writer can ascertain, no other versions are available. So, for the sake of the music and the specialness of Heifetz's playing, just make do with the very inferior sound, especially of the piano.

Pierre Boulez

(1925-   )

Livre pour cordes (1969)

String Orchestra

☐ Strings of the New Philharmonia Orchestra / Boulez (conductor) / Columbia M–32160

Boulez's *Livre* began as the string quartet *Livre pour quatuor* (discussed under *Chamber Music*, p. 264), which Boulez has now deleted. But the recording of portions of it lives on. Totally recomposed, the work presently exists in two parts for string orchestra (but with Boulez, who tends to constantly add and subtract from his published works, there may be more to come or less to have). These two parts are a Variation movement and another titled *Mouvement*.

Pungently and plangently serial and vigorously timbred, the music's philosophy is its science. A splendid presentation.

Instrumental

Piano

Piano Sonata No. 2 (1948)

☐ Pollini (piano) / Deutsche Grammophon 2530803

Boulez's imposing sonata may sound like a fleeting improvisation, but it is planets removed from the unpredictable. The structures here do not reflect the thesis-antithesis found in the traditional sonata format, yet parallel conflicts are maintained, albeit in a widely different manner. In the Boulez manner these pertain to speeds, rhythms (regularity versus independence of metrical signification), textures, and the highly motivic material itself. The general tempo definition of each of the four movements bears out a further affinity with what the term "Sonata" calls to mind: *extrêmement rapide* ("extremely fast"), *lent* ("slow"), *modéré, presque vif* ("moderate, almost lively"), and *très librement, avec de brusques oppositions de mouvement et de nuances* ("very freely, with brusque oppositions of movement and nuances").

This work is fearfully difficult to play from a technical point of view, and just as horrendous in interpretative demands. Throughout, there are various types of tension, and in realizing their differences the performance is very good. The falseness of playing music of this type in piecemeal fashion has been totally avoided. For these matters alone Maurizio Pollini deserves first-rank billing. That one can argue about a few other matters does not detract from this high rating.

Chamber Music

Sonatine for Flute and Piano (1946)

☐ Gazzelloni (flute); Rzewski (piano) / RCA VICS–1312

The *Sonatine* is a compound of serial and rhythmic elements outlining a fully drawn sonata within a single unit. This is twelve-tone music to be sure, but minus any smug conformity to rules of dodecaphonic textbooks. Technical and dramatic ingredients are mixed. Though there are restrictive functions because of the compositional system employed, these do not interfere with the commentary of Boulez's musical tale.

His twelve-tone world communicates with a language of extreme line-skipping and violent register-changing; the flute is unharnessed so that it growls, shrieks, and rolls its sounds as much as it sings them. This drains out the usual intimacy of chamber music and replaces it with fevered instrumental dialogue.

Interpretation? Performance? As far as flute playing of contemporary music is concerned, Severino Gazzelloni sits astride the world. Frederic Rzewski has the same stature.

Livre pour quatuor (excerpts) (1949)

☐ Parrenin Quartet / Musical Heritage Society MHS–1228
☐ Parrenin Quartet and Hamann Quartet / Mainstream 5009

As noted above (under *String Orchestra*), this "Book for Quartet" has been eliminated from Boulez's catalogue. The prerogative is his, of course, but the music is fascinating and fantastically strong; it defines, in its serial chemistry, loud and bold, soft and spidery generative sound elements. Let us enjoy what we have minus his permission.

The *Livre* is divided into "chapters," which in turn are subdivided into "parts." Each part concentrates on a certain musical element. Thus part 1 is in two sections, in fast and slow tempi; part 3 is divided into three portions, and so on. Chapter 1 deals with serial application to timbres, part 1 of chapter 3 covers durations serially constructed, and part 3 of chapter 3 details intensities and attacks based on twelve-tone structuring.

Both of these issues are splendid. In the Musical Heritage album the Parrenins play parts 1-a and 1-b, 3-a, 3-b, and 3-c, and part 5. On the Mainstream album they perform parts 1-a and 1-b, but add part 2, which is the only portion not available on the MHS release. Finally, Mainstream's issue is most interesting in that part 5 is played by a different quartet team.

Le Marteau sans maître (1955)

☐ Ensemble Musique Vivante / Minton (mezzo-soprano) / Boulez (conductor) / Columbia M-32160

Despite its scoring for only seven performers (a solo voice and six instrumentalists) Boulez's work has imposing symphonic qualities.

Boulez's opus comprises nine movements; four are settings of three surrealistically styled poems by René Char. The other portions are instrumental commentaries on the texts. These commentaries are matters before and after the vocally stated facts; once employed, they are disassembled. Each movement is scored differently, ranging from the third movement for voice and flute duo, to the final movement, which calls for the complete ensemble. The dream-world interchange of the poems sets the key for the composition. The French language is quite syllabic, but in Boulez's hands the words turn into sound images as their meaning is deliberately disintegrated, making a seventh instrument, as it were.

Marteau can be considered neo-impressionistic serialism. Though it is a far cry from the music of Schoenberg and Webern, it is remotely related to the former by fantasy, and somewhat to the latter by the use of sonic pulverization. The peripatetic, dissected rhythms are also reminders of the nervousness found in the Stravinsky domain. However, there are no intrusive recognizable duplicates of any of these composers; the fluid result is pure Boulez—a music of perpetual variation in color and pitch. *Le Marteau sans maître* is a plastic transformation of strict serial composition. Its music stings while it expresses a Freudian world in sound.

With Boulez conducting, "The Hammer Without a Master" is displayed in a definitive fashion. The disc is far superior to both the other versions that are current and those out-of-print issues that might be obtained. The sound is extremely bright—a Boulez decision?

Pli selon pli (1960)

☐ B.B.C. Symphony Orchestra / Lukomska (soprano); Bergmann (piano); Stingl (guitar); d'Alton (mandolin) / Boulez (conductor) / Columbia M-30296

There is almost unanimous opinion that Boulez's *Pli selon pli* ("Fold by Fold") is one of the major works of the twentieth century. It consists of a huge five-part structure in which the central section is a set of three *Improvisations sur Mallarmé*, for voice and chamber ensemble, heavy on the percussion. Both part 1 (*Don*) and part 5 (*Tombeau*) contain a smidgen of vocal participation and are for full orchestra.

Major to the conception is the tintinnabular quality, particularly in the central sections with voice. The soprano part, mostly in fragmented phrasing, projects the *formal* essence of the Mallarmé texts, but does not define their meaning—Boulez does not musically set the poems. Not only does this partially explain the *Pli selon pli* title (voice

Vocal

*Voice
and
Instrumental
Ensemble*

*Voice
and Orchestra*

line folded, as it were, on words), but it describes the piecemeal situation that builds the composition by consecutive layering of orchestra-voice-orchestra, as well as by the constant transformation of shapes and timbres. A bit of mysticism—expressed in some of the numerical devices Boulez used when composing the piece—gets wrapped into the concept. However, the total effect of the composition is far beyond mysticism in the Debussyan, somewhat Messiaenistic, world that Boulez takes over for himself.

Boulez, the expert conductor of things contemporary, is fully at home with the dynamic poetry and driven complexity of Boulez, the composer. An authoritative recording, without a single doubt. Halina Lukomska is very good, having mastered the excruciatingly difficult vocal part. The sound is brilliantly sharp, defining every timbre nuance of this quite remarkable score.

Cantata and Oratorio

Le Soleil des eaux (1948)

☐ B.B.C. Symphony Orchestra and Chorus / Nendick (soprano); McDaniel (tenor); Devos (bass) / Boulez (conductor) / Argo ZRG–756

The two pieces that comprise *Le Soleil des eaux* were written to poems by René Char, the first for soprano and orchestra, the other for three solo voices, chorus, and orchestra. The voices (solo and concerted) form a miniature body of a special type, including speaking, shrieking, and glissandi which move from normal vocal attack to speaking. The orchestration is super-detailed, most often fragmented but with a difference from Webernian depiction, since Boulez uses a much greater heaviness in his instrumental dispositions. The rhythmic limpidity, plus the flow and ebb, define the work as of the spiked-fence Debussy world.

Despite the fact of Boulez conducting Boulez, a few details are buried and glossed over. Nevertheless, this is an important performance of important music.

Paul Bowles   (1910-   )

Instrumental

Piano

Six Preludes

☐ Johannesen (piano) / Golden Crest S–4065

Lyrical wisdom for the most part, jazzy obedience in Nos. 4 and 5. The more one hears Paul Bowles's music, the more one regrets he has shifted his creative talents to the writing field.

Chamber Music

Music for a Farce (1938)

☐ Glazer (clarinet); Mueller (trumpet); Masselos (piano); Bailey (percussion) / Columbia Special Products AML–4845 (monaural)

A breezy entertainment, this. At times it is a reminder of music rasped out by a three-piece combo from the dim past, accompanying a silent film (not the drama, but the comedy on the bill). In one place old palm-garden music is brought to mind (the waltz in movement 5). Always the shadows of Satie and the early *Les Six* days come to mind. Bowles's pieces are so artistically corny they're gorgeous and beautiful.

The players must have had real fun producing Bowles's great spoof. It sounds like it.

Blue Mountain Ballads

☐ Gramm (baritone); Cumming (piano) / Desto 6411/2

A set of four—*Cabin, Heavenly Grass, Lonesome Man,* and *Sugar in the Cane*. Pedants and chi-chi sophisticates will probably criticize the sequential equality of phrase lengths in these songs. Further, they doubtless will argue that art songs shouldn't be made up of *tunes,* with thesis responded to by balanced antithesis. These qualities will be found in this set of exquisite songs to words by Tennessee Williams. Would that more composers of art songs were similarly guilty!

The true point in this case is that Bowles's lyrical meditations succeed marvelously in fulfilling his objective. Ballads they are, and real ballads remain pertinent only when simple style is maintained (as Bowles has done) minus any overly anxious creative curiosity.

The Gramm performance is fully understanding of this precept. Together with his pianist he treats these songs properly, as composed folk songs. Two of the group (*Cabin* and *Heavenly Grass*) are included in a Duke University Press album, *The Art Song in America,* sung by the tenor John Hanks, with Ruth Friedberg at the piano (DWRM-7501, a monaural release). However, not only in terms of better sound and greater coverage is the Desto recording the preferred one. Gramm's voice is fuller and warmer than Hanks's, and his delivery is far steadier.

Once a Lady Was Here

Song of an Old Woman

☐ Gramm (baritone); Hassard (piano) / New World Records NW-243

Interestingly, Bowles wrote the words for *Once a Lady,* and his late wife wrote the text for the other song. Hearing these examples and remembering that Bowles turned away from composition and achieved success as a writer, one realizes that the literary world's gain was music's loss. The poignancy of the songs reflects Bowles's superb gift for vocal composition.

Scènes d'Anabase (1932)

☐ Hess (tenor); Marx (oboe); Masselos (piano) / Columbia Special Products AML–4845 (monaural)

Five songs with a slight use of Moroccan intonations. No texts offered.

William Boyce (1711-1779)

Overture to His Majesty's Birthday Ode 1769

Overture to His Majesty's Birthday Ode 1775

Overture to *Peleus and Thetis*

Overture to The Birthday Ode 1768

Overture to The New Year's Ode 1758

Overture to The New Year's Ode 1772

☐ Lamoureux Orchestra / Lewis (conductor) / Oiseau-Lyre 60041

Interesting Boyce material edited by Gerald Finzi. The Lamoureux Orchestra's performance is an appropriate account of the music.

Symphony

No. 1 in B flat major / No. 2 in A major / No. 3 in C major / No. 4 in F major / No. 5 in D major / No. 6 in F major / No. 7 in B flat major / No. 8 in F major

☐ Menuhin Festival Orchestra / Menuhin (conductor) / Angel S-36951

Boyce's symphonies (all in three movements, except No. 6) are, for the most part, cheerful and extrovert. There isn't a minor tonality that defines any of them. Handel comes to mind, but it is worth remembering Burney's statement that Boyce's works had "original and sterling merit," and that he "neither pillaged nor servilely imitated Handel."

The symphonies were fashioned from the overtures Boyce had composed for various odes and operas. Thus the first of the set was originally the overture to a 1756 New Year's Ode; the fourth of the group was initially the overture to an operetta, *The Shepherd's Lottery*. Basically, the scoring is for strings and continuo, with interspersion of two flutes, two oboes, one or two bassoons, and occasionally a pair of horns. In the fifth of the set two trumpets and timpani are utilized.

Of the integral sets now available the Menuhin-led collection possesses beautiful flow and healthy contrast without any pendantism. Balances are all they should be, and above all there is the textural truth the music demands, including a properly pronounced continuo. *See below* for a partial selection of these works.

Symphony

No. 1 in B flat major / No. 4 in F major

☐ English Chamber Orchestra / Hurwitz (conductor) / London STS-15013

Those who prefer less than the total set of Boyce's symphonies would do well to consider these. The playing is ideal. In comparison with the Menuhin performances (*see above*), the tempi are brisker but just as propitious.

Hurwitz uses the Constant Lambert editions, which were the first modern ones. Menuhin utilizes an edition prepared by Neville Boyling.

Chamber Music

Trio Sonata

No. 2 in F major / No. 8 in E flat major / No. 9 in C major / No. 12 in G major

☐ Latchem and Brown (violins); Ryan (cello); Lumsden (harpsichord) / CMS/Oryx 1729

Stanley Sadie's statement that these works "stand unchallenged at the head of English chamber music of the eighteenth century" cannot be challenged.

There is no dry formal repetition in Boyce's Trio Sonatas. The Sonata No. 12 has only two movements, the others four. Among the latter a *Siciliana* and a brisk Minuet are used in No. 8, a *Fuga* and a canonic movement are contained in No. 9, and a *Bourrée* (marked *Tempo di gavotta!*) concludes the last of the set.

Acceptable performances, though more tension and a slightly increased drive would not be out of place.

Martin Boykan (1931-)

String Quartet No. 1 (1967)

Chamber Music

☐ Contemporary Quartet / Composers Recordings S–338

An exploration of serial devices in which the sentiments are very coolly displayed. Boykan's solutions are responsible ones though the language is never bold, consisting principally of static and dynamic tension points. We can, at this point, call some serialism classic, other serialism romantic. Boykan's is an ascetic offshoot of the latter.

Eugène Bozza (1905-)

Aria

Instrumental

Saxophone

☐ Brodie (saxophone); Brough (piano) / Golden Crest 7028 (monaural)

An example of the lyrical qualities of the saxophone. Deftly accomplished.

***Sonatine* for Flute and Bassoon**

Chamber Music

☐ Skowronek (flute); Grossman (bassoon) / Crystal 351

Ibertian alertness illustrating French-styled flexibility. Everything is appropriate for the instruments in their single parts and in their skeletonic combination.

These are two superb woodwind-instrument artists. They provide the happiest of performance situations.

***Sonatine* for Brass**

☐ New York Brass Quintet / Golden Crest S–4023

Bozza treats his five brass instruments as though they were woodwinds. No problem for the New York team. Bozza's language is crystal clear (French crystal), tight, musical, and hell-bent for virtuosity. His work is in the genre of Francaix's and Ibert's output. It would be difficult to imagine a performance as slick (properly so) as this one.

Variations sur un thême libre

☐ New York Woodwind Quintet / Counterpoint/Esoteric 505 (monaural)

No variational ambiguity in this case. Each of the compartments of the structure is clearly defined. The performance, even with the slightly dated sound, is styled to perfection, serious when it should be, elsewhere colored by typical French *savoir-faire*.

Johannes Brahms (1833-1897)

Academic Festival Overture, Op. 80

Orchestra

☐ Cleveland Orchestra / Szell (conductor) / Columbia MS-6965

Rhythmically etched to the finest detail but without oversharpening the edges. The mellowness remains in the music's flow. The inner lines move organically, and the entire production is a Brahmsian beauty. Second choices are Bruno Walter's accounts on Odyssey Y–32225 (with the Symphony No. 3) and on Odyssey Y–30851 (with the Variations on a Theme of Haydn and the Tragic Overture).

Hungarian Dances: Nos. 1-7, 10-12, 15, 17-21

☐ London Symphony Orchestra / Dorati (conductor) / Mercury 75024

There are five transcribers, including Brahms himself, involved in this orchestral compilation, which covers sixteen of the total twenty-one Hungarian Dances Brahms composed for piano duet. (See under *Instrumental: piano, four hands* for a discussion of the works and the data covering transcribers.)

The orchestral versions make key shifts in three instances: Nos. 5, 6, and 10. In each case the original tonality has been raised a half tone, thus permitting a more open sonority (for example, D major, with two sharps, rather than D flat, requiring five flats).

Not that a Hungarian is guaranteed to be the best conductor of Hungarian-styled music, but in Dorati's case interpretative empathy is fully realized. He deals with the music with a masterful hand, and with a feeling that warms the ear. There is vitality in the playing that is irresistible. There is subtlety as well. Reiner, and he alone, comes close (another case of a Hungarian understanding this music!), but on London STS–15009 he offers less than half the number of Dances available on the Mercury release. Reiner directs Nos. 1, 5-7, 13, 19, and 21. Only one of these Dances (No. 13) is not represented on the L.S.O. disc (*see below*).

Hungarian Dance No. 13

☐ Vienna Philharmonic Orchestra / Reiner (conductor) / London STS–15009

Not on the Dorati Hungarian Dances assortment (*see above*). Warm results—in fact, perfect ones.

Serenade No. 1 in D major, Op. 11

☐ London Symphony Orchestra / Kertész (conductor) / London 6567

Ah, sweet mysteries of symphonic-program-making life! Why the neglect of this truly masterful work in favor of the four symphonies? Perhaps listening to this outstanding demonstration will set the record straight. Istvan Kertész's spaciously masterful portrayal displays Brahms's autumnal colorations perfectly, and the word is not used unguardedly. The music has seldom, if ever, been expressed so beautifully. Triply recommended.

Serenade No. 2 in A major, Op. 16

☐ London Symphony Orchestra / Kertész (conductor) / London 6594
☐ Berlin Philharmonic Orchestra / Abbado (conductor) / Deutsche Grammophon 139371

Both are delightfully perceptive presentations. There is little choice between these two performances, with the exception of a slightly weightier texture in the *Adagio non troppo* of the Abbado edition. Both conductors hold the Scherzo to a comfortable, vivacious speed instead of giving it a breakneck tempo, and wend their way through the final Rondo with a light touch, keeping the sounds on the move.

These performances being at an equal level, the couplings may decide the choice. In that case, Kertész moves well up front. An unbeatable performance of the Dvořák wind instruments–cello–bass Serenade in D minor, Op. 44, is his companion work. On D.G. the much shorter Academic Festival Overture is the offering, and it has certain faults, especially limp rhythmic playing.

Symphony

No. 1 in C minor, Op. 68 / No. 2 in D major, Op. 73 / No. 3 in F major, Op. 90 / No. 4 in E minor, Op. 98

☐ Berlin Philharmonic Orchestra / von Karajan (conductor) / Deutsche Grammophon 27121002
☐ Cleveland Orchestra / Szell (conductor) / Columbia D3S–758

Obviously, no integral set can be all things for all people, but if one wishes the four Brahms symphonies in one package, these two choices are choice in most respects.

There is fine immediacy, precision, and vividness in the von Karajan readings. Although there are touches of overemphasized contextual points rather than blended balances, these do not negate the basic stylistic discipline of the performances. Breadth there always is—in phrase scale as well as tempi.

Precision can always be expected in George Szell's conducting, and it does not take away fluency. His performances of the Brahms symphony cycle are wholesomely rich. Especially significant is that counterpoints *are* counterpoints and not strongly urged to become leading voices. The textures are not filed but rounded, and *non troppo* aspects are maintained. Under Szell's direction the narrative-dramatic element in the Brahms scores is cultivated expertly and beautifully.

Symphony No. 1 in C minor, Op. 68

☐ Philharmonia Orchestra / Klemperer (conductor) / Angel S–35481
☐ Vienna Philharmonic Orchestra / Kertész (conductor) / London 6836
☐ Concertgebouw Orchestra / Haitink (conductor) / Philips 6500519

A healthy parcel of editions is on hand for this work, separate from its inclusion in the many complete offerings available of the four Brahms Symphonies. Klemperer's version is ideal—voiced big and remarkably steady, so that the inner pulses are provided by the music itself rather than by anxiety about tempi; the quality is deep, impressed into the texture, and most impressive. There is no question that Klemperer is the first interpretative choice. Through his command one hears a remarkable documentation of Brahms's masterpiece.

Kertész's rendition is beautifully shaped, with verve and fervor—this is a more emotional Brahms. Haitink's entry is powerful and consistent, obtaining a spaciousness in the music by broad tempi though avoiding any pedestrianism. The rhythmic smartness in the playing is a special adjunct to this fine performance.

Here are reactions to some of the other editions in the catalogue that are not included in the complete sets of the symphonies. Horenstein (Vox 510690): good conducting, undernourished orchestra. Krips (London STS–15144): steady as steady goes but causes no excitement. Levine (RCA ARL1–1326): mannerisms and un-Brahmsian effects galore, noisy beginning and twice as noisy ending. Munch (RCA VICS–1062): smooth sometimes, but superficial always. Steinberg (Westminster Gold 8166): full reliance on tradition but aloof, and sometimes tired. Stokowski (London 21131 and London 21090/91): this is a joining of two live performances, and it shows in the sound quality; otherwise it's Stokowski making great music even though it's not always great Brahmsian music.

Symphony No. 2 in D major, Op. 73

☐ Concertgebouw Orchestra / Haitink (conductor) / Philips 6500375

No overexpansive processes. Haitink plays warmly, engendering a golden-brown coloration for this symphony. The warmth breaks out into radiance when required. Importantly, the finale is taken at a pace that is outward looking and never tight-fisted in pace.

Symphony No. 3 in F major, Op. 90

☐ Concertgebouw Orchestra / Szell (conductor) / Turnabout THS–65003E (monaural)

This symphony emphatically needs, in its initial movement, a Klemperian type of breadth of line and moderated tempo so that it unfolds properly. Excessive vigor is defeating. The mensural accents belong *in* the sounds, not inserted from the top, as it were. Szell's authority reveals these points beautifully. Expansivity and spaciousness remain constant throughout and thus provide an account that is one of the best versions in the catalogue.

Symphony No. 4 in E minor, Op. 98

☐ Columbia Symphony Orchestra / Walter (conductor) / Odyssey Y–32373

Subdued excitement brings the greatest returns in Walter's dignified conception of Brahms's final symphony. The tempo depiction in the Passacaglia should be given concentrated listening time by all young conductors. This *might* have helped Stokowski, who turns in a beautifully erratic performance with the New Philharmonia on RCA ARL1–0719.

Tragic Overture, Op. 81

☐ Columbia Symphony Orchestra / Walter (conductor) / Odyssey Y–30851
☐ Berlin Philharmonic Orchestra / von Karajan (conductor) / Angel SB–3838

Either way is satisfactory: in the more restrained manner (classical) or in the more extrovert way (romantic). For the former choose Walter, whose pace gives the central section a beautiful burnished quality. For the latter your man is von Karajan, who opens up the music and is slightly more passionate about it.

Walter's performance is packaged with other Brahms music (the Variations on a Theme of Haydn and the Academic Festival Overture). On Odyssey Y–31924 it is coupled with the Symphony No. 2, and on Columbia MS–6158 it is included with the Concerto for Violin, Cello, and Orchestra.

Variations on a Theme of Haydn, Op. 56a

☐ Cleveland Orchestra / Szell (conductor) / Columbia MS–6685
☐ London Symphony Orchestra / Monteux (conductor) / London STS–15188

Within this Brahms piece one finds that conductors are good only here and there, since the piece is of sectional formation and mood differences. However, Szell masterfully structures the components of the piece but still provides an entity in which the effect builds from the very start to the concluding sound. His performance is together with the third symphony. On Columbia MS–6965 it is part of a triple bill, the other works being the Tragic and Academic Festival overtures.

Monteux's reading is lighter-scaled, yet supple. At the same time there is never any loss of definition of content or form.

See also under *Instrumental: two pianos.*

Concerto No. 1 in D minor for Piano and Orchestra, Op. 15

*Solo
Instrument
and
Orchestra*

Piano

☐ London Symphony Orchestra / Curzon (piano) / Szell (conductor) / London 6329
☐ Cleveland Orchestra / Rudolf Serkin (piano) / Szell (conductor) / Columbia MS-7143

Most pianists storm the score of this work. Notwithstanding, the total effect falls far short of presenting the meaty dramaticism of the piece. But placidity is not the way either, since that is also empty of the Concerto's firm proposals.

A properly proportioned mixture of the two viewpoints gives the Brahms opus its proper setting. Both Curzon and Serkin (with Szell conducting, which is far better than Serkin's partnership with Ormandy, who does not furnish the richest balance) exhibit a juxtaposition of the emotive substance and resoluteness of the work. Thereby they avoid the stereotyped blustery response mentioned at the beginning of this note.

Szell is the superb conductor for both of these chosen performances that exhibit balanced song and strife. He is certainly out front in the competition, since he is the conductor for a third edition that comes quite close to the pair listed, with Leon Fleisher as the soloist on Odyssey Y–31273. Again, the incomparably polished Cleveland Orchestra is concerned.

Serkin's performance, with Szell, is also obtainable on Columbia MG–31421, where it is paired with Brahms's second piano concerto. (The Serkin-Ormandy presentation mentioned above is on Columbia D3S–741.)

Concerto No. 2 in B flat major for Piano and Orchestra, Op. 83

☐ Royal Philharmonic Orchestra / Gelber (piano) / Kempe (conductor) / Connoisseur Society 2088
☐ Berlin Philharmonic Orchestra / Gilels (piano) / Jochum (conductor) / Deutsche Grammophon 2530259
☐ Philadelphia Orchestra / Rubinstein (piano) / Ormandy (conductor) / RCA LSC-3253

Good performances of this concerto remain as constant as the audiences that make haste to hear still another presentation of Brahms's masterpiece. It is well to bear in mind that this concerto is heard at its best when its virtuosic material is calmly presented, thereby underscoring its poeticism. This poses no paradox. There is more dazzle brought forth by implication in this case than by a direct, highly charged approach. Thus the virtuosity in Gelber's playing is full-steamed but channeled through a luminous singing tonal quality. Great warmth results, and the poetic temperature is splendid. Kempe's direction blends perfectly. The performance of this team is one of the very best ever recorded.

The above does not negate the value of the large-scale announcement. It is present in Gilels's edition, containing full identification with Brahmsian style and excellent sentiment. Metronomic cohesion that stymies flow is absent; the natural momentum of the music is maintained.

The special points in this performance (also on Deutsche Grammophon 2707064, where it is coupled with Brahms's first piano concerto) are the manner in which the second subject of the second movement is sung forth, the dreamy discourse that braces the slow movement, and the rhythmically polished drive of the finale. All these elements are beautifully and cogently produced without negating the grand design that covers Brahms's monumental concerto. (Not listed but to be remembered is another Gilels performance, with Reiner and the Chicago Symphony Orchestra, on RCA VICS–1026. It has more ardor but less poetry than the essay with Jochum.)

Rubinstein formulates the music clearly in the Brahms tradition, with no reluctance for full and free flow in the lyrical passages and no evidence of strain in the dynamic ones. The naturalness of the latter are ideal and very appealing. The soft dynamic planes are beautiful, with no timbre fuzz, and the lines are sung with aliveness. Both of the corner movements are portrayed with grandeur. This is a truly magnificent solo edition matched by Ormandy's masterly conducting.

Here too there are two packages of the same rendition. The other is a jumbo seven-disc affair on RCA CRL7-0725. Again there is also the chosen soloist with another conductor, in this case Krips, but the momentum is not maintained when it should be, and the orchestra is not as deep-toned as one would wish. This version covers two different packages on the RCA label (VCS-7088 and VCS-7071).

Violin

Concerto in D major for Violin and Orchestra, Op. 77

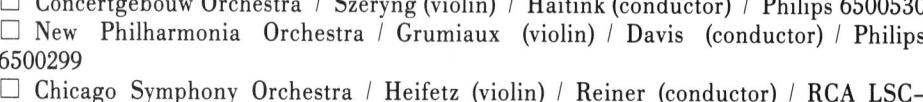

☐ Concertgebouw Orchestra / Szeryng (violin) / Haitink (conductor) / Philips 6500530
☐ New Philharmonia Orchestra / Grumiaux (violin) / Davis (conductor) / Philips 6500299
☐ Chicago Symphony Orchestra / Heifetz (violin) / Reiner (conductor) / RCA LSC-1903

All the romantic confidences are relayed by Henryk Szeryng and without pompous *rubati* and rhapsodic excess. His tone is winy rich, and the interpretation is deeply felt and rich. An older Szeryng production is still on the lists, with Monteux and the London Symphony (on RCA VICS-1028), which is almost the new edition's equal.

What is enticing about Arthur Grumiaux's reading is its nobility, and like Szeryng he avoids fluctuations in his interpretation. The Brahms masterpiece sounds best when the tone is creamy, not when it is either chicken-fatted or severely Germanic and restrained. Grumiaux finds the proper ingredients. In both his case and that of Szeryng the orchestral support is beautifully clear and of undeviating musicality.

Heifetz's greatness is made compellingly clear in his inspired playing of this work. Add to that the word "unerring." Without any cloying or any sugar coating, the performance has a sweet strength that is captivating—and, further, bravura that is controlled. Reiner's part in the proceedings is ideal.

The Heifetz-Reiner contribution is also available in a two-disc release, together with the Mendelssohn and Tchaikovsky violin concerti on RCA VCS-7058. Another coupling is with the Brahms second piano concerto (Rubinstein, with Krips and the RCA Symphony on RCA VCS-7088). Finally, the Heifetz-Reiner rendition is obtainable in a six-disc anthology (CRL6-0720) with nine other concerti, all played by Heifetz with various orchestras and conductors. Take your pick.

Violin and Cello

Concerto in A minor for Violin, Cello, and Orchestra, Op. 102

☐ Philadelphia Orchestra / Stern (violin); Rose (cello) / Ormandy (conductor) / Columbia MS-7251

Composers have tried, but the only successful double concerto for violin and cello remains the Brahms. There are no weaknesses in the score. It has fine writing that fits each of the solo instruments, colorful give-and-take between the pair, meaningful contrapuntal data, and eminently suitable orchestration.

Every detail and every nuance in the work are beautifully printed in this version, but not at the expense of the score's muscle and lyrical beauty. Further, there's Ormandy and the marvelous Philadelphia Orchestra; the result is a musical event of profound importance and meaning. The only near competitors are Szeryng and Starker with Haitink conducting the Concertgebouw (Philips 6500137). But sometimes Szeryng is a bit subdued, and at other times Starker is a bit too forward.

The above Stern-Rose-Ormandy recording is coupled with Mozart's double solo work for violin and viola (K.364). In another issue the Brahms is combined with a trio also by Brahms and the Beethoven triple concerto. The release is, of course, Columbia— D2S–720.

Chorale Prelude and Fugue on *O Traurigkeit, O Herzeleid*

Eleven Chorale Preludes, Op. 122

Fugue in A flat minor

Prelude and Fugue in A minor

Prelude and Fugue in G minor

☐ Rapf (organ) / Turnabout 34422

Instrumental

Organ

The above comprises the complete organ output of Brahms. The special sustained personal lyricism found in his music is evident in some of the Opus 122 set; the G minor Prelude and Fugue is dramatically outstanding.

Stylistic sincerity is present throughout Kurt Rapf's playing. He performs on the grand organ of the Ursulinenklosters of Vienna. Good engineering.

Ballades, Op. 10

☐ Katchen (piano) / London 6444

Piano

Katchen offers solid pianism in his portrayal of these four pieces, with emphatic bravura in the second and third of the set. He delineates the stylized intensity, even in the poetically sad initial piece of the group, that is the primary point in Brahms's early composition (he had just turned twenty-one).

Fantasien, **Op. 116**

☐ Walter Klien (piano) / Vox SVBX–5431

A mix of capriccios and intermezzi, two of the former and one of the latter in the first set, with three of the latter and one of the former in the second set.

Walter Klien gives full devotion to the vitalized lyrical details within the music's shapes. This provides the most propitious performance climate. Gilels (Deutsche Grammophon 2530656) is a feasible second choice, but his commentary has less graphic color.

Hungarian Dances, Nos. 1–10

☐ Katchen (piano) / London 6473

Key changes were made in other composers' transcriptions of these dances, and that is Brahms's procedure in his edition of the first ten for solo piano. In comparison with the keys listed for the original piano-duet version (see under *piano, four hands* for the list and a discussion of the works), No. 4 here is in F sharp minor and No. 7 is in F major.

Excellent musical presentations are made by Katchen. They are stylishly projected and sensitively nuanced.

Rhapsody

In B minor, Op. 79, No. 1 / In G minor, Op. 79, No. 2

☐ Katchen (piano) / London 6444

Illuminating performances. The G minor flares with fire, but the use of fluid *rubati* keep matters under control. The closest competition comes from Rubinstein (RCA LSC-3186), but there is a certain aloofness from him that just doesn't jell with the Brahms data.

Scherzo in E flat minor, Op. 4

☐ Arrau (piano) / Philips 6500377

Arrau's performance is unbuttoned in mood, tightly pointed in the delivery of the motival play. There is careful but not dull attention to dynamics and accentuation. Arrau's articulative keyboard touch makes this music doubly alive.

Sonata

No. 1 in C major, Op. 1 / No. 2 in F sharp minor, Op. 2

☐ Katchen (piano) / London 6410

Superb playing that has Brahmsian eloquence and strength plus subtlety of vocabulary. Both works emerge with their structures made more impressive through Katchen's dynamic investigation.

Sonata No. 3 in F minor, Op. 5

☐ Curzon (piano) / London STS-15272

The spontaneous tone of this performance lingers long after the recording has stopped revolving. There is full breadth and splendor in the first movement, the violet-like colors a subtle underlay for the magnificent portrayal. Superb legatos are displayed in the *Andante espressivo*. The definitions in the remaining movements are just as assured, especially the manner in which the Scherzo is characterized.

Theme and Variations in D minor from the Sextet in B flat for Strings, Op. 18

☐ Barenboim (piano) / Deutsche Grammophon 2530335

It's hard to find this curio in *Schwann*. It is there, but hidden in a listing that features Brahms's Variations and Fugue on a Theme by Handel, Op. 24. The solo work is a real oddity that few pianists know about, and if they do, never perform. The setting follows the original note for note, but Brahms transcribing Brahms is quite interesting in any event.

Variations and Fugue on a Theme by Handel, Op. 24

☐ Walter Klien (piano) / Turnabout 34165

Walter Klien provides a compelling and splendid performance of one of the great masterpieces structured in variational plan—compelling and splendid in the way he delineates the twenty-five Variations and in the manner in which he powers the concluding Fugue while clarifying all of its lines. Variational character is artistically determined; examples are No. 7, played with martial totality, the romantic flavor of No. 11, the somber facts of No. 13.

Tempi are realized in a definitive fashion. Some pianists (Barenboim, for example) dawdle, and that's bad reasoning for a work which should move with urgency (outwardly and inwardly) from one section to the next. This is vital, since Brahms planned the Variations with a feeling for growth to climax.

Variations on a Theme by Paganini, Op. 35

☐ Ohlsson (piano) / Angel S–37249

Virtuosic technique can be taken for granted in the major leagues of pianists. But extra ingredients mark the stars. This is star-studded playing. It has needle-sharp precision of attack, intense color and variety, immaculate gradations of timbre and dynamics, and communication throughout. The total is excitement.

Variations on a Theme by Schumann, Op. 9

☐ Barenboim (piano) / Deutsche Grammophon 2530355

There's a great deal of poetry in this opus, and Barenboim realizes every bit of it, without mishandling the contrastive situation pertinent to a set of variations. At the same time he does not lose sight of the improvisation-like quality that streams through the work. Highly recommended.

Waltzes, Op. 39

☐ Katchen (piano) / London 6444

If one prefers Brahms's Waltzes with two hands on one keyboard rather than four, then here they are, in a sparkling performance with countless felicities. The original piano-duet version is considered below (see under *piano, four hands*).

Hungarian Dance

Piano, Four Hands

No. 1 in G minor / No. 2 in D minor / No. 3 in F major / No. 4 in F minor / No. 5 in F sharp minor / No. 6 in D flat major / No. 7 in A major / No. 8 in A minor / No. 9 in E minor / No. 10 in E major / No. 11 in D minor / No. 12 in D minor / No. 13 in D major / No. 14 in D minor / No. 15 in B flat major / No. 16 in F minor / No. 17 in F sharp minor / No. 18 in D major / No. 19 in B minor / No. 20 in E minor / No. 21 in E minor

☐ Walter and Beatrice Klien (piano) / Turnabout 34068

This, the setting for one piano, four hands, is the original issue of the work from which a variety of transcriptions, arrangements, and recolorings have been made. The most passionate popularity, of course, belongs to No. 5. In that case the range has gone from mouth organ to full organ, from two violins to large symphonic band.

Brahms himself arranged Dances No. 1 through No. 10 for solo piano and Nos. 1, 3, and 10 for orchestra. Also for orchestra: Dvořák transcribed Nos. 17 through 21, and Paul Juon transcribed No. 4. Further, Andreas Hallén made orchestral versions of Nos. 2 and 7, and Albert Parlow receives credit for transcribing the famous No. 5 and No. 6 Dances, as well as Nos. 11 through 16. This leaves only the eighth and ninth apparently untouched for orchestra, but surely the pair could be found hidden in some obscure publisher's catalogue.

The Kliens play with stylish know-how, avoid excessive *rubati*, and choose effective tempi. A listener need not force himself to try to enjoy all these fine performances, though. That's a lot of Hungarian dances—twenty-one of them. If a listener prefers half of them, then a satisfactory edition (but not as topflight as the Kliens') is available on London 6473, played by Julius Katchen and Jean-Pierre Marty. It does have one advantage, being paired with Katchen's excellent performance of Hungarian Dances Nos. 1 to 10 in the solo-piano setting that Brahms made (see under *piano*). A recording of Joachim's arrangement of the complete set of dances for violin and piano is discussed below (see under *Brahms/Joseph Joachim: Instrumental: violin*). For orchestral performances see under *Orchestra*.

Waltzes, Op. 39

☐ Walter and Beatrice Klien (piano) / Turnabout 34041

Coherent playing with a nice swing about it for these sixteen waltzes for piano duet. Viennese climate with some Magyar wind blowing in the fourteenth of the set. The one following is *the* famous Brahms waltz.

Two Pianos

Sonata in F minor for Two Pianos, Op. 34a

☐ Eden and Tamir (pianos) / London 6533

This work constitutes the second step in a three-part creative documentation. The work began as a string quintet, then went into the two-piano format, and finally turned up as the famed piano quintet. It works quite well in the two-piano medium. Played with excellent pianism and musicianship.

Variations on a Theme of Haydn, Op. 56b

☐ Gold and Fizdale (pianos) / Odyssey 32160334

To deny this work because of the stunning orchestral setting (see under *Orchestra*) is to deny one of the greatest works in the two-piano repertoire. Neither can one deny that this team obtain a happy balance of form and color in their conception.

Chamber Music

F-A-E Sonata: Movement 3, Allegro

☐ Yehudi Menuhin (violin); Hephzibah Menuhin (piano) / Angel S-36234

The F–A–E Sonata—whose initials stand for the great violinist Joachim's motto *Frei aber einsam* ("Free but lonely")—was a creative adventure, including charade overtones, composed as a greeting for Joachim by Brahms, Schumann, and Albert Dietrich. Joachim was to guess which composer had written each of the four movements. (Brahms had signed his contribution "Joh. Kriesler.") It was not difficult for Joachim to identify Joh. Brahms's favorite mix of duple and triple pulsations, set in many pedal formations.

The Menuhins present a satisfactory reading of the movement (a scherzo formation in the key of C minor).

Sonata for Cello and Piano
No. 1 in E minor, Op. 38 / No. 2 in F major, Op. 99

☐ du Pré (cello); Barenboim (piano) / Angel S-36544

By and large the dangers in the cello-piano combo are conquered. The string instrument's thicker quality can be easily submerged in the wealth of rolled-wave piano tone, especially with the sustaining pedal of the piano aiding sound prolongation. The string instrument must have air to breathe in its low register. The dark and gloomy beginning of the E minor opus suffers to a certain extent from the cramped quarters of the cello voice, but these performers solve the problem fairly well. They do less well with the beginning of the fugal finale.

Opus 99 is clear sailing. Tempi are set excellently, and the phrasing is a joy. There's romantic juice all over the place, but no skidding about. One notices the cello's vibrancy and the rich pianism in the slow movement, as well as the impeccable tracing of the Scherzo's design, with its Brahmsian polyrhythmicizing of the fundamental beat so that three and two notes fall together in two simultaneous lines. No other style but the free and relaxed fashion in which these two performers play the Rondo that concludes the work would be fitting.

Sonata for Clarinet and Piano, Op. 120
No. 1 in F minor / No. 2 in E flat major

☐ David Glazer (clarinet); Frank Glazer (piano) / Vox SVBX-578

An intimate warmth covers the playing of these two mellow works. This is a treasurable collaboration. Especially compelling is Glazer's control of the clarinet line in all of its registers. Tempi, which often mar Brahms's music in performance by translating breadth into sluggishness or obliterating important inner detail by too speedy a pace, are perfectly realized here.

Sonata in E flat major for Clarinet and Piano, Op. 120, No. 2 (Transcribed for Violin)

☐ Stern (violin); Zakin (piano) / Columbia M-32228

This is Brahms's concluding chamber-music composition, which he transcribed, together with the companion work (Op. 120, No. 1), for both violin and viola. Most often the viola setting is heard, not the violin. Brahms made certain alterations in the transfer from clarinet to violin, and some further changes have been made by Stern. Musicological quibbling might be in order, but Stern's editing really doesn't amount to a great deal.

What does is the rather neutral style of the playing. Still, this is the only recorded performance available for those who want to have the Brahms (Stern) transcription. The performance is also included in a two-record release, together with the three violin and piano sonatas (Columbia MG-33713).

Sonata for Violin and Piano
No. 1 in G major, Op. 78 / No.2 in A major, Op. 100 / No. 3 in D minor, Op. 108

☐ Stern (violin); Zakin (piano) / Columbia MG-33713

Brahms's marvelous architectonic workmanship is fully conveyed by these artists. All three of these duo sonatas are solid in their structural portrayal, with each movement within a sonata of proper individual strength and relationship to the others. Stern's tone is of romantic coloristic robustness, but avoids any tinge of sentimentality. His use of natural harmonics to pigment phrase points in a few places is a mark of interpretative genius.

The second sonata is available separately on Columbia M-32228.

Sonata No. 3 in D minor for Violin and Piano, Op. 108

☐ David Oistrakh (violin); Richter (piano) / Melodiya/Angel S-40121

A totally different conception from the Stern-Zakin performance, and just as worthy. Richter, first of all, plays with big, bold impact. Oistrakh utilizes *rubati* to emphasize parentheses and emphatic points in the musical statement. There are also marked differences of tempi (especially in the opening movement) to define the thematics. The energetic and emphatic reading tends toward symphonicism, but this is not out of place in the Brahms chamber-music canon.

Trio in A minor for Piano, Clarinet, and Cello, Op. 114

☐ Frank Glazer (piano); David Glazer (clarinet); Soyer (cello) / Vox SVBX-578

The genial color of the clarinet influences this work considerably, controlling the mood, not the themes. There is determined reticence to be noted. Of the four movements, the first three end softly.

Accordingly, this team seeks out the lyricism of the piece, pushes the tempi down a bit, and opts for a quiet type of intimacy instead of emphasizing matters. It works beautifully and serves Brahms perfectly.

Trio in B major for Violin, Cello, and Piano, Op. 8

☐ Katchen (piano); Suk (violin); Starker (cello) / London 6611

Like the Rubinstein-Szeryng-Fournier team (on RCA ARL3-0138), the Istomin-Stern-Rose combine (on Columbia M2S-760), and the Mannheim Trio (on Vox SVBX-591), this threesome has recorded all three of the Brahms trios. However, unlike those of the other groups, the Katchen-Suk-Starker renditions are not contained in a single edition. London has produced the first and third trios on one disc (6611) and issued the second trio in a separate release (6814).

It is worth obtaining the separate London recordings. In contrast to the first group mentioned above, which is piano-dominated and has considerable string-instrument roughness, the second team, which tends to be obedient to the electrical personality of Stern, and the third combine, which lacks personality and is not in the same league as any of the others, London's representatives present truly sublime, perfectly balanced versions. And, where and when needed, Katchen, Suk, and Starker engage in diplomatic give-and-take. They provide a lyrically enthusiastic conception. Here one realizes the musicians have recognized the germinal material that fires the Scherzo statement, the measured thematic differences in the finale, and so on. It is consistently warm and beautiful trio music that this trio team produces. That's what makes their edition the very best.

Trio in C major for Violin, Cello, and Piano, Op. 87

☐ Katchen (piano); Suk (violin); Starker (cello) / London 6814

Interpretative reportage that is a triumph of chamber-music playing. The restraint of a sheer static dynamic level is maintained in the Scherzo. The rigidity of the muttering rhythm against the piano's swirling figures in a tight frame of *pianissimo sempre* provides marvelous musical excitement. All the other movements are always lovely-toned and idiomatically absolute. This team offers superb Brahms.

Trio in C minor for Violin, Cello, and Piano, Op. 101

☐ Katchen (piano); Suk (violin); Starker (cello) / London 6611

In this trio Brahms lights a fire at both ends, with less fire in between to facilitate balance and to cause musical felicity. But fire doesn't mean the rough and sometimes crude sounds that are heard elsewhere, especially in the cello playing of Fournier in his performance with Szeryng and Rubinstein, on RCA ARL3-0138. The London edition is beautifully modulated, catching the stress and the calmness that combine in a work wherein Brahms the artisan clutches the hand of Brahms the colorist.

Trio in E flat major for Horn, Violin, and Piano, Op. 40

☐ Tuckwell (horn); Perlman (violin); Ashkenazy (piano) / London 6628

Nary a weakness in this realization of Brahms's music for the special combination of a horn (or cello or viola, though these are indeed poor substitutes), violin, and piano. For rightness of phrasing, tempi, and style, the performance cannot be bettered. Tuckwell is a supreme artist, and Perlman proves his cooperative ability as a chamber-music participant—witness the sensitive merging they accomplish in the darkness of the minor-keyed slow movement. Ashkenazy is just as sensitive and musical.

Piano Quartet
No. 1 in G minor, Op. 25 / No. 2 in A major, Op. 26 / No. 3 in C minor, Op. 60

☐ Members of the Guarneri Quartet / Rubinstein (piano) / RCA LSC-6188

Interestingly, there are three different personnel situations in the three recorded sets of Brahms's complete works for piano, violin, viola, and cello. In the Philips edition (674768) the permanent pianist, violinist, and cellist of the Beaux Arts Trio are augmented by the violist Walter Trampler. On the Vox Box release (SVBX-592) the organization involved is an actual piano-quartet team, the Eastman Quartet—Frank Glazer, piano; Millard Taylor, violin; Francis Tursi, viola; and Ronald Leonard, cello. The RCA release (LSC-6188) combines three members of the Guarneri Quartet (democratically, the first violinist, Arnold Steinhardt, plays in the second and third quartets, and the second violinist, John Dalley, performs in the Opus 25) with Artur Rubinstein as the guest pianist.

The performance results vary as much as the different arrangements that governed the choice of personnel for making the recordings. The strings in the Philips release rarely dig into the music (Trampler is not to be included in this indictment), and as a result the balance between piano and the three stringed instruments is false, for the greater part. There is also a tendency for rephrasing long lines. In comparison the Vox performances are much better, but they are marred by engineering that in no way can match either the superb Philips surfaces or those provided by RCA. In the last instance the productions are the most convincing interpretatively, are assiduously balanced texturally, and display commanding partnership between Rubinstein and his Guarneri colleagues. There is refinement where it should be and there is sonorous impetus where it should be, but always in harmony with chamber-music objectives. There is also an interpretative romantic glow (and blaze where it is required) in the Rubinstein-Guarneri collaboration.

Piano Quartet No. 3 in C minor, Op. 60

☐ Silverstein (violin); Fine (viola); Eskin (cello); Frank (piano) / RCA LSC-6167

No cakes-and-ale sections in Brahms's final piano quartet. The few lighter sections do not relieve the dark mood of the opening portion, and the Scherzo is as feverish in its pace as the preceding movement is inquiet. There is no contrastive trio division in the Scherzo; it presents the unification of a basic duple-pulsed idea.

The blend of the strings with the piano is beautiful throughout and brings out all of the Brahmsian beauties. Special mention must be made of the performance of the magnificent song, dimmed with tears, that marks the slow movement.

String Quartet
No. 1 in C minor, Op. 51, No. 1 / No. 2 in A minor, Op. 51, No. 2 / No. 3 in B flat major, Op. 67

☐ Quartetto Italiano / Philips 6703029

This quartet gives performances that linger in the memory, performances that can be noted as definitive, performances with rich sound and exquisite realization of the Brahms text. Above all, this foursome understands the intense matter of tempo—paramount to proper tonal translation of the Brahms literature. Brahms's tempi, at best, tend toward the slower side. His *allegros, vivaces,* and the like are warm and more stately than speedy. With too fast a speed rate in Brahms's blocks of rhythm, the currents of counter, interallied rhythms are lost. Not only the tempi of the Quartetto Italiano are splendid; the total playing is sheer magic.

Quintet in B minor for Clarinet and Strings, Op. 115

☐ Tel-Aviv Quartet / Ettlinger (clarinet) / Oiseau-Lyre 146

There is no more distinctive identity in chamber music than this Brahms quintet. A gentle autumnal quality moves throughout its measures. It is Brahms's warmest music.

The feeling is always one of *diminuendo;* regardless of certain passages which seem to storm, all storms are under control. The course of the dynamic is always downward, lessened. In fact, every one of the movements ends softly—rare in any work, rare for Brahms.

This performance is one of mellow mellifluousness. It is just what the playing of this work should be. There is a sense of relaxation and affection. Ideal, indeed.

Quintet in F minor for Piano, Two Violins, Viola, and Cello, Op. 34

☐ Budapest Quartet / Rudolf Serkin (piano) / Columbia MS-6631

It is especially the clarification of the exciting rhythmic rhetoric that fills Brahms's work that makes this a choice performance. The playing is polished but never at the expense of decisive vitality. Two strong personalities (the pianist and the stringed-instrument team) must blend in playing a piano quintet, and the collaboration in this case is artistically intelligent and interpretively dynamic. Result: an inspired, memorable recording.

String Quintet

No. 1 in F major, Op. 88 / No. 2 in G major, Op. 111

☐ Budapest Quartet / Trampler (viola) / Columbia MS-6025

The playing of the famed Budapest team with the masterful Walter Trampler as guest violist cannot be faulted. The Budapest Quartet may have faltered in their last days but not here, and Trampler is a splendid extra strength. The musicianship heard here is penetrating, the tone one of golden consummation. Tremendous chamber-music playing that puts the competition in the distant shade.

Sextet in B flat major for Two Violins, Two Violas, and Two Cellos, Op. 18

☐ Menuhin and Masters (violins); Aronowitz and Wallfisch (violas); Gendron and Simpson (cellos) / Angel S-36234

This performance discharges all the artistic responsibilities contained within the score. Though at times Menuhin is a bit reticent, the admirable cello pair are careful to adjust their dynamic sights correctly. This all-star lineup gladdens the ear with its reading of the waltz swing in the first movement, containing a chain of melodies that is captivating. The Scherzo is kept at a moderate speed, rather than the designated *allegro molto,* but this editing of Brahms's metronomic marker seems perfectly fitting. And the carefree quality of the finale is retained, minus any attempt to create a fever in place of eighteenth-century-like fervor.

Sextet in G major for Two Violins, Two Violas, and Two Cellos, Op. 36

☐ Heifetz and Baker (violins); Primrose and Majewski (violas); Piatigorsky and Rejto (cellos) / RCA LSC-2739

While the voices of six string instruments offer half as much again as the string quartet, and much more opportunity for intricacies of counterpoint, fundamentally the string sextet offers an opportunity to enhance and enrich the sonorous objective. It is this value that often turns into a fault as a sextet burgeons into a minuscule string orchestra. This is not the case here. This group (and notice the bigger-than-bigs who hold the first desk in each of the three sections) plays Brahms's music as chamber music, and the sonorous glow is captivating.

There is a further danger in string sextet performance. With the same number of cellos as there are violins, there may be too much bass and textures can become muddy unless adjustments in balance are made. Again, all requirements are met in this recording.

Five *Lieder*, Op. 94

☐ Shirley-Quirk (baritone); Isepp (piano) / Argo ZRG-664

Fairly good portrayals.

Liebeslieder Walzer, Op. 52

☐ Valente (soprano); Kleinman (alto); Connor (tenor); Singher (bass); Rudolf Serkin and Fleisher (piano) / Columbia MS-6236

Brahms's first set of "Love-Song Waltzes," with its unusual scoring for mixed vocal quartet and piano duet, is given a fine performance. For this delightful work the cast is super and, as will be noted, star-studded, with such names as Rudolf Serkin, Martial Singher, and Benita Valente.

Two Songs with Viola Obbligato, Op. 91

☐ Flagstad (soprano); Moore (piano); Downes (viola) / Seraphim 60046 (monaural)

Meaning and incandescence are only part of the Kirsten Flagstad contribution here. There is also magnificent musicianship. Her understanding rendition of these Brahms songs, enriched by the artistic strength of Gerald Moore and the splendid viola playing of Herbert Downes, is the finest on record.

Vier ernste Gesänge, Op. 121

☐ Fischer-Dieskau (baritone); Barenboim (piano) / Deutsche Grammophon 2707066
☐ Forrester (contralto); Newmark (piano) / London STS-15113

Brahms's "Four Serious Songs," settings of texts from the Bible and the Apocrypha, was his last published work. No doubt Brahms planned the set to be sung by a male voice (the score used the bass clef, which is foreign to female vocalists), but it has been just as convincingly presented by both contraltos (Kathleen Ferrier's striking performance is still available on Richmond 23183 in monaural form) and sopranos (specifically Helen Traubel).

Both Fischer-Dieskau and Forrester provide searching and inspired performances. The subtlety of Maureen Forrester's phrasing deserves special mention.

Vocal

*Voice
with
Accompaniment*

Voice and Orchestra

Alto Rhapsody, Op. 53

☐ Vienna Philharmonic Orchestra and Vienna Singverein / Ludwig (alto) / Böhm (conductor) / Deutsche Grammophon 2536396

Ludwig's marvelous vocal instrument comes forth with impeccable musicianship and that means emotive understanding. A rich and moving interpretation that realizes the stoic resignation in the music.

Choral

Chorus Alone

Abendständchen, Op. 42, No. 1

☐ Leipzig University Choir / Rabanschlag (conductor) / Nonesuch 71081

Brahms's "Evening Serenade" is sung simply and effectively. It is a short example of intimate choral music.

Ach, arme Welt, Op. 110, No. 2

Das Mädchen, Op. 93a, No. 2

Ich aber bin Elend, Op. 110, No. 1

O süsser Mai, Op. 93a, No. 3

☐ Canby Singers / Canby (conductor) / Nonesuch 71115

The Opus 93a pieces are from Six Songs and Romances for Mixed Chorus, and the other two compositions are from the Opus 110 Three Motets (*see below*).

Subtle readings, yet with proper dynamism. All four are delightful fantasies within neatly conceived forms, and yet each sounds as though it were improvised on the spot.

Deutsche Fest- und Gedenkspruche, Op. 109

☐ Boy's Choir of the Church of St. Michael, Hamburg / Brinkmann (conductor) / Nonesuch 73003

These "Festival and Commemoration Proverbs" receive a fairly competent performance. Brahms's little-known opus moves with scrupulously arranged harmonic content. However, its textures are somewhat stabilized and bypass contrast.

Seven Part Songs for Mixed Voices, Op. 62 (Excerpts)

☐ Camerata Vocale, Bremen, and Leipzig University Choir / Blum, Kopf-Endres, and Rabanschlag (conductors) / Nonesuch 71081

Performed are Nos. 2, 3, 4, and 5 of the set. Three different conductors with two different groups are involved in the program. The Leipzig group, conducted by Friedrich Rabanschlag, sings Nos. 2 and 5; the Camerata Vocale, the other two. Of these, No. 3 is directed by Klaus Blum, and No. 4 by Willy Kopf-Endres. All the performances concerned are equally good.

Six Songs and Romances for Mixed Chorus, Op. 93a, Nos. 2, 3, and 4

☐ Gächinger Kantorei / Rilling (conductor) / CMS/Oryx 3C–324

In order the titles are *Das Mädchen, O süsser Mai,* and *Fahr wohl.* The singing is good, and Brahmsian decorum rules.

For another edition of Nos. 2 and 3 *see above,* under *Ach, arme Welt.*

Three Motets, Op. 110

Two Motets, Op. 74

☐ New English Singers / Preston (conductor) / Argo ZRG–571

Opus 110 has four- and eight-part writing. The first work in Opus 74, *Warum ist das Licht gegeben,* is the major piece on this program. Its emotive quality is beautifully conveyed by Preston's group.

The odd situation is to be noted that the New English Singers include countertenors rather than contraltos. This, of course, changes the timbre balance of a mixed chorus from its fixed division of female vocal qualities (soprano and alto) and male voices (tenor and bass). One is hard put to recall other choral groups having adopted such substitution. It is successfully realized in this case.

Deutsche Volkslieder

Deutsche Volkslieder (for Four-Part Chorus)

Volks-Kinderlieder

Chorus with Accompaniment

☐ Leipzig Radio Choir / Mathis (soprano); Schreier (tenor); Engel (piano) / Neumann (conductor) / Deutsche Grammophon 2709057

Folk-song settings and children's folk-song settings. Limited appeal, perhaps, but these are beautifully proportioned performances that will hit home with their simplicity and immediacy. The Brahmsian characteristics are fully detailed.

Four Part Songs for Female Voices, Two Horns, and Harp, Op. 17

☐ Gächinger Kantorei / Lohan and Ludwig (horns); Cassedanne (harp) / Rilling (conductor) / CMS/Oryx 3C-324

There is nocturnal vocal radiance with attractive instrumental colors here, especially in the strategic use of the horns, which are played exquisitely. The harp, on the other hand, is heard rather *sotto voce.* Rilling knows how to draw out every particular nuance in a choral piece, even when he is not blessed with a fine group of singers. This handicap does not apply to the Gächinger personnel, however, which adds considerably to this performance.

Four Quartets with Piano, Op. 92

☐ Gächinger Kantorei / Galling (piano) / Rilling (conductor) / CMS/Oryx 3C-324

Originally written for four solo voices (soprano, alto, tenor, and bass) but most often sung, as here, by multiple voices. The first three are of time and the seasons. The opening quartet is set to Daumer's *O schöne Nacht* ("O Beautiful Night"); the second is set to Allmers's *Spätherbst* ("Late Autumn"); the third is an *Abendlied* ("Nocturne") with words by Hebbel; the last quartet, set to a text by Goethe, is titled *Warum?* ("Why?").

All the singing is first-class, and at no time is there a striving for special effect; rather there is a stress on emphasizing the poetical nuances of the music.

Geistliches Lied, Op. 30

☐ New English Singers / Preston (organ) / Preston (conductor) / Argo ZRG-571

Brahms's sacred song for accompanied chorus, *Lass dich nur nichts dauern,* doesn't surface often, so it's good to have it on disc.

Neue Liebeslieder Walzer, Op. 65

☐ Gächinger Kantorei / Uhde and Werner (piano) / Rilling (conductor) / Turnabout 34277

This performance can be criticized only for the use of an expanded vocal group rather than the mixed vocal quartet Brahms had indicated. Nicely styled and enthusiastically delivered.

Six Quartets with Piano, Op. 112

☐ Gächinger Kantorei / Galling (piano) / Rilling (conductor) / Nonesuch 71228

Nos. 3, 4, 5, and 6 of this opus constitute a work within a work titled *Four Zigeunerlieder*. These should not be confused with the eleven-part *Zigeunerlieder*, Op. 103, mentioned *below* under Three Quartets with Piano, Op. 31.

The singing is dynamic and has tonal richness. This is certainly to be preferred to the much blander rendition by the Stephane Caillat Vocal Quartet. They perform the Opus 103 and the Four *Zigeunerlieder* from Opus 112 as a unit on Turnabout 34300.

Three Quartets with Piano, Op. 31
Zigeunerlieder, Op. 103

☐ Gächinger Kantorei / Galling (piano) / Rilling (conductor) / Nonesuch 71228

Regarding the Opus 103, *see above*, under Six Quartets with Piano, Op. 112. The remarks made there regarding performance apply here likewise.

The Three Quartets have rhythmic clarity, exact pitch, effective balance, and warmth. A joy to hear.

Chorus and Orchestra

Schicksalslied, Op. 54

☐ New Philharmonia Orchestra and Ambrosian Chorus / Abbado (conductor) / London 26106

It is not that Claudio Abbado has a better interpretation than Bruno Walter's on Columbia (MS-6488). It is simply that Abbado has a much better chorus than the college group Walter directs and that the Columbia Symphony Orchestra lacks the timbred body and personality of the Philharmonia. Both conductors color the "Song of Destiny" sensitively, though the first part is a bit brighter in Abbado's version.

Cantata and Oratorio

A German Requiem, Op. 45

☐ Philharmonia Orchestra and Chorus / Schwarzkopf (soprano); Fischer-Dieskau (baritone) / Klemperer (conductor) / Angel S-3624

While traditional expertise is to be expected from Klemperer, his conception of Brahms's *Ein deutsches Requiem* offers much more. It is one of his richest contributions to recorded literature. There is a special spontaneity of pulse providing a sufficiency of romantic freedom, with such enthusiasm tempered to present clear, detailed textures and not minimize or interfere with the music's basic, expressive strength. The breadth of tempi that sometimes cools down the music Klemperer conducts is nowhere evident.

Klemperer's statement is illumined by intelligence, depth, and affection. One can hardly imagine it being bettered. Ansermet's performance (on London 1265, the soloists being Giebel and Prey) has sensitivity and strength but is rather straight-laced in many sections. Von Karajan's edition on Deutsche Grammophon 2707018, with Janowitz and Wächter as the soloists, is restrained, and his later version on Angel SB-3838, with

Tomowa-Sintow and van Damm in the solo spots, is only marginally better. The other essays in the catalogue are informed but inflexible.

Rinaldo, Op. 50

☐ New Philharmonia Orchestra and Ambrosian Chorus / King (tenor) / Abbado (conductor) / London 26106

Brahms's cantata for tenor, male chorus, and orchestra (text by Goethe) concerns Rinaldo, who has left a Crusade in the Holy Land, together with his followers, and fallen under the spell of an enchantress, Armida. But strangely she never appears in Brahms's conception. Thus there is only a stream of dialogue between the chorus (the Crusaders) and Rinaldo—dialogue that is somewhat bland because of the lack of vocal contrast, all the participants being male.

James King is in control, even though his singing smacks of Wagnerian heroics rather than Brahmsian lyricism. Good singing by the chorus, firm playing by the orchestra.

Brahms / **Joseph Joachim (1831-1907)**

Hungarian Dances, Nos. 1-21

Instrumental

☐ Gerle (violin); Shetler (piano) / Westminster Gold 8118

Violin

The keys in the original version are indicated under *Brahms: Instrumental: piano, four hands,* where there is a discussion of Brahms's composition. Joachim made a number of tonality shifts. Here is a list of the changes with the original key in parentheses: No. 4, B minor (F minor); No. 5, G minor (F sharp minor); No. 6, B flat major (D flat major); No. 10, G major (E major); No. 15, A major (B flat major); No. 16, G minor (F minor); No. 19, A minor (B minor); and No. 20, D minor (E minor).

A pleasing recorded presentation. It has been marred, however, by recording the Dances in six groups (three of four Dances in each and three of three Dances in each) ''as they might be performed in a concert program.'' A person listening to a recording shouldn't be captive to concert-hall program arrangement, and it is most annoying not to have the original continuity basic to any recording. To hear particular Dances or compare them with the piano-duet settings, for example, means jumping from the A side to the B side. Thus Dances 1 and 2 are in group II on side A; for No. 3, one moves back to group I on the same side. For Dances 4 and 5 the record must be turned over, since these are in group IV on side B, and one must again go back to the other record side to hear No. 6, which is in group III, and so on.

Brahms / **Edmund Rubbra (1901-   )**

Variations and Fugue on a Theme by Handel, Op. 24

Orchestra

☐ Philadelphia Orchestra / Ormandy (conductor) / Columbia MS-7298

Of course not for purists, but really there's nothing wrong with having a listen. Rubbra's version is quite good. The Ormandy rendition of Rubbra's version is very good. (It is also available in a two-record set as the ''filler'' for the Brahms Requiem on Columbia M2S-686.)

Brahms / Arnold Schoenberg (1874-1951)

Orchestra **Piano Quartet in G minor, Op. 25**

☐ Chicago Symphony Orchestra / Craft (conductor) / Columbia M2S–752

What makes a great composer transcribe the work of another master creator? No guesswork in this case, since we have Schoenberg's own thoughts, stated in a letter he wrote to the critic Alfred Frankenstein. Some of the reasons: he admired the Brahms piece, thought it was seldom played, and when it was, the strings were not properly heard.

Schoenberg also stated, "I wanted once to hear everything, and this I achieved." True—and in an orchestrational style that one would swear was by Brahms himself.

The transcription is truly a fine achievement and deserves the widest hearing (which it doesn't get). Craft's tempi for the outer movements are too fast (though the claim for the speed of the first movement is Schoenberg's own specific metronomic indication). Otherwise, a good achievement.

Roger Brange / *Maurice Ravel.* See Ravel / Brange.

Henry Brant (1913-   )

Orchestra ***Kingdom Come, for Two Orchestras and Organ (1970)***

☐ Oakland Symphony Orchestra and Oakland Youth Orchestra / Brant (organ) / Samuel and Hughes (conductors) / Desto 7108

Kingdom Come is true-blooded spatial music. In live performance one orchestra is on stage and the other in the balcony. For this disc each orchestra was recorded individually and the results were then joined.

There is a great deal of snideness in the piece. This is to be expected, since Brant describes the organ cadenza in the middle of the work as "an improvisatory soap-box statement," and a short soprano solo as the impersonation of "a psychotic Valkyrie." But there is much more, represented by superb polyphony derived from the irreconcilable elements that make up the context. To this end the balcony orchestra is an instrumental catch-all that includes slide clarinets, slide trumpets, slide whistles, sirens, klaxons, buzzers, electric bells, ratchets, and even air compressors! The massive thrust of *Kingdom Come* opens the ears (Charles Ives would have loved this music, and not just because it is Ivesian to the core).

Brant has produced a brilliant tour de force. The orchestras go all out with gutsy extrovert playing. They provide a definitive performance (prepared by the premiere of the work which they gave on April 14, 1970, followed by repeats on April 15 and 16). The composition is not listed by its title in *Schwann*, but is identified as "Music 1970" (the Desto album's explanatory heading, since both *Kingdom Come* and the companion piece on the disc, *Machinations*, were written in 1970).

On the Nature of Things, after Lucretius (1956)

☐ Louisville Orchestra / Mester (conductor) / Louisville LS–765

A gentility permeates this Brant work. The strings (violins, violas, and cellos, without double basses) quietly declaim in a long-lined cantilena (always in unison); the other instruments (flute, oboe, clarinet, bassoon, horn, harp, and glockenspiel) interpose, but also always gently. Brant has a huge output, but none of his works have the cohesive warmth found in this chamber-orchestra score. To many listeners, ready for the complexes of Brant's use of simultaneous polyphonic tempi and material, further defined and emphasized by varied separation of the performing forces, *On the Nature of Things* will be a surprise. Such timbred elegance is the epitome of cultivated workmanship.

Jorge Mester is to be congratulated for a meticulous interpretation of Brant's score. The music flows; the seamlessness of the conception offers the listener an ideal sonic translation.

Brant has a habit of adding instruments to his scores for specific performances (a type of open-ended-instrumentation concept). For this piece additions were made of a second flute and a piano playing isolated, single, extremely low pitched sounds. Neither of these instruments are included in Mester's recorded performance.

Symphony No. 1 (1931)

☐ Vienna Symphony Orchestra / Swarowsky (conductor) / Desto 6461E (monaural)

Brant represented by an early tonal piece, titled Symphony No. 1. Its basic key is B flat. It illustrates his sure hand with the orchestra, rhythmic courage, and use of jazz-derived and ballad-shaped themes. Worth a listen anytime, though posterity will doubtless remember Brant for his amazingly individual music utilizing stereophonic instrumental distribution which includes magnificent tempi and thematic polyphony.

Verticals Ascending (1967)

Band

☐ Northwestern University Symphonic Wind Ensemble / Paynter and Colnot (conductors) / New World Records NW-211

Indeed, two conductors. Brant's piece, subtitled *After the Rodia Towers* (an architectural sculpture located in the Watts section of Los Angeles), calls for two separated groups. Oboes, bassoons, saxophone, trumpets, trombone, and piano are in one formation, the piccolo, flute, various clarinets, horns, tuba, percussion, and electric organ are in the other. Throughout, the mensural totals ply against each other: triple pulses per measure for one unit, quadruple for the other.

Dichotomous impact and feeling, therefore, and the method produces a message of conviction. Listening to Brant's clearly designed music (his linear detail is never involved) is complex—requiring the identification of the compound of contrast and merger of the two groups simultaneously. The performance is meticulously balanced and expertly defines the score. It presents the auditor with perfect documentation of an adroit, effective, and highly special conception.

For once, New World Records, which offer superb packaging and information for all its releases, has slipped. Nowhere is any credit indicated for Cliff Colnot. However, a note covering his career is given. Since two conductors are mandatory for *Verticals Ascending*, obviously he collaborated with John P. Paynter (director of bands at Northwestern University), but research should not be required to find the names of personnel of a recorded performance.

Orbits (1978)

Brass Ensemble

☐ Bay Bones Trombone Choir and Assisting Artists / Brant (organ); Snyder (voice) / Samuel (conductor) / Composers Recordings SD-422

Brant's *Orbits* is termed "A Spatial Symphonic Ritual." But that word "symphonic" is a far cry from orchestral maneuvers. No less than eighty trombones form the sonorous ingredients for this blockbuster, plus an organ that mostly lets all the decibels hang out, and a sopranino voice (smothered in this recording and hardly recognizable, but it doesn't really matter).

Hearing this music, which shuns any attempt to be gentle, makes one a Brant believer. Mind you, the opus runs for close to twenty-one minutes and yet each part of the total is constantly exciting as the sounds punch out, jab, and crisscross. Traditional trombonistic patterns are avoided in this healthy, wealthy, and extremely wise contemporary music.

Brant states that he understands the problem of having a work for eighty trombones performed. But he needn't worry in this case, for permanently imbedded in CRI's record grooves is a magnificent documentation of his score. The playing is superexcellent and full credit must be given to Will Sudmeier and Billy Robinson, the directors of the basic performing forces, the Bay Bones Trombone Choir. This group was augmented by members of the San Francisco and Oakland Symphony Orchestras and the San Francisco Ballet Orchestra. CRI's engineering is consummate.

Solo Instrument and Orchestra

Flute

Angels and Devils: Concerto for Flute Solo with Flute Orchestra (1932)

☐ Wilkins (flute) / Brant (conductor) / Composers Recordings 106 (monaural)

A classic among the flutist fraternity and performed a considerable number of times per season. There's nothing else like it. No reason there should be—Brant has said it all in music that has a sonority unlike any other, with contrapuntal confirmations, candent coloristic devices, jazzy twists, bird simulations, and other aural fascinations.

The flute orchestra consists of three piccolos, five flutes, and two alto flutes. In the middle movement the last, plus the third piccolo, are eliminated.

Angels and Devils is a flute player's dream. For a listener it's a delectable treat that doesn't bog down for a moment. The performance is in the definitive class.

Trumpet

Concerto for Trumpet and Nine Instruments

☐ Schwarz (trumpet) / Brant (conductor) / Desto 7133

Brant's Concerto was written in 1941 and was then revised a number of times; the final version appeared in 1970. Brant has also made a rendering for solo clarinet in place of the trumpet, combined with the same nine instruments—flute, four clarinets, two bass clarinets, tuba, and percussion.

The music moves in and out of a lyrical and dance stance in a soft, classical-jazz style. No schmaltzy or syrupy stuff in the piece; the tunes are quietly sophisticated, the rhythms are spicy.

Gerard Schwarz is a master musician. His conception of Brant's work presents great playing for easy listening.

Viola

Hieroglyphics 3 (1957)

☐ Glick (viola); Satterlee (mezzo-soprano); Brant (organ); Pearson (vibraphone and piano); Finckel (harpsichord); Calabro (timpani and chimes) / Composers Recordings S-260

Over a background of constant transparent imageries, mysterious and chimerical, the solo viola declaims, rhapsodizes, and intones in a doleful quasi-folkloric manner. Whether Brant is indulging in musical Freudianism or is simply delineating musical mockery cannot be answered. What is certain and clear is the pastel-colored nightmare of sonorities in the piece. These are always gripping and, in a certain way, almost frightening.

The drama of the solo part is beautifully portrayed by Jacob Glick; the rest of the cast in this special instrumental proposition is totally supportive.

Quombex, for Viola d'Amore, Music Boxes, and Organ (1960)

Instrumental

☐ Zukofsky (viola d'amore) / Desto 6435/37

Viola d'Amore

No better man in the business than Henry Brant for marshaling creative speculations mixed with the most affirmatively damnable imagination. *Quombex* is a prime example. Notice the combo: the rare string instrument to begin with, an organ (very lightly dusted into this complex), and music boxes! Of course, such a mix is only usable in a one-shot deal.

Inspired by a sculpture, *Bird with Passenger*, it has avian chirps. There are also strong reminders of organ-grinder sounds (not tunes!). All of it is imaginative, all of it is a fascinating exploration of timbre.

Paul Zukofsky makes his recording debut as a viola d'amorist here. The organist receives no credit: could it have been Brant himself?

Hieroglyphics (1966)

Violin

☐ Kobialka (violin); Brant (percussion) / Advance S-6

Stringed-instrument depiction (with some percussion) of "secret writings." Nothing secretive about Henry Brant's creative immersion in the use of unusual sonorities, structures, and scoring. He never repeats himself. Each work is a fresh attack on conventional dogma, each of unsuppressed individuality and keen invention.

One such discovery is presented here, including some dual-tracked sound.

Crossroads, for Four Violins (1971)

*Violins
and Viola*

☐ Kobialka (violins and viola) / Desto 7144

That is no typographical error next to the soloist's name. Daniel Kobialka played each of the four parts and then aided in mixing, editing, combining, and synchronizing the quadruple project. A perfect parallel, a gutsy undertaking for gutsy music.

The title is Brant's, but actually (and this again relates to the point that the instrumental identification next to the performer's name is correct) there are not four violins. Only one regular violin is utilized. The other instruments are a treble violin, a mezzo violin, and a viola. Each runs on an independent line.

The criss-cross for *Crossroads* produces fantastic imagery in its shifts. It follows a canon of beauty all its own.

The Fourth Millennium (Millennium IV) (1963)

*Chamber
Music*

☐ American Brass Quintet / Nonesuch 71222

A telling example of Brant's speciality: spatial separation of the utilized sound sources. In this case a duo (horn and euphonium) are pitted against a trio (two trumpets and a trombone). A program frames the music, picturing the trio as survivors of a "Grand Thermonuclear War" and the duo as visitors from another planet. No loss of the sense of the dynamic work occurs if one doesn't read the story line.

Opera and Dramatic Music

Machinations (1970)

☐ Brant (various instruments) / Desto 7108

It may well be that Brant will disagree with the dramatic-music category in which his work has been placed in this survey. Certainly that area comes closest to describing music that is produced by use of an outline of procedures that eliminates musical notation. Brant's "instant composing," as he terms it, means *Machinations* could only be played by Henry Brant. Further, it can only be heard via the mechanics of a recording, since four separate recordings were made and then combined to form the single stereo disc. In this respect alterations were made by way of variable speed, but there is no electronic sound in the mix.

Ten instruments are used in this mass improvisation. Of these, four are extremely rare: an E flat flute, a ceramic flute, a double ocarina, and a double flageolet; the others are timpani, chimes, xylophone, glockenspiel, organ, and harp. The assortment holds aural interest, though listening for an entire record side means much totals less in the long run. Nonetheless, stopping the disc after a period of time or sampling portions causes no harm, and certainly Brant wouldn't object to such improvisational listening since it would match his improvisational performance.

Brant describes his work "as a sort of last warning from the natural world to the human species—a kind of organizational underground meeting of animate and inanimate objects." A further warning applies to *Schwann*, which lists this work under the rubric Desto has used for the disc, namely, "Music 1970," rather than indicating the *Machinations* title as well as the title of the companion piece on the disc, *Kingdom Come*.

Yehezekiel Braun   (1922-   )

Choral

Chorus with Accompaniment

Psalm 98

☐ David Tilman Choir / Lam (baritone) / Serenus 12039

Fervent presentation of *Let Us Sing unto the Lord a New Song*, from the *Shabbat Mitzion*, the Israel Sabbath service. The solo interpolations by Nathan Lam, a cantor, are sensitively crafted, and the modal glories of Braun's piece are beautifully set forth. (No credit is given the organist who accompanies.)

Julian Bream / Benjamin Britten. *See Britten* / Bream.

Alvin Brehm   (1925-   )

Chamber Music

Dialogues for Bassoon and Percussion (1963)

☐ Pachman (bassoon); Price and Little (percussion) / Golden Crest 7019 (monaural)

The sheer opposition of bassoon and assorted percussion qualities is like adding a variety of sauces and garnishes to a solidly cooked steak. However, Brehm is careful and select with his combinations. In the second movement (Adagio) the xylophone is the principal flavor that is mixed with the bassoon timbre, and in movement 3 the wood block is the main tasty addition. The bassoon colors itself, as it were, by playing microtone curves in parts 3 and 4.

There is no real lack of geniality in Brehm's Dialogues, but the repartee is somewhat serious. Eavesdropping is extremely worth while, particularly with the excellence of the three participants.

Quintet for Brass (1967)

☐ American Brass Quintet / Nonesuch 71222

Virtuosity of the most dynamic type, yet not nullifying the concept of integrated musical construction. The designs are clear, and the *modus operandi* is of post-Webern detail. An exciting work for brass and played to bring out the white heat that pervades the composition.

Cycle of Six Songs on Poems of García Lorca

Vocal

☐ Composers Festival Orchestra / DeGaetani (soprano) / Brehm (conductor) / Trilogy CTS–1002

Voice and Orchestra

Only the fourth of this cycle, *The Little Mute Boy,* has a lightsome demeanor. All the others have the depth of expressionistic detail. These are evocative songs with clear textures and natural rhythmic contours applied to the texts.

One cannot fault Jan DeGaetani. She is a singer with a conscience. That needs no explanation. Her interpretation of Brehm's songs is spotless.

Martin Bresnick   (1946-   )

B's Garlands (1973)

Chamber Music

☐ Selmi, Ravenna, Mascellini, De Luca, Lanzilotta, Mastromatteo, De Girolamo, and Mori (cellos) / Composers Recordings SD–336

Bresnick's work was composed for a cellist, Bonnie Hampton, and her pupils, hence the title. Most of the time the writing is a harmonic collage, percussively oriented in the beginning. Most effective are the more relaxed middle section and the world-record-breaking sustained unisoned pedal (never disturbed and hardly opposed) that concludes the piece. It runs for more than two and a half minutes!

Hyman Bress   (1931-   )

Fantasy (Electronic)

Instrumental

☐ Bress (violin); Reiner (piano) / Folkways 3355 (monaural)

Violin

Bress's rhapsodic twelve-tone vocabulary is punctuated not only by the piano's phrases and chords but occasionally by some rough electronic sounds. Two points: the superabundance of activity threatens the stability of the music; the formal purpose served by the few tape entrances is not clear, and therefore is questionable. No questions as to Bress's abilities as a violinist, however.

Havergal Brian   *(1876-1972)*

Orchestra   **Symphony No. 6:** *Sinfonia Tragica* **(1948)**

Symphony No. 16 (1960)

☐ London Philharmonic Orchestra / Fredman (conductor) / Musical Heritage Society MHS-3426

Kaikhosru Sorabji, John Foulds, Havergal Brian—names that only a paltry few recognize, and not all of that small, select group have seen, let alone heard, any of the music by these composers. As for the great conductors, their total avoidance of this music (that they do not know of it is no excuse) makes them deserving of badges of black. For Musical Heritage, therefore, huzzas and hurrahs for the transfer of the English recording on Lyrita, thereby making possible the first domestic release in the United States of Havergal Brian's music—a pair of works drawn from his prodigious production of thirty-two symphonies, the final twenty-one composed after he had reached the age of eighty!

Hugh Wood, the English composer-critic, has put forth the substantial and highly intriguing idea that perhaps an alternative history of music might be written based on such forgotten names. If so, there are many others that would be as important as the three mentioned.

But is is not the prolificness of Brian that demands attention. Malcolm MacDonald describes him perfectly: "not a parochial minor figure, but a composer of truly European stature: Brian's achievements as a symphonist, in particular, seem scarcely less impressive than those of Mahler, or Sibelius." And there is more: the marvelous sense of orchestration and its pigmentation as pertinent to the structural unfolding of the material, the driving potency even in slower-paced sections, the ability to form long-line melodic statements (especially exemplified in Symphony No. 6), and, above all, the refusal to imitate and to concoct mannerisms. This is an individual composer of high rank, a man who practiced creative exploration.

Thomas Briccetti   *(1936-   )*

Orchestra   **Overture:** *The Fountain of Youth* **(1972)**

☐ Louisville Orchestra / Briccetti (conductor) / Louisville 733

The stylistic spectrum is Hindemith with less chromatics and more jazz waves. Glissando jets color Briccetti's sonorous fountain. It is clearly portrayed by the orchestra, and the sound is bright.

Frank Bridge   *(1879-1941)*

String   **A Christmas Dance:** *Sir Roger de Coverley* **(1922)**
Orchestra
☐ English Chamber Orchestra / Britten (conductor) / London 6618

One of the oldest of all English country dances, somewhat in sound like the American Virginia reel. Bridge posits an introduction, dismembers the melody, and puts it through various paces and developments, all without losing the charm of the melody itself. He is not oblivious to possible rhythmic monotony, and makes certain rhythm is purposefully disturbed, so that one finds duple meters cutting against the grain of the trinomial dance. Be on the lookout for an interweave of *Auld Lang Syne*.

A snappy, full-hearted performance, conducted by the onetime pupil of the composer.

Sonata for Cello and Piano (1917)

Chamber Music

☐ Rostropovich (cello); Britten (piano) / London 6649

A dark romantic rhetoric fills this work, even in the fastest-tempoed conclusion (a *Molto allegro e agitato*). Further, a rhapsodic, fragmentary approach covers the development of the principal themes. This poses a difficulty in performance, but the intelligent realization by these master musicians makes everything turn out with a seamless sense of coverage.

String Quartet

No. 3 (1926) / No. 4 (1937)

☐ Allegri String Quartet / Argo ZRG-714

No warm Englishness in these fine quartets, but heated motival detail, fully chromaticized, peripherally loyal to tonality but consistently arguing against it. The titling is a clear guide: Bridge's first quartet was in E minor, his second one in G minor, these bear (properly) no key locale. But passionate attention to shapes and balances marks every measure of the two late quartets. The music travels over Bergian territory but there are fewer potholes.

The playing is splendid and the Allegri group produces a compelling documentation of the scores. It is certainly time that our many quartet teams direct their attention to Frank Bridge's strong compositions.

Houston Bright   *(1916-   )*

Three Short Dances

Chamber Music

☐ American Woodwind Quintet / Golden Crest S-4075

Short and mostly sweet, but especially tastefully tart in the Little Quick Dance. Bright has a nice way with curling a tune. Tonal all the way but not academically overdriven. Splendidly played.

George Frederick Bristow   *(1825-1898)*

Six Pieces for Organ, Op. 45: No. 1 in F major, No. 4 in G minor, No. 6 in C major

Instrumental

☐ Beck (organ) / Musical Heritage Society OR A-263

Organ

All the sounds are formed quite correctly, knitted by solid Germanic fibers, and arranged in the right place. Measured by the individuality slide rule, Bristow is found wanting; estimated by the rod of constructive workmanship, his music is certainly acceptable. Ditto for the performance.

Dream Land, Op. 59

Piano

☐ Davis (piano) / New World Records NW-257

Of the days when gentility was in full flower. The piece still has a flavor for our machine-drummed ears, even though rather lengthy (seven minutes). Nevertheless, Bristow's historic strength of place deserves current sonic documentation, and this piece will do as well as any. Its arpeggio ubiquity is not poverty of invention, but a way of expression fashionable at the time it was written (1885). Then, most piano music of this kind was produced for the home, where it could be played by respectable, corseted young women.

Benjamin Britten (1913-1976)

Orchestra

Four Sea Interludes, Op. 33a, and Passacaglia, Op. 33b, from *Peter Grimes*

☐ London Symphony Orchestra / Previn (conductor) / Angel S-37142

The pieces are of varying formal shape and in their characterizations achieve the status of a balanced five-movement suite conveying the general mood, tone, and effect of the opera.

Previn's performance is tops and certainly is to be preferred to Britten's version (London 6179), which is simply edited down by excerpting the complete operatic recording (see under *Opera and Dramatic Music*). As a result, two short vocal passages are included. When listening to the recording, these are slightly annoying.

Sinfonia da Requiem, Op. 20

☐ New Philharmonia Orchestra / Britten (conductor) / London 25937

The argument here is leisurely disclosed: a solemn consideration of symphonic form, set in a quasi-programmatic frame of reference. The three connected parts (two slow movements embrace the middle portion) refer to the moods of the Requiem Mass: Lacrymosa, Dies Irae, and Requiem Aeternam. Though Britten has a long chain of colors at his command, the orchestration is scrupulous, and this scrupulousness is the most interesting facet of this work.

Britten's composition was ordered by the Japanese government to celebrate the twenty-six hundredth anniversary of the Mikado's dynasty, but was refused after completion on religious grounds.

Britten made the initial recording of his Opus 20 with the Danish State Radio Symphony Orchestra in the monophonic days (also for London on 1123). This later version has all the necessary ingredients, most especially the sense of formal integration and avoidance of the individual coloration found in the pair of Previn-led recordings. (One of these is with the St. Louis Symphony Orchestra on Odyssey Y-31016; the other is with the London Symphony Orchestra on Angel S-37142.)

The Young Person's Guide to the Orchestra, Op. 34

☐ Philadelphia Orchestra / Ormandy (conductor) / RCA ARL1-2743
☐ London Symphony Orchestra / Britten (conductor) / London 6671

The compound of vaudeville, musical midway, and didactic consideration known as the "children's concert" has brought to the repertoire a few genuine pieces—from the Soviet Union, Prokofiev's best-seller *Peter and the Wolf*; from America, *Tubby the Tuba* by George Kleinsinger and Don Gillis's *The Man Who Invented Music*; and from England, Britten's Opus 34, a set of variations plus fugue on a Purcell theme. Except for the last, none of these compositions prevail as absolutes. Conceived with commentary, they cease to exist without it.

Britten's published score allows for the elimination of the narrator's part. Opinions are divided about this; a number of critics insist that the narration is superfluous. The vote from this corner is all for having the narrator. Once one has heard the music in that form, it is frustrating and annoying to have the narrator lacking. (For the narrator-and-orchestra version see under *Opera and Dramatic Music.*)

Britten's version for orchestra alone has long been rightfully considered definitive, and no one can argue that point, and in addition Britten is no scholastic conductor. Still, he doesn't have the flair that Ormandy shows in his new recording, the old one he made for Columbia (5183) having gone into the delete department. As a back-up and for documentation get the Britten by all means. But for color, action, instrumental typing, and virtuosity, all presented with golden tone and sound, get the Ormandy edition.

Prelude and Fugue for Eighteen-Part String Orchestra, Op. 29

□ Royal Philharmonic Orchestra / Del Mar (conductor) / Argo ZRG–754

The title is traditional and academic, and though the music is tonally buttoned-down conservative, Britten's Prelude and Fugue is dramatic and emotional from the opening cohesively powered introduction to the concluding chord. Moreover, there is no compartmentalizing of the two sections, and their interlocking forms a further creative strategic success, with a great fugue spread over the eighteen parts.

A performance of punch and pungence, a brilliant execution.

Simple Symphony, Op. 4

□ English Chamber Orchestra / Britten (conductor) / London 6618

Early music, written between Britten's ninth and twelfth years, later reformulated, edited, and polished by the hands of the composer come of age. The profound emotion of the third part, a *Sentimental Sarabande,* is the peak of the opus.

Britten as conductor portrays the essentials of this music far better than the others (Marriner and Somary) represented in the catalogue. It is noteworthy that he takes, for the greater part, slower tempi. In the case of the *Sarabande,* for example, Marriner's timing (on Angel S–36883) is a minute and one-quarter faster. The difference in pace makes the Britten-led setting much more convincing.

Variations on a Theme of Frank Bridge, Op. 10

□ English Chamber Orchestra / Britten (conductor) / London 6671

Britten's basic means of variation is to rely on a freedom of departure from the thematic base and represent the principal idea more in spirit than in its individual characteristics. The ten variants here are mainly patterned on specific nonclassical propositions, and some of the variations have a wonderful sense of parody—the fourth, *Aria Italiana,* is snide Rossini; the sixth, *Wiener Waltz,* pulls the tail of that musical form. Other variants have an engaging color and textural plan. The embellishments do not twine around or flow out of the theme, but disport by themselves in the form of new settings. More sharply and clearly, myriad activity and change point up that Britten's engaging piece is essentially made up of diversions.

It is surprising that this work, which has become one of the few contemporary standards in the string-orchestra repertoire, has been bypassed by the recording companies. London's release is the only one currently available. It has superb sound, propelling playing, and decisive interpretative depth.

String Orchestra

297

*Solo
Instrument
and
Orchestra*

Symphony for Cello and Orchestra, Op. 68

☐ English Chamber Orchestra / Rostropovich (cello) / Britten (conductor) / London 6419

Cello

The "Symphony" in the title indicates instrumental equality, but solo virtuosic energy abounds in this work. So do sonorous hammer and tongs (movement 1), telegraphic motility (in the *Presto inquieto*), declamation, cadenza spotlighting, and variations. No soft ground in Britten's work, but plentiful rock-weighted, rock-sized solidities.

That the performance is a distinguished one is to be expected. It again proves Britten's fine ability to conduct his music (no easy matter in this case) and reflects Rostropovich's constant willingness to expand the cello repertoire. In this respect he outdistances every cellist in the world.

Piano

Concerto for Piano and Orchestra, Op. 13

☐ English Chamber Orchestra / Richter (piano) / Britten (conductor) / London 6723

No preoccupation here with formality. Britten gives the Concerto a modern perspective. A dynamic twelve-minute Toccata is contrasted to a four-and-one-quarter minute Waltz and an eighteen-minute Impromptu and March. The evocations (bits of Prokofiev and Shostakovich provide some borrowed flavors) are powerful. There are no light pop-musical turnovers.

Excellent performance, containing all of the music's sense of expectancy and drama. The sonics are ideal.

Diversions on a Theme for Piano (Left Hand) and Orchestra, Op. 21

☐ Baltimore Symphony Orchestra / Fleisher (piano) / Comissiona (conductor) / Desto 7168

Piano compositions designed for the left hand alone sometimes have the objective of specialized virtuosic display. This reminds one of Paganini's deliberately playing on one string of his violin; it is acrobatic fun, little more. But in the case of piano music written for a one-armed virtuoso the limitation is a virtuous requirement.

This concerto-sized piece was composed for Paul Wittgenstein, a concert pianist who had lost his right arm during World War I. In order to continue his career, Wittgenstein rebuilt his technique from scratch and acquired the ability to play music with his one hand that would tax the unhandicapped average performer with two. Assured of his artistic capabilities once more, he ordered works from a number of outstanding composers—Prokofiev, Richard Strauss, and Ravel among others. Britten's commission, fulfilled in 1940, reflects its title in consisting of a set of eleven diverting variations. Nothing profound is presented; what is presented is a thoroughgoing display of expert variational technique.

Natural and vivid playing are exhibited.

Violin

Concerto for Violin and Orchestra, Op. 15

☐ English Chamber Orchestra / Lubotsky (violin) / Britten (conductor) / London 6723

Britten probes a different concerto plan than usual in this darkly colored work for solo violin and orchestra. The first movement discourses around suspenseful rhythmic motives. A virtuosic Scherzo follows. The influence of Shostakovich is pertinent, but the music refuses to take on a gay air. In the final, solemn part of the concluding movement (a Passacaglia) the Concerto reaches its finest moment.

A highly expressive, deeply conveyed performance by Mark Lubotsky. It has more colored atmosphere and stronger playing than is heard on the monaural issue available from Louisville 626 (Kling as soloist, Whitney as conductor).

Suite for Cello, Op. 72

Second Suite for Cello, Op. 80

☐ Rostropovich (cello) / London 6617

Music for an unaccompanied string instrument quite often falls into a pseudo-contrapuntal frame of reference, in an attempt to compensate for its basic homophonic restrictions. Britten does not agonize in that way. Quite often in these two suites there are sections where Britten doesn't sound like Britten. However, the deftness of design and the coloristic management display a Britten who proves again his genius and mastery by solving the complex problems in conceiving two large-scale works for an unaccompanied cello.

There is some polyphony—a fugue is included in both suites. More pertinent is the use of a wide variety of color, dynamized but never reaching for outré effects. The complete timbre scale of the cello is utilized, with good portions of pizzicati, a fair amount of harmonics, and some *col legno*. Startling is the major use of monodic pitch progress, and this device more than anything else is the evidence of a creative mastermind.

In the first Suite, a *Canto* serves as a ritornello that divides the total of six movements into three major groups. The *Canto* is differently detailed in its various appearances and is always followed by a pair of movements. After a *Canto primo* there is a *Fuga* and a *Lamento;* then follows a *Canto secondo,* which is succeeded by a *Serenata* and a *Marcia.* The *Canto terzo* precedes a drone-laden *Bordone* and a virtuosic *Moto perpetuo.* The latter is linked to still another statement of the dominating *Canto* theme (indicated as *Canto quarto*), which concludes the work.

The formal plan of the Second Suite embraces five movements, beginning with a *Declamato* and concluding with a *Ciaconna.* Movement 2 is a *Fuga* and movement 3 is a Scherzo constructed from a pair of principal ideas. The only untitled movement is the fourth, an *Andanta lento* (an odd juxtaposition of speeds generally appearing separately).

It was Mstislav Rostropovich's mastery that stimulated the composition of the two cello suites. The cellist's recorded performances are truly inspired. One doubts that when a competitive edition appears on disc, it will be able to supersede what is heard on these two record sides.

Instrumental

Cello

Nocturnal, Op. 70

☐ Bream (guitar) / RCA LSC-2964

Britten's procedure will remind one of d'Indy's *Istar,* also a set of variations which appear before the theme is stated. The constructive process is undoubtedly more subtle thus, since the permutative progress cannot be considered in terms of thematic relationship until the subject is finally exposed. Here is the reverse of variational method, arriving at a thematic resolution instead of departing from it.

Aside from the technical process, Britten's sizable opus—seven variations and a passacaglia which ends with the theme *Come Heavy Sleep* by John Dowland, No. 20 in his *First Book of Songs or Ayres of Four Parts,* composed in 1597—is drenched with color and meaning. Each section is sharply outlined in mood, such as "Musingly," "Uneasy," and "Gently Rocking." The imagery is truly superb.

Bream considers *Nocturnal* to be the greatest single work written for the guitar. Made by an eminent musician, such a statement must be respected. Whatever the opinions of

Guitar

others may be, *Nocturnal* is certainly one of the most important compositions for the solo guitar. Bream's portrayal is, naturally, authoritative. It is, as well, poetically and emotively communicative.

Oboe

Six Metamorphoses After Ovid for Solo Oboe, Op. 49

☐ Gomberg (oboe) / Vanguard C–10064

Clarity of form without rigidity of design, definition of descriptive generalities without nullifying the broader concept of pure music, and virtuosity in using a homophonic instrument without technical trickery mark Britten's opus. The cello has its Bach Suites, the violin its Paganini Caprices, the flute its *Syrinx*. With Britten's Metamorphoses the oboe finally has its special piece.

Harold Gomberg's playing is sensational. It is splendidly rich, seamlessly phrased, and fully responsive to the creative document. Such oboistic enticement is the quintessence of artistry.

Organ

Prelude and Fugue on a Theme of Vittoria (1947)

☐ Preston (organ) / Argo 5BBA–1013/5

A minor item in Britten's catalogue. This, his only work for solo organ, is based on a theme from Vittoria's motet *Ecce Sacerdos Magnus*.

Chamber Music

Lachrymae, Op. 48

☐ Thomas (viola); Akst (piano) / Counterpoint/Esoteric 5605

This work is subtitled *Reflections on a Song of John Dowland* (the Dowland title being *If My Complaints Could Passion Move*). There are ten *Reflections,* which combine variational procedures with partial, quasi-symphonic development of themes.

A strongly colored reading. It is substantially structured by the performers.

Sonata in C for Cello and Piano, Op. 65

☐ Rostropovich (cello); Britten (piano) / London 6237

Britten's Sonata in C ("major" or "minor" are intentionally lacking in Britten's title and properly so, since the "C" marks a tonal polarity, not a specific mode) avoids any cut-to-fit formal procedure. First, it embraces five movements, and second, each of these has a pertinent descriptive heading.

What virtuosity Rostropovich and Britten display in their performance! A better one may appear on disc in the future, but the odds are against it.

A *Dialogo* ushers in the work. The motival concentration found in this *allegro*-tempoed movement exemplifies still another kind of virtuosity—the creative brand. Movement 2 is a Scherzo-pizzicato, a self-explanatory title that nevertheless can only hint at the colorful and exciting use of high-register piano writing against low-colored plucked sound. Movement 3 is an *Elegia;* a *Marcia* follows. It is snide music, covered with a good share of Prokofiev fallout. Britten (who wrote the liner note) succinctly describes the main theme: "The cello plays a rumbustious bass to the jerky tune on the piano." The fittingly fast finale is extremely colorful, with a consistent use of *saltando* bowing that carries out the *Moto perpetuo* title.

Suite for Violin and Piano, Op. 6

☐ Tarack (violin); Grubb (piano) / Lyrichord 7195

Tasteful neoclassic sandwiches for the instruments. Some of the ingredients are a mild March and a peppery *Moto perpetuo*. Everything is well prepared and well served.

(Britten revised this work in the latter part of his career. The version recorded is the original edition.)

Fantasy Quartet for Oboe, Violin, Viola, and Cello, Op. 2

☐ Gomberg (oboe); Raimondi (violin); Zaslav (viola); Stuch (cello) / Vanguard C-10064

Britten's talents were in early evidence. His second opus was composed in two months in 1932, before he had reached voting age.

Though it is a fantasy, the form of this oboe quartet is circular, passing through varying tempi and semisections determined, in part, by the use of free variation. When these are completed, the main theme returns, followed by the original introduction. Toward the end, the instruments drop out one by one, just as they entered.

This is the second time Harold Gomberg, who is a phenomenal oboist, has recorded the work. The initial execution is still available: a monaural disc released on Counterpoint 5504E. There Gomberg is supported by members of the Galimir Quartet. The Vanguard later setting is superior, better integrated, despite the fact that the strings are not drawn from a permanent team. It has fully detailed coloration, a fine sense of atmosphere, and a perspective that details all the points in the score.

String Quartet
No. 1 in D major, Op. 25 / No. 2 in C major, Op. 36

☐ Allegri String Quartet / London STS-15303

The first movement of Opus 25 obtains its stimuli from the vibrant secundal chord that opens the work. It is reiterated and spread horizontally to begin the main theme; it occurs not less than four times in the first movement. There is a similar process of germinal construction in the vehement second movement, with a triplet figure intruding on tightly repeated eighth-note rhythms. It finally lights the fuse, and the main theme bursts forth completely bordered with triplets. Movement 3 is cast in Britten's favorite variational design; the finale shows the composer again constructing his plot from a unitary idea.

The construction of the opening part of Opus 36 includes the important utilization of contrapuntal devices to unfold a clear sonata form. Movement 2, a Scherzo, is dulled and thereby made more mysterious by tutti use of mutes. Further, this music of the Scherzo is worried and full of theatrical dynamic shocks. At times the four string instruments sound tripled, so resourceful is Britten's scoring. A huge finale is offered, with eighteen variations on the opening unison theme.

Fine performances here. The Allegri team makes emotional as well as musical sense in both works. The competitive edition of String Quartet No. 1, available on Counterpoint/ Esoteric (5504E), is souped-up stereo, and aside from that point it is played in an only passable manner by the Galimir Quartet.

Canticle I: *My Beloved Is Mine*, Op. 40

☐ Pears (tenor); Britten (piano) / Argo ZRG-5277

The equivalent of a four-movement design is used here. Britten's form is as identifiable as a Haydn minuet, his language merely more sophisticated. The poem, by Francis Quarles (1592-1644), consists of six verses, each of seven lines. Britten balances verses 1

Vocal

*Voice
with
Accompaniment*

301

and 2 with the final pair in slow tempi, and contrasts these with recitative and quasi-scherzo sections.

A deeply felt conception by this famous performing partnership.

Canticle II: *Abraham and Isaac,* Op. 51

☐ Hahessey (alto); Pears (tenor); Britten (piano) / Argo ZRG–5277

An archaic beauty hovers over Britten's version of Abraham's submission to God's will to the point of being willing to kill his only son. It is described by music that is tender as well as profound.

Abraham is represented by the tenor, Isaac by the boy alto (at the first performance the part was sung by Kathleen Ferrier). By combining the voices to represent the character of God, Britten invents a third type of voice. A magnificent performance of the work; the singing of John Hahessey is both charming and poignant.

Canticle III: *Still Falls the Rain,* Op. 55

☐ Pears (tenor); Britten (piano); Tuckwell (horn) / Argo ZRG–5277

Variational treatment is utilized in the third of Britten's five canticles. The text is a wartime poem by Edith Sitwell. This black-bordered music, marked by an intervallic descent, can be described as a secular *Kol Nidre*.

A beautifully clear and balanced performance. When this was recorded, Pears was at his peak.

The Holy Sonnets of John Donne, Op. 35

☐ Pears (tenor); Britten (piano) / London 26099

Britten employs the poetic form of the sonnet in the nine parts of this cycle devoted to the general theme of death. The prose elements serve as intensifications of the vocal line and the composer further reacts to these by being creatively free.

With Pears and Britten no interpretative errors occur. Their performance has all the intrinsic truths.

Seven Sonnets of Michelangelo, Op. 22

☐ Stewart (tenor); Katz (piano) / Desto 7127

Britten, according to most critics, was a determinedly English composer. In Opus 22 he used an Italian text but maintained his stylistic Anglicism. This may seem impossible, but the sensitive loveliness of the cycle is artistic proof. Some of the word-handling is odd (and Stewart's diction doesn't always help), but the music gives sufficient compensation by its inspiring warmth of conception. A full piano background is utilized; it is scaled properly but the use of patterns is overdone.

Forthright delivery by John Stewart, though not matching the nobility that Pears displayed in his old London (No. 1204) monophonic recording.

Songs and Proverbs of William Blake, Op. 74

☐ Fischer-Dieskau (baritone); Britten (piano) / London 26099

☐ A continuous cycle consisting of six of Blake's *Proverbs of Hell* as preludes to six of his *Songs of Experience.* The seventh section consists of an aphorism and text drawn from Blake's *Auguries of Innocence.*

The dark overtones of Britten's cycle are perfect for Fischer-Dieskau's voice. The artistic conviction he displays is thrilling.

Les Illuminations for Tenor or Soprano Solo and String Orchestra, Op. 18

Voice and Orchestra

☐ English Chamber Orchestra / Pears (tenor) / Britten (conductor) / London 26161

One of Britten's most sensitive compositions gives listeners an opportunity to hear large-scaled vocal music shaped by intimate reasoning. Instead of presenting a big-sounding spectacle, Britten concerns himself with a tight, concentrated, and thrilling drama in his ten settings of poems by Arthur Rimbaud. Regardless of mood the details are pictured by chamber-music adaptations. Romantic passion and symphonic amplitude are always kept in balance. The orchestra of strings becomes an instrumental chorus of many divided voices. In its splendor this work is akin to a heady wine.

An enchanting performance and a fine example of recording art. (A version with soprano voice is available on Angel S–36788; the writer prefers the setting with a male voice.)

Nocturne for Tenor Solo, Seven Obbligato Instruments and String Orchestra, Op. 60

☐ Strings of the London Symphony Orchestra / Pears (tenor); Murray (flute); Lord (English horn); de Peyer (clarinet); Waterhouse (bassoon); Tuckwell (horn); Blyth (timpani); Ellis (harp) / Britten (conductor) / London 6179

When a composer binds himself to writing a song cycle with a precise, interlocked subject, it is a difficult task to reconcile such a concentrated plan with the demands of structural balance. If the design includes instrumental color individuality to substantiate the narrative, the problem increases unless some technical factor overcomes these clashing conditions.

The Nocturne embraces eight songs of different mood by as many poets (including Shelley, Wordsworth, Keats, and Shakespeare), and each is scored for strings with a different obbligato instrument. Since every poem is concerned with the subject of sleep and dreams, Britten attains his objective and the necessary formal stability by the original plan of his scoring and without any eccentric instrumentational behavior. The opening part uses muted strings; they are joined by the bassoon in the second song, by the harp in the next portion, and so on, until the full tutti reigns in the eighth and final section. The poetic subject matter becomes dramatic through the musical and orchestrational context.

Two editions are currently available. The one chosen has certain advantages to begin with: the tenor who participated in the premiere (at the Leeds Festival in October of 1958), the composer conducting, and a super set of musicians including the clarinetist, Gervase de Peyer; the hornist, Barry Tuckwell; and the harpist, Osian Ellis. Beyond these it has Pears's fuller upper range and his freer and steadier tone, plus more sensitive and convincing orchestral playing.

Serenade for Tenor Solo, Horn, and String Orchestra, Op. 31

☐ London Symphony Orchestra / Pears (tenor); Tuckwell (horn) / Britten (conductor) / London 26161

In the Serenade Britten's power to fit musical line to the poetry of Tennyson, Blake, Jonson, Keats, and Cotton is magical; the scoring is no less evocative.

The haunting six major sections of the Serenade (in addition to a Prologue and Epilogue) are like a synthesis of archaic yet fresh sound. Sweetened with the bouquet of horn tone, the composition has a gentle nocturnal breath throughout its measures. It defines the essence of musical beauty. In fact one realizes how Benjamin Britten might have been a younger Ralph Vaughan Williams.

The ways of the recording industry have long been unfathomable. Currently there are five issues of Britten's *A Ceremony of Carols* and fourteen of his *Young Person's Guide to the Orchestra,* but of Britten's gorgeous hunk of music, the Serenade, only a pair!

This release is projected beautifully by Pears (a huge improvement over his initial recording of Britten's music on a London 5358 monaural disc, with Brain as the hornist and Goossens as the conductor). The strings are topflight, and Barry Tuckwell is the equal of any player of the instrument. London's recording is richly engineered. The only criticism of the release is the lack of a text.

Choral

Chorus Alone

Choral Dances from *Gloriana,* Op. 52

☐ Chorus of the London Symphony Orchestra / Malcolm (conductor) / Oiseau-Lyre 60037

Music for a chorus to accompany an Elizabethan masque that appears in the second act of the opera Britten composed for the coronation festivities in 1953 for Elizabeth II.

In this instance, however, purpose does not change method. These a cappella choruses are styled in differing tempi and contrasting harmonic and polyphonic style. As usual, the choral medium shows Britten to advantage.

A lusty performance, far better than the subdued competitive recording made by Louis Halsey's Elizabethan Singers on Argo ZRG–5424.

Chorale (After an Old French Carol) (1944)

☐ Elizabethan Singers / Halsey (conductor) / Argo ZRG–5424

Balanced (ternary) form binds this choral statement, described by Eric Roseberry as music "of religious belief for a post-Freudian generation." It is a companion piece to A Shepherd's Carol (*see below*). Both pieces have words by W. H. Auden, and both were composed for a B.B.C. program called "Poet's Christmas." Neither work is listed among the bibliographic details in either *Grove's Dictionary of Music and Musicians* or *Benjamin Britten—a Commentary on His Works from a Group of Specialists,* edited by Donald Mitchell and Hans Keller.

Five Flower Songs, Op. 47

☐ Elizabethan Singers / Halsey (conductor) / Argo ZRG–5424

Music pertinent to the words. No sound-for-word descriptions, however. Thus in the second of the set (*The Succession of the Four Sweet Months*) Britten uses a fugato, and he chooses slightly prickly-pungent harmonies to describe *Marsh Flowers* (No. 3). Bouncy extroversion with catchy choral accompaniment against a solo voice, and other operetta devices, are found among the light notions of the finale, *Ballad of Green Broom.*

Not too often performed, for no sane reason. The recording is a gem and may awaken choral directors to what they have overlooked. The Elizabethan Singers prove to be marvelous advocates for Britten's splendid work.

Hymn to St. Cecilia, Op. 27

☐ Chorus of the London Symphony Orchestra / Malcolm (conductor) / Oiseau-Lyre 60037

Quite often choral music merely sets the text per se. In the Hymn to St. Cecilia Britten *translates* the music inherent in the beautiful words Auden wrote. It is as though the music and poems were inseparable, created simultaneously—a blending of sensibility of structure and sensitivity of prose meaning and mood. This is a work for unaccompanied five-part (divided sopranos) chorus with incidental solos. Especially appealing are the varied colors of the voices, to a degree imitative of instrumental timbres, plus a scherzo section that is as close to light string-instrument style as a chorus can come.

The London group is splendid—vocally clean, properly incisive—and has accomplished a fine rendition.

A Hymn to the Virgin (1930)

☐ Chorus of the London Symphony Orchestra / Malcolm (conductor) / Oiseau-Lyre 60037

Spearheaded by modality rarely employed by the composer, this little composition, which predates Britten's official Opus 1 (the Sinfonietta for chamber orchestra), was written in 1930 and revised four years later.

Churchly but not conventional, an anthem but not academic, the music contains keen differences of texture with neat antiphonal effects. Some four minutes of real beauty in the better of the pair of performances currently available on records.

A Shepherd's Carol (1944)

☐ Elizabethan Singers / Halsey (conductor) / Argo ZRG-5424

The text, by Auden, is given alternating solo and chorus consideration. Composed in 1944, Britten's choral charmer is listed neither in *Benjamin Britten—a Commentary on His Works from a Group of Specialists*, edited by Donald Mitchell and Hans Keller, nor in the latest edition of *Grove's Dictionary of Music and Musicians*. See also *above*, under Chorale (After an Old French Carol).

The Ballad of Little Musgrave and Lady Barnard (1943)

☐ Elizabethan Singers / Parry (piano) / Halsey (conductor) / Argo ZRG-5424

Chorus with Accompaniment

Britten the choral composer treats his tale of adultery and revenge in a quasi-operatic manner. Following the text supplied is mandatory to understand the story. Only male voices are utilized by Britten; the Elizabethan gentlemen do sing well but enunciate otherwise.

A Ceremony of Carols, Op. 28

☐ Choir of St. John's College, Cambridge / Turner, Bennett, and Matthews (trebles); Robles (harp) / Guest (conductor) / Argo ZRG-5440
☐ Robert Shaw Chorale of Women's Voices / Endich (soprano); Kopleff (contralto); Newell (harp) / Shaw (conductor) / RCA LSC-2759

To write purposefully for extremely concentrated forces—especially, in this case, for only treble voices and a mere harp as instrumental support—is difficult. Britten's gentle and genuine result is unique vocal chamber music. Devotional in content and with hardly a dot of contemporary inflection, Britten's music has the effect of turning the clock back. But simplicity of style is not entirely absent from contemporary music.

Britten's employment of plainchant is sensitive and atmospheric. The effect is paradoxical—secular music with religious feeling.

The Cambridge youngsters perform magnificently. Theirs is a distinguished (and distinguishing) intimacy that is "wolcum" to the ears. Since Britten wrote his work for "treble voices," the use of a female chorus is certainly not out of place. In that respect (and offering a different timbre totality for those who prefer it), Shaw's group is excellent. However, it does not have the youthful freshness of the boys' choir.

Festival Te Deum, Op. 32

☐ King's College Choir, Cambridge / Channing (treble); Lancelot (organ) / Ledger (conductor) / Angel S-37119

Religious-musical truthfulness with colorful choral symphonicism whether its texture is simple or full-bodied. It is this factor that epitomizes the freshness found in Britten's choral writing.

Ledger's singers are splendid, more balanced than the Shaw group (on RCA LSC-2759), who in turn give a richer-voiced reading than that presented by the St. John's College Choir (on Argo 5340). The dynamic documentation on the Angel release is masterfully set forth technically.

Jubilate Deo (1935)

☐ Choir of St. John's College, Cambridge / Runnett (organ) / Guest (conductor) / Argo ZRG-5340

A closeness to brass fanfares will come to mind when one hears this proclamatory choral piece. Further, the organ is an equal, not a junior partner in Britten's enterprise. A well-knit and clear performance.

Missa Brevis, Op. 63

☐ Choir of St. John's College, Cambridge / Runnett (organ) / Guest (conductor) / Argo ZRG-5440

Related to *A Ceremony of Carols*, since it calls for boys' voices and one instrument. The *Ceremony* uses harp with the voices, the *Missa Brevis* an organ. A medieval atmosphere is reincarnated in Britten's opus. Its direct stylistic simplicity shows that Britten is fully aware of the depth and meaning (and value!) of tradition, but it all turns out to be truly Brittenesque in the long run, with neo-plainchant and neo-Palestrinian conditions.

Old Abram Brown (1935)

Oliver Cromwell (1942)

☐ Elizabethan Singers / Parry (piano) / Halsey (conductor) / Argo ZRG-5424

The ostinato background of *Old Abram Brown* is matched by the repetitiveness of the tune covering the four lines of text. The ending, with an augmentation of the melody sung against itself in regular pulse, may be an academic procedure, but it is an inspirational one when, as here, a composer knows when to use it. *Old Abram Brown* is from a collection Britten produced in 1935 titled *Friday Afternoons*, for children's voices and piano. *Brown* is the last of the dozen items, published in two books, six in each.

Oliver Cromwell is a choral runoff in forty seconds flat. The text is a nonsense ditty; the setting is a mintage that brings the house down every time. Thus it is the real stuff to use for an encore. Hearing the recording, one is certain the listener will encore the encore. It is one of a group of fourteen folk-song settings that Britten turned out in 1942.

Te Deum in C major (1935)

☐ King's College Choir, Cambridge / Phillips (treble); Lancelot (organ) / Ledger (conductor) / Angel S–37119

Straightforward objective, clear tonality, motivic development. Those are the descriptive points for Britten's praise to God.

Two Part Songs for Mixed Voices and Piano (1934)

☐ Elizabethan Singers / Parry (piano) / Halsey (conductor) / Argo ZRG–5424

The above title which Britten indicated will not be found on the single recording available for these choral pieces. They are listed individually: *I Lov'd a Lass* and *Lift Boy*. Properly, however, they are to be heard in succession on the disc.

Especially cogent performance in the case of *Lift Boy*, with its declamatory vocal style and keyboard-instrument staccato background.

Spring Symphony, Op. 44

*Chorus
and Orchestra*

☐ Orchestra and Chorus of Royal Opera House, Covent Garden, and Chorus of Boys from Emanuel School, London / Vyvyan (soprano); Proctor (contralto); Pears (tenor) / Britten (conductor) / London 25242

To Britten, symphonic form does not mean relying on past conformations, and he freely departs from them in this work. It is true that words can disturb symphonic purity, but in the Spring Symphony the text is integrated with the formal concept. The poems, written as far apart as the thirteenth and twentieth centuries, deal with a concentrated theme, the spring season, and give birth to a large, four-movement design, with contrasts and relationships as beautifully invested as in an instrumental symphony.

Britten orchestrates with vividness (and conducts similarly); various groups are chosen for their specific qualities, and instruments with special colors are emphasized: the alto flute, bass clarinet, and a wholly extraordinary cow-horn. As a result, the restricted use of orchestral tutti becomes that much more effective. This is paralleled by an instrumentalized approach to the vocal forces of three soloists (all of whom sing here with immaculate tone, impelling feeling, and technical discipline), a mixed chorus, and a boys' chorus, who whistle and hum.

Purists may argue that this work is no symphony, since Britten avoids substantiated practices. Never mind! This vivid creation, presented in perfect collaboration by all concerned, has substantial symphonicism even though it skirts the usual areas.

War Requiem, Op. 66

☐ London Symphony Orchestra and Chorus, Melos Ensemble, Bach Choir, and Highgate School Choir / Vishnevskaya (soprano); Pears (tenor); Fischer-Dieskau (baritone) / Britten (conductor) / London 1255

The precept of this imposing work is found in the quotation on the title page of the score: ''My subject is War, and the pity of War./ The Poetry is in the pity./ All a poet can do is warn.'' These lines were written by Wilfred Owen, a poet who served as an officer in the British Army during World War I and was killed in action at the age of twenty-five.

Britten's War Requiem is no vocalized fanfare for measuring manhood by battle, no orchestral song about the circumstances of "glorious" combat. It is an antiwar manifesto of overwhelming power, within which words and music are equally potent and important.

To define his document (almost eighty-five minutes in performance time), Britten requires an imposing array: a very large orchestra with plentiful percussion, piano, and organ, a chamber orchestra of a dozen players performing on eighteen different instruments, a harmonium (or portable organ), mixed chorus, boys' choir, and three vocal soloists. These sing a combination of the Latin words employed for the Mass of the Dead and the modern English lines of nine of Owen's poems; the texts are contrasted, intermingled, and joined. The juxtaposition of the traditional liturgy for mourning and Owen's words of protest is conveyed by a triple disposition of instruments and voices. Styles and sonorous contexts of these three groups contrast yet fuse subtly. The first group—consisting of the solo soprano, mixed chorus, and orchestra—represents the liturgical element and is dramatic and brilliant; the second, with the tenor, baritone, and chamber orchestra, identifies worldly quality and is dry and almost gritty in sound; the third section (boys' voices and harmonium) is always veiled and ethereal in content and defines the heavenly innocent.

In the wake of performances of Britten's Requiem a number of critics have hailed the opus as the greatest of the century. Some may not term this a masterful composition, but they cannot deny that Britten's technical achievement is masterful. Even though it is derivative in spots (the Dies Irae recalls the stylistic manner of Carl Orff), it is one of his greatest achievements, worthy of company with the famed requiems by Mozart, Berlioz, and Verdi. In the War Requiem Britten proved that tonal music was not a dead language.

This is a distinguished recording. It would be difficult to imagine a presentation that could better this superb and moving performance, supported by brilliant engineering.

The three solo voices have a U.N. type of disposition, with Pears from England, Fischer-Dieskau from Germany, and Vishnevskaya from the Soviet Union. It had been Britten's hope to have these three for the premiere, given in England on May 30, 1962. Since Vishnevskaya could not arrange her schedule to accomplish this, it was not until London's recording was made that Britten's solo-voice plans were fulfilled.

Cantata and Oratorio

Cantata Academica (Carmen Basiliense), Op. 62

☐ London Symphony Orchestra and Chorus of the London Symphony Orchestra / Vyvyan (soprano); Watts (contralto); Pears (tenor); Brannigan (bass); Lester (piano) / Malcolm (conductor) / Oiseau-Lyre 60037

Fittingly titled and constructed to fit a contemporary depiction of cantata form, Britten's thirteen-sectioned cantata was written in 1960 as a result of a commission from the University of Basel, to help celebrate its quincentenary.

Academic, yes, though not strictly conventional. Britten puts on formal cap and gown, but they are dodecaphonically fashioned. Each of the movements is based on a different pitch for its key span, and thus the work encompasses twelve tones (the thirteenth section returns to the polarity of the opening). Serial organization is thereby considered, and accepted peripherally, but otherwise the work casts its lot tonally. The tone row is used as a row only in the eighth part, and even there it is disguised as E flat major harmony. The forms are a dictionary of devices, such as chorale, canon, recitative, arioso, scherzo, and fugue, combined with techniques galore—ostinato, inversion, retrograde, *stretto*, pedal points, imitation, and so on.

While all this is professional, it is also professorial, perhaps because Britten considered his scholastic commission scholastically. Measured strictly by the formal slide rule, Britten's cantata is quite resourceful.

The performance is a triumph.

Cantata Misericordium, Op. 69

☐ London Symphony Orchestra and Chorus / Pears (tenor); Fischer-Dieskau (baritone) / Britten (conductor) / London 25937

The *Cantata Misericordium* was composed for the centenary of the Red Cross, and first performed "at the solemn ceremony" in Geneva on the day commemorating the centenary, September 1, 1963. It is a sober work, proper for the occasion, and just as fitting was Britten's textual choice—a Latin dramatization of the parable of the Good Samaritan. Coloristic greed would be out of place, an aesthetic error. Accordingly, the orchestration bypasses winds and brass and calls for solo string quartet and string orchestra, harp, piano, and timpani. It is specialized and profitable for this piece, which is soaked in beauty and spirituality.

The recording provides maximum impact. It has the special value of the composer conducting and the same pair of vocal soloists who participated in the premiere performance. These stars make possible the highest rating possible.

Rejoice in the Lamb, Op. 30

☐ King's College Choir, Cambridge / Channing (treble); Bowman (countertenor); Morton (tenor); Creed (bass); Lancelot (organ); Corkhill (percussion) / Ledger (conductor) / Angel S-37119

A cantata in ten sections, which is, in the apt description of H. F. Redlich, a composite of "cloudy and mystical religiosity." Britten's music is most moving in its simple *Allelujah* portions (parts 3 and 10), most curious in a division devoted to the poet's cat, Jeoffry. (The text is by Christopher Smart, 1722-1771.) This latter division includes a motive in the organ which politely delineates feline characteristics.

Richer sound and slightly better solo voices dictated choosing this issue above the other two available (on RCA LSC-2759, with Robert Shaw conducting, and on Argo ZRG-5440, with George Guest conducting).

Saint Nicolas, Op. 42

☐ Academy of St. Martin-in-the-Fields, Cambridge Girls' Choir, and King's College Choir, Cambridge / Russell (treble); Tear (tenor); Davis and Hare (pianos) / Willcocks (conductor) / Seraphim S-60296

It is noteworthy that Britten, more than any other contemporary composer, has utilized the touching quality of children's voices for cogent artistic effect. In *Saint Nicolas* the young voices enhance, with contrapuntal color, the manifold forces of a solo tenor, a mixed chorus, and a four-ply instrumental aggregate of string orchestra, percussion, organ, and piano duet.

Dealing with nine episodes in the legendary tale of the patron saint of children, seamen, and travelers, Britten planned his work to include audience participation in the singing of hymns at the conclusion of the fifth and final sections. The score lives up to the composer's statement that the instrumental parts are "not very sophisticated." Lyrical, colorful, unassuming, this attractive work is easy to listen to.

It is good to have an updated recording of this work, let alone fill the gap since the deletion of the old London mono disc (No. 1254).

*Opera
and Dramatic
Music*

Albert Herring (1947)

☐ English Chamber Orchestra / Fisher (soprano); Pears and Ward (tenors); Terry (treble); Noble (baritone); Brannigan (bass); Peters, Evans, Cantelo, Wilson, Rex, Amit, and Pashley (vocalists) / Britten (conductor) / London 1378

Based on a Guy de Maupassant story in which one Albert Herring is honored as the only virginal person in the town. He loses that dubious honor when he drinks what he thought was lemonade and it turns out to be much stronger. Britten's comic opera is full of brashness and guile and swings along with a smiling vulgarity.

Fine ensembles and splendid singing all around. Pears as Albert Herring and Sylvia Fisher as Lady Billows, an elderly autocrat, star in the show.

Billy Budd, Op. 50

☐ London Symphony Orchestra, Ambrosian Opera Chorus, and Boys from Wandsworth School / Pears, Dempsey, Tear, and Rogers (tenors); Glossop, Shirley-Quirk, and Luxon (baritones); Langdon and Brannigan (basses); David and Robert Bowman, Bryn-Jones, Bush, Coleby, Drake, Garrett, Kelly, Lumsden, Newby, and Read (vocalists) / Britten (conductor) / London 1390

In the operatic world audiences tend to shy away from creations that don't give equal time to the sexes in the cast. Understandable, therefore, but not acceptable is the failure thus far of Britten's *Billy Budd* to become a stable repertory piece. Its all-male *dramatis personae* have the proverbial two strikes against them. Certainly not the music and plot. Both combine to project incidents of direct focus and splendidly pointed characterizations. These would be expected from the Herman Melville story (the libretto was made by E. M. Forster and Eric Crozier). No less would be awaited from Benjamin Britten, who was master of the creative strategy necessary for writing a successful opera. Special pleading doesn't bring a work into the opera house; only time can—and, in this case, one prophesies it will.

Melville's tale of good that is heavily laced with evil receives a triumphant recording. *Billy Budd*'s sweep, grandeur, and dramatic immediacy jump off the grooves and will keep a listener's attention concentrated throughout its two-and-a-half-hour length. Granting cast honors is difficult—there isn't a single weakness in London's cast of twenty-four. As a sampling, one can mention the imposing work of Peter Glossop in the title role, Peter Pears's vivid characterization of the ship's captain, and the evil wonder that Michael Langdon brings to the John Claggart role. Magnificent all around, with unbelievable diction, and sonics that provide the fullest scope.

Curlew River (1964)

☐ Pears (tenor); Shirley-Quirk, Blackburn, and Drake (baritones); Webb (boy soprano); Bohan, Boniface, Healy, Kehoe, Lemming, McKinney, Reed, Stern, and Tasman (vocalists); Adeney (flute); Sanders (horn); Aronowitz (viola); Knussen (double bass); Ellis (harp); Blades (percussion); Ledger (organ) / Britten and Tunnard (conductors) / London 1156

The first of Britten's "parables for Church performance" is based on a medieval Japanese Nō-play. The action concerns a mad woman who has been searching for her lost child only to find that he has died. The pace is muted, the sound tapestry is of subdued colors. But from the very first intonation of the plainsong hymn *Te lucis ante terminum* through its repetition at the end (over an hour later) Britten's atmospheric music holds one in its spell.

A Midsummer Night's Dream, Op. 64

☐ London Symphony Orchestra and Choirs of Downside and Emanuel Schools / Harwood, Watts, and Harper (sopranos); Veasey (mezzo-soprano); Deller (countertenor); Pears and Tear (tenors); Shirley-Quirk and Hemsley (baritones); Brannigan (bass); Alder, Clark, Dakin, Kelly, Lumsden, Macdonald, Pryer, Raggett, Terry, and Wodehouse (vocalists) / Britten (conductor) / London 1385

A compilation of all the music that has been written that is based on the Shakespeare tales would probably result in a fair-sized volume. But there's always room for more, and this opera is truly a welcome addition. Its three acts are based on a libretto written by both Britten (here the conductor) and Peter Pears (here singing the role of Lysander), without altering the basic Shakespeare story. A contemporary tone does drift through the work, but in no sense are there twists or gimmicks in an attempt to update the concept of the story line.

Tonality is the foundation for the technical style of the music. However, it will not escape the perceptive listener that some atonality has been included here and there for spice. The orchestration is deftly supportive and always subtly picturesque. The vocal writing, as always with Britten, is perfectly set for the different voices. The singers do magnificently in what is certainly a definitive performance. Top honors must go to Josephine Veasey as Hermia (in love with Lysander), Owen Brannigan in the role of Bottom, and above all to Alfred Deller in the role of Oberon, the King of the Fairies.

Noye's Fludde, Op. 59

☐ English Chamber Orchestra, East Suffolk Children's Orchestra, and Children's Chorus / Brannigan and Anthony (basses); Rex (alto); Alexander, Angadi, Clack, O'Donovan, David Pinto, Marie-Thérèse Pinto, Garrod, Hawes, Petch, and Saunders (vocalists) / Del Mar (conductor) / Argo ZNF-1

Compositions for children, but artistically acceptable to any age, form a special part of music's history. Britten's *Noye's Fludde* is the most ambitious and significant work of his total output in this category. In his setting of a Chester miracle play of the Middle Ages Britten has succeeded in making a union of disparities. He calls for a cast that combines adults with children—meaning professionals with amateurs—and the result is enchanting magic art.

God, Noah, and his wife are the only adult voices, the first being a narrator's part. Noah's sons and their wives, all other parts, and the chorus call for young people. The orchestral division is also largely assigned to children, playing string and percussion instruments (including the clean sound of handbells), recorders, and bugles, contrasted to a professional chamber combination of string quintet, piano duet, recorder, percussion, and organ.

The tale is presented with expressive simplicity, intensified by the colorful Middle English text, and includes three hymns sung at key points by cast and congregation (the opera is meant for church performance). Sheer inspiration marks the processional march of the animals into the ark, heralded by bugle calls and interspersed with the singing of a *Kyrie eleison*. No less inspired is the subtle storm scene, set in passacaglia form, followed by the scene of the dove's flight and return with an olive branch. The bird is represented clearly by a dulcet recorder, flutter-tonguing included.

This is music of tremendous charm and effect, and it is set forth on this disc in a captivating manner. The performance is so vivid that a listener will not miss the visual part whatsoever.

Owen Wingrave, Op. 85

☐ English Chamber Orchestra and Wandsworth School Boys' Choir / Harper, Fisher, and Vyvyan (sopranos); Baker (mezzo-soprano); Pears and Douglas (tenors); Luxon (baritone); Shirley-Quirk (bass-baritone) / Britten (conductor) / London 1291

Owen Wingrave was commissioned by the Television Service of the British Broadcasting Corporation and was first shown on TV on May 16, 1971. It is just as viable in live performance, though Britten identifies his score as "an opera for television in two acts."

Based on a short story by Henry James, *Owen Wingrave* is described by Donald Mitchell as a tale "of a young man haunted by his ancestral past, a past against which he determines to take a stand and from which he almost escapes (in one sense he does escape, but at the cost of his life)." Each of the characters is strongly defined in the libretto, and this definition is interlocked with coloristic orchestral definition. The scoring is extremely exciting to hear. In some respects the instrumental portion alone is Britten's greatest orchestral score. The all-star cast gives a five-star performance.

Peter Grimes, Op. 33

☐ Orchestra and Chorus of the Royal Opera House, Covent Garden / Claire Watson, Studholme, and Kells (sopranos); Elms (mezzo-soprano); Jean Watson (contralto); Pears, Nilsson, and Lanigan (tenors); Evans (baritone); Pease, Kelly, and Brannigan (basses) / Britten (conductor) / London 1305

Britten's opera is grim and powerful. It concerns a violent and sadistic fisherman whose two apprentices meet with suspicious deaths. The villagers do not believe the facts; only one person, a widowed schoolteacher, whom Grimes wishes to marry, offers understanding. When she discovers Grimes's harshness and irresponsibility, she realizes there is no hope for him. Grimes takes to the sea and scuttles his boat.

The *dramatis personae* are distinguished by superbly contrasted characterizations: among others, a retired sea captain, a constable, a nerve-frazzled widow, a druggist. The chorus plays an important role. It represents the "crowd," the unified protagonist pitted against one personality who will not merge with the others.

Britten's music is free of artificialities that might disturb the story line. *Peter Grimes* is a continuous drama, although it contains all the usual ingredients—arias and duets; storm, crowd, pub, and church scenes; plus the serious techniques of canon, passacaglia, and fugue. The orchestra is especially significant in the interludes that link what has preceded with what is to follow. And in this stage work the text is set without any marking of time; there are no scene-setting recitatives.

The musical profits of *Peter Grimes* are gigantic, one reflection of which is that some of the music has been recorded for orchestra (see under *Orchestra* [Four Sea Interludes, Op. 33a, and Passacaglia, Op. 33b, from *Peter Grimes*]). Once the listener is caught up in the plot he will experience a virtuoso operatic experience. The conventions of large-scale opera are not smashed, but neither are they painfully followed. They have been given a fresh scope of tremendous excitement.

London's performance is monumental, especially with Pears giving marvelous reality to the part of Grimes. Claire Watson, as the schoolteacher, is excellent; the work of Owen Brannigan makes him one of the stars of this production. The others are no less impressive.

The Rape of Lucretia, Op. 37

☐ English Chamber Orchestra / Harper and Hill (sopranos); Bainbridge (mezzo-soprano); Baker (contralto); Pears (tenor); Drake and Luxon (baritones); Shirley-Quirk (bass) / Britten (conductor) / London 1288

Operatic impact of startling response obtained by the most minimal means. Large choral forces are replaced by one man and one woman who offer the commentary (magnificently conveyed here by Peter Pears and Heather Harper, the former having been recorded at the peak of his career and the latter producing buttery lyricism), together with concentrated instrumental framework.

Those that predict dire bankruptcy for contemporary opera are triumphantly over-borne by this outstanding creation. The fine moments are many in the two acts—among them the nocturnal mood of the opening, Tarquinius's statement before the rape, and Lucretia's confession. All are covered by ravishing music that makes Britten's second opera as outstanding as the one that preceded it, *Peter Grimes*.

The huge opportunity given Janet Baker as Lucretia is met with artistic conviction, passionately so. It is one of her greatest triumphs.

The Turn of the Screw, Op. 54

☐ English Opera Group Orchestra / Vyvyan, Dyer, Cross, and Mandikian (sopranos); Pears (tenor); Hemmings (treble) / Britten (conductor) / Richmond 62021 (monaural)

The rarest of all operatic types is a ghost story packed with quiet, psychological terror. Britten's composition, based on the bone-chilling Henry James tale, holds the attention as it relates the supernatural grip of a man and a woman on two children in the care of a governess. The nature of this evil power is not precisely disclosed, and the tale becomes more frightening in the play on the listener's imagination. The effect is heightened further when ghosts are seen and heard—an important difference from the original story.

With uncanny ability, Britten conveys the horror of this ghastly domination. Despite the inclusion of some children's tunes, the score retains a sombre, threatening polyphonic quality from prologue to completion. The technique of thematic variations is still another binding device, but is handled freely so that it does not stem the flow. These variants are formal weights that aid the musical equilibrium. The theatrical impact of this opera gains by the use of compressed instrumentation. Britten uses five strings, four woodwind players (performing on eight instruments), horn, harp, piano, celesta, and percussion to produce the tragic, macabre totality of this work.

Under the composer's direction the performance is a study in subtle coloring and meaningful vocal inflections. Though at times Vyvyan is somewhat in cold, rather unpleasant voice, she fulfills her role admirably. Pears is magnificent, and the two young singers are exceptionally well cast. *Turn of the Screw* remains a triumph for Benjamin Britten.

The Young Person's Guide to the Orchestra, Op. 34

☐ London Symphony Orchestra / Previn (narrator) / Previn (conductor) / Angel S-36962

This work presents a variational survey (six thematic statements and thirteen variations) of a Purcell theme (from *Abdelazar,* or *The Moor's Revenge*) with the purpose of identifying the orchestra's components. This is followed by a fugue which displays the entire apparatus in sections and full tutti. All this is done with the assistance of an M.C. who points out the instrumental landmarks.

Initially conceived as the sonic data for a documentary film, *Instruments of the Orchestra, The Young Person's Guide* undeniably has rich effectiveness without pictorial support but with the original commentary. The narrator serves a dual purpose. He identifies the timbre differences and is the liaison between orchestra and audience (program notes in the flesh).

Though all the instruments are given a place in the spotlight, this is not a mere tone-color catalogue. Allowing that Britten's guide was educationally conceived, this is music that never forgets its artistic conscience. (The version without narration, authorized by the composer, is discussed under *Orchestra*.)

Previn, fulfilling the double role of conductor and narrator, follows others who did likewise on older recordings, including Sir Adrian Boult and Loren Maazel. Previn is very good. His diction is fine, his voice clear and effective, and there is no condescending attitude of the pedantic, schoolmarm kind that has been used by some narrators. The playing of the orchestra is totally brilliant.

Ballet

The Prince of the Pagodas, Op. 57

☐ Orchestra of the Royal Opera House, Covent Garden / Britten (conductor) / London STS-15081/2

Britten's ballet tale is overloaded with characters and situations. There are some good portions of music. Most of it is a mixture of material to fit balletic requirements, with overtones from earlier (meaning Tchaikovsky) and later (meaning Prokofiev) ballets.

Britten and Lennox Berkeley (1903-)

Orchestra

Mont Juic (1937)

☐ London Philharmonic Orchestra / Berkeley (conductor) / Musical Heritage Society MHS-1919

A suite of four Catalan dances produced as a collaborative project. More important for the joint effort by two important composers than for the result. However, it is apparent that only in light music would creative partnership have any chance for success. As far as that premise is concerned, one can therefore give a passing grade for this jointly composed work. (Britten indicated it as his Opus 12.)

Britten / Julian Bream (1933-)

Chamber Music

The Courtly Dances from *Gloriana*, Op. 53

☐ Bream Consort / RCA LSC-2730

Six sections from Britten's opera, the first a March which is repeated at the end, thereby forming a seventh part and giving a cyclic design. The sextet instrumentation covers lute (played by Julian Bream, of course), violin, tabor, two bass viols, and one performer tripling on piccolo, flute, and alto flute.

This is a delightful performance of Elizabethan dances in an excellent transcription.

Franz Xaver Brixi   (1732-1771)

Solo Instrument and Orchestra

Organ

Organ Concerto in F major

☐ Stuttgart Soloists / Lehrndorfer (organ) / Turnabout 34244

A work to be liked by those who like plainly stated Haydn. The form follows the traditional pattern of moderate, slow, and fast-paced movements. The organ playing is fine, the registration totally appropriate.

314

Carel Brons (1931-)

String Quartet No. 2 (1969)

☐ Gaudeamus String Quartet / Donemus Audio-Visual Series 7071/4

Chamber Music

The hard pizzicati, the glissandi, and the aphoristic gestures heard at the beginning reflect the entrance to the post-Webernian world in which Brons's pithy (nine-minute) quartet resides.

Its colors and procedures are both vivid and varied. The structure is interesting. There are thirteen connected sections. Parts 6, 8, 10, and 12 are totally aleatoric. They are recognizable by the absence of pulsatile definition; the other sections, though extremely fragmented, convey a demarcative, albeit disquieted, sense of rhythm. The chance portions are each repeated, but are dissimilar because of the permissiveness involved.

The Gaudeamus players are as snugly at home with this style of music as the old Budapest four were with Beethoven. Their playing makes for avant-garde believers.

Hans Bronsart von Schellendorf (1830-1913)

Piano Concerto in F sharp minor, Op. 10

☐ Westphalian Symphony Orchestra, Recklinghausen / Ponti (piano) / Kapp (conductor) / Candide 31076

Solo Instrument and Orchestra

Piano

Still another valid contribution to our knowledge of what the great romantic-music bank contains. Bronsart's three-movement concerto is a stringent investigation of piano virtuosity, reminding one of Liszt a great deal, and sometimes concerned with Brahmsian contours. The finale especially defines the former, the slow movement the latter.

That the composer is so little known does not decrease enthusiasm for the piece. And any sharp critical appraisal cannot deny Ponti's proven abilities in this instance.

Alfonso Broqua (1876-1946)

El Tango

☐ Averino (soprano); Slonimsky (piano) / Orion 7150 (monaural)

Vocal

Voice with Accompaniment

A song about a tango, but not in tango rhythm. It is taken from a collection, *Trois Chants de l'Uruguay*.

Sébastien de Brossard (1655-1730)

Four Airs for Soprano and Basso Continuo

☐ Selig (soprano); Schaeffer (harpsichord); Farlet (viola da gamba) / Musical Heritage Society MHS-792-CC-13

Vocal

Voice with Accompaniment

Taken from a six-volume anthology Brossard produced for one, two, and three voices. An Italianate flavor permeates the songs.

Leo Brouwer   (1939-   )

Instrumental

Two Guitars

Four *Micro-Plezas*

☐ Ito and Dorigny (guitars) / Delos FY–008

Slightly percussive and totally polytonal expressions. Of special enjoyment is the avoidance of average-formationed guitar writing, and yet the music is not radically styled in far-out, avant-garde fashion.

Earle Brown   (1926-   )

Orchestra

Available Forms I **(for Chamber Ensemble) (1961)**

☐ Rome Symphony Orchestra / Maderna (conductor) / RCA VICS–1239

To miss the visual performance of Brown's work is to be deprived. The basic material for the piece consists of very short "events" notated ambiguously for the greater part on six score pages. The conductor makes a choice from these, designating his/her wishes to the players by means of an arrow attached to a placard that displays the page numbers of the score. The number of the event to be played is given by the conductor's left hand. Relative tempo and dynamic intensity are free, being partially suggested by the speed and length of the conductor's beats.

It is the *availability* of the material that ends the composer's task. The conductor's role then begins in terms of sequence, arrangement, and formal totality, resulting in re-creative, free-hearted freethinking, therefore. In a recording, the realization (akin to the figured bass technique, but at many a remove!) becomes fixed and permanency is substituted for aleatoric heterodoxy. Should then such compositions never be recorded? The answer may well be the issue of a recording of a number of realizations, made by one or several conductors with one or more ensembles (a competition for the best version springs to mind!). In any event, Maderna, as the creative surrogate, produces an excellent result. A composer himself, he has advantages that other conductors would not have.

Novara **(1962)**

☐ Hartsuiker (piano and leader); Jurriaanse (flute); Floore (trumpet); Sparnaay (bass clarinet); Walta and van Driesten (violins); Oldeman (viola); Ruijsenaars (cello) / Brown (conductor) / Composers Recordings S–330

Novara is set in the free-formed *modus operandi* that marks most of Brown's music. Thus events are noted, but their use, placement, tempi, combination, and the like are left to the spontaneous consideration of the conductor. Control is vested in the conductor but the composer is always in remote control since the sound events he has fashioned remain permanent. In performance the results are always distinctly different, save when fixed in a recording.

Like Calder's mobiles (which greatly influenced Brown), the music quivers as it moves and attaches one event to another, or moves away from one. The shadows and lights that are pertinent to the motility of mobiles are to be recognized in this, a musical representation of the idea. It is beautifully planned, beautifully stated, and beautifully recorded, providing music of the highest level.

Four Systems, for Four Amplified Cymbals

Percussion

☐ Neuhaus / Columbia MS–7139

The notation for this piece consists of vertical and horizontal lines of assorted length and thickness. The performer reacts to these so that actually "psychological" improvisation becomes the composition, and although the stimulus is to be credited to Earle Brown, the product is the creative property of Max Neuhaus.

A constant spray of cymbalistic sound is the result, with little contrast. No discredit to Brown. What Neuhaus fails to indicate in his notes is that *Four Systems* is "for any number of any instruments." A contrastive choice of timbre would have avoided the coloristic nondescriptness of the metallic belaborment provided. However, if you like the sounds of cymbals, here is a five-minute helping.

Corroboree (1964)

Instrumental

☐ Takahashi (piano) / Mainstream 5000

Piano

Corroboree is for three pianos but performed in this case by Yuji Takahashi by superimposing one part on the other. There is more than that involved, however. In a live performance spontaneous exchanges (chance conclusions, therefore) occur between the players. In the recording, after taping part 1, Takahashi, while playing the second piano part, was reacting to his own initial reactions, and, again following the same pattern when taping the final (third) part. The result is less "mobile" and less fluid than when three performers counteract by counterworking on the composer's material.

Nonetheless, the materials of this three-into-one performance are most evocative, including the plucking and muting of the strings of the instrument. The mixed sonorities provide a special beauty.

December 1952

☐ Tudor (piano) / Composers Recordings S–330

This is David Tudor's realization of Brown's score chart "for one or more instruments and/or sound producing media." Graphic notation is the basis for such creative partnership, with the performer determining and defining his individual reactions to the concentrated material he is offered in the outline.

Brown emphasizes that what is heard on this recording is as much Tudor's as it is his. And what is heard is most effective: a music of light diction, colored swatches, and of unconventional expressivity.

Music for Cello and Piano (1955)

Chamber Music

☐ Soyer (cello); Tudor (piano) / Mainstream 5007

Graphic notation with certain composer-made controls is the basis for Brown's duo. It is subject "to numerous different but inherently valid realizations." These, which cannot be defined statistically, are set into rhapsodic figments and fractioned sounds. Though they never blend, they give a truthful continuity. The music is nervous, to be sure, but it excites by its specific irregularity, freed of metrical bondage and linear stiffness. The performers become creative participants and identify themselves in their successful playing.

Hodograph I (1959)

☐ Hammond (flute); Tudor (piano and celesta); Kraus (orchestra bells, vibraphone, and marimba) / Mainstream 5007

Music derived from both explicit and non-explicit notation. The performers pass over their frontier to the creative area, aided in certain technical procedures by the composer. Dull-eared diehards have called such music unnatural, the product of an eccentric. But the freed content of this musical mobility fascinates the ear and titillates the intellect. *Hodograph* is ripe music that is the result not of technical rigidity but of discovery. The playing of Don Hammond, David Tudor, and Philip Kraus is acute, colorful, and seductive.

Music for Violin, Cello, and Piano (1952)

☐ Raimondi (violin); Soyer (cello); Tudor (piano) / Mainstream 5007

Tone rows are applied here, but "no other rules of twelve-tone writing" are followed. The music shifts, radiates, and rhapsodizes. It is a mark of Brown's astute creativity that whereas many who stay within any set of systemized rules produce music that stumbles and straggles, his music, freed of blueprinted strictures, has the mystery of creative success.

String Quartet (1965)

☐ New York String Quartet / Mainstream 5009

Controlled material and free particulars are combined in Brown's fertile quartet, concerned with unsettled dream sounds and percussionlike seizures, as well as some of the most tenacious clusters in musical literature (not to speak of glissandi species that scream forth).

The music of these four stringed instruments thunders into the ears (and, intellectually, thunders into one's head). A remarkably dramatic conception; it has been recorded no less than three times! The other versions differ through the offering of the players' "spontaneous realization" of certain material, proportional durations, and sequence choice of events. All three editions are prime realizations of this passionately exciting quartet. The others are played by the Concord String Quartet, on Vox SVBX–5306, and the La Salle Quartet, on Deutsche Grammophon 2543002.

Times Five (1963)

☐ Jurriaanse (flute); Moore (trombone); Tieu (harp); Walta (violin); Ruijsemaars (cello) / Brown (conductor) / Composers Recordings S–330

Five instruments (coincidentally, the work is in five sections) freely performing (at the will of the conductor) and partnered with four channels of tape sound. Thus an electronic constant with the reverse, permitting different results at each performance. The logic is irrefutable, the rhetoric of manifold variety.

Electronic Music

Octet I for 8 Loudspeakers (1953)

☐ Composers Recordings S–330

This music is aroused and sustained by a variety of disassociated sound segments. The complexities and complexions of this work result in a kaleidoscopic array of sonic gestures, twitches, and scratches. All very positive if not very emotive. The sense of offhandedness is the Octet's most personal point.

Newel Kay Brown   *(1932-   )*

Poetics (1970)   *Instrumental*

☐ Robert Levy (trumpet); Amy Lou Levy (piano) / Golden Crest RE–7045   *Trumpet*

A ternary-designed piece "composed deliberately for effective realization by the student performer." This is nonetheless music that need not be hidden in teaching studios. It is clean and tuneful, and miles beyond the general trash published for "the student performer." Levy's interpretation and warm tone, of course, helps the composer to achieve more-than-academic creative success.

Pastorale and Dance   *Chamber Music*

☐ Brown (flute); Umiker (alto saxophone); Evanson (trombone); Stone (clarinet); Levy (trumpet) / Capra 1201

The contemporary attitude of using mixed-bag instrumentation in chamber music is illustrated by Brown's quintet of wind and brass. It is light of texture, and clear melodic and rhythmic devices are used. Easily digestible music.

Rayner Brown   *(1912-   )*

Five Pieces for Organ, Harp, Brass, and Percussion (1963)   *Orchestra*

☐ Los Angeles Brass Society / Thomas (organ) / Remsen (conductor) / Avant 1001

An example of orchestral transmutation, the organ replacing the winds and the harp replacing the strings. The combination offers an interesting sonorous verdict. Brown varies his forces, contrasts group mass with solo highlighting. The forms, in turn, are of traditional lineage: a Toccata, Adagio, Scherzo, Passacaglia, and Fugue. The penultimate movement is the major one in scope, its performance time just under a minute less than the other four movements combined.

All the players are topnotch. That also goes for the balance, sound, and packaging.

Fantasy-Fugue   *Brass Ensemble*

☐ Los Angeles Philharmonic Brass Ensemble / Remsen (conductor) / Avant 1005

By enclosing the fugue with fantasy sections, the composer has created a formal balance. Conjunct motion drives the music, which is fundamentally homophonic. This is a sensitive rendition of the work, directed by a man who has done much for the furtherance of worthy brass music of all types in this country.

Concertino for Piano and Band   *Solo Instrument and Band*

☐ WIM Symphonic Wind Ensemble / Davis (piano) / Henderson (conductor) / Wim WIMR–13

Piano

Brown's five-movement opus bypasses any tortured theorizing in a suite-like compilation. Examples: modal chatter in movement 1, jazzy idiom in the Scherzo and Fugue (artistically honky-tonk gestures in the latter). Conservative music, yes; academic music, no; entertaining music, yes.

*Solo
Instrument
and
Orchestra*

Two Pianos

Concerto for Two Pianos, Brass, and Percussion

☐ Los Angeles Brass Society / Davis and Stepan (pianos) / Remsen (conductor) / Wim WIMR-8

This Concerto is written in classic order, with two slight differences. The movements total six, and the instrumentation consists of six trumpets, four horns, four tenor trombones, two bass trombones, tuba, timpani, and percussion.

The performance sounds assured, with all details clear. Brown's work rewards repeated listening.

Instrumental

Clarinet Choir

Symphony for Clarinet Choir

☐ Los Angeles Clarinet Society / Henderson (conductor) / Wim WIMR-8

Four movements in the normal formal repertory (Prelude, Fugue, Scherzo, and Allegro); the novelty is the combination of six clarinets, and one each of alto, bass, and contrabass clarinets. A score using only a basic timbred family of woodwind instruments is always of interest; the result in this case is more than ordinary.

*Chamber
Music*

Sonata for Flute and Organ (1970)

☐ Shanley (flute); Thomas (organ) / Wim WIMR-2

A composer who decides to combine a flute with the organ is risking defeat if he goes around the textural curves without using his scoring brakes. It is to Brown's credit that he has handled his material (set in one movement but outlining four parts) with intelligence and has created a satisfactory work. Fully tonal and fully clear, the atmosphere disclosed is quietly colorful. Credit must be given to Thomas for a perceptively selected registration.

Dave (David) Brubeck   (1920-   )

*Cantata
and Oratorio*

The Light in the Wilderness

☐ Cincinnati Symphony Orchestra and Miami University A Cappella Singers / Justus (baritone); Brubeck (piano); Hancock (organ); Proto (string bass); Frerichs (jazz drums and tablas) / Kunzel (conductor) / MCA 10009

Deductions drawn by combining classical and jazz techniques make up this music. Brubeck's gifts make the sections devoted to jazz style the most personal and the most successful, and the improvisations included are excellent. However, the "straight" music is derivative and one can spot the influences, which include Honegger and Vaughan Williams. Brubeck's aesthetic manipulation between the two forces is nothing new, of course, but it has taste and effect, especially when uniquely applied to a full-scale oratorio.

All of this means that sacred music doesn't have to sound like Bach or Handel in order to register. Some critics imbued with more than ordinary enthusiasm have termed Brubeck's opus one of the most important pieces of recent years. This reviewer registers a large dissent. The *Light* is successful, no doubt about that, and worth listening time. To give it a higher place is exaggeration.

There is a fine imaginative vigor to the presentation, with a lively chorus and clearly defined playing by the Cincinnati musicians. William Justus is a fine vocal soloist. The jazz juxtapositions are so brilliantly styled that they should get top billing.

Max Bruch   (1838-1920)

Symphony No. 2 in F minor, Op. 36   *Orchestra*

☐ Louisville Orchestra / Mester (conductor) / Louisville S–703

The creation of a persevering romantic composer. If there is more Brahms than there is Bruch, it does not detract from music written with a constancy of design and purpose.

Mester shows he is a master of this score. The sound is especially warm and rich.

Kol Nidre, Op. 47   *Solo*
                                                        Instrument
☐ Monte Carlo Opera Orchestra / Walevska (cello) / Inbal (conductor) / Philips 6500160   *and*
                                                        Orchestra
A rich, beautiful, and extraordinary performance. Christine Walevska's priceless
presentation pushes all others (including Starker's) to the bottom of the heap. Her   *Cello*
seamless phrasing is emotively exquisite and the support given by Eliahu Inbal is of sensitive understanding.

Given playing of this kind and with full orchestral color it would not be expected that one would prefer the cello-piano version. But, if that is the case, a fairly decent recording is available (see under *Instrumental: cello*).

Concerto for Two Pianos and Orchestra, Op. 88a   *Two Pianos*

☐ London Symphony Orchestra / Berkofsky and Twining (pianos) / Dorati (conductor) / Angel S–36997

Granted that Max Bruch did not have an audacious imagination, he did possess fine craftsmanship. The double concerto shows a fine sense of fitness for the medium and deserves to be heard as much as the G minor violin concerto.

This is the first recording ever of the work. It is so good that no others need apply.

Concerto No. 1 in G minor for Violin and Orchestra, Op. 26   *Violin*

☐ New Philharmonia Orchestra / Grumiaux (violin) / Wallberg (conductor) / Philips 6500780
☐ New Symphony Orchestra of London / Heifetz (violin) / Sargent (conductor) / RCA LSC–2652

After at least two hundred performances, in which I have personally played this Con-
certo, conducted it, heard it live and on records, I am of the opinion that it is difficult to match the superbly beautiful and stylistically knowledgeable Grumiaux rendition. The warmth, the absence of any Russianized portamento, and the impeccable bowing and phrasing are miracles of violin playing. Heifetz digs in but he too evinces a poetical blaze, which is what this concerto requires. To conquer the juicy thirds in the finale with Paganini thrust is all wrong and to sentimentalize the slow movement is just as bad a condition. Heifetz is so beautifully controlled in his playing that the Bruch turns out to be one of his greatest recordings.

The Heifetz performance is also available with a different coupling on RCA LSC–4011. The Grumiaux should not be confused with a foreign disc edition in which he is supported by Haitink and the Concertgebouw Orchestra.

There are two others that are very close runners-up and deserve mention. One is Kyung-Wha Chung with the Royal Philharmonic Orchestra, conducted by Rudolf Kempe (London 6795) and the other is Itzhak Perlman with the London Symphony Orchestra, conducted by André Previn (Angel S–36963).

Concerto No. 2 in D minor for Violin and Orchestra, Op. 44

☐ London Symphony Orchestra / Menuhin (violin) / Boult (conductor) / Angel S-36920

Everyone plays the Bruch "G minor," practically no one pays attention to the "D minor." True, it isn't as juicy as the first Concerto but it has its points, especially a very fine, deeply delineated first movement.

Menuhin plays most persuasively and can only be called to account for the few forced sounds on the upper G string in the *Recitativ* (movement 2). Boult is no neutral in this recording. He supports and is always with the music's grain.

Konzertstück for Violin and Orchestra, Op. 84

☐ Gewandhaus Orchestra, Leipzig / Accardo (violin) / Masur (conductor) / Philips 9500423

Practically unknown but worthy of this, its initial recording, Bruch's "Concert Piece" consists of two movements, an *Allegro appassionato,* set in F sharp minor, with an Adagio in the enharmonic major key (G flat major). The scoring of the accompaniment is instrumentally full (but not heavy in application) with ten woodwinds, nine brass, timpani, and strings.

Salvatore Accardo is to be thanked for making this fine piece available. He gives a probing performance.

Scottish Fantasy for Violin and Orchestra, Op. 46

☐ London Symphony Orchestra / David Oistrakh (violin); Ellis (harp) / Horenstein (conductor) / London 6337
☐ Royal Philharmonic Orchestra / Chung (violin) / Kempe (conductor) / London 6795

Two opposite viewpoints, but both have the taste and thrills of artistic solo playing at its finest. David Oistrakh is poetical. His soprano violin has alto qualities quite often as he reads the score as though the sounds were to be mauves and brick reds. Kyung-Wha Chung's coloration is brighter. Her playing is effable and elegant. No need to look elsewhere for other than either of these two versions.

Instrumental

Cello

Canzone, Op. 55

☐ King (cello); Leviev (piano) / Orion 7287

Not the most profound music but Terry King brings out every bit contained in the piece. Impressive tone and top-grade musicality are exhibited by this young cellist.

Kol Nidre, Op. 47

☐ Goodman (cello); Bogin (piano) / Orion 75181

Goodman takes the big, assertive approach to this cello evergreen. It registers far better than the rather neutral style of du Pré (on Angel S-36338). (If you insist on the English cellist, be warned that the labeling on the disc has been reversed.)

Nevertheless, *Kol Nidre* is heard at its best with orchestral framework. It is in that medium that the most outstanding performance on disc is available (see under *Solo Instrument and Orchestra: cello*).

Six Pieces, Op. 12

Two Pieces, Op. 14

Piano

☐ Berkofsky (piano) / Angel S–36997

If you are one of those who want the complete works of a composer in a specific medium, here you have the opportunity. These two sets constitute Bruch's complete solo piano output. (Two other works for the keyboard instrument were composed, one for one piano, four hands, the other for two pianos.)

Swedish Dances, Op. 63

*Piano,
Four Hands*

☐ Berkofsky and Hagan (piano) / Turnabout 34732

Exceedingly rare Bruch music presented in an assured manner. The Swedish Dances also exist in versions for violin and piano and for orchestra. *Grove's Dictionary of Music and Musicians* fails to include the latter in its listing of Bruch's output.

Fantasy for Two Pianos, Op. 11

Two Pianos

☐ Berkofsky and Hagan (pianos) / Turnabout 34732

This is the only recording of this work, with sound musicianship on the part of this team.

Eight Pieces for Clarinet, Viola, and Piano, Op. 83 (Nos. 2, 6, and 7)

*Chamber
Music*

☐ Perahia (piano); Kroyt (viola); Wright (clarinet) / Turnabout 34615

With rich, golden-brown sounds bathing in warm romantic melodies and harmonies, Bruch's music, especially the *Night-Song* (the second of the three pieces played), is most eloquent.

The performers are expert, the recording is very good, despite being made ''live'' (including some audience shuffling and light applause at the conclusion).

Anton Bruckner   *(1824 - 1896)*

Symphony No. 0 (*Die Nullte*) in D minor

Orchestra

☐ Concertgebouw Orchestra / Haitink (conductor) / Philips 802724

The symphony is not included in the integral group of nine. Bruckner himself tagged this early work with its zero identification; it was composed in 1864 and then revised in 1869. But it certainly avoids zero qualities. There is plenty of Schubertian coverage within the four movements and Wagner does not take a back seat, either.

There is a decided affinity for this stylistic combination in Haitink's reading. There is also a belief in the worthiness of the work that comes through in the performance. Refinement and spirit are all they should be.

Symphony No. 1 in C minor

☐ Vienna Philharmonic Orchestra / Abbado (conductor) / London 6706

Brucknerian content is fully substantiated on the part of this conductor. The music is stated broadly but with convincing tempi, especially in the Scherzo. It becomes apparent that our younger conductors have made an unwritten agreement to play Bruckner's music with solid proportions rather than display individual sections. All to the good.

Symphony No. 2 in C minor

☐ Concertgebouw Orchestra / Haitink (conductor) / Philips 602912

Haitink uses the full Haas edition as does Stein with the Vienna Philharmonic Orchestra, on London 6879. (Some conductors, for example, Giulini, persist in using the severely cut version made by Nowak.)

The Adagio is heard with elegiac beauty, a magnificence that never lessens despite the music's length. The sensitivity and knowledge of Haitink's conducting permeate the entire symphony, providing a sumptuous statement of the work.

Symphony No. 3 in D minor

☐ Concertgebouw Orchestra / Haitink (conductor) / Philips 835217

The processes of this symphony boggle the mind. It was composed in 1873, revised in 1874, then extensively rewritten and in that form finished in 1877, first published in 1878, further rewritten between 1888 and 1890 and then again published. But this last edition (made with gratuitous advice by others) is considered, rightly, a corrupt one, especially with the violent slashes that were made in the finale. Bruckner scholars accept only the 1878 edition (and I agree with them). It is this version that Haitink uses and which he performs with evenness and great style. He particularly avoids the fussy tempo changes that plague so many parts of the other recorded editions.

If, however, one wishes the later (1890) version, known as the Nowak edition (Nowak was the editor of the Bruckner Society, succeeding Robert Haas) with structural imbalance and all, the best performance is Karl Böhm's on London 6717. Incidentally, Szell (on Columbia MS-6897) also uses this spurious edition.

Symphony No. 4 (*Romantic*) in E flat major

☐ Chicago Symphony Orchestra / Barenboim (conductor) / Deutsche Grammophon 2530336
☐ Columbia Symphony Orchestra / Walter (conductor) / Odyssey Y-32981

Quite a difference between the youthful vigor of the more recent Barenboim edition and the sagacious consideration represented by Bruno Walter at the time he recorded this Bruckner work. Quite a difference also between the virtuosic Chicago band and the free-lance line-up of the Columbians. But both are special and can be certified as the best.

Barenboim goes for the dramatic approach, displaying a fine sense of dynamic range and sensitivity to the variety of moods but nonetheless retaining structural solidity. Color it a vivid red. Walter considers the score in a more poetic manner, is quite often gentle and tender, and creates a decidedly Brucknerian persuasiveness. Color it garnet.

Symphony No. 5 in B flat major

☐ Concertgebouw Orchestra / Haitink (conductor) / Philips 6700055

A control of shape in the first movement profiles the music magnificently. Many conductors (one recalls a Jochum recording) indulge in excessive tempi manipulation that destroys the whole for the sake of its divisions. That same premise of seamless sweep pertains to Haitink's conception of the slow movement. And such directness (an asset in playing any Bruckner work) carries over to the huge scherzo. This is grand orchestral playing of a work that has grandeur.

Symphony No. 6 in A major

☐ Chicago Symphony Orchestra / Barenboim (conductor) / Deutsche Grammophon 2531043

Though probably the least admired of the Bruckner symphonies, it has an intensity that is quite striking, even though the finale sags somewhat. Barenboim probes this music with exceptional skill. The pace in the opening movement clarifies the important rhythmic detail, the scherzo has fine motoric power, and the eloquence brought to the slow movement is unmistakable. Barenboim's Bruckner expertise is proven in this exceedingly fine account, certainly number one on the list.

Symphony No. 7 in E major

☐ Vienna Philharmonic Orchestra / Solti (conductor) / London 2216

A highly charged conception that does not overlook the telling lyricism of the work, so specially colored by the use of a quartet of Wagner tubas. The tempi have a declarative point about them (in comparison, for example, with the streamlined consideration of this matter by Ormandy [RCA LSC–3059]). Above all is the radiance that Solti obtains.

Symphony No. 8 in C minor

☐ Vienna Philharmonic Orchestra / Solti (conductor) / London 2219

Solti uses the Nowak edition which contains a number of cuts. (For the Haas edition the choice would be Haitink on Philips 6700020.) There is little toying with outer details, but plenty attention is given the inner ones, to the betterment of the performance. This negates the tempi fluctuation that haunts so many Bruckner performances, though a bit of this re-creative headache is to be heard in the slow movement. The total result is one of intensity and power, with richness involved as well.

Symphony No. 9 in D minor

☐ Berlin Philharmonic Orchestra / Jochum (conductor) / Deutsche Grammophon 2707024

A performance that even the dead-centered Brucknerite will doubtless admit is the cream of the lot, and that covers the conceptions of such stalwart maestros as Klemperer and von Karajan, Mehta and Bernstein.

Bruckner's "Ninth" is, of course, unfinished and is represented by a *Feierlich, Misterioso* opening, a Scherzo, and an Adagio (the longest portion of the three movements). The scoring is for triple winds, the usual triple trumpets and trombones, plus tuba, timpani, and strings. The only enlargement is the use of eight horns, four changing to Wagner tubas in the third movement.

Jochum's eloquent poeticism in the opening part of the symphony is paced and sustained in a remarkable manner. The Scherzo has a robustness and tinge of grotesqueness that is absolutely fitting and no conductor has obtained the radiance Jochum finds in the slow movement.

Some remarks on a few of the performances that lack the totality of Jochum's artistry. Mehta (on London 6462) plays the finale with a sweet-toothed baton and it makes one squirm. Bernstein's reading (on Columbia M–30828) has power but never goes into the music's inner muscle. There's strength in von Karajan's performance (on Deutsche Grammophon 139011) but not much soul.

String Quartet in C minor

☐ Keller Quartet / Musical Heritage Society MHS–1363/1364

Chamber Music

Classic forms, with sonata design in movement 1 and large ternary plotting in part 2, followed by a Scherzo and a Rondo. The imprint of this early work, composed a few years after Bruckner had begun the study of composition, is heavily Schumannesque.

The playing is adequate. Most of the Keller Quartet's tempi are on the slow side.

Intermezzo for String Quintet

Quintet in F major for Two Violins, Two Violas, and Cello

☐ Keller Quartet / Schmid (viola) / Musical Heritage Society MHS–1363/1364

The Intermezzo is in the slow waltz tempo of *Ländler* style. No Bruckner heaviness.

The Quintet was the result of a request by a well-known organization to compose a quartet. Bruckner delivered a quintet instead, from which inference can be drawn that he had trouble in thinking in concentrated terms.

A system of leitmotivs prevails in the four movements. The Scherzo is heavy and built on an intervallic condition of a quartal leap. In the slow movement two themes are given variated treatment. In the final section, the writing is rather weighty; it is the symphonic Bruckner composing for five instruments.

Choral

Chorus Alone

| *Ave Maria* | *Locus Iste* |
| *Christus Factus Est* | *Virga Jesse* |

☐ John Alldis Choir / Alldis (conductor) / Argo ZRG–523

Superlative singing by this group; the quality is one of warmth and with a balanced blend that is most satisfying.

The *Ave Maria* is not to be confused with an earlier one written in four parts and with organ. The one heard here is a seven-part setting and is quoted in Bruckner's Symphony No. 0. Duplicate use of the *Christus Factus Est* also should be borne in mind. That recorded here is also of later-date composition, and like the *Ave Maria* is in seven-part voicing. The earlier setting is for six-part chorus plus three trombones.

Cantata and Oratorio

Mass No. 2 in E minor

☐ Schütz Choir of London and Philip Jones Brass Ensemble / Norrington (conductor) / Argo ZRG–710

A beautiful conception for eight-part chorus and brass instruments. A Wagnerian fragrance slightly permeates the atmosphere, adding sparkle to the solemnity. The performance is a dynamic, direct one.

Mass No. 3 (*Great*) in F minor

☐ New Philharmonia Orchestra and Chorus / Harper (soprano); Reynolds (mezzo-soprano); Tear (tenor); Rintzler (bass) / Barenboim (conductor) / Angel S–36921

The *Grosse Messe* displays Barenboim as a fine Bruckner conductor. All the detail is apportioned and still the total structure is totally placed in perspective. There is sweep to the performance and a properly temperated excitement. The soloists are fine.

Te Deum

☐ Concertgebouw Orchestra and Netherlands Radio Chorus / Ameling (soprano); Reynolds (mezzo-soprano); Hoffmann (tenor); Hoekman (bass) / Haitink (conductor) / Philips 802759/60

Ecstatic music matched by a blazing performance. Haitink's care in presenting the emotive side of Bruckner's work does not make him overlook the productive power of the motif that binds its structure. There is no doubt that Haitink establishes himself as one of the top Bruckner conductors with the evidence of this issue and his interpretation of a number of the symphonies.

Nicolaus Bruhns (1665-1697)

Prelude and Fugue

Instrumental

☐ Sherman (organ) / Crystal S–700

Organ

Bruhns, a Buxtehude pupil, later earned the reputation of being, next to his teacher, the best organist in northern Germany. His music, played very sensitively by Roger Sherman, is quite imaginative. A pedal-point section highlights a design that is anything but pat with fantasylike indentations probed into the fugal division.

Ignaz Brüll (1846-1907)

Overture to *Macbeth*, Op. 46

Orchestra

☐ Nürnberg Symphony Orchestra / Deàky (conductor) / Genesis 1015

The creative personality is a reflection of Wagner and Brahms (some Schumann, but much less so); the product is incisive and compact, and is effectively performed.

Piano Concerto No. 2 in C major, Op. 24

Solo Instrument and Orchestra

☐ Nürnberg Symphony Orchestra / Cooper (piano) / Deàky (conductor) / Genesis 1015

Piano

A delightful Schumannesque excursion. Brüll's structural concepts are straightforward but enriched with tasteful ideas. There is no sense of exploration; he was a follower of tried and true classic-romantic practices. As Frank Cooper (the excellent soloist and rediscoverer of this composer) states, the concerto is "carefree, grand and warm—suffused with poetry and song from first to last." The statement is herewith certified. The performance bears it out as well.

Louis Brunelli / *Morton Gould.* See Gould / Brunelli.

Gaetano Brunetti (1744-1798)

Symphony No. 23 in F major

Orchestra

☐ Angelicum Orchestra of Milan / Jenkins (conductor) / Nonesuch 71156

This suave four-movement work has a nice coloristic contrast in the *Quintetto: Allegro* third movement, wherein the outer sections are for the winds alone, the inner portion for the strings.

Breadth of spirit marks the playing. Give Jenkins credit as well for moving the work out of the dusty archives and producing it.

Mark Brunswick (1902-1971)

Instrumental

Piano

Six Bagatelles (1958)

☐ Helps (piano) / Composers Recordings S-288

Laced with Viennese atonalism of the 1920s, this set of pieces (four of the half-dozen are in *allegro* tempo) remains fresh to the ears. It is given a finely made performance.

Chamber Music

Seven Trios for String Quartet

☐ Galimir Quartet / Composers Recordings S-244

Varying scoring formations are used. Each of the trios is based on a poem by the composer (the texts are furnished with the recording), but nothing more than a general mood pertains to this programmatic device. The first six trios are very short and probably for that reason are played twice as a unit. (No mention is made of this, however, in the liner notes or on the label.) The final trio is the longest, its serene contrapuntal ordering making it a most satisfactory conclusion.

String Quartet (Contrabass)

☐ Galimir (violin); Rhodes (viola); Arico (cello); Levine (contrabass) / Composers Recordings S-244

Two movements, free of the aleatoric dogma, percussive block assemblages, and serialistic statistics that are associated with expressionism.

The idea of replacing the second violin in the string quartet formation with a double bass is novel but certainly makes it more difficult to obtain performances. The permanency of a recorded setting is therefore apparent.

Septet in Seven Movements (1957)

☐ Baker (flute); Kaplan (oboe); Listokan (clarinet); Froelich (horn); Newman (bassoon); Lynch (viola); Kougell (cello) / Jahoda (conductor) / Composers Recordings 170

Serial syntax is employed but with an extrovert demeanor. Pithy totals, except for movement 5 (a *Fantasia sopra "Christ lag in Todesbanden"*). Interesting touches: the tonal embroidery stitched onto the dodecaphonic patterns in movement 5 and the ostinato harnessing at the beginning of movement 3.

Most fascinating is the color of the miniature orchestra Brunswick chose: a woodwind quintet with a pair of the darker string instruments. A decidedly expert performance is to be heard.

Bjarne Brustad (1895-1978)

Orchestra

Symphony No. 2 (1951)

☐ Oslo Philharmonic Orchestra / Fjeldstad (conductor) / Composers Recordings 160 (monaural)

It would pay conductors to give heed to this powerful work, a combination of ruddy, romantic reportage with contemporary synonyms. A sense of violence pervades the composition. A vivid work, vividly recorded.

Mark Bucci (1924-   )

Concerto for a Singing Instrument (Movements 2 and 3: *Vocalise* and *Tug of War*) (1959)

***Tale for a Deaf Ear* (*Summer* Aria and *Spring* Aria) (1956)**

☐ Addison (soprano); Payne (piano) / Composers Recordings 147 (monaural)

Vocal

Voice with Accompaniment

The Concerto (part 1, *Promenade,* is not recorded) is a unique conception. The solo line is so conceived that performance is possible by any kind of voice or instrument from a piccolo to a marimba. Utilitarian objectives do not cancel sheer musical benefits in this case. There is a huge difference between pioneering for the market place and pioneering for artistic confirmation. In the *Vocalise* the triple-metered flow is haunting. In the other movement the sonorous contest is achieved by phrase and tonal opposition.

The pair of arias from the opera *Tale for a Deaf Ear* are self-contained propositions containing dramatic gravity. There is symmetry in the arias but with elastic conditions similar to the vertical and linear elements. This taste from the complete work raises the hope for full-scale productions and a recording to follow. Meanwhile one can enjoy Bucci's arias through the marvelous artistry of Adele Addison.

Dudley Buck (1839-1909)

Festival Overture on the American National Air, *The Star-Spangled Banner*

☐ Louisville Orchestra / Mester (conductor) / Louisville LS–755

Orchestra

This is just what it says. The "S.S.B." forms the second (lyrical) theme, enjoys separate responsibility, is combined with the initial theme, is the major hemstitching for Buck's piece, and even appears in a minor tonality. A period piece that uses a tune everyone knows but does not indulge in thematic assassination in order to flesh out a full-scale conception.

Grand Sonata in E flat major, Op. 22

☐ Morris (organ) / New World Records NW–280

Instrumental

Organ

There are no new twists in the formal make-up of this nineteenth-century piece until the final movement where the fugue is built on a subject that is a reshaped-ornamented setting of *Hail Columbia.* The climax of this movement is a powerful chunk of sound.

Morris plays with good interpretative quality, except in the Scherzo. Marked *vivace non troppo,* it comes out fully *non troppo,* and with hardly any *vivace.*

Rock of Ages

☐ Harmoneion Singers / Stewart (soprano); Skrobacs (harmonium) / New World Records NW–220

Choral

Chorus with Accompaniment

An anthem aspect of the well-known text in traditional musical language but not pedestrian. The three verses (six, four, and eight lines, respectively) are substantiated by using a tri-partite textural plan: chorus in the opening and closing, solo soprano in between. The recording shows clean projection and excellent musicianship.

Harold Budd   (1936-   )

Instrumental   *. . . only three clouds . . .* (1969)

Trombone   ☐ Anderson (trombone) / Avant 1006

This is the very far-out style of the far out. As with the one-pitch or one-drone composers, Budd's slow-ejected sounds inactivize pulse, line, contrast, and continuity. In comparison, Christian Wolff, whose static music is drastically restricted to a very few pitches, sounds like a Schubertian melodist. Tape growls, noises, and other unctions fill and support the trombone. (The unsigned liner notes speak of "no coordination points; each part is mobile relative to any of the others.")

This music is actively devoted to inaction. There's nothing wrong with such an urge except that it lasts almost twelve minutes. Still, this sort of sonorous narcotization is basic to inert musical style.

Trumpet   *New Work #5*

☐ Stevens (trumpet); Grierson (piano) / Crystal S–361

(One assumes that this piece is by *Harold* Budd. Nowhere in the release is the composer's first name indicated.)

Chance music from start to finish with sixty-four events given to the participants, each going about his business freely, depending on "whim, improvisatory skill, accident, timing," etcetera. One restriction: the playing is to be as soft as possible. Good enough. So are the extremely concentrated dips, dots, drops, and droops that represent the "events."

Naturally, like all aleatoric conditions, no performance is the definitive one and in chance music this is not the objective. The one recorded here is consistent in its single-minded convictions.

John Bull   (1562?-1628)

Instrumental   *The Duchesse of Brunswick's Toye*

Harpsichord   *The Duke of Brunswick's Alman*

☐ Payne (harpsichord) / Vox SVBX–572

Variational devices that charm the ear. The playing follows suit.

Organ   *In Nomine* [No. 1]

In Nomine [No. 2]

☐ Payne (organ) / Vox SVBX–572

Fantasy proportions based on plainsong. The second *In Nomine* is a ten-minute contrapuntal gem, twice the length of the first one, set in unusual undecennary meter. Meaningful playing.

David Burge   (1930-   )

Sources IV (1969)   *Instrumental*

☐ Burge (piano) / Composers Recordings SD–345   *Piano*

  Decisive and extrovert percussiveness plus dynamic smash mark Burge's piece. The
phrase separations add a breadth to the fragmented angularity. It may be Stockhausen-
inspired, but the positiveness and logical conclusions of Burge's piano essay are no sheer
imitations to be heard and then forgotten.

Johann Friedrich Franz Burgmüller   (1806-1874)

La Péri   *Ballet*

☐ London Symphony Orchestra / Bonynge (conductor) / London 6627

  This music is tuneful, with just the slightest fade on the coloration, and is romantically
elegant in character. Definitely worthwhile unsophisticated music that even the sophisticates might like. Bonynge, who edited the score, conducts a warm performance. He has a
way with music of this sort.

Norbert Burgmüller   (1810-1836)

Sonata in F minor, Op. 8   *Instrumental*

☐ Ruiz (piano) / Genesis 1018   *Piano*

  As an occasional change from the standard romantic diet, Norbert Burgmüller's
Sonata is worth placing on the menu. It's always poetic in demeanor, even when the music
is marked *con fuoco*.
  Ruiz's performance is sympathetic and stylishly stable.

Eldin Burton   (1913-   )

Sonatina for Flute and Piano (1946)   *Chamber*
                                                            Music
☐ Pellerite (flute); Webb (piano) / Coronet S–1713

  The Sonatina is Burton's most successful work. Since it won the New York Flute Club
Contest in 1948 it has achieved a huge number of performances and is firmly entrenched
in the repertory.
  The music is in Burton's fully tonal style. It is graced here with elegant lines, and
especially in the first pair of movements, with Ravelian diction and accent. The finale is
fast, happy music, indicated as *quasi fandango*. It is a paraphrase, actually, of the Spanish
dance, containing more duple pulse than the basic triple time of the form.
  Pellerite's performance is exceptional, clean and clear. His tone is rich and warm.

Geoffrey Bush   (1920-   )

Orchestra **Music (1967) for Orchestra**

☐ London Philharmonic Orchestra / Handley (conductor) / Musical Heritage Society MHS-1672

Bush's blueprint has a six-part plan. The work is set in four-part symphonic layout, each of which is apportioned to feature soloistic elements, and the cyclic system prevails. Within, the well-known ''Bach'' motive (translated musically in the German equivalents of B flat, A, C, and B) is used alone as well as in further linkage with the pitches C–A–E (which spell ''Caebach'' the name of Bush's Welsh cottage where he composed *Music*). Finally, the technical scope is a display piece, but for players of ''modest technical equipment.''

The last is not apparent from the colorful effect of the work. However, all the other structural points are quite apparent. And they work quite well. Yes, a nice bill of fare and served up nicely by the L. P. O.

Antoine Busnois   (?-1492)

Choral *Chansons*

Chorus Alone ☐ Nonesuch Consort / Rifkin (conductor) / Nonesuch 71247

Eight examples of fine fifteenth-century music by this extremely talented composer. The singing is well done and sensitive.

Ferruccio Busoni   (1866-1924)

Orchestra *Berceuse élégiaque*, Op. 42

☐ New Philharmonia Orchestra / Prausnitz (conductor) / Argo ZRG-757

The special orchestrational blend Busoni used (three flutes, one oboe, two clarinets, one bass clarinet, four horns, a gong, celesta, harp, and a small body of strings) carries over into a blend of major and minor tonality, consonance and dissonance, and a through-composed use of form.

Such dualism is not blatant at any time. A sense of veiled semi-mysticism hangs over the music (aided by the muted string body) marked by a suspended sense of pulsatile arrangement. Thereby, rhythmic definition is purposely debilitated, vague, and the poetical narrative is more intensified.

Rondo Arlecchinesco **for Orchestra with Tenor, Op. 46**

☐ Berlin Symphony Orchestra / Moser (tenor) / Bünte (conductor) / Candide 31003

That heading ''with tenor'' sounds very imposing, but the vocal part is so skeletal as to make one wonder why it is mentioned at all. It covers only a bit over forty seconds toward the very end of the piece, which runs some thirteen and a half minutes. Another odd point is the very soft, solo percussion conclusion. Writers tend to classify Busoni as a neo-classicist. With such unorthodox moves as these, the stylistic assignment is much more one of neo-romanticism. Regardless, this is a finely designed piece of music that has colorful juxtapositions and deserves revival. The recording might help.

Sarabande and *Cortège*, Op. 51

☐ Royal Philharmonic Orchestra / Revenaugh (conductor) / Angel S-3719

Busoni composed these pieces as preliminary studies for his opera *Doktor Faust*. Condensed, they were used in the stage work as orchestral interludes. Busoni left the opera unfinished. It was completed by his pupil Philipp Jarnach.

The dark contours of these pieces are effectively presented.

Concertino for Clarinet and Small Orchestra, Op. 48

☐ Berlin Symphony Orchestra / Triebskorn (clarinet) / Bünte (conductor) / Candide 31003

Solo Instrument and Orchestra

Clarinet

All the required formal logic is here, but there is little that is marked by moving and thrilling ideas. Busoni's Opus 48 music is effective in its minimal demands on a listener. It progresses along its one-movement path, clean and easily managed, and clear and easily heard.

The rendition tends to hang in a bounded area and follows suit with almost scholastic consideration of dynamics. Otherwise it is a good performance.

Divertimento for Flute and Orchestra, Op. 52

Flute

☐ Berlin Symphony Orchestra / Klemeyer (flute) / Bünte (conductor) / Candide 31003

The fantasy interlocks of this music bring to mind Busoni's statement that the creator "must not accept a traditional law" and his Opus 52 bears out this precept. What binds the music is the neo-classic harmonic syntax. What propels the performance is the fine playing of the soloist; the orchestra (two each of oboes, clarinets, bassoons, horns, and trumpets, plus a bit of percussion and strings) does well, if you don't mind pinched oboe sound.

Konzertstück for Piano with Orchestra, Op. 31a

Piano

☐ Berlin Symphony Orchestra / Glazer (piano) / Bünte (conductor) / Candide 31003

Brahms hangs heavy over this music and to a slightly lesser degree so does Liszt, and later in the work so does Beethoven. Oddly enough, it all fits. Don't underestimate the strength and the advantages of such creative company.

Frank Glazer plays with stunning command. There is a fine, coordinated relationship between orchestra and soloist.

Piano Concerto, Op. 39

☐ Royal Philharmonic Orchestra and John Alldis Choir / Ogdon (piano) / Revenaugh (conductor) / Angel S-3719

No ordinary concerto, this, but a big affair of five movements with the terminal part using a chorus (it is supposed to be hidden from view). Movements 2 and 4 contrast in their scherzo and tarantella aspects with the other parts; the entire matter reflects a duality of full-blown Germanic romanticism and pyrotechnical fustian patterns.

The bold writing is covered by masterly playing on the part of the soloist, and Daniell Revenaugh is an understanding collaborator.

Ballet-Scene No. 4, Op. 33

☐ Jones (piano) / Argo ZRG–741

Busoni's score consists of a series of waltzes with a bravado conclusion. Jones gets full credits for his playing.

Berceuse (Elegy No. 7)

☐ Jones (piano) / Argo ZRG–741

Some confusion exists in regard to the number of Busoni's Elegies. Some reference sources (*Schwann*, for example) list six; others (such as *Grove's Dictionary of Music and Musicians*) give the total as seven. The explanation is simple. A set of six was completed in 1907 and published in 1908. The *Berceuse* is an arrangement of the orchestral piece *Berceuse élégiaque: Des Mannes Wiegenlied am Sarge Seiner Mutter* ("Elegiac Lullaby: The Man's Cradle-Song at His Mother's Coffin"), which was written in 1909. Still later, Busoni made and then added his piano transcription to the set of Elegies.

Nonetheless, most pianists have disregarded the *Berceuse* and used the initial published version of six (Edward Steuermann, for example, in his recording: *see below*, Six Elegies). Actually, the lullaby can stand alone (as can any of the Elegies, for that matter) or can be added to the other six, which is the procedure followed by Jones in Argo's issue. Busoni is not harmed either way.

The preferable performance of the original group of six is by Steuermann. However, to repeat, for those who wish the entire set of seven pieces, the Argo release will serve, and without great interpretative loss. The best of both worlds is to obtain both Steuermann's and Jones's recordings. This makes it possible to have not only the better performance by Steuermann plus the *Berceuse,* but a wide assortment of other Busoni works as well: the Toccata and Sonatinas Nos. 1 and 6 on the Steuermann program; the Ballet-Scene No. 4 on the Jones disc.

Indianisches Tagebuch (1915)

☐ Manes (piano) / Orion 74154

In translation, Busoni's title for this work reads "Indian Diary: First Book, Four Piano Studies on Motives of the Red-Skinned Americans." Busoni had been given Indian themes by one of his pupils (Natalie Curtis, an ardent investigator of the songs and legends of the North American Indians) and turned out a group of four improvisational-like responses. The Indian element (except for a bit in part 3) is exceedingly peripheral. (Incidentally, Busoni indicates *Erstes Buch* [volume one], but no further volume appeared.)

Stephen Manes proves to be a fine pianist in his playing of Busoni's work.

Sechs kurze Stücke zur Pflege des polyphonen Spiels (1922)

☐ Jacobs (piano) / Nonesuch 71334

Busoni's "Six Short Pieces for the Practice of Polyphonic Playing" may lead one to expect cold, didactic essays, but they are completely opposite to such teaching studio material. The music exudes an artistic dimension that neatly finesses any overemphasis on contrapuntalism. There is plenty of that: imitation in inversion, counterpoint galore, canon and double canon. The last piece, *Nach Mozart,* is mainly devoted to the chorale used in the finale of *The Magic Flute.*

With Paul Jacobs's skills and marvelous musicianship the performance is ideal in all respects. What with codes applied to motion pictures it might well be apt to do the same for recordings. In that case the PG of the movies, meaning "parental guidance," would change to a PG for recordings to define "potent guidance," which applies to this interpretation.

Six Elegies

☐ Steuermann (piano) / Contemporary 8501

Never mind the romantic expansion of harmony or the fanciful titles, Busoni's music has the stability of classicism. All expansiveness of material is formally controlled but permitted to roam expressively. The elegies are visionary essays, far from lamentations. Here again, Busoni transfigures—a Neapolitan melody in the second piece and *Greensleeves* in the fourth one. The strangely luminous quality of this tune as it becomes divested of its haunting lilt and turns into exotic, quasi-macabre music highlights the set of six pieces.

Sonatina

No. 1
No. 2
No. 3 (*Ad Usum Infantis Madeline M. Americanae pro Clavicimbalo Composita*)
No. 4 (*In Diem Nativitatis Christi MCMXVII*)
No. 5 (*Sonatina Brevis in Signo Joannis Sebastiani Magni*)
No. 6 (*Sonatina super Carmen—Kammer-Fantasie über Bizet's "Carmen"*)

☐ Jacobs (piano) / Nonesuch 71359

Busoni's objective was to create a new classic art. These fascinating works exemplify such neo-classicism functioning within freed structural formations. He also warred against program music schemes. The former is illustrated in the first work, which is in three connected parts with a fugal scheme set within a delicately moving initial section and a closing scherzo-like concept. As for the latter, from the subtitle indications of four of the Sonatinas it would seem that picture-painting is involved, but the opposite is true. There are no narratives, merely suggestive overtones that relate to the descriptive idea. Thus No. 3 "for the use of the American child," structured as a suite, has a more relaxed manner than the others. The "for Christmas Day 1917" work (the fourth of the set) does not carol forth but does have a poetic spirituality.

It should not be believed that the music is intellectualized away from all emotion. In the "Short Sonatina under the Banner of the Great Johann Sebastian" the Bachian contours are apparent, and by such indirect hommage the music represents a type of emotional contact.

The final work of the set is probably the most important and, in its particular slant, the most powerful. An especially fascinating point in Busoni's writing was his enormous interest in the reconsideration of another composer's ideas. The Bizet transmutation does not swim in an ocean of tittle-tattle grace notes and cruising runs up and down the keyboard. In place of Lisztian verbiage we have an essay of new line, of new detail, of an afterpiece of musical drama. The re-animation here is not animated, but quiet and dark for the greater part (more or less the atmosphere that applies to the other five works in the group). No one can deny that Busoni's introspective analysis of some of the *Carmen* melodies is of commanding creativity. The mysterious independent variable brought to the Habanera is positively great art.

Great re-creative art is also manifested in these performances by Paul Jacobs. There are no doubts raised as to this musician's quality. He knows this music thoroughly and communicates his knowledge. In short, this is superb piano playing and thereby equals superb Busoni portrayals. (Jacobs can also write. His essay on the man and the music is beautifully styled and totally informative.)

Sonatina

No. 1

No. 6 (*Sonatina super Carmen—Kammer-Fantasie über Bizet's "Carmen"*)

☐ Steuermann (piano) / Contemporary 8501

This disc presents a more introspective consideration of these two works than in Jacobs's performances (*see above*). This does not necessarily mean better ones, but simply represents a poised inwardness that also marks great art.

Toccata

☐ Steuermann (piano) / Contemporary 8501

Busoni believed that all music written should be "elevated to the rank of classic art." In this way one would reach ever deeper into the intellectual concepts of the classic masters. This essentially objective precept did not mean a carbon-copy productiveness. It defined classicism as music built from contrasts but chiseled from one unit. Organic totality, within which line writing becomes amplified without overlooking formalism and logic, is exhibited in the Prelude, *Fantasia,* and *Ciaccona* of this opus.

Steuermann was a Busoni pupil and presents a most convincing performance. The Toccata is included in an unbanded recording, which is unwise as much as it is annoying.

Chamber Music

Sonata for Violin and Piano

No. 1 in E minor, Op. 29 / No. 2 in E minor, Op. 36a

☐ Bress (violin); Johnsson (piano) / Oiseau-Lyre S–296

It is to be expected that a prize-winning work, composed at the age of twenty-five, would fulfill academic standards as well as fit within the general, imitative work-period of a composer. These are the facts for Busoni's Opus 29, a work that imitates Beethoven and Brahms. The classical manners, with romantic colorings, are precise, exact, and ordered.

In the second work, four movements are combined in one, the last of which is a set of nine variations on a Bach chorale. Throughout, the style is broadly classical, which means that the emotive, romantic thrust given by the performers is not out of place.

Bress endeavors to whip up more vigor than exists intrinsically in the Opus 29 score, but such demeanor can't be faulted. This violinist's constant seeking of unordinary repertoire deserves special mention.

Busoni / *Franz Liszt.* See *Liszt* / Busoni.

Busoni / *J. S. Bach.* See *J. S. Bach* / Ferruccio Busoni.

Busoni / Kurt Weill (1900-1950)

Divertimento for Flute and Piano, Op. 52

Instrumental

Flute

☐ Gazzelloni (flute); Canino (piano) / Wergo WER–60029

An interesting affiliation is represented here in Weill's arrangement of Busoni's orchestral background for piano. In fact, one doesn't overly miss the original accompanimental setting what with the neat neo-classic spirit of Busoni's writing and Weill's idiomatic transfer. (For the original version, see under *Busoni, Solo Instrument and Orchestra: flute.*)

Hearing Severino Gazzelloni play other than super-contemporary music is rare. He is just as masterful with Busoni as he is with Bussotti or with Messiaen, Maderna, and Matsudaira.

(Wergo's liner note is given in German, French, and English. All three carry the same error. The Divertimento was composed in 1920, not 1922, and of course was not composed "for piano and orchestra," but for flute and orchestra.)

Henri-Paul Busser *(1872-1973)*

Prélude et Scherzo, Op. 35

Instrumental

Flute

☐ Hoberman (flute); Stannard (piano) / Avant 1015

The usual favorable flute solo situation—a nicely flowing part 1, sharply segregated from the antithetical Delibesian section. Busser's style is a commitment to well-groomed romantic writing. The performance is also well-groomed.

Busser / *Claude Debussy.* See Debussy / Busser.

Sylvano Bussotti *(1931-   )*

Coeur pour batteur – Positively Yes

Percussion

☐ Neuhaus (percussion) / Columbia MS–7139

Neuhaus's realization from a graphically designed score mainly covers reiterative punctuations of cymbals and tam-tams, with some glockenspielish taps and sweeps. Neuhaus's special addition is the amplification of his own voice sounds (mostly heavy grunts) and body movements (not light ones). These are not particularly special attractions. They simply thicken the textures.

Rara (eco sierologico)

Instrumental

Cello

☐ Hornung (cello) / Wergo WER–60048

Cage is the point of departure for this piece, an "echo" of another Bussotti composition. (Many of his compositions quote from each other or comment and reflect on previous ones.) Here there are overlays with the cello of voices, speech, laughter, motor-starting noises, and a certified erotic situation delineated at the conclusion, all montaged within the recording.

Chamber
Music

Couple for Flute and Piano

☐ Gazzelloni (flute); Canino (piano) / Wergo WER-60029

In this translation of a graphic score the players proceed to toss the sounds around and accompany a great deal of it with percussive sounds on and inside the piano and on the flute itself. The resultant effect is not beyond comprehension, it is merely difficult to provide more than passing interest. That's the result of leaving it to the performing boys to do a creative man's job.

———

Phrase à trois (1960)

☐ Trio della Società Cameristica Italiana / Wergo WER-60048

The *Phrase* for violin, viola, and cello was inspired by a passage in Proust but its fragmentary and slithering movement avoids any literary affiliation. Bussotti's score is notated in the most enigmatic fashion with a series of interlocked and cross-patched geometric patterns. This music purposefully designed for the eye then becomes freely translated into music for the ear, heard here in a slow-paced continuity of iced sensuality.

———

Il Nudo

☐ Quartetto della Società Cameristica Italiana / Poli (soprano) / Wergo WER-60048

This consists of four fragments from *Torso,* a large work for voices and orchestra. Though taken out of context each of the pieces retains its own conclusive identity. The style is a combination of pointillism, *Sprechstimme,* Webernian fragmentation, and expressionistic reminders of Berio's vocal works. That description sounds like crude eclecticism but the assimilation is successful.

Liliana Poli joins the small, select group (including Beardslee, DeGaetani, and Berberian) that can cope with avant-garde vocal demands. She negotiates the excruciatingly difficult vocal part with technical and interpretative panache. Pitches are hammered home exactly, style is perfectly formulated, and cohesion with the string quartet is masterly. Quite a performance.

Vocal

Voice
with
Accompaniment

Frammento (1958-1959)

☐ Berberian (soprano); Berio (piano) / Mainstream 5005

A fragment of a fragment, presented in a total method of fragmentation. (Explanation: it is titled *Voix de femme* in *Pièces de chair,* a cycle for piano, baritone, and instruments in various degree, in some cases the total of a chamber orchestra. Bussotti's decision to extract it was simply to isolate the piece and have it take on an "autonomous compositional genre.")

Only a Berberian could shape the Morse code quality of this work into any meaning. And it is Morse code stated in slow motion. There are many silences and these become powerful in framing the discontinuity of the sounds and language. The latter is like French smothered in English and mixed with Esperanto. Actual word meaning doesn't matter. It's the musical collage that counts, itself fractioned and fractured. An experience not easily forgotten and one in which the heroine is Berberian. A vocal genius, this woman.

Choral

Chorus Alone

Ancora odono i colli

☐ Chor der Schola Cantorum, Stuttgart / Gottwald (conductor) / Wergo WER-60048

This is the first of *Cinque frammenti all'Italia,* scored for two sopranos, one falsetto voice, tenor, baritone, and bass. (Nos. 3 and 5 of the set are also for vocal sextet, Nos. 2 and 4 call for chorus.) It is a linear-splintered madrigal, of contemporary sensitivity and of nocturnal expression, though one writer describes it as a *Liebesmadrigal 'erotico sentimental.'* However, if Bussotti's *Ancora* is sentimentally erotic, it is soft-cored to its core. The performance is unbelievable in its pitch exactness and balanced perfection, realizing that total disjunctiveness marks every part of the structuring.

Nigel Butterley   *(1935-   )*

The White-Throated Warbler, for Sopranino Recorder and Harpsichord (1965)

Instrumental

☐ Dolmetsch (sopranino recorder); Saxby (harpsichord) / Orion 74144

Recorder

Impressionism–quasi-realism–serialism are represented in Butterley's short piece. This bird in the hands of the recorder will, of course, remind one of Messiaen. As a miniature, it can hold its place against the Frenchman's output.

It is rare to hear a solo for the mini-representative of the recorder family. Difficult to handle, but not in the case of this excellent soloist.

George Butterworth   *(1885-1916)*

A Shropshire Lad

Orchestra

The Banks of Green Willow

Two English Idylls

☐ Academy of St. Martin-in-the-Fields / Marriner (conductor) / Argo ZRG–860

Music of an impressionist–modalist, as well as a composer concerned with the inculcation of folk song. Butterworth's limpid melodicism conveys warm and sincere emotions. Gorgeous performances by the Academy group.

The Banks of Green Willow

☐ London Symphony Orchestra / Previn (conductor) / Angel S–37409

A delicious folk-tuned piece, termed by the composer an "Idyll for small orchestra." It's a pleasure to have in this expressively breathed and affectionately tinged performance.

Dietrich Buxtehude   *(1637?-1707)*

Sonata in F major for Four Viols and Continuo

String Orchestra

☐ Camerata Lutetiensis / Nonesuch 73014

This is skillfully articulated music even if it overemphasizes a conceptual gravity. The relentless determination of the serious mood might perhaps have some programmatic reference, but that remains unknown. Whatever, Buxtehude's score has a consecutive and cumulative sense that is especially communicative.

The continuo is provided by an organ. This means both good and bad news. The former means there is excellent stabilization, the latter describes an occasional imbalance so that the continuo holds first place to a secondary counterpointed movement of the strings. However, don't overlook this work, it is one of Buxtehude's most striking pieces.

Instrumental

Lute

Suite in C minor

☐ Gerwig (lute) / Nonesuch 71229

The customary dance movements embracing one of Buxtehude's many keyboard suites, here played on the lute. It is a most satisfactory and acceptable substitution. Gerwig has a natural feeling for phrasing and his performance is sufficiently flexible and well-controlled. Dynamic coloration is rather bland, however.

Organ

Ach Gott und Herr

☐ Kraft (organ) / Vox SVBX-529

Fine color and fine clarity in this performance.

Ach, Herr, mich armen Sünder

☐ Kraft (organ) / Vox SVBX-527

Buxtehude's chorale treatment is played with a simplicity that is never overregistered. It is dark-timbred, totally beautiful and telling.

Auf meinen lieben Gott

☐ Biggs (organ) / Columbia MS-6944

An imposing title for a five-part Partita. This consists of a Chorale, a *Double,* followed by three dances: *Sarabande,* Courante, and Gigue.

This illustrates a lighter Buxtehude, though still not desirous of casting away all seriousness. Biggs's performance is neatly done and the coloring is most appropriate.

Canzon in C major

☐ Kraft (organ) / Vox SVBX-527

An absolutely beautifully balanced consideration of this stunning polyphonic piece. Though plenty of color variety is present, it fits the design and does not sectionalize the music.

Canzona
In D minor / In G major / In G major

☐ Kraft (organ) / Vox SVBX-528

The music is played with clarity and sensitive (which means sensible) registration and is totally effective.

Canzonetta in C major

☐ Kraft (organ) / Vox SVBX-527

(The same remarks apply as noted directly above.) The only (slight) difference here is a more compact format.

Canzonetta in E minor

☐ Hansen (organ) / Nonesuch 71188

This beauty in the usual polyphonic dress is considered one of Buxtehude's finest small pieces. The playing is wonderfully clear, informative in every nuance.

Canzonetta in G minor
Ciaccona in C minor
Ciaccona in E minor

☐ Kraft (organ) / Vox SVBX-528

The stunner in this group is the E minor "Chaconne." It is this work that Carlos Chávez transcribed so magnificently for orchestra. Kraft's playing is firm and sound, and certainly brings admiration.

Christ unser Herr zum Jordan kam

☐ Kraft (organ) / Vox SVBX-527

Nicely dimensioned playing.

Danket dem Herrn, denn er ist sehr freundlich
Der Tag der ist so freudenreich
Durch Adams Fall ist Ganz verderbt
Ein Feste Burg ist unser Gott
Erhalt uns Herr bei deinem Wort (Two Settings)
Es ist das Heil uns kommen her

☐ Kraft (organ) / Vox SVBX-528

Fine conceptions. Nothing is overemphasized, the lines are firmly in place and the playing is most compelling. Nothing is to be faulted in these performances.

Es spricht der Unweisen Mund wohl

☐ Kraft (organ) / Vox SVBX-529

(See remarks directly above.)

Fugue

In B flat major / In C major

☐ Kraft (organ) / Vox SVBX-527

As has been pointed out quite often, a Buxtehude fugue consists of more than one fugue within the totality and that is the case here with the B flat item. The C major polyphonic opus is nicknamed the "Jig" fugue (Bach's *Fugue à la gigue* will come immediately to mind). Kraft plays it beautifully and decisively. In his performance Kraft approaches the music with much more seriousness and *much* slower tempo than does Biggs (on Columbia MS-6944). The latter *moves!*

Fugue in G major

Gelobet seist du, Jesu Christ

Gott der Vater wohn uns bei

Herr Christ, der einig Gottes Sohn (Two Settings)

☐ Kraft (organ) / Vox SVBX–529

Herr Christ, der einig Gottes Sohn appears in different aspects. *Gelobet seist du* is also so available—the other setting appearing on Vox SVBX–528—as part of the nine-record release in three Vox boxes of Buxtehude's organ music.

Herr Jesu Christ, ich weiss gar wohl

☐ Kraft (organ) / Vox SVBX–527

Another fine chorale prelude that shows Buxtehude as equal to Bach in this particular form. It also shows the fine musical understanding of the performer.

Ich dank dir, lieber Herre

Ich dank dir schon durch deinen Sohn

☐ Kraft (organ) / Vox SVBX–528

(See remarks directly above.)

Ich ruf zu dir, Herr Jesus Christ

☐ Kraft (organ) / Vox SVBX–527

(See remarks above, under *Herr Jesu Christ, ich weiss gar wohl.*)

In Dulci Jubilo

☐ Kraft (organ) / Vox SVBX–528

The performance is faithful to the fine reputation Kraft holds. Tempo is fine, the inner voices function as substantially as Buxtehude's bass and soprano lines. Above all, Kraft's sense of color is ideal.

Jesus Christus, unser Heiland

Komm, Heiliger Geist, Herre Gott (Two Settings)

☐ Kraft (organ) / Vox SVBX–529

Smooth-flowing and thus thoroughly ingratiating playing. Polyphony and chorale wrap around each other in perfect equality. The registrational choice is perfect for.this.

Kommt her zu mir, spricht Gottes Sohn

Lobt Gott, ihr Christen allzugleich

Magnificat Primi Toni

☐ Kraft (organ) / Vox SVBX–528

Very little of Gregorian chant data in the last work listed. Still, the music has an ongoing dramaticism portrayed in Kraft's performance, and when he opens the swells, the music soars. A strong performance. A second setting of this work is on Vox SVBX–529.

Magnificat Noni Toni

Mensch, willst du leben seliglich

Nun bitten wir den Heil'gen Geist (**Two Settings**)

☐ Kraft (organ) / Vox SVBX–529

In the opinion of this reviewer Walter Kraft can do no wrong. Here is perfect articulation, care of the voicing, and sensible consideration of the registration. These are qualities that give emotional depth to Buxtehude's pieces. This is imaginative organ playing without the least doubt.

Nun freut euch lieben Christen g'mein

Nun komm, der Heiden Heiland

☐ Kraft (organ) / Vox SVBX–528

(See comments made directly above.)

Nun lob mein Seel den Herren (**Three Settings**)

☐ Kraft (organ) / Vox SVBX–529

No fewer than three settings of this chorale prelude are presented here, all with faultless clarity.

Passacaglia in D minor

☐ Hansen (organ) / Nonesuch 71188

This remarkably strong piece is played in a totally impressive fashion, even better than the more reticent projection of the score by Walter Kraft (on Vox SVBX–529). Virtuosity in this instance is the marshaling of the structural details and not simply delivering drivingly paced figurations and the like. This is significant organ playing that contains an inner passion that is quite rare.

Prelude and Fugue

In A major / In A minor / In A minor

☐ Kraft (organ) / Vox SVBX–528

Most of Buxtehude's Preludes are far from mere quiet prefaces to the linear syntax of the Fugues. Toccata urgency is included, and so is polyphony. In a sense the two parts are linked, therefore, even though there is contrast.

The separation of the preludes and fugues below has been made to maintain exact alphabetization and specifically to identify the records on which they are contained.

Walter Kraft's performances are of the highest standard throughout. There is impressive definition, and the fugal dispositions are models of precision.

Prelude and Fugue

In A minor / In C major / In D major

☐ Kraft (organ) / Vox SVBX–527

(See above, under *Prelude and Fugue in A major, in A minor, and in A minor.*)

Prelude and Fugue in D minor

☐ Kraft (organ) / Vox SVBX–528

(See above, under *Prelude and Fugue in A major, in A minor, and in A minor.*)

Prelude and Fugue
In E major / In E minor / In E minor / In F major

☐ Kraft (organ) / Vox SVBX–527

(See above, under *Prelude and Fugue in A major, in A minor, and in A minor.*)

Prelude and Fugue
In F major / in F sharp minor

☐ Kraft (organ) / Vox SVBX–528

(See above, under *Prelude and Fugue in A major, in A minor, and in A minor.*)

Prelude and Fugue in G major

☐ Kraft (organ) / Vox SVBX–529

(See above, under *Prelude and Fugue in A major, in A minor, and in A minor.*)

Prelude and Fugue
In G major / In G minor / In G minor / In G minor

☐ Kraft (organ) / Vox SVBX–527

(See above, under *Prelude and Fugue in A major, in A minor, and in A minor.*)

Prelude and Fugue in G minor

☐ Kraft (organ) / Vox SVBX–528

(See above, under *Prelude and Fugue in A major, in A minor, and in A minor.*)

Prelude, Fugue, and Chaconne in C major

☐ Biggs (organ) / Columbia MS–6944

This is a combination of cogent music and sheer virtuosity. Bach and Buxtehude do go together, as history indicates. Here there is a relationship to Bach's "Toccata, Adagio, and Fugue" in the same tonality. Biggs plays splendidly and the music is vividly portrayed.

Prelude in B flat major (fragment)
Puer Natus in Bethlehem

☐ Kraft (organ) / Vox SVBX–529

The concentrated *Puer Natus* is not considered a masterpiece, but its poetic yield could well nominate it for that category. The music is played with assurance and bright color. The fragment is a gay bit. Apparently a fugue was to be attached, although the Prelude does have a firm final cadence and by itself seems complete.

Te Deum Laudamus

☐ Kraft (organ) / Vox SVBX-527

Kraft has applied modest registration and the music gains thereby.

Toccata in D minor

☐ Kraft (organ) / Vox SVBX-529

A performance of impact.

Toccata

In F major / In F major

☐ Kraft (organ) / Vox SVBX-527

There is a strong Bachian affinity in this music, particularly in one of these two F major toccatas. The music has the same impetus, forwardness, and virtuosity as Bach's Toccata and Fugue in F.

Toccata in G major

☐ Kraft (organ) / Vox SVBX-528

A wonderfully clear portrayal with a depth and breadth of organ sonority.

Toccata in G major

Vater unser in Himmelreich **(Two Settings)**

Von Gott will ich nicht lassen **(Two Settings)**

Wär Gott nicht mit uns diese Zeit

Wie schön leuchtet der Morgenstern

☐ Kraft (organ) / Vox SVBX-529

The music is brilliantly played: robust where it should be and sensitive where it should be. Kraft especially probes the combination of poetry and power found in the chorale fantasia *Wie schön.*

Wir danken dir, Herr Jesu Christ

☐ Biggs (organ) / Columbia MS-6944

A wonderfully clear exposition.

Sonata in D major for Violin, Viola da Gamba, and Continuo, Op. 2, No. 2

Chamber Music

☐ Schlupp (violin); Dommisch (viola da gamba); Ruth Ristenpart (harpsichord); Hindrichs (cello) / Nonesuch 71119

There are two additional sections to this six-part work which are omitted from the recording. The highlight is the final movement performed here, an Arietta set in variation form. This is a thoughtful presentation, showing a thorough identification with the idiom.

Sonata in E minor for Violin, Viola da Gamba, and Continuo, Op. 1, No. 7

☐ Bünte (violin); Dommisch (viola da gamba); Ruth Ristenpart (harpsichord); Hindrichs (cello) / Nonesuch 71119

An eight-sectioned work, five of which are on the fast side of the tempo ledger. The playing stresses baroque style, which means incisive depictions of the speedier portions and an airy forwardness in the slow-paced divisions.

Cantata and Oratorio

Alles, was Ihr tut mit Worten oder mit Werken
Befiehl dem Engel, dass er komm

☐ Berlin Bach Orchestra and Greifswald Cathedral Choir / Kunzel (bass) / Pflugbeil (conductor) / CMS/Oryx 3C–303

The Bible supplies most of the text for *Alles, was Ihr.* The shorter *Befiehl* work has a text by the sixteenth-century writer Erasmus Alber. This disc offers fine singing by the four-part choir and intelligent singing by the bass, whose voice is of lightweight timbre. He is heard only in the first of the two cantatas.

Das neugeborne Kindelein

☐ Instrumentalists and Freiburg Student Choir / Knall (conductor) / Vanguard C-10045

Buxtehude's Christmas cantata calls for four-voice choir, strings, and continuo. There are four sections, each prefaced by a string ritornello. The performance deserves applause—there is nothing amateurish in the singing of the Freiburg group. It is forthright, firm, and totally professional.

The Final Judgment

☐ Heidelberg Chamber Orchestra and Mannheim Bach Choir / Grünewald, Lerche, and Rattunde-Würtz (sopranos); Kirchner (alto); Gilvan (tenor); Schmohl (bass); Müller (chamber organ); Schmidt (harpsichord and organ) / Göttsche (conductor) / CMS/Oryx 1702/3

The Final Judgment is divided into five episodes, four of which are prefaced by an orchestral sonata, interlude, or overture. This structural definition is matched by a fairly familiar chorale concluding each section. To work hand in hand with the text each voice portrays a character: the Voice of God, the Righteous Soul, the Wicked Soul, Pride, Avarice, and Lust. These are underlined by specific instrumental assignments: two oboes and a bassoon for the Wicked Soul, two violins and a cello for the Righteous Soul, and so on.

A commanding interpretation is given of this rarely heard Buxtehude composition. The soloists are fine, especially Traugott Schmohl representing the Voice of God and Raimund Gilvan as the Wicked Soul. Fine work by the chorus.

Herr, ich lasse dich nicht

Ich suchte des Nachts

☐ Bach-Collegium, Stuttgart / Altmeyer (tenor); Stämpfli (bass) / Rilling (conductor) / Nonesuch 71258

Musical triumphs both. Contrasting subjects are involved: the struggle and dialogue between Jacob and the angel (from Genesis) in *Herr, ich lasse* and a section from The Song of Songs with poetic interpolations in *Ich suchte.* The dramatic coloration of the former is intensified by the use of three trombones (played here by Willy Walther, Josef

Feck, and Lothar Zinke). There is more poetic sentience in *Ich suchte* but this too has its own type of drama.

The portrayals carry out the aesthetic emotion of the music. Rilling's direction obeys stylistic requirements but, more to the point, it brings with it artistic significance. Rarely have Buxtehude's cantatas been detailed in so clear and satisfactory a way.

Mein Herz ist bereit

☐ Bach-Collegium, Stuttgart / Stämpfli (bass) / Rilling (conductor) / Nonesuch 71258

This is a particularly outstanding exhibition of Buxtehude's music. The singing of Jakob Stämpfli excites with its solidity and natural beauty. Rilling's colleagues support perfectly (the scoring is for three violins, violone, and continuo).

Mit Fried und Freud ich fahr dahin

☐ Berlin Bach Orchestra and Greifswald Cathedral Choir / Pflugbeil (conductor) / CMS/Oryx 3C–303

This work is based on the Lutheran chorale by the same name. It is given a comfortable but far from exciting performance.

O Gottes Stadt

☐ Bach-Collegium, Stuttgart / Donath (soprano) / Rilling (conductor) / Nonesuch 71258

Buxtehude's solo cantata calls for two violins, viola, violone, and continuo. It is performed with a high sense of style and Helen Donath's voice is perfect for this type of music. Excellent liner notes, too, which is usual with Nonesuch.

William Byrd   (1543-1623)

Fantasia   *Instrumental*

☐ Davis (organ) / Argo ZRG–659   *Organ*

This piece is contained in an album of superbly performed *Ceremonial Tudor Church Music*. The problem is to find the work within the many on the disc (a total of twenty-one items, six of which are readings from the Bible, and with only three bands represented on each side). For such worthy music "needle research" brings rewards.

A Gigg

☐ Jesson (organ) / Lyrichord 7156

Byrd's keyboard music not only has been performed on the harpsichord, but also has been transferred to the lute, the piano, and the organ. These are, of course, purer definitions than the many transcriptions that include settings for two pianos, brass ensembles, strings, and full orchestra.

A Gigg is one of Byrd's contributions to the *Fitzwilliam Virginal Book*. What is lost in sharpness of outline, due to the heavier organ timbre, is gained in terms of sound sustainment. (Two other pieces from the *Fitzwilliam* collection are noted below in their alphabetical place in this section.)

Pavan and Galliard

Prelude and *Miserere*

☐ Jesson (organ) / Lyrichord 7156

(For details see above, under *A Gigg.*)

Verse

☐ Davis (organ) / Argo ZRG–659

(For details see above, under Fantasia.)

Choral

Chorus Alone

Assumpta Est Maria

Ave Verum Corpus

☐ Saltire Singers / Lyrichord 7156

The four-part *Ave Verum Corpus* is the better-known of this pair of motets, but the five-voice *Assumpta Est Maria* certainly is deserving of equal listening time.

The Saltire group (a quintet of soprano, contralto, two tenors, and a bass) conveys the spirit and creative powers of this music perfectly. The climactic points in both pieces are exceedingly well-managed.

Ave Verum Corpus

☐ Choir of King's College, Cambridge / Willcocks (conductor) / Argo ZRG–5226

This motet, one from a set of sixty-three published in 1605, is beautifully sung with every shade of meaning depicted.

Civitas Sancti Tui

☐ Saltire Singers / Lyrichord 7156

One of Byrd's noblest creations, *Civitas Sancti Tui* is a five-part motet contrasting polyphonic with chordal style. It is attractively sung with proper delicacy where needed.

Is Love a Boy?/Boy, Pity Me

I Thought That Love Had Been a Boy

Lord, Hear My Prayer

☐ Saltire Singers / Lyrichord 7156

All three are from Byrd's *Songs of Sundrie Natures.* Sundry they are—and persuasively sung in their diversity. The first two are madrigals, the third is an anthem, its text from Psalm 102.

The Nightingale

☐ Saltire Singers / Lyrichord 7156

Fruitful liveliness is displayed in Byrd's three-part madrigal. Hearing it sung by this group is a delight.

Wounded I Am

☐ Saltire Singers / Lyrichord 7156

The constant highlighting of a solo phrase, now in one voice and then in another, throughout this four-part polyphonic gem is judiciously accomplished.

Bow Thine Ear, O Lord

Chorus with Accompaniment

☐ Choristers of St. Paul's Cathedral and Purcell Chorus of Voices / Davis (organ) / Burgess (conductor) / Argo ZRG-659

This is described in Argo's liner note as a "contemporary English version of Byrd's motet *Civitas Sancti Tui* (see under *chorus alone*). The performance provides compelling listening.

An Earthly Tree, a Heavenly Fruit / Cast Off All Doubtful Care

☐ Saltire Singers / Jesson (organ) / Lyrichord 7156

An example of Byrd's undeniably sensitive attention to textural contrast and attendant color. *An Earthly Tree* is a Christmas piece, with the verse sung in duet form and supported by organ, and the refrain (*Cast Off All Doubtful Care*) set in unaccompanied four-part polyphony.

A warmly blended presentation, highly recommended.

Have Mercy upon Me, O God

☐ Saltire Singers / Jesson (organ) / Lyrichord 7156

This is a setting of Psalm 51, constructed as an accompanied solo alternating with five-part chorus. The Saltire Singers are excellent.

Christ Rising Again from the Dead

Chorus and Instrumental Ensemble

☐ Choristers of St. Paul's Cathedral and Purcell Chorus of Voices; Elizabethan Consort of Viols / Bowman and Deller (altos); Davis (organ); Burgess (conductor) / Argo ZRG-659

The text deals with St. Paul's reflection on the Resurrection. Byrd's emphasis is on a pair of solo voices responded to by the chorus.

Honest if not great solo singing retains the atmosphere of the piece. The string group is excellent.

From Virgin's Womb

☐ Choristers of St. Paul's Cathedral and Purcell Chorus of Voices; London Cornet and Sackbut Ensemble; Elizabethan Consort of Viols / Bowman (alto); Davis (organ) / Burgess (conductor) / Argo ZRG-659

A setting of *A Carowle for Christmas Day* by Francis Kindlemarsh. The solo voice (styled nicely here) sings the verse; the refrain is delivered by the chorus (beautifully detailed in the performance).

Make Ye Joy to God

☐ Choristers of St. Paul's Cathedral and Purcell Chorus of Voices; London Cornet and Sackbut Ensemble / Davis (organ) / Burgess (conductor) / Argo ZRG-659

The words are from Psalm 100, for which Byrd's sonorities are designed effectively, made more exciting by use of counterpoint in the high register. The entire conception fulfills the title completely.

349

Byrd's work is expertly sung and set forth in a sprightly tempo that helps obtain a winning interpretation.

Praise Our Lord, All Ye Gentiles

Sing Joyfully Unto God

This Day Christ Was Born

Turn Our Captivity, O Lord

☐ Choristers of St. Paul's Cathedral and Purcell Chorus of Voices; London Cornet and Sackbut Ensemble / Davis (organ) / Burgess (conductor) / Argo ZRG-659

Praise Our Lord and *This Day* are Christmas pieces, *Sing Joyfully* tells how God is to be praised with musical instruments, and *Turn Our Captivity* concerns the jubilation of Easter with Christ's triumph over death.

All are clearly sung and with an enthusiasm that provides the proper zest for these choral pieces.

Cantata and Oratorio

Magnificat* and *Nunc Dimittis* from *The Great Service

☐ Choir of King's College, Cambridge / Willcocks (conductor) / Argo ZRG-5226

This is a disc with beautiful sound and atmosphere. The singing reveals complete idiomatic penetration.

Mass for Five Voices

☐ Choir of King's College, Cambridge / Willcocks (conductor) / Argo ZRG-5226

Byrd's *Mass in Five Parts* (another title) is a superb example of his talents. The singing is sensitive, particularly in the mysterious *Et Incarnatus* section.

C

Juan Bautista José Cabanilles   (1644-1712)

Batalla imperial   *Pasacalles* **in G major**   *Instrumental*
Pasacalles **in D major**   *Toccata de ma esquerra*

Organ

☐ Rilling (organ) / Turnabout 34097

This is proclamatory music for the most part. Exceedingly majestic sound is provided by Rilling, who does not opt for much contrast. Still, in general the registration fits.

Antonio de Cabezón   (1510?-1566)

Diferencias sobre "La dama le demanda"   *Instrumental*

☐ Hogwood (harpsichord) / Nonesuch 71326

Harpsichord

These *Diferencias,* meaning "Variations," are continuous and firmly sustained in their thematic relationship. The playing is neat and totally clear.

Pavana   *Organ*

Variaciones sobre "El canto del caballero"

☐ Rilling (organ) / Turnabout 34097

De Cabezón was considered the greatest of the Renaissance organists. The examples of his music heard here have a quiet gentility that is quite moving. Rilling emphasizes this quality by choosing warm, soft sonorities. His playing is most telling in the *Pavana*.

Peter Cabus   (1923-   )

Variaties   *Chamber Music*

☐ Annapolis Brass Quintet / Crystal S-207

Tightly formationed, *Variaties* consists of a theme with nine short variations (the entire piece lasts six minutes). The piece is written in a lightly dissonant style, though (as with Hindemith) all ends well with a resolute tonic chord conclusion.

The Annapolis Quintet gives a fine depiction. This is an excellent brass team that provides finely calculated sounds throughout this Belgian composer's work.

John Cacavas / *Morton Gould.* See Gould / Cacavas.

Charles Wakefield Cadman   **(1881-1946)**

Vocal

*Voice
with
Accompaniment*

At Dawning, Op. 29, No. 1

☐ Garden (soprano); Dansereau (piano) / New World Records NW–247

Art songs don't make more than some loose change these days. It wasn't that way way back when. A song could be picked up by a famous singer, propelled into a hit, and the composer went off singing his way to the bank. *At Dawning* is a prime example. It represents Cadman's most famous song and it is available in a remastering of a 1926 recording, made by the famous Mary Garden.

Four American Indian Songs, Op. 45

☐ Parker (baritone); Huckaby (piano) / New World Records NW–213

Beautifully turned-out, utterly unsophisticated but with a skillfully organized continuum of melody, Cadman's songs are only cheap when they are cheapened by sentimental singing, which is not the case here. Included is the very famous example in the genre, *From the Land of the Sky-Blue Water.*

John Cage   **(1912-   )**

Percussion

Amores (1943)

☐ Cage (piano); Price, DesRoches, and Boberg (percussion) / Mainstream 5011

Timbre, rhythm, and special colors are combined in Cage's four-movement composition. The outer movements are for prepared piano (the composer performing). The inner pair are for percussion, each requiring three players. Movement 2 is for nine tom-toms (three each of high, medium, and low pitch) and a pod rattle. Movement 3 is for seven wood blocks (three high-pitched and two each of medium and low sound).

Cage's percussion alchemy produces a real, specialized music. It is richly strange and fascinates as it captures the ear. The piece is flawlessly performed with flawless reproduction. A better performance would seem impossible.

First Construction (in Metal) (1939)

☐ Les Percussions de Strasbourg / Philips 6526017

Only metal instruments—both pitched and unpitched—are used. In the latter case different sizes produce simulated pitch variables. Cage's choices are: four thundersheets; orchestra bells; string piano (playing therefore inside the instrument and also requiring an assistant performer who presses a heavy metal cylinder firmly against the strings while the pianist plays normally); a dozen sleigh bells of varying sizes (oxen bells may be substituted); suspended sleigh bells; four brake drums; eight cow bells; three Japanese temple gongs; four Turkish cymbals; eight anvils (pipe lengths can be used instead); four Chinese cymbals; four muted gongs; suspended gong; tam-tam, and a water gong (the pitch changes as the gong is lowered into the water or is raised up from it).

Sometimes there is metallic fervency, sometimes the timbre combination has poetic resonance. Always, the music moves with constant phrase fluidity.

The writer conducted this work at a contemporary music festival in Mexico, where the audience demanded an encore. The same will apply to this performance of finesse.

(Correction: Philips's liner note gives the year of composition as 1937. This should read 1939.)

Another (much earlier) monaural issue of this work (on Avakian S–1) deserves attention for two reasons. First, Cage's intrepid musical exploration is presented with remarkable rhythmic control (and most of the patterns are not simplistic by any means). Second, the performers include the composer Michael Colgrass and the pianist-composer David Tudor. His assistant is the famous dancer Merce Cunningham.

She Is Asleep (Part a, Quartet) (1943)

☐ Price, Colgrass, Smith, and Brown (percussion) / Avakian S–1

Twelve tom-toms are used in this piece, which is considered an entity here, but which really is only the initial part of a two-part work (for Part b, see under *Vocal: voice with accompaniment*). The piece has chantlike details, sensitively executed by four top percussionists.

Concert for Piano and Orchestra (1958)

☐ Tudor (piano) / Cunningham (conductor) / Avakian S–1

*Solo
Instrument
and
Orchestra*

Piano

There is singular method in this creative madness. The pianist is given a "book" containing eighty-four different kinds of compositions. He is free to play any elements of his choice, wholly or in part and in any sequence. The orchestral accompaniment "may involve any number of players or more or fewer instruments." (As recorded here the maximum number of instruments is employed: three violins, two violas, one cello, one bass; one performer doubling on alto flute, flute, and piccolo; one clarinet; a bassoonist doubling on baritone saxophone; five types of trumpet (in F, E flat, D, C, and B flat) used variously by one player; one trombone; and two types of tuba (in F and B flat), also handled by one player).

However, the orchestra can be totally dispensed with, or reduced to a chamber ensemble. Also, the work can be performed "in whole or part." The players, whatever their number, can play a few notes and then stop or play nothing at all!

Naturally, with such free ejection and rejection there is no form, no temporal pulse, no beginning, no end. It's a gigantic improvisation that can even turn on itself and eradicate its own existence. Since the players have the choice not to play at all if they so choose, it is possible to assemble a group and a solo pianist and have a "rendition" of total silence! Indeed, Cage's *Concert* is Cage uncaged as he passionately indulges in no-matter-whatever.

Ten thousand recordings would give ten thousand different results. (Play the game as I did—jump around the recording, back and forth; Cage won't mind, believe me.) There are no criteria for what I term a marvelous example of neo-Dadaism. Put another way, it is a prize work of communication by noncommunication.

Concerto for Prepared Piano and Orchestra (in 3 Parts) (1951)

☐ Buffalo Philharmonic Orchestra / Takahashi (piano) / Foss (conductor) / Nonesuch 71202

This is the sweet land of John Cage liberty. Temporal pulse is obviated and so is tension. An assembly line of fragmented entrances and exits are heard, with many sounds decaying before they can become definite. Cage knows what he is about, and it is fascinating (and enormously instructive!) to realize that the purpose of the music is *not* to claim any objective; the goal seems to be musical reflux. Some may find the lack of sonorous impact and pulse annoying and be reminded of the act of imaginary coitus. But after all, this is no hit-and-miss affair; it is precisely the reaction Cage wanted.

According to Cage, the concerto was composed with the aid of charts of rhythmic structures. These, he states, ''gave me the first indication of the possibility of saying nothing.''

Accordingly, the sharp and clear image of nonmusic. It works and works well. Only a chump would dare to criticize the type of performance recorded here, for what is involved here must be considered admirable.

Instrumental

Music for Carillon (1954)

Carillon

☐ Tudor (electronic carillon) / Avakian S–1

Cage's negation of a positive structure is worthy of quotation, since it describes this music of abstract bell-tolling: ''The objective was not to make a composition, but rather to bring about a situation in which the sounds themselves would be autonomous.'' There is a strange specialness to the result.

Clarinet

Sonata for Clarinet (Solo) (1933)

☐ Rehfeldt (clarinet) / Advance 4

This music is almost serial in terms of nonrepetition of pitches until all the chosen pitches have been covered. The piece consists of three movements that sound like improvisations. They are partially so, actually, since phrasing and dynamics are chosen by the performer.

Double Bass

26′ 1.1499″ for a String Player (1955)

☐ Turetzky (contrabass) / Nonesuch 71237

The music, if these sonic indulgences are to be termed ''music,'' is by Cage; the style is Dada's. One hears lots of sensory impacts (no pain) including mouth noises, yells, hisses, whistles, toy-piano sound, and sonorous jockeying of the bass as it slides, glides, slurps, swishes, goes behind the bridge, is struck. Turetzky works from a graphed score and therefore one hears an improvisational response. He cries ''Hey'' several times and certainly makes hay of this opportunity to be sonically histrionic.

Cage has written a number of time-titled pieces, the most famous being the totally silent *4′ 33″*. The most wondrous of these is *0′ 00″*, which exists only as a title to be read since the ''composition'' is a cipher. The longest is for prepared piano, due to come in at *34′ 46.776″*. Which leads one to ask why the work reviewed, *26′ 1.1499″*, is recorded at a total of 16′ 17″. Just curious, mind you, no complaint.

Organ

Variations I, for Any Kind and Number of Instruments (1958) (Realization for Organ by Gerd Zacher [1967])

☐ Zacher (organ) / Wergo 60033

Zacher's realization is derived from a set of transparent sheets coded in a certain manner. Of course, Zacher does not make the error of making the organ sound like an organ in his performance. He makes much of intonational drop-off, obtained by key pressures, which disorganizes the sound levels and pitch. The deliberate distortion is deliciously disordered.

This is the second time Zacher has recorded a realization of Cage's Variations I (mislabeled here as "Variations III"). The other is on a Deutsche Grammophon disc (139442) no longer available.

Bacchanale **(1938)**   *Piano*

Dream **(1948)**

Metamorphosis **(1938)**

Music for Marcel Duchamp (1947)

Prelude for Meditation **(1944)**

Root of an Unfocus **(1944)**

Tossed as It Is Untroubled **(1943)**

Two Pieces (1935)

Two Pieces (1946)

A Valentine out of Season **(1944)**

☐ Kirstein (piano) / Columbia Special Products CM2S–819

This is a mini-encyclopedia of John Cage's piano compositions. Even though ten works, composed between 1935 and 1948, are represented, the amount is minuscule compared to Cage's total output for solo piano. (The most recent catalogue of contemporary music put out by Cage's publisher, C. F. Peters, lists fifty-one such works.)

Some of the pieces are for "straight" piano, others are for the "prepared" instrument. All have the Cage profile, which belies those who claim his music is faceless. The largest pieces are *Metamorphosis* (sixteen minutes), serially constructed, and the twelve-minute Two Pieces (1946), a music of small paragraphs spread out between silences.

Of course, the creative visage varies according to mood and objective sought. Motival variation is used in Two Pieces (1935), percussive splashes spark the *Root of an Unfocus,* isolated bell-like formations function in the *Prelude for Meditation,* and resonating arpeggios are important to *A Valentine out of Season.*

The toccata power in the *Bacchanale* is carried along by prepared-piano sonorities; this is the first time that Cage used the method. As is so often the case with Cage's output, other versions exist for the same material. *Dream* is a case in point, available also for solo viola and viola ensemble (made by Karen Phillips). *Dream* was originally composed for dance use; Music for Marcel Duchamp was initially conceived for a sequence in a film called *Dreams That Money Can Buy.*

Columbia's album containing these pieces as well as *The Perilous Night* (see below) and the Suite for Toy Piano (see below) is most attractive. The liner notes (by Richard Kostelanetz) are well accomplished, though lacking in sufficient technical information. The listings are all precise, except for *Tossed as It Is Untroubled,* which does not indicate Cage's parenthetical subtitle *Meditation.* It is not quiet by any means as it examines a pentatonic idea during its two-and-one-half-minute span.

The performances by Jeanne Kirstein are ideal. It must be borne in mind that Cage's music does not leave much room (if any) for a performer's personality. Still, the temper of each of the pieces is conveyed ideally, and the textural conditions and dynamic states are clearly and cleanly defined.

The Perilous Night, **Suite for Prepared Piano (1944)**

☐ Bunger (piano) / Avant 1008
☐ Kirstein (piano) / Columbia Special Products CM2S–819

John Cage's sonorous, kaleidoscopian arabesques both taunt and caress the ear. *The Perilous Night* (in six movements) is certainly one of his most exquisite explorations. Subtle fragments and peppery repetitive figures move in and out of the music. The former characterize the silences and rebeginnings of part 3 and the conclusion of the suite; the latter are emphasized in the ostinati in part 4, the dynamic ictus that prevails in movement 5, and the boogie-woogie-like stability of the finale.

These two performances are as different as can possibly be imagined. Richard Bunger covers the work in ten and one-half minutes, Jeanne Kerstein takes thirteen and one-quarter minutes. Some movements are played so slowly by Kerstein that a completely different music emerges. Bunger's rendition emphasizes soft colors, Kerstein's, flat, hard surfaces. With music of this type such contrary orderings are both in order. The suggestion here is to obtain the two versions and to enjoy the double take, each viable and acceptable.

What is not in order or enjoyable is the lack of bands in both cases. This type of aggravation prevents ease of precise comparison or finding a specific section for replaying. Further, the liner notes give no details about the music itself, indicating only generalities about the preparing of the piano. Not even a mention is made of the number of movements.

Sonatas and Interludes for Prepared Piano (1948)

☐ Ajemian (piano) / Composers Recordings 199 (monaural)
☐ Ajemian (piano) / Avakian S-1 (monaural)

This music is written for a piano that is transfigured into an assortment of sounds that make of it a sensitive, twilighted orchestral instrument. No mere caprice, this, or a creative wise guy trying to focus attention on himself. Cage's changing of the piano, "preparing" it with mutes of differing type—slats of bamboo, bolts, screws, erasers, and the like—is an honest determination to add to the timbre palette.

The Sonatas and Interludes is a work of tintinnabular timbre and riverine rhythm. Cage once wrote me about his string quartet and some of his words can serve to describe this prepared piano work as well. He said of his music that "such means will bring to the familiar that same quality of freshness and never-having-been-heard-before-ness that characterize[s] a discovered sound."

The Sonatas and Interludes is, indeed, a fascinating conception, but best heard in portions. Already the Avakian release, which only embraces half of the total opus, is very much of a muchness.

There are no competitive editions in terms of performance. The Avakian production was released before the CRI recording, though the latter was put on disc much earlier. The former forms part of a three-record album which had been recorded at a concert at Town Hall in New York City, in May of 1958. The performance covers Sonatas I–IV, the First Interlude, Sonatas V–VIII, and the Second Interlude. The initial recording of the complete work was made by the now defunct Dial Records firm in 1951. It covered four record sides. The Composers Recordings version is a remastering of this on two sides and presents the total opus: sixteen Sonatas and four Interludes (the first of these follows Sonata IV, the second and third are placed after Sonata VIII, and the fourth one precedes Sonata XIII). The sound quality in both albums is practically the same: fair but sufficiently satisfactory for thoroughly enjoying Cage's unique composition in whole or in part.

Suite for Toy Piano (1948)

☐ Kirstein (toy piano) / Columbia Special Products CM2S-819

Who but John Cage would conceive of writing for the toy piano? And this isn't his only example. Twelve years after composing this suite, Cage produced his Music for Amplified Toy Pianos (as many as desired).

There are only nine "white key" pitches on the toy instrument, from E below middle C to the F above. The tingling and tinkling bell sounds ting and tink their way through various sprightly combinations and often scalic situations in Cage's cute composition. It has its particular fascinations, even though it is somewhat restricted. Lou Harrison, the composer, thought sufficiently of the piece to transcribe it for a large orchestra including twelve woodwinds, eleven brass, percussion, harp, celesta, piano, and strings.

Toy pianos never have the fullness of sound heard on this recording, unless there are Steinway toy pianos in existence. (I've never seen or heard one.) In this case, the resonance and reverberation quotient is so perfect that one suspects some special microphoning and/or some tinkering with the instrument's mechanism. No matter. It is enjoyable to the ear and, naturally, is played to the hilt by the (toy) pianist.

TV Köln (1958)

☐ Bunger (piano) / Avant 1008

A smidge of a smidgen, equivalent to a composer writing his signature in a fan's autograph book, this piece runs thirty-two seconds, and in order to accomplish aural surety Bunger plays it twice on this recording made "live" at a public concert. Very much live, since the first runthrough is followed by applause, followed by Bunger announcing the replay, succeeded by laughter, and completed by the second rendition and second round of applause.

The title simply identifies the television station in Cologne, Germany, which commissioned the piece.

Three Dances for Two Prepared Pianos (1945)

Two Pianos

☐ Thomas and Grierson (pianos) / Angel S–36059

The prepared-piano timbres that Cage developed produce a gamelan-like expressivity. Nicely assorted music is drawn from this delicate palette, heard in a charming performance by Michael Tilson Thomas and Ralph Grierson. Indeed, the former is as expert at the keyboard as he is on the podium. His colleague is just as musically efficient.

Winter Music (Version for Four Pianos) (1957)

Four Pianos

☐ Flynn (piano) / Finnadar 9006

Cage states that Winter Music is "to be performed, in whole or part, by 1 to 20 pianists." This is the first clue that chance music will be heard. Only a series of chords and harmonic sounds are offered—twenty pages of them. Flynn presents twenty minutes' worth (it could, of course, be exceedingly less or more).

The listing of only one pianist is no error. Flynn's version is the equivalent of four pianists performing simultaneously. He played the work four times, "picking the pages of the score indeterminately for each run." Each of the performances was then dubbed with the previous one (in this manner, of course, Flynn could have covered the work a lesser or greater number of times).

The fragmentation and elusiveness of the piece are so intense that the result sounds like a single run-through rather than the equivalent of a simultaneous performance by four pianists.

Both the creative and the operational procedures are, therefore, of total chance. One supposes that Cage realized there would be a further (different type of) chance that a listener would or would not be interested or like his product. Response to music, like almost all aspects of human endeavor, depends on probabilities.

Viola

Dream (1974)

☐ Phillips (viola) / Finnadar 9007

A great surprise! This is as un-Cage-like as possible. Without composer identification one might say it was by Barber or Fauré.

Dream was originally for piano. With Cage's okay Karen Phillips made this transfer, with the accompaniment for an ensemble of violas. All the parts of the latter are played by the soloist as well, and the magic of recording techniques has done the rest.

Chamber Music

Nocturne for Violin and Piano (1947)

☐ Zukofsky (violin); Kalish (piano) / Desto 6435/37

Despite its date (Cage was a ripe thirty-five years of age when he wrote this short piece), the Nocturne seems to have been an attempt to conceal Cage from Cage. Its quiet account is almost romantic but without rhetoric, impressionistic but without coloristic glamour. What color is used is concentrated in character (a great deal of harmonics for the violin). One of the most sensitively beautiful bits John Cage has written.

Six Melodies for Violin and Keyboard (1950)

☐ Zukofsky (violin); Kalish (piano) / Mainstream MS-5016

This is ascetic, hermetic music. No vibrato is to be used; most of the dynamics are for the piano only; and the phrases are simplistic, conveying a type of artistic monotony. The Melodies are in the same frame of reference as the String Quartet in Four Parts (*see below*).

To achieve this stasis artistically demands top performance, especially from the violinist whose entire instinct is to use vibrato and not be confined in his playing. It is a mark of Paul Zukofsky's mastery that he can accomplish all there is to accomplish with Cage's music. Gilbert Kalish's task is easier, but his performance is of equal skill.

String Quartet in Four Parts (1950)

☐ Concord String Quartet / Vox SVBX-5306

In Cage's peerless and unparalleled quartet, interpretation is taboo, and artistic response by the performers is off limits. The duplicate possibilities of producing the same pitch are eliminated. The precise string to be used for each and every sound is indicated. The usual freedom of choice of producing a flutelike harmonic tone is canceled and each harmonic is specified as to type and string. Further, Cage controls the minuscule fractioned-to-the-last-degree dynamic scale, as well as types of attack and bowing. Every single sound in his quartet is calculated, maintained as a static isolate without change permitted even of the subtlest kind. With such dogma, any free intensification would tear this carefully knitted fabric. The players are, therefore, to "play without vibrato and with only minimum weight on the bow." This is horrendously difficult since it is totally opposite to the norm of string-instrument performance. That the Concord players achieve a complete adherence to Cage's requirements is miraculous.

Principal to the piece are phraseological patterns grouped from exclusive concentrates of particular tones. The quartet is therefore athematic, nondeveloped; one hears no tonal pieces against subtle rhythms and timbres.

Cage wrote this work for the now defunct New Music String Quartet, who recorded it for Columbia. Their performance (long deleted) was of total perfection. The Concord String Quartet matches it in this fresh version.

Six Short Inventions for Seven Instruments (1934)

☐ Ajemian (violin); Fisch and Gromko (violas); Brockway (cello); Lolya (alto flute); Broiles (trumpet); Kaufman (clarinet) / Avakian S-1 (monaural)

This piece is so carefully (and nicely) organized that one does not realize that only twenty-five sounds within a two-octave range are employed. There is no harmonic structure per se; the concept should be regarded as a series of designs made from a deliberately restricted number of pitches. (Originally, Cage composed these without instrumentation; the scoring was done in 1958.)

Aria with *Fontana Mix* (1958)

☐ Berberian (soprano) / Mainstream 5005

A mix with a "mix." *Fontana Mix* can stand alone (see under *Electronic Music*). It is also available for other negotiable, reproductive imagination, as will be noted. That is simply the home of the Cage and the land of his free imagery. Thus, combining the Aria with *Fontana Mix* in simultaneous performance is a further realization. The complications do not disturb. They live happily together. There are further partnerships available, since the Aria forms one of the "orchestral" parts of Cage's Piano Concert. One is certain that if *Fontana Mix* were thrown into the Piano Concert score as well, Cage might not be too upset. To Cage, art is irrational and mad in its potentialities.

The voice line encompasses orientalisms, jazzy snippets, jargonistic bits, and clips that kid the pants off operatic arias, twelve-tone style, pointillism, etcetera, etcetera, etcetera. The tape music gurgles, squeals, goes to the bathroom, showers, and samples an unmapped world.

Mainstream's record does not assign any specific category to Cathy Berberian save "voice." A correct premise. She is soprano, contralto, and mezzo-soprano, female tenor, girl bass, and everything else that amounts to a remarkable artist. A grand recording. A grand Berberian document.

She Is Asleep (Part b, Duo) (1943)

☐ Carmen (contralto); Cage (piano) / Avakian S-1

The second part of a work, performed separately (for Part *a*, see under *Percussion*). The vocalist is encouraged to employ unconventional methods of voice production; the piano is "prepared" but simply so: four pieces of rubber are placed between the strings of four high piano keys. This is a *Vocalise*. Notwithstanding the poetic title there are no words for the vocal part.

The Wonderful Widow of Eighteen Springs (1942)

☐ Carmen (contralto); Cage (piano) / Avakian S-1

No pitches are included in the piano part. The pianist-turned-percussor strikes different resounding parts of the totally closed grand piano, including the under part as well as the top of the instrument and various parts of the keyboard's lid. Cage indicates that his piece "followed from impressions received from the text." (The lines were adapted from a page of Joyce's *Finnegans Wake*.)

Vocal

Voice
with
Accompaniment

Choral

Chorus Alone

Solos for Voice 2 (1960)

☐ Brandeis University Chamber Chorus / Mumma and Tudor (electronic realization) / Lucier (conductor) / Odyssey 32160156

There is an array of assorted sounds in this work. The equivalents are determinable: a steamboat whistle, a baby's cry, a kazoo (for the purists this can be termed a mirliton or a eunuch flute!), the rip of a window shade, even the reaction of a woman to being goosed! Neo-Dadaism or musical nihilism: either way one can have fun with Cage's games.

Here live sound becomes mechanically channeled. Throat, lip, and cup microphones feed these sounds into "a complex configuration of electronic equipment." Thus, the credits for Gordon Mumma and David Tudor, who developed the electronic version heard on this disc.

Opera and Dramatic Music

Indeterminacy

☐ Tudor (music); Cage (narrator) / Folkways 3704 (monaural)

This consists of Cage telling tales—serious and nonserious, important and nonimportant, while Tudor interjects, accompanies, and frames the narration (in no sense coordinating with it) using material from Cage's Concert for Piano and Orchestra and *Fontana Mix*.

In manner this monologue and its approach tell much more about Cage than the mostly fascinating anecdotes he relates. Regardless of how complicated a Cage work may be, it is always entertaining. These four record sides covering ninety stories are always entertaining. You don't have to hear them in their order. You can skip around and if the needle drops in the middle of a tale you can try elsewhere on the disc or wait it out—it won't be long, since each account takes one minute. I'm sure Cage won't mind your doing this; in fact, I'm certain that being John Cage he'd heartily approve of such freedom.

Electronic Music

Cartridge Music (1960)

☐ Cage and Tudor / Mainstream 5015

This is a bold entry into the world of noises: special, scrappy, and scratchy. The beauty of this long exploration occupying an entire record side is its sheer ugliness, and that's special too.

Special also is the method. Phonograph cartridges are used, not for needles, but for toothpicks, matches, wires, feathers, etcetera. Contact microphones are applied to anything handy: chairs, tables, waste baskets, and so on. Both cartridges and microphones are connected to amplifiers which go to loudspeakers, since most of the sounds would not be heard without amplification. Additional sound qualities are included by the removal of an item and the insertion of a different one in the cartridge, taping, and superimposition of one tape on another.

It is thus apparent why performer credit is given here for a work in the electronic category. Cage and Tudor not only produce but also shape the progress ("form"?) of this "Noise Passion According to John Cage."

(Be sure your volume control is set fairly high; the recording is at a level lower than average.)

Fontana Mix (1958)

☐ Turnabout 34046

Cage's score for this work makes possible his usual penchant for creative (and re-creative) re-inquiry. The score traces possible hints of action, that is, the actual or exact realization is thereby indeterminate. The magnetic-tape setting was prepared by Cage. Other versions have been made by David Tudor (for electrically amplified piano), by Max Neuhaus (using percussion instruments to produce electronic feedback), and by Cornelius Cardew (for guitar). (For the Neuhaus "solution," *see below;* for still another setting, see under *Vocal: voice with accompaniment* [Aria with *Fontana Mix*].)

The above facts show a partnering of the aleatoric objective with the aleatoric subjective. Cage's own realization of his own creation is a montage–collage of snatches of words, laughter, midget-sound injections, hints rather than even short statements. It turns out to be a fun piece—a true sound tease and almost as titillating as a human strip scene. Just as one is ready to hear a full tune, a march phrase, or a melody, the "music" shifts gears. All you get are two or three beats of something you would be certain to recognize if you were given at least ten or twelve beats' worth. You never do, and this is probably Cage's idea of disordered clarity and a way of waging creative war. In its bastard way of hiding things, *Fontana Mix* carries its own special insignia of authority. You don't have to like it, but it's worth every bit of listening time involved.

Fontana Mix-Feed

☐ Neuhaus (electronic realization) / Columbia MS-7139

Max Neuhaus's realization represents still another handling of Cage's tape work. (See under *Vocal: voice with accompaniment* [Aria with *Fontana Mix*], and see above, under *Fontana Mix.)* The tactic this time is the use of Cage's graphically notated score as the springboard for a totally different realization, one without any relationship to what Cage produced. But that's exactly what aleatoric anarchy is all about.

In *Feed* the sounds result from "the interaction and mixture of feedback channels set up by resting contact microphones on various percussion instruments that stand in front of loudspeakers." What have we? The sonic disturbances of feedback, that's what. All rather unyielding serious stuff.

Imaginary Landscape No. 1 (1939)

☐ Avakian S-1 (monaural)

This is a recording of a recording. Although the piece requires four performers, a public performance must be from a recording made in a studio. Obviously a radio broadcast would also fit the bill. Unstated therefore is the premise that live performers are required to make things heard but are not to be seen.

The sound is made up of commercially issued audio research items (two frequency records and one constant note record), played on variable-speed turntables, together with a large Chinese cymbal and a piano, in which the bass strings were swept with a gong beater and the strings were muted with the palm of the hand while the keyboard was being played.

Variations II (1961)

☐ Tudor (piano) / Columbia MS-7051

Normal piano sound is slaughtered by the substitution of contact microphones attached to the instrument and phono cartridges, both connected to such materials as plastics, pipe cleaners, and toothpicks, that are "stroked, scraped and struck on the strings." This is, of course, an overkill of "normal" sonorities.

Quite a creative verdict is obtained. In the person of David Tudor, however, one can be certain the best man in the business is available to keep the faith—and to preach it.

Variations IV (1963)

☐ Cage and Tudor / Everest 3132

Cage's Variations (I prefer the title "Interdigitations") is a recording excerpted from a live performance at the Feigen-Palmer Gallery in Los Angeles. It is "performed" by John Cage, who is assisted by David Tudor, but actually theirs was merely a matter of supervision of the event (read "happening" or, since many of the participants didn't realize they were being included, read "musical bugging").

The "concert" was drawn from electronic equipment distributed in two rooms, each containing amplifiers, speakers, record players, tape machines, mixers, radio tuners, and so on. These were placed in very odd positions so that microphones could pick up sounds from every direction, including an exit leading to the street (for outside noises and traffic counterpoints), and over the bar (for glass tinkling and conversation).

The catalogue of sounds covers the gamut: abstract and improvisational, disordered and conversional impulsations, sibilations, stridencies, ululations, interlocutions, noises, and so on. These are shuttled, mixed, imposed, trapped, split into the sonic equivalent of a giddy, happy type of delirium tremens. *The* Bolero links up with bus announcements, traffic noises share the stage with trumpet riffs and typewriter keys, and there is talk, talk, talk.

Cage dishes up an aural banquet of chatter, snorts, and laughs. The daffy, daring, dash of Dada is the daddy of Cage's piece. Whether heard in sampling bits or all at once, the production always works. It also entertains. Such a capering candor has a built-in guarantee to amuse.

Variations IV — Volume II

☐ Cage and Tudor / Everest 3230

A sequel to the madcap squeals, squeaks, and squibs found in Variations IV (*see above*). That recording excerpted the data detailed in a six-hour performance. This disc gives you additional portions.

Bear in mind that actual sounds (inside and outside) are mixed with "loaded" sounds (the game is fixed). By way of prerecorded tapes, snips and loops are mashed into the collage. Thus one can hear particles from the *Nutcracker* Suite, the march from *Aida*, a Strauss waltz, the *Hallelujah* Chorus, the *Dies Irae*, and so on.

Williams Mix (1952)

☐ Avakian S-1 (monaural)

Williams Mix is a montage of eight tapes of assorted sounds—urban and suburban, electronic, composer-created sounds—in a totally mixed mixture that becomes mishmashed at times. The *Mix* is a vivid electronic grotesquerie.

Cage and Lou Harrison (1917-   )

Percussion

Double Music (1941)

☐ Manhattan Percussion Ensemble / Cage (conductor) / Mainstream 5011

Double Music is an example of creative collaboration paralleled by creative instrumentation: all forty-four instruments are made of metal. In the gong family, six are muted, three are Japanese temple gongs, two are the closely related large tam tam, and one is the so-called water gong (the instrument is struck and is immediately lowered into a large basin of water, which causes a change of pitch).

Cage and Lejaren Hiller (1924-   )

HPSCHD for Harpsichords and Computer-Generated Sound Tapes (1969)

☐ Vischer, Bruce, and Tudor (harpsichords) / Nonesuch 71224

Instrumental

Harpsichords

HPSCHD (the word is "harpsichord"; the letter deficit is explained by the fact that in computer transmission six letters are the limit and computers are the basic soul-source of this twenty-one minute hunk of music) is (in the recorded version) a compote (I leave that Freudian typo just as is) of a composition for three "live" performers combined with a composite of fifty-one tapes. In its original "concert" (the proper word has yet not been formulated) version HPSCHD combined seven harpsichordists heard over fifty-nine amplified channels, together with assorted films, slides, and light spectacles, lasting more than five hours. Perhaps for this type of sound-stuff only a huge armory is satisfactory. (The Assembly Hall of the University of Illinois, where *HPSCHD* had its premiere, seated 18,000 people, with others standing and prowling about. Compressed on a disc, even with reduced forces, the noise captivates the ear and the effect is sonic laceration, a perfect musical zero, a sonorous mess.

The harpsichordists play Mozart and items drawn from Chopin, Beethoven, Busoni, Schoenberg, and others. It doesn't matter who plays what since nothing whatsoever is made clear. One sound smothers another and is in turn smothered by others, further penetrated and covered by still others. An insistent plucked noodling is heard combined with chattering telegraphic and microphonic mutations of the tape sounds. What a gorgeous imbroglio! What a nifty mess! What negation! Such explicit unexplicitness has never been heard before.

However, as with sex there are all kinds of music. There may be some who will want to avoid HPSCHD's aural angina. Others might like its emphatically nonexpressive jagged jumble of jingle-jangle.

Lucien Cailliet / Claude Debussy. *See Debussy / Cailliet.*

Louis de Caix d'Hervelois   (ca. 1680-1760)

Suite in G major for Cello and Harpsichord

☐ Heurtier (cello); Boulay (harpsichord) / Nonesuch 73014

Chamber Music

As one of the foremost viola da gamba performers of his time, this French musician concentrated in his compositions on music for that string instrument.

This five-movement example is rich with melody, and contrapuntalism is almost absent. This is a charming conception and the playing is equally graceful.

Louis Calabro   (1926-   )

Environments

☐ Eastman Brass Ensemble / Schonbeck (clarinet) / Calabro (conductor) / Composers Recordings S–260

Solo Instrument and Brasses

Clarinet

The principal clarinet part is backed up by twelve brass instruments, but the clarinet is

363

amplified and shakes loose from the brass mass. Firm color and interesting sonorities develop through the cluster compacts that mark the six trumpets and six trombones. Calabro uses creative sense in not overstating what he has firmly defined. His piece covers a seven and one-half minute span, which is just right. The performance, too, is just right.

Giovanni Giuseppe Cambini (1746-1825)

Chamber Music

String Quartet, Op. 40, No. 3

☐ Schäffer Quartet / Vox SVBX-5300

Prolificacy, thy name is Cambini. In the string quartet medium alone his output equaled one gross. If only some of the others match this serious work, there are rediscoveries to be made.

The recording is excellent in respect to playing and reproduction.

Wind Quintet No. 3 in F major

☐ Philadelphia Woodwind Quintet / Columbia Special Products CMS-6799

Cambini's Quintet for flute, oboe, clarinet, horn, and bassoon is easygoing and by no means unattractive music. Everything flows nicely, and the performance does this piece justice.

Alda Caminha (20th cent.)

Instrumental

Violin

Preludio, Op. 16

☐ Szeryng (violin); Maillols (piano) / Philips 6500016

The *Preludio* is an offshoot of Kreisler's *Praeludium and Allegro* without the prelude portion. Caminha dedicated her short piece to Szeryng, who plays it with interpretative savvy—meaning straightforwardly in Handelian style.

Thomas Campion (1567-1620)

Vocal

Voice with Accompaniment

The Cypress Curtain of the Night

It Fell on a Summer's Day

☐ Patterson (tenor); Spencer (lute) / Philips 6500282

Campion wore three hats: those of composer, poet, and doctor of medicine. The texts of both these songs are by Campion. They are beautifully realized by both vocalist and instrumentalist, with a special melting quality in the first of the pair.

Never Weather-Beaten Sail

☐ Brown (tenor); Channon (lute) / Nonesuch 73010

This song combines sacred and secular meanings. It is somewhat placidly sung here—one wishes for more voice to denote contrast.

Shall I Come, Sweet Love, to Thee?

☐ Patterson (tenor); Spencer (lute) / Philips 6500282

The intimacy and almost casual viewpoint of Elizabethan song style is represented in Campion's *Shall I Come*. The performance has satisfying direction and shape.

Frank Campo   (1927-   )

Times (1971)

☐ Stevens (trumpet) / Avant 1003

Campo's piece has a different slant: unaccompanied music covering a semi-programmatic basis. Thus we have *Good Times (alla marcia)*, *Hard Times (Interrupted Blues)*, and *Time to Go*, offering full-range virtuosic possibilities. The middle movement, naturally, is muted.

Stevens gives a convincing account of Campo's difficult work. It includes some exceedingly low notes one won't find listed as possible in orchestration treatises.

Instrumental

Trumpet

Commedie for Trombone and Percussion, Op. 42

☐ Anderson (trombone); Peters (percussion) / Avant 1006

This divertimento-like conversation is deftly carried out. Campo uses instrumental soft-sell, and little produces much. Quips, growls, stutters, and fast talk are all heard in a sophisticated manner. Miles Anderson and Mitchell Peters are expert musical conversationalists.

Chamber Music

Duet for Equal Trumpets

☐ Plog and Kidd (trumpets) / Crystal S-362

The word "equal" in the title of this work conveys a sense of the material's scope, not the actual similarity of instrumental types. Sharp-pointed musical diction is delivered with emphatic clarity.

Kinesis (1950)

☐ Atkins (clarinet); Davis (piano) / Wim WIMR-1

This is mostly motoric music, its rhythmic attitude kept from becoming overbearing by a lyrically nuanced portion. The details of the score are presented with authority.

Sonata for Violin and Piano, Op. 21

☐ Granat (violin); Herbst (piano) / Orion 73128

Campo's two-movement piece gives the effect of nineteenth-century lines put through the wringer of the twentieth century. Tonality thereby expands and intervallic progress is mainly disjunctive.

Endre Granat is a fine violinist. His tone is full and never saccharine, but he flaws in some octaves, and with the music liberally sprinkled with sevenths, it is crucial to be precise. Erwin Herbst is apparently a fine pianist, but he is not heard with the proper balance in Orion's recording, and the remoteness is disconcerting.

Concertino for E flat, B flat, and Bass Clarinets and Piano (1965)

☐ d'Antonio (E flat clarinet); Atkins (clarinet); Spear (bass clarinet); Davis (piano) / Wim WIMR-7

There are no preconditions of medium in the field of chamber music. Campo's clarinet trio (encompassing a range of about five octaves) combined with the piano is still another attempt to work away from the traditional groupings of string quartet, piano trio, wind quintet, etcetera. The piece is written in concerto grosso style, with pantonal syntax.

Five Pieces for Five Winds (1958)

☐ Philharmonic Wind Quintet, Los Angeles / Wim WIMR-9

Campo covers the past and the present in this piece, placing it in the category of neo-classicism, and shows apt workmanship. The recording is first-class—to be expected from these major-league performers.

Madrigals for Brass Quintet

☐ Los Angeles Brass Quintet / Crystal S-821

Campo's three-movement piece not only has to offer much of interest theoretically, but also offers creativity in its tightly fractioned scoring, which is sure-fire, well-sounding, well-proportioned, and of brilliant logic in its pitch permutations. The latter follow serial methods but avoid academic strictures.

The titles of the madrigals—*Indifference, Unrequited Love,* and *Aria perduta*—are more diplomatic than precise. No matter. In the last part, some swishing sounds toward its conclusion may be part of the piece or some erratic tape editing. This one bit (if in the score) is the only negative point in an otherwise totally affirmative piece of brass quintet writing, played in a positively virtuoso manner by the Los Angeles five. Their richly decisive and well-balanced performance deserves an individual credit listing: Thomas Stevens and Mario Guarneri play trumpets, Ralph Pyle is on the horn, Miles Anderson mans the trombone, and Roger Bobo is the tuba man.

Edward Tatnall Canby (1912-   )

Choral

Chorus Alone

The Interminable Farewell

☐ Randolph Singers / Randolph (conductor) / Composers Recordings 102 (monaural)

Humor is the main ingredient of this madrigal, structured on a basso ostinato over which such phrases as "so long," "good-bye," "good night," and "so nice of you to come again" and other leaving-at-the-door clichés are mingled. It's fun, even if one doesn't hear each and every word pronounced carefully.

Richard Cann (20th cent.)

Electronic Music

Bonnylee (1972)

☐ Odyssey Y-34139

This short (one and one-half minute) piece is whimsical if not sweet. Cann writes about

Bonnylee: "This song was sung by an IBM 360 Model 91." This opens up a whole new tradition, if not a whole new kind of music.

Thomas Canning   (1911-   )

Fantasy on a Hymn Tune by Justin Morgan for Double String Quartet and String Orchestra   *String Orchestra*

☐ Houston Symphony Orchestra / Stokowski (conductor) / Everest 3070

This piece offers luscious modalism that runs a close course to Ralph Vaughan Williams's Fantasia on a Theme by Thomas Tallis, which is also for strings with string quartet and incidental solos. The work is made to order for Stokowski's idea of uncloistered string tone.

(In a work of this type one feels that it is only just and proper to give credit to the string quartets' personnel. Everest, however, has decided otherwise.)

Marie-Joseph Canteloube de Malaret   (1879-1957)

Chants d'Auvergne   *Vocal*

Baïlèro	**Malurous Qu'o Uno Fenno**
Brezairola	**Passo Pel Prat**
L'Aïo dè Rotso	**Pastourelle**
L'Antouèno	

Voice and Orchestra

☐ American Symphony Orchestra / Moffo (soprano) / Stokowski (conductor) / RCA LSC-2795

Canteloube produced four sets of the alluring Auvergne songs, performable with piano or orchestra. Of the several recordings that have been issued, the most historic was made by Madeleine Grey back in the 1930s covering eleven of the songs. Her version is now a collector's item. Anna Moffo's interpretation of a group of seven comes closest to Grey's definitive realization of Canteloube's magical evocations.

Although a considerably larger selection is available in Netania Davrath's performance (thirty on Vanguard 713/4) and by Victoria de Los Angeles (on Angel S-36897, with the second volume of the songs on Angel S-36898), the enticement of Moffo's singing is complete compensation for having a smaller total. The sheer beauty of her tone, the exquisite phrasing, and the linear seamlessness produce vocal poetry that can hardly be surpassed.

André Caplet   (1878-1925)

Deux Divertissements pour la harpe   *Instrumental*

☐ Zabaleta (harp) / Deutsche Grammophon 139419   *Harp*

Floating *fiorituras* and rich color without any outlandish effects mark these Debussy-like pieces. The first is *A la Française;* the second, crammed full of harpistic delicacies, including some rubbed and tremolo sounds, is titled *A l'Espagnole.*

There is no debate as to the playing by this master. In Zabaleta's hands one hears a soloized orchestration.

Cantata and Oratorio

Mass

☐ Girls' Choir of the O.R.T.F. / Jouineau (conductor) / Musical Heritage Society MHS-1658

Caplet's Mass is written for three-part unaccompanied female chorus and covers five movements, with the *Credo* omitted and replaced by the Eucharist prayer *O Salutaris Hostia.*

Mystical sentiment is represented here with sufficient dramatic force. The Mass represents one of Caplet's best works; his most important contribution was in the field of choral music. It is good to have it on disc in this finely presented execution.

Caplet / *Claude Debussy.* See Debussy / Caplet.

Giacomo Carissimi (1605-1674)

Cantata and Oratorio

Balthazar

☐ Instrumentalists and Choir of the Kirchenmusikschule, Münster–Westfalen / Speiser and Friesenhausen (sopranos); Altmeyer and Jochims (tenors); Wenk (bass) / Ewerhart (conductor) / Turnabout 34172

Balthazar is set for five solo voices, five-part choir, and basso continuo. A flexible structure and textural stolidity prevail. The singing is confident, all the voices being of good oratorio quality. One ingredient Ewerhart does not supply: dynamic differences.

There are no liner notes, but the original Latin text is printed on the back of the record jacket.

Abel Carlevaro (1918-   )

Instrumental

Guitar

Preludios Americanos

☐ Benítez (guitar) / Nonesuch 71349

This music was composed during the late 1960s and early 1970s but, like most guitar music, does not reflect any contemporary language. Carlevaro's five pieces (*Evocación, Scherzino, Campo, Ronda,* and *Tamboriles*) are self-absorbed in a traditional, conservative demeanor. Obviously, the word *Americanos* refers to Latin America.

The playing of Baltazar Benítez shows nice character, and the same pertains to the sound qualities.

Walter Carlos (1939-   )

Instrumental

Flute

Variations for Flute and Electronic Sound (1964)

☐ Heiss (flute) / Turnabout 34004

In these six variations on a theme severe contrast is obtained by the flute voice traveling on the rough terrain of the electronic surroundings. A special feature is the superimposition of flute sound on top of flute sound (sometimes tripled) as well as echoes.

Heiss, a fine composer in his own right, does well with his fellow-composer's music.

Dialogues for Piano and Two Loudspeakers (1963)

☐ Ramey (piano) / Turnabout 34004

Piano

A blend of simply formed piano material (scalic, chromatic, chordal, and even sequential) in an almost totally subsidiary electronic framework provides the old-fashioned solo-with-accompaniment idea with new packaging.

John Alden Carpenter (1876-1951)

Adventures in a Perambulator (1914)

☐ Eastman-Rochester Symphony Orchestra / Hanson (conductor) / Eastman-Rochester Archives ERA–1009

Orchestra

A lengthy chronicle describes the events in the six movements. The script notwithstanding, the music is mostly in the absolute category. Part 3, *The Hurdy-Gurdy,* and part 5, *Dogs,* have more obvious detail. No matter how one considers the suite, a French impressionistic decor surrounds the perambulatory scenes.

There can be nothing but approval for Hanson's performance. It is further proof of his conductorial ability to provide a true-disposing conception no matter what style is involved. The E-R group may not be considered big-time but they play in major-league fashion. One criticism is the lack of bands on the disc, which is most annoying when one wishes to hear a specific movement.

Concertino for Piano and Orchestra (1915)

☐ Göteborg Symphony Orchestra / Mitchell (piano) / Strickland (conductor) / Composers Recordings 180 (monaural)

Solo Instrument and Orchestra

Piano

With a performance time of over twenty-five minutes, Carpenter's title is an understatement, but the content is enjoyable. The composer described his work as a "light-hearted conversation between piano and orchestra as between two friends." It was first played in 1916 by Percy Grainger and the Chicago Symphony Orchestra. Hardly heard in concert, the piece is certainly welcome on record.

Impromptu: July 1913

☐ Johannesen (piano) / Golden Crest S–4065

Instrumental

Piano

American impressionism pervades this work, with its moods ranging from matinal to nocturnal hours. Jon Morton, in his note on the work, states that as one listens one can "almost feel the heat of the Middle Western sun." Good enough, but there is also a pervading melancholy in the music, outlined in Grant Johannesen's poetic playing.

Sonata for Violin and Piano (1912)

☐ Gratovich (violin); Benoit (piano) / Orion 76243

Chamber Music

Franckian language is strong in Carpenter's G major duo sonata. Some Grieg accents will be noticed as well.

The lack of concert performances of this Sonata is a pity. Surely, there is much to be offered a listener in this work. Fortunately, Orion's recorded performance enables listeners to be exposed to some of Carpenter's very best music.

Vocal

Voice with Accompaniment

Jazz-Boys

☐ Gramm (baritone); Cumming (piano) / Desto 6411/2

A finger-snapping rhythm matches the Langston Hughes text, which itself has a fox-trotty lilt.

Light, My Light (No. 6 from *Gitanjali*) (1913)

☐ Bampton (contralto); (*no pianist credited*) / New World Records NW-247

The *Gitanjali* cycle is Carpenter at his very best in the vocal part of his output. The texts are by Rabindranath Tagore. (No. 1 in the cycle, *When I Bring You Colored Toys,* is discussed below.)

Looking Glass River

☐ Gramm (baritone); Cumming (piano) / Desto 6411/2

There is some impressionistic quality to the piano accompaniment for this song. The vocal line, however, has a restrained declamatory quality. Gramm sings in an expressive, intimate manner. Such simplicity gives the music a quiet dignity.

When I Bring You Colored Toys (No. 1 from *Gitanjali*) (1913)

☐ Hanks (tenor); Friedberg (piano) / Duke University Press DWRM-7501 (monaural)

This is undoubtedly Carpenter's most important song. It is also the most beautiful. The fragile imagery and the warmth covered in the three textual sections are conveyed with interpretative limpidity in this release. (No. 6 in the cycle, *Light, My Light,* is discussed above.)

Ballet

Krazy Kat (1921)

☐ Los Angeles Philharmonic Orchestra / Simmons (conductor) / New World Records NW-228

There is no doubt that this ballet is a delicious dish of classy jazz (Carpenter called it a "jazz pantomime") that hasn't a dated measure despite its 1921 composition date. The story is based on the once famous newspaper comic strip by George Herriman, and the music conveys, move by move, Krazy Kat's antics and adventures during an extremely busy day.

Playing this score too squarely is to invite disaster, but the Los Angeles Philharmonic catches the fantasy behind the notes. This record is a delight to have. Some composer should take a crack at Hairbreadth Harry.

Benjamin Carr   (1768-1831)

Instrumental

Piano

The Federal Overture

☐ Mandel (piano) / Desto 6445/7

Carr put together a nosegay of tunes, including *Yankee Doodle, O Dear What Can the*

Matter Be, Ça Ira, The Irish Washerwoman, and five others, with taste and craftsmanship and no monkeyshines. No small amount of talent was needed to accomplish a patchquilt of this type.

Mandel does wonders with the simplicity of this piece. He does not approach it as a cheap medley which would require a campy attitude, sentimental rubati, and the like. He plays it straight and with sensitive regard for the phraseology. For the objective involved it's a stunning account.

Julián Carrillo   (1975-1965)

Preludio   *Instrumental*

☐ Szeryng (violin) / Philips 6500016   *Violin*

This example of Carrillo's music was written long before the days of microtones, which absorbed him for the greatest part of his career. The *Preludio* is strictly tonal to the last eighth note. Szeryng, of course, has a field day negotiating the conjunct lines and the juicy thirds and sixths the piece contains.

Elliott Carter   (1908-   )

Concerto for Orchestra   *Orchestra*

☐ New York Philharmonic / Bernstein (conductor) / Columbia M–30112

Carter's orchestral concerto was commissioned by the New York Philharmonic for its one hundred and twenty-fifth anniversary and given its premiere by that organization on February 5, 1970. In 1974 a distinguished jury named it as one of the outstanding orchestral works produced by an American composer.

A valid judgment, indeed. Massiveness and Ivesian montage are fundamental to the work, which consists of four large continuous movements. Although individually formulated, the data and character of each movement are echoed in each of the others. The rational construction of the work is obvious, its effect one of virtuoso declaration but without any attempt at exhibitionism. Carter's work completely bypasses eclecticism and depicts a new consideration of the use of musical materials.

The sonorous mixtures give a brilliant edge to Carter's orchestration, even, paradoxically, when low registers are involved. The polyphonic lines and blocks follow the law of simultaneous contrasts, and one needs to bear this in mind when listening.

Only a handful of orchestras can cope with Carter's complex opus. The New York Philharmonic does well, of course, thanks to Bernstein's command.

Symphony No. 1 (1942)

☐ Louisville Orchestra / Whitney (conductor) / Louisville 611 (monaural)

This represents what might be called pre-Carter music. Metrical modulation, instrumental personality by intervallic identification, and the like would be future developments. Composed in 1942, Symphony No. 1 is devoted to a detail of motif that "suggests the folk-lore of the American rural past." Quiet continuity marks the three movements, even in the fast-paced finale. In the latter there is no blatancy but flexibility, with textures open, clean, and clear.

The piece is effectively played, though there is little dynamic differentiation.

Variations for Orchestra (1955)

☐ New Philharmonia Orchestra / Prausnitz (conductor) / Columbia MS-7191

None of the usual catch-alls of variation design are present in Carter's Variations (written to fulfill a Louisville Orchestra commission and first recorded by that group; the monaural disc is still available—Louisville 58-3). The variants grow out of each other, thereby negating the sectionalism that often weakens variation structure.

The eleven variations are conceived as though each one was first composed and then discarded in favor of a variation written on the variation. Two sections are extremely novel and fascinating. Variation 4 consists of a rigid four-measure idea that is metamorphosized eleven times, each portion in a specific, slower speed, metronomically ruled. Variation 6 is built on a six-measure unit, variated a dozen times, each section precisely defined in terms of accelerating speed. Such bare tempo modification (modulation) may seem to be primitive and cold formal testimony yet turns out to be aurally imaginative, musically individual, and properly fits the overall design.

The performance produces full evidence of contemporary instrumental and conducting virtuosity. One listens with admiration.

Solo Instrument and Orchestra

Double Concerto for Harpsichord and Piano with Two Chamber Orchestras (1961)

☐ Contemporary Chamber Ensemble / Jacobs (harpsichord); Kalish (piano) / Weisberg (conductor) / Nonesuch 71314

Harpsichord and Piano

Carter's concerto was called "a masterpiece" by Stravinsky. I cannot recall such praise from Stravinsky for any other work by an American composer.

The thesis of instrumental color defines solo identity. The harpsichord has one woodwind, three brass, and a tenor–bass coupling of strings as its orchestra. The piano is supported by the reverse: three woodwinds and one brass instrument, with two stringed instruments again contrasted in terms of gamut reach. Both ensembles are supported by a huge assortment of percussion.

There are additional mnemonics: specific intervals are emphasized—minor, perfect, and augmented types for the harpsichord and instrumental group, mainly major spans for the piano and instrumental ensemble. Specific rhythms are likewise used to identify the paired components. The form is dictated by conflicts and their compromises. No song has ever been as rugged as the tunes Carter spins in this virtuosic accumulation.

The concerto has been recorded three times. It was first released on Epic and went the way of unwelcome deletes. The second issue made (Columbia MS-7191) is still available, with Jacobs as the harpsichordist, a role he duplicates on the Nonesuch disc. The pianist on the Columbia release is Charles Rosen, and there is much to say for his perceptive handling of that difficult solo part. However, Weisberg's group is better controlled and deeper into the music than the English Chamber Orchestra, conducted by Frederick Prausnitz, on Columbia.

Instrumental

Pastoral

☐ Russo (clarinet); Ignacio (piano) / Orion 77275

Clarinet

Carter originally wrote this work for English horn and piano, but later transcribed it for both clarinet and viola. This early Carter piece offers a fusion of material that avoids the concentrate of small form in favor of an expansive and free consideration of sonata design.

It is good to have this work available on records. John Russo plays it rather neutrally.

Sonata for Piano (1946)

☐ Webster (piano) / Desto 6419E (monaural)

Some Copland and some Stravinsky can be heard in this work, but they are fully modulated and mitigated in Carter's instrumental fibers and figurations, rhythms and roborant creativity. This is an exciting opus, one for virtuosi only. In part 1, both affirmative and toccata-like propulsions are heard. Movement 2 divides into a triptych, with lyricism in the outer panels and an imposing fugue in between. The Sonata for Piano is highly involved music, but it is stated with intense lucidity. (Carter's composition was cited by the Music Library Association as the best work for piano by an American composer published in 1948.)

Beveridge Webster is the ideal interpreter for music of this magnitude and difficulty. All its intensity and dramaticism are conveyed in his superb performance. This is, indeed, distinguished playing of distinguished music.

Eight Pieces for Four Timpani (One Player)

☐ Lang (timpani) / Odyssey Y–34137

Carter's rhythmic specialties (including the technique he developed of metrical modulation) are expectedly given the fullest opportunity in the restricted language that applies to an unaccompanied set of kettle drums. Still, there are some extra highlights such as the accentuations in the *Moto Perpetuo,* the glides and vibrati in the Adagio, the special color of snare-drum beaters in the *Canto,* and the relationship obtained by use of two rhythms in the final March. These are fascinating inventions, best heard a few at a time.

(Originally Carter's work consisted of six pieces, written in 1949. In 1966 two more were composed. The first group were numbered 1, 2, 4, 5, 7, and 8, with the two later pieces designated as Nos. 3 and 6.)

This is not easy to perform, of course, but Morris Lang does everything that is essential. Indeed, Carter's fancies are well-served.

Canon for 3 – *In Memoriam Igor Stravinsky*

☐ Schwarz, Ranger, and Rosenzweig (trumpets) / Desto 7133

This is one of seventeen canons and epitaphs written specifically to appear in *Tempo* (a quarterly review of modern music published by Boosey & Hawkes) as memorial tributes to Stravinsky. Among the other composers represented are Boulez, Copland, Milhaud, Sessions, Berio, Maxwell Davies, and Tippett.

Although the original score indicates muted trumpets and the piece is so performed here, with each player using a different type of mute (straight, solotone, and cup), the slow-tempoed twenty-six-measure piece can be played by any three equal instrumental voices. Accordingly, a second version is on the same disc, using the flügelhorn, cornet, and trumpet (the specific instruments Schwarz, Ranger, and Rosenzweig each play in this second version is not indicated). Both editions are viable, and sensitively stated by the performers.

Duo for Violin and Piano (1974)

☐ Zukofsky (violin); Kalish (piano) / Nonesuch 71314

Instrumental counteraction or dichotomous dissertation (a favorite device that Carter has creatively sharpened to the point where it is his special trademark) characterizes this work. The "double" music provides a sense of seemingly intense improvisation, but this style is as far from the aleatoric arena as possible—Carter's notation is controlled and ultra-precise. The different tonal qualities of the keyboard and stringed instruments are emphasized and the rhythmic detail is also adapted to the instrument. Thus the lyrical violin is much looser than the percussive piano.

Merely to negotiate the notes of a Carter score is a tremendous task. To regulate its balances and to define its spiritual and structural meanings are agonizingly difficult. Even the new type of virtuoso, who has sharpened his technique on the music of Schoenberg, Berg, Webern, Boulez, and Stockhausen, has to confront considerable problems. Zukofsky and Kalish have all the technical and artistic equipment. Theirs is a prodigious accomplishment.

Sonata for Cello and Piano (1948)

☐ Krosnick (cello); Jacobs (piano) / Nonesuch 71234
☐ Greenhouse (cello); Makas (piano) / Desto 6419E (monaural)

In place of instrumentational cohesiveness, Carter here successfully opposes the cello timbre (basically lyrical) with that of the piano (basically percussive). As he indicates in the liner note of the Nonesuch publication, rather than concealing these differences "as had usually been done in works of the sort" he applies the disparity as "one of the points of the piece." Such instrumental characterization has been constantly developed in his later works.

The first movement is the freest. A scherzo contour is defined in the second movement, with an unbound rondo depiction following the slow-tempoed third movement. With Carter design is not subject to formal disciplines. His language is flexible, and the structural representations follow suit. The piece is acutely organized and yet is fluidly natural. It is a creative feat.

The performance clarity of the duo on the Nonesuch recording and the naturalness of their playing is an achievement of top order. No wonder that Carter thought of it not only as acutely faithful to his text but also as "lively, novel, and fresh as if they [the performers] were improvising."

Carter's work was written for Bernard Greenhouse, the cellist on the Desto disc. His interpretation is perfect and is recommended. However, the newer, stereo production with Joel Krosnick and Paul Jacobs is preferred. Desto's sound is not bad by any means, but it doesn't have the warmth found on the other disc.

Eight Etudes and a Fantasy for Woodwind Quartet (1950)

☐ Members of the Dorian Quintet / Candide 31016

By concentrating on a single line, an etude formulates its own coherence. The great majority of etudes are products of technical apprenticeship; only the brilliant masters of musical composition have been able to combine craftsmanship with creative meaning in this form. The contemporary composer has not been much inclined to enter this field of endeavor; in chamber music the possibilities have hardly been touched. Carter's Fantasy is a contrapuntal summation of the previously stated eight-chapter text, and here too the etude style prevails. Heard separately, this ninth movement might be defined as a *quodlibet*; as a postscript, it gives the work a valid conclusion.

The performance is superb.

Sonata for Flute, Oboe, Cello, and Harpsichord (1952)

☐ Sollberger (flute); Kuskin (oboe); Sherry (cello); Jacobs (harpsichord) / Nonesuch 71234

The form of the Sonata can be aptly described by the German *Fortspinnung*. This process of continuity by dynamic compactness rather than symmetrical disposition is constructively uncompromising. Not that Carter is unyielding. He is simply creatively outspoken, refuses to repeat himself or repeat dogma that can be catalogued under the usual headings.

The importance of the piece is proven by four current editions: an old Columbia release (now in the Columbia Special Products catalogue as AMS-6176), Serenus's reissue (No. 12056) of the original Decca recording (with Sylvia Marlowe, who commissioned the work, as the harpsichordist), a Deutsche Grammophon production (No. 2530104), and the one noted above, which is also the best. The music sings and dances; its text is made totally meaningful. The sound is also magnificent. Carter himself calls the performance "remarkable."

String Quartet
No. 1 (1951) / No. 2 (1959)

☐ Composers Quartet / Nonesuch 71249

The highlight in the first quartet is permutative rhythm, functioning with the thematic content as a second dimension of continuity. This rhythmic empathy is developed alongside the basic items of line, vertical and horizontal detail, design, and color, thus giving rise to a tremendous sense of freedom, as though exploratory improvisation were involved. A delineation of individual personality for each instrument is slightly present. This typing is totally and intensely developed in the second quartet. (In the first quartet the individuality is pointed toward linear latitude rather than instrumental profile.)

In the second quartet not a single one of its 633 measures has four-instrument metrical coincidence. For the greatest part the music consists of four solo lines each going its own way. In order to control this linear persistency, Carter characterizes the instruments. The first violin is "fantastic, ornate, mercurial," a bravura body. The second violin is anti-lyrical, the viola, sentimental (in an Elliott Carter sense), and the cello is rhapsodic. As is Carter's habit, the instruments are assigned specific intervals and individual rhythmic plans. Further, the second violin emphasizes plucked sound, and the viola, *portamenti*.

This kind of writing makes for soloistic opulence. The four voices are unaccompanied projections that climb on and around each other. The effect is similar to four string quartets simultaneously playing four different kinds of music, with each of the foursomes compressed into one instrument.

The Composers Quartet has translated Carter's scores into sound with unimpeachable artistry and virtuosity. Not only do they play each and every note in its proper setting, but they convince with their understanding. The words "sensitive" and "supple" perhaps do not apply to the muscle and dynamism found in Carter's quartets but they truly describe the documentation of these horrendously difficult pieces.

String Quartet No. 3 (1972)

☐ Juilliard Quartet / Columbia M-32738

Further evidence of Carter's original thinking is presented in this quartet. There is no precedent for the *modus operandi* of this work, in which the usually unified string quartet is splintered into duos; one, first violin and cello, the other, second violin and viola. The intricacy is further served by having each group cover separate, individual material; one duo playing six movements, the other, four, with interaction between them. The style is also mixed, so that one duo performs in rubato, the other in strict mensural application.

The complex montage has affinity with Charles Ives's music but in a super-sophisticated manner.

Naturally, there are considerable technical disciplines followed in the quartet, especially specific individual intervallic importance in each of the movements. To the listener unconcerned with analysis, the Carter quartet will add up to music that is lyrically acrid, beautifully argumentative, and, profoundly individual.

The recording is especially convincing since engineering techniques offer the definite separation of the two instrumental pairs. This separation is not as fully feasible in a live performance if the players are to make contact with each other. Regardless of the independent activity within the work, the performers must, paradoxically, maintain ensemble identification.

That the performance of this quartet deserves superlatives goes without saying. It certainly marks a glorious high point in the long recording history of the Juilliard Quartet.

Brass Quintet (1974)

☐ American Brass Quintet / Odyssey Y–34137

Carter's quintet is based on a script that deals with part individualization, governed by his favorite device of defining instrumental personality through specific intervallic assignment. The action of the instruments is sometimes presented in partnered arrangement, but most often there is oppositional exchange between them. Carter's style here (as in the third quartet and the violin and piano duo) is predicated on the rupturing of timbre affiliation as it exists in the brass quintet (or string quartet). It is as though the instruments no longer talk to each other but persistently argue among themselves.

Such a creative condition does not lead to easy listening and demands aural conditioning. The challenge is worthwhile. Performing the work is also a hefty challenge. In this respect the American Brass Quintet has met it head on and is victorious. Theirs is an amazing performance. One doubts that any group will be able to do better.

Woodwind Quintet (1948)

☐ Dorian Quintet / Candide 31016

Emphasis on timbre differences is paramount in the first of the pair of movements. This objective paradoxically gives a neat balance to the phrases and motives that structure the initial part of the piece. The finale, in rondo design, is marked *Allegro giocoso.* At the speed the Dorian five play it it is extremely exciting.

The Dorian edition is also available in a more recent three-record set, *Twentieth-Century American Music for Woodwind Quintet,* issued by Vox on SVBX–5307. That's the heading on the leaflet inside the Vox Box. On the box cover the collection is titled differently: *The Avant-Garde Woodwind Quintet in the U.S.A.* The clarinetist on Vox is Jerry Kirkbride. On the Candide issue the clarinetist is William Lewis.

Choral

Chorus Alone

Heart Not So Heavy As Mine (1939)

Musicians Wrestle Everywhere

☐ Canby Singers / Canby (conductor) / Nonesuch 71115

The quality of the English madrigal school is heard here, especially in the interweave of *Musicians Wrestle Everywhere.* There is nothing scholastic about the polyphony in these pieces set to texts by Emily Dickinson.

Choral finesse is the hallmark of Canby's group. The singing is both airy and springy and is beautifully effective.

To Music (1937)

☐ University of Michigan Chamber Choir / Hilbish (conductor) / New World Records NW-219

A setting of a lyric poem by Robert Herrick, Carter's piece was composed in 1937. At that date his music was neo-classical in style. This part of his output does not have the clear personality of the works written since 1948, beginning with the Woodwind Quintet and the Cello Sonata. Nevertheless, *To Music* defines effective choral writing, strong in its textures and rhythmic elements. It is also an eminently singable work.

Carter / *Henry Purcell.* *See Purcell* / Carter.

Ferdinando Carulli (1770-1841)

Concerto in A major for Guitar and Orchestra

Solo Instrument and Orchestra

Guitar

☐ Kammerorchester der Wiener Festspiele / Scheit (guitar) / Boettcher (conductor) / Turnabout 34123

The clear, traditional architecture of eighteenth-century music, with a single moderately fast movement, is represented in this Concerto. The playing is distinguished. The recording is duplicated on a Bach Guild disc (5043) with a different name for the orchestral group.

Twelve Romances for Two Guitars

Instrumental

Two Guitars

☐ Duo Company-Paolini / Turnabout 34341

Simple salon expressions. The Paolini team plays it straight, which is the proper way. Such unaffected manner and restraint bring out the best side of Carulli's conventionalities. (The performance is also included in Turnabout 34195/9, a collection of music for lute, guitar, and mandolin.)

Six Serenades for Flute and Guitar, Op. 109

Chamber Music

☐ Bolotowsky (flute); Karpienia (guitar) / Orion 78303

Light assurances, well played. One of the pieces has a Mozart melody as its theme. This music does not have a sharp profile, but nonetheless has sufficient character to be given attention.

Robert Casadesus (1899-1972)

Sonata No. 2 for Piano, Op. 31

Instrumental

Piano

☐ Johannesen (piano) / Golden Crest S-4060

There are two recordings of this bright neo-classic opus, but there is no problem as to choice. Grant Johannesen (to whom the work is dedicated) performs with panache and vitality, while Carol Colburn (on Orion 7174) plays unsmoothly for the most part. When rhythm is the lifeline of the music (the hopscotch patterns in the cool-jazz properties of movement 3) Johannesen sails along with ease while Colburn consistently struggles and never conquers.

Trois Berceuses, Op. 8

☐ Johannesen (piano) / Golden Crest 4099

This isn't somniferous music at all. The performance of these poetic preludes, the first with a blues contour and with sadness drenching the other pair, is exquisite, sensitive, and worth the price of the entire record, even though the piece is a mere filler for two full-sized cello and piano sonatas (by Hindemith and Casadesus).

Two Pianos

Six Pieces for Two Pianos

☐ Judith and Doris Lang (pianos) / Golden Crest S-4070

These pieces are musical postcards including depictions listed as *Algérienne, Russe, Sicilienne, Française, Espagnol,* and *Anglaise.* To Casadesus's credit there are no downright, mundane imitations but rather subject essences that are conveyed. A presentable performance but rather superficial.

Chamber Music

Sonata for Cello and Piano, Op. 22

☐ Nelsova (cello); Johannesen (piano) / Golden Crest 4099

Music that has the emotional durability, the fundamental warmth, the flow, spirit, and clarity of the work of Ravel. Every sound in this sonata glistens. The instrumental utterances have a straightforward sonority; the piano and violin sing. And the performers follow suit. Casadesus's cello and piano sonata is still another example of the debt many French composers owe to Maurice Ravel.

Pablo Casals   (1876-1973)

Chamber Music

Les Rois Mages from *Oratorio de la Crèche*

☐ Members of I Cellisti / Orion 7037

A fugue for six cellos that sounds like church music. The playing suits the piece quite well.

Sardana for Violoncelli (1951)

☐ I Cellisti / Kessler (conductor) / Orion 7037

Music celebrating Catalonia through the rhythm of its national dance. Some contrastive devices are used, but mainly this is folk music scored for eight celli. The simple and expressive content is made more important by the composer who produced it.

Choral

Chorus Alone

Canco a la Verge Eucaristica	*O Vos Omnes Recordare*	*Salve Montserratina Tota Pulchra*
Nigra Sum	*Rosari*	

☐ Choir of the Montserrat Capella / Segarra (conductor) / Everest 3196

There is a fair amount of variety in this music though all of the material comes under the heading of conventional sacred music. Two of the pieces are for four-part chorus, three are for the same with organ (no credit is given the organist), a pair are for two-part voices with organ (one of these is designated incorrectly as for unison voices and organ), and one is for unison singing with organ.

Aside from some soprano wavering here and there the singing is competent and of acceptable spiritual vitality.

El Pesebre (1960)

☐ Casals Festival Orchestra and Puerto Rico Conservatory Chorus / Iglesias (soprano); Forrester (alto); Saharrea (tenor); Serrano (baritone); Elvira (bass-baritone) / Casals (conductor) / Columbia M2-32966

Cantata and Oratorio

El Pesebre ("The Manger") was Casals's most important creative entry. It has a stylistic neutrality, but in no way is it faceless, fleshed out as it is with Catalan folklorisms. The eclecticism is manifold but persuades with its truthful ring.

A fine performance in all respects and certainly a definitive one. Since it is doubtful that there will be repertory life for Casals's opus, the recording documentation is to be welcomed.

Romeo Cascarino   (1922-   )

Sonata for Bassoon and Piano (1950)

☐ Schoenbach (bassoon); Cascarino (piano) / Columbia Special Products AMS-6421

Chamber Music

Cascarino has realized the importance of pithiness in a medium that has certain restraints. In form, the first movement is a sonatina. In place of development, a trinal design is used; the same structural factor holds true in the slow movement. The final part has a pert, mildly kinetic section, which takes advantage of the bassoon's special ability to skip nimbly, with fastidious deftness, from one register to another.

Cascarino's pocket-size sonata is just a bit sophisticated. It is a pleasure to hear. It was composed for and dedicated to Schoenbach and performed many times by him. The recording he made with the composer can be fully vouched for as being in the definitive class.

Alfredo Casella   (1883-1947)

La giara (1924)

☐ Orchestra of L'Accademia di Santa Cecilia, Rome / Luzi (tenor) / Previtali (conductor) / London STS-15024

Orchestra

This is a symphonic suite covering the first and last sections of Casella's ballet. It is marked by quartal and quintal harmonic formations, includes a love song about a girl who had been captured by pirates, and contains a great deal of simulated folk melodies. The last are so well done that one would swear actual quotations are being used.

The Italian composer's gay and lively piece is done to a turn by the expert Italian musicians and fine Italian tenor, with a first-class conductor completing the all-Italian cast.

Paganiniana (1942)

☐ Philadelphia Orchestra / Ormandy (conductor) / Odyssey Y–31246

This is a juicy workout of Paganini items in opulent orchestral summations. The first movement is bottled with heady pyrotechnical foam (the concoction is made from four of the solo violin *Caprices*). The Philadelphia Orchestra knocks the hell out of the work.

Instrumental

Harp

Sonata for Harp, Op. 68

☐ McDonald (harp) / Klavier KS–507

Hindemithian language is translated into Italian in Casella's three-movement piece. The initial sonata design, *Sarabande,* and marchlike Finale represent formality slightly freed and with contemporaneously enriched content. No technical tricks are called on for the encitement of effects or special colors. Casella's Sonata exemplifies straightforward musical expressiveness. It is one of the most substantial works in the literature for the plectral instrument. The recording is excellent.

Chamber Music

Five Pieces for Two Violins, Viola, and Cello (1920)

☐ New Music Quartet / Bartók 906 (monaural)

An example of a special Casella pose, one concerned with the grotesque, the semi-sarcastic, the fellow who can speak multilingually. An eclectic tour de force (and sometimes "de farce") so well done that it is not by any means "dated" music. Rather, it is music that is alive, exceedingly clever, and of great fun and entertainment.

The Prelude speaks of the 1920s with barbarous kinetic rhythms repeated until the rhythmic blister is near the bursting point. Though semi-impressionistic, *Ninna-Nanna* has the same predilection for repetitive rhythms. *Valse ridicule* contains a mixture of keys in a waltz tempo. No title is needed to recognize the tongue-in-cheekness of Casella's attitude. The music for the *Notturno* is almost frightening with its deadness, another example of how Casella was master of tone colors. The last movement is a Fox Trot, a depiction of the old "ragtime" days. It is a rollicking stylization of the old dance-floor bands for four stringed instruments.

One is grateful for this performance, the only time the work has been recorded. This kind of quartet playing makes one regret that the New Music team went out of existence and its members went their separate ways. The violinist, Broadus Erle, now deceased, was with the Yale Quartet; Matthew Raimondi, who played second violin, is now with the Composers Quartet; Walter Trampler, one of the great violists, enjoys a multifaceted career as both soloist and chamber-music performer; and the cellist, Claus Adam, until recently was a member of the famed Juilliard Quartet.

Gaspar Cassadó / Luigi Boccherini. See Boccherini / Cassadó.

Mario Castelnuovo-Tedesco   (1895-1968)

Orchestra

Overture to Much Ado About Nothing, Op. 164

☐ Louisville Orchestra / Whitney (conductor) / Louisville 545-4 (monaural)

Castelnuovo-Tedesco had a creative hobby rare among composers—writing music tied in with one author. This opus is the tenth in the series of overtures to Shakespeare's plays. Like all the others, traditional form is pertinent, with a slight touch of the flavor of the play as a quasi-programmatic link. This one has warm tunes and nice directness in its active passages.

The Louisville Orchestra plays exceptionally well in this case, which is only proper since the overture was dedicated to it and to its conductor at the time, Robert Whitney.

Concerto in D major for Guitar and Orchestra, Op. 99

□ I Solisti di Zagreb / Diaz (guitar) / Janigro (conductor) / Vanguard 71152

A revelatory performance of this beautiful work, one of the best of the very few existent in the medium. All the details are presented meticulously; the hauntingly nostalgic *Andante alla romanza* has rarely been so moving. Above all, the sensitive interplay of solo voice and small orchestra represents a joining of music and personality that is to be treasured.

Concerto for Two Guitars and Orchestra (1962)

□ English Chamber Orchestra / Sérgio and Eduardo Abreu (guitars) / Asensio (conductor) / Columbia M–32232

Not as pastoral-minded as Castelnuovo-Tedesco's well-known concerto for one guitar but almost as good. He knew how to write for the instrument. Here there is a fine swing to the melodic patterns, with a Hispanic twist to the finale.

The Abreu brothers play with precision and a nice touch, and in the cadenzas are exceedingly impressive.

Concertino for Harp, String Quartet, and Three Clarinets, Op. 93

□ Stockton (harp); Arno and Dieterle (violins); Dinkin (viola); Schnier (cello); Neufeld and Bambridge, Jr. (clarinets); Ulyate (bass clarinet) / Crystal S–107

A mini-orchestra is used to frame the solo voice of the harp. Melodious and harmonious music, reflecting in movement 1 the modal motility of Debussy's *Danses sacrée et profane,* which also uses the harp as the solo instrument. Such fundamental reexamination of style pertains to the *Ritmo di Malegueña* which braces the finale. The middle movement is reflective, nocturnal, quasi-Hispanic.

Of the four available recorded performances reviewed, Stockton's is the most clearly articulated and balanced. Crystal's sound is nicely resonant.

Concerto No. 2 (*The Prophets*) for Violin and Orchestra (1933)

□ Los Angeles Philharmonic Orchestra / Heifetz (violin) / Wallenstein (conductor) / RCA LM–2740 (monaural)

Despite its glamorous debut (on April 12, 1933) with Heifetz as the soloist, Toscanini as the conductor, and the New York Philharmonic as the orchestra, *The Prophets* has not turned out to be prophetic of repertoire acceptance. Nevertheless, its characterizations of *Isaiah, Jeremiah,* and *Elijah* are well stated with romantic rhetoric and some Hebraic touches. It deserves occasional exposure.

As a Jascha Heifetz exhibit it is tops. Heifetz recorded this in the mid-fifties and he was in fine form. The mono sound is solidly balanced and as good as you would want.

Canción Argentina (on the name "Ernesto Bitetti")

□ Bitetti (guitar) / Westminster Gold 8149

Solo Instrument and Orchestra

Guitar

Two Guitars

Harp

Violin

Instrumental

Guitar

Mostly gentle music based on sound equivalents for the guitarist's name. Efficient use of such data and played sensitively.

Sonata: *Homage to Boccherini*

☐ Segovia (guitar) / MCA 2523

Castelnuovo-Tedesco was one of Segovia's favorite composers, particularly because of his special ability to produce guitaristic music, in addition to basically fine romantic plotting. This opus is all Castelnuovo-Tedesco; there are no quotations. His bow to Boccherini is found in the elegance and graciousness of the musical lines, with dance-style bravura to seal the sonata.

Segovia's identification with the work, written at his suggestion, is total. His playing is only slightly marred in the finale by close miking that picks up some of the slight percussive sounds that haunt many a guitar recording.

Piano

Cipressi (1921)

Le danze del Re David (1925)

☐ Dominguez (piano) / Orion 74137

Cipressi later turned into an orchestral work. There the chromatic syntax is clearer than it is in the keyboard version. Some traditional themes are wrapped up in the "King David Dances."

Violin

Figaro from Rossini's *The Barber of Seville*

☐ Steiner (violin); Berfield (piano) / Orion 78313

The basis for this is, of course, the famous *Largo al factotum* aria Figaro sings in the first act of Rossini's opera. This *buffo* segment is one of the best operatic smashes in the literature, and in the violin take-off that Castelnuovo-Tedesco designed (dedicated to Heifetz) a good percentage of the humor is retained by the application of technical glitter. Nothing can equal, naturally, the rapid vocal declamation of the original, but there are sufficient merits to the paraphrase.

First-rate work by Diana Steiner; the sonics are extremely dry.

Vocal

Coplas (1915)

Voice and Orchestra

☐ Orchestra of the Vienna Volksoper / Nixon (soprano) / Gold (conductor) / Crystal S-501

Eleven songs set to the poetic form indigenous to Spain, each *Copla* consisting of five lines. There's some slight Spanish inlay but not enough to blemish the music with pseudoism. (The date of composition noted above covers the original version for voice and piano; the orchestral accompaniment was made in 1967.)

Marni Nixon's voice retains its smooth, rich quality. There is never any forcing and neither is there any unmusical realization. These are shapely realizations of the composer's score.

Castelnuovo-Tedesco / **Jascha Heifetz (1901-   )**

Instrumental **Sea Murmurs**

Violin

☐ Heifetz (violin); Smith (piano) / Columbia M2-33444

One of a pair of *Études d'ondes,* muted and suavely colored by Heifetz's fabulous tone. Recorded live, so expect applause to shatter the effect at the end.

Niccolò Castiglioni   (1932-   )

Gymel (1960)

Instrumental

Flute

☐ Gazzelloni (flute); Kontarsky (piano) / Mainstream 5014

Castiglioni's piece is predicated on a tightening of the textures, with resultant tensility. The keyboard instrument is treated percussively, mainly in chordal clumps.

Pellerite (on Coronet S-1713) is almost as good as Gazzelloni, but the piano that partners his playing sounds as though it were in a different room. One plus and one minus equal zero.

Alef – Composition for Oboe (1965)

Oboe

☐ Holliger (oboe) / Philips 6500202

A sensitive blend of oboe coloration, including some two-pitched sounds. Sectioned structuralism is used, arranged by the performer. It is to Castiglioni's credit that it does make possible, as heard in Holliger's realization, a firmly stitched fabric.

This oboe virtuoso presents uninhibited playing. Every pitch gesture is a pure delight.

Tropi (1959)

Chamber Music

☐ Hamann (violin); Palm (cello); Otto (flute); Irmisch (clarinet); Priegnitz (piano); Hinze (percussion) / Travis (conductor) / Mainstream 5006

Tropi exemplifies discontinuous continuity by acute, careful differentiation of sounds shot forth onto a background of silences. The last are so intense that they furnish a backlash of strength to the snippeted sounds. There is no diffuseness in this spidery texture, cleverly balanced in the middle of the piece by the longest sound of all.

The playing of the subtle, fluctuating changes of Castiglioni's work is truly exciting. The fullest credits must be given to Francis Travis and his splendid instrumentalists. (It is, of course, indicative of the way the composition market is set up these days that a conductor is required for chamber music.)

Gyro for Chorus and Nine Instruments (1963)

Choral

Chorus and Instrumental Ensemble

☐ Ars Nova Ensemble and the Chamber Choir of the O.R.T.F. / Couraud (conductor) / Musical Heritage Society MHS-1687

Castiglioni uses a biblical text, which is, however, secondary to the musical side of his project, the words being smothered and disintegrated. The chorus totals thirty-two, with eight each of soprano, alto, tenor, and bass; the nine instruments are of unusual disposition, consisting of four flutes, four trumpets, and a tam tam.

A superb realization; the use of hissing chorus sounds emphasize the objective of Castiglioni's score which uses words only to hang sounds on. The substantial understanding of the conductor is apparent.

Juan José Castro   (1895-1968)

Sonatina Española (1953)

Instrumental

Piano

☐ Somer (piano) / Desto 6426

Title notwithstanding, there is as much neo-classic syntax in Castro's three-movement piece as there are Spanish synonyms. The melorhythmic essence is definitely Hispanic, but form and harmony reflect no national specific. The merger is a healthy one. Hilde Somer's projection of this work is salubriously re-creative.

Alfredo Catalani (1854-1893)

Opera and Dramatic Music

La Wally

☐ Monte Carlo Opera Orchestra and Coro Lirico di Torino / Tebaldi and Marimpietri (sopranos); Malagù (mezzo-soprano); Del Monaco (tenor); Cappuccilli (baritone); Diaz (bass); Mariotti (vocalist) / Cleva (conductor) / London 1392

This is a strong cast, and in the case of Renata Tebaldi there has never been anyone that has bettered her conception of the Wally role. As Richard Osborne has vividly stated, "Tebaldi *is* Wally." The London recording proves Tebaldi's vocal radiance and dramaticism. Mario Del Monaco sings attractively, and Piero Cappuccilli is admirable in defining the character of Gellner, who is in love with Wally.

La Wally deserves a firm place in the repertory, but has not done well except in Italy. Toscanini's admiration of the score was such that he thought Catalani a better composer than Puccini. (Toscanini actually chose two of the names of the *La Wally* characters for his children: Wally and Walter.)

Charles-Simon Catel (1773-1830)

Orchestra

Introduction and *Air basque* from *L'Auberge de Bagnères*

☐ Jean-François Paillard Orchestra / Couraud (conductor) / Musical Heritage Society MHS-794

An utterly charming bit that would be among the top ten if Arthur Fiedler had taken hold of it. The Basque melody that Catel uses in his comic opera "The Inn of Bagnères" is a tune triumph.

Norman Cazden (1914-1980)

Orchestra

Three Ballads from the Catskills, Op. 52

☐ Oslo Philharmonic Orchestra / Buketoff (conductor) / Composers Recordings 117 (monaural)

Neo-modality set at the service of folk material. Each ballad has an obbligato string-instrument voice; thus: *The Lass of Glenshee* (viola), *The Dens of Yarrow* (cello), and *The Old Spotted Cow* (violin).

Professionally executed, but a bit hampered by somewhat dated sound.

Maurizio Cazzati (1620?-1677)

Chamber Music

384

Sonata (*La pellicana*) in D minor for Trumpet and Continuo

☐ Schwarz (trumpet); Sharrow (bassoon); Fuller (harpsichord) / Nonesuch 71274

This is no picture painting; the descriptive title is simply concerned with the dedicatee: Giovanni Battista Sanuti Pellicani. Cazzati gave him a neat and pithy work, brilliantly conceived for the brass instrument, topped by a fast-paced conclusion that moves from *presto* to *prestissimo*.

As always, top-flight playing from Gerard Schwarz and perfectly expressive partnership from his colleagues.

Sergio Cervetti (1940-)

Aria suspendida for Clarinet and Pre-Recorded Clarinet (1974)
Instrumental

☐ Hayes (clarinet) / Composers Recording SD-359
Clarinet

Thirteen and one-half minutes of the perpetual-drone type of composition, with retention of single pitches or sustained chords (all basic to A minor), occasionally scratched with a different sound here and there. Expect nothing more to happen (it doesn't!). In music of this type structural continuity ceases to exist since there are no rhythmic denominators, no pulse demarcations, no metrical fields.

Guitar Music (*The Bottom of the Iceberg*)
Guitar

☐ Fox (guitar) / Composers Recordings S-359

Static music, frozen on top by single-pitch ostinati. Eventually some additional material enters below, itself promulgating repetition. Running time: ten minutes and forty seconds.

Carlo Francesco Chabran (1723-?)

Sonata in G major, Op. 1, No. 5
Chamber Music

☐ Luca (violin); Richman (harpsichord); Bogatin (cello) / Nonesuch 71361

The suggestion is to listen and to listen well. Chabran's music is replete with harmonics, double stops, and the performance territory is that of virtuosity rather than chamber music. None of this prosaic, opened-up, fit-the-hand figurations. The playing matches the brilliance of Chabran's writing. Fine continuo partnership.

Emmanuel Chabrier (1841-1894)

Danse slave and *Fête polonaise* from *Le Roi malgré lui*
Orchestra

☐ Orchestre de la Suisse Romande / Ansermet (conductor) / London 6438

Efficient performances. This may sound like damning with faint praise but 'tis not so. Both are presented with warmth and spirit, which reflect on the comic opera source from which they were extracted.

España (1883)

☐ London Symphony Orchestra / Argenta (conductor) / London 6006

Full-blooded, snappily pointed rhythms, with marked attention to solo colors, give this reading high marks. Best of all there are no exaggerations in order to force a so-called idiomatic presentation.

Habanera (1885)

☐ Paris Conservatoire Orchestra / Dervaux (conductor) / Seraphim S–60108

This is Chabrier's orchestral transcription of a piano piece. Only fair-to-middlin', but here it is if you want it. It is also included in an album of Chabrier's orchestral music, with Louis de Froment conducting the Orchestra of Radio Luxembourg on Turnabout 34671, but Dervaux has a bit more zing in his direction.

Joyeuse Marche (1888)

☐ Philadelphia Orchestra / Ormandy (conductor) / Columbia MS–6979

This fairly popular piece was originally titled *Marche française*. Ormandy's sparkling rendition is also included in a two-record set, *The Philadelphia Orchestra March Album* (Columbia MG–32314).

Overture to *Gwendoline* (1884)

☐ Detroit Symphony Orchestra / Paray (conductor) / Mercury 75078

This is all that's left of the work Chabrier composed in 1884 and rarely surfaces in live performance. The overture is a good piece and Paray proves it with his pertinently pointed presentation. He is close to a minute faster than Dervaux's performance on Seraphim S–60108 (with the Paris Conservatoire Orchestra) and almost a minute and one-half speedier than Louis de Froment on Turnabout 34671 (conducting the Orchestra of Radio Luxembourg).

Suite pastorale (1880)

☐ Detroit Symphony Orchestra / Paray (conductor) / Mercury 75029

Four of Chabrier's *Dix Pièces pittoresques* for piano, which he orchestrated and then retitled. All four—*Idylle, Danse villageoise, Sous Bois,* and *Scherzo-Valse*—are in clearly compact tripartite designs. For music of such simplistic security Paray provides nicely toned sonorities, firmly shaped lines, and a convincing poetic quality for a maximum of artistic sense required.

Instrumental

Piano

Air de ballet (1888)	**Impromptu (1860)**
Bourrée fantasque (1891)	*Marche des Cipayes*
Capriccio	*Pièces pittoresques* (1880)
Cinq Morceaux pour piano	*Suite de valse*
Habanera (1885)	

☐ Kyriakou (piano) / Vox SVBX–5400

For the greatest part this music is totally unknown and unheard in the concert halls. Nonetheless, there are a few goodies worth being tasted now and then. The *Idylle,* for example, in the ten-part *Pièces pittoresques,* has an appealing old-lavender-and-torn-lace quality. The *Bourrée fantasque* (transcribed for orchestra by Felix Mottl) has rhythmic spice, with strong beats not where one usually expects them in this duple-pronged dance. For the rest, the going is pleasant enough, saturated with salon-style ease, with the ploy of blending Schumannesque turns of phrase with Offenbachian rhythms. The playing of Rena Kyriakou has the proper naturalness and vitality.

Though listed above as a stereo release, most of the five record sides are indicated by Vox as "remastered stereophonic." (Elsewhere in this survey any recording electronically reprocessed for stereo is termed monaural to differentiate the matter clearly. In this case the problem of the mix [extremely rare in a total release] makes monaural classification impossible.)

Cortège burlesque for Piano Duet

Souvenirs de Munich for Piano Duet

Piano, Four Hands

☐ Kyriakou and Walter Klien (piano) / Vox SVBX–5400

Colorful and dashing describe the *Cortège*, which is a good reason for Paul Lacombe to choose it for an orchestral transcription. Parody is available in the *Souvenirs de Munich*, a five-sectioned Quadrille, mixed from a batter of prosaic tunes and excerpts from Wagner's *Tristan und Isolde*.

There's plenty of panache in Rena Kyriakou's and Walter Klien's playing. (The label reads "Klein" incorrectly.) Vox has also made this performance available on its Turnabout label (No. 34241).

Trois Valses romantiques for Two Pianos (1883)

Two Pianos

☐ Kyriakou and Walter Klien (pianos) / Vox SVBX–5400

A subtle symphonicism surrounds Chabrier's waltzes, compellingly played by this team. ("Klien" incorrectly becomes "Klein" on the label copy.)

The performance is also available on Turnabout 34241.

Chabrier / Felix Mottl (1856-1911)

Bourrée fantasque (1897)

Orchestra

☐ Detroit Symphony Orchestra / Paray (conductor) / Mercury 75078

Chabrier wrote his *Bourrée fantasque* for solo piano in 1891. The date noted above is when Mottl made his transcription. It is splendid and enjoys a steady use on concert programs.

A stimulating and very alive execution. It would be difficult to do better.

George Whitefield Chadwick   (1854-1931)

Euterpe: Concert Overture for Orchestra (1903)

Orchestra

☐ Louisville Orchestra / Mester (conductor) / Louisville LS–753

An example of Chadwick's fine Germanic style (*echt* Brahms). One must fully disagree with the record annotator's statement that the overture "is keenly American in its sweeping folk-oriented melodies." I didn't hear any. But I did observe that the labels were reversed on the review copy of the disc (the Chadwick is coupled with a pair of Converse works, reviewed below).

Symphonic Sketches, Suite for Orchestra (1904)

☐ Eastman-Rochester Symphony Orchestra / Hanson (conductor) / Mercury 75050

A symphony with titles for the movements. *Jubilee* contains first-movement pep, with some Negro Americanese. *Noël* represents the slow movement, *Hobgoblin* equals the scherzo, and has parallel Mendelssohnian lightness. The finale (*A Vagrom Ballad*) is fantasy-shaped, more bitter than sweet.

In this type of music Hanson is a conductorial master.

Tam O'Shanter – Symphonic Ballad (1915)

☐ Vienna Symphony Orchestra / Schoenherr (conductor) / Desto 6421E (monaural)

Program music based on the Robert Burns poem, performed with rewarding understanding. This is an old recording but the sound is quite good.

Band

Tabasco

☐ Goldman Band / Cox (conductor) / New World Records NW–266

Catchy, as a really good march should be. This is from Chadwick's burlesque opera of the same name, first produced in Boston in 1894.

Instrumental

Organ

Pastorale in E flat major

☐ Beck (organ) / Musical Heritage Society OR A–263

Simple melody propped up with romantically tinged harmonies. The "head" of the main subject is the spitting image of the beginning of the theme in the Nocturne of Borodin's second string quartet.

Theme, Variations, and Fugue (1908)

☐ Ellsasser (organ) / Nonesuch 71200

Chadwick's large organ piece does not, like his other productions, break any new ground already well-tilled. It is always worth realizing that professionally ordered, sound creations, traveling well-traversed roads, still have their place.

The performance stresses vivid changes of dynamics, color, and playing style. The detail is always clear, unhindered by fussiness in registration, and, in the louder portions, never noisy.

Chamber Music

String Quartet No. 4 in E minor (1895)

☐ Kohon Quartet / Vox SVBX–5301

Considered to be Chadwick's most important chamber music work, this opus graphically indicates youthful vigor, classical scholarship, and idiomatic use of native characteristics (the inner movements are tinged with Negroid and Indian elements). These, by being adapted and shaped into materials for formal treatment, produce a clearly national feeling that one can type as non-European, if not truly "American."

Vocal

Voice with Accompaniment

O, Let Night Speak of Me

☐ Hanks (tenor); Friedberg (piano) / Duke University Press DWRM–7501 (monaural)

The favorite poet for the more than one hundred songs Chadwick wrote was Arlo Bates. It is his text that is used for this broadly lyrical song.

Nikolai Chaikin   (1915-   )

Concerto for Accordion

☐ Symphony Orchestra of the Moscow Region / Kazakov (accordion) / Dudarova (conductor) / Monitor S-2074E

Solo Instrument and Orchestra

Accordion

This work is of tonal and formal orthodoxy; the greater interest is the use of the accordion, played with praiseworthy musicianship by Yuri Kazakov, one of the Soviet Union's greatest accordion virtuosi. Folk turns fill the music and only a scornful snob would deny the haunting sadness that fills the slow movement with unmistakable Russian sentiment. It is the heart of Chaikin's concerto.

David Chaitkin   (1938-   )

Etudes (1974)

☐ Burge (piano) / Composers Recordings SD–345

Instrumental

Piano

The panchromatic syntax with a romantic patina belies neither the music's contemporary birth nor its link to the traditional past.

Burge's reading of this work offers the maximum artistic results. His insight into the composer's creative objectives is splendid.

Stephen A. Chambers. *See Talib Rasul Hakim.*

Cécile Chaminade   (1857-1944)

Concertino, Op. 107

Instrumental

☐ Hoberman (flute); Stannard (piano) / Avant 1015

Flute

Every flutist plays this just as every fiddler sharpens his technique on Kreutzer and Rode and moves onto *the* Mendelssohn Concerto. "Hackneyed," of course, is the word for it, but in the hands of a master flutist it has lavenderish charm.

There isn't a current recording around covering the original setting with orchestral accompaniment. One must make do with Hoberman's performance with piano partnership. It is acceptable—no more. For those interested there is a listing of a release by Coronet (S-1724) with band accompaniment. The transcription is not by Chaminade, of course. The idea of supporting a single flute with a band seems strange, but the recording proves that it can be done with adequate results.

Autrefois

Piano

☐ Kramer (piano) / Orion 7261

Short but not overly sweet. It is determined in exact ternary form, and Selma Kramer denotes the contrastive sections capably.

Gavotte, Op. 9, No. 2

La lisonjera

Pierretté (Air de ballet), **Op. 41**

Serenade in D major, Op. 29

Sonata in C minor, Op. 21

Valse caprice, **Op. 33**

☐ Pines (piano) / Genesis 1024

It is the short piece that shows this composer in the best light. She was immersed in the salonistic style and it brings the most rewards in this program.

The Gavotte is one of the very best, bringing in its thematic head-shape reminders of Rameau's *Tambourin. La lisonjera* ("The Flatterer") has a lissome Latin contour; the *Valse* glides gracefully. The single large-scale work (the Sonata) has neither poverty nor riches; it falls in the middle class of musical wealth. It does substantiate the initial sentence in these remarks.

Doris Pines is in perfect command throughout. She knows the style that should apply to this type of music.

John Barnes Chance   *(1932-1972)*

Instrumental

Credo

Trumpet

☐ Hickman (trumpet); Soderholm (piano) / Crystal S-363

This tonally bright, motivally structured work is given a clear and musical performance.

Theodore Chanler   *(1902-1961)*

Vocal

***The Children* (excerpts)**

Voice
with
Accompaniment

☐ Gramm (baritone); Hassard (piano) / New World Records NW-243

This is a cycle of nine songs, of which four are heard here: *The Children, Once Upon a Time, The Rose,* and *Moo Is a Cow.* With the exception of *The Rose,* prosy pitter-patter pertains, to which Chanler has deftly set singy sing-song lines that shake hands with the text. Although the music is a number of cuts above the poetry, the way Donald Gramm sings and the preciseness of his diction make these songs totally enjoyable.

The vocal line of *The Rose* is emphasized by piano doubling. The doubling process is also applied to *Moo Is a Cow.* An optional second voice part is included in the score, set in precise rhythmic duplication. By overdubbing, Gramm takes on two parts of the trio.

I Rise When You Enter

☐ McCollum (tenor); Biltcliffe (piano) / Desto 6411/2

Rhythmic commitment in the piano part, proper for the lively text. The rhymed lines do not have much depth, but it does not really matter, what with the liquid effortlessness of the vocal part.

Nine Epitaphs (1937)

☐ Curtin (soprano); Edwards (piano) / Columbia Special Products AMS-6198

Here displayed is classical balance, strengthened by sensitive harmonic language. The piano functions as a total duet with the voice, thus creating a form of chamber music. Properly simple in format, each of the set is a concentrate of form, the music a proof of the words. This is healthy art.

Nary a moment of excess in the recorded performance. Both Curtin and Edwards are eloquent and cogent and illustrate re-creative scholarship of the most advanced kind.

These, My Ophelia

☐ Beardslee (soprano); Helps (piano) / New World Records NW-243

Chanler's first song composition is a sad, restrained piece with text by Archibald MacLeish. It is beautifully sung.

The Pot of Fat

Opera and Dramatic Music

☐ CRI Chamber Orchestra / Stewart (soprano); Burrows and Abel (baritones) / Mester (conductor) / Composers Recordings 162

Chanler's *The Pot of Fat* is a six-scene opera, plus prologue and epilogue, based on the Grimm fairy tale *The Cat and the Mouse in Partnership*. It has an acceptable philosophical point of view in equating the cat and mouse characters with human beings, makes many a witty point, and conveys fine lyrical interest. Chanler's forte for vocal writing is reproven, and he deftly handles the orchestral forces (small: four winds, two brasses, percussion, piano, and strings). Mester's direction is also deft.

Gustave Charpentier (1860-1956)

Impressions d'Italie (1892)

Orchestra

☐ Paris Conservatoire Orchestra / Balout (viola); Cordier (cello) / Wolff (conductor) / London STS-15117

Five programmatic attestations, once over lightly. *On Muleback* trots along with symmetrical enunciation, the orchestral path lighted by bells. Unison song and off-stage recapitulation by a solo viola confirm the objective of the opening *Sérénade;* Italian *brio* travels through *Napoli*. Throughout, instrumental vocalism is paramount. That's the way the music is played: tonally delicious, rhythmically gay, entirely refreshing.

Jacques Charpentier (1933-   )

Lalita, for Ondes Martenot and Percussion

Instrumental

Ondes Martenot

☐ Loriod (ondes Martenot); Duclos (percussion) / Musical Heritage Society MHS-821

This work expresses "the act of Sacred Love" between the earth and the sun. The music moves from a nocturnal quality into a full brightness and then recedes. Mysticism pervades Charpentier's subject matter, and the electronic monophonic timbre chosen to express it captures the mood perfectly.

Jeanne Loriod is considered to be the greatest performer on the ondes Martenot. The expression she obtains in her performance of *Lalita* proves it.

Marc-Antoine Charpentier   *(1636-1704)*

Orchestra

Concert à quatre parties

☐ La Grande Ecurie et la Chambre du Roy / Malgoire (conductor) / Candide 31066

The *Concert à quatre parties* is one of two works by Charpentier that are purely instrumental and not affiliated with a stage piece or sacred concerns. A Prelude and a Passacaglia are represented in the outer movements with dance divisions in between. Shifts in the timbre apportionment add to the composition's flavor.

Everything is presented for the sake of stylistic clarity, but not in an academic way. Malgoire makes certain that nothing interferes with the easy-going charm of Charpentier's music.

Dances from *Médée*

☐ Caen Chamber Orchestra / Dautel (conductor) / Turnabout 34101

There are six dances in all, including the *Air, Menuet, Loure et Canarie, Passepied*, and *Passecaille*, in a faithful presentation. Another dance, *Rondeau pour les Corinthiens*, is listed *below*.

Marche de triomphe
Second air de trompettes

☐ Consortium Musicum / Lehan (conductor) / Nonesuch 71217

This is pomp with a special flavor, so that brilliant trumpet timbre (four parts played on baroque instruments) is contrasted with paired flutes, two baroque oboes, timpani, and two violins. The comparison between simplicity and bright finish represents a delightful period piece and it is presented in an admirable way.

Overture to *Le Malade imaginaire*

☐ La Grande Ecurie et la Chambre du Roy / Malgoire (conductor) / Candide 31066

This utterly charming two-minute piece—its "official" title is *Ouverture du prologue (à la gloire de Louis XIV) à "Le Malade imaginaire"*—is available in two versions (the other played by the Caen Chamber Orchestra, conducted by Jean-Pierre Dautel, on Turnabout 34101).

There are no doubts that Malgoire's setting takes first place. He uses the full original scoring of winds and strings, and color division separates the first part from the second one by the elimination of the strings in the latter. The music flows in linked continuity from measure to measure. In the Caen production only the strings are used and the styling is constantly articulative—"staccatoish." This relentless duplication of timbre and bowing is stodgy in comparison with the Candide edition.

Rondeau pour les Corinthiens from *Médée*

☐ La Grande Ecurie et la Chambre du Roy / Malgoire (conductor) / Candide 31066

Other dances from the lyric tragedy Charpentier composed in 1693 are on disc (*see above:* Dances from *Médée*). This presentation, however, is far richer and brighter in its scoring and peppier in its nippy rhythmic thrust. Malgoire knows how to snap-to in his tempi.

Salve Regina

Choral

☐ Peloquin Chorale / Hokans (organ) / Peloquin (conductor) / Gregorian Institute S-205

Chorus with Accompaniment

Within the general mood of sadness there are coloristic contrasts including operatic sighs and a bit of pitch picture painting (example: chromatic descent to fit "in this valley of tears"). The performance conveys the proper atmosphere, even though the dynamics are a bit restrained.

Grand Magnificat

Cantata and Oratorio

☐ Orchestra Jean-François Paillard and Chorale des Jeunesses Musicales de France / Angelici and Chamonin (sopranos); Mallabrera (countertenor); Corazza (tenor); Abdoun (baritone); Alain (organ) / Martini (conductor) / Vanguard HM-12

The adjective *Grand* is truly proper for this mostly sober work calling for a double choir, used antiphonally, soloists, and orchestra. The devotional range and polyphonic substance bear out the description. There is also room in Charpentier's music for praising the Lord in bright homophonic fashion, as in the active duple-pulsed *Gloria Patri, et Filio, et Spiritu Sancto.*

All the soloists are fine. Louis Martini directs with a fine sense of supple pace, and there is never any dogmaticism in his consideration of the music, which is all to the good. The chorus could certainly have been recorded closer.

Messe pour plusieurs instruments au lieu des orgues

☐ La Grande Ecurie et la Chambre du Roy / Malgoire (conductor) / Candide 31066
☐ Ancient Instrument Ensemble of Paris and Instrumental and Vocal Ensemble / Steinkopf (serpent) / Chailley (conductor) / Nonesuch 71130

Though to a certain extent a comparison can be made to arrive at a performance choice, for this composition the wide difference in editions makes a firm decision unwise. Though not noted, it is apparent that Jean-Claude Malgoire, the conductor of Candide's disc, is to be credited with the version heard. Nonesuch indicates that in the absence of a modern published edition of Charpentier's Mass the music was prepared jointly by the conductor of the performance, Jacques Chailley, and Roger Cotte, the director of the Ancient Instrument Ensemble of Paris.

There are a number of parallel performance decisions in regard to the *Kyrie* and the *Gloria.* Still, in the latter, on Nonesuch the movement ends with a vocal Amen passage. On Candide the Amen is followed by an instrumental section. Both recordings retain the instrumental totality for the entire *Offerte.* However, at its conclusion the realizations part company.

The Nonesuch edition includes a concluding *Agnus Dei* not performed in Malgoire's rendition. In the preceding movement, a *Sanctus*, Chailley uses voices plus instruments; Malgoire employs instruments only. In the latter case Charpentier's subheading for the movement, *pour tous les instruments,* is thus followed.

If one must make a choice, the more brilliant and dynamically projected one is on the Candide label. This does not negate Nonesuch's entry, which moves on a quieter track.

Te Deum

☐ Orchestra Jean-François Paillard and Chorale des Jeunesses Musicales de France / Angelici and Chamonin (sopranos); Mallabrera (countertenor); Corazza (tenor); Abdoun (baritone); Mars (bass); André (trumpet); Alain (organ) / Martini (conductor) / Vanguard HM-12

This is an exceedingly expressive presentation, notwithstanding bad engineering in some of the choral portions (the sound has been recorded at a low level and is rather distant). Maurice André is as much a star as the vocal soloists, performing the liberal trumpet part with dramatic vigor yet always with high polish. Warmly recommended, despite some low-key projection of the soloists.

Ernest Chausson   (1855-1899)

Orchestra

Symphony in B flat major, Op. 20

☐ Detroit Symphony Orchestra / Paray (conductor) / Mercury 75029

Extreme refinement of expression is heard in Paray's depiction of this César Franck–soaked work. Particularly satisfactory is the manner in which the ecstatic moments are shaped within the spiritual visions that permeate the music. The chromatic emotions that seethe within the harmonies can make sentimental mush of Chausson's piece if they are not tended to carefully. This conductor has done an excellent job of avoiding this pitfall.

Solo Instrument and Orchestra

Violin

Poème for Violin and Orchestra, Op. 25

☐ Orchestre de Paris / Perlman (violin) / Martinon (conductor) / Angel S-37118

Itzhak Perlman offers here the rare quality of special artistry: taste and intelligence partnered with magnificent technical skill. The dynamic palette is minutely proportioned; the differences displayed in the *piano, mezzo piano,* and *mezzo forte* planes illustrate how a master performer maintains control of the running commentary within a musical line.

Chausson's piece can be oversweetened if care is not taken with its intertwined modulations. Perlman offers sufficient emotional sensuousness but stops short of sentimentality, an ever present danger in this music of chromatic coalescences.

Instrumental

Piano

Quelques Danses, Op. 26

☐ Doyen (piano) / Musical Heritage Society MHS 1155-57

This work consists of a short and expressive *Dédicace,* followed by a *Sarabande, Pavane,* and *Forlane.* That these charming conceptions have been relegated to the department of music of no consequence is ridiculous. The set is as delightful as Ravel's *Le Tombeau de Couperin.* Truly one agrees with Harry Halbreich's statement that the dances ''will be a real revelation to most, and it is unthinkable that they should have been thus ignored.'' Nevertheless, most surveys do. Examples: Cooper fails to mention the work in his *French Music,* and the usually excellent and thorough *Music for the Piano* by Friskin and Freundlich likewise ignores it.

Doyen's playing of the suite is vital and perfectly tempoed, and displays elegance and rhythmic warmth in proper apportionment. Vladimir Pleshakov's reading (Orion 6906) is acceptable for the first half, then becomes ridiculous in part 3. He ruins the *Pavane* by playing it at a dizzy speed, quite opposite to the description of the piece as "wistful," a word he seems to think means "whiz-bangful." Further, the keen outlines of the *Forlane*, exactly realized in Doyen's performance are overpedaled and thereby blurred in Pleshakov's portrayal.

Quartet in A major for Piano, Violin, Viola, and Cello, Op. 30

☐ Richards Piano Quartet / Oiseau-Lyre S–316

Chamber Music

The interconnective method (the cyclic system of composition) is used in this piano quartet, a work more optimistic than most of Chausson's compositions, which carry the burden of almost foretelling doom and death.

The first movement proceeds along the usual lines, with extensions of material in the recapitulation and augmentation of the theme (cyclic expansion). Both inner movements are governed by the familiarity of three-part form, giving, respectively, noble sentiment and light folk viewpoints. In the final movement, the unfolding of bow-knotted transference and transmutation occurs.

This is a nicely conceived consideration of the score, not too weighty in its textural decisions, which is all to the good.

String Quartet (Unfinished), Op. 35

☐ Via Nova Quartet / Musical Heritage Society MHS–1351

Because of his death, Chausson's Opus 35 remained incomplete. The most devout of all Franck's disciples, Vincent d'Indy, completed the third movement by adding some seventy measures to the score.

Continuity of line is paramount in the work. In the slow movement the avoidance of cadential rest gives a spaciousness that does not require the listener to attempt identity of themes. The music moves in its calm shell, pregnant with emotion and intensity. The final movement displays rondo architecture; the rhythmic bite of scherzo demeanor mostly clenches on the music. A section in $\frac{5}{8}$ time forms the principal coda element, from which point d'Indy musically surmised what Chausson (dead with a crushed skull in a bicycle accident) never had the opportunity to do himself.

The Via Nova Quartet plays with marvelous richness and total understanding of Chausson's style. In the score there is solid work for every instrument and very little light shines through the thickness of writing. But by their artistic consideration they make certain that nothing is minimized and they still codify the lines to produce organic musical thought. Bravo!

Concerto in D major for Piano, Violin, and String Quartet, Op. 21

☐ Pascal String Quartet / Kaufman (violin); Balsam (piano) / Orion 73134 (monaural)

This is not a concerto in the solo or double-solo sense at all. There are no virtuoso features. There is no special highlighting of either the violin or the piano. It is a sextet in which the three voices of violin, piano, and massed quartet share equally, and further exploitation is made of the last in regard to its four components.

The Concerto is considered to be one of Chausson's greatest works. The cyclical device is used only once when a theme from the slow movement is recalled in the finale with the power of a full-blown tutti. The last movement is written following the principle of integral variation, not in the form of embroideries or the like, but in the constant development of the theme itself. This development emphasizes the larger aspects of the theme, not small portions within it.

There are two main themes in the opening movement. The first of these is most important and is presented in three different fashions. There is kinship with Corelli and Bach in the *Sicilienne,* a pastoral dipped into and made from the tenderest of musical sounds. Short-spaced chromatic intervallics dictate the sobriety of the slow movement, desolated in its individual emotion.

Not the playing, but the sound defeats the Heifetz-Sanromá-Musical Art Quartet recording (on RCA ARM4-0945), made in May 1941. The playing is a bit less suave on the disc noted above, but the sound is ten times better. Schwann lists the performance as conveyed on stereo. However, the Orion release is strictly monaural, "enhanced for stereo," but this survey considers all such as mono recordings. In spite of the engineering hankypanky, the results (certainly in this instance) confirm the monaural designation.

The facts covering the how, when, and where are somewhat vague on the Orion package. They read: "The Pascal String Quartet . . . in this recording made its initial appearance on Concert Hall Society records." The date was about 1951.

Vocal

Voice and Orchestra

Poème de l'Amour et de la mer, Op. 19

☐ Lamoureux Concerts Orchestra / de los Angeles (soprano) / Jacquillat (conductor) / Angel S-36897

Chausson's expansive "Poem of Love and the Sea" concludes with the once well known *Le Temps des lilas.* For that alone Victoria de los Angeles's rendition is worth obtaining. For the most part her singing in this symphonic song cycle is quite good, except that the upper part of the range is not always clear or always on pitch. Still, the intensity of the music is relayed beautifully and with expressive vocalism. Jean-Pierre Jacquillat's conducting gets a passing grade; more vitality would not have been improper for Chausson's score.

Louis Chauvin / Scott Joplin. *See Joplin / Chauvin.*

Eduardo Lopez Chavarri   (1871-1970)

Instrumental

Harp

Legenda del Castillo Moro

☐ Robles (harp) / Argo ZRG-5457

Originally written for piano, this is a gentle melody with the usual Spanish contours. Robles defines its essential simplicity.

Carlos Chávez   (1899-1978)

Orchestra

Sinfonía de Antígona (1932)

☐ Orquesta Sinfónica Nacional de México / Chávez (conductor) / Columbia Special Products C32310002

Contemporary music that reminds one of archaic solidity and austerity characterizes this ten-minute, one-movement symphony. In 1932 Chávez composed music for a Cocteau production of Sophocles's *Antigone*. It was from this score that he drew (in 1933) the material for the symphony. There is no programmatic basis; the symphony expresses a harsh, almost bitter pessimism. It is acrid and has a power that is eloquent. The prickling iciness of this work is an important contribution to this century's music.

Himself a first-rate conductor, Chávez gives a superb performance. The coloring so vivid in the score (including alto flute, heckelphone, and eight horns) is defined with superexcellence; the sound is brilliant and rich. Chávez's previous recording of the work is still available (Everest 3029). There he conducts the Stadium Symphony Orchestra of New York (alias the New York Philharmonic). It is good, but the Mexican organization responds even better.

Sinfonía India (1935)

☐ Stadium Symphony Orchestra of New York / Chávez (conductor) / Everest 3029

A single-movement symphony (the second of Chávez's six symphonies). It has design, it has formal balance; neither is dependent on textbook formulas. There is a complete absence of fussy figuration, ornaments, or padding in this music. The *Sinfonía India* has flaming color and a sonorous salvo that can only be described as Igor Stravinsky in the land of Mexico, but this is not to question Chávez's originality in any way. No work produced in Mexico can match this one for its indigenous honesty, its superb native graphology.

Chávez himself has thrice recorded the work. The old Decca version is, of course, deleted. The best recording is the one noted above. It has magnificent sound and represents a virtuoso performance. The only competition is from Bernstein's version with the New York Philharmonic on Columbia MS–6514. Chávez's setting has much more pulsatile punch.

Suite from *Horsepower* (1926)

☐ Louisville Orchestra / Mester (conductor) / Louisville 713

Back in the early thirties, when I attended the world premiere of *HP* (as the ballet *Horsepower* is generally referred to), I was struck by its combination of urbanistic musical detail with the northern-based rhythm of the fox trot and southern dances represented by the *huapango, sandunga,* and tango. The suite drawn from the ballet retains not only this partnership but also its contained power and direct color. *Caballos de vapor* (as Chávez always insisted the work be subtitled) draws its dimensional vitality from the shrewd collation of nonprogrammatic and native materials.

Symphony

No. 3 (1951) / No. 4 (*Sinfonía romántica*) (1953)

☐ Orquesta Sinfónica Nacional de México / Chávez (conductor) / Columbia Special Products C32310002

Chávez's lean textural style is illustrated in the third symphony, its dramatic timing aided by the orchestration. Freely classical in its formal shapes, with no ethnical Mexican specifics, the concept of the scherzo is especially individual. There is no retention of triple-pulsed forward drive. Instead, Chávez designs a fugue, developed from a perky but disjunct subject. Quite novel, it parallels the strongly colored aspect of the work as a whole.

The fourth symphony has the usual Chávezian strong sonorous setting. His rhythmic slant actually slants. The melodic lines are somewhat short, save in the aria-like middle movement; they have an urban drive with a suburban spaciousness.

This is the first recording of Symphony No. 3. The other symphony was previously recorded, also under the composer's direction, and is still available on Everest 3029. However, there is more warmth and spaciousness in the Columbia release, which contains all six symphonies that Chávez produced. (A seventh symphony was underway at the time of his death.)

Symphony No. 6 (1962)

☐ Orquesta Sinfónica Nacional de México / Chávez (conductor) / Columbia Special Products C32310002

The sixth symphony is important in the Chávez corpus, because it indicates a reconciliation between his own aesthetic and classic principles. It will be noted that in the final movement (close to sixteen minutes in length, just a bit shorter than the two previous movements combined) the Mexican quality prevalent in the music of Chávez's early period is manifested by sharp coloration and rhythmic circumstance.

The performance is vigorous, virile, and explores the score totally. Chávez is a fine conductor, so the guidance is better than most composer-led performances.

String Orchestra

Symphony No. 5 for Strings (1953)

☐ Orquesta Sinfónica Nacional de México / Chávez (conductor) / Columbia Special Products C32310002

This symphony for string orchestra has a lean sonority of taut percussiveness. Top-rank performers are required since the instrumental demands are of virtuoso order. Chávez's instrumentational directions are always for musical purposes and nothing else. All the requirements are met here.

Percussion

Tambuco (1964)

☐ Les Percussions de Strasbourg / Philips 6526017

Freer in form and larger in scope than Chávez's other all-percussion piece, Toccata (*see below*). In some respects the latter is "tonal," the former "atonical." There are subtly interrelated patterns and norms that are fully developed in this work, and a patina of native coloration gives it luster.

The Strasbourgians play expressively and definitively.

Toccata for Percussion Instruments (1942)

☐ Los Angeles Percussion Ensemble / Temianka (conductor) / Columbia Special Products AMS–6447

A membraneous group of instruments is used exclusively in the first part; the dynamic power is tremendous, and ostinati drawn from Mexican-Indian rhythmic patterns prevail. Bell and metal instruments hold the stage in the middle movement; the music is quasi-threnodic and beautifully mysterious. Instrumental mixtures are the elements of the exciting fugal finale. Chávez is extremely resourceful in this work and has set a mark that it is difficult to imagine being excelled.

This magnificent work belongs in every representative library of recorded music. No fewer than nine different disc issues have been made of the Toccata. The best of the pair remaining on the market is Columbia's. Fortunately, it delivers a brilliant execution, with sonic depth and acutely balanced resonance. The Los Angeles team (William Kraft, the composer-percussionist is its director) is major league in every way and it responds perfectly to Temianka's conducting.

Concerto for Piano and Orchestra (1938)

☐ Vienna State Opera Orchestra / List (piano) / Chávez (conductor) / Westminster Gold 8324

A big virtuosic work in which the keyboard instrument and the orchestra are equal partners producing a barbaric richness of color. It also joins sharp lyricism with native accentuations.

With Chávez conducting and Eugene List playing the solo part (he had introduced the work in 1942 with Dmitri Mitroupoulos conducting the New York Philharmonic) the recording is truly a definitive one.

Polígonos (1923)

☐ Somer (piano) / Desto 6426

Abstract, black-and-white music, its constant ongoing gestures guided by percussive instincts. Somer plays with proper antiromantic response.

Sonata VI for Piano (1961)

☐ Ruiz (piano) / Genesis 1008

Classical style reincarnated to the utmost, *not* neo-classic music. It is as though Haydn or Mozart were using Chávez's writing pen. Though nothing is left out in this repicturing of classic order, one factor is added: symmetry gives way to a *durchkomponiert* flow. It does not hamper the balanced clarity, which is styled as far from Chávez's ethnic sensations as Haydn's writing is from Xenakis's.

The recording is a discerning one and played in the Mozartian manner but without mannerisms. Ruiz is most impressive.

Unidad (1930)

☐ Somer (piano) / Desto 6426

"Unity" is no political musical tract, but a cohesive chunk of music. It has organic form with almost total concentration on line. Specific color is extremely sparse. Somer sustains the internal force of the music's style. Any other type of approach would be false.

Soli IV, for Horn, Trumpet, and Trombone (1964)

☐ Zarzo (horn); León (trumpet); Sanabria (trombone) / Chávez (conductor) / Odyssey Y-31534

Nonrepetitiveness is the axiom for *Soli IV*. The atonical continuity in this case becomes tremendously fragmented and includes some antiphonal touches. The piece is excellently played and framed in excellent engineering.

Soli I, for Oboe, Clarinet, Bassoon, and Trumpet (1933)

☐ Van Den Berg (oboe); Flores (clarinet); Salomons (bassoon); León (trumpet) / Chávez (conductor) / Odyssey Y-31534

Solo Instrument and Orchestra

Piano

Instrumental

Piano

Chamber Music

The first of the *Soli* cycle (*see above* and *below* for Nos. IV and II; No. III has not been recorded) has primitive color and rhythm and a straightforward and terse sonority of dry and taut percussiveness. Its action is free, eliminating any development of thematic material.

The performers are among the top professionals in Mexico; their playing proves their right to such status.

Soli II, for Wind Quintet (1961)

☐ Islas (flute); Van Den Berg (oboe); Flores (clarinet); Salomons (bassoon); Zarzo (horn) / Chávez (conductor) / Odyssey Y–31534

Despite formal designations that would lead one to expect proportional balances, the Sonatina, Rondo, Prelude, and Aria movements proceed otherwise. The blueprint is drawn in terms of nonrepetitiveness. The linear tissue of the work, with the pitches fractured into disjunctive apportionment remind one of expressionism; formally there is no reminder whatsoever.

There is a deep thrust to this music that doesn't caress the ear, but certainly stimulates it. It is simply a matter of a differing effect. The sharply contoured performance under Chávez's direction is superlative.

Ballet

Los cuatros soles (1925)

Pirámide (Acts III and IV) (1968)

☐ London Symphony Orchestra and Ambrosian Singers / Chávez (conductor) / Columbia M–32685

Both of these stark and dramatic scores have the gutsy rhythms, sharply pointed color, and orchestration (instrumental and vocal) that reveal the Chávez of the highly individual early style. The primitiveness and the austerity of the music bring to mind the *Sinfonía de Antígona* and the *Sinfonía India,* but there are no folkloric quotations or interminglings.

Los cuatros soles was composed as a ballet but first heard as a concert work. It took some twenty-six years before it was staged.

Pirámide includes a hair-raising section for unaccompanied chorus. Using a declamatory, nonsinging technique, this section highlights the composition. One does not need choreography in order to be caught up in the pair of exciting dramas Chávez produced and excitingly performed on this disc.

Charles Chaynes (1925-   )

Solo Instrument and Orchestra

Four Illustrations for *The Jade Flute* for Flute and Chamber Orchestra (1960)

☐ Chamber Orchestra of Radio-Luxembourg / Rampal (flute and piccolo) / De Froment (conductor) / Musical Heritage Society MHS–829

Flute

Musical transmutations of the mysterious quality of a set of ancient Chinese poems translated into French. A Prelude for flute alone prefaces the four movements, which have such titles as *Pavillion of Sadness* and *I Wander.* Chaynes's piece combines direct panchromaticism with filmy impressionism, and the hybrid is a comfortable one. It is made more so with some Honeggerisms that solidify the structure while simultaneously giving it contrast.

Rampal's golden tone (the piccolo is used in the opening movement, *The Two Flutes*) is heard with proper interpretative atmosphere. Actually, there is less solo instrument use than one would expect from the title. The flute in this piece has an obbligato function.

Concerto in C for Trumpet and Orchestra (1958)

Trumpet

☐ Symphony Orchestra of Radio-Luxembourg / André (trumpet) / De Froment (conductor) / Musical Heritage Society MHS–829

Atonalism, but not hard and dry, its chromatic pepper flavoring the result. Neo-classic rhythmic patterns define all the ideas and their developments.

Nicolas Chédeville *(1705-1783)*

Sonata (*L'Allemande*) in C minor for Two Flutes without Bass, Op. 8, No. 3

Chamber Music

☐ Rampal (flute) / Everest 3180

This is the third of a set of six sonatas titled *Les Galanteries amusantes*. It has seven movements with such characteristic titles as *L'Impératrice* and *La Palatine*.

No more perfect equality between the two parts can be imagined, since Rampal plays both by means of overdubbing. And plays them with perfect creative spirit.

Luigi Cherubini *(1760-1842)*

Overture to *Anacréon*

Orchestra

☐ Vienna Philharmonic Orchestra / Münchinger (conductor) / London STS–15076

Far from the dynamic performances one remembers given by Toscanini, this is simply a standard statement of the score. However, it's the best there is at present.

Symphony in D major

☐ New Philharmonia Orchestra / Boettcher (conductor) / Philips 6500154

This symphony is no less a triumph than any of the late Haydn or the first pair of Beethoven symphonies. Especially high art is found in the contrastive material to the principal data of the movements: the poetic introduction to the opening Allegro, and that movement's beautiful second subject, canonically framed; the romantically touched world of the trio in the *Minuetto;* and the linear impress in the finale.

Toscanini favored this symphony, but it is hardly heard these days, for no sensible reason. Aside from playing the end movement *Allegro* without the instructive *assai* that follows Cherubini's tempo designation, there is only praise possible for Boettcher's direction. The clarity of the voicing and the balances are excellent; the sonics perfect.

Sonata No. 2 in G major for Horn and Strings

Solo Instrument and Orchestra

☐ Academy of St. Martin-in-the-Fields / Tuckwell (horn) / Marriner (conductor) / Angel S–36996

Horn

This work is a little on the scholastic side, although contrasting dark and light atmospheres give it some color. Without Tuckwell, or an artist of similar strength and creamy tone, the music would die on the score page.

401

Chamber Music

String Quartet

No. 1 in E flat major / No. 2 in C major / No. 3 in D minor / No. 4 in E major / No. 5 in F major / No. 6 in A minor

☐ Melos Quartet of Stuttgart / Deutsche Grammophon Archiv 2723044

Guided by classical procedures, Cherubini was composing at the full height of romanticism, and one can perceive these elements clashing in his music. This lends a definite individuality to the six string quartets he composed after he had passed the mid-point of his career.

The compositions impart a large number of fine details. In the first quartet, for example, full-scale variation treatment serves for the slow movement; the mixture of French refinement (Cherubini spent a long time in France) is full of Italian overtones, all in a well-ordered unfolding of the classic form. This mixture of source feeding is not at the expense of stylistic integration. The finale of this quartet shows symphonic spirit, from the opening unison to the broad vigorous writing. In sonata design, the music is swept by a diatonically stimulated pace, climaxed by a speed rate that is constantly moving forward. In the C major opus the scherzo is in typical Beethoven style, but with a trio that excites rather than, as usual, lending less agitative contrast to the main body of the movement. The symphonic element of Cherubini's writing is evident in most of his quartets. They are long, powerful, and bold. The finale of the C major work follows suit, including the powering stimulus of a *fugato* occurring in the middle of the movement. In the D minor quartet the scherzo contains an imposing section of material separate in key, style, and character. The fact that the scherzo theme and material return shows how amalgamation of tendencies leads to resurveyal of the form. The other quartets exemplify similar creative aliveness and freshness.

Recordings of these works have been long overdue. I cannot recall any of the older organizations like the Pro Arte, Lener, and London Quartets performing any of these compositions. It is statistically clear that the same sad fact pertains to the current elder statesmen and newer-wave quartet teams such as the Juilliard, Guarneri, Amadeus, Cleveland, etcetera. More power therefore to the Melos foursome and congratulations to them for producing these "hidden" quartets and offering readings of the most convincing fidelity. The playing is flawless and so is the engineering.

Cantata and Oratorio

Missa Solemnis in D minor

☐ Clarion Concerts Orchestra and Chorus / Wells and Lee (sopranos); Forrester (contralto); Shirley and Shadley (tenors); Diaz (bass) / Jenkins (conductor) / Vanguard 10110/11

Size is no substantiation of value, but Cherubini's Mass parallels its large scope with true musical substance. The *Kyrie,* for example, is in three parts, the last an imposing fugue; the *Gloria* that follows (occupying more than a third of the total score) has five sections, exhibiting imposing creativity.

The mastery, musicianship, and artistic taste of soloists, orchestra, chorus, and conductor are stimulating. This is a responsible undertaking and the result is most responsive.

Requiem in D minor

☐ New Philharmonia Orchestra and Ambrosian Singers / Muti (conductor) / Angel S-37096

Listening to this magnificent Requiem Mass for male chorus and orchestra bears out Beethoven's high estimate of Cherubini. It has grandeur (the *Offertorium*), sensitive restraint (the unaccompanied *Graduale*), and terrific thrust (the *Dies Irae*).

This is an artistically honest and musically pertinent portrayal. Muti's skill in shaping the score is outstanding; the chorus (trained by its director, John McCarthy) is superb. In the crucial matters of pitch and diction the singers score a perfect one hundred mark. *Variety* would term this performance "socko." A substitute for this vernacular word is "memorable."

Medea

Opera and Dramatic Music

☐ Orchestra and Chorus of the Accademia Nazionale di Santa Cecilia, Rome / Jones and Lorengar (sopranos); Cossotto (mezzo-soprano); Prevedi (tenor); Diaz (bass); Foiani, Tavolaccini, and Carral (vocalists) / Gardelli (conductor) / London 1389

The pickings are not very propitious in this case. Callas with Serafin directing on Everest/Cetra (S–437/3) is passable, but the conducting doesn't do very much to arouse one's interest in the score. Callas again, this time with Bernstein conducting, is represented on a Turnabout issue (THS–65157/9) and this time she sounds much better. But the recorded sound is poor. There is a Hungaroton release (SLPX–11904/6) this reviewer has not heard—and in any event this foreign label is not covered in this survey.

We are left with the London edition. Most of the singing is quite accomplished, though Gwyneth Jones is a number of cuts below Callas. However, Lamberto Gardelli (who also conducts the Hungaroton release mentioned above) is a very consistent conductor and doesn't fluctuate the way Bernstein does; he thereby provides a better overall consideration of the score. The sound is excellent. Giving consideration to all matters involved, the safest recommendation is London.

Paul Chihara   (1938-   )

Willow Willow (1968)

Orchestra

☐ Stokes (bass flute); Bobo (tuba); Watson, Ervin, and Chihara (percussion); Kupka, Ose, and Sawhill (trombones) / Composers Recordings S–269

This is one piece of Chihara's *Tree Music*, which he explains as a sonorous translation using free-flowing rhythms that have a relationship to the shapes of trees. (For other *Tree Music*, see under *Instrumental: double bass* [*Logs*], under *Chamber Music* [*Branches* and *Driftwood*], and under *Electronic Music* [*Logs XVI*].)

Extremely low-key, the music practically doesn't breathe. It is as if there were no sound. We must credit Chihara, but equal credit must be given for this superb performance.

The Beauty of the Rose Is in Its Passing, for Solo Bassoon, Two Horns, Harp, and Percussion (1976)

Solo Instrument and Orchestra

☐ Los Angeles Group for Contemporary Music / Breidenthal (bassoon) / Crystal S–352

Bassoon

Chihara's poetic piece uses the title of a fourteenth-century Japanese poem. All but one section concerns a sensitive care for sensitive soliloquy. The spontaneity is most affecting, and so are the playing and the microtonal fall-offs that prompt the final sounds.

Cello

Wind Song for Cello and Orchestra (1972)

☐ American Symphony Orchestra / Solow (cello) / Samuel (conductor) / Everest 3327

Rhapsodic declamatory material is assigned to the solo instrument, which is bombarded with orchestral assertions. These contacts intensify the detail through which peeps suggestive imagery, though Chihara indicates there is no formal program or attempts at specific description. (Chihara has habitually titled his works with earthly designations such as *Redwood, Branches, Driftwood,* and *Willow Willow.*)

Solow meticulously represents the composer's intentions and Samuel does likewise. Combined, they realize the magical essence of the piece.

Instrumental

Double Bass

Logs (1970)

☐ Turetzky (string bass) / Composers Recordings S-269

Color functions as a dissecting process here. The initial phrase becomes generated by change via *rubato,* accent, or fractional pitch. Quiet fantasy is involved, and it is sensitively and poetically declared in the playing of Turetzky, the giant performer of double bass music written by the avant-garde.

Chamber Music

Branches (1966)

☐ Weisberg and MacCourt (bassoons); Watson (percussion) / Composers Recordings S-269

Color sweeps in the flitting sounds in *Branches.* Paramount is a set of eight differently tuned tenor drums. The bassoons "follow and react to the motion of the drum sound." Deep beauty registers in this suggestive impressionism.

Ceremony II (Incantations) (1972)

☐ Dunkel (flute); Eddy and Sherry (cellos); Fitz (percussion) / New World Records NW-237

This work has a tripartite structure in textural terms. Thus we hear flute fantasizing, with many expressive phrase endings concluded by a microtonal dip; dark-toned support by the pair of cellos; color additions by the percussion. This provocative choice of sonority produces a subtly sophisticated neo-impressionism.

Driftwood (1969)

☐ Philadelphia String Quartet / Composers Recordings S-269

The emphasis is on mid-range color, with the quartet formation having two violas rather than two violins. Incantatory diffusion is included in a sonorous thin rain of sound that floats, moves, and is practically pulseless.

This is extremely difficult to express but the Philadelphians do beautifully and with the fullest effect.

Electronic Music

Logs XVI (1970)

☐ Turetzky (string bass) / Composers Recordings S-269

This version of *Logs* takes the solo-bass *Logs* (see under *Instrumental: double bass),* electrically transforms it, and mixes it with other material. A sonorous magnificence results that is fascinating.

Barney Childs

37 Songs (1971)

☐ Bunger (piano) / Avant 1008

A catchy title to cover the bits and pieces of the piece, softly punctuated with silences. Such disconnectiveness paradoxically results in a connective totality. The latter part of Childs's five-minute work emphasizes a ritualistic-chant demeanor. It is quite moving and grabs a listener's attention. So does the conclusion—a nonmusical one, the pianist delivering a few short thoughts relating to man and the stars.

Bunger's playing is of ultimate lucidity.

Sonata for Solo Trombone (1961)

☐ Anderson (trombone) / Avant 1006

Though laced with aleatoric processes in its three movements: *Recitative, Double,* and *Rondo,* Childs's Sonata has a firm structural organization. Especially convincing is the interplay formation of the two-sectioned second movement (hence its title). However, the credits must be shared. Indeterminacy moves a performer into the dual re-creative and partially creative role. In this respect Miles Anderson displays superb insight.

Duo for Flute and Bassoon (1963)

☐ Middleton (flute); Weil (bassoon) / Composers Recordings S–253

Free-pitched, nonthematic, and containing a very small amount of performer freedom of choice, Childs's duo exemplifies sensitive and telling balance without using a codified, set form. The performers deserve congratulations for an accomplished presentation.

Music for Two Flute Players (1963)

☐ Harvey and Sophie Sollberger (flutes) / Composers Recordings S–253

Properly the title should read "Music for Two Flute Players Using Four Instruments," since one player doubles on piccolo, the other on alto flute.

The score gives procedures, directions, instructions, timings, notes, dynamics, and rhythms, and then hands the job of structuring all the data to the two players.

Such music, composed with extreme remote control, defines a new kind of chamber music intimacy for the players. Traditional teamwork is now expanded to cover the fullest type of exploratory re-creation and codification of the composed blueprint. The Sollbergers are experts in this field of performance–proxy composition.

Variations sur une chanson de canotier

☐ Modern Brass Ensemble / Advance FGR-2

The theme is the French-Canadian song *V'la l'Bon Vent.* By featuring one of the five brass instruments each of the variational observations is defined. Childs's music is termed "more relaxed" than usual in the liner note. Translated, this means it is more tonal than usual. The playing is nicely scaled.

Frédéric Chopin   *(1810-1849)*

Solo
Instrument
and
Orchestra

Piano

Hexaméron. See *Franz Liszt, Solo Instrument and Orchestra: piano (Hexaméron).*

Andante spianato and *Grande Polonaise brillante* in E flat major for Piano and Orchestra, Op. 22

☐ London Philharmonic Orchestra / Arrau (piano) / Inbal (conductor) / Philips 6500422

There is great depth in Arrau's playing of the first part of these two greatly contrasted pieces. Lighter appraisals of the unaccompanied Andante are more generally the rule but Arrau's probing portrayal of the contents is to be preferred. Nothing really can go wrong with the Polonaise and it doesn't. Anyway, it's all Arrau and that would be the case even if the orchestra would have something to do, which it hardly does. It is for that reason that the work can be performed (and more often is) in the piano-alone form. (For a recording of that version see under *Instrumental: piano.*)

This performance is also contained in a three-disc set of the complete works for piano and orchestra by Chopin on Philips 6747003.

Concerto No. 1 in E minor for Piano and Orchestra, Op. 11

☐ Philharmonia Orchestra / Pollini (piano) / Kletzki (conductor) / Seraphim S–60066
☐ Philadelphia Orchestra / Gilels (piano) / Ormandy (conductor) / Odyssey Y–32369

You can trot out all the adjectives in the book to describe the playing of Maurizio Pollini, who won the First Prize at the International Chopin Competition, held in Warsaw, in 1959. It is subtle and poetic, magnificently sensitive to light and shade, phrased to uncover every nuance in the lines, and with the most revelatory rubati. If one can term a performance "perfect," this is it.

Of the other scads of renditions available the choice would be Gilels. He, too, has an affinity for Chopin, and his performance has a textural delicacy and an aristocratic demeanor that are ideal.

Concerto No. 2 in F minor for Piano and Orchestra, Op. 21

☐ Symphony of the Air / Rubinstein (piano) / Wallenstein (conductor) / RCA LSC–2265
☐ London Symphony Orchestra / Ashkenazy (piano) / Zinman (conductor) / London 6440

The glowing lyrical light that permeates Rubinstein's playing makes for a handsome portrayal of this concerto. The tempi flow with a correctness of musical honesty that never deviates. Thus the finale is set forth as an *Allegro vivace* and the playing bears out the tempo designation exactly. Rubinstein does not imitate those pianists who succumb to the temptation to drive the music for the sake of brilliance. Alfred Wallenstein's masterly consideration of the orchestral part is no minor matter.

The London issue is poetically sensitive, particularly in the idyllic slow movement. The dramatic element is defined in a compelling, intimate manner that adds power to the performance.

The Rubinstein-Wallenstein issue is coupled with Chopin's *Andante spianato* and *Grande Polonaise.* The same coupling, plus the first piano concerto, with a different conductor and orchestra, is found on RCA VCS–7091.

Grand Fantasy on Polish Airs in A major, Op. 13

Krakowiak (Concert Rondo in F major), Op. 14

Variations on Mozart's *Là ci darem la mano*, Op. 2

☐ London Philharmonic Orchestra / Arrau (piano) / Inbal (conductor) / Philips 6747003

Although of lighter substance, these pieces display the Chopin personality every bit of the way. There are nice tunes in the *Krakowiak* and expert variational procedures elsewhere. Arrau's playing belies the content, and he brings out from the scores many effective points that other soloists have passed by. This is an example of topflight musicianship, warm and brilliant playing, with a strong personality that is as attractive as it is unexpected.

One quibble: four minutes of Opus 13 are on one side of the disc, the remaining ten minutes on the reverse. Surely this could have been planned better so that reminders of 78-rpm days wouldn't surface.

Introduction and Polonaise, Op. 3

☐ Rostropovich (cello); Dedyukhin (piano) / Monitor S-2119E (monaural)

The opening piano flourish gives the clue as to what sort of piece Chopin produced. He minced no words in describing it: "a brilliant drawing-room piece suitable for the ladies." With Rostropovich's golden tone and revealing phrasing fleshing out the piece, it is suitable to both sexes.

Andante spianato and *Grande Polonaise brillante* in E flat major, Op. 22

☐ Graffman (piano) / RCA VICS-1077

For the version with orchestra, see under *Solo Instrument and Orchestra: piano.* However, there is so little for the orchestra that it can be dispensed with and the two pieces played in straight solo form. The *Andante spianato* has no orchestra accompaniment whatsoever, so orchestral participation is only fifty percent of the total work to begin with, and in the Polonaise it only amounts to a dab here and there.

Chopin is suave in part 1 and energetic in part 2. Graffman is properly suave in part 1 and transfers some of the same to part 2 with excellent results.

(Graffman has also recorded this work for Columbia, on M–31934.)

Ballade

No. 1 in G minor, Op. 23 / No. 2 in F major, Op. 38 / No. 3 in A flat major, Op. 47 / No. 4 in F minor, Op. 52

☐ Rubinstein (piano) / RCA LSC-2370
☐ Vásáry (piano) / Deutsche Grammophon 136455

Ravishing playing by Rubinstein. There is marvelous intimacy in the second and fourth pieces; the colors and sweep in the G minor opus add up to extraordinary pianistic magnificence. (No. 1 is available separately on RCA LSC-4000; No. 3 is also obtainable separately, on RCA LSC-4016.)

Clarity and depth combined with both sensitivity and bravura make Tamás Vásáry's performances of these four works outstanding.

Etude

In C major, Op. 10, No. 1 / In A minor, Op. 10, No. 2 / In E major, Op. 10, No. 3 / In C sharp minor, Op. 10, No. 4 / (*Black Keys*) in G flat major, Op. 10, No. 5 / In E flat minor, Op. 10, No. 6 / In C major, Op. 10, No. 7 / In F major, Op.

Instrumental

Cello

Piano

10, No. 8 / In F minor, Op. 10, No. 9 / In A flat major, Op. 10, No. 10 / In E flat major, Op. 10, No. 11 / (*Revolutionary*) in C minor, Op. 10, No. 12 / In A flat major, Op. 25, No. 1 / In F minor, Op. 25, No. 2 / In F major, Op. 25, No. 3 / In A minor, Op. 25, No. 4 / In E minor, Op. 25, No. 5 / In G sharp minor, Op. 25, No. 6 / In C sharp minor, Op. 25, No. 7 / In D flat major, Op. 25, No. 8 / (*Butterfly*) in G flat major, Op. 25, No. 9 / In B minor, Op. 25, No. 10 / (*Winter Wind*) in A minor, Op. 25, No. 11 / In C minor, Op. 25, No. 12

☐ Pollini (piano) / Deutsche Grammophon 2530291

Pollini catches the essence of each of the pieces. He realizes and relays the total two dozen with nuance, color, and virtuosity that define great pianism. There are plenty of technical cruelties in these sets, but it is the matter beyond the performing mechanics that one awaits—the poetic imagery. The rhythmic lilt in Op. 10, No. 7, the whirl of the double thirds in the sixth of the second set, the spontaneous motion of the A minor piece in the first group are only a few examples. Everything is superbly and stunningly detailed. No critical qualifications apply to this release.

Etude

(*Revolutionary*) in C minor, Op. 10, No. 12 / In C sharp minor, Op. 25, No. 7

☐ Horowitz (piano) / Columbia MS-6541

These are landmarks of piano playing. The lyrical continuity in the C sharp minor Etude is unique; the dimensions of power and emphasis that are maintained in the C minor Etude are never blurred or staccato-pointed. The playing is tonally free-flowing, supple yet dynamic.

Fantaisie-Impromptu in C sharp minor, Op. 66

☐ Rubinstein (piano) / RCA LSC-7037

Rubinstein communicates this Chopin opus in a beautiful, natural way that emphasizes the appealing lyricism of the piece. Indeed, an outstanding issue.

Fantaisie in F minor, Op. 49

☐ Rubinstein (piano) / RCA LSC-2889

An imaginative performance, flexible, but sensitively styled.

Impromptu

In A flat major, Op. 29 / In F sharp major, Op. 36 / In G flat major, Op. 51

☐ Rubinstein (piano) / RCA LSC-7037

Rubinstein's way with Chopin has never been better detailed. The superb instinct this pianist has for Chopinesque ebb and flow, the admirable poise and delivery of phrases, and interpretative flexibility are all found here. Atmosphere, brilliance, warmth, and great technical élan are other particulars that bring enthusiastic response. It would be quite a task to surpass these performances.

Mazurka

No. 1 in F sharp minor, Op. 6, No. 1 / No. 2 in C sharp minor, Op. 6, No. 2 / No. 3 in E major, Op. 6, No. 3 / No. 4 in E flat minor, Op. 6, No. 4 / No. 5 in B flat major, Op. 7, No. 1 / No. 6 in A minor, Op. 7, No. 2 / No. 7 in F minor, Op. 7, No. 3 / No. 8 in A flat major, Op. 7, No. 4 / No. 9 in C major, Op. 7, No. 5 / No. 10 in

B flat major, Op. 17, No. 1 / No. 11 in E minor, Op. 17, No. 2 / No. 12 in A flat major, Op. 17, No. 3 / No. 13 in A minor, Op. 17, No. 4 / No. 14 in G minor, Op. 24, No. 1 / No. 15 in C major, Op. 24, No. 2 / No. 16 in A flat major, Op. 24, No. 3 / No. 17 in B flat minor, Op. 24, No. 4 / No. 18 in C minor, Op. 30, No. 1 / No. 19 in B minor, Op. 30, No. 2 / No. 20 in D flat major, Op. 30, No. 3 / No. 21 in C sharp minor, Op. 30, No. 4 / No. 22 in G sharp minor, Op. 33, No. 1 / No. 23 in D major, Op. 33, No. 2 / No. 24 in C major, Op. 33, No. 3 / No. 25 in B minor, Op. 33, No. 4 / No. 26 in C sharp minor, Op. 41, No. 1 / No. 27 in E minor, Op. 41, No. 2 / No. 28 in B major, Op. 41, No. 3 / No. 29 in A flat major, Op. 41, No. 4 / No. 30 in G major, Op. 50, No. 1 / No. 31 in A flat major, Op. 50, No. 2 / No. 32 in C sharp minor, Op. 50, No. 3 / No. 33 in B major, Op. 56, No. 1 / No. 34 in C major, Op. 56, No. 2 / No. 35 in C minor, Op. 56, No. 3 / No. 36 in A minor, Op. 59, No. 1 / No. 37 in A flat major, Op. 59, No. 2 / No. 38 in F sharp minor, Op. 59, No. 3 / No. 39 in B major, Op. 63, No. 1 / No. 40 in F minor, Op. 63, No. 2 / No. 41 in C sharp minor, Op. 63, No. 3 / No. 42 in G major, Op. 67, No. 1 / No. 43 in G minor, Op. 67, No. 2 / No. 44 in C major, Op. 67, No. 3 / No. 45 in A minor, Op. 67, No. 4 / No. 46 in C major, Op. 68, No. 1 / No. 47 in A minor, Op. 68, No. 2 / No. 48 in F major, Op. 68, No. 3 / No. 49 in F minor, Op. 68, No. 4 / No. 50 in A minor, Op. Posth. / No. 51 in A minor, Op. Posth.

☐ Magaloff (piano) / London STS-15146/8

The clarity, subtle dynamic gradations, and just as neatly contoured *rubati* make Magaloff's set ideal. Of course, as with any integral set of this scope, one can testify to differences of interpretative opinion regarding a few of the pieces. However, the overall average is truly impressive.

What is special to Magaloff's playing is the complete lack of overstudied reshaping (in the name of that escape term—*rubati*) that destroys the poetic simplicity of Chopin's instrumental dance formations.

Mazurka

No. 19 in B minor, Op. 30, No. 2 / No. 20 in D flat major, Op. 30, No. 3 / No. 22 in G sharp minor, Op. 33, No. 1 / No. 25 in B minor, Op. 33, No. 4 / No. 34 in C major, Op. 56, No. 2 / No. 43 in G minor, Op. 67, No. 2 / No. 45 in A minor, Op. 67, No. 4 / No. 46 in C major, Op. 68, No. 1 / No. 47 in A minor, Op. 68, No. 2 / No. 49 in F minor, Op. 68, No. 4

☐ Michelangeli (piano) / Deutsche Grammophon 2530236

If a listener's preference is for a smaller number of Chopin Mazurkas, this group of ten cannot be faulted. Compared to Magaloff, Michelangeli considers those he performs with a wider range of reference. He is more engrossed in differing dynamic judgments than in describing the true pulse for Chopin's mazurka beat. These are of distinctive variance from Magaloff's versions of the same pieces but both pianists provide superior results.

Mazurka

No. 25 in B minor, Op. 33, No. 4 / No. 31 in A flat major, Op. 50, No. 2

☐ Rubinstein (piano) / RCA LSC-3339

Simply superb. Rubinstein's playing gives fascinating listening returns. In these two mazurka examples no one can equal him.

Nocturne

In A flat major, Op. 32, No. 2 / In B flat minor, Op. 9, No. 1 / In B major, Op. 9, No. 3 / In B major, Op. 32, No. 1 / In B major, Op. 62, No. 1 / In C minor, Op. 48, No. 1 / In C sharp minor, Op. 27, No. 1 / In D flat major, Op. 27, No. 2 / In E flat major, Op. 9, No. 2 / In E flat major, Op. 55, No. 2 / In E major, Op. 62, No. 2 / In E minor, Op. 72 / In F major, Op. 15, No. 1 / In F minor, Op. 55, No. 1 / In F sharp major, Op. 15, No. 2 / In F sharp minor, Op. 48, No. 2 / In G major, Op. 37, No. 2 / In G minor, Op. 15, No. 3 / In G minor, Op. 37, No. 1

☐ Rubinstein (piano) / RCA LSC–7050

Rubinstein performs the "standard" set of nineteen Nocturnes; the two published posthumously are noted immediately below.

The dynamic differences portrayed here are manifold, which is amazingly meaningful in the structural schemes of the pieces. The phrasing is defined and yet gives the feeling of seamless continuity; the textures are of assorted weights and qualities. Such pianistic resource is amazing. The way to discover the basic nature and meaning of Chopin's Nocturnes is to listen to Rubinstein play them.

Nocturne

No. 20, Op. Posth. / No. 21, Op. Posth.

☐ Weissenberg (piano) / Angel S–3747

This pair is outside the regular canon of Chopin's nineteen Nocturnes. Good enough playing.

Nouvelle Etude

No. 1 in F minor, Op. Posth. / No. 2 in A flat major, Op. Posth. / No. 3 in D flat major, Op. Posth.

☐ Ashkenazy (piano) / London 6422

Subtle sensitivity and vitality combine and contrast in the performances of this set of three pieces.

Polonaise Fantaisie, Op. 61

☐ Brendel (piano) / Vanguard C–10058

Totally idiomatic and brilliantly characterized.

Polonaise

(*Military*) in A major, Op. 40, No. 1 / In A flat major, Op. 53 / In B flat major, Op. 71, No. 2 / In C minor, Op. 40, No. 2 / In C sharp minor, Op. 26, No. 1 / In E flat minor, Op. 26, No. 2 / In F sharp minor, Op. 44

☐ Brailowsky (piano) / Columbia MS–6305

Brailowsky's close identification with Chopin's music is tellingly revealed in this selection of Polonaises. There is a musical command that even makes the hackneyed *Military* opus come to the ears with a refreshing cleanliness and aliveness. All of the accounts are stimulating, dynamic, and tonically poetical as required. The total conviction and presence of these performances are undeniable.

For those who wish, the complete Polonaises are available in several recordings, the best of these being Peter Frankl's performances on Turnabout 34254/5.

Prelude

In C major, Op. 28, No. 1 / In A minor, Op. 28, No. 2 / In G major, Op. 28, No. 3 / In E minor, Op. 28, No. 4 / In D major, Op. 28, No. 5 / In B minor, Op. 28, No. 6 / In A major, Op. 28, No. 7 / In F sharp minor, Op. 28, No. 8 / In E major, Op. 28, No. 9 / In C sharp minor, Op. 28, No. 10 / In B major, Op. 28, No. 11 / In G sharp minor, Op. 28, No. 12 / In F sharp major, Op. 28, No. 13 / In E flat minor, Op. 28, No. 14 / In D flat major, Op. 28, No. 15 / In B flat minor, Op. 28, No. 16 / In A flat major, Op. 28, No. 17 / In F minor, Op. 28, No. 18 / In E flat major, Op. 28, No. 19 / In C minor, Op. 28, No. 20 / In B flat major, Op. 28, No. 21 / In G minor, Op. 28, No. 22 / In F major, Op. 28, No. 23 / In D minor, Op. 28, No. 24 / In C sharp minor, Op. 45 / In A flat major, Op. Posth.

☐ Arrau (piano) / Philips 6500622

An outstanding survey of all the Preludes, plus the splendid ruminative one that bears a separate opus designation and the posthumous item that did not reach publication until 1918. Arrau's playing is beautifully focused, sensitively integrated, and above all never oblivious (within style) of romantic personality. There is admirable control that subtly probes all the elements in these Chopin essays.

Other rewarding choices are Eschenbach (Deutsche Grammophon 2530231) and Pollini (Deutsche Grammophon 2530550). (The latter, however, performs only the Opus 28 set.) Arrau is number one because of his sensible tempi and refusal to fidget with the basic pace of any one of the pieces.

Scherzo

No. 1 in B minor, Op. 20 / No. 2 in B flat minor, Op. 31 / No. 3 in C sharp minor, Op. 39 / No. 4 in E major, Op. 54

☐ Rubinstein (piano) / RCA LSC-2368

In these powerful presentations the phrases flow and *rubati* do not disfigure the material. The bravura is vivid—an ingredient that is in itself a color within the music's colors.

(No. 2 of the group is included in a miscellaneous Chopin program on RCA LSC-4016.)

Scherzo No. 1 in B minor, Op. 20

☐ Horowitz (piano) / Columbia MS-6541

Mercurial pianism with a touch that has penetrating softness. Dramatic dynamic contrasts are scaled musically and still afford the most pertinent communicative power.

Sonata No. 2 (*Funeral March*) in B flat minor, Op. 35

☐ Perahia (piano) / Columbia M-32780
☐ Ashkenazy (piano) / London 6794

The sheer musicality and technical command of both of these performances are of brilliant order, realizing completely exciting experiences. Perahia's handling of the polyphonic detail is magnificent, the contrasts in the scherzo are splendidly shaped, and in the finale the enigmatic atmosphere is perfectly conveyed.

Power and eloquence also mark Ashkenazy's rendition. It is dramatic but in the process the romantic stimulus is not eliminated; the *rubati* are magical.

Sonata No. 3 in B minor, Op. 58

☐ Hungerford (piano) / Vanguard VSD-71214
☐ Simon (piano) / Turnabout 34272

Hungerford's playing goes from strength to strength. There is considerable freedom but it is musically inclined, Chopinesque in its travel. The rhythms are supple, the agogical depiction subtle; everything is integrated and provides a totally persuasive account.

Simon's portrayal is sharply focused, romantically warm, and totally apt at the same time. Add to that "impact," which is beautifully weighted in the scherzo and eloquent in the slow movement. Both of these performances are highly recommended.

Tarantelle in A flat major, Op. 43

☐ Rubinstein (piano) / RCA LSC-2889

A brilliant affair even if the substances of the piece are not overwhelming. When Rubinstein projects it, one overlooks the substances and enjoys pianistic panache.

Waltz

No. 1 (*Grande Valse brillante*) in E flat major, Op. 18 / No. 2 in A flat major, Op. 34, No. 1 / No. 3 (*Valse brillante*) in A minor, Op. 34, No. 2 / No. 4 (*Valse brillante*) in F major, Op. 34, No. 3 / No. 5 (*Two-Four Waltz*) in A flat major, Op. 42 / No. 6 (*Minute*) in D flat major, Op. 64, No. 1 / No. 7 in C sharp minor, Op. 64, No. 2 / No. 8 in A flat major, Op. 64, No. 3 / No. 9 (*L'Adieu*) in A flat major, Op. 69, No. 1 / No. 10 in B minor, Op. 69, No. 2 / No. 11 in G flat major, Op. 70, No. 1 / No. 12 in F minor, Op. 70, No. 2 / No. 13 in D flat major, Op. 70, No. 3 / No. 14 in E minor, Op. Posth.

☐ Rubinstein (piano) / RCA LSC-2726
☐ Lipatti (piano) / Odyssey 32160058E (monaural)

Poetry and aristocratic demeanor are represented in Rubinstein's playing. The tenderness, musical honesty, and understanding that Lipatti displays make one realize anew the great achievements of this young musician, who only lived a short thirty-three years. Of different temperament, both men are scrupulously authoritative pianists. Both provide a warmth that is maintained throughout the narrative progress of Chopin's triple-pulsed gems.

There is another version that Lipatti made, recorded live at the Besançon Festival on September 16, 1950 and released by Angel. This was his last public appearance—he died two months later. It is no better than the other one listed, but it is historically important and a collector might want it. It lacks the second waltz because Lipatti did not have enough stamina to complete the traditional set of fourteen waltzes. The Angel disc is a monaural production, No. 3556.

Waltz No. 1 (*Grande Valse brillante*) in E flat major, Op. 18

☐ Rubinstein (piano) / RCA LSC-4016

In case only a few of the Waltzes as played by Rubinstein (*see above*) are desired, they are excerpted in two different RCA albums (*see also below*).

Waltz No. 2 in A flat major, Op. 34, No. 1

☐ Rubinstein (piano) / RCA LSC-4000

(See note immediately above.)

Waltz No. 5 (*Two-Four Waltz*) in A flat major, Op. 42

☐ Rubinstein (piano) / RCA LSC-4016

Another excerpt from Rubinstein's performance of the basic fourteen waltzes. Beautifully realized.

Waltz

No. 6 (*Minute*) in D flat major, Op. 64, No. 1 / No. 7 in C sharp minor, Op. 64, No. 2

☐ Rubinstein (piano) / RCA LSC-4000

The tempo for the *Minute* is a musical one and there is no attempt to set speed records. Most significant is the beautiful tone registration. Tempo also plays a vital part in the ideal statement of the C sharp minor waltz. It is set close to the *moderato* mark; the line moves beautifully and is not sentimentalized into dull progress.

Waltz

No. 9 (*L'Adieu*) in A flat major, Op. 69, No. 1 / No. 14 in E minor, Op. Posth.

☐ Rubinstein (piano) / RCA LSC-4016

Chopinesque brightness in both cases and all the dazzle that properly clothes the posthumous waltz.

Waltz

No. 15 in E major, Op. Posth. / No. 16 in A flat major, Op. Posth. / No. 18 in E flat major, Op. Posth. / No. 19 in A minor, Op. Posth.

☐ Ciccolini (piano) / Seraphim S-60252

These are four of the five posthumously produced Chopin waltzes, not counting the final example in the traditional set of fourteen, also published after his death (actually nineteen years later).

All are as worthy as the standard fourteen waltzes. The playing is dandy and crisp, meaning that Ciccolini provides a thorough and totally sympathetic exploration of the music. The one waltz lacking (No. 17) is included in Abbey Simon's execution on Turnabout 34580 of all the Chopin waltzes: the "fourteen" and the five posthumously published ones. But Simon's waltzes are not convincing in comparison with those listed above played by Rubinstein and Lipatti, and the ones presented here by Ciccolini. The reason is the coolness of the playing, a formal politeness, as it were.

Sonata for Cello and Piano, Op. 65

☐ du Pré (cello); Barenboim (piano) / Angel S-36937

The premise that this sonata is second-rate music and not to be considered in the same

Chamber Music

413

class as Chopin's piano compositions is incorrect. It is true Chopin. The faults pertain to instrumental distribution, indicating a seeming reticent attitude to permit another instrument to enter the sacred keyboard domain. There are a few weak moments, mainly the usual ones that surface when combining a low string instrument with the piano. Further, the piano melodicism is just a bit overdone, though Barenboim does well in adjusting this, and the string timbre is used too often as a counterpoint to the piano.

Trio for Piano, Violin, and Cello, Op. 8

☐ Oistrakh (violin); Knushevitzky (cello); Oborin (piano) / Monitor S-2069E (monaural)

Considered separately, the musical material of this trio is good. But its scoring machinery is not effective; the strings fill in—they plug the gaps. This problem is emphasized by the rare use of the upper tessitura of the violin, creating even a duller aspect than is really the case.

Chopin having given the piano undivided attention, the performance problem is to check its overcommand and attempt to achieve a closer integration. Lev Oborin's suave playing almost miraculously achieves this. This is especially so in the final movement which resembles a marathonlike exercise for the piano. The playing of his partners is singularly musical. They almost bring Chopin's trio into textural balance.

The stereo sound on Philips 6500133, with the Beaux Arts Trio performing, is better, naturally. Still, Monitor's electronically processed issue is even a bit above the average obtained by such method, and the playing of the Soviet threesome accomplishes a warmth and a performance strategy that the Beaux Arts Trio does not match.

Ballet

Les Sylphides

☐ Philharmonia Orchestra / Mackerras (conductor) / Angel S-35833

The Prelude, Nocturne, Waltzes, and Mazurkas that make up this ballet are all Chopin's; the orchestration, of course, is not. There have been a number of orchestrators, beginning with Glazunov, who produced a four-part suite titled *Chopiniana* (see below, under *Chopin/Glazunov*). His objective was a purely orchestral one but his score was later chosen by Fokine as the basis for a ballet using Glazunov's title. A revision followed, in both plot, title, and musical expansion.

Nice sound and excellent rhythmic subtlety make this the preferable recording. Ormandy's old edition still stands up strong. Its tone is warm, the emphasis being on the lyrical side. It is available both on Columbia MS-6508 and M-31845.

Chopin / Alexander Glazunov (1865-1936)

Ballet

Chopiniana, Op. 46

☐ Orchestra of the Bolshoi Theater / Žuraitis (conductor) / Melodiya/Angel S-40231

If you like this sort of thing, here it is—the entire matter from A to Z, including additions scored by Maurice Keller. The basic guts of the score are the four pieces Glazunov chose: the Polonaise, Op. 40, No. 1; a Nocturne, Op. 15, No. 1; the Op. 50, No. 3 Mazurka;

and the *Tarantelle*, Op. 43. The Russian felt strongly about his work, assigning it a definite opus number: 46.

Chopin / **Leopold Godowsky** (1870-1938)

Badinage   *Instrumental*

Etude for the Left Hand Alone, Op. 10, No. 6   *Piano*

☐ Pines (piano) / Genesis 1000

This is Chopin viewed through re-creative bifocals. Heard here are two of Godowsky's superbly clever *53 Studies on the Etudes of Chopin*.

The Op. 10, No. 6 example takes the E flat minor two-hand original and reworks it for a one-hand setting to delightful effect. Chopin never wrote a *Badinage*. This is the name of a tasty Godowsky sandwich made from the G flat major (*Black Key*), Op. 10, No. 5 Etude and the G flat major (*Butterfly*), Op. 25, No. 9 Etude. Only diehards will block their ears to this striking combination.

Virtuosic stride is mandatory. Doris Pines has it, with plenty to spare. We could have been spared the bits of applause at the end of each piece. It was left in, apparently, to prove the playing was recorded at a "live" presentation. It's annoying.

Chou Wen-chung   **(1923-   )**

And the Fallen Petals, **a Triolet for Orchestra**   *Orchestra*

☐ Louisville Orchestra / Whitney (conductor) / Louisville 561 (monaural)

Music of decided individuality, combining within it concepts of Chinese music, impressionistic sound foliage, and pungent dissonances. The last element is part of what the composer terms "melodic brushwork." It produces an instrumental commentary that alternately smacks and caresses the ear.

Chou's flexible textures are carefully handled by the Louisvillians. The requirement that the orchestrational bits and wisps, crimsons and browns, not sound like effects but as part of a poetic continuum is well realized.

Landscapes (1949)

☐ Peninsula Festival Orchestra / Johnson (conductor) / Composers Recordings 122

A number of inventive, fresh sonorities mark the piece, but there is an overabundance of the tam tam and cymbal combination. Though the liner note stresses that the composer has united "the disparate cultures of East and West," he seems to favor the latter.

Pien (1966)

Yü Ko (1965)

☐ Group for Contemporary Music at Columbia University / Sollberger (conductor) / Composers Recordings S-251

Sound curves and loops are the patterns in *Yü Ko*, scored for alto flute, English horn, bass clarinet, two trombones, percussion, violin, and piano. In its delicacy and lack of fervor the piece is an abstraction of drama. It is all implied, an expert depiction of vitality in its quietest manner. (Some may term this a manifestation of Eastern non-emotionalism. Whatever, the immaterial character of the work is beautiful.)

Pien (requiring five wind players covering seven instruments, the same total of brass players using six instruments, four percussionists, and piano) lives up to its meaning: "transformation and change." Its textures are rarefactive, the subject matter single-stranded, with parenthetical material in place of development.

Both performances are significant, precise, and expressive.

Solo Instrument and Orchestra	***Soliloquy of a Bhiksuni***

☐ Los Angeles Brass Society / Stevens (trumpet) / Henderson (conductor) / Crystal S-361

Trumpet

Chou's piece (which includes percussion) is based on a scene from a sixteenth-century Chinese drama and consists of transparent textures oscillating in antiphonal contrast. In view of the background of the composer this is no Hollywoodish or Western make-believe but stylistic authenticity.

Clear impressions of the music's content are given by the performers. Apparently the dynamic monotony that prevails is built into the score.

Instrumental

Cursive (1963)

Flute

☐ Sollberger (flute); Wuorinen (piano) / Composers Recordings S-251

Chou's music has the expressivity of the East by manipulation of Western instruments. The discourse is thereby mostly symbolic and not direct. The flute in *Cursive* oscillates in minute motion (microtonal shifts obtained by rolling the instrument), glides variously, and vibrates in changing speeds. This is insular communication without the organic outwardness most common to music.

Piano

The Willows Are New (1957)

☐ Chang (piano) / Composers Recordings S-251

Central climax is not used in Chou's music, its material being intensely concentrated. Though disjointed metrically (there is constant change), the sense of one line from the opening *rubato* to the closing, shortened *rubato* section is maintained. The composer describes his piece as "a continuum of motion and tension in spatial equilibrium." A well-stated point of view, even though the tensions are not recognizable since there are no releases.

Chamber Music

Suite for Harp and Wind Quintet

☐ Otis (harp); Dunkel (flute); Taylor (oboe); Blackwell (clarinet); Morelli (bassoon); Rose (horn) / New World Records NW-237

These gentle and simple, plain and not fancy settings of five traditional Chinese melodies are exquisite perceptions, never brutally dynamic, always tender, which results in their being dynamic after all. Tastefully performed.

Domenico Cimarosa *(1749-1801)*

Overture to *I traci amanti*

Orchestra

☐ New Philharmonia Orchestra / Leppard (conductor) / Philips 802901

Mozartian delight and spirit. Leppard delivers Cimarosa's commentary marvelously.

Concerto in G major for Two Flutes and Orchestra

Solo Instrument and Orchestra

☐ Stuttgart Chamber Orchestra / Aurèle and Christiane Nicolet (flutes) / Münchinger (conductor) / London 6739

Two Flutes

Not only is this performance beguiling and shaped with sensitive grace, as well as true and strong character, it is also more authentic structurally than the Turnabout (34307) edition. Cimarosa indicated places in the first and last movements for cadenzas. Although Turnabout offers one in the opening part, it bypasses the soloistic disclosure in the concluding movement. The Nicolet team plays a cadenza by one Werner Speth in movement 1 and a shorter conception by the important Swiss composer Willy Burkhard (1900–1955) in the terminal Rondo. Both cadenzas are attentive to proper style and one is certain they would have had Cimarosa's blessing.

For some reason Turnabout is ambivalent about the title of this work. On the reverse of the jacket and in the liner notes the heading is "Concerto." On the front of the cover and on the record label the title is noted as "Concertante." Just a statistical note; the choice is strongly for the London release.

Sonata in B flat major

Instrumental

☐ Sgrizzi (harpsichord) / Nonesuch 73008

Harpsichord

Cimarosa's harpsichord sonatas are among those works that musicians have always known about but few have ever heard. They are very succinct items and most often as lively and bubbly as this one. Spirited response, with the utmost clarity, on the part of the performer makes this release a pleasure.

Sonata

In C major / In C minor

☐ Sgrizzi (harpsichord) / Nonesuch 71117

Just enough music to cover the formal plots, with timings of one and one-half and two and one-half minutes, respectively. Pinpointed articulation and bright recorded sound.

Sonata

In D minor / In E flat major

☐ Sgrizzi (harpsichord) / Nonesuch 73008

The D minor opus jogs along like the B flat major item (*see above*); the other work is more moderately poised. Both are played with fetching grace and skill.

Sonata

No. 23 in A minor / No. 24 in C major / No. 29 in C minor / No. 31 in G major

☐ Kipnis (harpsichord) / Columbia M3X–31521

Kipnis identifies the numbers of the Cimarosa sonatas he performs, whereas Sgrizzi does not (*see above*). It was these four sonatas that Arthur Benjamin used as the basis for his Concerto for Oboe and Strings (see under *Cimarosa/Benjamin: Solo Instrument and Orchestra: oboe*).

The harpsichord art of Igor Kipnis is beautifully illustrated in this group of works. His technique is effortless, his playing combines grace with power. Cimarosa could not be better served.

Cimarosa / Benjamin

Solo Instrument and Orchestra

Concerto for Oboe and Strings (1942)

☐ Chamber Orchestra of the Vienna State Opera / Lardrot (oboe); Nordberg (cembalo) / Prohaska (conductor) / Vanguard 2036

Oboe

Not exactly what the title describes, thereby nullifying the belief that Benjamin transcribed a concerto by Cimarosa and that's that. What Benjamin did was to adapt material from Cimarosa's piano sonatas and design a four-part work covering an alternation of slow movements (*Introduzione* [*Larghetto*] and *Siciliana*) with two fast-paced divisions (Allegro and *Allegro giusto*).

In honoring Cimarosa, Benjamin brought special honor to himself through this splendid reconstruction, which has become a standard oboe repertory piece. The honors continue with this performance in which André Lardrot plays with splendid tone and impeccable control, ably supported by a sensitive realization on the part of Felix Prohaska.

Anthony Cirone (1941-   )

Percussion

Double Concerto

Triptych

☐ Sonic Boom Percussion Ensemble / Crystal S–140

Once totally bare, the percussion-music worktable is now overcrowded. Unfortunately, much music scored for percussion is nothing more than a bunch of old shavings and leftovers from the aforesaid worktable. However, there are the exceptions. Here is a pair, of coloristic vitality and musical viability.

The Double Concerto also exists with orchestral partnership. In this case another setting, with piano, is offered. It works, aided by the chit-chat of jazzy diction. The *Triptych* is geared to and emphasizes the trinal total. Not only are there three movements, but such concepts as three major ideas in part 1, a three-part accompaniment to a timpani solo, and a triple-sectioned movement 2 as well as movement 3 (with exclusive use of three-note groups in the latter) further bear out the design. It isn't Cage, Harrison, Varèse, or Stockhausen, since it isn't radically inventive in any way, but it has a musicality that demands respect. It is played with first-class comprehension.

Israel Citkowitz (1909-1974)

Five Songs from *Chamber Music* (1930)

Vocal

Voice with Accompaniment

☐ Beardslee (soprano); Helps (piano) / New World Records NW–243

Citkowitz produced very little after 1936. This is unfortunate, considering the creative talent shown in these songs, composed in 1930. They are in the lyrical, not declamatory vein, matching Joyce's poetry. (A little roughness in the upper part of Beardslee's range will have to be overlooked for the sake of the music.)

Avery Claflin (1898-1979)

Fishhouse Punch (1948)

Orchestra

☐ Vienna Orchestra / Adler (conductor) / Composers Recordings 107 (monaural)

Fancy titles never harmed any art work. Claflin's simply identifies a scherzo that has tempo moderation. The performance is temperately spirited.

Teen Scenes for String Orchestra (1955)

String Orchestra

☐ Orchestra of the Accademia Nazionale di Santa Cecilia, Roma / Antonini (conductor) / Composers Recordings 119 (monaural)

This is light-cased music that has its more serious moments, as a sampling of the titles outlines: *Confident Freshman, Baby Sitting, Job in Supermarket,* and *Delinquent.* There are seven movements in all, which the Italians play with freshness and clean sound.

Concerto for Piano and Orchestra (*Concerto giocoso*) (1957)

Solo Instrument and Orchestra

Piano

☐ Iceland Symphony Orchestra / Magnússon (piano) / Strickland (conductor) / Composers Recordings 178 (monaural)

A compact eighteen minutes' worth of well-ordered music, save for some severe cadences. Innocent orchestration. Don't expect surprises.

Design for the Atomic Age

Choral

Lament for April 15

Chorus Alone

The Quangle Wangle's Hat

☐ Randolph Singers / Randolph (conductor) / Composers Recordings 102 (monaural)

Delightful settings of words by Edward Lear for the first and last titles listed. Regretfully, CRI does not include a text leaflet with the recording so one cannot catch every point in the pitter-patter delivery of the "Quangle" madrigal.

More delightful in terms of textual choice is the unique setting of the income-tax instructions. This flippant idea is carried out in a quasi-serious manner and it comes across perfectly by the simple and direct way in which the Randolph group sings.

La Grande Bretèche (1947)

Opera and Dramatic Music

☐ Vienna Orchestra / Brinton and Jones (sopranos); Blankenship and Gilmore (tenors); Owens (baritone); Harms, Nurmala, and Hartzell (vocalists) / Adler (conductor) / Composers Recordings 108X (monaural)

A gruesome tale made to order for opera order. A husband, who rightly suspects that his wife has hidden her lover in their bedroom closet, calls for a mason and has the closet walled up as she watches in horror. She finally admits the truth and he kills her.

Heavy, heavy drama and to go with it full romantic musical diction, minor and diminished chords, and the like. If Claflin's one-act opera, covering a prologue and two scenes, is not particularly individual it is always adroit in its vocal writing, orchestral color, and design.

Artistry on the part of the cast, with the honors to Patricia Brinton as the unfaithful woman and Richard Owens as the cuckold. Regretfully, no text is offered by CRI.

Herbert L. Clarke (1867-1945)

Instrumental

Cornet

The Bride of the Waves—Polka brillante

The Débutante

From the Shores of the Mighty Pacific—Rondo Caprice

☐ Schwarz (cornet); Bolcom (piano) / Nonesuch 71298

Cadenzas, showy passages, double and triple tonguing, trills, coloratura registers—all are displayed in these old cornet showpieces that used to wow 'em in the long lost days of summer band concerts. Such documentation is a joy to have, since you can't hear this wonderful stuff any more than you can expect to see silent movie serials starring Pearl White or Harry Houdini.

It may seem like campy music to some, but a listener becomes a believer when he hears the manner in which Gerard Schwarz tosses off these pieces. Conscious of his mission (it is that), Schwarz plays it straight without any hoke (the word applies to running silent films at a faster speed than originally planned), and the music is heard with freshness or with fresh nostalgia. There are few brass practitioners that can match this musician. No minor credit goes to William Bolcom. His piano accompaniments are idiomatically in the groove. It would have been quite simple to play these plain harmonic settings in a mundane, neutral manner. Not Bolcom. He adds the proper symbols to the melodic characters.

The Maid of the Mist—Polka

☐ Schwarz (cornet); Cooper (piano) / Nonesuch 71341

After an introductory section, *The Maid* moves onto a sentimental tune and then displays rhythmic gestures. It is to Schwarz's credit that even when sentiment rules he never permits the slightest bathos to candify his playing.

Sounds from the Hudson—Valse brillante

☐ Schwarz (cornet); Bolcom (piano) / Nonesuch 71298

Clarke's waltz avoids any Viennese sensuousness. His is outdoor waltz music, right on the button with its pulse demarcation. It is played with totally revealing style.

Twilight Dreams—Waltz Intermezzo

☐ Schwarz (cornet); Cooper (piano) / Nonesuch 71341

A light-hearted period piece, with a tinge of sadness and some cadenza exposure. Through his most elegant playing Schwarz is certain to make a convert of even the most sophisticated listener.

Cousins

☐ Schwarz (cornet); Barron (trombone); Cooper (piano) / Nonesuch 71341

Florid and fancy, the prototype of the display duo from ye olde days of outdoor band concerts. The authority with which this is played and the impeccable partnership, even in triple tonguing, are simply marvelous.

Robert Keyes Clark (1925 -)

Concerto for Clarinet and Chamber Orchestra (1970)

☐ Composers Festival Orchestra / Bunke (clarinet) / Brehm (conductor) / Trilogy CTS–1002

Two moods run through this fine piece—jazzy (extrovert) and declamatory (introvert). The spicy orchestration is at times a bit harsh, but it is always becoming.

The soloist, Jerome Bunke, is a fully informed musician.

Aldo Clementi (1925 -)

Triplum (1961)

☐ Gazzelloni (flute); Faber (oboe); Deplus (clarinet) / Mainstream 5008

This music sounds serialistic but is ruled by an opposite system, that of intervallic logistics. The music is therefore athematic and devoid of development or repetition. The opposing of the intervals is the attraction.

These three musicians are top experts in the performance of avant-garde music. Their account proves their right to that description.

Muzio Clementi (1752 - 1832)

Concerto in C major for Piano and Orchestra

☐ Prague New Chamber Orchestra / Blumental (piano) / Zedda (conductor) / Turnabout 34375

Presentable music in all respects. The thematic material is nicely differentiated, and if the aural reminders are those of Mozart this does not mitigate the concerto's values.

The fast movements are heard with stimulating results; more inner motility could be applied to the lyrical center piece of the work.

Sonata in F sharp minor, Op. 26, No. 2

☐ Goldsand (piano) / Desto 6200

Goldsand does not pass lightly over seeming lightnesses in Clementi's Sonata but probes and finds considerable depth in it, especially in the poignant *Lento e patetico*. The dynamic colors applied in the exhilarating final Presto are admirably suited to the composition.

Sonatina

Op. 36, No. 1 / **Op. 36, No. 2** / **Op. 36, No. 3** / **Op. 36, No. 4** / **Op. 36, No. 5** / **Op. 36, No. 6**

☐ Entremont (piano) / Columbia MG–33202

Used for over a century as standard teaching fare, Opus 36 is matched by other Sonatinas in Clementi's Opus 37 and Opus 38, but the lowest-numbered group is the best of the three. This always respectable music, which if not inspired displays impeccable workmanship, is beautifully crafted by Entremont in his recorded performances. He deserves thanks for placing on disc what has been heard only in the teaching studio or by students practicing in the home.

Chamber Music

Sonata in G major, Op. 2, No. 1

☐ Wilson (flute); Fuller (harpsichord) / Orion 7283

A fine musical performance of this charming two-movement work. Wilson's weight of tone (and color) in the low register is especially appealing. The partnership with Fuller is topflight.

Sonata in D major for Flute, Cello, and Piano, Op. 22, No. 1

☐ New York Camerata / Turnabout 34575

Attractive music with the piano sitting at the head of the trio table. Even though the end movements are in fast pace (*allegro di molto* and *vivace assai*, respectively) the effect (artistically portrayed in the performance) is one described in the second word of the central movement's tempo: *allegretto innocente.* Clementi's lack of adventure is compensated by the direct and refreshing playing of these musicians.

Louis Nicolas Clérambault   **(1676-1749)**

Instrumental

Organ

Suite du deuxième ton

☐ Hansen (organ) / Nonesuch 71170

A large-scale work in seven movements: *Plein jeu,* Duo, Trio, *Basse de Cromorne, Flûtes, Récit de Nazard,* and *Caprice sur les grands jeux.* (Nonesuch does not offer any data for the work itself, simply a fine but general article on the release in which this composition is included, titled "Master Works for Organ—Volume 5." Neither do they mention that this suite is from Clérambault's *Premier Livre d'orgue.*)

Jørgen Ernst Hansen's performance provides precise color in accordance with the movement designations which indicate the clues to registration. Thus the full organ is heard in part 1 and part 7, two registers are used in the Duo, and so on. (A performance of the finale, and a very good one, is available on Columbia MS-7438, in a miscellaneous program embracing the music of seven composers played by E. Power Biggs.)

This suite is most representative of Clérambault's output. Notwithstanding the oft-repeated but erroneous theory that most organ compositions are for organists only, this work deserves broad attention. It is secure music that should not be overlooked because of the still prevalent bias against the medium by otherwise intelligent music lovers.

Robert Clérisse   *(1899-   )*

Introduction et Scherzo

☐ Nova Saxophone Quartet / Crystal S–153

Well-played, well-mannered music, meaning traditionally conventional music.

Chamber Music

Eric Coates   *(1886-1957)*

London Suite (1933)

☐ Orchestra name not given / Gould (conductor) / RCA LSC–2719

This Boston Pops–type music is a solid success under Gould's baton.

Orchestra

Arthur Cohn   *(1910-   )*

Kaddish for Orchestra (1964)

☐ Royal Philharmonic Orchestra / Lipkin (conductor) / Composers Recordings S–259

The *Kaddish*, the ancient Jewish prayer, has always been intoned with reserve and acquiescence. I consider it quite differently. In this instance the *Kaddish*, translated into orchestral terms, is principally a depiction of protest against the unfairness of death, while understanding the requirements for its acceptance.

Orchestra

Samuel Coleridge-Taylor   *(1875-1912)*

Danse nègre

☐ London Symphony Orchestra / Freeman (conductor) / Columbia M–32782

For a time, this light, bracingly rhythmic piece enjoyed pops-concert popularity. It is rarely heard nowadays so Paul Freeman's revival in Columbia's Black Composer Series focuses justifiable attention on the work once again.

Orchestra

Onaway! Awake, Beloved from *Hiawatha's Wedding Feast* (1898)

☐ London Symphony Orchestra / Brown (tenor) / Freeman (conductor) / Columbia M–32782

This luminous, lyrical love song is an extract from a three-part work. *Hiawatha's Wedding Feast*, composed in 1898, is the initial portion of Coleridge-Taylor's trilogy *Song of Hiawatha* for solo voices, chorus, and orchestra. Part 2, *The Death of Minnehaha*, was written the following year; the concluding piece in the set, *Hiawatha's Departure*, was composed in 1900. *Onaway! Awake, Beloved* is beautifully contoured and emerges with a spontaneity that is most compelling.

Brown has a glorious voice and he is supported by a finely detailed orchestral accompaniment.

Vocal

Voice and Orchestra

Michael Colgrass   (1932-   )

Percussion

Fantasy-Variations (1961)

☐ New Jersey Percussion Ensemble / Passaro (chromatic drums) / DesRoches (conductor) / Nonesuch 71291

There are a small number of compositions for a solo percussion instrument (usually the timpani) with orchestra, band, or chamber group. Colgrass's Fantasy-Variations is quite unique, calling for a solo percussion *with* percussion. The principal voice covers eight chromatically pitched drums, the "orchestra" consists of six players performing on various types of cymbals, triangles, cowbells, marimba, vibraphone, etcetera.

A lyrical overlay colors this piece. It is performed with a clear and sturdy control on the part of soloist and the assisting performers. Their secure technique matches that of the composer.

Percussion Music (1953)

☐ Price, Colgrass, Brown, and Smith (percussion) / Orion 7276

It is regrettable that Colgrass has given up the writing of percussion music despite a long series of successes in the medium. Himself a percussion virtuoso, which role he has also abandoned, he has an advantage that few composers of percussion music possess.

The concentration of means in Percussion Music is the equivalent of a work for four stringed instruments. Each of the four performers is assigned a single timbre, itself divided into four representations by a graduated set of sizes that give differing pitches. Thus the pitch range of the work is kept strictly to the sixteen sounds involved. These are obtained from four temple blocks and twelve membranous instruments: four each of toy drums, high tom-toms, and deep tom-toms. The harmonic and contrapuntal simulation is of vivid imagery; the four movements contrast, with a cyclic tie to regulate the total form. It is an outstanding contribution and is played with memorable artistry.

Three Brothers

☐ Kraus (conductor) / Golden Crest 4004 (monaural)

One of the most popular works in the repertoire for percussion ensemble, Colgrass's piece is an exciting, very individual essay in a difficult medium in which few composers have been successful.

The title refers to the highlighting of a trio of solo voices: bongo drums, snare drum, and timpani (the names of the performers are not given), supported by six other percussionists using maracas, cow bell, tambourine, cymbal, tom-toms, and a second set of timpani.

While the performance is only fair and the sound likewise, even a sampling of this superb work is worth owning. *Three Brothers* is truly a three-star conception.

Solo Instrument and Orchestra

Three Violins

Concertmasters, for Three Violins and Orchestra (1976)

☐ American Symphony Orchestra / Rudié, Yanagita, and Oakland (violins) / Akiyama (conductor) / Turnabout 34704

Colgrass's medium is exceedingly rare. One thinks immediately of Vivaldi with his concerti for two, three, and four violins, but only the equality of the solo voicing and some passing Vivaldian imitation toward the end of the work offer any relationship. Despite his admiration for the Venitian, Colgrass has other priorities.

There is a sense of serialism in the syntax but Colgrass avoids academic attitudinizing in all of his work and *Concertmasters* follows suit. Color temperament is principal to the music, which is dominated by full-blooded contemporaneous lyricism, and metaphorical virtuosity rather than the direct, blatant kind is required of the soloists.

Concertmasters avoids circusy capers as do the best of twentieth-century concerti. It does meet a listener head on with colorful material and instrumentational savvy. The effective performance documents these facts.

Variations for Four Drums and Viola (1957)

Chamber Music

☐ Fine (viola); Firth (drums) / RCA LSC-6184

A solid portrayal that fills the gap left by the deletion of the old MGM disc (E-3714) on which the composer played the drums with Emanuel Vardi, who commissioned the piece for recording, as the violist.

RCA's liner note gives no information whatsoever about the composition. Counting the introduction, there are eight divisions in the work. The drums are tunable with cardboard shells (like timpani). Esoteric in timbre combination, Colgrass's duo has a cleanness, an *ease* of sonority that is stimulating and refreshing. The lines are tonally clear-cut and sufficiently intense without going through the dramatics of the ultrachromatic cult. Naturally, rhythmic values are exploited, but such vitality is not a preoccupation. Contemporary to the hilt, unusual in coloristic formation, Colgrass's Variations are conceived in the same meaningful manner as any worthy variational set in the classic-romantic catalogue.

New People (1969)

Vocal

Voice and Instrumental Ensemble

☐ Bonazzi (mezzo-soprano); Basquin (piano); Schulman (viola) / Grenadilla GS-1010

Quietly simmering within the seven poems of *New People* (written by the composer who matches his unique musical abilities with just as unique poetic ones) are outlined the complications of twentieth-century life and its problems with I.D. cards, the CIA, computer directives, science, etcetera. Colgrass avoids the usual symbols to mark the clearly pointed text and moves it coloristically within his musical prose, a prose of intense lyricism without pat progressions and cadences and yet embracing tonality (but the harmonic approach is fully of the twentieth century).

A fine performance backed with splendid sound, good notes, and complete text. The featured star is Elaine Bonazzi. She is never anything but superb.

The Earth's a Baked Apple (1968)

Cantata and Oratorio

☐ New Orleans Philharmonic Symphony Orchestra and Xavier University Chorus and Students from Booker T. Washington High School and Cohen High School / Nice (conductor) / Orion 7268

Colgrass explains that his work is meant "to give people a musical opportunity to speak their thoughts on moral issues to their elders." He does so with his own poetry (rare for a composer to have such talent) in a dramatic synoptic comprehension of what goes on in life these days with its hustle, bustle, lunch gulping, speed, drink, being glued to the boob tube, stock market gambling, computerization, mechanization, and so on. The heartbeat of the piece can be found in these lines: "I'd never kill purposely/ It's those reflexes/ That worry me."

To tell this tale, an orchestra, jazz group, choral singing and speaking, and theatrical plotting are used. Written for youth concert presentation, *Baked Apple* is as powerful for swanky subscription audiences. Its message is terribly important, and it is perfectly partnered with the music.

Colgrass's work has remarkable consistency and concentration. Its compelling vitality (theatrically proper because of its objective) make it a small masterpiece. One must listen to it.

Marc-Antonio Consoli   (1941 -   )

Instrumental	***Sciuri novi***
Flute	☐ Szlek-Consoli (flute) / Composers Recordings SD–359

Sciuri novi means "New Flowers." And, "New Flowers" means new sounds: multiphonics, wobbling pitches, microtones, windy glissandi, and pizzicati-like ejaculations. A smidgen here and there reflects melodic folk tune curvatures.

Loaded to the full with effects, Consoli's piece is fascinating and not for a split second does it lose artistic significance. The trick here is no trickery at all, but musical meaning in depth from first sound to last. A rarity in the avant-garde flute literature.

The fantasy is realized magnificently by the fantastic playing of Elizabeth Szlek-Consoli.

Vocal	***Tre canzoni***
Voice and Instrumental Ensemble	☐ Charlston (soprano); Szlek-Consoli (flute); Tsutsumi (cello) / Composers Recordings SD–359

A combination of abstract, expressionistic musical gestures with poetry of the opposite type. The slight use of declamation by the vocalist is compelling.

Frederick Shepherd Converse   (1871 - 1940)

Orchestra

Endymion's Narrative: **Romance for Orchestra, Op. 10**

***Flivver Ten Million: A Joyous Epic* (1926)**

☐ Louisville Orchestra / Mester (conductor) / Louisville LS–753

Endymion is robustly romantic with some Wagnerian rhetoric. The other Converse piece (and that Converse has been recorded is a fat credit in Louisville's ledger) bears this complete proclamatory title: *Flivver Ten Million: A Joyous Epic Inspired by the Familiar Legend, "The Ten Millionth Ford is Now Serving Its Owner."* It does not avoid the programmatic course, but drives right on it, with such parts as *The Call to Labor, The Din of the Builders,* and *The Joy Riders.* To sharpen the orchestrational focus percussion is important, including a wind machine and a Ford auto horn. (If these were used they were not clearly recorded.)

The *Flivver* score does not move away from Converse's basic romantic stance, notwithstanding its motoristic requirements (a *Pacific 231* it isn't!). It does have a few constrained modern gestures.

Mester's direction of both these pieces conveys warm assertions. The Louisville group has advanced considerably since he took over the controls.

Arnold Cooke (1906-)

Sonata for Recorder, Violin, Violoncello, and Harpsichord (1965)

Chamber Music

☐ Dolmetsch-Schoenfeld Ensemble / Orion 73104

Cooke's music is clearly caught up in the stylistic world of Hindemith. This means, first, excellent and consistent controls that work out of tonal polarities. It also means contrapuntalism, especially apparent in the first pair of movements.

Fine achievement by this ensemble, which plays this arresting music with a happy assurance. The recorder player (Carl Dolmetsch) for the most part plays an alto instrument, but in the finale he changes to a sopranino type.

Deryck Cooke / Gustav Mahler. *See Mahler / Cooke.*

Paul Cooper (1926-)

Symphony No. 4 (*Landscape*) (1975)

Orchestra

☐ Houston Symphony Orchestra / Austin (trumpet); Crouse (viola); Hester (flute) / Jones (conductor) / Composers Recordings CRI-347

The outer movements have a mysterious format, a music that Sibelius might have written if he were a young composer living today. Pivotal to these divisions is the dynamic thrust of the central movement. Cooper's scoring (clearly defined in this expertly recorded performance) is fascinating in its subtleties of coloratives, spacings, combinations, aleatoric additives, and the use of concertino highlighting. Intense music, this.

Variants for Organ

Instrumental

Organ

☐ Craighead (organ) / Crystal S-858

The determination to avoid traditional practice (not to be confused with traditional harmonic practice) of writing for the organ is the insignia of Cooper's piece. There is a cross-examination of crumpled and crunched sounds, derived from the objective of using ''the totality of the instrument'' and employing ''a counterpoint of timbres rather than of successive pitches.''

Shed no crocodile tears over the fact that romantic browsing (which is what so many compositions for the organ are all about) has been eliminated. There are no mistakes or inadequacies in this musical cross-fire. The organ can certainly make a gorgeously powerful sound, and Cooper knows how to obtain it. So does Craighead, as he demonstrates in his excellent performance.

String Quartet No. 5 (*Umbrae*) (1973)

Chamber Music

☐ Shepherd Quartet / Composers Recordings SD-369

The coloristic commitment makes for a quality of kaleidoscopic sound motility. Although movements can be discerned, it is the diversified and stimulating use of timbre that captivates. Additional pigmentation is brought by the almost constant use of mutes.

The Shepherd Quartet are a deft performing team; their performance is certainly to be recommended.

David Cope   (1941-   )

Orchestra

Margins (1972)

☐ Performance Group / Baker (conductor) / Orion 75169

Pointillistic and shadowy detail applied to a mini-orchestra of trumpet, cello, percussion, and two pianos. The concentration of the material and the flitting aspects of the timbre play are intensely articulated.

Instrumental

Cello

Arena, for Cello and Tape (1974)

☐ Cope (cello) / Orion 75169

Tape with a single instrument is a category that has a substantial literature at this date. Most of the pieces, however, tend to overlay the tape on a sharply contrastive level. In Cope's piece the integration is specific. The beginning of *Arena* indicates the premise on which this partnered structural coloration will be applied.

Cope's impressive contribution demonstrates the possibilities existent in the duo medium of instrument and tape and deserves special attention (and praise).

Clarinet

Three Pieces for Unaccompanied Clarinet

☐ Russo (clarinet) / Capra 1203

The title brings to mind Stravinsky's similar one. The difference here is Cope's chromaticism and his greater reliance on rhythmic manipulation.

Piano

Iceberg Meadow

☐ Cope (piano) / Capra 1201

Iceberg Meadow is for a partially prepared piano. The materials used are pairs of nuts, wood screws, and bolts, a metal washer, and a coin (a dime). Pictorial expressivity is, of course, aided by this as well as by the use of a wet finger for a glissando on the strings and by applying the fingernail to simulate a scream. All of it, including tone clusters and a section using a mid-E pitch as a pedal, produce the proper musical temperature.

No doubt that Cope is a virtuoso in the field of contemporary piano music. No doubt either that he provides a definitive performance of his own music.

Piano Sonata No. 4

☐ Ignacio (piano) / Capra 1204

Opposites are focused strongly in Cope's Sonata. The first part has Bartókian urgency and vigor. A bit of this filters into the remainder which has principal allegiance to Webernian disjunctiveness.

Chamber Music

Triplum

☐ DiMartino (flute); Garst (piano) / Capra 1203

Cope's *Triplum* is a magnificent realization for the medium—an inspired contribution to its literature. Many works using special techniques are found to be containers in which the effects are so much gas being pumped into them. Not here. There is no special pleading in calling for the plucking, pinching, and striking of the piano strings, the hitting of the piano's crossbar, the bent flute pitches, the singing and whispering of the performers, and so on. All are justified qualities in terms of the tale, convincing synonyms that keep the ears concentrated, from the initial part built out of doublings of contrasted timbres to the concluding four measures which consist only of whisperings.

Cope's piece is given a rich, glowing, and perfectly balanced performance by Linda Marie DiMartino and Marilyn Mangold Garst. The work was written for and dedicated to them and they have repaid the composer in full with their masterly presentation.

Aaron Copland (1900-)

Appalachian Spring, **Ballet Suite (1945)** *Orchestra*

☐ New York Philharmonic / Bernstein (conductor) / Columbia MS-6355

If any one work exemplifies Copland, typifies the man's facts and fancies; if one wishes to know *what* is Copland's music, his general creative method, *Appalachian Spring* will supply the answers. It is music that vibrates from beginning to end with Coplandesque spirit. The musical prose of the composer, as well as his rhythms, the nostalgic open-air quality of his retrospections, and their homespun tenderness, all come to the fore. *Appalachian Spring* is American to the core. Copland's music flows like a *Moldau,* its tunes breathe the simplicity and spirit of folklore, absorbed to such an extent that it has become the composer's own.

Composed in 1944 as a ballet for Martha Graham (see under *Ballet*), this work was originally for thirteen instruments. In its transformation into concert music, through orchestral amplification, it has gained much yet the tissuelike transparency of the original has been preserved. It stands as Copland's number one work.

Bernstein's rendition is super in quality with magnificent playing that blends tension with repose. With other Copland music (here it is coupled with *El Salón México*), it is available on Columbia MS-7521 and MG-3007. With works by Barber, Gershwin, Ives, and Piston it is included in a fourth packaging on Columbia MG-31155.

Billy the Kid, **Ballet Suite (1940)**

☐ London Symphony Orchestra / Copland (conductor) / Everest 3015

True Copland flavor and American savor. The connecting link here is native speech rendered in Copland's own type of slang. One is reminded of the relationship, for example, between New Orleans barrelhouse and Stan Kenton's "progressive" style; pure folk data are just as apposite to what emerges from Copland's artistic strainer. Aside from its indigenous subject, and a scenario made for rootin', tootin', and shootin', the musical veracity and the verve of *Billy* make it a unique contribution to musical Americana.

Not the most recent edition, Copland's still rides into first place by its avoidance of overregistration (found in Bernstein's version in three different issues on Columbia MS-6175, M-31823, and MG-30071), indication of Westernese (not heard in Ormandy's reading on RCA LSC-3184), and lean smoothness (lacking in the Abravanel disc on Westminster Gold 8170), and by its clean and direct dimensions. Nothing is roughed up or made blatant. In that manner *Billy* under Copland finds its greatest strength.

Connotations **(1962)**

☐ New York Philharmonic / Bernstein (conductor) / Columbia MS-7431

Connotations was commissioned by the New York Philharmonic to help celebrate its opening season at Lincoln Center. The work shared the program that baptized the hall with works by Beethoven, Mahler, and Vaughan Williams. Recorded live, Copland's piece was included in a special album, *First Performance–Lincoln Center* (on Columbia L2L-1007). This recording is its re-issue and even contains the applause at the end. It serves no purpose here and what was true to the original occasion is only distracting on a straightforward recording.

Copland's scoring is for a Strauss-sized orchestra of fourteen winds, fifteen brasses, six percussionists, piano, and strings. The Philharmonic and Bernstein, to whom the work was dedicated, return the compliment with a thorough performance that brings out Copland's use of serialism in his general style.

Dance Symphony (1925)

☐ London Symphony Orchestra / Copland (conductor) / Columbia MS-7223

Copland's work is an extract from the unpublished ballet *Grogh*. The symphonic detachment was a result of expediency. RCA Victor had offered a $25,000 (!) prize for a new symphonic work. Copland had not completed the composition he wished to enter and therefore extracted three dances from *Grogh* and titled them collectively Dance Symphony. The judges found their task somewhat difficult and split the prize money among four composers, with Copland receiving $5,000.

The opus is a commixture of Debussy impressionism and Stravinsky ballet. Not until the final section does the composer's individuality break through; it does so there by way of jazz infiltrations, heard in the nervous, asymmetric rhythms. Even though the music does not display what has come to be recognized as Copland's personality, it is far from being a student opus.

The terms of the 1929 Victor contest included the recording of the prize-winning work. None of the five pieces (two by Robert Russell Bennett, and one each by Ernest Bloch and Louis Gruenberg, in addition to Copland's) ever received this promised reward. It took thirty-one years before just one of these five works received recorded documentation, and then not in the United States but Japan!

The Japanese performance is creditable; the engineering plays tricks, however, with the heavy and loud passages. (It can be heard, for the curious, on Composers Recordings 129, with Akeo Watanabe conducting the Japan Philharmonic Orchestra.) Copland's version of Copland's Dance Symphony is thrice superior.

Danzón Cubano (1944)

☐ New York Philharmonic / Bernstein (conductor) / Columbia MS-6514

Originally for two pianos (see under *Instrumental: two pianos*), the work represents Copland the transcriber (not too often his practice) and Copland the temporary creative expatriate. It has no hyperbole and requires a tightness of statement. The performance is satisfying.

(Also in a collection conducted by Bernstein on Columbia MS-6871.)

Down a Country Lane (1962)

John Henry (1940)

Letter from Home (1944)

☐ London Symphony Orchestra / Copland (conductor) / Columbia M-33586

Short pieces, recognizable from the opening measures as being by Aaron Copland. All give a pleasing sense of immediacy. A folksy rhythmic urge surrounds *John Henry,* the other two pieces have the Coplandesque outdoor climate.

Fine recordings in all cases.

El Salón México (1936)

☐ New York Philharmonic / Bernstein (conductor) / Columbia MS-6355

A colorful essay in Latinate-Coplandesque virtuosity which has always tempted the conductors (and their E flat clarinet players). The music is a "pops" positive, but is not merely fanciful, displaying the composer's ability to synthesize any ingredient that he desires to use. Though not "American" and not one of his most impressive works, Copland's transmutation of Mexican colloquialisms is comparable to the foreign musical temper beautifully illustrated in the Frenchman Chabrier's well-known *España.*

Rather than being a mere functionary with a baton, Bernstein functions almost as a proxy creator. In music as graphic as this, such individuality is permissible. Stunning reproduction.

Columbia offers the work in four other packages. Two are all-Copland (MS-7521 and MG-30071) as is the disc listed above, which is coupled with *Appalachian Spring.* The other two are of the miscellaneous type (MS-6441 and MGP-13).

Inscape (1967)

☐ New York Philharmonic / Bernstein (conductor) / Columbia MS-7431

Inscape, suggesting a "quasi-mystical illumination, a sudden perception of that deeper pattern, order and unity which gives meaning to external forces," partakes of variational treatment. Here, serialism is bound in with Copland's nonserial mannerisms: sparse spacings, woodwind verticalities, tightly punctuated chords, and pandiatonic-like spaced intervallic movements. Lyricism is the great strength in *Inscape;* the serial slang merely serves as a coadjuvant enrichment of its language.

It is in this work that twelve-tone procedures become more attuned to Copland's fundamental style, or perhaps Copland is here more attuned to twelve-tone processes. Either way, *Inscape* is worthwhile and gains support from an excellent presentation.

Music for a Great City (1964)

☐ London Symphony Orchestra / Copland (conductor) / Columbia M-30374

An accommodation to programmatic detail, not of the inch-by-inch pictorial variety but by balancing it (assuagement, it might be called) by the reverse. Thus *Skyline* and *Subway Jam* are direct and urbanistic in tone, clank and clang, while *Night Thoughts* and *Toward the Bridge* are of general content.

Such creative diplomacy does not play false with cohesive style or with Coplandesque language, especially in movements 1 and 3. The playing by the Londoners (the work was commissioned by that outfit in celebration of its sixtieth anniversary season and is dedicated "to the members of the orchestra") is gratefully sympathetic.

Music for Movies (1942)

☐ New Philharmonia Orchestra / Copland (conductor) / Columbia M-33586

All of Copland's motion-picture music retains his personal flavor and creative quintessence, even though there is a sparseness of texture. The reasons for his success as a movie composer are here illustrated. The once functional music is haunting and cannot easily be differentiated from his concert-hall compositions; indeed quite an achievement. All of the settings—sections from one documentary and two commercial film scores (including music from the famed score for *Of Mice and Men*)—are real jewels.

The playing has fine distinction. Copland conducting Copland requires no apologies.

Music for the Theatre (1925)

☐ New York Philharmonic / Bernstein (conductor) / Columbia MS-6698

Read: "for the imaginary theatre," since no actual dramatic occasion is involved but simply a view of jazz onstage. The opus shows Copland working from the source and amalgamating the sound marks of the racy twenties into his music. It is his analogy to the period, written with no cold, academic attitude. The syncopations and other rhythmic flashes make an exhilarating essay including delineations of "burley-cue" and the night-club *viveur* (though the movement titles are very staid: Prologue, Dance, Interlude, Burlesque, and Epilogue).

This is the kind of music that is made to order for Bernstein. He directs it so that it has everything a person would want to hear.

Orchestral Variations (1957)

☐ London Symphony Orchestra / Copland (conductor) / Columbia M-31714

A transcription of the 1930 Piano Variations (see under: *Instrumental: piano*), made twenty-seven years after the fact. While a certain uncompromising hardness of piano texture is lost by the nonpercussiveness of woodwind and string instruments, the orchestral version is convincing. Copland's scoring has massivity, tensility, and strength. An assertive work.

The Variations served to fulfill a Louisville Orchestra commission and was recorded by that organization. (It is still available in a monophonic setting on Louisville 59-1.) As would be expected, this stereo performance with the composer at the helm is far superior to the initial recording.

Our Town — Suite (1940)

☐ Utah Symphony Orchestra / Abravanel (conductor) / Vanguard 2115

Music from the score for the film based on the famous Thornton Wilder play. The hymnodic beauty of Copland's work haunts the listener by its simple artistic truths. Abravanel shapes the score impeccably. (It is also included on Vanguard S-348.)

An Outdoor Overture (1938)

☐ Utah Symphony Orchestra / Abravanel (conductor) / Vanguard 2115

Copland style that hits the ears right from the proclamatory initial phrase. Juicy and fresh—and thoroughly outdoorish. Abravanel's performance is clean-colored, poetically effective, rhythmically tight. (It is also on Vanguard S-348.)

Preamble for a Solemn Occasion

☐ London Symphony Orchestra / Copland (conductor) / Columbia M-31714

The first version of Copland's *Preamble* (composed on commission from the National Broadcasting Company for the United Nations to mark the first anniversary of the adoption of the Declaration of Human Rights) included a narrator's part with words chosen from the Preamble to the United Nations Charter. The recording heard here is an alternate version without any text.

The *Preamble* is proclamatory, with large-phrased stately statements. One is reminded of the *Fanfare for the Common Man*, accompanied by an enveloping lyricism.

Rodeo — Suite from the Ballet (1943)

☐ London Symphony Orchestra / Copland (conductor) / Columbia M–30114

(Occasionally, another title is used for this work: Four Dance Episodes from *Rodeo*.)
Of all Copland's ballets *Rodeo* has the most inventive orchestration. The play of textures through the thickening and thinning of chordal combinations, together with the dovetailing and juggling of accents on the thematic lines is acutely perceptive. In this way Copland dressed his rowdy music for Agnes de Mille's lightly humorous ballet.

Copland's performance takes top place and marks one of the very best realizations of his music that he has recorded. The boldness and striking quality of the work demand that a conductor fully unbend. Copland does exactly that. (The release is also included in a jumbo all-Copland package on Columbia D3M–33720.)

Short Symphony (1933)

☐ London Symphony Orchestra / Copland (conductor) / Columbia MS–7223

The Short Symphony was completed in 1933. Its exceedingly difficult rhythms were not (and still, at this very late date, are not) attractive to most conductors, who so often deprive a new work of sufficient rehearsal time in order to polish and repolish their own interpretation of a hackneyed item in the orchestral repertory. The Short Symphony is one of Copland's consummate compositions and it is pitiful and frustrating that this work remains pushed to the side, hardly ever performed. This release marks the initial and sole recording. The big-league conductors are guilty of artistic indifference on the concert stage as well as in the recording studio.

Germinal material is paramount in the construction. The music is motivally synthesized from the start, not developed into strung-out thematic statements or led to associated themes. Quite often, the main impetus is rhythmic, the very opposite of grandiose. In the final part Copland exhibits jazz in long pants. Relentless rhythmic virtuosity (magnificently projected by the Londoners) stems from his study of this musical vernacularism. Conclusive music of significance, performed in a superclass manner. This is an important recording from every point of view.

(For a transcription by Copland of this work, see under *Chamber Music:* Sextet for String Quartet, Clarinet, and Piano, p. 440.)

Statements for Orchestra (1935)

☐ London Symphony Orchestra / Copland (conductor) / Columbia M–30374

Copland's six-movement Statements is a real adventure. But it has not met many adventurous conductors and almost repeats the ''stay away from the score'' history of his Short Symphony.

This is truly an abstract work, despite the titles—*Militant, Cryptic, Dogmatic, Subjective, Jingo,* and *Prophetic*—given by Copland ''as an aid to the public in understanding what the composer had in mind.'' All the musical elements, from pitch level to dynamic intensity, are as poised as the many steel cables that separately and together hold a suspension bridge in place. It is a music of impressions, without the exterior effects and influences this word usually connotes. The descriptions are *general*, the arena and décor against which the music performs.

This is Copland's second recording of the work (he has been the only one to record it). The first time was also with the London Symphony Orchestra and goes back to 1958 (Everest 3015). Just as efficient a performance, but understandably, not as good a sound.

Suite from the Film *The Red Pony* (1948)

☐ New Philharmonia Orchestra / Copland (conductor) / Columbia M–33586

The music from the film *The Red Pony* (not as successful as Copland's other motion-picture scores) is in summer-afternoon Copland style; the sonorities captivate but are restrained. Nevertheless, such musical economy does not mean simple black-and-white playing, with loud or soft dynamic planes and nothing else. What this music needs—tenderness and strength with discreet handling of the varying weights (disposed either dynamically or texturally)—Copland, the conductor, obtains. These were absent from the only previous recording (an old Decca disc, made by the Little Orchestra Society, conducted by Thomas Scherman). The call number of this old monaural item was DL–9616; the title, incidentally, was Children's Suite from *The Red Pony*.

Suite from the Opera *The Tender Land* (1954)

☐ Boston Symphony Orchestra / Copland (conductor) / RCA LSC–2401

The Tender Land has zig-zagged its way all over the musical map but not into the repertoire. It began as a two-act affair, premiered by the New York City Opera in that form, then underwent revisions (in the first act) and with that refurbishing was produced in Tanglewood. Further revisions and expansion into three acts followed, and was so presented at the Oberlin Conservatory.

At one time an abridgment of the final version was on Columbia (MS–6814). With its deletion the only music on disc is this three-part orchestral suite: Introduction and Love Music (the Introduction pertains to Act III), *Party Scene,* and Finale: *The Promise of Living.* It is sufficient to show Copland in his American stance, with reminders of the style of *Appalachian Spring*.

Symphonic Ode

☐ London Symphony Orchestra / Copland (conductor) / Columbia M–31714

The Symphonic Ode was composed for and dedicated to the Boston Symphony Orchestra on the occasion of its fiftieth anniversary. It was first performed in February 1932 with Koussevitzky conducting. Copland then revised the work for the orchestra's seventy-fifth anniversary and rededicated it in memory of Koussevitzky. The new version also was premiered by the Boston Symphony Orchestra in February 1956, with Munch conducting.

Formal pigeonholing in a large sense makes this Copland piece fall into trinal divisions, slow-fast-slow, but actually one can discern five sections knitted together in alternate speed rates. The dominating mood is declarative, proclamatory, punctuatively blocked.

The performance has guts, but it also raises some questions as to pitch perfection in the upper register. Nonetheless, for the frictional scoring characteristic of the work a bit of intonational impurity doesn't do too much harm. Then too, the Ode is one of Copland's major works, and this represents the only recording.

Symphony No. 3 (1946)

☐ London Symphony Orchestra / Copland (conductor) / Everest 3018
☐ New York Philharmonic / Bernstein (conductor) / Columbia MS-6954

The Third Symphony is Copland's major production in the area of absolute music and displays his desire to be other than a folk-symphonic statistician. It has staying power; it reveals a composer who has the knowledge to write in a classical-romantic manner though still with quiet virtuosity. This music is tightly bound, at the same time it has length; it is not shallow, and is without the usual glittering sheen which rubs off easily. In a word, this *is* a symphony. It is Copland's example of expansively wrought music, written without stage directions or a motion-picture scenario to constrain him. (The beginning of the finale of the symphony is based on Copland's *Fanfare for the Common Man*, which exists as a short, separate piece (see under *Brass Ensemble*).

Despite the composer-conductor surety, Everest's release is not the final word on the symphony, nor can any one version be that for a work of comparable breadth and importance. Bernstein has a thrilling way with this work and yet where Copland moves he applies the brakes and vice versa. The disparity indicates that no important symphony has its single interpretational answer.

Three Latin-American Sketches

☐ New Philharmonia Orchestra / Copland (conductor) / Columbia M-33269

A good, somewhat subtle understanding of Latinate idiomatic inflections. Though of minor importance in the Copland catalogue the set has distinctive values, realized in this well-balanced essay.

Two Pieces for String Orchestra (1928)

String Orchestra

☐ London Symphony Orchestra / Copland (conductor) / Columbia MS-7375

The initial version of this work (see under *Chamber Music,* Two Pieces for String Quartet, p. 440) was first heard in New York on May 6, 1928. In the following summer Copland expanded the work for string orchestra. In that form it was first presented on December 14, 1928, with Koussevitzky and the Boston Symphony Orchestra. In Copland's straightforward transcription nothing is changed; the work is telling in either setting.

Of course, the composer should know best. Still, there are plenty of arguments that in terms of interpretation he often doesn't or that he changes his mind after the creative fact. You make your choice. When comparing the two recorded performances available, the one for quartet and the one above for string orchestra, the writer found both excellent and satisfying, well-played and well-realized. However, a substantial time difference (more emphasized because the work is not of huge size) exists between Copland's direction and the quartet's tempi decisions. The quartet comes in at 8:59, Copland's at 10:09. Since the scoring is different, the best decision is to obtain both recordings! (One final point. The heavier textural weight of a string orchestra could well lead to a composer taking a slower tempo in his conducting.)

Fanfare for the Common Man (1942)

Brass Ensemble

☐ Members of the Philadelphia Orchestra / Ormandy (conductor) / Columbia MS-6684

Eugene Goossens, the conductor of the Cincinnati Symphony Orchestra, during World War II commissioned a number of American composers to write fanfares to begin his con-

435

certs. Copland's contribution (written in the fall of 1942) was one of the most successful, and he thought sufficiently well of the piece to incorporate it into his Symphony No. 3 (see under *Orchestra*). There the *Fanfare* serves as the basis for the introduction to the finale of the work.

Ormandy's is a tremendously exciting execution. The dynamic differences in the percussion, especially in regard to the gong (precisely registered in Copland's score), are very telling here.

The *Fanfare* is included in three other Columbia albums: MS–7289, MS–7521, and MG–31190, which is a two-record issue.

Solo Instrument and Orchestra

Clarinet

Concerto for Clarinet and String Orchestra (with Harp and Piano) (1948)

☐ Columbia Symphony Orchestra / Goodman (clarinet) / Copland (conductor) / Columbia MS–6805

Copland derives the concerto from lyrical, jazz, and south-of-the-border materials. The form of the work is interesting, as it consists of slow and fast movements, joined by a cadenza for the solo instrument.

The work was commissioned by Benny Goodman, so he is fully at home in playing it. (In this release it is programmed with works by Bernstein, Gould, and Stravinsky, all featuring Goodman as soloist. It has also been issued on Columbia MS–6497, where it is paired with Copland's *Old American Songs*.)

Organ

Symphony for Organ and Orchestra (1924)

☐ New York Philharmonic / Biggs (organ) / Bernstein (conductor) / Columbia MS–7058

There are some who will insist that Copland's Symphony (completed in 1924) is a youthful indiscretion. That Copland himself had second thoughts about the piece is proven by the version he made four years later for orchestra without organ (titled First Symphony). In 1934 a setting of the first movement (Prelude) was made for small orchestra. However, the redraft would only seem to emphasize the practical conclusion: symphonies for orchestra and organ (Saint-Saëns notwithstanding) are not very movable merchandise.

The temper, harmonies, orchestral diction, and rhythms are full of Coplandesque spice, especially the rhythm, which is drenched in tensile, springy, beautifully nervous juices.

The slightly disappointing report is the rather uninspired use of the organ. It mainly serves as a contrastive coloration, but when it appears it is like a poor relative of the orchestral winds. Biggs's performance is certainly satisfactory, but because of the organ's neutrality it gives him as much highlighting as a second fiddler in a large symphonic ensemble.

Perhaps Copland will make a disc of the work, since he is presumably recording his complete output for Columbia. Until such time, this release will have to serve.

Piano

Concerto for Piano and Orchestra (1926)

☐ Symphony of the Air / Wild (piano) / Copland (conductor) / Vanguard 2094

Written in 1926, Copland's Concerto does not have the imitative, *Mittel-Europa* jazz flavors that attend much music written in the 1920s, especially the products of the French school. This music was partially bankrupt, a parallel to the economic depression of the same period. It falls very flat to ears attuned to more sophisticated jazz styles. Copland's opus proves that jazz is best served in its birthplace.

Within Copland's creative spirit is a synchronistic method that gives the meaning of traditional jazz new gloss. Below all of this music is a composer "taking off," with no pretensions. Copland's pleasures include very exciting timbres—a beautifully raucous soprano sax, and a horseplay piano cadenza that equals a huge jazz "break" given a free head of steam. Copland's piano concerto is novel and daring, a completely nationalistic composition, moistened with the dewdrops of international musical language.

Earl Wild is one of the great naturals in the pianistic world and his playing has always displayed beauty and imagination. He depicts the score in the most polished and convincing manner, aided by guaranteed orchestral playing. This triple combination of talents is a real winner.

Quiet City (1940)
Trumpet

☐ Chamber Orchestra of Copenhagen / Ghitalla (trumpet) / Moriarty (conductor) / Cambridge 2823

This searching, nostalgic, almost threnodic music, originally served as a piece of incidental music for Irwin Shaw's play of the same name. The play passed into oblivion after a pair of performances, but Copland's sensitive score has proven its lasting qualities. It receives a peak performance here. (The fine English horn player certainly deserves being given credit.)

The Cat and the Mouse (1919)
Instrumental

☐ Silverman (piano) / Orion 7280
Piano

Early-early Copland, his first published work (1920), when he was studying with Rubin Goldmark. The title gives the story line; the subtitle, *Scherzo humoristique,* makes further briefing unnecessary. Silverman knows exactly what to do with Copland's piano cartoon.

Four Piano Blues (1949)

☐ Copland (piano) / New World Records NW–277 (monaural)
☐ Silverman (piano) / Orion 7280

Copland's consideration of his own music (in the first three parts) is cool and slightly more intimate than Silverman's. In the last piece (marked *with bounce*) Copland delivers sharper and more telling ejections. It's all a matter of performance staging since the timings are almost identical (a total of a mere fifteen seconds faster in Silverman's case). The sound is a smidgen better on Orion; to be expected, since Copland's performance was recorded in 1949 and originally released on Decca/London.

However, if you want *the* very best performance ever recorded of this open-hearted music with light kick, then seek out the Dot Records album *The Masters Write Jazz,* with Leo Smit at the keyboard. This deleted issue (DLP–3111) has even better sound than the two listed above, and Smit's playing is top-flight all the way.

Night Thoughts – Homage to Ives

☐ Fierro (piano) / Delos DEL–25436

This is the premiere recording of the piece Copland composed for the Van Cliburn Competition. It has Copland's usual poetic penetration with the slightest touch of Ivesian timbres.

Passacaglia (1922)

☐ Silverman (piano) / Orion 7280

Not counting discarded juvenilia, this composition, written in 1922, is Copland's fifth recognized opus. An eight-measure subject is the basis for eight variations, each considered clearly and differently in textural terms.

Silverman grasps the aesthetic unrest of the piece, illustrated by a mélange of romantic and latter-day sounds.

Piano Fantasy (1957)

Piano Variations (1930)

☐ Masselos (piano) / Odyssey 32160040

The Fantasy is a huge work. It has tremendous power and does not diligently court its listeners with snug tunes and harmonies. This steely-strong stuff is the "other" Copland, its intentions nonrepresentational, its sheer musical shapes the sole documentation. Copland speaks of the composition's "spontaneous and unpremeditated sequence of 'events.'" In no way does this result in cold technical manipulation. Within a thirty-minute scope the "events" produce an event as rich and meaningful as a late Beethoven opus. It is a masterpiece.

The intensity and luminosity that William Masselos brings to this work exemplifies interpretative mastery. No other pianist has been able to match it.

The earlier Piano Variations are in the same category. It is a view of Copland in a very austere and uncompromising attitude, the composition being the epitome of concentration and logic. Each sound is part of the argument; there are no ornamental fillers. Though not making use of serial technique, dealing with twelve tones, Copland reminds one of the Schoenbergian system, with a single unit of four sounds giving all the substance for the work's dyestuff. (Copland made a symphonic setting of the opus, under the title Orchestral Variations. See under *Orchestra*.)

Again, Masselos is magnificent in his conception. His logic is just as effective as Copland's.

Sonata for Piano (1941)

☐ Somer (piano) / Composers Recordings 171

Compared to the sternness of the Piano Variations, this is warm, rich-hued music, with a nice assortment of rhythmic spicing in the jazzy middle movement. There are a good number of contemporary piano sonatas and a fair total have been recorded, but few have touched the high point Copland's achieves. The sonata shows Copland, the sophisticated folklorist, being assimilated by Copland, the composer of profound absolute music.

Therefore, a merely good performance is not sufficient. The pianist must be sensitive to this subtle creative condition and Hilde Somer is, and then some. Her performance vibrates at the proper velocity and she can turn a phrase that is acutely sculpted and fully meaningful. The recording represents pianism of real presence.

Two Pianos

Danzón Cubano (1942)

☐ Copland and Smit (pianos) / New World Records NW–277 (monaural)

This is the original setting, created in 1942, to commemorate the twentieth anniversary of the League of Composers. Copland then orchestrated the piece two years later (see under *Orchestra*).

Despite the monaural setting and with second-class sound (the recording is a transfer originally issued by Concert Hall in 1947), this is the performance to own. The tight pilotage of the sounds and the rhythmic conduct are just what they should be. Enjoy!

Ukelele Serenade (1926)

☐ Steiner (violin); Berfield (piano) / Orion 74160

Semi-sophisticated jazz (Copland at the age of twenty-six), the second of a pair of pieces written in Paris between January and April of 1926. A Negro blues song is connoted by slides and slithering quarter-tones. Steiner and Berfield do the piece to a turn.

Duo for Flute and Piano (1971)

☐ Shaffer (flute); Copland (piano) / Columbia M–32737

Like the early ballet works, *Quiet City* and *Appalachian Spring,* Copland's Duo (written in 1971) expresses contiguity with the classical school in respect to its harmonic continuums. However, there are many touches more affiliated with the later works. Regardless, the basic material of the outer movements proclaims the "made exclusively by Aaron Copland" label.

The late Elaine Shaffer's tone quality is somewhat pinched and not fully satisfactory in outward spill. However, this is the only recording available.

Sonata for Violin and Piano (1943)

☐ Stern (violin); Copland (piano) / Columbia M–32737
☐ Glenn (violin); Somer (piano) / Composers Recordings 171

Positives first. Stern's tone is open-hearted, his playing intense. Copland's part in the performance is beyond any criticism (and not only because he's the composer but also because of his pianistic understanding of that part in his duo sonata). Carroll Glenn's playing is even better in style (of cooler temperature) than Stern's and Hilde Somer's keyboard work is set at the highest level for concentrating on the musical purpose. Now, negatives. This music represents a chamber music medium and Stern's forwardness is sometimes out of bounds. In the finale Stern's rhythmic sets are punched (Glenn's are much better, projected in a trampolinish manner). However, the piano sound of the CRI disc is edgy and clangy. It is this matter of engineering that puts the Glenn-Somer edition in second place.

Some points on two other versions that are available. The better of these is by Myron Sandler and Lowndes Maury on Crystal S–361. Sandler does quite well, but his broad conception does not meet approval when it is applied to outlining the pulsatile points of the finale; Maury is only an average pianist. Crystal's sound is good, its production is annoying, with one movement on side A, requiring a turn over of the disc for the balance of the sonata. Jaime Laredo and Ann Schein play the work on Desto 6439. Laredo plays in an intimate fashion and that's all to the good, but the finale is not sharply pointed and the rhythmic shapes lack the sharp bite needed for clarity. The piano sound is not full and when it is at a high dynamic, lacks body. Further, Desto's disc has no band separating movement 1 from the remainder of the work (movements 2 and 3 are played without pause.)

Vitebsk, Study on a Jewish Theme – Trio for Piano, Violin, and Cello (1929)

☐ Silverstein (violin); Eskin (cello); Frank (piano) / RCA LSC–6167

Despite the fact that a creative artist will always, in some manner, show his heritage, Copland has never deliberately drawn upon his Jewish ancestry, save in this one work. The rhapsodic emanation, the declamation, cantillations, and shofar of the synagogue are stated overtly and by implication. Although any musical work keyed to idiomatic expression has certain limitations, this does not keep it from having formal unity. Nor are biting dissonances stylistically incorrect in a composition in the Jewish manner around 1929.

There have been five recordings of Copland's trio. A vibrantly projected performance was on the Decca label (DL–10126), given by the New Amsterdam Trio. If it can be found in the byways of the out-of-print specialty shops, grab it, since it is the best of the lot. Still available is the mono University of Oklahoma Trio edition (University of Oklahoma Recordings-1). Don't grab it, since it is the poorest of the lot. The CRI release (171), played by Glenn, Somer, and McCracken, never gets off the ground because of the smoothed-out, reticent string playing, and the sound engineering is way below par.

Copland and two members of the Juilliard Quartet (Earl Carlyss and Claus Adam) join in a performance of the trio on Columbia M–30376. Granted that a composer's performance participation (as an instrumentalist or as a conductor) makes available permanent interpretative documentation, nonetheless there is no obligation to accept such and rule out exceptions. Inner discovery is part of the re-creative art process. It is in this respect that the trio from the Boston Symphony Chamber Players communicates much more vividly the intensity, passion, and percussive disturbances that are fielded in Copland's score. Put it this way: the Copland-Carlyss-Adam team gives a fervent rendition, the Bostonians' performance is of boiling registration.

Quartet for Piano and Strings (1950)

☐ Members of the Juilliard Quartet / Copland (piano) / Columbia M–30376

Although this work has precise formal details, it is not austere, nor is it forbidding and introverted, or hedonistic and extroverted. It is difficult to play and asks almost as much from the listener as from the performers. Copland employs a modified tone-row technique and each movement derives from a single theme. He relishes color in this piano quartet; in fact, he employs more instrumental techniques here than in any of his other chamber pieces.

This is a major-league recording. It offers persuasive evidence that Copland's work is a significant addition to contemporary chamber music.

Two Pieces for String Quartet (1928)

☐ Kohon Quartet / Vox SVBX–5305

One of the results of the *volte-face* that took place after the compositional thicknesses of the late romantic period and the evocative leanness of impressionism was a refurbishment of musical materials in the direction of simplicity and nonscholastic classicism. In the twenties this produced music sharply engrossed in contemporary manners, morals, and postwar freedom. Copland was conscious of these elements, and jazz was one of the ways of affirming a new structural force.

In 1923 Copland composed his quartet *Rondino*, pairing it with the *Lento molto*, written in 1928. In this format the work received its first performance in New York in May of the same year. Both pieces have the rhythmic precipitance (quieter in the *Lento molto*) that defines jazz. The first of these short pieces is an excellent example of sparseness; the effect is of a concert blues. The *Rondino* has jazz implications joined with a slightly nervous quality.

The performance on this release is efficient and efficacious. (For another version see under *String Orchestra:* Two Pieces for String Orchestra.)

Sextet for String Quartet, Clarinet, and Piano (1937)

☐ Juilliard Quartet / Wright (clarinet); Copland (piano) / Columbia M–30376

This is the alternative version Copland made of his Short Symphony (see under *Orchestra:* Short Symphony). Since the orchestral work was being bypassed because of its extreme rhythmic difficulties, Copland prepared another creative solution. Not that any of the problems of performance were phased out, but six instrumentalists could cope more readily with the technical problems than one hundred players and a conductor. Shifting to the intimate democracy of chamber music proposed a more optimistic potential. Copland judged correctly.

Columbia's star-studded cast polishes off the work with zest and understanding. An exciting presentation. (This is the second time around for the Juilliard foursome. Back in the mono days they recorded the work—they had a different second violinist then—with Leonid Hambro, pianist, and David Oppenheim, clarinetist. It, too, was a first-rate recording. If it can be located in any of the shops that specialize in out-of-print recordings it's worth owning as another edition—Columbia ML-4492.)

Nonet for Strings (1960)

☐ Columbia String Ensemble / Copland (conductor) / Columbia M-32737

It's Copland, all of him in triadic and polytriadic discourse, yet a Copland more somber and turgid than he's ever been. Part of this is due to the emphasis on nonsoprano instruments, the Nonet's formation consisting of three each of violins, violas, and cellos. But the heavy textural nub—so opposite from the usual open-airiness and leanness of Copland's music—is the result of the harmonic weights. And harmony is dominant, especially in the terminal divisions, forming a continuity of chordal timbre that is seamless. There is lighter, motile contrast in the central section, but the heart of the piece is found in the outer sections.

The performance impresses by its emphasis on the dark-tinged quality of the work, but it disappoints in that it overemphasizes the disparity of the instrumental weights and is bottom-heavy. If that is what Copland wants, one accepts it, though it does partly falsify what is seen on the score page. Nevertheless, the Nonet recording is important Copland, if only for the special individuality it represents in his catalogue.

Dirge in Woods (1954)

☐ McCollum (tenor); Biltcliffe (piano) / Desto 6411/2

Vocal

Voice with Accompaniment

This piece was composed in honor of Nadia Boulanger to mark the fiftieth anniversary of her teaching career. Despite the title, it is not threnodic but rather philosophic. Importantly, the piano part is no mere peg on which the voice part is hung. It fulfills Ned Rorem's astute precept that the piano must give "sustenance," provide "a fresh dimension," and form "a twin" of equal importance to the voice.

Song (1927)

☐ Beardslee (soprano); Helps (piano) / New World Records NW-243

Copland's Song (the text is by E. E. Cummings) is exceedingly expressive but does not convey the Copland style as it is generally recognized. One writer has tagged the piece as an "atonal experiment," which is nonsense. It is chromatic but not of tonal vacuity.

The sensitive severity that covers the song is given full justice by Beardslee and is beautifully understood in the piano playing of Helps.

Twelve Poems of Emily Dickinson (1950)

☐ Addison (soprano); Copland (piano) / Columbia M-30375

This is an exceedingly attractive song thesis of both earnestness and almost fragile beauty. One prophesies a long life for this cycle.

Addison sings with pitch precision and ideal intonation. She is never guilty of dissolved diction. (Yes, one knows texts should be supplied with recordings; but why one *must* follow printed words in order to understand a vocalist is beyond comprehension.) Good vocal style and, naturally, Copland's aid at the piano is not to be overlooked. Credit Columbia for especially high fidelity.

Choral

Chorus Alone

In the Beginning (1947)

☐ New England Conservatory Chorus / Miller (mezzo-soprano) / Copland (conductor) / Columbia M-30375

The creation of the world according to Copland. Although the music forms a single extended movement, each of the six days involved in the tale is marked by a different mood, introduced by a solo mezzo-soprano who serves as a singing narrator. The style is Coplandesque, including some light jazz touches, with integration of material from the old American school of hymnody.

There are three recorded performances of this music of almost objective detachment; yet by its reticence it conveys a sense of religious belief, if not an especially deep belief. Columbia's is by far the fullest in meaning, the warmest and most resonant. Gregg Smith's group (on Everest 3129) is good, but the soloist is too contained; the Whikehart organization (on Lyrichord 7124) comes in last place and so does the mezzo. Proper justice, perhaps, since only Columbia gives complete individual credit to the solo voice (none whatsoever on Lyrichord, while Marjorie MacKay's name is hidden in the liner notes on the Everest album).

Lark (1939)

☐ New England Conservatory Chorus / Hale (baritone) / Copland (conductor) / Columbia M-30375

Text by Genevieve Taggard set to point up its affirmative tone. Excellent choral singing and a bow to the similarly excellent vocal soloist.

Las Agachadas (1942)

☐ New England Conservatory Chorus / Copland (conductor) / Columbia M-30375

A Copland reconditioning of a Portuguese folk tune. Nice to hear, nicely done.

Opera and Dramatic Music

A Lincoln Portrait (1942)

☐ Philadelphia Orchestra / Stevenson (narrator) / Ormandy (conductor) / Columbia MS-6684

Though music can express the general aspects of specified emotions, it is, without an accompanying program that sets associations into mental motion, an abstract art. When joined with an expression of ideas (in this case, a great man's ideas culled from his speeches and letters), music becomes a representational but no less pure art. Copland's score is not a literal exposition of Lincoln's pronouncements but an extraordinarily skilled way of applying and combining free-sounding music with specific prose meanings. It is as moving and significant as the words Lincoln wrote.

There are no reservations in regard to Ormandy's production. In Adlai Stevenson Columbia chose the ideal interpreter of the narrator's part for Copland's monodrama (only partly so, because of the lengthy orchestral portion at the beginning). This viewpoint is not because both hero and narrator were from Illinois, but because of Stevenson's beautiful voice, his sense of phrasing, and his complete assimilation of the score. The playing of the orchestra is truly magnificent, the combination with the speaker stirring.

Though Copland's essay may be considered one of his lesser pieces by some, it does not lessen its dramatic impact or the astuteness with which he conceived the work through motival play and the use of ritornello in the narration.

Appalachian Spring (1944)   *Ballet*

☐ Columbia Chamber Orchestra / Copland (conductor) / Columbia M–32736

This is the original from which the orchestral suite was drawn (see under *Orchestra*). Its haunting beauties are even more fervently exposed in this concentrated group of flute, clarinet, bassoon, piano, and eleven strings. Two additional violins are used in the recording; the string-instrument part of Copland's original score for the ballet totaled only nine: two each of first and second violins, violas, and cellos, plus a double bass.

A great performance that every Copland buff should have. The Columbia pick-up group (including some great names) plays as though they've been in existence for years. Included with the release is a seven-inch rehearsal disc with its inside stuff that is always fascinating. But do listen to it only after hearing the entire performance.

Dance Panels (Ballet in Seven Sections) (1963)

☐ London Symphony Orchestra / Copland (conductor) / Columbia M–33269

A ballet without a story but not without all the Copland earmarks—the open-faced yet nostalgic melodic contours, the spare orchestration, and the athletic rhythms. Copland borrowing from Copland as it were and Copland conducting Copland—a perfect situation.

(The recording is duplicated in a big Copland edition on Columbia D3M–33720. Including *Dance Panels,* there is a total of eight works.)

Roque Cordero   *(1917-   )*

Eight Miniatures (1948)   *Orchestra*

☐ Detroit Symphony Orchestra / Freeman (conductor) / Columbia M–32784

Expressionistic ferment (almost twelve-tone) spread onto Latin and Panamanian documentation. The merger has fascinating results, especially in the *Pasillo* (a waltz shape), the *Danzonete* (hung on a duple rhythm split into a pair of equally long sounds followed by a slightly shorter one), and the *Mejorana* (a Panamanian dance).

This type of writing is quite new, and its possibilities need and deserve both consideration and development. The light Cordero has shed on this hybrid mode of music is certainly bright and distinctive.

It's nice to have the Detroiters on disc, even though not all of them are playing in this work, scored for chamber orchestra. Paul Freeman, as the conductor, shows dynamic control of the proceedings.

Symphony No. 2 in One Movement (1956)

☐ Louisville Orchestra / Mester (conductor) / Louisville LS–765

Cordero's symphony is constructed by way of serial devices but avoids being frozen to systematic hard-nosed procedures. The themes are strongly characterized; the developmental processes are clear, direct, and meaningful; and the orchestration is fittingly fused to the material. Cordero's expression is of total stylistic integrity; the result he brings is successful and imaginative. This is, indeed, impressive music, fully representative of this most important Panamanian composer.

The symphony won the Caro de Boesi Prize, given in connection with the Latin American Music Festival, held in Caracas in 1957. It was premiered in that city in 1957 and a year later was first heard in the United States. That it is now available on disc is a matter for which Mester is to be congratulated. His reading is excellent, and the orchestra responds with the stamina and technique required. Once again the Louisville Orchestra has produced a winner.

Solo Instrument and Orchestra

Violin

Concerto for Violin and Orchestra (1962)

☐ Detroit Symphony Orchestra / Allen (violin) / Freeman (conductor) / Columbia M–32784

A freely serial work of good size (close to thirty-two minutes). Especially there is an avoidance in the solo instrument's lines of severe disjunct intervallic successions in order to match serial style. Cordero's violin writing gives strong reminders of tonal days past in the layout of passages. The advantage becomes his, since there is no disturbing of style, and the clarification of the music is strengthened thereby. Shape is aided further by strong rhythmic definition. In all a lively and attractive addition to the contemporary concerto repertoire.

I'm fairly certain that this is Sanford Allen's recording debut. It is most impressive. Though it is not Paul Freeman's recording "first," his part of the proceedings is similarly impressive if not surprising.

There are few twentieth-century violin concertos that have made the grade. Given some attention on the part of our violin virtuosi, there will be no need to "rediscover" Cordero's opus a half century hence.

Arcangelo Corelli   *(1653-1713)*

String Orchestra

Concerto Grosso

In D major, Op. 6, No. 1 / In F major, Op. 6, No. 2 / In C minor, Op. 6, No. 3 / In D major, Op. 6, No. 4 / In B flat major, Op. 6, No. 5 / In F major, Op. 6, No. 6 / In D major, Op. 6, No. 7 / (Christmas) in G minor, Op. 6, No. 8 / In F major, Op. 6, No. 9 / In C major, Op. 6, No. 10 / In B flat major, Op. 6, No. 11 / In F major, Op. 6, No. 12

☐ Academy of St. Martin-in-the-Fields / Marriner (conductor) / Argo ZRG 773/5

While the most famous concerto in this set is the eighth (*Fatto per la Notte di Natale*) there are plenty of other beauties to be found. Performance skill is plentiful here; the music is played with rich enthusiasm and the listener can only be enthusiastic as to the results.

The Op. 6, No. 8 is available separately in several editions. A good pick is Münchinger conducting the Stuttgart Chamber Orchestra on London 6206.

Corelli / **Francesco Geminiani (1687-1762)**

Concerto Grosso

String Orchestra

In D major, Op. 5, No. 1 / **In B flat major, Op. 5, No. 2** / **In C major, Op. 5, No. 3** / **In F major, Op. 5, No. 4** / **In G minor, Op. 5, No. 5** / **In A major, Op. 5, No. 6** / **In D minor, Op. 5, No. 7** / **In E minor, Op. 5, No. 8** / **In A major, Op. 5, No. 9** / **In F major, Op. 5, No. 10** / **In E major, Op. 5, No. 11** / **(*La follia*) in D minor, Op. 5, No. 12**

☐ Gli Accademici di Milano / Biffoli and Magnani (violins); Gasperini (cello); Canino (harpsichord) / Eckertsen (conductor) / Vox SVBX–538

These are well-crafted versions made by Geminiani of Corelli's *XII Suonate a violino e violone o cembalo.* Eckertsen also did some editing, using the Corelli original, changing some of the embellishments, and adding some elaborations. Regardless, everything is in perfect taste and has no stylistic insults in either the music or its performance.

Not as well-known as the dozen Corelli Concerti Grossi that appeared fourteen years after the *Suonate,* the set has nonetheless innumerable delights in addition to the theme and twenty-two variations of the twelfth work (*La follia*). The playing is thoroughly skilled and sincere in every respect.

John Corigliano (1938-   )

Oboe Concerto (1975)

Solo Instrument and Orchestra

☐ American Symphony Orchestra / Lucarelli (oboe) / Akiyama (conductor) / RCA ARL1-2534

Oboe

When you start this recording don't think the tape hadn't been edited properly and some preliminary tuning got on the master reel. It did, rightfully, since it's noted in Corigliano's score, the first movement being a *Tuning Game* which is a tour de force of both imitation and individual realization about the procedure. In its way it's a show-stopper. Hellishly clever and devilishly musical.

A Song and an Aria separated by a diabolical Scherzo using oboe multiphonics that negate harmonic stability in a percussion framework—this describes the next three parts. The finale is a dance called a *Rheita,* a Moroccan double feature in its structural detail and in the sound of the oboe, as it is played in a special, pungent non-Western manner.

Corigliano's concerto fulfills concerto requirements but on his own special terms, and the results fascinate and excite. To combine in one work normal qualities, avant-garde coloration, and nationalistic esotericism and yet not produce a stylistic mishmash is quite a feat. Further, all the expected concerto soloism is made available with extremely virtuosic massaging from the orchestra, and with some concerto grosso detail as well.

The soloist, Bert Lucarelli, is magnificent in all respects. His shifts in color and phrasing, his technical expertise, as well as his articulative processes mark him as a giant among oboists. Kazuyoshi Akiyama shows a genuine feeling for, and total response to, the score. His conductorial alertness is obvious throughout.

Concerto for Piano and Orchestra (1968)

Piano

☐ San Antonio Symphony / Somer (piano) / Alessandro (conductor) / Mercury SRI-75118

Corigliano's work was commissioned by the San Antonio organization and Hilde Somer was the soloist at the world premiere, given on April 7, 1968, with the late Victor Alessandro conducting.

True soloism in a concerto vehicle is most often a minor fringe benefit these days. This one is a virtuosic crackerjack, a lulu that dazzles while it speaks musically in a contemporary romantic language. A real, honest-to-God concerto, and that's the way Hilde Somer plays it, demonstrating a dazzling technique and irresistible power.

Chamber Music

Sonata for Violin and Piano (1963)

☐ Corigliano, Sr. (violin); Votapek (piano) / Composers Recordings S-215

A gem of persuasive chamber music, a perfect example of tonality in the broadest sense. Corigliano's neo-classic (sometimes Stravinsky-sharpened) chisel carves not only with precision but with direction to the representation. The first movement is the most concentrated and with the most dynamic thrust. Movement 2 is the melodic peak of the opus—the D major theme is a real inspiration. It is contrasted by the generally brooding, recitative quality of the third part, and in turn by the somewhat peripatetic finale.

The performance is top-flight.

Cantata and Oratorio

Poem in October (1969)

☐ American String Quartet / White (tenor); Nyfenger (flute); Lucarelli (oboe); Rabbai (clarinet); Peress (harpsichord) / Peress (conductor) / RCA ARL1-2534

If one thinks of all the frantic compilations that have appeared on the contemporary music scene these last three decades it is important to remember that there have also been composers who have avoided such creative services. In his cantata (part 2 of a trilogy based on Dylan Thomas poems) Corigliano opts, and magnificently so, for sheer lyricism. It describes (in marvelous registral placement for the voice and splendidly delivered by way of Robert White's rich tenor) the poet's thoughts on his thirtieth birthday. Such rich romanticism proves again Corigliano's important creative stature.

The supporting ensemble plays with passionate enthusiasm. RCA's issue is a considerable asset to American music recordings.

William Cornyshe   (ca. 1468-1523)

Choral

Ah Robin, Gentle Robin

Chorus Alone

☐ Clark and Thomas (sopranos); Phillips (contralto); English (tenor); Keyte (bass) / Leppard (conductor) / Nonesuch 73010

A discovery that will haunt the listener with its canonic, minor-pitched emotional quality. The quintet that sings this work refreshes the ear for which equal credit is due this fine conductor.

Francisco Correa de Arauxo   (1576?-1654)

Instrumental

Tiento in A

Organ

Tiento in D

Tres glosas sobre de Canto Llano de la Immaculada Concepción

☐ Rilling (organ) / Turnabout 34097

These are three pieces from the seventy contained in this Spanish composer's *Facultad orgánica*. Bold music that anticipates Bachian grandeur in the case of the last piece. Rilling's playing opens the ears. It is colorful, clear, and direct.

Gaspard Corrette   *(?-ca. 1733)*

Fond d'orgue   *Instrumental*

☐ Hansen (organ) / Nonesuch 71170   *Organ*

By opting for an airy character in his playing Hansen infuses this placid music with a seductive charm.

Michel Corrette   *(1709-1795)*

Concerto in G major for Flute, Op. 3, No. 6   *Solo Instrument and Orchestra*

☐ Chamber Orchestra of Versailles / Bourdin (flute) / Wahl (conductor) / Nonesuch 71080

A fine piece of playing. No sense of strain, no attempt to break tempo records in the terminal Allegro movements. It is so recorded that one can hear the supportive harpsichord.   *Flute*

Concerto in D minor for Harpsichord, Flute, and Strings, Op. 26, No. 6   *Harpsichord*

☐ Mainz Chamber Orchestra / Ruf (harpsichord); Pohlers (flute) / Kehr (conductor) / Turnabout 34010

Especially Vivaldi will come to mind in the opening and closing movements, but such creative similarity does not nullify the value of Corrette's conception. Accordingly, the players go into the music with fine action and use brisk tempi. The music has some little surprises such as the soloistic turns of the harpsichord in the final part of the finale.

Corrette indicated that an organ could be used in place of the harpsichord. It is so performed with the Württemberg Chamber Orchestra, Faerber conducting, and Helmuth Rilling as the organist. However, it cannot compare either with the harpsichord setting or with the recorded performance using that instrument. There is instrumental heaviness where there should be the opposite, and the playing is flat-footed and half-masted in tempo. It is best avoided but if you insist on having it ask for Turnabout 34135.

Le Phénix for Four Bassoons and Continuo   *Instrumental*

☐ Zukerman, Gode, Wolken, and Steinbrecher (bassoons); Galling (harpsichord) / Turnabout 34304   *Four Bassoons*

What is better than one bassoon? Try four. This is the type of medium to be expected from a twentieth-century composer not from one who worked in the eighteenth century. True, it is simplistic vertical writing, and the nubby content doesn't include even a single polyphonic parenthesis, but it's all charming and exceedingly persuasive.

High-quality playing by the bassoonists, somewhat subdued playing by the harpsichordist.

*Chamber
Music*

Sonata (*Les Délices de la solitude*) in D major for Cello and Harpsichord

☐ Braunholz (cello); Ruf (harpsichord) / Turnabout 34010

Some Couperin borrowings in this five-movement affair shouldn't bother anyone. As Turnabout's liner note explains, Corrette "either revived older themes in new polished settings or recomposed them with buoyant original variations."

If the borrowings are accepted, the verdict is that Corrette is most successful in shaping and handling this small composition. Its proclamatory passions are quite evident and are given properly sympathetic statements by Bernard Braunholz and Hugo Ruf.

Sonata (*Les Jeux Olympiques*) in D major

☐ Wilson (flute); Fuller (harpsichord) / Orion 7283

The sport of imitation is heard in movement 1 and the light gymnastics of a gigue are detailed in movement 3, but to believe that Corrette had picture-painting in mind would be stretching the truth. This is lightly faceted eighteenth-century fare for which the title is simply that used by another composer from whom Corrette openly appropriated some of the thematic material. (*See below* for another instrumental version which gives the facts.)

No matter, the material flows most naturally and is delightfully communicative in this rhythmically flexible, tonally true, and convincing rendition.

Sonata (*Les Jeux Olympiques*) in D major for Harpsichord and Violin

☐ Kehr (violin); Ruf (harpsichord) / Turnabout 34010

The material for Corrette's Sonata was derived from music written by Jean-Joseph Mouret for a *comédie héroique.* No plagiarism, since title credit is given by Corrette to show his source, borrowing having been a perpetual habit of his. If not deep ones, nice values result. The playing of the duo is clean and incisive.

(Another version using the flute in place of the violin is discussed *above.*)

Les Sauvages et La Fürstenberg

☐ Pohlers (flute); Kehr and Karolyi (violins); Sichermann (viola); Braunholz (cello); Ruf (harpsichord) / Turnabout 34010

A chamber-music setting with individual instrumental highlighting based on creative borrowing. Movement 1 is variationally built on a theme by Rameau and the violin is in the solo spot. Movement 2 sets in motion a moderately stated stately idea by J.-J. Rousseau, and the flute and harpsichord are featured. An old *contredanse* (titled *La Fürstenberg*) completes matters with dash, colored and principally activated by having the violin again in the driver's seat. All goes well with the performance.

Ramiro Cortés   (1933-   )

*Solo
Instrument
and
Orchestra*

Cello

Chamber Concerto for Violoncello and 12 Wind Instruments (1958)

☐ Contemporary Chamber Ensemble / McCracken (cello) / Weisberg (conductor) / Composers Recordings 181 (monaural)

There have been a goodly number of partial successes by composers applying serial procedures to tonal properties. Cortés's warm music (a far different matter from sweetly heated affairs) obliterates the word "partial." It has a variational air as it progresses through its thirteen-and-a-half-minute length, the warmth moistened by a solo cello line that binds the material with its consistency.

To be exact, the "twelve wind instruments" represent nine woodwinds (played by eight players, the piccolo being an alternate instrument with one of the flutes), and four brass.

No flaws can be perceived in this expert rendition with the expert Arthur Weisberg in control.

Duo for Flute and Oboe (1967)

☐ Shanley (flute); Christ (oboe and English horn) / Crystal S–812

Cortés uses as much color as possible in this five-movement work, with the oboe (despite the title) doubling on English horn. Further, timbre is emphasized in movements 3 and 4 respectively for unaccompanied flute and oboe. The style is freely twelve-tone, but it is not serially applied.

Three Movements for Five Winds (1968)

☐ Westwood Wind Quintet / Crystal S–812

This work is panchromatically styled, with formal freedom used for the structural shape of the first movement. Tri-sectional detail applies to the other pair of pieces. The total pitch spectrum makes the music sound like it is dodecaphonically oriented, but it is simply "twelve-tone without there being a row per se."

The Westwood group (Shanley, Christ, Atkins, Brightman, and Henderson) play with a flair that enhances Cortés's music considerably. Cogent balances as well.

François Couperin   *(1668-1733)*

La Sultane, Sonade en quatuor

☐ Caen Chamber Orchestra / Dautel (conductor) / Turnabout 34101
☐ Oberlin Baroque Ensemble / Vox SVBX–5142

This is the work from which Milhaud took the first two of its six movements to make an arrangement for full orchestra. (The conception is noted on the score as being "freely transcribed and orchestrated." The published title is "Overture and Allegro from *La Sultane* Suite." In Milhaud's book *Notes Without Music* it is referred to and listed as "Introduction and Allegro.")

The Caen group plays with a clarity in the lower register that is lacking in the Oberlin performance. On the other hand, the Ohioans use authentic period string instruments in greatly reduced forces: two quintons (Baroque violins), two bass viols, and a harpsichord. There is something to be said for both presentations.

Pièces de clavecin

   Ordre No. 8 in B minor
   Ordre No. 11 in C minor and major
   Ordre No. 13 in B minor
   Ordre No. 15 in A minor and major
   Prélude No. 6 in B minor from *L'Art de toucher de clavecin*

☐ Puyana and Hogwood (harpsichords) / Philips 6700035

There are twenty-seven *Ordres* (Couperin's term for Suites) in the four volumes he produced in 1713, 1717, 1722, and 1730. The huge compilation includes close to 250 movements, most of them with descriptive titles. The wide range is to be noted in these examples: the *Passacaille* in *Ordre* No. 8, music of tremendous power, considered to be one of the masterpieces of all baroque keyboard music; *La Morinéte,* also in the eighth group, a Corelli-like gigue, presumably a portrait in sound of a composer friend's daughter; the satirical quality to be heard in the five parts of *Les Fastes de la grande et ancienne Ménestrandise,* the final section of the eleventh *Ordre;* the twelve couplets (No. 4 in *Ordre* No. 13) comprising *Les Folies françaises ou Les Dominos,* each representing a different human passion and sporting a symbolically colored costume.

Expectedly, recorded attention to this music has not been slim by any means. The great harpsichordists are represented in the catalogue, including Dart, Fuller, Kipnis, Leonhardt, Marlowe, Malcolm, and Puyana. (The latter's release, noted above, includes a second harpsichordist, but his contribution is exceedingly minor, limited to furnishing drone colorative background for the tunes in the *Musète de Choisi* and *Musète de Taverni* of *Ordre* No. 15.)

The two issues chosen (for the second one *see below*) not only provide a broad selection but playing of the utmost clarity and a sense of pace that is positively pertinent to each of Couperin's creations. Indeed, Rafael Puyana and George Malcolm offer memorably stylish music making. Not a chord, a phrase, or an ornament is out of place.

Pièces de clavecin

Ordre No. 8 in B minor
Ordre No. 14 in D major and minor
Ordre No. 21 in E minor

☐ Malcolm (harpsichord) / Argo ZRG–632

(For comments regarding the *Pièces de clavecin* and this performance, *see above.*)

Malcolm's recorded program only duplicates Puyana's in *Ordre* No. 8. However, Puyana prefaces the suite of ten parts with one of the *Préludes* Couperin wrote that may be used to introduce any of the *Ordres* in the appropriate key.

The world of nature is represented in the eight-movement *Ordre* No. 14 with *The Nightingale in Love* (No. 1), *The Frightened Linnet* (No. 2), *The Mournful Warblers* (No. 3), and *The Victorious Nightingale* (No. 4). The five parts of *Ordre* No. 21 include *The Leaper* and *La Couperin,* a rare musical example of a self-portrait that furnishes a superb example of Couperin's polyphonic writing.

Oboe d'Amore

Les Gôuts réunis (Concerto No. 9, *Il ritratto dell' amore,* in E major)

☐ Holliger (oboe d'amore); Jaccottet (harpsichord); Cervera (viola da gamba) / Philips 6500618

The ten works in this group were designated as "playable" by a number of instruments, including the oboe. Holliger states that while Couperin did not precisely specify the oboe d'amore he could have had that deeper-timbred instrument in mind. If he didn't, no matter; the oboe d'amore fits beautifully. It is played to perfection in all eight movements.

Organ

Pièces d'orgue consistantes en deux messes

Messe à l'usage des couvents
Messe solennelle à l'usage des paroisses

☐ Noehren (organ) / Lyrichord 7130

These two pieces are the only organ works that Couperin produced. A Mass for the organ (here one "for the Convents" and the other "for the Parishes") needs only the explanation that it provided the interpolation of organ pieces between the choir's plainsong chants. In Couperin's hands these have an imaginative and inspirational depiction that go far beyond the pedestrian works that cram available organ literature.

These compositions are performed with excellence and with full stylistic identification. Noehren's clean and fresh depictions are marked by telling registrations and dynamic levels.

Each of the two masses can be obtained separately—on the Lyrichord label, of course. The first listed title is on number 7129, the other on number 7128.

Pièces d'orgue consistantes en deux messes (excerpts)

☐ Darasse (organ) / Turnabout 34074

Organists have not overlooked Couperin's organ masses (*see above*). Six performers have dealt with the music on disc, two in total form, the others choosing to record one of the pair of works or excerpting from them, as in this case.

Darasse's edition covers eight parts from *Messe à l'usage des couvents* and five versets from the Gloria section of the *Messe solennelle à l'usage des paroisses*. This defines an excellent cross-section and is magnificently realized. The colors are an aural feast as produced on the organ of Notre Dame de St. Etienne.

Concerto in G major for Two Bassoons

☐ Zukerman and Gode (bassoons) / Turnabout 34304

This work may or may not have been written by Couperin. No listing of this work has been found in the bibliographical data on the composer. Let it be, it's a nice five-part (ten and one-half minutes) essay. To call it a concerto can be argued. A suite, yes, and a duo better yet. It is played with geniality and spirit to match.

Concert royal No. 4 in E minor for Flute and Continuo

☐ Le Rondeau de Paris / Nonesuch 73014

Couperin's set of six dances, preceded by a *Prélude*, emerges in this rendition as adequately performed, with one reservation. The technical side is excellent, and the continuo of cello and harpsichord is fluent. The single element lacking is a French personality, the playing having a neutrally Baroque cast.

La Steinquerque, Sonade en trio

☐ Oberlin Baroque Ensemble / Vox SVBX–5142
☐ Collegium Musicum de Paris / Douatte (conductor) / Nonesuch 71009

Couperin's piece, unbanded in the Vox release, consists of eight movements; on the Nonesuch disc the *Sonade en trio* (not included in the titling, and for that matter, the main title is there spelled "La Steinkerque") is divided into five banded segments. Since the work was composed to celebrate a military victory, one understands the reason for the subtitle of the first part, *Bruit de guerre* (not listed in the Nonesuch data), and the fanfares in part 5. The other movements have both spirit and a ceremonial quality.

The performance by the Oberliners consists of oboe, quinton (the baroque violin), harpsichord, and bass viol in support of the harpsichord. The Nonesuch edition is with modern instruments, with a larger group involved, plus oboes and bassoons. Style is good in both cases, but for textural quality and instrumental authenticity the preference is for

Chamber Music

the Vox Box in which Couperin's work is included. For those who like fatter and fuller instrumentation, Nonesuch must be the choice.

Louis Couperin (1626?-1661)

Instrumental	**Allemande grave** **Courante**
Harpsichord	**Branle de Basque** *La Piémontaise* **in A minor**
	Chaconne in D minor *Pavane* **in F sharp minor**
	Chaconne in G minor **Prelude in F major**

☐ Fuller (harpsichord) / Nonesuch 71265

The two Chaconnes are also recorded in organ settings and are discussed below, under *Instrumental: organ.* In the case of the D minor opus the tonality denomination is a slippery matter. Biggs terms it as ''D major,'' Hamilton lists it as plain ''D,'' and Froidebise (probably the most authentic) defines it as ''en ré.'' This variability also pertains to *La Piémontaise.* On Blandine Verlet's Telefunken release (641264) the music is titled ''Suite in D major (*La Piémontaise*).'' The *Pavane* is also duplicated in the Verlet program.

These are all fine renditions including a brawny style that is most fitting in the instances where it is applied. This approach is particularly effective in the playing of *La Piémontaise.*

Le Tombeau de M. de Blancrocher

☐ Fuller (harpsichord) / Nonesuch 71265

A winner but far from overly threnodic, the piece is beautifully expressed in Albert Fuller's performance.

Suite

In C major / In F major

☐ Verlet (harpsichord) / Telefunken 641264

Skillful playing on a fine instrument, providing more evidence of the abilities of this composer, the uncle of the famous Couperin. Verlet's ornamentation is sensible and finely styled.

Organ

Chaconne

In C major / In C minor / In D major

☐ Biggs (organ) / Columbia MS-7438

Orthodox but in no way ordinary music. The free invention found in these pieces is built on strong thematic contours and denies any note of academic procedure. No commonplace performance either. Biggs moves into this music with lusty activity. In fact, in the D major piece he clips more than a minute off the performance time in comparison to the drag that marks Froidebise's playing of the work (on Nonesuch 71020); Froidebise also matches his slow pace with dull coloring. Hamilton's performance (on Orion 73133) is even slower (!) and also lacks viable timbre reasoning.

Chaconne in F major

☐ Hamilton (organ) / Orion 73133

Another in the series of Chaconnes (*see above* and *below* for the others recorded) showing the fine inventive powers of this lesser known member of the Couperin family. Rather gruff organ sound but it is the only example available on disc.

Chaconne in G minor

☐ Biggs (organ) / Columbia MS-7438

A brilliant execution, matching Biggs's performance of three other Chaconnes by Louis Couperin (*see above*). This is the best version in the recorded books, far better accomplished in pace and color than Pierre Froidebise's on Nonesuch 71020.

Cinq Sinfonies pour les violes et basse continue

☐ Oberlin Baroque Ensemble / Vox SVBX-5142

Chamber Music

These works are scored for a treble viol and bass viol, with the latter instrument also duplicated to double the bass line of the continuo (harpsichord). A completely authoritative performance of this music.

Henry Cowell   *(1897-1965)*

Hymn and Fuguing Tune No. 3 (1944)

Orchestra

☐ Louisville Orchestra / Mester (conductor) / Louisville S-682

Cowell produced a large number of hymn-and-fugue combinations in a variety of settings, ranging from a trio for paired clarinets and saxophone to full orchestra. No. 3 is one of the best and contains a good portion of "up and at 'em" quality. The recording must be given a very high mark for its clarity, balance, and stylistic know-how.

Music 1957

☐ Japan Philharmonic Symphony Orchestra / Watanabe (conductor) / Composers Recordings 132

Music of wit, good fun, and a healthy devotion to treading lightly (with folk slippers) in the halls of orchestral composition. Music 1957 is informative in two ways—it gives both title and year of composition. (It was conceived in Japan.) The working material is a jiggy tune, sometimes given a sophisticated touch by being surrounded with a dissonant, calliope effect. Cowell contrasts this idea with a lyrical theme, a hybrid of Irish-Western U.S.A. culture, dunking it into a sonorous sauce that is sometimes sweet, sometimes sour.

There are no inhibitions in this music. Watanabe and his musicians follow this premise perfectly. The plentiful percussion is further evidence of this, as it is used not only as rhythmic support but as a solo-functioning group. Henry Cowell's "Music Made in America–Composed in Tokyo" is healthy art. Don't overlook it.

Persian Set (1957)

☐ Orchestra (name not given) / Stokowski (conductor) / Composers Recordings 114

Still another in Cowell's long list of explorations. However, indulging in a cardinal point of technique with overzealous attention to the one stylistic speciality may breed monotony. The *Persian Set* is almost canceled by its emphasis on the Iranian blueprint to the point of overemphasis. Yet, credit Cowell with an honest preoccupation. And add another credit to the long list in the Stokowski recorded ledger. How many conductors have displayed his extensive interest? And then proven it?

Sinfonietta (1928)

☐ Louisville Orchestra / Mester (conductor) / Louisville S–681

This illustrates the Cowell of secundal harmony, of tone-cluster stress. The concluding chords of two of the movements represent the type of traffic signs found on Cowell's musical freeway: a G minor triad plus a raised and lowered seventh, and a combination of minor and diminished triads which results in triple-sectioned seconds.

Mester conducts an intensely cogent performance. In two instances (a major one made by Cowell; the other, made by Mester, is of minor significance), his performance does not follow the published score that appeared in 1932, which consists of three movements and is scored for one each of the woodwinds and brass, and seven strings (two each for violins 1 and 2, one each of viola, cello, and bass). A fourth movement is added, played before the original final movement. It is for strings alone, an example of monophony, using either straight unisons or amplified octaves. Originally, this was a piece for unaccompanied cello, so Cowell's expansion was strictly limited to instrumental weighting. Mester's other change is that to a great extent the string body is expanded to full strength.

Symphony No. 5 (1949)

☐ Vienna Symphony Orchestra / Dixon (conductor) / Desto S–6406E (monaural)

Somewhat conservative music, far from Cowell's usual searching investigations. Only a part of the slow movement departs from the tonal norm as it contains some clusterized harmonies in the strings. More Cowellian is the Scherzo, which is colored by the Celtic touch often found in this composer's work. Dixon leads only a fair presentation of the score.

Symphony No. 7 (1952)

☐ Vienna Symphony Orchestra / Strickland (conductor) / Composers Recordings 142 (monaural)

A work of moods. Rather than full-spanned symphonic development Cowell uses a chain of melodic ideas. Some composers counter-attack formalism. Henry Cowell certainly displays it. The avoidance here of a square-cut, four-part symphonic essay provides its own type of excitement.

The recording is a re-issue of a very old MGM disc (E–3084), where it was coupled with music by Robert Ward. Not the greatest sound in the world, but Strickland displays an unerring sense of relationship to Cowell's design.

Symphony No. 16 (*Icelandic*) (1962)

☐ Iceland Symphony Orchestra / Strickland (conductor) / Composers Recordings 179

Cowellian chemistry with little-known native material. Included are melodic turns and accents from Icelandic folk-tune language. Included, also, is an actual Icelandic melody in the second movement of the five-part work. Highlights: the haunting beauty of the slow movement and the catchy dance that follows (its orchestration samples a large number of solo colors).

Strickland does well with this vividly scored music. He shapes the phrases neatly and he projects Cowell's sweetly dissonant voice with clarity.

Synchrony **(1931)**

Variations for Orchestra

☐ Polish National Radio Orchestra / Strickland (conductor) / Composers Recordings S-217

One of Cowell's finest works is represented by *Synchrony.* It is a dissonant blockbuster with grapnelized orchestral tone clusters that grip the ears. For the time being, this, the only recorded performance, will have to satisfy but it lacks the full-blooded tone ambiance the music demands. One of our major orchestras should give this outstanding creation the attention it deserves.

The Variations are only fair Cowell; the playing is just average which doesn't stimulate aural response.

Thesis **(Symphony No. 15) (1962)**

☐ Louisville Orchestra / Whitney (conductor) / Louisville 622 (monaural)

Since the extremely short liner note (by the composer) says nothing about the matter, it is important to point out that Cowell borrowed the music for the first four of the six movements of Symphony No. 15 from his *Mosaic Quartet* (see under Movement for String Quartet, p. 460). The quartet is transferred in a different sequence after the opening part. Thus the *Mosaic* second, third, and fourth movements become movements 4, 2, and 3 in the symphony. One other change: the quartet's fourth movement was in $\frac{5}{8}$ time, and in the shift to the orchestral version (as movement 3) the meter is changed to $\frac{5}{4}$.

The best playing of the Louisvillians is heard in the outer movements, markedly so for distinguishing the dissonant pungency of the opening part of the symphony. Otherwise, only a fair performance. Two major criticisms: the unison cello line in movement 2 wavers in pitch and Whitney is far too slow in the third movement, a Presto. The score reads 192 to the quarter note; he is considerably below this metronomic indication.

Ballad (1955)

☐ Louisville Orchestra / Mester (conductor) / Louisville S-682

String Orchestra

The transfer from the third movement of Cowell's Sonata for Violin and Piano (see p. 459) is a beauty—a sort of American *Londonderry Air*—haunting the ear long after it is over.

The recording is rich, but properly not over-rich, and appropriately warm in feeling. No mention is made anywhere that the piece is for string orchestra. Neither is there a single word about the Ballad in the liner notes.

Hymn and Fuguing Tune No. 2 (1944)

☐ Louisville Orchestra / Mester (conductor) / Louisville S-682

The music soars with sweet strength in this contemporary transplant of eighteenth-century New Englandish polyphony.

It is nice to have this work on a recording—the version on the old Unicorn label (in two issues: UNLP-1011 and UNLP-1045) having gone the way of many deletes. It is given a wonderfully sonorous performance, so it is twice welcome. (There is no indication on the label that the work is for string orchestra.)

Ostinato pianissimo **(1934)**

☐ Manhattan Percussion Ensemble / Price (conductor) / Mainstream 5011

Percussion

Cowell's piece is pressed in and simultaneously stimulated by the ostinato patterns. The coloristic motivation of this refined music gives the lie to those who still contend that percussion music equals "arranged noise," or those who, giving a half-inch, call it "noisy music." The score's delicacy (somewhat oriental in quality) is superbly set forth by the seven players of the ensemble.

Instrumental

Piano

Advertisement

Aeolian Harp

☐ Cowell (piano) / Composers Recordings 109 (monaural)

Listening to *Advertisement* one realizes again how Cowell's special tone cluster technique (practically his invention) is common property today in the work of the advanced coterie.

Listening to *Aeolian Harp* one realizes that its employment of the strings of the piano and not the keys became the source book from which Cage, Bussotti, Kagel, and many others have drawn.

Despite versions in stereo (Doris Hays on the Finnadar label, No. 9016) and without giving biased credits because the performer is the composer, there is no doubt as to these being the choice performances. Hays uses unbecoming *rubati* and is highly overmannered in her rendition of *Advertisement*. In *Aeolian Harp* there is more proper and telling vibrancy in Cowell's portrayal. Further, Hays drags the tempi and the music loses its flow. (Cowell plays the piece in 1:34, Hays takes 2:20.)

Amiable Conversation

Anger Dance

Antinomy

☐ Hays (piano) / Finnadar 9016

The *Conversation* is a burlesque of a dispute heard in a Chinese laundry. *Anger* is equated with insistent repetitive phrases. Clusters abound in *Antinomy*, a corroborant confirmation of Cowellian style.

All three are heard here to their best advantage.

The Banshee

☐ Cowell (piano) / Composers Recordings 109 (monaural)
☐ Hays (piano) / Finnadar 9016

An extraordinary example of alluring sonorities, so organized as to depict the wailing of the legendary female who in this manner warns that death is approaching. All the sounds are drawn directly from the piano strings, with inferential polyphony created by overtones. Manifold color is produced as well, obtained by string glides and plucking, and by permitting the strings to vibrate.

Cowell's performance is extraordinary. It has to be heard to be believed. On the other hand, because there are certain variables due to the piano string technique involved, subtle differences can (and do) occur in separate performances. The outcome of Doris Hays's playing of the work is somewhat dissimilar from Cowell's. It is not only totally satisfactory, but especially interesting for comparison with Cowell's performance so that a listener can hear the alterability inherent in the *Banshee* score.

Dynamic Motion

☐ Hays (piano) / Finnadar 9016

Cluster language and lesser dissonances, dynamically played.

Episode

☐ Rogers (piano) / Composers Recordings S–281

A purely diatonic miniature. And cute. A mini-type of perpetual motion.

Exultation

☐ Cowell (piano) / Folkways 3349 (monaural)

Exultation, an Irish melody with tone-clustered support, rejoices through a pentatonic setting.

Folkways's album covers twenty of Cowell's piano pieces. It is a re-release of a very old (deleted, of course) Circle recording (for the curious the number was L–51–101), with the composer discussing his music at the conclusion of the second side. Six of these pieces were freshly recorded by CRI, with Cowell again at the piano. Though monaural, CRI's sound is excellent. On the other hand, one must accept what Folkways offers despite antiquated sonics that make the piano register like a cheap spinet without any depth whatsoever, because it accomplishes availability for four Cowell piano compositions otherwise not recorded thus far.

At a later date, CRI issued three other Cowell piano creations and most recently Finnadar and New World Records have added to the list. The total piano works recorded, therefore, is twenty-six, and all these are discussed above and below.

Fabric

☐ Hays (piano) / Finnadar 9016

The tri-colored weave in *Fabric* is manufactured by three-ply rhythms. As each voice goes its own mensural way it produces a sharply contrasted contrapuntal design. The linear pattern is clearly defined in this recorded performance.

Fairy Answer

☐ Cowell (piano) / Folkways 3349 (monaural)

Polychrome antiphony is the intriguing communication here—a phrase is played on the keyboard and freely echoed by contact with the piano strings. This is still another of Henry Cowell's entrancing ideas.

The Harp of Life
The Hero Sun

☐ Hays (piano) / Finnadar 9016

The Harp of Life has a folksy tune surrounded and supported by healthily incessant and optimistically seething tone clusters. Cowell's *Harp* is far from small-sounding as it is creatively amplified. Registral contrast is the plan for the other piece. It is in turn bright with fanfarelike phrases and clouded with low-pronged clusters.

Invention

☐ Rogers (piano) / Composers Recordings S–281

As bubbly as champagne and as delightful a seventy seconds of music as one can wish to hear. Light-faceted, of course. The perfect encore piece, better in effect than dozens of the standard bits that recitalists toss off after the regular program.

Jig

☐ Cowell (piano) / Folkways 3349 (monaural)

An Irish folk-tune stylization, with dissonant paprika.

The Lilt of the Reel

☐ Cowell (piano) / Composers Recordings 109 (monaural)

A Celtic evocation with punchy harmonies. Cowell never followed those who insist that music of folk quality requires a do-re-mi setting.

Not that a composer always knows best how to play his own music, but the dash of Cowell's performance is preferable to the more refined conception of Hays (on Finnadar 9016).

Maestoso

☐ Hays (piano) / Finnadar 9016

Chunky counterpoints and potent polyharmonies adding up to a majestic utterance. Doris Hays presents the picture with proper bravura.

Piano Piece (1924)

☐ Miller (piano) / New World Records NW–203

Tone clusters dominate this piece, both as melodic, rhythmic, and percussive agents. The power is enticing. The playing is similar—Robert Miller is a master performer of contemporary piano music.

Sinister Resonance

☐ Cowell (piano) / Composers Recordings 109 (monaural)

Music such as the *Sinister Resonance* was the forerunner of John Cage's compositions for "prepared" piano, in which the instrument's strings are re-timbred by way of slats of bamboo, bolts, pennies, and so on. Cowell uses the simple but powerful effect of choking the sonority by such special muting and adds delicate, arpeggiated bits. Despite its title, *Sinister Resonance* is music of pervading beauty.

Cowell's playing of this piece is more resonant and more sinister as well than the competitive edition on Finnadar 9016. Above all, the coloring in the bass gamut is superb in Cowell's performance, of neutral effect in the other issue.

Six Ings Plus One

☐ Rogers (piano) / Composers Recordings S–281

Seven action sketches, each title ending with the suffix "ing." Thus: *Floating, Frisking, Fleeting,* and so on. They couldn't be played better.

The Snows of Fujiyama

☐ Cowell (piano) / Folkways 3349 (monaural)

Pentatonic clusters framing a pentatonic melody. In settings such as this one a tone cluster changes almost into a creamy consonance.

The Tides of Manaunaun

☐ Cowell (piano) / Composers Recordings 109 (monaural)

Once more the tone cluster; this time to picture the sea god Manaunaun. The music consists of a folk tune embedded in and surrounded by tone clusters that enhance and place the melody (a real tune!) in perspective.

Tides is one of the most often played of Cowell's smaller pieces. Cowell's performance, therefore, is of historic importance, but aside from that fact it is magnificently accomplished and sweeps aside the competitive issue available.

Tiger   The Voice of Lir
The Trumpet of Angus Og   What's This?

☐ Hays (piano) / Finnadar 9016

With nary a chromatic, *The Trumpet of Angus Og* contrasts forcibly with the dissonant diction employed in the first and last pieces listed above. The Irish folk accent is fully expressed (and percussed with bass-zone clusters) in *The Voice of Lir*.

Air and Scherzo

Saxophone

☐ Robert Black (alto saxophone); Patricia Black (piano) / Brewster 1216

Organic melodic spinning in both movements, curvaceous in the slow-paced Air, jiggly and kinetic in the Scherzo. Cowell aims to please with simplistic behavior, and he does.

Robust performance. Black's ability to project pitches at the extreme top of the register (and there are a number of instances here) and still maintain a firm tonal lucidity is special to his playing.

Prelude for Violin and Harpsichord (1955)

Chamber Music

☐ Brink (violin); Pinkham (harpsichord) / Composers Recordings 109 (monaural)

Cowell in a suave diatonic frame of mind. No novelty, except for the harpsichord instead of the usual piano. Brink does his part with tonal liquidity.

Six Casual Developments

☐ Russo (clarinet); Ignacio (piano) / Capra 1204

A series of casual toss-'em-off pieces that Henry Cowell produced so nicely and with a sure touch for acceptable stylistic mixture. The flight of fancy includes a brashly keening high clarinet section with swoops, sweeps, and glides, a jig, and a pithy polyphonic bit. Difficult not to like. The recording is faithful to the score.

Sonata for Violin and Piano (1945)

☐ Szigeti (violin); Bussotti (piano) / Columbia Special Products AML-4841 (monaural)

Although it has certain suite-like connotations instead of the more formal outlines of a sonata, Cowell's work has cohesive style, and there is even thematic transformation in the two outer movements. Melodicism is paramount, without odd twists or furbelows. This can be considered a kind of "homey" music, but it is far short of being banal. The folksy quality is highlighted by the third-movement Ballad. As a preliminary to the coda of the last movement, Cowell employs one of his "percussion" ideas for the piano, resulting in an effect akin to muted gongs. An independent, artistic mind, we realize gratefully, is never reformed.

The violin plays close-up, and some extraneous sounds mar the performance.

Homage to Iran (1959)

☐ Avakian (violin); Andrews (piano); Bahar (Persian drum) / Composers Recordings 173 (monaural)

This is really a work for violin and piano. The sonority of a Persian drum is required of the pianist in some portions (by "pressing the strings of the indicated notes near the bridge while playing the keys"). Leopold Avakian went the composer one better and obtained the services of an actual Persian-drum player.

The duo-turned-into-trio is a resounding celebration of freshness, matching alternate movements of the violin and drum with the violin and piano. Movement 2 highlights the piece; its whirling dervish toccata contrasts vividly with the metrical reconnoitering of the finale. All of it is potent, and further proof that Henry Cowell retained his belief that for a composer there were no divine, rigid laws.

Trio for Violin, Cello, and Piano (1965)

☐ Philharmonia Trio / Composers Recordings 211 (monaural)

This is Cowell's last completed composition. It is no essay in the usual three-or-four-movement total or of the synthesized one-movement type. Divisionally formed, the opus is explicitly coded in its instrumentation. The strings play as solo, unaccompanied voices or as a duo team. When the piano is combined with the strings it supports and does not seize control because of its textural identity. Thus through instrumentational influence coherence is given to each of the nine variationlike short stories that comprise Cowell's trio volume.

Further, each section is computed by a specific technique. Examples: movement 4 has antiphonal instrumentation and some gentle clusters; the movement following is hymnodic with sweet acridity; part 6 represents a Scherzo with dessicated sonority. Cowell's Trio proves again that originality on the part of the composer always produces further originality.

Quartet Euphometric

☐ Emerson String Quartet / New World Records NW–218

A two-minute polymetrical dissertation. The result belies the technical premise; the music sounds gently late romantic!

The Emerson group is a splendid (unfortunately, very little known) string quartet that was founded in 1972. Its playing is warm and cohesive, its tone quality deep and rich.

Quartet

No. 2: Movement for String Quartet (1934)
No. 3: Mosaic (1935)
No. 4: United (1936)

☐ Beaux Arts String Quartet / Composers Recordings 173 (monaural)

Tone clusters, modified by wide spacing, are the harmonic backbone of the Movement. There is no relinquishing of the clustered sounds' probity and bite; the quality is merely more lubricated.

Mosaic concerns improvisational design. There are five short movements and these can be performed in any manner. This produces a fusion of internal order (there is no choice as to the material within any single movement) and outward (structural) improvisation. The Beaux Arts foursome proceed rather regularly, playing the movement sequence 1-2-4-3-4-5.

According to Cowell, the *United Quartet* was "an attempt toward a more universal style." Whatever the objective, the result exemplifies a type of neo-primitivism. This is emphasized by the use of ostinati in each of the five movements, the polyrhythm in movement 3, and the percussive treatment of the instruments.

In these quartets there is much for the listener—newness, a holiday of sounds not commonly heard. To say that the Beaux Arts gentlemen have done well is not really sufficient praise. They deserve a five-star rating. I can back this assertion up with some special testimony. The quartet which I had organized in Philadelphia in 1932 (the Stringart Quartet), and of which I was the second violinist, gave the world premieres of both the *Mosaic* and the *United* quartets; the latter work was dedicated to my quartet group. Further, after presenting the first Philadelphia performance of the Movement for String Quartet, the Stringart Quartet featured it several dozen times in its programs.

Toccanta (1938)

☐ Smith (flute); Boatwright (soprano); Parisot (cello); Kirkpatrick (piano) / Columbia Special Products AML-4986 (monaural)

This is pure Cowell plunging into the uncharted seas of musical creation. His *Toccanta* is neither a toccata nor a cantata, but a Thorne Smith turnabout; the instruments play vocally and the voice sings instrumentally, without words. The performance is one of absolute truth.

The Donkey

☐ McCollum (tenor); Biltcliffe (piano) / Desto 6411/2

Henry Cowell's reputation isn't identified with solo voice composition. According to a catalogue issued in 1965 by BMI, Cowell produced only nine songs with piano (including *The Donkey,* which is not on the BMI list), plus four other vocal works with instruments. Indeed, very meagre, when compared to his output of fifty-nine works for orchestra, fifteen for solo instrument or instruments with orchestra, and fifty-two chamber compositions. (According to information I possess there are gaps in the BMI lists, but such data would only enlarge the totals for the instrumental compositions.)

However, Cowell has left a special mark in the solo voice literature with this splendidly dramatic contribution. *The Donkey* is great theatre in its concentrated time length and McCollum presents a marvelous vocal projection. His is an exciting account.

. . . *If He Please* for Chorus and Orchestra (1955)

☐ Members of the Oslo Philharmonic Orchestra and Norwegian Choir of Solosingers / Strickland (conductor) / Composers Recordings S-217

Cowell's most emotive piece for this combination and doubtless one of the most deep-felt in all of his output. The text is by Edward Taylor (1645-1729). It brings the lesson that whatever God has done he can undo.

Vocal

Voice with Accompaniment

Choral

Chorus and Orchestra

461

The powerful writing is clearly portrayed. The singing is impeccable, though the diction (as so often occurs with massed voices) is blurred. Nevertheless, a performance that is expressive and impressive.

Johann Baptist Cramer (1771-1858)

*Solo
Instrument
and
Orchestra*

Piano

Piano Concerto No. 5, Op. 48

☐ Orchestra of Radio Luxembourg / Sagara (piano) / Cao (conductor) / Turnabout 34608

Preoccupation with the larger figures in the classical school is a danger, since the music of the lesser composers should be heard and considered if the period is to be understood in its full perspective. In no sense a great composer, Cramer was a very good one, fulfilling the requirements of classical style and taste, as this concerto exemplifies. It is all plain sailing (but not plain music), with attractive material in its dramatic opening part, in the nocturnal Larghetto, and in the rhythmically defined finale (a *Rondo à l'hongroise*). It is not unduly elaborate and is not weighed down by scholarship devices.

The worthiness of the piece is honored by a performance that is clear and convincing and without flaws.

Ruth Crawford. See Ruth Crawford Seeger.

Paul Creston (1906-   )

Orchestra

Corinthians XIII, Op. 82

☐ Louisville Orchestra / Whitney (conductor) / Louisville S-655

An orchestral meditation on the words of St. Paul to the Corinthians. Romantically considered by Creston, even lushly so, and cast in a large ternary design. Included is the Gregorian melody *Salve Regina.*

The Louisville Orchestra does itself proud, with fine bassoon playing by its first desk man. Don't be surprised, since no mention of it appears on program leaflet or label copy, but the music is prefaced by a reading (by an anonymous individual) of the complete text of Corinthians XIII.

Dance Overture (1954)

☐ Oslo Philharmonic Orchestra / Antonini (conductor) / Composers Recordings 111 (monaural)

Creston's Overture, rather than following the prescribed academic forms, is a four-ply set of variations on a theme. In uninterrupted continuity profiles of national dances are projected: a bolero from Spain, a country dance from England, followed by a French *Loure,* and concluding with an American square dance.

This is systematized music-making, but it is incidental to the smooth, pleasant sounds that result. Written to specific scale and played accordingly.

Invocation and Dance, Op. 58

☐ Louisville Orchestra / Whitney (conductor) / Louisville 545–1 (monaural)

Musical blueprints may seem well-organized on paper, but actual sound and aural reception are still required for complete substantiation. Creston here proposes a study in rhythmic technique (he emphasizes this principle in his music to a point just short of becoming a burdensome cliché). It works. But it works in spite of the metric ratiocination. If the listener cannot follow the composer's architectural-rhythmic plan, has the plan been successful? Perhaps Creston's disposition of meter is a logical device to defeat logicians. A well-informed, controlled piece of music, notwithstanding.

A fair performance. At the time this was recorded the Louisville group lacked string strength. However, it was good enough for Columbia to have issued it later (ML-5039). Eventually it fell into the delete category but not due to quality.

Partita for Flute, Violin, and Strings (1937)

☐ Vienna Symphony Orchestra / Hendl (conductor) / Desto 6424E (monaural)

A neo-classic chronicle. Each of the five movements—*Preamble, Sarabande, Burlesk, Air,* and *Tarantella*—is an excellent facsimile of a certified design.

An elegant and entertaining opus. It is nicely played. Unfortunately, Desto fails to give credit to the soloists.

Solo Instrument and Orchestra

Flute and Violin

Concertino for Marimba and Orchestra (1940)

☐ Philadelphia Orchestra / Owen (marimba) / Ormandy (conductor) / Columbia MS–6977

Affinity of material with the solo instrument is fully supplied in this instance. The marimba softly trips its way along a rhythmic path. It's a once-over lightly, little jazzy piece, and its attractiveness is its simplicity.

Expertly played by Owen and with the proper sense of proportion—which includes Ormandy.

Marimba

Sonata for Saxophone and Piano, Op. 19

☐ Sinta (saxophone); True (piano) / Mark 22868 (monaural)

There are those who still feel the saxophone is not a legitimate instrument, and that if it is to be accepted it should not be permitted in the domain of chamber music. The saxophone is only illegitimate in the hands of the badly tutored; the whining tone produced by the semi-professional is not real saxophone playing. Donald Sinta's playing exemplifies the liquidity and fluidity, the authentic special timbre beauty of the instrument.

There are certain Parisian influences in Creston's work, but its forthrightness makes it matter little where its ancestral deposits lie. Melodic spontaneity and jazz-strapped rhythms give life to the music, especially in the metrical subtleties that color the final movement. Sinta plays with sensitivity and suppleness. Where it is needed he supplies the necessary verve.

Chamber Music

Suite for Violin and Piano, Op. 18

☐ Steiner (violin); Berfield (piano) / Orion 74160

Strong counterpointed voicing in the outer movements (Prelude and Rondo). The drive of these parts of the work contrast with the balladic curves of the central movement, an Air. Creston's opus is well-made for the instruments, and the effect of the performance is one of solidity.

Henri-Jacques de Croes   (1705-1786)

Solo Instrument and Orchestra

Concerto No. 6 in B flat major for Flute, Violin, and Strings

☐ Solistes de Liège / Isselee (flute); Koch (violin); Koch-Pichon (harpsichord) / Le maire (conductor) / Musical Heritage Society MHS–793 CC–11

Flute and Violin

In this, the penultimate work in a set of seven concerti, Vivaldi characteristics are clear, and so is a second violin within the solo group, but no credit is indicated. The play ing is smooth and the interpreters fulfill the responsibility of style. Magnificent sounc (this is a transfer from an original Erato issue).

Lowell Cross   (1938-   )

Electronic Music

Three Etudes for Magnetic Tape

☐ Composers Recordings S–342

Conventionalized patterns in these electronic turns, though Cross does project a keenness for neat contrasts.

Gordon Crosse   (1937-   )

Orchestra

***Some Marches on a Ground* (1970)**

☐ Louisville Orchestra / Mester (conductor) / Louisville LS–741

An Ivesian approach that combines seriousness of format with keen musical wit. March tunes with drum support are pitted against string-instrument sounds and other commentary. By its maintenance, the severe opposition paradoxically gives a colorful blend to the sharp individuality. Dynamited chords against a soft string ostinato at the end prove Crosse's ear for fine-grained sonority and his ability to prepare and shape a splendid climax.

Mester has this orchestra playing at top level. Excellent trumpet execution by the first desk player who deserves program credit.

Solo Instrument and Orchestra

***Concerto da camera*, Op. 6**

☐ Melos Ensemble / Parikian (violin) / Downes (conductor) / Argo ZRG–759

Violin

This is a first cousin of dodecaphonic music. A basic series is used, but only of seven notes and these avoid craggy chromaticism. Taken from the row for special use is a vertical arrangement that clamps minor and diminished thirds together.

Crosse's piece travels on lyrical lines in the first-movement Prologue and third-movement *Canto*, twines around jagged curves in movement 2 (Scherzo) and movement 4 (Finale). Colors suggest themselves in terms of the instrumental conditions heard. The melodic flow has the settled white of sunlight about it, the spiky details of movements 2 and 4 envelop the timbres so that their gradations are the grey of dusk and the black of night.

This bears out Crosse's statement that the piece "can be heard as a drama of contrasts—of oppositions between 'characters,' instrumental and musical."

Played with impeccable attention to all details, with telling balances throughout. The recording itself is superbly engineered and Argo's documentation is of significant detail.

Changes

Cantata and Oratorio

☐ London Symphony Orchestra and Chorus, Orpington Junior Singers, and Highgate School for Boys Choir / Vyvyan (soprano); Shirley-Quirk (baritone) / Del Mar (conductor) / Argo ZRG-656

A large-scale work with large forces required but not offering complications for the listener. There is a variety of moods, based on texts from a number of poets, including Blake, as well as prayers. The link in the lengthy work which fills two record sides is the use of bell sounds and meanings.

A confirmed performance.

George Crumb (1929-   )

Echoes of Time and the River (Echoes II) (1968)

Orchestra

☐ Louisville Orchestra / Mester (conductor) / Louisville S-711

A prime example of George Crumb's special world of music (it won him the Pulitzer Prize in 1968). It is a world where the sounds are the themes, where the sonorities shimmer and blast, strike and undulate, where sounds are of intensity and expansion, subtlety and vigor.

The scoring calls for flutes, clarinets, horns, trumpets, two pianos, harp, mandolin, strings, and six percussionists dealing with a variety of qualities. The instruments are handled traditionally and untraditionally (the strings, for example, also strike antique cymbals and glockenspiel plates). Moreover, the players become vocalists stating certain phrases (nonsense, a Latin motto, a Spanish phrase) and whistle in chordal form. The philosophical program behind the work is really less important than the total evocative effect which provides a new music of inventive power that in its color surfaces is directly opposite the absolutes of neo-classicism, neo-romanticism, serialism, and the other style camps. If anything, Crumb stands alone.

The performance can be classified as being extremely good. That no major orchestra has seen fit to record this work produces an exactly contrary reaction.

Sonata for Solo Cello (1955)

Instrumental

Cello

☐ Sylvester (cello) / Desto 7169

Atypically, this music is without any special sonic pigmentation or special ways of playing ordinary or unordinary instruments. With an almost classical-romantic stance the music moves through a motivally engendered *Fantasia*, a set of variations on a *Tema pastorale*, and a Toccata.

Sylvester defines the cleanness of this work. It may not sound the most important messages, but it does impart precise, dramatic ones.

Five Pieces for Piano (1962)

Piano

☐ Burge (piano) / Advance 3 (monaural)

Crumb's palette is super-adventurous: strings are plucked with the finger tip, with the finger nail (the contacts are made at various locations), and the strings are also brushed.

There are other ideas included in this individual conception: finger nail vibrati, a special metallic vibrato, and meticulous use of the pedal. This inventory goes beyond statistics—it is set to obtain evocative eloquence akin to Debussy walking through an aleatoric world that suddenly is under strict controls.

Burge's re-creation makes him a super performer–partner. He brings out the sensibility of the music to sound as though one were enveloped in a bath of delicately perfumed water. His fidelity to the score is impressively secure; the phrases cling and lap against each other, the *forzati* become astringent adductions. Even those who may not fully agree with Crumb's thesis will not deny this stimulating performance.

(A slight negative report must be added. The sound engineering often brings no distinction between keyboard and direct finger contacts with the strings. This makes delicate pizzicati turn into light-scaled, ordinary piano sound, neutralizing some of the special colorations of the score.)

Makrokosmos, Volume I—Twelve Fantasy-Pieces After the Zodiac, for Amplified Piano (1972)

☐ Burge (piano) / Nonesuch 71293

Having poked his creative nose into a special coloristic world of sound, Crumb is not likely to pull it back. This big work of slightly over thirty-four minutes is another striking example of why he shouldn't pull back. No one has been able to match his particular creative conquests though innumerable young composers have attempted and are still trying. Crumb remains one of the great adventurers in fashioning timbres to make other timbres.

He always has a scenario for his music that in itself is smeared with color. The effects here require the use of an amplified piano. Each of the twelve pieces has its own suggestive title, each is linked with one of the Zodiac signs, and each, with enigmatic courage (his right, though annoying because we can't solve the puzzle), bears the initials of a person born under the sign. Further, the individual pieces are tri-grouped in sets of four each.

So much for the overall design. Inside it the features include the pianist playing on keyboard and within the instrument, plucking the strings, picking at them with a plectrum, using thimbles ("to evoke the image of a spectral mandolinist"), and, as he is theatrically required to do, shouting, singing, grunting, hissing, whispering, and whistling. A huge order, which this amazing pianist covers with great flair, precision, and artistry. There are also some dreamlike quotations, drawn from Chopin and Berlioz, set in the score as naturally as though they were conceived by Crumb himself.

David Burge is, expectedly (the cycle was written for him), accorded one of the subscripted initials and Crumb gives himself one. Just for the sake of the record we guess that G.R. (No. 1) represents George Rochberg, that A.W. (No. 6) is Arthur Weisberg, while P.Z. (No. 7) stands for Paul Zukofsky, and B.W. (No. 12) defines Bea Wernick, the bassoonist and wife of composer Richard Wernick.

Chamber Music

Four Nocturnes (Night Music II) for Violin and Piano (1964)

☐ Zukofsky (violin); Kalish (piano) / Mainstream MS-5016

Crumb's noctivagant chronicles have the startling beauty of stating their tales without beginnings, middles, or ends. The music floats, full of its own discoveries, of uncommon dedication to dots and dashes of sounds. Overall is the sense of weightlessness that only George Crumb seems capable of achieving with instruments. It is a music that haunts as it convinces.

The Zukofsky–Kalish team has recorded this work twice, as above for Mainstream, and for Desto (6435/37). Oddly enough the timings given for the total work vary considerably. On Mainstream it is 10:30, on Desto it is 8:55. The latter's shorter span may be due to the fact that there are no bands separating the four movements. However, aside from this (a minus point, nevertheless), the sound is better on the Mainstream release.

Voice of the Whale (Vox Balaenae) (1971)

☐ Aeolian Chamber Players / Columbia M–32739

Crumb's trio (for flute, piano, and cello, the performers of the first and last also playing antique cymbals) is indicated "for Three Masked Players." The masks, Crumb explains, "are intended to represent, symbolically, the powerful impersonal forces of nature." On a recording, naturally, this staging direction is meaningless. However, the total introspectiveness of the music relating strongly to this masked-performer concept is intensely apparent.

Crumb and special sound pigmentation are synonymous. In this work the flutist introduces the piece by simultaneously playing and singing into the instrument. A marvelous newness is thereby exhibited. The unmistakable originality of this prologue sets the tone for the composition, leading to a set of variations and an epilogue. Further colorations are the *scordatura* of the cello applied to the three lower strings and the amplification of the instruments by the use of contact microphones. (Other subtle effects result thereby.)

Since this edition has been recorded under the supervision of the composer, one may be certain of its definitiveness. Music of this kind depends on superb performers for its success. The Aeolian group (Erich Graf, flute; Walter Ponce, piano; and Jerry Grossman, cello) is superb.

Black Angels (Images 1): Thirteen Images from the Dark Land for Electric String Quartet (1970)

☐ New York String Quartet / Composers Recordings S–283

The detail of *Black Angels* is based on the hybrid of the traditional (programmaticism) and the new (electrically amplified string instruments). The work portrays a voyage of the soul, which, according to Crumb, represents three stages: *Departure* (fall from grace), *Absence* (spiritual annihilation), and *Return* (redemption).

Each instrumentalist also plays a variety of percussion instruments. Such additions in the realm of the string quartet have surfaced occasionally in avant-garde scores, but none can match Crumb's ingenious choices, including maracas, crystal glasses, metal thimbles, and tam-tams. Further, the players take on the roles of nontextual vocalists, providing tongue clicks, whispers, shouts of phonetic sounds, and whistling. The thesaurus of coloristic exploration includes special pedal sounds, a "viol consort" quality, playing behind the bridge, and striking the bow near the pegs. Tonal-styled music quotation is also heard. Truly, Crumb's combination of concord and discord, sibilation and stridency, resonance and mutescence, form a consensus that has never before appeared in the literature of chamber music.

Given the bizarrerie of the score, its artistic infraction of chamber music conduct, its beautiful violations of sound *qua* sound, it stands to reason that a performance using emphasis and pertinent exaggeration is mandatory. The New Yorkers are best in this respect. The version by the Concord String Quartet (on Vox SVBX–5306) shows more politeness than one wishes. The third recording of the work (by the Gaudeamus String Quartet on Philips 6500881) is sufficiently dynamic but the balances are not always clearly put forth (this applies more to the engineering than the performance itself). Sound in Crumb's work is equivalent to sonic vomiting. The CRI disc also provides the best resonant disgorgement.

Eleven Echoes of Autumn (1966)

☐ Aeolian Chamber Players / Composers Recordings S-233

Another of Crumb's instrumental revelations. Structure is built out of a motive but the sublime meaning of these eleven linked sections is color—fresh, new, violent, frightening, faint, loud, and chilling. It is a music that remembers nightmares in its daydream echoes. The timbral review is a Shangri-la of effects: rubber slid along the piano strings, vibrations bubbling from playing an alto flute and clarinet into the piano strings, harmonics, special bowing, chorded whistling, choked and released sounds that have and do not have identity. Surrounding the echoes is a softly spoken quote from García Lorca (a potent influence in the engenderment of a goodly number of Crumb's compositions).

A memorable visionary fantasy emerges from hearing this music. It is certain to grip a listener's imagination if the composition is approached fairly and without preconceived bias, and if one realizes that no contemporary composer can match Crumb's inspired type of instrumental individuation.

Crumb's work was written for the Aeolian Chamber Players so their performance is an understanding one that fully identifies with the score in all of its details. The recording of the variety of special sounds and of the many sympathetic vibrational partnerships that criss-cross the score has been successfully accomplished.

Vocal

*Voice
and
Instrumental
Ensemble*

Ancient Voices of Children (1970)

☐ Contemporary Chamber Ensemble / DeGaetani (mezzo-soprano); Dash (boy soprano) / Weisberg (conductor) / Nonesuch 71255

Crumb's magical sound images provide stunning beauties in this cycle of songs to García Lorca texts. It is a timbre highball whose recipe cannot be completely listed here but includes such things as Tibetan prayer stones, a chisel used on the piano's strings, two types of piano (electric and toy), tuned tom-toms, Japanese temple bells, and a musical saw. The voice part is not tied down to words. Additionally, its phonetically designed melismatic content projected onto the amplified piano strings, together with flutters and tongue clicks, forms a mini-orchestra by itself. When combined with the instrumental group (which also occasionally sings, whispers, and shouts), the total may be unconventional (for anybody but Crumb) but it is of the most significant expressivity.

Jan DeGaetani is phenomenal in this recording, as she was at the world premiere. (This was given in 1970 at the Coolidge Festival held at the Library of Congress. It brought the greatest ovation in the history of these festivals.) The boy soprano is superb, his part of haunting content. Arthur Weisberg and his musicians reveal every nuance and subtlety in Crumb's score. Nonesuch is to be congratulated for producing one of the great contemporary music recordings.

Madrigals

☐ Suderburg (soprano); Shrader (percussion); Skowrcnek (flute, piccolo, and alto flute); Vokolek (harp); Warner (double bass) / Turnabout 34523

Another work in the several that Crumb has written based on García Lorca texts. The Madrigals are divided into four Books (the first two were composed in 1965, the other pair in 1969). Each has a different instrumentation in combination with the soprano. Thus:

vibraphone and double bass (in Book 1); flute, doubling on alto flute and piccolo, and percussion (in Book 2); harp and percussion (in Book 3); and flute, harp, double bass, and percussion (in Book 4). The emotional effusion of the music is obtained by virtuoso singing of the involved and difficult microtones, whispering, stratospheric registration, and disjunct picturesque patterns, together with instrumentational effects that are almost the private property of George Crumb (or, at least, his copyrighted ownership). These are on-surface colors but penetrate with inner emotional vividness.

The difficulties for the voice are conquered totally by Elizabeth Suderburg who maintains a fine vocal quality. All the instrumental details are expertly set forth by members of The Contemporary Group of the University of Washington.

Night Music I (1963)

☐ Toth (soprano); Parmelee (piano and celesta); Burge and MacCluskey (percussion) / Crumb (conductor) / Composers Recordings S–218

Seven nocturnes (Crumb's term), two of which include the voice, with texts by García Lorca (a favorite of the composer). The musical dynamic is obtained by the special sounds that mark all of George Crumb's music. These are arranged for the most intense luminosity by impressionistic dabs and colors that contrast and punctuate sharply. Examples: the piano is mainly played inside its mechanism, a gong is lowered into and out of water accomplishing a unique type of pitch glide. (In all fairness, this instrumental color was first used by John Cage.)

The execution is beautifully conveyed and extremely sensitive. Louise Toth colors her voice with proper interpretive strategy.

Night of the Four Moons (1969)

☐ Aeolian Chamber Players / DeGaetani (mezzo-soprano) / Columbia M–32739

The only familiar aspect of Crumb's music is his own recognizable style—a style that is color-drenched, mystical, and dynamically narrative. In each of Crumb's works there is never exactly the same use of timbre individualities or combinations. Only the texts here repeat Crumb's preoccupation with the poetry of García Lorca.

Crumb's resourceful color impulse is never traditional. In this case the quartet of instruments includes a cello, but it is an electric type; a banjo, but it is played with a glass rod; and percussion that embraces such esoteric representatives as Tibetan prayer stones, Japanese Kabuki blocks, an alto African thumb piano (a *mbria*), and a Chinese temple gong, as well as the usual tambourine, suspended cymbal, etcetera. The flute family is only drawn on, in the normal sense of things, with the use of an alto flute and piccolo. However, even the vocalist is in new territory, playing finger cymbals, castanets, a glockenspiel, and a tam-tam in addition to singing.

All concerned with this performance realize the captivating fantasy of Crumb's conception. Thus far the Columbia issue is the only one that is on the market. There is no need for another, really.

Songs, Drones, and Refrains of Death for Baritone and Chamber Orchestra (1968)

☐ Philadelphia Composers' Forum / Weller (baritone) / Thome (conductor) / Desto 7155

Crumb's private and terrifying colors are on exhibit here again in a set of four songs to García Lorca poems, each prefaced by instrumental concentration, called "refrains." There is no doubting the power of his coloristic intelligence, intensified by having all the instruments, save the percussion, electrified (guitar, contrabass, harpsichord, and piano). The percussion—if different representatives of a single type are each counted—totals fifty-nine. In addition, the baritone supplements his singing with ten percussion instruments, and the guitarist, bass player, and pianist each have three. Thus a grand total of seventy-eight qualities supplement the many others.

Such rich compost could easily threaten the very existence of the subject matter, but it is carefully dovetailed with the dark character of both text and music.

The performance of Thome's musicians is totally assimilative. One doubts that a better version would be possible. Every nuance, variation, and mutation is controlled and yet the entire work sounds free, fluid, and thereby forceful.

César Cui   (1835-1918)

Instrumental

Piano

Berceuse in E flat major, Op. 20, No. 8

Etude in F major

☐ Tarnowsky (piano) / Genesis 1004

A pair of examples of Cui's best creative side: light-faceted, Schumannesque music. Genesis's listing assigns the notation Op. 40, No. 6 to the Etude. This is incorrect, since Op. 40 covers an orchestral work in five movements, *Suite IV: "À Argenteau."*

Richard Cumming   (1928-   )

Instrumental

Piano

Twenty-Four Preludes

☐ Browning (piano) / Desto 7120

An interesting thesaurus that moves through all of the major and minor keys, including one example each for right hand and left hand alone, and covering assorted lengths and styles "ranging from the café to strict twelve tone." The formal blueprint may not be original, but the working out of the details is penetrative and imaginative.

Browning's interpretations offer no disadvantages to Cumming's music. Each one of the stylistic hats he puts on while he plays fully fits.

Arthur Cunningham   (1928-   )

Orchestra

Lullaby for a Jazz Baby **(1969)**

☐ Oakland Youth Orchestra / Hughes (conductor) / Desto 7107

Jazz—yes, baby! Both idiomatic and imaginative. All the makin's: screaming trumpet, pit-patter, wa-wa mute color, blues, perky percussion, trombone gliss.

Top pros could, of course, knock off this score with no trouble. Still, young people having a go at it do it with much more class, simply because they are not as sedate. So, chalk one up for the Oakland Youth Orchestra and its conductor, Robert Hughes.

Instrumental

Piano

Engrams

☐ Hinderas (piano) / Desto 7102/3

The composer explains the title as "memory tracings." The remembrance is serialism, which is the functional equipment for the work. Certainly given a fine performance by this splendid musician.

Curtis O. B. Curtis-Smith (1941-   )

Rhapsodies

☐ Burge (piano) / Composers Recordings SD–345

Instrumental

Piano

Four extremely colorful pieces, titled from lines taken from Joyce's *Ulysses,* and with tolerance of the words in the musical conceptions. These are all rich sonorous sensations and most inventive ones, even with reminders of the creative world of George Crumb. Curtis-Smith uses the keyboard and the piano's insides, including bowing of the strings. The information in part 4 (*Listen! The spiked and winding cold seahorn*) sounds as though the production were made in an electronic music studio.

David Burge's playing cannot be challenged. Music of this kind demands as much virtuosity as do the large tonal compositions. No critic can fault Mr. Burge in this respect.

Five Sonorous Inventions

☐ Fischbach (violin); Curtis-Smith (piano) / Composers Recordings S–346

Chamber Music

Violin and piano changed to different identities by specially devised bows threaded at various points through the piano's strings; use of a flat-bridged violin with the pianist turning the violin's pegs, producing varying microtones and glissandi; a special mute that provides filtering (intermittent) sounds; a guitar pick (worn on the thumb) by the pianist to obtain special plucked timbres: and so on and so forth.

The inventions are skillful but the attenuated results deflate the surprise factor. All of the opus can be classified as a surrealistic type of impressionism.

Such passionate attachment by the composer for specialized timbre esoterica is to be respected. It is certainly worth taking the aural excursion into these strange realms of sonority.

Arthur Custer (1923-   )

Found Objects No. 3, for Contrabass and Tape

☐ Turetzky (contrabass) / Serenus 12045

Instrumental

Double Bass

Free and loose sounds, improvisationally based and improvisationally determined. A program exists (fully described on the liner note) but it concerns live performance. On disc there's little to hang on to. But no matter what Bertram Turetzky does, it's always interesting, so just listen to his sounds and those additional ones that surround his playing. The free and loose material is not deprived of originality.

Found Objects No. 6, for Flute and Tape

☐ Shansky (flute, alto flute, and piccolo) / Serenus 12045

Flute

The title should properly read "for flutes and tape" since the music is described by Custer as "a series of moods expressed via the differing 'personalities' of flute, alto flute and piccolo.'' The duo term applies by the use of the tape which combines with as well as contrasts to the wind instruments' plus synthesizer sounds which expand the timbre spectrum even further.

Custer's piece is involved with a variety of dispositions—none are obvious or trite. As such the compositional freeway twists and turns but the landscape is always interesting. The scoring of the tape material is exceedingly effective.

Piano

Four Ideas for Piano

Rhapsodality Brown! (1968)

☐ Peltzer (piano) / Serenus 12024

Plenty of dynamism in the *Ideas* without any formalistic problems. In *Rhapsodality* both ''rhapsody'' and ''sodality'' can be recognized. As for *Brown*, recognition occurs only when the total title is suddenly vocalized by the pianist, midway in the piece. A golden performance by this skilled, contemporary-minded musician.

I Used to Play by Ear, for Two Pianists, One Piano, and Selected Objects (1971)

☐ Peltzer (piano) / Serenus 12031

Jazzy and with a plentiful supply of special effects applied to the inside and outside of the instrument. The ''selected objects'' include a plastic bottle, a rubber snake, a large toothbrush, and a stuffed rubber chicken. In addition, percussion instruments are used.

While probably more fun to watch than to hear on a recording, *I Used to Play* (four movements of the total seven in the work are covered here) is still worth listening time. Thanks to tape science Peltzer performs both parts and is thus a (duo-) pianist. And a damn good one (or two)!

Chamber Music

Found Objects No. 8, for Violin and Tape

☐ Kobialka (violin) / Serenus 12045

Mostly tonal segments that represent a free-floating quality that is assisted (gently) by the tape. Improvisation is included but Kobialka's abilities along that line can be questioned since he seems to be bounded by standard-traditional fiddlistic patterns. Be that as it may, the Custer work falls gently on the ears in a way that is related to the impasto technique of painting.

Parabolas, for Viola and Piano (1970)

☐ Sackson (viola); Peltzer (piano) / Serenus 12031

Jekyll-and-Hyde character. The quite serious projection is four times interrupted with the flash of a mighty surprise. Twice this produces singing on the part of the violist and twice Bach is mangled by Custer inventing on top of Bach's *Invention*. What objective was planned is not explained (nothing is indicated in the liner notes about any of these happenings). Nonetheless, the sense of jest layered on the musical polemic is strong. More proof: in public performance at a specific point in movement 2, if there is a page turner ''he is expected to rise and conduct this section.''

Sackson and Peltzer are an excellent team. Theirs is a beautifully honed and inwardly animated performance.

Permutations

☐ Douglas (violin); Gray (clarinet); Davis (cello) / Composers Recordings S-253

Rhapsodic rhetorical structural elements give the three movements a split personality. The music moves from preambles to transitions to contained perorations.

String Quartet No. 2 (Concertino for Second Violin) (1964)

☐ St. Louis Quartet / Serenus 12024

A quartet "intended to do honor" to the second violinist. A worthy democratic thought but only successful if observed on stage. On a recording it is difficult to ascertain which fiddler is being honored. Aside from the hop-skip-and-jump of microtonal glides and percussive pizzicati in movement 2, actual percussion instruments are used by the players. These strengthen the entertaining syntax of the music. So does the mock waltz section that suddenly pokes its way into the final movement.

Concerto for Brass Quintet

☐ New York Brass Quintet / Serenus 12031

This vivid and theatrical music is vivacious and trenchant, and is played so excitingly as to have one think fiddles are being bowed rather than brass instruments blown. A mighty fine piece of work including the usual special coloration that marks Custer's output. In this case percussive effects are made by striking the music stands with mutes.

Two Movements for Woodwind Quintet (1964)

☐ Interlochen Arts Quintet / Composers Recordings S–253

Contrastive commentary with textural differences in part 1 and frisky figurations of woodwind quintet writing in part 2. A performance of excellence.

Three Pieces for Six Brass Instruments (1958)

☐ American Brass Quintet / Happe (horn) / Serenus 12024

Direct and spontaneous contemporary music, which gives all the pluses necessary. A finely finished performance by a top-class organization.

Cycle for Nine Instruments (1963)

☐ Francis Chagrin Ensemble / Farberman (conductor) / Serenus 12024

Notwithstanding the directorial role of Harold Farberman in this performance, Custer's nonet represents large-sized chamber music. The scoring calls for four strings, two brass, and a trio of oddly assorted winds: a flute alternating with piccolo, an alto saxophone, and a bass clarinet. A light and colorful quadruple-partitioned piece, with motility and clarity throughout. Custer's keen spacing plans define the assorted timbres, which are cogently displayed in a fine performance.

Comments on This World (1967)

☐ Phoenix String Quartet / Forrester (contralto) / Serenus 12031

Texts by Abbie Huston Evans; parts 1 and 3 are nature poems, the second poem is more expressionistic. There is a neat affiliation—a dramatic one, actually—between voice and quartet, making the cycle a true quintet.

A performance that spells out once again Forrester's marvelously pure and artistically applied voice.

Vocal

Voice and Instrumental Ensemble

**Opera
and Dramatic
Music**

Found Objects No. 5, for Five Instruments and Tape

☐ Poularikas (violin); McClintock (clarinet); Pellegrino (trumpet); Pezzullo (trombone); Preston (contrabass); Custer (piano) / Custer (conductor) / Serenus 12045

Subtitled *A Little Sight Music* since it is strongly structured by improvisational sound reactions to two- or three-dimensional visual objects. Custer's piece is fun and games and the players seem to be enjoying themselves if the auditor isn't (or can't, because visual response is necessary for this type of piece to be really successful). No shapes emerge, but there are a variety of vaudevillian or circusy sounds and some verbal commentary that the performing personnel pass around.

One minor question. Custer's title states that the piece is for five players, but six instrumentalists are credited.

Francis Cutting   (fl. 1583 - 1596)

Instrumental

Lute

Galliard in G minor

☐ Spencer (lute) / Philips 6500282

An example of one of Cutting's forty-five solos for the lute.

Carl Czerny   (1791 - 1857)

Hexaméron. **See under** *Franz Liszt: Solo Instrument and Orchestra: piano (Hexaméron).*

**Solo
Instrument
and
Orchestra**

Piano

Piano Concerto in A minor, Op. 214

☐ Vienna Chamber Orchestra / Blumental (piano) / Froschauer (conductor) / Turnabout 34389

Though the creative flame does not burn high, Czerny's Concerto is sufficiently reasonable to be heard from time to time. There is nothing gauche about the writing, it is simply scrupulously imitative. The grammar is correct, and the forms are well presented.

The piano sound is somewhat brittle, for which the blame is to be applied to the instrument used and not the engineers. The proof is that the orchestra is heard with satisfaction.

**Piano,
Four Hands**

Concerto for Piano - Four Hands and Orchestra in C major, Op. 153

☐ Camerata Symphony Orchestra / Jean and Kenneth Wentworth (piano) / Kaplan (conductor) / Desto 7149

Despite the fact that nothing in Czerny's work can vaguely be termed individual, it offers a good quotient of enjoyment. Czerny studied with Beethoven and it is the great man's influence that is well-applied to this three-movement work.

Of course, a four-hand piano with orchestra piece is not standard repertoire, so it offers that specialness. The Wentworth team do well by the score.

Fantaisie et variations brillantes sur un motif très favori chanté par Mme. Malibran   *Instrumental*
dans l'opéra "Ines de Castro de Persiani," Op. 377

Sonata No. 1, Op. 7   *Piano*

☐ Somer (piano) / Genesis 1057

Make no mistake—there is no scholastic advice carried over to Czerny's early Sonata. This is a fine example of creativity that makes one indebted to Hilde Somer for uncovering it and making it available in a top-flight recorded performance. The work is structurally solid and of size to match: five movements, including a steamy Scherzo in *prestissimo agitato* tempo and a final *Capriccio fugato* that is a lesson for those who persist in viewing fugal writing through academic lenses.

The much later work shows a healthy appetite for brilliance and variational panache, as conveyed through an introduction, the main tune, and a half-dozen permutations. Thus: purple musical prose in the form of runs, roulades, ripples, and let-fly Lisztian pianistic liberalism.

Hilde Somer has all the virtuosity and then some to be the interpretative trustee of the *Fantaisie et variations*. But more—the playing is imbued with an artistic perception, which is the only fair way of dealing with this type of music. In the Sonata the thrust required in the dramatic sections and the fast-moving portions is fully supplied and in the polyphonic conclusion the linear clarity is superfine.

Alphons Czibulka   *(1842-1894)*

Love's Dream After the Ball, Op. 356   *String Orchestra*

☐ London Symphony Orchestra / Bonynge (conductor) / London 2232

Love's Dream is an oldie that was a café music perennial. It's good to have this sentimental intermezzo available in a modern top-flight recorded performance.

D

Entries on composers whose surnames are preceded by particles beginning with d (such as d', da, dall, de, and so on) are arranged alphabetically according to the surname; however, entries on composers generally known by prefixed names (such as Dello Joio and Del Tredici) are alphabetized according to common usage.

Ingolf Dahl   (1912-1970)

The Tower of Saint Barbara (1955)   *Orchestra*

☐ Louisville Orchestra / Whitney (conductor) / Louisville 56-2 (monaural)

Subtitled *Symphonic Legend in Four Parts,* this music functions as peripheral programmaticism; the picture painting is hinted at rather than boldly defined. Its movements—*Barbara, The King, The Tower,* and *The Martyrdom*—are particularly concerned with an advanced polyphonic style in which free dissonant counterpoint rules.

The Louisville recording provides a sympathetic reading of Dahl's score, though the orchestra's string strength is less than it should be.

Fanfares (1958)   *Instrumental*

☐ Helps (piano) / Composers Recordings S-288   *Piano*

A short neoclassic essay, structurally clarified by ternary division. Impeccable piano playing by this soloist.

Hymn (1947)

Sonata pastorale (1959)

Sonata seria (1953)

☐ Fierro (piano) / Orion 76209

Dahl's neoclassic assurance is illustrated in these three works. However, there is no cold preaching of technical dogma—the range of expression within the style is extremely wide. The music has no romantic afflatus (one cannot find a superfluous note in Dahl's scores); there is a cultivation of rhythmic life, coloristic range, and a naturalistic narrative. The dissonant polyphony and polyharmonies contribute measurably to the textual meaning of the music.

Both of the sonatas (served well by the soloist) have big gestures; the *Sonata pastorale* is of more balletic type and simpler constructions, including a Scherzino and *Fête champêtre.* The *Sonata seria* has fast and slow movements flanking a pair of Fantasias. The Hymn has baroque solidity projecting fantasia expressivity.

Saxophone

Concerto for Alto Saxophone (1949)

☐ Hemke (alto saxophone); Granger (piano) / Brewster 1203

Although originally Dahl's work was scored for solo saxophone with wind ensemble, this version stands by itself, the piano part not being a reduction of the instrumental score. For the duo arrangement there was a total recasting of the music.

Dahl's work is a sophisticated stylization of harmonic and contrapuntal construction. It represents the neoclassic technique in its most advanced state. Emphatic tonality is employed, but it is fructified by dynamic dissonance and fertile polyharmonies. Emotionalism is not avoided, but it is not sentimental, proclamatory, or of archaic origin. It is freshly contemporary and cleanly powerful, proving that many potent areas still exist in tonal music.

Notwithstanding Dahl's viewpoint concerning the saxophone-piano version, it does not have the coloristic punch of the setting with wind ensemble (which includes double basses). Nonetheless, this performance, even with only fair piano sound and some off-balance engineering, will have to serve until the larger (in instruments) and slightly larger (in content) edition has been recorded.

Chamber Music

Duettino concertante for Flute and Percussion (1966)

☐ Dwyer (flute); Firth (percussion) / RCA LSC–6189
☐ DiTullio (flute); Ervin (percussion) / Crystal 641

Dahl's work is an instrumentational curiosity, for there are exceedingly few duos for a wind instrument with percussion. However, in no case is the percussion a mere dictatorial accenting agent. It simulates neat (pulsatile) melodic swirls and twirls and is a totally real polyphonic companion. The *Duettino* exemplifies tonalized serialism. It is not only diversified but diverting as well.

There is little to choose between the two performances, save a slightly brighter tone on the RCA release. It is only proper to indicate that Dahl had expressed to the author some reservations about the percussion treatment in the RCA performance. He was to give the details "next time I speak to you." His unfortunate death prevented learning what criticisms he had.

Concertino a tre (1946)

☐ Lurie (clarinet); Shapiro (violin); Gottlieb (cello) / New World Records NW–281 (monaural)

Dahl's trio for one woodwind and two stringed instruments combines set forms of classicism with the tenor of valid musical sense. The principle of relating basic tonalities with respect for their clarity and the renewing of the traditional characteristics of the classic school with contemporary attractions is constant. Thus, the frictions within the assertive tonal demeanor of this work are neoclassic, not neoacademic.

Sharply convincing playing is exhibited by this team. The work was recorded in 1950, originally released by Columbia. Its reissue is good news.

Allegro and Arioso for Five Wind Instruments (1942)

☐ New York Woodwind Quintet / Concert-Disc 216

An interplay of brilliance and lyricism, further contrasted by differing formal patterns. Although this is a composition without superemotional heat (put together by the hand of a master), this type of music has its sensual appeal too.

First-rate performance with reproduced sound of excellence. (The label copy is a mess, since side 2 is duplicated. Dahl's work should be noted as side 1, to be recognized as the first band of a pair. The correct side 2 has four bands, covering a work by Alvin Etler.)

Music for Brass Instruments (1944)

☐ Canadian Brass / Vanguard VSD–71253

Wealthy, original, serious, and bold music. The pace and style of the three movements parallel the modern prelude (Chorale Fantasy), scherzo (Intermezzo), and vigorous-finale (Fugue) pattern. The opening is based on *Christ Lay in the Bonds of Death.* Three-part form encloses the variational treatment afforded the subject. The Intermezzo is pert, profane as it were, in relation to the semisacred facture of the preceding movement. The logic of this rondo-delineated scherzo is asymmetry—of meter, accentuation, and color application. The arguments of the finale's contrapuntalism are not from the textbook.

This is no work for any but first-class players, technically analogous in brass literature to the late Beethoven string quartets, and requiring just as expert musicians to work their way through the pitfalls. Such credit belongs to this brass-instrument team.

Luigi Dallapiccola *(1904-1975)*

Due pezzi (1947)
Orchestra

☐ Louisville Orchestra / Whitney (conductor) / Louisville 641 (monaural)

This is an orchestral version Dallapiccola made of his violin-and-piano *Due studi.* Correlativism is found between the two settings. In the comments for the *Due studi* (see under *Instrumental: violin*) it is noted that the muscle and vitality of the second piece are better displayed in the orchestral version (in a performance that adds substantially to the Louisville Orchestra's reputation). Conversely, the first of the two pieces loses a considerable amount of its shadowy, whispery flexibility in the enlarged scoring.

Heard as separate entities, both the instrumental and orchestral versions are successful. However, to secure the best of two worlds, the auditor should secure both recordings. Aside from considering the findings noted here regarding the two musical castings, the *Due pezzi,* when compared with the *Due studi,* offer a special insight into the orchestrational art and science of a master composer.

Piccola musica notturna (1954)

☐ New Philharmonia Orchestra / Prausnitz (conductor) / Argo ZRG–757

Music impregnated with Debussyan sensuousness, darkly orchestrated, fused by a twelve-tone row organized by different interval totals between each pitch. But its sixty-eight measures in *molto tranquillo, ma senza trascinare* tempo prove that dodecaphonic status does not mean an emotional stasis constantly found in the *Weltschmerz* category.

Important to the piece are the bell-like, percussively ictused measures that split the textural softness. These punctuations occur five times and provide a radiant effect.

Prausnitz produces a five-star performance. The sensitivity of the colors and phrasing he obtains are beautiful.

Due studi for Violin and Piano (1947)
Instrumental

☐ Gross (violin); Grayson (piano) / Orion 74147
Violin

These *Due studi* exemplify a totally fresh twelve-tone sound not to be found either within the severity of the older practitioners of Schoenbergian ideology or within the abstruseness of the younger composers.

The first of the pair of pieces is a freely formed *Sarabande*. In this instance Dallapiccola refused to follow the ordinary strict measurements of the stately dance. Neither development nor recapitulation is cut to fit, but both have refined subtlety. The violin is muted, the music haunted by a *quasi parlando* main subject. Gross's portrayal of this movement is of exquisite sensitivity and complete musical insight. Immediately following is a *Fanfara e fuga,* as vibrant in character as the previous piece was introspective. Gross does well with this portion, though the dynamism is better projected in the orchestral version Dallapiccola made under the title *Due pezzi* (see under *Orchestra*).

Vocal

*Voice
and
Instrumental
Ensemble*

Concerto per la notte di Natale dell'anno 1956

☐ Philadelphia Composers' Forum / Lamoree (soprano) / Thome (conductor) / Candide 31021

Dallapiccola's form of musical worship is not marked by commonplace hymn singing in this "Christmas Concerto for the Year 1956" for soprano voice and seventeen instruments. The voice is employed in the second and fourth movements, and the translated tempi (animated, jubilant and impetuous, violent) underline the apodictic tone of vehemence that shows the worship of God is as powerful (if not as sweet) as ever. The poetry consists of three excerpts (a total of twenty-two lines) from the thirteenth-century mystic writer Jacopone da Todi. An instrumental prologue initiates the composition, and the second vocal section is preceded by an intermezzo and concluded with an epilogue. It is possible to describe these divisions as *cantus lateralis,* literally "song side by side," since the continual growth of the material not only reaches new points of information but provides constant fresh ideas of instrumental color.

The composition is heard with dramatic direction. Apparently chamber ensembles with local identity do not always use home talent. Most of the members of Joel Thome's group are New York–based.

Goethe Lieder (1953)

☐ Ensemble Amsterdam / Dorow (soprano) / de Leeuw (conductor) / Telefunken 642350

The language of these seven concise pieces illustrates how potent twelve-tone speech can be in place of the overgushing conversations of the postromantic tonal elite. Regardless of the total polyphony (the harmony results from the juxtaposition of moving lines; it is not measured to fit specific vertical arrangement), there is no harshness. Dallapiccola's active support of dodecaphonic language is warmed by his Mediterranean accent; it speaks with passion, but passionate neatness.

The "Goethe Songs" constitute lyrical chamber music for the unusual combination of a voice and three different clarinets: the small (E flat), normal, and bass. Although the aid of the score is required to decipher the assorted tone-row permutations, this is unnecessary; musical content and merit need not be determined or proved by technical premises. This music glows; it is also very moving.

Dorothy Dorow's voice is beautifully adapted to this type of music, and her understanding of the style is patently clear in every measure. Good support by the instrumentalists. It is very good to have this work restored to the record catalogue, the old Epic (No. 3706) issue having gone to rest.

Nos. 2, 3, 5, and 6 are included in RCA LM-6092. Good, but one shouldn't choose this at the expense of missing Nos. 1, 4, and 7.

Parole di San Paolo (1964)

☐ Philadelphia Composers' Forum / Valente (mezzo-soprano) / Thome (conductor) / Candide 31021

The Italianate quality of the *Parole* persuades one that he is listening to richly chromaticized music, not expressionistic dodecaphonicism. Thus the special talent of this composer is to furnish music with clear textures and an emotive condition that is not scratched by *Weltschmerz*. A quiet and smooth performance with alert sensitivity to color.

Sicut Umbra (1970)

☐ London Sinfonietta / Michelow (mezzo-soprano) / Bertini (conductor) / Argo ZRG–791

Three songs, preceded by a very short introduction, set to poems in Spanish by Juan Ramón Jiménez. The instrumentation parallels the poetic totality by use of timbre triplicity. Dallapiccola uses piccolo, flute, and alto flute as one unit; E flat clarinet, B flat clarinet, and bass clarinet as another group; three stringed instruments (violin, viola, and cello); and a bell-like combine of vibraphone, celesta, and harp. The flutes play in the prelude. Clarinets and strings join the voice in *El olvido;* these are amplified by the flute combination in *El recuerdo.* The total twelve instruments and voice are heard in the *Epitafio ideal de un marinero.*

The music is restrained, acutely sensitized by the instrumental commentary. The delicacy of the writing only emphasizes the inner strength that pervades the cycle, to be considered as "a contemplation of death." There are composers who can be considered only as dodecaphonic diehards. Luigi Dallapiccola again confirms in his *Sicut Umbra* (the title drawn from the Book of Job: *Sicut umbra dies nostri sunt super terram*—"Our days on earth are but a shadow") that he stands supreme in managing serialism to convey the most telling romantic expressivity.

Preghiere (1962)

Voice and Orchestra

☐ New Philharmonia Orchestra / McDaniel (baritone) / Prausnitz (conductor) / Argo ZRG–757

Preghiere joins dark, dramatic lyricism with an orchestra of nine woodwinds (including alto saxophone and double bassoon), two brass instruments, celesta, piano, vibraphone, xylomarimba, and a solo string quintet. Power and demand match music with the text's objective as perceived in the concluding lines of the work: "Before the Crucifix/ I stand, pale and/ Trembling:/ 'Thou who art the true son of God/ Unnail humanity from this Cross.'"

Barry McDaniel's full voice is perfect for this music. His diction is fine, his understanding of the structure apparent. Prausnitz's directing of the score is of high artistic order. Indeed, everyone connected with this recording deserves a superb rating.

Sex Carmina Alcaei (1943)

☐ New Philharmonia Orchestra / Harper (soprano) / Prausnitz (conductor) / Argo ZRG–757

The striking fact about these *Sex Carmina Alcaei* is the sheer musical beauty that is derived from the most rigorous technical substantiation. All types of dodecaphonically based canons are utilized—simple, double by contrary motion, crab, etc. What generally results from such conduct is quite ordinary musical exercise. In Luigi Dallapiccola's hands the evidence is magnificent artistic expertise.

The natural impulse of these songs is certainly proof of creative genius going beyond stylistic method, since all the technical trappings are fully proven in the score. The performance is of genuine musicality.

Choral

Chorus Alone

Due cori di Michelangelo Buonarroti il Giovane (1936)

☐ Monteverdi-Chor, Hamburg / Jürgens (conductor) / Telefunken 641011

More sunny than most of Dallapiccola's choral compositions. One hears the breakdown of straightforward tonality in these two pieces, a shadowing of the pantonal technique that would appear later in Dallapiccola's work and finally end in serialism. Another outstanding performance by this organization. The Monterverdi Chorus has the sensitivity of a super string quartet.

Tempus Destruendi/Tempus Aedificandi (1971)

☐ BBC Singers / Kennard (soprano); Milburn-Fryer (contralto) / Poole (conductor) / Argo ZRG–791

A diptych of opposites: a *Ploratus* ("Lamentation") titled *Tempus Destruendi* ("A Time to Destroy") and an *Exhortatio* ("Exhortation") titled *Tempus Aedificandi* ("A Time to Build"). Dallapiccola's work was the outcome of a commission that was to be concerned with the city of Jerusalem. Accordingly, the significance of "the building of a new civilization, with new or renewed values, on the ruins of an old, outmoded one."

The vehemence of the laments and urgencies of this music are fully detailed in the performance. Pitch clarity in the chromatic diction utilized is not easy to come by; the BBC group accomplishes it though with some strain, but paradoxically that is an assist to a successful portrayal.

Chorus and Instrumental Ensemble

Canti di prigionia (1941)

☐ Monteverdi-Chor, Hamburg / Jürgens (conductor) / Telefunken 641011

A massive work in three movements—the first for six-part chorus, the middle one for four-part women's voices, the final one moving from four to eight parts for the mixed chorus. An array of bell-like instruments frame, move with and against the voices. Never accompanimental, the scoring covers two pianos, paired harps, vibraphone, xylophone, six timpani, ten bells, plus tripled tam-tams, cymbals, and some other percussion.

Pantonal mostly, panchromatic partly, this work is Dallapiccola before serialism became his total language. As dramatic as an operatic tragedy, as frightening in its restraint as a dark mystery, the music never releases a tension that is both moving and exciting.

Jürgens directs the music impeccably. The intonation is fantastically maintained, and the group is amazing in its projection of the varied dynamic range. Perfect balances pertain. One of the best contemporary choral recordings ever made.

The credits give no indication as to the instrumentalists. Doubtless, a free-lance group assembled for the concert given in the Hamburg Music Hall, May 13, 1964, at which the recording was made.

Opera and Dramatic Music

Il prigioniero (1948)

☐ National Symphony Orchestra and University of Maryland Chorus / Barrera (soprano); Emili and Carelli (tenors); Harrell (baritone); Mazzieri (bass) / Dorati (conductor) / London 1166

Il prigioniero is a story of persecution, of a man's escape being aborted when the jailer who aided him turns out to be the Grand Inquisitor. Constructive symbolism wraps itself around the score by the use of tone rows to express prayer, hope, and freedom, by triadic harmony equating liberty, and by choral writing in sixteenth-century style.

There is an undertoned harshness in the score, but it is matched (not tempered) by Verdian vocal verity as well as enriched by Bergian instrumental fervor. This is no mix; the identifications outlined are simply an approach to technical description. In *Il prigioniero* Luigi Dallapiccola is his own creative man.

The performance is genuine, meshed beautifully and kept at a point of intensity that never lessens. Maurizio Mazzieri as the Prisoner is fully forceful and emotively truthful. Romano Emili's two-faced characterization of the Jailer and the Grand Inquisitor covers the role's subtle and dynamic scope admirably. Dorati is truly in command and clarifies every measure in the forty-six-minute length of the work. It is one of the superb operatic documents of the twentieth century.

Jean-Michel Damase (1928-   )

Sonata for Flute and Harp

Chamber Music

☐ Rampal (flute); Laskine (harp) / Musical Heritage Society MHS–1345

Damase's duo proves that certain composers have an impersonality in their music yet convey a well-balanced vitality. Though Damase has no dominant individuality, the tunefulness of his piece (commissioned for the recording) is immediately recognizable. There are agile themes, and dissonances are arranged in the milder conventions of the present century. One wishes for just some more harmonic naughtiness. No need to wish for a better rendition, however.

Jean-François Dandrieu (1682-1738)

Les Caractères de la guerre

Orchestra

☐ Angelicum Orchestra of Milan / Jenkins (conductor) / Nonesuch 71146

Subtitled *Suite de symphonies, ajoutée à l'Opéra.* The Dandrieu war characters disport gaily and persistently in one key. The picture painting is reflected solely in the titles, not in the music for a pair of marches, a pair of fanfares (the second one cast as a minuet!), "The Charge," etc. The only militaristic colorations are some broken-chord trumpet calls and a handful of timpani flourishes.

Dandrieu promises more than he delivers, though as a festive piece the conception has its moments.

Dialogue

Instrumental

☐ Hansen (organ) / Nonesuch 71170

Organ

The duo sense is obtained by differences of registration. These are precisely met in the performance of this short bit.

Noël with Variations

☐ Biggs (organ) / Columbia MS–7438

The tune is *Or nous dites Marie;* the variants avoid the deadliness of mechanical calculations. Played on a fine eighteenth-century organ at the Abbey Church of Ebersmunster, in France, with a natural but fully alert consideration of the music.

Pierre Dandrieu   (?-1733)

Instrumental

Organ

Noël with Variations

☐ Biggs (organ) / Columbia MS-7438

A "song of the people" (as Columbia describes it): *Quand le Sauveur Jésus-Christ fut né de Marie* developed with persuasively clear variations. The playing is fresh-colored (with emphasis on a variety of flute stops) and thoroughly well balanced (using an old French organ at the Abbey Church of Ebersmunster). Splendidly recorded.

Mabel Daniels   (1878-1971)

Orchestra

Deep Forest (1931)

☐ Imperial Philharmonic of Tokyo / Strickland (conductor) / Composers Recordings 145 (monaural)

Herewith romantic chromaticism embellishing classical solidity. An intimate mood picture originally scored for chamber orchestra and then recast for normal-sized symphony orchestra. *Deep Forest* has an imposing performance record over the years; the recording is, indeed, welcome. It is exceedingly well done.

Chamber Music

Three Observations for Three Woodwinds (1945)

☐ Roseman (oboe); Rabbay (clarinet); McCord (bassoon) / Desto 7117

In turn, Daniels's woodwind look-sees are *Ironic, Canonic,* and a coined title *Tangonic.* Especially cute in the latter case, and not boring at all in the other two instances.

These free-lance musicians play the pieces perfectly, pungently, and with gorgeous sound.

Franz Danzi   (1763-1826)

Solo Instrument and Orchestra

Cello

Concerto in E minor for Cello and Orchestra

☐ Berlin Symphony Orchestra / Blees (cello) / Bünte (conductor) / Turnabout 34306

Well, perhaps not a masterpiece, but Danzi's Concerto has lyrical compactness in its Larghetto, with compelling and enjoyable flow in its faster-tempoed sections. It always follows vocal objectives, and so the feeling of string-instrument song is fundamental.

Thomas Blees is thoroughly efficient, never allows the tone to be forced, and keeps the pace moving.

William B. Ober, who furnished the jacket notes, asks "why such delightful music is not heard more often." Indeed, why?

Concerto No. 2 in D minor for Flute and Orchestra, Op. 31

Flute

☐ Vienna State Opera Orchestra / Meylan (flute) / Prohaska (conductor) / Vanguard C-10010

Light romantic phraseology and syntax mark the three movements. A serenade aspect covers the slow (middle) movement, mild motility is defined in the *Polacca*.

Bassoon Quartets, Op. 40
No. 1 in C major / No. 2 in D minor

Chamber Music

☐ Grossman (bassoon); Friedmann (violin); Figueroa (viola); Orazi (cello) / Lyrichord 7154

Facile interest can be expected from these four-movement works. Both are disarming in their rhythmic simplicity and melodic grace. Save for some chaste considerations (the bassoon "replacing" the first violin of the string-quartet formation doesn't permit unrestricted action), the performances are adequate.

Wind Quintets, Op. 56
No. 1 in B flat major / No. 2 in G minor

☐ New York Woodwind Quintet / Nonesuch 71108

Fluent and graceful music, a type of wind-instrument commentary totally friendly to pat classical forms with romantic touches. Healthy playing, productive ensemble, and always musical.

Wind Quintet in E minor, Op. 67, No. 2

☐ New York Woodwind Quintet / Concert-Disc 205
☐ New York Woodwind Quintet / Nonesuch 71108

Such a minute difference that the result is a tie score for playing Danzi's score. The tempo of movement 1 on the Concert-Disc disc is a little faster than the speed on the other release, and in the following movement the Concert-Disc edition is slower than the Nonesuch issue, etc. Brighter sound on Concert-Disc, but warmer sonority on Nonesuch.

So the choice has to consider what goes with the Danzi. On Concert-Disc there is Hindemith (*Kleine Kammermusik*); on Nonesuch there are two other Danzi wind quartets, Op. 56, No. 1, in B flat major, and No. 2 in G minor (*see above*). The personnel differ for three-fifths of the same-named ensemble performing for two different recording companies. Samuel Baron (flute) and David Glazer (clarinet) retain their roles in both recordings. On Concert-Disc the oboe is Jerome Roth, the bassoon, Bernard Garfield, and the horn, John Barrows. On Nonesuch these instruments are played, respectively, by Ronald Roseman, Arthur Weisberg, and Ralph Froelich. Tie score again, since all are magnificent musicians individually and in their ensemble contributions.

Wind Quintet in F major, Op. 56, No. 3

☐ Soni Ventorum Wind Quintet / Lyrichord 7216

Praise is due this group for their superb ensemble, together with the suavity and vigor of their playing. Danzi's music can be extremely dull if the highlighting of specific instruments within its structural concepts is overlooked. The handling of this important point is both assured and brilliantly achieved by the Soni Ventorum, and their tonal quality is most impressive. A definitive Danzi documentation.

Wind Quintets, Op. 68

No. 2 in F major / No. 3 in D minor

☐ Soni Ventorum Wind Quintet / Crystal 251

No abolition of conventional detail in Danzi's music. It is all clear and straight, with hardly any differences in the structures: a fast or moderately fast opening movement, a slow movement, a Minuet, and a lively finale.

The skill and experience of this fine quintet produce as convincing performances of these works as might be possible.

Louis-Claude Daquin   *(1694-1772)*

Instrumental

Organ

Noël suisse

☐ Hansen (organ) / Nonesuch 71170

The usual sequence of variations of music praising Christmas. The recording is of excellent fidelity, but Hansen's fidelity to similar registration can be pointedly questioned.

Noëls

☐ Biggs (organ) / Columbia M-32735

These comprise a dozen sets of variations on Christmas folk tunes. Warmth and color in the playing bring out all the charm that is bound into the music.

Piano

Le Coucou

☐ Entremont (piano) / Columbia D3S-791

Lively pitch massage based on the call of the cuckoo. Played neatly and with impeccable clarity.

Alexander Dargomyzhsky   *(1813-1869)*

Vocal

*Voice
with
Accompaniment*

I Am Grieving

Look, Darling Maiden

☐ Davrath (soprano); Werba (piano) / Vanguard VSD-71115

Elegiac in the first case, light and folksy in the other. Davrath is superb in these contrasting attitudes.

Louis-François Dauprat   *(1781-1868)*

*Chamber
Music*

Grand Trios, Op. 4

No. 2 / No. 3

☐ Grieve, Lott, and Meek (horns) / Avant 1013

Just on the other side of teaching material. Gentle classicism even at its most energetic. The playing is exemplary.

Carl Davidov   (1838-1889)

At the Fountain, Op. 20, No. 2

☐ Krosnick (cello); Grant (piano) / Orion 7291

For long a favorite encore item by the important Russian cellist-composer. A little more tasty than the usual musical lollipop and played with stylistic quality.

Instrumental

Cello

Mario Davidovsky   (1934-   )

Synchronisms No. 5, for Percussion Ensemble and Electronic Sounds (1969)

☐ Des Roches, Fitz, Heldrich, Marcone, and Van Hyning (percussion) / Sollberger (conductor) / Composers Recordings 268

Total association in the combine of the electronic sounds and the percussion instruments. The former color, modulate, and inculcate the latter, thereby taking on elements of ictus as part of their personalities, while the latter retain their basic melodic importance. The merger is sensitively formulated, so that it is difficult to separate the ingredients as one might in the case of a piano associated with a full orchestra. Davidovsky's fifth of his group of *Synchronisms* does mesh successfully and fruitfully.

Another edition on Turnabout 34487 is certainly worth considering, though the CRI issue has slightly better detail to offer.

Percussion

Synchronisms No. 3, for Cello and Electronic Sounds (1965)

☐ Moore (cello) / Opus One 6

A real meeting of the twain. The live instrument's pitch being picked up and precisely matched by the tape is only one of the many fascinations of Davidovsky's very successful piece. Another example is a disjunctly upward passage of the cello being completed by tape sound, which merely gives two clues to the prosperous condition of Davidovsky's work. The tape part is much more than squeals, thuds, and white noise, etc., effective by itself but often simply anticontextual when combined with live-performance material. The colors and rhythms, the forms and textures, the total design are structurally sound, compact, beautifully organized, artistically unarguable. This is what one hopes for in the use of tape and rarely obtains.

The values of Davidovsky's work have been recognized, and competitive recorded editions are available. Delos (on its 25406) has Jay Humeston playing the cello part, and CRI's entry (S–204) has Robert L. Martin as the "live" performer. Neither one has the tonal amplitude of David Moore or can match his bravura approach, a prime ingredient in performing Davidovsky's *Synchronisms*.

Instrumental

Cello

Synchronisms No. 1, for Flute and Recorded Electronic Sounds (1962)

☐ Baron (flute) / Nonesuch 71289

Duo fusion of disparate materials. The three possibilities of the partnership are utilized, with sections for flute alone, tape solo, and the two together. An unconventional company of timbres, and for that alone there is aural interest here.

A deeper flute tone in general favors this performance over the other one that is available on Composers Recordings (S–204), with Harvey Sollberger as the flutist.

Flute

Piano

Synchronisms No. 6, for Piano and Electronic Sounds (1970)

☐ Miller (piano) / Turnabout 34487

As is usual with Davidovsky's synchronal style, the music is far less a duo than it is a two-into-one formation. By use of intertextural procedures the electronic sonorities channel into the keyboard sounds. Primary, therefore, is the point the composer describes and then proves: "the electronic sounds in many instances modulate the acoustical characteristics of the piano, by affecting its decay and attack characteristics."

The piano part is of fantasy, and its proportions need a performer who can combine poetry with virtuosity. Robert Miller is that man and this disc demonstrates why. The music also demonstrates why Davidovsky was awarded the Pulitzer Prize in 1971 for his composition.

Chamber Music

Junctures for Flute, Clarinet, and Violin

☐ Sollberger (flute); Blustine (clarinet); Benjamin (violin) / Nonesuch 73028

Mostly reticent in its gestures so that the short, sharply contrasted sections produce double the effect. The material gives the impression of a twelve-note structure, but that merely mistakes specific intervallic movement for dodecaphonic style. The playing is passionately accented, not by extroverted qualities, but by subtle dynamic motivation. This is one of the best pieces in Davidovsky's catalogue.

Synchronisms No. 2, for Flute, Clarinet, Violin, Cello, and Electronic Sounds (1964)

☐ Sophie Sollberger (flute); Drucker (clarinet); Zukofsky (violin); Martin (cello) / Guigui (conductor) / Composers Recordings S–204

Cohesion of tape sounds with instrumental ones to the point that the former take on a complete instrumental personality. Granting that objective, Davidovsky's second in his large set of *Synchronisms* is a superfine work and one of the best in the medium that partners live-played instruments with tape material.

True, there is hardly any stress on comparing and individualizing the components (instruments and electronic), but Davidovsky's handling of this combine is more artistically focalized than setting instruments against or with smacking pops, whistly whirrs, and fluttering ping-pongs of sound from the tape machine.

The light and shade plus thickness and thinness of the score are ideally realized by the quartet of virtuosi.

Synchronisms No. 8, for Woodwind Quintet and Tape

☐ Dorian Quintet / Vox SVBX–5307

The title is apt. The tape is not used as an overlay or for a sharp contrastive timbre. While it does have its individuality, just like all the instruments of the woodwind quintet, it is of bridged quality, expanding the quintuple sounds to sextuple totality by equal participation in the rhapsodic statements of the music. A further expansion concerns the flute and oboe parts. The former alternates with alto flute as well as piccolo, the latter doubles with the English horn.

Electronic Music

Electronic Study No. 1 (1964)

☐ Columbia MS–6566

The composer explains that the Study is created from five sound mixtures. These work as a series "which is inverted, transposed and interpolated, and the sound mixtures are changed in density and intensity from the original.'' Nonetheless, there is a general neutrality that pervades the composition, since the fundamental color pattern does not change.

Electronic Study No. 3 (1965)

☐ Finnadar 9010

By its sparseness, filigree detail, and light touch, Davidovsky's short work (timed at 5:20) may be termed impressionistic electronic music. The piece is ''in memoriam Edgard Varèse,'' and enjoys a duplicate release in the recorded catalogue, on Turnabout 34487.

Peter Maxwell Davies. See under Maxwell Davies.

Sharon Davis (1937-   )

Vocal

Though Men Call Us Free, Op. 2

Voice and Accompaniment

☐ Stevenson (soprano); Atkins (clarinet); Davis (piano) / Wim WIMR-13

Astute lyricism in an extrovert manner contrasts with declamatory instrumental force in this dramatic piece. The text is excerpted from Oscar Wilde's *The Young King.*

Little known, on the basis of this work Sharon Davis's creative output bears close attention. Delcina Stevenson's vocalism deserves everyone's listening time.

Richard Davy (ca. 1467-ca. 1516)

Cantata and Oratorio

St. Matthew Passion

☐ Purcell Consort and Choir of All Saints, Margaret Street / Partridge (tenor); Keyte (baritone) / Flemming (conductor) / Argo ZRG-558

One of the earliest settings of the Passion. Its austerity mostly utilizes plainsong, its style superbly covered by Ian Partridge as the Evangelist. Christopher Keyte's singing of the Jesus role is both dignified and dramatic. Though little-known, Davy's St. Matthew Passion is more than simply a historic document. This sensitive recording is proof of his excellent creativity. It is a welcome contribution.

Claude Debussy (1862-1918)

Orchestra

Images pour orchestre

☐ Boston Symphony Orchestra / Thomas (conductor) / Deutsche Grammophon 2530145

Thomas's conducting leads to an issue that combines precision with coloristic power. The former proportion is most expertly carried out in the case of Boulez (on Columbia MS-7362 or Columbia D3M-32988), but the latter gets cancelled in the process. A merged balance is also represented in the case of Stokowski, but he only performs the second piece of the three, *Ibéria* (on Seraphim S-60102). (The other two pieces are *Gigues* and *Rondes de printemps*. Debussy began writing *Images* in 1906 and completed the three-part work in 1912.)

Incidental Music for *King Lear* (1904)

☐ French National Radio Orchestra / Martinon (conductor) / Angel S-37068

A welcome recording, since Debussy's *King Lear* music is a rarity on concert programs. It consists of two very short pieces. The first one is a one-and-a-half-minute *Fanfare,* scored for four horns, three trumpets, timpani, drum, and two harps. The second piece is titled *Le Sommeil de Lear* ("Lear's Slumber"), runs three minutes, and calls for two flutes, four horns, timpani, harp, and strings.

The *Fanfare* offers no surprise. However, "Lear's Slumber" registers significantly. It is no ordinary berceuse, but a music that is mystically touched and is touchingly played by the French orchestra.

La Mer (1905)

☐ New Philharmonia Orchestra / Boulez (conductor) / Columbia MS-7361

Boulez does wonders with this piece. Here the music has been wiped clean of super-colored abandon sometimes invoked in the name of proper (?) style, and instead emerges in a clear architechtonic statement. By his purgative approach, Boulez makes apparent a huge amount of detail lost in readings that are nothing more than sonorous swellage. The effect is uncanny, for *La Mer* is for once shown to contain decided symphonic development—something little suspected when it is heard without the sharp (almost classically pristine) definition of this performance.

Some will decry the objective demeanor proposed here—which means firm tempi, balanced textures, and transparent sonorities—because they would rather have subjective virtuosity and orchestrational flair and to hell with formalism (meaning a really truthful analysis of Debussy's score). Too bad, I say, for the finesse and foresight of Boulez prove that *La Mer* is music of an even higher order than we had realized before.

Columbia has also packaged Boulez's performance in a Debussy anthology covering six record sides in D3M-32988.

La Plus que lente (1910)

☐ London Philharmonic Orchestra / Herrmann (conductor) / London 21062

Debussy's own orchestration of his piano piece (see under *Instrumental: piano*). The waltz (neatly described by David Simmons as a "wry little dialogue in waltz time") is scored for a very small group. The piano is used as an orchestral instrument (it was rarely used in that manner in Debussy's time) and contrasted with the Hungarian national instrument, the cimbalom, a close relative of the zither. The other instruments are flute, clarinet, and strings.

Good, sensuous pace, Herrmann taking it really "more than slow" but keeping it moving within that tempo boundary.

Marche écossaise, sur un thème populaire (1908)

☐ French National Radio Orchestra / Martinon (conductor) / Angel S-37068

Debussy's *Marche écossaise* was composed for piano duet in 1891. (A recorded performance using two pianos is available—see under *Instrumental: two pianos*). He later (in 1908) transcribed the work for orchestra, whereby it gains measurably by the color support.

Debussy's march "on a popular tune" is Scottish, but it bubbles like champagne in this first-rate presentation.

Nocturnes (1899)

☐ Philadelphia Orchestra and Temple University Women's Chorus / Ormandy (conductor) / Columbia MG-30950

That old Philadelphia Orchestra magic produces a splendid atmosphere for these three pieces. That bothersome detail of the central section in *Fêtes* being taken too slowly is resolved—the tempo is what one feels is exact and moves on thin electrical wires until the music blazes. *Sirènes* is lean and not too languid. Throughout, there is timbred detail that lights up the material or sheds reflected light on it. A five-star recording.

There are some versions which only cover the first two of the three movements. The best of these is by Bernstein, who does both *Nuages* and *Fêtes* on Columbia MS-6271 and does *Fêtes* alone on Columbia MS-7523.

Prélude à l'Après-midi d'un faune (1894)

☐ New Philharmonia Orchestra / Boulez (conductor) / Columbia MS-7361

There is no argument that the orchestral eclogue Debussy fashioned in his "Prelude to the Afternoon of a Faun" contains the evocative colorism, the timbred delicacy that marks musical impressionism. There *is* argument, however, that most performances of the piece falsify Debussy's intent. Though the indication *expressif* appears constantly in the score (in measures 1, 15, 21, 37, 51, 55, 63, 74, 75, 79, 86, 94, and 95 of the 110 measures), the instruction most often is translated to mean a voluptuous sighing, a kind of inhalation-exhalation, as though the faun were a client in a whorehouse. These dynamic bulges (which make exotic that which is suave and poetic) are absent in the Boulez reading. Here *L'Après-midi* has its true pastoral nature; the colors are delicate and yet firm; the statements are truly *expressif*. It is an ear-opener.

Columbia's engineering is noteworthy throughout every measure of the piece. (This performance is also included in a three-record Debussy album, Columbia D3M-32988.)

Printemps (Symphonic Suite) (1887)

☐ French National Radio Orchestra / Sendrez and Boury (pianos) / Martinon (conductor) / Angel S-37124

This piece was originally for orchestra and chorus; the score was destroyed in a fire. However, a reduction for two pianos with the voices was fortunately safe. From this a new score was made by Henri Busser with Debussy's blessing. It is a just and discriminating reproduction of Debussyan methods. (Though it can be argued, the writer considers this a restoration, not a full-scaled transcription. For that reason it is listed and discussed in this place.)

Martinon's edition has a trenchant, virile viewpoint on the work. The music is shaped cohesively, and he does not overemphasize the coloristic orchestral detail that gives the score its richness.

Solo Instrument and Orchestra

Clarinet

Première Rapsodie for Clarinet and Orchestra (1910)

☐ Philadelphia Orchestra / Gigliotti (clarinet) / Ormandy (conductor) / Columbia MS–6977

It is, after all, a rhapsody, but conductors try to smooth and bind the sectional material. The desire, apparently, is to tighten the structure, but such procedure makes the music cool and almost forbidding. Both Gigliotti and Ormandy let the music run its diversified course, and it thrives that way.

Gigliotti has dexterous expertise. His ability to regulate *crescendi* and *decrescendi* evenly is one feature of his Debussy portrayal. Another is the special ability to play staccatos musically and not checkmate proper style by spiky sounds. His performance is not merely successful, but a striking one.

Harp

Danses sacrée et profane for Harp and Orchestra (1904)

☐ Cleveland Orchestra / Chalifoux (harp) / Boulez (conductor) / Columbia MS–7362
☐ Philadelphia Orchestra / Costello (harp) / Ormandy (conductor) / Columbia MS–6977

It is in the handling of the string-orchestra partnership with the solo instrument that the differences appear. Boulez's coloration is like white and light blue, Ormandy's one of ruddiness. The French conductor emphasizes tight dynamic planes, Ormandy lets them hang looser and fuller. In a sense Boulez plays the music cool and aloof, and this is Debussy as he is rarely (if at all) exhibited.

The Boulez version is also included in a three-record set of Debussy music (on Columbia D3M–32988). Ormandy's performance is also duplicated, in a two-record Debussy package (Columbia MG–30950).

Piano

Fantaisie for Piano and Orchestra (1889)

☐ London Symphony Orchestra / Kars (piano) / Gibson (conductor) / London 6657

Though there are not too many of Debussy's mature harmonic mezzotints in this early work, much of the orchestration will be immediately recognizable as his.

Jean-Rodolphe Kars turns in a fully representative portrayal of the solo part. It has quality and proper finesse, matched by the orchestral framework.

Saxophone

Rhapsody for Saxophone and Orchestra (1905)

☐ Orchestra of Radio Luxembourg / Londeix (saxophone) / de Froment (conductor) / Candide 31069

Debussy's work was completed and orchestrated by Roger-Ducasse. It is a relatively minor item in Debussy's catalogue, but due to the paltriness of worthy literature for the instrument, it has achieved a higher rating than would generally apply.

But if the Rhapsody is second-rate Debussy, it is given first-class playing by Jean-Marie Londeix. Nowhere during the progress of the concentrated piece (9:45 in time) is there a flabby quality to the sax tone, and at no time is there any evidence of the flappy vibrato that haunts so many saxophonists.

Instrumental

Cello

Intermezzo

☐ Solow (cello); Vallecillo (piano) / Desmar 1006

French romanticism, not French impressionism. Debussy's early work was issued posthumously, the manuscript having been found by Gregor Piatigorsky in Paris, 1938. It has charm and moves in a nicely businesslike manner. Solow shows that it works well and proves it by robust playing.

Syrinx for Flute Solo (1912)

☐ Dwyer (flute) / Deutsche Grammophon 2530049

This is *the* classic work in the literature for unaccompanied flute. It can be considered the inspirational force for the many works in the medium that later appeared, especially just prior to and after World War II.

The playing has compelling persuasiveness; the dynamic scale is magnificently apportioned. Great performance!

Flute

Children's Corner Suite (1908)

☐ Michelangeli (piano) / Deutsche Grammophon 2530196

There's plenty of coloristic opportunity in Debussy's six-part affair and all of it is negotiated to the fullest in this portrayal. Examples: the motility in *Doctor Gradus ad Parnassum* is seamlessly run off, *The Snow Is Dancing* is a blizzard of lightness, and the *Golliwog* has a proper strut. (See under *Debussy/Caplet: Orchestra* for the orchestral transcription.)

Piano

Clair de lune from *Suite bergamasque* (1905)

☐ Entremont (piano) / Columbia MS–6886

A large number of choices for this evergreen. Naturally it is to be secured as part of the entire suite in the recommended performance by Vásáry (*see below* under *Suite bergamasque*), with a second pick being Ciccolini's complete suite presentation (Seraphim S–60253). However, Entremont's playing of *Clair de lune* alone has this writer's fullest advocacy and deserves consideration as a single entry since he has not recorded the entire suite. Debussy's sensual language for this masterful short piece is exquisitely presented.

Entremont's performance is also in another Debussy collection on Columbia MS–6214 and also in a grab-bag three-record set titled by Columbia *Clair de lune* (D3S–791).

Estampes (1903)

☐ Beroff (piano) / Angel S–36874

Playing that is not only expert (to be expected from Beroff) but evocative (not always to be expected from our piano virtuosi). The kaleidoscopic spectrum of this three-part work is full of *Pagodes* (exquisitely concluded by Beroff); a genuine picturing of Spanish atmosphere and quality is accomplished in *Soirée dans Grenade;* and gorgeous technique is displayed, with fantastic power, in *Jardins sous la pluie.*

Etudes for Piano (1915)

☐ Jacobs (piano) / Nonesuch 71322

Pianists have two different approaches to these dozen works (studies in thirds, fourths, opposed sonorities, composite arpeggios, etc.). In Anthony di Bonaventura's performance (Connoisseur Society CSQ–2074) he attempts (rather successfully if you agree with his viewpoint) to turn the clock back a bit and play these pieces in a Debussyan, earlier, colorful manner. He softens them up, as it were. However, this is late, very late Debussy, and matters are more direct. The material is lean and tight (far from the enfeebled creations one would expect from a man dying of cancer). Played leanly and tightly, the pieces have much more validity.

And, that's the way Paul Jacobs plays this music. It is kept clean, and each piece is depicted as a stable architechtonic statement. It is a purgative approach, minus any sonorous swillage, achieving a truthful musical objective.

Images pour piano, Books 1 (1905) and 2 (1907)

☐ Michelangeli (piano) / Deutsche Grammophon 2530196

Superb. Every measure in each of the three pieces in the two sets is sensitively colored. Every detail is audible. Weights, textures, outlines, colors, and rhythmic patterns are all as perfect as could be. Truly a magical performance.

La Plus que lente (1910)

☐ Vásáry (piano) / Deutsche Grammophon 139458

Tamás Vásáry finds more in this waltz (see also under *Orchestra*) than any other pianist. It probably is that he considers it of higher order than his colleagues.

Pour le piano (1901)

☐ Vásáry (piano) / Deutsche Grammophon 139458

Precise balancing and refinement of keyboard attack mark the playing. Vásáry's conception of this suite is lucid and an illuminative accomplishment. Beroff (on Angel S–36874) is another fine choice.

Preludes for Piano, Books I and II

Brouillards (Book II)
Bruyères (Book II)
Canope (Book II)
Ce qu'a vu le Vent d'ouest (Book I)
Danseuses de Delphes (Book I)
Des Pas sur la neige (Book I)
Feuilles mortes (Book II)
Feux d'artifice (Book II)
General Lavine — Eccentric (Book II)
Hommage à S. Pickwick Esq. P. P. M. P. C. (Book II)
La Cathédrale engloutie (Book I)
La Danse de Puck (Book I)
La Fille aux cheveux de lin (Book I)
La Puerta del vino (Book II)
La Sérénade interrompue (Book I)
La Terrasse des audiences du clair de lune (Book II)
Les Collines d'Anacapri (Book I)
Les Fées sont d'exquises danseuses (Book II)
Les Sons et les parfums tournent dans l'air du soir (Book I)
Les Tierces alternées (Book II)
Le Vent dans la plaine (Book I)
Minstrels (Book I)
Ondine (Book II)
Voiles (Book I)

☐ Jacobs (piano) / Nonesuch HB-73031

Debussy's subjects range, as will be noted from the titles, from the legend of *La Cathédrale engloutie* ("The Sunken Cathedral") to dances (*La Danse de Puck* and *Les Fées sont d'exquises danseuses* ["The Fairies Are Exquisite Dancers"], for example), from water pieces (*Ondine*—she is a water spirit—and *Voiles* ["Sails"]) to music concerned with the evening hours (*Les Sons et les parfums tournent dans l'air du soir* ["The Sounds and Perfumes Swirl in the Evening Air"]), from personality sketches (*General Lavine—Eccentric* and *La Fille aux cheveux de lin* ["The Girl with the Flaxen Hair"] are two in this group) to nature depictions (examples are *Brouillards* ["Fogs"], *Feuilles mortes* ["Dead Leaves"], and *Le Vent dans la plaine* ["The Wind on the Plain"]).

In such an assortment, though a single basic style is strongly confirmed, effects and special colorations abound within the music. If italicized, they are thrown out of context, but Paul Jacobs refuses to add a single interpretative footnote to any note and thus break the extraordinary totality of each of the two dozen pieces. Each setting is allowed its pictured setting in proper relationship, and no self-conscious expressions are included. The dynamic scope is minutely arranged, the phrasing is impressively expressive, and in no place is virtuosity forced into the principal place, despite the virtuosity necessary to bring off the technical demands made by Debussy. None of the quiet rhapsody and impressionistic fantasy within the music escapes Jacobs's performance, certainly the most outstanding in the catalogue.

Preludes for Piano, Book I. *For individual titles,* **see above, under** *Preludes for Piano, Books I and II.*

☐ Gieseking (piano) / Angel 35066 (monaural)

Great, definitive performances. All the timbre differences and yet no waywardish interpretations in the name of impressionistic effect, color wash, and the like. Gieseking gets to the point of each piece in a way that creates a perfection of structure combined with the pictorial idea. The harmonic materials are both detailed and blended in a masterful way that only a mere handful of pianists (in fact, that's being overgenerous) have been able to accomplish with the Debussy Preludes.

Preludes for Piano, Book II. *For individual titles,* **see above, under** *Preludes for Piano, Books I and II.*

☐ Gieseking (piano) / Angel 35249 (monaural)

(For discussion, see above, under *Preludes for Piano, Book I.)*

Rêverie (1890)

☐ Frankl (piano) / Vox SVBX-5433

Once the pops boys got ahold of this one, it got played out, and its standard popularity has waned. Still, it's a fine little piece, and Peter Frankl proves it.

Suite bergamasque (1905)

☐ Vásáry (piano) / Deutsche Grammophon 139458

Beautifully conceived playing. A fine blend of structural detail and color. There are other viable versions that can be considered, of course. The best of these would be that recorded by Ciccolini, on Seraphim S-60253.

Clair de lune from this suite has been separately issued (*see above,* under *Clair de lune* from *Suite bergamasque*).

Two Pianos

Two Arabesques (1888)

☐ Entremont (piano) / Columbia MS-6214

An ingratiating and unpretentious account. That's just right. For only the first of the pair, get Columbia MS-6398.

En blanc et noir (1915)

☐ Walter and Beatrice Klien (pianos) / Turnabout 34234

Fortunately not played in black and white and allowed to rest at that. Each of the three pieces is colored with pastels and bright shades as well.

Lindaraja (1901)

☐ Joy and Robin-Bonneau (pianos) / Musical Heritage Society MHS-849/850

The fundamental music that when reshaped later became the *Soirée dans Grenade* as the second of the three-part *Estampes*. The pianists provide a fine dimensional relationship in their playing, notwithstanding an overemphasis on the whole-tone chordal passages.

Marche écossaise, sur un thème populaire (1891)

☐ Alfons and Aloys Kontarsky (pianos) / Deutsche Grammophon 2707072

The initial conception of this charmer was for one piano, four hands, composed in 1891. In 1908 Debussy arranged it for orchestra (see under *Orchestra*). More groovy in that form.

The Kontarsky gentlemen play this rather coolly, though clearly. It is to be noted that the performance is a two-piano affair rather than two performers at one piano. In a live presentation it would really be improper to play the work in that manner (the intimate partnership of two pianists using one keyboard has certain pictorial advantages, not to overlook the practicality of only requiring a single instrument for performance). Providing the two pianos are perfectly matched instruments, recording a one piano, four hands composition by the use of two pianos doesn't matter whatsoever. There is also the bonus of more room for each pianist.

Petite Suite (1889)

☐ Eden and Tamir (pianos) / London 6754

Four movements: *En Bateau, Cortège, Menuet,* and *Ballet.* There is an especially suave portrayal of the first movement ("In the Boat"), and cool grace in the performance of the dance movements. This is totally distinguished two-piano playing. (See under *Debussy/Busser: Orchestra* for the orchestral transcription.) (The two-piano use for this performance is valid in terms of a recording, where one only hears and does not see. Originally Debussy's *Petite Suite* was composed as a piano duet.)

Six Epigraphes antiques (1914)

☐ Walter and Beatrice Klien (pianos) / Turnabout 34235

Debussy's exotically modal pieces, swimming in a sea of whole tones, played extremely atmospherically and extremely dynamically downgraded. However, this is far better than the heavier statements on the part of the Kontarskys, on Deutsche Grammophon (2707072).

Sonata for Cello and Piano (1915)

☐ Harrell (cello); Levine (piano) / RCA ARL1-1262
☐ Solow (cello); Vallecillo (piano) / Desmar 1006

The first movement, a Prologue, is based on an embellished *lento*, paralleled and contrasted in turn by a suave (faster) sweetly designed idea. Here the depiction of exact score specifications places the second-listed duo in the first position, especially by their following and clearly contrasting the elements of ornate data and the buttoned-down, settled rhythm that comprise the sum and substance of the opening section.

The second and last movements are joined (*Sérénade et Finale*). The first of the pair mainly emphasizes the rich possibilities of pizzicati (without Bartókian findings). Technically conservative, this movement has completely vagrant tempi; there are twenty-two changes in the total sixty-four measures. Thus Debussy is subjective in the framework of sonata objectivity. Here the first-listed performers deserve to retain first place—this not only by stylistic discipline but by their disclosures of tempi. The playing is of utmost significance and superb color, the latter not lacking in the semi-sonata design of the finale.

The differences in the conceptions of the two teams define both as authentic. The bright and vivid presentation of the RCA gives that release some extra points.

Sonata for Violin and Piano (1917)

☐ Silverstein (violin); Thomas (piano) / Deutsche Grammophon 2530049

A sense of improvisation marks this work, and at times there is almost shaky bridgework as the principal subjects are connected. Nevertheless, the trestles of this three-movement sonata are sufficiently strong.

This team outpaces all others in the recorded catalogue with a performance that is passionate, colorful, and alert to every rhythmic pinch and Debussy-bred phrase.

The "Silverstein" is Joseph Silverstein, the concertmaster of the Boston Symphony Orchestra. The "Thomas" is Michael Tilson Thomas, who rivals his pianistic self as a superb conductor.

Sonata for Flute, Viola, and Harp (1915)

☐ Melos Ensemble / Oiseau-Lyre 60048

Quietness of dynamism is present in Debussy's trio sonata, even though the play of color and light is more to the fore in this piece than in any of Debussy's other chamber-music compositions. In regard to the timbre qualities and the manner in which Debussy designed his scoring, the three instruments are equal to several dozen players, speaking, however, without bugles.

Sensitive styling and impulsive playing where it should be are heard in the first movement. This is matched by beautifully realized simplicity of the middle division and a determinative buoyancy in the finale. Proper atmospheric sound marks Oiseau-Lyre's recording.

String Quartet, Op. 10

☐ La Salle Quartet / Deutsche Grammophon 2530235

No wishy-washy approach in this case. No opting for a false type of gentility for the sake of impressionistic definition and forsaking the sonorous paging of this great work. The La Salle team emphasizes the linear strength of voice movement rather than chordal pigmentation to convey the meaning of the music. It is playing of clarity and brilliance, but above all it is playing that gives you Debussy direct and honest.

Among the competitive editions the best is that of the Quartetto Italiano (on Philips 835361). It is brilliant and satisfying. The most disappointing rendition comes from the Guarneri Quartet (RCA ARL1-0187). Their view of this music is aloof and not well integrated; it lacks passion.

Vocal

Voice with Accompaniment

Chansons de Bilitis (1897)

☐ Crespin (soprano); Wustman (piano) / London 26043

Crespin is exceedingly expressive in this cycle. And being expressive, her conception of the style is in tune (and, of course, so are her pitches). Indeed, Crespin's technique is most impressive. The necessary passion is heard clean and clear in *La Chevelure,* and expressive subtlety is reflected in *Le Tombeau des Naïades.* Beautiful balances add another credit to the list.

Choral

Chorus Alone

Trois Chansons de Charles d'Orléans (1908)

☐ John Alldis Choir / Alldis (conductor) / Argo ZRG-523

Debussy's only music for unaccompanied chorus. Delights, each and every *Chanson.* Why, then, are they so rarely heard?

Argo heads them as ''Part Songs,'' which they are, but the failure to give the over-all title can lead to confusion.

High-standard singing, and the best of the two performances available on records.

Opera and Dramatic Music

Chansons de Bilitis (1900)

☐ Ensemble ''Die Reihe'' / Escribano (speaker) / Cerha (conductor) / Candide 31024

This exquisite set of twelve Pierre Louÿs poems to be recited with just as exquisite accompaniment for two flutes, two harps, and celesta should not be confused with the three-part *Chansons de Bilitis* song cycle Debussy wrote. Both compositions utilize texts from the same Louÿs collection, but none are duplicated.

Though Darius Milhaud wrote the liner notes for Candide's recording, he gives practically no information on the work. Debussy had extracted some music from the score of his *Epigraphes antiques* for two pianos as the basis for the *Chansons,* but the composition remained unfinished. Pierre Boulez completed it in the late 1950s with admirable perceptivity (it is utterly impossible to pinpoint where Boulez substitutes for Debussy. Boulez also supplied the celesta part, which had been lost.

The music is not conceived as narration with sound-over. In a few cases the instrumental group links the sections, but otherwise it is distinctly separate and impressionistically processed. The quintet plays beautifully and sensitively, producing velvety-soft textures. The work is rarely heard in concert, and the Cerha-led performance is therefore a special entry in the annals of recorded music.

Pelléas et Mélisande (1902)

☐ Orchestra and Chorus of the Royal Opera House, Covent Garden / Söderström (soprano); Britten (treble); Minton (alto); Shirley (tenor); McIntyre (baritone); Ward and Wicks (basses) / Boulez (conductor) / Columbia M3-30119

Pelléas et Mélisande, one of the greatest of all operas and a landmark in twentieth-century musical literature, regardless of medium, is represented by two principal recordings, severely contrasted in their interpretative conditions. Ansermet (London 1379) sets the work in a half light; the effects are muted, the scenario played to the full but interpretatively underplayed, the timbre differences decreased in a manner to stress monochromic qualities and textures. This also affects tempi, which are exceedingly checked. Paradoxically, however, smothering the impressions increases the potency of the music and the characterizations.

Boulez is diametrically opposite. The gradations of colors, dynamics, textures, and tempi are precise (not academic)—the total is heavied and therefore made even more potently dramatic than by Ansermet. Boulez's definition of the orchestral score is the opposite of reticence. He permits the usually smothered instrumental forces in Debussy's lyric drama (as he called it) to register clearly, thereby interweaving a fascinating lacework. This patterned variety moves among the human voices, which are styled like a gigantic unending recitative. *Pelléas et Mélisande* has no stop-action formed from arias and set numbers. Its special continuity (of which a greater portion is formed in the orchestra and the remainder by the characters) *is* the most direct type of drama.

Indeed it is the orchestra by means of the conductor that comes first in Debussy's operatic cast. Understanding this is mandatory if Debussy's masterwork is to make proper impact on its audience. Boulez fully understands the opera's objective and directs a performance that is vivid and thrilling from beginning to end. It results in one of the finest things Boulez has ever put on disc. The singers (not a single one is French) are outstanding. A great recording.

Jeux (1912) *Ballet*

☐ New Philharmonia Orchestra / Boulez (conductor) / Columbia MS-7361

A complete understanding of the deeper implications of Debussy's music is evidenced in Boulez's performance of this "dance poem." Despite the composer's concern with balletic requirements, this score has a strong motival element within its sectional structure. The latter often has caused a choppiness in performance. Boulez avoids sectionalism by viewing the work as a totality, though its divisions are solidified by textural and tempi contrasts. Again, one realizes that there is much more in Debussy than the surface values (call them "color") usually exhibited. Boulez proves that the score is, after all, one of Debussy's best. The endless variation within *Jeux* also represents a new Debussy, far different from the composer of the piano Preludes and *La Mer*.

In the presence of such sensitive insight as that of Boulez one considers again the theory that, provided they possess the necessary baton techniques, composers make the best conductors.

A duplicate of this performance is included in a three-record Debussy program: Columbia D3M-32988.

La Boîte à joujoux (Ballet for Children) (1913)

☐ French National Radio Orchestra / Martinon (conductor) / Angel S-37124

"The Toy Box" is a Debussyan delight. Debussy only sketched the instrumentation; the definitive orchestration was made by André Caplet. It contains the standardized characters Punchinello, Pierrot, and Harlequin. It also contains a mock march that pokes some fun at Gounod and self-quotes some Golliwoggian rhythms. But there are no toy-music platitudes, and the conception is always witty and colorful.

Jean Martinon's conducting of this work is precisely right. This means a display of masterful technique that extracts exactly balanced and minutely modulated sounds from his orchestra. It's marvelous.

Debussy / Henri-Paul Busser (1872-1973)

Orchestra **Petite Suite**

☐ Orchestre de la Suisse Romande / Ansermet (conductor) / London 6227

Absolutely delightful playing, delicate when it should be, firm when the lyricism is more resolute. Ansermet's rhythmic chronicling is no less than superb.

Debussy's *Petite Suite* is better known in Busser's orchestral costuming than the original setting for piano duet (see under *Debussy: Instrumental: two pianos*).

Debussy / Lucien Cailliet (1891-   )

Orchestra **Clair de lune from Suite bergamasque**

☐ Philadelphia Orchestra / Ormandy (conductor) / Columbia MS-6478

There are versions of this wondrous small piece in the record stores for organ (shades of Radio City Music Hall style), guitar (sounds very picky), two guitars (sounds very picky-picky), and violin (makes for a melodic definition which should not be stressed). If an arrangement is to be acquired, there are two better orchestral choices—this one and another by Caplet, discussed under *Debussy/Caplet: Orchestra.*

Both are very good. They do not blemish the original piano conception with orchestrational overload or stylistic slang. They are, at the same time, totally different. Cailliet (once the bass clarinetist of the Philadelphia Orchestra in Stokowski's days and the orchestra's official transcriber, without portfolio, of a number of compositions, including works by Bach and Ravel) chooses to use thin textures, and the weights are restrained.

The arrangement is played with sensitive blend and the slightest use of valuable *rubati*. Ormandy's splendid edition of Cailliet's transcription is on hand in no less than eight assortments: six others on Columbia—MS-6575, MS-6883, MS-7523, MS-6934, M-30064, and MG-30950—and one on RCA LSC-3284.

Debussy / André Caplet (1878-1925)

Orchestra **Children's Corner Suite**

☐ French National Radio Orchestra / Martinon (conductor) / Angel S-37064

Debussy's piano suite (see under *Debussy: Instrumental: piano*) was transcribed by his very close friend André Caplet, and the result was given full approval by the composer. Caplet orchestrated the opus three years after Debussy had completed the original setting. His translation (using two flutes [with the second alternating with piccolo], two each of oboes, clarinets, and bassoons, four horns, two trumpets, harp, percussion, and strings) is evidence of his orchestrational wisdom.

Martinon provides an excellent issue of the transcribed work. There is fine atmosphere and clear detail, and the textures are naturally balanced.

Children's Corner Suite
> **No. 2, *Jimbo's Lullaby***
> **No. 5, *The Little Shepherd***
> **No. 6, *Golliwog's Cake-Walk***

☐ Stadium Symphony Orchestra / Stokowski (conductor) / Everest 3327

A production with the special Stokowski treatment applied to the score. If you're satisfied with only half of Debussy's suite, then choose this over the complete representation (*see above*). This has it all: marvelous character and color plus stylistic expressiveness.

Everest's vividly recorded release gives no credits to Caplet. And its liner note has no facts whatsoever regarding his transcription. (*See above,* under *Children's Corner* Suite, for the background.)

Clair de lune from Suite bergamasque

☐ London Philharmonic Orchestra / Herrmann (conductor) / London 21062

Caplet's setting is rarely heard (it has not been published). It is richer, slightly heavier than Cailliet's arrangement of the piece (see under *Debussy/Cailliet: Orchestra*). Caplet emphasizes vibrant dabs of color in his orchestral substantiation.

Since it was sanctioned and approved by Debussy, the Caplet transcription can be considered an official and authoritative version. This does not deny, in the slightest, the worthiness of Cailliet's version. One is certain that Debussy would have approved of it as well, since Cailliet's pigmented parallelization respects every nuance within the original piano creation. Both versions are equally worthy.

Bernard Herrmann's conducting can only be praised in every respect. His shaping of the color patterns is masterly.

Debussy / Charles Koechlin (1867 - 1950)

Khamma (1912)   *Ballet*

☐ L'Orchestre de la Suisse Romande / Ansermet (conductor) / London 6437

Debussy had neither time nor inclination for the task of orchestrating this ballet, once having finished the piano score. Thus Koechlin's affiliation with the work.

It is not top-drawer Debussy by any means, embracing wisps of ideas hardly defined, full of brass mutterings and whole-tone progressions. Koechlin's scoring is neat, but his orchestrational adjectives are not attached to any cogent musical nouns.

Played quite well. Still, only for those who are Debussy buffs or simply curious.

Debussy / Maurice Ravel (1875 - 1937)

Danse   *Orchestra*

☐ French National Radio Orchestra / Martinon (conductor) / Angel S-37064

This work was originally composed in 1890 for piano and published with the title *Tarentelle styrienne*. Ravel made his transcription in 1922; the first performance of his setting took place the year following.

The pliable consideration of the pulse continuity makes Martinon's edition the preferable one among those available. Oddly, Ansermet's performance (London STS-15022) is often misbalanced; the playing is not always clean.

M. de la Barre / Louis XIII. See *Louis XIII* / de la Barre.

Adam de la Halle. See *Halle.*

Michel-Richard Delalande. See *Lalande.*

Lex van Delden   (1919-   )

Orchestra

Piccolo Concerto, Op. 67

☐ Utrecht Symphony Orchestra / Hupperts (conductor) / Donemus Audio-Visual Series DAVS-6602 (monaural)

This is not a concerto for piccolo but a "small" concerto lasting 9′ 15″. To a certain extent, average instrumental proportions pertain: double winds, horns, and trumpets, plus piano, timpani and percussion. However, the eight woodwinds are divided in their positioning. In "mono," a certain amount of the antiphony of these wind quartets goes by the board, but the clarity of the neoclassicism remains.

String Orchestra

Trio per Orchestra d'Archi, Op. 44

☐ Netherlands Chamber Orchestra / Hupperts (conductor) / Donemus Audio-Visual Series DAVS-6301 (monaural: 10-inch disc)

"Trio" here means three movements: two slow-paced divisions surrounding an *Allegro marcato*. The string orchestra scoring represents a second version of three of four piano pieces. The technical device is pantonalistic, providing stimulating music and showing stylistic cohesion.

Instrumental

Harp

Impromptu for Harp Solo, Op. 48

☐ Berghout (harp) / Donemus Audio-Visual Series DAVS-6102 (monaural: 10-inch disc)

Any type of musical travail is out of place within the lightweighted scope of the harp. It needs careful music to suit its delicacy. This doesn't mean weak music. The French school, especially, has realized this expertly. Van Delden does not err, either, with his free-rondo presentation.

Léo Delibes   (1836-1891)

Orchestra

Entr'acte to Act III of *Le Roi l'a dit*

☐ London Symphony Orchestra / Bonynge (conductor) / London 6744

Occasionally the overture to *Le Roi l'a dit* surfaces. This never. There's always a place for charming and unpretentious music such as this, especially when played, as here, with polished professionalism.

Intermezzo from *Naïla*

☐ London Symphony Orchestra / Bonynge (conductor) / London 2232

The Intermezzo (*Pas de fleurs*) is from the first Delibes ballet score, *La Source*. Later, this three-act ballet was produced under the title *Naïla, die Quellenfee*.

La Source: Ballet Suite

☐ Paris Conservatoire Orchestra / Maag (conductor) / London 6026

A good part of the total score. Faultlessly presented with sensitive music making for this traditionally sound material.

Suite from the Ballet *Coppélia*

Suite from the Ballet *Sylvia*

☐ Philadelphia Orchestra / Ormandy (conductor) / Columbia MS-6508

Auditors who want some of the best highlights from these two ballets will not be disappointed. The Philly players are in top form and so is Ormandy. Where strength and color are demanded, they are fully supplied, and where daintiness is the requirement (the *Pizzicati* movement in *Sylvia*), it is heard without any excess.

Lakmé

☐ Monte Carlo Opera Orchestra and Chorus / Sutherland, Annear, and Clément (sopranos); Berbié (mezzo-soprano); Sinclair (contralto); Vanzo and Belcourt (tenors); Bacquier and Calès (basses) / Bonynge (conductor) / London 1391

Oh yes, the famous "Bell Song," but much, much more. *Lakmé* deserves permanence in the repertoire if only for its exceedingly strong melodic profile. Oh yes, a plot that is really ten-twent-thirt about a Brahmin priestess and a British army officer, with the gal saving the man's life only to commit suicide when he is going to desert her.

Sutherland's ravishing voice is a great bonus. Hers is a commanding conception, and she is splendidly sensuous. Vanzo's tenor voice is a bit light but sufficient for his role. All the others are excellent, with special mention deserved for Monica Sinclair, who gives all in her part as a governess and produces a belly-laughish result. Bonynge is in fine control, which keeps things moving nicely and all the textures clear. There is cohesion in the chorus, but the group sounds just a bit tired. With Sutherland and Vanzo as the leads in London's edition, the other version available on Seraphim (S-6082) must take second place. It also is placed in the second slot in terms of its sound.

Coppélia

☐ Minneapolis Symphony Orchestra / Dorati (conductor) / Mercury 2-77004

The long conducting experience Dorati had with the Ballet Russe de Monte Carlo is exhibited in this prime recording. It is deft, has finesse, and moves with impeccable dance tempi. (One comparison may be informative: Bonynge on London 2229 covers the ground in ninety-six minutes, Dorati's time is eighty-four minutes, and there are no cuts.)

A plus in the Dorati recording is the twenty-six bands that separate the sections so that it is very easy to find a portion one would like specifically to hear.

Sylvia

☐ London Symphony Orchestra / Fistoulari (conductor) / Mercury 77005

Graceful and delicate, strong where strength is needed—all the ideal requirements for a ballet score are here. The playing is polished and is disciplined by tempi that provide a vitality and inner pulse that would please the most finicky ballet company.

Just to hear the admirable sensitivity applied to the *Valse lente,* the grandeur of the *Marche et cortège de Bacchus,* and the delicacy of the *Pizzicati* section in the third act offers sufficient rewards for having this highly recommended recording.

Frederick Delius   *(1862-1934)*

Brigg Fair: An English Rhapsody (1907)

☐ Hallé Orchestra / Barbirolli (conductor) / Angel S-36756

Barbirolli conducts a glowing presentation of Delius's set of variations on an old English folk song. Those who will remember (or have) Beecham's recordings of this work will realize that Sir John provides as much poetry in his reading. He also has stereo, which is a decided plus in defining specific colors, such as the short, atmospheric passage for the bass clarinet and the use of the bells which ring clear and true—words that describe this recording as a whole.

Dance Rhapsody No. 1 (1908)

☐ Royal Liverpool Philharmonic Orchestra / Groves (conductor) / Angel S–36870

Variational design on and around a folksy tune, British locale. Delius's Rhapsody is clear-cut compared with the atmospheric chromatic chain of command of most of his work. Chromatics are here, to be sure, but they are used to flavor the harmonic essence, not to define it.

Charles Groves directs a bright and polished performance, without attempting to negate any roughnesses that hype Delius's delightful creation. Excellent playing and tone quality by the solo violinist. It's also nice to hear the solo sound of a "bass oboe" (Delius's term), which is actually a baritone oboe in range and which is correctly called a Heckelphone.

Dance Rhapsody No. 2 (1916)

☐ Royal Philharmonic Orchestra / Beecham (conductor) / Seraphim S–60212

Mature Delius and thus the structural content is strongly built from the rhythmic gracefulness that is thematically pertinent.

Beecham playing Delius is always an expressive experience. Here the results are of incandescent loveliness. The reconception and re-creation are perfect. Beautiful playing by the orchestra's woodwinds.

Eventyr: Once upon a Time (1917)

☐ Royal Liverpool Philharmonic Orchestra / Groves (conductor) / Angel S–36870

Eventyr (the Norwegian word for "fairy tale") deals with the world of trolls, demons, and giants. Delius's tale is pixy-laden and spooky in a wholesome way. Its instrumentation includes a pair of shouts delivered by the orchestra.

Groves shows a special conductorial gift for clarifying color imagery. The score is realized with full Delian rapport and is as good a version as the old Beecham performance, still available in its monaural form on Odyssey Y–33284.

Florida Suite (1887)

☐ Royal Philharmonic Orchestra / Beecham (conductor) / Seraphim S–60212

The monothematicism, the simplistic melodicism, and the general conduct of Delius's four-movement piece (with spliced dance sections in parts 1 and 3 this equals a six-part suite) strongly remind one of Grieg. Even in its more active portions there is the sensation of serenity in Delius's evocation of a day from dawn to sunset on to night in his Florida Suite.

Delius composed the work in 1886 and revised it the year following. This setting bears Sir Thomas's full consideration in terms of being "edited and revised" by him. His consideration of the music is charming, relaxed, and includes substantial excisions in the first movement.

In a Summer Garden (1908)

☐ Hallé Orchestra / Barbirolli (conductor) / Angel S–36588

Labeled a *Fantasy* by the composer. It has Delius's usual supervertical structure; the harmonies sweeten or make more tart, surround or counteract the melodic line as desired.

Without important tempo changes and free from all representational thematicism, the music articulates an essay of expressive meaning. *In a Summer Garden* is freely formed but has determinate shape. Its colors flash in a score that is underscored so that the style can be termed orchestral chamber music.

Barbirolli is superb. He interprets Delius as if he were Delius.

Intermezzo from *Fennimore and Gerda* (1910)

☐ Royal Philharmonic Orchestra / Beecham (conductor) / Seraphim S–60185

Knowledge of the opera is not necessary to enjoy this twilighted music. The sweet melancholy sadness that permeates its measures presents Delius in his most representative manner. Beecham obtains the utmost in delicate and expressive playing from the Royal Phil.

Life's Dance (1911)

☐ Royal Philharmonic Orchestra / Groves (conductor) / Angel S–37140

A certain amount of propulsiveness is contained in Delius's *Life's Dance* (a revision of a work titled *The Dance Goes On*), but the principal tone is introspective. The performance is informed and finely tempered.

Marche caprice (1888)

☐ Royal Philharmonic Orchestra / Beecham (conductor) / Seraphim S–60185

The first of a pair of early pieces Delius produced at the age of twenty-six. The piece is totally different from the subtle tone painting of his later work. Eric Fenby calls it a "pleasant trifle." Pleasant it is, but certainly a few cuts above being a musical knick-knack.

For the second of the pair, *Sleigh Ride,* see below.

North Country Sketches (1914)

☐ Royal Philharmonic Orchestra / Groves (conductor) / Angel S–37140

Eric Fenby, the Delius expert, states there is no program to these *Sketches.* Nevertheless, the titles are there for stimulating the imagination: *Autumn—the Wind Soughs in the Trees* (movement 1), *Winter Landscape* (movement 2), *Dance* (movement 3), and *The March of Spring—Woodlands, Meadows and Silent Moors* (movement 4). So if the *Dance* is considered as summer, then the four seasons are represented. Whatever the interpretation (and Sir Charles Groves's interpretation is a pliable one, stressing timbral pastels and never forcing dynamic stresses from the orchestra that might tear the music's tissue), the quality is impressionistic, achieving a degree of depth with minimal sound weights. All in all this is an outstanding Delius work.

On Hearing the First Cuckoo in Spring (1912)

☐ Royal Philharmonic Orchestra / Beecham (conductor) / Seraphim S–60185

Delius's famous short piece: the first of Two Pieces for Small Orchestra, written in 1912 (for comment on the second, *Summer Night on the River,* see below). It is given a magical performance touch by the Delian master of them all. The way Beecham presents the music, its pulse melts into a seamless continuity. And with no apologies to Beethoven, Delius presents the full expression of feeling through sound painting.

On Hearing the First Cuckoo is also in another Seraphim package: S–60134.

Over the Hills and Far Away (1895)

☐ Royal Philharmonic Orchestra / Beecham (conductor) / Seraphim S-60212

One commentator has stated the work is a "contemplation of the moors and uplands of the composer's native Yorkshire, an impression of open country." Whatever the response, the music is less ephemeral in its constitution than usual with Delius, with packed golden sonorities achieved in the orchestration.

The work was edited by Beecham, who plays the piece with a certain majesty which is most becoming. The R.P.O. is suitably responsive; its horns, especially, play splendidly.

Paris: The Song of a Great City (Nocturne) (1899)

☐ Royal Philharmonic Orchestra / Beecham (conductor) / Odyssey Y-33284 (monaural)
☐ Royal Liverpool Philharmonic Orchestra / Groves (conductor) / Angel S-36870

Delius supplied a double subtitle to his twenty-minute urban exposition. A third one is in order, "Rhapsody." This suggestion because *Paris* includes an interplay of moods and picturization—matinal and nocturnal responses, simulations of street cries and the sound of a goatherd's pipe, plus impressions of Parisian spirit and temper.

The problem with performing *Paris* is not instrumental difficulties (it is easier than any of the Strauss tone poems, for example). The difficulty for the conductor is to balance the network of relationships within the piece. Delius's production is highly articulate and very often ebullient. Natural spontaneity, in addition to sensitive phrasing, makes Beecham's statement so true as to place it as the number one choice. Such compelling insight into a composer's conception is a rarity.

Groves does splendidly, though two matters must be set forth. At times the details mesh instead of being placed in contrast. In other places loudness and textural heaviness are substituted for linear excitation. However, the sonics of the Angel disc are exceedingly persuasive, and on that count Groves's entry must be considered.

Prelude to Irmelin (1932)

☐ London Symphony Orchestra / Barbirolli (conductor) / Angel S-36415

The opera *Irmelin* was finished in 1892. The Prelude was redrafted in 1932 with the aid of Delius's amanuensis, Eric Fenby. It is a haunting six minutes of music equaling a miniature symphonic poem.

A beautifully moving performance.

Sleigh Ride (1888)

☐ Royal Philharmonic Orchestra / Beecham (conductor) / Seraphim S-60185

Delius's *Schlittenfahrt*, subtitled *Winternacht* ("Winter Night"), is a companion piece to the *Marche caprice* (see above). Written in the same year (1888), it features a gorgeous glitter of upper-soprano flute-and-violin timbre, modalistically motivated and stabilized by a pedal point. It is unlike Delius's mature blend of impressionistic music and yet clearly shows his future creative habits in its gossamer sentiments.

Beecham's consideration for this little-known piece results in an outstanding performance, especially in the intense feeling realized in the principal central section. The colorful dynamic contrasts are quite dramatic.

A Song Before Sunrise (1918)

☐ Hallé Orchestra / Barbirolli (conductor) / Angel S-36588

No syllabification in Delius's musical prose. The words are run together, forming luminous images in the strings, with wind arabesques forming another color layer. Activity in this short tone poem is restrained.

With the apparent arrest of pace a sense of forward motion in performance is crucial. Barbirolli achieves this far better than Sargent (on Angel S–36285) and does not blur the mainly vertical structure as does Beecham (on Seraphim S–60185).

A Song of Summer (1930)

☐ London Symphony Orchestra / Barbirolli (conductor) / Angel S–36415

Delius's *A Song of Summer,* written in 1930, used material from his *A Poem of Life and Love,* begun in 1918 and completed the year following. It is music that shifts from the quality of a humid nocturne to blazing orchestral song. Barbirolli's players deliver a glory of controlled golden sound.

Summer Evening (1890)

☐ Royal Philharmonic Orchestra / Beecham (conductor) / Seraphim S–60000

A curvaceously marked motive moves in and out of this piece, the first of a pair of short orchestral works that Delius wrote in 1890. Beecham, having edited and touched up the music, is best equipped to summarize its summery gentility.

Summer Night on the River (1912)

☐ Royal Philharmonic Orchestra / Beecham (conductor) / Seraphim S–60185

Summer Night is the second of Two Pieces for Small Orchestra, written in 1912. The first is the well-known *On Hearing the First Cuckoo in Spring* (see above).

A statement Eric Fenby made applies vividly to this piece: "In the best of Delius we are made one with Nature. No man has given musical utterance to all her moods, but in the expression of her tranquillities he excelled all others." And in the performance translation Beecham excels all others.

The Walk to the Paradise Garden (1906)

☐ London Symphony Orchestra / Barbirolli (conductor) / Angel S–36415

Played with depth and spaciousness. The richness of this piece is maintained without a flaw.

The Walk forms an intermezzo in the opera *A Village Romeo and Juliet,* though it was actually composed five years after the opera itself. Its poetry needs no operatic affiliation.

Concerto for Cello and Orchestra (1921)

☐ Royal Philharmonic Orchestra / du Pré (cello) / Sargent (conductor) / Angel S–36285

Delius's Concerto bypasses technical ballyhoo for lyrical appeasement. There is no cadenza in the single movement, which has five major tempo progressions. The music represents an idyllic soliloquy, its character expressed in minute changes, its texture transparent. It is all purity and serenity, and the wonder of this all is that despite the absence of specific contrasts, it holds the interest for its total twenty-five minutes. Only an obstinate creative independence could make this possible.

The magnificent cellist Jacqueline du Pré, now extremely ill, made her recording debut with this work a little more than a dozen years ago. She is positively brilliant in her

*Solo
Instrument
and
Orchestra*

Cello

golden-toned conception and seamless delivery of the solo line. The control needed (and supplied) for this type of music represents a special type of virtuosity. It doesn't bring the same audience reaction that occurs when a violinist sets off the fancy fireworks in a Paganini concerto, but it truly is no less demanding for the soloist.

Sargent always was sympathetic to Delius's music and was a topflight accompanist. The combination of du Pré and Sargent with the Royal Philharmonic Orchestra makes possible a totally definitive representation.

Piano

Concerto in C minor for Piano and Orchestra (1906)

☐ London Symphony Orchestra / Kars (piano) / Gibson (conductor) / London 6657

Delius's only piano concerto began as a three-movement work which he completed in 1897. Revision and compression into one movement then took place in 1906.

The concerto is not so Delian in its minimal chromatic contours, though the general *cantabile* characteristics of the work partake of the ruminative personality of this composer. However, there is a fair amount of elaborate writing for the solo instrument: double-note technique, powerful octaves and harmonic statements. All of these are fully mastered and smoothly played by Jean-Rodolphe Kars. Gibson's direction proves he is a fully dedicated and sure-handed accompanist.

Violin

Concerto for Violin and Orchestra (1916)

☐ Royal Philharmonic Orchestra / Menuhin (violin) / Davies (conductor) / Angel S-37262

In most concerti the solo instrument flexes its virtuosity. Even when it is restrained (as in Mozart), one is aware of the outward continuity of the music in terms of soloism. Though some of this does filter into the Delius Concerto, most of the work is the opposite of display or singlistic prominence. The *élan vital* is subdued; the concerto is formed from poetic statements.

Menuhin is masterly in this one-movement piece. His tone is clear, and though there is a total avoidance of overstress, a nice portion of Delian glow suffuses the production.

Violin and Cello

Concerto for Violin, Cello, and Orchestra (1916)

☐ Royal Philharmonic Orchestra / Menuhin (violin); Tortelier (cello) / Davies (conductor) / Angel S-37262

Indeed, there are a few other double concerti for violin and cello besides the Brahms, but not a single one has entered the repertoire. Delius's should. It doesn't have pulsatile drive, but it does have vocal thrust in its extended one-movement structure.

The playing must be smooth and lovely, and these two musicians provide these qualities. Their musically engaged performance can help draw an audience into involvement and understanding of the work. It is only by the style of playing heard here that Delius's richly endowed but non-showy meanings are manifested. Truly, conductors and soloists ready to schedule the Brahms "double" should give thought to pairing it with the Delius "double."

Instrumental

Five Piano Pieces (1921)

Piano

Three Preludes (1923)

☐ Jones (piano) / Argo ZRG-727

Here are all of Delius's piano compositions. Save for the Lullaby (the fourth of the Five

Piano Pieces), it would be difficult to recognize Delius's creative personality. None offers any technical difficulties (even the Toccata, which is the concluding item in the Five Piano Pieces).

Martin Jones is most successful with his interpretations. His playing is perfectly suited to the style of the music and is totally engaging.

Cello Sonata (1917)

Chamber Music

☐ Isaac (cello); Jones (piano) / Argo ZRG-727

A sonata only in the broad sense, not in the formal one, since there is no impulse to dramatize by juxtapositioning strongly contrastive material and there is a total refusal to structure themes and develop them. Unity is derived from a constancy of Delian rumination and Delian "cantabilian" writing assigned to the string instrument.

For this type of writing a seamlessness must be projected by the cellist. George Isaac's accomplishment is excellent, especially so since he produces, at all registral points, an even weight from bass to soprano. This is significant, since Delius often favors the difficult upper tessitura. Here this is heard without strain and minus pinched sound, and the bass zone is covered without any brashness or gruffness.

Midsummer Song (1908)

Choral

On Craig Ddu (1907)

Chorus Alone

The Splendour Falls on Castle Walls (1924)

☐ Louis Halsey Singers / Halsey (conductor) / Argo ZRG-607

Little-known Delian gems. There is a springy quality in *Midsummer Song*; a dark evocation, chromatically chronicled, fulfills the subtitle, *An Impression of Nature*, of *On Craig Ddu*; and a deep response to the Tennyson text is heard in the last part song.

Though word definition is not full, the singing is otherwise without fault and has a very generous quality.

To Be Sung of a Summer Night on the Water (1917)

☐ Louis Halsey Singers / Partridge (tenor) / Halsey (conductor) / Argo ZRG-607

Two wordless part songs, the second including a solo tenor. Their charming images led Eric Fenby to set them for strings, and in that translation the music enjoys much more attention (see under *Delius/Fenby: String Orchestra* [*Two Aquarelles*]). The attention given to the instrumental translation should not be at the expense of the original edition, which deserves equal performance time.

The recorded performance is absolutely beautiful.

Appalachia (1902)

Chorus and Orchestra

☐ Hallé Orchestra and Ambrosian Singers / Jenkins (baritone) / Barbirolli (conductor) / Angel S-36756

The subtitle indicates the structure: Variations on an Old Slave Song, with Final Chorus. But, though the variants belong to formal tradition, the style, with its magnificent orchestrational flux, belongs solely to Delius. Wilfrid Mellers has stated that there is no human population in Delius's music, only Delius himself and solitude. This describes the essence of this beautiful, unnervous work. There is only a bit of solo voice and chorus in its nearly forty-minute length. When these enter, there is no dynamic blaze, but there certainly is an emotional one.

Barbirolli does not play the score with impressionistic finger touches. Solidity is present; the music is full and radiant. With such direction the underlying power comes through.

Sea Drift (1903)

☐ Royal Liverpool Philharmonic Orchestra and Liverpool Philharmonic Chorus / Noble (baritone) / Groves (conductor) / Angel S–37011

Delius's music is a music of the sea and of birds, based on a portion of Whitman's *Out of the Cradle Endlessly Rocking*. The canvas is saturated with vibrant color slabs that mark one of the composer's most moving musical paintings.

The performance is a combine of heady textures and secure transparency. Noble is on stage practically throughout. He sings with splendid dignity and musicality.

A Song of the High Hills (1912)

☐ Royal Liverpool Philharmonic Orchestra and Liverpool Philharmonic Chorus / Bowen (soprano); Bingham (tenor) / Groves (conductor) / Angel S–37011

Noting a chorus and two vocal soloists, one expects a note on the textual basis. There is none. *A Song of the High Hills* is mainly orchestral. When the chorus is used, it sings its way in wordless form, with the solos as an incidental part of the design. A yearning mysticism pervades the music, and both material and scoring fit the mysticism like a hand in a glove. In this music the intensity is always on the rise, for even when the dynamic plane is lowered, a soft stress remains. One final remark: the set-in of the chorus long after the music has begun is an example, a highly positive one, of creative inspiration.

A gorgeous performance, personifying perpetual radiance.

Songs of Farewell for Double Chorus and Orchestra (1932)

☐ Royal Philharmonic Orchestra and Royal Choral Society / Sargent (conductor) / Angel S–36285

Five verses from Whitman's *Leaves of Grass* serve as the text for the Songs of Farewell. Here again is the Delian penchant for symbolistic color rather than tonal explanation of the text, with an emphasis on introspectiveness.

A fair enough performance, though the diction is not of the type that draws raves.

Cantata and Oratorio

Idyll (Once I Passed Through a Populous City)
Requiem (1916)

☐ Royal Philharmonic Orchestra / Harper (soprano); Shirley-Quirk (baritone) / Davies (conductor) / Seraphim S–60147

A nonreligious Requiem—rather, a lament for the human race misled by orthodox religion. Still, the titles of the work's five sections, such as *Our Days Here Are as One Day* and *Hallelujah*, have sacred overtones. The orchestration is tight: the pastel colorations of a typical Delius score are absent. In some respects the vocal writing is close to the instrumental; the voice lines are not curvaceous, but somewhat angular. Both soloists produce clear-cut delivery, and Shirley-Quirk's voice is richly toned.

In the *Idyll* the more familiar Delius is present; the music has poignance and moves in a Tristanesque climate. The *Idyll* is given an ideal performance, with beautiful singing and complete orchestral involvement.

Delius / Thomas Beecham (1879 - 1961)

Intermezzo and Serenade from *Hassan* (1920)   *Orchestra*

☐ Hallé Orchestra / Barbirolli (conductor) / Angel S–36588

Two brilliantly effective pieces from the incidental music composed for a production of *Hassan: The Golden Journey to Samarkand.* The tenor becomes an orchestral instrument, singing in vocalise style. Yes, the arranger is *the* Sir Thomas. He has not rescored, but simply amplified the string-instrument portion.

Delius / Eric Fenby (1906 -   )

La Calinda from *Koanga* (1897)   *Orchestra*

☐ Hallé Orchestra / Barbirolli (conductor) / Angel S–36588

In the opera this is a choral dance. Fenby's arrangement transfers the vocal parts to orchestral instruments. Here is Delius in a lighter frame of reference and aptly realized by Barbirolli.

Late Swallows (1917)   *String Orchestra*

☐ Hallé Orchestra / Barbirolli (conductor) / Angel S–36588

Late Swallows is an amplification of the final (third) movement of Delius's string quartet (actually his second; the first he ultimately rejected). Practically the entire score is intact, with merely a duplication of the voices and a solidifying of the lowest gamut by use of the double bass.

The music is in the form of implied programmaticism, with no hint save the undulation of certain accompaniment figures suggestive of winged movement. The pallid shimmering casts a glow as if the piece were a humid nocturne. Pace and mood constantly prod each other; the effect is one of remoteness, with only occasional attempts to be vigorous.

Barbirolli's performance is warm, rich, and beautifully balanced. This release deserves the highest rating.

Two Aquarelles

☐ Academy of St. Martin-in-the-Fields / Marriner (conductor) / Angel S–36883

A transcription of a pair of unaccompanied part songs (see under *Delius: Choral: chorus alone* [*To Be Sung of a Summer Night on the Water*]). The primary color of the strings is shaded by use of *divisi* of the voices, and its effect is a warm blend.

It is translucency that is the music's main means of expression, and Marriner and his players achieve this beautifully. The music does not fail to breathe, though in its totality it sounds like a single phrase.

Norman Dello Joio   *(1913 -   )*

Epigraph (1951)   *Orchestra*

☐ Vienna Symphony Orchestra / Swarowsky (conductor) / Desto 6416E (monaural)

Dello Joio describes his *Epigraph* as "simply a piece written in memory of a man." It was the result of a commission to compose such a commemorative piece. The music is in a large ternary form and is in no sense threnodic, though it has emotive overtones in the outer sections, with a more lively division, for contrast, in the middle portion.

Homage to Haydn (1969)

☐ Louisville Orchestra / Slatkin (conductor) / Louisville 742

Homage, yes. Thematic identity, no. Dello Joio's three-movement piece is gay (therefore, one supposes, Haydnesque). It is also a bit jazzy in the finale and bluesy in the preceding movement. Dello Joio mentions his affinity for Haydn's communicative directness. In that respect this eighteen-minute piece follows suit.

The recording is one of the rare instances of a guest at the helm of the Louisville organization. No problems, of course, with this young fellow's conducting.

New York Profiles (1949)

☐ Oslo Philharmonic Orchestra / Lipkin (conductor) / Composers Recordings S–209

The four-movement opus is for an orchestra with reduced brass forces—calling only for two horns and two trumpets. In other words the classical orchestral format, matching the neoclassic style of the music. The finale (*Little Italy*) is kin to the finale of Mendelssohn's well-known *Italian* Symphony. Imitative reasoning leads clever composers into good conclusions. The recording comes off with good grades.

Serenade for Orchestra (1948)

☐ Vienna Symphony Orchestra / Swarowsky (conductor) / Desto 6413/4E (monaural)

In reduced orchestration Dello Joio's work is heard more often as the score for Martha Graham's ballet *Diversion of Angels* than on symphonic programs. More's the pity, for the music is healthy, rich in its neoclassic outpour, and needs no choreography for substantiation.

In performance and sound this is one of the best of the Desto reissues of the old American Recording Society releases.

The Triumph of St. Joan Symphony (1951)

☐ Louisville Orchestra / Whitney (conductor) / Columbia Special Products AML–4615 (monaural)

One cannot type Dello Joio either as a pure classicist or as a through-and-through disciple of Paul Hindemith. Either definition might point to a composer of the pastiche. Yet Dello Joio forms his three-part symphony on the classic tradition, and with the implications of the looking glass through which all Hindemith's music is seen. The influence of the first is seen in the dynamic development of expressive thematic ideas, the method which builds a structure from small materials rather than fully stated melodies; the Hindemith parallel is in the series of sounds generated by free tonal harmony together with chunky, choired orchestration. But it is Dello Joio's spontaneous creative imagination that makes his symphony a successful opus, not a shallow imitative show of technique. Though the *Saint Joan* music displays both classic and Hindemithian influences (and the two are not as divergent as many believe), the symbolism is not derivative. In this sense Dello Joio is a "new" traditionalist.

The movements are designated *The Maid,* wherein variational treatment covers the thoughts of the girl of Domremy and the hearing of voices that summon her to fight the English; *The Warrior,* music of emotional force and drive; and *The Saint,* a perorative section. This symphonic debate achieves classic form in its total three-movement contrasts.

Both performance and recording are very good.

Meditations on Ecclesiastes (1956)

☐ Oslo Philharmonic Orchestra / Antonini (conductor) / Composers Recordings 110 (monaural)

Variation form is a favorite device of this composer. But Dello Joio's employment of variation does not lead him to survey melodic dimensions braced by filigrees and patterns. In this set of *Meditations,* of which there are ten, the variations develop the subject in a type of cumulative design; it is apparent where each portion begins and ends, and what its texture weighs.

Antonini does a professional job, and the Oslo group plays with good sound and ensemble. The technical part of the recording is satisfactory.

Fantasy and Variations (1961)

☐ Boston Symphony Orchestra / Hollander (piano) / Leinsdorf (conductor) / RCA LSC–2667

The Fantasy and Variations move along the channels of specific tonality, derived from a compact motive. The pithy pivot is allowed to swing in all directions, but tight construction is evident in all parts of the work. This kind of structuring is basic to the give-and-take, play, and development of the Fantasy. Clear profile is present in the Variations, the well-sharpened tools of nineteenth-century composers being the technical apparatus that Dello Joio utilizes.

Hollander is a facile technician, and there is no doubt that he confirms all that should be confirmed in the piece. (He gave the world premiere of the work with the Cincinnati Symphony in March 1962.)

Sonata No. 3 for Piano (1948)

☐ Glazer (piano) / Concert-Disc 217

Classical procedures hold first place in this meaningful work. The Sonata opens with a set of recognizable variations, five in number; each successive variation undergoes changes of shade and shape, but the subject's core remains. The remaining movements are symmetrical in their arrangement: a scherzo-like movement with a *presto e leggiero* tempo, an Adagio, and a vigorous *Allegro vivo e ritmico.* No dichotomy exists in regard to formal clarity.

Dello Joio's sonata has enjoyed countless concert-hall performances. The published score has had three printings, and for a contemporary American piano composition this is a record in itself. The work further enjoys a splendid realization in this recorded performance. Glazer plays with ardor and full understanding; his tone is luminous, and his technique is vividly exemplified.

Variations and Capriccio for Violin and Piano (1949)

☐ Travers (violin); Dello Joio (piano) / Columbia Special Products AML–4845 (monaural)

String Orchestra

Solo Instrument and Orchestra

Piano

Instrumental

Piano

Violin

513

Music arranged with simplicity, evidence of the craft found in Dello Joio's art. In a way, this composer gives the lie to the view that a composition requires big lush sounds. The formula here is a set of variations that do not overburden the theme (the ear is permitted its chance to understand all moves), plus a neat final part, minus instrumental blood-letting. Dello Joio explains his work as "charming intellectually unproblematical." *Touché!*

The performance is gentle, sweet, of high quality.

Vocal	*Eyebright*
Voice with Accompaniment	***Meeting at Night***

☐ Hanks (tenor); Friedberg (piano) / Duke University Press DWRM–7501 (monaural)

In *Meeting* musical shapes suggest the action of Browning's poetic monologue. *Eyebright* is fluid, with a divisional design to match the four stanzas of John Addington Symonds's poem.

Hanks is at his very best in this pair of songs.

Choral	**A Jubilant Song (1946)**
Chorus with Accompaniment	

☐ Mormon Tabernacle Choir / Ottley (soprano); Cundick (piano) / Ottley (conductor) / Columbia M–34134

Whitman's words piloted on a jazzy course. The triumphant flush of the music is exceedingly becoming. Dello Joio's piece, thirty years old, still remains fresh.

David Del Tredici   (1937-   )

Instrumental	**Fantasy Pieces**
Piano	

☐ Bennette (piano) / Desto 7110

Dark-colored expressionistic essays that remind one of Schoenberg prior to his serial days. Expert performance.

Vocal	***Night Conjure-Verse***
Voice and Instrumental Ensemble	

☐ Players from the Marlboro Festival / Valente (soprano); Burgess (mezzo-soprano) / Del Tredici (conductor) / Composers Recordings S–243

Two Joyce poems, *Simples* and *A Memory of the Players in a Mirror at Midnight,* in which refractional technique is used. Thus one voice merges into the other by retrograde echo and other imitative uses. The same applies to the instrumental groups, one a wind-septet combine (piccolo, flute, oboe, clarinet, bass clarinet, bassoon, and horn), the other a string quartet.

The mesh provides expressionistic music with colorful nervous vitality. One assumes the performance meets the composer's requirements.

Christoph Demantius   (1567-1643)

Chamber Music	**Five Polish and German Dances**

☐ Recorder Ensemble of the Concentus Musicus of Denmark / Irmgard Knopf Mathiesen (conductor) / Nonesuch 71064

Of course unpretentious items but a delight to the ear, surpassingly played and with richly toned sound.

Echo! Responsum si Vis

Jungfrau, Ich het ein Bit

☐ Accademia Monteverdiana / Stevens (conductor) / Nonesuch 71272

Both appear in an interesting collection of pieces termed *Amorous Dialogues of the Renaissance.* Both are set for "equal but opposing four-part groups." The music is a masterpiece of its own genre, and the renditions are faithful to the material.

Prophecy of the Sufferings and Death of Jesus Christ

☐ Spandauer Kantorei / Behrmann (conductor) / Turnabout 34175

The text is from the fifty-third chapter of the Book of Isaiah. Similar to the St. John Passion (*see below*), the *Prophecy* is a motet Passion.

The Spandauer group is fuller-bodied (the sopranos especially so) than the N.C.R.V. Vocal Ensemble that performs the work on Nonesuch (71138). Behrmann's broader-tempoed concept is also preferable.

St. John Passion

☐ N.C.R.V. Vocal Ensemble, Hilversum / Voorberg (conductor) / Nonesuch 71138

Demantius's setting of the Passion *nach dem Evangelisten S. Johanne* tells the story entirely in contrapuntal-motet style, without accompaniment, solo sections, or recitatives. Austerity is thereby emphasized.

Finely styled singing.

Robert Dennis

Improvisation and Variations for Cello and Piano (1962)

☐ Moore (cello); Thomas (piano) / Opus One 6

A method of *duo interruptus* is employed. The unaccompanied cello covers the first half of the work with more than a dozen aphoristic announcements, split by silences. The latter, by sheer contrast, give weight to the former and are of potent import by themselves. The piano joins the cello for the second half of the piece, which moves in the same kind of society as the initial division. This produces a very effective conception, with slight jazzy tones heightening the effect of the music's vivid colorations.

David Moore is the star of this one. He plays with zest and with totally fluent coverage of all the technical difficulties—and there are many.

Three Views from The Open Window: No. 3, Pennsylvania Station

☐ Louisville Orchestra and The Open Window / Mester (conductor) / Louisville S–691

The tale Dennis tells concerns the demolition of the Pennsylvania Railroad Station. The plentiful narration includes material from *The New Yorker* magazine and Thomas Wolfe's *You Can't Go Home Again.* Contrasted to this, there is some eerie music from an unknown source that is heard over the public-address system. There is also some close-harmony singing by The Open Window gentlemen, in this and the other parts of the three-part cycle recorded by the Louisville Orchestra. (See under *Peter Schickele* and *Stanley Walden*, respectively, *Opera and Dramatic Music*, for comment on the other two parts.) This full-scaled piece of programmaticism is presented with nice quality.

Alfred Desenclos (1912-)

Chamber Music

Quartet for Saxophones

☐ Marcel Mule Saxophone Quartet / Musical Heritage Society MHS–817

Bittersweet harmonies are handled in a virtuosic manner in Desenclos's Saxophone Quartet (for soprano, alto, tenor, and baritone representatives). The chromaticism is insistent, but nothing is static because of the voicing of the individual instruments. Rhythmic plotting, particularly in the finale, avoids ponderous primitive textures. Guts there are in Desenclos's piece, but there is also plenty of air in the form of instrumental spacing. The playing is totally communicative.

Josquin Des Prez (ca. 1440-1521)

Choral

Chorus Alone

Absalon Fili Mi

☐ University of Illinois Chamber Choir / Hunter (conductor) / Nonesuch 71216

"Absalom My Son" is music of passionate immediacy that stirs the emotions. It bears out Joshua Rifkin's description of it as "a work of unprecedented power and vision." The statement by this fine university organization is one of phraseological grace and emotional warmth.

Ave, Christe, Immolate

☐ Kaufbeurer Martinsfinken / Hahn (conductor) / Nonesuch 71084

A four-voice motet given an understanding performance that offers liquid, melting sound.

El grillo

☐ Sine Nomine Singers / Saltzman (conductor) / Turnabout 34485

Des Prezian patter that rhythmically sounds as though written just the other day. *The Cricket* is excellent choral humor. Once it's heard, you'll keep returning to it. Finding's keeping, when it comes to such pleasurable music.

Mittit ad Virginem

Salve Regina

Tu Solus, Qui Facis Mirabilia

☐ University of Illinois Chamber Choir / Hunter (conductor) / Nonesuch 71216

Entrancing motets, each and every one. The *Salve Regina*, in five-part writing, is supported by an ostinato played by a trombone. The performances of these three motets are of fused beauty.

Missa Ave Maris Stella

Cantata and Oratorio

☐ University of Illinois Chamber Choir / Hunter (conductor) / Nonesuch 71216

One of the very best of Des Prez's imposing number of masses. Superlatively styled and authoritatively directed. This university group is a remarkably proficient group.

R. Nathaniel Dett (1882-1943)

In the Bottoms (A Characteristic Suite) (1913)

Instrumental

☐ Hinderas (piano) / Desto 7102/3

Piano

Five romantic vignettes, including the famous *Juba Dance*. Full involvement on the part of this excellent pianist.

François Devienne (1759-1803)

Concerto

No. 5 in G major / No. 7 in E minor / No. 8 in G major

Solo Instrument and Orchestra

☐ Jean-François Paillard Chamber Orchestra / Rampal (flute) / Paillard (conductor) / Musical Heritage Society MHS-1127

Flute

Some Haydn and much Mozart coupled with formal authority, plus soloistic writing that bespeaks excellent creative imagination. This music will surprise and greatly satisfy those who do not know it. Devienne does not practice rote designs. The fifth and eighth concerti are in two parts each; they have fast initial movements and quite different final divisions (a set of variations in the former, an *Adagio et Tempo di polonaise* in the latter). In the finale *Rondo* of the seventh concerto one can hear several times an exact replica of the famous Paganini Caprice No. 24 theme!

Rampal's playing is so musicianly and sound that no challenges are possible. Paillard's support is excellent.

Sonata No. 1 for Clarinet and Piano

Chamber Music

☐ Russo (clarinet); Ignacio (piano) / Orion 77275

The patented imitative Haydn package. Still, the recording deserves its place in the catalogue. Nice clarinet tone, less nice piano sound.

Quartet in C major for Bassoon and String Trio, Op. 73, No. 1

☐ Zukerman (bassoon); Lautenbacher (violin); Beyer (viola); Blees (cello) / Turnabout 34304

Most stimulating because of its exceedingly rare instrumental combination. Quite often the bassoon takes over the solo role and the strings are accompanimental hand-servants.

A satisfying performance.

David Diamond *(1915-   )*

Orchestra

Music for Shakespeare's *Romeo and Juliet* (1947)

☐ Polish National Radio Orchestra / Krenz (conductor) / Composers Recordings 216

There is much to be admired in the work of David Diamond, especially in the classical convictions of his chiseled musical prose. This is not to say that he is blatantly conservative. Chromaticism is entwined in his music, used as a dramatic formulation, but it is never aggressive. The *Romeo and Juliet* music (five movements: *Overture, Balcony Scene, Romeo and Friar Laurence, Juliet and Her Nurse,* and *Death of Romeo and Juliet*) has long-breathed lines beautifully portraying the different moods of the suite.

The Polish group performs competently if not with great finesse.

Symphony No. 4 (1947)

☐ New York Philharmonic / Bernstein (conductor) / New World Records NW-258

David Diamond here presents a symphony of depth, and Bernstein's performance has done the score full justice. (Originally issued by Columbia, paired with a Sinfonietta by Jacob Avshalomov; the reissue by New World Records is a matter for which New World should be congratulated.)

No floridity here. Diamond is a composer devoted to classicism in its largest sense. The orchestration is derived from the Mahler school, dusted with a touch of the neoclassic Stravinsky. All the structures of the three movements are furbished and furnished with plentiful color, without sacrificing stability. This is good music. This is important music.

Timon of Athens: A Symphonic Portrait After Shakespeare (1949)

☐ Louisville Orchestra / Whitney (conductor) / Louisville 605 (monaural)

Diamond terms his piece "a psych-orchestral study," going on to state that his symphonic portrait is "of a munificent man whose false generosity betrays him." Thus no programmatic veneer to this portrait, but a deeply considered, powerful canvas. There is a strong romantic bias in the style and full emphasis on the orchestrationally directed analysis of the character. *Timon* is a brilliant conception with all of its arguments most persuasively related.

A musicianly recording, but one would hope for some major organization to pick up Diamond's piece and give it the top-league setting it deserves. Meanwhile, credit to the Louisvillians for a performance worthy of full respect, at the very least.

The World of Paul Klee (1957)

☐ Portland Junior Symphony / Avshalomov (conductor) / Composers Recordings 140 (monaural)

Musico-pictorial technique, but while the orchestral narratives clearly distinguish the subjects—*Dance of the Grieving Child, The Black Prince, Pastorale,* and *Twittering Machine*—a broader musical identification is presented rather than specific programmatic evidence. This follows Klee's idea of a "process of formation" rather than a direct (here musical picture-painting) product.

The suite is played fairly well. It doesn't have much subtlety, however.

Quintet for Clarinet, Two Violas, and Two Cellos (1950)

☐ Sobol (clarinet); Schulman and Moss (violas); Eddy and Sherry (cellos) / Grenadilla GS-1007

A russet instrumental combination (chosen, as Diamond states, ''to capture a quality of Rembrandtian, Brahmsian, even Regerish autumnal richness of texture and emotions'') is utilized here with a sensitive concentration of musical resources. Diamond's Quintet is illustrative of musical objectivity, its structure the twentieth-century façade of classical cognizance. The lines are long-breathed. Regardless of the special instrumentation there is no coloristic virtuosity. This is a music that, because of its strength, solidity, and profile, does not need such superficialities.

Quintet in B minor for Flute, String Trio, and Piano (1937)

☐ Gilbert (flute); Kooper (violin); Doktor (viola); Sherry (cello); Boehm (piano) / Turnabout 34508

Though Diamond's work is rather vigorous, it has a divertimento flavor—again showing the proclivity of this composer for seeking classical cap and gown for his music's dress. The tempo indication of the opening part is a favorite one (composers have their tempo habits, as well as harmonic mannerisms)—*Allegro deciso e molto ritmico*. The last two words describe the movement, one incited by a theme that is toccata-draped. The *Romanza* breathes long lines and sings while so doing. Diamond's *Finale* never stops moving, first to last. Some vivacious music can be dry, notwithstanding the forward drive. This example is of unslaked joy.

An all-star cast plays this work. Each member lives up to his reputation.

Brigid's Song

David Mourns for Absalom

☐ Miller (mezzo-soprano); Biltcliffe (piano) / Desto 6411/2

Diamond's gift for vocal settings is strongly illustrated with this pair of songs. The first is by James Joyce, the other from the Bible. Assured singing.

Alphons Diepenbrock (1862 - 1921)

Elektra: Symphonic Suite (1920)

☐ Concertgebouw Orchestra / Haitink (conductor) / Donemus Audio-Visual Series DAVS-6203 (monaural: 10-inch disc)

Passionate, lushly scored music. It *sounds*. In sections quite exciting, using an idiom that does not go beyond 1899. The orchestration is compelling, and I do not know of another composer who includes a duet passage for oboe d'amore and English horn in his output.

Excellent performance.

Grigoras Dinicu (1889-1949)

Instrumental

Violin

Hora staccato

☐ Heifetz (violin); Bay (piano) / RCA ARM4–0944 (monaural)

Well, here it is! The piece that Heifetz made famous, that brought its New York publisher much silver, and that made certain the permanent place of a composer of light music in the gypsy manner in the biographical dictionaries.

Heifetz made his own virtuoso edition of the original. I've heard dozens of violinists play it, but no one, *but no one,* can devour this Rumanian palatable popsicle the way Heifetz does. No one!

Karl Ditters von Dittersdorf (1739-1799)

Solo Instrument and Orchestra

Double Bass

Concerto in E major for Double Bass and Orchestra

☐ Württemberg Chamber Orchestra, Heilbronn / Hörtnagel (double bass) / Faerber (conductor) / Turnabout 34005

Style, text, and technical requirements are posited in the usual Dittersdorfian manner. Georg Hörtnagel's tone is not golden, but neither is it overly thick, so that its registration is acceptable, especially in the upper register, where it has a nice crispness. The cadenza in the first movement is a highlight. The orchestra of pairs of flutes and horns plus strings is consistently stable.

Double Bass and Viola

Sinfonia Concertante in D major for Double Bass, Viola, and Orchestra

☐ Württemberg Chamber Orchestra / Hörtnagel (double bass); Lemmen (viola) / Faerber (conductor) / Turnabout 34005

Far from the unlikely instrumental coupling one might expect. The russety color of the soli provides an example of Dittersdorf's originality and adds to the enjoyment of his four-movement essay.

Only recently there were three versions to choose from, but now only Turnabout's edition remains. It is sufficient, indicating fine soloistic imagination and complete stylistic awareness.

Harp

Concerto in A major for Harp and Orchestra

☐ Paul Kuentz Chamber Orchestra / Zabaleta (harp) / Kuentz (conductor) / Deutsche Grammophon 139112

A transcription of the Concerto for Harpsichord (see under *harpsichord*). Just as ingratiating on the harp as it is on the keyboard instrument. Zabaleta remains the masterful performer even with the reduced scope of the music he performs. For his performance alone the harp setting might be the preferable one.

Harpsichord

Concerto in A major for Harpsichord

☐ Hungarian Chamber Orchestra / Sebestyen (harpsichord) / Tatrai (conductor) / Turnabout 34325

Dittersdorf's gentle, merry style with a central movement of more breadth, including a short cadenza, and a fine closing section. A little wooden playing in the beginning, but matters improve, so that by the middle of the first movement everything is well in hand. This is music to listen to with no need to probe deeply.

The concerto has been transcribed for harp (see under *harp*).

String Quartet No. 1 in D major

Chamber Music

☐ Stuyvesant String Quartet / Nonesuch 71114

A fairly intelligent performance. However, one can question the speed of the initial Moderato, which is just as fast as the final Allegro.

String Quartet No. 5 in E flat major

☐ Sinnhoffer String Quartet / Orion 75170

The best known and the best of Dittersdorf's quartets. Usually played with four movements, including a slow movement, which Dittersdorf did not write for this quartet. He had no voice in the matter, since publication occurred after his death. The inserted slow movement (to fulfill the publisher's objective of matching the usual four-movement plan of most classical quartets) was taken from his B flat major Quartet, transposed in tonality (from F to G) in order to obtain a better key relationship, all the other three movements being in E flat. Nor should it be overlooked that the final two measures of the finale are not Dittersdorf's, but are by some editor who could not see his way clear to permitting the original to stand, which concludes with an extremely high solo first-violin note.

The E flat opus is a "quartet *buffa*." Only the Sinnhoffers come close to realizing this spirit. The Schäffer Quartet (on Vox SVBX-5300) mistake speed for lightness. Neither they nor the Weller team (on London STS-15168) are as graceful in delivering the minuet as the Sinnhoffer four. The question remains: why haven't such quartet groups as the Amadeus, the Griller, the Guarneri, and the Juilliard tackled this one?

Tod Dockstader   *(1932-   )*

Apocalypse (1961)

Electronic Music

☐ Owl ORLP-6

Dockstader calls his productions "organized sound," since they combine everything: electronic source material, *musique concrète*, straightforward natural sounds (unchanged), plus choices from anything that sounds, noise, etc.

In *Apocalypse* some things will be easily recognized: a trombonish timbre, voices, bells. Others are not so easily identified in the design. According to Dockstader, the mix he used in his piece includes guns, chimes, wind, cats, drums, and the ragged voice of a sawtooth oscillator. The aural totality consists of producing textural tensions and then their releases.

The four-part piece originally had two other sections, but these were cut away and have a separate life (see below: *Quatermass*). A still further reduction of *Apocalypse* has been made: see below, *Two Fragments from "Apocalypse."*

Drone (1962)

☐ Owl ORLP-7

Clear sound, that of a guitar, blended with and manipulated by electronic sound, that of a muted sawtooth oscillator. The twain having met, Dockstader shows a fine capacity to deal with the mating. Perhaps the conception is a bit attenuated, but it does have a fine sense of tidy balance.

Luna Park (1961)

☐ Owl ORLP-6

There are three interlinked parts to *Luna Park*. The principal sonic evidence consists of a type of laughing motive and a splash of pitches in tertial arrangement. Dockstader's unorthodox material fills an orthodox design of a fast, then a slow, then again a fast division.

Quatermass (1964)

☐ Owl ORLP-8

Large-scale "organized sound" (as the composer calls it: see above, *Apocalypse*), forty-six minutes worth. Metaphorical content is used to convey the simplicity of movement headings such as *Song and Lament, Tango, Parade, Flight,* and *Second Song.* Electronic metaphoricalness, indeed! From the suggestions derived from the metamorphosis of such items as a balloon, gongs, a cymbal, an oscillator, white noise, and adhesive tape, one cannot expect the drive of a Sousa two-step or a syncopative melody to ride over a duple pulse.

Traveling Music (1960)

☐ Owl ORLP-6

Deep-throated pulsations, sound gushings, and corrugated punctuations. Good frictions and good vitality.

Two Fragments from "Apocalypse" (1961)

Water Music (1963)

☐ Owl ORLP-7

Dockstader's *Apocalypse* (see above) was of considerable length ("in its original form it ran for hours"). He therefore reduced it and then further reduced the reduction by making the two *Fragments* a separate entity. It is closely related to the mother work, save that the finale of the second *Fragment* is highly colored by a pitch-defined ostinato.

Water Music acutely derives from aqueous sounds, electronically dictioned in many ways. There are six parts to the eighteen-minute composition, in which, in addition to the basic water-sound source, Dockstader has used "equivalent sounds of metal and glass, and a sine-wave oscillator." The composer treads water most capably.

Charles Dodge   (1942-   )

Electronic
Music

Synthesized Speech Music

    In Celebration
    Speech Songs
    The Story of Our Lives

☐ Composers Recordings S–348

Pseudo-vocal sounds placed on tape by computer synthesis. The effect is startling at first but diminished in the long span of *The Story of Our Lives*. Best are the short ("designed to entertain in a light vein") *Speech Songs* titled *When I Am with You, He Destroyed Her Image, A Man Sitting in the Cafeteria,* and *The Days Are Ahead.*

The unique inventiveness of this special technique cannot be denied; neither can Charles Dodge's special creativity and artistry. Nonetheless, a little bit goes a long way. For that reason it is suggested that the four *Speech Songs* be heard first.

Stephen Dodgson (1924-)

Suite for Brass Septet

Chamber Music

☐ Philip Jones Brass Ensemble / Argo ZRG–655

Bright sonorities mark Dodgson's four-movement work for three trumpets, three trombones, and tuba. It embraces contemporary tonality, which means rich harmonic condiments are used. No dizzying sensations are offered in this music, which is structured with solidity. That describes the performance as well.

Ernst von Dohnányi (1877-1960)

Ruralia Hungarica, Op. 33b

Orchestra

☐ Hungarian State Symphony Orchestra / Lehel (conductor) / Westminster Gold 8290

Nationalistic all the way. Excellently performed all the way. Originally *Ruralia Hungarica* was for piano (Opus 33a: see under *Instrumental: piano, Etude de concert*). Dohnányi later made still a third version, including three of the five pieces, for violin and piano (Opus 33c). (These opus designations are correct. For some reason Dohnányi used Opus 33 also for a major-sized composition, his String Quartet No. 3 in A minor. Indeed, many a composer is the author of confusion.)

Suite in F sharp minor, Op. 19

☐ Seattle Symphony Orchestra / Katims (conductor) / Turnabout 34623

The libraries are full of romantic-music inventory, much of it worthy of remaining on the shelf, some undeserving of such a fate. That Dohnányi's Opus 19 doesn't appear on concert programs is the whim of conductorial fashion. To every action there is ultimate reaction—Dohnányi's Suite is bound to return to the repertory. It has melodic flair and colorful orchestration, and it has expressive and impressive accents, especially in the beguiling set of six variations of movement 1 and in the warmly aggressive *Scherzo* of movement 2.

Its return to the recorded catalogue bears out the reaction noted above. Save for an occasional imbalance (noticeable in important phrases for the English horn and bass clarinet), the Turnabout edition is good.

*Solo
Instrument
and
Orchestra*

Piano

Concerto No. 1 in E minor for Piano and Orchestra, Op. 5

☐ New Philharmonia Orchestra / Vázsonyi (piano) / Pritchard (conductor) / Genesis 1022

Most of Dohnányi's music is a mixture of slight modal suavity and a healthy portion of Brahmsian expression, with a tincture of Hungarian melos and rhythms. It has been said that he was a poor man's Brahms. Having known and admired the latter, Dohnányi carried over his esteem into his own productions and suffered little for it (though some disagree). But the second hand aesthetic is made of first-class means.

An early opus is represented here, but it illustrates the vitality and drive of a masterful young composer. These qualities Dohnányi retained throughout his career.

The performance by the soloist Bálint Vázsonyi and the New Philharmonia directed by John Pritchard is splendid. It is a welcome addition to the small list of recorded works by this composer. Where are the superfine second piano quintet and the three colorfully dramatic string quartets?

Concerto No. 2 in B minor for Piano and Orchestra, Op. 42

☐ Royal Philharmonic Orchestra / Dohnányi (piano) / Boult (conductor) / Angel S-35538

Brahmsian shapes and treatment are the appurtenances which brace the Concerto. It has the important ingredients of balance, elastic tensions of impeccable instrumentation, and the mature weapon of cyclic fusion. All these are sure-fire pronouncements, especially since the melodic lines are of felicitous vocalization.

A definitive performance, emphasized by Dohnányi's expressive phrasing of Dohnányi's music.

Variations on a Nursery Song for Piano and Orchestra, Op. 25

☐ New Philharmonia Orchestra / Ortiz (piano) / Koizumi (conductor) / Angel S-37178

Dohnányi's Brahmsogenetic (Nicolas Slonimsky's apt adjective) and clever variations on the tune *Ah, vous dirai-je, maman* (for the French kiddies)—*Twinkle, Twinkle, Little Star* is the title known by American small fry—are available in a number of recorded versions.

The work is dedicated "to the enjoyment of lovers of humor and to the annoyance of others." So be the recordings. Angel's edition is the most enjoyable, with no compromise in regard to precise and refined perception. Turnabout's edition becomes annoying when soloist and orchestra don't mesh exactly in the *Finale (Fugato)*. Not the best sonically, though the playing is certainly what it should be, is the edition with the composer playing the solo part with Boult conducting, on Angel S-35538.

Instrumental

Piano

Etude de concert in B flat minor, Op. 28, No. 4

Etude de concert in E major, Op. 28, No. 5

Etude de concert (Capriccio) in F minor, Op. 28, No. 6

Five Pieces from Ruralia Hungarica, Op. 33a

Rhapsody in F sharp minor, Op. 11, No. 2

Three Pieces, Op. 23

☐ Dohnányi (piano) / Everest 3061

The *Etudes de concert* are the last three of the set; the Rhapsody is the second of a group of four. *Ruralia Hungarica* (see under *Orchestra* for the orchestral version) has seven movements from which Dohnányi plays Nos. 1, 3, 4, 5, and 7 (the label copy is correct; the movement sequence noted on the sleeve is incorrect). Except for some infiltration of native musical contours in Opus 33a, we have here music of a late-nineteenth-century type, most often of Brahmsian influence.

Dohnányi recorded this program at the age of eighty-two. It presents tasteful and vigorous playing worthy of a man half his age. Everything is right in the groove. (The opposite pertains to the incorrect Opus number 32a assigned the *Ruralia Hungarica* excerpts.)

Sonata for Violin and Piano, Op. 21

☐ Steiner (violin); Berfield (piano) / Orion 76244

Chamber Music

More is heard of the first movement of this sonata than is heard in the movement itself. Some of the opening unit is used in the second movement, and both principal themes of the initial part appear as the coda seal to the final movement. Secure in its conservative shell, Dohnányi's opening movement has dignified warmth, preserved and projected by the classic form Brahms employed for his head movements, including the figurations and arpeggios so dear to him. The middle movement is variational, with the theme anchored at both flanks, though varied on its reappearance. Five treatments develop all the subject's essentials; of these the most picturesque is the last, a pizzicato duet in which the piano imitates the string plucking as closely as possible. In rhythm and shape the last movement is a scherzo species, including the more relaxed middle section as well, but has larger detail and scope than denoted by the scherzo formula.

The performance is excellent. Diana Steiner sings beautifully on her four-stringed instrument. David Berfield is a fine pianist and sensitive to chamber-music teamwork. They play every phrase and every turn in Dohnányi's Brahmsian opus with musicality.

Serenade in C major for String Trio, Op. 10

☐ Heifetz (violin); Primrose (viola); Feuermann (cello) / RCA LVT–1017 (monaural)

The Serenade is a fine work, as beautifully constructed as any classic masterpiece, in which Dohnányi's dreams are of the estates of Brahms and Wagner, not the domains of his native land. Indeed, the Serenade does not depend on any Hungarian nationalistic music qualities. The qualities that are provided are wit and technique, the latter as expert as that of any of the classic or romantic master composers.

A variety of forms is included in the trio; these have serenade, suite, and sonata propensities. These forms are mixed together as a whole, and elements of them are combined within the individual movements. The resultant modern transcription of the classic serenade form is just as ordered as its ancestral use.

The "VT" in the recording's call letters signifies that this release is termed a "vault treasure" album in RCA's catalogue. A well-chosen designation, not only for its chronology in the RCA inventory but because of the actual performance. These artists are a marvelous team, and the major-league tone of their performance is heard and maintained from the opening tutti six-part C major chord of the *Marcia* to the tutti twelve-part C major chord that concludes the *Rondo,* the final (fifth) movement.

Quintet in C minor for Piano, Two Violins, Viola, and Cello, Op. 1

☐ New London Quintet / HNH Records 4072

There have been few men whose Opus 1 can match Dohnányi's first numbered work. While the initial published composition may not be the very first one the composer has written, it is generally very imitative. Dohnányi's is a strict Brahms sequel, but it illustrates the vitality and drive the former had as a masterful young composer, which he retained through the years. While some composers spring into the limelight with their early works, many of these soon bog down into silence because they lack true imaginative power. Dohnányi is not to be included among those composers who exhaust their small creative lungs with their first full cries.

The C minor Quintet retains its validity, though it pays no heed to any other than romantic methods, excludes novel color devices, sets no new harmonic blaze, is not a symphony cut to quintet size. The playing is handsomely delivered.

Franco Donatoni   (1927-   )

*Chamber
Music*

String Quartet IV (*Zrcadlo*) (1963)

☐ Società Cameristica Italiana Quartet / Wergo WER–60053

A chamber-music game, unlike any other avant-garde entry. There is no score, only individual parts containing graphic indications. These are translated with the help of titles and illustrations printed in a newspaper. Thus double chance weaponry. What the players wish to do they do as they react to the newsprint and music-print data. The discipline is freedom, which is quite different from the total disorder that would result minus any visual triggering.

What one hears is seeming chaos, but that's exactly what this music of the absurd is all about. The Wergo disc offers two different versions, since no two performances could ever be the same. If the music intrigues, a third version is obtainable from CBS-Sugar in Milan, Italy (No. 61285). It is played by the same organization but with different violinists.

Gaetano Donizetti   (1797-1848)

*String
Orchestra*

String Quartet in D (arranged for String Orchestra)

☐ Academy of St. Martin-in-the-Fields / Marriner (conductor) / Argo ZRG–603

Numerical identification is not given, though Donizetti produced eighteen quartets (not twelve as *Schwann* has it). D major is the tonality for Nos. 4, 14, and 17, and it is the last named that is performed here. That it is in fleshed-out instrumental format is especially acceptable since none of the quartets appear to have been recorded.

The music has a sweet-tooth type of operatic melody, with Haydnesque harmony and Rossinian *joie de vivre*. While the instruments are given some opportunity to behave as equals titular control is granted the first violin. Though not indicated, movement three, a Presto, is a straightforward ternary-patterned scherzo.

Marriner's presentation is a model of how this type of music should be played. Tempi are not hurried and there is a relaxed condition that shows off Donizetti's tunes to their best advantage without negating sensibility as to line and shape.

Concertino in G major for English Horn and Orchestra

☐ Bamberg Symphony Orchestra / Holliger (English horn) / Maag (conductor) / Deutsche Grammophon 139152

The highlight of the piece is the set of variations that hold the middle place in the three movements. Oboe or English horn, the mastery of Heinz Holliger is immediately apparent.

Solo Instrument and Orchestra

English Horn

Anna Bolena

☐ Vienna Opera Orchestra and Chorus of the Vienna State Opera / Souliotis (soprano); Horne and Coster (mezzo-sopranos); Alexander and de Palma (tenors); Ghiaurov and Dean (basses) / Varviso (conductor) / London 1436

Anna Bolena is finely constructed and its sound-poetry is lyrical and intense. The choice of this performance of the two available bears on the fact that the objective is directed to achieving a dramatic stress rather than emphasizing vocal importance. (And, in the latter instance, the London singers are better anyway.) Thus Elena Souliotis, in the title role, has a thin, somewhat pointed voice, and it certainly is not as good as Beverly Sills's (appearing in the competitive edition on ABC ATS-20015/4) but she totally outshines Sills in the creation of the important character she portrays. Marilyn Horne and Nicolai Ghiaurov (as Jane Seymour and Henry VIII, respectively) are outstanding, whereas Shirley Verrett and Paul Plishka as their parallels in the ABC edition are otherwise. Vocally, Verrett pushes and Plishka doesn't push enough. Donizetti's opera fares better under Varviso's direction. There is a welcome sense of excitement in his conducting. Rudel (on ABC) is in no way as acute.

Opera and Dramatic Music

Don Pasquale

☐ Vienna Opera Orchestra and Chorus / Sciutti (soprano); Oncina and Mercuriali (tenors); Krause (baritone); Corena (bass) / Kertész (conductor) / London 1260

Don Pasquale was written in less than three weeks and such creative agility rubbed off on the sparkling comedy that Donizetti produced.

This is a bright performance, and the entire opera sparkles under Kertész's knowledgeable conducting. Of course, the male singers are in command for the most part in this tale and all of them are splendid. Fine singing and an alive characterization from Graziella Sciutti.

La Fille du régiment

☐ Orchestra and Chorus of the Royal Opera House, Covent Garden / Sutherland (soprano); Sinclair (contralto); Pavarotti (tenor); Bruyére, Malas, Garrett, Coates, Jones, and Godknow (vocalists) / Bonynge (conductor) / London 1273

"The Daughter of the Regiment" mixes neat (sometimes broad) comedy with some downright human emotions. Bonynge knows his Donizetti and knows it well. His handling of this stage work justifies Donizetti all along the line. Sutherland also knows her Donizetti and she projects her tomboyish role with ease, command, and plenty of splendid vocal touches. She is certainly at top form here. Finely wrought singing on the part of Pavarotti and Sinclair. They are outstanding among a generally competent cast.

L'elisir d'amore

☐ English Chamber Orchestra and Ambrosian Opera Chorus / Sutherland (soprano); Pavarotti (tenor); Malas (bass); Casula and Cossa (vocalists) / Bonynge (conductor) / London 13101

Thin-plotted but sufficiently frothy to hold interest. It is well cast, and Joan Sutherland as a minxish character scores a success with her interpretation. Pavarotti, of course, is in fine shape and carries off his part with dispatch and marvelous singing. Lively control from the conductorial end.

Lucia di Lammermoor

☐ Orchestra and Chorus of L'Accademia di Santa Cecilia, Rome / Sutherland (soprano); Satre (mezzo-soprano); Cioni, MacDonald, and Pelizzoni (tenors); Merrill (baritone); Siepi (bass) / Pritchard (conductor) / London 1327

Sutherland is, of course, the imposing personality in this dynamic production. She has both the voice and the dramatic authority for the title role. Her voice shows remarkable range, with a special sweetness in the middle register; she produces an authentic trill and is just as authentic a magnificent prima donna, so tellingly illustrated in the famous Mad Scene. Renato Cioni has a vocal size that fits the Edgardo part perfectly. The others in the cast are thoroughly excellent.

There is a later recording that again stars Sutherland with Pavarotti, Milnes, and Ghiaurov in the cast, and conducted by Bonynge (also on London–13103). It has the advantage of containing none of the cuts in the London 1327 recording, but Sutherland doesn't have the youthful purity she provides in the edition made ten years earlier. One also senses a better fix on the score by John Pritchard. Finally, the Italian chorus is more polished than its English counterpart.

Maria Stuarda

☐ London Philharmonic Orchestra and John Alldis Choir / Sills and Farrell (sopranos); Kern (mezzo-soprano); Burrows (tenor); Quilico and du Plessis (baritones) / Ceccato (conductor) / ABC ATS–20010/3

The only recording available but fully sufficient. Beverly Sills is highly accurate in her projection of the leading character and is both dramatically and colorfully contrasted by Eileen Farrell in the role of Queen Elizabeth. The other parts are covered with excellence, especially the treasurable artistry displayed by Stuart Burrows. Ceccato keeps things on a spirited, well-paced level and is aided by persuasive engineering.

Richard Donovan   (1891-1970)

Orchestra   **Epos (1963)**

Passacaglia on Vermont Folk Tunes (1949)

☐ Polish National Radio Orchestra / Krenz (conductor) / Composers Recordings S-203

The Passacaglia title would seem to grant opportunity to hear some nice folksy effects and tunes. However, though some evocative native data blends in or counterpoints, the music avoids both the light and quotable touch. It rides on serious rails bearing heavy sonorous merchandise. Straightforward music it is (and that includes *Epos*, which is subtitled *Communication—Message*), dealing with absolute statements. They are performance relayed by an almost tough certainty.

Antiphon and Chorale

☐ Krigbaum (organ) / Composers Recordings S-262

Rightfully the title should read "Antiphon, Chorale, and Antiphon," since Donovan's work is securely set in a ternary frame. The texture is moderately dissonant for the greater part, which, on the organ, becomes nubbier, and consequently makes that much more of an impact. The Chorale is somewhat more of a chorale fantasia in its makeup.

Charles Krigbaum is one of our finest organists. There are no miscalculations here; everything is fluent, and the coloring choices fit the compact structure of Donovan's music.

Music for Six (1961)

☐ Columbia Chamber Ensemble / Schuller (conductor) / Composers Recordings S-290

Music for Six sounds improvised but is contained in a free rondo framework. It's a dancy denomination for oboe, clarinet, trumpet, and piano trio, with a bit of Ivesian quote-a-tune adventure, including a play on *East Side, West Side*. Brisk, extroverted playing by this pick-up group.

Five Elizabethan Lyrics for Soprano and String Quartet (1957)

☐ Galimir String Quartet / Addison (soprano) / Composers Recordings S-290

It took a quarter of a century for Donovan to complete these simple reflections mirrored in a romantic type of harmony. They were begun in 1932 and finished in 1957. Suitable playing by the Galimir group, which changes its personnel like the weather. Adele Addison's singing is average in this case.

Magnificat

☐ Battell Chapel Choir, Yale University / Harbach (organ) / Krigbaum (conductor) / Composers Recordings S-262

All too much sacred music, save by the greatest of the great, is either overwrought and/or monotonous. Such damage is avoided in Donovan's piece, which is compelling in its noble state and concentrated in a seven and one-half-minute length.

Charles Krigbaum had commissioned the work, and directs a clearly marked dynamic presentation. (Neither record label nor liner copy mentions the name of the organist. It is taken for granted that Barbara Harbach fills this role since she was the organist in another Donovan work on the same disc.)

Mass (1955)

☐ Battell Chapel Choir, Yale University / Nagel, Dean, and Holland (trumpets); Emerson (timpani); Harbach (organ) / Krigbaum (conductor) / Composers Recordings S-262

No reticence in Donovan's sacred work. It is bright with triadic popular appeal, to which are added colorful fanfarric trumpets.

CRI's recording is fine except that the timpani is hardly heard.

Instrumental

Organ

Chamber Music

Vocal

Voice and Instrumental Ensemble

Choral

Chorus with Accompaniment

Cantata and Oratorio

Matt Doran   *(1921-   )*

*Chamber
Music*

Sonata (1963)

☐ Atkins (clarinet); Davis (piano) / Wim WIMR-1

Fully indebted to traditional practice, but minus any academic ennui. Good playing, good recording.

Sonatina for Flute and Cello

☐ Shanley (flute); Davis (cello) / Wim WIMR-2

This concentrated work of three movements is in the very telling manner of neoclassicism. The general reserve of the music is abandoned somewhat in the Burlesque finale. A strongly delineated presentation by the duo performers.

Bill Douglas   *(20th cent.)*

Instrumental

Clarinet

Improvisations III (1969)

Vajra (1972)

☐ Stoltzman (clarinet); Douglas (piano) / Orion 73125

Music concerned with constant motion and unconcerned with contrast. There is a formal agenda but it is one related to the freedom of sonorous continuity. This is a type of music that gives up its secrets very quickly. For those who like it and want it the playing is tops.

John Dowland   *(1562-1626)*

Instrumental

Lute

Air

☐ Noad (lute) / Orion 72102

Dowland's slow-tempo Air is in contrast to the greater part of his lute music which uses dance forms. The playing is somewhat restrained.

Dowland's First Galliard   ***The Earl of Essex Galliard***
The Earl of Derby His Galliard   ***The Frog Galliard***

☐ Bream (lute) / RCA LSC-2987

Some of Dowland's lute pieces are duplicated in the form of songs (the last two of this group, for example).

The playing deserves a superlative rating. Bream's ability to differentiate dynamic planes and always retain a balance in the harmonic voicing marks his special artistry. The tonal resonance of the recording is superexcellent.

***Galliard* in D**

☐ Spencer (lute) / Philips 6500282

Short and sweet—fifty seconds in length. Spencer's tone is not as full as Julian Bream's but it has a delicacy and pointedness that is very appealing.

Lachrimae Antiquae
Lachrimae Verae

☐ Bream (lute) / RCA LSC–2987

Two of the most famous pieces in Dowland's lute output. The emotive authority of the music is matched by Bream's matchless playing.

Lady Hammond's Alemaine

☐ Noad (lute) / Orion 72102

Another short item, lasting fifty-two seconds. The *Alemaine* is also spelled *Almaine*, and is the four-pulse-per-measure Allemande dance.

Lady Rich Her Galliard
Lord d'Lisle's Galliard
Melancholie Galliard
Mrs. Vaux's Gigge
My Lady Hunsdon's Puffe

☐ Bream (lute) / RCA LSC–2987

All tastefully portrayed. The *Gigge* is especially cute. It is made more charming by the color and inflections Bream applies with quasi-ponticello sounds contrasted to normal ones.

The last-titled piece concerns sprightly music, delivered in a tempo faster than most of Dowland's other lute compositions. It is a pure delight.

The Round Battle Galliard

☐ Noad (lute) / Orion 72102

Noad plays this Galliard a bit faster than the usual tempo that applies to performing this dance form. No reason not to accept Noad's tempo opinion. Dynamically, the piece is heard unvaried which is not as acceptable.

Semper Dowland, Semper dolens
The Shoemaker's Wife (A Toy)
Sir Henry Gifford's Almaine
Sir John Smith's Almaine

☐ Bream (lute) / RCA LSC–2987

Like other Bream performances of Dowland's music (*see above*), there is lutenistic perfection for this group. The playing is imaginative and sensitive. Captivating, therefore.

Tarleton's Resurrection

☐ Noad (lute) / Orion 72102

Never mind the title. This is as gentle as a lullaby and Noad plays it simply, which is sufficient.

Unnamed Piece (Almaine)

☐ Bream (lute) / RCA LSC–2987

Dowland's untitled work (of one and one-quarter minutes total) is in the allemande dance form. Usual Breamian performance quality is to be heard.

*Solo
Instrument
and Strings*

Lute

Captain Digorie Piper's Galliard

Mr. George Whitehead's Almand

☐ Viols of the Schola Cantorum Basiliensis / Channon (lute) / Wenzinger (conductor) / Nonesuch 73010

The gentleman (?) honored by having his name attached to this Galliard for the lute was a young pirate. Regardless, the music sings sweetly and moves moderately. The *Almand* is in all probability an amplified arrangement of a solo lute piece.

*Chamber
Music*

Pauan

☐ Musica Reservata / Morrow (conductor) / Argo ZRG–572

Processional dignity marks this work, indicated *à 4*, and performed by three violins and continuo. A short harpsichord scale phrase used in ritornello form as well as strong counterpoint are coloristic supports for the piece, which is accorded a full-scale and dynamic statement.

M. Thomas Collier His Galliard

☐ Musica Reservata / Morrow (conductor) / Argo ZRG–572

A five-voice setting using viols. The work is taken from Dowland's *Lachrimae*, subtitled *Seven Teares Figured in Seven Passionate Pavans with divers other Pavans, Galiards and Almands*, published in 1604.

Vocal

*Voice
with
Accompaniment*

Awake, Sweet Love Thou Art Return'd

Away With These Self-Loving Lads

☐ Patterson (tenor); Spencer (lute) / Philips 6500282

Intimacy is the prime direction of Dowland's lute songs. Frank Patterson and Robert Spencer provide a splendid conception covering this objective.

Can She Excuse My Wrongs

Come Again, Sweet Love Doth Now Invite

Come Away, Come Sweet Love

☐ Blanchard (tenor); Noad (lute); Adams (viola da gamba) / Orion 72102

Excellent exploration of the sensitivity that lies within Dowland's songs. Hayden Blanchard's lyric tenor timbre is warm and most pleasing and he provides that great plus, excellent diction. The lutenist and gamba player are effective partners.

Come, Heavy Sleep

☐ Angadi (boy soprano); Channon (lute) / Nonesuch 73010

While it is true that the yearning that is found in *Come, Heavy Sleep* might be best expressed by a mature voice, the use of a boy soprano lends a type of silken courtesy to the sounds.

Farewell, Unkind, Farewell
Fine Knacks for Ladies

☐ Noorman (soprano); Brown (tenor); Channon (lute); Kessler (bass viol) / Nonesuch 71167

The first song is for soprano, the other for tenor. Both are impressive illustrations of Dowland's lyrical style. The singing has freshness and spontaneity, especially so in the lightsome *Fine Knacks for Ladies*.

Fortune My Foe

☐ Cuénod (tenor); Cohen (lute); Jaccotet (virginals) / Turnabout 34510

Skillful singing, excellent phrasing, and a particular insight into word meaning make Cuénod's rendition exceedingly communicative. Perhaps not a great voice but there are no doubts that he is one of the most musicianly of vocalists.

Go, Crystal Tears

☐ Brown (tenor); Channon (lute); Kessler (bass viol) / Nonesuch 71167

As in other songs on this disc (*see above* and *below*), a bass viol supports the lute. A bit more lower-gamut resonance results but also a trio effect, for the string instrument does have linear life. Brown's voice is steady, with an attractive timbre—excellent for Dowland's music.

In Darkness Let Me Dwell
I Saw My Lady Weep

☐ Patterson (tenor); Spencer (lute) / Philips 6500282

The fervent lament of *In Darkness* is one of the special Dowland songs. The inexpressibly lovely *I Saw My Lady Weep* is just as noteworthy and has sensitive balances in its construction. Patterson's projection of these pieces is clear, unforced, musical, and meaningful.

Lady, If You So Spite Me
Love, Those Beams that Breed

☐ Brown (tenor); Channon (lute); Kessler (bass viol) / Philips 6500282

Sung smoothly, and accomplished with real affection for the music. The trio ensemble of voice and two instruments is beautifully balanced.

Now, O Now
Orlando Sleepeth

☐ Cuénod (tenor); Cohen (lute); Jaccotet (virginals) / Turnabout 34510

Cuénod sings with sensitive quality and a superb sense of phrasing. Dowland's lute songs thrive when heard in the concentrated world of the recorded performance, whereas public performance tends to make them small-scaled, which they are not.

Rest Awhile You Cruel Cares

☐ Blanchard (tenor); Noad (lute); Adams (viola da gamba) / Orion 72102

Dowland's *Rest Awhile* is one of his larger conceptions. (The Orion release consists of nine Dowland songs and six lute solos. *Rest Awhile*, covering 6:20 in performance time, is the longest.) Blanchard's control of the long phrases that mark this song is exceedingly expressive; the diction crystal clear.

Robin Is to the Greenwood Gone

☐ Cuénod (tenor); Cohen (lute); Jaccotet (virginals) / Turnabout 34510

Communicative singing which means that even if the vocalism may be considered straightforward the musical results are totally expressive.

Say, Love, If Ever Thou Didst Find
Shall I Sue?

☐ Brown (tenor); Channon (lute); Kessler (bass viol) / Nonesuch 71167

Further proof of Dowland's mastery in the composition of lute *ayres*. Sung with a fresh lyrical voice, and with stylistic intelligence. Add to that the word "spirit." Excellent diction adds further to the credits.

Stay, Time, Awhile

☐ Cuénod (tenor); Cohen (lute); Jaccotet (virginals) / Turnabout 34510

A song title that fits the beautiful interpretation and the artistic delivery by Hugues Cuénod. It fits uniquely because the Swiss tenor was just seventy years of age when he made this recording in 1971.

Tell Me, True Love

☐ Vocal Ensemble / Noorman (soprano); Channon (lute); Kessler (bass viol) / Leppard (conductor) / Nonesuch 71167

There have been some critics who believe that the best results in presenting Dowland's lute songs are achieved when the singer is a male. This reviewer has never agreed with that premise. The captivating example here listed is sufficient evidence that a female voice is as propitious as a male voice in these songs.

A special extra bit is used in this case, not found in other recordings of the lute songs. A vocal quartet is brought in to support matters at the conclusion. It is very effective.

Think'st Thou Then by Thy Feigning

☐ Blanchard (tenor); Noad (lute); Adams (viola da gamba) / Orion 72102

Perhaps a trifle more seriously presented than is necessary for this lute song, but any minus points for that approach are canceled by the pulsed ongo that Blanchard projects. And additional points for splendid diction.

Weep You No More, Sad Fountains

☐ Brown (tenor); Channon (lute); Kessler (bass viol) / Nonesuch 71167

Beautiful vocal delivery and fine negotiation of the long-lined phrases of this Dowland song. Indeed, lovely in all respects, with a caressing quality applied to the interpretation.

What If I Never Speed?

☐ Patterson (tenor); Spencer (lute) / Philips 6500282

Patterson's crisp vocalism makes this light song a delight.

When Phoebus First
White as Lilies

☐ Cuénod (tenor); Cohen (lute); Jaccotet (virginals) / Turnabout 34510

In general impressively styled, though lacking the finesse of tonal variety in *White as Lilies*.

Wilt Thou, Unkind, Thus Reave Me

☐ Blanchard (tenor); Noad (lute); Adams (viola da gamba) / Orion 72102

This song is presented with infallible taste and fine intelligence. Blanchard is imaginative in his singing.

An Heart That's Broken and Contrite
If That a Sinner's Sighs

Voice and Instrumental Ensemble

☐ Consort of Instruments / Cantelo (soprano); Baker (contralto); English (tenor); Keyte (bass) / Leppard (conductor) / Nonesuch 71167

Melancholic statements sung with beauty. The consort of instruments includes lute, recorder, cittern, bandura, treble viol, and bass viol.

In This Trembling Shadow   Sorrow, Stay
Lasso Vita Mia   Welcome, Black Night

☐ Musica Reservata and Purcell Consort of Voices / Morrow and Burgess (conductors) / Argo ZRG-572

Sorrow, Stay is credited to Dowland, since it is a song included in his *The Second Booke of Songs*. However, the arrangement recorded is anonymous. The other three pieces are from Dowland's *A Pilgrimes Solace*.

Presented with the best of taste and splendid feeling for style.

Were Every Thought an Eye
Where Sin, Sore Wounding

☐ Consort of Instruments / Cantelo (soprano); Baker (contralto); English (tenor); Keyte (bass) / Leppard (conductor) / Nonesuch 71167

Expert singers, fine direction. The characterizations are apt and the sound fully responsive.

It Was a Time
The Lowest Trees Have Tops

Choral

Chorus Alone

☐ Sine Nomine Singers / Saltzman (conductor) / Turnabout 34485

A good number of Dowland's "Songes or Ayres" were written for either solo voice and lute (known therefore as "Lute Songs" even when sometimes amplified by use of a keyboard or a bass string instrument) or four voices. The latter, of course, is the situation in this case. The pacing and the vocal flexibility as well as the ensemble are ideal. Saltzman's group deserves state-of-art rating.

Psalms for Four Voices

Psalm 51 / Psalm 100

☐ Cantelo (soprano); Baker (contralto); English (tenor); Keyte (bass) / Leppard (conductor) / Nonesuch 71167

Two prime examples from Dowland's set of hymn tunes. Sung with infallible taste. The quality of the disc adds considerably to the listener's enjoyment.

John Downey   (1927-   )

Instrumental

Two Pianos

Adagio lyrico (1953)

☐ Anthony and Joseph Paratore (pianos) / Orion 77267

The appropriate niche for Downey's earlier piece is neoromantic. But this does not exclude a proportionate amount of sharply focused hard-crusted chromaticism that marks the central part of the music and which verges on atonalism. This does not cripple the structural cohesion based on a concept of continuous free variation.

Chamber Music

Octet for Winds (1954)

☐ Rydz (flute and piccolo); Covelli (oboe); Talbert (clarinet); Hibler (bass clarinet); Basson and Babinec (bassoons); Treviranus (horn); Sodke (trumpet); DeRusha (conductor) / Orion 77267

Harmonic pungency becomes doubly candid when expressed solely by wind and brass instruments. The more fundamental such use in chamber music the more such type of composition becomes a type of musical algebra, manifested by its concern with pure relationships and with proving them. Downey uses his chosen resources with unequivocal definition. The product is a music that has power of sonority, and pungency of free tonal correlativity.

The sharp, black-white quality of performance matches the score's objective.

Vocal

Voice and Instrumental Ensemble

A Dolphin (1974)

☐ Nelson (tenor); Bourachoff (alto flute); Zaslav (viola); Burda (vibraphone and percussion); Downey (piano) / Downey (conductor) / Orion 77267

No mere instrumental accompaniment to an engaging test written by the composer's wife. In actuality the work is the equal of chamber music for five performers, the instrumental voices integrated with and responding to the voice and vice versa. At the same time there is no abstract textual condition whereby the words are utilitarian pegs on which to hang pitches and other organized relationships simply because the voice must have something to sing and because musical translation of their meaning has little or no bearing on the result. Every part of Downey's richly colored contemporary score buttresses the text, both in its outward and inward meanings.

With the composer as the pianist-conductor one can be certain the performance is all it should be.

What If? (1973)

☐ University of Wisconsin in Milwaukee Concert Choir with Alumni / Granatella and Cook (trumpets); Fraederich and Davies (horns); Howlett and Kling (tenor trombones); Ruck (bass trombone); Neesley (tuba); Burda (timpani and percussion) / Balko (conductor) / Orion 77267

Powerful prose (by E. E. Cummings), set forth with maintained choral intensity, swinging around a strong tonal polarity and framed by a timpanic ritornello. The quality of Downey's writing indicates a distinct musical personality.

Sem Dresden (1881-1957)

Oboe Concerto (1939)

☐ Radio Philharmonic Orchestra / van Slogteren (oboe) / Travis (conductor) / Donemus Audio-Visual Series 7374/2

A three-pitch motive embracing a seventh in its total span is the prime material for the composition. Its general mood is reflected in the initial tempo: *Allegretto pastorale.* The middle movement is divided between a *Recitativo* and an *Arioso;* variations complete the concerto. Pandiatonic integration smooths the way for Dresden's piece, acceptably played, though with not much depth in the recording (taken from a live performance).

Violin Concerto No. 2 (1942)

☐ Concertgebouw Orchestra / Juda (violin) / Haitink (conductor) / Donemus Audio-Visual Series DAVS-6702

Dark-stranded music, tonally firm. In the first movement, sonata form is contemporaneously edited by inverting the two principal themes in the recapitulation. The peak of the concerto is the funereal content of the slow movement. A fair recording, but for Donemus one of the better ones they've issued.

Alexander Dreyschock (1818-1869)

Concert-Piece in C minor for Piano and Orchestra, Op. 27

☐ Nürnberg Symphony Orchestra / Cooper (piano) / Deàky (conductor) / Genesis 1013

Technically demonstrative information contrasted to a nice second subject tune. The music exactly defines what is meant by nineteenth-century romantic virtuosity. There are no earth-shattering gestures in this piece but it certainly is worth hearing—and more than once.

Cooper's playing is clearly spirited, beautifully styled, in all a positive declaration and most enjoyable.

Riccardo Drigo (1846-1930)

Pas de trois from Harlequin's Millions

☐ London Symphony Orchestra / Bonynge (conductor) / London 2213

Not the once-famous Serenade or the similarly once-popular *Valse bluette,* but an equally telling segment from *I milioni d'Arlecchino.*

Ballet

Pas de deux from Le Corsaire

☐ London Symphony Orchestra / Bonynge (conductor) / London 6418

Adolphe Adam was the composer for this ballet. Drigo's entry onto the scene and into the score was in the form of this dance added to a later version of the work. It has all the expected melodic turns and is performed to do the music complete justice.

Jacob Druckman   (1928-   )

Orchestra

Incenters (1968)

☐ Contemporary Chamber Ensemble / Weisberg (conductor) / Nonesuch 71221

Druckman's geometric-semantic title is carried out in his thirteen-instrument work (coincidentally almost thirteen minutes in length) by approaching the objective mainly through application of the scoring distribution. As Eric Salzman perceptively points out in his liner notes, "the brass dominate, and they set in motion each chain of musical events by upsetting the equilibrium established by the other instruments." A brilliant and stimulating piece.

Weisberg's performance (the work was specifically written for the conductor and his group) is firm and spacious, and always on the right lines.

Instrumental

Clarinet

Animus III, for Clarinet and Tape (1969)

☐ Bloom (clarinet) / Nonesuch 71253

Bloom is his own duo partner in *Animus III.* The tape part consists of his voice and clarinet, transformed totally, and combined with his "live" performance; the latter, further heard in conjunction with a microphone connected to a feedback device. Thus the duo becomes a pseudo-trio. It produces a score that has swagger, bounce, and a good amount of subtle humor. (Druckman's theatrical result was recognized and was used for the ballet *Solarwind.*)

Double Bass

Valentine

☐ Brehm (contrabass) / Nonesuch 71253

A cousin (several ranks removed) to *Synapse* (discussed under *Electronic Music*). *Valentine* treats the double bass with astonishing disregard for traditional practice. It requires percussing the instrument much more than playing on its strings. The instrument is struck with the bow and timpano stick, and drummed on its body. A variety of plucked timbres are used; the bassist as vocalist sustains pitches, sings, and whispers along, and vocally accents instrumental accentuations.

It's indeed a double bass bash and when seen in performance, even more effective. The score serves, with the same title (*Valentine*), as a most successful ballet, with the bassist on stage as part of the dance action with his own instrumental actions.

Its relationship to *Synapse* is indicated in the commentary on that work.

String Quartet No. 2 (1966)

☐ Concord String Quartet / Vox SVBX–5306

That Druckman's quartet radiates influences from the music of Elliott Carter is meant to be a compliment, since he has not absorbed and thereby boldly imitated him. The Americanized angst in this work may not be identifiable as being Druckman's and Druckman's alone, but it certainly does not resemble the mood of Carter's music, notwithstanding some reminder by the use of assigning each instrument "something of a theatrical character role that determines to some extent what each instrument is assigned to play" (from the notes by Lejaren Hiller).

Druckman's quartet excites simply by its total dramatic thrust regardless of the quoted characterization outline. It is serial music, but neither academic nor so freely quirky that it loses definable shape. It is a substantial and ever-expanding documentation drawn from a specific compositional plan, but needs no following of the plan to make sheer musical sense and impact. In short, the writing does not avoid emotional indulgence in favor of technical discipline.

There's plenty of color to prime the sonorities. This includes cadenzas, cluster compacts, controlled (pitchwise) improvisational sections, *col legno* glides, and finger contacts on the body of instruments. All these fascinate the ear but are integrated in the stuff and substance of a thrilling work.

And the performance is thrilling as well. Druckman's opus is for virtuosi who understand, believe in, and enjoy playing twentieth-century music. Those words describe the Concord Quartet.

Delizie contente che l'alme beate for Woodwind Quintet and Tape

☐ Dorian Quintet / Vox SVBX–5307

A strange dream-haunted state exists in Druckman's creation. For half of the piece, tape scribblings of a Cavalli operatic aria (hence the name of the work) filter in and out. They are barely recognized, giving the sense that the snippets are simply illusory. Eventually the quotation takes on sufficient distinguishability though never without sonic adumbration and interlardation. The textures are ravishing especially in the tape content, made of both electronic and woodwind quintet material. The interlock produces a music of excitable gifts.

Animus II (1968)

☐ DeGaetani (mezzo-soprano); Fitz and Gottlieb (percussion) / Composers Recordings S–255

Druckman's contemporary voice speaks loud and clear in *Animus II*. It speaks not only by way of the human voice and percussion timbres but with the addition of an electronic tape, which includes *concrète* sounds. No dubious adherence to a specified system is found in this work. It has complex patterns but none of subterfuge, though *Animus II* registers more vividly in live presentation than on disc. But there is enough to hold the ears of a listener as one imagines the actions of the performers, which Druckman describes as being "the celebration of a sybaritic ritual." That one can become involved totally in a *musical* experience without the support of the theatrical counterpart speaks highly for this talented composer. One speaks highly also for the quality of CRI's engineering.

Electronic Music	**Synapse** ☐ Nonesuch 71253

On Nonesuch's recording *Synapse* leads into *Valentine* (discussed under *Instrumental: double bass*). However, they are two separate pieces, even though *Synapse* "assumes the stance of *Valentine*." *Synapse*, Druckman explains further, "functions as avant-propos, paraphrase, setting for *Valentine*."

There is special color in *Synapse* but much more so in the companion string-instrument piece. However, the major premise is that the electronic work includes simulations of sounds found in the string-instrument creation (plucks and glides), while the latter contains implied imitations of the tape piece (odd vocal effects and percussive productions).

John W. Duarte   (1919-   )

Instrumental

Guitar

Variations on a Catalan Folk Song, *Canco del Llabre*, **Op. 25**

☐ Williams (guitar) / Everest 3195

Duarte, a well-known guitar pedagogue, has composed important didactic material, and is included among John Williams's teachers. His tonally conceived "Variations" have a light contemporary flavor with neat cohesion between harmony and melodic line. There are seven variations, the tonality changing for each, with balance obtained by matching the key of the first and last of the variations.

Two Guitars

Six Friendships

☐ Ito and Dorigny (guitars) / Delos FY–008

Sociable music, indeed. There is rapport with defined forms: a *Chanson*, a twenty-nine-second Ostinato, a compact Gavotte, and a movement titled *Cantando*. Jazz amity is heard in *Offset;* comradeship with the perpetual motion idea is displayed in *Sans Cesse*.

Duarte specializes in writing for the guitar and in teaching the instrument. His compositional style is beautifully related to the instrument. (The *Chanson* is listed as Opus 14; the *Sans Cesse*, as Opus 34; the remaining pieces are all drawn from Opus 26.)

Gustaf Düben   (1624-1690)

String Orchestra

Three Dances

☐ Camerata Lutetiensis / Nonesuch 73014

Music by this Swedish court composer. The Allemande, Courante, and Sarabande are all reasonable pieces, friendly and communicative, if not at all original.

Arcady Dubensky / Sergi Rachmaninoff. See Rachmaninoff / Arcady Dubensky.

Pierre-Max Dubois (1930-)

Concerto for Flute and Orchestra

☐ English Chamber Orchestra / DiTullio (flute) / Howarth (conductor) / Crystal S-503

The neoclassic pursuit of balance (formally and harmonically) is exhibited here, and successfully. Dubois's creative ethos concerns light-hearted pathos, especially in the outer movements. In between, a more sober pair of dances gives expressive contrast.

Concerto for Alto Saxophone and String Orchestra (1959)

☐ Paul Kuentz Chamber Orchestra / Rousseau (alto saxophone) / Kuentz (conductor) / Deutsche Grammophon 2530209

There is some wit in this Frenchman's music, but for the most part it has the solid qualities of serious expression.

This performance is utterly engaging. Rousseau's saxophone tone doesn't flutter with excessive vibrato, and Kuentz's collaboration is excellent.

Quartet

☐ Paul Brodie Saxophone Quartet / Golden Crest 4131

Dubois is extremely partial to compositions utilizing a basic timbre. Accordingly, he has produced quartets for horns, flutes, trombones, and clarinets, additional to this one for saxophones. The last instrument is also a decided favorite, as witness its use in a *Divertissement* for Saxophone and Orchestra (1952), a *Concertstück* for Saxophone and Piano (1955), the Concerto for Alto Saxophone and String Orchestra (see under *Solo Instrument and Orchestra: saxophone*), and a Concertino for Four Saxophones and Orchestra (1961).

In his Quartet Dubois opts for Ibertian lightness plus the bitter-sweet of a French *chanson* in the *Doloroso* (second) movement. Rhythmic vitality and the clearest type of form make Dubois's quartet for soprano, alto, tenor, and baritone saxophones a gem. A handsome performance.

Solo Instrument and Orchestra

Flute

Saxophone

Chamber Music

Théodore Dubois (1837-1924)

Fantaisie in E major

Toccata in G major

☐ Lehrndorfer (organ) / Vox SVBX-5314

Natural formal explanations, especially good in the vital rhythm of the Toccata. The performances are well organized and perceptively colored.

Instrumental

Organ

Jean Dubuffet (1901-)

Musical Experiences (1961)

Cry and Clap	*Futile Diligences*	*Uncertain Humor*
Deliberators	*Joyful Wisdom*	*Water*
Enticements	*Sunken Ship*	

Electronic Music

☐ Finnadar 9002

In his attempt to hurl a slingshot and wipe out every (no matter how remote) stylistic affiliation, cancel any vestige of tradition or of contemporaneous affiliation, totally destroy meaning and balance, Dubuffet is a representative of Dadaism. His music has the same objective as the Dadaists who made pictures out of rubbish or displayed a urinal as an art object.

Dubuffet states that he "ignores everything about Western music and invents a music for himself without any reference, without any discipline." Accordingly, he has improvised on a considerable number of instruments (most of which he cannot play "correctly"), recorded his performances, and worked on these with the usual electronic music composer's techniques of mixing, superimpositioning, editing, etc. etc. Some of the instruments played are of the standard variety (piano, flute, trumpet, cello, cimbalom, drum, bassoon, etc.). Some are extremely rare (Chinese mouth organ, Geisha drum, balafon, etc.). Certain timbres will be recognized from time to time, others hardly ever, if at all. The *pasticcio* is a sonic stew of mishmash, hotchpotch, and *disjecta membra*. It sounds like Scarlatti's famous cat in drunken action—out-of-whack synthesizers, backstage warm-ups, and front-stage tune-ups.

Of course, like any art work, confusion to one may be a masterpiece to another. Ilhan Mimaroğlu, who supervised this recording and wrote the liner notes, is a master in the electronic music field, and no one's fool or patsy. He states that the criteria for Dubuffet's performance should not be "of the musical performance, but of musical creativity in all its vastness." He considers the music to be "among the purest products of imagination, unadulterated by conceptual thinking." All of his detailed notes deserve the closest attention and thought. From this critical remove, there is no comment.

William E. Duckworth (1943-   )

Percussion

Gambit for Percussion and Tape

☐ Youhass (percussion) / Capra 1201

An interesting concept is developed in Duckworth's piece. Sometimes the tape accompanies the percussion detail, other times the tape is soloistic and the percussion accompanies by punctuation. Sensitive sensibilities in this music, conceived in impressionistic style.

Instrumental

Saxophone

A Ballad in Time and Space

☐ Hemke (saxophone); Granger (piano) / Brewster 1204

A nocturnal beauty that includes key percussion and two-part chords for the saxophone. But, these do not represent an obsessional desire to play tricks or to engender effects. Their use is always meaningful (the chordal conclusion is a masterful touch).

Hemke is one of the great saxophonists. His control is superb, his tone full and musical. For a performance of this quality, the composer should be everlastingly in his debt.

Guillaume Dufay   *(ca. 1400-1474)*

Vergine Bella

☐ Early Music Consort of London / Bowman (countertenor) / Munrow (conductor) / Nonesuch 71326

One of the most beautiful examples in Dufay's output. The *chanson* is a warm piece of music, with a medieval fiddle and a crumhorn supporting the voice. A small marvel and sensitively executed in this program of *The Pleasures of the Royal Courts,* covering twenty-eight works from the thirteenth, fifteenth, and early sixteenth centuries.

Apostolo Glorioso

Fulgens Iubar Ecclesie

Nuper Rosarum Flores

☐ Capella Cordina / Planchart (conductor) / Lyrichord 7190

These three isorhythmic motets illustrate the special strengths of this Burgundian master composer. The textural syncopations and cross rhythms (sometimes flowing, other times driving) found in these pieces provide a strength and imagery of remarkable creativity.

The singing is imaginative and of unfailing taste. Instruments are used (recorder, English horn, one or two violas, trombone, and bassoon) and are integrated with discrimination.

These motets are also available on Lyrichord 7233. Here, on Lyrichord 7190 they are coupled with Dufay's *Missa Caput.* On Lyrichord 7233 they are recorded along some hymns and the *Missa Ave Regina.*

Missa Caput

☐ Capella Cordina / Planchart (conductor) / Lyrichord 7190

Dufay's *Missa Caput* has been described as his simplest Mass. It has a tenderness and a sweetness that are derived from an absence of ornateness.

This is a fine recorded conception. The singing is clear and the rhythms are shaped succinctly. It is a work that excites by its elegant musicality.

Missa L'Homme Armé

☐ Instrumental Ensemble and Vokalensemble Pro Musica, Köln / Hömberg (conductor) / Candide 31094

A finely set performance that need not be considered only by the Dufay scholar. The singing is warm and better integrated than in the competitive edition issued by Lyrichord.

Paul Dukas   *(1865-1935)*

The Sorcerer's Apprentice (1897)

☐ Philadelphia Orchestra / Ormandy (conductor) / RCA ARD1-0002
☐ New York Philharmonic / Bernstein (conductor) / Columbia MS-6943
☐ L'Orchestre de la Suisse Romande / Ansermet (conductor) / London 6367

With Ormandy the Dukas programmatic scherzo is given an all-out, brilliantly animated performance, the rhythms spitfired. The listed catalogue number covers a collection with a colorful, yet truthful title: "The Fantastic Philadelphians." Dukas's "Sorcerer" is also included in a three-record album (RCA CRL3-0985), again with the same sales-pitch title, as one of twenty "stereo spectaculars." Ormandy recorded the work earlier on the Columbia label (on MS-6624 and MS-7437), but it doesn't have the same sonic punch.

Similarly brilliant allocation pertains to Bernstein's reading; the Philadelphians, however, are heard as having produced a slightly more rounded tone. Actually, almost a dead heat for these entries. (The Columbia firm offers Bernstein's depiction in a different program on MS-7165 and in a three-record compilation on D3S-785.)

A different kind of brilliance is found in Ansermet's performance—within the music rather than on top of it—and it is extremely positive. It is very lyrical yet contains all the needed vitality. The rhythmic snap is jabbed, rather than punched, and this tactic is an exciting procedure for this orchestral tale of an apprentice's mischief.

Brass Ensemble

Fanfare to precede *La Péri* (1912)

☐ L'Orchestre de la Suisse Romande / Ansermet (conductor) / London STS-15022

This has no thematic connection whatsoever with *La Péri* (discussed under *Ballet*). Calling for four horns, three trumpets, three trombones, and tuba, it is quite often played as a pithy prelude by itself. Little known is the reason for Dukas composing the Fanfare. Since *La Péri* began with extremely low dynamic levels, and ballet audiences were not often known to be quiet, the objective for the brass preliminary was to silence chattering audiences so that the atmospheric opening of the ballet could register effectively.

Instrumental

Piano

La Plainte, au loin, du faune . . . (1920)

☐ Pleshakov (piano) / Orion 7266

A poetically delicate, fugitively phrased lament conceived as a memorial piece for Debussy. Pulverized wisps of turns from Debussy's *L'Après-midi d'un faune* float in Dukas's expressive impression.

This is another plus for the world of recorded music, since the concert world doesn't seem to know of this piece's existence. It is played with total musical understanding. But the very opposite pertains to Orion's hiding Dukas's miniature gem by failing to list it anywhere on the jacket of the disc.

Sonata in E flat minor (1901)

☐ Pleshakov (piano) / Orion 6906

Franckian syntax is the chief resource in Dukas's large-scale work (its four movements weigh in at forty and one-half minutes, though Martin Cooper in his study of French music claims the work covers one hour). The dramatic conception, however, goes beyond chromatic meandering and has Beethovenesque decisiveness, especially the third (Scherzo) movement. A structural weakness develops in the last movement, because the theme is not strongly profiled and the development thereby is of weak communication.

The writing for the piano is full, intense in detail, and demands highly honed technique and meticulous musicianship. Vladimir Pleshakov meets every challenge head on and his rendition deserves the highest praise.

Variations, interlude et finale sur un thème de Rameau (1903)

☐ Johannesen (piano) / Candide 31059

Dukas chose to retain the basic mood of the Rameau minuet theme in the eleven variants rather than introduce a creative spree exploiting technical know-how. Plenty of virtuosity for the pianist (including some cogent contrapuntalism), but all of aural interest.

Johannesen provides a well-knit presentation of the score, more so than Pleshakov's on the Orion label. The sound is also far better in the Candide release.

La Péri: poème dansé (1912)   *Ballet*

☐ L'Orchestre de la Suisse Romande / Ansermet (conductor) / London STS-15022

Ansermet plays this chromatically punched score (a blend of ballet and tone poem) with intensity. Others opt for more atmospheric conditions, but the harmonic shifts begin to pall if inner motility is not maintained.

London properly prefaces *La Péri* with the Fanfare that Dukas composed as a special strategy (see under *Brass Ensemble*). Yet, there is no separation band. That's poor strategy. If a listener is in the mood to hear the ballet score and *only* the ballet score, he may be jolted out of it by placing the needle in the grooves of the Fanfare.

John Duke   (1899-)

I Carry Your Heart   *Vocal*
In Just Spring

Voice with Accompaniment

☐ Hanks (tenor); Friedberg-Erickson (piano) / Duke University Press DWR-7306 (monaural)

E. E. Cummings's texts set in the first case with lyrical let-go and in the other with *scherz* stipulation. The latter has a neat "bring-down-the-house" ending; it's exceedingly short and it fits.

Loveliest of Trees

☐ Hanks (tenor); Friedberg (piano) / Duke University Press DWRM-7501 (monaural)

Totally extrovert expression. One of the best of this composer's songs and Hanks knows how to deliver it.

Luke Havergal
Miniver Cheevy

☐ Gramm (baritone); Hassard (piano) / New World Records NW-243

Personality studies in song. *Havergal* mourns for words from his deceased beloved; *Cheevy* is an ambivalent chap. The ingrained humor of the latter song leads Duke to utilize some Mickey-Mouse tactics. For a text of this type it is stylistically on target.

Gramm does marvelously with both songs, especially *Miniver Cheevy*. Keep your ears open for the textless coda!

The Mountains are Dancing

☐ Hanks (tenor); Friedberg-Erickson (piano) / Duke University Press DWR–7306 (monaural)

The title is informative: Duke's song is one of gaiety. The title is the composer's; the text is by E. E. Cummings, and his title is *when faces called flowers*. Either way, a very effective song.

Richard Cory

☐ Gramm (baritone); Hassard (piano) / New World Records NW–243

Like *Luke Havergal* and *Miniver Cheevy* (see above), a character study. The conclusion offers a surprising twist. Duke is a top expert in conveying this type of musical short story; the large number of performances of his songs (stylistically middle-of-the-road-toward-the-right) certify the statement.

There Will Be Stars White in the Moon
Viennese Waltz Yellow Hair

☐ Hanks (tenor); Friedberg (piano) / Duke University Press DWRM–7501 (monaural)

The metrical plan in the Viennese Waltz is as expected, but the writing is not mundane. Neither is it in any of the other songs; the simply conceived piano part reflects a chamber-music quality in *White in the Moon*, and a polyphonic framework of contrastive elements imparts drama to *Yellow Hair*.

Certified performances in all respects.

Vernon Duke. *See Vladimir Dukelsky.*

Vladimir Dukelsky *(1903-1969)*

Solo Instrument and Orchestra

Oboe

Variations on an Old Russian Chant for Oboe and Strings (1955)

☐ Roth Chamber Players / Gassman (oboe) / Roth (conductor) / Contemporary 7024

(Vladimir Dukelsky used the pen name Vernon Duke for a good part of his life, but only for his popular-music compositions. From 1955 on, there was no further use of the name Vladimir Dukelsky, regardless of the type of composition.)

The Variations on an Old Russian Chant are non-adhesive permutations of the eighteenth-century chant that Dukelsky uses for his thematic resource. All six variants are free, specified by moods. Thus: scherzo-type in the second variation, mysterious in the next one, *alla burlesca* in the fourth, a waltz in the fifth variation.

Instrumental

Piano

Parisian Suite (1955)
Souvenir de Venise (Piano Sonata No. 2) (1950)

☐ Ryshna (piano) / Contemporary 8007

The "Parisian" cycle consists of ten pieces, all engagingly titled. Some embrace the descriptions very closely; others, less closely. So Dukelsky's music ambulates in A.M. tempo in *A Morning Stroll,* pedals quite vigorously in *A Spinster on a Bicycle,* includes some pianistic barks in *My Grocer's Dog,* and waltzes along in the *Sunday Outing.* All these and the others are aurally diverting and all are performed with impressive pianism.

Souvenir de Venise was written for the harpsichordist Fernando Valenti, who quickly decided never to play it. His loss. The work is just as effective on the piano, consisting of baroque-like sections surrounding a Scarlattiesque, chatty Toccata.

Surrealist Suite (1939)

Three Caprices for Piano (1944)

☐ Vernon Duke (piano) / Contemporary 7024

In the Caprices Dukelsky first outlines a mood of decisiveness, then continues with a nocturnal reference, and concludes with a waltz movement.

Intriguing titles such as *Cherrystones in Love, The Frolicking Sardines,* and *Rhumba Danced by a Wilting Telephone* are in the nine-part suite. As a musical spoof of the modern school of painting, Dukelsky applies a light but guileful hand. Examples: *The Exploding Giraffe* has a distended range, *The Headless Glamour Woman* has both feet on the ground in a spastically arranged tango, and the *Parade of Paranoiacs* is a rag using ragtime.

Etude for Violin and Bassoon (1931)

☐ Baker (violin); Christlieb (bassoon) / Contemporary 8007

The genre of Dukelsky's short work is the rhapsody. The violin introduces matters alone; the bassoon enters with accompaniment; a fugato follows, from which the main ingredients are taken for what then occurs. Chromaticism does not interfere with harmonic clarity.

An oddball combination that does please the ear. The playing is on the ball.

Chamber Music

Sonata in D for Violin and Piano (1949)

☐ Baker (violin); Vernon Duke (piano) / Contemporary 8007

Conservative romanticism; meaning, always tonally lucid and containing some rhapsodically expressive moods. A clean and direct performance.

String Quartet in C (1956)

☐ Roth Quartet / Contemporary 7024

Fluid tonalities, lyrical constancy, and black and white moods define Dukelsky's quartet as both neoclassic and leaning on the neoromantic fence. An engaging individual quality results.

The Roth foursome underwent a considerable number of changes over the years. When this work was recorded in 1959 the personnel consisted of Feri Roth and Thomas Marrocco, violins; Laurent Halleux, viola; and Cesare Pascarella, cello.

John Dunstable (ca. 1385-1453)

Choral

Chorus and Instrumental Ensemble

Alma Redemptoris Mater

☐ Purcell Consort of Voices and Elizabethan Consort of Viols / Davis (organ) / Burgess (conductor) / Argo ZRG-681

Sacred music in which neither scholasticism nor grey-bearded sobriety enters.

Ave Maris Stella

☐ Purcell Consort of Voices and Elizabethan Consort of Viols / Burgess (conductor) / Argo ZRG-681

Beautiful simplicity flows through every part of this piece. It is cleanly sung with a moderate dynamic appropriateness that matches the purity of the conception.

O Rosa Bella

☐ Purcell Consort of Voices and Elizabethan Consort of Viols / Brenner and Goodwin (sackbuts) / Burgess (conductor) / Argo ZRG-681

O Rosa Bella is one of the three exceptions in Dunstable's compositions that are not in the category of Latin church music. The piece is a pseudo-ballata dealing with rejected love.

Sancta Maria Succurre Miseris

☐ Member of Purcell Consort of Voices and Elizabethan Consort of Viols / Burgess (conductor) / Argo ZRG-681

An antiphon from a Magnificat, beautifully engraved by Dunstable and beautifully sung by an uncredited female vocalist.

Veni Sancte Spiritus, Veni Creator Spiritus

☐ Purcell Consort of Voices and Elizabethan Consort of Viols / Davis (organ); Thomas (shawm) / Burgess (conductor) / Argo ZRG-681

Gothic-like splendor is to be heard in this polytextual motet, one of the largest of Dunstable's works. The performance has the velvety smooth texture that does full justice to sacred polyphonic music. Dynamic levels are thereby given no false ramifications.

Jean-Louis Duport (1749-1819)

Chamber Music

Sonata in G minor for Cello and Harp

☐ Klaus Storck (cello); Helga Storck (harp) / Telefunken 641020

Just as the name Kreutzer means (or represents) more to violinists than others, ditto for Duport in respect to cellists. Both men produced etudes that are still required material for mastery for those who want to make the grade or even go on to vaunted virtuosity.

Duport's piece is run-of-the-mill and yet has sufficient interest, mainly through its combination of instruments. Of course, no special use of the harp is made—too early for that. Performance is good.

Marcel Dupré   *(1886-1971)*

Carillon, **Op. 27, No. 4**

☐ Noehren (organ) / Delos 24201

More carillon pieces (the Dupré example is from his Seven Pieces) are found in organ literature than in any other medium. Understandable, considering the opportunities the organ makes available to a single player. Dupré's massive mix of simulated bells and strong-willed material cutting across the sounds and mingling with them shows his faultless ear for organ composition. It is a big piece and played in a big manner by Noehren on the organ of the historic First Presbyterian Church, Trenton, New Jersey. Built in 1974, it is a grandiose instrument and proven so by the dazzling sounds Robert Noehren has produced on this recording.

Cortège et litanie, **Op. 19, No. 2**
Evocation, **Op. 37**

☐ Cochereau (organ) / Delos FY–020/021

The composition began as one of Dupré's free improvisations (his amazing ability to improvise formed a part of his more than two thousand public performances). It then took shape as a ballet suite for eleven instruments; after that, it was incorporated into Four Pieces for Piano. After transcription for organ solo, still another setting was made for organ and orchestra.

Two themes are basic to the work, the second one strengthened by its ostinato persistence. The performance on the *grand-orgue* of Notre-Dame de Paris is magnificent and contains striking imagery on the part of Pierre Cochereau. It is more heated than Noehren's version on Delos 24201.

The *Evocation* is in three large movements, of symphonic length (almost twenty-five minutes). Its shifts between nobility and drama are solidly realized, with the latter of exhilarating thunderous sound. Mundane organ comforts are not to be expected in the music of Marcel Dupré.

Fileuse, **Op. 21, No. 2**
In Dulci Jubilo

☐ Noehren (organ) / Delos 24201

"Spinner" is from Dupré's *Suite bretonne,* a picturesque repetitive use of figuration in perpetual-motion style. *In Dulci Jubilo* is one of a set of Seventy-Nine Chorales, Op. 28.

No disturbing registrations punctuate the musical plots, and Robert Noehren evokes the backgrounds in effective fashion.

Symphonie-Passion, **Op. 23**
Trois Préludes et fugues, **Op. 7**
Variations sur un Noël, **Op. 20**

☐ Cochereau (organ) / Delos FY–020/021

These three differing conceptions can be offered as a rebuttal to Saint-Saëns's negative remark that the organ (and thereby its music) "furnishes a harmonious noise rather than precise music." The Preludes and Fugues (in B major, F minor, and G minor, though Delos's bold listing on the back cover of the album incorrectly lists all as being in a major tonality) are, in each case, testimony to rich polyphonic development as well as colorful chromatic harmonies. The contrasts between the three in the set are marked.

The Variations (based on a Dorian tune) cover twelve sections ending with a Fugato and a Presto of toccata type. The Opus 23 is based on Gregorian chants. Its religious ceremony is sumptuous and details a beautiful form of organ worship in its four movements: *The World in Expectation of the Saviour, Nativity, Crucifixion,* and *Resurrection.*

Vivid registration follows suit, especially for the last work mentioned. Full-scale organ virtuosity and mastery are displayed. The five-manual Notre-Dame organ is, of course, no friend of a small room in recorded reproduction, so the disc has the proper effect only when played in a large room. Otherwise, leave the power on high and retreat to a different room. Cutting down the volume negates the wonderment of the sound of these pieces.

Another recording of the Preludes and Fugues is available on Delos 24201. That performance by Noehren is fine. So is Biggs's version (on Columbia MS–6307) of the Variations, though the contrasts are not as vivid as in Cochereau's edition. This work is also in a Vox Box (SVBX–5315) played by Franz Lehrndorfer. In order he ranks number three on the list. Incidentally, Biggs's performance is much, much faster—two and one-half minutes faster—than Cochereau's, and close to three minutes faster in the case of Lehrndorfer's rendition.

Marie-Auguste Durand *(1830-1909)*

Instrumental

Piano

Valse **in E flat major, Op. 83**

☐ Bauer (piano) / Klavier 121

Durand's most popular piece. Bauer beautifully demonstrates all its elements: whirling that reminds a listener of Chopin's Minute Waltz, Viennese lilt, and sections that would apply to silent-movie "hurry" situations.

Francesco Durante *(1684-1755)*

Instrumental

Harpsichord

Sonata in G minor for Harpsichord

☐ Sgrizzi (harpsichord) / Nonesuch 73008

One of a half-dozen *Sonate per cembalo divisi in studii e divertimenti.* Accordingly, a *Studio* in duple pulse contrasted to a *Divertimento* in triple meter. Sgrizzi plays with a light, pointed manner and thereby neatly frames the musical ideas.

Maurice Duruflé *(1902-   )*

Instrumental

Organ

Prélude et fugue sur le nom d'Alain, **Op. 7**

☐ Cleobury (organ) / Argo ZRG–787

Musical quotation (from Alain's *Litanies*) and simulated notation (to equate the spelling of Alain's name) are utilized in Duruflé's Prelude and Fugue. The act of homage produces music of delicate harmonic coloring, somewhat related to Ravel and Fauré.

Isoir (on Vox SVBX–5315, issued in a collection, and on Turnabout TV–S–34319, released on a single disc) plays this work. (In the latter recording it is one of eight pieces by seven composers. Unfortunately, Turnabout has listed all the composers represented, except for Duruflé, on the front of the album cover. Proper information is on the reverse side, and there is correct labeling.) However, Isoir's dark registration, especially in the Prelude, does not provide the stimulus exhibited by Cleobury. The latter allows all the material to unfold with the proper textural weights.

Quatre Motets

☐ Choir of St. John's College, Cambridge / Guest (conductor) / Argo ZRG–662

Plainsong themes for this delicately framed but richly colored set of four motets. Magical singing that brings out all the subtle strands in the contents.

Requiem, Op. 9

☐ Choir of St. John's College, Cambridge / Keyte (baritone); King (treble); Cleobury (organ) / Guest (conductor) / Argo ZRG–787

This sensitively dark, Gregorian-injected work spins its spell by persuasive understatement. There are some bursts in terms of dynamic decibels, but it is the exact reverse that furnishes the dramatic commentary. The inspirational and ancestral clue is found in Fauré's Requiem, but Duruflé's is more tragic.

This edition is a special view of the work with boy trebles instead of female sopranos; the ache of its measures is thereby intensified. Although given in the organ reduction of the score one does not especially miss the orchestral support. However, there is that version in the Musical Heritage Society's catalogue (Number 1509), conducted by the composer, for those who are interested. It has not been heard by this writer.

Jan Ladislaus Dussek (1760-1812)

Concerto in B flat major for Piano and Orchestra

☐ Berlin Symphony Orchestra / Kyriakou (piano) / Bünte (conductor) / Turnabout 34362

This three-movement work by Dussek (or Dusík, as Turnabout has it; Dušek and Duschek are other spellings) is one of the twelve piano concertos he wrote. It prefigures romantic style. (The picturesque titles attached to much of Dussek's music provide another sign of such romantic view, emphasized by the fact that no programmaticism is involved.)

Nothing arbitrary here in this presentation. There is a confirmed fidelity to style in the playing.

Concerto in B flat major for Two Pianos and Orchestra

☐ Orchestra of the Vienna Volksoper / Toni and Rosi Grünschlag (pianos) / Angerer (conductor) / Turnabout 34204

A precision of classical fluency with good *brioso* in the first and last movements. The soloists play with clean articulation, defined rhythm, and care of dynamic levels. Nothing more can be asked. The orchestra is especially alive and interested and warms the music's spirit thereby.

Instrumental	**Sonata**
Harp	**In B flat major, Op. 2, No. 1** / **In B flat major, Op. 34, No. 2** / **In C minor, Op. 2, No. 3** / **In E flat major, Op. 34, No. 1** / (*The Lass of Richmond Hill*) **in F major** / **In G major, Op. 2, No. 2**

☐ McDonald (harp) / Orion 7153

No complexities; the range and scope have traditional identification. The melodic ideas are simple and polite, the forms cover strict patterns. But, pleasurable music.

So, it seems a shame that complications surround the recording of these sonatas. First, *Schwann* lists six sonatas and another set of non-existent six sonatinas, using the latter heading incorrectly for this Orion group. For the former set, *Schwann* indicates "number one" as the only one recorded (on Nonesuch 71098). However, it is not number one, but the third of the set of six McDonald performs (Op. 2, No. 3).

Second, Orion gives the tonality for the Op. 2, No. 3 piece as C major—it is actually C minor. Though Nonesuch gives the proper key identification, it bypasses the opus and number. As far as the duplicate performance of the Op. 2, No. 3 sonata is concerned, Jamet's (on Nonesuch) is exceedingly dull compared to McDonald's.

Further, for some reason, Orion has reversed the chronology, placing the later works on side one. These are listed with their separate movements, whereas the earlier sonatas on side two (Op. 2, Nos. 1, 2, and 3) are minus movement identification.

Fortunately, such sloppiness does not pertain to Susan McDonald's playing. It is fluent, nicely contrasted dynamically, and exceedingly well recorded.

Harpsichord	***Within a Mile of Edinburgh***

☐ Kipnis (harpsichord) / Angel S–3816

Variations on a ballad tune performed beautifully and most resonantly by this superb artist.

Piano	***La Consolation***

☐ Pleshakov (piano) / Orion 75178

A respectful consideration of salon music, distinguished by sections that strive for larger, more important quarters. Pleshakov plays it as it exists, not overemphasizing either quality. It's relaxed but it does fit.

Sonata (*Le Retour à Paris*) in A flat major, Op. 70

☐ Pleshakov (piano) / Orion 7296

The subtitle, which is just a fancy handle, clues in the romantic congeniality of this four-movement work. No academic verbiage lessens Dussek's contribution, played with a unified and consistent style by this fine pianist.

Sonata in B flat major, Op. 35, No. 1

☐ Marvin (piano) / Genesis 1068

The greatest emphasis in Dussek's early-period composition is on its vertical dimensions; the material is developed with skill and if not inspiring, it is, at the very least, interesting.

Frederick Marvin's fine musicianship and his belief in the music's values are most apparent.

Sonata in C minor, Op. 35, No. 3

☐ Marvin (piano) / Genesis 1069

The C minor opus represents Dussek's twenty-first of approximately forty piano sonatas and is one of the very best of that output. One critic indicates that it might have been the model for Beethoven's *Pathétique*. It certainly has excellent structural stability and incisive solidity. If it is less impressive than the Beethoven it still remains impressive. Marvin's performance is certainly a distinguished contribution. It convinces.

Sonata (*The Farewell*) in E flat major, Op. 44

☐ Pleshakov (piano) / Orion 7296

Dussek's Opus 44 is dedicated to Clementi, with whom he has been compared, but there is no doubt that the former is more skillful and has greater profile. Nothing sad about Dussek's *Farewell* which runs rather cheerfully through its four movements, including the *Molto adagio e sostenuto* section, though there, tempi dictates a quieter description. The force of contrary motion is fundamental to the finale.

What is admirable about Pleshakov's playing is its attention to structural definition, aided considerably by clear articulation and pedalling of the passagework within the sonata.

Sonata (*L'Invocation*) in F minor, Op. 77

☐ Firkusny (piano) / Candide 31086

In practically every instance Dussek's titles are really forms of creative salesmanship, but in this case there is a dramatic stir and line within the four movements, in addition to the directing minor-key tonality. A further situation is the reflection of Schumann and Brahms within the music.

This sonata is stunningly defined by Firkusny simply by avoiding overt pianism. Interpretative oversubscription would mar Dussek's fine music, which is played with fitting open-heartedness, marked by artistic phrasing and beautiful tone.

Sonata (*Elégie harmonique sur la mort du Prince Louis Ferdinand de Prusse*) in F sharp minor, Op. 61

☐ Marvin (piano) / Genesis 1069

Almost full-scale romanticism is displayed, containing some Lisztian luster and syncopative drive. Marvin presents a fine performance as part of his recorded series of the Dussek piano sonatas (*see above*).

Sonatina, Op. 20, No. 1

☐ Entremont (piano) / Columbia MG–33202

Conventional form: an Allegro and a Rondo. Entremont imbues the music with a delicate charm that enhances the simplistic data.

Trio in F major for Flute, Cello, and Piano, Op. 65

☐ Pittsburgh Musica Viva Trio / Turnabout 34329

Chamber Music

Certainly one of Dussek's best chamber pieces (here Turnabout uses the accentless ''Dusik'' spelling; elsewhere it adds the accent). The piano is given a bit more attention than is appropriate for the true balance of chamber music, but the formal shape and the material within it are meaningful.

The recording balance also favors the piano—the cello is fairly well suppressed in many instances. (An error in the otherwise good liner notes gives the tonality as F minor.)

Henri Dutilleux   *(1916-   )*

Orchestra

Métaboles

☐ French National Radio Orchestra (O.R.T.F.) / Munch (conductor) / Musical Heritage Society MHS–981

Musical metabolism (the rhetoric via large orchestra) in five connected essays. The processes and substances are assimilated and incorporated, and their changes are, of course, equivalent to continual variation. In turn, the subjects are incantational (motivally engendered), linear (strings only), obsessional (passacaglia), torpid (developed from a single chord), and flamboyant (scherzo outlook). The orchestration is vivid, the style freely dissonant.

Munch's projection of the score is brilliant and shows a distinguished manner of clarifying Dutilleux's complexities. Magnificent sound.

Symphony No. 2, *Le Double*

☐ Lamoureux Orchestra / Munch (conductor) / Musical Heritage Society MHS–3022

Rousselian doctrines pushed to the extreme and introspectively conditioned. *Le Double* means an orchestra of two groups, one of twelve players (soloists, yet mainly functioning as a group), the other consisting of the full orchestra. Collective independence rules as well as partnership and superimposition of the small on the large. This, of course, expands neoclassicism into polytonal territories. But, never any Ivesian onslaught of the combine; Dutilleux maintains a positive significance (the meaning is always clear) to his stereophonic structure. Three movements: the usual (read: classical again) fast-slow-fast situation.

Munch gave the world premiere of the symphony (Boston, December 11, 1959). He then performed it in New York, Washington, and throughout Europe. Repetition of a composition does not prove mastery, of course. Nevertheless, it is difficult to imagine a more masterly performance than the one heard here.

**Solo
Instrument
and
Orchestra**

Cello

Concerto (*Tout un Monde lointain*) for Cello and Orchestra (1970)

☐ Orchestre de Paris / Rostropovich (cello) / Baudo (conductor) / Angel S–37146

Inspired by Baudelaire (hence the subtitle "An Entire Distant World"). Structured by fragmented material which is then developed into totalities. This process typifies variational system in reverse but is just as formationally clear. The contents of these transformational accommodations utilize a crackling contemporary language as the stimulant for a colorful solo-orchestra essay.

Rostropovich tosses off the difficulties with dazzlingly clear sonorities and with an athleticism that is truly ear-opening. You've got to present the laurel wreath to this great cellist. Unlike every other big-time soloist he has maintained a full-hearted and unstinting interest in new music for his instrument (if not for his conducting, though that may be because he's too new to the podium game). Compare his record with the sporadic attention to contemporary music of others. Statistic the Dutilleux work, which he commissioned, was the fifty-second world premiere he has presented. Bravo!

(Of interest is the fact that due to this outstanding recording Dutilleux was the recipient of the 1976 Koussevitzky Award.)

Sonata (1948)

☐ Siegel (piano) / Orion 7299

Instrumental

Piano

Dutilleux's composition is a pagination of select and solid designs and nicely filamented textures. The last is especially cogent in the *Lied* (movement 2). A strong opening movement (containing a lyrical section that has a blues-like content) is matched by an even stronger variational finale. Quite often sets of variations achieve technical distinction, but lack integration. Many the variational-filled barrel that nonetheless gives off an empty sound. Dutilleux's *Choral et variations* is proof of structural cause with perfect effect. In this instance, the permutations become a single, thoroughly composed piece of music, not simply technical elaborations. Dutilleux's achievement is not too common.

Siegel's choice of this work is to be commended. His brilliant performance is recommended.

Sonatine for Flute and Piano (1943)

☐ Anne Diener Giles (flute); Allen Giles (piano) / Crystal S-312

Chamber Music

A sunny melodic brilliance is portrayed in Dutilleux's work. The transparency of this *Sonatine* is full indication of the high level lighthearted music can attain. Two cadenzas are included for formal enumerative distinction: one leads to the slow section, the other precedes the coda of the final section.

The Giles' conception is fine, presenting a rendition of agreeable and nicely filamented textures.

Le Loup (1953)

☐ Orchestre de la Société des Concerts du Conservatoire / Prêtre (conductor) / Angel S-35932

Ballet

Carnality of a different kind characterizes this ballet fantasy. A young bride is abducted by a wolf. She eventually succumbs willingly to him. They are pursued by the townspeople only to die in their final love embrace. Dutilleux's powerful score, particularly the final sections—Dance of Love and Dance of Death—a heavily colored. It is far removed from prissy romantic style or neutral neoclassic manners in its Rousselian rhythmic thrust.

The seven sections are handled with verve by Prêtre. Special credit belongs to the percussion.

Antonin Dvořák (1841-1904)

Carnival Overture, Op. 92

☐ London Symphony Orchestra / Kertész (conductor) / London 6574

Orchestra

The choicest reward is found in this conception. No one has produced the linear equality and yet maintained the required transparency as well as István Kertész. The pastoral gorgeousness of the section that features the English horn and solo violin is poetry at its most telling sensitivity. Throughout, the rhythms and sounds, the stresses and phrasings are golden-toned.

In this package Dvořák's Opus 92 is companioned with two other overtures and the *Scherzo capriccioso.* On London 6495, it is coupled with Dvořák's Symphony No. 6.

Czech Suite, Op. 39

☐ English Chamber Orchestra / Mackerras (conductor) / Philips 6500203

An absolutely perfect performance in terms of proper tempo, style, balance of colors, and especially the knowledge of where agogic and accent are to be placed.

Why this work, which is Dvořák speaking his pure native tongue, remains off programs is an enigma. The Suite in D (its other title) is delicious music from its beginning (*Preludium: Pastorale*) on to the Polka and the savory (and heartwarming as well) *Sousedská: Minuetto,* and its completion by the Romance and Finale: *Furiant.* A magnificent release.

The Golden Spinning Wheel, Op. 109

☐ London Symphony Orchestra / Kertész (conductor) / London 6721

Another of the morbid "Fancy Dan" tales Dvořák spun with winds, brass, percussion, and strings. This one has the gal killed and mutilated by her stepmother. Fully expressed in the tale's program and musically fully expressed in Kertész's direction.

Husitská Overture, Op. 67

☐ London Symphony Orchestra / Rowicki (conductor) / Philips 6500286

This "dramatic" overture, as Dvořák termed it, includes a pair of traditional Hussite battle hymns and part of a medieval chant. The "Hussite" opus has dynamic propulsion and it is fully furnished in the sharply indicated recording. Kertész has also recorded it with the L.S.O. (on London 6525 and also issued on London 6746) but while his portrayal is as fluid, it is not as animated.

In Nature's Realm, Overture, Op. 91

☐ London Symphony Orchestra / Kertész (conductor) / London 6526

Dvořák indicated three choices on his sketches for the title of this composition: *Ouverta Lyrica, In Nature's Realm,* and *A Summer Night.* Certainly, while the first of these matches the contents, there is more activity in the music than one thinks of in relationship to nocturnal hours. (*Schwann*'s listing of *Amid Nature* fits well and comes closest to the title on the original Simrock published score: *V přírodě.*) In any case, the recorded account is warm and poetic.

(The above London issue is the filler for the major work on the disc, Dvořák's fourth symphony. On London 6574, Opus 91 is found with two other Dvořák overtures and his *Scherzo capriccioso.*)

Legends
Series I, Op. 59 / Series II, Op. 59

☐ London Philharmonic Orchestra / Leppard (conductor) / Philips 6500188

The recording is split exactly, with the five numbers of each group covering one side of the disc. Originally, when Simrock published the *Legenden* in their orchestral dress (the first version was for piano duet; see under *Instrumental: piano, four hands*), it divided what is really a single created work into two: *Erste Sammlung* ("First Series") and *Zweite Sammlung* ("Second Series"). This commercial procedure, which was intended to obtain wider sales and performance and thus almost double income, gave tacit approval to the notion that each set could stand by itself.

Fortunately, all ten pieces are recorded in a substantially acceptable presentation. They are in tripartite or rondo form, and the orchestration adheres to the directed boundaries. Basically, the pieces are scored for double woodwinds, two or four horns, and strings. A bit of timpani and some triangle color is used; two trumpets appear in the fourth piece; a harp is used in Nos. 5 and 6.

Othello Overture, Op. 93

☐ London Symphony Orchestra / Rowicki (conductor) / Philips 6500124

There can be viable arguments offered as to the calculations in Dvořák's overture being far from inspired though none about his orchestrational workmanship. However, no one would want to argue against what Rowicki provides in his recording detail. The music is always stimulatingly colored with a special deep hue by the woodwinds' playing and is given a sure sense of pace. The full-scale send-off scores further points for Rowicki's edition.

Overture, *My Home*, Op. 62

☐ London Symphony Orchestra / Rowicki (conductor) / Philips 6500287

Nationalistically injected by the use of a pair of folk tunes and combined with Dvořák's individual native musical accent, *Domov Můj* (most often identified in German as *Mein Heim*) demonstrates full-blooded Czech identity. Rowicki's playing is fully committed to displaying this factor and the music is heard with spontaneity. It is also heard with pertinently coiled precision—marvelous, indeed.

Scherzo capriccioso, Op. 66

☐ London Symphony Orchestra / Kertész (conductor) / London 6538

This is a capital *Capriccioso*. Any way one looks at Dvořák's piece it's a grand Slavonic dance, and that feeling permeates Kertész's viewpoint. This is a beautifully tonally-grained recording.

London's release is coupled with Dvořák's Symphony No. 8 (new numbering). In another packaging (London 6574) the *Scherzo capriccioso* is included with three Dvořák overtures.

Serenade in D minor for Winds, Cello, and Bass, Op. 44

☐ London Symphony Orchestra / Kertész (conductor) / London 6594

Kertész represents perfection with his handling of this music of amiability and optimism. Tempi are relaxed and phrasings are polished. The tone of the winds (two oboes, two clarinets, two bassoons, contra bassoon, and three horns) is fully ingratiating. This is the only recording listed at this date. No other is needed.

Slavonic Dances (Series I), Op. 46

No. 1 (*Furiant*) in C major / No. 2 (*Dumka*) in E minor / No. 3 (*Polka*) in A flat major / No. 4 (*Sousedská*) in F major / No. 5 (*Skočná*) in A major / No. 6 (*Sousedská*) in D major / No. 7 (*Skočná*) in C minor / No. 8 (*Furiant*) in G minor

☐ Bamberg Symphony / Dorati (conductor) / Turnabout 34582

Toward Dvořák's total work (the sequel, Series II, Op. 72, is discussed below) the recorded catalogue is filled with good intentions. However, there are many decisions to make before considering any of the performers. Should the original piano duet edition (see under *Instrumental: piano, four hands*) be obtained and/or the vivid orchestral settings Dvořák produced? Shall one opt for the complete sixteen dances in one issue (as on Odyssey Y2–33524, with Szell conducting the Cleveland Orchestra) or obtain the same performer or totally different ones where the two sets have been produced separately? And finally, there are the vast numbers of recordings which include choices from the two series, from a single dance (Stokowski directing the Czech Philharmonic on London 21117), to two, four, five, six, eleven, or as many as twelve of the dances (the complete Opus 46 and four of the total in Opus 72, on Vanguard S–189, with Rossi conducting the Vienna State Opera Orchestra). Only then, when the choice of scope and packaging has been made, can the all-important matter of the performer involved be considered.

Dorati has a way with this music that never falters. (It is duplicated, more or less, here and there, in the performance he gives of the two sets on Mercury 77001.) The playing is fine, the rhythms extremely secure, and especially noteworthy are the exemplary tempi. A very idiomatic reading that deserves the highest rating.

Slavonic Dances (Series II), Op. 72

No. 1 (No. 9) (*Odzemek*) in B major / No. 2 (No. 10) (*Dumka*) in E minor / No. 3 (No. 11) (*Skočná*) in F major / No. 4 (No. 12) (*Dumka*) in D flat major / No. 5 (No. 13) (*Spacírka*) in B flat minor / No. 6 (No. 14) (*Polonaise*) in B flat major / No. 7 (No. 15) (*Srbské Kolo*) in C major / No. 8 (No. 16) (*Sousedská*) in A flat major

☐ Bamberg Symphony / Dorati (conductor) / Turnabout 34583
☐ Bavarian Radio Symphony Orchestra / Kubelik (conductor) / Deutsche Grammophon 2530593

Beautifully sculpted performances by Dorati that match those of the first set of eight dances (*see above*). Kubelik's readings are just as good, just as sensitive, just as rhythmically viable, and even, in some places, more plastic. However, Dorati's orchestra has better string players, and that gives points to his recording.

Slavonic Rhapsody, Op. 45

No. 1 in D major / No. 2 in G minor / No. 3 in A flat major

☐ Czech Philharmonic Orchestra / Neumann (conductor) / Telefunken 3635075

All the Dvořákian virtues are illuminated in these conceptions.

Suite (*American*) in A major, Op. 98b

☐ Berlin Radio Symphony Orchestra / Thomas (conductor) / Columbia M–34513

Composed in 1894 for piano (a recording is available: see under *Instrumental: piano*). The Suite was orchestrated the next year and first performed six years after Dvořák's death. Publication followed. Such are the bare facts. The music itself is middle-road

Dvořák, lacking the individual temperament found in his major works. No fault with the performance, which does its part with surety and robustness.

Symphonic Variations, Op. 78

☐ London Symphony Orchestra / Kertész (conductor) / London 6721

Kertész's empathy for and understanding of Dvořák is again shown in this beautifully conceived performance. Each of the twenty-seven variations has its color and shape and yet all are bound so that piecemeal statement is avoided; the fugal finale is beautifully proportioned.

Not to replace the above but as a duplicate, it is worth finding the deleted Philips (839706) disc, again played by the L.S.O., with Colin Davis conducting. It provides eloquent lyricism and dynamic coloration, totally proportioned with skill and apparent affection for the piece.

Symphony No. 1 (*Bells of Zlonice*) in C minor, Op. 3

☐ London Symphony Orchestra / Kertész (conductor) / London 6523

The statistics covering the first hundred years of Dvořák's initial symphony are fascinating. It was composed in 1865, lost until the score surfaced in 1923, first performed in 1936, and initially published in 1961. It then reached the recorded stage, but because of its length (and there *is* a good amount of padding) there were cuts made in the Supraphon edition, conducted by Václav Neumann.

Kertész covers the score completely. It offers the opportunity of hearing the young composer and his affinity, at that time, for some Schumann and some Wagner, and just the slightest bit (movement 3) of affinity for Dvořák. Splendidly played and minus any fussy attempt to imply what is not present.

Symphony No. 2 in B flat major, Op. 4

☐ London Symphony Orchestra / Kertész (conductor) / London 6524

Despite seriously shaped introductions to all four movements, including the Scherzo (an odd business, at that place), Dvořák's second symphony travels optimistically, with his individuality most apparent within the Scherzo.

This is another lengthy essay, but in Kertész's performance decision time does not hang heavily. In this manner also lies true conductorial scholarship.

Symphony No. 3 in E flat major, Op. 10

☐ London Symphony Orchestra / Rowicki (conductor) / Philips 6500286

The only one of Dvořák's symphonies in three movements. It has a long slow movement, but Rowicki's pacing keeps matters on the move without upsetting the mood. Dvořák's coloristic intensities are minimal, but they are deftly commanded. In the competitive edition (same orchestra, Kertész directing, on London 6525) the patterns unfold, but no special conductorial investments are made to highlight the communication.

Symphony No. 4 in D minor, Op. 13

☐ London Symphony Orchestra / Rowicki (conductor) / Philips 6500124

A fine Scherzo invested by Witold Rowicki with a proper amount of *feroce* quality. Of course he can't do anything about removing the extremely strong Wagnerian resemblance (the Pilgrims' music in *Tannhäuser*) in the Andante movement.

Rowicki controls the symphony expertly. Where there is vigor required, it is refined; where there are static sequences, he doesn't drag; and all the curved melodies are brightly alive. Let's face it—the Opus 13 is not one of Dvořák's major compositions, but in this reading the auditor gets the most creative presence that is possible.

Symphony No. 5 in F major, Op. 76

☐ London Symphony Orchestra / Kertész (conductor) / London 6511

Dvořák's Opus 76 (originally Opus 24) has not had much concert association. It remains to be rediscovered, and hopefully conductors will soon recognize the worth of the work. It offers, in its Bohemian Wagnerisms, a splendid slow movement and a typical masterly Dvořákian scherzo. The panoramic array in the finale is perhaps overdone, but that shouldn't negate attention to a generally fine work.

Kertész's consideration of the Symphony is splendid in all respects. His performance has clarification of detail and outline and an eloquent sense of the music's narrative.

Symphony No. 6 (old No. 1) in D major, Op. 60

☐ London Symphony Orchestra / Kertész (conductor) / London 6495
☐ Berlin Philharmonic Orchestra / Kubelik (conductor) / Deutsche Grammophon 2530425

Both orchestras produce glowing sounds. There is more deliberation on Kertész's part but both conductors provide the right amount of structural tension in the first movement. In the Scherzo (*Furiant*), both men go for a steady, strutting lilt and are totally successful. The geniality in this case neatly falls between softness and spinyness. Kubelik deals with subtle tempi definitions in the slow movement which are just as convincing as the more literal statement made by Kertész. The Brahmsian finale is engagingly defined in both performances.

Symphony No. 7 (old No. 2) in D minor, Op. 70

☐ London Symphony Orchestra / Rowicki (conductor) / Philips 6500287

The inner motility heard in this recording exemplifies a unique textual understanding on Rowicki's part unmatched by any other edition. Attention to this does not convey an overemphasis that interferes with a mellow sound containing succulent woodwind and golden-brown horn colorations. The commitment to a forward-moving tempo in the slow movement brings perfect results, as does the pulsed flow in the *furiant* (third) movement. With this single performance as evidence it can be said that no one has bettered Rowicki's interpretation of the Dvořák dynamic.

Symphony No. 8 (old No. 4) in G major, Op. 88

☐ London Symphony Orchestra / Kertész (conductor) / London 6358

Couldn't be better. Kertész contrasts the moods of this beautiful piece perfectly. Moreover, the structuring of the material for each part of the symphony is most impressive. Further, he knows how to handle climaxes so that the smaller ones enroute don't overshadow the final one. No blundering. The orchestral playing is superfine.

A second choice might well be Walter conducting the Columbia Symphony Orchestra on Odyssey Y–33231.

Symphony No. 9 (old No. 5) (*From the New World*) in E minor, Op. 92

☐ London Symphony Orchestra / Kertész (conductor) / London 6527
☐ Philharmonia Orchestra / Giulini (conductor) / Seraphim S–60045

Habits die hard and those of conductors are not exempt. The bad habits concerning this symphony include: (a) failing to take the important repeat of the exposition in the first movement and thereby mismeasuring its structural proportions; (b) taking the second subject of the first movement slower than the first when it is not so marked and thereby nullifying a suave motility that is important to the music's atmosphere; (c) sentimentalizing the slow movement, which is what also happens when point *b* is adopted; (d) not finding the proper *quality* for the Scherzo, which is far more important then speed; (e) inserting ritards before the principal subject of the finale, especially at the movement's beginning; and (f) being pompous about the same movement, which is a fiery affair, plus (g) permitting the brasses to blow their guts out and thereby destroy the acutely beautiful orchestrated balances of Dvořák's tutti scoring.

The performances listed have none of these bad habits and, furthermore, have many additional special good points. Kertész's is a combination of fervent lyrical outpour and a golden-brown sound, and when he wishes to drive the music, it has dynamite energy. The greatest compliment that one can pay this great conductor is that under his direction one hears the symphony as a fresh experience. This spontaneity also pertains to Giulini's edition. The phrasing under his direction is truly superb and the balances that include the usually ubiquitous brass are marvelous. Some may consider his performance just a bit restrained. That's because they've become habituated to the Stoky rock-'em and pull-it-out school. For Dvořák's "New World" that's horrible.

Notturno in B major for String Orchestra, Op. 40

String Orchestra

☐ Czech Philharmonic Orchestra / Neumann (conductor) / Nonesuch 71271

Almost Wagnerian but with the chromaticism uncreased. There is more threnodic content than there is nocturnalism and that's the way Václav Neumann portrays this moving music.

Serenade in E major, Op. 22

☐ English Chamber Orchestra / Barenboim (conductor) / Angel S–37045

A perceptive presentation to which one can add the expected finding of being technically immaculate. More to the point is the lyrically beautiful effect brought to the fourth (Larghetto) of the five movements. Barenboim shifts his interpretative temperature flawlessly, with a higher one for the more dramatic Finale, for example, than for the sad-like quality of the *Tempo di valse*. All this, however, without nullifying Dvořákian style.

Concerto in B minor for Cello and Orchestra, Op. 104

Solo Instrument and Orchestra

Cello

☐ Royal Philharmonic Orchestra / Rostropovich (cello) / Boult (conductor) / Seraphim S–60136

The problems of architectural detail, its elaboration, and attendant projection are always a concern for the composer of a cello concerto. The balance of a baritone-tenor string voice pitted against an orchestra needs a special décor. Dvořák's fruitful contribution is no mere solo-plus-accompaniment affair; the orchestral part is the equal of the leading string voice, and defeat is the result for the conductor who misunderstands this.

The stature of Rostropovich's artistry has never been so emphatic as in this performance. From beginning to conclusion it is a magnificent display of musicianship, tonal beauty, and string vocalism that is a refreshment from sheer virtuosic delivery. The orchestra projects a properly strong personality when it should and is a subsidiary agent in the proper places. Together Rostropovich and Boult let the music breathe in natural rhythms, permit it to have flow. The result is a captivating exemplification of great art. Played otherwise—aluminum-bright, stereo-soloistic, or overbearing—it would be false documentation.

Rondo in G minor for Cello and Orchestra, Op. 94

Silent Woods, for Cello and Orchestra, Op. 68

□ St. Louis Symphony Orchestra / Nelsova (cello) / Susskind (conductor) / Vox QSVBX-5135

Every cellist plays *the* Dvořák Concerto. None ever presents these two short pieces in concert, though du Pré has recorded (on Angel) the Opus 68, and Opus 94 is represented (on Orion) with piano reduction of the orchestral part.

The dreamy song of *Silent Woods* is sharply contrasted by the Bohemian *brio* in the Rondo. Impressively played by the soloist with superlative support from Susskind.

Piano

Concerto in G minor for Piano and Orchestra, Op. 33

□ St. Louis Symphony Orchestra / Nelsova (cello) / Susskind (conductor) / Vox QSVBX-5135

The statistics are boldly clear: Rudolf Firkusny has been the loyal standard bearer for Dvořák's piano concerto. Rare attention is given the work by other pianists because of its sense of enlarged chamber music and its lack of virtuoso display. It is their loss. To have this superb example of musical beauty and involvement is an auditor's gain.

An earlier Firkusny recording of an edited version of the score is still available on Westminster 8165. In addition to its use of this version, the Westminster disc suffers from lack of depth in the orchestral interpretation. Another edition of the score, prepared by Vilém Kurz and further revised by Firkusny, has also been recorded. Vox's release represents the initial recorded example by Firkusny of Dvořák's original conception. Thus a double value is offered in the Firkusny-Susskind recording on Vox: complete authenticity and a matchless performance.

Violin

Concerto in A minor for Violin and Orchestra, Op. 53

Romance in F minor for Violin and Orchestra, Op. 11

□ Czech Philharmonic Orchestra / Suk (violin) / Ančerl (conductor) / Vanguard SU-3

Double errors afflict this concerto, one of the finest of Dvořák's works. First, it is bypassed too often. Second, when it is played, most violinists tend to overdo its passions, pressing in and on with a Tchaikovskian scale of ponderosity which is unbecoming to the work, its style, and its meaning (Itzhak Perlman, for example, on his Angel S-37069 recording).

Whether it is sheer artistry or understanding through blood relationship (Dvořák was Josef Suk's great grandfather) that produces the outstanding conceptions heard here cannot be decided. In his performances of these two works Suk presents the ideal interpretations. His tone is gorgeous, the music comes off his bow in the concerto's slow movement with the most lucious beauty. And, when necessary, Suk can dig in, as in the finale, but when so doing the tonal quality does not diminish.

The Romance is no mere bagatelle; it lasts some twelve and a half minutes. It is a development from the slow movement of a string quartet composed in 1873. Like the slow movement of the concerto it has a haunting tenderness in its sad overtones.

Mazurek in E minor for Violin and Orchestra, Op. 49

☐ St. Louis Symphony Orchestra / Ricci (violin) / Susskind (conductor) / Vox QSVBX–5135

Some gentility but mostly double-stop fiddle excitement. Ricci presents auditory drama. As usual, perfect support from Susskind—a master at accompaniment.

Polonaise in A major, Op. Posth.

Instrumental

Cello

☐ King (cello); Leviev (piano) / Orion 7287

There are some fancy un-Polonaise turns in Dvořák's piece. When the music permits, King plays in a lush manner. (Dvořák's posthumous cello piece exists with orchestral accompaniment, made by one Anton Modr—unrecorded however.)

Humoresques, Op. 101

Piano

Mazurkas, Op. 56

☐ Firkusny (piano) / Candide 31070

Eight of the former, seven of the latter. Yes, *the* Humoresque is there; it's the seventh of the group and despite its hackneyed life it is still in good health, thanks to the clarity with which Firkusny presents it. It is this particular *unaffected* naturalness of manner that makes listening to all of these short pieces a pleasure.

Suite (*American*) in A major for Piano, Op. 98

☐ Kvapil (piano) / Genesis 1025

A minor page in Dvořák's ledger. The orchestral version was published posthumously as Opus 98b (for a discussion of that version, see under *Orchestra*).

Kvapil's performance is a natural one, containing as much color as the score contains.

Legends, for Piano Duet, Op. 59 (Nos. 1, 2, and 3)

*Piano,
Four Hands*

☐ Walter and Beatrice Klien (piano) / Turnabout 34041

Three of the ten original pieces; the orchestral setting is discussed above (see under *Orchestra*).

Except for the elision of some *ritards* and some slight tempo tampering the playing does not deny authentic fulfillment.

Slavonic Dances (Series I), Op. 46

No. 1 (*Furiant*) in C major / No. 2 (*Dumka*) in E minor / No. 3 (*Sousedská*) in D major / No. 4 (*Sousedská*) in F major / No. 5 (*Skočná*) in A major / No. 6 (*Polka*) in A flat major / No. 7 (*Skočná*) in C minor / No. 8 (*Furiant*) in G minor

Slavonic Dances (Series II), Op. 72

No. 1 (No. 9) (*Odzemek*) in B major / No. 2 (No. 10) (*Dumka*) in E minor / No. 3 (No. 11) (*Skočná*) in F major / No. 4 (No. 12) (*Dumka*) in D flat major / No. 5 (No. 13) (*Spacírka*) in B flat minor / No. 6 (No. 14) (*Polonaise*) in B flat major / No. 7 (No. 15) (*Srbské Kolo*) in C major / No. 8 (No. 16) (*Sousedská*) in A flat major

☐ Brendel and Klien (piano) / Turnabout 34060

The original settings for the more-often-heard orchestral versions (see under *Orchestra*). Indeed, so well crafted are these pieces that they display special delights not supplanted by the beautiful orchestral canvases Dvořák created. Not only the Dvořák buff will want to have both editions of the total sixteen dances.

Alfred Brendel and Walter Klien form a fine team. Their projection is sensitive and precise. Perhaps the greatest compliment that can be given them is that while listening to their playing one does not wish for the richer orchestral palette.

Comparison between this keyboard version and the orchestral one shows a slight difference in the order within Opus 46. Movements 3 and 6 in the former are respectively 6 and 3 in the latter. There are three errors in Turnabout's labeling of the dance titles for Opus 72: the second (No. 10) is not a Mazurka, but a *Dumka;* the fourth (No. 12) is also a *Dumka,* and not a *Sousedská.* A further error concerns the tonality for Number 5 (No. 13): the key is B flat minor, not D flat major.

The performances of the two sets are faster than the orchestral ones, not because of tempi motility but because some of the repeats are omitted. Finally, the very definite stereo separation makes one suspect that two pianos were used rather than a single one. No harm. Visually, there is a difference and it's always interesting to watch a piano duo adjust for *lebensraum* at the keyboard. In a recording studio two keyboards not only solve the matter of playing space and ease but give each pianist his own pedal mechanism.

Violin

Four Romantic Pieces, Op. 75

☐ Temianka (violin); Robbins (piano) / Orion 7020

Highly satisfying playing with romantic sound detail on the part of Henri Temianka, but fortunately not oversweetened.

For an obvious reason, but not an acceptable one, Temianka reverses the third and fourth movements. This is done so that the group does not conclude with the single slow movement (a Larghetto), the three others being Allegros with different modifiers: *moderato, maestoso,* and *appassionato.*

Chamber Music

Sonata for Violin and Piano, Op. 57

Sonatina for Violin and Piano, Op. 100

☐ Temianka (violin); Robbins (piano) / Orion 7020

The sonata is refined and delicate, sequential in its opening movement, with a theme that spins around a pedal point. Repetition of figures on varying tonal levels rides herd in the slow movement. A Rondo is used for the finale, likewise (the birds-of-a-feather wisdom) blocked out from neat four-measure ideas that appear repetitively. Temianka and Robbins play this companionable piece of music with full responsibility as to its style. Here, Temianka completely avoids a stylistic approach that slightly mars the other work.

The so-called *Indian Lament,* which was a favorite encore piece for Fritz Kreisler (in his edited version) is the second movement of the Sonatina. However, Dvořák neither tabbed the music as "Indian" nor "Lament," but merely indicated the formality of a tempo: *larghetto.* Orion even goes further and revamps Kreisler's title choice and terms the movement (a G minor, beautiful conception) an "Indian Canzonetta."

If one accepts the Indian idea for the second movement, the Sonatina is mostly Bohemian in its other three sections. All is stated simply, the work having been composed for two of the composer's children as a sort of celebration on reaching the century opus mark.

All the forms are presented in the most direct manner—sonata design preceding the slow movement; scherzo and Finale as the two last sections.

If you want this performance you will have to accept a few drops of schmaltz and a number of fiddle *portamenti* in either direction. No reason for these erroneous ideas of *espressivo* playing but there they are. Otherwise, there is clear and clean delivery.

Terzetto for Two Violins and Viola, Op. 74

☐ Dalley and Tree (violins); Steinhardt (viola) / RCA ARL1-0082

It is the lack of bass tone that gives Dvořák's trio its rare charm. The essential sweetness of the work, set in a miniature frame is expressed by the introductory movement, one almost in the form of sonatina contraction. This leads into the slow movement: superb, angelic-moving music, conveyed in three-part form. The Scherzo uses the plan of major-minor keys to postulate contrasts, further colored by the wheeze of *ponticello*. A set of variations in various points of departure—rhythmic, lyric, dramatic, *recitando*, plus final tutti—completes the work.

The performance is ideal, intimate, with superbly mellow reproduction that adds a special quality to the warm tone of the performers. They will be recognized as three-quarters of the Guarneri Quartet. In this case the lodge membership acts very democratically without any artistic loss whatsoever. The regular first violinist (Arnold Steinhardt) has shifted to viola; the permanent violist (Michael Tree) has moved over to second fiddle; and John Dalley, who sits in the quartet formation at the second violin desk, here takes over the first violin position. It reminds one of the old Pro Arte Quartet days, when early in its career the violinists alternated in their roles.

Trio for Piano, Violin, and Cello
In B flat major, Op. 21 / In G minor, Op. 26 / In F minor, Op. 65 / (*Dumky*) in E minor, Op. 90

☐ Beaux Arts Trio / Philips 6703015

The *Dumky* is the most famous of these trios, one of the most perfect conceptions of folk art in chamber music. The initial opus in the medium (the B flat, Opus 21) is rather academic, since Dvořák was not free with his forms as yet; the G minor (Opus 26) is hardly better; the proportions are somewhat strained. The F minor, however, indicates that at the age of forty-two, Dvořák was beginning his period of maturity—fame would soon follow. He would be invited to England and then to the United States. This trio was the new and prophetic sign: complete evidence that his technique had been sharpened to its finest point.

Richly romantic is the approach taken by the gentlemen of the Beaux Arts, rather than a restrained, subtle approach. However, generally, the playing is of rich variety and no important point is overlooked. No listener will become dissatisfied with these performances—a magnificent inheritance from Antonin Dvořák.

Trio in B flat major for Piano, Violin, and Cello, Op. 21

☐ Dumka Trio / Vox SVBX-571

A good issue. The Dumka team validates the key changes in the slow movement with fine definition. In the Scherzo they modify the pace to a *scherzando*, which is all to the good.

Trio (*Dumky*) in E minor for Piano, Violin, and Cello, Op. 90

☐ Beaux Arts Trio / Philips 802918

Available separately from the integral edition discussed *above*. The Beaux Arts portrays the shifts from the melancholic to the exuberant with finesse. Gorgeous tone from the group.

Trio in F minor for Piano, Violin, and Cello, Op. 65

☐ Yuval Trio / Deutsche Grammophon 2530371

A worthy entry, though the balance between the violin and the cello places the latter in a subsidiary role occasionally. The playing of the pianist is sensitive; ditto the violinist, though he is slightly guilty of some rough bowing in the second movement. Nonetheless, this work offers a worthwhile choice if one wishes a single example of the Dvořák piano trios, rather than the integral set performed by the Beaux Arts.

Piano Quartet

In D major, Op. 23 / In E flat major, Op. 87

☐ Beaux Arts Trio / Trampler (viola) / Philips 6500452

Warm song liquidity in the playing of the first movement of the Opus 23 is paralleled by precise distinction in the variations. In the later quartet there is a danger of swinging out of chamber-music style into the error of trying to impress by power. Dvořák does not make it easy when tutti unisons are combined with tremolo insistence until finally the quartet could become a seething miniaturistic orchestra. But, these fine musicians will not have it that way. Their playing has strength, sonority, and tonal impact but it always remains within chamber-music boundaries. Further, the tempi are beautifully registered, with a graceful air in the Scherzo and the proper percentage of *ma non troppo* in the finale.

String Quartet in A flat major, Op. 105

☐ Guarneri Quartet / RCA LSC–2887

Firm formal features in which the introduction of the work is used as the basis for the main theme of the first movement, as well as (in altered form) the opening theme of the slow movement. Despite the classical contours, the rhythmical elements are those of popular Bohemian tunes cast in the company of serious quartet formations.

A musical performance throughout, with special agogical subtleties portrayed in the Scherzo and suavity expressed in its Trio section. The rather lengthy final movement is strategically planned so that interest never lags.

String Quartet in C major, Op. 61

☐ Guarneri Quartet / RCA ARL1–0082

Here stated, in no uncertain terms, is a performing impact of dramatic flux, of wide color application from the four instruments. The Guarneri group not only plays the notes and confirms the dynamics but probes the seething expressivity within the score. Superb.

String Quartet in D minor, Op. 34

☐ Janáček Quartet / London STS–15207

Dvořák's technique in writing for the string quartet made a transversion of affinity in the four voices, and yet did not, with such conduction, create undue heaviness of structure or textural thickness. He gave the most optimistic opportunity for a quartet to sound *good* and not have to fight to clarify the voicing. There is little adjustment a quartet team has to do in order to make a Dvořák quartet "sound." And sound beautifully, therefore, the Janáček foursome do in this work. The *Alla polka* movement is a beauty; the Adagio (colored by muted timbre) is sung out with simplicity, and beauty follows. Zip in the energetic finale completes a splendid performance.

String Quartet (*American*) in F major, Op. 96

☐ Budapest String Quartet / Columbia M–32792

Still the most stunning consideration of this repertoire staple. The first movement is, for once, taken *ma non troppo*. (Compare how rushed and *troppo* the Quartetto Italiano takes this movement and makes it sweat, whereas it should only be comfortably warm.) The *Molto vivace* is pulsed and not percussed. Finally, when the Budapest spreads the pace for a second subject (in the finale, for example), it is registered significantly within the structural plan and does not tear it by metronomic exaggeration. One fault: the failure to repeat the exposition in the opening movement.

String Quartet in G major, Op. 106

☐ Prague Quartet / Deutsche Grammophon 2530480

Dvořák's treatment in the opening movement is as organic as anything found in Beethoven's late-period quartets. The details are clearly focused in the playing of the Prague team, which also fully understands Dvořák's handling of thematic elements in the slow movement, defining the textural weights and variational contrasts so that a balanced ternary-shaped structure is provided. Fine rhythmically pointed delivery is given the Scherzo.

This is certainly a better conceived and more graphic performance than the one offered by the Kohon Quartet on Vox SVBX–550.

Piano Quintet, Op. 81

☐ Guarneri Quartet / Rubinstein (piano) / RCA LSC–3252

In this quintet Dvořák uses the two forms that have become associated with him (more than with any other Czech composer). Thus: the *Dumka,* with its Jekyll-Hyde form of somber, threnodic seriousness opposed to the lightness of the dance; and the *Furiant,* a Bohemian dance, though strictly metered, which alternates within a rigidity of bar-lined notation, changing accents so that one has now triple, then duple rhythms, thereby conveying the spice of differentiation.

The playing is ideal. It has the exact inflections of the two forms mentioned, and breathes the pastoral relaxation of the opening part of the quintet with the greatest spontaneity. Immediacy and impact are the profits here. A better version cannot be obtained.

Sextet for Two Violins, Two Violas, and Two Cellos, Op. 48

☐ Members of the Vienna Octet / London STS–15242

The playing is fine throughout. It is at its very best in the two movements that most generously offer Bohemian culture—the *Dumka* (movement 2) and the *Furiant* (third movement). In the former, the definition of the elegiac rectitude of the two different moods, posited by two speed rates, is well-nigh perfect. The *Furiant* is permitted to proceed on its straight, gay-speeded, trinal-metered road. The trio section is given neat and fluid contrast. Thereby, all of the movement's strengths are maintained. Everything is in good focus in the other parts of the work.

Cantata and Oratorio

The American Flag, Op. 102

☐ Berlin Radio Symphony Orchestra, St. Hedwig's Cathedral Choir, and RIAS Chamber Chorus / Evans (tenor); McDaniel (baritone) / Thomas (conductor) / Columbia M-34513

One might call *The American Flag* an example of proxy chauvinism, but this would overlook Dvořák's well-meaning tribute to the country in which he worked for a period of time. Actually, Opus 102 was composed in 1892 before Dvořák's departure for the United States and was planned to be used in celebrating the quatercentenary of the discovery of America. The timing did not work; it was not until 1895 that the work was first heard.

The text is pompously patriotic, the music avoids the obvious for the greater part. However, there is some pictorialism to match the words, and a march sequence. In short a slab of Dvořák creative history but not sublimely important.

Michael Tilson Thomas will not agree for he has produced a work which shows his entire belief in its validity. However, the belief of the soloists in overstressing their delivery at times is not valid.

Mass in D major, Op. 86

☐ Choir of Christ Church, Oxford / Ritchie (treble); Giles (alto); Byers (tenor); Morton (bass); Cleobury (organ) / Preston (conductor) / Argo ZRG-781

Though Dvořák provided an orchestral accompaniment at the insistence of his publishers the original version was as is recorded here: four solo voices, choir, and organ. However, there is a slight change that Simon Preston makes by using boys' voices for the upper two solo parts, replacing the female soprano and contralto timbres. The decision brings a tie score. There is a loss in the body of sound, with a gain in the obtaining of sweet-flowing vocal delicacy.

Those that must have the orchestral version can find it in the foreign Supraphon catalogue. Still, the chamberized refinement of Dvořák's Mass has a finesse and a simple loveliness that fulfill the composer's original objectives far better than the fleshed-out setting he was required to produce.

Requiem Mass, Op. 89

☐ London Symphony Orchestra and Ambrosian Singers / Lorengar (soprano); Komlóssy (contralto); Ilosfalvy (tenor); Krause (bass) / Kertész (conductor) / London 1281

A quietly dramatic work, Dvořák's Requiem Mass makes its point without theatrical vibrations. Compared to the operatic demeanor that colors Verdi's contribution to the form, Dvořák's is intimate, more poetic.

The only one in the recorded catalogue, London's edition meets all requirements. Kertész, a Dvořák specialist, formulates a cohesiveness and a stylistic balance throughout the thirteen sections of the work. The solo vocalists are a joy to the ear, especially Pilar Lorengar, whose musicality does not exhibit a single flaw. And kudos to the beautiful and expressive instrument represented by the chorus.

Dvořák / Fritz Kreisler (1875 - 1962)

Slavonic Dance   *Instrumental*

No. 1 in G minor / No. 2 in E minor   *Violin*

☐ Elman (violin); Seiger (piano) / Vanguard SRV–367SD

Elman at his very best and Kreisler at his best as an authentic transcriber. Students of agogic matters should have a listen.

The numbering is, of course, Kreisler's. Actually, the G minor dance corresponds to Dvořák's Op. 46, No. 2, and the E minor piece is the transcription of Dvořák's Op. 72, No. 2.

Judith Dvorkin   *(1930 -   )*

Maurice (1955)   *Choral*

☐ Randolph Singers / Randolph (conductor) / Composers Recordings 102 (monaural)   *Chorus Alone*

Light and neat and sung with character by the five singers (two sopranos, contralto, tenor, and bass).

E

Brian Easdale   (1909-   )

Cantilena

☐ Modern Brass Ensemble / Advance FGR-2 (monaural)

The clear melodic purpose of Easdale's three-movement piece (*The Nativity, The Shepherds,* and *The Magi*) for two trumpets, horn, trombone, and tuba produces a respectable music. Though no individualized impulse guides the conception, it is shaped well and it is so played.

Chamber Music

Music from *The Red Shoes*

☐ St. Louis Symphony Orchestra / Golschmann (conductor) / Odyssey 32160338

This is the ballet music that was included in the score for this very successful film, now considered a classic in its particular genre.

Ballet

Michael East   (1580?-1648)

O Metaphysical Tobacco   Weep Not, Dear Love
Poor Is the Life   Your Shining Eyes

☐ Musica Reservata and Purcell Consort of Voices / Morrow (Musica Reservata) and Burgess (Purcell Consort of Voices) (conductors) / Argo ZRG-572

The singing is warm and sweet throughout and especially well-turned in the first of the group, a five-part setting contained in East's *The Second Set of Madrigales,* composed in 1606. Only one of these madrigals (*Poor Is the Life*) has some instrumental backing.

Choral

Chorus and Instrumental Ensemble

John Eaton   (1935-   )

Concert Piece for Syn-Ket and Symphony Orchestra

☐ Dallas Symphony Orchestra / Johanos (conductor) / Turnabout 34428

Not much is heard from the orchestra, which has a defined orchestrational personality, but which here rather has an electronic-sound profile. Further, to blend with the fractional pitch simulants of the portable sound system, the orchestra is split into two sections, which are tuned a quarter-tone apart. This further cuts off specific orchestral-sound identity.

Solo Instrument and Orchestra

Syn-Ket

The effect is one of solidity, with little light and shade differences or contrast brought by sonic projection and recession. This is apparently a performance approved by the composer. Question: why no credit for the person who operated the Syn-Ket? We are informed that the Syn-Ket "is performed by pushing buttons, tuning dials, playing keyboards, depressing a volume pedal, and every now and then patching." Certainly, all that deserves a credit indication.

John Edmunds (1913-   )

Vocal

Voice with Accompaniment

Adam's Lament

☐ Langstaff (baritone); Crowder or Garvey (piano) / Desto 6430

For eleven of the thirteen songs by Edmunds noted here and below, all eleven on Desto 6430, two pianists are listed on the front and back of the album cover: Charles Crowder and David Garvey. Neither are indicated on the record label. It's anyone's guess (Desto doesn't have the answer) whether one or both played this set of songs, and if both, how the credits should be distributed. The problem is compounded since these songs are coupled with a set by William Mayer that suffers from similar (and other!) lack of information.

The poem *Adam's Lament* is from a medieval Coventry miracle play. A neat polyphonic concept engages the voice and the piano.

As Dew in Aprille

☐ Renzi (soprano); Crowder or Garvey (piano) / Desto 6430

Edmunds's text, indicated as "Anonymous Fourteenth Century," refers to the Incarnation of Christ. The song is framed by chordal ostinati.

The Drummer
The Faucon

☐ Gramm (baritone); Cumming (piano) / Desto 6411/2

Death is the subject of both songs. The textural contrast of the piano is further evidence of John Edmunds's special ability in fusing the voice with a keyboard instrument, without making the latter a mere accompaniment.

Gramm is a musicianly singer, projecting these settings with intelligence and taste.

The Fish   Milkmaids
The Isle of Portland   Molly Samways
The Magi

☐ Langstaff (baritone); Crowder or Garvey (piano) / Desto 6430

Edmunds has produced well over five hundred songs, with every type included. In this group of five, the last two are in a rollicking vein. Declamatory style marks the symbolistic words of Yeats used in *The Magi*; a lament-like concept marks *The Isle of Portland* (to a text by Housman). The last-named is one of Edmunds's most moving pieces.

Langstaff's delivery is fine, his diction impeccable.

O Death, Rock Me Asleep

☐ Renzi (soprano); Crowder or Garvey (piano) / Desto 6430

A processional type of song to a poem written in 1536.

On the Nature of Truth

☐ Langstaff (baritone); Crowder or Garvey (piano) / Desto 6430

One of Edmunds's strongest pieces, constructed with the use of a ground bass. (Desto, which does well with its engineering, but not with its packaging, eliminates a key preposition in the title.)

O Sweet Everlasting Voices

Why Canst Thou Not

☐ Renzi (soprano); Crowder or Garvey (piano) / Desto 6430

Modal style is used for both songs. This colors the highly mystical Yeats text of *O Sweet* and intensifies the mood of the other song. (For the first of this pair, Desto's sloppy editing indicates two different titles on album cover and label; the complete, correct listing is noted above.)

George Edwards (1943-)

String Quartet (1967)

Chamber Music

☐ Composers String Quartet / Composers Recordings S-265

This prize-winning piece (one of four in a string quartet contest, sponsored by the New England Conservatory of Music) is of concentrated length and format (in one movement). The complexities of the music derive from the music of Elliott Carter whose special style has pervaded the consciousness of many a young American composer.

The difficulties are made easy by the Composers String Quartet.

Exchange-Misère (1974)

☐ Persichilli (flute, alto flute, and piccolo); Incenzo (clarinet and bass clarinet); Coen (violin and viola); Uitti (cello); Saperstein (piano) / Composers Recordings SD-336

Fragmentation linked in "an attempt to regain some of the expressive and structural possibilities of tonal music, but without allowing any single tone or sonority to be as ultimately stable as a tonic would be." Chromaticism naturally applies, with equivalent restlessness in the figures and rhythms.

Kreuz und Quer (1971)

☐ Boston Musica Viva / Pittman (conductor) / Composers Recordings SD-323

That a conductor is required to control the intricacies of Edwards's work for flute, clarinet, violin, viola, and cello, is indicative of its involved instrumental details. The style is the internationally accepted convictions of the post-Webern school that deals with fragmented clauses, telegraphic color interchanges, and declarative registral settings.

Pittman's group is as fully at home with this type of music as the major orchestras are with the three B's.

Cecil Effinger (1914-)

Little Symphony No. 1 (1945)

Orchestra

☐ Columbia Symphony Orchestra / Rozsnyai (conductor) / Columbia Special Products CMS-6597

Effinger's "Little" symphonic work embraces the classically proportioned four movements but says as much in its eleven-minute length as works thrice its length. The concentration carries over to the scoring, which calls for seven wind instruments (six players, one doubling), three brass, and strings.

There is no pretense or belabored contrivance in the piece. The music sings and moves, and has fine emotive meaning in the slow movement. A touch of Roy Harris will be recognized here and there.

The playing is clean and clear, properly proportioned, and full credit should be given to Zoltan Rozsnyai for his perceptive realization of a fine piece of music.

Klaus Egge   (1906-1979)

Orchestra

Symphony No. 3 (Louisville Symphony) (1959)

☐ Louisville Orchestra / Whitney (conductor) / Louisville 602 (monaural)

A one-movement conception marked by a slow-fast-slow tempo pattern. Such sectionalism carries over to the thematic detail, which is stated in blocks and tied together by a metamorphic technique. The music is both mysteriously evocative and rhythmically hard-driven.

Whitney's production of Egge's Symphony (commissioned by the Louisville Orchestra and first performed by them on March 4, 1959) is clean and quite spacious.

Solo Instrument and Orchestra

Piano

Piano Concerto No. 2, Op. 21

☐ Members of the Oslo Philharmonic Orchestra / Riefling (piano) / Fjeldstad (conductor) Composers Recordings 184 (monaural)

Egge has always flirted with folk materials. In this heady concerto, the generative item is an ancient folk tune and thus the music's subtitle: Symphonic Variations and Fugue on a Norwegian Folk Song. Leading from such strength is a set of free variations and fugue.

The pianistic directness of Egge's writing is a boon for the soloist, and Robert Riefling offers a skillful and arresting translation of the solo part. Good support from the orchestra, which has an attractive sound.

Jesse Ehrlich   (1920-)

Chamber Music

Six Short Pieces for Three Cellos

☐ Members of I Cellisti / Orion 7037

Here one finds purity of timbre through instrumental equality and purity of style through dodecaphonic involvement. A defined agreement with Ehrlich's serial seriousness is conveyed by the rich playing of the three cellists (the composer, Raymond Kelley, and Jerome Kessler).

Gottfried von Einem   (1918-)

Orchestra

Meditations: Two Movements for Orchestra, Op. 18

☐ Louisville Orchestra / Whitney (conductor) / Louisville 545-9 (monaural)

Von Einem's *Meditations* exemplifies a composer not looking in any new directions but staying within late-romantic territory.

Whitney directs his outfit in a performance that offers both forms and textures in a lucidly consistent manner. Neat sonorous fullness.

Johann Jakob Löwe von Eisenach (1629-1703)

Capriccio for Two Trumpets and Continuo

No. 1 / No. 2

Instrumental

Two Trumpets

☐ London Brass Players / Rifkin (conductor) / Nonesuch 71145

Baroque perceptions played clearly and distinctly. No more is required or would be possible.

Hanns Eisler (1898-1962)

Klavierstücke, **Op. 3**

Instrumental

Piano

☐ Colburn (piano) / Orion 7298

A set of four pieces in the expressionistic intermedium freed from any clinging vine of tonal locution. Miss Colburn presents these pre–twelve tone era examples with expertise.

Third Piano Sonata (1943)

☐ Rzewski (piano) / Finnadar 9011

Music of the very late romantic period. The piece descends from the pre-twelve tone manner of Schoenberg, but turns on such luxuries and dries them out with stylizations of the expressionistic school. Lushness is rejected; the material moves in dissonant strands.

Rzewski is as splendid a pianist as he is a composer. His performance demonstrates total stylistic sympathy for Eisler's music.

Will Eisma (1929-)

World Within World, **for Oboe, Violin, Viola, and Cello (1966)**

Chamber Music

☐ Netherlands Oboe Quartet / Donemus Audio-Visual Series 7071/4

No pastoral piping for the oboe in this athletic avant-garde piece. All the instruments work in the "world" (sustained sounds), the "within" represented by rapid figures, slides, glides, and behind-the-bridge smashes. Midway, the viola enjoys cadenza-like, extemporization-like highlighting. In comparison to this type of music, Schoenberg's twelve-tone works sound pristine.

Halim El-Dabh (1921-)

Leiyla and the Poet, **for Tape-Transformed Voice and Instruments (1962)**

Electronic Music

☐ Columbia MS–6566

Pure electronic sounds are used sparingly here. Most of the effects are created by tape manipulation (speed transposition and electronic reverberation) of the vocal and instrumental materials prepared and then recorded by the composer. A great deal of ostinati is used.

Edward Elgar *(1857-1934)*

Orchestra

Carissima

***Chanson de matin**, Op. 15, No. 1*

***Chanson de nuit**, Op. 15, No. 2*

☐ English Chamber Orchestra / Barenboim (conductor) / Columbia M–33584

The salonistic objectives of these pieces are well-expressed. Responsible workmanship throughout. The two *Chansons* were originally for violin and piano, then, after publication, were transcribed for orchestra.

Cockaigne Overture, Op. 40

☐ Philharmonia Orchestra / Barbirolli (conductor) / Angel S–36120

Barbirolli's version stands up through the slightly more than twenty years since it was issued. The rhythmic detail of the overture (subtitled *In London Town*) is not sharply ejaculated, so it fits much better with the lucent warmth of the *nobilmente* melody, which has the mark of great Elgarian authority. The naturalness of statement and breadth of the whole production are a fine achievement.

Enigma Variations, Op. 36

☐ London Symphony Orchestra / Monteux (conductor) / London STS–15188

It is not hard to pick the choice performance for Elgar's masterwork. Monteux's understanding of tempi differences, so essential to the fabric of the music, cannot be questioned. The entire essence and interrelated structure of the composition are made magnificently clear. There is no juggling of dynamics and all the proportions are ideal. One example is the *Nimrod* variation, which builds to an open-powered condition and not the usual blatant, brassy one. (The beginning of this section has magnificent dynamic influence.)

Jochum's version (Deutsche Grammophon 2530586), with the London Symphony Orchestra, is a fine second choice. So is Stokowski conducting the Czech Philharmonic Orchestra on London SPC–21136. No editorial manipulation for once!

Falstaff (Symphonic Study), Op. 68

☐ London Philharmonic Orchestra / Barenboim (conductor) / Columbia M–32599

Falstaff is surely a symphonically designed piece, but within its structure it has defined moods and character illustrations. These are what Barenboim stresses, and the resultant sonorous proliferation brings the largest benefits in his essay.

Froissart Overture, Op. 19

☐ New Philharmonia Orchestra / Barbirolli (conductor) / Angel S–36043

Elgar's concert overture is one of his early works (written in 1890). It is full of Germanic romanticism. Full-spirited playing displays this work advantageously.

Pomp and Circumstance March
No. 1 in D major / No. 2 in A minor / No. 3 in C minor / No. 4 in G major / No. 5 in C major (1930)

☐ Philharmonia Orchestra / Barbirolli (conductor) / Angel S–36043

Now, of course, everybody plays and everyone knows the first of these (composed together with Nos. 2, 3, and 4 in the period 1901–1907), especially because of the "Land of Hope and Glory" trio section. And there are plenty of recordings of it: Bernstein (Columbia MS-7271), Fiedler (RCA VCS-7068), Davis (Philips 6502001), and Ormandy (Columbia MS-6474). More or less, they're all satisfactory—how can anyone go wrong with this ceremonial piece of perfection? In addition, total sets of the marches are available, conducted by the composer Arthur Bliss (on London STS-15112) and on Columbia M–32936, directed by Daniel Barenboim. Here again, both are assured readings.

It is time that more attention is given to the other marches. There are some internal similarities, but Elgar's creative behaviorism did not brook carbon copies. Each is sufficiently different to hold the interest and it is patently incorrect to place the second, third, fourth, and fifth marches in a secondary category. The trio to the second march, for example, has an odd affinity with Dvořák; the fourth march is truly optimistic, and the fifth one has a gay jiglike element. Throughout, there is variety and contrastive creative decisions.

Bliss does well with the pieces but tends to flatten out the tempi. The finest consideration is to be found in Barbirolli's interpretations. He shows he knows when to be spirited and brisk and when to relax and let the instruments sing. At no time is he sentimental. Certainly his performances are the best of the lot.

Rosemary
Salut d'amour, Op. 12

☐ English Chamber Orchestra / Barenboim (conductor) / Columbia M–33584

Salut d'amour has been played to death in every combination and solo form possible. However, Elgar's tidbit (which also describes the other work noted above) is tedious and banal, boring and commonplace only when badly played (or overplayed). Heard as it is here it offers two and one-half minutes of refreshing salon music.

Rosemary is small beer compared to *Liebesgruss* (the published German title for *Salut d'amour*). But there it is if it is wanted, performed with unforced simplicity.

Symphony No.1 in A flat major, Op. 55

☐ London Philharmonic Orchestra / Solti (conductor) / London 6789
☐ London Philharmonic Orchestra / Boult (conductor) / Musical Heritage Society MHS-1285

It has long been argued that only an Englishman can truly conduct this symphony (and the second one as well). It's not true. While Boult's masterly authority with this work has long been one of the special highlights of his career and his version cannot in anyway be ruled out, Solti has also produced a masterful reading of the piece, drenched with its full emotional and spiritual content.

In only one place can one question Boult's reading—the reticence in the coda to the slow movement. This is not the case with Solti. The breadth and grandeur of the first movement are expressed to the fullest; the aggressiveness that is required to push the Scherzo through its unific pulse depiction $\frac{1}{2}$ time) is fully displayed, and throughout there is a romantic panache that is thrilling; the music glows in its melodic grandeur.

What makes Boult's interpretation so viable is the Elgarian temper that is totally apparent, whereas Solti's viewpoint is that some unbuttoning of the composer's vest is fully in order. Boult is a bit more delicate in certain places than Solti. The latter brings a freshly new conception; the former's long and close relationship with the score gives him a knowledge that cannot be discounted in any respect. Both recordings are recommended.

Symphony No. 2 in E flat major, Op. 63

☐ London Philharmonic Orchestra / Boult (conductor) / Musical Heritage Society MHS-1335

This is the fourth time that Boult has recorded Elgar's Opus 63, spanning close to fifty years of association with the work. It is the wealth of that knowledge and the cognizance of Elgarian tradition that make Boult's the most glorious interpretation of the several available. Barbirolli (on Seraphim S-6033) produced a distinguished performance but tended to slower tempi in many parts of the symphony (his timing is five minutes longer than Boult's). Barenboim's conception (on Columbia M-31997) is essentially inflexible and some of the long lines (especially in the finale) just move along without detailing crucial points. Solti has a very dynamic viewpoint of the music and is quite persuasive in his reading (on London 6941), but he does not equal Boult's grasp of contour. Without it a sense of occasional meandering takes over.

There is no doubt that Boult's presentation of the slow movement will be difficult to match. It has a grandeur and a pathos without the type of emotive overplay that can ruin elegiac content. Throughout the symphony the music is completely alive, flexible, naturally expressed; yet total attention is paid to structural weights. Above all, there is a spontaneity that makes the music alive. Boult has never been better. This is conducting that gives impressive evidence in favor of both creator and re-creator.

String Orchestra

Elegy for Strings, Op. 58

☐ Academy of St. Martin-in-the-Fields / Marriner (conductor) / Argo ZRG-573

This is a miniature work, but the expressiveness of the muted strings fully compensates for its size. The playing is lovely, fully involved, more so than what is heard on the competitive presentations by Angel on S-36403 (Barbirolli conducting) and by Columbia on M-33584 (Barenboim conducting).

Serenade in E minor for Strings, Op. 20

☐ Academy of St. Martin-in-the-Fields / Marriner (conductor) / Argo ZRG-573

A large number of recordings of the Serenade (one of Elgar's favorite works) proves its intimate charm, melodic pensiveness, and beauty. Some conductors overstress agogic particulars (Barenboim, for example, sharply impressing *forzati* indications in movement 2 of his Columbia M-33584 recording); others somehow mistake wistfulness to mean profundity, and the music becomes heavy (Barbirolli on Angel S-36101). There is no question as to Marriner's warmly lyrical, luminous performance. It may be surpassed by another release in terms of sound engineering, but I very much doubt that its performance will be bettered.

Sospiri, Op. 70

☐ English Chamber Orchestra / Barenboim (conductor) / Columbia M-33584

Elgar's *Sospiri* ("Sighs") is an intensely elegiac piece, embracing strings, harp, and organ. Barenboim probes it more deeply than Barbirolli on his recording for Angel (S–36403) or Marriner on his all-Elgar disc (Argo ZRG–573).

Suite from *The Spanish Lady*

☐ Academy of St. Martin-in-the-Fields / Marriner (conductor) / Argo ZRG–573

Three pieces from Elgar's unfinished opera: a *Burlesco*, a *Sarabande*, and a Bourrée, edited by Percy Young. Middle-of-the-road music, sympathetically played.

Romance for Bassoon and Orchestra, Op. 62

Solo Instrument and Orchestra

Bassoon

☐ English Chamber Orchestra / Gatt (bassoon) / Barenboim (conductor) / Columbia M–33584

This reflective, somewhat somber music is without much contrast, and only an Elgar aficionado will want this recording.

Concerto in E minor for Cello and Orchestra, Op. 85

Cello

☐ London Symphony Orchestra / du Pré (cello) / Barbirolli (conductor) / Angel S–36338

This is the Concerto that sparked the career of Jacqueline du Pré, now no longer able to play because of a crippling disease.

What extraordinary playing this young lady offers! She phrases with freedom and yet includes a neat balance between thesis and antithesis. Her tone is light and delicate or deep and rich in accordance with the score; the coloristic gamut is huge. But greater than anything else is her imaginative power, proclaimed by a spontaneity that is thrilling. No one, but no one has matched her conception of the Elgar. This is memorable musical mastery.

Introduction and Allegro for String Quartet and String Orchestra, Op. 47

String Quartet

☐ Strings of the Sinfonia of London and Allegri String Quartet / Barbirolli (conductor) / Angel S–36101
☐ Academy of St. Martin-in-the-Fields / Maguire, Keenlyside, Essex, and Heath (string quartet) / Marriner (conductor) / Argo ZRG–573

Interestingly, the Argo release lists the tonality of the work as "in G minor and major" which is a dovetailing of the principal keys that parallel the interlacing of the sound resources Elgar used. This work has often brought remarks of an Elgarian concept of *concerto grosso*. Opus 47 is definitely not in that category any more than it is a concerto vehicle with string orchestra accompaniment. The quartet functions as a unit itself, is drawn from for solo voices, and used for colorative points within the total score. The black–white positiveness of the concerto grosso design is absent.

The use of an actual string quartet organization, rather than first-desk players in the string orchestra definitely adds to the integration and tonal solidity of the Barbirolli-led performance. The St. Martin rendition is almost as good and in certain of the tutti passages, more resonant and warm. Both conductors prove why Elgar's richly inventive and gorgeously scored work is a mainstay in the string orchestra repertory.

Concerto in B minor for Violin and Orchestra, Op. 61

Violin

☐ New Philharmonia Orchestra / Menuhin (violin) / Boult (conductor) / Angel S–36330

Menuhin has been associated with Elgar's concerto ever since he performed it with the composer as the conductor and then recorded it with him. He performs it with majestic profile and with a superb insight into the style of the piece.

The matter of editing has entered into the picture. A few harmonics have been altered to solid-sounding timbres and some single notes have been expanded to octaves. In view of Elgar's manifold and precise tempi indications some may term the *rubati* that slow the traffic a few times interpretative impiety. Nonetheless, these do not blatantly spoil a warmly persuasive rendition with superfine support from that Elgarian master, Sir Adrian Boult.

Instrumental

Violin

La Capricieuse, Op. 17

☐ Ricci (violin); Lush (piano) / London STS–15049

Elgar termed this a *morceau de genre*. Ricci plays this tidy and tuneful music with simple statement and does not oversweeten it. Heifetz recorded the piece twice; in 1917 and again in 1934. Though the later setting is a bit faster, it is just as mannered as the initial presentation. In both cases the music is overfed with *rubato*. The attempt to be cute harms Elgar's miniature.

Chamber Music

Sonata for Violin and Piano, Op. 82

☐ Weiss Duo / Unicorn RHS–341

Elgar's hallmarks were the spun melody enobled by majestic profile, a vigorous and resolutely determined type of writing in the fast movements, and a warm romantic urge in the slower-paced sections. It takes temperament as well as a fine creative ability to form a theme with the beautiful proportions of the one that opens this sonata. As an answer to criticism of Elgar's being mainly scholastic, it should be indicated that in this opening theme the home tonality of E minor is not stated immediately. Further, note the modal spirit over Bach figurations for the string instrument in the middle section.

In the second movement (Romance) the music seems to turn on itself. It begins improvisatorally, and it takes considerable time before the general idea of undulating figures settles into a theme of quartal and quintal intervals. The tonic major to the home key's minor dominates the last movement.

The playing by this husband-and-wife team is masterly, the blend of the instruments perfect, and so is the style. This is a revelatory chamber-music performance.

String Quartet in E minor, Op. 83

☐ Aeolian String Quartet / Dover 7259
☐ Claremont Quartet / Nonesuch 71140

The main clue to Elgar's quartet is the $\frac{12}{8}$ meter chosen for the opening—a broader concept of four pulse units per measure than the affinitive $\frac{4}{4}$. The former is more articulatively majestic and close to the essence of this composer, with his oft-met instruction *nobilmente* (though the quartet is more vernal than it is noble).

There isn't a flaw in the Aeolian performance. They know Elgar's style and every sixteenth note in the score. They do not add any schmaltz or editorial condiments. This is certainly a definitive interpretation.

Neither is there any arguing the excellence of the Claremont version. The expertise of this team is beautifully documented in their approach: robust yet careful to present the bittersweet essences of the score, and dynamically powerful in the finale. One notices that they avoid being either sentimental or strait-laced. Theirs is a fully Elgarian documentation.

Piano Quintet in A minor, Op. 84

☐ Aeolian String Quartet / Cassini (piano) / Dover 7260

Elgar writes with restraint, expressing a type of creative mystery. The quintet is overcast and brooding, fraught with an introverted quality rare in this composer's output. One senses an unexplained programmatic significance in the opus. Indeed, the troubled thinking within the music makes it Elgar's "Enigma" in the field of chamber music.

The performance of the quintet (one of the master works in the medium) is exceedingly probing, with a blend of the string voices that is a pure delight. Just a more distinct piano registration—not so much of contrast but of individual color—would have produced a truly memorable recording.

As Torrents in Summer

Deep in My Soul, Op. 53, No. 2

The Fountain, Op. 71, No. 2

Go, Song of Mine, Op. 57

Love's Tempest, Op. 73, No. 1

My Love Dwelt in a Northern Land

O Wild West Wind, Op. 53, No. 3

Owls

The Shower, Op. 71, No. 1

There is Sweet Music, Op. 53, No. 1

Choral

Chorus Alone

☐ Louis Halsey Singers / Halsey (conductor) / Argo ZRG–607

An assortment that conveys an Elgarian variety that will bring surprise to those who still think of E. E. as only of the *nobilmente* school.

The harmonic complex in *Love's Tempest* provides dramatic association with the text. In *Owls* one hears a hallucinatory quality that is totally gripping. Profound depth is found in the setting of Byron's *Deep in My Soul*. In the remainder there is very little that is conventional.

The Louis Halsey group deserves a special credit for making this music available with an additional credit for utterly communicative choral singing which is of top quality and complete artistic capacity.

The Apostles, Op. 49

Cantata and Oratorio

☐ London Philharmonic Orchestra and Choir, and Choir of Downe House School / Amstrong (soprano); Watts (alto); Tear (tenor); Luxon (baritone); Grant and Case (basses) / Boult (conductor) / Connoisseur Society CS–2094

This is the first of a group of three oratorios Elgar planned to compose on the subject of the founding of the Christian Church. It is a grand-scale conception, including instrumental programmaticism, with the material constructed from a huge number of leitmotifs. However, the structure is totally Elgarian in breadth and has a fine dignity, though the dignity is retained at great length. The Boult-directed conception guarantees proper interpretation and authenticity to the last degree.

The Dream of Gerontius, Op. 38

☐ Hallé Orchestra, and Hallé and Sheffield Philharmonic Choirs / Baker (mezzo-soprano); Lewis (tenor); Borg (bass-baritone) / Barbirolli (conductor) / Angel S–3660

Some conductors stress the spiritual side of Elgar's score; others prefer to emphasize a fuller dramatic reasoning (and edit the score accordingly). One is reminded of George Bernard Shaw's consideration of the work: "Here was no literary paper instrumentation, no muddle, and noise, but an absolutely new energy given to the band by a consummate knowledge of what it could do and how it could do it." And so the Barbirolli viewpoint for both voices and orchestra is always dynamic and always impressive. A fitting operatic climate surrounds Elgar's work.

The Kingdom, Op. 51

☐ London Philharmonic Orchestra and Choir / Price (soprano); Minton (alto); Young (tenor); Shirley-Quirk (bass-baritone) / Boult (conductor) / Connoisseur Society CS-2089

This is the second of a trilogy of oratorios Elgar planned (for the first, see above: *The Apostles*); the third work was never written, though a good part of the libretto had been prepared as well as a few musical sketches. Most critics claim there is a great unevenness in Elgar's work, but spiritual containment and sufficient diversity can be offered as counterclaims. In terms of the meaning and drama of the text the work does strike deep.

Boult's performance is truly an inspiring one. He achieves a sense of motility that nullifies the additional criticism that the music is overweighted with its sentiments and is therefore somewhat static. Not here. This is certainly one of Boult's major conductorial achievements. Never mind the critics!

Merrill Ellis   (1916-   )

Orchestra   **Kaleidoscope, for Orchestra, Synthesizer, and Soprano**

☐ Louisville Orchestra / Wall (mezzo-soprano); Ellis (composer) / Mester (conductor) / Louisville S-711

Ellis's fascinating conception is a smorgasbord of sounds produced by the winds, brass, and strings of the orchestra, an electronic sound synthesizer, a solo violin, and a voice. The voice is heard in self-duet, a shadowing echo of most of the words and pitches being intoned. Glides and growls coalesce. Sound intoxications are constant. They prove Ellis's impressive ability to make a successful continuity out of his fantasy.

No credit is given for the synthesizer performer. However, Ellis is noted in the *performer* credits as "composer." That's one for the book that isn't explained. Does a composer get credit for standing around while a recording is being made? Or does Ellis man the synthesizer? Did he direct the aleatoric detail that forms the second part of the work? Whatever, this is an alluring creation for which he fully deserves the double credit of composer and composer-performer in whatever manner the latter is meant.

Jean-Claude Eloy   (1938-   )

Orchestra   **Equivalences (1963)**

☐ Domaine Musical Ensemble and Strasbourg Percussion Group / Boulez (conductor) / Everest 3170

Color is the dominant factor in this work, conducted by the man who was once a teacher of the composer. There are six percussionists, three separate wind groups, a harp, and a piano doubling on celesta. Form? The color changes make the form.

Equivalences is partly indeterminate in terms of registral placement and instrumental coordination. The performance is vivid and convincing.

Herbert Elwell   (1898-1974)

A Child's Grace	*Service of All the Dead*	*Vocal*
I Look Back	*This Glittering Grief*	
The Ouselcock	*Wistful*	*Voice with Accompaniment*

☐ Maxine Makas (soprano); Anthony Makas (piano) / Composers Recordings S-270

Fully romantic examples without any unexpected deviations by this former teacher-music critic-composer. CRI offers no texts for the songs, but that is the only thing lacking in the recording.

Georges Enesco   (1881-1955)

Rumanian Rhapsody No. 1 in A major, Op. 11

Orchestra

☐ London Symphony Orchestra / Dorati (conductor) / Mercury 75018
☐ Philadelphia Orchestra / Ormandy (conductor) / Columbia M-31846

Dorati is terrific. Under his direction the music glows and is fresh and clean. Peeled away are all the interpretative crusts that have been piled on by an army of conductors. Most recently Enesco's piece has been relegated to the pops concert repertory but its thematic beauties and fantastic orchestral colors belong rightfully on top-rung concert programs.

Dorati is here a master of orchestral luminosity and tempo choice and controls. In this respect he is several points ahead of Ormandy, who governs beautifully but a bit more conservatively. Both bring out details that other conductors regard as minor and parenthetical. So, from the many choices on the market, Dorati is first and Ormandy an exceedingly close second. Only the fatter tone of the solo violist of the Philadelphia Orchestra, in the very short portion involved, places that version ahead of the Dorati-London edition.

The Ormandy setting is also included in Columbia MS-6018. The same conductor-orchestra team has recorded Enesco's rhapsody for RCA (CRL3-0985) where it is part of "20 Stereo Spectaculars" covering six record sides.

Rumanian Rhapsody No. 2 in D major, Op. 11

☐ London Symphony Orchestra / Dorati (conductor) / Mercury 75018

Compared to the extroversion of the well-known first Rumanian rhapsody, Enesco's second one is totally introverted. It is a dark, quiet music—of russet brown musing compared to the scarlet scintillation of the initial work of the pair. But beautiful it is.

That it has not reached any popularity status is understandable if not acceptable. It does not have catchy tunes or orchestrational blaze. But its quiet intensity is sufficient to prove its right to be ranked with the A major companion work.

Dorati's performance is a beautifully committed one. It is truthfully shaped and in the concluding part masterfully colored. A five-star release.

Instrumental

Cantabile et presto

Flute

☐ Hoberman (flute); Stannard (piano) / Avant 1015

Contrastive pace is the creative strategy here, underscored by the articulated figures that carry forward the Presto section. This is a fine work for the flute that displays Enesco's usual artistic stability.

Arthur Hoberman is in fine fettle here. The seamlessness of his playing, especially in the Presto, deserves special mention. A short bit where the piano is raucous is the only criticism.

Violin

Prelude for Solo Violin, Op. 9

☐ Rosand (violin) / Candide 31064

Not many violinists know this short earnest piece, and those who do don't play it. Their loss and our gain thanks to Rosand.

Chamber Music

Sonata in F minor for Violin and Piano, Op. 6

☐ Enesco (violin); Lipatti (piano) / Monitor 2049 (monaural)

This is a brooding and restless work that only partially avoids being on the stormier side in the last third of its total. Cyclic formation is the technical pin that clasps this composition together. However, Enesco does not stubbornly state his cyclic facts. He reiterates but colors his arguments. No detailed nationalism, save for the melancholic, partial-gypsy air (in its most subtle sense) of the second movement.

Do not expect the brightest type of engineering. The recording has some hiss and even with the use of a filter there is a good amount of surface noise. Never mind. It is a rare treat not only to have Enesco's music on disc but to enjoy the artistry of two of the greatest performers of the century.

Sonata No. 3 in A minor for Violin and Piano, Op. 25

☐ Yehudi Menuhin (violin); Hephzibah Menuhin (piano) / Angel S–36418

The clue to this work is its informative subtitle: "In the Popular Rumanian Style." It is chock-full of it, as expressed by melancholy curves and brooding, restless colorations. Enesco stubbornly states his nationalistic facts. Still, while he reiterates he colors and recolors his arguments.

Menuhin and Menuhin make Enesco's meanings fully clear. However, for Yehudi there are some fuzzy sound points as though there were too much rosin on the strings. Otherwise, plenty of rhapsody and *rubati*.

String Quartet in G major, Op. 22, No. 2

☐ Rumanian Radio String Quartet / Monitor 2049 (monaural)

A brooding, magnificent essay that has the depth of late Beethoven, the soul stirring of Mahler, and the exquisite workmanship of Mozart. There are no native (Rumanian) synonyms in the quartet's vocabulary. It has the sober design of classical ancestry but not once does Enesco follow the academic line of least resistance. Balances apply to the sonata, song-form, scherzo, and rondo designs, but the feeling persists that the quartet is a *durchkomponiert* conception. Thus the grand line, which never once departs from the dark-colored mood of Enesco's *Quartetto serioso*.

The playing of the Rumanian team is beautiful and sensitive.

Seven Songs, Op. 15

    Aux Demoiselles paresseuses d'écrire à leurs amis

    Changeons propos, c'est trop chanté d'amour

    Du Confict en douleur

    Estrene à Anne

    Estrene de la rose

    Languir me fais

    Présent de couleur blanche

Vocal

*Voice
with
Accompaniment*

☐ Marcoulescou (soprano); Phillabaum (piano) / Orion 75184

In this imaginative responsibility to the texts by Clément Marot, court poet to François I, each song is sensitively cohesive in a melodic climate that is beautifully warm and memorable.

Orion's recording furnishes a real find in both music and vocalist. Yolanda Marcoulescou is a soprano of the highest caliber and a musician of top distinction. This is masterly singing, and certainly a recording every one should own.

Manuel Enríquez   *(1926-   )*

Diptico I (1969)

*Chamber
Music*

☐ Gilbert (flute); Hübner (piano) / Mainstream MS–5017

A great deal of the work is to be done by the performers. According to the composer, the interpretation "must be ambivalent and of equal importance." In this case there is a strong sense of instrumental individuality as well as interplay of the fractured sound dabs and percussive punctuations.

Apparently the performers are those listed. Mainstream's disc (covering six works) is very unclear about the entire matter.

David Epstein   *(1930-   )*

Vent-ures (1970)

Band

☐ Eastman Wind Ensemble / Hunsberger (conductor) / Desto 7148

Virtuosity, contemporaneously conditioned and contemporaneously unshackled as rarely found in the literature for the wind ensemble (not a band, since there are no multiple duplications of any single-voiced instrument in the score, covered by the hit-and-miss basis that pertains to the majority of concert bands; the voicing and therefore the textures are strictly controlled by the composer, matching the specificity of an orchestral score).

The title is, of course, a word play on the use of wind instruments (*vent*). It also codifies the work as concerned with particular undertakings: poly-tempi in movement 1, timbre exploration in movement 2, and so on.

A dynamically true performance, showing that the abilities of this school organization can match those of top professionals.

Chamber Music

String Trio (1964)

☐ Pacific Trio / Desto 7148

Contemporary syntax need not interfere with a classically derived structural solidity. It doesn't in this instance. An intensely dramatic and colorfully select (but never outré) four-movement work for violin, viola, and cello, Epstein's opus is a dynamic example of such cross-breeding.

The forms of the four movements are each strongly particular but do not create a pastiche because of these differences. Movement 1 is quasi–toccata-mannered, movement 3 is a type of impressionistic *Anhang*. Part 2 of the trio emerges as a large ternary frame of reference. Though unbound by strict measured lengths which are basic to the form, the architectural clarity of the end movement (*Passacaglia fantastica*) is undisturbed by the mensural differences of the permutations. It is a cogent blend of passacaglia shape, both with a fantasy inlay and overlay.

This is a well-shaped performance by the Pacific team (Annette Levi, violin; Morris Sutow, viola; and William Harry, cello).

String Quartet (1971)

☐ Philadelphia Quartet / Desto 7148

The principal purpose of Epstein's quartet (his second work in the medium) is concerto-line virtuosity, without traditional concerted rapport. The four instruments are considered as four individuals, although there is some consolidation. It is quartet dialogue that is the objective, during which the instruments "respond *to* one another and at other times play *against* each other, almost as if unaware of the others' thoughts." Listened to without this premise of individuation, utter confusion reigns. Heard (rather overheard!) as several simultaneous conversations the musical sense becomes clear.

Extremely difficult, but the Philadelphians clarify the formulations of this work expertly. Only praise can be forthcoming for their performance.

Vocal

Voice with Accompaniment

The Seasons (1955)

☐ DeGaetani (mezzo-soprano); Freeman (piano) / Desto 7148

Settings of five poems by Emily Dickinson. The grammar of the music relates to German expressionism; the textures are just a bit lighter.

The performance is a distinguished one. This partnership defines consummate artistry.

Donald Erb   (1927-   )

Brass Ensemble

Sonneries

☐ Members of the Cleveland Orchestra Brass Section / Bamert (conductor) / Crystal S-531

A dozen brass instruments do not a band make and certainly would expand the meaning of the term "chamber music." Best is to place Erb's *Sonneries* in the brass ensemble category.

Clear, well laid out virtuosity is on display in this piece. Movement 1 contains plenty of jazz atmospherics, packed as it is with flutters, rips, and glisses. Lyricism (emphasized by muted timbre) is the contrast found in the central movement. The finale has a robust flair and contains flares and bent tones as well. It's all delivered with conviction. The performers carry out with seeming ease Erb's blend of music and brass-instrument effects.

Basspiece for Contrabass and Tape (1969)

☐ Turetzky (double bass) / Desto 7128

Four movements with virtuosity for the string instrument made to order for Bertram Turetzky. Catch the *col legno* memoranda in part 2, especially. The tape itself is a manipulation of double bass sounds—zestful and titillating. Nothing subtle in this suite, everything ferociously up to date and most enjoyable.

In No Strange Land for Trombone, Double Bass, and Electronic Sounds

☐ Dempster (trombone); Turetzky (double bass) / Nonesuch 71223

Erb's title is the title of a poem by Francis Thompson. His music reveals nothing about that affiliation but it fully reveals a colorful and sensitive application of electronic ideas in connection with instrumental timbres. The degrees of sound are superbly contrasted. For example, in movement 1 of the total four the qualities are glutinous, in movement 3 they emerge as velutinous. Form is of elasticity; the trombone and double bass spit and spurt, enter and depart in a rhapsodic continuity. Some vocalism is tossed into the sound mass.

The live musicians are virtuosi, the integration of all the material is virtuosic. In adding electronic synonyms to his vocabulary Donald Erb is a masterful speaker in the instrumental-tape medium.

Diversion for Two (Other than Sex) (1966)

☐ Murtha (trumpet); Lesbines (percussion) / Opus One S–1

A jazzy duologue, spiced with crisp fragments, and flavored with trumpet bends and glides. Virtuoso performance.

Trio for Two (1968)

☐ Bertram Turetzky (bass); Nancy Turetzky (alto flute and timpani) / Finnadar 9015

A collage of strikes, glides, zig-zag tones, and even some human voice shouts, providing a jazz-percussion hybrid. Nothing representational, simply direct color effects which, as they occur, create a sense of expectancy for the next one. In that regard, quite successful.

Harold's Trip to the Sky

☐ Ferritto (viola); Benedict (piano); Williams (percussion) / Crystal S–531

Whether Erb's idea is a spoof of far-out techniques or not, the result is a pixilated bunch of sound effects, especially emphasizing glides. All kind of tricks are utilized: harmonicas are tapped together, people blow into tuned soda bottles, etcetera. Erb's objective: "to give a small ensemble as wide a color spectrum as possible." Well achieved, sir!

Instrumental

Double Bass

*Trombone
and
Double Bass*

*Chamber
Music*

587

String Trio (1966)

☐ Pollikoff (violin); Tekula (cello); Hall (electric guitar) / Opus One S-1

Virtuoso use of the electric guitar, and probably the first time the instrument has been used in such an intimate combination. Splendid idea. There are some touches of jazz that match the hybrid instrumentation by combining guitar licks with weird string glissandi.

Erb is clearly his own man. His structural design is excellent and his conception interesting. The performers deliver what he wants, the balances of color and musical importance are ideal.

Phantasma (1965)

☐ Nancy Turetzky (flute, alto flute, and piccolo); Korman (oboe and English horn); White (harpsichord); Bertram Turetzky (contrabass) / Opus One S-1

Erb states he is uninterested in any pertinent style and avoids any specific system. He is quoted as writing "what by instinct appeals to me."

Here his instinct leads to a swatch card of various chunks of material; the sum and substance form a catalogue of effects. A somewhat thickly populated score but one that holds the interest.

Reconnaissance for Violin, Double Bass, Piano, Percussion, Moog Synthesizer, and Moog Polyphonic Instrument (1967)

☐ Douglas (violin); Forbes (double bass); Grierson (piano); Watson (percussion); Thomas (Moog synthesizer); Stein (Moog polyphonic instrument) / Erb (conductor) / Nonesuch 71223

Five movements that integrate a sextet of four conventional instruments (not always used in the strict conventional sense) with a pair of electronic instruments played by live musicians. (And, to be noted, though all the performers are excellent, two are of specially high reputation: Michael Tilson Thomas, the conductor at the synthesizer, and Leonard Stein, the Schoenbergian scholar at the other Moog representative.)

The Moog synthesizer is, by this date, standard electronic equipment. The polyphonic instrument has a keyboard with a range of four octaves, each octave, however, divided into forty-three parts in place of twelve.

With a pair of soprano and bass string instruments, piano, percussion, and two different Moogs a new kind of chamber music is offered here. It is not startling, but it certainly is freshly interesting in its colorative, collective, and contrastive actions.

Three Pieces for Brass Quintet and Piano (1968)

☐ New York Brass Quintet / Smolko (piano) / Bamert (conductor) / Composers Recordings SD-323

Fragmented lyricism is heard in movement 2 and jazzy densities are presented in movement 3, but the peak of the work is the witty, snide, and meaningfully distorted contents of the opening movement. Erb says it all by describing this section as using "many things one can do with a brass instrument without actually 'playing' it." Meaning: fancy Dan breathing, percussing, and other weirdly wonderful effects that serve as superb aural stimulants.

Quite a performance is necessary to put all of this across. It is fully realized in this instance.

Robert Erickson (1917-)

Chamber Concerto (1960)

Orchestra

☐ Hartt Chamber Players / Shapey (conductor) / Composers Recordings S-218

A four-movement work scored for seventeen players. It calls on Webern securities, with fragmentation and a variety of timbred shapes. The sharp angles of the structures are expertly delineated by Ralph Shapey, an expert conductor of this style of music.

Oceans

Instrumental

☐ Logan (trumpet); Erickson (percussion) / Orion ORS-7294

Trumpet

Unceasing long sounds bathing in a quiet sea of attenuation. A sense of static absorbs the music. The work is "a mix down of six over-dubbed tracks, four of trumpet and two of percussion." A sonic berceuse.

End of the Mime

Choral

☐ NMCE I / Gaburo (conductor) / Composers Recordings S-325

Chorus Alone

The text (a total of 105 lines) is from James Joyce's *Finnegans Wake*. The music amazingly characterizes the fantastic prose, with an assorted amalgam of choral procedures that equate the multiple levels of the words. Such handsome newness in the use of unaccompanied voices is rare. It is to be enjoyed, for it always remains musical though its result is unseen theatre.

By all means listen with text in hand, otherwise the uniqueness is mitigated and the listener will miss the complete effect of hearing such as "Rendningrocks roguesreckning reigns. Gwds with gurs are gttrdmmrng" pronounced by this virtuoso choral ensemble.

Philipp Heinrich Erlebach (1657-1714)

Siehe, ich verkundige Euch grosse Freude

Cantata and Oratorio

☐ Instrumentalists and Freiburg Student Choir / Graf (soprano); Brinkmann (alto); Schmidt (tenor) / Knall (conductor) / Vanguard C-10045

Probably only a handful know the name of Erlebach, but merely on the basis of this short Christmas cantata he deserves attention. It is beautifully crafted, the text being a combination of Biblical verses and free poetry. The singing has both flexibility and a rich quality. Superb instrumental back-up of two trumpets (incorrectly listed by Vanguard as "clarinets" in place of "clarini"), bassoon, strings, and continuo.

Don't overlook this disc.

Heinrich Wilhelm Ernst (1814-1865)

Concerto in F sharp minor for Violin and Orchestra, Op. 23

Solo Instrument and Orchestra

☐ Orchestra of Radio Luxembourg / Rosand (violin) / de Froment (conductor) / Candide 31054

In this principally lyrical, one-movement piece there is far less of the pyrotechnical

Violin

detail found in most of Ernst's other violin works. Rosand emphasizes the quality described in the Concerto's subsidiary title, *Allegro pathétique*.

Instrumental

Violin

Fantasy on Airs from Rossini's *Othello*, Op. 11

☐ Steiner (violin); Berfield (piano) / Orion 78313

Brilliant and effective disposition of a pair of tunes given vivid variations by the violin. Consistently good playing, though the resultant sound quality is not of the distinguished variety.

Rudolf Escher (1912-   )

Orchestra

Musique pour l'esprit en deuil, Op. 6

☐ Concertgebouw Orchestra / van Beinum (conductor) / Donemus Audio-Visual Series DAVS–6403 (monaural: 10-inch disc)

A gigantic threnody that is paced to a shattering climax within its tripartite textural plan. Escher uses a large orchestra including seventeen individual woodwind parts plus two types of saxophone, twelve brass, plentiful percussion, piano, two harps, in addition to the strings. Completed in 1943, it proves that Straussian speech is not passé.

The performance, a "live" one, is only worthy as a sonic example of the work. It is not well balanced and some of the detail is lost. Still, it represents important music and until an up-to-date recording is issued it will have to serve. Escher's powerful score, regardless of this second-class recording, makes its point.

Chamber Music

Wind Quintet (1967)

☐ Danzi Wind Quintet / Donemus Audio-Visual Series 7071/4

Aside from the expansion of the five timbres by alternating the flute with an alto flute and the clarinet with a bass clarinet, the coloration of Escher's work is special in the use of an oboe d'amore throughout.

Though chromatically full-scale, tonal centers are quite apparent. The continuity is comprehensive and yet after the first time signature no less than 258 metrical changes take place in the total 381 measures. Within these are eighteen major tempo shifts. To have meaningful flow while the material is rhapsodic and grained with color fantasy proves the expert craftsmanship of the composer.

This expertise also applies to the Danzi group. Their playing is utterly captivating and achieved with crystalline clarity.

Oscar Esplá (1886-1976)

Instrumental

Guitar

Antaño

☐ Segovia (guitar) / MCA 2526

Folk-styled, but not of regimented order. Esplá's harmonies have individual resources and *Antaño* is no trip down a lane of folk-tuned memories. Segovia's "orchestration" of this piece toward its conclusion is singular and lovely.

Cinco canciones playeras españolas

☐ Paris Conservatoire Orchestra / de los Angeles (soprano) / Frühbeck de Burgos (conductor) / Angel S–35937

Esplá's "Five Spanish Seashore Songs" are set in the native idiom but bypass the rhythmic clichés that tend to decrease individual credibility.

This type of music is made to order for both de los Angeles and Frühbeck de Burgos. Both obtain a unique plasticity in their joint performance and prove their stylistic understanding of Esplá's music.

Vocal

Voice and Orchestra

Alvin Etler   *(1913-1973)*

Triptych (1961)

Orchestra

☐ Louisville Orchestra / Whitney (conductor) / Louisville S–674

Etler's early work contained some sophisticated Broadway echoes, not actual jazz, but rhythmic raciness and serious-shaped pop tunes. The *Triptych* is sterner, stronger stuff—symphonic stuff and no nonsense. Etler's contrapuntal habits in this piece are excellent; counterpoint is achieved not by lines but by chunks of sound pitted against each other. The effect is athletic; the vigor and body contacts of the textures are exhilarating. Good punch and vitality in this performance.

Concerto for Brass Quintet, String Orchestra, and Percussion (1967)

Solo Instrument and Orchestra

Brass Quintet

☐ Members of the Alumni of the National Orchestral Association and American Brass Quintet / Barnett (conductor) / Composers Recordings S–229

Except in the slow movement there is considerable merging of the soli group with the strings and percussion, thereby almost constituting the normal orchestral totality. Etler's piece has considerable rhythmic merging as well, with articulating groups of seven, six, five, and four at times simultaneously focused against the five solo brasses. This has the impact of gravitational attraction, and frictional though it may be, the sonorous stuffing has sufficient and worthy identity.

The Concerto was commissioned by the American Brass Quintet (the members in this case are Edward R. Birdwell, horn; Gerard Schwarz and John W. Eckert, trumpets; Robert Biddlecome and Arnold Fromme, trombones). It has become a major repertory piece for them, and the solidly integrated playing on the recording proves it.

Concerto for Wind Quintet and Orchestra (1960)

Wind Quintet

☐ Louisville Orchestra / Fuge (flute); McAninch (oboe); Livingston (clarinet); D'Attilio (bassoon); Ball (horn) / Whitney (conductor) / Louisville 651 (monaural)

That the decided influences of Bartók and Hindemith are found in Etler's Concerto doesn't mean his is a type of second-hand and thereby second-rate creativity. The emotional power derived is to be credited to Etler. Nowhere is the chic French style of woodwind writing in evidence. Seriousness, even in the brilliant finale, is the keyword, keyed to frictioned tonality.

The Louisville Orchestra (without winds—not used in Etler's instrumentation in order to highlight the solo colors) plays with command. Their contribution is matched by elucidative and attractive five-ply soloism.

Chamber
Music

Sonata for Bassoon and Piano

☐ Schoenbach (bassoon); Levine (piano) / Columbia Special Products AMS–6421

Etler's work shows excellent concentration of resources. Mainly a study in black and white, this work's four movements are illustrative of musical objectivity, its structure the twentieth-century façade of classical cognizance. The lines are long-breathed, the music sings. It has, however, little of some of the lighter allocations that marked Etler's *Six from Ohio* or his earlier music.

These are superb musicians and they prove it. However, the remote piano sound makes a weak frame in relation to the bassoon's striking fullness of sonic impulse.

Quintet for Winds (1955)

☐ New York Woodwind Quintet / Concert-Disc 216

Etler knew his winding way with the woodwinds—he was a first-rate oboist. Most of his earlier music has cheerful temper; this work is much more seriously propounded. It has intense colorations and glistening liquidity; its sonorities are a constant joy of fresh discovery. Above all, it bypasses the generally predictable chit-chat that marks so much music for the wind quintet.

The New Yorkers give a first-rate execution of the score; the sound is full and resonant, and with excellent depth.

(Both labels of the disc indicate the Etler work. The side with four bands *is* the Etler. The other side with two bands is really Side 1 and begins with Dahl's *Allegro and Arioso* and is followed by Barber's *Summer Music*.)

Sonic Sequence (1967)

☐ American Brass Quintet / Composers Recordings S–229

Etler's chromatically laced music moves in small spans, the result of the development of a quadruple pitch pattern that embraces only a tone and one-half span. There are no smiles in Etler's grim, tone-cluster-styled music.

Sonic Sequence had not been publicly performed before being recorded. It was expressly written for inclusion on the CRI disc with another work by Etler, companioned with three pieces by Wallingford Riegger.

Franco Evangelisti   *(1926-1980)*

Instrumental

Flute

Proporzioni (1960)

☐ Gazzelloni (flute) / Mainstream 5014

Music in perpetual change, proposed with the freedom that is the badge of the post-Webern sound draftsman. Evangelisti's score consists of fragments that the performer puts together in any order he wishes. Tempo decisions are left to the flutist as well and so are repetitions.

Gazzelloni is a magician in presenting the new type of flute glides and defining the no-pitch land of flutters. He is also an excellent proxy composer or musical structuralist.

Robert Evett (1922-1975)

Harpsichord Sonata

☐ Parris (harpsichord) / Composers Recordings S–237

A favorite instrument of this talented composer. It was used in three other compositions: a Concerto for Harpsichord and Orchestra, a Sonata for Cello and Harpsichord, and a Sonata for Oboe and Harpsichord.

The style of the Harpsichord Sonata can be described as mild neo-classicism. There are four movements in alternate speeds that might remind a listener of the music of Jean Françaix without its sophistication. The final part, *My Papa's Waltz*, is inspired by a Roethke poem (it is included on the liner copy) and touches the light fantastic with a fantasy-rondo built out of *For He's a Jolly Good Fellow*. A compulsive use of squared phrases sometimes blocks meaningful flow, but in the main Evett's piece, somewhat attenuated, has intelligent simplicity.

Robert Parris, a composer in his own right, premiered Evett's work and is in full command in his recorded execution.

Instrumental

Harpsichord

Chaconne (1950)

☐ Gowen (piano) / New World Records NW–304

This music exemplifies updated Bach but with even less harmonic pungency than is found in Stravinsky's neo-classically styled scores. Evett's pithy work (a little under four minutes) has cogency and lucidity. It is a little gem and should be picked up by our concert pianists.

Bradford Gowen, the winner of the 1978 John F. Kennedy Center-Rockefeller Foundation International Competition for Excellence in the Performance of American Music, gives a vivid and well-stated interpretation.

Piano

Victor Ewald (1860-1935)

Symphony (Quintet) for Brass, Op. 5

☐ Philip Jones Brass Ensemble / Argo ZRG–655

Unproblematic music, bathed in Russian-scented waters. Ewald's complacent acceptance of traditionalistic formulae produces, of course, tuneful, reasonable, and lightly relaxing music, with well-balanced writing for the brass instruments.

Competing with the other edition available (by the American Brass Quintet, on Desto 6474/7), the Jones Ensemble version earns the right to first choice. It has a warmer manner and less pointed attacks, which is more fitting for this kind of music, and better sound reproduction. A plus is that Argo's release bands the three movements; Desto's does not. A still further plus is that Desto's issue can only be obtained in a jumbo four-record package.

Chamber Music

Manuel de Falla   *(1876-1946)*

El amor brujo (1915)

☐ Philadelphia Orchestra / Verrett (mezzo-soprano) / Stokowski (conductor) / Odyssey Y–32368

In *El amor brujo,* a young gypsy girl finds love, but her romance is haunted by the ghost of her former paramour. Attempts to exorcise the phantom (the music for this portion is the famed *Ritual Fire Dance*) are unsuccessful. Another girl accompanies the lovers to their next meeting; the ghost is distracted, succumbs to the new face, and the couple finds peace and happiness.

Despite the conception of *El amor brujo* as a one-act ballet, it is rarely seen in that form; the huge number of performances as an extracted suite of a baker's dozen numbers has led to the adoption of Falla's inspired work as a symphonic piece with or without voice, or with instrumental substitutes for the latter. The music displays moods ranging from the starkly primitive to the mournfully evocative. Brilliant and alive with color, the score is fundamentally Andalusian (considered the most characteristic region of Spain). The orchestration is a marvel of effect, though the instrumental forces are restrained—only pairs of horns and trumpets are used in the brass section.

Stokowski's performance offers a fantastic auditory experience. Not a single measure is permitted to go by casually. It is a glorious illustration of a conductor in pursuit of white-heated orchestral volatility.

Interlude and Dance No. 1 from *La vida breve* (1905)

☐ L'Orchestre de la Suisse Romande / Ansermet (conductor) / London 6224

Poignant atmosphere and ethnic veracity are contrasted in this double portion from Falla's opera, his first creation for the stage. The Interlude covers a scene in which the heroine, forsaken by her lover, approaches the villa of his new sweetheart, where a wedding party is being held. This leads into the companion piece which forms a part of the festivities. Evocative sensualism permeates the dance. The effect is eloquent.

It takes clear insight, magnificent color shaping and the right tempo to reveal the magnetism of Falla's operatic portions. All these and a rhythmic excitement that jumps right out of the record grooves are supplied by Ansermet's superb performance.

Ritual Fire Dance from *El amor brujo* (1915)

☐ New York Philharmonic / Bernstein (conductor) / Columbia M–31816
☐ Philadelphia Orchestra / Ormandy (conductor) / Columbia MS–7673

This is the piece that caused Manuel de Falla to become a household name. The orchestral setting is straight from the original ballet. No brave, new arrangement (and there have been a few dozen) can match its original color and fire.

Any orchestra of professional standing can play this exciting bit blindfolded. Naturally, all the readings are contained within miscellaneous collections or as a filler with the recording of a major-sized work. Choice is thus mainly conditioned by what comes with what, and very little by who is interpreting Falla's excerpted dance.

Those listed will cause no argument as to worth. However, the best of all performances of the *Ritual Fire Dance* remains that contained in the recording of the complete work by Leopold Stokowski on Odyssey Y–32368 (*see above* under *El amor brujo*).

The Three-Cornered Hat, Suites Nos. 1 and 2 (1919)

☐ New York Philharmonic / Bernstein (conductor) / Columbia M–31816

Here is the fullest promulgation of Hispanic sensations and the criteria for authenticity in nationalistic art. The liberating folk force not only shapes the profile of Falla's composition, but it also gives it stamina while serving as a point of departure.

If wit is paramount in the story of *El sombrero de tres picos* (see under *Ballet*), the orchestral suites form a crescendo of color and rhythmic bewitchment that ravishes the senses. Inspired by traditional native dance forms, the music is stylized by discriminating sophistication. No one-two-three-four pulsed monotony blemishes Falla's measures. In *The Neighbors,* Mozartian motility contrasts with *seguidilla* snap. The *farruca*-styled Miller's Dance is mild and also violent, a flamenco both tamed and untethered—its heel-stamping conclusion raises the temperature. And no better illustration of rhythmic ambivalence can be given than the final dance of the ballet composition, where ideas whirl along sometimes in duple and sometimes in triple beat. Presumably this is a *jota,* but no national dance remained static in Manuel de Falla's hands.

Neither does it in Leonard Bernstein's hands. A rightful aggressiveness and highly hammered rhythmic friction are on display. Great!

The Three-Cornered Hat (Suite No. 2) (1919)

☐ Paris Conservatoire Orchestra / Wolff (conductor) / London STS–15057

A performance of good intensity, in case one wishes a disc that has only the more widely performed second suite (for details *see above*). If it can be found, the deleted Reiner recording (RCA LSC–2230) is even sharper and more dynamic.

London labels this "Three Dances," which is a very loose heading and neither precise nor authentic. This follows the indicatory freedom recording companies have exhibited in the past—a practice that oversteps their prerogatives. The designations have included "Ballet Suite," "Dances," "Three Dances" (as here), "Suite," and Suite No. 2. The last is the only correct one, covering the compilation consisting of *The Neighbors,* The Miller's Dance, and a Final Dance.

Solo Instrument and Orchestra

Piano

Nights in the Gardens of Spain, Symphonic Impressions for Piano and Orchestra (1915)

☐ National Orchestra of Spain / Soriano (piano) / Argenta (conductor) / London 6046
☐ L'Orchestre de la Suisse Romande / de Larrocha (piano) / Comissiona (conductor) / London 6733

Paradoxes pile up in this triple set of nocturnal impressions. *Noches en los jardines de España* is a concerto without exhibitionism, conceived in terms of concentrated chamber music. It is orchestrated in French pastels that trace Spanish contours. If combines coolness with sensual warmth. It indicates picturesque titles but tells no story.

De Falla's "Nights" was written with no pretension of being descriptive. The composer said the music was "merely expressive," meant to evoke "sensations and sentiments." Nevertheless, many annotators have foolishly attempted to wrap the piece in a purple cloth of programmaticism. *Nights in the Gardens of Spain* grows increasingly rhythmic and excited as it progresses; but, whatever the mood or tempo, it contains all the elements and persistencies that make for impressionism—meaning that it is suggestive and not positive. De Falla's themes are too langorous, too dipped in color, and are not squared sufficiently to be developed methodically. In this colorful instance Hispanic impressionism clearly produces its own brand of clarity and powerful effect.

Recordings of this composition come and go with regularity. In a book published some fifteen years ago I discussed eleven recorded performances of Falla's work. Of these, eight are no longer in the current catalogue, covering performances by Casadesus, Ciccolini, Curzon, del Pueyo, Haskil, Loriod, Soriano (with Frühbeck de Burgos conducting), and one uncredited pianist. Three remain from that group (one in mono: Novaes) and there have been four additions.

Regardless of the recorded traffic, the presentation of Gonzalo Soriano with the late Ataulfo Argenta conducting has remained through all these many years in first place and no edition has appeared to remove it. These musicians portray the most defined Spanish character, color, and atmosphere. Theirs can be classified as *the* definitive version. Coming very close is the Alicia de Larrocha–Sergiu Comissiona partnership. Their performance has a sensitive atmosphere and warm poetry. Additionally, the subtle intensity portrayed by both soloist and orchestra is strikingly idiomatic.

Homenaje: Pour le tombeau de Debussy (1920)

☐ de la Torre (guitar) / Nonesuch 71233

An elegiac mood is maintained within a basic habanera metrical design. By employing an instrument most representative of his native land, Falla paid further homage to Debussy's evocative Spanish-styled and colored music.

At a later date Falla incorporated his "To the Memory of Debussy" in a *Suite sinfonica* for orchestra titled *Homenajes* ("Homages"). Not an important work, it was once available in two editions on RCA Victor and Angel—both eventually deleted.

Nonesuch titles Falla's work in an abbreviated form: "Homenaje a Debussy." A statistical fault. There is no fault with Rey de la Torre's playing. His instrument sings with effortless grace, beautiful clarity, and comprehensive knowledge of line.

Cuatro piezas españolas (1908)

Fantasia Baetica (1919)

☐ de Larrocha (piano) / London 6881

In the "Four Spanish Pieces" the harmony is woven and the color applied in representative Falla style, while the indigenous authenticity of the forms remains unaltered. Except for the third piece (*Montañesa*), where the sounds are wrapped in a perfumed, impressionistic cloth, the music has the fullest Spanish identity.

De Larrocha presents with the greatest clarity the guitar imitations of the *Andaluza*, the *jota* patterns of the *Argonesa*, and the irresistible beat of the *Cubana*. Her playing represents an enthusiastic combining of formality with native illumination. She illustrates how to interpret the simplest domestic elements and still propound forceful artistic logic.

Instrumental

Guitar

Piano

The *Fantasia Bética* (or *Baetica,* the ancient Roman name for Andalusia, where Falla was born) has the identifiable slant of folklore but is unlocalized. It is not a sonorous postcard for a tourist in search of a picturesque snapshot. The *Fantasia* (Falla's last and longest composition for solo piano, twelve and one-half minutes in length) is a musical mural that portrays a cross-section of Hispanic sensations. Agitated merging rhythms, guitar sound synonyms, broad lines, and keyboard song provide a compendium of Falla's creative credo.

Fantasy though it is, Falla's work must not sound like a potpourri. De Larrocha understands the basic purity, depth, and continuity of the piece. Her performance of it is stunning.

Homenaje: Pour le tombeau de Debussy (1920)

☐ Richard (piano) / Nonesuch 71135

Originally for guitar (see under *guitar*). Jean-Charles Richard plays "To the Memory of Debussy" acceptably, but the sound is hard-edged.

Nocturno
Pour le tombeau de Paul Dukas (1935)

☐ Achúcarro (piano) / RCA AGL1–1967

The *Nocturno* is stylistically in the Chopin manner, with not even a modicum of Falla's usual accent. The performance of this tuneful music, colored by its minor tonality, is sensitive.

The forty-two-measure "To the Memory of Paul Dukas" is not comparable in size to its emotional cogency. The music has no Spanish slant, no contrapuntal communication, merely dark, paean-like harmonies set in F minor, which conclude in a poignant, unresolved addition to the tonic chord. Another sensitive portrayal by Joaquín Achúcarro.

Serenata Andaluza

☐ Richard (piano) / Nonesuch 71135

This piece is not to be confused with the *Andaluza* that constitutes the last of the "Four Spanish Pieces" (see above under *Cuatro piezas españolas*). Pahissa, the composer's biographer, makes no mention of this lollipop. No shame for Falla, no credits either. If there are any, give them to the pianist, who tosses the work off acceptably.

Suite from El amor brujo (1915)
Three Dances from The Three-Cornered Hat (1919)

☐ de Larrocha (piano) / London 6881

The ebullient rhythms of Falla's ballet *El sombrero de tres picos* have sufficient strength to register in his keyboard arrangement. On the other hand, the piano version of *El amor brujo,* also arranged by the composer himself, is felt by some to blight Falla's catalogue.

If they heard de Larrocha's performances, they would change their opinion. She provides stunning conceptions in both cases. In the famous *Ritual Fire Dance* she plays the warhorse straight on, without the three errors so many make in an effort to draw more out of it on the piano than it has. There is no dynamic poking about, no teasing of phrases, and no false tempo shifts. The color she provides in *El amor brujo* almost makes one forget the orchestral setting.

Valse capriccio

☐ Achúcarro (piano) / RCA AGL1–1967

An early pianistic snapshot, in style a salon daguerrotype. Absolutely unimportant, but still good to have on disc as documentation of Falla's output.

Concerto for Harpsichord (or Piano), Flute, Oboe, Clarinet, Violin, and Cello (1926)

Chamber Music

☐ Members of the New York Philharmonic / Kipnis (harpsichord) / Boulez (conductor) / Columbia M–33970

The title of Falla's work has led to severe differences of opinion as to whether it is a solo vehicle accompanied by five players, or a work for six players *in toto*. In form, content, and instrumental style, the conception harks back to the days of the *sonata da camera* or *concerto da camera,* that is, a chamber work in sonata or concerto form. The Concerto is certainly ensemble music, not only because it is limited to six players but because the composer has indicated that all are "soloists" (read: equal to each other). Furthermore, although more grandiloquent speech is given to the keyboard instrument, the balances of the piece are those of chamber style.

De Falla's three-movement work is less Spanish than broadly neo-classic. The composer lives in the twentieth century and muses in retrospect. Notwithstanding the formula of free tonality and shifting harmonic roots, with some chordal brushing that uses the paints of combined keys, these deliberations do not interfere with the refined quality that cannot be termed other than classic. The Concerto becomes as much a hybrid of means (in harmony, form, and color) as is its title.

The basic compositional style can be recognized at the very start. The harpsichord plays in clear D major, but its rhythm is complicated by two rates of combined periodicities. To this, sharp string chords are pinned, one instrument being in the distinctly opposed key of E flat minor. Thus tradition mingles with modernity. In the final Vivace, a pertinent Spanish rhythm is employed, combining duple with triple patterns. Casting such rhythmic binomials in an eighteenth-century tonal setting shows the neo-classic hand at its best. De Falla connects his own art with those of his forebears in a composition singular in his entire output.

This performance is direct and pungent. In the middle movement both pace and explanation follow the *energico* in Falla's tempo indication, a matter somewhat edited in other recorded performances. Balances are perfect and so are the sonics.

Seven Popular Spanish Songs (1914)

Vocal

Voice with Accompaniment

☐ de los Angeles (soprano); Soriano (piano) / Angel S–35775

De Falla did not want his music to be called "delicate." Regardless, the integration within these songs illustrates a delicate fusion between free will and folk winnowing. Neither is emphasized. Mirroring the native ethos and remaining himself at the same time, Falla creates a fresh music, honestly Spanish, totally removed from the pseudo-provincial shallowness that marks self-conscious "Spanish style."

The songs contain the procedures Falla used from the start of his career: an enlargement of triadic harmony, a romantically blended *cantabile* undertone, intensely proportioned rhythm framed in designs that display the contents without rigidity. Clear and powerful, the songs speak of Spain with the individual diction of Falla. In this manner indigenous art has universal effect.

Each one of the performances of the *Siete canciones populares españolas* is a recreative gem. The recording deserves a place in every collector's library.

Opera and Dramatic Music

El retablo de Maese Pedro (1919)

☐ National Orchestra of Spain / Bermejo (soprano); Munguia (tenor); Torres (baritone) / Argenta (conductor) / London STS–15014

Operatic conventions take a holiday in this one-act marionette musical play with grand opera trimmings. De Falla's "Master Peter's Puppet Show" is an adaptation of classical Spanish idiom into neo-nationalism, mixed with *authentica* (such as street cries) and a tinge of secularized liturgicalism. Everything is concentrated and intimate, even the orchestra, which includes a harpsichord.

The tale is based on a section from Cervantes's *Don Quixote*. Don Quixote and Sancho Panza are watching a puppet group act out a Castilian adventure dealing with a captive fair lady, freed by her man in armor from the villainous Moors. Thinking the puppets to be real, Don Quixote attacks them, destroying the little theater of Master Peter. Two sizes of puppets are required: miniature ones for the show and larger ones for the onlookers—the singers are in the orchestra pit. De Falla was meticulous in his instructions, indicating that the singers must avoid all theatrical mannerisms, and minutely specifying the exact way each of the puppet characters was to be vocally portrayed.

The unusual format of *El retablo* has limited its presentation. However, the crystal-clear, picturesque music offers plenty of interest even if no staging takes place. In its avoidance of clichés Falla's score represents an ideal of musical purity, without forsaking operatic dramatics.

The pointed exactness of Argenta's direction, the precise following of Falla's vocal instructions (particularly by Julita Bermejo as the one who describes the action), and the performance's declarative quality make this a superior recording.

La vida breve (1905)

☐ Orquesta Nacional de España and Orfeon Donostiarra / de los Angeles and Higueras (sopranos); Rivadeneyra (mezzo-soprano); Cossutta, Higuero, and de Andia (tenors); Moreno and Villarejo (baritones); de Narké (bass-baritone); Tena (castanets); Monge (guitar) / Frühbeck de Burgos (conductor) / Angel S–3672

Active and assertive, *La vida breve* is a tragedy that fits in the operatic cubbyhole neatly and comfortably. Salud, a blacksmith's daughter, is in love with Paco. He deserts her for a girl of the upper class. Salud breaks into the wedding celebration, reproaches her seducer, and then falls dead.

There's plenty of Spanish lace in Falla's creation, and it is produced with great beauty in this recorded version. There is also plenty of Italian fringework. Nevertheless, the stylistic merger is neatly made and is acceptable. De Falla was a young composer when he wrote his opera, but no cheap compositional histrionics interfere with the music's progress.

The orchestral color (except for the famous Dance—see under *Orchestra:* Interlude and Dance No. 1 from *La vida breve*—and a choral-dance section) has a subdued quality. Even in the most native-tempered sections Falla generally avoids a "big guitar" sound. The dark timbres employed fit this score, which unfolds like a gigantic set of Lieder.

This is an impressive cast. There isn't a weak singer in the total group. Victoria de los

Angeles as Salud delivers her part with exquisite taste and projects perfectly styled vocalism, while Carlos Cossutta's dark quality fits as a perfect contrast for the plot's good and evil basis. Gabriel Moreno, as El Cantaor, deserves special credit for his emotive singing of the Andalusian songs that open the second act. The colorful choral scenes are fully integrated and the resultant clarity of dramatic action is rare in operatic recordings. The touches are many: for example, the rhythmic hand clapping accompanying the Dance, the sense of activity, and the guests' cries of *Viva!* and *Olé!* In all, an eloquent and exciting production.

The Three-Cornered Hat (1919) *Ballet*

☐ New York Philharmonic / DeGaetani (mezzo-soprano) / Boulez (conductor) / Columbia M–33970

A ballet tale about a flirtatious miller's wife, the attempts of the old *corregidor* of the province to seduce her, the seeming compromise of the wife, and confusion by mistaken identity. With the eventual clearing of the village air all ends happily and the old roué gets his just deserts. It is almost like a Viennese operetta transplanted to Spain.

Though the excerpted set of three dances so often heard (see under Orchestra, [*The Three-Cornered Hat*, Suite No. 2]), is exhilarating, the complete ballet (first produced in the summer of 1919) is thrice so. Here we have the total that enhances the sections commonly known. Most ballets gain by excerpting, Falla's great score for *El Sombrero de tres picos* does not.

Boulez displays the proper temperament for this score. Exuberance and vitality are all they should be, and his rhythmic realism and virtuosic-timed discipline bring out all of the ballet's richnesses. Though Berganza has more earthy sexuality in her contributions to the Ansermet-led edition (London 6224), DeGaetani makes up for the difference by her impeccably styled vocal luminosity. Columbia's is the best in the catalogue.

Falla / **Paul Kochanski (1887 - 1934)**

Suite populaire espagnole *Instrumental*

Violin

☐ Szeryng (violin); Janopoulo (piano) / Everest 3153E (monaural)

The quality of these miniatures makes them perfect vehicles for string vocalism.

Some fancy titling on the label. The *Drap mauresque* is actually *El paño moruno* ("The Moorish Cloth"); The *Berceuse* originally was called *Nana*, and *Asturienne* should properly read *Asturiana*.

Good playing by Szeryng, only fair sound from Everest.

Falla / **Fritz Kreisler (1875 - 1962)**

Spanish Dance from *La vida breve* *Instrumental*

Violin

☐ Szeryng (violin); Janopoulo (piano) / Everest 3153E (monaural)

Fritz Kreisler's *La vida breve* transcription is probably the most famous of any made from Falla's catalogue. The sensuousness of the music lends itself to multicolored violin sound. Kreisler was a master of musical resetting, avoiding cheap effects and unstylistic bargains.

Falla / Maurice Maréchal (1892 - 1964)

Instrumental

Cello

Suite populaire espagnole

☐ Starker (cello); Pommers (piano) / Everest 3222E (monaural)

This is the secondary title for Falla's Seven Popular Spanish Songs, chosen when transcription of six of the group was made first by Paul Kochanski, for violin, and then by Maréchal, for cello.

Starker gives Falla's musical outpour its full head in his rendition. Not the best of sound, but the super playing comes through nonetheless.

Harold Farberman   (1929-   )

Orchestra

Elegy, Fanfare, and March

☐ Stuttgart Philharmonic / Farberman (conductor) / Serenus 12016

There is plenty of direct contrast in forms, moods, and colors in this three-part piece. The Elegy calls for strings alone; the full orchestra is used for the other two movements. Serialism is at work here, coupling Schoenbergian restlessness with vividly direct orchestration. The performance is assured. With the composer on the podium it is definitive.

Percussion

Alea, A Game of Chance, for Six Percussion Players

☐ Pugwash Percussion Ensemble / Farberman (conductor) / Serenus 12064

Not much of the pings and pit-a-pats of the pulsatile instrumental family, but much more of its stubby and stuffy sounds. In addition, there is some handclapping and some whispering. All of it is percussively poetic. All of it is executed with proper scale and sensitive relationship. (The Pugwash group is described in the liner notes as "six of the finest percussionists to be found in the area of the New York Philharmonia.")

Solo Instrument and Orchestra

Saxophone

Concerto for Alto Saxophone and String Orchestra

☐ Strings of the Stuttgart Philharmonia / Estrin (saxophone) / Farberman (conductor) / Serenus 12016

The effect of Farberman's concerto—and an extremely powerful one it is—is one of a sax player improvising in a late-night jam session. It is an uncanny, written-down statement but it sounds free of notated documentation. The sax solo part includes glides, gushes, gusts, wails, whips, bent and brazen sounds, as well as punch-it-home virtuosity.

Tough to play, fascinating to listen to. Harvey Estrin's soloistic personality is superb. The string orchestra adds its own quota of color and what they have is handled with the same certainty that the soloist displays.

Trio for Violin, Piano, and Percussion

Chamber Music

☐ New York Studio Trio / Serenus 12016

Lots of action and lots of color, but they are always in partnership with clear thematics and rhythmic patterns. Lots of percussion, with the special colors being drawn from a dozen antique cymbals, graduated sets of cymbals (three), wood blocks (four), and a Chinese bell tree.

High-standard playing. The Serenus organization tabs the performers with a name for its one-time recording gig, which is rather silly. Accordingly, here is the personnel: Gerald Tarack, violin; Robert Miller, piano; and the composer, Harold Farberman, as the percussionist.

Three States of Mind (for Six Musicians)

☐ New York Studio Sextet / Serenus 12016

The "six musicians" play violin, piano, trumpet, cello, flute, and percussion. Again (*see above:* Trio for Violin, Piano, and Percussion) Serenus gives a name for the group though it is obvious that it came together solely to tape the piece for its later disc release. Individual credit would have been more appropriate. The sextet includes Gerald Tarack, violin; Robert Miller, piano; Joe Newman, trumpet; Charles McCracken, cello; Hubert Laws, flute; and Harold Farberman (the composer), percussion.

This is rhapsodically nervous music. It is full of sound jabs and fragments, weaving in asymmetric rhythms, very much alive and not music to slumber by. Expertly played.

Ferenc Farkas (1905-   )

Chanson de l'aube

Choral

Chorus Alone

☐ Budapest Madrigal Ensemble / Szekeres (conductor) / Monitor S-2054

Farkas masks his Hungarian creative profile in this supple and savory setting, the words being pinned onto an old French troubadour air. The "Dawn Song" is a very short item so one had best play it twice or three times successively in order to soak in the flavor and enjoy mighty fine music-making by a group of sixteen beautifully balanced voices.

John Farmer (16th-17th cent.)

Fair Nymphs I Heard One Telling

Choral

Chorus Alone

☐ Purcell Consort of Voices / Burgess (conductor) / Turnabout 34202

A six-part madrigal that Farmer (an Irish or English sixteenth- or seventeenth- century composer) contributed to the famous collection *The Triumphs of Oriana*, a set of twenty-five madrigals written to honor Queen Elizabeth I. Farmer's piece is gaily testimonial in character, ending with the same words as all the others in the collection, "Long live fair Oriana," Oriana being the poetic title for the Queen. Beautiful singing by the group of two sopranos, countertenor, tenor, baritone, and bass.

Giles Farnaby (ca. 1565-1640)

Instrumental

Harpsichord

Giles Farnaby's Dream — His Rest — Farnaby's Conceit — His Humour

The New Sa-hoo

The Old Spagnoletta

Tell Me, Daphne

A Toye

Up Tails All

☐ Kipnis (harpsichord) / Angel 3816

A selection of pieces that illustrate the lively, fresh imagination of this composer. In Kipnis's keen and sympathetic performances the music registers splendidly.

Lynnwood W. Farnam (1885-1930)

Instrumental

Organ

Toccata on *O Filii et Filiae*

☐ Harmon (organ) / Orion 76255

This is presumably the only organ composition by this famous organ virtuoso. And virtuosic is the descriptive word for the piece. It's a powerhouse that brings down the house.

Arthur Farwell (1872-1952)

Instrumental

Piano

Navajo War Dance

Pawnee Horses

☐ Basquin (piano) / New World Records NW-213

The Dance is much more respectable than warlike. *Pawnee Horses,* music that keeps moving through a gentle, syncopated rhythm, is based on an Omaha melody. Neither piece represents the most important Indian music Farwell wrote, but for small recorded gifts one must be grateful.

(The version Farwell made of the *Navajo War Dance* for chorus [see under *Choral: chorus alone*] stems from the same material, but the creative decisions are different and take a bit longer to be made.)

Navajo War Dance **No. 2, Op. 29**

☐ Johannesen (piano) / Golden Crest S-4065

This is an example of this composer's pioneer efforts to promulgate native ideas for American music. Johannesen conquers all the demands, which include a driving pace and bravura octaves and chords.

(The numerical designation is not indicated on either jacket or label.)

Quintet in E minor for Piano and Strings, Op. 103

Chamber Music

☐ James (piano); Erickson and Rosenberger (violins); Kissling (viola); Warkentin (cello) / Musical Heritage Society MHS-3827

Farwell is one of America's overlooked composers. No folk stuff here but the style of solid late romanticism. However, the material flows freely with large lyrical phrases so there is no stolidity, therefore, and for that matter no sentimentality either. The color of the second movement, derived from a reiterative pitch point, is most individual.

Good playing. No vestige in this instance of the excessive symphonicism that haunts so many piano quintet performances.

Three Indian Songs, Op. 32

Vocal

Voice with Accompaniment

☐ Parker (baritone); Huckaby (piano) / New World Records NW-213

This is the real thing, with Farwell's harmonizations; the melodies are transcribed from songs of the Omaha tribe. The version of the third of the set, The Old Man's Love Song, for unaccompanied chorus (see under *Choral: chorus alone*), while based on the same material, is an entirely different conception.

Navajo War Dance, Op. 102, No. 1

The Old Man's Love Song, Op. 102, No. 2

Choral

Chorus Alone

☐ New World Singers / Miner (conductor) / New World Records NW-213

Masterly transmutations that retain the original source data. Not self-conscious (meaning naïve) but artistically integrated Indian music.

There isn't much depth in the singing. There is apparently a small total of vocalists in the New World group. A few pitch problems are also noticeable. However, Farwell on disc is better than no Farwell at all.

Johann Friedrich Fasch   *(1688-1758)*

Sinfonia

In A major / In G major

String Orchestra

☐ Jean-François Paillard Chamber Orchestra / Paillard (conductor) / RCA FRL1-5468

Telemann all over again, but with slightly less color. The usual structures are detailed by the usual good playing of this organization.

Concerto à 8 for Trumpet, Strings, and Continuo

Solo Instrument and Orchestra

Trumpet

☐ Consortium Musicum / Tarr (trumpet); Müller-Dombois (lute); Thoene (harpsichord); Bickbach (positive organ) / Lehan (conductor) / Nonesuch 71217

This is music depicted by the conventional three-movement plan, including the high trumpet in apt antiphonal address with the strings. The mood and the material are heard in a good musical presentation.

Concerto in D major for Trumpet, Two Oboes, and Strings

☐ Academy of St. Martin-in-the-Fields / Wilbraham (trumpet); Tilney (harpsichord) / Marriner (conductor) / Argo ZRG–585

A brilliant specimen of high trumpet playing. John Wilbraham tosses off the flourishes and filigrees in the extreme register with a spontaneity that is striking. Give full credit for the logic applied to the dynamic planes to Neville Marriner. There is no doubt that the interaction of the soloist and the orchestra in this performance makes a major musical exhibit from Fasch's made-to-pattern baroque piece.

Chamber Music

Sonata in B flat major for Recorder, Oboe, Violin, and Continuo

☐ Concentus Musicus of Denmark / Nonesuch 71064

A highlight among the plethora of baroque music literature. The instrumentation is already larger than the usual trio sonata format, with viola da gamba, violone, and harpsichord as the continuo. The second movement fugue is a gem; the following Grave has Bachian intensity.

The performance is constant in its expressivity—a fine achievement.

Gabriel Fauré   (1845-1924)

Orchestra

Masques et bergamasques, Op. 112

☐ L'Orchestre de Paris / Baudo (conductor) / Seraphim S–60273
☐ L'Orchestre de la Suisse Romande / Ansermet (conductor) / London 6227

Neo-classic music set (with the exception of a harp) for a classic instrumentation of double winds, two each of horns and trumpets, timpani, and the usual strings.

There are four movements: *Ouverture, Menuet, Gavotte,* and *Pastorale.* There is little difference between the two orchestras that have recorded this fine, little-known work. Ansermet presses onward in the *Ouverture* and this is more propitious for the music. On the other hand, Baudo brings out more in the *Pastorale,* which incidentally is not as well scored as the other movements in the suite.

Pavane, Op. 50

☐ L'Orchestre National de la Radiodiffusion Française / Beecham (conductor) / Seraphim S–60000

Beecham moves it along, which is a plus compared to the snail's pace so often applied to this sensitive bit of beauty. (For the version with chorus, see under *Choral: chorus and orchestra.*)

Pelléas et Mélisande, Op. 80

☐ L'Orchestre de Paris / Baudo (conductor) / Seraphim S–60273
☐ L'Orchestre de la Suisse Romande / Ansermet (conductor) / London 6227

The four-part suite Fauré drew from the incidental music he wrote for the Maeterlinck play has a fervency in the first and last movements that is highly eloquent. Ansermet reverses movements 3 and 4 and thereby ends the suite on a more "up" mood with the *Sicilienne,* rather than with the tragic atmosphere of *The Death of Mélisande,* which is the original (and relevant) conclusion. Complete disagreement with this must be registered.

Otherwise Ansermet's treatment of the suite is good, especially the dignity he imparts to the *Prélude,* and despite the questionable restrained pace he applies to the music of *The Spinner.*

Baudo's tempi are all fine, and his orchestra plays with a subtlety that is extremely profitable. However, Ansermet's performance of the death music is the best ever registered on disc. It has a forward movement that gives an emotional impetus to the music rather than dragging the pulse because of its tragic climate.

The Munch version (Odyssey Y–31017) is played to the hilt by the lusciously toned Philadelphia Orchestra and thereby receives a negative verdict. Fatness does not fit the frame of this ultra-sensitive music. The Orchestra of Radio Luxembourg, conducted by Louis de Froment (Turnabout 34587), is a poor fourth. Not bad average quality, but the oboe's tone is pinched, the clarinet breaks lines, and there is some question as to rhythmic definition in a few places.

Prelude to *Pénélope* (1913)

☐ L'Orchestre de la Suisse Romande / Ansermet (conductor) / London 6227

Ansermet plays this dark-lined introduction to *Pénélope* (subtitled *Lyric Poem*)—a three-act work with text by René Fauchois—with balanced intensity. The sections featuring the trumpet are well conceived.

Elégie for Cello and Orchestra, Op. 24

☐ Philadelphia Orchestra / Rose (cello) / Ormandy (conductor) / Columbia M–30113

Rose plays Fauré's C minor beauty with eloquence. Ormandy's accompaniment is as sympathetic as one could possibly expect.

Ballade in F sharp minor for Piano and Orchestra, Op. 19

☐ City of Birmingham Symphony Orchestra / Ogdon (piano) / Fremaux (conductor) / Klavier 527

This is the second consideration Fauré made of this work (for the initial one, see under *Instrumental: piano*), with the scoring calling for woodwinds, horns, and strings, and the same opus number in both cases.

The sense of elegance combined with clarification of detail that John Ogdon brings to the score makes his recording superior to the other performances available on disc. Casadesus with Bernstein conducting the New York Philharmonic on Columbia MS–6377 offers a somewhat subdued conception, but it is still better than the one offered by Devetzi, with Baudo conducting the Paris Conservatory Orchestra, on Nonesuch 71178—which is a rather pedantic affair.

Fantaisie for Piano and Orchestra, Op. 111

☐ London Philharmonic Orchestra / de Larrocha (piano) / Frühbeck de Burgos (conductor) / London 6878

What is appealing in this Fauré piece is the subtle virtuosity of its piano writing—elaborate, but far from the drive and hustle school of inscription. Plenty of cantilena also. It takes aristocratic playing to produce the required effect and this is warmly represented by Alicia de Larrocha.

The competing issue features Grant Johannesen (on Turnabout 34587), and he delivers a faultless conception. However, his orchestral back-up is dry and dull. Though

Solo Instrument and Orchestra

Cello

Piano

the orchestra isn't given much to say, nonetheless the L.P.O. plays what it does have with vitality and tonal pith. (Turnabout's orchestra is the Orchestra of Radio Luxembourg, conducted by Louis de Froment.)

Instrumental

Flute

Fantaisie, **Op. 79**

☐ Hoberman (flute); Stannard (piano) / Avant 1015

Two-sectioned in tempo and laced with the usual Fauré lyrical largesse, this is the only work he wrote for the instrument. Performance: O.K.

Harp

Impromptu, Op. 86

Une Châtelaine en sa tour, **Op. 110**

☐ McDonald (harp) / Klavier KS–525

Opus 110 was inspired by a Verlaine poem. Its lyrical view is similar to the Impromptu. The Impromptu has the effect of a line drawing embellished with harpistic material. It is played with lively elegance.

Piano

Ballade **in F sharp minor, Op. 19**

☐ Doyen (piano) / Musical Heritage Society MHS–1770/71

This is the original version, which later was redrafted for piano and orchestra (see under *Solo Instrument and Orchestra: piano*). The larger setting did not replace the initial one, and both have complete viability.

It is impossible to understand Liszt's remark about Fauré's piece that it was "very difficult." Musically, perhaps, but certainly not in terms of technical requirements. Musically and, of course, technically, Jean Doyen illuminates every note in the score. His is a broadly stated conception, making more transparent the charm of this spacious composition. Ogdon, the soloist in the version with orchestral accompaniment, plays it a bit tighter, with more emphasis on its chromatic colors.

Barcarolle

No. 1 in A minor, Op. 26 / No. 2 in G major, Op. 41 / No. 3 in G flat major, Op. 42 / No. 4 in A flat major, Op. 44 / No. 5 in F sharp minor, Op. 66 / No. 6 in E flat major, Op. 70 / No. 7 in D minor, Op. 90 / No. 8 in D flat major, Op. 96 / No. 9 in A minor, Op. 101 / No. 10 in A minor, Op. 104, No. 2 / No. 11 in G minor, Op. 105, No. 1 / No. 12 in E flat major, Op. 105, No. 2 / No. 13 in C major, Op. 116

☐ Collard (piano) / Connoisseur Society 2078

A number of pianists have recorded the entire set of Fauré's *Barcarolles*. There are quibbles to be raised in each case, including about Collard's statements. Still, the highest average is his. No one has as much warmth or matches his probity of the music. It is sharply defined, both in the design (the musicality of the accompanying figures in No. 1 and the rhythmic detail in No. 5 are but two examples) and in the specific mood (for instance, the austerity in the seventh piece and the wistfulness of the tenth of the group).

Grant Johannesen's playing (on Golden Crest) comes closest to Collard's point of view. However, the G. C. sound is not tops and it is a doubtful privilege to have to purchase three separate two-disc albums in order to obtain Johannesen's performances of the entire set of thirteen.

The Golden Crest tri-album release of the "complete works for piano" ("complete" with one missing, the *Ballade,* Opus 19) is very poorly planned. Although it is true that three sets (the Impromptus, *Pièces brèves,* and *Préludes* are complete in S-4030 and the three *Romances sans paroles* are played as a unit in S-4048, not only the group of thirteen *Barcarolles* but the thirteen Nocturnes, and the four *Valse-Caprices* are scattered in three albums (S-4030, S-4046, and S-4048). Not only are they scattered, but in no case have they been recorded in any chronological order within the individual albums.

Impromptu No. 1 in E flat major, Op. 25

Impromptu No. 2 in F minor, Op. 31

Impromptu No. 3 in A flat major, Op. 34

Impromptu No. 4 in D flat major, Op. 91

Impromptu No. 5 in F sharp minor, Op. 102

Mazurka in B flat major, Op. 32

☐ Doyen (piano) / Musical Heritage Society MHS-1773/74

There is a stability in Doyen's playing that provides the enduring substances of these pieces. From the nature of their playing there is always the suspicion that pianists approach Fauré with the sense that only a light, somewhat lacy style is in order. At least, that's the result and it does frustrate Fauré's purpose and meaning. Full credit, then, to Doyen, whose playing is matched by golden, resonant sound.

Nocturne

No. 1 in E flat minor, Op. 33, No. 1 / No. 2 in B major, Op. 33, No. 2 / No. 3 in A flat major, Op. 33, No. 3 / No. 4 in E flat major, Op. 36 / No. 5 in B flat major, Op. 37 / No. 6 in D flat major, Op. 63 / No. 7 in C sharp minor, Op. 74 / No. 9 in B minor, Op. 97 / No. 10 in E minor, Op. 99 / No. 11 in F sharp minor, Op. 104, No. 1 / No. 12 in E minor, Op. 107 / No. 13 in B minor, Op. 119

☐ Doyen (piano) / Musical Heritage Society MHS-1770/71

The eighth of Fauré's Nocturnes forms the last of the *Pièces brèves,* which is discussed below. This is understandable, since the "Short Pieces" are grouped under one opus, while the other Nocturnes, aside from the three in Opus 33, were each assigned an individual opus number. Evelyne Crochet, in her survey of Fauré's complete piano music (in two volumes, each containing three discs, on Vox SVBX-5423 and SVBX-5424), likewise plays the eighth Nocturne as part of the *Pièces brèves.*

The significant differences in this group of pieces range from the dark-toned contour of the first and the serenity of the next pair to the tensions heard in the final one. Though Fauré's intellectual processes differ, the capacity of Doyen to match his conceptions accordingly provides a fine re-creative experience.

Pièces brèves, **Op. 84**

Préludes, **Op. 103**

Romances sans paroles, **Op. 17**

☐ Doyen (piano) / Musical Heritage Society MHS-1773/74

The eight "Short Pieces" cover a variety of formal patterns, including a Capriccio, an Improvisation, and a pair of fugues. The last of the group is a Nocturne in D flat major and is numbered eight among Fauré's thirteen Nocturnes (*see above*). There are nine different-keyed preludes and a total of three "Songs Without Words" in Opus 17.

Fine portrayals, sensitive to Fauré's harmonic meanings, with vocalized lyricism exhibited in Opus 17, plus all the smooth technique to make music from the etude-manifests found in several of the preludes. At all times Doyen beautifully probes matters of texture related to movement.

Theme and Variations, Op. 73
Valse-Caprice No. 1 in A major, Op. 30
Valse-Caprice No. 2 in D flat major, Op. 38
Valse-Caprice No. 3 in G flat major, Op. 59
Valse-Caprice No. 4 in A flat major, Op. 62

☐ Crochet (piano) / Vox SVBX–5423

Crochet provides graceful and elegant conceptions of the salonistic waltzes. This is matched by fine flexibility in the playing of the eleven variations, apparently written in 1910 for a competition under the aegis of the Paris Conservatoire.

Piano, Four Hands

Dolly, for Piano Four-Hands, Op. 56

☐ Jean and Geneviève Doyen (piano) / Musical Heritage Society MHS–1773/74

Light Fauré, a little more substantial than a musical bonbon. The rendition is a felicitous one. (For the orchestral version, see under *Fauré/Rabaud: Orchestra.*)

Violin

Berceuse, Op. 16

☐ Elman (violin); Seiger (piano) / Vanguard 71173

A muted miniature that floats into the ear with artistic simplicity. A number of violinists have been drawn to the work, but Elman's consideration is the most sensitive.

Chamber Music

Sonata in A major for Violin and Piano, Op. 13

☐ Heifetz (violin); Smith (piano) / RCA LM–2074 (monaural)

If one word were required to describe Fauré's music, most especially this work, that word would be "elegant." But together with this is the most demarcated clarity and sense of unified style. Balanced proportions, immaculate translation of spiritual values into music make this a light composition, but one never bordering on a state of triviality.

Heifetz is in fine form here, with playing of marked warmth in the first pair of movements. Both performers scamper through the *Allegro vivo* via its single pulse per measure with immaculate feathery percussiveness and complete the Sonata with fluid tonal partnership.

Sonata No. 2 in G minor for Cello and Piano, Op. 117

☐ Kessler (cello); Carmen (piano) / Orion 73124

The reflective austerity of this sonata is due mainly to the fact that Fauré refused to use a baritone instrument in mezzo-soprano regions. As a result, the music is given a grave quality by the color of the cello homophonically singing its way throughout. There were no Straussian *Don Quixote* supercilious supererogations in Fauré's make-up. He considered a cello sonata as a vehicle for an instrumental baritone-tenor to sing his poetry.

Fauré's type of lyricism demands subtle recitation, and in that respect the Kessler-Carmen team is not always successful. However, when the material is straightforward, stated in a sustained manner, they are fully convincing.

Trio for Piano, Violin, and Cello, Op. 120

☐ Eymar (piano); Kehr (violin); Braunholz (cello) / Vox SVBX-5100

The durability of sobriety, of tempered writing, relaxed and yet grounded with as much strength as any work making thrice the sound, is to be heard in this expressive trio. Fauré's stylistic, rhythmic habit—only to be indulged in by those who can carry off the difficult matter of cloistering the metrical impulse—is heard throughout.

In addition to the Vox disc, another recording is available, on Oiseau-Lyre S-289. Neither is the last word, and both tend to brashness. The Vox release has a lesser percentage of the latter.

Piano Quartet in C minor, Op. 15

☐ Members of the Guarneri Quartet / Rubinstein (piano) / RCA ARL1-0761

For those who still think of Fauré as a cool, detached composer, the rebuttal lies in the outer movements of his C minor piano quartet. The entire work is still another example of this man's cultured music that has a freshness that never stales.

The performers give full justice, with erudite sense of balance, to this warm and expressive work. The playing of the Scherzo is delicate and yet makes neatly clear Fauré's sensitive combinations of binomial and trinomial pulses within specific beats or their non-symmetrical assortment within the measures. The Rubinstein-Guarneri is about the best recording around now; the old monaural Columbia (ML-5343), made by Alexander Schneider, Milton Katims, Frank Miller, and Mieczyslaw Horszowski, was even a bit more fluent.

Piano Quartet in G minor, Op. 45

☐ Eymar (piano); Kehr (violin); Sichermann (viola); Braunholz (cello) / Vox SVBX-5100

A fluent and well-crafted performance. Especially fine in presentation is the second movement, an *Allegro molto*. There, the main theme sounds syncopatively over a "noodling" repetitive *Alberti bass*, never quite deciding whether it will swim in duple or triple metrical channels. The slow movement is delivered with good style. This movement builds into a Siciliano-like theme, one engendered with the warmth and delicacy of a *great* melody. Though the performers don't recognize and define all the inner pendants of Fauré's writing, there is sufficient exposure to prove that this movement is one of the most expressive in the entire Fauré literature.

String Quartet, Op. 121

☐ Guarneri Quartet / RCA ARL1-0761

The poetic diction and certain of the techniques one observes, for instance, in Schumann's quartets will be felt in this Frenchman's music. The use of syncopation, which instigates a quiet drive without recourse to frenetic *allegro* writing, and a gentle, semi-sad, romantic quality combine with the *élégance* that is French.

This style demands sensitive response to the variations in harmonic nuance that fill the pages of Fauré's work—in which one may observe the harmonic simmering that finally was fulfilled in the neo-classically formed works of Stravinsky. It is this recognition that is so beautiful in the Guarneri conception. A richer tonal quality also makes the Guarneri Quartet's edition preferable to the Loewenguth Quartet's summary on Vox (SVBX–5100).

Piano Quintet

In D minor, Op. 89 / In C minor, Op. 115

☐ Eymar (piano); Kehr and Neuhaus (violins); Sichermann (viola); Braunholz (cello) / Vox SVBX–5100

Not well known music at all. Performances of these works are rare, and this is the only recording of the pair of quintets. To such inattention, discontent can be the only reaction. The urbane beauty of these quintets can be observed in every one of the seven movements (three in Opus 89, four in Opus 115). Inspired workmanship can be found in every measure. Two examples, one each from the two quintets, are offered as substantiation.

In the last movement of the D minor work a simple yet vocal four-measure idea is used eighteen times in succession. However, by its unlabored treatment it becomes diffused and elevated into an effusion of truly articulate meaning. In the opening movement of the C minor opus, kinetic sixteenth notes are used with a vigorously sustained subject, and contrastive vigor through blocked string-instrument motion as well as gentle pulsed curves provide the legato style of the second theme. Later, the rhythms interchange and become combined—development is taking place.

The music is heard with excellent advantage in these recorded performances by a fine foursome. They produce a good chamber-music blend. Above all, their understanding of Fauré's style is first-rate.

Vocal

Voice with Accompaniment

Cinq Mélodies de Venise, **Op. 58**

Dans la forêt de septembre, **Op. 85, No. 1**

La Chanson d'Eve, **Op. 95 (Nos. 6 and 10)**

La Fleur qui va sur l'eau, **Op. 85, No. 2**

La Rose, **Op. 51, No. 4**

Le Jardin clos, **Op. 106 (Nos. 1 and 4)**

L'Horizon chimérique, **Op. 118**

Madrigal from *Shylock*, **Op. 57, No. 2**

Mirages, **Op. 113**

☐ Souzay (baritone); Baldwin (piano) / Philips 835286

This program of Fauré songs displays his refinement and supple subtlety as a song writer. Gérard Souzay is an ideal interpreter.

Choral

Chorus with Accompaniment

Ave Maria, **Op. 93**	*Maria Mater Gratiae*, **Op. 47, No. 2**
Ave Verum, **Op. 65, No. 1**	*Messe basse*
Cantique de Jean Racine, **Op. 11**	*Tantum ergo*
En Prière	

☐ Gabriel Fauré Chorale / Turnabout 34486

The lack of information furnished by Turnabout concerning these choral pieces is most annoying. There are no opus designations. As a result, score comparison was necessary in order to determine which of the composer's two *Ave Marias* had been used.

Without a score it is also impossible to determine whether *Tantum ergo* is Opus 55, the second of *Two Offertories* in Opus 65, or still another work bearing no opus number whatsoever.

With the exception of the quiet radiance of the *Cantique* (dedicated, incidentally, to César Franck), these pieces for female chorus are calm and a bit sweet, their emotional temperature at its most moderate point. The *Messe basse* is the longest (nine and a half minutes). A bit of variety is included: the first title is for a duo; *En Prière* is for a single voice.

However, Turnabout gives no credits. None for any conductor, either. Nor any credit for the organist, who accompanies everything with the utmost discretion. It is important that he or she do so, since the singing is always low-scaled and slightly muted—although fairly appealing.

Pavane, Op. 50

Chorus and Orchestra

☐ L'Orchestre de Paris and Edinburgh Festival Chorus / Barenboim (conductor) / Angel S–37077

The ad libitum chorus designation is evidence of Fauré's practicality, but its exclusion offers far less striking music, notwithstanding the generous beauty of the version for orchestra alone. Still, chorus–orchestra performances are quite rare and recordings even more so. The *Pavane* is short and has sometimes been used as a filler when orchestra and chorus have been assembled to record Fauré's Requiem. Strange therefore, that in at least two instances the *Pavane* has been recorded just for such filling-out purposes, but without the available chorus!

Barenboim's performance is the only one in the recorded catalogue at the present time. It is satisfactory. (For the version without chorus, see under *Orchestra.*)

Requiem, Op. 48

Cantata and Oratorio

☐ New Philharmonia Orchestra and Choir of King's College, Cambridge / Chilcott (treble); Case (baritone); Wells (organ) / Willcocks (conductor) / Seraphim S–60096

This gentlest of all requiems is matched by the small orchestral forces Fauré chose. It must have a continuity of flowing detail in its performance, but this does not mean that solidity is to be swept aside. But meaningful solidity does not mean heaviness, which squashes expressivity.

Willcocks's reading uses the proper amount of weight and it places the Fauré work in a healthy interpretative climate. In the ethereal *Pie Jesu* Willcocks opts for a boy soprano and it is extremely effective, as is John Carol Case's ideal voice.

Fauré / **Henri Rabaud** (1873-1949)

Dolly Suite, Op. 56

Orchestra

☐ L'Orchestre National de la Radiodiffusion Française / Beecham (conductor) / Seraphim S–60084

Fauré completed his six-movement piano duet (see under *Fauré: Instrumental: piano, four hands*) in 1896; Rabaud made his orchestral setting in 1906. Fully orchestrated (double winds, with piccolo alternating with the second flute, four horns, two trumpets, three trombones, timpani, percussion, harp, and strings) but never overdone and retaining the charm and light elegance of the original.

This is the sort of music that was Sir Thomas's musical cup of tea. Beecham loved this type of music, and it can be recognized in his beautiful portrayal. He called it one of his "lollipops," but the playing does not contain any undue amount of sugar.

Richard Felciano (1930-   )

Orchestra

Chöd, for Six Players and Electronics (1975)

☐ Philadelphia Composers' Forum / Thome (conductor) / Composers Recordings SD–349

Chöd is the title of a Tibetan mystery play and means "cutting off." As the composer defines it, this is "the absorbtion of personality in the universal order of all created matter."

The quiet reiterations within the score arouse a counteractive type of writing consisting of rhythmic spurts and wailing figures. The aesthetic sense is a merge of East–West styles, sometimes attaining a bitter violence. (The mini-orchestra consists of violin, cello, contrabass, piano, and percussion.)

Thome's group is expert. The content of *Chöd* is characterized most informatively.

Crasis, for Seven Instruments and Electronic Sounds

☐ Subke (flute); O'Brien (clarinet); Bloch (violin); Hampton (cello); Bellows (harp); Sparrow (piano); Blackshere (percussion) / Felciano (conductor) / Composers Recordings SD–349

This is an attempt to simulate the sonorous climate of a Noh drama, hence oscillating, gliding, and wail-like sounds punctuated and criss-crossed by ictus jabs and explosive thrusts. By themselves, without any philosophical or imitative objective, Felciano's sound shapes are fresh, mobile, and inventive. No doubts about the performance, especially with the composer directing the proceedings.

Instrumental

**Piano,
Four Hands**

Gravities, for Piano, Four Hands

☐ Milton and Peggy Salkind (piano) / Composers Recordings SD–349

Most of Felciano's material is percussive, with registral opposition emphasized. The discourse also includes repetitive sounds that bind the structure and give contrast.

This difficult music is clearly displayed in the hands of this two-at-one-piano team.

**Chamber
Music**

Spectra, for Piccolo, Flute, Alto Flute, and Contrabass (1967)

☐ Nancy Turetzky (piccolo, flute, and alto flute); Bertram Turetzky (contrabass) / Composers Recordings SD–349

Five sections, with three duos, one for each of the three flute types with the stringed instrument and two solo sections for the latter. In terms of the instrumentation, color was paramount in the conception, and color remains the principal factor in the assortments heard in the piece. The transformations are fascinating.

The liner note states the Turetzkys have performed *Spectra* over two hundred times. Their belief in the work is a listener's rich gain, for the delivery of the music is superb.

Jindřich Feld   (1925-   )

Quintette (1970)

☐ Annapolis Brass Quintet / Crystal S–206

Dodecaphonic spit and quasi-tonal polish combine in Feld's four-movement brass quintet. Of course, in such a procedure motivic manipulation pertains and, as with Schoenberg's music (though Feld has much brighter rhythmic interlocutions), the music's progress is within serious territory.

Nothing soggy in the playing of this group (Robert Suggs and David Cran, trumpets; Calvin Smith, horn; Tim Beck, trombone; and Robert Posten, bass trombone).

Jan Felderhof   (1907-   )

Concerto for Flute and Strings (1955)

☐ Radio Chamber Orchestra / Barwahser (flute) / van den Berg (conductor) / Donemus Audio-Visual Series DAVS–6703 (monaural)

Chromatic distillations, but this does not make the nicely suave melodic lines impure. Felderhof gives most attention to the solo voice (played warmly and with velvety tone). He also gives some attention to a bit of percussion used in a couple of the movements, though one would not expect such sounds from the title of the composition.

Morton Feldman   (1926-   )

The King of Denmark (1964)

☐ Neuhaus (percussion) / Columbia MS–7139

Gloved sounds, as usual with Feldman. The quietness of the music and its subtle progress are like peeling the clothes off timbres and hearing them in stark nudeness. Perhaps six and one-quarter minutes worth is a bit too much, but it is difficult to deny the sensibility and sensitivity of the conception. (Like most of Feldman's titles, this one has no programmatic meaning.)

The extremely soft character of the music (Feldman's usual soft-sell style) is made more effective by a recording. In a concert hall a considerable amount of Feldman's wispy sounds would decay at their source.

The Viola in My Life (1970)

☐ Phillips (viola); Ajemian (violin); Barab (cello); Tudor (piano); Robison (flute); Bloom (clarinet); Des Roches (percussion) / Feldman (conductor) / Composers Recordings S–276

These are the first three of a number of separate pieces for viola with a varied instrumental ensemble. No bombastic irritation or excitation in this music or, for that matter, in any of Morton Feldman's output. What satisfactions are derived from the extremely low-key quality of this music are ascetic ones. With Feldman's trance-induced music a *piano* dynamic is like an explosion.

Karen Phillips is the star but only has the opportunity to produce sounds that are on their way into evaporation before they identify themselves.

(For a remark regarding crediting the composer as a conductor, see under *Chamber Music: False Relationships and the Extended Ending*.)

Instrumental

Piano

Piano Piece (to Philip Guston) (1963)

Vertical Thoughts IV (1963)

☐ Hays (piano) / Finnadar SR 2-720

Piano Piece is another example of Feldman's cloudy-soft music, minus linear life, alive only to short chordal segments (almost breathless, minus an anchored pulse). The music needs a keyboard touch equivalent to lightly pressing a wad of absorbent cotton. Doris Hays has that required touch.

Vertical Thoughts is a pithy piece (one and a half minutes in length). It lives up completely to its title, being a succession of mild clusters (counterpoint doesn't exist here) of extreme softness (*fortes*, or *mezzo-fortes*, or even *mezzo-piano*s don't exist here either). It typifies fully Feldman's super-introspective attitude.

Doris Hays doesn't interfere with the ascetic situation and plays the work straight, minus a single stress. That's exactly the way it should be.

Chamber Music

Vertical Thoughts 2, for Violin and Piano (1963)

☐ Zukofsky (violin); Kalish (piano) / Desto 6435/37

Slonimsky's description of Feldman's music as being "on the threshold of audibility" could not be more accurate. With Feldman, the few sounds here and there amount to an anticlimax. Bits appear and disappear. Musical line has been flushed away like waste. The delicacy and reticence are powerful in their ability to function by understatement.

Structures, for String Quartet (1951)

☐ Concord String Quartet / Vox SVBX-5306

Music wrapped in a dream state, within which some textural contrasts apply. However, even when the sounds are more active they are singularly lightweight.

Intense luminosities are absent in the closet impressionism that styles Feldman's piece. Marvelously played, though recorded, for no good reason, at an extremely low level. Turn up the volume!

Durations (1961)

☐ Hammond (alto flute); Butterfield (tuba); Tudor (piano); Kraus (vibraphone); Raimondi (violin); Soyer (cello) / Mainstream 5007

Four parts cover *Durations* here (the fifth was not recorded). Though requiring six instruments, the work is never a sextet. Each of the movements varies, with one duet for cello and piano, two different trios: one for violin, tuba, and piano, the other for violin, cello, and vibraphone, plus a single quartet consisting of violin, cello, alto flute, and piano.

The music is typical Feldman, meaning it is flat-surfaced and totally restrained. It is music without skin and bones, and only the marrow showing.

False Relationships and the Extended Ending (1968)

☐ Raimondi (violin); Barab (cello); Jacobs and Takahashi (pianos); Fromme (trombone); Fitz (percussion) / Feldman (conductor) / Composers Recordings S-276

There are two groups within this total sextet. Though they are independent of each other, the static use of sound patterns, in Feldmanish sounds of choked vibration, makes it impossible to distinguish one from the other.

CRI should watch its production details. Nowhere save on the label is there mention of a conductor. Even then one is not sure there is a conductor, since the credit reads "under direction of the composer." Does that mean supervision or actual on-podium beating of time, cueing, and direction?

For Frank O'Hara

☐ Blum (flute); Blustine (clarinet); Hudson (violin); Eastman (piano); Gibson (cello); Knaack and Kahle (percussion) / Williams (conductor) / Odyssey Y–34138

Feldman's memorial piece (for O'Hara, the great New York poet who died after being struck by a car) is not for audiophiles. Like almost all of Feldman's music, it is stated at an extremely low dynamic level, musical time is *in absentia,* pitches are arranged *in abstracto,* and sounds *as* sounds are the total construction. Since there is no dynamic pulse the emotive condition is found to exist completely in the intellectualization. If one agrees with that viewpoint, Alfred Frankenstein's remark that Feldman is "the great monotonist of modern music" is unacceptable, even though the famous critic wants this read as meaning "high praise."

Christian Wolff in Cambridge (1963)

Choral

Chorus Alone

☐ Brandeis University Chamber Chorus / Lucier (conductor) / Odyssey 32160156

Don't try to fathom the title. It is, like most of Feldman's, decorative—quite often an acknowledgment of a friend or an event (a back door method of dedication?). There aren't many of the usual Feldman silences in this short piece; there is almost total sonic continuity. However, there is the usual Feldman dynamic gentility; the loudness ceiling is pegged at the *mezzo-piano* mark.

Chorus and Instruments (II) (1967)

Chorus with Accompaniment

☐ Brandeis University Chamber Chorus / Phillips (tuba); Bergamo (chimes) / Lucier (conductor) / Odyssey 32160156

Vertical inserts of wordless choral sound are situated among silences. Weight shifts are minimal, at times anchored with a tuba, sometimes with the barely audible association of a chime note. The performance is ultra-sensitive.

Rothko Chapel

☐ Gregg Smith Singers / Phillips (viola); Holland (percussion) / Smith (conductor) / Odyssey Y–34138

This work was composed for performance in the Rothko Chapel (constructed in 1971 in Houston, Texas), which contains fourteen large canvases by Mark Rothko. Feldman's objective was to parallel Rothko's "imagery [which] goes straight to the end of his canvas." Flat-surfaced continuity, therefore, with slight timbred changes which give minute movement to Feldman's usual stylistic sequestered set of sequences.

Rothko Chapel has a magnetic, hypnotic effect. Some may not like Morton Feldman's music but they must admit its singularity. *Rothko Chapel* is one of his best creations.

Vittorio Fellegara (1927-   )

Chamber Music

Serenata (1960)

☐ Hamann and Köhnsen (violins); Doberitz (viola); Palm (cello); Otto (flute); Irmisch (clarinet); Diestel (bass clarinet); Priegnitz (piano); Hinze (percussion) / Travis (conductor) / Mainstream 5006

Fellegara's opus has all the habits of the intervals-out-of-their-sockets school, but it will be found that his total organization (not only of pitch, but of dynamic, duration, color, and register) has jelled into emotional sense. Of course, no sentimentality is left for Tchaikovskian thinkers. That Fellegara's music is of an unsentimental type does not bring disfavor.

The performers (as a group known as the Hamburger Kammersolisten) reveal every subtle point within the score. Certainly, a first-rate presentation.

Eric Fenby / Frederick Delius. See *Delius* / Fenby.

Brian Fennelly (1937-   )

Chamber Music

Evanescences (1969)

☐ Members of Da Capo Chamber Players / Composers Recordings S–322

Electronically generated material combines with a quartet consisting of equally paired winds (alto flute and clarinet) and strings (violin and cello). Interplay of the tape music with the instruments as well as both units heard alone provide the music's environment. Naturally, music of this type doesn't live in a diatonically furnished household.

By the action and play-on and play-off of the musical characters, Fennelly's piece can, in a sense, be considered as chamber theatre totally concerned with sound. *Evanescences* is finely crafted and performed with judicious perspective.

Prelude and Elegy for Brass Quintet

☐ Empire Brass Quintet / Advance FGR–19S

The black and white of pithy-punched phrases in the *Prelude* and tensiled threnodic thoughts in the *Elegy* are sensitively scored with a masterful knowledge of what to do with the brass medium—exciting and touching in relation to the material, and always personal.

The disc presents convincing playing that is well-contrived in sonorities, weight, and balance.

Wind Quintet (1967)

☐ Dorian Woodwind Quintet / Composers Recordings S–318

Twelve-tone organization, detailed by extremely rhapsodic formal totality. Especially potent are the relationships of changing speed ratios and the simultaneous different tempi.

Fennelly's music is uncompromising for the listener. Its performance requirements are similar and call for the highest perceptivity and honed technique of the players. The Dorian group fulfills every demand.

618

Howard Ferguson (1908-1961)

Sonata No. 1 for Violin and Piano (1931)

☐ Heifetz (violin); Steuber (piano) / RCA LSC-2909

Chamber Music

Music of romantic expression, but without any of the fussiness of that school. The outer movements are, respectively, sonata-designed and fantasy-impelled; the middle movement is the most interesting, a fast-tempoed, hearty and hardy furious scherzo representative.

Heifetz is in top form. He deserves credit for choosing to play the music of a contemporary composer, even if that composer is of the conservative wing, since it brings special performance values to the listener.

Oscar Lorenzo Fernandez (1897-1948)

Batuque

☐ New York Philharmonic / Bernstein (conductor) / Columbia MS-6514

Orchestra

An illustration of Bernstein and his colleagues in rip-roaring, rip-snorting, top colorful form as they play this Afro-Brazilian dance. The constancy of the sharply syncopated rhythm is built-in showmanship. (The *Batuque* is considered as an individual piece though it forms part 3 of Fernandez's orchestral suite *Reisado do pastoreio*.)

Canção do mar

Samaritana da floresta

☐ Averino (soprano); Slonimsky (piano) / Orion 7150 (monaural)

Vocal

Voice with Accompaniment

The Brazilian identity, with nostalgia surrounding both songs, is more intensely realized in the haunting disposition of the *Samaritana* item. Averino knows how to style songs of this kind.

John Fernström (1897-1961)

Concertino for Flute, Women's Chorus, and Chamber Orchestra, Op. 52

☐ Stockholm Radio Orchestra and Chorus / Holmstedt (flute) / Frykberg (conductor) / Turnabout 34498

Solo Instrument and Orchestra

Flute

Modal pentatonicism pervades this one-movement work. It brings strong reminders (in terms of its repetitive procedures) of the music of Orff. Sound musicianship is provided in the performance.

Alfonso Ferrabosco, the Younger (1575?-1628)

O Eyes, O Mortal Stars

☐ Brown (tenor); Channon (lute) / Nonesuch 73010

Vocal

Voice with Accompaniment

A spiritual quality pervades Ferrabosco's song, one that is quite different from the gay tunes that highlight music of the Elizabethan age.

Luc Ferrari   (1929-   )

Solo
Instrument
and
Orchestra

Piano

Société II (et si le piano était un corps de femme) for Piano, Three Percussionists, and Sixteen Instruments

☐ Ensemble Instrumental de Musique Contemporaine de Paris / Frémy (piano); Drouet, Gualda, and Sylvestre (percussion) / Simonovitch (conductor) / Deutsche Grammophon 2543004

Yes! That subtitle reads "and if the piano were a woman's body." But you must read the program to know the action. This is music that requires the listener to collaborate and become an "actor," in order to "charge the exposed material with meaning," thereby becoming stimulated to obtain "tangible erotic fantasies." It presents the listener with plenty of time to achieve this "high"—twenty-eight minutes' worth.

In this sound massage there are lots of glides and plunges, flutters and contacts, instrumental cries (ecstatic and otherwise), orgasmic (?) whimpers, human shouts, and an entire catalogue of sheer noises. By using one's imagination and experiences, the product is musical porn, but no parental guidance is required.

There are some special touches: a sudden major chord which is then attached to a semi-lush melody (someone has obtained full sexual satisfaction?), a healthy quote from Liszt's *Liebesträume* (the famous one, of course), some carnival music toward the end, and a final set of detumescent sounds.

Ferrari states that if anyone considers his *Société II* in bad taste, he would agree. I wonder how Masters and Johnson would evaluate this music.

Electronic
Music

Présque rien No. 1 (Lever du jour au bord de la mer)

☐ Deutsche Grammophon 2543004

It all hangs out in Ferrari's nude (unmanipulated and undistorted) *musique concrète* depiction of "Daybreak on the Beach." Conversation fragments, chirps, engine roars, distant children's voices, the sound of a pump, a little laughter, a woman singing a tune are heard in this tape collage.

Ferrari calls this "anecdotal music." It meets its objectives. You will not need to contact your travel agent.

John Ferritto   (1937-   )

Vocal

Voice with
Accompaniment

Oggi, Op. 9

☐ Pilgrim (mezzo-soprano); Blustine (clarinet); Oppens (piano) / Composers Recordings S–325

The composer's own text, he tells us, is "often meaningless in the sense of linear thought." Thus, the voice part becomes a simulated instrumental line through the effect and quality of the words and sounds used. This is quite different from music for voice with defined text framed by clarinet and piano. An interesting concept and fairly well-realized.

Alexander Ernst Fesca   (1820-1849)

Chamber
Music

Septet No. 1 in C minor for Oboe, Horn, Violin, Viola, Cello, Double Bass, and Piano, Op. 26

☐ Collegium con Basso / Turnabout 34493

Fesca liked this medium and wrote a second work as his Opus 28 (unrecorded; versions for piano quartet of both works were published). The music is clear and nicely colored, without adventurousness of any kind.

No *apologia* is required for this performance. A commendable contribution is made by the pianist, Helmuth Barth, who blends nicely with his half-dozen partners.

Joseph Fiala (1748-1816)

Concerto in E flat major for English horn and Orchestra

□ English Chamber Orchestra / Holliger (English horn); Pearson (harpsichord) / Leppard (conductor) / Philips 839756

Solo Instrument and Orchestra

English Horn

Granting a conventional composition format, the interest here lies in the unusual use of the English horn as a solo voice. Further, the instrument does not portray a bucolic or threnodic character, as is so often its lot. There is full-scale use which Heinz Holliger translates magnificently; he even tosses in a large-scale cadenza of his own making. Fiala's kind of writing belies the nonsense that still appears in instrumentation texts that the English horn has "limited playing potentials," and has "limited versatility." Creamy sound from Philips.

Jacobo Ficher (1896-1978)

Palabras a mama

□ Averino (soprano); Slonimsky (piano) / Orion 7150 (monaural)

This children's song is Ficher's sole representation in the current recorded literature.

Vocal

Voice with Accompaniment

John Field (1782-1837)

Concerto No. 2 in A flat major for Piano and Orchestra

□ Berlin Symphony Orchestra / Kyriakou (piano) / Bünte (conductor) / Candide 31006

Solo Instrument and Orchestra

Piano

The heart of Field's work is its short (three and one-half minutes in length) *Poco adagio* which prefigures Chopin style. It is in that movement that Rena Kyriakou does her best work. The balance of the concerto resides in Hummel-like territory. Steady playing with agreeable taste.

Concerto No. 3 in E flat major for Piano and Orchestra

□ Vienna Chamber Orchestra / Blumental (piano) / Froschauer (conductor) / Turnabout 34389

Two movements in expected forms for the period: Sonata and Rondo; the latter is a modified polonaise. The aspirations of balanced design are met, the inspirations are professional, even if not awe-inspiring.

Blumental covers the somewhat attenuated opus (just a bit under a solid half-hour) with a quality performance.

Instrumental	**Nocturne**
Piano	

No. 1 in E flat major / No. 2 in C minor / No. 3 in A flat major / No. 4 in A major / No. 5 in B flat major / No. 6 in F major / No. 7 in C major / No. 8 in A major / No. 9 in E flat major / No. 10 in E minor / No. 11 in E flat major

☐ Boehm (piano) / Turnabout 34349

Mary Louise Boehm performs Field's Nocturnes (for the remaining eight, *see below*) with clear articulation and an acceptable romantic gentility, preferring a more complacent climate than Noël Lee's (*see below*). Boehm's tempi are all slower than Lee's and in some instances considerably so. In No. 10 (which, by the way, is listed incorrectly as being in E major on Turnabout's liner copy) her timing is 4:07, while Lee covers the piece in 2:20, and exactly the same difference exists in the performances of Nos. 13 and 17.

Whereas there is greater luminosity in Lee's performances, there are two points in Boehm's favor that must not be overlooked. She plays the entire set of nineteen Nocturnes and in exact sequence, though rather than in a single two-record set Turnabout has issued the Nocturnes in two separate albums. Lee only plays twelve of the total and mixes the assortment chosen so that, for example, one finds No.13 following No. 6, which was preceded by No. 3, and so on.

Nocturne

No. 12 in G major / No. 13 in D minor / No. 14 in C major / No. 15 in C major / No. 16 in F major / No. 17 in E major / (*Midi*) No. 18 in E major / (*Le Troubadour*) No. 19 in C major

☐ Boehm (piano) / Turnabout 34350

(For a complete discussion *see above*: Nocturnes Nos. 1–11.)

Nocturne

No. 2 in C minor / No. 3 in A flat major / No. 4 in A major / No. 5 in B flat major / No. 6 in F major / No. 9 in E flat major / No. 10 in E minor / No. 12 in G major / No. 13 in D minor / No. 15 in C major / No. 17 in E major / (*Midi*) No. 18 in E major

☐ Lee (piano) / Nonesuch 71195

(For a discussion *see above*: Nocturnes Nos. 1–11.)

As pointed out, Lee's tempi are faster than Boehm's. In the other competitive edition of a group of Field's Nocturnes (Nos. 1, 2, 3, 4, 7, 10, and 11 played by Rena Kyriakou on Candide 31006) Kyriakou plays even faster than Lee in two instances and in two other cases paces the music faster than Boehm. The poetry gets lost in the tempo shuffle.

Henry Fillmore   *(1881-1956)*

Band	***His Excellency***

☐ Goldman Band / Goldman (conductor) / New World Records NW–266

Take the word of the great expert on band music, the late Richard Franko Goldman, who stated that Fillmore was "one of the best march writers of his time." *His Excellency* shows such excellence.

Irving Fine (1914-1962)

Symphony (1962) *Orchestra*

☐ Boston Symphony Orchestra / Fine (conductor) / Desto 7167

Dramatic in exposition and in technical demonstration, Fine's opus is "almost operatic in gesture," according to Aaron Copland. To which should be added the fact that without obviating the requisite formal balances of the three movements (*Intrada,* Capriccio, and *Ode*) Fine brings a continuity of fantasy-rhapsody that handsomely colors the designs.

The style is an amalgamated one: tonalism exploring dodecaphonic territory (or twelve-tone procedures applied to tonal doctrines). Here too the plan is dramatically convincing.

Originally, Pierre Monteux was to have performed and recorded Fine's symphony (premiered by Munch and the Bostonians previously). Sudden illness prevented Monteux's direction and Fine was offered the opportunity. The loss of a recording under Monteux is offset by a definitive reading of the piece by the composer. It contradicts the opinion that composers are their worst interpreters.

Toccata concertante (1947)

☐ Boston Symphony Orchestra / Leinsdorf (conductor) / Desto 7167

The skin-tight neo-classical style bears out the hybrid title. Kinetic motility and fanfare-like persistence characterize the *Toccata* part and solo instruments as contrasting voices within the texture define the *concertante* part.

An impeccable performance. The surprising appearance of the famed B.S.O. on the Desto label is simply a matter of Desto obtaining the re-release rights from RCA, which first issued and eventually deleted Fine's work.

Serious Song: A Lament for String Orchestra (1955) *String Orchestra*

☐ Boston Symphony Orchestra / Leinsdorf (conductor) / Desto 7167

Fine described his piece as "an extended aria." Its flexible lyricism and warm severity, plus a mood of demanding asceticism, mark it as a miniature symphonic poem for strings.

The best is last in terms of recorded performances. The initial one was by the Louisville Orchestra, but it is currently not available. RCA Victor then released the work in 1966 and later on deleted it from its lists. The Desto recording is a transfer from the RCA masters. It has the Boston Symphony strings and the word for that group is "outstanding."

Music for Piano (Excerpts) (1947) *Instrumental*

☐ Fine (piano) / Composers Recordings 106 (monaural) *Piano*

Movements 3 and 2 (recorded in that order) of the total four, played with the authority of the composer's own interpretation. Prokofievian sarcasm and Stravinskian neatness of thought are heard here. However, Fine's music is no mere carbon copy; it is filtered through a lighter cloth.

Fantasia for String Trio (1957) *Chamber Music*

☐ Silverstein (violin); Burton Fine (viola); Eskin (cello) / RCA LSC-6167

Fine's Fantasia represents a hybrid of dodecaphonic technique applied to freed tonality; the twain meet successfully. The outer movements are both in slow tempo, the first lyrical, the other more rhapsodic. The middle movement (marked *scherzo* but of mordacious content) is nervous, driven by cross-accents, an example of virtuosity in motival criss-cross. The passion that drives the music proves Fine's inspiration; the performance by these members of the Boston Symphony Chamber Players is equal to it.

String Quartet (1952)

☐ Juilliard Quartet / Composers Recordings SRD-395 (monaural)

Twelve-tone technique essentially is not far removed from the architectural soundness that marks Beethoven's towering musical structures. The motival unfolding of the classic master is matched at its analytical peak (no emotional premise is being considered) by the unity and variety of serial procedure. Fine's quartet furnishes important evidence to support this statement.

His use of dodecaphonic technique takes on new meaning, for his twelve tones are clothed with the royal purple of classic design. And within his music there is the necessary freedom that must be enjoyed by good art, unless it is to be a mere laboratory report. On top of all this the quartet has a tonal center. The twain have certainly met and embraced each other! Fine's heady rhythms are not bounded by a serial blueprint; they hammer the spikes into the quadruple lines, strengthening and thereby clarifying the work as a whole. In this way the Bartók heritage makes its presence felt.

Though these formal purposes would seem to be served by eclectic choice rather than true serial technique, the facts are the opposite. Fine's quartet has clear positiveness; it is his own music, exhibiting a codification of rare sensibility and sensitivity.

The Juilliard performance (the personnel is from the 1952 days: Robert Mann and Robert Koff, violins; Raphael Hillyer, viola; and Arthur Winograd, cello) is magnificent, styled with minute scrupulousness. Originally this recording was issued by Columbia in a monaural setting (ML-4843). CRI's reissue of Columbia's deletion is most welcome. In the transfer the disc has been electronically rechanneled for stereo.

Partita for Wind Quintet (1948)

☐ Dorian Quintet / Vox SVBX-5307

Fine's Partita tends mainly to use this generic title in its truest meaning; although the word "partita" is used frequently to identify a miscellaneous group of movements in suite form and of that character, it means actually a set of variations. The first three and the last sections of this work are definitely in the variation category, while the penultimate part is only subconsciously related to the variation principle. Regardless, the five movements establish a specific unit in one stylistic groove, especially in the neo-classic manner, refined (if one may be permitted the pun) with crystal-clear workmanship and a neutral (black–white) viewpoint of instrumental colors. There is no attempt at establishing a basic timbre design; the instruments share equally in promulgating the essentials of the music. The organic instrumentation of the music's eighteenth-century ancestry is in direct opposition to any pictorial or decorative luxuriance.

This is one of the best wind quintets that have been produced in the last half-century. It is played by one of the best groups devoted to such literature.

Romanza for Wind Quintet (1963)

☐ Musical Arts Quintet / Now 9362

One of the pair of works that Fine wrote for this medium. The *Romanza* has an engaging sonority plan, set as it is in a syntax whereby the intervallic elements of twelve-tone technique are reconciled to quasi-tonality. A fresh approach, this, with a refreshing aural result. First-class presentation.

The Frog and the Snake

☐ Miller (mezzo-soprano); Biltcliffe (piano) / Desto 6411/2

This song is from the set of *Childhood Fables for Grownups*. A pert and piquant text, with a pingy parallel in the neo-classic music-play. Miller's diction enhances listening enjoyment.

Mutability (1952)

☐ Alberts (contralto); Fine (piano) / Composers Recordings 106 (monaural)

Each of the six songs is of sensitive musical essence. Each shows scrupulous regard for the poetry of Irene Orgel.

Eunice Alberts's voice has a good timbre, her diction is not memorable. No text is provided. This is always valuable but rarely available when needed.

Polaroli

☐ Miller (mezzo-soprano); Biltcliffe (piano) / Desto 6411/2

Another song from the delightful group titled *Childhood Fables for Grownups* (see above: *The Frog and the Snake*). The remarks made there apply here as well.

Alice in Wonderland, First Series (1949)

☐ Gregg Smith Singers / Beegle (piano) / Smith (conductor) / Composers Recordings SD–376

This set of three choruses (together with the second set: *see below*) is among the most successful contemporary choral music in terms of sales of the printed edition. The prosperity naturally carries over to performance—choral music is not purchased to adorn the coffee table. Fine's music is choral probity at its best, with dancing light counterpoint, exuberant rhythmic dash, neo-classic harmonic spice, and texts that are sharply stimulating to begin with.

These are powerfully convincing performances. The piano is somewhat edgy; it must be overlooked if one wishes this exhilarating creative invention, since it is the sole recording available.

Alice in Wonderland, Second Series (for Women's Chorus) (1949)

☐ Gregg Smith Singers / Coons (soprano); Beegle (piano) / Smith (conductor) / Composers Recordings SD–376

Fine's second set of *Alice* choruses (for women's voices) contrasts with the first (*see above*), which is for mixed voices. Otherwise, the same elements are to be found: elegance of style, rich harmonic choices, and the special ability to write *for* the voice without sacrificing any creative integrity. For such "choral individualism" parallels are difficult to find.

All the telling touches and the phrased finesse in Fine's music are well displayed in Gregg Smith's performance.

Vocal

Voice with Accompaniment

Choral

Chorus with Accompaniment

The Hour-Glass Suite (1949)

☐ Gregg Smith Singers / Smith (conductor) / Composers Recordings SD–376

Fine's *Hour-Glass* consists of six pieces, all set to poems by Ben Jonson. All represent the type of choral craftsmanship that is rare, despite the plethora of compositions produced in the medium. There is brilliance here. It is never top-surface but always inwardly trenchant, which gives the music an emotive frame.

Gregg Smith's group of vocal virtuosi have the merits of vocal clarity, solidity, balance, and beauty.

McCord's Menagerie (for Men's Chorus)

☐ Gregg Smith Singers / Morrow and Lee (solo voices) / Smith (conductor) / Composers Recordings SD–376

The menagerie of David McCord consists of *Vultur Gryphus, Jerboa, Mole,* and *Clam.* Light humor, of course, but sophisticated. By all means read the texts before listening and then catch the matching of the poet's wit in Fine's clever, fluidly capricious music.

The performance follows suit.

Vivian Fine   (1913-   )

Orchestra

Alcestis (1960)

☐ Imperial Philharmonic of Tokyo / Strickland (conductor) / Composers Recordings 145 (monaural)

The terms offered here are of abstract conditions. Simply, this means eliminating overt romanticism and substituting clear antiromanticism. Fine thus avoids any super-colorful fallout that destroys meaning. The structures and lines of this piece are precisely detailed and very exciting. The unity in the four movements relates a complete story in a few paragraphs.

Good enough playing, but less than good enough sound.

Solo Instrument and Orchestra

Piano

Concertante for Piano and Orchestra (1944)

☐ Japan Philharmonic Orchestra / Honsho (piano) / Watanabe (conductor) / Composers Recordings S–135E (monaural)

Fine's opus contrasts a slow movement with a fast-paced one. There is the air of Charles Stanford about the music. This makes it healthily academic but not dull, fortunately.

There is fine musicianship displayed by soloist, orchestra, and conductor. However, the disc is only fairly resonant.

Cantata and Oratorio

Paean (1969)

☐ Eastman Brass Ensemble and Bennington Choral Ensemble / Baker (tenor and narrator) / Fine (conductor) / Composers Recordings S–260

Part of this piece offers quotations from Keats's *Ode to Apollo.* The other part offers push-and-poke vocalism, fractured sounds, effects, twitters, sighs, whistles, and cheerleaderlike repetitions. Both of these contrast with the brass pungency (trumpets and trombones).

Not easy to perform, but the Bennington women have the requisite virtuosity for Fine's piece. The soloist, Frank S. Baker, has a nice voice, splendid diction, and matches the chorus with his abilities in the special-vocal-effects department.

Gottfried Finger *(1660-1723)*

Sonata in D minor

Chamber Music

☐ Rampal (flute); Duschenes (recorder) / Orion 75199

Neither Orion nor Everest (which duplicates the duo's performance on 3194) gives any data concerning this four-movement piece. One suspects it is from A Set of Sonatas in Five Parts for Flutes and Hautboys.

Better resonance in Orion's sound; Everest's is a bit flat and subdued.

Ross Lee Finney *(1906-   )*

Symphony No. 1: *Communiqué* (1943)

Orchestra

☐ Louisville Orchestra / Whitney (conductor) / Louisville 652 (monaural)

Finney is here represented by music in tonal wrappings, a style that he maintained for the first half of his career before moving into serialism. More or less traditional structures brace the symphony, though mood indications are specific: *Introduction, Dramatic Statement,* Elegy, Scherzo, Interlude, and Fanfare. But tonality does not mean conservatism. Finney's use provides a sharp, formal sense without negating freer dramatic scope. It also provides proof that tonal tidiness has not lost its strengths because of the more fashionable hide-and-seek permutative involvements of the twelve-tone composers and the catch-as-catch-can of the aleatoric advocates.

The Louisville organization does very well with Finney's music. They play with suitable expressive power and are well disciplined.

Symphony No. 2 (1960)

☐ Louisville Orchestra / Whitney (conductor) / Louisville 625 (monaural)

Classical proportions applied to twelve-tone processes. There are four movements: a vigorous first movement, a somber slow movement, a *scherzo* manifestation, and a capricious conclusion. Rich orchestration and rich creativity are evident. There is no discrepancy between serial procedures and plotting them within the forceful contours that have served composers prior to the Schoenbergian dictum.

The Louisville Orchestra rendition only gets a passing grade—there are places that could stand some "wood shedding."

Symphony No. 3 (1964)

☐ Louisville Orchestra / Whitney (conductor) / Louisville S-672

Proof that no technically crusading compass is required to guide a contemporary symphony through a successful journey. Finney's conception consists of the traditional three movements (two fast-tempoed corner movements with a central Adagio). Traditional also is the work's authoritative sense of balance. But it is totally of the present in its language.

The Symphony is sober and dark colored (a threnodic tone persists even in the fast-paced sections), and serially syntaxed. Yet there are no ghostly (and ghastly) echoes of the note spinning prevalent in so many (all too many) twelve-tone compositions.

The performance is authoritative. Whitney clearly outlines the motives that tighten the structure and give tension to the outer movements, and sensitively and meaningfully translates the long-spun lines of the slow movement. A significant recording of important music.

Solo Instrument and Wind Orchestra

Saxophone

Concerto for Alto Saxophone and Orchestra of Wind Instruments

☐ Northwestern University Symphonic Wind Ensemble / Hemke (saxophone) / Paynter (conductor) / New World Records NW–211

Persuasive music in a medium extremely limited in quality within the small quantity available. Textures and tone colors are choice; the solo voice is allowed space in which to be heard and never smothered by overscoring.

Movement 1 sings, movement 2 is trimly vigorous. No matter what shapes emerge, they come from a stream of strong melodicism. Hemke's clear musical playing proves that the only things wrong with the saxophone are the overabundance of inept saxophonists.

Instrumental

Cello

Chromatic Fantasy in E for Violoncello Solo

☐ Jelinek (cello) / Composers Recordings S–311

"Chromatic" in terms of the serial syntax, "Fantasy" in regard to the employment of the pitch language rather than the form itself. Still, there are varying moods, especially those dealing with dynamic thrust, all demonstratively proven by the soloist.

Organ

So Long as the Mind Keeps Silent (1967)

☐ Noehren (organ) / Lyrichord 7191

Dissonant blood and atonic sweat pours healthily out of this major contribution to a repertory that still seeks viable contemporary conclusions, Messiaen notwithstanding. Finney has an infallible ear for balance and texture for an instrument that often makes a travesty of a composer's good intentions. All too often organ music is either excessively swollen or falls flat on its choir-loft face. This is a damn good music. It is also damn good music for the organ.

Chamber Music

Second Sonata in C for Violoncello and Piano

☐ Jelinek (cello); Gurt (piano) / Composers Recordings S–311

The "in C" is a key polarity that stabilizes the work—Finney's expressive and dynamic piece is fully chromatic but remains firmly and pertinently tonal. It also remains beautifully written for the combination of a cello and piano, a medium always beset with balance problems (fully conquered in this performance). Noteworthy is Finney's structure, anchored at its extremes with slow-tempoed, pensive statements. Here, too, the playing is especially convincing.

String Quartet No. 6 in E

☐ Stanley Quartet of the University of Michigan / Composers Recordings 116 (monaural)

Finney's tone row begins on E (hence its use in the title), and in its initial presentation the row is completed by stepwise progression to the E tonal point. Consistently drawing from this basic material, the quartet employs the horizontal mannerisms of the twelve-tone school but with the classic inlay of clear rhythm so that the imprint is sharp. There are four movements—Sonata, Scherzo, Intermezzo, and Fugue—preceded and completed by slow-paced data.

With such traditional links every part of the work becomes readily clear. The performers, of course, deserve a good portion of credit for providing such favorable listening weather.

Drinking Song   *Vocal*

Wedlock   *Voice with*
                                                                    Accompaniment
☐ Hanks (tenor); Friedberg (piano) / Duke University Press DWRM–7501 (monaural)

A pair of songs from Finney's *Poor Richard*. The words are meaningful. To be expected, since they are by Benjamin Franklin. With Hanks's excellent diction, listening pleasure is increased.

Gerald Finzi (1901-1956)

Intimations of Immortality (1950)   *Vocal*

☐ Guildford Philharmonic Orchestra and Choir / Partridge (tenor) / Handley (conductor) / Lyrita SRCS–75   *Voice and Orchestra*

Full-scale works are few in Finzi's catalogue. *Intimations of Immortality* is one of his major compositions. It is concerned with the Wordsworth poem (all but two of its eleven stanzas) and the result is a combine of Delian reticence and the more forthrightedness found in Vaughan Williams.

The fact that less than a major orchestra is concerned does not lessen the viability of the disc. Rising to the need, the Guildford organization does extremely well; the soloist, Ian Partridge, is in glorious form.

Irwin Fischer (1903-   )

Overture on an Exuberant Tone Row (1964)   *Orchestra*

☐ Louisville Orchestra / Whitney (conductor) / Louisville S–676

A scherzo-like opus: clean and clear, healthy twelve-tone music. It nullifies those who still argue that dodecaphonic style can apply only to neurotic subjects.

No questions can be raised regarding the performance. Fischer's tone row remains alive and kicking throughout.

Johann Christian Fischer (1733-1800)

Concerto No. 2 in E flat major for Oboe and Orchestra   *Solo Instrument and Orchestra*

☐ Wiener Solisten / Lardrot (oboe) / Böttcher (conductor) / Vanguard 2138

Strictly classical in format but not academic. Movement 1 has the complete exposition, development, recapitulation, and coda, plus a worthy cadenza. This is followed by an aria-   *Oboe* like slow movement and a final *Rondeau.* All of it meaningful. It is not surprising that Johann Christian Bach thought so highly of the work that he made a piano arrangement of the score.

André Lardrot plays with personality and style. Such a classical presentation cannot be bettered.

Johann Caspar Ferdinand Fischer (ca. 1665-1746)

Instrumental

Harpsichord

The Nine Muses

> **Suite I:** *Clio*
> **Suite II:** *Calliope*
> **Suite VI:** *Euterpe*
> **Suite IX:** *Urania*

☐ Roberts (harpsichord) / Klavier 506

Fischer's *Musikalischer Parnassus* (not so identified on Klavier's release) consists of suites of varying assortment (here the total movements are seven, five, six, and nine, respectively). The compilations include defined forms: *Ouverture,* Toccata, Passacaglia, etc.; dances: Allemande, Courante, Gigue, etc.; and some fanciful designs, such as *Balet Anglois,* and a *Praeludium Harpeggiato,* which is nothing more than a broken-chord affair. The suite titles are simply creative window dressing for charming music that prefigures Bach style.

Roberts displays the highest level of musicality in his playing. A prime assist to his performance is the crystalline sound.

Luboš Fišer (1935-   )

Orchestra

Fifteen Prints After Dürer's "Apocalypse" (1965)

☐ London Symphony Orchestra / Buketoff (conductor) / RCA LSC–3181

Serialism based on a basic six-pitch mode is used in this suite. The orchestral colors include a harpsichord, and they are exquisitely effective. A first-rate presentation of the score under Igor Buketoff's direction.

Nicolas Flagello (1928-   )

Orchestra

Lautrec: Suite for Orchestra in Four Movements (1965)

☐ Orchestra Sinfonica di Roma / Flagello (conductor) / Serenus 12014

A mixture of colorful sympathy. Stravinsky and Ibert images are to be noted flitting about in Flagello's sketches: *Paris—La Belle Epoque, Histoires naturelles, Elles,* and *Moulin Rouge.* The orchestration is bright and healthy; the harmonic framework mostly side-slips in the "traditional" contemporary manner.

Good orchestra, though one wonders how extensive the rehearsals were prior to making the recording. Flagello is an excellent conductor, and doubly so in his own music.

Concerto for Strings (1959)

☐ Orchestra Sinfonica di Roma / Flagello (conductor) / Serenus 12002

Classically oriented in terms of form, with two outer fast movements enclosing an *Andante languido*. Bold music, rhythmically exciting and penetrating. But it never pants because it is breathless. Strongly tonal, like all of this composer's music, but not of academic retrocedence. A crisp performance.

Capriccio for Violoncello and Orchestra (1962)

☐ Orchestra Sinfonica di Roma / Koutzen (cello) / Flagello (conductor) / Serenus 12003

The length (sixteen minutes) and content (dark-toned) belie the title. Still, there are no restrictions on a composer's choice of a caption. The music has a brooding personality, reminding one of a *Schelomo* without a Hebraic beard. Like Bloch's cello writing, Flagello's is beautifully arranged and especially informative in the bass gamut. It is beautifully performed by Koutzen, a confirmation of his artistic reputation.

Concerto Antoniano for Flute and Orchestra (1953)

☐ Orchestra Sinfonica di Roma / Sigurdson (flute) / Flagello (conductor) / Serenus 12004

Not many contemporary flute concertos have been produced. Of those that have, most are not necessarily a joy forever. The *Antoniano* (no clue is given as to this title) is a creditable contribution. Its initial movement contains a cadenza that truly climaxes the working material and is followed by a warm, slow movement and a bouncy finale. The last perfectly fits the flute's personality.

Sigurdson's playing evidences well-disciplined fluency. The rapport between soloist and conductor-composer is excellent.

Concertino for Piano, Brass, and Timpani (1963)

☐ Members of Orchestra Sinfonica di Roma / Marshall (piano) / Flagello (conductor) / Serenus 12003

Since it is crossfired with rhapsodic devices, Flagello's pithy (nine-minute) opus could well be described as *quasi una fantasia*. Like most of his other works, the composer displays a stimulating ingenuity in his organization of harmonic materials.

Prelude, Ostinato, and Fugue (1960)

☐ Marshall (piano) / Serenus 12004

The greatest interest is found in the final section. So many fugues are stiff in their thematic opinions. This sort of quirk is absent here. Flagello's fugal subject is individual, of cogent identity, and has a pert tag. The polyphonic workout is vigorous, confident, impressive, and concludes with virtuosic pepper. Marshall is most impressive in her presentation.

Sonata for Piano (1962)

☐ Marshall (piano) / Serenus 12002

Music that does have both luster and passion. Somewhat free structures, though it is much more a suite than a sonata. It *sounds* either way, with rhapsodic modulations in part 1, neoromantic sighs and furbelows in part 2, and perpetual-motion kinetics in the finale. Elizabeth Marshall does her work well. This recording totally partners composer (and teacher) with performer (Marshall having studied with Flagello).

Three Dances for Piano (1945)
Three Episodes for Piano (1957)

☐ Marshall (piano) / Serenus 12003

Well made, nothing adventurous (which is not to imply a negative report), utilitarian classification. The Three Episodes are four minutes in length, comprising a March, a Lullaby, and a character depiction: *Pulcinella*. The first two dances are defined as "abstract" and "ceremonial"; the final one is a Tarantella.

First-class playing and reproduction. Serenus's packaging is most attractive, but the liner copy doesn't give a single word about the compositions on the recording.

Chamber Music

Burlesca for Flute and Guitar (1961)

☐ Sigurdson (flute); Garzia (guitar) / Serenus 12004

There are hints of folk sounds here (the guitar can well breed this type of reaction even if it is not true). Neat scoring that is a compelling, constructive part of the piece. It shows that Flagello never postures, never attempts to write for the sake of mere effect.

Philos for Brass Quintet

☐ American Brass Quintet / Serenus 12041

Contrastive tempi but parallelistic moods. The heart and voice of this piece are concerned with dark-toned sentiments. Flagello's music is definitely tonally based but colored and stimulated by chromatic adjuncts. These provide the tensions that are not released until the conclusion. A substantially conveyed presentation with Serenus's usual fine sound.

Chorale and Episode for Ten Brass Instruments (1948)

☐ Members of Orchestra Sinfonica di Roma / Flagello (conductor) / Serenus 12003

These days the barrier that separated chamber music from the chamber orchestra has been breached. Ten players are probably one more than the farthest extent of chamber music and yet, with the broadest definition, below the minimum limits of a chamber orchestra. The fact that a conductor is used (not always required in conditions such as this, but a safeguard for performance control) does not negate placement in the chamber music category.

However, no matter how one might argue proper classification (a category must be assigned) there is no arguing the strength of Flagello's short (four and three-quarter minutes) piece. His dectet has Hindemithian craginess, with engaging dry sonority and taut chordal percussiveness. Importantly, the scoring articulates awareness of the special distinctions that must pertain when writing for brass ensemble.

The performance Flagello directs is lucid, sensitively balanced, and neatly colored.

Vocal

Voice with Accompaniment

As I Walked Forth
Good English Hospitality
Leave, O Leave Me to My Sorrows

☐ Reardon (baritone); Herbert (piano) / Serenus 12019

Conservative music, but fitting for the William Blake lines. Serenus fails to include any texts, but fortunately John Reardon's diction needs no improving.

William Flanagan *(1923 - 1969)*

A Concert Ode (1951)

Orchestra

☐ Imperial Philharmonic of Tokyo / Strickland (conductor) / Composers Recordings 143 (monaural)

Lyricism of this sort has been smothered by attention to serialism, pointillism, and other isms. This music is warm with melodic curves and not obvious ones. On the basis of the recorded evidence, Flanagan's work deserves a place on concert programs. The playing is rather bland but it will (have to) get by.

Good-Bye, My Fancy

Vocal

Voice with Accompaniment

☐ Bogard (soprano); Preble (flute); Sullivan (guitar) / Desto 6468

Whitman's text colorfully set with flute and guitar supporting the voice. Neither label nor jacket copy indicates the scoring or gives specific performer credit. In fact, from the label designation one would think the song was for soprano and piano.

Horror Movie	*See How They Love Me*
If You Can	*Time's Long Ago*
Plants Cannot Travel	*The Upside-Down Man*

☐ Bogard (soprano); Del Tredici (piano) / Desto 6468

(All of the single songs are to texts by Howard Moss, *Time's Long Ago* is a cycle of six songs to poems of Melville.)

A few people have realized the special talent Flanagan had for song composition. Proof awaits those who listen to these half-dozen pieces and the cycle called *The Weeping Pleiads* (see under *voice and instrumental ensemble*). Flanagan has brought out the poetry within the poetry. He avoids any exaggeration, word picturization, or academic balances. The music flows, perhaps a bit reticently at times, but in the main there is a technical and intellectual projection that make his songs a major creative experience.

The Weeping Pleiads

Voice and Instrumental Ensemble

☐ Beattie (bass-baritone); Preble (flute); Wrzesien (clarinet); Goldman (violin); Esch (cello); Del Tredici (piano) / Desto 6468

A cycle of five song settings of poems by A. E. Housman. (See under *voice with accompaniment* [*Horror Movie*] for remarks that apply to this cycle as well.)

Another August

Voice and Orchestra

☐ Royal Philharmonic Orchestra / Barton (soprano); Lee (piano) / Jenkins (conductor) / Composers Recordings S–250

A richly neoromantic conception. The very high tessitura was used as a requirement in a commission given the composer. However, he rightfully warns that the extreme range "makes [the] words all but incomprehensible." This applies even when following the printed text supplied by CRI. The suggestion is to abandon textual meaning and listen to this music as a vocalise with piano obbligato and small orchestra.

The Lady of Tearful Regret (1958)

☐ Members of the Oslo Philharmonic Orchestra / Larsen (soprano); Krogh (baritone) / Strickland (conductor) / Composers Recordings 163 (monaural)

Flanagan's music has a searing quality in its clearly tonal, clearly constructed phrases. There are no fussy figurations, obnoxious ornaments, or poky padding. The score, set to an early unpublished poem of Edward Albee, is of poetic motility. *The Lady* should enjoy a long life.

Marius Flothuis (1914-)

Orchestra   **Symphonic Music for Large Orchestra, Op. 59**

☐ Concertgebouw Orchestra / van Beinum (conductor) / Donemus Audio-Visual Series DAVS-6101 (monaural: 10-inch disc)

A four-movement-in-one composition. It begins with a stunning, compulsive five-measure idea that is treated like a thematic ostinato. The succeeding sections present an expressive slow-tempoed portion, an agitato that deals with tight bands of sound, incisive rhythms, and moving lines, and a set of variations (the least interesting and, coincidentally, the most dissonant). Flothuis reminds one of Honegger, especially in terms of musical vigor. The total result of his Symphonic Music is a product of contemporary alertness, crispness, and saltiness.

Choral   ***Round,* Op. 50**

Chorus Alone   ☐ Netherlands Chamber Choir / de Nobel (conductor) / Donemus Audio-Visual Series 6903

Choice text, taken from the dedication of Orlando Gibbons's *First Set of Madrigals and Mottets of 5 Parts,* issued in London in 1612. Flothuis's setting for eight-part chorus, with equally scored proportions between the sopranos, altos, tenors, and basses, is somewhat imitative of Gibbons's writing.

Exceedingly fine singing. The Hollanders enunciate the English words as nicely as their choral colleagues in England and America.

Carlisle Floyd (1926-)

Orchestra   ***In Celebration:* An Overture for Orchestra**

☐ Louisville Orchestra / Mester (conductor) / Louisville 716

The principled operations of overture form are exhibited. Floyd's creative celebration includes some folkish turns.

Vocal   ***The Mystery*—Five Songs of Motherhood for Soprano and Orchestra**

Voice
and Orchestra   ☐ Louisville Orchestra / Curtin (soprano) / Whitney (conductor) / Louisville 635 (monaural)

Five parts with texts by the Chilean poetess Gabriels Mistral, translated by Anita Fleet, serve for this song cycle. In turn the set portrays the wonder of the woman carrying a child, her awareness of kinship with other mothers, asking her husband for understanding, the pain and ecstasy of bearing the child, and finally rocking her newly born baby.

Floyd's score fulfills the highly keyed emotional subject. It embraces a rich vocal line (he is a master in the medium) and fine orchestration. A worthy performance in all respects.

Three Sacred Songs from *Pilgrimage* (1955)

☐ New Orleans Philharmonic Symphony Orchestra / Treigle (bass-baritone) / Torkanowsky (conductor) / Orion 7268

A huge volume could be produced merely listing the titles of vocal and choral works set to Biblical texts. But only a small number of pages would be required to indicate those compositions that go beyond care of the text, that produce creative discovery.

Carlisle Floyd's songs (the first, third, and last in the set) are of such artistic significance. They are beautiful, they are dramatic, and they are magnificently set forth by this vocalist.

George Flynn   (1937-   )

Wound   *Instrumental*

☐ Flynn (piano) / Finnadar 9006   *Piano*

Music of protest—and a violent protest it is as massive percussiveness detonates off the instrument. If Flynn does not protest too much he certainly protests for a long time—twenty-three minutes of unremitting chordal heavyweights, in response to the composer's "perception of the violence both in Vietnam and at home in the streets and on the college campuses."

Josef Bohuslav Foerster   (1859-1951)

Symphony No. 4 (*Easter*) in C minor, Op. 54   *Orchestra*

☐ Prague Symphony Orchestra / Smetáček (conductor) / Nonesuch 71267

Foerster's Symphony combines the traditional melos of Czech music (especially the second movement) with Mahlerian qualities. The four parts of the work picture the Easter season, culminating in a celebration of Christ's resurrection. As the liner notes aptly declare, the composition (styled beautifully on the recording produced by Supraphon in Prague) "can be readily grasped as pure music."

Quintet, Op. 95   *Chamber Music*

☐ Boehm Quintette / Orion 76254

Slovakian melorhythms are combined with Germanic formalism and procedures in Foerster's wind quintet. It is given a beautifully polished and meaningful performance.

David Foley   (1945-   )

Four Pieces for Saturday Afternoon (1966)   *Orchestra*

☐ Composers Festival Orchestra / Brehm (conductor) / Trilogy CTS-1002

Foley in Colorland. Sometimes stark, sometimes static, always interesting. The set (apparently the third and fourth parts are linked; this reviewer could not distinguish more than three and there are only three bands covering the recording) calls for an increasing number of instruments, beginning with the first as a duo for bassoon and harp.

Giovanni Battista Fontana   (?-1630)

Chamber Music

Balletto e pass'e mezzo for Trumpet and Continuo

☐ Schwarz (trumpet); Sharrow (bassoon); Fuller (harpsichord) / Nonesuch 71274

A short, slow-paced dance followed by a racy tempoed one. Unpretentious, and to be enjoyed for the scintillating passage work for the trumpet and bassoon. It offers the type of virtuosity that cleanses the ears of jaded listeners.

Sonatas Nos. 1, 2, 3, 4, 5, and 6 for Trumpet and Continuo

☐ Schwarz (trumpet); Feves (bassoon); Katz (harpsichord) / Desto 6481

A half-dozen from the dozen and one-half Sonatas Fontana produced for *violono o cornetto, fagotto, chitarone, violoncino o simile altro instrumento.* The performance of these works on modern trumpets (Nos. 1, 5, and 6 on a trumpet in C and Nos. 2, 3, and 4 on a D instrument) can be argued only by musicological scholiasts. Listeners realize that the validity of the music is not besmirched by such deviation from stern instrumental truth.

Plenty of virtuosic opportunities in these early baroque pieces, containing slow-tempoed, polyphonic, and dancelike sections. The playing is exemplary, the realizations and ornamentations expertly detailed.

Sonata No. 10 for Trumpet and Continuo

☐ Schwarz (trumpet); Sharrow (bassoon); Fuller (harpsichord) / Nonesuch 71274

Formal embodiment similar to that shown in the other sonatas by this composer (*see above*). There are different performers for the continuo, but the performance is just as thoroughly tidy.

Arthur Foote   (1853-1937)

Orchestra

Francesca da Rimini (1893)

☐ Louisville Orchestra / Mester (conductor) / Louisville LS-754

No more padding than to be found in Tchaikovsky's work of the same name, and with the similar amount of passionate involvement. Initial response may be biased because it's Foote and not Tchaikovsky, but given its chance, Foote's music (which he termed a *Symphonic Prologue*) proves to be of substance.

Instrumental

Organ

Canzonetta in A minor, Op. 71, No. 4

☐ Beck (organ) / Musical Heritage Society OR A-263

From a set of Seven Pieces for Organ. The simplicity of an A-B-A pattern is effectively colored with darker registration in the central portion.

Sonata in G minor for Piano and Violin, Op. 20

Chamber Music

☐ Silverstein (violin); Kalish (piano) / New World Records NW–268

Rich, romantic expressions here, and sensitively stated, especially in the outer movements. The home key of the opening provides a type of tonal dramaticism. However, the stimulant of the minor key is balanced by the temporal use of $\frac{9}{8}$ meter—akin to the pulsatile broadness of a Brahms Allegro. In the finale the determinative aspects expected are present. However, strategically, it is the second theme that becomes principal to the design and provides the piece's peroration. At the age of thirty-seven Foote knew how to create dramatic suavity.

With the appearance of this recording the Gratovich-Benoit presentation on Orion (76243) moves into a firm second place. Silverstein and Kalish are musicians of marvelous accuracy and formidable authority. This is chamber music playing of the highest order.

String Quartet in D major, Op. 70

☐ Kohon Quartet / Vox SVBX–5301

The lyrical flow that relates to Brahms is present. No clamor of dissent can rise for such richnesses. There are four movements (an Allegro, a *Scherzo capriccioso,* an *Andante espressivo,* and a fast-paced finale, introduced by a section in slow tempo). A truly romantic and easily digested string quartet. Full command by the performers.

Piano Quintet in A minor, Op. 38

☐ Boehm (piano); Kooper and Rogers (violins); Maximoff (viola); Sherry (cello) / Turnabout 34556

Despite his American training, Foote's music was wrapped in Germanic paper. It reminds one of Daniel Gregory Mason's remark that "Music hath Brahms to soothe the savage breast." Principally so, in the case of Foote, though the Scherzo has some Mendelssohnian distillations. The preceding movement, an Intermezzo (there is no slow movement, the outer pair of movements being in the expected *allegro* tempo), especially shows Foote's full-nurtured romantic style of writing.

The playing is stylistically confirmed and neatly balanced. These are all solid musicians and one can expect a worthy performance from them.

Christoph Förster *(1693-1745)*

Concerto in E flat major

Solo Instrument and Orchestra

Horn

☐ Academy of St. Martin-in-the-Fields / Tuckwell (horn) / Marriner (conductor) / Angel S–36996

Late baroque music, rather unknown even to hornists, I am told. Tuckwell's performance makes more of the music than it actually contains.

Lukas Foss *(1922-   )*

Baroque Variations (1967)

Orchestra

☐ Buffalo Philharmonic Orchestra / Foss (conductor) / Nonesuch 71202

To the passions of the avant-garde for multimedia, aleatoric adventure, and vellicating vocalisms within mini-dramas, Foss has introduced malconformative music in his *Baroque Variations*. This is music written by others, for the most part, which has been manipulated, fragmented, and artistically distorted. The composers serving as proxies in this essay are Handel (a Larghetto from a Concerto Grosso), Scarlatti (a Sonata), and Bach (a Prelude from a Partita). The title of the third movement, *Phorion*, is especially appropriate—it translates as "borrowed." A smidgen of music here and there is original.

The score combines exact passages with a plan that is improvisational and yet under control. The paradox occurs because certain sounds are to be "played" inaudibly. Where and what will emerge in actual sound is uncertain. The conductor cues the players in and out. This cueing procedure is also free of preciseness, but whether heard or not the line involved is maintained by the player. The surprise is what reaches the ear when sounds are heard, since the notated continuity of each part is maintained, whether sounding out or soundless.

Sweet teachers of traditional composition will doubtless recoil in horror at this treatment of revered composers. But no impiousness is implied. What Foss has accomplished is a surrealistic, dreamlike consideration of classically styled music. The keyword here is variations, which exactly describes the procedure even if it be of diabolic disordering.

It remains to say that the *Baroque Variations* has achieved a considerable number of performances throughout the world, and this acceptance is being maintained. (Movement 3 has been choreographed by one dance company with the ballet title *Aves Mirabiles*.) The Nonesuch release is, without question, not only definitive but marvelously engineered and packaged.

Elytres (1964)

☐ Members of the New York Philomusica Chamber Ensemble / Wummer (flute); Galimir and Rhodes (violins); Levin (piano) / Foss (conductor) / Turnabout 34514

An example of Foss's multiple-choice-formationed music. This is not aleatoric or chance music at all, but is devised for multivariety that is to be obtained from a score arranged with multidiverse solutions. The fully composer-controlled data means that he is taking no chance with chance music but has diagrammed a large number of performance possibilities. A neat creative trick.

Elytres ("Wing Sheaths") calls for a solo flute, two solo violins, distant violins and percussion, harp, vibraphone, and piano—the latter to be played both on the keyboard and on the strings. The percussionist sometimes plays inside the piano with covered mallets.

Tiny sounds titillate the ear, and in one sense the creative game is played with impressionistically designed cards. In another (paradoxical) sense it is exactly the attenuated substances that give Foss's piece its substantial strength.

Geod, for Orchestra (1969)

☐ Buffalo Philharmonic Orchestra / Foss (conductor) / Candide 31042

In some telepathic-testing checks the subject is not given any object to look at during the examination. In *Geod* (an abbreviation for "Geodesics") there is a parallel for the listener. He is given, according to Foss, "a music without beginning or end, without development, without rhetoric, without 'events.'" He also is given choices made by the performers of clusters, sustained sounds, mixtures, figments and fragments, and snips of almost recognizable tunes. Above all, there is a process in this collage of music bits (whatever their formation) of submerging into inaudibility only to reappear later (connected remotely or not all) into audibility.

Indeed, though *Geod* lacks pulse demarcation, and the traditional measurements of pitch arrangement divided into contrasts and formal sequence, it is *a* music. It is a music of clouds and of nebulae that avoids any gravitational center or decisiveness—no matter its statistical uniformity to such identities as bells, hymns, triads, *tremolandi*, glissandi, cymbals, fiddles, and the like.

Many will scream their way away from Foss's work; others (like myself) will be fascinated by the conjectures raised, for there is nothing definite but eclipsed variables in *Geod.* That is the finding after following the composer's direction not to *listen* to the sounds but to *listen in* on the sounds.

Concerto for Oboe and Orchestra (1948)

Solo Instrument and Orchestra

Oboe

☐ Crystal Chamber Orchestra / Gassman (oboe) / Endo (conductor) / Crystal S–851

A Fossian product long before he was self-injected by Darmstadtian creative blood. Classic allegiance is saluted here waving a romantically colored flag. The music compares the bright with the subdued as is proper to classical applicability, with the quieter division based on a Sicilian folk song.

The performance brings honor to a flawless oboist. This is the way an oboe should sound. Seamless smoothness, tasteful tone, incontrovertible interpretation describe the playing of Bert Gassman. Foss must have been pleased. The auditor will be also.

Piano Concerto No. 2

Piano

☐ Los Angeles Festival Orchestra / Foss (piano) / Waxman (conductor) / Varèse Sarabande VC–81052E (monaural)

Four points are to be noted for Foss's Piano Concerto No. 2. He completed the work in 1951 and was the soloist at the world premiere, given in Venice, on October 7, 1951. He then revised the composition two years later. In 1954 Foss's Concerto was given the New York Music Critics' Award.

This is music of romantic casing with some barbed hooks. Foss's Concerto is made to order for a virtuoso, but has no Rachmaninovian music-for-the-keyboard characteristics; rather, it is of tighter cast. No tiny dimensions are considered. The music has brilliance, is almost overdramatic in its manners. It can be considered as a written-down, fantastic improvisation. Throughout, the writing exemplifies a skilled contemporary composer's way of displaying a solo piano without imitating the crisp regulations of the traditional concerto.

Originally this was issued as a Decca monaural disc (DL–9889). Its sound was below average and the balances were capricious. They've been bettered by the remastering done by Varèse Sarabande. Anyway, Foss overrode the sound problems by the force and artistry of his performance.

Capriccio for Cello and Piano

Instrumental

Cello

☐ Piatigorsky (cello); Foss (piano) / New World Records NW–281

A frothy work, making the piano almost a subsidiary voice to the mosaic virtuosity of the stringed instrument. Foss does not peep into the salon; his music is of concert-hall variety, informally glancing at Coplandesque Westernese style and New England square dancing. A fancy as lighthearted as a Haydn finale, superbly tossed off by this pair of creative performers.

Piano

Ni bruit ni vitesse (1973)

☐ Foss (piano); Williams (percussion) / Turnabout 34514

An account of timbred effervescence produced by piano and percussion, the latter all obtained by playing inside the piano and using large cow bells, small Japanese bowls, and tape-covered triangle beaters as contacts. Development of the novel sound material is a throwback to traditional devices, such as canon, transposition, rhythmic augmentation, et cetera.

Ni bruit ni vitesse ("Neither Noise nor Speed") is actually for two pianists and two percussionists. As noted above, only one of each category is credited. Foss and his colleague recorded one part and then added the other while listening with earphones. Good show.

Chamber
Music

Echoi (1963)

Non-Improvisation (1967)

☐ Foss (piano); Yadzinski (clarinet); Davis (cello); Williams (percussion) / Wergo WER-60040

In *Non-Improvisation* a conflict arises in order to break through solid, sustained sound with other, vigorously contrasted material. *Echoi,* on the other hand, sounds serialistic (but is not) and improvisatory simultaneously. There is improvisation, but the controls are defined by the composer so that one hears both coordinated and noncoordinated rhythms, and a process of fade-out and fade-in in the textures. Plenty of echos: canonic, imitations, from a distance, and through the imitating of a previously played bit by the use of prerecorded tape tracks. But the echoes one hears are strictly Fossian.

One writer has termed *Echoi* "one of the most significant works of contemporary chamber music." High praise, which is confirmed by the Wergo recording.

String Quartet No. 1 (1947)

☐ American Art Quartet / Columbia Special Products AML–5476 (monaural)

This work (published as String Quartet in G) followed productions that were initially influenced by Hindemith and then by Copland. The first movement exemplifies aliveness through moving lines, spiced with lyrical themes, assorted in a neo-Hindemithian fashion. But the stringencies here are less ascetic than Hindemith's. Foss filters his through a more luscious cloth. Movement 2, a theme and variations, comprises some eleven peregrinations on the main subject. The variants are free, dovetailing, as it were, several movements in one; harking back (only slightly) to the free form of late Beethoven—thus, a polyglot of variation form itself and slow-scherzo-fast form.

The American Art group performs with tonal beauty and sharply focused ensemble.

The Cave of the Winds (1972)

☐ Dorian Quintet / Vox SVBX–5307

Foss's score is titled *La Grotte des vents* because it was issued by a French music publisher, but it is best known by its English title. The work emphasizes the newest findings for the wind group. Pointedly, the most important point concerns multiphones, whereby two or more pitches (chords, therefore) are sounded simultaneously on a single wind instrument. The *Cave* swarms with these. The initial eleven measures of the piece consist entirely of poly-dissonant mixtures of three-, four-, five-, and six-part chords for the flute, oboe, clarinet, and bassoon. Multiphoned chords occupy the end of the first part, are found in the middle, and in practically every measure of the concluding section. However, this technique is not as yet perfected and the sounds produced are often not of top reliability as to intonation, control, and total balance within a chord. The Dorian group manages quite well, if not perfectly. No matter—the general effect (if not the purity) is unique.

The Cave of the Winds has three distinct sections. A variety of chordal polyphony leads to a mix of figuration, *ad libitum* material, textural shifts, and the like. It is finalized by mass chordal patterns indicated "repeat (à la Morse code)." The next major section is some eight minutes of aleatoric material outlined and "controlled" by the composer. Foss describes it as "strident, pauseless, merciless." (So much for a composer's quasi-sadistic approach to wind-instrument performers!) The final part of the quintet returns to the slow tempo of the beginning (classical ternary form rears its head!); the writing for these thirteen measures is severely vertical. And in one place totally in *pianissimo* unison! Such effect, coming among the "merciless" chordal corrugations, is like a sudden *Mutterakkord* crashing into an elementary Czerny C major exercise.

The Dorian Quintet commissioned Foss's piece and naturally gave it its baptism in public. Thereby being thoroughly acquainted with its excruciating problems, it can be taken for granted that their performance is top class. The composer has "lovingly dedicated" the work to them. Indeed, to have mastered the stupendous problems of Foss's score, a wind quintet team must be lovingly dedicated to its work.

Paradigm (1970)

☐ Williams (percussion); Silverman (electric guitar); Roseman (oboe); Levine (viola); Foss (electric harpsichord) / Williams (conductor) / Turnabout 34514

Still another side of the creative personality of Lukas Foss. Here it is chance music. *Paradigm* (which is subtitled *For my Friends*) allows free choice of instrumentation, manner of performance, and materials. The last not only covers music but textual matter which is fragmented, declaimed, hummed, whispered, or shouted. Whether or not all this makes sense is immaterial; when it does, it is happenstance, and when it doesn't it still makes sense in a sort of theatrical fun-form manner.

Foss's *Paradigm* is conjugated quite well. Within, it includes a jazzy section and one that is dreamy. Fore and aft this musical voyage is extremely entertaining.

Time Cycle (1960)

Vocal

Voice and Orchestra

☐ Columbia Symphony Orchestra and Improvisation Chamber Ensemble / Addison (soprano) / Bernstein (conductor) / Columbia Special Products AMS–6280

Time Cycle represents an interlinking of texts, each referring to time, clocks, or bells, balanced with language, the Auden and Housman poems in English, the Kafka and Nietzsche words in German, and all synchronized in a blend of style that has the attenuativeness of Webern with the rhythmic ictus of Bartók. Running through all of the creation is a poetic eloquence that is an outcome of the basic lyrical talent of Lukas Foss. It proves that given the hand of a master composer atonal music can sing as heartwarmingly as a Schubert *Lied*.

In discussing Foss's *The Song of Songs* (see under *Cantata and Oratorio*) I refer to it as a masterpiece. *Time Cycle* is one as well. It has orchestral sounds that are fantastically inventive, tied to a profound inner beauty. It is the result of a true inspiration.

The recorded performance is an eloquent representation—a repeat of the premiere concert performances by the same forces, though for some unexplained reason the New York Philharmonic is here called the Columbia Symphony Orchestra. The three interludes that are heard between the songs (played by Foss at the piano; Richard Dufallo, clarinet; Howard Colf, cello; and Charles DeLancey, percussion) are simply an added attraction and do not form part of Foss's composition. They are excellent by themselves but do not add very much to the work. Adele Addison sings with an all-conquering artistry that shows that even those habituated to tonal music can imbue serial sounds with parallel depth and beauty. Her singing is perfection itself.

Choral

Chorus with Accompaniment

Behold! I Build an House (1950)

☐ Roger Wagner Chorale / MacInnes and Foss (pianos) / Wagner (conductor) / Composers Recordings S-123

An example of Foss's favorite method (when he practiced tonalism) of using a Biblical text. Because of the fluid writing there is no retreat into strict formalism. Regardless of Foss's classic adaptations, this is the work of a romanticist.

The performance is splendid in every aspect, and since Foss is one of the participants it can be considered definitive.

Psalms (1956)

☐ Roger Wagner Chorale / Gordon, Levitt, and Wyatt (vocalists); MacInnes and Foss (pianos) / Wagner (conductor) / Composers Recordings S-123

Although the texts of four Psalms are used, the music is not partitioned; the forceful idea of contrast within continuity guides the conception.

There is less significant temper in this version than in the one which calls for symphonic partnership, with its stimulating plectral and pungent orchestration. No recording exists, however, of the second setting. The Wagner people give a good reading.

Chorus and Instrumental Ensemble

The Fragments of Archilochos (1965)

☐ Crane Collegiate Singers, State University College at Potsdam / Betts (tenor); Abramowitsch and Strauss (speakers); Rantucci (mandolin); Marcus (guitar); Williams, Burnham, and Harbold (percussion) / McElheran (conductor) / Wergo WER-60040

The text used is based on the poetry of Archilochos (714–676 B.C.). The text heard is segmented and distributed. It is so arranged that many choices are available, with the results most often meaningless. But the wild dynamic temper of the piece, with its decomposition of the textual composition, is meaningful.

Brock McElheran directs magnificently. The expertise he displays is vivid proof of his abilities in conducting extremely difficult avant-garde works.

Cantata and Oratorio

The Song of Songs (1947)

☐ New York Philharmonic / Tourel (mezzo-soprano) / Bernstein (conductor) / Composers Recordings S-284E (monaural)

This writer prophecies that the future will prove that this Biblical Cantata is Foss's greatest work, though Foss no longer considers this style in his creative practice. (The Cantata predates the period when Foss moved into the avant-garde circle in a desire to shed his tonal past fully and reside in the territory of what he once termed "dangerous music.")

The Song of Songs is a combination of pure love music and sonorous sensuality, and its style is also a combination—neo-Bachian (semi-Hindemithian) material decorated with cantillative embroideries. The music rises into its third section with a passionate probe that is then finalized with one of the most beautiful sections in the vocal literature (part 4: *Set Me as a Seal upon Thine Heart).*

When Foss wrote this work he was past the *Wunderkind* period during which he was composing music at an age when most youngsters hardly know the alphabet. Nevertheless, *The Song of Songs,* written at the age of twenty-five, shows an emotive depth that one rarely expects from a composer in his twenties.

The performance is a glowing one. Jennie Tourel was at her peak when the work was originally recorded in 1961. Her voice is rich and full, her diction and phrasing are exemplary, and the extremely low notes are nicely resonant. Bernstein has the work fully in hand. The recording was released in 1962 by Columbia, then deleted (truly an artistic error, regardless of what the financial report on sales may have shown). CRI wisely picked up the masters and released an edition within its "program of reissuing contemporary music of extraordinary historical interest." What has been reissued is a masterpiece.

Jean Françaix *(1912-)*

Concerto for Piano and Orchestra (1937)

☐ Orchestra of Radio Luxembourg / Calude Paillard-Françaix (piano) / Jean Françaix (conductor) / Turnabout 34552

Solo Instrument and Orchestra

Piano

Hedonistic easy-come, easy-go music in Françaix's bright neoclassic style. There are four movements, precisely balanced, with parts 1 and 3 minus any tempo indication, the second movement an Andante, and the fourth an Allegro.

This utterly French music, down to the last flippant sixteenth note, receives a joyful and (naturally) a definitive performance by father-composer, daughter-pianist, and their most cooperative colleagues.

Rhapsody for Viola and Small Orchestra (1946)

Viola

☐ Orchestra of Radio Luxembourg / Koch (viola) / Françaix (conductor) / Turnabout 34552

Though in this case somewhat more mellow in keeping with the timbre of the solo string instrument, Françaix's witty and fluid neoclassic writing is never in danger of dying out. The Rhapsody is proof. It provides civilized music, covering ideas that never belabor the point or are ever a bit labored.

The recording is a profitable presentation. With Françaix conducting the commentary is properly paced and balanced. With Ulrich Koch the various colors are defined and the solo line published clean and clear. Good show.

Suite for Violin and Orchestra (1934)

Violin

☐ Orchestra of Radio Luxembourg / Lautenbacher (violin) / Françaix (conductor) / Turnabout 34552

Françaix owns the franchise for the lighter facets of neoclassicism. Here is a perfect example: scalic twists in the first movement, simple melodic warmth in movement 2, square-dancey rhythms in movement 3, and a bouncy finale.

The recording personnel render the athletic prose and exuberant humor that pervade the music with artistic intelligence.

Instrumental

Piano,
Four Hands

Danses exotiques (Excerpts)

☐ Joy and Robin-Bonneau (pianos) / Musical Heritage Society MHS–849/850

Some of the dances are recognizable types such as a *Mambo* and a *Sambe lente,* and others strongly suggest formal discovery, such as the opening *Pambiche* and No. 3: *Nube gris.* Six are performed, two are omitted: *Malambeando* and *Rock 'n' Roll.*

To be sure it's Françaix and his neoclassical syntax, but there are also the high delights of good tunes, pointed rhythms, and alluring textures. The piano team presents the music with warmth, splendid rhythmic vigor (but never overdone), and taste.

Chamber
Music

Sonatine for Violin and Piano (1934)

☐ Steiner (violin); Berfield (piano) / Orion 75195

Compared to Stravinsky's neoclassic discourse, Françaix writes limericks. His lines are ruled off, bisected. For example, practically the entire first movement is formed from two- and four-measure phrases in capricious language. It is played by these artists with the fullest confidence in conveying the jigs and joggles of the pert scherzo idea over and over again. It equates with minute outlined Stravinsky, decidedly *not* in the grand manner.

The short Andante is expressed by a plan of antiphonal scoring in triplex denomination. A set of pithy variations completes the work. Here again structure and style are well defined.

Divertissement for Oboe, Clarinet, and Bassoon (1947)

☐ de Lancie (oboe); Gigliotti (clarinet); Schoenbach (bassoon) / Columbia Special Products AMS–6213

Music conceived in the tonal-yet-not-throttled technique of neoclassicism. This is music similar to an acrobat on a tightrope; he makes all the gestures of falling off, creates much excitement, but keeps everything under control.

The playing by these superb musicians is a delight, marked with elastic finesse. They understand Françaix's style and his harmonic ropes and know full well how to sway on them. Indeed, they have all it takes.

At the time this recording was made these three musicians with two others constituted the Philadelphia Woodwind Quintet. John de Lancie and Sol Schoenbach were solo wind players in the Philadelphia Orchestra but have departed for musical administrative posts. Anthony Gigliotti still functions as the principal clarinetist of the Philadelphia organization.

Gaguenardise

☐ Paul Brodie Saxophone Quartet / Golden Crest 4131

The first movement of Françaix's *Petit Quatuor.* It illustrates his usual role as the bright boulevardier of the neoclassic musical lodge.

Quintet for Flute, Violin, Viola, Cello, and Harp

☐ Marie-Claire Jamet Quintet / Musical Heritage Society MHS–883

As usual Françaix cannot be accused of harmonic incuriosity in this work, but the probing is strictly within neoclassic boundaries. Tonalities (F major, D minor, G major, and G major again) cover the four movements but do not block a lightly-paced freshness throughout and, for comparison, a gentle expressivity. The swift and witty finale is Haydn dressed in smart twentieth-century clothes. And there's a smart performance by this group named after the harpist.

Quintet for Winds (1948)

☐ New York Woodwind Quintet / Concert-Disc 222 (also listed as Everest 3080)

Mostly verve and go for this fellow, a member of the neoclassic group. Only the slow movement has a serious demeanor. There are assorted delights (and all probed deftly by the performers) in Françaix's Quintet, including the thumb-to-the-nose gestures in the first movement, and the snide clownish steps in the final *Tempo di marcia francese*. This sort of musical sweet is Françaix's specialty of the house.

Divertissement for Bassoon and String Quintet (1944)

☐ Melos Ensemble / Angel S–36586

The usual candid light dissonances of this composer. These are used for unequivocal definition of his neoclassic correlativity. Totally pleasant music performed with excellence.

Françaix / *Francis Poulenc*. See Poulenc / Françaix.

Petronio Franceschini (ca. 1650-1680)

Instrumental

Sonata à 7 for Two Trumpets, Strings, and Continuo

Two Trumpets

☐ Consortium Musicum / Tarr and Bodenroder (baroque trumpets); Müller-Dombois (lute); Thoene (harpsichord); Bickbach (positive organ) / Lehan (conductor) / Nonesuch 71217

Well recorded and characteristically presented by the use of baroque trumpets. The soloists are almost perfect (one measure wavers in pitch, and in this clean and open writing is impossible to overlook but should be forgiven) and realize the imitative conversation with panache.

Arnold Franchetti (1906-   )

Orchestra

Three Italian Masques (1953)

☐ New York Brass Ensemble / Hanson (piano); Sankey (bass); Gould (percussion) / Baron (conductor) / Composers Recordings 125 (monaural)

A puppet-show tale about a cuckolded husband is the springboard for this work, subtitled Concertino for Piano, Brass, Percussion, and Bass. The brass group consists of three trumpets and two trombones.

Sprightly twelve-tone derivations are used both in the Variations of movement 1 and the *Imbroglio e baruffa* of movement 3. A squared-to-the-last-chord Serenade (the central part) is in direct contrast, being set in E flat major. Its tonal state—almost a prosaic one—cleverly serves to brighten and ready the ear for the truly rhapsodic ventures surrounding the finale's total chromaticism.

Without score reference it can be taken for granted that the performance well serves the composer's conception.

César Franck   (1822-1890)

Orchestra

Le Chasseur maudit (1882)

☐ L'Orchestre de la Suisse Romande / Ansermet (conductor) / London 6222

Ansermet paces this work magnificently and presents a dramatic address that simply outclasses the competition. Vivid, dynamic interchanges and sharpened ictus in the rhythms make this performance of "The Accursed Huntsman" exciting.

Les Eolides (1876)

☐ Budapest Philharmonic Orchestra / Martin (conductor) / Turnabout 34626

Les Eolides shivers with chromaticism and the outlines can easily get blurred. Martin gives an expressive reading of Franck's symphonic poem, and realizing that pedestrian pace would kill the work, keeps the measures on the move. This also removes stickiness from the harmonic tissue.

Rédemption (1874)

☐ Budapest Philharmonic Orchestra / Martin (conductor) / Turnabout 34626

Franck at his most religious. *Rédemption*, Franck stated, was to evoke "the joy of the world as it becomes transformed and blossoms through the Word of Christ." And the Word is some seraphic brass, with a great many devotionally chromatic phrases. Indeed, the work is full of Franckian habits, but these melodic, harmonic, and textural features are what make Franck great and identify him.

Martin permits the idiom to speak for itself without overstressing or overreproducing, which might heighten the color but infringe on the style. This does not mean the performance is nerveless. Rather, it is heard as an authoritative interpretation of Franck's piece. (It was written in 1871, and a second version—the one heard here—was completed in 1874.)

Symphony in D minor (1888)

☐ Chicago Symphony Orchestra / Monteux (conductor) / RCA LSC-2514

The outward tonal splendor of this essay is truly magnificent. Yet there are muscle and guts holding the inner material together, and that is where Franckian strength lies; namely, in the fractional conjunct movement of his lines and harmonies. Every specific in the score is identified by Monteux, but never at the expense of the big line.

This tonal splendor is available in Ormandy's performances (one on Columbia MS-6297, the other on Odyssey Y-33922), but it blots out the detail, and how much golden sound and just golden sound can one take?

Symphonic Variations for Piano and Orchestra (1885)

☐ Philadelphia Orchestra / Casadesus (piano) / Ormandy (conductor) / Odyssey Y-31274

For stylistic demeanor and musical efficiency, without a single arbitrary interpretative decision, this remains the top performance. It is not a sparkling new recorded edition and the sound is far from creamy rich, but the definition of Franck's style is preferable to anyone else's. The Casadesus-Ormandy team deliver it beautifully and completely.

Six Pièces pour grand orgue

No. 1—*Fantaisie* in C major, Op. 16

☐ Demessieux (organ) / London STS-15104

One applauds the registrational decisions made to bear upon the content of Franck's beautiful piece. Thus the delicacy of the *Allegretto cantando* section is a stunner. No fanciful indulgence by this superb organist.

Six Pièces pour grand orgue

No. 6—*Final*, Op. 21

☐ Demessieux (organ) / London STS-15105

A vigorous and brilliant performance to match the Franckian conception. But there is more—everything is conceived in an extremely musical manner and therefore, despite the powerful colors and heavy textures, falls easily on the ears.

Six Pièces pour grand orgue

No. 2—*Grande pièce symphonique*, Op. 17

☐ Dupré (organ) / Mercury 75059

Franck's longest piece in the half dozen of the set (close to twenty-six minutes in performance time) is essentially music cast in sonata form. It needs a big hand and a big thrust, and Marcel Dupré provides it in full. Of the competition, only Jeanne Demessieux (on London STS-15104) comes closest. The others do release the instrument's vast color range, but while this displays the organ they play it does not offer much help in codifying the structural sense of the work. Dupré's selection processes in "scoring" are of the best blend and provide the most notable result.

Six Pièces pour grand orgue

No. 4—*Pastorale*, Op. 19
No. 3—*Prélude, fugue et variation*, Op. 18
No. 5—*Prière*, Op. 20

☐ Demessieux (organ) / London STS-15105

The *Prière* has been described as one of the most intensely expressive organ pieces ever written. In this splendidly clear portrayal there is substantiation. The *Pastorale* ranges wide of its title, including scherzo and fugato properties. Demessieux effectively binds all the material in a rich presentation; the conclusion is particularly effective.

Demessieux's ability to endow each piece with its particular character makes her playing of this program beyond praise.

Solo
Instrument
and
Orchestra

Piano

Instrumental

Organ

647

Trois Chorals (1890)

No. 1 — in E major / No. 2 — in B minor / No. 3 — in A minor

☐ Dupré (organ) / Mercury 75006

Listening to these pieces, one must remember that Franck was a church organist for over thirty years. Undoubtedly, there is a creative subconscious offshoot in the music, the result of improvising, modulating, and filling in sections of church services.

Variational in concept, the pieces have highlights such as the fugal section in the second of the set and the beautiful *cantabile* portion in the A minor piece. Dupré's playing shows rich imagination in his performance translation and brings a rediscovery of the music that minimizes its chromaticism. In other presentations that element becomes terribly cloying. The organ used is housed in St. Thomas's Church in New York City.

Trois Pièces pour grand orgue (1878)

No. 2 — Cantabile
No. 1 — Fantaisie in A major
No. 3 — Pièce héroïque

☐ Demessieux (organ) / London STS–15103

The greatest attention by organists is given to the third of this group. Overstatement becomes a prime defect, but Jeanne Demessieux, playing the organ of the Church of the Madeleine in Paris, gauges matters perfectly, using well-chosen registration, and thereby makes the piece artistically vivid. The *Fantaisie* hops, skips, and jumps a great deal, but that's Mr. Franck and not Miss Demessieux speaking. Nice quality and finely poised performance of the B major *Cantabile*, admirably covered at a *non troppo lento* pace.

Piano

Prélude, aria, et final (1887)

☐ Chodos (piano) / Orion 73122

Music from Franck's final period of work. Rarely performed and represented in the record catalogue by this entry only. Sympathetic playing, with especially fine momentum in the finale.

Prélude, choral, et fugue (1884)

☐ Moravec (piano) / Connoisseur Society S–2062

The harmonic ski turns in Franck's music (especially on the piano) need a very careful adjustment and balance; otherwise the performer goes off course to defeat. In this case Moravec makes a perfect schuss. It is a distinguished performance.

Chamber Music

Sonata in A major for Cello and Piano (transcription of the Violin and Piano Sonata) (1886)

☐ du Pré (cello); Barenboim (piano) / Angel S–36937

If you look just for sheer performance beauty, then naturally this transcription of the original for violin will provide good values (a number of cellists do play the piece—there are two other recordings). But if it's Franck's music you want to hear, choose the original listed and discussed *below*.

Sonata in A major for Flute and Piano (transcription of the Violin and Piano Sonata) (1886)

☐ Galway (flute); Argerich (piano) / RCA LRL1–5095

An oddball. Listening to the Franck violin and piano sonata in an instrumental transcription to which one is not accustomed takes some adjustment. Bearing in mind sales potentials, the publishers of the Franck opus did issue versions for cello or viola in place of the violin, and the cello version does get a fair amount of play (*see above*), while the viola version is hardly heard. Now comes Galway, who probably made this transcription.

James Galway plays the work magnificently, but his glorious tone notwithstanding, the flute doesn't have string-instrument muscle. Even with the considered reticence of Martha Argerich the balances are often iffy, and when they are not, the textural impulse is toned down and thus wanting. But you want Galway notwithstanding? Understandable, so the Franck arrangement is your ticket for Galway front and center and for Franck in the back rows. But, with apologies to Franck, the sheer musicality of this flutist chap show him to be a great master of his instrument.

Sonata in A major for Violin and Piano (1886)

☐ Nadien (violin); Hancock (piano) / Monitor S–2017
☐ Perlman (violin); Ashkenazy (piano) / London 6628

In addition to those listed above, run down the list of the teams that have recorded this great work and whose performances are currently available: Heifetz-Rubinstein, on a monaural disc, Seraphim 60230; Heifetz-Smith, on Columbia M2–33444; Stern-Zakin, on Columbia MS-6139; Oistrakh-Richter, on Melodiya/Angel S–40121 (the major league representatives); and Wilkomirska-Barbosa, on Connoisseur Society CSG-2050, plus Zsigmondy-Nissen, on Klavier 534 (these last two situated a few rungs below). Certainly it would be expected that one of these (at least from the first group) would be represented in this entry. But none can compare to the superb revelation of the Sonata made by David Nadien and David Hancock. It is, without doubt, the *ne plus ultra* of any recorded performance of Franck's opus. Its interiority is minutely delineated, its exteriority is blazing and yet its surfaces are not roughed but polished to a high gloss of emotive outpour. The legati are satiny, the balances of such order that for once the piano articulates and doesn't become muddy, fouling the violin's homophonic line. The music's immensity comes through without two-instrument symphonicism. This is ideal chamber-music playing of elegance and dynamism.

The Perlman-Ashkenazy account has passion and conviction and also refuses to enter by instrumental aggressiveness a domain in which the music does not belong. Nonetheless, it is heavier, with more volume and movement than described by Nadien-Hancock.

Of the two Heifetz performances the one with Rubinstein is far better than the one with Brooks Smith. In the latter case the dynamic dips and the use of harmonics that weaken agogic weights are just too much to accept. The performance is not well recorded either, and since it was done live one is subjected to applause at start and finish. (Why can't such noise be deleted from the tape, or is it left in to prove the recording was made live and therefore please forgive all the errors and imbalances?) There is applause at the end of the Oistrakh-Richter live-recorded affair but none at the beginning. However, there are audience shuffles and undertones that interfere with listening. Though the playing is rich and impressive it tends to personalize the piano part too often and balances go awry.

Piano Quintet in F minor (1879)

☐ Quartet of the Bolshoi Theatre Orchestra / Richter (piano) / Monitor 2036 (monaural)

The closest competition for this great work for string quartet and piano is with a recording (on RCA LSC-2739) resultant from the Heifetz-Piatigorsky Concerts. However, despite Monitor's less robust sound, its performance takes first place, for it is performance that must take precedence over sound, providing the latter is adequate. The Heifetz-led reading is just that—too much Heifetz and too slurpy Heifetz. There's plenty of chromatic intervallic agitation in Franck's work without adding to it the protesting matter of portamenti and indulgent phrasing.

Further, the Bolshoi four and their notable pianist never try to play as a symphonic hand-me-down, scaling the five instruments to resemble thrice that amount. At all times the work is considered as a chamber-music composition. No matter the texture, the clarity of the part writing is made clear. And they play the slow movement as the *lento* it is, not the Heifetz-led *moderato* it isn't.

Cantata and Oratorio

Psyché (1888)

☐ Orchestre de Liège and Belgian Radio Chorus / Strauss (conductor) / Connoisseur Society 2096

The best performance of Franck's mix of sensuality and mysticism. And truly the most authentic, since Paul Strauss presents the complete score. Barenboim (on Deutsche Grammophon 2530771) presents only the orchestral sections.

Melchior Franck   (ca. 1579-1639)

Brass Ensemble

Intrada II

☐ Brass Ensemble / Masson (conductor) / Nonesuch 71111

Franck's short piece comes from a collection titled New Musical *Intradas* for All Sorts of Instruments. It fits the brass group perfectly especially because of its neat proclamatory tone, spiced with gentle frictions.

Choral

Chorus Alone

Ihr Lieben

☐ Canby Singers / Canby (conductor) / Nonesuch 71026

''Beloved'' has hymnodic contours. It needs nothing more to make its point, one that is conveyed by the just proportions of the singing.

Johan Franco   (1908-   )

Orchestra

Symphony No. 5 (Cosmos) (1958)

☐ North Holland Philharmonic Orchestra / Arends (conductor) / Composers Recordings S-135E (monaural)

Somewhat mystical in its main title and subtitles, which deal with *The Beginning, Nocturne, The Planets,* and *The Earth and Man.* Cyclic technique is used, which tightens the work served up by sections and aesthetic unrest.

The Hollanders are in the category of our top community orchestras. This makes possible an adequate consideration of Franco's score, if not a fully realized one.

José Maria Franco   (20th cent.)

Cancion y danza   *Instrumental*

Lullaby   *Harp*

☐ Robles (harp) / Argo ZRG–5457

Everything is poetic, even the "Dance." Robles plays these pieces in typical Basque style, gently and clean in phrase.

Andrew Frank   (1946-   )

Orpheum (**Night Music I**)   *Instrumental*

☐ Lois Burge (piano) / Composers Recordings SD–345   *Piano*

Frank's piece represents freely developed motival material. The evidence of structural control makes *Orpheum* a composition of solidity. Lois Burge makes certain that this is retained in her playing, avoiding any episodic delineation in her interpretation.

Benjamin Franklin   (1706-1790)

Quartet for Three Violins and Cello   *Chamber Music*

☐ Kohon Quartet / Vox SVBX–5301

Maybe spurious, maybe not. (The composition was found in Paris in 1945 and was published there the following year.) Musically primitive, musically amateurish. But if by the philosopher, writer, musical amateur, statesman, educator, inventor, and humanitarian, then its sheer curiosity value outweighs all other arguments and to have a recorded performance is invaluable.

But double curiosity is offered. Franklin's odd "string quartet" makeup is *totally*, from first sound to last, in F major, and all pitches are heard via open strings. Accordingly, retuning is required of all four instruments (called *scordatura*) and no two are alike. Minus modulation or chromatic intercession (the fingers of the left hand are not used in a single instance), Franklin's five-movement suite of simple forms is the first complete work in musical history using solely open strings. Regardless of its restricted artistic result, it is a worthy experiment.

Frederick II of Prussia   (1712-1786)

Sonata in C minor   *Chamber Music*

☐ Rampal (flute); Veyron-Lacroix (harpsichord) / Everest 3180

The greatest interest in Frederick the Great's piece applies to the end movements. The Sonata opens with a Recitativo linked to an Arioso and concludes with a Fugato.

Everest gives the tonality as C major, but the piece begins with the key of C minor.

Girolamo Frescobaldi (1583-1643)

Brass Ensemble

Canzon Quarta

☐ Brass Ensemble / Masson (conductor) / Nonesuch 71111

An ensemble *canzon* included in Frescobaldi's first published book of ensemble *canzoni*.

Instrumental

Harpsichord

Balletto Terzo

☐ Kipnis (harpsichord) / Columbia M3X–31521

From Frescobaldi's *Toccate e partite d'intavolatura di Cimbalo* and set in three parts: *Balletto, Corrente del balletto,* and *Passacagli*. Rather sober music and Kipnis follows suit.

Organ

La Frescobalda from Arie Musicale a Più Voci

☐ Zanaboni (organ) / Everest 3173

Fastidious polyphony and vertical arrangement. It is played on a beautifully sounding organ housed in St. Guiseppe's Church in Brescia, Italy. The registration is ideal, defining the clear, sensitive nature of the music.

Chamber Music

Canzoni per Sonar

☐ Schwarz (trumpet); Feves (bassoon); Katz (harpsichord) / Desto 6481

Each of the five *canzoni* is multisectionally structured. The performance stresses this factor and still achieves a tidy coherence. Versatility and virtuosity and fully exemplified.

Peter Racine Fricker (1920-)

Orchestra

Symphony No. 1, Op. 9

☐ Louisville Orchestra / Whitney (conductor) / Louisville S–675

The outer divisions of the four movements are basically controlled by Sonata designs; the textures carefully proportioned for contrast. A lighter touch is found in the third movement, Tableau and Dance, in direct contrast to the rhythmical vitality found for the greater part in Fricker's work.

Whitney produces this opus with firm ability and sparkling spontaneity. (The listing of the movements on the liner note reverses the last two movements.)

Chamber Music

Wind Quintet, Op. 5

☐ London Wind Quintet / Argo 5326

There is gaiety and wit in Fricker's pantonal work that reflects both Hindemith and

Bartók style. Canonic variations and fugal sections highlight the piece but there is neither academicism nor padding. Fricker picks his sounds carefully and doesn't waste a single one.

Nothing but praise for the splendid playing, a lesser amount for Argo's failure to list the headings of the four movements of the opus—a rare slip-up for this fine recording firm.

Géza Frid *(1904-)*

Symphonietta for Strings, Op. 66

□ Limburg Symphony Orchestra / Rieu (conductor) / Donemus Audio-Visual Series DAVS–6703 (monaural)

String Orchestra

No reticence on Frid's part. The strings don't play behind the bridge or slap their instruments—there are no avant-garde exuberances, but simply a colorful approach to sonority scale and minute attention to registral possibilities. In movement 1, the percussive pizzicati and polyphonic glissandi blocks are enticing, entrancing, and exciting. The movement ends in the lowest voices, preceded by a huge double bass solo. Movement 2 is Bartók revisited; movement 3 is a sectionally designed delight of sound, motility, and rhythm.

Excellently performed, cogently balanced. This is a work deserving of attention by major orchestras.

Ignaz Friedman *(1882-1948)*

***Elle danse*, Op. 10, No. 5**

From *Estampes*, Op. 22

***Minuetto Vecchio*, Op. 76, No. 6**

Viennese Waltz No. 1 and Viennese Waltz No. 2 on Themes by Gaertner

□ Friedman (piano) / Klavier 115

Instrumental

Piano

If you're interested in comparing Ignaz Friedman the concert pianist to Ignaz Friedman the composer, here are some good examples. The music resides in salon land but the temperature is not tepid but temperate. More of the Viennese dances are to be found listed *below*.

Need it be said that Friedman plays Friedman enchantingly?

Viennese Waltz

No. 3 on a Theme by Gaertner / No. 4 on a Theme by Gaertner

□ Friedman (piano) / Klavier 119

More waltz music developed from melodies given the pianist-composer by the Austrian baritone Eduard Gaertner. (*See above* for the first two in the set.)

Five Waltzes for Piano Four-Hands

□ Friedman (piano) / Klavier 115

Piano, Four Hands

A full one-man show. Friedman plays his own music and plays both *primo* and *secondo* parts via the dubbing process. Originally, this was accomplished on the Steinway Duo-Art piano. The technique works nicely, the music sounds sweetly. All that's missing are potted palms.

Johann Jakob Froberger (1616-1667)

Instrumental

Harpsichord

Fantasy No. 2 in E minor

Lamentation in C major

☐ Goldstein (harpsichord) / Pandora 101

Authentic playing using authentic (nontempered) tuning of the harpsichord.
The Fantasy is in the Phrygian mode. The Lamentation is from Froberger's C major Suite.

Herbert Fromm (1905-)

Instrumental

Organ

Partita: *Let All Mortal Flesh Keep Silent* (1940)

☐ Noehren (organ) / Lyrichord 7191

Variation tactics applied to a liturgical fundament. The recording is splendid; the liner notes, an abrogation of responsibility. Nary a word about Fromm's work, and the same goes for the other half-dozen pieces included in the release (*20th Century American Organ Music*).

Chamber Music

String Quartet

☐ Pro Arte Quartet / Lyrichord 7203

A quartet with a divertimento slant, with its seven movements in variation form. The variational progress samples assorted designs: *scherzo, recitative, arioso, march, ländler,* and *rondo*. Serious music, minus floridity, a music devoted to classicism in the large sense, with perceptive regard for harmonic order.

Fromm's Quartet is clearly indited. The manner in which the Pro Arte foursome play it is certainly the way it should go.

William Henry Fry (1813-1864)

Instrumental

Piano

Adieu (Song for the Piano)

☐ Davis (piano) / New World Records NW–257

Fry's only completed piano piece; short and in a pensive mood. It is excellently presented.

Julius Fučik *(1872-1916)*

Donausagen **Waltz**

Entry of the Gladiators

Florentine **March**

Herzogewina **March**

Marinarella **Overture**

The Old Bear with a Sore Head

Winter Storms **Waltz**

☐ Czech Philharmonic / Formacek (bassoon) / Neumann (conductor) / Quintessence PMC-7038

Great pop stuff. Included is one of the most famous circus marches, *Entry of the Gladiators,* played as no one has ever heard it in public. Fučik was a Czech and that native tang flavors both the Overture and the *Herzogewina* March. *The Old Bear* is a light brew that is fortified with special bassoon seasoning (the bassoon was the composer's instrument).

Neumann sharply colors each piece and like Arthur Fiedler, the conductor of the Boston Pops Orchestra, the phrasing and colors are heard with immaculate representation. The superficiality that has so often ruined worthy light music is absent from these performances of stylistic fidelity.

Carl Fuerstner *(1912-   )*

Nocturne and Dance, Op. 36

☐ Pellerite (flute); Webb (piano) / Coronet S-1713

The Nocturne has hazy impressionistic curves. Contrastive and equalized expressivity is heard in the grotesque points of the Dance. Extremely well conceived for the flute and well executed by the flutist. The piano sound is below par.

Kazuo Fukushima *(1930-   )*

Hi-kyò for Flute, Piano, Strings, and Percussion

☐ Soloists of the Rome Symphony Orchestra / Gazzelloni (flute) / Maderna (conductor) / RCA VICS-1313

Fukushima's *Hi-kyò* (meaning "flying mirror"—the Japanese word for the moon) comprises three sections. Microtones predominate and a type of squared percussion sonority.

No one can play contemporary flute music the way Severino Gazzelloni can. All the tricky techniques are tossed off with ease and all of them with impeccable musicality. It's simply marvelous and so is Maderna's part in the performance.

Chamber Music

Three Pieces from *Chū-U* for Flute and Piano (1964)

☐ Sollberger (flute); Wuorinen (piano) / Nonesuch 73028

Concentrated in every respect. Pitch movement is restrained. Rhythms have a sense of arrested motion, with isolated chordal insets by the piano, while the flute line can be described as being mostly the equivalent of pulselessness, its formations curving in and out and around a pitch point. The textures are sparse—in movement two the piano is silent. While there is more motility to the dynamics, they, too, tend to a demarcative (thus concentrated) arrangement.

One is reminded in this music of the flat color washes of Japanese prints. The playing emphasizes this parallel and provides a fascinating quality akin to persistent immobility.

Wilhelm Furtwängler (1886-1954)

Chamber Music

Sonata in D major

☐ Müller-Nishio (violin); Dennemarck (piano) / Musical Heritage Society MHS-3026

Here is your opportunity to assuage your curiosity as to what sort of music this great conductor wrote. Be prepared for massivity rare in the world of the duo Sonata: close to fifty minutes worth! Stylewise, the music binds late Beethoven (the middle movement) with Brahms (the outer movements). It plays well and is well played, but the listener might want to make his own cuts by lifting the record needle and replacing it. (This, though not noted, is the second of Fürtwangler's violin and piano Sonatas. The first, published two years prior, in 1938, is of similar length.)

Charles Fussell (1938-   )

Orchestra

Three Processionals for Orchestra (1973)

☐ Springfield Symphony Orchestra / Gutter (conductor) / Opus One 21

Powerful scoring (a kinship with Berg) and a certain heaviness of weight (a reminder of Ives) permeate Fussell's orchestrational prose. The composer states there are "many textures which recall Debussy." If so, then it is Debussy with a stern visage. Regardless, there is a liberated activization in this music that has significant meaning.

The Springfield Symphony Orchestra is a very pliable instrument and an expert one. It proves that all the action is not necessarily in the big towns. Credit for this goes to the conductor, Robert Gutter. Fussell's score is of advanced essences. That the Springfielders can field such music so expertly makes one sit up and take notice.

Johann Joseph Fux (1660-1741)

Orchestra

Concentus Musico Instrumentalis

    Rondeau à 7
    Serenada à 8
    Sonata à 4

☐ Vienna Concentus Musicus / Harnoncourt (conductor) / Telefunken 641271

Further proof that nullifies any statement that Fux only produced dry, academic music. The three Partitas (suites) move with agility and sparkle, particularly the *Serenada à 8*, the most sizable work of those recorded here. (There are seven suites in all in the *Concentus Musico Instrumentalis*—another representation [the final one in the set] is discussed under *Chamber Music.)*

The performance is a spontaneous and naturally directed one.

Concentus Musico Instrumentalis: **Partita in F**

Chamber Music

☐ Camerata Musicale / Nonesuch 71085

Fluid and nicely inventive chamber music for flute, oboe, and a continuo of cello and harpsichord. Fux's ability as a contrapuntalist is proclaimed in the third part where melodies representing Italian and French styles are partnered. It highlights a work that includes a three-part Sinfonia and two picturesquely titled movements (*La Joye des fidels sujets* and *Les Ennemis confus*). The former heading has some relationship to the triple-beat pulse of the music but the other one, also Minuet-like (as Joshua Rifkin indicates in his expert notes), is totally healthy and refreshing, and even gentle, so apparently Fux's ''confused enemies'' is simply a humorous title tactic.

Lightness of execution, smoothly localized. Good tone, if the slightly nasal timbre of the oboe is accepted.

G

Pierre Gabaye (1930-)

Sonatine for Flute and Bassoon

Chamber Music

☐ Skowronek (flute); Grossman (bassoon) / Crystal 351

Poulencian patter and lyricism, with all its intonations modulated neatly. Gabaye shows a vivid and intuitive imagination in his wind duo. Topflight playing by the soloists.

Harley Gaber (1943-)

The Winds Rise in the North (1975)

Chamber Music

☐ Cummiskey, Goldstein, and Seplow (violins); Reynolds (viola); Gibson (cello) / Titanic 16–17

Clustered sonority bands in constant, slow-moving discharge. Gaber's raw-blistered music; absent of melody, counterpoint, rhythm, related motion, and form, concentrating only on sheer staticness, derives from the composer's metaphysical approach, which he describes as "trying to reach an understanding of things." The macerated metamorphosis that results probes but does not produce a solution in documentation that comes close to an hour and three-quarters in length.

Andrea Gabrieli (ca. 1510-1586)

Ricercare IX del XII tono

Brass Ensemble

☐ Brass Ensemble / Masson (conductor) / Nonesuch 71111

A fine example of the choir writing of this composer, the elder of the Gabrielis (Giovanni, his famous nephew, studied with him). Masson's group consists of four trumpets and four trombones. The instrumental blend is significant.

Tirsi morir volea

Choral

Chorus Alone

☐ Accademia Monteverdiana / Stevens (conductor) / Nonesuch 71272

Stunning reproduction of a score set in seven-part writing. Split texture, with a quartet of an alto, tenor, and two basses set in contrast to a trio of soprano, alto, and tenor. This is memorable choral writing—its singing by Denis Stevens's chamber-total vocal group cannot be second-guessed.

Domenico Gabrieli   (ca. 1650-1690)

Chamber Music

***Ricercare* for Cello and Harpsichord**

Sonata in G major for Cello and Harpsichord

☐ Brancaleon (cello); Zanaboni (harpsichord) / Everest 3173

Two rarities that present close-knit intensity. Both are finely poised and well-balanced works of art. Our concert cellists are advised to give their attention to this music, here recorded in well-paced and expressive readings.

Giovanni Gabrieli   (ca. 1555-1612)

Brass Ensemble

Canzon I, La Spiritata

☐ Brass Ensemble / Masson (conductor) / Nonesuch 71111

Dignified and powerful music. The playing shows a good blend.

Sonata pian e forte

☐ London Gabrieli Brass Ensemble / Nonesuch 71118

A beautifully shaped and golden-toned performance of this famous Gabrieli piece. The dual dynamic levels are expertly stated.

Choral

Chorus and Instrumental Ensemble

Angelus ad Pastores

Jubilate Deo

***Jubilate Deo* in B flat major**

Magnificat

Nunc Dimittis

Regina Caeli

Surrexit Christus

***Intonation* on the Second Tone**

***Intonation* on the Third and Fourth Tones**

***Intonation* on the Eleventh Tone**

☐ Edward Tarr Brass Ensemble, Gregg Smith Singers, and Texas Boys Choir / Biggs (organ) / Negri (conductor) / Columbia M-30937

A Gabrieli cross section that is impressive in all accounts, the performances beautifully integrated and stylistically focused. The cast of performers carries the insignia of authority and the presentations substantiate that designation.

The three organ *Intonations* are short introductions that are linked respectively to the first, sixth, and third pieces listed above. All but the *Magnificat* and *Surrexit Christus* (both arranged by Denis Stevens) are motets. These are in eight, ten, twelve, and fourteen parts, some for double choir, and one (*Nunc Dimittis*) for three choirs.

Kenneth Gaburo (1926-   )

Mouth-Piece (1970)

☐ Logan (trumpet) / Orion ORS–7294

The transfer of words into musical statement by pronouncing them through the trumpet's mouthpiece. Or, to put it another way, as Gaburo describes it, the "diverse explorations of the acoustical, physiological, and structural properties of language in a musical context." There is a major gain in actual public performance since the listener (spectator) is able to follow the poem (shown on large slide projections) which is being "trumpeted." Without the words no sense is possible; instead one hears a lot of polyglottonic monologue. What sounds! Zounds!

Logan's performance cannot, naturally, be brought into comparison. Taken for granted, it will startle and dazzle the listener as well as confound and bewilder him.

Line Studies (1957)

☐ Trampler (viola); Baker (flute); Glazer (clarinet); Price (trombone) / Columbia Special Products AMS–6421

Gaburo's *Line Studies* for a truly mixed instrumental bag of flute, clarinet, trombone, and viola is dodecaphonic music with class and cogency. The divided translations of the basic row—fragmented, spatially redesigned, harmonically emphasized, et cetera—are in constant reactivation, but the subject's core remains. No stunt man, this fellow. The sounds he has created are those of honesty and meaning.

Antiphony IV (Poised) for Voice, Piccolo, Bass Trombone, Double Bass, and Electronics (1967)

☐ Dalheim (voice); Howell (piccolo); Fulkerson (bass trombone); Fredickson (double bass) / Gaburo (conductor) / Nonesuch 71199

Isolates of sounds, electronic punctuations and horizontalistic short statements, fractured voice dabs, and jabs. Together they form a heated fantasy. The complexity makes its own sense. A superb statement by all concerned with the performance.

Two (1963)

☐ Turetzky (contrabass); Sudock (soprano); Purswell (flute) / Meier (conductor) / Advance FGR–1 (monaural)

Fractured vocalized prose drawn from a poem by Virginia Hommel with an overlay and wraparound that are strong reminders of the vibrant dabs marking impressionistic style. The twain do work well together. Minutely structured according to Gaburo's description on the liner copy. However, the effect the music achieves goes far beyond the technical blueprint and can be enjoyed and thoroughly appreciated without ever reading the composer's explanation.

Choral

Chorus Alone

Antiphony III (*Pearl-white Moments*) for 16 Voices and Electronics (1962)

☐ New Music Choral Ensemble / Gaburo (conductor) / Nonesuch 71199

Gaburo's composition relies on textual fracturing (the text is by Virginia Hommel) and the use of phonemes thereby creating an individual layer of response with a dramatic (if not direct, poetic) meaning. The interplay of the voices, divided into four groups, each covering a soprano-alto-tenor-bass alignment, creates a jargonic contrapuntalism that is coherent in its own sonorous right. Their shift and combination with the electronic sounds are so sensitively accomplished as to form an inner ingredient of coloristic excitement to Gaburo's unique piece. Though antiphony means, according to the composer, "the state of fluctuation between the total music and the poem as poem," there is this further antiphony between the live sonorities and the electronic ones, as well as those that result from having the four choral groups spatially arranged.

Opera and Dramatic Music

Lingua II: Maledetto (*Composition for 7 Virtuoso Speakers*) (1968)

☐ Members of the New Music Choral Ensemble III / Gaburo (conductor) / Composers Recordings S–316

Coldly pigeonholed, Gaburo's three-quarters-of-an-hour work can be termed "speaking music." Analytically described, it is a soloistic-polyphonic-polyrhythmic-human sound effects discussive composition on the word "screw." The word's etymological and semasiological facts, and the types and uses of the screw, are explored in depth, all basically laced with double entendre and inlaid (the pun is unintentional) with vivid scatological detail (sometimes poetically implied, elsewhere realistically articulated), and further colored by Joycian polyglottic splintering.

Gaburo explains his concepts and objectives in a lengthy essay that forms the liner note. There, too, his cloud of words has a style of its own, but sufficient information comes through to give meaning to this extraordinary work.

The performance by the NMCE III (described by Gaburo as "a group concerned with gesture, action, talk, and theatre music") is one of mastery. Putting it differently, the performance is of the highest type of "screwmanship."

Electronic Music

Exit Music I: *The Wasting of Lucrecetzia* (1964)

Exit Music II: *Fat Millie's Lament* (1965)

☐ Nonesuch 71199

Forget the titles for these two pieces, consisting of *musique concrète* and electronic sounds. The first is a wild, uproarious blast against the young and their life-style (then the predisco crowd). It has the texture of rock-and-roll music without its beat. *Fat Millie's Lament* is quieter and less meaningful. Though a short, dirty poem about the gal is printed in the liner notes, there is no connection between verse and sound.

Jacob Gade   *(1879-1963)*

Orchestra

Jalousie **(1925)**

☐ Boston Pops Orchestra / Krips (violin) / Fiedler (conductor) / Quintessence PMC-7018 (monaural)

The Tango that made this composer's name famous, and brought him a sizeable amount of income. Originally for piano, Fiedler, who "discovered" the piece, had an orchestral version prepared and has played it to a fare-thee-well. (Such special transcriptions are not included in this survey, but this representative of artistic schmaltz is a deserving exception.)

Niels Gade (1817-1890)

Symphony No. 1 *On Sjølund's Fair Plains,* in C minor, Op. 5

Orchestra

☐ Royal Danish Orchestra / Hye-Knudsen (conductor) / Turnabout 34052E (monaural)

Aside from some nationalistic auxiliary tunes that are interwoven, the Symphony is commanded by Mendelssohnian procedures. Such creative obedience can't hurt and does lead to a fair success. As does the performance.

Aquarellen (Books I and II), Op. 19

Instrumental

Arabeske in F major, Op. 27

Piano

☐ Ruiz (piano) / Genesis 1003

Gade's "Watercolors," subtitled *Little Tone Pictures* (five in each set, with such clear titles as Elegie, Scherzo, and Novellette) are explicit character pieces, drawn in the vocabulary used by Mendelssohn and Schumann. The *Arabeske* is larger-scaled but in a parallel text.

It's pleasurable to have this music available on disc. It's pleasurable as well to have it played with care for its style. Ruiz's attention to harmonic meanings brings further credit.

String Quartet in D major, Op. 63

Chamber Music

☐ Copenhagen String Quartet / Turnabout 34187

Thirty-seven years separate this work from the earlier quartet discussed below, but hardly any difference in style separates the two. Again, Mendelssohn is embraced and it does no harm to Gade to adopt such aesthetic patronage.

The work is written beautifully for the strings and therefore sounds with the fullest coherence. Even an amateur quartet could make fair sense of this work. In the hands of the professional Copenhagen four (Givskov, Lydolph, Bruun, and Christiansen) the fullest truths of Gade's material are presented. They are truly a fine quartet team.

String Quartet in F minor (1851)

☐ Copenhagen String Quartet / Turnabout 34270

Totally Mendelssohn-tinted and so performed. Both of the outer movements have introductions before the fast-paced major divisions. In the central place Gade has an *allegretto* and a playful movement. The latter, however, does not have the feathery travel of the great Felix. Otherwise, Gade is faithful to him and produces a worthy work. The Danish team play with warmth and good tonal quality.

Marco da Gagliano   (ca. 1582-1643)

**Opera
and Dramatic
Music**

La Dafne (1608)

☐ Camerata Accademica of Hamburg and Monteverdi Choir of Hamburg / Lerer, Schlick, and Kollecker (sopranos); Rogers, Partridge, and Possemeyer (tenors); Thomas (baritone) / Jürgens (conductor) / Deutsche Grammophon ARC-2533

The characters are those found in the traditional and dramatically fashionable pastoral setting of the very early seventeenth century: Daphnis, Cupid, Apollo, Venus, and nymphs. It was Parry who stated that a work like *Dafne* was only "very effective to minds which were absolutely free from any experience whatever of theatrical representation accompanied by music throughout." However, that statement was made at the turn of the present century. It must be revised, since Gagliano's music is a delight to fully experienced contemporary ears and deucedly effective.

Fine singing, good diction, splendid choral work, together with instrumental authenticity give this production a top rating. That said, it must be indicated that an edition listed in *Schwann* on Command 9004 was not heard by this reviewer.

Johann Ernst Galliard   (1680-1749)

**Chamber
Music**

Sonata No. 6

☐ Pachman (bassoon); Maxin (piano) / Golden Crest 7019 (monaural)

The last of a set of Sonatas written for bassoon or cello and harpsichord. The authenticity of using a piano in this case may be questioned but really nothing is harmed, especially in Jacob Maxin's carefully regulated playing. Pachman's assets are a solid tone and excellent dynamic differentiation.

Jacobus Gallus   (1550-1591)

Choral

Chorus Alone

Egredietur Virga/Radix Jesse

☐ Kaufbeurer Martinsfinken / Hahn (conductor) / Nonesuch 71095

Name confusion for this composer. His real name was Jacob Händl (or Handl or Hähnel). There is no confusion as to giving him a high rating as a polyphonicist.

This two-part piece is strong evidence of his fine flexible technique. Sensitively sung.

Mirabile Mysterium

O Admirabile Commercium

☐ Canby Singers / Canby (conductor) / Nonesuch 71026

O Admirabile Commercium is scored for double chorus with registral definition. Canby indicates that the text "is a somewhat doctrinal account of the Christmas mystery but the music makes it persuasive." True, mainly because it is presented with fine expressivity under his direction.

However, a far different music is pictured in the key shifts and harmonies of *Mirabile Mysterium*. These are quite extraordinary, anticipatory of matters harmonic of a much later period. It is sung beautifully with consummate sensitivity, especially in the way the vocal stresses and agogic content are portrayed.

Baldassare Galuppi *(1706-1785)*

Concerto in G major for Flute

Solo Instrument and Orchestra

Flute

☐ Ensemble Instrumental Jacques Prat / Marion (flute) / Turnabout 34566

Baroque steadiness with the spirit of Vivaldi hovering about the Andante. The performance of the outer sections has fine solidity with an excellent transparent delicacy conveyed in the slow movement.

Sonata No. 4 in C minor

Instrumental

Harpsichord

☐ Kipnis (harpsichord) / Columbia M3X-31521

Perfectly styled playing. One example: The manner in which Kipnis produces the arpeggio plunges that highlight the opening Larghetto. All the beauties of this fine music are persuasively detailed and elegantly stated. They shouldn't be missed.

Sonata No. 9 in F minor

☐ Sgrizzi (harpsichord) / Nonesuch 71117

Elegantly played and clearly registered in terms of touch, pitch, and dynamic differentiation.

Sonata in D major

Piano

☐ List (piano) / Musical Heritage Society MHS-733

One of the biggest of Galuppi's keyboard Sonatas. Four movements including a Gigue, which List plays at roller-coaster speed to the music's benefit. The indication of a fifth movement marked *Quasi presto con fuoco* is an error, simply being the tempo indication for the Gigue.

Sonata No. 5 in C major

☐ Michelangeli (piano) / London 6446

In three movements of ascending speed rate. Michelangeli's sound in the first (slow) movement especially is what one expects from a violinist in terms of "spun tone." The virility of the other pair of movements is maintained without sacrificing vocal quality on the keyboard. Magical playing, indeed.

Trio in G major

Chamber Music

☐ Camerata Musicale / Nonesuch 71085

Three movements for this trio Sonata using flute, oboe, and harpsichord, with a cello supplementing the last. Solidly played, if a bit dynamically fixed.

Herman Galynin   (1922 - 1966)

Solo Instrument and Orchestra

Piano

Concerto for Piano and Orchestra

☐ Moscow Radio Symphony Orchestra / Bashkirov (piano) / Svietlanov (conductor) / Orion PGM–6902 (monaural)

A real sleeper. Galynin had studied with Shostakovich, and especially in the two outer movements it is a spitting stylistic resemblance that one hears. Indeed, *tel maître, tel valet*. But, in some respects this work is better than Shostakovich's second piano Concerto, or, at least, worthy of standing equally alongside of it.

Bashkirov re-creates the piece with a good whiff of virtuosity and warmly sings the lines of the inner, slow movement. Good support from the Svietlanov-led orchestra.

Gerardo Gandini   (1936-   )

Solo Instrument and Orchestra

Piano

Fantasie-Impromptu for Piano and Orchestra (1970)

☐ Louisville Orchestra / Gandini (piano) / Mester (conductor) / Louisville LS–714

Use of quotations and quotationary collages are found in some works of the avant-garde. Gandini goes whole hog in this fashion. Bits and pieces of Chopin pieces are disengaged, dissected, distrained, and thrown about. Recognition is not the objective, but simply a means to an end (of Chopin!). The climax is the combination of dozens of fragments from Chopin's music played simultaneously. Where Ives was subtle, Gandini is blunt.

The assumption is that the performance is in order. If it isn't it would be too difficult to give the reasons.

Chamber Music

Soria Moria (1968)

☐ New Sound Composers-Performers Group / Lanza (conductor) / Mainstream MS–5017

Textural innerplay and overplay. Gandini does not wallow in his chosen qualities but carefully distinguishes them. Principal typologies are a single pitch (varied in timbre), and glissandi. A music of subtly etched demarcation, performed with fine-grained attention.

Louis Gaston Ganne   (1862 - 1923)

Instrumental

Flute

Andante et scherzo

☐ Hoberman (flute); Stannard (piano) / Avant 1015

No dealing with subtleties here. Nice squared tunes and balletic pace are compared. The *et* is equaled by a flute cadenza. Encore category.

Roberto García Morillo. *See under Morillo.*

Florian Leopold Gassmann (1729-1774)

Overture to *L'Amore artigano*   *Orchestra*

☐ English Chamber Orchestra / Bonynge (conductor) / London 6735

Still another overture that exemplifies the simmering of actual symphonic style. Good tunes and workmanship mark the prelude to one of Gassmann's most successful operas.

Remi Gassmann (20th cent.)

Electronics: Music to the Ballet (1961)   *Electronic Music*

☐ Westminster Gold 8110

To finish off the title by proper explanation: *as produced by the New York City Ballet Company under the direction of George Balanchine.* The Studio Trautonium, designed and developed by Oskar Sala, is the basic instrumentation for the work. It covers eleven sections with some ordinary titles such as *Curtain Music,* Overture, Waltz, et cetera, and some unordinary ones such as *Echo-Stretta* and *Stretta-Coda.*

Giovanni Giacomo Gastoldi (?-1622)

Three Fantasias for Two Violas   *Chamber Music*

☐ Phillips and Trampler (violas) / Musical Heritage Society OR–398

Music written for voices or instruments—violas in this case. Polyphonic, of course, and mainly in imitative counterpoint. Fine playing by this team.

Crawford Gates (1921-   )

***Oh, My Luve's Like a Red, Red Rose* (1956)**   *Choral*

☐ Mormon Tabernacle Choir / Ottley (conductor) / Columbia M–34134   *Chorus Alone*

Gates's setting of a text by Robert Burns is nostalgically "luverly." The excellent diction of the chorus, together with the warmth and earnestness of their singing, add up to a distinguished performance.

Philippe Gaubert (1879-1941)

Fantaisie   *Instrumental*

☐ Hoberman (flute); Stannard (piano) / Avant 1015   *Flute*

Plenty of gushing passages and flute travel but, notwithstanding all the action, a self-reflexive type of writing. Hoberman encompasses this two-section piece with panache.

Nocturne and Allegro Scherzando

☐ Robison (flute); Sanders (piano) / Vanguard 71207

Gaubert was more known for his flute playing and conducting abilities than as a composer. Accordingly, these short pieces are not overly important music, but are decidedly nice to hear, especially for the superb writing for the solo wind instrument. The performance is suave and perfect. Mouth-watering tone by this consummate artist.

Ennemond Gaultier (ca. 1580-1651)

Instrumental	**Allemande** *La Polonoise*
Lute	**Courante** *La Belle Homicide*

☐ Satoh (lute) / Klavier 528

Characteristic baroque dance pieces with fanciful titles. Both simply articulated and both in the same A minor tonality.

Francesco Geminiani (1687-1762)

Orchestra

The Enchanted Forest

☐ Angelicum Orchestra of Milan / Hammond (harpsichord) / Jenkins (conductor) / Nonesuch 71151

Imposing size, with twenty-two movements covering the two parts of the piece. Written for a stage spectacle presented in pantomime form, one would expect descriptive portions, but the opposite pertains—Geminiani's work is absolutely absolute music. And it is fluently musical, assured and always entertaining, though this decreases in ratio to the length of the piece. Fine playing with sensitive attention to dynamics and phrasing.

*String
Orchestra*

Concerto Grosso, Op. 3, No. 3

☐ Academy of St. Martin-in-the-Fields / Marriner (conductor) / Oiseau-Lyre S-277

A forthright account and a stylish one.

Concerto Grosso in D minor, Op. 2, No. 3

☐ London Soloists Ensemble / Nonesuch 71052

Almost completely satisfactory. Geminiani's Opus 2 music needs only proper motility, since the phrasings and instrumental relationships are immediately apparent in the score. The London group move the opening Presto but not to the point that it is simply pell-mell—complete clarity is linked from one note to the next. Sound balances are good throughout. So much for the pluses. Two minuses regarding tempi: a rather pedantically moving Adagio and a slowed-down Allegro finale.

*Chamber
Music*

Sonata in D

☐ Rampal (flute); Gilbert (harpsichord) / Everest 3194

Four movements in *adagio, allegro, largo,* and *vivace* tempi. Even though the patterns offer no surprises, the music, if compared to that of his teacher, Corelli, is a bit more adventuresome.

Nothing tentative about Rampal's performance. He is well supported by Kenneth Gilbert.

Watch the labeling. The Marcello Sonata listed first is actually the second work on the record; the Geminiani precedes it.

Geminiani / *Arcangelo Corelli.* See Corelli / Geminiani.

Harald Genzmer (1909-)

Concerto for Organ and Orchestra (1971)

☐ Bochum Symphony Orchestra / Krapp (organ) / Maga (conductor) / Turnabout 34627

Solo Instrument and Orchestra

Organ

Genzmer is a composer who knows full well that controlled dissonance will not deface the essential representation of positive tonality, and that, conversely, interference will not take place with the placing of dissonance into more than a supporting role. Refutation of tonality is obviated when the core is strongly delineated. Dissonance then serves to soften undue tightness and constrictedness of key without its tonal frontiers being overrun. Genzmer's music is free, yet is not deluded into misbelief of tonality by complete heterodoxical dissonance. The fruits of this type of research were first gathered by Hindemith, from whom Genzmer has learned much.

The Concerto is in four movements, the second a graphic type of grotesque Scherzo. The final movement is based in part on a theme by Pachelbel.

Balance between the organ and orchestra is made an easier task by Genzmer's elimination of woodwinds; the score calls for brass, timpani, and strings. The orchestra is a new name to this writer as is the conductor. They do exceedingly well. The soloist is very, very good. All of it comes across with power and meaning. A first-rate achievement.

Sonata for Trumpet and Organ

Chamber Music

☐ Bilgrim (organ); André (trumpet) / Musical Heritage Society MHS-3340

Hindemithian for the greater part but with some extra pepper added for taste. Topflight playing.

Roberto Gerhard (1896-1970)

Alegrias — Suite from the *Ballet-Divertissement Flamenco* (1944)

Orchestra

☐ Louisville Orchestra / Whitney (conductor) / Louisville S-646

The concert data drawn from the original ballet constitutes about two-thirds of the total. Initially, the ballet was written for two pianos, the orchestration was developed for the concert setting. It calls for seven woodwinds, four brass, percussion, harp, piano, and strings; the format covers two movements, each split: a *Preámbulo-Jácara* and a *Farruca-Jaleo*.

Alegrias represents light-faceted music, using Falla-like Andalusian quality. It may not be representative of Gerhard's late style but it is a highly colorful and satisfactory example of national music. Substantial performance.

Concerto for Orchestra (1965)

☐ BBC Symphony Orchestra / Del Mar (conductor) / Argo ZRG-553

The title is not simply a neat, neutral one. Gerhard's work, in one continuous movement, is virtuosity rigged onto the total orchestra with exciting constancy maintained throughout. To obtain the desired effect, thematic substances as principal identification points are eliminated. Instead, material is presented that concentrates in its place on timbre combinations, or pulsatile force, or static ("constellationlike") patterns.

Obviously, instrumental pigmentation is primary, and in this area Gerhard is a master. String instruments imitate percussion, the latter draws from the former as well (the use of cello bows on cymbals). At times the colorations remind a listener of electronic music. All of it is of dazzling brilliance, the product of superb creative thought.

The BBC Orchestra meets the technical problems head on and triumphs in spectacular fashion.

Symphony No. 4 (New York) (1967)

☐ BBC Symphony Orchestra / Davis (conductor) / Argo ZRG-701

The parenthetical title must not be misunderstood. This is neither a programmatic work nor a composition that has any detail pertinent to New York City. It is simply an identification of a New York Philharmonic commission (for its 125th anniversary)—first performed by that orchestra in 1967. The music is sectional in its structure, freely serial, highly colored by sound projections and recessions. It is a music that is tight, nervous, and explosive.

Davis and the BBC give a solid account of the piece. It makes extraordinary demands in its constant and radical challenges, all thoroughly met in the recording.

Solo Instrument and Orchestra

Violin

Violin Concerto (1945)

☐ BBC Symphony Orchestra / Neaman (violin) / Davis (conductor) / Argo ZRG-701

Our violinists flirt with the Berg Concerto, seemed to have forgotten the Schoenberg, and do pay some attention to "the" Bartók. They don't seem to know the existence of this high-flavored, intensely formulated work (or does the fault belong to the conductors?).

Virtuosity is available in Gerhard's work for soloist, orchestra, and, thereby, for the conductor. It is laid out in three movements, each split into two parts. Some of the material is serial but applied with Gerhardian serialism which means that Hispanic warmth is dovetailed with introspectivism. Color differences are constant—a parallel to the vitality that seethes within the work.

The free sensibility of this music is given a stimulating and intelligent performance. Yfrah Neaman is an absolute master of the solo part.

Chamber Music

Wind Quintet (1928)

☐ London Wind Quintet / Argo 5326

The world of serialism will be immediately apparent after merely hearing the first few measures of Gerhard's opus. But, the contextual direction is different. Row development is used but the row is not twelve-tone. Repetitions are utilized and so are ostinati. There are other transplants from Schoenbergian territory that make Gerhard's a fresh view of dealing with serial nursing. Any modicum of cold and forbidding results that cram the literature of serialism by the twelve-tone academicians are not to be heard here. This is fine music defined with full confidence in the recording.

The Plague (1964)

*Opera
and Dramatic
Music*

☐ National Symphony Orchestra and Chorus / McCowen (narrator) / Dorati (conductor) / London HEAD-6

Dorati says that *The Plague* is "not a pleasant piece." It isn't. How can a story that concerns the outbreak of disease due to plague-infested rats overrunning a city be otherwise? But if not pleasant it is of burning power. Gerhard's adaptation of Camus's novel *La Peste* has a text that frightens and a musical score (including choral singing and choral speech, mostly solo narration, and a small amount of orchestral individuality) that matches it. The frenzy of the population is graphically translated into directional orchestral explanation—there are both prime and subtle programmatic symbols in the progress of this melodrama.

The recording is masterly. Alec McCowen's British accent is different from the American one used by the chorus, but since he is the solo narrator and the chorus is the "crowd," the difference doesn't cause concern, though it will indeed be noticed.

Friedrich Gernsheim (1839-1916)

Sonata No. 1 in D minor for Cello and Piano, Op. 12

*Chamber
Music*

☐ Smith (cello); Jensen (piano) / Genesis 1060

Assured proportions and a music of well-turned and well-sounding romanticism. If Gernsheim's music does not have the specialness of the grand line, it does have style and the proper gestures belonging to it.

The playing spells out the score clearly. A few spots of imbalance are not the fault of the performers.

George Gershwin (1898-1937)

An American in Paris (1928)

Orchestra

☐ Philadelphia Orchestra / Ormandy (conductor) / Columbia MS-7258
☐ New York Philharmonic / Bernstein (conductor) / Columbia MS-6091

The Philadelphians play with their usual golden tone, but this does not prevent the required vitality and exuberance from coming through. This is Ormandy's best Gershwin performance and is also available on Columbia MS-7518 and in a two-disc set on Columbia MG-30073.

Gershwin is a specialty of the house for Bernstein, and he conducts a cracking depiction, with nice swing in the blues portion and pace in the score's travels. Here, too, there are other duplications in releases by Columbia; on M-31804 and in an all-American program with music by Barber, Copland, Piston, and Ives on MG-31155.

Catfish Row (Suite from Porgy and Bess)

☐ St. Louis Symphony Orchestra / Liberman (piano); Mortland (banjo) / Slatkin (conductor) / Turnabout 34594

In no way to be confused with the "standard" orchestral potpourri made by Robert Russell Bennett (see under *Gershwin/Bennett*). There are differences in the total material chosen, in placement of whatever music is duplicated in the two editions, orchestration, and total length. Further, Bennett's synthesis is undivided; *Catfish Row* is structured as a five-part suite.

Most importantly, and without repudiating the top expertise proven by the Bennett "symphonic picture," it simply represents Gershwin seen through Bennett's eyes, whereas *Catfish Row* is Gershwin reworking Gershwin.

The Suite was made by Gershwin after the initial ambivalent response to his *Porgy and Bess*. The setting was premiered in Philadelphia on January 21, 1936, and then dropped out of sight. It was rediscovered in 1958 and given the title *Catfish Row* by Ira Gershwin to distinguish it from the Bennett version and other miscellaneous compilations and arrangements of material from the opera. Slatkin's recording is the first one made. It deserves a place in the collection of anyone interested in Gershwin's music.

Cuban Overture (1932)

☐ St. Louis Symphony Orchestra / Slatkin (conductor) / Vox QSVBX-5132

First called *Rhumba* and then renamed in order to avoid any Broadway pops-tune connotation and provide a symphonic slant to the piece. But, rhumba rhythms it has and a good amount of Cuban percussion, both supplied in ample quality in this recorded version. A bit noisy, but that's G. Gershwin and not L. Slatkin.

Promenade

☐ St. Louis Symphony Orchestra / Silfies (clarinet) / Slatkin (conductor) / Turnabout 34594

The *Walking the Dog* sequence from the score for the motion picture *Shall We Dance*. According to the liner note, the work was "reconstructed from sketches, the soundtrack of the film, and the memories of Gershwin devotees by Ira Gershwin." That's a lot of sources for a little bit, but worth it.

Promenade (the title given the music when it was published) was, therefore, Gershwin's final instrumental composition.

Finely played and well styled, especially by George Silfies in his little interludes. (Also available in a three-disc set on Vox QSVBX-5132.)

Solo
Instrument
and
Orchestra

Piano

Concerto in F (1925)

☐ Boston Pops Orchestra / Wild (piano) / Fiedler (conductor) / RCA LSC-2586
☐ Boston Pops Orchestra / Nero (piano) / Fiedler (conductor) / RCA LSC-3319

Arthur Fiedler had the touch for this work and combines it with his choice of soloist that make his recordings the top selections. There is more dynamic appeal in Earl Wild's playing than in Peter Nero's, which relies more on a lyrical poetic slant. Nonetheless, either of the pair of discs is all it should be, and in both instances the orchestral coloring is deftly applied.

(The Wild version is also duplicated in an RCA compilation, VCS-7097.)

I Got Rhythm, **Variations for Piano and Orchestra**

☐ Boston Pops Orchestra / Wild (piano) / Fiedler (conductor) / RCA LSC-2586

For all the other versions in the book you can trot out all the negative descriptive words: academic, square, heavy-handed, stodgy, falsely pretentious, and they all fit. And, don't blame foreigners who aren't cognizant of the style. Included in the thumbs-down vote are such American pianists as Leonard Pennario and Jeffrey Siegel and such American conductors as Leonard Slatkin and Alfred Newman. Old as it is, the best recording is still with Wild at the piano and Fiedler on the podium. It's racy and motile, fluid and nonmetronomical. The last means the all-important matter of eliminating a rigidly architectural direction. In that manner Gershwin's theme (it was the hit of the Broadway show *Girl Crazy*) and its developments register with idiomatic pleasure.

(Also available in a two-record all-Gershwin edition on RCA VCS-7097.)

Rhapsody in Blue (1924)

☐ Columbia Symphony Orchestra / Bernstein (piano) / Bernstein (conductor) / Columbia MS-6091

Some play the Gershwin piece too square, some overintellectualize, others muddy the lines with exaggerations. One point is apparent: The ability to play Beethoven, Brahms, and Rachmaninoff concerti doesn't mean a piano soloist can stylistically master the Gershwin opus. Neither is being an American a shortcut to success, as witness the number of American pianists who serve up a cold stew.

The elusivity of improvisation must pervade the conception, the music must paradoxically be rhythmically anchored and phrased with airborne freedom. It must, above all, come off the symphonic orchestra stage and onto the dance bandstand.

Of the more than a dozen pianists who have recorded the Rhapsody (for the single version using the jazz-band instrumentation, *see below;* and for Gershwin's own solo piano recording see under *Instrumental: piano*) only Leonard Bernstein meets these demands. He achieves them by taking on the double role to make certain that not only the solo part is relayed with proper panache and styling, but that the orchestra follows suit. It is the best in the book. (It is also obtainable on Columbia M-31804 and in a Gershwin assortment that Columbia provides in its MS-7518.)

Rhapsody in Blue [jazz band score] (1924)

☐ Berlin Symphony Orchestra / List (piano) / Adler (conductor) / Turnabout 34457

Used here is the original scoring for "jazz band" made by Ferde Grofé, calling for flute, oboe, two clarinets, bassoon, three saxophones, two horns, two trumpets, trombone, timpani, percussion, banjo, and strings. It is a smart, sharply pointed consideration of the score, especially interesting because of the orchestration. List is fluent and Adler meets all the challenges.

(*See above* for the full symphonic setting and see under *Instrumental: piano* for the solo piano version.)

Second Rhapsody for Piano and Orchestra (1931)

☐ St. Louis Symphony Orchestra / Siegel (piano) / Slatkin (conductor) / Vox QSVBX-5132

The best performance of this lesser Gershwin work is an oldie, with Oscar Levant soloing and Morton Gould conducting, on Columbia ML-2073, a ten-incher and mono, of course. Worth the search even if the sound is quite dated.

For those that want this work without hunting in the byways this issue is adequate.

Instrumental

Piano

Clap Yo' Hands **from** *Oh, Kay!* **(1926)**

Do Do Do **from** *Oh, Kay!* **(1926)**

Do It Again from *The French Doll*

☐ Bolcom (piano) / Nonesuch 71284

All three are from the piano settings in *George Gershwin's Song Book.* The only competitive version is for the third song (in the collection made by André Watts on Columbia M-34221). Competitive only statistically. Watts doesn't have Bolcom's directness, which equals expressivity.

Drifting Along with the Tide **from** *George White's "Scandals of 1921"*

☐ Gershwin (piano) / Klavier S-122

Ragtime played as it was and should be played, and yet no bangy, noisy consideration.

Fascinating Rhythm **from** *Lady Be Good* **(1924)**

I Got Rhythm **from** *Girl Crazy* **(1930)**

I'll Build a Stairway to Paradise **from** *George White's "Scandals of 1922"*

Impromptu in Two Keys

☐ Bolcom (piano) / Nonesuch 71284

The pair of *Rhythm* pieces are great Gershwin gems. Bolcom's is the only edition available for the first of the two, while Watts has also recorded the other one, as well as *I'll Build a Stairway* (on Columbia M-34221). But, he isn't "with it" the way Bill Bolcom is.

The Impromptu sounds forbidding but is no Milhaudian bitonal thing. It is soft-shoeish and played suavely. Bringing it to life brings special credit to Bolcom.

I Was So Young, You Were So Beautiful **from** *Good Morning Judge*

Kickin' the Clouds Away **from** *Tell Me More*

☐ Gershwin (piano) / Klavier S-122

Gershwin's published songs are quite a different matter compared to Gershwin performing them at the piano. In that case they sometimes tripled and quadrupled in length as Gershwin improvised within and around the tune, embellished and rung variations on it. (David Hamilton, the well-known critic, has aptly described this as a "distillation process.")

Two fine examples herewith, both offering perfect documentation.

Liza **from** *Show Girl* **(1929)**

The Man I Love

Merry Andrew

My One and Only **from** *Funny Face* **(1927)**

Nobody But You **from** *La La Lucille*

Oh, Lady Be Good **from** *Lady Be Good* **(1924)**

Piano Playin' Jazzbo Brown

Promenade

☐ Bolcom (piano) / Nonesuch 71284

Gershwin's *The Man I Love,* in its miniature way (two and one-quarter minutes), is great Gershwin. The performance is ideal, slow but with a compelling continuity. In comparison, Bolcom covers the staccato snap within *Oh, Lady Be Good* and the contrastive elegance in the most effective manner.

Merry Andrew is as little known as the *Piano Playin'* item. The former was used as a dance number in the show *Rosalie;* the latter was meant for *Porgy and Bess* but was not included. It is published as *Jasbo Brown Blues.* The very catchy *Promenade* exists in an orchestral version (see under *Orchestra* for discussion).

Rhapsody in Blue (1924)

☐ Gershwin (piano) / Klavier 124

This is an ear-opening performance that clears away all the interpretative foliations that have smothered the work. Gershwin plays it clean, plays it straight, plays it as it is. All of that makes for musical health rather than the blight resultant from soloists who feel required to ''do something'' with Gershwin's work. Not that there aren't insinuations and insouciancies in the way Gershwin plays. But, it is always musical and convincing, and minus a single exaggerated note. One doesn't need (or miss!) orchestral partnership. In this staging the solo piano is totally sufficient.

(For those that wish the original 1924 version with Ferde Grofé's jazz band scoring or his later, most usually heard symphonic setting, see both under *Solo Instrument and Orchestra.* The initial version published in 1925 was a two-piano arrangement; the setting for solo piano, heard here, appeared in print in 1927.)

Rialto Ripples

☐ Bolcom (piano) / Nonesuch 71284

Ragtime. Gershwin was seventeen when he wrote it. Bolcom plays it precisely and not noisily.

So Am I from *Lady Be Good* (1924)

☐ Gershwin (piano) / Klavier S-122

A charming piece with Gershwin's usual rhapsodizing—in this case quietly accomplished.

Somebody Loves Me from *George White's "Scandals of 1924"*

Strike Up the Band from *Strike Up the Band* (1927)

☐ Bolcom (piano) / Nonesuch 71284

A pair of Gershwin evergreens. Pithy depictions—a minute and a fraction for the first title, forty-eight seconds for the other one.

Swanee (1917)

☐ Bolcom (piano) / Nonesuch 71284
☐ Gershwin (piano) / Klavier 124

This is the famous song that Gershwin wrote at the age of 19. It was a smash hit, the sheet music sales went over the million mark, and as a single disc more than 2,250,000 copies were purchased.

The "once-through" method of Gershwin's published songs in piano transcription is exemplified in Bolcom's thirty-seven-second performance. Gershwin's special treatment takes two and a quarter minutes. Get both.

Sweet and Low Down from *Tip-Toes* (1925)
'S Wonderful from *Funny Face* (1927)

☐ Bolcom (piano) / Nonesuch 71284

Especially fascinating is the way Bolcom handles the hesitation bass in *Sweet and Low Down*. (The setting on Klavier S–122 is a large-scale compound. It covers three minutes and twenty seconds in Gershwin's performance; Bolcom's playing of the same tune but obviously not the same score[!] is clocked at forty-seven seconds.)

Tee-Oodle-Um-Bum-Bo from *La La Lucille*

☐ Gershwin (piano) / Klavier S–122

Ragtime contour and catchy breaks with the full Gershwin spirit. Included in a wonderful program that is as musically satisfying as it is historically important. The title of the release is *George Gershwin Plays Gershwin and Kern*. (Not exact: There is one work by Walter Donaldson.) All the Gershwin titles are covered in the above commentaries and Kern's under his entries.

That Certain Feeling from *Tip-Toes* (1925)

☐ Gershwin (piano) / Klavier 124
☐ Bolcom (piano) / Nonesuch 71284

No stronger evidence of the difference between Gershwin's recorded conceptions of his songs (transferred from the Steinway Duo-Art piano rolls) and the concentrated piano versions published in *George Gershwin's Song Book* can be displayed. Gershwin's approach was a full improvisational delivery, in this case with engaging motility and more than twice the length of Bolcom's balladlike presentation. (Most interestingly, the latter begins with the same triple upbeat pitches that announce the "big tune" in the Rhapsody in Blue.)

Accordingly, it is not a matter that involves duplicate performance comparison. Bolcom and Gershwin are really not playing the same material. So—get both!

Three Preludes (1926)
Three-Quarter Blues
Who Cares? from *Of Thee I Sing* (1931)

☐ Bolcom (piano) / Nonesuch 71284

The Three Preludes are played with a *rubato* that neither robs the music of its subtle bluesy feeling (in number two) nor denies the catchy, faster-paced syncopatives that frame it.

The Three-Quarter Blues is a nice pithy item. It has also been called Irish Waltz. As in his other Gershwin representations, Bolcom is fully responsive to this piece as he is to the choice tune from *Of Thee I Sing*.

Lullaby

☐ Juilliard Quartet / Columbia M–32596

A charmer. Gershwin's miniature eight-minute item surfaced in the 1960s, having been shelved since its composition about 1920. Unidentified, it would recall (in part) Dvořákian flow. No matter, reminder of another composer or not, the piece has a sensitive stimulus. Its technical flame is low but the Lullaby has compelling warmth.

This represents the "world premiere recording," as Columbia describes it. The Kohon Quartet has since recorded it in a Vox box (SVBX–5305), but it is oversentimentalized and far too slow, resulting in a performance time of eleven and one-half minutes. Indeed, the music drags and loses its liquidity.

Porgy and Bess (1935)

☐ Cleveland Orchestra, Cleveland Orchestra Chorus, and Children's Chorus / Mitchell, Hendricks, and Floyd (sopranos); Quivar, Conrad, and Jones (mezzo-sopranos); Clemmons, Pickens, Hagan, and Brown (tenors); White and Thompson (baritones); Boatwright and Deane (basses) / Maazel (conductor) / London 13116

No watered-down, no excerpted production, but the whole thing. What a joy it is to hear, finally, all the music Gershwin composed for his masterpiece. A considerable amount was excised prior to the initial stage presentation but all of it (almost a good thirty minutes' worth!) is contained in Maazel's (now definitive) edition. That some of it has a make-do padding is not to be denied, but to overprotest the matter is to overlook the basic mastery and inspiration that concern *Porgy*.

The performance is dramatic, beautifully colored, and the sound vivid. As Porgy, Willard White's dark-timbred voice is splendid, displaying a sensitivity for phrasing and rhythmic definition that is matched by the vibrant delivery of Leona Mitchell in the Bess role. François Clemmons as Sportin' Life sings with great skill and verve. The cast's diction is of such clarity that one can cast the libretto aside. In charge is the dazzling conducting of Loren Maazel.

This release is a triumph. As the initial recording of the complete score it is a blessed event for which all of us should remain thankful.

Gershwin / **Robert Russell Bennett**

Porgy and Bess — A Symphonic Picture for Orchestra

☐ Utah Symphony Orchestra / Abravanel (conductor) / Vanguard C–10023

The well-known, widely played, largely recorded orchestral synthesis that Bennett constructed from Gershwin's operatic score. Choice of material, its structuring, and orchestration were solely made by Bennett. (Gershwin's own orchestral suite is titled *Catfish Row* — for a discussion see under *Gershwin*.)

A number of conductors have recorded the Symphonic Picture, including such top names as Ormandy and Fiedler. Probably due to his special experience as an operatic conductor, Abravanel's conception (also available on Vanguard 345) is just that amount freer and more fluidly played to warrant its placement in the top slot.

Robert Gerster   (1945-   )

Instrumental

Flute

Bird in the Spirit for Solo Flute

☐ Skowronek (flute) / Crystal 351

Neither the few flutter tongues and microtoned pitches nor the use of the flute's extreme register change the poetic declamatory range of Gerster's piece. The music is mystically targeted, and its spare, evocative style is quite affecting. Felix Skowronek plays admirably and, indeed, he provides a notable performance.

(*Schwann* incorrectly lists this as a duo for flute and bassoon and, to double its error, names the performers as Skowronek [flutist] and Grossman [bassoonist].)

Don Carlo Gesualdo   (ca. 1560-1613)

Choral

Chorus Alone

Aestimatus Sum

Ave, Dulcissima Maria

Hei Mihi, Domine

O Vos Omnes

☐ Cappella Vocale Hamburg / Behrmann (conductor) / Candide 31036

The first and last titles are responsories, the other two works are motets. Excellently presented, and, in the case of *O Vos Omnes,* superbly so.

Madrigals

Ancide sol la morte (Book VI, No. 15)
Chiaro risplender suole (Book VI, No. 5)
Deh, com invan sospiro (Book VI, No. 9)
Dolce spirito d'Amore (Book III, No. 7)
Ed ardo e vivo (Book III, No. 13)
Meraviglia d'Amore! (Book III, No. 12)
Moro, lasso, al mio duolo (Book VI, No. 17)
Non mai non cangerò (Book II, No. 18)
Non mi toglia (Book II, No. 20)
O dolce mio tesoro (Book VI, No. 8)
O mal nati messaggi (Book III, No. 9)
S'io non miro non moro (Book V, No. 2)
Sospirava il mio core (Book III, No. 8)
T'amo, mia vita! (Book V, No. 21)
Tu piangi, o Filli mia (Book VI, No. 3)

☐ Cappella Vocale Hamburg / Behrmann (conductor) / Candide 31036

A set of fifteen Madrigals drawn from Books II, III, V, and VI of those published. (These are known as the Italian Madrigals.) The singing is eminently stylish and warm. A distinguished release that clearly proves Gesualdo's individuality.

Chamber Music

Gagliarda à 4

☐ Jaye Consort of Viols / Nonesuch 71277

A delicate construction and played in a manner to emphasize its fragility.

Emmanuel Ghent (1925-   )

Helices for Violin, Piano, and Tape (1969)

Chamber Music

☐ Golub (violin); Cobb (piano) / Desto 7124

Finely balanced sound complexes that twirl, lightly colored by the tape. A fluency of tender tartness surrounds Ghent's work. Catalogue it as avant-garde minus fragmentation.

Surprises: the almost-total section for violin harmonics; the tonal pedal-pointed passage by the violin.

The performance is entirely convincing, as is the composition itself.

Dinu Ghezzo (1941-   )

Thalla for Piano, Electric Piano, and 16 Instruments (1974)

Solo Instrument and Orchestra

Piano

☐ Contemporary Direction Ensemble of the University of Michigan, Ann Arbor / Tipei (piano and electric piano) / Mayer (conductor) / Orion 75172

Three quintets: string quartet plus double bass, woodwind (including an alto saxophone), brass (two horns, two trumpets, and trombone), plus vibraphone support the solo instrumental voice. Ghezzo's *Thalla* (a shortening of the Greek *thallassa*, meaning "the sea") is athematic but has a cogent sonorous continuity. It is derived from aleatoric stipulations but so put together in this performance as to sound exactly figurated and structured.

Music for Flutes and Tape (1972)

Instrumental

Flutes

☐ Andrus (flutes) / Orion 75172

Color is the thesis and antithesis of Ghezzo's Music. Its athematic sweep and enchantment are all derived by instrumental pigmentation, via use of four flute types: piccolo, flute, alto flute, and bass flute together with tape and the extension of timbres by utilizing amplification, echo devices, and contact microphones. Special sensual effects result from slow bent-pitch tones. Throughout there is a sense of an ecstatic anthem being sung in this music—it is indeed a beautiful and moving sonorous exhibit.

Gretel Shanley Andrus gives a seductive performance. Nevertheless, she does not neglect meaningful phrasing and structural definition.

Ritualen (1969)

Piano

☐ Tipei (piano) / Orion 75172

Ritualen calls for a hybrid instrument, normal and "prepared"; the latter concentrated in scope. Glissandi on the strings are used in addition. The rituals of contrastive instrumentation are matched by poetic rituals providing a music that most often has contemporary lyrical curves.

Listening to this sensitively conceived work is unquestionably a pleasure.

Kanones for Flute, Cello, and Harpsichord (1972)

Chamber Music

☐ Andrus (flute); Shapiro (harpsichord); Hurford (cello) / Orion 75172

Ghezzo uses prerecorded taped sounds, which are mirrored by actual performer statements, plus electronic handling of the flute and cello, for amplification purposes and to obtain echo effects. The structuring is sectional. The playing is fine.

Luis Gianneo   *(1897-1968)*

Solo
Instrument
and
Orchestra

Mandolin

Suite Argentine for Mandolin and Orchestra (1956)

☐ Heidelberg Chamber Orchestra / Thomas (mandolin) / CMS/Oryx 40

Argentinian data, naturally. This covers the *Chacarera* and the sadly profiled *Vidala*. The third part (*Zapateado*) is a tap dance.

General liner data—nary any pertinent facts concerning Gianneo's opus. A passable performance.

Vittorio Giannini   *(1903-1966)*

Orchestra

Divertimento No. 2 (1961)

☐ Louisville Orchestra / Whitney (conductor) / Louisville 642 (monaural)

Three movements of compelling romantic order spruced up with some modern orchestral touches, without which one would be back in the world of such men as Paul Graener, Max Trapp, Italo Montemezzi, and Arrigo Boito.

A worthy performance, best when the music is bright.

Symphony No. 3 (1958)

☐ Eastman Wind Ensemble / Roller (conductor) / Mercury 75010

Because Vittorio Giannini was concerned with the wealthy, emotional aspects of music, he was a romanticist. Since his structures were imitative of the Beethoven-Brahms school, he was a classicist. No paradox—a normal combine, actually. The Symphony exemplifies his ability to create fertile, frank melodies (his Italian heritage certainly helped), with the support of fully tonal harmonies. Conventional? Yes. But the viability of diatonic harmony will never wear out. He was simply a twentieth-century composer using the well-sharpened tools of the nineteenth.

Giannini had an acute sense of scoring balances. The Symphony is proof. It includes a gem of a third movement, with an exquisite theme. Roller's performance is finely detailed, projected *con amore*.

Opera
and Dramatic
Music

The Taming of the Shrew

☐ Kansas City Lyric Theatre / Christensen, Davis, Harris, Holloway, Hook, Jennings, Jones, Latimer, Knott, McGowen, Nelson, Powers, Steele, and Weedman (vocalists) / Patterson (conductor) / Composers Recordings S-272

An adaptation of the Shakespeare play, with additional texts from his sonnets and *Romeo and Juliet*. The book is by the composer and Dorothy Fee. The music is opulently clear, generously eclectic in a merger of Verdi (major total) and Wagner (minor amount). Hence, melodies and vocal lines that singers like to prepare, and most opera buffs like to hear.

Certainly a spirited performance. However, CRI doesn't offer a text, indicate how the additions to the libretto were used, or even list the voice types of the cast.

Orlando Gibbons (1583-1625)

Fantazia of Foure Parts

☐ Anderson (organ) / Crystal S–180

This is from the historically famed *Parthenia,* the first collection of music for the virginals published in England. It consisted of eight works by William Byrd, seven by John Bull, and six by Gibbons. The *Fantazia of Foure Parts* is number seventeen in the collection.

The virginal (or virginals) was the earliest and simplest form of the harpsichord. Playing Gibbons's virginal music on the organ is fully appropriate, thereby enhancing the marvelous and magnetic polyphony of this masterful composer.

Instrumental

Organ

Allemande (Italian Ground)

Fantasy in C

Lord of Salisbury—Pavan and Galliard

☐ Gould (piano) / Columbia M–30825

Perhaps not displaying authenticity in terms of the instrument used but modern piano timbre does not harm Gibbons's music. Gould's choices are very choice and so are his executions which are minus any of the habitual Gouldian verbal and/or musical fomentations.

Piano

Miriam Gideon (1906-   )

Symphonia Brevis (1953)

☐ Radio Orchestra of Zurich, Switzerland / Monod (conductor) / Composers Recordings 128 (monaural)

In two movements but substantiating a four-part structure; the second division telescoping slow-*scherzo*-finale proportions. Like form, so content. Everything is concentrated, strongly wired by the scoring, avoids unhealthy abandon for a terse point of view. Monod's direction is as succinct as the score requires.

Orchestra

Lyric Piece for String Orchestra (1942)

☐ Imperial Philharmonic Orchestra, Tokyo / Strickland (conductor) / Composers Recordings 170 (monaural)

A bit of stylistic differences. The music ranges from suave chromaticism to agile quartal-banked measures onto tertial patterns.

Gideon's music receives only a fair performance. There is more in the score than Strickland has found. No issue is taken with him in regard to tempo details or phraseology. It is simply a matter of a somewhat note-laden performance that prevents the music from singing out fully.

String Orchestra

Piano Suite No. 3 (1963)

☐ Helps (piano) / Composers Recordings S–288

Concentrated to the hilt, chromatically packaged. The tempi designations are fully

Instrumental

Piano

descriptive: "Restlessly," "Tenderly," and "Vehemently." This is a handsomely executed performance.

Vocal

Voice and Instrumental Ensemble

The Adorable Mouse

☐ Members of the Ariel Quintet / Reardon (baritone); Spiegelman (harpsichord); Venuto (timpani) / Heller (conductor) / Serenus 12050

Miriam Gideon has written the libretto and composed the music for this fable. A witty combine results which also describes using the voice for both singing and narrating. As they say, Gideon has furnished colorful copy.

As usual, John Reardon walks off with the top honors in the performing forces. The instrumental group fills in most acceptably.

The Condemned Playground (1963)

☐ Bryn-Julson (soprano); Cassolas (tenor); Galimir and Shapiro (violins); Tolomeo (viola); Arico (cello); Dunkel (flute); Heller (bassoon) / Jahoda (conductor) / Composers Recordings S-343

Imaginative use of three texts by Horace, Gary Spokes, and Baudelaire, each heard in two languages and their distribution acutely balanced. Thus, the first song, *Pyrrha,* is sung initially in English translation and then in the original Latin; in the second piece, *Hiroshima,* the reverse occurs: The first part is in the original English and its translation into Japanese follows. Two languages also are utilized in the final *Litanies of Satin,* but in this instance the English translation is constant, interspersed only four times with the repetition of one line in the original French as a refrain device. Accordingly, three subjects in four languages, for two voices and six instruments. It is apparent that Miriam Gideon has not overlooked the high percentage gain of inner variety within her conception. However, musically, there is fine formalistic cohesion. The same goes for the sureness of the recording. There are no critical reservations by this writer.

The Hound of Heaven (1945)

☐ Metcalf (baritone); Roseman (oboe); Cohen (violin); Phillips (viola); Sherry (cello) / Jahoda (conductor) / Composers Recordings S-286

Gideon's seven-minute piece utilizes a portion (twenty-two lines) from the Francis Thompson poem. It implies the use of tonality in its scope, yet is not hidebound by conventional dictates. The music is excited by impressive and inventive instrumental colorations (a few spots in the performance are pitch wavery), with the voice part constructed to obtain textural clarity. (The baritone, William Metcalf, delivers the text accordingly.)

Questions on Nature (1965)

☐ DeGaetani (mezzo-soprano); West (oboe); Lipman (piano); Jekofsky (percussion) / Composers Recordings S-343

Gideon uses an unusual type of text, one that is not continuous but consisting of a series of topics propounded by Adelard of Bath in the early twelfth century. (Examples: "Why we hear echoes." "Why, as one can see from darkness into the light, one cannot see from light into the darkness." "Why men are not born with horns, or other weapons." Now then, this sort of textual framework is not easy to pin onto sounds but Miriam Gideon has accomplished it by a creative modus vivendi that finds the most pertinent pitch choice for the word involved. The effect is not sing-song narration but a series of musical paragraphs that engage the attention with their warm chromatic character.

Diction is always paramount. In this situation it is absolutely crucial. Jan DeGaetani provides performance truth for both pitch and verbiage.

Rhymes from the Hill (1968)

☐ DeGaetani (mezzo-soprano); Bloom (clarinet); Des Roches (marimba); Sherry (cello) / Gilbert (conductor) / Composers Recordings S–286

Sensitive instrumentation combines with a lyrical voice line that is expressionistically imprinted. The use of the marimba, especially, is extremely telling throughout Gideon's beautifully formed and articulated five-part cycle.

Though the main title is in English, the texts are sung in the original German (from Christian Morgenstern's *Galgenlieder*). (Full texts are supplied with translations.)

The ensemble and quality are expert; the voice of Jan DeGaetani is fluent, musically intelligent.

The Seasons of Time (1969)

☐ Mandac (soprano); Arico (cello); Jahoda (piano); Kraber (flute) / Desto 7117

Ten settings of Tanka poetry of Ancient Japan. Most are cryptic and reserved in totality, though covered by complete musical statements. Gideon's music here has a Bergian warmth color-spliced with impressionistic instrumental material.

The spirit of the music is keenly felt by the soprano and three instrumentalists and as keenly conveyed to the listener with a lucid performance.

Nicolas Gigault   *(1624?-1707)*

Instrumental

Prélude du 3ᵉ et 4ᵉ Tons

Organ

☐ Hansen (organ) / Nonesuch 71170

One solid swath of full organ sonority. Imposing, indeed, but drawn to the limits (two and one-quarter minutes) of static sound poundage.

Eugène Gigout   *(1844-1925)*

Instrumental

Scherzo in E major

Organ

☐ Biggs (organ) / Columbia MS–6307

A mini-charmer. Three-part form, as expected, with a catchy principal section and cute pomposity for contrast. Of course, Biggs whips through it *con amore*, which is another way of saying he plays it enchantingly.

Toccata

☐ Raynaud (organ) / Vox SVBX–5314

Touch and go and no drawing back for the entire two and three-quarter minutes, save for a few fanfarelike matters at the very end. Excitingly played by splitting the work in half and designing a black-white depiction of moderately soft figurations and then insistent dynamic ones.

David Gilbert   *(1936-   )*

Instrumental

Alto Flute

Poem VI (1966)

☐ Gilbert (alto flute) / Opus One 13

Phrases constantly alternating with qualities obtained by blowing through the embouchure opening, producing nonpitch air sounds. The constancy neutralizes total formal stability, though there is an identity with consonance-dissonance brought to bear by the pitch-nonpitch patterns.

Gilbert plays his own music splendidly and deserves congratulations. So does Opus One for making Poem VI available on disc. However, Opus One has mislabeled the "A" side of its disc. Poem VI is listed first whereas it covers the third band.

Oboe

Poem VII (1970)

☐ Lucarelli (oboe) / Opus One 13

Unification in a fixed position. Gilbert's piece is extremely static, consisting mainly of long-held sounds, punctuated by multiphonics and some breathing sounds. Technical science is the creative religion here. Interesting, always, even though all of it is recognizable as data that is firmly part of twentieth-century instrumental practice. As his performance shows, Lucarelli is an interpretative master of the style.

(The labeling is run backwards. Thus, Shields's Wildcat Songs covers band one, not band three, on the "A" side and Poem VII pertains to band two [correctly noted], while Gilbert's Poem VI occupies the third cut, not the first one.)

Henry F. Gilbert   *(1868-1928)*

Orchestra

The Dance in Place Congo, Op. 15

☐ Los Angeles Philharmonic Orchestra / Simmons (conductor) / New World Records NW-228

French Creole tunes are basic to Gilbert's tone poem describing the street revels of off-duty New Orleans slaves. There's considerable charm remaining in this only slightly dated piece which relies on straight melodic statements and rhythmic clarity rather than any internal subtleties. It is played in that manner.

(When Pierre Monteux conducted this work with the Boston Symphony Orchestra in the 1920s, he made substantial cuts. These, totaling some fifty-seven score pages, reduced the performance time approximately fifty percent. The same cuts have been retained in this recording.)

Alberto Ginastera   *(1916-   )*

Orchestra

Estancia—Ballet Suite (1941)

☐ London Symphony Orchestra / Goossens (conductor) / Everest 3013

An exciting reading of music containing the very essence of folk *materia*. Ginastera does not tuck in his sonority ideas, and displays an extrovertism that is most appealing.

The final dance is a thriller—defined for popularity once conductors get wise to its existence. It outthrusts the Khachaturian Sabre Dance twenty times over. Everest's sound is magnificent.

Ollantay, A Symphonic Triptych (1947)

☐ Louisville Orchestra / Mester (conductor) / Louisville S–696

Programmatic musical property, concerning an Inca soldier who ravishes a priest's daughter in the temple of the virgins and is then killed. The orchestrational deportment is both somber and exciting. In the middle portion ''Sacre du printemps'' styled shapes are stimulative utilities for a warrior's dance. The music breathes burning phrases throughout, even when the dynamic level is quiet.

Mester has full control of this score and the playing is one of clear expression.

Pampeana No. 3, A Pastoral Symphony (1953)

☐ Louisville Orchestra / Whitney (conductor) / Louisville 545–10 (monaural)

Despite the picturesque title, Ginastera's work is held together logically by the subjective inspiration of the Argentine pampas and by its formal unity, with arch-designed and ternary structures in the end movements.

No criticism of Whitney's performance or the sonics, which have all the brightness required.

Panambi – Suite from the Ballet (1940)

☐ London Symphony Orchestra / Goossens (conductor) / Everest 3003

Ginastera began as an impressionist, but soon assimilated folkloristic properties in his work. The specialness of Argentinian *melos* is very strong in the *Panambi* music. And, this acquiescence is maintained. Neither glib nor superpowered, Goossens's portrayal is just. Music of this type can be faulted by overstatement. Not here.

(Everest also issues Goossens's performance on its number 3041 as well as including it in a two-disc collection [3107/2].)

Variaciones concertantes (1953)

☐ Boston Symphony Orchestra / Eskin (cello); Zighera (harp); Dwyer (flute); Cioffi (clarinet); Fine (viola); Gomberg (oboe); Walt (bassoon); Ghitalla (trumpet); Gibson (trombone); Silverstein (violin); Stagliano (horn); Portnoi (double bass) / Leinsdorf (conductor) / RCA LSC–3029

A novel plan with the music just as enticing. Each of the eleven variants employs a different instrumental scheme, the orchestra, as an entity, being reserved for the end. It can be termed Ginastera's ''Guide to the Orchestra.'' And, as played by these experts, no better one could be secured.

Concerto for Harp and Orchestra

☐ Orchestre ORTF, Paris / Zabaleta (harp) / Martinon (conductor) / Deutsche Grammophon 2530008

Ginastera is off and running in his earlier folkloric style in the first part. Included are much bigger orchestral sentences and footnotes than usually contained in an essay for the small-toned harp with orchestra. So, plenty of percussion. Contrast is applied by the impressionistic wash of movement two.

Solo Instrument and Orchestra

Harp

685

As the occasion, so the behavior. Accordingly, the concluding division begins with a very long cadenza. It connects to music of zip, pep, and dash. Again there is plenty of the percussion's punctuative power.

Anyone interested in the harp will want this recording. Those that aren't should take the opportunity of hearing a new way of solving the problem of pitting a harp against an orchestra. Of course, Zabaleta charges through his solo part with magnificent virtuosity. Martinon has his players right there with him.

Piano

Concerto for Piano and Orchestra (1961)

☐ Vienna Philharmonia Orchestra / Somer (piano) / Maerzendorfer (conductor) / Desto 6402

Ginastera's concerto is a bit warmed by Schoenbergian gospel. It has a magnetic appeal because it has a brash freshness. The scherzo is most fascinating. It is drawn from (but is away from) Webern. The checking and stifling, the sonorous choking of Webern's style is father to Ginastera's *scherzo allucinante*, though the results are far from the sonic isolationism of Schoenberg's disciple.

Masterful playing by the soloist. Hilde Somer's pianism is no mere note-grubbing display, but a rendition that indicates abiding knowledge of what makes the score tick, plus love and respect for the music. She was a truly impressive artist.

Instrumental

Pampeana No. 2 (Rhapsody for Cello and Piano) (1950)

Cello

☐ Gabor Rejto (cello); Alice Rejto (piano) / Orion 7282

The melorhythms of the Argentine pampas are used to evoke the essence of Ginastera's countryside. Lyrical and dance qualities are vividly contrasted. Gabor Rejto catches the special spirit of the work admirably.

Piano

Sonata for Piano (1952)

☐ Somer (piano) / Desto 6402

A few rhythmic and melancholic nationalistic tinges permeate the work. Mostly, however, it contains Ginastera's mysterious scherzo writing and stamping, stomping toccata urgency.

Hilde Somer's playing is totally communicative, powerful without bluster, and passionately intense even in the music's quieter portions.

Suite de Danzas Criollas (1946)

☐ Somer (piano) / Desto 6426

Folkloristic fellowship is realized in Ginastera's five-movement work. No actual tunes are quoted—Ginastera sets his own songs and sings them with individual accent.

This is a splendid rendition. Hilde Somer brings out to the full the abundance of fancy in these musical creations. There is full interpretative nourishment here.

Twelve American Preludes (1944)

☐ Ruiz (piano) / Genesis 1008

With didactic determination but without relaxing artistic responsibility, Ginastera achieves the same goals pertinent to the preludes for piano composed by Chopin and Debussy. Thus, technical situations (accents in No. 1, octaves in No. 7); qualities

("Sadness" in the second prelude, "Pastoral" in the tenth of the set); and compositional methods (canonic imitation, modes), and so on. Though held within set boundaries, each piece has compelling interest. Never do the formal factors interfere with the sheer musical end result.

There are no errors of judgment in Ruiz's performance. All details are clearly delineated.

Duo for Flute and Oboe (1945)

☐ Shanley (flute); Christ (oboe) / Crystal S–812

From the neoclassic orbit, with the terminal movements concerned with sonata and fugue designs; the central Pastorale following choral style. Shanley and Christ present a sensitively balanced consideration of the score.

Cantos del Tucumán for Voice, Flute, Violin, *Cajes,* and Harp

☐ Dal Segno Ensemble / Reid-Parsons (mezzo-soprano) / Critics Choice cc–1703 (monaural)

Early Ginastera (written at the age of twenty-two and therefore sounding with native resonances. And very native in regard to the *cajes,* a pair of wood drums utilized by the Indians in the northern province of Tucumán. Only the voice and percussion are used in the third of the set, providing a music of gentility and warmth; the same quality embraces the first two songs. The last Canto offers a lively conclusion.

Not the choicest recording by any means but since it is the only one available it will have to serve until something better comes along.

Cantata para América Mágica (1961)

☐ Los Angeles Percussion Ensemble / Adonaylo (soprano) / Temianka (conductor) / Columbia Special Products AMS-6447

Music of terrifying power, calling for fifty-three percussion instruments partnered with a dramatic soprano. The incantational texts are drawn from Mayan, Aztec, and Inca poetry.

The vocal soloist is magnificent; the percussion orchestra (William Kraft is its director) consummate artists.

Mílena, Cantata No. 3 for Soprano and Orchestra, Op. 37

☐ Denver Symphony Orchestra / Curtin (soprano) / Priestman (conductor) / Desto 7171

Heated and intense prose adapted from Kafka's *Letters to Mílena* bound by equivalent heated and intense vocal-instrumental music, honed with percussion. There are six parts—the first, *Prelude—Ghosts* for voice alone, with Nos. 3 and 5, *Cantus I—On Love* and *Prosa II—Jealousy and Despair,* set in the form of narration with orchestra.

Curtin as vocalist and narrator is a double star. Her voice is beautiful, her delivery communicative, and her temperament for this dramatic music thrilling. The text is in Spanish and her diction in the long declamatory portions impeccable. She makes the strongest case possible for Ginastera's opus.

Umberto Giordano   (1867-1948)

*Opera
and Dramatic
Music*

Andrea Chénier

☐ National Philharmonic Orchestra and John Alldis Choir / Scotto and Ewing (sopranos); Killebrew (alto); Domingo, Sénéchal, and de Palma (tenors); Milnes, Dara, and Monk (baritones); Sharpe (bass); Beavan, Brand, Bushkin, Harling, King, and Kraft (vocalists) / Levine (conductor) / RCA ARL3-2046

Opera in the fullest melodramatic sense is represented here. The blood-curdling story is portrayed by three principal characters—Maddalena (sung by Renata Scotto), Gérard (sung by Sherrill Milnes), and the title role sung by Placido Domingo. There is a sizable cast in addition but they have little to do, and, in fact, so little that their characterizations lack profile. While the chorus is also not given much importance, the orchestra is a virile and important voice in whipping up excitement.

But the three principal singers are sufficient to carry the ball and satisfy any opera buff. In this rich recording they score vocal and artistic smash successes. Domingo is in stunning voice; Scotto has never been better—her range of expression is magnificent; and Milnes's beautifully focused voice is ideal, his interpretation of the role bold and exceptionally so. James Levine's conducting is masterful—his sense of pace superb.

This outstanding issue, providing unreserved success, eliminates all the competition which is of good total. The London 1303 production includes Tebaldi in the cast; Corelli is one of the leads in the Angel S-3645 edition. There are two monaural releases still available, both fairly good but, of course, in no way to be compared to the RCA entry. Tebaldi is again represented (on Everest/Cetra S-412/2) and Caniglia is the female star in a Seraphim 6019 production.

Giovanni Francesco Giuliani   (18th cent.?)

*Chamber
Music*

Quartet in A major for Mandolin, Violin, Viola, and Lute

☐ Bauer-Slais (mandolin); Pichler (violin); Baierle (viola); Hladky (lute) / Turnabout 34016

A different type of string quartet, which, through its combination of paired bowed and plucked instruments, produces a hearty and bright sound. And so it is addressed in terms of two movements that bypass any tempo slower than a moderate one. Some may find Giuliani's piece small beer, but given a fair chance it will project a Viennese charm that is most enjoyable.

Some confusion in *Schwann*, which lists this piece as one of a set of *Quartetti*, proceeds to name five instruments: mandolin, violin, viola, cello, and lute, and then reverses itself by listing correctly four performers' names. Ditto the misunderstanding in the liner notes for the disc. These mention the work having been drawn from "four quartets for mandolin, viola, violoncello and lute." Later this is totally canceled by indicating that "the violin plays the leading role" and in mentioning "the absence of a low-pitched bass (violoncello)."

Mauro Giuliani   *(1781-1829)*

Concerto in A major for Guitar and Strings, Op. 30

☐ Melos Ensemble / Bream (guitar) / RCA LSC-2487

*Solo
Instrument
and
Orchestra*

Guitar

One of the best of the considerable number of guitar concerti of the classic period written by this Italian guitar virtuoso. Full-scale formulation: Sonata construction, a warmly melancholy *Siciliano*, and a rondo-promulgated *Alla polacca*, with musical cadenzas of pithiness in the opening movement.

The genuine quality of the piece has led to a number of recordings: the soloists include Behrend (Deutsche Grammophon 139417), Diaz (on Angel S-36496), Pepe Romero (on Philips 6500918), Scheit (on Turnabout 34123 and 34195/9), Williams (on Columbia MS-7327 and M3X-31508), and Bream. Because of a compound of interpretative grace and tempi choice that keeps the music moving, Bream is the definite choice. He retains the maestoso feeling of the initial movement without resorting to the more or less plodding pace used by his colleagues. This carries over to a more direct viewpoint of the other movements, without nullifying their proper conduct. (In terms of performance time one example will suffice: Bream plays the Concerto in 22:45 minutes; Scheit requires 26:34.) Furthermore, the very small ensemble accompanying Bream produces a textural refinement of chamber-music effect that is most appealing.

Introduction, Theme, Variations, and Polonaise for Guitar and Orchestra, Op. 65

☐ Academy of St. Martin-in-the-Fields / Romero (guitar) / Marriner (conductor) / Philips 9500042

Music of average merit and rather obvious in what course it will take. Played with an alertness and a genuine feeling for its contents.

Grande ouverture, Op. 61

Instrumental

Guitar

Gran sonata eroica

La Melanconia

☐ Romero (guitar) / Philips 9500513

La Melanconia is slight fare; the others, especially the *Gran sonata*, are more substantial. No quirkiness in the playing by Pepe Romero. His clarity is ideal.

Le Rossiniane

Op. 119 / Op. 121

☐ Bream (guitar) / RCA ARL1-0711

Two of the six *Rossiniane* suites Giuliani wrote. These twirl and variate on themes from Rossini's operas. In turn, Julian Bream has done some judicious editing, including cuts. No harm results to these musical bantamweights which are stunningly performed.

Sonata in C major, Op. 15

Sonatine in D major, Op. 71, No. 3

☐ Yepes (guitar) / Deutsche Grammophon 2530871

Everything meshes beautifully in these performances, especially the slow movement in the Sonata. The coloristic concepts are additional assets.

Variations on a Theme of Handel, Op. 107

Variations on _I bin a kohlbauern bub_, Op. 49

☐ Romero (guitar) / Philips 9500513

The artistry displayed by Pepe Romero helps to cover the patchwork that covers the structures of Giuliani's pieces. Excellent sound.

Chamber Music

Sonata in A major for Flute and Guitar, Op. 85

☐ Linde (flute); Ragossnig (guitar) / Klavier 505

Gentility and equality for the pair of instruments. The liner notes speak of the "tremendous" virtuoso technique required in the piece but it never surfaces. Of course musicianship that makes something of the simplicity of this composer's music equates a certain type of virtuosity and that the performers do display.

Glen Glasow (1924-   )

Instrumental

Violin

Rakka for Violin and Tape

☐ Kobialka (violin) / Desto 7144

In terms of importance the tape is in first place, consisting mainly of Japanese temple-bell and wind-chime timbres electronically processed as well as other electronic processes. A great deal of the piece makes the violin subsidiary and accompanying the tape procedures. Little matter what comes first, since _Rakka_ (a title taken from a tenth-century Haiku) is of abstract imagery, just a bit hallucinatory around the edges.

Alexander Glazunov (1865-1936)

Orchestra

Ballet Suite from _Raymonda_ (1896)

☐ Bolshoi Theatre Orchestra / Svetlanov (conductor) / Melodiya/Angel S-40172

Perhaps overly sweet, but that's the way it is. In any event the playing can't be faulted.

Cortège solennel

☐ Moscow Radio Symphony Orchestra / Rozhdestvensky (conductor) / Melodiya/Angel S-40225

The recording of this work is clear. The data concerning it is not. Glazunov produced two works with the title _Torshestvennoye Shestvie_ ("Solemn Procession"). One, written in 1894, is his Opus 50, the other composed in 1909, is marked Opus 91. M/A shows a date of 1907. Take your choice.

Finnish Fantasy, Op. 88

☐ Moscow Radio Symphony Orchestra / Svetlanov (conductor) / Melodiya/Angel S-40119

An extreme rarity in Glazunov's large orchestral output. Composed in 1910, the very next opus, produced two years later, was a related work, titled _Finnish Sketches_.

From the Middle Ages, Suite, Op. 79

☐ Moscow Radio and Television Symphony Orchestra / Fedoseyev (conductor) / Columbia/Melodiya M–34522

Glazunov's *Iz Srednikh Byekov* has four movements. Two of these are formal: Prelude and Scherzo, the other pair are picturesque: Troubadour's Serenade and *The Crusaders*. The most interest is to be found in the last. Richly larded orchestration is the reason.

Fine performance. From the rich sound I am not certain whether the ad libitum pianino was used.

Marche de noces, Op. 21

Pas de caractère, Op. 68

☐ Moscow Radio Symphony Orchestra / Gauk (conductor) / Melodiya/Angel S–40119

Glazunov's "Wedding March" unmistakably fulfills its objectives, though it will never replace Mendelssohn's. The "Characteristic Dance" is in Slav-Hungarian style. Both have similar scoring detail, the only (extremely slight) difference is the use of the harp in the March.

Poème lyrique in D flat major, Op. 12

☐ Moscow Radio Symphony Orchestra / Rozhdestvensky (conductor) / Melodiya/Angel S–40225

Glazunov's "Lyrical Poem" is subtitled more prosaically as an *Andantino for Full Orchestra*. Displayed are the melodic virtues and firmly sound orchestration of this minor composer who deserves a little more attention.

Scènes de Ballet, Op. 52

☐ Moscow Radio Symphony Orchestra / Rozhdestvensky (conductor) / Melodiya/Angel S–40225

Trust a romantic-nationalist Russian composer to bring insight to a Dance score. This is finely organized in its eight parts and well delivered.

Stenka Razin, Op. 13

☐ L'Orchestre de la Suisse Romande / Ansermet (conductor) / London STS–15240

Sure-fire old-Russian-style orchestration for this symphonic poem, which means built-in fat middle register sounds, good space in the bass, and upper movement don't provide much of a challenge for a top professional orchestra so as to convince listeners with this symphonic poem. Accordingly, Ansermet convinces, and adds enough to bring a blazing climax.

Symphony No. 5 in B flat major, Op. 55

☐ Moscow Radio and Television Symphony Orchestra / Fedoseyev (conductor) / Columbia/Melodiya M–34522

The main features of Glazunov's Opus 55 (the best of his eight symphonies) are a substantial melodic depiction and an assured hand at interlocking the instrumental voices. The scoring is sure-fire, well sounding, well proportioned, and of brilliant logic. No masterpiece, but there is no doubt as to the symphony's worth. It receives an excellent presentation here.

Valse de Concert
No. 1, Op. 47 / No. 2, Op. 51

☐ L'Orchestre de la Suisse Romande / Ansermet (conductor) / London 6509

The Straussian format of an introduction, a chain of waltzes, and a coda is followed by Glazunov. The formula remains viable especially in the manner in which Ansermet highlights solo colors, harp, and percussion touches, and the like.

(*Schwann* incorrectly combines these works under one opus number.)

Solo Instrument and Orchestra

Cello

Chant du Ménestrel, Op. 71

☐ Moscow Youth Orchestra / Rostropovich (cello) / Kondrashin (conductor) / Monitor S-2119E (monaural)

Glazunov's haunting "Song of a Troubador" is a miniature in length but one of the composer's best inspirations. Rostropovich's playing (beautifully partnered with sensitivity by the orchestra) is emotion laden, yet with such sustained control as to make one hold one's breath. A performance to be treasured.

Melody, Op. 20

☐ State Radio Orchestra / Rostropovich (cello) / Anosov (conductor) / Monitor S-2119E (monaural)

Since Monitor does not supply any notes for the works in the "encore" album of nine compositions in which this eight-minute piece appears, it is propitious to indicate it is from a set of "Two Pieces." (For that matter, Monitor does not indicate on the front or back of the album's cover the names of the three pianists, two orchestras, and two conductors that assist Rostropovich.) Glazunov set his Opus 20 in versions for cello and piano as well as cello and orchestra.

Piano

Concerto No.1 in F minor for Piano and Orchestra, Op. 92

☐ Moscow Symphony Orchestra / Richter (piano) / Kondrashin (conductor) / Monitor S-2131E (monaural)

Opus 92 shows the technical facility of this composer, providing a polished prose with balanced emotional appeal. There are but two movements, the first in free sonata form, the other displaying Glazunov's favorite variational structure. Sequential patterns abound, but that's part of the conservative game.

Richter's performance is stunning. He has the fullest insight to Glazunov's music. Our other piano soloists have steered clear of this Concerto. A purge of their repetitive repertoire might be a worthy undertaking.

Concerto No. 2 in B major for Piano and Orchestra, Op. 100

☐ Westphalian Symphony Orchestra, Recklinghausen / Ponti (piano) / Landau (conductor) / Turnabout 34621

Through in one movement, four principal sections can be noted in the Concerto. Also to be observed is the cyclic touch and more polyphony than usually found in Glazunov's music.

Sustained romanticism, of course, and it is this which is conventionally displayed in the performance.

Concerto in E flat major for Alto Saxophone and String Orchestra, Op. 109

☐ Paul Kuentz Chamber Orchestra / Rousseau (alto saxophone) / Kuentz (conductor) / Deutsche Grammophon 2530209

This was Glazunov's final work. It embraces a single movement in trisectional ordering. Engaging material structurally, including a Fugato, and interesting data for the solo voice, including a florid cadenza opportunity.

Concerto in A minor for Violin and Orchestra, Op. 82

☐ New Philharmonia Orchestra / Milstein (violin) / Frühbeck de Burgos (conductor) / Angel S-36011

Slipping a little on the current concert schedules, but this is a good romantic-nationalistic fiddle concerto and there's no reason to consider the Glazunov has worn out its welcome. The finale, if naught else, has all the requisite juices.

This is a solid presentation, and Milstein delivers the Glazunovian goods. Frühbeck de Burgos does outstanding work in the orchestral accompaniment.

Mazurka-Oberek for Violin and Orchestra

☐ State Radio Orchestra / David Oistrakh (violin) / Yudin (conductor) / Monitor 2136E (monaural)

Nice rhythmic details and all made for solo violin highlighting, including two colorful short paragraphs in harmonics. David Oistrakh shows his usual high standards in projecting all the details.

Meditation for Violin and Orchestra, Op. 32

☐ Philharmonia Hungarica / Ricci (violin) / Peters (conductor) / Turnabout 34621

Meditative pathos but no sugary elements. It is beautifully stated by Ricci. (See also under *Instrumental: violin*.)

Gavotte in D major, Op. 29, No. 3
Prelude in D flat major, Op. 49, No. 1

☐ Tarnowsky (piano) / Genesis 1004

Straightforward sensibility of form geared to lightly romantic syntax. Not outstanding Glazunov, but not lacking in average character.

(Genesis assigns the incorrect Opus number to the Gavotte as 49. It has been corrected in the title listing above.)

Gavotte in D major, Op. 49, No. 3

☐ Prokofiev (piano) / Klavier 125

The pianist is far more important than the piece he plays here. The Gavotte in D, from *Trois Morceaux*, expectedly follows conventional form. It serves as an example of this composer's miniatures for the piano, which include Waltzes, Mazurkas, Preludes, Etudes, Impromptus, and so on.

Meditation for Violin and Piano, Op. 32

☐ Heifetz (violin); Arpád Sándor (piano) / RCA ARM4-0943 (monaural)

Among the first electrical recordings, but that Heifetz flawless tone is all there—rich and round. Just the thing needed for Glazunov's communicative miniature. (See also under *Solo Instrument and Orchestra: violin.*)

Chamber Music

Quartet, Op. 109

☐ Paul Brodie Saxophone Quartet / Golden Crest 4131

A Kremlinesque modal melody (doubtless the best part of the work) is the basis for a set of five variations (the third is omitted in this performance).

Played with rich tone and excellent balance. The performance is keyed to chamber music demands with the Brodie group displaying the sensitiveness of a fine string quartet.

In modo religioso, **Op. 38**

☐ American Brass Quintet / Desto 6474/7

Introspective, formulated on chorale precepts which give a full romantic cast to the music. A gorgeously balanced example of brass-instrument playing.

Vocal

Voice with Accompaniment

Oriental Romance, **Op. 27, No. 2**

☐ Davrath (soprano); Werba (piano) / Vanguard VSD-71115

No doubt about the adjective in the title. Plenty of the orientalistic augmented step in the vocal line. A touch of cantillation also.

Ballet

The Seasons, **Op. 67**

☐ Moscow Radio Symphony Orchestra / Khaikin (conductor) / Melodiya/Angel S-40088

Vivid and with active definition of dynamic contrasts. The enunciations depicted in this case are not to be heard in the competitive editions. The surprise in that regard is the muddiness that pertains to Ansermet's London (6509) rendition, especially in the fourth tableau (*Autumn*).

Khaikin's performance is also available on Melodiya/Angel S-4114, a six-record release of ballet music.

Glazunov / Frédéric Chopin. See Chopin / Glazunov.

Reinhold Glière (1875-1956)

Orchestra

Suite from the Ballet *The Red Poppy*, Op. 70

☐ Bolshoi Theater Orchestra / Fayer (conductor) / Melodiya/Angel S-40089

Some simulated Chinese atmosphere and some downright schmaltz. The best of what this ballet represents. Best of all, of course, is the darn good set of variations that cover the famous *Yablochko*, the "Russian Sailors' Dance."

This performance is also included in a big Russian-Soviet compilation on Melodiya/Angel S-4114. Be warned: The competitive edition on Turnabout 34218 has only fair playing, little profile, and atrocious sound.

Suite from the Ballet *The Bronze Horseman* (1949)

No. 1 / No. 2

☐ Bolshoi Theater Orchestra / Žuraitis (conductor) / Melodiya/Angel S-40103

Twenty-two minutes and twenty-four minutes of music, respectively, from Glière's four-act ballet (sometimes called *The Bronze Knight*). One needn't know the story, since its generalities are in the composer's full-blown romantic style that has nicely turned tunes framed in mellifluous harmonies and sonorities. These are not stalemated by antiquated musical law and order but are simply in the conservative orbit.

The playing is properly weighted and positively balletic.

Symphony No. 3 *(Ilya Murometz)* in B minor, Op. 42

☐ Moscow Radio Symphony Orchestra / Rakhlin (conductor) / Columbia/Melodiya MG-33832

Currently, the complete transmittal of Glière's score is still to be recorded. Stokowski's edition on Seraphim (S-60089) is severely truncated, Ormandy's on RCA (LSC-3246) is also excised though much less so, while Rakhlin's is cut the least of all, but cut it is. (The last also applies to Scherchen's monaural measurement of the work on Westminster Gold 8235.)

One agrees with the purists. Let's have it all. Still, Rakhlin's edition is sufficient for the listener not to miss anything of great importance in the orchestral grandiloquence covering the legendary career of this folkloristic character. Plenty of panache and color in his translation of Glière's outsize orchestration, which includes quadruple woodwinds, eight horns, four each of trumpets and trombones, tuba, timpani, plentiful percussion, two harps, celesta, and strings. Indeed, Rakhlin's viewpoint is extremely persuasive.

Concerto in E flat major for Harp and Orchestra, Op. 74

Solo Instrument and Orchestra

Harp

☐ London Symphony Orchestra / Ellis (harp) / Bonynge (conductor) / London 26110

Not an especially harpistic work but tuneful and with Glière's romantic nationalism everything is put down nice and easy. The scoring withholds the heavy brass (only three horns) so with double winds, timpani, and percussion, plus strings, there's no problem in achieving a fine balance. High standards by all concerned.

Tarantella, Op. 9, No. 2

Instrumental

Double Bass

☐ Azarkhin (double bass); Alexandrova (piano) / Columbia/Melodiya M-33593

An example of high-grade double bass playing by the Soviet musician Rodion Azarkhin. The Tarantella is the only original work on the recording—all the nine other pieces are transcriptions made by the soloist (including the Bach Chaconne and Sarasate's *Zigeunerweisen!*).

O Do Not Braid a Flower, Op. 18, No. 7

Vocal

Voice with Accompaniment

☐ Davrath (soprano); Werba (piano) / Vanguard VSD-71115

Davrath phrases this two-minute song with charm. Glière's flower does not bloom in Russian fields, but in neutral, romantic territory.

**Voice
and Orchestra**

Concerto for Voice (Coloratura) and Orchestra, Op. 82

☐ London Symphony Orchestra / Sutherland (soprano) / Bonynge (conductor) / London 26110

Glière's wordless voice concerto represents a "first." There have been a few vocal concerti composed since but the only rival in the jumbo vocalise category is a stunning, pyrotechnical conception by the Croatian composer Boris Papandopulo. Until that appears on disc, Glière's opus stands in first place.

A performance is also available on Monitor 2030. However, the mono sound is less than fair-to-middlin', though Valentina Maksimova's singing style is quite good.

Mikhail Glinka   (1804-1857)

Orchestra

A Night in Madrid (1848)

Jota Argonesa (1845)

Kamarinskaya (1848)

Overture to A Life for the Tsar

☐ Bamberg Symphony / Perlea (conductor) / Vox 510600

Schwann does not consider the first title sufficiently important to be given a specific heading in its Glinka listings. This, despite performances by Bernstein (on Columbia MS-7014 and M-31844), Solti (on London 6944 and 6785), Svetlanov (on Melodiya/Angel S-40081), and Perlea. The last-named is certainly excellent. As usual, he does not surrender to the balcony crowd to make proper effect. His documentation is always musical, containing a subtlety that offers much super dynamic drive and thrust as well. (Glinka's quadruple-themed *A Night in Madrid* bears the full title of *Summer Night in Madrid*. It was subsequently indicated as Spanish Overture No. 2.)

Care and excellent attention to detail and balance are found in the *Jota*. Moreover, it is not overdone, which makes a blatant work from one that is a sensitive cultural transfer. (The "official" title of Glinka's piece is *Capricio brillante on the Jota Argonesa*. He later renamed the piece Spanish Overture No. 1.)

Kamarinskaya is perfectly paced. Perlea does not permit the vivacious dance tune to get out of hand and thus lose its proper contour, which it so often does. His authoritative imprint makes Perlea's interpretation the best of those published.

The Overture is done neatly. Vox's release with Perlea conducting is the only recording now available. It would repay conductors to give it a whirl instead of their constant choice of *Russlan and Ludmilla*.

Overture to Russlan and Ludmilla

☐ New York Philharmonic / Bernstein (conductor) / Columbia D3S-818

Performed with a style that comes from understanding that the greatest profits result from clarity. The music sparkles and excites under Bernstein's baton (also available in single-disc Russian music collections on MS-7014 and M-31844; and a two-record album, *Joy of Music*, M2X-795—all on the Columbia label). Some conductors plod (Perlea on Vox takes more than five and one-half minutes; Bernstein's timing is a crucial fifteen seconds faster). Some conductors (notably Solti, of all people) choose an extravagant tempo that may claim orchestral virtuosity but produces only a horrifying mess of note bleed. If you want an example of such conductorial impudence you can try Solti with the London Symphony (London 6730 or 6785). Just listen to what happens when this Overture is knocked off in four minutes and fifty-five seconds!

Valse-Fantaisie (1839)

☐ Bamberg Symphony / Perlea (conductor) / Vox 510600

Managed in an engaging fashion and minus any *rubati* trickery.

Nocturne

Instrumental

Harp

Variations on a Theme by Mozart

☐ McDonald (harp) / Klavier KS–543

Rarities, both of them. Musical memories identify Glinka's work. The two pieces are visibly patterns of German models, well wrought, stated in a simple, nondiscursive language. (Another edition of the Variations [the theme is from *Don Giovanni*] is available on Oiseau-Lyre S–308, played by Osian Ellis.)

Nocturne in F minor

Piano

☐ Tarnowsky (piano) / Genesis 1004

One can readily apply a syllogism here: The nocturne form relates especially to Chopin, Glinka writes a Nocturne, therefore Glinka sounds like Chopin. This deduction is proven by the sonic evidence.

Variations in A minor on *In den fernen Tälern*

☐ Schwarz (piano) / Musical Heritage Society MHS–1147

The native tune (''In the Distant Valleys'') is treated to five unsophisticated variations. No half measures in these measures; the tune is there to be heard. Short, sweet, and satisfying.

Trio pathétique (1827)

Chamber Music

☐ Oistrakh (violin); Knushevitsky (cello); Oborin (piano) / Monitor S–2068E (monaural)

Glinka's trio (originally cast for piano, clarinet, and bassoon, but just as often played in this version) possesses interesting incidents worthy of performance. It is traditionally paced rather than an example of nationalistic composition. At the age of twenty-three Glinka had not yet dressed his music in Russian style.

Soloists all, the three artists do not repudiate the special needs of chamber-music performance. A rich, clean bill of sound that needs no stereophonic setting to obtain proper effect.

Doubt

Vocal

Voice with Accompaniment

☐ Davrath (soprano); Werba (piano) / Vanguard VSD–71115

An example of fine vocal art. Glinka's song contains the recognizable curves of Russian melody.

Doubt

Vain Temptation

☐ Tourel (mezzo-soprano); Levine (piano); Karr (string bass) / Desto 7118/9

Double artistry, and, if you include James Levine, the accompanist, it truly is triple. Jennie Tourel is strongly sympathetic to these examples of Russian self-counsel and Gary Karr imparts a luscious string sound frame that is as vocal as a double bass could ever be. Recorded live so you'll have to accept the extra sounds and applause thrown in, but the musicianship of these artists is worth it.

Glinka / Mily Balakirev (1837-1910)

Instrumental

Piano

The Lark

☐ Pleshakov (piano) / Orion 73111

A very tasteful arrangement of Glinka's song and a standard repertoire item. Pleshakov presents it with utter smoothness and pearly figuration.

Christoph Willibald Gluck (1714-1787)

Orchestra

Overture to *Iphigénie en Aulide*

☐ Philharmonia Orchestra / Klemperer (conductor) / Angel S-36175

The ending was made by Wagner, for concert purposes. A strong-toned performance, the lines demarcated with fine balance.

String Orchestra

Chaconne

☐ Stuttgart Chamber Orchestra / Münchinger (conductor) / London 6206

Stunning portrayal of this three-part work, with a charming Gavotte as the middle-section contrast to the principal material. Beauty of tone, stylistic spirit, and impeccable playing.

Solo Instrument and Orchestra

Flute

Dance of the Blessed Spirits from *Orfeo ed Euridice*

☐ Vienna State Opera Orchestra / Baker (flute) / Prohaska (conductor) / Vanguard 71170

When it is decided to have a Hall of Fame for melodies this will be voted in on the first ballot. Every flutist, young and old, student, and concert professional plays it. But, no one like Julius Baker. He shows what is meant by seamless projection of a musical line.

Opera and Dramatic Music

Iphigénie en Aulide

☐ Munich Radio Orchestra and Bavarian Radio Chorus / Moffo and Auger (sopranos); Schmidt (mezzo-soprano); Spiess (tenor); Fischer-Dieskau, Stewart, and Weikl (baritones); Hillebrand (bass) / Eichhorn (conductor) / RCA ARL2-1104

Fact: This is Gluck by way of Wagner, the latter revamped the score by fleshing out and enriching the harmony, recoloring and enlarging the orchestration, revising the text, adding and subtracting material, and changing the ending of the opera.

Fact: This RCA release is an American reissue of the original recording released by Eurodisc in Germany on their 86271-XR.

So much for specific data. The production is splendid, and the biggest names—Dietrich Fischer-Dieskau (as Agamemnon) and Anna Moffo (as Iphigenia)—are matched by the lesser ones. Wagner's objective confuses Gluck, but it certainly does not confuse Wagner, and disregarding all the changes the opera provides, in its own right, a splendid piece of work. Purists should leave and Wagnerians remain. One is positive of the applause of the latter.

Orfeo ed Euridice

☐ Orchestra and Chorus of the Royal Opera House, Covent Garden / Lorengar and Donath (sopranos); Horne (mezzo-soprano) / Solti (conductor) / London 1285

The extraordinary beauty of this masterpiece receives a full and unblemished profile in the Solti-led performance. Style and character are immaculate; the articulation and pace are firmly controlled. There is a profound consideration of the score yet there is no disturbing of requisite classical purity. Full-bodied singing is obtained from the chorus, and the orchestral playing could not be bettered in regard to precision and clarity.

Marilyn Horne's Orfeo is most expressive. The *Chiamo il mio ben cosi* is colored with poignancy, the *Che farò* is beautifully accomplished because it is delivered with telling simplicity. Both Pilar Lorengar (though just a bit tight in the upper register at times) and Helen Donath are substantial members of the cast.

The only real competition is in RCA's version (LSC–6169) and that is only fractional, solely due to the stunning singing of Shirley Verrett in the Orfeo role. Moffo as Euridice does not project much feeling for what she is doing and Judith Raskin as Amor is adequate and no more. Chorus and orchestra are good but not equal to the tonal depth that Solti summons from his musicians. The RCA takes three discs and runs over the two-hour mark; London's two-record version clocks in at less than one hour and three-quarters.

Don Juan (1761)

Ballet

☐ Academy of St. Martin-in-the-Fields / Preston (harpsichord) / Marriner (conductor) / London STS–15169

There are some dry spots, but the greater part of Gluck's score holds up quite well, thank you. Marriner's statement of the content is excellent, minus any overemphasis that would equate distortion.

Benjamin Godard   (1849-1895)

Concerto Romantique in A minor, Op. 35

Solo Instrument and Orchestra

☐ Sinfonie Orchester Radio Luxembourg / Rosand (violin) / de Froment (conductor) / Turnabout 34466

Violin

The liner note author downgrades Godard's piece by terming it "drawing-room music for solo violin and orchestra." Objection! True enough, movement 3 is a Canzonetta that for many decades was performed by the gifted and sensitive as encore data and mauled by the untalented and bored in the teaching studio. And, certainly that movement's flowery bed of melodic ease seems out of place in a concerto document. However, the rest of the work (fast-paced outer movements and a second movement of Adagio articulation) is as good and as musical and as serious as the concerti in the repertoire by Bruch, Paganini, and Saint-Saëns, none of which has ever been libeled by being denigrated as belonging in the "drawing room."

So much for the defense. The music is delightfully unmannered, interesting, and perfectly designed for the solo voice. There are plenty of juicy thirds and sixths, proper amounts of fiddle technicalities, and no padding. Especially interesting is the recitative-type cadenza in the first movement.

Rosand is not the household name of a Stern or a Menuhin, but he's as good as any violinist on the scene today. If he isn't a violinist's violinist, he certainly is many critics' violinist, including this one. He tosses off this music in an expressive, precisely timed, and stylistically flashy manner. Such a virile presentation helps prove that Godard's Concerto is one of the best finds in the current romantic music revival.

Instrumental	**Suite de trois Morceaux, Op. 116**
Flute	☐ Robison (flute); Sanders (piano) / Vanguard 71207

Sure, lightweights all three: *Allegretto, Idylle,* and *Valse.* But, the graciously songful *Idylle,* especially as it is so compellingly presented here, adds to the small credits Godard has on the books. The *Valse* is witty and in one place beautifully snide (a quote from Waldteufel's most famous Waltz).

It takes a top artist to make an impression with music of this type. No doubts that Paula Robison fills the bill. One is also certain no one else could do better and most not as well.

Leopold Godowsky (1870-1938)

Instrumental	**Chattering Monkeys on the Sacred Lake of Wendit** from ***Java Suite***
Piano	**Gamelan** from ***Java Suite***
	Sonata in E minor (Movement One)
	Wienerisch from ***Walzermasken***
	☐ Pines (piano) / Genesis 1000

Music bound to its chromatically consonant romantic past. In the case of the Sonata there are no shortcuts; the movement recorded covers fifteen and one-half minutes and is only the first of five. In the excerpts from the twelve pieces descriptive of Javenese scenes (in turn, part of a large project titled *Phonoramas,* subtitled *Tonal Journeys for the Pianoforte*) general programmaticism applies.

Especially in the *Java* pieces, Doris Pines produces technically and musically superior readings.

Piano,	**Humoresque from *Miniatures for Piano, Four Hands***
Four Hands	☐ Pines and Friedman (piano) / Genesis 1000

An example from the total of forty-six Godowsky produced. Very simple writing for the upper part, the opposite for the lower part. A neat tidbit.

Godowsky / Frédéric Chopin. See Chopin / Godowsky.

Roger Goeb *(1914-   )*

Concertino II for Orchestra (1956)

☐ Louisville Orchestra / Whitney (conductor) / Louisville 58–5

In place of orchestral integration, Goeb's work exposes the various individual choirs and exploits their personalities as specific units. Often, a melodic line will be split between the groups. Such color motility also applies to the rhythmic climate of the piece.

Only a small string section (the performance was put on disc in the early days of Louisville's recordings) can be criticized in the presentation.

Symphony No. 3 (1950)

☐ Leopold Stokowski and His Orchestra / Stokowski (conductor) / Composers Recordings 120 (monaural)

Extrovert music, cleanly orchestrated, with a motility of linear action that reminds one of the practices of Walter Piston, but with a lighter touch. An outdoorish quality covers the outer movements.

One can be certain there is more in the score than Stoky and his pick-up group present. However, the possibility of another recording in the immediate future seems rather remote.

Concertino for Trombone and Strings (1950)

☐ WQXR Strings / Shuman (trombone) / Golden Crest 7011 (monaural)

To begin with, the medium is far from ordinary. Goeb takes advantage accordingly. Thus, long trombone lines against packed string ingredients, counterpoint underlined by color contrast, dialogue between the brass instrument and the strings—staccato in the former, pizzicati in the latter, and so on.

The rendering of Goeb's fine piece is excellent.

Prairie Songs for Woodwind Quintet (1947)

☐ Five Wind Ensemble / Desto 6422E (monaural)

Goeb has indicated his music uses "rhythmic and melodic characters of American folk music without actually borrowing directly from . . . folk literature." Folksy it is, indeed. *Evening* is covered by a semipolyphonic section, followed by soloism backed up with accompanimental ostinati. Syncopation and rhythmic tidbits brighten the *Dance.* In *Morning,* flute roulades are a preliminary to a moderately paced dancelike expression.

The playing of Goeb's work is worthy, even though the dynamic differences are rather casual. No names are noted for the players of the Five Wind organization.

Quintet No. 2 for Woodwinds (1956)

☐ New Art Wind Quintet / Composers Recordings 158 (monaural)

A fascinating wind quintet. Goeb's conception is one of fluid regard for timbre conduct and shows an acute ear for sound choices. Instrumental distinction is called on to accentuate the dissonant style of the four movements, each concerned with rhapsodic imagery. In Goeb's hands form is also originated by instrumental handling. And his scoring is far from the pert French brand of saucy sauce or the brittle Germanic type of acidic acuteness. Goeb's winds sound with resinous tartness and the tartness is very telling.

This is truly a special composition, one with its own woodwind writ. Wind quintet teams should be grateful and so should listeners.

Alexander Goehr (1932-   )

Vocal

Voice with Accompaniment

Four Songs from the Japanese, Op. 9a

☐ Nixon (soprano); McCabe (piano) / Nonesuch 71209

Aphoristic style, related to Schoenbergian expressionism. Much smoother detail in the vocal line than in the keyboard part. Nixon sings these songs without destroying their introverted mood.

Choral

Chorus Alone

Two Choruses, Op. 14

☐ John Alldis Choir / Shaw (baritone) / Alldis (conductor) / Argo ZRG-758

Settings of a passage from Milton's *Paradise Lost* and Ulysses's speech in Shakespeare's *Troilus and Cressida*. The writing, dovetailing and contrasting solo voices with full chorus, thrives on weights and spacings of instrumentallike definition. Ultrachromatic, fed by serial potencies, each portion develops a terse, logical fundament.

Goehr's Opus 14 was completed in October 1962, and a little more than a month later Alldis and his group gave the premiere in London. The recorded performance is, expectably, an expert one and fully realizes all that the score contains.

Hermann Goetz (1840-1876)

Orchestra

Frühlingsouvertüre, Op. 15

Overture to *Der Widerspänstigen Zähmung*

Overture to *Francesca da Rimini*

Symphony in F major, Op. 9

☐ Orchestre National de l'Opéra de Monte-Carlo / van Remoortel (conductor) / Genesis 1031

The Opus 15 "Spring Overture" chatters away with romantic anecdotes, especially light-keyed and fluent in the handling of the wind instruments. The Symphony shows some formal problems (it lacks the fullest persuasive continuity), but has a fine melodic source in the slow movement and stands up well in the second movement (its quality is similar to the "Spring Overture").

Goetz wrote two operas and the overtures are represented on this disc. *Francesca da Rimini* isn't in the Tchaikovsky class, but it does display dramatic publication. The other opera overture preludes Goetz's version of *The Taming of the Shrew*. Shrewdly, Goetz did not attempt to storm the heavens and produced an attractive curtain raiser.

Average performances from the Monte Carlo ensemble.

Solo Instrument and Orchestra

Piano

Piano Concerto in B flat major, Op. 18

☐ Beromünster Radio Orchestra / Baumgartner (piano) / Schmid (conductor) / Genesis 1010

Romantically drenched music, with contained virtuosity. The principal objective is lyricism, maintained in the several solo piano passages and even in the cadenza in the first movement.

That two editions of this rare work are available should be a matter of satisfaction. However, only partly so. The version on Candide 31076 (Ponti is the soloist) is best avoided. The sound is poor, the tempi restless, and apparently, in a determination to get the Concerto to fit on one side of the disc, the work is slashed. Twenty-seven measures are cut in the *Mässig Langsam* (second movement) and seventy-one measures are tossed away in the final *Lebhaft* movement.

Genrebilder, **Op. 13**

Lose Blätter, **Op. 7**

Sonatina in E flat major, Op. 8, No. 2

Sonatina in F major, Op. 8, No. 1

☐ Ruiz (piano) / Genesis 1023

Nine parts in the Opus 7 "Loose Leaves." The collection is a sharp reminder of the romantic Songs Without Words syndrome. Sample titles give the clue: *Through Field and Halls of Beech, With You!,* and *Spring's Greeting.* Goetz's speech was derived from good influences; the technique and manner of the six "Genre Pictures" have eclectic authority: Chopinesque in Nos. 2 and 4, Schumannesque in No. 3, and Brahmsian in No. 5. The pair of Sonatinas are of lesser weight; the style is similar to the "Loose Leaves" miniatures.

Ruiz's playing is clean and honest. He is thoroughly cognizant of the style involved in these pieces and does handsomely by this little-known nineteenth-century composer.

Drei leichte Stücke **for Violin and Piano, Op. 2**

☐ Dicterow (violin); Robbins (piano) / Genesis 1037/8

No special personality but impeccably constructed and efficiently organized. No criticism, since the objective is clearly defined in the title. The "Three Easy Pieces" are a *Marsch,* a *Romanze,* and a Rondo. No criticism for the recording, either.

Piano Trio in G minor, Op. 1

☐ Dicterow (violin); King (cello); Robbins (piano) / Genesis 1037/8

Despite the influence of Mendelssohn and Schumann (also a bit of Brahms here and there) a good piece, and for a first published work, a very good piece. Crystal clear in layout, with introduction and dynamic first movement, slow movement, Scherzo, and finale.

Genesis labels the performer credits incorrectly, thereby leading one to believe the instrumentation is for violin, viola, and piano.

Piano Quartet in E major, Op. 6

☐ Dicterow (violin); de Veritch (viola); King (cello); Robbins (piano) / Genesis 1037/8

Dedicated to Brahms and fully worthy of bearing his name. Goetz's quartet is as rich and as technically wise as the three piano quartets Brahms produced. Laurence Vittes in his sleeve note calls it "one of the masterpieces of the literature," and he is absolutely correct in his opinion.

The highlights of the opus are the variational slow movement and the Scherzo with a fine canonic trio for contrast.

Instrumental

Piano

Violin

Chamber Music

A well-integrated performance, spoiled only by consistent intonational problems in octave doublings.

Quintet in C minor, Op. 16

☐ Dicterow (violin); de Veritch (viola); King (cello); Trembly (bass); Robbins (piano) / Genesis 1037/8

Mostly dark-colored music, emphasized still further by a piano quintet instrumentation that includes a double bass rather than two violins. Movement 1 has a Goethe motto to set the mood: *"Und wenn der Mensch in seiner Qual verstummt, gab mir ein Gott zu sagen, was ich leide."* The third part of the work is fast-paced but "quasi menuetto," and the contrastive trio has the flow of a Ländler.

Goetz's quintet has the general romantic arguments but is never platitudinous. The playing of the group is well done, the sound beautifully clear.

Ernest Gold   (1921-   )

Vocal

Voice and Orchestra

Songs of Love and Parting

☐ Orchestra of the Vienna Volksoper / Nixon (soprano) / Gold (conductor) / Crystal S–501

Seven full-bodied songs enriched by the lucidity of Marni Nixon's singing. Gold dresses his texts—by Emily Dickinson, Edna St. Vincent Millay, Shakespeare, Burns, Shelley, and James Thomson—in romantic relevance. Expect much in these fine conceptions; you won't be disappointed.

Edwin Franko Goldman   (1878-1956)

Band

The Chimes of Liberty

The Pride of America

☐ Goldman Band / Richard Franko Goldman (conductor) / New World Records NW–266

Edwin Franko Goldman is an illustrious name in America's band history. He was the founder of the famed Goldman Band which has been giving an annual series of summer concerts in New York City for more than a half century.

Goldman was a prolific creator of Marches. Of the more than one hundred he produced, *On the Mall* is the most popular, but these two are just as brilliant, especially *The Chimes of Liberty* with its piquant, pipey piccolo obbligato in the trio section.

Richard Franko Goldman   (1910-1980)

Chamber Music

Sonata for Violin and Piano (1952)

☐ Senofsky (violin); Mack (piano) / Composers Recordings SD–353

Each of the three movements is based on a tone row but is no more rigidly calculated or coldly academic than if developed from a triadic theme. The forms are clear and the music has stuff and fiber. It also has heart and voice. Played with bright finish.

Sonatina for Two Clarinets

☐ Cole and Falcone (clarinets) / Composers Recordings SD–353

Expectedly, the music is contrapuntal, helping, therefore, to deter the merging of the lines, and thus, a loss of interest. The three movements are built on perky (close-spaced) and slowly unwinding (wide-spaced) themes. Goldman obtains the maximum of contrast; with boundaries of sevenths and ninths prevailing in style with the bipartite writing. The last movement is jumpy with rhythm, and in strict canonic form for the first quarter of its length.

Karl Goldmark *(1830-1915)*

Orchestra

Symphony, *Rustic Wedding*, Op. 26

☐ New York Philharmonic / Bernstein (conductor) / Columbia MS–7261

One widely played, but nowadays rarely. It is a minor masterwork, more of a suite than a symphony. Either way, a romantic joy. No performance matches Bernstein's warm and loving approach.

Concerto No. 1 in A minor for Violin and Orchestra, Op. 28

Solo Instrument and Orchestra

☐ Philharmonia Orchestra / Milstein (violin) / Blech (conductor) / Seraphim S–60238

Violin

No one plays Goldmark's second fiddle Concerto, and little by little fewer are performing the first one. Too bad regarding such situation. The A minor has fine romantic material and shows off the violin in its best vocal manner. All the evidence is here in Nathan Milstein's fully in-the-groove performance with fine support from Blech. The idea for a listener is to be fully indifferent to fashion and not bypass genuine, if not great, music.

Stan Golestan *(1872-1956)*

Instrumental

Ballade Roumaine (1932)

Harp

☐ Laskine (harp) / Musical Heritage Society MHS–602

Nationalistic imagery, with marked attention to the augmented intervallic span. A bit of the improvisatory character of folk material creeps in without disturbing the formal discipline. Not too much of this type of music has been written for the harp, so it is especially welcome. And, since Golestan's name is absent from *Schwann,* this single example of his work becomes doubly welcome.

G. Gombau-Guerra *(20th cent.)*

Instrumental

Apunte Bético

Harp

☐ Robles (harp) / Argo ZRG–5457

A prize-winning work—in the 1952 contest held by the Harpists' Association in America. Hispanic vitality and buoyancy in the music and so presented in the very smooth playing of Marisa Robles.

Joseph Goodman (1918-   )

Chamber Music

Jadis III (Hommage a la Serenade Interrompue)

☐ Skowronek (flute); Grossman (bassoon) / Crystal 351

Retrospective inspiration (*Jadis* meaning "in times gone by") tied in with the character of the Debussy Prelude. Suave and vocal music, a music of uninterrupted poetic content even when it explores rhythmically. The strength of the music is brought out to the full by the duo performers.

Quintet for Wind Instruments (1954)

☐ Soni Ventorum Wind Quintet / Lyrichord S-158

Tonality that is freed of traditional cultures is apparent in all three movements. Sonata style is also freed in the first movement, though there are the usual pair of principal contrasting ideas. Movement 2 is shaped like a scherzo. Symmetrical in total pulses (eight to the measure), these are disclosed in a variety of beat patterns: 3-2-3, 2-3-3, and 3-3-2. The metrical keenness of the middle movement becomes exceedingly sharper in the final one—a set of introspective variations. Derived from Boris Blacher's variable meter technique, precise arithmetical progressions structure the music. The musical results justify the act.

The Soni Ventorum five are a fine group and exhibit a finesse that is captivating. Their blended tone is, for the mix pertinent to a woodwind quintet, most unusual. And the balances are perfect throughout.

Frederic Goossen (1927-   )

Instrumental

Piano

Fantasy, Aria, and Fugue (1973)

☐ Gowen (piano) / New World Records NW-304

Tonality reigns supreme in Goossen's finely shaped three-part work. There is a strong Regerian reminder in the textural weights and activity of line in the first two pieces. The Fugue has Hindemithian features. But in no way does this music represent watered-down eclectic formalism. It may not be strikingly new, but it certainly registers clear and immediate; the Reger-Hindemith identifications do not nullify writing of character and lucidity.

Gowen's playing is fresh and full of life, extremely strong and bountifully clear.

Chamber Music

Clausulae

Temple Music

☐ Steinerius Duo / Composers Recordings S-371

Pantonal music with clear dissonant grammar. The forms are neat: seven pieces comprising the suite design of *Clausulae,* sonata format for the other work, which concludes with a fugue. (Temple Music does not signify any special picture. It was written for the dedication of Temple Emanu-El in Tuscaloosa, Alabama, hence its title.) The joinery in the works is unobtrusive and there is a good amount of rhythmic variety.

Otar Gordeli   (1928-   )

Concerto in D major for Flute and Orchestra, Op. 8

☐ State Radio Orchestra / Korneyev (flute) / Svetlanov (conductor) / Monitor 2030 (monaural)

Solo Instrument and Orchestra

Flute

Romanticism tossed around in rhapsodic figurations is the prime detail in Gordeli's work. Folkloric melodic turns are also presented. Effective orchestral background and a cadenza near the conclusion that is also effective.

François-Joseph Gossec   (1734-1829)

Sinfonia Concertante in D major from the Ballet *Mirza* for Two Harps and Orchestra

☐ Jean-François Paillard Chamber Orchestra / Laskine and Le Dentu (harps) / Paillard (conductor) / Musical Heritage Society MHS-CC-1

Solo Instrument and Orchestra

Two Harps

Compositions for two harps are in very short supply, still fewer for two harps and orchestra. This lovely melodicized three-part work is a superb find. The playing is a marvel of balance and harpistic coordination. It is truly delicious.

Arthur Gottschalk   (1952-   )

Substructures for Ten Tubas

☐ University of Michigan Tuba Ensemble / Mayer (conductor) / Golden Crest CRS-4145

Instrumental

Ten Tubas

An original medium if not original music. I know of no other work recorded for such a group, with eight bass tubas and two tenor tubas, scored in a three-choir disposition. Lots of clusters but plenty of air in the texture so that the sound image is not obscured.

Louis Moreau Gottschalk   (1829-1869)

Suite from the Ballet *Cakewalk*. See under *Hershy Kay.*

Orchestra

Symphony No. 1—*La Nuit de tropiques*

Symphony No. 2—*A Montevideo*

☐ Vienna State Opera Orchestra / Buketoff (conductor) / Turnabout 34440/2

Nocturnal substances mark the first movement of the initial Symphony, twice the length of the concluding part which has dance piquancy. The simplistic romantic folksy data of the second movement is thoroughly engaging, instrumentally engraved with tropical drums.

The other symphony is actually innocent of symphonic form and is basically a Fantasia, and, at that, a lightly scoped one. It contains patriotic tunes—typical Gottschalkian in its viewpoint.

The conductor, Igor Buketoff, edited the first symphony in which the Vienna ensemble is augmented with a band and extra percussion.

Solo Instrument and Orchestra

Piano

Variations on the Portuguese National Hymn

☐ Vienna State Opera Orchestra / List (piano) / Buketoff (conductor) / Turnabout 34440/2

You can't miss the tune since it is heard before each of the variations and is clearly laced into each of the set of four. List's super-fine clean playing is a further aid to definition. Buketoff gives excellent support.

This work was originally for piano solo (Opus 91). In its orchestral partnership it was edited by the soloist.

Instrumental

Piano

America, Op. 41

☐ Mandel (piano) / Desto 6470/3

Take it as it sounds—a variational twist on the tune. Originally it was titled *God Save the Queen*. It has the effect of an improvisation and Mandel tosses it off as though he were doing just that—and doing it magnificently.

Bamboula—Danse des Nègres, Op. 2
The Banjo—Fantasie Grotesque, Op. 15

☐ List (piano) / Vanguard 485 (monaural)

Two of the most famous pieces from the vast amount of music Gottschalk produced. The nineteenth-century freshness delights twentieth-century ears and Eugene List's playing likewise. More definitive conceptions can't be imagined.

Battle Cry of Freedom: Grand Caprice de Concert, Op. 55
Berceuse, Op. 47
Brazilian National Anthem—Grand Fantasie Triomphale, Op. 69
Chant du soldat, Op. 23
Danza, Op. 33

☐ Mandel (piano) / Desto 6470/3

Pan-American patriotism applied to music in the first and third pieces and some north- and south-of-the-border examples. Gottschalk covered all the categories in his creative deliberations. Mandel approaches the music with a serious stance and the results are extremely beneficial.

The Dying Poet—A Meditation, Op. 110

☐ List (piano) / Vanguard 485 (monaural)

List tells us that this sentimental bit initially sold some 35,000 copies and then went through at least twenty-eight editions. Well, then, it had other values since it must have been played more than a million times in the silent movie houses throughout the country.

But, truly, its salonistic turns have a flavor that can only be termed "campy" when played in that manner. In List's performance, minus parlor-piano affectations, the music has proper grace and charm.

El Cocoyé

Forget Me Not **(Mazurka Elegante)**

Grand Scherzo, Op. 57

Impromptu, Op. 54

Jeunesse: **Mazurka Brillante, Op. 70**

La Gallina, **Op. 53**

La Jota Aragonesa, **Op. 14**

☐ Mandel (piano) / Desto 6470/3

Emphasis on the dance in these pieces, with Cuban nationalistic touches coloring *El Cocoyé* and the catchy considerations of *La Gallina* ("The Hen"). Mandel is in full command, never trying to elevate the music to a style other than what it possesses.

La Savane – **Ballad Créole, Op. 3**

☐ List (piano) / Vanguard 485 (monaural)

It was Eugene List's and Jeanne Behrend's recordings that led to the Gottschalk revival, now in full swing with numerous other recordings, books about the composer, magazine articles, and reprints of his music. Playing with the superb artistry and finesse exhibited here was a fundamental stimulus.

La Scintilla

☐ Mandel (piano) / Desto 6470/3

Gottschalk touched all the bases in his compositions: patriotic, Latin-American, pictorial, poetic, sweet, and neutral. "The Spark" is termed a "Mazurka sentimentale." Gracefully depicted by this first-class musician.

The Last Hope – **Méditation Religieuse, Op. 16**

Le Bananier – **Chanson Nègre, Op. 5**

☐ List (piano) / Vanguard 485 (monaural)

Salon music represented by *The Last Hope,* which became a smash hit and even was turned into a Presbyterian hymn. But, if it is a sentimental sample List avoids sentimental *shtick* in his marvelous performance. The other work is brightly detailed and its rhythmic spice is perfectly depicted by List.

Le Mancenillier

☐ Davis (piano) / London 6943

If you wish this neat West Indian Serenade (played with snap and splendid style), you will have to secure Davis's album titled *Great Galloping Gottschalk* (it contains eleven other Gottschalk items). "The Machineel Tree" is not contained in either of Eugene List's or Alan Mandel's recordings of Gottschalk's piano music (*see above* and *see below*).

Love and Chivalry: Caprice elegant en forme de Schottische, Op. 97
L'Union, Op. 48

☐ Mandel (piano) / Desto 6470/3

"The Union" (see also under *Gottschalk/Adler*) is high-class potpourri that swatches into the score *The Star-Spangled Banner, Yankee Doodle,* and *Columbia.* Great fun and ear-catching counterpoint and colorations. Mandel plays the hell out of the piece just in the extroverted way it should be heard.

Gottschalk's Opus 97 is hamstrung by its conventionality. In short, a commonplace entry in his catalogue. Mandel does his best with the music.

The Maiden's Blush — Le Sourire d'une jeune fille

☐ List (piano) / Vanguard 485 (monaural)

A *Grand Valse du concert* is the composer's subtitle for this work with a lengthy and bilingual title. "The Smile of a Young Girl" is Chopin-derived Gottschalk music. In List's hands it is a gem; he dispels any prejudices the mid-Victorian title may have aroused before hearing the performance.

Manchega, Op. 38
Marche de nuit, Op. 17
Minuit à Séville, Op. 30

☐ Mandel (piano) / Desto 6470/3

More Gottschalk that represents, in turn, rhythmic aliveness, a finely crafted march (no banging in the playing and subtly defined by Mandel), and a variationally designed opus.

Ojos criollos — Les Yeux Créoles, Op. 37

☐ List (piano) / Vanguard 485 (monaural)

Gottschalk's *Danse Cubaine* was originally a piano duet and then redone by him for solo piano. *Ojos criollos* ("Cuban Eyes") represents again List's magnificent rapport with Gottschalk's music and his sensitive realization of its style.

O! Ma Charmante, epargnez moi!
Ossian, Op. 4

☐ Mandel (piano) / Desto 6470/3

Both compositions have interesting profiles. "O, My Charmer, Spare Me!" is Creole styled; Gottschalk composed the other piece, subtitled *Deux Ballades,* at the age of fourteen. As to be expected, it has a sentimental surface.

Pasquinade-Caprice, Op. 59

☐ List (piano) / Vanguard 485 (monaural)

"Lampoon" was one of Gottschalk's most popular works. Its light character needs special attention, and List's deft playing, spiced with the most engaging *rubato,* is certain to charm the listener.

Pensee Poetique, Op. 62

Radieuse, Op. 116

Ricordati, Op. 26

Sixth *Ballade,* Op. 85

Souvenirs d'Andalousie, Op. 22

Souvenir de la Havane, Op. 39

☐ Mandel (piano) / Desto 6470/3

    The rhythmic vitality of the dance was a constant stimulus to Gottschalk. Opus 22 and Opus 39 are evidence of this. Another stimulus was Chopin. Evidence of that is also included in this group. Mandel styles his playing accordingly and plays convincingly.

Romance

☐ Davis (piano) / New World Records NW–257

    Simple but charming. No exoticisms here, just a few well-pressed chromatics to color the material.

Souvenir de Porto Rico — Marche des Gibaros

Suis-Moi — Caprice, Op. 45

Tournament Galop

☐ List (piano) / Vanguard 485 (monaural)

    The first piece is based on a tune sung by Puerto Rican peasants. List's dynamic control in this work is superb. The *Caprice* has a note in the score that the performer should give the music as much care in his playing as the composer took in conceiving it. List does. His sensitive phrasing represents elegant pianism. The *Galop* is delivered on target with smash but not impolite percussiveness.

Two Mazurkas, Op. 6

☐ Mandel (piano) / Desto 6470/3

    Also titled *Colliers D'Or.* Played simply and thereby honestly.

Escenas Campestres

Opera and Dramatic Music

☐ Vienna State Opera Orchestra / Paniagua (soprano); Estevés (tenor); Garcia (baritone) / Buketoff (conductor) / Turnabout 34440/2

    Gottschalk terms his "Cuban Country Scenes" an "Opera in One Act," but that's stretching matters considerably. First the baritone offers his love to the soprano, then the tenor does likewise. Later both men join in their appeal. All appeals are rejected. If no plot, there is, at least, gentle and attractive nationalistically accented music. All of it is presented with utter smoothness.

Gottschalk / Samuel Adler (1928-   )

The Union, Concert Paraphrase on National Airs, Op. 48

Solo Instrument and Orchestra

☐ Vienna State Opera Orchestra / List (piano) / Buketoff (conductor) / Turnabout 34440/2

    A fleshed-out version of the solo piano work (see under *Gottschalk: Instrumental: piano*

Piano

711

[*Love and Chivalry: Caprice elegant en forme de Schottische*]). Eugene List, the soloist, commissioned this version because he felt it "practically cried out for a larger frame." Excellent idea. That objective has been well met by the composer-conductor Samuel Adler. This represents a fine performance of a fine transcription.

Gottschalk / Hershy Kay (1919-   )

Solo Instrument and Orchestra

Piano

Grande Tarantelle for Piano and Orchestra

☐ Vienna State Opera Orchestra / List (piano) / Buketoff (conductor) / Turnabout 34449

Various versions were made of this work but were lost and spurious editions surfaced. Eugene List uncovered a two-piano score and from this a full reconstruction and orchestration were made by Hershy Kay.

Basic Tarantella information rides through the music; the orchestration is solid but lightly applied and deftly so. List plays with stylistic panache and receives magnificent partnership from Buketoff.

The recording is also available in a three-record set released by Turnabout (34440/2) of Gottschalk music.

Gottschalk / Gunther Schuller (1925-   )

Orchestra

Ojos criollos

☐ New England Conservatory Ragtime Ensemble / Schuller (conductor) / Golden Crest CRS–31042

Ojos criollos, which is subtitled *Danse Cubaine, caprice brilliant*, has a tango swing with a march-like overlay. It was originally for either piano solo or piano four-hands. Schuller's transcription is color supervised to bring out the details without intruding on the style. Good show by the school musicians.

Morton Gould   (1913-   )

Orchestra

American Salute

☐ Utah Symphony Orchestra / Abravanel (conductor) / Turnabout 34459

Everybody but everybody has played, at one time or another, Gould's variational jamboree on the Civil War tune *When Johnny Comes Marching Home*.

Abravanel's reading has all the clarity and vitality one desires in this pops best seller. Arthur Fiedler's performance with the Boston Pops outfit on RCA VCS–7068 is a close second.

Columbia (Broadsides for Orchestra on Columbian Themes) (1967)

☐ Louisville Orchestra / Gould (conductor) / Louisville 716

A Gouldian workout (as only he is capable) on *Hail Columbia* and *Columbia, the Gem of the Ocean.* He describes it as formed from "pronouncements, airs, dances, memorials, hymns, parades, and flourishes." It's skillful, colorful, and exceedingly clever. Above all, it makes musical sense as a thematically rhapsodic parallel to formalized variations on a theme. Only snobbery refuses to accept the former, while not denying the latter.

Gould's notes on the work indicate that his recorded performance is "in the composer's shortened version." It is this writer's considered opinion that the nine-minute length used here should remain the definitive rendering.

Fall River Legend (Ballet Suite) (1948)

☐ Morton Gould and His Orchestra / Gould (conductor) / RCA LSC–2532

This is the symphonic suite Gould drew from his ballet score, based on the historic Lizzie Borden parricide case. It covers six parts: a *Prologue and Waltzes, Elegy, Church Social, Hymnal Variations, Cotillion,* and *Epilogue.* Of course it is played with understanding, but there is the added matter of orchestral assurance and distinction that make the product more than just another composer-led performance.

Latin-American Symphonette (1941)

☐ Utah Symphony Orchestra / Abravanel (conductor) / Vanguard S–275

Four movements: Rumba, Tango, Guaracha, and Conga. Satisfactory in all respects, but even better when directed by Gould. However, only the second and third movements are so available (on RCA LSC–2532).

(The Guaracha movement has achieved a special popularity as noted by the many performances it receives separate from the complete Suite.)

Soundings (1969)

☐ Louisville Orchestra / Gould (conductor) / Louisville 716

A far cry from Gould's savory and spicy Latin-American Symphonette or the Broadway bounciness of his *Interplay.* Which is not to say that it isn't good. At the least, it's damn interesting. This music represents a Morton Gould who has breathed Darmstadian air and has come away remembering its sonic segmentation, fracturing, and fractioning. Its two parts (*Threnodies* and *Paens*) are vividly colored (part two splits the strings into muted and unmuted groups and the "general character of the instrumentation moves the musical patterns from 'open' to 'echo' effects"). Orchestrational enterprise has always been Gould's forte and in this respect he scores (pun intended) a success. As a conductor of his own music, he doubles that success.

Spirituals for String Choir and Orchestra (1941)

☐ London Symphony Orchestra / Susskind (conductor) / Everest 3002

Gould at his very best. Gould speaking in his most original manner. The hymnodic, jazzy, and glossy convictions of this work are given a captivating performance by one of the finest conductors in the field.

There are no spirituals as such in the opus. Gould calls them Spirituals since he planned "to use the strings as if they were a vocal choir." He's done this so well that one can almost believe that Negro Spirituals are included. A great piece with especially effective use of the percussion as well as—of course—the strings.

Symphonette No. 2 (1939)

☐ Louisville Orchestra / Mester (conductor) / Louisville LS–751

Slick, sure! In its genre, a masterpiece. Gould's work (when it was premiered it was titled Second American Symphonette) contains the famous *Pavane*, a fusion of swing in the framework of a classical court dance. And many-splendored orchestral touches. Music that still works in the class, top-entertainment category.

The Louisville team, with Mester directing, sparkles. The playing projects precise phrasing, brings out all the color and shape of the three parts of the piece. Exceedingly bright sound, and just what this opus should have.

Venice (Audiograph for Double Orchestra and Brass Choirs) (1967)

☐ Seattle Symphony Orchestra / Katims (conductor) / RCA LSC–3079

The result of a commission calling for a work for two orchestras. Accordingly, much emphasis in terms of instrumental separation, with each orchestra comprising full woodwinds, horns, percussion, harp, and strings, plus paired brass choirs. Oddly, for Gould, a great deal of restrained dynamic intensity. Expectedly, for Katims, a worthy performance.

Band

Battle Hymn of the Republic (1951)

Formations (1964)

Santa Fé Saga (1956)

☐ Knightsbridge Symphonic Band / Gould (conductor) / Everest 3253

Total cultivation of American subject matter and music to fit. Bountifully brilliant in scoring and inculcating musical vernacularism. This is especially apparent in the *Saga*, which covers four sections: *Rio Grande, Round-Up, Wagon Train,* and *Fiesta,* and just as marked in the eight-part *Formations*. Some of its titles will clue in the potential listener: *March On, Rally, Strut,* and *Slink*.

The *Battle Hymn* is another one of the many Gould adaptations, reworkings, and repackaging of well-known tunes. It was originally for orchestra (made for Toscanini and the NBC Symphony!).

Gould can score like hell, whether it be for orchestra or band. He is equally fully at home on the podium. The performances are splendid, bright and brash when they should be, more chaste in other instances. Not only for band music devotees.

Solo Instrument and Band

Clarinet

Derivations for Clarinet and Band

☐ Columbia Jazz Combo / Goodman (clarinet) / Gould (conductor) / Columbia MS–6805

A miniature survey of jazz speech in slightly formalistic dress. The boogielike huffs and puffs of the finale *Ride-Out* make it the most spectacular. The *Contrapuntal Blues* and *Rag* are self-explanatory; the opening is a *Warm-Up*. All the styles are presented honestly, and there's none of that special orchestrational pretentious hamming that is all effects and no music.

The playing is polished, warm, wise, and classy. Goodman as the spotlight man is magnificent, reaffirming his individual artistic stature. Columbia's sound is something special.

Solo Instrument and Horns

Tuba

Tuba Suite for Solo Tuba and Three French Horns

☐ New York Horn Trio / Phillips (tuba) / Brehm (conductor) / Golden Crest 4122

A quartet in total but not chamber music. The star is the tuba, and Harvey Phillips, who plays it, fulfills every bit of the many requirements in this charming and melodious and sometimes virtuosic compendium. There are five movements: Prelude, Chorale, Waltz, Elegy, and Quickstep.

Vivaldi Gallery (for Divided Orchestra and String Quartet on Vivaldi Themes)

☐ Seattle Symphony Orchestra / Siegl and Kardalian (violins); McInnes (viola); Davis (cello) / Katims (conductor) / RCA LSC–3079

The stereophonic syndrome galore. In addition to two wind choirs, a brass choir, and harp, Gould splits his strings three ways: two tutti groups and a solo string quartet. The Concerto Grosso dialectic is sure-fire. Actually not Vivaldi-Gould, but the reverse—actual Vivaldi shapes flit in and out, some are *almost* identifiable, others totally so. But always the Gouldian impress.

Solo Instrument and Orchestra

String Quartet

Rag–Blues–Rag

☐ Helps (piano) / Composers Recordings S–288

No attempt here to sustain the reputation brought Gould by such compositions as *Interplay, Latin-American Symphonette, American Salute,* and so on. Two-thirds of the work is introverted in its statements, and even the other portion (the second Rag) has an unordinary semiausterity. Most Rags are pedestrian and most Blues are just as cliché ridden. These three pieces propose Gouldian qualifications of the forms and as such are very individual expressions. Such aspects turn Gould's set of pieces into a real "sleeper." Small-scaled but nevertheless a distinguished contribution to contemporary piano literature.

Instrumental

Piano

Interplay

☐ Morton Gould and His Orchestra / Gould (piano) / Gould (conductor) / RCA LSC–2532

Originally conceived as "a little Concerto" for piano and orchestra, the great success of *Interplay* as a ballet score (to choreography by Jerome Robbins) has given the piece permanent balletic identity, though concert performances are still of fair number. Regardless, Gould's work, with its jaunty, jazzy, tuny turns, is a solid fixture in lighter-faceted American music and is as worthy as dozens and dozens of heavier-hefted productions.

Gould is tops here in his triple capacity as composer, conductor, and soloist. It's an irresistible release and should last forever as *the* performance. Who could do better?

Ballet

Gould / **Louis Brunelli (1925-   )**

Revolutionary Prelude (1965)

☐ Knightsbridge Symphonic Band / Gould (conductor) / Everest 3253

Music from Gould's score for a TV series, *World War I*. The evocation of a pre-Bolshevik Russian atmosphere is professionally typed by Gould's piece which is in the Glière-Glazunov vein. The scoring by Brunelli (from the original orchestration) was made with the composer's approval. (Another section of Gould's *World War I* music has also been arranged for band; see under *Gould/Cacavas* [Prologue].)

Band

Gould / John Cacavas (1930-   )

Band

Prologue (1965)

☐ Knightsbridge Symphonic Band / Gould (conductor) / Everest 3253

Originally, the musical signature for a TV series, *World War I*. Monothemed and thereby direct as required for identification by viewers. Full-scoped scoring developed from Gould's music. (For another excerpt from Gould's TV score, see under *Gould/Brunelli* [Revolutionary Prelude].)

Charles Gounod   (1818-1893)

Orchestra

Ballet Music from *Faust*

☐ Berlin Philharmonic Orchestra / von Karajan (conductor) / Deutsche Grammophon 2530199

Perhaps V. K. doesn't let his hair down enough (this *is* a French ballet score, after all); but nonetheless, the score twinkles and sparkles sufficiently under his direction. In comparison with the performance of this section in the complete opera recording (see under *Opera and Dramatic Music*), von Karajan is the winner hands down and baton up.

Danse Grècque from *Le Tribut de Zamora*
Grande Valse from *La Reine de Saba*

☐ London Symphony Orchestra / Bonynge (conductor) / London 6744

Little survives from "The Queen of Sheba" save the ballet music from which Bonynge has chosen the Waltz. The other dance is from Gounod's last opera, a five-act affair which didn't last long after its opening night.

Funeral March of a Marionette (1873)

☐ Philadelphia Orchestra / Ormandy (conductor) / Columbia MS–6474

The *Marche funèbre d'une marionette* is a diverting item and Ormandy captures all of the qualities requisite for the success of Gounod's make-believe.

Cantata and Oratorio

Messe solennelle (St. Cecilia)

☐ Orchestre de la Société des Concerts du Conservatoire, Paris and Choeurs René Duclos / Lorengar (soprano); Hoppe (tenor); Crass (bass); Puig-Roget (organ) / Hartemann (conductor) / Angel S–36214

The primary interest is the antithesis Gounod's Mass represents to his *Faust*. Differing objectives, naturally, but respect for the spirituality of his sacred subject did not prevent Gounod from injecting theatricality into his work.

The talents of the singers are nicely exhibited in this recorded statement. No blind spots in the direction.

Opera and Dramatic Music

Faust

☐ Orchestra and Chorus of the Théâtre National de l'Opéra / de los Angeles (soprano); Berton (mezzo-soprano); Gorr (alto); Gedda (tenor); Blanc and Autran (baritones); Christoff (bass) / Cluytens (conductor) / Angel S–3622

It's become quite fashionable to downgrade *Faust*. That's shameful, since the score is filled with absolute beauties, such as the Waltz, the Jewel Song, the Flower Song, the Cavatina, and so on. *Faust* may not be dramatically subtle but it's on target. In all, Gounod's music is a healthy handmaid for the drama, dated though the storyline may be. No downgrading Gounod's ability considering the fine manner in which the voices and orchestra are treated. And there's a fine tuny ballet (separately available, see under *Orchestra*).

Good organization to all matters in this recording, with choice tempi, and acute but well-rounded characterizations. Boris Christoff's Méphistopheles is clear-cut and convincing, voiced with darkly dramatic definition, Victoria de los Angeles is splendid in all respects (her singing of the Jewel Song is outstanding), Gedda's Faust is richly conceived and thus totally commanding. Though the conventions (and cuts, of course) are all followed by Cluytens, that doesn't deny the worthiness of this recorded edition.

Percy Aldridge Grainger *(1882-1961)*

Orchestra

Children's March

Colonial Song (1913)

Country Gardens

Handel in the Strand (1913)

Immovable Do

Irish Tune (1909)

Mock Morris (1911)

Molly on the Shore (1913)

My Robin Is to the Greenwood Gone (1921)

Shepherd's Hey (1913)

Spoon River

☐ Eastman-Rochester Pops Orchestra / Fennell (conductor) / Mercury 75102

A healthy and invigorating sampler of Grainger's music, familiar and unfamiliar. Grainger's harmonic and contrapuntal conversions on such tunes as *Molly on the Shore* and the *Londonderry Air* (Irish Tune from County Derry, to give Grainger's complete title) ring as true today as they did sixty or seventy years ago when most of these pieces were written.

Fennell is a master of this musical style and furnishes impeccable performances, paced properly, and affording the ultimate in enjoyment for the auditor. Delightful!

Faeroe Island Dance

Band

☐ Cornell Wind Ensemble / Stith (conductor) / Cornell University 8

A little more than a tidbit, which, by virtue of Grainger's uncanny harmonic and color abilities, becomes larger and more important than the trifle it seems to be.

Lads of Wamphray March

☐ Cornell University Symphonic Band / Stith (conductor) / Cornell University 10

717

A March of artistic nourishment that has the beat expected but has unexpected subtleties. That's Percy Grainger—a personality all too little known.

Instrumental

Piano

Paraphrase on the Waltz of the Flowers from Tchaikovsky's *Nutcracker* Ballet

☐ Ponti (piano) / Turnabout 34560

Grainger: tasteful and in good taste. Ponti: sometimes fleet, sometimes heavy-handed performance.

Enrique Granados (1867-1916)

Orchestra

Andalusia—Danza Española **No. 5 in E minor, Op. 37**

☐ London Symphony Orchestra / Argenta (conductor) / London 6006

The genuine article, even though on the lighter side and which has led to its pops concerts' popularity.

Neatly played and properly paced. London's liner note does not include the important fact that the orchestration is not by Granados. Three of the dozen *Danzas Españolas* (of which this one was the fifth) were made into a set and orchestrated by Juan Lamote de Grignon. In this new dress the *Andalusia* forms the central part, preceded by an *Oriental* and followed by a *Rondella*.

Instrumental

Piano

Danzas Españolas **(Numbers 1, 2, 3, and 5), Op. 37**

☐ Beatriz Klien (piano) / Turnabout S-34327

Granados produced a dozen "Spanish Dances," issuing them in four sets of three each. Number two was subtitled *Oriental,* while the fifth is unofficially known as *Andalusia,* and has also been called *Playera.* (For an orchestral transcription of the last see under *Orchestra* [*Andalusia—Danza Española* No. 5 in E minor, Op. 37].)

Klien styles the pieces, especially the second one, with excellent *rubato* contours. Overdoing this, especially at cadential points marks the semiprofessional, which this pianist is not. Also neatly accomplished is the subtle soft thrusts in the ostinato that anchors the fifth dance.

Vocal

Voice with Accompaniment

Canciones amatorias

☐ Badia (soprano); de Larrocha (piano) / Everest 3237

An eight-part collection, of nostalgic mood for the greater part. The appeal of Badia's singing pertains more to her fine sense of style, rather than matters of depth and beauty.

La maja dolorosa **from *Tonadillas***

☐ de los Angeles (soprano); Soriano (piano); Sagu (English horn) / Angel S-35775

Three songs (the first with English horn as well as piano) that tell of a dead lover. "The Grieving Lady" has a searching intensity. Inspired singing by this artist.

Tonadillas

☐ de los Angeles (soprano); Soriano (piano) / Angel S-3672

A set of nine songs of folkloric quality, set to texts by Fernando Periquet. They have in their nonblatant national tinges the suavity of a Scarlatti, the beauty of a Mozart. To be expected when the explanatory title is considered: *escritas en estile antiguo.*

Sung by this artist with simplicity and elegance and beautifully supported by a fine pianist.

The set is duplicated by Conchita Badia on Everest 3237, also with the aid of a super-fine pianist, Alicia de Larrocha. The quieter classicism of Victoria de los Angeles's singing is to be preferred. Incidentally, following the order she uses, the sequence is completely different in Badia's edition, in comparison reading: 7-1-9-6-2-8-4-3-5.

Dante, **Symphonic Poem, Op. 21**

Voice and Orchestra

☐ Louisville Orchestra / Maull (soprano) / Mester (conductor) / Louisville 713

Romantic persistence with Wagnerian colorations and chromatic drift. The latter especially in the richer, second part (*Paolo e Francesca*) where the voice is used. Part one, *Dante e Virgilio* is a much darker picture.

Maull's voice is pleasing and effective. (Louisville has failed to include the text, which is not pleasing.)

Two Canciones Amatorias

☐ Paris Conservatoire Orchestra / de los Angeles (soprano) / Frühbeck de Burgos (conductor) / Angel S-35937

These songs from the *Colección de Canciones Amatorias* are articulated in a pleasant folkloric manner that fits the subjects of ungrateful love (*Weep My Heart*) and a happier situation telling about dancing and shelling pine nuts (*They Have Gone to the Pines*). The orchestration is by Rafael Ferrer.

Marcel Grandjany *(1891-1975)*

Aria in Classic Style for Harp and Strings

Solo Instrument and Orchestra

☐ Louisville Orchestra / Kling (harp) / Mester (conductor) / Louisville S-701

Harp

Quietly simple neo-Handelian music; the theme promulgated by variation. Expressive, no pomposity, and easily digestible. Played with charm and proper style.

The Children's Hour

Instrumental

Rhapsodie pour la Harpe

Harp

☐ Grandjany (harp) / Seraphim S-60142

Friendly spontaneity is impressionistically detailed in the "Rhapsody." The same sentiments, with a touch of humor, are to be found in the six pieces for which Grandjany gave both French and English titles: *Espiègle—Into Mischief, Très sage—Little Angel, Au trot—Giddap Pony, Jeux dans le jardin—Playing in the Garden, Militaire—Parade,* and *Le Marchand du sable—The Sandman.*

The playing is of prime quality, neatly phrased and balanced. And, no extraneous sounds that mar so many harp recordings.

Noël Provençal

☐ Remsen (harp) / Avant AV–1000

A modal-framed tune and some pithy variations on it.

Rhapsodie

☐ Vito (harp) / Orion 7039

Music attentive to the coloristic style of impressionism. Calm and connected by numerous broken chord figurations. Gracefully played.

Parks Grant (1910-   )

Chamber Music

Essay for French Horn and Organ, Op. 25

☐ Jones (horn); Held (organ) / Coronet 2738

Colorful strength and a fine counterpoint of ideas are presented in this tonal piece. The combination is rarely used but makes a very effective one.

Prelude and Canonic Piece for Flute and Clarinet, Op. 51

☐ Owen (flute); Hite (clarinet) / Coronet 2738

The second part exhibits scholarly endeavor but avoids any pedantic dryness. There are nine connected sections in the Canonic Piece, with a variety of imitations including inversion, retrograde, and diminution.

Brevities, Op. 44

Laconic Suite, Op. 31

☐ Love and Wolford (trumpets); Wagnitz (horn); Keller (trombone) / Coronet 2738

The virtue here is simplicity. All of it is light-framed music with no intellectual ax to grind. Grant doesn't muddy the formal waters in any of the seven movements that cover the two works, with such designs as a Fanfare, Canon, Chorale, and March.

Victor A. Grauer (1937-   )

Electronic Music

Inferno

☐ Folkways 33436

Considerably pedal-layered, dark toned throughout. A low-pitched male voice (electronically modified obtaining thereby a spectral quality) is used in one place. Totally a threatening atmosphere. Hell, in this case, is pictured with goodly realized intentions.

Carl Heinrich Graun (1704-1759)

Surely He Hath Borne Our Griefs

☐ Concordia Choir / Christiansen (conductor) / Concordia S-1

Neatly stated sacred music, of tonic response to the text that is concentrated in a total of two lines (eleven words in all).

Johann Gottlieb Graun (1703-1771)

Concerto in B flat major for Bassoon

☐ Württemberg Chamber Orchestra, Heilbronn / Zukerman (bassoon) / Faerber (conductor) / Turnabout 34278

The most delightful morsel from this three-movement affair is the final Rondo. Zukerman dashes it off with pulsatile articulation. The accompaniment, for string orchestra and continuo, is clean and natural.

Thomas Greaves (16th or 17th cent.)

Come Away Sweet Love

☐ Purcell Consort of Voices / Burgess (conductor) / Turnabout 34202

The last of a set of six madrigals included in a collection titled *Songs of Sundrie Kindes*. (The remainder consists of twenty-one pieces and fifteen songs.) This example of Greaves's work (an English sixteenth-seventeenth century lutenist and composer) is a delight of speedy, gay music, almost of pitter-patter type. The Purcell singers delight the ear with their deft projection of words and music.

George Green (1930-   )

Triptych for Trumpet Alone

☐ Stith (trumpet) / Golden Crest S-7042

Three facets of trumpet personality: martial, melodic, and rhythmic. A tinge of the last permeates the Aria (part two) for punctuative purposes. The containment of writing for unaccompanied trumpet raises many difficult creative issues. Without using any special effects (often a means of avoiding the problem by diversionary tactics), Green has produced a convincing piece of music.

Stith presents a meaningful statement of the work. Fine tone and depictive phrasing are additional credits.

Ray Green   (1909-   )

Orchestra   **Sunday Sing Symphony (1946)**

☐ Vienna Symphony Orchestra / Schoenherr (conductor) / Desto 6420E (monaural)
☐ Hessian Radio Symphony Orchestra / Van Vactor (conductor) / Composers Recordings 169 (monaural)

Green's symphony incorporates the happy-go-lucky elements of the early American fuguing tunes. The lyricism is of the exultant type, the harmonies circulate modally, the rhythms are invigorating. No virtuoso piece, but certainly a strong and skillful exploitation of homespun materials.

Its effectiveness has led to two recordings. Though the CRI release is a smidgen better than Desto's re-release of the American Recording Society's version (made in 1953), the companion work (Haieff's Piano Concerto) on Desto gives it first place. Van Vactor's performance is coupled with Van Vactor's creativity: a decidedly conservative Symphony No. 2. The playing of both orchestras is just average. Incidentally, Desto lists the five movements properly, but has only four bands on its disc, joining movements two and three without any explanation.

Noah Greenberg   (1919-1966)

Opera
and Dramatic
Music   **The Play of Daniel (1958)**

☐ New York Pro Musica and Boy Choristers of the Church of the Transfiguration, New York / Baker, Bohn, Bressler, Ehrlich, Hakes, Lewis, Myers, Oberlin, Sien, Squires, Tripp, and Wilson (vocalists) / Greenberg (conductor) / MCA 2504

Noah Greenberg's edition and scoring of this beautiful, twelfth-century liturgical music drama led the way for two other versions by David Wulstan and Mark Brown that have since appeared. Recorded performances of these have respectively been issued in England, the former on the Calliope label, the other on Argo. It is difficult to imagine that Greenberg's famous recording (originally issued on Decca and then transferred to MCA when the former firm's activities ceased) will be supplanted. Of course, each edition differs. Nonetheless, Noah Greenberg's sensitive realization can be deemed definitive. Whatever some graybearded critics may think, they cannot deny its beauty, glow, and gorgeousness.

The recreative forces for Greenberg's surrogate setting include a large cast of splendid voices and an instrumental group of nine playing such instruments as a rebec (a medieval fiddle), a minstrel's harp, miniature highland bagpipes, a straight trumpet (*buisine*), tiny kettle drums, and so forth. They make a joyful sound and an exceedingly special one. The edition is well documented, including various articles and texts. Indeed, this is a five-star recording.

Joel Gressel   (1943-   )

Electronic
Music   **Points in Time (1974)**

☐ Odyssey Y-34139

Tone-row methodology transferred to pitch and rhythmic permutations. A few sections bring a solo piano to mind, but naturally that's only instrumental memory survival. *Points in Time* is a hard-core electronic piece that authenticates the chosen technical system.

André Ernest Modeste Grétry (1741 - 1813)

Ballet Suite from *Céphale et Procris*

Orchestra

☐ Solistes de Liège / Lemaire (conductor) / Musical Heritage Society MHS–793 CC–11

Most often (better stated, really, as ''always'') the version heard of this stunning music—so described because of its special charm—is the Felix Mottl arrangement of the *Tambourin, Ménuet* (listed by the publisher as Minuet [The Nymphs of Diana]), and Gigue, set for double woodwinds, two each of trumpets and horns, timpani, triangle, tambourine, and strings. Nothing wrong with Mottl's transcription which prudently avoids any evil of overscoring. Still, the original is a gem and a richer one, with two additional movements (Entrée and Gavotte) (and using the full original title of the Gigue mentioned above, as *Gigue Légère*), and Grétry's scoring for flute, two oboes, two horns, and strings.

Lemaire's soloists play exquisitely and in a thoroughly disciplined manner. They impressively declaim Grétry's music. Under Lemaire's direction there is no stylistic haze or nonsense. The dynamics are allowed their full way, there are no special ritards or *accelerandi,* the music is permitted its natural manifestation and warmth. Highly recommended.

Overture to *Le Magnifique*

☐ English Chamber Orchestra / Bonynge (conductor) / London 6735

The lively overture to Grétry's three-act Opera is a little thin harmonically, but has some excellent counterpoint. It also has some colorful orchestration.

Concerto in C major for Flute and Orchestra

Solo Instrument and Orchestra

☐ Academy of St. Martin-in-the-Fields / Monteux (flute) / Marriner (conductor) / Oiseau-Lyre S–279

Flute

Though not of the greatest importance, Grétry's music is presented in the best possible manner here.

Edvard Grieg (1843 - 1907)

Lyric Suite, Op. 54

Orchestra

☐ London Symphony Orchestra / Black (conductor) / London 21046

Engaging playing of this suite of four pieces Grieg orchestrated from his piano originals.

Peer Gynt: Suite I, Op. 46

☐ Cleveland Orchestra / Szell (conductor) / Columbia MS–6877

A distinguished performance that truly leaves all others far behind. The music glows under Szell's baton, and the only regret is that he did not record the second suite as well. In addition, Szell shows an understanding of these pieces that, for some unknown reason, is generally absent from other conductors' readings. *Anitra's Dance* is *not* paced as a fast waltz and becomes more convincing thereby. Further, the terraced *accelerando* of the repetitively sectioned *In the Hall of the Mountain King* is perfectly proportioned. Most often the speed rate moves up too soon, or when it doesn't it reaches a point where clarity is muddied. For this Szell production only continual bravos are proper.

(Szell's edition is also released on Columbia MS-7505.)

Peer Gynt: Suite II, Op. 55

☐ Hallé Orchestra / Barbirolli (conductor) / Angel S-36803

Well proportioned, communicative performance of this less popular *Peer Gynt* music, though one can argue that the lesser popularity is chiefly due to in-the-rut programming. Witness the recording field: Though currently six performances are available of the first suite coupled with other material, the second suite cannot be obtained in a parallel manner. If you want Suite II, you're captive to one of seven different releases containing Suite I.

Sigurd Jorsalfar: Suite, Op. 56

☐ Berlin Philharmonic Orchestra / von Karajan (conductor) / Deutsche Grammophon 2530243

Grieg's orchestral suite, drawn from the incidental music he composed for a stage work by Bjørnstjerne Bjørnson, is given an exciting performance. This work has been overlooked by the many conductors who have flocked to the Peer Gynt materials. It's just as good as can be realized in this, the only recording available.

Symphonic Dances, Op. 64

☐ Vienna Pro Musica Orchestra / van Remoortel (conductor) / Vox 510330

Large-scaled in their designs, though overemphasizing sequential depiction (a Grieg habit). The specialness of Grieg's work is marked by the Norwegian themes that spark the music. Not the most flavorsome performance but the only one presently in the domestic catalogue. If you can find the English HMV SXLP-30105 disc (the late Walter Susskind conducting the Philharmonia Orchestra), get it—it's much better.

String Orchestra

Holberg Suite, Op. 40

☐ Netherlands Chamber Orchestra / Zinman (conductor) / Philips 6580102

A brilliant characterization by the simple expedient of not playing to the gallery (not easy to accomplish but still possible in a work for string orchestra). Zinman lights up every phase and phrase of Grieg's five-part work. The situations are relatively pat, but by weighing the sections properly and with proportionate contrasts, Grieg's music sings at its fullest. And sounds completely fresh.

This work was originally written for piano (see under *Instrumental: piano*).

Two Elegiac Melodies, Op. 34

☐ Philadelphia Orchestra / Ormandy (conductor) / Columbia MS-7103

Not surprisingly, the Philadelphia Orchestra's gorgeous string body does the fullest justice to these two pieces. The Melodies were originally composed for voice and piano, as part of a set of twelve, designated as Opus 33. A pair from the set is available (see under *Vocal: voice with accompaniment* [*Efteraarsstormen*]).

Concerto in A minor for Piano and Orchestra, Op. 16

☐ Monte Carlo Opera Orchestra / Richter (piano) / Matačić (conductor) / Angel S-36899

☐ BBC Symphony Orchestra / Bishop-Kovacevich (piano) / Davis (conductor) / Philips 6500166

☐ Philharmonia Orchestra / Lipatti (piano) / Galliera (conductor) / Odyssey 32160141 (monaural)

Solo Instrument and Orchestra

Piano

First things first. Those pianists who approach the Grieg Concerto with their gloves off and have their thunder machines at the ready are barking up the wrong keyboard. Sure, there's plenty of rock 'em and sock 'em in this opus, but there's much more, *very* much more—poetry. When the latter is stressed it gives the proper frame to the virtuosic discourse. Those pianists who realize that refinement *is* the bravura within the piece constitute the more daring because of their resistance to the overeagerness and technical idolatry that have mangled the composition over and over again. The same applies to the orchestral part of the work.

It is the acceptance of these factors that makes the three performances listed the choicest of the choices available. Richter plays the Concerto with the warmest poeticism, and a radiance surrounds the bigger statements. The spontaneity, suavity, and ease (even in the pyrotechnical divisions) of the Bishop-Kovacevich-Davis version is ideal. Finally, Lipatti's sensitivity brings a poetic lyricism that is captivating. His monaural recording in no way shows its age. Truly, there's no need to seek further than these choices.

Album Leaves, Op. 28

☐ Mourão (piano) / Vox SVBX-5458

Instrumental

Piano

No titles as in Grieg's Lyric Pieces, but key identifications for these *Album Leaves*. Vox does not note these (A flat major, F major, A major, and C sharp minor), but instead gives the individual tempo headings.

The longest and best is the last of the group—the only one that affords much opportunity for interpretative projection. Understandably, it is there that Isabel Mourão does her best playing.

Ballade, Op. 24

☐ Walter Klien (piano) / Turnabout 34365

Continuous rhapsodicism due to the compositional procedure Grieg applied. Actually (Turnabout avoids mentioning it), the complete title for this work is *Ballad in the Form of Variations on a Norwegian Folk Song*. Klien deliberately stresses the structural sectionalism of the music.

Four Pieces, Op. 1 (Excerpts)

☐ Mourão (piano) / Vox SVBX-5458

Since this is an Opus 1, it is not a surprise that Edvard Grieg does not come through in this music but rather someone else, in this case Robert Schumann, a composer the nineteen-year-old Norwegian admired. (Mourão plays two of the four pieces, though the program-note insert states three as the total.)

Holberg Suite, Op. 40

☐ Walter Klien (piano) / Turnabout 34365

This is the original setting of the work best known in the string orchestra transcription Grieg made (see under *String Orchestra*). It sounds considerably better and richer in the transfer, but that does not deny keyboard plausibility for the conception.

Klien plays a little roughly and unclearly and with too much pedal at the very beginning, but makes a sharp improvement after a dozen measures or so and thereafter is fine. In fact, his performance is much finer and richer in imagery than Isabel Mourão's (on Vox SVBX-5458).

Humoresques, Op. 6, Nos. 1, 2, 4
Improvisations on Norwegian Folk Songs, Op. 29

☐ Mourão (piano) / Vox SVBX-5458

Three of the four Humoresques are a Waltz, a *Menuet,* and an *Alla burla* in fast pace. Principal title and subtitles notwithstanding, Norwegian flavor permeates the set. The pair of Improvisations on Norwegian Folk Songs do not indulge in understatement of their nationalistic content. Accordingly, Mourão very conscientiously underlines the Griegian replicas so that the weave of the music does not hide the fundamental folk outlines.

Lyric Pieces

Book I, Op. 12, Nos. 1, 2, 3, 4, 5, 6, 7 / Book II, Op. 38, Nos. 1, 2, 4, 5, 6, 7, 8

☐ Mourão (piano) / Vox SVBX-5457

The final piece in Opus 12 (National Song) and the third item in Opus 38 (*Melodie*) are eliminated. Focused playing, prominently in the *Halling* and *Springdans* in the Book II compilation. (On the label copy these are each titled Norwegian Dance.)

Lyric Pieces, Book III, Op. 43

☐ Walter Klien (piano) / Turnabout 34365

Splendidly nuanced performances of the entire half-dozen pieces. Hearing Klien play *To the Spring* provides an artistic rebirth for a piece of music long violated by students and betrayed by schmaltzed orchestration.

Lyric Pieces

Book IV, Op. 47, Nos. 1, 2, 3, 4, 5, 6 / Book V, Op. 54 / Book VI, Op. 57, Nos. 1, 2, 4, 5, 6 / Book VII, Op. 62

☐ Mourão (piano) / Vox SVBX-5457

Of the twenty-five pieces in these four assortments, two are not included: the seventh of the Opus 47 set (*Elegie*) and the third in the Opus 57 group (*Illusion*).

The simplicity of the ideas is enhanced by natural coloring on Mourão's part. There is no interpretative oversell to mar such well-known pieces as *Shepherd Boy* or *March of the Dwarfs* or *Notturno* (all in Book V). Pianism on a high level.

Lyric Pieces, Book VIII, Op. 65

☐ Mourão (piano) / Vox SVBX-5458

Though the program notes state that Isabel Mourão includes only three of this set, actually the entire half dozen (including the best known, *Wedding Day at Troldhaugen*) are played, and very well played they are.

Lyric Pieces, Book IX, Op. 68, Nos. 2, 3, 4, 5, 6

☐ Mourão (piano) / Vox SVBX-5457

This set contains the charming *Grandmother's Minuet* and the individually atmospheric *Evening in the Mountains*.

Lyric Pieces, Book X, Op. 71, Nos. 1, 2, 3, 4, 5, 7

☐ Mourão (piano) / Vox SVBX-5758

Faithfulness to the text marks all of Mourão's playing of Grieg's miniatures. However, here and in the other sets (*see above*) the material unfolds naturally, bypassing any sophistication but minus any scholasticism.

Interestingly, the one piece in the suite that Mourão does not include (No. 6: *Forbi* ["Gone"]) is found in Gilels's program devoted to the Lyric Pieces (*see below*).

Lyric Pieces

Books I, Op. 12 / II, Op. 38 / III, Op. 43 / IV, Op. 47 / V, Op. 54 / VI, Op. 57 / VII, Op. 62 / VIII, Op. 65 / IX, Op. 68 / X, Op. 71

(Excerpts)

Album Leaf, Op. 47, No. 2	*Homesickness*, Op. 57, No. 6
Arietta, Op. 12, No. 1	*Homeward*, Op. 62, No. 6
At the Cradle, Op. 68, No. 5	*In Ballad Vein*, Op. 65, No. 5
At Your Feet, Op. 68, No. 3	*Lonely Wanderer*, Op. 43, No. 2
Brooklet, Op. 62, No. 4	*Melodie*, Op. 47, No. 3
Butterfly, Op. 43, No. 1	*Notturno*, Op. 54, No. 4
Cradle Song, Op. 38, No. 1	*Once Upon a Time*, Op. 71, No. 1
Gone, Op. 71, No. 6	*Puck*, Op. 71, No. 3
Grandmother's Minuet, Op. 68, No. 2	*Remembrances*, Op. 71, No. 7
Halling, Op. 47, No. 4	**Scherzo**, Op. 54, No. 5

☐ Gilels (piano) / Deutsche Grammophon 2530476

Grieg's Lyric Pieces comprise sixty-six compositions, distributed over ten volumes. In Emil Gilels's program he has chosen twenty examples, which cover representatives from each set. All are also recorded by either Isabel Mourão or Walter Klien, except one: *Gone*, Op. 71, No. 6.

Yes, otherwise available (*see above*), but none can match the sensationally (that's the word) smooth and knowing artistry of the Soviet pianist. The musical probity displayed is productive mastery. If just a sampling is what you want, then *this* is the single recording you will need. This does not negate the coverage and values to be recognized in the recordings discussed above from Grieg's five and a half dozen piano pieces.

Moods, Op. 73, Nos. 2, 3, 4, 5, 6

Norwegian Dances and Songs, Op. 17

Norwegian Folk Melodies, Op. 66

☐ Mourão (piano) / Vox SVBX-5758

It is the succession of colorful folk items that's alive with musical news. Listen to the third of the nineteen Folk Melodies and you hear *Greensleeves* Scandinavian style! Indeed, a large dose of nationalism but an exceedingly healthy one.

Norwegian Peasant Dances, Op. 72

☐ Mourão (piano) / Vox SVBX-5457

Revitalized folk music that speaks baldly but not primitively, since Grieg reshaped and polished the basal data. There are eleven pieces. Notwithstanding the main title two are bridal marches, one is a *Bridal-ride of the Girls from the North*, and still another is a Funeral March.

Poetic Tone Pictures, Op. 3, Nos. 1, 5, 6

Scenes from Peasant Life, Op. 19

☐ Mourão (piano) / Vox SVBX-5458

Opus 19 contains in its three *Scenes* one of Grieg's finest piano pieces, a *Norwegian Bridal Procession*. It is played with bright detail and resonant rhythm. The other music is heard to good effect.

Sonata in E minor, Op. 7

☐ Gould (piano) / Columbia M-32040

It is commonplace to state that Grieg was a miniaturist and that his music in the larger forms gets minus points for its sectionalism. Because of this, his critics have insisted that his large works have substance but no craft. Nonsense. That is, if you are as pro-Grieg as this writer. The freshness of the melodic spans, the creative rhythms, and the individuality of his harmonies are sufficient. It is the sectionalism that *is* Griegian and that makes him deserve his special creative place.

Glenn Gould emphasizes the darker aspects of the opus. It convinces. What doesn't is the strange tempo assignment for movement 3, marked *Alla menuetto ma poco più lento*. Gould erases any dance sense by playing the movement *molto più lento* and so the result is a Sonata of outer fast movements and two inner slow movements. Strange, but not for Gould, who makes a habit of mandating such tempi reversals. Nonetheless, the playing of the balance of the work is a most convincing exposition of pianistic art.

Piano,
Four Hands

Four Norwegian Dances, Op. 35

☐ Walter and Beatrice Klien (piano) / Turnabout 34041

This music for a pair of pianists at one keyboard is far better known in its orchestral setting, made by Hans Sitt (see *Grieg/Sitt: Orchestra*). This is only so because piano duo concerts, for which Grieg's original edition could be scheduled, are practically nonexistent.

The Kliens give Grieg's fully national music a spontaneous depiction. All practical problems are totally solved, naturally, and what emerges is a fine artistic focus on the music.

Sonata in A minor for Cello and Piano, Op. 36

☐ Reese (cello); Linsley (piano) / Crystal S–134

Much of the first movement sounds like portions of Grieg's Piano Concerto. In the second movement, the main theme (first stated by the piano alone and then by the cello with rolling piano arpeggios) sounds like Grieg's *Sigurd Jorsalfar* march. One would rather believe that this is not so much self-quotation as it is the composer speaking his own personal language, just as it is fully declared in the finale's genuine, supple dance.

The playing is on the bravura side and it fits the symphonic outlook of the work. However, the cello is never covered by the piano. Further, Grieg's zeal for rhythm in the final movement is fully respected by Reese and Linsley without toppling over any of the balances in this climactic part of the Sonata.

Sonata for Violin and Piano
No. 1 in F major, Op. 8 / No. 2 in G major, Op. 13 / No. 3 in C minor, Op. 45

☐ Temianka (violin); Fields (piano) / Orion 75193

Though there is an absence of ostentation in Grieg's Opus 8, Temianka (who slightly overshadows his partner, but for most of that bias the fault is Grieg's) is finely forthright in his portrayal. It must be borne in mind that the music is romantic, but not of pale-moon variety; its scope is rather of the stronger midnight sun.

The assurance as well as the fine contrastive highlighting that mark the second sonata's performance remove a point of criticism regarding Grieg's Opus 13. Every one of the movements is in triple meter, the pulse of the most popular of Norwegian dances, the *Springar* or *Springdans*. The only exception is the introduction to the first movement (the only time Grieg used a formal introduction in any of his four chamber sonatas), where the recitative quality slightly foreshadows the theme of the opening movement proper. This similarity of meter can be criticized especially since such leveling gives a similar cast to the movements. However, Temianka shapes his playing so that such cadenced rhythmic neutrality is considerably lessened.

The broad dramatics in the C minor opus (most opinions designate this work as the greatest of the three violin and piano sonatas) are strongly characterized. There is again more violin than there is piano and once more most of this is due to Grieg's scoring, but in this instance a bit of the blame is to be handed to Temianka. This is especially critical in the many imitative points that guide the animated finale.

Sonata No. 2 in G major for Violin and Piano, Op. 13

☐ Heifetz (violin); Bay (piano) / RCA ARM4-0944 (monaural)

Discounting the lackluster sound, this is a beautiful performance that emphasizes fluidity over vitality. It is the lovingly handled matter of phrasing that provides an intimacy that is not present in Temianka's playing (*see above*).

String Quartet in G minor, Op. 27

☐ Guarneri Quartet / RCA LSC-2948

Discounting the unfinished (two-movement) quartet, Opus 27 represents Grieg's single attempt at four-string writing. At one time the work was subjected to abuse, with the word "orchestral" (an ugly term in quartet analysis) being bandied about. We are far from such nonsense. Dramatic the Grieg quartet is; at times it is also heavily scored. By translating the string quartet idiom into his characteristic language, Grieg is not guilty of any creative error, and to have his work summarily dismissed because of its textural weight is a critical misunderstanding of and indifference to his individuality.

If one wishes to criticize, one can point out that Grieg's music is based on the sequential pronouncement of thematic material, with a fondness for the small thought restrung and repeated, rather than developmental musical inquiry. In defense it must be stated that Grieg was a poet, not an orator. Melody and supporting harmony rather than contrapuntalism mark his music.

The Guarneri group's depiction is stunning. It shows passionate regard for Grieg's dissected thoughts. Movements 1 and 4 are taken at a speed that intensifies the agitation of the former and the lustiness of the latter. The Copenhagen String Quartet reading of these movements (on Turnabout 34270) is slower and the playing style is looser, both dulling the impact of Grieg's work.

Vocal

Voice with Accompaniment

Efteraarsstormen, Op. 18, No. 4 **Langs ei aa, Op. 33, No. 5**
Fyremaal, Op. 33, No. 12 **Mens jeg venter, Op. 60, No. 3**

☐ Flagstad (soprano); Moore (piano) / Seraphim 60046 (monaural)

An outstanding program. Trot out all the superlatives—this is miraculous vocalism. Sung in Norwegian, Grieg's songs register far better than in the usually heard translations.

Though Seraphim offers translations of texts and titles (in respective order for the latter: "The Autumn Storm," "The Goal," "Along the River," and "While I Wait"), it gives no further data. The excerpt from Opus 18 is the final song in a set of four comprising a first volume; a second volume of five songs completes the opus. The two songs from Opus 33 are set to texts by the peasant poet Aasmund Olafsen Vinje (issued in two volumes, six songs in each). Opus 60 comprises five songs set to poetry by Vilhelm Krag. All the songs are excellent; those from Opus 33 are the most striking. (The two songs from Opus 33 are available in a transcription for string orchestra: see under *String Orchestra*, Two Elegiac Melodies.)

Opera and Dramatic Music

Peer Gynt—Incidental Music for Ibsen's Drama, Op. 23 (Excerpts)

☐ Hallé Orchestra and Ambrosian Singers / Clark and Armstrong (sopranos) / Barbirolli (conductor) / Angel S-36531

Of the three available recordings not only is Barbirolli's the most evocative; it offers a greater portion of the twenty-three numbers that comprise the whole score. A dozen items are presented, including the greater part of the two more familiar orchestral suites (all of No. 1 and three of the four movements of No. 2. The missing music is Solvejg's Song). (See under *Orchestra* [*Peer Gynt*: Suite I and Suite II].)

Beecham's version (on Angel S-35445) totals ten numbers, as does Fjeldstad's (on London STS-15040). Beecham and Fjeldstad duplicate seven pieces. Of course, the orchestral suites are covered: both completely in Fjeldstad's version, with the same suite coverage chosen by Barbirolli included in the Beecham edition.

Grieg / Hans Sitt (1850-1922)

Orchestra

Four Norwegian Dances, Op. 35

☐ Hallé Orchestra / Barbirolli (conductor) / Angel S-36803

Fully splendid performances of the set (the first and fourth in D minor, the middle pair in A and G major, respectively). Why is there constant failure to give open and clear credit to Hans Sitt for the excellent orchestral transcription he made?

Charles Tomlinson Griffes (1884-1920)

The Pleasure-Dome of Kubla Khan, Op. 8

Orchestra

☐ Boston Symphony Orchestra / Ozawa (conductor) / New World Records NW–273

This is a discerning presentation of Griffes's orientally laced, colorfully compounded piece. History repeats itself in a slightly different form; the first concert performance of Griffes's work was also given by the Boston Symphony Orchestra on November 28, 1919, with Pierre Monteux as the conductor.

Three Tone-Pictures, Op. 5

☐ New World Chamber Ensemble / New World Records NW–273

These three impressionistic pieces (*The Lake at Evening, The Vale of Dreams,* and *The Night Winds*) were initially written for piano (see under *Instrumental: piano*). Griffes then transcribed them for woodwinds and optional harp, and made still a third setting for a chamber orchestra consisting of a string quartet, double bass, wind quintet, and piano. It is the last version that is recorded here.

With such musicians as Gilbert Kalish (piano), Felix Galimir and Isidore Cohen (violins), Ronald Roseman (oboe), and David Glazer (clarinet), in the ensemble, one can expect an authoritative performance. Considering that eleven performers are involved and there is no conductor, the playing is beautifully cohesive; the effects of changing light and movement in the score are well presented.

Poem for Flute and Orchestra (1919)

Solo Instrument and Orchestra

☐ Eastman-Rochester Symphony Orchestra / Mariano (flute) / Hanson (conductor) / Mercury 75020

Flute

Sensitive flute poetry, impressionistically patterned, with an oriental overlay. Griffes's *Poem* has become standard fare for flutists everywhere. Mariano's playing is authentic and has good atmospheric coloring. He receives excellent support from Hanson.

This is the sole stereophonic recording on the lists today. Odd fact, considering the importance of the work in the literature. A monophonic version (electronically reprocessed) is on Desto (6424E). It has dated sound, bad balances, and a heavy-handed performance (the parties involved are the Vienna Symphony Orchestra, Walter Hendl conducting, and Camille Wanausek as the soloist).

Roman Sketches, Op. 7

Instrumental

Sonata (1921)

Piano

☐ Hambro (piano) / Lyrichord 105 (monaural)

The sensitively fluent first piece (*The White Peacock*) in the *Roman Sketches* has become the most favored of Griffes's piano compositions. Still, the other three parts of the suite (*Nightfall, The Fountain of the Acqua Paola,* and *Clouds*) are no less impressionistically evocative. Hambro's presentation is the only recording available.

Totally opposite in style is the three-movements-in-one Sonata. It is powerfully dramatic, sharply pulsed, fertilized with ostinati and cross-rhythms.

Three Preludes

☐ Mandel (piano) / Desto 6445/7

Alan Mandel defines the dark atmosphere of these short pieces most perceptively. The Preludes are Griffes's last completed work.

Three Tone-Pictures, Op. 5

☐ Jochum (piano) / Golden Crest CRS-4168

This is the original setting of the work (for a discussion, see under *Orchestra*). The performance here is very good.

Chamber Music

Two Sketches (based on Indian Themes) for String Quartet (1922)

☐ Kohon Quartet / Vox SVBX-5301

The *Sketches* is Griffes's sole chamber music composition. It is an attempt to combine Griffes's impressionistic ideas with an elementary postulate of Americanism. Most pertinent is the second movement—a pure war dance. It shows Griffes with his feet directly on Indian ground. In this case he is reporting rather than observing.

When chamber music was not enjoying the boom it is these days, this work was in every quartet's repertoire. Nowadays our quartet teams (playing for large audiences which would have wider tastes) have relinquished the delights found in Griffes's piece. It seems that slowly but surely most of our string quartet teams are imitating our major symphony orchestras with their restricted programming. Listeners should not forgo the opportunity of obtaining this tasteful recording.

Vocal

Voice with Accompaniment

An Old Song Re-Sung (1920)

☐ Hanks (tenor); Friedberg (piano) / Duke University Press DWRM-7501 (monaural)

This is the first of a pair of songs titled *Two Poems by John Masefield*. It contains graphic vigor and chromatic vehemence.

Four German Songs

☐ Milnes (baritone); Spong (piano) / New World Records NW-273

The above title is a convenient superscript chosen by the New World outfit to cover a selection of four songs from the total of twenty Griffes wrote between 1903 and 1911. *An den Wind, Am Kreuzweg wird begraben, Meeres Stille,* and *Auf geheimem Waldespfade* are all products derived from German romanticism, defining the conservative period of Griffes's creativity.

Four Impressions

☐ Stapp (mezzo-soprano); Richardson (piano) / New World Records NW-273

Griffes used Oscar Wilde poetry for these four songs: *Le Jardin* ("The Garden"), *Impression du Matin* ("Early Morning in London"), *La Mer* ("The Sea"), and *Le Réveillon* ("Dawn"). They are impressionistically detailed.

The performers adjust their sights to this style; the result is gratifying.

Song of the Dagger

☐ Milnes (baritone); Spong (piano) / New World Records NW-273

A dramatic song, displaying the balance between voice and piano Griffes always maintained in his vocal compositions. A performance of impact.

Symphony in Yellow, Op. 3, No. 2

☐ Hanks (tenor); Friedberg (piano) / Duke University Press DWRM-7501 (monaural)

There are many impressionistic devices in this song, the second of three *Tone Images*. (*Grove's Dictionary of Music and Musicians* incorrectly indicates that this opus has only two songs. Lacking from *Grove's* list is the first song, *La Fuite de la Lune. We'll to the Woods, and Gather May* is the third song in the opus.)

Waikiki, Op. 9, No. 2

☐ Steber (soprano); Biltcliffe (piano) / Desto 6411/12

Waikiki is the second of Griffes's *Three Poems,* set to a text by Rupert Brooke. Steber's vocal timbre and delivery are excellent.

Three Poems of Fiona MacLeod, Op. 11

Voice and Orchestra

☐ Boston Symphony Orchestra / Bryn-Julson (soprano) / Ozawa (conductor) / New World Records NW-273

This song cycle is undoubtedly one of the most outstanding in the vocal literature that has been produced by American composers. The expressivity of *The Lament of Ian the Proud, Thy Dark Eyes to Mine,* and *The Rose of the Night* is totally gripping. The architectonic detail is no less decisive.

Phyllis Bryn-Julson has a very expressive voice, not heavily weighted, but most appropriate for this work. More important, she conveys a range of sensibility of the words she is singing that is quite rare in the vocal world. Ozawa and the Bostonians back up her singing in an engrossing partnership and deliver sumptuous tonal color.

Peter Griffith (1943-)

Classic for Clarinet (1969)

Instrumental

☐ Rehfeldt (clarinet) / Advance 15

Clarinet

Don't let the word "classic" mislead you. Griffith's piece is ruled by a sectional plan (it was originally designed to accompany the use of a laser beam apparatus that would flash on a screen "an ever-fluctuating pattern governed by the physical characteristics of the sound produced by the clarinet"). The expressive necessities are drawn from registral opposition and nervous rhythmic patterns.

It is extremely difficult to negotiate this music. However, the communication of Rehfeldt's playing proves his stunning abilities to cope with and conquer all the problems.

One String Quartet

Chamber Music

☐ Composers String Quartet / Composers Recordings S-265

Impressively serious in its objectives, this quartet derives from the serialistic world and the style of Elliott Carter. The energetic detail provides the most interest.

As usual, this virtuoso quartet delivers a stunning realization of the music.

Nicolas de Grigny   (1671 - 1703)

Instrumental   **Mass (excerpts)**

Organ   ***Pange Lingua***

                   Veni Creator

☐ Saorgin (organ) / Turnabout 34054

René Saorgin plays five portions from the Mass, culminating in an imposing *Dialogue de flûtes pour l'élévation.* Another "Dialogue" completes the five sections of the hymn piece *Veni Creator,* while three divisions mark the other hymn composition, *Pange Lingua.* All of this music depicts liturgical and polyphonic austerity; the latter is common to most of the pieces but is specifically highlighted in the fugues that appear (à 5) in the hymn works.

There is acceptable fluency in Saorgin's playing, with an emphasis on the heavy reeds of the unidentified organ he uses. The recording is spacious and without any echo.

Ragnar Grippe   (1951 -   )

Electronic   ***Musique douze* (1975)**
Music
                   ☐ Composers Recordings SD–364

A thoroughly interesting conception in which electronic sonorities are joined to, contrasted with, as well as combined with, instrumental sounds that have been electronically processed (the instrumental choices are unidentified). A comparative diapason results, with more linear, less active action relating to the electronic material, and rhythmically vertical action pertaining to the other sonic class.

The weights, densities, and velocities are cogently proportioned. *Musique douze* represents advanced electronic composition, with artistic profits to be derived from its sensitive creative-feeling.

Ferde Grofé   (1892 - 1972)

Orchestra   ***Grand Canyon* Suite (1931)**

☐ New York Philharmonic / Corigliano (violin) / Bernstein (conductor) / Columbia MS-6618

All the makin's of this pops-popular, large-scaled item are detailed to a stunning, stirring fare-thee-well. This produces intoxicating results, since Bernstein plays it for all it is worth and doesn't look down his baton the way most conductors do when they play Grofé's score because they're required to do so.

O.K., so it is a poor man's Strauss, but it is, simultaneously, a coloristic music drama that has plenty to offer the unbiased and unsnobbish. If that be protesting too much, so be it. Listening to Bernstein's magnificent portrayal reconfirms the evergreenish viability of Grofé's programmatic project. (Also available on Columbia M–31824.)

Concerto for Piano and Orchestra

□ Rochester Philharmonic Orchestra / Sanromá (piano) / Grofé (conductor) / Everest 3044

Solo Instrument and Orchestra

Piano

This is pops concert piano fare. All the paraphernalia: Lisztian glittering passages and arpeggiandi, and booming octaves à la Rachmaninoff and Tchaikovsky bound onto the lush style of Addinsell's Warsaw Concerto.

If this is what you want, you won't be disappointed.

Robert Gross (1914-   )

Epode for Solo Cello (1955)

□ Rejto (cello) / Composers Recordings 208 (monaural)

Instrumental

Cello

Gross describes his piece (concentrated: six and one-quarter minutes) as "a very free lyric poem in the nature of an incantation." At the start, a Blochian impress hovers over the music; later on, the influence turns toward Hindemith.

This is a fine performance, striking just the right note of lyricism or dynamism as required.

Louis Gruenberg (1884-1964)

Polychromatics, Op. 16

□ Shaulis (piano) / Composers Recordings S–295

Instrumental

Piano

Though titled with such headings as *The Lady with the Damask-Mantle, The Knight of the Black Pool,* and *A Rag-Time Fragment,* none of these eight items are pianistic chit-chat or representative of prittle-prattle music. Gruenberg mixes the lighter with the more serious in this graphic suite. Hardly known these days and practically unperformed, the music of Gruenberg needs to be rediscovered. No better start could be made than with these evocative pieces, superbly stated by the winner of the 1971 Naumburg Piano Contest.

Camargo Guarnieri (1907-   )

Dansa Brasileira (1941)

□ New York Philharmonic / Bernstein (conductor) / Columbia MS–6514

Orchestra

This is the third in Guarnieri's set of dances, although this is not indicated on the release. The dance is part of the *Tres Dansas para Orquesta* (*see below*), but each dance is an entity. A bit of choice playing is offered here.

Suite IV *Centenario*

☐ Louisville Orchestra / Whitney (conductor) / Louisville 561 (monaural)

Modern injections into Brazilian materials for the most part. Thus the *Introdução* ("Introduction") is built on a theme of African-Brazilian character; the *Toada* ("Song") is concerned with a Brazilian lyrical air of Portuguese derivation; and the *Interludio* ("Interlude") is set as an *embolada*—a melody with some syncopative kick. An *Acalanto* ("Lullaby") and a *Baiao* ("Dance") complete Guarnieri's homage to the city of São Paulo, commemorating its four centuries of existence.

More thrust would have been welcomed in the Louisville performance. The neutrality portrayed pays attention to the pitches and rhythms but does not honor the inner spirit of the piece.

Tres Dansas para Orquesta (1941)

☐ Louisville Orchestra / Mester (conductor) / Louisville S–702

Brazilian musical folklore simulated in a masterly fashion. All original, however, all Guarnieri-made. The colors do mingle and the features do join but there is sufficient contrast between the *Dansa Selvagem* ("Forest Dance"), the *Dansa Negra,* and the samba contours of the *Dansa Brasileira* ("Brazilian Dance"). Certainly, the last of Guarnieri's dances is far more exciting in its orchestral dress than in its original piano make-up (composed in 1931).

The projection of the music is accomplished with professional satisfaction; *Schwann* errs in listing only the last dance as representing the total Louisville performance. However, for a more colorful and decisive rendition of this particular dance, *see above* (*Dansa Brasileira*) for a recording directed by Leonard Bernstein.

Instrumental

Piano

Ponteios (Nos. 1, 2, 3, 5, 6, 7, 22, 24, 26, 29, 30, 41, 42, 43, 44, 45, 46, 48, 49, 50)

☐ Johannesen (piano) / Golden Crest S–4098

This is a selection from fifty *Ponteios* ("Preludes") Guarnieri composed in the 1950s (ten of the *Ponteios* were transcribed for orchestra). Some are colored with American jazz feeling, all have Brazilian sentiments, but they are not blatantly stated.

Violin

Cantiga lá de longe

☐ Szeryng (violin); Maillols (piano) / Philips 6500016

The minutest infiltration of nationalistic turns is found within the "Song from Afar." Otherwise, almost a Mahlerian affinity is found in Guarnieri's style here. This is a short piece but it is rather special in Guarnieri's output. Szeryng's playing is eloquent, especially in the terminal, muted sections.

Carlos Guastavino   (1912-   )

Instrumental

Violin

Llanura

☐ Szeryng (violin); Maillols (piano) / Philips 6500016

The Argentinian composer wrote his "Plains" (or "Prairies") especially for Szeryng. It has a text of romantic relevance. Beautifully played.

Jean-Pierre Guézec (1934-1971)

Reliefs Polychromés **for Twelve Vocal Parts (1969)**

☐ Chamber Choir of the O.R.T.F. / Couraud (conductor) / Musical Heritage Society MHS-1687

Choral

Chorus Alone

Guézec's piece is a series of musical abstractions, presumably nonobjective in style. Notwithstanding its disjunct lines, plastic textures, and concentrated color, it outlines, according to the composer, "a reflection of the unrest of the world of today." Even though the piece was composed in 1969, the unrest has been maintained, so there is no dated retrospective condition.

All the functions are clearly expressed by the O.R.T.F. group, though the singing represses the dynamic scale to a great extent. It reminds one of a picture that consists only of a black square on a white ground. But that, too, has expressive meaning as well as a clear disposition of space.

Alexandre Guilmant (1837-1911)

March on a Theme of Handel

☐ Preston (organ) / Argo ZRG-5448

Instrumental

Organ

This is characteristic organ writing in an uncharacteristic form. Where the contrastive trio is expected, a full-scale fugue is disclosed. There is nothing like a polyphonic structure to spruce up a march! The outer parts of this tripartite piece are also contrasted in terms of size and dynamic decibels.

Subtlety and clarity, refinement and proper perorative perspective are found in Simon Preston's playing of this fine example of organ composition. He is in control of every organistic situation that arises.

Prière et Berceuse

Sonata ("Final" movement)

☐ Raynaud (organ) / Vox SVBX-5314

Clear actions by both composer and performer in these representations. The finale from one of Guilmant's eight organ sonatas (Vox gives no identification, no liner notes on any of the works in the box, and not even the first names of the composers!) is clean and positive; the other piece is quiet. It is also positive in its thematic borrowing from Mozart's A major Piano Sonata—strange that Guilmant didn't notice it. Or did he?

Ernest Guiraud (1837-1892)

The Fantastic Hunt **(Symphonic Poem) (1887)**

☐ Louisville Orchestra / Mester (conductor) / Louisville 743

Orchestra

All the ingredients are here: horn calls and echoes, chromatic passages, diminished seventh "mystery" chords, and sequences that accompany orchestral "hurry" music. It's based on a story about a man drawn by the devil into a mad chase.

Sophisticates will point out that Guiraud's music is similar to the background scores that frame innumerable Hollywood and made-for-television films. They'll be correct. Good enough. The music's fun to hear, in a campy way. The playing is up to the hilt and with all the best intentions possible, which is as it should be.

Jesús Guridi (1886-1961)

Instrumental

Harp

Agura Zarkilun
Aritz Adarean
Ator, Ator Mutil
Garizuma Luzerik

Nere Maitea
Viejo Zortzico
Zorabitatua Naiz

☐ Robles (harp) / Argo ZRG-5457

Basque folk music was Guridi's specialty. All seven pieces are drawn from this resource. With the exception of *Viejo Zortzico*, the miniatures were originally part of a collection of twenty-two Basque songs based on folk melodies that Guridi set for voice, then arranged for orchestra, then for piano. The versions for harp, therefore, represent the third (though partial) transcription of the work.

The simplicity of the music is charming. Robles's playing is flawless.

Cornelius Gurlitt (1820-1901)

Instrumental

Toy Symphony (Kindersymphonie) in C major, Op. 169

☐ Lewenthal (piano); Ross (violin); Aller (cello); McNab (toy trumpet) / Lewenthal (conductor) / Angel S-36080

The average instrumentation (call it the "standard") for the toy symphony medium is: piano, violin, and cello, backed up by quail, cuckoo, and nightingale imitation instruments, plus triangle, drum, and toy trumpet. Gurlitt retains the classical form, with a fast initial movement, a Scherzo, and a finale titled *Rondo Burlesco*. This is as good as Leopold Mozart's Toy Symphony, so long credited to Haydn.

Gene Gutchë (1907-)

Orchestra

Genghis Khan, Op. 37

☐ Louisville Orchestra / Mester (conductor) / Louisville S-722

A general, not analytical orchestral portrait of the Mongol conqueror. Thus, in order to obtain a harder texture, violins, violas, and cellos are not used in the score. Otherwise, the music reflects a neo-romantic attitude.

Gutchë's opus is no great masterpiece, but it is well planned and intelligently shaped. Very decently performed.

String Orchestra

Fifth Symphony for Strings, Op. 34

☐ Cincinnati Symphony Orchestra / Rudolf (conductor) / Composers Recordings S-189

Not many major-league orchestras are found on the CRI label, where subsidy is a major factor in its budgeting. This does not lessen the value of most of its recordings. When, therefore, an organization such as the Ohioans appears under CRI's auspices, it is a sign of special esteem for the music performed.

Rudolf chose well. Gutchë's motile lines, tight, intervallic frictions, rhapsodic turns, and uncontroverted flux of fluidic rhythms are matters to enjoy.

Elizabeth Gyring *(1886-1970)*

Piano Sonata No. 2 (1957)   *Instrumental*

☐ Andrews (piano) / Composers Recordings S-252   *Piano*

This is a traditional four-movement conception, traditional as well in its late romantic style gestures. Mitchell Andrews articulates the material in a clearly defined manner, though the dynamic identifications are made rather placidly.

H

Jae Eun Ha *(1937-   )*

Three Pieces for Tuba

Instrumental

Tuba

☐ Cummings (tuba) / Crystal S–391

Unaccompanied tuba picture-painting, even though lightly detailed, is attempted here. It is not overly successful in the delineatory terms of parts 1 and 2, respectively titled *Abstract Vision* and *Morning Calm,* but it is quite interesting if considered as absolute aspects. Aleatoric rhythms are found in the *Abstract Vision,* and also to be observed are fractional pitches and pitchless sounds. There is more rhythmic aliveness in the *Morning Calm* movement and still more in the unstudied construction of the final Etude.

Not only tuba buffs will approve Barton Cummings's playing. It is super secure.

Alois Hába *(1893-1973)*

Fantasy for Violin Solo in $\frac{1}{4}$ Tones, Op. 9a

Instrumental

Violin

☐ Bress (violin) / Folkways 3355 (monaural)

In this piece there are twenty-four pitches to the octave rather than the semitonal dozen sounds. Hába's piece has a Bachian drive. So does Bress's playing. Bress's intonation sounds correct, though it takes more than a single run through the recording to become familiar with the larger pitch spectrum.

Louis Haber *(1915-   )*

Six Miniatures for Violin and Flute

Chamber Music

☐ Sackson (violin); Wummer (flute) / Serenus 12018

A divertimento of pert and colorful ideas. It's rarely serious—a violin-flute combination could not make the grade. It is fun to listen to; all the ploys are brought out neatly by two fine performers.

Trio for Flute, Violin, and Piano

☐ Musical Arts Trio / Serenus 12018

This light material is presented with serious formality: a bit of padding and a bit of sectionalism. Yet it is sufficiently colorful to deserve occasional hearing. Firm ensemble and textural clarity as well as balance help considerably.

Glenn Hackbarth (1949-)

Solo Instrument and Orchestra

Trumpet (doubling on Flügelhorn) and Tuba

Double Concerto

☐ Illinois Contemporary Chamber Players / Hickman (trumpet and flügelhorn); Perantoni (tuba) / Zonn (conductor) / Crystal S–394

The significant stylistic link in Hackbarth's Concerto is panchromaticism working out of small cell fermentation. Concerto emphasis there is, but an intimacy of instrumental conversation between the solo voices gives rise to an intense type of *Nachtstück*. Quickly, however, dismiss any *Eine kleine Nachtmusik* from the mind. Hackbarth's imposing essay doesn't describe sweet serenades but reminds a listener of Goya-like dreams.

The orchestra backup is made up of winds, brass, piano, and percussion. Heard in live performance (the tape transfer is excellent), the Illinois group deserves firm credit for their work. The soloists are of the highest standard. Crystal has chosen a winner with this one.

Don Haddad (1935-)

Chamber Music

Blues Au Vent

☐ American Woodwind Quintet / Gordon (dance band drums) / Golden Crest S-4075

The main title and the subtitles, *Three by Four, Twist,* and *Ad Libitum,* tell the tale. Not disco stuff, but clean jazz of the pre-rock days, far from rewarmed cold turkey.

It is played with distinctive style and zip. Special honors go to the splendid handling of the extremely difficult soloistic horn sections in the last part by the famed Philip Farkas. He hasn't lost his touch.

Henry Hadley (1871-1937)

Chamber Music

Piano Quintet in A minor, Op. 50

☐ Kohon Quartet / Byman (piano) / Vox SVBX–5301

Only the minutest deviations from accepted practice are found in the four movements of this work. The inner pair have special values: one a poetic slow movement, the other a piquant yet restrained Scherzo. Best of all, Hadley does not try to storm the symphonic heights with his piano and four stringed instruments and always retains a chamber music ambience.

The performers follow suit, which is a matter of congratulation. It is a suave, integrated and polished reading without any semi-orchestral simulation. Byman blends her part beautifully with the strings.

Manos Hadzidakis (1925-)

For a Little White Seashell — Preludes and Dances for the Piano, Op. 1

☐ Constantinidis (piano) / Musical Heritage Society MHS–3055

Instrumental

Piano

There are five parts, each containing a prelude and dance. The preludes include a fine imitation of Prokofiev; with cute honesty it is titled *Conversation with Serge Prokofiev*. Among the dances (all Greek) are a *Tsamikos* (triple metered), a *Calamatianos* (seven-ply time, with the pulse pattern consisting of 3–2–2), and a final robust *Big Sousta*.

This is the other side of the coin of Greek serious music, illustrative of the tonal (mostly nationalistically concerned) school as compared to the stochastic music of Xenakis, the total serialization processes of Tsouyopoulos, and the polymorphic graphs used for symbolic musical notation by Logothetis. Hadsidakis proves (again) that neither tonality nor nationalism are exhausted.

Richard Hageman (1882-1966)

Do Not Go, My Love (1917)

☐ Bampton (contralto); (no pianist credited) / New World Records NW–247 (monaural)

Vocal

Voice with Accompaniment

Hageman was a prolific composer of songs. This example, written in 1917, is one of his best.

Reynaldo Hahn 1874-1947)

Si Mes Vers

☐ Tourel (mezzo-soprano); Levine (piano) / Desto 7118/9

Vocal

Voice with Accompaniment

Hahn in his sweet and simple mood. Tourel completely captures the spirit of the song and doesn't tamper with its neat phrases. It turns out beautifully.

Alexei Haieff (1914-)

Divertimento (1944)

☐ Louisville Orchestra / Whitney (conductor) / Louisville 611 (monaural)

Orchestra

The beauties of neoclassicism have rarely been so pleasurable. The melodies that Haieff distributes are delicate and durable, savory and succinct. Of course, these days Haieff's music is not heard in the leagues where Ligeti, Penderecki, Maxwell Davies, and others play. Only a temporary matter, one may be assured.

An absolute charmer in every one of its five movements.

Solo Instrument and Orchestra

Piano

Concerto for Piano and Orchestra (1952)

☐ Vienna Symphony Orchestra / Smit (piano) / Desto 6420E (monaural)

The peppy, controlled kineticism of this Concerto would make a wonderful ballet. Haieff's score, with its tonally leveled dependency and staccato rhythms, relates it to the Stravinsky of the pre-twelve-tone days. No romantic dilly-dallying, just persuasive architecture.

Beautifully played by Smit—also a composer belonging to the neoclassic lodge. The sound is among the best I've heard in Desto's series of re-releases of the old American Recording Society's issues.

Chamber Music

Three Bagatelles for Oboe and Bassoon (1955)

☐ Gomberg (oboe); Walt (bassoon) / RCA LSC-6184

Since homophonic instruments are being used, Haieff's three-part set (begun in 1939 and completed in 1955) is naturally contrapuntal, with lightly salted dissonances helping to deter the merging of lines and accordingly increasing aural interest. Mainly perky, close-spaced items, they are examples of musical hedonism. Exemplary clarity is produced in the playing.

Edmund Haines (1914-1974)

Solo Instrument and Orchestra

Septet

Concertino for Seven Solo Instruments and Orchestra (1959)

☐ Oklahoma City Symphony Orchestra / Harrison (conductor) / Composers Recordings 153 (monaural)

It may be because of the obbligato-integrated principle involved, rather than the steadfast soli highlighting, that the solo instruments are not listed nor are the players given individual credits. And they deserve it. Democratically, across the board, the solo representatives are two winds, flute and clarinet; two brass, horn and trumpet; and three strings, violin, viola, and cello.

Contemporary tonalism and bright orchestral colors give Haines's work a good sense of direction within its sonata, scherzo, Intermezzo, and Rondo statements.

Instrumental

Harp

Sonata for Harp

☐ Chertok (harp) / Orion ORS-75207

Haines's Sonata comprises outer movements with an unusual title for the initial one (Constant), and a common one for the other (Finale). In between are a set of six *Mosaics* that the performer can play in any number (but no less than two and no more than six) and in any sequence. Chertok has chosen Nos. 2, 3, 5, and 6. The contrastive ingredients of these tend to be minimal, the quality introverted, reticent. More punch is derived from the Finale, though Haines's drive is obtained without any high-decibel spicing and glissandi glossaries that usually have scanty substance. Avoiding the *réchauffé* tricks of harp playing that give little musical benefits and bypassing the angelic contours of the romantics that apply only to Muzak-conditioned ears, Haines has found a happy medium and produced a telling work without concerto-span pyrotechnics. It is given a recorded performance of high artistic fidelity.

Quartet No. 4 (1957)

☐ Oxford String Quartet of Miami University / Composers Recordings 188 (monaural)

Haines's music has a romantic center of gravity that spins in a contemporary orbit. Melodic juice gives a tang to his ideas, which are intent on song and rhythm. The quartet is structured on a variational basis. The grouping of its nine parts (the third is not recorded, being optional) is made so that sets of variations provide the composite parallel of a movement. Thus the fourth, fifth, and sixth variants (titled Dance, Second Dance, and Scherzo) equate "movement 2" of the total work. One drawback is the choice of all-pizzicato timbre for the Scherzo division. The seminal source for this is, of course, Bartók's fourth quartet. There have been dozens and dozens of imitations, but almost all of them suffer when compared to Bartók's magnificent original invention. Indeed, comparison with his famed pizzicato movement brings woe to the imitator.

If you wish this quartet—and it deserves attention—the listener will have to accept a flawed performance. There are intonational lapses, a less-than-professional polish, and a deep-set tonal quality is lacking. The opus would be thrice effective if it were presented by a first-class foursome.

Toccata for Brass Quartet

☐ Members of the New York Brass Quintet / Golden Crest S-4023

Haines's music generally displays a racy rhythmicity and this piece follows suit, even when the dynamic level is relaxed. It has bite—the opening chord is plugged with a second and marks well the harmonic language that will follow. Ternary framework holds the music in place.

The performance is ideal. The failure to list the personnel of the New York group is regrettable.

Talib Rasul Hakim [*Stephen A. Chambers*] (1940-)

Shapes, for Orchestra (1965)

☐ Oakland Youth Orchestra / Hughes (conductor) / Desto 7107

Shapes—written eight years before the composer converted to the philosophy of Sufism and changed his name to Hakim—is a collection of random materials that hold the attention by its disparateness. These swatches (the same thing Hakim terms "shapes") are timbre assortments that show his fondness of jazz colorations as well as the wide contemporary school. Eclectically concerned with such recent events, Hakim has turned out a satisfactory and responsible piece of work.

The piece is well-played, and one hopes that this group will continue its recording career.

Visions of Ishwara (1970)

☐ Baltimore Symphony Orchestra / Freeman (conductor) / Columbia M-33434

Hakim's piece is inspired by Hindu mysticism, but no nationalistic melorhythms are included. This dramatic piece displays fine expertise.

There is excellent playing here. Paul Freeman is a conductor who can be depended on for a stimulating and illuminating response to a contemporary score.

Instrumental

Piano

Sound-Gone (A Poetic-Philosophical Sketch) (1967)

☐ Hinderas (piano) / Desto 7102/3

A compound of unthematic fragments, lyric figments, ostinati, and Cowellian inside-the-piano explorations. There is a charm to Hakim's irregular procedures. His explanatory words (in the notes supplied with the recording) are faintly mystical and quite unclear—as is the music. Nonetheless, it's an interesting work; its indirectness evokes a direct response.

Hinderas masters whatever there is to master. The excellent engineering of the recording helps Hakim's music.

Adam (or Adan) de la Halle (or Hale)　(ca. 1237-ca. 1287)

Vocal

Voice and Instrumental Ensemble

Fines Amouretes Ai

Tant Con Je Vivrai

☐ Early Music Consort of London / Bowman (countertenor) / Munrow (conductor) / Nonesuch 71326

Fascinating representations. A countertenor is heard in both pieces. A recorder and portative organ are used in the first-listed piece, a *Virelai;* a medieval fiddle, viol, and nakers (small kettle drums) are used in the other example, a *Rondeau.*

A more authentic focus could not be obtained. The only problem will be digging this music out of the single band covering six works, the others being a *Chansonnette* by Colin Muset, and three by the ubiquitous "Anon."

Ernesto Halffter　(1905-　　)

Solo Instrument and Orchestra

Guitar

Concerto for Guitar and Orchestra (1968)

☐ Orquesta Sinfonica of Spanish Radio-TV / Yepes (guitar) / Alonso (conductor) / Deutsche Grammophon 2530326

Neoclassic style with nicely woven polyphonic coloration. Still, a hint or two of Spanish nationalism can be ascertained. Effective guitar writing, effectively played.

Rodolfo Halffter　(1900-　　)

Orchestra

Ballet Suite La Madrugada del Panadero (1940)

☐ Louisville Orchestra / Whitney (conductor) / Louisville 625 (monaural)

"The Early Awakening of the Baker" is a fifty-second cousin to Falla's "Three-Cornered Hat." The seven sections are an Introduction, a Scene and Habanera, and a number of separate dances, including within them a Nocturne. All of it is rational national academicism.

Pastorale

☐ Szeryng (violin); Janopoulo (piano) / Everest 3153E (monaural)

Tonal, but slightly salted with dissonance. The Pastorale is no relaxed sing-song item but has rhythmic verve, well-supplied by this fine violinist.

Johan Halvorsen *(1864-1935)*

Triumphant Entry of the Boyars

☐ Philadelphia Orchestra / Ormandy (conductor) / Columbia MG–32314

Halvorsen produced three symphonies, a pair of Norwegian rhapsodies, a violin concerto, and a considerable number of suites. However, his name has been erased from concert programs, with the one exception of the March noted above, which deservedly surfaces on pops programs.

The full and correct title should be followed. An old Fiedler recording, for example, lists the piece as "Entry of the Boyars." In this Columbia release it is indicated as "March of the Boyars."

Ebbe Hamerik *(1898-1951)*

Quintet for Winds (1942)

☐ Soni Ventorum Wind Quintet / Desto 6401

It would be no exaggeration to describe Hamerik's work as a set of four chorale-styled movements. Vertical designations predominate, and the counterpoints are harmonic offshoots rather than true linear statements. Still, these remarks do not negate an interesting, if somewhat gray-colored, wind quintet that reflects a brighter shade only in the finale.

The Soni Ventorum opt to leave the score alone. As a result the dynamic levels become leveled. Their tone quality is superb as is the mesh of their ensemble.

Iain Hamilton *(1922-   )*

Scottish Dances, Op. 32

☐ Louisville Orchestra / Whitney (conductor) / Louisville 625 (monaural)

Five of 'em, based on traditional songs and dances and flavored with some contemporary-branded salt and pepper. Best of the set is the urge of No. 3, the acceptable sentimentality of the fourth piece, and the Reel set against a beguine rhythm that provides the finale. Satisfactory performance.

Solo Instrument and Orchestra

Horn

Voyage for French Horn and Chamber Orchestra (1970)

☐ London Sinfonietta / Tuckwell (horn) / Atherton (conductor) / Composers Recordings S-280

Though Hamilton refers to three specific poems dealing with voyages that relate to his opus, his musical journey is "an inner one."

Barry Tuckwell guides the virtuosic cruise decisively with the assistance of flute (sometimes piccolo), oboe, clarinet (doubling on the smaller E flat type), two trumpets, trombone, piano, percussion, string quartet, and double bass. Sharp, contemporary-colored incidents are observed en route.

Instrumental

Organ

Threnos: In Time of War (1966)

☐ Anderson (organ) / Crystal S-180

Ordinary models of organ writing are not followed in this powerful exposition of sonority. The days of sweet sounds or meshed counterpoint are very remote indeed.

Hamilton's work is in four sections, played without pause, with the sections titled *Dawn, Holocaust, Elevation, Purgatory,* and Requiem. Tone clusters abound, impacts rebound, and whatever sobriety is made available is vehement.

This music of protest—described as Hamilton's "personal reaction to war in general and to the Vietnamese tragedy in particular"—is heard in a power-laden performance.

Trumpet

Five Scenes for Trumpet and Piano (1966)

☐ Stevens (trumpet); Grierson (piano) / Avant 1003

The management and command of Hamilton's suite are drawn from the dodecaphonic system. But line movement is clear and textural density is avoided. Artificial academic rigidity is absent without vacillating style. The wild, declamatory, brilliant, and nocturnal moods of the work are clearly illustrated.

Thomas Stevens proves he has technical marksmanship together with musical mastership. All very exhilarating. There are no doubts that Hamilton's *Five Scenes* are an illustrious addition to the limited repertory of the trumpet.

Cantata and Oratorio

Epitaph for This World and Time (1970)

☐ Choirs of Cathedral Church of St. John the Divine, New York City, Trinity Church, Princeton, N.J., and Trinity Church, New York City / King, Agler, and Jones (organs) / Wyton (conductor) / Composers Recordings S-280

Blockbuster forces perform this work, consisting of the more alarming sections of the Book of Revelation—*The Seven Plagues, The Fall of Babylon, The End of Heaven and Earth,* and *The Descent of the Celestial City,* with a *Prologue* and *Epilogue* framing the four sections.

Awesome sounds are employed to press home the awesome meaning, with the voices not only singing, but also shouting, screaming, whispering, and declaiming, and the organs supplying centers of opposition and resistance as well as support.

Naturally one doesn't need hugeness to cause attention, but it certainly helps. Hamilton's work *is* frightening, not only by the terrible sense of the text but by its flogging sounds. (The CRI firm has a sticker on the shrink wrapping of the album that states "Avant Garde Album of the Year—*Time,* 1972." It is a deserving recommendation.)

Andreas Hammerschmidt   *(1612-1675)*

Sonata super "Gelobet Seist Du Jesu Christ"

☐ London Brass Players / Cable (alto) / Rifkin (conductor) / Nonesuch 71145

Like the work discussed immediately below, this is from Hammerschmidt's *Kirchen-
und Tafel-Musik,* with the same instrumentation as the other Sonata. The text is Luther's
Christmas hymn "Praised be Thou, Jesus Christ."
Warm vocal delivery and fine instrumental support.

Sonata super "Nun Lob Mein Seel den Herren"

☐ London Brass Players / Clarke (soprano) / Rifkin (conductor) / Nonesuch 71145

A Fantasia on a paraphrase of the 103rd Psalm ("Now Praise the Lord, My Soul") with
two trumpets, four trombones, and continuo supporting the voice.
Joshua Rifkin controls a perceptive performance. The rhythms are especially firm and
help project a sturdiness that is telling. Christina Clarke has a light voice but it is not over-
balanced by the instruments.

Don Hammond   *(1917-   )*

Quintet for Brass

☐ New York Brass Quintet / Golden Crest S-4017

Hammond's five-movement suite is from the hothouse of jazz, a still respectable conception despite the fact that it wears its slightly dated style very clearly. Terrific performance even if the music doesn't make older folk nostalgic.

George Frideric Handel   *(1685-1759)*

Ballet Music from *Il Pastor Fido*

☐ Academy of St. Martin-in-the-Fields / Marriner (conductor) / Argo ZRG-686

This is the Hunting Scene music and has a true Handelian ring. It also rings true in
the performance.

Ballet Suite *Terpsichore*

☐ Orchestre de l'Association des Concerts Pasdeloup / Devos (conductor) / Nonesuch
71164

This piece is faithfully executed with considerable professionalism. Nice oboe quality
in the second movement, a Chaconne. It is to be noted that Gérard Devos favors slow-
scaled tempi until he reaches the final Gigue.

Concerto a Due Cori No. 1 in B flat major

☐ La Grande Ecurie et la Chambre du Roy / Malgoire (conductor) / Columbia MG-
32813

This is a sturdy interpretation, though tending to be on the speedy side in the fast portions. A strong characterization as well, brought by use of authentic period instruments. Such crisp instrumental tokens of Handel's creativity sit well though they are not heard too often; they fit extremely well in this case.

Concerto a Due Cori

No. 2 in F major / No. 3 in F major

☐ English Chamber Orchestra / Richter (conductor) / Deutsche Grammophon ARC–2533151

Double choirs of winds, each consisting of two oboes, bassoon, and two horns, with strings, explain the title. The plan, therefore, permits solo group definition, combinations, and naturally the strong contrast of concertino and ripieni. The disc offers rich-grained playing and a minimum of editorializing on the part of the conductor, who recognizes that all that is necessary is built into Handel's scores.

Concerto Grosso

In B flat major, Op. 3, No. 1 / In B flat major, Op. 3, No. 2 / In G major, Op. 3, No. 3 / In F major, Op. 3, No. 4 / In F major, Op. 3, No. 4 bis / In D minor, Op. 3, No. 5 / In D major, Op. 3, No. 6

☐ English Chamber Orchestra / Leppard (conductor) / Philips 6500050

Among the variety of scoring plans in this set (always stabilized with strings and continuo) there are pairs of recorders, oboes, and bassoons in No. 1; flute and a solo violin in No. 3; organ, two oboes, plus bassoon in No. 6; etcetera. The formal plans show as much assortment.

Of the several editions of these concerti grossi, Leppard's is the most elegant, and his conceptions embrace dignity and grace as well. Further, his sense of pace is a lesson on how to manage the crucial matter of obtaining motility within the sustainment of slow movements. In the contrapuntal portions the linear perspective is ideal.

Concerto Grosso in C from *Alexander's Feast*

☐ English Chamber Orchestra / Leppard (conductor) / Philips 6700050

Clarity is the pulse beat of this performance. Each of the four movements is beautifully detailed.

Concerto

In D major / In F major / In F major

☐ English Chamber Orchestra / Pearson (organ and harpsichord) / Leppard (conductor) / Philips 6500369

These orchestral pieces each vary in their orchestral makeup. The closest are the pair in F, one calling for four horns, the other for but two, the remainder in each case consisting of two oboes, bassoon, and strings. The D major is a hefty affair, with four horns, two trumpets, two oboes, bassoon, timpani, strings, and organ. Its instrumental coverage carries over to the dimensions of the work, which consists of three movements; the other works have two movements each. Finally, an organ supplements the larger F major work, while a harpsichord supports the other Concerto in the same key.

Sprinkled throughout are sections that are used with or without change in the *Water*

Music and the *Music for the Royal Fireworks.* This doesn't mean that one can't consider Handel's concerti as having individual rights. These are dynamic performances, rich in sound and in meaning.

Overture and Ballet Music from *Alcina*

Overture and Ballet Music from *Ariodante*

☐ Academy of St. Martin-in-the-Fields / Tilney (harpsichord) / Marriner (conductor) / Argo ZRG-686

Musicological truth notwithstanding, many of us have enjoyed the several ballet suites Beecham compiled, arranged, and orchestrated from Handel's music. Some of the original material he used will be recognized in this pair of appealing treasures.

Alcina includes a Sinfonia as well as a number of dances, one of which is a *Tamburino* (a "drum dance"), and a four-part ballet scene, termed "Dream Music," covering such connotations as "Pleasant Dreams," "Bad Dreams," and a combat between them. Even the Overture includes dance sections.

Ariodante includes a "Pastoral Symphony," as well as a series of seven dances.

The playing of every part of these twenty total pieces belongs in the superlative category. Marriner's detailing of the color and dynamic issues is simply unbeatable. For those who prefer only the overtures, *Alcina* is available on Philips (6599053) and *Ariodante* is included in an album of Handel overtures and sinfonias on London 6586.

Overture and Minuet from *Giulio Cesare*

☐ English Chamber Orchestra / Bonynge (conductor) / London 6711

The Minuet is from the first act. First-rate playing.

Overture in B flat major

Overture in D major

☐ English Chamber Orchestra / Leppard (conductor) / Philips 6700050

Contrastive tempi plans embrace these overtures. The D major piece is marked by increasing speeds in its three movements. In the other Overture two slow movements embrace an Allegro.

Character and impulse are superlative in both cases. The colorations of the oboes and solo violin in the B flat major work are delectable; the solo strings, flute, and arch-lute in the D major opus are just as delightful. Tonal beauty and personality mark the playing of the orchestra as a whole.

Overture to *Admeto*

☐ English Chamber Orchestra / Pearson (harpsichord) / Leppard (conductor) / Philips 6599053

A rich and rewarding portrayal.

Overture to *Arminio*

Overture to *Belshazzar*

Overture to *Deidamia*

☐ English Chamber Orchestra / Bonynge (conductor) / London 6711

751

Even though Bonynge uses a certain amount of editorial license that might be argued by musicological patriarchs, the end result is a performance vitality that gives him sufficient points to win the debate. Such feathering of the Handelian nest makes one glad Bonynge does it his way.

Overture to *Esther*

☐ English Chamber Orchestra / Pearson (harpsichord) / Leppard (conductor) / Philips 6599053

A presentation of the Overture is also on London 6586, in a program of overtures and sinfonias by Handel. The Philips edition, especially for the supportive oboe playing, gets the top slot.

Overture to *Faramondo*

Overture to *Judas Maccabaeus*

☐ English Chamber Orchestra / Bonynge (conductor) / London 6711

Not a murmur of discontent for these lively performances.

Overture to *Lotario*

Overture to *Orlando*

Overture to *Ottone*

Overture to *Partenope*

Overture to *Poro*

☐ English Chamber Orchestra / Pearson (harpsichord) / Leppard (conductor) / Philips 6599053

Totally well-ordered presentations. There is a tendency to double-dot to the most finite length, which is like italicizing an italic; no matter, this is the only slight minus point in the whole set. Minus points, however, for Philips which doesn't say a single word about any of the compositions or about the composer. Exceedingly rare for this firm.

Overture to *Radamisto*

☐ English Chamber Orchestra / Bonynge (conductor) / London 6711

Thoroughly enjoyable music in a splendid, sonorous statement.

Overture to *Rinaldo*

☐ English Chamber Orchestra / Bonynge (conductor) / London 6586

Everything you always wanted in a Handel performance: good and sharp entrances, pointed dynamic controls, and stylistic tempi.

Overture to *Scipio*

☐ English Chamber Orchestra / Bonynge (conductor) / London 6711

Satisfying in all respects. This is further proof that Bonynge is certainly a brilliant Handelian conductor.

Overture to *Solomon*

Overture to *Sosarme*

Overture to *Teseo*

☐ English Chamber Orchestra / Bonynge (conductor) / London 6586

The *Teseo* Overture is a work of special breadth and is in the nature of a find. The spontaneous way in which it is played is a delight. So are the depictions of the other two Overtures.

Sinfonia from *Jeptha* (Act 3)

Sinfonia from *Rinaldo* (Act 3: *March and Battle*)

☐ English Chamber Orchestra / Bonynge (conductor) / London 6586

Bright and lively yet keenly balanced performances, especially in the *Rinaldo* excerpt.

Sinfonia from *Semele* (Act 2)

☐ English Chamber Orchestra / Bonynge (conductor) / London 6711

An excellent statement.

Sinfonia from *Solomon* (Act 3: *Arrival of the Queen of Sheba*)

☐ Academy of St. Martin-in-the-Fields / Marriner (conductor) / Argo ZRG–5442

What makes this performance ideal is the pace that Marriner sets for this famous excerpt from Handel's Oratorio. The decision to be more majestic (Bonynge on London 6586) negates the excitement that is absorbed into the music.

***Water Music* (Complete)**

☐ English Chamber Orchestra / Pearson (harpsichord) / Leppard (conductor) / Philips 6500047

An important point that makes Leppard's edition so choice is his avoidance of the big orchestra sound as in the case of Boulez, Kubelik, and Scherchen. However, if instrumental quantity is disregarded, quality and style naturally are the prime premises. The shaping of the assorted pieces (divided, as the case is generally, into three suites) is ideal, and that pertains both to the best-known and to the not-so-well-known numbers. Speed rates are alive, meaning definitive; dynamic planes are richly registered. The brass playing is unforced, of golden sound. This is a recording that will delight music lovers and will equally be accepted by Handelian scholars.

Undoubtedly there are those who still prefer the updated arrangement that remains standard program material. They are referred to the listing discussed under *Handel/ Harty*.

Concerto Grosso

String Orchestra

In G major, Op. 6, No. 1 / In F major, Op. 6, No. 2 / In E minor, Op. 6, No. 3 / In A minor, Op. 6, No. 4 / In D major, Op. 6, No. 5 / In G minor, Op. 6, No. 6 / In B flat major, Op. 6, No. 7 / In C minor, Op. 6, No. 8 / In F major, Op. 6, No. 9 / In D minor, Op. 6, No. 10 / In A major, Op. 6, No. 11 / In B minor, Op. 6, No. 12

☐ English Chamber Orchestra / Hurwitz and Keenlyside (violins); Harvey (cello); Pearson and Leppard (harpsichords) / Leppard (conductor) / Philips SC71AX302

An outstanding, if not the best, version of these extraordinary masterpieces that range from four to six movements, from fugues to gigues to movements that almost defy classification. Leppard has edited with light and shade, but not with thick crayon and colored chalk as, for example, Max Seiffert in the *Gesamtausgabe.* He has avoided overdressing the natural beauty of the twelve works, and has maintained a stylistic quality that makes a notable contribution to Handel literature.

The performance is of enthusiastic response, a joy to the ear. I have no criticisms save for those that don't take the opportunity of owning this set.

Hornpipe in D major

☐ English Chamber Orchestra / Leppard (conductor) / Philips 6700050

This is an exuberant delight which Handel composed ''for the concert at Vauxhall, 1740.'' This was the name of the famous pleasure-garden of London where Handel's music was often performed at the summer concerts.

In the stimulating way in which it is played it is worth triple repetition of its one and a half minute length.

Largo in F major for Two Horns and Strings

☐ English Chamber Orchestra / Leppard (conductor) / Philips 6700050

This is a recasting of a movement from one of the oboe concerti. Tonality change and some different material are involved. It is extremely short but as rewarding as grand-scale Handelian music.

The performance, also, is as rewarding as one might wish. (Philips changes the title only on its label where it is termed a ''Concerto Grosso in F!'')

Overture to *Berenice*

☐ Academy of St. Martin-in-the-Fields / Marriner (conductor) / Argo ZRG–5442

A lively and well-articulated presentation of the Overture to one of Handel's last operas. It is also included in an all-Handel program on London 6586, but Marriner's account is to be preferred.

Wind and Brass Ensemble

Music for the Royal Fireworks

☐ Augmented Wind Ensemble of the English Chamber Orchestra / Somary (conductor) / Vanguard 71176

If it's authenticity that you want, here it is, with Handel's complete and original scoring (for a smaller orchestral version, see under *Handel/Harty*). The inventory is tremendous: twenty-four oboes, a dozen bassoons, no less than a pair of double bassoons (is there any orchestra in the world that has more than one?), two serpents, nine horns, nine trumpets, timpani, and two snare drums! Authentic indeed, but, more to the point, tremendously spectacular—a great sound show. This is a thrilling offering, superbly played, and magnificently realized by Johannes Somary.

Concerto in B flat major for Harp and Orchestra, Op. 4, No. 6

☐ Paul Kuentz Chamber Orchestra / Zabaleta (harp) / Kuentz (conductor) / Deutsche Grammophon 139304

This is *the* Concerto that all harpists play. Zabaleta performs with full commitment and without any of the pedantic rigor that pops up constantly in the playing of this work because of certain square phrasing situations. Fine, full tone, also.

Concerto for Oboe and Strings

No. 1 in B flat major / No. 2 in B flat major / No. 3 in G minor

☐ English Chamber Orchestra / Holliger (oboe) / Leppard (conductor) / Philips 6500240

There is plenty of competition for this set of concertos, some recorded complete, others individually, and still others with timbre substitution (trumpet in one case, tuba [!] in another). But, you will search far and wide to match the sweet, fresh, and heart-filling oboe tone of Mr. Holliger. With that you will have to accept plenty of embellishments and ornamentations, but why not?

Sonata a Cinque in B flat major

☐ English Chamber Orchestra / Holliger (oboe); Sillito (violin) / Leppard (conductor) / Philips 6500240

A decent recording, with fine soloistic partnership and steady back-up by the E.C.O.

Concerto for Organ and Strings

No. 1 in G minor, Op. 4, No. 1 / No. 2 in B flat major, Op. 4, No. 2 / No. 3 in G minor, Op. 4, No. 3 / No. 4 in F major, Op. 4, No. 4 / No. 5 in F major, Op. 4, No. 5 / No. 6 in B flat major, Op. 4, No. 6 / (The Cuckoo and the Nightingale) No. 7 in F major, Op. 6, No. 1 / No. 8 in A major, Op. 6, No. 2 / No. 13 in B flat major, Op. 7, No. 1 / No. 14 in A major, Op. 7, No. 2 / No. 15 in B flat major, Op. 7, No. 3 / No. 16 in D minor, Op. 7, No. 4 / No. 17 in G minor, Op. 7, No. 5 / No. 18 in B flat major, Op. 7, No. 6 / No. 19 in D minor / No. 20 in F major

☐ London Philharmonic Orchestra / Biggs (organ) / Boult (conductor) / Columbia D3M-33716

These concerti are splendidly played, with special quality on two counts: the solo instrument, which is the Aylesford organ at Great Packington (Handel's own organ), and the strength of Boult's conducting. The music is always illuminated with understanding and reflects a splendid consideration that shows Boult to be a first-class Handelian. Biggs's organ prose is never strained even if he sometimes does not probe deeply.

Pastorale, Theme and Variations

☐ DeCray (harp) / Coronet 2508

Presumably this is authentic Handel though intense checking does not bring affirmation. If it isn't Handel he deserves being credited with the work, a sizable affair that shows fine creative responses.

Marcella DeCray's playing is sensitively colored and has full character. By all means bypass the performance by Marie-Claire Jamet included in her miscellaneous program on Nonesuch 71098. There titled "Theme and Variations," Handel's music is triply trun-

Solo Instrument and Orchestra

Harp

Oboe

Oboe and Violin

Organ

Instrumental

Harp

cated. First, the title is incorrect. Second, the Pastorale is totally eliminated. Third, there is a huge excision in the variation section. One assumes that DeCray's version *is* responsible and there's no reason to believe otherwise. The timings, therefore, are most informative and, as far as Jamet is concerned, damning. The Pastorale she eliminates runs 2:50 in DeCray's presentation at the beginning and 0:52 in its concentrated recapitulation. The Theme and Variations section covers 7:50 in DeCray's performance, while Jamet produces it in 4:42! Even if one accepts Jamet's decision to play only the Theme and Variations, her boiled-down version is completely suspect. The unknowing choice of a spurious published edition can only be used as an alibi. Certainly no explanation is to be obtained from the liner notes (this pertains to both albums) which are totally vague and simply fill space.

(Coronet's number is listed as above in *Schwann* and on the disc. On the album cover it is noted as 2745.)

Harpsichord

Chaconne in G major

☐ Hamilton (harpsichord) / Delos 15322

The Chaconne is listed on the recording as "No. 1," since there are two in the second set of Handel's eight harpsichord suites. A "number one" work it is, indeed, with its twenty-one variations. The splendid performance by this fine harpsichordist can also be listed as "number one." Hamilton establishes a proper playing diplomacy in defining the variations and yet somehow managing a seamlessness of continuity.

Forest Music

☐ Kipnis (harpsichord) / Angel S-3816

Forest Music was edited by Kipnis from a manuscript held in the Royal College of Music in London. It is an absolute delight, high-gamuted, bellish. Kipnis plays it with open-hearted imagery. The musical common sense of this artist is not commonly found in the world of keyboard-instrument performers.

The Harmonious Blacksmith from Suite No. 5

☐ Kipnis (harpsichord) / Columbia MS-7326

This familiar and delightful set of variations is contained, of course, in the harpsichord suites (*see below:* Suite for Harpsichord). If you wish it as a single, here it is, played by a master. (The work is also included on Columbia MS-7515.)

Suite for Harpsichord

No. 1 in A major / No. 2 in F major / No. 3 in D minor / No. 4 in E minor / No. 5 in E major / No. 6 in F sharp minor / No. 7 in G minor / No. 8 in F minor

☐ Tilney (harpsichord) / Deutsche Grammophon ARC-2533168/9

This well-documented discourse avoids any bucking bronco character in order to add color. Though there is a minimum application of ornamentation, Colin Tilney fully conveys the sense of the music's historical period in his playing. He also demonstrates an intuitive sense of the proper pace for the various parts of these suites.

The suites are not recorded chronologically. The order in the first disc is Nos. 2-4-5-8 and in the second, Nos. 1-3-6-7. There is a specific reason for this: Tilney uses two different instruments, a single-manual instrument for the first sequence and a double-manual harpsichord for the other.

Suite for Harpsichord

No. 1 in A major / No. 2 in F major / No. 3 in D minor / No. 4 in E minor

☐ Gould (harpsichord) / Columbia M–31512

A recording of the complete first book of Handel's harpsichord suites is covered *above*. Here and immediately *below* are excerpts from the eight works in the group that deserve the fullest attention.

It may be the restrictions of the instrument ("restrictions" in comparison to the modern piano) that force his hand but Glenn Gould has rarely been so positive and so musically *rational* as in his playing here. There are no slipslaps, no interpretative flimflammery, and thus no style indiscretions. This is a display of representational skill relevant to every measure in the four suites and yet with no cloistered academicism.

Suite for Harpsichord

No. 3 in D minor / No. 7 in G minor

☐ Hamilton (harpsichord) / Delos 15322

Handel is played here with a dynamism that produces the utmost in clarity. The vigor that infuses Hamilton's performances does not interfere with the seriousness of the music or its sonorous accuracy. It rather reports Handel refreshingly aright with a harpsichord sound that has both weight and depth. Great!

Suite No. 8 in F minor for Harpsichord

☐ Kipnis (harpsichord) / Angel S–3816

The sensitivity of this musician and his impeccable artistry are of as much bravura as Paganinish pyrotechnics. This statement holds one spellbound throughout.

Sonata for Violin and Continuo

Chamber Music

In A major, Op. 1, No. 3 / In G minor, Op. 1, No. 10 / In F major, Op. 1, No. 12 / In D major, Op. 1, No. 13 / In A major, Op. 1, No. 14 / In E major, Op. 1, No. 15

☐ Lautenbacher (violin); Ruf (harpsichord); Koch (viola da gamba) / Nonesuch 71238

The usual performance of these works finds the violin with a piano, much less often with a harpsichord, and still less often with further support to the continuo. In this recording the ideal is presented.

There are no infractions of style in the solo part. Though not played with cold calculation, the works are not marred by *rubati* or that horror of horrors—the italicizing of cadences by portamenti. Handelian order and personality are unmistakably stamped upon each of the six Sonatas.

Trio Sonata in C minor for Alto Recorder, Violin, Violoncello, and Harpsichord

☐ Dolmetsch-Schoenfeld Ensemble / Orion 73104

This is one of the best of Handel's trio sonatas, from the Opus 2 group. Its slow movement is a special gem. You can't go wrong with this consistently stylish performance.

Care Selve **from** *Atalanta*

Vocal

☐ English Chamber Orchestra / Baker (mezzo-soprano); Leppard (harpsichord) / Leppard (conductor) / Philips 6500523

Voice and Orchestra

Ten words form the text of this excerpt. A hundred words would be needed to describe the exquisite vocal delivery of Janet Baker. The best advice is to get the disc and hear it.

Where Shall I Fly from *Hercules*

☐ English Chamber Orchestra / Baker (mezzo-soprano); Leppard (harpsichord) / Leppard (conductor) / Philips 6500523

Baker's performance of this broadly extended accompanied recitative, dramatized by tempi shifts, is clear in diction and artistic in substance. The accompaniment is just as sensitive.

Choral

Chorus and Orchestra

Anthems for the Coronation of King George II and Queen Caroline

> *The King Shall Rejoice*
> *Let Thy Hand Be Strengthened*
> *My Heart Is Inditing*
> *Zadok the Priest*

☐ English Chamber Orchestra and Choir of King's College, Cambridge / Dart (harpsichord); Langdon (organ) / Willcocks (conductor) / Argo ZRG–5369

Handel's Anthems represent music of extrovert directness. They remain as fresh today as when first heard at the Coronation of King George II and Queen Caroline in Westminster Abbey on October 11, 1727. With typical practicality Handel later transferred a considerable part of this music to his oratorios *Esther, Deborah, Athalia,* and the Occasional Oratorio.

When first performed, this music, containing golden brass references and as golden polyphony, was sung by a group of about fifty voices and an orchestra of a little over one hundred and fifty. Such prodigious orchestral personnel is not necessary, indeed would cause a severe imbalance, whether it be presented in the concert hall or in the making of a recording. Actually, more choral power would be welcome in this otherwise excellent edition, the better of the pair on the market.

Chandos Anthems
No. 6, *As Pants the Hart* / No. 10, *The Lord Is My Light*

☐ Academy of St. Martin-in-the-Fields and King's College Choir / Cantelo (soprano); Partridge (tenor); Davis (organ) / Willcocks (conductor) / Argo ZRG–541

Handel wrote eleven of these anthems for the Duke of Chandos. These two are most representative, make no compromise with rote creation, and have Handelian first-rate values. An excellent recording in all respects.

Dixit Dominus (Psalm 109)

☐ Bach Orchestra of Berlin and Choir of the School for Church Music, Halle / Reichelt (soprano); Wolf-Matthäus (alto) / Wenzel (conductor) / Vanguard S–249

This performance has vitality (but is always musically weighted). The contrast between large and small groups is well maintained. The floridity of Handel's writing is beautifully translated throughout; the smooth focus of the chorus's work is admirable.

Ode for St. Cecilia's Day

☐ Academy of St. Martin-in-the-Fields and Choir of King's College, Cambridge / Cantelo (soprano); Partridge (tenor); Heath (cello); Adeney (flute); Izen (trumpet) / Willcocks (conductor) / Argo ZRG–563

There is much to enthuse about in this performance; it provides a directness that is compelling. The soprano displays full-powered lyricism; the tenor supplies bright vocalism.

Belshazzar

☐ Orchestra of the Stuttgart Kirchenmusiktage and Choir of the Stuttgart Memorial Church / Stahlman (soprano); Raab and Ankersen (contraltos); Jochims (tenor); Birkeland (bass); Haas (organ); Brachmann (cello) / Rilling (conductor) / Vox SVBX-5209

Although this work is an oratorio, its drama and music make it yearn for operatic identification.

There is a twist in that the chorus is a German aggregation but sings in English. As with American choral groups, not much comes through without the aid of the libretto furnished. Of the five soloists, two are German and one is Norwegian. The words are clearer in this department.

Be ready for some heavy cuts, even though the recording covers six sides. On Telefunken 4635326 the coverage is complete and totals eight sides. There it is also authentic in terms of style and instruments (Harnoncourt conducts). Nevertheless, the Vox edition has more life and better singing.

Cantata No. 17, *Pensieri Notturni di Filli*

☐ Collegium Aureum / Ameling (soprano); Linde (recorder); Leonhardt (harpsichord) / RCA VICS-1275

This account effectively captures the pastoral element of the piece, especially the shepherding of the content through the obbligato recorder, the instrument of shepherds. A considerable part of the vocal line lies in the higher register but there is never a problem with voicing, and throughout the piece the atmosphere of poetic relevance is maintained. (The performance is also available on BASF 21687.)

Cantata No. 22, *Tu Fedel? Tu Costante?*

☐ New York Chamber Soloists / Bressler (tenor) / Nonesuch 71159

The usual Handelian delights of mingled moods, with recitatives and arias in equal number, are found in this Cantata. It is given a worthy account by Charles Bressler, although the cantata was originally written for soprano. The instrumental support, consisting of violin, viola, cello, and harpsichord, is efficient.

Cantata No. 26, *Ah, Che Troppo Ineguali*

☐ Collegium Aureum / Ameling (soprano); Koch (viola da gamba); Leonhardt (harpsichord) / RCA VICS-1275

This semisecular Cantata sings the praise of the Queen of Heaven. It is here sung with deeply moving, expressive strength and with touches of subtlety that are a model of its kind. A completely clear-sighted, clear-voiced performance. Superb. (Also available in a BASF release—No. 21687.)

The Dettingen Te Deum

☐ Telemann Society Festival Orchestra and Chorus / Wheeler and Laurence (sopranos); Pavlides (alto); Ferrante (tenor); Dennison (bass) / Schulze (conductor) / Nonesuch 71003

Handel's sixteen-part work includes a number of fine solos, the most important one being the penultimate section for solo bass: "Vouchsafe, O Lord!" It is sung acceptably, but one would wish for more weight in John Dennison's voice. In fact, all the soloists, while steady and accurate, do not have commanding voices. The chorus, on the other hand, is quite capable.

Cantata No. 46, *Lucrezia: O Numi Eterni*

☐ English Chamber Orchestra / Baker (mezzo-soprano); Leppard (harpsichord) / Leppard (conductor) / Philips 6500523

The musical sweep is magnificent, the story line dramatic, the singing enthralling, rich, and powerful. *Lucrezia* concludes with a novel *furioso* recitative. For this alone the disc is worth owning.

Jephtha

☐ English Chamber Orchestra and Amor Artis Chorale / Grist (soprano); Woolf (boy soprano); Watts and Forrester (contraltos); Young (tenor); Lawrenson (bass); Lester (harpsichord) / Somary (conductor) / Vanguard C-10077/9

This is Handel's good-bye to the oratorio medium. Based on the text of the ninth chapter of *Judges, Jephtha* has a wealth of Handelian credits. As Winton Dean indicates (his notes on the composition are a healthy bonus that Vanguard offers), "there is no decline in invention, range or power of composition."

A wealthy performance matches the score. This offers phrasing that has meaning, impeccable accuracy by the fine team of soloists, and acute balances between chorus, orchestra, and vocalists.

Messiah

☐ English Chamber Orchestra and Ambrosian Singers / Harwood (soprano); Baker (mezzo-soprano); Esswood (countertenor); Tear (tenor); Herincx (bass) / Mackerras (conductor) / Angel S-3705
☐ Philharmonia Orchestra and Chorus / Schwarzkopf (soprano); Hoffman (contralto); Gedda (tenor); Hines (bass) / Klemperer (conductor) / Angel S-3657

There has been a continual insistence on placing heavy editorial hands on Handel's great Oratorio. A bit of the blame falls on Handel himself, who constantly made different settings of various numbers in both the Christmas and Easter sections of the work. Today, there are so many published editions of the vocal score that one loses count. Orchestrally, Mozart made some additional accompaniments for the work, then Prout stuffed it full of romantic weight.

Performance-wise, there is the old traditional approach, somewhat deadly though very churchly. It is preferable to pass that depiction by. Several steps above this is the big production viewpoint, unmannered and spacious, almost ultra-dramatic, represented by Klemperer's edition. The opposite is the leaner and more Handelian-sounding version, conducted by Charles Mackerras. The textures are clear and fluid, the rhythms are crisp, there is excellent ornamentation that doesn't get in the way of the music, and the whole presents a very compelling over-all freshness. The soloists are superb.

Theodora

☐ English Chamber Orchestra and Amor Artis Chorale / Harper (soprano); Forrester and Lehane (contraltos); Young and Fleet (tenors); Lawrenson (baritone); Lester (harpsichord) / Somary (conductor) / Vanguard C-10050/2

This Oratorio is not on the usual Old Testament subject but about a Christian martyr. The three-act story is suitable window dressing for some fine Handel music.

One can only praise this release. The soloists are top-flight; all enjoy true vocal richness and a fine understanding of what they are singing and how to style it. For that the fullest praise descends on Johannes Somary. His expertise and musicianship are very evident in this publication.

Alcina

□ London Symphony Orchestra and Chorus / Sutherland, Scutti, and Freni (sopranos); Berganza (mezzo-soprano); Sinclair (contralto); Alva (tenor); Flagello (bass); Malcolm (harpsichord); Heath (cello) / Bonynge (conductor) / London 1361

This is superfine Handel; the score is full of material that provides a field day for the singer of the exacting title role and not much less for the supporting characters. Joan Sutherland has never been better; her voice is full and clear, her interpretation is of expressive substance. What appeals in the case of the other members of the cast is their auditory clarity, their stylistic understanding. The orchestra furnishes an excellent palette of sound and the continuo is not buried.

It is, indeed, a lovely work, with a plot that includes the special gambit of magic so helpful to operatic stage existence. Plot or not, the joy of listening to Handel's music will be sufficient for any opera buff.

Bonynge, who prepared and edited the score (tastefully and knowingly, let it be emphasized) was also the supervisor for the variants and cadenzas that the singers have inserted. His conducting is excellent and there is never any tendency to drag tempi, which seems to be a fondness of many conductors when they are involved with a Handel work.

Julius Caesar

□ New York City Opera Orchestra and Chorus / Sills (soprano); Wolff (mezzo-soprano); Forrester (contralto); Cossa and Beck (baritones); Treigle and Devlin (bass-baritones); Malas (bass); Earle and Rudel (harpsichords) / Rudel (conductor) / RCA LSC-6182

The New York City Opera's production is a viable one but the scalpel has been wielded—cleanly but very deeply. Of course, Handel operas are far from pithy and cuts are expected but there's plenty of the score not here, despite the fact that the six sides of the recording embrace some two and one half hours. The excisions cover complete arias as well as the elimination of da capo repeats. Cuts necessary for an audience in order to avoid backside travail are one thing, but in the relaxed home atmosphere with opportunity to move about if so desired or just to hear certain scenes the matter of an incomplete recording can be vigorously argued. Regardless of extra rehearsal and preparation time for the sake of the recording, extra expense for musicians, and a higher purchase price, the matter should be accorded serious consideration.

Rudel's direction is excellent. Yet, one cannot understand his shifting scenes, and making other changes and additions, even though his contention is that *Julius Caesar* was conceived "for [your] enjoyment rather than for [your] reverence." It is a perfected personal approach but must be heard as Handel–Rudel rather than as Handel–Handel.

The singing is never heavy, is always focused, and is styled properly. This is especially so in the case of Beverly Sills (as Cleopatra). *Caesar* was composed for a *castrato*. Solving that insurmountable problem was the task of a bass-baritone, and Norman Treigle's accomplishment is far above par.

Still, Handel operas not being big box office, recorded availability cannot be sneered at even with the check marks on the minus side mentioned above. There is, after all, a win-

Opera and Dramatic Music

ning temperament to the totality (considered *as* a totality) and there isn't another recording on the market, just excerpts.

Serse

☐ Vienna Radio Orchestra and Vienna Academy Chorus / Popp (soprano); Forrester, Lehane, and Miller (altos); Hemsley and Brannigan (basses); Isepp (harpsichord) / Priestman (conductor) / Westminster Gold 8202

Xerxes, Serse being the Italian title, is an odd opera since it wavers between being serious and semi-comic; regardless, it has a vitality worth knowing. It is from *Serse* that the famed Largo has been extracted. In the opera it is a Larghetto, and it is not the prayer practically everyone thinks it is, but an apostrophe to a tree!

Fine singing all the way, sumptuous in the case of Maureen Forrester, beautifully characterized in the comic role taken by Owen Brannigan. The score has been properly embellished by Brian Priestman, whose conducting is absolutely top-drawer, avoids any stodginess, and is fully in stylistic control. There is not a single blemish. Martin Isepp, the harpsichordist, certainly cannot be bypassed in terms of special credits. In his hands the continuo sparkles with life, as do his improvised passages.

Handel / Hamilton Harty (1879-1941)

Orchestra
Music for the Royal Fireworks

☐ Philadelphia Orchestra / Ormandy (conductor) / Columbia MS-6095

This is the boiled-down (not meant to be a derogatory term) version that is the one usually heard at concerts. (For the original wind scoring setting, see under *Handel: Wind and Brass Ensemble.*) Thanks to Harty, matters are brought within reason by a scoring calling for pairs of oboes and bassoons, four horns, three trumpets, timpani, snare drum, and strings.

If some of the blare is missing, none of the flair is in Ormandy's sumptuously sounding performance.

Water Music (Suite)

☐ London Symphony Orchestra / Szell (conductor) / London 6236
☐ London Symphony Orchestra / Dorati (conductor) / Mercury 75005

For a long time (since 1918, when Harty's transcription was first made and given its first performance) this has been "the" *Water Music* played at concerts (see under *Handel: Orchestra* for complete score). With the introduction of long-playing records the situation has changed a bit, but only a bit. One occasionally hears in concert the complete version, but it still is a rarity save on the record turntable, where one of the dozen available editions on disc are to be heard.

Harty's transcription covers six movements and is scored for double woodwinds, four horns, two trumpets, timpani, and strings. It is lovely, and only snobbish purists can object to a beautiful, fully acceptable setting of beautiful Handel music.

Szell's performance is bright and virile, a substantiation of classical style with quasi-romantic coloring. Dorati plays it with full justice to style but a bit gentler.

Handel / **Arnold Schoenberg (1874-1951)**

Concerto for String Quartet and Orchestra (after the Concerto Grosso, Op. 6, No. 7)

☐ London Symphony Orchestra and Lenox Quartet / Farberman (conductor) / Desto 7170

Schoenberg's consideration of Handel's music is more than just several cuts above transcription of a string work for soli with orchestra. The latter calls for double wood-winds, two each of horns and trumpets, a trombone, percussion, harp, piano, and strings. What has been done makes the listener wonder whether the work should be listed as Schoenberg–Handel rather than the reverse. Indeed, there is a huge amount of twentieth-century interpositioning and interpenetrations of Handel's eighteenth-century opus. There are doubts as to this freely expanded translation. But, raising such doubts does not mean a critic is a purist.

Some cramped sound in places brings doubt as well concerning the performance. For this, Schoenberg is partially to blame due to his textural quantities.

Solo Instrument and Orchestra

String Quartet

Stephen Hanna *(1950-   )*

Sonic Sauce

☐ Hanna (percussion) / Crystal S-140

Recognized here is the traditional affiliation with the world of jazz. Hanna's style is thoroughly consequent and competent. He is a top performer as well. In this case he plays all the parts, using multi-track overdubbing.

Percussion

Howard Hanson *(1896-   )*

Elegy in Memory of My Friend Serge Koussevitzky (1955)

☐ Eastman-Rochester Symphony Orchestra / Hanson (conductor) / Eastman-Rochester Archives ERA-1010

Finely tempered, fully threnodic music. The music enunciates the Hanson character, a parallel to the darker side of Elgar's and Vaughan Williams's musical prose. It is cogently designed, rising to an intense climax and then subsiding to the warm quiet with which it began. The performance is exemplary.

Orchestra

For the First Time

☐ Eastman Philharmonia Orchestra / Hanson (conductor) / Eastman-Rochester Archives ERA-1015

A dozen snapshots with engaging orchestrational color photography. Examples: the slightly moist tints for *Mist*, the royal and crimson hues for *Fireworks*. All the characterizations are apt: mischievous in *Kikimora*, optimistic in *Dreams*, ticked off nicely in the *Eccentric Clock*. Though critics contend program music is dead, Hanson's example surely denies it.

Merry Mount Suite (1937)

☐ Eastman-Rochester Orchestra / Hanson (narrator) / Hanson (conductor) / Eastman-Rochester Archives ERA–1005

Gutsy and lusty music from the one opera Hanson has written. It survives in the excerpted format for orchestra with a transcription for band.

It will be noted that Hanson is listed as a narrator as well as composer. There is no narration in the music for *Merry Mount*. Hanson's narrative pertains to a recorded lecture on orchestration, based on the *Merry Mount* music. This covers the working tools (the individual instruments), the product these produce (combination of sound qualities), onto the final structure (the musical composition itself). As one example of orchestrational science the project is successful. Of course, to consider fully orchestration in relation to its role within multitudinous aesthetics would take hundreds of discs.

Mosaics (1957)

☐ Eastman-Rochester Symphony Orchestra / Hanson (conductor) / Eastman-Rochester Archives ERA–1006

Subtle variation within the principal theme, with further relationship existing within the variations of the work itself as they appear, defines the mosaic plan of Hanson's piece. For the greater part the modally conceived music is dark-stranded.

No super-duper technical revelations from Howard Hanson, simply original poetic music, with the meanings clear upon first hearing. But that's good enough for anyone's money. Hanson is an honest composer, and *Mosaics* is further proof.

Symphony No. 2 (*Romantic*), Op. 30

☐ Eastman-Rochester Orchestra / Hanson (conductor) / Mercury 75007

Plenty of Hollywoodism used in the days when Bette Davis was in flower. Don't mind them and remember that such gambits appeared first in Hanson (and others) around the late 1920s. The orchestration is both powerful and lush. Hanson knows how to arrange a huge sound; he wears the full romantic crown and is not ashamed of it. He turns out a beauty of a melody to spark the slow movement. (Speaking of this melody, a British critic wrote me that he didn't know the number of the Hanson Symphony he was seeking, but could clue me in by stating it was the one with the "famous" tune in it!)

Symphony No. 5 (*Sinfonia Sacra*) (1954)

☐ Eastman-Rochester Symphony Orchestra / Hanson (conductor) / Eastman-Rochester Archives ERA–1014

As Hanson's first two symphonies were related through their subtitles (*Nordic* and *Romantic*), so his Fifth Symphony relates to the Fourth (*Requiem*) Symphony. Classical ideology, romantic enlargement of harmony, and a broad murallike sweep of sound and formal arrangement characterize this work. This is an example of a free yet controlled voice in the sophisticated welter of musical styles of the current century. The engineering is superb and the interpretation is, of course, definitive.

Symphony No. 6 (1968)

☐ Music for Westchester Symphony Orchestra / Landau (conductor) / Turnabout 34534

The golden glow of romanticism lights up Hanson's Symphony of six movements. A motto theme knits the music together as the linked movements proceed through alternating slow- and fast-paced sections.

Landau's organization does fairly well with the colorative dissonances and the invigorating rhythms, which are Hanson's particular trade mark.

Serenade for Flute, Harp, and Strings (1946)

☐ Eastman-Rochester Symphony Orchestra / Mariano (flute); Malone (harp) / Hanson (conductor) / Eastman-Rochester Archives ERA–1001

In its most common form a serenade is a song to a lover's lady. But the term also applies to instrumental music associated with entertainment and happy events (an example: Mozart's *Haffner Serenade,* written to celebrate the wedding of a friend's daughter). Hanson's Serenade is a romantic outpouring that fits both categories; it was written in 1946, as a wedding present to his bride.

The artistry of the principal soloist, Joseph Mariano, and the high level of insight this flutist shows in making his instrument one of multicolor sensitivity are accomplishments worth hearing.

Pastorale for Oboe, Strings, and Harp (1949)

☐ Eastman-Rochester Symphony Orchestra / Sprenkle (oboe); Malone (harp) / Hanson (conductor) / Eastman-Rochester Archives ERA–1001

An oboe evokes a pastoral and rustic setting: thus precedents create unilateral rules. Hanson follows the dictum with a fluent and concentrated work, particularly as to the color of the woodwind voice. The Pastorale was originally conceived for oboe with piano accompaniment; in the bowed and plucked stringed instrumental setting the solo oboe is enriched by a warmer background.

All parties involved play beautifully in this single recording available.

Fantasy Variations on a Theme of Youth for Piano and String Orchestra (1951)

☐ Eastman-Rochester Symphony Orchestra / Burge (piano) / Hanson (conductor) / Eastman-Rochester Archives ERA–1002

The "theme of youth" in the title is not a philosophical topic but describes the subject of the variations, since it was written by Hanson when he was a student at Northwestern University. The "fantasy" aspect does not disturb the clear projection of its development.

Burge plays with obvious commitment and total clarity. Of course Hanson is completely in charge and provides superb support.

Piano Concerto, Op. 36

☐ Eastman-Rochester Symphony Orchestra / Mouledous (piano) / Hanson (conductor) / Eastman-Rochester Archives ERA–1006

This is a perfect example of Hanson's romantic ideology producing a music where form and application to content are clearly proposed and where the thematic material is of deep-felt sensitivity. The Concerto is more an integrated symphony for a solo instrument with orchestra than a showpiece. That may not please many virtuosi but it will please listeners on the lookout for expressive, emotive music. The word is "communication."

An ideal performance.

Quartet in One Movement, Op. 23

☐ Kohon Quartet / Vox SVBX–5305

Dual thematic evolution is the basis of Hanson's single chamber music work. The two ideas are clearly presented in terms of contrastive mood and tempo. Alternative representation follows, each time varied in thematic presentation, background, and coloring.

A secularized-liturgical climate surrounds the work. The Kohon Quartet ably defines this in its interpretation.

Choral

Chorus with Accompaniment

The One Hundred Fiftieth Psalm (1958)

☐ Mormon Tabernacle Choir / Schreiner (organ) / Ottley (conductor) / Columbia M–34134

Hanson has always been successful in communicating simply and yet effectively in the choral medium. If evidence is required, the Mormon Tabernacle Choir's vibrantly telling performance is all that is necessary.

Choral and Orchestra

The Cherubic Hymn for Chorus and Orchestra, Op. 37

☐ Eastman-Rochester Symphony Orchestra and Eastman School of Music Chorus / Hanson (conductor) / Eastman-Rochester Archives ERA–1014

The text is taken from the Liturgy of St. John Chrysostom. There is no better force for projecting a choral-orchestral work than a composer's ability to create sustained lines. This factor is present here and illustrates Hanson's compelling strength as a writer of dynamic as well as colorful choral music.

A recording of exultant sound and sensitive performance.

The Lament for Beowulf, Op. 25

☐ Eastman-Rochester Symphony Orchestra and Eastman School of Music Chorus / Hanson (conductor) / Mercury 75007

A distinctive Northern element is found in many of Hanson's works. Influential in this opus are tenebrous and sombrous Sibelian colors that aid in achieving the austere quality required for the Anglo-Saxon text.

This especially convincing portrayal is due chiefly to Hanson's control of dynamic contrast and relationship—the mark of the expert conductor as well as the top professional composer.

Song of Democracy (1957)

☐ Eastman-Rochester Symphony Orchestra and Eastman School of Music Chorus / Hanson (conductor) / Eastman-Rochester Archives ERA–1010

Without a doubt this is the most-often-performed work by an American composer in the medium of chorus and orchestra. The *Song of Democracy* has achieved over 1,000 performances since it was completed in 1957—not counting about twice that total in presentations with piano, organ, or symphonic band as a substitute for the orchestral forces. The work is deserving, containing breadth and compulsion; its modal flavors have full romantic urge. The text is drawn from Walt Whitman.

The performance is a brilliant collaboration between orchestra and chorus.

Songs from Drum Taps (1935)

☐ Eastman-Rochester Symphony Orchestra and Eastman School of Music Chorus / Meyers (baritone) / Hanson (conductor) / Eastman-Rochester Archives ERA–1007

Hanson's composition of three settings from Walt Whitman is eloquent, warm-blooded music. It illustrates the cleanly romantic school of composition with nary a false step.

The performance standards of the Eastman Chorus have always been very high; in this case they must be classified as superlative. Their tone is magnificently full and resonant; precise and meaningful enunciation enhances the patriotic feeling of Hanson's work. The clarity of diction makes the following of the text on the liner unnecessary. The recording is a choral joy: a brilliant achievement of a stunning work.

Merry Mount (Excerpts) (1937)

*Opera
and Dramatic
Music*

☐ Eastman-Rochester Symphony Orchestra and Eastman School of Music Chorus / Cullen (soprano); Schadema and Shellhammer (mezzo-sopranos); Nason and McDevitt (tenors); Fleck and Cullen (baritones); Crawford (bass-baritone) / Hanson (conductor) / Eastman-Rochester Archives ERA–1013

It is absolutely unguessable why *Merry Mount* has not found its way into the operatic repertory. It has all the ingredients: a story of the conflict between Puritan and Cavalier colonists in New England and the struggle of a fanatic Puritan clergyman beset by carnality, dramatic arias and choruses, and sumptuous orchestral narration. Yet, after fantastic audience and critical response to its premiere by the Metropolitan Opera Company (fifty curtain calls at the conclusion!) and ten performances in four cities during the 1934 season, only a few sporadic presentations have been given since.

This thirty-five-minute sampler is prime evidence of top achievement. The organic coherence of Hanson's style and his dramatic power are felt throughout every measure of the nine parts presented. The recorded documentation is rich and exciting in all respects.

Johannes Hanssen *(1874 - ?)*

Valdres March

Band

☐ Eastman Wind Ensemble / Austin (trumpet) / Fennell (conductor) / Mercury SRI–75099

Valdres March is concert fare, though no laws are being broken if one marches to it rather than only listens. Really very good, with a spirit of folk song permeating the contrastive trio portion.

Jan Hanuš *(1915-   )*

Symphony No. 2 in G major, Op. 26

Orchestra

☐ Czech Philharmonic Orchestra / Ančerl (conductor) / Serenus 12046

The spirit of Dvořák is very strong in Hanuš's four-movement Symphony, completed in 1951. The tonal orderliness and rhythmic flow in the first movement, the *Spindle* Dance outlines in the Molto vivace, and the folksy theme on which variations are rung in the finale are all evidence. There is more.

It's nice to hear neo-Dvořákian music, especially in the beautiful way it is presented here.

The Czech Year for Chorus of Treble Voices and Small Orchestra, Op. 24

Choral

☐ Chamber Ensemble of the Czech Philharmonic Orchestra and Prague Radio Symphony and Jan Kühn Children's Choir / Šidlo (piano) / Kühn (conductor) / Serenus 12047

*Chorus
and Orchestra*

The four seasons: *Spring, Summer, Autumn,* and *Winter,* are celebrated by a variety of folk texts. Gentle and gay for the most part, the music has an engaging tonal simplicity; no lushness at any time and no disturbing musical fluorescence. Music of such description holds warm promise for a listener. It is fully provided by a fine performance; the voices of the choir are of excellent (and delightful) substance.

John Harbison (1938-   )

Orchestra

Confinement (1965)

☐ Contemporary Chamber Ensemble / Weisberg (conductor) / Nonesuch 71221

Various shapes are tightly blocked in and contrasted with looser ones in *Confinement.* Through the use of a very tensile blend of instrumentation the music has homogeneous totality. All of it adds up to attractive, civilized contemporary music, valid if not highly original.

A well-turned-out performance.

Carter Harman (1918-   )

Choral

Chorus Alone

A Hymn to the Virgin (1956)

☐ Randolph Singers / Randolph (conductor) / Composers Recordings 102 (monaural)

This short work is by the major domo of Composers Recordings. No nepotism—it certainly deserves discing and is neatly organized in a duple-layered manner: three voices (soprano, alto, and bass) sing a background for the principal material by another soprano and a tenor.

Arthur Harris (1927-   )

Chamber Music

Four Moods for Brass Quintet

☐ Metropolitan Brass Quintet / Crystal S-208

This work consists of a Chorale setting of *Komm Süsser Tod,* a *Waltz,* followed by a *Lyric Piece,* and a *Finale.* The music is nicely brushed with refined dissonance. The Metropolitan five play with spirit and a nice sense of style.

Donald Harris (1931-   )

Chamber Music

Fantasy for Violin and Piano (1957)

☐ Zukofsky (violin); Kalish (piano) / Composers Recordings S-307

Harris describes his objective as "lyric and romantic." That it is, in an expressionistic sense combined with serial technique. Despite the many changes of tempi and moods the duo narrative is direct. Its performance is likewise.

Roy Harris *(1898-1979)*

Elegy and Dance (1958)

Orchestra

☐ Portland Junior Symphony / Avshalomov (conductor) / Composers Recordings 140 (monaural)

Harris defines his binary work as putting forth "dream" music and "action" music. Melodic temper is paramount and the sonorous combinations are of discreet pungency. This harmonic piquancy is a colored ingredient within Harris's usual open-breathed, strongly lyrical statements. Avshalomov's young musicians provide a workmanlike job.

Epilogue to Profiles in Courage: JFK (1964)

☐ Louisville Orchestra / Whitney (conductor) / Louisville S-666

Because of its resemblance to portions of Harris's famous third symphony the thought persists that that work must have been permanent and enduring in Roy Harris's mind. Nevertheless, the piece is of interest exactly because of its similarity of conception.

Only a poor performance would make this resemblance a liability. Fortunately, though Whitney's rendition is not fully contrasted in dynamic relationships, the playing provides a good scale of color and linear detail for effective results.

Kentucky Spring (1949)

☐ Louisville Orchestra / Whitney (conductor) / Louisville 602 (monaural)

The format is Scherzo, but a strict symmetry is not followed. The usual Harris sonic fullness is found here.

Symphony 1933

☐ Boston Symphony Orchestra / Koussevitzky (conductor) / Columbia Special Products AML-5095 (monaural)

Harris's "1933" work was never quite such a success as Harris's later symphonies; the composer's grasp of form was too studied, the orchestration somewhat dull. However, the very roughness (crudeness) of Harris's unpolished musical speech has an individual appeal and is worth anyone's listening time. Further, the seed of the later symphonies can be recognized in this work.

Based on the importance of the above, one must overlook the sound of this LP transfer from a very old recording.

Symphony No. 3 (1938)

☐ New York Philharmonic / Bernstein (conductor) / Columbia MS-6303

This is *the* great contribution of the composer. There is practically unanimous opinion that this Symphony will be one of the works that will last through the centuries. Depth of meaning, expressive power, glowing orchestration, all are contained in musical discourse that has a completely individual sound. Yet the music is of such consequence that very few listeners will remain unmoved. Make no mistake—Harris does not seek the popular path in this one-movement composition; no unconditional surrender to academic rules is made, nor any other concession.

This is one of Bernstein's most inspired performances. There is a spontaneity and a flowing connection between the tragic, lyric, pastoral, and dramatic situations in the work that represent re-creation in its most telling sense. It is truly beautifully conducted and executed.

Symphony No. 5 (1943)

☐ Louisville Orchestra / Whitney (conductor) / Louisville S–655

A step-brother in sound, style, melodic curves, and orchestration to Harris's famed third symphony. Some writers term the three movements a Prelude, Chorale, and Fugue. The published score does not indicate anything other than metronomic speeds for movements 1 and 2, and *Appassionato* for the concluding one. However, the essence of these descriptions does apply to the music.

Louisville's program leaflet (unsigned), although mentioning that the Symphony was composed during World War II, does not indicate that the dedication was "to the heroic and freedom-loving people of our great ally, the Union of Soviet Socialist Republics, as a tribute to their strength in war, their staunch idealism for world peace, their ability to cope with stark materialistic problems of world order without losing a passionate belief in the fundamental importance of the arts." Neither does this dedication appear in the published score. Did Harris change his mind?

Not much attention, actually practically none, has been given the Harris "fifth" since it was premiered by Koussevitzky and the Boston Symphony Orchestra in February 1943. This is rather unbelievable. Although the recording by the Louisvillians is presentable, it is not top class. Harris's work needs a larger orchestra and deeper conductorial research than is exhibited here.

Symphony No. 7 (1952)

☐ Philadelphia Orchestra / Ormandy (conductor) / Columbia Special Products AML–5095 (monaural)

Harris's consistent concern for the polyphonic stimulant may be heard in this huge one-movement work. The initial passacaglia displays the melodic scope peculiar to this composer. As the permutations of the generator are displayed, they reflect the polyphonic devices common to all composers who have utilized the technique. Here, the result is new and daring.

Ormandy's performance, with its clean depiction of the lean score, stands as a definitive version.

Chamber Music

Sonata for Violin and Piano (1942)

☐ Shapiro (violin); Johana Harris (piano) / Contemporary 8012

This is one of Harris's most inspired works. Spontaneity is difficult to achieve in set forms, yet each of the four movements gives the impression of complete freedom with an outpouring of noble themes and a balance between lyricism and virtuosity without negating proper chamber music instrumental equality. A splendid performance by Eudice Shapiro, a consummate artist, and the composer's wife, just as fine a musician.

Trio for Piano, Violin, and Cello (1934)

☐ New England Trio / HNH Records 4070

Rather than in the standard sonata form, the themes are engendered by rhythm, expansion, turns, and twists. This essence of continuity is also found in the slow movement and finale. In the former, Harris illustrates the principle of sustained form, without considering recapitulation even in a semiliteral sense. The latter is a fugue.

It is good to have this recorded performance. The only other edition is an old mono disc released by University of Oklahoma Recordings (their No. 1) which offers only extremely cool-hearted playing and below-par sound qualities.

Three Variations on a Theme (String Quartet No. 2) (1933)

☐ Emerson String Quartet / New World Records NW-218

The theme for the Variations is a two-pitch motive, heard at the beginning of each of the three movements. Each movement is a grand varied development on this musical unit. It is only natural that, with such restricted means, the composer's imagery must be somewhat free and rhapsodic, even though provoked germinally. The woven polyphony is stimulated by counterpointed rhythms; melodic principles stem from the compact thought.

Most string quartet teams bypass Harris. Neither this fine work nor the third quartet, consisting of four preludes and fugues, deserve such disregard. New World is to be thanked for their penetrative decision to record this quartet. The Emerson four acquit themselves with intelligence and insight.

Quintet for Piano and Strings (1936)

☐ Johana Harris (piano); Shapiro and Ross (violins); Schonbach (viola); Lustgarten (cello) / Contemporary 8012

Harris's full-measured involvement with contrapuntal methods is vividly displayed in this large-scaled work, consisting of a Passacaglia, a Cadenza, and a Fugue that are heard without interruption. This virile quintet, both a landmark in Harris's career and one of the most important contemporary examples in the medium, has as the root of all matters a twenty-eight measure opening theme.

The Cadenza (properly this should read "cadenze" since there are four separate ones) develops the Passacaglia theme. There is deliberate use of pyrotechnically ordered virtuosity. This approach is common to much modern chamber music, but not in the sense of cadenza interpolations in the infrapolarities of a work.

The final movement, titled simply Fugue, is actually a double fugue with three subjects. While no triple associations occur (to be called a *real* triple fugue the piece should have a combination of the triple subjects), there are all possible partnerships of two subjects (first and second, then second and third, and finally the first and third).

The functional, architectural lines of Harris's Quintet are laid out to produce creative beauty. In this work there is drama and mastery within a medium that offers symphonicism in a chamber music totality. The performance was recorded under the composer's supervision, so it is authentic. It has fine power and color; the cadenzas are artistically negotiated and only a few pitches are out of focus.

Concerto for Piano, Clarinet, and String Quartet, Op. 2

☐ Basquin (piano); Sobol (clarinet); Webb and Weller (violins); Schulman (viola); Eddy (cello) / Grenadilla GS-1007

Though this work is an early production, it has all the ingredients and means of Harris's later works—his usual long-swept lines and free polyphony. It was this work that catapulted Harris into public prominence, and it still is, a half-century after its composition, a fresh and worthy piece.

The opening Fantasia lives up to its titled freedom. Movement 2 is the Scherzo representative. There is no trio, the two parts of the movement being separated by a Lento (in the uncommon time of $\frac{12}{2}$), with the meter usually shifting and, when it does not, being marked by fluctuating phrase lengths. The clarinet has an important role, colored by the piano working octavially above and below it. The spirit is of the Scherzo, the form is personal.

Although there are monothematic characteristics in the slow movement, the use of imitation is applied to the chromatic vacillation of the movement's main motive. The Finale is a very free fugue, with a long preliminary statement and a development into varying metrical divergencies of the very important short (sixteenth) note in the subject.

The performers represent the Long Island Chamber Ensemble of New York with Lawrence Sobol as its artistic director. They're very good. It has been a very long time since this work was on disc. It's good to have it back again, especially in this well-crafted performance.

Vocal	*Fog*
Voice with Accompaniment	☐ Hanks (tenor); Friedberg (piano) / Duke University Press DWRM–7501 (monaural)

Textual sentiment is relayed by musical parallelism in this song. The tempo is slow, the chordal background is foggy, the vocal line is remote (though sung clearly and nicely by the tenor).

Choral

Symphony No. 4 (*Folksong* Symphony) (1940)

Chorus and Orchestra

☐ Utah Symphony Orchestra and Utah Chorale / Abravanel (conductor) / Angel S–36091

Music for the masses from the masses. Five movements for chorus and orchestra, and a pair of interludes without the voices. The folk melodies are not patchy, spasmodic fragments developed à la textbook, but full and complete, spun out healthily and organically. The orchestral painting is sound, folksy.

A solid performance, with much more polish than presented in the competitive version (by the American Festival Orchestra and Chorus, conducted by Golschmann, on Vanguard S–347). Incidentally, *Schwann* lists the performers on this Vanguard disc incorrectly as Abravanel and the Utah Symphony.

Lou Harrison   *(1917-   )*

Orchestra

Pacifika Rondo

☐ Oakland Youth Orchestra / Colvig (sheng and fang-hsiang); Harrison (miguk piri) / Hughes (conductor) / Desto 6478

The "Pacific Round" is for "an orchestra of Western and Oriental instruments," and the exotica of percussion, wailing Gamelanish, fricative and sibilantic sounds immediately identify the instrumental climate.

Harrison is an original in practically every one of his pursuits and the music he writes follows suit. Thus his seven-part essay embraces reflections of the music of the Chinese Tang Dynasty and old Mexico as well as a remarkable ripoff of twelve-tone sounds and smears to represent *Malamo pri la malpuregaj bomboj* (the title is in Esperanto, like all the others, Harrison being fluent in that language), meaning " A Hatred of the Filthy Bomb."

Each of the other movements refers to a section surrounding or in the Pacific Ocean. Some of the instruments used include a reed mouth organ (sheng), psalteries, one made of steel tubing (fang hsiang), small vertical Indian flutes, slabs of heavy hardwood (pak), etc.

A fascinating array and a fascinating aural rendition by this highly proficient orchestra of high-school students.

Suite for Symphonic Strings

☐ Louisville Orchestra / Whitney (conductor) / Louisville 621 (monaural)

Lou Harrison will always be Lou Harrison. If twelve tones can be used, he uses them, as in parts of this work. If primitivistic mono-theme rotation is viable, he opts to use it, as in this composition. These do not form a pastiche, but are included here in a Suite that rhapsodizes in its various shapes. In the nine movements there are an *Estampie,* a Round, a set of Canonic Variations, a Nocturne, and so on.

Healthy individuality brings rewards. Only strings are used and yet one doesn't miss color variety, since it is built in by harmonic and contrapuntal procedures.

Fine originality is matched by a fine portrayal. Whitney's direction is most convincing.

Canticle No. 1 (1939)

☐ Manhattan Percussion Ensemble / Price (conductor) / Mainstream 5011

Harrison exemplifies percussion composition at the most positive level, meaning that there is tension and release, juxtaposition and opposition, proposition, development, and climax. Above all there is a sensitivity rare to the percussion medium. The work is carried out beautifully by the quintet of performers, who use a total of forty instruments, including such rarities as dragon's mouths (wooden bells without clappers), an Indian rasp (known as a morache), windbell, brake drum, and thundersheet. These give further evidence of Lou Harrison's creative sensitivity.

Song of Queztecoatl (1941)

☐ Brown, Price, Smith, and Colgrass (percussion) / Orion 7276

The bombast that comes to mind when percussion music is mentioned is far from what is written by composers who know their way around the pulsatile mines. Explosive force is simply one element; the free power of glassy and opalescent sounds is a far different matter. It is the last that make Lou Harrison's composition a thrilling percussion experience.

The Song is based on Aztec melodies, set in a persistent sextuple meter. Harrison's instrumentation is offbeat. It includes five each of dragon's mouths, suspended brake drums, and muted brake drums, one each of guiro, windglass, and contrabass drum. The remainder is more traditional: five wood blocks, five bells, sistrums, maracas, five cowbells, rattle, snare drum, triangle, gong, tam tam, and five tom-toms. Of course, the quintal totals of the types listed are far from traditional and afford a pitch range within each of the timbres. (Song of Queztecoatl was originally included in an old Period recording, released with the title *Song Adventure*.)

Suite for Percussion (1940)

☐ Manhattan Percussion Ensemble / Price (conductor) / Composers Recordings S–252

Lou Harrison's percussion music (it embraces a good-sized total) has always been clearly detailed, and in such manner expresses more sophistication in the medium than the large-instrumentated sock 'em and rock 'em school. Further, Harrison does not pursue serialization of simulated pitches (or defined ones for that matter).

Each of the three movements of this work (*Moderato, Slow,* and a *Recitative* linked to a *Moderato allegro*) clearly differentiate its expressive intent by instrumental choice.

Metallic qualities predominate in part 1, temple block clanks and percussive swishes mark the slow movement, and a mix that includes chimelike sounds is used in the finale. (No instrumental list is given on the liner copy, and information concerning the work is limited to the cryptic statement that it "is a late work of his 'San Francisco period.'")

Paul Price's ensemble has always been a first-rate group, despite shifting personnel drawn from students at the Manhattan School of Music. Musical finesse and sensibility are exemplified in this case.

Solo Instrument and Orchestra

Organ

Concerto for Organ with Percussion Orchestra

☐ Los Angeles Percussion Ensemble / Craighead (organ) / Kraft (conductor) / Crystal S-858

Harrison's poetic prosody, flavored by a type of neo-medievalism that he favors, is not only expressive and superbly structured, but also always inventive. The organ is combined with the two generic types of percussion: unpitched (which includes such maculations as wooden drums—very large cubelike instruments suspended from a large rack and a set of large gas cylinder bells) and pitched, the latter covered by a team of piano, glockenspiel, vibraphone, celesta, and tube chimes.

Special points to intrigue the ear are Harrison's tone cluster formations. These, of course, are old-hat in terms of the piano, but fairly new in regard to the organ. The freshness and absoluteness of their ictus expand Harrison's percussion orchestra into tripartite totality.

The performance brings into focus all the moods and special qualities of the score. David Craighead shows himself to be not only a superb technician but also a sensitive artist. The emotional expression of the work as well as its excitement are magnificently achieved.

Violin

Concerto for Violin and Percussion Orchestra (1959)

☐ Los Angeles Percussion Orchestra / Shapiro (violin) / Kraft (conductor) / Crystal S-853

Harrison's *Koncherto por la Violino Kun Perkuta Orkestra* (to use the Esperanto the composer favors) is formally traditional (in the very clear fast-slow-fast three-movement division). Coloristically, both for solo voice and orchestra, it is totally the opposite. The violin only uses three intervallic spans, which give six possible (ascending and descending) moves. The percussion orchestra includes such unique utensils as two different sizes of washtubs, resonated clock coil chimes, five differently pitched coffee cans, muted pipe lengths, etcetera.

Harrison justifies his individuality; celebrating a combination of string-instrument monophony and percussive rhythm, his music sings. Everything works and results in a colorful success. The performance is sensitive, smooth, subtle, and silhouettes the contrastive elements magnificently.

Concerto in Slendro

☐ Daniel Kobialka (violin); Machiko Kobialka and Barbagallo (tack pianos); Jennerjohn (celesta); Marconi and Neff (percussion) / Hughes (conductor) / Desto 7144

The title refers to five-pitched Indonesian modes; gamelanlike sounds mark the style. The accompaniment, as will be noted, is principally tinkly and metallic, with the percussion covering six pitch-simulated triangles, a half-dozen graduated-in-size gongs, four galvanized garbage cans, with claves and iron pipes used by the pianists in the dreamy slow movement.

The playing of this flat-surfaced music is delicately neat and sonorously pure.

Suite for Violin, Piano, and Small Orchestra (1957)

☐ Leopold Stokowski and His Orchestra / Anahid Ajemian (violin); Maro Ajemian (piano) / Stokowski (conductor) / Composers Recordings 114 (monaural)

Music of warmth in its synthesis of western and eastern elements—a codification that can be termed exotic but is without any vulgarization. In all six parts of the Suite Harrison is not indifferent to the matter of making his instrumental lines sing through the most gentle filamented textures.

A duplicate of an old RCA Victor issue (LM-1785), even though this is not mentioned on the record liner. Stokowski's performance, directing a group of two flutes, oboe, piano, celesta, harp, percussion, two cellos, and double bass is neat and nicely shaped. The Ajemian sisters follow suit.

Four Pieces for Harp

☐ Bellows (harp) / Desto 6478

The casualness of this music is to be guessed by the titles: *Serenade for Frank Wigglesworth* (written in a letter to the dedicatee and originally for guitar which Wigglesworth was learning to play), *Beverly's Troubador Piece* (composed at a party for immediate performance), *From Music for Bill & Me* (an example of house-music), and *Avalokiteshvara* (an extract from a larger work).

Everything is simply stated, mostly harpistic monody. The *Troubador* piece is accompanied by tambourine and some other light percussion; bells are combined in *Avalokiteshvara*. Simple but beautifully defined music, reflected in playing of unfailing auditory delight.

Two Pieces for Psaltery

☐ Harrison (psalteries) / Desto 6478

A *Psalter-Sonato*, meaning a "Sonata for Psaltery" (but pocket-size, lasting just two and one-half minutes), and *The Garden at One and a Quarter Moons*. Both provide in full amount the tweak and twang, the glide and glyph, as well as the microtonal melodics that identify this instrument. Who is to argue?

Music for Violin with Various Instruments, European, Asian, African

☐ Bouton (violin) / Desto 6478

Exotic in all three movements, but totally exoteric through the studiedly simple melodic spans of the violin. A great deal is heard over the persistent drone of a specially tuned reed organ. In the Largo (middle) movement, microtonal violin glides add their specific color to the psalteries and quartet of mbiras (African thumb-pianos) used in Harrison's suite.

Non-exoteric is Desto's mix-up on the violin soloist. On the album liner it is Thomas Halpin, on the record label it is William Bouton. (We're crediting the latter as a guess.) No specific acknowledgments are given for the players of the "various instruments."

Suite for Cello and Harp

☐ Barab (cello); Lawrence (harp) / New World Records NW-281 (monaural)

Economy of material makes for a light-weight texture. Harrison slightly colors his work with some xylophonic sounds for the harp and binds it by making a literal repeat of the initial movement as the finale (part 5). The idiom is simplistic, like a monody expanding on and within itself. The effect is fresh, the result one of immediacy.

Seymour Barab and Lucille Lawrence deserve special mention for their playing. Each is a skilled technician (Barab is a fine composer as well) and their partnership displays keen musical understanding. This issue offers splendid aural privileges for the listener.

Vocal

*Voice
and Orchestra*

Four Strict Songs for Eight Baritones and Orchestra (1956)

☐ Louisville Orchestra and Members of the Southern Baptist Theological Seminary Choir / Bingham (baritone) / Whitney (conductor) / Louisville 58-2 (monaural)

These songs are "strict" in the sense that special tuning derived from mathematically pure intervals is used in place of equal temperament, bounded by a specific fivefold scale for each of the songs. These scales are formed on G, E, E flat, and C. The scalic formations are different in every instance—herewith two examples showing the number of semitones between the pitches: 2-2-3-2-3; 4-1-2-4-1.

The text, by Harrison, is innocently direct and powerful, dealing with matters of Holiness, Nourishment, Tenderness, and Splendor, in turn containing references to plants, animals, the heavens, and minerals. A spiritual reverence that eradicates a kinship with rites of any kind covers the work. It is a conception of tender beauty, thrillingly evocative, of telling enchantment that casts a spell from its opening measures.

Whitney's direction of Harrison's work is a sensitive one. The orchestra of strings, two trombones, piano, harp, and percussion (timpani struck with the fingers, a set of water bowls, and maracas) plays expressively, and the singing is fully responsive. There is fine mono sound that fulfills all the requirements of a unique and all-important work.

Harrison and John Cage. *See Cage and Lou Harrison.*

Tibor Harsányi   *(1898-1954)*

*Opera
and Dramatic
Music*

L'Histoire du petit tailleur (1939)

☐ Paris Conservatoire Orchestra / Ustinov (narrator) / Prêtre (conductor) / Angel S-36357

"The Story of the Little Tailor" is a thirteen-part suite for seven instruments and a goodly amount of percussion. It was originally conceived as a background score for marionettes, but it works just as well as a chamber orchestra concert piece with or without the narration.

With Peter Ustinov at the narrator's desk this work is heard at its most colorful advantage. Prêtre's conducting is knowledgeable and nicely colored; the important percussion effects register vividly.

Célestin Harst   *(1698-1776)*

Instrumental

Harpsichord

Suite No. 3 in F major for Harpsichord

☐ Schaeffer (harpsichord) / Musical Heritage Society MHS-792-CC-13

The French school influenced the music of this Benedictine monk as can be heard from its detail. Like Couperin, Harst uses picturesque titles for the movements. Here, for example, movement 2 of the six-part Suite is headed *Le Bon Garçon* (" An Agreeable Young Man"), and movement 5 is termed *La Flatteuse* ("A Beguiling Girl").

Harst found the language of his time and, having located it, copied it neatly and correctly. He shows the probity of a good musical mind. Marc Schaeffer proves to have the same insight. There is a fine sense of nuance in his playing with a strongly controlled feeling for line and rhythm.

Walter Hartley (1927-   )

Concerto for Saxophone and Band (1967)

Solo Instrument and Band

☐ Ithaca College Band / Sinta (saxophone) / Beeler (conductor) / Golden Crest S–4077

Saxophone

This medium has a large play among composers who write for the band. For the most part no dangerous courses have been taken by composers. That's the case here, with contemporary romantic tonalism holding the fort in the three movements. Good playing by the collegians and top-flight soloism by Donald Sinta.

Poem for Tenor Saxophone and Piano

Instrumental

☐ Hemke (tenor saxophone); Granger (piano) / Brewster 1204

Saxophone

Romanticism that has immediate accessibility is heard in this case. Ternary format, with suave lines predominating. Golden-brown tone color from Hemke, whose purity of playing is impressive and masterly.

Orpheus

Chamber Music

☐ Annapolis Brass Quintet / Crystal S–206

A fine "white" sound covers this fully tonal piece conceived as a madrigal. Not knowing the composer's name one would never guess it wasn't from the fifteenth century. It is played with clarity, balance, and expressive euphony.

Hamilton Harty / *Georg Frideric Handel.* See *Handel* / Harty.

Johann Adolph Hasse (1699-1783)

Concerto in G major for Mandolin and Orchestra

Solo Instrument and Orchestra

☐ Heidelberg Chamber Orchestra / Thomas (mandolin) / CMS/Oryx 40

Mandolin

The outer fast movements are cut to scale, but the Largo is a real inspiration, with significant depth inculcated with the minor-key procedure. One might say that with this work a minor talent found its proper *métier*.

Sonata in D minor, Op. 1, No. 11

Chamber Music

☐ Rampal (flute); Veyron-Lacroix (harpsichord) / Everest 3180

The tempos here can be questioned. The *un poco vivace* is paced rather moderately and the *arioso* rather quickly. However, both the tone quality and the ensemble are unquestionably good.

Alphonse Hasselmans (1845-1912)

Instrumental

Harp

Will-o'-the-Wisp (Follets)

☐ McDonald (harp) / Klavier KS–525

Musically, a half of a bonbon, but technically, as an exhibit of *bisbigliando* technique on the harp, well worth the little over two minutes' listening time. McDonald tosses it off with satiny sleekness.

Hans Leo Hassler (1564-1612)

Choral

Chorus Alone

Cantate Domino

O Aufenthalt meins Lebens

☐ Canby Singers / Canby (conductor) / Nonesuch 71115

Light but completely expressive singing. The quality is enhanced by excellent diction.

Mein Lieb will mit mir kriegen

☐ Accademia Monteverdiana / Stevens (conductor) / Nonesuch 71272

''My Love Will Wage War upon Me'' is for eight-part unaccompanied chorus. It is sung with pitch exactitude, excellent balance, and stylistic sweetness.

Johann Wilhelm Hässler (1747-1822)

Instrumental

Piano,
Three Hands

Sonata in C major for Three Hands

☐ List and Kirkpatrick (piano) / Musical Heritage Society MHS–733

Straightforward and patterned classic style, covering one movement (Allegro). However, an added novelty commands attention. The music requires two players, one using only one hand, which plays the uppermost voice.

Roman Haubenstock-Ramati (1919-   )

Instrumental

Flute

Interpolation, Mobile for Flute (1, 2, and 3) (1958)

☐ Gazzelloni (flute) / RCA VICS–1312

Haubenstock-Ramati's short piece is here performed by Gazzelloni playing together with Gazzelloni, by the superimposition of previously recorded sections. The key word in the title is ''mobile''; it immediately describes the aleatoric condition of the music. There are six melodic hunks (a classier word is ''formants'') to be performed according to certain rules and score directions. These are then mixed with realizations of the same half-dozen items by a second and then a third flutist, or two can cover for the total of three; or, still more insular, one flutist can play all three "solutions," as is the case with this recorded version.

Whereas one performer is more economical, this does not give as free a conduct of the music as when three are concerned. But in the long run it really doesn't matter. Gazzelloni playing all three parts is a wealthy dose of Gazzelloni, and who is to quibble with this decision, considering his phenomenal ability?

Charles Haubiel   (1892-1978)

Pioneers—A Symphonic Saga (1956)   *Orchestra*

☐ Hamburg Philharmonia Orchestra / Walther (conductor) / Orion 75197

A type of folkloric, homespun entry. (Haubiel wrote *Pioneers* in 1946 and totally revised the work ten years later.) The nine connected sections draw on Catholic chants (in the portion titled *Father Marquette*), American Indian melodies (expectedly covering such designations as *Scalp Dance* and *The Peace Pipe*), plus Ohioan folk songs (used in four movements).

Fair performance and fair sound for this fair music.

Portraits for Symphony Orchestra (1935)

☐ Hamburg Philharmonia Orchestra / Walther (conductor) / Orion 74143

These Portraits were originally for solo piano, than orchestrated by the composer. Three friends of Haubiel are sketched in personalities equivalent to a *Capriccio,* an *Idillio,* and a Scherzo. All very nice people they turn out to be, all of romantic disposition and tonally polite.

Elves Spinning   *Instrumental*

Noche en España   *Piano*

☐ Kramer (piano) / Orion 7261

A delicate Scherzo (can elves move other than delicately?) and a neat Spanish imitation with proper, moderately lively pace.

Metamorphoses (Variations on *Swanee River* by Stephen Foster) (1948)

☐ Dowis (piano) / Orion 75188

This is one of those variational anthologies that touch base with stylistic imitations of assorted composers. The greatest fun is to see whether you can guess the composer without following the score card supplied by liner note data. Haubiel does fairly well with such as Hucbald, Bach, Mozart, Wagner, and Gershwin. The style samplings total twenty-nine, representing nine periods from the Medieval right through to the Americans (Ellington and Gershwin).

Orion, again, is guilty of a puzzling production. On the record label the spelling is "Swanee," on the liner notes it is "Suwannee," and on the cover one guesses that the *Old Folks at Home* (sometimes referred to as *Swanee Ribber*) theme is used since it says, "Variations on a Theme by Stephen Foster." It shouldn't be necessary to check bibliographical tools (which are not always easily available) for the authentic title of a work or its proper spelling.

Chamber
Music

Sonata in C minor for Cello and Piano (1944)

☐ Mannucci (cello); Haubiel (piano) / Orion 74165

Classical designs—sonata, song form, and rondo—are used by Haubiel but his language is expressively romantic. The growth and unity of each part of the work are nicely detailed by the performers.

Herbert Haufrecht   *(1909-   )*

String
Orchestra

Square Set (1941)

☐ Orchestra of the Accademia Nazionale di Santa Cecilia, Roma / Antonini (conductor) / Composers Recordings 111 (monaural)

Here is a Reel, followed by a *Clog Dance,* which has some pepper dusted on the harmonies, a bit of raggedy jazz, and some wood block ictus. The finale is a *Jig Tune.*

Excellent stylization of square dance musical data. Though one won't hear country fiddlin', banjo twangs, and the like, Haufrecht's string instrument realization of square dance formations fully avoids "squareness."

Joseph Haydn   *(1732-1809)*

Orchestra

German Dances

☐ Academy of St. Martin-in-the-Fields / Marriner (conductor) / Argo 5498

These half-dozen Dances from the goodly number that Haydn produced are played deftly and graciously.

German Dances

No. 4 in C major / No. 10 in C major / No. 11 in F major

☐ Orchestra of the Vienna Volksoper / Angerer (conductor) / Turnabout 34156

The entry discussed *above* covers six of the dozen *Deutsche Tänze* Haydn composed. If that's too many, this set of three is just as good and of undoubted performance.

Menuetti Ballabili, Nos. 1 and 14, Hob. IX/7

☐ Vienna State Opera Orchestra / Angerer (conductor) / Nonesuch 71141

There is balance in Angerer's performance choice of the first and last of a set of Minuets *ballabili* ("for dancing"). Since minuets are not being danced anymore, one can enjoy them as light concert music. Very nicely played.

Nocturne

In C major / In G major (Excerpt)

☐ Chamber Orchestra of the Sarre / Ristenpart (conductor) / Nonesuch 71024

These are two of the eight Nocturnes Haydn composed, the C major opus in three movements and the other represented by two of its movements (a Presto and an Andante). They are neatly published here and every Haydn lover should have them.

Overture in D major (Hob. Ia, No. 7)

☐ Academy of St. Martin-in-the-Fields / Marriner (conductor) / London STS–15172

The D major Overture is often heard as the finale to Haydn's Symphony No. 53 (*L'Impériale*) in D major (*see below*). The music rolls off the instruments with delightful pace.

Overture to *Acide e Galatea*

☐ Academy of St. Martin-in-the-Fields / Marriner (conductor) / Argo 5498

This Overture is like a miniature three-part symphony. The blend of the oboes, horns, and strings is significant. The playing a stylistic delight.

Overture to an English Opera

☐ Little Orchestra of London / Jones (conductor) / Nonesuch 71197

This Overture is also known as the Introduction to the Haydn opera *L'anima del Filosofo*. This is a stylish performance, with the Allegro held at a reliable pace to bring out all the flavors of the work.

Overture to *L'isola disabitata*

☐ Orchestra of the Vienna Festival / Janigro (conductor) / Vanguard 703/4

A discriminating viewpoint that gives proper proportions to Haydn's Overture. Best of all is the pace that defines the cohesiveness of this fine orchestral prelude.

Overture to *Lo Speziale*

☐ Vienna State Opera Orchestra / Goberman (conductor) / Odyssey 32160006

Italian overture form is used for this Overture. The music is in two fast sections (*presto*-tempoed) that embrace a slow (*andante*) section. Goberman's tempi levels are acute and the music swings along with a natural impact.

Overture to the Opera *Armida*

☐ Little Orchestra of London / Jones (conductor) / Nonesuch 71032

Music that is cozily appealing. Jones eliminates any great dynamic differences between the sections, though some consideration is given in terms of tempo.

The Seven Last Words of Christ

☐ Little Orchestra of London / Jones (conductor) / Nonesuch 71154

The Seven Last Words of Christ was composed for performance in the Cádiz Cathedral to serve as the musical interludes between the bishop's seven sermons, delivered as part of the Good Friday proceedings. An *Introduzione* is followed by seven Sonatas in *lento, grave, adagio,* and *largo* tempi, and a concluding *Il Terremoto* ("The Earthquake"). Admittedly, the last part is a little naïve. Haydn then made a string quartet transcription (see under *Chamber Music*, p. 803) and later a choral version.

Notwithstanding a lack of intrinsic contrast in the score, Jones manages to emphasize whatever relative minute values are within it. This provides eloquence even if it is subdued.

Symphonies — *Special Versions*

"A" in B flat major / "B" in B flat major / No. 22 (*The Philosopher*) in E flat major (*second version*) / No. 53 (*L'Impériale*) in D major (*three alternate finales*) / No. 63 (*La Roxolane*) in C major (*first version*) / No. 103 (*Drumroll*) in E flat major (*alternate finale*)

☐ Philharmonia Hungarica / Dorati (conductor) / London STS–15316/7

The importance of Antal Dorati's survey of the entire Haydn symphonies is obvious. His performances are of high caliber and as integral sets (in nine volumes on the London label, five of which include six discs each, and four covering eight-record sides each) will not disappoint. (Three of these collections are included in the discussions of the Haydn symphonies—*see below*.)

However, the most important point of Dorati's project is an "extra" (tenth) album of "Appendices" totaling four-record sides. The material in that volume is detailed above. Notwithstanding the fact that the primary value is musicological, the secondary values are not to be overlooked, especially the pair of Symphonies without specific number.

Symphony

No. 1 in D major / No. 2 in C major

☐ Vienna State Opera Orchestra / Goberman (conductor) / Odyssey 32160006

These are appetizers for the great symphonies that would follow. Though not overserious in his approach, Goberman does not play down the works but strikes a fine balance.

The rhythmic pointing in the first work is ideal and that includes the slow movement. In the C major opus the special way the *Andante* is proportioned removes a stolidity that would otherwise prevail. Indeed, keen conductorial scholarship is at work here.

Symphony No. 3 in G major

☐ Little Orchestra of London / Jones (conductor) / Nonesuch 71096

Light-scaled but far from flimsy, this Symphony presents its best event in the pleasingly expressive Andante moderato movement, which flows deftly under Jones's direction. Jones also knows how to pace and phrase the Menuetto to bring clarity to its canonic arrangement.

Symphony

No. 4 in D major / No. 5 in A major

☐ Vienna State Opera Orchestra / Goberman (conductor) / Odyssey 32160034

These performances of simplicity and breadth match the contents. It is true that the sound quality is better in Dorati's presentation (on London STS–15310/15), but certainly Haydn's manner and allure are at the highest level in these Goberman-directed performances.

Symphony

No. 6 (*Le Matin*) in D major / No. 7 (*Le Midi*) in C major / No. 8 (*Le Soir*) in G major

☐ Prague Chamber Orchestra / Klee (conductor) / Deutsche Grammophon 2530591

Haydn's symphonic trilogy evocative of the hours 'round the clock ("Morning," "Noon," and "Night") have many scoring delights including violin and cello concertante parts in *Le Matin,* and two violin and cello concertante parts in *Le Midi* and *Le Soir.*

There is competition aplenty (Dorati [on London STS–15310/15], Böttcher [on Turnabout 34150], Ristenpart [on Nonesuch 71015], and Goberman [Odyssey 32160034]). All offer definite values, to be sure, and there is no need to indicate any prefatory warning as to interpretative mishaps. Goberman's renditions are especially sensitive. However, there is a suppleness to Klee's presentations, together with superb sound, that give him the nod. Plenty of spirit, too.

Symphony No. 12 in E major

☐ Little Orchestra of London / Jones (conductor) / Nonesuch 71083

Compact, as Haydn's early symphonies tended to be (Jones's playing time is twelve minutes flat), this Symphony is played with snapped confidence and is right on the button in phrasing and tone. This is a finer-grained definition than Goberman displays in the competitive disc on Odyssey 32160116.

Symphony No. 13 (*Jupiter*) in D major

☐ Little Orchestra of London / Jones (conductor) / Nonesuch 71121

Four horns in place of the usual pair swell the sonority, and Jones takes advantage of the enlargement with a performance of sonorous energy and clear-cut distinctions. An alive, stimulating presentation, offering the specialness of hearing Haydn's use (in the Finale) of the same four-note figure that Mozart immortalized in *his Jupiter* symphony.

Symphony

No. 20 in C major / No. 21 in A major / No. 22 (*The Philosopher*) in E flat major / No. 23 in G major / No. 24 in D major / No. 25 in C major / No. 26 (*Lamentatione*) in D minor / No. 27 in G major / No. 28 in A major / No. 29 in E major / No. 30 (*Alleluja*) in C major / No. 31 (*Horn Signal*) in D major / No. 32 in A major / No. 33 in C major / No. 34 in D minor / No. 35 in B flat major

☐ Philharmonia Hungarica / Dorati (conductor) / London STS–15257/62

Once again, listening to these symphonies elicits the persistent desire to query our conductors as to why, oh why, they play the very same few Haydn symphonies. There isn't a single work among the sixteen listed above that doesn't deserve programming. For the home listener there is no need, of course, to fret. He can obtain every single Haydn symphony if he so wishes (all are recorded) and let futility surround the concertgoer who is captive to someone else's choice of what he can hear.

The variety here is constant, regardless of the structural parallels. The snappy fun that subtly carries the Minuet in Symphony No. 28, the festive brilliance that surrounds the *Alleluja* Symphony, the virtuosity of the horn quartet within the *Horn Signal* Symphony, the vibrant colorations in Symphony No. 33 are but a few samples. Several dozens more could be given.

Not only are the performances that Dorati directs splendid, but they bring a chain reaction, so that hearing one work urges the listener to hear the next one, and so on. Rarely has performance of a group of works of chronological succession been without some flaw. In this set one can be hard put to find even minor imperfections.

Symphony No. 21 in A major

☐ Chamber Orchestra of the Saar / Ristenpart (conductor) / Nonesuch 71101

Ristenpart understands this symphonic drama and he understands how to play the Haydn game. The opening Adagio pulses onward and yet is never hurried, the following Presto and later the Finale swing out and away, but every point of sound is gathered in and concentrated. This is a vivid Symphony that is brought on stage with invigorating freshness—in great part due to Ristenpart's rare sense of the exact pace required. Beautiful sound quality from the orchestra.

Symphony No. 22 (*The Philosopher*) in E flat major

☐ Vienna State Opera Orchestra / Goberman (conductor) / Odyssey 32160374

There is an unconventional view at work here, with the use of a pair of English horns instead of the customary oboes and an initial slow rather than a moderately fast movement. Played with plenty of fine vitality; when the poetic touch is required it is applied.

Symphony No. 26 (*Lamentatione*) in D minor

☐ Little Orchestra of London / Jones (conductor) / Nonesuch 71083

One hears strong music in movement 1 powered by syncopations, choralish in the Adagio, and a releasing of the mood in the final *Menuett.* A performance of high order throughout.

Symphony No. 29 in E major

☐ Little Orchestra of London / Jones (conductor) / Nonesuch 71121

The best part of this Symphony is the last half, from the trio of the *Menuet* through the Finale (a *presto*-tempoed matter, naturally). Jones's orchestra responds magnificently to his shaping of the music, a shaping that is most assured.

Including Haydn's Symphony No. 13 (*Jupiter*) in D major and Symphony No. 64 in A major, this issue of Symphony No. 29 is indeed most impressive.

Symphony No. 34 in D minor

☐ Little Orchestra of London / Jones (conductor) / Nonesuch 71106

A critic has the right to his subjective opinions, but the statement that this Symphony covers "emotionally pretentious music" (made by C. G. Burke, whom this writer fully respects) cannot be accepted. On the other hand, Edward Tatnall Canby describes the Symphony as a "suave, eloquent work." My full vote goes to the illustrious Mr. Canby. From the opening Adagio to the closing Presto assai this is certainly eloquent music. It is performed with certainty and a fine devotion to detail.

Symphony No. 35 in B flat major

☐ Little Orchestra of London / Jones (conductor) / Nonesuch 71131

The sun shines very bright in this Symphony. In the slow movement Haydn sings quietly; there is not the slightest hint of *Sturm-und-Drang* atmosphere. The finale is marked by motile figurations, colored and punctuated by chordal material that "kicks" the music. Jones's application of differing weights in this movement exemplifies fine interpretative sense. Elsewhere there is total stylistic perceptivity and splendid Haydnesque discipline. Nowhere is there anything but splendid orchestral sound and playing.

Symphony No. 39 (*The Fist*) in G minor

☐ Little Orchestra of London / Jones (conductor) / Nonesuch 71096

An affirmatively crafted performance. Particularly, Jones provides the proper dramatic depiction of the opening movement, which has been considered the model for Mozart's "little G minor" symphonic opus (No. 25). It is the concentrated scope of the thematic material of this movement that has given rise to the nickname of *The Fist* for Haydn's work.

Symphony No. 43 (*Mercury*) in E flat major

☐ Academy of St. Martin-in-the-Fields / Marriner (conductor) / Philips 9500159

The remarkably deft and solid classicism of this performance makes this a prime representation of the work. Every part of the music is detailed with the fullest understanding.

Symphony No. 44 (*Trauer*) in E minor

☐ English Chamber Orchestra / Barenboim (conductor) / Deutsche Grammophon 2530708

This performance offers a meaningful tempo selection and a marvelous tonal quality. Barenboim convinces in all aspects, with stress and positiveness that underline the emotive depth of the Symphony.

Symphony No. 45 (*Farewell*) in F sharp minor

☐ Zagreb Radio Symphony Orchestra / Janigro (conductor) / Vanguard 703/4

Not being cut to an exact pattern, the *Farewell* has the elusiveness of a mystery. Most of the stories about this Symphony have a central point but few have the more important formal moral that Haydn drew from the shaping of his extremely individual opus. The final movement only is necessary to documentate this highly individual method of the composer. The ending of this movement is a listener's reward.

Responsive and expert playing. A decidedly fine version. (Jones conducting the Little Orchestra of London, on Nonesuch 71031, is an excellent second choice.)

Symphony No. 47 (*The Palindrome*) in G major

☐ Philharmonia Hungarica / Dorati (conductor) / London STS–15249/54

Currently, Dorati's performance in the third volume (twelve record sides) of the entire sequence of Haydn's symphonies is the only one available. A finely-wrought performance it is, as are the others (the album covers Symphonies 36–48).

If Philips 839796 can be found (Raymond Leppard conducting the English Chamber Orchestra; the other works are Symphonies 22 and 39), economy is served and a fine performance is obtained.

Symphony No. 48 (*Maria Theresia*) in C major

☐ Academy of St. Martin-in-the-Fields / Marriner (conductor) / Philips 9500200

There's more pomp in the circumstances of this work than is commonly found in the Haydn symphonies (a visit of Maria Theresia, Holy Roman Empress and ruler of Hungary, to Esterház was the stimulant for the Symphony's production). There are, of course, contrastive data, but it is to Marriner's credit that he strikes a sensitive balance between the two elements. Sure-fire playing.

Symphony No. 49 (*La Passione*) in F minor

☐ English Chamber Orchestra / Barenboim (conductor) / Deutsche Grammophon 2530708

Like Leslie Jones (on Nonesuch 71032), Barenboim pairs this Symphony with Haydn's forty-fourth Symphony (*see above*). Jones also includes the Overture to *Armida* (*see above*). Though quantity gives Jones the edge, the edge moves over to Barenboim in regard to quality. He provides the music's energy in full but offers it with a neat refinement that makes him the winner. Deutsche Grammophon's sound means additional percentage points. It is of rich, glowing texture.

Symphony No. 53 (*L'Impériale*) in D major

☐ Academy of St. Martin-in-the-Fields / Marriner (conductor) / Philips 6500114

Pace and precision are all one would want, and the scale is beautifully proportioned by Marriner. The Andante moves and doesn't languish. There are three finales for the work and Marriner chooses the second one, also known as an Overture in D major. This piece is also available on a separate recording (*see above*).

Symphony No. 54 in G major

☐ Little Orchestra of London / Jones (conductor) / Nonesuch 71106

The performance problem for this Symphony rests with the Adagio, as lengthy as movements 3 and 4 combined. Jones manages fairly well, though some neutrality in handling the dynamic situations does make the music drag. Indeed, a rare minus sign in the many first-rate performances of Haydn's symphonies Jones has placed on disc. However, his handling of the balance of the work cannot be criticized.

Symphony No. 55 (*The Schoolmaster*) in E flat major

☐ Academy of St. Martin-in-the-Fields / Marriner (conductor) / Philips 9500198

Where suavity and suppleness constitute the name of Haydn's symphony game, it is so covered, and where there should be flair it is likewise fully accomplished. A beautiful Haydn experience in all respects.

Symphony

No. 57 in D major / No. 58 in F major / No. 59 (*Fire*) in A major / No. 60 (*Il Distratto*) in C major / No. 61 in D major / No. 62 in D major / No. 63 (*La Roxolane*) in C major / No. 64 in A major

☐ Philharmonia Hungarica / Dorati (conductor) / London STS–15131/4

Haydn's Symphony No. 60 has the unusual format of six movements, otherwise four-movement plan prevails in this group of eight Symphonies. No. 60 has a delightful finale, set in *prestissimo* tempo, which illustrates Haydn's musical wit. This fact doesn't escape Dorati's interpretation which is of responsive understanding throughout. His minute tempo differentiation is marvelous—compare this *prestissimo* with the *presto* conclusion in the F major opus. A further plus is Dorati's adherence to minuet speed stipulations rather than conceiving of them as disguised scherzi. The effective and strong dynamic differentiations that are employed in Symphony No. 62 are also treated with the utmost sensitivity. This is a set of five-star performances.

Symphony No. 59 (*Fire*) in A major

☐ Academy of St. Martin-in-the-Fields / Marriner (conductor) / Philips 9500159

Marriner's total commitment invites a committed response. This is great Haydn in every respect. Tempi move forward, not necessarily fast but fluid, and that makes Haydn sing with charm.

Symphony No. 61 in D major

☐ Little Orchestra of London / Jones (conductor) / Nonesuch 71168

Meticulous care was taken in shaping the materials, all devoted to delivering the essence of this fine work. A cohesive yet transparent performance is the result.

Symphony No. 63 (*La Roxolane*) in C major

☐ Little Orchestra of London / Lester (harpsichord) / Jones (conductor) / Nonesuch 71197

This is perceptive Haydn playing, especially in the variations which unfold with cogency. Although the *prestissimo* finale is not taken at that speed, the performance clearly displays all the details that distressingly are passed by when the tempo designation is considered too literally. Totally competitive with the Dorati performance on London STS-15131/4 (*see above*).

Symphony No. 64 in A major

☐ Little Orchestra of London / Jones (conductor) / Nonesuch 71121

Well-tooled playing and a well-toured, four-part consideration of Haydn's fluent work. The Largo is quiet and restrained but its tempo never gets dragged into the area of inertia. The full-scale *presto* finale is not so quick-triggered that the definition of sounds and shapes gives way to mere pace.

Symphony No. 70 in D major

☐ English Chamber Orchestra / Leppard (conductor) / Philips 6500194

This Symphony has four movements, as usual, but the slow movement has unusual content. It consists of a quiet processional music designed in double counterpoint, a technical trick that can be mastered but does not often result in real musical meaning. Trust Haydn, of course.

The performance validity cannot be questioned. Leppard's handling of the contrapuntalism (not only in the slow movement) is ideal in balance, contrast, and meaning.

Symphony No. 73 (*La Chasse*) in D major

☐ Philharmonia Hungarica / Dorati (conductor) / London STS-15182/5

For the best extant recorded performance the choice is certainly Dorati. However, in order to obtain his edition of the Symphony, one is captive to purchasing London's four-record set. Only in England (on the Decca Ace of Diamonds label) is the *La Chasse* Symphony available separately (coupled with Symphony No. 74). However, all of the Dorati performances in the set (Symphonies 73–81) are splendid and there is no gamble involved.

No. 73 is available, together with Haydn's third and thirty-ninth symphonies, on Nonesuch 71096, played by the Little Orchestra of London, conducted by Leslie Jones. Whereas Jones has produced fine recorded performances of these and other Haydn symphonies, the playing of the *La Chasse* is pedestrian in the first three-quarters of the piece. In the finale, matters are reversed and the brass picturesqueness of the score (originally used by Haydn as a prelude to a hunting scene in an opera, hence the cognomen *La Chasse* ["The Hunt"]) triggers ripe and bright playing.

Symphony No. 75 in D major

☐ Little Orchestra of London / Jones (conductor) / Nonesuch 71106

A fine, alert performance. As usual with this conductor, everything is appropriate stylistically. The dynamic contrasts are sharp and the tutti resonances always solid, never blatant; the wind blend (Haydn uses flute, two oboes, and two bassoons) is excellently balanced.

Symphony No. 77 in B flat major

☐ Little Orchestra of London / Jones (conductor) / Nonesuch 71168

Beautiful realization of Haydn style, fluent and with precise attention to all details. Jones emphasizes the warmth in this music, which is filled with a Haydn temper that is powerful yet orderly.

Symphony No. 78 in C minor

☐ Little Orchestra of London / Lester (harpsichord) / Jones (conductor) / Nonesuch 71197

Some may consider the Adagio a trifle fast but one must agree with Jones's tempo decision. The music takes on a subtle propulsion that is most stimulating. All the other movements are finely graded as to dynamics, tempi, and phrasing.

Symphony No. 80 in D minor

☐ Philharmonia Hungarica / Dorati (conductor) / London STS-15182/5

A critic once described this Symphony as "mixing bubbles and forebodings, suavity and prankishness." Good prose and an excellent description. If one wishes these elements to be present in a recorded performance, only Dorati supplies it in one of his big albums covering Haydn's entire output of symphonies.

Jones, who is represented a good number of times in this Haydn chapter, strikes out in this case. The playing in the first movement (the Symphony is on Nonesuch 71131) is patently out of tune and the tempi is neither *allegro* nor *spirituoso*. The Adagio has no dimension and the *Menuetto* is heavy and tired. Only the Finale has proper range but by that time it's too late.

Symphony

No. 82 (*L'Ours*) in C major / No. 83 (*La Poule*) in G minor / No. 84 in E flat major / No. 85 (*La Reine*) in B flat major / No. 86 in D major / No. 87 in A major

☐ Philharmonia Hungarica / Dorati (conductor) / London STS-15229/34

These are the *Paris* symphonies, so termed because they were written for production in France. That explains the French nicknames as well.

The first work illustrates the fine artistic disciplines that will be found throughout. Dorati's sharply defined performance of "The Bear" has vigor and is sensitive to the textural changes that mark the Symphony. Let not the auditor be confused by the fancy nickname assigned this work. There is no programmatic intent. Nonetheless the pedal insistence that brought the cognomen to be fastened to the piece is drawn and quartered properly.

"The Hen" has rhythmic firmness, and Dorati opts for a breadth in his tempi that does not deny the form and meaning of the music. Similar rhythmic virtues and a coloristic cogency make the Symphony No. 84 totally successful.

Haydn's music is monumental by way of its simplicity and genuineness. Symphony No. 86, rarely performed (what reasons can our conductors supply?), is no smattering of trivia. The performance here, like those of the other works in this edition, is completely profitable, played with power and intelligence. Never is the art of Haydn short-changed—its wit, its homophonic gaiety, its refreshing musical manners are all beautifully depicted. There is brilliance, excitement, and marvelous musicality in the playing of all six symphonies.

A second choice representing fine performances, if at times a bit too refined, in the fast-paced movements is on Nonesuch 73011, with the Little Orchestra of London, conducted by Leslie Jones. The production throughout is characteristically clean.

Symphony No. 85 (*La Reine*) in B flat major

☐ Academy of St. Martin-in-the-Fields / Marriner (conductor) / Philips 9500200

This performance is beautifully paced and beautifully shaped. What is most apparent is Marriner's insight into Haydn's symphonic structuring. He does not centralize his interpretation and emphasize sections. The performance flows. It is as though the materials were created together and not merely fitted together. And within is a constant aliveness regardless of tempo. This is a stunning performance.

Symphony No. 88 in G major

☐ Vienna Philharmonic Orchestra / Böhm (conductor) / Deutsche Grammophon 2530343

The music is paced clearly and naturally. All the detail is immaculately projected, and that's what is needed to display the eloquence of Haydn's work. The fine points in the Minuet are most impressive, and Böhm doesn't permit the slow movement to lag.

Symphony
No. 90 in C major / No. 91 in E flat major

☐ Esterhazy Orchestra / Blum (conductor) / Vanguard C-10044

Blum doesn't bother with, and thereby emphasizes, the wispiness that darts through the C major Symphony. He is not heavy-handed but neither is he overdelicate. This direct and precise playing is just right. In the E flat major opus the strongest competition is from Böhm (Deutsche Grammophon 2530524), but a bolder Blum is far better than a conservative, too serious Böhm.

Symphony No. 92 (*Oxford*) in G major

☐ Vienna Philharmonic Orchestra / Böhm (conductor) / Deutsche Grammophon 2530524

Haydn's symphonies are so full of freshets of inspiration that only a volume of commentary could do them full justice. The *Oxford* Symphony is one of the perfect gems in the jewel case of Haydn. Its hybrid flow of joy and seriousness require the attention of a disciplined conductor, and as disciplined an orchestra. That combination is here provided to the fullest extent. Böhm's tempi are fitting; the tone of the orchestra is a delight. The style fits the music, and the music fits Haydn's score.

Symphony

No. 93 in D major / No. 94 (*Surprise*) in G major

☐ Cleveland Orchestra / Szell (conductor) / Columbia MS-7006

Both are luminous and strong Symphonies and are presented thus by this master conductor. These recorded editions are models of beautifully interpreted proportions in all facets.

Believe it or not, in this age of know-how it is still fashionable for many conductors to consider Haydn with simple regard, but this disregards the essence of the composer's thought. A damn-the-Papa-Haydn edict could well be a watchword for some conductors. The man had real and intense creative juice—it must emerge in performance. It does in these instances.

Symphony No. 95 in C minor

☐ Cleveland Orchestra / Szell (conductor) / Columbia M-30366

This is, indeed, a Haydn banquet, served by that royal group of orchestral musicians in the Cleveland organization under the *chef d'orchestre*, George Szell himself. There is a continuity of beauty in every movement, and not once is a phrase distorted. In choice of tempi alone, the performance makes the release the definitive one. Quite often Haydn's *allegros* are merely furiously flamboyant instead of being fluidly fast, and the *andantes* are paced to the point of being almost paralyzed. Szell's tempi are so proper that he transforms the well known into discoveries.

Symphony No. 96 (*Miracle*) in D major

☐ London Philharmonic Orchestra / Jochum (conductor) / Deutsche Grammophon 2530420

Jochum's performance with the Londoners can well go to the top of the list. His tempi are correct, with fine motility in the outer movements; his Haydn demeanor is not patronizing; and neither does he consider the composer to be of namby-pamby disposition. The clarity of the voices is precise. Jochum employs the full apparatus, for the sound is of the total variety—no mere fractioned orchestra here!

Symphony

No. 97 in C major / No. 98 in B flat major

☐ Cleveland Orchestra / Szell (conductor) / Columbia M-30646

Szell's ability with Haydn matches his other successes. What brings this ability? It is a simple matter: the mark of the true re-creative artist is the ability to stay within style and not blend varying sources. One bows to the profuse inspiration of a conductor who maintains the inexhaustible attention to all details without permitting one minuscule portion of style change. Following these instructions is the motto of the Cleveland Orchestra. There is no doubt that its performances of these Symphonies are number one on the books.

Symphony

No. 99 in E flat major / No. 100 (*Military*) in G major

☐ London Philharmonic Orchestra / Jochum (conductor) / Deutsche Grammophon 2530459

Jochum's impressive concern for shading, style, and dynamic balance places the Deutsche Grammophon release ahead of all others. The sensitivity of change, requisite to any large-scaled work's performance, is not absent—note well the relaxed feeling of the trio to the Minuet in the E flat major opus and the golden glow that suffuses its slow movement. (Krips portrayal on London [STS–15085] is methodical and lacks the viewpoint of the colorist. Since when was Haydn a study of only black and white and neutral grey?)

No false step, no miscalculated point or direction, and no pedantry in the playing are heard in the *Military* Symphony. Crisp sprightliness most effectively clothes the composition. Other editions are fair to middlin'. In Scherchen's case (Westminster Gold 8134) the orchestra is earthbound; the music is heard as if it were aged with creases.

Symphony No. 101 (*Clock*) in D major

☐ Symphony Orchestra / Reiner (conductor) / RCA AGL1–1275
☐ Vienna State Opera Orchestra / Wöldike (conductor) / Vanguard S–187

Reiner understood classical fashions. All the grace and substance of this work are exhibited in his reading with a pick-up, unnamed orchestra. Fine tempi and an enthusiastic demeanor bring out all the music's tastes. (This is the same issue that originally appeared as LSC–2742.)

Wöldike's version has long been in the catalogue. It deserves its long life. The natural and relaxed performance that he provides has splendid sound as well as perfect tempi choices. Thus it must be emphasized that he reads the *presto* tempo indicated for the opening movement as *presto,* not as a *presto possibile,* which is an interpretative sin so many other conductors enjoy committing.

The above therefore rules out such conductors that have recorded the work as Dorati, Bernstein, von Karajan, Klemperer, Monteux, and Richter. Each has something to say, but none portrays Haydn's great work with the total dimensional quality of Reiner and Wöldike. There is also always the nagging realization that Haydn is number two in the pecking order.

Symphony No. 102 in B flat major

☐ Vienna State Opera Orchestra / Wöldike (conductor) / Vanguard S–211

No color-me-romantic on this conductor's part. This is classical style one hears. Optimum conditions for making great music obtain here, and Wöldike takes advantage accordingly.

Klemperer conducting the New Philharmonia on Angel S–36364 comes close to being the first choice. It is only his too firmly grounded tempi that make that performance second to the earlier-produced Vanguard edition.

Symphony

No. 103 (*Drumroll*) in E flat major / No. 104 (*London*) in D major

☐ London Philharmonic Orchestra / Jochum (conductor) / Deutsche Grammophon 2530525

The introduction to the *Drumroll* Symphony proclaims the thrilling place in symphonic literature this composition holds. The picture is almost gloomy, weighted with sadness; it verges on the tragic. It is a clue to a conductor's ability when he can make this preamble more than heavy, dark, and bass-colored. The performance must intrigue and be related to the severe contrast that follows. Throughout the work Haydn's audacious creative slant makes the work one for only the very special conductors. The only candidate that best fulfills these needs and never falters in a single measure is Eugen Jochum.

Again, it is Jochum who furnishes a magnificent performance of the *London* Symphony. It is true to Haydn, played with tonal beauty, correct style, and pertinent sensitivity. No one does better.

Toy Symphony

☐ Philharmonia Orchestra / von Karajan (conductor) / Angel S–35638

Habit dies slowly. It is now confirmed that the Toy Symphony is part of a larger Leopold Mozart work. On the basis of composer marriage by title and repute the work remains firmly in the Haydn camp. So be it; he deserves the credit.

The number of times this writer has heard this work murdered, the toy instruments (cuckoo, quail, nightingale, toy trumpet [played in rhythmic doubling with a simple drum], rattle, and triangle) sounding like hit and miss, and the strings playing without style cannot be counted. Treating the music as a fun-bash piece for children's and pops concerts is unfair. Expect, therefore, that the fun should come from the special sounds and not from the players' antics or amateurism. In von Karajan's handling of this work, the music is treated respectably and is played with proper gracefulness and gaiety.

Twelve Minuets (Nos. 4, 6, 8, and 12)

☐ Boskovsky Ensemble / Boskovsky (conductor) / Vanguard 2096

Haydn wrote a number of sets of minuets (most of which totaled an even dozen). From one of these, composed in 1792 for a grand ball to be held in the Imperial and Royal *Redoutensaal*, Boskovsky has chosen four (played in an order that makes the final numbered one the second of the set). Though known as the *Redouten* Minuets, they are called *Katherinen-Tänze* in this release.

The original for strings has been arranged in assorted settings. Boskovsky's version calls for two violins, viola, double bass, flute, clarinet, and two horns.

Zingarese (Nos. 1, 6, and 8)

☐ Boskovsky Ensemble / Boskovsky (conductor) / Vanguard 2096

These are three examples from a set of eight "Gypsy Dances" Haydn composed. They consist of primitive harmonies, Hungarian-contoured folk melodies scored for a pair of violins, double bass, guitar, flute, and clarinet, and fall in precise place. Unimportant though they may be, they have their simple charms for a listener.

Wind and Brass Ensemble

March for the Derbyshire Cavalry Regiment, No. 2 in C major, Hob. VIII, No. 2
March for the Prince of Wales, in E flat major, Hob. VIII, No. 3

☐ Netherlands Wind Ensemble / Philips 6599172

Haydn *Gebrauchsmusik*, performed with alacrity and stated with beautiful timbre and clarity.

Concerto in C major for Cello and Orchestra

Solo
Instrument
and
Orchestra

Cello

☐ English Chamber Orchestra / Rostropovich (cello) / Britten (conductor) / London 6419

It was not until the early 1960s that this Concerto was discovered. Although it has not fully moved ahead of the until then single Haydn cello Concerto in D major, its attractions will probably lead it to that point. In any event, the D major affair is Haydn and then some, since the standard edition used is the one "edited, newly orchestrated, and with cadenzas" by François Auguste Gevaert. The cadenzas in the C major opus heard here are by Britten—fine ones, indeed, but otherwise this essay is Haydn with some dynamic and phrasing editing that does not interfere with the authenticity of the work.

Rostropovich plays the piece with less romantic oil than the other editions available. For that matter, on a later issue (Angel S–37193, with Marriner conducting) even he tends to deviate from classical style. In this instance the text is enthusiastically detailed but in a manner that cannot be categorized other than classical. One point: the final Allegro molto is just on the verge of falling into *presto* territory.

Concerto in D major for Cello and Orchestra, Op. 101

☐ English Chamber Orchestra / Walevska (cello) / de Waart (conductor) / Philips 6500381

It's rather unbelievable to hear this work romanticized in the recordings by such cellists as Rostropovich (on Angel S–37193) and du Pré (on Angel S–36580), or portamentoized by Navarra (on Nonesuch 71071). Most of the orchestral accompaniments are in the range of being really dull (Paumgartner on Nonesuch 71071, for example). The best choice falls on that listed above. Christine Walevska plays with luminiferous tone and still keeps the style from crawling into foreign territory. Edo de Waart's alive accompaniment is the best on disc. The cadenza is by the famed Emanuel Feuermann.

Concerto in D major for Harpsichord and Orchestra, Hob. XVIII, No. 11

Harpsichord

☐ Academy of St. Martin-in-the-Fields / Malcolm (harpsichord) / Marriner (conductor) / London STS–15172

Superb unity between content and style. A fresh and illuminating conception, with perfectly proportioned sound. Most often heard, as is to be expected, with piano (see under *Solo Instrument and Orchestra: piano*).

Concerto for Horn and Orchestra

Horn

No. 1 / No. 2

☐ Academy of St. Martin-in-the-Fields / Tuckwell (horn) / Marriner (conductor) / Argo 5498

Plenty of fancy work for the horn soloist, and the demands are increased by the cadenzas written by Tuckwell. Good Haydn, even though he may be getting credit where credit is not due—there is not absolute proof that the second Concerto is by Haydn. Scoring: oboe and strings in the first work, strings only in the other one.

Beautiful in all respects and gorgeous sound by Argo. Marriner sets the tempi at the best points of fluency.

Two Liras

Concerto No. 1 in C major for Two Liras and Orchestra, Hob. VIIh, No. 1

☐ Ruf (lira); Lautenbacher and Nielen (violins); Beyer and Berndt (violas); Uhl (cello); Koch (viola da gamba); Hoffmann and Irmscher (horns) / Turnabout 34055

The lira (here fully *lira organizzata*) was in the hurdy-gurdy class, performed by turning a wheel which caused the strings to vibrate and which also was used to operate a small bellows that fed air to a row or rows of organ pipes. Its sound was woodwindy. Edward Tatnall Canby, a writer of encyclopedic knowledge, indicates that *organizzata* should not be read as meaning "organized" but "organ-ized." This properly relates the basic lira instrument (the string hurdy-gurdy) with its "organwork" addition.

It will be noted that the title indicates two liras and yet there is only one soloist. In Haydn's time the performer turned the crank with one hand and pressed the fingerboard's keys with the other. The instrument used for the recording was generated electrically. Thus freed of wheel turning, the player was able to play both parts himself, turning a duo into a solo. The timbre of this modernized instrument is akin to the sounding of the upper pipes of a baroque organ.

The first of the five concerti Haydn wrote for the instrument (Canby states that "a sixth was perhaps lost") is in three movements and that design is maintained in the four other works, with outer fast-paced movements and a slow-tempoed movement in between. It is performed with skill and stylistic appropriateness. The sound is admirable and natural.

Instrumental substitutes for the liras have been used in performances of the Concerto. A recording replacing one voice by a flute, the other by an oboe can be heard on Nonesuch 71067, with Rampal and Pierlot together with the Collegium Musicum of Paris, directed by Roland Douatte.

(Disregard Turnabout's listing of the keys of the three concerti in the album; all three are incorrect. No. 1 *is* in C major.)

Concerto No. 2 in G major for Two Liras and Orchestra, Hob. VIIh, No. 2

☐ Ruf (lira); Lautenbacher and Nielen (violins); Beyer and Berndt (violas); Uhl (cello); Koch (viola da gamba); Hoffmann and Irmscher (horns) / Turnabout 34418

Another delightful lightweight. For details *see above:* Concerto No. 1 in C major for Two Liras and Orchestra.

Concerto No. 3 in G major for Two Liras and Orchestra, Hob. VIIh, No. 3

☐ Ruf (lira); Lautenbacher and Nielen (violins); Beyer and Berndt (violas); Uhl (cello); Koch (viola da gamba); Hoffmann and Irmscher (horns) / Turnabout 34055

Haydn didn't overlook the beauty of the second movement, a *Romanze*. Eight years later he lifted it into his Symphony No. 100 (nicknamed *Military*) to serve as its slow movement. Good thinking, that; otherwise we would have lost this beautiful piece of music, since performances of lira concerti just don't happen, save on recordings.

(For details covering the lira concerti, *see above:* Concerto No. 1 in C major for Two Liras and Orchestra.)

The key listed on the album cover is incorrect. G major *is* the tonality of the third concerto.

Concerto No. 4 in F major for Two Liras and Orchestra, Hob. VIIh, No. 4

☐ Ruf (lira); Lautenbacher and Nielen (violins); Beyer and Berndt (violas); Uhl (cello); Koch (viola da gamba); Hoffmann and Irmscher (horns) / Turnabout 34418

(*See above:* Concerto No. 1 in C major for Two Liras and Orchestra *for details.*)

Concerto No. 5 in F major for Two Liras and Orchestra, Hob. VIIh, No. 5

☐ Ruf (lira); Lautenbacher and Nielen (violins); Beyer and Berndt (violas); Uhl (cello); Koch (viola da gamba); Hoffmann and Irmscher (horns) / Turnabout 34055

As with the third concerto, Haydn transferred material from this work to a Symphony (No. 89), this time twice as much: both the slow movement and the finale. (For other details *see above:* Concerto No. 1 in C major for Two Liras and Orchestra.)

Instrumental substitution for the two lira parts is found in two recordings. Rampal (flute) and Pierlot (oboe) perform the solo parts on Nonesuch 71067; Dwyer and Legrand (both flutists) are heard on Orion 75198.

(All the keys listed for the three lira concerti on Turnabout's album cover are incorrect. No. 1 is in C, *not* F; No. 3 is in G, *not* C; and No. 5 noted as in G, is, as listed above, in F.)

Concerto in C major for Oboe and Orchestra

Oboe

☐ Chamber Orchestra of the Vienna State Opera / Lardrot (oboe); Nordberg (cembalo) / Prohaska (conductor) / Vanguard 2036

It is not certain that this is by Haydn, but its élan and quality make it proper to give him credit until it can be proven otherwise. No surprises but surety in the playing which is always musically intelligent.

Concerto for Organ and Orchestra

Organ

No. 1 in C major, Hob. XVIII, No. 1 / No. 2 in C major, Hob. XVIII, No. 5 / No. 3 in C major, Hob. XVIII, No. 8

☐ Columbia Symphony Orchestra / Biggs (organ) / Rozsnyai (conductor) / Columbia MG–32985

All are in C major and all have three movements but the scoring varies. The first is for two oboes, two horns, and strings; No. 3 is for two trumpets, timpani, and strings; and the second Concerto calls for strings only. Note, however, that what Columbia lists as "No. 2" is properly "No. 3" indicated above and their "No. 3" is correctly "No. 2." In the Chorzempa recording (on Philips 6700052) no specific Arabic numbers are indicated but the sequence follows the Hoboken numbering in proper order.

Irresistibly attractive conceptions—all of them. The brilliant quality of the organ is special in this release and thus makes it the preferable one.

Concerto in D major for Piano and Orchestra, Hob. XVIII, No. 11

Piano

☐ Vienna Chamber Orchestra / Brendel (piano) / Angerer (conductor) / Turnabout 34073

For young pianists who have the opportunity to appear with orchestras this Concerto has been a permanent and enduring choice. For no valid reason, the Haydn D major rarely appears on the programs of the major organizations. The big boys have the piece in their repertoire but that's where it sits. Too bad, for it smiles all the way through and is a delight.

Brendel presents the music with crispness and conciseness, and the orchestra matches this with clear and conclusive playing. Together, the moderately scaled reading is an ideal realization. For those who prefer the solo part on the harpsichord, a marvelous recording is available (see under *Solo Instrument and Orchestra: harpsichord*).

Trumpet

Concerto in E flat major for Trumpet and Orchestra

☐ Solisti di Zagreb / Wobisch (trumpet) / Janigro (conductor) / Vanguard 703/4
☐ Bamberg Symphony Orchestra / André (trumpet) / Guschlbauer (conductor) / RCA CRL2-7002

Once a rarity, now this Concerto is every trumpet player's helping of brassy food. The writer recalls when there was but one copy of the score in the country, jealously guarded by the solo-chair member of one of the major orchestras. Then another copy was uncovered, also in manuscript form, in a New York radio station's library. From then on the gates were opened wide, concert performances multiplied, and now the number of recordings is plentiful and then some. And the publishers have made haste to issue their versions—four thus far, and another arranged for trombone, plus a transcription with band accompaniment! Surely, a home without a copy of the trumpet Concerto is not a place of artistic balance. The Haydn music is good (for the trumpet), but naturally it is restricted by the instrument for which Haydn composed.

Helmut Wobisch plays with panache and yet with a tonal "brassed" delicacy that is exemplary. He is a musician of great skill and sensitivity. His recorded edition is also obtainable on Bach Guild 5053.

Maurice André is brilliant and somewhat jaunty in his conception. He displays fine articulation and offers an excellent cadenza as a bonus. The other André performance is on Deutsche Grammophon (ARC–198415), but with a different orchestra and conductor. One prefers the RCA release because of better balance between soloist and the accompanying orchestra.

Concerto for Violin and Orchestra

Violin

No. 1 in C major, Hob. VIIa/1 / No. 3 (*Melk*) in A major, Hob. VIIa/3

☐ Toulouse Chamber Orchestra / Gotkovsky (violin) / Auriacombe (conductor) / Nonesuch 71185

The first Concerto is for string orchestra accompaniment, the other includes oboes and horns. Both are in three movements and have cadenzas—No. 1 by Carl Flesch, No. 3 by the soloist. (The nickname for the A major work is due to the work having been discovered in the Benedictine monastery at Melk.)

Nell Gotkovsky is not a Heifetz or a Stern, but she is a sound violinist and one cannot fault her realizations of this pair of works; the accompaniment is good.

Concerto No. 2 in G major for Violin and Orchestra

☐ South West German Chamber Orchestra, Pforzheim / Terebesi (violin) / CMS/Oryx EXP-24

Satisfactory playing, though the dynamic differences are rather bland. Gyorgy Terebesi's tone is clear and full. The best is heard in the central Adagio.

Violin,
Cello, Oboe,
and Bassoon

Sinfonia Concertante in B flat major for Violin, Cello, Oboe, Bassoon, and Orchestra, Op. 84

☐ English Chamber Orchestra / Hurwitz (violin); Harvey (cello); Graeme (oboe); Gatt (bassoon) / Barenboim (conductor) / Angel S-36582

This work deserves programming as much as any of the best known of Haydn's symphonies. The music has depth and wit and offers wonderful opportunities to all four soloists.

This writer has cherished for a long time a Columbia edition (now deleted) of this work (MS–6061), made by Ormandy and four Philly Orchestra first-desk men. If it can be found, grab it. It is a masterly conception of Haydn's inspired work. If not, the Angel release comes closest. It is an impressive performance, with the solos within the tuttis artistically understood, especially by the cellist. Barenboim shows a fine ear for sonority balance and tends his Haydn property properly.

Piano Sonatas (*The numbering of Haydn's Sonatas for Piano follows H. C. Robbins Landon's definition, with the Hob. number indicated in parentheses.*)

Piano Sonata No. 1 in G major (Hob. 8)

☐ McCabe (piano) / London STS–15352/4

Of the more than sixty Haydn piano sonatas, an excellent cross-section in terms of coverage is available in the third and fourth volumes London has issued. In terms of performance one can only praise the sense of sparkle and the warmth of communication John McCabe offers in his playing. McCabe is known as a composer-pianist, but from these Haydn essays that designation might well be reversed to read pianist-composer. Indeed, as will be heard in this and the other sonatas (noted below in numerical sequence and separated according to placement in the individual albums, each covering six-record sides), it is rather difficult to find performances that can match these for sensitivity, impeccable proportions, and total beauty.

Piano Sonata
No. 2 in C major (Hob. 7) / No. 3 in F major (Hob. 9)

☐ McCabe (piano) / London STS–15368/70

(See commentary above under Piano Sonata No. 1.*)*

Piano Sonata No. 4 in G major (Hob. G1)

☐ McCabe (piano) / London STS–15352/4

(See commentary above under Piano Sonata No. 1.*)*

Piano Sonata
No. 5 in G major (Hob. 11) / No. 7 in D major (Hob. 1) / No. 11 in B flat major (Hob. 2) / No. 13 in G major (Hob. 6)

☐ McCabe (piano) / London STS–15368/70

Further exceptional Haydn playing marks this group of four Sonatas. There isn't a smidgen of artificiality in McCabe's playing.

Piano Sonata
No. 20 in B flat major (Hob. 18) / No. 30 in D major (Hob. 19) / No. 32 in G minor (Hob. 44)

☐ McCabe (piano) / London STS–15352/4

Especially top-polished achievement in the G minor opus. No estentatious display or looseness of revamped Haydn is to be heard. The contrasts are not extreme, yet they offer as much explanation as the bombastic method of a virtuoso. In this respect McCabe *is* the pure virtuoso.

Piano Sonata No. 34 in D major (Hob. 33)

☐ McCabe (Piano) / London STS-15368/70

A substantial and transparent production that emphasizes McCabe's sensitive playing.

Piano Sonata No. 35 in A flat major (Hob. 43)

☐ McCabe (piano) / London STS-15352/4

The playing is controlled, elastic where it should be, and the tempi in general keep matters moving with proper care. There is no question that McCabe's Haydn is a clear response to the order of classical design.

Piano Sonata No. 40 in E flat major (Hob. 25)

☐ McCabe (piano) / London STS-15368/70

(See commentary above under Piano Sonata No.1.)

Piano Sonata

No. 41 in A major (Hob. 26) / No. 42 in G major (Hob. 27)

☐ McCabe (piano) / London STS-15352/4

(See commentary above under Piano Sonata No. 1.)

Piano Sonata

No. 44 in F major (Hob. 29) / No. 49 in C sharp minor (Hob. 36) / No. 51 in E flat major (Hob. 38)

☐ McCabe (piano) / London STS-15368/70

Clarity, formal outlines, and the total sonority become etched with clear perspective in the performances of these Sonatas. Freshets of inspiration on the part of Haydn and magnificent re-creations by the soloist.

Piano Sonata

No. 53 in E minor (Hob. 34) / No. 57 in F major (Hob. 47)

☐ McCabe (piano) / London STS-15352/4

The ill-conditioned realization of a composer's work often stems from an overbearance on the personal views of the performer. This does not mean that the performer has to be cool, impersonally detached, but it does demand a warm kind of communication. John Mc-Cabe fulfills the demand.

Piano Sonata No. 58 in C major (Hob. 48)

☐ McCabe (piano) / London STS-15368/70

McCabe is not a hyperorthodox pianist—the type of musician who clings to the religious devotion of detail without meaning. Though there is restraint, it is restraint with affection for the music. This makes a worthy recorded artistic experience.

Piano Sonata No. 59 in E flat major (Hob. 49)

☐ McCabe (piano) / London STS-15352/4

Playing of sheer beauty, wealthy with musical virtue, and devoid of sham. Truly, great Haydn playing.

Duet in D major for Violin and Cello

☐ Alice Schoenfeld (violin); Eleonore Schoenfeld (cello) / Orion 7267

In the opinion of some, this work is not by Haydn. If so, it is nevertheless excellent. The only point that can be criticized is that, throughout, the D major key is stationary. Give-and-take occurs between the two voices in the opening ornamentated Adagio, an energetic Allegro, and a final set of three variations on a minuet theme.

The work is played intelligently, though dynamic differentials are not very acute. The Schoenfelds opt to change the order of movements, giving the variations the central place.

Duo in B flat major for Two Violins

☐ David and Igor Oistrakh (violins) / Monitor S-2058

The duet form, without keyboard instrument, was not too favorable a medium for Haydn. Numerous duets attributed to him can be found, but most of these are the handiwork of transcribers.

This one is a transcribed reduction of the first and last movements of the B flat major String Quartet, Op. 9, No. 5, but the rigged-up (one should really say rigged-down!) result is far from a *reductio ad absurdum*. Credit Haydn or Anonymous for a fine duo concept that produces a nice, full sound. Credit the father and son team for a performance worthy of the fullest endorsement.

Sonata for Flute and Piano

In C major, Op. 87 / In G major, Op. 90

☐ Rampal (flute); Veyron-Lacroix (piano) / Nonesuch 71045

Transcriptions (extremely valid ones) of two Haydn string quartets without the minuet movements; Op. 87 is from the Op. 74, No. 1, quartet and Op. 90 is drawn from the first of the pair in Op. 77. Whether Haydn actually prepared the arrangements is arguable. If he didn't, he deserves credit anyway.

O.K., but not a star-studded performance. Rampal is a bit breathy in some places.

Sonata No. 1 in G major for Violin and Piano, Hob. XV/32

☐ Salzburg Mozarteum Duo / CMS/Oryx 55

Presumably, this is the only original Sonata Haydn wrote for violin and piano—the seven others that have been published are transcriptions drawn from his piano sonatas and string quartets. There is still a great deal of haze about this work, even with its official Hoboken catalogue identification. First, it is still unresolved as to whether it actually is a Haydn original or a Haydn transcription from an unidentified piano trio. Whatever the answers, the musical value of the duo cannot be downgraded.

If it weren't for gritty sound, and imbalance between the instruments to boot, the preferable recording would be the Staryk–Boucher performance on Orion (7027/2). Accordingly, even with the rather slow-paced viewpoint of the opening Andante, and some chords changed from bowed to plucked sound, the recommended choice must be given to the Karlheinz Franke–Paul v. Schilhawsky team. There is no question as to their portrayal of the Allegro part of the piece or of their tonal quality and ensemble throughout the two-movement composition.

Cassation for Lute Obbligato, Violin, and Cello

☐ Tryssesoone (baroque violin); Podolski (lute); Terby (bass viol) / Orion 7032

Light quality, simple vocabulary, cast in four movements. Using the baroque violin and bass viol in place of the standard violin and cello in this performance means little, though the soprano sonority is less bright than it would be otherwise.

More important, however, the end movements, both marked presto, are played much below that speed.

Divertimento for Baryton, Viola, and Cello

No. 45 in D major / No. 49 in G major / No. 60 in A major / No. 64 in D major / No. 113 in D major

☐ Salzburger Baryton Trio / Schwamberger (baryton) / Nonesuch 71049

For this combination Haydn produced a flood of one hundred and twenty-five compositions. There is a definite reason for this. Haydn's patron, Esterházy, played the baryton, a bass affair of six strings supplemented by an unfixed number of metal strings that sounded in sympathetic vibration.

This program gives the general blueprint Haydn followed—three movements and always a minuet, sometimes as the central movement, other times as the finale. All of it is bread-and-butter music, for general and comfortable, top-surface listening. If an auditor wants more, Nos. 44 and 70 are to be found with duplicates of Nos. 45 and 60 on RCA VICS–1425.

The baryton is the featured instrument. It is for that reason that special credit is given on the release to the barytonist: Karl-Maria Schwamberger. The playing proceeds in a kind of honorable constancy. That's the way the music is made.

Piano Trio

No. 18 in A major / No. 19 in G minor

☐ Beaux Arts Trio / Philips 6500521

Regardless of the autocracy of the piano in Haydn's trios—the violin is permitted only intermittently to hold the stage and then only in restrained form, while the cello steadfastly thickens but does not enlarge the bass section of the keyboard voice—the wealth of ideas and the workmanship make it impossible to shunt them to one side as representing second-class chamber music.

Refined playing from an impeccable ensemble. Menahem Pressler as the pianist is, of course, the star.

Piano Trio No. 20 in B flat major

☐ Beaux Arts Trio / Philips 6500522

The spacing of the piano in the first movement is most interesting. Separation of voices is not usual with Haydn; in fact, one must look to the Beethoven piano sonatas for such textural perspective. Together with the width of spacing there are certain intervallic jumps, adding an inner agility to the movement. More emphasis is given to the dominant piano by opening the slow movement with a solo for the keyboard instrument.

A clear and fluent performance in all respects, with an excellent tempo choice for the finale.

Piano Trio No. 21 in C major

☐ Beaux Arts Trio / Philips 6500401

The middle movement, variational in concept, takes advantage of the difference of the instrumental resource between violin and piano. This is rather unusual in Haydn's piano trios. The final Presto bounces along on a basic rhythm of sixteenth notes. Pressler, the pianist, covers this virtuosic-keyed material beautifully.

Piano Trio No. 22 in E flat major

☐ Beaux Arts Trio / Philips 6500521

Some have found a certain gentility in the Beaux Arts playing of Haydn, but it is just such a style that is truest to the music. Heavier playing would only re-emphasize what is already emphasized in terms of the cello, which is a reinforcement of the piano's line; and more intensification in the violin's tone would reflect a Beethovenistic concept, which Haydn's trio music is not. No, this is another top-drawer Haydn performance by a magnificent trio team.

Piano Trio No. 23 in D minor

☐ Beaux Arts Trio / Philips 6500401

The main characteristic of this Trio is the succession of two slow movements, both using variation technique. With the fluidity of Haydn's hand there is no overbalance by such similar types. The fast-tempoed finale resembles a concerto conclusion.

Piano Trio No. 24 in D major

☐ Beaux Arts Trio / Philips 6500522

The opening movement is in sonata form, with robust themes displayed almost symphonically. The slow movement (played with poignant conviction) is short, a preamble to the final Allegro, which bears the additional reminder of *ma dolce* ("with suavity"). The slow movement, therefore, prepares the optimistically lifted mood of the outer movement, not only by contrast of key (D minor followed by D major), but by the gentle insistence of its drooping pessimism.

Piano Trio
No. 25 in G major / No. 26 in F sharp minor / No. 27 in C major

☐ Beaux Arts Trio / Philips 6500023

The finale (*Rondo all'Ongarese*) of the G major Trio has achieved the household popularity plane, with resultant necessity of transcription to make ready availability. Its hurry-scurry is neatly controlled in this performance, and the sectional design is clearly identified, as it should be. Improper tempo recognition has often marred otherwise excellent playing but no such guilt applies to the Pressler-Cohen-Greenhouse team. In the rosy-hued finale of the F sharp minor Trio there is full respect for the *tempo di minuetto* designation and as a result the music's lilt is buoyantly conveyed. The same pertains to the finale of the C major work.

These are superb performances.

Piano Trio No. 28 in E major

☐ Beaux Arts Trio / Philips 6500401

Color and formal individuality appear in this trio, in the former by the use of string pizzicati, in the latter by shaping the middle movement as a Passacaglia, with almost wholesale elimination of the string instruments. The playing is ideal.

Piano Trio
No. 29 in E flat major / No. 30 in E flat major / No. 31 in E flat minor
☐ Beaux Arts Trio / Philips 6500400

The second movement of the twenty-ninth Trio begins in the key of B major and passes into E flat major where it ultimately settles on an unresolved chord to prepare for the immediate entrance of the last movement. Its tempo is somewhat rare for Haydn: *andantino ed innocentemente.* The Beaux Arts gentlemen fully carry out this indicated *desideratum* of romantic intent. The last movement is another Haydn rarity—an Allemande. Even after its amalgamation as a stylized dance, its tempo was moderate. However, Haydn indicates a *presto assai,* which if taken literally could make a shambles of the terpsichorean fancy of the music. The performers opt for a middle-course between moderate pace and exceedingly fast tempo, and it works beautifully.

The E flat minor Trio has only two movements having contrasting tonalities that provide parallel dark and bright colorations. In the last part the violin is given the opportunity to work much more freely than is usual in Haydn's trios.

As with all the recorded performances in the Beaux Arts coverage of the Haydn piano trios, these are expert and outstanding realizations.

Piano Trio No. 32 in G major
☐ Beaux Arts Trio / Philips 6500522

This beguiling two-movement Trio is an arrangement of a violin sonata. It is played with grace and a sensitive nuance for its simple details.

Trio in F major for Flute, Cello, and Piano, Hob. XV, No. 17
☐ New York Camerata / Turnabout 34575

This is a trio that Haydn indicated could be for flute or violin, with piano and cello. It has two movements—an Allegro and a *tempo di minuetto.* The Camerata threesome play it almost casually, but it falls nicely on the ears.

Trio for Violin, Viola, and Cello
In G major, Op. 53, No. 1 / In B flat major, Op. 53, No. 2 / In D major, Op. 53, No. 3
☐ Grumiaux Trio / Philips 802905

Entertaining settings of the Piano Sonatas Nos. 40, 41, and 42. It is a feast mainly for the violin with sonorous submission by the viola and cello. A feast for the ears also with Grumiaux's rich tone. When necessary, he can be delicately deft, and the totality is authoritative artistry worth hearing.

Quartet in D major for Lute and Strings, Hob. III/8
☐ Scheit (guitar); Kamper (violin); Weiss (viola); Benesch (cello) / Vanguard S-295E (monaural)

Haydn's quartet is performed in this edition with guitar in place of the lute. Although this substitution is musicologically arguable, it is musically satisfactory, with the plucked instrument set apart from the strings in a quasi-soloistic manner. Karl Scheit clearly identifies the timbre's personality in his capable playing. The strings give adequate support in this formally direct, early-period Haydn example, with two outer fast movements and two minuet apportionments separated by an Adagio. While the stately motion of the minuets is acceptable, the opening Allegro is rather cooled by performance in a very moderate tempo.

Not the most sophisticated sound. This recording was made almost two decades ago and is a transfer from the original issue, VRS–1044.

The Seven Last Words of Christ, Op. 51

☐ Amadeus Quartet / Deutsche Grammophon 2530213

This is the quartet version of the original orchestral work (see under *Orchestra*). (Haydn only assigned an opus number to the quartet setting.) The performance here is informative though somewhat scholarly. It must be borne in mind that because of the sacred requisite of the original the music does not (cannot) break away from its solemn pace into secular, slow-movement style. Nevertheless, the conception is of moving quality and worthy of being heard.

String Quartet (*Serenade*) in F major, Op. 3, No. 5 (by Hofstetter attrib. Haydn)

☐ Janáček Quartet / London 6385

Musical detectives have proven that this work was written by one Romanus Hofstetter (1742–1815; a German cleric as well as a composer), not by Haydn. It's difficult to let the credit go elsewhere. Habit being what it is, it remains listed as part of the Haydn string quartet canon. Anyone wanting this Quartet would not think of looking under Hofstetter and in lieu of a cross-reference it is considered here with the above explanation and the same parenthetical note as listed in *Schwann*: "Hofstetter attrib. Haydn."

No deep investigation is required to recognize the artistic naturalness of the Janáček's performance. It is utter grace. In turn, the muted song of the first violin over the plucked other instruments is a silky delight. A very highly recommended essay.

String Quartet

In C major, Op. 9, No. 1 / In E flat major, Op. 9, No. 2 / In G major, Op. 9, No. 3 / In D minor, Op. 9, No. 4 / In B flat major, Op. 9, No. 5 / In A major, Op. 9, No. 6

☐ Dekany Quartet / Vox SVBX–563

The best skills of this quartet are displayed in the fast end movements of Op. 9, No. 1. If the other portions are not as beautiful, style is not given secondary position. In the second work of the group the quartet shines by realizing that pace must be regulated for the final movement, so that all the spicy syncopations are clearly exposed. Again, the skills of this foursome are best pronounced in the speedy movements of Op. 9, No. 3. Their recognition of the Haydn brand of fun is displayed in the final portion of the work. This is musical sly wit and new coinage in quartet literature. Haydn's joke book never repeated any stale stories.

In the other works one notices that the Dekany four play best when the tempo is speedy, otherwise they perform acceptably but are in need of seasoning. In the fourth work in the set their playing is richer than in any of the other five works in the opus. Only a little more intensity is required. Thus, good performances but not by any means definitive ones.

String Quartet

In E flat major, Op. 20, No. 1 / In C major, Op. 20, No. 2 / In G minor, Op. 20, No. 3 / In D major, Op. 20, No. 4 / In F minor, Op. 20, No. 5 / In A major, Op. 20, No. 6

☐ Lenox Quartet / Desto 7152/4

These are the *Sun* quartets. This would fit the golden glow and warmth of the music but the nickname derives from the publisher's trademark on the original edition, which was a picture of the sun. There are wonders everywhere in this half-dozen Quartets, but especially important are the fugues used in three of the works. The first in the set appears in Op. 20, No. 2. It is a fugue with four subjects, not the exceedingly rare form of a quadruple fugue that takes four separate subjects through paces and combines them, but a fugue with four themes that, as it were, accompany and jostle each other. The second fugue is in the F minor opus, this time with two subjects; the third fugue appears in Op. 20, No. 6, and has three subjects.

There are many virtues in this set of performances, one of them being the balanced proportions of the four instruments. One need only hear the simply enchanting set of variations in the fourth Quartet of the group. Rhythmic bite is always held within chamber music bounds, as the ''zing'' given in the *alla zingarese* minuet movement of the same Quartet. There is heartiness, but of Haydnesque quality, with the proper amount of gusto. The Lenox gentlemen are sensitive to proper tempi and to avoidance of irrational and unmerited braking or pushing of speedrates.

Desto furnishes notes by the famed Donald Francis Tovey, but it does not furnish the keys for the Quartets anywhere. As for the movement designations, they can only be found on the label copy, an annoyance for the listener if he wishes that information while the recording is playing.

String Quartet

In B minor, Op. 33, No. 1 / (*Joke*) in E flat major, Op. 33, No. 2 / (*Bird*) in C major, Op. 33, No. 3 / In B flat major, Op. 33, No. 4 / (*How Do You Do?*) in G major, Op. 33, No. 5 / In D major, Op. 33, No. 6

☐ Dekany Quartet / Vox SVBX–556

Healthy playing in the first quartet, with neat and cohesive contrasts. This sense of registration and coloration is also heard in Op. 33, No. 2, similarly in the C major Quartet. However, there is some pedestrian playing in the B flat major work.

The Dekany Quartet does not overlook the importance of the unison work that gives impulse to the slow movement of the fifth work in the set. They plan their proportions nicely to emphasize this in contrast to the first violin's soloistic song. The playing in the final composition in the opus is dynamic and most convincing.

String Quartet (*Joke*) in E flat major, Op. 33, No. 2

☐ Janáček Quartet / London 6385

The prognosis here is mellow tone, much more so than the Dekany foursome in their performance of the work in their complete edition of Haydn's Opus 33 (*see above*). The delicate warmth in the *Largo sostenuto* and the clear tonal reasoning in the opening *Allegro moderato cantabile* represent enticing chamber music playing. Here is a first violinist who commands but does not unduly overshadow his colleagues. If you are satisfied with but a single example in the Opus 33 group, take this.

String Quartet

In B flat major, Op. 50, No. 1 / In C major, Op. 50, No. 2

☐ Tokyo Quartet / Deutsche Grammophon 2530440

Memorable chamber music playing. Every point in the score is brought to light: the tensile rhythmic condition in the first movement of the B flat major opus, the dramatic coloration of the key changes in its slow movement, the phrasing defining the somewhat flowery manifestation in the slow movement of the C major work, and the perfection of the linear situation in its finale.

String Quartet

In E flat major, Op. 50, No. 3 / In F sharp minor, Op. 50, No. 4 / (*Dream*) in F major, Op. 50, No. 5 / (*Frog*) in D major, Op. 50, No. 6

☐ Fine Arts Quartet / Vox SVBX–595

Fluid playing. The fugal data in the F sharp minor Quartet are a bit cautious but the structural power is hardly diminished. In the finale of the last work in the set, the first violin's *bariolage* registers cleanly. It is this effect that gave the Quartet its nickname. (There are two other, less used nicknames: "House on Fire" and "Row in Vienna." Though the vigor of the repeated pitches suggests a brawl to a degree, it is *only* to a degree.)

String Quartet

In G major, Op. 54, No. 1 / In C major, Op. 54, No. 2

☐ Amadeus Quartet / Deutsche Grammophon 2530302

Haydn's set of three Quartets under this opus opens with brilliance and a very alive theme. The ideas are sprightly. Both this portion and the following movement are played with beauty of finish by this team. Especially compelling is their realization that the "slow" movement is in quickened state: an *Allegretto* is taking its place. The first violin delivers the melodic statement with exquisite taste. The Amadeus plays with decision throughout; their sound is a gem; only a pinched tone, now and then, from the first violin, can be criticized.

Oddly, the voicing is not always in balance in the C major composition. This results from a more romanticized Haydn than one generally hears. Some may prefer it that way.

String Quartet in E major, Op. 54, No. 3

☐ Dekany Quartet / Vox SVBX–559

If you wish this Quartet, you are captive to purchasing the Vox box containing the other two Quartets in the opus, the three comprising the Opus 55, and the single work that is designated Opus 42. Not a bad bargain at all, but it must be pointed out that other recommendations are given for three of the works of the total seven in Vox's package.

This is a fair performance, best displayed in its recognition of the reticence of the dynamic plan in the finale. The Dekany four carefully control their *sotto voce* speech in order to permit the effect of the dissimilarity brought by the full-blown *fortes*.

String Quartet in F minor, Op. 55, No. 2

☐ Stuyvesant String Quartet / Nonesuch 71114

An honorable appraisal, which, stated in a different way, means professionally competent.

String Quartet

In C major, Op. 64, No. 1 / In B minor, Op. 64, No. 2 / In B flat major, Op. 64, No. 3 / In G major, Op. 64, No. 4 / (*Lark*) in D major, Op. 64, No. 5 / In E flat major, Op. 64, No. 6

☐ Fine Arts Quartet / Vox SVBX–597

The playing is a little on the light side in Op. 64, No. 1, but fine vivacity governs the performance of the second Quartet of the group. The line of the slow movement of the third Quartet is superbly shaped, with the Fine Arts team carrying it from start to finish without sectional depiction. It exemplifies the finest type of chamber music playing, as does the fluidic manipulation of the finale.

The *Lark* is the most famous work in the Opus 64 set. The performance here is fine, with a proper mood of relaxation in the opening part, not too percussive a stress in the minuet, and a sensible speed applied to the kinetic formation of the last movement. This has led to calling the work the "Hornpipe" Quartet, but the finale's music is certainly not in hornpipe style.

(A rather odd cognomen is also attached to Op. 64, No. 6—namely, "Railwayman." A rather ridiculous idea since it can apply only, and even then it is somewhat forced, to the last five measures of the first movement.)

String Quartet

In B flat major, Op. 71, No. 1 / In D major, Op. 71, No.2 / In E flat major, Op. 71, No. 3

☐ Griller String Quartet / Vanguard HM–41

These three Quartets (and great ones they are) usher in the last fifteen of Haydn. Although oveshadowed somewhat by the Opus 76 set, they are not of less importance. They show how, with the melodic impetus being fed from an inexhaustible source, Haydn was able to mix the profound with the light, and how he continually tried his hand at the new.

For the most part the Griller ensemble is persuasive in its readings, with good sense of dynamic controls. The quartet's sound is not lush but clean and clear, and tends to be chamber-intimate rather than big-hall lustrous. One prefers the former.

String Quartet

In C major, Op. 74, No. 1 / In F major, Op. 74, No. 2 / (*Horseman*) in G minor, Op. 74, No. 3

☐ Griller String Quartet / Vanguard HM–42

Sound dicta and classical wisdom are displayed in the playing of these three Quartets. The slow movement in the C major opus is not simply slow-paced; it is swept with the breeze of a moving *Grazioso*. Depicted just as expertly is the syncopative and polyphonic sport of its finale. The famous *Horseman* (or *Rider*) Quartet is played with stylish consistency. A fine set of quartet performances.

String Quartet

In G major, Op. 76, No. 1 / (*Quinten*) in D minor, Op. 76, No. 2 / (*Emperor*) in C major, Op. 76, No. 3 / (*Sunrise*) in B flat major, Op. 76, No. 4 / (*Largo*) in D major, Op. 76, No. 5 / In E flat major, Op. 76, No. 6

☐ Fine Arts Quartet / Vox SVBX–596

Music of such commentary as in these half-dozen works demands performers of imagination and with ears that can hear beyond the refinements of intonation and ordinary balance. The readings of these works are particularly lucid and worthy of high praise. The Fine Arts is (was—there have been large changes in personnel since these recordings were made) especially well-balanced from first violin to cello; its second violin (thank heavens) is a sensitive voice. The tempi cannot be argued; there is only a slight hesitancy of moving forward in some of the slow movements. But what a delight to hear Haydn's minuets played in normal tempo! The Fine Arts four give testament to the golden beauties of Haydn and bring praise to themselves simultaneously.

String Quartet (*Quinten*) in D minor, Op. 76, No. 2

☐ Janáček Quartet / London 6385

The corner movements of this exhilarating Quartet are given a superb reading. The variations are smooth but just a mite stiff in mensural depiction. In the *Menuetto* the peasantlike dance pulse is again stiff but properly so, with the tone quality firmly rounded. Overall, a performance worth having.

Divertimento for Two Oboes, Two Horns, and Two Bassoons
No. 1 in F major / No. 2 in F major / No. 3 in C major / No. 5 in D major / No. 6 in G major / No. 7 in G major / No. 8 in D major

☐ London Wind Soloists / Brymer (conductor) / London STS–15078

Haydn lightweights but Haydn delights nonetheless. The greatest amount of virtuosity is demanded of the horns—hear especially the finale of the sixth of the set.

Fastidious playing in every measure in every piece.

Arianna a Naxos, Hob. XXVIb, No. 2

☐ Baker (mezzo-soprano); Leppard (fortepiano) / Philips 6500660

A sustained dramatic solo cantata, with an interplay of song and recitative in interwoven contrast and thereby unbroken sequence.

Janet Baker has never been better. Every word with its emotional essence is characterized and significant. Truly a memorable performance. Raymond Leppard accompanies with good effect. However, his instrument is a fortepiano (following Haydn's definition that his cantata is "with harpsichord or fortepiano accompaniment") and its sound is hard, its resonances somewhat aborted.

Berenice che fai, Hob. XXIVa, No. 10

☐ English Chamber Orchestra / Baker (mezzo-soprano) / Leppard (conductor) / Philips 6500660

The *Scena di Berenice* is a brilliant solo cantata. It is a mature Haydn piece, written during the time he was producing the magnificent "London" symphonies. It can be described as exciting music with operatic thrust. The *Scena* is superbly crafted in a vocally precise and dramatically responsive manner by Janet Baker. It represents magnificent singing.

The Creation

☐ New York Philharmonic and Camerata Singers / Raskin (soprano); Young (tenor); Reardon (baritone) / Bernstein (conductor) / Columbia M2S–773

Cantata and Oratorio

Some performances use five soloists, others, as Bernstein's, use the three that were satisfactory to Haydn. Thus Judith Raskin combines the roles of Gabriel and Eve, John Reardon sings the Raphael and Adam parts, with Alexander Young as Uriel. All are rich in voice and project vivid vocal personalities. Striding over the entire production is conducting that is a joy. This is no oratorio of churchly squareness, but one that is an exultation and exaltation of lyrical imagery. Understandably, Bernstein displays the music with a magical brightness, his orchestra and chorus could not be better.

The closest competition for *Die Schöpfung* is an edition conducted by Münchinger (London 1271) but it has been deleted. Still available is von Karajan's (Deutsche Grammophon 2707044). It's good, but it also has a seeming holy obligation to precise patness. It's warm in many places but only outwardly so. The minute polish given the score dams rather than uncovers it. Bernstein, on the other hand, is decisive even to the most minute point. It is one of his top achievements.

Mass No. 7, *Missa in Tempore Belli (Paukenmesse)*

☐ Vienna State Opera Orchestra and Vienna Chamber Choir / Davrath (soprano); Rössl-Majdan (alto); Dermota (tenor); Berry (bass) / Wöldike (conductor) / Vanguard HM–28

All the components are effectively matched in this edition of Haydn's "Mass in Wartime," thereby producing an absorbing recording. The soprano has vocal purity, the bass soloist is especially significant, and his singing of the *Qui tollis* is thrilling in its artistry. Balances are provided so that proper equality is obtained between orchestra, chorus, and solo voices. The smooth discipline of Wöldike's conducting is apparent; it avoids the slightest oversentimentalizing that can be so irritating even with the best of performing forces. Such directness and distinctiveness provide the equal dimensions of lyricism and dramaticism that command Haydn's score.

Mass No. 8, *Missa Sancti Bernardi von Offida (Heiligmesse)*

☐ Academy of St. Martin-in-the-Fields and Choir of St. John's College, Cambridge / Cantelo (soprano); Minty (alto); Partridge (tenor); Keyte (bass) / Guest (conductor) / Argo ZRG–542

The parenthetical identification of a "Holy Mass" is because of Haydn's inclusion of an old hymn tune *Heilig, heilig, heilig* as the basis for the Sanctus section. The mass is dramatically tempered, made stronger by cogently planned and developed fugal sections.

Guest opts for a big-scaled conception but never sacrifices clarity and solidity for sonorous force. The positiveness of the conception brings its own vivid rewards.

Mass No. 9 in D minor — *Missa in Angustiis (Nelson Mass)*

☐ Vienna State Opera Orchestra and Chorus / Stich-Randall (soprano); Casei (mezzo-soprano); Equiluz (tenor); Simkowsky (bass) / Swarowsky (conductor) / Nonesuch 71173

Though the choral work on the Argo disc (5325) is better (the sopranos in the Nonesuch entry struggle a bit), the vote for the orchestral playing and the fine soloists in this issue brings the necessary majority. The total quality is dramatic; the passions are splendid in both Haydn's music and in the performers' sonorous realization.

Mass No. 12 (*Harmoniemesse*) in B flat major

☐ Academy of St. Martin-in-the-Fields and Choir of St. John's College, Cambridge / Spoorenberg (soprano); Watts (contralto); Young (tenor); Rouleau (bass); Runnett (organ) / Guest (conductor) / Argo ZRG–515

The healthy spirit of Haydn's work as expressed in its scoring (an orchestra of two each of flutes, oboes, bassoons, horns, and trumpets; timpani, strings, and organ) has extended to this re-creation directed by George Guest who plots the dynamics artistically and obtains a precision and an excitement proper to the work. In comparison, Bernstein (on Columbia M–33267) plays direct to the gallery and thereby overplays. His accentuations are too pointed, and most of the tempi are overloaded. This negative response compares to a completely affirmative one in terms of the Argo release.

The vocal foursome is well-balanced and beautifully blended. The same applies to the chorus.

The Seasons

☐ Royal Philharmonic Orchestra and Brighton Festival Chorus / Cotrubas (soprano); Krenn (tenor); Sotin (bass); Vignoles (harpsichord) / Dorati (conductor) / London OSA–13128

Perfectly clear proof is given here that Haydn's *Die Jahreszeiten* should not be approached as music of epic dimensions but rather as music of congeniality. Heavy-handed consideration is out of place though it can be recognized in other available recorded editions.

Dorati strikes a fine balance and achieves a flexibility to the music that is of warmth and freshness. Ileana Cotrubas's voice is at its loveliest, and the same testimony applies to the other soloists. Distinctive choral and orchestral work.

Il Mondo della Luna

☐ Lausanne Chamber Orchestra and Chorus of the Radio Suisse Romande / Auger and Mathis (sopranos); von Stade and Valentini-Terrani (mezzo-sopranos); Alva and Johnson (tenors); Trimarchi (baritone); Dorati (harpsichord) / Dorati (conductor) / Philips 6769003

"The World of the Moon" is opera buffa in the fullest sense—comic situations, a mixed-bag plot that turns and twists, plus plenty of secco-recitative. All of it is glorious and unstintingly top-drawer Haydn, with an impulsiveness that is entrancing.

There is a fine overture (Haydn used it in his Symphony No. 63 in C major), and the score is thoroughly sprinkled with spontaneously sounding instrumental gems.

The cast presents an absolutely splendid view of the score. The voices are all beautiful and the character representations are strong and believable. Full compliments for Antal Dorati's artistic management on the podium and at the harpsichord. One point regarding the latter: the arpeggiated style he uses does get a bit boring.

La Fedeltà Premiata

☐ Lausanne Chamber Orchestra and Chorus of the Radio Suisse Romande / Cotrubas and Lövaas (sopranos); von Stade (mezzo-soprano); Valentini (contralto); Landy and Alva (tenors); Titus and Mazzieri (baritones); Perret (harpsichord) / Dorati (conductor) / Philips 6707028

Haydn's plot is, in its criss-cross, quasi–*La Ronde*. A loves B, B loves C, C loves D, E loves F, and G plays the field. It is laced with the traditional misconceptions, intrigues, and so much of a somersaulted story that one might as well just listen to the music. There are delineated personalities so that it is possible to tell the good from the bad, the serious from the light. Still, never mind. The music is first-class, a number of the arias are special, and the finales have real power.

A fine cast, best of all Frederica von Stade. A fine job by Dorati. Haydn's operas don't

*Opera
and Dramatic
Music*

enjoy a place on the stage. Again, no matter. A beautiful response can be obtained by listening to this one in the privacy of one's home.

Michael Haydn   (1737-1806)

Orchestra

Symphony in G major

☐ Saint Paul Chamber Orchestra / Davies (conductor) / Nonesuch 71323

Special interest attaches to this Symphony. Its three movements are preceded by a twenty-measure *Adagio maestoso* written by Mozart when he decided to perform Haydn's Symphony, which he admired.

The buoyancy of the playing under Davies's direction is a delight. Furthermore, the clear diction of the slow movement is especially compelling. This is a fine orchestra with a splendid musician on the podium.

Wind and Brass Ensemble

Turkish March in C major

☐ Netherlands Wind Ensemble / Philips 6599172

The Turkish flavor is defined by drum pulsations—otherwise M. Haydn's repetitive idea moves along with jolly bounce and decided performance good will.

Solo Instrument and Orchestra

Organ and Viola

Concerto in C major for Organ, Viola, and Strings

☐ Academy of St. Martin-in-the-Fields / Shingles (viola); Preston (organ) / Marriner (conductor) / Argo ZRG–631

Those on the lookout for double concerti (listeners or performers) should give this fine work full attention. A nicely turned classical opening movement is followed by a nobly spun Adagio, and the conclusion is a high-spirited Prestissimo. And equal time is given to the soloists.

This release is far superior to the competitive edition on Philips 6700052 with Daniel Chorzempa (organ) and Bruno Giuranna (viola), backed by the German Bach Soloists conducted by Helmut Winschermann. Marriner takes brighter tempi, the quality of the players is better, the sound fuller, and a more definite profile exists for the total.

Argo titles this work *Duo concertante*. However, the manuscript reads *Concerto per l'Organo ó Clavicembalo è Viola./ con 2 Violini, Viola Rip: e Basso.* Argo should revise its headings when new discs are prepared.

Trumpet

Concerto in C major for Trumpet and Orchestra

☐ Chamber Orchestra of Copenhagen / Ghitalla (trumpet) / Moriarty (conductor) / Cambridge 2823

Faithful high trumpet playing, including a cadenza for each of the two movements. The accompaniment is finely organized.

Violin

Concerto in A major for Violin and Orchestra

☐ Concertgebouw Orchestra, Amsterdam / Grumiaux (violin) / de Waart (conductor) / Philips 839757

Haydn's work did not surface until 1964, when a set of parts was found in Prague. The first performance in recent times was given by Grumiaux and the Rotterdam Philharmonic Orchestra at the Holland Festival of 1968.

There are three movements, all of which are delivered with violinistic seduction. Every note is clean, clear, and styled in a natural manner. Grumiaux has supplied musical cadenzas for the first pair of movements.

String Quartet No. 3 in A major

☐ Schäffer Quartet / Vox SVBX–5300

Chamber Music

The expected format: fast-tempoed outer movements, Minuet, and slow movement. A worthy eighteenth-century affair and played with stylistic respect.

String Quintet

In F major / In G major

☐ Vienna Philharmonic Quintet / London STS–15309

Divertimentoish in style—six movements, for example, in the F major piece. The format is for two violas together with two violins and cello. Sound performance all the way.

Ave Regina

☐ Choir of St. John's College, Cambridge / Guest (conductor) / Argo ZRG–634

Choral

Chorus Alone

A setting of the antiphon *Ave Regina* for two four-part a cappella choirs. Nice order and continuity in the singing of this motet.

Richard Hayman (1920-)

Pops Hoe-down

Orchestra

☐ Cincinnati Pops Orchestra / Kunzel (conductor) / Turnabout 34714

This composer of lighter fare is not to be confused with the composer of the same name belonging to the extreme avant-garde movement.

Hayman's "Pops" derives from the fact that the work was especially written for Arthur Fiedler and the Boston Pops Orchestra. The "Hoe-down" says it all. Popsy, peppy, precipitous tunes, plenty of square-dance fiddlin' and Yankee temper. Couldn't be better played. (The Cincy Pops outfit is, of course, the Cincinnati Symphony Orchestra doing moonlighting work in the recording studio.)

Bernhard Heiden (1910-)

Sonata for E flat Saxophone and Piano (1937)

Chamber Music

☐ Sinta (saxophone); True (piano) / Mark 22868 (monaural)

While there are pertinent Hindemithian influences in the work, Heiden's music has validity. There is a source of natural energy in the three movements, and note-spinning is kept out of the picture. Fast tempi cover parts 1 and 2 and most of part 3. The last telescopes both slow and speedy sections, not only in tempo but also in terms of relationship of theme, the *presto* material a working out of the fluency of the *adagio*. The two sections, therefore, interlock as one—an indication of musical-engineering efficiency.

Quintet for Horn and String Quartet (1952)

☐ Philadelphia String Quartet / Leuba (horn) / Olympic OLY-102

The shadow of late, late romanticism falls heavily on Heiden's Quintet. That isn't bad at all, since it is, in fact, descriptive of music that is civil and urbane, and freely tonal. Heiden's work (a stunning muted Vivace must be stressed) may be in romantic dress, but it walks with the security that marks classical gait.

The playing presents a secure sense of style, and the ensemble is absolute.

Sinfonia for Wind Quintet (1949)

☐ Musical Arts Quintet / Now 9362

Heiden's ternary-shaped six-minute piece is superbly neo-Hindemithian. No monkey business; it says what it has to say directly, cleanly, and holds the attention. It is the work of a craftsman who has something to relate even though with a borrowed accent. The impersonality of the playing does not harm the music.

Jascha Heifetz/Mario Castelnuovo-Tedesco. See Castelnuovo-Tedesco / Heifetz.

Irwin Heilner   (1908-   )

Vocal

**Voice
and Orchestra**

Chinese Songs (1947)

☐ Imperial Philharmonic of Tokyo / Maki (soprano) / Strickland (conductor) / Composers Recordings 143 (monaural)

Heilner is one of the many American composers who received a fair amount of attention in the late 1920s and early 1930s and then got lost in the shuffle of the creative crowd. On the basis of these four fine songs, his absence from the concert scene is to be regretted. The audible sensitivity, the craftsmanship, and the coloristic simplicity of this song cycle, which makes much from little, are worth anyone's listening time. Truly, this is beautifully written music. It is given a character-filled performance.

Anthony Philip Heinrich   (1781-1861)

Instrumental

Piano

Yankee Doodle Waltz

☐ Mandel (piano) / Desto 6445/7

Heinrich is an interesting historical figure in American music. Posterity paying every man his just honor, Heinrich's music remains untouched and unheard. No argument from this corner. However, this little example, the work, one might say, of a professional amateur, is worth listening to. Its form is very loose, but it has a quaintness and a honky-tonk flavor that will bring a chuckle.

John Heiss (1938-)

Inventions, Contours, and Colors (1973) *Orchestra*

☐ Speculum Musicae / Fitz (conductor) / Composers Recordings SD–363

Color fragmentation displaying a nice sense of assorted timbre tastes. Heiss's piece represents the way a fantasy or rhapsody is written in the latter part of the twentieth century—and the way such forms are now titled.

One expects impressive music making in a performance by the Speculum Musicae group. Such virtue is found in this case.

Stephen Heller (1813-1888)

Nocturne, Op. 103 *Instrumental*

***Solitary Rambles*, Op. 78** *Piano*

Tarantella in E minor, Op. 53

Thirty-three Variations on a Theme of Beethoven, Op. 130

***Valses-Rêveries*, Op. 122**

☐ Puchelt (piano) / Genesis 1043

Mostly Schumannesque adaptive behavior, especially in the half-dozen pieces of Opus 78 (*Spaziergänge eines Einsamen*). A touch of Schubert as well, as in the Opus 122.

The most interesting is the set of variations. Based on the theme of Beethoven's Thirty-two Variations in C minor, Heller deftly incorporates minute bits from Beethoven's fifth and ninth symphonies and his Op. 1, No. 3 Trio. Double homage therefore, by use of theme and quotation.

Gerhard Puchelt plays adequately. There is not too much depth, but neither is there much depth in this music.

William Hellermann (1939-)

***Passages 13 — The Fire* (1971)** *Instrumental*

☐ Schwarz (trumpet) / Nonesuch 71275 *Trumpet*

That the prose that is somewhat splintered and electronically modified on the tape that partners the solo trumpet in this work mostly cannot be understood does not negate the basic effect of Hellermann's piece. The other surrounding tape sounds and the phrased waywardness of the trumpet part create a mystical and unreal quality. William Bolcom, who wrote the liner notes, says the music "exudes an air of great pathos." That subjective response is no less valid than this writer's different reaction. What is clear in this powerful essay (of sizable length, amounting to twenty-five minutes) is that mood and technique are married in a blend that intrigues as well as fascinates.

The subtle trumpet style in this work is far removed from the usual rich cantilena, the rhythmic flourish, and the brassy impetuosity most common to the instrument. Only a master musician such as Gerard Schwarz has the technique to master it. His playing adds still another fat credit to the many he has received throughout his career.

For those who may want to follow the text by Robert Duncan, or whatever part of it is clear through the tape modifications, it is indicated as part of the liner-note copy.

Chamber Music

On the Edge of a Node (1974)

☐ Street (violin); Uitti (cello); Hellermann (guitar) / Composers Recordings SD–336

Timbre experimentation by "preparing" all three stringed instruments with clips. The best results are from the guitar; results from the violin and cello are much less felicitous. The composer says "the notes have a lot to do with a reworking of received material mostly Bach." Once in a while in the constantly uncoiling sounds a reminder of this basis comes through. Credit: good idea by Hellermann. Debit: too much of a muchness.

Charles-Joseph van Helmont (1715-1790)

Orchestra

Overture in D major for Two Choirs

☐ Solistes de Liège / Koch-Pichon (harpsichord) / Lemaire (conductor) / Musical Heritage Society MHS–793 CC–11

Odd title for what is actually a sinfonia since there are three movements—Allegro, Largo, and Presto. And what delightful, meaningful music! One orchestra consists of an oboe and strings with a bassoon supporting the fundamental bass. The other group includes an oboe, two horns, strings (without double basses—an odd point), and a harpsichord serving as the basso continuo.

Fine presentation with special marked rhythm in the corner movements.

Robert Helps (1928-   )

Instrumental

Piano

Image (1958)

☐ Helps (piano) / Composers Recordings S–288

Impressionistic concept with an expressionistic overlay. It produces a short piece of depth and nocturnal feeling.

Portrait (1960)

☐ Bennette (piano) / Desto 7110

Black and white contrast within this pianistic picture. Both moods have finely chiseled textures. The soprano pedal ostinato that rides over the concluding material for a full minute is as dramatic as an orchestral peroration.

Quartet (1971)

☐ Helps (piano) / Desto 7122

The *Quartet* title neatly shows the total number of movements of Helps's meaty work. But it is far from a suite, since its four sections (Prelude, *Confrontation*, Intermezzo, and Postlude) equate a full-scale sonata conception. It is an expressionistic essay, considerably involved with Sessions-like massivity, but for individual invention and imagination Helps does not want. A number of the paragraphs glitter with a pianistic prose that indicate

Helps the composer has drawn on the vast knowledge of Helps the concert pianist and piano pedagogue.

The imposing ability of the latter personality is displayed in this recorded performance, marred only by thinnish sound.

Recollections (1959)

☐ Masselos (piano) / Desto 7122

A slight affinity to Ravel in the *In Memoriam* and *Epilogue,* but with additional impact. The thrust is given full head in the central *Interlude.* The stylistic pigeonholing is simply convenient. Helps's *Recollections* have individual imagery and show a total mastery in the handling of their subject matter.

Performance poetry where it should be, performance vitality where it is required. One would not expect less from this pianist.

Three Etudes

☐ Del Tredici (piano) / Desto 7122

Helps calls these pieces "criminally difficult." This self-impeaching statement should be corrected. "Difficult," absolutely, but musically honest, so no apology is required for the technical obstacles as long as they serve artistic demands. And they do. In Nos. 1 and 3 the music is feverish—motoric. The other study is mainly an impressionistic rough diamond.

David Del Tredici is something of a pianist! He moves through the music like a hard-boiled keyboard-instrument veteran, impervious to the supervirtuosic profusions Helps has conceived.

Saccade for Piano, Four Hands (1967)

Piano, Four Hands

☐ Chinn and Brings (piano) / Composers Recordings SD-383

Helps's piano duo achieves a cogent style without technical dogma and without striving. It has a sense of rhapsody in its six-minute span, but its chunky sentences are naturally and neatly shaped.

The Running Sun

Vocal

Voice with Accompaniment

☐ Beardslee (soprano); Helps (piano) / New World Records NW-243

Five poems (by James Purdy) run continuously as a cycle. The songs are dramatically expressive in an improvisational way. Most interesting: the three lines of the second song, set to an unchanging single pitch.

Beardslee seems to be struggling (not with her diction which has special clarity), but one assumes with the composer at the piano all goes well.

Oscar van Hemel (1892-   )

Violin Concerto No. 2 (1968)

Solo Instrument and Orchestra

☐ Concertgebouw Orchestra / Krebbers (violin) / Haitink (conductor) / Donemus Audio-Visual Series 7374/2

Violin

A Concerto with a distinct formal difference, subtitled *Four Scherzandi with Four Instrumental Groups.* The design is given contrast through the instrumentational plan.

Movement 1 uses only the woodwinds with the solo instrument. In part 2 the strings are exclusively employed. Movement 3 calls for percussion and harp, and tutti coalescence takes place in the final division. The style is atonal—on the light side, meaning no dark expressionism.

Recorded live. The soloist is fine, the orchestral playing exact (scores come with the Donemus recordings and offer the critic the opportunity for the closest reference check in regard to the performances). Some concert-hall sounds between movements are to be heard.

Robert Henderson (20th cent.)

Instrumental

Trumpet

Variation Movements (1967)

☐ Stevens (trumpet) / Avant 1003

Not a serial work though sounding like one since the basis is pitch choice drawn from an initial configuration that covers nine sounds. The simulation of a three-part fugue for a single homophonic instrument can be deemed interesting if not entirely successful. That last word does not fully apply to Stevens's performance, however.

Hans Henkemans (1913-   )

Orchestra

Partita per Orchestra (1960)

☐ Concertgebouw Orchestra / Haitink (conductor) / Donemus Audio-Visual Series DAVS-6401 (monaural: 10-inch disc)

Neoclassic syntax, but with no hesitation to use Straussian orchestral dialect for driving home the message. The performance is dynamic.

Solo Instrument and Orchestra

Four Flutes

Elégies for Four Flutes and Orchestra (1967)

☐ Concertgebouw Orchestra / Vonk (conductor) / Donemus Audio-Visual Series 7002

The dedication "à la mémoire de Pierre Monteux" underscores Henkemans's objective. The language is one of expanded tonality, and concerto mannerisms are avoided even to the extent that the flutes may choose to perform either *in* the orchestra or in front of it. But if there is little soloism, there is ample emotive depth in the piece, structured from the use of a sighing, minor-second interval.

Apparently because of this negation of soloistic liberality (though the four flutes are in no way merely obbligato), no credits are given the flutists. They certainly deserved credits, for their playing is fluid and sensitive. Good orchestral support particularly from the brass.

Instrumental

Piano

Sonata for Piano Solo (1958)

☐ Henkemans (piano) / Donemus Audio-Visual Series DAVS-6102 (monaural: 10-inch disc)

The Sonata is a virtuoso affair (and the composer plays it like one). It has ornate textures and shows a love of expansive sounds; it is thick with charged movement, making this fellow a Dutch prototype of Richard Strauss. Any affinity to Wagnerian language stops at that point. There is the same belief in rhetorical grandeur and a verbose manner of statement, but Henkemans's accent is less guttural. Nevertheless, we have heard this type of music before, and so has Henkemans.

Villonnerie (1965)

Vocal

*Voice
and Orchestra*

☐ Radio Philharmonic Orchestra / Kruysen (baritone) / Fournet (conductor) / Donemus Audio-Visual Series 6903

Villonnerie consists of settings of three texts by François Villon. Plausible musical solutions in each case, stated by conventional (but still expressive) romanticism.

Bernard Kruysen sings with sincerity and musicality and with a fine grasp of the texts. Music that one can investigate profitably.

Adolph von Henselt   (1814-1889)

Etude, Op. 2, No. 6

Instrumental

Piano

☐ Rachmaninoff (piano) / Klavier 107

This is listed with its subtitle "Were I a Bird," which is the translation of the original *Si Oiseau j'étais,* minus identification anywhere that it is the sixth of Henselt's Twelve Etudes. It is the most popular of the set, and its delicacy carries out the title perfectly. And Rachmaninoff carries out the re-creation perfectly, as well.

Trio in A minor for Piano, Violin, and Cello, Op. 24

*Chamber
Music*

☐ Mirecourt Trio / Genesis 1058/9

The textural and textual facets of romantic scoring, with fully resonanced piano writing. Henselt's writing is all intelligent and skillful even though it breeds conventionality.

Romantic-music collectors will want this. The performance sounds "right" and catches all the urgency of the music.

Hans Werner Henze   (1926-   )

Ode an den Westwind

*Solo
Instrument
and
Orchestra*

Cello

☐ Orchestra of the Bavarian Radio / Palm (cello) / Henze (conductor) / Deutsche Grammophon 139382

A concerto concept that relatively images the five stanzas of the Shelley poem. Not a virtuosic essay in the commonly understood sense, though it takes a virtuoso to negotiate its fragmented verbiage, as Siegfried Palm does successfully. The orchestra mostly colors in and around the solo voice.

Concerto No. 2 for Piano and Orchestra (1968)

Piano

☐ London Philharmonic Orchestra / Eschenbach (piano) / Henze (conductor) / Deutsche Grammophon 2530056

Henze carries a big stick in this three-movements-in-one work—twice the average length of a concerto. This splurge is matched by big romantic sounds, especially in the wild dance atmosphere of the second section. The finale was inspired by words from Shakespeare: "The expense of spirit in a waste of shame." No stinting here either on sonorous celebrations.

With Henze conducting and the person for whom the work was written at the piano, plus the orchestra that participated in the London premiere of the work, there is no doubting the authenticity of the Deutsche Grammophon recording.

Violin
Concerto for Violin and Orchestra (1948)

☐ Luxembourg Radio Orchestra / Lautenbacher (violin) / Köhler (conductor) / Candide 31061

Early Henze, hardly touching on twelve-tone procedures and extremely freely rhapsodic. Just as freely structured in its four movements.

The soloist is admirable, meeting all challenges contained in the score.

Instrumental
Drei Tentos from Kammermusik 1958

Guitar
☐ Bream (guitar) / RCA LSC–2964

These are three interludes drawn from a work that calls for a tenor, guitar, and eight other instruments. High-register coloration is emphasized in the first part, activity in the second of the set, and a Neapolitan flavor is recognizable in the final piece.

Piano
Sonata per pianoforte (1959)

Variationen für Klavier, Op. 13

☐ Floyd (piano) / Advance S–10

Intense lyricism in the *Sonata* that is counterpointed by expressionism that peeps out of the clouds for the greater part. The "Variations" are abstracts minus a thematic springboard. Finely prepared playing.

Chamber Music
Quintett (1952)

☐ Dorian Quintet / Candide 31016

Drollery, with a sense of parody is exhibited in the pithy *Galopp* finale. An opaque quality marks the opening, variations follow. In the second movement sectionalism shapes the structure.

Free dodecaphonicism is blended with direct polytonality in Henze's woodwind quintet. To clarify this offers performance problems. However, the playing is well balanced and lucidly discloses all the pertinent detail of the score.

Robert Heppener   (1925-   )

Vocal
Cantico delle creature di San Francesco d'Assisi (1954)

Voice and Orchestra
☐ Radio Chamber Orchestra / Ameling (soprano) / Hupperts (conductor) / Donemus Audio-Visual Series DAVS–6604 (monaural)

A twentieth-century conception of a hymn from the early Italian Renaissance period.

The music is mostly concentrated in the voice part (effectively sung by Elly Ameling), with the support of a string orchestra plus harp.

Victor Herbert (1859-1924)

American Fantasia

Orchestra

☐ Cincinnati Pops Orchestra / Kunzel (conductor) / Turnabout 34714

The stuff movie orchestras used to present as the overture preceding the newsreel. American tunes in medley form, written at the request of the famed Anton Seidl for use at his summer concerts. As far as can be ascertained this is the premiere recording, made eighty-one years after the work was published.

The President's March

Band

The Serenade

☐ Goldman Band / Goldman (conductor) / New World Records NW-266

The name of Victor Herbert means we're in the operetta world. But Herbert wrote more than a dozen marches. The recording of this pair (*The Serenade*, taken from an operetta with the same name, does not bear the descriptive formal word) will be a premiere performance for most people. They will ascertain that Herbert could turn out as good marches as those that enjoy the greatest popularity.

Concerto No. 2 for Cello and Orchestra, Op. 30

Solo Instrument and Orchestra

☐ Eastman-Rochester Symphony Orchestra / Miquelle (cello) / Hanson (conductor) / Eastman-Rochester Archives ERA-1014

Cello

Instrumental vocalism of charm and tastefulness, and considerably more of that than of pompous virtuosity, is contained in Herbert's concerto. The lines of the solo voice are shaped in long phrases and are extremely profitable.

It's good to have this work recorded (and recorded with taste and style) just to document that Herbert could turn his refreshing melodic hand to other than operettas and light music.

By no means consider the Bernard Greenhouse performance with the Vienna Symphony Orchestra conducted by Max Schoenherr (on Desto 6417E). The orchestral playing is just downright bad, the sound atrocious, rough, grainy, scratchy, noisy, and unbalanced.

Johannes Herbst (1735-1812)

I Will Go in the Strength of the Lord

Vocal

☐ Moravian Festival Orchestra / Kombrinck (soprano) / Johnson (conductor) / Odyssey 32160340

Voice and Orchestra

Handel revisited in this aria.

Choral	**God Was in Jesus**
Chorus and Instrumental Ensemble	☐ Gregg Smith Singers / Smith (conductor) / Vox SVBX–5350

An example of the most prolific of the American Moravian composers. Herbst's anthem is accompanied by strings and is framed with a long-short rhythmic figure that is typically Handelian. Fine, vigorous singing by Gregg Smith's expert group.
(No credits are given for the instrumentalists.)

Chorus and Orchestra

O Sacred Head, Now Wounded

☐ Moravian Festival Orchestra and Chorus / Johnson (conductor) / Odyssey 32160340

The melody of Herbst's chorale-anthem was first written by Hassler and later used in Bach's St. Matthew Passion. First-rate choral work on this recording.

Louis-Joseph-Ferdinand Herold   (1791 - 1833)

Orchestra

Overture to *Zampa*

☐ New York Philharmonic / Bernstein (conductor) / Columbia D3S–818

The Overture to *La Fiancee de Marbre* (to give its secondary title) is currently available in ten issues, with Bernstein and the New York Phil. in five different assortments all on Columbia (MS–6743, MS–6988, M–31815, and M3X–31068), Albert Wolff and the Paris Conservatory ensemble in two (on London STS–15021 and STS–15223), and Ansermet (Suisse Romande on London STS–15217), Bonynge (London Symphony on London 6486), and Ormandy with his Philadelphians (on RCA ARL1–0453) each on the market in single releases.

This entire output can be indicated as acceptable, save that in each case except Bernstein's there is a minus point: insufficient punch in Wolff's reading, overheaviness in the tuttis in Ormandy's, etc. Clarity in the dynamic portions and sensitivity in the lyrical portions place the Bernstein edition in first place. His performance, as catalogued above, falls in a three-record combine that covers eighteen overtures. Of the other four albums (all Columbia) which include "his" *Zampa,* one is still another three-record affair; the remainder cover single records.

Ballet

La Fille mal gardée

☐ Orchestra of the Royal Opera House, Covent Garden / Lanchbery (conductor) / London 6252

One of the oldest of 'em all still in the international repertory. It is performed with innate respect for the idiom.

Johann Wilhelm Hertel   (1727 - 1789)

Solo Instrument and Orchestra

Double Concerto in E flat major for Trumpet, Oboe, Strings, and Continuo

☐ Consortium Musicum / Tarr (trumpet); Hucke (oboe) / Lehan (conductor) / Nonesuch 71270

Trumpet and Oboe

While the format is usual—three movements, with a pair of fast movements embracing an Arioso—the playing is not. Edward Tarr's tone is not brassy or edgy. It has a delicacy that is as impressive as any heavy virtuosity or laying into the notes. This is a special type of trumpet virility that makes Hertel's work a delight to hear. The oboist, Helmut Hucke, is a fine partner.

820

Partita III in D minor

☐ Haselböck (organ); Riessberger (flute) / Turnabout 34612

Hertel's Partitas were written for organ or cembalo with flute or oboe. The choice represented here is efficacious, resulting in soft-sell, amiable music. (There are three movements, no tempi given, and no bands on the disc.)

Concerto a cinque

☐ Academy of St. Martin-in-the-Fields / Wilbraham (trumpet); Tilney (harpsichord) / Marriner (conductor) / Argo ZRG–585

Matters of title first. *Schwann* lists this work as "Concerto in D," which follows Turnabout's listing in its two packages that include Hertel's extremely appealing work, the rubric for the Turnabout 34090 album being "German Baroque Trumpet Concerti." Argo's definition is practically the same, its heading being "Baroque Trumpet Concertos." However, the medium is set straight in Robin Golding's expert liner note, which states, "It is not really a concerto at all, but a quintet, scored for the unlikely combination of trumpet, two oboes and two bassoons." Only Desto (6438) is exact with its "Baroque Chamber Music" album designation. A chamber-music work this is, even with the word "concerto" included, and a quintet it is, notwithstanding the use of a harpsichord for continuo purposes.

The four movements include one minus the trumpet (the *Cantabile*) and another (*Plaisanterie*) which contains a delightful trio section for the bassoons alone. But here again production matters are sloppy. Nonesuch does not list the movements and gives zero data concerning the work. Desto names three oboists on the liner copy and properly only two on the label. The contradiction is quite suspect, since one of the listed oboe players, Virginia Brewer, disappears entirely from the label copy on both sides of the disc covering three different compositions (Albinoni and Telemann, additional to the Hertel). Then why is her name on the jacket? Questionable editorial decision also extends to Desto's recording, since movements 3 and 4 are interchanged; the original, as on Argo, ending with the peppier *Plaisanterie* is certainly to be preferred, both for performance honesty and actual effect.

Both the Argo and the Desto performances are excellent. The former is chosen because it not only is a mite smoother but has far better sound. The playing on Nonesuch's release is pedestrian.

Henri Herz *(1803 - 1888)*

Hexaméron. **See under *Franz Liszt: Solo Instrument and Orchestra: piano.***

Etude in A flat major (*Au Bord du lac*), Op. 153, No. 2
Variations on the March from Bellini's *I Puritani*
Variations on the National March *La Parisienne*, Op. 53

☐ Cooper (piano) / Genesis 1006

High-class salon music and most worthy. The sets of variations are extremely colorful and contain some effects (in the *La Parisienne*) in which the piano becomes a mini-band.

Frank Cooper is responsible for rescuing a great deal of forgotten music and is a driving force in the current romantic-music revival. Any way, apart from this, he's a fine pianist, and the literate notes he has written about the music are worth everyone's time.

Philip Heseltine. See Peter Warlock.

Richard Heuberger (1850-1914)

Orchestra

Overture to *Der Opernball*

☐ Vienna Philharmonic Orchestra / Kempe (conductor) / Seraphim SIB-6109

Whatever success Heuberger enjoyed was due to his operettas, though his orchestral Variations on a Schubert Theme (which *Grove's Dictionary of Music and Musicians* doesn't even list) is a fine work. *Der Opernball* was the most successful of the half-dozen operettas he wrote. The Overture is an example of its fine qualities.

George Heussenstamm (1926-   )

Chamber Music

Tubafour, Op. 30

☐ New York Tuba Quartet / Crystal S-221

A mainly dark, somewhat turgid quality embraces this work. Within the instrumental limitations of sonority chosen, Heussenstamm has resorted to a somewhat fragmentary style. Virility there is, though no gaiety.

James Hewitt (1770-1827)

Instrumental

Organ

Yankee Doodle, with Variations

☐ Ellsasser (organ) / Nonesuch 71200

Hewitt was doubtless the first to ring variations on the well-known tune. A fair number of composers have been doing it ever since. Hewitt's set is best when it rolls over to the minor-key side. Ellsasser gives it the big treatment. No harm.

Piano

The Fourth of July: A Grand Military Sonata

Grand March and Tammany Quick Step

☐ Mandel (piano) / Desto 6445/7

In the days before radio (and even for a time afterwards) programs of summer band concerts often included a descriptive potpourri covering such topics as "A Day in the City," Down on the Farm," "The Hunt," etc. It mattered little that the titles of the "action" promised considerably more than the music could deliver. The story line was a peg on which to hang an auditor's interest and maintain his concentration on material that for the most part was undifferentiated or primitively imitative.

It is this type of old-timey music that Mandel plays with the same spirit, intensity, musicianship, and color that he would apply to a deadly serious contemporary opus. Hewitt's Americana souvenir runs for a bit over twelve minutes, during which there are nineteen depictions, such as "Day break," "Assembling the people," "Firing small arms," etc., concluding with *Hail Columbia* and a tag finale. Americana, yes. Historic, yes. Bringing nostalgia, yes. Corny, yes. But amusing.

There is a competitive edition, which is interesting, worthy, and played to the hilt, but one must be warned that it is not authentic and must be considered an arrangement. This is Richard Ellsasser's performance on Nonesuch 71200. First, Hewitt's piece is "for the pianoforte"; Ellsasser plays it on the organ. Second, his edition is a bit more than three and one-half minutes shorter. While Ellsasser's cutting does not in any way disturb the balance or continuity, nevertheless it is a condensation. The big plus is that no matter Mandel's expertise, the imitative possibilities of a piano are not in the same league as an organ.

Hewitt's Grand March is solemn, in keeping with its purpose—for use at a funeral procession. The Tammany Quick Step is, naturally, the other side of the mood coin.

William Hibbard   *(1939-   )*

Bass Trombone, Bass Clarinet, Harp (1973)

Chamber Music

☐ English, West, and Forman (instrumentalists) / Hibbard (conductor) / Composers Recordings S–324

Has any other composer written a trio for this combine? I doubt it. Incidentally, it is titled exactly as listed above. "Trio for" does not precede the named instruments.

The mode of free-formed communication is special, inventive, and telling. The trombone provides a direct impression of timbre, principally by emphasizing ictus quality for its entries; the more spontaneously quiet use of the bass clarinet is in direct contrast, and the harp inserts add fluidity.

Hibbard's three-voice "orchestration" is sensitively registered in this recording. (The names of the performers are without instrument identity. The guess here is that Jon English plays the bass trombone, Charles West is responsible for the bass-clarinet part, and the harpist is Motter Forman.)

String Quartet (1971)

☐ Stradivari Quartet / Composers Recordings S–322

Within are Babbittesque procedures (rhythmic serialism) and Carterian processes (though not rigidly applied, specific personality character having been assigned each of the four instruments). Though developed from ritornello data, Hibbard's work is constructed by tight serial structuring. A rational music it is, fully validating twelve-tone style. The playing is excellent.

Edward Burlingame Hill   *(1872-1960)*

Sextet for Flute, Oboe, Clarinet, Horn, Bassoon, and Piano, Op. 39

Chamber Music

☐ New York Woodwind Quintet / Kallir (piano) / Columbia Special Products AML–4846 (monaural)

Hill was in his sixties when he composed this prize-winning work (selected by the

Society for the Publication of American Music in 1937, after being commissioned by Elizabeth Sprague Coolidge); yet it definitely bears the mark of a young man, in the jazz shrugs of its opening movement, spliced with syncopation, especially in forming a $\frac{4}{4}$ measure so that it has ratioed pulsations of $1\frac{1}{2}$, $1\frac{1}{2}$, and 1. The first movement's germination carries over into the effectively wrought Scherzo, alive with movement, with each instrument sharing matters.

Hill was not an impressionist, but he more than glanced at such methods. The opening of the slow movement, with the spacing of hollow timbre is New England impressionism if not of France. The Finale is gay and includes the main theme expressed in fugato.

Ferdinand Hiller (1811 - 1885)

Solo Instrument and Orchestra

Piano

Concerto in F sharp minor for Piano and Orchestra, Op. 69

☐ Radio Luxembourg Symphony Orchestra / Ponti (piano) / de Froment (conductor) / Candide 31058

As good an example as any of the style of this prolific composer (with an output including three symphonies, five string quartets, five piano trios, five piano quartets, three piano concertos, and more than a hundred songs. Rich Mendelssohn-like content, solid form, and clear orchestration comprise music that is certainly worthy of revival.

Michael Ponti does well with the dynamic opening movement (*Moderato, ma con energia e con fuoco*), sings nicely in the *Andante espressivo,* and nimbly tosses off the *Finale* (in *allegro con fuoco* tempo). Good support from the orchestra.

Not always good production details from Candide. Hiller's work in coupled with a Piano Concerto by Joachim Raff. The jacket boldly gives the soloist credit for both works in the issue, but only credits the orchestra and the conductor for the Raff piece. Totally misleading unless one checks the label copy carefully, not to mention the total unfairness to the conductor and orchestra that perform Hiller's work. Two other errors: major—no liner notes whatsoever and thus no information concerning the music; minor—a typo in the tempo for movement 1 on the label copy.

Lejaren Hiller (1924-   )

Orchestra

Algorithms I

Version I (1968) / Version IV (1968)

☐ Kotik (flute); Kirkbride (clarinet); Reynard (bassoon); Collura (trumpet); Falcāo (harp); Burnham (percussion); Haupt (violin); Verberne (cello); Kurzdorfer (double bass); Ritscher (tape recorder) / Hiller (conductor) / Deutsche Grammophon 2543005

Computer application was used by Hiller in writing this work, heard in two of the four versions existent. Serial procedures are included, though the results are like sound chips off the Xenakis block. Even the titles of the three parts of the piece have a Xenakis tinge: *The Decay of Information, Icosahedron,* and *The Incorporation of Constraints.*

The technical difficulties are extreme. However, these young virtuosi, from the Center of Creative and Performing Arts at the State University of New York at Buffalo, are superb.

Sonata No. 4 for Piano (1950)

☐ Frina Arschanska Boldt (piano) / Orion 75176

Hiller does not attempt to identify Hiller here, but to mimic specific styles. Movement 1 equals late romantic procedures, the second part is a look at pop that includes blues and a bit of bash. In movement 3 march outlines are outlined and just a bit of Ivesian reminder slithers in. The finale is "folk derived" and uses a registral plan to frame a tarantella.

It is all meant, says Hiller, "to be rather humorous." Interesting, indeed, but only possibly humorous in the way interruptive clash of material occurs in movements 2 and 3.

The playing is a bit rough. That's acceptable in the middle sections, not so much so in the corner movements. The piano's tone is also not very rich. Again, that's serviceable for movements 2 and 3, below par for movements 1 and 4.

Sonata No. 5 for Piano (1961)

☐ Kenwyn Boldt (piano) / Orion 75176

Diversity plays a great part here. An all-interval row is basic to movement 1; evaporative sound, limited to the upper range of the piano and including considerable use of silence, is the plan for movement 2. Motility arrives in movement 3, and a design of increasing speed covers the finale. Diversity also is found in the purposeful imbalance of the time lengths for these four sections, namely, 8:09, 12:31, 3:33, and 1:35.

Boldt is meticulously consistent in his playing. In that respect there is a freshness that cannot be denied. There are no doubts that all the musical problems of Hiller's piece have been musically solved.

Five Appalachian Ballads for Voice and Guitar (1958)

☐ Simpson (soprano); Sussman (guitar) / Orion 78287

The tunes are taken from the famous Cecil Sharp collection *English Folk Songs from the Southern Appalachians.* They are *Lord Randall, Barbara Allen, The Three Ravens, The Cruel Mother,* and *The Two Sisters.* They are slightly sing-song in effect but are joined to tart and dissonant harmonies. The acridity produces a yield, as though the composer were imitating on-the-spot amateur music making to fit a homespun atmosphere.

Winifred Simpson's voice is somewhat light but satisfactory. David Ethan Sussman manages nicely, but the recording has picked up a lot of finger swishes.

Jesse James for Vocal Quartet and Piano (1950)

☐ Bane (soprano); Rosenberg (alto); Daniel (tenor); Schultze (bass); Cary (piano) / Orion 78287

Once-over-lightly style, some pitter-patter, and some "wrong note" chording in this imitation of a mixed vocal quartet performing in quasi-vaudeville atmosphere. Perhaps one reads Hiller incorrectly in making this statement, but such is the response to his honky-tonk-highbrow blend. Quite enjoyable. Patly styled in the performance. Great lyrics by William Rose Benét.

Hiller and Robert Baker (20th cent.)

Electronic Music

Computer Cantata for Soprano, Instrumental Ensemble, and Two-Channel Tape Recorder (1963)

☐ University of Illinois Contemporary Chamber Players / Hamm (soprano) / McKenzie (conductor) / Composers Recordings S–310

The instruments comprise two each of woodwind, brass, and strings, a guitar, and ten percussion (two of which are pitched). The electronic sounds include a theremin and a tape that includes sine, square, and sawtooth waves, white and ''colored'' noise, and computer-generated sounds. Computer-generated sequences of English phonemes are used by the voice.

Computer programming for musical composition just cannot be dismissed—it will not go away—but we are far from the nonexperimental stage, regardless of all the tracts, the explanations, and the copious theory. The Hiller-Baker eleven-section work is a supreme didactic piece of evidence. Included in the Cantata are studies in rhythmic organization, ''totally organized'' serial music, and composition in even-tempered scales that range from nine to fifteen tones per octave. The published score shows the magnificent mathematical conceptions that can be derived from computerized musical programming. That is the most positive evidence. The opposite is the lack of identification of a style, in contrast to Xenakis's music, for instance, which has its own recognizable profile. It remains true that the machines are only as good as the people who run them; the moral is obvious. Still, the Hiller-Baker Computer Cantata is fantastically functional and beautifully braintrusted. It should be experienced.

Hiller and John Cage. *See Cage and Lejaren Hiller.*

Paul Hindemith   (1895-1963)

Orchestra

Concert Music for String Orchestra and Brass Instruments, Op. 50

☐ Philharmonia Orchestra, London / Hindemith (conductor) / Seraphim S–60005

Organized with discrimination. There is a reshuffling of classic order, with sensible elimination of all superficialities. Five divisions are spliced into the two parts of the work. The inner contrasts of the pair of movements produce an equilibrium of finesse, with a ''rondo'' alternation of speeds.

The best of the recordings available. The sonic blend will make any recordphile very happy.

Der Dämon: Concert Suite, Op. 28

☐ Stuttgart Solisten / Grüber (conductor) / Candide 31044

''The Demon,'' a ballet pantomime, was written in 1924. The story deals with a prehistoric character, an exemplification of evil, who seduces two young girls and then practices sadism on them.

The scoring is for a dectet of flute doubling on piccolo, clarinet, horn, trumpet, piano, and a string quintet. In a note in the score Hindemith is very clear that the entire ballet is not to be performed in concert. However, he states, ''Parts of it would . . . be suitable for concert performances. It is left to the conductor's judgement to make an appropriate choice.'' This has been done, but with vague identification on Candide's part and little differences between the dances to begin with, it is difficult to know what has been selected for performance.

The playing is adequate. Sufficient it is, since this score is by no means top-drawer Hindemith.

Kammermusik No. 1 (with Finale: 1921) for Twelve Solo Instruments, Op. 24, No. 1

☐ Concerto Amsterdam / Telefunken 3635008

The best known of Hindemith's *Kammermusik* anthology. It is music of wit, irony, and violent vitality, with twenty-one instruments utilized by the dozen performers. Toccata drive and heat mark the end movements, and a dance tune of 1921 vintage is woven into the Finale, plus the wail of a siren.

This is music of muscle and tone, and it is played with exultant energy. No conductor is utilized—never thus on the concert stage, but the Amsterdam players don't need one from the evidence heard here.

Nusch-Nuschi-Tänze, Op. 20

☐ Berlin Symphony Orchestra / Grüber (conductor) / Candide 31044

Das Nusch-Nuschi is a one-act musical play for Burmese marionettes that Hindemith composed in 1920. The premiere took place on June 4, 1921, in Stuttgart, with Fritz Busch conducting. A bit of a scandal followed, since a quotation from *Tristan und Isolde* is used in a castration scene in the work. (The prudish reaction did not pertain to the action, but to the Wagnerian use.)

Despite a full orchestra (only two horns and two trumpets but four clarinets) the music has a rewarding flexibility. The playing displays this nicely, as well as the Hindemithian brand of clear-cut rhythmic designs.

Sinfonietta in E (1950)

☐ Louisville Orchestra / Whitney (conductor) / Louisville 605 (monaural)

Hindemith's artistic calligraphy shows in this work. Movements 2 and 4 combine a slow section with a fugato and a recitative with a spicy rondo. The opening is fast, the third movement based on ostinato. The initial part is Hindemith *en rapport* with Bach, a factor that distinguishes most of the motoric allegros; ostinato and fugue are two of the major forces of Hindemith's technical arsenal—very few of his pieces omit either.

Symphonia serena (1947)

☐ Philharmonia Orchestra / Hindemith (conductor) / Angel S-35491

No pat summations. Hindemith is mindful of not calling back all old yesterdays in his formal treatment. Transmutation-translation methods are used in the second movement, molded from a Beethoven march. In the third movement, for double string orchestra alone, themes are stated separately, then combined, and further interstices occur with solo instruments. The entire work is crammed with a divertimento atmosphere. The recording is masterful in all respects, with beautiful sound.

Symphonic Metamorphosis of Themes by Carl Maria von Weber (1943)

☐ Chicago Symphony Orchestra / Kubelik (conductor) / Mercury MG 3-4501 (monaural)
☐ Philadelphia Orchestra / Ormandy (conductor) / Columbia MS-6562

There is no error in the above listings. The preferable delineation of Hindemith's score is that conducted by Rafael Kubelik. It is in monaural form, indeed, but the opinion here is that top performance quality comes first, and that all that is necessary is a satisfactory sonic reproduction to accompany it. A monophonic disc does not diminish interpretative values. Of course, stereo is better, but there isn't a recorded performance of this piece in stereo that can match the Chicago-Kubelik version. However, if the auditor insists on a stereophonic release, then Ormandy's performance with the Philadelphians is the best choice.

Symphony, *Die Harmonie der Welt* (1951)

☐ Festival Symphony Orchestra / Hindemith (conductor) / Everest 3226E (monaural)

Akin to the Symphony, *Mathis der Maler*, this suite is drawn from an opera, *The Harmony of the Universe*. The subject matter is the life of Johann Kepler, a seventeenth-century philosopher and astronomer, and emphasizes his speculations concerning the music of the spheres.

There are some who contend that while polyphony is an intense factor in compositional technique, it is not the most dramatic means of expression. Hindemith's three-part Symphony (especially the compelling final passacaglia) argues against such a theory.

Symphony in E flat (1940)

☐ New York Philharmonic / Bernstein (conductor) / Columbia MS-7426

For the key of "E flat," read tonal polarity. In his later period Hindemith is not concerned with constrained keys, but employs tonality centers. All sounds are related by the measurement of the distance from one center to other points, which affords (depending on the distance) tension or repose, stability or motility; furthermore, modulations from one area move to another and, in turn, give a particular tensility contrasted to release. Thus Hindemith "keys" his music in terms of new controls. It is the contemporary manner of tonal etiquette.

Formally, the Symphony follows the traditional four-movement procedure. The vigorous opening portion is followed by a dirge-like slow movement, then a scherzo that avoids the light hop-skip-and-jump of Mendelssohnian style, and a summational finale. In content, the paramount technical element is polyphony. Hindemith refuses to disguise his love for horizontal construction.

No problem as to recorded-performance choice. Bernstein is in his element here, and the entire work is worked out and presented with grand eloquence. Boult and the London Philharmonic Orchestra are available on Everest 3008. He keeps things moving, but the effect is somewhat aloof, almost distressingly ascetic.

Symphony, *Mathis der Maler* (1934)

☐ London Symphony Orchestra / Horenstein (conductor) / Nonesuch 71307
☐ Philadelphia Orchestra / Ormandy (conductor) / Columbia MS-6562

Proof of Horenstein's abilities, somewhat overlooked in the conductorial scheme of things. Clean and clear, direct and dynamically proper. Ormandy's reading is as superb. He has rarely surpassed it with any other work. A golden glow suffuses his conception.

Five Pieces for String Orchestra, Op. 44, No. 4

☐ I Solisti di Zagreb / Janigro (conductor) / Vanguard 71118

The pieces are a synthesis, a concentrate of Hindemith's early style representing the richest segment of his output. The small and precise settings of these pieces make perfect art jewels. Especially compelling is the final movement with a solo violin riding on top of the full string body. It is Hindemith's creative trademark all the way. And the Zagreb players' special performance qualities shine throughout.

Konzertmusik für Blasorchester, Op. 41

☐ University of Michigan School of Music Wind Ensemble / Reynolds (conductor) / University of Michigan Records SM-0003

Composed in 1927. In those days Hindemith didn't avoid the smirk, the tongue in cheek, the sardonic crease in his notes. And a lot of that will be found, plus healthy doses of militaristic rhythms, in the three movements. Mixed in is a quote from popular Austrian music: the six variations of movement 2 are based on the song *Prinz Eugen, der Edle Ritter* ("Prince Eugene, the Noble Knight").

The university musicians knock the hell out of this music. Their performance is stunning. If it is realized that such an ensemble is subject to constant turnover due to graduation, then one feels more appreciation. H. Robert Reynolds's conducting is superb; his projection of the score shows all the big-league music making is not centered in the cities of New York, Chicago, Boston, and Philadelphia.

Symphony in B flat for Concert Band (1951)

☐ Eastman Symphonic Wind Ensemble / Fennell (conductor) / Mercury 75057
☐ Philharmonia Orchestra, London / Hindemith (conductor) / Seraphim S-60005

None of the restrictive orthodoxy that plagues 99 percent (and more!) of band compositions. This work is Hindemithian to the core, and there is resourceful use of colors (one illustration: the counterplay between the alto saxophone and cornet in the middle movement of this twenty-minute opus). Open a Hindemith score, and of course you will find polyphonic empathy. This is strongly and admirably reflected in the work.

There is little choice between the pair of performances listed. Hindemith moves his music a bit more slowly and his conception is less athletic than Fennell's. Both conductors do not overindulge themselves (Hindemith certainly wouldn't!). It is really worth owning both recordings.

Kammermusik No. 3 (Cello Concerto) for Obbligato Cello and Ten Solo Instruments, Op. 36, No. 2

☐ Concerto Amsterdam / Bylsma (cello) / Telefunken 3635008

There is a breadth in this opus not duplicated in any of the other *Kammermusik* works. The opening movement sets the style: it is a majestic portion that along the way presents the metrical definitions utilized later. In movement 2 the $\frac{9}{4}$ time signature makes possible wide-spanned mensural patterns. The same applies to the sextuple-beat measurement of movement 3. A *comodo* pace in the finale certifies that the general mood of the music is not disturbed.

Balance and tonal sheen are as close to perfection as one could wish in this performance.

Trauermusik for Cello and Strings (1936)

☐ I Solisti di Zagreb / Janigro (cello) / Vanguard 71118

The original setting was for viola as the solo instrument. A recording in that form is also noted—see under *viola* (*Trauermusik* for Viola and Strings [1936]). This performance is just as ideal, and the version is absolutely "official." With Hindemith's approval, the work was published for solo viola or solo cello or solo violin. Even a setting for solo trombone was sanctioned for recording, at least by the publisher's American agents if not by the publisher's home office.

Horn

Concerto for Horn and Orchestra (1950)

☐ Philharmonia Orchestra / Brain (horn) / Hindemith (conductor) / Angel S–35491

Music *for* the horn, not transferred to it from initial, neutrally colored creativity. None of this monkeying with fanfare-like data, *à la chasse* material, etc. The instrument sings. And it is impossible to imagine a better performance, or one with a more potent quality of tone. Brain recorded this soon before his untimely death in an auto accident.

Organ

Kammermusik No. 7 (Concerto for Organ and Chamber Orchestra), Op. 46, No. 2

☐ Concerto Amsterdam / de Klerk (organ) / Telefunken 3635008

The dogmatism of Hindemith's musical speech is well suited to the organ, and so are the gritty harmonic synonyms that season his language. Motoric style is the plain-speaking objective of movement 1. The finale is just as unequivocal—a fugue that concludes matters properly with rousing toccata energy. A great performance in all respects.

Piano

Kammermusik No. 2 (Piano Concerto) for Obbligato Piano and Twelve Solo Instruments, Op. 36, No. 1

☐ Members of the Louisville Orchestra / Luvisi (piano) / Mester (conductor) / Louisville S–684

Hindemith's four-movement "Chamber Music" (the titling of the recording eliminates the parenthetical subtitle as well as the explanatory "for obbligato piano and twelve solo instruments") has not dated, though at the time this is being written Hindemith is not terribly fashionable. (This writer is of the opinion that this is but a temporary lapse in appreciation. Critics, after all, must believe in their convictions.)

Machinelike, unemotional, the work is nonetheless exciting, and the sheer music-making that takes place is a joy to both performer and auditor. (And this covers the recorded performance as well.) In its way, Hindemith's serious contemporary Bachian conspectus is quite unserious. Even in its more quiet moments (movement 2) there is a smart, crisp underlay.

Trumpet and Bassoon

Concerto for Trumpet, Bassoon, and String Orchestra (1949)

☐ Los Angeles Group for Contemporary Music / Breidenthal (bassoon); Guarneri (trumpet) / Kraft (conductor) / Crystal S–352

Hindemith's gingery drive did not lessen throughout the years. The vagrant waltz idea included in this work is in evidence. The bright and dark colors of the soli are contrasted beautifully (and played similarly) in a modern translation of concerto grosso design. A rare contribution to the limited literature of double concerti.

It is good to have the work back in the recorded catalogue—the Fantasy disc (5001), conducted by Millar, with Haug and Ojeda as the trumpet and bassoon soloists, respectively, having long been out of print. A few more in the Los Angeles orchestra would not have been amiss—the strings total just three each of first and second violins, violas and cellos, with two double basses.

Concert Music for Solo Viola and Large Chamber Orchestra, Op. 48

Viola

☐ Louisville Orchestra / Hillyer (viola) / Mester (conductor) / Louisville S–694

Hindemith's tonal chromaticism used in long, romantically fused lines and in note-busy passage work, with generous opportunities for the virtuosity that Raphael Hillyer displays aptly here. Absent is the pinched sound heard from many a violist. Hillyer's tone is exceedingly bright, in the high range very close to sounding like a violin. It is playing of this quality that makes one overlook some of Hindemith's shopworn formulae.

Der Schwanendreher (1935)

☐ London Philharmonic Orchestra / Doktor (viola) / Downes (conductor) / Odyssey 32160368

There are two special points to be made about this "Concerto for Viola and Small Orchestra." First, the three movements are based on four folk tunes with which Hindemith makes polyphonic sport, though there are sufficient homophonic sections to give relief and contrast. Second, there are neither violins nor violas in the orchestra, and this places the solo instrument in bold outline.

There are also two special points concerning the chosen recording. First, Paul Doktor's tone has none of the somewhat coarse, somewhat nasal, somewhat heavy-handed negative qualities generally heard in performances of Hindemith's piece. Second, the playing is totally convincing because it has just the correct amount of aggressiveness.

Kammermusik No. 5 (Viola Concerto), Op. 36, No. 4

☐ Concerto Amsterdam / Doktor (viola) / Telefunken 3635008

Music of quite motoric impetus, very exciting in the first movement, very ornate and somewhat recitative-like in the second. The finale is a set of variations and includes one of the few cadenzas Hindemith used in his *Kammermusik* set.

Paul Doktor's is a rave performance. It falls in a three-record set forming a major release and in totality deserving of a special award. However, Doktor's exposition can be secured separately (together with *Kammermusik* No. 6) on Telefunken 641291.

Trauermusik for Viola and Strings (1936)

☐ English Chamber Orchestra / Aronowitz (viola) / Barenboim (conductor) / Angel S–36484

"Music of Mourning" was begun the day after the death of King George V of England and performed the following evening. A short four-movement piece in full Hindemithian voice. Its performance is with viola (the original solo voice), or cello, or violin.

A release using the cello as the solo instrument is also noted—see under *cello* (*Trauermusik* for Cello and Strings [1936]).

Kammermusik No. 6 (Concerto for Viola d'Amore and Chamber Orchestra), Op. 46, No. 1

Viola d'Amore

☐ Concerto Amsterdam / Vermeulen (viola d'amore) / Telefunken 3635008

Creativity in the average Hindemith manner, with no special coloristic pleading for the solo voice employed. The usual four-movement plan, including a set of variations in the third part.

Joke Vermeulen's capable performance is also available on Telefunken 641291, paired with *Kammermusik* No. 5.

Violin

Concerto for Violin and Orchestra (1939)

☐ London Symphony Orchestra / David Oistrakh (violin) / Hindemith (conductor) / London 6337

No angry, bleak, icy, cutting music here. Hindemith's Concerto is not illustrative of the heedlessness that so often makes modern pieces for the violin a stifling of the instrument's personality. Instead, it proclaims a romantic contemporaneity that sings with liquescence (and therefore conviction), making the fiddle sound like a violin.

For the most part the music is un-Hindemithian, but this does not damn him; rather, these delights have beautiful persuasion. The Concerto is lyrical, a scrutiny of *cantilena* that is as exciting as all the flying-trapeze technique required by music of the note-loose, virtuosic school. This ardent vocalism is even present in the third movement, the most rhythmic and spirited portion of the piece.

David Oistrakh's performance is brilliantly styled, and his tone is marvelous. His consideration of the Hindemith score is in the nature of a sleeper if there ever was one, since one would not expect Oistrakh to be favorably disposed to music of Hindemithian cut. However, if anything this further supports the finding that a romantic inlay supports Hindemith's structure.

Oistrakh's impeccable violin diction backed by orchestral playing of substance receives competition only from Turnabout's 34276 (originally on Vox 11980) with Ivry Gitlis as the soloist and Hubert Reichert conducting the Westphalia Symphony Orchestra. It is totally rewarding, but the sound quality is not what is offered by the London firm.

Fuchs, with Goossens conducting (on Everest 3040), is not in the running because of an academic depiction. Stern, with Bernstein conducting (on Columbia MS-6713), has all the notes right on target, but the music is styled with waywardness, and this disturbs the lyrical positiveness of the Concerto's lines. There are also some questionable balances.

Kammermusik No. 4 (Violin Concerto) for Solo Violin and Large Chamber Orchestra, Op. 36, No. 3

☐ Concerto Amsterdam / Schröder (violin) / Telefunken 3635008

The solo voice is silent in the opening *Signal*, but elsewhere it is in command: vigorous in movement 2, lyrical in the *Nachtstück*, and fugally peppery in the finale, a section which is a marvel of perpetual-motion excitement.

Superb solo rendition, superb orchestral partnership by Jaap Schröder and his colleagues. Incidentally, the orchestral scoring does not include violins, which highlights the solo string voice. However, Hindemith specifies that four each of the violas, cellos, and basses are to be used. The recording group shaves these totals, utilizing three violas and two each of cellos and basses.

Instrumental

Cello

A Frog He Went A-Courting: Variations on a Nursery Song (1941)
Three Easy Pieces (1938)

☐ Steiner (cello); Berfield (piano) / Orion 73117

The Three Easy Pieces should not be confused with the Three Pieces, also for cello and piano, Hindemith's Opus 8, dating from 1917 and representing his first published work. The *Drei Leichte Stücke* are *Gebrauchsmusik* and, though bounded by the cello's first position, sound as if they were not written with any technical or range restraint whatsoever.

Steiner exhibits an expressive insight into both pieces, especially the earlier-composed one.

Sonata for Cello Alone, Op. 25, No. 3

☐ Sylvester (cello) / Desto 7169

Five concentrated movements; the fourth of which is a snappy, speedy, scherzoish sketch of thirty seconds that highlights the work. Hindemith's post-Brahmsian style involves a principal process of horizontal (melodic) selection and a minimal amount of vertical (chordal) adjustment.

I have always remembered some lines by the critic Edwin Evans in which he stated that Hindemith's unaccompanied string-instrument sonatas were "scarcely suitable for concert performance." If he had heard Robert Sylvester's demonstration, he would have had to admit his error.

Echo for Flute and Piano (1942)

Flute

☐ Di Tullio (flute); Mayorga (piano) / GSC–3

A one-minute sampler of the composer's style.

Sonata for Harp (1939)

Harp

☐ Zabaleta (harp) / Deutsche Grammophon 139419

Composing for the harp demands a milder dynamic speech, but with no lessening of intensity. Regardless of the instrument Hindemith chose, there was creative rapport; accordingly, he utilized ratioed simplicity to companion the harp's restricted chromaticism. Since there is a touch of medievalistic modalism within its three movements, the Sonata has softer impact than most of Hindemith's other music.

Sonata

Organ

No. 1 (1937) / No. 2 (1937) / No. 3 (1940)

☐ Noehren (organ) / Lyrichord 53 (monaural)

Excluding the output of Messiaen, and with the exception of an occasional short piece, music for the organ is not characteristically found in the catalogues of the important contemporary composers. However, Hindemith put his acute instrumental knowledge to work. His three organ Sonatas are imaginative, modern without unsuitable aggressiveness. Above all, the organ is made to order for his linear language. One exception: the *Phantasie* (movement 3 in the first sonata) is somewhat removed from Bachian postulates.

Each of the three movements in No. 3 is based on an old German folk song. The tunes are used as the basis over and under and around which polyphony is woven with neo-archaic coloration and intertwined with mild lyricism.

Exemplary performance, sound, and excellent registration mark the Lyrichord disc. It is far better in its monaural setting than any of the stereo integral releases. Noehren's bright conception of this music is telling. His playing can hardly be bettered, and his phrasings especially show a musician of deep understanding. In contrast, George C.

Baker's version, released under the FY label in France and re-released by Delos (026), is lacking in coloristic explanation and is altogether too neutral. E. Power Biggs has also recorded the three-ply set, but the first two are played rather soberly; the third one turns out better. Biggs can be heard on Columbia Special Products CMS-6234. (For those interested, Preston has also recorded the three sonatas on Argo ZRG-663.)

Piano

Kleine Klaviermusik, Op. 45, No. 4

☐ Stevens (piano) / GSC-1

The commercial music world (especially the publisher) has always sought compositions that represent the composer's style and yet are capable of being played by students in the early grades of development. For every work of worth by a recognized composer, a few hundred are issued that are exactly the opposite, only because it is virtually impossible to fulfill this objective. To scale down technically is a simple matter, to retain simultaneously one's personal style is horrendously difficult.

Hindemith was a realist and a composer of extraordinary skill. He neither changed nor renounced his doctrines—merely edited them to fit. These "Little Piano Pieces," which Hindemith termed "Easy Five-Tone Pieces," offer the proof. They total a dozen tidbits limited to a five-tone gamut, but are as Hindemithian as his symphonies.

Ludus Tonalis (1942)

☐ Tetley-Kardos (piano) / Orion 75189

Subtitled "Studies in Counterpoint, Tonal Organization and Piano Playing," this extensive opus could well be called "The Processes of Tonal Order According to the Rules of Paul Hindemith," since the music defines his theoretical principles (spelled out in a number of textbooks). *Ludus Tonalis* consists of a dozen fugues, including such polyphonic attractions as inversion, *stretto,* and palindrome. Eleven interludes are interspersed in the fugal cycle. These make a variety of statements; they include a waltz, a pastorale, a perpetual-motion affair, and a solemn march. The suite is completed by a Prelude and a Postlude, the latter a mirror inversion of the former.

Ludis Tonalis is a contemporary *Well-Tempered Clavier,* with some modern glances at Bach's *Art of Fugue.* It tempers didacticism with down-to-earth good music. Though it is not in the best-seller class as yet, it may be expected that time will define Hindemith's imposing undertaking as one of the most important piano works of the twentieth century.

Reihe Kleine Stücke, Op. 37, Part 2

☐ Billeter (piano) / Musical Heritage Society MHS-1884

Nine of the thirteen total parts in the collection. (*See below* for the remainder.) Hindemith's "Set of Little Pieces" requires dexterity (which Bernhard Billeter has in sufficient amount), but most of the bravura is in the polyphonic detail.

Musical Heritage's failure to band the nine items is a disservice to the listener. Individual pieces should be distinguished on a record.

Reihe Kleine Stücke, Op. 37, Part 2

☐ Billeter (piano) / Musical Heritage Society OR H-423/424

The remaining four parts of Hindemith's compilation. (*See above* for the other nine.)

Sonata No. 1, *Der Main* (1936)

Sonata No. 2 (1936)

☐ Laugs (piano) / Musical Heritage Society OR H–291

A competent realization of the first Sonata, even though one still seeks a performance that at least can match the deleted issue on Westminster (initially No. 18200, reissued as 9309), played by Badura-Skoda. The presentation by Glenn Gould (on Columbia M–32350) is rather bewildering principally because its tempo and style are undisciplined and there is hardly any finesse.

Laugs does well with the cool colorations of the much shorter second Sonata. Best of all is his documentation of the scherzo temper of the second movement. Here again, in the only competitive version (by Gould), the preferred-performance salute goes to the lesser-known soloist.

Sonata No. 3 for Piano (1936)

☐ Siegel (piano) / Orion 7299

Horizontalism explodes in every direction of this Sonata's four movements, culminating in a tremendous double fugue. Hindemith presents pure black and white values in his Sonata. Many times the voices are spaced widely, a very literal way of avoiding any romantic descant.

Siegel styles his playing to define the frictions in the work. Sometimes gruff, sometimes grim, only sounding unconventional to conventional listeners, Hindemith's Piano Sonata No. 3 is vitally effective in Seigel's hands.

Suite: *1922*, Op. 26

☐ Kubalek (piano) / Golden Crest 7050

Some hot jazz, written in a tight and hard, intensely syncopated style. Some serious composers turn out feeble specimens when they try their hands at this special art; as usual, Hindemith is quite expert. The Shimmy and Ragtime constitute parts 2 and 5; a March, a lyrical *Nachtstück*, and a slow, slightly dismembered waltz titled *Boston* complete the opus, as parts 1, 3, and 4.

Kubalek plays it all as it should be. He snubs any fussiness in the March, makes the Shimmy sound like the sexy and properly uncivilized item it is, knocks out the Ragtime with excellent brittle percussiveness.

***Tanzstücke*, Op. 19**

☐ Billeter (piano) / Musical Heritage Society MHS–1884

Mostly tight, mostly mechanistic in their rhythmic depiction. Billeter's playing is properly *secco* and minus any disturbing *rubati*.

***Uebung in drei Stücken*, Op. 37, Part 1**

☐ Billeter (piano) / Musical Heritage Society MHS–1884

Despite the title "Exercise in Three Pieces," this was not written for the didactic trade. All the items provide a stringent technical work-out, especially in terms of rhythmic detail. Hindemith's motile obduracy is paramount. It can be readily understood, therefore, how the third piece, a Rondo, easily lent itself to a version Hindemith made for mechanical piano.

Piano,
Four Hands

Sonata for Piano, Four Hands (1938)

☐ Yaltah Menuhin and Ryce (piano) / Everest 3130

Formal clarity and thematic warmth are the artistic working tools of this three-movement piece. Within are contrasted elements, such as the dramatic drive and keen kick of the middle part (representing the scherzo) and the gentle polyphony of the final movement, which is a synthesis of slow and fast divisions.

Advantageously presented by this team.

Two Pianos

Sonata for Two Pianos (1942)

☐ Katia and Marielle Labeque (pianos) / Musical Heritage Society MHS–1766

Hindemithian ratifications are present. This means polyphonic designs: movement 2 is a Canon, movement 3 has two parts of which the last is a Fugue. The latter is preceded by a Recitative, consisting of a musical paraphrase of a medieval English poem, *This World's Joy.* Hindemith follows both the meaning and the phonetic rhythms of the verses. Unfortunately, no text is included with the recording, which would have provided greater insight for the listener and increased his enjoyment considerably. Nonetheless, the musicianship of the performers makes possible a viable result if not a fully comprehensive one.

The opening Allegro is also sturdily contrapuntal. It is prefaced by a division titled *Glockenspiel,* primed by a three-pitch ostinato that bears out the "Chimes" caption.

Viola

Sonata for Unaccompanied Viola, Op. 11, No. 5

☐ Wallfisch (viola) / Musical Heritage Society OR H–294

Classically ordered, Hindemith-clothed. The work culminates with a movement *In Form und Zeitmass einer Passacaglia* that equals in size the preceding three. The nobility of this variational movement is especially compelling in Ernst Wallfisch's presentation. His clear portrayal of the previous part (a Scherzo) is similarly distinguished.

Sonata for Unaccompanied Viola, Op. 25, No. 1

☐ Trampler (viola) / RCA LSC–2974

Music of imposing length. This is especially so in the slow-tempoed third movement, but its length is proper for explanation of the material on which the movement is based. Above all, the material of the work is violistic; the intrinsic thought of the composition is for the tenor string instrument, not conceived merely for another string instrument and then transferred.

Trampler's performance removes all the harshness I recall displayed by Hindemith when he performed his own music. Hindemith, one will remember, played a number of instruments, but his speciality was the viola.

Violin

Sonata for Violin Solo, Op. 31, No. 1

☐ Ricci (violin) / London STS–15153
☐ Tarack (violin) / Nonesuch 71149

Suave and delightful. Hindemith proves that unaccompanied string-instrument music need not become craggy and complex because of the lack of supporting voices. The Sonata's main characteristic is its melodic flow, carried forth in five movements that alternate in tempo. Special color and quality are present in the finale, a *prestissimo* excited by muted sound.

Ricci approaches the music with chamber-music intimacy. His consideration has a special purity that gives the material extra warmth. (He has performed the Sonata for Violin Solo, Op. 31, No. 2, similarly: *see below*.) Tarack's formulation is much more dramatic, as though planned for large-concert-hall presentation. It has all the required neatness and clarity of playing desired, plus special sonorous prosperity.

Sonata for Violin Solo, Op. 31, No. 2

☐ Gross (violin) / Orion 74147
☐ Ricci (violin) / London STS–15153

The precept is simple: four strings on one instrument do not make a string quartet. The boundaries stare one in the face. To enlarge these only modestly, without monotony, demands the most subtle methods of changing the demarcations and refurbishing the ground.

Hindemith is not found wanting. The four movements of the Sonata follow the motto affixed to the score: *Es ist so schoenes Wetter draussen* ("It's such beautiful weather outside"). It is certainly "such beautiful" music—lyrical and songlike throughout, including the all-pizzicato third movement and the variations on a Mozart tune employed in the finale.

Robert Gross's large, rich tone and its projection in forthright playing total a decidedly sympathetic consideration of Hindemith's score. The full-scale information that prevails does not yank Hindemith's work out of proper proportions. Ricci plays the piece with the same restraint that he applies to the first of the pair of Sonatas (*see above*). It is fitting, though more sonic depth seems appropriate in this instance.

Duet for Viola and Cello (1934)

☐ Lynch (viola); Kouguell (cello) / Nonesuch 71149

Chamber Music

Without preidentification, just hearing a few measures will make clear the profile of Paul Hindemith. Thus: succinct linear energy with metrically assorted rhythmic zip, both coloring the motival underpinning of the three-part structure.

The first recording ever made of this work was in the time-honored days of short-play, and that on a 10-inch disc. Hindemith's work was then listed as Scherzo, not incorrect in terms of the music's mood, but misleading for those who may not realize this modern long-play interpretation covers the same piece. The initial recording paired no less than Hindemith and Feuermann. (It was in Volume V of Columbia's *History of Music*.) The best compliment that can be paid Messrs. Lynch and Kouguell is that their playing is just as good and, in the case of the former, much smoother.

Sonata for Alto Horn and Piano (1943)

☐ Jones (alto horn); Gould (piano) / Columbia M2 33971

An extra added attraction, and indeed a special one, changes Hindemith's usual four-movement design (broad-tempoed, scherzo-like, expressively slow-paced, and lively, in turn) into a five-part total. Before the final movement the instrumentalists speak lines written by the composer, which are an intrinsic part of the composition. Hindemith made two versions of his prose—one in German, *Das Posthorn (Zwiegespräch)*, and one in English, *The Posthorn (Dialogue)*. Jones and Gould use the English, as would be expected.

The Sonata is also playable on an alto saxophone (*see below*) or on the usual French horn. Choice of the latter is at the expense of the intrinsic special timbre of the alto instrument; the saxophone version is certainly worthy as a substitute setting.

There is no quibbling with the beauty of sound that a master like Mason Jones obtains. However, there is certainly a great difference in the tempo realizations between this version and that recorded in the alto-saxophone setting. By and large, all the tempi (especially in movement 2, most significantly) that Jones and Gould use are slower than those employed by Pfeifer and Laugs. One senses the fine hand of Glenn Gould in the pace decision making. Be that as it may, one is urged to obtain both the alto-horn and the alto-saxophone settings and enjoy different timbres and different realizations. Both are valid.

Sonata for Alto Saxophone and Piano (1943)

☐ Pfeifer (alto saxophone); Laugs (piano); Geldner and Lang (speakers) / Musical Heritage Society OR H-296

See above for remarks regarding the Sonata for Alto Horn and Piano (1943), which also apply to this work and its recorded performance.

The playing and the sound quality of the MHS disc are on target. But be warned! As with film that ends up on the cutting-room floor, the copy I reviewed listed the speakers and indicated the text (in both German and English), but the entire tape section containing the dialogue had apparently been snipped off during the mastering procedure.

Sonata for Bassoon and Piano (1938)

☐ Grossman (bassoon); Hokanson (piano) / Coronet 2741

Here, Hindemith reverses the usual elements of style whereby faster, more dramatic elements are the bridgework that straddles and contains the more relaxed, dancelike sections. Thus most of the rhythmic content is held centerwise, and the more resigned sections become the principal strengths of the structure. There is no instrumental contradiction—the bassoon is used properly for the truly lyric voice it represents.

Of the versions currently available on GSC-1, Mark 5-32286, and Musical Heritage OR H-292, Grossman's is the most effective, the best balanced. His tone is impressive.

Sonata for Bass Tuba and Piano (1955)

☐ Torchinsky (tuba); Gould (piano) / Columbia M2 33971

Torchinsky's playing of this work is sheer brilliance. He makes the heavy brass, low-gamuted instrument sound like velvet, and he tosses off the figures Hindemith has created with featherweighted finesse. Rüdiger Augustin's performance on Musical Heritage Society (OR H-290) is just not in the same league. Abe Torchinsky must, of course, share the plaudits with his partner, Glenn Gould.

Sonata for Cello and Piano, Op. 11, No. 3

☐ Steiner (cello); Berfield (piano) / Orion 73117

Music with backlash and recoil, full of violent reaction compared with the earlier works that share the same opus number (*see below:* Sonata in E flat major for Violin and Piano, Op. 11, No. 1). The energy and drive of the first movement show an athletic composer pitchforking his sounds to propel them off the ground. A slow march occupies the first half of the second movement and progresses into the finale. Rhythmic action with free-conducted lines persists in this instance.

Sonata for Cello and Piano (1948)

☐ Nelsova (cello); Johannesen (piano) / Golden Crest 4099

"Dynamic" best describes the opening Pastorale, central movement, and concluding Passacaglia. The word may seem odd when used in connection with a Pastorale. But the noiseless tenor of quiet music has its own predominant strength. The bold simplicity of this portion is one of the most attractive parts of the Sonata.

Zara Nelsova and Grant Johannesen give a strongly characterized performance. Tonally, there is no comparison with the rather pinched and contained viewpoint demonstrated in the Steiner-Berfield setting issued by Orion (73117). The Musical Heritage release (Taube and Dennemarck performing, on OR H-295) is a close second. It has excellent sound, and there are no quibbles tonally speaking. However, the performance does not have the inner *brio* represented in the Nelsova-Johannesen portrayal.

Sonata for Clarinet and Piano (1939)

☐ Klöcker (clarinet); Genuit (piano) / Musical Heritage Society OR H-292

Notwithstanding four distinct and concrete patterns in this composition, there is an interlink that gives a duodimensional reality to the utilized balanced conventions of a four-movement-sonata plan. The first, second, and fourth portions conclude in a *pianissimo* dynamic, the third in *piano*. The natural intensities of the fast, scherzo, slow, and pertly demeanored divisions have minute but communicable effect on the general reticence of the final cadences.

The clear designs of Hindemith's Sonata require no interpretative paraphrase. Klöcker and Genuit understand their roles as functionaries and avoid any personal regulation of the music's conduct.

Sonata for Double Bass and Piano (1949)

☐ Karr (double bass); Lewis (piano) / GSC-6

Virtuosity is possible but is not the best profit to be derived from the double bass; a ponderous instrument is not the paragon for fiery pyrotechnics. But Hindemith's Sonata is strictly in chamber-music style. The piano writing carefully avoids smear in regard to the tonal physiognomy; the bass does not struggle with distress.

In this Sonata the double bass is pitched differently from its usual *accordatura*. Each of the strings is raised a whole tone in order to achieve a slightly greater brilliance.

The recording catches the meaning of the music perfectly. It is distinguished by a fidelity of interpretation and a high quality of execution. There is a certain amount of poetry in the performance that brings advantages. The edition available on Musical Heritage Society (OR H-295) is played by Nestle (double bass) and Klemann (piano). It is of fitting taste, but the sonics are a bit dry.

Sonata for English Horn and Piano (1941)

☐ Germann (English horn); Laugs (piano) / Musical Heritage Society OR H-296

Though Hindemith does not belabor the most common methodical use of the instrument (to depict suburban facets of music, the shepherd's voice, and so on), neither does he miss such opportunity. He balances all possibilities so that a melancholic atmosphere is compared with a more cheerful view. In addition, the spice of variety stems from the shifting commentary basic to variational form.

Germann's playing is rich and smooth, a reminder of Louis Speyer's marvelous artistry on the instrument when he was a member of the Boston Symphony Orchestra and, at that time, recorded the work for the old Unicorn firm on their number 1028.

Sonata for Flute and Piano (1936)

☐ Bryan and Keys Duo / Lyrichord 7185

Virtuosity is not lacking in Hindemith's music, but he never indulges in it for sheer pretension. The use of the agile flute in connection with the exposition of a sonata might lead some to make such an error—Hindemith does not. The content explains the instrument's character and type of personality. It is not simply conventional, but exercises proper discrimination for the charming wind instrument. Thus geniality and light niceties dot the surface of the music's conversation.

A beautifully styled performance. Only a lack of crispness where the music should be so detailed eliminated listing a second choice (on Musical Heritage Society OR H–296, with Joachim Starke, flute, and Richard Laugs, piano).

Sonata for Horn and Piano (1939)

☐ Jones (horn); Gould (piano) / Columbia M2 33971

Music wherein brass vocalism pervades the entire atmosphere. It is a warm-blooded work with no lack of proper musical corpuscles. This is a further exemplification of Hindemith's special ability to attune his writing to the soul of each instrument, not merely to paraphrase in symbolistic regard for it.

The performance choice is difficult. Mason Jones's sound is nonarguable—fresher, cleaner, and far more beautiful than the competitive issue on Musical Heritage Society (OR H–290). However, Jones and Glenn Gould expand their tempi in a manner that brakes the flow and breaks into the line movement. Erich Penzel (horn) and Richard Laugs (piano) on the Musical Heritage Society issue mentioned adopt acceptable speeds. The timings are substantial evidence: 16:41 for the MHS issue, 21:38 for Columbia's. One wishes that the quality of the latter were accompanied by the speed rates of the former. That not being the case, one opts for top quality above proper speed.

Sonata for Oboe and Piano (1938)

☐ Roseman (oboe); Kalish (piano) / Desto 6484

Hindemithian orthodoxy is illustrated: motival coordination, fluctuating tonal polarity, and cleverly disposed rhythm.

Of the several issues on the market, this one is the very best, with Roseman's expressive tone a feast for the ear. Desto's disc is sensitively engineered.

Sonata for Trombone and Piano (1941)

☐ Smith (trombone); Gould (piano) / Columbia M2 33971

No indulging in fantasies foreign to the majestic breadth and stability of the most sonorous of all brass instruments. Firmness and a declamatory quality cover this one-movement work that is parceled into definite quadruple sections. Wide-spaced intervals are used, giving the enthusiastic and healthy "well-to-do" quality of most brass-timbred thematics.

In Smith's hands the trombone is like a prancing instrument (but retains its footing). He plays the Sonata with a dominating and resolute style but without a theatrical manner, which would be unfitting.

Sonata for Trumpet and Piano (1939)

☐ Johnson (trumpet); Gould (piano) / Columbia M2 33971

Trumpet music equals music of authoritative character. Most often, determined clarion intervals are used in its subject matter, together with short jets of simulative bugle calls (as in part 1 here) plus proclamation (movement 3). This Sonata is conceived instrumentally *à la mode;* harmonically and rhythmically it is completely under Hindemith's control. With Gilbert Johnson, all the points involved are perfectly attained and with a tone that is golden-showered.

Sonata for Viola and Piano, Op. 11, No. 4
Sonata for Viola and Piano (1939)

☐ Trampler (viola); Turini (piano) / RCA LSC-3012

Within the Opus 11 Sonata, one finds a Brahms-Hindemith partnership. Harmonically they clasp hands. In rhythmic and structural matters Hindemith is the senior member. Especially pertinent is the use of a formal plan that is both graphic and forcible. Hindemith charts his work so that the variational concepts contained in the sonata format of the third (final) movement become a continuation of the Theme and Variations design of the previous movement. The section most flattering to Brahms is the opening Fantasy, quietly eloquent and somewhat improvisational music, designed monothematically.

In the other Sonata, composed seventeen years later, Hindemith rides his creative horse alone. The first movement dips vigorously into fugal territory and just as strongly in the concluding movement, a Finale with Two Variations. It is fascinating to hear how the tonal-polarity magnet permits Hindemith to chromaticize afield yet retain the most punctilious clarity of key center.

The performances of these works by Trampler and his associate Turini are distinguished, clothed with authority. Trampler's tone is superb, a fully true viola voice, crisply clear. The musicianship of both artists is completely at the service of the composer.

Sonata in E flat major for Violin and Piano, Op. 11, No. 1

☐ David Oistrakh (violin); Yampolsky (piano) / Monitor 2009 (monaural)

Hindemith's first violin and piano Sonata shows that he will have none of the schematics proposed by dry and stuffy textbooks. Notwithstanding that Hindemith at this early period cannot be false to his love of Brahms, he begins to shake loose from him. It is most apparent in the little harmonic spikes that are thrust into the romantic tissue of the music. Later in the same opus Hindemith's self-assertiveness goes further (*see above:* Sonata for Cello and Piano, Op. 11, No.3).

The playing takes care of all of Hindemith's harmonic stresses without disturbing the general romantic temper of the Sonata. Oistrakh's tone is round and mellow, Yampolsky's keyboard touch blends beautifully with it. The performance of this team is one of full commitment and admirable clarity.

Two Canonic Variations for Two Violins (1929)

☐ Shure and Douglas (violins) / GSC-1

Hindemith illustrates the creatively spontaneous gift he possesses in this work. He is able to write in defined formal structures of length and yet not be forced even once to break away from canonic strictness. The two pieces prove Hindemith's amazing abilities as a contrapuntalist. Both of the duets make good musical, artistic, and technical sense, and possess emotional qualities as well.

Two Duets for Violin and Clarinet (1932)

☐ Shure Raimondi (violin); Hugo Raimondi (clarinet) / GSC-1

Both duos are in ternary form; the first one is moderately paced, the second of the pair is in slower tempo. Throughout, Hindemith's music is gentle in character and typically linear.

Trio for Viola, Heckelphone, and Piano, Op. 47

☐ Kestenbaum (viola); Ellis (heckelphone); Stevens (piano) / GSC-5

The instruments in this trio are a rare combination, even if the baritone-type oboe is replaced by a tenor saxophone, as Hindemith permits. The trio is in two parts—the first in three sections, the second in four. Sequential instrumental strength marks part 1: the Solo is for piano, the Arioso is for the wind instrument and piano, and, notwithstanding the subtitle *Duett,* the complete trio force is used in the third section.

Part two is a *Potpourri.* It varies a primary idea in a dozen different ways in its initial division and mixes and tosses three items in its second. This is followed by a duple-pulsed allotment, bounced and rocked by jazzy, irregular accentuation, and the opus is concluded by a *Prestissimo* presenting rhythmic automatism and lyrical abandon simultaneously.

Trio for Violin, Viola, and Cello, Op. 34

☐ Rainer Kussmaul (violin); Jürgen Kussmaul (viola); Wolf (cello) / Musical Heritage Socity OR H-297

A composition of transcendent power; the working material is handled freely, the horizontal impulse being the paramount objective. Strength of color predominates in the third movement. Save for the last few measures (where the cello changes to bowed sounds), the three instruments are completely muted and fully concerned with pizzicato throughout.

The playing is acceptable, with enough muscularity. If, however, it can be found in one of the speciality shops, obtain the old Westminster (18593) mono release; the instrumentalists (Pougnet, Riddle, and Pini) play Hindemith's piece with exceptional solidity and tonal resonance.

Morning Music (1932)

☐ Members of the Los Angeles Brass Quintet / Crystal S-102

Hindemith's *Morgenmusik* is from a group of nine miscellaneous works in his *Plöner Musiktag* ("A Day of Music at Plön"), composed in 1932.

The composition is a modern equivalent of baroque-tower music. It calls for trumpets in two divided parts (flügelhorns, etc., may be added at will to each of these), and horns and trombones also combined in two parts, with an ad libitum tuba. Though conceived originally for a massed combination of performers, the three movements are written strictly in four parts throughout.

The Los Angeles group plays the work with paired trumpets (Thomas Stevens and Mario Guarneri), trombone (Miles Anderson), and tuba (Roger Bobo). The American Brass Quintet on Desto 6474/7 performs it with this group's full membership: two trumpets, horn, tenor and bass trombones. It is not the different instrumentation (just as fitting as the Los Angeles choice, within the freedom Hindemith permits) which makes the difference and leads to the decision that the Crystal edition is the preferable one, but tempi and style. The Los Angeles four use an alive pace in the proclamatory initial part, for example, but their speed better fits the quality of the music. Further, throughout, they play in a warmer, more refined chamber-music manner, while the American ensemble simulates an outdoor ambience.

Whatever choice is made, be ready for unacceptable liner notes. Crystal says nothing about the work save that it is in three movements, and even there overlooks the title of movement 2, *Lied* ("Song"), simply giving the tempo indication. Far worse is the program note for the Desto release which is packed full of misinformation.

Quartet for Clarinet, Violin, Cello, and Piano (1938)

☐ Klöcker (clarinet); Karolyi (violin); Braunholz (cello); Genuit (piano) / Musical Heritage Society OR H-289

As is so often the case, the use of the clarinet by Hindemith gives his quartet mellow properties of mixed string, woodwind, and keyboard-instrument timbre. This fact is especially noticeable in the first movement, where a romantic glow (shining in the composer's style) suffuses the music. The middle movement is obedient to ternary form; the finale is a diversified variational type.

The opus benefits from the excellent team of performers.

String Quartet No. 1, Op. 10

☐ Stuyvesant String Quartet / Nonesuch 71006E (monaural)

Hindemith's very early Quartet demonstrates the attempt of a young composer to whittle down the confines built up by insular growth and study. The tendency to length is one piece of evidence that romanticism still breathes in Hindemith's ear. There is the additional point that tonality (notwithstanding the use of the rubberbanded stretching that Brahms and especially Reger had begun) is a determined factor; the Quartet is based in F minor. Thickness of writing is still another sign that indicates this Quartet is an early Hindemith opus. However, the astute skill of the instrumental writing shows the working hand of a string player.

Counterpoint is an important element in the Quartet's testimony, and the seething, stamped-from-iron rhythms also show that Hindemith, though young, is bound to get off the old-fashioned scholastic chair in which he sits. The tail end of romanticism begins to vanish in this work; in Hindemith's next string quartet he departs for other regions.

The Stuyvesant team play with guts where they should and temper their vigor where lesser force is needed. The ensemble is a fine one, and it is a shame the quartet disbanded. The recording originally appeared on the very old, long since gone Philharmonia label (No. 100—a 10-inch disc). It was very perceptive thinking that caused Nonesuch to reissue it.

String Quartet No.2, Op. 16

☐ Schaeffer Quartet / Musical Heritage Society OR H-297

Melodic material does not have timid diffidence here. Hindemith uses motivally cast dynamic themes; he employs warm subjects rounded by song and has some lengthy topics plus several robust ideas in the Quartet. The last mark both of the outer movements. Chromaticism is a major point in the slow movement.

Why one never hears this Quartet in the concert hall is a mystery. That it deserves a high place in the string-quartet repertoire is apparent after hearing the recorded performance available.

String Quartet No. 3, Op. 22

☐ Fine Arts Quartet / Concert-Disc 225

Of all the Hindemith string quartets the third one had a place that matched those compositions of classical distinction in the confirmed repertoire. The absence of this work from present-day concert programs is simply one of those temporary matters of fashion. Hindemith's work will outlast most of the jerry-built, jellyfish-like, aleatoric quartets that have been turned out in great numbers during the past twenty years.

Each part of Opus 22 displays clarity of form and theme and melodic potency. All of the formal patterns are based on reconstituted classical ordering. The first movement is a free fugato. Movement 2 is a total stream of power channeled through the most violent and barbaric kind of string sonorous action. The third movement is the most captivating of all. In muted loveliness this movement progresses dissonantly but intimately—its nocturnal mood is impressionism coded by bitonality. The fourth section is a wild toccata-like affair, improvisational in its course through free fantasy and proceeding into the final Rondo. There, Hindemith serves up a fugal movement of almost chaste quality.

Save for a tempo that could (and should) move faster in part 2, the performance is absolutely authoritative, sensitive in all respects, and a commanding realization of Hindemith's score. The reproduction deserves the same high praise.

String Quartet No. 6 (1945)

☐ Karolyi Quartet / Musical Heritage Society OR H–295

Fully realized voice movement with calm but elocutionary power is found in movement 1. A short conception (two and one-half minutes), it is matched in its concentrated length by the quiet scherzo that follows. Movement 3 is designed by a ternary division of tempi (slow, fast, slow); the work is concluded by a moderately fast-paced Canon.

A divertimento doctrine is reflected in Hindemith's final String Quartet. The liner notes speak of "fine strokes of humor" and "unproblematical *Spielmusik*." Apt descriptions, and realized in the first-rate performance by the Karolyi organization.

Clarinet Quintet, Op. 30

☐ Karolyi Quartet / Klöcker (clarinet) / Musical Heritage Society OR H–289

Motoric motility in abundance here; the work was composed in 1923, when Hindemith was twenty-eight, and still in his *sehr schnell und wild* creative period. Even in quieter tempi the immoderation comes through, as in the fourth-movement Arioso where one glissando after another decorates the solo violin's recitative, framed only by simple drummed pizzicati. The clarinet has nothing more than what amounts to three snide interruptions, each a sustained sound in the low register.

Two other special points: in the *Ländler* the small and shrill E flat clarinet replaces the basic B flat instrument, and in the finale there is perfect formal symmetry as the first movement is run through in retrograde (crabwise) fashion.

The performance is first class, properly brash when it should be, with special sensitive playing by Sandor Karolyi in the Arioso.

Kleine Kammermusik for Five Wind Instruments, Op. 24, No. 2

☐ Westwood Wind Quintet / Crystal S–601

One of the most widely played of all contemporary works for wind instruments. It is scored for the traditional forces of the woodwind quintet—flute, oboe, clarinet, bassoon, and horn—with a piccolo being substituted for the flute in the second movement. This is without doubt one of Hindemith's most charming pieces.

The Quintet embodies humor, parody, and irony; some of the pasages must have been written with acid. Its dancy attitude, in typical post-World War I style, equals a musical hedonistic view of life presented in cameo fashion. The dissonant chordal bite of the very first beat outlines and sketches the type of aesthetic axiom that the composer will propound; the Quintet's tonality is to be free, and friction harmony will persist.

In proper place, soft sounds have as much influence as the bombastic explanation. For example, it is a quiet dynamic use that implies the most concentrated and pungent detail in musical parody. This fact is demonstrated in the second movement (*Walzer*), not related to any "Blue Danube." And the same relish is obtained throughout this music with spiculated texture.

There is no question as to the choice of recorded performance. The Westwoodians cast the proper smartness on the music, provide peppery pungency as required, and display fine ensemble. What is surprising is the lack of choice for a work which at one time had seven editions listed in *Schwann*. At this date of writing there are but two: this one and another by the Oberlin Faculty Woodwind Quintet on Coronet (S–1408).

Three Pieces for Five Instruments (1925)

☐ Spear (clarinet); McNab (trumpet); Baker (violin); Neidinger (bass); Carno (piano) / GSC–6

Instrumental democracy is observed in this quintet, with representatives from the woodwind, brass, string, and keyboard families. Plenty of color, therefore, used for tonal material handled in a plastic manner.

Strange it is that neither the first edition of *Cobbett's Cyclopedic Survey of Chamber Music* nor the update volume issued in 1963 mentions Hindemith's Three Pieces.

Octet (1958)

☐ Members of the Fine Arts Quartet and Members of the New York Woodwind Quintet / Siegel (double bass) / Concert-Disc 218

The instrumentation for the Octet represents attention to timbre variance in the larger media of chamber music. Semidiaphanous qualities predominate, with the darker, mellower winds (clarinet and bassoon) and horn associated with a string quintet of violin, two violas, cello, and double bass definitely pitched toward smoky colors. The consanguinity of form and content integrates the richness of the composer's varied, masterful modern polyphony. Counterpoint is almost the whole means of regulating the expression, yet the linear bargain is not overdriven into boredom. The contrapuntalism in each of the five movements has a different point to explain: a sonata-styled initial part, variations, a slow-paced division, a gingered, dry scherzo description, and a novel twist to a fugue that intertwines "*drei altmodische Tänzer*" (waltz, polka, and galop).

Performance rating is tops. The sound is less so.

Das Marienleben, Op. 27

Vocal

Voice with Accompaniment

☐ Bonini (soprano); Dahl (piano) / GSC–7

A most important and excellently realized recording, making available exceedingly valuable documentation. For the details involved, *see below: Das Marienleben* (1948).

Das Marienleben (1948)

☐ James (soprano); Brough (piano) / Lyrichord 97 (monaural)

Hindemith's huge song cycle was originally composed in 1923. In 1939 he set four of the fifteen songs with orchestral accompaniment. Then, in 1941, he announced a completely revised version. It was completed seven years later. No slight redraft, this. Only one song remained as it was originally; the others were totally rewritten for the most part.

The initial edition (*see above*) has the urgency of youthful restlessness; the second one, a much smoother projection. Indeed, roughhewn musical sculpture had been changed into a polished engraving. But such gains were balanced by equal losses. The instinctive veracity and heated virility of the young composer were replaced by carefully considered, even comfortable, and a bit cautious writing by the older man. Dynamic creativity at the age of twenty-eight was substituted by calculated care (and theoretically direct guideposts) at the age of fifty-three. Still, *Das Marienleben* remains at the peak of contemporary vocal writing, first *or* second draft.

Why the recording companies have given sparse attention to Hindemith's magnificent work is unexplainable. Tourel's version on Columbia 196, made in 1954, is no longer on the lists. Neither is Gerda Lammers's rendition, which had been on the Bärenreiter-Musicaphon label (30–1514/15). At this time the only execution of Hindemith's first and second editions are those in the GSC and Lyrichord catalogues, respectively. James's assets are excellent intonation and aesthetic understanding. The dynamic range is only a bit confined. This should not deter ownership.

Motets for Soprano and Piano (Nos. 1, 2, 9, and 11)

☐ Feuerhake (soprano); Meckies (piano) / Musical Heritage Society OR H–293

Four of the total thirteen motets Hindemith produced for either soprano or tenor. No sacred definition is served. Secular sunshine streams over these Motets. Gospel texts are utilized (from Luke for Nos. 1, 2, and 9, from John for No. 11), but these furnish the only ecclesiastical touch. Otherwise, each of the Motets sounds like a canzonetta, or an ordinary art song.

Margot Feuerhake's sweet voice is fitting for these items.

Voice and Instrumental Ensemble

Des Todes Tod, Op. 23a

☐ Dal Segno Ensemble / Reid-Parsons (mezzo-soprano) / Critics Choice cc-1703 (monaural)

An exceedingly rare Hindemith song cycle, "The Death of Death" has three movements: *Countenance of Death and Misery, The Death of God*, and *The Death of Death*. The poignancy of the text is emphasized by the scoring for a quartet of paired violas and cellos. The work is truly one of Hindemith's masterpieces, and why it has not achieved its proper importance is still another of the mysteries of musical literature.

Susan Reid-Parsons is the star of this performance. Her voice is beautiful, dark-hued, fully expressive, and she knows how to shape a phrase. Extra plaudits are due her for bringing to light this exquisite opus.

Martinslied, Op. 45, No. 5

☐ Bressler (tenor); Lynch (viola); Fuller (harpsichord); Kaplan (oboe); Kouguell (cello); Tarack (violin) / Nonesuch 71149

An example (and a good one) of *Gebrauchsmusik*. Accordingly, the voice part can be solo as here, or delivered by two vocalists, or even a unison chorus. The instrumental background is for anything! Hindemith merely indicated high, middle, and low parts, and these can be amplified, as desired, by octaval doublings. The group performing here has made an excellent realization of Hindemith's blueprint.

Frauenklage (1943)

☐ Canby Singers / Canby (conductor) / Nonesuch 71115

One of the Five Songs on Old Texts that Hindemith designated as his Opus 33. The "Woman's Lament" (at losing her man) exemplifies choral writing without floridity. The Canby group is excellent (to be expected when the conductor is the first-class musician Edward Tatnall Canby).

Landsknetchtstrinklied (1943)

Vom Hausregiment (1943)

☐ Chorus of Radio Berlin / Koch (conductor) / Monitor 2047 (monaural)

Both are drawn from the Five Songs on Old Texts. (This recording also includes the *Frauenklage* from the same cycle: *see above*, where the preferable recording is discussed.)

The perceptive regard for Hindemith's neatly tailored harmonies produces a performance of compact delight. The second piece, "Of Household Rule," is set to a Luther text. The other one, "Mercenary's Drinking Song" (an alphabetical gem in the German), is not assigned any textual credit.

Mass (1963)

☐ Whikehart Chorale / Whikehart (conductor) / Lyrichord 7161

No smug (meaning picturesque) religiosity here. Hindemith is exceedingly sober and ascetic. Polyphony is the functioning organism creating, for the greater part, a picture of harmonic suspense. This is a complex yet not complicated work and does not propose to give up its secrets without repeated aural exposure.

Lyrichord's labeling is reversed. In order to hear the Hindemith, begin on side 2 and continue with bands 1 and 2 on side 1. Bands 3 and 4 on side 1 are *Dreimal Tausend Jahre* and *De Profundis,* unaccompanied choral pieces by Schoenberg, available in much better (*very* much better) editions on Everest 3182 and Columbia (M2S–709 for *Dreimal Tausend Jahre,* M2S–780 for *De Profundis*), the very best being on the former label.

Six *Chansons* (1939)

☐ Canby Singers / Canby (conductor) / Nonesuch 71115

Settings of poems by Rainer Maria Rilke, using clear chromaticism to dovetail into diatonic purity.

A truly elegant performance; the voices are beautifully blended.

Die Serenaden: Kleine Kantate nach romantischen Texten, Op. 35

☐ Winter (soprano); Roseman (oboe); Tuttle (viola); Goberman (cello) / Desto 6484

Hindemith's "Serenades" is truly a serenade of forms and assorted colors. The "Little Cantata on Romantic Texts" has eight parts, the second one prefaced by a solo-cello Toccata. Each portion is scored differently, the gamut being four duet combinations, three trio settings, and one portion calling on the entire quartet. This is not an example of forced instrumentation feeding; the combines both set and carry out the moods of the texts.

The warmer and brighter quality of Desto's release ranks it above those available on Nonesuch 71149 and from GSC-2. I also find the tempo decisions far more acceptable on Desto's presentation.

Opera and Dramatic Music

Hérodiade (1944)

☐ Columbia Chamber Ensemble / Zorina (narrator) / Craft (conductor) / Columbia Special Products AMS–6571

At its world premiere as a ballet, the Mallarmé poetry joined to Hindemith's music was not used. Hérodiade has since been performed and once recorded (by the MGM Chamber Orchestra, with Arthur Winograd conducting, on MGM 3683) without the extremely emotional text, but I am firmly convinced that narration of the poem is essential. One cannot overlook the fact that Hindemith subtitled his work *Récitation orchestrale*. He did not mean a reciter *with* orchestra, but a *blend* of poetry and music. The blend is crucial. As pure orchestral fare *Hérodiade* is only half rations. This fine performance provides full supply.

Hin und Zurück, Op. 45a

☐ Berlin Symphony Orchestra / Miller (soprano); Bock (tenor); Schaible (baritone); Kühnle (bass) / Grüber (conductor) / Candide 31044

A great spoof. All the action runs forward and at the midway point runs backward. So the adulteress who had been killed by her husband returns to the living, the husband puts his gun back in his pocket, the physician who had been called backs out of the door, etc., until the very short opera ends *status quo ante.*

Far better seen than only heard, naturally. However, a recording is still worth while. This is the only one available.

Wells Hively   (1902-1969)

Orchestra

Icarus (1961)

☐ Polish National Radio Orchestra / Wodiczko (conductor) / Composers Recordings S–254

Programmaticism concerned with the mythological tale. Hively's music strongly reminds one of the symphonic poems of Saint-Saëns, which is no back-handed compliment.

Well scored and well played. The liner copy incorrectly credits William Strickland as the conductor. It is Vohdan Wodiczko.

Summer Holiday (Rive gauche) (1944)

☐ Orchestra of the Accademia Nazionale di Santa Cecilia-Roma / Antonini (conductor) / Composers Recordings 111 (monaural)

Lucid, light-faceted music. The holiday is not hectic but a fully relaxed one that Hively describes. Nicely orchestrated, minus fuss. However, the performance is not minus a few pitch waverings. Apparently "takes" were taboo in the mono days when this disc was made.

Tres Himnos

☐ Eastman-Rochester Symphony Orchestra / Hanson (conductor) / Eastman-Rochester Archives ERA–1015

Mainly modal style surrounds the "Three Hymns." Included is a reliable reaction to Mexican scenes, such as "the ancient Indian pyramids and the colonial churches of the high valley of Mexico."

In this type of music one can rely on interpretative authenticity from Howard Hanson.

Vinzenz Hladky / *Johann Hoffmann.* See *Hoffmann* / Hladky.

Alun Hoddinott   (1929-   )

Trio for Violin, Cello, and Piano, Op. 77

☐ Barton (violin); Isaac (cello); Jones (piano) / Argo ZRG–691

Chamber Music

Serial syntax, as clearly determined in its application as music conceived with steadfast tonalism. Such classical lucidity and poise applied to twelve-tone style provide an ordered continuity to Hoddinott's Trio. The music is expertly scored and just as expertly performed by three members of the Cardiff Festival Players.

Roman Dream, Op. 54

☐ Cardiff Festival Players / Price (soprano); Lockhart (piano) / Argo ZRG–691

Vocal

Voice and Instrumental Ensemble

Hoddinott's *Roman Dream* is a *scena* for voice and instruments (piano, harp, and three percussionists). Expressionistic style surrounds the music based on a narrative poem of macabre content by Emyr Humphreys. Indeed, more than once Schoenbergian influences are clearly heard. Unfortunately, the clarity of the text is muddied in this performance and use of the printed text becomes mandatory.

The instrumental colorations are sensitively projected. James Lockhart's role is no more important than those of the others and he is only credited because he is the director of the Welsh group. In all fairness one should, therefore, indicate the other participants: David Watkins, harp; and Tristan Fry, Keith Millar, and Alan Suttie, percussionists.

André Hodeir   (1921-   )

Around the Blues

☐ Modern Jazz Quartet / Schuller (conductor) / Atlantic S–1359

Chamber Music

Indeed, chamber music! Intimately cool, heated with an irresistible beat. The diction and tone of Hodeir's piece are heard with the slick virtuosity that only the M.J.Q. possess.

Anna Livia Plurabelle

☐ Aldebert and Croisille (voices); Rostaing (clarinet); Guiot (flute); Ponty (violin); Guerin (flügelhorn); Portal (alto saxophone); Lubat (vibraphone); Cullaz (guitar); Mochelot and Pedersen (basses); Garros, Humair, Manzecchi, and Fugen (drums) / Hodeir (conductor) / Philips 900255

Opera and Dramatic Music

A goodly part of the famous section from Joyce's *Finnegans Wake*. Quite atonal for the greater part, considerable jazz framework. Hodeir's musical transformation does not ease the matter of total understanding of the text, but the sounds and novel framework do hold the attention of an unbiased listener.

Sydney Hodkinson (1934-   )

Instrumental

Organ

Megalith Trilogy (1973)

☐ Albright (organ) / Composers Recordings SD-363

Deliberately planned static constructions, aided by the special uninterrupted, unemphasized sound continuity available only from the organ. Each of the three parts is purposefully pitch-constricted. In *Dolmen* a limited segment is utilized in place of the total chromatic range, in *Menhir* only six sounds are employed, and in *Talayot* all the sonorities are derived from the components of two intervals.

This is programmatic music, therefore, at its most fundamental basis: the working material itself equating the program rather than a developed detailing of the material. No free curves or zigzags or rhetoric rampant in Hodkinson's telling trilogy, but an organic solidity producing solidity of picture and structure. The very opposite of coloristic vividness here, paradoxically, provides extremely vivid music.

Johann Hoffmann (late 18th cent.)

Solo Instrument and Orchestra

Mandolin

Concerto in D major for Mandolin and Orchestra

☐ Vienna Pro Musica Orchestra / Kunschak (mandolin) / Hladky (conductor) / Turnabout 34003

Total conformity to the classic pattern, marked with a use of spare accompanimental portions in the final Rondo. Kunschak's tone is less pointed than that of most other mandolinists on the recorded lists. (The work is also available in a jumbo release of five records devoted to music by eighteen composers for the lute, guitar, and mandolin on Turnabout 34195/9.)

Hoffman / Vinzenz Hladky (?-?)

Chamber Music

Quartet in F major for Mandolin, Violin, Viola, and Lute

☐ Kunschak (mandolin); Pichler (violin); Baierle (viola); Hladky (lute) / Turnabout 34016

Effective simplicity, attentive to the narratives found in early Haydn and Mozart. Any pedantic postures are eradicated by the colorful combination of bowed and plucked string instruments.

What Hladky's role was in arranging Hoffmann's work is not explained. And only a typographical omission can explain the listing in *Schwann*, which notes the work as a "Quartet" but names only three instruments—mandolin, violin, and lute.

Franz Anton Hoffmeister (1754-1812)

Concerto in D major for Piano and Orchestra, Op. 24

☐ Prague New Chamber Orchestra / Blumental (piano) / Zedda (conductor) / Turnabout 34285

Authentic classical forms, and what is to be expected takes place within such structures, including a nicely pat cadenza toward the end of the first movement. There's a truthful ring to the work, and a depth to the slow movement that makes Hoffmeister rate full consideration.

Felicja Blumental does well. The orchestra doesn't have much to worry about, and what it does is not worrisome. There are no bands on the disc and no tempo indications anywhere.

Duo in G major

☐ Grumiaux (violin); Pelliccia (viola) / Philips 839747

A splendid imitation of Mozart's duos for violin and viola. Worthy, absolutely. Played in a manner that exposes the themes and their presentations with absolute clarity.

Lee Hoiby (1926-   )

After Eden

☐ London Symphony Orchestra / Foster (conductor) / Desto 6434

Hoiby describes his five-movement ballet as "the moment after Eden—two figures in a landscape, a tragic landscape of despair, guilt and deep need." But the strong point about this strong, color-dosed work is that it can stand firmly on its absolute legs without functional choreographic partnership. It also proclaims the effectiveness of neo-romantic tonality, the syntax used for Hoiby's exciting score.

Foster directs a distinctive appraisal of the music, with vitality and rhythmic significance. Top quality all around.

Anthony Holborne (?-1602)

Five Pieces for Instrumental Ensemble

☐ London Gabrieli Brass Ensemble / Nonesuch 71118

The title is not Holborne's, but is by Thurston Dart, who edited the work. The pieces (*Galliard, The Choice, As It Fell on a Holy Eve, The Fruit of Love,* and *The Fairie Round*) are from Holborne's *Pauans, Galliards, Almains, and Other Short Airs,* which contains all the music discussed here under this composer. A setting for viols of the fifth piece is noted below: see under *Chamber Music (The Fairie Round).*

Purists may be annoyed by hearing this music played by three trumpets, three trombones, and a tuba, but why not? Holborne included "wind instruments" in the allowable scope of instrumental performance in his work's title, and a brass group in no way disfigures or clouds the part writing. This was recognized by Dart. His 1959 edition allows even further coloration, the heading reading "Suite for an Ensemble of Brass or Other Instruments."

Instrumental

Recorders

The Marie-golde
Pavan

☐ Dolmetsch Consort / Nonesuch 73010

These are taken from Holborne's *Pauans, Galliards, Almains, and Other Short Airs.* Since the music was composed for "Viols, Violons, or other Musical Winde Instruments," the use of a recorder consort is certainly in order. This is especially propitious, since equal voicing is in the great majority.

Clean and clear recorder playing that never falters in texture or intonation.

Chamber Music

Almain

☐ Viols of the Schola Cantorum Basiliensis / Wenzinger (conductor) / Nonesuch 73010

All the compositions in this Chamber Music section are contained within the same total work from which the pieces discussed in the Brass Ensemble and Instrumental sections (see under *Brass Ensemble* [Five Pieces for Instrumental Ensemble]) were drawn. They have been purposely placed under the Chamber Music heading since all the performances are on viols.

As usual, an intimacy surrounds this well-played dance-derived piece.

The Fairie Round

☐ Musica Reservata / Morrow (conductor) / Argo ZRG–572

In the brass transcription (see under *Brass Ensemble* [Five Pieces for Instrumental Ensemble]) the tempo is much brighter. Still, this presentation by a seven-voice group of viols is perfectly satisfactory.

Galliard: The Sighs

☐ Viols of the Schola Cantorum Basiliensis / Wenzinger (conductor) / Nonesuch 73010

A subdued tempo and a moderated dynamic plane provide a recommended portrayal of the piece. For the collection from which it comes, see under *Brass Ensemble* (Five Pieces for Instrumental Ensemble).

Heigh Ho Holiday
The Honie Suckle
Pavana Ploravit

☐ Musica Reservata / Morrow (conductor) / Argo ZRG–572

Holborne used *The Honie Suckle* in another collection of pieces titled *The Cittarn Schoole.* There it is termed an *Almayne.* Another use also was made, as a lute solo called *Heartsease.*

By and large the performance of Holborne's music by the Morrow-directed group is brighter in tempo and smoother in texture than that of the three pieces represented by the Basiliensis organization—see the other entries under *Chamber Music.* For the source of all these works see under *Brass Ensemble* (Five Pieces for Instrumental Ensemble).

Pavan: Paradizo

☐ Viols of the Schola Cantorum Basiliensis / Wenzinger (conductor) / Nonesuch 73010

Well paced. This account presents the best playing by Wenzinger's group of the three Holborne pieces it has recorded that are discussed in this Chamber Music section.

Karl Höller   (1907-   )

Choral Variations on *Jesu Meine Freude*, Op. 22, No. 2   *Instrumental*

☐ Bilgrim (organ) / Musical Heritage Society MHS–3340   *Organ*

The heavy, heavy what-hangs-over of twentieth-century romanticism. No Bergian syntax, Pfitznerian more so.

Heinz Holliger   (1939-   )

Trio for Oboe (Alternating with English Horn), Viola, and Harp (1966)   *Chamber Music*

☐ Heinz Holliger (oboe and English horn); Collot (viola); Ursula Holliger (harp) / Philips 6500292

Free fantasy, especially in the aleatoric second part. Acrobatically shaped; the principal interest is in the association and disassociation of the colors.

Stanley Hollingsworth   (1924-   )

Stabat Mater (1957)   *Choral*

☐ Syracuse Music Festival Chorus / Bowman (piano) / Brown (conductor) / Desto S–102   *Chorus with Accompaniment*

An impressive blend—a mild twentieth-century impress on neo-ecclesiastical style. The singing is fairly good, though at the beginning of the work it is rather short-breathed and doesn't have depth. If you wish this piece, you will have to accept a piano sound that is dull and further is not fully in tune.

Vagn Holmboe   (1909-   )

Symphony No. 8 (*Sinfonia boreale*), Op. 56   *Orchestra*

☐ Royal Danish Orchestra / Semkow (conductor) / Turnabout 34168

Classically oriented only in its four-part formal structure. Otherwise, within, tonal polarities hold and release the pitch direction, always solidly balanced and permitting a fine coloristic glow to permeate the solid orchestration. The thematic detail is developed in Holmboe's habitual metamorphoic manner.

Strongly contrasted playing. Semkow coordinates matters clearly, and there is no doubt that this is a distinctive performance.

Chamber
Music

String Quartet No. 8, Op. 87

☐ Copenhagen String Quartet / Turnabout 34217

A strong five-movement work with Bartókian streaks, especially in the pivotal central movement (*Presto volante et robusto*). The cellular developmental process is particular to Holmboe's writing and is fully defined in the splendid performance the Copenhageners give of this Quartet.

Gustav Holst   *(1874-1934)*

Orchestra

Ballet Music from *The Golden Goose*, Op. 45, No. 1

Capriccio (1932)

☐ English Chamber Orchestra / Imogen Holst (conductor) / Musical Heritage Society MHS-1452

The Capriccio is as quietly expressive as it is jaunty. The ballet turns are from a choral ballet which Holst indicated could be performed in a shortened form minus chorus. Holst's daughter has made further excisions. The ballet music runs nicely if it does run a little long.

Egdon Heath, Op. 47

☐ London Symphony Orchestra / Previn (conductor) / Angel S-37152

A pastoral study, but entirely without bucolic gentility. *Egdon Heath* represents desolation at its gloomiest. Loneliness, despair, and the effect of limitless space are brought to mind by its measures, inspired by a quotation from Hardy's novel *The Return of the Native*.

The introspectiveness of Holst's composition is obtained by an intensely checked orchestral condition. Despite a full instrumentation (but no percussion, not even timpani), the entire orchestra is used in only one measure. Elsewhere, there is fractional scoring; the strings are divided for the greater part, and further thinned by being split into muted and nonmuted groups.

Although none of the books dealing with Holst points it out, a subtitle exists for Opus 47, *Homage to Thomas Hardy*. Holst wrote his piece for the New York Symphony Orchestra, which gave the premiere in February of 1928, under the direction of Walter Damrosch.

Good mood is provided in Previn's performance. It is certainly darker than the deleted Boult recording (London 9324). However, Boult was able to ice the sonorities in such a way as to create an orchestral sound of isolation that was quite special.

A Fugal Overture (1923)

☐ London Philharmonic Orchestra / Boult (conductor) / Musical Heritage Society MHS-1229

Note well Holst's adjective. This is no austere depiction of a fugue, but a fugal toss-around of the theme. All of it is sport and spark, and the fragmenting makes jolly good musical sense. It demands exact orchestral cohesion. Boult puts it all together with a firm hand and yet permits the music its head. Above all the overture has an English tang of outdoors healthiness about it.

Japanese Suite, Op. 33

☐ London Symphony Orchestra / Boult (conductor) / Musical Heritage Society MHS-1919

Six movements, four of which are dances. The last, *Dance of the Wolves,* has the most drive. Holst's music was written for a Japanese dancer who supplied him with all of the thematic material save for one of the dances. Holst's daughter Imogen, his most severe critic, calls the opus "disappointing." Not quite. Certainly an attractive performance.

The Perfect Fool: Ballet Music, Op. 39

☐ London Symphony Orchestra / Previn (conductor) / Angel S-37152

Though Holst's oddly parodistic opera on opera lies in peaceful rest, the Ballet remains one of his better-known pieces and is truly exciting fare. It is certainly unusual to open an opera (let alone one in a single act) with a ballet. The three dances—representing the spirits of earth, water, and fire—initiate Holst's stage piece. Thus it has come to pass that with the opera's demise its beginning has become its entire representation.

Despite the similar melodic shapes of the principal tunes of the work, their contours are varied expertly. A clever septuple metrical plan is employed in the first part, cool orchestration surrounds the middle section, and the final division has powerful thrust. There is no stock response to any of the ideas, and the orchestration is handsomely alive.

Previn's view of the music raises no questions; the score is realized in all of its virtuosic brilliance. The sonics are marvelous.

The Planets: Suite for Large Orchestra, Op. 32

☐ New Philharmonia Orchestra and Ambrosian Singers / Boult (conductor) / Angel S-36420
☐ London Philharmonic Orchestra and John Alldis Choir / Haitink (conductor) / Philips 6500072

Holst's magnificent essay for a huge orchestra (including alto flute, bass oboe, six horns, tenor and bass tubas, large percussion array, two harps, organ, and so on, plus a six-part female offstage chorus in the seventh movement) represents instrumental painting that can also be defined as absolute music. The suite can be judged as an astrological whole, or its structures can be considered separately. Each movement has a set design (sometimes framed by ostinati), pertinent subject character, and undeceptive allegiance to both pattern-scoring and composition.

The subject of each movement specifies a mood that Holst carries out vividly. *Mars, the Bringer of War* is a battering ram of quintuple rhythm framing parallel chordal violence; tender and quiet ideas symbolize *Venus, the Bringer of Peace.* Other divisions indicate the contrasts of speed and jollity, then desolation (*Saturn, the Bringer of Old Age*), followed by magic (plus grotesqueness and comedy), and finally quietude (*Neptune, the Mystic*). These seven images represent an anthology of Holst's ideas of orchestration, texture, and speech (a small parcel of Elgar and Vaughan Williams samplings is contained in the music).

It is strange that the success of this work distressed Holst. But it is not strange that this music of opulence and grandeur has retained its popularity. Originality makes its way—Holst's music of the outer spaces is not stamped with the hallmark of any particular *schola.*

The conductor should understand that the imagery is paramount, that the dramatic thrusts must be pinpointed, that every juicy and subtle nuance must be given its full quota of registration. This exactly describes the Boult recording—truly a beautiful musical feat. The man knows every slur and dynamic of Holst's opus and knows it better than any conductor who has tackled the work. Others get more excitement here and there, but it's top surface. Boult gets excitement from the guts of the score without overstress. His portrayal is fluent, solid, dynamic, and terse in turn as the need may be, and when it should be there he provides a John Bullish quality that no one else achieves.

There is a glowing nobility to much of Haitink's realization of the score. At the same time he does not overlook the high-minded vigor of the music or its coloristic legibility. No mispersuasion is allowed in order to make the *big* sound.

Two Songs Without Words, Op. 22

☐ English Chamber Orchestra / Imogen Holst (conductor) / Musical Heritage Society MHS-1452

These two pieces (*Country Song* and *Marching Song*) for small orchestra sound derived from folk songs, but the folk character is totally Holst-made. Both are knit like Vaughan Williams casual garments. Properly dedicated, therefore, to R.V.W.

I. Holst conducts these pieces by G. Holst in a fit and trim manner, tempoed so that they have nice articulation.

String Orchestra

Brook Green Suite for String Orchestra (1933)

Nocturne for String Orchestra (1928)

☐ English Chamber Orchestra / Imogen Holst (conductor) / Musical Heritage Society MHS-1303

Three movements in the Brook Green work: Prelude, Air, and Dance. Folk-song twists make their appearance. The Nocturne (not to be confused with the same-titled work for piano) is Holst's arrangement for strings of a movement from his Moorside Suite for brass band. Such delicate music belongs in the string medium rather than in any brass combination, be it ever so carefully arranged, especially in the telling way it is played by the English Chamber Orchestra's personnel.

St. Paul's Suite, Op. 29, No. 2

☐ Academy of St. Martin-in-the-Fields / Marriner (conductor) / Angel S-36883

In listening to this work, one notices its allegiance to the spirit of the dance. (The title has no religious connection; the Suite was composed in 1913 for the orchestra of the St. Paul's Girls' School, where Holst was in charge of music from 1905 until 1934.)

Rhythm and folk melody mark the music. The modal jig of the first part, the ostinato whip of movement 2, and the sixteenth-century country-dance tune of the finale (*Dargason*), cleverly counterpointed by *Greensleeves*, furnish the proof. Contrast is provided with the more majestic contours of the Intermezzo. Though Holst's suite uses catchy themes, there is nothing trivial about a single one of them.

Only praise can be stated for this recording. The Englishry of the music (totally exportable!) has been caught in every one of its measures. The performance brings honor to Marriner and his colleagues.

Band

First Suite in E flat major, Op. 28a

Second Suite in F major, Op. 28b

☐ Eastman Symphonic Wind Ensemble / Fennell (conductor) / Mercury 75011E (monaural)

More effective band writing is difficult to imagine. Holst's scoring gives an organic totality to his "bandstration"; the organlike sonorities illustrate expertise in a medium that few composers have mastered artistically. The March in the first Suite is a special humdinger. The finale in the other work illustrates magnificently timbred contrapuntalism, combining *Greensleeves* with the principal theme.

Though both Suites have been recorded by other school organizations (Ithaca Alumni Concert Band and Cornell University Wind Ensemble) in stereo, they cannot compete with Fennell's magnificent statements. The playing could hardly be bettered.

Hammersmith: **A Prelude and Scherzo, Op. 52**

☐ Eastman Wind Ensemble / Fennell (conductor) / Mercury SRI–75028

Music dealing with implied programmaticism. Aside from the proper noun of the title, which describes a London borough where quiet and noise, respectability and hedonism, homes and machine shops are in jagged counterpoint, there is the contrasted impact of the two moods of the subtitle.

The Prelude can be termed a humid nocturne; it can also reflect (as suggested by Holst's daughter, Imogen) the Thames that flows through Hammersmith. It is the Scherzo that makes a thousand picture possibilities spring to life. Pace and musical character constantly prod each other, chameleonlike, in this earthy movement. This is rather unusual in that the final portion of a large-scaled work is usually definite. It can be argued that Holst had absolutism in mind while composing this band masterpiece, but the soft-hardness of texture is further evidence of the music's multifarious (programmatic) character.

Magnificent is the rating for both performance and engineering of the record.

Fugal Concerto for Flute, Oboe, and String Orchestra, Op. 40, No. 2

Solo Instrument and Orchestra

☐ English Chamber Orchestra / Bennett (flute); Graeme (oboe) / Imogen Holst (conductor) / Musical Heritage Society MHS–1303

Flute and Oboe

Fugal in part 1, and ultimately the third movement (finale) becomes a double fugue by incorporating a seventeenth-century country-dance tune, *If All the World Were Paper*, with the original subject.

Polyphonic, but with a light touch of Holst's expert contrapuntal hand, and that is the way it is performed here. Expressive solo work by William Bennett and Peter Graeme.

Lyric Movement for Viola and Small Orchestra (1933)

Viola

☐ English Chamber Orchestra / Aronowitz (viola) / Imogen Holst (conductor) / Musical Heritage Society MHS–1303

One of Holst's most deliciously expressive pieces, with the solo voice accompanied by a quartet of winds plus strings. The piece was written in the last months of his life and at a time when he was physically weakened by illness, and there is a mood of autumnal resignation in the music.

The playing of Cecil Aronowitz has sustained warmth. This is a most convincing presentation of the score.

Double Concerto for Two Violins and Orchestra, Op. 49

Two Violins

☐ English Chamber Orchestra / Hurwitz and Sillito (violins) / Imogen Holst (conductor) / Musical Heritage Society MHS–1452

A bit austere in its content—three linked movements: Scherzo, *Lament*, and *Variations on a Ground*—but never dry, though the commitment is principally contrapuntal.

One commentator has described Holst's piece as "gritty." It's difficult to justify such reaction.

It requires a special sensitivity to Holst's objectives to avoid academicism in the Concerto's performance. The soloists, Emanuel Hurwitz and Kenneth Sillito, are extraordinarily perceptive, and the result is a superb rendition.

Instrumental

Two Pianos

The Planets, Op. 32

☐ Bennett and Bradshaw (pianos) / Delos DEL-25442

Holst's own boil-down of his great orchestral work. No argument as to the sincerity that dictated making this draft, but the results are problematic. Without orchestral color the music remains very, very cold. Only for those who are curious or for Holstians.

Chamber Music

Terzetto for Flute, Oboe, and Viola (1925)

☐ Adeney (flute); Graeme (oboe); Aronowitz (viola) / Argo ZRG-5497

Holst's two-movement trio is entirely written polytonally (flute in A major, oboe in A flat major, and the viola in C major; later, respectively, in E, A flat, and E flat). The effect is stimulating.

Naturally, polytonality requires polyphony for its best registration. It is counterpoint that is used, therefore, in both the Allegretto and the faster second movement. A large ternary form is employed in the first section, with some intersticed chorale-like sections. The second movement is fugal, more relaxed intermedial portions giving flux and contrastive pace. The entrancingly correlated polytonality of the final measures is a gem. There, the shifts as well as the meeting on common tonal soil disprove the nonsense that polytonality is always dissonance.

The performance is beautifully tailored, beautifully balanced, beautifully engineered.

Vocal

Voice with Accompaniment

Four Songs for Voice and Violin, Op. 35

☐ Catherine Malfitano (soprano); Joseph Malfitano (violin) / Musical Heritage Society MHS-1976

Texts from a medieval anthology, music of beautiful modal claim, qualities of exquisite enunciation. And "exquisite" also describes the performance, a magnificent blend of Catherine Malfitano's golden-pitched voice and her father's sensitive violin.

Since the titles of the Songs are not given, they are listed here: *Jesu Sweet, Now Will I Sing; My Soul Has Nought but Fire and Ice; I Sing of a Maiden;* and *My Leman Is so True.*

A close competitive edition is in the Argo catalogue (ZRG-5497), sung by Pears, with Brainin as the violinist.

Twelve Songs, Op. 48

☐ Pears (tenor); Britten (piano) / Argo ZRG-512

Pears in top form, meaning a rich, golden voice, artistic phrasing, and clear diction. Britten is a marvelous partner and expressively colors the content of each song. Prime examples of Britten's sensitivity can be heard in the sound currents of the eighth of the set, *The Dream City,* and the feathery pattering patterns of *The Floral Bandit,* the sixth of the group.

These are two of the best of the dozen. But there are others that deserve attention. Holst's songs are rarely heard, but reward the listener when they are. Most of them have an economy of expression that frames the words with impeccable style and aptness.

Ave Maria, Op. 9b

The Song of the Blacksmith, Op. 36, No. 4

Three Welsh Folk Songs (1931)

Two Carols

Two Part Songs

☐ Purcell Singers / Imogen Holst (conductor) / Argo ZRG–512

A fascinating program of Holst's choral music, covering a creative span of three decades from the *Ave Maria,* begun in 1899 and finished the year following, to the Three Welsh Folk Songs, started in 1930 and completed in 1931. The music represents three types of choral formation—female voices alone, male voices alone, and mixed (S–A–T–B) chorus—and there are further differences in the format and vocal writing of the various pieces.

The *Ave Maria,* for female voices in eight parts, is Holst under the influence of Byrd and Gibbons. In The Song of the Blacksmith (from a set of Six Choral Folk Songs) the male chorus is split so that percussion-like accompaniment rides along with the Hampshire folk song. The three Welsh Songs—*The Dove, My Sweetheart's like Venus,* and *The Lover's Complaint*—are from a group of twelve that Holst arranged. They are not small scale, yet they do not go beyond the proper style of folk-song settings. The title of the first of the pair of part songs, *Pastoral,* describes the quality of the second song, *The Swallow Leaves Her Nest.* The construction of the pair of Carols indicates Holst's unwillingness to work in set patterns. *Of One That Is So Fair and Bright* is in three sections. In the first a solo male voice alternates with the mixed chorus; in part 2 a solo female voice is responded to by the chorus; in the final portion the entire chorus is used for textural contrast. *Bring Us In Good Ale* is brought to conclusion by speed-up of tempo.

Choral

Chorus Alone

The Evening-Watch, Op. 43

Jesu, Thou the Virgin-born, Op. 20b

This Have I Done for My True Love, Op. 34

☐ Purcell Singers / Imogen Holst (conductor) / Argo ZRG–5497

The Evening-Watch for eight-part choir is a setting of Henry Vaughan's *Dialogue Between the Body and the Soul.* Sixteenth-century plainsong is the guiding plan for the *Jesu* piece, sung with superb sensitivity and immaculate balance. *This Have I Done* is a motet and a setting of a medieval Cornish poem. Its optimistic exaltation is truly convincing. The music is given a marvelous rendition by this first-class group of singers led by the composer's daughter.

Canons for Equal Voices (1932)

☐ Purcell Singers / Tunnard (piano) / Imogen Holst (conductor) / Argo ZRG–5497

Chorus with Accompaniment

The recording presents a half-dozen canons. (Basic identifications of their sources are not given.) The first four—*If You Love Songs; Lovely Venus; The Fields of Sorrow;* and *David's Lament for Jonathan*—are for three unaccompanied voices. These are from a set of six; Nos. 5 and 6 (not recorded) are, respectively, for three choirs of nine voices and two choirs of six voices. The last two heard here, *Evening on the Moselle* and *If 'twere the Time of Lilies,* are for two voices—*Evening* for voices alone, the other with piano accompaniment. Holst titled this pair Two Canons for Equal Voices and Piano.

The use of combined keys in these pieces is sharply different from the polytonality of Darius Milhaud, where every attempt is to maintain individual-key independence, almost ruthlessly. Holst's tonality method is a compromise (but without artistic compromise) between exact key individuality and relationship.

Two Carols for Sopranos and Altos, Oboe, and Viola

☐ Purcell Singers / Selwyn (oboe); Aronowitz (viola) / Imogen Holst (conductor) / Argo ZRG–5497

Originally for mixed voices with accompaniment for oboe and cello. The adaptation was specifically made for the recording. Whatever the reason, one is grateful. The pair of carols, especially the first, *A Welcome Song*, are of entrancing polyphonic beauty. A better performance can hardly be imagined.

Chorus and Orchestra

148th Psalm (1912)

☐ Philadelphia Orchestra and Mormon Tabernacle Choir / Schreiner (organ) / Ormandy (conductor) / Columbia MS–6068

Actually, Holst titled this piece *Lord, Who Hast Made Us for Thine Own*. It forms the second of *Two Psalms* for chorus, string orchestra, and organ, which he composed in 1912 (as in a great number of his works, no opus number was assigned).

When the principal tune (based on a sixteenth-century hymn melody) is set in augmented time values and counterpointed above, the effect is telling. This builds to a neat climax that is gently thrilling.

Seven Part Songs for Women's Voices and Strings, Op. 44

☐ English Chamber Orchestra and Purcell Singers / Longfield (soprano) / Imogen Holst (conductor) / Argo ZRG–5495

Holst's blend of triadic harmony and polymodalism gives a memorable beauty to this group of part songs. The partnership is maintained in the dual expressions found in a number of the songs, such as the blend of irony and tenderness in the second one, *O Love, I Complain*. The strings are used with reticence, but play a positive role. They enhance and never ensnare the vocal texture. For example, a simple pedal at the terminal points of the first song, *Say Who Is This?*; the solo violin overlay that counterpoints *When First We Met*, No. 4; the plucked timbre that frames *Sorrow and Joy*, the fifth in the set, and so on. All these touches parallel the subtlety of the word setting and the utter smoothness and flow of the vocal writing.

This is a splendid presentation. It is fully translucent. The voices are a joy to the ear, and the sound is similar.

Six Medieval Lyrics for Men's Voices and Strings

☐ English Chamber Orchestra and Purcell Singers / Imogen Holst (conductor) / Argo ZRG–5495

Choral simplicity styled in a neo-Elizabethan manner. The polyharmonic and slightly polytonal data produce a mellowed austerity in Holst's writing. He was, of course, creative light years distant from academically programmed harmony.

Opera and Dramatic Music

The Wandering Scholar, Op. 50

☐ English Chamber Orchestra / Burrowes (soprano); Tear (tenor); Rippon (baritone); Langdon (bass) / Bedford (conductor) / Angel S–37152

A tiny tale about a young, lusty wife not beyond looking into having a bit of sex in the hay with a friar. The other characters are her husband and a young student. The ending can be guessed but not the music, which is light and rather un-Holstian. Not the most important Holst but worth some attention.

Too ill to hear the first performance (it was held during the final three months of his life), Holst left the score of his one-acter unrevised. It has been edited by Benjamin Britten and Imogen Holst.

The performance is nicely gutsy and nicely fluid; the voices are certainly up to snuff, and the orchestral playing is smart and well finished. A no-defects performance of this light, bawdy-toned comic opera.

Samuel Holyoke (1762-1820) / Daniel Pinkham (1923-   )

Masonic Processional March   *Orchestra*

☐ Members of the New England Conservatory Collegium Musicum / Pinkham (conductor) / Golden Crest/N.E. Conservatory NEC-111

A delightful find of a short piece "preserved in a print in the Yale University Library." Pinkham arranged the work tastefully, and it is played with warmth and conviction.

Arthur Honegger   (1892-1955)

Pacific 231 (Mouvement symphonique No. 1) (1924)   *Orchestra*

☐ Utah Symphony Orchestra / Abravanel (conductor) / Vanguard S-274

Mention of Honegger generally brings this work to mind. *Pacific 231*, a fascinating description of an American locomotive, is now rarely performed, but during the 1920s and the modern *verismo* period of musical composition it was a program best-seller. The piece does not concern itself with the locomotive in static grandeur, but with the dramatic drive of the machine in motion. It starts with scratching slowness, moves gradually into full speed, and then reverses the process as it slows down and finally stops. In total, the music is like a rhythmic bibliography.

Abravanel engineers the music with a vigorous, detailed performance, with the polyphony allowed to be heard at full throttle. That produces the greatest effect.

Pastoral d'été (1921)

☐ New York Philharmonic / Bernstein (conductor) / Columbia MS-6659

For Honegger, this is a rare example of relaxed music. Nevertheless, his quiet rustic rumination does not meander; there is a well-balanced demeanor in the score between purpose and the formal plan chosen. Thematic consideration is emphatic, the working material based on a pair of subjects. Honegger's "Summer Pastoral" (for four woodwinds, horn, and strings) is neither breezy nor stormy—simply gentle.

Bernstein gives a nicely colored presentation.

Prelude to Aglavaine et Sélysette (1917)

☐ Louisville Orchestra / Mester (conductor) / Louisville S-693

An example of early Honegger set in impressionistic format. This provides orchestrational convenience and profit for the subject matter.

Rugby (Mouvement symphonique No. 2) (1928)

☐ New York Philharmonic / Bernstein (conductor) / Columbia MS–6659

Rugby is a vigorous, sonoric abstraction replete with blocked counterpoint and motile part activity. The interlocking and the interweaving of the voices produce a polytonal web, which could be descriptive of something or nothing at all. It is the music *plus* the significant name of the piece that provides mental levers for the auditor. Without title, no rugby match. With title, suggestion translates the music into images of the teams dashing up and down the field, the contact of player against player, etc.

Bernstein scores all the necessary goals with this score. He doesn't thin out the texture, and digs in with conductorial cleats.

Suite archaïque (1951)

☐ Louisville Orchestra / Whitney (conductor) / Louisville 615 (monaural)

Honegger proves that linear style is successful only if it has clear form and clean, direct counterpoint. The color surfaces in this suite are indices to the forms. The outer movements complement each other: the stark, brass-dressed hymn tune in the *Overture* becomes the march resource of the *Processional*. In the *Pantomime*, flutter-tongued flute sound is primary, and in the *Ritournelle et sérénade,* solo string variants are focused on.

The piece was commissioned by the Louisville Orchestra, which does satisfactory work. Honegger's piece is not great music, but it is an example of excellent creative skill.

Symphony No. 3 (*Liturgique*) (1946)

☐ L'Orchestre de la Suisse Romande / Ansermet (conductor) / London 6616

Honegger's Symphony is colored by the Latin subtitles given its three movements: *Dies Irae, De Profundis Clamavi,* and *Dona Nobis Pacem.* These definitions are expressed dramatically by a quality of nihilism and fear combined in the opening movement, by the sense of anxiety and pleading in the second part, and through a mood of militancy that climaxes in a hymn of aspiration in the final portion. However, if there are almost sacred objectives in this composition, they are more mystical than spiritual.

Ansermet always had an uncanny insight into Arthur Honegger's music, and here is proof positive. Balance and precision clarify all the textures; the broad strokes Honegger applied to his orchestrational canvas are reflected in every measure of this performance. More than one conductor has relayed a sense of struggle when directing Honegger's music. Ansermet shows how it can have all the required emotive impact with virtuoso effortlessness.

Symphony No. 4 (*Deliciae Basilienses*) (1947)

☐ French National Radio Orchestra (O.R.T.F.) / Munch (conductor) / Musical Heritage Society MHS–981
☐ L'Orchestre de la Suisse Romande / Ansermet (conductor) / London 6616

Honegger mainly in a lyrical mood. More athletic concern is found in the concluding third movement, which combines rondo, passacaglia, and fugue designs. The "Delights of Basel" subtitle derives from the composer's honoring the Swiss city, a place of warm memories of important first performances and the residence of a very close musical friend, Paul Sacher, the founder of the Basel Chamber Orchestra. (Sacher gave the initial performance of *Deliciae Basilienses* with his orchestra on January 21, 1947.)

Honegger's chamber-orchestra piece includes an old Basel tune in its second movement (*Z'Basel an Mim Rhy*) and another in the finale (*Basler Morgenstreich*).

Both conductors are Honegger experts. Both exhibit full knowledge and rapport with the emotional range of Honegger's music. Both realize that the textures of his scores need care and attention, else their special color credits are heard as dilated debits. The only difference between these recordings is the brighter sound tissue in the Musical Heritage issue; London's disc is more fine-grained in its sonic response. There are no doubts that Munch and Ansermet present fully detailed and successful performances of Honegger's serenade to a city.

Symphony No. 2 for Strings (1942)

String Orchestra

☐ L'Orchestre de la Suisse Romande / Ansermet (conductor) / London 25320

The succinct theorem of the work is constant activity, the parts knitted tightly into the sound fabric. (There is an ad libitum trumpet portion, used at the conclusion of the Symphony. That it is ad libitum makes possible indexing the work in the string-orchestra category. As would be expected, Ansermet includes the trumpet in his performance.)

The music moves from strength to strength in a parade of somber, emotional intensity. Only in the finale is some of the intensity removed. But even there the sense of struggle is maintained, as harmonies and rhythms are set in opposition.

The performance is ideal. The vitality and inspiration of the playing are of intense eloquence. Ansermet reinforces the view that Honegger's Symphony is one of the most dramatically probing in the literature for massed strings.

Concertino for Piano and Orchestra (1925)

Solo Instrument and Orchestra

Piano

☐ Vienna Pro Musica Orchestra / Klien (piano) / Hollreiser (conductor) / Turnabout 34130

In this approximately ten-minute piece one can enjoy a lighter opus from the Honegger catalogue. In comparison with most of his other compositions, the Concertino is a wonderful conceit, a delicious delicacy. The style is Parisian low-down; the music sounds like a jazzy Mendelssohnian prospectus. It has the proper décor: snide tunes, stop-and-go rhythms, blue notes, wail, and rag scale. Really fun.

It is good to hear Viennese performers play Honegger's music without schmaltz and slickness. (The recording was initially issued on the Vox label [10840].)

Danse de la chèvre

Instrumental

Flute

☐ Duschenes (flute) / Orion 6911

The outer portions are akin to a soliloquy rather than a dance, while the main middle section is a delicate scherzo, smoother in flow than one would expect from music titled "Dance of the Goat."

Deux Esquisses

Piano

Hommage à Albert Roussel (1928)

Le Cahier Romand (1923)

Prélude, arioso, et fuguette sur le nom de Bach (1932)

Sarabande

Sept pièces brèves

Souvenir de Chopin

Toccata et variations (1916)

Trois pièces

☐ von Vintschger (piano) / Turnabout 34377

The most substantial in this collection of Honegger's piano works, complete save for a pair of very short pieces and a three-movement suite, is the *Toccata et variations*. All the rest are of short length, including the *Romand*, which is a five-part set. The *Trois pièces* (*Prélude, Hommage à Ravel,* and *Danse*) should not be confused with an earlier work with the same principal title, covering a Scherzo, Humoresque, and *Adagio espressivo*.

Jürg von Vintschger makes a fine case for this music, consistently absent from concert programs. There are represented Honegger's polychordal strength, polyphonic jurisdiction, and peripheral impressionism. Rhythmic guts, which always provide musical gusto, are available in the repetitive intervallic conditions in the *Danse* (the end piece in the *Trois pièces*), and are especially prominent in the tango-like concept of part 5, the staccato format of part 6, and the brusque percussiveness of the finale of the *Sept pièces brèves*.

Not only does von Vintschger make known the fine values of this music, he also convinces with his interpretations. He understands the style, displays clean execution, and discloses all the substances within Honegger's texts.

Chamber Music

Sonata No. 2 for Violin and Piano (1919)

☐ Novšak (violin); Weisbrod (piano) / Musical Heritage Society MHS-1869

The opening subject is a swinging and sensuous "*echt* Brahms" item (in meter only!) fitted by triple- and quadruple-pulse patterns. A fugato neatly substitutes for the development section. The slow movement is monothematic. In the finale, Honegger shapes his rondo prototype by introducing the two principal themes in the extreme bass zone of the piano.

Sonatine for Cello and Piano (1922)

☐ Solow (cello); Vallecillo (piano) / Desmar 1006

An alternate setting of Honegger's *Sonatine* for Clarinet and Piano (for details *see below*).

It works almost (two-thirds) as well for the cello as it does for the clarinet. It is the finale with its gangbusters activity that comes off better with the wind instrument. However, if you wish the cello version, it's a fully official Honegger opus and can be heard here in a suitable frame of reference.

Sonatine for Clarinet and Piano (1922)

☐ Drucker (clarinet); Hambro (piano) / Odyssey Y-30492

This composition for clarinet or cello (*see above* for the latter version) represents relaxed Honegger. The compressed and concentrated three movements define a residue of true sonata form. There is such condensed depiction that if one is not aurally quick, the subtle Honeggerian order will pass by all too swiftly. In the first part the composer uses a lazy type of theme, a short fugato (wherein the subject is heard in augmented rhythm), and a recapitulation. A synthesis of ternary form is employed in the *Lent et soutenu*. The finale consists of thirty-seven measures and includes some nimble jazz glides. Actually, this work is a "sonatinette."

An alert performance giving superb results.

Sonatine for Two Violins (1920)

☐ David and Igor Oistrakh (violins) / Monitor S-2058

Proof that proper climax can be obtained even with the minimal means of two-voiced polyphony is ably presented in the opening movement of this work. Thematic relationship is made clear by alternating homophonically coupled statements, and by four-part writing. Contrasts are also detailed by color (muted timbre in the middle movement). Fugal design defines the final movement.

The premiere (in 1921) was certainly a historic affair, since two famous twentieth-century composers were the instrumentalists—Honegger himself and Darius Milhaud, to whom the work is dedicated. True and totally befitting partnership is maintained in this richly cogent and balanced performance by the father-and-son team. (A further link is that the latter was the pupil of the former.)

Sonatine for Violin and Cello (1932)

☐ Schoenfeld Duo / Everest 3243

In this duet, artful contrapuntalism is linked with smart rhythmic ideas. Though the first movement begins in unisoned G major, assorted tonal interlacement quickly appears from within. The slow movement is in aria style; its first part is followed by a fugal section and then a return to the initial manner. Whimsicality is found in the finale. The stop-and-go of some rhythms is somewhat Stravinskian, but the gay E major theme is decidedly French.

The performance by Alice and Eleonore Schoenfeld is preferable to the only competitive release, by Primož Novšak and Susanne Basler, on Musical Heritage (MHS-1869), even though the latter is clearer and much richer. The reason is unarguable. Novšak and Basler play with such deliberation that the music seems to be sticking in the grooves, rather than flowing freely. Their idea of an *allegro* is an extremely checked, moderate metronomic pulse. The spirit of the music becomes so dulled and prosaic as to deaden all the joys within the conception. Thus movement 1 is played in a properly fitting four-minute span by the Schoenfelds; the MHS team take seven minutes to travel over the same ground. The same pertains to the last movement: 4:23 for the gals, 5:17 for the mixed team.

A Christmas Cantata (1953)

Cantata and Oratorio

☐ L'Orchestre de la Suisse Romande; Le Choeur des Jeunes de Lausanne; Le Choeur de Radio-Lausanne and Children's Chorus: Le Petit Choeur du Collège de Villamont / Mollet (baritone) / Ansermet (conductor) / London 25320

Not merely a seasonal work. The *Cantate de Noël* contains both Yuletide and concert music. It displays a magnificent clarity of polyphonic thought (honest-to-goodness polyphony, not simply harmony turned on its stomach and stretched horizontally). This is set in a true Bachian manner, with the abrasiveness usual to Honegger's strong contrapuntal language honed down to the minimum. Utilized in the Cantata are French and German carols, including a fascinating, laced weave of *Silent Night*. There are also a pair of Latin hymns. All this is accomplished with taste and stylistic tact.

Reacting to the persuasiveness manifested in the work, the performers are sympathetic and deeply convincing in their interpretation. London's vivid sound serves the composition especially well.

Le Roi David (1921)

☐ Utah Symphony Orchestra and University of Utah Chorus / Davrath (soprano); Preston (mezzo-soprano); Sorenson (tenor); Singher (narrator); Madeleine Milhaud (speaker) / Abravanel (conductor) / Vanguard 2117/8

An oratorio in concept, termed a "dramatic psalm" by the composer, this powerful piece combines chorus, solo voices, and narrator with orchestra in a work of operatic sweep and purity of thought. A composition of mixed genre, Honegger's oratorio-opera is divided into three major sections, and consists of twenty-eight different numbers.

"King David" is stark music, both radiant and brutal because of its subject. It is like a huge mural as it traces David from shepherd to king by way of psalms, fanfares, incantations, lamentations, marches, and dances. Because of its varied scope the contrasts are extremely vivid, obtained by chord and discord, Bachian classicism compared with audacious *Le Sacre du printemps* coloristic and rhythmic types, pure harmonic constructions set off from polytonal counterpoint. Though each scene has its individual evocative power, the extremes of style and content do not make a hodgepodge. The sections are related one to the next no matter how different. Nothing artificial, nothing mannered. *Le Roi David* shows how an abundance of variety can serve dramatic purposes and create its own colorful balance. The rewards are eloquent.

Abravanel has turned out a thrilling representation of Honegger's fascinating musical fresco. He has the advantage of a magnificent narrator in the person of Singher, the best of any I have heard in this part. Another exquisitely delineated segment is the chilling *Incantation* for speaking voice and orchestra, narrated by Madeleine Milhaud, the composer's wife. This release is a triumph.

Antony Hopkins   (20th cent.)

Chamber Music

Suite for Soprano Recorder and Piano (1953)

☐ Dolmetsch (soprano recorder); Saxby (piano) / Orion 74144

Four short movements. The second is a reminder of Britten's *Peter Grimes* (one of the Interludes). The comparison is not meant to be odious. Gaiety and spirit are here.

The Dolmetsch-Saxby team zip through this music with marvelous control. Especially clean is the rhythmic vivacity.

James Hopkins   (1939-   )

Chamber Music

Diferencias sobre un tema original

☐ Western Arts Trio / Laurel LR-104

No prosaic formal cant in the "Variations on an Original Theme." The variations, preceded by an introduction and the generating subject, are followed by a section of cadenzas, and the trio is completed by a return to the thematic idea and the introduction. Repetition of a core section is accompanied by a change in its statement to help solidify the music's arch form.

Symphonic operations are paramount in Hopkins's handling of the piano-trio medium. The Western Arts team applies the required robustness and weight.

Francis Hopkinson (1737-1791)

Beneath a Weeping Willow's Shade

My Generous Heart Disdains

☐ Members of the New England Conservatory Collegium Musicum / Golden Crest/N.E. Conservatory NEC-111

Vocal

Voice with Accompaniment

Gentility exhibited in a pair of songs historically important and musically valuable. No individual credits given for the renditions, one by a male singer (good), the other by a female (fair), both with harpsichord partnership.

Joseph Horovitz (1920-   )

Music Hall Suite

☐ Metropolitan Brass Quintet / Crystal S-208

Chamber Music

Scintillating subjects given the proper pops touch, reminding one of Morton Gould in his younger days. Best: the rhythmic play in *Trick Cyclists* and the very effective brass-sound translation of *Soft-Shoe Shuffle. Les Girls* concludes the work in the form of a modernized Offenbachian galop. (The other movements are *Soubrette Song* and *Adagio—Team.*)

Anthon van der Horst (1899-1965)

Réflexions sonores, Op. 99

☐ Concertgebouw Orchestra / Haitink (conductor) / Donemus Audio-Visual Series 6804 (monaural)

Orchestra

Program music dealing with a twelfth-century Indian tale and including a medicant, vampires, magic events, etc. The style deals with Bartók, Stravinsky, and Ravel. Lots of exotic touches and virtuosic orchestration, but unfortunately no exact delineation of the story is given in the data that accompany the recording. No documentation is necessary, however, to realize that Haitink conducts an exciting performance.

Jacques Hotteterre (ca. 1684-1762)

Instrumental

Flute

Ecos for Unaccompanied Baroque Flute

☐ Shanley (baroque flute) / Orion 73108

Each and every phrase from the start of the Adagio to the conclusion of the Allegro is repeated at a softer dynamic level; thus the title "Echoes." Admirably done, with Orion noting that "no artificial echo or equalization" was added. A novelty piece, but in close to five minutes it almost wears out its welcome.

First Book of Pieces for the Transverse Flute

☐ Stastny (baroque flute); Harnoncourt (bass viola da gamba); Fischer (harpsichord) / Vanguard C-10029

A half-dozen charming dances (saraband, branle, etc.) with quaint titles such as *Le Depart, La Mitilde,* etc. The performance by members of the Concentus Musicus is highly recommended. Leopold Stastny colors the sounds of the middle-eighteenth-century flute he uses as though he had the advantage of playing on a modern instrument.

Chamber Music

Suite in D major for Flute and Continuo

☐ Murray (baroque flute); Goldstein (harpsichord) / Pandora 103

Typical music of the very early part of the eighteenth century, with a Prelude followed by four dance movements. Paramount performance authenticity: Murray plays an eighteenth-century instrument, and Goldstein uses an Italian harpsichord originally built in 1600 and restored in 1974. The baroque flute utilized provides a heavier texture than the recorder, but in turn produces a grayish neutrality of color when compared with the modern flute. However, this unpretentious music is well worth hearing with the only instrumental qualities that were available to the composer. Considered in that light, this is a first-rate, true-tongued performance.

Suite in C minor for Flute and Continuo

☐ Le Rondeau de Paris / Nonesuch 73014

In this performance, more emphasis is given the cello support of the continuo than usual. This almost makes for trio equality, though the flute stays in command.

Nicely articulated performance by the group, and exceedingly well balanced.

Alan Hovhaness (1911-   )

Orchestra

And God Created Great Whales, Op. 229, No. 1

☐ Orchestra / Kostelanetz (conductor) / Columbia M-34537

No orchestral imitations of the aquatic mammal. The real thing, obtained by including the recorded sounds of great humpback whales as part of the instrumentation. It can only be done once, and Hovhaness has done it. The orchestra produces pitch shivers, and freely rhythmic conjunct sounds are in the strings. This is meant to "suggest waves in a vast ocean sky," and so on. But what are important are those whale sounds.

Hovhaness has a good ear for blending these into the score, and Kostelanetz produces an impressive statement of the music.

Concerto No. 7, Op. 116

☐ Louisville Orchestra / Whitney (conductor) / Louisville 545-4

Repetitive figures, odd timbre combinations, and forthright Eastern melos set partially with Western-style techniques distinguish this beautifully sensitive music. Hovhaness's polyphonic mixtures result in unburdened, intoxicating sonorities. And he can be very zealous: a Hindustanian scherzo and a final double fugue lead to an epilogue in the form of a hymn. The last is for the citizens of Louisville, Kentucky, in acknowledgment of the Louisville Orchestra's commission for this work.

It is played with complete understanding, matched by full-scale recording and plenty of fidelity. If Hovhaness is your taste, this disc could well be your best choice of all.

Floating World, Op. 209

☐ Orchestra / Kostelanetz (conductor) / Columbia M-34537

There are some neat effects in this three-sectioned work, proceeding from glides in the trombones to a march that is especially percussively stimulated. Naturally, the objective is music of picturesque detail rather than a music developed formally. Development in most of Hovhaness's music consists of restatements that are considered with different-colored instrumentational glasses.

Kostelanetz keeps things alive and produces a statement of a convincing whole.

Fra Angelico: **Fantasy for Orchestra,** Op. 220

☐ New Orleans Philharmonic Symphony Orchestra / Torkanowsky (conductor) / Orion 7268

An orchestral tribute to the mystical fifteenth-century artist who "painted his visions of angels playing celestial trumpets." And "celestial" is delineated by Hovhaness through division of massed colors: the five-part strings spread into sixty-six voices, the woodwinds are set in a dozen lines, and the brass in a total of eleven. Density of totality is filtered by such apportionment. It produces a truly seraphic sonority supported by chanting modal motivity.

Hovhaness's highly evocative music receives a stunning performance.

The Holy City, Op. 218

☐ Royal Philharmonic Orchestra / Howarth (trumpet) / Lipkin (conductor) / Composers Recordings S-259

Lots of Hovhanessian graphic glides contrasted to modal declamation. The latter is sensitively carried out by Elgar Howarth.

Meditation on Orpheus, Op. 155

☐ Orchestra / Kostelanetz (conductor) / Columbia M-34537

Central to this work, as to so many others by the same composer, is the element of timbre. Some timbres are clearly identifiable—in a horn line, an oboe or trumpet statement. But there are others—heard, for instance, in rushing configurations formed from a rhythmic mixture, or pizzicato murmurs not enclosed in metrical fences. These elements—"traditional" and the reverse—alternate to specify the shape of this piece. It is beautifully played by the orchestra—an indication of personal involvement with the music.

Kostelanetz's newer edition pushes the older monaural Composers Recordings 134 issue (played by the Japan Philharmonic Orchestra, conducted by Strickland) deep into second place.

Mysterious Mountain, Op. 132

☐ Chicago Symphony Orchestra / Reiner (conductor) / RCA LSC–2251

In terms of performance by the major-league orchestras, this is the composer's most successful symphonic piece. Again, most of the music represents Hovhaness intoning the descant of bygone centuries, but in one portion of this work there are reflections which indicate that, despite the composer's renunciation of his early music (that written prior to 1940, which, for the most part, he destroyed), something of it has remained with him. These are to be heard in the middle section, which has the Sibelian dash and defined Northern climate of the early output. No harm done: this provides relief from the persistent triadic neosacred sound that otherwise permeates the opus.

Reiner's performance is sensitive. The recorded sound is beautiful.

Sunrise

☐ Orchestra / Kostelanetz (conductor) / Columbia M–34537

Thin, cluster-like sounds blended with and contrasted to a lush melodic line. Nice warmth supplied by the score and generated by the performance.

Symphony No. 9 (St. Vartan), Op. 80

☐ National Philharmonic of London / Hovhaness (conductor) / Poseidon 1013

A huge work in twenty-four sections, these grouped in five major parts; it is named for a fifth-century Armenian national hero. This music is symphonic in scope; in form it is rather a mural of canonical description. In presenting his picture of Armenian religion via chants and dances, Hovhaness has a sectarian attitude. Despite a large variety of instrumental colors, not once does he depart from his apostolic music making.

This is a work of originality, but its scope can tax the listener. However, one can hear a single section or sections without disturbing the unity, for Hovhaness's *St. Vartan* is organized in a multi-insular way. This music sounds unlike any other composer's. Hovhaness's so-called unsophistication is actually a new sophistication.

Symphony No. 11 (All Men Are Brothers) (1960)

☐ Royal Philharmonic Orchestra / Hovhaness (conductor) / Poseidon 1001

A rich, radiant score (first performed in 1961 and then completely rewritten in 1969). Some of Hovhaness's stark neoprimitivism is included, plus expansive melodic lines. The scoring is of the juicy type.

Symphony No. 15 (Silver Pilgrimage), Op. 199

☐ Louisville Orchestra / Whitney (conductor) / Louisville LS–662

As in so many Hovhaness works, the hypnotic use of rhythmless murmuring string sounds is basic, in this case to the first three of the four movements. The Symphony is named after the Indian novel by M. Anantanarayan, with movements titled *Mount Ravana, Marava Princess, River of Meditation*, and *Heroic Gates of Peace*. Modalism and canonic arrangement support the musical texts, nourished by the free-pulsed ostinati. Tonal restriction is major to the piece, with seven pitches used in movement 1, six in movement 2, and seven in movement 3.

Hovhaness's Symphony is not difficult to play but requires equilibrium and balance. Whitney supplies it. Fine trumpet playing.

Armenian Rhapsody No. 1, Op. 45

☐ Crystal Chamber Orchestra / Gold (conductor) / Crystal S–800

Music catalogues are crammed with so-called Oriental music, Chinese music, Hindu music, and the like, making a great deal of ordered confusion, for in most cases the music is strictly sham exotica, an imitation made from an imitation. Hovhaness does not compose from rote observation. Though he is not an Easterner (he was born in Somerville, Massachusetts, and studied piano and composition at the New England Conservatory of Music), his Eastern-designed music is stated with authority. This (a plow song sung before dawn and three dance tunes) is the real thing, the result of study, research, orientation, and conviction of purpose.

Hymn to Yerevan, Op. 83

☐ North Jersey Wind Symphony / Brion (conductor) / Mace MXX–9099

Hovhaness explains his title: "The ancient city of Yerevan, at the foot of majestic, towering Mount Ararat, is the home of Armenians who found refuge there from many massacres."

Much more Oriental commentary than otherwise found in Hovhaness's work is to be heard in this tripartite piece. Thus, a conspicuous use of the augmented interval that is the credit card for acquiring this type of simulated indigenous character.

Requiem and Resurrection, Op. 224

☐ Members of the North Jersey Wind Symphony / Hovhaness (conductor) / Poseidon 1002

Scored for a brass group of four horns, two trumpets, three trombones, and tuba, with timpani and percussion requiring three players. No wind instruments temper the vigor of this persuasive score.

The superlative sound produced by this little-known recording firm deserves special comment.

Symphony No. 4, Op. 165

☐ Eastman Wind Ensemble / Roller (conductor) / Mercury 75010

The hothouse world that Hovhaness occupies has become familiar territory. The same ostinati, the analogous sectional architecture, the overprotestation of bell sonorities, the fluidic metrical sprawl heard in his other pieces are heard here. But there are some fresh particulars that are spiced seasoning for the ear. In movement 1 one hears the murky colors of solo bass clarinet and solo double bassoon, with butterfly smashes of percussive sounds against them. In movement 3 there appear a record number of successive trombone glissandi that are frightening, fascinating, and magical. And set in that same part are the most gorgeous, unrefined trombone pedal sounds this reviewer has ever heard.

Roller scores a triumph with his understanding projection of this Hovhanessian splendor. The playing is superb, the sound richly rewarding.

Symphony No. 7 (*Nanga Parvat*), Op. 178

Symphony No. 14 (*Ararat*), Op. 194

☐ North Jersey Wind Symphony / Brion (conductor) / Mace MXX–9099

The first work is Hovhaness's "Alpine Symphony." Nanga Parvat is a Kashmir mountain and is depicted in two of its aspects—in its ferocity and at sunset. A March is the pivotal middle part. But no Straussian experiences. Lost of rhythm, primitive scoring and plenty of the ostinato detail that is Hovhaness's trademark.

Ararat is another mountain. Its music is fierce, sequential, with an enthusiasm for cantillative phrases and lengthy mensural patterns that eradicate strong and weak pulses in such meters as $\frac{13}{8}$, $\frac{19}{8}$, $\frac{23}{8}$, and $\frac{13}{4}$. There are echoes here, not of other men's music, but of Hovhaness's own: bells clanging, drums beating, trumpets blaring. Here is a blend of earthiness and sonic delirium that is quite unique in the band medium.

Solo Instrument and Orchestra

Clarinet

Talin, Op. 93

☐ Orchestra da Camera di Roma / Sobol (clarinet) / Flagello (conductor) / Peters International PLE–071

Those who like modal-styled music will find more than enough of it in this haunting three-movement conception. There are no pyrotechnics; the middle section is fast-paced, but *Talin* is not a display piece.

This is a second edition of Hovhaness's work. Originally it was for viola and string orchestra and in that form was recorded by the MGM String Orchestra, with Emanuel Vardi as the viola soloist and Izler Solomon as the conductor, on MGM E–3432—a monaural issue. Since that fine disc performance has long been deleted, it is a pleasure to have this splendid presentation in the clarinet version Hovhaness made specifically for the soloist, Lawrence Sobol. Sobol performs with consistent beauty of tone and grace of phraseology that deserve a rave notice. Flagello's body of strings deserves equally high praise. The disc has gorgeous sound.

Flute and Violin

Tzaikerk ("Evening Song") for Solo Flute, Solo Violin, Timpani, and String Orchestra

☐ Crystal Chamber Orchestra / Shanley (flute); Shapiro (violin); Peter (drums) / Gold (conductor) / Crystal S–800

A festival of combined pitch-concentrated ostinati and long-lined melodies. The web of repetitive sound is Hovhaness to the core.

The performance is acutely in style. Though scored for timpani, the percussion part was played on Roto-toms for this recording.

Piano

Lousadzak: Concerto No. 1 for Piano and String Orchestra

☐ Ajemian (piano) / Hovhaness (conductor) / Folkways 3369 (monaural)

It is a singular event when a piano (especially in a designated "Concerto") is heard homophonically, minus its usual chordal and polytextural cast. Hovhaness indicates he is imitating various Armenian instruments. Melisma and sound curves revolving around themselves are the main features. The piano ripples and is in practically constant use.

Maro Ajemian is the paramount interpreter of Hovhaness's piano works, and so, with the composer conducting, this is certainly a definitive performance. I've heard better sound qualities from Folkways.

Prayer of St. Gregory for Trumpet and String Orchestra

Trumpet

☐ Crystal Chamber Orchestra / Stevens (trumpet) / Gold (conductor) / Crystal S-800

Intense concentration on incessant modal harmonic contours is displayed in this very sonorous outpouring of religious atmosphere. Performance: gorgeous.

Fantasy on Japanese Woodprints, Op. 211

Xylophone

☐ Orchestra / Hiraoka (xylophone) / Kostelanetz (conductor) / Columbia M-34537

Gentle touches that twirl pentatonically. The sense of quiet that pervades the music is its prime asset. Hovhaness's enthusiasm for static sounds in a variety of patterns fulfills his objective of "mood pictures inspired by old Japanese woodcut prints." The performance is properly gentle and delicate.

Return and Rebuild the Desolate Places (Concerto for Trumpet and Wind Orchestra), Op. 213

Solo Instrument and Band

Trumpet

☐ North Jersey Wind Symphony / Schwarz (trumpet) / Brion (conductor) / Mace MXX-9099

The scenario begins with a mystical prelude, followed by a furious avalanche of sound. It ends with a long hymnodic section of restrained modalistic motility. The ear is hypnotized, especially by the suave trumpet tone of Gerard Schwarz.

Sonata for Flute, Op. 118

Instrumental

Flute

☐ Baron (flute) / Composers Recordings 212 (monaural)

Of course exotic, shamelessly so. Still, whatever Hovhaness does he does without a sense of striving and with natural structuring. A different mode or raga is used in each of the three movements. Languid microtonal slides are heard in parts 1 and 3; the center movement has metrical malleability in its pulse arrangement of $\frac{3}{8}-\frac{3}{4}-\frac{3}{8}-\frac{4}{4}$.

Nocturne, Op. 20, No. 1

Sonata for Harp, Op. 127

Harp

☐ McDonald (harp) / Klavier KS-507

Despite the chronological disparity between these two works, they are remarkably similar: poetic and somewhat pentatonic, and without the doctrinaire exoticisms that permeate most of Hovhaness's music. Hovhaness is always alert to what will carry well via the harp. Use is made of a few basic ideas, and these are repeatedly renewed.

Allegro on a Pakistan Lute Tune, Op. 104, No. 6

Piano

☐ Helps (piano) / Composers Recordings S-288

Hovhaness's usual worship of ostinati, which frame a simple tune given repetitive statements.

Duet for Violin and Harpsichord (1954)

Chamber Music

☐ Brink (violin); Pinkham (harpsichord) / Composers Recordings 109 (monaural)

Hovhaness can bat 'em out! This duo was commissioned on May 16, 1954, composed the very next day, and two weeks later given its first hearing in Frankfurt, Germany.

Three short movements: a Prelude, *Haiku,* and an Aria. Ordinary, but worth an occasional hearing.

Sonata for Trumpet and Organ (Movement 1), Op. 200

☐ Plog (trumpet); Thomas (organ) / Crystal S-362

A hymn without words. A melody abjuring marked rhythm. Hovhaness in his usual evangelical manner writing music "which might be sung among high mountain peaks." The brass instrument "becomes the voice of the cantor, the messenger of God, who sings blessings and hope to the people."

With Anthony Plog's beautiful trumpet voice and his commanding golden tone, listeners will certainly become believers.

Firdausi for Clarinet, Harp, and Percussion, Op. 252

☐ Sobol (clarinet); Agostini (harp); Boyar (percussion) / Grenadilla GS-1008

Firdausi was a tenth-century Persian poet. Hovhaness delineates him as a "magical singer" who describes mystical and magical events. There are eighteen of these, beginning with an *Invocation,* concluding with a *Love Song.* In between there are four dances, three sections concerned with an avatar, etc. The textures are fragile, the sounds on the sweet side, the percussion restrained. Nonviolence rules.

Hovhaness's complete unpretentiousness makes his piece almost forceful in effect, despite the restricted and exceedingly rarefied instrumentation. The playing is sensitively controlled. However, with the gentle-pulsed continuity, it is suggested that you listen in small segments.

Suite for Violin, Piano, and Percussion, Op. 99

☐ Anahid Ajemian (violin); Maro Ajemian (piano); Bailey (percussion) / Columbia Special Products AML-5179 (monaural)

Repetitive oscillative patterns plus the effect of unending improvisation on and around the same sound-course typify this Eastern music in Western instrumental translation (save for the microtoned violin, which occasionally plays sixth tones; but these are not clearly defined on the recording, which is otherwise worthy).

The six movements contain many other devices: improvisatory and meterless designs, plus rhythmic patterns that range in cycles from as few as six beats to as many as fifty-nine. Color is paramount; the pianist simulates a gong by striking the bass strings inside the piano with a timpani stick, and in the fifth movement (a canon) an effective sonorous impact is made by utilizing tritonality.

Tumburu, Op. 264, No. 1
Varuna, Op. 264, No. 2

☐ Macalester Trio / Composers Recordings S-326

Both titles are the names of ancient Indian gods. Both works have the Hovhaness hothouse brand of repetitive phrases, drones, cantillative sections, and ostinato rhythms. His timbre arrangement always charms the ear, even when it overemphasizes by remaining static, minus changes of velocity, weight, density, pressure, and resistance. Where another composer develops, Hovhaness poetizes on a theme and then repoetizes on it.

Koke No Niwa ("Moss Garden"), Op. 181

☐ Kaplan (English horn); Rosenberger and Bailey (percussion); Negri (harp) / Composers Recordings S–186

The result of a commission by a Tokyo television station to create a musical tribute to the Moss Temple in Kyoto, called *Koke Dera*. The title was predefined for Hovhaness as *Koke No Niwa*, which means "Moss Garden."

Hovhaness's exoticism is made to order for this type of subject, including the almost rhythmically static statements by the English horn and slight punctuations by the timpani, tam-tam, glockenspiel, marimba, and harp that we hear here.

Upon Enchanted Ground, Op. 90a

☐ Baron (flute); Lawrence (harp); Adam (cello); Bailey (tam-tam) / Hovhaness (conductor) / Columbia Special Products AML–5179 (monaural)

The music, though of fairly enchanting character, makes no thematic gestures, avoids harmony as we know it, and diffuses its rhythms. Thus with gentle-pulsed motility Hovhaness defines his personal idea of Hindu music.

Notwithstanding a conductor on the podium, *Upon Enchanted Ground* remains in the chamber-music category. Gorgeous performance.

Sharagan and Fugue for Brass Choir, Op. 58

☐ New York Brass Quintet / Desto 6401

Hovhaness's penchant for a baroque quality of sound is expertly set forth in this hymn (the meaning of *Sharagan*) and Fugue. Modalism is the technique, fully utilized, with hardly any exotic overhang.

The playing is a marvelous example of brass fluidity. These performers have the subtlety and sensitivity of superfine string players.

Six Dances, Op. 79

☐ Dallas Brass Quintet / Crystal S–203

Hovhaness's faith in cantillative and Eastern exotic colors is maintained in this set, scored for horn, two trumpets, trombone, and tuba. Imaginative music and imaged with the support of ostinati. The liner note mentions that the work is in his "usual listenable style." That it is, particularly in the Dallas Quintet's strong execution.

Hercules for Soprano and Violin, Op. 56, No. 4

Vocal

Voice with Accompaniment

☐ Catherine Malfitano (soprano); Joseph Malfitano (violin) / Musical Heritage Society MHS–1976

Practically nothing to do with the Greek hero, but an evocation of ancient rituals, "of pre-Christian, Armenian or Greek civilizations." Melismatic vocalism and microtonal pitches are the teammates that Hovhaness uses for his esoteric composition. It is beautifully expressed by the Malfitanos.

Avak, the Healer: Cantata for Soprano, Trumpet, and Strings, Op. 65

Cantata and Oratorio

☐ Louisville Orchestra / Farris (mezzo-soprano); Rapier (trumpet) / Mester (conductor) / Louisville LS–735
☐ Crystal Chamber Orchestra / Nixon (soprano); Stevens (trumpet) / Gold (conductor) / Crystal S–800

The intoxicating juices of modal melismaticism flow through most of Alan Hovhaness's work. These are represented here in constant abundance, conjuring up the image of music written by an Armenian Vaughan Williams.

Avak tosses in hot sonorities, even though these are only made from fatty string sounds (expressing, according to the composer, the prayer of the people), and a martially sensual trumpet timbre (symbolizing, again according to Hovhaness, the voice of the inspired messenger, the cantor, the singer-prophet). The format for this ethnic religiosity consists of four parts for the voice and two for the trumpet and strings (an Overture and a Processional). The material is a music of crimson and bishop's purple.

Three reasons dictate placing the Louisvillians in first-choice position, before the Californians. The string body of the former group has more of the corpulence needed to represent the score than the total of twenty-four strings used by the latter assemblage. Second, Leon Rapier's trumpet sound is more penetrating than Thomas Stevens's. Last, the thicker, over-all sound force on the Louisville disc is more propitious. However, it is only proper to point out that Marni Nixon is the superior vocalist, in terms both of control and of projection of diction.

Triptych: Ave Maria - Christmas Ode - Easter Cantata

☐ Members of the Bamberg Symphony and Bay Rund Singers / Valente (soprano) / Antonini (conductor) / Composers Recordings S–221

Hovhaness's devotional sincerity needs no question. It permeates his output and is shown by the three parts of this work, composed in 1956, 1952, and 1953, respectively. Each is designed differently and paralleled by a varied scoring. The *Ave Maria* is a motet for womens' chorus with two oboes, two horns, and harp. The Christmas Ode is for soprano, strings, and celesta. Largest of all is the Easter Cantata, which calls for soprano, chorus, two oboes, two horns, harp, celesta, and strings.

Hovhaness has found his formula and has found it works. The ear is caressed by his idea of "celestial joyousness," detailed by modalities. It is an ecclesiastical climate that Hovhaness favors, and he does not move out of it in his *Triptych*.

I would consider this to be the finest recording made thus far by Alfredo Antonini. Benita Valente's singing is warm and proficient.

Opera and Dramatic Music

The Rubáiyát of Omar Khayyám

☐ Orchestra / Fairbanks, Jr. (narrator); Carrozza (accordion) / Kostelanetz (conductor) / Columbia M–34537

A liberal person will overlook the distilled sentimentality of this work. It celebrates the Orientalish clichés that Hollywood made famous (or infamous) and that are now carried over to TV. One section is a blind carbon copy of some phrases from the well-known *Caucasian Sketches* by Ippolitov-Ivanov. All of it is surrounded and linked by very sweet narration (meaning overserious) by Douglas Fairbanks, Jr. Included is some fine featuring of the accordion, sensitively played by Carmen Carrozza.

Mary Howe   (1882-1964)

Orchestra

Sand (1928)

☐ Vienna Orchestra / Strickland (conductor) / Composers Recordings 103 (monaural)

Scherzo-like kinetics build this short piece. Nothing gritty, all filamented and gossamer. The composer states it is music dealing with "the substance itself—its consistency, grains . . . and . . . scattering quality."

Spring Pastoral (1936)

☐ Imperial Philharmonic of Tokyo / Strickland (conductor) / Composers Recordings 145 (monaural)

A nicely gentle piece, and nicely eclectic. Worth occasional listening time.

Stars (1937)

☐ Vienna Orchestra / Strickland (conductor) / Composers Recordings 103 (monaural)

If chromaticism equals romanticism, *Stars* is that. Melodic shapes are determined, the harmonies shifting these subtly in varied directions. These fulfill the composer's focus, "the gradually overwhelming effect of the dome of a starry night—its peace, beauty, and space."

Herbert Howells   (1892-   )

Phantasy Quartet, Op. 25

Chamber Music

☐ Richards Ensemble / Lyrita SRCS-68

Fantasy means which are applied to simulate a four-movement composition. Sensitive textures, with creamy modalism the principal ingredient. In the last third of the twentieth-century, music of Howells's ductility may be an old-fashioned recipe, but only to those whose diet begins with Berio and ends with Xenakis. A nourishment for the ears, with the aid of a finely arranged performance.

Quartet in A minor for Piano, Violin, Viola, and Cello, Op. 21

☐ Richards Piano Quartet / Lyrita SRCS-68

There are several very odd facts concerning this Piano Quartet, one of the best of Howells's productions. It has single specialness by being partly dedicated to a place in nature ("To the Hill at Chosen and Ivor Gurney who knows it"), and therein lies the second matter. Although the work is issued without a program, and titles for its three movements are absent, the composer has elsewhere described it with such poetic words as to imply a definite story. Yet (in view of its published form), the Quartet must be considered at the opposite pole—a work in the "absolute music" category.

It will be found that the music is gray and white in its colorations, that it is a picture and an abstraction of the effect of nature, that it seems to probe folk song and yet it has none. It is all that and more—a composition conveying tender emotions that produce a chamber-music "pastoral symphony."

The performance is a totally committed one.

Rhapsodic Quintet for Clarinet and Strings, Op. 31

☐ Richards Ensemble / King (clarinet) / Lyrita SRCS-68

This work in one movement puts more emphasis on polyphony than will be found in other chamber works by Howells. The structure is built on variational development of the thematic data. Satisfactory playing, though balanced integration is not at its best in the very early part of the piece.

Choral

Chorus Alone

Magnificat and Nunc Dimittis

☐ Choir of St. John's College, Cambridge / Guest (conductor) / Argo ZRG-621

Superb English impressionism that represents extremely significant sacred music. The work was written for the choir that sings it with magnetic artistry.

Chorus with Accompaniment

Like as the Hart

☐ Choir of St. John's College, Cambridge / Runnett (organ) / Guest (conductor) / Argo ZRG-5340

The third of a set of four anthems for chorus and organ. A slightly romantic intensity colors this church-music piece.

Jenö Hubay   *(1858-1937)*

Solo Instrument and Orchestra

Violin

Concerto No. 3 in G minor for Violin and Orchestra, Op. 99

☐ Orchestra of Radio Luxembourg / Rosand (violin) / de Froment (conductor) / Candide 31054

Deeply sincere romantic music, minus any fussy and clouded harmonic content. The Scherzo is a Mendelssohnian-styled delight, the slow movement (Adagio) is a *cantilena* with a unifying introspectiveness. The finale is spirited, with an admirable opening: a short theme is announced which then is set in fugato and followed by a short cadenza, after which the main idea is given a thorough workout. Throughout Hubay's fine Concerto there is no technical hocus-pocus for the violin; the virtuosic demands are the demands of the total design.

As so often, Rosand here deals with off-beat repertoire, and for this alone he deserves the fullest attention and commendation. However, he backs up his choice of music with a fully convincing solo portrayal. His playing most persuasively carries out the special responsibility involved because the music performed is practically unknown.

Hejre Kati for Violin and Orchestra, Op. 32

☐ Orchestra of Radio Luxembourg / Rosand (violin) / de Froment (conductor) / Candide 31064

Hejre Kati (translate it "Heigh-ho Kitty") is the fourth in a set of fourteen pieces Hubay wrote for violin and orchestra in the Hungarian manner, titled *Scènes de la Csárda*. Each piece was assigned a separate opus number.

Once upon a time every violin student tackled this one, and every concert violinist played it. Once upon a time, that is. Musical fashion having its entrances and exits, *Hejre Kati* has been shelved. One wonders why. After all, the somewhat sweet and sentimental-longing character of the first part (the *lassu* of the Hungarian czardas), contrasted to rapid motility (the *friss* or *friska* of this dance form), provides all that is necessary for juicy fiddlin'.

Rosand's recording, therefore, is in the nature of a revival. It is most welcome. With his stylistic rapport, it is doubly welcome.

Instrumental

Violin

The Violin Maker of Cremona

☐ Ricci (violin); Pommers (piano) / MCA 2537

A violin aria with nostalgic classification. Ricci's tone can fully be described as warm and rich. It is also projected with fervor and intensity; the sounds come from the very depths of the instrument.

The Zephyr, Op. 30, No. 5

☐ Ricci (violin); Lush (piano) / London STS–15049

The Hungarian violinist-composer's miniature essay describing a gentle breeze is registered with superb bowing, phrasing, and technical control. It lasts just as long as it should.

Hubay / *Franz Liszt.* See *Liszt* / Hubay.

Klaus Huber (1924-   )

Noctes Intelligibilis Lucis for Oboe and Harpsichord (1961)

Chamber Music

☐ Holliger (oboe); Wyttenbach (harpsichord) / Philips 6500202

The fascination of the intense luminosity of the oboe timbre, ranging totally over its pitch span, is matched by the harpsichord sounds, which are removed from the tinkly tingles common to this instrument. Among other things, hearing punched deep-bass clusters on the keyboard instrument is aurally fascinating.

In certain respects form is secondary to the dialogue undertaken by the instruments; the improvisation-like conversation animates and shapes the design. There is expert sensibility in this piece, and exquisite sensitivity. The playing is perfection itself.

Joe Hudson (1952-   )

Reflexives for Piano and Tape

Instrumental

Piano

☐ Burge (piano) / Composers Recordings SD–345

Contemporary rhapsodicism. Sometimes the tape part is infused with the basic soft insides of the piano's material, adding thereby a colorful crust. At other times it expands the color of the keyboard sound in a tinctured reflection.

John Huggler (1928-   )

Quintet No. 1 for Brass Instruments (1955)

Chamber Music

☐ Cambridge Brass Quintet / Crystal S–204

Compounded from classical design and serial technique but not scholastically weighted in either case. Huggler's four movements flow from one relationship to another and yet are each totally balanced. There is fine depth in this music, which the Cambridge team (Robert Pettipaw and Peter Chapman, trumpets; Michael Johns, horn; Norman Bolter, trombone; and Gary Ofenloch, tuba) probe to perfection.

Robert Hughes (1933-)

Chamber Music

Sonitudes (1971)

☐ Millard (flute); Brown (cello) / Arch S–1760

We're not at the stage of "seeing" a recorded performance (would that still be counted as a "recording"?), so we miss a few visual aspects of this sensitive-sounding duo, well conceived by Hughes, well performed by Janet Millard and Loren Brown, and well produced by Arch Records.

The cellist beats the D and A strings of the instrument with a drumstick to begin the piece (pitch changes only apply to the higher string). Later the cello is laid on the floor and the two upper strings are hit with the drumstick and also slapped against the fingerboard. The flutist has no histrionics to match these actions, except blowing through the instrument to simulate what the composer terms a "wind shriek." This effect opens the second part of the work, a Recitative, which is linked to the first section, titled *Scene* and subtitled *Introduction*. A Serenade, with *rubato* as its principal essence, and a peripatetic Caprice (the tempo designation is *As fast as possible*) conclude *Sonitudes*.

There's little been written for the flute-cello combination. Hughes's contribution is a fruitful addition.

Tobias Hume (?-1645)

Instrumental

Viola da Gamba

Captain Hume's Galliard from The First Part of Ayres

☐ Sampson (viola da gamba) / Orion 74162

A small unaccompanied string-instrument delight by this English violist-composer. The variations are simple and decidedly musical. Peggie Simpson's playing is neat and likewise decidedly musical.

Vocal

Voice with Accompaniment

Fain Would I Change That Note

☐ Brown (tenor); Muller (tenor viol) / Nonesuch 73010

As neat an English *ayre* as you would want to hear, sensitively sung and colorfully accompanied.

Gerald Humel (1931-)

Instrumental

Flute

Preludium und Scherzo

☐ Baron (flute) / Composers Recordings S–237

The disciplines of writing for unaccompanied flute are maintained here in sober outlines. Humel avoids external effects save for some flutter-tonguing in the *Scherzo*. Actually the material is of standard panchromatic color, meaning constructive development and no flamboyance. Samuel Baron plays in the same meaningful manner.

Sonata (*Journey to Praha*) for Violin and Piano

☐ Gross (violin); Hewitt (piano) / Composers Recordings S-237

Chamber Music

Style and forms are quite clear. The former is twelve-tone, the latter define fantasy proportions in the corner movements and a scherzo atmosphere in the central one. What is special is the use of the Czech national anthem as the basis for the tone row that is the springboard for the work.

Humel's piece is craggy but tightly formationed, and if its sentiments are not mellifluous, they are secure. The playing of Robert Gross, an expert in matters of contemporary music, and Peter Hewitt seems properly intense (which Humel's work requires) if not luminous.

Johann Nepomuk Hummel (1778-1837)

Octet-Partita in E flat major

☐ Wind Section of the Little Orchestra of London / Jones (conductor) / CMS/Oryx 1830

Wind and Brass Ensemble

The scoring is for two each of oboes, clarinets, bassoons, and horns, plus a contrabassoon substituting for the original serpent. Of course, that means nine instruments are playing an "octet." However, only eight voices are involved, since the double bassoon merely doubles the second bassoon to give more bass depth.

Lightly conceived outdoorish music, even in its moderately paced inner movement. Hummel's work is handsomely produced by CMS/Oryx.

Concerto in F major for Bassoon and Orchestra

☐ Württemberg Chamber Orchestra, Heilbronn / Zuckerman (bassoon) / Faerber (conductor) / Turnabout 34348

Solo Instrument and Orchestra

Bassoon

Here's a bassoon Concerto as good as Mozart's, and, with the lack of literature for the instrument with orchestra, both listeners and bassoonists should take immediate notice.

Fine music and fine initiative for the bassoon, with arpeggios, use of the top and bottom register, trills, and fiddlistic passage work. And fine cadenzas in the first two movements, though one wagers they are not by Mr. Hummel. Query: why is cadenza information most often omitted from liner copy?

The playing of George Zuckerman is an established success. He is a master of the instrument. Turnabout's sound is especially good in achieving an ideal balance between the solo voice and the orchestra.

Concerto in G major for Mandolin and Orchestra

☐ Vienna Pro Musica Orchestra / Bauer-Slais (mandolin) / Hladky (conductor) / Turnabout 34003

Mandolin

No unusual features, with a fast first movement, a set of variations, and a rondo. In the last, a pair of smidgen solo spots covers the cadenza factor. But no pyrotechnical splurge in either case. Hummel's Concerto has total formal respectability and is less striking than his Sonata in C major for the same string instrument and the piano (see under *Chamber Music* [p. 884]).

An interesting point: the conductor is himself a mandolinist and in that role is represented in the recorded-music catalogue (see under *Schlick* [Divertimento in D major for Two Mandolins and Continuo]).

The Concerto in G major disc is also available in a ten-side anthology covering lute, guitar, and mandolin compositions on Turnabout 34195/9.

Hummel composed a piano version of the Concerto in G major—see under *piano* (Concertino in G major for Piano and Orchestra, Op. 73).

Oboe

Adagio-Theme and Variations in F minor/major for Oboe and Orchestra

☐ English Chamber Orchestra / Holliger (oboe) / Leppard (conductor) / Philips 839756

The interest here is contained in the strong preludial portion; the variations are simplistic. However, throughout one can thoroughly enjoy marvelous and supple oboe playing by this technically and musically superior soloist.

Piano

Concertino in G major for Piano and Orchestra, Op. 73

☐ Berlin Symphony Orchestra / Galling (piano) / Bünte (conductor) / Turnabout 34348

Here termed a Concertino, this is Hummel's piano version of his Concerto in G major for Mandolin and Orchestra (see under *mandolin*).

Interestingly, the pace is much better chosen in this case. There is more vitality in completing the Concertino in 17:47, whereas Hladky conducting the solo-mandolin edition takes 20:06. Galling's touch is nicely pointed, and if one must choose between the two settings, the vote goes to the keyboard performer.

Concerto in A minor for Piano and Orchestra, Op. 85

☐ Stuttgart Philharmonic Orchestra / Galling (piano) / Paulmüller (conductor) / Turnabout 34028

Finely structured and with equally fine thematic offerings. The slow movement leans into Chopinesque territory, described with warm liquidity in Martin Galling's playing. Otherwise good formal expositions and all relative values firmly fixed. Paulmüller gives splendid support.

Concerto in B minor for Piano and Orchestra, Op. 89

☐ Innsbruck Symphony Orchestra / Galling (piano) / Wagner (conductor) / Turnabout 34073

Beethoven-like environment for the long opening movement, with a Chopinesque quality to the slow movement, which precedes an entrancing rondo finale.

Martin Galling communicates, the orchestra a bit less so. Another minus sign is the questionable playing of the horns at the beginning of the Larghetto.

(The opus number has never been defined. The Concerto is also listed as Opus 90 and as Opus 91.)

Grand Concerto (*Les Adieux*) in E major for Piano and Orchestra, Op. 110

☐ Hamburg Symphony / Kann (piano) / Beissel (conductor) / Turnabout 34561

Wholesome classic music, especially in the cute and bouncy measures of the rhythmic finale, set in rondo design. No pretentiousness in Hummel's work. It's been said before, but it's worth retelling even though we realize what the melodic and harmonic punch lines will be.

Hans Kann plays with unforced tone and a welcome avoidance of exaggerated *rubato,* with the exception of the use made of *rubato* in the contrasting lyrical theme of the final movement.

Concerto in G major for Piano and Violin with Orchestra, Op. 17

Piano and Violin

☐ Stuttgart Philharmonic Orchestra / Galling (piano); Lautenbacher (violin) / Paulmüller (conductor) / Turnabout 34028

Democratic handling of the soloism, with alternative highlighting and very little combining of the principal instrumental characters. This does not limit enjoyment of Hummel's music organized in traditionally patterned particulars: fast-tempoed music, a set of variations, and a Rondo.

Well-organized playing. The orchestra is somewhat subdued during its accompanimental chores.

Concerto in E flat major for Trumpet and Orchestra

Trumpet

☐ Lamoureux Orchestra, Paris / André (trumpet) / Mari (conductor) / RCA CRL2–7002

Creamy tone in the poetic slow movement applied to musical sensitivity. There is impeccable technical range as André ranges through the fairly elaborate opening movement and the racy *Rondo alla Polacca.* Jean-Baptiste Mari controls the orchestra but does not deter required aliveness to back up the super performance of the soloist.

Etudes, Op. 125

Instrumental

No. 1 in C major / No. 2 in C minor / No. 3 in G major / No. 4 in G minor / No. 5 in D major / No. 6 in D minor / No. 7 in A major / No. 8 in A minor / No. 9 in E major / No. 10 in E minor / No. 11 in B major / No. 12 in B minor / No. 13 in F sharp major / No. 14 in F sharp minor / No. 15 in D flat major / No. 16 in C sharp minor / No. 17 in A flat major / No. 18 in G sharp minor / No. 19 in E flat major / No. 20 in E flat minor / No. 21 in B flat major / No. 22 in B flat minor / No. 23 in F major / No. 24 in F minor

Piano

☐ Boehm (piano) / Turnabout 34562

Don't be turned off by these titles. Hummel's two-dozen pieces offer a pianist the opportunity to sharpen his technique, but they also provide, for the most part, fine little items that deserve life outside the studio. Grace and entertainment are in many of them, dramatic and colorful conceptions are represented in other instances.

Clean playing but with meaning as well. This provides of a set of stylish performances minus any dead spots.

Fantasie and Rondo, Op. 19

Sonata in F minor, Op. 20

☐ Pleshakov (piano) / Orion 75178

The Sonata has teeth and is vividly dramatic, its recitation bringing to mind Beethoven. Three movements, with the last pair attached. In the Opus 19, tempo comparison matches formal shapes, with a Larghetto and an *Allegro con spirito.*

Pleshakov provides a compelling sense of the music. Clear phrase substantiation and clean rhythmic precision.

Grand Sonata in F sharp minor, Op. 81

☐ Sagara (piano) / Turnabout 34608

One will hear Schubertian references in the first movement and plenty of Beethoven in the three parts of Hummel's "grand" opus. Yet there is to be recognized convincing proof of Hummel's reliable creativity, meaning nondidactic writing, distinctive ideas—true music making.

Akiko Sagara has the music fully in hand, using extremely well-judged tempi, certifying the clarity of the polyphony (the fugal section in the finale), and being uniformly fluent.

La Galante (Rondeau) for Piano, Op. 120

☐ Galling (piano) / Turnabout 34348

Simple expressivity marked by a lilting main tune. Galling is not prisoner to the bar lines, using an expert *rubato* that flavors the work without overusing the ingredient.

Chamber Music

Sonata in C major for Mandolin and Piano

☐ Scivittaro (mandolin); Veyron-Lacroix (piano) / Nonesuch 71227

An inspired collaboration. Maria Scivittaro plays with suavity and impeccable control. Robert Veyron-Lacroix is simply superb in his phrasing, delivery of figurations, and marvelous rhythmic control.

Hummel's work will surprise. It is no run-of-the-mill, bland opus. It contains formal clarity and variety. It also shows full knowledge of mandolin technique, with *tremolando* chords and with repetitive sounds coloring the material.

For Hummel's Concerto in G major for Mandolin and Orchestra, see under *Solo Instrument and Orchestra: mandolin.*

Sonata in D major for Flute and Piano, Op. 50

☐ Robison (flute); Sanders (piano) / Vanguard 71207

Music scrupulously devoted to material that fits the wind instrument like a glove, without negating equality to the keyboard instrument. And music beautifully structured in its three movements.

Thanks to these performers for choosing to record Hummel's substantial Sonata. They play it with exquisite ensemble, beautiful tone, and significant meaning. A rich delight!

Adagio, Variations, and Rondo on Schöne Minka for Flute, Cello, and Piano, Op. 78

☐ New York Camerata / Turnabout 34575

The seriousness and length of the slow-tempoed beginning contrasts strongly with the half-dozen variants on the Russian tune, which are pleasantly relaxed and unforced and clearly show their parenthood.

The New York Camerata (Paula Hatcher, flute; Charles Forbes, cello; and Glenn Jacobson, piano) are a fine group. They achieve a splendid ensemble, and their balance is perfect.

Quintet in E flat major, Op. 87

☐ Melos Ensemble / Oiseau-Lyre S–290

Hummel's setting of the piano-quintet formation subtracts the second violin and adds a double bass. Looking at it another way, the medium he uses is the standard piano quartet plus double bass. This combination gives more solidity to the texture.

There is the usual front-to-back arrangement of movements that offer Mozartian spirit with Weberian lacings. The Melos group (Hurwitz, violin; Aronowitz, viola; Weil, cello; Beers, double bass; and Crowson, piano) considers the music dynamically. Such benefits bring a scherzo impetus to the Menuetto.

Grand Military Septet in C major for Flute, Clarinet, Trumpet, Violin, Cello, Double Bass, and Piano, Op. 114

☐ Collegium con Basso / Turnabout 34493

The use of the trumpet indeed gives the Hummel work its name, there being no militaristic tone to the opus. The brass instrument is used sparingly, though it is the featured color in the closing cadence of the Menuetto, an incorrect designation for a speedy scherzo.

The Collegium outfit provides an authentic ring to its performance. Nice blend to the ensemble.

Septet in D minor, Op. 74

☐ Melos Ensemble / Oiseau-Lyre S-290

Hummel's "grand" Septet calls for flute, oboe, horn, viola, cello, double bass, and piano. Nice compact sound combinations without featuring specific timbres. Impressively shaped and balanced in this presentation.

Engelbert Humperdinck *(1854-1921)*

Hansel and Gretel

Opera and Dramatic Music

☐ Bavarian Radio Orchestra and Tölzer Boys Choir / Donath, Moffo, Auger, and Popp (sopranos); Ludwig (mezzo-soprano); Fischer-Dieskau (baritone) / Eichhorn (conductor) / RCA ARL2-0637

What is specially productive in this production is the assured sense of dramatic timing on the part of every member of the cast. And, not a single miscalculation in the actual singing. Anna Moffo is beautiful to listen to as Hansel, and Christa Ludwig is realistic as the Witch. Her dynamic range is splendidly registered, and there is flair and gusto in her portrayal.

Good sonorities, lively qualities, and expert direction make this a first-class release.

Franz Hünten *(1793-1878)*

Etude in C major, Op. 81, No. 1

Instrumental

Galop in A major (*Un Moment de recreation*)

Piano

Grand Valse brillante (*Les Bords du Rhin*), Op. 120

Variations on an Aria from Donizetti's *L'Elisir d'amore*

Variations on the Duo from Donizetti's *Belisario*, Op. 148

Variations on the March from Bellini's *Norma*, Op. 94

☐ Cooper (piano) / Genesis 1006

Topflight light concoctions, every one. Clarity right on the button. Not Carnegie Hall music, but damned pleasurable in its nineteenth-century conventionality. So the Etude flies with the speed of wind and reaches its destination in forty-two seconds; the Waltz clearly retains its triple-beat swing; the variations embellish and don't get lost in dense developmental depositions, and the Galop is cute and swingy.

The performances are clean, clear, and always musical. Cooper realizes the fun in this type of music, but he does not ham it up, nor does he approach it as musical camp. Give him extra credit for such honesty.

Karel Husa   (1921-   )

Orchestra

Mosaiques for Orchestra (1961)

☐ Stockholm Radio Symphony Orchestra / Husa (conductor) / Composers Recordings S-221

A *thematisches verzeichnis* of orchestral impressions. Husa has a passion for sonorous passions that inhale and exhale very quickly. They appear, mingle, contrast, and occasionally break into a fine flame. These are clear-cut contemporary colorations, applied with an unprejudiced approach to matters of dissonance.

Music for Prague 1968

☐ Louisville Orchestra / Mester (conductor) / Louisville S-722

This work was originally for wind ensemble. Husa prepared a second version for orchestra which has achieved a huge performance record. Music for Prague is no neo-Dvořákian exercise, but a potent essay that mainly pictures the dark anguish that has been principal to the history of the city's existence.

Dark, frenetic, and fractured scoring are frontal in the piece; the concept is totally muralistic in its four movements. The third part (Interlude) is for percussion alone. Important are the collective improvisations that occur in the terminal movements, producing a thrust that bypasses effect for symphonic structural meaning.

Husa's piece has a convulsive energy no matter its varied tempi. Mester's control of this factor and his shaping of the score are quite significant.

Two Sonnets from Michelangelo

☐ Louisville Orchestra / Mester (conductor) / Louisville S-725

A pair of orchestral songs that substitute for words by the use of orchestrational devices. The dramatic outlines of the sonnets are relayed quite vividly. In *La notte*, for example, quarter tones, glides, and saxophone and marimba timbres equate peripheral Pendereckian precepts and produce the mysterious atmosphere of the sonnet.

A good performance. (The liner-note copy includes the texts of the sonnets.)

Band

Al fresco

☐ Western Illinois University Wind Ensemble / Husa (conductor) / Mark MC-5405

No programmatic content, the title indicating the composer's "admiration for the arts of painting, in this case the mural painting on wet plaster." Husa mentions, in this connection, the importance of "pictures dealing with primitive life, wars and pageantry." The music is a forceful parallel of the last statement, and with a scoring that is minus strings, its textural definition has a significative hardness that is quite telling.

Concerto for Alto Saxophone (1967)

Instrumental

Saxophone

☐ Robert Black (alto saxophone); Patricia Black (piano) / Brewster 1216

Husa's work was written for alto saxophone and band. The piano reduction is the composer's, who approves the setting for actual performance.

There are three movements—a Prologue, *Ostinato,* and Epilogue, forming a triptych of reflective content in the outer parts with motility within. Freely chromatic, Husa's work tends to circle the periphery of tonality. It is extremely coloristic and treats the saxophone in a virtuoso manner.

Brewster has issued the work in two editions, the other being by Frederick Hemke with the pianist Milton Granger. Black's performance is preferable—more direct and more decisive.

Sonata for Violin and Piano (1973)

Chamber Music

☐ Oliveira (violin); Oei (piano) / Grenadilla GS-1032

Grim music and paramount tensility in Husa's Sonata. Strong medicine, indeed, and one of the bitterest pieces of music for violin and piano in the literature. The sound qualities of the instruments are used for continual attack even in the middle (slow) movement, with glisses, microtones, frictions, clusters, and percussive plucked sounds by both the violin and the piano. No one should expect affable and amiable tinkles from music "influenced . . . by . . . wars, senseless destruction of nature" and the "killing of animals," as Husa explains.

Generally, contemporary music is played competently, but rarely with the inner depth identified with this performance. Elmar Oliveira won the coveted gold medal in the 1978 Tchaikovsky Competition in Moscow, and one doesn't expect other than the standard repertoire from competition winners. That he chose to record Husa's piece shows an artistic integrity that is not common among our top virtuosi. His partner, David Oei, is also a prize winner at a lower level. However, his terse and vital playing is just as technically brilliant and emotionally powerful as Oliveira's.

Evocations de Slovaquie for Clarinet, Viola, and Cello (1951)

☐ Sobol (clarinet); Schulman (viola); Eddy (cello) / Grenadilla GS-1008

The externals of Slovakian folk material rekindled by stylistic preparation in the warmth (and heat) of Husa's creative oven. According to the composer, the instruments chosen recall "some of the small dance ensembles used by the musicians of Slovakia." The product is a real fruit from the native vine.

Lawrence Sobol, Louise Schulman, and Timothy Eddy play in a very enjoyable and enlightening manner; the interpretative climate is ideal.

Two Preludes for Flute, Clarinet, and Bassoon (1966)

☐ Members of the Dorian Quintet / Vox SVBX-5307

In the now wholly familiar "traditional" contemporary style. No outlandish fancies for this composer. The Dorian ensemble describes the music in a firm and clear way.

Quartet

No. 2 (1959) / No. 3 (1968)

☐ Fine Arts Quartet / Everest 3290

Bartókian technique remains a staple contemporary argument. In his second Quartet Husa is heart and soul a Bartókian as much as Webern was a devout follower of Schoenberg and Piston believed in the neoclassic Stravinsky. No folk material, however, in this rhythmically meshed, percussively driven composition. It is of composite order, of essentially concentrated primitive style but organic as a whole.

The Bartók reference is much less in the later Quartet. Instrumental individuality invigorates the work, with featured spots given to the viola in part 1, to the cello in movement 2, and to both violins in part 3. Movement 4, Husa indicates, "is an epilogue, when all the instruments come together." To which must be added that motility and color effects are incessant, forming the cartography of the work as a whole.

Both quartets demand virtuosi, a requirement met in the full by the Fine Arts foursome. The sense of their full involvement with the music prevails in every measure.

Scott Huston (1916-   )

Brass Ensemble

Sounds at Night for Thirteen Brass Instruments (1971)

☐ Indianapolis Brass Ensemble / Akins (conductor) / Serenus 12066

The personality here is that of a neo-impressionist sketching with the usual pictorialism. This is conveyed by part 1, *Mutation–Dusk Toward Midnight*, balanced by part 2, *Transformation–Dark of Night Until Dawn*.

Satisfactory presentation by the Indianapolis group, consisting of four trumpets (two in C and two in B flat), four horns, three trombones, baritone, and tuba. The harmonic clusterization that colors the score is particularly effective.

Chamber Music

Lifestyles for Clarinet, Cello, and Piano (1972)

☐ Plasko (clarinet); Miller (cello); Loewy (piano) / Serenus 12064

Instrumental simmerings and shifting tempi and meters are the particulars for Huston's four-movement opus. The first pair is termed *Introspective, Reflective: Calm and Cool*, the second pair is again of combined title: *Nervous, Frustrated: Energetic, Unpredictable*. The sonorities, colors, and textures are stylistic splinters from the Donaueschingen and Darmstadt workbenches. Huston puts them together fairly well, though his glue has little thematic substance.

Music in this style is not the most comfortable to play. The musicians involved seem fully at ease.

Suite for Our Times for Brass Sextet (1973)

☐ Indianapolis Brass Sextet / Serenus 12066

The sextet scoring covers two trumpets, a horn, two tenor trombones, and one bass trombone. General programmatics cover the three parts—*Brilliance of Bells, Thoughtful Solitude*, and *Tempered Animation*. Tempo situations follow the sense of these titles, as does the broadly tonal syntax.

I

Giuseppe Maria Iacchini   (ca. 1665-1727)

***Tratenimento per camera* in D major**   *Orchestra*

☐ Academy of St. Martin-in-the-Fields / Smithers (trumpet); Preston (harpsichord) / Marriner (conductor) / Philips 6500110

This "chamber entertainment" matches the potency and enthusiastic coverage of Purcell. It is braced by a soloistic trumpet voice riding with the strings and backed by a continuo, well realized in this instance.

Anthony Iannaccone   (1943-   )

Partita for Piano (1967)   *Instrumental*

☐ Gurt (piano) / Coronet LPS-3038   *Piano*

Classical designs (Prelude, Sarabande, and Gigue) and a *Burlesca* using neoclassic material, knit with pantonal colors. Music not only for the intellectual crowd. Brilliantly played by Joseph Gurt.

***Bicinia* for Flute and Alto Saxophone (1974)**   *Chamber Music*

☐ Hill (flute); Plank (alto saxophone) / Coronet LPS-3038

In its segmentation, controlled by wire-thin connections, *Bicinia* (the sixteenth-century term for a vocal composition in two parts) is like a mobile with slightly nervous linear intensity. Part 1 is slow, the second movement is twice as fast.

The playing is exceptional.

Rituals for Violin and Piano (1973)

☐ Pignotti (violin); Mehta (piano) / Coronet LPS-3038

Iannaccone's chamber-music rite is both direct—rhapsodic and virtuosic—and symbolistic, incorporating a pair of chants from the ritual of the Roman Mass—*Victimae paschali* and the *Dies Irae*. The latter are crunched into the texture with the related twelve-note theme of the piece. Though the spontaneous effect of the work sounds like an improvisation, the expressive vitality and flux are strictly the consequence of Iannaccone's creative discipline.

The players realize the imagery of the piece most creditably. While Mehta is not *the* Mehta of international renown, he brings honor to the name.

Sonatina for Trumpet and Tuba (1975)

☐ Eggers (trumpet); Smith (tuba) / Coronet LPS-3038

The combination itself is sufficiently unusual to draw interest. But there is more. The music is a bit snide, has some sophisticated humor, and is aided by chatty, caustic counterpoint.

Hades for Tuba Quartet

Three Mythical Sketches for Tuba Quartet

☐ University of Michigan Tuba Ensemble / Mayer (conductor) / Golden Crest CRS-4145

The medium is more compelling than the material. Nonetheless, there is no "Tubby the Tuba" mischievous attitude. Iannaconne's idea of the abode of the dead is hellishly serious in its serialized pitch activity. The same demeanor applies to the three P's (*Pluto, Persephone,* and *Poseidon*) covered in the Mythical Sketches. Identifications and contrast are made specific: *Persephone* features a solo voice, and *Poseidon* is programmed by fugal writing. Contrapuntalism for four tubas might sound absurd, but both in the writing and playing it cannot be dismissed as absurd.

Jacques Ibert (1890-1962)

Orchestra

Bacchanale (1958)

☐ Louisville Orchestra / Mester (conductor) / Louisville S-702

Ibert's usual rhythmic zip, basically with syncopated forwardness, the music gift-wrapped with attention-grabbing colors. The French Morton Gould. It satisfies as does the Louisville's expert rendition.

Ballade de la Geôle de Reading (1922)

☐ Louisville Orchestra / Mester (conductor) / Louisville LS-736

Ibert sets forth the general moods of Oscar Wilde's famous poem in three connected sections, styled with dark-veined impressionism. Mester colors the score of "The Ballad of Reading Gaol" with avid attention to all its details.

Divertissement (1930)

☐ Paris Conservatoire Orchestra / Martinon (conductor) / London STS-15093

Doubtless the most typical work in Ibert's output. An orchestration of caustic wit, its zip governed by tonal and harmonic bite and full of the musical wisecrack. Watch for the spoofing of Mendelssohn's Wedding March amidst some jazz and a mock procession; catch the thumb-to-the-nose Viennese waltz, listen to the pianist simply bang the instrument, and laugh with the graphic vulgarisms (including a police whistle) that mark this parody.

Ibert's suite is an assortment of succulent Parisian bonbons. Originally written as music for a farce (*Le Chapeau de paille d'Italie*), it fulfills this titillative objective in the concert hall.

At one time it was available in performances conducted by Désormière, Fiedler, Ormandy, Slatkin, Swoboda, and Surinach. All are now gone, though there are no regrets for the last three. Martinon displays a cleanness of delivery and a complete recognition of Ibert's extrovert style. One fault is that the opening movement is not as chiseled in its contours as it should be.

Escales (1922)

☐ Boston Symphony Orchestra / Munch (conductor) / RCA VICS–1323

Ibert's best-seller. The "ports of call" are *Palermo, Tunis-Nefta,* and *Valencia.* Munch is the best tour guide at the present time.

A Louisville Concerto (1954)

☐ Louisville Orchestra / Whitney (conductor) / Louisville 545–5 (monaural)

An opus mainly devoted to activity of line. Aside from a pastoral-like section, the Louisville piece is mostly what is called "busy" music.

Ouverture de fête

Tropismes pour des amours imaginaires (1957)

☐ Orchestre National de l'O.R.T.F. / Martinon (conductor) / Angel S–37194

Ibert has been damned as a serious composer of light music and, flipping the coin, as too light in his serious music. Nonsense, confusion will arise and matters will never be sorted out until it is realized that even in meaningful musical matters there is a place for a sense of humor and that important connotations can be realized in the decor of bright, yes, even slick, orchestration.

The *Tropismes* (conceived as a ballet but not so limited) are picaresque and episodic and contain a strong sense of rhapsodic detachment and attachment. The "Festival Overture" is placidly pleasant and light-hearted, but, again, not "light" music as the term is generally understood and has been greatly misunderstood in the case of Jacques Ibert.

Martinon directs the music with knowing consideration of its nimble style. Where the scores require sparkle and fizz, it is supplied fully.

Paris 32 (1932)

☐ Leningrad Philharmonic Chamber Orchestra / Rozhdestvensky (conductor) / Westminster Gold WGS–8310

A suite drawn from incidental music Ibert wrote for a Jules Romains play, *Donogoo.* Concise, flexible music that can be classified as extremely high-class pops material.

Concerto for Flute and Orchestra

☐ English Chamber Orchestra / Di Tullio (flute) / Howarth (conductor) / Crystal S–503

Though Ibert's chromatically incised diatonic music avoids empiricism as well as sensationalism, it just as emphatically seeks the expression of pleasure and comes gift-wrapped in catchy melodies and marvelous colors. The Flute Concerto is what can be called healthy, well-dressed neoclassic music. There isn't a dull measure in the entire twenty-minute span of the work.

The pleasure to be obtained from Ibert's Concerto is fully exhibited in the single recording available. Louise Di Tullio plays the solo part with Mozartian clarity. By performing it straight, she permits all the elasticity and wit of the music to emerge.

Solo Instrument and Orchestra

Flute

891

Saxophone ### Concertino da camera (1935)

☐ Abato (saxophone) / Shulman (conductor) / Nonesuch 71030E (monaural)

Still considered the most important solo work for the alto saxophone. The *Concertino* summarizes fascinating triple aesthetic qualities of high spirits, fun in proper style, and polyphonic expertise. It also exhibits the essentials of concerto format, splitting two movements into three parts and giving additional solo privileges (magnificently exploited by Vincent Abato) by reducing the accompaniment to six instruments plus strings (the eleven-instrument group is not given name credit). The syncopations and melodic curves are typical of Jacques Ibert.

Chamber Music ### Entr'acte for Flute and Harp (1935)

☐ Rampal (flute); Laskine (harp) / Musical Heritage Society MHS-1345

The special coloring of certain instruments would draw a composer of picturesque intent to them. Ibert's short piece creates a definite mood of romantic poesy. It courses its way by busy figurations, its tunes creating the effect of an idealized dance.

A version for flute and guitar has been recorded on Angel S-36050 by Ruderman and Almeida, but cannot be compared with the brilliant work of Rampal and Laskine. Further, for what Ibert has written, the harp is a better timbre partner with the wind instrument, despite the Spanish cast of the piece.

Trio for Violin, Cello, and Harp (1944)

☐ Sanchez (violin); Degenne (cello); Jamet (harp) / Musical Heritage Society MHS-883

In this trio Ibert does not use long-strung classical forms, since his themes will not permit undue development. Excellent and impressive music results because it is placed in simple frames that match its character.

Measures containing extra beats inserted at strategic points in the thematic line give additional kick to the first movement. Compared with the outer movements, the middle one is rather serious. A breezy type of scherzo is called on for the finale. Ibert's magnificent sense of color is exhibited in this section (which is the best-played portion of the work, incidentally). His symphonic works display orchestrational perception just as acutely.

Trois Pièces brèves (1930)

☐ New York Woodwind Quintet / Everest 3092

With the exception of Hindemith's *Kleine Kammermusik,* Op. 24, No. 2, this is the most favored contemporary work in the wind-quintet category. Ibert's tuneful themes do not require enlargement by argument. These pieces, for a delightful and frolicking pocket-sized orchestra, are examples of true hedonistic music; they combine paprika with soda pop—a pleasure to the ear, a delight to play.

The New York outfit first recorded the work for the Counterpoint label, No. 505, in a monaural version. (It is still available.) With the exception of the flute (Samuel Baron), the New York group's membership had entirely changed by the time the stereo recording was made for Everest. It is not only stereo that leads to the choice indicated above, but better stylistic insight, with more spirit and sparkle in the playing.

Toshi Ichyanagi (1933-   )

Extended Voices for Voices with Moog Synthesizer and Buchla Associates Electronic Modular System (1967)

☐ Brandeis University Chamber Chorus / Lucier (conductor) / Odyssey 32160156

Static conditions are primary, with sustainment of sounds and slow glides in both directions as the means. (Ranges are expanded by the use of slide whistles.) The electronic apparatus colors the timbres and expands the dynamics. As a further layer on these textural components, a prerecorded tape is utilized, adding its own purely electronic sounds to the others. Ichyanagi's obsession not to cut away into contrast can be considered the realization (and, indeed, a very successful one) of a musical deep freeze.

Choral

Chorus with Accompaniment

Alexander Ilyinsky (1859-1920)

Berceuse from *Noure and Anitra*

☐ Tarnowsky (piano) / Genesis 1004

A charming tune—a whistlable one. The uninformative Genesis notes require facts being stated. This piece was originally an orchestral work (the seventh of eight movements). The transcription, one assumes, is by the composer. If it isn't, it still carries as much validity.

Instrumental

Piano

Andrew Imbrie (1921-   )

Symphony No. 3 (1970)

☐ London Symphony Orchestra / Farberman (conductor) / Composers Recordings S-308

Imbrie stays away from any fashionable "isms" in this well-crafted three-movement piece. The style is panchromatic, the scoring, save for some special attention given the clarinet in the second movement, is well balanced but minus any special technical effects. The syntax reminds one of the music of Roger Sessions.

Orchestra

Concerto for Violin and Orchestra (1958)

☐ Columbia Symphony Orchestra / Glenn (violin) / Rozsnyai (conductor) / Columbia Special Products CMS-6597

The writing is mainly linear, the tonal sphere is fluctuatory; however, there are polarity points for regulating—another prime necessity in the freeness of the diatonic-semichromatic which is the practice of the neoclassicist. But there is more. A Berg-like dark mood embraces the piece. Now, this may mean no sounding of sweet messages, but it does promise precise, dramatic, and deeply emotive ones.

Carroll Glenn's playing is beautiful, her stylistic constancy impeccable. The entire production deserves the highest rating.

Solo Instrument and Orchestra

Violin

Chamber Music

Impromptu for Violin and Piano (1960)

☐ Gross (violin); Grayson (piano) / Orion 73107

A sizable work in three parts, which Imbrie describes as "essentially similar to movements of a brief sonata." Though it does not lack some direct dynamism, tension is the principal ingredient in Imbrie's close-to-fifteen-minute work. This tension is more the result of linear activity than vertical enunciation.

Fine fluency by both musicians, displaying especially a sensitive warmth in the inner section of the piece.

Sonata for Cello and Piano (1966)

☐ Sayre (cello); Bogas (piano) / Desto 7150

Classically refurbished materials will be recognized in the Sonata. Handling of the duo medium is colorfully alive, but there is no striving for auditory awe-striking. The concept is supple, sometimes austere, but totally balanced.

The tone of the piano is somewhat hard; Sayre's tone is not.

Serenade for Flute, Viola, and Piano (1952)

☐ Di Tullio (flute); Trampler (viola); Brandwynne (piano) / Desto 7150

Imbrie avoids light facets in his Serenade. Each of the three essays has a serious demeanor. This includes the middle movement, a *Siciliano,* which bypasses its traditional dance derivatives but not its duple rhythmic reliance. It contains successive cadenzas for the flute and the viola. Another mark of special distinction is the last movement. No gay flyweight affair, this. In place is an Adagio—exceptional as the concluding division of a Serenade. Its introverted tone is the antithesis of the extroverted quality of the opening movement.

Substantial performance acumen is displayed by the group that presents Imbrie's piece.

Second String Quartet (1953)

☐ California String Quartet / Contemporary 7022

The traditional link of the neoclassicist is here retained—declarative, clear form, and the use of pitch centers as the basis for free diatonicism. However, these substantially true and proven considerations are expanded—stylistically bridged from the past into the present. Tonality is now hard-boiled, laced with dissonant counterpoint, chromaticized with a no-nonsense diction. Imbrie is not endeavoring to charm. The string voices take the ear into custody and retain attention with rich polyphonic detail. This is a rhythmically stable music—not a single metrical change is made from beginning to end within each of the three movements, though the inner designs are of virtuosic order. Again, this shows a dovetailing of classic stability with contemporary activity. All superficiality is banished. The Quartet is a web of enthusiastic detail, all finely defined in the performance.

Third String Quartet (1957)

☐ Walden String Quartet / Contemporary 7022

For the greater part, row technique applies to the first movement, with portions of the system used in the other two divisions of the work. But as Imbrie adds, he also retains. Tonality is not dispossessed. It functions in certain areas as an overlay to the influence of the row. Since tonalism is chromatically administered, Imbrie has accomplished a neat combine of classical contours with a total chromaticism which is both twelve-tone-controlled and the opposite. It makes for beautiful logic.

Dandelion Wine for Oboe, Clarinet, String Quartet, and Piano (1967)

☐ Lucarelli (oboe); Bloom (clarinet); Kooper and Rogers (violins); Maximoff (viola); Sherry (cello); Boehm (piano) / Turnabout 34520

A short, expressionistic piece. The intriguing title is the name of a novel by Ray Bradbury, concerning memories of a boyhood spent in a small town. The tale includes the bottling of dandelion wine, with each bottle dated. Imbrie indicates that these bottles "become symbols of memory, since each date recalls a particular summer day and its activities."

Nothing graphic is included in Imbrie's *Dandelion Wine*. It is the essence of the novel's basis that is utilized. The musical ideas are presented in fantasy arrangement, and then at the end certain of them are recalled "in new contexts to give, if possible, the effect of poignant reminiscences, all 'bottled' in a very brief container." The relationships of these recalls are rather free. In over-all examination, *Dandelion Wine* is an absolute piece of absolute music.

Vincent d'Indy   (1851-1931)

Symphony on a French Mountain Air for Orchestra and Piano, Op. 25

Solo Instrument and Orchestra

Piano

☐ Philadelphia Orchestra / Casadesus (piano) / Ormandy (conductor) / Odyssey Y-31274

Full-blown romanticism pervades the Gallic thematicism, and the spirit of Wagner is still to be exorcized in d'Indy's exuberant piece. But tunefulness wins over bombast, and the use of the piano as a solo voice and yet as an integrated part of the texture brings its special appeal.

The buoyancy of the performance and the Casadesus-Ormandy partnership are expressively responsive to the needs of the score. D'Indy's finale is constantly on the verge of being fustian. Podium rule and care here make certain that it is not.

Le Poème des montagnes, Op. 15

Instrumental

Piano

☐ Doyen (piano) / Musical Heritage Society MHS 1155–57

A large-scaled piece, with prologue and postlude, three major sections, each further divided so that the subsections total sixteen (there is no pause within the sections of each main movement), linked by a generative motive. Semiprogrammatic material partners absolute data. Thus in movement 1 "The Song of the Heather" is followed by *Brouillard* ("Mist"), etc., the movement ending with *Lointain* ("Far Away").

The opus has the chromatic sweetness of César Franck and is rather poetic. Rarely does the music dip into showmanship virtuosity, though a first-rate pianist is required.

Sonata in E major, Op. 63

☐ Pleshakov (piano) / Orion 7266

Luxurious constancy of sound marks this work. Likewise it is luxurious in terms of chromaticism. It is in three movements but not classically structured. A set of variations covers the opening part, and in d'Indy's usual method its theme is transferred to the concluding variation-like movement. The principal definition of the middle movement is a quintuple-metered rondo.

Pleshakov plays this Frenchman's Germanically heavy work commendably. (Orion incorrectly classifies the work in E minor.)

Chamber Music

Sonata in C for Violin and Piano, Op. 59

☐ Temianka (violin); Dominguez (piano) / Orion 73105

The music of a classicist in the Franck tradition. The Sonata illustrates d'Indy's method of constructing music from generic motives that are reshaped as the work progresses through its four parts. The most individual movement is the Scherzo, with its Trio set in septuple meter.

Trio for Clarinet, Cello, and Piano, Op. 29

☐ Montagnana Trio / Delos DEL-25431

In this Trio, patent use is made of transformational thematic technique. The unison subject of the first movement is the musical dictator of the composition. It powers the Overture, serves as the theme for the *Divertissement,* and is found in the "Elegiac Song," where it is somewhat hidden in its transference. In the finale the Franckian device is used for development, including the augmentation of its rhythmic values in various ways.

The performance is a good one.

Mikhail Ippolitov-Ivanov   (1859-1935)

Orchestra

Caucasian Sketches, Op. 10

☐ Utah Symphony Orchestra / Abravanel (conductor) / Vanguard C-10060

Once gracing the programs of the major symphonies (it was a Stokowski speciality), Ippolitov-Ivanov's four-part suite has become a museum piece. Granted it has simple tunes and four-square constructions. Still, the *In the Village* movement, with its pictorial English horn and viola antiphonies and Orientalish sensual dance section, and the *Procession of the Sardar,* with its catchy principal tune, provide vivid impressions—unless snobbery persists.

Bernstein does the best of all, but only does the two movements mentioned above (on Columbia MS-7014 and on M-31844). Abravanel gives you the entire work, and though he doesn't pull out all the stops (and one wishes he had), it is a clear portrayal, solidly characterized, with fine playing on the part of the solo voices in the second movement and excellent pacing in the finale.

Stay away from the Turnabout edition (34218). The orchestra cannot compare with the Utah group, its solo voices lack character, and the sound is an abomination. The Melodiya/Angel version (S-40119) is better, but it lacks vitality and forcefulness.

John Ireland (*1879-1962*)

Epic March (1942) *Orchestra*

☐ London Philharmonic Orchestra / Boult (conductor) / Musical Heritage Society MHS-1498

There's nothing that can equal the Englishry of a march composed by an English composer. Don't expect the pep, blaze, and gait of a Sousa march. Instead, there is a ceremonial flavor to the initial part and a nobility in the contrasting portion. Two different worlds are of course represented by the composers, but more pertinent is the fact that two subtly opposite stylistic approaches are used. Both are special and definitive and equally good. To compare one type with the other is odious.

Ireland's is British to the core and a splendid entry in English march literature. Naturally, it's played just the way it should be.

A London Overture (1936)

☐ London Symphony Orchestra / Barbirolli (conductor) / Angel S-36415

Sharp contrasts between introspectiveness and perkiness. The theme of perkiness was suggested by a London bus conductor's cry of "'Dilly: Piccadilly."

Barbirolli has always been very sympathetic to Ireland's neo-romantic music. With uncanny perception he has realized what Ireland intended in his overture—some hints of musical journalism (the tread of a policeman's footsteps, an outlined elegy for a friend, etc.) but with the maintenance of flow so that the design is not sectionalized. It is a superb production.

Overture: *Satyricon* (1946)

Prelude: *The Forgotten Rite* (1913)

☐ London Philharmonic Orchestra / Boult (conductor) / Musical Heritage Society MHS-1317

Ireland's *Rite* was composed the same year (1913) that Stravinsky's *Rite of Spring* was produced in Paris. The coincidence means nothing save that many years later Ireland stated he heard in Stravinsky's work musical ideas that called up from the subconscious "things long hidden and belonging to a remote and forgotten past." This description applies just as aptly to Ireland's work. But only in terms of objective: the expression of mysticism and the spirit of pagan ritual. The romantic and partially impressionistic style of Ireland's music is so violently different from Stravinsky's that no comparison is possible.

The *Satyricon* Overture (the score also has the parenthetical "after Petronius" indicated) is properly light-hearted, containing a warm second subject that features the clarinet.

Both performances are adequate; a little more pep in the Overture would not be amiss.

Symphonic Prelude: *Tritons*

☐ London Philharmonic Orchestra / Boult (conductor) / Musical Heritage Society MHS-1481

Early Ireland, which he used some forty years later as the basis for a military-band work, *A Maritime Overture,* composed in 1944. No personal fancies for this hardly known piece (it isn't even listed in *Grove's Dictionary of Music and Musicians).* Its large ternary design plus coda is pat, but not annoyingly so.

Symphonic Rhapsody: *Mai-Dun* (1921)

☐ London Philharmonic Orchestra / Boult (conductor) / Musical Heritage Society MHS-1317

A tone poem epitomizing the strenuous life and struggles of a primitive community. The aggressiveness depicted in most of the work is not usually met in this composer's output.

String Orchestra

Concertino Pastorale (1939)

Elegy and Minuet from *A Downland Suite*

The Holy Boy (a Carol of the Nativity)

☐ London Philharmonic Orchestra / Boult (conductor) / Musical Heritage Society MHS-1498

The *Eclogue* of the Concertino has the expected rustic response; the final Toccata has neo-romantic carpeting, fringed by ostinato, the inlaid designs sharply contoured. In between is a *Threnody,* emotively tender but also rich in its harmonic syntax.

It is difficult to realize that originally the Elegy and Minuet were for brass band (movements 2 and 3 of the four-part *A Downland Suite,* written in 1932), so gentle are their contents. This is a second transcription; the first one was for piano. (On the recording the Minuet precedes the Elegy.)

The Holy Boy also represents a second arrangement. It was originally the third of a set of four Preludes for piano. Ireland then transcribed it for organ and much later made the setting for strings.

Solo Instrument and Orchestra

Piano

Concerto in E flat major for Piano and Orchestra (1930)

☐ London Philharmonic Orchestra / Parkin (piano) / Boult (conductor) / Musical Heritage Society MHS-1429

Two movements, the second of large trisectional arrangement. Cyclic transfer binds the work as a whole, one of unabashed lyrical outlook save for *martellato* glitter in the latter portion of the piece. Neat colorations there, with percussion punctuations and muted trumpet parentheses. Modal sections that contrast with this are poignant and present their own special color.

Where poetry is demanded, Eric Parkin portrays it. Always considered one of John Ireland's most authoritative interpreters, Parkin proves it with his playing. Expressive support from Boult.

Legend for Piano and Orchestra (1933)

☐ London Philharmonic Orchestra / Parkin (piano) / Boult (conductor) / Musical Heritage Society MHS-1317

Dialogue procedures mark this work, and so do dusky colors. There is an unstated tale behind the notes. The Legend was written during time spent in a lonely part of the Sussex Downs, where there are few inhabitants. Ireland has written of some mysterious moments during his stay and visits to a church that had a "squint" through which lepers had watched the proceedings without contaminating the congregation, plus examination of relics from Neolithic flint-mines. The response can be felt in this work, which Ireland neither confirmed nor denied.

The comprehensibility of the performance leaves no doubts. There are no faults in execution, and Boult commands the score so that the single driven climax registers magnificently. Fine playing by the soloist and special kudos to the English hornist in the L.P.O.

Aubade (1930)

Ballade (1929)

☐ Rowlands (piano) / Musical Heritage Society MHS–7001 (monaural)

Clear-cut romantic music, but not smudged by mushy harmony. *Aubade* is the second of Two Pieces. *See below* for the first of the pair, *February's Child.*

Equinox (1922)

☐ Rowlands (piano) / Musical Heritage Society MHS–7002 (monaural)

Rhythmic vitality applied to constant figuration defines Ireland's equinoctial picture. Rowlands plays effectively, equally weighting the continuous five-note rotational patterns.

February's Child (1929)

For Remembrance (1921)

☐ Rowlands (piano) / Musical Heritage Society MHS–7001 (monaural)

Both are the first parts of two different sets of Two Pieces. *Aubade* (*see above*) partners *February's Child. For Remembrance* is sharply contrasted by *Amberley Wild Brooks* (unavailable presently in recorded form).

Greenways Suite (1937)

London Pieces (1920)

On a Birthday Morning (1922)

☐ Rowlands (piano) / Musical Heritage Society MHS–7002 (monaural)

Responses to a pair of picturesque places (*Chelsea Reach* and *Soho Forenoons*) and a little boy whistling a tune (*Ragamuffin*) are depicted in Ireland's London Pieces. No attempt is made to get involved with sharp programmatic contracts; analogies carry out the titular themes, with Sohoesque sophisticated harmonies for the *Forenoons,* a rollicking rhythmical tune to move the *Ragamuffin* along his way, and soft chordal blends to picture *Chelsea Reach.*

The responses in the suite are to poems by Housman (*The Cherry Tree*), Shakespeare (*Cypress*), and Thomas Nashe (*The Palm and May*). Rowlands clearly outlines the motival transfer that binds this set.

Holiday vivacity is heard in *On a Birthday Morning,* but the performance is just a bit slower than preferred. Otherwise Rowlands plays with full understanding, displaying clean tonal balances and clean rhythmic outlines.

Sarnia (1941)

☐ Rowlands (piano) / Musical Heritage Society MHS–7001 (monaural)

Sarnia is parenthetically titled *An Island Sequence,* and consists of *Le Catioroc, In a May Morning,* and *Song of the Springtides.*

Purely lyrical style is used, but the last of the set has a bouyant virtuosity, nicely projected by the soloist.

Soliloquy (1922)

Sonatina (1927)

☐ Rowlands (piano) / Musical Heritage Society MHS–7002 (monaural)

Ireland packs variety into his Sonatina. A feeling of irony pervades the first movement, the finale is thoroughly extrovert music. In between is a *Quasi lento* in which whole-tonish atmosphere brings reminders of the type of background music that was used for movies like *The Phantom of the Opera.* Ralph Hill says this movement "has something of the queer atmosphere of a nightmare." The liner-note writer (only the initials R.M.W. are given) terms it "alarmingly eerie." However Rowlands considers it, he colors it beautifully.

The short *Soliloquy* is one of Ireland's minor pieces. It was suggested to the composer by one of Masefield's shorter poems.

Chamber Music

Fantasy-Sonata for Clarinet and Piano (1943)

☐ de Peyer (clarinet); Parkin (piano) / Musical Heritage Society MHS–1610

Ireland's somewhat rhapsodic work (bearing a very natural relationship to the clarinet, an instrument that possesses in its rather full gamut and varying color registers such inherencies) sets forth the variety of three movements, but, in addition, relates the primary material. For example, the second theme of the major first part serves as a cell from which grows the second section's theme, and in the last portion the opening subject is both augmented and changed ornamentally. As a result, the work is a unit, even with its punctuated fantasy. Freedom is conveyed by changes of mood, but formal amalgamation is not left in the lurch.

Sonata for Cello and Piano (1923)

☐ Navarra (cello); Parkin (piano) / Musical Heritage Society MHS–1610

Ireland's sonata is of the rugged-music type. Logical shaping of material is displayed in the three movements, with the details presented without lushness or mere pursuit of luxuriant sounds. The scoring is clear, so that the cello does not fight nubby piano textures and overdetailed material.

The playing is marked with fine style; the interpretation is ideal.

Sextet for Clarinet, Horn, and String Quartet

☐ Melos Ensemble / Musical Heritage Society MHS–1610

Ireland wrote his Sextet at the age of nineteen. Stanford, his teacher, did not approve of the work, but nevertheless Ireland retained the score. He first heard it when he was eighty years of age.

At this remove one realizes that Stanford erred and that Ireland was wise in not destroying the piece. Yes, it is patently a Brahms imitation, but there's not a measure that would cause composer embarrassment in the four movements of the work. There is fine unity, and all the shapes have firm and healthy musical flesh covering them.

One can always trust performances of truth, resource, and coloristic relish from the Melos Ensemble. That trust is fulfilled in this case.

Greater Love Hath No Man (1912)

Choral

Chorus with
Accompaniment

☐ Choir of St. John's College, Cambridge / Runnett (organ) / Guest (conductor) / Argo ZRG-5340

A blend and balance of church-music steadfastness with lyrical intensity. These offer a union of total assent.

These Things Shall Be (1937)

Chorus
and Orchestra

☐ London Philharmonic Orchestra and London Philharmonic Choir / Case (baritone) / Boult (conductor) / Musical Heritage Society MHS-1429

The text is by John Addington Symonds—the "things" a faith in the ultimate brotherhood of man. The music was written in 1937, and Ireland's expectations are yet to be fulfilled.

However, the music fulfills itself as one of the finest products to be found in the English choral tradition. There are some Elgarian echoes, especially the concluding portion, but Ireland's work has its own personal romantic resources, emphasized by a sinister rhythmic motive that binds the entire first part of the composition.

Ireland's sole large-scale choral opus is produced by authoritative interpreters; the chorus is an expressive body of singers.

Heinrich Isaac   *(ca. 1450-1517)*

Isbruck, ich muss dich lassen

Vocal

Voice and
Instrumental
Ensemble

☐ Early Music Consort of London / Bowman (countertenor) / Munrow (conductor) / Nonesuch 71326

A long, very long time ago, this touching little piece was first recorded in *L'Anthologie sonore*, a historical survey. It proved to be one of the hits of the many items covered in the series. It still is, in this bright new issue, with a recorder, a medieval fiddle, and a viol supporting the voice. Superlatively presented.

Missa Carminum

Cantata
and Oratorio

☐ Neidersächsischer Singkreis, Hannover / Trader (conductor) / Nonesuch 71084

Isaac's "Song Mass" has a lighter tone than is usually heard in the form's sacred specifications. Joshua Rifkin describes it aptly: "The intimacy, grace, and beauty of this Mass are well nigh irresistible."

The performance is likewise. It is full but not overloaded. One of Isaac's best works could not fare better.

Ion Ivanovici   *(1845-1902)*

The Waves of the Danube Waltz (1880)

Orchestra

☐ Philadelphia Orchestra / Ormandy (conductor) / Columbia MS-7032

The one remaining Ivanovici work of the approximately 150 published that rings a bell for this Rumanian bandmaster-composer. *Valurile Dunării* deserves to be kept in the waltz repertory.

Any listing found that credits this work to Waldteufel (listed below in this guide) is in error. Waldteufel prepared the orchestration that is most often used, however.

Charles Ives   (1874-1954)

Orchestra

Ann Street (1921)

☐ New England Conservatory Ragtime Ensemble / Schuller (conductor) / Golden Crest CRS-31042

An example of Ivesian transfer. *Ann Street* was first for voice and piano (see under *Vocal: voice with accompaniment*) and then scored for a pithy instrumental ensemble. It is cross-sectioned with brashness and sentiment. Excellently played.

Central Park in the Dark (1898-1907)

☐ New York Philharmonic / Ozawa and Peress (conductors) / Columbia MS-6843

Central Park (Ives's titles are sometimes most confusing; officially the piece should be called *Central Park in the Dark Some Forty Years Ago*) is a companion to *The Unanswered Question*. The latter was first titled "A Contemplation of a Serious Matter" or "The Unanswered Perennial Question." On the other hand, *Central Park in the Dark* was initially called "A Contemplation of Nothing Serious" or "Central Park in the Dark in the Good Old Summer Time."

This is a fully original example of orchestral picture-painting—of quiet nocturnal sounds and active urban night noises in which Ives combines melodies, harmonies, keys, and rhythms in a dazzling array. The poetry of this polydimensional montage (the strings maintain a rigid *adagio* while all the other instruments ride herd in a constant *accelerando*) is an extremely sensitive depiction.

Totality of effect is mandatory for the success of this music. The resultant blend, so that the specific ingredients are not italicized, is excellent on the selected disc, and where slight emphasis is required, the stereophonic realization is ideal. 'Twas not so with the old CRI 163 monaural disc or the previous (initial) recording of Ives's work on the very, very old Polymusic label, No. PRLP-1001.

Seiji Ozawa in this case was still in the apprentice stage. Both he and Maurice Peress join in conducting, but "under Mr. Bernstein's supervision."

Circus Band March (1894)

☐ Royal Philharmonic Orchestra / Farberman (conductor) / Vanguard C-10013

This was the initial recording of this quick-step; Bernstein's (in a three-disc Columbia set, M3X-31068) followed. The first is first choice. Full-steam march, with some Charles Ives bitters for seasoning. Farberman did some editing but no harm. He turns out a real zinger in the performance.

Decoration Day from A Symphony: Holidays (1912)

☐ New York Philharmonic / Bernstein (conductor) / Columbia MS-6843

Decoration Day begins slowly with vague motives zigzagging through the tonal fabric (an extra violin line merges with the basic ten-part string orchestra, conceived at a lower intensity and shadowing the other string voices). This is followed by gaudy parade music, as hostile a difference as one would want. Then, as suddenly, the music plunges from quadruple *fortissimo* to quadruple *pianissimo* and brakes into a very slow tempo for the concluding four measures.

Sure, this is program music but at the highest level, and it attempts to pinpoint only general characterizations. Bernstein is most convincing in his depiction. In the suave sections there is no attempt to produce a lush sound, which would destroy the homespun quality. And in the faster-paced section the statements are crisp and thereby of conclusive cogency.

Bernstein's edition is of course also to be heard in his recording of the complete *Symphony* (a fanciful term for the actual suite form the four parts represent). This is presented on Columbia MS-7147.

The Fourth of July from A Symphony: Holidays (1913)

☐ New York Philharmonic / Bernstein and Lipkin (conductors) / Columbia MS-6889

A luxuriant vision of what the holiday meant to Ives. One thousand percent American in gusto and because fractionalized patriotic tunes are crammed into the orchestrational package, including and highlighting *Columbia, the Gem of the Ocean.* Raucous, rambunctious, and with marvelous roborant textures. Nothing subtle, and written with all stops out, which is the way Bernstein lets it loose.

The performance is also in a miscellaneous program on Columbia MG-31155 and is included in the one-hundredth-anniversary package Columbia issued in Ives's honor (M4-32504). There it is the first cut in the first of the five discs that constitute the edition. (It is also in the complete four-part *Holidays* on Columbia MS-7147.)

The Gong on the Hook and Ladder or Fireman's Parade on Main Street (1911)

☐ New York Philharmonic / Bernstein (conductor) / Columbia M3X-31068

The usual fabric Ives knitted—knotty but colorful. Plenty of gong and plenty of counterpoint. A small opus but worth consideration. Bernstein rings the bell with his vivid presentation.

The Indians (1912-1921)

☐ Boston Chamber Ensemble / Farberman (conductor) / Cambridge 1804

A lament that is another example of an Ives "song without voice," originally for voice and piano and then arranged for English horn, bassoon, Indian drum, and strings. The opening with solo drum offers no surprise; the final cadence, leaving the line up in the air, is a surprise.

Orchestral Set No. 2 (1915)

☐ London Symphony Orchestra and Chorus / Stokowski (conductor) / London 21060

Music in the typical unfrightened, unshrinking, totally original Ivesian manner. The usual passionate advocacy of mass dissonant and pulsatile combinations is paramount; the merge of over twenty different rhythms for an orchestra going hell-bent for effect is representative. Quite often the score appears to be a mishmash of miscalculation, but with Ives the result shows this to be a calculated miscalculation, for it is mass, density, and spread-eagled orchestration that he wishes and not academic, prissyish balances. For Ives's music, orchestral mud paradoxically is the cleanest of sounds.

In the first movement the superpolytonal panorama contains some Stephen Foster snippets, with the special attraction of a zither framing the orchestral combine. Movement 2 is a species of ragtime run through the Ives wringer. Movement 3 splits the orchestra into uneven units, one a "distant choir" (mainly a few violins, piano, harp, and basses); the other gathers strength as the movement progresses until a large orchestra is at work, including plentiful percussion and multiple *divisi* in the strings, plus organ and accordion.

Stoky is at his best in this recorded statement. There is an excellent realization of the music's character; the dynamic eloquence he draws from the score provides the necessary proof. Nonetheless, if you can find Morton Gould's performance with the Chicago Symphony Orchestra that once was in the RCA catalogue (LSC–2959), don't hesitate. It's even better, simply because there is greater dramatic stress and more attention to coloristic detail.

Over the Pavements (1913)

☐ Boston Chamber Ensemble / Farberman (conductor) / Cambridge 1804

A scherzo design (using piccolo, clarinet, bassoon, trumpet, trombone, bass drum, cymbal, and piano), utilizing flavorsome polyrhythms, suggested to Ives by the hurry of city dwellers. The jazzy, nervous accents convey a Shavian-Ivesian humor. The percussionized music is extremely well played.

The Pond (1906)

☐ Boston Chamber Ensemble / Curry (soprano) / Farberman (conductor) / Cambridge 1804

Threnodic, impressionistically dusted music illustrating the genius of the composer in a mere twelve measures of *largo* tempo.

Ives's piece is for a small combination with voice as part of the instrumentation. He allows an instrumental substitution, but the haunting blend with the voice is preferable. Those who have a contrary opinion can obtain the work as conducted by Gunther Schuller on Columbia MS–7318 or in the mammoth album celebrating Ives's one-hundredth anniversary which Columbia released (M4–32504). The quality of the English horn that substitutes for the voice in Schuller's performance is exceedingly special and has the realism of a trumpet.

The Rainbow or So It May Be (1914)

☐ Boston Chamber Ensemble / Farberman (conductor) / Cambridge 1804

Music termed "a song without voice" and calling for flute, strings, and piano and featuring a woeful English horn. Still another of a type of multiple choice for a Ives piece. Originally the work was for voice and instruments, later it was set for voice and piano, and somewhere along the way the full instrumental conception was produced.

Robert Browning Overture (1911)

☐ Royal Philharmonic Orchestra / Farberman (conductor) / Vanguard C–10013

Important statistic: the Ivesian habit of quotation is not found within the main body of the Overture. There are some hymn inserts at the very end, but these are merely slight and light postscripts.

Ives's Overture is a solid unit, even with its punctuated fantasy. There is an introduction, a fast-paced section which is in contrast to the former (in terms of dynamics and texture, as well as speed), variations, a return to the second division, and a fugal-shaped coda.

Above all (especially in the *allegro* sections) Ives's artistic autograph shows clearly in the signature of his chunky counterpoints.

Farberman's portrayal is one of conviction and full authority. His ability to specify the detail, place in perspective what should be in command, and artistically monitor the fierce, fightin', on-the-offensive fast sections marks conducting of major distinction.

Among the competitive editions Strickland's conception on CRI (S-196) comes very close. However, the Polish National Radio Orchestra he conducts isn't in the same league with the R.P.O., and CRI's engineering can't compare with Vanguard's.

The See'r (1913)

☐ New England Conservatory Ragtime Ensemble / Schuller (conductor) / Golden Crest CRS-31042

A scherzo for small combo with full Ivesian presence and conduct. All of it is revealed in forty-eight seconds and with efficacy by Schuller's ensemble.

Set for Theatre Orchestra (1904-1911)

☐ Royal Philharmonic Orchestra / Farberman (conductor) / Vanguard C-10013

A set of three pieces with full Ivesian creative criteria and complete depiction of the titles. *In the Cage* excellently illustrates constricted movement; *In the Inn* doesn't relax into neutrality, but is maintained with ragtime jabs and syncopative punches. The final piece, *In the Night,* is Ives's idea of a nocturne—mysterious, never direct, always undertoned.

Totally expressive playing marks all three parts; the interpretation is positive and certain, and reflects all the Ivesian touches and special colors perfectly.

A Symphony: Holidays. See Decoration Day; The Fourth of July; Thanksgiving and/or Forefathers' Day; Washington's Birthday.

Symphony No. 1 in D minor (1896-1898)

☐ Chicago Symphony Orchestra / Gould (conductor) / RCA LSC-2893

A delight, a savory delight, a sentient work that one relishes for its scrupulous sensitivity and sensibility. Now, this is totally eclectic music—music without a measure of discovery, but complete with rediscovery. This melic musical memory book that Ives put together at an early age is not the sort of thing one would expect from a composer who in the same year would produce a piece for chorus divided into two groups each singing in a different key, or would shortly thereafter pour out creations totally devoid of romantic stylizing and academic formulas.

The first movement breathes the melodic grace of Schubert and the rhythmic *cordiale* of Dvořák, its principal theme a haunting one. There are no rhetorical gestures. Within this movement as all others—except for some places in the concluding movement, where the brass take off their jackets—the orchestration is clean and neat, with no tricks or gimmicks; the instrumental procedures are governed entirely by the material and are stylistically fitting. Movement 2 is a music of pathos, but free of sentimentality. The Scherzo is precise, no whirl and twirl of cross-rhythm, its fugal deportment being properly framed by the slower-paced Trio. Only the finale is out of proportion, though the most dramatic part. It is weakened by its wide range of ideas that escapes from symphonic stability.

Gould's was the initial recording of Ives's work. Since then Ormandy, Farberman, and

Mehta have followed with their recorded versions. Gould's remains the best because of its beautiful weave and retainment of youthful freshness. A sense of striving after something more (and better) than the Symphony offers is apparent in all other cases. To make a packaged passion of this work is to miss its honest imitation of romantic simplicity. Gould makes a small cut and so do the other conductors; Mehta outdistances the field with additional cuts. This recording is the highest point in Morton Gould's conducting career. No one has thus far matched the caressing sweetness of his interpretation.

(For those interested, Ormandy's performance, conducting the Philadelphia Orchestra, is on Columbia MS–7111; Mehta directing the Los Angeles Philharmonic is on London 6816, and Farberman with the New Philharmonia Orchestra of London can be found on Vanguard C–10032/4.)

Symphony No. 2 (1897-1902)

☐ New York Philharmonic / Bernstein (conductor) / Columbia MS-6889

The Symphony consists of five movements, all (save movement 2) originally parts of completely other compositions. Such musical interchange had nothing to do with laziness; it was simply proof of Ives's ever-seeking consideration of his working materials. The second symphony is not only an illustration of this criss-cross, creative scrapbook system of composition, but illustrative of interwoven Americana—a favored Ives procedure. Orchestral hymnody plays an important part, as do patriotic and college songs. Some of the themes sound like gospel hymns, and others suggest (as Ives described them) "Steve Foster." These are displayed in a nineteenth-century showcase of austere romanticism. But wait—Ives's daring contrapuntalism (the use of *Columbia, the Gem of the Ocean* with a Brahms-like melody is but one example) is the opposite of mid-Victorian musical sanctimony.

Bernstein plays this symphony to the hilt and plays it with professional mastery. It has polish, and yet it has the correct amount of Yankee drawl and the tobacco juice which covers some of the sounds. Bernstein's devotion to the composition shows—it was he who gave the first performance in 1951, almost exactly just a half century after the symphony was completed.

Symphony No. 3 (1901-1904)

☐ New York Philharmonic / Bernstein (conductor) / Columbia MS-6843

From first note to last the spirit of a church service of bygone days is nostalgically implied and reflected in this work (secularly speaking there is no programmatic definition whatsoever). It is as though Ives were writing a huge anthem for small orchestra. Though the tonality range is restricted and the sounds are based on memories of hymn singing and tent meetings held in New England, there is no academic constraint and thereby nullified effect. But nullification of another kind comes to mind—the 1947 Pulitzer Prize was awarded Ives for this work forty-three years after its composition!

Bernstein's performance is properly grained and states the quaint spiritual essence with sympathetic style. And avoiding too much extrovertism makes the Philharmonic's playing of the Symphony more effective.

Symphony No. 4 (1910-1916)

☐ London Philharmonic Orchestra and John Alldis Choir / Serebrier (conductor) / RCA ARL1-0589

A work of monumental significance. The opening Prelude is mystical, nocturnal, and introspective simultaneously. It incorporates hymns gently smothered by polyphony that give off iridescent refractions. Movement 2 is an orchestral colossus, but virtue goes with its size. Full independence is manifested in terms of direct meter (for example, the beginning combines $\frac{5}{8}, \frac{6}{8}, \frac{2}{4}, \frac{4}{4}, \frac{7}{4}$, and zero pulse definition). Further on an *allegro* (that moves into *accelerando*) is partnered with an *adagio*. Diatonic clings to chromatic, chromatic clutches clusters, clusters blend with ad libitums. Movement 3 is simplest of all. It is a majestic fugue, warm with impact, restrained in its scoring. The finale is just as majestic, but restlessness is apparent. It is the heaviness of sound (*heaviness,* not loudness) that exemplifies an individual type of muscular music.

The first recording was made by Stokowski (available on Columbia MS–6775), who used two associate conductors. That version, as expert as it was, has been replaced by Serebrier's edition (he was one of the assistants in the Stokowski performance). The parts for the players offer withering difficulties. For a single conductor the demand to control groups metrically disoriented from the already principal refractory rhythms is almost beyond human ability. Sererbrier does it miraculously and magnificently. But it is not this feat that gives his the nod as the preferred performance. It is the uncanny ability to clarify the repulsions and divergences within the score, provide the declarative tempo changes, and convey the general excitement pervading the music that makes Sererbrier's rendition the positive choice.

Thanksgiving and/or Forefathers' Day from A Symphony: Holidays (1904)

☐ New York Philharmonic and Camerata Singers / Bernstein (conductor) / Columbia MS–7147

There is fervent austerity in Ives's creation, and that's the way it is heard in this case. Nor does Bernstein play down or attempt to temper the superpolytonality of the piece, built from an initial combine of C major and D minor and concluding in choked tonality employing all the twelve sounds save G natural. The greatest effect occurs when the music brakes into pure G major (it is framed by bell sounds intoning the raised fifth and leading tone, but these do not deny the purity of key).

The choral portion is a simple hymn, *Duke Street,* and is but seventeen measures long. It is relatively unimportant and is fully doubled in the orchestra.

The spiritual fervor Bernstein obtains in this recorded setting represents fine music-making. But to hear it, one must obtain the entire Symphony. *Thanksgiving* (and only *Thanksgiving* among the four parts) is unavailable as a separate recording in Bernstein's or any other stereo version, despite the fact that Ives stressed that the four parts of the work "may be played as separate pieces" (which most often they are) as well as "lumped together as a symphony" (which most often they are not). The piece is available singly in mono (Composers Recordings 180), but it is played with a note-heaviness that dries up the emotional content.

Three Places in New England (Orchestral Set No. 1) (1903-1914)

☐ Boston Symphony Orchestra / Thomas (conductor) / Deutsche Grammophon 2530048

Contrapuntal and harmonic artificialities never existed for Charles Ives. The occasional four-square bits in his music were utilized for either direct picture-painting or pseudo-politenesses among antitraditional musical obscenities. Ives carried forth, at all dynamic levels, a totality of sonorous splendor contrasted to bends and twists of improvisation-like sonic doodlings.

The sense in Ives's music that everything is up for grabs is very strong. Exactness in combining the exact with the inexact in the *Three Places* (initially Ives called his work

"Three Corners in New England") makes Thomas's performance memorable. Everything in the score—evocations of Negro rhythms, American Revolutionary material in polymetrical status, impressionistic colorations—is made clear in a continuity that exemplifies marvelous music-making. Sectionalization can pop up at a quarter note's notice in Ives's scores, but it never does in this reading. The rhythmic layers, the metrical convolutions, and the pulsatile give-and-take are stated to perfection. This makes available one of the greatest of all Ives performances. One is tempted to say it is *the* greatest.

Tone Roads
No. 1 (1911) / No. 3 (1915)

☐ Boston Chamber Ensemble / Farberman (conductor) / Cambridge 1804

The first is for three winds and strings, the other is for two woodwinds, two brass, chimes, piano, and strings. Each is a thesaurus of heavily textured free lines, causing an excitement that makes superpolyphonic Milhaud sound like a Czerny exercise. *This* is what is meant by honest-to-God counterpoint!

Farberman's direction of these complex pieces deserves plaudits beyond the ordinary. He has established (here and elsewhere) the right to be known as an Ives expert.

The Unanswered Question: A Cosmic Landscape (1908)

☐ Chicago Symphony Orchestra / Gould (conductor) / RCA LSC-2893

More and more performances are being given of this program music, based on a philosophical essay of the composer. In fact, it has become *the* Ives piece of the present day. The strings play out of sight, and a wind group and a solo trumpet are on stage. According to Ives, the strings represent "The Silences of the Druids—Who Know, See, and Hear Nothing"; the trumpet propounds "The Perennial Question of Existence," and the winds (flutes here) attempt to give the answer but never succeed. As Ives conceived the piece, it is not to be performed with exactitude; tempi and meters are in opposition to one another. Therefore the conductor must regard one group (the strings), playing in extremely slow tempo, and another (the winds), playing at ever-faster speed, and the declamatory trumpet, as separate entities meeting only by happenstance. The more the blend of these three instrumental components, the less effective the result. This is neither a joke nor a trick. With three different levels at work simultaneously, it is amazing how easily the tridimensional facts are followed by the ear.

Conductorial regulation to avoid disparity is an error, a big one actually. One suspects that Foss's reading, on Turnabout 34154E (originally on Unicorn UNLP-1037), is guilty of this. Morton Gould's careful distinction of timbre noncoincidence, with absolute noncrystallization of the three instrumental elements, is the best on the books. Who no credit is given the fine solo trumpeter is something only RCA can explain.

Washington's Birthday from A Symphony: Holidays (1913)

☐ New York Philharmonic / Bernstein (conductor) / Columbia MS-7015

Washington's Birthday utilizes a handful of instruments—a flute that changes to piccolo, a horn, bells (for the most part totally free in rhythmic counteraction, the use of six-ply and five-ply phrase units paradoxically unifying the polyphonic and polyharmonic lines), strings—and introduces a Jew's harp into the field of serious music. The last is employed in the central section, which is severely in contrast to the outer divisions and is as American as a New England boiled dinner. The rustic ramifications of this portion caress the ear with spit and dissonance, including interwoven Ivesian transmutations of

Old Zip Coon and a sailor's hornpipe. (It was this section that was recorded separately for the old New Music Quarterly Recordings more than forty years ago, becoming the first Ives work ever recorded for release. It can be heard [minus the Jew's harp] on Orion's *History-Making Premieres,* conducted by the indefatigable Nicolas Slonimsky, No. 7150. The spirit is fine, the sound extremely poor, but there it is: Ives's introduction to the recording world.)

The end parts of *Washington* are a luxuriant conglomerate of the polyphony, metrical unrest, improvisational bravado, noise scoring, and all the rest that marked the individuality and beauty of Charles Ives's inventions. The score also drips with some irony—*Ave Maria* is twisted inside the final measures, followed by *Good Night Ladies.*

Bernstein's exciting performance has no competition in single-recorded form. There are other editions to be heard within the releases of the entire four parts of the *Symphony,* but none compares with his conception—a fascinating, on-the-mark delineation in every respect. It is coupled here with two other Ives works. On Columbia MG–31155 it is joined by Ives's *The Fourth of July* and works by Barber, Copland, Gershwin, and Piston. It is also available in Bernstein's portrayal of the complete *Holidays* (on Columbia MS-7147).

Hallowe'en (1911)

String Orchestra

☐ Boston Chamber Ensemble / Farberman (conductor) / Cambridge 1804

This piece (for strings without double basses, piano, and bass drum) is no musical gambol on the green! The sensations are direct, obtained by meaningful cacophony. The fourteen measures of the piece are played several times around, progressing from slow to fast to faster still, from soft to loud to louder still, with each instrument in a different key. Hail music, well met (and meant).

Farberman is direct and clear-cut in his depiction of Ives's raw and rampant musical caricature. He permits the swaggering bravado of the conception but takes care that no linear cancellation occurs and results in a mucky, meaningless texture. His solution concerning the ad libitum peremptory bass-drum part that contrasts with the diagonal crosscut accents that pepper Ives's quinary construction is ideal.

Hymn (*Largo cantabile*) for String Orchestra and Solo Cello (1904)

☐ Boston Chamber Ensemble / Farberman (conductor) / Cambridge 1804

No conventional four-square-hymn format. Church deacons and ministers could be expected to state that Ives was in need of harmonic exorcism. Their mistake, however. The music is slightly, ever so slightly, touched with atonality. Mainly it is of late-romantic style, as the cello (intoning the hymnodic text) takes its soloistic place or floats within the texture.

Farberman's version is a warmer reading than Schuller provides (on Columbia MS-7318 and in the big album honoring Ives's one-hundredth anniversary on Columbia M4-32504). Schuller's has an ascetic quality.

March Intercollegiate (1895)
March II

Band

☐ Members of the New England Conservatory Wind Ensemble / Battisti (conductor) / Golden Crest/N.E. Conservatory NEC-111

Young Ives. Interesting music because it *is* by Ives and due to its un-fleshed-out scoring—like that of the town band of the nineteenth century, flavorsomely unbalanced.

Frank Battisti is one of the best band conductors in the country, and he has his young musicians right on top of things. (Another performance of the March Intercollegiate is on Columbia XM–33513, conducted by Gunther Schuller.)

Omega Lambda Chi

☐ Columbia All-Star Band / Schuller (conductor) / Columbia XM–33513

Another Ives march in the same style category as the pair noted above. March titles mostly mean nothing at all. However, this one, according to Schuller, was named "after a fictious fraternity created as a hoax by some Yale sophomores."

Instrumental

Organ

Adeste Fidelis, a Prelude (1891)

☐ Ellsasser (organ) / Nonesuch 71200

A vibrantly colored performance. The piece has the usual Ivesian overlay—nocturnal, misty, and mysterious, tonally clashing with prejudice—and that's where the beauty lies.

Nonesuch's label and liner listing title this work *"Adeste Fidelis" in an Organ Prelude.* Jason Farrow's notes speak of "the prelude on *Adeste Fidelis.*" The title used for this discussion is that indicated in the Cowell book on Ives.

Variations on *America* (1891)

☐ Biggs (organ) / Columbia M4–32504

There's so much flounce, frisk, and frolic in Ives's piece that the utmost definition must be sought for the pigmentations applied to the score. This concerns not only the bitonal byplay but the blockblustering mimicry found in parts of the music. The organists who have recorded the piece all differ in their approach, and each has something individual to offer. The greatest returns in terms of color choice, clarity, and pace are present in E. Power Biggs's solution.

The record number listed above covers a jumbo release of eight record sides, two of which have Ives playing Ives. In addition there is another two-face disc presenting verbal reminiscences of Ives by "relatives, friends and associates," plus a sumptuous 52-page multicolored booklet containing all types of material, pictures, reprints, etc. Those who can fit the cost into their budget would do well to obtain this marvelous release. If not, the Biggs performance is available on single-disc releases (Columbia MS–6161 and MS–7269).

Piano

Allegretto (Invention)

Anthem-Processional

The Anti-Abolitionist Riots (Study No. 9) (1908)

Bad Resolutions and Good

Baseball Take-off

The Celestial Railroad (1919)

March in G and D: *Here's to Good Old Yale*

Rough and Ready

Scene Episode

Seen and Unseen

Some Southpaw Pitching (Study No. 21) (1908)

☐ Mandel (piano) / Desto 6458/61

Ives's piano works are bracing music for a listener, provided he braces himself and doesn't expect anything but the unexpected or, better still, expects anything and everything. It's all there and provides an anthological situation that is fascinating.

The Anti-Abolitionist Riots, for example, is quiet music of protest, though powerful in effect. Written without bar lines, the opus is of severe, urgent tensility and includes tone clusters. Polyrhythms excite the material in *Rough and Ready;* quotes from Stephen Foster and others are in *Some Southpaw Pitching* (so named because of its virtuosic left-hand part), which seals matters with a plagal thumb-to-the-nose final cadence. The Allegretto (Invention) is as Bachian as can be and as un-Ivesian as can be. It is not a spoof, but the March in G and D is one.

Mandel makes all the pieces exciting, provides scrubbed definition for every measure (many of which sound as though they were reductions of unwritten orchestrations). Thicknesses, heavy part writing, finger-cracking figurations, and cannonaded rhythmics matter not: each composition emerges clear. Such high-polished music-making among other pianists who tackle some of Ives's shorter pieces is the exception.

For more of Ives's shorter piano works *see below* (Song Without [Good] Words).

Sonata No. 1 (1902-1910)

☐ Masselos (piano) / Odyssey 32160059 (monaural)

Of massive five-movement length, with an imposing coloristic scope and a great deal of mixed motival impetus. In typical Ives fashion, borrowed tunes, both sacred and profane, are knitted into the score. And, a typical Ives conception, the score weight is heavied with thrusting and packaged lines, harmonies, and counterpoints. Some are rough and muddy, some are not especially pretty, but all of them are strong. It all adds up to an amazing keyboard piece that comes out of the instrument sounding like a continually heated improvisation that lasts more than half an hour.

Only a few pianists have attempted to cope with this vast changing sonorous landscape. If a record collector has the means, he should have Alan Mandel's conception (on Desto 6458/61) as well as Noël Lee's (on Nonesuch 71169). These vary considerably one from the other and from the Masselos performance, but be assured these differences are valid, an outcome of the Ivesian ideal of alternate versions and formal flexibility. Max Wilcox has pointed out that "each pianist's performance will vary according to the choices he makes," and Masselos has stated that each presentation of the Ives Sonata has a "character of its own" and that, further, he "can never predict how [he] will play it on any given night."

If but one edition is to be chosen, then it is the Masselos performance. Ives had written his work between 1902 and 1910, but it was Masselos who brought it into the public arena, giving the premiere on February 17, 1949. There is a remarkable and exciting ecstatic sweep to Masselos's playing, and he gives a fundamental inner pulse to the material, despite its free-wheeling and incessant motility.

The fact that the Odyssey disc is monaural should not deter anyone. Its sound is fine. However, if stereo it must be, and with Masselos at the keyboard, one will have to search for the RCA edition Masselos made (LSC-2941), now deleted.

Sonata No. 2 (*Concord, Mass., 1840-1860*)

☐ Kalish (piano); Baron (flute); Graham (viola) / Nonesuch 71337

Lawrence Gilman termed this Sonata, composed in the years 1909 to 1915, "the greatest music composed by an American, and the most deeply and essentially American in impulse and implication." In technical difficulty of performance and in the scope of its concentrated expressiveness plus forcefulness, the *Concord* is the equal of the greatest of the late Beethoven piano sonatas. Ives intended in his Sonata to express the spirit of transcendentalism as represented by Emerson, Hawthorne, the Alcotts, and Thoreau. The Sonata contains such an immense amount of detail that it can be regarded as objective music, paradoxically composed subjectively. It is a work that demands repeated hearings. Then, and only then, do the tumultuous intensities of its music register.

By the breadth of his playing Kalish defines and thereby magnificently clarifies the freedom of Ives's formal realization. Kalish's playing is akin to a microscopic examination of the score, and the aural gain is amazing. This approach does not nullify the persistent sense of dramatic *strain* (purposeful) in the music, even within its quieter, more relaxed moments. The delineation of this is articulated perfectly, without interfering with the hymnody and sentimentality pictured in the third movement (*The Alcotts*) or the salted-and-peppered barn dances and march steps heard in movement 2 (*Hawthorne*). The pair of electives that Ives included are utilized: the minute insert for viola in the first (*Emerson*) movement and the flute bit toward the end of the concluding movement (*Thoreau*).

Mandel (on Desto 6458/61) plays the Sonata with technical power but without grasping the continuity that one hears accomplished by Kalish. Kontarsky (on Mainstream 5013, originally on Time 8005) tends to go for impact (Teutonic?), and though the improvisation-like amalgam of the score does not suffer when it is delivered with dramatic determination, he misses the Ivesian poetry that is laced into the measures. On the other hand, on CRI 150 Pappastavrou (CRI just can't make up its mind how to spell his name, it also appears as Pappa-stavrou, on the disc's label, and on the back album cover as Pappa·Stavrou!) is poetically eloquent, but nullifies the heavier material by a lack of textural clarity. The mono sound is only fair. Finally, CRI presents the four movements in alternation, justifying its procedure by saying that the sound might become distorted through crowding of the longest movements on one side. CRI should have called on Nonesuch's engineers.

Worth having for historical reasons is the John Kirkpatrick recording. It was Kirkpatrick who gave the first performance of Ives's masterwork (in 1939), and he was the first to record it. His version is available on Columbia MS-7192. Bear in mind that no one understands better than Kirkpatrick the spiritual climate of this masterpiece.

Song Without (Good) Words

Storm and Distress

Studies No. 2, 5, 6, 7, 8, 15, 18, 20

Three-Page Sonata (1905)

22 (Study No. 22) (1912)

Varied Air and Variations (*Six Protests*) (1914)

Waltz-Rondo

☐ Mandel (piano) / Desto 6458/61

More of Ives's compact piano wonders (*see above*, under Allegretto [Invention]). More of Ivesian montaged quotations (in Study No. 20, for instance), with ragtime sprinkled all over the place (see Study No. 18), and polytonality (Study No. 7 and elsewhere). All the other creative habits are illustrated also—screaming difficulties, thick, artistically disordered part-writing, humor, and so forth.

The Three-Page Sonata (the title descriptive of the length of Ives's manuscript) is akin to a stark-naked picturization of Ives's methods: ragtime, march-like assertions and insinuations, odd voicings and mixed tonalities. After what has preceded, the final, unexpected C major chord provides the emphatic proof that the whole piece is a satire.

As in the other pieces in this album discussed above, Alan Mandel proves himself to be a marvelous pianist. Indeed, his ability to clarify the sometimes vague detail and elsewhere to balance the checkerboarded counterpoints that smother so much of Ives's writing is exceptional. His technique is just as special and is matched by a sensitivity that perfectly projects both the spirituality and the bravado of this American composer. Every detail is illuminated, even such a matter as the duo between celesta and piano in the Three-Page Sonata.

Three Quarter-Tone Pieces for Two Pianos (1903-1924)

Two Pianos

☐ Pappastavrou and Lanning (pianos) / Odyssey 32160162

Somewhat academic, though the central section has Ivesian rashness. The quarter tones fade in and out, are most potent when adjacent to the familiar half-step distances. Catch some fragmented hints of *My Country 'tis of Thee* in No. 3, titled *Chorale.*

Largo for Violin and Piano (1901)

Chamber Music

☐ Zukofsky (violin); Kalish (piano) / Columbia M–30230

The initial version of the Largo for Violin, Clarinet, and Piano. For a discussion *see below.*

Paul Zukofsky indicates his preference for the duo setting. However, the listener can make his own decision, since fortunately (and wisely) both versions are on the same disc.

Largo from the "Pre-First Sonata" for Violin and Piano (1899-1902)
Sonata No. 1 for Violin and Piano (1903-1908)
Sonata No. 2 for Violin and Piano (1902-1910)
Sonata No. 3 for Violin and Piano (1905-1914)
Sonata No. 4 (*Children's Day at the Camp Meeting*) for Violin and Piano (1906-1915)

☐ Zukofsky (violin); Kalish (piano) / Nonesuch 73025

In the Sonata No. 1 tonality stays rooted for only a fraction of time and then takes off on a ride of unhinged rhapsody. There is no pretense of specific dissonant arrangement in the music; the tensions intermingle, as well as the rhythms, developing into a fresco of solid power. Sacred swatches (hymn-contoured) are stitched to popular materials (ragtime-outlined).

A similar kaleidoscope of design is used for the Sonata No. 2. In the second movement (*In the Barn*) there is pulsatile snap and much sonic sport. There are recollections of the whining tone and improvising, plus the "dips" and "scrapes," of the typical country-dance performer. (Here is the only criticism of Paul Zukofsky's playing. He re-creates the music with tonal polish and impeccable bow artistry, whereas for stylistic truth it is better to be a *fiddler* than a *violinist* in presenting this portion of the Sonata.) It's truly real fun to listen and identify the quotes as they are tossed about athletically in this Ivesian gambol: quadrille snips, a bit of a hornpipe, *Till Eulenspiegel* as a counterpoint, a terse quotation from *Pagliacci,* two-step dance snatches of *Old Zip Coon, Dixie,* and *Marching Through Georgia,* plus a maze of syncopation. These clippings are all in place, not pasted on—it is just such treatment that makes Ives's quotations so enthralling. In direct contrast, the finale (*The Revival*) is set in a contemplative frame.

The seriousness of the Sonata No. 2 carries over to the opening and closing movements of the Sonata No. 3, fashioned by long lines transported and transmuted from the classic-romantic heritage. Here the harmony, for the greater part, is triadic and modal, polyharmonized and polymodalized, creased and joined to heady, zigzag rhythms. Contrast is produced in the middle movement, where ragtime makes the governing points of order. In the final Sonata No. 4 the source is hymnody, plunged into a bath of salty tonal brine containing polyrhythmic and polytonal substances. It illustrates a composer considerate of sacredness but just as cognizant of being free of dogma.

Aside from the one point mentioned above, the executions of Zukofsky and Kalish are positively superb. The element of phrasing in compositions such as these is especially vital. Ives's thoughts are far from four-square, and the agogic punctuations required to define all the subtle meanings within the music demand musicians of the highest order. The last five words describe Paul Zukofsky and Gilbert Kalish. The radiant understanding they bring to these compositions is a magnificent accomplishment.

Largo for Violin, Clarinet, and Piano (1902)

☐ Zukofsky (violin); Kalish (piano); Russo (clarinet) / Columbia M–30230

Here, Ives's music (originally set for violin and piano—*see above*—and then instrumentally amplified) is in almost a stark-naked state: no hymn tunes, no march snippets, nothing but the sounds of strange voices, formed from mixed tonalities. This pithy work of sixty-two measures grows upon the auditor after repeated hearings. Except for the first measure and a fraction, where Zukofsky's tone is unanchored, the performance is splendid.

Trio for Violin, Cello, and Piano (1911)

☐ Pacific Art Trio / Delos 25402

This is one of Ives's finest pieces, especially in its outer movements, more especially the initial division. The combination of lines which give rise to pointed, honest-to-goodness counterpoint can only be achieved by acute independence. Such nonchordal, freed-pitch polyphony clothes the opening movement. Climax in this part is obtained by duo formations linking into a total trio statement. The final coalescing factor is a surprising major chord. The other outer movement is just as introspective and ends with the hymn *Rock of Ages* in an unresolved state. Inside these two parts is the typical Ivesian robust bill of health. It is a fast, chirpy, gossipy scherzo. The rock-and-sock-'em music is filled with the snippets of familiar tunes that are part of Ives's creative trademark. Among them is an augmentation of *My Old Kentucky Home;* another is a retempoing of *Marching Through Georgia;* and still another is an Ivesian "disagreement" with *Rally Round the Flag, Boys.*

There are sharp differences in the performances available. In turn these are in contrast to the deleted Decca recording (DL–10126) by the Nieuw Amsterdam Trio. Best of all is the less extroverted and darker-tinged coloration the Pacific group brings to the outer movements. The playing of the Beaux Arts Trio (Philips 6500860) is slightly restless in the opening movement, and with plenty of up-and-go to follow in the second movement this is disturbing. In the scherzo, titled TSIAJ (the telescoped letters stand for "This Scherzo Is a Joke"), the joke has much greater point in its telling by the Pacific team (Alice Shapiro, piano; Israel Baker, violin; and Edgar Lustgarten, cello). This is accomplished by dynamic reticence, which clarifies the general textural chaos and collage-like character. The other teams bust the movement wide open; the Pacific Trio performers clip the music's hairs short, consider the conception in chamber-music character as far as possible, and avoid a symphonicism which only adds weight to what is already exceedingly heavy.

The Innate (1908)

☐ New York String Quartet / Brehm (bass); Kalish (piano) / Columbia M–30230

Quietly emotive music planned dynamically in arch form. The piece has an alternate title, *Adagio cantabile*.

Scherzo for Two Violins, Viola, and Cello (1903)

☐ Kohon Quartet / Vox SVBX–5305

Real raggy, flip, and funny are the descriptions of this fifty-measure item. The tail end of the first part is a musical yak—a canonic snippet quoting the famous (infamous?) hootchy-cootchy, that pseudo-Oriental, cheap carnival dance tune. The second section is a scalic and rhythmic salmagundi, properly belonging in this short and sweet-sour piece which is brazen, musical sass.

As good a performance as one can find.

String Quartet No. 1 (*A Revival Service*) (1896)

☐ Concord Quartet / Nonesuch 71306

The spirit of the church service of bygone days in reflected (with some unpious speaking) in Ives's quartet. In fact, basically, the harmonies are of the choir loft; few Ives issues are at stake as he rolls out his anthems for four stringed instruments. Simple, elementary, for the most part correctly resolved harmonies (some cutely clever inappropriate-appropriate voice-leadings salt the texture) reflect Ivesian academicism. In the third movement, the coming Ives peeps out when combined triple and quadruple meters are used, one of the former for a theme drawn from the opening movement. The work terminates in correct cadential style, via a plagal formation.

Comparing the three editions available, the Juilliard Quartet (Columbia MS–7027) play with an exceedingly classic demeanor, too tidy and even too serious for the free-ranging impetus of the piece, regardless of its safe-sane structure. The Kohon Quartet (Turnabout 34157) overdramaticizes, viewing the composition through varicolored glasses. The no-nonsense interpretation of the Concord group presents the music in its truest light, neither counterfeiting the style to make the work what it isn't (Juilliard) nor placing a dramatic gloss on it which doesn't belong (Kohon).

String Quartet No. 2 (1913)

☐ Cleveland Quartet / RCA ARL1–1599

Ives's heterodox formulas are not cramped by the limitations of four stringed instruments, but his musical intensity and fervor (notwithstanding the fact that the basic reasoning may well seem that of madness, to some) belong to no fanatical school. One may call this quartet atonal, polyrhythmic, of linear counterpoint, built partly of folk materials, sarcastic, happy, moody, or even skeptical. It is all these. The resultant combination is Charles Ives, *his* style, and in that manner he writes purely.

Though all three movements have titles, the work is not programmatic. The "themes" of this quartet are those of conversation, expressed in the give-and-take of free counterpoint. But the music is of diabolic origin. It is no sham, however; rather, it is prophetic art displayed in the pantheistic visions of this composer.

The Cleveland team consists of master performers and tosses off the pyrotechnics with ease. Extremely difficult though this may be, these performers also triumph in obtaining a balance between perfect ensemble and individual definition of the lines Ives wove in his work.

Chromatimelodtune (1913-1919)

☐ American Brass Quintet / Kaplan (field drum); Marcus (bass drum); Fontanella (cymbals) / Nonesuch 71222

Dogged dissonance here, its canonic consistency a prefigurement of twelve-tone style. The light percussion colors, aids the climax, and adds gust to the gusto.

From the Steeples and the Mountains (1901)

☐ American Brass Quintet / Nonesuch 71222

The sounds of two brass instruments (each doubled) are surrounded and penetrated in Ives's piece by two pairs of church bells, playing scalic, sustained, and arpeggiated figures. Ordinary orchestral bells or tubular chimes do not cover Ives's demands (as heard in the Turnabout performance on 34398, otherwise satisfactory). In this release the demands are met by using the carillon of New York's Riverside Church, one of the largest church carillons in existence. The ending is sheer sonic liberation—a joy for those who don't wince at strong music.

In Re Con Moto Et Al for Piano Quintet (1908)

☐ New York String Quartet / Kalish (piano) / Columbia M–30230

The *Re* in the title has nothing to do with tonic sol-fa notation. Ives's "with regard to" pertains to five-instrument music drawn and quartered by the sharpest possible rhythmic knife. Of concentrated length, but much more would be too much. The specialness of Ives's piano quintet is its mallet-and-chisel style. He described it as "studies in rhythm, time, duration, space, pulse, meter, accent, together and in various ways. . . ."

The metrical definition has no brotherly love for convention with such arrangements as $\frac{33}{8}$, $\frac{11}{4}$, $\frac{33}{16}$, and $\frac{15}{16}$. Further, the more common measure separations are just as inner-competitive, with cross accentuations plus such as five or eleven direct units to be set evenly across four beats.

There is excitement in this music of pent-up energy. Have a listen and have a unique experience. It's all set forth by these five expert musicians in a masterful manner.

Largo risoluto for String Quartet and Piano

No. 1, The Law of Diminishing Returns (1908)
No. 2, A Shadow Made—a Silhouette (1908)

☐ New York String Quartet / Kalish (piano) / Columbia M–30230

For the first-listed work, Ives's enigmatic title is a humorous ploy. The developmental procedure that follows the first nine measures—a granity, rocky, superdissonant quasi-prelude—in its command and individuality is creative money in the bank, with compounded interest. A more apt subtitle would be "The Proof of Profitable Returns."

On the other hand, the subtitle for the second work is exact. The quintet is timbre-split. Thereby, the work is heard twice as a delineated outline with shadowed background. The first time the piano plays *forte,* the strings *piano.* (Ives indicated the latter "as if heard in the distance.") On the repeat (minus the last ten measures) the dynamic roles are exactly reversed.

The playing documentation is clean, the tone full and robust.

Vocal

Voice with Accompaniment

Afterglow (1919)

☐ Puffer (tenor); Tenney (piano) / Folkways 3345 (monaural)

Ives's muted song is available only in this monaural edition. Most satisfactory.

Ann Street **(1921)**

At the River **(1916)**

The Cage **(1906)**

☐ DeGaetani (mezzo-soprano); Kalish (piano) / Nonesuch 71325

Ann Street and *The Cage* are also available in Ives's instrumental settings. (For the former, see under *Orchestra* [*Ann Street*]; for the latter, listed as *In the Cage,* see also under *Orchestra* [Set for Theatre Orchestra].) *Ann Street* is a short item set to a text found in the New York *Herald Tribune. At the River* is still another illustration of the composer's penchant for musical interchange. The song (exquisitely sung here as are the others) was fashioned from the end portion of a movement of the Violin and Piano Sonata No. 4.

Canon **(1894)**

☐ Boatwright (soprano); Kirkpatrick (piano) / Columbia M4–32504

One of Ives's early-period songs. The imitative polyphony is natural and apt for this charming light-faceted piece, which bears the subtitle *Not Only in My Lady's Eyes.*

Charlie Rutlage **(1921)**

☐ Nixon (soprano); McCabe (piano) / Nonesuch 71209

A keen portrayal of this lusty cowboy narrative, sometimes sung, sometimes delivered like an Ivesian form of *Sprechstimme.*

A Christmas Carol (1900)

The Circus Band **(1894)**

☐ DeGaetani (mezzo-soprano); Kalish (piano) / Nonesuch 71325

Ives termed his Christmas Carol a "traditional" piece. It certainly is, beginning with the words "Little star of Bethlehem"! It is sung with the simplicity that marks high art. The other song is at the opposite end of the spectrum. DeGaetani adapts her style perfectly to suit its snap and swagger. (Another setting, which is given the title Circus Band March, is discussed under *Orchestra.*)

The Collection for Solo Voice, Chorus, and Organ (1920)

☐ Berkeley Chamber Singers / Brubacher (soprano); Gilchrist (organ) / Gilchrist (conductor) / Musical Heritage Society MHS–1240

The traditional side of Ives with traditional hymnodic use of the solo voice, chorus, and organ. The order run through, twice, is organ introduction, solo voice, and choral response. It fits the text, which Ives notes as "stanzas from old hymns." Nicely done by all involved.

Disclosure **(1921)**

☐ Nelson (soprano); Gilchrist (piano) / Musical Heritage Society MHS–1240

The text is by Ives. The song has a craggy line, and the lyrics are rather mundane. Nelson gives an artistic performance with good shading.

Down East (1919)

☐ Boatwright (soprano); Kirkpatrick (piano) / Columbia M4–32504

A cross between folk and sacred style. Boatwright, however, does not depend on middle-road neutrality in her conception, but emphasizes each element by subtle changes in her singing.

Evening (1921)

A Farewell to Land (1925)

☐ Nixon (soprano); McCabe (piano) / Nonesuch 71209

Evening is a segment (Book 4, line 598) from Milton's *Paradise Lost*. The tonal prospectus is as usual with Ives; the dynamic range is not—ranging from *piano* to triple *piano*. A chromatic mysticism envelops the other song.

Marni Nixon sings superbly. John McCabe plays superbly.

Feldeinsamkeit

☐ Boatwright (soprano); Kirkpatrick (piano) / Columbia M4–32504

A poetically reflective example. Completely un-Ivesian in its romantic syntax, on top of which the text is in German!

From Lincoln the Great Commoner (1912)

☐ Puffer (tenor); Tenney and Corner (piano) / Folkways 3344 (monaural)

Ives's songs (which total more than 140) cover a huge range, from satire to engineering, from musical doggerel to expressive art pieces. This one is declamatory, akin to a concentrated dramatic scene in an operatic work.

From Paracelsus (1921)

☐ DeGaetani (mezzo-soprano); Kalish (piano) / Nonesuch 71325

Music of severe difficulty. Presented here with dramatic power and minus any stress or strain. This is certainly an outstanding achievement for both musicians.

From The Swimmers (1921)

☐ Nixon (soprano); McCabe (piano) / Nonesuch 71209

Ives translated word meanings into symbolistic musical equivalents in this song. *The Swimmers* is music of impassioned declaration, despite the sounds' clinging to the precise descriptive meaning of the words (by Louis Untermeyer).

Fine singing by Marni Nixon. The exceedingly difficult piano part is played with technical perfection and meaning by John McCabe.

Grantchester (1920)

☐ Puffer (tenor); Tenney (piano) / Folkways 3345 (monaural)

Ives constantly quoted Americana in his scores. Here he pins in a quote by Debussy.

The Greatest Man (1921)

☐ Nixon (soprano); McCabe (piano) / Nonesuch 71209

A poem found in a newspaper forms the text. This piece presents declamation set to song with amusing results. Ives's creative scrapbook comes in handy as he writes in a semivernacular way. Like a blackout on the old burlesque stage, this song has a "tag" ending ("They're lots o' great men, George Washington 'n Lee,/but Dad's got 'em all beat holler, seems to me!"). Nixon adapts her style perfectly to suit.

The Housatonic at Stockbridge (1921)

☐ DeGaetani (mezzo-soprano); Kalish (piano) / Nonesuch 71325

One of the most sensitive songs Ives produced, clinging to impressionistic coloring. DeGaetani's interpretation has such poetic quality as to make her rendition a required point of reference for all future singers of this music.

Ich grolle nicht (1899)

☐ Curry (soprano); Vosgerchian (piano) / Cambridge 1804

"I'll Not Complain" is Ives in a Schumannesque disguise. Thus the German text (by Heine). Satisfying music despite its un-Ivesian content.

Immortality (1921)

☐ Puffer (tenor); Tenney (piano) / Folkways 3345 (monaural)

Hymnodic, the text treating of the death of a child. Puffer's pitch control is not always firm.

Incantation (1921)

☐ Boatwright (soprano); Kirkpatrick (piano) / Columbia M4–32504

Another example of the diversity and originality of Ives's vast song collection. *Incantation* (also known as From the *Incantation*) emphasizes narrow intervallic spans for his setting of Byron's mystical words.

The Indians (1921)

☐ DeGaetani (mezzo-soprano); Kalish (piano) / Nonesuch 71325

A quiet, simple song, with a sensitive meaning of lament. The performance is memorable for its subtle gradations and mood positiveness.

In Flanders Fields (1919)

☐ Stewart (baritone); Mandel (piano) / Columbia M4–32504

In Flanders Fields fulfills an unusual idea, that of setting John McCrae's well-known poem. This is a war song and integrates a snatch of *America*, as well as a larger segment of *Columbia, the Gem of the Ocean*. Additionally, there is a quotation of the *Marseillaise* which is very moving. Morbidity is absent; proper dissonance and optimism are present.

The Innate (1916)

In the Mornin'

☐ DeGaetani (mezzo-soprano); Kalish (piano) / Nonesuch 71325

The first song is one of tender sentiment, as enchanting in its way as the songs composed in a more fanciful, extroverted manner. *In the Mornin'* is Ives's consideration of a Negro spiritual.

DeGaetani's interpretation of these songs provides a depth that one would not expect to be present from examining the music itself. She is a singer with a crystalline voice, but more, she is a consummate artist with a rare understanding of the music she performs.

Judges' Walk (1898)

☐ Boatwright (soprano); Kirkpatrick (piano) / Columbia M4–32504

Mixed circumstances concern this song. (This is maintained in the titling by Columbia. The record label uses "Judge's," the liner notes are headed "Judges," and within the notes themselves the word is spelled "Judges'"!) *Judges' Walk* is set to a poem by Arthur Symons. Later (in 1902) Ives adapted his music to a different text, Shelley's *Rough Wind* (the title used for the song's publication). It also served as the principal theme in Ives's first symphony.

The song has a soft dramatic thrust. Boatwright supplies it in full.

Majority (or The Masses) (1921)

☐ DeGaetani (mezzo-soprano); Kalish (piano) / Nonesuch 71325

The solo-voice-and-piano version of the same piece for chorus and orchestra (see under *Choral: chorus and orchestra* [*Lincoln, the Great Commoner*]).

Maple Leaves (1920)

☐ Puffer (tenor); Tenney (piano) / Folkways 3345 (monaural)

Chromatic tonal chemistry gives the song *Maple Leaves* a beauty rare in the Ives corpus. The half-tone descent that marks the last of the four lines of Thomas Bailey Aldrich's poem provides vivid musical illustration.

The whole song is only eleven measures in length.

Memories (1897)

☐ DeGaetani (mezzo-soprano); Kalish (piano) / Nonesuch 71325

Bounce and reticence in this two-part song. The section designated Very Pleasant moves like an express train and includes whistling by the soloist. Part 2 (marked Rather Sad) moves wistfully. DeGaetani is truly marvelous, shifting from the one extreme to the other and making each portion an artistic winner.

Mists (1910) No More (1897)
The New River (1921) Old Home Day (1920)

☐ Boatwright (soprano); Kirkpatrick (piano) / Columbia M4–32504

Mists is but an average vocal piece, set in ternary form. It is marked by fitful chromaticism. There is more individuality in the other songs—for instance, the syncopative violence in *The New River*, which Ives later turned into an instrumental piece for trumpet, clarinet, saxophone, piano, and four ad libitum violins.

1, 2, 3 (1921)

☐ Curry (soprano); Vosgerchian (piano) / Cambridge 1804

1, 2, 3 is almost as short as the title and a real vocal quip. Ives's words merely ask the question why a Yankee prefers "one, two" to "one, two, three." The answer can be surmised: because he'd rather walk than waltz! One cannot find such a vocal delight in any other composer's song stock.

The One Way **(1923)**

Peaks

Pictures **(1906)**

☐ Boatwright (soprano); Kirkpatrick (piano) / Columbia M4–32504

Pictures is washed by Wagnerian style, but *Peaks* has the recognizable mysticism that marks so much of Ives's work. The other song is standard stuff, cooly conservative but tuneful.

Boatwright can certainly sing Ives with conviction and understanding, and Kirkpatrick matches her achievements.

Religion **(1920)**

☐ Curry (soprano); Vosgerchian (piano) / Cambridge 1804

A pithy, hymn-like setting, slightly creased chromatically. Effectively sung with excellent diction.

Requiem **(1911)**	*September* **(1920)**
Resolution **(1921)**	*The Side Show* **(1921)**
A Sea Dirge **(1925)**	*Slow March* **(1887)**
The Sea of Sleep **(1903)**	

☐ Boatwright (soprano); Kirkpatrick (piano) / Columbia M4–32504

Ives recognized no restrictions as to text. The authors whose lines he chose to set include Emerson, Longfellow, and Whittier; other texts are by Ives himself or his wife, and a number are by unknowns. In this group, for example, the words for *Requiem* are by Robert Louis Stevenson, while Shakespeare was the source for *A Sea Dirge.*

The song listed last, *Slow March,* may be Ives's earliest-known composition, written at the age of twelve.

Soliloquy **(1907)**

☐ Nixon (soprano); McCabe (piano) / Nonesuch 71209

A fifty-one-second item, written to a text by Ives, consisting of two philosophical sentences. It is subtitled *A Study in 7ths and Other Things.* The first eighteen words are almost static in pitch statement, the antithesis of twenty-three following words that are wildly disjunct, the intervals being yanked completely out of their sockets.

Masterful summary by the performers.

There Is a Certain Garden **(1893)**

☐ Boatwright (soprano); Kirkpatrick (piano) / Columbia M4–32504

A song in the Cadman (*At Dawning*)–Mana-Zucca (*I Love Life*)–Rasbach (*Trees*) style, meaning as un-Ivesian as Ives would ever be.

The Things Our Fathers Loved **(1917)**

Thoreau **(1915)**

☐ DeGaetani (mezzo-soprano); Kalish (piano) / Nonesuch 71325

Thoreau is a chip from the *Concord* piano sonata. In its concentrated format of spoken introduction and sung lines from *Walden* it is one of Ives's most moving vocal essays.

Jan DeGaetani's portrayal is superb.

Tom Sails Away (1917)

Two Little Flowers (1921)

☐ Puffer (tenor); Tenney (piano) / Folkways 3345 (monaural)

Like a refrain hidden within, the spiritual *Deep River* is implied, and the war tune *Over There* is defined, in *Tom Sails Away,* one of three World War I songs. No subtle disguise—*Over There* is utilized when the words appear in Ives's own text. *Two Little Flowers* is in a tender mood—a rare emotion for Ives. The text is by Harmony Ives.

Puffer's vocalism is less important than his musicality. His scrupulous attention to the manifold detail deserves plaudits, and his ability to phrase and color in the style required is excellent. While he does not project glowing warmth, he has impeccable intonation, equality in all registers, plus fine diction.

Walking (1902)

☐ Puffer (tenor); Tenney (piano) / Folkways 3344 (monaural)

There are two lines of semisong, which can be described as Ives's version of *Sprechstimme,* in *Walking.* The harmonies are rather simple, but their use in relation to the text shows true invention. A song of moving sentiment, free of banality.

West London (1921)

☐ Nixon (soprano); McCabe (piano) / Nonesuch 71209

This is an arrangement of a section from an incomplete orchestral overture. The text is by Matthew Arnold. Keenly depicted by Marni Nixon.

Where the Eagle (1900)

☐ Mortimer (tenor); Gilchrist (piano) / Musical Heritage Society MHS-1240

Expressive vocal music. For Ives, however, rather conventional.

The White Gulls (1921)

☐ Puffer (tenor); Tenney (piano) / Folkways 3345 (monaural)

The very close reflection of the text fundamental to Ives's songs is seen in *The White Gulls* (on a Russian text translated by Maurice Morris)—an excellent illustration of poetry conveyed by song.

Yellow Leaves

Widmung (1902)

☐ Boatwright (soprano); Kirkpatrick (piano) / Columbia M4–32504

John Kirkpatrick's statement concerning *Yellow Leaves* is worth quoting: "direct, though its end evokes Debussy." *Widmung* (to a German text) is romantically spaced and tinged.

Voice and Instrumental Ensemble

At Sea (1921)

☐ Columbia Chamber Ensemble / Feuerstein (baritone) / Smith (conductor) / Columbia MS–7321

Illustrative of chromaticism in embellishing tonal solidity. Feuerstein sings with quiet, simple, and therefore proper effect.

The Children's Hour (1901) The Last Reader (1921)
From the Incantation (1921) Like a Sick Eagle (1920)

☐ Columbia Chamber Ensemble / Albert (mezzo-soprano) / Smith (conductor) / Columbia MS–7321

The first and fourth songs listed have tremendous individuality and produce the most responsive performances. That the severe contrast demanded stylistically is perfectly accomplished shows the convincing artistic adaptability of the soloist.

The Children's Hour is one of the most exquisite songs Ives composed. A great many of his songs are quite unorthodox, but in this case orthodoxy rules, with subtle beauty marking the styled clarity. Albert's sensitive phrasing, her warm voice, and her diction are a joy to hear. In *Like a Sick Eagle* the opposite of warmth is required. It is a slithering conception, italicized by quarter-tone progressions, to emphasize the pessimistic text (by John Keats). Ives's programmatic approach in his music is apt. Albert's ability to change her vocal timbre to match and to shift character in her delivery is just as dynamic as the calid conviction with which she invests *The Children's Hour.*

A lyrical line is supported by oppositional mensural patterns in *The Last Reader.* Rhythmic dichotomy is also the precept in the *Incantation* (also known as From the *Incantation*). The vocal performances are totally authoritative, and Smith handles his back-up chamber forces with finesse. (Only a piano is used in *The Children's Hour.*)

General William Booth Enters into Heaven (1914)

☐ Columbia Chamber Orchestra and Gregg Smith Singers / Drake (bass) / Smith (conductor) / Columbia MS–6921

A lusty, block-buster conception. Ives's ripsnorting music deals with the general whose reforming zeal continued under the very eyes of Jesus. It is a real inspiration, based in part on the Salvation Army hymn *Are You Washed in the Blood of the Lamb?*

Ives's virile piece is performed with potent vigor by all the forces involved. (The orchestral back-up was written by the American composer John J. Becker.)

The recording is duplicated in Columbia's M4–32504, a five-record compilation released in observance of the hundredth anniversary of Ives's birth.

Luck and Work (1920)

☐ Columbia Chamber Ensemble / Feuerstein (baritone) / Smith (conductor) / Columbia MS–7321

Polyrhythmic detail which contrasts with the rhyming text. (Sung with piano accompaniment by Helen Boatwright on Columbia M4–32504.)

The Pond (1906)

☐ Columbia Chamber Ensemble / Albert (mezzo-soprano) / Smith (conductor) / Columbia MS–7321

In exactly one minute and six seconds (to a fourteen-word text) Adrienne Albert, with Gregg Smith conducting a chamber group, registers maximal art decisiveness. Ives's delicate miniature has the concentrated scope of a work twenty times its length. Only a master could have created from a complex rhythmic plan the beautifully startling impressionistic filigree of *The Pond*.

The Rainbow (1921)

Tolerance (1921)

☐ Columbia Chamber Ensemble / Feuerstein (baritone) / Smith (conductor) / Columbia MS-7321

Ives drew the contents of *Tolerance* from an early orchestral piece. He then used a text taken from a university lecture! Unorthodoxy is an undeviating tenet in his career. The build to climax is negotiated with proper "let go" by the vocalist. He does as well with the overt romantic expressionism of the other song. (Columbia does not indicate the alternate title for *The Rainbow: So May It Be.*)

Song of the Harvest Season (1894)

☐ Members of the American Brass Quintet / DeGaetani (mezzo-soprano) / Nonesuch 71222

The usual Ivesian informative inventory, with a hymn text supported by a bare three-part brass combine (here cornet and tenor and bass trombones). The quadruple totality is further colored by quadruple tonalities. Short (one and three-quarter minutes) and sweetly pungent. The music is presented with the fullest artistic response by this superb vocalist and her brass-instrumental colleagues.

Choral

Chorus Alone

Psalm 14

☐ Gregg Smith Singers / Smith (conductor) / Columbia MS-7321

The technical premise of musical changes for each of the seven stanzas in no way falsifies the consistent continuity of the whole. Ives's harmony is only a bit salted. Heavier seasoning was unnecessary for the cumulative effect he sought.

Gregg Smith's group obtains the maximum heightening of expression within the piece. Further, the singers' stressing of certain pitches gives a subtle coloration as well as inner strength to the work.

Psalm 24

Psalm 67 (1898)

☐ Gregg Smith Singers and Ithaca College Concert Choir / Smith (conductor) / Columbia MS-6921

Both a cappella. Both exemplify sensitive choral writing. *Psalm 67* is especially compelling in Ives's setting by the use of polyharmonic juxtaposition, the chorus being divided into two groups. The duodimensional effect is enhancing, and Smith's direction of his choral personnel is striking.

Chorus with Accompaniment

Let There Be Light (1901)

☐ Gregg Smith Singers / Beegle (organ) / Smith (conductor) / Columbia MS-7321

A processional (so subtitled by Ives) calling for male voices with organ.

On the Antipodes (1923)

☐ Gregg Smith Singers / Smith (conductor) / Columbia MS-7321

Ivesian shouted substantiation is primary in this mostly unison choral piece, with words by the composer. Antithetical material gives a black-white dramatic effect, ably presented here. (The chorus is not supported with organ as listed on the recording, but with piano, four hands. No credits are given for the keyboard performers.)

Psalm 25

Psalm 54

Psalm 135

☐ Gregg Smith Singers / Beegle (organ) / Smith (conductor) / Columbia MS-7321

Ives rarely took advantage of the creative ease of formal repetition. These three psalms are individual reinvigorations. The first listed has hardly any organ-part importance, save sustained stability. There is much counterpoint; the opposite device of vertical validity serves for climactic points.

Antiphonal vocal scoring marks *Psalm 54.* Dissonance is the rector here. Not fat and pockmarking the harmony, but lean and thereby subtly pungent—and extremely telling.

There is no arguing the primacy of *Psalm 135,* no disputing its powerful thrust and powerful musicality. It is Ives at his best and at his noblest. It is, in this initial recording, a find. There is timpani and a bit of brass added to the score. (There are no credits on Columbia's otherwise exact documentation.)

The performances are truly exciting ones, convincing evidence of Charles Ives's great imagery. Gregg Smith is to be credited in this case with achieving the highest state of choral performing art.

Psalm 90

☐ Gregg Smith Singers and Ithaca College Concert Choir / Martinez (soprano); Brown (tenor); Beegle (organ) / Smith (conductor) / Columbia MS-6921

Music of clear, sacred force. And no fuss. But far from academic, if you please. The majestic conception is colored with bells in addition to the organ.

Psalm 100

Psalm 150

☐ Gregg Smith Singers, Ithaca College Concert Choir, and Texas Boys Choir of Fort Worth / Beegle (organ) / Smith (conductor) / Columbia MS-6921

Unchallengeable performances of masterful choral settings. Ives indicates here that he knew how to portray a psalmodic text as expertly as he designed music of heterodox formula.

Turn Ye, Turn Ye (1889)

☐ Berkeley Chamber Singers / Gilchrist (organ) / Gilchrist (conductor) / Musical Heritage Society MHS-1240

Tonal music with no research into chromatic fields. However, the result is *not* academic, though the progressions move according to basic harmonic disciplines. The singing is first rate, soundly blended.

Vita (1921)

☐ Gregg Smith Singers and Texas Boys Choir of Fort Worth / Beegle (organ) / Smith (conductor) / Columbia MS-7321

The partner to Ives's *Duty* (see under *chorus and orchestra*). Six words by Manlius are intoned in unison by female and boys' voices. A short, short item. Its monkish quality sounds as un-Ivesian as it is possible to imagine.

*Chorus
and Orchestra*

An Election (It Strikes Me that) (1921)

☐ American Symphony Orchestra, Gregg Smith Singers, and Ithaca College Concert Choir / Stokowski (conductor) / Columbia M4–32504

A unison chorus dealing with what John Kirkpatrick calls Ives's "angry outburst of biting satire," written after the United States had rejected supporting Woodrow Wilson and the League of Nations.

The impact in text and music is clear. However, the singing is slightly rough, and the rhythmic scanning is not precisely defined.

The Circus Band (1894)

☐ Gregg Smith Singers and Columbia Chamber Orchestra / Drake (bass) / Smith (conductor) / Columbia MS–6921

A typical example of Ivesian creative shifting. *Circus* was sketched for piano, scored for small orchestra, then used as a song. Later Ives made additions to the scoring. The sonorous parade-music ambience is typical Ives as well.

Three additional points are necessary. First, the entire latter part of the text listed on Columbia's insert is not utilized in this presentation. One supposes Ives wouldn't have minded. Second, the bass-solo credit is hardly noticeable in the recording. Last, this performance is also included in a jumbo (ten-side) Columbia release (M4–32504) commemorating the hundredth anniversary of Ives's birth in 1874.

December (1920)

☐ Gregg Smith Singers and Columbia Chamber Orchestra / Smith (conductor) / Columbia MS–6921

Vigorous and pithy (one minute flat in performance time). The first of the two settings (for unison men's voices garnished with woodwinds and brass) is heard here. Some seven years later Ives made a voice-and-piano version.

Duty (1921)

☐ Gregg Smith Singers and Columbia Symphony Orchestra / Smith (conductor) / Columbia MS–7321

Ives crams power into *Duty* and crams it with a less than ten-measure concentrated totality. Only male voices are required.

The companion piece is titled *Vita* (see under *chorus with accompaniment*). It is not companioned in discussion here because it is for a different medium. According to Gregg Smith the two pieces were subtitled *Two Slants, or, Christian and Pagan*.

Lincoln, the Great Commoner (1912)

Majority (or The Masses) (1914)

☐ American Symphony Orchestra, Gregg Smith Singers, and Ithaca College Concert Choir / Stokowski (conductor) / Columbia M4–32504

Unison chorus projected against heavy instrumental detail. There are patriotic-song quotations in *Lincoln*. Some of the detail in these recordings, made in October of 1967, is a bit blurred. Good spirit is displayed otherwise.

For a version of *Majority* for solo voice and piano see under *Vocal: voice with accompaniment.*

The New River (1921)

☐ Gregg Smith Singers and Columbia Chamber Orchestra / Smith (conductor) / Columbia MS-6921

Especially vivid in its concluding measures as the music winds down and then zooms into the final cadence.

Serenity (1919)

☐ Gregg Smith Singers and Columbia Chamber Orchestra / Smith (conductor) / Columbia MS-6921

A simple unison chant with minute instrumental framework.

They Are There! (1917)

☐ American Symphony Orchestra, Gregg Smith Singers, and Ithaca College Concert Choir / Stokowski (conductor) / Columbia M4-32504

A "War Song March" (Ives's description) for unison chorus with orchestra. The quotes are there—*Columbia, the Gem of the Ocean* and *Battle Hymn of the Republic* principally, others less so.

Three Harvest Home Chorales (1898-1912)

☐ Gregg Smith Singers and Columbia Chamber Orchestra / Beegle (organ) / Smith (conductor) / Columbia MS-6921

Traditional nineteenth-century hymn texts realized in an advanced twentieth-century manner (but all completed by 1912!). Powerful contrapuntal activity guides these three pieces, not only horizontally but rhythmically.

Walt Whitman (1921)

☐ Gregg Smith Singers and Columbia Symphony Orchestra / Smith (conductor) / Columbia MS-7321

Despite some critics' opinions Ives was no harum-scarum, cigar-ash-on-the-paper composer. The forceful quintary harmony shows how carefully Ives organized his material.

Choral sonorousness at its best is represented here.

The Celestial Country (1899)

Cantata and Oratorio

☐ Columbia Chamber Orchestra and Gregg Smith Singers / Rees (soprano); Eckard (alto); Boydan and Perry (tenors); Fifer (baritone); De Ruiter (bass) / Smith (conductor) / Columbia M4-32504

Safe and sane, with hardly a speck of the Ives personality. Not to negate the work, but to place it properly—"the epitome of what he learned from Horatio Parker," as John Kirkpatrick, the great Ives scholar, explains. Tonal sentimentality is paramount.

There are seven sections, including arias for baritone and tenor and a charming Intermezzo for string quartet. Gregg Smith competes with Harold Farberman (on Composers Recordings S-314) in this work. Better singing on the Smith production.

Ives / **William Schuman (1910 -   )**

Orchestra

Variations on *America*

☐ Chicago Symphony Orchestra / Gould (conductor) / RCA LSC–2893

In the fun and games that constitute these variations on *God Save the King* (excuse me, *America*) the tongue-in-cheek of Ives is paralleled by the smart, follow-the-leader orchestration of the original organ version by William Schuman. (The solo organ setting is discussed above.) The buffoonery is apparent: old brass-band-in-the-park figurations, thumping scalic passages for the trombones, polytonality, unadulterated academic harmony.

Though I prefer some of the tempi a little slower (and thereby the particular variational joke is savored longer), this is a prime rendition. It's the kind of thing that Morton Gould, a composer of intrinsic Americana, can understand far better than our virtuoso conductors, such as Ormandy, who has a squarer version on the market (Columbia MS–7289).

Jean Eichelberger Ivey   **(1923-   )**

Instrumental

Viola

***Aldebaran* for Viola and Tape**

☐ Glick (viola) / Folkways 33439

A semiprogrammatic consideration, noted by the composer as suggestive of the mood in which one "contemplates the sky on a starry night." Accordingly the title, "named after a star, whose name is Arabic for 'the follower.'" Fundamentally, Ivey's *Aldebaran* is built from impressionistic soundshots for the viola with similar partnership by the electronic tape.

Jacob Glick's unwavering service in the halls of contemporary music has shown him to be an expert artist. He proves it here.

Vocal

Voice with Accompaniment

***Terminus* for Mezzo-Soprano and Tape**

☐ Bonazzi (mezzo-soprano) / Folkways 33439

Ivey has mated here a unique and telling sound experience to define the plaint of Emerson's poem. One would be tried to find a better framework for the voice than the tape discoveries Ivey has utilized.

Elaine Bonazzi is a singer of power and status. She is also that rarity, a vocalist with triumphant diction. The words come off the recording with naturalness, clarity, and meaning, and one can listen without the disturbance of following the text supplied.

Voice and Instrumental Ensemble

Three Songs of Night for Soprano, Instruments, and Tape

☐ Peabody Conservatory Contemporary Music Ensemble / Rowe (soprano) / Pearlman (conductor) / Folkways 33439

The colors of the instrumental quintet (alto flute, clarinet, viola, cello, and piano) are enhanced by the tape, forming a second dimension functioning in contrast to the voice and framing it. The firm sense of color again demonstrates the filigreed beauty that can exist in electronic scoring.

Catherine Rowe's diction is super. There's no need to use the text supplied by Folkways.

Hera, Hung from the Sky (1974)

Voice and Orchestra

☐ Notes from the Underground / Bonazzi (mezzo-soprano) / Thomas (conductor) / Composers Recordings S–325

Ivey has produced a dramatic realization of the text (by Carolyn Kizer) which deals with the goddess Hera, wife of Zeus, "who for her presumption of equality with him was punished by being turned into a constellation, still hanging in the sky."

The full emotional implications of the poem are carried out by both subtle and direct strokes, via the combination of the voice with winds, percussion, and tape. This is alertly imaginative music, slightly expressionistic in style but not beclouded by a musical syntax that gets in the way of direct meaning. Ivey's handling of the entire project makes one believe she could create a successful opera.

Credit to all concerned in the performance; doubly so for the expressive voice and musicality of Elaine Bonazzi.

Cortege: **For Charles Kent**

Electronic Music

☐ Folkways 33439

Dark-pitched, with special savor obtained by sounds like keening. The threnodic mood is sustained throughout.

Pinball (1965)

☐ Folkways 33436

Entirely derived from sounds recorded from pinball machines. Ivey modified and reassembled the sounds, forming new qualities, pitches, and rhythms. *Pinball* has achieved a type of popular success in the electronic-music field. There's no gamble for those interested in the medium in picking this one. It has a bracing individuality and yet is not overly serious like the greater bulk of electronic music.

J

Gordon Jacob   (1895-   )

William Byrd Suite
Band

☐ Eastman Wind Ensemble / Fennell (conductor) / Mercury SRI–75028

Jacob has dipped into the wealthy holdings of Byrd and fashioned a beauty for winds and brass. Six delights including a *Marche*, a *Wilde*, *The Mayden's Song,* and a set of variations called *The Bells*. This is a honey.

Byrd's genius and Jacob's scoring talent form a best-seller in the medium, and Frederick Fennell knows how to sell. There is no doubt that this musician in the wind-ensemble-and-band field is the equal of such as Maazel, von Karajan, and Bernstein in the orchestral domain.

Five Pieces
Solo Instrument and Orchestra

☐ Academy of St. Martin-in-the-Fields / Reilly (harmonica) / Marriner (conductor) / Argo ZRG–856

Harmonica

An exceedingly rare and delightful instrumental combination productive of delightful music. This work is worthy for its special color alone. Just as worthy due to the fine artistry of Tommy Reilly and Neville Marriner.

For an even rarer combination of harmonica with other instruments see under *Chamber Music* (p. 932).

Rhapsody for English Horn and Strings (1948)
Instrumental

☐ Stenberg (English horn); Wolf (piano) / Golden Crest S–7039

English Horn

It is worth having this work on records, even though in a version for piano in lieu of strings. The piano version was sanctioned and approved by the composer. It was made by the English composer John Addison.

Patricia Stenberg plays this melodious, harmonically clean romantic music with appropriate style and finish.

Variations for Recorder and Harpsichord (1963)
Chamber Music

☐ Dolmetsch (recorder); Saxby (harpsichord) / Orion 74144

Jacob is a contemporary classicist, but does not believe stubbornly that meaningful directness must be secondary to formal requirements. The ten Variations on a Scottish-type theme are all clear, and minus any bedeviled webs of mere technique called on to fulfill the design.

Saxby exhibits superfine playing—his part is totally removed from simple, subsidiary support. Of course, Dolmetsch is not in second place. His intonation (a matter that plagues 99.99 percent of all recorder players) is impeccable.

The Variations were recorded live. This results in a few spots that are below par.

Divertimento for Harmonica and String Quartet (1954)

☐ Hindar Quartet / Reilly (harmonica) / Argo ZDA-206

There are at least a good half-dozen worthy pieces for harmonica and orchestra (for example, see under *Solo Instrument and Orchestra: harmonica* [Five Pieces]), but that total is far from being equaled in the harmonica–string quartet medium. This is a most attractive entry and receives a worthy account.

Jacob / *Charles Lecocq.* See *Lecocq* / Jacob.

Frederick Jacobi (1891-1952)

Solo Instrument and Orchestra

Cello

Concerto for Cello and Orchestra (1932)

☐ Members of the Oslo Philharmonic Orchestra / Vecchi (cello) / Strickland (conductor) / Composers Recordings 174 (monaural)

Without knowing the underlying structural plan of Jacobi's concerto, one realizes its meditative objective. It is covered by an outpour of melody, touched with melancholy, minus spiritual tumult. No dramatic acme is proposed in an introspective style that eloquently expresses the lines of Psalms 90, 91, and 92 that preface the three movements. Jacobi's concerto stands as a huge *cantilena*, of gorgeous curve and quiet intensity. It is realized superbly by Guido Vecchi's quietly passionate playing.

Why is this work so totally neglected?

Instrumental

Viola

Fantasy for Viola and Piano

☐ Rood (viola); Irene Jacobi (piano) / Composers Recordings S-146

Illustrative of Jacobi's excellent craftsmanship. This denies mere academicism. The Fantasy is of high accomplishment in a neo-romantic manner. The ultracontemporary will call it old-fashioned music, and the average contemporary's ears will not be shocked. Both should be able to recognize a creative voice very much alive and interesting.

Violin

Ballade for Violin and Piano (1942)

☐ Lack (violin); Irene Jacobi (piano) / Composers Recordings S-146

Jacobi uses romantic enlargement of harmony with a pinch of present-day salt. The resultant musical dish is an excellent one.

Chamber Music

Quartet No. 3 (1945)

☐ Lyric Art Quartet / Composers Recordings S-146

Movement 1 shows the classical attitude of preserving the elements of sonata form, yet is redesigned in terms of the present century. Important within this movement is a stepwise intervallic progression, and it reappears as an important point in the other three movements. Muting of fast sections (a Bartók original) is followed in the scherzo.

Hagiographa: Three Biblical Narratives for Piano and Strings (1938)

☐ Claremont String Quartet / Irene Jacobi (piano) / Composers Recordings 174 (monaural)

Hagiographa (meaning ''Holy Writings'') pertains to depictions of Job, Ruth, and Joshua. Despite the piano-quintet formation, which generally expands the chamber-music total into miniature symphonicism, the conception is concentrated, intimate. Though Jacobi ''endeavored to reproduce the dramatic intensity of the Book of Job,'' this section of the music is under wraps, and likewise the lyrical second part. In the finale the emotional climate is much warmer, and a quality of percussive barbarism appears.

The performance is of high quality. Irene Jacobi (the composer's widow) has been associated with the work since it was completed. With the Kolisch String Quartet she participated in the premiere, in 1938, and later she recorded the work on 78-rpm discs with the Coolidge Quartet. A fully definitive performance is realized, one of deeply articulated repose that matches the endowments of Jacobi's fine creative voice.

Leoš Janáček (1854-1928)

Orchestra

Lachian Dances (1890)

☐ London Philharmonic Orchestra / Huybrechts (conductor) / London 6718

A half-dozen folkloric exemplifications (the only title used is noted above, but Janáček's published score clearly indicates *6 Lašske tance*); bright, gay, and with none of the compositional doodads that create havoc with simple utterances. The dances are in the Dvořák ''Slavonic'' tradition, with just enough variety to sustain the naturalness of the music.

Huybrechts is a grand talent and proves his perspicacity in this performance. He lets the music ride on without interference. It makes its own impact minus any intrusive embellishment. That type of understanding is the sign of a good conductor, and a talented one.

Sinfonietta (1926)

☐ London Symphony Orchestra / Abbado (conductor) / London 6620

Urban refinement and sophistication combine with rural earthiness in this singular work, containing a range of orchestration that is bewitching. Janáček's spacing methods give weirdly wonderful personal sounds that haunt the mind. The other processes of the composition are as select. With this composer, development procedures were as special as his consideration of harmony (all chords had emotional clues—of calmness, of agitation, and so on).

The many brass instruments (twelve trumpets, two bass trumpets, no fewer than four trombones, and a pair of tenor tubas) caused Janáček sometimes to refer to his piece as a ''Military Sinfonietta,'' but the martial quota is extremely small. Nevertheless, the coolness of classical order is foreign to the essence of the Sinfonietta. Lushness (in correct proportion), richness, and coloristic fantasy are its related objectives. They make the composition a rhapsody of themes, though some relationship and recapitulation exist. This five-sectioned composition is powerful evidence of Janáček's significant creative voice.

Abbado's reading is a triumph of understanding. He realizes the pathos of the third section with intense emotive response. The difficult final (fifth) movement, with its almost outlandishly grotesque scoring, is particularly clear under his baton. The only minus item (an extremely slight one) is the overmicrophoning of the timpani.

Suite from *The Cunning Little Vixen* (1923)

☐ Toronto Symphony Orchestra / Andrew Davis (conductor) / Columbia M-35117

Janáček's opera was once represented in the domestic catalogue on Artia 88B/L. With that firm's demise the gap has never been filled. This orchestral suite, therefore, is most welcome.

The music furnishes a fine anthology of Janáček's deep-felt sensitivity to the communications of native musical sounds. He described these as ''the eternally young rhythm of nature.''

Taras Bulba, Rhapsody for Orchestra (1918)

☐ London Philharmonic Orchestra / Huybrechts (conductor) / London 6718

The profile of nationalism (a Moravian comprehends a Russian story by Gogol about a seventeenth-century war with Poland in which a Cossack leader and his two sons meet death) is very strong in Janáček's programmatic three-movement suite. The music is spontaneous and not formally stiff so that it loses its urgency. Story detail is clear, but not to the point of a minute inventory. Janáček's orchestration is especially inventive, including a fine use of the organ as a special timbre.

Huybrechts emphasizes the richly scored sonority scheme. Any attempt to be subtle at the expense of the music's theatricality would diminish its strength. This is the most truthful version on the market.

String Orchestra

Idyll for String Orchestra (1878)

☐ Southwest German Chamber Orchestra, Pforzheim / Angerer (conductor) / Turnabout 34532

Hardly known, but as worthy as any romantic piece for the medium. It breathes Dvořák (he was present at the first performance) throughout its seven connected movements, which have sixteen major tempo changes. Angerer leads a sensitive performance, shaping all the contours of the work neatly.

Suite for String Orchestra (1877)

☐ Los Angeles Chamber Orchestra / Marriner (conductor) / Argo ZRG-792

Early Janáček (his post-student period), pro-Dvořák in concept and content. Despite the use of set classical designs, the native idiom is not completely subsurface. A romantic outlook (and that includes a bit of later Janáčekian outlook as well) permeates the suite.

Richly and handsomely played. The warmth of sound of Marriner's ensemble in the upper register says a great deal for the quality of his conducting.

Solo Instrument and Orchestra

Piano

Capriccio for Piano (Left Hand) and Chamber Orchestra (1926)

☐ Caramoor Festival Orchestra / Somer (piano) / Rudel (conductor) / Desto 6427

Unusual facts surround the work. It would be expected that music for but eight players would fit easily into the category of chamber music, but the Capriccio is for piano with seven wind and brass players. This places it in the rare area of a concentrated solo vehicle, not with chamber-orchestra accompaniment (despite the title heading), but with a distinctive septet group.

The full scale of the four movements approaches concerto style but falls just short of it. Janáček's extremely odd coloration (a flute and alternating piccolo are the only woodwind representatives; the other instruments are a pair of high trumpets, three trombones, and a tenor tuba) and his avoidance of virtuosity turn the Capriccio into an eight-timbred sonata for concerted instruments. Thereby, it fully straddles the fields of chamber and solo-accompaniment music.

All the discovery and invention of the composer are brought out by this ensemble. Hilde Somer understands and realizes the tense emotional condition of the work. She defines the succinct melodic curves and cryptic motives of the score to the fullest.

Concertino for Piano and Chamber Orchestra (1925)

☐ Caramoor Festival Orchestra / Somer (piano) / Rudel (conductor) / Desto 6427

A hybrid plan of concerto (prominence of the piano), chamber music (seven instrumentalists), and symphonic elements (despite the opening pair of movements calling only for two instruments each) makes this work unique. The sound is expressly and expressively nationalistic with a tough accent—not by way of tunes and dances, but by naturalism in the lines, which are never cut to fit squared phrase lengths or smoothed to ordinary balances. A maximum sonority is obtained by minimal means. The frictions are mild but powerful. Janáček's Concertino is an example of Moravian musical philology set within an extraordinary concerto design.

Since Janáček's music gains if it is presented for the realistic substance it is rather than for the smooth-grained romanticism that it is not, a performance that is almost unrounded and slightly spiky is truer than one of graduate-school polish. Desto's release fits this theorem. Somer is a powerful pianist, and she applies the required clear-cut roughage in her portrayal.

In the Mist (1912)

☐ Kubalek (piano) / Golden Crest 7050

Poetic, nocturne-like music. Just a few of Janáček's special pitch contours are contained here, though the music has a folk-contour interlay. A sense of quiet improvisation hangs over the four movements (only the last is in speedy tempo; the others are Andante, *Molto adagio,* and Andantino).

Kubalek's pianism commands undivided attention. His playing is perfectly styled.

Instrumental

Piano

Sonata for Violin and Piano (1913)

☐ Bloch (violin); Brandwynne (piano) / Redwood S-3

Janáček's primitive (but extraordinarily knowledgeable) style will be noted in the Sonata, composed in 1913, revised during World War I, and completed in 1921. The opening movement, with abrupt changes from a single fast theme to a completely opposed tempo, conveys the subtleties of Moravian language. The *Ballada* that follows alternates two subjects, in unadorned style, with the final statement in ad libitum manner. There is no sense of *two* instruments; the combination is *one.* The final portion of the work has a special fascination in terms of rhythm. It is charged with elongation, contraction, and attendant irregularity. This is characteristic Janáček.

In the domestic catalogue at the present time this is the only recording of the opus. It

Chamber Music

fills the gap left with the deletion of the monaural Westminster disc (W–18750), on which the Sonata was performed by Barylli and Holetschek, and the monaural Mercury album (MY–50090), which featured Druian and Simms.

String Quartet
No. 2 (1923) / No. 3 (*Intimate Letters*) (1928)

☐ Austrian String Quartet / Turnabout 34471

Janáček indicated the motivation for his second quartet was "an unfortunate woman, suffering, beaten, ill-treated, just as Tolstoy describes her in his *Kreutzer Sonata*." In no sense is there a scene-by-scene portrayal of Tolstoy's novel. What Janáček depicts are the furtiveness, cruelty, and passion of the tale. One need not know the story. The listener shares in a chamber-music drama that requires no precise thematic analysis, since it is conveyed by the power of perfectly integrated music.

Intimate Letters (termed "Intimate Pages" on Turnabout's release; the deleted Artia recording [by the Smetana Quartet] used "Secret Pages") was originally titled "Love Letters" by the composer (Janáček's mistress, Kamila Stössel, thirty-eight years his junior, was the inspiration for this quartet). It is interesting that Janáček's intensely intimate musical document was initially scored for a viola d'amore in place of the viola. This choice of the fourteen-string instrument, with its lovely, passionate tone, further underlines the composer's feelings.

The entire quartet is pervaded with transient thoughts and fleeting ideas, bound by determined pronouncements, articulations, and punctuations. Technically speaking, these are obtained by changing meters, dislodged accents, and other refractional permutations. (Janáček's music is as seen through mirrors giving various shapes.) Throughout, there is intertwined a Tristanesque emotionalism without Wagnerian overtones.

The performance of the third quartet is adequate. What one wishes for is more focused heat and drive. In the second quartet the Austrian ensemble plays with sensitivity. (The Smetana Quartet's magnificently exciting presentations of these works are worth searching for in those shops that specialize in deleted issues. For those who want to make the effort, the Smetana team's performances were recorded in Prague by Supraphon and released in the United States on the Artia label, No. 109.)

There is some confusion about the numbering of Janáček's quartets, and it is not clarified by Turnabout's liner notes. Sometimes the second and third quartets are incorrectly listed as Nos. 1 and 2. However, Janáček produced his first string quartet in 1880, though the manuscript has not been found. Based on this fact, the listing of the extant quartets as Nos. 2 and 3 is correct.

Mládí: Suite for Flute (alternating with Piccolo), Oboe, Clarinet, Horn, Bassoon, and Bass Clarinet (1924)

☐ Monteux (flute and piccolo); Schuman (oboe); Silfies (clarinet); Tillotson (horn); Nakagawa (bassoon); Simonelli (bass clarinet) / Desto 6428

Janáček's creed that one develops national music by listening to the voices of the birds and by drawing from nature is fully developed in *Mládí* ("Youth"), a suite for wind sextet. The country of Moravia is expressed in this musical travelogue of the forest—the creatures that inhabit it, the land, and the people speaking. The only bow to musical form (in the classic sense) is the increasing speed of the four movements—but only in general terms, since the tempi constantly change within each section. Janáček's ideas of wind scoring are as far from the traditional as possible, including the rare chamber-music use of the flabby-toned bass clarinet.

The $\frac{4}{4}$ beat of the second movement, interrupted eight times and stretched an extra sixteenth, is a delightful rhythmic anachronism. And the catchy march (movement 3) is a pert parody.

If you can find the old Columbia recording (CO-4995) of this work (by the Philadelphia Woodwind Quintet with Leon Lester as the bass clarinetist), grab it. It's exceptional. If not, this Desto release will serve adequately.

The Diary of One Who Disappeared (1916)

□ Tear (tenor); Ledger (piano); Gale (soprano); Bainbridge and Creffield (mezzo-sopranos); Biggar (contralto) / Argo ZRG–692

An unusual conception which can be classified either as a monodrama or a miniature concert opera. (Janáček wanted dim lighting throughout a performance, unobstrusive entrances and exits, and no breaks within the twenty-two "stanzas," or divisions, of the work.)

The score calls for a tenor, who has the major role in the cycle, an alto (here this part is taken by Elizabeth Bainbridge, a mezzo-soprano), and a piano (of solo proportions), plus three female voices. The story (a true one which came to light when poems were found in the room of a young man who had mysteriously disappeared) is extremely concise and simple, of high moral tone. It kindled an intensive reaction on Janáček's part after he had read it in a newspaper, and triggered one of his most powerful works. It concerns a farmer's son who falls in love with a Gypsy girl, who has a child from the affair. The boy cannot forget her. After much inward struggle he runs away from home to join the girl, despite his intense love for his parents and though this means leading a nomadic life.

Janáček's music has the same fundamental artistic truth as the tale it describes. The contrast between the emotional conflict of the youth and the sensuality of the woman is telling, underlined by the commentary-like color of the miniature chorus and piano. Exciting and unusual music set for a unique combination.

The performance is thrillingly set forth in English translation. If possible, however, it is worthwhile to search for the old Artia recording (No. 102) which presented the work in Czech, giving the music an additional vital rhythm. The tenor for this deleted issue is Blachut, the pianist Palanicek.

Vocal

Voice with Accompaniment

Czech Legion
The Evening Witch (No. 3 from Four Moravian Male-Voice Choruses)
Leavetaking (No. 4 from Four Moravian Male-Voice Choruses)
Maryčka Magdonova
Schoolmaster Halfar
Seventy Thousand
The Soldier's Lot (No. 3 from Four Male-Voice Choruses)
Our Birch Tree

□ Moravian Teachers' Choir / Tučapský (conductor) / Nonesuch 71288

Janáček's special personality is magnificently portrayed in these unaccompanied choruses for men's voices. Especially significant are the musical resonances that are attuned to the rhythmic and accentual outlines of the texts. The subject matter is extremely varied. *The Evening Witch* has folksy vitality, while *Leavetaking* has dark-toned aspects, its tonality the extremely rare one of A flat minor. But this is just another example of Janáček's keen vocal sense. Other choruses have either a patriotic view (the dramatic

Choral

Chorus Alone

direction of *Czech Legion*) or fervent social consciousness displayed (*Seventy Thousand*).

All of the music is beautifully executed. Only a group totally grounded in Janáček's special style, which describes the Moravian Teachers' Choir, can perform these pieces properly and so effectively. The precision and blend are masterly.

Nonesuch has provided just as masterly liner notes by Jack Diether, together with complete texts and translations. In regard to the latter, there are variances, naturally. In the matter of titles, for example; *Grove's Dictionary of Music and Musicians* lists *Alas the War!* for *The Soldier's Lot* and *The Twilight Goblin* rather than *The Evening Witch*, and designates *Leavetaking* as *The Parting*.

The Wandering Madman

☐ Moravian Teachers' Choir / Syková (boy soprano); Jokl (tenor); Firley (baritone) / Tučapský (conductor) / Nonesuch 71288

Interlay and interplay of the solo voices with the chorus produce a vocal coloration that equates orchestrational inventory. *Potulný Šílenec* is a ballad set to the translation of a poem by no less than Rabindranath Tagore, the Bengali poet, who drew Janáček's admiration when he visited Prague in the early days of the Czechoslovak Republic.

The work is not only special in its scoring, but truly one of the most magnificent pieces in the literature for unaccompanied male voices. The perfection of the performance deserves a five-star designation. A special credit applies to the exquisite silvery voice of Běla Syková, the boy soprano.

Chorus and Orchestra

Nursery Rhymes (*Říkadla*) (1927)

☐ Caramoor Festival Orchestra and Chorus / Rudel (conductor) / Desto 6428

Janáček's *Říkadla* consists of an introduction and eighteen very short sections produced here with English translation, which doubles aural enjoyment. Children's material is presented in a sophisticated manner, typically Janáčekian with its pithy phrases, darting pitch swoops, and the special colors of his palette. The orchestra is small and includes an ocarina and a toy drum.

Rudel's eight-part chorus gives a clear, meticulously enunciated performance. The instrumentalists do very well; George Silfies as principal clarinetist does extremely well. (The liner notes do not jell with the listing of the performers and instruments involved.)

Cantata and Oratorio

Slavonic (Glagolitic) Mass (1927)

☐ Bavarian Symphony Orchestra and Bavarian Radio Chorus / Lear (soprano); Rössi-Majdan (mezzo-soprano); Häfliger (tenor); Crass (bass); Bedřich Janáček (organ) / Kubelik (conductor) / Deutsche Grammophon 138954

Not music for religious purposes, but rather a composition celebrating God in a secular, self-determined, quasi-pagan manner (one of the reasons why this work is also known as a "Festival Mass"). Though Janáček's Mass follows the usual format, it interlards several features uncommon to the plan, in addition to being set in the old ecclesiastical Slavic language rather than the usual Latin. The Credo divides into several sections of pure instrumental character, and after the final Agnus Dei there is a brilliant organ solo plus an Intrada. There is no simple psalmodic tone or even pulse; the rhythms are restless, irregular, bold, the mood tense and charged with vocal electricity.

Probably no single piece better explains and illustrates Janáček's technique and aesthetic courageousness than this Mass, one of the last compositions he wrote. It is the product of an individualist, a composer stating truths, even though these are of nonliturgical order paradoxically set in a sacred musical form. (Janáček's score is headed with the remark "God is gone up with a shout.")

High praise must be accorded everyone concerned with the presentation. Kubelik has his forces keyed to the emotional sincerity that fills the work; the solo voices (with very taxing parts) and chorus, the organist, and the orchestra are all magnificent.

Jenůfa (1894-1903)

☐ Orchestra and Chorus of the Prague National Theatre / Krasova, Jelinkova, Fidlerova, and Subrtova (sopranos); Vesela, Musilova, and Hanzalikova (mezzo-sopranos); Cadikovicova and Kourimska (altos); Blachut and Zidek (tenors); Kalas (baritone); Jedenactik (bass) / Vogel (conductor) / Angel S-3756

Jenůfa is Leoš Janáček's *opéra de résistance*. Its dramatic tempo persistently moves forward in the Mussorgsky tradition, and in addition it has all the intensity of Debussy's *Pelléas et Mélisande*. The story treats of lust and infanticide, enmeshed in jealousy, resolved by expiation and hope. In *Jenůfa* expressiveness is paramount. There is no massive retardation of action by formal cut-to-pattern constructions. Janáček projects his opera by way of declamation woven into song—a potent method maintaining urgency and yet meeting lyrical demands. Plot and musical shape become correlative; the expression of the former defines the latter. The design therefore permits, without irritating static stage representation, the inclusion of a mad scene, an *Ave Maria,* a splendid climactic duet. However, unlike Debussy's operatic orchestra, Janáček's does not become part of the *dramatis personae,* though it is far from mere accompaniment.

This is a powerful recording, sung in Czech, of course. At times it is a little too frenzied, but this is a minor dissent to an otherwise outstanding performance.

Opera and Dramatic Music

Paul Jeanjean   (1929-   )

Carnival of Venice, for Clarinet and Piano

☐ Campbell (clarinet); York (piano) / Crystal 331

The old tune has been an inexhaustible mine of sympathy for composers—good, bad, and indifferent. This entry is in the first-named class, especially because of the sensitive *rubati* and color applied by Campbell and York to the variations Jeanjean has invented.

Instrumental

Clarinet

Donald Jenni   (1937-   )

Musique printanière

☐ Mather (flute); Simms (piano) / Composers Recordings S-329

Most of the writing is percussive in tone. Jenni does not hunt with the hounds of flute tradition in their pastoral-nocturnal habitats.

He explains that *printanière* means "both 'primeval' and 'having to do with springtime.'" Clearly, most of the former with only a little bit of the latter. An admirably pointed (which for a romantic work would be written as "rounded") performance.

Chamber Music

___

Cucumber Music (1969)

☐ Mather (alto flute and piccolo); Hibbard (viola and toy piano); Avery (piano and celesta); Parsons (percussion) / Composers Recordings S–324

Structurally, Jenni's piece is loosely analogous to binary formation. Massed blocks of isorhythmic materials are followed by quiet, moody data. White/black, extrovert/introvert, and thesis/antithesis come to mind in the aural reaction.

The scoring is well documented. The title *Cucumber Music* "has no symbolic significance." Actually it's a poor choice leading thoughts totally astray regardless of the composer's disclaimer.

Adolf Jensen   (1837-1879)

Instrumental

Piano

Sonata in F sharp minor, Op. 25

☐ Ruiz (piano) / Genesis 1005

A sizable composition, covering close to thirty-three minutes. Plenty of Schumann-esque juice and a good portion of virtuosity. Ruiz does very well with this yellowed romantic document.

Joseph Joachim   (1831-1907)

Solo Instrument and Orchestra

Violin

Concerto in D minor (*In the Hungarian Style*) for Violin and Orchestra, Op. 11

☐ Louisville Orchestra / Treger (violin) / Mester (conductor) / Louisville LS–705

Currently, violinists are not interested in Joachim's striking Concerto—or should this read "conductors"? Well, then, if it is a matter of box-office draw, is Wieniawski, Bruch, or Glazunov a stronger name? One doubts it. The Joachim Concerto is totally neglected (as are a dozen others that could be named), and for no good reason.

It consists of a large-spanned *Allegro maestoso,* a rich *Romance,* and a bracing *Finale à la Zingara.* Hungarian sentiments, accents, and rhythms pervade the piece. More to the point is that even with a sizable cadenza in the first movement there is no attempt to impress by the force of fiddling histrionics. Musical, not theatrical content is the prime objective of Joachim's undeniable creative integrity; the technical fancies are fittingly blended into the total.

The approach by the performer must therefore combine musical pertinency with a bravura overlay. Treger provides the combination with great skill. The other recorded entry is on Candide 31064, with Aaron Rosand as the soloist. It is fine, but is trimmed down from the music's actual forty-two-minute length.

Bengt-Emil Johnson   (1936-   )

Instrumental

Piano

Disappearances, for Piano and Tape (1974)

☐ Persson (piano) / Composers Recordings SD–364

The tape consists of prerecorded piano sounds, arranged and transformed. Thus we hear a clearly structured two-dimensional piano duet (despite the totally unpianistic sound of the tape), with the quiet conclusion exactly opposite to the character of the first half of the piece.

Mats Persson does very well with the architectonically bare piano part.

Hunter Johnson (1906-)

Trio for Flute, Oboe, and Piano (1954)

Chamber Music

☐ Baker (flute); Bloom (oboe); Nordli (piano) / Composers Recordings 125 (monaural)

Classical orientation does not lead to dogmatic propriety. The shifting and freeing of the materials in Johnson's three-movement work are illustrative of a twentieth-century romantic viewpoint. No effects spoil the polished texture of Johnson's trio; the substances are all musically (and stylistically) meaningful.

Execution by this ensemble is top-drawer.

John Johnson (?- 1594)

Lavecheo

Instrumental

Two Lutes

☐ Channon and Poulton (lutes) / Nonesuch 73010

Lavecheo consists of two pieces, a *Pavan* and a *Galliard*. The edition used was made by Diana Poulton, who joins with David Channon in playing that has artistic conviction.

Robert Johnson (ca. 1583- ca. 1634)

Full Fathom Five

Vocal

Where the Bee Sucks

Voice and Instrumental Ensemble

☐ Angadi (boy soprano); Walton and Ring (recorders); Kessler (bass viol); Channon (lute) / Nonesuch 73010

Johnson was a Jacobean composer, and included in his output was music for plays by Shakespeare. Both of these texts will be recognized as being from *The Tempest*. The music is totally flavorsome, especially because of the special timbre of the voice and the instrumental quartet.

Robert Sherlaw Johnson. *See under S.*

Roger Johnson (1941-)

Suite for Six Horns

Chamber Music

☐ Horn Club of Los Angeles / Kraft (conductor) / Angel S–36036

No technical polemics illustrated here. Johnson's three-movement piece is richly consonant and presents three formats. The first is totally a delicate two-voice canon (Prologue), the imitation always in echo (muted) form. The Chorale is followed by a medieval-like Fugato that is concluded in homophonic style.

Johnson doesn't write like this anymore. Atonality, electronic instrumentation, and some aleatoric concepts are his current creative interests—all a far cry from this fresh tonalism.

The playing of the group is clean, the pitch marksmanship is impeccable, and the balances perfect. Angel has provided splendid sonics for this recorded performance.

Ben Johnston (1926-   )

Instrumental

Double Bass

Casta Bertram (1969)

☐ Turetzky (contrabass) / Nonesuch 71237

A stockpile of fun (probably better if seen) with material heard to be recorded "then and there" and played back later in accompaniment to the continuing performance. On a recording, what is what is totally lost. Nevertheless, a stockpile of not uncomfortable noises, vocalizing, applause, typewriter timbres, and microbic extracts from such as *Für Elise, Greensleeves, Eine kleine Nachtmusik,* and the finale tune from "the Ninth."

It's all undignified, which makes it absolutely correct. To enjoy, be quite serious about taking the piece unseriously.

Piano

Sonata for Microtonal Piano

☐ Miller (piano) / New World Records NW-203

For understanding the pitch detail of Johnston's piece (totally opposite to the standard piano's tempered tuning, with twelve equally divided pitches in each octave and duplicated in lower and higher equivalents), the composer's descriptive explanation is mandatory: "Only seven of the eighty-eight white and black keys of the piano have octave equivalents, one pair encompassing the distance of a double octave and the remaining six pairs separated by almost the entire length of the keyboard. Thus there are eighty-one different pitches, providing a piano with almost no consonant octaves." There are, of course, many intricacies in the handling of such a both subtle and vivid sound spectrum. These are clearly described by the composer in the very detailed notes that accompany the recording (a sumptuous production covering music by Cowell, Cage, and Nancarrow, in addition, with six solid pages of written matter furnishing a variety of information).

This writer finds Johnston's activization of the available and yet dormant state of pitch much more than casually interesting and simply experimental. It is validated by music of vital consequence in its four movements. The forms cohere and bear out Johnston's statement that his opus is "a tissue of familiarity in radically strange garb." With nonprejudice, a listener should have an affirmative response to the very telling accentuations heard in Johnston's specially pitched speech.

Chamber Music

Duo (1963)

☐ Bertram Turetzky (double bass); Nancy Turetzky (flute) / Advance FGR-1 (monaural)

Lyric serialism that holds fast throughout the three movements—*Prelude, Interim,* and *Flight.* Strongly colored by the contrastive properties of the flute and double bass to begin with, the music provides additional sonorous sensation by the use of microtones.

Johnston's Duo was expressly written for the Turetzkys. They respond beautifully in their playing.

String Quartet No. 2 (1964)

☐ Composers Quartet / Nonesuch 71244

Johnston's Quartet utilizes pure intervals (the opposite of the well-tempered dozen) plus minute microtones. Such pitch distinctions define a very lucid and bright new sound world. With this method, enharmonics (D sharp equals E flat, A equals B double flat, etc.) don't exist, and in fact the term is a technical abomination. Fluctuations in intervallic movement create an intense quality, as in the finale's beginning, where a line curves up and down a quarter tone and then dips a three-quarter-tone distance. Pitches one-tenth of a tone below "normal" and sounds a fifth of a tone apart have a fascinating color, but the principal objective of these pitch choices is not decorative, but integral to the music.

There are three movements in the close-to-fifteen-minute total of the Quartet. The first is a whimsical, wispy scherzo with extremely contrastive portions. Movement 2 sounds contrapuntal, but this is the result of vertical dismemberment. Fantasy rules the finale. It is in this division that the micropitches reflect their greatest impact.

The playing of the Composers Quartet (Raimondi, Ajemian, Zaslov, Barab) is truly amazing. The problems of intonation are monstrous. They are completely conquered.

Betsy Jolas *(1926-)*

Tranche   *Instrumental*

☐ DeCray (harp) / Coronet 2508   *Harp*

Jolas avoids harp clichés such as glissando "broomsweeps," chords, arpeggios, and harmonics. Pitch separation is emphasized, giving the equivalent of flat-plane painting. Such cubistic-like music shows how effective harp writing can be without the gushing romanticism that fills so much of the harp repertoire.

A special effect of one-finger trilling is used. Its timbre-rubbing coloration is dramatically effective and technically difficult. Indeed, Jolas's *Tranche* is positively demanding. Positively, Marcella DeCray meets all the demands.

Coronet has No. 2745 on its record jacket. On the label and as noted in *Schwann* the number is 2508.

André Jolivet *(1905-1974)*

Five Ritual Dances (1939)   *Orchestra*

☐ National Orchestra of the O.R.T.F. / Jolivet (conductor) / Musical Heritage Society MHS–1371

No lace cuffs on this orchestral dress.The rituals are, in turn, of initiation (with an insidious gamut), of heroes (with heavy-laden content), of nuptials (with nuncupative Oriental-like emotions), of rape (rapt in unfervent and repulsive timbre blocks), and of funerealism (with fury contained). No pose, no pedantry, no picayune gestures in this work. Jolivet's orchestral dances are plashy at times, rich elsewhere, yearning in some sections, unshackled in other places. Always of fertile realization, to the point, his set of dances have vibrational beauty in their emphasis on elemental force.

Jolivet the conductor makes certain that all the creative discoveries of Jolivet the composer are made clear. It is certainly a performance that expresses the dramatic continuity of each dance, specifying its form and content. The results obtained by many composers in their conductorial efforts are like the semiliterate language of an uneducated person. As proven here, André Jolivet is one of the exceptions.

Suite transocéane (1955)

☐ Louisville Orchestra / Whitney (conductor) / Louisville 57-2 (monaural)

In the words of the composer, the title has no significance save that it "symbolizes a liaison between the two continents of Europe and America." The composition is not clarified by this vague description.

Despite its line and detail, the music's activity is somewhat hyperactive, and some might even term it fussy. Jolivet's writing is unmistakably highly expert, but does show a fanatical *idée fixe* of wholesale contrapuntalism. The Louisvillers do the best they can with this polyphonic cant.

Brass Ensemble

Fanfare: *Narcisse*

☐ Philip Jones Brass Ensemble / Howarth (conductor) / Argo ZRG-731

Part of the incidental music Jolivet wrote for Racine's play *Britannicus*. Not the average occasional bit, but music that can stand on its firm brass legs. Played expressively.

Solo Instrument and Orchestra

Bassoon

Concerto for Bassoon, String Orchestra, Harp, and Piano (1954)

☐ Jean-François Paillard Chamber Orchestra / Allard (bassoon); d'Arco (piano); Cotelle (harp) / Jolivet (conductor) / Musical Heritage Society MHS-1405

The athletic tone of the music is its cardinal point. Jolivet is insistent that the demeanor of a concerto be (soloistically) extrovert. Accordingly, the bass wind instrument is treated with dogmatic virtuosity—its testimony remains constantly fresh and exciting.

Like the majority of Jolivet's scores, this one is linear, with moderately heavy textures modified by motoric rhapsody. Formally balanced by alternative slow- and fast-tempoed music, it embraces recitative, a concentrated sonata section, a plaintive nocturnal poem (one of the most moving of all Jolivet's creations), and a snappy, multitonal fugue. The bassoonist fraternity will welcome this lusty addition to their very slim repertoire. So should the public, since Jolivet writes a contemporaneously cultured, solidly constructed music that bypasses the latest fads and fashions.

Another welcome is deserving from listeners to the performers. Maurice Allard's playing displays a firm balanced tone quality throughout the entire range of the instrument. Plenty of bassoonish fireworks, but these are not overemphasized to nullify a genuine musical statement. Phenomenally rich sound (originally released by Erato).

Cello

Concerto for Cello and Orchestra (1962)

☐ Orchestra de l'Association des Concerts Lamoureux / Navarra (cello) / Jolivet (conductor) / Musical Heritage Society MHS-1647

Sharply different situations are described in Jolivet's devilishly difficult work (for both soloist and orchestra). The *Méditatif* finds the cello mainly in violinistic registral territory; this essay is a nervously worded polemic. In the *Heeratique* movement the percussion storms alone and against the principal voice. The *Cursif* finale has vigor and raciness, its atmosphere peripatetic for the main part.

Credit on a modest level would be unfair to André Navarra. This is no Lalo or Saint-Saëns situation, and there are no shortcuts to the technical discipline and stamina that must be maintained. Navarra's vitalism is expert.

Second Cello Concerto (1966)

☐ National Orchestra of the O.R.T.F. / Rostropovich (solo cello); Quatrocchi and Emanuele (violins); Lemoine (viola); Zanlonghi (cello); Primentens (double bass) / Jolivet (conductor) / Musical Heritage Society MHS–1371

A cellistic triumph of pyrotechnical abandon over plot, despite five connected movements which begin with *Allant* and end with *Animé*. Jolivet is completely indifferent to the rigors he demands of his soloist, accompanied by a string orchestra and five soloists within it. Only a Rostropovich would be interested in conquering an atonic, violent work like this one, since he, contrary to the top international soloists, is receptive to *fully* contemporary music similar to the Jolivet (Foss's *Cello Concert*, for example, which no other cellist has dared to perform). No wonder that Jolivet said that "no audacity in writing would frighten Rostropovich" and therefore he gave "free vent" to his imagination when he composed his Second Cello Concerto in 1966.

Jolivet's creation is extremely loose and tends to loosen and lose itself in daredevil cello writing, but that offers its own brand of artistic excitement.

It is impossible not to mention the world record for a *single* liner-note sentence in the MHS release. The original text was by Bernard Gavoty, with English translation by Harry Halbreich. The sentence occupies twenty-two lines of type; the word count covers a staggering total of 103! Remember it for future trivia contests.

Chant de Linos for Solo Flute, Violin, Viola, Cello, and Harp (1944)   *Flute*

☐ Lardé (flute); Sanchez (violin); Lequien (viola); Degenne (cello); Jamet (harp) / Musical Heritage Society MHS–883

Originally Jolivet composed the *Chant de Linos* for a competition at the Paris Conservatoire. It called for flute and piano. Later it was reset for solo flute with harp and string trio as the accompaniment, though this support is never mundane.

The writing can be classified as non-Germanic postromantic poematicism, but in Jolivetian fashion rhapsodic fantasy becomes the creative haberdasher. There are sections that blend one into the other—the piece moves from a cadenza-recitative into a "Funeral Lamentation," which is followed by a portion described as "the mourning song interrupted by cries," another cadenza, and so on.

Candid exposition is furnished by the performers, with Christian Lardé turning in a very spectacular interpretation.

Concerto for Flute and String Orchestra (1949)

☐ Lamoureux String Orchestra, Paris / Rampal (flute) / Jolivet (conductor) / Musical Heritage Society MHS–1015

A four-movement work telescoped into two parts in which chromatic expansiveness reaches the ultimate point. Jolivet's landscape is full of action. There is in his depiction a rhetorical grandeur and verbosity, almost Germanic (once over lightly), but the French accent is, naturally, much less guttural. The flute rides herd over the strings, but the strings are not gentle, polite, refined color spokesmen; *divisi*s abound, pizzicato and arco doublings give percussion plus smoothness, and there is a plentiful supply of textural shifts.

Rampal glides through the pyrotechnics of the piece. He hits extreme D's, runs through flutter-tongue passages and bitter registral changes as though he were zipping off a simple one-octave scale. His dynamic control is startling.

Suite en concert for Flute and Percussion (Second Flute Concerto) (1965)

☐ Rampal (flute); Casadesus, Drouet, Masson, and François (percussion) / Jolivet (conductor) / Musical Heritage Society MHS-1015

A triumph of color in this four-movement work. Lyrical panchromaticism is evidenced in parts 1, 2, and 4, fully conveyed by the principal tempo indications: *Modéré, Stabile*, and *Calme*. The only vehemence is in the third movement, marked *Hardiment*. Though this has violent musical verbiage, never does Jolivet depart from poetic expressivity. The music is spontaneous and not formally designed.

Any music performed by Jean-Pierre Rampal will be done so in a distinguished and expressive manner. Here again this is proved. The quartet of percussionists parallel him in their technical endowments.

Harp

Concerto for Harp and Chamber Orchestra (1952)

☐ French Radio-Philharmonic Orchestra (O.R.T.F.) / Laskine (harp) / Jolivet (conductor) / Musical Heritage Society MHS-1079

Because of the harp's inability to command his usual ultrachromatic language, Jolivet utilizes a variety of modes which result in a diversity as close to his harmonic style as possible. This makes feasible a less parochial music than would otherwise result.

Laskine's performance is a heady one (the demands are of Paganini-like order). More percussiveness would be welcome in places, but this need is minor within the major triumph she enjoys.

Ondes Martenot

Concerto for Ondes Martenot and Orchestra (1947)

☐ French Radio-Philharmonic Orchestra (O.R.T.F.) / Loriod (ondes Martenot) / Jolivet (conductor) / Musical Heritage Society MHS-1079

No facile methods in Jolivet's output. There is a kinship with expressionism here, a partial devotion to Scriabin-like tonal tautology, and a total devotion to cosmic musical philosophy. One must be patient while the initial movement unfolds, and cast aside memories of movie scores aroused by the special sepulchral sonorousnesses of the solo instrument. Then the extraordinary affirmation of Jolivet's score will be revealed—by way of the fantastic scherzo-minded, diabolical musical montage of the middle movement.

Both performance and recording are true to every point of measurement. Every note on the packed score staves is registered correctly. Liner notes tend to puff up performances beyond truth. Not in this case. When it is stated that Loriod "gives a fresh aspect to the concerto" and that it is "masterfully played," a square-dealing statement is being made.

Trumpet

Concertino for Trumpet, Piano, and String Orchestra (1948)

☐ English Chamber Orchestra / Thibaud (trumpet) / Constant (conductor) / Deutsche Grammophon 2530289

Despite free tonality Jolivet's structure is as carefully organized as that of those who use pandiatonic orientation. It is as controlled as works employing fluid tonality which sprays from a central source. The form of an introduction, a theme, and a set of variations exemplifies neat and concentrated design. Within are the potentials today's composer expects from a brass instrument.

No nineteenth-century-concerto décor here. Jolivet abhors that tradition. He describes the soloist's role in such music as that of "a virtuoso chatterbox." His viewpoint is proven by the expert contemporary logic of the Concertino. It does not include one measure of small talk.

Effective contributions from soloist, orchestra, and conductor.

Concerto No. 2 for Trumpet (1954)

☐ Orchestre de l'Association des Concerts Lamoureux / André (trumpet); d'Arco (piano) / Jolivet (conductor) / Westminster Gold 8108

All the packin's of jazz (which have led to a number of ballet settings of the Concerto), with the trumpet using the "wah-wah" mute, blueing the notes, growling, and prancing in top-class, dancy-acrobatic fashion. The slow movement is cool-jazz stuff, the finale wild and even a bit low-down-primitive, though it is indicated as a "Hommage to Chabrier."

The title on the Westminster release is false. It reads that, in addition to the trumpet, there is "brass, piano and percussion." The last, yes! Fourteen instruments divided among two players. The piano, also yes! But no brass. The balance of the instrumentation is for two flutes, clarinet, English horn, two saxes, harp, and double bass.

Maurice André's playing has uninhibited spontaneity and, where it should, splendid warmth. He has an unfailing ear for the style that Jolivet has adopted for his piece, and everything rings true. The supporting cast is just as bravura-tuned in its playing.

Incantation

☐ Rampal (alto flute) / Musical Heritage Society MHS–1015

The freedom of unencumbered improvisation, but contained in its essence. Jolivet's *Incantation* is quiet, seamless, as if formed from one single phrase in its performing-time length of two minutes and forty seconds.

Nowhere is the original subtitle of the piece indicated—*Pour que l'image devienne symbole*—though the liner notes give its translation, "that the image may become the symbol." Liner notes, front- and back-cover headings, and label copy are in unified error in calling this piece an "Incantation in G major" for flute solo. It is an "Incantation," but for a flute *in G*—the alto flute. Jolivet's spiritualistic piece is in no way "in G major." (Alternate versions were made by Jolivet for solo ondes Martenot and for unaccompanied violin.)

Instrumental

Alto Flute

Suite en concert for Cello Solo (1965)

☐ Navarra (cello) / Musical Heritage Society MHS–1030

It has seemed that the law surrounding the writing of unaccompanied string works commands preludes, fugues, simulated contrapuntalism, neobaroque concepts, and the like. Good enough, but there is room (and it is rarely realized) for more colorful, freer supports for the medium. Thus Jolivet's *Suite en concert,* with its meditative *Improvisation,* the pizzicato decorations of the *Sérénade* (marked *Fantasque et désinvolte*), and the final *Sonata* (marked *Véhément*) with its registral virtuosity as parts of the work's five-part span.

André Navarra plays this coloristic personification of the medium with captivating élan and command. There are few who can match the way he presents his performance.

Cello

Five Incantations for Flute Solo (1936)

☐ Rampal (flute) / Musical Heritage Society MHS–1015

Flute

Jolivet's constant and passionate belief in the incantatory properties of music is here again illustrated—and magnificently documented. To hear Rampal's playing is to be won over to Jolivet's credo.

Each of the set is basically descriptive: "To welcome the negotiators . . ."; "That the child to be born may be a son"; "That the harvest that will grow . . ."; "For a serene communion . . ."; and "At the funeral of the chief." Contrastive colorations help clarify these pieces: flutter tonguing in the first, repetitive and "bent" tones in the second, curved lines in the next two pieces, and a synthesis of all the previous conduct in the final piece. No musical memory identifies Jolivet's fascinating five-part flute essay. It is strictly his own invention—a fresh conception of what is possible to convey with a homophonic instrument playing alone.

Guitar

Comme un Prélude

☐ Santos (guitar) / Musical Heritage Society MHS-1916

The first of a pair of *Etudes de concert. Comme un Prélude* consists of quiet, reticent short phrases, as though Jolivet considered the instrument capable only of muted timbre. The conception is restrained but rewarding.

Two Guitars

Serenade (1956)

☐ Ito and Dorigny (guitars) / Delos FY008

No pedantic response to instrumental demeanor or mechanical regard for form is to be expected from André Jolivet. The Serenade addresses separate national styles in each of the four movements, but in directing his attention thus, Jolivet retains his own creative personality.

Only the first movement's heading gives any hint of the music's contents, a *Praeludio e canzona* that evokes Italy; the material is colored by harmonics. Movement 2 (*Allegro trepidante*) and movement 4 (*Con allegria*) are concerned with Spain and America. Both are percussive and dissonant; a borrowing from Falla appears in the former, while the latter luxuriates in jazz. The *Andante malinconico* (part 3) has a bitter-sweet cordiality toward French melody.

The performers convey the passion that pervades the entire score. Rhythms are never loose; this is a fully integrated presentation. Delos, however, should look to its liner notes; the translation of the original French is horrible. What is one to make of a statement that reads "rythmic [sic] subtleties which the apparent simplicity of the $\frac{4}{4}$ time in which it is written"? And, for the record, Jolivet studied with Paul Le Flem, not "Le Flen."

Organ and Trumpet

Arioso barocco for Trumpet and Organ (1969)

☐ Bilgrim (organ); André (trumpet) / Musical Heritage Society MHS-3340

Significantly successful in its timbre combination. There are exceedingly few contemporary works in this medium. Sensitively colored by the performers.

Choral

Chorus and Instrumental Ensemble

Suite liturgique (1942)

☐ Female Chorus of the O.R.T.F. / Pierlot (oboe and English horn); Bex (cello); Laskine (harp) / Jouineau (conductor) / Musical Heritage Society MHS-1658

Orientalistic modalism and sacred motivation combine in Jolivet's eight-movement work for female chorus and instrumental trio. Three of the movements are for the instruments alone.

The style is much simpler than found in Jolivet's orchestral compositions and various concerti.

Charles Jones (1910-   )

Sonatina for Violin and Piano (1942)

☐ Zukofsky (violin); Kalish (piano) / Composers Recordings S–283

Jones' short work shows that he has reaped the benefits of the swirling tonal combines and rhythmic riches of Darius Milhaud. This is a Canadian-born, naturalized American's view of French pantonality and rhythmic freedom.

The team of Zukofsky and Kalish is excellent here, especially in fluidly presenting the rhythmic permutations within the piece.

String Quartet No. 6 (1970)

☐ New York String Quartet / Composers Recordings S–283

Fantasy proportions in this one-movement work. The father of it all is neoclassic diction, but here extended into enlarged chromaticism and the use of jagged intervallic punctuations. Nicely colored with pizzicati and nicely flavored with harmonics.

Collier Jones (20th cent.)

Four Movements for Five Brass (1957)

☐ New York Brass Quintet / Desto 6401

Jaunty partnership of jazzy rhythmics with Stravinskian neoclassic syntax. Nice music-making to be listed on the lighter side of the brass-music ledger. The playing of the New Yorkers is excellently calculated with finely scaled dynamics and balances.

Jeffrey Jones (1944-   )

Pièce mouvante (1974)

☐ Hiraga (piano) / Composers Recordings SD–336

Beginning with the repetitive statement of a raw (small-formationed) set of pitches, Jones's music then bursts out of its shell. Though variation tactics are recognizable, they are irregular ones, and the mosaic produced is extremely effective. Freely structured as the music is, order—fresh order, that is—can be perceived in this fine nine-minute creation. It is extremely well presented by Noriko Hiraga.

Kelsey Jones (1922-   )

Rondo for Flute (1963)

☐ Duschenes (flute) / Orion 6911

Clear form, as proposed. The piece is minus any special effects, but beautifully contoured with registral differences that give off flashes of light and splendor. The Rondo is just as beautifully played by Mario Duschenes.

Robert Jones II (late 16th cent.)

Vocal

Voice with Accompaniment

Sweet Kate

☐ Poulter (soprano); Brown (tenor); Channon (lute) / Nonesuch 73010

The duo is written in imitative style to heighten the light-laced text concerning—what else?—a man and a maid. Excellent diction on the part of the vocalists.

Samuel Jones (1935-)

Orchestra

Let Us Now Praise Famous Men

☐ Houston Symphony Orchestra / Jones (conductor) / Composers Recordings S-347

Jones's deeply expressive work is based on folk hymns associated with the Shenandoah Valley. These are developed into a strong interweave within a contemporary modal fabric. In great part the orchestration (regardless of dynamics) is declamatory and includes the special color of off-stage flutes.

The composer-led performance has conviction. It marks the return to the recording field of the Houston organization after a long absence.

String Orchestra

Elegy for String Orchestra

☐ Houston Symphony Orchestra / Jones (conductor) / Composers Recordings S-347

The composer's reaction shortly after the assassination of John F. Kennedy. Jones's piece is sorrow-shot music with a nobility within it that makes it one of the most telling musical works produced in the wake of the horrible event, if not *the* most telling.

Joseph Jongen (1873-1953)

Instrumental

Flute

Danse lente for Flute and Harp

☐ Vito (harp); Roberts (flute) / Orion 7039

The presence and urbanity of Debussy is heard in this Belgian composer's piece, a pure solo for the flute, with harp back-up. It is played persuasively.

Léon Jongen (1884-1969)

Instrumental

Piano

Campéador (1932)

☐ Berman (piano) / Monitor MCS-2135 (monaural)

Campéador was originally for orchestra. The piano version was made by the composer.

Lazar Berman colors his performance beautifully. With such masterful musicianship one prefers the piano version to the larger setting.

Scott Joplin *(1868 - 1917)*

The Easy Winners

Wall Street Rag

Instrumental

Piano

☐ Bolcom (piano) / Nonesuch 71257

Wall Street Rag has a gentle tenderness. The other piece is termed *A Ragtime Two-step*. It has bounce. The skill of William Bolcom in styling his playing has as much impressiveness as Joplin's creations.

Treemonisha (1911)

*Opera
and Dramatic
Music*

☐ Houston Grand Opera Orchestra and Chorus / Balthrop (soprano); Allen and Johnson (mezzo-sopranos); Rayam, Hicks, and Ramson (tenors); Bazemore (bass-baritone); White, Harney, Duckens, and Pierson (basses) / Schuller (conductor) / Deutsche Grammophon 2707083

There has been much ado about Joplin's opera, but don't expect something that isn't forthcoming. *Treemonisha* may be called an opera, but actually Joplin's work is a musical and sharply imitative of styles that range and meander from MacDowell to Lehár and from Gilbert and Sullivan to Victor Herbert. It touches bases with rag, barber-shop harmony, folk tunes, hymns, and even (according to Gunther Schuller) Handel and Weber.

Be this as it may, the concept hangs together loosely, with its episodic content cutting into dramatic continuity (further proof that it is a musical or at best an operetta), but it doesn't fall apart. And it is mostly entertaining in its unblended blend.

Perhaps if it hadn't been for the American Bicentennial fever *Treemonisha* might never have achieved the sumptuous production that eventually reached Broadway. And to realize that a German company issued the recording is still another oddity in the history of the piece—exceedingly odd when Joplin discs of all types by Angel, Columbia, Vanguard, RCA, and others glut the market.

The production is excellent, and Gunther Schuller's direction (he is also to be credited with the orchestration) is first-class throughout. The singing is, for the greater part, likewise. Diction? The usual lack of definition.

Joplin / **Louis Chauvin (1883 - 1908)**

Heliotrope Bouquet

Instrumental

Piano

☐ Bolcom (piano) / Nonesuch 71257

A slow-drag two-step for which the younger man provided most of the material. Simply a delightful presentation that has full style know-how.

Werner Josten   (1885-1963)

Orchestra

Jungle

☐ American Symphony Orchestra / Stokowski (conductor) / Composers Recordings S-267

Despite use of African drums and a lion's roar, Josten's piece has a fancier title than the music itself, which derives from Germanic romanticism. Nice colors, however, and the sort of stuff that Stoky always liked. In this case he played the work several times over his career. Performance is O.K.

Symphony in F (1936)

☐ Polish National Radio Orchestra / Strickland (conductor) / Composers Recordings S-225

Josten's pithy (fifteen and a half minutes) Symphony in F, first heard in Boston in 1936, deserves revival in the concert hall. The two movements are full of the neat dissonances that signal the accents of neoclassic speech. The inner conjunction of rhythmic vitality is an asset in Josten's work, as is the very appropriate orchestration. No thick, fatty substances inside the texture. All the colors are concentrated, the weights distributed in a manner equating huge chamber music. It is very telling.

Strickland has produced here one of the very best performances of the many he has to his credit of music by American composers.

String Orchestra

Concerto sacro I (1925)

Concerto sacro II (1925)

☐ American Symphony Orchestra / Del Tredici (piano) / Stokowski (conductor) / Composers Recordings S-200

Each concerto is in two movements. Those of the first are *The Annunciation* and *The Miracle; Lament* and *Sepulchre and Resurrection* are those of the second concerto. There are further subdivisions in the former composition: eight uninterrupted sections (*Mary's Dream; Dialogue Between Mary and the Angel,* etc.) within *The Annunciation* and five in *The Miracle.* For the greater part the titled references become musically merged. Josten's neoclassic religious sentiments can well be considered as an absolute piece without any aesthetic discords arising.

Stokowski treats the music as a total chunk and bypasses specific definition. Little harm, especially with the usual special string warmth that only Stoky can engender. Since the works are for string orchestra with piano obbligato, the credits should rightfully read ''members of'' or ''the strings of'' the American Symphony Orchestra. Buried in the liner notes is the fact that David Del Tredici (a fine composer as well as pianist) is at the keyboard. Neither the jacket nor the label copy gives mention of this fact.

Chamber Music

Canzona seria

☐ Dunkel (flute); Krilov (oboe); Shifrin (clarinet); Scribner (bassoon); Cooper (piano) / Composers Recordings S-267

Canzona seria was originally composed for first and second violas, first and second cellos, and double bass. It was written in 1937, not 1940 as the CRI note indicates. The second setting was made in 1957, and first performed in the same year.

The music is less serious than the title implies. Presented acceptably; noted as having been recorded under the supervision of Leopold Stokowski.

Adoration

☐ Hanks (tenor); Friedberg (piano) / Duke University Press DWRM-7501 (monaural)

A John Keats text set in late German romantic style. Acceptably sung.

Joseph Julian (1948-   )

Akasha for Contrabass and Electronic Tape (1972)

☐ Turetzky (bass) / Finnadar 9015

Pointillism fragmented and fractured, an attempt to musically parallel a painting style found in north India termed *Akasha*. The demonstration gives off an improvisational quality.

Gilles Jullien (ca. 1650-1703)

Prélude du 5ᵉ ton

☐ Hansen (organ) / Nonesuch 71170

A trisectioned work which mixes stateliness with a good amount of imitative antiphony. Good playing in terms of textural clarity and color values.

Paul Juon (1872-1940)

Berceuse from Four Pieces, Op. 28

☐ Heifetz (violin); Chotzinoff (piano) / RCA ARM4-0942 (monaural)

Juon is one of the many composers in the "overlooked school." I believe him ready for rediscovery and urge examination, especially, of his chamber music.

This example, the third piece in the suite, is sensitive and inventive without an iota of sentimentality. Heifetz plays it with the proper warmth but does not overdo a single note. The recording is an old acoustic affair, but don't let that keep you away.

K

Dmitri Kabalevsky (1904-)

The Comedians, Op. 26

Orchestra

☐ RCA Victor Symphony Orchestra / Kondrashin (conductor) / RCA LSC-2398
☐ Vienna State Opera Orchestra / Golschmann (conductor) / Vanguard S-207

Kabalevsky's ten-part suite is for small orchestra. The score is a bit sardonic, the wit bathing in watered sugar for the most part.

Though lightweight in scope, there is opportunity for varied realizations of it. Kondrashin, with a pick-up orchestra, drives the music at high speed, and paramount are the vim, vigor, and vitality of the performance. More theatrical, thereby. Golschmann's conception is more chaste, slower in tempo for the most part, and yet its refined factor has its own appeal. Both interpretations present a sense of rightness even though they have different objectives. RCA has brighter sound.

Overture to Colas Breugnon, Op. 24/90

☐ Chicago Symphony Orchestra / Reiner (conductor) / RCA VICS-1068

The best possible portrayal. Good zip, clean as a whistle, and at a tempo that defines each note without letting go of speed. (Toscanini used this piece as an encore during his tours with the NBC Orchestra and recorded it; it was released as part of a 78-rpm album. If there has been any transfer to long-play, this writer has not been able to locate it.)

Romeo and Juliet, Op. 55

☐ State Radio Orchestra / Kabalevsky (conductor) / Monitor S-2078E (monaural)

There are ten sections in these "musical sketches to Shakespeare's tragedy." This is flavorsome, tuneful, nice-to-listen-to, nice-to-read-by music, the weave of its material made mostly from Tchaikovskian yarns. One can consider the performance a professional one. The sound is only fair.

Symphony No. 4 (1956)

☐ Leningrad Philharmonic Orchestra / Kabalevsky (conductor) / Monitor 2007 (monaural)

Large-scaled (forty minutes), Kabalevsky's Symphony No. 4 displays a tight emotive waist throughout its first three movements, even in its Scherzo, which features a seven-ply metrical format (alternating $\frac{4}{4}$ and $\frac{3}{4}$ measures). In the finale the atmosphere brightens after, once again, a sombre introduction, with march pace and contrapuntal optimism in the form of a fugato.

Kabalevsky scores solidly—in terms of orchestration and his symphonic scenario. The Leningrad outfit does well with the piece, though its sound only has limited depth.

*Solo
Instrument
and
Orchestra*

Piano

Concerto No. 3 (*Youth*) in D major for Piano and Orchestra, Op. 50

☐ Westphalian Symphony Orchestra / Preston (piano) / Freeman (conductor) / Orion 74149

One of a set of three concertos (the others are for violin and cello respectively) dedicated to Soviet youth, hence the subtitle. But the work's emollient harmonies and tonal charm and gaiety do not pigeonhole the work for youth concerts (where it most often appears anyway) or to be played only by the young (though they do considerably). Tchaikovsky it ain't, in power or depth (but related in its melos), so it isn't played by the soloistic bigwigs. Too bad, for audiences are being deprived of a fine work by such bias and snobbishness.

Perhaps Robert Preston's communicative and colorful performance will trigger a response that will correct this situation. His is top-drawer playing, and the high standard he sets is matched by Paul Freeman's dynamic direction of the orchestra.

A most interesting old mono recording must be mentioned, with Gilels as soloist, on Monitor S–2061E. Unfortunately, the sound isn't good, but Gilels is worth anyone's listening time.

Violin

Violin Concerto, Op. 48

☐ Royal Philharmonic Orchestra / Zukerman (violin) / Foster (conductor) / Columbia M–30644

Kabalevsky wrote a trilogy of concerti; the second is for cello, and the third is the widely played Piano Concerto (see under *Solo Instrument and Orchestra: piano*). All are dedicated to Soviet youth, but not specifically directed for young peoples' performance. The Violin Concerto, fluent and succinctly tonal, clear and precise, needs a first-class artist, like Zukerman, who proceeds to polish off the work with the greatest élan. There are three movements. Note the final movement's cadenza, with its twinkling glance at the cadenza section in Mendelssohn's fiddle concerto.

Instrumental

Piano

Children's Pieces

☐ Kabalevsky (piano) / Monitor 2039 (monaural)

Music of color and balance, tonal tact and conclusive charm. Four of the pieces (including *A Short Story* and *Toccatina*) are from Fifteen Children's Pieces, Op. 27; one, *The Clown*, is drawn from Twenty-four Little Pieces, Op. 39; the Little Rondo stands by itself, and is minus opus identity.

There isn't a false note in the music. All of it is unsophisticated but will not bore sophisticated ears. Kabalevsky plays his creative inventions with perfect skill, diversified color, and strongly shaped rhythm.

(*Schwann* lumps all the pieces under Op. 27 and also gives an incorrect total of pieces in the recording.)

Sonata No. 3, Op. 46

☐ Drake (piano) / Orion 75168

Conventional but never dull, with a touch here from and a nod there to Prokofiev, especially in the outer movements.

Drake plays the Sonata with nice suavity and with good rhythmic bite, as required. A bit more motion in the slow movement would not be amiss. Otherwise very little alteration could well be made.

Sonatina in C major, Op. 13, No. 1

☐ Kabalevsky (piano) / Monitor 2039 (monaural)

This piece has reached the status of a teaching classic, combining the values of worthy music and not too difficult didactic source material. It has just the exact amount of contemporaryism for the student who must be led carefully into twentieth-century territory. The last movement, marked Presto, is like a heady toccata. Kabalevsky matches his creative skills with pianistic ones.

Improvisation, Op. 21, No. 1

Violin

☐ Ricci (violin); Pommers (piano) / MCA 2537

After some introductory sectional material, Kabalevsky touches bases with full-fledged melodic sweep. It's not difficult to identify Kabalevsky's residence from this piece's somewhat Tchaikovskian consanguinity.

Shakespeare Sonnets, Op. 52 (Excerpts)

Vocal

Voice with Accompaniment

☐ Reizen (bass); Kabalevsky (piano) / Monitor 2020 (monaural)

Slavic Shakespearean examples, with the music contours of the former matching the texts of the latter. The use of a bass voice emphasizes the Russian ethos found in Kabalevsky's three songs, the second, fourth, and sixth of the total ten in the cycle.

The performance is a faithful one, marked by the specialness of having the composer as the pianist.

Colas Breugnon, Op. 24/90

Opera and Dramatic Music

☐ Orchestra and Chorus of Stanislavsky–Nemirovich–Danchenko Musical Theater / Kayevchenko and Chitikova (sopranos); Isakova (mezzo-soprano); Mishchevsky and Gutorovich (tenors); Maximenko (baritone); Boldin (bass-baritone); Dudarev (bass) / Zhemchuzhin (conductor) / Columbia/Melodiya M3–33588

Kabalevsky's opera, based on a Romain Rolland story, is old history in terms of its overture. The complete work is little known, but is worthy, and has all the necessary operatic ingredients—unhappy marriage, other romance, a plague, destruction of the hero's life work (he is a French wood carver), etc. The treatment is lively, sharply tonal, and rhythmically clear in style; the score includes some quotations from authentic French melodies.

A well-made recorded production, though the voices are only average—except for Leonid Boldin as Colas Breugnon, who gets top honors.

Miloslav Kabeláč (1908-)

Scherzo from Eight Inventions, Op. 45

Percussion

☐ University of Michigan Percussion Ensemble / Owen (conductor) / Golden Crest CRS–4145

As structurally clear as any scherzo for totally pitched instruments (two in this instance, both xylophones). Also clear in its performance. The other instruments are cymbals, temple blocks, field and snare drums.

Mauricio Kagel (1931-)

Instrumental

Organ

Improvisation ajoutée (1961)

☐ Tudor (organ), assisted by Lucier, Mumma, and Sahl / Odyssey 32160158

The title leads one to expect formal freedom and here it is. This is a real fun piece that would be spoiled if it had form. The content is akin to a compilation of organ vocabulary set forth in slang, with sonic puns—a Mardi Gras shindig on an organ console. Every organ cliché is heard: the Vox Humana spirit, the mixture stops further mixed, crawly sounds, the old Roxy thunder. The gamut is all the way from peaches-and-cream quintupled triads to all-devouring tone clusters that seem a mile long in tonal scope.

The three assistants (Kagel calls them "registrants") make changes of registration during Tudor's performance. They also add "business" to Tudor's playing by handclapping, laughing, shouting, humming, and whistling. In one place one of the assistants emits a midget vocalise. Truly a real *jeu d'orgue*.

Choral

Chorus Alone

Hallelujah (1967)

☐ Schola Cantorum, Stuttgart / Gottwald (conductor) / Deutsche Grammophon 137010

A complete crusade against ordinary choral statements, even those used in far-advanced styles. *Hallelujah* is here recorded in one of its variety of versions by sixteen unaccompanied voices, with the singers occasionally blowing on organ pipes. There are touches of vocal violence as well as screeching, shouting, accordion effects, and cantillated portions snidely delivered.

Let it be said that whatever Kagel has in mind as the function of his work, it is theatricality that predominates. However, if there is a hidden, mystical purpose here, it is technically postulated by colorful, irrational vocal methods and one need not seek for the meaning.

Electronic Music

Transición II for Piano, Percussion, and Two Magnetic Tapes (1959)

☐ Tudor (piano); Caskel (percussion) / Mainstream 5003

Stockhausen's splintering of tempo in his *Zeitmasse* is seized on by Kagel in his composition. The tempo unrest is changed by accumulation in a manner that equates tense (i.e., classifies time) in terms of music. The past is signified by recordings of material made prior to the actual performance; the present is the performance itself, and the future blends with the present since sections are taped during performance for later use simultaneously with the then-current performance. Simple? Yes! Chance? Yes! Valid? Why not!

Erich Itor Kahn (1905-1956)

Instrumental

Piano

Ciaccona dei tempi di guerra, Op. 10
Eight Inventions, Op. 7 (Nos. 1, 2, 3, 5, 6)
Short Piano Piece (1951)

☐ Kahn (piano) / Composers Recordings 188 (monaural)

The beautifully observing creativity of Kahn's music deals with positive matters: a merging of the classical tradition with Schoenbergian freedom (though the exactness of dodecaphonic technique is not bypassed).

Kahn's music has tremendous power, especially the *Ciaccona,* which combines a freely treated twelve-tone bass theme with strong frictions that are derived from free-roving tonality. This kind of fusion is not easy to accomplish, but the forty variations are fruitfully exposed with structural balance and colorful dramaticism.

The Short Piano Piece (from Op. 12) depends almost solely on serial procedures. This method is also utilized in the Inventions, but is contrasted here with bitonality (No. 1) and with major and minor companionship and tonality in serial statement (No. 3, based on a Brahms theme). Especially compelling are Kahn's rhythms. These do not backbite with Bartókian ferocity, but have similar incisiveness in their play within the designs.

Kahn's reputation as a sensitive and technically expert pianist is proven by the playing heard on this recording. Aside from the value of definitive statements of his music, his spontaneity, marvelous shaping of textural weights and changes, and expressivity produce musical statements of singular poetic-dramatic strength. The sound is amazingly good, considering that the recording was made from a tape of a German (Hessischer Rundfunk) broadcast in June of 1955.

Vassili Kalinnikov   *(1866-1901)*

Symphony No. 1 in G minor (1897)   *Orchestra*

☐ Moscow Philharmonic / Kondrashin (conductor) / Melodiya/Angel S-40173

This used to grace many major symphony programs, then dropped down to the top minor orchestras' programs and, in turn, to the low minors (the community-orchestra league). Now even the last seem to have turned their backs on this nicely turned, nicely orchestrated, nicely imitative (à la Borodin and Tchaikovsky) symphony.

Unfair. The first movement has a swell main theme and a beautifully flourishing contrasting idea. There are nice bell-like sounds in the slow movement, and a tightly laced Scherzo. The only minus sign applies to the lengthy and redundantly structured finale, which marks the major problem with so many composers of the old Russian school. But it isn't sufficient to cancel the values of the preceding portions.

The symphony has a built-in playing ease. It can fail only if a conductor tries to juice it up and overdefine by interpretative bargaining. No such criticism applies here.

Symphony No. 2 in A major (1898)

☐ U.S.S.R. Symphony Orchestra / Svetlanov (conductor) / Melodiya/Angel S-40132

Rarely performed, but just as viable as the once fairly often heard initial symphony. Kalinnikov's creative beat is in the same rhythm as Glazunov, Glière, and Gretchaninov. Svetlanov styles the symphony superbly; the sound is marvelous.

Friedrich Kalkbrenner   *(1785-1849)*

Concerto No. 1 in D minor for Piano and Orchestra, Op. 61   *Solo Instrument and Orchestra*

☐ Hamburg Symphony / Kann (piano) / Beissel (conductor) / Turnabout 34561

The common currency of virtuosity pays the way in the opening *Allegro maestoso.* In the slow movement the solo voice is front and center practically throughout, and ditto for the light-hearted *Rondo vivace.*

Piano

Hans Kann delights with the quality of his playing—warm here, flashy there, and always sound. And always a performance with authority. The orchestra is an adequate helpmate.

Instrumental

Grande sonate brillante **in A flat major, Op. 177**

Piano

☐ Ruiz (piano) / Genesis 1016

Classical form with romantic radiation. This joining brings considerable attention to scintillating passage work and melismatic embroidery that mark salonistic speech. There is less attention to inherent development and more emphasis on the flowery enlargement of miniature propositions. Nonetheless, the piece is magnificently written for the instrument and in that respect most convincing.

Ruiz has all the technical facility and delivers a spontaneous-sounding presentation. He fully understands the essential feelings of Kalkbrenner's period piece.

Chamber Music

Grand Quintet for Piano, Clarinet, Horn, Cello, and Bass

☐ Boehm (piano); Bloom (clarinet); Howard (horn); Sherry (cello); Levine (bass) / Turnabout 34506

''Grand'' in terms of attention to the piano; the paired strings and single wind and brass instruments are subsidiary in this conception of chamber music. Not an unexpected viewpoint from a composer who was a piano virtuoso (a piano manufacturer as well!).

The playing is beautifully polished, and Boehm's consideration of the leading part is very musicianly.

Johann Wenzel Kalliwoda *(1801 - 1866)*

Orchestra

Symphony No. 1 in F minor, Op. 7

☐ Prague Symphony Orchestra / Rohan (conductor) / Candide 31073

No secret genius or fancy is disclosed here, but this is certainly a respectable and always interesting nineteenth-century orchestral work. Four movements, naturally, with the outer ones avoiding anything but serious demeanor. The *Menuetto* is played with the throttle closed, which does not carry out the *allegro assai* tempo designation, but otherwise the performance is first class. A hearing of Kalliwoda's symphony, written at the age of twenty-five, forces a change in the general opinion that he is a faceless composer without even minimal stature.

Jan Kapr *(1914-   )*

Chamber Music

Dialogues for Flute and Harp: Nos. 1, 3, 4, 9, 10 (1965)

☐ Baron (flute); Platilova (harp) / Serenus 12064

Music that is a product of subtle folkloric weave in a cloth of modal and twelve-tone design. Always colorful. Always different. One of the pieces is for a single instrument, the flute (No. 3). Most fascinating and truly unforgettable is the finale, containing wailing, crying, and gliding sounds in the flute. The effect is probing; Baron's performance of this concluding movement is of uncommon significance.

For the remaining set of Dialogues *see below*.

Dialogues for Flute and Harp: Nos. 6, 7, 8, 2, 5 (1965)

☐ Baron (flute); Platilova (harp) / Serenus 12042

The remaining set of Kapr's Dialogues for Flute and Harp (*see above*). The last of the set, No. 5, is dainty-dancy; the next to last piece, No. 2, is stimulated by bent flute sounds. "Dialogue" No. 7 is actually a monologue for the harp. Most colorful is No. 8, with whistling and flutter tones for the flute and an ingenious effect for the harp, produced by small wooden paddles attached to the fingers of gloves worn by the performer.

Superb playing by this team. Theirs is a captivating rendition framed by magnificent sound (in both sets of the Dialogues).

Rotazione 9 (The Crystal) (1967)

☐ Bohuslav Martinu Piano Quartet / Serenus 12042

The form derives from the concept of a rotating nine-angled crystal. As a result there are many gliding and sweeping sounds (the various angles and intensities of light falling upon the crystal's planes). The incessant motion of Kapr's piece bears out the crystal's rotation.

Applause at the end, indicating live performance. It took place at the 1969 Czech Festival of New Music.

String Quartet No. 6 for Baritone Voice and Strings (1962)

☐ Novak Quartet / Jedlicka (baritone) / Serenus 12042

Kapr's use of the voice is principally devoted to a broad declamatory style; the voice is woven into and around dramatic string writing with a predilection for the darker side of the palette. There is no sense of accompaniment in this moving quintet—moving despite the fact that no text is supplied, not even a précis of what is being expressed by the vocalist. Never mind, just sit back and enjoy the work on an absolute basis. It has dignity and pathos and a controlled grandeur.

Dalibor Jedlicka's voice is a rich instrument with a viola-like burnished quality that blends beautifully with the expressive playing of his Czech colleagues.

Woodcuts: Four Pieces for Eight Instruments (1973)

☐ Edward Tarr Brass Ensemble / Serenus 12066

A tight packaging of timbre using four trumpets and four trombones. The tightness carries over to the harmonic data, which involve bruising contact, but contact always of musical consequence. There's some chance throwing about, glides, and the like, but a jug of hot effects is not thrown over the auditor. Kapr's four-part music has contemporaneous meaning as it avoids all gimmickry.

The playing of Tarr's group is technically astute and musically tasteful. It is also extremely fluid, which makes the compact style that much more successful.

Sigfrid Karg-Elert *(1877-1933)*

Marche triomphale (Now Thank We All Our God)

Instrumental

☐ Preston (organ) / Argo ZRG–5448

Organ

Karg-Elert minus involved chromaticism or pictorial portrayal. The *Marche* is in the standard organ tradition. Nothing ventured, with standard gain.

M. William Karlins   (1932-   )

Instrumental   **Solo Piece with Passacaglia (1964)**

Clarinet   ☐ Rehfeldt (clarinet) / Advance 15

Variational format but with a difference. Karlins has no desire or yearning for playing the fancy permutative game. The continuity is tight, the feeling is that full-scale and full-display variations were written and then most of the notes erased. What remains is direct and sparse, a pithy totality that brings forth more meaning than hundreds of sounds.

Rehfeldt's playing is commendably clear.

Saxophone   **Music for Tenor Saxophone and Piano (1969)**

☐ Hemke (tenor saxophone); Granger (piano) / Brewster 1204

A superbly crafted work, musically as a whole and in terms of defining the true substances of the saxophone. The prejudices against this instrument are thinning out, fortunately, but musicians' anti-comments are still not negligible. A few more works like Karlins's and this instrumental racism will finally disappear.

Declamatory and kinetic-nervous details are found in the first movement. A slow jazz style, of genuine expressivity, marks part 2, dedicated "to the Memory of Coleman Hawkins." In the finale jazz also directs some of the passages—a little dirty jazz it is, with sax growls. The main point develops into an unaccompanied cadenza.

Hemke's presentation of Karlins's artistic documentation is exceptional. One recognizes his complete belief in the music he is playing, and that is something far more special than the total technical coverage one expects to hear and does.

Chamber   **Variations on *Obiter Dictum* (1965)**
Music
☐ Krosnick (amplified cello); Bucheri (piano); Siwe (percussion) / Composers Recordings C-329

The theme is Karlins's—the first seventeen measures of a work for organ. There is no complacent tolerance for serial or structured systemization (a huge inventory of dull music is covered by those terms). Karlins's six variations are each decisively clear and yet there is no partitioning; the emotion and fantasy cohere as a solid, total free-pitched essay. There are power bursts that are in strong contrast to the predominant, intensely tight and provocative lyricism of the amplified cello part. This music exemplifies compelling creative imagination.

Joel Krosnick is a splendid cellist. His playing is firm (the amplification doesn't mean very much and hardly changes the timbre), and he is very sensitive in conveying the internalization of the winding cello lines. His colleagues play securely.

Jeffrey Kaufman   (1947-   )

String   **Pastorale for Strings (1977)**
Orchestra
☐ Orchestra da Camera di Roma / Flagello (conductor) / Peters International PLE-071

A finely adjusted statement, its inflections completely tonal and enjoyable. The playing is fresh and marked by delicacy of phrasing. Beautifully balanced creatively and performance-wise.

Reflections for Clarinet and Piano

☐ Sobol (clarinet); Basquin (piano) / Grenadilla GS–1009

This composer's neoclassic manner, his devotion to pure instrumental music, written as a ''homage'' to Poulenc, with tonality dynamized by fan-wise spread, are all evidenced by the pithiness and the sunny nature of this duo. It is by realizing he does not want to go beyond the fluidic limits of twentieth-century classicism that Kaufman brings stylistic unity and balance to his work. Kaufman's aim is to be intelligible, and he is.

Sobol's playing commands the full attention of the listener, and his partner is deserving of equal credit. Splendid sound.

Walter Kaufmann *(1907-   )*

Partita

☐ American Woodwind Quintet / Golden Crest S–4075

Firm neoclassic music but not coloristically or rhythmically repressed. Kaufmann provides a good mix of serious and witty data.

A dynamic performance and furnished with bright sound, among the best this label has provided.

Hershy Kay *(1919-   )*

Suites

From the Ballet *Cakewalk* (after Louis Moreau Gottschalk)
From the Ballet *Stars and Stripes* (after John Philip Sousa)

☐ Boston Pops Orchestra / Fiedler (conductor) / RCA AGL1–1271

Catalogue and credit problems! Neither is a straightforward transcription as in the case of the Mussorgsky–Ravel *Pictures at an Exhibition* or the Bach–Stokowski items, etc. Kay's works are three-ply: adaptation, arrangement, and orchestration. Of course, all the music is by Gottschalk in the first case and by Sousa in the other instance. Listing it in the traditional manner, Gottschalk–Kay, is not totally correct considering the extent of Kay's conception. But neither is RCA's extremely confusing reverse designation, Kay–Gottschalk, which reads at first glance as if Gottschalk has transcribed Kay's music—not to speak of the fact that Gottschalk (and Sousa) have long been dead. The fairest titling method is to follow the publisher's decision, which is duplicated above. (Cross-reference indications appear under the respective composers' names.)

O.K. As to the music itself, Kay has accomplished a superb free translation (that's another way of looking at it) in each case. Charm, zest, and vitality are present, and not a single eighth note is cheapened or stylistically crippled. Fiedler is a master of presenting music of lighter weight with the same finesse and minute attention that attends a Brahms or Tchaikovsky symphony. He deserves substantial applause.

Ulysses Kay *(1917-   )*

Orchestra

Fantasy Variations (1963)

☐ Oslo Philharmonic Orchestra / Lipkin (conductor) / Composers Recordings S-209

Commissioned by Lipkin and given its baptismal performance under his direction when he was conductor of the Portland, Maine, Symphony Orchestra.

Kay's work is much more a rhapsody than it is a fantasy, or better still, it is a fantasy with rhapsodical qualities. Either way it bypasses the patch-quilted sectionalism of many variation designs. One of Kay's best pieces and played with sensitive regard.

Markings (1966)

☐ London Symphony Orchestra / Freeman (conductor) / Columbia M-32783

The title is taken from the volume of Dag Hammarskjöld's writings published after his death. It is undoubtedly Kay's most potent piece, the materials moving and interpenetrating within a single movement which has defined sections that are nevertheless interrelated. There are quieter elegiac sections that provide relief from the tensile conditions of other sections.

Markings is one of Paul Freeman's repertoire pieces, and he has performed it with a number of orchestras. This background results here in a powerful and colorful interpretation which proves that Freeman has delved far below the score's surface. It is without doubt his best recorded performance.

A Short Overture (1946)

☐ Oakland Youth Orchestra / Hughes (conductor) / Desto 7107

Kay's overture (winner of the third annual George Gershwin Memorial Award) is in the neoclassic frame of reference. It moves swiftly and tonally, its vocabulary contemporaneously enriched. An adequate performance is given by the young musicians.

Sinfonia in E (1950)

☐ Oslo Philharmonic Orchestra / Barati (conductor) / Composers Recordings 139 (monaural)

Framed in four sections, alternating slow and fast movements. The third part is highlighted by a sensitive, deeply felt, yet tuneful middle portion. It is a conceptual gem. Kay's rich palette, a romantically significant one, is handsomely realized by George Barati, a composer as well as a conductor.

Umbrian Scene (1964)

☐ Louisville Orchestra / Whitney (conductor) / Louisville 651 (monaural)

Only some pitch disagreements in line doublings in the first minute of Kay's orchestral scene interfere with its general mood of sobriety. The bell-type sounds color and lighten the austerity and nobility of this twilit music.

String Orchestra

Six Dances for String Orchestra (1954)

☐ Westphalian Symphony Orchestra / Freeman (conductor) / Turnabout 34546

A set of semi-sweet neoclassic items. This is the first time the entire work has been recorded. Way back when, two parts (Round Dance and Polka) were produced by the New Symphony Orchestra of London, conducted by Camarata and released by London (LL-1213). This was then transferred to Composers Recordings (119) and in its monaural form is still available. Of course, for these two parts or the whole thing the Turnabout issue is the one to get.

Organ Suite No. 1

Instrumental

Organ

☐ Harmon (organ) / Orion 76255

Superbly crafted for the organ. Sometimes polyharmonic, sometimes polytonal, always poetic even when it poses dynamic thrust, as in the Finale, a toccata with a stunning mysterious section. The preceding movements are a Prelude and a Pastorale.

Aside from a tendency to suddenly change registration at the beginning of *crescendi*, Thomas Harmon's playing is first-rate.

Brass Quartet for Two Trumpets, Tenor Trombone, and Bass Trombone (1950)

Chamber Music

☐ Members of the American Brass Quintet / Folkways 3651 (monaural)

The first movement (Fantasia) pays attention to the medium with fanfare-like jets and exciting rhythmic repetitions. The Arioso is reflective, an example of how brass instruments can portray a warmth of expression as sensitive to the ear as the winds or strings. By use of some fanfare patterns and pitch repetitions, the finale (a Toccata) relates to and thereby balances the initial part of the quartet.

How Stands the Glass Around? (1954)

Choral

What's in a Name?

Chorus Alone

☐ Randolph Singers / Randolph (conductor) / Composers Recordings 102 (monaural)

Lucidly expressive contrapuntalism defined in five-part madrigal style. Both pieces were written for the performing group, who, naturally, gave them their premieres.

Roland Kayn   (1933-   )

Cybernetics III (1969)

Electronic Music

☐ Deutsche Grammophon 2543006

An extended continuity of original vocal sounds, transformed, of course, as well as animal noises, also transformed. Conscious meaning is difficult to perceive, since the mass totality does not offer much contrast. Kayn's point that the sonic density corresponds "to certain entropy values" brings unprejudiced admiration for his objectives even though the sonorous result persistently remains fixed in a repetitive state.

Donald Keats   (1929-   )

String Quartet No. 2 (1965)

Chamber Music

☐ Beaux Arts Quartet / Composers Recordings S-256

Keats adopts a serialist attitude in this three-movement work, but is not devoted to the technique. His second quartet avoids the fixations of twelve-tone style with its hexachordic hobnobbing. Well-crafted playing by the Beaux Arts team.

Wendell Keeney (1903-)

Instrumental

Piano

Sonatina (1943)

☐ Gowen (piano) / New World Records NW–304

The fast-paced music could be described as Scarlatti dressed in bright twentieth-century clothes (movement 1 is an *allegro*, movement 3 is in *presto* pace). Each covers the territory in the most direct manner, with performance times of 2:32 and 2:02 respectively. The *Quasi adagio* (movement 2) is even shorter (1:37), a lyrical relaxation between the bounce-and-go of the other parts of the work.

Listening to this clean and healthy music is proof that neoclassicism is still in flower. It offers no surprises anymore but it's fully welcome and as refreshing as cool spring water.

Bradford Gowen is a splendid pianist. He presents Keeney's music in a brilliant, committed, and totally definitive performance.

Gunild Keetman / Carl Orff. *See Orff* / Keetman.

Ronald Keezer (1941-)

Percussion

For Four Percussionists

☐ Sonic Boom Percussion Ensemble / Crystal S–140

It was bound to happen—lighter-faceted percussion music. Stimulating and provocative rhythms in *Fours* is followed by a bluesy *Ballad for Mary*, and then follows dance action: Less than a Minute Waltz and a Rondo Samba. Made to order for ballet picturization, just as enjoyable as tuneful (yes!) music scored for percussion instruments.

Milko Kelemen (1924-)

Orchestra

Floréal (1970)

☐ Norddeutscher Rundfunk Symphony Orchestra, Hamburg / Slothouwer (conductor) / Philips 6500314

As a title *Floréal* reminds one of flowers, but there is no programmatic basis for Kelemen's sound sculptures. The sonorous equivalents are thoroughly clusterized among riotous color schemes. This may prove the composer's objective of showing the "interaction between 'density' and 'rhythm' of tone color."

This is one of three versions Kelemen made of the work, begun in 1969 and completed the following year. (There is no indication given as to which version was recorded.) Slothouwer provides a strong performance of Kelemen's avant-garde sonorism. The playing clearly demarcates the sequences of the material.

Improvisations concertantes **for String Orchestra (1955)**

☐ I Solisti di Zagreb / Janigro (conductor) / Vanguard 71118

Folkloristic facets and rhythmic recoil are the appurtenances that brace Kelemen's kaleidoscopically colored suite. It is exciting music which bites as it drives forward, commanded by tremendous power.

The performance is split-second in accuracy and persuasively heated. It should be, since the work was composed for and dedicated to Janigro and his colleagues. There are actually six movements; the third and fourth are not included in this recording.

Surprise **(1967)**

☐ Radio Symphony Orchestra, Berlin / Kelemen (conductor) / Philips 6500314

If you've heard Penderecki, there's no surprise in *Surprise*. Thus, here to hear are fragmented sound blocks, harsh colors, sound masses, dessicated harmonics, and sound thrusts. The cluster harmonies are surrogates for thematic detail. The colors are the contours. These are expertly spread over the string-instrument canvas in this composer-directed performance.

Changeant **for Cello and Orchestra (1968)**

☐ Westdeutscher Rundfunk Symphony Orchestra, Cologne / Palm (cello); Gawriloff (violin) / von Dohnányi (conductor) / Philips 6500314

Kelemen signifies *Changeant* as "the interplay between various colors." No argument. The music is of desperate timbre abstraction. A passion for yawps and shrieks, sonorous angles, percussive rents, textural tears, and abrasive textures is declared and never diminishes. The work concludes with the most violent cadenza this writer has ever heard. The cellistic regurgitation is simply fantastic. Don't turn the volume down!

Of course, there's no cellist alive that can do this sort of thing and toss if off with its special panache the way Siegfried Palm can. For his soloism alone the recording deserves high recommendation. Though Saschko Gawriloff is given special credit his role is extremely minor.

Composé **for Two Pianos and Orchestral Groups (1967)**

☐ Südwestfunk Orchestra / Alfons and Aloys Kontarsky (pianos) / Bour (conductor) / Philips 6500314

A zest for the lust of fricative sound embraces *Composé*. There is no decay in impetus here—the music has force, fire, and frenzy. No thematicism of direct importance, and some improvisation, but the logic and rhetoric are still unmistakable: a music of strongly patterned colors and lines—on the dark side and exciting. And preponderant in its percussiveness. The final cadence is the throwing of heavy chains on a gong.

The performers seem to be in full control and thoroughly enjoying their rambunctiousness.

Etudes contrapuntiques **(1959)**

☐ Otto (flute); Nordbruch (oboe); Irmisch (clarinet); Franke (bassoon); Lind (horn) / Travis (conductor) / Mainstream 5006

Kelemen's set of four studies considers the matter of integrated variation by color and rhythm simultaneously, and the product is dynamic. The metrical halter is disengaged in this instance, but, in its pertinent way, the flow is just as neatly adjusted as music based on classical-style precepts. The fluidity (sensitively considered in this performance) of

Kelemen's delicate timbres makes much of the music function like an unbroken line as the sound portions pass from one instrument to the next.

Choral

Chorus Alone

Hommage à Heinrich Schütz (1964)

☐ Gächinger Kantorei / Cianella (soprano) / Rilling (conductor) / Philips 6500314

Although this was inspired by the study of motets by Schütz, there is no carryover influence whatsoever. Kelemen begins his choral homage with whispered sounds, develops it by full vocal liberation, and returns to the whispering timbre. The intensity and the full texture provide a tension without letup. It is ear-filling. The recapitulation then furnishes the required release. Beautifully performed.

Roger Kellaway (1939-   )

Chamber Music

Esque for Trombone and Contrabass (1971)

☐ Anderson (trombone); Nadel (double bass) / Avant 1006

Cutting the light jazz bit with expertise, Kellaway opts for the subtle touch rather than the thigh-slapping approach. Combining a slide trombone with a bull fiddle may seem to be a poor choice of partnership but it works, works very well, especially for the saucy musical strips Kellaway has put together. The piece is played with an undeniable flair for the style involved.

Homer Keller (1915-   )

Solo Instrument and Orchestra

Clarinet

Serenade for Clarinet and Strings

☐ Eastman-Rochester Symphony Orchestra / Osseck (clarinet) / Hanson (conductor) / Eastman-Rochester Archives ERA–1001

Romantic lyricism as exhibited by simplistic means, but containing coloristic subtlety and impression.

Keller's work is on a program for solo winds and string orchestra in an album called *Americana*. It was originally available on Mercury, then deleted, and since reissued by ERA. Neither the original nor the re-release gives any liner notes on Keller's piece, though the other six works are covered. Strange.

Robert Kelly (1916-   )

Orchestra

Symphony No. 2 (1958)

☐ Japan Philharmonic Symphony Orchestra / Watanabe (conductor) / Composers Recordings 132 (monaural)

Kelly's Symphony No. 2 is based on a passage from Genesis, from which the key words, used as subtitles, are *Seedtime, Summer, Harvest,* and *Winter.* A germinal, dodecaphonic line sparks the work, from which Kelly wanders nicely afield. The subtitles, as noted above, are general descriptions, the arena and décor in which the music passes and performs. They are mental lean-tos. Actually, the symphony is a four-movement, classically oriented work in design, and carefully plotted as to developmental processes. Little-known, Kelly's symphony should be given attention. It is an excellent composition of crystal-clear conception; its fricative harmonies are used sensitively to point up the music's interweave. Beautifully played under Watanabe's direction.

Kent Kennan (1913-   )

Three Pieces for Orchestra

Orchestra

☐ Eastman-Rochester Orchestra / Hanson (conductor) / Eastman-Rochester Archives ERA–1004

These three pieces—*Promenade, Nocturne,* and *Il campo di fiori* ("The Field of the Flowers")—belong to the Respighi school (movements 1 and 3), and as far as the middle section is concerned, to the Pizzetti heritage. Wide-open brasses blend with and contrast to zippy diatonic string ostinati. Good eclectic work and full-blooded playing by Hanson and his musicians.

Night Soliloquy for Flute and String Orchestra

Solo Instrument and Orchestra

Flute

☐ Eastman-Rochester Symphony Orchestra / Mariano (flute) / Hanson (conductor) / Eastman-Rochester Archives ERA–1001

Kennan's reputation was achieved by this piece, which has been given hundreds of performances, including one directed by Toscanini. The style is Debussy's impressionism from start to finish. This does not harm Kennan's keen exploration of flute color, beautifully delivered by Joseph Mariano's playing. (The strings do not include double basses and there is a short bit for the piano as well.)

Two Preludes (1951)

Instrumental

Piano

☐ Helps (piano) / Composers Recordings S–288

Tonally based but with considerable chromaticism that gives dramatic tension.

Sonata for Trumpet and Piano (1956)

Chamber Music

☐ Stith (trumpet); Bilson (piano) / Golden Crest S–7042

Kennan's Sonata for Trumpet and Piano (no matter what residue of previous composers' talk will be found in his speech) breathes creative healthiness without brassy brashness. Sonata, ternary, and rondo designs constitute the neoclassic format.

Jerome Kern (1885-1945)

Mark Twain Portrait (1942)

Orchestra

☐ Cincinnati Pops Orchestra / Kunzel (conductor) / Turnabout 34714

Commissioned by André Kostelanetz as one of three musical portraits of important Americans. One of the results has become a real hit: Aaron Copland's *Lincoln Portrait.* Neither of the others—Virgil Thomson's The Mayor LaGuardia Waltzes nor Kern's piece—have come close to acceptance, though the latter deserves occasional hearing. The tuneful conception is realized in fine form by Kunzel and his musicians. (The full title of the Kern work is Portrait for Orchestra of Mark Twain.)

Instrumental

Piano

Land Where the Good Songs Go

☐ Gershwin (piano) / Klavier 124

Don't miss it. George Gershwin playing Jerome Kern is irresistible. O.K.—it isn't "serious," but it's good music wrapped around a great tune. Just listen to the way Gershwin runs into the initial part of each phrase. That's artistry.

The recording is "reenacted" from the "Steinway Duo-Art Reproducing Piano" original. Not bad sound at all.

Left All Alone Blues from *The Night Boat*

Whip-Poor-Will from *Sally* (1920)

Whose Baby Are You? from *The Night Boat*

☐ Gershwin (piano) / Klavier S-122

All vintage 1920 and evidence of Kern's abundance of talent. Gershwin drives it all home nice and free.

Transfers from piano rolls made more than four decades ago, but beautifully engineered with clean resonance.

Kern / **Charles Miller (20th cent.)**

Orchestra

Showboat: **A Scenario for Orchestra**

☐ Utah Symphony Orchestra / Abravanel (conductor) / Vanguard C-10023

They used to call this sort of compilation a "medley." Now the titles are more sophisticated—thus, a "Scenario." No matter what you call it, all the best tunes from this evergreen musical (category: American light opera), including the famous *Old Man River.*

The only current version in the catalogue—none other is needed. (Vanguard also lists this recording as obtainable under No. 345.)

Harrison Kerr   *(1897-   )*

Solo
Instrument
and
Orchestra

Violin

Concerto for Violin and Orchestra (1951)

☐ Imperial Philharmonic Symphony of Tokyo / Stavonhagen (violin) / Strickland (conductor / Composers Recordings 142 (monaural)

An independent voice writing independent dissonant music. This means freely chromatic devices, neither systematized nor twelve tone. The free formula continues in the avoidance of symmetry of content and consequential formal repose. Only in terms of what one expects in a concerto prospectus does Kerr follow the usual enthusiasms. The work highlights the fiddle and takes care to agitate the specialized string sonority against the opposing mass. But Kerr follows these points with modern virtuosity, which means color power and, at times, violence. Even in its quiet moments Kerr's concerto is exciting.

The soloist is first-rate. Both orchestra and conductor display worthy credentials. The total is extremely stimulating.

Trio for Violin, Cello, and Piano (1938)

☐ University of Oklahoma Trio / University of Oklahoma Recordings 1 (monaural)

Though there is some flirting with tonality (the work begins and ends in A minor) for the greater part it is the power and ofttimes violence of free concantenated dissonance that surrounds Kerr's Trio. Firm textures and active horizontal progress match this style.

Sound ensemble performance but little attention is given to highlighting and line give-and-take. The engineering is not exceptional. However, if you want Kerr's work this is the only edition.

Otto Ketting   (1935-   )

Due canzoni per orchestra (1957)

☐ Concertgebouw Orchestra / Leinsdorf (conductor) / Donemus Audio-Visual Series 7002

Soberly sensitive music that finds its roots in Webern. The chamber orchestra scoring is for five winds, four brass, harp, celesta, and percussion.

The performance by this fine orchestra is excellent. Leinsdorf has never been known as an expert in dealing with serial music but the poetic manner in which he displays Ketting's piece is a denial of that reputation.

Nelson Keyes   (1928-   )

Suite: Music for Monday Evenings (1959)

☐ Louisville Orchestra / Whitney (conductor) / Louisville 631 (monaural)

Music inspired by an aim to meet the technical caliber of college and community orchestras by writing in a relatively uncomplicated manner. However, the word "some" should have preceded these categories, for there are a good number of such groups that have tackled (and acceptably) complicated contemporary scores. In any case, Keyes's objective helps make his five-movement suite of discriminating clarity using middle-of-the-road contemporary language.

A lucid though not terribly exciting performance.

Abysses, Bridges, Chasms for Ten Rock-Jazz Soloists and Orchestra

☐ Louisville Orchestra / Members of the Philharmonic Bridge / Mester (conductor) / Louisville S–712

Fusion of classical and pop music is nothing new. However, their successful partnership is rare. Keyes's work belongs to that select category. His craft is superb. Strategically, he has found one *modus operandi* of amalgamating the two styles by using strong contrasts built into a design similar to a five-movement symphony: a very slow introduction, a fast jazz-like section, a slow movement followed by an improvisational division, and a rock-like finale. The colors and styles both contrast and blend. Unlike most such duo-dimensional pieces, this doesn't give one the impression of being present at some junky musical sideshow.

Fine playing, vigorously styled, all around. The decuple group consists of saxophone, horn, two trumpets, two trombones, electric bass, guitar, keyboard, and percussion. Keyes knows how to write short-hair music as brilliantly as he conceives serious music. Mester knows how to conduct both similarly.

Aram Khachaturian (1903-1978)

Orchestra

Masquerade Suite (1944)

☐ RCA Victor Symphony Orchestra / Shumsky (violin) / Kondrashin (conductor) / RCA LSC-2398

Khachaturian's suite alternates dances with slow-paced Tchaikovskian conduct. Kondrashin conducts the music of his countryman with taste, dazzling vigor, and impeccable clarity. The credit to Oscar Shumsky (only indicated on the record label) concerns his sympathetic projection of the solo violin part in the second movement, a Nocturne.

Music from the Ballet *Spartacus* (1953)

☐ State Radio Orchestra of the USSR / Gauk (conductor) / Monitor 2025 (monaural)

Khachaturian prepared no less than six suites from his huge ballet for concert performance. Three of these are titled; the other three are identified by scene numbers. These compilations cover twenty-eight different numbers from the stage work. Though Monitor relates the ten excerpts on its release to their place in the ballet's four acts, no mention is made of how these selections apply to the suites.

One excerpt, Dance with the Shields, is not included in any of the concert selections Khachaturian designed. Four movements are found in the first suite; one each is included in suites Nos. 2 and 3; and three pieces are in the suite titled *Scenes Nos. 4 and 5.* Not represented in Gauk's recorded edition is material from *Scene No. 3* or *Scene No. 9.*

Khachaturian himself conducted excerpts from *Spartacus* with the London Symphony Orchestra, released on Angel S–37411, but now deleted. Again (with some differences) he recorded portions from the ballet with the Vienna Philharmonic Orchestra, found on London 6322. There are also available the Dance of the Shields and Adagio of Spartacus and Phrygia on Philips 6585012, with Edouard van Remoortel conducting the National Opera Orchestra of Monte Carlo. Both of these pieces are included in the Monitor disc.

Notwithstanding the values of Khachaturian as conductor of his own music, Alexander Gauk's portrayal is preferable. It has more depth, and despite its monaural setting the playing is sharper. Gauk's performance edge shows the hand of the professional conductor in comparison to the composer-conductor hybrid. Further, there's more to hear on Monitor if one wishes a good chunk of the ballet. Of course, it's a small bit compared to the full ballet, which is available on eight fat sides (see under *Ballet*).

Suite from the Ballet *Gayane* (1942)

☐ Vienna State Opera Orchestra / Golschmann (conductor) / Vanguard S–207
☐ Boston Pops Orchestra / Fiedler (conductor) / RCA LSC-2267

Confusion reigns in the listing, titling, subtitling, and compilation of material drawn from *Gayane* (spelled also "Gayne," but less preferable). Fiedler's release is indicated as

"Gayane Ballet Suite." Golschmann's version is called "Suite from Gayane" on the cover; the liner heading is slightly false since "Gayane Ballet" implies the complete score. The label copy is closest to the basic fact, reading: Suite from the Ballet *Gayane*.

There are actually *three* suites that Khachaturian drew from his complete ballet. Eight movements are in the first suite, and six each in suites Nos. 2 and 3. Of course the Sabre Dance enjoys considerable currency as a single. Unfortunately, the American representatives of the Soviet publishers have issued two other versions. One is absolutely spurious since it is called "Suite No. 1-A," and it includes five pieces from the three suites, a compilation conceived for sales purposes, being 18 minutes in length, whereas the three authentic suites are, respectively, 36, 30, and 26 minutes in length. The other American offering is simply (and properly) called "Three Pieces from the Ballet *Gayane*," and includes the three most popular sections (one, naturally, being the Sabre Dance).

To set all data in order, the subtitle "Dance of the Rose Maidens" used in both recordings should correctly be identified as Dance of the Young (Rose) Maidens. The indication "Dance of the Kurds" (again found in both releases) eliminates the main title of the movement and lets stand only the parenthetical indication. Properly, therefore, it should read Mountaineers' Dance (Dance of the Kurds). Finally, on Vanguard's list, instead of "Dance of Ayshe," the full title in Khachaturian's score stands as Ayshe's Awakening and Dance.

It is important to realize that neither of the worthy available recordings embrace any single total suite. Golschmann's "realization" begins with No. 5 from Suite No. 3, then covers Nos. 5, 2, 3, and 4 from the first suite, extracts the second number from the third suite, and is completed by the *Lesginka*, which is the eighth and final part of Suite No. 1. Fiedler's four excerpts begin with Nos. 8, 2, and 4 from the first suite and conclude with the Sabre Dance, the fifth of the six parts in Suite No. 3.

As will be apparent, no single piece from Suite No. 2 is included in these recommended recordings. In any event, Suite No. 2 is the weakest of the compendiums, and as such has not received much performance attention, but *see below*.

Khachaturian's modern Armenian music, especially block-scored, is given expert performances by both Golschmann and Fiedler. The former deletes some introductory material and makes some shortcuts in a few of the pieces. The auditor's choice depends on how much he wants of *Gayane:* seven numbers (22 minutes, 11 seconds net playing time) from Vanguard; four numbers (8 minutes, 52 seconds net playing time) from RCA Victor.

Suite No. 2 from the Ballet *Gayane* (1942)

☐ London Symphony Orchestra / Fistoulari (conductor) / Everest 3052

Includes the choice two numbers in the second suite which are not represented in the best-played compilations (*see above*). These are the Russian Dance (No. 3 in the second suite) and *Fire* (the sixth and final movement of the second suite). Well-projected and well-balanced playing.

Symphony No. 3 (1947)

☐ Chicago Symphony Orchestra / Stokowski (conductor) / RCA LSC-3067

Khachaturian's one-movement third symphony, which he described as a "Symphony-Poem," is an instrumental blockbuster. In addition to the ten woodwinds, eleven brasses, percussion, harp, and strings, there are fifteen additional trumpets (making eighteen in all), plus an organ part of concerto amplitude.

Stoky's meat and potatoes, of course. It's a luscious performance, even if it is concerned with less than fabulous music.

Cello

Concerto for Cello and Orchestra (1946)

☐ National Opera Orchestra of Monte Carlo / Walevska (cello) / Inbal (conductor) / Philips 6500518

An example of Khachaturian's usual melismatic vocality, but a penetrating restraint in its use is observed in comparison with his concerti for violin and piano.

Christine Walevska maintains fine control of the solo line, though the tendency for a wide vibrato is noticeable in parts of the slow movement and the final set of variations. There's good orchestral support.

Rhapsody-Concerto for Cello and Orchestra

☐ Moscow Radio Sympony Orchestra / Shakhovskaya (cello) / Khachaturian (conductor) / Orion PGM-6902 (monaural)

Much Russian Orientalism focused on lengthy exhibition of the solo cello (after a two-minute introduction by the orchestra, the solo instrument stays in the spotlight alone for almost four minutes). The emphasis on soloism fulfills the "concerto" part of the work; the high-fantastical personality of the piece carries out the "rhapsody" designation. Khachaturian certainly shaped his music for the great Rostropovich, for whom it was written, and who premiered the composition in London on December 21, 1963.

Natalia Shakhovskaya is a persuasive advocate, even though her tone is somewhat small. A monaural record with that gambit "electronically enhanced for stereo."

Piano

Concerto for Piano and Orchestra (1936)

☐ Boston Symphony Orchestra / Kapell (piano) / Koussevitzky (conductor) / RCA LM-2588 (monaural)

☐ Moscow Radio Orchestra / Oborin (piano) / Khachaturian (conductor) / Monitor 2079E (monaural)

One of the great Soviet concertos and the one on which William Kapell in a huge number of performances rode to glory and fame before death in a plane crash ended his career.

Forget the stereo releases. Alicia de Larrocha (on London 6818) just is not with it. The slow movement doesn't resemble the Russian *melos* that sing forth and the finale has no impact and dynamism, without which it becomes a namby-pamby scherzo type—all wrong. Philippe Entremont (on Columbia M-31075) is much better, but he's always on top of the notes instead of crushing them in his pianistic paws. This music needs blood, guts, fire, and heavy saliva. Kapell understood this, and it was the reason for his and the concerto's simultaneous success. The famed performance with Koussevitzky is, fortunately, still on the lists. The sound isn't great, but the playing of Kapell and the Bostonians makes one forget this and one is caught up with the excitement and beauty (a haunting slow movement) of the music. This is the definitive version.

Oborin's version with the composer conducting is very good—Kapell's is far better. The tempo of the Monitor edition is much faster than RCA's, but even though the composer is the conductor of Monitor's release, the RCA disc is to be preferred, just because of the fabulous Kapell. One wonders if such a penetrating conception of Khachaturian's macho-indigenous concerto will ever be duplicated anywhere, on disc or on stage.

Violin

Concerto for Violin and Orchestra (1940)

☐ Boston Symphony Orchestra / Kogan (violin) / Monteux (conductor) / RCA VICS-1153

Plenty of pedal points, plenty of luscious tunes fluffed and flavored by Khachaturianistic nationalism. The music is full of the stuff made to order for fiddling and fits the fingers—just the material violinists love to play. But very few can play the piece the creamy elegant way this Russian virtuoso can. In the lyrical sections Kogan's quality is of highly polished artistry. In the technical passages the effect is brilliant without strain—a natural delivery which is always musical. Monteux's conducting is a marvel of accompanimental accomplishment.

Dance in G minor	**Sonatina**	*Instrumental*
Fughetta	**Toccata**	
Poem	*Valse caprice*	*Piano*
Sonata		

☐ Dubal (piano) / Genesis 1062

These piano compositions fill a gap in the Khachaturian discography. The Toccata is the best-known and its sonorous drive is asserted here with a fine amount of bravura. No subtle significances mark the music. These are all Khachaturian-brand staples, with his characteristic use of rhythm and sonority in place of deeply planned developments.

Solid playing, if somewhat metronomic at times. But there's no distortion; the pieces are played straightforwardly and are thereby acceptable.

Toccata in E flat minor

☐ Berman (piano) / Columbia M–34545

Go, man! Not terribly important music, but for what it represents it has a pianistic knockout punch. The selection is difficult to locate on the disc but it's there. Finding it is worthwhile.

Trio for Clarinet, Violin, and Piano (1932)

Chamber Music

☐ Sorokin (clarinet); Grach (violin); Kaplan (piano) / Monitor 2059 (monaural)

One of Khachaturian's best pieces, a product of his early period of work. It has vital rhythmic excitement, sonorous percussiveness, and a typical nationalistic flair. The timbre of the clarinet results in excellent creative strategy as it stirs the embers of native intonational fires. None of the themes are in any way a drug on the musical market. Their worth is generously set forth by excellent harmonic dress and a semi-cantillatory melodic style.

An expert performance of a work that deserves more attention than is given it in the concert field.

Spartacus (1953)

Ballet

☐ Bolshoi Theater Orchestra and Chorus / Zhuraitis (conductor) / Columbia/Melodiya D4M–33493

All of the ballet, including a few numbers that were eliminated after the world premiere, given December 26, 1956. A good number of the best portions can be heard in the orchestral excerpts (see under *Orchestra*). However, if you wish "Spartak" with every blood-sweat-and-tears sound, here 'tis. Sure, a great deal of it is obvious and sentimental but it's impressively sentimental—the pluses cancel the minuses. Topflight playing in on-the-mark Russian ballet style.

Khachaturian / **Jean-Pierre Rampal (1922 -   )**

Solo
Instrument
and
Orchestra

Flute

Concerto for Flute and Orchestra

☐ Orchestre National de l'ORTF / Rampal (flute) / Martinon (conductor) / Odyssey Y-33906

You won't find this work listed in Khachaturian's catalogue. Reason? Rampal had requested that Khachaturian write him a concerto. K. replied in the negative, suggesting that if R. wanted a flute concerto to go ahead and transcribe K.'s violin concerto, which R. did, in 1968. It is practically the same as the original, minus double stops, and with a cadenza by Rampal.

To a degree the transcribed work succeeds. However, only in the slower and lyrical portions. Otherwise no flute can project the forceful rhythmic pungency that a violin can. And, the work has a considerable amount of that type of writing. All that one need do is to compare this wind-instrument setting with the original (*see above*). For those who wish Rampal, regardless, this is the only version and it can't be bettered. For that matter no other flutist has performed the concerto, though anyone could make his own transcription if he so desired, since the composition is in the public domain, having been composed and published in the Soviet Union long before that country subscribed to the international copyright convention.

Indeed, this is the third release of the sole recording. In was initially issued by Erato; then it was remastered and released in 1972 on the Musical Heritage Society label (MHS-1186), which is still available. Odyssey's edition went on the market in 1976.

Karen Khachaturian   *(1920 -   )*

Chamber
Music

Sonata for Violin and Piano, Op. 1

☐ Heifetz (violin); Steuber (piano) / RCA LSC-2909

A garland of nineteenth-century musical facts—no fancies appear. In the conclusion of the initial movement there is some muted sonority, a little flavoring of pizzicato is used in the middle portion, and the finale has some Scotch-snap folksy turns that turn into a tarantella.

Heifetz knocks off the piece as one expects—this sort of semi-lush, semi-Tchaikovskian material is his meat and potatoes. (But, mind you, he is guilty of some slightly creased octaves in one place!)

Ivan Khandoshkin   *(1747-1804)*

Solo
Instrument
and
Orchestra

Viola

Concerto in C major for Viola and Orchestra (1801)

☐ Moscow Chamber Orchestra / Barshai (viola) / Barshai (conductor) / Monitor 2018 (monaural)

Composed in 1801 but not published until 1947. There are Haydnesque particulars in the opening Moderato and the final Rondo, *La Chasse*. One perceives some editing (or, if not, some remarkable stylistic anticipation) in the romantic diction of the slow movement, a Canzona. For that matter, there is apparently some downright and forthright editing throughout the work, and one can wager that the cadenzas are not by Mr. Ivan Khandoshkin. Probably these are the work of Rudolf Barshai (there is no information furnished). The three cadenzas (one for each movement) are colorful, but leap totally into late-nineteenth-century style.

A strong performance by the soloist, with a consistent bravado that is also of romantic character.

Variations on a Russian Folk Tune

Chamber Music

☐ Kogan (violin); Rostropovich (cello) / Monitor 2019 (monaural)

A fine example of the output of this composer (Monitor spells his name "Handoshkin"), who was the first to write instrumental music based on Russian folk themes. His string duo is built on the melody "I Lose What I Love."

Since Monitor's liner note is biographical and otherwise rather bland it is well to indicate that Khandoshkin's duo was published in Amsterdam in 1781 with the title *Chansons russes variées pour violon et basse.*

Unaccompanied and uncomplicated music. It is played to the hilt by these two masters.

Tikhon Khrennikov   *(1913-   )*

Symphony No. 1 in B flat minor, Op. 4

Orchestra

☐ State Radio Orchestra / Gauk (conductor) / Monitor S–2077E (monaural)

More advanced by a few notches than Glazunov, as darkly covered as Miaskovsky, and considerably less adventurous than Shostakovich or Prokofiev—those phrases describe Khrennikov's three-movement symphony. The aspirations are strictly traditional. The performance is a musically assured one.

Olav Kielland   *(1901-   )*

Concerto Grosso Noregese, Op. 18

String Orchestra

☐ Olso Philharmonic Orchestra / Kielland (conductor) / Composers Recordings 160 (monaural)

A set of folk-music forms, with *Bruremarsj, Springar, Kjempevise,* and *Halling* representing respectively a march, a dance, a ballade, and another dance. A considerable amount of the music imitates native instrumentation.

The performance is adequate. However, the packaging is not up to snuff. Neither cover nor liner notes indicate that the *Concerto Grosso* is for string orchestra and a pair of horns. Further, Op. 80 is given on the album cover. However, the correct opus designation for this piece, composed in 1952, is noted on the record label and liner copy.

Earl Kim   *(1920-   )*

Two Bagatelles

Instrumental

Piano

☐ Helps (piano) / Composers Recordings S–288

The first of the pair (*Allegro scherzando*) was written in 1950; the other (*Andante sostenuto*), in 1948. Both survey Bergian horizons. (Surprisingly, this is the only instrumental music by this composer recorded at this date of writing, despite concrete recognition including commissions from the Fromm Foundation, the Prix de Paris, and awards from the Guggenheim Foundation and the National Institute of Arts and Letters.)

Vocal

Voice with Instrumental Ensemble

Earthlight

☐ Sargon (soprano); Potter (violin); Kim (piano) / New World Records NW-237

Earthlight is subtitled *Romanza* for Violin *con sordino*, High Soprano, Piano, and Lights. The last are used to go up on the individual musicians when they are performing and fade out when they are not. The requirements (demands!) for the soprano deserve a footnote that she is to sound like an amplified flute and possess the technical scope of a Paganini on the violin.

The text consists of lines from eight works by Samuel Beckett which are mostly narrated and are contrasted to wordless soprano instrumentalization. (The term ''vocalise'' would be incorrect, since not only is the technique used sectionally rather than totally in this case, but the vocalise form implies a writing of cursive quality.)

Merja Sargon is the star of this trio, and she deserves all the stars in the book for her stunning conception. It takes courage (and a voice of huge range) to attempt this part. It is as taxing as a huge operatic role in its concentrated, quarter-hour length.

George Kirbye   (1565?-1634)

Choral

Chorus Alone

Sorrow Consumes Me

☐ Purcell Consort of Voices / Burgess (conductor) / Turnabout 34202

A double madrigal. Part 1 (as titled) tells of a poet who is troubled by fearful dreams. Part 2: *O Heavens! What Shall I Do?* concerns his conclusion that he will die of grief.

The five-part writing has a rich harmony that convincingly sets forth the text. A madrigal that matches the accomplishments of such composers as Byrd and Morley.

Leon Kirchner   (1919-   )

Orchestra

Toccata for Strings, Solo Winds, and Percussion (1955)

☐ Louisville Orchestra / Mester (conductor) / Louisville S-683

Representative of Kirchner's ambivalent expressions of rhapsody and introversion. Despite the title there is no grandiloquent orchestration. The scoring has innumerable beauties: the celesta doubling high string-harmonics; soprano and tenor percussion providing pithy duos; xylophonic doubling of the low bassoon, affording aeration; and exciting brass scoops. In its nervousness, the piece is a toccata; in its motival astrictions, it is much more a fantasy.

The performance is fair; more string strength would have given this disc a higher rating.

Piano Concerto No. 1 (1956)

☐ New York Philharmonic / Kirchner (piano) / Mitropoulos (conductor) / New World Records NW-286 (monaural)

Kirchner makes the piano both a solo and symphonic instrument in his concerto. Nor does the instrument discourse with frenzy when it takes the limelight. The motival development of the opening movement is a deterrent to unbridled soloism. There is no direct, impulsed theme; the music debates on specific points: a conjunct interval and a snapped-rhythm idea. Movement 2 is restless: its frictions, rhapsody, and inner agitation might be termed super-romantic, but the décor is of the present. Violence marks the final section.

A thrillingly alive performance, with the mono sound still holding up exceedingly well. (The reissue was made from the original Columbia edition: ML-5185.)

Sonata concertante for Violin and Piano (1952)

☐ Jaime Laredo (violin); Ruth Laredo (piano) / Desto 7151

In this work Kirchner casts off certain technical aids; the values are integrated, rather than arrived at eclectically. The interval of a third, triadic stimuli, and conjunct moves are the principal devices used in this duo. These occur as inlays and overlays, creating the matrix on which the music rests.

The sonata lives up to its title: concerted elements rival one another, though cooperation is fully at work. Integral cadenzas are given each of the instruments, and contrast emerges from the breadth of the violin's lines and the sense of qualified violence in the piano, making the work in effect a concerto grosso with orchestral adjuncts eliminated.

The *Sonata concertante* requires that rarely found combination of artistry and virtuosity; no others need apply—its cool fires will not appeal to lesser lights. The performance is truly masterful. That it is makes one finally accept the loss of the superb, but long-deleted presentation (on Epic LC-3306), where Kirchner, no ordinary pianist, teamed with Eudice Shapiro, a violinist with extraordinary insight into contemporary music.

Quartet No. 3 for Strings and Electronic Tape (1967)

☐ Concord String Quartet / Vox SVBX-5306

An ideal marriage of string quartet and tape sounds. Kirchner's work displays an excellent contrast and blend of the two sound-production types. The electronic tape does not frame or merely oppose; it both colors and enlarges the string spectrum. Example: the tape hinges to the violins and the range moves upward and outward. Here, the sonorous territory seems endless and the string quartet becomes a gigantic entity rather than four instruments punctuated or orchestrated by the tape collation.

The opus has the type of form whereby its design is made apparent by the firmly knit content. Kirchner avoids the strictly formal response, which so often is actually a formal defect. In his third quartet there is no formula, the use of which is most often just as bad as formless music. The inlay and overlay of this work (beautifully performed) is the integration of its materials. It deserved the Pulitzer Prize given it in 1967.

String Quartet No. 1 (1949)

☐ American Art Quartet / Composers Recordings SRD-395 (monaural)

Kirchner's quartet is derivative only in its nervous asymmetries; it is scarcely so as to form, or in its manner of painting colors and measuring sonorities. The first movement's

Solo Instrument and Orchestra

Piano

Chamber Music

979

rhythms are exceedingly plastic, the pulse rhapsodic, and the same emboldening of the rhythm applies to the form. In the slow movement the negotiation of the intervallic second is all-important—vertically, horizontally, embellishing, or gliding chromatically. The third movement, a Divertimento, is the only symmetrical one of the entire quartet. It has the graphic design of a large Beethoven scherzo (tempoed faster than that style, however). Though harmonies, inner pulsations, color, and vocabulary are a far cry from Beethoven, the aid of that composer's acute balances cannot be overlooked. The last part is like a cadenza in slow motion. Throughout, Kirchner's keen exploration of rhythm is paramount.

The performance by the American Art Quartet is equal to the playing of any quartet on the concert scene. Columbia initially released this recording on ML–4843. Then followed the period of deletion. CRI's reissue of the original mono setting has been electronically rechanneled for stereo. It makes available an outstanding documentation of contemporary musical art.

Theodor Kirchner   (1823 - 1903)

Instrumental

Piano

Allegro con passione, Op. 30, No. 17

Aquarellen, Op. 21, No. 3

Days Gone By, Op. 73, No. 4

Elegy, Op. 73, No. 16

Moderato, Op. 30, No. 8

Moderato, Op. 71, No. 100

Nocturne, Op. 73, No. 12

Romanze, Op. 73, No. 6

Spring-Greeting, Op. 73, No. 2

☐ Ruiz (piano) / Genesis 1032

Two examples are from the Opus 30 *Studies and Pieces*. The Opus 71 representative is the final item in Kirchner's *100 Little Studies*. One quarter of the entire Opus 73, *Romantic Poems*, is included in Ruiz's program.

Kirchner was a miniaturist and as such gives proof of unpretentious ease in stating his Schumannesque-light Brahms ideas. Ruiz's playing is rather well managed, only limited by the material he is presenting.

Lothar Klein   (1932-   )

Orchestra

Musique à go-go

☐ Louisville Orchestra / Whitney (conductor) / Louisville S–672

A peppy divertimento, this. Klein is reticent in his description, stating that the impetus for composition was nothing more than a "desire to attempt a virtuoso orchestral piece." This virtuosity the music displays. But it also projects humor in sweet-sour harmonies, framed by dance-bandish percussion. The total absence of mishmashed gobbledygook and the clean-cut, clear-cut hedonistic tone of the piece are equivalent to what *Les Six* might be turning out if they were composing nowadays.

The recording is directed with roguish authority. Be sure to catch the puns on Ravel's *Bolero* and Gershwin toward the close!

George Kleinsinger   *(1914-   )*

Pan the Piper for Narrator and Orchestra (1946)

Opera and Dramatic Music

☐ Philharmonic-Symphony Orchestra of New York / Tiller (narrator) / Pelletier (conductor) / Columbia CL–671 (monaural)

One of the numerous narrator-orchestra pieces that used to be featured on so many children's concerts. More serious and creatively solid stuff is fed the younger set these days, such as Britten's *A Young Person's Guide to the Orchestra* and Prokofiev's perennial *Peter and the Wolf.* Many of these works "introduced" the orchestral instruments, with their illustrations wrapped around a fancy tale. Thus Don Gillis's *Alice in Orchestralia,* this Kleinsinger opus, et cetera. *Pan* remains one of the very best of this fairly large literature (many composers jumped into the market—mostly second-rate ones, however).

Ted Tiller narrates his lines with no campy smirks, and there's fine playing by the orchestra. You can probably tell from the catalogue number how old this recording is, but don't let that deter you if you want this disc for the little ones—or yourself. Columbia's sound is monaural but very good.

Tubby the Tuba (1942)

☐ Boston Pops Orchestra / Child (narrator); Schmitz (tuba) / Fiedler (conductor) / Polydor 5032

Presumably, some might place this work in the *Peter and the Wolf* category. This writer is inclined to classify *Tubby* in the lower classification where Don Gillis's *Alice in Orchestralia* and his *The Man Who Invented Music* are found. No insult is being made.

Like most lightly faceted narrator-with-orchestra pieces, *Tubby* has the objective of teaching the kiddies that music is quite digestible. This doesn't bar adults from enjoying it as well, since *Tubby* is music for children of all ages.

Julia Child fields this work like a pro. The famous TV chef is as successful here as she is concocting mouth-watering recipes.

Henri Kling   *(1842-1918)*

Kitchen Symphony, Op. 445

Instrumental

Piano and Percussion

☐ Lewenthal (piano); McNab (trumpet and funnel trumpet) / Lewenthal (conductor) / Angel S–36080

In the toy symphony category, but with items used from the parlor and dining room as well as the kitchen, the score calling for piano, trumpet, funnel trumpet, wine glass, bottle, saucepan, fire irons, milk jug and tin covers! A harmless but nice six-minute bit of whimsy that is split between a Viennese waltz and a gentle galop.

August Klughardt   *(1847-1902)*

Chamber Music

Quintet, Op. 79

☐ Boehm Quintette / Orion 76254

Romantic syntax merging into well-crafted textures. This provides an agreeable example of standard woodwind quintet music. Fine musicianship by the Boehm organization.

Jan Klusák   *(1934-   )*

Orchestra

First Invention (1961)

☐ London Symphony Orchestra / Buketoff (conductor) / RCA LSC–3181

The technical principle of Klusák's piece is twelve-tone; the performing energy is supplied by seventeen solo players (five strings and twelve winds). An ingratiating invention is the result.

Morris Knight   *(1933-   )*

Instrumental

Clarinet

Refractions for Clarinet and Tape (1962)

☐ Sweetkind (clarinet) / Golden Crest S–4092

Classically designed in its three movements: sonata, ternary form, and rondo. However, the formal procedures are not academically shaped and a sense of quiet rhapsody surrounds the music, with all the tape data borrowed from the clarinet's material and then transformed.

David Sweetkind is mentioned in the liner notes but is given no specific credit there and none whatsoever on album cover or record label. He is herewith credited, therefore, with giving a sensitive performance.

Chamber Music

Cassation for Trumpet, Horn, and Trombone

☐ Florida State University Brass Trio / Golden Crest S–4081

Seven sections, the first an *Introduction* and the last an *Epilogue*. Rhythmic ball-tossing figures are in *Catch;* solo colors are highlighted in the Song for Horn and Trumpet Minstrel, but not at the loss of ensemble conditions. Slippery floor conditions exist in the glisses heard in the Waltz for Trombone. The penultimate movement is titled *Three in Two,* a nice duple-sprung tidbit.

Splendid playing in every respect. Knight states that his music would sound well out-of-doors. It sounds just as fine indoors spinning off a disc.

Opera and Dramatic Music

The Origin of Prophecy, for Speaker and Tape (1964)

☐ Knight (narrator) / Golden Crest S–4092

Based on a part of a poem by Chan Sieg, the text sometimes delivered straightforwardly and at other times electro-mutated. Effective because of the textual clarity and effective because the sound materials that partner the narration sensitively fit the subject.

982

Luminescences (1967)

☐ Golden Crest S-4092

Ballet

Electronic music for ballet purposes, and perhaps a little static therefore when heard separately from stage action. There are five movements, each probing a different sound situation: e.g., high-frequency pitches subjected to rapid reverberation in the first part, white noise in section 3, and "highly percussive non-pitch sound" in movement 4.

After Guernica (1969)

☐ Golden Crest S-4092

Electronic Music

Knight's reaction to the famous Picasso canvas. The starkness of the painting (it may be well to recall that it was entirely conceived in black, white, and gray) is translated in Knight's essay, especially in the first half of the music. It then increases in dynamic totality and textural activity and is followed by a release.

Lev Knipper   *(1898-1974)*

Youth Overture

☐ State Radio Orchestra / Gauk (conductor) / Monitor 2038 (monaural)

Orchestra

Knipper was once attracted to contemporary dissonance and ostentatious orchestration, but no longer. His overture is as gay and untroubled as a Strauss waltz, but far more dynamic and peppier.

Gauk has the knack for setting forth this type of music with suitable pace and letting it run its course unhampered. That's the way it should be.

Frederick Koch   *(1928-   )*

String Quartet No. 2 (with Voice)

☐ Cleveland Orchestra String Quartet / McMurray (mezzo-soprano) / Crystal S-531

Chamber Music

Serial music with a strong sense of avoiding the dry and schematic. The voice is heard in movement 2, the text of which is Carl Sandburg's *Wind Song*. It is excellently delivered by the warm mezzo voice of Peggy Anne McMurray.

Paul Kochanski / *Manuel de Falla.* See *Falla* / Kochanski.

Zoltán Kodály   *(1882-1967)*

Ballet Music (1925)

☐ Philharmonia Hungarica / Dorati (conductor) / London 2313

Orchestra

One of Kodály's most irresistible pieces, which for some reason is not too well known.

It is a Hungarian mini-mini-*Sacre du printemps* in part. Originally it figured as the Dragon's Dance in *Háry János,* but then was moved into its own individual place. The grotesquerie and the mechanistically light rhythmic detail are entrancing. So is the clever timbre of the saxophone.

The piece is played with such infinite preciseness that it mesmerizes the listener into hearing it two or three times in succession. (The performance time is five and one-half minutes.)

Concerto for Orchestra (1940)

☐ Philharmonia Hungarica / Dorati (conductor) / London 2313

All the frictions and dynamism of the Hungarian master are found in this work, commissioned for the fiftieth anniversary of the Chicago Symphony Orchestra (first performed by them in February of 1941). The native idiom is unmistakable, as are the neoclassically defined rhythms. Dorati performs this one-movement piece with assurance, knowledge, and keen balances.

Dances of Galánta (1933)

☐ Philharmonia Hungarica / Dorati (conductor) / London 2313

Kodály's attractive themes were chosen from a book of gypsy dance tunes issued in the early nineteenth century. He thus preserves tradition and envisions true Hungarian music in terms of quantitative apportionment.

The Dances of Galánta were composed to commemorate the eightieth anniversary of the Budapest Philharmonic Society. Kodály's neo-Magyar document was a fitting gift. It also shows that one does not need to be a creative exhibitionist to write exciting music.

Dorati considers the dances almost tenderly and they gain much by such underplaying. The music obtains considerable warmth in that manner.

Háry János Suite (1926)

☐ Philadelphia Orchestra / Ormandy (conductor) / RCA ARL1–1325

The suite Kodály fashioned from his opera "in four adventures with a prologue and an epilogue" (see under *Opera and Dramatic Music* [*Háry János*]) is little concerned with virtuosic posturing of the full orchestra. More pertinent are specialized timbres and orchestrational picture-painting: the instrumental simulation of a sneeze, clock imitations, *secco* military music, the rarely heard cimbalom, a healthy quota of percussion, and enlarged brass, with three cornets as well as three trumpets in the finale (though I defy anyone to hear the difference in the way these closely allied instruments are employed).

The balances of this score are built-in; a conductor need only be careful that in the heavier tutti sections glitter is not replaced by bombast. Ormandy meets all the requirements and then some. This edition is a delightful definition of the score's colors.

Hungarian Rondo (1917)

☐ Philharmonia Hungarica / Dorati (conductor) / London 2313

A little-known piece for an orchestra of strings plus paired clarinets and bassoons. Native charm, native melos, native emotion. The Hungarian ensemble and Hungarian conductor are the perfect interpreters.

Marosszék Dances (1930)

☐ Philharmonia Hungarica / Dorati (conductor) / London 2313

Authentic Hungarian folk materials from the Transylvanian district of Marosszék form this set. They were collected by Kodály and later (1929) made the basis for a piano work (see *Instrumental: piano*). The following year, at the request of Toscanini, they were transcribed for orchestra.

No matter how nationalistic Kodály's feelings, he never permits his folk indoctrination to outweigh his interest in proportional balance. The dances illustrate this. By using the introductory subject as a link between the various sections, Kodály composes a set of delightful dances with rondo overtones. There is no pyrotechnical posturing, but there is quiet excitement in his amalgam of native elements and formal logic.

Dorati plays the dances naturally, understanding the rhythmic joys to be found in the score. That gives the exact amount of interpretative lighting for the music.

Minuetto serio

☐ Philharmonia Hungarica / Dorati (conductor) / London 2313

An extract from Kodály's stage work *Czinka Panna* (composed in 1948), which was somewhat extended (into ternary form) and became an independent piece. It is straightforward—an example of Kodály minus Hungarian diction and accent.

The orchestra is suitably responsive, providing a well-balanced and truthful depiction.

Summer Evening (1930)

☐ Philharmonia Hungarica / Dorati (conductor) / London 2313

Kodály's tone poem was written in 1906 and then totally revised in 1930. It received its first performance by the New York Philharmonic, with Toscanini conducting, in April 1930.

Intimacy pervades Kodály's warm-weather nocturne. There are no perplexing arguments in the suave score. Dorati's execution of this chamber orchestra work (calling for seven woodwinds, two horns, and strings) is one of musicianship and taste. The sound is gorgeous.

Symphony in C (1961)

☐ Philharmonia Hungarica / Dorati (conductor) / London 2313

Though not as strong as his earlier orchestral compositions, Kodály's Symphony is well-oiled with folk elements and moves without creative squeaks. The work is dedicated to the memory of Toscanini.

The Philharmonia Hungarica is a finely tuned instrument in every phase of this piece. Dorati's recording naturally places high above the monaural setting made by the Louisville Orchestra, with Robert Whitney as the conductor (on Louisville 631). Give Whitney credit, however, for having been the first in a recording studio with Kodály's last major orchestral work.

Theatre Overture (1927)

☐ Philharmonia Hungarica / Dorati (conductor) / London 2313

A proxy operatic overture, composed to precede the comic opera *Háry János* (see under *Opera and Dramatic Music*). It is faithful to native reflections, containing a heady czardas among its several themes. Styled well, performed likewise.

Variations on a Hungarian Folk Song (*The Peacock*) (1939)

☐ London Symphony Orchestra / Kertész (conductor) / London 26186

Kodály set this song (also known as *Fly, Peacock, Fly*) for men's voices (see under *Choral: chorus alone*) before writing the orchestral Variations.

There is a difference between variations on a theme and thematic modifications. In the former case, the principal idea or one of its components becomes reorganized and totally developed; in the latter, the main characteristics of the theme are retained within defined statements.

Kodály's set of orchestral Variations illustrates the values of controlled modification. The theme is treated to varying types of development—scherzo, funeral march, dance type, and so on—producing an orchestral showcase of colorful gems.

Kertész's forces match Kodály's exhilarating, constructivistic expansion of theme with tremendous color and change of pace. There is no lukewarm *savoir-vivre,* which would be far from the pointedness of this work.

Instrumental

Cello

Sonata for Cello Solo, Op. 8

☐ Varga (cello) / Vox SVBX–560

Among all of the contemporary literature for a solo string instrument, no work can come close to matching Kodály's fabulous contribution for the cello. Not only does the composer exploit the instrument's technique, but he never departs for a single measure from his distinctive Magyar personality.

The sonata consists of three movements, beginning with a majestic emphasis on declamatory lines. In the slow part, melodic urgency (sustained thoughts preceded most often by fast-jetted sounds) is contrasted to savage cadenzas. Varga is in top form here. Pedal insistence, simultaneous pizzicato with bowed ideas, gives further color, sometimes banking the melodic stream above and below. This is extremely difficult to perform, but Varga sends it forth with prime smoothness. The barbaric finale is an ingrained transmutation of Kodály's study of his country's melodies. The weavings of this movement are not only those of aural excitement; they are its language.

Piano

Marosszék Dances (1929)

Méditation sur un motif de Claude Debussy (1907)

Nine Pieces for Piano, Op. 3

Seven Pieces for Piano, Op. 11

Valsette (1909)

☐ Sándor (piano) / Candide 31077

The Marosszék Dances for piano are rarely heard these days, since Kodály transcribed them for orchestra (see under *Orchestra*). They are pleasant enough, even in the restricted black and white range of the keyboard instrument. Opus 11 is somewhat ordinary music from this extraordinary creator. The compositional manner is akin to light and shadow; folk moods accompany impressionistic inclinations à la Debussy. The last situation is fully defined in the *Méditation,* based on an idea in *Pelléas et Mélisande.*

Full folk flavor is to be found in the Opus 3 set, containing an improvisatory quality. Sándor does his best work here, with playing marked by sensitive *rubati,* flexible rhythm, and re-creative imagination.

Adagio for Violin and Piano (1905)

☐ Steiner (violin); Berfield (piano) / Orion 74160

A rich, soaring melody, composed in 1905. Eleven years later Kodály revised the piece for viola or cello and piano. It has very little Hungarian quantity, but contains real quality.

Duo for Violin and Cello, Op. 7

☐ Heifetz (violin); Piatigorsky (cello) / RCA LSC–2550

The minimal means with which Kodály is concerned cause him to employ a striking new technique, one in which he writes for the instruments to produce at times sonorities of twice their number. This is not merely textural enlargement, but enlargement to substantiate and emphasize the truthfulness of the creative idea.

Most of the first movement is of broad continuity, perfectly balanced between the two instruments, which often break into exultant song. The extent of Kodály's rhapsodic vocalizations doesn't matter. The movement's form and its allied tonalities are as clear as his allegiance to Hungarian style. The result is one of the two greatest works (the other is Ravel's Sonata) instrumentally limited to a violin and a cello.

The Magyar feeling in the slow movement is somewhat subdued. The final Presto (with a *parlando* preamble, presented antiphonally) is in huge binary form, twice surveyed, with the addition of a coda that seals the work with a wild conclusion.

The beautiful virtuosity of these players and the vastly superior sound make the RCA disc the first choice of the editions available. However, less teeming passion than is displayed by Heifetz and Piatigorsky strengthens Kodály's music. This is found, to some degree, in the performance by the Schoenfeld Duo, on Orion 7267, but the sound is not good at all, and some of the balances the producer permitted are against the grain. One must point out that Heifetz occasionally indulges in solo display rather than chamber-music style. One example: string changes on repeated sounds accentuating what should remain subtle.

Sonata for Cello and Piano, Op.4

☐ Shapiro (cello); Wild (piano) / Nonesuch 71155

Movement 1 is a Fantasia. It proposes the mood of the work by dialogue and loosened rhythmic exhortations; it also sketches the composition's warmth and Hungarian manner. Movement 2 integrates and tightens the rhythm, sweeping along with dance motility, which confirms ("develops") the spirit of the initial part of the sonata. At the end of the second movement the first section reappears, in a concentrated manner; thus there is formal recapitulation. Sonata terms have been fulfilled, yet this is less a sonata of two movements with semicyclic inference than it is a work of one panel drawn in colors that complement each other.

The recording is a supple and subtle delineation of the first movement. The second part is performed without Bartókian hammer and tongs, and the music benefits by this approach.

Serenade for Two Violins and Viola, Op. 12

☐ Lautenbacher and Schaefer (violins); Koch (viola) / Vox SVBX–560

The three movements of the Serenade could well have titles affixed—"Activity," "Dialogue," and "Dance." The most individual part of the trio (and the very best played) is the middle movement. Kodály's unerring manipulation of instrumental detail is beautifully expressed as the first violin and viola converse with each other in an example rare to chamber music, one akin to operatic recitative of the boldest order. Such declamatory writing is program music in spirit, without detail.

―――――

String Quartet

No. 1, Op. 2 / No. 2, Op. 10

☐ Chicago Symphony Quartet / Vox SVBX–560

Although Kodály's initial quartet shows great interest in the terms and turns of old Hungarian music, his characteristic method of portraying it beyond the arbitrary, classic-romantic manner is not as yet displayed. Nevertheless, his later personality is present; future possibilites and solutions are simmering.

In the later quartet the speech of the four stringed instruments is produced from indigenous Hungarian musical dialect, which accents "open-air" intervals; its rhythms move through the Magyar slow *lassu,* the frenetic *friss,* and the *alla zoppa* of limping syncopation, its vocabulary extended by the *rubati* of rural gypsy melisma. There is no better identification of Kodály's art, which conveys the subtleties of idealized musical folklore. It has all of the fertile and mysterious variables that make a sensitive composer independent of scholastic calculations.

Satisfactory productions by the Chicago team.

Vocal

Voice with Accompaniment

Hungarian Folk Music (Excerpts) (1917 - 1932)

☐ Magda (soprano); Hambro (piano) / Bartók 927 (monaural)

Refinement of the crude, basal musical stuff that Kodály found in his researches. The styling is superbly artistic, a gentle editing of the native materials with pastel-colored crayons. All the songs manifest superb craftsmanship.

László Magda sings six songs from the volume and sings them with taste. Perfect delights, each and every one.

Hungarian Folk Music (Excerpts) (1917 - 1932)

☐ Chabay (tenor); Kozma (piano) / Bartók 914 (monaural)

A total of ten in this issue (*see above* for details). The fourth is titled *The Bad Wife,* the sixth is a Song of Doberdo, and the seventh of the set is *Huszárnóta* ("Hussar's Song"). The tenth song is a duplicate of the first of the group of six that Magda sings.

Recruiting Song

Soldier's Song

☐ Chabay (tenor); Kozma (piano) / Bartók 904 (monaural)

Folk items not stylistically dressed to kill the primordial quality of the tunes. Simply sung with taste.

Two Songs from Twenty Hungarian Folk Songs (in collaboration with Béla Bartók) (1906). (See also *Bartók: Vocal: voice with accompaniment* [**Two Songs from Twenty Hungarian Folk Songs**].)

☐ Chabay (tenor); Kozma (piano) / Bartók 904 (monaural)

A pair of examples from the fascinating results of Kodály's partnership with Bartók in the field of Hungarian folklore, a tremendous untapped resource before their research took place. The results of the project were first made known in this collection, issued in 1906; independent publication of folk materials followed. Though given professional polish, the beauty of the native melodies is not hindered by worldly technique. Both Bartók and Kodály reserved that for their own music, which stems from the indigenous background they probed.

Two Songs from Twenty Hungarian Folk Songs (in collaboration with Béla Bartók) (1906). (See also *Bartók: Vocal: voice with accompaniment* [Two Songs from Twenty Hungarian Folk Songs].)

☐ Chabay (tenor); Kozma (piano) / Bartók 914 (monaural)

(See above for details.)

Akik Mindig Elkésnek (1934)

Choral

Chorus Alone

☐ Budapest Madrigal Ensemble / Szekeres (conductor) / Monitor S-2054

One of the characteristics of Hungarian music is the wide intervallic descent (quite often of a fourth). This tonal birthmark is quite plain and markedly important in Kodály's very haunting *Akik Mindig Elkésnek* ("Those Who Are Always Late"), a short choral piece, written to a poem of the revolutionary Hungarian poet Endre Ady.

Sung with chilling effect. Monitor's release, contained in an album titled *Madrigals & Motets,* is slightly marred by the fact that although the original Hungarian text is contained on an inserted page in the record envelope, no translation is offered. This is odd, since English versions are given for thirteen of the other twenty-one pieces in the album, a number of the thirteen so chosen being of much lesser importance than Kodály's conception.

A Christmas Carol

☐ Whikehart Chorale / Whikehart (conductor) / Lyrichord 7170
☐ Concordia Choir / Christiansen (conductor) / Concordia S-1

Kodály's carol is bedecked with colorful counterpoint, moving in imitation, excited by use of minute syncopation. Though one loves the well-known carols, a new one is like pure, fresh air.

Whikehart's group has a fuller and more resonant sound than Christiansen's. However, the latter conductor uses a slightly different setting, which warrants having both recordings.

Communion   I Will Go Look for Death
Evening (1904)   An Ode for Music
Hymn to King Stephen (1938)

☐ Whikehart Chorale / Whikehart (conductor) / Lyrichord 7170

Choral fluency with hardly a hint of nationalistic mannerisms. In *An Ode for Music,* tonal amplitude results in salty harmonic command. Less harmonic flirting with dissonance is to be noted in the other works. Romantic cosmopolitanism is present in all cases and with no academic concession, even in *Communion,* an anthem "preparing the worshipper for the Eucharist."

The execution and interpretations leave nothing to be desired.

Jesus and the Traders (1934)

☐ Whikehart Chorale / Whikehart (conductor) / Lyrichord 7144

A moving, fascinating work that interweaves baroque austerity with some plainchant brought up to date, colorful polyphony (more than one usually finds in Kodály's music), and Hungarian tints. *Jesus and the Traders* is a motet of split personality and split divisions, yet paradoxically it creates a clear conception because of its sensitive contrasts.

The scoring for unaccompanied chorus is anything but foursquare. There are telling spaces, especially the splitting away of top voices from the lower ones. Kodály's textures are in constant change. They are truly exciting.

This is the single recorded choice at the present time of writing. While it is satisfying, clean, and generally stylish, it lacks vocal weight. A more impressive recording (if it can be found) is the Thomanerchor's performance on Cantate 640217.

Norwegian Girls (1940)

☐ Whikehart Chorale / Whikehart (conductor) / Lyrichord 7170

Kodály's *Norwegian Girls* use Hungarian make-up. A juicy, folksy item, performed with the clearest conception.

The Peacock (1937)

☐ Chorus of the London Symphony Orchestra / Kertész (conductor) / London 26186

The folk song (sung here by unaccompanied male voices) on which Kodály based his orchestral variations (see under *Orchestra*, Variations on a Hungarian Folk Song [*The Peacock*]). In this instance it is recorded as a preliminary to the orchestral work and illustrates keen programming.

Psalm 121 (1936)

☐ Whikehart Chorale / Whikehart (conductor) / Lyrichord 7170

There is minute nationalistic scripture in Kodály's sacred choral piece. It is subtly stressed in this fluid performance.

The Ruins

☐ Male members of the Whikehart Chorale / Gray (baritone) / Whikehart (conductor) / Lyrichord 7208

A patriotic bit but not jingoistic. That sort of strutting can never be found in the native colorations that permeate the text of any Kodály piece, large or small. Here Kodály expresses pride and love of his country in noble terms.

The music is heard in a commendable presentation. Tone and pitch are unimpeachable.

Songs from Karád (1934)

☐ Male members of the Whikehart Chorale / Moss (bass-baritone) / Whikehart (conductor) / Lyrichord 7208

A lusty Hungarian pub song (''Hey, there, girl . . . Fill my mug, fill it higher!'') based on three Hungarian folk songs. Zestful male singing.

Stabat Mater
Veni, Veni Emmanuel

☐ Budapest Madrigal Ensemble / Szekeres (conductor) / Monitor S-2054

The first work is a fully chordal chorale, hymn-styled; the same music states each of the four stanzas. Simple, yes; recognizable as the work of Zoltán Kodály, no. Clearly a historical item, written when the composer was a youth, but compelling nevertheless.

Veni, Veni Emmanuel is a simple setting of a melody Kodály found in a French missal. It is modal, and minus any national fingerprints. Kodály matches the mood and flow of his music to the solemn Latin words. A minor work in his catalogue but of major effect.

The singing of Szekeres's group is prize-worthy.

Tavern Song

☐ Male members of the Whikehart Chorale / Rudzinski and Dial (tenors); Jackson (baritone) / Whikehart (conductor) / Lyrichord 7208

Brewed with bounce. The use of ostinato choral accompaniment in parts of the song adds effervescence. The small solo parts are designated as "Revelers." An attractive piece, attractively done.

Psalm 114

Chorus with Accompaniment

☐ Whikehart Chorale / Whikehart (conductor) / Lyrichord 7170

Hymnodic retentivity in Kodály's forthright effectuation. The organ is important in framing, supporting, and coloring the joyous music but, alas, is given no performer credit.

Psalmus Hungaricus, Op. 13

Chorus and Orchestra

☐ London Symphony Orchestra, Brighton Festival Chorus, and Wandsworth School Boys' Choir / Kozma (tenor) / Kertész (conductor) / London 26186

The 1923 commemoration of the fiftieth anniversary of the unification of Buda and Pest proved to be a red-letter event in music. Commissions by the Hungarian government produced Bartók's colorful Dance Suite and Kodály's powerful *Psalmus Hungaricus,* the text of the latter an adaptation of Psalm 55 by the sixteenth-century Hungarian poet Michael Vég. The nonliturgical interpolations and extensions that Vég made amount to a paraphrase of the biblical prose.

Kodály's nationalistic temper is tenacious. Formality is secondary to the aesthetic truth of his piece—a one-movement symphony for tenor solo, two choruses, and orchestra that portrays music of Hungarian substance. However, the scope and emotion of the *Psalmus Hungaricus* could not be evoked by a provincial composer. It is steeped in native melos, but also contains the direct expressiveness and dramatic strength that are understood universally.

Kertész's viewpoint and conducting are splendid and so is the tenor soloist. Fervor and excitement give special point to the unfolding of the score. There is neither dilution nor transformation that would bleed off the intensity of Kodály's writing.

The version on Everest 3200 offers the text in English. It receives an uneven performance, however, though the engineering is flawless.

Te Deum (1936)

☐ Hungarian Concert Orchestra and Budapest Chorus / Szecsody (soprano); Tiszay (alto); Udvardy (tenor); Farago (bass) / Kodály (conductor) / Turnabout 4351

In spite of the devoutness and a richness of traditionally telescoped polyphony, the true characteristics of Hungarian peasant music are present in the Te Deum (sometimes called *Budavári Te Deum*). Vivid and forceful alternations of mood occur, combining religious praise with national spiritualism. This does not constitute superficial compromise but a modern "duologue." Kodály proves in his work (written to commemorate the two hundred and fiftieth anniversary of the freeing of Budapest from the Turks) that kinship with folk sources need not be of mere outward reference in the medium of sacred music.

This is only a fair-quality recording, but still most important because it is the only one available and is under Kodály's direction.

Cantata and Oratorio

Missa Brevis (in Tempore Belli) (1945)

☐ Peloquin Chorale / Hokans (organ) / Peloquin (conductor) / Gregorian Institute S-205

Despite the fearful days of World War II, Kodály remained in Budapest continuing his creative work. It was during this period that he wrote the *Missa Brevis* ("in time of war"). It has as much conviction as his *Psalmus Hungaricus*, but is far simpler in formulation. In this contemporary mass Kodály's methods are never extravagant; the dominating effect of the music is its subtle, native characteristic, with a bit of intermingled quasi-Gregorian qualities.

Kodály's piece has ecclesiastical meaning without loss of individual style. The *Missa Brevis* is a self-sufficient art work, no less fitting, however, for liturgical use. Kodály worships God in his own special way. It is as sincere, respectful, and correct as the cheerfulness by which Haydn paid homage to the Deity in his masses.

Neither of the two performances available fulfills the work's strengths or its emotive consolations. The Peloquin's is the better of the pair, given with organ in place of orchestra. It is a restrained consideration. So is the one available on Lyrichord (7144), but the sound is not as cogently balanced. It is also done with organ, but no credit is listed for the performer involved.

Opera and Dramatic Music

Háry János, Op. 15

☐ London Symphony Orchestra, Edinburgh Festival Chorus, and Wandsworth School Boys' Choir / Komlóssy, Pálocz, Melis, Bende, Szönyi, and László (vocalists); O'Shea and Holland (choir soloists); Leach (cimbalom); Ustinov (narrator) / Kertész (conductor) / London 1278

The bald fact is that *Háry János* is far less than an opera; it is a play, with background music—talk is the major element. Listening to it, one will find that the picturesque sections used in the orchestral suite (see *Háry János* Suite under *Orchestra*) are mere aural hinges in the stage work and offer no surprise. All of it fits very well; it fits even better when it exists orchestrally apart and does not support stage action. The fair amount of music that was not used in the orchestral suite is neat, folksy, and quite lovely, but incidental.

Still, the orchestral suite from *Háry János* being so well known, there has always been curiosity about the complete work. But it is not exportable. (I can only recall one American stage performance, presented thirty-four years after the Budapest première in 1926.) This is largely because of the language barrier, since, as previously stated, talk is the major element.

However, London's edition has solved the problem. Members of the Hungarian State Opera do the singing in Hungarian. Peter Ustinov narrates the tale in English in piecemeal fashion in order to link the many scenes, and, wearing many hats, also provides the dialogue of assorted characters in the play. He's marvelous. Everything else is top quality, but Ustinov steals the show.

Charles Koechlin (1867-1950)

Cinq chorals dans les modes du Moyen-Age, Op. 117 bis

Orchestra

☐ Louisville Orchestra / Mester (conductor) / Louisville S-682

A principally restrained survey of modality. Apparently, the piece was an outgrowth of Koechlin's intense study of the style, resulting in a large tome titled *Treatise on Modal Polyphony*. With an occasional impressionistic turn in the orchestration, there is no academic dryness. The recording follows appropriately.

Les Bandar-Log, Op. 176

☐ BBC Symphony Orchestra / Dorati (conductor) / Argo ZRG-756

A violent, explosive essay (based on Kipling's *Jungle Book*) that describes the actions of the monkey kingdom with a background of jungle sounds and moods. Koechlin's orchestra is a sonorous moving-picture of black, violet, and screaming crimson colors as it utilizes an instrumentation from the stinging piccolo and small clarinet to the pulpified double bassoon.

Argo's recording (beautifully packaged and supplied with excellent documentation) is a five-star production. Dorati and his musicians cover all the kinetic requirements and lush colorants of Koechlin's symphonic poem to perfection.

Partita for Chamber Orchestra, Op. 205

☐ Louisville Orchestra / Mester (conductor) / Louisville LS-736

Whenever Koechlin's music has been heard (most of it remains unpublished, though the total output went over the two hundred mark), it has proven to have a specific personality of its own. Koechlin remains one of several creative figures for whom the musical world at large has not lived up to its responsibilities.

The Partita reproduces varied sensations. The *Basse donné* is for strings alone—its modal conclusion is a fine inspiration. Contrapuntalism marks both the *Divertissement à 5 parties* and, of course, the final Fugue, but neither is processed academically. In his counterpoint Koechlin was a free-lance. The *Sarabande* is significantly also polyphonic, a hybrid of dance and fugue; a smooth *Calme sur la mer* quietly sets sail as the music prior to the finale.

Any conductor who performs Koechlin's music deserves commendation. The same would apply if any one of them would only open his scores for examination. Mester is to be congratulated not only for the existence of this recorded performance, but for a sensitively organized and expressive musical achievement. This is said without bias, because it should be apparent that I am biased in favor of the work of Charles Koechlin.

Koechlin / Claude Debussy. See *Debussy* / Koechlin.

Karl Kohaut   (1738-1793)

Solo Instrument and Orchestra

Guitar

Concerto in F major for Guitar and Orchestra

☐ I Solisti di Zagreb / Diaz (guitar) / Janigro (conductor) / Vanguard 71152

Originally for lute, but the transfer to the guitar offers no argument. Three movements, with a rondo-minuet combination as the concluding part. An integrated and idiomatic performance.

Karl Kohn   (1926-   )

Chamber Music

Little Suite (1963)

☐ Los Angeles Wind Quintet / Orion 7263

Kohn's work is economical in its thinking, with open textures and tart harmonies. There is a laconic type of humor in the dance portions. Perfectly fit for winds and fittingly performed by the Di Tullio–Benno–Raimondi–Decker–Christlieb team.

Serenade (1962)

☐ Bernhard (flute and piccolo); LeRoux (oboe); O'Brien (clarinet); Barber (bassoon); Sprung (horn); Kohn (piano) / Desto 7166

There is a freshness and a vigorous voice expressed in Kohn's piece. The sense of freedom in the designs is apparent, and so is the panchromaticism that emphasizes the fricative intervals of seconds and sevenths. Rhapsody moves through the music, but the plots of the five movements are clear. To a great extent the colors (the instrumental writing is full of verve and exhilaration) and densities provide the necessary balance for each movement.

The six musicians play this music with expertise. But Desto's production department lacks that element. There is no indication anywhere that the Serenade is for wind quintet and piano. Neither is there specific performer credit. The only information given is a list of the eight musicians that participate in the three works that comprise the release.

Choral

Chorus with Accompaniment

Madrigal

☐ Gregg Smith Singers / Fink (piano) / Smith (conductor) / Composers Recordings S–241

Kohn combines neo-Elizabethan voice lines with a strong piano obbligato part that he describes as "in a flamboyant *concertante* style." They fit with complete success.

The text chosen (the first stanza of a poem by Robert Chester of the seventeenth century)—with such lines as "Your eares having hard the Nightingall soe long,/ I feare will blame my hoarse throat ravens song"—is of a type to demand the circumstance of music. Kohn has accomplished the matter beautifully.

Ellis B. Kohs   (1916-   )

Orchestra

Symphony No. 1 (1950)

☐ Vienna Orchestra / Adler (conductor) / Composers Recordings 104 (monaural)

Music of contemporaneously expressive power and poetic distinction. Add to these a passionate eloquence throughout, whether in the outer fast-paced movements or in the Moderato central part.

The performance is far from an outstanding one. The effect is as though there had been a single runthrough, after which the work was taped. Enough comes through, however, to recognize a music of special accomplishment.

A Short Concert for String Quartet (Quartet No. 2) (1948)

☐ Shapiro and Ross (violins); Schonbach (viola); Rejto (cello) / Composers Recordings S-176E (monaural)

Chamber Music

Illustrative of an interesting working plan. The Concert consists of a sonata movement followed by five short pieces in varied dance designs (save for the fourth part, titled *Farce*). Except for the first of these five divisions, all are for three players, each in turn differing in make-up of instrumentation. The quartet is completed by a fantasy titled *Dreams and Recollections*.

Only a fair performance by this group of excellent West Coast musicians. But this is the only recording available, and Kohs's work deserves to be heard.

Psalm 23 (1958)

☐ Mid-America Chorale / Dexter (conductor) / Composers Recordings 191 (monaural)

Choral

Chorus Alone

Kohs's motet for double mixed chorus, with solo sections for soprano, alto, tenor, and baritone, is of substantial length and of substantial substance. There are six parts, with the full chorus heard in the terminal divisions. There is an eloquence in the work that reminds one of Brucknerian seriousness, but with considerably more passion.

Barbara Kolb *(1940-   )*

Trobar Clus (1970)

☐ Contemporary Chamber Players of the University of Chicago / Kolb (conductor) / Turnabout 34487

Orchestra

Here is a fascinating exhibit of sound swatches. The array is quietly kaleidoscopic—a plectric ingress here, plush flute sounds there, tight trumpet inserts, glides, a twisting harpsichord soundball, a bell bit, a splash of pizzicato, a tremolo on the xylophone, and so on. However, this is no instrumental sampler, but a collage individually detailed in horizontal progress rather than combined in vertical array.

Trobar Clus (on the liner notes the title is followed by "to Lukas"—one assumes Lukas Foss) is poetic, sensitive, beautiful music. This type of separative style could simply have turned out to be a sonic investigation. Kolb has, however, produced music of discriminating taste. She leads a fine performance of her work.

Figments for Flute and Piano (1967)

☐ Herlinger (flute); Seltzer (piano) / Desto 7143

Chamber Music

Though occasionally a line starts a linear journey, it is always interrupted to form still another of the assorted sound objects that pertain to Figments. One is reminded of *frottages* (designs composed of rubbings of a variety of rough surfaces). Kolb's Figments may not have exquisite emotivity but they do have secure sensibility.

The performers toss off the difficulties. It is quite certain that they project all the minute values of the score.

Solitaire for Piano, Vibraphone, and Tape

☐ Seltzer (piano); Fitz (vibraphone) / Turnabout 34487

A type of quiet, consonantlike perpetual-motion piece that turns the vibraphone into a clangy sound by the use of echo and filter devices for the tape. There are precise performance schemes "giving variety (without chance) to each performance." However, the game is rather lengthy for the amount of similar material.

Vocal

Voice and Instrumental Ensemble

Chansons bas for Soprano and Chamber Group (1966)

☐ Lamoree (soprano) / Kolb (conductor) / Desto 7143

Six settings of Mallarmé poems with an instrumental interlude before the final one. Kolb's voluntary or involuntary aestheticism relates to the Boulez of *Marteau sans maître*, with slightly more gentleness. That in itself produces values.

Opera and Dramatic Music

Three Place Settings for Narrator and Chamber Soloists (1968)

☐ Eastman (narrator) / Kolb (conductor) / Desto 7143

Milhaud set descriptions of agricultural machinery in his *Machines agricoles* and was inspired by a florist's catalogue to create his *Catalogue de fleurs*. The Soviet composer Alexander Mossolov wrote a work using newspaper advertisements as his texts. In the same genre, Barbara Kolb considers three aspects of food. The first is to words by Irving Diamond, the second is an amazing roast peacock recipe, and the last, by Ron Costa, is about the death of the Automat, with the title coinage aptly describing the matter as *Automort*.

The wry humor of the lines is entwined with the instrumental data, which is not in any manner a simple accompanimental background. At times the text gets buried, but with the aid of the printed lines on the record jacket a listener can find his way. It's worthwhile, especially because of the meaty lines Kolb has chosen.

Karel Komzák (1823-1893)

Orchestra

Badner Mäd'n, Op. 252

☐ Johann Strauss Orchestra of Vienna / Boskovsky (conductor) / Angel S-36887

Komzák was a Czech, but his twenty years' service as a bandmaster in the Austrian army gave him sufficient stylistic influence to turn out a good Viennese waltz. It therefore finds proper place in Boskovsky's recorded album titled *Music of Vienna*, Vol. 2.

Peter Jona Korn (1922-   )

Orchestra

Variations on a Tune from *The Beggar's Opera,* Op. 26

☐ Louisville Orchestra / Whitney (conductor) / Louisville 58-2 (monaural)

The "tune" is *Over the Hills and Far Away.* Korn's variations total nine plus a Finale. In this recording Variations 3 and 4 have been eliminated.

Korn's neat neo-romantic structures are sometimes bent backward and forward, so to speak, as in the neoclassic seventh permutation (Gavotte). Such stylistic shifts are acceptable in a set of variational exploits.

Whitney, always competent if not brilliant, does a fine presentation in this instance.

Erich Wolfgang Korngold (1897-1957)

Suite from the Music to Shakespeare's *Much Ado About Nothing*, Op. 11 *Orchestra*

☐ Westphalian Symphony Orchestra, Recklinghausen / Landau (conductor) / Candide 31091

Korngold's score (for a chamber orchestra including a harmonium and with the string body minus cellos) consists of fourteen numbers. From these, five were selected for the suite performed here. Later on, Korngold made a transcription of the last four numbers in the suite (the opening Overture was eliminated) for violin and piano, which was titled Four Pieces from *Much Ado About Nothing* for Violin and Piano. (For a discussion of the recording of this version, see under *Instrumental: violin.*)

The movements that follow the Overture are: *Maiden in the Bridal Chamber;* a humorous march, *Dogberry and Verges,* subtitled March of the Sentinel; a lyrically polished Intermezzo, also with a subtitle, *Garden Scene;* and a boisterous Hornpipe (sometimes called *Mummery*).

The economy of Korngold's means exemplifies the craftsmanship of this former prodigy. Landau's performance is adequate and the better of the pair on the market. (The other issue is on Angel S-36999.)

Symphony in F sharp major, Op. 40

☐ Munich Philharmonic Orchestra / Kempe (conductor) / RCA ARL1-0443

All the earmarks of the full romantic. Impassioned cantilena and exemplary structural logic mark Korngold's opus. It is a bit more serious than most of his other works. The performance is clear-cut and fully carries out all the subtleties contained in the score.

Theme and Variations, Op. 42

☐ Stuttgart Radio Orchestra / Mattes (conductor) / Angel S-36999

Formal fitness, defined by a good performance.

Korngold's strong affinity for writing in the style of Richard Strauss is illustrated here. One could wish that some of the clichés of that composer were not present, but whatever the criticism at the very least the writing is clear and makes its point, and the orchestration avoids sonorous overcrowding.

Concerto in D major for Violin and Orchestra, Op. 35 *Solo Instrument and Orchestra*

☐ Los Angeles Philharmonic / Heifetz (violin) / Wallenstein (conductor) / RCA LM-1782 (monaural)

Violin

Heifetz commissioned this work, gave its premiere performance (on February 15, 1947) with the St. Louis Symphony Orchestra, Vladimir Golschmann, conducting, and then recorded it on January 10, 1953. It remains *the* recording to have, despite an excellent rendition given by Ulf Hoelscher on Angel (S-36999).

The statement Korngold made says it all about the piece: "The work was contemplated for a Caruso of the violin rather than for a Paganini.'' There is, nonetheless, sufficient technical force in the concerto, particularly in its finale. One cannot agree with the critic who made a prose play on the composer's name by stating there was more corn than gold in the concerto.

Instrumental

Märchenbilder, Op. 3

Piano

Sonata No. 2 in E major, Op. 2

☐ Kubalek (piano) / Genesis 1055

A commitment to rich romantic detail, with luxuriant orchestralike textures in Sonata No. 2, as though the work were a keyboard reduction of an orchestral work. A special essay by Glenn Gould discusses this in an individually styled prose that adds to the value of the release. Kubalek's playing, however, while candid, is not overloaded in any attempt to make more of a muchness.

The seven *Märchenbilder* (with such delineations as *The Princess and the Pea, The Ruler of the Spirits,* and *The Fairy King's Ball*), though necessarily drawn a little lighter, are far from lightweight. One of the best of the suite is *Wichtelmännchen* (''The Gnomes''). Kubalek offers some of his finest playing to match.

Violin

Four Pieces from *Much Ado About Nothing* for Violin and Piano

☐ Granat (violin); Gray (piano) / Orion 74166

For the background pertaining to this work, see under *Orchestra* (Suite from the Music to Shakespeare's *Much Ado About Nothing*). There are slight differences here in the movement titles, with some confusion arising from further differences between the liner notes and the record label. *(The) Maiden in the Bridal Chamber* is termed *Bridal Morning* by the producer and liner-note writer of the present disc. The orchestral Intermezzo heading is not listed here by that title, but outlined as an ''intermezzo in form,'' with the label calling the piece *Scene in the Garden,* the liner note changing this to *The Garden Scene.* Again, titling is shifted to formal description as the last piece is termed ''a horn-pipe,'' but designated as *Masquerade.* Perhaps these comments may be considered mere quibbling, but production ambivalence is unfair to the record buyer, who should be given information that matches wherever it may appear.

This being said, the performance itself is a stimulating one. Granat avoids what could easily have been some schmaltzy salonistic solutions, and that adds to the credits.

Chamber Music

Sonata for Violin and Piano, Op. 6

☐ Granat (violin); Gray (piano) / Orion 74166

There is abundant power in the thick lines of the passionate opening movement. The Scherzo gives an example of birthright infiltration. While the first theme is driven by the impulses of the form, the second one is an idealization of the Viennese waltz. Interestingly, the main theme of the Adagio includes both the rise and fall that define the two subjects of the opening movement. The finale runs through modified sonata form, and contains a fugato. But the *Sturm und Drang* of the sonata ends in the opposite manner.

This is a polished, well-defined performance. (Orion and *Schwann* both list this as Opus 4, which correctly is the designation for Korngold's *Schauspiel* Overture.)

Piano Trio, Op. 1

☐ Pacific Art Trio / Delos 25402

Korngold composed his first official opus at the age of thirteen. It has definitive workmanship and provides fine aural communication in its ringing affirmation of quasi-Straussian language. Even in a composer thrice that age it would be becoming. Here it is a vivid conspectus of what a creative prodigy was able to produce.

Alice Shapiro, Israel Baker, and Edgar Lustgarten make a fine team. They have an unerring ear for this robust music and prove it in their playing.

The Adventures of Robin Hood

Film Music

☐ Warner Bros. Orchestra / Rathbone (narrator) / Korngold (conductor) / Delos DEL/ F–25409 (monaural)

If not a cause for celebration, at the very least a cause for nostalgia is represented by this release. It illustrates the status of film music in the 1930s with its whammy romantic characterization. The score presented here consists of ten of the sequences in the film, with the story line outlined between each portion by Basil Rathbone.

The original recording was made in 1938 (on four 78-rpm discs). The present disc is an acceptable transfer, providing one doesn't expect top-drawer sound.

Karl Korte   (1928-   )

Concerto for Piano and Winds

Solo Instrumental and Orchestra

Piano

☐ University of Texas Wind Ensemble / Perry (piano) / Lee (conductor) / Turnabout 34704

Despite its hard-bitten musical verbiage and heated dissonances, Korte's work is firmly related to classical formal balances, with an aggressive first part, an introspective middle division, and a lighter-framed, somewhat jazzy end movement. But there is no mishmash of contemporary maxims in this solidly conceived fantasy. One of the important points is the equalized strength of the solo voice and the wind ensemble.

Since the soloist gave the premiere, his knowledge of the work is special and his playing is most convincing. The university group sounds totally professional.

Remembrances for Flute and Synthesized Processed Sound (1971)

Instrumental

Flute

☐ Baron (flute, alto flute, and piccolo) / Nonesuch 71289

A trisectional piece, each section matched by a different type of flute—in turn, alto flute, flute, and piccolo—and each of these paralleled by a specific tempo frame: *slow, moderate to fast,* and *very fast.* It will be noted that the size of the instrument is akin to the speed rate. Coloristic rhetoric is primary. The flute includes microtones and other subtle effects. In turn, the tape part has the sense of instrumental well-being, its rhythmic figures and patterns avoiding the usual (and now academic) electronic vocabulary.

Matrix (1968)

Chamber Music

☐ Baron (flute); Roseman (oboe); Glazer (clarinet); Weisberg (bassoon); Hamme (saxophone); Des-Roches (percussion); Elizabeth Korte (piano) / Composers Recordings S–249

Music of serialized sum and substance. However, no technical dry rot will be found in *Matrix.* Motival rhapsody carries the music forward, without the expressionistic coldness that pervades so many serial explanations. The balances are derived from juxtapositions of material. In this, color plays a strong role, though for the greater part the percussion is used for ictus, punctuation, and framing. The pedal roll that combines with the solo saxophone portion is, indeed, a neat bit. So is the jocularity just before the final portion of the piece. *Matrix* has the substance of real musical matter.

There are no doubts as to the performance. But do doubt (in part) the credits on the back of the album cover and on the record label. In both cases the New York Woodwind Quintet is given credit. But there is no horn in the personnel, and only four-fifths of the New York group is involved—the horn being replaced by a saxophone. On the label, "with piano and percussion" is found. The only way to locate the performer credits for these two instruments is to dig into the liner notes.

Martin Scot Kosins   *(1947-   )*

Chamber Music

Love Letters—A Dialogue for Flute and Piano

☐ Shostac (flute); Swearengin (piano) / Crystal S–314

Tonal music with engaging romantic gestures. There is an overlay of nostalgic (almost nocturnal) sadness to Kosins's three-part piece, described as "a work of melodies . . . a work of feelings . . . a work of hopes."

The playing fits the mood and the music.

Vocal

Shadows of the Heart for Soprano, Flute, and Strings

Voice and Orchestra

☐ Members of the Detroit Symphony Orchestra / Gordon (soprano) / Resnick (conductor) / Orion 78287

Kosins's work is large scale, inhabiting the territory of intense romanticism, its atmosphere slightly permeated with Bergian temperature. The quality of invention is rich, the pantonal sweep codifying the text. Shadows of the Heart, which depicts "a woman's confrontation with the passage of time," marks the work of a practically unknown composer. On the strength of this score that negative point will change.

Majorie Gordon trenchantly explores every phrase. The range demanded is huge, but she conquers every difficulty, while giving infinite care to phrasing and diction, including the one section where narration replaces song. Keep an eye on this composer.

Wlodzimierz Kotoński   *(1925-   )*

Orchestra

Canto for Chamber Orchestra (1961)

☐ Internationalen Kranichsteiner Kammer-Ensemble / Maderna (conductor) / Mainstream 5008

In Kotoński's Canto the sustained nature of the basic material kills off the underlying pulsed inserts and the definition that these provide. Variety is obtained by instruments (a total of eighteen) and a dynamic assortment that individually regulates the strength of each pitch as it enters. This forms the music's special mystery.

A score of this type provides no easy answers for a conductor. However, Maderna (who was a splendid composer) proves with this special advantage his complete understanding of every note in the work.

Serge Koussevitzky

Concerto for Double Bass and Orchestra (1905)

☐ Oslo Philharmonic Orchestra / Karr (double bass) / Antonini (conductor) / Composers Recordings S–248

Solo Instrument and Orchestra

Double Bass

Koussevitzky composed his concerto with the aid of the Russian composer Reinhold Glière. It has a simplistic type of ternary design, with the outer portions the same, spliced with a slower section. But even in the terminal Allegro parts the name of the piece is lyricism, a ballade masquerading (though effectively and prettily) under the concerto title. There are no cadenzas, no pyrotechnical flourishes—all string song.

The performance is unbelievable. Karr makes his bass sound like a cello. (Some may criticize this—where is the *true* bass sound, therefore?) But sensitive ears will realize that Karr is not trying to imitate a cello. In his playing he has simply removed all the ordinary gruffness and common lugubriousness of the instrument. The richness and sonority is powerfully vocal; a seamlessness of bowing and acute phrasing enriches this composition far more than one would think possible. If stars are to be assigned, Karr deserves a dozen or so.

Valse miniature

☐ Karr (double bass); Siegel (piano) / Golden Crest RE–7012

Instrumental

Double Bass

Limited musical values, but the highest standards of playing by this virtuoso who makes a bull fiddle sound like a ripe cello.

Boris Koutzen

Concertino for Piano and Strings (1959)

☐ Orchestre Lamoureux / Guralnik (piano) / Barzin (conductor) / Serenus 12010

Solo Instrument and Orchestra

Piano

Koutzen deemed himself a romanticist. Acceptable. His Concertino has not so much suave song from above as it has weighted counterpoint from within. The music moves but moves through thick passages. At times the shrubbery surrounding an idea makes viewing difficult, but the general combined-movements design is clear.

The piano sound is sharp, slightly percussive; the orchestal sound is full and resonant.

Eidólons

☐ Maxin (piano) / Serenus 12010

Instrumental

Piano

Highly chromatic material, but in Koutzen's hands the treatment is both fastidious and sophisticated. The fantasy proposition of this work (subtitled Poem for Piano) is based on the poem by Walt Whitman. Secure playing.

Sonatina (1931)

☐ Guralnik (piano) / Serenus 12010

Entirely characteristic of this composer's music by way of its persistent chromaticism. At times the tonality span almost expands into a split personality.

Unfortunately, Serenus fills its unsigned liner notes with general background on the composer (twenty-nine lines), data regarding the performers on the all-Koutzen disc, of which this is one of four works (thirty-eight lines), and some *generalia* about his music that is a puff but still says nothing (nine lines). Only one of the four works—*Eidólons* (*see above*)—is given a single line and a poetic quote. The other compositions don't even get that amount of space.

The Sonatina has a length that goes beyond that usually applied to this type of structure. Its eleven-and-one-quarter-minute span portrays an unbroken continuity but traces three-movement division. Robert Guralnik demonstrates a sure-fire technique, presenting the music with fine tone in its slow-lyrical inflections and a dynamic thrust in its kinetic portions. Fine music, if not presented with proper information for the consumer.

Two Pianos

Sonatina for Two Pianos

☐ Maxin and Guralnik (pianos) / Serenus 12010

Koutzen avoids any tune with accompaniment in his two-piano work. Like most of his output, the textures are solidified by contrapuntalism, though something akin to simpler bell-imitations comes through the middle of the work. The action of the opus explodes in the final section (a three-in-one structure is apparent), which has a type of joyous animalism about it, avidly executed by the performers.

Violin

Sonata for Solo Violin

☐ Rosand (violin) / Serenus 12062

The problem in unaccompanied violin music is not only one of requisite harmonic notification, but a tendency to congestion in the attempt to fulfill such a requirement. Koutzen's music is texturally nicely calculated; the harmonic content is detailed cleanly without pseudo-linear action competing for attention.

Four connected sections, in contrasting tempi, cover the opus. In the second part (in fast pace) cadenza circumstances are in play, with pedal points, ponticello sounds, simultaneous bowed and plucked timbre, and flying left-hand pizzicati. The final part is sunny and dancy.

There are not many twentieth-century solo violin sonatas that are artistically realized or maintain interest by using technical tact and cunning. Koutzen is especially successful in all respects. Aaron Rosand's playing is of high distinction. He displays a steady musicality, projects illuminating clarity, and tosses off the technical difficulties as though they were trifles.

Hans Kox (1930-   )

Orchestra

Cyclophonie V (1966)

☐ Utrecht Symphony Orchestra / Schreuder (oboe); Vink (clarinet); Westerveld (bassoon) / Hupperts (conductor) / Donemus Audio-Visual Series DAVS–6903

There are no halfway measures in Kox's scoring choice, or neutrality, for that matter. Three winds (oboe, clarinet, and bassoon) are combined and contrasted against thirteen violins, four cellos, and two double basses, each with an individual part, always chordally concerned, save for ten measures.

Communicative use is made of this colorful combine for contrasts of starkness and cuteness and for rhythmic thrust both intense and light.

All the proportions of the score are realized in a fine statement by Hupperts's musicians. The sound is excellent, some of the very best heard in the Donemus series.

Cyclophonie I (1964)

Solo
Instrument
and
Orchestra

Cello

☐ Radio Chamber Orchestra / Werner (cello) / Hupperts (conductor) / Donemus Audio-Visual Series DAVS-6602 (monaural)

Kox's piece in *voor Violoncello en Klein Orkest*. Indeed, for "small orchestra," and a special one that banishes the usual for the extremely novel scoring of three flutes, twelve violins, and four double basses all playing individual parts. Indeed, also "for cello"—and how! Declamatory under sustained chords, exhortative passages, and a very sizable cadenza. The nineteen instruments are entirely subsidiary.

Let it be known that though color is emphatically in first position here, it is not achieved at the expense of musical reasoning that has value and more than average interest. The density combinations of the violins, basses, and flutes are apportioned well, and the soloist is most communicative.

Leopold Anton Koželuch   (1747 - 1818)

Piano Concerto in D major

Solo
Instrument
and
Orchestra

Piano

☐ Prague New Chamber Orchestra / Blumental (piano) / Zedda (conductor) / Turnabout 34279

Rococo attunement, reflective of grace and melodic elegance. No deep probing here, but most certainly a lovely duet between the piano and the accompanimental oboes, horns, and strings.

Fine presence in the recording. Blumental is best in the set of variations of the third movement.

Leo Kraft   (1922-   )

Concerto No. 3 for Cello, Winds, and Percussion (1969)

Solo
Instrument
and
Orchestra

Cello

☐ New Wind Quintet / Kouguell (cello); DesRoches (percussion) / Serenus 12037

Though Kraft's primary proposition is immediately made clear by the contemporary virtuosity of the solo instrument (quite different, of course from patterns that fit the hand trained in the major-minor tonal orbit), there is a secondary network of logistics. These include extensions of pitch designs from cello onto percussion and the thrust of wind colors against string timbre, as well as the pulsatile punctuation of the percussion. Further, the use of the horn offstage defines another dimension.

These involved interlucents provide a stunning colorful conception of concerto writing and form one of Leo Kraft's finest works. It is performed magnificently by soloist, wind players, and percussionist. The music itself is exciting; the playing equally so.

Allegro giocoso (1957)

Instrumental

Piano

☐ Helps (piano) / Composers Recordings S-288

Constructive and imaginative, aurally justifying Kraft's title objective. To this can be added: compelling and effective. And the last statement describes Robert Helps's pianism.

Statements and Commentaries (1965)

☐ Peltzer (piano) / Serenus 12037

Separate structural duality forms a set of unitary divisions in Kraft's piece. Each statement is followed by a commentary. While the relationships are elusive, the total content is highly charged in these expressionistic, nontonal fragments.

Chamber Music

Trios and Interludes (1965)

☐ Baron (flute); Sackson (viola); Peltzer (piano) / Serenus 12037

Alternative disposition of the instrumental totality is basic to the design, with the full trio being used in parts 1, 3, and 5, and a pair of Interludes covering divisions 2 and 4. This sets up a rondo design of color and textural proportions that can be basically coded as A–B–A–B–A. However, the use of the solo piano for the first Interlude and the flute and viola for the second one lends more contrast to the design, so that the code can be revised and refined to A–B–A–C–A. Further, the statements of the Interludes are sharply opposite in tempo and mood.

The blueprint is clear and so is the detail that Kraft has placed in his structure. Virtuosity is mandatory to define it in sound and these expert musicians are in that category.

Partita No. 3 for Wind Quintet (1964)

☐ New Wind Quintet / Serenus 12037

Mostly spiky and punctuative. Kraft avoids the long line until the Finale of his five-part work. Still, in these jabs of atonal wind play there is an urgency and directness—and a firm stylistic balance. The quintet (Levy, Schumann, Rabbai, Chapin, and Nakagawa) is deft in handling the athletic rhythms of Kraft's text.

William Kraft   (1923-   )

Orchestra

Contextures: Riots – Decade '60 (1967)

☐ Los Angeles Philharmonic Orchestra / Sachs (violin); Bunker (snare drum and drums); Guarneri (trumpet); Kelley, Jr. (bass); Nash (soprano saxophone) / Mehta (conductor) / London 6613

Extrovert music—a music of almost horrible fear and concern, governed by black horizons. It disturbs. It should. There are five movements: the first of decided conflict; a jet-flighted second part that includes random metrical designs plus multilayered sound chunks that contain neo-Ivesian data; a more introspective section; and a final pair of linked divisions in which there is, at first, a sense of rhapsodic recitative combined with forceful punctuation and multipolyphony, and, finally, a more pulsating verticalistic section. Between the first and second movements a jazz duo (violin and snare drum) gives a lower-case footnote to Kraft's fiery collisions. In the final movement jazz is used again (by means of an offstage quartet this time). This jazz group merges with and then comes out of the full orchestral mass soloistically.

Contextures lingers long in the ear after it is heard. Though the scoring is packed with instrumental placements, there is repose and tension, direction, plan, and climax. It is a powerful document, fastidiously drawn under Mehta's direction.

Games: Collage No. 1 (1969)

☐ Horn Club of Los Angeles / Kraft (conductor) / Angel S–36036

Kraft's *Games* is placed in the band category merely as a convenience, since all but four of the twenty-six instrumentalists involved play brass instruments. The total is divided into two equal antiphonal groups, each consisting of three trumpets, four horns, three Wagner tubas, one tuba, and two percussionists.

This sonic inventory is utilized for musical sportsmanship in a series of eight games, including chess and poker moves. Such gambling passion lurks in the heart of every composer who tests his aleatoric luck, and a number of works by Kraft fall in that classification. His winnings have been huge, however, if one equates them with artistic and creative viability.

The eight games in the present work are all fully detailed on the recording's jacket. Whether one can follow some of the intricate plays and ploys is immaterial; the music is the thing, and it's a stimulating eight-minute affair, containing ripe and rash sonorities, intricate and imperative rhythms, all placed in neat correspondence between coloration and matter. Kraft's gamble pays off for himself and the listener.

Fanfare 1969

☐ Los Angeles Brass Society / Remsen (conductor) / Avant 1001

High-charged, tightly textured, metrically compounded. All in one minute flat.

Momentum for Eight Percussionists

☐ Pacific Percussion Ensemble / Kraft (conductor) / Crystal S–104

Forty individual instruments are included in Kraft's pulsatile orchestra: five are pitched mallet types, seven are wood, eight are metal (including a set of five varied-sized iron pipes and a pair of anvils), one is a string drum (known as the "lion's roar"), and nineteen are membrane representatives.

Kraft's octet (an octet in terms of performer totality) builds from a generating figure. It is elongated and compressed and then contrasted to more data, in which rhythmic counterpoint is stated in high style. The speed differences, tensions, and releases within this are eventually combined with elements drawn from the initial part, and thus, by association, the music obtains its "momentum."

Percussion music has its own cult following. The majority feel that their pet medium has special qualities that most others would not fully appreciate. A hearing or two of Momentum will prove that other than percussion music cultists can enjoy its contemporary *musical* drama and discover a new world of titillating timbres.

Morris Dance (1963)

☐ Ervin (percussion) / Wim WIMR–5

A contemporary cross-pollinated view of the old English folk dance. In the hands of this jointly expert composer-percussionist (or percussionist-composer!) rhythmic straightforwardness is replaced by swordlike excitation.

The instrumentation is for three membraneous representatives: snare drum, field drum, and bass drum. Karen Ervin handles these with expertise and artistic realization.

Theme and Variations for Percussion Quartet

☐ Pacific Percussion Ensemble / Kraft (conductor) / Crystal S–104

A mini-anthology of percussion detail for four players performing on twenty-seven instruments. These are all of standard identity, including timpani, bass drum, triangle, wood block, chimes, and so on. There is a pair of exceptions: a mouth siren and a bulb horn (a French-style taxi horn).

In the hands of this percussion magician the conduct of the music is clear and comprehensive. Kraft is also meticulous in taking care of the formal sense and, as a result, the sections of the piece have musical significance. When composers such as this master craftsman (pun intended but a factual description at the same time) produce music like the Theme and Variations, there is no doubt of the robust survival of this medium, once considered merely experimental or existing for didactic purposes.

Solo Instrument and Orchestra

Flute, Bassoon, Violin, and Cello

Concerto Grosso (1962)

☐ Louisville Orchestra / Fuge (flute); Nelson (bassoon); Kling (violin); Grace Whitney (cello) / Robert Whitney (conductor) / Louisville S–653

A superb entry in an unusual medium. The soprano and bass members of the wind and string families (here discriminately defined by first-rate soloists) give a strongly typed concertino which strengthens the arguments deployed in this music of serial organization. The rhythmic firmness and terseness in the composition (here cogently realized by Robert Whitney) show how a free-lance creative voice can deal with Schoenbergian syntax without imitative gestures.

Percussion

Triangles, A Concerto for Percussion and Ten Instruments (1969)

☐ Members of the Los Angeles Philharmonic / Silverman (percussion) / Kraft (conductor) / Crystal S–104

The solo voice handles a huge array of six different types of drums, metallophones (including varied sized cymbals, tam-tams, triangles, antique and finger cymbals), lignophones (that is, wooden instruments, in this case, temple and wood blocks), as well as marimba, vibraphone, and glockenspiel. The instrumental body that supports and complements the solo percussionist consists of a dectet (four woodwinds, three brass, and three stringed instruments).

The title of the work arises from instrumental placement. The percussion is deployed in two triangles facing each other to the left with another triangular arrangement to the right; the conductor is in between these. In front of him there are two groups as well (also both in three-sided disposition): the winds and brass to the left, the strings to the right. It should be noted that no such precise disposition is conveyed by the recording, but it does not matter a whit in terms of musical significance.

The invention in the work is thrilling. Through Kraft's appropriate radical solo instrumentation for his radical design, all the complex details and shuttling montages become defined. There is coloristic paragraphing in the essay to highlight specific solo particulars within the solo instruments' totality, but the music is never segmented. Triangles is prime evidence of the maturation of percussion music.

Percussion Quartet

Concerto for Four Percussion Soloists and Orchestra (1964)

☐ Los Angeles Philharmonic Orchestra / Kraft, Goodwin, Delancey, and Clark (percussion) / Mehta (conductor) / London 6613

Kraft's Concerto might well be called a partita, since his formal plan is a collation of diverse ideas. These, however, project a definite unity. Movement 1 is recitative in nature; movement 2 presents the scurry and brimming briskness of a scherzo; and the final movement proceeds from a pithy theme to a cadenza and twelve variations.

The soloists are masters of their instrumental craft. Their playing is handsomely realized and of exceptional artistry. Mehta balances matters beautifully in this work of aural fascinations.

Encounters II (1966)

☐ Bobo (tuba) / Crystal S-215

Excruciatingly difficult, but Roger Bobo is no ordinary musician, and tuba conquers all.

The music has extremely wide compass, its dynamic range is kaleidoscopic, its colors complex. Glissandi are special within the piece; so are duple lines (the player sings one part while playing another). Though rather free in its design, the form of *Encounters II* is clearly defined by the multitudinous tempo changes.

The composition "was written especially for Roger Bobo." Still, a tie score. Kraft's individuality is matched by Bobo's virtuosity.

The recording in question was made in 1969. Nine years later, Bobo again recorded the work, again for Crystal. Bobo explains: "Since the first recording my concept of the work has significantly changed." Both interpretations are splendid. The newest one is on S-392.

Encounters III for Trumpet and Percussion (1971)

☐ Stevens (trumpet); Peters (percussion) / Avant 1003

Kraft indicates that *Encounters III* "is conceived of as a medieval battle; the trumpet represents the attacking force, the percussion the defending." With contemporary administration Kraft lets loose a colorful arsenal of material intensely picturing the chosen creative premise. In part, what the performer chooses to play is basic to the structuring of this duo embroilment. Actually, listening to the piece without any consideration of the scenario is totally satisfactory, indicating how a talented composer goes beyond self-imposed restrictions.

There is no gibblegabble in Kraft's liner note. And, to continue the accolades, there is intense technical-musical passion on the part of the performers.

Encounters IV, A Duel for Trombone and Percussion

☐ Thomas Ervin (trombone); Karen Ervin (percussion) / Crystal 641

A different version of *Encounters III* (for details, *see above*), with the same objectives and similar concepts dictating the titles of the movements: *Strategy* (the processes of the battle Kraft is picturing by way of musical attacks and counterattacks); *Truce of God* (referring to the medieval custom of Sabbath respite during war)—Crystal's label indicates "Peace of God," though the liner copy speaks of the title correctly; and *Tactics* (battle in totality leading to denouement). Here, not only is a different brass instrument used, but there is a tape collage of war speeches, songs, and so on made by William Malloch. (The album notes make no mention of the kinship between *Encounters III* and *Encounters IV*.) Again, as in *Encounters III*, the auditor can bypass Kraft's musical simulation of a medieval battle plan and just listen. Fantastic and fascinating duo music is thus "encountered."

Cadenze (1972)

☐ Kobialka (violin); Bernhard (flute); LeRoux (oboe); Ellis (viola); Sprung (horn); Barber (bassoon); O'Brien (clarinet) / Kraft (conductor) / Desto 7166

Here, the composer is partnered in both re-creation and creation by the performers. The method as explained by Kraft: "The players must be involved with one another in various free (non-directed) interdependent areas, and in some of the cadenzas"—meaning, of course, the *modus operandi* of chance operations. Since the basic quality of a cadenza (there are eight in succession in Kraft's opus) has the sense of an improvisation, Kraft's decision to have performer participation in cadenza formation is quite apt.

This "eight-voiced" creative counterpoint, with its continuant and contrastive degrees of color, includes some parenthetical references to other composers. Just a bit, but enough to add a flavorsome touch.

Nonet for Brass and Percussion (1958)

☐ Los Angeles Brass Quintet and Los Angeles Percussion Ensemble / Kraft (conductor) / Crystal S–821

Kraft's Nonet is dodecaphonically detailed and developed but has unprejudiced and unconstrained individuality within the twelve-tone premise. Its colors make the syntax scintillate.

Many a serial-styled piece has an impersonality while conveying a well-balanced technical order. The missing element is vitality. Kraft's Nonet has dominant singularity as well as stability, and, as is so usual with this composer, the percussion writing is a constructive gem.

This is a music neither imitative nor of narrow outlook. It is twelve-tone music brought into the fullest artistic balance.

Opera and Dramatic Music

Des Imagistes

☐ Los Angeles Percussion Ensemble / Geer and Kermoyan (readers) / Kraft (conductor) / Delos 25432

If one were to write a history of percussion music, consideration of William Kraft's *Des Imagistes* would occupy one of its most intriguing sections. This work is both a drama intertwined with percussion and music for percussion alone. In the former, the percussion plays on and against and colors within and about the texts (five in total, by Cummings, Pound, Everett, Frost, and Barbara Kraft). By itself, the pulsatile array is dynamically magical.

The impact of Kraft's music is enormous; this may turn out to be his major piece.

The personality of the work is wonderfully exposed by the ensemble; the diction of Ellen Geer and Michael Kermoyan is beautifully controlled, beautifully delivered, and clear in every syllable. The text supplied was found to be unnecessary.

A. Walter Kramer (1890-1969)

Vocal

Voice with Accompaniment

Swans, Op. 44, No. 4

☐ McCormack (tenor); Schneider (piano) / New World Records NW–247 (monaural)

The only representation in the recorded catalogue of music by this composer-publisher. Despite the age of the recording—the original was made in September of 1923—McCormack's voice rings clear and true. And beautiful it surely is.

Joseph Martin Kraus (1756-1792)

Overture: *Olympia*

☐ English Chamber Orchestra / Bonynge (conductor) / London 6735

As fine an overture as any Mozart (Kraus's contemporary) produced. It has a wonderful introduction and is fully symphonic in its format.

Symphony in C minor

☐ Angelicum Orchestra of Milan / Jenkins (conductor) / Nonesuch 71156

A real find. Every portion spells potent creativity and meaning. The Symphony begins with a Larghetto that instantly recalls the *Iphigénie en Aulide* overture by Gluck and moves into a dramatic Allegro. The slow movement is variational-like. Though it is lyrical, a depth of emotive consequence surrounds the material. The finale is energetic, a partner to the inner urgency of the initial fast movement.

Newell Jenkins produces an admirable and substantial presentation, emphasizing the dark quality of the music. This Symphony should be given attention by the conductorial fraternity. Truly, a find.

Funeral Cantata for Gustave III of Sweden

☐ Clarion Concerts Orchestra and Chorus / Moynagh (soprano); Meyer (mezzo-soprano); Ulfung (tenor); Borg (bass) / Jenkins (conductor) / Vanguard C-10065

The possibility that Kraus's name, let alone his music, is known to even the consistent concert-goer is worth a hefty wager on the negative end. Yet this contemporary of Mozart produced some worthy pieces, especially this one. It has the regular format of arias, choruses, a vocal quartet, and the usual fugue. It has, also, the shaping force of threnodic emotivity.

It receives here a thoroughly prepared performance, with good feeling and lyrical sense. The male voices are solid, and some female vocal vibrato does not disturb the communicative quality of the total production.

Johann Ludwig Krebs (1713-1780)

***Fantasia à 4* in F major**

Herr Jesu Christ, mein's Lebens licht

☐ Haselböck (organ); Hertel (oboe) / Turnabout 34612

The oboe in *Herr Jesu Christ* is used as a coloristic ritornello with the organ's chorale. This alternation provides a continuous thesis-antithesis. There is no chorale in the *Fantasia*, but there is a surprising oboe flourish near the conclusion.

Treuer Gott, ich muss dir klagen

☐ Haselböck (organ); Hertel (oboe d'amore) / Turnabout 34612

An appealing example of a practice popular in church music, especially in Central Germany, in the middle eighteenth century; that is, the partnering of the organ with a wind instrument. The use of the old type of oboe for this purpose is quietly colorful.

Organ and Trumpet

In allen meinen Taten

Wachet auf, ruft uns die Stimme

☐ Haselböck (organ); Spindler (trumpet) / Turnabout 34612

Gorgeous amplification of the polyphonic material, with golden streamlined trumpet timbre. Especially ideal is *Wachet auf.* Both pieces are imaginative conceptions that warm the ear.

Six Chorales

Es ist gewisslich an der Zeit
Gott der Vater wohn' uns bei
Herzlich Lieb hab' ich dich, o Herr
Liebster Jesu, wir sind hier
Wachet auf, ruft uns die Stimme
Was mein Gott will, das g'scheh' allzeit

☐ André (trumpet); Bilgram (organ) / RCA CRL2-7001

Precise timbre differentiation of the material applies here: the chorale melody is played by the trumpet; the organ entwines it with a contrapuntal texture. Obedience to this is certainly the way to success. However, monotony creeps into some of the pieces that are substantial in length: for instance, *Gott der Vater* runs five minutes and fifteen seconds, and *Wachet auf* is four and one-half minutes in length.

The unsigned liner note mentions the music's "beauty and invention." A fair verdict. The playing is fully up to standard, though there is little attempt to seek out dynamic differences.

Chamber Music

Fantasia for Transverse Flute, Two Keyboards, and Pedal

☐ Rampal (flute); Alain (organ) / Musical Heritage Society MHS-1277

It is rare in combinations of this type that the wind instrument does not hold the upper hand, supported as it moves about by the keyboard instrument. But such is the case here: the organ dominates, the flute plays second fiddle. Akin to this condition is the form; no fast-slow-fast blueprint, but a fantasy that constantly unfolds new details. Alain and Rampal do themselves honor with a superb statement of the work.

Sonata in G major

☐ Rampal (flute); Gilbert (harpsichord) / Orion 73114

Krebs's Sonata is regulated by suite terms, comprising a *Siciliano,* two *Menuetts,* and a *Polonaise* within its six movements. The *Finale alla breve* partakes of dance character as well.

Orion lists it incorrectly as in G minor on its jacket. Its sound is fuller than the duplicate performance that is contained in Everest's jumbo collection of Rampal performances (No. 3194). No data whatsoever is given concerning any of the music in that release.

Arthur Kreiger (20th cent.)

Electronic Music

Short Piece (1974)

☐ Odyssey Y-34139

Kreiger's Short Piece consists of phrase contrasts ("articulated in a highly pungent manner"). Academicism is bypassed in Kreiger's reportage. A sense of impressionistic style pervades the conception. It is a pithy piece (two and one-half minutes), and that modesty in length is one of the best ways of electronic music life.

Fritz Kreisler (1875-1962)

Allegretto in the Style of Boccherini

☐ Elman (violin); Seiger (piano) / Vanguard SRV–367SD

A few swoops to harmonics do not spoil this fine performance.

Andantino in the Style of Padre Martini

☐ Grumiaux (violin); Hajdu (piano) / Philips 6599373

One of the Kreisler simulations. An appealing viewpoint of the miniature, because it is performed without *rubati* and thereby intelligently projected.

Caprice viennois
Chanson Louis XIII and Pavane in the Style of Couperin
Gypsy Caprice

☐ Kreisler (violin); Lamson (piano) / RCA VIC–1372 (monaural)

No one, but no one, can ever match Kreisler playing Kreisler's *Caprice viennois*. Indeed, as played, there is separation between parts of phrases and all that sort of thing, but what would be disjointed in the hands of X is stylistically enthralling in the hands of this wonder violinist. That kind of string-instrument magic special to Kreisler is a lost art. It should be cherished.

The *Pavane* is another one of Kreisler's originals modeled from another source style. It is captivating in its creative skill and recreative spirit.

La Chasse in the Style of Cartier

☐ Heifetz (violin); Smith (piano) / Columbia M2-33444

One of those delightful Kreisler bits that is all Kreisler, all double stops, and has nothing to do with Mr. Cartier, though his name as stylistic godfather looks very effective on the program listing. (The claimed style source is Jean Baptiste Cartier [1765-1841], and the only connection with Kreisler's "imitation" is that he was a violinist as well as composer.) Of course, Heifetz is dynamically positive. Such playing could hardly be bettered.

La Gitana

☐ Elman (violin); Seiger (piano) / Vanguard SRV–367SD

Kreisler in a gypsy mood. Like all of his style simulations it has everything required. So does Elman's playing in this clean cut, animated presentation.

La Précieuse in the Style of F. Couperin

☐ Elman (violin); Seiger (piano) / Vanguard 71173

Another charming Kreisler stylistic transfer. Elman perfectly translates its simple elegance.

Liebesfreud

Liebeslied

☐ Grumiaux (violin); Hajdu (piano) / Philips 6599373

A pair of perennials, both presented with lovely, pure tone and without the portamenti and Viennese schmaltz that they have too long suffered.

The Old Refrain

☐ Kreisler (violin); Lamson (piano) / RCA VIC-1372 (monaural)

Recorded in 1924 but as fresh-sounding to the ears as if it were made today.

Praeludium **and Allegro in the Style of Pugnani**

Preghiera **in the Style of Martini**

☐ Elman (violin); Seiger (piano) / Vanguard SRV-367SD

Violin playing that exhibits perfect control over both the medium and material. And, importantly, Elman does not rush the Allegro section, so the figurations can be identified and enjoyed.

Rondino on a Theme of Beethoven

☐ Grumiaux (violin); Hajdu (piano) / Philips 6599373

Styled nicely. One of the best Kreisler shorts.

Schön Rosmarin

Shepherd's Madrigal

☐ Kreisler (violin); Lamson (piano) / RCA VIC-1372 (monaural)

Fiddle playing of the most elegant taste. And that's the way it should be.
The first piece is very well known, the other is a Kreisler rarity. However, its delicately adjusted lines make one wonder why it is so little heard.

Sicilienne **and** Rigaudon **in the Style of Francoeur**

☐ Elman (violin); Seiger (piano) / Vanguard SRV-367SD

Richly phrased in part 1 and lacy legati plus pointed spiccati in part 2. A splendid exhibition and, indeed, a sensitive one by this great violinist.

Tambourin chinois

☐ Kreisler (violin); Lamson (piano) / RCA VIC-1372 (monaural)

Transcriptions of Kreisler's music are in the many dozens. None of the pieces, however, have the great variety that has been applied to this one, covering all types of solo instruments and piano, small orchestra, large orchestra, and solo instrument with band accompaniment! Listening to the original played by its creator makes all other special colorations fade away. This is *it* and is the way one should hear the work. Fresh as the day it was written, with a performance that is, of course, sheer perfection.

Kreisler / *Antonin Dvořák.* See Dvořák / Kreisler.

Kreisler / *Manuel de Falla.* See Falla / Kreisler.

Kreisler / *Niccolo Paganini.* See Paganini / Kreisler.

Kreisler / *Giusseppe Tartini.* See Tartini / Kreisler.

Ernst Krenek (1900-)

Drei Lustige Märsche, Op. 44 **Band**
Kleine Blasmusik, Op. 70a

☐ Louisville Orchestra / Mester (conductor) / Louisville LS–756

Opus 70a is a reworking of Krenek's Four Bagatelles for Piano, Four Hands, once recorded by the composer and Maro Ajemian (on Music Library Recordings 7014). There the parenthetical title Sonata appeared. However, the *Kleine Blasmusik* ("Little Suite for Wind Instruments") is hardly a "sonata" as the term is defined. Still, these "Bagatelles" must not be considered in the French meaning of the word ("trifles"), but in the pure musical sense of short pieces; they are compact but not of short importance. Rarely has Krenek been so lyrically engaging. The performance is fluid without reaching the danger point (overzealousness) that so often appears in wind-brass-percussion pieces.

The *Drei Lustige Märsche* ("Three Merry Marches") is a vintage from the days when "modren" music was in flower, but is still wonderful fun and highly enjoyable. Krenek's band sound (made up of six winds, six brass, timpani, and percussion) is peppy, properly brassy; the pieces are flavored with a zestful, dissonant icing. The conception here is far better than the performance on the quite old disc once issued by Boston Records, No. 411.

Toccata (1962) *Instrumental*

☐ McMahan (accordion) / Orion 75204 *Accordion*

It is sufficiently rare to find serious composers being serious about writing music for the accordion. More rare are those pieces that go beyond sharpening the taste and technique of an accordionist and are worth hearing. Krenek's Toccata is one, especially because it speaks with acute accordion vocabulary and thus fits the medium beautifully.

I doubt the Toccata can be played better than it is here. McMahan displays a well-honed technique, but more importantly exhibits a musicianship that is hardly found in the accordion performance world, where the key words are sentimentality and exaggeration.

Monologue for Clarinet Solo (1956) *Clarinet*

☐ Rehfeldt (clarinet) / Advance 4 (monaural)

Five short and to-the-point sections, each cogently structured so that the lines trace a beginning, middle, and end. Played rather in a bland manner, however.

Flute

Flute Piece in Nine Phases

☐ Batschelet (flute) / Orion 78295

The system of compositional preordering is major to this work. It is an intelligent conception, though it imitates the severe side of expressionistic musical speech.

Harp

Sonata for Harp, Op. 150

☐ McDonald (harp) / Klavier KS–507

Harpistic husbandry is practiced here—a few glides and nothing else are exhibited in the way of harp habits. As a result the work gains in sheer musical concentration. The harmonic language is serially derived; the content (especially in the outer movements) is quite rhythmic.

Organ

Sonata, Op. 92

☐ Andrews (organ) / University of Oklahoma 2 (monaural)

The organ does not thrive on heavily packed writing, or without resulting in a puzzling cipher of unidentifiable sounds. Krenek's one-movement, twelve-tone work is shaped well as a successful conception for this restricted and difficult medium; its slow section is especially appealing.

Recommended to those who believe that organ literature began with Bach and ended with Reger by way of Franck. Recommended also for the transpicuous definition given by the performer.

Piano

Piano Sonata No. 4 (1948)

☐ Burge (piano) / Musical Heritage Society MHS–3874

In this work, as in the third piano sonata written in 1943, Krenek pursues the serial muse differently from Schoenberg. The basic twelve-tone row turns into a dozen different series as the original row is splintered into three-note groups, permutated by the rotation of the sounds within each. The entire sonata is drawn from combinations of these sets.

There are four movements: the first rather free in form, the second in ternary design, the third a rondo, and the last a set of variations.

Burge's recording is thrice welcome. The only sonic documentation of the Krenek opus was on an old (and terribly poor-sounding) Music Library recording (No. 7014). That it now can be removed from the shelf is a pleasure so that one can have the far greater pleasure of listening to Burge's splendid conception.

Two Pianos

Tape and Double for Two Pianos and Electronic Tape (1970)

☐ Marcus and Tracy (pianos) / Orion 75204

Making special color assurance double-sure, Krenek differentiates between the two pianos by "preparing" one, modifying the timbre by stretching a light metal chain across its strings. Further, the tape is no mere peripheral accessory but mostly integrated, and, at times, used in imitation of phrases with the piano. A long, tensile piece, but worth the required listening time, especially for the fine climax.

The players do not deny the encompassment found in Krenek's score. Neither do they cede any of the fundamental violence contained in the conception. This is one of Krenek's best pieces, no matter the huge number he has produced in a variety of styles.

Five Pieces for Trombone and Piano

☐ Dempster (trombone); Krenek (piano) / Orion 78295

Elsewhere I have stated that Krenek is always on the lookout for what is the "latest" being done in the compositional field, and most often he has immediately followed suit. Thus, this piece, with its total emphasis on the expanded technique of the trombone, including chordal sounds, coloristic twists, and multitudinous technical seductions. It is interesting no matter what, though totally imitative of the instrumental work of such men as Ligeti, Zimmermann, Kagel, Cage, and Bussotti.

Stuart Dempster's abilities are miraculous. For that alone the disc is worth owning.

Sonata No. 2 for Violin Solo (1948)

☐ Gross (violin) / Orion 73107

Some critics speak of music as being "safely tonal." In this case the three movements are "safely (and superbly) twelve-tonal"—despite rigorous blueprinting: three contrastive ideas in movement 1, developed from the basic series and its inversion; ten appearances of the retrograde form of the row, each interlaced with a pitch transposition of itself, in movement 2; and so on. Krenek's seven and one-half minute work has meaning in addition to its high technical competence. In Krenek's liner note only the coldly analytical is noted, but the listener can expect music of a high emotional temperature, expertly defined by the recorded performance.

Vier Stücke for Oboe and Piano (1966)

☐ Holliger (oboe); Wyttenbach (piano) / Philips 6500202

One can trust Krenek to try his hand at every twentieth-century style. This responsivity has been proven by creative responsibility. In the "Four Pieces" the melodic and harmonic expressionism of the Bergian type is expanded to include percussive gestures, bent oboe tones and multiphonics, and pitch glides. The blend is new though the ingredients are not.

The performers premiered Krenek's work at the Zagreb Musical Biennale in 1967. Their recorded rendition is distinguished by its smoothness and perfection of detail.

Pentagram for Winds (1957)

☐ Soni Ventorum Wind Quintet / Lyrichord S–158

Twelve-tone music, but not devoted to dark expressionistic tenancy of *Sturm und Drang* expressions. There is a casual, lightly diverting aspect to all of the four compact movements.

All these special advantages are displayed in the Soni Ventorum's deft and flexible playing.

O Lacrymosa (1926)

☐ Weide (soprano); Dare (piano) / Orion 75204

Late romantic examples, set to texts by Rainer Maria Rilke. No emotional turbulence, but songs of deep sense and expressivity.

The soprano is sure, but her diction is the exact opposite. One surmises Weide is singing in German, but the results offer no proof.

Voice and
Instrumental
Ensemble

Sestina for Voice and Instrumental Ensemble (1958)

☐ Instrumental Ensemble / Beardslee (soprano) / Krenek (conductor) / Orion 78295

Compared to his other music, Krenek's Sestina is as driving rain to sunlight. In this work there is a brute and unshaken belief in the rigid organization and regulated distribution of all elements. Tones, textures, spacings, time values, tempi, dynamics, and even the text are determined by the row system. All the art is in the serial science. Any free thinking is disallowed. The condition is dogmatic—that of ordered order; a totalitarian form of the art process.

Thus, this is an example of the unharnessing of twelve-tone technique, and in its way is as different from Schoenberg's work as his was from the tonalists. There is formal discipline in the Sestina even though the control is completely different from its traditional meaning. The forms of the triadic world of harmony are predicated on key relationships and the premise of consonance and dissonance. Using one of the ''standard'' forms here would be like trying to construct a limerick in free verse.

However, the technique in the Sestina is not original. Krenek has never been very late in trying his hand at the newest fashion, and in this instance he imitates the Boulez-Stockhausen methods. Undeniably, there are aural portions of this piece that are remarkably fascinating. The structural implications are twice as intriguing.

The recording is not a new one. It was originally issued on the Epic label (3509). The sound qualities we hear today are much better, but, in the long run, there's little loss of sonic quality in this resurrected edition.

Choral

Chorus Alone

The Santa Fe Timetable (1945)

☐ California State University–Northridge Chamber Singers / Alexander (conductor) / Orion 75204

Krenek here hangs his creative cap on an unusual text: a timetable of the Santa Fe Railroad. He comes up with an engaging, tightly and bitingly harmonized and polyphonicized work. All stops between Albuquerque and Los Angeles are covered, and a fugue marks ''entering California at Needles.''

It is all very serious no matter how one might joke about singing the names of towns in staid style. The performance can be termed an assured one though it furnishes little of color values.

Adam Krieger   (1634-1666)

Vocal

Voice and
Instrumental
Ensemble

Student Songs

☐ Members of the Little Orchestra of London / Le Sage and Clarke (sopranos); Rogers (tenor); Shaw (baritone); Rifkin (harpsichord) / Rifkin (conductor) / Nonesuch 71204

Delightful and invigorating, to which one can add enchanting and lovely. Melodies that sparkle and words that are full of beans, the subjects covering comradeship, drinking, fun, and, of course, girls. Especially girls, with their give and nongive and their charms and noncharms (one song concerns a lack of breasts, which are ''a maiden's pride and glory'').

There are ten items in this collection, with such titles as *Rhine Wine Is All Too Lively, Maidens Care Only About Appearances,* and *She Lacks but One Ornament* (the last is the song about flat-chestedness). Most are heard in solo form, these only by the male singers.

There are some duets but the sexes are kept strictly separate. The voices are admirable, the texts delivered with wonderfully clear enunciation. Joshua Rifkin's direction is a considerable asset to the entire production.

Vladimir Kriukov   *(1902-1960)*

Concerto-Poem for Trumpet and Orchestra, Op. 59

Solo Instrument and Orchestra

☐ Bolshoi Theater Orchestra / Dokschitser (trumpet) / Žuraitis (conductor) / Melodiya/Angel S-40149

Trumpet

Romantic in a Hollywoodish way, which is not meant to denigrate the work, but to describe it as simply as possible.

The lush playing is therefore responsible.

William Kroll   *(1901-1980)*

Banjo and Fiddle

Instrumental

☐ Heifetz (violin); Bay (piano) / RCA LM-2382 (monaural)

Violin

Mostly fiddle, but sufficient banjo (via pizzicato) for contrast, in addition to some lush double-stopping. Razor-edge playing that sets Kroll's lightweight piece in the strongest light. Fine pizzicato, too. (Does anyone ever discuss a violinist's pizzicato tone, its dynamic subtlety, and so on?) Compliments also to Emanuel Bay for a rare example of accompanimental blend and support.

Question to RCA: Why treat small pieces with production snobbery? There are plenty of liner words about Heifetz and some of the other composers included on the program, but not a word about Kroll or his music—not even the politeness of giving his full name!

(Another version, in stereo, is available on London STS-15049. It is played by Ricci and is almost as good.)

Juanita

☐ Elman (violin); Seiger (piano) / Vanguard 71173

Light, as all Kroll music is, and with a slight Latin twist. Meat and potatoes for Mischa E.

Franz Krommer   *(1759-1831)*

Concerto in E flat major for Clarinet and Orchestra, Op. 36

Solo Instrument and Orchestra

☐ Vienna State Opera Orchestra / Brymer (clarinet) / Prohaska (conductor) / Vanguard 71167

Clarinet

The clarinet Concerto by František Vincenc Kramář (to give his name in another setting one might run across) is a Mozartian gloss. No discredit, thereby, simply worthy of being heard (especially because of the restricted clarinet concerto repertoire), but with the facts to be known beforehand. The usual fast-slow-fast format pertains.

Johann Baptist Krumpholtz   *(1742-1790)*

Instrumental

Harp

Air et variations

☐ Zabaleta (harp) / Deutsche Grammophon 139419

Brilliant writing by this harpist-composer. The Haydnesque variations fall interestingly even on hardened and sophisticated ears, due to Zabaleta's colorations and dynamic strategy.

Chamber Music

Sonata in F major for Flute and Harp

☐ Rampal (flute); Laskine (harp) / Musical Heritage Society MHS-1345

Lightweight music conveyed in the set forms of a fast-paced section, a *Romanze,* and completed by a rondo with a *Tempo di minuetto* heading. Krumpholtz gave an alternate instrumentation of violin and piano. The recorded setting is, of course, more colorful. Regardless, the playing is the important matter in this case.

Ton de Kruyf   *(1937-   )*

Percussion

Séance, for Percussion, Op. 25

☐ Concertgebouw Orchestra–Percussion Group "Amsterdam" / Donemus Audio-Visual Series 7002

A fancy fantasy that relies a great deal on the combined sound sprays from marimba, harp, and piano four-hands. Sectional divisions are marked by a ship's bell. Special timbres are a frog call, two sandpaper boxes, and five bottles. But the best is heard at the very end of the work—a hand saw cutting through a piece of hard board.

The recording is quite good, considering it was made at a live performance. The playing is extremely good, and so is Ton de Kruyf's composition.

Gail Kubik   *(1914-   )*

Orchestra

Divertimento No. I for Thirteen Players (1959)

☐ Cleghorn (flute and piccolo); Gassman (oboe and English horn); Smith (clarinet and bass clarinet); Marsh (bassoon); Decker (horn); Boltuch (trumpet); Marstellar (trombone); Clark (percussion); Dahl (piano and harpsichord); Shapiro (violin); Thomas (viola); Gottlieb (cello); Kestenbaum (bass) / Kubik (conductor) / Contemporary 8013

There are musical gags galore in this music and in the companion work (see under *Chamber Music:* Divertimento No. II for Eight Players, p. 1020). Kubik's cool humor is rare in contemporary music so the opportunity shouldn't be missed. Great, bouncy score, and great orchestrational and rhythmic punch lines. A splendidly pointed performance conducted by the composer who knows his way on the podium.

Symphony No. 2 in F (1956)

☐ Louisville Orchestra / Whitney (conductor) / Louisville 58-5 (monaural)

Kubik attempted ''to achieve a contemporary, personal expression within the tight framework of the early nineteenth century symphony form." He succeeded, and vividly so, especially in the orchestration which is boldly attractive, while keeping faith with the formal objectives.

Whitney presents a convincing case for the work in this recording. There is an occasional lack of tension but this doesn't nullify an otherwise basically good performance.

Symphony Concertante (1952)

☐ French Radio Orchestra / Hanneuse (trumpet); Chailley (viola); Glazer (piano) / Kubik (conductor) / Composers Recordings S–267E (monaural)

Neo-classic meat garnished with jazz mustard. Further seasoning comes from asymmetrical rhythms. Despite the honor of the Pulitzer Prize in 1952, Kubik's work has not entered the repertory. The evidence of the music itself does not warrant such unfair treatment.

Originally this was an RCA-Victor release. CRI has electronically rechanneled it for stereo purposes. The sound is not bad and it is certainly clean enough. Good playing by the trumpet soloist, especially.

Celebrations and Epilogue (1938-1950)

Sonata for Piano (1947)

☐ Maxin (piano) / Contemporary 8006

In the Sonata the musical organism is persistently alive, the harmonic forms clinching and reinforcing the designs of the four movements. In no case does Kubik sentimentalize into a romantic stance, even in the slow division, constructed in variational form around a hymnlike tune. As is habitual with Kubik, the finale is toccata-driven, its tempo "fairly fast," and it is to be played "hard, bright, mechanical."

The ten parts in the other work cover general picture painting, including a *Birthday Piece, Wedded Bliss,* and *Movies–Saturday Night.* Simplicity is laced with sophistication in this case and meanings are never fouled up. Trim and tasteful short subjects in every instance.

Maxin has all the solutions necessary for the work. His playing has commanding attention.

Sonatina for Piano (1941)

☐ Dahl (piano) / Contemporary 8013

One finds here the typical salutations to neo-classicism: irregular meters, some caustic inserts, and lean textures. In the final Toccata (played with on-the-button preciseness, but a little less "hard and brittle" than required by the composer) Kubk displays a true manifesto of contemporary fast music.

The pianist is the splendid musician, Ingolf Dahl, equally expert in the fields of composing, conducting, and teaching.

Sonatina for Clarinet and Piano (1959)

☐ Smith (clarinet); Dahl (piano) / Contemporary 8013

The balances of this work are as clear as the timing proportions that pertain to the piece itself, in which each movement covers four minutes, or a shade more. Kubik's harmonies and counterpoints are biting and his rhythmic continuity is asymmetric, but the solidity of updated classicism is evident. This means allegiance to triadic coloration

Solo Instrument and Orchestra

Trumpet, Viola, and Piano

Instrumental

Piano

pigmented with polyharmonic inculcations and shaded often with bitonality. It also means rhythms that are not merely of motoric drive but that are infused with American jazz.

Five Theatrical Sketches (Divertimento No. 3) for Piano, Violin, and Cello (1971)

☐ Pacific Art Trio / Desto 7172

Kubik is decidedly at home among the assorted goodies that mark the divertimento design as it is considered these days. An expert instrumentator, Kubik applies his technique to the piano trio combination, making it function as a mini-orchestra to maxi-effect. This bravura handling of the instruments is paralleled by a bravura compositional attitude and a bravura performance.

In movement 4, a *Trialogue* (Fantasy-Scherzo), a mixture of light and heavy pitches, of delicate and ripping bowing, of vacillating rhythms and clipped lines, the pianist doubles as percussionist, striking the edge of the instrument's console with a pencil. Cute and effective. So is the finale, a Waltz and Circus March. The latter is principally pinned onto a striding, civilized type of boogie-woogie.

Divertimento No. II for Eight Players (1959)

☐ Cleghorn (flute and piccolo); Gassman (oboe); Smith (clarinet); Marsh (bassoon); Boltuch (trumpet); Marstellar (trombone); Thomas (viola); Dahl (piano) / Kubik (conductor) / Contemporary 8013

Kubik's intent is to be "diverting and gay." That he is. One will recall *Les Six* in their heyday in this music. One will also recall jugglery animated-cartoon style, the tightly spare music of Aaron Copland (the work is dedicated to him), and the spastic nervousness of Stravinsky's *Histoire*.

A definitive performance that presents the score with full-bodied quality.

(See also Divertimento No. I for Thirteen Players under *Orchestra*.)

Choral

Chorus Alone

Scholastica: A Medieval Set (1972)

☐ Concert Choir of Claremont Men's, Harvey Mudd, Pitzer and Scripps College / Lilley (conductor) / Desto 7172

Scholastic? No! Kubik's settings cover a pair of texts from *Carmina Burana* (but Orff is not mimicked), a clever and humorous disputation by Duns Scotus, lines derived from a French poem from the tenth century, and the German University drinking song, titled *Gaudeamus Igitur* (with a preludial quote of the tune that Brahms used in his Academic Festival Overture and a postludial quote as well, this time dissonantly supportive).

Kubik colors part 4 by using women's voices alone. In the preceding (and longest) part the chorus is punctuated by apostrophizations by a solo tenor (seven different times), a solo baritone (in eight places), and the combined tenor and baritone three times. The scoring is appetizing to the ear, the words are a delight, the choral pedal adjuncts are meaningful.

It all makes for a masterly disquisition on how to handle the unaccompanied choral medium. A choice piece and extremely accomplished in its presentation.

Friedrich Kuhlau   (1786-1832)

Orchestra

Incidental Music from Elf-Hill, Op. 100

☐ Royal Danish Orchestra / Hye-Knudsen (conductor) / Turnabout 34230

A stunning portrayal of the Overture, the Prelude to the first act, the three sections of the Ballet Music to Act IV, the eight parts covering the Ballet Music to Act V, and the final Royal Song, *Protect our King* (a version of the royal anthem *Kong Christian Stod*), which Kuhlau composed for the festival play *Elverhøj*. Romantic in sum and substance, the music is built on Danish and Swedish folk tunes. Brilliantly orchestrated and performed.

Concerto in C major for Piano and Orchestra, Op. 7

☐ Salzburg Symphony Orchestra / Blumental (piano) / Guschlbauer (conductor) / Turnabout 34375

Solo Instrument and Orchestra

Piano

Despite a confirmed didactic consideration of form, Kuhlau's three-movement opus has the virtues of positive subject matter and development. The pleasant and well-balanced performance places the work in the best light possible.

Grand Solo for Flute and Piano, Op. 57, No. 3

☐ Louise Di Tullio (flute); Virginia Di Tullio (piano) / Genesis 1048

Instrumental

Flute

Though there is more pleasure in music of this type for the flutist (the pianist is made a second-class musical citizen), a good amount can be enjoyed by a listener. This is especially so because of the musical taste and distinctive smoothness that Louise Di Tullio displays.

Sonatina

Piano

Op. 20, No. 1 / Op. 20, No. 2 / Op. 20, No. 3 / Op. 55, No. 1 / Op. 55, No. 2 / Op. 55, No. 3

☐ Entremont (piano) / Columbia MG–33202

Long known as staples in the teaching studio, these sonatinas offer some worthy music. Not great by any means, they are perfectly satisfactory and as good as the dozens of pieces that have surfaced in the romantic revival.

Entremont plays them sympathetically and without trying to register more than is contained within the music. What a great stimulus for those studying the piano as well as those that did and gave it up!

Duet in G minor, Op. 39

☐ Rampal and Duschenes (flutes) / Orion 7149

Chamber Music

An intensely emotive duo consisting of a single movement headed *Lagrimoso*. The amount of dramatic continuity that Kuhlau was able to engender with a pair of homophonic instruments whose lowest pitch is middle C marks a striking achievement.

The music is given an absorbing reading. It catches every inflexion of Kuhlau's work.

This performance is included in Everest's seven-record set that features Rampal (3194) and is further duplicated on Everest 3299. In the last instance Mario Duschenes is not given any credit, only Rampal.

Grand Trio Concertant in G minor, Op. 13, No. 2

☐ Jean-Pierre Rampal, Larrieu, and Marion (flutes) / Musical Heritage Society MHS–876

Kuhlau produced seven flute trios. Of these the G minor is a delight and rivals the B minor, Op. 90, Trio, which has gained the most popularity only among flutists. However, such insularism is not to be blamed on the flute fraternity. It has been due to a lack of outlets for public performance of any quantity and a lack of recordings. This recording provides the listener with a chance to hear music of geniality and charm, with hop-skip-and-jump flute-weighted robustness and perennial freshness.

There are two movements and both are Allegros. They are played with impeccancy and with golden tone. Who plays is not clear, however. The Kuhlau is coupled with music by Reicha for four flutes and a pair of five-flute concerti by Boismortier. No distinction is made as to which flutists play in the Reicha and Kuhlau works. Those indicated above are the first three noted on the disc. The others playing on the program are Joseph Rampal and Marius Beuf. Whatever, the three who do play deserve kudos.

Meyer Kupferman   (1926-   )

Orchestra

Chamber Symphony (1950)

☐ Prisma Chamber Players of Copenhagen / Farberman (conductor) / Serenus 12017

In addition to the fundamental compositional balance derived from the use of twelve-tone technique, Kupferman's total structure achieves a tight cohesion by the tempo pulse interlock of its movements. The two slowest divisions are Nos. 1 and 3, the pair of faster-tempoed movements are Nos. 2 and 4. The sonorous lengths are similarly balanced. Movements 1 and 3 total 7:00 and 6:10 respectively, parts 2 and 4 in turn total 3:50 and 3:45.

Aside from the neatly precise blueprint, the music has quality and solidity and reaches a fine conclusion in an almost chirpy finale.

Farberman controls his eightfold forces effectively (the instruments in the group are flute doubling on piccolo, oboe, clarinet, bass clarinet, bassoon, horn, violin, and double bass). The recorded sound is somewhat dry.

Divertimento for Orchestra (1948)

☐ Stuttgart Philharmonia / Farberman (conductor) / Serenus 12017

This work is directly dissonant, containing a kind of shadow-boxing with twelve-tone style. The orchestration is clearly colored. Kupferman's directness is also very effective, and that applies to the performance under Harold Farberman as well.

Instrumental

Cello

Evocation for Cello and Piano (1951)

☐ Moore (cello); Thomas (piano) / Opus One 6

A music of opposites that jells through the sheer opposition involved. The cello is dramatically lyrical, the piano dynamically percussive. A condition of horizontalism punctuated by sharp percussiveness is realized, even when the latter rolls over its boundary lines.

The performers project the music with spontaneity and are totally involved in their inventive realization of Kupferman's creation.

Flute

Line Fantasy from *Infinities One* (1961)

☐ Baron (flute) / Composers Recordings 212 (monaural)

Impassioned attention to color in this, the fifth work of the eight in Kupferman's *Infinities One*. This is declared by slow, sometimes "dirty" jazz-blues slides and extreme

registral leaps and high dives. The length of the work might be questioned (7:30) in relation to the concentrated material involved. However, Baron's sensuous and athletic playing holds the interest.

Superflute for Flute and Tape

☐ Baron (flute) / Nonesuch 71289

By use of tape techniques Kupferman has conceived a duo for three different instruments—a triple color bargain that requires only solo salesmanship, in this case by
Samuel Baron. Baron first taped the material for piccolo and alto flute and then combined
it with the flute music composed for live performance. Thus we have *Superflute,* engaging
the flute family at one fell swoop in a thoroughly engaging piece. (Obviously, all the parts
could be taped and there would be no need for any live playing, but in that case the result
would be a tape piece, something a bit different from music designed "for flute and
tape." The other difference to be emphasized is that the tape part is not made of the usual
electronic (synthesized) materials, but is fully concerned with defined music.

Variations for Piano (1948)

Piano

☐ Estrin (piano) / Serenus 12017

Strictly dodecaphonic music: the theme presents the tone row and six variations
follow. So much for the foundation and the plan. Kupferman keeps his documentation
firmly united and in the process creates a music of poetical power.

The Variations were written for Estrin, who gave the piece its premiere performance.
His recorded essay is of top-drawer quality.

Three Ideas (1967)

Trumpet

☐ Robert Levy (trumpet); Amy Lou Levy (piano) / Golden Crest RE–7045

One scherzoish part and a pair of slow-paced sketches, containing some microtoned
pitches and a slight jazz overlay. The Levy team provides a communicative performance.

Fantasy Concerto for Cello, Piano, and Tape

*Chamber
Music*

☐ Varga (cello); Hersh (piano) / Serenus 12059

The tape is not electronically formulated. Instead, it consists of pre-recorded tracks,
two each for the cello and piano; the duo thus turns into a sextet. During the progress of
the piece, more insistently tonal than most of Kupferman's output, a variety of stylistic impressions are presented. The assortment is apportioned colorfully. Such keen methodology
makes aural comprehension immediate.

Fantasy Sonata (1970)

☐ Mann (violin); Masselos (piano) / Desto 7142

Using both tone row and tonal arrangement, Kupferman not only maintains stylistic
equilibrium but also obtains a contrastive force in his one-movement Sonata. Basic instrumental personality is also confirmed: the violin principally sings, the piano mainly executes rhythmic plans, and horizontal and vertical regions thus are clearly identified.

Robert Mann and William Masselos express everything in a very clear and satisfactory
way. Thus Kupferman's internal relationships are defined externally in an artistic
manner.

Madrigal for Brass Quartet

☐ Indiana Brass Quartet / Serenus 12066

Don't be put off by the equivalent of a put-down for the composer and nonsensical information on the work in the liner note. To say that Kupferman "is too well known" to be given "much space here" and to refer to other Serenus issues for such information is unfair to both the record buyer and the composer. The statement that the Madrigal is "intended for those who like madrigals for brass quartets" not only begs the question but also is moronic hogwash.

The Madrigal is guided by both motival use and the antiphonal device of imitation. Tightly structured and tightly textured, the music is always alive and brassy-warm. As such it has the proper performance climate.

Brass Quintet

☐ American Brass Quintet / Serenus 12041

This is twelve-tone music to the hilt, but it is color-charmed by virtuosic throwing of the pitches. Jazzy stuff as well as a fugue are included. The brassy flashes prove that twelve-tone passion can be combined with brashy scoring. The performance has stuff and fibre. It is impressive.

Robert Kurka   *(1921 - 1957)*

Orchestra
Serenade for Small Orchestra, Op. 25

☐ Louisville Orchestra / Whitney (conductor) / Louisville 632 (monaural)

The title hides the fact that the work covers orchestral documentations that broadly translate lines from Walt Whitman. These are planned to equate the four movements of a symphony. Accordingly, an *Allegro molto* with proclamatory music is based on *Song of Myself*. Then follows a slow movement (marked *Adagio molto espressivo*), its objective derived from *When Lilacs Last in the Dooryard Bloom'd*. Movement 3 represents the scherzo element, indicated by a *Presto* prefaced by lines from *Song for Occupations,* with the finale, *allegro* in tempo, drawing from Whitman's lines in *A Song of Joys*.

A moderately acceptable rendering. Lack of string depth is, however, noticeable.

Symphony No. 2, Op. 24

☐ Louisville Orchestra / Whitney (conductor) / Louisville 616 (monaural)

Steadfast neo-classicism stalks through the measures of Kurka's Opus 24. The primary tonalities are balanced, with D for the outer movements (an *Allegro molto* and a *Presto gioioso*) and B flat for the inner portion, an especially significant and beautiful slow movement marked *Andante espressivo*. But there is no formal austerity in the entire work. Kurka's music obeys structural checks and balances but this does not interfere with a *savoir-faire* that is a delight to hear.

Clean-cut orchestration without any instrumental sloppiness provides an ideal score for an orchestra to sound at its best. Whitney takes advantage of the opportunity.

Band
Suite from *The Good Soldier Schweik* (1957)

☐ Louisville Orchestra / Whitney (conductor) / Louisville S–656

A partnership of the snide side of Prokofiev and the humor of Kodály (as found in his *Háry János*) comes to mind when listening to Kurka's six-movement suite. Clean and clear, the *Schweik* music is never slick, its bouncy tunes and bubbly rhythms being the product of a musician of individual profile.

Wisely, Whitney does not fall into the trap of exaggerating any portion of the score. Such interpretative therapy would be a disaster.

(It will be noted that the category assigned this work is "band," but actually the multiple forces of that medium, with loose totals for the various instruments, which vary greatly from one performing group to the next, would be contrary to the composer's wishes. *Schweik* is scored for the modern wind ensemble, where each instrumental voice is covered by one player and is never multiplied. The ensemble required here parallels the average orchestral forces without strings.)

L

Felix Labunski   *(1892 - 1979)*

Canto di Aspirazione (1963)   *Orchestra*

☐ Louisville Orchestra / Mester (conductor) / Louisville S-721

The "Song of Aspiration" moves quietly but has a demanding intensity. This is obtained by use of declarative unison writing. When harmonically framed, the music gives the effect of contrapositive balance.

Richly played with handsome attention to phrasing.

Ezra Laderman   *(1924-   )*

Concerto for Orchestra   *Orchestra*

☐ Baltimore Symphony Orchestra / Comissiona (conductor) / Desto 7168

Orchestrational generosity bears out Laderman's title. Though soloism—single, grouped, and total—is prevalent, the diversification does not negate a firm symphonic document. Although there are some eclectic reflections, Laderman is mostly very much his own man in this ardently acrid, tellingly dissonant, compactly shaped work.

The liner notes include some discussion as to the validity of orchestral composition these days. Orchestral good health is substantially proven in this case.

Stanzas for Chamber Orchestra

☐ Orchestra / Mester (conductor) / Desto 7129

This music is dodecaphonic with panchromaticism mixed in and with strong tendencies to circle around tonal centers. Plenty of counterpoint and rhythmic action are provided. There is plenty of color, also, proving that Laderman's orchestral manipulations are never less than interesting. There are five movements for a good-sized orchestra: two flutes, oboe, two clarinets, bassoon, horn, trumpet, trombone, tuba, four percussionists, three violins, two violas, cello, and bass, plus the odd inclusion (only in terms of rarity in music of this style) of an organ.

No orchestra credit. The pick-up group makes a fairly well-polished transaction.

Duo for Violin and Piano   *Chamber*
                                                     Music
☐ Jaime Laredo (violin); Ruth Laredo (piano) / Desto 7125

Dramatic consistency is found throughout Laderman's Duo, a work in three movements. Where there is sentiment, it is never sentimental; where there is strength, it does not negate lyrical intensity. A sense of defiance, however, is pertinent to Laderman's opus.

This is not easy music for performers, not only in technical demand but also in balancing its proportions. No problem here, since the Laredos play with taste and polished detail.

String Quartet (1959)

☐ Beaux-Arts String Quartet / Composers Recordings 126 (monaural)

Laderman's style is stinging; it has an invigorating rhythmic life that moistens any dry-as-dust quartet writing. Above all, Laderman handles the four stringed instruments as a medium of virtuosity, and this brings volatile excitement.

Performance: a red-blooded affair.

String Quartet No. 2

☐ Cohen and Yajima (violins); Rhodes (viola); Sylvester (cello) / Composers Recordings S–244

A big, bold, and stimulating piece. The uncompromising use of the basic working material is only one of its fascinations; the virtuosic handling of the instruments (without any trick fripperies) is another. The musical logic is a further bonus. The tight, boldly driven consolidations of Laderman's opus remind one that classical procedures are not totally lost in the music of some contemporaries.

Laderman's Quartet is a marvel of construction, dramatic drive, and intensity. The playing of the foursome is excellent, though the sound tends to be on the harsh side.

Opera and Dramatic Music

Magic Prison (1967)

☐ Louisville Orchestra / O'Brien and Jory (narrators) / Mester (conductor) / Louisville S–712

The text for this work for two speakers and orchestra was drawn (by Archibald MacLeish) from poems and letters of Emily Dickinson and from an essay by Thomas Wentworth Higginson that appeared in the *Atlantic Monthly* in 1891.

Declamation with orchestra poses difficulties. The composer is always confronted with problems of how far his music should blend with, separate from, contrast to, supplement, and further define the spoken word. Mickey-Mousing is a terror to be avoided, though there are times (in descriptive data designed for the very young) when even that style is necessary. Laderman has turned his back on musical affiliation with the text. Instead, for practically the entire work the music bridges, ties in, sets the scene. It is beautifully and basically true to content, never intrudes, and is conceived in a richly romantic style. Paradoxically, it is always subsidiary and yet retains its own strength.

Both speakers deliver their lines with clarity and proper expression. Though the full text is supplied by Louisville it is not needed. Mester provides sensitive orchestral support. A success in all respects.

László Lajtha   *(1892-1963)*

Choral

Rondel

Chorus Alone

☐ Budapest Madrigal Ensemble / Szekeres (conductor) / Monitor S–2054

The infectious scoring for this choral piece has a tiered plan as though written with instruments in mind. Deft, bouncy consecutive triads sound like vocal trumpets. This fine composer, who remains to be discovered, knows choral neatness. The accuracy on the part of this quadruple quartet of singers is wholly admirable.

Michel-Richard de Lalande   (1657-1726)

Orchestra

***Symphonies pour les soupers du roi*, No. 1**

☐ Collegium Musicum de Paris / Douatte (conductor) / Nonesuch 71009

Lalande's "Symphonies for the King's Supper" are not symphonies but an eight-part collection of airs and dances, written to be played at court dinners. Sufficiently tasteful for occasional listening.

Cantata and Oratorio

De Profundis (1689)

☐ Vienna State Opera Orchestra and Vienna Chamber Choir / Thomas and Sheppard (sopranos); Deller (countertenor); Tear (tenor); Bevan (baritone); Tachezi (organ); Opalensky (flute); Kautzky (oboe) / Deller (conductor) / Vanguard S-296

Considered, and properly so, as one of the masterpieces of French church music, Lalande's noble nine-part work (composed in 1689) receives an outstanding presentation.

Edouard Lalo   (1823-1892)

Orchestra

Namouna Ballet (Excerpts) (1882)

☐ L'Orchestre de la Suisse Romande / Ansermet (conductor) / London STS-15293

These excerpts are enough to give the flavor of this stage work, a two-act Ballet Lalo wrote in 1882, especially the colorful aptness of its orchestration.

Overture to *Le Roi d'Ys* (1887)

☐ Monte Carlo Opera Orchestra / Almeida (conductor) / Philips 6500297

A good consideration of the score, with natural diction and fine emphasis on coloration.

***Rapsodie Norvégienne* (1881)**

☐ L'Orchestre de la Suisse Romande / Ansermet (conductor) / London STS-15293

Lalo wrote this work, but it might as well have been Rimsky-Korsakov. Breezy stuff, played with a fitting balletic swing to the rhythms.

Scherzo for Orchestra (1883)

☐ L'Orchestre de la Suisse Romande / Ansermet (conductor) / London 6615

Ansermet makes as good a case for this light-weight piece as can be. The principal strength and interest are found in the outer sections of the composition.

Symphony in G minor (1885)

☐ French National Radio Orchestra / Beecham (conductor) / Seraphim S-60192

Since the Franck symphony seems to be going out of style (or is already in that category) perhaps our conductors will have a look at this fine work. Not that Lalo's piece is Franckian—merely a suggestion to replace an overplayed symphony with an overlooked one. Lalo's opus (especially the opening movement) has a commanding, declamatory, dramatic quality.

Beecham's performance (the only recorded one available) is stunning and rich. The man had taste and knowledge. Take advantage of it.

Solo Instrument and Orchestra

Cello

Concerto in D minor for Cello and Orchestra (1876)

☐ Philadelphia Orchestra / Rose (cello) / Ormandy (conductor) / Columbia M–30113

One listens to Lalo's Concerto and realizes that, even though it is conservatively romantic, well-built, and well-ordered, it is also very wise music. It is always in good taste and represents lasting art.

There is no opportunity in this piece for roustabout, virtuosic tactics, but in the hands of a soloist like Leonard Rose the results are of similar convincing impact. The dignity and nobility of Rose's playing are vivid. The fluency of his conception is matched by a gem of immaculate backing by Ormandy.

Piano

Concerto in F minor for Piano and Orchestra (1889)

☐ Orchestra of the Vienna Volksoper / Frugoni (piano) / Gielen (conductor) / Turnabout 34423E (monaural)

Facts first. In his record sleeve notes John S. Weissmann indicates the proper tonality for this work as F minor and not C minor. He is correct. Why then does Turnabout continue the error he describes, which has been perpetuated by all writers because of someone's initial mistake in designating the key? The matter does not end there. Checking the Heugel published score one finds the key of F indicated!

It is obvious from its neutral profile why Lalo's work has not entered the repertoire. Further, it does not offer much for the soloist, the piano part having an obbligato contour. There are no cadenzas, of course. However, recorded earnestness deserves attention. Without it few would know this work. The playing is good enough, mostly clean and flexible. It is best in the last movement, expectedly, since that's where the best music is.

Violin

Symphonie Espagnole for Violin and Orchestra, Op. 21

☐ New York Philharmonic / Francescatti (violin) / Mitropoulos (conductor) / Odyssey Y–33229

Silken suavity and ringing rhythms confirm a performance of perfection. Like most violinists, Francescatti omits the Intermezzo, but it is no great loss not to have it. This recording represents Francescatti with his rich, singing tone at the height of his career. That special sound is in full bloom in this stunning performance, first released by Columbia in 1957 as ML-5184 (coupled with the Vieuxtemps Concerto No. 4 in D minor), then reissued by Columbia (on MS-6201) but with a fresh coupling: Walton's Concerto for Violin and Orchestra. Finally, it was placed on the budget-price Odyssey label (again with the Walton piece). It has not lost its freshness in its travels.

Chamber Music

Sonata for Violin and Piano, Op. 12

☐ Temianka (violin); Dominguez (piano) / Orion 73105

Rhythmic activity through scale scamperings lends excitement to the otherwise romantic, melodic conception of the first movement. The variations that follow are planned to increase the texture and inner-voiced ornamentations as they move forward, providing variational treatment by weight as well as development. The rondo finale has balletic finesse and grace within its rhythmic content.

The distinct French spirit of the work is carried on in an excellent performance. Especially fully measured is the playing in the last movement.

Constant Lambert / Giacomo Meyerbeer. See Meyerbeer / Lambert.

John La Montaine (1920-)

Birds of Paradise

☐ Eastman-Rochester Symphony Orchestra / La Montaine (piano) / Hanson (conductor) / Eastman-Rochester Archives ERA-1006

Pastoral exotica, but firmly avoiding exotic trickery. *Birds of Paradise* is no Messiaenic catalogue. It is based on "sounds of nature heard in remote places: in woods and forests, at the ocean shore, in the mountains." There are plenty of simulations of birds but they are stated in a sense of formal conclusiveness. The score is rich with invention; the performance with the composer at the piano is compelling. ERA provides excellent reproduced quality.

Concerto for Piano, Op. 9

☐ Oklahoma City Symphony Orchestra / Keys (piano) / Harrison (conductor) / Composers Recordings S-189

This work is also available in a monaural edition (CRI-166), but with a different companion piece (Symphonic Dances by Halsey Stevens). This version of the Concerto gets the vote, not so much for the stereo recording, as for the companion composition (Symphony No. 5 for Strings by Gene Gutché), which is more interesting. Both La Montaine and Gutché won prizes (La Montaine, the 1959 Pulitzer; Gutché, the 1962 Oscar Esplá International Composition Award). Why La Montaine's rich neo-romantic, lyrically drenched piece has not become standard fare is a puzzle. The sensitive performance here proves the strong credits of the work.

Stopping by Woods on a Snowy Evening

☐ Steber (soprano); Biltcliffe (piano) / Desto 7411/2

Some recitativelike statements and a great deal of high treble accumulations support the voice. Ostinato governs this song.

Marcel Landowski (1915-)

Concerto for Ondes Martenot, String Orchestra, and Percussion

☐ Chamber Orchestra for Contemporary Music / Loriod (ondes Martenot) / Bondon (conductor) / Musical Heritage Society MHS-988

Whether the solo instrument dictated the style of Landowski's piece or the style dictated the proper timbre is immaterial. The two are not mutually exclusive. To wit: melan-

*Solo
Instrument
and
Orchestra*

Piano

Vocal

*Voice with
Accompaniment*

*Solo
Instrument
and
Orchestra*

Ondes Martenot

cholic mysticism is bound into the timbre of Maurice Martenot's invention (it has other qualities but this is the principal one) and Landowski does not pull away from this quality, so that his music and its color choice blend into one. It is a choice performance.

Guillaume Landré   (1905 - 1968)

Orchestra   ### Anagrammen (1960)

☐ Limburg Symphony Orchestra / Rieu (conductor) / Donemus Audio-Visual Series DAVS–6703 (monaural)

The material that is presented at the start of Landré's "Anagrams" is pertinent to the balance of the work. Portions are differently arranged, combined, inverted, and rhythmically changed. The same goes for the harmonic content.

Texturally compact, the score is not easy in performance translation. The Limburg group gets a fair mark. What is lacking is some air in the sound structure and a little less tensility on the part of the occupants.

Symphony No. 3 (1950)

☐ Concertgebouw Orchestra / Jochum (conductor) / Donemus Audio-Visual Series DAVS–6403 (monaural: 10-inch disc)

Late-romantic style marks Landré's Symphony. It has dark commentary, save for a lighter viewpoint in the third movement.

The performance is "live," made in 1961.

Variazioni Senza Tema (1967)

☐ Concertgebouw Orchestra / Haitink (conductor) / Donemus Audio-Visual Series DAVS–6902

In this piece variational processes and procedures are drawn from a pair of chordal combinations and a few rhythmic figures. Since there is no theme, a multiplicity of events takes place, with a striking use of coloration. Tonality is freely disposed of and in many instances it vanishes.

Landré's work was commissioned by the Netherlands Government and is dedicated to the orchestra and conductor who perform it here in a live recording made in 1968. Fair sound.

Peter Erasmus Lange-Müller   (1850 - 1926)

Orchestra   ### Incidental Music from *Once upon a Time*, Op. 25

☐ Royal Danish Orchestra and Royal Danish Opera Chorus / Hartmann (tenor) / Hye-Knudsen (conductor) / Turnabout 34230

The music Lange-Müller wrote for the festival play *Der Var Engang* has folk tinges among its romantic determinations. The plot derives from *The Taming of the Shrew* infused with a Hans Andersen fairy-tale atmosphere. The piece, which has nine sections, concludes with a *Midsummer Song* that has achieved perpetual popularity in Denmark.

A definitive rendition of the score.

Jean Langlais   *(1907-   )*

Chant de paix

Chant héroïque

Deux Poèmes évangéliques **(1932)**

☐ Noehren (organ) / Lyrichord 7187

> *(For remarks see below: Hymn d'Actioan de Grace, Te Deum, etc.)*
> (The *Deux Poèmes* are from a set of three.)

Evocation from *Hommage à Jean-Philippe Rameau*

☐ Raynaud (organ) / Turnabout 34319

This is one of a half-dozen pieces in a suite commissioned on the occasion of the 200th anniversary of Rameau's death. It has toccata thrusts that explode in contrast to the very opposite of chant-characterized passages. Excitingly colored, nicely fricative.

Jean-Claude Raynaud plots his playing to fit the schematized plan of the music, doubly, as it were, emphasizing the dynamic and registral differences. A fine presentation that is also included in a Vox Box (SVBX–5315).

Hymn d'Actioan de Grace, Te Deum

La Nativité

Les Rameaux

Pistaccio

☐ Noehren (organ) / Lyrichord 7187

The chromatic impulse is strong in Langlais's music but it is disciplined, confirming the spiritual or the poetic content as the case may be. He can use a light hand, as in *Pistaccio,* and not hide his stylistic profile—a further evidence of creative discipline. All the designs are clear and the textures avoid overload.

Langlais's exceedingly interesting organ music is played with full insight by Noehren. He uses the organ of St. John's Cathedral in Milwaukee—a splendid-sounding instrument.

Messe solennelle

☐ Choir of St. John's College, Cambridge / Cleobury (organ) / Guest (conductor) / Argo ZRG–662

There is an athleticism that surrounds the passionate urgency of this "Solemn Mass" that makes for special aural impact. Langlais mixes a plainsong quality into his modalism and flavors it with twentieth-century punctuations. There is no reluctance to sing out in this sacred essay and the choir does so with incisiveness and a rhythmic springiness that are most exhilarating.

Instrumental

Organ

*Cantata
and Oratorio*

Joseph Lanner   *(1801-1843)*

Die Schönbrunner, **Op. 200**

☐ Johann Strauss Orchestra of Vienna / Boskovsky (conductor) / Angel S–36887

Orchestra

1033

Lanner turned out 112 waltzes. Authorities agree that the late works are his best examples. Mosco Carner, the important Viennese musicologist and conductor, lists a half dozen of Lanner's waltzes as "true masterpieces of the species." *Die Schönbrunner* is one of the six. It has melodic catchiness, engaging harmony, and deft rhythmic conditions.

This waltz authenticity is matched by a performance that is ideal.

Jagd Galop

☐ Johann Strauss Orchestra of Vienna / Boskovsky (conductor) / Angel S–36956

Of Lanner's total output of 207 works, only three are polkas. The *Jagd* has wonderful flavor and Boskovsky makes certain it is prepared properly.

Mitternachtswalzer, Op. 8

Regata Galop, Op. 134

☐ Vienna State Opera Orchestra / Angerer (conductor) / Nonesuch 71141

In the waltz there is a little off-beat coda—just a little, but interesting. Midnight strikes and its sounds are joined to a minor-keyed section that preludes a quiet close. Prior to that the usual linked set of Viennese waltzes swings through.

The *Galop* observes the expected pointed duple rhythm. It's sincere but very standard music. The performance is O.K. for both pieces, particularly for that special coda.

Sommernachtstraum-Galop

Trennungswalzer

☐ Orchestra of the Vienna Volksoper / Angerer (conductor) / Turnabout 34156

The "kick" beats in the "Parting Waltz" are a delight of stylistic integrity—and authenticity as well. The "Summer Night's Dream" is played quickly but not with can-can speed, thus allowing for more of the flavor to come through. The solo spots in both works are admirable. For Paul Angerer, admiration.

String Orchestra

Abendsterner Walzer, Op. 180

Neue Wiener Ländler, Op. 1

☐ Boskovsky Ensemble / Boskovsky (conductor) / Vanguard 2096

Rapturous old Viennese dance music played with love, devotion, and all the finesse possible. Both the "New Vienna" opus and the *Abendsterner* ("Evening Stars") piece use a four-ply group of three violins and a double bass.

Paul Lansky   (1944-   )

Instrumental

Piano

Modal Fantasy (1970)

☐ Miller (piano) / Composers Recordings S–342

For "modal" read combinations and progressions of certain intervals rather than scalic or rhythmic arrangement. A triptichal balance pertains, with the central *Ludus* section preceded by a Prelude and followed by a Postlude, with the development of the materials of the outer divisions found in the central one.

Lansky's concentrated work (six-minute length) has a decided personal quality. It is shown off to its best advantage by Robert Miller's musicianship and technical dexterity.

Mild und Leise (1974)

Electronic Music

☐ Odyssey Y–34139

This richly colored music has within it and surrounding it a sense of relaxed *Klangfarbenmelodie*. There are chordal complexes that relate to and then deviate from tonal combinations. The sounds are soft and easy, sometimes zitherlike. One is reminded of emanations from a slow-motioned kaleidoscope. This represents a refreshingly revitalized consideration of the medium. Compared to the snap-crackle clichés and twaddled chatter of most electronic music, Lansky's work sounds like a muted, humid nocturne. It's a beauty—a delight to the ear.

Electronic music will live only when there are experts composing in the medium, not merely advocates of it. Paul Lansky is one of those experts.

Pierre Lantier (1910-   )

Sicilienne

Instrumental

Saxophone

☐ Brodie (saxophone); Brough (piano) / Golden Crest 7028 (monaural)

Saxophone-timbred simplicity conveyed in a French romantic manner.

Alcides Lanza (1929-   )

Penetrations II (1969)

Electronic Music

☐ New Sound Composers/Performers Group / Lanza (conductor) / Mainstream MS–5017

Penetrations II is scored for wind, string, percussion, and keyboard instruments, together with voices, electronic sounds, and electronic extensions. Lanza indicates that the work was specifically created for "a recording studio situation." Initially the "live" players react to taped sounds and each other; the performance itself is taped and is then "transformed, distorted, fed back and overlapped," which forms the "final" (definitive) presentation. The result follows the now quite familiar electronic liturgy.

Lars-Erik Larsson (1908-   )

Concerto for Violin and Orchestra, Op. 42

Solo Instrument and Orchestra

Violin

☐ Stockholm Radio Orchestra / Gertler (violin) / Frykberg (conductor) / Turnabout 34498

Most of Larsson's three-movement opus, even in its faster-tempoed portions, is like a Vocalise. This Concerto sings rather than stings. Pyrotechnicalia are at a minimum.

Gertler's tone is rich and, when it should be, silky. Sensitive backing from the orchestra.

Concertino, Op. 45, No. 7

Instrumental

Trombone

☐ Sauer (trombone); Carno (piano) / Crystal S–384

One of a series of a dozen concertini, each for a different solo instrument. Though

Larsson's primary aim was didactic, his music crosses the boundary line into concert fare. What one misses is the orchestral accompaniment which gives the solo voice a far better frame than does piano support. The presentation in this case is worthy.

Orlandus (Roland de) Lassus   (1532-1594)

Choral

Chorus Alone

Ave Regina Coelorum

☐ Pro Cantione Antiqua / Turner (conductor) / Deutsche Grammophon Archive 2533290

A four-voice motet in an expert and most direct rendition. Turner's conducting exemplifies excellence of style.

Cum Essem Parvulus/Nunc Cognosco
Factus Est Dominus
Nunc Cognosco

☐ Kaufbeurer Martinsfinken / Hahn (conductor) / Nonesuch 71084

The first is a double motet, exceedingly rich in texture. Hahn's direction makes both works more than sympathetically schooled in style, meaning they sound most expressive. Nothing is left to be desired here save more music of the same performed in the same way.

Der Wein, der schmeckt mir also wohl
La Terre les eaux

☐ Sine Nomine Singers / Saltzman (conductor) / Turnabout 34485

The first is a lighthearted drinking song; the other a rationalization for drinking. Fine, clear, full-toned singing by this group of fifteen. Turnabout's issue is live and spacious.

O doux parler
Que dis-tu, que fais-tu?

☐ Accademia Monteverdiana / Stevens (conductor) / Nonesuch 71272

Denis Stevens's group, consisting of pairs of sopranos, contraltos, tenors, and basses, fits perfectly for performing Lassus's settings of a pair of sonnets by Pierre de Ronsard. Each calls for two four-part choirs or soloists. These songs are further proof of the magnitude and wonder of this sixteenth-century composer's work.

Uncommon musicianship projects the essence of this music and its particular style. Indeed, impressive.

O Mors, Quam Amara Est
Salve Regina

☐ Pro Cantione Antiqua / Turner (conductor) / Deutsche Grammophon Archive 2533290

Warmly sonorous performances, especially in regard to the six-voice setting of the *Salve Regina*. Special subtlety is not required for it is built into Lassus's motets.

Penitential Psalm-*Domine Exaudi Orationem Meam*

☐ Choir of Christ Church Cathedral, Oxford / Preston (conductor) / Argo ZRG-735

This is the final work in Lassus's set of seven Penitential Psalms. Its sixteen parts cover a great amount of ground but Simon Preston keeps one's interest by his open and bright performance.

Prophetiae Sibyllarum

☐ Prague Madrigal Choir / Venhoda (conductor) / Nonesuch 71053

These are the Sibylline Prophecies according to the chromatic realization of Orlandus Lassus. The twelve sections are prefaced by a three-line *Carmina Chromatico,* which deserves quotation here in its translation: "Chromatic songs, which you hear in a modulatory manner;/These are they, in which the secrets of our Salvation/Were sung, with undaunted voices, by the twelve sibyls." That tells all and the glorious expressivity of the writing fulfills the premise.

This work has seemingly escaped notice in favor of Lassus's madrigals and motets. The breadth of the performance, with its immaculately balanced voicing, may serve as a stimulant to other choral conductors. Unfortunately, the work has been omitted in *Schwann.* Though the Mass with which it is coupled (*Ecce Nunc Benedicite Dominum*) is fully listed, the *Prophetiae,* which is the larger work (by more than seven minutes), draws a blank.

Resonet in Laudibus

☐ Canby Singers / Canby (conductor) / Nonesuch 71026

This elaborate motet is a setting of the old Christmas tune *Resonet in Laudibus, Josef Lieber, Josef Mein.* Canby's group has a chamber quality that is most fitting for this sensitive narrative. Large choruses may better propel the joy inherent in the text but can bring an overweight to the magical simplicity of words and music pertaining to the birth of Jesus Christ.

Sacrae Lectiones ex Propheta Job

☐ Prague Madrigalists / Venhoda (conductor) / Telefunken 641274

There are nine motets in this example of noble and most affecting music. The singing is alive and there is no cut-and-dried coverage that is the deadly norm that choral groups so often follow.

Penitential Psalms

Chorus and Instrumental Ensemble

Domine, Ne In Furore Tuo
Miserere Mei, Deus

☐ Hamburger Bläserkreis für Alte Music and Pro Cantione Antiqua / Turner (conductor) / Deutsche Grammophon Archive 2533290

These are two of the seven Penitential Psalms Lassus composed. Though they are lengthy works, there's plenty of beauty that twines within. Rather staid presentations, nonetheless.

Missa "Bell' Amfitrit' Altera"

Cantata and Oratorio

☐ Choir of Christ Church Cathedral, Oxford / Preston (conductor) / Argo ZRG–735

The Venetian style with double choirs makes possible octuple sonorities as well as antiphonal quality. Single choirs are used as well as split voicing (the lower voices of the second choir combined with the basses of the first group, for example).

Golden music is heard here with golden-voiced vocalism. The blends achieved by Simon Preston provide the most affecting type of communication of Lassus in the recorded catalogue.

Missa "Ecce Nunc Benedicite Dominum"

☐ Prague Madrigal Choir / Venhoda (conductor) / Nonesuch 71053

The six-part writing in this mass produces a strong inner textural cohesion. Splendid, high-standard singing, with excellently blended tone quality. There is clear proof in the recorded performance that Miroslav Venhoda has the style of Lassus's idiom fully absorbed in his system.

Antonio Lauro (1917-   )

Instrumental

Guitar

Dos Valses Venezolanos

☐ Diaz (guitar) / Everest 3155

Two hearty dances by this Venezuelan guitarist and composer. Diaz plays them intensely throughout. Such sacrifice of subtlety is not aided by the exceedingly bright sound.

Everest deserves to be criticized for its production. Its album, titled *400 Years of the Classical Guitar,* includes the above work and a few other premieres in the recorded catalogue. However, no first names are given for the composers, no dates for them, and not a single word for any of the thirteen works included on the disc, only some background on Alirio Diaz plus a great amount of press agentry puffs. If, understandably, financial returns are wanted, this ain't the way to do it. In the recording field, Everest, you must describe and give information on the product.

William Lawes (1602-1645)

Choral

Chorus Alone

See How in Gathering of Their May

☐ Sine Nomine Singers / Saltzman (conductor) / Turnabout 34485

This is a "catch," meaning a form of round with word juxtaposition that offers some ribald connotation. The music is pleasant and charming and it doesn't matter whether one "catches" all the words or not. Saltzman's group is very, very good.

Pamela Layman (20th cent.)

Instrumental

Violin

Gravitation I

☐ Oliveira (violin) / Grenadilla GS-1032

Layman's solo violin composition is constructed from free-formed material, strongly controlled, however, in terms of its pitches. Abstract though it may be, the segments offered the performer to use in shaping the design are neo-romantically compatible.

Oliveira provides an illuminating projection of the music. His proportions are fine. The performance time span can be anywhere from five to eight minutes. Grenadilla's recording clocks him at 5:26.

Billy Jim Layton   (1924-   )

Three Studies for Piano, Op. 5

Instrumental

☐ Wyner (piano) / Composers Recordings S-257

Piano

Schoenbergian chromaticism and vertical order, crossed with freed horizontalism, give Layton the best of both worlds in these pieces. The music is controlled by its structural clarity, including a fugue in the final study.

The vitality of Yehudi Wyner's playing freshens this music. The poor proofreading of the liner note provides humor (as well as annoyance) when one reads: ''is most obvious n the hrid study, whetre a kind of sarabande.''

Five Studies for Violin and Piano, Op. 1

Chamber Music

☐ Raimondi (violin); Wyner (piano) / Composers Recordings S-257

Each study separately outlines a subject but there is no cold technical dogmatism though there is clear objectivity. Thus we hear rhythmic modulation and opposed rhythms in the first piece, the implied jazz in No. 3, the percussive dialoguing of the final study.

Layton's creative confidence (note the opus number!) is total, his musical reasoning superb. The performers are positive and their interpretation is deserving of the boldest praise.

String Quartet in Two Movements

☐ Claremont String Quartet / Composers Recordings 136 (monaural)

Layton's Quartet is high-powered, high-geared, high-pressured. It is a splendid composition, representing inexhaustible invention, keen color sensitivity, and a creative boldness. In certain respects, Layton equals Webern with his compactness of timbre presentations, but the sonorous freeway is much bigger and recalls Berg. Romanticism in its formalistic flogging sense is the clue here. It represents the ferment and its capitulation as Layton is done with it. No instrument plays a neutral role as each partakes of the persuadableness of fluid characterization, changing its personality dozens of times.

There are great difficulties for any quartet in covering the technical and color scale of Layton's work. The challenges are many but the Claremont group meets all of them. They magnificently exhibit the exciting and architectonically brave new world represented by Layton's two-movement Quartet.

Henri Lazarof   (1932-   )

Espaces (1966)

Orchestra

☐ Los Angeles Chamber Ensemble / Lazarof (conductor) / Composers Recordings S-263

Lazarof follows his favorite practice in the repetitive formations, each instrumentally identified, within *Espaces,* a dectet for four winds (two flutes, clarinet, and bass clarinet), four strings (two violas and two cellos), and two pianos. *Actes* and *Entr'actes* alternate to a quintal movement total. Tutti use marks the former and different combinations cover the latter. Busy though the music may be, it is lucid in its eclectic contemporary idiom.

Structures sonores (1966)

☐ Utah Symphony Orchestra / Abravanel (conductor) / Vanguard C-10047

Scoring variety is the method Lazarof uses to mark the six sections of his work: Introduction, *Polyphonie I*, Etude I, *Polyphonie II*, Etude II, and *Polyphonie III*. Thus, there are strings only in the second "Polyphony," woodwinds with harp, celesta, and vibraphone in the first Etude, et cetera. This is matched by stylistic variety that touches bases with Bartók, Varèse, Cowell, and Berg, but hangs together nonetheless, though it takes some thirty-one minutes for the knitting to be accomplished.

Credit Lazarof with virtuosity of scoring and eclectically styled virtuosity. Credit Abravanel with a virtuosic presentation. Credit the judges who gave Lazarof the International Prize of the City of Milan, La Scala Award, for this composition.

(See also Concerto for Cello and Orchestra under *Solo Instrument and Orchestra: cello.*)

Third Chamber Concerto for Twelve Soloists

☐ Lazarof (conductor) / Avant AV–1019

The *raison d'être* is color: blatant, thin, heavy, and mixed. From this disparateness (a purposeful disunity) comes unity. From this textural shifting of intersecting sonorous lines and shapes come the form and the balance. It is exciting.

Solo Instrument and Orchestra

Cello

Concerto for Cello and Orchestra (1968)

☐ Oakland Symphony Orchestra / Lesser (cello) / Samuel (conductor) / Desto 7109

Formal reconstruction applies here. Lazarof's Concerto begins with the traditional cadenza. This is not of traditional content, of course. Neither is it of traditional length, covering a record-breaking eight and one-quarter minutes! (It is not to be wondered that Lazarof also considers the cadenza to be an independent piece and that as such it has been given many performances.) Then, as in Lazarof's *Structures sonores* (see under *Orchestra*) a pair of designs are intertwined: an Invention being followed by two Variations, then a second Invention, three more Variations, and a final third Invention. Similarly, differing concentrated and large instrumentation formats pinpoint the divisions within the work.

Contemporary harmonic freedom sets off the virtuosity of the conception. It is a work that rockets forth its modern tunes and turns. Laurence Lesser is mostly superb and he is never less than very good. There is occasional harshness from the orchestra.

Flute

Concerto for Flute and Orchestra

☐ New Philharmonia Orchestra of London / Galway (flute and alto flute) / Lazarof (conductor) / Composers Recordings SD–373

Lazarof's Concerto consists of two movements separated by a flute monologue. One part has a nocturnal mood, the other is disturbed by oppositional temper. Though there is more activity in the second section, here again the music breathes neo-impressionistic night air. It is important to realize that the solo voice part has breadth—fragmentation pertains to the orchestra only.

Galway's performance is exceedingly impressive. His tone is warm and full. An exciting artist.

Piano

Textures for Piano and Five Instrumental Ensembles (1970)

☐ Utah Symphony Orchestra / Ogdon (piano) / Lazarof (conductor) / Candide 31072

Lazarof explores here variation and development not of theme or motive but of textural material. The piano is considered a total personality in the contemporary sense: it is played on the keyboard as well as inside the instrument by plucking and brushing the strings. Urbanistic evocative auditory responses are produced. Everything is heard strong and confident. This is to be expected. *Textures* was commissioned by the London Sinfonietta for Ogdon and premiered by him with the London organization in London (January 1971).

Concertazioni for Solo Trumpet, Six Instruments, and Tape

☐ Stevens (trumpet and flügelhorn); Giles (flute and alto flute); Buxbaum (clarinet and bass clarinet); Pyle (horn); Rothmuller (cello); Remsen (harp) / Lazarof (conductor) / Avant 1009

The solo voice in Lazarof's work (for a high D trumpet and sometimes a flügelhorn) rhapsodizes against a parallel color-mindedness and timbre hustle in the other instruments.

The statistics seem confused. A count of the instruments shows seven, not six as noted in the title. If the flute–alto flute and clarinet–bass clarinet are each considered as one, since each pair is from the same instrumental family, then there are only five. Further, the liner notes mention the six instruments as "flute, clarinet, harp, vibes, horn, cello." If so, where are the vibes?

Major credit must be given to the healthy virtuosity of the soloist, Thomas Stevens.

Spectrum for Solo Trumpet, Orchestra, and Tape

☐ Utah Symphony Orchestra / Stevens (trumpet and flügelhorn) / Lazarof (conductor) / Composers Recordings SD–373

High-colored sonority patterns churn though the work. There are flourishes and proclamations on the part of the solo voice, with enmeshments and conflicts by the orchestra and the tape; the latter is solely of prerecorded trumpets (mind the plural!). Even in its quieter moments (not many) Lazarof's *Spectrum* is a music of interweaving climaxes. Exciting.

Tempi Concertati (1964)

☐ Everest Chamber Ensemble / Plummer (violin); Johnson (viola) / Lazarof (conductor) / Everest 3160

Tempi Concertati calls for solo violin and solo viola, with an instrumental septet that requires only a quartet of musicians: flute, one performer for vibraphone and xylophone; harp, and one player who covers piano, celesta, and harpsichord. The arrangement of the work's three parts varies. The violin solo voice in part 1 is featured with the support of the three keyboard instruments and the xylophone. In movement 2, the viola is in the limelight with the aid of the flute, harp, and vibraphone. The entire forces take part in the third and final division.

Lazarof's chromaticism is clarified by diatonic data. The linear detail is clarified by fluid rhythms, there being no bar lines though a basic metronomic pulse is maintained.

Cadence V

☐ Galway (flute, alto flute, and bass flute) / Composers Recordings SD–381

Cadence V always sounds like a duo and sometimes as music for more than a pair of performers. This is due to the use of a prerecorded tape part consisting of the sounds of three different wind instruments (the "normal" C flute, in addition to alto and bass flutes) which the instrumentalist also plays. Thus, an inventory of six timbres that delineate reflections and refractions, hot and cool colors, as well as softness and ebullience. A fascinating conception in which James Galway proves himself to be a virtuoso artist.

Piano

Cadence IV (1970)

☐ Bunger (piano) / Avant 1008

In this piece of ultrachromatic and atonical syntax, colored by some hand-plucked and hand-damped string sounds, free-formed and virtuosic, Bunger passionately displays all there is to display.

Tuba

Cadence VI for Tuba and Tape

☐ Bobo (tuba) / Crystal S-392

Lazarof's tape association is not purely electronic sound supplementing and contrasting the brass voice but is a complete, second tuba-timbred part. 'Tis clever, this "two-for-the-price-of-one," where the tuba plays a duet with itself.

It is very dramatic, very colorful, very expert. Probably the most exciting tuba duo in existence. For Bobo's perception, skill, and tone quality, bravos.

Viola

Cadence II for Viola and Tape (1969)

☐ Thomas (viola) / Desto 7109

This is neo-baroque material for the greater part, with toccata turmoil. All of it is very exciting, made more so in a Thomas and Thomas duo formation, Thomas having pre-recorded the second part. The tape doesn't include any electronic sounds but consists of pantonal material that matches, supplements, contrasts, and counterpoints the "live" material.

All of it is also played very excitingly, some of it moving at a fantastically fast speed. The opus was written especially for Thomas, hence the subtitle "Cadence for Milton." He certainly is not found wanting in his performance and repays the honor in full.

Violin

Cadence III for Violin and Two Percussion Players (1970)

☐ Plummer (violin); Watson and Bunker (percussion) / Candide 31072

It is possible to define *Cadence III* as having kinship with recitative procedures. The violin presents virtuosic statements, the percussion interjects or accompanies.

Plenty of bravado in the playing.

Chamber Music

Adieu for Clarinet (Bass Clarinet) and Piano (1974)

☐ Gray (clarinet and bass clarinet); Vallecillo (piano) / Avant AV-1019

This piece has an introspective quality, with restrictive tempi. It is considerably fragmented but the fragments are placed in relief. The consistent mood holds the material together. An honest work without any note spinning.

Duo-1973 for Cello and Piano

☐ Gabor Rejto (cello); Alice Rejto (piano) / Avant AV-1019

Lazarof's Duo moves into the territory of the avant-garde with its respect for effects. The diffuse infusions partake of improvisational procedures but there is always a musical shape for each. Underlying all of this is a romantic emotion in spite of the contemporary gusto. To paraphrase the TV commercial, if you're out of gusto you're out of music. Be sure to catch the pithy Beethoven quote that ends the piece.

The technique, intelligence, and musical strength of the Rejtos provide an exceedingly rewarding recording.

Inventions for Viola and Piano (1962)

☐ Thomas (viola); Akst (piano) / Everest 3160

This is twelve-tone music with the row marked by pivotal tertial intervals within it. Tempo alternations (for example: a march-like second part, a recitative-like third part) clarify the structure; such advantages are immediately apparent at the initial hearing of the composition.

One hears vigorous playing even within the lyrical portions. The music can take it. (The performance is also available on Counterpoint/Esoteric 5605.)

Rhapsody for Violin and Piano

☐ Plummer (violin); Steinhardt (piano) / Everest 3160

Though it is not sequestered, Lazarof does not liquidate tonality in his opus. There are temporary compromises with atonality but a return is always made to tonal centers. Exciting directions are observed in this rhapsodic opus but all are neatly balanced through its contrasts; the overall form is strongly imagined.

The violinist of the recording team, Stanley Plummer, commissioned the work, and gave the premiere performance in October 1966. His recorded version with Victor Steinhardt's support is excellent.

Continuum for String Trio (1970)

☐ Plummer (violin); Thomas (viola); Lesser (cello) / Desto 7109

This music is mostly thickly textured with both hectic and restrained contrasts. The massed bluntness of the piece massages the instruments and exemplifies chamber music falling into string-orchestra territory. Maximum returns from the performers.

Partita for Brass Quintet and Tape (1971)

☐ Los Angeles Brass Quintet / Candide 31072

In the hands of a keen composer the changed environment that occurs when tape sounds are combined with instrumental ones offers fascinating possibilities. A tuba growling with (or at a) tape overhang is one example; oscillating packed muted sounds is a second one. Still another: the spitting, spiculated rhythmic dots immersed in the texture.

Because of the nature of the material it is not possible to ascertain which sounds are "live" and which are on the tape pre-recorded by the quintet. It doesn't matter; the final result is a heady discovery.

Octet (1967)

☐ Members of the UCLA Wind Ensemble / Lazarof (conductor) / Composers Recordings S–263

The variations in this piece focus mainly on matters of timbre arrangement. The commentary is serialistic but of free disposition. Lazarof's enthusiasm for color receives a careful appraisal from the musicians he directs.

Nicolas-Antoine Lebègue (1631 - 1702)

Instrumental

Organ

Magnificat

☐ Isoir (organ) / Turnabout 34074

This is the first of nine Magnificats by this composer, a colleague of François Couperin. A well-known melodic friend is included—a fugue on the theme that begins Bizet's *L'Arlésienne*.

There are some pungent, low, reedy sections in the registration. Captivating they are and somewhat uncommon. The slight coarseness of the organ is actually fine for this music. (Isoir plays the organ of the Cathédrale d'Auch.)

Symphonie en ré majeur

☐ Hansen (organ) / Nonesuch 71170

Lebègue's organ composition is a proclamatory prelude and in no sense a symphony as one understands the term. There are fully vertical sonorities and very imposing ones. Jørgen Ernst Hansen wisely plays it straight, with no registral change, just the full organ sound of the instrument in St.-Merry Church, Paris.

Hugh Le Caine (1914-   )

Electronic Music

Dripsody (1955)

☐ Folkways 33436

A mouthwatering two-minute bit. Le Caine's work, An Etude for Variable Speed Recorder, is derived entirely from the sound of the fall of a single drop of water. Indeed, fresh, clear, and delightful.

Leonhard Lechner (ca. 1550 - 1606)

Cantata and Oratorio

History of the Passion and Sufferings of Our Savior and Redeemer, Jesus Christ

☐ Spandauer Kantorei / Behrmann (conductor) / Turnabout 34175

A five-part plus one-line *Conclusio* motet passion. Well accomplished though the diction is blurred. However, Turnabout offers text and translation. No notes whatsoever.

Jean Marie Leclair (1697 - 1764)

Orchestra

Suite from *Scylla et Glaucus*

☐ English Chamber Orchestra / Leppard (conductor) / Oiseau-Lyre S-303

Off-beat literature but, of course, not off-beat style. However, the music has more to offer than mere passing interest. Leppard directs a stimulating performance.

Sonata in G minor for String Orchestra

☐ Chamber Orchestra of Versailles / Wahl (conductor) / Nonesuch 71080

Wahl performs this work with warmth and the proper amount of élan. It makes for pleasureable listening. Fine reproduction.

String Orchestra

Concerto in C major for Oboe, Strings, and Continuo, Op. 7, No. 3

☐ Members of the Dresden State Orchestra / Holliger (oboe); Jaccottet (harpsichord) / Negri (conductor) / Philips 6500413

Leclair's work is one of a set of six performable by either violin, flute, or oboe as the solo voice. The distinguished, rich, burnished sound of Heinz Holliger, not to mention his exceptional articulation and seamless continuity, are a delight. The eloquence of the phrasing especially enriches the splendid inspiration defined by Leclair's Adagio movement.

Solo Instrument and Orchestra

Oboe

Concerto for Violin and Orchestra

In A minor, Op. 7, No. 5 / In G minor, Op. 10, No. 6

☐ Concerto Amsterdam / Schröder (violin) / Schröder (conductor) / Telefunken 642180

These are bold, energetic presentations. Fine dynamic boosts as required and sensitive work by Jaap Schröder in his double-feature role.

Violin

Sarabande and *Tambourin*

☐ Bress (violin) / Folkways FM-3351 (monaural)

Hyman Bress plays these two dances with admirable coherence. His tone is warm and full. Full credit to him. Some acknowledgment should be given to the accompanist but he's not listed.

Instrumental

Violin

Sonata in D major, Op. 9, No. 3

☐ Oistrakh (violin); Yampolsky (piano) / RCA VICS-1058

David Oistrakh plays the most familiar of Leclair's violin sonatas with ingratiating beauty. Every part of the work *sounds,* including the final festive *Tambourin* which too many fiddlers rough up, as does Staryk on Orion (7027/2).

Chamber Music

Sonata in D major for Violin, Viola, and Continuo, Op. 2, No. 8

☐ Schlupp (violin); Kempen (viola); Ruth Ristenpart (harpsichord); Hindrichs (cello) / Nonesuch 71119

This Sonata is no boneless baroque example. There is superb creativity and meaning in Leclair's work and one can certainly mark it as one of his finest.

The playing is excellent. It is shaped with full niceties of pulse and phrase in the pair of slow movements (the second one a *Sarabanda*) and has strength and tempo honesty in the pair of Allegro movements.

Trio Sonata in D minor for Recorder, Violin, Violoncello, and Harpsichord

☐ Dolmetsch-Schoenfeld Ensemble / Orion 73104

Movements of nicely flecked contrapuntal engagement surround an *Aria* which too has polyphonic merits and a *Sarabanda*. The playing is well-bred, perhaps a bit businesslike, but it deserves more than a mere passing grade.

Charles Lecocq (1832-1918)

Orchestra

Overture to *La Fille de Madame Angot*

☐ New Philharmonia Orchestra / Bonynge (conductor) / London 6643

A typical operetta overture: four and one-half minutes of buoyancy. The performance swims right with the tide.

Lecocq / Gordon Jacob

Orchestra

Suite from the Ballet *Mam'zelle Angot*

☐ Royal Opera House Orchestra / Fistoulari (conductor) / London STS-15191

The Suite consists of the Overture, a Mazurka, and a *Tempo di Marcia* from the first act, a Gavotte and another excerpt from Act II, and the Finale of the third act.

A sparkling and zippy account. This is not a new production, simply a transferred release, the original (now deleted) having been issued on RCA LSC-2285.

Dai-Keong Lee (1915-   )

Orchestra

Polynesian Suite (1959)

Symphony No. 1 (1947)

☐ Nürnberg Symphony Orchestra / Barati (conductor) / Composers Recordings S-195

Direct opposites here. Lee's Symphony is neoclassically propelled with a full head of pandiatonic-Hindemithian steam. It includes a strong Passacaglia and Fugue. In the other work, the Hawaiian-born composer pays ethnic homage in a Tahitian Dance (*Ori Tahitian*), a *Hula*, and a *Festival*. Throughout, there is plenty of rhythm and plenty of percussion.

Thus the serious and the light are contrasted in these examples of Lee's music. The greater interest naturally lies in the use of the Polynesian musical idiom.

The performances are but fair, with a lack of positiveness here and there as well as a few intonational slips. However, if you want Lee's music this is the sole recording of the two works.

Noël Lee (1924-   )

Vocal

Five Songs on Poetry by Federico García Lorca (1955)

Voice with Accompaniment

☐ Addison (soprano); Baron (flute); de la Torre (guitar) / Composers Recordings 147 (monaural)

These songs are dodecaphonically styled but not at all with the wide intervallic leaps, melodically diffused lines, and dab-patched sound of so much serial music. Lee is not fearful of symmetry. The second song of the set (*Arbrisseau*) is an enchanting example of ritornello technique.

The ensemble of the performers is of intoxicating beauty. Addison presents silky smoothness. This is a magnificent presentation in all respects.

Norman Lee (1895-)

Temple Song

Instrumental

☐ Gozesky (piano) / Capra 1203

Piano

A revival of salon music, filled with sequences, diminished chords, some whole-tone excursions, and all the proper tonal harmony resolutions. It is incomprehensible why this old-fashioned work was included on a record with avant-garde music. One might as well couple Czerny with Stockhausen.

Benjamin Lees (1924-)

Concerto for Orchestra (1962)

Orchestra

☐ Louisville Orchestra / Whitney (conductor) / Louisville S–665

Full-scale thematic evolution makes Lees's work as much a symphony as a concerto. The latter covers the virtuosic treatment of the instruments and the prepossessing orchestration. The performance substantiates the excellent ability of this orchestra to master new scores and present them with definition and proper meaning.

Prologue, *Capriccio*, and Epilogue (1959)

☐ Portland Junior Symphony / Avshalomov (conductor) / Composers Recordings 140 (monaural)

It is the *Capriccio* that highlights this work. There is presence in the terminal portions but the *Capriccio* is where the action is. It communicates through tight rhythm and sharply colored scoring. Constructively played if not with finesse.

Symphony No. 3 (1968)

☐ Louisville Orchestra / Orton (tenor saxophone) / Mester (conductor) / Louisville LS–752

Lees is no extrovert experimentalist. Nonetheless, he persistently refuses to stick closely to tried (tired?) and true formal facts. His third Symphony shows that individual gamble (and a winning of the stakes). It will be noted that in the credits given above the tenor saxophonist is singled out. Properly so. The work is stitched and knitted with that instrument, prefacing each of the three movements (described as interludes) and appearing within the work. A dramatic bitterness pervades the entire symphony. It truly is an untempered consideration of the temper of the times in which it was written (1968).

Instrumental

Piano

Odyssey (1970)

Sonata Breve

☐ Mandel (piano) / Desto 6445/7

There is no less acute formal stability (non-academic, however) in the romantically pro-visioned (and titled) *Odyssey* than in the *Sonata Breve*. Both are richly contemporaneously tonal, the former more extrovert, more emotionally portentous, the latter guided so that its drama is allied to the design. These are compositions of pianistic courage and Mandel has all the equipment to deal with them, exhibiting the depth, passion, and personality of Lees's music.

Chamber Music

Sonata No. 2 for Violin and Piano (1973)

☐ Druian (violin); von Alpenheim (piano) / Desto 7174

Lees's duo luxuriates in the harmonic pincers of sevenths and ninths, with the tensions thus set up further intensified by the metrical shapes. This is a music of sharp black and whites. There is no textural glutting but there is a power-laden progress straight forward, not only in the outer *allegro*-paced movements, but also in the slower-tempoed central division. Tempo reflects the differences here, but there is no watering-down or relaxing for the sake of achieving needed contrast. This does not produce a cold running of music. There is sentiment though it is delivered with clenched fists.

All of the positiveness of the work is conveyed in the recording by superb recreative musicianship. Rafael Druian plays with powerful intensity and yet his tone is always clean and clear, without any roughage. Ilse von Alpenheim provides a magnificently tooled quality and partners Druian in sharply bitten metrical accentuation. Indeed, such a per-formance deserves a rave notice.

Ton de Leeuw (1926-   )

Orchestra

Ombres (1961)

☐ Concertgebouw Orchestra / Haitink (conductor) / Donemus Audio-Visual Series DAVS-6301 (monaural: 10-inch disc)

Ombres is full of dodecaphonic diction, abounding in extremely busy and disconnec-tive phrases. Above all is the composer's enthusiasm for orchestral colors, kept separate or bleeding into each other. Though de Leeuw tills the twelve-tone soil in the same manner that many other composers have long since plowed it, everything is not barren, especially the flowery brass detail in movement 1.

This is a well-stated performance, exceedingly well held together. The sound is only fair but it must be realized that these early Donemus discs were made from ''live record-ings''—this one taped on October 21, 1962.

Spatial Music I (1966)

☐ Radio Chamber Orchestra / Hupperts (conductor) / Donemus Audio-Visual Series 7001

Mostly chance music with certain elements fixed into the working plan (extremely com-plicated) to insure that all performances will fall, a bit more or less, in the same style. The players are distributed throughout the hall and the material they play depends on where they are individually located.

The shapes produced in this performance remain sympathetic to the usual contours of quietly swaying aleatoric music. The passions, however, are in the maneuvers rather than in the results. Profound statements, even light emotional ones, cannot be expected to be heard and they aren't. Still, de Leeuw's experimentation is worth examination.

Symphonies of Winds (1963)

Band

☐ Radio Philharmonic Orchestra / Bour (conductor) / Donemus Audio-Visual Series DAVS–6604 (monaural)

This is an apt title for a work that bears the indication "An Homage to Igor Stravinsky." De Leeuw's scoring is acutely balanced with four each of the winds and brass, the only exception being a single tuba.

A tightly banded insularism marks the style. Clusters of varying type are used: vertical, pyramided, antiphonally drawn, rhythmically engendered, and implied by the disintegration of single pitches sounding in concentrated chromatic conjunctiveness. A mystical penumbra hangs over the music, which does not move into other contrastive areas.

Ernest Bour controls the score admirably. Dynamic levels are crucial in the work and he makes certain they are precisely registered.

String Quartet No. 2 (1964)

Chamber Music

☐ Gaudeamus String Quartet / Philips 6500881

A thematic continuity is the plan for this Quartet. There are some thirteen sections, completed by a chorale-like, simplistic, and very moving portion based on a motto from Dylan Thomas, "And death shall have no dominion." The jurisdiction of each section is governed by specific technical pigmentation. Thus: microtones and glissandi in part 2, scoop chords in the fourth section, string tuning (polyphonic and subtly originated) in the eighth segment, fragmented fragments in the tenth, and so on.

The compilation hangs neatly together, with a type of free variational process, but acutely free it is. The work is enormously difficult to perform, but the group (Verkoeyen, Wittenberg, Neuburger, and Werner) are masters of this type of contemporary musical fare. Every compositional gesture is fulfilled. This version is "without electronic equipment." Although it would be interesting to hear the second setting, there is sufficient electricity in the way de Leeuw treats the four instruments. A stunning work and a marvelously communicative performance.

Louis James Alfred Lefébure-Wély *(1817-1869)*

Offertoire in D minor

Instrumental

☐ Lehrndorfer (organ) / Vox SVBX–5314

Organ

This large and heavy chunk of organ music spins on a firm tonal base, with constant cadential reminders throughout its fifteen and one-quarter minutes' length. Nicely padded with urgent sequences.

Lehrndorfer pitches in and meets the composer in proper manner, meaning full registration and dynamic tenacity. Indeed, this is as it should be.

Jean Xavier Lefèvre   *(1763-1829)*

Chamber Music

Sonata No. 7 in G minor

☐ Campbell (clarinet); York (piano) / Crystal S-333

Lefèvre's Sonata is set in classical style, partially leaning backward in technical procedure. The piano part was written as a bass line and had to be filled-out (the contribution of one Jacques Lancelot). In length a sonatina, the entire work covers a seven-minute span. The interpretation is intelligent and the playing is without any fuss—whatever expressive range the music contains is conveyed.

Ethel Leginska   *(1886-1970)*

Instrumental

Piano

Three Victorian Portraits **(1959)**

☐ Dowis (piano) / Orion 75188

A *Nostalgic Waltz, A Dirge,* and *Heroic Impromptu* are the titles of these pieces. The waltz does not stick in the rut of triple accompanimental meter. *A Dirge* glances at Chopin and benefits thereby. Both pieces have a deeper quality than the more ordinary and salonistically framed Impromptu.

It's good to have something recorded by this important musician, who was courageously practicing Womens' Lib long before it was in flower. Jeaneane Dowis's playing is of effective substance and nicely styled. She deserves extra applause for choosing to record the Leginska pieces.

Johannes Legrant   *(ca. 1419-ca. 1446)*

Vocal

Voice and Instrumental Ensemble

Entre vous, noviaux mariés

☐ Early Music Consort of London / Bowman (countertenor) / Munrow (conductor) / Nonesuch 71326

Be curious and discover creativity that is singularly different. Legrant's *Ballade* is performed with a styled intelligence and quality that are totally captivating.

Giovanni Legrenzi   *(1626-1690)*

String Orchestra

Sonata

☐ Camerata Lutetiensis / Nonesuch 73014

Sectional fantasy is involved in the design of Legrenzi's string-instrument opus. Dark-colored, it thrives mainly on harmonic urgency. An impressive piece, effectively played.

Franz Lehár   *(1870-1948)*

Orchestra

Gold and Silver **Waltz, Op. 79**

☐ Vienna Philharmonic / Boskovsky (conductor) / London 6791

The playing of this beautiful Waltz is entirely perfect, wanting nothing. The dynamic differences applied are only one of the superexcellences of Willi Boskovsky's conducting.

Merry Widow — Czardas

☐ André Kostelanetz and His Orchestra / Kostelanetz (conductor) / Columbia MS-7087

A cute bit, rewardingly played.

Merry Widow Waltz
Waltzes from *The Count of Luxembourg*
Waltzes from *Eva*

☐ Vienna State Opera Orchestra / Paulik (conductor) / Vanguard S-205

The Waltz from *Die lustige Witwe* (officially titled *Ballsirenen*) is, of course, one of the great ones. The Waltzes from two of Lehár's operettas are of no less stature.

Paulik is an old hand at this type of music and directs it enchantingly, and with an élan that is captivating.

Paganini

☐ Bavarian Symphony Orchestra and Bavarian State Opera Chorus / Rothenberger and Miljakovic (sopranos); Gedda, Lenz, and Zednik (tenors); Kusche and Wichartz (baritones); Sachtleben, Dieberitz, and Wagner (speakers) / Boskovsky (conductor) / Angel SBLX-3863

Opera and Dramatic Music

If you can swallow this soppy-corny story you will enjoy some good tunes, including (naturally!) a fine waltz. If you like the tunes you will find that the best singing is by the lesser lights. Nicolai Gedda doesn't tune up exactly as Paganini. Willi Boskovsky is professionally competent but no interpretative ecstasy can be expected.

Hans Ulrich Lehmann (1937-)

Quanti for Flute and Chamber Orchestra (1962)

☐ Soloists of the Rome Symphony Orchestra / Gazzelloni (flute) / Maderna (conductor) / RCA VICS-1313

Solo Instrument and Orchestra

Flute

Quanti has some aleatoric portions as well as interplay between the solo flute and the ubiquitous vibraphone (and marimba). It thus contains the bell-like sounds that are the celestial fantasies of so much contemporary writing for flute and instrumental combinations. Nevertheless, the manipulation of the solo wind instrument is dramatically dazzling and will maintain a listener's interest. So will the pyrotechnical magic of which only Severino Gazzelloni is capable.

Spiele for Oboe and Harp (1965)

☐ Heinz Holliger (oboe); Ursula Holliger (harp) / Philips 6500202

Chamber Music

Lehmann's fundamental style of neo-classic language intertwined with dodecaphonic connotations is absent here. *Spiele* is as much composed by the performers as by the composer. The former are offered the basic musical material and in playing react to each other, thereby, as Lehmann states, "entering into a performing 'competition.'" This interesting exercise is carried out with flair but with little definitive shape.

Jón Leifs   (1899-1968)

Orchestra

Iceland Overture, Op. 9

☐ Iceland Symphony Orchestra / Strickland (conductor) / Composers Recordings 179 (monaural)

Leifs's Iceland Overture (also known as Icelandic Overture) was written in Oslo in 1926. It is considered his most successful work. It is designed more like a rhapsodic fantasy than an overture. As expected the data are folkloristic; the scoring is never heavy and mixtures of unrelated timbres predominate. In terms of handling the orchestra Leifs reminds one of Janáček. The pleasure of listening is aided by Strickland's excellent reading.

Claude Le Jeune   (1528-1600)

Choral

Chorus Alone

Chansons

☐ Jean-Paul Kreder Ensemble / Nonesuch 7001

Just listen to the first of these fourteen delicacies, *La Belle Aronde,* and you won't let go. All of them offer incontestable proof of this sixteenth-century composer's great talent. Tenderness and lightness are the key words to describe both Le Jeune's writing and the beguiling singing of the Kreder ensemble.

Guillaume Lekeu   (1870-1894)

Chamber Music

Sonata in G major for Violin and Piano (1891)

☐ Grumiaux (violin); Varsi (piano) / Philips 6500814

Coached in his work by César Franck, Lekeu, not surprisingly, adopted Franckian methods. These draw on the formal concepts of thematic tie-up (and tie-in) of that composer, and to a degree, his harmonic vocabulary. However, Lekeu's harmonies are clearer than Franck's since the chromaticism shifts less. Lekeu pins the chromatics; he does not permit them to sideslip and sequentialize themselves. Further, Lekeu's phrasings are longer than Franck's—his music *sings* more.

These points are exemplified in the Sonata (Lekeu's most frequently performed composition) which embraces the cyclian system of the Franck school. Thus the opening theme not only casts its shadow on the two succeeding movements (the first of this pair is in septuple meter, its middle section being in the form of a Walloon folk song) but is also used in practically the same form in the final movement.

This is a richly toned performance, with keen balance between the instruments—not easy since the piano part is filled to the brim. Music in this style is always in danger of being heard in a slushy dialect. None of that here—the playing is romantic but clean, clear, and detailed with finesse.

Leonardo Leo *(1694-1744)*

Concerto in A major for Cello and Strings

☐ Stuttgart Soloists / Blees (cello) / Turnabout 34236

Solo Instrument and Orchestra

Cello

Nice spontaneity of melody. Leo gives evidence of a fine grasp of what works with a solo string voice pitted against massed strings. There are more than lingering traces of Vivaldi and Domenico Scarlatti in Leo's music but such influences do not strike the work down in any way. Blees's account of the solo part is firm and convincing as is that of the Stuttgart group.

Ruggero Leoncavallo *(1857-1919)*

I Pagliacci

☐ Orchestra and Chorus of La Scala, Milan / Amara (soprano); Corelli, Mercuriali, and Spina (tenors); Gobbi, Zanasi, and Piva (baritones) / von Matacic (conductor) / Angel S-3168

Opera and Dramatic Music

Leoncavallo's two-act *Pagliacci* turned out to be his one-shot deal to fame. It was first performed on May 21, 1892. Its factual story of passion and murder was an instantaneous success and has maintained that status unceasingly. Its "veristic" style has traditionally made it a perfect part of a twin bill with Mascagni's one-act *Cavalleria Rusticana* that all opera fans know as "Cav" and "Pag."

Strong stuff, this opera is, in lusty Italian style. The Angel production has long been available but it stands up against later editions because it doesn't attempt to refine the details. *Pagliacci* should have clout (and not tempered refinement as on Deutsche Grammophon 2709020 under von Karajan, for example) and this cast provides it to the full. None of the singers strain but they are dramatically effective and vocally dynamic. Lucine Amara is fine, Tito Gobbi is a splendid Tonio, and Franco Corelli is superb. The style is just the way "Pag" should be heard.

Raymond Leppard. *See C. P. E. Bach / Raymond Leppard.*

Fred Lerdahl *(1943-   )*

Piano Fantasy (1964)

☐ Miller (piano) / Composers Recordings SD-319

Instrumental

Piano

Music of impassioned conviction that zigs and zags but never sags within the style of post-Webernian rhetoric. The wide leaps and fragmentation, the total disjunctiveness have a nervous eloquence—it is a music always emotionally alive and never coldly ascetic. The conclusion has special dramatic effect by its sheer use of dynamic contrast to what has preceded.

Robert Miller furnishes a distinguished performance. His consideration of Lerdahl's music is one of total involvement and understanding.

Chamber Music

String Trio (1966)

☐ Raimondi (violin); Dupouy (viola); Rudiakov (cello) / Composers Recordings SD–319

Lerdahl mentions being influenced by Schoenberg's work for three stringed instruments. In that respect the affinity is recognizable. However, the concise and strongly imagined music of Lerdahl's Trio is strongly characterized by phrases that are on the threshold of pre-dodecaphonic Schoenberg style—a reconciliation with late-romantic cultivations. Above all, the expressionistic writing is pulsed strongly and there are no superfluous or decorative sounds. This is a strong work, the product of a composer of fertile imagination.

The playing by Raimondi, Dupouy, and Rudiakov is sensitively projected. These musicians form, with another violinist, the Composers String Quartet.

Adrian Le Roy   (ca. 1520 - 1599)

Instrumental

Guitar

Allemande

J'aymeroy mieux dormir

Passemèze

☐ Santos (guitar) / Musical Heritage Society MHS–1916

These are sixteenth-century lute pieces transcribed for the modern guitar. One can consider the process as similar to lighting up the area in which a painting is hung. Turibio Santos plays with positive clarity.

Frederick Lesemann   (1936-   )

Chamber Music

Sonata for Clarinet and Percussion

☐ Lurie (clarinet); Ervin (percussion) / Crystal 641

Contrastive sharpness—short clarinet phrases, rarely overmotile, many in the high register, and punctuative percussive sentences—is the formal objective of Lesemann's sound piece. Plenty of invention and potency, even in the less energized clarinet part, provide interesting aural stimulation.

Mitchell Lurie's tone is somewhat hard as though it were influenced by the sounds of the percussionist.

John Lessard   (1920-   )

Solo Instrument and Orchestra

Concerto for Flute, Clarinet, Bassoon, String Quartet, and String Orchestra (1952)

☐ Peninsula Festival Orchestra / Krell (flute); Marcellus (clarinet); Kilburn (bassoon); Cohen and Adams (violins); Kahlson (viola); Ehrlich (cello) / Johnson (conductor) / Composers Recordings 122 (monaural)

Lessard's composition of seven soli has an affinity with baroque period concerti. It is well knit and well played.

Wind Trio and String Quartet

Toccata for Harpsichord

Instrumental

Harpsichord

☐ Spiegelman (harpsichord) / Serenus 12032

Tonal lights are not dimmed in this work and neither is there any preoccupation with gentility. Lessard treats the harpsichord with respect but shows its ability to make big gestures and a big sound. The performance by Joel Spiegelman is in total agreement and has a panache that registers with impact.

Sonata for Cello and Piano (1955)

Chamber Music

☐ Greenhouse (cello); Pressler (piano) / Composers Recordings 208 (monaural)

Lessard follows the fruitful line of neoclassic style, so the three movements of his duo parallel tempered pitch with tempered form. The latter is determined specifically in the fantasy schematic of the central movement. A sonata design and a motile finale surround it.

This Sonata requires a lot of work for the players but they deftly toss it off in fine chamber music style.

Trio in Sei Parti

☐ Zukofsky (violin); Eddy (cello); Kalish (piano) / Serenus 12032

All but two of the mathematical possibilities for using the three instruments are contained in Lessard's trio. The missing combinations are movements for violin and piano and cello with piano. The others are represented: a duo for violin and cello, separate solo sections for each instrument, and two trio divisions.

Panchromatic language that has its roots in serialism styles the "Trio in Six Parts." In the hands of these fine musicians it receives a direct and clear presentation.

Brass Quintet No. 1

☐ American Brass Quintet / Serenus 12041

The common tautness of serial style is avoided in Lessard's opus through fluid shapes and crisp phrases. An aristocratic temper is to be found in this music and it is fully displayed in the performance.

Quintet for Woodwinds

☐ New York Woodwind Quintet / Serenus 12032

All the moves would seem to stem from the land of dodecaphonism but there is a strong tonal polarity in every part of the three movements of Lessard's second wind Quintet (not so identified anywhere save once in the liner notes). The punctuative pointillism of the writing establishes keen nuances of thought. This is an extremely colorful work that doesn't use any special effects and has expressive originality. Fine-grained playing by the New Yorker group.

Daniel Lesur   *(1908-   )*

Elegie

Instrumental

Two Guitars

☐ Ito and Dorigny (guitars) / Delos FY-008

Nocturnal as well as elegiac music. Lesur or, as he liked to be called, "Daniel-Lesur," shapes his piece in a dynamic curve. Sensitively played.

Alfonso Letelier   *(1912-   )*

Orchestra   **Aculeo, Suite for Orchestra (1957)**

☐ Louisville Orchestra / Whitney (conductor) / Louisville 59–1 (monaural)

Aculeo is the name of the place where the composer was born. There is nothing exotic or remote to be found on this musical horizon, described in two parts: *Horcon de Piedra* (a huge rock mountain) and *El Lago* ("The Lake"). A heavy-laden, chromatically geographic harmony is the sonorous simulant.

The Louisville organization is diligent as to the pitches but the playing is somewhat rigid and lacks flexibility.

Burt Levy   *(1936-   )*

Instrumental   **Orbs with Flute for Flute Solo**

Flute   ☐ Sollberger (flute) / Nonesuch 73028

This is an assorted package of new flute colors: multiphonics, bent tones, pitchless key clicks, glissandi, and so forth. But even though effects seem primary, they are put to work with quality and taste if not tradition. The way Harvey Sollberger tosses off these techniques and binds them so that the music has structural cohesion is to his credit as much as to the composer. In the hands of a lesser musician sectionalism could well be the negative result.

Louis Lewandowski   *(1821-1894)*

Choral   **Zocharti Loch**

Chorus with   ☐ David Tilman Choir / Lam (baritone) / Serenus 12039
Accompaniment

Music used in the synagogue service held during the Jewish High Holy Day, *Rosh Hashanah*. There is less German romantic style in this piece than in most others by this eminent composer of sacred Jewish music.

Impeccable singing by the Cantor (Nathan Lam) as well as the chorus. (No credit for the organist who supplies the instrumental background.)

Peter Todd Lewis   *(1932-   )*

Electronic   **Gestes (1973)**
Music
                    ☐ Composers Recordings S–324

This is a nocturnal type of electronic music. The composer terms it "electronic chamber music" since it uses "only a few clearly identifiable" materials. So much for "chamber music" totality; there is a sonic environment of calm and of brashlessness that suggests the nocturnal designation.

Robert Hall Lewis   *(1926-   )*

Monophony VII (1972)   *Instrumental*

☐ Stevens (trumpet) / Crystal S-361   *Trumpet*

This is a fascinating exploration of trumpet properties, not merely of what can be done on the instrument nowadays (pedal tones, micro pitches, variable vibrati, hand muting, etcetera), but also of their artistic accession. Lewis's piece has form and balance, tension and release, and fully fulfills its expressive purposes. It proves how contemporaneously beautiful an unaccompanied homophonic instrument can be when handled with creative intelligence and requisite talent.

Thomas Stevens is a name to remember in the world of the trumpet. His playing is both delicate and diabolic. He performs like a master.

Toccata for Solo Violin and Percussion   *Violin and Percussion*

☐ Banat (violin); Goodman (timpani and percussion); Rosenberger (percussion) / Composers Recordings S-263

Lewis chooses not to be rigid in his large three-part Toccata. His structural flexibility merges with a fluid use of pantonality and chromatic modifications. This is matched by the neat instrumentation that has the violin as the dominating voice with a graded subservience on the part of the percussion (mainly timpani with considerable xylophone). However, do not read the last statement to mean cold accompaniment.

A clear, crisp, and finely characterized recording. Gabriel Banat and Walter Rosenberger are excellent musicians, and Saul Goodman is to percussion what Heifetz has been in the violin world.

Divertimento for Six Instruments   *Chamber Music*

☐ Aeolian Chamber Players / Composers Recordings S-263

Chamber music with a nonintimate personality. Lewis enthusiastically commandeers color by way of "continuity-discontinuity, complexity-simplicity and the juxtaposition of static sound with gestures of more intense rhythmic activity." This assorted contemporary garden is nicely cultivated. Nicely performed as well.

Anatoly Liadov   *(1855-1914)*

Baba-Yaga, Op. 56   *Orchestra*

☐ L'Orchestre de la Suisse Romande / Ansermet (conductor) / London STS-15066

Most conductors have a tendency to propel this Russian ogre's flight as though it took place in the twentieth century and via jet transportation. Granted the excitement of the score, the *presto* tempo, as marked, is sufficient to bring out all the colorful delicacies that Liadov has included. Performed in *molto prestissimo* speed it just is an ordinary work-out for the orchestra players. Ansermet opts for the former and brings home the witch without tempo sweat. In this case less is considerably more.

Eight Russian Folk Songs, Op. 58

☐ London Symphony Orchestra / Previn (conductor) / RCA AGL1-1265

Previn's performance of this beautiful example of nationalistic music miniatures is especially sensitive, warm, subtle, and expressively phrased. The songs are treated not as a collection of folk sweets and casually served in that manner. The numerous solo passages laced in the score are far better in this case than in any of the other issues on the market.

The Enchanted Lake, Op. 62

From Days of Old, Op. 21b

From the Apocalypse, Op. 66

☐ U.S.S.R. Symphony Orchestra / Svetlanov (conductor) / Melodiya/Angel S-40159

Liadov's legendary water picture is nicely framed in this recording. Op. 21b represents an orchestral translation of a piano work (the instrumentation includes an upright piano). Svetlanov's performance is definitely first-class.

Kikimora, Op. 63

☐ L'Orchestre de la Suisse Romande / Ansermet (conductor) / London STS-15066

A nicely detailed and atmospheric performance. The dynamic relationships are especially expressive.

Instrumental

Piano

Prelude

In B minor, Op. 11, No. 1 / In D flat major, Op. 11, No. 2

☐ Tarnowsky (piano) / Genesis 1004

A touch of Russian melos in the minor-keyed piece. Miniature business as usual in reference to the other one.

Sergei Liapunov   (1859-1924)

Instrumental

Piano

Etudes d'exécution transcendante, Op. 11 (Nos. 1-9)

☐ Kentner (piano) / Turnabout 34469

In terms of performance demands, Liapunov's "Transcendental Etudes" approach the technical virtuosity built into Liszt's piano music. Properly, therefore, the dozen pieces (*see below* for Nos. 10, 11, and 12) were dedicated "to the memory of Liszt."

Bearing out the principal point of a specific technical objective, such as legato and simultaneous figuration in the same hand (No. 5), exploitation of tremolandi (No. 9), as well as a different tonality for each piece, which is another ingredient in sharpening performance technique, Liapunov goes one step further. Each étude portrays a specific mood or general descriptive viewpoint, so that a true hybrid is produced: music for both rich, super-advanced study and for performance on the concert stage. Thus No. 2 is called *Ronde des Fantômes*, No. 4 is *Térek* (the name of a river, with the music simulating the wild rushing of its waters), No. 8 is a *Chant Epique*, etc.

Naturally, there is much to show off in this music and Kentner has all the technical know-how and bravado. However, everything is presented with sensitivity and sensibility. None of the pieces is overplayed or underplayed.

Etudes d'exécution transcendante, Op. 11 (Nos. 10-12)

☐ Kentner (piano) / Turnabout 34470

For details *see immediately above* where the composition and Kentner's performance are discussed.

Fittingly, Liapunov concludes his Etudes with a further gesture to Liszt. The title of the twelfth piece is *Elégie en mémoire de F. Liszt.*

Goddard Lieberson   *(1911 - 1977)*

Piano Pieces for Advanced Children or Retarded Adults (1963)

Instrumental

□ Previn (piano) / Columbia Special Products CMS-6586

Piano

Sophisticated spoofery, which does not deter some nice (as well as clever) music to be heard in the nineteen sections. These are divided into "Five Songs Without Mendelssohn," "Six Technical Studies (Which Will Teach You Nothing)," and "Eight Studies in Musicology (Which Will Teach You a Great Deal)." All the titles furnish objective clues: *My Father Plays Pizzicato* (in the "Songs"), *Safe on Third* (within the "Technical" group), *How to Handle a Bach Violin Solo,* and *Aaron Copland Shakes Hands with Abe Lincoln* (parts 2 and 7 of the "Studies in Musicology").

Previn plays it straight and thereby delineates Lieberson's subtleties and humor in the best possible manner.

String Quartet (1938)

Chamber Music

□ Galimir Quartet / Columbia Special Products AMS-6421

This is music by a conservative twentieth-century composer, not unaware of the need for string music to sing its tunes above all else. The motival coherence of the initial part, the savage incisiveness of the central movement, and the acid etching portrayed by the final, slow movement show Lieberson as one who knew all the tricks of the trade but avoided trickery as a gimmick.

This worthy contribution is given a worthy statement by the Galimir four. Since the personnel of this quartet has changed over the years it is well to indicate the players in this recording: Felix Galimir and Marvin Morgenstern, violins; Samuel Rhodes, viola; and Charles McCracken, cello.

Peter Lieberson   *(1946-   )*

Concerto for Four Groups of Instruments

Orchestra

□ Speculum Musicae / Lieberson (conductor) / Composers Recordings SD-350

The explosively nervous sounds in Lieberson's piece are made by a string quartet plus double bass, a woodwind quartet, piano, and harp. There is little relaxation in this music, which spans the total pitch spectrum. It cultivates pungency and intensity and is unconstrained. This makes for an excitement equating a climax in every one of its measures. No failure of balance, however. Lieberson's Concerto needs no contrastive shelters as it detonates.

Instrumental

Piano

Piano Fantasy

☐ Oppens (piano) / Composers Recordings SD–350

Ideas are determined, lengthened, and developed in this huge panchromatic composition of rhythmic vitality, sonority, and granitic contour. Lieberson's piece is intense, a music with Bergian flame.

The Fantasy demands a virtuoso for its technical bravado and one that can cope with the contemporary syntax that gives it meaning. High-tension playing is a further demand. Ursula Oppens supplies all the requirements perfectly.

György Ligeti   (1923 -   )

Orchestra

Atmosphères (1961)

☐ New York Philharmonic / Bernstein (conductor) / Columbia MS-7176

Ligeti opts for the destruction of line, harmony, counterpoint, and form by absorption of the entire orchestral mass. Texture is the sole device in this powerful score, sounding as though electronic means have been reversed and turned into a music sounded by ordinary winds, brass, and strings. The tensions of the hunks and chunks of sound create the structure. Ligeti has understood how to dress his ideas without considering any inherited method and has produced a magnificently individual piece. In a way this music is an abstraction made by sonorous contraction, not in the sense of a lowered dynamic level, but by coalescence. It would seem impossible not to pay full attention to its cold-sweated message. (See also discussion of *Lux Aeterna* under *Choral*.)

Bernstein's recording first appeared in an album devoted to "Music of Our Time." The other items (by Austin and Feldman and four improvisations by the New York Philharmonic, all on MS-6733) are in the delete pile. In the present instance the recording appears in a collection titled "2001." Lenny B. moves the music with more impetus than Ernest Bour does with the Southwest German Radio Symphony on a Wergo disc. Bernstein's performance time is clocked at 6:49, Bour's at 8:01. The Bernstein pace is a better choice for this unornamentalized conception.

(Linking each piece in the "2001" collection is an electronic interlude by Morton Subotnick. For no worthy reason the Subotnick links onto the Ligati before it has been totally completed. Stupid monkeyshines, that idea.)

Chamber Concerto for Thirteen Instrumentalists (1970)

☐ Ensemble "Die Reihe" / Cerha (conductor) / Wergo WER-60059

The baker's dozen performers use more than thirteen instruments—four winds: flute (doubling on piccolo), oboe (tripling on oboe d'amore and English horn), two clarinets (the second alternating with bass clarinet); two brass: horn and trombone; five strings: a string quartet plus double bass; and two keyboard instrumentalists, playing between them piano, celesta, harpsichord, and Hammond organ.

Typical Ligeti, with background merging into foreground as melodic, harmonic, and rhythmic elements are eradicated and the focus is reset on sound particles changing in kaleidoscopic differentiation. This is a montage of varied densities formed by micro sound-dots. In its way Ligeti's music is music that holds its breath but does not choke.

Ligeti composed his work for Friedrich Cerha's ensemble. They premiered the work in Berlin on October 1, 1970. One can be assured the recorded performance is everything it should be. (This is, actually, a revised version of the piece. Originally it was only three movements and was so performed for the first time on April 2, 1970. The definitive four-movement version heard here followed.)

Lontano for Full Orchestra (1967)

☐ Südwestfunkorchester, Baden-Baden / Bour (conductor) / Wergo 60045

A centrospheric system binds *Lontano* in which ictus and punctuation are foreign to Ligeti's style. Attacks of entering instruments are eliminated. In the opening, for example, it is simply impossible to realize that what sounds like a sustained unison is the result of fourteen entrances on the same pitch by a succession of four flutes, four clarinets, three bassoons, and three horns! Sound inlay and interlacement (rhythmically spaced in both coordinated and uncoordinated fashion) with multi-division of single colors (strings split into forty-two voices, for example) define the vocabulary. There is no linear identity. It is like a dream of sound divested of definition by the absence of the usual corporeal parts of melody, chords, and rhythms.

Lontano (meaning "distant") begins, so to speak, from nowhere and gains strength with its multi-layered groups of sound, and eventually thins out until only a pair of clarinets and bass clarinet remain. It provides a sensuous, stimulating aural massage, caressing the ear, and even in its lengthy application, never lessens in interest. It is magnificently performed by the orchestra and conductor to whom Ligeti dedicated his work.

Ramifications for String Orchestra (1969)

String Orchestra

☐ Südwestfunkorchester, Baden-Baden / Bour (conductor) / Wergo WER-60059

Ramifications is a twelve-voiced work for multiple strings or one each to a part (*see immediately below*) wherein the shifting blocks and fissures are intensified by micro-pitch division. One group is tuned at 440 vibrations per second, the other at 453. The constant stream of sounds has no relationship to tonality, atonality, serialization, or any other technique of pitch arrangement. Ligeti is very much his own man. In the aural fascinations of *Ramifications* it is as though the guts of a few sounds have been dissected and redissected into their manifold multi-fractional elements and are "seen" through the ears.

Ramifications for Twelve Solo Strings (1969)

☐ Kammer Orchester des Saarländischen Rundfunks, Saarbrücken / Janigro (conductor) / Wergo WER-60059

This is the alternate version Ligeti made of *Ramifications* for String Orchestra (*see immediately above*). Sometimes the solo decision occurs also in the multiple string setting, with passages prescribed for single players.

Continuum for Harpsichord

Instrumental

☐ Vischer (harpsichord) / Wergo 60045

Harpsichord

Since sustained sound chunks—Ligeti's trademark—cannot be obtained on a harpsichord he has substituted the consistency of ostinati. The repetition of similar pitches and clusters to equate bands of sound creates a rhythmic stir and excitation within the texture. Some will say it scratches the ear rather than strokes it. Still, *Continuum* lasts only four minutes.

To produce the incessant action requires vast stamina. The Swiss harpsichordist Antoinette Vischer stands up to the demands of the music she had commissioned.

Organ

Etude No. 1, *Harmonies* (1967)

***Volumina* (Original Version 1961/62)**

☐ Zacher and Adamidis (organ) / Candide 31009

Both works are concerned with textures—socko textures, as foreign to any specific design as may be imagined. Globs of sounds, practically all tone clusters of varying poundage and intensity, in *Volumina* and pale, unearthly, boxed-in qualities in the Etude provide the entire "themes" and "developments" if one insists on using such words. Changes occur, but the variances are not contrastive in a structural sense. In *Volumina* a huge cluster is treated like a bunch of bound rubber bands that is expanded and contracted and in the Etude a sustained sound combination is shifted by registration and by switching the organ's motor on and off to obtain what Ligeti calls "discolored sounds."

Hypnotic music, this. Total serialism is do-re-mi stuff compared to Ligeti's approach in writing for the king of instruments. Such gusty primitivism is truly highly sophisticated.

Gerd Zacher is the organist. The other name in the credits is simply an assistant who helped push register knobs and the like while all of Zacher's ten fingers were occupied on the keys.

Chamber Music

Ten Pieces for Wind Quintet (1968)

☐ Wind Quintet of the Südwestfunk, Baden-Baden / Wergo WER-60059

A network of woodwind gestures that cover color, cohesion, and concertino application. Not only the usual flute, oboe, clarinet, horn, and bassoon are used, but English horn, oboe d'amore, and piccolo as well. The ten movements alternate with full ensemble and highlighting of one of the five instruments. A type of elastic technique is applied: one hears a static plane of sound and before it settles into the ear there enters Ligeti's "color of movement," and before that coheres, rhythmic karatelike chops are used. Nothing dogmatic in these mini-pieces. Everything rivets the attention.

Of course the work demands chilling virtuosity to deal with the technical acrobatics. (Small wonder Ligeti calls the quintet one of his "tightrope pieces.") The Baden-Baden based group does wonders and keeps its balance firmly throughout.

Vocal

Voice and Instrumental Ensemble

***Aventures* for Three Singers and Seven Instrumentalists (1962)**

***Nouvelles Aventures* for Three Singers and Seven Instrumentalists (1965)**

☐ Ensemble "Die Reihe" / Charlent (soprano); Cahn (alto); Pearson (baritone) / Cerha (conductor) / Candide 31009

A startling and fascinating vocal orchestration is backed by flute, horn, cello, double bass, percussion, piano alternating with celesta, and harpsichord. Both "Adventures" (composed in 1962) and the sequel, "New Adventures" (completed in 1965) represent a nontextual state of theatrics of the absurd for the singers. The fractured nonsense and the implosive and explosive sounds are often a reminder of vocal infantiloquy but they are always fascinating, fresh, and surprising.

Ligeti's sonic syllabic rumbles and screams, oral ejaculations and noises, vocal groans and moans have no individual meaning, but put together they are meaningful. For the unbiased listener these vocal inventions will be difficult to resist.

It was disappointing when the Helidor recording of this work (2549003) disappeared from the market. The singers on the Helidor disc turned in a truly hair-raising performance. On Candide the very same vocalists are used and they repeat their magnificent presentation.

Lux Aeterna (1967)

Choral

Chorus Alone

☐ Gregg Smith Singers / Smith (conductor) / Columbia MS–7176

The explorative condition of tone cluster writing as applied to sixteen-part mixed voices forms a parallel to the same creative strategy that Ligeti used in his *Atmosphères* (see under *Orchestra*). It is an intriguing concept that works beautifully and is most satisfactory in this realization, especially by maintaining the inner tensions generated throughout the score.

(Columbia's "2001" album in which this work is included "joins" the pieces with electronic interludes by Morton Subotnick. His work is good enough but the interlude does not permit complete silence at the end of the Ligeti piece. Beware, therefore.)

Requiem for Soprano, Mezzo-Soprano, Two Choirs, and Orchestra (1965)

Cantata
and Oratorio

☐ Hessian Radio Symphony and Bavarian Radio Chorus / Poli (soprano); Ericson (mezzo-soprano) / Gielen (conductor) / Wergo 60045

In the first two parts of this magnificent work Ligeti uses *Klangflächenkomposition* (composition with blocks of sound) as heard in his *Atmosphères* and *Lontano* (for both works see under *Orchestra*). In part 3 a fascinating and unexpected type of contrast occurs. In place of granitic and tidal waves of sound, a violence of solo voice against chorus against orchestra and an inner play among all three take place. Here too is the excitement of activated play within unified mass groupings (clusters moving side-saddle, as it were, and slow-motioned voice combinations).

This is truly vocal virtuosity of a new kind. It is given a memorable presentation in all respects, with vivid assists from Liliana Poli and Barbro Ericson. Both display magnificent vocal artistry.

Artikulation (1958)

Electronic
Music

☐ Wergo WER–60059

The curves, zig-zags, corrugations, and other individual types of the electronic music vocabulary are now almost as familiar as chords in set tonality. Ligeti, however, arranges them in a special way. Thanks to his choice and disposition of small particles, the effect resembles that of speech. Of course, the language spoken is nontranslatable Ligetian.

Norbert Linke   (1933–   )

Violencia

Instrumental

Violin

☐ Edinger (violin) / Orion 75171

Linke states that his title is an association of "violin" (yes, of course), "violent" (no argument there), and "Valencia" (hardly a reminder of Spain will be heard). One rarely writes unaccompanied fiddle music with simplistic contours these days, and Linke doesn't. His work of eight and one-half minutes is athletic and dynamic, of demanding virtuosity, as well as quotational. Included are some massaged entries from Mozart and Strauss (his claim, difficult to spot) plus Paganini and Rimsky-Korsakov (easy to spot, especially the *Scheherazade* snip).

A brilliantly sharp performance. Christiane Edinger is some fiddler. She belongs in the top-brass category.

Robert Linn (1925-)

*Solo
Instrument
and
Orchestra*

Concertino for Violin and Wind Octet

☐ Winds of the Crystal Chamber Orchestra / Shapiro (violin) / Kraft (conductor) / Crystal S–853

Violin

On this, the sunny side of the neoclassic street, Linn has taken his cue from the Haydn and Mozart wind octets and serenades and attempted a twentieth-century parallel. Instrumentation-wise the winds remain the same: pairs of oboes, clarinets, bassoons, and horns; the contemporary enlargement is the solo violin. The latter functions vividly against the wind band.

Tonal confession is still a good cleansing agent for a composer and Linn has produced a work that is crystal-clear. Crystal-clear also are the words to describe Eudice Shapiro's gorgeous playing, William Kraft's direction, and the wind octet's performance. Again, the same description covers the sound.

*Chamber
Music*

Dithyramb for Eight Celli

☐ I Cellisti / Kessler (conductor) / Orion 7037

The ternary design is one of the balances in Linn's probing work for cello octet. The other balance comes from the use of a twelve-note series, although tonal polarities tighten the chromatic scope, as is aurally apparent.

Eight celli do not usually make for lightness. Linn's *Dithyramb* has dynamic depth but is always clear in the heightening and transmutation of its materials. It is a fine success and the playing is most appropriate.

Dinu Lipatti (1917-1950)

*Solo
Instrument
and
Orchestra*

Concertino in Classical Style, Op. 3

Rumanian Dances for Piano and Orchestra (1943)

☐ Milan Philharmonia Orchestra / Blumental (piano) / Cillario (conductor) / Everest 3166

Piano

Lipatti as a composer was well-trained (he studied with Paul Dukas and Nadia Boulanger), and it shows in the neoclassic fertility of his writing in the first work, which leans very heavily on J. S. Bach, and in the much stronger set of dances. In the latter there is less leaning, though Enesco could be given some credits.

Performance on the part of the pianist is good, on the part of the orchestra not as good. You'll also have to accept some funny pitch differences between piano and orchestra.

Kurt List (1913-1970)

Choral

Remember (1956)

Chorus Alone

☐ Randolph Singers / Randolph (conductor) / Composers Recordings 102

Attractive use of a motto phrase balances and links List's lightly accented five-voice madrigal. This is a demonstration by the Randolph quintet of well-realized singing.

Franz Liszt   *(1811-1886)*

Ce qu'on entend sur la montagne (*Bergsymphonie*) (Symphonic Poem No. 1 after   *Orchestra* Victor Hugo) (1854)

☐ London Philharmonic Orchestra / Haitink (conductor) / Philips 6500189

Haitink knits the manifold details of Liszt's first symphonic poem (originally conceived for piano, then changed into orchestral form) in such a way that only a few of its many seams show. For that alone, approbation.

(Also available in a release covering the entire thirteen symphonic poems by Liszt on Philips 6709005.)

Die Ideale (Symphonic Poem No. 12 after Schiller) (1857)

☐ London Philharmonic Orchestra / Haitink (conductor) / Philips 6500191

Quite often Liszt's *Die Ideale* is on the verge of sentimentality, especially in the *Andante maestoso* section ("Disappointment"). To Haitink's credit this is held in check, and the phrases in full romantic diction come through cleanly and clearly.

This is the only current recorded performance. It is duplicated in Philips's album 6709005, which contains the other twelve symphonic poems.

A Faust Symphony (1854)

☐ Royal Philharmonic Orchestra and Beecham Choral Society / Young (tenor) / Beecham (conductor) / Seraphim S-6017

(*Eine Faust-Symphonie* was completed in 1854. However, the choral finale was added three years later.)

All the demands of Liszt's Goethe-based triptych are met in this stunning performance. Bernstein's edition (Columbia M2S-699) has a great deal of flair but it doesn't have the poetry of Beecham's interpretation.

Festklänge (Symphonic Poem No. 7) (1853)

☐ London Philharmonic Orchestra / Haitink (conductor) / Philips 6500191

There is not even a remote story line for this work. Festive it is, including march and polonaise characteristics. No problem for any competent conductor and certainly not for Bernard Haitink. (Philips has issued the total thirteen symphonic poems on 6709005.)

Hamlet (Symphonic Poem No. 10) (1858)

☐ London Philharmonic Orchestra / Haitink (conductor) / Philips 6500046

Beautifully shaded, perfectly paced. Haitink has recorded all of Liszt's symphonic poems. This is one of the very best of his performances. (Also contained in the set of the complete symphonic poems, on Philips 6709005.)

Héroïde Funèbre (Symphonic Poem No. 8) (1854)

☐ London Philharmonic Orchestra / Haitink (conductor) / Philips 6500190

The only representation in the recorded catalogue, and a damn good one. Liszt's piece (titled *Symphonie révolutionnaire* when first sketched) is dark-jacketed, its rhetoric contained. The performance is beautiful and sensitive.

(Also on Philips 6709005, with all the other symphonic poems.)

Hungaria (Symphonic Poem No. 9) (1854)

☐ London Philharmonic Orchestra / Haitink (conductor) / Philips 6500046

With its gypsy style paramount, this symphonic poem tends to be more rhapsodic than poematic. Although Haitink's conception is perhaps a bit too well-tailored in places, it gets more than a mere passing grade. (It is paired here with *Hamlet* and *Mazeppa*. If you want these three plus the other ten of Liszt's symphonic poems, they can be obtained in Philips's five-record set 6709005.)

Hungarian Rhapsody No. 1

☐ New York Philharmonic / Bernstein (conductor) / Columbia M-30645

Bernstein sinks his teeth into this one (the original piano version is No. 14) but doesn't mangle the work, letting it hang out neatly and nationalistically.

Hungarian Rhapsody
No. 2 / No. 3

☐ London Symphony Orchestra / Dorati (conductor) / Mercury 75018

Yes, that's the famous one on top. The orchestral No. 3 is No. 6 in the piano set.

Dorati's way with these rhapsodies, especially No. 2, is ideal. There's no *rubati* buccaneering, but just the right amount in the right place. Fine sound supports the splendid playing.

Hungarian Rhapsody No. 4

☐ New York Philharmonic / Baker (flute) / Bernstein (conductor) / Columbia M-30645

Fine style and control make this recording the best of the several presentations in the catalogue. Julius Baker is, of course, one of our great flutists, and the opportunity to hear him in special solo spots within the work adds a fat bonus to the Columbia release.

Hungarian Rhapsody
No. 5 / No. 6

☐ Vienna State Opera Orchestra / Fistoulari (conductor) / Vanguard S-160

The fifth orchestral Rhapsody is also No. 5 in the piano original, the sixth is No. 9 in the initial piano setting. It bears the subtitle "Carnival at Pest."

Full-natured playing in both works, with proper amounts of paprika, and pitched and paced sensibly at all times.

Hunnenschlacht (Symphonic Poem No. 11 after Kaulbach's painting) (1857)

☐ Los Angeles Philharmonic Orchestra / Mehta (conductor) / London 6738

The more the bravado in the playing of this piece, the better. It's Mehta's cup of Liszt tea, and his brew is strong and more flavorsome than any of the competing editions.

Les Préludes (Symphonic Poem No. 3 after Lamartine) (1850)

☐ Vienna Philharmonic / Mehta (conductor) / London 6529

This once great favorite on concert programs was dropped as dated, but it is now slowly resuming its popular place. No shift in the currents of fashion for the recording industry, however. Constant releases have been made. First, there were the ten-inch discs (the conductors were André, Ludwig, and Ormandy), then the full-sized discs with Mengelberg, Monteux, Paray, and Stokowski and less important conductors: Dixon, Fistoulari, Galliera, Schwarz, and Van Otterloo.

The latest availability maintains this track record. Represented are Bernstein (on Columbia M–30306 and M2S–699), Fiedler (on RCA, ARL1–0111), Fricsay (on Deutsche Grammophon 136226), Haitink (on Philips 839788), von Karajan (on Deutsche Grammophon 139037), Mehta, and Silvestri (on Angel S–35636).

Mehta's conception is a rousing one; the orchestra plays brilliantly. It can be argued that he takes liberties, but *Les Préludes* is just the sort of work that cries for that type of treatment, with its assortment of sonic scenes: the vigorous string action, the storm sequence, the pastoral flow, the militaristic rhythm. Square-to-center readings of this opus can never be convincing.

Mazeppa (Symphonic Poem No. 6 after Victor Hugo) (1851)

☐ Los Angeles Philharmonic Orchestra / Mehta (conductor) / London 6738

A varied number of steps preceded the first performance of *Mazeppa* (in Weimar, on April 16, 1854, with Liszt conducting). It was originally composed (in 1826) as an Etude for piano, then expanded (in 1837), published as one of the *Grandes Etudes* for piano (in 1839), further enlarged (in 1841), and finally orchestrated in 1851.

In *Mazeppa* the obviousness of the material is best delivered by vigorous and direct playing. Any sophisticated reasoning with the score interferes with its bald salesmanship. The conductor should just ride along with the "death ride," and showcase the "triumph." Of the four conductors on the current lists performing *Mazeppa*, Mehta most fully realizes this concept.

Mephisto Waltz No. 1 (1860)

☐ London Philharmonic Orchestra / Haitink (conductor) / Philips 6500190

Haitink's conducting of this subtle piece (the first of "Two Episodes from Lenau's Faust") is emphatic, beautifully styled; he knows how to control a climax so that it can cut through further, though one thinks the ultimate point has been reached. It's done without roughness and always has depth. This is the best of the Mephisto waltzes Liszt wrote, whether for piano or for orchestra.

Orpheus (Symphonic Poem No. 4) (1854)

☐ London Philharmonic Orchestra / Haitink (conductor) / Philips 839788

This is the most vocal of all of the Liszt symphonic poems, set in a three-part design. Haitink presents an expressively lyrical performance. So does Mehta (with the Los Angeles Philharmonic on London 6738). However, the London Philharmonic is the superior outfit.

(The complete symphonic poems, conducted by Haitink and, of course, with the same organization, is on Philips 6709005.)

Prometheus (Symphonic Poem No. 5) (1855)

☐ London Philharmonic Orchestra / Haitink (conductor) / Philips 6500190

Carefully apportioned textural balances are realized here. That is not simple to achieve, since the heaviness of the scoring could easily cause trouble. Not with Haitink. And, no brass blast. (Also in the five-record set Philips has issued on 6709005 of the complete symphonic poems.)

Tasso, Lamento e Trionfo (Symphonic Poem No. 2 after Byron) (1854)

☐ Orchestre de Paris / Solti (conductor) / London 6925

Liszt's *Tasso* was written in 1849, revised in 1850, and again in 1854. Both versions were first performed in Weimar, with Liszt conducting.

Solti obtains a burnished color from the orchestra in the "Lament" portion that matches the mood of somberness to perfection. In the "Triumph" section there is plenty of theatricality, but it is never vulgar. That a masterly hand is directing matters is apparent in every measure of Liszt's score.

Von der Wiege bis zum Grabe (Symphonic Poem No. 13) (1882)

☐ Orchestre de Paris / Solti (conductor) / London 6925

The choice is between Solti and Haitink and there is no doubt that the vote goes to Sir George. In "The Cradle" both orchestras respect the extremely low-pronged dynamic plane, but Solti achieves a depth in the softness of the texture, whereas Haitink (on Philips 6709005) permits the tone to float, which decreases the evocative effect materially. In "The Struggle for Existence" more drive is heard in Solti's reading—it is diminished to an almost neutral quotient in the Philips entry. Again, breadth of contour makes the exquisite finale, "To the Grave: The Cradle of the Life to Come," superbly rendered by Solti. The eloquence of this performance is a high mark in the total Liszt discography.

Solo Instrument and Orchestra

Piano

Concerto for Piano and Orchestra

No. 1 in E flat major (1856) / No. 2 in A major (1861)

☐ London Philharmonic Orchestra / Brendel (piano) / Haitink (conductor) / Philips 6500374

☐ London Symphony Orchestra / Richter (piano) / Kondrashin (conductor) / Philips 835474

Both these pianists sit squarely, comfortably, and magnificently in the virtuoso class, and they prove why by their performances. In Brendel's case Liszt's rhetoric is stated with dynamic decision and conviction. In Richter's instance the consideration is a bit more elegant, but not at the expense of the dramaticism that spills over most of the measures.

Those who don't wish this coupling can get a good version of the E flat major opus in Martha Argerich's performance (on Deutsche Grammophon 139383). She belongs in the class of pianists who try to play the Concerto with more attention to expansiveness than impacted insularity. It is very successful in this instance.

Hexaméron (1837)

☐ Westphalian Symphony Orchestra, Recklinghausen / List (piano) / Landau (conductor) / Turnabout 34541

This is one of those collaborative works on a basic theme that pop up once in a while. There are twelve parts, and half of them were Liszt-made: the Introduction and setting of the thematic statement (by Bellini), a variation, a *Ritornello*, two separate Interludes, and a Finale. Thalberg, Pixis, Herz, Czerny, and Chopin contributed one variaton each.

This creative sampler is very interesting and most entertaining. It is played by Eugene List with passion and authority—and panache as well.

One fault and that's not his. There are no bands so if a listener wants to hear Chopin's or Czerny's variation, for example, there's nothing to do but keep trying to guess where to put the needle into the grooves. In a work of this type, banding must be mandatory.

Hungarian Fantasia for Piano and Orchestra (1852)

☐ New Philharmonia Orchestra / Entremont (piano) / Ozawa (conductor) / Columbia M-31075

Brilliance and color mark this performance. What makes Entremont's version so acceptable is that he generates excitement and produces the requisite ratio of bravado without ever attacking the instrument. Pianistic percussion on top of key-to-string percussion is just too much percussion. Extra credits here are Entremont's supple phrasing and the fine playing of the orchestra. So, full acknowledgment to Ozawa.

Malédiction for Piano and String Orchestra

☐ Vienna Symphony / Brendel (piano) / Gielen (conductor) / Turnabout 34518

There's more lyrical diction than malediction in Liszt's piece. Brendel's playing is of the highest caliber; the piano tone is overly resonant.

Totentanz for Piano and Orchestra (1859)

☐ London Philharmonic Orchestra / Brendel (piano) / Haitink (conductor) / Philips 6500374

Liszt's "Paraphrase on the 'Dies Irae'" is projected with sharply controlled playing that offers the double gift of finessed contrast. There is no pussyfooting in the dynamic sections which are depicted without any crude force. Neither is there any sectionalized treatment, which often occurs. Brendel and Haitink measure this music perfectly and it achieves proper momentum and sweep—and powerful security.

Am Grabe Richard Wagners (1883)

Andante Maestoso

Andante Religioso

Angelus, Prière aux anges gardiens

Ave Maria

Ave Maris Stella

Chorale *Nun danket alle Gott*

Instrumental

Organ

☐ Sebestyen (organ) / Vox SVBX-5328

Liturgical incense hangs somewhat heavy over practically all these pieces. Somewhat sentimental musing in the organ loft at twilight constantly comes to mind as one listens to the various pieces.

Save for the last work listed, all the compositions represent secondary creative decisions by Liszt. The *Am Grabe* was written for string quartet and harp (it also exists for solo piano). The *Andante Maestoso* is an organ setting of a piece for male chorus; the "Angelus, Prayer to the Guardian Angels" is a transfer from a piano work; *Ave Maria* originally was a vocal solo, et cetera.

Janos Sebestyen plays these compositions in a rather placid manner. Still, essentially that's best for Liszt as he is represented in this case.

Dante (Einleitung, Fuge und Magnificat)

☐ Sebestyen (organ) / Vox SVBX-5329

This is a partial transcription of the symphonic original made by an organist and then thoroughly revised by Liszt so that it can certainly be considered Liszt's own handiwork.

The version stands up quite well compared to the original conception. It could even be better if more color were applied by the performer than was chosen in this case.

Evocation à la Chapelle Sixtine

☐ Chorzempa (organ) / Philips 6500376

A Lisztian fantasy based on Allegri's *Miserere* and Mozart's *Ave Verum Corpus*. The contrastive details of the originals stand out clearly without undue elaboration and the paraphrase-transcription is clearly a success.

Chrozempa opts for a rather slow tempo (five minutes more [!] than Sebestyen's performance on Vox SVBX-5329) but succeeds by the use of rich voicing and perfect textural clarification.

Fantasy and Fugue on the Chorale Ad nos, ad Salutarem Undam (1850)

☐ Preston (organ) / Argo ZRG-503

With the exception of one other work, possibly two, Liszt was like an errand boy in delivering items to the organ medium. Here he is master of the domain. Based on a Meyerbeer theme (from *Le Prophète*), the "Fantasy and Fugue" is an imposing work of over half an hour's length, encompassing three divisions. The invention displayed is intense, the technical display is brilliant. It is one of the outstanding contributions to the literature.

Of the three versions considered, Simon Preston's rates first place. Crystalline playing is apparent from beginning to end, the pedaling is magnificent, and the proportions are ideally defined.

Gebet (1879)

Hosannah

Introitus (1884)

☐ Sebestyen (organ) / Vox SVBX-5328

This is more Liszt organ music contained in sacred shelters. The *Introitus* is the first of *Zwei Vortragsstücke*. *Gebet* ("Prayer") was first written for chorus and organ ad lib. and arranged for piano before the organ setting appeared. *Hosannah* also falls in the transcribed category.

Missa pro Organo (1879)

Offertorium

☐ Sebestyen (organ) / Vox SVBX-5329

Though no characteristic Lisztian profile can be identified in the accompaniment to a Mass that Liszt produced, it does have an astute formal arrangement. An arch structure is defined by dynamic engagement and Sebestyen tastefully and intelligently chooses the registration to distinguish this. Imitations are also colored skillfully.

Ora pro Nobis, Litanei (1864)

☐ Sebestyen (organ) / Vox SVBX-5328

Meditative music, a bit sentimentalized by passages in thirds. The performance is clean but overly slow.

Prelude and Fugue on B.A.C.H. (1870)

☐ Preston (organ) / Argo ZRG-503

Music with the technical brilliance of Bach's D minor Toccata and Fugue and with a chromaticism in the fugal section that is deliciously exhilarating. (Humphrey Searle considers it a direct link between Bach and Schoenberg.)

Preston provides marvelous interpretative juice. Everything is clear to the nth degree, flexibility is used to demarcate the material, and the registration is applied so as to distinguish the design. It is beautifully recorded and not once is it marred by distortion in the loudest passages.

Preludium

☐ Sebestyen (organ) / Vox SVBX-5328

Proclamatory music, dynamically packed. Sebestyen fittingly plays the piece with weight and power.

Requiem for the Organ (1883)

☐ Sebestyen (organ) / Vox SVBX-5329

This piece is based on a work for voices and choir accompanied by organ, four brass instruments, and timpani ad lib. The solo organ transcription delineates the varied moods pertaining to such as the *Dies Irae, Recordare,* and *Sanctus,* found in the Requiem format.

Sebestyen's performance is excellently balanced, coloristically clear and fitting.

Resignation (1877)

☐ Sebestyen (organ) / Vox SVBX-5328

A tidbit of twenty-nine measures, covering one and one-half minutes of quiet music. Quiet, yes, but with some alluring chromatic harmony.

Rosario (1861)

☐ Sebestyen (organ) / Vox SVBX-5329

This work presents three conceptions of an *Ave Maria:* "gaudiosa," "dolorosa," and "gloriosa." Sebestyen paces himself accordingly and presents a nicely registered performance.

Salve Regina

☐ Sebestyen (organ) / Vox SVBX-5328

Liszt has handled a Gregorian antiphon without erasing the basic source data. A dependable realization by this Hungarian organist.

San Francesco

☐ Sebestyen (organ) / Vox SVBX-5329

This is material drawn from Liszt's *Cantico del Sol di San Francesco* (for baritone solo, male chorus, and orchestra), thus providing both an independent composition and a Prelude for use with the original work. It covers four sections and begins and concludes with consequential power.

A nicely balanced presentation.

Trauerode (1860)

Tu es Petrus

☐ Chorzempa (organ) / Philips 6500376

The "Funeral Ode" is powered by harmonic ramifications and dynamic climax. The contrast between "churchified" and dramatic moods adds to the vividness of the piece. *Tu es Petrus* is an organ arrangement drawn from the oratorio *Christus*.

Chorzempa's playing is a delight: airy when it should be, fully resonant otherwise. It is never muddy regardless of the dynamic totality and that is, by itself, a special virtue.

Ungarns Gott

☐ Sebestyen (organ) / Vox SVBX–5328

This work is in two sections: the first section is short-phrased and quietly declamatory, the second part is more optimistic and proclamatory. The romantic syntax is recognizable though Liszt's diction is not.

Variations on Bach's *Weinen, Klagen, Sorgen, Zagen*

☐ Chorzempa (organ) / Philips 6500215

One hears Liszt in a stance that is both potent and virtuosic, supported by telling chromaticism. Dark music, this, and most emotively probing. It is one of the few important organ pieces Liszt produced.

The opportunity of exploiting timbre differences and fast registration shifts are offered the organist in the Variations and Daniel Chorzempa doesn't miss a single possibility. His playing is not only of the utmost clarity but it portrays a dramatic insight that places this musician at the top of the organists' heap. This is exciting music-making.

Weimars Volkslied

Zur Trauung

☐ Sebestyen (organ) / Vox SVBX–5329

The first piece is not a folk song, but merely a fancy title for a short piece that Liszt based on music by Peter Cornelius (versions were made for piano two- and four-hands, string quartet, as well as organ). A meditative mood pervades the *Zur Trauung*. Confidential romanticism is heard in both works, which are mild, run-of-the-mill contributions within the total that Liszt wrote for the organ.

Piano

Années de Pèlerinage: Première Année, "Suisse"

Années de Pèlerinage: Deuxième Année, "Italie"

Années de Pèlerinage: Troisième Année

Venezia e Napoli (Supplement aux Années de Pèlerinage, 2d volume)

☐ Rose (piano) / Vox SVBX–5454

Joint congratulations are in order for Jerome Rose and Vox for providing in one package the entire *Années de Pèlerinage,* plus the three-part supplement to the "Second Year." (Brendel's performance noted *immediately below* does not include the supplement.) To have the 26 pieces in one place is already a listener's gain; to have them in performances of skill and artistry, coupled with good sound and excellent notes (by Richard Freed) is a rare pleasure.

In the flowing parade of diversified material one finds Liszt's reaction to nature scenes, poetry, painting, gondola songs, and so forth. Those that prefer samplings of these can find them in the discussions that follow. (*See below* under: *Années de Pèlerinage: Deuxième Année, "Italie"; Les Jeux d'eaux à la Villa d'Este; Sonetto 104 del Petrarca;* and *Vallée d'Obermann.*)

Années de Pèlerinage: Deuxième Année, "Italie"

☐ Brendel (piano) / Philips 6500420

The extraordinary piano playing conveys the implications of the various seven titles of the Lisztian sojourn. Brendel's pianistic sculptures are poetic pieces beautiful in their perspective and beautiful in their faith to the Lisztian data that made them possible. (See the discussion on Rose's rendition *immediately above.*)

Ballade No. 2 in B minor (1853)

☐ Arrau (piano) / Philips 802906

Arrau's playing is on an epical scale. Even in the quieter sections the dynamism is retained.

Bénédiction de Dieu dans la solitude (No. 3) from Harmonies poétiques et religieuses) (1852)

☐ Arrau (piano) / Philips 6500043

This is rightfully acclaimed as one of Liszt's finest works. Arrau's realization of its peace and mystical contemplation is of the purest musical truth.

Berceuse (1862)

☐ Curzon (piano) / London 6371

This represents the second version of Liszt's piece, the first (composed in 1854) having been too closely modeled on Chopin's Berceuse, Op. 57. Curzon wisps and whisks through the piece, the wisping representing the Chopin influence that remained, the whisking covering Liszt's linear embellishments and ornamentations.

Concert Paraphrases on Operatic and Dramatic Music: Bellini, Réminiscences de "Norma" (1841)

☐ Campanella (piano) / Philips 6500310

Stylishly accomplished and with good tone as well as the requisite flair for this category of piano music. Certainly an impressive performance.

Concert Paraphrases on Operatic and Dramatic Music: Donizetti, Funeral March from Dom Sébastien (1844)

☐ Lewenthal (piano) / Angel S–36079

Powerful! Paraphrases as good as this one are hard to come by. No wonder Donizetti waxed enthusiastic about Liszt's transmutation of his *Marche Funèbre*. Such keyboard orchestration! The soloist calls it "a dark and proud epic." That it is. Lewenthal's performance of this trump-card paraphrase deserves five-star rating. It has great musicianship and great pianistic panache.

Concert Paraphrases on Operatic and Dramatic Music: Donizetti, *Réminiscences de "Lucia di Lammermoor"* (1856)

☐ Brendel (piano) / Turnabout 34581

This is Liszt's reordered evocation of the famous sextet, *Chi Mi Frena?*. It is a brilliant realization that does not destroy the stylistic point of the original and yet proclaims the inventive imagery of Liszt's voice.

Brendel's playing is strong and the music's spirit is allowed full play.

Concert Paraphrases on Operatic and Dramatic Music

Gounod, Waltz from *Faust* (1861)

Mendelssohn, Wedding March and Dance of the Elves from *A Midsummer Night's Dream* (1850)

☐ Kentner (piano) / Turnabout 34163

The melodies are there, within a new format. In the case of the Mendelssohn there is a very interesting jazzy contour at times. The performances are good, the sound is sometimes tubby.

Concert Paraphrases on Operatic and Dramatic Music: Meyerbeer, *Illustration No. 2* from *Le Prophète* (1850)

☐ Campanella (piano) / Philips 6500310

Liszt produced three *Illustrations* from the Meyerbeer opera in the paraphrase category. Michele Campanella does well with this one.

Concert Paraphrases on Operatic and Dramatic Music: Mozart, *Réminiscences de "Don Giovanni"* (1841)

☐ Kentner (piano) / Turnabout 34163

Considered one of the best of the large number of Liszt's paraphrases, operatic transcriptions, et cetera, the work is akin to a miniature suite in three parts, each concerned with a different aspect of Mozart's great drama. Kentner is extremely impressive in delineating the various moods of the piece. His choice of tempi makes good musical sense.

Concert Paraphrases on Operatic and Dramatic Music: Pacini, *Divertissement sur la Cavatine "I Tuoi Frequenti Palpiti"* from *Niobe* (1836)

☐ Trenkner (piano) / Orion 77278

Brilliance comes first; still, the work is not devoid of musical interest. The fine technique that it needs is evidenced by this pianist who provides a stimulating presentation.

Concert Paraphrases on Operatic and Dramatic Music: Tchaikovsky, Polonaise from *Eugene Onegin* (1880)

☐ Ponti (piano) / Turnabout 34560

This is the only paraphrase Liszt made of Tchaikovsky's music. A standard presentation.

Concert Paraphrases on Operatic and Dramatic Music:

Verdi, *Coro di Festa e Marcia Funèbre* from *Don Carlos* (1868)

Verdi, *Danza Sacra e Duetto Finale* **from Aïda (1879)**
Verdi, *Ernani* **(1859)**
Verdi, *Miserere* **from** *Il Trovatore* **(1859)**
Verdi, *Réminiscenes de "Simone Boccanegra"* **(1883)**
Verdi, *Rigoletto* **(1859)**
Verdi, *Salve Maria de Jerusalem* **from** *I Lombardi* **(1848)**

☐ Arrau (piano) / Philips 6500368

The highlight of this collection is the paraphrase on the famous quartet in the fourth act of *Rigoletto*. The well-known *Miserere* is a close second. Whether well known or not, these are fine expressions and cheap medley procedures are absent.

There's plenty of opportunity to play to the gallery in these pieces but Arrau negates such approach and in each case the music is presented to bring out its poetic information. Such cultivated consideration makes a deep effect.

Concert Paraphrases on Operatic and Dramatic Music: Wagner, *Spinning Chorus* from *The Flying Dutchman* (1860)

☐ Kentner (piano) / Turnabout 34163

Kentner exhibits a fine sense of color in his authoritative reading.

Consolations (1850)

☐ Rose (piano) / Vox SVBX-5475

If it's any consolation to Jorge Bolet, he plays these half-dozen *Consolations* much better than Mr. Rose and Mr. Katin on London (STS–15123). Bolet is not listed here for the very fundamental reason of extremely poor sound. His performance is released by RCA (CRL2-0446) but was produced by Ensayo in Spain. It should have stayed there. It is absolutely tinny anywhere above the keyboard's center and sometimes is so nonresonant that a quarter note drops off to a sixteenth-note length. And so on. If you wish the best insight and are willing to suffer senseless sound then get the RCA album. Beware, however! Do bear in mind that Vox isn't that bad and does have worthy sound.

Deux Légendes

St. Francois d'Assise. La Prédication aux oiseaux
St. Francois de Paule marchant sur les flots

☐ Kempf (piano) / Deutsche Grammophon 2530560

Two decidedly interesting piano stories, especially interesting because of the splendorous piano writing that poetically describes and never overdrives the points to be made. "St. Francis of Assisi preaching to the birds" is discreet in its musical sermonizing; "St. Francis of Paola walking on the waters" is in direct contrast in its pianistic programmaticism.

Wilhelm Kempf is master of this music. The vitality and precision, the coloring, and the expressivity exemplify artistry at the highest level. There is a duplicate of this release on Turnabout 34385E. (The "E" being the code identification that the performance is from a monaural setting produced in "compatible stereo.") Deutsche Grammophon makes no such statement and in fact the D.G. sound is better.

Harmonies poétiques et religieuses

☐ Rose (piano) / Vox SVBX-5475

Examples of some of the titles in this ten-part work define further the motivating force indicated in the main title. No. 1 is an *Invocation;* No. 2 is an *Ave Maria;* the third part, *Bénédiction de Dieu dans la solitude* (*see above* for a separate performance) is followed by *Pensée des morts;* No. 9 is an *Andante lagrimoso;* and No. 10 is titled *Cantique d'amour.* The seventh part of the cycle, *Funérailles, Octobre 1849,* is a blend of profundity and virtuosity. In the notes by Priam Clay the piece is described as having "few equals among Liszt's works."

Rose does full justice to the virtues contained in this music. In the case of the *Invocation,* the smoothness he projects makes more of this piece than one would expect to be possible. His sense of line also strengthens the *Pensée des morts.* Performances only of the *Bénédiction* and *Funérailles* are not uncommon. To have the balance of Liszt's cycle on disc makes the Vox issue worthy of attention.

Hungarian Rhapsody

No. 1 in E major (1846) / No. 2 in C sharp minor (1847) / No. 3 in B flat major / No. 4 in E flat major / (*Héroïde funèbre*) No. 5 in E major and E minor / No. 6 in D flat major / No. 7 in D minor / (*Capriccio*) No. 8 in F sharp minor / (*Carnaval de Pest*) No. 9 in E flat major (1848) / (*Preludio*) No. 10 in E major / No. 11 in A minor / No. 12 in C sharp minor / No. 13 in A minor / No. 14 in F minor / (*Rákóczy March*) No. 15 in A minor / No. 16 in A minor (1882) / No. 17 in D minor / No. 18 in F sharp major (1885) / No. 19 in D minor (1885)

☐ Szidon (piano) / Deutsche Grammophon 2709044

Dazzling technical brilliance is supplied throughout. Szidon exhibits great command and does not falter in any of the nineteen works.

If a listener prefers just a sampling, Nos. 2, 5, 9, 14, 15, and 19 are played by Szidon on Deutsche Grammophon 2530441.

As would be expected, the record catalogue is crammed with performances of these works. Some issues only include a single rhapsody, others embrace a selected group from the total. Performances by twenty-one pianists are available in a total of twenty-eight releases. Two of these deserve attention. Brendel's playing of Nos. 2, 3, 8, 13, and 15 on Vanguard C-10035 is a superior edition and so is Entremont's excellently styled and commanding performance of the famous Hungarian Rhapsody No. 2. This is on Columbia MS-6938 and D3S-791. It is also on Columbia MS-6723 together with No. 15 of the set of rhapsodies.

La Lugubre Gondola (1882)

☐ Brendel (piano) / Turnabout 34518 (monaural)

Brendel plays this moody piece, not a perennial on concert programs, with unchallenged conviction and superb musical intelligence. Especially cogent is the way he considers the music's declamatory phrases.

Les Jeux d'eaux à la Villa d'Este (No. 4) from *Années de Pèlerinage:* Troisième Année (1877)

☐ Arrau (piano) / Philips 802906

This is the Lisztian relative of Ravel's famous *Jeux d'eaux.* The recording provides an impressive delineation by Arrau of the music's impressionistic content. The color scale he applies is both subtle and powerful. (See also discussion *above* under *Années de Pèlerinage: Première Année,* "*Suisse.*")

Liebesträume (1850)

☐ Ohlsson (piano) / Angel S–37125

The Liebestraum so often heard is the third of a set of three. Though the first two are rarely heard, there is no valid reason for that fact. Originally all were songs that Liszt transcribed for piano and termed *Liebesträume, 3 Notturnos*.

The fact that Garrick Ohlsson plays all three is a pleasure and that he plays them beautifully doubles that response.

Rhapsodie Espagnole

☐ Berman (piano) / Columbia/Melodiya M2–33928

When Berman gets into the heavy technical stuff in this work he leaves the others behind. Octaves whizz off the keyboard, silvery runs glitter, rhapsody turns into an artistic precision that holds one on the edge of the chair.

Kentner (on Turnabout 34444 and repeated in a Vox Box SVBX–5453) comes close, but the treble register sounds tinny, and in the antiphonal clauses that is very annoying. I find Szidon (on Deutsche Grammophon 2709044) uneven, not in his playing, but in shaping the structure. The work is sectioned somewhat to begin with. Not to stitch these parts together makes musical black holes. Take Berman.

(See the discussion of Busoni's transcription of this work under *Liszt/Busoni: Solo Instrument and Orchestra: piano*.)

Rhapsody in A minor on Hungarian Songs

☐ Kentner (piano) / Turnabout 34444

This is a setting from Liszt's Hungarian music research. Though Liszt had taken material from his *Magyar Dallok* ("Hungarian National Melodies") containing eleven pieces, with its slow-fast tempi shifts, the A minor opus properly belongs in the ten-part *Magyar Rhapsodiák* ("Hungarian Rhapsodies" group—not to be confused with the formal set of Hungarian Rhapsodies).

Effectively played and with only a dab or two of *rubato*—sufficient for what there is to color in this minor item.

(*Schwann* indicates that the work is also included in Vox SVBX–5453 but it is not.)

Rumanian Rhapsody

☐ Kentner (piano) / Turnabout 34444

At best, there are only exceedingly minor pleasures in this rather academic idea of nationalism. The work never takes off to offer stimulation. If the best Hungarian Rhapsodies were written by Liszt then it is only fair to state that the best Rumanian Rhapsodies were written by Enesco.

No blame on Kentner. What there is to do, he does. The piece appears also in a Vox Box (SVBX–5453).

Sonata in B minor (1853)

☐ Berman (piano) / Columbia/Melodiya M–33927

This is a prodigious representation of Liszt's huge work. Within however, Berman doesn't overlook coloristic differences in the technical splash of the music. If he doesn't always sing as does Horowitz (in a most worthy mono version on Seraphim 60144) he is never short of eloquent. There are quibbles that one can bring to the critical table, but far fewer than pertain to others in the recorded lists. Berman is ahead of all others in putting a foamy head on Liszt's strong pianistic brew.

Two other performances are worth considering—that is, in a different light: Curzon's (London 6371) gentler and more poetic essay and an oldie by Barere (a mono, hyped with "stereo" on Turnabout THS-65001E), presenting old-fashioned bravura, but Lisztian to the very last sound.

Sonetto 104 del Petrarca (No. 5) from *Années de Pèlerinage: Deuxième Année, "Italie"*

Sonetto 123 del Petrarca (No. 6) from *Années de Pèlerinage: Deuxième Année, "Italie"*

☐ Arrau (piano) / Philips 802906

Masterful declamatory playing in *Sonetto 104*, with a fully expressed emotional quality that is not spoiled by overstressed overt depiction. *Sonetto 123* is as confirmed in its lyrical imagery. (See also discussion *above* under *Années de Pèlerinage: Première Année, "Suisse."*)

Three Concert Etudes

Il Lamento (No. 1)
La Leggierezza (No. 2)
Un Sospiro (No. 3)

☐ Kentner (piano) / Vox SVBX-5453

The poetic insight of *Il Lamento*, the lucid tactility of *La Leggierezza*, and the soft-spoken flowing lines of *Un Sospiro*, the most popular of the "Etudes de Concert," are expressed with warmth and lucidity of production, thereby offering total conviction (*see also* discussion of Cliburn's rendition *immediately below*). This represents one of the best Kentner performances on disc.

Three Concert Etudes: *Un Sospiro* (No. 3)

☐ Cliburn (piano) / RCA ARL1-1173

A spacious and yet deeply ingrained interpretation. If (metaphorically) Kentner's playing of this beautiful bit (*see immediately above*) sounds "violinistic," Cliburn's sounds like a viola.

Transcendental Etudes (1851)

Allegro agitato molto in F minor (No. 10)
Chasse-neige (No. 12)
Eroica (No. 7)
Feux follets (No. 5)
Harmonies du soir (No. 11)
Mazeppa (No. 4)
Paysage (No. 3)
Preludio (No. 1)
Ricordanza (No. 9)
Study in A minor (No. 2)
Vision (No. 6)
Wilde Jagd (No. 8)

☐ Ashkenazy (piano) / London 6719

One cannot find fault with this prodigious playing, which provides, with panache and with poetry where it fits, the fullest exploration of what is to come out of the notes. Ashkenazy also produces an assortment of colors to confirm the variety in the moods Liszt has outlined. Above all, there is no sheer exhibitionism—fully-powered musical meaning is produced in this playing of flawless precision.

Lazar Berman, on Columbia/Melodiya M2-33928, is impressive but the sound is not equal to his technical and stylistic bravado.

Transcendental Etudes after Paganini (1838)

In E flat major (No. 2)   *La Chasse* **(No. 5)**
In E major (No. 4)   *Preludio* **(No. 1)**
La Campanella **(No. 3)**   **Theme and Variations (No. 6)**

☐ Kentner (piano) / Vox SVBX-5453

Three of these (Nos. 3, 5, and 6) are quite familiar; No. 6 is, of course, the one with the famous tune that many composers have used for their own variational viewpoint. All save *La Campanella* are taken from Paganini's solo violin *Caprices*.

There is plenty of bravura in this music but it finds better effect if it is enmeshed with refinement. That's the way Louis Kentner approaches the set and that's why he is most successful. Otherwise, constant exhibitionism with Liszt's music becomes extremely tedious.

Two Concert Studies (1863)

Gnomenreigen **(No. 2)**
Waldesrauschen **(No. 1)**

☐ Arrau (piano) / Philips 6500043

One hears bravura of an exceptional type both in the timbred sensitivity of the delicate first piece and in the remarkable dynamic control exhibited in the dance study. Arrau shows how it should be done and nothing in the recorded lists can match his performance.

Two Polonaises (1851)

☐ Katin (piano) / London STS-15123

A bit brash but it's fitting. The touch balance, dynamic differentiation, and buoyancy serve as full credits.

Vallée d'Obermann (No. 6) from *Années de Pèlerinage:* **Première Année, "Suisse"**

☐ Arrau (piano) / Philips 802906

A beautifully colored response to Liszt's mountain portrait. The manner in which Arrau shapes this piece and powers its climax exemplifies high pianistic art. (*See* also discussion *above* under *Années de Pèlerinage: Première Année, "Suisse."*)

Valse Oubliée No. 1 in F sharp minor (1883)

☐ Arrau (piano) / Philips 802906

This is a poetic portrayal that nevertheless does not meander away into dreamland. Arrau's combination of delicacy and controlled power make his performance outstanding.

Weihnachtsbaum (1876)

☐ Rose (piano) / Vox SVBX-5475

    Light-scaled but oh-so-delightful Liszt is the way to describe the set of dozen pieces that comprise the "Christmas Tree" suite. Hung on the staves of the score are music based on Christmas carols, nationalistic tidbits, bell pieces, and other genre representations. Just to hear what Liszt does with *Adeste Fideles* and a sketch titled *Carillon* is worth the price of the entire edition.

    Jerome Rose plays everything with distinction. His statements of the substances of the pieces are perfect. A highly satisfying recording of this charming opus.

Two Pianos

Concerto Pathétique in E minor for Two Pianos

☐ Kentner and Havill (pianos) / Turnabout 34444

    Though there's sufficient virtuosity in this music, the performers stress its more poetic aspects. One minor snag is the muddled sound that creeps in in a few places. The competitive edition (Argo ZRG-721) is even worse.

Vocal

Voice with Accompaniment

Comment, disaient-ils

Mignon's Lied

O quand je dors

Über allen Gipfeln ist Ruh

Vergiftet sind meine Lieder (1842)

☐ Tourel (mezzo-soprano); Levine (piano) / Desto 7118/9

    These are five of Liszt's best songs: *Comment* is one of the most telling of his Victor Hugo settings, as is *O quand;* the dramatic spill of *Vergiftet* is apparent from its first measures.

    The sound is full and the voice is excellent, but it is the musicality that is the greatest here. Don't be disturbed by the applause. The recording was made live and it's a small price to pay for these examples of keen artistic understanding.

Choral

Chorus Alone

Ave Maria

O Salutaris Hostia

☐ Budapest Madrigal Ensemble / Szekeres (conductor) / Monitor S-2054

    These are two examples from the vast choral catalogue Liszt produced. Both show an abiding affection for conservatism. Worth having, nevertheless.

Cantata and Oratorio

Missa Choralis (1865)

☐ Vienna Kammerchor / Thomann (soprano); Jahn (mezzo-soprano); Wing (tenor); Kawamura (baritone); Buchsbaum (bass); Nebois (organ) / Gillesberger (conductor) / Turnabout 34201

    Liszt's short liturgical mass, which includes a number of Gregorian themes, receives a finely detailed performance. There is some low-level recording in regard to the organ, but it is a minor blemish.

Liszt / *Jacob Arcadelt.* See Arcadelt / Liszt.

Liszt / *Ludwig van Beethoven.* See Beethoven / Liszt.

Liszt / **Ferruccio Busoni**

Rhapsodie Espagnole for Piano and Orchestra

☐ Prague Chamber Orchestra and Vienna Wind Ensemble / Blumental (piano) / Froschauer (conductor) / Turnabout 34372

This is Liszt's tribute to Spain in variations and dance: *Folies d'Espagne* (*"La Follia"*) for the former and a *Jota Argonese* for the latter. Brilliant, naturally, made more so with the instrumental amplification included in Busoni's arrangement.

A respectable result, though one would welcome more *vino* in the orchestral playing. (Liszt's original work is discussed under *Liszt: Instrumental: piano* [*Rhapsodie Espagnole*].)

Solo Instrument and Orchestra

Piano

Liszt / **Jenö Hubay**

Hungarian Rhapsody for Violin and Orchestra

☐ Westphalian Symphony Orchestra, Recklinghausen / Glenn (violin) / Landau (conductor) / Turnabout 34541

This is not one of Liszt's Hungarian Rhapsodies transcribed for violin and orchestra but a recasting of a violin and piano item that Liszt turned out, called *The Three Gypsies.* Hubay's setting is excellent and so is his choice of title.

It has all the nationalistic investments of gypsy music and Hubay gives the soloist plenty of opportunities to show off. Carroll Glenn proves her expertise in this entertaining concoction.

Solo Instrument and Orchestra

Violin

Gaston Litaize   *(1909-   )*

Prière from *Douze Pièces pour Grand Orgue*

☐ Raynaud (organ) / Turnabout 34319

In the arch form used by Litaize the music builds from a chromatic long-spun line into a section of finely calculated, imposingly weighted sonority, and then recedes. It is all clearly formulated in Jean-Claude Raynaud's interpretation.

(The same performance is also available in the sixth volume of "A Survey of the World's Greatest Organ Music," issued by Vox on SVBX–5315.)

Instrumental

Organ

Henry Charles Litolff   (1818-1891)

Solo Instrument and Orchestra

Piano

Concerto Symphonique No. 4 in D minor for Piano and Orchestra, Op. 102

☐ Monte Carlo Opera Orchestra / Robbins (piano) / van Remoortel (conductor) / Genesis 1035

The title indicates the interfused factors of Litolff's work. This is not an example of piano soloism backed up with an orchestra, but a full two-sized, equalized conception. Such partnership is maintained in the music's scope: four symphonically shaped movements running thirty-seven minutes.

The vigorous assertiveness of the fiery first movement and the impetuous finale are fully commanded by the performers; the brilliant Scherzo,Presto (this movement is Litolff's best-known music) is beautifully colored and is in sharp comparison to the slow movement.

The soloist and conductor give witness of an excellent imaginative penetration of the score. (If one merely wishes the Scherzo movement, it is included on Klavier 527, with John Ogdon supported by the City of Birmingham Symphony Orchestra, conducted by Louis Frémaux. Ogdon's tempo is less scintillating, however.)

Chamber Music

Piano Trio No. 1 in D minor, Op. 47

☐ Mirecourt Trio / Genesis 1058/9

Litolff's Opus 47 is the first of three Trios and it is most deserving of no longer being neglected. It can hold its own with the strong competition of trios in the same romantic vein by Mendelssohn, Schubert, Schumann, and Brahms.

The very idiomatic reading is propelled by very good balance and sound.

Pietro Locatelli   (1695-1764)

String Orchestra

Concerto Grosso, Op. 1, No. 9

☐ Academy of St. Martin-in-the-Fields / Marriner (conductor) / Oiseau-Lyre 60045

This performance is another example of Neville Marriner's ability to shape a baroque work with perfection of style. The ensemble cohesion is a joy to hear.

Introduzione Teatrale No. 5 in D major, Op. 4, No. 5

☐ New Philharmonia Orchestra / Leppard (conductor) / Philips 802901

Full use of strings within strings in this zestful work. Locatelli uses a string quartet, a solo violin, as well as the full string body.

The work is styled characteristically and performed with deftness from the opening fanfare-like build of the home key to the concluding pair of tutti chords.

Solo Instrument and Orchestra

Violin

Il Pianto d'Arianna, Op. 7, No. 6

☐ Angelicum Orchestra of Milan / Biffoli (violin); Hammond (harpsichord) / Jenkins (conductor) / Nonesuch 71151

This work is no facsimile copy of the usual concerto or concerto grosso idea. Locatelli's last of his set of six *Concerti a Quattro* has vocal-based influences in its design. It sharply outlines an operatic *scena* in its nine varying sections beginning with a large recitative and aria.

"The Plaint of Ariadne" deserves a special place and attention in Locatelli's output. It destroys Burney's remark dismissing Locatelli as "a voluminous composer of music that excites more surprise than pleasure." There is some surprise in *Il Pianto,* but much more pleasure.

Fine playing by soloist and orchestra. Jenkins understands how to arrive at fine textural colorations by basing these on dynamic balances.

L'Arte del Violino, Concerto, Op. 3

No. 1 in D major / No. 2 in C minor / No. 3 in F major / No. 4 in E major / No. 5 in C major / No. 6 in G minor

☐ Mainz Chamber Orchestra / Lautenbacher (violin) / Kehr (conductor) / Vox SVBX–540

Do not expect the usual early eighteenth-century (pre-classical) concerto structure in these works. Indeed, there are decided differences in the designs as compared to the concertino-tutti textural pattern of the concerto grosso. True there are certain elements carried over, but these are of minor totality. In these concerti the only exact link is the use of strings and harpsichord as the tutti body—squared phraseology begins to be loosened, and the usual slow-movement solo aria likewise.

It is Locatelli's title that is the clue to the decided differences. In 1733 he wrote his *L'Arte del Violino, 12 Concerti cioe Violino Solo con 24 Capricci* ("The Art of the Violin, 12 Concertos for Violin Solo with 24 Capriccios"). He defines that the emphasis is on the solo voice and makes a formal breakthrough by including sizable *capriccios* for the unaccompanied violin for each of the outer movements in each Concerto. Though technically matters of display, every *capriccio* has musical relevance. Certainly, the later all-out Paganini method has its roots in this Locatellian device.

But the actual musical content does not suffer because of this new plan. Fertile creativity and colorful spirit mark all of the concerti. The playing is splendid, with fine attention to dynamic weights, phrasing, and coloration. Susanne Lautenbacher as the soloist is the star of the proceedings. She is a musician of the highest quality.

L'Arte del Violino, Concerto, Op. 3

No. 7 in B flat major / No. 8 in E minor / No. 9 in G major / No. 10 in F major / No. 11 in A major / No. 12 in D major

☐ Mainz Chamber Orchestra / Lautenbacher (violin) / Kehr (conductor) / Vox SVBX–541

(For details see immediately above.)

Sonata (*Au Tombeau*) in F minor, Op. 6, No. 7

☐ David Oistrakh (violin); Yampolsky (piano) / RCA VICS–1058

Chamber Music

Oistrakh uses the Ysaÿe edition for this significant dramatic work. He plays it with the intensity that would apply to a late Beethoven opus—Locatelli's music deserves this kind of attention. *Au Tombeau* does not have the easy-come, easy-go character of so many eighteenth-century compositions. This is music of undenied depth performed with artistic mastership.

Sonata in G minor for Flute and Organ

☐ Linde (flute); Rapf (organ) / Klavier 545

This Sonata is tuneful and completely unpretentious in its four parts, concluded with a sprightly gigue. Linde plays it gracefully and generally with full tone. Rapf is rather reticent.

Matthew Locke   (1630?-1677)

String Orchestra

Music from *The Tempest*

☐ English Chamber Orchestra / Hurwitz (conductor) / London STS-15013

These three examples have more unity of tempo than the titles (Introduction, *Curtain Tune,* and *Martial Jigge*) reflect. The edition (by W. G. Whittaker) is played straight. That's the way it should be, for though in other cases Locke has been unfairly overshadowed by the great Purcell, this music has only antiquarian interest.

Normand Lockwood   (1906-   )

Choral

Chorus Alone

Sing unto the Lord a New Song (1952)

☐ Mid-America Chorale / Dexter (conductor) / Composers Recordings 191 (monaural)

There is rhythmic punch in this pithy setting for unaccompanied voices of the opening verse of *Psalm 96.* Nice singing by the Mid-America group.

Charles Martin Loeffler   (1861-1935)

Orchestra

A Pagan Poem (1906)

☐ Leopold Stokowski and His Symphony Orchestra / Hunter (piano); Kosinski (English horn) / Stokowski (conductor) / Seraphim S-60080

Inspired by the Eighth Eclogue of Virgil, Loeffler's *Poem* romantically impresses with the aid of impressionistic devices and with a special coloristic use of obbligati instruments: piano, English horn, and three off-stage trumpets. Back in 1908, the erudite critic Philip Hale called the diagnostic shot perfectly when he said that Loeffler's work ''is a masterpiece of musical eloquence.'' That it is, and it is eloquently detailed in Stokowski's rich performance.

The sound is not the best ever, but this is a fine conception and one welcomes it.

Chamber Music

Deux Rapsodies for Oboe, Viola, and Piano (1905)

☐ Basile (piano); Sprenkle (oboe); Tursi (viola) / Eastman-Rochester Archives ERA-1011

Though based on poems by Maurice Rollinat (1853-1903) (for which Loeffler made vocal settings and then discarded them), the *Rapsodies* avoid the dogma of program music. Mood essences flavor both *L'Etang* (''The Pool'') and *La Cornemuse* (''The Bagpipe''). Though a slight drone is incorporated in the last, no picture-painting is involved. Both of the poems that inspired Loeffler contain dark overtones, and they are retained in the conduct of the music and its scoring. "The Pool" has spectral definition; the other piece is more tightly constructed and is more astringent in tone. Discounting the ease of the second guess, one can fully agree with Loeffler's decision that the (wordless) chamber music setting of Rollinat's lines produced a greater effect. One agrees with the effect of the performance also.

Music for Four Stringed Instruments (1917)

☐ Kohon Quartet / Vox SVBX-5301

Music for Four Stringed Instruments was dedicated to the memory of Victor Chapman, an American aviator who was killed in the World War I. The dedication is the clue to the entire feeling of the work, which is also expressed by the main musical motivation, drawn from the Gregorian chant dealing with the *Resurrexi.*

There are almost religious aspirations in Loeffler's composition, but they are more of a mystical affinity than of the spiritual type. Loeffler's semiprogrammatic quartet (movement 2 is titled "The Holy Day of Easter") has a unique place in the history of American chamber music. It is a memorial testament bound up with the qualitative philosophical and sober delineations that permeate practically all of Loeffler's work.

A very restrained consideration of the music is important and is most telling. The Kohon ensemble shows proper understanding of this need.

A Dream Within a Dream

☐ Hanks (tenor); Friedberg (piano) / Duke University Press DWRM-7501 (monaural)

The text is by Edgar Allan Poe; the musical style is a blend of chromaticism with impressionistic touches. An expert performance.

Vocal

Voice with Accompaniment

Jean-Baptiste Loeillet   *(1680-1730)*

Sonata in A minor for Recorder and Continuo, Op. 1, No. 1

☐ Irmgard Mathiesen (recorder); Alstrup (viola da gamba); Aksel Mathiesen (harpsichord) / Nonesuch 71064

This is an illustration of meeting the formalistic objective without defining any vivid personality. Loeillet's music is an integration of late seventeenth-century tradition. Nice melodies are fitted neatly to apt harmonies; the continuo remains subsidiary as a support and chordal prop to the homophonic curves.

The performance is somewhat bland and at times the recorder is shriller than one would expect possible from this dulcet instrument.

Trio in G minor for Flute, Recorder, and Continuo, Op. 1, No. 3

☐ Rampal (flute); Duschenes (recorder); Gilbert (harpsichord) / Orion 75199

Loeillet's trio sonata is represented in three different releases triplicating the same, comfortable performance. The choice is for Orion because it is included on a single disc. Everest has included it in its seven-record set (3194), but the production is sloppy, the mastering of the tape is not as good, and there are no program notes. The third choice is also by Everest, on an all-Rampal album (3229). Again, there are no notes on the piece, the sound is just as compressed, and the production is even worse. Not a single credit is indicated *anywhere* for the other performers.

Chamber Music

Carl Loewe   (1796-1869)

Choral

Chorus Alone

In der Marienkirche, Op. 81, No. 4

☐ Camerata Vocale, Bremen / Kopf-Endres (conductor) / Nonesuch 71081

"In St. Mary's Church" illustrates the gentle romantic style this composer practiced. Nonesuch's issue is an attractive presentation.

Edwin London   (1929-   )

Choral

Chorus with Accompaniment

Bjørne Enstabile's Christmas Music

☐ The Ineluctable Modality / Udwo (bells); Maddox (organ); London ("Irish" tenor) / London (conductor) / Advance FGR-18S

A Christmas mix to end all Christmas medleys. London has artistically corrupted snatches of carols, and has woven fantastically, sensitively violent bits between, on, and around these, with bells tinkling along and occasionally an organ sounding ponderous and sweet; some dialogue has been included as well. It produces a surrealistic dream content, highly original and marvelouly irritating.

The whole matter results in a spoof, emphasized by the funniest liner note that has ever appeared on a serious (sic!) music disc. Of course, there is no "Bjørne Enstabile." If this name is examined carefully, it will soon be apparent that this really reads "born in a stable." 'Nuff said.

Nikolai Lopatnikoff   (1903-1976)

Orchestra

Music for Orchestra, Op. 39

☐ Louisville Orchestra / Whitney (conductor) / Louisville 596 (monaural)

Lopatnikoff never abandoned his loyalty to neoclassicism. Opus 39 exemplifies this creative balance of tonal power. The core of the work is found in the drive of the *allegro molto* middle section of this one-movement piece. The cleanness of the music may not sound four-square nice but it does impart honed, no-nonsense messages.

The Louisville playing is best in the fast tempi portions; the other sections lack coloration.

Variazioni Concertanti (1958)

☐ Louisville Orchestra / Whitney (conductor) / Louisville S-654

I find Lopatnikoff a composer of Rousselian order, with perhaps just a little less of the Frenchman's preciseness. The *Variazioni Concertanti* do not stagger into split sections. With fully realized power of variational technique Lopatnikoff defines theme, four variants, and a conclusion. The performance is to the point, which means that it is not only an intelligent surveyal but a conclusive one.

Antonio Lora   *(1899-1965)*

Concerto for Piano and Orchestra (1948)

☐ Vienna Orchestra / Wollman (piano) / Adler (conductor) / Composers Recordings 113 (monaural)

Solo Instrument and Orchestra

Piano

No mistaking the stylistic climate of Lora's Concerto. This is the discriminating work of a neo-romantic, without milk and buttered toast, providing a *real* concerto ambience, including the old-reliable cadenza. Eva Wollman gets first-rate credits for her solo playing; F. Charles Adler supports cogently.

Raymond Loucheur   *(1899-   )*

Quatre Pièces en Quintette

☐ Marie-Claire Jamet Quintet / Musical Heritage Society MHS–883

Chamber Music

Loucheur's work for flute, string trio, and harp has a tonal flush throughout. A scherzo conception is followed by a poetic Lento, a moderate-paced interlude, and a finale that has a few slightly Spanish turns.

Louis XIII   *(1601-1643)*

Ballet de la merlaison

☐ Instrumental Ensemble / Chailley (conductor) / Nonesuch 71130

Orchestra

A set of eleven numbers constitutes the French King's "Ballet of the Blackbird." Though there is little difference between the music and the assigned descriptive titles, the simple tunes and rhythms are totally engaging.

History tells us that Louis XIII had a melancholy and retiring personality. It doesn't show in this music.

Chanson "Tu crois O beau soleil" (Amaryllis)

☐ Roblot (soprano); Fauchet and Husson (tenors); Cottret (bass); Cotte (lute) / Nonesuch 71130

Vocal

Voice with Accompaniment

This is the tune that became well-known through Fritz Kreisler's variational arrangement under the title *Chanson Louis XIII*. A sweet and lovely item, appropriately sung. (An instrumental version appears on the same disc; see under *Louis XIII/M. de la Barre: Instrumental: harpsichord* [Diminutions].)

Psalm V

☐ Petit (mezzo-soprano); Cottret (bass); Jean-Pierre Cotte (theorbo) / Nonesuch 71130

The *Psalm* is another extremely short example of the French King's abilities as a composer. Very simple and nicely tuned. (The note by Roger Cotte states that apparently only the melody was written by Louis.)

Psalm CXXX

☐ Fauchet (tenor); Cottret (bass); Jean-Pierre Cotte (theorbo) / Nonesuch 71130

(For data see immediately above.)

Louis XIII / M. de la Barre (17th cent.)

Instrumental

Harpsichord

Diminutions on *"Tu crois O beau soleil"* (Amaryllis)

☐ Charbonnier (harpsichord) / Nonesuch 71130

For "Diminutions" read "ornamental variations." For "variations," expect clear-squared depictions. The vocal version minus "diminutions" is on the same disc (see under *Louis XIII: Vocal: voice with accompaniment [Chanson]*).

The complete realization of de la Barre's variational plan (de la Barre was the King's spinet player and organist) has been carried out by Roger Cotte, the director of the Ancient Instrument Ensemble of Paris.

Vincentius Lübeck   (1654-1740)

Instrumental

Organ

Prelude and Fugue

No. 1 in D minor / No. 2 in E major / No. 3 in F major / No. 4 in G minor / No. 5 in C minor / No. 6 in C major

☐ Andrews (organ) / University of Oklahoma 2 (monaural)

These are the complete preludes and fugues that are extant. Lübeck's music is in the Buxtehude vein and has a strength fully recognizable in Mildred Andrews's playing.

Alvin Lucier   (1931-   )

Choral

Chorus Alone

***North American Time Capsule 1967* for Voices and Sylvania Electronic Systems Vocoder**

☐ Brandeis University Chamber Chorus / Lucier (conductor) / Odyssey 32160156

Lucier's contribution belongs to the farthest left section of the left wing of the avant-garde. It employs a Vocoder, which is a machine that converts, that is, scrambles material for secret transmission over narrow band widths via telephone lines or radio channels. The singers (it wouldn't be necessary to use a specifically organized chorus actually) produce any sounds they wish (no written score for the composition exists) and these are "fed into the Vocoder and are modified during the performance both by the sounds acting as control signals and by the manual alteration of the vocoder components."

The sounds one hears in this performance are like one might expect from a chorus of dolphins and wasps. The mixture produces some other goodies such as the effect of an out-of-tune toy trumpet (which, it is to be noted, is off-pitch to begin with!). Sure, musical impropriety for the prudes. Everything has its place and values, however. This ten-minute (plus) item is heady expertimentalism that represents a type of unseen musical vaudeville.

Vespers (1968)

Electronic Music

☐ Mainstream 5010

The sound source is a "Sondol," an echolocation device that surveys the environment by emitting clicks. The means of echolocation make possible the location of objects via sound waves that are reflected back to the point of emission.

On the recording the clicks and clacks mean very little. *Vespers* requires live performance. Each participant is blindfolded and has a Sondol, by means of which he or she attempts to avoid colliding with any of the others. In a very far-fetched way, listening to *Vespers* is like "seeing" an opera by listening to a recording of it.

Otto Luening   *(1900-   )*

Kentucky Rondo (1951)

Orchestra

☐ Vienna Orchestra / Adler (conductor) / Composers Recordings 103 (monaural)

Originally, this was the finale of Luening's *Louisville Concerto,* hence the "Kentucky" in the title. There is no connection with regional music. The main theme is jocular and it is taken through assorted paces with contrasting material.

The Viennese catch the spirit of the music and deliver a well-estimated presentation of the score.

Prelude to a Hymn Tune

☐ Vienna Symphony Orchestra / Dixon (conductor) / Desto 6429E (monaural)

Luening's orchestral piece presents a rich workout on a William Billings tune (*Hymn to Music*). The borrowed subject appears as prelude and epilogue; in between, scoring shifts accompany variational treatment including a fugal depiction. A bit of dissonant style intersects and adds color.

There is utter confusion as to Luening's title. The one used above appears in the special catalogue issued by BMI in observance of the composer's seventieth birthday and is so listed in *Grove's Dictionary of Music and Musicians* and in an article on Luening written by Jack Beeson. The Desto release uses the preposition "on" in place of "to." This would seem to make much better sense, especially since Desto expands the title to read *Prelude on a Hymn Tune by William Billings.* ("By" is eliminated on the front part of the album and on the label!) However, one must take for granted that Luening's wishes were followed when his "official" catalogue was prepared.

Schwann edits the designation, listing the work as *Prelude to a Hymn Tune (after William Billings).* However, *Schwann* errs in defining the piece as being "for piano and small orchestra." Small orchestra, yes, including the piano, but the piano has no more importance than any other instrument in the total orchestration (the scoring is for flute, oboe, clarinet, bassoon, horn, piano, and strings).

Symphonic Fantasia (1924)

☐ Vienna Orchestra / Adler (conductor) / Composers Recordings 103 (monaural)

The varied material that is found in Luening's opus is made from partially polyphonic threads that are often stitched vertically. This permits ideas, organic within themselves, to move with the avoidance of severe cadential impressions. Thus the piece, made of pieces, is held together. Adler's rendition makes certain of this.

Synthesis for Orchestra and Electronic Sound (1960)

☐ Hessian Radio Symphony Orchestra / Van Vactor (conductor) / Composers Recordings S-219

In some respects the most effective use of electronic sounds is when they are combined and contrasted with traditional ones and when they expand the gamut and registral colorations of winds, brass, and other timbres. There are those who declare that this type of partnership holds the only future for electronic detail. (As proof, witness the large number of duos, trios, and other chamber music totals where one of the "instruments" is the tape machine.)

Strong evidence in support of this premise is offered by Otto Luening's *Synthesis*. A fascinating rhetoric results from the orchestra-electronic combination. The composition begins with dismembered phrases. In turn, this segmentation leads into solo electronic events for strong contrast. The tape sounds are then joined to the percussion, and finally the twain meet in totality.

Two Symphonic Interludes (1936)

☐ Vienna Symphony Orchestra / Dixon (conductor) / Desto 6429E (monaural)

The power and sometimes violence of the free concatenation of dissonance pervade Luening's pieces. Tempo and meter are contrasted in this pair of succinct declarations.

Solo Instrument and Orchestra

Flute

Lyric Scene for Flute and Strings

☐ Oslo Philharmonic Orchestra / Øien (flute) / Serebrier (conductor) / Desto 6466

Composed in memory of Busoni with whom Luening studied, this work is most effective when a duo-dimensional result is obtained by combining string contrapuntalism with a lyrical, soaring flute line. Well played. (See *Legend* for Oboe and Strings under *Solo Instrument and Orchestra: oboe,* which also appears on this disc.)

Oboe

Legend for Oboe and Strings (1951)

☐ Oslo Philharmonic Orchestra / Øien (flute) / Serebrier (conductor) / Desto 6466

Bottled with vernal ingredients and flavored with folksy fizz, this work is coupled with another Luening piece (see under *Solo Instrument and Orchestra: flute*) and a half-dozen tape music productions. Listening to this work immediately after the tape program is too swift a submission to traditionalism and offers no advantages. To be fair to Luening's *Legend,* one must wait a while and ready the ears to become accustomed to orthodox properties.

Instrumental

Organ

Fantasia for Organ (1929)

☐ Kneeream (organ) / Composers Recordings S-219

An example of music segmented in its material, dynamic, and instrumental style. Ralph Kneeream does wonders with the piece, specifying each and every portion clearly and yet (paradoxically) blending the total. In this performance Luening's piece acquires its proper profile.

Fugue and Chorale Fantasy with Electronic Doubles for Organ and Tape (1973)

☐ Wyton (organ) / Composers Recordings S-334

Two pieces that Luening wrote for organ (the Chorale Fantasy almost sixty years ago, in 1922, and the more recent Fugue, a product of 1971), have been "updated" by being placed in a duo-dimensional setting.

Each work is sectionalized, with the organ material followed by an electrocized version—the so-termed "double." This manipulation produces a kaleidoscopic variation of the original, a development Luening terms "in effect, electronic echoes." Of course, the "echo" must not be taken literally. There is only a frail reflection of the organ fragment, originally tape-recorded, with slight variations to begin with, and subsequently converted and organized into the electronic double. But, whereas the sonic territory is widely divided between the organ sound and that of the double, there is a bridge of reflective relationship that results in formal continuity (of subtle exteriority rather than interiority). The use of solo statements, the contrast between the two elements, and their combination give a sensitively controlled partnered relationship.

The effect of this real and dream-world musical marriage is dramatic and colorfully exciting. Its twenty-two-minute length is possibly a bit much.

Sonata for Piano (*in memoriam Ferruccio Busoni*) (1966) *Piano*

☐ Oppens (piano) / Composers Recordings S-334

A substantial work, one of Luening's largest and certainly one of his most important. There are four movements: Introduction, Dramatic Scene, Burlesque, and Fantasia.

The Sonata was planned and completed for the 1966 Busoni centenary (Luening studied with Busoni in 1917). There are a number of hints in the composition to stimuli Luening received from Busoni's music, as described in Luening's very thorough and detailed liner notes for the recording. The structural detail represents music of involved yet compact particulars, strengthened by inner relationships—a *sui generis* contemporary classicism.

Ursula Oppens has a dazzling technique. She also has the special ability to understand the varied cadences of creative speech that crisscross the output of contemporary composers. Her performance is on target and is therefore totally revelatory of the meanings and relationships within Luening's exciting piece.

Gargoyles for Violin Solo and Synthesized Sound (1962) *Violin*

☐ Pollikoff (violin) / Columbia MS-6566

Those who have not accepted electronic music creation have argued that its validity exists only in partnership with human-produced sound. And one must consider such a premise. Perhaps the real strength of the tape world is found in the multi-structure that combines an instrumental or vocal performance with the machine. Otto Luening's *Gargoyles* is a demonstration of such a successful hybrid formation.

Luening has a solo violin pitted against and joined to synthesized sound. In variation form, the design is cogently delineated and beautifully projected; the violin functions as a lyric contrast to the synthetic statements, which are mostly dramatic and brilliant.

Solo Sonata No. 3 (1971)

☐ Pollikoff (violin) / Composers Recordings S-303

Some works for an unaccompanied instrument do not profit by confinement. Not this one. Luening's eight-part Sonata has well-balanced melodic and virtuosic elements as well as vitality.

Max Pollikoff produces a definite profile of the music. His skills remain unimpaired.

Chamber Music

Trio (1962)

☐ Sollberger (flute); Sherry (cello); Wuorinen (piano) / Composers Recordings S–303

In this, a type of structural tease, phrases dart in and out and are punctuated by silences that have a strong effect on what has been heard and what will be heard. The effect leans on the improvisational, but the tactics are thoroughly organized in terms of registration, weights, dynamics, and colors.

With musicians like Harvey Sollberger, Fred Sherry, and Charles Wuorinen a composer can have no better proponents.

String Quartet

No. 2 (1922) / No. 3 (1928)

☐ Sinnhoffer Quartet (Munich) / Composers Recordings S–303

It took forty-three years for Luening's second quartet to receive its first performance. This is difficult to understand for a one-movement work that has clear syntax, even though it escapes from a tonal anchorage.

Three movements cover Quartet No. 3; the first two are telescoped. A variational design is used in the first part, its diagram covering partnered ideas developed in alternation. In the final part of the work, a twelve-note theme furnishes the basic material. Again, the method of operation is one of continuous variational development, but the *sounds,* the manner, and the purpose are totally non-decaphonic. It proves that Luening is a composer open to technical suggestion but who draws his own conclusions.

The Sinnhoffer Quartet is little-known. They deserve to be well-known on the basis of their fine-toned and integrated playing. Superb balances.

Vocal

Voice with Accompaniment

The Divine Image

Love's Secret

☐ Miller (mezzo-soprano); Biltcliffe (piano) / Desto 6411/6412

Simple, but very natural settings of the texts, both by Blake.

Electronic Music

Fantasy in Space

Invention in Twelve Notes

Low Speed

Moonflight

☐ Desto 6466

Manipulation of the sounds of a conventional instrument—the flute—is the source-stuff for the four works noted above. New colors and fresh timbres are produced by the special resources available from the tape recorder: varying speeds, superimposition, reverberation, echo, controlled distortion, and so on. Quite different from the recorded sonations of urban and suburban life, factory and home, and what have you, combined and developed as *musique concrète,* Luening's tape pieces are not bizarre, irrational, or sheer laboratory conceits. Totally different in their sonorous dress, they retain a comprehensible relationship to works composed for conventional instruments either in a conventional or unconventional manner.

A new type of virtuosity is found in the *Fantasy.* In *Low Speed* the normal limits of range of the instrument's sounds are stretched—an expansion that does not deny the timbre's identity. Complex patterns, including augmentation and diminution, will be heard in the *Invention,* and *Moonflight* is described as "an astronautical adventure," which thereby is a parallel to old-fashioned program music.

In the Beginning from Theater Piece No. 2 (1956)

☐ Ethel Luening (soprano) / Composers Recordings 268

Three components are combined in this music conceived for the opening part of a ballet: electronic sound, instrumental sounds manipulated on tape, and a recorded human voice.

There is no lubricity in Luening's effective recipe. Sounds as though emerging from the bowels of the earth are later joined to a disembodied type of vocalise (originally from Luening's *Night Piece* in his Suite for Soprano and Flute). The glutinous consistency of the former alone and as an underlay and contrast to the voice create a fertile communication.

Luening and Vladimir Ussachevsky (1911-   )

A Poem in Cycles and Bells for Tape Recorder and Orchestra (1954)

Orchestra

☐ Members of the Royal Danish Radio Orchestra / Luening (conductor) / Composers Recordings 112 (monaural)

Development of the basic material by the orchestra and tape recorder development of the orchestral material, with the electronic idiom coloring the instrumental one, provide a fascinating use of such combination. The variational transformations are not sectionalized and the music flows from beginning to conclusion. At the time this collaborative work was written (1954) it could have been a mere experiment. However, both Luening and Ussachevsky kept expressive intent in view constantly, and their opus proves that fresh invention can have artistic permanence.

Concerted Piece for Tape Recorder and Orchestra (1960)

☐ Oslo Philharmonic Orchestra / Serebrier (conductor) / Composers Recordings S–227

The twain (instrumental and electronic music) meet in this work, but more of a concerto and concerto grosso structure guides the creative tactics. The soloism of a tape recorder cadenza is used, and the antiphony between instruments and tape sounds reminds one of the *concertino-ripieni* responses found in the baroque form. Amalgamation, of course, does occur, but mainly the two sound elements are partitioned, as it were, for emphasis.

Bernstein commissioned this piece and premiered it with the New York Philharmonic in 1960 (the year it was composed). Serebrier does very well with the opus, having conducted it in a number of cities before making the recording.

Incantation

Electronic Music

☐ Desto 6466

The piece heard here is a hybrid of bell sonorities, wind instruments, and the human voice. The blend of the diverse materials with tape treatment produces a high-seasoned sound concoction. This short piece is not music to relax by.

1093

Suite from *King Lear* (1955)

☐ Composers Recordings 112 (monaural)

These are two excerpts from the background score for a production of the Shakespeare play. The episodes covered are the "Storm Scene" and "Lear's Madness." Tape recorder music provides a perfect medium for portraying such moods and Luening and Ussachevsky deliver with dynamic expressivity.

Alexandre Luigini (1850 - 1906)

Ballet

Ballet Egyptien (1874)

☐ London Symphony Orchestra / Bonynge (conductor) / London 2232

The single work by which this composer is remembered. And one remembers quite well its popularity in the silent movie days when it was used for a variety of situations on the screen. Pseudo-styled it is, but nicely so. Bonynge and the L.S.O. bring it neatly into focus.

Ray Luke (1928-   )

Orchestra

Symphony No. 2

☐ Louisville Orchestra / Whitney (conductor) / Louisville S-634

No decorative frivolities here, no adventurous aleatoric devices. Luke has simply, and in a well-directed fashion, written a fast–slow–fast, three-part Symphony, wrapping it around contemporary tonalism. This has its own appeal. Whitney meets all the requirements successfully.

Solo Instrument and Orchestra

Bassoon

Concerto for Bassoon and Orchestra

☐ Crystal Chamber Orchestra / Sharrow (bassoon) / Gold (conductor) / Crystal S-852

Luke's Concerto is presented in the very telling manner of neoclassicism. The harmonies group themselves around and are guided by pandiatonic controls, though this does not deter chromatic condimental flavor. The constructions are meticulous, there is a brilliant spirit to the outer fast movements, and the slow introduction to the first movement and the inner division (an Andante) are poetically phrased.

Leonard Sharrow is a powerful soloist. The orchestra is no small affair, totaling forty-six players, and it does its part admirably.

Jean-Baptiste Lully (1632 - 1687)

Orchestra

Soldier's Air

☐ Collegium Musicum de Paris / Douatte (conductor) / Nonesuch 71002E (monaural)

No sweet sing-along, but a fanfare-march item. Very much alive, of course.

Fanfares for the King's Tournament of 1686

March of the Grey Musketeers

March of the Turenne Regiment

*Wind
and Brass
Ensemble*

☐ Collegium Musicum de Paris / Douatte (conductor) / Nonesuch 71009

The feature here is the last piece, which uses a melody that Bizet included in his *L'Arlésienne* music. Lully's is in major tonality, Bizet's is in minor. The Fanfares retain their brassy personality, though parts 2 and 3 are a slow-paced Menuet and Gavotte. Movement 4 is a moderately tempoed Gigue.

Use of a small group makes these pieces most effective. A swollen, full-size band would ruin their charm.

Marche royale

☐ Brass and Wind Ensemble / André (trumpet); Cochereau (organ) / Birbaum (conductor) / Turnabout 34232

The "full-works" treatment by use of organ plus the wind and brass group is not out of place. For this occasional music Lully wouldn't have minded the change in instrumental décor.

March of the King's Musketeers

Percussion

☐ Collegium Musicum de Paris / Douatte (conductor) / Nonesuch 71009

Some eighty seconds of pomposity delivered first by one drum and then two. Watch the recording since the piece is unbanded and almost blends in with the following composition on the disc which is for winds and brass.

Plaude, laetare Gallia

Choral

☐ Orchestre de la Société des Concerts du Conservatoire / Croisier and Felix (sopranos); Paquet (alto); Lecocq (tenor); Vessières (bass) / Blanchard (conductor) / Nonesuch 70139

*Chorus
and Orchestra*

Plaude, laetare Gallia ("Rejoice and be glad, O France!") is a festive, bright motet. It was written for the baptism of the French *Dauphin* in 1668.

This is an engaging, spirited performance given by fresh-toned voices with excellent instrumental support. Roger Blanchard keeps the music moving even in its more reticent moments. Full credit belongs to Lully for a splendidly eloquent piece of music. No credit is to be given Nonesuch for failing to name the vocal ensemble that is part of these successful proceedings.

Erik Lundborg   (1948-   )

Passacaglia (1974)

Orchestra

☐ Light Fantastic Players / Shulman (conductor) / Composers Recordings SD–350

Lundborg's work is not in the usual passacaglia form but is a complexion within the fabric, woven tightly into the design. Lundborg explains: "the passacaglia in *Passacaglia* is a guide, not an absolute criterion for listening comprehension."

There are involved variants and developments, organized in accordance with serial procedures. This is a fine formal achievement producing a music with undercurrents of nervous anxiety.

The performance is a wealthy one, CRI's engineering is warm and immediate.

Chamber Music

From *Music Forever No. 2* (1972)

☐ Holzman and James (piano); Heldrich and Passaro (percussion) / Shulman (conductor) / Composers Recordings SD–350

This tightly organized serial music emphasizes its percussive content by percussive instruments: piano four-hands, vibraphone, marimba, xylophone, glockenspiel, twelve drums, six cymbals, and six wood instruments (temple blocks in the case of this recording).

The performers are from the Light Fantastic Players and expose the details of the score clearly.

Witold Lutoslawski (1913-   )

Orchestra

Concerto for Orchestra (1954)

☐ Warsaw National Philharmonic Symphony Orchestra / Rowicki (conductor) / Philips 6500628

When a contemporary work achieves the status of three separate recordings, that statistic already proves importance. Lutoslawski's Concerto distinctly deserves its success. It is fueled by folk materials, transported into freely molded classical shapes. *Intrada, Arioso,* Passacaglia, Toccata, and Chorale forms make their appearance in the three movements, as well as a *Capriccio Notturno* that is a scherzo of beehive activity. The orchestrational culture is controlled, never outré, but of blast-furnace impact.

That last statement means virtuosity. The Suisse Romande with Kletzki (London 6665) (who incidentally makes a cut in part 2 of the work) and Ozawa with the Chicago Symphony (Angel S–36045) can cope with the score without the least trouble. However, both lack what Rowicki, with a shade lower-category orchestra, has to offer. This is due to a long artistic marriage. Rowicki asked Lutoslawski for a work for what was then (in 1950) his new orchestra. In 1954 the composition was completed, and the Warsaw ensemble gave the first performance on November 26 of that year; the work has since remained in their repertoire. Such deep familiarity carries over to the recording, which possesses a responsiveness and a quality that are not found in the other editions.

Mala Suita (1955)

☐ Berlin Symphony Orchestra / Grüber (conductor) / Candide 31035

The titles of the four movements of Lutoslawski's "Little Suite" give away the stylistic secret: *Fujarka* ("Little Joke" with the alternate title "Wooden Flute"), *Hurra Polka* ("Jolly Polka"), *Piosenka* ("Small Song"), and *Taniec* ("Dance"). The opening music confirms it, with a piccolo melodically curling up and down, a snare drum (without the snares) supporting it here and there, and with light chordal accompaniment by solo violins. Indeed, folkloristic music, deftly colored and true to the source. It is backed up by a true-to-scale rendition.

Venetian Games (1961)

☐ Warsaw National Philharmonic Symphony Orchestra / Rowicki (conductor) / Philips 6500628

The title *Jeux Vénitiens* is simple to explain. Lutoslawski's use of aleatory technique covers the "games" description, and the fact that the first performance took place in Venice (April 24, 1961) applies to the "Venetian" designation.

Closed-form, traditionally notated music is a composer's private possession. Aleatoric material, no matter how much force of direction is built in by the composer, becomes a shared musical possession, considerably more than the interpretative re-creation that applies to music without aleatoric specifications. The scope it gives to individuals to play freely means that the composer places his reputation on the line each time his aleatoric work is performed. Only in performances as good as this one is there no danger of creative loss of standing.

Funeral Music (1958)

☐ Warsaw National Philharmonic Symphony Orchestra / Rowicki (conductor) / Philips 6500628

Musique Funèbre is dedicated to the memory of Béla Bartók. It conveys its dramatic energy by twelve-tone totality, but it is not bound to dodecaphonic strictures. Four successive sections are connected by canonic interlocking in the terminal sections (Prologue and Epilogue), between which development is covered in the *Metamorphoses*, culminating in a thrillingly raw *Apogeum*.

Dynamited sounds are heard in this score; even in the quieter moments they are quivering to explode. This is a music that was written from the guts. It is so played, with extremely fine-honed balance of the ten-part string orchestra (the violins are in four sections, the violas, cellos, and basses in two each).

There is a competitive issue on Candide 31035, performed by the Hamburg Symphony Orchestra, conducted by Arthur Grüber. Should that edition be selected (it is second best), be sure to bypass the misinformation that the program note gives, indicating that the Funeral Music juxtaposes "'live' and recorded string sounds which are distorted, stratified and overlap[ped]." No way!

Overture for String Orchestra (1949)

☐ Berlin Symphony Orchestra / Grüber (conductor) / Candide 31035

These Bartókian penetrations are rhythmically hypnotic, melodically sometimes snide. The playing is rough at times, but it fits the conception.

Concerto for Cello and Orchestra (1970)

☐ Orchestre de Paris / Rostropovich (cello) / Lutoslawski (conductor) / Angel S–37146

Lutoslawski's use of controlled aleatoric materials is included in this four-movements-in-one concerto. The sectional depiction is clear with unitary pitch development balancing the much more outgoing finale and a pair of movements in the contrastive application of episodes and instrumental song in between. A strong performance in all respects.

Five Dance Preludes for Clarinet, String Orchestra, Harp, Piano, and Percussion (1955)

☐ Berlin Symphony Orchestra / Masseli (clarinet) / Grüber (conductor) / Candide 31035

This is the second setting of Lutoslawski's sparkling suite born of folk parentage—his last significant work in that style. The initial setting was for clarinet and piano and has been recorded (see under *Instrumental: clarinet*). Still a third version appeared (in 1959) in nonet form for wind quintet, violin, viola, cello, and double bass.

String Orchestra

Solo Instrument and Orchestra

Cello

Clarinet

All the color and affirmative folk accents come through clearly in the rendition. That the clarinet tone is sometimes rough is O.K. since, when that quality occurs, it is in the accentuated peasantlike sections and it fits. Not fitting is the lack of bands, a gripe I will always make when they are lacking in the recording of a composition consisting of distinctly separated movements or pieces.

Instrumental

Clarinet

Five Dance Preludes for Clarinet and Piano (1954)

☐ Milosovich (clarinet); Dresden (piano) / Musical Heritage Society MHS-1473

For a discussion of this work, see under *Solo Instrument and Orchestra: clarinet.*
Chester Milosovich's playing is most congenial. However, Musical Heritage Society's usual care with liner information is absent this time. First, the Five Dance Preludes were written in 1954 not 1955. Second, this is the original version, not the edition with string orchestra, et cetera.

Two Pianos

Variations on a Theme of Paganini (1941)

☐ Eden and Tamir (pianos) / London 6434

What, again? Indeed, yes. Paganini's famous subject is variationally inexhaustible. When worked into the design of a contemporary-styled, two-piano composition, it retains its uniqueness while permitting the creativity of the composer to come through as well. Lutoslawski's purpose is exhibitionistic, but it is always musical.
The pianists play with splendid spirit; a classy performance throughout.

Vocal

Voice and Instrumental Ensemble

Die Strohkette (1951)

☐ Miller (soprano); Sowlak (mezzo-soprano); Dohn (flute); Schnell (oboe); Stute and Klose (clarinets); Steinbrecher (bassoon) / Grüber (conductor) / Candide 31035

An absolute folk delight. *Die Strohkette* ("A Straw Chain") is a set of rural songs. It is all crystal-clear, all simple, with an instrumental introduction, six songs, and then the final one from which Lutoslawski drew the title for his song cycle: *Słomkowy Łańcuszek,* itself divided into seven parts. This is basal creativity with no extra flesh on the music. Thus we have a 34-second introduction, and songs of such minimal lengths as "Tiny Little House in the Countryside" (25 seconds), "A Pear Tree Stood in the Field" (22 seconds), and *Pies* ("Dog") which takes 12 seconds.
The performance is an absolute delight.

Voice and Orchestra

Paroles tissées (1965)

☐ London Sinfonietta / Pears (tenor) / Lutoslawski (conductor) / London HEAD-3

Paroles tissées is not really a song cycle but rather a four-part work in which the voice irradiates, twines among, and coloristically amplifies the symphonicism of the orchestra (piano, harp, seventeen solo strings [ten violins, three violas, three cellos, one double bass]). "Controlled" aleatoricism prevails but it is an asset to the shadowy filaments that are major to the score. Clustered chromaticism is at the heart of things but the dramatic output is obtained by gentle input.
A slight vibrato does not undo the sincerity of Peter Pears's performance. One admires the expressivity which does equal credit to singer and composer–conductor.

Elisabeth Lutyens (1906-   )

Ô Saisons, Ô Châteaux!, Op. 13

☐ Royal Philharmonic Orchestra / Tyler (soprano) / Del Mar (conductor) / Argo ZRG–754

Music guided by twelve-tone impressionism, thus belying the premise that only extreme expressionism is serialistically successful. ''O Seasons, O Castles'' provides a rare emotional experience.

Marilyn Tyler's singing, covering a huge range, is fresh and exciting. The strings, including mandolin, guitar, and harp, of the Royal Philharmonic Orchestra are convincingly sensitive. A brilliant achievement.

Donald Lybbert (1923-   )

Sonata Brevis (1962)

☐ Rogers (piano) / Composers Recordings S–281

Heard here is a fusion of serialism with enlarged tonality, and it is percussively minded even in its more relaxed sections. There are no stale rhetorical gestures in Lybbert's score. The power and vigor of his conception are matched by Rogers's re-creative strength and vitality.

Lines for the Fallen (1967)

☐ Bryn-Julson (soprano); Pappastravrou and Lanning (pianos) / Odyssey 32160162

Quarter tones are paramount here. Not only are the pianos so tuned (thus there are twenty-four pitches within the octave) but the vocalist produces microtonal differentiations. The music is superbly realized and superbly performed; the text is drawn from the Mass for the Dead and the poetry of Blake.

M

Robert MacDougall   (1941-   )

Anacoluthon: A Confluence (1972)

Chamber Music

☐ Contemporary Music Ensemble / Weisberg (conductor) / Composers Recordings SD-323

An octet for flute, oboe, two clarinets, trumpet, violin, viola, and cello. Thematic material is bypassed in favor of closely knit materials that are brought ''into conflict with one another.'' The greatest fascination pertains to the score's coloristic aspects, whereby the combining of instrumental opposition is of vital consequence.

Be assured that you can expect top-quality playing from Weisberg's group. The stamp of authority is most evident in this recorded issue.

Edward MacDowell   (1860-1908)

Suite

Orchestra

No. 1 for Large Orchestra, Op. 42 / No. 2 (*Indian*), Op. 48

☐ Eastman-Rochester Orchestra / Hanson (conductor) / Mercury 75026

MacDowell's Opus 42 (in D minor), in totality, actually was completed after the better-known second Suite, which bears the later opus number 48 and which was composed in 1892. MacDowell wrote his D minor Suite in 1890 and 1891. As then constituted (movements 1, 2, 4, and 5 of the final work) it received its first performance. The *In October* movement (now movement 3) was composed in 1893.

Opus 42 includes the designation *grosses Orchester* in its title, but actually the orchestra is of normal size (piccolo and double woodwinds, four horns, two trumpets, three trombones, tuba, timpani, bass drum, cymbals, and strings); two of the movements (movements 2 and 4) are for a much smaller instrumentation of winds, horns, timpani, and strings. Each of the five divisions creates a definite mood of romantic poesy. Thus: refined delicacy in movement 2 (*Summer Idyll*); a light-fast, fancy-free scherzo depiction serving for the finale (*Forest Spirits*).

Motives of the Iroquois, Iowa, and other tribes are used in the five-movement second Suite. A Kiowa tune, a chant of mourning, is the basis for the fourth movement (Dirge), the composer's favorite among his total output. It is, indeed, music of intensity and emotive depth.

MacDowell has been described by Hanson as both ''a remarkable man'' and the ''American romantic supreme.'' As a present-day romantic composer, Hanson, the conductor, would fully understand MacDowell, an older-period romantic creative voice. It shows in these warmly projected performances: full-throated, beautifully shaped and balanced, with the colors subtle where they should be, fully defined elsewhere.

Solo Instrument and Orchestra

Piano

Concerto No. 1 in A minor for Piano and Orchestra, Op. 15

☐ Vienna State Opera Orchestra / List (piano) / Chávez (conductor) / Westminster Gold 8156

The forgotten MacDowell Concerto. While there is no doubt the second work in the medium (*see below*) is a better property (certainly a more popular one), there are values in the earlier opus, even though Grieg is not far away throughout the end movement.

Eugene List's performance may help to refocus proper consideration of the work. He is fully at home in the idiom and displays complete knowledge of the composer's creative objectives. Good support from Chávez.

Concerto No. 2 in D minor for Piano and Orchestra, Op. 23

☐ Chicago Symphony Orchestra / Cliburn (piano) / Hendl (conductor) / RCA LSC–2507
☐ Westphalian Symphony Orchestra, Recklinghausen / List (piano) / Landau (conductor) / Turnabout 34535

Though List commands the music with more brilliance and thrust than Cliburn, he is placed second because Turnabout's recorded sound lacks sufficient depth and the piano tone suffers accordingly. The go-ahead, no-nonsense sort of way that List adopts goes well wth MacDowell's all-stops-out Concerto. Cliburn covers the sounds with a softer touch. Finally, as to giving the RCA edition first place, one perceives better attention to the accompanimental undercurrents by Hendl.

Instrumental

Cello

Romanze, Op. 35

☐ Krosnick (cello); Grant (piano) / Orion 7291

It's worth having this short, hardly known piece that MacDowell composed for cello and either orchestra or piano accompaniment. Especially so, in this genuine performance.

Piano

Sea Pieces, Op. 55

Second Modern Suite, Op. 14

Shadow Dance, Op. 39, No. 8

☐ Swem (piano) / Orion 75175

Swem does well with the poetical ingredients found in the set of eight Sea Pieces. No Lisztian storms in these, each prefaced by a motto or verse by MacDowell, who so often used such semiprogrammatic material to define his music's inner significance.

The same pertains to the first of the six parts in the Second Modern Suite, which bears an explanatory quotation from Byron's *Manfred*. Swem offers accomplished performances of both suites and zips neatly through the Shadow Dance, an extract from Twelve Etudes for the Development of Technique and Style. (Some of the pieces in this opus go beyond hard-crusted, didactic boundaries and are viable concert music.)

Sonata

No. 2 (*Eroica*) in G minor, Op. 50 / No. 3 (*Norse*) in D minor, Op. 57

☐ Takahashi (piano) / Orion 75183

MacDowell indicated the Sonata *Eroica* as "not exactly programme music." Nevertheless, while disavowing that objective, at the same time he stated he "had in mind the Arthurian legend when writing the work," continuing with a single-sentence précis for each of the four movements. Sonata No. 3 takes its *Norse* nickname from the semiprogrammatic poem derived from Norse mythology that MacDowell wrote as a preface to the score.

Both sonatas are played with superb artistry and a sense of color that does much for the compositions. Miss Takahashi bypasses the one point that has played havoc with MacDowell's piano music (miniatures or sonatas), namely sentimentality, the outcome, so often of an over-indulgence in *rubato* phrasing. It is that point that mars Lythgoe's playing of the second Sonata on Philips 9500095.

Mandel avoids the *rubato* syndrome, but his conception of the *Norse* Sonata (on Desto 6445/7, in *An Anthology of American Piano Music*) lacks requisite breadth. It was not surprising, when checking the timing of Mandel's performance with that of Takahashi's, to find that his was considerably faster (by almost four and three-quarter minutes).

Twelve Virtuoso Studies, Op. 46

☐ Jochum (piano) / Golden Crest CRS–4168

Veronica Jochum plays these Etudes (to follow the exact word used in MacDowell's title, though the English word is most often used) capably and sympathetically. She is at her best in the speedy, light-faceted pieces such as the *Moto Perpetuo* (No. 2), *Wild Chase* (No. 3), Elfin Dance (No. 5), and the tenth number, *March Wind*.

Witches' Dance, Op. 17, No. 2

☐ Swem (piano) / Orion 75175

The second of MacDowell's Two Fantastic Pieces and the one most often played, usually called by its German title, *Hexentanz*.

Woodland Sketches, Op. 51

☐ Lythgoe (piano) / Philips 9500095

MacDowell is at his best in these ten miniatures, which include the charm of *To A Wild Rose* and such characteristic sketches as *Will o' the Wisp* and *From Uncle Remus*.

America's Bicentennial has come and gone and practically no attention was given MacDowell during the celebration. The fact that the only complete recorded version of the *Woodland Sketches* was made by an English pianist for a non-American firm is a shameful statistic. Praise for Lythgoe, therefore, and praise for a good presentation.

Long Ago, Op. 56, No. 1

☐ Hanks (tenor); Friedberg (piano) / Duke University Press DWRM–7501 (monaural)

Special to this song (also fully titled *Long Ago, Sweetheart Mine*) is that the text is by MacDowell.

New World Records has included this expressive song in an album, *When I Have Sung My Songs*. It is beautifully interpreted by Alma Gluck. However, one must overlook the sound quality of the edition, made from a disc recorded over a half-century ago.

Vocal

Voice with Accompaniment

A Maid Sings Light, Op. 56, No. 3

☐ Gluck (soprano); Bourdon (piano) / New World Records NW-247 (monaural)

Also called *Merry Maiden Spring*. Gay and graceful and very compact. (New World's release is a transfer of a recording made for Victor on June 10, 1912.)

The Sea, Op. 47, No. 7

☐ McCollum (tenor); Biltcliffe (piano) / Desto 6411/2

The Sea (the seventh of the eight songs in the set) has been described as "the strongest song of the sea since Schubert's *Am Meer*," by no less a critic than the famed James Gibbons Huneker. The piano's role is a subtle one, but most important, and it is cogently realized in this instance, partnering the excellent projection by John McCollum.

Thy Beaming Eyes, Op. 40, No. 3

☐ Hanks (tenor); Friedberg (piano) / Duke University Press DWRM-7501 (monaural)

From a set of Six Love Songs. John Kennedy Hanks eloquently carries out the impulsive quality of the song.

Thomas Mace   (ca. 1613-ca. 1709)

Instrumental

Lute

Suite in D minor

☐ Gerwig (lute) / RCA VICS-1362

A six-movement work extracted from Mace's historically important *Musick's Monument*. A special attraction is the final part, *Tattle de Moy*, a lighter-faceted Sarabande concoction.

Gerwig's lute touch is sensitive and fluid.

Teo Macero   (1925-   )

Orchestra

***One-Three Quarters* (for Chamber Ensemble and Two Pianos)**

☐ Chamber Ensemble from Syracuse University School of Music / Pappastravrou and Lanning (pianos) / Macero (conductor) / Odyssey 32160162

A piece absorbed with improvisational fantasy, including innumerable coloristic ideas. The pianos are tuned in quarter tones, and further color is projected by these mini-intervallic spans.

Guillaume de Machaut   (ca. 1300-1377)

Cantata and Oratorio

Missa Notre-Dame

☐ Medieval Chamber Ensemble and Deller Consort / Deller (conductor) / Bach Guild 5045

Fourteenth-century polyphony containing vigorous pulsatility, striking pitch combinations, and a fascinating early example of motivic construction. The performance has a rough-edged quality that well fits Machaut's starkly expressive music.

The choice of instruments is excellent, their very colorful disposition aiding the intense quality of the score. They consist of two violins, a zink (an instrument producing delicate trumpet-timbred sounds), two blockflötes (recorders), a discantpommer (an early European double reed instrument), two regals (portable organs with single sets of reed pipes), a tenorpommer (lower-pitched in relation to the discantpommer), a trombone, and a krumhorn (an oboe type).

The Deller Consort's work deserves individual credit. The group consists of Alfred Deller, countertenor; Wilfred Brown and Gerald English, tenors; and Maurice Bevan, baritone.

Elizabeth Maconchy   (1907-   )

Overture, *Proud Thames* (1952)   *Orchestra*

☐ London Philharmonic Orchestra / Handley (conductor) / Musical Heritage Society MHS-1672

Motival management used with utter plasticity and fluid persistency builds this sonorous piece. This is a music quite different from Maconchy's Bartókian chamber music, but just as welcome. It receives a fine statement by the L.P.O.

String Quartet No. 5 (1948)   *Chamber Music*

☐ Allegri String Quartet / Argo ZRG-5329

Among England's women composers it can well be said that if Elisabeth Lutyens is the female counterpart of Schoenberg, then Elizabeth Maconchy is the female Bartók. No more powerful music can be written than the tight, baldly driven consolidations of this chamber work, a representative example of her output. As in her other quartets, there is a terse, uncompromising use of generating material, akin to both late Beethoven and Bartók. It is splendidly set forth in the Allegri's playing.

Ariadne   *Vocal*

☐ English Chamber Orchestra / Harper (soprano) / Leppard (conductor) / Oiseau-Lyre 331   *Voice and Orchestra*

A dramatic monologue to a poem by Cecil Day Lewis. The style verges on declamatory depiction, though the entire work is sung by Heather Harper with fluidic concern for the music and thorough clarity as to the text. Leppard's direction is extremely perceptive.

Clarence Mader   (1904-1971)

Prelude, Tune, and Eight Masquerades   *Instrumental*

☐ Calligaris (piano) / Orion 7142   *Piano*

The Masquerades are variations on the preceding tune, a Loggers' Song. Romantic syntax and fine-scaled sonorities provide a decently eclectic result. Sergio Calligaris colors the music with taste.

Bruno Maderna (1920 - 1973)

Orchestra

Il Giardino Religioso

☐ Schuller (conductor) / Odyssey Y-34141

Mystical pronouncements are contained in the ten sections of Maderna's "The Religious Garden." Its religion is concerned not only with mood but with aleatoric, improvisatory technique. Maderna's images are matched by Schuller's performance facts.

Serenata No. 2 (1954)

☐ English Chamber Orchestra / Maderna (conductor) / Mainstream 5004

A clever simulation of serenata formation compressed into one piece. Thus, a classical section moves into pointillism, is succeeded by rhythmic rhapsody, and concludes with nocturnal effect. Four movements in one, thereby fulfilling the title objective.

The playing is minute, particular, sensitive, and strongly controlled at the same time.

Solo Instrument and Orchestra

Flute

Hyperion III for Flute and Orchestra

☐ Symphony Orchestra of the Südwestfunk, Baden-Baden / Gazzelloni (flute) / Maderna (conductor) / Wergo 60029

A collage made from two other Maderna works: *Hyperion I* (Aria for Soprano and Orchestra) and *Hyperion II* (*Stele per "Diotima,"* Serenata for Orchestra), with solo flute interstices that range from long-lined, curvaceous, noncadenced material to ear-splitting sopranino-ranged ejaculations. The orchestral packing consists of sharply frictioned sounds and short, spiny thrusts, plus qualities similar to electronic music. A powerful work, intense, typical of the composer, and magnificently presented.

Oboe

Concerto for Oboe and Chamber Orchestra

☐ Soloists of the Rome Symphony Orchestra / Faber (oboe and English horn) / Maderna (conductor) / RCA VICS-1312

This is neither a concerto as one knows the form nor extrovert in communication. The construction consists of six cadenzas (again, of unexpected format—they are not the circusy type). The solo statements are declarative, with the orchestral group contrasting or supporting. A sense of quiet improvisation and restraint persists; the lyricism is entrancing because it is fresh. The final portion is for English horn with the sole support of tuned drums.

Super-convincing music, this, but not for those in whom rote listening has ruled for so long. Nonetheless, Lothar Faber's amazing oboe playing will be immediately recognized, and one can be assured that Bruno Maderna's direction is superb.

Instrumental

Flute

Honeyrêves

☐ Gazzelloni (flute); Kontarsky (piano) / Mainstream 5014

A nocturnal rhapsody with flute glides and key tappings, principally supported by piano percussion—striking of the bass strings, plucking, and a harmonic or two.

Gazzelloni gives an uninhibited reading. His technique itself provides excitation. Kontarsky's keyboard pigmentation is sensitively applied.

Viola (Closed-form Version)

Viola (Open-form Version)

☐ Phillips (viola) / Finnadar 9007

Viola for viola alone is a mosaic (nervously put together but nevertheless not losing basic continuity) of vividly contrasted fragments. The studied rejection of declarative lines produces its special type of dramaticism because of the discursive detail.

The first setting follows the composer's structure. The open-form version gives the performer freedom to choose as he wishes from the score: to start at any point, jump to another place, repeat, omit, terminate wherever desired, and so on. In this manner Karen Phillips elongates Maderna's *Viola* from its set six minutes twenty seconds basis to a total of seven minutes seventeen seconds. Both versions will maintain an auditor's interest.

Dedication (Widmung)

Pièce pour Ivry (1971)

☐ Edinger (violin) / Orion 75171

A high degree of serial fantasy is proposed in the *Dedication* (written for the opening of an art gallery). The movement does not fit into the textbooks, with its sharp contrastive relay from extremely high-pitch sections, to violent chordal work, on to plucked string action, with assorted continuation. Its ending is climactic by reverse means, as the music simply disintegrates.

Pièce pour Ivry represents creative definition with performance choice. Sixteen fragments are composed, their sequence being at the will of the violinist. The version Edinger delivers ratifies the unhallowed formalism that develops from such freedom. She also ratifies her magnificence as a virtuoso, already indicated in her playing of the *Dedication*.

Albéric Magnard   *(1865-1914)*

Symphony No. 3, Op. 11

☐ L'Orchestre de la Suisse Romande / Ansermet (conductor) / London 6615

Magnard plots his four-movement Symphony with touches of the picturesque, so that the first movement has an Overture preceded by an Introduction, and movement 2 is termed Dances, with a musette tinge in the contrasting section. Movement 3 is titled Pastorale. Identification processes are dropped for the last movement, simply called a Finale.

The best point of the work is that despite study with Vincent d'Indy, Magnard has avoided Franckian practice, which in the disciples of the Belgian (and the Frenchman) can be (and has often been) much too much chromatic. What has not been avoided is the sense of center-of-the-road academic reasoning. However, Ansermet does his best to color the work and thereby obtain an ebb and flow that spruces up matters considerably.

Promenades (Pièces pour le Piano), Op. 7

☐ Doyen (piano) / Musical Heritage Society MHS–1155–57

Pianistic excursions covering Parisian excursions. The first movement is *Envoi* and then follow the locales: *Bois de Boulogne, Villebon, Saint-Cloud, Saint-Germain, Trianon,* and *Rambouillet.* The detail is strongly contrasted. Thus, waltz rhythm in the *Bois de Boulogne,* variations over a bell-like ostinato in *Villebon,* a scherzo pace in *Saint-Cloud,* a fugue in *Trianon,* and so on.

More expressive than representative, the differing colors of these pieces function as part of the individual structures rather than mere decoration. These are finely wrought conceptions that come close to the work of Debussy. The emotive sincerity of Magnard's music is extremely impressive.

Gustav Mahler *(1860-1911)*

Orchestra

Symphony No. 1 in D major (1883-1888)

☐ Bavarian Radio Symphony Orchestra / Kubelik (conductor) / Deutsche Grammophon 139331

This is a classic Mahler performance, containing poetry, wonderful color (demonically depicted, especially in the Scherzo), and full drama. And, when Kubelik lets out, Mahler's score instructions (and, as usual, there are many) are still respected to the fullest extent. There is attention to the finite detail and a grasp that is ultrasensitive to the content: the grotesquerie in the Funeral March and the exultancy of the finale's finale are examples.

There are several other choices of recordings, particularly Solti's evocative and magnificent account (London 6401) and Levine's expertly exciting essay (RCA ARL1-0894). However, if a second choice is to be made, it is suggested that Ormandy's (*see below*) be the edition, in view of his inclusion of the *Blumine* movement.

Finally, it will be noted that the cognomen *Titan* does not appear here, but does with the Ormandy performance. This follows the reasoning of the Mahler scholar and expert, Jack Diether, who has written that "a recording that does *not* include the *Blumine* movement should not carry the old subtitle *Titan* either."

Symphony No. 1 (*Titan*) in D major (with *Blumine* movement) (1883-1888)

☐ Philadelphia Orchestra / Ormandy (conductor) / RCA LSC-3107

This version (*see* immediately *above*) includes the *Blumine* movement, thereby returning to the original sequence of five movements. The performance has strength and a thoroughly idiomatic tone.

Symphony No. 2 (*Resurrection*) in C minor (1887-1894)

☐ London Symphony Orchestra and Edinburgh Festival Chorus / Armstrong (soprano); Baker (mezzo-soprano) / Bernstein (conductor) / Columbia M2-32681

The initial shattering triple-*forte* plunge of the lower strings is a mark that Bernstein will be in command of this mighty symphony—and he is. He takes the first movement slower than the metronomic indication, but the interpretative strategy becomes quite clear—to highlight the two tempi territories, so that slow-paced material is drawn out and the reverse drawn in. It is most exciting in its results, though Mahler academicians may object.

Delicacy, but not innocent of agogic coloration, marks the second movement. The third moves in a dynamicized atmosphere; the dynamic controls are virtuosic. The vocal section (*Urlicht*) is sensitive and beautiful. And the finale? Give Leonard Bernstein a finale of this type and you've got the best man in the business in charge. He conquers its vastness and explains all of its details in a fully acceptable, histrionic manner.

A second choice is Ormandy's edition (he was the first conductor to record the work, some forty years ago). It is a strong realization (on RCA LSC-7066) and matches the scope of Bernstein's finale.

Bernstein's performance is also coupled with the Mahler Third on Columbia M4X-31432.

Symphony No. 3 (*Ein Sommermorgentraum*) in D minor (1893-1896)

☐ London Symphony Orchestra, Ambrosian Singers, and Wandsworth School Boys' Choir / Proctor (contralto); Georgiadis (violin); Lang (flügelhorn); Wick (trombone) / Horenstein (conductor) / Nonesuch 73023

The tension in the orgiastic first movement has a power that dazzles as it almost frightens. In comparison, the final (sixth) part, so important in the Symphony's structure and totally opposite to the initial section in its antithetical mood, has an unsurpassed radiance. As performed, there are no false enunciations in this music of *innigkeit*. Tempo seems to stand still as Mahler's eloquently gorgeous music unfolds. Horenstein never distorts a single beat here, as a number of conductors feel they must, to impress and stress (Solti, especially).

I do not believe there is a more revelatory performance on disc, despite fine editions on the part of James Levine (RCA ARL2-1757) and Bernstein (Columbia M2S-675). The assists here from Norma Proctor and the choral groups are splendidly focused. This disc is very highly recommended. Horenstein has given us one of the great Mahler representations.

Symphony No. 4 in G major (1889-1901)

☐ Vienna Philharmonic Orchestra / von Stade (mezzo-soprano) / Abbado (conductor) / Deutsche Grammophon 2530966

Claudio Abbado has produced a stunning rendition of this radiant romantic work. In the first movement the detail is strongly outlined, and yet over it all there is a *gemächlich* contribution, which includes a warm energy that flows into every measure. The slow movement is as marked, extremely *Ruhevoll,* and yet one is not aware of how checked the pace is—as though the pulse has been erased. The final measures of this movement are wondrously serene.

Frederica von Stade sings with an openness that is totally captivating. She offers a quality of simplicity that is, in its way, as ravishing as a vocal delivery of huge dramatic input.

I have always favored Szell's (Columbia MS-6833) and Horenstein's (Monitor S-2141) editions of this Symphony. They now take second place to the Abbado entry. His performance truly parallels the final words of Mahler's song-finale: *Dass alles für Freuden erwacht* ("making everything awaken for joy").

Symphony No. 5 (*The Giant*) in C sharp minor (1901-1902)

☐ New Philharmonia Orchestra / Barbirolli (conductor) / Angel S-3760
☐ Berlin Philharmonic Orchestra / von Karajan (conductor) / Deutsche Grammophon 2707081

The breadth of Barbirolli's conception and his pulsatile control are unique among the many editions of this work. Every distinction in the score is made precise, but more important is the depiction of the music's inner imaginative meanings. Pulse control reacts against a loosening of the content but is applied to obtain special character. The *Trauermarsch* thus remains both foreboding and of splendor; the slow movement (for strings and harp) is seamless and yet marked by its agogic stresses and dramatically dynamic suppressions. This is a focused Mahler that provides a perfect equilibrium between specific content and meaning. It has soul.

Von Karajan's reading has a tension in the opening movement that adds a mysterious overlay to Mahler's music. The closing portion of the Adagietto is superb. He eliminates the join to the Rondo-Finale, but achieves in that Finale one of the most exhilarating Mahler readings in the recorded music catalogue.

Haitink's version (Philips 6700048), though well-balanced, is too objective for this style of music. Solti (London 2228), of course, provides a brilliant exposition, but that palls when it simply produces emotional responsibility, and there's much more than that element in Mahler's Fifth. Bernstein's statement (Columbia M2S–698) of the slow movement is better than any of the dozen recordings reviewed. But otherwise his performance never passes the line between score signals and cogent realization.

Symphony No. 6 in A minor (1903-1905)

☐ Stockholm Philharmonic Orchestra / Horenstein (conductor) / Nonesuch 73029

This profoundly disturbing work (which "blends hope and despair," as one critic has described it) is magnificently detailed by Horenstein. That the recording was made from a live performance does not lessen full acceptance of its value. The innermost points are thrillingly detailed, and in the matter of tempi Horenstein (an unsurpassed Mahler interpreter) cannot be faulted. Thus, the opening movement has a moderated speed that does not negate but rather underlines the tone of menace in the music. (Bernstein, on Columbia M3S–776, is too energetic, as is Solti, on London 2227.) The slow movement is not too slow, and its breadth is made even more pertinent by finely culled *rubati*. The Scherzo is weighted, not pitched forward (Bernstein, again, I feel, drives too fast, and, for that matter, so does Solti). The finale has a stalwart nobility that I find matched only in a version by Haitink (Philips 839797/8).

Symphony No. 7 in E minor (1904-1906)

☐ New York Philharmonic / Sabinsky (mandolin) / Bernstein (conductor) / Columbia M2S–739

A fine-turned balance of the lyrical and the dramatic, especially espousing the romantic spread of color in the two *Nachtmusik* movements and in the Scherzo, which Jack Diether has cogently termed "sinister and parodistic." In the Rondo-Finale the robustness is as compelling as it is intriguing, since its Mahlerian syntax and orchestration are to be classified as reflecting a classical link (discussed in Jack Diether's magnificent notes that accompany the recording).

The performance uses the Ratz edition, published in 1960, which includes orchestrational changes and correction of errors that had not appeared in the initial edition of the Symphony.

(This edition is also available in combination with Bernstein's conducting of Symphony No 8 on Columbia M4X–31441.)

Symphony No. 8 (*Symphony of a Thousand*) in E flat major (1906-1907)

☐ London Symphony Orchestra and Chorus, Leeds Festival Chorus, Orpington Junior Singers, Highgate School Boys' Choir, and Finchley Children's Music Group / Annear,

Jones, and Spoorenberg (sopranos); Proctor and Reynolds (altos); Mitchinson (tenor); Ruzdjak (baritone); McIntyre (bass); Vollenweider (organ) / Bernstein (conductor) / Columbia M2S-751

Mahler's Symphony No. 8 is of no small matter, either on stage or in a recording studio, what with five choruses, eight vocal soloists, large orchestra, plus organ. A *Symphony of a thousand* problems, but Bernstein has solved them, in a blazing, magnificent rendition. The minor quibbles one might raise are like a thimble of dust lost in the Milky Way, considering the scope of this mighty Symphony.

Mahler's score exults in God, and Bernstein exults in Mahler. Bernstein's rapport with the score leads him to tempi that burst and move forth, and his understanding leads him to the proper atmosphere and colors for Mahler's opus. The soloists and choruses are superfine and the L.S.O. is brilliant. In sum, this is a recording that dominates all others.

(The performance is also included with Bernstein's conducting of Symphony No. 7 on Columbia M4X-31441.)

Symphony No. 9 in D major (1908-1910)

☐ Bavarian Radio Symphony Orchestra / Kubelik (conductor) / Deutsche Grammophon 2707038

☐ London Symphony Orchestra / Solti (conductor) / London 2220

Both recordings belong in the highest category. Solti is excitingly alert in the first movement, Kubelik a bit less so, but he keenly depicts the thrust and release of the music. Both are superb guides in the central pair of movements, with Solti implying more snideness in the *Rondo Burlesque*. The rhythmic stability is never tampered with, and there is sharp focus to the metrical designs. Perhaps the Londoners don't feel the pace of the *Ländler* in the same manner as do the Bavarians, but the effect is not minimized.

Of course, it is the finale which reaches a sublime conclusion that is a test for all conductors. Its penetratingly spiritual beauty is gently portrayed by Kubelik, more outwardly by Solti. Musically and technically both of these accounts are vivid and faithful Mahler essays—imposing ones as well.

(Solti's performance is included in the integral edition of the Mahler symphonies he made, obtainable on London CSP-7.)

Symphony No. 10 (*Unfinished*) (Adagio) (1909)

☐ New York Philharmonic / Bernstein (conductor) / Columbia M-33532

The single movement of the Mahler Tenth Symphony that is authenticated as totally Mahler's. Matters are complicated plus. Bernstein uses the critical edition by Erwin Ratz. Other conductors who have recorded the movement (Boulez, on Columbia M2-30061 and Szell; *see below*) have utilized an earlier, less confirmed edition. Further, Szell also performs the *Purgatorio* section, which had been edited (together with the Adagio) by Ernst Krenek. Last in this saga is the completion of the entire Symphony by Deryck Cooke, also performed and recorded in several versions (see under *Mahler and Cooke: Orchestra*).

The quiet and then the soaring climax of this music is made extremely vivid in Bernstein's reading. Boulez (using, as indicated, a different, less "official" edition) provides a deeply earnest, quiet, burning performance, well worth having, despite the criticism of total authenticity.

Symphony No. 10 (*Unfinished*) (Adagio and *Purgatorio*) (1909)

☐ Cleveland Orchestra / Szell (conductor) / Columbia M2-31313

The Adagio of Mahler's Symphony No. 10 is equally strong in its vertical arrangement as in its linear progress (*see above* for Bernstein's recording); the *Purgatorio* is typical Mahlerian grotesquerie with a dance turning within it.

Szell plays these two movements (which were edited by Ernst Krenek) beautifully, placing a glowingly rich quality on the Adagio and guiding a proper sneer to the *Purgatorio* movement. Originally this account was released on Epic 3568 (it was the first recording ever of any portion of the unfinished work), where it was coupled with William Walton's *Partita for Orchestra*. In its transfer to Columbia the partnership was dissolved and Walton was replaced by Mahler, in the form of his sixth symphony.

Vocal

Voice with Accompaniment

Lieder und Gesänge aus der Jugendzeit (Excerpts) (1880-1892)

☐ Fischer-Dieskau (baritone); Bernstein (piano) / Columbia KM–30492

Performances of numbers 4, 6, 10, 11, 12, 13, and 14 of the total fourteen are given here. Intelligent singing with fine vocal phrasing and splendid backing by Leonard Bernstein.

Additional songs from the set are available on another release (*see below*).

Lieder und Gesänge aus der Jugendzeit (Excerpts) (1880-1892)

☐ Reynolds (mezzo-soprano); Parsons (piano) / Oiseau-Lyre S–327

Pertinent values are presented by this release, since performance by a female voice can be chosen and heard in contrast to the performance by a male voice (*see above*). There is the further benefit that Anna Reynolds duplicates only three of the songs included in the Columbia album (numbers 6, 12, and 13). Her program therefore offers unduplicated numbers 1, 2, 3, 5, 7, and 9. It becomes obvious that if both discs are obtained, the only song lacking is number 8.

This represents good singing, if not great singing. The piano accompaniment reaches the same average.

Songs from Rückert (1902)

☐ Fischer-Dieskau (baritone); Bernstein (piano) / Columbia KM–30492

A heady team, combining the great baritone and the great Bernstein, who is as good at the keyboard as he is on the podium.

The entire set has also been produced magnificently with orchestra and Janet Baker as soloist (see under *Voice and Orchestra*). The value here is the different type of voice, the different type of accompaniment, and the different performance personality. All is as valid as Baker's version, though with a keyboard instrument there is, of course, less color, but Bernstein does command a wide spectrum in his playing. One song is not covered: *Liebst du um Schönheit*.

Voice and Orchestra

Das Lied von der Erde (1907-1910)

☐ Philharmonia Orchestra / Dickie (tenor); Fischer-Dieskau (baritone) / Kletzki (conductor) / Seraphim S–60260
☐ Berlin Philharmonic Orchestra / Ludwig (mezzo-soprano); Kollo (tenor) / von Karajan (conductor) / Deutsche Grammophon 2707082

One of the most profound explorations in musical literature. Very few performances measure up to its compelling emotive radiance. Among Mahler devotees, a large number retain as their number-one choice a recording still available in the monaural category, namely, Bruno Walter conducting the Vienna Philharmonic, with Kathleen Ferrier and Julius Patzak as the soloists (Richmond 23182). Its sonic stability must be considered, however.

For color and superb imagery the Kletzki version is undoubtedly a triumph. It has the alternative use of the male voice sanctioned by Mahler. The other recorded choice is Mahler approached from a different point of view. Von Karajan uses a tensile subtlety in conducting this Symphony (that's what Mahler called it). It produces a powerful dramatic confrontation. The singing of the soloists is rich.

Des Knaben Wunderhorn (1888)

☐ London Symphony Orchestra / Schwarzkopf (soprano); Fischer-Dieskau (baritone) / Szell (conductor) / Angel S-36547

A Mahler accomplishment that reveals refined controls and orchestral subtleties. There is effortless singing on the part of Schwarzkopf, save in one place where she fights the tempo and roughens her timbre. Fischer-Dieskau is at his best.

Kindertotenlieder (1901-1904)

☐ Concertgebouw Orchestra / Prey (baritone) / Haitink (conductor) / Philips 6500100
☐ Vienna Philharmonic Orchestra / Ferrier (contralto) / Walter (conductor) / Odyssey 32260016E (monaural)

These "introverted monologues of a solitary soul" are presented with a penetrating interpretation by Hermann Prey, joined with an amazing concept of the orchestral background by Bernard Haitink. Fischer-Dieskau (who has recorded the work on Deutsche Grammophon 138879) has a great voice and his conceptions are fine, but Prey has a special affinity for this cycle—an intensity of expression that doesn't overstress and yet penetrates emotively to the greatest extent.

The other version gives the most self-revelatory essence of Mahler's music. Kathleen Ferrier's ripe, vibrant vocal instrument is perfect for this song cycle, and she has as the conductor the masterful Bruno Walter, who is sensitive to every agogic point in Mahler's score. The sound of this monaural disc is good.

Songs from Rückert (1902)

☐ New Philharmonia Orchestra / Baker (mezzo-soprano) / Barbirolli (conductor) / Angel S-36796

Singing that communicates and brings out in these five songs the entire Mahler personality. A critic has indicated that "no Mahlerian should miss hearing this." He is absolutely correct—these songs are gorgeous and gorgeously portrayed. They are coupled with Elgar's *Sea Pictures*. On another release (Angel S-3760) they are issued with Mahler's Symphony No. 5.

(For another version, see under *Voice with Accompaniment*.)

Songs of a Wayfarer (1883-1885)

☐ Bavarian Radio Symphony Orchestra / Fischer-Dieskau (baritone) / Kubelik (conductor) / Deutsche Grammophon 2707056

No accusation of male chauvinism will be acknowledged in stating that this work needs a man's voice to relate the heartaching tear of Mahler's cycle. To emphasize the point, it is contended that not even a tenor voice will do justice to this set of four songs. Fischer-Dieskau it is, and marvelous he is, and so is Kubelik. They present a richness that matches Mahler's beauties.

Cantata and Oratorio

Das Klagende Lied (Complete Version) (1880-1899)

☐ London Symphony Orchestra and Chorus / Soederstroem and Lear (sopranos); Hoffman (mezzo-soprano); Haefliger and Burrows (tenors); Nienstedt (baritone) / Boulez (conductor) / Columbia M2-30061

A music critic has no right to attempt Freudian or any other type of psychological analysis, and may use analytical science only in terms of notes, bar lines, and other symbols on score paper. Therefore, there will be no probing here of why Mahler withdrew the original part 1 of his dramatic work (*see below*), which is included in this release. It certainly belongs to and fits with the other two sections. One thought, which is a question: since Mahler did not destroy the score, was the excision only to be a temporary one?

This initial Mahler work (written at the age of twenty) unbelievably typifies a mature Mahler in most respects, and so a conductor's interpretation must bear witness to a positive understanding of Mahler's style. Boulez's performance is dynamic and he shows himself a thoroughly knowledgeable Mahlerian. However, the solo female voices are not nearly as good as those that Haitink has for his production (*see below*).

Das Klagende Lied (Two-Part Version) (1880-1899)

☐ Concertgebouw Orchestra and Netherlands Radio Chorus / Harper (soprano); Proctor (contralto); Hollweg (tenor) / Haitink (conductor) / Philips 6500587

This represents parts 2 and 3 of the original, part 1 having been deleted (but, significantly, not destroyed) by Mahler. The original complete version has also been recorded (*see above*).

Haitink's reading is a free-wheeling one, heartily colored, and emphasizes sharp contrasts. Harper's singing is pure silver-gold, Proctor is excellent, and Hollweg is satisfactory. The chorus is tremendous and has a solidity of timbre that is wonderful to hear.

Mahler and Deryck Cooke   (1919-   )

Orchestra

Symphony No. 10

☐ New Philharmonia Orchestra / Morris (conductor) / Philips 6700067

Like the complex variances in the single movements of the Tenth Symphony (see under *Mahler: Orchestra*), the completion of the entire work by Deryck Cooke (aided by others—the complete story is included in the booklet with the recording) has been followed by various changes in his version. Actually, there have been three editions of the completed setting. The second of these has been recorded by Eugene Ormandy and the Philadelphia Orchestra (Columbia D3S-774). This Philips disc represents the third (and last?) setting.

On the strength of this disc one pays full respect to the conductor Wyn Morris for a splendid rendition and triple congratulations to Deryck Cooke for his reconstitution of a fine Mahler symphony.

Martin Mailman (1932-)

Autumn Landscape   *Orchestra*

☐ Eastman-Rochester Symphony / Hanson (conductor) / Eastman-Rochester Archives ERA–1003

Radiant, traditional romantic music, powered by a section of rich and juicy counterpoint. The spontaneity is what makes the piece tick.

George Malcolm (1917-)

Variations on a Theme by Mozart for Four Harpsichords   *Instrumental*

☐ Malcolm, Aveling, Parsons, and Preston (harpsichords) / London STS–15075   *Four Harpsichords*

An effective, lightly-strung piece by the famous harpsichordist. The theme is taken from a Mozart violin and viola duo. The all-star quartet does well, as expected.

Pierre van Maldere (1729-1768)

Symphony in B flat major, Op. 4, No. 3   *Orchestra*

☐ Solistes de Liège / Lemaire (conductor) / Musical Heritage Society MHS–793 CC–11

Maldere's Symphony, one of thirty-seven he produced, provides enough good music to state that it is as good as any of Haydn's middle-period symphonies. Scored for two oboes, two horns, and strings, it is a splendid contribution. With music of such finish and meaning it is time to reassess this Belgian composer's output.

M.H.S.'s issue illustrates the excellence of Lemaire's ensemble. There is a vocal ease provided in the slow movement; the enunciation of the material in the final Presto is heady music-making.

Ivo Malec 1925-)

Oral (1967)   *Opera and Dramatic Music*

☐ French Radio Philharmonic Orchestra / Rousseau (speaker) / Brück (conductor) / Musical Heritage Society MHS–1082

In *Oral* the voice becomes a new orchestral instrument, in its cubistic delivery of fractured fragments taken from André Breton's poem *Nadja*. (For that reason the omission of a printed text was a worthy decision. The text would be unrecognizable for the greater part, and without it the listener can concentrate on its surrealistic manipulation.) The instrumental part of this composition is similar, as Malec splits his basic x-rayed type of scoring of sound paroxysms and sonic regurgitations. *Oral* is dramatic and ambiguous by intention. Its startling sound surfaces will remind one of electronic music and of *musique concrète,* but the simulation is not intended. The music's effective sensitivity reflects the individuality of the composer and is in no sense a direct imitation.

Pierre Rousseau's delivery of his exceedingly difficult part headlines this relese. He is a superb combination of actor-musician. Brück and his musicians fulfill their roles beautifully, but it is Rousseau's performance that grips the ears.

Gian Francesco Malipiero   (1882-1973)

Orchestra

Fantasie di Ogni Giorno (1954)

☐ Louisville Orchestra / Whitney (conductor) / Louisville 545-11

Solitary formal titles are the exception in Malipiero's catalogue. Most often these are accompanied by a parenthetical, semipictorial explanation. Such combinations bypass detailed musical reportage and paradoxically hint at a story. Thus this work, a Louisville Orchestra commission, has no programmatic intent but is merely a set of thoughts rolled into one. One idea moves into the next—a series of inferences shuffled into a musical huddle, but yet not a pastiche. This is Malipiero's method of order in his ''Fantasies of Every Day.''

On a performance-judging scale from one to five, this rates a three.

Notturno di Canti e Balli (1957)

☐ Louisville Orchestra / Whitney (conductor) / Louisville S-664

The ''Nocturne of Songs and Dances'' follows Malipiero's precept of plastic continuity, architectonically formed, and directly stated by sectional composition. It poses a difficulty for a conductor to ensure that the independent sections do not seem separative and that they are led smoothly one into the next. Whitney does well by the opus. He also accomplishes a success with the textural problem, since Malipiero uses the instruments for their particular individuality and rarely binds them together for purposes of sheer mass.

Solo Instrument and Orchestra

Piano

Concerto No. 3 for Piano and Orchestra (1949)

☐ Louisville Orchestra / Owen (piano) / Whitney (conductor) / Louisville 604 (monaural)

This work, which is in one piece, is defined by differentiated degrees of tempo for its three linked sections. The solo piano is considered as a basic, chordal personality, and when it is given melodic lines these are in a form it can sustain successfully. Malipiero does not attempt to duplicate a fully singing string or wind instrument.

Throughout there is a neobaroque positiveness, with the sunny side up. Malipiero looks to the end result of a Concerto without showy capers, cadenza spotlighting, or virtuosic gimmicks. The Concerto is a celebration of composition without rigid system, producing music in a vocalized style.

Plaudits for Benjamin Owen. He plays with a richly resonant tone and is in full command within the style of Malipiero's work, always finding the proper proportions for the solo voice he represents. Whitney and his orchestra afford him excellent support.

Violin

Violin Concerto

☐ Prague Symphony Orchestra / Gertler (violin) / Smetáček (conductor) / Supraphon 1-10-1120

Malipiero's opus defines a modern spelling of concerto design, in lightly tart linear style, pandiatonic as to harmonic vocabulary, with a spontaneity of sonorous instrumental flow. The violin alternates in its role: it is a homophonic character and a contrapuntal resource.

There is not a single weakness in this performance, not even one that might be pardoned. The playing of soloist and orchestra is excellent, nicely colored, and stylistically on the button.

Rispetti e Strombotti for String Quartet (1920)

☐ Stuyvesant String Quartet / Nonesuch 71006E (monaural)

Chamber Music

Malipiero hardly ever considered predicated structural designs, but this did not consequently signify formlessness. His system amounted to a series of strophiclike conceptions, of total montage effect, but which are observed as if through a slow-motion lens, since each part of the whole is readily identified. Prose forms, which dot the titles of Malipiero's library of works, were often employed to effectuate the plan and to give fixed contour to the sectional technique. In this quartet the *Rispetti* (short poems of ancient folkloric character) are contrasted to *Strombotti* (rustic love songs).

The *Rispetti* consist of eight lines each, and are not of the poetic type taught in staid scholastic circles—the authors are unknown as behooves folk creation—while the *Strombotti* are best described as verbal ammunition for a man to woo a maid. Malipiero translates these very freely in his musical parallel.

It must be emphasized that *Rispetti e Strombotti* is a quartet in the field of absolute, not program music. The only items that style the quartet are the Tuscan forms with their peasant character, plus the verve and exhilaration of outdoor life, pointed up by the composition's individual sound, outlined by the earthy alfresco instrumentation with its jangle of open strings.

Until the last decade this work was one of the most widely played of twentieth-century quartets. Suddenly it disappeared from programs. There is no valid reason for this rejection. The recording situation parallels the present concert stage situation. There is no valid reason for that state of things either. Fortunately, the old Philharmonia recording was reissued by Nonesuch. It does not show any age whatsoever, and the Stuyvesant foursome (no longer in existence) do quite well with the score.

Ursula Mamlok   (1928-   )

Variations for Solo Flute (1961)

☐ Baron (flute) / Composers Recordings 212 (monaural)

Instrumental

Flute

The continuing tradition (that's what it is at this date) of twelve-tone music. The roots here are found in Schoenberg rather than Webern.

Baron sheds all the light necessary in his playing.

Alexander Manevich   (1908-   )

Concerto for Clarinet and Orchestra

☐ Leningrad Philharmonic Orchestra / Roginsky (clarinet) / Rabinovich (conductor) / Monitor 2030 (monaural)

Solo Instrument and Orchestra

Orientalistic folk melos colors Manevich's work, based on a single thematic idea.

Clarinet

There is nothing organically wrong with this middle-of-the-road Soviet conception. Nicely played, with a nicely negotiated cadenza included.

Francesco Manfredini (ca. 1680-1748)

Solo Instrument and Orchestra

Piano

Concerto in B flat major for Piano and Orchestra

☐ Mozarteum Orchestra of Salzburg / Blumental (piano) / Inoue (conductor) / Turnabout 34495

It would be abysmal nonsense to say this three-movement affair was a great work. But, it is an interesting one and deserves the fine recording it has received from Felicja Blumental. Especially cogent are the embellished operatic-like turns in the slow movement and the jaunty finale.

Two Trumpets

Concerto in D major for Two Trumpets and String Orchestra

☐ Württemberg Chamber Orchestra, Heilbronn / Schneidewind and Pasch (trumpets) / Faerber (conductor) / Turnabout 34057

Splendid affirmation of seventeenth-century style. The middle movement (as usual) is for strings alone and is buttressed on either side, with the duo soloists and strings presenting brilliant figurations and fanfare-like detail. A powerful performance. (The Concerto is also in a collection of ten record sides on Turnabout 34295/9.)

Robert Mann (1920-   )

Opera and Dramatic Music

Tales

☐ Lyric Trio / Bartók 928 (monaural)

Compositions for narrator with orchestra exist in fair number, but the use of a narrator in a chamber music formation is exceedingly rare. Mann (the first violinist of the Juilliard Quartet and the violinist of the Lyric Trio with Leonid Hambro, as pianist, and Lucy Rowan [Mann's wife] as narrator) has chosen two tales by Hans Christian Andersen—*The Emperor and the Nightingale* and *The Princess and the Pea*—and a pair by Rudyard Kipling: *How the Whale Got his Throat* and *How the Rhinoceros Got his Skin* for his contributions.

To Mann's credit, there is the smallest amount of Mickey-Mousing. What there is is extremely subtle. A free weave, of almost impressionistic tinction, surrounds or responds to the spoken material.

One should not be prejudiced because of the texts chosen. Mann's work is as good for grown-ups as it is for kiddies. However, it is best heard one or two stories at a time. Four in a row tend to bring decreasing interest.

Giacomo Manzoni (1932-   )

Chamber Music

Quadruplum

☐ American Brass Quintet / Desto 6474/7

Bits and pieces, placed together by informal communication, derived from aleatoric stipulations. Continuity is not desired; discontinuity is the internal force of the style of *Quadruplum*. Harmony and counterpoint are erased from this piece made up of timbres smashing against each other. Thereby one sonority crisis follows another; tensions are never resolved.

Marin Marais   *(1656-1728)*

Variations on *Les Folies d'Espagne*   *Instrumental*

☐ Wilson (flute) / Orion 7289   *Flute/Oboe*
☐ Holliger (oboe); Jaccottet (harpsichord); Cervera (viola da gamba) / Philips 6500618

The famous dance melody on which diverse modifications have been rung by Corelli, Scarlatti, C.P.E. Bach, and others, in later days by Liszt, and still later by Rachmaninoff. (Wilson terms his selection Variations, Holliger calls them Couplets.) Marais produced thirty-two variants, indicating that his set for viola da gamba could be played on other instruments with the performer "choosing whichever pieces best suit" his instrument (see under *Chamber Music*, [*Allemande l'Asmatique*]).

Two completely different versions are here represented: one for unaccompanied flute, the other for oboe backed with a two-instrument continuo. In the former case, Wilson presents twenty-five continuous variations; in the other edition, eighteen sections have been chosen.

The coloristic variety of Heinz Holliger's playing demands acceptance. Such superb artistry is what is known as perfection. At the same time, Wilson vividly exposes Marais's transfigurings in a performance that cannot be faulted either technically or artistically. No question—both versions should be in every record collector's library.

Allemande l'Asmatique   **Chamber**
                                                                                  Music
Couplets des Folies d'Espagne

La Sincope

Prélude in D minor

Suite No. 4 in A minor

Suite No. 5 in A major

Tombeau de M. de Sainte-Colombe

Tombeau pour M. de Lully

☐ Heinitz (viola da gamba); Hamilton (harpsichord) / Delos 25403

A healthy selection of music by a contemporary of Couperin. The suites are sizable affairs, No. 4 consisting of eight movements with two repeated in other positions, No. 5 comprising nine divisions, with the eighth part repeated to bring the total also to ten. *La Sincope* is a witty gavotte, and light spirits are again present in the *Allemande*. The *Couplets* (variations) are based on the famous 17th century melody *La Follia*, which Marais indicated could be played by any one of a number of instruments (see under *Instrumental: flute/oboe*).

These are all cultured performances. Moreover, the stylistic intelligence is outstanding even though the tone quality falters here and there. But that is a small penalty to pay for the musicianship displayed and the opportunity of hearing music written for this elegant six-string instrument.

Suite in G minor for Viola da Gamba and Harpsichord

☐ Sampson (viola da gamba); Shapiro (harpsichord) / Orion 74162

A ten-movement work. The writing throughout is clear and telling. Both performers exhibit a smooth and flowing technique.

Suite in B minor, *Pièces de Violas*, Book II

☐ Oberlin Baroque Ensemble / Vox SVBX–5142

A collection of eleven pieces, including an *Allemande,* a *Courante,* a *Gigue,* and pairs of *Sarabandes* and *Menuets.* The trio scoring uses a bass viol, with a second viol partnering the harpsichord continuo. The concluding piece, a *Tombeau pour Mons'r. de Lully* (*see* also *above,* p. 1119), portrays a moving expression of grief.

The playing is sensitive throughout, stylistically satisfying, and tonally lovely. (Mary Anne Ballard's notes, clear and literate, indicate that the B minor Suite includes thirteen pieces in all, with a second *Allemande* and another *Gigue* having been eliminated from the recorded performance.)

Suite in D major for Flute and Continuo

☐ Le Rondeau de Paris / Nonesuch 73014

A *Prélude,* then a *Bourrée paysanne* (played on the slow side), a *Petit rondeau* (played with tempi naturalness), and a *La Brillante* constitute this lovely suite. Robert Erich Wolf's description of the last is perfect: "cheerful whistle-down-the-street" music. A naturally shaped performance by this team of flute, cello, and harpsichord.

La Gamme en forme de petit opéra

☐ Oberlin Baroque Ensemble / Vox SVBX–5142

Marais's "The Notes of the Scale in the Form of a Small Opera" is a connected traversal through conjunct keys upward from C through B on to C, then reversing the direction. Each tonality is represented by one or more pieces, mostly defined by tempo. Of the little more than forty total, thirty-one are heard in this thirty-four minute presentation. The instrumentation is for flute, quinton (the baroque violin), bass viol, harpsichord, and a second bass viol in support of the continuo.

Any expectations that Marais's strict, prestructured, formal recipe would be a matter for oblivion are laid to rest by the performance manner, the attention to mood changes, the coherence of the ensemble, and their playing finesse, which maintain the attention throughout. Though thoroughly and properly styled, there is no deadly academic attitude in the Oberlin Ensemble's interpretation.

Alessandro Marcello (1669-1747)

Solo Instrument and Orchestra

Oboe

Concerto in C minor for Oboe and Orchestra

☐ Philadelphia Orchestra / de Lancie (oboe) / Ormandy (conductor) / Columbia MS–6977

A consummate rendition. The exquisite phrasing and extremely subtle *rubati* implants in the slow movement constitute great art—and great theatre at the same time. It goes without saying that John de Lancie's articulations in the outer, fast-paced movements parallel this high artistic competence.

(Columbia notes the composer as Benedetto Marcello, but correctly it is the *other* Marcello who should be credited.)

Benedetto Marcello   *(1686-1739)*

Sonata in B minor, Op. 2

☐ Rampal (flute); Gilbert (harpsichord) / Orion 73114

One of a series of twelve sonatas that Marcello composed for the recorder. The transfer to the fuller-toned modern flute only enhances the beauty of the opus. This is especially pertinent in the slow movement, a Largo that is shaped like a Saraband, in which Rampal's embellishments in the repeats of the sections are stylistically deft and becoming.

The performance is also available in Everest's seven-disc release (3194). No program notes are offered with that compendium, however. Further, the Marcello there is mislabeled. It is not the first work on the fourth disc (side H) of the set, but correctly the second one, beginning with band 4.

Sonata in D minor for Recorder and Organ

☐ Linde (recorder); Rapf (organ) / Klavier 545

Recorder and organ are not a commonly heard combination. But this performance is authentically realized, with the blockflöte's sweetly thin timbre used for the wind instrument part and the continuo covered by the organ. Linde's ability to toss off sprightly passages (parts 2 and 4) deserves special notice.

Sonata in G major for Flute and Organ

☐ Rampal (flute); Alain (organ) / Musical Heritage Society MHS–1277

Marvelous tone from Rampal, and sensitive intelligence in handling the organ part by Marie-Claire Alain, make this a very special recording. Not simply a reasoned approach to the matter of balancing the flute against the organ, but one that illustrates a perfect solution.

The Sonata was originally for flute or oboe and harpsichord. Giuseppe Martucci transcribed the keyboard part for piano, which in turn served for the organ realization heard here.

Sonata No. 2 in E minor for Cello and Continuo

☐ Dommisch (cello); Ruth Ristenpart (harpsichord) / Nonesuch 71119

A musically valid performance, with fine supple tone from the cellist and an excellently detailed continuo partnership that can be heard as an equal to the string instrument.

Louis Marchand   *(1669-1732)*

Dialogue sur les grands jeux

Récit et Plein jeu en Ré (No. 1)

Récit et Plein jeu en Ré (No. 2)

☐ Froidebise (organ) / Nonesuch 71020

Differences of tone quality on *les grands jeux* ("the grand organ") are the principal communications in Marchand's *Dialogue*. There are brilliant projections of lights and shades in Pierre Froidebise's playing of this fine work on the organ of the Church of Saint-Laurent d'Alkmaar.

Plein jeu has the same pertinence regarding tone color, and in both cases the organ is opened wide but with stylistic rationaltiy. In the *Récit* portions much more confined timbre weights mark these thematic statements, sensitively portrayed in the performance.

These works appear in a collection titled *French Organ Masterpieces of the 17th and 18th Centuries*. Marchand's name does not appear in *Schwann*, but on the basis of the evidence he deserves individual listing.

Maurice Maréchal / *Manuel de Falla*. See Falla / Maréchal.

Giovanni Battista Marella (18th cent.?)

Instrumental

Two Guitars

Suite in A major for Two Guitars

☐ Duo Company–Paolini / Turnabout 34341

Chastely tuneful, sometimes slightly Handelian, at other times slightly and lightly derived from Haydn. There are four movements in Marella's Suite, an Overture and Fugato, a slow-paced movement, and a *Minuetto*. Nice to listen to once in a while, especially because of the musicianly control of the Paolini twosome.

Biagio Marini (1597-1665)

Chamber Music

Romanesca for Trumpet and Continuo

Sonata in D minor for Trumpet, Bassoon, and Continuo

☐ Schwarz (trumpet); Sharrow (basson); Fuller (harpsichord) / Nonesuch 71274

Alternating slow-paced and polyphonic sections cover the Sonata, in which the virtuosic dexterity of Schwarz and Sharrow is displayed with uninhibited flair. The variations on *Romanesca* show less contrast, but this is due to Marini's flat-surfaced conception.

Frank Martin (1890-1974)

String Orchestra

Etudes for String Orchestra (1956)

☐ Strings of L'Orchestre de la Suisse Romande / Ansermet (conductor) / London STS-15270

A five-sectioned work, thus: an Overture followed by divisions concentrated on precise aspects—chained lines, plucked sound, sustained writing (scored for violas and cellos alone), and fugal play. The performance, sonics, and entire concept are splendid.

Concerto for Cello and Orchestra (1967)

☐ Louisville Orchestra / Kates (cello) / Mester (conductor) / Louisville 731

A vivid tonal expressionism pours out of this work. It is a learned music that grips the ears with its philosophy, derived from pantonalism and quasidodecaphonic chromaticism. There is no dissent; the two can join without stylistic irrationality. The music convinces with its dark and introverted brooding. The total experience gives testimony that Martin's Concerto is one of the most important of the century and deserves permanence in the repertoire.

The orchestration is open, of chamberized styling, and includes the special color (beautifully handled) of the saxophone. Its facts are disclosed beautifully. Mester deserves all the plaudits possible.

Kates presents a well-nigh perfect performance. It is dynamic, intensely communicative, beautifully toned, and delivered with rich, garneted tone. His phrasing is sensitive and meaningful. There is great artistry here by this musician—it should not be missed.

Ballade for Flute, String Orchestra, and Piano (1939)

☐ English Chamber Orchestra / Di Tullio (flute) / Howarth (conductor) / Crystal S–503

Martin first wrote his Ballade with piano backup in 1939; it was orchestrated two years later. Recordings of the earlier setting are available on Telefunken (641011) and on Monitor (S–2120).

The work has a fine sense of form and, indeed, a very subtle method of implanting climax by the opposite of instrumental force. The central section is for flute alone, and its monodic delivery is, in this case, more telling than a swollen sonority concerned with perorative action.

There is delectable playing by the soloist. Her tone is warm, full, and without even the slightest hint of vibrato. Add: admirable phrasing.

Concerto for Seven Wind Instruments, Timpani, Percussion, and String Orchestra (1949)

☐ Soloists and Strings of L'Orchestre de la Suisse Romande / Ansermet (conductor) / London STS–15270

A frictional tonal work, the harmonic grammar flavored and punctuated with the assorted solo timbres of flute, oboe, clarinet, bassoon, horn, trumpet, and trombone. The rhythmic element (showing a kinship with Honegger) is very marked and emphasizes the neoclassical contours of this refurbishment of concerto form. Especially expert is the thematic affinity for the instrument to which it is applied.

The recording is superb in every respect. It is welcome news that London has restored this once-deleted disc.

Concerto for Harpsichord and Small Orchestra (1951-1952)

☐ Chamber Orchestra of Lausanne / Jaccottet (harpsichord) / Martin (conductor) / Candide 31065

Given a chance, this composition might rival Martin's most popular (and quite often performed) piece, the *Petite Symphonie Concertante* for string orchestra, piano, harp, and harpsichord. (Unbelievably, as this is being written, the *Symphonie Concertante* is not listed in *Schwann!*) The textures are a joy, the orchestral colors (two flutes, oboe, clarinet, and bassoon; two horns, trumpet, and strings) transparent, the solo part one of brilliance, but always musically intrinsic. There is a Ravelian touch to some of the music—but that reminder does not negate a stylistic certitude typically identified with Frank Martin.

The performance is a handsome and authoritative one. Candide's sound deserves special mention.

Piano

Ballade for Piano and Orchestra (1939)

☐ Chamber Orchestra of Lausanne / Benda (piano) / Martin (conductor) / Candide 31065

Poetic suppleness describes Martin's Ballade, with sufficient rhythmic detail to emphasize one of the strong elements in this composer's style. There is fine feeling and expression in Benda's explication of the music.

Piano Concerto No. 2 (1969)

☐ Symphony Orchestra of Radio Luxembourg / Badura-Skoda (piano) / Martin (conductor) / Candide 31055

In comparison with Martin's Concerto for Violin and Orchestra (see under *violin*), this is the other side of the coin. Energy dominates the outer movements; a big elegiac construction contrasts. Reflected is orchestral color that has its own poetry and special timbre in the form of a saxophone. Within the devilish drive of the sounds there is a film of mystery that adds to the excitement.

This is not an easy work by any means. Badura-Skoda had asked Martin to write him a "big" Concerto. He got it. And he lives up to all the demands.

Trombone

Ballade for Trombone and Orchestra (1940)

☐ Chamber Orchestra of Lausanne / Rosin (trombone) / Martin (conductor) / Candide 31065

Melodic broadness framed with nice orchestration, far preferable to the alternative version with piano accompaniment. The writing fits the brass instrument most aptly. Though the piece does not have the hot colors and pointed rhythms that are found in most of Martin's output, the detail of the seven connected divisions is always interesting. The piece is well played here.

(The version for trombone and piano can be heard on Golden Crest 7011, performed by Davis Shuman with the pianist Leonid Hambro. The disc is monaural.)

Violin

Concerto for Violin and Orchestra (1952)

☐ Symphony Orchestra of Radio Luxembourg / Schneiderhan (violin) / Martin (conductor) / Candide 31055

Formally neat and classically clear. This is not music devoted to voracious virtuosity; it has plenty of dark lyricism. There is some bravura in the piece, but the idea of violinistic fireworks to define concerto display is far from Martin's objective. It is the long-lined statement, the continuity of melodic shapes that make this Concerto individual and of powerful meaning and beauty (compare Piano Concerto No. 2—see under *piano*).

The performance is thrilling because of the beauty of tone by Wolfgang Schneiderhan and his phrasing narrative. It is far superior to the Louisville Orchestra edition (with Paul Kling as soloist and Robert Whitney conducting) on Louisville S-636.

Instrumental

Quatre Pièces Brèves (1933)

Guitar

☐ Bream (guitar) / RCA LSC-2964

For some reason RCA has eliminated the lead title, *Guitare* for these "Four Small

Pieces.'' This is music of contemporary vintage designed with lace cuffs. Accordingly, neoclassical harmonic colors are used in Martin's *Prélude, Air, Plainte,* and *Comme une gigue* patterns.

Here again Bream proves his major status in the guitar field. The playing is beautifully styled.

Passacaille (1944)

Organ

☐ Krapp (organ) / Turnabout 34627

A favorite piece of the composer's. Its organ setting represents the original version. Martin later arranged the work for string orchestra (in 1952) and then made a third edition in 1962 for full orchestra.

Its powers are classically formalized, as though Bach were writing in the twentieth century. No anachronism. The contrapuntal grandeur (a polychromatic brilliance) of the piece and the structural cohesion match Bachian tenets moved up two hundred years. The powerful concluding section is gripping.

Sonata da chiesa for Flute and Organ (1941)

Chamber Music

☐ Rampal (flute); Alain (organ) / Musical Heritage Society MHS-1277

Tonality permitted freedom and combined in degree with the dodecaphonic ethos. The exuberant chromaticism is mainly dark-colored, a point emphasized in the recorded presentation.

Martin's work was written in 1938 for oboe and organ. He transcribed it in 1941 for flute and organ.

Golgotha (1948)

Cantata and Oratorio

☐ Symphony Orchestra and Chorus of the University of Lausanne / Staempfli (soprano); de Montmollin (alto); Tappy (tenor); Mollet (baritone); Huttenlocher (bass-baritone); Zanlonghi (piano); Luy (organ) / Faller (conductor) / Musical Heritage Society MHS-1337/1338

A weighty affair, with ten sections, divided equally between the oratorio's two major parts, covering close to a ninety-minute span. Each dramatic episode (taken from the Bible) is in most cases followed by a meditation (taken from Saint Augustine).

The ideal of purity that marks Martin's compositional style—even when dusted with dissonance it remains clear and direct—makes the choice of subject matter excellent. A fine balance exists between the musical waves of power and unadorned lyricism. The latter is not squarely phrased but set in a continuity made more compelling by the framework surrounding it.

The performance displays an intimate involvement with Martin's material. There is a fine sense of nuance and a strongly controlled rhythmic feeling.

Donald Martino

(1931-   )

A Set for Clarinet (1954)

Instrumental

☐ Webster (clarinet) / Composers Recordings SD-374

Clarinet

A convincing way of depicting statements for unaccompanied clarinet. Thus: fast music to show definition of registers, slow tempo for lyrical assignment. Contrastive disjunct voicing (especially in the final part) simulates a pair of instruments. The forms of Martino's Set of three pieces are clearly writ: ternary in parts 1 and 2 (complementing each other with reciprocal speeds—fast-slow-fast and slow-fast-slow) and binary in the last part.

The piece receives a top-flight performance on this disc. The soloist is the son of the well-known pianist Beveridge Webster.

(The first recording of this work is still available, in a monaural setting on Advance 4, where it is played by Phillip Rehfeldt. His performance is not as clean as Webster's, especially in the extreme register. The release is mentioned, however, because along with Martino's Set it includes a program entirely devoted to unaccompanied clarinet pieces, most of definite interest.)

Flute

Quodlibets for Flute (1954)

☐ Baron (flute) / Composers Recordings 212 (monaural)

Structured in three-part totality, with a *Studio* in *adagio* and then *allegretto* tempo, an Arietta, and a *Burla*. Pleasantly chromatic music and, aside from a few clearly heard breath intakes, pleasantly depicted by Baron.

Violin

Fantasy-Variations

☐ Kobialka (violin) / Advance S-6

Genuine contemporary music never guilty of false directions. Martino's piece is no humdrum of variational normalcy. It moves in its fantasy in rhapsodic ways. It is superbly performed.

Chamber Music

Cinque Frammenti (1962)

☐ Marx (oboe); Turetzky (contrabass) / Advance FGR-1 (monaural)

The language is Schoenbergian. But the extra touch (and difference) is that Martino's "Fragments" are sunnier and more enthusiastically depicted than music represented by general Viennese expressionism. The luminosity of this duo is kin to the atmosphere of Dallapiccola's twelve-tone music.

The playing is finely conceived, though one must be ready to accept a type of brash oboe sound.

Concerto for Wind Quintet (1964)

☐ Contemporary Chamber Ensemble, sponsored by Rutgers University / Weisberg (conductor) / Composers Recordings S-230

Martino's Concerto is in one movement, basically divided into five principal sections, each introduced by a solo or cadenza. The influence of Elliott Carter pervades the piece, in terms of its density, contrapuntalism, metrical modulation, and above all its uncompromising character.

The difficulties for the performers are immense. Having a conductor for the five instrumentalists is a great aid, and it is proved by this clearly outlined recording.

Notturno (1973)

☐ Speculum Musicae / Shulman (conductor) / Nonesuch 71300

Martino's *Notturno* honors twelve-tone style and honors it with magnificent long-lined content. (Further honor for Martino's *Notturno* was its choice for the 1974 Pulitzer Prize for Music.) No spasmodic fragments are here, though this does not mean the absence of sharp decisive contrasts within the sound fabric. It is a dark-tinged work. One might wish to accept the description by Michael Steinberg that the Martino work represents a "nocturnal theater of the soul." This writer finds in it a mood overcast by melancholy mixed with hallucinatory overtones. No matter what the depths and meanings of Martino's piece, it remains strong in the memory and is a memorable contribution.

The playing of the Speculum Musicae group (consisting of flute alternating with piccolo and alto flute, clarinet alternating with bass clarinet, violin alternating with viola, cello, piano, and percussion) is truly marvelous. This is not easy music and yet every note in the score is clearly detailed with finesse and utter smoothness. This is a performance of advanced contemporary music that is stimulating.

Seven Pious Pieces

Choral

☐ John Oliver Chorale / Oliver (conductor) / New World Records NW-210

Sacred music that is rarely heard in sacred surroundings and even less often chosen for inclusion in a church service. (Why not?) Martino's set of choruses has a structural exuberance obtained from the mosaic character pertinent to tonality freedom. They are clearly sung, especially in textural definition.

Jean Martinon

(1910-1976)

Concerto No. 2 for Violin and Orchestra, Op. 51

Solo Instrument and Orchestra

☐ Orchestra of the Bavarian Radio / Szeryng (violin) / Kubelik (conductor) / Deutsche Grammophon 2530033

Violin

Martinon studied with Roussel, and some of the hard-fisted harmonies in this fine Concerto reflect Roussel. They also include just a bit of Stravinskian spice. But the work is no pastiche; it has sufficient individuality not to be termed a work of bald eclecticism. It is fantastically well-directed for the violin, and such violinistic ambience rubs off in a spectacular performance.

The Concerto is dedicated to Szeryng, who gave the premiere in May of 1961.

Doménon, Op. 21

Chamber Music

☐ Soni Ventorum Wind Quintet / Crystal S-253

Richly voiced, beautifully chorded, especially for the upper instruments. Martinon's romantically timbred treatment is linked to French classicism. Further, the freer scope of the tonal contours represents an expansion of French classicism. It is sufficient to heighten interest without breaking faith with requisite formal identity.

The work receives fine styling by this supertalented group of players. They provide a full-scaled response to the score. It couldn't be bettered.

Three *Chansons*

Choral

☐ Grenoble University Choir / Giroud (conductor) / Musical Heritage Society MHS-1078

Fresh tonal expressions in five-part neotroubador style. Imaginatively subtle in the settings of texts by Fernand Marc. A splendid performance, particularly appropriate in regard to the wit of the final song, *On croyait entendre.*

Bohuslav Martinů   (1890-1959)

Orchestra

Estampes (1959)

☐ Louisville Orchestra / Whitney (conductor) / Louisville 596 (monaural)

Martinů's three-part work exemplifies the art of stylistic borrowing (from impressionism), but it is accomplished with such surety that the eclectic sonorous result wins acceptance. The playing is nicely controlled under Whitney's leadership.

Symphony No. 5 (1946)

☐ Louisville Orchestra / Whitney (conductor) / Louisville S-663

Dissonant conflicts, both softened and clarified by keen block scoring, mark Martinů's work. The rhythmic detail is asymmetric but unnervous, holding the material in a solid format. The finale shifts from a lamentlike mood to a dynamic antithesis. Whatever one thinks of Martinů, the healthy robustness of his writing shows creative common sense, and nowhere in his orchestration is there a gelatinous combination.

There is no doubt that this performance represents one of the very best that Robert Whitney achieved during his long tenure with the Louisville Orchestra. The playing is of conviction, the outlines of sharply-honed contact. Splendid.

Instrumental

Piano

Etudes and Polkas, Book III (Excerpts) (1945)

Etude in F

Etude in F

Polka in A

☐ Kubalek (piano) / Golden Crest 7050

Sure-fire vitality in the pair of studies, one based on arpeggio figures, the other on asymmetric rhythms. These are concentrated inspirations that rivet the attention; they are played with gusto by the Czech pianist. He empathizes as succinctly in regard to the dance piece, with its procession-like beginning.

Two Pianos

Fantasy for Two Pianos (1929)

Three Czech Dances for Two Pianos (1949)

☐ Katia and Marielle Labeque (pianos) / Musical Heritage Society MHS-1766

The Czech Dances are not to be confused with Martinů's suite for solo piano bearing the same title, written in 1926. These are steamy virtuosic pieces (played dynamically) that have little folk allegiance, save in terms of rhythmic scanning. Striking fancies, these.

The Fantasy is cold steel in comparison. It has toccata tensility, propulsive and frenetic action as though attached to a motor. The rhythmic action is juiced up by driving dissonances, mainly secundally formed. Great piece. Great performance. Great sound. Grab it.

Chamber Music

Duo for Violin and Cello (1927)

☐ Heifetz (violin); Piatigorsky (cello) / RCA LSC-2867

Everything in this musical twosome is paired: two instruments, two movements, two formal aspects. The method of part 1 is chromatic and linear, that of part 2 is more clarified and straightforward. The first (*Preludium*) evolves from a cross-relationship of two centers of harmonic flux; the second, a Rondo, is clearly defined by its harmonic-contrapuntal delivery.

Granted a bit of roughage in the second movement, the playing is in the whiz-bang category. This is the way it should be, since Martinů's Duo is chamber music, but with its intimate guard down. Good sound, including the bit between the movements when the ear is treated to Heifetz tuning his fiddle.

Sonata No. 1 for Flute and Piano (1945)

☐ Bryan and Keys Duo / Lyrichord 7185

Style falls into neat, contrasting casings in this display. Martinů does not spread his wings, but writes very competent and pleasant neo-romantic music. This does not mean a cancellation of pointed polyphonic detail, nor that contemporary touches are absent from the Sonata. Certainly, this is lucid, convincing music.

The work receives a secure performance by Lyrichord's team: Keith Bryan, flute, and Karen Keys, piano.

Sonatina for Clarinet and Piano (1956)

☐ Campbell (clarinet); York (piano) / Crystal S–333

Martinů's harmony is transparent, spaced for the air to come through. Chords in a pandiatonic cloth dress the ternary form of the opening movement and the fast-flowing, Czechish rhythmic patterns of the last part. The essentials of sonata form are cut to the bone; likewise in the slow portion, which is more a preliminary to the terminal movement than a section by itself. Martinů may be imitating a generally moderate contemporary style, but his formulations are sound, agreeable ones.

The piece is fetchingly played, and that includes warm and clear sounds with proper proportions observed. It's good to have this work back on the lists, filling the gap left by the long-deleted Oiseau-Lyre disc (50197), a monaural production played by de Peyer and Preedy.

Trio for Flute, Cello, and Piano (1944)

☐ Dingfelder (flute); Carrington (cello); Gordon (piano) / Composers Recordings SD–362

Music with a vivid Czech feeling, with its attention to melodies that are tuneful and of nostalgic remembrance. The finale, a happy-go-lucky, large, three-part, rondo-styled music, is prefaced with a solo flute introduction and contains a stylization of a waltz that glides syncopatively. The action of this triple meter against the duple meter of the *Allegretto scherzando* gives an appetizing contrast. The Adagio is one of pure song, only somewhat elaborated in its middle section. The opening movement is no less cheerful, dancelike, and relaxed. And that's the way the music is presented, which is all to the good.

Piano Quartet No. 1 (1942)

☐ Richards Piano Quartet / Oiseau-Lyre S–316

Those who contend Martinů is an incorrigible rhythmist make a valid point, but only when he commits the sin of overemphasis. When the pulse patterns are as spontaneous as in this work, technique becomes secondary to artistic effect. Strong and virile rhythm is characteristic of this composition and the man who conceived it.

In any chamber work that includes the piano, symphonicism is always a danger—but there is no mishap in this case.

Nonet (1959)

☐ Dwyer (flute); Gomberg (oboe); Cioffi (clarinet); Stagliano (horn); Walt (bassoon); Silverstein (violin); Fine (viola); Eskin (cello); Portnoi (double bass) / RCA LSC-6189

Martinů wrote two nonets and did not number them. The work under discussion should not be confused with the earlier nonet, completed in 1925, calling for almost the same combination of instruments—the difference being the use of a piano instead of the double bass.

Typical Martinů: the blocked rhythmic patterns, the textural churning, a sort of quiet automotive drive, and a melodic mood that avoids lushness. This mood is best displayed in the central, slow-paced movement. The whole is played with artistic conviction.

Choral

Chorus and Orchestra

Field Mass, for Male Chorus, Baritone, and Orchestra (1939)

☐ Soloists of the Czech Philharmonic Orchestra and Chorus of the Vít Nejedlý Army Ensemble / Srubář (baritone); Sýkora (piano); Kampelsheimer (organ) / Liška (conductor) / Everest 3329 (monaural)

A compound of secular and sacred moods, in neoecclesiastical and folksy style, including modal choralism and fancy brass fanfares. Composed in Paris at the start of World War II, and conceived as a testimonial to the composer's countrymen who volunteered for service in the French army, it partly lives up to its title by being militaristic in tone. (There are no strings in the small orchestra, which contains nine wind and brass instruments, piano and organ, plus plentiful percussion.) On the other hand, the design of the piece is much more a cantata than it is a mass.

The material matches the formal hybrid, with robust sounds flattened against somber ones. It is strung out, more melodic than generative, with continuums of nice, rich sonorities.

Everest's release is strictly mono—a transfer from the original Supraphon release (10387). The rendition is certainly satisfactory.

Salvatore Martirano   (1927-   )

Instrumental

Piano

Cocktail Music (1962)

☐ Burge (piano) / Advance 3 (monaural)

The concoction is described as having certain "external" influences (including Art Tatum and Domenico Scarlatti). In a way these filter through the music. A jazz fling spins in between the notes combined with a classical clarity projecting the material. The music is like a scherzo that splinters itself into raw edges, with hunks and chinks, chunks and hoists of sound.

Burge orchestrates this piece with beautiful excitement. He displays authority and convinces that Martirano's piece is a substantial addition to the literature.

Vocal

Chansons innocentes (1957)

☐ Nightbay (soprano); Marchand (piano) / Composers Recordings S-324

Martirano partially treats three E.E.Cummings texts (*in Just-, hist whist,* and *tumbling hair*) in simulation of their graphic arrangement on the printed page. Accordingly: severe registral separations for disparate word spacings and fast articulated pitches for words run together and to be read with fast continuity. The second song is a symbolistic scherzo; the first and last songs have exact textural balance. In the first the piano plays alone and then the voice is heard unaccompanied. In the third of the set the voice is unaccompanied at first, then the piano is solo. A tag end for both voice and piano completes the piece.

One of Martirano's best productions. Candace Nightbay is a most responsive vocalist, her range is big, her voice has quality, and her diction is super.

Mass

Cantata and Oratorio

☐ The Ineluctable Modality / London (conductor) / New World Records NW–210

Striking contrapuntal power is illustrated here—a spontaneously sounding documentation of the Mass. In Martirano's terms there is a grandeur within the mystical temper that is as telling as a Palestrinian opus. A sensitivity to the spacing of the voices is one of the prime beauties of Martirano's splendid work (listen especially to this in the *Agnus Dei*).

Pietro Mascagni   (1863-1945)

Cavalleria Rusticana

Opera and Dramatic Music

☐ Maggio Musicale Fiorentino Orchestra and Chorus / Tebaldi (soprano); Dani (mezzo-soprano); Corsi (alto); Bjoerling (tenor); Bastianni (baritone) / Erede (conductor) / London 12101

Mascagni's one-act tale of village passion rescued him from obscurity. This took place after *Cavalleria Rusticana* was awarded the first prize in a competition held in 1889 by the publisher Sonzogno. The premiere followed in Rome on May 17, 1890. It has retained its robust good health and will probably be in the same state a century hence.

"Cav" is one of the leading products of the Italian "verismo" school—the principal objective being stark realism with dramatic development cut to formulate this goal. Accordingly and fittingly, this recording is a heated compendium; decisive and exciting. The cast is choice, providing all the score's emotional lubrications and its luscious effects.

Daniel Gregory Mason   (1873-1953)

Chanticleer Overture (1928)

Orchestra

☐ Vienna Symphony Orchestra / Dixon (conductor) / Desto 6409E (monaural)

Mason's piece was inspired by passages from Thoreau's *Walden*. The stylistic inspiration stems from the German romantic school. The reportage of this source is harmonically neat, orchestrationally neutral. Dixon's portrayal follows the latter and it is a somewhat placid performance, probably due in part to the rather low-key engineering.

Prelude and Fugue for Piano and Orchestra, Op. 20

Solo Instrument and Orchestra

☐ Westphalian Symphony Orchestra, Recklinghausen / Boehm (piano) / Landau (conductor) / Turnabout 34665

A well-wrought creation in the school of classical-romantic scholarship. Cultivated music making by soloist and orchestra.

Piano

Instrumental	***The Whippoorwill*, Op. 9a**
Clarinet	☐ Reynolds (clarinet); Gilbert (piano) / Musical Heritage Society MHS–3143

A romantic charmer. Originally, the third of the four pieces in Mason's second book of *Country Pictures* for piano. Self-transcribed, it has greater effect in its second setting.

Chamber Music	**Sonata for Clarinet and Piano, Op. 14**
	☐ Reynolds (clarinet); Gilbert (piano) / Musical Heritage Society MHS–3143

Three movements in fashionably fat neo-Brahmsian style. Mason's Sonata has historical specialness—it was the first work selected for publication (in 1919) by the very important Society for the Publication of American Music. A wise choice, for the piece has retained its solid place in the literature for the clarinet.

Pastorale, Op. 8

☐ Wehlan (violin); Reynolds (clarinet); Gilbert (piano) / Musical Heritage Society MHS–3143

Romantic regulations of the instrumental lines (including a fugue) do not negate the traditional balances that are found in all of Mason's music. Nevertheless, a nice quota of richness is heard here, minus any excess.

String Quartet on Negro Themes, Op. 19

☐ Kohon Quartet / Vox SVBX–5301

Mason's most successful chamber music composition. Not only is the element of the Negro folk theme at the heart of the work, but its spiritual quality is caught when it becomes necessary to transfer to purely original thematics. Such shift shows no change in style, an all-imporant matter in the use of outside influences, as well as pure, personal ideas in a musical work. The composer's personality must necessarily be in terms of the borrowed material. Mason works with the spirit of his choice—capably, authoritatively.

Clarity, definition, and proper style mark the Kohon's performance. In addition to its availability in the three-record Vox Box (with works by Griffes, Foote, Chadwick, Hadley, Loeffler, and Benjamin Franklin [!]), indicated above, it can be obtained on a Turnabout release (34398) where it is companioned with compositions by Copland, Ives, and Ruggles.

William Mason (1829-1908)

Instrumental	***A Pastoral Novellette***
Piano	***Silver Spring*, Op. 6**
	☐ Davis (piano) / New World Records NW–257

A pair of examples of this Bostonian's music, exemplifying the refinement of his writing, even though of academic propriety.

Tiburtio Massaino (ca. 1550-ca. 1609)

Instrumental	***Canzona* for Eight Trombones and Continuo**
Eight Trombones	☐ London Brass Players / Rifkin (conductor) / Nonesuch 71145

Organically compact and organ-like in sound. It is played "straight," without what would be improper dynamic gradations.

Jules Massenet *(1842-1912)*

Ballet Music from *Le Cid*   *Orchestra*

☐ Israel Philharmonic Orchestra / Martinon (conductor) / London STS-15051

The sound of this edition is full and resonant and it is just what this music requires. No tricky fiddling with the work; it stands well and is performed with bright character, precise rhythms, and excellent pace.

Entr'acte to Act III of *Chérubin*

Entr'acte (*Sévillana*) to Act III of *Don César de Bazan*

Invocation (*Elégie*) from *Les Erinnyes* (1873)

Prelude to Act V and *Valse* from *Le Roi de Lahore*

☐ London Symphony Orchestra / Cummings (cello) / Bonynge (conductor) / London 6744

Save for the once-hackneyed (hardly heard these days) *Elégie* (with Cummings featured), which is part of the incidental music Massenet composed for Leconte de Lisle's ancient tragedy, background similarity binds the other pieces. All of them represent excerpts freed from operas covered with library dust. Good pieces they are and deserving of recorded time.

Le Dernier Sommeil de la vierge from *La Vierge* (1880)

☐ City of Birmingham Symphony Orchestra / Frémaux (conductor) / Klavier 522

The oratorio *La Vierge* was a flop and all that remains is this excerpted bit, "The Last Sleep of the Virgin." That bit deserves life. It has its expressive point even though not so expressively declared in this instance.

Overture to *Phèdre* (1900)

☐ Detroit Symphony Orchestra / Paray (conductor) / Mercury 75078

The only part that survives of Massenet's incidental music for Racine's tragedy and, at that, hangs by a hair. Paray's exhilarating performance may direct attention to a piece that deserves revival.

Scènes Alsaciennes (Orchestral Suite No. 7) (1881)

Scènes Pittoresques (Orchestral Suite No. 4) (1874)

☐ L'Orchestre de la Société des Concerts du Conservatoire de Paris / Cordier (cello); Boutard (clarinet) / Wolff (conductor) / London STS-15033

Only snobs would decry or deny the refreshing tunes and snug dance measures contained in the eight movements of these suites. And, adding fuel to the melodic material is the expressive orchestration. No better demonstration than to listen to the *Angélus* (third movement of the *Scènes Pittoresques*).

The latter was once an evergreen in the pops program field, but it is hardly heard these days. It is shameful to place these works on the shelf. A hearing of Wolff's warmly resonant readings will certainly be convincing.

Fantasy for Cello and Orchestra (1897)   *Solo Instrument and Orchestra*

☐ L'Orchestre de la Suisse Romande / Silberstein (cello) / Bonynge (conductor) / London 6750

The adjective "lyrical" should precede the title. Massenet's three-parts-in-one piece is   *Cello*

1133

so posed, avoids any overload of virtuosic pomposity. There is a small cadenza that links parts 1 and 2 but it too is simply vocalistic.

Massenet's piece is practically unknown. Having the recording is a positive addition to the cello literature.

Opera and Dramatic Music

Esclarmonde

☐ National Philharmonic Orchestra and John Alldis Choir / Sutherland (soprano); Tourangeau (mezzo-soprano); Aragall and Davies (tenors); Quilico (baritone); Grant and Lloyd (basses) / Bonynge (conductor) / London OSA-13118

Another operatic rescue by Richard Bonynge. Due to his efforts, *Esclarmonde* was revived in San Francisco (1974) and eventually reached the Met's stage two years later.

Massenet's Wagnerian mix (Verdi will also be recalled and even Berlioz) is used to convey a plot brewed from magic, religion, and sex. It features Joan Sutherland in the leading role (it's made to order for her), who gains good footholds into her ascents into the vocal stratosphere. There is this to indicate: her interpretation is more powerful than it is slitheringly sensuous—more of the latter would be better. Giacomo Aragall sings sweetly and sensibly and all the others in the cast provide sympathetic interpretations. A strong vote for Bonynge who knows how to put over an opera of this type. His respect for the score cannot be doubted and neither can his understanding of its semi-Wagnerian flavor. The recording itself is vividly rich.

La Navarraise

☐ London Symphony Orchestra and Ambrosian Opera Chorus / Popp (soprano); Vanzo and Sénéchal (tenors); Souzay and Sardinero (baritones); Meloni (bass-baritone) / de Almeida (conductor) / Columbia M-33506

Massenet's two-act *épisode lyrique* is not found in Met territory (why not?) but it has been honored by two recorded editions. This, presumably, is evidence of a commercial know-how lacking in opera house management.

The score conforms to the norms of operatic behavior, meaning distinguished melody, dramatic guts, and a good tragic story line. Lucia Popp as Anita, the heroine, is superb and brings a flaming intensity to her interpretation of the role. In comparison with Marilyn Horne on the competitive RCA release (ARL1-1114), Popp is certainly the victor, with a balanced range and a steadiness of projection that Horne fails to supply. The other members of the cast balance out.

By an odd situation both the orchestra and the chorus are the same for the two editions. This leaves only the conductors to consider and in that case Antonio de Almeida structures the work with more character and command than RCA's Henry Lewis. There is a recognized authority with de Almeida's view of the score that is lacking in Lewis's direction. Massenet's *La Navarraise* is an exciting addition to operatic recordings; don't overlook it.

Le Cid

☐ Opera Orchestra of New York and Byrne Camp Chorale / Bumbry and Bergquist (sopranos); Domingo and Ingram (tenors); Gardner and Adams (baritones); Plishka, Voketaitis, Hodges, and Lightfoot (basses) / Queler (conductor) / Columbia M3-34211

This can be typed as grand-styled grand opera. All of the makings are included (even though this is a cut version of the score): duels, battles, visions, invocations, prayers, et cetera, and color galore. There is a sense of stop-go procedure, doubtless because Columbia's release is based on the taping of a live performance and any applause has been edited out, thus sharply snipping some conclusions. The cast is star-checked, with Grace Bumbry, Placido Domingo, and Paul Plishka, all of whom respond splendidly—Domingo's singing is extremely heroically styled; Plishka's has fine nobility, and Bumbry's fine depth.

The orchestral playing cannot be faulted and the well-known ballet music is heard with exceptional flexibility.

Le Jongleur de Notre-Dame

☐ Monte Carlo Opera Orchestra and Chorus / Rossi (soprano); Cassini (mezzo-soprano); Vanzo and Raffalli (tenors); Frémeau and Carey (baritones); Bastin, Vento, and Doumène (basses) / Boutry (conductor) / Angel SBLX-3877

Massenet's three-act miracle play concerns a monk who has nothing substantial to offer in celebration of the Virgin so he simply sings and dances in front of her statue. He is repaid: the statue comes to life and blesses him. He dies of ecstasy, certain of a special place in heaven.

Save for the Angels, Massenet's Opera covers an all-male cast. The singers make a strong appeal for this little-known work which is given a totally substantial representation. Coincidentally, the Opera recorded by Monte Carlo forces had received its world premiere in Monte Carlo, on February 18, 1902.

Manon

☐ New Philharmonia Orchestra and Chorus / Sills (soprano); Gedda (tenor); Souzay (baritone) / Rudel (conductor) / ABC ATS-20007

This represents Beverly Sills's peak interpretation of Manon. She is brilliant and dazzling and in the lyrical portions she is as lovely as any soprano who has negotiated the role. Gedda is in fine voice. It is an informed production from beginning to end and represents peak operatic recording documentation.

There are two mono editions available. The one on Seraphim 6057 features Victoria de los Angeles. Pierre Monteux is the conductor and the elegant production is worth anyone's attention. The other one is a Richmond release RS-63023. The singing is not bad (Janine Micheau is Manon), but the work is heavily cut, and the recording has a narrator (speaking in French no less) to aid the listener as to what is going on. God!

Thaïs

☐ New Philharmonia Orchestra and John Alldis Choir / Sills, Connors, and Burrowes (sopranos); Murray and Kern (mezzo-sopranos); Gedda (tenor); Milnes and Ethridge (baritones); Van Allan (bass); Maazel (violin) / Maazel (conductor) / Angel SCLX-3832

There are three editions currently available for Massenet's exotic Opera. The great flaw in the RCA release (ARL3-0842) is Anna Moffo's singing of the Thaïs role. It is simply unbelievable that Rudel (who conducts with authority and actually brings more color to the work than the other conductors) permitted and approved her work. It is mannered to begin with, the voice is uncontrolled and in the few places where it is in place it has no freshness or warmth. The Westminster Gold version (8203) is somewhat excised and its sound favors the highs and is sometimes extremely shrill. Renée Doria is the Thaïs in that production and dramatically covers the role of the courtesan with assurance. Her voice, however, lacks roundness and quite often is tightly compressed.

These flaws do not appear in the Angel edition, though Beverly Sills is not the Sills she was in the early days. Her voice shows traces of fatigue. Still, she is far ahead of the competition and sings with stylistic conviction. Milnes as Athanaël (the monk who falls in love with Thaïs) is in substantial voice and his portrayal is both of depth and proper subtlety when required. Gedda (as Nicias) sings with elegance and is in full control. He is especially sensitive to the varying nuances that are contained within his role.

Lorin Maazel conducts with a straightforwardness that sometimes results in tempi being dragged. However, he compensates for this by bringing a fine cohesion and temper to the strategic dramatic places. He plays the famous "Meditation" that made this Opera famous in thousands of violin teachers' studios.

Thérèse

☐ New Philharmonia Orchestra and Linden Singers / Tourangeau (mezzo-soprano); Davies and Calley (tenors); Quilico, Taylor, and Opie (basses) / Bonynge (conductor) / London 1165

Two acts covering the familiar triangle aspect for its plot. Finale: wife sends lover away and marches to the guillotine with husband. But the score has a good amount of intensity even if it has no memorable themes.

Perhaps there is more that could meet the ear in this Opera but it doesn't seem possible. All the singing and playing are appealing, though some of the pacing seems to be loose. But it isn't cricket to be ungenerous, what with Richard Bonynge again rescuing a work from total oblivion.

Jean Matelart   (?-?)

Instrumental

Two Guitars

Ricercare Concertate

☐ Duo Company–Paolini / Turnabout 34341

A hybrid. Part 1 is the fourth lute Fantasy of Francesco Milanese (a sixteenth-century composer), set for one guitar. Part 2 for two guitars is a repeat of the melodic loan combined with Matelart's own polyphonic coin.

William Mathias   (1934-   )

Orchestra

Dance Overture, Op. 16
Invocation and Dance, Op. 17

☐ London Symphony Orchestra / Atherton (conductor) / Oiseau-Lyre S–346

Opposite in mood but the stylistic features join. Rich neoclassic language is used in the peppy Overture, which has exciting and informative scoring, and in the folksy-like contours of the Invocation and Dance.

The playing under David Atherton's baton is rich-toned, on target, and beautifully controlled.

**Solo
Instrument
and
Orchestra**

Harp

Harp Concerto, Op. 50

☐ London Symphony Orchestra / Ellis (harp) / Atherton (conductor) / Oiseau-Lyre S–346

A careful adjustment between the far-from-heavy-toned solo instrument and small orchestra does not nullify vigor and robustness in Mathias's Concerto. Dynamic scale is always a problem for a composer using the harp-orchestra medium, but here it is sufficiently wide to produce needed balance and plentiful color. At the same time there is a cosy comfort to the tonal syntax Mathias employs.

Splendid performance by Ossian Ellis and just as splendid support from David Atherton. No one can quibble about a single spot in this release.

Three Harp Improvisations

Instrumental

Harp

☐ Ellis (harp) / Oiseau-Lyre S–308

Early-period work by this Welsh composer. Mathias's fluent neoclassic language is related with sensitivity and nice tone.

Chorale

Organ

Invocations, Op. 35

Jubilate, Op. 67, No. 2

Partita, Op. 19

Postlude

Processional

Toccata Giocosa, Op. 36, No. 2

Variations on a Hymn Tune, Op. 20

☐ Herrick (organ) / Oiseau-Lyre S–342

A mix of types but no confusion of stylistic intention. This is a most impressive organ program ranging from the vim of the *Jubilate* to the tougher perspectives of the larger works such as the Partita and the Variations.

Nothing academic in a single measure. Mathias's music is hardly known in the United States but recordings of this type will change the record, one is sure. Everything is superbly played by Christopher Herrick using the organ of the Hereford Cathedral.

Ave Rex – A Carol Sequence, Op. 45

Choral

Chorus and Orchestra

☐ London Symphony Orchestra and Welsh National Opera Chorale / Atherton (conductor) / Oiseau-Lyre S–346

Strong reminders here of Benjamin Britten's Ceremony of Carols. However, there's always room for more carol delectations and Mathias's offering is most welcome. His delights totally avoid the pseudoproportions of both the educational (read: commercial) and pops markets.

Yori-Aki Matsudaira   (1931-   )

Rhymes for S. Gazzelloni for Flute and Percussion (1966)

Instrumental

Flute

☐ Gazzelloni (flute) / Wergo WER–60029

No rigidly architectonic direction to this piece, simply a delight of sounds that course through its fantasy. The flute has bent tones, glissandi, non-pitch (noise) sounds, wind-in-the-embouchure projections, key clicks, and the flutist not only makes some chocked vocal sounds but syllabicates and plays a sound simultaneously. It's a grand double feature though the percussion is disposed very lightly, save in one place where a siren and a fire bell enter.

Matsudaira's music represents a light touch—as avant-garde divertimento in one movement. It is written for Severino Gazzelloni and played to a fare-thee-well by this magnificent virtuoso. Who plays the percussion cannot be told—no credits.

Yoritsuné Matsudaira (1907-   )

Instrumental

Flute

Somaksah (1961)

☐ Gazzelloni (flute) / Mainstream 5014

Small pitch groups, set in a kind of dot-dash method. No flamboyance in this cantillative frame of reference. The music has individuality without being too remote in style.

As to be expected, Gazzelloni is in magnificent form in his performance. He does full justice to the special facts in Matsudaira's *Somaksah*.

Johann Mattheson (1681-1764)

Chamber Music

Sonata in A minor, Op. 1, No. 12

☐ Rampal (flute); Duschenes (recorder) / Orion 75199

Short and sweet is a cliché but it perfectly describes the four dance pieces that comprise Mattheson's opus. The *Capriccio, Air en Rondeau, Rigaudon,* and *Gigue* cover a four-and-one-half minute performance span. All of it is pleasant and savory and played in equal manner.

While the Rampal-Duschenes performance is also represented in Everest's jumbo collection of Rampaliana (number 3194) it is less preferable there than here on Orion. The latter has processed the tape at a higher and fuller level, giving the unaccompanied duo sound much more richness.

William Matthews (1950-   )

Orchestra

Letters from Home

☐ Ensemble of the Center for New Music, University of Iowa / Dixon (conductor) / Composers Recordings SD–375

Composites of improvisational-like sound portions that produce a free fantasy. There is an enthusiasm for sonorous contrasts that enliven this music for eleven players antiphonally arranged into four groups. The recording does not define this so acutely.

Electronic Music

Field Guide

☐ Composers Recordings SD–375

A quiet essay as electronic music goes. Matthews describes his work as "a bit like walking through a woods in which each species of flora is found only in its particular habitat, while interloping fauna are more free to put in surprising appearances here and there."

Roger Matton   *(1929-   )*

Concerto for Two Pianos and Orchestra (1964)

☐ Toronto Symphony / Morrisset and Bouchard (pianos) / Susskind (conductor) / Composers Recordings S–317

Motoric vitality is the principal ingredient of both the opening Allegro and the concluding Toccata. Given two pianos and orchestral power, nothing is lacking. This carries over to the slow movement where inner tightness is the passion of the music.

A stunning performance, this.

*Solo
Instrument
and
Orchestra*

Two Pianos

Ludwig Maurer   *(1789-1878)*

Lied

Scherzo

☐ Berlin Brass Quintet / Crystal S–201

Tempi are opposite here, with the *Lied* faster and even gayer than the light-hearted Scherzo.

Maurer is known amongst violinists who know the byways of the instrument's literature as the composer of a very interesting *Symphonie Concertante* for Four Violins and Orchestra. While the brass pieces don't have the depth of the multiple violin work, they clearly display the expert workmanship of this little-known composer.

Three Pieces

☐ Metropolitan Brass Quintet / Crystal S–208

Maurer lives in music history only for his very fine work, *Symphonie Concertante* for four solo violins and orchestra. (It's time for revival and recording!) The brass suite is strictly traditional with a touch or two of Schumann.

*Chamber
Music*

Paule Maurice   *(1910-1967)*

Tableaux de Provence

☐ Pittel (alto saxophone); Grierson (piano) / Crystal S–105

Semi-programmatic relevance. *Farandole des jeunes filles* is a light dance; *Chanson pour ma mie* is serenade-shaped; *La Bohemienne* is rhythmically gestured; a lament is pictured in *Des Alyscamps l'ame soupire* and hopscotching movement marks *Le Cabridan*. The last is described as a "great buzzing, flying creature, turning and bustling...." All comfortably described but minus buzz and with reduced bustle. However, all five pieces are very efficient tonal sketches that reflect good values without challenging the intellect.

Pittel's reputation as a master of the saxophone is deserving. The authority of his playing is not to be argued, but it is the control, coloristic differences, and quality of the tone he produces that are rarely duplicated by others in the international saxophone fraternity.

Instrumental

Saxophone

Lowndes Maury   *(1911 - 1975)*

*Chamber
Music*

Sonata in Memory of the Korean War Dead (1952)

☐ Sandler (violin); Maury (piano) / Crystal S-361

Maury's Sonata is a compound of loosened form within established tenets. In being related to the old, the new is not shining bright, but neither is it hackneyed. It totals a combination of recognizable elements and those that are not obsequious to pedantic strictures. The eclecticism is satisfying, never annoying. Especially compelling is the second movement, a "blues," but smoothed down and unsquared. The finale, an Elegy, tells the story of this opus—a music of deep emotional content that never departs from positive, musical sense.

Aside from first movement octaves that do not exactly reach that intervallic measurement, the performance can be considered worthy.

Nicholas Maw   *(1935-   )*

*Chamber
Music*

Chamber Music for Wind and Piano (1962)

☐ Music Group of London / Argo ZRG-536

Non-serial Schoenbergian syntax with lines that are a mix of astriction and distention cover Maw's work for oboe, clarinet, bassoon, horn, and piano. The forms are also combinative. These are quinquepartitioned: an Introduction and Sonata; a *Complaint* tied to a Scherzo and Trio; a *Phrase; Dialogue and Lied,* and a final set of Variations. This emphatic sense of interlock is maintained in specific timbre associations: these feature the oboe in the *Complaint,* the horn in the *Phrase;* highlight the clarinet and bassoon in the *Dialogue;* and pinpoint the bassoon in the *Lied.*

The Londoners play this quite serious divertimento assortment with fastidiousness and impeccable style.

Vocal

*Voice
and Orchestra*

Scenes and Arias (1962)

☐ BBC Symphony Orchestra / Manning (soprano); Howells (mezzo-soprano); Proctor (contralto) / Del Mar (conductor) / Argo ZRG-622

A virile and a powerfully colored work. Maw's text is an anonymous fourteenth-century two-part poem, "Lines from Love Letters," in the form of a letter from a man to his loved one: *De Amico Ad Amicam* and her reply: *Responcio.*

The orchestration is brilliant and large-scaled, the vocal parts long-lined and intense. Maw works on a big canvas and within that space uses panchromatic pigmentation. The richness and emotionalism produce an aural delight made more entrancing by the combination of three different vocal qualities. The recording is superbly produced.

Richard Maxfield   *(1927 - 1969)*

*Electronic
Music*

Night Music (1960)

☐ Odyssey 32160160

Night Music sounds like a direct, unedited recording of bird chirps and insect tones. It isn't whatsoever. It was conceived indoors basically "from the interaction of an oscilloscope and a tape recorder." Maxwell then realized that the electronic sounds "were identical in feeling to those made by birds and insects on summer nights." Be assured the first sentence was written after hearing the disc and before reading a word of the liner notes.

There are some diehards that claim electronic music can never be sensitive, let alone "beautiful." It is suggested they listen to Maxfield's Night Music, which is not only beautifully sensitive and sensitively beautiful, but a delight throughout its total nine minutes.

Peter Maxwell Davies *(1934-   )*

Points and Dances from *Taverner* (1972)   *Orchestra*

☐ Fires of London / Maxwell Davies (conductor) / Argo ZRG-712

These sixteen sections have specific place in Maxwell Davies's Opera but they can well stand alone. Various colors are combined, exceedingly contrastive, and include regal and positive organ. The ancient timbres are applied to contemporaneous glosses on the material—a neo-medievalism that strikes the ear with its specific individuality.

The playing is superb. One can take for granted this is a definitive performance.

Second Fantasia on John Taverner's *In Nomine* (1964)

☐ New Philharmonia Orchestra / Groves (conductor) / Argo ZRG-712

A postscripted realization of ideas from Maxwell Davies's Opera *Taverner*. This developed from the Opera's first act which the composer felt had "many ideas . . . capable of a more symphonic development than was possible within the confines of the dramatic context."

Thematic transformation set in linked continuity results. The polyphony is intense, the dramaticism similarly but never outwardly declarative. Maxwell Davies's' Fantasia is always internal, slow-motioned in its punch but nevertheless a music of impact. It requires careful listening and rehearing for there are no sweet-toothed, easy to digest paragraphs in this stunning symphonic document. The playing is completely convincing.

Saint Michael Sonata (1957)   *Wind and Brass Ensemble*

☐ Louisville Orchestra / Mester (conductor) / Louisville LS-756

The fundamental material of this work for seventeen wind instruments is derived from the chants of the Requiem Mass. But, no dedication to quotation, since atonic absorption makes identity vanish. Continuous small details form the structure, dogmatically nervous in action, colorfully violent at the same time.

Mester conducts a brilliant performance of this exceedingly difficult piece. His scrupulous sensibility to the individual sounds, his maintenance of tension are a notable achievement.

Sonata for Trumpet and Piano (1955)   *Chamber Music*

☐ Schwarz (trumpet); Oppens (piano) / Nonesuch 71275

Here there is none of the fury and theatricality that are to be heard in Maxwell Davies's later works. This early representation, however, offers special color in the sharp-pointed handling of the trumpet's timbre. The upper register is favored, and the music is restless and tense even in the central Lento movement that is balanced by the opening movement (*Allegro moderato*) and the closing one (*Allegro vivo*). There aren't many worthy sonatas for the trumpet in the available literature. The qualities of this work make for a fine contribution.

However, such contribution demands a virtuoso to negotiate the trumpet part. Gerard Schwarz, who is now concentrating his conductorial talents in place of a soloistic career, is exactly that kind of virtuoso. He plays with remarkable clarity, amazing projection of color, impeccable technique, and complete musical conviction. This is a stunning issue and he has fine support from Ursula Oppens.

Nonesuch's liner notes have always been excellent. Less so in this instance. This is the complete note on the work: "While not employing the various trumpet mutes, Peter Maxwell Davies' early Sonata forcefully demonstrates the advances in sheer playing technique in the last decades." As far as it goes, O.K., but background and data concerning the music itself?

Antechrist (1967)

☐ Pierrot Players / Maxwell Davies (conductor) / Mainstream 5001

Let it be said immediately—*Antechrist* is a small (six-minute) masterpiece. Utilizing five players, it takes a thirteenth-century motet *Deo Confitemini Domino,* tears it apart, and then reglues it with contemporary stitching and colors. No cloistered convocation takes place but a Janus-like situation, since the music looks back to its origins as it simultaneously looks at the present. The motet is therefore composed in a recomposed manner and the effect is bold, dynamic, lit by nonaccommodating scoring (piccolo, bass clarinet, violin, cello, and percussion, including pitched handbells, etc.), and singed with vertical-horizontal heat.

The performance of the Pierrot Players is totally definitive, the group having presented Maxwell Davies's piece innumerable times. It has both frenetic drive and controlled excitement as it proceeds artistically to tear up the sounds. This is brilliant recorded documentation of Maxwell Davies's masterpiece.

Vocal

Dark Angels for Soprano and Guitar

☐ DeGaetani (mezzo-soprano); Ghiglia (guitar) / Nonesuch 71342

The text for *Dark Angels* is a pair of poems, one dealing with the drowning of the last two children in the then almost deserted Orkney Islands, the other describing the desolation after the few inhabitants left, considering the tragedy as a sign that the area was doomed. A short interlude for guitar alone serves as a center piece between the two parts, set for voice and guitar.

The concentration on the mood of the work is intense and Maxwell Davies's control and domination of his material is masterly. Such meaningful fusion between prose and music is extremely rare. The tension to be felt in the score chillingly continues after the total seventeen minutes of music has been completed.

Perhaps there will be other singers that will match Jan DeGaetani's naturalness and distinguished realization. It is rather difficult to imagine. A similarly consummate, innate technique is exemplified in the playing of Oscar Ghiglia.

Vocal

Leopardi Fragments for Soprano, Contralto, and Chamber Orchestra (1961)

Voice and Orchestra

☐ Melos Ensemble / Thomas (soprano); Phillips (contralto) / Carewe (conductor) / Argo ZRG–758

Music of the post-Webern world, but reordered to be minus the pitch splintering that one has grown weary of hearing. It conveys an extremely sensitive poematicism that has the mixed colors of Webern and Boulez. There is none of the rhythmic agitation of the Frenchman here, but the music always *moves*. The five sections of the piece (one each for the soprano and contralto and three in duo format) frame the voices with an octet utilizing eleven different instrumental timbres. The style is dodecaphonic but far from systematized, showing again that this technique is as flexible in its flux and reflux as any other.

A superb conception, superbly represented in this recorded performance.

Eight Songs for a Mad King (1969)

Opera and Dramatic Music

☐ Fires of London / Eastman (voice) / Maxwell Davies (conductor) / Nonesuch 71285

This is Maxwell Davies's recasting of the madness of George III, made into a theatrical piece. It is based on the specific historical fact that George III had pet birds and attempted to teach them songs with the aid of a miniature mechanical organ. Maxwell Davies indicates that the songs "are to be understood as the King's monologue while listening to his birds perform."

In performance the instrumentalists sit in cages and the action is vivid. On a recording the hallucinatory aspects are concentrated in the vocal part which staggers the mind (and ears), requiring a technique that makes *Pierrot Lunaire* sound like a C major vocalise.

On stage this piece is violently effective. On a recording there is the visual loss, much more than in an operatic transfer to disc because the instrumentalists are themselves actors. (They have mechanical birdsong devices, operated by clockwork, and the percussionist has a collection of bird-call instruments.) Nonetheless, as a concert piece the score's raw power is unmistakable. So is the fantastic ability of the soloist, Julius Eastman.

Vesalii Icones (1969)

Ballet

☐ Fires of London / Maxwell Davies (conductor) / Nonesuch 71295

It is difficult to categorize *Vesalii Icones*. There are fourteen parts to the work, each based on illustrations contained in Andreas Vesalius's *De humani corporis fabrica*. These drawings, issued in 1543, are both bold and ugly (some are reproduced on Nonesuch's album cover) and Maxwell Davies has translated their individual content as being identified with one of the stations of the Cross. The music is scored for a principal cello (here played by Jennifer Ward Clarke), supported by flutes, basset clarinet, viola, percussion, piano, and autoharp, and to be presented with a solo dancer. Each of the dances is to be of abstract configuration, not, as the composer explains, "an attempt literally to act out the Vesalius drawing or the 'Station'" situation.

As is the multiformity of the producing forces and the translation of the pictorial representation, so likewise the musical detail. Triple combination occurs of plainsong, a sampling of popular music, and a blend of the previous two mixed with the composer's own. The effect is a continuum of linear criss-cross, reverberating styles, and surrealistic-like sound assortments. With a dancer to observe there would be much more clarity and identification. From only a recording the responses can only be limited. But there is this to say: whatever the responses they will be derived from exposure to extraordinary ideas of timbre combinations and timbre-zoned polyphony.

One can be assured of the authenticity of this performance directed by the composer. The Fires of London are a superb group of musicians and they prove it in this very individual and exceedingly difficult music.

William Mayer   *(1925-   )*

Orchestra

Overture for an American (1958)

☐ London Philharmonic Orchestra / Stanger (conductor) / Composers Recordings S–185

The American in the title is Theodore Roosevelt—a result of the commission Mayer received to compose a work for the Theodore Roosevelt Centennial in 1958. The piece shows that Mayer is fully aware of contemporary currents, but maintains an equilibrium that is quite refreshing.

The performance marks Russell Stanger's recording debut. It is excellent and the rhythmic suppleness is a matter of congratulation.

Two Pastels (1960)

☐ Minnesota Orchestra / Skrowaczewski (conductor) / Desto 7126

The stylistic security of this music is basically impressionistic but with the gloves off. Stated differently the music is warm but has poised alertness.

Mayer's score is given a brilliant and comprehensive statement by the Minnesotians.

String Orchestra

Andante for Strings (1955)

☐ Minnesota Orchestra / Skrowaczewski (conductor) / Desto 7126

A redo of an early string quartet movement. Threnodic thrust moves within the measures. The gestures are big—romanticism with contemporary resistance. It is a masterly expression derived from an emotional source and naturally communicated. The playing of the orchestra is masterly and meaningful.

Solo Instrument and Orchestra

Octagon for Piano and Orchestra

Piano

☐ Milwaukee Symphony Orchestra / Masselos (piano) / Schermerhorn (conductor) / Turnabout S–34564

Contemporary liberation of design is exemplified here. While Mayer does not break down the contrastive unity of the concerto conformation, the construction is duodimensional, so that both piano and orchestra share equally in virtuosic definition. It is like introducing different materials, such as glass, metal, and wood, into a single unit, thereby obtaining totally opposite expressive values.

Mayer's work has variational direction, with the sections (eight, of course) each displaying a different mood, experience, or rationale. Plastic continuity, however, marks these regardless of change.

Though the piece is undisturbed by egoistic solo pretensions, William Masselos's projection of his part is especially brilliant, dynamic, and marvelously conceived. Kenneth Schermerhorn's direction and control of the proceedings are first-class. In all a three-star release.

(A comparison has been made of two separate releases of this work. Both, musically, are the same. The only difference is that the later one has a different cover and some slight revisions in the liner notes. In the course of the last, the author's name—Joseph Braunstein—has been deleted.)

Instrumental

Appalachian Echoes

Harp

☐ Chertok (harp) / Orion ORS–75207

The reverberations described are general (Prelude) and more specific (*Wild Horses*). A French twist within this music, especially strong in the second piece which is alive and not wild. Ravel comes to mind most often in it.

Thoroughly tasteful rendition. Thoroughly annoying errability in the packaging. Mayer is ill-treated in the misspelling of his name on cover and label as "Meyer."

Piano Sonata (1960)

Piano

☐ Masselos (piano) / Composers Recordings 198E (monaural)

Most of Mayer's music is freely tonal. In the case the climate of the serial world is present. The format consists of three movements—actually the central part can be considered a duple movement as well—with rhapsodic ingredients, but not of the sort to destroy strength of design.

Masselos is to the manner born when it comes to contemporary music. His empathy is a talent rarely found in the pianistic world. In a performance such as this Masselos reproves his superstar status.

Concert Piece for Trumpet

Trumpet

☐ Robert Levy (trumpet); Amy Lou Levy (piano) / Golden Crest RE-7045

This is a second version of the work, the first calling for solo trumpet, string orchestra, and percussion. The diction is neoclassic, the trumpet personality beautifully communicated in the music. A good performance from both musicians.

Country Fair (1957)

Chamber Music

☐ Robert Nagel Brass Trio / Composers Recordings S-185

A healthy quibble, but a good one. This is a hunk of *Gebrauchsmusik* for a pair of trumpets and a trombone, and is one of the best of its type I've heard. The jocular rhythms of the piece are smart and intriguing.

Brass Quintet

☐ Iowa Brass Quintet / Composers Recordings SD-291

Most of the time Mayer's Quintet is pulsed with jiggery-pokery figures which have a nervousness that keeps a listener's attention tightly concentrated on the sounds. This totals authoritative contemporary brass writing, the constant motility and urgency only singly contrasted in the second part of the work, described in the liner notes as "an elegy."

The playing by the group to whom the work is dedicated is first-class. CRI's failure to include bands is annoying.

Essay for Brass and Winds (1954)

☐ New York Brass and Woodwind Ensemble / Composers Recordings S-185

In Mayer's general style: tonality slightly swabbed with colored acid. Neat sonorous impact from the double quintets utilized plus percussion in the second of the pair of movements.

Always, Always Forever Again

Vocal

☐ Renzi (soprano); Crowder or Garvey (piano) / Desto 6430

Voice with Accompaniment

See preliminary note under vocal compositions by John Edmunds. It covers the discussions of Mayer's recorded vocal works as well.

And, more. While it is obvious which two singers are concerned with "Barbara" (see below), *no proper individual identification is noted for any of the three vocalists relating to the performance of the six other songs on Desto's release.*

A song of life's endless renewal. Mayer indicates the interweave between flute (there is one on the recording, played by an anonymous individual) and voice "reflects, in part, this theme of eternal movement."

Renzi (apparently, since specified credits are absent from this disc) does beautifully with this sensitive song.

Barbara

☐ Renzi and Crader (sopranos); Crowder or Garvey (piano) / Desto 6430

A pithy vocal drama of a girl's morbid attachment for her sister that leads to tragedy. One of Mayer's most moving compositions and sensitively depicted by the performers.

Five Miniatures

For a Young Man

☐ Renzi (soprano); Crowder or Garvey (piano) / Desto 6430

The *Miniatures* are short, unheavy philosophical statements; the texts of the first pair by Mayer himself, the last three by Dorothy Parker. In Mayer's conceptions simplicity of expression rules—the attention of the listener will not wander. In the other song, the myth of Icarus is fundamental to the text's meaning.

Khartoum

☐ Langstaff (baritone); Crowder or Garvey (piano) / Desto 6430

Mayer's description of this song: "It expresses the longing for someone who has disappeared." Further: "The soft rise and fall of chords at the end . . . suggests . . . great reaches of distances—both in space and in the heart."

Paradox

That Purple Bird

☐ Renzi (soprano); Crowder or Garvey (piano) / Desto 6430

Tender poetic examples. *That Purple Bird* was the composer's "first serious song," written to his own text.

Voice and Instrumental Ensemble

Khartoum

Six Miniatures

Two News Items

☐ Ensemble / Rowe (soprano) / Weisberg (conductor) / Composers Recordings SD-291

There is novelty here, musically and textually. In the latter case six of the nine texts are by the composer. Nos. 1, 2, and 4 of the *Miniatures* are set to words by Elizabeth Aleinikoff, Alfred Noyes, and Dorothy Parker, respectively. Mayer is a fine prose creator; in each case the text possesses its own logic and vivid meaning. The music is always suitable, the novelty mentioned appearing in *Fireworks* (the third of the *Miniatures*) which consists of fracturing and fragmenting of words and sounds.

This interesting collection is most effectively presented. Catherine Rowe styles her singing in fine fashion and Arthur Weisberg conducts with discretion, obtaining neat colors from his unlisted group of musicians.

Brief Candle (1964)

Opera and Dramatic Music

☐ Princeton Chamber Orchestra / Renzi and Crader (sopranos); Langstaff (baritone) / Harsanyi (conductor) / Desto 6430

Six minutes of performance time equals a mini-opera. And, the idea is cute and pointed: the three most important phases in a female's existence—as a baby, getting married, and death. For each situation a one-liner is stated and thrown about ("Isn't she the cutest thing?" "I don't think I ever saw a lovelier bride!" and "Poor dear, doesn't she look natural?")

Live, of course, there is some mimed stage business but it isn't required to enjoy Mayer's jest. Acceptable performance given by first-rate vocalists.

(Johann) Simon Mayr   (1763-1845)

Concerto No. 1 in C major for Piano and Orchestra

Solo Instrument and Orchestra

Piano

☐ Hamburg Symphony / Littauer (piano) / Springer (conductor) / Turnabout 34526

A rarely performed work (perhaps that should read "never performed") but it should be. Many concerti that are imitations of the Mozart-Beethoven category are flat and expressionless, but not this one. Its *Andantino grazioso* is not merely a convenient contrast to the outer brightly tempoed movements, but has a warm tenderness in its melodic contours that is quite appealing, while the final Rondo sails along on a conjunct breeze.

The playing of Maria Littauer is fluent, has spontaneity, and is well-phrased. Springer's backing is musical. Both should be thanked for making Mayr's work available. It is a real find.

Walter Mays   (1941-   )

Six Invocations to the Svara Mandala

Percussion

☐ Wichita State University Percussion Orchestra / Combs (conductor) / Composers Recordings SD–344

The statistics are imposing: ten percussionists covering sixty-five instruments, with three other players used for celesta, piano, and electric bass guitar. Plenty of unusual timbres: chromatic toy piano, brake drums, tuned glasses, musical saw, etc.

The *Svara Mandala* is a rare type of harp used in Indian classical music. Each of the six *Invocations* are titled to show the feature of specific timbres, thus: *Brass and Steel, Bowed Bronze, Bowed Glass, Bowed Aluminum,* etc. "Bowed" in this reference is the use of double bass bows on the vibraphone, bass guitar, flexatone, etc. (It is the sound of the *Svara Mandala* that influenced Mays's use of bowed percussion.)

Of course Mays's piece is rich with snaps, rolls, resonances, sibilations, and stridencies, in never-ending array. It is a fine work and contains fascinating additions to percussion's vibrational vocabulary.

Toshirō Mayuzumi   (1929-   )

Orchestra   **Bacchanale**

☐ Tokyo Symphony Orchestra / Mori (conductor) / Angel S–36577

Not a dance, but an orgy of assorted sounds. Themes almost begin but die aborning; the primary emphasis is on rhythm and color. These formations collide and recoil and collide and recoil again and again.

The playing fits the kaleidoscopic coloration of the piece. Indeed, the performance speaks well for the inherent musical strength of the Tokyo musicians. Angel has supplied full-bodied sound.

Mandala Symphony (1960)

☐ NHK Symphony Orchestra / Iwaki (conductor) / Odyssey 32160152

Those that understand Buddhist philosophy can judge whether Mayuzumi has succeeded in expressing in sound the Buddhist view of an omnipotent universe. Those that do not can hear his abstract use of "only pure collections of sounds" in this two-movement work. Those that are technically able can consider the composition in the terms by which Nicolas Slonimsky describes the *Mandala* Symphony as "based on a series of 10 notes derived from two sets of overtones of sacred bells of Japanese temples, each forming a pentatonic scale, with the tonics of the two sets distanced by a minor ninth." Those who hear a relationship to the work of Varèse in Mayuzumi's composition will not have an incorrect opinion.

Nirvăna Symphonie (1958)

☐ NHK Symphony Orchestra and Mixed Chorus of Tokyo Choraliers and Nippon University Chorus Group / Takei, Harada, Srta, and Komatsu (voices) / Schüchter (conductor) / Mainstream 5012

Two precepts direct this large work. First, bell repercussions and reverberations. Second, imitation of the recitations of Buddhist priests. The major impetus of the second point is repetitively static, chant-like singing. The other detail throbs throughout Mayuzumi's piece and in fact the three parts are not each termed a movement but a *Campanology*. The titles of the first two are tintinnabulant themselves: *Sūramgaman* and *Mahāprajñāpāramitā*, the last is prosaically traditional, a Finale.

The Nippon Hoso Kyokai performers play well and the resonances ring with spine-tingling veridity.

Phonologie symphonique (1957)

☐ Tokyo Symphony Orchestra / Mori (conductor) / Angel S–36577

Serial technique applied to a fundamental rhythmic plan which is then translated into assorted sound combinations. The effect is almost a set of musical graffiti.

Samsara, Symphonic Poem (1962)

☐ Louisville Orchestra / Whitney (conductor) / Louisville S–666

Samsara, meaning the cycle of birth, death, and rebirth, is "the world itself with all the variety of creatures whose souls intermingle in the web of the past and future."

The sweet essences of the piece are the exoticisms that permeate the score. But, there are splices into these of different stylistic shape. Mayuzumi states that the philosophical idea of his work is "too complicated to express in all its subtleties." However, the horn exultations, the primitive rhythmic beatings, the xylophonic twirling amidst a pentatonic-dodecasemitonical mélange, plus solo percussion, timpani, and wind counterpoints are not overly subtle though they have esoteric entrancement. *Samsara,* therefore, without arguing Mayuzumi's thesis, is a colorful orchestral travelogue. As such it is enjoyable. Nothing else, really, is required to buttress enjoyment. Or, for that matter, understanding.

Concerto for Percussion

Band

☐ American Wind Symphony Orchestra / Boudreau (conductor) / Point Park College KP-101

Not actually soloistic, but percussion highlighted, with practically an equal amount of winds and brass data. A contrastive rationale of gentility and severity guides the music. There is a further relationship of Japanese-like ornamentation and rhythmic drive.

Boudreau's outfit supplies the requisite sensitivity and power for the elements involved.

Pieces for Prepared Piano and Strings

Solo Instrument and Orchestra

Piano

☐ Louisville Orchestra / Owen (piano) / Whitney (conductor) / Louisville S-636

Three-pieces-in-one for the John Cagian piano format whereby pieces of rubber and screws are placed within the strings, i.e., a "prepared piano," or better still an "orchestrated piano." Mayuzumi's music quivers, shudders, rustles, and shimmers. Exoticism is the goal, of course. As much a novelty for the ears as hot ice cream would be for the palette.

Owen's performance brings out every nuance and coloration, and fulfills the contrastive dynamic details. This type of music requires a special kind of virtuosity. Owens meets all of the demands.

W. Francis McBeth (1933-)

Four Frescoes for Five Brass

Chamber Music

☐ Annapolis Brass Quintet / Crystal S-206

Trumpetic bravado in the finale, a "crippled waltz" in the penultimate movement give an idea of McBeth's coloristic emphasis in his Suite. Clear and satisfying twentieth-century music but firmly related to traditional practice. A clear and satisfying performance as well.

Robert McBride (1911-)

March of the Be-Bops (1948)

Orchestra

☐ Polish National Radio Orchestra / Szostak (conductor) / Composers Recordings S-228

First performed as a radio novelty, McBride's little piece of musical marshmallow retains its taste. It represents his third example in the bebop style; the others: Bop Pizzicato and Bop Sophisticate.

Mexican Rhapsody (1934)

☐ Eastman-Rochester Symphony Orchestra / Hanson (conductor) / Eastman-Rochester Archives ERA–1012

All the required pops stuff applied to popular Mexican songs such as the Mexican Hat Dance, *Alla en el Rancho Grande,* and *La Cucaracha* and given a Broadway show and nightclubbish treatment, with flared muted trumpets, swishing maracas, and pingy woodblocks.

The recorded performance vividly captures the spirit of the whole affair.

Panorama of Mexico (1960)

☐ Polish National Radio Orchestra / Szostak (conductor) / Composers Recordings S–228

A light jangle in the light-music field, Simply organized: melodic curves contrasted to nationalistic recognizable rhythms. McBride has gone down the Mexican route in a number of other instances, especially the successful Mexican Rhapsody.

Workout for Small Orchestra (1936)

☐ New Symphony Orchestra of London / Camarata (conductor) / Composers Recordings 119 (monaural)

Workout runs its course in the well-informed, well-formed means of jazz. The three movements represent a transfer of a cocktail lounge idiom in terms of a concert chamber orchestra. A bullseye performance.

String Orchestra

Pumpkin Eater's Little Fugue (1952)

☐ New Symphony Orchestra of London / Camarata (conductor) / Composers Recordings 119 (monaural)

Cute and flippant. A short morsel that has less fugue and considerably more take-off on *I Love Coffee, I Love Tea* and *Peter, Peter, Pumpkin Eater.* Worth anyone's listening time if they're not intellectually uptight. Zippy performance. (The data on cover, liner copy, and label make one expect a work for orchestra. Not so—only strings.)

Solo Instrument and Orchestra

Violin

Concerto for Violin and Orchestra (1954)

☐ Vienna Symphony Orchestra / Wilk (violin) / Hendl (conductor) / Desto 6417E (monaural)

Originally titled "Variety Day," the adjective has a double meaning. Music-wise, it describes an assortment of slick lines with snap-finger rhythms, honey-tongued lush tunes, all tied onto jazz style, with blues, honky-tonk bass lines, and snappy fiddlin' virtuosity. Title-wise, the three movements use the inimitable show-biz headlines of the *Variety* mag: *Sock 10–G; Lush Pix Nix* (not "Wix" as the typo has it on Desto's liner copy); and *B.O. Hypo.*

For some, perhaps slightly dated. For others, just as snappily fresh as it was when written in 1954. The sound is not of the best but the solo playing is.

Ballet

Punch and the Judy (1941)

☐ Vienna Orchestra / Adler (conductor) / Composers Recordings 107 (monaural)

The third version (for full orchestra) of McBride's serious-jocose, blazingly professional dance score. The first setting (for Martha Graham) was for piano. It was then scored for ten instruments. The edition performed here is somewhat truncated but contains the ballet's six principal sections: *The Three Fates,* Overture, *Soliloquy of Judy, Pony Express, Pegasus,* and *Punch.*

McBride's work stands on its own without benefit of choreography. It is one of his strongest creations and is notably imaginative as will be recognized in Adler's finely sculptured presentation. Here is still another score that awaits rediscovery. It is considerably long overdue.

William McCauley (1917-   )

Five Miniatures for Flute and Strings (1958)

□ Aitken (flute) / McCauley (conductor) / Composers Recordings S–317

Solo Instrument and Orchestra

Flute

Atonal music but translated into neat lyrical statements. For no good reason CRI fails to indicate the *Miniatures* are coded: *Adventurous, Dolorous, Dextrous, Languorous,* and *Capricious.* All these moods are ably conveyed.

Nice flute playing and likewise acceptable representation by the pick-up string combine.

Staggering

□ Canadian Brass / Vanguard VSD–71253

Chamber Music

A sketch (the timing is one minute and a few seconds) using pitch layering and soft rebounds. Gorgeous brass sounds by this great quintet.

Joseph J. McGrath (1889-1968)

Six Brevities for Brass Quintet, Op. 81

□ New York Brass Quintet / Desto 6401

Chamber Music

Variational off-shoots of a choralish theme. Mainly staid and always tonal. Clear definition in the playing.

Jack H. McKenzie (1930-   )

Nonet

Three Dances

□ Kraus (conductor) / Golden Crest 4004 (monaural)

Percussion

The Nonet is in tripartite form, with a literal recapitulation of the first section. While ostinati patterns prevail in great number, the textural situation is not static. The Three Dances are linked together, proceeding from a Samba, to a Tango, onto a Bolero. Each dance pattern is clearly exposed. (The work calls for three players but no credits are noted on the disc, save Phil Kraus who ''presents'' the works. He is therefore indicated here as the conductor.)

Barton McLean   (1938-   )

Electronic Music

Spirals **(1973)**

☐ Composers Recordings S-335

A very mobile and inventive piece, without ever being overburdened with electronic clichés. McLean adapts melodic and rhythmic strategies in terms of electronic timbres; the shapes of the former are quite clearly recognized in the latter. This is not a hybrid since no instrumental transfer is utilized but a creative linkage that produces a strong style and results in fuller auralistic understanding.

Priscilla McLean   (1942-   )

Instrumental

Two Pianos

Interplanes **for Two Pianos**

☐ Hamilton and Douberteen (pianos) / Advance FGR-19S

McLean states that her work "is a collage of superimposed contrasts." It is a music of thick fabric. It is also highly colored by a forceful personal language.

Electronic Music

Dance of Dawn (1974)

☐ Composers Recordings S-335

McLean's essay is based on such lines as "thunderous sun roaring away the abyss/ riotous life-noises scream the air...." It contains a candor of utterance and a rhapsodic structural significance of detail.

The composer offers a detailed analysis of the technical layout of her piece which clarifies what procedures were involved. However, there is a much warmer intensity of expression in the music itself than would be expected if the notes are read prior to the listening process.

Colin McPhee   (1901-1964)

Orchestra

Nocturne (1958)

☐ Hessian Radio Symphony Orchestra / Van Vactor (conductor) / Composers Recordings S-219

McPhee's night piece is spiced by the influence of xylophone color and warmed by fluidal marimba sounds. These add to the general exotic content. Fair performance.

Symphony No. 2, *Pastoral* **(1957)**

☐ Louisville Orchestra / Whitney (conductor) / Louisville 592 (monaural)

Based largely on pentatonic scale forms and making considerable use of Balinese melodic material. This includes the middle Elegy movement.

However, no special exoticism exists but rather an expansive statement of lyrical musical poetry, which is heard in a fine rendition by the Louisville organization.

Solo Instrument and Orchestra

Piano

Concerto for Piano with Wind Octet Accompaniment (1928)

☐ Johannesen (piano) / Surinach (conductor) / Composers Recordings S-315

Pungent neoclassicism with "wrong" pitches stylistically in the right place. This is especially so in the steely-pronged, vertical arrangements of the Chorale. The Coda (an odd title for a movement almost as long as each of the preceding two) is a flourishing, motoristic toccata. It is a development and unification of the materials of movements 1 and 2. (A typo in CRI's liner note causes the nonsensical analytical statement that this structural procedure pertains to the opening movement of the three. Utterly impossible, of course!)

Surinach deftly leads the group consisting of piccolo, flute, oboe, clarinet, bassoon, horn, trumpet, and trombone, and Grant Johannesen performs with distinction. The CRI disc is a transfer of the deleted Columbia ML–5105, and is "electronically re-channelled for stereo."

Kirke Mechem (1925-   )

Make a Joyful Noise Unto the Lord (Psalm 100), Op. 2, No. 1

☐ Mormon Tabernacle Choir / Ottley (conductor) / Columbia M–34134

Choral

Chorus Alone

Contemporary harmonic inculcation but without any abnormal privileges. Mechem's present-day touches provide fringe benefits for his sacred music piece. In a medium suffering from a superfluity of academic, pedantic, and commercial products, its artistic professionalism is a welcome exception.

Nikolai Medtner (1880-1951)

Concerto No. 3 (Ballade), for Piano and Orchestra, Op. 60

☐ Orchestra of Radio Luxembourg / Ponti (piano) / Cao (conductor) / Candide 31092

Solo Instrument and Orchestra

Piano

A close-knit work, with three connected movements. Tonality is always present but manipulated in a forceful vertical and linear way that makes the textures not heavy but very active. And activity is the name of the game for the piano which practically is front and center from beginning to end. The orchestral coloration becomes emphasized by its secondary role.

Ponti's playing is always vivid and he provides the uninhibited vitality that Medtner's Concerto demands.

Fairy Tale, Op. 8, No. 1

Fairy Tale, Op. 20, No. 1

Fairy Tale, Campanella, Op. 20, No. 2

Four Pieces, Op. 4

Sonata-Ballade in F sharp major, Op. 27

☐ Pleshakov (piano) / Orion 7019

Instrumental

Piano

Medtner's catalogue is stuffed with groups of "Fairy Tales." There are eleven such sets, ranging from a single example to six in an opus—thirty-three pieces in all. (He even composed a Fairy-Tale Sonata.) The selection Pleshakov plays is representative of their romantic, somewhat Rachmaninoffian style. (Orion indicates that four of the "Tales" are included, and in his notes Nicolas Slonimsky speaks of the pair in Opus 8 but only the first one is on the disc.)

The Opus 4 set is of the same cut. Number 3 is titled *The Gnome's Lament* in this release, whereas *Grove's Dictionary of Music and Musicians* lists it as *Moment Musical*.

Pleshakov's performances of these pieces, as well as the rhapsodically turned Sonata-Ballade, are of undeviating honesty. Certainly, there is more in the music than one hears in the latter work's performance, but meanwhile we must be grateful for what we have on disc.

Mood Picture, Op. 1, No. 3

☐ Tarnowsky (piano) / Genesis 1004

The last of a set composed in 1902. A bit lighter in character than most of Medtner's music, but just as romantically stated.

Sonata in G minor, Op. 22
Sonata Tragica, Op. 39

☐ Ponti (piano) / Candide 31092

There is a passionate insistence on dramatic enthusiasms in these works. No bombast but intensity works at full pressure most of the time. If some Rachmaninoff peeps through, so does some Scriabin.

Ponti's conception is accurate in terms of notes, rhythms, and signs. It is rather lax in contrastive coloring.

Three Fantastic Improvisations, Op. 2

☐ Pleshakov (piano) / Orion 7019

Romantic generalized picture painting consisting of a *Mermaid, Reminiscences of a Ball,* and a *Scherzo Infernale.* The personality of each of these pieces is nicely defined by Pleshakov. He is also especially successful in conveying the dreamy quality that swings in and out of the second of the set.

(According to *Grove's Dictionary of Music and Musicians,* the title of the initial piece is *Nixie.*)

Violin

Nocturne in D minor, Op. 16, No. 1

☐ Oistrakh (violin); Yampolsky (piano) / Monitor 2003 (monaural)

The first of a set of three, all in minor keys. Romantic decor, romantic exactitude, played with romantic *brio.*

Vocal

Voice With Accompaniment

Dawn, Op. 24, No. 7	*The Rose,* Op. 29, No. 6
Day and Night, Op. 24, No. 1	*Signs,* Op. 52, No. 4
The Echo, Op. 32, No. 1	*Sleeplessness,* Op. 37, No. 1
Elegy, Op. 28, No. 5	*Spanish Romance,* Op. 52, No. 5
Elegy, Op. 45, No. 1	*Twilight,* Op. 24, No. 4
Heavy, Empty and Bleak, Op. 28, No. 4	*Verses Written During Insomnia,* Op. 29, No. 3
Midday, Op. 61, No. 6	*Waves and Thoughts,* Op. 24, No. 3
The Muse, Op. 29, No. 1	

☐ Del Grande (baritone); Pleshakov (piano) / Orion 7157

Fifteen of the more than one hundred songs Medtner produced. The program embraces selections from eight different sets of songs. Though most of the songs are within the darker side of the spectrum, the general feeling of each poem is conveyed, minus any word painting in sound. Important piano parts (played with characteristic insight by Vladimir Pleshakov). Peter Del Grande is adequate; his interpretative range restricted.

Étienne-Nicolas Méhul   (1763-1817)

Overture to *Les Deux Aveugles de Tolède*   Orchestra

☐ Jean-François Paillard Orchestra / Couraud (conductor) / Musical Heritage Society MHS-794

"The Two Blind Men from Toledo" is as fine an Overture as the standards by Auber, Suppé, Rossini, et cetera. Splendid truth in this performance.

Sonata in A major, Op. 1, No. 3   *Instrumental*

☐ Kramer (piano) / Orion 7261   *Piano*

No heavy bulk in this work that covers a flowing opening movement, a *Menuetto* with the usual trio, and a bright Rondo to finish matters. A fairly efficient account by the soloist.

Ouverture Burlesque   *Piano, Violin, and Percussion*

☐ Lewenthal (piano); Ross (violin); McNab (toy trumpet) / Lewenthal (conductor) / Angel S-36080

Musical fun, the monkeyshines due to the use of three mirlitons, which are kin to kazoos and sound just as wavery in terms of pitch control. Add the noisy, purposeful discordant conclusion with everyone involved (including drum, ratchet, and whistle) and Méhul's objective is fully realized. (The additional instruments in the score are piano, violin, triangle, and toy trumpet.)

Joyce Mekeel   (1931-   )

Planh (1975)   *Instrumental*

☐ Cirillo (violin) / Delos 25405   *Violin*

Mekeel's work for solo violin (the Provençal title means plaint or lament) has a five-part formation, clearly recognizable though the sections are joined. Development of material proceeds from the initial statement. An improvisational quality hangs over the music brought about by the use of repetitive patterns. Though impressively formed and well-conceived for the violin the monochrome color of the medium is not aided by the work's length.

Nancy Cirillo does well with the music's phrases, less so with its dynamic contrasts.

Corridors of Dream (1972)   *Vocal*

☐ Boston Musica Viva / Curtis (mezzo-soprano); Pittman (percussion and recitation) / Pittman (conductor) / Delos 25405

Voice and Instrumental Ensemble

There is extraordinary dramaticism in this work, obtained by a minimum of means but used in such a way as to draw off the greatest amount of color and contrast. While the instrumental group consists only of alto flute, clarinet, viola, cello, and harp, it is augmented by percussion and recitation supplied by the conductor. Not all of the texts (by Kandinsky,

Hein, Schnurre, Stramm, and Enzensberger) are sung by the vocalist—the flutist also sings words, through the instrument (a telling effect). Further, to broaden the spectrum, the text is juxtaposed (three lines by Kandinsky, for example, are followed by ten lines by Hein, then a return to Kandinsky, and so forth) and, for further qualities within the score, both German and English are used.

The counteractions continue in the use of various vocal methods: straight song, recitation, and *Sprechstimme*. It is this coloristic fantasy on all levels that produces a chilling emotional musical document, superbly conceived and as superbly realized in the performance by Jan Curtis as the solo vocalist, Richard Pittman as the conductor, percussionist, and reciter, and the five instrumentalists.

John Melby   (1941-   )

Chamber Music

91 Plus 5 for Brass Quintet and Computer (1971)

☐ Contemporary Brass Quintet / Pawlowski (conductor) / Composers Recordings S–310

The title is explained thus: *plus 5* represents the brass group, *91* from the fact that the electronic tape was realized on an IBM 360/91 digital computer. The latter is not utilized as a compositional aid or short cut, but is programmed to achieve performance of material almost impossible with live players ("such as accurate rendering of passages in simultaneous different tempi") plus making available certain timbral possibilities. In Melby's hands the results are interesting if not exceptional.

Vocal

Two Stevens Songs for Soprano and Computer-Synthesized Tape (1975)

☐ Bryn-Julson (soprano) / Composers Recordings SD–364

Chamber-music definition applied to the tape part, with a romantically warm and outgoing vocal line that does not deny the time of its creation. Indeed, a thoroughly intelligent and artistic solution of the problems of composing for voice with an electronic partner.

Phyllis Bryn-Julson dazzles with her execution. Melby's vocal writing is not of the yanking-the-intervals-out-of-their-sockets type but he demands a huge range. Not only is the performance dazzling, but beautifully dramatic, keyed by a voice of full body.

Jacques de Menasce   (1905-1960)

Instrumental

Piano

Instantanés (1959)

Sonatina No. 2 (1942)

☐ Bloch (piano) / Composers Recordings 154 (monaural)

The "Snapshots" are a set of six *Enfantines* which were composed for the children of some of the composer's friends. They are a delight. Despite the mixture of ideas the music stays within the basic neoclassic diction of the composer.

The Sonatina No. 2 has a grotesque air in part 1, a Scherzo contrasted to a waltz section in movement 2, a slow movement, and a vivacious conclusion. All provide a well-balanced vitality.

Excellent and sensitive playing throughout. (CRI incorrectly spells the performer's name as "Block" on the cover.)

Sonata for Viola and Piano (1955)

☐ Fuchs (viola); Balsam (piano) / Composers Recordings 154 (monaural)

A one-movement conception, divided into five sections. One is reminded of Roussel, especially in the directness and drive of the piece, with the material heightened by the artful use of tension, plus the foil of tight counterpoint. Instrumentally, de Menasce retains a neutral and sober viewpoint—there are no special exploitations of the sonorous means.

First Sonata for Violin and Piano (1940)

☐ Fuchs (violin); Balsam (piano) / Composers Recordings 154 (monaural)

Though without a dominant individuality, the tastefulness of de Menasce's music is immediately recognizable. His choice of forms can be traced easily to formal classical proportions, but the remolding is neat and the quality extremely elegant. Harmonically, the dissonances are arranged in the milder conventions of the present century. De Menasce could spin a noble line of length, as illustrated in the Aria of this work.

Fanny Mendelssohn *(1805-1847)*

Trio in D minor for Violin, Cello, and Piano, Op. 11 (Posth.)

☐ Martin (violin); Bloemendal (cello); Taussig (piano) / Crystal S-642

As far as can be ascertained this is the only domestic recording of music by Mendelssohn's sister. It is extremely viable chamber music, full of romantic *esprit,* and has a strength that does not falter throughout its four movements. These include a fine Lied and a very colorfully scored Finale.

It is a welcome addition to the recorded catalogue, especially in this performance of lively intelligence and thorough musicianship.

Felix Mendelssohn *(1809-1847)*

The Hebrides (*Fingal's Cave*) Overture, Op. 26

☐ London Symphony Orchestra / Maag (conductor) / London STS-15091

Sensitively colored, not overcome with overemphasized dynamic punctuations. The contrasts are subtle and thereby much more effective. Smoothness that provides the required brilliance and delicacy. A superb Mendelssohn performance.

A Midsummer Night's Dream – Suite from the Incidental Music, Op. 61

☐ Cleveland Orchestra / Szell (conductor) / Columbia MS-7002

Various suite compilations are offered from Mendelssohn's magical music. The largest is presented by Szell and it forms a perfect design, beginning with the Overture, and then, in sequence, are the Scherzo, Nocturne, Intermezzo, and Wedding March. And perfect playing also.

Overture *Calm Sea and Prosperous Voyage,* Op. 27

☐ Vienna Philharmonic Orchestra / Münchinger (conductor) / London STS–15076

A rewarding, tone-worthy execution. "Meeresstille und Glückliche Fahrt," a most responsive, but infrequently performed Overture, is accorded fine conductorial rudder-ship.

Overture *The Fair Melusina,* Op. 32

☐ Royal Philharmonic Orchestra / Beecham (conductor) / Quintessence PMS–7004

Mendelssohn's concert Overture is played in a dazzlingly clear way, with good thrust and with incisive lyricism where required. The two faults of many Mendelssohn performances are oversentimentality and playing to the balcony. Neither is represented here. Beecham produces a sonorous transfer of complete fidelity.

Overture to *A Midsummer Night's Dream,* Op. 21

☐ London Symphony Orchestra / Frühbeck de Burgos (conductor) / London STS–15246

Of course, all the suite combinations chosen from Mendelssohn's *Midsummer Night's Dream* music include the Overture, and one can obtain that gem in that manner (*see above*). It is also, naturally, in the complete incidental music package (*see below*). However, if one wishes the Overture alone then this choice is as fine as one would desire.

Overture to *Ruy Blas,* Op. 95

☐ New Philharmonia Orchestra / Sawallisch (conductor) / Philips 802858

Warm brass playing, sweep in the strings that gives meticulous definition, and unerring tempi. There is fine excitement and tone to the entire production.

Symphony No. 1 in C minor, Op. 11

☐ Leipzig Gewandhaus Orchestra / Masur (conductor) / Vanguard VCS–10133/6

The particular identity, the full musicality of this work makes one fail to agree with its status as a nonevent on concert programs. Granting passages that seem to offer only filler utilities there is a majority of fine creativity that demands acceptance and a place in the repertory. The sextuple-metered Menuetto, the fine fugue that sits in the *Allegro con fuoco* finale, the symphonic appropriateness of the first movement are some examples.

The discourse here is superb. There is no interpretative analogy. Masur measures Mendelssohnian style and content perfectly and the music glows under his direction. Super it is.

Symphony No. 2 (*Lobgesang*) in B flat major, Op. 52

☐ Leipzig Gewandhaus Orchestra and Leipzig Radio Chorus / Casapietra and Stolte (sopranos); Schreier (tenor) / Masur (conductor) / Vanguard VCS–10133/6

Critical confidence with conviction has not fully been applied to Mendelssohn's "Hymn of Praise," simply because its structure doesn't fit the chapters and verses of formality. The *Lobgesang* is not just a Symphony with a choral finale (a plan which is not severely uncommon). It begins with a three-part Symphony and then moves into a sacred cantata that is double the size of the purely instrumental division. Thus, Mendelssohn's heading that his opus was "A Symphony-Cantata to Words from the Holy Scriptures." Simply by proportional measurement the imposing symphonic section becomes compressed into a prelude to a major work for solo and massed voices. However, there are relationships and links to the cantata in the purely instrumental section that unify the entire opus. So much for the accusation of formal dichotomy.

The playing is beautifully focused and in the first part to such extent that the music could (with a proper conclusion) stand on its own as a symphonic piece. The singing has the full ring of truth. One can only extend high praise to this recorded "Hymn of Praise." Vocally, it is knitted better than Sawallisch's edition on Philips 802856/7, though both conductors are equally expert in the purely instrumental part of the Symphony.

Symphony No. 3 (*Scotch*) in A minor, Op. 56

☐ London Symphony Orchestra / Maag (conductor) / London STS-15091
☐ New Philharmonia Orchestra / Muti (conductor) / Angel S-37168

If there is a better consideration of Mendelssohn's score than Maag's on disc, I haven't heard it. Plenty of performances to choose from but, with one possible exception, the response perception in all instances lacks the fluidity and freshness of Maag's performance. Peter Maag has developed a reputation for Mozart interpretations. On the strength of this rendition that should read Mendelssohn as well.

Muti's version is listed because it is pliable, avoids being overdramatic (the minor tonality draws conductors into that interpretative syndrome), and has a very desirable flexible footedness. His realization of the final coda is especially choice.

Symphony No. 4 (*Italian*) in A major, Op. 90

☐ New Philharmonia Orchestra / Muti (conductor) / Angel S-37412
☐ Philharmonia Orchestra / Klemperer (conductor) / Angel S-35629

What makes these two performances choice is the choice matter of *not* taking tempi with the throttle wide open—a temptation to show off an orchestra's virtuosity that is rarely avoided. In the opening and closing movements, the music can seduce a conductor to let go and richochet the sounds into the auditor's ears. But, that doesn't produce a true temperatured emotional fire.

Muti's direction shows the mysterious strength that applies to certain tempi where a lesser pace brings more potency. The opening sings as it moves fluidly, the finale beats properly on the sonorous ground but still is not anchored. That's the way a Saltarello's rhythms are tastefully salted.

Klemperer obtains as much glee and atmosphere in his reading of the first movement, though his tempo choice is slower. He obtains this result by shrewdly tightening the phrasing. Such concentration produces the equivalent of speed. The same genuine virtue applies to the finale. *Con moto* is an important designation in this work—movement two is an *Andante con moto* and the following movement is a *Con moto moderato*. Both Muti and Klemperer read the instruction to mean inner motility and not super speed sense; the results are ideal.

Other positives, but none that surround the entire Symphony: Szell (Columbia MS-6975), fine first and last movements, but no give-and-take in the middle pair; Solti (London STS-15008), splendid until the finale which is just of such riotous speed that the musical meaning evaporates, and Mazur (Vanguard VCS-10133/6), actually excellent throughout but only providing you will accept elegance in place of thrusted positiveness, bearing in mind the latter is a far different matter than mere speed.

Symphony No. 5 (*Reformation*) in D minor, Op. 107

☐ Leipzig Gewandhaus Orchestra / Masur (conductor) / Vanguard VCS–10133/6

Despite good intentions, most performances of the *Reformation* Symphony are overblown and overdriven and the softer spots made sentimental. Masur's has fine resplendency, with the brass rounded and resonant and not hard-packed and brass-bandy. Most critics tend to sell this Symphony short, but this is doubtless due to their having been subjected to inflationary performances.

War March of the Priests from *Athalia*, Op. 74

☐ Philadelphia Orchestra / Ormandy (conductor) / Columbia MG–32314

An excerpt from the incidental music Mendelssohn composed for Racine's tragedy.

String Orchestra

Symphony Movement in C minor for Strings

Symphony

No. 1 in C major for Strings / No. 2 in D major for Strings / No. 3 in E minor for Strings / No. 4 in C minor for Strings / No. 5 in B flat major for Strings / No. 6 in E flat major for Strings / No. 7 in D minor for Strings / No. 8 in D major for Strings / No. 9 in C major for Strings / No. 10 in B minor for Strings / No. 11 in F minor for Strings / No. 12 in G minor for Strings

☐ Amsterdam Chamber Orchestra / Voorberg (conductor) / Telefunken 4635025

The only integral set on the market of these examples of very early Mendelssohn. Some of the Symphonies mark time (with student pulse) but the last five are all together excellent, beautifully accomplished works. Professional performances in all cases.

Solo Instrument and Orchestra

Piano

Capriccio Brillant for Piano and Orchestra, Op. 22

☐ Boston Symphony Orchestra / Graffman (piano) / Munch (conductor) / RCA VICS–1030

A splendid exhibition of controlled virtuosity in the glittering principal part of Mendelssohn's initial work for solo piano with orchestra. The slow-tempoed introduction has silken quality. It is played naturally without fussy *rubati*, thereby providing all the meaning within the content. The orchestral integration is perfect.

Concerto in A minor for Piano and Strings

☐ Academy of St. Martin-in-the-Fields / Ogdon (piano) / Marriner (conductor) / Argo ZRG–605

Mendelssohn at the age of thirteen but a Concerto as deftly wrought as the later, well-known pair. Particularly the depth of the slow movement is evidence of impressive mastery.

There is no comparison between this performance of effortless grace and superb soloism and the heavier one issued on Vox SVBX–5413 and repeated on Turnabout 34170. The orchestral playing on the Vox-Turnabout recording is choked, dull, labored, and at a bad community-orchestra level. Marriner's conception is perfectly charming and John Ogdon plays with unerring taste.

Concerto No. 1 in G minor for Piano and Orchestra, Op. 25

☐ Philadelphia Orchestra / Rudolf Serkin (piano) / Ormandy (conductor) / Columbia M–31837

Some may prefer a little less detrusion and a little more lighter-toned delivery but the intentness of Serkin's playing is fully attentive to the passions that seethe in Mendelssohn's score. The orchestral support is magnificent, again proof of how Ormandy is tops in providing full-scale backing for a soloist rather than merely a solicitous one.

Columbia offers this work in other issues: with the Schumann Piano Concerto in MS–7185 (the same coupling as for the catalogue entry listed above), in MS–6128 with the second Mendelssohn Piano Concerto, in D3S–741 with both Brahms piano concerti plus the Schumann, and in MG–32042 with other Mendelssohn works and once again the Schumann.

Concerto No. 2 in D minor for Piano and Orchestra, Op. 40

☐ Academy of St. Martin-in-the-Fields / Perahia (piano) / Marriner (conductor) / Columbia M–33207

If the critic who described this work as largely containing music of "labor and repetitiousness" were to hear the recording made by Murray Perahia and Neville Marriner, he would have second thoughts. It is a performance that is a beautifully natural one and yet provides pertinent contrastive content that strongly colors the work. Indeed, Perahia and Marriner convey splendid proof that Mendelssohn's music is rich with both poetry and drama. The latter is the reference point that Rudolf Serkin overstresses at the expense of the former in his performance with Ormandy (on Columbia MS–6128 and also on Columbia MG–32042).

Rondo Brillant for Piano and Orchestra, Op. 29

☐ London Symphony Orchestra / Ogdon (piano) / Ceccato (conductor) / Klavier 531

Light purity. Ceccato never forgets that this music is a matter of sparkle above everything else; natural orchestral back-up.

Serenade and *Allegro Gioioso* in B minor for Piano and Orchestra, Op. 43

☐ Pro Musica Symphony, Vienna / Kyriakou (piano) / Swarowsky (conductor) / Vox SVBX–5412

Mendelssohn's last work for piano and orchestra but his usual sense of freshness covers the music. Not too much to do for the orchestra, but what it has been given is fairly well stated, though of luster it isn't. Rena Kyriakou obtains a different report. From her one hears a secure, well-directed account.

Concerto in A flat major for Two Pianos and Orchestra

Two Pianos

☐ Chamber Orchestra of the Saar / Billard and Azaïs (pianos) / Ristenpart (conductor) / Nonesuch 71099

A Mendelssohn work that remained unpublished and did not receive a concert-hall performance for some 130 years. One is not always grateful for discoveries of music that the composers would have placed in a shredding machine if it had been available to them. The reverse pertains in this case. There are no mixed blessings to discuss. Mendelssohn's work is totally as Edward Tatnall Canby describes: "easy and fluent; it sings its own story."

The solo parts are set off stunningly, and Ristenpart's contribution is no minimal attraction. The sound is somewhat contained and the pianos could have been more assertive, but the stylistic authority and musicality of the playing demands naming this as the choice edition. Be assured one can live with the sound quality.

Concerto in E major for Two Pianos and Orchestra

☐ Academy of St. Martin-in-the-Fields / Ogdon and Lucas (pianos) / Marriner (conductor) / Argo ZRG-605

This Concerto remains a rarity though Argo's edition is one of three in the current recorded catalogue. Great Mendelssohn it may not be, but confident and charming it is throughout its three movements. What it says it says directly, clearly, and constructively. Anyway, it's time to start looking out for the music that deserves to be in the standard repertoire but due to concert manager and conductorial politics is kept outside of it. The plea of "not box office" is bunk.

Superbly played by the soloists (Brenda Lucas is John Ogdon's wife). The performance is searching, stimulating, and beautifully expressed, for which credit applies as well to Neville Marriner and his expert musicians.

Violin

Concerto in D minor for Violin and String Orchestra

☐ New Philharmonia Orchestra / Grumiaux (violin) / Krenz (conductor) / Philips 6500465

Though this early work (written when Mendelssohn was twelve) will never supplant *the* Mendelssohn Violin Concerto it certainly does not deserve museum shelf residence. If only for the line motion of the slow movement, the Concerto is a winner, overall representing a handsomely and well-organized composition.

Grumiaux plays the work with lucidity and does not clutter the sounds with interpretative makeout. The figurations in the finale are bowed with exceptional accuracy; the entire disc is a model of clarity and Mendelssohnian definition.

Concerto in E minor for Violin and Orchestra, Op. 64

☐ Vienna Philharmonic Orchestra / Milstein (violin) / Abbado (conductor) / Deutsche Grammophon 2530359
☐ London Symphony Orchestra / Perlman (violin) / Previn (conductor) / Angel S-36963

Everybody, but everybody, plays and records this Concerto. There is a hefty quota of current recorded editions by the old masters (Heifetz, Francescatti, and Milstein, etc.) and by the young ones (Zukerman, Perlman, and Kim, etc.) from which to choose. It's rather easy to rule out certain of these (rejoicing in a critic's right of subjectivism no matter what). I find (on RCA LSC-3304, VCS-7058, and CRL6-0720) Heifetz's tempi too fast, (on Columbia MS-6062, M-31835, D3S-721, and MS-7516) Stern's fat sound out of place when it doesn't permit contrastive dynamics to color the music, and Grumiaux's playing (on Philips 6500465) all very graceful but with a certain lack of romantic commitment. And, so it goes.

There is no doubt about Milstein's inspired playing. His depiction is lithe and expressive. Mendelssohn's linguistics have never sounded better. Abbado's support is exemplary and eloquent where it has to be. This comment on Milstein does not hold true in the version he made with Leon Barzin (on Angel S-35730).

Perlman's playing is rich and of a wonderful depth that adds a special quality rarely heard in performances of Mendelssohn's work. Everything is bowed and fingered naturally; the music resonates. Truly, a superb performance.

Instrumental

Cello

Song Without Words for Cello and Piano, Op. 109

☐ Schuster (cello); Balsam (piano) / Vox SVBX-582

This *Lied ohne Worte* is pure song for the stringed instrument; the piano is the harmonic housekeeper. Nice, unassuming playing of simple music.

Sonata No. 1 in F major for Organ, Op. 65, No. 1

Organ

☐ Biggs (organ) / Columbia Special Products AMS-6087

Especially good presentation, neatly contrasted in weight and tempo, keenly dynamic where it should be, and correctly colored. The interpretative behavior is splendid.

(The disc also contains the sixth sonata in D major.)

Sonata No. 2 in C minor for Organ, Op. 65, No. 2

☐ McVey (organ) / Orion 74161

Split tempo and tonal personality in Mendelssohn's work (the second of his six organ sonatas); the first two parts are slow-paced and in C minor, the final pair of movements are in the opposite speed and in C major.

Playing the Smith Memorial Organ at Pomona College (in Claremont, California), David McVey is sensitive to the structural demands and displays fine phrasing. Only one quibble, and that pertains to the sustained heaviness in the latter part of the fugue. Excellent organ sound.

Albumblatt in E minor, Op. 117

Piano

☐ Barenboim (piano) / Deutsche Grammophon 2709052

Used as a filler in Barenboim's production of the complete Songs Without Words (*see below*). A good choice, since it is in the same genre.

Andante Cantabile and *Presto Agitato*
Capriccio in E major, Op. 118
Capriccio in F sharp minor, Op. 5

☐ Kyriakou (piano) / Vox SVBX-5414 (monaural)

Strong and clearly articulated performances. The variety of technical requirements in the Opus 5 piece are demanding but Kyriakou prevails at the highest level.

Do not think there is mislabeling for the first-named work. Its first part is Mendelssohn borrowing from himself, with the closest carbon copy of the introductory section of the *Rondo Capriccioso*. However, it is impossible to find any substantiation for Vox subtitling this work *Two Musical Sketches*.

Etude in F minor

☐ Kyriakou (piano) / Vox SVBX-5413

Full-scale playing matching the urgency of the piece. Little breath spots provide excellent performance strategy.

Fantasy in F sharp minor, Op. 28

☐ Kuerti (piano) / Monitor 2128

Mendelssohn subtitled his opus *Sonate écossaise* but there seems to be no relationship whatsoever to that description, with three movements that begin in an agitated manner, followed by a moving song division (marked *Allegro con moto*), and completed by a peripatetic Presto.

So much for constructive detail. The playing is of strength and sweep and these determine an eloquence that carries the auditor along in full stride. Certainly exciting pianism.

Fantasy on *The Last Rose of Summer,* Op. 15
Gondellied in A major

☐ Kyriakou (piano) / Vox SVBX-5412

Striking proportions to the Opus 15 with the Irish melody (which sparked a fine aria in Flotow's Opera *Martha*) used to bind the work in its terminal parts. It is played with zest and sympathy. The other piece is not to be confused with the three others in the Songs Without Words.

Perpetuum Mobile, Op. 119
Preludes and Etudes, Op. 104

☐ Kyriakou (piano) / Vox SVBX-5413

There are two books to Opus 104, with three Preludes in the first and the same number of études in the second one. Virtuosity is the objective. Virtuosity it obtains in the playing.

Prelude and Fugue in E minor

☐ Kyriakou (piano) / Vox SVBX-5412

Not to be confused with the first of the Six Preludes and Fugues, Op. 35, also set in E minor (*see below*). Mendelssohn wrote the Fugue first and then fourteen years later added the Prelude. Kyriakou nicely colors the first part but is less effective with the polyphonic piece because of the similarity of the dynamic design.

Rondo Capriccioso, Op. 14
Scherzo a Capriccio
Scherzo in B minor

☐ Kuerti (piano) / Monitor 2128

Mendelssohn's Opus 14 (sometimes listed as *Andante and Rondo Capriccioso* which does describe its binomial design) shows him at his most wonderful, sound brimming best. Anton Kuerti's *rubati* and vocalism in the first part and the glistening tactility of the second portion are splendid. It is a singular example of artistry.

No time is wasted by Kuerti in the *a Capriccio,* the other *Scherzo* is slightly toned down in its speedrate. Both are exhilarating experiences of music that is fruitful material for use within a regular program as well as in an encore situation.

Seven Characteristic Pieces, Op. 7
Six *Kinderstücke,* Op. 72

☐ Kyriakou (piano) / Vox SVBX-5413

By titling the Opus 7 as plain Seven Pieces on box cover and label copy, the Vox release (played with finesse and spirit) does not lead from descriptive strength. This is detailed in Mendelssohn's music with rare (for him) headings such as: *Sanft und mit Empfindung* (number 1), *Ernst und mit steigender Lebhaftigkeit* (for the *Fuga* in the fifth slot), et cetera, plus the *Sehnsüchtig* heading for the sixth piece. Fortunately, such haphazardness only reflects on production details and not in Rena Kyriakou's consideration.

The Opus 72 (known in England as Christmas Pieces) is well executed. The same pertains to Barenboim's conception on D.G. 2709052. However, if you can locate André Previn's edition on Columbia Special Products CMS-6586, you'll have the best there is.

Six Preludes and Fugues, Op. 35

☐ Kyriakou (piano) / Vox SVBX-5412

Careful playing, which means more outgoing spirit, would be worthwhile. If a listener would be satisfied with half the set, Kuerti fulfills that viewpoint meaningfully in his Mendelssohn program on Monitor 2128, where he includes numbers 1, 2, and 3, in E minor, D major, and B minor, respectively.

Sonata in B flat major, Op. 106

☐ Kyriakou (piano) / Vox SVBX-5412

Early Mendelssohn, posthumously published. Expectedly indeed, the key spot is the second movement Scherzo, though the rhythmic kicks in the finale hold one's interest, especially the off-beat inserts. There is clear detail in Kyriakou's presentation of the music.

Sonata in E major, Op. 6

☐ Karl Ulrich Schnabel (piano) / Sheffield S-8

No great masterpiece, though it is amazing to realize that this Sonata is the creation of a seventeen-year-old. Those who are not musically convinced will not be able to deny the conviction of the performance.

Sonata in G minor, Op. 105

☐ Kyriakou (piano) / Vox SVBX-5414 (monaural)

Posthumously issued. Rather repetitive in its opening movement, attenuated in the slow movement, but very alive in the Presto finale. Written at age 12 and in that respect worth attention historically.

Fair playing not helped by clangy sound.

Songs Without Words
Book I, Op. 19 / Book II, Op. 30 / Book III, Op. 38 / Book IV, Op. 53 / Book V, Op. 62 / Book VI, Op. 67 / Book VII, Op. 85 / Book VIII, Op. 102

☐ Barenboim (piano) / Deutsche Grammophon 2709052

All of them, all forty-eight, with six in each set. No words but titles, some by Mendelssohn, some by traditional attachment.

Barenboim plays them with fine sentiment but not a wisp of sentimentality. No histrionics, either. In his hands the music charms the ear—best, of course, not heard four-dozen at a crack but sampled here and there.

Songs Without Words
Duet (Book III, Op. 38, No. 6)
***Elegie* (Book VII, Op. 85, No. 4)**
***The Fleecy Cloud* (Book IV, Op. 53, No. 2)**
***The Joyous Peasant* (Book VII, Op. 102, No. 5)**

May Breezes (Book V, Op. 62, No. 1)
Sadness of Soul (Book IV, Op. 53, No. 4)
Song of the Traveller (Book VII, Op. 85, No. 6)
Spinning Song (Book VI, Op. 67, No. 4)
Spring Song (Book V, Op. 62, No. 6)
Sweet Remembrance (Book I, Op. 19, No. 1)
Tarantella (Book VIII, Op. 102, No. 3)
Venetian Gondola Song No. 1 (Book I, Op. 19, No. 6)
Venetian Gondola Song No. 2 (Book II, Op. 30, No. 6)
Venetian Gondola Song No. 3 (Book V, Op. 62, No. 5)

☐ Novaes (piano) / Turnabout 34245

A fine sampling. Novaes has included all the "hits" and simultaneously has representations from each of the eight books.

Fine playing to match the sampling. Clear style, and like Barenboim (*see above*) there is no vestige of sugariness added to Mendelssohn's sweet poetry. And, at the same time, no overintellectualizing.

Three Capriccios, Op. 33

☐ Kyriakou (piano) / Vox SVBX-5414 (monaural)

The first and third pieces are prefaced by matters of gravity then proceed to nimble music with an underlining of dramatic guidance, brought by the use of minor keys. The second of the set is all charm and grace as fits the major tonality. The playing is decent though not overpowering and where it is careful it does avoid pedestrianism.

Three Fantasies or Caprices, Op. 16

☐ Kyriakou (piano) / Vox SVBX-5412

Mendelssohn described this work as embracing "three of my best piano pieces." Truth, especially for the second one, a Scherzo, with crisp little trumpet-like figures. The world of the *Midsummer Night's Dream* is there revealed again. And it is there that Kyriakou plays with exemplary style. Elsewhere her piano voice is of acceptable clarity and order.

Two *Clavierstücke*

☐ Barenboim (piano) / Deutsche Grammophon 2709052

In the Songs Without Words category.

Variations

In B flat major, Op. 83 / In E flat major, Op. 82

☐ Kyriakou (piano) / Vox SVBX-5413

The B flat set was arranged by Mendelssohn for piano duet as Opus 83a and is often titled *Andante tranquillo con Variazioni*. (A recording is available of the latter—*see below*.) Likewise, the other set of variations has a second title: *Andante con Variazioni*.

Variations Sérieuses, Op. 54

☐ Simon (piano) / Turnabout S-34460

Certainly the most important of any of the variations Mendelssohn produced and in scope worthy of placement with the major sets composed by Beethoven and Brahms.

This is a splendid depiction. Simon plays with a light touch that makes such as the fourth and thirteenth of the total seventeen variations absolute delights. When energy is demanded (the third and seventh permutations, as examples) it is forthcoming but his tone is always mellow and never forced or overdemanding. An important point—the continuity Simon obtains is the strongest of all the available editions.

Allegro Brillante, Op. 92

Piano,
Four Hands

☐ Kyriakou and Klien (piano) / Vox SVBX–5413

Vitally vivacious music. It is played with a becoming snappy tempo and excellent staccati touch. A fine example of writing for four hands at one piano.

Andante tranquillo con Variazioni, Op. 83a

☐ Menuhin and Ryce (piano) / Everest 3112

Mendelssohn's own version for piano four-hands of a set of variations in B flat major for solo piano (Opus 83). Brilliance is the main point in the eight variations and coda. Convincingly presented by Yaltah Menuhin and Joel Ryce.

Sonata in B flat major for Cello and Piano, Op. 45

Chamber
Music

☐ Soyer (cello); Wingreen (piano) / Monitor S–2045

Soyer and Wingreen take advantage of the broad style of the outer movements, permitting the cello voice to spin fully its *cantilena*, doubly enhanced by the framed balance of moving piano tone. This represents astute chamber music making. They also, significantly, understand that although there is motival preoccupation in the slow movement, it is melodically unfurled and not organically developed. Therefore, they play the music in the pure simplicity of a gentle mood, rather than emphasize structural particulars. It provides beautiful effect.

Sonata in D major for Cello and Piano, Op. 58

☐ Harrell (cello); Levine (piano) / RCA ARL1–1568

In the third movement, Harrell's opportunity to be not a classical gentleman but rather a rich declaimer of full romantic estate is met by beautiful lyricism. Though the finale's material is brilliantly stated, contains oppositional gamuts in its setting, as well as active figurations and the like, the playing of these musicians achieves a perfect transparency. One is never lulled into casual background listening in this perceptive presentation of Mendelssohn's masterful creation.

Variations Concertantes for Cello and Piano, Op. 17

☐ Schuster (cello); Balsam (piano) / Vox SVBX–582

Formal clarity with warm subjectivity. Neat equality of instrumentation and fully convincing in the valorization by the duo team.

Piano Trio
No. 1 in D minor, Op. 49 / No. 2 in C minor, Op. 66

☐ Beaux Arts Trio / Philips 6580211

Finely detailed, beautifully toned representations. The original Beaux Arts team (this recording was made when Daniel Guilet was the violinist) understands that, while classical designs are present, for the most part the style is freer and is so displayed in their playing.

The slow movement of the D minor is presented in a serene fashion. It is detailed with unquestioned emotion but it is kept at a quiet level. Similarly, the Beaux Arts retain a dark concentration in the finale and only open up their conception when the major tonality enters in the coda. Both scherzi are masterfully balanced; the playing of the fugato in the C minor work represents perfection.

No reservations. These are infinitely the best performances of Mendelssohn's trios in the record catalogue.

Piano Quartet
No. 1 in C minor, Op. 1 / No. 2 in F minor, Op. 2

☐ Trio Dell'Arte / Koch (viola) / Vox SVBX–585

There are points about these early Mendelssohn works that need to be stressed. In Opus 1 the harmonic shifts of the slow movement are clues to the romantic liquidity of the vertical aspects of the music. In addition, the movement breathes a fairly long line, sufficiently difficult for any composer. In the case of a boy (Mendelssohn was thirteen when he composed his first piano quartet), it is *wunderkind* magic. The trio of the Scherzo is actually a trio, scored for the esoteric combination of viola, cello, and the left hand alone for the piano.

In Opus 2 the strings perform quite often as a trio unto themselves, or with slight accompaniment from the piano. The reverse method is also used, wherein the string threesome act as a resonanting body to support the moving agility of the piano. Romantic leaning is apparent in the third movement where an Intermezzo is introduced into chamber music. This fast-type barcarolle had never been used by any of the classic school.

The performances have fine clarity and a romantic passion that is very telling. Total impressive translations of these scores are presented.

Piano Quartet No. 3 in B minor, Op. 3

☐ Haas (piano); Malecek (violin); Tsuchiya (viola); Steiner (cello) / Philips 6500170

Certainly the richest of Mendelssohn's three piano quartets. He thought the slow movement "rather cloying," but this team of performers (the string-instrument players are members of the Berlin Philharmonic Octet) adopts a tempo that avoids such criticism. Nice lightness in the right-on-the-button Mendelssohnian scherzo. In the finale the pianist is given a miniature type of concerto with which to play ball. Werner Haas doesn't miss the opportunity yet does not forsake chamber-music atmosphere. Five-star performance and engineering.

String Quartet in E flat major

☐ European String Quartet / Vox SVBX–582

Known as the *Jugendquartett,* composed in 1823, and posthumously published. It is for that reason that it is not included in the chronologically numbered quartets, three of which have their own catalogue problems.

But this does not deter enjoying a comfortable, fairly resourceful work, consisting of an *Allegro moderato,* a slow-paced division, a *Menuetto,* and a fugal finale. The performance is a disciplined one, though a bit dry. For the latter, the blame is partly to be shouldered by Mendelssohn.

String Quartet No. 1 in E flat major, Op. 12

☐ Fine Arts Quartet / Concert-Disc 224

Composed in 1829, this is Mendelssohn's second quartet, the first (Opus 13, *see below*) having been written two years earlier, but later publication reversed the opus numbers.

Fine playing by the first violin in the slow movement, a music that belies true quartet character, with most of the work given to the leading violin. The *Canzonetta* (quite often serving as encore fare) is light as a scherzo, but slower-scaled. The Fine Arts team plays it with mercurial, light deftness.

(The performance is also included in Concert-Disc 505, with other Mendelssohn quartets and his Octet.)

String Quartet No. 2 in A minor, Op. 13

☐ Guarneri Quartet / RCA LSC–2948

Mendelssohn was eighteen when he wrote this work, actually his first string quartet, though published as the second in the sequence of opus identities (*see above*).

The Guarneri are aware of the characteristic, personal sentiments of a romantic composer in this work. They play accordingly and are beautifully successful. The storm, strife, and blazing actions of the first movement proper (an Adagio is situated in prelude and epilogue positions) are strongly depicted but with no roughage of tone. The effect is quartetish-sonorous to the extreme. The childlike dance of the Intermezzo which connects to scherzo sprightliness and the ultradramatic moves of the finale (propounded by recitative passages) are played with sensitive color and distinctive excitement. The textures are always clear and immaculate—a difficult matter with the amount of material crossing and being tossed among the instruments.

String Quartet

No. 3 in D major, Op. 44, No. 1 / No. 4 in E minor, Op. 44, No. 2

☐ Fine Arts Quartet / Concert-Disc 505

There is no doubt that Mendelssohn's quartets are coarser than the finer-grained examples of the classic school, but when properly performed, as in this case, the so-called orchestral qualities are not overevident. Lush and yet controlled playing mark the D major's slow movement and there is a full quantity of *brio* applied to its finale.

The turbulencies in the E minor opus come through but minus any thickness that would cancel voicing identity. The playing of the Scherzo is tissue-textured but there are no tears in the fabric.

(Concert-Disc has also released the Opus 44, Number 2 quartet in two other albums: Numbers 224 and 260.)

String Quartet No. 5 in E flat major, Op. 44, No. 3

☐ European String Quartet / Vox SVBX–581

This quartet contains one of the greatest of Mendelssohn's scherzi. It is a filament of four threads that spins into the aural consciousness. Even when the hand of the technician appears (fugato sections), the mood is retained. It is played fairly well, a bit lighter style would be even more appropriate. The European team covers the balance of the work with an above-average performance.

String Quartet No. 6 in F minor, Op. 80

☐ European String Quartet / Vox SVBX–582

Tragedy stalks this work, its tonality, color, and sound, and in the circumstances that were prelude and postlude to it. Mendelssohn had not written any quartets for some nine years when his beloved and most devoted sister, Fanny, died. Turning to the string quartet as the medium of most intimacy, he poured into it as touching a threnodic message as he was capable of writing. A few months later Mendelssohn died. The mysticism is almost frightening.

The European Quartet plays in a fine manner, even though the slow movement is rather neutrally depicted. However, they score a real success in the second movement, a music uncompromising in its somber scherzo mood and that has overtones of a sickly waltz.

String Quartet No. 7 (*Unfinished*), Op. 81

☐ European String Quartet / Vox SVBX-581

A real mix. Opus 81 is also known (and so titled in at least one printed edition) as Andante, Scherzo, Capriccio, and Fugue. It consists of three works put together by Mendelssohn's publisher. The first two of these pieces were planned for inclusion in a full-sized quartet. The last two are individual pieces written four years and twenty years, respectively, before Mendelssohn's death.

Wisely, the European team changes the order in its rendition and secures a much better balance. The outer movements in the recording are the Fugue and the Capriccio, which passes through slow, fugato, and vivacious sections. Within these are the pair of movements Mendelssohn had completed for his seventh quartet: an Andante (a set of variations) and a Scherzo. This arrangement provides a very effective format and is portrayed in a pronouncedly skillful manner.

Quintet in A major for Two Violins, Two Violas, and Cello, Op. 18

☐ Laredo and Kavafian (violins); Ohyana and Kashkashian (violas); Robinson (cello) / Columbia M-35110

Mingling the yarns of the scherzo with fugue and creating a cloth that is both transparent and plastic is quite a feat. For while the scherzo concept of agility can use the flighted qualities of the fugue, the parts must be disposed with deft instrumental touches. Mendelssohn achieves this amalgam in the third movement. The ensemble headed by Jaime Laredo is inspired by the Mendelssohn invention; they carry off the performance with grace and rhythmic point. Similar quality playing is displayed in the other movements.

Quintet in B flat major for Two Violins, Two Violas, and Cello, Op. 87

☐ Vienna Philharmonia Quintet / Musical Heritage Society MHS-1865

Compared to this work, the earlier string quintet is light; in this instance, the meshed writing is dramatic. Even the *Andante scherzando* is leaded with heaviness on first beats and cross-accentuations. But, of course, in Mendelssohn's hands, scherzo charm cannot be completely obliterated, no matter what its organization.

It is the greater lyrical and dramatic intensity the Vienna Philharmonia group brings to this music, especially in the profound *Adagio e lento,* in scope a symphonic essay, that makes theirs the preferable recorded performance. (The competitive renditions are by the Bamberg String Quartet with Paul Hennevogl assisting, on Vox SVBX-585 and a Marlboro ensemble, on Columbia M-35110.)

Sextet for Piano, Violin, Two Violas, Cello, and Double Bass, Op. 110

☐ Members of the Berlin Philharmonic Octet / Haas (piano) / Philips 6500170

The opus number is no clue to the time of composition because this work dates from the composer's fifteenth year. The instrumentation, it will be noted, is out of the ordinary in that the string group gamut tends toward the lower regions, only one violin being used.

Only occasionally do the strings break away from the dictatorship of the piano. Otherwise, they give blend to the piano, with tutti treatment of the simple material for purposes of emphasis.

Werner Haas is in good form and is amply supported by the five string players from the Berlin group.

Octet for Four Violins, Two Violas, and Two Cellos, Op. 20

☐ Maguire, Marriner, Brown, and Connah (violins); Shingles and Essex (violas); Heath and Vigay (cellos) / Argo ZRG–569

A miracle of fine-spun music—youthful, lively, and considered the greatest of all works written in string octet form. There is nothing more integrated in all of Mendelssohn's music than this mature work written at the age of sixteen.

Of the recorded versions, this one, performed by members of the Academy of St. Martin-in-the-Fields, rates the highest. The ensemble is of the sharpest cohesion. It is strange that merging two first-rate quartets doesn't seem to work on stage or in recording studio as well as a miscellaneous group. There is no four-instrument unified personality, of course, in the latter situation, whereas putting two quartets together does cause some conflict (conscious or subconscious) since there are *two* first violinists, *two* "first" cellists, etc. Whatever, no group shows the sympathetic understanding and brimming sound mingling of these eight stringed-instrument players. Since they have performed as part of a total unit within the Academy's string section, they do not have to overcome the problems that concern partnering two separate concertizing string quartets.

Vocal

Voice and Orchestra

Infelice!, Op. 94

☐ Leipzig Gewandhaus Orchestra / Moser (soprano) / Masur (conductor) / Angel S–37016

Mendelssohn's single concert aria. Not a major work but certainly deserving of a listing in *Schwann*, which it doesn't have, even though it is a filler for the major issue of *Die Erste Walpurgisnacht* (*see below*). Edda Moser sings with distinction.

Choral

Chorus Alone

Abschied vom Wald, Op. 59, No. 3
Der Erste Frühlingstag, Op. 48, No. 1
Die Nachtigall, Op. 59, No. 4
Es Fiel ein Reif, Op. 41, No. 3
Im Wald, Op. 41, No. 1

☐ Camerata Vocale, Bremen / Blum and Kopf-Endres (conductors) / Nonesuch 71081

Two conductors share these choral pieces sung by a group of soprano, two altos, a tenor, and a bass. Klaus Blum conducts Op. 41, No. 3 and Op. 48, No. 1; Willy Kopf-Endres the other three items.

Cantata and Oratorio

Die Erste Walpurgisnacht, Op. 60

☐ Leipzig Gewandhaus Orchestra and Leipzig Radio Chorus / Burmeister (mezzo-soprano); Buchner (tenor); Lorenz (baritone); Vogel (bass) / Masur (conductor) / Angel S-37016

Mendelssohn's richly wrought score concerning paganism and Christianity has a substantial overture followed by nine sections. The romantic registration is wealthy and the writing between solo and massed voices has rewarding balance.

This is a fine recorded publication. It pushes completely aside a rather flawed performance (poorly paced and badly balanced) on Everest 3229, coincidentally also by Leipzig personnel under the banner of the Leipzig Bach Festival, without any credits whatsoever save to the conductor (Lorenzo Bernardi). Masur conducts a lusty execution that peaks in the exciting sixth part. This includes such colorful thoughts as "Owls and Ravens/ howl with us/ and scare the cravens!"

Elijah, Op. 70

☐ New Philharmonia Orchestra and Chorus and Wandsworth Boys' Choir / Jones (soprano); Baker (contralto); Gedda (tenor); Fischer-Dieskau (baritone); Woolf (vocalist) / Frühbeck de Burgos (conductor) / Angel S-3738

Vivid storytelling is wrapped around and built into *Elijah,* one of Mendelssohn's greatest inspirations. Worth noting is that it is conceived as a balanced structure, with no favoritism to either solo voices, chorus, or orchestra.

Superb direction that doesn't miss a detail. The singing of the soloists is pliant and naturally delineated. Dietrich Fischer-Dieskau as Elijah is very imposing, though his diction is not always on center. Little matter considering the total communication of this issue.

Paulus (St. Paul)

☐ Düsseldorf Symphony Orchestra and Chorus of the Düsseldorf Musikverein / Donath (soprano); Schwarz (mezzo-soprano); Hollweg (tenor); Fischer-Dieskau (baritone) / Frühbeck de Burgos (conductor) / Angel SC-3842

Concert hall performances of this work have lapsed but in the church world it maintains a healthy life. Since it is a composition of some length, a number of presentations consist of the first part of the work and this makes a most satisfactory excerpt.

This performance is impressively firm and disciplined.

Opera and Dramatic Music

Incidental Music to *A Midsummer Night's Dream,* Op. 61

☐ New Philharmonia Orchestra and Ambrosian Singers / Van Bork (soprano); Hodgson (mezzo-soprano) / Frühbeck de Burgos (conductor) / London 26107

There are fifteen numbers that Mendelssohn composed for *A Midsummer Night's Dream.* Only on disc is there the opportunity of hearing them. In concert halls the offerings are either the overture (*see above*) or a suite of three to five parts (*see above*). But even recorded editions have cuts. Most of these omit six numbers; one recording reviewed only consisted of seven parts.

The recording listed is complete and includes such novelties as a *Fairy March,* a *Funeral March,* and a *Dance of the Clowns,* etc.

Peter Mennin   (1923-   )

Concertato (*Moby Dick*) for Orchestra (1952)   *Orchestra*

☐ Vienna Symphony Orchestra / Swarowsky (conductor) / Desto 6416E (monaural)

The parenthetical title (not noted, incidentally, on album cover or label of the recording) is the clue to the emotional character of the piece. Read, then, Mennin's reaction to Melville's novel, rather than creation of any picture-painting. The contrapuntal drive of the main portion, set mainly in massive block scoring, is orchestrational excitation at peak registration.

An old recording, electronically reprocessed, but it sounds good and is played graphically.

Symphony No. 3 (1946)

☐ Philharmonic-Symphony Orchestra of New York / Mitropoulos (conductor) / Composers Recordings S-278E (monaural)

Mennin's style is clearly identified in the third of his eight symphonies. The rhythms are motoric but not rough, of intense strength to the structure. These carry the neo-classic lines that quite often revolve around a tonal polarity instead of depending on tonics, dominants, etc., and their equivalents. Thus the C minor focus of the opening *Allegro robusto*. His scoring is mainly in block formation, and this, too, in its concentration of totals, is another element of dynamism.

In these days of faddism it is invigorating to hear music tonally headquartered and yet contemporaneous in its detail. Written over thirty years ago, Mennin's work remains fully fresh and has lasting values.

Symphony No. 5 (1961)

☐ Eastman-Rochester Orchestra / Hanson (conductor) / Mercury 75020

Mennin's brand of vitality (he can move an Allegro with great electrical motility, as well as any twentieth-century composer) is present in the outer movements. The first of these is tempoed *Con sdegno*, which means "with scorn," but there is nothing snide here; rather, there is severity. The slow movement, a *Canto*, was once a separate orchestral piece, but Mennin revised it and placed it in this opus. It is of imposing size—almost ten minutes in length.

The Louisville Orchestra has recorded this work in a monaural setting (613). It does not have the compelling playing (or the sound values, of course) of Hanson's production.

Symphony No. 6 (1953)

☐ Louisville Orchestra / Whitney (conductor) / Louisville 545-3 (monaural)

Traditional forms—a *Maestoso* introduction to the opening Allegro, a Grave movement, and a combination of Scherzo and Finale for the concluding movement—do not deter Mennin's clear, resilient contemporary spirit. And what spirit! This is especially heard in the bold, aggressive, spiculated dissonances of the composer's neoclassic diction. Mennin's Symphony is dynamic, zippy, controlled to the last note to make sense but never to lose its excitement.

The Louisville group, when it recorded this work, was not the fully honed aggregation it is nowadays. Nonetheless, it gives a powerful reading, styled well, and with the details fully polished.

Symphony No. 7 (*Variation-Symphony*)

☐ Chicago Symphony Orchestra / Martinon (conductor) / New World Records NW–258

Mennin's Symphony has five connected movements; the variational aspect is totally different from the sectionalism that so often pertains to variation systems.

The Symphony is athletic and lyrical, and when Mennin lets loose in a fast-paced section with all the orchestral stops in full blast, he makes much excitement, but never of the cheap kind. His lyricism is acrid—lightly sweet, based on free (almost atonic) harmony. The tautness of twentieth-century nervousness creeps into the slow-moving lines, so that flabby relaxation never occurs. The clarity and zest of the music are conspicuous.

Martinon conducting Mennin is very productive. Indeed, Martinon proves his excellence as a conductor, especially for such a contemporary score. That New World Records has chosen to reissue this recording, originally released by RCA (companioned with Martinon's Symphony No. 4), shows a keenness of discernment.

Solo Instrument and Orchestra

Cello

Concerto for Cello and Orchestra (1956)

☐ Louisville Orchestra / Starker (cello) / Mester (conductor) / Louisville S–693

Mennin has no compulsion to bypass the traditions of concerto composition in his work. He indulges the soloist with a lengthy, extremely difficult, but fully musical cadenza in the first movement. He heeds the fact that a cello is a rich, singing instrument and gives it plenty of opportunity, especially in the Adagio. At the same time he does not confine its range, providing a full-blown lyrical disposition. The finale is also of full-blown disposition, this time in Mennin's favorite toccata-like tracking.

Starker plays this music with authority and clarity. The orchestra performs with vigor and accuracy.

Piano

Piano Concerto

☐ Royal Philharmonic Orchestra / Ogdon (piano) / Buketoff (conductor) / RCA LSC–3243

Traditional format, contemporary combustion, and an authentic balance between solo voice and orchestra without nullifying the special spotlight for the former describe this Concerto. Of course no lush details or cozy possibilities for *rubati*, and so, once again, by overlooking this piece, our virtuosi are guilty of lack of broad perception. There is no doubt that Mennin's work deserves repertoire recognition.

John Ogdon plays with all the energy required. When poetic response is demanded, he supplies it. Four-star, this performance.

Instrumental

Piano

Canto (1950)

Toccata (1950)

☐ Johannesen (piano) / Golden Crest S–4065

These are the last two of Mennin's Five Piano Pieces. (The previous three are a Prelude, Aria, and Variation-Canzona.) The pieces can be performed separately or as a unit.

Neoclassic erudition and pianistic virtuosity are combined in these conceptions. Mennin's usual rhythmic vitality and drive make the Toccata a block-buster for performer and auditor.

Sonata concertante for Violin and Piano (1956)

☐ Zukofsky (violin); Kalish (piano) / Desto 6435/37

Chamber music with a virtuosic array of armament. Save for the middle, slow movement, where the objective is introspective, and a very short introduction to the total work, Mennin's piece is all extrovert dash, pep, and energy, with tumultuous, frenzied emotionalism.

Though only a pair of instruments are involved, the work dazzles because of its toccata-like qualities which furnish a rapport between the corner movements. The only difference is that the outer one blazes a bit more.

The *Sonata concertante* is ultrabravura chamber music. It is a music only for elite performers. That describes Paul Zukofsky and Gilbert Kalish.

String Quartet No. 2 (1951)

☐ Kohon Quartet / Vox SVBX–5305

Although there are four distinct movements, there are inner relationships (not thematic) within Mennin's high-voltage quartet. Neoclassically styled, the first pair of movements has vivid kinetic impetus, with Bartókian percussive precepts, exceedingly asymmetric layout, and a strong contrapuntal sense of architecture. Both the slow and final movements also have polyphonic strengths. Fugal developments parallel the devices in the outer movements as well.

Mennin's quartet is one of stunning virtuosity. The Kohon Quartet meets all of its demands in terms of style, color, and vigorous rhythmic intensity.

Symphony No. 4, *The Cycle,* for Chorus and Orchestra (1948)

☐ Camerata Symphony Orchestra and Camerata Singers / Kaplan (conductor) / Desto 7149

Vigorous athleticism in the outer of the three movements; the middle movement, somewhat mysterious, is displaying the opposite of the outwardness of the former. A Symphony in title, this work has more kinship with choral-orchestral music of symphonic character (the text is by the composer).

A performance of clarity, and powerful when it should be. The Camerata Singers are several shades better than their orchestral colleagues.

Gian Carlo Menotti *(1911-   )*

Concerto in F for Piano and Orchestra (1945)

☐ Symphony of the Air / Wild (piano) / Mester (conductor) / Vanguard 2094

Questioned about his concerto at the time of its premiere, Menotti indicated he was influenced by the preromantic style of the Italian school, especially that of Scarlatti's keyboard works. Accordingly, the initial movement is ignited by neoclassic activity, especially confirmed by the cleanliness and white-black quality of the piano part. Vocal style predominates in the middle movement, but the opposite marks the temper of the finale. There Menotti's plan is of positive instrumental order—tertial and quartal harmonies in blocked array define the martial mood. Tonality is consolidated, but does not wither away in the underbrush of its vocabulary. The music is stark and concentrated, but just as starkly devoted to chordal frictions even though all the harmonic percussion is sounded within a tonality. This method is the true philosophy of neoclassic technique; and here is the most up-to-date brand of the style, paradoxically utilized by a contemporary romanticist. It fully serves Menotti's needs, and should satisfy the listener who demands the excitement promised by the concerto medium.

Earl Wild is a pianist of refinement and sensitivity besides being a virtuoso of top caliber. These qualities are fully evident in this recording. Wild's performance is a model one, and the support he receives from Jorge Mester has generous understanding.

Opera and Dramatic Music

Amahl and the Night Visitors (1951)

☐ Orchestra and Chorus / Allen (boy soprano); Kuhlmann (mezzo-soprano); Aiken and Monachino (baritones); Lishner (bass) / Schippers (conductor) / RCA VIC-1512 (monaural)

Menotti's one-act Opera, the first ever composed expressly for television, has become a classic. The number of performances it receives each year is tremendous.

Menotti's sensitive tale was suggested by the Bosch painting *The Adoration of the Magi.* It relates a visit by the Three Kings on their way to Bethlehem to find the Christ Child. They meet the crippled shepherd boy Amahl, and in return for his generosity the Kings perform a miracle and restore him to perfect health. Menotti's score is extremely moving, has unusual character in that every nuance and color fits the story. *Amahl* illustrates the composer's cardinal gift for setting words to music that can stir the senses without moving outside the frame of its chosen style.

This recording was made by the original (1951) cast of the Opera, and this fact gives it extra value, especially since the important part of Amahl can no longer be sung by Chet Allen (a problem that arises when a lead role calls for a boy soprano). No one has ever bettered Allen's colorful treble. Rosemary Kuhlmann is superb, as are the three singers representing the Kings. This is a potent recording, and its sound is extremely good.

RCA has made a stereo version (LSC-2762) with Kurt Yaghjian as Amahl and Martha King as his mother, together with the others of the NBC Opera Company's cast who presented the work on television in December of 1963. This version is indeed first class, but it still must take second place (stereophonic sound notwithstanding) to the earlier recording, which has a greater sense of depth and more defined characterization. It is most interesting that RCA lists the mono recording in its numerical catalogue as a "steady best-seller." The later release does not enjoy this special identification.

The Medium (1946)

☐ Orchestra / Keller, Dame, and Mastice (sopranos); Powers (contralto); Rogier (baritone) / Balaban (conductor) / Columbia OSL-154 (monaural)

A powerful piece of theater. A fake medium (Madame Flora) has an assistant (Toby), a deaf mute, who is in love with her daughter (Monica). During a séance Madame Flora feels a clammy hand at her throat. She believes Toby to have been the culprit, but of course cannot make him talk. The medium, caught between the real and unreal, is driven to near insanity. She beats her assistant and drives him out of the house. When Toby returns to be with Monica, she shoots him. The story ends with Toby, "the dead ghost," holding the answer to the riddle. Who was it?

Not for a moment does the tragic tale lapse from the macabre. It is steeped in gruesomeness despite the few bright moments used for relief. Menotti writes with dramatic expertness. He models his work on the *verismo*-Puccini school. It serves him well despite having served many times before.

No composer has been better served than Menotti by his star—Marie Powers, who takes the role of the tragic heroine, Madame Flora. Her singing on the recording matches her dramatic ability in the flesh. This does not mean the remaining roles make a minor contribution. Everyone in this production is an accomplished vocalist, and with a perfectly paced performance under the late Emanuel Balaban's baton, the result is a fascinating and exciting recording. The music speaks with substantial power and proves Menotti's dramaturgical talent.

The Saint of Bleecker Street (1954)

☐ Orchestra and Chorus / Marlo, de Gerlando, and Ruggiero (sopranos); Akos and Lane (mezzo-sopranos); Poleri (tenor); Aiken (baritone); Lishner (bass) / Schippers (conductor / RCA CBM2-2741 (monaural)

All the ingredients in the recipe for proven (not original) Grand Opera are here. This has a logic all its own, since opera with a capital "O" means the past has been summoned up in full. Yes, Menotti's *Saint,* with all of its cogent effectiveness, is eclectic to its Puccinian core. Menotti rarely alters his Italian stops; the idiom is quite familiar and intensely nondebatable, in the sense that one knows what to expect. The ending is pat theater—how else describe the heroine's taking the veil to the background of choral counterpoint? The reproduced recipe turns out an excellent morsel—any dry eyes in the house? Let not this mixed metaphor confuse. Menotti sets out to trace a story of sacred-quasi-profane pattern, and the music is cut to fit, from models no longer fashionable but still very serviceable.

The cast is excellent—here one can find nothing to quibble about—and its performance finds its just reward in an excellent recording, made in 1954, first released in its mono setting on RCA Victor LM-6032, then deleted, and finally reissued with brighter sound. The voices are beautiful, and Schippers keeps the entire score alive.

The Telephone (1947)

☐ Cotlow (soprano); Rogier (baritone) / Balaban (conductor) / Columbia OSL-154 (monaural)

An amusing one-act Opera, in form closer to a skit, with high-class but unaffected music. Though the work calls for only two characters, there is actually a third, the mechanical sound of a telephone. The instrument imperiously rings and constantly frustrates the man whenever he is ready to "pop the question." He finally uses the telephone himself, calling from the corner drugstore and asking the girl to marry him. And they probably lived happily ever after.

Perfectly performed, and magnificently suited for mechanical reproduction, since no visual element is needed in order to follow the simple story line.

The Unicorn, the Gorgon, and the Manticore, or The Three Sundays of a Poet (1956)

☐ Paul Hill Orchestra and Chorale / Hill (conductor) / Golden Crest CRS-4180

Menotti describes his three-quarter-hour work as "a madrigal fable." It is unique in having no solo parts, merely a chorus that relates the story in madrigal style, while all the action is colored by a nine-piece instrumental group (four winds, a trumpet, two strings, percussion, and harp). The moral of this allegory, according to the composer, is, "Although the world may not suspect it,/All remains intact within/The Poet's heart." Menotti's tale discloses the stupid pretenses of affected respectability and the adoption of the passing whims of fashion.

The entire work has the fragrance of very old wine, in bottles of much newer make. Menotti's musical suavity and humor make his fable a sensitive and genuine art piece. It need not be seen to be enjoyed.

The first recording was led by the late Thomas Schippers and released on Angel 35437. The delete curse followed, and only recently the disc listed above appeared to fill the gap. It serves to make the music available, but presents only a fair performance.

Ballet

Sebastian (1944)

☐ London Symphony Orchestra / Serebrier (conductor) / Desto 6432

Menotti not only writes the libretti for his operas, he has written the scenario for this ballet. His vocal flair is exemplified instrumentally to a marked degree in the score, especially in the haunting and poignant *Barcarolle,* representing the second of the baker's dozen of sections in the work. Here is a tune to whistle.

Serebrier does very well. He informs the score with good taste. This is the first (and thus far only) integral recording of the ballet. A suite from the stage work was once available on RCA Victor LM-1858 with Stokowski conducting the defunct NBC Symphony.

For those who wish the *Barcarolle* alone, it can be found in a miscellaneous program on RCA LSC-2747, performed by the Boston Pops Orchestra, with Arthur Fiedler conducting. The name of the RCA album is *Slaughter on 10th Avenue.* That odd album title is the name of the lead piece of the assortment on the disc.

Saverio Mercadante   (1795-1870)

Solo Instrument and Orchestra

Flute

Concerto in E minor for Flute and Strings

☐ I Musici / Gazzelloni (flute) / Philips 6500611

An excellent introduction to the music of a composer given full scope in musical dictionaries, otherwise bypassed.

Severino Gazzelloni is a phenomenal flutist in the field of avant-garde flute literature. He is just as much the great artist in music of this songful type. It has simple operatic curves in the slow movement, sprightly spirit in the *Rondo russo,* "Russian" only in its dotted rhythms and light syncopations.

Olivier Messiaen   (1908-   )

Orchestra

Chronochromie (1960)

☐ BBC Symphony Orchestra / Dorati (conductor) / Argo ZRG-756

Chronochromie (which Messiaen indicates may be translated as "Color of Time") marks a wholesale use of bird song and orchestrally pictured water sounds. Basic to the work plan of the score is a set of thirty-two different durations. These are arranged and contrasted by use of melodic counterpoints, metallic percussion, and differently tinted chordal streams. The complexity is fascinating.

Dorati controls this score so that a constant tension is maintained, with cadential suppression and relentless textural weight. It is, indeed, tremendously difficult to accomplish, but accomplish it he does. It is a tour de force.

Couleurs de la cité céleste (1964)

☐ Orchestre du Domaine Musical and Groupe Instrumental à Percussion de Strasbourg / Loriod (piano) / Boulez (conductor) / Columbia MS-7356

The "Colors of the Celestial City" are drawn from five quotations from the Apocalypse. A granitic instrumentation prevails. There are no strings whatsoever; the winds are restricted to three clarinets. Ten brass instruments are used, plus a soloistic piano part, and the percussion is strictly metallic: xylophone, xylorimba, marimba, tuned cow bells, tubular bells, four gongs, and two tam-tams. Still, a large-scale type of chamber-music writing is utilized; densities are in the minority. This is due to the formal plan, which derives from a symbolistic use of color—shift of idea is underlined by shift of timbre combination.

There can be no doubts about the performance; everything is precise and clear, and all the textures are positive, for which both Boulez and the engineers deserve credit. Too bad Columbia does not provide separation bands on the disc, making impossible thereby the definition of the five quotations which comprise the opus.

Et Exspecto Resurrectionem Mortuorum (1964)

☐ Orchestre du Domaine Musical and Groupe Instrumental à Percussion de Strasbourg / Boulez (conductor) / Columbia MS-7356

No string instruments in this neotheopneustic musical document. There are five movements in Messiaen's piece, and all are based on texts from Holy Scripture. Avoidance of calidity is furthered by the restriction of the percussion to metallic instruments (three sets of tuned cow bells, tubular bells, six gongs, and three tam-tams).

Force is the paramount device in "And I Await the Resurrection of the Dead." This gives a plus to Messiaen, since he states he intended the work "for vast spaces: churches, cathedrals and even performances in the open air and on mountain heights." Because of the appropriateness of the scoring, the end movements are another plus for the composer. In these places the setting is totally tutti-threaded—embroidery is absent from the heavy tonal garment.

This disc marked Boulez's debut on the Columbia label—an extremely successful one.

L'Ascension (Quatre Méditations symphoniques) (1934)

☐ London Symphony Orchestra / Stokowski (conductor) / London 21060

With the exception of the third of these "Four Symphonic Meditations," this cycle was originally composed for organ, in 1933, and transcribed for orchestra the following year. The scoring shows the hand of Messiaen the organist. (Oddly enough the last movement is scored for strings alone.) And the program furnished shows the hardcore philosophy of Messiaen the devout, the text being drawn from the Catholic liturgy. "The Ascension" reflects a good part of Messiaen's general creative conduct—it is low-keyed ecstatic music.

Stokowski's performance is properly detailed to bring out the score's coloration, and he avoids any oversumptuousness in his portrayal. (For the organ version see under *Instrumental: organ.*)

Seven Haïkaï (1962)

☐ Orchestre du Domaine Musical and Groupe Instrumental à Percussion de Strasbourg / Loriod (piano) / Boulez (conductor) / Everest 3192

Plenty of bells and percussion. The music is full of Messiaen's ''hang-up'' with bird calls. Some fifteen different birds are listed in Messiaen's liner note. However, this avian guide is not followed precisely. Certain birds in part 3 are heard again in movement 6, but their ''tunes'' have such maximal differences that one is hard put to hear a relationship between the two statements.

The percussion and the piano are the principal progenitors in Messiaen's work; the other instruments support, frame, or adumbrate the percussion. Top credits belong here to Yvonne Loriod, Messiaen's wife. She plays magnificently.

Turangalîla Symphony (1949)

☐ London Symphony Orchestra / Beroff (piano); Loriod (ondes Martenot) / Previn (conductor) / Angel SR–3853

A Symphony, yes; but forget all average ideas of the form. *Turangalîla* (meaning freely ''song of love'') is an impassioned musical document for the brave and patient only. It embraces ten movements that cover almost an hour and a half of playing time. This mammoth projection is full of fervent sound surges, violent colors, and rhythmic counterpoint. Messiaen's piece is the equivalent of *Tristan und Isolde* converted into orchestral fantasies by way of Hindu-promulgated metrical plans. (The Symphony is an outgrowth of three *Talas* for piano, ondes Martenot, and large orchestra.)

Some of the movements are titled, but no storytelling is attempted. Type characterizations are used, based on four cyclic themes: a fierce ''statue'' subject, a supple ''flower'' motive, a very important love theme, and a chordal idea. The cycles are interwoven and developed, as well as restated. They are supercharged by a huge orchestra plus a smaller group within it of glockenspiel, celesta, vibraphone, piano, and metallic percussion that lends a sonority like a Balinese Gamelan ensemble. The staggering piano part is almost a solo role.

Turangalîla poses a set of paradoxes. It is heated, pagan music, yet devout. It is complex in construction, yet totally understandable. It is exciting and volatile, but its relentless paroxysms are also irritating. It has tuned balance and orgiastic climaxes, but seems to be in a constant tumescence.

Véga, in France, produced the first recording (No. 35–339/340). This was followed by an Ozawa-led production (on RCA LSC–7051). This, the very latest, is the most vivid not only in actual playing definition but in terms of recorded sound. Altogether, Angel's release is a block-buster.

Instrumental

Flute

Le Merle noir (1952)

☐ Brook (flute); Levin (piano) / Candide 31050

Although it bears a descriptive title (''The Blackbird''), Messiaen's piece is not a musical chronicle. The skittering passages (for the unaccompanied flute) may remind one of the feathery tribe, but mainly the music bathes in soaring, disjunctly curved canons. There is a grace to these measures, but they are not graced by cut-and-dried metrical patterns—no time signatures compress this contemporary music. Because of his detailed and unique research into the subject, one cannot quarrel with Messiaen's devotion to birdsong interpretation. It is a kind of ''my bird music, right or wrong, but my bird music.''

There is also no quarrel with Paige Brook's suave way with Messiaen's opus. The closest competition comes from Gazzelloni (on Mainstream 5014), but with the Italian virtuoso the music is driven rather than soars. (Incidentally, Mainstream's release titles the work incorrectly in the plural—''Merles Noir.'') There are two other recordings available: Nicolet (on Telefunken S–43098), which can be assigned third place, and Pellerite (on Coronet S–1713), which is a firm last, due to the horrible piano sound.

Fête des belles eaux for Ondes Martenot Sextet

Six Ondes Martenot

☐ Caron, Matagne, Recoussine, Trow, Chanforan, and Loriod (ondes Martenot) / Musical Heritage Society MHS–821

"The Festival of Beautiful Water" was conceived as a musical background for a festival of sound, water, and lights given in Paris in 1937. The sounds were amplified through loudspeakers placed on buildings bordering the Seine.

There is, of course, a great loss of effect in the transfer to a recording. However, Messiaen's Martenot *Fête* can be enjoyed for its main function of presenting repose. There isn't a single trace of any feverish writing. And for the ears, six ondes Martenot are no more problematic than six flutes.

Apparition de l'église éternelle (1932)

Organ

☐ Krigbaum (organ) / Lyrichord 7297

In its slow pace and incessant progression of block chords, this is music of stolidity, without contrast. The coalescence is shaped by an arched dynamic plan. Messiaen's mystical organ picture is not restricted in appeal by its constraint.

Krigbaum is totally at one with the composer's vision. The naturalness of the playing provides a gripping result.

La Nativité du Seigneur (Neuf Méditations pour Orgue) (1935)

☐ Klinda (organ) / Everest 3330

Messiaen has been quoted as saying that "God being present in all things, music dealing with theological subjects can and must be extremely varied." And "varied" means in this case a formal relaxation for each of the composition's nine parts (divided into four books, three "Meditations" in the first and three in the third, two in the second, and one in the last). The style of "The Birth of the Lord" resembles improvisation but is actually motival repetition. While the rhythmic accent and the rise and fall of the pulsatile figures are very flexible, none of the music is rhapsodic. Each of the "Nine Meditations" has a specific mood. Some examples: pastoralism is the flush that colors *Les Bergers* ("The Shepherds"), a hazy nocturne defines *Desseins éternels* ("Eternal Purposes"), fanfare-like optimism marks the final *Dieu parmi nous* ("God Among Us").

The cycle gains strength on repeated hearings. Messiaen's representation of Christ's birth must be considered as a whole montage. To expect to recognize every small documentary detail is to lose sight of the essential grandeur and positive depth of the music.

The recorded choice is between performances by Ferdinand Klinda, Simon Preston (Argo 5447), and Charles Krigbaum (Lyrichord 7225). All are expert organists. All play this music with expertise. The preference depends partly on the instrument used. A very large and powerful organ is less desirable (Krigbaum uses the Woolsey Hall organ at Yale University, Preston plays the gigantic Westminster Abbey instrument) than the one on which Ferdinand Klinda performs—the organ of the St. Nicholas Church in Prague. It fits Messiaen's prose a bit better than the two others mentioned. But above all stands the fine sense of continuity and superb registration that Klinda exhibits in his most distinguished performance.

L'Ascension (Quatre Méditations symphoniques) (1933)

☐ Preston (organ) / Argo 5339

The "Four Symphonic Meditations" were inspired by passages from scripture, such as

St. John's gospel (parts 1 and 4 of Messiaen's music) and verses from St. Paul's Epistles to the Colossians (the toccata impetus of movement 3).

However, regardless of Messiaen's apparent craving for programmatic delineation, most of Messiaen's music does not follow any story. Instead, it codes a specific emotional experience. The background of unceasing chordal movement in movement 4 (*Prière du Christ montant vers Son Père*), for example, presents a decisive image of beseeching, fully bearing out the mood: "Prayer of Christ Ascending Toward His Father." It is a music of muted florescence and shadowed inquiry that becomes the sound of service in the church of Olivier Messiaen. It is strangely moving.

Movement 3, *Transports de joie d'une âme devant la gloire du Christ que est la sienne*, is entirely different from that of the orchestral version (see under *Orchestra*). It utilizes the full dynamism of the organ and is a tour de force of instrumental injunction in its sonic expulsions.

Preston's playing is impressive. He performs on the organ in the Chapel of King's College in Cambridge. The instrument is smaller than that used by Krigbaum in his Lyrichord recording (7297)—the Newberry memorial organ in Woolsey Hall at Yale University—and the music benefits thereby.

A duplicate of Preston's performance is included in Argo's jumbo release *Four Centuries of Organ Music* (5BBA-1013/5).

Le Banquet céleste (1928)

☐ Preston (organ) / Argo ZRG-633

It was this short work that brought Messiaen to the attention of the European music world. Composed in 1928, before he had attained voting age, *Le Banquet céleste* exhibits the usual symbolism that prevails in all of Messiaen's compositions. (The music represents the Last Supper, the "celestial banquet of Holy Communion.") The hermetic harmony gives a desolate and sad tinge to the slow motion of the piece, bound further by motivic constancy. Notwithstanding, it is as purely ecstatic a declamation as Messiaen's pyrotechnic orchestral pronouncements.

It is not easy to place music of static quality in proper perspective, especially when the texture is thick. The tendency to involve dynamic change and thereby seemingly intensify the motility makes Krigbaum's rendition (Lyrichord 7297) less satisfying than Preston's. Preston's retention of the quiet that pervades the piece provides all the strength the music requires.

Les Corps glorieux (1939)

☐ Krigbaum (organ) / Lyrichord 7224

Messiaen's full-scale hieratic gestures are displayed in the seven movements of *Les Corps glorieux*, subtitled *Sept Visions brèves de la vie des ressuscités*. The quiet and the exultant moods, together with plainsong and Hindu rhythms are involved in a compounding of scriptorial spirituality, with a highly individual feeling for color.

Movement 4, *Force et agilité des Corps glorieux*, is often heard out of its suite context and has been recorded in several miscellaneous programs. Its dogmatic majesty combined with inner struggle is a masterpiece among the many Messiaen masterpieces that represent the most important organ music of the twentieth century.

Charles Krigbaum's performance is strong, rich, and vital—phrased to register all the pulses and impulses of the music. It has greater power than Simon Preston's conception on Argo (ZRG-633). It also conveys slightly better articulation.

Messe de la Pentecôte (1950)

☐ Krigbaum (organ) / Lyrichord 7226

Despite its title, the *Messe* is a gigantic fantasy stuffed with the composer's favorite plainchant shapes, embroidered with counterpoints, and amorphic rhythmic patterns. Included are countless bird songs, transformed and reinterpreted.

The interposition and mass combination of Messiaen's sound complexes, though exceedingly long in performance time, are not tautological. Here is sonority that captivates regardless of the method. Messiaen's statement is worth recalling: "It is a glistening music we seek, giving to the aural sense voluptuously refined pleasures." Nonetheless this is raw music, despite the pious garb worn by the composer.

The Woolsey Hall organ at Yale University that Charles Krigbaum uses is ideal for this five-movement opus. His performance is marvelous, exciting, dynamic, and faithfully precise to the last note. Heavy sections emerge full-weighted, but thoroughly clear. This is absolutely a musically informative presentation—and tremendously stimulating. It is recommended without qualification.

Catalogue d'oiseaux (1956–1958)   *Piano*

I. *Le Chocard des alpes*	VIII. *L'Alouette Calandrelle*
II. *Le Loriot*	IX. *La Bouscarle*
III. *Le Merle bleu*	X. *Le Merle de roche*
IV. *Le Traquet Stapazin*	XI. *La Buse variable*
V. *La Chouette Hulotte*	XII. *Le Traquet rieur*
VI. *L'Alouette Lulu*	XIII. *Le Courlis cendré*
VII. *La Rousserolle effarvette*	

☐ Oliveira-Carvalho (piano) / Vox SVBX–5464

Musical coinage that communicates Messiaen's passionate sincerity and enthusiasm for birds, landscapes, flowers, and the colors of nature. The forms are free, presumably based on the passing of the day's hours. Thus, as a specific example, the fourth piece, "The Black-eared Wheatear." This is a setting in the month of June, the design dictated by the hours from 5 A.M., with "the red disc of the sun rising from the sea," to 10 P.M. and "total night."

This type of explanation is not sheer verbal extravagance—programmatic property equates a creative freehold. What can be imaged or imagined by a composer can be heard (and translated) just as freely. The visions in this music are almost apocalyptic. Indulge the ears—the writing is of fantastic originality and goes beyond, far beyond, the trills, turns, and tweets of birds.

The performance of Jocy de Oliveira-Carvalho (the wife of the conductor) is expert, producing a wide range of sonorities and exhibiting consummate technical efficacy.

Preludes

La Colombe
Chant d'extase dans un paysage triste
Le Nombre léger
Instants défunts
Les Sons impalpables du rêve
Cloches d'angoisse et larmes d'adieu
Plainte calme
Un Reflet dans le vent

☐ Bennette (piano) / Desto 7110

The sophistications of this music reflect the style of Claude Debussy. Not surprising, since these eight Preludes represent young Messiaen, having been composed at the age of twenty-one. Still, the Messiaen-to-be is already apparent, with mystical title impressions and the use of special scalic designs that depart from major-minor schemes.

Well-stated playing by George Bennette. Especially cogent is the clarity of the involved rhythmic designs.

Vingt Regards sur l'Enfant Jésus (1944)

☐ Peter Serkin (piano) / RCA CRL3-0759

Messiaen enmeshes his doctrines with occult definitions which practically require a concordance to understand. In this huge work (twenty movements, covering five record sides, with a performance time of a bit over two hours) he is describing the "Contemplation of the Child-God of the Crib and the Glances which fall on Him." He utilizes certain harmonies to simulate the design of stained glass, the heavenly rainbow, and so on. In part 14, *Regards des anges* ("Contemplation of the Angels"), his remarks begin, "Flickering, throbbing; powerful blast from the trombones...." These directions are translated into overly charged chordal combinations thrown about in semitortured ecstatic melodic lines. The atmosphere is heavily concentrated and heavy with musical incense. The effect is close to stifling.

Constantly astir and severely untempered in contrast, the "Twenty Contemplations on the Infant Jesus," like Messiaen's other lengthy compositions, are taxing for a listener. The point is offered that too much Messiaen defeats him. For best results, his exhortations in sound should be heard in small portions.

The Messiaen performer of all performers has been Yvonne Loriod. Her performance of the cycle on two old Westminster mono discs (18469/70) is not replaced by Peter Serkin's amazing portrayal of this music. He has one special asset that no one has been able to duplicate (least of all John Ogdon in his performance on Argo ZRG–650/1), and that is a sense of spontaneity within which is a total involvement. In some places his rhythmic controls are more certain even than Loriod's. The quieter pieces are served the best (positively clean and without sonorous waste), but there is a most satisfactory equilibrium between those and the more fiery sections. I said that Loriod's performance has not been replaced. Indeed not, but it has been matched.

Two Pianos

Visions de l'amen (1942)

☐ Peter Serkin and Takahashi (pianos) / RCA ARL1-0363

Seven movements which are symbolic of the act of creation. Included in the sonorous plans (always crowded with content and motile rhythms) is a movement concerned with the heavenly bodies as the insensible objects of creation. Another recalls the agony and sorrow of Christ in the garden of Gethsemane. Again, in this ecstasy of sound and movement, it is apparent that religious data and belief can no more be separated from the pulse and veins of Messiaen's music than speech can be separated from the mouth.

In this depiction of "amens" (the word itself implying finality and completeness of a divine act) the act of performance is brilliantly conceived and carried out. There are other versions —one on the Véga label, No. 8509, another in the Musical Heritage catalogue, No. 1762, and still another on Argo, ZRG–665. The RCA edition is number one on this writer's list.

Quatuor pour la fin du temps (1941)

☐ Tashi / RCA ARL1–1567

Messiaen's work is in eight movements, so purposefully totaled because, he says, "Seven is the perfect number, namely, the creation of six days hallowed by the Divine Sabbath; the seventh . . . extends into eternity and becomes the eighth of the indefectible light, of unalterable peace." Various instrumentation plans effect a fluidic texture in the eight movements. The third part is for clarinet alone, the fourth eliminates the piano, No. 5 is for cello and piano, while the final movement (very oddly) is for violin and piano only. Thus solo, duet, and trio media are included in a composition for four instruments.

The work is filled with rich invention. The unaccompanied-clarinet solo in movement 3 is truly remarkable. This section, *Abîme des oiseaux* ("Abyss of the Birds"), is meant to speak of "time with its gloom, weariness." Movement 6, *Danse de la fureur, pour les sept trompettes* ("Dance of Fury for the Seven Trumpets"), is the most amazing division of the entire quartet, a true tour de force. Although the music includes the freest type of rhythmic patterns, a pyrotechnic type of writing, and fantastic use of plastic motival and permutative development, it is scored entirely in unison.

There have been a number of recorded performances, but none can match the one presented by Tashi (Richard Stoltzman, clarinet; Ida Kavafian, violin; Fred Sherry, cello; and Peter Serkin, piano). Messiaen's work has become this organization's speciality, and they present the score with a rich subtlety that fully projects the mystical and visionary ideas of this master composer. Each member of the group produces a sound that details both the finesse and the emotionalism within the score. There are constant technical challenges, one of the most enormous being the control required in the solo-clarinet section. Stoltzman's playing is a masterpiece in itself.

Chants de terre et de ciel

☐ Barker (soprano); Johnson (piano) / Argo ZRG–699

The cycle reflects Messiaen's usual love of worship of his God ("Anthem of Silence," dedicated to the Feast of the Guardian Angels; "Resurrection," for Easter; and one other song) and also includes a pair of songs "for my little Pascal" and one for his first wife.

The "Songs of Earth and Heaven" are sung with conviction, though with less than the extroverted exalted positiveness which these songs require. Noelle Barker's voice is clearly pitched, but her restraint drains some of the impact that is contained in the music.

Poèmes pour Mi (1936)

☐ Arséguet (soprano); Messiaen (piano) / Everest 3269

Nine songs devoted to a constantly evolving commentary. This is early Messiaen (composed in 1936), minus the superconstructivistic approach but with an intense indifference to traditional *Lieder* format. The harmonic flow is sensuous, nullifying cadential punctuation; the rhythms are just as fluid.

The performance is certified by the composer's being half of the duo. Be warned—this is proxy stereo, a transfer from a mono French release. (The correct spelling of the soprano's name is on the record label; elsewhere it is misspelled.)

See under *Voice and Orchestra* for Messiaen's version for soprano and orchestra.

Poèmes pour Mi (1936)

☐ BBC Symphony Orchestra / Palmer (soprano) / Boulez (conductor) / Argo ZRG–703

There is also a version of this work for voice and piano (see under *Voice with Accom-*

paniment). The coloristic instrumental background expands the impact of these songs in both versions, but doubly so in the present one, since the orchestral qualities bind in, counterpoint and highlight, the harmonic colors. Splendid singing. (It is important to stress that Messiaen considers as "official" *both* the piano-and-voice setting and the orchestra-with-voice setting. The piano edition is not the usual orchestral reduction made for rehearsal purposes for the singer's benefit.)

Choral

Chorus Alone

Cinq Rechants (1949)

☐ John Alldis Choir / Alldis (conductor) / Argo ZRG–523

Neo-medievalism rules in these "Five Refrains" (*rechant* being the sixteenth-century French word for "refrain"). Make-believe also rules in the occasional use of pseudo-Hindu language. Further, vocal effects are ruled into the score, via articulation of such items as "t k t k t k t k" and "la li la li la li." The choralstration is compelling, though at this date Messiaen's inventions have become a firm fixture with the advanced contemporary school of composers, who have added dozens of other effects to the choral vocabulary.

The twelve voices conquer all the many difficulties Messiaen has included. Certainly this is exceptional singing of an exceptional score.

Chorus with Accompaniment

O Sacrum Convivium (1937)

☐ Choir of St. John's College, Cambridge / Cleobury (organ) / Guest (conductor) / Argo ZRG–662

Textural simplicity that embraces sensuous harmonic coloring. Messiaen celebrates his "Sacred Communion" with a quiet vocal ceremony that knowingly moves up to one high pitch and dynamic point and then recedes. Exceedingly moving singing by this fine choir, reflecting every nuance of the score in its proper dimension.

Cantata and Oratorio

La Transfiguration de Notre Seigneur Jésus Christ (1969)

☐ National Symphony Orchestra and Westminster Choir / Sylvester (tenor); Aquino (baritone); Loriod (piano) / Dorati (conductor) / London HEAD–1/2

A huge work of fourteen movements that is in Messiaen's richly ornate style. Here the sermon is a set of meditations on various texts, with the religious exaltation intensely set forth in timbre perception, chant-like detail, and vivid pulsatile designs.

The performance has passion even when it throws overripe combinations of sound into imbalance.

Josep Maria Mestres-Quadreny   (1929-   )

Chamber Music

Divertimento La Ricarda for Flute, Clarinet, and Double Bass

☐ Turetzky (double bass) / Desto 7128

Fractured sounds, bits and pieces thrown against each other. First the bass, then the flute (not credited on the recording) with a screaming high-pitched sound. Later the clarinet (also nameless) enters the arena. Stage business is part of the score: the flutist starts by playing sitting in the auditorium, then moves on stage; later the double bass leaves the stage. Of course all this is out of sight totally as far as a recording is concerned. The theatrical gestures probably would add some flavor to this odd trio recipe.

Giacomo Meyerbeer (1791-1864)

Coronation March from *Le Prophète* (1843)   *Orchestra*

☐ Philadelphia Orchestra / Ormandy (conductor) / Columbia MS-6474

A resonant, fully articulated statement of the old warhorse.

Cantique du trappiste   *Vocal*

Der Garten des Herzens   *Voice with*

Die Rose, die Lilie, die Taube, die Sonne   *Accompaniment*

Die Rosenblätter

Hör'ich das Liedchen klingen

Komm'

Le Chant du dimanche

Le Poète mourant

Menschenfeindlich

Mina

Sicilienne

Sie und ich

Ständchen

Südwind

☐ Fischer-Dieskau (baritone); Engel (piano) / Deutsche Grammophon ARC-2533295

A large sampler from Meyerbeer's song settings, which total a bit more than sixty. While none of these songs will quicken the pulse, in most cases the vocal writing is sound and the accompaniments appropriate.

Fischer-Dieskau gives well-considered renditions, though in some instances he bears down much more than required so that neither Meyerbeer nor Fischer-Dieskau benefit. Yet for vocal literature otherwise hardly heard, it is good to have this program available.

Les Huguenots   *Opera
                                                                and Dramatic
☐ New Philharmonia Orchestra and Ambrosian Opera Chorus / Sutherland and Arroyo   Music*
(sopranos); Tourangeau (mezzo-soprano); Vrenios (tenor); Bacquier (baritone); Ghiuselev
and Cossa (basses) / Bonynge (conductor) / London 1437

Perhaps the tendency to underestimate Meyerbeer is disappearing. It would be proper to realize this composer's special command of the orchestra and his excellent choice and handling of vocal devices. It also should be restated how he influenced Berlioz, Verdi, and Wagner. But even without such documentation *Les Huguenots* proves it can stand on its complete five acts as fine opera.

The London recording followed a full-scale London concert performance in 1962 and is excellent. Martina Arroyo is brilliant; the tenor, Anastasios Vrenios, has a magnificent voice, and its quality is matched by a splendid ability to negotiate high-pitch embroideries of quite some difficulty. Sutherland is fine, though her diction is less impressive. Bonynge's line of action is accomplished. There are some cuts.

Meyerbeer / Constant Lambert (1905-1951)

Ballet

Les Patineurs

☐ Israel Philharmonic Orchestra / Martinon (conductor) / London STS-15051

Formed from excerpts taken from Meyerbeer's operas *Le Prophète* and *L'Étoile du nord.* Martinon goes at it on the strong side, but even if subtlety is secondary, the results provide balletic truth. Profits for a listener thereby.

Nikolai Miaskovsky   *(1881-1950)*

Band

Symphony for Band (Symphony No. 19), Op. 46

☐ Moscow State Band / Petrov (conductor) / Monitor 2038 (monaural)

A suite-like opus, with rhythmically folksy, waltz, meditative, and festive moods embracing the four movements.

Miaskovsky's work is for military band, which differs (by its emphasis on brass instruments and a minimal number of woodwinds) from the symphonicized make-up of American band instrumentation. Bearing this in mind, the performance is especially clean, clear, and well balanced.

Solo Instrument and Orchestra

Cello

Concerto in C minor for Cello and Orchestra, Op. 66

☐ Philharmonia Orchestra / Rostropovich (cello) / Sargent (conductor) / Seraphim S-60223

Miaskovsky's Concerto (first heard in 1945) has stayed out of the repertoire because it does not deal with melodramatics and is far from a display piece. It consists of a pair of movements which emphasize lyricism of a subdued nature. Rostropovich is as warm-hearted and masterful as usual, and there is fine partnership between himself and the orchestra. The recording dates back some years, but its sound is certainly good.

Instrumental

Piano

Grillen, Op. 25, (Nos. 1 and 6)

☐ Prokofiev (piano) / Klavier 125

The neglect of this composer, both in the concert hall and in the recorded catalogue, is artistic injustice. There is no doubt that he will eventually be "discovered." There is sufficient in his voluminous output from which to choose. This pair of extracts from his "Whimsies," a set of "six sketches," composed in 1922, has its romantic style refreshed by a nationalistic touch.

Chamber Music

Sonata No. 2 for Cello and Piano, Op. 81

☐ Rostropovich (cello); Dedyukhine (piano) / Monitor 2145 (monaural)

A composition that displays magnificent workmanship and rich themes, without overindulgences or extravagances of any kind. Miaskovsky's classically shaped, romantically tonal music (the outer movements of the Sonata are in A minor, the central movement is in F major) remains little known, save to a handful, yet the Cello and Piano Sonata No. 2 further bears out the eloquence of this composer.

The playing here is discriminating and significant. It is also significant that this is still another work not logged in *Schwann* (neither in the No. 2 catalogue, where it properly belongs since Monitor's disc is "re-recorded to simulate stereo," nor in the No. 1 listings). One understands the impossibility of listing everything in *Schwann* (disregarding the multitudinous small pieces in assorted collections, which are another story), but surely an important composer such as Miaskovsky deserves a complete listing of the few works that have been recorded.

Donal Michalsky   *(1928-1975)*

Chamber Music

Partita piccola for Flute and Piano (1962)

☐ Shanley (flute); Davis (piano) / Wim WIMR-2

Twelve-tone musical order set into very live existence by cogent designs: *Preludio*, Toccata, *Variazioni,* and *Giga alla rondo.* What is stimulating in this case is the Mozartian dress (without the eighteenth-century wig) of the composition.

A quiet virtuosity is demanded to make this music register. Gretel Shanley and Sharon Davis meet all the requirements.

Divertimento for Three Clarinets (1952)

☐ Atkins (clarinet); d'Antonio (alto clarinet); Spear (bass clarinet) / Wim WIMR-7

Michalsky treats the instruments, each of definite color, mostly as a compact unit, akin to the string trio with which they are in close equivalence. There are six movements, balanced by march divisions at the terminal points.

Francisco Mignone   *(1897-   )*

Instrumental

Piano

Prelude No. 6, *Caiçaras*

☐ Calligaris (piano) / Orion 7286

Emotional expressivity in terms of a lament. The scope demonstrates the soloist's full command.

Violin

Noturno Sertanejo

☐ Szeryng (violin); Maillols (piano) / Philips 6500016

The sentiments here revealed can be described as a slow blues, Brazilian style. Szeryng's sensuous delivery is totally fitting.

Vocal

Canção Brasileira

Voice with Accompaniment

☐ Averino (soprano); Slonimsky (piano) / Orion 7150 (monaural)

The plaintive content found so often in slow-tempoed Brazilian songs. This is a real beauty and sung to emphasize every nostalgic nuance in the piece.

Georges Migot   *(1891-1976)*

Chamber Music

Trio for Piano, Violin, and Cello (1935)

☐ Trio Courmont / Harmonia Mundi HMU-458

The absence of this composer (with an output of close to 300 works) from recorded literature constitutes an outrage. This seems to be the only issue available. It is undeniable proof of the singularity of his art. Just to name a few, why no attention to such creative strengths as the Six Small Preludes (each descriptive of a bird) for two violins, the *Five Movements of Water* for string quartet, the deeply felt and deeply moving oratorio *Le Sermon sur la Montagne,* and the orchestral *The Lacquered Screen with Five Images,* with its soft brush-work instrumentation?

Migot's music provides a modern rejuvenation of *ars antiqua,* with freedom of voices and a substance of sonorous refinement. In Migot's work there are neither the development processes used in the classic-romantic-school sense nor the pictorial landscaping of the impressionists. Metaphorically, the use of phonetics in his musical style is a far cry from chordal words. A parallel to the field of graphic art will make this clearer: Migot avoids fresco painting and portraiture. His line engravings are three-dimensional super-etchings. His melodic detail is neither square- nor round-shaped, but of curved traction. Combined, the lines still proceed freely, each on its own way, establishing individual logic, every voice supple and expressive, separate yet in its pith and moment in the total mass.

This polylineal style is represented in the Trio (Migot gave it the alternate title *Suite à trois*). It consists of four sizable movements covering forty-one minutes: *Prélude, Allègre, Danse,* and *Final.* One is grateful to the Trio Courmont (Marie-Claude Chevalier-Dumé, piano; Claude Bardon, violin; and Alain Courmont, cello) for producing this work on disc. They deserve plaudits for this recording breakthrough. They also deserve plaudits for a superb performance.

Marcel Mihalovici (1898-)

String Orchestra

Esercizio per Archi, Op. 80

☐ Jean-François Paillard Chamber Orchestra / Paillard (conductor) / Musical Heritage Society MHS–1405

Mihalovici studied with Vincent d'Indy, and to a certain extent the thicker writing of the Frenchman was never removed from the Rumanian's composition paper. However, Mihalovici's harmonic language would have shocked his teacher. This is not because the idiom is atonal, atonic, or of linear freedom (the polarity tonal moderative is evident here), but because it has certain chromatic extravagances which are of foreign nature if set beside d'Indy's already heavy chromatic accents. This may very well have been caused by the more rhapsodic nature of an expatriate Rumanian working and composing in France.

Paillard's musicians clarify the chromatic and polyphonic details of this two-part work expertly. There is fine string sound as well.

Solo Instrument and Orchestra

Piano

Etude en deux parties, Op. 64

☐ "Ars Nova" Ensemble of the O.R.T.F. / Haas (piano) / Constant (conductor) / Musical Heritage Society MHS–1405

Horizontal chromatic spread is constant in the melismatic opening movement of Mihalovici's "Study in Two Parts." Vertically percussive, toccataish progress marks the *Tempo giusto* of part 2. The scoring avoids softish strings, calling for three woodwinds (two clarinets and bassoon), four brass (two trumpets, trombone, and tuba), two percussionists, and celesta.

Monique Haas, the composer's wife, is the prime interpreter of his music and certainly proves it here.

Luis Milán   (ca. 1500 - ca. 1565)

Instrumental

Guitar

Pavana

No. 1 in A minor / No. 2 in B minor / No. 3 in C major / No. 4 in D major / No. 5 in D major / No. 6 in D major

☐ Segovia (guitar) / MCA 2501

Milán's music was for the vihuela, the Spanish relative of the lute. Performance on the modern guitar gives far less of a color exchange than playing harpsichord music on the piano.

Modal style and staid demeanor are represented. Segovia's restrained playing brings out all the simple qualities of the music. This recording was once in the Decca catalogue, which company was taken over by the Music Corporation of America, which has reissued a few of Decca's releases on its own (MCA) label.

Ellsworth Milburn   (1938-   )

Chamber Music

String Quartet (1974)

☐ Concord Quartet / Composers Recordings SD–369

Though there is definable form and Milburn makes no attempt to conceal the quintuple sectionalism, the great passion here is the generously involved sound spectrum. It is cogently organized and sensitively outleted. It produces a quartet of quality, freshness, and ingenuity.

The Concord four play this music of dissonance and spongy percussiveness with complete virtuosity.

Darius Milhaud   (1892 - 1974)

Orchestra

Cortège funèbre (1940)

☐ Louisville Orchestra / Mester (conductor) / Louisville S–685

Originally this was background music in a section of a film titled *Espoir,* portraying a funeral procession honoring a group of Spanish Republican soldiers. It is set in Milhaud's usual polytonal language. The use of the saxophone highlights the heavy orchestration.

Protée: Suite symphonique No. 2 (1919)

☐ Utah Symphony Orchestra / Abravanel (conductor) / Angel S–37317

The high spirits of this five-sectioned Suite (drawn from the incidental music Milhaud wrote for Paul Claudel's play) are most apparent. *Protée* is devoid of any pose; it is fresh and sometimes arrogant—sophisticated, with a devil-may-care attitude about it, yet never cheap. The music is chatty but not gibberish, nervous but not strained.

Our norms of behavior differ widely, and no law dictates how we should behave at concerts. Nowadays it is rare to have spontaneous disapproval registered at an artistic affair. In 1920, when this work was first produced in Paris, it incited behavior comparable to a gang fight. Milhaud describes the brawl in his book *Notes Without Music;* the brawl included everything from musicians slapping each other to police intervention. Disapproval by reactionaries tends to make a work significant instead of producing artistic sanctions against it. We listen to Milhaud's opus today wondering what sort of climate there was in Europe that could cause such a *succès de scandale*.

This is a welcome issue, filling a gap made long ago by the deletion of Pierre Monteux's recording with the San Francisco Symphony Orchestra. This was a 78-rpm transfer onto the economy Camden label (No. 385); its only deficiency was the sound, and that was not even too bad. Monteux's reading made a listener overlook the sonics. Now that Abravanel has done this good performance deed, an important twentieth-century composition is again available. His conception and his orchestra are first rate.

Saudades do Brasil (Excerpts) (1920-1921)

☐ Orchestre National de France / Bernstein (conductor) / Angel S-37442

Milhaud transcribed this suite of dances, originally composed for piano, at the request of the conductor Vladimir Golschmann (see under *Instrumental: piano*). The fertile polytonality that covers the score is clarified by the instrumental color streams, and the rhythmic chic is likewise enhanced by the varied timbres.

Bernstein conducts four of the set. They glow under his direction, and as a result one wishes he had done the entire dozen.

Symphony

No. 1 (*Le Printemps*) for Small Orchestra (1917) / No. 2 (*Pastorale*) for Small Orchestra (1918) / No. 3 (*Sérénade*) for Small Orchestra (1921) / No. 5 (for Ten Wind Instruments) (1922)

☐ Orchestra of Radio Luxembourg / Milhaud (conductor) / Candide 31008

Milhaud duplicated the numbering of the first six of his dozen symphonies. Though this is confusing, there is a difference in the two groups. Initially composed was a set of six *petite* symphonies (meaning not only small in size and scope but chamber-styled in instrumentation), each scored for a different combination; then followed the symphonies Nos. 1 to 12 for large orchestra (the third with chorus).

The first three of the *petite* group are subtitled as noted above. *Le Printemps* calls for piccolo, flute, oboe, clarinet, harp, and string quartet; the *Pastorale* requires three winds (flute, English horn, and bassoon) and four strings (violin, viola, cello, and double bass); the same strings and the same number of winds are used in the *Sérénade,* but the wind trio this time consists of flute, clarinet, and bassoon.

The fourth of the set is discussed under *String Orchestra* (Symphony No. 4 [for Ten Stringed Instruments]). The sixth of the group is found under *Vocal: voice and instrumental ensemble* (Symphony No. 6 [for Soprano, Contralto, Tenor, Bass, Oboe, and Cello]). Number 5 is for a dectet of eight woodwinds (piccolo, flute, oboe, English horn, clarinet, bass clarinet, and two bassoons) and two horns.

The only regularities in these delightful pieces—performed delightfully as well—are the three movements for each Symphony and the wholesale bitonality, tritonality, and polytonality that are the Milhaudian signature. Like the instrumentations, distinct formal differences mark the individual movements.

Symphony No. 4 (1947)

☐ Philharmonic Orchestra of the O.R.T.F. / Milhaud (conductor) / Musical Heritage Society MHS-1089

In 1947 Milhaud received a request from the Minister of Education of France for a work to celebrate the centenary of the 1848 Revolution. (The subtitle of the work has appeared at times as simply *1848*.) As usual, it took little time for Milhaud to compose the piece. He set his Symphony in the common four-movement arrangement, subtitling the divisions *The Insurrection, To the Dead of the Republic, The Peaceful Joys of Regained Freedom, Commemoration 1948.*

As usual with Milhaud, polyphony is presented here to a very large degree. It denotes an abstract, cold compositional logic, though within the woven lines and conjugated melodies the ideas of each movement (with an assist from the descriptive titles) are clear. Nevertheless, the feeling remains that the Symphony is successful only in its fine linear musical arrangement. None of the themes remain in the memory. This may be due to the performance, which is somewhat docile in terms of power and neutral in color.

Symphony No. 6 (1955)

☐ Louisville Orchestra / Mester (conductor) / Louisville S–744

Strongest in its two slow movements, where the composer's cultured lyricism is indented by neatly colorful dissonances. Throughout, Milhaud's usual love of polyphony is present, but not to the usual large degree. An important point in the work is the interplay of textures.

Symphony No. 8 (*Rhodanienne*) in D (1958)

☐ Philharmonic Orchestra of the O.R.T.F. / Roques (violin) / Milhaud (conductor) / Musical Heritage Society MHS–1089

Milhaud's musical celebration of the Rhone River. The material conveys the moods of the river's birth, its serenity, and then its impetuosity, with the finale "inspired by the approach of the Mediterranean Sea, when the divided Rhone encloses in a delta the Camargue."

The "in D" signifies a pitch polarity. Milhaud branches his river into polyharmonies and polytonalities. It is much less fervent in its linear convolutions than is habitual with this composer. Classy portrayal by the orchestra with pungent violin playing on the part of Max Roques, who has opportunities in the second movement: *Avec Sérénité et nonchalance.*

Symphony No. 4 (for Ten Stringed Instruments) (1921)

*String
Orchestra*

☐ Orchestra of Radio Luxembourg / Milhaud (conductor) / Candide 31008

Milhaud's *Dixtuor à cordes* calls for four violins, and two each of viola, cello, and double bass, though the parts may be multiplied. Like all the other *petite* symphonies—see under *Orchestra* (Symphony No. 1 [*Le Printemps*] for Small Orchestra)—it has three movements.

This is music of utopian timbre intensity, with Bachian strength and contrapuntal mobility in the *Ouverture*, an umbrageous Chorale, with uncompromising harmonic acidity, and a breathtaking polyphonic acrostic in the concluding Etude. This final section is doubly contrapuntal by sheer force of individual line and direct fugal sensibility. It may be criticized as mechanically conceived music, but it is magnificently apportioned.

The playing is clear-cut, with great muscle in the finale and fine strength of texture in the second movement. Those who are curious as to another approach to this music might try Lukas Foss's direction of the Zimbler Sinfonietta in Milhaud's work. It is on Turnabout 34154E, the *second* reissue of his performance, this time hyped into stereo. Initially

Unicorn released it on its No. 1037, then the performance went over into the Siena catalogue, numbered 100-2.

Band

Suite française (1944)

☐ Ohio State University Concert Band / McGinnis (conductor) / Coronet S-1502

Originally composed for band but very often heard in transcription for orchestra—an unusual reversal of matters. Milhaud's purpose was to write for the average school group, but technical boundaries do not suffocate art. The product, including some contemporaneously dressed folk tunes, is a work of brilliance and virtuosity without requiring virtuosi.

**Solo
Instrument
and
Orchestra**

Les Quatre Saisons ("The Four Seasons"). See below (under individual instruments with orchestra) for Concertino d'automne; Concertino d'hiver; Concertino d'été; and Concertino de printemps.

Since Milhaud, in his recording of this cycle, approved the above title, we must accept it. However, it should be realized that this was a decision made long after the creative facts. The composition of the works, covering a twenty-year period, did not follow the solstitial order. Milhaud's conceptions of the seasons began with spring, then after many years jumped to autumn, which was followed by summer and winter. The years of composition are 1934 for the first, 1951 for the next two, and 1953 for the last. The parallel to Vivaldi's famous "Seasons" occurred to Milhaud later, accounting for the lack of such a heading in any of the individually published scores.

The four concertini are distinct, and are usually performed separately. Each calls for a different solo voice, and various groups of instruments are used in support. "Autumn" is for two pianos with two winds, three horns, and three strings; "Winter" is scored for trombone and strings; "Summer" calls for viola accompanied by four winds, two brass, two cellos, and double bass; and "Spring" is set for violin and chamber orchestra.

As is the method in this survey, each of the four concertini is discussed separately, though the cycle is covered as a unit on a single recording. This, now available on Philips, was originally released on the Epic label, No. 3666.

Cello

Suite cisalpine sur des airs populaires piémontais (1954)

☐ Orchestra of Radio Luxembourg / Blees (cello) / Kontarsky (conductor) / Turnabout 34496

Give Darius Milhaud folk tunes and he's off to the races. A listen to his Suite provençale and the Suite française is all the proof required. And here is more, for cello and orchestra. The most interest is found in the outer fast movements of this Suite cisalpine (cisalpine meaning "on the Roman side") built on piemontais tunes (meaning "from the Piedmont region," which is just over the Franco-Italian frontier in Italy).

These are moderately short and sweet—also slightly bitter and sweet but always suave and sweet—inventions. Only a moderately fair recording. There's some pinched sound in the Modéré section to begin with, and it's not helped by Thomas Blees's hard-driven tone quality in the upper register, where most of the cello writing in that movement is situated. Milhaud's work was composed for Piatigorsky in 1954. I doubt that he gave it any special attention (in fact, the world premiere was given by Reine Flachot), and he certainly never recorded it.

Percussion

Concerto for Percussion and Small Orchestra (1930)

☐ Orchestra of Radio Luxembourg / Daniel (percussion) / Milhaud (conductor) / Candide 31013

All Milhaud had to do was to rub his creative lamp and music jumped to his command. In this unique Concerto one percussionist plays timpani, five types of drums (one with cymbal attachment), metal and wood blocks, cymbals (clashed and suspended), triangle, tam-tam, castanets, slapstick, and rattle. The orchestral back-up consists of four woodwinds, two brass, and a small group of strings.

Faure Daniel, the soloist, is super. He proves that if a soloist takes care of the sense of a work, the sounds will take care of themselves. His rhythmic commentary and obbligato points match his colorful soloism. A bright and appealing performance of a delightful work that does not contain a single measure of mundane make-do.

Concerto No. 2 for Piano and Orchestra (1941)

Piano

☐ Orchestra of Radio Luxembourg / Johannesen (piano) / Kontarsky (conductor) / Turnabout 34496

One can consider this Concerto as three essays about three different things, though through the hedonistic writing of this smart composer they fit and go together. So note a kinetic first-part piece, a bluesy-blue (reminders of Ravel) middle movement, and a south-of-the-border (reminders of *Saudades do Brasil*) end piece.

Grant Johannesen does as smart a presentation. He is in full control, adjusting perfectly to the stylistic content. The conductor is less flexible here and there, but in the long run the playing works.

Le Carnaval d'Aix (1926)

☐ Orchestra of Radio Luxembourg / Seaman (piano) / Milhaud (conductor) / Candide 31013

The subtitle of this work denotes the original source of the material: *Fantaisie pour piano et orchestre d'après "Salade."* Milhaud took twelve sections from *Salade* (a choral ballet he wrote for Leonid Massine and first produced in Paris on May 17, 1924) and turned them into a witty and scintillating work for piano and orchestra. It has no pyrotechnical premises, no momentous musical moralizing; it is highbrow honky-tonk. The carnival of characters (including a peppy Polichinelle) and dance turns (such as a polka, tango, maxixe, and waltz) form a real frolic that is rarely sober, quite often ribald. Milhaud's music travels between light limericks and the brash musical revues to be seen in Parisian cafés.

This is a sparkling rendition. This, combined with excellent sound and beautiful balance between solo voice and orchestra, make it a four-star production. A must, even for other than dyed-in-the-wool Milhaud believers.

Concertino d'automne ("Autumn") for Two Pianos and Eight Instruments (1951)

Two Pianos

☐ Ensemble de Solistes des Concerts Lamoureux / Joy and Bonneau (pianos) / Milhaud (conductor) / Philips 6504111

The main theme is simple and gentle. Then the music develops into contrasting, cross-patched counterpoints, the fresh tunes swimming in a bath of dissonant colors and lathered lines.

Concertino d'hiver ("Winter") for Trombone and String Orchestra (1953)

Trombone

☐ Ensemble de Solistes des Concerts Lamoureux / Suzan (trombone) / Milhaud (conductor) / Philips 6504111

"Winter" is adumbrated by the trombone's low range—it growls. General timbre disassociation from the supporting string body indicates a partial pictorial realization that

Milhaud undoubtedly sought. Thus the coolness and aloofness; the thematic material could apply to any time of the year.

The performance by Maurice Suzan is healthy and seasonally apt.

Viola

Concertino d'été ("Summer") for Viola and Nine Instruments (1951)

☐ Ensemble de Solistes des Concerts Lamoureux / Wallfisch (viola) / Milhaud (conductor) / Philips 6504111

Patterned thinking and a ternary design are manifest here. The first is a codification of style heavily drawn from clichés in Milhaud's own inventory.

Concerto for Viola (1929)

☐ Orchestra of Radio Luxembourg / Koch (viola) / Milhaud (conductor) / Candide 31013

Despite terminal consonant harmonies in several of the four movements, Milhaud's polytonal worship exists in this case. Nothing difficult to catch in this music flowing with sound and energy. It is so constructed that it falls with ease on the ear—a hunk of evidence that combined keys are as normally natural as totally single-tonal music. This is proof that harmonic complexity can be ordered (without compromise) to produce the paradoxical matter of harmonic simplicity in effect.

In obtaining the recording watch that the promised program notes by the composer are included. This writer's copy did not have them. Here are some basic statistics (whether Milhaud mentions them or not): this is Milhaud's 108th work. It was written for and dedicated to Paul Hindemith and was given its baptism on December 15, 1929, by the Concertgebouw Orchestra in Amsterdam, with Monteux conducting and, of course, Hindemith in the solo spot. Certainly a star-studded lineup in all respects. At this remove it remains fresh and warms the ear that can appreciate key mixes with a kick. Captivating spirit describes Koch's solo performance; this musician displays viola playing with impact and knowledge. A superb issue.

Violin

Concertino de printemps ("Spring") for Violin and Chamber Orchestra (1934)

☐ Ensemble de Solistes des Concerts Lamoureux / Goldberg (violin) / Milhaud (conductor) / Philips 6504111

A charming example of concentrated music; its solidity contains no extraneous packing. What is particularly enchanting is the manner in which Milhaud symbolizes the vernal atmosphere while retaining his style of carefully combined tonalities. A number of thoughts are discussed in the piece: each is stated, reconfirmed, quickly concluded, and then the music skims off to the next idea. The coda, which disassembles one of the themes while the solo violin skitters like a bird, is a marvelous way of clinching a proposition without long-winded musical oratory.

From every point of view Szymon Goldberg's performance is just superb. Milhaud must have been overjoyed to have this artistry applied to his own music.

Concerto No. 2 for Violin and Orchestra (1946)

☐ Prague Symphony Orchestra / Gertler (violin) / Smetáček (conductor) / Supraphon 1-10-1120

Milhaud substantiates Milhaud here. The method employed combines classical clarity with polytonal address. It is observed in the opening theme, which is embraced with chordal counterpoint that touches various keys. It continues with the clear and somber (yet limpid) melodic line of the inner movement against a shifting gray-colored background, with all individual points carefully stating their tonal affiliation. It is certified by the impetuosity of the last movement.

The bracing technique of the composer offers rewards when it is so clearly utilized. These rewards are increased when disclosed by the secure playing of André Gertler. It is the epitome of both stylistic correctness and musical understanding. This also applies to the conducting of Václav Smetáček.

Segoviana

Instrumental

Guitar

☐ Santos (guitar) / Musical Heritage Society MHS–1916

Improvisation-like substances mark *Segoviana*. Harmonic vitalities, in the expected Milhaud manner, define the sectional specifications of the music.

The liner note, written by Claude Chauvel, questions whether Segovia has ever played the piece that bears his name. If he hasn't, he's missed a fine, special, certainly out-of-the-ordinary example of guitar music. The more welcome, therefore, to Turibio Santos's portrayal. It has a fine unity of technical sureness and coloristic beauty.

Suite for Martenot and Piano

Ondes Martenot

☐ Loriod (ondes Martenot); Philips (piano) / Musical Heritage Society MHS–821

A five-part sampler of some of the possibilities of the ondes Martenot—its wide range, power, and special timbre. This is the musical reality of Milhaud's piece, originally written to serve as incidental music for a play, scored for Martenot and small orchestra.

Neuf Préludes (1942)

Pastorale

Petite Suite (1955)

Sonata

Organ

☐ Baker (organ) / Delos FY–016

It was characteristic of Milhaud's incessant instrumental curiosity not to overlook the organ, though other composers just as curious about timbre have done so. This recording offers a complete collection of Milhaud's output for the instrument. Included are "organistic" conceptions, such as the *Entrée, Prière,* and *Cortège* of the *Petite Suite,* written for Milhaud's son's wedding and first performed in the synagogue as part of the ceremonies. The joy-soaked content is unmistakable, even in the quiet song of the *Prière.* A different type of charm is found in the vernal Pastorale, written in *bel canto* style and avoiding the curse of much organ music: pedantic and dusty voice couplings.

These works, and some of the "Nine Preludes" (the shortest 0:55, the longest 2:23), are restrained and economical in comparison with the thrust, strength, and textural weight of the Sonata. This piece (three movements: *Etude, Rêverie,* and *Final*) exemplifies the full measure of Milhaud's harmonic energy.

Playing on the *grand orgues de la Cathédrale de Chartres,* George C. Baker presents excellent rhythm and phrasing and, for the most part, vitality. There is a tendency to flatten out the dynamic range and to use a neutral registration plan, but these are not sufficient to deny well-ordered performances. The notes are not the best even in the original French. In the translation offered they are horrible.

Piano

L'Album de Madame Bovary (1933)

☐ Johannesen (piano) / Golden Crest S-4060

Seventeen extracts from the score Milhaud composed for the film *Madame Bovary,* produced by Jean Renoir. A compendium of Schumannesque melody, sensitively colored by Milhaud's special harmonic synonyms, the suite gives full evidence of the composer's lyrical gift, reminding one of the clarity of the French clavecinists.

Grant Johannesen perfectly realizes the fundamental warmth, flow, and spirit of the score.

La Muse ménagère (1944)

☐ Johannesen (piano) / Turnabout 34496

Musical representation is the method in ''The Household Muse,'' manifested by the use of very specific descriptive titles. However, Milhaud's picture-painting is more idealized than actual. It is exciting to await a composer's tonal realization of *La Cuisine* or *Le Chat* (''The Cat''), for example, but these particular movements sound almost the same as others named *Les Soins du ménage* (''Household Chores'') and *La Lessive* (''Washing''). There is no doubt that Darius Milhaud is no Richard Strauss in portraying his fifteen-part ''domestic symphony.''

However, program music is exceedingly difficult to accomplish with a keyboard instrument. The existing orchestral setting is a slightly better guide. Even there, however, Milhaud's explanations are still rather vague. The only recording of the orchestral version is a real oldie, difficult to find even in the ''we specialize in deleted classical rarities'' shops. If you want to try, it was on the Spa label, No. 12, played by the Vienna Philharmonic Orchestra, conducted by Haefner.

Le Printemps (1919)

☐ Bolcom (piano) / Nonesuch 71316

Early Milhaud, consisting of two sets of three pieces each, their style somewhat impressionistic with Fauré-like touches. Bolcom plays them in a proper intimate and relaxed manner.

Saudades do Brasil (1920-1921)

☐ Bolcom (piano) / Nonesuch 71316

One of the most enjoyable of Milhaud's multitudinous compositions. Completed in Paris in 1921, after he had returned from a stay in Brazil, the pieces reflect his memories of Brazil's musical climate. Each of the dozen items is distinctly Latin American in rhythm, but folk tunes are not used at all. No fiery, passionate mannerisms are exhibited, but rather uninhibited Parisianism (festooned with Milhaud's picturesque harmonic combinations) frames the native elements. The various titles (colorful by themselves, such as *Sorocabo, Botofogo,* and *Copacabana*) mean nothing. They simply identify municipal districts in Rio de Janeiro.

These salty and swingy ''Recollections'' are full of surprises. One example is the final cadence of *Laranjeiras,* which offers a musical O. Henry twist.

Bolcom's surveyal of the score is simply marvelous, the textures are clarified, the rhythmic chic perfectly realized. His liner notes are excellent, save two points concerning the violin-and-piano transcription of the *Saudades.* Milhaud did not make the transcription, but Claude Lévy. Further, the complete set was not so arranged, but only six of the total dozen pieces.

Milhaud did transcribe the *Saudades* for orchestra (see under *Orchestra*).

Three Rag Caprices (1922)

☐ Bolcom (piano) / Nonesuch 71316

Milhaud traces ragtime's rhythmic reflexes and charts these with his own type of harmonic crayon. The textures are economical, the music elastic, with primal style and hedonistic tone.

Bolcom plays these cute and colorful pieces neatly and with stylistic realization.

Scaramouche (1937)

Two Pianos

☐ Eden and Tamir (pianos) / London 6434

The title may recall Sabatini's novel of the same name. This is purely coincidental. Milhaud's choice is predicated on the word's meaning—"buffoon" or "scamp"—borne out by the music's entertaining, diverting representation, for the most part, of mischief-making temper. One of the "classics" of contemporary two-piano literature, *Scaramouche* was actually derived from music written for two plays. Such self-helping is found in a number of places in Milhaud's catalogue. All to the good, since only a fraction of incidental music has lasting properties, whereas *Scaramouche* is one of Milhaud's triumphs.

Scaramouche is cross-sectioned by brashness. This is especially noticeable in the music-hall potpourri of the opening, which carries strains of many light tunes, including the old radio chorus "We want Cantor." Movement 2 has a bitter-sweet pertness. Dash and flash return in the final portion, a Brazilian souvenir that rocks and rolls (officially a samba).

The Bracha Eden and Alexander Tamir team play with eloquent spirit and expertise. Milhaud's sparkling wit clearly emerges from their ensemble dynamism.

First Sonata—on Unpublished and Anonymous Themes of the Eighteenth Century for Viola and Piano (1944)

Chamber Music

Second Sonata for Viola and Piano (1944)

☐ Zaslav Duo / Orion 75186

Though Milhaud considers eighteenth-century style in his treatment of the themes used in his *Première Sonate,* in the faster movements the tonality scheme is a far cry from the 1700s. In the *Entrée* (movement one of the First Sonata) a strict canon marks its opening section. A French-style country dance (*Française*) shapes the second part. A muted, simple *Air* and a *Final* follow. The three sections of the latter are represented by placing fugal expositions on either side of a more homophonic portion.

Compression is to be noted in the second work. The three movements cover eleven and three-quarter minutes in performance time. Contrast, of course, prevails. In *Champêtre* the "rustic" imagery swings with abandon. However, the pulsatile excitement is kept in check so that the music as a whole is not distorted. Tertial and quartal intervallic ascents are the important basis for the second movement (*Dramatique*). In the finale the temper of the title *Rude* is conveyed by rhythm and acid-sounding secundal harmony.

Milhaud's Second Sonata for Viola and Piano is in direct antithesis to the First Sonata for the same pair of instruments. The husband-wife performers (Bernard and Naomi Zaslav) are mindful of this and their playing shows understanding, depth, and feeling. Where some dynamic roughage is required, it is made available.

Sonata No. 2 for Violin and Piano (1944)

☐ Voicou (violin); Haas (piano) / London STS-15175

In this early work (written at the age of twenty-five) Milhaud concludes his adolescent romanticism and goes on to examine tonality.

The first movement of the Sonata (dedicated to André Gide) is a Pastorale—a mood present often in Milhaud's works. It includes the harmonically salty use of unrelated keys such as the triple combination of B flat, D, and A flat major. Partnered tonality is very marked in sections of the slow movement, with C major triads cascading against pentatonic sharped tones. The last part is free in form and implies a bitonal conclusion.

The music is played expertly and diagnostically.

Sonatine for Clarinet and Piano (1927)

☐ Drucker (clarinet); Hambro (piano) / Odyssey Y-30492

Milhaud's music is devoid of any pose; it is fresh and arrogant, sophisticated with a devil-may-take-you air about it. The clarinet furnishes the perfect instrumental voice for such frolicking. That covers the outer pair of movements, both marked *Très rude*. The slow movement is directly opposite. It has a succinct and beautiful songlike line decorated with piano arabesques. Its dramatic central section is, again, in direct contrast. Here Milhaud employs the darker register of the clarinet and marks out a three-part design by the return of the opening theme.

The talents of Drucker and Hambro provide a convincing display of Milhaud's brash-introspective-brash compendium.

Suite for Violin, Clarinet, and Piano (1936)

☐ Compinsky Ensemble / Sheffield S-3

Contemporary chamber music not only differs from that of the earlier periods in form, harmonic style, and rhythm. Very often it delights in using a combination that consists entirely of mixed timbres.

Milhaud's trio is a study of some of the color and sonority possible in the combination of a string, wind, and keyboard instrument. Matching these textural shifts is the French manner of Milhaud's musical illuminations. Rarely has this composer been as charming and gracious.

Fine style and fine tone by this ensemble, consisting of Manuel Compinsky, violin; Kalman Bloch, clarinet; and Sara Compinsky, piano. The third movement, *Jeu,* exclusively scored for the violin and clarinet, is particularly excellent in its suavity.

String Quartet No. 6 in G (Movement 2)

☐ Juilliard Quartet / RCA LM-6092 (monaural)

This portion (*Très lent*) is irregular in pulsation, toasted to a contrapuntal turn.

Isn't it time to have Milhaud's eighteen string quartets available in recorded form?

La Cheminée du Roi René (1939)

☐ Philadelphia Woodwind Ensemble / Columbia Special Products AMS-6213

Milhaud's seven-movement opus is nonnarrative in form though it has the feelings of the times it celebrates (the king of this chamber piece lived in the fifteenth century in Aix-en-Provence, Milhaud's birthplace). The poetic moods and engaging rhythmic swing of these miniatures describe, in a general way, such things as a *Cortège, Jousts on the Arc, Hunting at Valabre,* etc.

The enlightened performance by the golden-toned Philadelphians (also known as the Philadelphia Woodwind Quintet) enriches Milhaud's vocabulary.

Two Sketches for Woodwind Quintet

☐ New York Woodwind Quintet / Counterpoint/Esoteric 505 (monaural)

Deeply felt short pieces (a Madrigal and Pastoral), with the composer exceptionally restrained. Sketch 1 casts off formal anchors. The rhythmic flow of the second sketch is animated by combining duple- and triple-pulse points within the steady flow of two beats per measure.

Septet for Strings (1964)

☐ Milhaud Ensemble / Milhaud (conductor) / Everest 3176

The principal designs are those of the two-part variety, with the second of the pair utilizing invertible counterpoint. Within are the usual matters of polyphonic talkee-talkee—imitation and canon, fugato and *stretto*, which aid (by giving individual identity to sections within the total structure), but actually thicken, the polytonal prittle-prattle.

The Septet, for 2 violins, 2 violas, 2 cellos, and 1 double bass, (commissioned by the Library of Congress, though the liner notes fail to supply this fact) contains a hybrid of defined and chance music. In movement 2 (*Etude de hasard dirigé*) duple-pulsed measures are to last one second, against which the aleatoric unbarred items are thrust at a faster tempo. Fun and games here, of course, but almost as much also in the other parts of this work with its twirling and whirling counterpoints.

Aspen-Serenade (1957)

☐ Milhaud Ensemble / Milhaud (conductor) / Everest 3176

The freeway traffic is carefully organized on Milhaud's polytonal road (the vehicle is built from a quartet of strings—violin, viola, cello, and bass—and a quartet of wind—flute, oboe, clarinet, and bassoon—plus trumpet). Thus binary form for the first pair of movements, ternary in the next, retrograde apportionment in part 4, and two simultaneous fugues in the finale. Within each, one perceives busybodies of pitch-tossing and note-wrestling.

The erudite critic Paul Collaer, who supplied the liner notes, failed to point out that the tempi of the five movements form an acrostic from the initial letters. Animé, Souple et printanier, Paisible, Energique; Nerveux et Coloré, spell "Aspen," with the abbreviation for the state appearing in the final word.

Milhaud monitors the performance as well as he controls his keys and their combinations.

Symphony No. 6 (for Soprano, Contralto, Tenor, Bass, Oboe, and Cello)

Vocal

Voice and Instrumental Ensemble

☐ Doemer (soprano); Klein (contralto); Arend (tenor); Koster (bass); Matern (oboe); Mallach (cello) / Milhaud (conductor) / Candide 31008

The last of the set of the *petite* symphonies and, like the others—see under Orchestra (Symphony No. 1 [*Le Printemps*] for Small Orchestra)—it is in three movements and, of course, succinct. It is unlike the others in its unusual six-ply combination of voices and instruments, and another difference is the completion of the work in a slow tempo.

The textures are solid, but the line writing is clear (the vocal parts are wordless). Charmingly, expressively, and effectively performed.

Voice and Orchestra

Quatre Chansons de Ronsard (1941)

☐ Louisville Orchestra / Seibel (soprano) / Mester (conductor) / Louisville S–744

Music originally written for a coloratura specialist (Lily Pons) with no holds barred. Positive differences appear in the four songs. The first is a Frenchy, nineteen-twenties number; the second, an ornately fashioned romantic bit, is followed by a vocally exhibitionistic concoction which reminds one of a whiz-bang operatic "stop the action" aria. The set concludes with a grand-scale quasi-folksy piece.

It is good to have these songs available again in recorded form. One of my old treasures is the deleted Angel (35441) disc, with Micheau as the vocalist and Milhaud conducting.

Choral

Chorus Alone

Eloge from Deux Poèmes (1919)

☐ Grenoble University Choir / Giroud (conductor) / Musical Heritage Society MHS–1078

The text is from Saint-Léger Léger's *Eloges*, dealing with exotic symbolism. (The liner notes on the work are very vague and do not mention that Saint-Léger Léger was better known under his pseudonym St.-John Perse.)

Chromaticism rules every measure, and pitch detail does pose problems. Nonetheless, the university group provides a fine sense of atmosphere lacking only quite enough vocal passion. There is one mishap by the sopranos, who lose their clutch on pitch at a crucial extremely high spot. Seriously convincing otherwise.

Cantata and Oratorio

Naissance de Vénus (1949)

☐ Modern Madrigal Singers / Desto 6483

While Desto doesn't, Milhaud classifies this four-part work as a cantata. There is rich harmony all the way, with a lesser amount of chromaticism only in the concluding *Les Heures* ("The Hours").

Fairly considerable demands are made on the chorus singing without accompaniment, but the eight-voice Modern Madrigal Singers conquer all problems and deliver a very effective chronicle.

Sabbath Morning Service (1947)

☐ Orchestre du Théâtre National de l'Opéra de Paris and Chorus of the Radiodiffusion-Télévision Française / Rehfuss (baritone) / Milhaud (conductor) / Westminster Gold 8281

Among the compositions related to Hebrew topics in Milhaud's catalogue, this is by far the strongest and most fervent. It is a major opus in four parts, divided into twenty sections.

In this production for the synagogue, Milhaud demonstrates his doctrines in more orthodox ways than usual. While choral thrust is matched by chordal incisiveness, diatonic disposition is called on for the greater part in Milhaud's setting of the text. Structural balance with warm, devotional feeling replaces uncompromising polytonal viscidity. Milhaud adapts his style to the eloquent content of his chosen subject.

The Westminster production is a transfer from the French Véga label (No. C 30 A 178). Full expertise is demonstrated by all concerned, and with Milhaud at the helm the performance is most definitely a definitive one.

Les Choéphores (1915)

☐ New York Philharmonic and Schola Cantorum of New York / Zorina (narrator); Jordan and Babikian (sopranos); Boatwright (baritone) / Bernstein (conductor) / Columbia Special Products AMS–6396

A musical blockbuster of sound and fury, containing one of the strongest doses of polytonality in this composer's inventory. The savage power of Milhaud's opus not only illustrates the vehemence of combined tonalities but is a compendium of vocal techniques, many invented by the composer. The versification has a remarkable puissance which is maintained from start to conclusion, especially in places where the narrator is surrounded by sonoric contrapuntal vocalized timbres and a battery of percussion principally combined in chordal components of varying tensility.

Les Choéphores ("The Libation Bearers") is the second part of Aeschylus's trilogy the *Oresteia,* with text arranged by Paul Claudel. It is divided into seven sections with varied scorings (one is for soprano and six-part mixed chorus alone; two others are for narrator, chorus, and fifteen percussion instruments). Structural heaviness surrounding the complex chordal textures predominates. The impact and emotional fierceness are stunning. Milhaud's score is as exciting and new today as it was when conceived in 1915.

Bernstein brings clarity to Milhaud's score. His direction is thorough, responsive, and responsible—the result of collaboration between a composer who is a brilliant conductor and a conductor who understands the purposes of a composer. A spectacular release (originally issued by Columbia on MS–6396, with a monaural setting on ML–5796), marred a bit by having almost twenty-three minutes of music on one side and a mere eleven-plus on the other. For a better bargain (and, as well, a superlative performance conducted by Igor Markevitch), the record collector might search for the deleted Decca edition (9956), which includes a five-star rendition of Honegger's Symphony No. 5 (Di tre re).

Suite de Quatrains (1962)

☐ Milhaud Ensemble / Madeleine Milhaud (speaker); Rampal (flute) / Darius Milhaud (conductor) / Everest 3176

Creative freedom here. The instruments (flute, bass clarinet, saxophone, harp, and three strings—and note the marvelous flutist in this ensemble!) overlay the speaking (simply and beautifully delivered by the composer's wife) with free lines, each without bothering about the rhythm of the others. The lack of friendship is interesting and holds the attention regardless of the aural complications, especially because each portion of the total ten-minute work is brief.

La Création du monde (1923)

☐ Orchestre du Théâtre des Champs-Elysées / Milhaud (conductor) / Nonesuch 71122

The easygoing assurance with which Milhaud usually fashioned his music into wholesale polyphony criss-crossed with multitonalism produced anything but a romantically lyrical result. The music becomes almost noisy, in the artistic sense. When the very same formula is disposed with subtlety, the effect is thrice powerful. Whereas scholasticism arguably can be heard in many of the symphonies and quartets because Milhaud cherished his own tradition, his usual techniques mingled with 1920-style American jazz make "The Creation of the World" one of the composer's most exciting and delicious pieces.

Milhaud's admiration for jazz (most of his research was done in New York's Harlem district) has been asserted by utilizing the idiom, either explicitly or as a metaphorical means, in many portions of his compositions. In *La Création du monde* the inventory includes a blues, a jazzy fugue, ragtime beat, trombone smears, and other sonic accouterments of the popular dialect. A dance-combo type of instrumentation makes a perfect frame for the structure; the score calls for sixteen soloists plus percussion, with an alto saxophone replacing the viola in the string quintet. The orchestrational lingo produces jazz as it should be spoken—properly improper. All this is decidedly apt for a ballet and just as fitting for concert listening.

The composer-conductor combine doesn't always work. In this case it does. All the pungency and swing inherent in the score are there; no fat is allowed to cling to the textures. This is a spirited, stylish reading. In this instance Milhaud playing Milhaud cannot be argued against.

Le Boeuf sur le toit (1919)

☐ Orchestre du Théâtre des Champs-Elysées / Milhaud (conductor) / Nonesuch 71122

Originally *Le Boeuf sur le toit* (its English title is "The Nothing Doing Bar") was conceived as a "cinema symphony" to be used as the accompaniment for a silent-movie comedy. Its high-class, honky-tonk, five-and-dime prattle would have served this objective admirably. Instead, it was "imagined and arranged" as a ballet by Jean Cocteau, who invented a mad stage concoction that anticipated the era of surrealism.

Made from Brazilian tangos, sambas, maxixes, and so on, with one tune binding the mélange (appearing fifteen times!), the score is sophisticated yet properly low-down. The cocktail tunes, spiked with polytonality, produce a wonderful sweet-and-sour jam session. Milhaud's marvelous farce music requires no dramatic action.

The performance has the kind of heated and swingy playing that the score requires. Milhaud was never a great conductor and never thought of himself as one. But quite often no one could do better directing his music than Milhaud could himself. This is such a case.

Les Songes

☐ Utah Chamber Orchestra / Abravanel (conductor) / Angel S–37317

Practically unknown Milhaud but not to Maurice Abravanel, who conducted the premiere of *Les Songes* ("Dreams") in 1933. That familiarity remained and now has carried over to an expert performance that discloses all the zest of the music. Though the reduced forces that are called for already thin out the usual Milhaud texture, there is to be noticed an additional transparency that gives the music an extra portion of directness.

L'Homme et son désir (1918)

☐ Utah Symphony Orchestra / Blanche Christensen (soprano); Nixon (mezzo-soprano); Ronald Christensen (tenor); Chartrand (bass) / Abravanel (conductor) / Vanguard S–274

This music is run on polytonal wheels within polyrhythmic wheels. Complete independence of material rules: melody, tonality, and rhythm each goes its own way. The musical media are just as individual: a wordless vocal quartet, five wind instruments, a string quartet, double bass, trumpet, harp, and fifteen percussion instruments.

The story of Milhaud's early ballet (his forty-eighth work) concerns the primitive strength of the Brazilian forest at night and the mystical forces that hold sway therein. Milhaud's sonorous texture is as complex as the jungle setting. His four-layered counterpoint of motival snippets, noises, and fractured and fractioned pulsations, framed by exotic instrumentation, is exciting. Traditional methods of producing cohesion are lacking, but in this superexpressionistic vehicle they are not required.

To give a critique of this recording, the best available in the catalogue, all one need do is to quote the composer. After receiving a copy of the disc, Milhaud wrote to the Vanguard firm, "It is *marvelous—perfect,* and the performance as well as the recording." Absolutely!

Charles Miller / *Jerome Kern.* See Kern / Miller.

Edward Miller   *(1930-   )*

The Folly Stone **(1966)**   *Chamber Music*

☐ New York Brass Quintet / Composers Recordings 302

Miller's consideration of a specific detail in five paintings by Hieronymus Bosch produced a vivid creative chain reaction. The free colorations of this ten-minute score are as acute as the grotesqueness, exuberance, and macabre qualities found in the feverish imageries of the Flemish painter. Thus inspiration begets inspiration.

The liner notes give sparse data—none for the sources that triggered Miller's composition. The main title (and that of the first movement), *The Folly Stone,* is a detail in Bosch's *The Cure of Folly. Monster with a Basket* is an item in *The Last Judgement* painting. The third piece, *Fool with a Bowl* is "taken" from Bosch's *The Ship of Fools* (Ivesian polyphony sparks this section). In *A Team of Demons* (a point from *The Hay Wagon*), vertical textures predominate. A pair of piccolo trumpets are used in *Paradise,* a reaction from Bosch's *The Garden of Earthly Delights.*

Miller's proficiency in the technique of musical simulation is stimulating. The performance is a superior one; the trumpet playing of fractional details in the stratospheric register in the last movement deserves special mention.

Malloy Miller   *(20th cent.)*

Prelude for Percussion (1956)   *Percussion*

☐ Percussion Ensemble / Price (conductor) / Orion 7276

Variational contrast controls Miller's piece. It is defined, for the greater part, by actual pitched instruments rather than depending on the "purer" (and, naturally, more difficult) method of simulated pitch content.

Karl Millöcker   *(1842-1899)*

Der Feldprediger: Traumwalzer   *Orchestra*

☐ Johann Strauss Orchestra of Vienna / Boskovsky (conductor) / Angel S-36956

A waltz from one of the composer's operettas (he composed more than twenty). Viennese romanticism in good supply here.

Charles Mills   (1914-   )

**String
Orchestra**

Prelude and Dithyramb (1954)

☐ Radio Orchestra of Zurich, Switzerland / Monod (conductor) / Composers Recordings 128 (monaural)

A huge dose of Roy Harris is included here (parts sound like sketches for that composer's third symphony). Also some modality and folksy bits tied by asymmetric rhythms, giving a nervous tick-off to unnervous melody.

CRI's production facts are awry. Though Mills's piece is for string orchestra, it is not so listed on the cover or the label, or so described in the liner notes. Fair playing. Fair sound.

Choral

Chorus Alone

The True Beauty (1950)

☐ Randolph Singers / Randolph (conductor) / Composers Recordings 102 (monaural)

An old English atmosphere is detailed in this expressive madrigal.

Ilhan Mimaroğlu   (1926-   )

Instrumental

Piano

Rosa (1978)

☐ Hays (piano) / Finnadar SR 2-720

Far different music from the electronic compositions that have resulted in a high-ranking reputation for this sensitive composer. On the basis of this fully powered musical document, Mimaroğlu deserves high-ranking status in the field of nonelectronic music as well.

Rosa (Rosa Luxemburg) is both a memorial piece and an explanation of the quality of her person—one might term her a "premature" freedom fighter, "murdered by fascist thugs, prototypes of Hitler's brown-shirts," as the composer explains. It is, indeed, a moving music that Mimaroğlu has produced, dramatic in every phrase, even in the quieter portions, containing an extrovert vehemence that grips the listener.

Doris Hays plays magnificently. Mimaroğlu wrote *Rosa* for her. Her performance is artistic repayment to the fullest extent. Finnadar's sound is of remarkable depth and roundness.

**Electronic
Music**

Agony (Visual Study No. 4, After Arshile Gorky) (1965)

☐ Finnadar 9012

Title notwithstanding, Mimaroğlu's piece is "totally autonomous in musical meaning." Dynamically fierce in contrast, it relies on impacted groupings for each point of climax.

Anacolutha: Encounter and Episode II (1965)

☐ Finnadar 9001

The main title signifies "a sudden change in grammatical construction." The music follows suit, using electronically detailed instrumental sources such as a viola, a basset horn, and percussion, as well as the human voice. Though rhapsodic in its totality, the sound image has a basic unity that is not fragmented thereby.

Bal des leurres from Music for Jean Dubuffet's *Coucou Bazar* (1973)

☐ Dubuffet (narrator) / Finnadar 9003

One of the eleven pieces in the set. (For the remaining ten and a discussion of Mimaroğlu's composition, *see below* [Music for Jean Dubuffet's *Coucou Bazar*].)

In *Bal des leurres* Dubuffet, the painter, reads his own poem of the same title, which has been recorded in multiple overdubs.

Bowery Bum (Visual Study No. 3, After Jean Dubuffet) (1964)

☐ Finnadar 9012

An electronic scherzo (no relationship to the standard form, of course), the sound source for the creation being a rubber band! This item's sounds are amplified, filtered, treated by speed variation plus superimposition. Mimaroğlu's great flair for the electronic language is exhibited here most vividly.

Hyperboles (1971)

☐ Finnadar 9001

Mimaroğlu's title "denotes the exaggerated utterance of the piece, and the intent is praise—meant to go to young activists everywhere." It is definitely dynamic, set in a ternary structure that includes the transformed sounds of an electric piano and a violin.

Interlude II from *Sing Me a Song of Songmy* (1971)

☐ Nha-Khe (narrator) / Finnadar 9001

Tripartite arrangement, including recitations of a Vietnamese poem (by the poet), in the first section, and a much shorter set of lines, in an English translation of the original Turkish (by Dağlarca), in the third part. The music strongly counterpoints the initial section, rises to soloistic intensity in the central division, and then subsides in the concluding portion. The last is sensitively moving creativity. It represents a high poematic point in Mimaroğlu's work.

Intermezzo (1964)

☐ Finnadar 9012

The neutral title of Intermezzo reflects the composer's objective for a piece of "pure music," one minus "any extra-musical implications."

Le Tombeau d'Edgar Poe (1964)

☐ Buri (speaker) / Finnadar 9012

A blend of the human voice with the electronic complex. This gives a solid complexion to the Poe study (based on a poem by Stéphane Mallarmé), though the effect is phantasmagoric. A prerecorded reading of the poem is totally transformed, the purpose being to reflect, not define, the meaning within and behind the lines. A fascinating realization.

Music for Jean Dubuffet's *Coucou Bazar* (1973)

Canine	*Reflections*
Double Mask and Deployment	*The Rose*
Fragmentation	*Swift Feet*
Hide and Seek	*Traffic*
Motors	*The Window*

☐ Finnadar 9003

These ten pieces, plus one with narrator (*see above* [*Bal des leurres* from Music for Jean Dubuffet's *Coucou Bazar*]), were composed for Jean Dubuffet's articulated painting *Coucou Bazar.* In no way do they parallel an electronic "Picture[s] at an Exhibition." Mimaroğlu's inventions, no matter their inspirational source, are absolute and make independent pronouncements.

Indeed, anecdotal or representational electronic music is not being propagandized in this instance. Relationship of the sound content to the titles is extremely ephemeral and noted here only in terms of a subjective reaction (which is possible with any kind of music and regardless of a programmatic or absolute title). Thus, some ohmic sounds in *Motors,* growl-like qualities in *Canine,* water (?) spray simulants in *Hide and Seek,* rhythmic freshlets in *Swift Feet,* etc.

Preludes for Magnetic Tape

No. 1 / No. 2 / No. 6

☐ Finnadar 9012

Concentrated fields of action are used in each case. In the first Prelude the composition is made from "the sounds of a piano torn apart for tuning practice." This nonelectronic fundament contrasts strongly with the modifications applied to the sounds of an organ in Prelude No. 2 and those of a guitar in Prelude No. 3. The virgin sound of the untampered guitar's open strings gives an important pithy coda to the latter. Such centralization of basic material in each piece makes the procedures used clear and direct—and successful.

Preludes for Magnetic Tape — Prelude No. 8 (*to the Memory of Edgard Varèse*) (1966)

☐ Finnadar 9001

Transparent and delicate electronic music. Mimaroğlu's choices of components are a celesta and a harpsichord. The music's quietness is extremely moving.

Preludes for Magnetic Tape

No. 9 / No. 11

☐ Finnadar 9012

Unbelievable reconstitutions of the basic sound of a clarinet (Prelude No. 9) and of a rubber band (Prelude No. 11). The flux of phenomena and experiences that result is expressive and inexhaustibly evocative.

Preludes for Magnetic Tape — Prelude No. 12

☐ Bozkurt (speaker) / Finnadar 9012

Mimaroğlu uses triple components in this two-and-one-half minute piece: electronic and nonelectronic (which he terms "natural") sound, plus narration of a poem. The last is by the Turkish writer Orhan Veli. The emotive consequences make one wish for more of such partnership of contrastive techniques.

Preludes for Magnetic Tape — Prelude No. 14 (*Face the Windmills, Turn Left*)

☐ Finnadar 9012

The composer's political orientation is patent in the title. The social protestation can be recognized in the music. Even without the title one would understand a music of unrest.

Preludes for Magnetic Tape—Prelude No. 16

☐ Siegel (vocalist) / Finnadar 9012

A rare combine of electronic-music invention with the special pop-styled voice (but highly individual, of soft-hard quality) of Janis Siegel. The opposites produce a rare adduction; Mimaroğlu's short piece lingers long in the ears (and mind).

Provocations (1971)
White Cockatoo (Visual Study No. 5, After Jackson Pollock) (1966)
Wings of the Delirious Demon (1969)

☐ Finnadar 9001

Mimaroğlu states that *Provocations* can be called "The Little Demon." Its *scherz* factor is prevalent in the use and manipulation of clarinet sounds as the source material; the same timbre serves for producing *Wings,* which obtains its fanciful title from a poem of Ilya Ehrenburg. Constant movement and unrest bear out the superscription.

If a concrete pictorial sensation can be transferred to electronic sound, Mimaroğlu apparently has succeeded in doing so in *White Cockatoo.* Certainly his music contains a parallel to the internal dynamics found in Pollock's work.

Alois (Louis) Minkus   (1826-1917)

Grand Pas de Deux from *La Bayadère* (1877)   *Orchestra*

☐ London Symphony Orchestra / Bonynge (conductor) / London 2213

A convincing illustration of Minkus's easily choreographable music. Bonynge provides an authoritative conception.

It is important to indicate that this recording and the two that follow in this section all are listed under the name of Ludwig Minkus. Complete misinformation marks biographical information concerning Minkus. For example, *Grove's Dictionary of Music and Musicians* lists him as Léon, with the immediate disclaimer that it is "actually Aloisius Ludwig." He is shown as being born in Vienna in 1827 and having died in St. Petersburg in 1890. *Schwann* follows the recording companies choice of name (Ludwig) but assigns the dates as 1826–189–?). Thanks to that musical Sherlock Holmes, Nicolas Slonimsky, the name and dates that head this section have been authenticated "from documentation available in the parish register and the burial records of the city of Vienna." Slonimsky correctly calls him an Austrian composer since he was born in Vienna, March 23, 1826, and died there, December 7, 1917. However, it is proper to split the credits and identify him as an Austro-Russian composer, since the major part of his career took place in Russia where he lived from 1853 to 1891.

Pas de Deux from *Paquita* (1846)

☐ London Symphony Orchestra / Bonynge (conductor) / London 6418

From the two-act ballet. All the prescribed patterns, but, with this nicely moulded playing by the Londoners, a true delight that illustrates the talents of this fine composer of old-fashioned ballet music.

Ballet   ***Don Quixote* (1869)**

☐ Elizabethan Trust Melbourne Orchestra / Lanchbery (conductor) / Angel S-37008

Music by this composer is solidly embedded in the ballet repertory, especially in the Soviet Union. Lanchbery, who knows his way around ballet music, dispenses clear information.

Lyndol Mitchell   (1923-   )

Orchestra   ***Kentucky Mountain Portraits***

☐ Eastman-Rochester Symphony Orchestra / Hanson (conductor) / Eastman-Rochester Archives ERA-1012

The traditional arsenal of folk tunes colored and sequenced and sent on their way. During the progress of the three pieces—*Cindy,* Ballad, and *Shivaree*—one will recognize *Pretty Polly* and *Skip to My Lou* and also hear *Come All You Fair and Tender Ladies* and *Paw Paw Patch.* Spontaneous and convincing music and played accordingly.

Akira Miyoshi   (1933-   )

Orchestra   **Concerto for Orchestra (1964)**

☐ NHK Symphony Orchestra / Iwaki (conductor) / Odyssey 32160152

Miyoshi favors bold rhythms with vehement exercise of the percussion in his outer movements (both in the *presto* speed zone). Delicately flowing, translucid transformations balance these in the *lento* central movement. The Concerto for Orchestra (*Kyoso Kyoku*) exemplifies virtuosic orchestration; the performance projects it with verve.

Ernest John Moeran   (1894-1950)

Orchestra   **Overture for a Masque (1944)**
             Rhapsody No. 2 (1924)

☐ London Philharmonic Orchestra / Boult (conductor) / Musical Heritage Society MHS-1411

The Overture is mostly lively and cleanly scored. There is more color in the E major Rhapsody, especially marked by a juicy tune in the center that has Irish personality. No artificiality to this music—it sings its way with wholesome musicality. The performances are nicely detailed, and Boult's tender, loving care is apparent in every measure, as is his understanding.

Sinfonietta (1944)

☐ London Philharmonic Orchestra / Boult (conductor) / Musical Heritage Society MHS-1229

A firm and lively work that combines classical formal security with modal color and folk-song flavor. The earnestness and robustness of the piece and its open-hearted freshness are undeniable. Why it is never performed in public remains a mystery. Moeran's music is still to be discovered, but thanks to this recorded performance (lucid, direct, clean, and clear), the record collector can have that favorable opportunity.

Symphony in G minor (1937)

☐ New Philharmonia Orchestra / Boult (conductor) / Lyrita SRCS-70

There seems to be an ill-founded theorem that folk-type themes cannot be expanded and developed. Moeran proves they can in his Symphony that deserves a place along with those of Walton and Vaughan Williams. Included as well is a great deal of initial fragmentation of material which is then cumulatively organized in a Sibelian manner. A fine example of this little-known (in America) composer's work. Boult's performance has everything required.

Concerto in B minor for Cello and Orchestra (1945)

☐ London Philharmonic Orchestra / Coetmore (cello) / Boult (conductor) / Musical Heritage Society MHS-1411

Solo Instrument and Orchestra

Cello

A human-interest story pertains to this recording. Moeran composed his cello Concerto in 1945, as a wedding gift for his bride, Peers Coetmore, the soloist performing on this disc. The composition was originally recorded in 1970 by Lyrita, two decades after Moeran's death.

It is quite apparent that Moeran's widow is emotively involved with the music she is playing. However, her tone is not especially big, and the darkish declamation that surrounds the first two-thirds of the work requires larger statements. Despite this criticism, the fine poetry and imagery of Moeran's Concerto make its acquisition worthwhile.

Prelude for Cello and Piano (1948)

☐ Coetmore (cello); Parkin (piano) / Musical Heritage Society MHS-1689

Instrumental

Cello

A broad string-instrument aria, simply backed up harmonically.

Bank Holiday (1925)
Prelude and Berceuse (1933)
Stalham River (1921)
Toccata (1921)
Two Legends (1923)
The White Mountain (1927)

Piano

☐ Parkin (piano) / Musical Heritage Society MHS-1689

This group offers a fine cross-section of Moeran's eighteen piano compositions. There is poetic romantic flow in *Stalham River;* the same applies to the simple outlines of *The White Mountain,* folk-based on an Irish tune. Catch the outline of *Tom, Tom, the Piper's Sun* in the Prelude that is paired with the limpid Berceuse. The *Two Legends* describe *A Folk Story* and a Celtic-flavored *Rune.*

Vigor and motility, of course, are present in the Toccata, which also has a folksy slant. In parallel mood is the hedonistic *Bank Holiday,* which reminds one of the music of Percy Grainger.

Eric Parkin gives sympathetic readings of these pieces. He is best in the quieter examples, perhaps a bit too polite in the two fast-tempoed works.

Chamber Music

Sonata in A minor for Cello and Piano (1947)

☐ Coetmore (cello); Parkin (piano) / Musical Heritage Society MHS-1689

This Sonata, one of the last chamber-music compositions Moeran wrote, follows the same path he pursued practically from the start of his career: the triadal flavor, the romantic *cantabille,* the modal folk cast. The opening movement has march-like connotations contrasted to a lyrical secondary theme, with the latter used in slightly different shape in the concluding movement. Differences of speed mark the structural sections of the slow movement. The finale is set in a rondo design, using the constant means of triads and sevenths.

The performers follow the meaning of the work and clearly define its style of refined romanticism, illustrated by a minting of tenderly reticent music.

Robert Moevs   (1921-   )

Orchestra

Musica da camera (1965)

☐ Contemporary Chamber Ensemble / Weisberg (conductor) / Composers Recordings S-223

Though sparsely textured, Moev's twelve-tone music moves with dramatic spirit. The technical plan makes the structure circular, with pitch and instrumental complements providing the balance. A sharply pointed and pivoted performance, which is what is to be expected from Arthur Weisberg's conducting.

Instrumental

Piano

Sonata per pianoforte (1950)

☐ Bloch (piano) / Composers Recordings 136 (monaural)

Lusty music with the difficult but fully pianistic text artistically detailed by Joseph Bloch. Each of the four movements is balanced yet free of academically rigorous form. Moevs is somewhat eclectic, as though he were investigating, in each movement, a pertinent objective out of memory. Thus the opening *Preludio* has the sweep of Hindemith's early music, dovetailed with chordal material; the Aria has the neoclassic coolness of Stravinsky, while the final two sections (*Canone* and Rondo) lean heavily on Prokofiev. In the last there are the structural dams that constrict constructive continuity: sequences and ostinati. However, there are tremendous climaxes and lots of keyboard fireworks.

Chamber Music

Variazioni sopra una melodia (1961)

☐ Glick (viola); Sylvester (cello) / Composers Recordings S-223

Dark-timbred and dark-detailed music. Moevs's duo fits securely into the expressionistic scheme of the Schoenbergian tradition.

The soloists are experts in matters contemporary, and again prove that reputation in this case.

Cantata and Oratorio

A Brief Mass

☐ Kirkpatrick Chapel Choir, Rutgers, The State University of New Jersey / Drinkwater (conductor) / Composers Recordings S-262

No argument that Moevs keeps the faith: his Mass *is* brief, covering eight minutes. (CRI is also concentrated with its credits, since the work also calls for organ, vibraphone, guitar, and double bass, but none of these performers receive a solitary credit.)

Moevs's work is an attempt to convince "the current *aggiornamento* of the Church" to solicit the best *avant-garde* composers to write liturgical music. His example, which includes spoken recitation (it even has words pronounced by the concelebrating priests on the occasion of its first performance as part of an actual service), is a sensible one.

I leave to the *aggiornamento* its utilitarian values. Structurally it has a tendency to avoid continuity for the sake of colorisms. Otherwise, it is sparse and ascetic in tone. Musically it is a Mass which has new shadows and lights. It needs no special pleading.

Richard Mohaupt (1904-1957)

Town Piper Music (1946) *Orchestra*

☐ Louisville Orchestra / Whitney (conductor) / Louisville S-645

A stylistic transfer, inspired by a mural picturing medieval musicians performing from a balcony. *Stadtpfeiffermusik,* Mohaupt's more colorful original German title, is nicely constructed semifestive music, but midway it gets quite serious for contrast—understandable only if simply in the absolute category. For this semipictorial objective the music flattens out, and this could be termed a possible structural error. Of course the return of the hedonistic principal material balances matters. Whitney directs an appropriately shaped performance.

Allen Molineux (1950-)

Encounter *Chamber Music*

☐ Annapolis Brass Quintet / Crystal S-207

An exciting bit of brass kineticism. Incessant drive for close to three and one-half minutes. Fine focused playing.

Wilhelm Bernhard Molique (1802-1869)

Concertino in G minor for Oboe and Orchestra *Solo Instrument and Orchestra*

☐ Frankfurt Radio Symphony Orchestra / Holliger (oboe) / Inbal (conductor) / Philips 9500070

Oboe

As a violinist-composer Molique is best represented by his nicely turned-out violin works. Does anyone know his fine fifth concerto in A minor for violin and orchestra? If you do, then you'll know what to expect from this nicely crafted opus. If you don't, expect, then, solid romantic facts of music composition. And expect, as well, a far above average performance.

John Christopher Moller (1755-1803)

Sinfonia *Instrumental*

☐ Harmon (organ) / Orion 76255 *Organ*

Two *Menuetto* portions balance a pair of spirited movements. Harmon's unerring sense of effect in his registration of this plain eighteenth-century musical example makes it all worth while.

Johann Melchior Molter (?-1765)

Instrumental

Clarinet

Concerto in G major for Clarinet and Strings

☐ Munich Chamber Orchestra / Michaels (clarinet) / Stadlmair (conductor) / Deutsche Grammophon AKC-198415

One of four concerti published in a modern edition almost 200 years after Molter's death. The descriptive heading says the music is for *clarinetto concertado, violino primo, violino secondo, violetta e cembalo*. As expected there are three movements, the end ones in moderate and fast tempi, respectively, balancing a finely defined slow division.

A good example of this composer's work and sufficient to recognize what abilities he had—average ones. The performance is ideal, with a well-chosen pace for all the movements and a solo-instrument tone of quality, considering that a considerable part of Molter's writing avoids the lower register of the clarinet.

Flute

Concerto in G major

☐ Jean-François Paillard Chamber Orchestra / Rampal (flute) / Paillard (conductor) / RCA CRL2-7003

Music of *brioso* character. Rampal in command all the way.

Four Trumpets

Symphony in C major for Four Trumpets

☐ Schwarz, Soper, Ranger, and Gould (trumpets) / Nonesuch 71301

Molter's engaging five-movement opus (written for either four horns or four trumpets) is "in symphony" rather than *a* symphony. But it little matters how it is titled, since this music is a feast for the ears with its golden illumination. No accompaniment. None is needed to enjoy the quadruple set of Allegro movements plus a *Menuet* as part 2 of the total of five.

The playing is immaculate, the heaven-pointed top register sounding as though dulcet flutes were involved. Especially, this is helped by perfect reproduction that is bright but not sharp.

Federico Mompou (1893-   )

Instrumental

Piano

Canción y Danza No. 6
Jeunes Filles au jardin (1915)

☐ Beatrice Klien (piano) / Turnabout S-34327

Evocative impressionistic enchantment. A marvel of gentility floats through Mompou's music, and at its most direct (rarely so) it is never heavy. If the sound of music can be termed perfumed, then Mompou's is exactly that.

Jeunes Filles is the last of the five pieces in *Scènes d'enfants*, written in 1915. The *Canción y Danza* is from a set composed between 1918 and 1928.

Praise can only be applied to the interpretation of the two pieces. Beatrice Klien fully understands these sensitive miniatures. One wishes there were more recorded examples of her playing Mompou's music.

Damunt de tú només les flors from *Combat del somni*

☐ de los Angeles (soprano); Soriano (piano) / Angel S-35775

A nostalgic gem. Sung with an exquisite sense of style.

Vocal

Voice with Accompaniment

Jean-Joseph Cassanea de Mondonville *(1711-1772)*

Sonata for Violin and Harpsichord
In G minor / In F major / In B major / In C major / In G major / In A major

☐ Fryden (baroque violin); Leonhardt (harpsichord) / Telefunken S-9497

The premises of accompaniment, harmonic fill-in, and the like are not present in these works. Equality reigns, and true duo-sonata climate warms the music. Performance certainty prevails; the lines are properly ornamented and are heard with a fine sense of rhythmic continuity.

Chamber Music

Georg Matthias Monn *(1717-1750)*

Concerto in G minor for Cello and Orchestra

☐ London Symphony Orchestra / du Pré (cello) / Barbirolli (conductor) / Angel S-36580

Vivaldian blocked-sound designs with solo replying to the orchestra are the fruitful situation here; the slow movement sings in the form of a *Siciliano*.

Warm and very stylish playing with admirable supportiveness from Sir John.

Concerto in D major for Harpsichord and Orchestra

☐ Hungarian Chamber Orchestra / Sebestyen (harpsichord) / Tatrai (conductor) / Turnabout 34324

Functional classicism arranged in the Allegro-Larghetto-Rondo sequence. The orchestra is rather pedestrian in spots; otherwise, feeling, sonority, and musical organization are satisfactory if not extraordinary.

Solo Instrument and Orchestra

Cello

Harpsichord

Monn / **Arnold Schoenberg (1874-1951)**

Concerto for Cello and Orchestra (After Monn)

☐ Columbia Symphony Orchestra / Lesser (cello) / Craft (conductor) / Columbia M2S-780

This is marked as a "free adaptation," but regardless of the creative flight from Monn's original or Schoenberg's flight of fancy, a transcription it remains. To consider it

Solo Instrument and Orchestra

Cello

a worthy project means accepting stylistic shifts and a type of total slickness. From this corner, Schoenberg's score does not score.

The soloist is given a real virtuosic opportunity. Aside from a thin tone, Laurence Lesser is only fairly successful. If the solo part is to mean anything, it needs more panache than is delivered in this case.

Marius Monnikendam   (1896-1977)

Orchestra

Arbeid ("Labor"), Symphonic Movement (1931)

☐ Hague Philharmonic Orchestra / van Otterloo (conductor) / Donemus Audio-Visual Series DAVS-6604

Monnikendam pictures a "dynamic tableau" of men at work in the port of Rotterdam. Monothematically proposed, with aggressive free variations. Van Otterloo paces the music nicely.

Jacques-Louis Monod   (1927-   )

Vocal

Voice and Orchestra

Cantus Contra Cantum I

☐ Chamber Orchestra / Sargon (soprano) / Monod (conductor) / Composers Recordings SD-358

Though the instrumentation covers flute, oboe, clarinet, bassoon, horn, tuba, mandolin, guitar, violin, harp, piano, double bass, and percussion, Monod's use of these colors is skeletonized, delicately embellishing the voice. Thus, with an expressively stripped instrumental background the vocal content achieves a very definite, almost lacy profile. These are soft passions, conveyed by two vocalises and settings of five French texts by Paul Eluard and Jean Sénac, but deeply felt ones.

Twelve rehearsals took place before the world premiere and the making of the CRI recording. The stylish and knowing results are proof.

Claudio Monteverdi   (1567-1643)

Vocal

Voice and Orchestra

Madrigals: Books IX, X, and Supplement—Madrigals, Canzonets, and Scherzi musicali

Alcun non mi consigli	*Ohimè, ch'io cado*
Alle danze	*O mio bene*
Bel pastor	*Perchè se m'odiavi* (Book IX)
Come dolce hoggi l'auretta	*Perchè se m'odiavi* (Suppl.)
Di far sempre gioire	*Più lieto il guardo*
Ecco di dolci raggi	*Quando dentro al tuo seno*
Eri già tutta mia	*Quel sguardo sdegnosetto*
Et è pur dunque vero	*Sì dolce è il tormento*
Io che armato sin hor	*Sì, sì ch'io v'amo*
La mia Turca	*Su pastorelli vezzosi* (Book IX)

Maledetto sia l'aspetto　　　*Su pastorelli vezzosi* **(Suppl.)**
Non voglio amare　　　　　*Taci, Armelin*
O come vaghi　　　　　　　*Zefiro torna*

☐ Strings of the English Chamber Orchestra / Armstrong (soprano); Hodgson (mezzo-soprano); Watts (contralto); Dickerson, Oliver, and Tear (tenors); Dean (bass); Leppard (harpsichord); Hall (cello) / Leppard (conductor) / Philips 6799006

A compilation of music for two and three voices, some works published posthumously (those in Book IX). The variety is just as colorful as in other sets of Monteverdi's madrigals. A few highlights are *Bel pastor,* a delightful seduction scene between a shepherd and a shepherdess that Leppard states should be presented as a stage piece; *Zefiro torna,* a duet for tenors and continuo which is one of the most famous of Monteverdi's compositions; and *Et è pur dunque vero,* which rates as a highly impressive piece for solo voice with strings and continuo.

Authentic evocations throughout. The performances are the equal of the other superb Monteverdi representations Leppard has conducted (see under *Choral: chorus alone* [Madrigals: Book III, and Madrigals: Book IV] and *chorus and orchestra* [Madrigals: Book VIII]).

Madrigals: Book III

Choral

Chorus Alone

Ch'io non t'ami **(No. 13)**
La giovinetta pianta **(No. 1)**
Lumi miei, cari lumi **(No. 18)**
Occhi un tempo mia vita **(No. 14)**
O come è gran martire **(No. 2)**
O dolce anima mia **(No. 4)**
O primavera **(No. 11)**
O rossignuol **(No. 6)**
Perfidissimo volto **(No. 12)**
Rimanti in pace **(Nos. 19 and 20)**
Se per estremo ardore **(No. 7)**
Sovre tenere herbette **(No. 3)**
Stracciami pur il core! **(No.5)**
Vattene pur, crudel **(Nos. 8, 9, and 10)**
Vivrò fra i miei tormenti **(Nos. 15, 16, and 17)**

☐ Chorus / Armstrong, Eathorne, and Watson (sopranos); Hodgson (mezzo-soprano); Collins (contralto); English and Partridge (tenors); Dean and Keyte (basses) / Leppard (conductor) / Philips 6703035

This recording is a superb achievement, important in its coverage of the two complete books of Monteverdi madrigals and in presenting performances characterized by the highest kind of artistry. There is a slight difference of soloists in the two sets of madrigals, as will be noted (*see* Madrigals: Book IV), including the fact that the Glyndebourne Opera Chorus sings only in nine of the madrigals in Book IV. In both books, when the chorus does sing, the heaviness that might result from such textural weight does not exist.

Monteverdi's madrigals run the gamut from the light to the passionate, from starkness to eroticism. Their quality is of privileged communication. Leppard's direction of these creative communications is simply superb. (Also see under *Vocal: voice and orchestra* [Madrigals: Books IX, X, and Supplement].)

Madrigals: Book IV

Ah, dolente partita (No. 1)
Anima del cor mio (No. 18)
Anima dolorosa (No. 17)
Anima mia, perdona (Nos. 6 and 7)
A un giro sol de'begl'occhi (No. 11)
Cor mio, mentre vi miro (No. 2)
Cor mio, non mori? e more (No. 3)
Io mi son giovinetta (No. 13)
La piaga c'ho nel core (No. 9)
Longe da te, cor mio (No. 19)

Luci serene e chiare (No. 8)
Non più guerra! (No. 15)
Ohimè, se tanto amate (No. 12)
Piagn'e sospira (No. 20)
Quel augellin che canta (No. 14)
Sfogava con le stelle (No. 4)
Sì, ch'io vorrei morire (No. 16)
Voi pur da me partite (No. 10)
Volgea l'anima mia (No. 5)

☐ Glyndebourne Opera Chorus / Armstrong, Eathorne, and Watson (sopranos): Hodgson (mezzo-soprano); Watts (contralto); Dickerson and Tear (tenors); Dean and Keyte (basses) / Leppard (conductor) / Philips 6703035

(For commentary see Madrigals: Book III.)

Chorus
and Orchestra

Madrigals: Book VIII

Canti amorosi:
Altri canti di Marte
Ardo, e scoprir
Chi vol haver felice
Dolcissimo uscignuolo
Il ballo delle ingrate
Mentre vaga angioletta
Ninfa che scalza il piede
Non havea Febo ancora
Non partir, ritrosetta
O sia tranquillo il mare
Perchè t'en fuggi
Su pastorelli vezzosi
Vago augelletto

Canti guerrieri:
Altri canti d'amor
Ardo, avvampo
Armato il cor
Gira il nemico
Hor che'l ciel e la terra
Il ballo (per l'Imperatore Ferdinando)
Il combattimento di Tancredi e Clorinda
Ogni amante è guerrier
Se vittorie si belle

☐ Strings of the English Chamber Orchestra, Members of the Glyndebourne Chorus, and Members of the Ambrosian Singers / Armstrong, Bostock, Fuller, Harper, Howells, and Watson (sopranos); Hodgson (mezzo-soprano); Collins (contralto); Alva, Davies, Oliver, Tear, and Wakefield (tenors); Dean and Grant (basses); Spencer (lute); Ellis (harp); Leppard, Pearson, and Ward (harpsichords); Hall and Heath (cellos); Beers (double bass) / Leppard (conductor) / Philips 6799006

Not all is as expected in these "Madrigals of Love and War." Monteverdi's *Canti amorosi* and *Canti guerrieri* madrigals range from solos and duos to heroic cantata and opera. And a sinfonia precedes the first of the *amorosi* set.

Il combattimento di Tancredi e Clorinda calls for special attention. This is a dramatic recitation illustrating the poem by Tasso by way of three characters: a reciter, Tancredi, and Clorinda. Though it is included in the madrigals, Monteverdi envisaged staged performances of this work, and it has thus become a totally viable operatic property.

Another of the madrigals has been staged as a one-act opera: *Il ballo delle ingrate*—the "ingrate" being the souls of females condemned to everlasting torment in Hell for having refused to give themselves to their lovers.

The performances are eloquent and in the memorable class.

See also under *Vocal: voice and orchestra* (Madrigals: Books IX, X, and Supplement).

Mass in Four Parts

Mass in Four Parts

☐ Strings from Academy of St. Martin-in-the-Fields and Choir of St. John's College, Cambridge / Turner and Odom (trebles); Birts and Bishop (tenors); Keene (bass); Hogwood (harpsichord); Bielby (organ) / Guest (conductor) / Argo ZRG-5494

One of these Masses was published in 1640, the other, posthumously, in 1651. However these dates do not relate to the years of composition which are unknown. Both works are performed in modern editions made by D. Arnold Gema (for the earlier Mass) and by H. F. Redlich (for the other Mass). The editings are mainly in terms of the instrumental support, in all cases stylistically fitting and never interfere with the Monteverdian beauties that surround these most impressive works.

One is struck by the exultant tone that permeates the music of the later-published work; the other Mass is much more restrained. Jerome Roche, Argo's editorial adviser, indicates, in regard to the latter, that "We are here listening to him at his most ascetic." But Monteverdi's ascetic demeanor (if that description is accepted) does not result in dull music whatsoever. Not too well known, these Masses are true finds. They are performed with excellence and eloquence.

Il ballo delle ingrate
> *See above:* **Madrigals: Book VIII**

Il combattimento di Tancredi e Clorinda
> *See above:* **Madrigals: Book VIII**

L'Incoronazione di Poppea

☐ Vienna Concentus Musicus / Gartner, Hansmann, Donath, and Söderström (sopranos); Berberian, Minetto, and Baker (mezzo-sopranos); Esswood (countertenor); Gaifa and Equiluz (tenors); Fissore (baritone); Luccardi (bass) / Harnoncourt (conductor) / Telefunken 635247

A rich production. And, importantly, a complete one (the release embraces ten record sides). There might be questions as to the instrumentation, but really only die-hards would argue the point. One matter of contention concerns the soloists, and that is Elisabeth Söderström as Nero. Originally this part was set for a high-voiced castrato, and a listener's unwillingness to accept her vocal quality for the character she portrays persists. But this is the only major criticism of a performance that has stylistic nobility.

Orfeo

☐ Hamburger Bläserkreis für Alte Musik, Hamburg Monteverdi Choir, and Members of the Hamburg Camerata Accademica / Petrescu (soprano); Reynolds (mezzo-soprano); Bowman (countertenor); Rogers and Partridge (tenors); Elwes (baritone); Dean and Malta (basses) / Jürgens (conductor) / Deutsche Grammophon ARC-2710015

Opera it is, but there isn't a great amount of action in this case. There are a great number of choruses, and that part of the production is exceedingly well done. However, this does not negate the fine work provided by most of the soloists, especially the tenor,

Nigel Rogers. He is Orfeo and so the Opera is his show, and he is truly outstanding in the delivery and delineation of a very difficult vocal assignment.

Bassols Xavier Montsalvatge (1911-   )

Vocal

Voice and Orchestra

Cinco canciónes negras

☐ Paris Conservatoire Orchestra / de los Angeles (soprano) / Frühbeck de Burgos (conductor) / Angel S–35937

These songs contain both lyrical charm and sinuous melodic turns. Throughout, the writing escapes from insular constriction, while being tinged by native color and slightly agitated by native rhythms.

The singing of Victoria de los Angeles is treasurable. Each song is defined, consistently re-created—for example, the exotic strain in the *Canto negro* ("Negro Song"), and the nostalgic quality and tawny color of the *Canción de cuna para dormir a un negrito* ("Cradle Song to Put a Negro Child to Sleep").

Douglas Moore (1893-1969)

Orchestra

Farm Journal (1947)

☐ Oslo Philharmonic Orchestra / Antonini (conductor) / Composers Recordings 101 (monaural)

Folksy, comfortable music. It has Moore's usual flowing lyricism. By fully avoiding any sentimentality, the composition gains strength.

Played cleanly and with a becoming fluidity.

In Memoriam (1943)

☐ Japan Philharmonic Symphony Orchestra / Strickland (conductor) / Composers Recordings 127 (monaural)

The memorial piece is for "those who die young," and the "irreconcilable loss to us and them." A finely detailed performance, and one of Strickland's best conductorial contributions.

Pageant of P. T. Barnum

☐ Eastman-Rochester Orchestra / Hanson (conductor) / Mercury SRI-75095

The melodic and harmonic aspects are completely tonal. No catch-as-catch-can in the shape of the tunes—all of them are catchy, matched by convincing orchestration that covers the objective of the subject matter. This includes such as *Jenny Lind* and *Circus Parade.*

Movement 2 describes *Joice Heth—161-year-old Negress.* But Mercury can't seem to agree. The liner notes make Joice 160 years old, and Mercury's record jacket listing of the titles of the five movements adds a year to her age. It is 161, "officially," according to the published score.

Hanson directing this type of music, with which he has full rapport, is unbeatable.

Symphony No. 2 in A major (1946)

☐ Japan Philharmonic Symphony Orchestra / Strickland (conductor) / Composers Recordings S–133E (monaural)

Moore's music was conservatively rounded and conservatively romantic, including the early music, such as this Symphony written in 1946, and the operas composed in the 1950s. This Symphony's profile is not sharp, but is that of a composer who believed in well-built structures. Such strength lends expressivity, and the expressivity is aided by sonorous textures and bypassing of busybody scoring. All this serves the listener well.

Orchestral precision is lacking in the performance from time to time, and the sound is rather dry. Otherwise acceptable.

Cotillion Suite (1952)

String Orchestra

☐ Oslo Philharmonic Orchestra / Antonini (conductor) / Composers Recordings 107 (monaural)

Dances, of course—five of them after an opening Grand March. Serious light music, played with assurance if not with freedom.

Quintet for Clarinet and Strings (1946)

Chamber Music

☐ New Music String Quartet / Oppenheim (clarinet) / Desto 6425

The clarinet-quintet medium tends to have autumnal moods, and Moore's mood follows suit. Though the finale (neatly stitched with shifting rhythms) has overtones of folk material, all of the thematic material is self-originated, and there is no attempt to clutter the musical mosaic with any other than original ideas. The Quintet is suave and breathes with a very gentle feeling that is wholesome and exceedingly healthy.

Originally this work was released on the Columbia label. Its return to the catalogue is welcome. So is the opportunity of hearing that magnificent string team, the New Music Quartet. What a shame they disbanded!

Come Away Death

Vocal

Voice Alone

☐ Gramm (baritone) / Desto 6411/2

Here Moore has produced a magnificent realization of the lines from *Twelfth Night.* Dignity and tone are striking, thrice so by choosing to use an unaccompanied voice. A short piece, but probably Moore's most telling creation.

Death Be Not Proud

Voice with Accompaniment

☐ Steber (soprano); Biltcliffe (piano) / Desto 6411/2

Moore's neo-romanticism is exhibited here, with a directness of expression. The climax of the song occurs on the very last word.

The Devil and Daniel Webster (1939)

Opera and Dramatic Music

☐ Festival Orchestra and Choir / Young, Dubin, Gayle, and Kondakjian (sopranos); Paul (alto); Weidner, de Groat, Douglas, and Eva (tenors); Winters and Harms (baritones); Blankenship and Hartzell (basses); Milstein, de Groat, and Hartzell (speakers) / Aliberti (conductor) / Desto 6450

Moore described his work as a "folk opera in one act" (the tale is by Stephen Vincent

Benét). Accordingly, folksy, homespun music, and there's plenty of straight dialogue. Not made for the Met's stage but serviceable fare for the college and university areas.

The recording has clear production. Synopsis and libretto are included.

Thomas Moore (1933-)

Instrumental

Piano, Four Hands

Metamorphosis for Piano, Four Hands

☐ Chinn and Brings (piano) / Composers Recordings SD–383

An overlay of Webern's Symphony for Chamber Orchestra, Op. 21, explains Moore's title. Webern's material is stated by augmentation and durational value changes. Moore's material inspissates and interlards Webern's to the extent that it is unrecognizable. There is this to say, however: the textures are shot with color and dynamic differences, even if Webern's *Klangfarbenmelodie* of necessity has disappeared, what with only a single timbre utilized.

As a creative offshoot one can congratulate Moore on his choice (many a composer has done likewise without acknowledgment!). The idea is undeniably effective, though what Moore has to say eliminates any of Webern's poised clarity, replacing it with energized athleticism.

François d'Assise Morel (1926-)

Orchestra

Antiphonie (1951)

☐ Louisville Orchestra / Whitney (conductor) / Louisville S–661

Not a superfluous note in the fifty-four measures. A neo-Gregorian opus, superbly harmonized and counterpointed with abrasive pitch selection and with intense motility without disturbing the quietness of thought. There are thirty-five metrical changes within the work. The Louisville's seamless performance neatly gathers these in and maintains the proper amount of tension. Another instance of the abilities of this orchestra, indicating its major-league status.

Federico Moreno Torroba (1891-)

Instrumental

Guitar

Castles of Spain

☐ Segovia (guitar) / MCA 2534

These eight short sketches are lightly impressionistic. Segovia plays the gentle music (dedicated to him) in a befitting graceful and reflective manner.

Roberto García Morillo (1911-)

Orchestra

Variaciones olimpicas, Op. 24

☐ Louisville Orchestra / Whitney (conductor) / Louisville 612 (monaural)

A dozen variations, each representing a character in Greek mythology. So *Zeus* is described with ferocious music, *Hermes* by a solo piano section, *Athena* by dynamic phrases to depict this goddess's warlike side of her personality. A pair of odd points are the parenthetical homages to Satie and Schoenberg.

Interesting instrumentational ideas that carry forward a fine creative intelligence using an expanded type of tonality. Strong playing. The music is exhibited with firm command and a fine sense of the coloristic differences.

Jean Baptiste Morin   *(1677-1745)*

The Deer Hunt Overture: *Le Réveil*   *Orchestra*

☐ Collegium Musicum of Paris / Douatte (conductor) / Nonesuch 71002E (monaural)

No danger of praising this piece out of proportion to its two-and-one-half-minute length. Still, its full-blooded joyousness gives us a fine instrumental prelude, sectionally arranged so that a trumpet proclaims and woodwinds respond. Appealingly stated, but no credit given the solo trumpet.

Thomas Morley   *(1557-1602)*

Three Pieces for Two Violas   *Chamber Music*

☐ Phillips and Trampler (violas) / Musical Heritage Society OR–398

Rich samplings from Morley's *First Booke of Canzonets to Two Voyces*. All three are fantasias. Especially compelling in its performance is the last one, titled *La caccia*.

Come, Sorrow, Come   *Vocal*

It Was a Lover and His Lass   *Voice with Accompaniment*

Thyrsis and Milla

☐ Patterson (tenor); Spencer (lute) / Philips 6500282

Examples of the richness to be found in Morley's songs with lute. The latter is no mere harmonic identifier, but an equal participant. First-class reportage by the performers involved.

Cruel You Pull Away Too Soon **from** *Canzonettes or Little Short Songs to Three Voyces*   *Choral*

                                     Chorus Alone

☐ Hest and Simone (sopranos); Shor (tenor); Turnabout 34485

Regarding a lover who chides his gal about quick kissing. Light as a feather.

Madrigals

April Is in My Mistress' Face   *Leave This Tormenting*
Arise, Get Up, My Dear   *Miraculous Love's Wounding!*
Besides a Fountain   *Now Is the Month of Maying*
Fire! Fire! My Heart!   *O Grief!*
Good Morrow, Fair Ladies   *Say, Gentle Nymphs*

Hard by a Crystal Fountain	*Shoot, False Love, I Care Not*
Hark, Alleluia Cheerly	*Though Philomelax Lost Her Love*
I Follow, Lo, the Footing	*When, Lo, by Break of Morning*
I Go Before, My Darling	*Whither Away, So Fast*
In Dew of Roses	

☐ Deller Consort / Deller (conductor) / Vanguard HM-4

Have aural joy in these madrigals, each and every one a delight in its setting and in its performance by this group of two sopranos, countertenor, two tenors, and a baritone. That there is pitch wavering in a few of the pieces by the female voices does not harm the production.

Jerome Moross (1913-   )

Instrumental

Clarinet Choir

Sonatina for Clarinet Choir (1966)

☐ Hacker, Ronchetti, Hambleton, and Reidy (clarinets); Trier (alto clarinet); Howes (bass clarinet) / Desto 6469

A clarinet sextet (comprising four of the B flat type, plus alto and bass representatives) is an unordinary medium for the concert-music stage but quite ordinary for the educational-music stage. Moross's Sonatina is one of the best. Its principal message is jazzy and perky.

Chamber Music

Sonatina for Contrabass and Piano

☐ Grey (contrabass); Pearson (piano) / Desto 6469

Jazz procedures are not too far away from most of Jerome Moross's output, and the bass-piano piece follows suit. Its characteristic feeling is of the dance floor, and the principal procedure is the bass's pizzicati, which one expects to break out in the rhythmic jive of slap-bass style. That it doesn't is no detriment to Moross's light-faceted but still solid piece.

Sonatina for Brass Quintet (1968)

☐ Wilbraham and Evans (trumpets); Busch (horn); Brenner (trombone); Jenkins (tuba) / Desto 6469

Two movements. The first is threnodic in rhythm, nocturnal in its horizontal course. It features the trombone and then the muted trumpet. A more bravura essay completes the piece.

Sonatina for Woodwind Quintet (1970)

☐ Taylor (flute); Morgan (oboe); Hacker (clarinet); Busch (horn); Gatt (bassoon) / Desto 6469

Diaphanous and amiable music, more serious in its bluesy slow (middle) movement. The outer movements resemble Poulenc with a little less salt and pepper.

Ballet

***The Scandalous Life of Frankie and Johnny* (1938)**

☐ Vienna Symphony Orchestra / Hendl (conductor) / Desto 6408E (monaural)

Six of the seven sections in Moross's ballet score (the second-part Blues is omitted in the recording). No fancy tricks, right down the pike with jazz zip and exactitude. The harmonies are both clean and dirty—both fitting without any dishonest sophistication.

A fair performance. No credits are given the gals who interject bits of the familiar folk tune on which the work is based. Their proper undercultured vocal delivery does not deserve the anonymity accorded them.

Franklin E. Morris (1920-)

Five Esoteric Pieces for Woodwind Quintet

Chamber Music

☐ Soni Ventorum Wind Quintet / Desto 6401

Don't be misled by the "esoteric" designation. Titlewise there is nothing unusual with Invention I, Invention II, *Introspection, Protestation,* and *Reflection.* And gentle chromaticism that stretches tonality is also not in the esoteric range. However, these reactions aside, Morris's suite has a vitality and a refined instrumentational condition that warrant some attention.

This quintet is made up of splendid musicians. Their sensitivity is reflected in the performance of Morris's piece. It is fresh and full of life.

Harold Morris (1890-1964)

Passacaglia, Adagio, and Finale

Orchestra

☐ Louisville Orchestra / Riesley (soprano) / Whitney (conductor) / Louisville 57-6 (monaural)

The soprano voice used in movement 2 is an orchestral instrument; no words are utilized, simply the formations "ah" and "la." This is the only deviation from a standard, neutral type of orchestration.

Robert Morris (1943-)

Phases

Instrumental

☐ Albright and Morris (pianos) / Composers Recordings S-346

Two Pianos

Linear styled material is the principal support of the music with rigorously pursued definition of the sounds from four locations. More successful, undoubtedly, in concert with the use of loudspeakers in front, in back, to the left, and to the right of the audience. This is accomplished by two additional performers who spatially locate the sounds by the use of photo-cell mixers. The composer suggests listening with earphones to compensate for the bounded difference in the recorded version.

In general outline one recalls Boulez's *Structures,* though minus the preordering of the Frenchman's piece.

Richard Moryl   (1929-   )

Orchestra

Chroma for Chamber Ensemble (1972)

☐ New England Contemporary Ensemble / Moryl (conductor) / Desto 7143

Color indeed, most of it sounding like electronic-music segments. Moryl explains it differently, but the thought persists that electronic music subconsciously (unconsciously?) was the source of these symbolic instrumental metaphors.

Multiples

☐ Contemporary Chamber Ensemble / Weisberg (conductor) / Desto 7121

Multiples is scored for a small string orchestra, with harp, piano, and percussion. And it is percussiveness that describes the varied pitch combinations (mainly clustered fists of sound) that style the work. These whirl about, separate, come together, and then move on to other settings. Such inner play and counter play provide the structure. A great deal of the music is like smaller-scaled Penderecki.

This type of music is a Weisberg speciality. One hears the disc with the fullest confidence.

Instrumental

Piano

Contacts

☐ Joanne Moryl (piano); Desroches (percussion) / Desto 7133

Music for piano and percussion involvement totally inside the piano. The latter is based on the keyboard instrument functioning ''as a sounding board and reverberation chamber, when struck on the strings, metal supports or wood frame.''

A fair number of new sounds are to be heard; others resemble sounds that have been obtained in other ways. Some composers cannot cut the percussive mustard and merely turn out a quantity of pure noise. Moryl's inventions are musical and deserving of substantial credits.

A keenly detailed performance.

Trumpet

Salvos (1969)

☐ Schwarz (trumpet) / Desto 7133

Unbelievable trumpet playing. Sensational trumpet writing. O.K.—after hearing flutter tonguing, wobble sounds, slow and fast glissandi, growls, microtones, cannon-ball tonguing, echo effects, wa-wa and jazz gushes, buzz-saw and vocal regurgitative imitations, passages that come off the grooves as though a piccolo were playing and instantly answered by a phrase one would wager was for a tuba bouncing around in its extremely low register, disjunct trampoline skips, and sounds that can't be pinned to a specific pitch—O.K. if one wishes to call this a type of musical yellow journalism. I'll buy it. Try it, it will be almost impossible not to be caught up in this display of blood-boiling virtuosity.

Chamber Music

Modules (1969)

☐ Nancy Turetzky (piccolo); Bertram Turetzky (string bass); Williams (trombone); Lesbines (percussion) / Serenus 12028

Modern chamber music as it is writ. One each of the four families (wind, brass, string, percussion) represented, and extreme disparity of timbre purposefully sought. Amalgamation of texture is bypassed in this piece independent of strict pulse or meter. The total formal uncertainty paradoxically produces a unity, obtained by a series of events. Music that stretches the ears through the authoritative command of these virtuoso performers.

Choralis

☐ Instrumentalists and Choruses from Western Connecticut State College / Moryl (conductor) / Desto 7121

No text for this work, written for two mixed-voice choruses, three trombones, two string basses, four percussion, jazz drummer, and organ. Moryl's piece is a choral happening, though planned within certain limitations, whereby there is whispering, hissing, talking, and the uttering of various sounds, including self-applause. As effects these are fairly effective, though attenuated. The ending offers a surprise: a fair portion of Handel's Hallelujah Chorus. As this emerges from a dissonant framework into a firm cadential close, it brings strongly to mind the arrival of the (pun intended) "tonal Messiah."

Fluorescents

☐ Instrumentalists and Chorus from Western Connecticut State College / Moryl (conductor) / Desto 7121

Moryl combines mixed chorus with percussion, chimes, and organ. He also mixes his sounds, sometimes in sets of intensely fractionalized rounds that smear the totality into clustered proportions. Some humor too from water-like sounds, mouth noises, and a sudden insert of a breathless solo female voice singing the opening of Schubert's *Die Forelle* unaccompanied.

Moryl's purpose, the unsigned notes state, "was to produce a galaxy of sound which would fascinate, both in its abstract aspect, and [in] its aural imagery." It does.

Illuminations for Soprano, Voices, Eight String Basses, and Chamber Ensemble

☐ New England Contemporary Ensemble / Stellato (soprano) / Moryl (conductor) / Desto 7143

Moryl's Illuminations are propped by a single-pitch pedal sustained by the octet of double basses. Over this come the pronouncements of diverse details: vocalise, brass bombardments, choral sound blocks (including a Gregorian imitation), and percussive detail. A compelling mix, all of it, and most illuminative of a strong creative voice.

Everyone taking part does excellently.

Ignaz Moscheles   *(1794 - 1870)*

Concertante in F major for Flute, Oboe, and Orchestra

☐ Frankfurt Radio Symphony Orchestra / Nicolet (flute); Holliger (oboe) / Inbal (conductor) / Philips 9500070

Handsomely executed in terms of Schumannesque stylization and color. Something else, however. There is an interpretative imagination that lifts this reading above the ordinary and thereby adds measurably to the enjoyment quotient.

Piano Concerto in G minor, Op. 58

☐ Philharmonia Hungarica / Ponti (piano) / Maga (conductor) / Candide 31010

Polished classic-romantic prose here. Three movements, with the slow central portion leading direct into the concluding movement. Though the finale is sprightly, there is a certain amount of dramaticism within it, and all fluff is avoided.

The playing of Michael Ponti is first class, delivered with conspicuous firmness, flair, and total responsibility to the music. In 1824 Moscheles gave Mendelssohn piano lessons. Ponti's vital performance helps prove that the teacher's piano concerto is as good as his pupil's using the same tonality.

Instrumental

Piano

Characteristische Studien, Op. 95

No. 2, Widerspruch / No. 4, Juno / No. 6, Bacchanal / No. 9, Terpsichore

Etudes, Op. 70, Nos. 5, 9, 12, 13, 14, and 24

☐ Ponti (piano) / Candide 31010

The two dozen Etudes contained in Opus 70, while concentrating in each instance on a pertinent technical problem, are all miniatures worthy of concert representation. The last of the group consists of a prelude and a fugue with three subjects. Small items, but all display Moscheles's creative largesse.

The "Characteristic Studies" bypass single technical objectives, displaying the romantic demeanor of the era in which they were composed by titling the general musical conduct. However, the Bacchanal, while spirited in tempo, is decorous in its note revelry. On the other hand, Terpsichore does fulfill balletic turns.

Ponti's playing of all these items is sensitive and of coloristic selectivity. He fully displays the métier they exploit.

Sonate caractèristique pour le piano, Op. 27

☐ Marvin (piano) / Genesis 1061

Optimistic reflections are described in the three parts displaying the composer's mood after the return of Emperor Francis II of Austria from France after Napoleon's defeat. (The score states, Composée pour le retour de S. M. l'Empereur d'Austriche dans sa Capitale.) Accordingly, a gay Allegro con brio, a group of variations on the Austrian folk song Freut' euch des Lebens ("Let All Enjoy Life"), and a waltz-propelled final Rondo.

There are a few superfluities but of small enough number not to harm the general sparkle of the music. Marvin plays the score with the required buffo aspect. A very informative and fluid performance.

**Piano,
Four Hands**

Grande Sonate symphonique, Op. 112

☐ Mary Louise Boehm and Pauline Boehm (piano) / Turnabout 34590

Full-scale, bearing out the "grand" designation. Moscheles's work for two performers at one piano has an introduction followed by a sonata movement, a florid slow-tempoed division, a Scherzoso alla tedesca, and a bracing finale. Aesthetically the spirit is Mendelssohnian. And there is good spirit in the playing of the sister team.

**Chamber
Music**

Grand Sextet in E flat major for Piano, Violin, Flute, Two Horns, and Cello, Op. 35

☐ Consortium Classicum / Musical Heritage Society MHS–1310

An odd combination that is simply a mixed quintet that supports the principal piano voice. Genial conditions prevail, with only a bit of a shift into a more serious situation in the slow movement. There the violin is given an opportunity to take the lead. He is the fairly well-known Sandor Karolyi. Werner Genuit, the pianist, plays splendidly and stylishly.

Grand Septet in D major for Piano, Violin, Viola, Clarinet, Horn, Cello, and Double Bass, Op. 88

☐ Consortium Classicum / Musical Heritage Society MHS–1310

"Grand" indeed—that is, for the piano. The keyboard instrument is in command; the narrative and characterization are controlled and directed by the piano. Not surprising, therefore, that when the score was checked, it was full of "tutti" and "solo" indications. Honest man, Mr. Moscheles! Yes, this is chamber music, since it calls for seven instruments, but really it is a concerto accompanied by a mini-orchestra of six performers.

This little-known group gives a fine portrayal of the score. On the basis of this recording the Consortium Classicum deserves to be recognized as a major-league organization.

Lawrence Moss   *(1927-   )*

Four Scenes for Piano (1961)

Instrumental

Piano

☐ Fink (piano) / Composers Recordings S–186

Pitch class groups are the syntactic means of behavior and feeling here. However, Moss does not structure these in terms of conventional cliché format.

The Scenes were commissioned by and dedicated to the soloist. He gives a fine performance, strongly characterizing the material.

Omaggio for Piano-Four Hands (1966)

Piano,
Four Hands

☐ Jean and Kenneth Wentworth (piano) / Desto 7131

Moss's "Homage" is no essay in fanfare style. Its accents and meanings derive from fluid phrases, contrastive registral development, and thinned sonorities. The testimonial material involves some Mozart quotes, but put through a fragmented wringer they are hard to identify. This is not important, since the music makes its own impressionistic impact.

Omaggio was written especially for the Wentworths, and they do it full justice in a splendid recording.

Sonata for Violin and Piano (1959)

Chamber
Music

☐ Raimondi (violin); Wyner (piano) / Composers Recordings S–186

Old habits die hard, but old habits die. The time-honored and time-worn factors of sonata form are updated in this case. Moss does not totally abolish the formal past—he simply capsulizes it. His Sonata covers three movements, played without pause (and played here with stage sense and complete musicianship). Its balances are mainly achieved by totality rather than emphasis on single-movement conception and comprehension.

In this Sonata household there is no diatonic furniture. The appurtenances are chromatically styled. Nevertheless, in the violin part, there is a decided reliance on the juicy romantic decor of sixths. The choice is fruitful and does not harm the fresh setting of Moss's Sonata.

Elegy for Two Violins and Viola (1969)

☐ Zukofsky and Teco (violins); Dupouy (viola) / Composers Recordings S–307

The trio medium for paired violins and viola has a very limited literature. Of the few works of the highest rank, none has the intensity, tensions, and feelings of this Elegy. None weaves into the fabric of the work the methods followed here (players perform both on- and off-stage).

The emotive plaintiveness is most cogently set forth in the opening Adagio and in the closing section of the fourth part. But even in the most violent portions of the trio, the feeling of personal loss in its most dissident sense prevails. (The work is dedicated to Moss's brother, who died the year this work was in progress.)

Paul Zukofsky had requested the composition of Moss's string trio. He and his colleagues provide a fine realization of the score. There is no doubt, however, that a live performance, with the performer placement procedure mentioned earlier, would provide a more exciting response for an auditor.

Timepiece for Violin, Piano, and Percussion (1970)

☐ Zukofsky (violin); Kalish (piano); Des Roches (percussion) / Composers Recordings S-307

The mix of proportional notation with metered pulse—improvised data with fixed material—is beautifully organized. The fluidity makes Timepiece sound as precise as totally measured music, due to Moss's subtle and sensible control of the parts graphically notated. Moss has described the music as concerning "time in the usual (chronological) sense as well as time flowing simultaneously at different rates." The success of the method is a strong argument on behalf of proportional notation.

The performers' execution is prime, displaying and proving the exciting continuity of Moss's sensitive score.

Auditions (1971)

☐ Dorian Woodwind Quintet / Composers Recordings S-318

The work is in two parts, the second turning into a sextet with the wind quintet augmented by tape. *Auditions* at first makes much of noodles, trills, and fractured, fractional figures suggestive of instrumental warm-up procedures. Within it a transmuted quote of Richard Strauss's *Till Eulenspiegel* motive appears. This off-shoot also appears in the second part of the work, which is of contrasting seriousness.

The number of wind quintet organizations concertizing and recording is more than ever before. Very few can match the breadth of substantiality and the general vitality of the Dorian team. Their playing of Moss's difficult music is proof.

Vocal

Voice with Accompaniment

Unseen Leaves (1975)

☐ Ostryniec (oboe); Drucker (soprano) / Orion 78288

A pair of Walt Whitman poems is the basis for Moss's trio for oboe, soprano, and tape. The texts function as well in the tape part—heard with electronic change—as in the vocal part. Moss does not use the tape in isolation but beautifully enmeshes it with the oboe and voice. The resultant artistic credits of the work mark it as one of the prime entries on the scene today. Its colors are fresh, and so is Moss's treatment. Everything is inventive. *Unseen Leaves* will go very far.

The singing and the playing are splendid. Both parts are quite difficult, but there is no sound of strain on the part of the performers.

Moritz Moszkowski (1854-1925)

Spanish Dances (Book I), Op. 12

Orchestra

☐ London Symphony Orchestra / Argenta (conductor) / London 6006

A professional performance, duly straightforward because that's the way the music was written. The liner notes fail to indicate that Moszkowski did not himself orchestrate the Dances; he originally conceived them for piano duet and later arranged them for solo piano because of their great popularity. Numbers 1, 3, and 4 (in C, A, and B flat major, respectively) were transcribed by Valentin Frank. The other two (numbers 2 and 5, in G minor and D major, respectively) were orchestrated by Philipp Scharwenka.

Suite No. 3, Op. 79

☐ Louisville Orchestra / Mester (conductor) / Louisville 734

Moszkowski's opus has not been subtitled (as noted in the liner notes) ''a symphony for salon orchestra.'' It could well be described as ''a salon example for symphony orchestra.'' There is light chemistry here: a lyrical Allegro; a catchy movement titled *The Obstinate Note* (a cute way of describing a pedal tone), a waltz, and a finale with a slightly more serious demeanor.

The Louisville folks project this music in an informed manner, meaning that they and Mester are fully sympathetic to the *modus operandi* and neither overplay nor underplay.

Concerto in E major for Piano and Orchestra, Op. 59

Solo Instrument and Orchestra

Piano

☐ Philharmonia Hungarica / Ponti (piano) / Stracke (conductor) / Candide 31030

Full-scale layout (moderate-paced music, slow-tempoed music, a Scherzo, and a vivacious conclusion) devoted to grateful and effective romantic parlance. The work is completely overlooked these days but certainly worth revival. Ponti produces the substantial evidence for this statement.

Violin Concerto in C major, Op. 30

Violin

☐ Louisville Orchestra / Treger (violin) / Mester (conductor) / Louisville 743

Charles Treger extracts all the juice contained in this little-known romantic concerto. Violinistic juices they are: lush tunes, rapid passage work, cadenza spurts, double stops. All made to order for enjoyable listening. The work has less turbulence than Vieuxtemps and much less than Paganini but is just as worthy a concerto as any these gentlemen produced. So why isn't it heard?

Blumenstück

Instrumental

Piano

☐ Kann (piano) / Musical Heritage Society MHS–1862

A typical example of superior salon style.

Caprice Espagnol, Op. 37

☐ Ponti (piano) / Candide 31030

Lightly virtuosic. The *Caprice* has retained its popularity and will not lose it if performances like that of Michael Ponti are accorded it. He zips it off, with high gloss, in a five-minute span that is healthy. Hans Kann, in his Moszkowski program on Musical Heritage

Society (MHS–1862), lingers over it (more than a minute and a half of lingering). Such slow pace makes the music pot-bellied.

Chanson napolitaine, Op. 83, No. 6

Course folle, Op. 73, No. 3

☐ Kann (piano) / Musical Heritage Society MHS–1862

Kann is especially effective in the dance pulse of the second piece.

Danse bohème (after Bizet's Carmen)

☐ Ponti (piano) / Candide 31030

Just a few M.M. additions to G.B.'s operatic extract. Thus: tactful and tasteful translation for the piano. The playing is indisputable.

Esquisse vénétienne, Op. 73, No. 1

☐ Kann (piano) / Musical Heritage Society MHS–1862

A touch of nostalgic Chopin precedes and succeeds the *Vénétienne* outline. One of Moszkowski's best poetic manifestations.

Etude in F major, Op. 72

Etinselles, Op. 36, No. 6

☐ Ponti (piano) / Candide 31030

A comparison of the Etude with another recorded version (Hans Kann on Musical Heritage Society MHS–1862) shows that Ponti is clearer and cleaner in his playing. Also, he chooses a faster tempo, which freshens the music.

''Sparks,'' from the set of *Eight Characteristic Pieces,* is considered (properly) as one of the best items Moszkowski turned out. Ponti's staccato playing is fastidious and delightful.

Etude pour la main gauche seule, Op. 22, No. 4

Guitarre, Op. 45, No. 2

La jongleuse, Op. 52, No. 4

Melodie, Op. 18

Pantomime, Op. 77, No. 8

Serenata, Op. 15

Thema, Op. 10

Valse d'amour, Op. 57, No. 4

Valse mignonne

☐ Kann (piano) / Musical Heritage Society MHS–1862

Some old favorites included here (*Guitarre* and the third piece ''The Juggler''). There is no arguing the salon genre, but the music is generous with fluid melodic lines and refreshing rhythmic patterns. Of course, it is not profound, but certainly not superficial either. Moszkowski's depositions have the ring of salonistic authenticity.

Venusberg Bacchanale (Paraphrase for Piano after Music by Wagner)

☐ Ponti (piano) / Candide 31030

A soft approach to the *Tannhäuser* material—no Lisztian fireworks. It's very becoming. Neatly accomplished by the composer and beautifully realized by the performer.

Felix Mottl. *See Chabrier / Felix Mottl; also, Richard Wagner / Felix Mottl.*

Leo Mouravieff   (1905-   )

Nativité for String Trio and String Orchestra   *String Orchestra*

☐ Württemberg Chamber Orchestra, Heilbronn / Faerber (conductor) / Turnabout 34545

Sometimes modal, sometimes polymodal language is used in *Nativité,* the first part of Mouravieff's *La Mère* ("The Mother"). There are sharp reminders of Tansman's linear practices in that composer's slow-tempoed music.

The fact that no sharp emphasis is given the solo trio in the score is probably the reason why no credits are noted for the three players. The performance is a creditable one, but Turnabout's heading is not, since it reads "for string trio and orchestra."

Jean-Joseph Mouret   (1682-1738)

Suite de Symphonies No. 1   *Orchestra*

☐ Collegium Musicum de Paris / Douatte (conductor) / Nonesuch 71009

The saying is that the devil is the author of confusion. Not necessarily. It is recording companies (and in this case the venerable *Schwann* as well) that sometime also produce glaring chaos.

Nonesuch titles this *Fanfares for Violins, Oboe, Bassoons, Trumpets, and Percussion,* though Edward Tatnall Canby speaks of it correctly in his liner note. A competing edition, on Turnabout (34232), designates the piece as *Sinfonies de Fanfares. Schwann* does not follow the error but peculiarly compounds it by listing that performance as *Fanfares pour trp., . . . av. une suite de symph.,* as though it were a different piece from its succeeding catalogue entry, where Douatte's reading is noted correctly as the first of two total *Suites de simphonies.* At least *Schwann* thereby corrects the improper Nonesuch title.

There is more, however. Though the titles for the first pair of movements agree in both versions, each goes its separate way in regard to movements 3 and 4. Nonesuch calls the third movement Fanfares, while Turnabout terms it a *Tambourin.* As to movement 4, what is a *Gigue* on Nonesuch is named *Gay* on Turnabout.

However, none of the above has any bearing on the choice of performance, where again one is faced with major differences. Douatte includes violins, winds, trumpets, and percussion. Turnabout's disc is conducted by Armand Birbaum, who not only directs a brass and wind ensemble (its make-up is not designated) plus a solo trumpet, but fleshes this out with full organ; perhaps that is why the performance plot thickens.

I have never heard a more lugubrious performance than Birbaum's. Movement 1 (*Rondeau*) has gained popularity by being the theme for television's *Masterpiece Theatre*. It will be recognized in Birbaum's setting, but it will be heard as though grapnel is attached to every note. He takes a full three minutes to cover the ground, whereas Douatte styles it in 1:53. This same sense of slow motion contaminates the other sections as well. The *Gracieusement* (part 2) is 3:11 for Douatte, 5:06 for Birbaum. The former covers the third movement in 2:02, the latter only five seconds longer; but in the brisk finale, he blocks forward motion by a 1:04 timing, while Douatte breezily conducts it home free in 48 seconds. The ceremonial content is certainly obliterated in Birbaum's complete performance, which takes almost three and one half minutes longer and which seems to go on for even more than that amount of time.

Charles Mouton   (17th cent.)

Instrumental   **Pièces du luth sur différents modes**

Lute   ☐ Schäffer (lute) / Turnabout 34137

A set of three dances: *Allemande, Sarabande,* and *Canarie.* Fancy subtitles with each, such as *La Dialogue des Graces sur Iris* for the first of the group. Mouton, a seventeenth-century French lutenist, used regulated forms but filled them with fresh music.

The piece is also obtainable in a five-record set issued by Turnabout on 34195/9.

Leopold Mozart   (1719-1787)

Orchestra   **Musical Sleigh Ride**

Sinfonia in D major

☐ Ensemble Eduard Melkus / Melkus (violin) / Melkus (conductor) / Deutsche Grammophon ARC-2533328

Of course there are the tinklings of sleigh bells and the crackings of a whip in the *Schlittenfahrt* piece. That's what one hears in the Württemberg Chamber Orchestra rendition on Turnabout (34134). But with Melkus there are some extra added sound-effect attractions that are not in the score. It's O.K. to have them in this amusing sketch.

The D major work is subtitled *Bauernhochzeit* ("Peasant Wedding"). A gay affair it is and played right up to snuff.

String Orchestra   **Sinfonia burlesca in G major**

☐ Ensemble Eduard Melkus / Melkus (viola) / Melkus (conductor) / Deutsche Grammophon ARC-2533328

Who or what Mr. L. Mozart is burlesquing is not clear. However, that's a small matter. The music moves along in an enthusiastic manner under the direction of Melkus, who doubles as one of the two violas in the piece.

Solo Instrument and Orchestra   **Concerto in D major**

☐ Academy of St. Martin-in-the-Fields / Tuckwell (horn) / Marriner (conductor) / Angel S-36996

Horn   Fair substances made into convincing ones by the playing of the distinguished soloist.

Concerto in D major for Trumpet

☐ Consortium Musicum / Tarr (trumpet) / Lehan (conductor) / Nonesuch 71270

A "standard" in the medium. Leopold Mozart's *Concerto per il Clarino Solo,* with a backing of two horns, strings, and continuo and cast in two movements (Adagio and *Allegro moderato*), makes no bones as to the trumpet's place in the registral scheme. It's up there and stays there, as befits late baroque practice.

There are a number of performances to choose from. Edward Tarr's conception is the freshest. It is up tempo but not rushed, poised but not forced, and one is not constantly reminded that the ear is hearing continual sounds in the treble territory. Tarr provides elegant precision with a matchless tonal quality. A second choice would be Wobitsch soloing with the Solisti di Zagreb on Bach Guild 5053.

Suite of the Year 1762

☐ Salzburg Mozarteum Duo / CMS/Oryx EXP-55

Papa Mozart was not in the same league as his illustrious son, but no shame pertains to his music, as this eight-part divertimento illustrates. All of its lightnesses are professionally written, and it is played by violinist Karlheinz Franke and pianist Paul v. Schilhawsky in a mellifluous manner.

Wolfgang Amadeus Mozart *(1756-1791)*

Ballet Music

Les Petits riens, K. 299b (K. Anh. 10)
From *Idomeneo,* K. 367

☐ Netherlands Chamber Orchestra / Zinman (conductor) / Philips 6500861

All the sections in *Les Petits riens* are minor Mozart, but Zinman's performance gives them a charm and grace that make them sound much better than they are actually. (*See below* [Gavotte in B flat major, K. 300, and *La Chasse,* K. 320f] for a discussion of music that may have been written for inclusion in this ballet.)

The *Idomeneo* music includes a splendidly strong Chaconne and a Gavotte that has achieved separate popularity. It is recorded with fine presence and stylistic clarity.

Cassation

In B flat major, K. 99 / In G major, K. 63

☐ Collegium Musicum, Zurich / Langbein (violin) / Sacher (conductor) / Turnabout 34373

No pretentions here, just a series of assorted movements—seven in K. 63 and one more than that in K. 99—that provide delectable listening, especially in these fine conceptions. The playing is faultless, with no relentless attempt to overfocus the details.

Cassation in D major, K. 62a

☐ Saint Paul Chamber Orchestra / Davies (conductor) / Nonesuch 71323

A model of Mozartean precision and this covers all nine movements. With a string group of sixteen, all the wind voices function with clarity.

Contredanses

> **Das Donnerwetter, K. 534**
> **Der Sieg vom Helden Koburg, K. 587**

☐ Vienna Mozart Ensemble / Boskovsky (conductor) / London STS-15280/4

Mozartean sweets, tastefully played. "The Victory of the Hero Coburg" was a tribute to a field marshal; the enemy he fought is represented by a short section in the minor key. Such a gentle smidgen of programmaticism is also found in the other piece, though no one will be frightened by this musical skimming of a thunder storm. (K. 534 was orchestrated by Erik Smith, the only documentation left being a piano score.)

Contredanses

> **Il trionfo delle donne, K. 607**
> **In B flat major, K. 123**
> **La Bataille, K. 535**
> **Les Filles malicieuses, K. 610**

Five *Contredanses Non più andrai*, K. 609

☐ Vienna Mozart Ensemble / Boskovsky (conductor) / London STS-15275/9

Whatever kind of dance was needed, Mozart was able to supply it. Here are a number of *contredanse* examples, all written and performed with cultured gentility.

Mozart produced K. 123 at the age of fourteen, while K. 610 represents his final dance contribution, composed nine months before his death. The titles mean practically naught, though a little piccolo, trumpet, and snare drum bit gives a militaristic touch to *La Bataille*.

Contredanses—Four *Contredanses*, K. 101

☐ Vienna Mozart Ensemble / Boskovsky (conductor) / London STS-15280/4

Erik Smith's contention, in his marvelous liner notes, is that two of the four pieces are by Leopold Mozart (if that is the case, the saying can be reversed: like son, like father). Make your own decision regarding this nice though unimportant music.

Contredanses

> **Four *Contredanses*, K. 267**
> **Six *Contredanses*, K. 462**

☐ Vienna Mozart Ensemble / Boskovsky (conductor) / London STS-15275/9

In K. 267 the music includes a gigue and a pair of gavottes, but to judge from the titling, it was doubtlessly used for *contredanses*. The music is of lighter cast in K. 462. Both sets are played with a deep loveliness that gently touches the heart.

Contredanses

> **Three *Contredanses*, K. 535a**
> **Two *Contredanses*, K. 603**
> **Two *Contredanses* for Graf Czernin, K. 270a**

☐ Vienna Mozart Ensemble / Boskovsky (conductor) / London STS-15280/4

The first and third works listed were edited and orchestrated by Erik Smith. In K. 603 both minuet and *ländler* shapes are included. Whatever strengths (somewhat limited) are in the music are fully portrayed in the performances.

Divertimento

No. 1 in E flat major, K. 113 / No. 2 in D major, K. 131

☐ Vienna Mozart Ensemble / Boskovsky (conductor) / London STS–15170

There is quite a difference in the scoring of these two divertimenti, proof again that no form or design ever enclosed Wolfgang Amadeus Mozart. The first has pairs of oboes, English horns, clarinets, bassoons, horns, and strings; the K. 131 cuts back to three winds, four horns, and strings.

The pieces are splendidly styled and executed. The music is beautifully molded in every phrase.

Divertimento

No. 10 in F major, K. 247 / No. 11 in D major, K. 251

☐ I Musici / Kühn (oboe); Kotulan and Peter (horns) / Philips 6500538

I Musici address this music directly, thus presenting it with its solid virtues. This is Mozart played with care and yet not academically. All to the good. In both cases the scoring calls for strings and two horns; an oboe is added in K. 247.

Divertimento No. 15 in B flat major, K. 287

☐ English Chamber Orchestra / Blum (conductor) / Vanguard 10082

Not as small-scaled as many performances of Mozart's larger-scoped divertimenti, but most fitting. Blum's full-alive attendance to rhythm is ideal.

Gavotte in B flat major, K. 300

☐ Vienna Mozart Ensemble / Boskovsky (conductor) / London STS–15275/9

Most of Mozart's dance music is scored without violas in the strings, but not this short and graceful item. Erik Smith says that the Gavotte was probably intended for the ballet *Les Petits riens*—*see above* (Ballet Music *Les Petits riens,* K. 299b [K. Anh. 10]) and then was "laid aside for some unknown reason."

German Dances—Four German Dances, K. 602

☐ Vienna Mozart Ensemble / Boskovsky (conductor) / London STS–15280/4

Solid scoring, including full winds, two horns, two trumpets, timpani, strings (without violas), and a special attraction—a hurdy-gurdy! A Boskovsky success, as would be expected.

German Dances—Six German Dances, K. 509

☐ Vienna Mozart Ensemble / Boskovsky (conductor) / London STS–15275/9

Symphonic brilliance and flexibility within the form that only a Mozart could create. Marvelous playing.

German Dances—Six German Dances, K. 536

☐ Vienna Mozart Ensemble / Boskovsky (conductor) / London STS–15280/4

Played enchantingly. Listen carefully and catch some Mozart quoting Mozart.

German Dances

Six German Dances, K. 567
Six German Dances, K. 571
Six German Dances, K. 600

☐ Vienna Mozart Ensemble / Boskovsky (conductor) / London STS–15275/9

No docile self-imitation by Mozart. Though the form of the dance is maintained there are special touches. Thus, the percussioned emphasis in the trio of the fifth of the K. 567 set and the conjunct canarylike climbs by flute and piccolo in the K. 600 group, also in the trio of the fifth dance.

German Dances—Three German Dances, K. 605

☐ Philharmonia Orchestra / Davis (conductor) / Seraphim S–60057

The second dance is specially colored in its trio with the color charm of sleigh bells backed up with a pair of post horns. Davis doesn't minimize his treatment of these light Mozart delights. He stands clear of pat tempi, subtly varying them in the separate dances. All is beautifully distinct and thoroughly convincing.

German Dances—Twelve German Dances, K. 586

☐ Vienna Mozart Ensemble / Boskovsky (conductor) / London STS–15275/9

A large set of dances, matched by a slightly larger amount of percussion (timpani, cymbals, and tamburino). Mozart calls for a fair amount of high horn writing that oddly is not always as clearly played as might be desired. Otherwise, of course, Willi Boskovsky is the usual expert practitioner of light dance delights such as these.

La Chasse, K. 320f

☐ Vienna Mozart Ensemble / Boskovsky (conductor) / London STS–15280/4

Mozart left *La Chasse* unfinished—it was completed by Erik Smith.
Of course, horns are featured, but so is an important bassoon voice. This short entry may have been written for inclusion in the ballet *Les Petits riens—see above* (Ballet Music *Les Petits riens*, K. 299b [K. Anh. 10]). It is presented with the usual Boskovsky performance panache, in a piece that covers less than a two-minute span.

Marches—March in C major, K. 214

☐ Vienna Mozart Ensemble / Boskovsky (conductor) / London STS–15280/4

A prancing item, with snapped rhythm. The performance is suavely detailed.

Marches

In D major, K. 189 / In D major, K. 215

☐ Vienna Mozart Ensemble / Boskovsky (conductor) / London STS–15275/9

The first of the pair has a bit of everything: good march tune, fine contrastive melody, tasteful counterpoint, and a cute, unexpected echo conclusion.

Marches—March in D major, K. 237

☐ Vienna Mozart Ensemble / Boskovsky (conductor) / London STS–15280/4

A familiar pattern but somewhat tonally fuller than most of Mozart's other marches. Accurate definition by Boskovsky's ensemble with sensitive voicing balance.

Marches—March in D major, K. 249

☐ Vienna Mozart Ensemble / Boskovsky (conductor) / London STS-15275/9

Mozart wrote this March to precede or succeed the complete *Haffner* Serenade—*see below* (Serenade No. 7 [*Haffner*] in D major, K. 250). It is never heard in that manner these days. No matter—the March has complete validity as a piece by itself.

Marches—March in D major, K. 290

☐ Vienna Mozart Ensemble / Boskovsky (conductor) / London STS-15280/4

Erik Smith terms this "one of the most beautiful of all the marches." There is full agreement here with that statement. The piece is played beautifully as well.

Marches—March in D major, K. 445

☐ Vienna Mozart Ensemble / Boskovsky (conductor) / London STS-15275/9

Assertive rhythm, of course, but there is more than a sharply defined pulse in Mozart's March. There is the excitation of syncopation, and there is the coloristic shift in key mode that makes this March much more dramatic than the others. Rhythm for such music must be steady, and that is provided here, but more to the point is the fine attention to agogic stresses. A superb performance.

Marches—March in F major, K. 248

☐ Vienna Mozart Ensemble / Boskovsky (conductor) / London STS-15280/4

The only Mozart orchestral March in a tonality other than C or D. Slightly delicate but positively played.

Marches—Three Marches, K. 408

☐ Chamber Orchestra of the Saar / Ristenpart (conductor) / Nonesuch 71194

All three marches enjoy sonata-styled formation. That equals, in a sense, a sophisticated approach to march design. There are unusual performance values, the music being stated with both tenderness and vibrancy. That's difficult to match.

Marches—Two Marches, K. 335

☐ Dresden State Orchestra / de Waart (conductor) / Philips 6500627

Ceremonial types, played with symphonic stability. One of the marches uses oboes, horns, trumpets, and strings; the other is the same save for flutes in place of the oboes.

Minuets
Eight Minuets, K. 315a / Fifteen Minuets, K. 176 / Five Minuets, K. 461 / Four Minuets, K. 601 / In C major, K. 409 / In E flat major, K. 122

☐ Vienna Mozart Ensemble / Boskovsky (conductor) / London STS-15280/4

How many minuets have come off composers' worktables? How many are more than merely competent, almost machinelike affairs? Mozart's superior examples deserve the fullest limelight. Don't play them one after the other, but sample them in any order. Be sure to check out the K. 601 group, with its use of the special timbre of a hurdy-gurdy.

With the above suggestion it seems niggling to indicate that for some reason the Fifteen Minuets, K. 176, are interrupted by the inserted performance of an isolated March.

The first four Minuets end side 1 of the five-record set. Then, instead of completing the group on side 2, the remaining eleven are split into totals of six and five, with the March intervening. Rather silly.

Minuets—Nineteen Minuets, K. 103

☐ Vienna Mozart Ensemble / Boskovsky (conductor) / London STS–15275/9

Scored for paired flutes, oboes, horns, trumpets, and strings without violas. (Most dance music of this type eliminated the violas to clear the middle way for emphasis on melody and bass support.)

The pieces are beautifully played—but not beautifully arranged on the disc, which is part of a five-record set. In place of complete continuity, a *Contredanse* succeeds the sixth minuet; then follow the seventh, eighth, ninth, and tenth minuets. Turn the disc over and the minuet sequence is again broken: first a March, then four more minuets, again an interruption (a set of five *Contredanses*), and finally the balance of the minuets. For what reason?

Minuets

Six Minuets, K. 61h
Six Minuets, K. 104

☐ Vienna Mozart Ensemble / Boskovsky (conductor) / London STS–15280/4

There's a little bit of borrowing from Michael Haydn in the K. 104 set, but the rest is by Mozart. Stylish playing by Boskovsky's splendid ensemble.

Minuets—Six Minuets, K. 105

☐ Vienna Mozart Ensemble / Boskovsky (conductor) / London STS–15275/9

Erik Smith states that he would not be surprised if these minuets were written by another hand, ''perhaps Leopold Mozart's, for the autograph is lost.'' Ours not to worry. The playing is of the highest Boskovsky standard, which means it couldn't be bettered.

Minuets—Six Minuets, K. 164

☐ Vienna Mozart Ensemble / Boskovsky (conductor) / London STS–15280/4

Although the scoring embraces flute, two oboes, two horns, two trumpets, and strings (with the violas omitted, as is generally the case), no full tutti use is made. Further, the flute constantly doubles the first violin line at the octave. This is a lesser entry in the Mozart minuet ledger.

Minuets—Six Minuets, K. 599

☐ Vienna Mozart Ensemble / Boskovsky (conductor) / London STS–15275/9

One of the most intriguing minuet sets Mozart produced. The music is entirely innocent of utilitarian make-do—a sense of symphonicism pervades the conception, as can be realized from the full-scale instrumentation used: piccolo and completely paired winds from flutes through bassoons, two each of horns and trumpets, timpani, and strings.

Boskovsky's portrayal is unquestionably of the highest artistry, and the stylistic decorum is perfect.

Minuets—Three Minuets, K. 363

☐ Vienna Mozart Ensemble / Boskovsky (conductor) / London STS–15280/4

Straightforward examples, save that there are no contrasting trios.

Minuets—Twelve Minuets, K. 568

☐ Vienna Mozart Ensemble / Boskovsky (conductor) / London STS–15275/9

A splendid essay on the subject of the minuet. The proportions are not small, considering that a dozen minuets in a row are concerned, but the discourse is derived from orchestral color arrangement that is always fresh. And, of course, there is that special Mozartean lyricism that wraps around any melody, whether it be in a symphony, a sonata, a concerto, or in a minuet.

Mozartean dance music is refreshingly heard when Boskovsky directs it. This is absolutely beautiful playing.

Minuets

Twelve Minuets, K. 585
Two Minuets, K. 604

☐ Vienna Mozart Ensemble / Boskovsky (conductor) / London STS–15280/4

Richly scored in the case of K. 585, with more mellow character in the K. 604 pair. First-rate performances in both instances.

Overture and Three *Contredanses*, K. 106

☐ Vienna Mozart Ensemble / Boskovsky (conductor) / London STS–15275/9

The performance time of this composition is five minutes fifty seconds; the Overture portion runs just fifty-eight seconds! That gives a general idea of the lightness of the introduction. This is not meant to throw a wet blanket on Mozart's mini-fanfarelike Overture, however.

The dances are filled with the usual Mozartean craft, and the playing is a sheer delight.

Overture to *Apollo et Hyacinthus*, K. 38

Overture to *Ascanio in Alba*, K. 111

Overture to *Bastien und Bastienne*, K. 50

☐ Württemberg Chamber Orchestra, Heilbronn / Faerber (conductor) / Turnabout 34628

Rarely-heard overtures performed with admirable texture and balance. Best of all is that there is no tampering to achieve a dynamic assortment unbecoming to the music.

Overture to *Così fan tutte*, K. 588

☐ Columbia Symphony Orchestra / Walter (conductor) / Odyssey Y–30048

Mozartean refinement sounds through every note. Comparison with recordings by Davis (on Seraphim S–60037) and Klemperer (on Angel S–36289) shows them both to be marginally less precise.

Overture to *Der Schauspieldirektor*, K. 486

☐ Academy of St. Martin-in-the-Fields / Marriner (conductor) / Angel S–36869
☐ Cleveland Orchestra / Szell (conductor) / Columbia M2X–787

Marriner's edition is a beautiful, ear-filling production, with his usual exactitude—but one that permits healthy Mozartean playing.

For those who understand German, the single word that fittingly describes Szell's performance is "Mozart." The Columbia release is on a double disc of "evergreens," such as *The Blue Danube,* and so on. (The Szell version is included also on Columbia MG–30841, also a two-disc package, in which everything is by Mozart.)

Overture to *Die Entführung aus dem Serail*, K. 384
Overture to *Don Giovanni*, K. 527

☐ New Philharmonia Orchestra / Klemperer (conductor) / Angel S–36289

As usual with this conductor, the overtures are not as fast-paced as a listener is accustomed to hearing; but wait—it works, and works with Mozartean presence. The result is most gratifying.

(K. 384 appears with other overtures and additional Mozart music in this album. It is also represented on Angel S–36128 with two Mozart symphonies [Nos. 35 and 36] and on Angel S–35945 with Beethoven's Seventh.)

Overture to *Idomeneo, Rè di Creta*, K. 366

☐ Royal Philharmonic Orchestra / Davis (conductor) / Seraphim S–60037

This is first-class Mozart, displaying a keen regard for the dramaticism in the work. A strong presentation.

Overture to *Il rè pastore*, K. 208
Overture to *Il sogno di Acipione*, K. 126

☐ Württemberg Chamber Orchestra, Heilbronn / Faerber (conductor) / Turnabout 34628

That Jörg Faerber has a special way with this music has already been observed (*see above* [Overture to *Apollo et Hyacinthus*, K. 38]). The opinion stands.

Overture to *La clemenza di Tito*, K. 621

☐ Royal Philharmonic Orchestra / Davis (conductor) / Seraphim S–60037

The Overture to the last opera Mozart composed. It requires the full-bodied view that Davis gives it. Altogether beautifully dressed, with clarity, detail, and fine orchestral tone.

Overture to *La finta giardiniera*, K. 196

☐ New Philharmonia Orchestra / Leppard (conductor) / Philips 802901

A two-movement work, consisting of an *Allegro molto* and an *Andantino grazioso*. But Leppard's performance offers two for the price of one, since he plays a third movement, an Allegro (coded as K. 121), and the end product is Mozart's Symphony in D major—not one of the "official" total of forty-one. Needing a symphony in a great hurry, Mozart cut corners and lifted his *La finta giardiniera* Overture for the first two-thirds of the Symphony, simply adding a third part to complete the opus.

The performance of the Overture in the complete opera (see under *Opera and Dramatic Music* [*La finta giardiniera*, K. 196]), directed by Hans Schmidt-Isserstedt, is totally opposite in tempi from Leppard's. The former chooses a much slower speed for the first part while adopting a markedly faster pace for the second part. Tie score: one prefers Leppard for the *Allegro molto* and Schmidt-Isserstedt for the *Andantino grazioso*. However, the availability of the complete Symphony is a plus that makes possible acceptance of this version of the Overture, despite the desire for more ongoing playing of its second part.

Overture to *La finta semplice*, K. 51

☐ Academy of St. Martin-in-the-Fields / Marriner (conductor) / Angel S–36869

This recording of the Overture to Mozart's *opera buffa* stands alone in the current recorded catalogue. No need for anyone to try to compete with it. Everything there is to say Marriner has said, in playing of utter naturalness.

Overture to *Lucia Silla*, K. 135

☐ Academy of St. Martin-in-the-Fields / Marriner (conductor) / Angel S–36869

Fresh, clean, and utterly charming Mozart playing. For that matter the same *almost* applies to Maag's edition (with the London Symphony Orchestra on London STS–15088). There's a bit more delicacy and grace in Marriner's performance.

Overture to *The Magic Flute*, K. 620

☐ New Philharmonia Orchestra / Klemperer (conductor) / Angel S–36289

A major-league performance by a major-league conductor. From the triple set-in chords at the beginning through the fugal Allegro, the Overture has the depth of a mini-symphony, and it is in that manner that Klemperer presents it. There is no doubt that his reading is in a class by itself.

Only Toscanini can match the depth realized. Two different releases of the Toscanini performance with the BBC Symphony are available in mono form: in a collection of overtures on Seraphim 60150, and in a three-record package of three overtures (the other composers being Beethoven and Brahms) plus the First, Fourth, and Sixth Symphonies by Beethoven, on Seraphim 6015. It is only Angel's better sound that gives a slender advantage to the Klemperer edition.

Overture to *The Marriage of Figaro*, K. 492

☐ Cleveland Orchestra / Szell (conductor) / Columbia MS–6858

The roll call of conductors who have recorded this delight extends from Bernstein and Beecham to Walter and Winograd. Most of them are very good. The choice falls on Szell simply because the discipline of the playing he obtains is perfect and because a sense of large chamber music is present that conveys a great deal about textures and weights.

Columbia must have recognized this also. They have issued the *Figaro* Overture in a total of five different albums. The numbers of the others are: MS–7507, MG–30841, MS–7435, and D3M–33261.

Overture to *Mitridate, rè di Ponto*, K. 87

☐ Württemberg Chamber Orchestra, Heilbronn / Faerber (conductor) / Turnabout 34628

The only representation in the catalogue. It is achieved with excellent character and phrasing.

Serenade No. 1 in D major, K. 100

☐ Vienna Mozart Ensemble / Boskovsky (conductor) / London STS–15301

The sonorities in this work for two flutes, two oboes, two horns, two trumpets, and strings are warm and full scaled, but never overdone. A true delight.

Serenade No. 3 in D major, K. 185

☐ Vienna Mozart Ensemble / Boskovsky (conductor) / London STS–15171

The same scoring as in Serenade No. 1 (*see above*). And the same Mozartean discipline and warmth—and delights.

Serenade No. 4 (*Colloredo*) in D major, K. 203

☐ Chamber Orchestra of the Saar / Hendel (violin) / Ristenpart (conductor) / Nonesuch 71194

The *Colloredo* Serenade is large-scoped, containing eight movements, within these there are three movements that feature the solo violin and as many movements set as minuets with the usual contrastive trios.

One cannot take issue with this fine conductor as to tempi details, phraseology, or expressivity within Mozartean style. The communication is ideal, and so is the solo violin playing of (read the name very carefully) Georg-Friedrich Hendel.

Serenade No. 7 (*Haffner*) in D major, K. 250

☐ English Chamber Orchestra / Zuckerman (violin) / Zuckerman (conductor) / Angel S–36915

In eight movements, the *Haffner* is as glorious as it is elaborate, with three of the divisions comprising a mini-violin concerto of maximum beauty. With Zuckerman doubling as conductor and solo violinist, the recording is a testament to his fine musicianship. Eloquence permeates every part of the work.

Serenade No. 9 (*Posthorn*) in D major, K. 320

☐ Dresden State Orchestra / Damm (post horn) / de Waart (conductor) / Philips 6500627

The nickname is derived from the use of a *corno di posta* in the sixth (*Minuetto)* movement. Its refreshing sound fits the felicity, even coziness of the total work.

This is an ideal presentation, well paced, with a seamlessness that is an exceedingly impressive accomplishment. An invitation to musical nourishment that one should not deny oneself.

Symphony in D major. *See above:* Overture to *La finta giardiniera*, K. 196.

Symphony

No. 1 in E flat major, K. 16 / No. 4 in D major, K. 19 / No. 5 in B flat major, K. 22

☐ Academy of St. Martin-in-the-Fields / Marriner (conductor) / Philips 6500532

Strong and supportive realizations, each and every one. Marriner tabs cogently the *buffa* style that dominates these symphonies. With such interpretative authenticity, he is as much the scholar as the musicologist sweating over original manuscripts to track down each faint appoggiatura and dynamic blur.

Symphony

No. 13 in F major, K. 112 / No. 14 in A major, K. 114 / No. 15 in F major, K. 124 / No. 16 in C major, K. 128

☐ Academy of St. Martin-in-the-Fields / Marriner (conductor) / Argo ZRG–594

The results are splendid, the tempi perfect. Marriner lets the music find its way to the most direct point. A pleasure.

Symphony

No. 21 in A major, K. 134 / No. 22 in C major, K. 162 / No. 23 in D major, K. 181 / No. 24 in B flat major, K. 182

☐ Berlin Philharmonic Orchestra / Böhm (conductor) / Deutsche Grammophon 139405

This writer cannot make a single critical quibble in regard to the playing of these four symphonies. In K. 134 the dynamic contrasts are especially expressive, in K. 162 telling emphasis is applied to the concertante episodes. The rhythmic impulses to be found in the other two works are ideally defined. Full command in all instances makes this issue one that offers splendid Mozart playing for the fullest enjoyment of a listener. (The disc is a separate release from Böhm's performances of the entire set of Mozart symphonies on Deutsche Grammophon No. 2721013 [Symphonies Nos. 1–24] and 2721007 [Symphonies Nos. 25–41].)

Symphony No. 25 in G minor, K. 183

☐ Academy of St. Martin-in-the-Fields / Marriner (conductor) / Argo ZRG–706

This is the "little" G minor. It is not little in its use of four horns (the "larger" famous G minor Symphony [No. 40, K. 550] calls for only a pair of horns [*see below* under Symphony No. 39 in E flat major, K. 543, and Symphony No. 40 in G minor, K. 550]). It is also far from little in its dark, emotive impact.

Marriner is a respectful master of Mozart's musical materials. There is no loose interpretative thinking. This is a performance that deserves to be the first choice among those available.

Symphony No. 26 in E flat major, K. 184

☐ Staatskapelle Berlin / Klee (conductor) / Philips 6500840

Mozart's three-movement Symphony is sparing in quantity but not in quality. Lasting but eight and one-half minutes, it also serves as the Overture (of average length, therefore) for the music Mozart wrote for the play *Thamos, King of Egypt* (see under *Opera and Dramatic Music* [Incidental Music to *Thamos, King of Egypt*, K. 345 (336a)]).

Bernhard Klee directs a well-proportioned statement of the work. It possesses fine Mozartean manners, which is all it requires.

Symphony No. 29 in A major, K. 201

☐ Academy of St. Martin-in-the-Fields / Marriner (conductor) / Argo ZRG–706

Marriner defines the full identity of this work. It is not academic (no prosaic trisquared pulse for the minuet), not timid (there is a let-go in the finale but never at a clip that misses the fun contained in the music), and it is not sterile (the playing has a personality but not at Mozart's expense).

Symphony
No. 31 (*Paris*) in D major, K. 297 / No. 32 in G major, K. 318

☐ Klassische Philharmonie Stuttgart / Münchinger (conductor) / London 6625

Beautifully controlled and natural performances. There is sheer enchantment from start to finish in both symphonies. Klemperer's performance of K. 297 (Angel S-36216) is not number one, but is a strong second choice for that work.

Symphony No. 34 in C major, K. 338

☐ Concertgebouw Orchestra / Szell (conductor) / Philips 802769

A Mozart delight played delightfully. Szell's rendition has transparent tone, but also body and phrasing that is not only graceful but breathes with full health.

Symphony No. 35 (*Haffner*) in D major, K. 385

☐ Philharmonia Orchestra / Klemperer (conductor) / Angel S-36128

Klemperer has been criticized innumerable times for stodgy preoccupations in the name of pedantic accuracy. Such criticism does not apply here. The performance he directs is one of sparkling classicism totally sensitive to all the facets in the score. In the first movement, and especially in the peripatetic Presto finale, the music must sweep along. The exact metronomic point is difficult to place, but the Klemperer performance is the one that sounds absolutely correct. It is clean, clear, and zestful. A fine second choice is Walter's reading (Columbia MS-6255).

Symphony No. 36 (*Linz*) in C major, K. 425

☐ Vienna Philharmonic Orchestra / Bernstein (conductor) / London 6499

Bernstein's Mozart is transparent, but it is mounted on a solid frame of performance. The rhythmic depiction is masterful; the whole Symphony has the performance solutions that spell Mozartean wisdom.

Symphony
No. 38 (*Prague*) in D major, K. 504 / No. 39 in E flat major, K. 543

☐ Philharmonia Orchestra / Klemperer (conductor) / Angel S-36129

Of course Klemperer has all the technical knowledge, but the conducting fraternity does not have many members with his artistic unselfishness. With him, it is Mozart (or whoever the composer may be) first and always. Such clarity and dimension are unusual. In the E flat Symphony it is Klemperer's warm breadth of conception that makes his version unique.

(*See below* for another recording of the Symphony No. 39.)

Symphony
No. 39 in E flat major, K. 543 / No. 40 in G minor, K. 550

☐ London Symphony Orchestra / Davis (conductor) / Philips 6500559

Divine expressivity and expressly divine performances that should not be passed by. No minor reservations, either.

The Philips issue for the E flat work should not be confused with another Davis-led (but only fair) performance: with the London Sinfonia on RCA VICS-1378.

(*See below* for additional recordings of the Symphony No. 40.)

Symphony No. 40 in G minor, K. 550

☐ Philharmonia Orchestra / Klemperer (conductor) / Angel S–36183
☐ Columbia Symphony Orchestra / Walter (conductor) / Columbia MS–6494
☐ London Symphony Orchestra / Davis (conductor) / Philips 6500559

The tempo choice Klemperer adopts for the outer movements gives Mozartean spirit and yet does not obviate the stripped-down elementalism that seethes within every movement. Throughout, there is a pulse that is both sensitive and sensible. The playing is superpolished but never prissy. (The *Jupiter* [*see below:* Symphony No. 41 in C major, K. 551] is coupled with this Symphony on this release. On Angel's catalogue No. S–35407 the "small" G minor Symphony [No. 25; *see above*] is the companion work.)

There is more constraint in Walter's edition, but it does not overlook depth and internal meaning. The orchestral blend is remarkably firm, and Walter's fierce ideal of styled purity pours out of every measure.

Davis's reading falls, as it were, between the versions of Klemperer and Walter. Textural clarity is a feature and the slow movement particularly rejects academic tempo progress.

Symphony No. 41 (*Jupiter*) in C major, K. 551

☐ Boston Symphony Orchestra / Jochum (conductor) / Deutsche Grammophon 2530357
☐ Berlin Philharmonic Orchestra / Böhm (conductor) / Deutsche Grammophon 138815

It's a tie score between these two releases, but no tie with other versions. There are, of course, many top-quality editions of this great work, but both of these are exceptional. The essential polyphony of the finale is sharply detailed, and neither conductor presses his tempo luck by attempting to fling the counterpoint rather than integrate it. These elucidations throw the greatest light on Mozart's masterpiece.

Symphony

No. 42 in F major, K. 75 / No. 44 in D major, K. 81

☐ I Musici / Kühn and Elshorst (oboes); Kotulan and Peter (horns) / Philips 6500535

Forget the numbers, though they are fully accepted in the bibliographic scheme of Mozart's music. These are *early* symphonies. The playing is neat and attractive.

Two Minuets with *Contredanses*, K. 463

☐ Vienna Mozart Ensemble / Boskovsky (conductor) / London STS–15275/9

The key word in the title is "with." This is not a pair of minuets followed by two *contredanses*. The minuet stands as the slower introductory portion to the faster *contredanse* in both cases. And further, the former is much slower than usual (the tempo is indicated as *Menuetto cantabile adagio*). A neat idea and played just as neatly.

Divertimento

In B flat major, K. 137 / In D major, K. 136 / In F major, K. 138

String Orchestra

☐ Chamber Orchestra of the Saar / Ristenpart (conductor) / Nonesuch 71207

Written in Salzburg when Mozart was sixteen, these Divertimenti have become known as the Salzburg Symphonies. They were originally scored for string quartet. But this writer agrees with the great Mozart authority Alfred Einstein (who accomplished the monumental task of totally revising the Köchel "bible" relating to Mozart's catalogue of works) that K. 136–138 are symphonies for multiple strings, not for four stringed instruments.

Others in addition to Karl Ristenpart have agreed with this finding and have recorded the set, including the I Musici group (on Philips 6500536) and Neville Marriner conducting the Academy of St. Martin-in-the-Fields (on Argo ZRG–554). However, the extra sparkle and idiomatic cohesion in Ristenpart's versions make them the prime choice. Further, his tempi for the Presto movements are of metronomic mastery. It remains to say that if one insists on having these works served as string quartets, an edition is in the catalogue that is of top quality. It is performed by the Quartetto Italiano on Philips 6500645.

Minuet

In C major, K. 61g / In D major, K. 94 (73h)

☐ Vienna Mozart Ensemble / Boskovsky (conductor) / London STS–15280/4

Both Minuets were orchestrated from piano scores by Erik Smith, the original orchestral versions being lost. These settings display good imitation of Mozart scoring habits. The task was made easier, of course, by the use of strings alone, minus violas.

Serenade *(Eine kleine Nachtmusik)* in G major, K. 525

☐ Philharmonia Orchestra / Davis (conductor) / Seraphim S–60057
☐ Academy of St. Martin-in-the-Fields / Marriner (conductor) / Argo ZRG–679
☐ Cleveland Orchestra / Szell (conductor) / Columbia MS–7273

The outstanding mastery and beauty of this work are possible to perform with either a string quintet or multiple strings (performances in string quartet form are in error, since Mozart's score clearly indicates *bassi,* meaning a coupling of cello and bass). Notwithstanding musicological diatribes about using the large string-instrument body of the twentieth-century symphony orchestra for the playing of eighteenth-century music, it is really a matter of manner rather than amount that is involved. Providing proper style is applied to the matter of weight, a conductor is never guilty of Mozartean foul play when utilizing a large string group for *Eine kleine nachtmusik.*

The music thrives when the outer *allegros* are not taken at dizzy speed and when the *Romanze* and Minuet are not creased with impertinent *rubati* and halted by cadential *ritards.* The recorded music catalogue is stuffed with such examples of performance malpractice. But there are a good number that have spontaneity, textural balance, and clear phrasing, are well paced and garnished with crisp rhythms.

Colin Davis and the Philharmonia and George Szell with the Clevelanders both provide, with a full string body, finely structured and fully Mozartean depictions. Szell's strings are, of course, radiant, but the garnet sound of the Philharmonia supplies a richness that is most appealing. While the Marriner-led presentation is smaller-scaled, it provides a beautifully stylish reading. Szell's edition is also available in a two-record Mozart compilation on Columbia MG-3084 and in a three-record Mozart program on Columbia D3M-33261. The choice recording in the string quintet form is discussed below (see under *Chamber Music*, p. 1274).

Serenade No. 6 *(Serenata notturna)* in D major, K. 239

☐ Philharmonia Orchestra / Davis (conductor) / Seraphim S–60057

For string orchestra plus—with timpani and with the strings split so that there is plentiful solo work. Performances are sometimes described as "effortlessly convincing." The description certainly fits here. The soloists are excellent, and Davis likewise. His view of Mozart is proof of special musical integrity.

Six *Ländler*, K. 606

☐ Chamber Orchestra of the Saar / Ristenpart (conductor) / Nonesuch 71207

The set is written with the simplest of simplicities—the scoring covers first and second violins, plus cello and double bass. There are no instrumental fattenings by dividing any of the four groups; strength is paradoxically obtained by minimal means.

Mozart's *Ländlerische Tänze,* or, as Nonesuch translates them, "Country Dances," receive an extraordinary performance directed by this consummate musician. There is no straightforward *ein-zwei-drei* procedure here. Without minimizing the requisite dance quality, attention is given to minute phrasing, dynamics, and the most sensitively artistic *rubati* at certain phrase introductions. It is a lesson on how to play utilitarian music of this type.

Divertimento No. 3 in E flat major, K. 166

Wind and Brass Ensemble

☐ Netherlands Wind Ensemble / de Waart (conductor) / Philips 6500002

A gentle performance, but that certainly means a good one of this ten-instrument piece, for winds that include two English horns and two (French) horns.

Divertimento No. 4 in B flat major, K. 186

☐ Netherlands Wind Ensemble / de Waart (conductor) / Philips 6500003

The same scoring as in the Divertimento No. 3 (*see above*). Modestly proportioned. The playing follows suit.

Serenade No. 10 in B flat major for Thirteen Wind Instruments, K. 361

☐ Netherlands Wind Ensemble / de Waart (conductor) / Philips 839734

This performance is what is meant by discipline that is not at the expense of spontaneity and finesse. De Waart's group produces magnificent Mozart.

Concerto in B flat major for Bassoon and Orchestra, K. 191

Solo Instrument and Orchestra

Bassoon

☐ Philadelphia Orchestra / Garfield (bassoon) / Ormandy (conductor) / Columbia MS-6451

The accompaniment for this work poses problems in concert performance because of the balance factor between solo voice and orchestra. Of course, performance in a recording studio, with mechanical adjustments available, nullifies the problem. All this is preamble to the fact that the meshed partnership between Bernard Garfield and Eugene Ormandy is perfection itself. The music is played with a refined vibrancy. Garfield's tone is colorful and invigorating.

Concerto in A major for Clarinet and Orchestra, K. 622

Clarinet

☐ London Symphony Orchestra / de Peyer (clarinet) / Maag (conductor) / London 6178

De Peyer has technical knowledge and artistic unselfishness to begin with and backs these matters with beautiful intonation. He has marvelous control, maintaining the dynamic ratios in balance regardless of the gamut involved. Maag does not play Mozart with prissiness. Nor does he mix any bran into the tuttis to get roughage. The fullest honors are due this release.

Flute

Andante in C major for Flute and Orchestra, K. 315

Concerto No. 1 in G major for Flute and Orchestra, K. 313

☐ I Solisti di Zagreb / Baker (flute) / Janigro (conductor) / Vanguard 71153

Natural performances, clearly set forth, unassuming and thereby placing the music in the best perspective. The sound is spacious.

(The Concerto is also included in a two-disc concerto compilation on Vanguard 709/10.)

Concerto No. 2 in D major for Flute and Orchestra, K. 314 (285d)

☐ Vienna State Opera Orchestra / Baker (flute) / Prohaska (conductor) / Vanguard 71170

A work that has received plenty of recorded performances. And why not? It is one of the Mozartean specials for which all flutists—and listeners—have been grateful. Though the work was transcribed by Mozart from his Concerto in C major for Oboe (see under *Solo Instrument and Orchestra: oboe*), that does not lessen its value one iota.

There are plenty of flutists to pick from, including such artists as Rampal (on Everest 3194), Shaffer (on Seraphim S–60123), and Claude Monteux (on London 6400). However, the elegance of Baker's playing, his immaculate tone quality, and his consistent adherence to *musical* honesty make his essay the choice.

Flute and Harp

Concerto in C major for Flute, Harp, and Orchestra, K. 299

☐ Berlin Philharmonic Orchestra / Zöller (flute); Zabaleta (harp) / Märzendorfer (conductor) / Deutsche Grammophon 138853

It is quite rare to find such matched pitch as obtains here, always a difficulty because of the opposed sonorous quality. There is nothing overbrilliant about the playing, and yet because of this the performance has unusual clarity and dimension. A minor work like this double concerto suddenly becomes almost an important one with such a sensitive partnership among soloists, conductor, and orchestra.

Harpsichord

Concerto

No. 1 in D major, arranged from Johann Christian Bach's "Sonata for Piano, Op. 5, No. 2," K. 107-I / No. 2 in G major, arranged from Johann Christian Bach's "Sonata for Piano, Op. 5, No. 3," K. 107-II / No. 3 in E flat major, arranged from Johann Christian Bach's "Sonata for Piano, Op. 5, No. 4," K. 107-III

☐ Stuttgart Solisten / Galling (harpsichord) / Turnabout 34312

Examples of practicality by the boy Mozart prior to composing his first end-to-end piano concerto. There are three movements in the first work and two movements in each of the others. Tuttis, accompaniments, and cadenzas (only in the first of the set) flesh out and structure the borrowed material.

The pieces receive smooth performances in all cases.

Horn

Concerto for Horn and Orchestra

No. 1 in D major, K. 412 / No. 2 in E flat major, K. 417 / No. 3 in E flat major, K. 447 / No. 4 in E flat major, K. 495

☐ Philharmonia Orchestra / Brain (horn) / von Karajan (conductor) / Angel 35092 (monaural)

Remarkable horn sound, beautiful rhythmic markings, and an elegance that captivates. This is a monaural recording, but it has much more to offer than the many that have contributed to the literature by stereo recordings of these works. The closest competition comes from Barry Tuckwell, who covers all four on London 6403, and Nos. 1 and 3 on London 6178; Maag is the conductor. The complete works are also played by Tuckwell on another label (Angel S–36840), for which the conductor is Marriner.

Concert Rondo for Horn and Orchestra, K. 371

☐ Academy of St. Martin-in-the-Fields / Civil (horn) / Marriner (conductor) / Philips 6500325

More important because of the playing than of the music. The big sound is from the soloist, not from the engineering.

Concerto in C major for Oboe and Orchestra, K. 314 (271k)

Oboe

☐ Academy of St. Martin-in-the-Fields / Black (oboe) / Marriner (conductor) / Philips 6500379

From Mozart's letters it was known that, in 1777, he had written an oboe concerto. However, while no trace of the music could be found, Mozart scholars considered the Concerto No. 2 in D major for Flute (see under *Solo Instrument and Orchestra: flute*) to be a reworking of the "lost" oboe concerto. In 1949 complete confirmation of this opinion was made—the music for the oboe concerto was found in the library of the Salzburg Mozarteum by the Austrian musicologist and conductor, Bernhard Paumgartner.

This is playing of superb estate. Every note has meaning, and the tone is exquisite. However, those who swear by Holliger and no other oboist will not go astray by choosing his performance with the New Philharmonia Orchestra (on Philips 6500174). Fewer advantages are available in an earlier recording Holliger made with the Munich Chamber Orchestra (Deutsche Grammophon ARC–198342).

Concerto in E flat major for Oboe and Orchestra, K. Anh. 294b

☐ Prague Chamber Orchestra / de Vries (oboe) / Kersjes (conductor) / Angel S–37534

Simply a curiosity, since it is one of those "attributed to" compositions. A general harmless harmonious state of affairs. The playing is good, though not overly striking.

Sinfonia Concertante in E flat major, K. 297b

Oboe, Clarinet, Horn, and Bassoon

☐ English Chamber Orchestra / Graeme (oboe); King (clarinet); James (horn); Gatt (bassoon) / Barenboim (conductor) / Angel S–36582

This work of grace and treasured invention is played ideally. The rhythms are supple and springy, cased in tempi that neither move too fast, nor too slow, in the name of an Adagio determination. The textures and balances are perfect, and all the solo voices are smooth and natural.

Sonata for Organ and Orchestra

Organ

No. 1 in E flat major, K. 67 / No. 2 in B flat major, K. 68 / No. 3 in D major, K. 69 / No. 4 in D major, K. 144 / No. 5 in F major, K. 145 / No. 6 in B flat major, K. 212 / No. 7 in F major, K. 224 / No. 8 in A major, K. 225 / No. 9 in G major, K. 241 / No. 10 in F major, K. 244 / No. 11 in D major, K. 245 / No. 12 in C major, K. 263 / No. 13 in G major, K. 274 / No. 14 in C major, K. 278 / No. 15 in C major, K. 328 / No. 16 in C major, K. 329 / No. 17 in C major, K. 336

☐ German Bach Soloists / Chorzempa (organ) / Winschermann (conductor) / Philips 6700061

Plenty of recorded attention has been given to these *Kirchensonaten*, also known as the *Epistle* Sonatas, and in several instances given the heading of *Festival* Sonatas. All are in one movement; fourteen call for only strings with the organ; one (K. 263) adds two trumpets to the strings; in another (K. 278) two oboes, two trumpets, and timpani are scored with the string body; and in K. 329 two horns plus the two oboes, two trumpets, timpani, and strings constitute the largest group.

The overall warmth and fullness of the playing by the German orchestra make this the favorite release. Chorzempa's contribution cannot be faulted, and the re-creative side is matched by beautiful sound. The organ used is the little choir organ (1746) of the Cistercian Stiftskirche Wilhering, near Linz.

One can consider the Columbia editions MS–6857 or MG–32985—the latter including the three Haydn organ concertos, with E. Power Biggs supported by the Columbia Symphony Orchestra conducted by Zoltan Rozsnyai. However, be prepared for the seventeen works on two record sides, where Philips takes four sides for the same compositions. This is not a matter of tempo, only that in the Biggs version "nonessential repeats are omitted." But the sonatas are short enough to begin with, and the repeats are there to be followed.

Piano

Concerto for Piano and Orchestra

No. 1 in F major, K. 37 / No. 2 in B flat major, K. 39 / No. 3 in D major, K. 40 / No. 4 in G major, K. 41

☐ Stuttgart Solisten / Galling (piano) / Wich (conductor) / Turnabout 34260

It was not until the Piano Concerto No. 5, K. 175 (*see below*), that Mozart produced a totally original work in the medium. These four, together with the three concerti for harpsichord (see under *Solo Instrument and Orchestra: harpsichord*), were patched from material by others and shaped by the young genius, especially with orchestral preludes, interpolations, and accompaniments. The composers Mozart leaned on in these *pasticci* (Mozart's term) range from the good (C. P. E. Bach) and the fair (Johann Schobert) to the rather insignificant (Johann Gottfried Eckard, Leontzi Honnauer, and Hermann Ferdinand Raupach).

Their blend becomes our gain, since there is a definite Mozartean personality to be recognized in the music. Martin Galling gives a fine account of the scores, expressively proportioned in all of the twelve movements.

Concerto No. 5 in D major for Piano and Orchestra, K. 175

☐ Vienna Volksoper Orchestra / Frankl (piano) / Fischer (conductor) / Turnabout 34313

No firm stamp of the Mozartean personality is to be found in this work. However, Peter Frankl probes the material wisely and turns in an excellent account.

Concerto No. 6 in B flat major for Piano and Orchestra, K. 238

☐ London Symphony Orchestra / Ashkenazy (piano) / Schmidt-Isserstedt (conductor) / London 6579

Style and spirit are fully provided here. K. 238 is small-scaled but has a gracious charm, which is the stimulant that covers the music in this performance.

Concerto No. 8 in C major for Piano and Orchestra, K. 246

☐ London Symphony Orchestra / Ashkenazy (piano) / Kertész (conductor) / London 6501

All that one wishes for in Mozart is accounted for in this performance: textural clarity that permits the fullest demarcation of detail, tonal glow, and a profitable choice of tempi. Kertész provides an excellent collaboration.

Concerto No. 9 in E flat major for Piano and Orchestra, K. 271

☐ I Solisti di Zagreb / Brendel (piano) / Janigro (conductor) / Vanguard 705/6

The K. 271 is Mozart in a brilliant mood and with a triumphantly bold approach. Though Brendel is fully cognizant of this and matches boldness with boldness, there is also noteworthy gracefulness and lyrical feeling in his playing.

Concerto for Piano and Orchestra

No. 11 in F major, K. 413 / No. 12 in A major, K. 414

☐ Marlboro Festival Orchestra / Serkin (piano) / Schneider (conductor) / Columbia M-31728

Truly convincing performances. Everything is beautifully accomplished and the internal balances are not rigid so that fluidity is particular to the playing. The orchestral support is splendid.

Concerto for Piano and Orchestra

No. 14 in E flat major, K. 449 / No. 15 in B flat major, K. 450 / No. 16 in D major, K. 451 / No. 17 in G major, K. 453 / No. 18 in B flat major, K. 456 / No. 19 in F major, K. 459

☐ English Chamber Orchestra / Peter Serkin (piano) / Schneider (conductor) / RCA ARL3-0732

Peter Serkin is young, but he has the sensitivity of a mature artist, and it is proclaimed in his playing of these half-dozen Mozart concerti. To be sure, there are points that could be argued, but the general, overall conceptions have Mozartean class written all over them and couldn't be improved on idiomatically. There is no sag to the lyricism and there is no cooling opposition to the *brio* within these works. Fine conducting—knowledgeable, that is—and scrupulously delivered by the E.C.O.

Concerto No. 17 in G major for Piano and Orchestra, K. 453

☐ RCA Victor Symphony Orchestra / Rubinstein (piano) / Wallenstein (conductor) / RCA LSC-2636

Rubinstein is at his best in this joyous work. Wallenstein is not one of the major-league conductors, but he truly has this work at his fingertips and delivers orchestral support that is authoritatively Mozartean.

Concerto No. 20 in D minor for Piano and Orchestra, K. 466

☐ English Chamber Orchestra / Barenboim (piano) / Barenboim (conductor) / Angel S-36430
☐ Academy of St. Martin-in-the-Fields / Brendel (piano) / Marriner (conductor) / Philips 6500533

Indeed the most played of the Mozart piano concerti, approaching, if not already at, the hackneyed stage. But the communication of these pianists removes ennui and refreshes the ears. The music sounds fresh, wholesome, and marvelous.

Barenboim does not overstress, but lets the romantic streaks in the classical work show, and the combine is one of clarity, taste, and an alive and exciting presentation. Brendel's idea of Mozart is more poetic, dreamy (but alive) in the slow movement, and he obtains a wonderful chamber-music sense in the finale.

Concerto No. 21 in C major for Piano and Orchestra, K. 467

☐ Cleveland Orchestra / Casadesus (piano) / Szell (conductor) / Columbia MS-6695

One of the top achievements this team has produced. The speed of the finale may disconcert some, but the passions for velocity never get out of hand. And the sensitivity for Mozart's conception endures even when (as in movement 1) one wouldn't expect it to appear because of the extroverted quality of the music.

(The performance is also catalogued as Columbia M-31814.)

Concerto for Piano and Orchestra
No. 22 in E flat major, K. 482 / No. 23 in A major, K. 488

☐ Columbia Symphony Orchestra / Casadesus (piano) / Szell (conductor) / Columbia MS-6194

The playing here is unfailingly accomplished, thoughtful, musical, and always Mozartean in its scope and conduct. Interpretation is applied entirely free of mannerisms and exaggeration. (Szell wouldn't permit that no matter who was at the keyboard.)

Concerto No. 24 in C minor for Piano and Orchestra, K. 491

☐ London Symphony Orchestra / Curzon (piano) / Kertész (conductor) / London 6580

There is plenty of competition in the recorded catalogue for this work but there is no one who plays it as beautifully, naturally, and knowingly as Clifford Curzon. Other pianists tend to overstress the tragic color and dramatic emphasis that surround and fill Mozart's score; Curzon perceptively does not. The orchestral part is conveyed with conviction and Kertész is an admirable accompanist. This is a memorable account.

Concerto No. 25 in C major for Piano and Orchestra, K. 503

☐ Vienna Pro Musica Orchestra / Brendel (piano) / Angerer (conductor) / Turnabout 34129

Brendel pays the keenest attention to clear textures, and the result is music of aristocratic elegance. In the finale there are the important ingredients of tossed wit and colorful sparkle which Brendel supplies. And more than average credit belongs to Paul Angerer, who supplies a full-hearted, supple, and Mozartean orchestral framework.

Concerto for Piano and Orchestra
No. 26 (*Coronation*) in D major, K. 537 / No. 27 in B flat major, K. 595

☐ Columbia Symphony Orchestra / Casadesus (piano) / Szell (conductor) / Columbia MS-6403

K. 595 marks the last of Mozart's glorious piano concerti. It does not finish the cycle with a bang; neither does it stay subdued. There are rich harmonic colors in the score, which are vividly reflected in the playing by soloist and orchestra. A better-styled *Coronation* concerto is difficult to imagine. A better-paced *Coronation* would also require considerable research. It certainly will not be found in the other recorded editions currently available.

Concert Rondo No. 1 in D major for Piano and Orchestra, K. 382

☐ Pro Musica Orchestra, Vienna / Brendel (piano) / Angerer (conductor) / Turnabout 34233

Chamber-music style that does not negate the medium of solo instrument with orchestral accompaniment. Brendel also subtly covers the three different tempi found in the piece without sectionalizing the composition.

Concert Rondo No. 2 in A major for Piano and Orchestra, K. 386

☐ London Symphony Orchestra / Ashkenazy (piano) / Kertész (conductor) / London 6501

A most appealing performance of this lesser-known of the two Concert Rondos.

Concerto in E flat major for Two Pianos and Orchestra, K. 365

Two Pianos

☐ Philadelphia Orchestra / Robert and Gaby Casadesus (pianos) / Ormandy (conductor) / Columbia MS-6274

This is the tenth of Mozart's piano concerti, the single one for two pianos. The performance is one of unfailing spontaneity, which means marvelous effectiveness. There is fine interplay between the soloists, total rapport between them and Ormandy. The closest competition comes from Alfred Brendel and Walter Klien on a Turnabout disc (34064), but the orchestra supporting them is far inferior to the super-polished Philadelphians.

Concerto in F major for Three Pianos and Orchestra, K. 242

Three Pianos

☐ English Chamber Orchestra / Ashkenazy, Barenboim, and Ts'ong (pianos) / Barenboim (conductor) / London 6937

Two family teams put up the No Trespassing sign and play the piece with insular soloism—namely, R., G., and J. Casadesus (Odyssey Y-31531) and H., Y., and J. Menuhin (Seraphim S-60072). But more respect and better results obtain from those combines that have a professional rather than a blood-line relationship. This applies to the above listing, as well as to the Gold–Fizdale–Bernstein threesome on Columbia M-32173.

Concerto No. 1 in B flat major for Violin and Orchestra, K. 207

Violin

☐ London Symphony Orchestra / Grumiaux (violin) / Davis (conductor) / Philips 835136

This deserves to be played more often than it is. Here the performance sounds beautifully unstudied, avoiding the sleek and forced style that results from overdetailed realization. Entirely relaxed playing with luminous sound make this production a gem.

Concerto No. 2 in D major for Violin and Orchestra, K. 211

☐ English Chamber Orchestra / Zukerman (violin) / Barenboim (conductor) / Columbia M-33206

A somewhat neglected work but certainly not deficient in the delights of melodic detail that only a Mozart could produce. The playing is well wrought and styled without any quirks. That cannot be said for the Francescatti performance on Columbia MS-7389 or even for David Oistrakh's conception on Angel S-36892. On the other hand, Grumiaux presents close competition on Philips 835256. Zukerman's substantial warmth and tonal roundness win the day, however.

Concerto No. 3 in G major for Violin and Orchestra, K. 216

☐ Academy of St. Martin-in-the-Fields / Loveday (violin) / Marriner (conductor) / Argo ZRG–729

Alan Loveday does not enjoy the status of such as Francescatti, Grumiaux, Oistrakh, Stern, and Zukerman who (among still others including Loren Maazel!) have recorded this beauty. However, his playing is certainly strong while beautifully intimate, warm and richly tuned and toned. His Mozart No. 3 goes to the top of the list. If violinists were seeded the way tennis tournament players are, then Loveday, on the basis of this performance, belongs in the top ten.

Concerto No. 4 in D major for Violin and Orchestra, K. 218

☐ New Symphony Orchestra of London / Heifetz (violin) / Sargent (conductor) / RCA LSC–2652

Stay with Heifetz on this one (also issued on RCA LSC–3265). All the juice in the music is found in the playing; no distortion of the pure lines is found. (In Zukerman's reading, for example, on Columbia M–30055, the purity turns into romantic privilege that is just not acceptable.) As a result the essential bravura (Mozartean-distilled) in the diatonic action is present in a vocal sense and the music takes on its proper brilliance.

Concerto No. 5 in A major for Violin and Orchestra, K. 219

☐ Berlin Philharmonic Orchestra / Mutter (violin) / von Karajan (conductor) / Deutsche Grammophon 2531049

This is quite a performance! Mozart sounds pure and real, and there is a registration of the content that is focused to the most finite point. And always with shipshape vocalism on the string instrument. The performance doubles in wonder when one considers that Mutter is a young girl (not yet fifteen at the time of this release) combining her artistry with an international jet-set conductorial star. The twin bounty is terrific.

Two Violins

Concertone in C major for Two Violins and Orchestra, K. 190

☐ Marlboro Festival Orchestra / Laredo and Tree (violins); Arner (oboe); Soyer (cello) / Schneider (conductor) / Columbia MS–6848

Convincing style that defines the content. The elegance of the *Allegro spiritoso* and the sensitivity of phrasing in the *Andantino grazioso* yield a Mozartean perfection. There is a fine finale also, with vivacity and no aggression. The oboist has a tight sound, but the unique spirit of the total overcomes this very minor blemish.

Violin and Viola

Sinfonia Concertante in E flat major for Violin, Viola, and Orchestra, K. 364

☐ Berlin Philharmonic Orchestra / Igor Oistrakh (violin); David Oistrakh (viola) / David Oistrakh (conductor) / Angel S–36892

One of the most perfect double concerti in the entire repertoire. It receives a sensitively flexible performance, with complete Mozartean charm and spirit. Naturally, there is a special rapport in the all-Oistrakh combination. The elder Oistrakh shows how fine a violist he was and is definitely the equal (at least in this instance) of any of the regular concert violists.

This performance is also included in a jumbo Mozart package (Angel S–3789), which embraces the five violin concerti, two other works for violin and orchestra, and the two-violin *Concertone*.

Adagio in C major for Glass Harmonica, K. 617a

☐ Hoffmann (glass harmonica) / Turnabout 34452

Before being assigned the new Köchel number this miniature was originally listed as K. 356 (not K. 326 as the liner listing states). The opportunity to hear it in its original format is special. Most often the piece is heard in transcription, as, for example, played on the organ by E. Power Biggs (on Columbia M–33514). (For still another rendition see under *piano*.)

Adagio and Allegro in F minor, K. 594

Andante in F major, K. 616

Fantasia in F minor, K. 608

☐ Biggs (organ) / Columbia MS–6856

Transfer of these pieces to the organ from their original setting "for a little clockwork organ" or "a small mechanical organ" makes little difference. All are played in a lyrical fashion that is most acceptable.

(The Fantasia and the Adagio and Allegro have also been recorded with piano, four hands, both under the title Fantasy in F minor, the former K. 608 and the latter K. 594; see under *piano, four hands* [under Andante and Variations in G major].)

Adagio in B minor, K. 540

☐ Klien (piano) / Vox SVBX–5407
☐ Bilson (fortepiano) / Golden Crest 4097

Arthur Hutchings, the important English critic, terms the Adagio Mozart's "finest single work for piano solo." Tonality (cause) and deep expressiveness (effect) can be used as supporting evidence, but there is much more. There is a total seamlessness to the introspective eloquence of the music that grips the attention and does not yield. The Adagio surely represents one of the great Mozart contributions.

Klien plays the work with impeccable taste, avoiding any move that would interfere with its organic concept. Thereby Mozart's voice is clear.

Bilson's performance is listed more for its special color than for its interpretative discernment. The fortepiano he plays is a copy of a late eighteenth-century instrument, of smaller compass than the modern piano, with two strings to each note. The sound is robust and somewhat harsh and at times akin to a harpsichord. It has its interest, especially because it represents the type of piano that Mozart knew.

Adagio in C major for Glass Harmonica, K. 356

☐ Klien (piano) / Vox SVBX–5407

Just a tidbit, beautifully focused by Klien, who does not pursue force in this concentrated soprano-range piece. Perfectly fitting in the instrumental translation heard. (See under *glass harmonica* for a performance on the original instrument.)

Allegro and Andante in F major, K. 533

☐ Gould (piano) / Columbia M–32348

Composed in 1788 as the first two movements of a sonata. Later, an earlier (1786) Rondo was attached as the finale (*see below* [Rondo in F major, K. 494]). In such three-movement form it is known as the Sonata in F major, K. 533. Nevertheless, performing the first two movements as a unit without the tacked-on finale has full validity, especially because of the stylistic difference and poweful data of the Allegro and Andante compared to the lightweighted Rondo. In the sense of historical correctness, the Allegro and Andante can be termed an ''unfinished sonata.''

The playing by Gould is fresh and strong.

Allegro and Rondo in F major, K. Anh. 135
Allegro in B flat major, K. 3
Allegro in C major, K. 9a

☐ Klien (piano) / Vox SVBX–5407

The Allegro and Rondo is Mozart's transcription of two movements from his final sonata for violin and piano. The other two short pieces show what a genius can do respectively at the ages of six and seven. The playing is fine, however, K. 3 and K. 9a were recorded at a higher level and a shift of the volume control will be required.

Allegro of a Sonata in G minor, K. 312

☐ Klien (piano) / Vox SVBX–5406

A real gem. With G minor Mozart can never do any wrong. Klien plays K. 312 with very fine personality and excellent dynamic coloration.

Andante für eine Walze in eine kleine Orgel, K. 616

☐ Klien (piano) / Vox SVBX–5407

Another of the pieces Mozart composed for the mechanical organ; it is just as viable on the piano. Stylish playing by Klien.

Capriccio in C major, K. 395
Eight Variations on a Dutch Song by Christian Ernst Graaf, K. Anh. 208

☐ Klien (piano) / Vox SVBX–5406

The delivery of the C major piece is swift and bright. The theme for the Variations is a patriotic song; the ornamental workout needs no formal analysis, and Klien's playing needs no criticism.

Eight Variations on Come un' Agnello, K. 460
Eight Variations on Ein Weib ist das Herrlichste Ding, K. 613

☐ Klien (piano) / Vox SVBX–5407

K. 460 is based on an aria from a Sarti opera; Mozart used it again in *Don Giovanni* (see under *Opera and Dramatic Music*). Klien's performance is a delight, Bernardo Segall's on Orion 73132 less so. (Segall, miscounting, indicates that the work has ten variations. Where did he find the extra two, since every one else only lists eight?). K. 613 is the last set of piano variations Mozart produced. No flimsy material, this. No run-of-the-mill performance, either. Klien's playing is beautifully articulated and his conceptions sensitively styled.

Eight Variations on the March from Grétry's Les Mariages samnites, K. 352

☐ Klien (piano) / Vox SVBX–5406

Thematic clarity reigns throughout, but this is far from a collection of bare-boned figurations. Klien plays the set with pure voicing and yet obtains a sense of freedom that is very engaging.

Eine kleine Gigue in G major, K. 574
Fantasia and Fugue in C major, K. 394

☐ Klien (piano) / Vox SVBX–5407

An impeccable performance of the *Gigue*—a contrapuntal delight. Klien's delicate staccato translates Mozart's music to perfection. Though the viewpoint in the fugal section of K. 394 is rather austere (not demanded that way, even if Mozart stated it should be played *Andante maestoso*), the retroactions in the fantasy division are vividly displayed.

Fantasia in C minor, K. 396

☐ Brendel (piano) / Vanguard C–10043

Actually an Adagio in sonata form. Continuity is far from easy to achieve in this long-lined conception, but Brendel readily solves the problem and communicates a totality of statement that is extremely impressive.

Fantasia in C minor, K. 475

☐ Moravec (piano) / Vanguard SU–11

Mozart's strongly contrasted piano drama receives a performance of possessing authority by Ivan Moravec. A compelling continuity is obtained by fastidious attention to dynamic planes so that minute gradations register in the clearest fashion. This presents a subtle keyboard orchestration and thereby of telling detail. Moravec's wonderful performance should not be overlooked.

(Do not be confused by the error on the reverse side of the record jacket. The key is C minor, not D minor. Mozart's Fantasia in D minor is covered by K. 397, discussed *below*.)

Fantasia in D minor, K. 397

☐ Kuerti (piano) / Monitor S–2133

Scaled to proper dimension, with exemplary clarity in the final cheerful section, which is in direct contrast to the expressive slow-tempoed beginning. A fine achievement by a very sensitive pianist.

Fugue in G minor, K. 401
Klaviersuite in C major, K. 399

☐ Klien (piano) / Vox SVBX–5406

The Fugue in G minor is also available in a version Mozart made for one piano four hands (see under *piano, four hands* [under Andante and Variations]).

The "Piano Suite" (incorrectly listed as "in G" on the table of contents Vox provides for its program of seventeen Mozart compositions) is also called "Overture in the Style of Handel" (the "Overture" meaning the Bach term for the Suite or Partita known as the French Overture). It opens with a slow movement; then follow a fugue, an Allemande, and a Courante. Accordingly, this is Mozart in a direct imitative vein, only partially successful because of tonality and style shifts. Klien is fully successful, however.

Kleiner Trauermarsch in C minor, K. 453a

Minuet and Trio in G major, K. 1

Minuet in D major, K. 355

Minuet in F major, K. 2

Minuet in F major, K. 4

Minuet in F major, K. 5

☐ Klien (piano) / Vox SVBX–5407

The formal device of a minuet (without a trio) primed with emotive chromaticism is exhibited in K. 355. The flexibility and logic of the harmony are exquisite. Klien subtly suggests the dissonances in some places and emphasizes them elsewhere. A fine achievement.

The short March is of less importance than the examples of Mozart's minuets, written in 1762 at the age of six.

Nine Variations on a Minuet by Duport, K. 573

☐ Brendel (piano) / Vanguard C–10043

This is no mere run-through of the simplistic variational structuring Mozart employed. Brendel shapes each section, classifies, depicts, and shows a re-creative sensitivity. This is marvelous artistry. The engineering is gorgeous.

Nine Variations on Dezède's Arietta *Lison dormait,* K. 264

☐ Klien (piano) / Vox SVBX–5406

Much more virtuosic demands, including cadenza sprays, are required in this set of variations than in any of the others Mozart produced. Walter Klien fulfills all requirements.

Piano Sonata in F major, K. 533. *See above:* Allegro and Andante in F major, K. 533. *See below:* Rondo in F major, K. 494.

Piano Sonata

No. 1 in C major, K. 279 / No. 2 in F major, K. 280 / No. 3 in B flat major, K. 281 / No. 4 in E flat major, K. 282 / No. 5 in G major, K. 283 / No. 6 in D major, K. 284 / No. 7 in C major, K. 309 / No. 8 in A minor, K. 310 / No. 9 in D major, K. 311 / No. 10 in C major, K. 330

☐ Klien (piano) / Vox SVBX–5428

A fine grasp of the music. Presenting a span of many works by the same composer demands artistic aliveness and variety from the performer (the findings to be within general style, of course) in order to avoid a monotonous run-off of the compositions. Klien judges exceedingly well, spelling out elegance where required and playing with disciplined rhythmic detail in the speedy movements in order not to jab into their flow. There is an absolute distinctness to Klien's pianism. Details are registered, and the danger of overrefined playing verging on bloodlessness is thoroughly avoided.

Above all, Klien affords as much attention and care to the earlier works as he applies to the later ones. That particular interpretative information is not totally available in other recordings of the integral set of Mozart piano sonatas. In every work one hears essential musicality. That further certifies the total success of this complete performance project (*see below* for Klien's rendering of Nos. 11–17).

(*See below* for other recordings of individual sonatas.)

Piano Sonata

No. 4 in E flat major, K. 282 / No. 5 in G major, K. 283

☐ Backhaus (piano) / London 6534

Mozart with a seriousness in the performance style that may not be to everyone's taste. But every note is clear and the structural shapes absolutely detailed.

(*See* immediately *above* for a different recording.)

Piano Sonata

No. 8 in A minor, K. 310 / No. 17 in D major, K. 576

☐ Ashkenazy (piano) / London 6659

The important Mozart scholar Arthur Hutchings names the eighth piano sonata as "one of the greatest" of Mozart's piano sonatas. This performance matches that statement in its re-creative skill. Hutchings writes that "few can let the music [of this Sonata] breathe its own life." Ashkenazy is to be included in that special group. Truly, a performance to be treasured.

In K. 576 the polyphony is immaculately balanced, the phrasings are natural, the lines clear, and the styling ideal. A splendid, special Mozart disc.

Piano Sonata No. 10 in C major, K. 330

☐ Eschenbach (piano) / Deutsche Grammophon 139318

A finely wrought performance. It is beautifully textured, beautifully characterized, with a superb rendition of the slow movement. Eschenbach's Mozartean wisdom is magnificently exhibited here.

Piano Sonata

No. 11 in A major, K. 331 / No. 12 in F major, K. 332 / No.13 in B flat major, K. 333 / No. 14 in C minor, K. 457 / No. 15 in C major, K. 545 / No. 16 in B flat major, K. 570 / No. 17 in D major, K. 576

☐ Klien (piano) / Vox SVBX–5429

(*See commentary above* for Piano Sonatas Nos. 1–10. *See below* for other recordings of individual sonatas.)

Piano Sonata

No. 12 in F major, K. 332 / No.13 in B flat major, K. 333

☐ Eschenbach (piano) / Deutsche Grammophon 138949

Eschenbach has recorded the entire set of Mozart piano sonatas (on Deutsche Grammophon 2720031). This pair is one of the several discs drawn off from that edition and released separately. It offers illuminating playing, slightly forceful but thoroughly acceptable.

Piano Sonata

No. 14 in C minor, K. 457 / No. 16 in B flat major, K. 570

☐ Moravec (piano) / Connoisseur Society S-2002

Clean and vital playing. Mozartean syntax is read with a superb regularity of impulse and an exhilarating pulse.

Piano Sonata No. 15 in C major, K. 545

☐ Entremont (piano) / Columbia MG–33202

Known as the "easy" piano sonata in the Mozart catalogue. It also became widely known when it moved onto the pop music charts after its initial theme was lifted and promoted as *In an Eighteenth-Century Drawing Room*. That hasn't spoiled its charm, especially in the well-ordered way Entremont presents the original and all that follows it. Everything is cool and collected, but charming, the way he does it.

Rondo in A minor, K. 511

☐ Arrau (piano) / Philips 6500782

A composition that many have recorded. Arrau excels for the freshness and elegance of his playing. The *legati* he projects and the dynamic contrasts he defines are superbly accomplished and are matters to be relished. And Arrau is a master of achieving the most infinitesimal *rubato*, in this most beautiful musical document Mozart has given us. It is a music that sounds very simple, it contains a palpitation that quietly surrounds the sounds. Arrau explains this sublime act of creativity better than anyone else.

Rondo in D major, K. 485

☐ de Larrocha (piano) / London 6866

Not the greatest of the shorter pieces in the Mozart canon, but the strong impetus Alicia de Larrocha gives to the music strengthens it and makes hers the recommended performance.

Rondo in F major, K. 494

☐ Gould (piano) / Columbia M–32348

A breezy elucidation. Mozart clipped this earlier opus onto a later larger work, Allegro and Andante in F major, K. 533 (*see above*), to form a sonata (Piano Sonata in F major, K. 533). This writer prefers to consider the Rondo as it was conceived—as a separate piece, and not as a proxy sonata finale.

Seven Variations on *Willem van Nassau,* K. 25

Six Pieces from the *Londoner Skizzenbuch* (1764)

☐ Klien (piano) / Vox SVBX–5406

The Six Pieces consist of a *Rondeau,* an Andantino, two *Contredanses,* an Andante, and a final movement of a Sonata. They show again the astonishing creative ability of a child prodigy. The *Willem van Nassau* tune probably dates from the early 17th century—the composer of this song is not known. Mozart's variations are simply written but never mundane or dully academic.

Klien tosses everything off with grace and with the utmost clarity.

Six Variations on an Allegretto in A major, K. Anh. 137

☐ Segall (piano) / Orion 73132

A version of the finale to the Quintet in A major for Clarinet and String Quartet, K. 581 (see under *Chamber Music,* p. 1273). It is included here simply because it is available on disc. The work offers little in comparison to the source from which it was taken, and the performance is presented on a harsh-sounding piano in an overly accented manner.

Six Variations on an Allegretto in F major, K. 54 (K. Anh. 138)

☐ Klien (piano) / Vox SVBX-5407

Taken from Mozart's concluding Sonata for Violin and Piano. Short and simple but sufficient to display Klien's graceful technique and appropriate musicality.

Six Variations on *Mio caro Adone* from Salieri's *La fiera di Venezia*, K. 180

☐ Klien (piano) / Vox SVBX-5406

Some writers apologize for the simplicity of Mozart's variations, belonging, as they did, to the earlier part of his career. Rebuttal: they are worth hearing when performed by a master, as represented by Walter Klien in this case. The whole set is heard at a wise tempo; the music flows beautifully.

Six Variations on *Salve tu, Domine,* K. 398

☐ Klien (piano) / Vox SVBX-5407

Bravura is fully in evidence in the variants Mozart based on a male chorus from Paisiello's *I filosofi immaginarii.* Klien, as expected, is in full command.

Sonata Movement and Minuet in B flat major, K. Anh. 136
Sonata Movement in B flat major, K. 400

☐ Klien (piano) / Vox SVBX-5406

Fine finesse and feeling are displayed in these pieces. The vigor of the dance portion in the first title is given the kind of healthy approach that proves the mincing playing of such Mozart music to be false. There's plenty of theatre in these works, and Klien stages them admirably.

Ten Variations on *Unser dummer Pöbel meint,* K. 455

☐ Klien (piano) / Vox SVBX-5407

One of the most important and brilliantly conceived sets of Mozart's variations. (The theme is a comic song from Gluck's comic opera *Pilger von Mekka.*)

A great deal of Mozart's ingenuity prefigures Beethoven, and it is to Klien's credit that he governs his playing accordingly.

There is a recording (on Orion 7269) that may interest some because of the use of the Siena Pianoforte by Kathryn Deguire. I am not convinced by the instrument—after a very short space of time its twang and tweak twist the ear.

Twelve Variations on *Ah, vous dirai-je, maman,* K. 265

☐ Previn (piano) / Columbia MS-7507

A truly inspired performance, with punch here and delicacy there that bring out all the enchantment of this music. The theme is, of course, that known among some of the nursery set as *"Baa, Baa, Black Sheep,"* and among others as *"Twinkle, Twinkle, Little Star."* Get it!

Twelve Variations on a Minuet by Johann Christian Fischer, K. 179

☐ Klien (piano) / Vox SVBX-5406

A crisply alert portrayal of this variational essay. The Haydnesque flair is expertly conveyed.

Twelve Variations on an Allegretto, K. 500

☐ Klien (piano) / Vox SVBX–5407

There is no certainty that the *Allegretto* of this variational composition is by Mozart. The actual working out is average Mozart.

Twelve Variations

On *Je suis Lindor* from Beaumarchais's *Le Barbier de Séville*, K. 354
On *La Belle Françoise*, K. 353

☐ Klien (piano) / Vox SVBX–5406

In K. 354, for the first time Mozart does not implant the entire theme in each variation. K. 353 exemplifies Mozart's usual charming way with variation form. The set contains a number of engaging permutations, especially the final Presto.

Klien shows fine musicianship and immaculate attention to phrasing in these performances.

Piano,
Four Hands

Andante and Variations in G major, K. 501

Fantasy in F minor, K. 594

Fantasy in F minor, K. 608

Fugue in G minor, K. 401

☐ Jean and Kenneth Wentworth (piano) / Desto 6440/1

The last three of these four piano duets are all transcriptions. Both F minor pieces were originally for mechanical organ; the Fugue was for piano, two hands (see under *piano*). The transfer of K. 594 and K. 608 is an absolute gain, since it saves good music from oblivion, the mechanical organ (also known as a musical clock) not being on the premises these days. It is especially good to have these recorded in this form, since most often both are heard in an organ setting. (K. 594 is also termed Adagio and Allegro; K. 608 is also known as Fantasia in F minor. See under *organ* [Adagio and Allegro].) The performances by the husband-wife team are dignified and precise.

The set of variations (improperly titled Theme and Variations on the release) fares well in the four hands of these pianists. It is enchanting music and far from a minor entry in the huge Mozart catalogue.

Sonata for Piano, Four Hands

In C major, K. 19d / No. 1 in G major, K. 357

☐ Haebler and Hoffmann (piano) / Vox SVBX–566 (monaural)

K. 19d is termed the *Jugend* Sonata, composed by Mozart at the age of nine. In the Desto release (No. 6440/1) by Jean and Kenneth Wentworth of Mozart's piano-four hands music this work is eliminated because "it is too full of 'bare spots' to be fulfilling as a complete piece of music." However, it has the nicest simplicity and it all works quite well. Its recording is welcome, bare spots and all.

The Wentworths also bypass the first of the five sonatas Mozart composed for four hands at one piano. Valid reason: both of its movements were left incomplete. Yet it is good to hear just what Mozart did conceive basically, with the completion made by Julius

André. Haebler and Hoffmann provide an especially well-conceived rendition. The only minus sign applies to the sound, still lacking depth and sounding a bit remote, despite being "electronically reprocessed to simulate stereo."

Sonata for Piano, Four Hands

No. 2 in B flat major, K. 358 / No. 3 in D major, K. 381 / No. 4 in F major, K. 497

☐ Jean and Kenneth Wentworth (piano) / Desto 6440/1

The D major is performed in a bright and vivacious manner. In the weightier, much larger-scaled F major Sonata the Wentworths play frankly if not too deeply. Still, the phrasing is well turned and the ensemble very tidy.

For some reason the numbering of the sonatas has been changed, despite the clear chronology of the Köchel enumeration. No. 2 is correct, but No. 3 (K. 381) is termed No.1, and K. 497 is moved up to No. 3.

Sonata No. 5 in C major for Piano, Four Hands, K. 521

☐ Eschenbach and Frantz (piano) / Deutsche Grammophon 2530285

An example of high artistry, with the players blending their temperamental differences so that Mozart's work is presented in the most definitive manner. There is no tear in the connective tissue of the music. Indeed, this is duo playing of a magical sort, it outclasses all the other versions of K. 521 on the market.

Fugue in C minor, K. 426

Two Pianos

Sonata in D major, K. 448

☐ Brendel and Klien (pianos) / Vox SVBX–566

These two works represent, aside from a few unfinished attempts, Mozart's complete music for two pianos alone.

Of course one expects perfect ensemble in a recording of this kind, but all too often in the concentration on this objective the interpretation becomes undernourished. Not here. The phrasing is excellent, the Sonata fluent, the Fugue serious and sharply cut in its polyphonic dress. The problem of fragmenting and thereby weakening Mozart's fugal inspiration is totally overcome. On a scale of one to five, five it is.

Duo in B flat major, K. 424

Chamber Music

Duo in G major, K. 423

☐ Grumiaux (violin); Pelliccia (viola) / Philips 839747

Handling Mozart's music as though it were made of Dresden china is a gross error. No problem here. The playing is probing, set at the proper dynamic level. Thus, all the high points of K. 423 are brought to the fore in vivid fashion: the marvelously calculated relationship in the slow movement between the semibrilliant ornamental quality of the violin and the less-favored viola, the merry let-go of the final rondo. In K. 424, again the violin takes charge in the slow movement; the writing is meticulous in its adherence to melody and accompaniment, the viola relegated to enriching but not demanding. There is an opportunity for a violin cadenza interpolation, but Grumiaux bypasses it. In the finale, Mozart's rich variational technique is manifested. Throughout, the music is performed with consummate artistry. The B flat major duo is a masterpiece set in a small frame, with the creative largesse of Mozart seen at every step.

Six Variations on *Hélas, j'ai perdu mon amant*, **K. 360**

☐ Szeryng (violin); Haebler (piano) / Philips 6500144

The developments drawn on the French song are neatly distributed. (The biographer, Georges Saint-Foix states that the theme is actually *Au bord d'une fontaine*.) For beauty of ensemble, sound, and stylistic fluency this team is perfect.

Sonata for Flute and Harpsichord

No. 1 in B flat major, K. 10 / No. 2 in G major, K. 11 / No. 3 in A major, K. 12 / No. 4 in F major, K. 13 / No. 5 in C major, K. 14 / No. 6 in B flat major, K. 15

☐ Hechtl (flute); Klien (harpsichord) / Turnabout 34314

In many listings K. 10–15 are noted as being for piano, violin, and cello (*see below* [Sonata for Piano, Violin, and Cello], p. 1269). The instrumentation here is based on Mozart's indication of his work as "Six Sonatas for the Harpsichord—which can be played with the accompaniment of Violin or Transverse Flute." A cello part was added later.

Composed when Mozart was very young, the sonatas have a simplicity (not to be downgraded) that is far better heard in the lighter-scaled orbit of a flute with harpsichord, dispensing with the continuo offshoot of the cello.

The performances have a fidelity of observation and a good quality of execution.

(*See below* for another recording of Sonatas Nos. 3 and 5.)

Sonata for Flute and Harpsichord

No. 3 in A major, K. 12 / No. 5 in C major, K. 14

☐ Wilson (flute); Fuller (harpsichord) / Orion 7283

Fine artistic conceptions. The only difference between them and those heard in the complete set (*see above*) is the quicker tempi adopted by Wilson and Fuller. Assuredly, both interpretative decisions are valid. The choice is really one of deciding whether to have the complete set or only a pair from it.

Sonata for Violin and Piano

No. 19 in E flat major, K. 302 / No. 20 in C major, K. 303

☐ Szeryng (violin); Haebler (piano) / Philips 6500145

The K. 302 is a two-movement work, from the set of six Mozart composed in 1778. The form of the first movement is vigorous in relation to the more contemplative view of the second. However, the performers realize that the reposed state of the rondo (movement 2) is almost a psychological affirmation of the inherent pathos cutting into the jollity of the opening movement. Thus, tempi are not merely foisted in terms of squarely fast and then rigidly slow. That shows great understanding and is conveyed in the playing.

The relationship of the violin to the piano is marked in the other Sonata. When the violin in the first-movement Allegro is freed from an affiliative texture it sings; otherwise it calmly serves as a figuration board. The performance is beautifully realized.

Sonata for Violin and Piano

No. 23 in D major, K. 306 / No. 28 in E flat major, K. 380

☐ Szeryng (violin); Haebler (piano) / Philips 6500144

The D major work is major-scaled. Careful listening will reveal that in the finale there are simmerings of cyclic form, and that Mozart has a coda of considerable size (beginning with an outright piano cadenza). The duo team shapes all the formalities with sense and sensitivity and skilfully blends the music into a bold concept of chamber-music style. Theirs is a correct artistic diagnosis.

Another performance of significance details the E flat major opus. Fine clarity covers the finale—a rondo in skittering duple meter. The key of the slow movement is the precious G minor of this composer. The intensity of the tragic haunts its dialogue.

Sonata for Violin and Piano

No. 32 in B flat major, K. 454 / No. 33 in E flat major, K. 481

☐ Szeryng (violin); Haebler (piano) / Philips 6500055

K. 454 is one of Mozart's most important violin and piano sonatas. The last movement is quite extraordinary. It has contrapuntal formation, stitched with a wonderful bass line. The entrance later of harmonic systems is, therefore, exceedingly fresh in contrast. The opening movement is prefaced by a broad Largo, followed by its antipode—an Allegro. Mozart's use of the violin is considerably freer than in his earlier works in the medium, thus bringing equality to the two instruments. This overflows into the slow movement, where the theme is announced by the violin, rather than the usual piano.

This attention to the stringed instrument is found in the later work. The finale starts with a duetted theme—a coloristic nicety of sonority since the violin remains one octave below the piano. Six variations follow, ending with Allegro for complete climax purposes.

Szeryng and Haebler make a marvelous team. She distinguishes her playing by assorted shades of meaning, his tone is smoothly silken, always of Mozartean character. The results are perfect duo playing.

Twelve Variations on *La Bergère Célimène*, K. 359

☐ Szeryng (violin); Haebler (piano) / Philips 6500145

Similar to the set of Six Variations on *Hélas, j'ai perdu mon amant* (*see above*), this group is based on a French song. Another superb example by these musicians of how to give and take and equalize in chamber music for violin and piano.

Adagio for Two Basset Horns and Bassoon, K. 410

☐ Netherlands Wind Ensemble / de Waart (conductor) / Philips 6500004

The only trouble with this piece is that there isn't more of it. This canonic item, colored in an unusual fashion, provides as autumnal a timbre as one can imagine. It is a choice bit, minute as it may be.

Divertimento in E flat major for String Trio, K. 563

☐ Stern (violin); Zukerman (viola); Rose (cello) / Columbia M-33266

Mozart makes no attempt to equal a larger medium by textural thicknesses. His is true trio writing. The composition is not in classic chamber-music form in its number of movements, since the spread of divertimento design is involved. Although a string trio is not the usual instrumentation for divertimenti, there is here, most importantly, no recourse to the lightness and entertainment properties of the divertimento form, which here consists of six movements in the split plan of fast–slow–minuet, then reversing the sequence to slow–minuet–fast. The depth of this work makes it incorrect to speak of Mozart's "ten great string quartets." This should be restated as Mozart's "eleven great works for string trio and quartet."

None of the four other recorded editions considered (by the Grumiaux Trio on Philips 802803, the Kehr Trio on Dover 5203, the Pasquier Trio on Musical Heritage Society MHS-623, and the Trio à Cordes Français on Nonesuch 71102) depict the light and shade and the power and Mozartean panache heard in the essay by these three soloists functioning as freelance chamber-music players. Their abilities to formulate an inspiring documentation of Mozart's composition are beyond reproach. Quite extra is the fact that Pinchas Zukerman, a violinist, plays the viola and does so as expertly as any full-time violist in the field.

Stern, Zukerman, and Rose combine their temperaments to present an interpretation of classic grandeur and with a centralism that strongly outlines the music's structures. There are some portamenti in Stern's playing but such romantic flavor is minimal. These finger links do not disturb the originality and strength of Mozart's masterwork.

Divertimento

No. 2 in B flat major, K. 439b / No. 4 in B flat major, K. 439b

☐ Stalder, Kubli, and Leuthold (basset horns) / Turnabout 34417

Music for home rather than hall, and, as such, music for sampling. The importance here is the unusual use of a trio of basset horns (not a brass instrument, of course, but a type of clarinet). As stated, a little bit goes a good distance for the five movements in each work.

The playing is fair in No.2, much better in No. 4.

Piano Trio

In B flat major, K. 254 / In G major, K. 496 / In B flat major, K. 502 / In E major, K. 542 / In C major, K. 548 / In G major, K. 564

☐ Beaux Arts Trio / Philips 6770017

The first trio finds the piano running matters with a firm and solo hand. But conditions change in the next trio, whereby the cello has obtained considerable freedom from the piano. There are Mozartean delights and wonders from then on: the chromaticism serving to color matters in K. 502, dynamic crisscross highlighting the slow movement in K. 542, and thematic juggling in K. 548.

The last trio was originally cast as a piano sonata. There is a certain naïveté that clings to the first movement, certainly almost primitive in comparison with the other piano trios. The middle movement consists of a very simple theme with six variations. But the winsomeness of the theme and its daintiness, as they are permitted to show themselves all the way through the variational treatment, are rather fetching—even though not heavenstorming.

The players are of notable accomplishment and their ensemble is faultless, as are the various balances throughout the entire set of works. They provide perceptive and musical documentation that is far better than the Mannheim Trio's competent but not outstanding presentation on Vox SVBX-568.

Six Preludes and Fugues (After Johann Sebastian and Wilhelm Friedemann Bach) for Violin, Viola, and Cello, K. 404a

☐ Trio à Cordes Français / Nonesuch 71112

The amalgamation of the work of two great composers is only possible in the various transcriptions made by one composer of another's music (Vivaldi–Bach, Schubert–Liszt, Mussorgsky–Ravel, for example). In this instance, it is possible to enjoy not only two but three composers together.

Four of the Preludes are original works by Mozart, the other two being arrangements of movements from J. S. Bach's organ sonatas. All the Fugues are Mozart's transcriptions, five originally by Johann Sebastian and a single one by Wilhelm Friedemann Bach.

The preferable performance (there are two editions currently available) is the one noted, played with classical relevancy. A more romantic approach is used by the Grumiaux Trio (on Philips 6500605). The Trio à Cordes Français plays the set in straight sequence. For no apparent reason, the Grumiaux team mixes the six pieces, the order being Nos. 1, 3, 4, 5, 2, 6.

Sonata for Piano, Violin, and Cello

No. 1 in B flat major, K. 10 / No. 2 in G major, K. 11 / No. 3 in A major, K. 12 / No. 4 in F major, K. 13 / No. 5 in C major, K. 14 / No. 6 in B flat major, K. 15

☐ Hokanson (piano); Diedrichsen (violin); Herzer (cello) / Musical Heritage Society MHS–1753

This set of six sonatas was composed when Mozart was eight. (For a different setting of these sonatas, *see above* [Sonata for Flute and Harpsichord], p. 1266.) M.H.S. calls them "trios," which they represent in all respects in a primitively anticipatory way. Where there are two movements, they contrast in slow-fast tempi. Where there are three movements, the sequence is fast, slow, and a pair of minuets.

The performance is made more "authentic" by the use of a Hammerklavier (the early nineteenth-century instrument) in place of the modern piano. The playing is characteristic. This album is principally for the Mozart lover who wants to hear everything he wrote. Others will prefer to sample a bit here and there once in a while.

Trio in E flat major for Piano, Clarinet, and Viola, K. 498

☐ Bishop (piano); Brymer (clarinet); Ireland (viola) / Philips 6500073

One of the most important of Mozart's trios, and in the opinion of some critics the very best. It took Mozart to realize first the beauties of the clarinet in the symphonic field, and he paralleled this uncanny judgement with use in chamber-music compositions. The beautiful expressiveness of this woodwind instrument becomes the focal purpose of a work that, while dusted with a deeper-tinged instrumental color, is nonetheless sheer delight.

This group plays Mozart's beautiful music with beautiful seasoning. Hearing them play the finale and feeling the surge of its twilight atmosphere is to understand fully the meaning of romanticism.

Adagio and Fugue in C minor, K. 546

☐ Quartetto Italiano / Philips 6500645

Though most often heard with the forces of a string orchestra (with several recordings in this form available), the work is for either string quartet or multiple strings (Mozart's definition: *"à 2 violini, viola, e basso"*).

The Fugue is bold and powerful, with a melodic drop in the center that serves to keynote its flux. The minor key helps the vehement development, which uses all the necessary fugal devices.

Tonal massiveness does not harm this small masterpiece, but the "little is more" precept is proven when the piece is played by only four stringed instruments. Hearing it in this recorded performance is exciting and dramatically moving. The Quartetto Italiano does not attempt to force their tone and yet the sound is magnificently full and of superb sonorous poundage.

The Adagio and Fugue has been given the transcription treatment—not unexpectedly. The setting for organ (Biggs on Columbia MS-6856) is fairly satisfactory.

Piano Quartet in G minor, K. 478

☐ Silverstein (violin); Fine (viola); Eskin (cello); Frank (piano) / RCA LSC-6184

The two piano quartets composed by Mozart are the first examples of the medium as we know it today. In this, the first work of the pair, Mozart shows a disposition to pit the three strings (written in string-trio formations) against the piano.

The members of the Boston Symphony Chamber Players with Claude Frank as "guest artist" approach the music with superior results. There is passionate urgency in the first movement, a more relaxed attitude in the B flat major slow movement, and a Haydnesque, joyous *brio* in the concluding rondo.

Quartet for Flute and Strings

In A major, K. 298 / In C major, K. 285b / In D major, K. 285 / In G major, K. 285a

☐ Grumiaux Trio / Bennett (flute) / Philips 6500034
☐ Trio à Cordes Français / Debost (flute) / Seraphim S-60246

What is wanted in these works is élan and not overbrisk tempi. William Bennett and the Grumiaux Trio (Grumiaux, Janzer, and Czako) supply both. The sonorities are kept transparent. In solo spots (the entire thirty-four measures of the slow movement in K. 285, which is for flute accompanied by plucked strings in simple, equated harmonies) Bennett plays exquisitely. So does Michel Debost.

Neither of these teams overburdens the music; rather they let it sing forth in its simple lyrical state. This makes their performances of the complete quartets Mozart wrote for flute, violin, viola, and cello the best in the catalogue.

(*See below* for another recording of K. 285.)

Quartet in D major for Flute and Strings, K. 285

☐ Dwyer (flute); Silverstein (violin); Fine (viola); Eskin (cello) / RCA LSC-6167

The longest and most substantial of the Mozart flute quartets and without doubt the most important. A fine portrayal in which Doriot Anthony Dwyer shows why she is one of the best in the flute league.

Quartet in F major for Oboe, Violin, Viola, and Cello, K. 370

☐ Gomberg (oboe); Galimir (violin); Rhodes (viola); Arico (cello) / Vanguard C-10064

Plenty of recorded performances of Mozart's K. 370 are available, but none of the oboists involved can match the fantastic artistry of Harold Gomberg. That artistry includes expressivity and delicacy, breadth and breath control. And, above all, a tone that is of a rounded, wealthy soprano timbre which remains golden-full at all dynamic levels. Listen to Gomberg, and so many other oboists will appear substandard, with their pinched and pointed, harsh and nasal tone production.

The piece is, of course, in the chamber-music category; but no matter how much attention is given to achieving balances, the three strings cannot cancel the highlighting of the wind instrument, because of the sharply contrasting timbres. It was because of this realization, perhaps, that Mozart conceived the slow movement (second of the total three) in the form of an oboe solo—a type of virtuoso demeanor for the instrument, but without cheapening the music.

This performance is paced without raciness, thus permitting a natural flow in the outer Allegro movements. Most of the other renditions tend to excessive speed. One example: Holliger and members of the Pascal String Quartet, in their Monitor (S-2115) release, play the work a bit more than two minutes faster than Gomberg and company. That's a great deal of Mo-tion and no (z)art.

Seven Minuets, K. 65a

☐ Boskovsky and Weller (violins); Scheiwein (cello); Rühm (bass) / London STS-15275/9

Played with cello reinforcement of the lower voice, the set having been written for two violins and bass. Composed the day before Mozart reached his thirteenth birthday. These minuets represent the first ones Mozart composed for dancing; hence the restricted instrumentation. They are delights nonetheless.

String Quartet

In G major, K. 387 / In D minor, K. 421 / In E flat major, K. 428 / (Hunt) In B flat major, K. 458 / In A major, K. 464 / (Dissonant) In C major, K. 465 / In D major, K. 499 / In D major, K. 575 / In B flat major, K. 589 / In F major, K. 590

☐ Amadeus Quartet / Deutsche Grammophon 2720095

Here in one package is what quartet players refer to as Mozart's "ten famous quartets"—the six dedicated to Haydn, the single D major work (K. 499), and the three quartets dedicated to the King of Prussia.

Within any group of ten works performed by the same ensemble there expectedly will be criticisms. Percentagewise there are not many here. The Amadeus team may overstate the decisive dynamic alternatives in the second movement of K. 387, but the effect of the floating *fiorituras* in the slow movement could not be stated any better. In K. 421 the emphasis on darker coloration (additional to tonality) is noticeable and specially significant. In the finale of the E flat major Quartet (K. 428) the finale is played with a Haydnish caper and bounce. Only the rather heavy statement of the minuet in the *Hunt* quartet (or *Hunting*, though the former is preferable) can be argued; the balance of the work is portrayed with excellent style and color.

The last three of Mozart's quartets favor the cello, but without disturbing the quartet design or the equalization of the voices. (The three works were written for Frederick William II, King of Prussia, who was a rather exceptional cellist.) The Amadeus retain a splendid balance without blemishing the special expressive beauty in these works. Their stress of chromatic inflection in K. 575 marks high artistry. On the other hand, the opening of K. 589 is rather bland and it takes a fair amount of time before the music gets going. The finale of the last work (K. 590) is played to a fare-thee-well. A delight it is, like a demon let loose on a drunken tear. The feeling is wild and disorderly, performed, paradoxically, in perfect order. While it is totally within a rondo form it shows music over technique, genius ahead of form. It is Mozart's *Till Eulenspiegel*.

(*See below* for other recordings of individual quartets.)

String Quartet in D minor, K. 421

☐ Yale Quartet / Vanguard C-10019

Ravishing quartet playing. The Yale team does not overlook a single point in this work, especially in the subtle interweave of the instruments. One example: maintaining the importance of the constant play of the rhythmic form of the accompanying voices in the first movement. From the opening Allegro to the concluding *Più allegro* there is a full display of the determinative mood and character of Mozart's sublime tragic-toned composition.

String Quartet

In E flat major, K. 428 / (*Hunt*) in B flat major, K. 458

☐ Guarneri Quartet / RCA ARL1-0762

Like the playing in the two following quartets (*see below*), the music here has freshness and sparkle and is delivered with the fullest knowledge. Moreover, the Guarneri play with emotional clarity. The listener is not confused by accepting other than truthful issue in this issue.

String Quartet

In A major, K. 464 / (*Dissonant*) in C major, K. 465

☐ Guarneri Quartet / RCA ARL1-1153

Tempi are admirable here, the fast-paced movements are not mere canters for virtuosic display. The difference between a dramatically thrust *forte* and its antithetical *piano* is realized in Mozartean terms (of true discriminative proportions, rather than the plunged obligatory that marks a Beethoven contrast).

The tension and oppression of the opening twenty-two measures in the glorious C major opus, followed by the typical classical lilt and charm of the Allegro proper, indicate that the Guarneri foursome have all the needed watchful and artistic senses.

String Quartet in D major, K. 575

☐ Yale Quartet / Vanguard C-10019

What makes this execution so ideal is the Yale foursome's conception of the chromaticism in the work. There is much dissimilarity between chromaticism per se, and the type that is merely invested in a basic, pure diatonic use. The entire quartet is formed from this latter element. The counterpoint, melodic lines, and the like are all stylistically Mozartean, yet the performers take heed (exceptionally so) of the coloration of the chromatic inflections, which are constantly bending the diatonic tones to and fro. Everything is shaped ideally: the nobility of the opening movement, the warmth given the slow movement, the lilting quality of the *Minuetto,* and the vim of the finale. The special role of the cello in this quartet is artistically defined by Aldo Parisot.

String Quartet

In B flat major, K. 589 / In F major, K. 590

☐ Guarneri Quartet / RCA LSC-2888

The Guarneri play, as usual, with elegance and crispness—which means Mozartean freshness. The strength of this quartet team is solid from the soprano to the bass. It is for that reason that inner voice activity (and personality) lend a new strength and meaning to these quartets.

Adagio and Rondo for Glass Harmonica, Flute, Oboe, Viola, and Cello, K. 617

☐ Hoffmann (glass harmonica); Ulrich (flute); Hucke (oboe); Nippes (viola); Plumacher (cello) / Turnabout 34452

The reverberation of the glass instrument is of a constant overflow that can result in too much of a muchness. Nonetheless, the music Mozart wrote for it as a highlighted aspect, with a quite subsidiary wind-string combine, has sufficient value to hold the listener. It contrasts tempo (the Rondo is an *allegretto*) and tonality; the Adagio a rich minor-keyed representation, the Rondo is in major.

There is no doubt as to Bruno Hoffman's ability. And no doubt as to the recording's clarity.

Adagio for Two Clarinets and Three Basset Horns, K. 411

☐ Netherlands Wind Ensemble / de Waart (conductor) / Philips 6500003

The Adagio has unique color equivalent to a quintet of clarinets, the basset horn (badly named) being an alto-range instrument belonging to the clarinet family. The ensemble is fine and the playing beautifully textured.

Quintet in A major for Clarinet and String Quartet, K. 581

☐ Melos Ensemble / de Peyer (clarinet) / Angel S–36241

In general, there are a number of fine performances of this warm and genial work, but they falter in terms of tempo selection. For some reason, most drag in the slow movement, denying its Larghetto indication and translating it into a Largo. On the other hand, too swift a speed for the finale, a set of variations, spoils the enjoyment of the give-and-take that includes the clarinet's bold leaps and swirling runs.

This team combines all the ingredients. Their performance has clarity, atmosphere, and tempi that fit the material.

(See under *Instrumental: piano* [Six Variations on an Allegretto in A major, K. Anh. 137] for a version of the finale.)

Quintet in E flat major for Horn and String Quartet, K. 407

☐ Fine Arts Quartet / Barrows (horn) / Orion 7281

When one realizes that the horn in Mozart's day was valveless, adequate performance by an eighteenth-century hornist of the difficult part assigned the instrument must have fallen in the realm of the miraculous. Even for the modern instrument the requirements tax the present-day virtuoso, with their gushing scales and tremendous changes of register. John Barrows fulfills every technical need with fine stylistic panache.

The string quartet is not the usual two violins, viola, and cello, but one violin, two violas, and cello. This centralizes midregister tone and sonority and makes the combination more compact. Employment of two violins (with resultant higher tessitura) would call more attention to the horn, since the quality of timbre would be drawn away from the basic center gamut. Wise Mozart.

And wise playing throughout. For the performance, Abram Loft, the second violinist of the Fine Arts group, moves to the second viola chair. The recording has also moved in the sense of reissue. It was originally a Concert-Disc release (CS–204).

Quintet in E flat major for Piano and Winds, K. 452

☐ London Wind Soloists / Ashkenazy (piano) / London 6494

The three winds and horn may call themselves the London Wind Soloists (and, indeed, include such imposing performing personalities as the clarinetist Jack Brymer and the superb hornist Alan Civil), but their blend here is memorable. No one can fault the exquisite playing accorded this great Mozart opus, touched with feelings of *concertante* style, yet not made to sound like a solo piano work framed with triple wind and single brass. And for this, credit must be given to Vladimir Ashkenazy. His ensemble sensitivity leaves an indelible mark on the performance. The keyboard instrument is absorbed in the total, not set off for soloistic egomaniac display. This is five-star Mozart playing.

Serenade (*Eine kleine Nachtmusik*) in G major, K. 525

☐ Budapest String Quartet / Levine (double bass) / Columbia MS-6127

Mozart's K. 525 may be played by either string quintet or string orchestra. (For a discussion of the work and performances by the latter, see under *String Orchestra*.)

The Budapest foursome with Julius Levine give a well-tailored surveyal. Tempi are on the slow side in the Minuet and somewhat deliberate; however, the fivesome's presentation is fine, clear, and tasteful and has full interpretative intelligence.

String Quintet in B flat major, K. 46

☐ Pascal String Quartet / Gerhard (viola) / Monitor S-2114

A version of four of the seven movements in the famous Serenade for thirteen winds, K. 361. It charms with its content; and save for a somewhat lame introduction, the playing of the Pascal team, with their second viola guest, does the same.

String Quintet

In B flat major, K. 174 / In C minor, K. 406 / In C major, K. 515 / In G minor, K. 516 / In D major, K. 593 / In E flat major, K. 614

☐ Danish Quartet / Collot (viola) / Telefunken 5635017

Mozart sensed the emotional as well as the color possibilities of warming the inside of the quartet body by doubling the viola voices. This brown-hued instrument, especially in its middle register, imparts a somberness that does not dull; rather it vibrates the sonority of the middle gamut against the brilliance of the top and the solidity of the bottom registers. Such enriched sound structure offers a wonderful vehicle to those composers who can organize their creative powers without voice doublings or merely enlarging the basic four parts into five. Mozart seized and solved all the possibilities. His quintets are technical, warm, garnet jewels without a flaw in them; the music itself no less so.

These performances are radiant and superbly crafted. In the C major (K. 515), where the music is relaxed, the performers follow suit but without slouching. They make certain to underline the counterpoint to keep its posture in place. Every part of the great G minor opus (K. 516) is consummately detailed; the playing combines intensity with lyricism, interwoven with subtle stresses and agogic impresses. This is exciting music-making, maintained through every movement in every work.

Divertimento

No. 8 in F major, K. 213 / No. 9 in B flat major, K. 240 / No. 12 in E flat major, K. 252

☐ Netherlands Wind Ensemble / de Waart (conductor) / Philips 6500002

Philips's colorful album cover, including a picture of the entire Netherlands group of ten players, completely hides the fact that three of the four works on the program are sextets for two oboes, two bassoons, and two horns. The fourth piece (Divertimento No. 3 in E flat major; see under *Wind and Brass Ensemble*) is for ten instruments, to be sure, but there is no mention save by remarks hidden away in the liner notes that three-quarters of the issue covers sextets. Notwithstanding a conductor on hand, these finely proposed and deftly played pieces are chamber music and are so categorized. There are special movements in K. 213 and K. 252: a *Contredanse en rondeau* in the former and a Polonaise in the latter.

Divertimento No. 13 in F major, K. 253

☐ Netherlands Wind Ensemble / de Waart (conductor) / Philips 6500003

Another Mozart Divertimento for sextet (two oboes, two bassoons, and two horns). This one is an outstanding example, emphasized by the fine set of variations that begins the three-part work, and confirmed by the grace and sparkle in the playing conducted by Edo de Waart.

Say, Philips, what sort of merchandising goes on? This isn't the first album cover that does not picture what the program covers. There are five instrumentalists shown playing. But that group is only involved in an Adagio piece, the other pieces (three full-scaled Divertimenti) call for sextets in two cases and ten players in the other. Without any scoring indication (and not even numbers assigned the Divertimenti), how is anyone to know what is truly contained on the disc?

Divertimento No. 14 in B flat major, K. 270

☐ Netherlands Wind Ensemble / de Waart (conductor) / Philips 6500004

One more in the many sextets for winds that Mozart produced, and one more in the many superb performances of this wind ensemble.

Ein musikalischer Spass, K. 522

☐ Kehr and Bartels (violins); Sichermann (viola); Gräser (double bass); Spach and Roth (horns) / Turnabout 34134

A gem of artistic tomfoolery. Satirical elements are caught by the subtle musical dig here, the oafish and clumsy writing there, together with a capering glint as well as fully rough horseplay. Enmeshed with all this is delightful brilliance special only to Mozart. It is wonderful to observe musical sounds acting quite foolishly in the right place.

The playing does not overdrive the satire. Everything is temperamentally in tune with the concept. The solo fiddle cadenza is perfect; so are the ''wrong'' sounds in the horns which are the right notes in the score.

Divertimento
In B flat major, K. Anh. 227 / In E flat major, K. Anh. 226

☐ Netherlands Wind Ensemble / de Waart (conductor) / Philips 6500004

The authenticity of these two divertimenti has not been fully established (hence the K. supplementary indications). Take your choice. Whether or not by Mozart, there is no doubt about the authenticity of the playing by de Waart's group.

Serenade No. 11 in E flat major, K. 375

☐ Netherlands Wind Ensemble / de Waart (conductor) / Philips 802907

Mozart has rightly been called the ancestor of the romanticists. Strong evidence is to be found in the opening movement of this octet for two oboes, two clarinets, two horns, and two bassoons. Substantiation of this was made by the important German music scholar Hermann Abert. He mentions that one is immediately struck by the "strong subjectivity, particularly in the romanticism of the B flat minor second theme," the use of "rests and pauses" in the movement, and "the dramatic ending of the coda."

No other recorded presentation on the books has the lovely tonal suavity and phrasing of this one. There is brilliance without edginess, textural consideration without overlooking a single dynamic possibility, and an ensemble that is equal to the most skilled group one might hear. An artistically drenched setting.

Serenade No. 12 in C minor, K. 388

☐ Marlboro Wind Ensemble / Schneider (conductor) / Columbia MS–7446

Serenade in title, but already the minor-key tonality prepares the listener for anything but light-hearted details. The dramatic effect of this work is intense, and there is no doubt that K. 388 is a dark-striped score. There is plaintiveness in the slow movement, and even the minuet (though in a major tonality) has inner agitation. Only the close of the work is optimistic.

All the positive points are made in this performance of what is considered to be one of Mozart's masterworks: passion and color and ensemble cohesion that is a joy to hear. The continuity of the playing is itself of virtuoso effect.

Vocal

Voice and Instrumental Ensemble

Six *Notturni* for Three Voices and Three Basset Horns

Due pupille amabili, **K. 439**
Ecco quel fiero istante, **K. 436**
Luci care, luci belle, **K. 439a**
Mi lagnerò tacendo, **K. 437**
Più non si trovano, **K. 549**
Se lontan ben mio tu sei, **K. 438**

☐ Speiser (soprano); Gohl (mezzo-soprano); Widmer (baritone); Stalder, Kubli, and Leuthold (basset horns) / Turnabout 34417

Odd combinations are not restricted to the avant-garde folk of the twentieth century, as witness Mozart's rare partnership of three voices and three basset horns. It offers a rich, if small-sized, Mozartean harvest. The singing and playing are warm and with real personality.

Voice and Orchestra

A questo seno deh vieni . . . Or che il cielo a me ti rende, **K. 374**

Basta, Vincesti . . . Ah, non lasciarmi, no, bell'idol mio, **K. 486a**

Voi avete un cor fedele, **K. 217**

☐ English Chamber Orchestra / Ameling (soprano); Pearson (harpsichord) / Leppard (conductor) / Philips 6500006

Each design is slightly different. The first title covers music embracing a recitative and a rondo, the second work has a recitative followed by an aria, while *Voi avete* is an aria structured by a pair of alternating subjects and bound by a coda.

The singing is impressive; it couldn't be bettered. The accompaniments are extremely sensitive.

Exsultate Jubilate, K. 165

☐ English Chamber Orchestra / Ameling (soprano) / Leppard (conductor) / Philips 6500006

Singing that provides all the poise and all the style for this famous solo motet. Ameling's pointing of words and phrases is impeccable, and in the *Alleluia* section there is tasteful jubilation expressed.

Alma Dei Creatoris, K. 277	**Regina Coeli, K. 276**	*Choral*
Ave, Verum Corpus, K. 618	**Sancta Maria, Mater Dei, K. 273**	
Inter Natos Mulierum, K. 72	**Veni, Sancte Spiritus, K. 47**	*Chorus*
Misericordias Domini, K. 222	**Venite Populi, K. 260**	*and Orchestra*

☐ Vienna Cathedral Orchestra, Wiener Sängerknaben, and Vienna Chorus / Resch (tenor); Buchbauer (bass); Boehm (organ) / Grossmann (conductor) / Philips 835396

This is a fine selection of Mozart's sacred music, among which are four Offertories, the beautiful motet *Ave, Verum Corpus,* and the *Sancta Maria, Mater Dei* Gradual. The earliest work (K. 47) was conceived by Mozart at the age of twelve; the latest is the motet, composed six months before he died. Odd (and startling) point: the Beethoven *Ode to Joy* theme is stated in the *Misericordias Domini.*

The performances are affectionate. However, exactly who is performing in each piece is confused no end; the label credits do not match the data on the album cover whatsoever. It is for that reason that, contrary to other commentary in this compendium, separate entries, limited to the exact performing personnel involved in each work or group of works, have been eliminated.

Benedictus Sit Deus, K. 117

☐ Pro Musica Orchestra and Vienna Oratorio Choir / Lavergne (soprano) / Grossmann (conductor) / Turnabout 34029

An offertory that divides in three parts with choruses embracing a movement for solo voice. The wealth of Mozart's invention is apparent even in this minor opus. The singing is skilled though lacking subtlety.

There is nothing subtle about Turnabout's omission of the title on the main side of the jacket and their failure to mention a single word about the composition in the unsigned liner notes. There can be no excuse about cramped space, since the notes covering the other two works on the disc appear in three languages.

Mass (*Coronation*) in C major, K. 317

Cantata and Oratorio

☐ Pro Musica Symphony, Vienna, and Vienna Oratorio Choir / Lipp (soprano); Ludwig (alto); Dickie (tenor); Berry (bass) / Horenstein (conductor) / Turnabout 34063

Mozart's lovely Mass is music of exquisite balance, purity, and a dramaticism that has a line of directness. It is never theatrically restless. Affirmative spirit serves all the needed dramatic purposes.

Save for this Turnabout issue, the performances available lack a dynamic expression that would exceed superficiality. Kubelik's on Deutsche Grammophon (2530356) is overdone (that fits the "theatrically restless" element mentioned above); the Grossmann-led edition on Philips (835187) is sometimes elegant, but its sweetness is nonchanging and becomes quite irritating. And so on. But everything one wishes in terms of line, color, and emotive weight is present in Horenstein's version. On top of that the soloists are outstanding and their rapport is ideal. The chorus is splendid. This is the best there is on disc and deserves that overworked but true phrase, "highly recommended."

Missa Brevis (Spatzenmesse) in C major, K. 220

☐ Bavarian Radio Symphony Orchestra and Regensburg Cathedral Choir / Mathis (soprano); Troyanos (mezzo-soprano); Laubenthal (tenor); Engen (bass) / Kubelik (conductor) / Deutsche Grammophon 2530356

The "Sparrow Mass" (so nicknamed due to the repeated violin figure in the Credo) is a sunny affair. It is presented with what it takes to fulfill Mozart's creation: pure, classical style, beautiful ensemble, and a relaxed delivery on the part of the vocal soloists.

Missa Brevis in C major, K. 259

☐ Vienna Cathedral Orchestra, Wiener Sängerknaben, and Vienna Chorus / Resch (tenor); Buchbauer (bass); Boehm (organ) / Grossmann (conductor) / Philips 835396

This is No. 13 of Mozart's masses and is known as the "Organ Solo" Mass because of the use of the keyboard instrument in the Benedictus. That section and the Agnus Dei that follows call for tenor and bass soloists plus high (soprano) and low (alto) voices, sung here by two members of the Vienna Choir Boys. However, no credits are given the boy soloists "in accordance with the policy of the Choir's controlling body." (One can understand and respect the democratic policies of this unique organization, bearing in mind that it has been in existence since 1498.)

The performance is inspired. Liquidity and body describe the tonal production of chorus and soloists. Perhaps K. 259 is minor Mozart, but it is heard under major auspices.

Missa Solemnis (Waisenhaus) in C minor, K. 139

☐ Vienna Philharmonic Orchestra and Vienna State Opera Chorus / Janowitz (soprano); von Stade (mezzo-soprano); Ochman (tenor); Moll (bass); Scholz (organ) / Abbado (conductor) / Deutsche Grammophon 2530777

The unbelievable musical depth of this work includes dynamic creative plotting, with (for its time) a large orchestra. The music features sharply paced fast movements and splendidly constructed fugues. "Unbelievable" because this is the product of a thirteen-year-old boy—a word for which "genius" should be substituted.

The participants deserve nothing but praise. Fluency and assurance mark the solo quartet of voices. Claudio Abbado holds matters together beautifully, with subtle changes of characterization marking the progress of the work. This is a substantial entry, better than the older recording that Philips issued (6500866).

Requiem Mass in D minor, K. 626

☐ Vienna Philharmonic Orchestra and Vienna State Opera Chorus / Mathis (soprano); Harmari (contralto); Ochman (tenor); Ridderbusch (bass); Haselböck (organ) / Böhm (conductor) / Deutsche Grammophon 2530143

☐ Vienna Philharmonic Orchestra and Vienna State Opera Chorus / Ameling (soprano); Horne (mezzo-soprano); Benelli (tenor); Franc (bass) / Kertész (conductor) / London 1157

Istvan Kertész presents a perfectly weighted, remarkably fluent reading of this masterpiece. Every measure is perfectly balanced in his entirely convincing direction, which is a strongly committed dramatic one. Böhm's consideration is no less dramatic and contains a real grandeur. It also has an onward pace and inner urgency that is rarely accomplished in performances of Mozart's work.

Both conductors achieve a truly apocalyptic fervency in the *Dies Irae* and the concluding double fugue. The choral work in each of the settings is excellent, though there is some slight strain in the soprano section in both the *Offertorium* and the Sanctus in the London release. The soloists are impressive and equally matched, with the exception of Ridderbusch, who is a shade better than Franc, especially in his phrasing in the *Tuba Mirum*.

Vesperae de Dominica, K. 321

☐ Camerata of Los Angeles Orchestra and Chorus / Stevenson (soprano); Hurwood (mezzo-soprano); Wyatt (tenor); Nehls (bass-baritone) / Mitzelfelt (conductor) / Crystal S-902

Stylistically there is a decided parallel in this work to the other Vespers Mozart composed (*see below*), in addition to the use of the same psalm text. Though somewhat illogically neglected, this music of sacred sensibility and stunning sensitivity should not be underestimated.

The *Laudate Dominum* is a highlight in the score, and in this performance it is beautifully negotiated by Delcina Stevenson. The orchestra of twenty-nine plays solidly and the chorus of forty-four sings expertly.

Vesperae Solennes de Confessore in C major, K. 339

☐ Pro Musica Symphony, Vienna, and Vienna Oratorio Choir / Lipp (soprano); Ludwig (alto); Dickie (tenor); Berry (bass) / Horenstein (conductor) / Turnabout 34063

Though there is a touch of severity in this, one of the two Vespers Mozart composed, Horenstein obtains a fine breadth in his conception. Never is the music anchored in solid observation—there is an inner motility that goes beyond the polyphonic specifics. The soloists are fine, especially Wilma Lipp, who sings the *Laudate Dominum* gently but convincingly.

The Abduction from the Seraglio, K. 384

Opera and Dramatic Music

☐ Royal Philharmonic Orchestra and Beecham Choral Society / Marshall and Hollweg (sopranos); Simoneau and Unger (tenors); Frick (bass) / Beecham (conductor) / Angel S-3555

An old recording (produced in the early 1950s) but so infused with Mozartean intelligence and style as to make it the prime choice of the recordings available. This is notwithstanding Beecham's obsession with changing details, realized by the transfer of a pair of sections and the omission of another.

There are no distractions to annoy in the accompaniments. All the balances are exquisite, the tempi totally justified. This is a graphic exhibition of great operatic conducting.

A strong cast is at work. Mozart's bravura passages for the sopranos are carried off with panache; Frick's voice is rich and golden; the tenors are never less than admirable.

Così fan tutte, K. 588

☐ London Philharmonic Orchestra and Chorus of the Royal Opera House, Covent Garden / Lorengar (soprano); Berganza and Berbié (mezzo-sopranos); Davis (tenor); Krause and Bacquier (baritones); Tate (harpsichord) / Solti (conductor) / London 1442

A stunning and totally perceptive production. Solti's molding of the performance is well-nigh perfect. There is an ease and a stylistic charm to the proceedings that are captivating. Nothing is cut and nothing is but alive in all respects, including the recitatives, which have point and substance in their delivery. The pace is ideal, and sensitivity to dynamic differences colors this opera in a particularly special way (too often a rare fact in operatic situations).

There is no quibbling as to the competence of the cast. It is a strong one, indeed, particularly Ryland Davis and Tom Krause—the latter subject in many instances elsewhere to uneven vocal delivery, but not in this case. Solti's *Così* sets a very high standard.

Don Giovanni, K. 527

☐ Orchestra and Chorus of the Royal Opera House, Covent Garden / Arroyo, Kanawa, and Freni (sopranos); Burrows (tenor); Wixell (baritone); Roni, Ganzarolli, and Van Allan (basses) / Davis (conductor) / Philips 6707022

The dramatic ambiguity of this work has entranced audiences since it was initially produced in October of 1789. Its blend of the comic and the tragic furnishes music of beauty and power, with passion and effervescence as well. *Don G.* contains the ingredients that help to make it an overwhelming experience: marvelous arias, rich ensembles, and action. It is one of the greatest masterpieces of the lyric stage.

Meaningful operatic characterization is as essential as the vivacity of action. It is this point that makes this performance a truly unforgettable one. There is no one recording that reaches perfection, but the Philips edition comes quite close.

Wixell, as the licentious Don, projects magnificently, and has the special ability to act with his voice. Arroyo's beautiful voice is a responsibly big one and is responsive to controls that fit the part of Donna Anna. Kiri Te Kanawa as Donna Elvira is no Schwarzkopf (if you want to hear *her,* you must get the Angel production [S–3605]), but she does magnificiently. Burrows provides an elegant vocalism, and there is no doubt that Mirella Freni makes the most enchanting Zerlina imaginable.

The Angel album mentioned is conducted by Klemperer. But no matter the great musician he represented, his ideas of tempi in this particular opera flaw the wit, humanity, and drama of Mozart's masterwork. To obtain as close to the ideal on records choose the Philips version. It is a decided success.

Idomeneo, Rè di Creta, K. 366

☐ BBC Symphony Orchestra and Chorus / Rinaldi, Tinsley, Jeanette Hill, and Valerie Hill (sopranos); Henshilwood and Harrison (contraltos); Shirley, Davies, Tear, Pilley, and Austin (tenors); Dean and Farrall (basses); Constable (harpsichord); Vigay (cello); Brinnen (double bass) / Davis (conductor) / Philips 83958/60

Great dramatic music is contained in many parts of this rather neglected opera. Thus: the three arias assigned Elettra (Pauline Tinsley), the trio in the second act, and a thrilling chorus that appears in the third act. There is considerably more than the sampling mentioned, but it is such theatrical expression that makes this opera outstanding.

The singing is excellent. George Shirley as Idomeneo is most eloquent, and Pauline Tinsley is likewise. Margherita Rinaldi (as Ilia) does not avoid edginess, but her conception of the part is fascinating. Colin Davis does not push tempi and blends his orchestra beautifully with the singers. The chorus is superlative, and the continuo well recorded.

Incidental Music to *Thamos, King of Egypt,* **K. 345 (336a)**

☐ Staatskapelle Berlin and Rundfunk-Solistenvereinigung, Berlin / Eickstaedt (soprano); Pohl (contralto); Büchner (tenor); Adam and Polster (basses); Weih (oboe) / Klee (conductor) / Philips 6500840

The music Mozart wrote for Tobias Philipp Baron von Gebler's play is far from the bread-and-butter concoctions that fill the incidental music larder. It fully accommodated the utilitarian purposes involved, but it offers much more—that Mozartean resource that is as splendid as any of the material found in his first thirty symphonies. Indeed, it opens with his Symphony No. 26 in E flat major, K. 184 (see under *Orchestra*), which serves as a proxy overture. Then follow three choruses, each including solo parts and five purely instrumental interludes.

Klee's interpretation provides clarity and understanding style. Though Karin Eickstaedt has skill and enthusiasm, her upper register is watery; the other vocalists are good; the chorus is excellent. The instrumental interludes are also included in a London release (STS–15088), without any of the choral-vocal material or the overture.

La clemenza di Tito, **K. 621**

☐ Vienna State Opera Orchestra and Chorus / Popp (soprano); Casula, Berganza, and Fassbaender (mezzo-sopranos); Krenn (tenor); Franc (bass); Fischer (harpsichord) / Kertész (conductor) / London 1387

Granting a plot that cannot stand up to close examination (but there are other operas that hold the boards with almost as stilted a story line), it would be difficult to argue against Mozart's superfine score. It is crammed with such riches as the arias *Parto, ma tu, ben mio, Deh per questo istante solo,* and *Non più di fiori;* striking choral writing; and superb ensembles, especially the vivid trio in the second act, *Se a volto mai.* Indeed, just from the emotional tone of the "Titus" music, the work deserves full reconsideration by our ultraconservative operatic impresarios.

London's cast is excellent, especially the persuasive stylistic fidelity exhibited in Teresa Berganza's singing. Werner Krenn performs elegantly, and for the most part Maria Casula handles her very difficult role admirably, with only a bit of vibrato and some forced tones reducing her credits a bit. The conviction of Kertész's conducting is apparent in every part of London's superb recording.

La finta giardiniera, **K. 196**

☐ Orchestra and Chorus of the Norddeutsche Rundfunk / Donath, Norman, and Cotrubas (sopranos); Troyanos (mezzo-soprano); Unger and Hollweg (tenors); Prey (baritone) / Schmidt-Isserstedt (conductor) / Philips 6703039

Mozart's opera is sung in German, in which language its title becomes *Die Gärtnerin aus Liebe.* Since the plot is one of cross-purpose that is further crisscrossed, it would be best to bypass it and just enjoy Mozart's music. Nevertheless, to synthesize the plot, herewith follows a précis, tightening the reading by substituting letters in place of names. A is in love with B (really a countess, but serving A as a maid). C (a count) is engaged to D, but formerly was in love with B. D, however, was first in love with E, prior to her betrothal to C. E is still in love with D, though abandoned by her. F is a chambermaid for and in love with A, while G (really a servant of the countess [B]) is working as a gardener for A and is in love with F!

Mozart's opera embraces twenty-eight set numbers, but is overloaded with twenty-three arias. Clear musical identity of the characters is not fully confirmed, so that the personalities get somewhat confused. There is a continual use of dialogue (in twenty-one instances). While the libretto furnished by Philips (in German, English, and French) is of great aid, additional listener-made assistance is required: since the spoken sections are recorded at an extremely low level, the volume control must be turned up (and then reset at their conclusions) in order to hear these portions.

No criticism pertains to the singers. All of them are fully in rapport with classical style. Schmidt-Isserstedt's conception, especially regarding tempi, is an excellent one.

The Magic Flute, K. 620

☐ Philharmonia Orchestra and Chorus / Janowitz, Pütz, Popp, Schwarzkopf, Giebel, and Reynolds (sopranos); Ludwig and Veasey (mezzo-sopranos); Höffgen (contralto); Gedda, Unger, and Liebl (tenors); Berry, Frick, and Crass (basses); Schmidt (glockenspiel) / Klemperer (conductor) / Angel S–3651

Klemperer's slow tempi mannerisms are legendary and it is this factor that has brought prejudicial guilt even before proof. However, there is not a bit of heavy-handedness here. In fact the pace of this *Zauberflöte* provides a welcome freshness. And much more from the maestro: an acute and loving care for matters of detail and balance, impeccable musicality, and absolute warmth to the phrasing of the singers. And what a great cast!

Some of the vocalists have become totally identified with their roles. Thus, Nicolai Gedda as Tamino, Walter Berry as Papageno, and Lucia Popp as Queen of the Night. Gedda's characterization is not only strong but rich, Berry's flexibility is a joy, and Popp is exciting. These qualities are matched by those of the others in the cast, all of whom capture the spirit of the opera to the fullest. The orchestral playing is beautifully clear and registers with full immediacy.

On stage, Mozart's great opera, properly mounted, has often dazzled the eye. It has never failed to dazzle the ear. This recording does exactly that.

The Marriage of Figaro, K. 492

☐ BBC Symphony Orchestra and Chorus / Norman, Minton, Freni, Watson, Palmer, and Clarke (sopranos); Casula (mezzo-soprano); Tear and Lennox (tenors); Wixell (baritone); Ganzarolli, Grant, and Hudson (basses) / Davis (conductor) / Philips 6707014

There is conclusive personality in this outstanding performance, which is free of irritating mannerisms made in the name of dramatic needs. Mirella Freni is radiant and sings with mouth-licking warmth. Yvonne Minton is totally terrific as Cherubino, and her arias not only have musical and dramatic substance but are completely believable in relation to her characterization. There is substantial flexibility in the way Jessye Norman defines the role of the Countess. She has a creamy voice that she uses with intelligence, and she is matched by Ingvar Wixell's commanding interpretation as the Count.

Truly, this is a stunning realization of *Figaro*. The ensembles breathe together and the orchestra is supple and subtle. Colin Davis's interpretation is fully idiomatic. He paces the opera so that its basic elements—the scheming of Figaro, Almaviva's lechery, the impertinence of Susanna, and the Countess's loneliness—are emphasized, not passed over in favor of a general lightweighted affair. A great Mozart production.

Robert Muczynski (1929-   )

Concerto No. 1 for Piano and Orchestra (1955)

☐ Louisville Orchestra / Muczynski (piano) / Whitney (conductor) / Louisville 56–5 (monaural)

Solo Instrument and Orchestra

Piano

Crystal clear concerto tactics and just as clear tonal presence and designs. Françaix comes to mind in the finale but that doesn't lessen the pronounced values of this smartly arranged work. Excellent playing by the soloist, and Whitney makes a fine partner. (All the participants took part in the first performance of the work, in Louisville, in January 1955.)

Suite for Piano, Op. 13

☐ Drake (piano) / Orion 75168

Instrumental

Piano

Not too much piano music like this is being written these days. Variety of sound and subject are heard here, with fascinating attention to musical rapport with the titles. Four of the pieces—*Festival, Flight, Labyrinth,* and Scherzo—are brightly tempoed and there is no guesswork involved; Muczynski's sound camera is impeccably focused. The same is true of *Vision* and *Phantom.*

Paulina Drake plays this music with great flair. There is a kind of animal warmth given the fast-paced pieces that is extremely stimulating.

Georg Muffat (1653-1704)

Concerto Grosso *Victoria Maesta*

☐ Mainz Chamber Orchestra / Kehr (conductor) / Turnabout 34324

String Orchestra

This is music that does not suffer from any identity crisis. Muffat's work (in five movements: Sonata, Aria, *Grave, Sarabanda,* and *Borea* [meaning *Bourrée*]) glows with its clear and rich themes and the detail within the movements. None of that academic utilitarianism here; this is a splendid example and makes one wish that more of Muffat's concerti grossi were available on disc.

Günter Kehr brings the correct rapport to the playing of his musicians. The tonal quality is fine, the tempi excellent, and the proper sense of atmosphere set forth in every one of the movements.

Jan Mul (1911-   )

Sinfonietta (1957)

☐ Utrecht Philharmonic Orchestra / Hupperts (conductor) / Donemus Audio-Visual Series DAVS–6203 (monaural: 10-inch disc)

Orchestra

Neatness of content and musical grammar mark Mul's work. It is freely tonal throughout and includes zones of colorful semicontrapuntal recording—all of which makes the former matter clear in delineation. It would make an admirable ballet, and has so been used.

Hupperts shows he knows how to bring out the detail in a score and yet keep matters in balance. The execution is very good.

Vocal

Voice and Orchestra

Lettre de M. l'Abbé d'Olivet à M. le Président Bouhier (1961)

☐ Limburg Symphony Orchestra / Kruysen (baritone) / Rieu (conductor) / Donemus Audio-Visual Series DAVS-6604 (monaural)

Attracted by its typical eighteenth-century manner of writing, Mul has vocalized a letter form an abbé to a president of parliament. Lightly lyrical and reflective, it is similar to an operatic *scena*. Comfortable music, performed with an alive manner most fitting to the musical content.

Johann Peter Müller   (1791-1877)

Chamber Music

Quintet

No. 1 in E flat major / No. 2 in C minor / No. 3 in A major

☐ Richards Wind Quintet / Crystal S-252

The pieces are practically unknown but worth the attention of anyone who enjoys wind quintet music. There is no deep emotional portent within the total of twelve movements that cover the customary classic forms. The music is played with intelligence and with bright sound.

Paul Müller   (1898-   )

Instrumental

Flute

Capriccio

☐ Anne Diener Giles (flute); Allen Giles (piano) / Crystal S-312

Müller (some catalogues incorrectly list his name as Müller-Zürich) shows Gallic spirit in this piece, commissioned for the 1973 *Concours international de Genève*. He is intent on song and rhythm and the performers follow suit nicely.

Gordon Mumma   (1935-   )

Electronic Music

Hornpipe (1967)

☐ Mainstream 5010

Live horn with cybersonic console (worn by the performer) providing the basic electronics. The horn is transformed, played by special double reeds and the slides rearranged so that its sound "is heard from different parts of the instrument." A variety of sonorities occur: horn with console, producing further electronic sounds, which then result in additional qualities.

Hornpipe doesn't dance, but it has definite sonorous rhythms and extremely novel ones.

Mesa, for Cybersonic Bandoneon (1966)

☐ Tudor (bandoneon); Mumma (cybersonic console) / Odyssey 32160158

The bandoneon (an Argentine variety of the accordion) is attached to an electronic circuitry that "determines the sound modifications and musical continuity by semi-automatic, or 'cybersonic,' means." *Mesa* consists of a succession of frozen sound chunks. This purposeful staticness naturally is devoid of rhythmic motility. In a way, the objective is a total cancellation of usual musical objectives. One must not endeavor to expect recognizable form and structure and the balances derived therefrom.

Karl Münchinger / *J. S. Bach.* See *J. S. Bach* / Münchinger.

Münchinger / *Johann Pachelbel.* See *Pachelbel* / Münchinger.

Santiago de Murcia   (19th cent.?)

Prelude and Allegro   *Instrumental*

☐ Segovia (guitar) / MCA 2523   *Guitar*

A short and good illustration of the work of this Spanish guitarist-composer. There are Scarlatti manifestations throughout. As usual, Segovia is in full command.

Bain Murray   (1926-   )

Three Songs for Tenor and Piano   *Vocal*

☐ McCoy (tenor); Shirey (piano) / Crystal S–532   *Voice with Accompaniment*

Simplicity, tonal clarity, and a fine type of urbanity are present. The texts are by Yeats, Frost, and Sandburg.
Seth McCoy has a rich voice. He also has a vibrato here and there that fractions pitch. (Crystal does not supply any texts.)

Herbert Murrill   (1909-1952)

Sonata for Alto Recorder and Harpsichord (1950)   *Chamber Music*

☐ Dolmetsch (alto recorder); Saxby (harpsichord) / Orion 74144

Handelian gusto invigorates this no-nonsense neoclassical item. It is difficult to think of recorder sounds as being crisp, yet Carl Dolmetsch achieves this rarity in his magnificent playing.

Thea Musgrave (1928-   )

Orchestra

Concerto for Orchestra (1967)

☐ Scottish National Orchestra / Pearson (clarinet) / Gibson (conductor) / London HEAD-8

Musgrave's piece is a solid chunk of powerful music, a dazzling essay in sound, with fricative sonorities one of the highlights. The other feature is the special objective of the work, which Musgrave explains is conceived "essentially on the struggle between the solo and tutti forces, which gradually develops into a virtuoso piece for the whole orchestra." Although the soloism is subtle in great part, the featuring of the clarinet (as noted in the credits) is much more direct. There is no catch-penny approach in Musgrave's writing. The qualities and weights vary in the five linked sections of the piece but specific tensions are always present. All of this equals virtuosity, therefore, in concept, realization, and demands on the performers. Those demands are fully met in this superb recorded performance.

Solo Instrument and Orchestra

Horn

Horn Concerto (1971)

☐ Scottish National Orchestra / Tuckwell (horn) / Musgrave (conductor) / London HEAD-8

No ordinary concerto, this, though soloistic virtuosity is on tap from first note to last. The horn line is a mosaic of declamatory, cryptic, and episodic materials. It is surrounded by instrumental informality that always stimulates by solo-instrument opposition or by providing a special coloristic framework for the solo voice. Spatial placement is used: in the last portion of the work the orchestral horns are "strategically placed round the Hall," the composer explains, "so as to surround the soloist." The percussion is spread around the back of the orchestra and the brass form a concertante group within the orchestra. These sonorous strategies are fairly well conveyed in the recording, though, understandably, such bold structuring would be more convincing in live performance.

No tunes in this piece but one doesn't miss them what with the powerful timbre details set off by the scoring. Musgrave has a hearty appetite for doing things with sounds *as* sounds and if the formality of the music is somewhat loose the effect is the opposite. Indeed, the reaction to the Concerto is immediate and exciting.

This is no easy score to conduct and Musgrave conducting Musgrave must be given fat credits for her work. That Barry Tuckwell plays with conviction and amazing control no matter what difficulties are demanded of him is to be expected.

Two Horns

Night Music for Two Horns and Orchestra (1969)

☐ London Sinfonietta / Tuckwell and Chidell (horns) / Prausnitz (conductor) / Argo ZRG-702

Sectionally disposed within its single movement, Musgrave's piece has an intelligible retentiveness of mysterious nocturnal mood, plus an instrumentational feature—the horns move about in a special condition of soloistic response, playing close together in lyric statements, being separated for more dramatic ones. This is not a marginal attempt for effect but one for significant formation.

Judged without score the performance certainly is relevant and the playing of the soloists is of prime quality.

Monologue for Piano

☐ Musgrave (piano) / Argo ZRG–704

Musgrave's *Monologue* is based on duodenary detail. She opts for freedom from the twelve-tone system, but the syntax is a constant strong reminder that serial language is being spoken. Rhythmic strengths are found in the conjunctions and juxtapositions of the detail. With Musgrave at the keyboard the interpretation is truly realistic.

Excursions for Piano Duet

☐ Musgrave and ? (piano) / Argo ZRG–704

Light-scaled and picturesque settings; all eight are closely drawn sketches. Thus: tipsy-addled rhythms for *The Drunken Driver*, carefully quiet shapes in *The Sunday Driver*, nagging antiphony in *Backseat Driver*, and so on. Splendid pieces, they would do well in orchestral dress.

There are lots of production errors. *Schwann* (in part not their fault) lists the suite as "Excursions, for Piano." Argo blithely labels and lists it on the back cover as "Excursions." Only a passing remark in the liner notes notifies that the work is for piano duet. Further, the identity of Musgrave's partner is guesswork. It is either Richard Rodney Bennett or Malcolm Williamson, the other performers in the six-work collection Argo has released with the description *Composers at the Piano*. Finally, in a descriptive suite especially, it should be possible to pick out any single piece in the group. Without separative spirals it means guess and hunt among the grooves. Annoyance turns off desire in such instances.

Chamber Concerto No. 2 (1966)

☐ Boston Musica Viva / Pittman (conductor) / Delos 25405

There is an *entente* in Musgrave's composition between abstract shapes and Ivesian-like interjections and overlays. Such a stylistic link carries over to the timbre enlargement of the basic performing forces, with the five players utilizing a total of nine instruments.

Expectedly, the syntax for music of this type relies on chromatic formations. However, reliance on shifting pitch phrases is no drawback. One admires the constant invention that results in a significant spontaneity that holds the interest. Musgrave states the piece is "in homage to Charles Ives," but the Ivesian echos one hears are sensitively and individually originated and most of the credit rightfully belongs to Musgrave rather than Ives.

And, full credit must go to the members of the Boston Musica Viva group: Paul Brittan (flute, alto flute, and piccolo); William Wrzesien (clarinet and bass clarinet); Nancy Cirillo (violin and viola); Jay Humeston (cello); and Evelyn Zuckerman (piano). Their solid performance matches the composer's solid craftsmanship.

Modest Mussorgsky   (1839-1881)

Intermezzo in B minor (1867)

☐ Munich Philharmonic Orchestra / Andreae (conductor) / BASF BC–22128

This is a work that Rimsky-Korsakov rescored after Mussorgsky's death. The title given here is "Intermezzo symphonique in Modo Classico" (see also under *Instrumental: piano* [Two Piano Pieces]), whereas the published score (by Bessel) is titled as noted above. Whatever the cognomen, it has more than academic, historic interest.

Introduction and *Hopak* from *The Fair at Sorochinsk* (1877)

☐ Bolshoi Theatre Orchestra / Nebolsin (conductor) / Monitor 2038 (monaural)

Mussorgsky never finished his opera based on Gogol's tale. (Eventually it was completed by César Cui and first performed in St. Petersburg on October 26, 1917.) The Introduction was edited from sketches and then orchestrated by Anatoly Liadov, who also orchestrated the Hopak. Both pieces are Russian to the core.

The Soviet musicians perform with appropriate knowledge of the style involved.

Introduction to *Khovanshchina*

☐ Berlin Philharmonic Orchestra / Solti (conductor) / London 6944

The character and atmosphere are of the finest, and the rendition is extremely sensitive to the style. Lush projection of this beautiful exposition of a dawn scene is to be avoided as a falsification. Trust Solti.

A Night on the Bald Mountain (1866)

☐ Berlin Philharmonic Orchestra / Solti (conductor) / London 6944
☐ L'Orchestre de la Suisse Romande / Kletzki (conductor) / London 6622
☐ London Symphony Orchestra / Stokowski (conductor) / London 21110

Mussorgsky's *A Night on the Bald Mountain,* or *A Night on Bald Mountain* (the English prefer the title "Night on the Bare Mountain"), was published posthumously after being edited, arranged, and reorchestrated by Rimsky-Korsakov. It is this long-standard edition that Solti and Kletzki use. Stokowski's performance is based on his own editing and is perfectly responsible. His response to this music of febricity is typical Stoky, and the ending is accomplished better than anyone in the business. The call number noted above covers an all-Mussorgsky disc. On London 21026 the "Bald Mountain" is coupled with Tchaikovsky and Stravinsky.

The snap, crackle, and color in the Solti-led performance is tops in the catalogue. The tempi shifts, the dynamic variegation, and above all, the beautiful control of the brass in his conception are deserving of a recording Oscar. Kletzki's version is highly recommended because he does not mistake brilliance to mean brass overkill; the balances are superb and the playing likewise.

Persian Dance from *Khovanshchina*

☐ Berlin Philharmonic Orchestra / Solti (conductor) / London 6944

Well-knit edition with full commitment to the creative details. (Mussorgsky's piece is often listed as "Dance of the Persian Slaves," thus describing the characters that perform the dance in the opera.)

Scherzo in B flat major (1858)

☐ Munich Philharmonic Orchestra / Andreae (conductor) / BASF BC-22128

Mussorgsky composed the Scherzo for piano in 1858. In the period 1882–1884 Rimsky-Korsakov orchestrated the work for double winds, two horns, two trumpets, three trombones, timpani, and strings. A standard item.

Turkish March in A flat major (1880)

☐ Munich Philharmonic Orchestra / Andreae (conductor) / BASF BC-22128

Bessel issued the published score of this work in 1883 with the title *Marche turque*, so-named because of its *alla turca* trio. Here again, as is so often the case with Mussorgsky, the orchestration was made by Rimsky-Korsakov.

On the recording the titling is quite different: "The Capture of Kars: Ceremonial March." According to Oskar von Riesemann, the trio section was intended as an accompaniment to a tableau vivant, *The Capture of Kars*, as "part of a projected gala performance to celebrate Alexander II's twenty-five years of reign." Whatever name is used, the March is a good example of the genre and there is no doubting the nationalistic flavor of both the principal section and the contrastive trio.

Au Village **(1880)**   *In the Crimea* **(1880)**   *Instrumental*
Gopak   *La Couturière* **(1880)**
Impressions of the Crimea **(1879)** *Meditation* **(1880)**   *Piano*
Impromptu passionné **(1859)**

☐ Krieger (piano) / Musical Heritage Society MHS–1130

Aside from the richly important *Pictures at an Exhibition* (*see below*), only the duple-pulsed *Gopak* dance is well-known. But apart from historical interest, Mussorgsky's piano miniatures contain sufficient musical values for occasional exposure. *Au Village* has a folksy quality; the *Impromptu* is altogether different, with Schumannesque outlines. Orientalisms spice the Crimean items; "The Dressmaker" (*La Couturière*) is a parallel to Mendelssohn's Spinning Song.

Pictures at an Exhibition (1874)

☐ Richter (piano) / Odyssey Y–32223 (monaural)
☐ Ashkenazy (piano) / London 6559

There is not much to choose from but what there is is very choice. Richter's playing is that of a re-creative genius. And it doesn't matter one whit that it is a monaural edition. Ashkenazy's is a very close second; the only defect concerns some phrasings that do not ring true or match the score objective.

(For orchestral transcriptions of this piece, see under *Mussorgsky/Ravel: Orchestra* and *Mussorgsky/Toushmalov: Orchestra*.)

Scherzo (1858)

Souvenirs d'enfance

☐ Krieger (piano) / Musical Heritage Society MHS–1130

The Scherzo (in C sharp minor) was intended for orchestra. Mussorgsky never scored it, though an orchestration exists made in 1917 by Vladimir Senilov (1875–1918). The "Childhood Recollections" are three in number: *Nurse and I; First Punishment: Nurse Locks Me in a Dark Closet;* and *Souvenir d'enfance*. The last has the specialness of being the earliest existing piano piece Mussorgsky wrote. (A *Porte-Enseigne* Polka, composed five years earlier, was lost.)

Two Piano Pieces

☐ Previn (piano) / Columbia Special Products CMS–6586

Keen depictions by any critical measurement.

Previn's title derives from the edition published by Belaiev. The first work (composed in 1859) is noted as *A Child's Joke*, the translation of *Ein Kinderscherz*. Mussorgsky's *scherz* is subtitled "Children's Games: Puss in the Corner." The second piece (written in 1867) bears the compressed title Intermezzo. Fully this should read *Intermezzo in Modo Classico* (see also under *Orchestra* [Intermezzo in B minor]). This was later transcribed for orchestra by Mussorgsky and still later totally rescored by Rimsky-Korsakov.

The *Intermezzo in Modo Classico* is also included in the album of Mussorgsky's piano music discussed *above* (see under *Au Village* and Scherzo) and *below* (see under *Une Larme*), performed by Günther Krieger. The tempo contrasts between Previn (4:46) and Krieger (7:25) tell the whole story. Such shocking differential puts the latter in the poorest light, though it is true that Previn tends to push forward just a bit.

Une Larme (1880)

Une Plaisanterie (1859)

☐ Krieger (piano) / Musical Heritage Society MHS-1130

Krieger's use of *rubato* makes "A Tear" palatable. The other title is indicated as it appears on the record sleeve. On the record label the proper designation is noted: *Ein Kinderscherz*. If one wishes this sprightly bit then by all means choose André Previn's far superior rendition (*see above* [Two Piano Pieces]).

Vocal

Voice with Accompaniment

The Nursery (1872)

☐ Dorlyak (soprano); Richter (piano) / Monitor 2020 (monaural)

Sung with a graciousness and a charm that validate the seven parts of Mussorgsky's cycle. Dorlyak's voice is light but is used with excellent sensibility. The piano part is colored beautifully, as one would expect from an artist of Sviatoslav Richter's stature. But though this is Richter (the soprano's husband), there is no taking over the No. 1 slot. His playing is pitched at a level of equality that provides further proof of his musicianship. A rare treat, this performance, with dimensions that always convince.

Songs and Dances of Death (1877)

☐ Arkhipova (mezzo-soprano); Wustman (piano) / Melodiya/Angel S-40198

An impressive portrayal. Irina Arkhipova's voice has a dark quality that matches the expressivity and content of this four-part song cycle. The delivery is not overrobust but sufficiently dramatic.

Opera and Dramatic Music

Boris Godunov

☐ Vienna Philharmonic Orchestra, Vienna State Opera Chorus, Vienna Boys Choir, and Sofia Radio Chorus / Vishnevskaya and Dobrianowa (sopranos); Miljakovic, Cvejic, and Lilowa (mezzo-sopranos); Maslennikov, Prelćeć, Spiess, and Paunov (tenors); Ghiaurov, Markov, Radev, Heppe, Talvela, Diakov, Kélémen, Frese, and Karolidis (basses) / von Karajan (conductor) / London 1439

This is the version edited by Rimsky-Korsakov, including the editing by Ippolitov-Ivanov of the first scene in the fourth act. Its performance is truly magnificent. Von Karajan's taste in defining the score's sonorous configurations is of impeccable taste, and both the orchestra and choruses are heard with opulent richness.

Nicolai Ghiaurov is splendid as Boris, his singing in the Death Scene unforgettable and hardly to be surpassed by George London's portrayal (on Columbia M4S-696). Boris Christoff (on Angel S-3633) is undeniably a stronger-voiced Boris Godunov and he has the role in his hip pocket. (Christoff was once hailed as the heir to the great Chaliapin.) But

Cluytens's orchestra in the Angel release cannot match the perspective that the Vienna outfit gives to this great opera, and in general the surrounding cast is stronger in London's edition. If there is any weakness in the last it is in the Coronation Scene which lacks sufficient display.

(Shostakovich's edition of the Mussorgsky opera is available on Telefunken AS-641290 on an import basis.)

Mussorgsky / Maurice Ravel (1875-1937)

Pictures at an Exhibition (1922)   Orchestra

☐ Philadelphia Orchestra / Ormandy (conductor) / Columbia MS-7148
☐ Berlin Philharmonic Orchestra / von Karajan (conductor) / Deutsche Grammophon 13910

Ormandy's fine sense of sonority discharges not only the usual obligations in this case but adds a sheen that demands a listener's special commendation. This is a performance with an amazingly wide range of expression and all the vitality (save overvitality for the tempo of *Bydlo*) to make dynamically clear Mussorgsky's musical canvases. The Philly brass sing beautifully.

The Berliners display similar virtues, though, indeed, their sound is different from the Philadelphians. A clever use of playing each *Promenade* at a slightly reduced tempo adds to the relish of the contrastive pace for each of the pictures.

Ormandy's version is also available on Columbia M–30448 and M–31826. He recorded the work later for RCA, and there are two different packages for his performance on that label (ARL1–0451 and CRL3–0984), but the Columbia edition is superfine and there is no advantage in opting for the RCA issue. Von Karajan also published this work for Angel (S–35430), but it offers no better returns and, in fact, somewhat lesser ones in terms of the engineering.

Among the many other products available some are certainly worthwhile and deserve consideration. A few have basic faults and it would be best to discount them. Thus: a rather academic bit of playing with Ansermet on the podium (London 6177), fine playing but fuzzy sound with Reiner at the helm (RCA LSC-2201), and the terribly mannered Stokowski. He does it both ways: Ravel's setting on London 2110 and his own transcription (which was aided in great part by Lucien Cailliet) on London 21006. One other entry falls into this thumbs-down list: Edo de Waart. His intentions are honorable but his tempi are not, as can be heard on Philips 6500882.

(For Mussorgsky's original piano setting of this work, see under *Mussorgsky: Instrumental: piano*.)

Mussorgsky / Mikhail Toushmalov (19th cent.)

Pictures at an Exhibition   Orchestra

☐ Munich Philharmonic Orchestra / Andreae (conductor) / BASF BC-22128

A performance included because of the special identity of its transcriber, rather than for its quality. It will be noted that the arrangement is not by Casella, Cailliet, Leonardi, Stokowski, Szell, Wood, or any of the several others who have transcribed the piece, including *the* version by Maurice Ravel (see under *Mussorgsky/Ravel: Orchestra*). It is by a totally unknown musician, whose orchestral translation was first heard in St. Petersburg in 1891. Despite the credit given on this release to Rimsky-Korsakov, indicating that he helped in the transcription, his role in the matter is sheer guesswork; there is no proof whatsoever that Rimsky had any hand in the matter.

Counting all the *Promenades,* there are fourteen divisions in Mussorgsky's *Pictures.* Toushmalov's realization begins with a *Promenade* and continues with seven of the movements. Eliminated are the additional *Promenade* sections, *Gnomus, Tuileries,* and *Bydlo.*

The recording is worth having as comparative documentation. It is a fair enough performance, and certainly full of the necessary sonorous impact.

(The writer is well acquainted with this first orchestral transcription of Mussorgsky's work, having conducted the initial American performance in the 1930s. It is interesting to note that the score—published by Bessel—makes certain to define that it is a "Suite" *from* the *Tableaux d'une Exposition.*

(For Mussorgsky's original piano setting of this work, see under *Mussorgsky: Instrumental: piano.)*

Robert Myers (1941-   )

Percussion

Percussion Piece

☐ University of Michigan Percussion Ensemble / Owen (conductor) / Golden Crest CRS-4145

Modest and well-crafted without attempting to simulate pitch patterns by choosing from the registral differences of the instruments involved (timpani, tom-toms, snare, field, and bass drums, triangle, gong, ratchet, and cymbals). Myers does not only use rhythmic facts to relate his six-minute piece. The images are equally derived from varying textural weights.

Charles Owen's group is excellent; it plays with spirit and with attention to balances.

Fredric Myrow (1939-   )

Vocal

Voice and Instrumental Ensemble

Songs from the Japanese (1965)

☐ Contemporary Chamber Ensemble / Bryn-Julson (soprano) / Weisberg (conductor) / Nonesuch 71219

These are no pseudo-Orientalistic imitations that adorn film and television scores. The creative strategy here is delicacy, a once-over-lightly brushworked collation of sounds that fascinate the ear and prove again that less is more. The instrumental formulation (flute and alto flute, clarinet and bass clarinet, violin, viola, cello, double bass, piano, harpsichord, and percussion) not only reveal relations in the vocal line but lightly massage as well as frame it.

The vocal demands are prodigious, but Phyllis Bryn-Julson is a total achiever and never at the expense of true music-making or quality. Weisberg's group includes some of the best musicians in the business (Arthur Bloom, clarinetist; Paul Zukofsky, violinist; Jacob Glick, violist; and the pianist, Gilbert Kalish, for example), so that the instrumental particulars are defined with the highest standards.

N

François Joseph Nadermann (1781-1835)

Sonatina, Op. 92, No. 2

Instrumental

☐ Jamet (harp) / Nonesuch 71098

Harp

Two movements, of which the second, a Toccata, is delicately touch-and-go. Nadermann's concentrated and most enjoyable piece is the second of a group of seven Progressive Sonatas.

The gleaming transparency of Marie-Claire Jamet's playing passes the severest critical test. Further, her singing tone is rare in the harpists' fraternity (or sorority).

Robert Nagel (1924-   )

March

Instrumental

☐ Swallow (trombone); Wingreen (piano) / Golden Crest 7015 (monaural)

Trombone

High marks for enunciation and trombone tonal freshness pertain to John Swallow's playing. The March is a movement from a suite for solo brass instruments accompanied by piano.

Conlon Nancarrow (1912-   )

Study for Player Piano

Instrumental

No. 1 / No. 27 / No. 36

Player Piano

☐ New World Records NW-203

Examples of composition achieved by the perforation of player-piano rolls. The intricacies of polymetrical designs and simultaneous tempi thus made mechanically available are unlimited, mechanically perfect, and totally beyond human performance even if it were possible to be duplicated in musical notation. Naturally, creation and locked-in permanent performance are thereby simultaneously accomplished.

Though somewhat dynamically static, these are fascinating inventions. The varied tempi curvatures in canonic layering in Study No. 27 highlight the set.

Eduard Napravnik (1839-1916)

Orchestra
Festive March

☐ Louisville Orchestra / Mester (conductor) / Louisville 734

Mostly Old Russian-styled pomp and circumstance. Damn good for what it wishes to accomplish.

Pietro Nardini (1722-1793)

Chamber Music
Sonata No. 1 in B flat major

☐ Luca (violin); Richman (harpsichord); Bogatin (cello) / Nonesuch 71361

Fine spirited music, with plentiful embroideries twirled around the pitch arrangement, and further ornamented by Luca in a telling and knowing manner.

String Quartet in E flat major

☐ Schäffer Quartet / Vox SVBX–5300

This is one of the six string quartets Nardini produced. Interestingly, the total of six is a constant in his output. His Opus 1 comprises six violin concertos; Opus 2 includes six sonatas for violin and bass; also numbered Opus 2 are six sonatas for two violins; and Opus 5 identifies six violin solos. In addition there are six flute trios and six *Duos pour deux violons.*

Only two movements in the quartet are recorded, the second shaped like a Minuet. They show constructive balance and far from first-violin dominance, with an especially goodly number of passages for the cello as the lead voice.

The work is in a three-disc album that Vox has titled *The Early String Quartet.* It contains fourteen works by as many composers. In the Nardini, the Schäffer team exhibits its very best playing, with intelligent exposition of the music's contents, compelling balance, and a warm sound.

Jean Jacques Naudot (?-1762)

Chamber Music
Sonata in B minor for Two Flutes

☐ Rampal and Duschenes (flutes) / Everest 3299

No reason for Everest not mentioning Mario Duschenes's name anywhere in connection with this performance. He is a perfect partner for the famous Rampal.

Not a remarkable piece of work by this eighteenth-century French flutist-composer, but certainly no less professional than that of the average composer of the same period.

Johann Gottlieb Naumann (1741-1801)

Orchestra
Ballet Excerpts from *Gustaf Wasa*

☐ Chamber Orchestra of the Drottningholm Theater / Björlin (conductor) / Nonesuch 71213

Nothing fancy, nothing swift paced in these two excerpts from Naumann's work which stayed in the Swedish operatic repertory for a considerable period of time after its premiere in January 1786. Instead there is a moving *Pas de deux* and a gentle-coursed *Pas de quatre*.

Both musical and performance substances are beautiful. So is the flute playing in the *Pas de quatre*.

Quartet in C major for Glass Harmonica, Flute, Viola, and Cello

Chamber Music

☐ Hoffmann (glass harmonica); Ulrich (flute); Nippes (viola); Plumacher (cello) / Turnabout 34452

Naumann's four-instrument work is in two-part form; an Andante and a Grazioso. Simplicity rules; the greatest interest is found, naturally, in the timbre of the glass instrument.

(The performance is also duplicated in a collection issued by Candide—No. 31007.)

Siegfried Naumann (1919-)

Risposte **No. 1 for Flute and Percussion (1963)**

Chamber Music

☐ Christiansson (flute, alto flute, and piccolo); Liljequist (percussion) / Caprice CAP-1034

There are subtle changes of timbre in the wind-instrument part of this duo (it will be noted that three different flute types are used), matched by fluid color change in the percussion. The latter includes a novel instrument, a jar filled with crushed glass, which is stirred with a stick. The quality of the music is improvisational, the effect one of finesse despite the dynamically intensive dialogue, beautifully defined by the two performers.

(Though not on the disc's liner information, *Risposte* ("Answers") is Naumann's Opus 6.)

Manuel Blasco de Nebra (ca. 1750-ca. 1784)

Sonata

Instrumental

No. 5 in F sharp minor / No. 6 in E major

Harpsichord

☐ Kipnis (harpsichord) / Columbia M3X–31521

A pair of rarities by a composer that won't be found listed in the usual music dictionaries. Each piece is in two movements, with an Adagio followed by a Presto. The former has aria testimony laced with fantasia demeanor. The latter blends Scarlatti with Soler. All very stimulating and certainly of individual cast.

Kipnis's recording is a premiere (if one doesn't count that it was originally issued by Epic on their BC–1374 and that Columbia's is a transfer into a new packaging that combines other Epic releases that Kipnis made). It represents fascinating playing.

Vaclav Nelhybel (1919-)

Etude symphonique (1949)

Orchestra

☐ Utah Symphony Orchestra / Abravanel (conductor) / Turnabout 34459

In this piece the orchestrational virtuosity knocks one in the aisles. (Keep ears open for a lusty, glissando-formation coda and, earlier in the work, for a section abounding in dynamic pizzicati.) All demands are met by the Utah group which plays superbly and shows its class. Yes, Nelhybel's work is derivative, and a footnote of thanks is due Stravinsky. Nonetheless, there is plentiful invention in addition, and the listener's interest will not languish. The Etude also contains one of the most exciting Fugues I've ever encountered.

Two Movements for Chamber Orchestra

☐ Members of Orchestra Sinfonica di Roma / Flagello (conductor) / Serenus 12007

Though styles shift in the two movements—chromatic and polymodal in the Adagio, *scherzo*ish and fugal in the other—the music hangs together by the use of rhythmic glue, i.e., ostinato. No reflection on the merit of the work as entertainment, though it is not a music for stylistic specialists. A robust performance throughout.

String Orchestra

Three Movements for Strings

☐ Members of Orchestra Sinfonica di Roma / Flagello (conductor) / Serenus 12007

Modal implications in the fugally shaped Ricercar. A pair of dances follow, the second an *Estampie*. The first of these is Bartókian with a clean shave on its countenance. Nelhybel's music is played rather neutrally and can take much more *brio* and subtlety.

Band

Slavic March

☐ Members of Orchestra Sinfonica di Roma / Flagello (conductor) / Serenus 12006

Short, sweet, and succinctly Slavic. However, while it is played by "members" of an "orchestra," it is strictly band scored. And no points for Serenus in not listing a solitary line of information as to the medium involved or anything about the work. Strictly a filler, yes, but not deserving of such production shortcoming.

Three Intradas for Brass

☐ Members of Orchestra Sinfonica di Roma / Flagello (conductor) / Serenus 12006

The guardian angel here is constant polyphony but it is never of the heavy-handed kind. Chunky brass sounds. However, deftly providing linear crisscrossing.

Probably recorded in one take, since some of the doubling of the lower instruments is a bit fuzzy.

Solo Instrument and Orchestra

Piano

Concertino for Chamber Orchestra and Piano (1949)

☐ Members of Orchestra Sinfonica di Roma / Flagello (conductor) / Serenus 12007

Rhythmically informative and always entertaining, the Concertino has moods of fantasy and rhapsodic change, with some jazzy turns being turned into the sounds as well. The piano, it will be noted, is not given top billing in the composition's title. Its role is not the pearly passions of soloism but strictly those of obbligato purpose. (Some catalogue listings title Nelhybel's work as a "Concertino for Piano and Chamber Orchestra," but it is incorrect to do so.)

No credit for the pianist. No notes about the work, just its timing. For the reader's information, it is 7:40.

Suite for Trombone and Piano

☐ McDunn (trombone); Eby (piano) / Golden Crest S-4091

Five musical snapshots covering a variety of moods. No riddles proposed. Made for easy listening and appreciation of fine trombone playing on the part of Mark McDunn.

Arco and Pizzicato

Three Miniatures for Three Strings

☐ Phoenix String Trio / Serenus 12062

Compared in timbre, tempo, and style, *Arco and Pizzicato* are engaging short essays. Slow and faster speeds, tight linear and dance considerations are two of the three contrastive factors. Oddly enough, Nelhybel inserts a bit of plucked sound into the *Arco* score. It does slightly spoil the clear compartmentalization that otherwise exists in the paired pieces.

The Three Miniatures are reminders of Nelhybel's orchestra blockbuster, *Etude symphonique*. The composer's itch for color is thereby further revealed.

Trio for Brass (1961)

☐ Members of Orchestra Sinfonica di Roma / Flagello (conductor) / Serenus 12006

The usual instrumentation: horn, trumpet, and trombone. The usual brass behavior patterns: bantering first movement, conversation-like bits in the Andante, and a set of variations. A nice pleasantry expertly conceived and played. (Flagello is credited as directing the matter. So be it, but did he actually conduct three brass players?)

Brass Piano Quartet (1959)

☐ Members of Orchestra Sinfonica di Roma / Flagello (conductor) / Serenus 12006

The instrumentation is for the usual brass trio (horn, trumpet, and trombone) with piano. (The above title is used on Serenus's release. Elsewhere, the writer has noted the title as being "Quartet for Piano and 3 Brass Instruments.") The music is not in Nelhybel's usual hedonistic style, but somewhat expressionistically conceived. No harmonic audacities but open polyphonic sport that creates interesting webs as the instruments cross and respond to one another. More than a trace or two of Hindemith colors the finale (an *Allegro vivo*). Well-detailed playing.

Quartet for Horns (1957)

☐ Members of Orchestra Sinfonica di Roma / Flagello (conductor) / Serenus 12007

Nelhybel's Quartet is matched by a quartet of movements: *Intrada, Danza,* Arioso, and Scherzando. The second of these doesn't drive fast and has scalic steps. A romantic, dreamy, textural close-fit marks the Arioso.

Horn quartets are no longer esoteric, and a fair number are available for hornists to play. Listeners can share in sampling the musical merchandise.

Impromptus for Six Woodwinds (1963)

☐ Members of Orchestra Sinfonica di Roma / Flagello (conductor) / Serenus 12006

Light and balletic (waltz meters are important). Nelhybel can certainly spin melodies. In this regard he can be termed the American Ibert, matching the Frenchman's style with this delightful nonphilosophical music. Once this piece gets around, every wind society will schedule it. Save for an expert but sometimes cramped-sounding oboist, it is played with vitality. But why a conductor for uninvolved music?

Vocal

Voice with Accompaniment

Four Readings from Marlowe's Doctor Faustus

☐ D'Armand (bass-baritone); Tanner (piano) / Serenus 12049

The affirmative diction of John B. D'Armand makes potently clear all the dialogue that is sung. There are no expansive arias as such but a continuity of conversation with a varying vocal quality to achieve the differences. The piano reduction of the full orchestral score is fairly adequate, but for a work of this type and length instrumental color is a necessity.

Voice and Instrumental Ensemble

The House That Jack Built

☐ Members of the Ariel Quintet / Reardon (baritone); Spiegelman (harpsichord); Venuto (percussion) / Heller (conductor) / Serenus 12050

A real delight with a tremendous assist from John Reardon, whose richly pliant declarative singing and absolutely perfect enunciation deserve rave notices. The instrumentation is choice, particularly the harpsichord sprinkle and the deft percussive inserts. The conductor, Marsha Heller, is the "missing" member of the Ariel group, the others (flute, clarinet, bassoon, and horn) participating.

Ron Nelson   (1929-   )

Orchestra

Sarabande: For Katherine in April (1954)

☐ Eastman-Rochester Symphony Orchestra / Hanson (conductor) / Eastman-Rochester Archives ERA–1003

A lush bit, but always in good taste. What's good is worth repeating, so Nelson made use of this piece in his opera *The Birthday of the Infanta*. There are very strong reminders in the *Sarabande* of Howard Hanson's style (one of Nelson's teachers).

Savannah River Holiday (1957)

☐ Eastman-Rochester Symphony Orchestra / Hanson (conductor) / Eastman-Rochester Archives ERA–1012

The "ground bass" of Nelson's piece is drive and pep, outdoorish tonal tunes, and block scoring. Clear departmentalization of large three-part form. Splendid extroverted definition by Hanson and his orchestra. Enjoy!

(Nelson's work has obtained such success that the publisher has issued a band version.)

Pomponio Nenna   (ca. 1550-ca. 1618)

Choral

Chorus Alone

Ahi, dispietata e cruda	L'amoroso veleno
Asciugate i begli occhi	Lasso, ch'io moro
Deh! scoprite il ben seno	Mercè, grido piangendo
Ecco, O dolce	Signora, io penso

Ecco, O mia dolce pena	*S'io taccio*
In monte Oliveti	*Tenebrae factae sunt*
La mia doglia s'avanza	*Tristis est anima mea*

☐ Accademia Monteverdiana, Trinity Boys Choir, Croydon, and Accademia Chorus / Stevens (conductor) / Nonesuch 71277

These madrigals and motets are drawn from six of the eight volumes of madrigals produced by this composer. They include one *Villanella a 3* (*Signora, io penso*) and three examples of a *Responsory a 5* (*In monte Oliveti* plus the two last titles noted).

There is a heartiness to Nenna's music; less so, of course, in regard to the motets. The singing is appealing, the sonorities refined and somewhat contained but nonetheless sweetly impressive. Substantial results from the direction of Denis Stevens who wrote the fine liner notes together with Glenn Watkins. (The latter is credited with transcribing and editing the music.)

Ricercare a 2 for Treble and Alto Viols

Chamber Music

☐ Francis Baines (treble viol); Elizabeth Baines (alto viol) / Nonesuch 71277

A three-minute bit of simple two-voice counterpoint. On the academic side.

Alberto Nepomuceno   *(1864-1920)*

Quartet No. 3 in D minor, *Brasileiro*

Chamber Music

☐ Brazilian String Quartet / Odyssey 32160176

The only recorded example of this Brazilian's music. It therefore serves as important historical documentation.

In its early stages, Brazilian music kept pace with European musical affairs. Not until the latter part of the nineteenth century did any Brazilian nationalism manifest itself. Nepomuceno (with Henrique Oswald) was the leader in this respect. However, the D minor quartet has only a smidgen of Brazilian turn of tune in it—found in the motival impetus of the slow movement.

Well played, even though a lighter approach might have been in order.

Franz Christoph Neubauer   *(1750-1795)*

Sinfonie (*La Bataille*), Op. 11

Orchestra

☐ Angelicum Orchestra of Milan / Jenkins (conductor) / Nonesuch 71146

Neubauer's battle starts slowly with the calm of the morning, reveille, followed by a speech to the troops (via a bassoon solo) and then picks up steam (tempo-wise) describing the battle which is far from bloody music-wise. The victory is celebrated by a *contredance*.

The events are a bit more colorful than the music attached to them. But it's a bit different from the average eighteenth-century conception and is pleasant enough. Newell Jenkins (who edited the piece) plays it straight and that's sufficient.

Robert M. Newell   (1940-   )

Choral

Chorus and Instrumental Ensemble

Ryo-nen

☐ Ineluctable Modality / Fonville (flute and bottle); London (percussion) / London (conductor) / Advance FGR-18S

All-pervasive orchestrational treatment of a chorus, mixed in with taped sounds, a flute, and some percussion in a montage of singing, speaking, sonorous scattering, and vocal streaming. That the English-set text used as a splintered springboard for this is by a Buddhist nun is a mere statistic. The abstract distillation is the important matter.

Dika Newlin   (1923-   )

Chamber Music

Piano Trio, Op. 2

☐ London Czech Trio / Composers Recordings 170 (monaural)

Newlin's opus is cast in one movement, holding hands with classical formality while kicking it to the side at the same time. The paradox is explained by the triple-ply exposition, with developments equaling the Scherzo and slow movements; the recapitulation reaching back only partly into earlier material. The music soaks in a full dodecaphonic bath, with little perfume or bubbly colors.

Otto Nicolai   (1810-1849)

Orchestra

Overture to *The Merry Wives of Windsor*

☐ New York Philharmonic / Bernstein (conductor) / Columbia MS-7085

Played as it should be, with a deft and quicksilver quality, and in a proper, agile tempo. (Bernstein's reading is almost a minute faster than the competing issues.)

This performance is also available in two- and three-record albums consisting of varied assortments on Columbia M2X-795 and D3S-818, respectively.

Opera and Dramatic Music

The Merry Wives of Windsor

☐ Bavarian Symphony Orchestra and Chorus of the Bavarian Radio / Donath and Sukis (sopranos); Schmidt (mezzo-soprano); Ahnsjö and Zednick (tenors); Brendel (baritone); Ridderbusch, Malta, and Sramek (basses) / Kubelik (conductor) / London OSA-13127

Die Lustigen Weiber von Windsor enjoys smooth sailing and production finesse in this recorded production. There are no cuts and only a minimum of spoken dialogue (in German). Whatever is not there will not be missed.

The female singers, especially Helen Donath as Frau Fluth, cover their roles quite well. Lillian Sukis, as Anna Reich, isn't above some vocal posturing that one could well do without. Karl Ridderbusch, as Sir John Falstaff, musters fine warmth and sprightliness. The orchestra is first class and provides unflawed pleasure. However, the star of this show is the conductor. The comprehension and conviction Rafael Kubelik displays are ideal. It is that finding that makes this issue to be favored over the one produced by Deutsche Grammophon (2740159). Another minus for that edition is the use of a narrator to link the scenes. Quite annoying.

Carl Nielsen *(1865 - 1931)*

Saga-Drøm, Op. 39 *Orchestra*

☐ New Philharmonia Orchestra / Horenstein (conductor) / Nonesuch 71236

Despite the detail in the old Icelandic legend on which *Saga-Drøm* (''Saga-Dream'') is based, Nielsen's score simply wends its way unceasingly in a pleasant pastoral fashion. There are no program music procedures per se. For example, important to the tale are attacks by wolves but Nielsen has eliminated them from his conception. As Richard Freed states: ''The dreamy quality is there, but the wolf-infested nightmare is not.''

But the gentle flow of the music with special scoring attention to the woodwinds is compelling. So are the Sibelius-like style and the poetical performance directed by Jascha Horenstein.

(Nielsen's work is also listed under the title *En Sagadrøm*.)

Symphony No. 2, *The Four Temperaments*, Op. 16

☐ New York Philharmonic / Bernstein (conductor) / Columbia M-32779

Faced with movements of a Symphony titled The Choleric, The Phlegmatic, The Melancholic, and The Sanguine (and all these emphasized by the tempi indications the composer placed in his score: *Allegro collerico, Allegro comodo flemmatico, Andante malincolico,* and *Allegro sanguinicu*), a conductor might be tempted to overexploit matters. To Bernstein's credit, he does not. The Symphony is given a rich, romantic patina of sound and the profiles are all clear with no false wrinkles.

One might give some consideration to the Turnabout (34049) edition. The Tivoli Concert Hall Symphony Orchestra is a surprisingly good organization, and Carl Garaguly, its conductor, comes off quite well in this entry. Aside from an unphlegmatic tempo in movement two, everything is quite convincing.

Symphony No. 3 (*Sinfonia Espansiva*), Op. 27

☐ Royal Danish Orchestra / Guldbaek (soprano); Møller (tenor) / Bernstein (conductor) / Columbia MS-6769

Bernstein's reading establishes a communication with Nielsen's work as it has never previously enjoyed on records. What clues this performance into one of transcendent fusion are the tempi. A true expansive consideration is given the first movement (marked *Allegro espansivo,* hence the subtitle of the work), the pastoral second movement sings and exults with its vocalise duetting in the concluding part, and the Scherzo is held in check so that all of its dark views are thus emphasized. Further, the finale is not treated as a down-the-road music, but with (again) an expansivity of heroic declaration that powers the work to a remarkable close.

Maybe not the definitive word on the work but exceedingly close to it.

Symphony No. 4, *The Inextinguishable*, Op. 29

☐ Royal Danish Orchestra / Markevitch (conductor) / Turnabout 34050

There are some that find a welter of stylistic events in this man's music. No one argues the Mahler and Sibelian insinuations in the score, but the integration of these by his own critical and selective process makes Nielsen very much his own man and the Symphony very much one of his greatest works.

No germinal credits, or very few are found in Mehta's performance (London 6848). Bernstein's (on Columbia M-30293) is infinitely better but Lenny tampers, and while it doesn't do the music much harm it doesn't do it any good either. It is Markevitch who sweeps through this symphonic document (in one large movement, close to thirty-three minutes) triumphantly. The balances are superb, the moods defined with articulate imagination, and no matter the intense sound there is never roughness or overtimbred orchestral weight.

Symphony No. 5, Op. 50

☐ New York Philharmonic / Drucker (clarinet); Bailey (snare drum) / Bernstein (conductor) / Columbia MS–6414

The powerful continuity Bernstein brings to this work makes his the preferable version. Horenstein (Nonesuch 71236) tends to sectionalize the music, even though within divisions there is fine power and a coloration that comes close to the way Bernstein timbreizes his conception. Kletzki's edition (London 6699) is in third place because his players cannot match the Philharmonic team.

(See also under *Solo Instrument and Orchestra: clarinet*.)

Symphony No. 6 (*Sinfonia Semplice*) (1925)

☐ Westchester Symphony Orchestra / Landau (conductor) / Turnabout 34182

Everything is relative but to consider this Symphony as one of simplicity just doesn't fit. The sound-stuff is easily ascertained: emancipative tonalism with good doses of dissonance, but the contents with its inner motility (as well as the more easily recognizable outward type) needs an orchestra that can conquer the harmonic disturbances and untraditional combinations within the score. The Westchester outfit play the notes competently and Siegfried Landau does fairly well, but it isn't just well enough. Principally, there is an inlay of tension in the piece that doesn't come across. However, it's a fine piece and with just this single recording one must take what one can get.

Solo Instrument and Orchestra

Clarinet

Concerto for Clarinet and Orchestra, Op. 57

☐ New York Philharmonic / Drucker (clarinet) / Bernstein (conductor) / Columbia MS–7028

A single-movement Concerto, its concentration applied to the fundamental exploitation of a basic theme that is, to quote from the splendid liner note of Charles B. Yulish, "subsequently torn apart, reworked, restated and again shredded, and finally changed into something quite malevolent." It is the last phrase that describes the core quality of this highly individual Concerto—undoubtedly the most important written for the instrument since Mozart's great contribution. A raucous tone (not Drucker's) filters through the music, partnered with a barbaric and violent undertone. Nielsen's Concerto is nervous, uneasy—its vital lines are never suave, its figures are never of virtuosic slickness (though it demands a virtuoso performer, which describes the soloist, Stanley Drucker).

The performance is magnificent. Bernstein knowingly not only accompanies but enters the concerto arena and rightfully competes with the solo voice. Credit must also be given the unnamed snare drum performer who does full justice to the important part for the instrument, similar to its quasi-soloistic role in Nielsen's Symphony No. 5. (Oddly enough, Columbia does give credit to the snare drummer in its issue of that work: see under *Orchestra*.)

Concerto for Flute and Orchestra (1926)
Flute

☐ New York Philharmonic / Baker (flute) / Bernstein (conductor) / Columbia MS-7028

The rhapsodic coil and recoil that mark Nielsen's music are present in his two-movement Concerto for Flute and Orchestra. (The first movement is an *Allegro moderato;* the second movement begins Allegretto, has an Adagio within it, and concludes with a *Tempo di marcia.*) The subsidiary type of soloism that is found in a number of Nielsen's works, especially in the fifth symphony and the clarinet concerto, is also present here, most vividly in the use of a bass trombone.

The Concerto has more than a fair amount of supple lyricism and a good amount of light-character sensations. The orchestra is fully detailed and is far from a subsidiary voice, notwithstanding the star role of the solo flute.

Columbia indicates that Julius Baker "is one of the world's foremost flutists." Indeed! In this case such promotional puff is fully acceptable since Baker lives up to it in his playing. However, not acceptable is the merchandising concept that includes a listing of this Concerto and the Concerto for Clarinet and Orchestra (see under *clarinet*) with the soloists' names in small print and the rubric "Bernstein Conducts Nielsen" given top billing in typeface twice the size and twice the boldness. There is no argument that Bernstein should be given credit, but the heading is a bit inappropriate considering that solo works are concerned and, accordingly, soloists are featured. Let it be said that Bernstein does conduct the Nielsen Flute Concerto with outstanding perception of its delicacy and humor.

Concerto for Violin and Orchestra, Op. 33
Violin

☐ Royal Danish Orchestra / Varga (violin) / Semkow (conductor) / Turnabout 34043

No preoccupation with pat patterns here. Composed in 1912, the freshness of the work remains clear, the reason for its neglect does not. This is superbly written music for the instrument and superbly realized in Tibor Varga's stunning rendition.

The form is keen. Nielsen's Concerto is split into two movements and further split by slow and fast divisions within each: a *Praeludium* in *largo* tempo (movement 1) and a *Poco adagio* (movement 2) are in turn followed by an Allegro and a Rondo. There is no stalling to get to the point. A crash-chord for the orchestra and the violin is off and running with musical spectacularism, set on a pedal stage. There isn't a dull measure in this work. So where are our violinists?

This is the only available domestic recording. Though it would be super if some of our great violinists recorded it, we are not being denied, for Varga's playing is beautifully proportioned, intensely sung, and technically juiced to the utmost. There is a HMV (His Master's Voice) foreign edition SLS-5027 (eight discs, all covering Nielsen's music) which contains a performance by Arve Tellefsen. Not having heard it, there is no comparison possible. None is really required, with the magnificent satisfaction to be obtained from this Turnabout edition. And full credit to Jerzy Semkow, who supports the soloist with outstanding understanding and musicality. Recommended without the slightest reservation.

The Children Are Playing from Incidental Music for *The Mother,* Op. 41
Instrumental

☐ Wion (flute) / Lyrichord 7155
Flute

A gentle Pastorale, despite the title. These "children" are well behaved.

Flute and Harp

The Fog Is Lifting from Incidental Music for *The Mother*, Op. 41

☐ Wion (flute); Kronberg-Brown (harp) / Lyrichord 7155

A Serenade concept covers this musical weather report. It's all for the flute; the harp is strictly accompanimental.

Flute and Viola

Faith and Hope Are Playing from Incidental Music for *The Mother*, Op. 41

☐ Wion (flute); Nickrenz (viola) / Lyrichord 7155

A minuetlike bit with Mozartean charm riding through it. The blend in the performance is beautiful.

Horn

***Canto Serioso* for Horn and Piano (1928)**

☐ Brown (horn); Lebon (piano) / Lyrichord 7155

Dark colored, most expressive and certainly music expressly conceived for the personality of the mellow brass instrument. The substitution of a cello for the horn was indicated by Nielsen but use of the string instrument would certainly not be as effective.

Oboe

Fantasias, Op. 2

☐ Lucarelli (oboe); Lebon (piano) / Lyrichord 7155

Simplistic content covering a lyrical Romance and a pert Humoreske. Lucarelli is a star-studded oboist, as proven here.

Organ

Commotio, Op. 58

Preludes, Op. 51 (Excerpts)

☐ Hansen (organ) / Turnabout 34193

Polyphonic stratification is the imposing matter that covers Opus 58, Nielsen's final major composition. *Commotio* is considered the greatest Danish work for the organ since Buxtehude's output. The clear articulations within the playing are no mean feat and represent truly glorious organ playing.

There are twenty-nine Preludes in Nielsen's Opus 51, Jørgen Ernst Hansen plays twenty of the group. Represented are numbers 2, 3, 4, 5, 6, 8, 9, 10, 11, 12, 13, 15, 16, 18, 21, 22, 23, 26, 27, and 28. However, they are not performed chronologically, but mixed in sequence. Thus, 27–8–11–6 forms one group, with four others in each of the other four groups. Banding separates the total group not the pieces within it. All these are played with clear textures and a becoming directness.

Chamber Music

String Quartet in G minor, Op. 13

☐ Copenhagen String Quartet / Turnabout 34187

Though bearing a higher opus number than Nielsen's F minor quartet, actually it precedes that work, marked as Opus 5. Later publication caused the improper chronological indication.

The two inner movements provide the greatest creative security—a warm lyrical conception and a gay Scherzo. Principally, Opus 13 is of historic interest though it is far from dull fare. The performance is well meshed and totally satisfying.

String Quartet No. 4 in F major, Op. 44

☐ Copenhagen String Quartet / Turnabout 34217

Lightly faceted as though it were running on folkloristic paths (though it is completely constructed from original material), but especially strong in its rhythmic content and vertically impacted sonorities. Nielsen knew how to write for strings; the euphonies that are heard in his fourth quartet are romantically colored, brightly clear and true.

The original title of the Quartet was *Piacevolezza* (translated in John W. Barker's splendid liner essay on the work as "Pleasantry"). The content follows suit.

This is a decidedly polished performance that has buoyancy, sharply gauged balances, and a depth of quartet sound that is quite enticing. Our quartet teams should examine the music of Nielsen and other Danish composers. They're missing some real beauties.

Serenata in Vano for Clarinet, Bassoon, Horn, Cello, and Bass (1914)

☐ Bloom (clarinet); Alan Brown (bassoon); William Brown (horn); Gardner (cello); Levine (bass) / Lyrichord 7155

An initial set of tunes moves into a slower portion, and continues with an irregular-paced march. Further balance is obtained by each of the three parts being subdivided into ternary sections. A quaint entry in Nielsen's catalogue.

The playing of this group is most impressive. They establish fine balances throughout and convey a total understanding of Nielsen's style.

Woodwind Quintet, Op. 43

☐ Lark Woodwind Quintet / Lyrichord 7155

Nielsen's Quintet has a personality habit of stating one specific idea and then passing on to another. Despite this, the music is not disconnected, since thematic threads stitch the sections together. Nonetheless, it is a test of performance to integrate the composition. The Lark ensemble solves this problem. Futher, their playing has a suavity that takes a bit of the edge off the austere outlines of Nielsen's work. The closest any of the other recorded releases come to this is that by the Westwood Wind Quintet, but their tone tends to be eruptive at certain places where it should not be. (The Westwood performance is on Crystal S-601.)

Alfred Nieman *(20th cent.)*

Sonata No. 2 (1963)

Instrumental

☐ Portugheis (piano) / Composers Recordings SD-333

Piano

Sound-piece totally, especially in the use of cluster formations in the finale, *Music of Changes*. Sonata form is not employed in Nieman's Sonata No. 2; twelve-tone structuring is. It is carefully controlled in movement two (Passacaglia), freer in the opening Fantasy. Method, thereby, accomplishes the titling objectives.

Nine Israeli Folk Songs

Vocal

☐ Lam (baritone); Walmer (piano) / Serenus 12039

Voice with Accompaniment

None of the set is in the "popular" category, but most have pervasive spirit. Nieman's harmonizations are romantically colorful. All are naturally sung.

Janko Nilovic (1941-)

Brass Ensemble

Double Concerto (Music for Seven Trombones)

☐ L'Ensemble de Trombones de Paris / Becquet and Demarle (trombones) / Nilovic (conductor) / Crystal S-223

Nilovic's work is for a richly timbred, unordinary septet of two solo trombones, three tenor trombones, and two bass trombones. In the recording four players are used for the three tenor trombone parts. The solo parts are not highlighted in the concerto sense but represent the soprano members of the ensemble. There are four movements in the work, one tightly enmeshed in ostinato.

Fastidious playing and impeccable balance.

Instrumental

Trombones and Percussion

Suite Balkanique (Music for Seven Trombones and Four Percussion)

☐ L'Ensemble de Trombones de Paris / Bauer, Lamare, Bercovitz, and Czerkinsky (percussion) / Nilovic (conductor) / Crystal S-223

Nilovic's seven-part Suite includes picturesque objectives such as *Occident, Voyage, Macedonien,* and *Orient.* The materials are folkloristic, placed in a slightly dissonant atmosphere. Rhythmic enlightenment is paramount.

The scoring is for seven trombones, but it is performed here by six tenor trombonists and two bass trombonists. Prime playing.

Bo Nilsson (1937-)

Orchestra

Frequenzen (1956)

☐ Hamburger Kammersolisten / Travis (conductor) / Mainstream 5008

Pulverization of sounds showing splendid resource and inventiveness within almost cruel self-imposed limitations. These include matters of duration, pitch, and ten different dynamic levels. Nilsson's choice of sensitive sound qualities is paralleled by Travis's sensitively concerned account.

Szene III (1961)

☐ Internationalen Kranichsteiner Kammer-Ensemble / Maderna (conductor) / Mainstream 5008

Nilsson's "Scene" is refined in its makeup of free instrumentation and form but gives dynamic attention to the role of the percussion. The music is a jest of sonority interchange and extemporizationlike detail. It then explodes into a tumultuous tornado of sound-weights whereby chaos becomes climax. Effective performance by this expert conductor of avant-garde music.

Chamber Music

Zwanzig Gruppen (1958)

☐ Christiansson (piccolo); Gillblad (oboe); Almgren or Kingstedt (clarinet) / Caprice CAP-1034

One of the very few aleatoric pieces for wind instruments that has established itself in the repertoire. "Twenty Groups" is precisely titled. Each player has a total of twenty fragments and plays them in any sequence. Although each instrument goes its own way, the montage that results is stylistically logical and affirmative. Of course, there is the shadow of Stockhausen hovering over the score but Nilsson's fragmented data comes out with a much lighter connotation than is to be heard in a Stockhausen opus. Yes, this is chance music but it is superbly intelligible and meaningful. Nilsson's work certainly lives up to its fame.

The playing is of the highest standard. Caprice has listed all the musicians performing on the disc (counting Nilsson's, there are seven works by as many composers, including Webern and Varèse) but unfortunately has not identified the specific names of the performers for each work. Twenty-two performers are involved in all. Since two are clarinetists, both are listed above.

Joaquín Nin   (1879-1949)

Chants d'Espagne   *Instrumental*

☐ Gabor Rejto (cello); Alice Rejto (piano) / Orion 7282   *Cello*

Beautiful documentation of Spanish folk music. This covers a Castilian *Montanesa,* a *Tonada Murciana* (from the region of Murcia), and two Andalusian types: a *Saeta* (which Gabor Rejto plays with the most telling sensitivity) and a fandango-like *Granadina.*

Nin's *Chants d'Espagne* was originally for violin and piano. However, he authorized and fully approved the edition for cello made by the violinist Paul Kochanski.

Joaquín Nin-Culmell   (1908-   )

Six Variations on a Theme by Milán   *Instrumental*

☐ de la Torre (guitar) / Nonesuch 71233   *Guitar*

The theme is a Pavane, repeated as the final variation in a modernized harmonic setting. On the credit side, Rey de la Torre's overall playing is superb; there is less enthusiasm for the dynamic constancy.

Marlos Nobre   (1939-   )

Tropicale (1968)   *Chamber Music*

☐ New Sound Composers/Performers Group / Lanza (conductor) / Mainstream MS-5017

Scored for piccolo, small clarinet, piano, and percussion. *Tropicale* is aleatorically notated but directed in such a way as to make certain a frenetic bite grips the music. A strong performance meets this objective.

Luigi Nono   (1924-   )

Polifonica-Monodia-Ritmica (1951)   *Orchestra*

☐ English Chamber Orchestra / Maderna (conductor) / Mainstream 5004

There is neither formal hesitancy on Nono's part nor difficulty with recognizing the contrastive detail of his three-part work (for flute, clarinet, bass clarinet, alto saxophone, horn, piano, and four percussionists playing xylophone, four different-sized cymbals, side drum, tom-tom, and two small drums, one with snares and one without). Part 1 is concerned with diassembled polyphony and is sparsely noted in a Webernian manner, part 2 is a *Monodia* devoted to the *Klangfarbenmelodie* principle, and part 3 stresses the jolt of percussive timbre.

Nono's piece has held its strong position among contemporary Italian music while he has moved away into a totally different style. There can only be praise for the undeniable creative resource of this work, now equating an almost classical stability. This recording does full justice to the composition. It is by far the most accurate I have heard and is perfect in its response to dynamic pertinency and textural clarity.

Uno Espressione (1953)

☐ Louisville Orchestra / Whitney (conductor) / Louisville S–665

An evocative, pointillistic-brush-work piece. Typically post-Webernian in its silences with the sound wisps making a *Klangfarbenmelodie* motility.

Acceptably played to present the special, fragile beauty of Nono's piece.

Solo Instrument and Orchestra

Flute

Y su sangre ya Viene cantando for Flute, Strings, and Percussion

☐ Soloists of the Rome Symphony Orchestra / Gazzelloni (flute) / Maderna (conductor) / RCA VICS–1313

This is part 2 (and the only exclusively instrumental section) of Nono's *Epitaffio per García Lorca,* consisting of programmatic episodes based on lines from a Lorca poem. Best are the first two episodes: one sensitively emotive (the flute rising as if from a music of silences), the other an ecstatic section.

Vocal

Voice, Piano, and Orchestra

Como una ola de fuerza y luz for Soprano, Piano, and Orchestra (1972)

☐ Bavarian Radio Symphony Orchestra / Taskova (soprano); Pollini (piano) / Abbado (conductor) / Deutsche Grammophon 2530436

Agitprop music or elegiac musical documentation, the category depending on whether one sits on the left or on the right. "Like a Wave of Power and Light" is another Nono work that has sharp political stripes. It mourns the death of a Chilean left-wing individual.

Strong, powerful present-day music is to be heard. The scoring includes tape sounds, and its sonic goal is as straight as the pull of a magnet. Great climactic section.

Choral

Chorus Alone

Y Entonces comprendio (1970)

☐ RAI Chamber Chorus / Lindsay, Poli, and Ravazzi (sopranos); Bove, Acevedo, and Vicini (speakers) / Antonellini (conductor) / Deutsche Grammophon 2530436

"And Then He Understood" combines speaking, singing, and electronic sounds. This compact has further compact in the text which is drawn from Ché Guevara (to whom the composition is dedicated) plus the work of Carlos Franqui. The aim is that which occupies Nono—music as a weapon in the class struggle. Concertgoers are last in importance in composing this type of work, being preceded by workers, farmers, and guerrillas.

Electronic Music

Contrappunto dialettico alla mente

☐ Coro da Camera della RAI / Poli (soprano); Bove, Mazzoni, Vicini, and Troni (voices) / Antonellini (conductor) / Deutsche Grammophon 2543006

Though individual vocalists are given credits, most of the material in "Dialectic Counterpoint for the Mind" is of antiindividual identification. The sounds are electro-translated and electro-transposed. With these there are mixed various noises, water sounds, bells, and other *musique concrète* data, also processed for total change.

This is another Nono piece of musical protest. There is some peripheral mention of (and reaction to) the death of Malcolm X and the "imperial aggression" in Vietnam, but specific identification relating to such is not brought to light. Power, dynamic perceptivity, and intense polyphonically percussive tone textures are.

Paul Nordoff *(1909-1977)*

White Nocturne

☐ Hanks (tenor); Friedberg (piano) / Duke University Press DWRM-7501 (monaural)

Vocal

Voice with Accompaniment

A neoromantic conception set to a text by Conrad Aiken. It typifies the style of this fine composer who for the last twenty years of his life devoted all his time to the field of musical therapy and working with mentally retarded children.

Per Nørgård *(1932-   )*

Iris (1967)

☐ Danish Radio Symphony Orchestra / Blomstedt (conductor) / Caprice CAP-1054

Orchestra

Nørgård describes his work as "a network of lines where each one represents a rather simple melody or rhythm." That reads as though one should expect to hear a heavy dose of counterpoint, but that is exactly opposite to the motile fluidity of the themeless combinations that structure the piece. *Iris* provides a paradox. There is always a lightness and transparency of texture, despite the use of massed sound complexes. The music breathes clearly though heavily a few times in its somewhat pulseless condition. This is a composition of definite originality and it is played with full involvement.

Voyage into the Golden Screen (1968)

☐ Danish Radio Symphony Orchestra / Vetö (conductor) / Caprice CAP-1054

The raw sound images in the first movement are stark reminders of Penderecki's layered clusters, together with the filtered noises, timbral alterations, and other sonorous ferocities found in the electronic music world. In movement 2 a type of motif is used, covered with timbre over- and underlays, with an occasional sharp-edged, single-pitched trumpet entrance. There is no developmental evolution in this music, which is formed from the refocusing of the same material.

Nørgård's "Voyage" has a primitive directness from which there is no deviation. Apparently, to be completely unsentimental such strong passivity was necessary.

The playing is excellent. There is no doubt that there is no compromise with the demands of the score.

Constellations, Op. 22

☐ Royal Danish Orchestra / Semkow (conductor) / Turnabout 34168

String Orchestra

Nøgård's *Konstellationer* is subtitled as a *Concerto for 12 String Groups*. However, this does not mean twelve different string bodies as though each has the full family of string instruments included. It signifies a total division into twelve: seven violins, two violas, two cellos, and one double bass. In this performance a complete string orchestra is utilized with different weights obtained by use of tutti and solo instruments. There are three movements: Constellations, Contrasts, and Alternations.

The atonical procedures of this music tend toward the highly charged Bergian world, the colors attracted by Bartók examples, especially in the middle movement. The performance is strong and distinct.

Spencer Norton   (1909-   )

Solo
Instrument
and
Orchestra

Two Pianos

Partita for Two Solo Pianos and Orchestra (1960)

☐ Oklahoma City Symphony Orchestra / Zaremba and Bell (pianos) / Harrison (conductor) / Composers Recordings 151 (monaural)

A composer's pleasing jaunt with a very professional eye for selecting eclectic markers on the way. Within the eighteenth-century forms Norton uses he refreshes them with some slight contemporary décor. The Sinfonia relates to the block chords of Bloch's Concerto Grosso No. 1 opening; the *Corrente* has some modified Shostakovich; the *Sarabande* clings to the perorative theme of Sibelius's Fifth Symphony. And to continue, the Gavotte leans heavily on Prokofiev, there is Fauré in the Air, and a number of creative reflections in the Toccata.

Well, then why bother? And since such fact-finding can be found in hundreds of pieces with numbing regularity, why even suggest listening to the piece? The point is that Norton has gathered his assimilations with a most convincing technique and for that alone he is worth listening to, even though his own contributions are exceedingly difficult to locate. Further, the performance is a handsome and striking one, and for that alone it is worth listening to.

Ottokar Nováček   (1866-1900)

Instrumental

Violin

Perpetuum mobile

☐ Perlman (violin); Sanders (piano) / Angel S–37003

Show-off time and why not? Nováček produced a good number of works in his short life (including a piano concerto and three string quartets) but only this virtuoso piece remains as a reminder of his output. It's a standard sweet for encore time and always goes down well. Couldn't be better served than in this case.

Another excellent version is available on Orion 7027/2, with Staryk as the soloist.

Lionel Nowak   (1911-   )

Solo
Instrument
and
Orchestra

Timpani

Concert Piece for Kettledrums

☐ Bennington String Ensemble / Calabro (timpani) / Nowak (conductor) / Composers Recordings S–260

A beautifully made nocturnal first part, in which the timpani act as subdued antiphonal qualities. Then follows a more active division, tightly bound in its rhythmic declaration, that brings to mind Honegger-Tansman partnership. This is a very telling piece without the composer indulging in any pseudointellectualized creative shell game. It's not easy to make a solo timpani piece lyrically interesting, but Nowak has done it.

Fine playing by the eleven strings. Superb playing by Louis Calabro (a composer in his own right as well). Some of the sounds he obtains are warmly sensual (and by a timpanist that's a tough bit of business). In the latter part of the work Calabro's playing on the shell of the timpanum displays a fine virtuosic passion.

José Mauricio Nuñes Garcia *(1767-1830)*

Requiem Mass

☐ Helsinki Philharmonic Orchestra and Morgan State College Choir / Davis (soprano); Allen (mezzo-soprano); Brown (tenor); Tuloisela (bass-baritone) / Freeman (conductor) / Columbia M–33431

Cantata and Oratorio

The composer is regarded as the father of Brazilian music. Most of his work was modeled after Gluck and Handel. The Requiem moves ahead into the Viennese (classical) orbit and contains solid polyphonic details. While there is some stylistic wandering in the finale it all fits nicely.

Outstanding proof is given here that the college group is absolutely first class and so are the soloists.

Gösta Nystroem *(1890-1966)*

Soul and Landscape

☐ Irving (soprano); Werba (piano) / Caprice CAP–1061

Vocal

Voice with Accompaniment

An important part of Nystroem's output consists of music for the voice, which includes some of the finest examples in Swedish vocal literature. The three songs in this cycle (to texts by Ebba Lindqvist), *White Land, The Wish,* and *Only with the One,* are most representative, marked by romantic style, tinged with some impressionistic colorations. The vocal side of the performance is quite good, though an occasional vibrato is present in the upper range; the piano playing of Erik Werba is fully convincing.

O

Kil-Sung Oak (1945-)

Amorphosis (1971)

Percussion

☐ New Jersey Percussion Ensemble / Moss (soprano) / DesRoches (conductor) / Nonesuch 71291

A philosophical program surrounds Oak's work, with pitched instruments (such as the glockenspiel, marimba, etc.) representing the sky and nonpitched identities (gong, sizzle cymbal, etc.) representing the earth. The liner notes explain that the piece "is symbolic of a drama between man and heaven and the earth." With this distribution the soprano is, of course, part of the pitched group. Since the vocal part is syllabic (drawn from three Korean words), it functions simply as another percussion timbre, albeit a warm legato one.

Eugene O'Brien (1945-)

Lingual for Soprano, Flute, and Cello

Vocal

Voice and Instrumental Ensemble

☐ Nuove Forme Sonore, Rome / Hirayama (soprano) / Crystal S–532

For Lingual read "equal." The voice here (given an extremely difficult role, superbly realized by Michiko Hirayama) is instrumentalized and forms part of the trio. A total ensemble is the objective and so the voice becomes integrated, with textual separativeness eliminated by the use of phonemes and snatches of words. Effective, though even the short length (5:45) seems a bit attenuated by reason of the severe concentration and insularity of the sound communications.

Johannes Ockeghem (ca. 1420-1496)

Ma Bouche rit

Ma Maîtresse

Vocal

Voice with Accompaniment

☐ Fay (soprano); Liddell (lute); Dunn (viola) / Lyrichord 7213

A pair of delicate and transparent *Chansons*. The melodic filigrees and the phrasing are finely set and accomplished.

Choral

Chorus Alone

Motets

Alma redemptoris Mater	*Gaude Maria Virgo*	*Salve Regina I*
Ave Maria	*Intemerata Dei Mater*	*Salve Regina II*

☐ Prague Madrigal Singers / Venhoda (conductor) / Telefunken 641878

Excellent impressions of the shape and character of these Motets. The intonation is fine and the singing is far above the average.

Cantata and Oratorio

Missa Caput

☐ Capella Cordina / Planchart (conductor) / Lyrichord 7213

A mass modeled after Dufay's Caput Mass, save for the Kyrie. Fine performance decorum for the greater part.

Jacques Offenbach   (1819-1880)

Orchestra

Overture to *Barbe-Bleue*

Overture to *The Grand Duchess of Gérolstein*

Overture to *La Belle Hélène*

Overture to *La Vie Parisienne*

☐ City of Birmingham Symphony Orchestra / Frémaux (conductor) / Klavier 517

Balanced performances; good sound. Properly approached without the slightest consideration of playing down in "pops concert" style.

Overture to *Orpheus in the Underworld*

☐ New York Philharmonic / Bernstein (conductor) / Columbia MS-7085

Orpheus in Hades (another way of considering the title) is also included in a collection of Offenbach overtures of which the four others are discussed above. However, it cannot compete with this richly colored, symphonically radiant reading. And right zippy when it should be.

Bernstein's conception is also available in a two-record set, *Joy of Music* (Columbia M2X-795), and in a three-record compilation (Columbia D3S-818).

Opera and Dramatic Music

Ba-ta-Clan

☐ Jean-François Paillard Orchestra and Philippe Caillard Chorale / Boulangeot (soprano); Amade and Corazza (tenors); Terrasson (bass); Desailly (speaker) / Couraud (conductor) / Musical Heritage Society MHS-794

Offenbach's one-act operetta (first produced on December 29, 1855), classified as a Musical Chinoiserie, is a delightful pseudo-Chinese concoction. Subtle spoofery of all sorts. One example: When the character Fé-Ni-Han sings "My friend, let's sing, as in 'Les Huguenots,' with rage and fury!" All sheer fun and entertainment with exultant soprano trills and roulades and that sort of thing that makes you believe all over again that when speeches are to be sung they should be sung in operetta form.

Clear singing by the cast and fine narrative delivery by Jean Desailly to connect the text and portray the plot. Everything in French, but Musical Heritage has it all indicated on a four-page insert that gives the French text and an excellent English translation.

Les Bavards

☐ Orchestra and Chorus of the O.R.T.F. / Boulangeot (soprano); Terrasson (bass); Benoit, Dachary, Destain, Doniat, Lenoty, Peyron, Pruvost, and Saugey (vocalists) / Couraud (conductor) / Musical Heritage Society MHS-897

There are ten numbers in Offenbach's two-act comic opera "The Gossips" and plenty of dialogue (in French, easily followed with the English translation in the booklet that comes with the disc). Not great Offenbach but with a good percentage of verve and parallel melodic invention. Satisfactory cast.

The Tales of Hoffman

☐ Royal Philharmonic Orchestra and Sadler's Wells Chorus / Bond, Grandi, and Ayars (sopranos); Sinclair (mezzo-soprano); Rounseville (tenor); Dargaval (bass) / Beecham (conductor) / Turnabout THS-65012/4 (monaural)

For this reviewer the strongest production remains the old monaural set, conducted by Beecham and sung in English. The absolute positivism of the performance has an appeal that cannot be found in competitive and newer stereo editions. However, if one demands the French language, the Cluytens-directed release on Angel S-3667 can be chosen.

Offenbach's opera (consisting of three acts with a prologue and an epilogue) is sung with vocal freshness and a musicality on the part of the cast that is rather special. There has been some editing of the score but it does not interfere with the success and rightness of this dramatically atmospheric work.

Le Papillon   Ballet

☐ London Symphony Orchestra / Bonynge (conductor) / London 6812

Offenbach's lone full-length ballet and not to be confused with compilations, such as *Gaîté Parisienne,* made for the stage by others. It has all the makings and fixings required for choreographic delineation, with waltzes and marches, tuny tunes and characteristic colors.

Richard Bonynge again proves his decided accomplishments as a conductor of this type of music.

Offenbach / Manuel Rosenthal (1904-)

Gaîté Parisienne   Ballet

☐ Boston Pops Orchestra / Fiedler (conductor) / RCA LSC-3308

This colorful sampler of waltzes and cancans plus other goodies gathered from various Offenbach operettas, is brilliantly played. Flexible, as it should be, and containing all the necessary panache. There are two different couplings. The one listed is paired with *Les Sylphides*. On RCA LSC-2267 the companion work is a four-part suite from Khachaturian's *Gayne.*

Will Ogdon   (20th cent.)

By the Isar for Soprano, Alto Flute, and Double Bass   Vocal

☐ Turetzky (double bass) / Desto 7128

Voice and Instrumental Ensemble

A lyrical vocal statement, pinpointed with tidbits of sound for the alto flute and double bass. For some reason neither the soprano nor the flutist are credited—an undeserved omission by design, since the album heralds Bertram Turetzky, and others are tossed into a group of nameless "assisting artists."

Maurice Ohana (1914-   )

Orchestra

Synaxis (1965)

☐ French Radio Philharmonic Orchestra / Joy and Ivaldi (pianos); Rollin (cithara) / Brück (conductor) / Musical Heritage Society MHS-1082

Eight connected divisions are presented in Ohana's exercise of sonorous worship, bypassing thematicism and development, solely making contact by freely disposed sonorous detail which brings vivid reminders of the music of Varèse, Jolivet, Messiaen, and Ligeti. A specific component is stressed in each section; thus, tessitura in *Diaphonie*, sustainment in *Organum*, harmonic specification in *Tropes*, etc. Intertwined are the soloizing of timbres: the pianos in *Diaphonie*, the timpani in *Tympanum*, the guitar in *Tropes*, etc.

A responsible presentation is given of this complicated score. Ohana subtitles *Synaxis: for 2 pianos, percussion, and orchestra.* However, these are definitions of three groups of equal consignment, and it is for that reason that the work is listed under the "orchestral" heading.

Solo Instrument and Orchestra

Concerto for Guitar and Orchestra (1950)

Guitar

☐ National Orchestra of Spain / Yepes (guitar) / Frühbeck de Burgos (conductor) / London 6356

Opposite to the traditional format of guitar material. The workstuff of this piece in three movements is drawn from the melorhythms of the Andalusian *cante hondo*, each movement transforming a basic design. These cover the *farruca, seguiriya,* and *buleria y tiento.*

The score leans percussively on the solo instrument and is more concerned with short color patterns than patterned phrases. The orchestra is indeed accompanimental, and mainly interjects pithy commentary.

Tres gráficos para guitarra y orquesta (1957)

☐ London Symphony Orchestra / Yepes (guitar) / Frühbeck de Burgos (conductor) / Deutsche Grammophon 2530585

Laced into this work are ideas that mark the Spanish descent of the composer. A fascinating conception brilliantly played.

Chamber Music

Signes (1965)

☐ Rollin (citharas); Debost (flute); Ivaldi (piano); Drouet, Gualda, de Vonogradov, and Sylvestre (percussion) / Constant (conductor) / Musical Heritage Society MHS-1087

A new model of Impressionism that flirts with dreamy, quasi-expressionistic content. Not until the fifth of the six parts of *Signes* does the dynamism become extrovert. Though the sound complexes are rarely incisive, the restricted, glovedlike contacts have an intensity that are just as compelling. *Signes* is still another instance of Ohana's involvement with music's incantatory properties.

Third tones play an important part here and their projection by the citharist and flutist, especially the latter is of uncanny precision. Debost's work is of the greatest virtuosity in terms of interpretation and pitch definition; his portamenti exemplify the highest and sharpest control possible. Truly, he is the star of a fabulous performance.

Cris for Twelve Voices a cappella (1969)

☐ Soloists of the Chorus of the O.R.T.F. / Ohana (conductor) / Musical Heritage Society MHS–1789

A huge mosaic. Ohana's *Cris* encompasses a montage of religious insinuations, tractlike incantations against man's inhumanity, sung-and-spoken slogans, revolutionary demands, etc. The fantasy force of the conception wipes out any pertinent vocal line per se. This is a music of ultrachromatic bits and snips, phonetics, glides and glisses, cries, sweeps, and a large use of thirds of tones that are striking in their contrast to the traditional, basic semitones. The effect is a percussion orchestra of voices.

The difficulties of the techniques used are hideous. Nonetheless, the dozen singers deliver a performance that is miraculous.

Cantigas (1954)

☐ Ars Nova Ensemble of the O.R.T.F. and Chamber Choir / Garcisanz (soprano) / Ohana (conductor) / Musical Heritage Society MHS–1789

Freely tonal pieces with direct dissonance that makes the music full-blooded. Ohana's six sacred monodies deal with exile, the Nativity, etc. Garcisanz's solo work in the fourth of the set, *Cantiga del ahazar* ("*Cantiga* of the Orange Flower") and the one following, *Cantiga de la noche santa* ("*Cantiga* of the Holy Night"), displays magnificent sensitivity. No less stimulating is the work of the chorus.

Pauline Oliveros (1932-   )

Outline for Flute, Percussion, and String Bass (An Improvisation Chart) (1963)

☐ Bertram Turetzky (bass); Nancy Turetzky (flute); George (percussion) / Nonesuch 71237

The parenthetical portion of the title tells the tale. Oliveros's chart includes pitches to be chosen "according to the given contour," rhythms to be stated "in the spaces provided," as well as no directions whatsoever but with the improvisation limited "within a given time length."

Expectedly, a convulsive set of transformations takes place. In music of this style, surprises can happen. Most here are of the gentle type, with the lion's share the result of the virtuosity of Bertram Turetzky. He makes a bass do things of many-splendored newness. Nonetheless, the performers produce for the composer (who assisted in the recording) what amounts to a nocturne, even though of unconventional structure.

Sound Patterns

☐ Brandeis University Chamber Chorus / Lucier (conductor) / Odyssey 32160156

The singers improvise pitches, click their tongues, pop their lips, snap their fingers, and produce other percussions. The premise to be unvocal (in the traditional sense) is fruitful (and acceptable) since these sounds cannot be obtained otherwise. For "patterns," read "disconnected discourse." Common plastic sensibility is replaced by uncommon provocative suppositions.

Exceedingly difficult to perform. Alvin Lucier's group meets all the demands.

Electronic Music	**I of IV (1966)**

☐ Odyssey 32160160

No editing or tape splicing. *I of IV* is a huge (twenty-minute) mural of neutrally defined electronic sound. Contrast is extremely minimal. If the analogy is permitted, this is a large piece of "absolute" electronic music, whereas most others could properly be contained in the programmatic category.

Julián Orbón   (1925-   )

Instrumental

Guitar

Preludio y tocata

☐ de la Torre (guitar) / Nonesuch 71233

By use of a Cuban rhythmic pattern an interlock is formed here with Spanish style, further colored by neoclassic diction in the "Prelude." A strong entry in guitar literature, written for de la Torre and dedicated to him.

Chamber Music

Partita No. 2

☐ Members of the Group for Contemporary Music at Columbia University / Dufallo (conductor) / Composers Recordings S-249

The modern mellowness of the combination Orbón uses in his Partita has a beautiful and fresh glow. Scored for string quartet, celesta, harmonium, vibraphone, and harpsichord, the music is warmed by its instrumentation. In variational style, especially marked by the use of the harpsichord, the composition has a unity rare to the balladry of rhapsodicism that usually marks variation writing.

Orbón is not a composer of aural polemics. His music is of contemporary romantic allegiance, with cheerful harmonic munificence. The Partita remains in the ears long after the final measure. What also remains in the ears is a definite Spanish cast (a music one would imagine Falla to be writing if he were Orbón).

Preston Ware Orem   (1865-1938)

Instrumental

Piano

American Indian Rhapsody

☐ Basquin (piano) / New World Records NW-213

Hokey perhaps, but no hoax. Authentic themes strung together and with a finale that is still stylistically fashionable in the musical backwaters of television when the Indian is in the cast of characters.

Give Peter Basquin special credit. By playing the score in a soft-sell manner, but with everything in place, he makes the music fairly decent for present-day ears. Overplaying music of this type brings laughter before the piece is smothered.

Carl Orff   (1895-   )

Orchestra

Entrata after William Byrd (1928)

☐ Vienna State Opera Orchestra / Scherchen (conductor) / Westminster Gold 8192

Beautiful obstinacy is the virtue of Orff's lone instrumental composition, a setting (composed in 1928 and fully revised in 1943) for quintuple orchestra, based on a keyboard piece (*The Bells*) by William Byrd. Actually, the quintuple orchestra is a set of five choirs—far from the staggering total the description would seem to indicate—comprising eleven woodwinds, sixteen brass, pairs of harps and pianos, strings, organ, and (for Orff) very moderate percussion.

The tonality is static, the bass generator a mere pair of chords. *Entrata* sticks to its unremitting point as bell sounds crisscross, engage, and reengage themselves. Its ostinato delights create the impression of a processional ceremony, and Scherchen is a most magnificent master directing the event.

Carmina Burana (Trionfi—Part I) (1936)

□ Boston Symphony Orchestra, New England Conservatory Chorus, and Children's Chorus of the New England Conservatory / Mandac (soprano); Kolk (tenor); Milnes (baritone) / Ozawa (conductor) / RCA LSC–3161

Opera and Dramatic Music

Orff's reputation stems from this scenic oratorio (or cantata). It defines his stylistic tenets.

For his text, Orff chose twenty-five poems from the thirteenth century, in all instances representing a revolt against the conventional prose of the times. The hour-long work is divided in three parts, covering *Springtime, In the Tavern, Courting and Love* (read: the restless season, drink, and sex), preceded and followed by a section titled *Fortune, the Empress of the World.* These generalities go into many matters of living, including the delights of feasting, wining, and wenching—especially the matter of love in its fullest physical sense. Nothing is taboo, even rousing singing about the joy of deflowering virgins. In toto, this is a musical Rabelaisian tale, quaintly described as "Profane chants, performed by singers and chorus accompanied by instruments and magical representations."

There is no cerebral speculation required, and Ozawa realizes the primitivism as Orff drives home his arguments in the simplest and most direct fashion. Any criticism of redundancy is canceled out by a plan which is totally based on supersaturation. Repetition and still more repetition is used for melodies, rhythms, words, and orchestration. The arch-primitivistic language of the composer is thoroughly in keeping with the musical plot; it may be called banal by those who wish a much more sophisticated method, but it is no more artificial than any other "system." *Carmina Burana* is a vivid example of musical pleonasm exploited to its fullest.

Ozawa's attention to minute dynamic distinctions, his control of pace and timbre make his the preferable recording. The vocalism is precise. This is a smooth, and fully dynamic, well-nigh perfect exposition of the score, beautifully engineered. Above all, Ozawa does not go constantly for the percussive element but integrates it with the euphonious data. It makes Ozawa's the most stunning (and musical) release of the several available.

Catulli Carmina (Trionfi—Part 2) (1943)

□ Members of the Leipzig Radio Symphony Orchestra and Chorus of Radio Leipzig / Mai (soprano); Büchner (tenor); Czapski, Philipp, Wappler, and Erber (pianos) / Kegel (conductor) / Philips 6500815

Catulli Carmina is the middle piece in the trilogy that opens with *Carmina Burana* (*see above*) and is completed by *Trionfo di Afrodite* (once available on Decca 9826, with Jochum conducting). Erotic poems by Catullus are the basis of the text for Orff's *Ludi Scaenici* ("Scenic Play"), which can be properly described as "for adults only." Because of its earthiness, most translations that are furnished for concert and recording purposes are edited. (The liner copy of Philip's disc states "libretto on insert card." There was none included in the review copy used. Be sure to check before purchasing.)

The setting begins with the pledging of love and devotion by groups of young men and women. Another group of older men dispute these vows as "unbounded foolishness." The story of the poet Catullus and Clodia (known as Lesbia) is reenacted as evidence (the method of a play within a play). Her faithlessness is offered as proof that promises of everlasting love are nonsense. The young people are not convinced and the play ends as it began, with their pledges of "In eternity I am yours."

Orff's music is vivid, violent, and frenzied. Its repetitive patterns remind one of super-propelled Gilbert and Sullivan. The instrumentation is a bath of spectroscopic timbres, with four pianos, four timpani, and approximately a dozen players for other percussion instruments (including two types of xylophones, stone sounds, maracas, cymbals, etc.) *Catulli Carmina* is a fascinating experience.

This is undoubtedly the best performance of the five editions (one a monaural disc) on the market. It is a stunning exposition of Orff's hot musical potion. The choral singing, representing the major part of the score, is electrifying and the dynamic strata intensely realized. Superb in all respects.

Der Mond (1938)

☐ Philharmonia Orchestra and Philharmonia Chorus / Christ and Kuén (tenors); Schmitt-Walter, Graml, Peter, and Hotter (baritones); Lagger (bass); Rösner, Holloway, Delcroix, Kurzinger, Harsdorff, Wisheu, and Hunkele (speaking parts) / Sawallisch (conductor) / Angel S-3567

Orff based *Der Mond* ("The Moon") on a Grimm fairy tale. In the main this is a piece of mnemonics: from the field of Wagner; from music-hall ditties; out of low-down jazz; out of Puccini, Strauss, and Mahler; by way of beer-cellar ditties and pop tunes; even to the inclusion of a nursery tune. The subtitle, *Ein kleines Welttheater*, may explain the assortment. This "small theatre of the world" or "theatrical microcosm" (as one writer has termed it) means that one must accept Orff in terms of a vaudeville show, music drama, oratorio-*cum*-symbolism, narrative opera; light, comic, and heavy.

There is something for everyone in this wacky tale of four chaps who steal the moon from a neighboring village and install it in their own hamlet. As each dies he takes a share of the moon with him. When the moon is reassembled St. Peter claims it and places it where it belongs, in the heavens. A tale of sheer nonsense, but with a sufficient frame for Orff's musical effigies. These are quite evocative, despite their differences. One either delights in the musical antics or becomes annoyed. No middle course is possible.

An absolutely exceptional portrayal is offered by Angel that has been *the* recording, even though it was the only one for twenty years. It remains *the* recording of the work, despite the stiff competition offered by Philip's edition (6700083) with Herbert Kegel conducting. There's just that extra bit of finesse in the Angel production that makes it deserving of the first slot. Although the singing in the Philips album is just as good and the sound plus recording clarity are even slightly better, that important matter of finesse tells the tale for Orff's tale.

De temporum fine comoedia: Vigilia (1973)

☐ Cologne Radio Symphony Orchestra, Cologne Radio Chorus, RIAS Chamber Chorus, and Tölz Boys Chorus / Ludwig (mezzo-soprano); Schreier (tenor); Greindl (bass); Boysen (speaker) / von Karajan (conductor) / Deutsche Grammophon 2530432

Not the Orff of the tonally toned and clearly cut *Carmina Burana* or *Der Mond* but a huge theatrical piece that is a mishmash of voicings, effects, primitivism, and mysticism. The "Play About the End of Time: A Vigil" calls for close to two dozen singers and speakers, three choruses, orchestra, and a huge percussion arsenal of nearly one hundred instruments. Greek, Latin, and German are the languages used, which tells the assorted approach to the work's unity.

No arguing the trueness of the recording, both in terms of performance and engineering.

Orff and Gunild Keetman (20th cent.)

Music for Children (*Das Schulwerk*)

Choral

☐ Instrumental Ensemble, Choruses of the Children's Opera Group and of the Bancroft School for Boys, and Speech Ensemble from the Italia Conti School / Orff, Keetman, and Jellinek (conductors) / Angel 3582 (monaural)

Chorus and Instrumental Ensemble

Music designed to train the young but a delight outside its didactic environment. The naturalness of the examples makes for wonderful joy in sheer listening. But for Orff's sake, listen in segments; this is not a continuous music drama! (The fully explanatory booklet issued with the four-side recording fully explains all the purposes, possibilities, and details.)

I wager that it will be difficult to turn away from this recording. The speech exercise, *Trees and Flowers,* is both magnificent poetry and heartwarming; the singing of *Sumer is Icumen in* is eye filling. The entire project is gladsome news for young and old, teacher, musician, and listener. Though Music for Children is truly an educational recorded textbook, it is also a marvelous auditory experience cut away from its prime goal.

There are two other releases dealing with and based on Orff's *Schulwerk.* Both are in the BASF catalogue: Nos. 20374 and 25122; the latter is practically all-instrumental. Plenty of values in both, but by far the very best is the initial, monaural album listed above, issued by Angel some two decades ago. There is sufficient music contained in it for all of the *Schulwerk's* purposes and objectives.

Leo Ornstein   (1892-   )

Nocturne and Dance of the Fates

Orchestra

☐ Louisville Orchestra / Mester (conductor) / Louisville LS-754

Not the Ornstein of the *Poems of 1917* or *The Wild Man's Dance.* These pieces, withal the rhythmic beating in the *Dance,* are polite in comparison, and Orientalized in their melodic turns. The *Nocturne* brings to mind Griffes, the *Dance of the Fates* calls up *Prince Igor.* Anyway, Ornstein's return after an absence for some forty years from the scene in any form (concerts or records) is deserving of a welcome, and some listening time.

Impressions de Notre-Dame I & II

Instrumental

☐ Hays (piano) / Finnadar SR2-720

Piano

The elements in Ornstein's *Impressions* are massive dissonant harmonies, smothered often by tone clusters. Perhaps the original boldness (the work was published in 1914) has lessened but the power has not. There are no sacred pictures in Ornstein's music, the suggestive silhouettes of these piano pieces are those of the gargoyled tops of cathedrals.

Doris Hays's response to this work is that it has "violence in it." This writer agrees. He also agrees that her performance is of definitive stamp.

Three Moods (1914)

☐ Westney (piano) / Composers Recordings S–339

Music composed in Ornstein's early days (1914), when he was tabbed as a "wild" personality, writing in a style dissonantly ahead of its time, but which is now part of settled contemporary language. However, this music is far from dated. It is strong, dynamic, and full-blooded.

Anger smacks into the ears, contains tone clusters. *Grief* and *Joy* are delineated with atonal sombreness and with an exuberant registral range, respectively.

The performance received high praise from the composer. It was justified.

Chamber Music

Quintet for Piano and Strings, Op. 92

☐ Stepner and Strauss (violins); Sacco (viola); Mansbacher (cello); Westney (piano) / Composers Recordings S–339

Ornstein approaches the piano quintet medium with the same scoring pungency and potency found in both the first string quartet and piano quintet of Ernest Bloch. The statement concerns only the motorium and compacted interjacency of Ornstein's work, composed in 1927. This covers the *barbaro* spikes and Hebraic flavor that permeate most of the work. To be added is a Russian ambience. These combine in a music of strength, passion, and fervor. In 1927 this quintet would have been regarded as "modern." It now belongs in the "traditional" contemporary category.

Effectively played.

Robin Orr   (1909-   )

Choral

Chorus Alone

They That Put Their Trust in the Lord

☐ Choir of St. John's College, Cambridge / Guest (conductor) / Argo ZRG–5340

A setting of the first pair of verses of Psalm 125. Traditional, but avoids the cul-de-sac of so much church music by some carefully honed harmonic punctuations. It is sung with sweet vitality.

Juan Orrego-Salas   (1919-   )

Orchestra

Serenata Concertante, Op. 40

☐ Louisville Orchestra / Whitney (conductor) / Louisville 56–5 (monaural)

Four movements, describing moods that are *Peaceful, Light, Simple,* and *Gay.* Vigor always, neoclassic clarity always. An impressive piece.

Symphony No. 2, Op. 39

☐ Louisville Orchestra / Whitney (conductor) / Louisville 624 (monaural)

The subtitle *To the Memory of a Wanderer* is explained by the death of a friend of the composer. This is, therefore, an "In Memoriam" piece, most potently indicated in the funereal and emotive disclosures in the central movement (a Maestoso). Elsewhere, Orrego-Salas, who claims no nationalistic ties to his music (neither does he negate them, simply does not discuss them), has laced his music with Latinesque particulars (the composer was born in Chile).

(Nationalism is an unpopular subject these days. Ridiculous situation. Heritage provides an important element for a composer's use, providing he believes that nationalism has not outlived its force and effect.) The Louisville Orchestra parallels that last phrase, playing with dynamism and producing a vital commentary.

Léon Orthel (1905-)

Cinq Etudes caprices, Op. 39

☐ de Haas (piano) / Donemus Audio-Visual Series 7071/4

Instrumental

Piano

That three of the movements are Ravelian does not minimize worthy qualities, interesting conceptions, and on-the-button piano writing. Movement one is a *Perpetuum mobile* that peppers forth sixteenth notes; the same type of kineticism marks the third piece, spiced by chromatic thirds. The *Foute Som* ("Faulty Sum") designation of the fourth piece remains an enigma, though its rondo structure is patently clear.

Virgil Thomson once cleverly described a pianist's playing as illustrative of a "wowing technique." It applies here to Polo de Haas.

Richard Orton (1940-)

Cycle for Two or Four Players (1967)

☐ Orton (piano and percussion); Welsh (cello) / Mainstream 5001

Chamber Music

Aleatoric government which produces excellent coloristic responses, aided doubtless by the fact that the composer is one of the two participants. Light-scaled fragmentation until the latter part when matters get more excited, the cellist tries out tuning and harmonics and quotes from a standard Concerto. A few mouth sounds also are heard. In all a type of chance-made Scherzo develops. Good show.

Hans Otte (1926-)

Touches (1965)

☐ Zacher (organ) / Wergo 60033

Instrumental

Organ

Neatly ironic. Thus, a combination of hymn progressions break-off and break-into clusters and other remote material. There are imitations of old-style movie organ and out-of-tune parlor harmonium sounds.

The piece offers a nice balance to organ music that still continues to advertise Wagner's and Strauss's wares.

Willem Van Otterloo   (1907-1978)

Wind and Brass Ensemble

Symphonietta for Wind Instruments (1943)

☐ Utrecht Philharmonic Orchestra / Van Otterloo (conductor) / Donemus Audio-Visual Series DAVS-6303 (monaural, 10-inch disc)

Otterloo's double octet calls for piccolo, two flutes, two oboes, English horn, two clarinets, bass clarinet, two bassoons, double bassoon, and four horns. The four movements are interlocked thematically and move in territories of expanded tonality.

Otterloo was a fine conductor and under his baton his own work is heard with telling effect.

Hall Overton   (1920-1972)

Orchestra

Pulsations (1972)

☐ Ensemble of New York / Davies (conductor) / Composers Recordings 298

An industrious affection for the jazz vocabulary is heard in Overton's final work. But the quality is never dynamically deadbeated in the center, but shifts, coalesces, implies, and has a strange smoke-filled room atmosphere about it.

Davies (a fine and sensitive conductor) directs a comprehensive realization. Pondered intent can defeat any work in any style, but his spontaneity is truly exciting. It presents Overton's music as it should be presented.

Symphony No. 2 in One Movement (1962)

☐ Louisville Orchestra / Whitney (conductor) / Louisville S-633

Heavy colors—crayoned browns, blacks, and bloodstone timbres—here (even with the Louisville's lack of string-instrument depth there is a vivid re-creation of Overton's non-pastel scoring). No luxuriances either. Lushness is rejected, the music moves in tight, dissonant strands as an attestation of expressionism. One must admire the way this composer pursued his own compositional research.

Instrumental

Piano

Polarities No. 1 (1958)

☐ Helps (piano) / Composers Recordings S-288

Expressionistic and in its intensity strongly related to the Schoenberg of the Six Little Piano Pieces. But, no ersatz product. Sensitively performed.

Chamber Music

Second String Quartet (1954)

☐ Beaux-Arts String Quartet / Composers Recordings 126 (monaural)

Overton's two-movement work is pleasing, greatly influenced by eclectic tenets drawn from the documents of Béla Bartók. The pizzicato section was born in Bartók's fourth quartet and the line writing is a cousin to the Hungarian's third quartet. But Overton, though he was a learned man and knew what to import, also blended in his own inventive voice. The quartet will be found to contain strong thematic transformations and motival ministrations. No faddy adherences in Overton's music to chance, or instrumental rape to obtain a peculiar effect.

Harold Owen *(1932-   )*

Chamber Music for Four B flat Clarinets

☐ Atkins, d'Antonio, Spear, and Raimondi (clarinets) / Wim WIMR-7

Very little worthy music has been written for this type of quartet. Owen has covered with fine sympathy the requirements of creating music for equal-timbred instruments. The suite consists of a Scherzo, Nocturne, and Fugue.

The ensemble of this team and its artistic behavior deserve special mention.

P

Wouter Paap (1908-)

Garlands of Music

String
Orchestra

☐ Radio Chamber Orchestra / van Otterloo (conductor) / Donemus Audio-Visual Series 6804 (monaural)

Paap's musical wreath is light and tidy (but not cheaply made) and is steadfastly tonal. There may be an absence of depth but that doesn't apply to the charm of the piece.

Luis de Pablo (1930-)

Iniciativas

Orchestra

☐ Symphony Orchestra of the Südwestfunk, Baden-Baden / Bour (conductor) / Wergo WER-60037

Some critic has termed de Pablo a "neoclassic abstractionist." The noun reads true, but not the adjective. *Iniciativas* is designed by percussively smashed sections and small polyphonic appulsions from generally non-percussive instruments. The stitching of the timbre swatches is contrasted by very thin, impressionistically styled fringes, but these, too, are cluster-colored. Such sonorous agglomerations have no affinity with neo-classic procedures, of course.

These ejections on the orchestral canvas are bold and fascinating. A virtuoso orchestra and a virtuoso conductor directing it are mandatory. It is supplied in the recording.

Modulos III (1967)

☐ Instrumentalgruppe Alea / Gil (conductor) / Wergo WER-60037

The orchestral forces are split into three groups in de Pablo's *Modulos*. Thus: four trumpets; two each of xylophone, piano, and harp; timpani, harmonium, celesta, glockenspiel, guitar, mandolin, and vibraphone. Though the instruments in group 2 are closely affiliated with those in group 3 and both of these are in direct contrast to the brass timbre in group 1, the interbreeding nullifies sectioned identification save by radical dispersion in the concert hall. On the recording one is hardly aware of divisional distinctions.

Intensities are subdued but such suavity does not interfere with high-keyed colorations of the improvisationally typed elements.

The performance seems totally responsive and responsible.

Tombeau pour Orchestre (1963)

☐ Symphony Orchestra of the Norddeutscher Rundfunk, Hamburg / Gielen (conductor) / Wergo WER-60037

Tombeau is dedicated to the memory of Wolfgang Steinecke, who founded and then directed the famous avant-garde music activities of the Darmstadt Festival. The piece is formed from pointillistic data and the pitches, tints, and short-coursed lines are developed accordingly. This does not nullify the sombre objectives of de Pablo's piece, proving that, in the hands of a creative expert, emotional suggestion is not bound to a specific style.

Chamber Music

Ejercicio para Cuarteto (Modulos IV) (1965)

☐ Società Cameristica Italiana / Wergo WER-60037

In the writing of this string quartet de Pablo has dispensed with harmony, counterpoint, specified form, and basic pulse. What remains is color of lavish application. This is splashed on by glides, a variety of plucked sounds, fusions of harmonics, and wood-of-the-bow contacts.

There is tangible meaning to such adventurous quartet terms, especially since de Pablo concentrates the size of his work. Virtuosity of the avant-garde type is required, and it is provided in this recorded exhibit.

Johann Pachelbel   (1653-1706)

String Orchestra

Suite

In G major for Strings / No. 6 in B flat major for Strings

☐ Jean-François Paillard Chamber Orchestra / Paillard (conductor) / RCA FRL1-5468

Nicely formed, average conceptions. The playing is well-defined.

Pachelbel / Münchinger

Orchestra

Kanon

☐ Stuttgart Chamber Orchestra / Münchinger (conductor) / London 6206

Here it is, the piece that made Pachelbel a household name and resulted in a financial goldmine. The *Kanon* has remained on the "charts" for over two years (135 weeks and still going strong when last checked in Billboard's "Best Selling Classical LPs"). With its glorious polyphony it is deserving of all the honors.

It is true that the edition that has been the hot sale is that performed by the Paillard Chamber Orchestra (RCA FRL1-5468). However, the version listed above is stronger in this critic's opinion and was the release that made Pachelbel's *Kanon* become known and famous in this country. Advertising being what it is and impulse buying being what *it* is, it is probable that the sales have been predicated on the music, not necessarily on the performance choice in this case.

Pachelbel's *Kanon* is a great miniature, arranged from the first part of an organ composition: *Kanon and Gigue in D*. You won't be too far off base if you take the RCA release, but you should try this rich London setting. A third choice is the suave presentation given by the English Chamber Orchestra, conducted by Johannes Somary on Vanguard SRV-344SD.

Ignace Jan Paderewski (1860-1941)

Piano Concerto in A minor, Op. 17

☐ Pro Musica Orchestra, Vienna / Blumental (piano) / Froschauer (conductor) / Turnabout 34387

This Concerto is perhaps a bit diffuse, but it is certainly sufficiently effective to be returned to the repertory. It's the type of Concerto you will either like because of its good themes or scoff at because of its traditional (old-fashioned, if you will) treatment.

An effective account by the soloist, except that the finale could have been given more bite.

Minuet in G major, Op. 14, No. 1

☐ Entremont (piano) / Columbia D3S-791

The performance is perhaps a bit mannered but it's good for this hackneyed bit. Playing to the grandstand maintains the spectator's interest.

Theme with Variations, Op. 16, No. 3

☐ Nicolaisen (piano) / Klavier 501

The *Thème varié* (in A major) consists of a half-dozen variations and a finale. Laura Nast Nicolaisen's performance contains no interpretative points one can argue about.

Sonata in A minor for Violin and Piano, Op. 13

☐ Granat (violin); Gray (piano) / Desmar 1004

The highlight of this three-movement work is the charming Intermezzo, enclosed by more dramatic movements, though these outer divisions are formerly shaped with all the i's dotted and all the t's crossed. Still, the urgency of the finale makes one overlook its precise design.

A solid rendition. Endre Granat has a small tone but it has a definite personality. Harold Gray is a fine partner: when strength is required he supplies it.

Solo Instrument and Orchestra

Piano

Instrumental

Piano

Chamber Music

Ferdinando Paër (1771-1839)

Overture to *Sargino*

☐ English Chamber Orchestra / Bonynge (conductor) / London 6735

Music that predates Rossini style (Rossini was twelve years of age when Paër composed his opera). The Overture to *Sargino o L'allievo dell' Amore* (to indicate the complete title) certainly deserves hearing. Good, professional presentation by Bonynge and his group.

Orchestra

Niccolò Paganini (1782-1840)

Sonata for Grand Viola

☐ Orchestra of Radio Luxembourg / Koch (viola) / Cao (conductor) / Turnabout 34606

All the Paganini rituals are here: luscious thirds and sixths and plenty of harmonics, all nicely dispatched by Ulrich Koch, with a paltry few wavering in the pitch wind. The

Solo Instrument and Orchestra

Viola

norm of sonata behavior is, however, not followed. This is a very sectional work, finally settling into a set of variations.

The "Grand Viola" (the words "Gran Viola" appear in the composition's title, though Paganini called the instrument a "contra viola") is nothing more than a special, large-sized viola that Paganini had in mind to use in performance when he composed his Sonata in 1834. Another interesting point is the use of the guitar in the orchestral accompaniment. In fact, the composition begins with two phrases for the guitar alone answered by string pizzicati.

Violin

Concerto for Violin and Orchestra

No. 1 in D major, Op. 6 / No. 2 in B minor, Op. 7 / No. 3 in E major / No. 4 in D minor / No. 5 in A minor / No. 6 in E minor, Op. posth.

☐ London Philharmonic Orchestra / Accardo (violin) / Dutoit (conductor) / Deutsche Grammophon 2740121

Some top choices of the individual concertos are noted below. However, if one wishes the whole Paganini concerto package here it is, and a juicy compilation it is. I say this while being mindful of a creative condition of non-growth. Paganini remains Paganini: what is in the first Concerto is heard in the second, and so on through the sixth work of the set. Still, sweetly turned melodies and an engaging collection of fiddle athletics are clear-cut values, even if the concertos cannot be compared with late Beethoven quartets or Mahler symphonies.

Salvatore Accardo raises no doubts. He is a musical violinist and a violin magician who can turn all the tricks and still make them sound musically responsible and responsive.

Two of the concertos are available singly on D. G.: the third (No. 2530629) and the sixth (No. 2530467—*see below*).

Concerto No. 1 in D major for Violin and Orchestra, Op. 6

☐ Orchestre National de l'Opéra de Monte-Carlo / Grumiaux (violin) / Bellugi (conductor) / Philips 6500411

There is no doubt that the younger violinists can parcel out the pyrotechnics of this work without strain. However, very few of them can match the thorough synthesis of musicality and technicality that is heard in Arthur Grumiaux's performance. He brings belief that everything is solidly bricked into the structure rather than just a matter of decorative trimmings. All is depicted with cohesiveness, warmth, and aliveness. Five stars for this one.

Concerto No. 2 in B minor for Violin and Orchestra, Op. 7

☐ Vienna Symphony Orchestra / Ashkenasi (violin) / Esser (conductor) / Deutsche Grammophon 139424

There's a certain amount of professional music in this work, but at best it's an attenuated *morceau de salon*. Of course, there are hair-raising technical conditions to hold the attention. It is played by Ashkenasi with pulverizing exactness. Every sound, chord, double stop, harmonic, and leap is heard with hammered preciseness like nails driven through a board with an electric machine. At the same time a good tonal quality is maintained. The final movement, the famous *Rondo* (*"La Campanella"*), is especially projected with a bravura that shows this soloist can match any in the field of fiddlistic fireworks.

Concerto No. 3 in E major for Violin and Orchestra

☐ London Symphony Orchestra / Szeryng (violin) / Gibson (conductor) / Philips 6500175

Szeryng is to be credited for the premiere recording of this work. He is also to be credited for creating the cadenzas. Above all, he is to be credited for a fine performance, opting for romantic color even in the more rousing passages. The vitality comes through clearly, but it codifies and binds the music rather than coats it. Szeryng receives excellent support from Gibson who makes the most of the purely orchestral sections.

Concerto No. 4 in D minor for Violin and Orchestra

☐ Orchestre National de l'Opéra de Monte-Carlo / Grumiaux (violin) / Bellugi (conductor) / Philips 6500411

This recording is artistically significant because of Grumiaux's bow and fingers even though the composition is not top-drawer Paganini (in comparison to the first two concerti). Grumiaux provides tonal warmth and smooth-as-silk playing in spite of the usual Paganinian technical hurdles. The balletic finale (a *Rondo galante*) sparkles. (The cadenza in the first movement is Grumiaux's.)

Concerto No. 6 in E minor for Violin and Orchestra, Op. Posth.

☐ London Philharmonic Orchestra / Accardo (violin) / Dutoit (conductor) / Deutsche Grammophon 2530467

Discovery of this work (*see* also *above*) was not earth-shaking but simply brought more of the special brand of technical goodies that Paganini designed for virtuoso fiddlers. That's all to the good, and they're all present and accounted for in Salvatore Accardo's display. The orchestration was especially prepared, and this non-Paganini realization is much better than any of Paganini's accompanimental originals.

Accardo knocks in all the runs (the pun is intentional) and makes no errors. Good orchestra back-up.

Romanze in A minor for Solo Guitar

Instrumental

☐ Scheit (guitar) / Turnabout 34123

Guitar

Italian *triste* character is displayed in beautifully delineated playing. (Also in a collection on Turnabout 34195/9.)

Cantabile and Waltz

Violin

☐ Ricci (violin); Pommers (piano) / MCA 2537

Both works are embellished considerably and any square-cut presentations of the designs have been removed. One gets the feeling that the performer is improvising the curlicues.

Caprices, Op. 1

☐ Rabin (violin) / Seraphim SIB–6096

Considerable attempts to outdo the doer have been tried on a number of Paganini's two-dozen marvels for the fiddle. Piano accompaniments have been added by Fritz Kreisler, Leopold Auer, Ferdinand David, Mario Pilati, and others; versions have been made for viola alone and viola with piano (some recorded by no less than William Primrose); a few have been scored with orchestral accompaniment (Nos. 17 and 21 are on

RCA VICS-1647); and there are transcriptions galore: for piano, string quartet, small orchestra, large orchestra, and even brass quintet! Such transfers and different consignments produce no substantial art income. The original, unaccompanied set is the acme of perfection. It needs no coloring, enlargement, or harmonic explanation.

Of course, composers have borrowed the famous twenty-fourth caprice theme (which Paganini used for eleven variations and finale), including Liszt, Brahms, Rachmaninoff, and others. No criticism there.

Rabin recorded these *Caprices* almost twenty years ago (he died in 1972, at the age of thirty-six). Seraphim's edition is a reissue of the original Capitol release (SPBR-8477). It's sensational. The entire technical gamut of spiccato and saltato, left-hand pizzicato, double and triple stops, flying tenths, and so on, is displayed with clarity and inevitability; the tone is always full and rich regardless of what finger or bow obstacles must be overcome, and the rhythmic conviction is beautiful. Musical finesse and conviction are of equal dominance. Rabin's lyrical depth in the twenty-first caprice is but one example and the dynamic thrust and retreat in an important motive in No. 13 are but two examples of many.

The competition is by Perlman (on Angel S-36860), Ricci (on London 6163), and Zukofsky (on Vanguard 10093/4). The order of these names gives their standing in relation to Rabin. There is no argument from this writer's point of view that Rabin outplays them all.

Nel Cor Più Non Mi Sento (Sonata Appassionata con Variazioni), Op. 38

☐ Fodor (violin) / RCA ARL1-1172

There is not much musical depth here—for some none at all. However, if one wishes to take a sonorous roller coaster ride, zinging all over the landscape with double harmonic flips, pizzicati twists, *sbalzato* dips, and other convolutions, this is the vehicle.

With Fodor at the controls satisfaction is guaranteed. There are a few notes that are out of tune, but so what?

Chamber Music

Cantabile

Centone di Sonate No. 1 in A major

☐ Perlman (violin); Williams (guitar) / Columbia M-34508

Though this work is more fiddle than guitar, you can't deny the splendid teamwork of this pair. The playing takes precedence over the music.

Centone di Sonate

No. 3 in C major / No. 4 in A major / No. 6 in A major

☐ Terebesi (violin); Prunnbauer (guitar) / Telefunken 641300

These are posthumous works with the violin in the lead. No surprises but merely comfortable and tuneful music. A little bit goes a long way but do take advantage of that little bit.

Sonata Concertata in A major

☐ Perlman (violin); Williams (guitar) / Columbia M-34508

Like other Paganini works for this combination, the Sonata is mostly music for violin with the guitar as a secondary personality. But the facts are that a bit more is assigned to the plucked instrument in this fairly sizable work. Another version is on Telefunken

641300 by György Terebesi, violin, and Sonja Prunnbauer, guitar. Perlman's tone wins the race.

Sonata

In A major, Op. 2, No. 1 / In C major, Op. 2, No. 2 / In D minor, Op. 2, No. 3 / (La Sinagoga) In A major, Op. 2, No. 4 / In D major, Op. 2, No. 5 / In A minor, Op. 2, No. 6 / In A major, Op. 3, No. 1 / In G major, Op. 3, No. 2 / In D major, Op. 3, No. 3 / In A minor, Op. 3, No. 4 / In A major, Op. 3, No. 5 / In E minor, Op. 3, No. 6

☐ Kohon (violin); Shaughnessy (guitar) / Orion 6907

Every one of the twelve sonatas is in two movements, a slow and a fast one. Twice, dance formations appear: a *Polonese*, a *Tempo di Walzer*. The scoring is stacked; the guitar is strictly like an unused third-string football quarterback and accompanies in every measure. The violin sings in the spotlight in every measure, though once in awhile a Paganini-like passage, such as left-hand pizzicati, flying thirds, *sbalzato* bowing, and *tremolandi* (the last in part 1 of Op. 2, No. 4), finds air space.

Two of these works (Op. 2, No. 6 and Op. 3, No. 4) are contained in a Telefunken release (No. 641300), and Staryk plays the last of the set in an Orion two-disc miscellaneous music edition (No. 7027) using piano instead of guitar. But the spoils belong to Harold Kohon who invests the music with all the nuances required. His tempos are always right, and when technique has to be let loose he lets loose. Above all, it's the clarity and the definition that make his playing a four-star performance.

Terzetto Concertante in D major for Viola, Guitar, and Cello

☐ Walker (guitar); Geise (viola); Tachezi (cello) / Turnabout 34322

A diverting four-movement work, with a bit more than usual attention given the guitar, in addition to its chief role as accompanimental support. The finale is a "Waltz" in rondo form, not Viennese, of course, but a *Danza Tedesca*.

This is acceptable guitar playing if you don't mind some swishes and glides and acceptable viola playing if you don't mind a few pitch displacements.

Quartet No. 7 in E major for Violin, Viola, Guitar, and Cello

☐ Walker (guitar); Roczek (violin); Geise (viola); Tachezi (cello) / Turnabout 34322

Turnabout emphasizes the word "guitar" in its packaging and in one place terms the work a "Guitar Quartet." Let's call the shots properly. An enjoyable work, this, but the violin is the major domo, the other stringed instruments are helpmates, and the guitar is low man on the totem pole. The guitar is assigned a few interludes in the first movement and has a solo snippet in the *Minuetto*, but otherwise it is the "continuo" to the string trio.

A rich slow movement in which the violin projects a beautiful aria-like conception is the peak of the work. Paul Roczek plays with a fine, full tone and his colleagues support him professionally.

Paganini / Kreisler

Concerto No. 1 in D major for Violin and Orchestra (in one movement)

☐ London Symphony Orchestra / Campoli (violin) / Gamba (conductor) / London STS-15142

In the past Kreisler's condensation was used much more than it is these days when

Solo Instrument and Orchestra

Violin

1333

violinists opt for the complete work. Plenty of the fireworks are still kept in and Campoli negotiates them smoothly. Recognize the conductor? Piero Gamba was a prodigy and made his podium debut at the age of nine.

John Knowles Paine   (1839-1906)

Instrumental   **Concert Variations on the Austrian Hymn in F major, Op. 3, No. 1**

Organ   ☐ Beck (organ) / Musical Heritage Society OR A-263

The "Hymn" means the melody *Gott erhalte Franz den Kaiser* ("God Save our Emperor") which became the Austrian national anthem. It has importance in chamber music history as the theme used for variations in the second movement of Haydn's Op. 76, No. 3 quartet. Haydn kept the theme untouched, surrounding it with new, rejoindering relationships. For most of his composition, Paine does the same. After the subject's announcement, the first four variants keep the thematic contour in place, the last one with extra strong bass action, played on the organ's pedals. A fugal variation then precedes the final declaration of the theme.

This is the recording to have. One is warned about Richard Ellsasser's rendition on Nonesuch 71200 (in an album titled *Yankee Organ Music*). Titled differently (Variations on "Austria"), a severely truncated version is heard. Janice Beck's complete reading runs just nine seconds under ten minutes; Ellsasser delivers his conception in five minutes plus ten seconds. Furthermore, critical editings and changes are made in the condensed setting, beginning with playing the theme unaccompanied!

Fantasie über "Ein' feste Burg," Op. 13

☐ Morris (organ) / New World Records NW-280

A contrast of elements gives co-extensive balance, with prelude material followed by fugal content. Morris plays the piece with full logical insight.

Prelude in B minor, Op. 19, No. 2

☐ Beck (organ) / Musical Heritage Society OR A-263

Paine's title belies the size of his work, which is close to the nine-minute mark. It is a large ternary affair, with textural weight and dynamic intensity marking the central part and strongly contrasting the quieter terminal portions.

This produces a music of poetry and drama, repose and strife. It is romantic, indeed. Janice Beck's coloring of the piece and her subtle registration are most convincing.

Prelude in D flat major, Op. 19, No. 1

☐ Harmon (organ) / Orion 76255

This is gentle, romantic music, gently chromatic, set forth in a gentle tempo. That Paine's formula is plainly clear should not spoil the enjoyment of his dreamlike sketch.

Piano   **Dance, Op. 25, No. 1**

A Funeral March

Under the Lindens, Op. 26, No. 3

☐ Mandel (piano) / Desto 6445/7

Comfortable miniatures. The March was written "in memory of President Lincoln." *Under the Lindens* is the third part of a suite, Ten Sketches for Piano. Mandel's playing is stylistically positive.

Giovanni Paisiello   (1740-1816)

Concerto in F major for Piano and Orchestra

☐ Torino Orchestra / Blumental (piano) / Zedda (conductor) / Turnabout 34495

This Concerto is immediately appealing in its very simplicity. Conventional, yes, but not unimaginative. The conception is solo-directed, the small orchestra, calling only for flutes, horns, and strings, is quite subsidiary. However, with confidence in the piece and with directly characterized playing, Felicja Blumental makes a good case for Paisiello's unassuming Concerto.

Solo Instrument and Orchestra

Piano

Alexandra Pakhmutova   (1929-   )

Youth Overture

☐ State Radio Orchestra / Beloussov (conductor) / Monitor 2038 (monaural)

Rhythmic élan and nice tunes (Russian folk-flavored), packaged with straightforward, Rimsky-Korsakovian orchestration. It can't miss and it doesn't in this spirited performance.

Orchestra

Concerto in E flat minor for Trumpet and Orchestra (1955)

☐ State Radio Orchestra / Popov (trumpet) / Svetlanov (conductor) / Monitor 2030 (monaural)

Not too much is available in this medium and a great deal of what there is doesn't warrant a second hearing. Pakhmutova's piece doesn't dig deep, but in its Boston Pops décor it is appropriate and charming. Clean playing.

Solo Instrument and Orchestra

Trumpet

Giovanni Palestrina   (1525?-1594)

Exsultate Deo

☐ Choir of St. John's College, Cambridge / Guest (conductor) / Argo ZRG–578

Exsultate Deo is a five-part motet, set to the first three verses of Psalm 81. Alan Brown's liner note points out that in contrast to the "cool atmosphere" of most of Palestrina's music this music is "joyous and brilliant." It is also rhythmically nimble, and this quality is carried out in the splendid performance conducted by George Guest.

Choral

Chorus Alone

Hodie Beata Virgo Maria
Senex Puerum Portabat

☐ Choir of King's College, Cambridge / Willcocks (conductor) / Argo ZRG–5398

These motets, both in five parts (two sopranos, alto, tenor, and bass) are grouped together since they were planned as paired works, though usually performed in the reverse order of the above listing. Both were written for the Feast of the Purification. The singing of Willcocks's group is rich and mellifluous.

Hymn—*Jesu Rex Admirabilis*
Hymn—*Tua Jesu Dilectio*
Hymnus in Adventu Dei

☐ Choir of St. John's College, Cambridge / Guest (conductor) / Argo ZRG–578

All three pieces are representative beauties from the Palestrina catalogue. All are exquisitely shaped in the performance, are sensitively balanced, and exhibit an enhancing depiction of style.

Both *Jesu Rex Admirabilis* and *Tua Jesu Dilectio* are termed "sacred madrigals." The Advent Hymn (*Hymnus in Adventu Dei*) is the first of a set of forty-five *Hymni totius anni*, which were published in 1589.

Lauda Sion Salvatorem
O Magnum Mysterium
Tu Es Petrus

☐ Spandauer Kantorei / Behrmann (conductor) / Turnabout 34309

Lauda Sion Salvatorem is in four parts, while the other two motets call for a six-part choir. Fine sound, fine blend, and a totally intelligent set of performances, the highest quality, therefore.

The Song of Songs

☐ Cantores in Ecclesia / Howard (conductor) / Oiseau-Lyre S–338/9

This is a cycle of twenty-nine motets all set to love texts taken from the *Song of Songs.* One need not fear stylistic confusion. Palestrina maintains his identity amidst the feverish pitch of the word images.

Howard's group sings with vibrancy and intelligency. There is a slightly antithetical quality to Michael Howard's conducting, since the lyrical surge if not exactly passion of his argument is not basically *echt*-Palestrinian. Nonetheless, the music never becomes vulgar; though it is romantically knit, it is always tasteful.

Stabat Mater

☐ Choir of King's College, Cambridge / Willcocks (conductor) / Argo ZRG–5398

Palestrina's *Stabat Mater* motet (probably composed in 1589 or 1590, that is, sometime during the last five years of Palestrina's life) is considered to be one of his finest compositions. The scoring is for a double choir, each in four parts (soprano, alto, tenor, and bass), and the music falls into four distinct, though combined sections. Antiphony is the dominating characteristic of the work; the combined choirs are heard in the third section beginning with the words *Juxta crucem.*

The performance is beautifully developed, the vocal quality of the best. A highly recommended edition.

Antiphon—*Assumpta est Maria*

Missa—Assumpta est Maria

Missa Brevis

☐ Choir of St. John's College, Cambridge / Hunt (treble); Tudhope (tenor) / Guest (conductor) / Argo ZRG-690

The *Assumpta est Maria* Mass is based on the Antiphon included in this recorded program. These examples of Palestrina's beautifully moving music are detailed with sonorous richness and splendid atmosphere. An expressively rewarding recording.

Antiphon—*Veni Sponsa Christi*

Mass—*Veni Sponsa Christi*

Motet—*Veni Sponsa Christi*

☐ Choir of St. John's College, Cambridge / Guest (conductor) / Argo ZRG-578

Complete relationship is operative here. The Antiphon consists of four phrases. Palestrina used each one for constructing the Motet, contrapuntally developing the transferred material. In turn, the material in the Motet supplied the basis for the Mass. This is most evident in the Kyrie, where all of the Motet's themes are used, but affiliation with the Motet is also to be recognized in the other sections of the Mass.

The singing is excellent, defining the musical details clearly and yet not bypassing flexibility. There are no reservations to be made for the performances.

Missa De Beata Vergine

☐ Spandauer Kantorei / Behrmann (conductor) / Turnabout 34309

Polished singing makes vivid Palestrina's Mass. However, the atmosphere is not disturbed—the serenity of the world of *plainchant* is maintained.

Missa Papae Marcelli

☐ King's College Choir / Willcocks (conductor) / Seraphim S-60187

This is the most famous of Palestrina's masses. The performance is of absolute melodic cohesion, with phrases defined and yet snugly blended, thus providing a superb continuity. The tonal blend is quite exceptional and Willcocks's direction is of the highest standard of interpretative statement.

Cantata and Oratorio

Robert Palmer (1915-   )

Toccata Ostinato

☐ Mandel (piano) / Desto 6445/7

Percussive and persistently energetic music. No dominating new situation is pictured here but this does not deflect a pertinent interest in Palmer's vitally communicative piece.

Quintet for A Clarinet, String Trio, and Piano

☐ Bloom (clarinet); Kooper (violin); Doktor (viola); Lash (cello); Boehm (piano) / Turnabout 34508

Instrumental

Piano

Chamber Music

The obsessive characteristic of this composer of virile voice is ingrained polyphony, which, promulgated by exceedingly strong rhythmic contours, bestows a freshness not usually associated with the contrapuntal.

Palmer's work is in four movements, with outward adherence to the standard forms. However, he does not revive classical achievements. At heart, Palmer is a romantic (a full-blown twentieth-century one), freeing the structures of the classicists on his individual terms.

Active line writing and fibrous textures are constant in the work, but Palmer avoids the symphonicism that is always on the periphery of the piano-quintet medium (in this case, a clarinet takes the place of the usual first violin).

The performance is of the highest grade with complete artistic understanding. It fulfills Palmer's integrity of purpose.

Andrzej Panufnik (1914-   )

Orchestra

Autumn Music (1965)

☐ London Symphony Orchestra / Peebles (piano) / Horenstein (conductor) / Unicorn RHS-306

Panufnik explains that his composition was written in memory of a friend "who, after a long, incurable illness, experienced her last autumn in 1960." (Autumn Music was composed in 1962 and then revised in 1965.) Understandably threnodic, there is a vernal cast to a number of the sections and some parcels of bell sounds.

Horenstein performs this mood music with full understanding, strongly contrasting the two interludes found within its tripartite construction. The credit to Anthony Peebles is apparently a contractual matter since the piano is of no greater importance than the rest of the orchestra of three flutes, three clarinets, harp, celesta, percussion, and strings—the latter not including any violins.

Heroic Overture (1969)

☐ London Symphony Orchestra / Horenstein (conductor) / Unicorn RHS-306

Bold music, slightly militaristic. Within the outbursts and stamping rhythms there is a noticeable disquiet. The posture of the work is well realized in this recorded performance.

Nocturne (1955)

☐ Louisville Orchestra / Whitney (conductor) / Louisville S-654

No dreamy decorum is practiced by this composer. A ternary plan is proposed by the application of dynamic levels and textural weights, starting with a solo, snareless drum (thereby of dulled timbre) until the forces are built up to a screaming *triple forte* with horns and trumpets zooming up to their upper limits in glissando; the music then returns to its quiet thinness.

For the most part the harmonies are raw; the ground-glass effect of seconds and ninths, augmented unisons and diminished octaves, slowly unwinding together and against each other, indicate that Panufnik's night piece comes from an icy climate. The orchestration is superb, tight, extraordinarily dry. Whitney's players keep it that way. One cannot find the *locus classicus* of this composition. Panufnik's Nocturne is determinedly related only unto itself. This is one of the most important of all the Louisville Orchestra's recordings.

Rhapsody for Orchestra (1956)

☐ Louisville Orchestra / Whitney (conductor) / Louisville S-671

A rather neglected composer in the United States, Panufnik, an expatriate Pole resident in England, does better abroad.

The Rhapsody (an apt title because of its elusive context) is pantonal but not in a doctrinaire sense. The binary design of the work is manifest. Whitney's reading colorfully clarifies the motoric content and clearly guides the restrained aspects.

Sinfonia Elegiaca (1966)

☐ Louisville Orchestra / Whitney (conductor) / Louisville 624 (monaural)

Panufnik's *Sinfonia* is a musical tract about war victims, designed in one continuous movement, sectioned in three parts. It embraces music of bitter draft with an antithetical section expressing music of protest. This strong essay exemplifies artistic agitprop documentation. Its ternary design revolves around the use of dynamics. A soft level is retained for the corner sections with the opposite force demarcating the central portion.

There's a lot of compacted guts (not blatantly stated) in the Louisville reading, fully defining the strengths of Panufnik's work.

Sinfonia Rustica (1948)

Sinfonia Sacra (1963)

☐ Monte Carlo Opera Orchestra / Panufnik (conductor) / Unicorn RHS-315

Important parallels are found in these two works. Stylistically both are neo-romantic in their subjective content, a romanticism that has colorful harmonic barbs with their edges rounded slightly. A tribute to the composer's land of birth is found in the *Sinfonia Rustica* (Panufnik's first symphony) by the use of Polish folk themes as the basis for the musical material. Panufnik composed the *Sinfonia Sacra* (representing his third symphony) "as a tribute to Poland's Millennium of Christianity and Statehood, and as an expression of my religious and patriotic feelings." A further relationship is the use in the *Sinfonia Sacra* of the first known hymn in the Polish language, the *Bogurodzica*, a truly magnificent Gregorian chant.

There are other affiliatory matters aside from national love and native flavor. Each work has four movements: three Visions and a Hymn in the *Sacra*, mood depictions (*con tenerezza, con grazia, con espressione,* and *con vigore*) defined in the *Rustica*. Even the disposition of the performers indicates a relationship. The four trumpets in the *Sinfonia Sacra* are stationed at the four corners of the orchestra; the smaller instrumental forces of the *Sinfonia Rustica* call for two string orchestras with five woodwinds and three brass instruments—the string orchestras are separated, with the eight winds and brass situated in between. A further affinity is the scope of the two pieces, each embracing about twenty-three minutes in length. Finally, both compositions were prize winners. The *Sinfonia Rustica* won the First Prize in the Chopin Competition in Warsaw in 1949; the *Sinfonia Sacra* won First Prize in the Prix de Composition Musicale Prince Rainier III de Monaco in 1963 (it was chosen from 133 total entries representing composers from 38 different countries).

With the composer conducting, the recorded editions are certainly definitive. The Monte Carlo Opera Orchestra is not one of the major league teams but it plays with fine credibility. A splendid issue in all respects.

Tragic Overture (1955)

☐ London Symphony Orchestra / Horenstein (conductor) / Unicorn RHS-306

The Tragic Overture was composed in Warsaw in 1942, "under the influence of the fear and horror of our daily life, and my agonizing sense of worse things to come," Panufnik explains. With the German onslaught Panufnik's prophecy came true and during it every note of music he had composed was destroyed. In 1945, after the war, he reconstructed the piece and then revised it in 1955.

The music is sparked by a four-note motif that propels the rhythmic and thematic material onto a contrasting section and then returns for recapitulatory emphasis as well as balance. Composed forty years ago, Panufnik's Tragic Overture is no dated document. It retains its power for today, defined by this dynamically recorded performance.

Cantata and Oratorio

Universal Prayer (1969)

☐ Louis Halsey Singers / Cantelo (soprano); Watts (contralto); Mitchinson (tenor); Stalman (bass); Watkins, Korchinska, and Bonifacio (harps); Kynaston (organ) / Stokowski (conductor) / Unicorn RHS–305

Panufnik's cantata is tightly constructed (various charts and analytical data are contained in the liner-note material) and as concentrated in its instrumentation of three harps and an organ. The text is by Alexander Pope.

It is a strong and colorful conception, especially in the use of the chorus which sings only one pitch throughout, though it is varied considerably in dynamic range and type of expression.

Stokowski's advocacy of the work is not to be doubted. He gave the premiere (May 1970), directing the work twice on the program, recorded it four months later, then performed the composition again in Princeton, New Jersey, and at St. Patrick's Cathedral in New York City; he later produced it specifically for television. There are no questions concerning the recorded performance. It not only fully realizes Panufnik's conception but presents it with passionate commitment.

Pietro Domenico Paradies   (1707-1791)

Instrumental

Harpsichord

Sonata No. 6 in A major

☐ Sgrizzi (harpsichord) / Nonesuch 71117

The Scarlatti dynamic is exhibited here, with a profitable closing Toccata. Sgrizzi's playing is a marvel of clarity and his registral editing is artistically organized.

Horatio Parker   (1863-1919)

Orchestra

Prelude to Mona

☐ Eastman-Rochester Symphony Orchestra / Hanson (conductor) / Eastman-Rochester Archives ERA-1013

This is the opening to the three-act Opera that won a $10,000 prize in a competition sponsored by the Metropolitan Opera Company. Premiered in 1912, it was short-lived (only four performances). On the strength of the Wagner-romantic Prelude it deserved better.

Allegretto (from Sonata in E flat, Op. 65)

Arietta in C minor, Op. 68, No. 4

Fugue in C minor, Op. 36, No. 3

Slumber Song in A flat major, Op. 68, No. 2

☐ Beck (organ) / Musical Heritage Society OR A-263

The Slumber Song (marked by melodic chromaticism) and the Arietta are from a set of Five Short Pieces for the Organ. The Sonata excerpt is codified by a Bachian rhythmic figure of two long and one short sounds. Parker's C minor Fugue follows the usual, decisive pattern. The ending is a proper confirmation of the previous building of the material rather than a mere dramatic confrontation.

Beck's playing is marked by her distinction of the different objectives of the pieces. She does not overemphasize color when it is not proper. Above all, her registral decisions certify the structural detail of the pieces being played.

The Lark Now Leaves His Watery Nest, Op. 47, No. 6

☐ de Gogorza (baritone); (*accompanist unidentified*) / New World Records NW-247 (monaural)

This is the last of a set of Six Old English Songs. Parker's handling of the cadences in this song, including repeats of portions of the text, is a special and very effective touch.

Emilio de Gogorza made this recording on May 18, 1908 (the same day his wife, Emma Eames, recorded another Parker song—*see below*) for the Victor company. Its modern reissue is to be appreciated.

Love in May, Op. 51, No. 1

☐ Eames (soprano); (*accompanist unidentified*) / New World Records NW-247 (monaural)

A song of light gaiety. The performance is a transfer of a recording made by the famous operatic star Emma Eames in May of 1908. Fine historic value and surprisingly quite clear.

Hora Novissima

☐ Vienna Symphony Orchestra / Hopf (soprano); Wien (alto); Kent (tenor); Berry (bass) / Strickland (conductor) / Desto 6413/4E (monaural)

Granted that there is a good mix of standard styles in Parker's work (Bach, Handel, and even some Mendelssohnian mannerisms), one cannot deny that it is first-class eclecticism. It is of historic importance in the history of American music, as well.

Parker's cantata divides into two parts, with six sections in the first division and five in the second. It is given a passably good performance in this release, electronically reprocessed from the original monaural tapes. (No credit is indicated for the chorus that appears in six of the eleven sections.)

Robert Parris (1924-   )

Concerto for Trombone (1964)

☐ Polish National Radio Orchestra / Siwek (trombone) / Szostak (conductor) / Composers Recordings S-231

Parris's Concerto is no square-phrased conception. The formal design consists of two

---

Instrumental

Organ

Vocal

Voice with Accompaniment

Cantata and Oratorio

Solo Instrument and Orchestra

Trombone

movements, sharply contrasted in structure and content. The Nocturne is a shimmering costume with black bituminous percussion pockets sewn into it, and the *Perpetual Motion* has a constant stream of impetuous energy. The trombone part is of wholesale virtuosity and no performance discount is made by the soloist, Roman Siwek.

Good trombone concerti are still few in number—the medium is not a gracious one for a composer. Robert Parris has provided a first-class entry.

Hubert Parry   (1848-1918)

Orchestra

Overture to an Unwritten Tragedy (1893)

Symphonic Variations (1897)

☐ London Symphony Orchestra / Boult (conductor) / Musical Heritage Society MHS-1483

The detail in the Symphonic Variations is designed in such a way that the variants are molded into a total shape with divisional contrast. Hence, the word "symphonic" is applied formally and not to describe the instrumental medium. This is no new departure, of course, but it certifies structural strength in place of a possible weakening through a continuity of juxtaposed portions.

Both works enjoy a solid performance, with special sonic clarity. (MHS's disc is a transfer from the Lyrita Recorded Edition, produced in England in 1971.)

String Orchestra

An English Suite

Lady Radnor's **Suite (1894)**

☐ London Symphony Orchestra / Boult (conductor) / Musical Heritage Society MHS-1483

Parry's string-orchestra compositions (An English Suite was posthumously published) represent cultured music, cultivating dance forms such as the Allemande, Sarabande, Minuet, Gigue, and Bourrée. The works are harmonically chaste yet removed from academic strictures, as in the compelling content of the muted Slow Minuet in *Lady Radnor's* Suite. (The name of Parry's work comes from its dedication to her. She premiered the composition with her own colorfully named group, Lady Radnor's String Band.)

Boult's reading is artistically apt; it cogently integrates form and content.

John Parry   (1710-1782)

Instrumental

Harp

Sonata in D major

☐ Ellis (harp) / Oiseau-Lyre S-309

Oiseau-Lyre's recording is most welcome, giving a listener the opportunity to hear a fine three-movement example of the work of this blind Welsh harpist–composer. The Sonata is one of four "Lessons," with single variations included in both the slow movement and the Gavotte. Ellis's playing is as smooth as the music.

Harry Partch   *(1901-1974)*

And on the Seventh Day Petals Fell in Petaluma (1966)

Instrumental

☐ Gate 5 Ensemble / Partch (conductor) / Composers Recordings S–213

In the unconventional world of Harry Partch conventional instruments are not to be found. Partch both designed and built his own instruments. They are beautifully shaped and named. *Spoils of War, Boo, Marimba Eroica, Bloboy,* and *Eucal Blossom* are among the more than thirty instrumental types Partch invented. Their tuning is based on a 43-tone-to-the-octave basis so that the resultant pitch shapes match the novel freshnesses of the timbres.

And on the Seventh Day uses a large number of these instruments, first in twenty-three consecutive sets of duos and trios and then through electronic synthesis in ten additional continuous sets of quartets and quintets with a concluding septet. The thirty-four total reflects the predominant Asian-African quality that permeates Partch's music.

Cloud-Chamber Music (1950)

☐ Ben Johnston, Betty Johnston, Pippin, and Partch (instruments) / Composers Recordings 193 (monaural)

Featured in this music, which does not deny its resemblance to Balinese gamelan sounds, are the Partch-invented Cloud-Chamber Bowls (tops and bottoms of Pyrex carboys) and the Adapted Viola (played like a cello and with a range one octave below the violin). A snippet of a Zuni Indian (New Mexico) tune is heard at the end. The twain of old music and new timbres meet, even if only momentarily.

Ulysses Departs from the Edge of the World for a Consort of Harry Partch Instruments, Baritone Saxophone, and Trumpet

☐ Logan (trumpet); Livingston (baritone saxophone and speaker); Mitchell (diamond marimba); Grimes (bamboo marimba and cloud-chamber bowls); Pluth (bass marimba and cloud-chamber bowls) / Orion ORS–7294

A beautiful partnership is involved here: cool jazz trumpet turns with short and calm sax phrases framed by the filigreed timbres of the Partch instruments. Very intriguing, very special, and very good. The performers are top-class.

Barstow

Opera and Dramatic Music

☐ Partch and Stannard (voices); McAllister, Mitchell, Ranta, and Schell (instruments) / Columbia MS–7207

Partch's work is subtitled "Eight Hitchhiker Inscriptions from a Highway Railing at Barstow, California." Each of the statements is prefaced by an instrumental ritornel, and followed by a play on the verbiage through an expansion which is sometimes sung and sometimes intoned. This is Americana at its most fundamental. (Partch called it his "Hobo Concerto." He knew, having spent some eight years during the Depression "riding the rails.")

Barstow has as much punch and kick and depth as a full-scale drama and, in its particular way, is a small masterpiece. The performance is positively entrancing.

The Letter (1943)

☐ Partch (narrator and instrument); Ben Johnston, Betty Johnston, and Pippin (instruments) / Composers Recordings 193 (monaural)

There's humor crossed with wry seriousness in the narrating of a letter that Partch received, including the place (Cincinnati, Ohio) and date (October 2, 1935) right through to the conclusion ("and tell me all the news," etc.). The accompaniment clearly introduces the sentences and is also used for punctuative purposes; the instruments are a Kithara, an Adapted Guitar, and two types of Partchian marimbas.

Partch is the star, reading the letter with precise diction and with no attempt to dramatize. The aloof effect is very good.

Ballet

The Bewitched (1957)

☐ University of Illinois Musical Ensemble / Schell (voice); Olson (marimba eroica and voice) / Garvey (conductor) / Composers Recordings S–304E (monaural)

In this a twelve-episode dance satire Partch deals with symbolism in parodies that are described, for example, as "Visions Fill the Eyes of a Defeated Basketball Team in the Shower Room" and "A Court in Its Own Contempt Rises to a Motherly Apotheosis." Partch aims in his ritualistic theatre piece for a "seeking for release—through satire, whimsy, magic, ribaldry—from the catharsis of tragedy." Even without stage action there is sufficient sonorous effect to hold the attention for most of the seventy-six-minute length of the work.

(The final [tenth] scene and the Epilogue are included in an all-Partch release on Composers Recordings 193. The title of the scene is "The Cognoscenti Are Plunged into a Demonic Descent While at Cocktails." Truly a demonic section.)

Castor & Pollux (1952)

☐ Coleman, Drummond, McAllister, Mitchell, Richards, Ranta, and Schell (instruments) / Columbia MS-7207

Castor & Pollux is described as *A Dance for the Twin Rhythms of Gemini* from *Plectra & Percussion Dances*. It begins with the encounter of Zeus with Leda and concludes with the hatching of the fertilized eggs—first Castor and then Pollux. Percussion sounds are paramount in this allegory, which mates instrumental timbres (Kitharas and Cloud-Chamber Bowls) to match the mating of the beautiful Leda and the male swan and parallels *"Conception"* by pairing a Harmonic Canon with a marimba type, etc.

(Another performance is available in monaural form, on CRI 193, by the Gate 5 Ensemble of Sausalito. Excellent sound, put on disc in 1953.)

Film Music

Daphne of the Dunes (1958)

☐ Partch (adapted viola) / Columbia MS-7207

This is the complete score (17:25 in length) of the music Partch wrote for the film *Windsong*, a modern rendering of the ancient myth of Daphne and Apollo, hence the title given for concert use. (For data concerning another recorded version *see below*.)

Twelve instruments are played by eleven performers, one (as credited above) by Partch himself. In addition, there is a prerecorded tape. However, a chamber music concentrate is produced since not more than a quartet of timbres is used simultaneously. Motivic coherence is strong in the haunting sound conjugations that result from Partch's rhythmic diction.

Windsong (1958)

☐ Partch (instruments) / Composers Recordings 193 (monaural)

An excerpted version (11:52 in length) of the music Partch wrote for the film *Wind-song*. The complete score is recorded (for details *see above*).

Not only is the score condensed in length but two of the dozen instruments used for the complete music are not required in this shorter edition. Partch plays "nearly all the parts, through the well-known device of adding sound track, one part at a time."

Bernardo Pasquini   *(1637-1710)*

Cuckoo **Toccata**

Three Arias

☐ Kipnis (harpsichord) / Columbia M3X-31521

Instrumental

Harpsichord

The *Cuckoo* Toccata (its full title is *Toccata con lo scherzo del cucco* or "Toccata on the Playfulness of the Cuckoo"), which naturally is based on the cuckoo call, is a cuckoo piece to end all cuckoo pieces. Talk about motival engenderment! The piece is a total delight and its intervallic affection is, in the long run, quite moving.

Kipnis captures the music's spirit to the fullest. He delivers the Arias (which he edited from a manuscript in the British Museum) in a moderated and thus most acceptable manner.

Jiří Pauer   *(1919-)*

Charaktery

☐ Annapolis Brass Quintet / Crystal S-207

Chamber Music

"Characters" delineates the "characters of trumpets, horns and trombones." The music is conceived in typical brass terms and would not have validity if transcribed for different timbres. All three movements are set in a civilized contemporary style. The disciplined playing by the Annapolis team works well for Pauer's interesting score.

Gustaf Paulson   *(1898-1966)*

Sonatine, Op. 136, No. 6

☐ Palsson (piano) / Caprice CAP-1069

Instrumental

Piano

The only recorded work by this little-known Swedish composer who deserves long overdue recognition. This piano composition was Paulson's last creation. Its opus identification is a clue to his extraordinary prolificity which resulted in thirteen symphonies, nineteen concertos for various solo instruments (including two for English horn, one for saxophone, and one for double bass), five string quartets, and so forth.

The *Sonatine* is dark-colored, Hindemithian in part, and strongly polyphonic. That it is available on disc should make one grateful to both Caprice for issuing it and Hans Palsson (to whom the work is dedicated) for an explicit and strongly contrasted reading.

Russell Peck   (1945-   )

Percussion

Lift-Off

☐ Hemphill, Van Geem, and Kvistad (bass drums) / Reference Recordings RR-3

These rhythmic varieties were conceived "to give exuberant physical release to the performers and to sweep the audience into an ever-expanding spiral of excitement and momentum." Three players percussing three bass drums are a plain way to achieve this.

Instrumental

Piano

Suspended Sentence

☐ Hays (piano) / Finnadar SR2-720

Peck states he wanted to write music that was "purely pornosonic." He defines the term as "titillation of the senses without any deeper significance." The extremism of definition turns out to be a little-more-than-nine-minute improvisation that whirls around trying to find a theme but never succeeds—deliberately it would seem. There's a little of this and a little of that: jazz turns, glissandi, a pitch here and a pitch there, and a good amount of tone clusters, small- and medium-sized. Listening to Peck's music the first time through may make little sense. Suspend your judgment on *Suspended Sentence* and hear it the second time. Ah yes, it does make sense and has a vitality that shows a genuine imagination.

Doris Hays plays this music with full interpretative wisdom. She understands that Peck's essay is really laced with light shock tactics and she lets them all hang out, nice and loose.

Vocal

Voice and Instrumental Ensemble

Automobile

☐ Ragains (soprano); Middleton (flute); Johnson (percussion); Calvetti (bass) / Composers Recordings SD-367

Truly, a chamber music vaudeville, with part 1 a sonic prophesy of "a lounge act in the year 2000, when supposedly Stockhausen–Boulez sounds will be *in,* as Chopin's are today." Actually, Peck's S-B complex is "in" right now, not in lounges but on university campuses. The sense of spoofery continues in the second part, as a result of chance operations. Included in the scenario are instrumental improvisation, fractured prose, grunts, hacks, snorts, jazz, ostinati, vocalise, and so on. Peck's aleatoric game is fun to hear.

Choral

Chorus with Accompaniment

Quotations from the Electric Chairman

☐ Ineluctable Modality / London (conductor) / Advance FGR-18S

Hot avant-garde sounds are curled around jazzy stuff. The amalgam is in a constant boil, exciting in its sophisticated search (fully realized) for relating "moderno and pop music."

Backed up with an amplified double bass, which can be substituted by a tape (used for the recording), the chorus performs free pitch selection, claps, finger snaps, foot stamps, mouth sounds, velar clicks, and kissing sounds. It is a feast of choral swing and "swingle" doings, constantly in action.

The work is extremely difficult to perform, but certainly London's group has managed extremely well with Peck's sonic saturation.

Carlos Pedrell (1878-1941)

Caballitos

☐ Averino (soprano); Slonimsky (piano) / Orion 7150 (monaural)

This one-and-one-half-minute simple folklike song is the only recorded music by the Uruguayan composer.

Flor Peeters (1903-   )

Toccata, Fugue, and Hymn

☐ Krapp (organ) / Turnabout 34627

The Toccata, Fugue, and Hymn is memorable organ music, its three parts based on *Ave Maris Stella.* This thematic pattern is clearly woven into the fabric, making for a music of gorgeous textures, consistent vigor, and illuminative tonality.

Edgar Krapp's playing shows integrated registration without any stiff conditioning of Peeters's music. Quite an achievement for this young organist (he was twenty-eight years when he recorded the Toccata, Fugue, and Hymn).

Jubilate Deo

☐ Peloquin Chorale / Hokans (organ) / Peloquin (conductor) / Gregorian Institutes EL–19 (monaural)

This is a fine, classically defined example of the work of a composer who has produced voluminous liturgical music. The recording is a robust one.

C. Alexander Peloquin (20th cent.)

Kyrie and Gloria from *Missa Christus Rex*

☐ Peloquin Chorale and Instrumental Ensemble / Hokans (organ) / Peloquin (conductor) / Gregorian Institutes EL–19 (monaural)

An example of straightforward liturgical music, mainly homophonic and with more than a touch of Vaughan Williams. Clean inserts by organ and brass instruments add color. The recorded account is good.

Krzysztof Penderecki (1933-   )

Anaklasis for Strings and Percussion (1960)

☐ Symphony Orchestra of the National Philharmonic, Warsaw / Markowski (conductor) / Philips 6500683

The orchestration does not include winds or brass, calling as it does for forty-two strings, harp, piano, celesta, and percussion. Weights play an important role in the three athematical sections that form the design. In this case the strings, used in a variety of massed communication, are heavy, the percussion is lighter and even more motile. This orchestrational concentration creates new contents and thereby new meanings. Markowski's statement of this music is exceptional.

De Natura Sonoris (1966)

☐ Buffalo Philharmonic Orchestra / Foss (conductor) / Nonesuch 71201

Penderecki's *De Natura Sonoris* is an exercise in sonority research (athematic, of course). In this instance, Penderecki includes a flavorsome jazzy bit and gives special attention to the percussion, though the eighteen winds, fourteen brass, piano, harmonium (a favorite instrument of Penderecki's), flexatone, and strings are often treated as and sound like percussion.

Foss's orchestra plays with more clarity than the Cracow Philharmonic (on Philips 839701). Nonesuch's sound is also far better identified. Fuzziness and imbalances mar the Philips disc.

De Natura Sonoris No. 2 (1968)

☐ Louisville Orchestra / Mester (conductor) / Louisville S-722

One hears the usual sonorous summary which is Penderecki's speciality and which he dispenses *summa cum laude*. This piece calls for a very large orchestra with integrated timbres that are rare but very fitting: flexatone, pennywhistle, musical saw, wind machine, and so on. A huge number of effects make this work exceedingly effective. Try it, you'll be intrigued.

Fluorescences for Orchestra (1962)

☐ Symphony Orchestra of the National Philharmonic, Warsaw / Markowski (conductor) / Philips 6500683

The sounds will mesmerize you if you do not draw back but meet this piece willingly. The timbres Penderecki includes here are particular, pronged, and percussive: typewriter (but in no way fun-fun stuff à la Leroy Anderson), siren (Varèse would have approved), electric bell, whistles, saw, file, and pieces of iron, wood, and glass.

The unsigned liner notes term these substances "Satie-like," but surely this is a false description for material used to affirm structural force, textural variation, and to frame color chunks.

The clarity of the recording is certainly magnificent. There is no doubt as to Markowski's reading. Penderecki's music is one of his specialties.

Fonogrammi for Flutes and Chamber Orchestra (1961)

☐ Polish Radio Symphony Orchestra / Penderecki (conductor) / Angel S-36949

Skip part 1 of the instrumental heading. The flutes (three of them) are very minor in this denial of traditional sounds. There's a great deal of percussion, plus strings and harpsichord. These timbres are split, fragmented, and passionately dissected. Accordingly, extremely high, almost pitchless sounds are matched against violent tam tam blasts and thus produce an excellent forgery of taped electronicized sound by instruments played by live musicians. No matter how you approach or consider it, the piece holds the attention.

String Orchestra

Emanationen for Two String Orchestras (1959)

☐ Polish Radio Symphony Orchestra / Penderecki (conductor) / Angel S-36950

This is a triumph of string refinement, in which dissonant luminosity is the end result. In the pitch sphere the two string orchestras move in secundal opposition since the second group is tuned an intervallic minor second higher, making for a midgeted cluster arrangement (reflecting Cowell). Microtones appear via third tones (reflecting Haba). The fragmentation of color devices is bound in (reflecting Webern). Even though the technical sources are easily identified, the totality is properly assigned to Penderecki, who has blended these close relationships into his own creative personality. Oddly, and speaking subjectively, I identify all this with a sensuousness that reflects Debussy.

A good performance is also available on the Candide label (31071). Penderecki's is to be preferred simply because he is the composer. Further, there is just a bit more forward action here than in the Candide edition, conducted by Alois Springer.

Kanon for Orchestra and Tape (1962)

☐ Polish Radio Symphony Orchestra / Penderecki (conductor) / Angel S–36949

The orchestra is a string body of fifty-two instruments, mostly individualized in their scoring. The tape is used in delay fashion, repeating material played by the strings while they move on in the score, thus presenting a new form of canonic enterprise. Whereas the distances between such *dux* (antecedent) and *comes* (consequent) make the imitation exceedingly difficult to comprehend, the preoccupation with heavying the textural content is obvious.

Penderecki's sound tapestry has the usual assortment of colors. The beginning outlines the style of the exposition: two bomblike thrusts, then a light sopranoish spray of pointillistic qualities, followed by a murmuring of pitches. It isn't profound but it is tremendously interesting throughout its nine-and-one-half-minute length.

Polymorphia for 48 String Instruments (1961)

☐ Cracow Philharmonia Orchestra / Czyz (conductor) / Philips 839701

These sound potencies are served up full and tight. The quality is varied so that one block is agitated, another is glided, another is bow-tapped, and so forth. If you know Penderecki's style, there will be no surprise until the sudden final C major chord. Such harmonic thaw doesn't match the clusterized cold abstractions that have preceded it.

Threnody for the Victims of Hiroshima (for 52 Strings) (1960)

☐ Rome Symphony Orchestra / Maderna (conductor) / RCA VICS–1239

Extraordinary string instrument mastery marks Penderecki's work. It is considered to be one of the most important ever produced in the medium and certainly the most powerful example in the literature for string orchestra. This instrumentational inventory was never previously attempted (though it has been since imitated). In this sonorous impressibility the snap pizzicato of Bartók is a delicate and almost noble gesture. The *Threnody* is a music of fastidious frenzy, a fury that moves slowly and in so doing purposely tortures the listener with remembrances of the Hiroshima horror. It is impossible to relinquish the thought that one is being musically returned to the scene of the crime. As such, the score becomes one of the classics of the twentieth century.

Maderna's performance is acute if a trifle analytical. Since Penderecki's work exemplifies cancellation of all musical elements except sound *as* sound (the textures do not follow the usual means of being either lean or fat), Maderna tends to be concerned more with the how of the technical means at the expense of the expressive content. Fortunately, the score is sufficiently strong to overcome this minor fault.

Band

Pittsburgh Overture (1967)

☐ American Wind Symphony Orchestra / Boudreau (conductor) / Point Park College KP-101

More than the usual amount of percussion is found in this band piece—"wind symphony orchestra" notwithstanding, the category involved is that of the band. The percussion stimulates the extremely colorful details used. Shapes rather than themes are Penderecki's processes. These produce an external arrangement rather than internal development. It all adds up to a blockbuster addition to the still restricted repertory of the band.

The work is played with striking virtuosity.

Solo Instrument and Orchestra

Cello

Cello Concerto (1972)

☐ Polish Radio Symphony Orchestra / Palm (cello) / Penderecki (conductor) / Angel S-36949

The solo part has a coldly forbidding technical content interspersed with steaming hot whirlwinded passages that make Paganini's demands a cinch by comparison. Explosive figures blast off the cello's strings, the music is hurt and angry; warmth and gentlemanly gentleness are absent and so are the inevitable ball-playing sequences between solo voice and orchestral forces. The latter explode in the usual Pendereckian manner, with tangled and transformed sonorities.

There are few cellists who would care about putting their fingers and bows to work on this monstrously difficult piece (they should). Those who might would have a difficult task bettering Siegfried Palm's execution. It was Palm for whom the work was written. It was dedicated to him and he gave the premiere at the 1972 Edinburgh Festival.

Sonata for Cello and Orchestra (1964)

☐ Orchestra of Radio Luxembourg / Blees (cello) / Springer (conductor) / Candide 31071

Here presented is avant-garde virtuosity without reticence, meaning that all parts (not only the strings) of the solo instrument are played with either bow or fingers. The nervous, improvisationlike second part of the work is akin to a concerted black mass. Put another way, Penderecki performs a rape of the instrument. To watch it in public performance equals musical voyeurism. On a recording there's no action but there are plenty of sounds. Those alone offer plenty of titillation.

This isn't music for those with delicate tastes. (For flutters and whispers, light prattle and sound trickles they will have to seek [and listen] elsewhere.) It is lusty and gutsy and it is played with incredible macho by Thomas Blees.

Harpsichord

Partita for Harpsichord and Orchestra (1971)

☐ Polish Radio Symphony Orchestra / Blumental (harpsichord) / Penderecki (conductor) / Angel S-36950

The harpsichord is not featured as a solo instrument but instead functions in group dialogues and units with harp, guitar, bass guitar, and double bass. The orchestra consists of nine winds, six brass, seven percussion (including celesta and glockenspiel), and strings. This is a typical Penderecki piece of color fibers banded together and separated, coming together again and moving on to another exhibit. The substance is the color, which in turn is the compositional process.

One can be assured of the artistic and technical success of the recording. This is a highly recommendable disc.

Capriccio No. 2 for Violin and Orchestra (1967)

☐ Buffalo Philharmonic Orchestra / Zukofsky (violin) / Foss (conductor) / Nonesuch 71201

This Capriccio's *raison d'être* is an avant-garde brand of virtuosity, and there's no mildness about it whatsoever. Included are all the tricks of the fiddle trade plus bowing behind the bridge, some freely notated lines, and the highest possible pitch that can be reached on a specific string. The piece is capricious in its color partnership with the big orchestra, which is treated like a huge chamber music ensemble, including four saxophones of three different types, contrabass clarinet, electric bass guitar, and harmonium, as well as the usual winds and brass (both enlarged, with four oboes and six horns), piano, harp, percussion, and strings.

The other edition on the market, Angel S–36950, can't be second-guessed readily since it is conducted by the composer, and neither the Polish Radio Symphony Orchestra nor Wanda Wilkomirska, the soloist, are strangers to this type of music. (Wilkomirska gave the premiere in Donaueschingen in October, 1967 and Penderecki had her abilities in mind when he wrote his Capriccio [sometimes, as *Schwann* lists it, known as "Capriccio No. 2" in order to differentiate it from another Penderecki work with the same title].) However, Zukofsky bypasses her by having less of the high seriousness that marks her interpretation. Should you choose W. over Z. you will not be stung. Nonetheless, you should realize that Zukofsky and Foss play the work in 10:12 and Wilkomirska and Penderecki cover the ground in 11:36. This difference is another sign of the seriousness of the one recording and the more capricious interpretation of the other.

Miniatures for Violin and Piano (1959)

☐ Banat (violin); Vered (piano) / Candide 31071

Tempting subtitles dealing with musical instruments are offered by Penderecki: *Okaryna* ("ocarina"), *Basetla* (a small string bass), and *Skrzypce* ("violin"). Forget it, since there are no imitations but simply an offering of fragmentary, quirky colors. Webern in Pops style, so to speak.

String Quartet (1960)

☐ Kohon String Quartet / Candide 31071

One does not find the substance of four-string instrument writing here, not even of the spidery post-Webern kind. A good part of the quartet consists strictly of percussion sounds produced by striking various parts of the instruments. (In this gentle S–M scoring approach normal bowing is off limits.) Then follows the use of raw timbre: playing on the tailpiece, performing between bridge and tailpiece, indefinite pitches (as high as one can reach on the top string), sophisticated forms of pizzicato, glisses, and the like. There are no particular formal connotations. The positives of color alone provide the compositional order. Pitch arrangement and the like would be an intrusion and would be a stylistic error.

Of course a quartet of this kind will never find its way into *Hausmusik* territory. The music demands prodigious professionalism and requires the fullest sympathetic understanding of the composer's objectives. The seriousness and the technique are provided by the Kohon team. Their versatility is tested and proven in this recorded report.

Miserere (1965)

☐ Schola Cantorum Stuttgart / Gottwald (conductor) / Candide 31071

The *Miserere* is an excerpt from Penderecki's St. Luke Passion (see under *Cantata and*

Oratorio: Passion and Death of Our Lord Jesus Christ According to St. Luke) which he has approved as having independent status as well. Accordingly, it has been published in that manner. The recorded publication here is sensitively executed by the three choruses plus boys' choir.

Stabat Mater (1962)

☐ Schola Cantorum Stuttgart / Gottwald (conductor) / Candide 31071

Three choruses, each in sixteen parts, furnish virtuosic vocalism in Penderecki's conception. The *Stabat Mater* was composed as an individual piece and then included in the St. Luke Passion which Penderecki completed in 1965 (see under *Cantata and Oratorio: Passion and Death of Our Lord Jesus Christ According to St. Luke*). It retains its validity as an independent entity as proven by this excellent performance.

Cantata and Oratorio

Dies Irae (Auschwitz Oratorio) (1967)

☐ Orchestra and Chorus of the Cracow Philharmonia / Woytowicz (soprano); Ochman (tenor); Ladysz (bass) / Czyz (conductor) / Philips 839701

Penderecki's *Dies Irae,* together with his St. Luke Passion are his two strongest works. The blood-chilling intensity of this score probes painfully deep with its reminders of the indescribable horrors of the Nazis' death camp. To form his essay Penderecki has drawn his texts from the Apocalypse, Aeschylus, Psalm 114, Louis Aragon, Paul Valéry, and a pair of contemporary Polish poets. From the first words (all translated into Latin, save for those sections in Greek which remain unchanged) "Fetters of death have entwined me . . ." to the final ones: "The wind rises. Let us try to live!" the music is a thunderbolt of an essay using Penderecki's orchestralized choralism with melismatically styled solo sections and vivid orchestration.

The performance is inspired. All of the technical data such as tone clusters, microtones, glissandi, and explicit contrastive registration are met with complete assurance and with dramatic coloration. Those who argue (rightfully) that places like Auschwitz and the events that placed it into history must never be forgotten have a power-laden sonorous document to use. There are not many lasting works of this type of musical protest. In the twentieth century Shostakovich's *Babi Yar* Symphony (see under *Shostakovich: Orchestra* [Symphony No. 13]) and Penderecki's *Dies Irae* are the two most important.

Kosmogonia for Soprano, Tenor, Bass, Mixed Chorus, and Orchestra (1970)

☐ Symphony Orchestra and Chorus of the National Philharmonic, Warsaw / Woytowicz (soprano); Pustelak (tenor); Ladysz (bass) / Markowski (conductor) / Philips 6500683

This is the world of outer space according to Krzysztof Penderecki. Stated another way, this is the way John Williams would have written the score for the film *Star Wars* if he had been Krzysztof Penderecki. Various texts are used: Copernicus, the Book of Genesis, Sophocles, Ovid, and so on, but the compression into the sonorous bands that strap the score makes word definition almost impossible.

A seamless rendition, nevertheless.

Magnificat (1974)

☐ Polish Radio National Symphony Orchestra, Polish Radio Chorus of Cracow, and Soloists and Boys' Chorus from the Cracow Philharmonic Chorus / Lagger (bass) / Penderecki (conductor) / Angel S-37141

Penderecki's creative behavior in this darkly toned work retains some of his habits: wails and glides, plus microtones and mild clusters, but in order to justify the objective, polyphonic determination prevails—freely but recognizable within the setting of the twelve verses. Thus there is a fugue with the usual devices of augmentation and diminution, inversion and retrograde, as well as a passacaglia. The pace is slow-moving but the music is enriched through the emphasis on the events.

This is a moving performance with magnificent sound locked into the recording.

Passion and Death of Our Lord Jesus Christ According to St. Luke (1965)

☐ Cracow Philharmonia Orchestra and Boys' Chorus and Mixed Chorus of the Cracow Philharmonia Orchestra / Woytowicz (soprano); Hiolski (baritone); Ladysz (bass); Herdegen (speaker) / Czyz (conductor) / Philips 802771/2

☐ Cologne Symphony Orchestra and Radio Chorus / Woytowicz (soprano); Hiolski (baritone); Ladysz (bass); Bartsch (narrator) / Czyz (conductor) / RCA VICS–6015

The Passion covers twenty-six sections, divided (as Bach's St. Matthew Passion) into the "Passion" and the "Death." In addition to the account of the Passion in Luke, passages are used from the Gospel According to St. John, Psalm excerpts, portions from the Lamentations of Jeremiah, and from the Liturgy for Holy Week. The basis of this material may be religious; the result is beyond sacred boundaries.

Penderecki's Passion is an example of strictly formal disembodiment, of sonorous data shaken ruthlessly out of their shell. Penderecki's choral and vocal techniques are especially dazzling. The use of microtones gives a freedom and scope to the gamut that create chromatic pitch of ingressive intensity. For once one feels the great power inherent in microtonal measurements. A large amount of cluster harmonies are employed as punctuations and bridges, and as flat surfaces for projecting secondary colors. The combination of these against the pithy "Bach" motive which highlights the tone rows that Penderecki uses, unifies the musical pigmentation.

The orchestration quite often turns into instrumentalized vocalization. In turn, the chorus becomes an orchestralized body, with rhythmic repetitions of indeterminate pitches, whispering, hissing, semi-whistling; slow, long glissandi; as well as speaking in strict time. Nothing is done for the sake of yellow-journalistic music. All of it is for expanding the expressivity of the work. All of it is totally genuine.

With the same three vocal soloists and conductor there is, naturally, much similarity between the two performances. However, Leszek Herdegen's narration is far clearer and much more compelling that that of Rudolf Jürgen Bartsch (Herdegen had the advantage of preparing his role for the world premiere and appeared in a number of subsequent performances). The choral diction is somewhat troubled in the RCA release, and even, at times, in the other recording, but for the greater part the Cracow choruses are better.

A further inducement for choosing the Philips version is the inclusion of Penderecki's *Threnody for the Victims of Hiroshima*. Though a far better performance is directed by Bruno Maderna (see under *String Orchestra*), its incorporation in the album is a bonus not to be overlooked. The packaging is of the deluxe variety in the case of Philips. (RCA shortens the title to *Passion According to St. Luke*. Philips doesn't telescope the heading, indicating the original, *Passio et Mors Domini Nostri Jesu Christi Secundum Lucam* plus the full English translation.) Both productions enjoy excellent sound, just below four-star rating. That rating belongs to the composer.

Utrenja (1971)

☐ Symphony Orchestra and Chorus of the National Philharmonic, Warsaw, and Pioneer Choir / Ambroziak and Woytowicz (sopranos); Szczepańska (mezzo-soprano); Pustelak (tenor); Denysenko, Carmeli, Ladysz, and Lagger (basses) / Markowski (conductor) / Philips 6500557

A massive work of almost seventy-six minutes, *Utrenja,* which means "morning prayer," divides into two parts: *The Entombment of Christ* and *The Resurrection of Christ.* It calls for soloists (only the mezzo-soprano and tenor listed above sing in both divisions, otherwise the vocal cast changes in part 2), two mixed choirs, and a large orchestra (quadruple woodwinds plus contrabass clarinet and four saxophones of two types, sixteen brass, and a huge percussion array of thirty different types, some duplicated and including such esoterica as hyoshigi, wood bells, Sanctus bells, a piece of train rail, and glass chimes, the usual string section, plus three different keyboard instruments as well as a bass guitar).

Utrenja bears the Penderecki trademark of bruised sonorities and clustered explosions. Some triadic contrasts are used but they only bring the fricative style more into relief. The last carries over to the choral writing (the most prominent particular in this work is that the individual solo voices are of lesser pertinence). The massed voices whistle, yell, and shriek, whisper, speak, and babble, and are an orchestration unto themselves. They form more than a fringe benefit to the colors of the large orchestra and are treated accordingly, so that division of the choirs reaches a total of forty-eight parts.

This extraordinary scoring solution is employed in such a way that part 1 has a gray tone with a slightly brighter quality found in part 2. Especially in the first section this is grim music. In the second part it is tinctured with sonorous dynamite, but a sense of aggressiveness never leaves.

This is the sole complete performance on records. At one time Ormandy and the Philadelphia Orchestra, plus soloists (two of whom appear on the Philips release: Stefania Woytowicz and Peter Lagger), and the Temple University Choirs recorded part 1 for RCA (LSC–3180). Since the essay directed by Andrzej Markowski is much stronger, tighter, and clearer in its details the deletion of the RCA disc is not really a loss.

Opera and Dramatic Music

The Devils of Loudun (1969)

☐ Orchestra and Chorus of the Hamburg State Opera / Troyanos, Thieme, and Kruger (sopranos); Ahlin (mezzo-soprano); Boese and Steiner (contraltos); Wilhelm, Marschner, and Melchert (tenors); Hiolski, Blankenburg, and Workman (baritones); Schultz (bass-baritone); Ladysz, Sotin, Wiemann, and Van Mill (basses); Hess, Mamero, and Eckhardt (speaking parts) / Janowski (conductor) / Philips 6700042

Penderecki's opera is drawn from the Aldous Huxley novella of the same title. Its three acts, split into thirty-two scenes, are an interfusion of the sacred and the profane, laced with sex accomplished and sex frustrated, leading to bigotry and hatred, continuing with the sadism and grinding torture that accompanies a witch trial, and concluding with a burning at the stake. (Nicolas Slonimsky's superbly succinct and exquisitely elliptical description of the plot demands quotation: "dealing with a *furor uterinus* among nuns of Loudun struck by a multifutuent incubus personified by a neighboring monastic youth.")

No operatic straightjacket constrains Penderecki's work. It is conventional only in its use of certain recitative projections. Otherwise, monologues and dialogues are freely pulsed or rhythmically defined, the music does not merely support but rather is as important to plot motivation as the words sung or spoken. The style is polyglot within the harmonic and linear scope, and Penderecki's graphic tone coloring includes fatty clusters, scraped fractional tones, stridencies and glides, and a pitch archery that zooms far up and way down.

The inventive yield is great and the recording is executed beautifully. Philips has supplied the full text in German (the language used in the performance), English, and French. A huge amount of very important prefatory material is also included.

William Penn   *(1943-   )*

Ultra Mensuram for Three Brass Quintets (1971)

Brass Ensemble

☐ Western Michigan University Wind Ensemble / Bjerregaard (conductor) / Composers Recordings S-340

The title is a direct clue to the contents. "Beyond Mensuration" means the use of some type of freely disposed arrangement, and Penn accordingly uses spatial and graphic notation. For these splashes of sound, with occasional compact smashes, even multi-asymmetrical pulsations would not fit. There is a convulsive energy within the fragments, consisting of color wisps, growls, and sprays of sound.

Penn's music exemplifies a liberated brass world. Its performance difficulties are beyond description, yet these college musicians provide a magnificent performance.

Fantasy

Instrumental

Harpsichord

☐ Louwenaar (harpsichord) / Composers Recordings SD-367

There is a paucity of valuable, valid, and viable contemporary harpsichord music. In this work musicianship and technique are joined in a blend that meets all the requirements for success. One can state that the future life of this piece is assured.

There is no chaste coverage in the *Fantasy*. There is no spiky contemporary revisiting of Baroque sequences, either. Penn's music is exciting, with an open-minded view of toccata turmoil punctuated with cluster credits. Such harpsichordic hospitality is rarely found in the literature for the instrument.

Karyl Louwenaar delivers all the gusto, vehemence, and heartiness of the score. This is stirring music presented in a stirring performance.

Four Preludes for *Leigh Howard Stevens*

Marimba

☐ Stevens (marimba) / Composers Recordings SD-367

This is technically difficult music to perform on an instrument that has a very restricted literature. Most marimba pieces are in the "ten-twent-thirt" category, with stock-in-trade patterns—a result of commercial music-publishing objectives. Penn's pieces demand virtuosity but are not outré, having for the greater part a nocturnal poetic subtlety.

The Preludes represent a challenging addition to the repertory and are given an exemplary performance by the musician for whom they were composed. There is no doubt that Penn has created music that is marimba box office.

Chamber Music II for Cello and Piano

Chamber Music

☐ Budd (cello); Penn (piano) / Advance FGR-19S

There is nothing intimate about this sky-rocketing and percussively layered piece, even with its contrastive lyrical material.

This difficult music receives a skillful production.

Clermont Pépin   *(1926-   )*

Monade for Strings (1964)

String Orchestra

☐ Brott (conductor) / Composers Recordings S-317

Monade (it should be precisely designated as *Monade I,* since Pépin has composed a second one for strings, a *Monade III* for violin and orchestra, and a fourth and fifth in the series, both for violin and piano) is for fourteen string instruments. These portray a solid yet inner-active totality somewhat suggestive of the play of sustained electronic sounds.

Johann Christopher Pepusch   (1667-1752)

Chamber Music

Trio Sonata in G minor

☐ Rampal and Duschenes (flutes); Gilbert (harpsichord) / Orion 73114

This was originally a *Sonata a Tre con Hautbois, Flauto e Basso.* Although the substitution of a flute for the oboe diminishes the contrast, it does not interfere with the musical content. The format is the pat one of alternate slow and fast movements. The piece is played with rhythmic vigor, lightness and clarity, as well as expressive phrasing. (The same performance is in a seven-record release on Everest 3194.)

Mario Peragallo   (1910-   )

Choral

Chorus Alone

De Profundis Clamavi ad te

☐ Monteverdi-Chor, Hamburg / Jürgens (conductor) / Telefunken 641010

Peragallo's motet covers four- to seven-part writing and leans on the traditional *Dies Irae* motive for its message. It shows the attitude of an antiromantic. The work is given a penetrating interpretation.

Ronald Perera   (1941-   )

Electronic Music

Alternate Routes (1971)

☐ Composers Recordings SD-364

Perera's objective is contrast between heavy and light material. However, textural punctuations create a subsidiary contrastive class, especially glides and oscillations.

Moses Pergament   (1893-1977)

Instrumental

Violin

Chaconne for Solo Violin (1941)

☐ Dekov (violin) / Bis LP-9

Serious music, this, and seriously tonal. It also is seriously patterned in its variational formation after Bach's famous Chaconne. But that does not result in love's labor lost since Pergament's opus is based on and integrates the use of the *Kol Nidre* motive that is sung in the synagogue to usher in *Yom Kippur,* the most solemn of the Jewish holy days.

The Chaconne (originally written for viola) is played in a communicative manner. The thought persists that it would be intriguing to hear Itzhak Perlman, or Pinchas Zukerman, or Isaac Stern tackle this piece.

Giovanni Battista Pergolesi *(1710-1736)*

Concerti Armonici

No. 1 in G major / No. 2 in G major / No. 3 in A major / No. 4 in F minor

☐ Stuttgart Chamber Orchestra / Münchinger (conductor) / London STS-15244

These Concerti (and the two others listed *below*) are also known as "concertinos." They also enjoy the rubric "attributed," so it is guess work whether they are by Pergolesi. However, worthy substances are here to hear and enjoy and there is a good percentage of invention. Münchinger is a fine stylist, and the music is presented in exemplary fashion.

Concerti Armonici

No. 5 in E flat major / No. 6 in B flat major

☐ Stuttgart Chamber Orchestra / Münchinger (conductor) / London 6395

(See remarks immediately above.)

Concerto for Flute

No. 1 in G major / No. 2 in D major

☐ Stuttgart Chamber Orchestra / Rampal (flute) / Münchinger (conductor) / London 6395

As with a certain number of his other works, musicologists and other researchers have not been able to confirm officially that these concerti are by Pergolesi. If not, the counterfeiter has produced beautiful copies, containing freshness and sequences that are sensitive and musical.

The performance is of the highest standard. Rampal has recorded the second work also with Ristenpart conducting the Saar Radio Chamber Orchestra on Musical Heritage Society MHS-976.

Sonata in C major

☐ Sgrizzi (harpsichord) / Nonesuch 71117

Short and sweet—a one-movement affair. Clear and healthy music, not great, but pleasurable. Sgrizzi plays it cool by playing it straight and without pretensions.

Sinfonia in F major for Cello and Continuo

☐ Dommisch (cello); Ruth Ristenpart (harpsichord) / Nonesuch 71119

This is really a sonata cast in the standard four movements. Don't look for dynamic wonders, though black–white weight differences do appear. Tempi in the pair of fast movements are on the slow side. It is the nice phrasing and the forceful harpsichord cohesion (a grateful point) that recommend this portrayal.

Magnificat

☐ Academy of St. Martin-in-the-Fields and King's College Choir, Cambridge / Vaughan (soprano); Baker (contralto); Partridge (tenor); Keyte (bass) / Willcocks (conductor) / Argo ZRG-505

Special use of *plainsong* in two of the choruses marks Pergolesi's work. The Magnificat is handsomely presented.

String Orchestra

Solo Instrument and Orchestra

Flute

Instrumental

Harpsichord

Chamber Music

Cantata and Oratorio

Stabat Mater

☐ Rossini Orchestra of Naples / Raskin (soprano); Lehane (contralto); Zanon (organ) / Caracciolo (conductor) / London 25921

Persuasively presented with fine playing on the part of the instrumentalists and with good singing. Diction is only fair; the slight revision and organ part by Zanon are acceptable.

John MacIvor Perkins   *(1935-   )*

Orchestra   **Music for Thirteen Players (1964)**

☐ Contemporary Chamber Players of the University of Chicago / Shapey (conductor) / Composers Recordings S-232

Perkins's work is guided by serial technique with sound layers and sound pulverization, but it is always soundly formationed. There is, of course, in music of this type a debunking of tonality with its attendant modulation. However, there is in Perkins's structure modulation of a different type, namely, by relationships of densities compared to thinner totalities. Development of material also takes place through the application of differing textural weights.

Shapey is an expert in handling complexities found in a score like this one. Be assured the performance is excellent.

Instrumental   **Caprice (1963)**

Piano

☐ Blackwood (piano) / Composers Recordings S-232

Authoritative, dynamic twelve-tone music. Clear formations define the sections derived from tempo differences. The thrust of the music is heard with virtuosic conclusions in the playing by Easley Blackwood, himself a composer, who had commissioned Perkins's *Caprice*.

CRI has forgotten to list the piece on the record's label. It is the second cut (or band) on the second side of the disc.

George Perle   *(1915-   )*

Orchestra   **Rhapsody for Orchestra (1954)**

☐ Louisville Orchestra / Whitney (conductor) / Louisville 545-9 (monaural)

Perle blocks out his material freely, massing and opposing its darks and lights to give the broadest and yet most pertinent expression to the total form. This is music with strength and yet it is remarkably sensitive in its individual character. It is informal and yet possesses stability. (For informality notice the final cadence.)

Instrumental   **Three Inventions for Solo Bassoon**

Bassoon

☐ Grossman (bassoon) / Coronet 2741

Arthur Grossman performs these connected pieces with an artistry that is to be envied. Perle's music contains immediately impressive ideas. The first piece is mainly declamatory, the second moves into more motility, and the set is completed by ostinato detail. Successful unaccompanied music for a homophonic instrument demands creative courage and mastery of the special medium. A number of composers have the former but lack the latter. George Perle has both.

Monody II for Unaccompanied Double Bass (1962)
Double Bass

☐ Turetzky (contrabass) / Advance FGR–1 (monaural)

The content of *Monody II* indicates serialistic investigation—meaning ordered pitch arrangement—but it is not hostile to tonal polarities within the writing. A generous use of pizzicati and some percussive punctuations are special color ingredients.

Mostly positive playing with the exception of some roughed tone passages in the upper register.

Monody No. 1 (1960)
Flute

☐ Baron (flute) / Composers Recordings 212 (monaural)

Perle's work lies in the twelve-tone orbit, but if one is permitted to coin a term, this exceedingly accessible work for unaccompanied flute is vernacular twelve-tone music. And the fellow knows how to begin and sign off magnificently.

Baron plays this fresh piece brilliantly and impresses once again with his technical and interpretative artistry.

Six Etudes for Piano (1976)
Piano

☐ Gowen (piano) / New World Records NW–304

Technically brilliant music. The rhythmic content has an aggressive approach and demands keen aural concentration in order to appreciate the many subtleties within the score. The individuality of Perle's inventions is completely sustained throughout the set of six pieces, the thinking always incisive. There is no doubt that these Etudes are a substantial contribution to contemporary piano literature.

Of course this is music for a virtuoso. Bradford Gowen proves his right to that designation in his superb performance.

Six Preludes, Op. 20B

☐ Helps (piano) / Composers Recordings S–288

The cogency and lucidity in this set of piano pieces are illustrative of Perle's modification of twelve-tone writing, in which certain tonal properties are partnered with it. This meaningful result produces music of strong profile. The Preludes are concentrated, the entire set taking a little less than four-and-one-half minutes in performance time.

Robert Helps (a composer as well as a pianist) gives an understanding and evidently well-prepared interpretation of the music.

Toccata (1969)

☐ Miller (piano) / Composers Recordings S–306

There is plenty of vitality and the touch-and-go of toccata design in this music, but there is just as much evidence of an acute ear for textural and temporal contrast. The avoidance of constant, naggingly blunt figurations is a decided plus to the success of Perle's piece.

Chamber Music

String Quartet No. 5

☐ Composers Quartet / Nonesuch 71280

Technically, Perle develops his quartet from serial premises that emphasize intervallic relationships rather than linear ones. In this work the generative emphasis is on the interval of a third. That the quartet sounds as though it were moving within a triadic climate is not surprising therefore, but there is no tonal traditionalism involved. Thus unified and articulated, the music has a neo-romantic thrust and a fully individual (truly independent) character.

The playing is warm and marvelously integrated. The Raimondi-led Composers Quartet has won constant acclaim for its performances. They deserve such plaudits.

String Quintet, Op. 35

☐ Beaux-Arts String Quartet / Trampler (viola) / Composers Recordings 148 (monaural)

Perle's two-viola quintet exemplifies the hot-house world of chromaticism. Expressionism is the fertilizing process used in its four movements, but without that style's overly heavy hand, thereby establishing a lucidity which makes for comprehensibility. Importantly, the impression that Perle's Op. 35 gives is a music of inexhaustible inner energy, which is far different from the motoric kind that rhythmically rides herd on top of the sounds.

The Beaux-Arts is a team of serious, cultivated, and experienced artists, and Walter Trampler is one of the world's greatest violists. Together they produce an intensity of expression in their playing that is ideal for Perle's opus. The immediacy of the performance could hardly have been bettered.

Julia Perry   (1924 - 1979)

Orchestra

A Short Piece for Orchestra (1952)

☐ Imperial Philharmonic of Tokyo / Strickland (conductor) / Composers Recordings 145 (monaural)

There is excellent cohesion in this seven-minute piece. Excellent cohesion is likewise displayed in the recording. The music is formed from differing concepts of a terse, logical fundament.

Percussion

Homunculus, C. F. for 10 Percussionists (1960)

☐ Manhattan Percussion Ensemble / Price (conductor) / Composers Recordings S-252

Homunculus is a creature produced by alchemy experimentation. The enigmatic "C. F." stands for a chord of the fifteenth on which Perry's work is built. Percussion in this instance leans heavily on pitched instruments: timpani, xylophone, and vibraphone, with two keyboard representatives: celesta and piano, and one string instrument: harp. (It is stretching matters in wholesale fashion to call the last three instruments "percussion" simply because keys are depressed and strings are plucked. One might as well term the violin a percussion instrument by reason of its sounds being produced by finger and bow contacts.) The unpitched percussion instruments are snare drum, bass drum, wood block, and cymbals.

Naturally, the pitched instruments provide a simplistic security for displaying the chordal pattern on which the music is based. This does leave little to the imagination. The performance is excellent.

Vincent Persichetti   *(1915-   )*

Serenade No. 5 for Orchestra (1950)   *Orchestra*

☐ Louisville Orchestra / Whitney (conductor) / Louisville 606 (monaural)

Healthy pandiatonicism and strong block scoring are the characteristics of Persichetti's contemporary conservatism. It is colorful in the play of intervals (the motile and juggling thirds of the Capriccio) and in dynamic pulse (the Prelude and the concluding *Burla*). Whitney does fine work with this piece.

Sinfonia: Janiculum (Symphony No. 9), Op. 113

☐ Philadelphia Orchestra / Ormandy (conductor) / RCA LSC–3212

Persichetti's ninth Symphony is persistently picaresque in its dynamic orchestration; it is constantly rhythmically appulsed and has a dramatically shimmering surface tone. The Symphony moves continuously, though it contains four sections. It was inspired by the Roman deity Janus, whose two faces looked in opposite directions. The philosophical questions the composer asks and discusses in his work are based on this duplexity ("the meaning of existence," what is life's beginning, and "what is its end?"). Whether the answer Persichetti projects is immutable and absolute can be argued. No matter. He has produced one of his major pieces in *Janiculum*. It has a breathtaking, dazzling quality. Ormandy re-creates this disposition in his splendidly convincing performance.

Symphony No. 8 (1967)

☐ Louisville Orchestra / Mester (conductor) / Louisville S–706

Persichetti appreciates the traditional law of four-movement symphonic design here. Thus there is an introduction that links to a sonata *allegro grazioso,* a moody but not constricting slow movement, an Allegretto, and a jaunty, final Vivace. Persichetti scores solidly, has a fine ear for harmonic contours, and has a good melodic flair. This is a middle-of-the-road Symphony, which Jorge Mester directs with a fine sense of style and exemplary balance.

Pageant, Op. 59   *Band*

☐ Northwestern University Symphonic Wind Ensemble / Paynter (conductor) / New World Records NW–211

The force of *Pageant* derives from the simple matter of thesis (stately music) and antithesis (rhythmic force). This type of formal purpose has sufficient merit.

There are exceedingly few top-rank band conductors. John Paynter is one of that select group. Furthermore, concert bands worthy of attention are similarly few. The partnership here provides proof in a performance that is both secure and impressive.

Symphony No. 6 for Band, Op. 69

☐ New England Conservatory Wind Ensemble / Battisti (conductor) / Golden Crest/ N. E. Conservatory 103

Symphonies for band that can hold their place as equals with symphonies for orchestra are frightfully slim in number. Persichetti is one of the few composers who has mastered the band art. It's all available in this piece: color, balance, together with proper stuff and substance for the medium. Persichetti's middle-road contemporary language is bright and alive, with a rhythmic tang. Battisti's young musicians do well; the sound is only fair.

Instrumental	***Parable IV* for Solo Bassoon (1969)**
Bassoon	☐ Grossman (bassoon) / Coronet 2741

This is a reflective parable for the greater part. The use of bent tones (thereby producing microtonal measurements) is a special color. A masterly performance by Grossman.

Cello

Sonata for Solo Cello, Op. 54

☐ Moore (cello) / Opus One 6

The priority in Persichetti's virtuosic, full-ranged opus is coloristic detail, though structurally the work realizes its solidity by thematic transference. Persichetti's cogent formal grasp is matched by telling choices made in terms of the cello's registral, dynamic, and timbre qualities. The proportions are impeccably balanced. This is a beautifully organized work.

David Moore details the piece (it is extremely difficult) with technical expertise, projects the inner nervous energy behind the notes, and obtains superb textural contrast in his playing.

Two Pianos

Sonata for Two Pianos, Op. 13

☐ Yarbrough and Cowan (pianos) / Composers Recordings S–279

In an effective disposition of form, this work is neo-romantically styled and is exceedingly well-designed for the two-piano medium. The initial movement that begins with a declamatory section and moves into orchestralike robustness is especially compelling. Persichetti's finale, peppered with salty harmonies, is rhythmically nervous and offers a superb conclusion.

This first-class team gives a dynamic performance throughout the four movements.

Trumpet

***The Hollow Men,* Op. 25**

☐ Plog (trumpet); Swearingen (organ) / Avant 1014

Persichetti's delineation of the meaning and mood of the T. S. Eliot poem on which his music is based is considered rightfully as one of the best pieces in his large output. Originally scored for trumpet and string orchestra, the work has also been set with organ or piano accompaniment. With the former, the effect is naturally closer to the orchestral environment. Accordingly, the Avant release is to be preferred to that on Golden Crest (RE–7045), which uses piano with trumpet. Further, the playing by Plog is of clearer discourse and Avant's sound is superior.

Tuba

Serenade No. 12 for Solo Tuba, Op. 88

☐ Phillips (tuba) / Golden Crest 7018 (monaural)

By mixing his six forms, including an expressive *Mascherata* (a type of sixteenth-century song that was used at masked balls and fancy-dress processions), a clever Capriccio, and a colorful *Marcia*, and keeping everything concentrated, Persichetti is most successful with his rare medium choice. One would expect difficulties to arrange musical interest for an unaccompanied tuba, but all are overcome with creative panache.

Harvey Phillips is to the world of the tuba what Rampal is to the flute population. Phillips is a tubistic Horowitz and proves it with this realization. There is strong metrical definition but no rigidity, dynamic differences are both subtle and clear, and tone and technique are perfect. An absolutely splendid musical document.

Serenade No. 10 for Flute and Harp (1957)

☐ Baron (flute); Maayani (harp) / Desto 7134

Persichetti's tenth in a series of serenades for a variety of media is in his freely tonal manner. There are seven movements, nicely contrasted in terms of the woodwind-plucked-string instrumentation. A fastidiously conceived work. It is beautifully played by the well-known Samuel Baron and by Ruth Maayani who deserves to be better known.

Serenade No. 3 for Violin, Cello, and Piano, Op. 17

☐ Temple University Trio / Golden Crest 4117

Persichetti's three-movement trio sings well but is more serious than most works concerned with serenade form. It is not the predominating polyphony that causes this but rather the tartness of the tonal combinations.

Satisfactory ensemble but a somewhat stiff performance.

Parable for Brass Quintet

☐ Dallas Brass Quintet / Crystal S–203

Persichetti explains his title as being "non-programmatic," defining a composition built from a "single germinal idea." He has produced a total of twenty *Parables* for various media. This one provides muscular music with extrovert energy. Even in the music's more relaxed moments the sonorous muscles are flexed. There are fricative beauties here, made more so by the pungency of brass timbre. All of it is clearly exhibited in the playing of this fine ensemble.

The Death of a Soldier / *The Snow Man*
The Grass / *Thou Child So Wise*
Of the Surface of Things

☐ Hanks (tenor); Friedberg-Erickson (piano) / Duke University Press DWR–7306 (monaural)

Straightforward stylistic statements are the crucial method that accurately define the texts in three songs from the song cycle *Harmonium: The Death of a Soldier, Of the Surface of Things,* and *The Snow Man.* The simplicity of the last song listed above exemplifies cognitive creativity. Less produces much more in this sensitive vocal translation of Hilaire Belloc's devotional poem. It is intellectually perfect and emotionally pertinent.

Sonatina to *Hans Christian*

☐ Miller (mezzo-soprano); Biltcliffe (piano) / Desto 6411/2

Offered here is the pleasure of a fine vocalized characterization of a Wallace Stevens poem. A lightly jogging rhythmic figure neatly ties the piece, which is taken from Persichetti's song cycle *Harmonium*. Well-stated singing.

Giovanni Battista Pescetti *(ca. 1704 - ca. 1766)*

Allegretto in C major
Presto in C minor

☐ Goldstein (harpsichord) / Pandora 101

A pair of representative examples of the work of this Venetian composer. Goldstein's playing is beautifully crisp and thereby intensifies the linear imitative writing style Pescetti favored.

Sonata in C minor for Harpsichord

☐ Sgrizzi (harpsichord) / Nonesuch 73008

Lucidity keys the final Presto, which speeds, but not at the expense of musical meaning; the dynamic dimensions are fruitfully exploited. Perhaps there is more melancholy in the slow movement than Sgrizzi depicts, but there is nice phrasing.

Johann Friedrich Peter   (1746-1813)

Vocal

Voice and Orchestra

It Is a Precious Thing

☐ Moravian Festival Orchestra / Estanislao (baritone) / Johnson (conductor) / Odyssey 32160340

An anthem for two solo voices and mixed chorus with orchestral background. A compelling performance.

I Will Make an Everlasting Covenant

☐ Moravian Festival Orchestra / Estanislao (baritone) / Johnson (conductor) / Odyssey 32160340

Contains a high degree of expressivity that exceeds the utilitarian purpose of its composition (for a service at the Moravian church where Peter was both ordained minister and organist). Aurelio Estanislao's voice is warm and full.

Choral

Chorus and Instrumental Ensemble

I Will Freely Sacrifice to Thee

☐ Gregg Smith Singers / Smith (conductor) / Vox SVBX–5350

A vigorous anthem, made more so by the motile accompaniment. Additional energy is provided by the instrumentational weight, which includes a pair of horns supplementing the strings. Discriminatingly sung and played.

Choral and Orchestra

Sing, O Ye Heavens

☐ Moravian Festival Chorus and Orchestra / Johnson (conductor) / Odyssey 32160340

An anthem for "Christmastide or General Use," worthy of any of the classic masters, and a worthy performance to match.

Wayne Peterson   (1927-   )

Instrumental

Flute

Capriccio for Flute and Piano (1972)

☐ Millard (flute); Peterson (piano) / Arch S–1760

Although much contemporary flute music includes all the techniques Peterson uses—glissandi, flutters, microtones, multiphonics, and registral skips of extreme contrast—many can be termed effects-but-not-much-else compositions. Exclude Peterson's

Capriccio from that category. His music has expressivity together with an intensity that is very compelling. The varied special colorations energize the lines. Peterson's Capriccio is certainly a success.

And the performance is a success as well. The work was written at the request of the flutist who performs and is dedicated to her. Janet Millard is a gifted musician and proves it in this recording. With the composer at the piano one can be certain the interpretation is all that it ought to be.

Pierre Petit *(1922-)*

Tarentelle   *Instrumental*

☐ Ito and Dorigny (guitars) / Delos FY-008   *Two Guitars*

Totally characteristic of the dance, but with a clever central episode that adumbrates Debussy's *Clair de lune*. The playing is properly rhythmically full.

Goffredo Petrassi *(1904-)*

Concerto No. 5 for Orchestra (1955)   *Orchestra*

☐ Louisville Orchestra / Whitney (conductor) / Louisville S-676

Two movements emphasizing concertante scoring. Whitney and his colleagues have produced an excellent reproduction of a score that merges Bartókian and Stravinskian rhythms with neoclassic formalism. The latter presents in each movement mystical, slow-paced material driven into the opposite type of power, geared by a faster tempo. Further balance is gained through the cyclic knot, the conclusion matching the temper and tempo of the opening. Petrassi does not flush out his tone row, but prefers to work principally from an *Urmotiv* which consists of the first four tones of the set.

Performance and content mark this as one of the best of all the Louisville releases. (The companion pieces are Ben Weber's *Dolmen*, an Elegy, and Irwin Fischer's Overture on an Exuberant Tone Row. Notes concerning these works are found under the respective composers' listings.)

Nonsense (1952)   *Choral*

☐ Monteverdi-Chor, Hamburg / Jürgens (conductor) / Telefunken 641010   *Chorus Alone*

The text is drawn from Edward Lear's *The Book of Nonsense*. The music is liquidy, even when it is texturally tight; gay, even when it is slightly scorched with tone frictions. Petrassi treats his unaccompanied voices like instruments and includes whispering, hissing, and speaking minus pitch. Additionally, long-sprung glissandi, monotoning, and unchecked, decrescendoed yawns are sprinkled throughout the work.

Petrassi's sonantized delight is given a graphically expressive performance. No problems even though the recording was made at a live performance.

Noche oscura, Cantata for Mixed Chorus and Orchestra (1950)   *Cantata and Oratorio*

☐ Louisville Orchestra and Choruses of the Southern Baptist Theological Seminary / Mester (conductor) / Louisville S-684

The text for Petrassi's work is by San Juan de la Cruz, a Carmelite monk of the sixteenth century. The prose is concerned with mystical meanings, somewhat sensually conveyed. Petrassi's design is of large ternary measurement, with serial procedures applied to motival projections. This quasi-dodecaphonic method strengthens the flexibility of the chromaticism. The orchestra is used sensitively; tuttis are the exception. Though choral conjunctions outline sections of the text, the vocal writing (containing many *divisis*) emphasizes contrapuntalism. Petrassi's fusion of constructional and emotive data produces a rich music. It is given a distinguished performance, one of the best offered in the Louisville catalogue.

Emil Petrovics (1930-)

Choral

Chorus Alone

Jatszik a Szél

☐ Budapest Madrigal Ensemble / Szekeres (conductor) / Monitor S-2054

"The Wind Plays" has undulating sounds to back up the words. It is something of a find. So is this group, which sings beautifully with first-rank style.

Gustaf Allan Pettersson (1911-)

Orchestra

Symphony No. 7 (1967)

☐ Stockholm Philharmonic Orchestra / Dorati (conductor) / London 6740

Essential middle-right-of-the-road contemporary music with some light Honegger touches and some mild Shostakovich syntax. Complexities: none. Strengths: long lines and strong rhythms. Form: contrastive blocks.

The Symphony is dedicated to Dorati, and he carries through in a definitive manner.

Johann Christoph Pezel (1639-1694)

Instrumental

Two Trumpets

Bicinium

No. 71 for Two Trumpets and Continuo / No. 74 for Two Trumpets and Continuo

☐ London Brass Players / Rifkin (conductor) / Nonesuch 71145

Effortlessly natural playing of these excerpts from Pezel's *Bicinia Variorum Instrumentorum.*

Chamber Music

Sonatina

No. 61 / No. 62 / No. 65 / No. 66

☐ Schwarz and Ranger (trumpets); Hindell (bassoon); Cooper (harpsichord) / Nonesuch 71301

Four pieces from Pezel's *Bicina Variorum Instrumentorum,* of which Nos. 61 through 66 are for the coupled brass instruments and continuo.

The delights of early baroque music are here displayed. Each Sonatina is a one-movement affair; two are in *andante* tempo, the other pair in *allegro* speed, and all are in binary form.

Schwarz and Ranger display consummate artistry. Their tones have solidity, and yet everything breathes. They achieve a beautiful flow of seamless continuity.

Allemande and Courante for Two Violins and Continuo
Ballo, Ciacona, and Gigue for Two Violins and Continuo

☐ Hess and O'Reilly (violins); Jones (cello); Walton (double bass); Rifkin (harpsichord) / Nonesuch 71204

Miniatures from Pezel's *Bicinia Variorum Instrumentorum.* Simple, communicative music. The performance is a responsible one.

Tower Music (Excerpts)

☐ Los Angeles Brass Quintet / Crystal S–102

The version performed is a recasting of the original for modern instruments with the parts edited as to voicing, dynamics, and phrasing. This doesn't nullify validity. These attractively shaped pieces sound just as stylistically effective on two trumpets (one a D instrument, the other a C type), horn, trombone, and tuba as the original combination calling for trombones and wooden cornets. The five excerpts are all dances.

John Pfeiffer   *(1929-   )*

Nine Images   *Electronic Music*

After Hours	*Pavone*
Drops	*Reflection of a String*
Forests	*Take Off*
Moments	*Warm-Up, Canon and Peace*
Orders	

☐ RCA VICS-1371

The praxis involved here is, in a way, related to a combine of tape organization, electronic detailing, and use of specific items which are electronically manipulated. Pfeiffer does not tell how he does it, save to call his anthology *Electronomusic* and describe his creations as "musically organized sound built from electronic technology." The electronic transformations utilized are hidden in the instrumentational descriptions given the nine pieces; for example, "sequential sines," "modes for alphormer and set," "duotonic transform," and so on.

It really doesn't matter how Pfeiffer originates his images. His objective is to blend traditional musical concepts with new sonic materials. Electroluminescence applied to basic musical structures is contrary to most electronic composers' views. Their belief is that new media cannot companion old structures. Now then, that's just as goosey as pretending that twelve-tone technique cannot be applied to classical forms.

Pfeiffer's concept of "holding onto a familiar feature of musical orientation" is certainly proven valuable in these pieces. Best are *Take Off,* similar to a *moto perpetuo* with jazz accompaniment, the clocklike coil sounds and rings in *After Hours,* and the scherzo properties that outline *Orders.* The toccata impact in *Warm-Up, Canon and Peace* is excellent, and so is *Drops,* with its whines and glides, zigs and zags, staccatos and glissandi. Real quality is found in *Reflection of a String,* with the effect of a solo fiddle traveling in a bind of *vox humana* sound. And there is no question as to past instrumental identification in the programmatic *Forests,* with its sound blocks both framed and laced by simulated bird and nature noises.

Hans Pfitzner   *(1869-1949)*

Instrumental

Piano

Five Piano Pieces, Op. 47

☐ Frieser (piano) / Musical Heritage Society MHS–1590

Take Schumann and add a slight bit of chromatic salt and one has Pfitzner's Opus 47. It pictures Schumannesque titles—*Last Effort, In High Spirits, Hieroglyphics,* etc. The playing is quite satisfactory.

Chamber Music

Sonata in F sharp minor for Cello and Piano, Op. 1

☐ Mantel (cello); Frieser (piano) / Musical Heritage Society MHS–1590

While basically the classical pillars of form support this duo sonata, the romantic tendency to embellish a design is in evidence. The harmonic basis of this sensible romanticist is that of Brahms; the music speaks with a fullness of declaration in all of its four movements.

The team of Gerhard Mantel and Erika Frieser give a beautifully proportioned performance. Matters of balance are perfect, and that can hardly be said about many a cello-piano rendition on disc or in the concert hall. As usual, the Musical Heritage sound is exemplary. Fine liner notes by Douglas Townsend.

Opera and Dramatic Music

Palestrina **(1917)**

☐ Bavarian Radio Symphony Orchestra and Chorus / Donath, Lampart, Hautermann, and Rüggeberg (sopranos); Fassbaender, Rosner-Greindl, and Freyer (mezzo-sopranos); Steinbach, van Kestern, Lenz, Kraus, Kreile, Rosner, and Gedda (tenors); Weikl, Fischer-Dieskau, Prey, Mazura, and Nienstedt (baritones); Ridderbusch, von Halem, Meven, and Weber (basses) / Kubelik (conductor) / Deutsche Grammophon 2711013

The arguments about *Palestrina* concentrate on its unexportability, due to its Germanic style, subject, and spirit. One refuses to argue that irrational point. Whatever its essences, *Palestrina* is an important opera, and there's no reason to acquiesce in the view that it has only insular acceptance. And, for further support of this statement, here is a fine recording, directed by Kubelik, who firmly believes in the work, and sung by a good cast, with Nicolai Gedda in the star title role.

Pfitzner's opera was first produced in 1917. It is conceived on a huge scale and covers a full evening plus. Pfitzner prepared the libretto, based on the life of the famous Italian composer. Some consider the work as the successor to *Parsifal.* Donald Mitchell, the important English critic, says it "provides an almost complete spiritual and musical experience." Edward J. Dent in his *Opera* criticizes the length of *Palestrina* but says that "it has much that is wonderfully beautiful, and its lofty idealism compels sincere respect."

André Philidor   *(1647-1730)*

Percussion

1368

March for Four Timbales

☐ Collegium Musicum de Paris / Douatte (conductor) / Nonesuch 71009

A rare example in a medium that is no longer rare in contemporary music. No chromaticism, of course, but this three-minute fancy for four timpani will not bore anyone.

Burrill Phillips (1907-)

Selections from McGuffey's Readers (1934) *Orchestra*

☐ Eastman-Rochester Symphony Orchestra / Hanson (conductor) / Eastman-Rochester Archives ERA–1009

Exemplifying Phillips's early concern with American scene-painting. He has since shifted to more abstract arguments. "Selections" means a three-part suite made from tonal coalescences that eliminate harmonic conservatism. Phillips's rhythms are simple but not square; the motility is fluid, minus the nervousness resulting from total asymmetry. Quasi-programmatic expositions: *The One Horse Shay* (trotting rhythms, aided by wood-block punctuations), *John Alden and Priscilla* (quiet romanticism), and *The Midnight Ride of Paul Revere* (richly colored in its excitingly paced formations).

There are two recorded choices, but there is no doubt that the listing noted is *the* one to obtain. (It was originally on the Mercury label MG–50136, now re-released by ERA with other Eastman-Rochester Symphony Orchestra recordings Mercury deleted.) Avoid the Schoenherr-led performance on Desto 6423. That depiction is sodden, without juice, and dynamically sluggish.

Sonata da Camera for Organ *Instrumental*

Organ

☐ Morgan (organ) / Pleiades P–101

A sharp difference from the initial purely tonal style of this fine craftsman. Row material based on a quadrate pitch arrangement is fundamental to the work, which consists of three movements. These are equilibrated and contrasted sharply, so that the sonority plans are heavy in the initial part, thinned in the central division, and filigreed in the finale. Morgan's registration is kept basic for each part of the work, essentially changing only with the beginning of a new movement.

First Piano Sonata *Piano*

Second Piano Sonata

☐ Sanders (piano) / Trilogy CTS–1003

Neo-classicism in both cases, with plenty of granitic edges. Fast outside movements surround an *Andante cantabile* in the first work. Variations (on a meter), fugue, scherzo, and ricercar are the structures for the other Sonata. But, no mere filling of old bottles here. Phillips pours in fresh and colorful liquids. Positive inventiveness (especially in the Second Sonata) illustrates the difference between Phillips's contributions and the uninspired inventory that fills the many bins of neoclassic music.

Sonata for Violin and Harpsichord (1942) *Chamber Music*

☐ van Bronkhorst (violin); Morgan (harpsichord) / Pleiades P–101

Twelve-tone writing that has a romantic bravura within it. The end movement maintains its power by way of a vigorous, somewhat rhapsodic, heat-flushed narrative. Convincing playing.

Canzona III

☐ Juilliard Ensemble / Basescu (reader) / Davies (conductor) / Composers Recordings S-286

Instrumental coloristic disciplines are applied to specific formats in Phillips's five-part work. Though each movement is introduced by a somewhat mood-descriptive set of verses (created by the composer's wife), the work can certainly stand by itself minus them.

The seven instruments (flute, clarinet, trumpet, piano, percussion, violin, and cello) set forth compressed blocks of sound in movement 1. This static formation is balanced by part 3's ostinati and the fragmented disposition heard in movement 5. Sections 2 and 4 are scherzi, one for low-pitched sonorities, the other for the opposite gamut.

That Webern comes to mind as this work progresses is not uncomplimentary. Worthy music doesn't need a prophet preaching a new gospel. *Canzona III is* a worthy contribution.

Alessandro Piccinini   (1566-ca. 1638)

Instrumental

Lute

Tenore detto il mercatello
Toccata IV
Toccata VI

☐ Satoh (lute) / Klavier 528

Examples by one of the last of the Italian composers who wrote for the solo lute and chitarrone. Gentility marks the style of the pair of toccatas. There's much more motility in the other piece, which is a set of three variations on a chordal subject.

Satoh's playing is good and clear, but with little dynamic change. He has been given lifelike sound reproduction.

Gabriel Pierné   (1863-1937)

Orchestra

Cydalise et le chèvre-pied: Suite No. 1 (1919)

☐ National Orchestra of the O.R.T.F. / Martinon (conductor) / Musical Heritage Society MHS-1489

Pierné's ballet *Cydalise et le chèvre-pied* is probably the best known and most successful of his large compositions. The first of two symphonic suites he extracted from the stage work comprises six connected sections, the fifth having a half-dozen divisions within it. Programmatic direction is nicely depicted in this tale of nymphs and satyrs, especially in *La Leçon de flûte de Pan;* the scoring is fresh and clean, and Martinon's performance is as delightfully clear.

For Suite No. 2, *see below.*

Cydalise et le chèvre-pied: Suite No. 2 (1919)

☐ Paris Opera Orchestra / Mari (conductor) / Angel S-37281

Five more sections from Pierné's ballet (for the first orchestral suite drawn from the work *see above*). Mari also performs the initial suite, but Martinon has more color in his conception.

Divertissements sur un thème pastoral, Op. 49

☐ National Orchestra of the O.R.T.F. / Martinon (conductor) / Musical Heritage Society MHS–1489

The *Divertissements* actually consist of two types of variations—some cover the subject with enlarged harmonies and decorative material, others are freed of thematic subjection.

Martinon's direction is distinguished by complete structural intelligibility.

Overture to *Ramuntcho* (1907)

☐ Paris Opera Orchestra / Mari (conductor) / Angel S–37281

The title noted above is inexact. The proper form is "Overture on Basque Popular Themes." It identifies one of two sections Pierné extracted from the incidental music he wrote for Pierre Loti's drama *Ramuntcho*. The other published section is a six-minute *Rapsodie basque*. (Passing thought: whatever happened to Deems Taylor's opera *Ramuntcho*, given its world premiere by the Philadelphia Opera Co. in 1942?)

Mari's direction provides a very idiomatic conception of Pierné's catchy-themed piece.

Konzertstück for Harp and Orchestra, Op. 39

Solo Instrument and Orchestra

Harp

☐ National Orchestra of the O.R.T.F. / Laskine (harp) / Martinon (conductor) / Musical Heritage Society MHS–1489

A golden, haunting, and luscious quality suffuses this opus. Pierné studied with both the operatic master Jules Massenet and the cleric-like composer César Franck. The former's discipline is heard in the colorful prose that is set forth, Franck's influence in just a tinge of the shifting chord, and the cyclic inference in the last section.

There is a flawless clarity in this recorded setting. There is also stunningly rich, spacious sound, and all in all it is a triumph for the composer and the performers. (In all fairness it must be stated that I have not heard another available performance on Angel [S–36290], with Challan as the soloist and Cluytens conducting the Paris Conservatory Orchestra.)

Concerto in C minor for Piano and Orchestra, Op. 12

Piano

☐ Stuttgart Philharmonic / Dosse (piano) / Kuntzsch (conductor) / Candide 31102

Another of the many piano concertos in the never-heard-in-public category. But really such an example of programming politics doesn't mean creative bankruptcy. There's plenty of life and dash in this concerto. It has real show'em trimmings, and though it doesn't often cut itself off from traditional patterns (Liszt, for example), it is not a stale imitation.

Marylene Dosse is no big name, but she does a big job here. The conductor is a new name to me, but he does quite well with his musicians.

Solo de concert for Bassoon, Op. 35

Instrumental

Bassoon

☐ Pachman (bassoon); Maxin (piano) / Golden Crest 7019 (monaural)

An adroitly conceived, utterly respectable piece for the wind instrument. Lyrical processes are dominant. Good playing, but the piano's tone is poor and has a fair amount of jangle.

Harp

Impromptu-Caprice, Op. 9

☐ Laskine (harp) / Musical Heritage Society MHS-602

Pierné's sole work for solo harp. Laskine performs with singing vitality even in the quiet sections contrastive to the centrally placed triple-metered dance.

Chamber Music

Introduction and Variations on a Popular Round for Quartet of Saxophones

☐ Marcel Mule Saxophone Quartet / Musical Heritage Society MHS-817

Pierné calls on four members of the sax family to equate a full gamut—namely, soprano, alto, tenor, and baritone. One has, therefore, the varying colors and weights of full-scale sonority, from the thinness of the soprano member to the reedy thickness of the baritone.

The theme is uncovered slowly, twice being interrupted by other material. It is only on its third entrance that the subject appears fully. The variational development (including a fugal section) is continuous; the theme is well oriented and to the fore.

Extraordinary clear, alert, and fully polished playing. Magnificently recorded.

Paul Pierné   (1874-1952)

Chamber Music

Trois Conversations

☐ Nova Saxophone Quartet / Crystal S-153

Music by the cousin of the better-known Gabriel Pierné. Music completely unconcerned and untouched by any special contemporary currents. Well scored, it scores a small success with its unassuming, tonally turned sax conversations, in turn *Amusante*, *Sentimentale*, and *Animée* (*Dispute*).

Superbly played and recorded. The balance of this group is as fine as that of any famous string quartet. The Nova gentlemen (Richard Lawn, Jay Vosk, Douglas Walter, and Kevin Boutote) provide a perfect depiction that permits every nuance to come through clearly and with its proper meaning.

Willem Pijper   (1894-1947)

Solo Instrument and Orchestra

Piano Concerto (1927)

☐ Radio Philharmonic Orchestra / Bruins (piano) / van Otterloo (conductor) / Donemus Audio-Visual Series 7374/2

Piano

Interesting facets: the use (and not hidden in the tutti) of an alto saxophone, the constant polyrhythmic and polymetric situations, and the three sizable solo-piano sections that divide the total canvas. That a Gershwin-inflected accent emerges (aided by the jazzy timbre of the saxophone) does not mean a mixed musical metaphor, but indicates the substantial tone of the work. No innuendo in the concerto concept; the work is primed for the soloist, but equal time is given the orchestra. A big piece in its twelve-minute span.

Produced from a live recording made in 1966. Not the greatest sound possible, but certainly adequate.

Passepied (1916)

☐ 't Hart (carillon) / Donemus Audio-Visual Series DAVS–6304 (monaural: 10-inch disc)

An extremely rare example of recorded carillon music, and not a hymn tune or some sentimental favorite, but an honest piece by an important contemporary composer! Not the sort of thing one hears on a Sunday A.M., though one wishes it could be heard then. Notwithstanding the restricted gamut and the everlasting clang color (the concentual upper partials and overtones are a constant built-in type of God-given counterpoint), Pijper's close-to-three-minute piece is worth listening time at any time.

The possibility of public performance is extremely remote. The recording thus becomes thrice valuable.

Halewijn **(Excerpts) (1933)**

☐ Utrecht Symphony Orchestra and Netherlands Chamber Choir / Lugt (soprano); van Sante (mezzo-soprano); van Kerkhof (contralto); Vroons (tenor); Bijnen (baritone); Willink (bass) / de Nobel (conductor) / Donemus Audio-Visual Series 6704 (monaural)

A good sampling (though the performance is but fair) of the nine scenes in Pijper's "Symphonisch Drama" based on a medieval Netherlands ballad. It concerns a Bluebeardish chap who lures girls to their death and in turn is killed by one of his intended victims.

The fifty minutes worth was recorded live, like all Donemus issues. While the voices are passably clear, the orchestra is not. However, this is the only recorded example of Pijper's work.

Boris Pillin *(1940-   )*

Duo for Percussion and Piano (1970)

☐ Davis (piano); Ervin (percussion) / Wim WIMR–5

Title equalization notwithstanding, an equalization emphasized by listing the percussion first, Pillin's Duo is more a work for solo piano, rhythmically colored and placed in perspective by the assisting percussion. The combination is interesting.

Sonata for Cello and Piano (1972)

☐ Douglas Davis (cello); Sharon Davis (piano) / Wim WIMR–11

Pillin makes all of the moves expected in a neoclassic essay. The three movements contain formal sincerity and a keen approach to instrumental equipoise between the cello and piano, which are always difficult to balance.

Sonata for Clarinet and Piano (1965)

☐ Atkins (clarinet); Davis (piano) / Wim WIMR–1

Alert and eager music in the fast outer movements, with the expected contrastive slow movement in between. Expert neoclassic music.

Skilled musicians are at work here—their playing is impeccable.

Tune in C minor for Piano and Percussion (1975)

☐ Davis (piano); Silverman (percussion) / Wim WIMR–11

Pillin's Tune is a three-sectioned essay that swings on the girders of jazz. The seasoning of the percussion is applied with taste. A secure, sensitive performance.

Serenade for Piano and Woodwind Quintet (1973)

☐ Westwood Wind Quintet / Davis (piano) / Wim WIMR-11

Neoclassic depictions, a little jazzy here, a little Poulenc there, balletic in the first and last movements, nocturnal in between.

A handsomely executed rendition, especially well balanced.

Karl Pilss   (1902-   )

Chamber Music

Capriccio

☐ Annapolis Brass Quintet / Crystal S-207

A response to light romantic dealings. The music is cast in ternary form, with the main theme representing a clean-shaven Hindemith profile. The Annapolis five are fully in command in their execution.

Solomon Pimsleur   (1900-1962)

Choral

Chorus Alone

Two Songs for Mixed Voices

☐ Gregg Smith Singers / Smith (conductor) / Composers Recordings S-241

Two settings of sonnets by John Masefield in a straightforward romantic manner.

Contradicting the label copy, notes, and printed texts, the performance order of the pieces is reversed. *There Are Two Forms of Life* precedes *I Never See the Red Rose.*

Daniel Pinkham   (1923-   )

Orchestra

Signs of the Zodiac (1964)

☐ Louisville Orchestra / McCord (narrator) / Whitney (conductor) / Louisville S-673

Pink-pilled by programmaticism, though not of the play-by-play variety. Each of the twelve signs is musically ascertained. Aries the "rambunctious Ram" is brassy, instruments are paired for Gemini, the twins, etc. For music of this sort the pinpointed subject lends enchantment, and Pinkham is successful.

Each of the movements is preceded by a clever poem by David McCord, written to accompany the music though it is not clear whether the texts were created before or after the music had been composed. The orchestra is good; the poet, reading his own words, does so in a dull monotone.

Symphony No. 2 (1963)

☐ Louisville Orchestra / Whitney (conductor) / Louisville 652 (monaural)

Definition of content meaning neither removes a work from the absolute-music category nor cancels the composer's decision to term it a symphony. One hears and recognizes the elegiac tone and symphonicism of Pinkham's twelve-tone work but is specifically aided by the subtitles: *Aria, Three Epigrams, Ballade,* and *Envoy.*

Pinkham's work speaks clearly and, more importantly, eloquently. That significant artistic result is evidence that practice must go beyond theoretical commitment and that when it does, it thereby proves the absolute validity of the latter. Point of evidence: the marvelous trumpet phrases edged by rhythmic persistence in the *Ballade.* There's plenty more.

There is maximum clarity in the playing. One wishes for greater string strength, but there is no doubting the effectiveness Whitney obtains from his musicians. Monaural recording notwithstanding, the sonics are first rate.

Concertante No. 1 (1954)

☐ String Ensemble / Brink (violin); Chiasson (harpsichord); Low (celesta) / Solomon (conductor) / Composers Recordings 143 (monaural)

Pinkham's work features the violin and harpsichord as the solo voices, with the celesta functioning as a part of the orchestral forces. The music is in turn thoughtful and robust; the creative recipe is classicism salted with neat frictions and peppered with sharply defined coloration. Deucedly attractive writing and played with zest. The sound is exceedingly bright and open.

Cantilena for Violin and Harpsichord (1954)

Capriccio for Violin and Harpsichord (1956)

☐ Pinkham (harpsichord); Brink (violin) / Composers Recordings 109 (monaural)

An expert harpsichordist, Pinkham has composed a large quantity of music using the instrument, including it in a dozen chamber and instrumental pieces. Contemporary classic diction defines Pinkham's *Cantilena* and Capriccio; the latter is athletically graceful, the former curvaceously lyrical. Engaging music engagingly played.

Concerto for Celesta and Harpsichord (1955)

☐ Pinkham (harpsichord); Low (celesta) / Composers Recordings 109 (monaural)

A unique combination. The suave sonorities match the scrupulous harmonic clarity, the guarantee of neoclassic style. "Concerto" notwithstanding, the intimacy of the work places Pinkham's communicative piece (three movements) in the chamber-music category. Expertly performed.

Folk Song: Elegy (1947)

Madrigal (1955)

☐ Randolph Singers / Randolph (conductor) / Composers Recordings 102 (monaural)

A pair of madrigals, both for four voices, sung with full confidence. The light dissonance that sprays the first of these pieces is a perfect example of creative good taste and stylistic reasonableness.

The liner notes fail to indicate that these are the first and last of *Four Poems for Music,* with texts by Robert Hillyer.

Glory Be to God: Motet for Christmas Day (1955)

☐ Mid-America Chorale / Dexter (conductor) / Composers Recordings 191 (monaural)

Solo Instrument and Orchestra

Violin and Harpsichord

Instrumental

Violin

Chamber Music

Choral

Chorus Alone

A refreshing approach to devotional music. Pinkham's Motet for unaccompanied double chorus uses imitation both of phrases and of bell-like sounds. The result is highly communicable.

Cantata and Oratorio

Christmas Cantata (1957)

☐ Wagner Chorale / Wagner (conductor) / Angel S–36016

Simple but strong contemporaneous music. Fine performance of this *Sinfonia sacra*.

Pinkham / Samuel Holyoke. *See Holyoke* / Pinkham.

Jesús Pinzón (1928-   )

Orchestra

Study for Orchestra (1970)

☐ Louisville Orchestra / Mester (conductor) / Louisville LS–714

A sketch-like composite of free sound choices, the rhythms sometimes regular, other times aleatory. The over-all organization emphasizes color. Music of this type reflects its emphasis on procedures rather than feelings. In that, it is interesting, of course.

The performance by the Louisvillians is a hearty one. The recording followed their first American performance of the work at the Fifth Inter-American Music Festival in Washington, D.C.

Lubomir Pipkov (1904-1974)

Chamber Music

String Quartet No. 3, Op. 66

☐ Bulgarian Quartet / Musical Heritage Society MHS–1889

The most stimulating ingenuity of Pipkov's Quartet is its ripe, rhythmic cogitation. The vitality of the mensurable patterns is exciting; there is a motility even in the slow-paced sections. Pipkov does not qualify his rhythmic clauses or modulate their bite within the Quartet's melodic springs. These are fed by Bulgarian musical waters. The results from this folk source give a rhapsodic stimulus of unequal metrical divisions and cross-accentuations.

The Bulgarian team play with a certain quotient of roughage. For Pipkov's type of musical language this is performance honesty.

Charles Piroye (early 18th cent.)

Instrumental

Organ

Dialogue

☐ Froidebise (organ) / Nonesuch 71020

Unific material, the *Dialogue* relating to the composer's specification that two different types of organ sonority be contrasted. That is done here by dividing the short essay and precisely defining the pair of colors and weights.

Paul Amadeus Pisk   *(1893 -   )*

Passacaglia, Op. 50   *Orchestra*

☐ Radio Orchestra of Zurich, Switzerland / Monod (conductor) / Composers Recordings 128 (monaural)

Straight out of Brahms via Wagner and Strauss. Not as powerful as the original sources, yet not too thin a substitute, furnishing music well constructed and never dull. The contrapuntal design is filled with full-nurtured romantic music, intensified by Viennese colors.

Monod shows his conductorial abilities in a rendition that obtains expressive playing from the Swiss ensemble.

Walter Piston   *(1894 - 1976)*

Concerto for Orchestra (1933)   *Orchestra*

☐ Polish National Radio Orchestra / Strickland (conductor) / Composers Recordings S-254

Movement 1 is the kind of music Vivaldi would probably be writing if he were working in the present era. Movement 2 hustles and bustles but never splutters; its second half is a retrograde consideration of the first half. Variational delights mark the finale, and instrumental probing colors its music vividly.

The performance is a responsible one, the sound sometimes cloudy.

The Incredible Flutist (Ballet Suite) (1938)

☐ Eastman-Rochester Orchestra / Hanson (conductor) / Mercury 75050

It is certainly a pity that Piston composed no program music other than this superb jaunty score. Of course it was his prerogative, but it is our loss that such a master of roguish, frisky entertainment saw fit otherwise to stay strictly within the bounds of serious, formal production. It is a rare gift that Piston displays in this single work that is diametrically opposed to his entire output of symphonies, suites, quartets, and other compositions.

The Incredible Flutist lives in its excerpted form for the most part, since the ballet never achieved repertory status. (One recording has appeared of the entire score—see under *Ballet.*) It lives in full lusty health. It has a little of the midway atmosphere about it; changes occur in rapid succession—a tango (a haunting $\frac{5}{8}$ tune that will stay with the listener), a minuet, a waltz, a polka, and so on. And for dessert a rousing circus march, with crowd noises, whistling, and so on let loose by the orchestra players. This was improvised at the first performance and has become a traditional addition, awaited by those in the know.

The Hanson setting has a freshness and resoluteness that injects proper pep into the proceedings. It is a model of what a performance of the work should be.

Serenata (1956)

☐ Louisville Orchestra / Whitney (conductor) / Louisville 58-6 (monaural)

A cross between a short symphony and a suite, Piston's *Serenata* is influenced by the divertimento form. A divertimento should give pleasure, and this piece is not found wanting. The themes are gay (even in the slow movement the seriousnesses are on the sweet side); the rhythms are refreshing and American in origin.

This is one of the best of the many recorded Louisville performances. The sound is white-bright and clear.

Symphony No. 2 (1944)

☐ Boston Symphony Orchestra / Thomas (conductor) / Deutsche Grammophon 2530103

Piston's neoclassicism remains here, but considerably warmed by a lyricism in the slow movement that has (despite his confirmed denial) an American flavor. It is one of his most telling symphonic movements. The jazzy effect in a section of the opening part is more evidence of native climate.

Thomas presents a telling, rich, and beautiful performance. This recorded edition is highly recommended and deserves the widest circulation.

Symphony No. 4 (1949)

☐ Philadelphia Orchestra / Ormandy (conductor) / Columbia Special Products AML-4992 (monaural)

Piston rarely wears his heart on his sleeve, but this work has no dryness about it whatsoever. In fact, it is almost refreshingly folksy at the start, vigorously red-blooded in the concluding movement. The inner divisions have a freshness of concept and are as bracing in their effect as any music of sheer gusto.

Ormandy keeps the flowing lines smooth, balances the counterpoint that moves with Pistonian confidence, and measures the bite of dissonance for the greatest effect. The tone of the Philadelphians is wondrous.

Symphony No. 5 (1956)

☐ Louisville Orchestra / Whitney (conductor) / Louisville S-653

Standard design for Piston—meaning a three-movement affair that he uses often, with fast movements embracing a central adagio. Piston's music is always learned, but not academic. Exceptionally, for him, the fifth symphony dips slightly into dodecaphonic resources in the slow movement. But unlike the neoclassicism of Stravinsky that jumped into the rougher territory of twelve-tone, Piston's essentially stays put. Serialism is only given a sideways glance. A thoroughly musical performance is produced by the Kentucky-based outfit.

Symphony No. 6 (1955)

☐ Boston Symphony Orchestra / Munch (conductor) / New World Records NW-286 (monaural)

Formally the symphony runs its course, as one has come to expect from Piston. The only exception is found in the pyrotechnical second movement, a veritable reincarnation of Mendelssohnian deftness and gossamer texture.

The music demands virtuosi, and the Boston men eat it up. Munch's performance was originally released on RCA LM-2083, paired there with Martinů's *Fantaisies symphoniques*. New World Records is to be thanked for putting the work in the recorded catalogue again.

Symphony

No. 7 (1961) / No. 8 (1965)

☐ Louisville Orchestra / Mester (conductor) / Louisville LS–746

The seventh of Piston's symphonies continues his neoclassic chronicle, with plentiful chromatic synonyms. It not only is respectable but exemplifies creative fitness—no flabbiness in the musical body. Three movements, the middle one an elegiac essay, the finale having the physical motility of a toccata.

However, the surprise is the eighth symphony. Here, at the age of seventy-one, Piston succumbed to the lure of dodecaphony, with the same type of design he so often used: a moderately fast movement, a slow-tempoed division (variationally proposed), and a propulsive, rhythmic finale.

Let it be clear: the Louisvillians are not in the same league with the Boston and Philadelphia teams, but they come quite close. These are more than merely respectable performances. They're responsive and responsible ones, and for this the Louisville Orchestra scores points. And do bear in mind that the majors (labels and orchestras) are far from ready to record such merely important but not money-making works.

Concertino for Piano and Orchestra (1937)

Solo Instrument and Orchestra

Piano

☐ Göteborg Symphony Orchestra / Mitchell (piano) / Strickland (conductor) / Composers Recordings 180 (monaural)

A concentrated concerto in Piston's usual neoclassic syntax. Quietly emotional, but properly virtuosic in an orderly way. The performance is very good, and Strickland again shows he is in command regardless of what style is involved.

Concerto for Viola and Orchestra

Viola

☐ Louisville Orchestra / Doktor (viola) / Whitney (conductor) / Louisville S–633

The solo instrument is presented as a strong *cantabile* personality. The harmonic frictional pungencies that lace the work thereby help define the relationship between orchestra and viola. Such a blend makes for good musical conversation rather than the usual solo-orchestra oppositional display. A decided addition to the still limited repertory of the instrument. Doktor's strong performance is a promotional plus to back up this statement.

Chromatic Study on the Name of Bach (1940)

Instrumental

Organ

☐ Noehren (organ) / Lyrichord 7191

Piston's piece is tightly knit by polyphony, in keeping with the minute intervallic span between the sounds of his theme. It is almost *too* contrapuntal, save that polyphony is manna for the organ.

Noehren's registration is accomplished, and his playing is clear. It is good to have this piece in the recorded catalogue; it was once available only on an old University Recordings 2 release.

Duo for Viola and Cello (1949)

Chamber Music

☐ Ilmer (viola); Teraspulsky (cello) / Coronet 1715

Piston's favorite ternary design, with corner movements in active tempo (the second one with more rhythmic kick) bracing a slow movement. Clear polyphonic organization is the major premise, and the music is presented in a clearly organized manner by these fine musicians.

Sonatina for Violin and Harpsichord (or Piano) (1945)

☐ Zukofsky (violin); Kalish (piano) / Desto 6435/37

There is splendid creative strategy here, displaying Piston's consummate knowledge of what will be instrumentally successful. The clean and uncluttered writing is especially productive for the harpsichord, but it is just as fruitful for the piano. The same clarity applies to the concentrated texture, which is thinner than in most of Piston's compositions. Two fast movements with intrinsic rhythmic vigor surround the slow-tempoed division. The "lacking" scherzo movement is compensated for capably by the inclusion of a *scherzando* quip in the first movement.

These are two of the finest musicians on the scene today. In their playing they combine a discipline and stylistic definition that is totally exhilarating. The timbral partnership is meticulous.

Piano Trio (1935)

☐ Temple University Trio / Golden Crest 4117

Rhythmic vitality is always an asset to a composer. It can be observed here in the way the rhythm gives life and tone to the contrapuntalism that permeates the four movements. All the polyphonic data of the linear-minded expert are on view—canon, imitation, augmentation, inversion, etc. Of course, such technical devices establish the composer's craftsmanship, but Piston makes them work as effective music.

Elsewhere I've mentioned that these players (Alexander Fiorillo, piano; Helen Kwalwasser, violin; and Michael Haran, cello) display excellent ensemble but are somewhat stiff in their playing. The same pertains here—there is a little too much ascetic regard for the notes and not sufficient dynamic differentiation. Perhaps a better way of saying this is to say that the Temple group is a bit square in its playing.

Three Pieces for Flute, Clarinet, and Bassoon (1925)

☐ Members of the Soni Ventorum Wind Quintet / Lyrichord S-158

This is very early Piston, his second composition (the first being a piano sonata). The pieces are squarely in confined forms, and the symmetry of each is unmistakable, all three being cast in ternary style. One will recognize the dryness of wit, controlled by use of ostinato rhythmic figures, in the first piece and the foggy chromatic haze that gives a nostalgic quality to the second item of the set; the final portion also runs on ostinato feet.

Piston stated that these pieces were like "concise pencil drawings." If so, the musicians (Felix Skowronek, William McColl, and Arthur Grossman) use hard-lead implements. No smudges occur.

String Quartet No. 5 (1962)

☐ Kohon Quartet / Vox SVBX–5305

Explicit classical architectural processes structure Piston's quartet. It comprises the composer's favored three-movement plan: sonata form in movement 1, a ternary design in the second part, and a marked emphasis on polyphony in the concluding fugue. Piston requires no novel devices to define the stability and full meaning of his work.

The Kohon Quartet team produces a top professional conception of the score. All of the merits of Piston's score are confirmed.

Quintet for Wind Instruments (1956)

☐ Boehm Quintette / Orion 75206

The "pingy" quality that is found in much of this neoclassicist's work is heard in this case. The texture of the Quintet is sparser than in most of Piston's compositions, but this is doubtless due to a desire to achieve clear instrumental definition rather than to the music's plan per se.

The Boehm group is excellent, displaying a true beauty of sound. These players make one wonder why so many wind-quintet ensembles sound as though their instruments were covered with thistles. This fivesome has a sweetness without being sonorously slick. This helps the Piston work considerably.

Divertimento for Nine Instruments (1946)

☐ Silverstein and Krips (violins); Fine (viola); Eskin (cello); Moleux (bass); Dwyer (flute); Gomberg (oboe); Cioffi (clarinet); Walt (bassoon) / RCA LSC-6167

Here French élan is mixed in with neoclassic syntax. The nonet medium is a rarity in chamber music and best balanced by combining two dissimilar color groups, as does Piston: four winds and five strings. Mainly, however, Piston builds his work as a blend of tone, using the composite nine-instrument force as an additional factor within his assured, pungent, and very orderly usual style. The diverting antagonisms of this music are more of harmonic and contrapuntal conflict than of color.

The performers are the Boston Symphony Chamber Players. However, because of their splendid conception of Piston's score they have been credited individually. This is, indeed, a unique performance conveying ultimate lucidity and artistry. In a recording, perfection of the technical requirements is to be expected but the superbly convincing manner of interpretation heard here is not too often encountered.

The Incredible Flutist (1938)

Ballet

☐ Louisville Orchestra / Mester (conductor) / Louisville LS-755

The only recording ever made of the complete score, all thirty-four minutes of it. This is about twice the amount of music in the orchestral suite (see under *Orchestra*). While Piston had taken the real guts out of the score for concert use, there is sufficient other material to provide listening returns beyond the mere satisfaction of curiosity.

Johann Peter Pixis   *(1788-1874)*

Hexaméron. See under Franz Liszt: Solo Instrument and Orchestra: piano.

Solo Instrument and Orchestra

Piano

Concerto for Piano, Violin, and String Orchestra

Piano and Violin

☐ Westphalian Symphony Orchestra, Recklinghausen / Boehm (piano); Kooper (violin) / Landau (conductor) / Turnabout 34590

The common denominators of romantic style, expressed in a brilliant opening movement, a lighter, more sprightly finale, and an *Adagio sostenuto* in between. The performers discharge their duties efficiently.

Jean-Robert Planquette   *(1848-1903)*

Overture to *Les Cloches de Corneville*

Orchestra

☐ New Philharmonia Orchestra / Bonynge (conductor) / London 6643

The Overture to this solidly-in-the-repertoire stage work (see under *Opera and Dramatic Music*) runs true to form and has such stuff as operetta orchestral prefaces are made of. It is played with the fullest effect.

Opera and Dramatic Music

Les Cloches de Corneville

☐ Opéra-Comique and Paris Opera Chorus / Mesplé, Stutzmann, Tallard, and Verlen (sopranos); Burles, Giraudeau, and Bussard (tenors); Sinclair and Benoit (baritones); Roeder (bass) / Doussard (conductor) / Connoisseur Society CS2-2107

The performance record of this operetta is amazing. Composed in 1877, by 1886 it had achieved 1,000 performances in France alone. As "The Chimes of Normandy," in its English translation, it has become an "evergreen," especially with nonprofessional groups. Never mind—*Les Cloches de Corneville* may be very light fare, but it is crafted within its genre with top expertise.

When top professionals apply themselves seriously to the music, the performance result is worth top attention. Perhaps one might have a quibble here and there, but this production is nicely focused and is a welcome contribution.

The Overture is available as a separate recording—see under *Orchestra*.

Giovanni Platti   (1697-1763)

Solo Instrument and Orchestra

Flute

Concerto in G major for Flute

☐ Ensemble Instrumental Jacques Prat / Marion (flute) / Turnabout 34566

The usual sympathetic and prevailing practice of eighteenth-century music by one of its rank-and-file composers. This isn't meant to downgrade Platti's work, which doesn't wear out its welcome by its quarter-hour length. Good marks for the soloist, who probably supplied the cadenzas for the three movements (no information is given about this). The Jacques Prat group provides an adequate backdrop for the solo character.

Piano

Concerto No. 2 in C minor for Piano and Orchestra

☐ Salzburg Symphony Orchestra / Blumental (piano) / Guschlbauer (conductor) / Turnabout 34495

There is a curious shift between the basic baroque situation of Platti's Concerto and less contrapuntal types of preclassical writing. This is illustrated in the middle movement. In the *Giga* of the finale, a full baroque head of steam is sent forth.

The performance is extremely expert, most compelling in the last part of the work.

Raoul Pleskow   (1931-   )

Instrumental

Piano, Four Hands

Three Pieces for Piano, Four Hands

☐ Chinn and Brings (piano) / Composers Recordings SD-383

A product of the style that derives from Henri Pousseur and Karlheinz Stockhausen. However, controls, as far as K. S. is concerned, are here fully vested in the performers, who give a brilliant and tidy reading. Pleskow concentrates his percussively fragmented ideas into four and a half minutes. For this type of technical physiognomy pithiness is an enhancement.

Movement for Oboe, Violin, and Piano (1966)

☐ Marx (oboe); Moore (violin); Rovics (piano) / Composers Recordings S-253

Intensity of change and intensity of data within each segment make Pleskow's intensely structured piece one of manic excitement. Indeed, this work can be described as manic-impressive. The performers conquer all the pitiless difficulties.

Three Movements for Quintet: *Of a November Morning 1970* (1971)

☐ Schulte (violin); Blustine (clarinet); Sollberger (flute); Sherry (cello); Miller (piano) / Wuorinen (conductor) / Composers Recordings 302

A preoccupation with rhapsodic events, tied together with the same pitch choices, pertains to Pleskow's piece. The textural order, especially in the last section, displays a very sensitive freedom of expression.

With these first-rank performers there is the assurance of a perfectly set reading.

Motet and Madrigal (1973)

☐ Allen (soprano); Sperry (tenor); Oppens (piano); Spencer (flute); Quan (violin); Blustine (clarinet); Sherry (cello) / Wuorinen (conductor) / Composers Recordings S-342

Pleskow emphasizes that the texts for his Motet and Madrigal (the former from the Good Friday liturgy, the other a vulgate Latin version of the *Song of Songs*) were chosen "for their evocative rather than their dogmatic content." Still, these superfine evocations have powerful neo-ecclesiastical effect. The fully chromatic communication, with antiphony and combines, is one of unfailing expressivity.

Ignaz Pleyel *(1757-1831)*

Symphonie periodique No. 6 in F major

☐ Collegium Musicum of the University of Strasbourg / Delage (conductor) / Musical Heritage Society MHS-792-CC-13

Scored for two oboes, two horns, and strings, heard in a "reconstruction" by Fernand Oubradous. No debate as to its Haydn conventions. No debate, either, as to the professional tone of its recorded performance.

Sinfonia Concertante in B flat major for Violin, Viola, and Orchestra, Op. 29

☐ English Chamber Orchestra / Stern (violin); Zukerman (viola) / Barenboim (conductor) / Columbia M-32937

The number of movements equals the number of soloists in Pleyel's comfortable, traditionally straightforward piece. Intense communication would be out of place for its somewhat neutral material, and Stern and Zukerman adjust accordingly. There is extra interest, of course, in hearing Pinchas Zukerman, a superb violinist, play the viola. From what one hears he is as solid a performer on the alto string instrument as he is on the soprano relative.

If you see a listing in some discographies of an E flat major Sinfonia Concertante by Pleyel, don't expect a different work. It's the same as the one above, with an incorrect tonality attached to it.

Chamber Music	**Trios for Flute, Cello, and Piano, Op. 16**

No. 1 in G major / No. 2 in C major / No. 5 in E minor

☐ Northwest German Chamber Trio / Musical Heritage Society MHS–1149

Not standard repertoire, though the format is strictly according to Haydn standards. Each Trio covers three movements, and each is played in a standard manner.

Anthony Plog (1947-   )

Vocal

Voice with Accompaniment

Two Scenes for Soprano, Trumpet, and Organ

☐ Bing (soprano); Plog (trumpet); Swearingen (organ) / Avant 1014

Plog begins gently and then proceeds to more dynamic considerations within his Scenes, both drawn from the single text *The Hills of Morning* by Daveda Lamont. Essentially romantic music with a fair amount of doubling the voice with the trumpet. Though this obliterates word meaning, it does offer a fine timbre partnership.

Alessandro Poglietti (?-1683)

Instrumental

Organ

Ricercar Septimi Toni

☐ Rapf (organ) / Klavier 545

Twelve *Ricercari* for organ, based on the Church (ecclesiastical) modes, constitute this composer's claim to fame. Somewhat severe and unyielding, the music is of sculptured solidity.

Poldowski (1879-1932)

Instrumental

Violin

Tango

☐ Heifetz (violin); Bay (piano) / RCA ARM4–0946 (monaural)

Poldowski is the pen name of Irene Regine Wieniawska. She was a daughter of the famous violinist-composer Henryk Wieniawski; by marriage, she was Lady Dean Paul.

Best known for her songs, she wrote two short pieces for violin and piano, the Tango achieving more play than the other, a lullaby item. Heifetz doesn't mince his bow strokes in this one.

Robert Pollock (1946-   )

Instrumental

Piano

Bridgeforms (1972)

☐ Pollock (piano) / Composers Recordings SD–333

Post-Webern serialism with an overlay of full-blooded romantic rhetoric—only in the music's inner gestures, since no hybrid technique is involved. There are eight parts identified by Bergian terminology: With Great Energy; Agitated; Melancholy; March; Expressively; Slow, Somber; Delicately; and Dance. No further relationship, however.

Naturally, Pollock plays his own music with understanding. Moreover, he conveys a virtuosity and sweep in his performance that provide a powerful asset.

Movement and Variations

☐ Composers String Quartet / Composers Recordings S–265

Strong echoes here of serialism, though basically the music is free of such technique, being supremely nontonal in its arrangement. There is strong unification between the sections of the work.

Finely gauged playing that overcomes all the technical difficulties involved.

Manuel Ponce   *(1882-1948)*

Concierto del sur (1941)

☐ Symphony of the Air / Segovia (guitar) / Jordá (conductor) / MCA 2522

Ponce wrote his Mexican impressionistic work for Segovia, and the two men joined in giving the first performance (in Montevideo, Uruguay, on October 4, 1941). But it is more than this artistic affiliation that makes the MCA (once Decca) edition preferred over the competitive one on Columbia M–31963, with Previn conducting the London Symphony Orchestra and John Williams as the soloist.

Ponce's concerto is like a nocturne even in its most rhythmic portion, the finale marked *Allegro moderato e festivo*. The quietness and gentleness of Segovia's conception, precise and neatly phrased, fit the music far better than the high-poweredness of the London's playing surrounding Williams's solo voice and the manner in which they have been recorded.

Allegro in A major (1923)

☐ Segovia (guitar) / MCA 2526 (monaural)

The first movement of Ponce's Sonata No. 1, often played as a separate piece by Segovia, for whom the complete work was written in 1923. It mixes modal bits with a Bach-like figuration and invigorates the process with folk-tune turns.

Also released in a six-record-side album on MCA 19000.

Sonata Clásica

Sonata Mexicana

☐ Segovia (guitar) / MCA 2532

The *Sonata Clásica* is set in the traditional format of four movements: Allegro, Andante, *Menuet,* and Allegro. It bears a subtitle *Hommage à Fernando Sor,* who has frequently been called the "Beethoven of the guitar." In most respects the neo-classical style used in the work is repeated in the four-movement *Sonata Mexicana,* its content slightly colored by indigenous rhythms. Though the usual tempi indications head the movements: *Allegro moderato, Andantino affettuoso,* etc., the music is based on descriptive subtitles furnished Ponce by Segovia, for whom the work was composed. These are *Bailecito del Rebozo* ("Little Dance of the Long Scarf"), *Lo Que Sueña el Ahuehuete* ("Dream of the Ahuehuete"), *Intermedio Tapatio* ("Tap Dancing Interlude"), and *Ritmos y Cantos Aztecas* ("Aztec Rhythms and Melodies"). Ponce's balanced forms, however, are not disturbed by these picturesque stimulants.

Segovia's playing of both works is ideal. There is great care for musical decorum even in the slightly less chaste measures of the *Sonata Mexicana*. In his playing the textures always remain soft—a delight to the ear. (MCA's recording is a reissue of the deleted Decca disc DL–710145.)

Sonata Romántica (1929)

☐ Segovia (guitar) / MCA 2530

Ponce indicates a subtitle for this four-movement work: *Hommage à Fr. Schubert qui aimait la guitare.* Expectedly, Schubertian turns are to be found in the composition, most vividly in the *Allegretto vivo* (movement three), and in the persistent figurations of the finale, marked *Allegro non troppo e serioso.*

Segovia's performance is splendid, with finely depicted dynamic differences and subtle color contrasts. The overall elegance of his playing is of specialness in the world of the guitar.

Sonatina meridional

☐ Bitetti (guitar) / Westminster Gold 8149

Folk-hued music, especially the improvisational contour of the second part, *Copla* ("Couplet"), which is based on an old Castillian song. The *Fiesta* that concludes the work is rather restrained. A discerning performance.

Theme, Variations, and Fughetta on a Theme by Antonio de Cabezón

☐ Benítez (guitar) / Nonesuch 71349

Extremely responsive variations on the stately theme Ponce selected for his permutations. There are nine variants and a dramatically drawn polyphonic closing section, colored by pedal points.

Ponce's work is splendidly conceived for the guitar. It is penetratingly presented by Baltazar Benítez with colorful narrative verve and sensitive contrasts. A truly superb entry in the field of recorded guitar music.

Three Mexican Popular Songs

☐ Williams (guitar) / Everest 3195

Plain and simple musical folklore, its innocence untouched by profound harmonic procedures. *La pajarera, Por ti mi corazon,* and *La valentina* are played without any fussy interpretation which would nullify their documentary significance.

Chamber Music

Sonata breve

☐ Szeryng (violin); Maillols (piano) / Philips 6500016

Mainly neoclassic in style, with some slight nationalistic interiority in the final movement, *Allegro alla spagnuola.* Indeed *breve,* with a playing time just under eight minutes. Szeryng's performance (with a different pianist) is also available on Everest 3153E (in monaural form). The Philips edition has cleaner sound.

Amilcare Ponchielli   (1834 - 1886)

Orchestra

Dance of the Hours from *La Gioconda*

☐ Philadelphia Orchestra / Ormandy (conductor) / Columbia MS-7437

Played with all the required flair and color. Not one measure is labored—the music moves, and moves in correct tempo.

Expectedly, this work is in a collection of various pieces here, and it is also in another Columbia collection (MS-6823). On the RCA label it is as well represented twice: in a two-record set (titled *Fantasia*), VCS-7079, and in a three-record program (titled *The Fantastic Philadelphians*), CRL3-0985.

La Giocanda

Opera
and Dramatic
Music

☐ Orchestra and Chorus of l'Accademia di Santa Cecilia, Rome / Tebaldi and Dominguez (sopranos); Horne (mezzo-soprano); Bergonzi and di Palma (tenors); Merrill (baritone); Maionica and Ghiusalev (basses) / Gardelli (conductor) / London 1388

Certainly this opera needs the strongest possible soprano in the title role. No side-stepping here. Renata Tebaldi, displaying all the temperament one wishes for, has competition only from Callas in the Seraphim (S-6031) edition. Just as certainly, the report is that the rest of the cast strongly favors the London release. Marilyn Horne's Laura characterization offers an intensively strong foil, and both Robert Merrill and Nicolai Ghiusalev, as head and spy of the Inquisition, are splendid.

Lamberto Gardelli's direction of the proceedings is a fine achievement. He probes the score, finds the proper pace for the tensions, and emphasizes Ponchielli's emotional communication thereby. Swell theatrics in this piece, and all of them are given their best display by the cast in the arias, duets, trios, and ensembles. Not *great* opera, it's been said, but *La Giocanda* has been a thoroughly successful one, and you can't argue with success.

Georges Poniridis   *(1892-   )*

Rythmes Grecs

Instrumental

☐ Constantinidis (piano) / Musical Heritage Society MHS-3055

Piano

For "Greek Rhythms" read "Greek Dances." Each of the six parts concerns a dance from a region of ancient or modern Greece. This artistic research covers *Smyrniote* ("Smyrna"), *Thessaliote* ("Thessaly"), *Pontique* ("Pontus"), *Thrace, Epirote* ("Epirus"), and *Cretois* ("Crete").

True substances presented without compositional trickery that hides the basal material, though neither is the music simply outlined primitively. Finely played, although most of it is dynamically neutral.

David Popper   *(1843-1913)*

Concerto in E minor for Cello and Orchestra, Op. 24

*Solo
Instrument
and
Orchestra*

☐ L'Orchestre de la Suisse Romande / Silberstein (cello) / Bonynge (conductor) / London 6750

Cello

Simple formality (sonata design, slow song movement, and a rondo) is matched here by an exceedingly highlighted cello part, but not one devoted to technical acrobatics. Popper, who was one of the great cello virtuosi in the last third of the nineteenth century, is totally concerned with the warm romantic voice of the instrument. This offers as much of a concerto document as one filled with fuming verbiage.

Instrumental	***Polonaise de concert* in D minor, Op. 14**
Cello	☐ Carr (cello); Kin (piano) / Orion 72106

Old-fashioned style, pitched toward the salon, but with plenty of opportunity for the string soloist to show off a virtuosic voice. The young cellist does fairly well; the sound is not as good.

Spinning Song, Op. 55, No. 1

☐ Krosnick (cello); Grant (piano) / Orion 7291

Krosnick whirls through the measures of this cello pops piece with flair.

Nicola Antonio Porpora   *(1686 - 1768)*

Solo Instrument and Orchestra

Concerto in G major for Cello and String Orchestra

☐ Southwest German Orchestra, Pforzheim / Blees (cello) / Angerer (conductor) / Turnabout 34574

Cello

Far above the usual baroque conception. There are four movements, and the two slow-tempo representations have lyrical depths that go beyond the narrow, straightened confines of formal tradition. The pair of fast-paced movements avoid, for the most part, continuity stitched by knitting-machine-like figuration. Really a fine, far-above-the-average opus.

Thomas Blees's cello playing is exemplary, always alert and always stylish. Good backing from Angerer.

Two Violins

***Sinfonia da Camera à 3* in D major for Two Violins and Continuo, Op. 2, No. 4**

☐ Instrumentalists of the Società Cameristica di Lugano / Scrosoppi (violin) / Nonesuch 73008

No sentimentality even where it might creep in very easily. Tempi and attacks are keen, and balances are realistic. The Lugano players are as good as any of the many groups specializing in the performance of baroque music. That only Antonio Scrosoppi is credited and not his violin partner is an odd bit of status symbolism.

Quincy Porter   *(1897 - 1966)*

Orchestra

***New England Episodes* (1958)**

☐ Polish National Radio Orchestra / Wodiczko (conductor) / Desto 7123

Porter has rarely been so serious. The music remains quietly solid, it never spurts into excitement, though the orchestrational weights are distributed sufficiently for contrast. The score seems to be cherishing hymnodic secrets. Interestingly, the unsigned liner note mentions that "New England is recalled with nostalgia." That statement can be accepted, for it is simply another way of describing the introspective quality of Porter's score.

It says something that a Polish orchestra initially records an American work. Credit this orchestra also with a good portrayal, for which the conductor, Vohdan Wodiczko, is to be thanked.

Symphony No. 2 (1962)

☐ Louisville Orchestra / Whitney (conductor) / Louisville 642 (monaural)

The heart of this Porter work lies in its quaint second movement and melancholic third movement. The former snaps the attention with opening duo colorations of solo viola and snare drum followed by trumpet and wood block. The third movement's mood of retrospection is also heard in the first movement. Only in the finale is the mood fully relaxed.

Whitney plays this piece of romantic draftsmanship professionally, but the sound is anything but of solid depth. The strings also sound pinch-penny.

Concerto for Harpsichord and Orchestra (1960)

☐ Polish National Radio Orchestra / Pleasants (harpsichord) / Krenz (conductor) / Composers Recordings S-226

Porter dresses up the solo harpsichord with orchestral garments of reason. There is no attempt to contrast the keyboard instrument with orchestral severity, and the careful coloristic faith produces benefits. The style is neobaroque with slight extensions of its boundaries that project some polytonal protuberances.

Granting the inevitable flattening out of dynamics in the harpsichord part and overlooking some slight balance variables in the orchestra, the performance is fairly good.

Solo Instrument and Orchestra

Harpsichord

Concerto for Viola and Orchestra (1948)

☐ Vienna Symphony Orchestra / Angerer (viola) / Schoenherr (conductor) / Desto 6410E (monaural)

Porter was a first-class violist, as well as violinist, so the writing for the solo instrument is very knowing. This cognizance sometimes allows the work to drift into a neutralized projection of timbre, and one hopes for some occasional roughage, merely for the contrastive effect it would bring. There are subtle shifts of weight and tension in the four movements. But in totality Porter's concerto is the opposite of dancing, driving, and dramatic music. The cadenzas are very few and have no Humpty Dumpty characteristics. Porter's concerto is indeed the product of a creative *gentleman.*

Good engineering surrounds Angerer's acceptable playing, backed by clear support from the orchestra. There are no bands—always an annoyance when one wishes to replay portions. Also, watch out for reverse labeling. (The companion piece is Piston's Symphony No. 2.)

Viola

String Quartet No. 3 (1930)

☐ Kohon String Quartet / Composers Recordings S-235

Porter has always been considered one of the most deft (and was one of the most prolific) of American composers in the writing of string quartets. His structures in the medium all have sonorous spontaneity. As a string player Porter understood from inside out what constitutes telling string-quartet scoring. All of his quartets display cohesive warmth and fluid textures, regardless of the musical idea being presented.

The third quartet is a music of intimate expression, simply stated with subtle shift of tensions. A satisfactory performance—a little less refined in places than one might wish and raising some questions about intonation in the first movement, but worth a passing grade nonetheless.

Chamber Music

String Quartet No. 7 (1943)

☐ Hungarian Quartet / Owl 10

Porter's pleasant-natured nonnationalistic music is mostly emphasized in the first movement, one with scherzo qualities. The finale is fast, powered by means of triplet rhythmic units in varied patterns. There are tarentella overtones to this semirondo movement.

The performance is well coordinated which is no surprise, considering the reputation of the Hungarian Quartet. What is surprising is to find that organization appearing on the Owl label.

String Quartet No. 8 (1950)

☐ Stanley Quartet of the University of Michigan / Composers Recordings 118 (monaural)

There are two movements in Porter's Quartet. However, as Ross Lee Finney has indicated, the composition is basically of single totality. He writes: "There are, of course, different tempos and different moods, but the formal design is found in the flow of one idea into the next and the lovely arch of the entire work, ending where it began." The scoring is ideal and Porter's ability to write a lyric postimpressionistic type of music with catchy rhythmic embroideries is reconfirmed here.

The Quartet (commissioned by the performing group who gave the premiere performance) is played with care, though the sound lacks depth and roundness.

Quintet (*Elegiac*) for Oboe and Strings

☐ Yale String Quartet / Bloom (oboe) / Composers Recordings S–235

Freer in form than most of Porter's music (in three parts, though the recording lists only two on the label). The threnodic mood is stressed by the preponderance of slow tempi. Accordingly, the balletic rhythms that Porter generally favored are eliminated in this, his last major work according to the unsigned liner note.

The music is performed beautifully.

Francis Poulenc *(1899-1963)*

Orchestra

Deux Marches et un intermède (1937)

☐ Louisville Orchestra / Mester (conductor) / Louisville S–685

Three succulent tidbits. The first is high-fashion Muzak music, the second has more dissonance and a dash of French popular song in the recipe. Part 3 mixes its rhythms and tonal modes and is crisp and crunchy. Mester's direction of Poulenc's music (composed to provide background music for a society banquet!) is perfect. He realizes the chamber-orchestra setting would be defeated if inflated.

Les Biches: Suite for Orchestra (1924)

☐ Orchestre de la Société des Concerts du Conservatoire / Prêtre (conductor) / Angel S–35932

Poulenc's *Les Biches* ("The Does"—in French slang, females that represent themselves to be innocent) is light-swinging, salonesque ballet music. It is totally relaxing, smart but not arrogant, whimsical but not flippant, lightly sexual—a French music-hall transplant of a Broadway musical.

Prêtre's conception is stylish and quite chic. Just fine.

Music for *Les Mariés de la Tour Eiffel* (1921)

☐ Orchestre de Paris / Prêtre (conductor) / Angel S–36519

What is most important (more than the music, which is snap-the-finger-stuff) is that for this mix of comedy and drama, pantomime and vaudeville, and a touch of opera, five-sixths of *Les Six* collaborated. The one of the six famed composers abstaining was Louis Durey. The project was planned by Cocteau and was first presented by the Ballets Suédois in Paris on June 19, 1921.

What remains as far as Poulenc is concerned? A couple of dances, that's all. Fair to middlin' and played middlin' to good. Historic value.

Sinfonietta

☐ Orchestre de Paris / Prêtre (conductor) / Angel S–36519

The Sinfonietta displays the bitter-sweet style of Poulenc's neoclassicism. Not one of his more important contributions, but for now-and-then listening. The performance is crisp for the most part.

Suite française (1935)

☐ Orchestre de Paris / Prêtre (conductor) / Angel S–36519

A British writer has accused Poulenc of "illiterate trifling" with the music of Claude Gervaise, a sixteenth-century composer, which is the genesis of the seven pieces making up the "French Suite." Though the content is simple, it is not trifling, and in his approach Poulenc certainly respects the stylistic source. The air of the old period is allowed full circulation in these dance pieces, ever so slightly channeled by neoclassic controls. (A piano version was also made by Poulenc—see under *Instrumental: piano.*)

This recorded statement by Prêtre is almost as good as the deleted Music Guild disc (No. 39), on which Poulenc conducted an "Ensemble of Soloists." "Almost as good" because the harpsichord is not registered sufficiently in some places. Otherwise profitable.

Concerto champêtre for Harpsichord (or Piano) and Orchestra (1928)

☐ Orchestre de la Société des Concerts du Conservatoire / van de Wiele (harpsichord) / Prêtre (conductor) / Angel S–35993

Solo Instrument and Orchestra

Harpsichord

Music that has direct eighteenth-century consanguinity. Classical diatonicism blends with harmonic pepper, resulting in a typical Parisian (Poulenc) concoction. It is seriousness laced with lightness—sugar with bitters.

This composer is more than capable of handling the difficult balance of a harpsichord and a modern orchestra. Themes and episodes are set off against each other, and when they are combined, the action has the pace of a speedy basketball game. No jollier example of fast-charged music can be heard in these days of serialized polyphonic shuttling. The end movements are as clear as Haydn. The orchestral quality is effervescent, a virtue in itself. And the relaxed, contrasting slow movement is an ingratiating *Siciliano*. The entire score offers genuine entertainment—many of the themes can be recalled long after performance.

Played with technical excellence and musical taste. The result is stunning.

Organ

Concerto in G minor for Organ, Strings, and Timpani (1941)

☐ French National Radio-Television Orchestra / Duruflé (organ) / Prêtre (conductor) / Angel S-35953

Although there is a plentiful supply of contemporary solo-organ music, little of it is outstanding. The same applies to the limited number of concerti that have been written for the instrument. Poulenc's is one of the standouts. His colorful opinions are a cultivation of things heard before and remembered. His eclectic "originality" has neither poverty nor riches, but is to be listed in the middle class of musical wealth. (For the record, Poulenc considered this composition to be one of his very best.)

The Concerto is attractive in its medieval nonpolyphonic Bachian seriousness plus refurbished Saint-Saëns and Delibes. This is quite a mixture, but Poulenc was always master of his kitchen, and the combination is appealing. The design of the music consists of varying sections tied into a single movement. Near the conclusion, continuity and balance are strengthened with the reprise of material heard earlier.

At one time the catalogue of recordings of this work was substantial, including the one listed above, which is still the most dramatic of the lot. Of the others, only the Ormandy-Biggs edition is still available (Columbia MS-6398). It is less dynamic as a totality, emphasizing the contrasted timbres of organ and orchestra. Gone are the performances of Munch with Zamkochian (on RCA 2567), Burgin and Biggs (on Columbia 4329), and Winograd with Ellsasser (on MGM 3361). No severe loss as long as Angel's edition is on the market.

Piano

Aubade, a Choreographic Concerto for Piano and Eighteen Instruments (1929)

☐ London Symphony Orchestra / Jones (piano) / Freeman (conductor) / Orion 74139

For discussion, see under *Ballet.*

Two Pianos

Concerto in D minor for Two Pianos and Orchestra (1932)

☐ Orchestre de la Société des Concerts du Conservatoire / Poulenc and Février (pianos) / Prêtre (conductor) / Angel S-35993

Poulenc's music is supertonal but festooned with dissonant cellophane. Facile and silky for the most part, the Concerto has the air of superstyled salon music, running the gamut from frank-hearted Mozartian imitation to spoofery.

Poulenc's double concerto is so disarming that by the time it has run its course one is willing to allow him all its artistic naïveté. In the long-hair musical world, successes of this kind of unabashed parody are very rare.

Well now, what kind of Poulencian bubbly water do you like? If a brilliant *sec,* the one you might choose is Gold and Fizdale with Bernstein and the New York Phil. (Columbia MS-6392). I prefer a mellower vintage, and that's why Poulenc and Février are listed above. On Seraphim S-60214 there's Whittemore and Lowe with Mitropoulos conducting the RCA Victor Symphony Orchestra. This team is less compelling only because its playing is more athletic than *galant.*

Instrumental

Guitar

Sarabande

☐ Santos (guitar) / Musical Heritage Society MHS-1916

A chaste and fragile short work, Poulenc's only composition for the guitar. Each sound is calculated to obtain the most emotively pertinent response from the listener.

Elégie   *Horn*

☐ Barrows (horn); Sanford (piano) / Golden Crest 7018 (monaural)

In the limited repertory of worthy horn music one must include Poulenc's *Elégie,* composed "in memory of Dennis Brain," one of the great horn virtuosi, who died in 1957 as the result of an automobile accident. Poulenc's piece illustrates the conviction that a lament need not be doleful sentimentality. Its ecstatic moments have raw, chromatic urgency, and its logical coherence and commanding sweep mark it as one of the best pieces for the brass instrument.

John Barrows's playing presents eloquent testimony for the *Elégie.* The piano support is intensely sympathetic. A highlight in the Golden Crest catalogue.

Humoresque (1935)   *Piano*

☐ Johannesen (piano) / Golden Crest S-4042

The stuff of encores, one notch above the salon category. Johannesen presents Poulenc's musical bonbon tastefully.

Improvisations: Books I and II (1932-1942)

☐ Kassman (piano) / Lyrichord 61 (monaural)

A sophisticated collection of twelve numbers, not virtuosic music but requiring more than a mere playing of the notes. There is no smart-alecky attitude in the Improvisations, but there is some salt. If impropriety is not the way of politeness, Poulenc proves it is the soul of wit. He remains the life of the contemporary-music party.

Poulenc's skill in shifting from Ravelian moments to Russian moods and yet remaining himself all the time is paradoxical but artistically successful. He illustrates how a composer can reshape conventional musical factors and make them his own. It is nothing more than musical plastic surgery.

If you want the entire set, you'll have to settle for Elly Kassman's rather neutrally grounded performance—it's the only one around. If half of the set will satisfy, then by all means obtain the disc noted *below* (Improvisations: Book II) or else get both and hear Kassman on mono for Nos. 1 through 6 and then shift to Johannesen on stereo for Nos. 7 through 12.

Improvisations: Book II

☐ Johannesen (piano) / Golden Crest S-4042

Grant Johannesen's playing gets inside every one of Poulenc's pieces. *See above* in regard to the entire set of Improvisations, and especially Book I.

Les Animaux modelés (1942)

☐ Johannesen (piano) / Golden Crest S-4042

In 1941 Poulenc completed his ballet *Les Animaux modelés,* based on six fables by La Fontaine in which animals possess human qualities. Obviously, a ballet cannot be produced without a musical outline. This is required for the choreographer and then serves for the pre-orchestral rehearsals of the ballet corps. As usual, therefore, Poulenc made a piano reduction of the orchestral score. From this Johannesen drew material for a solo piano suite. The deadly monotony (the music sounds like the background of an old silent movie) is not Johannesen's doing.

Schwann lists the orchestral version, conducted by Prêtre, on Angel S-36421.

Mouvements perpétuels (1918)

☐ Tacchino (piano) / Angel S–36602

The most frequently played of Poulenc's piano compositions, these pieces display a waggish demeanor on Poulenc's part. Like an acrobatic clown prancing on a tightrope, his music makes all the gestures of falling on its face, but everything is controlled during the excitement.

The attenuated, unchanged rhythmic doodling of "perpetual motion" pieces is completely absent from Poulenc's designs. The material is concentrated, the action alive (as is the playing), the effect one of slyness with an engaging smile.

Suite française (1935)
Valse in C from *Album des Six* (1918)
Villageoises (1933)

☐ Johannesen (piano) / Golden Crest S–4042

Poulenc's piano text of the orchestral *Suite française* (see under *Orchestra*) displays the neat contours of its neo-archaic contents, though, naturally, the orchestral setting adds timbred sharpness. While the black and white of instrumental antiphony can only be hinted at by a keyboard instrument, Johannesen manages quite well with his keyboard coloring of the seven picturesque movements that comprise the Suite. (The titles are: *Bransle de Bourgogne, Pavane, Petite March Militaire, Complainte, Bransle de Champagne, Sicilienne,* and *Carillon.*)

The waltz is short-hair music written by a young long-hair. Poulenc's light caricature is café music for the concert hall—catchy, concentrated, with no oom-pah-pah monotony.

Villageoises (taken from music written for Jean Giraudoux's play *Intermezzo*) consists of tunes for whistling, with slightly salty harmonies, placed in pithily defined forms—a waltz (titled *Valse Tyrolienne*), a march (titled Staccato), a melody, repeated in three different registers (called *Rustique*), a ternary-formed Polka, and a succinct round dance (titled *Petite Ronde*). Though this music is simple (Poulenc described the product as "little pieces for children"), it is packed with Poulencian sophisticated wit, and this is recognized in Johannesen's presentations.

Piano,
Four Hands

Sonata for Piano Duet (1918)

☐ Eden and Tamir (piano) / London 6434

Sometimes a young composer provides music of profit and delight. Poulenc's concise and witty three-movement piece, written at the age of nineteen (then revised twenty-one years later), caresses the ear with its nicely colored ideas and filamented textures. The surfaces are crystal clear; the dissonances are slight scratches thereon. There are no complex curvatures or heavy gravities in the Sonata; it simply floats.

Ernest Ansermet, the conductor, spoke of this piece with admiration, mentioning its subtlety, joviality, and occasional spirit of abandon. One notes other points that decorate the concentrated designs: pentatonic touches, childlike tunes, and cadences that smirk. Poulenc's four-handed piano sonata displays typical French *savoir-faire.*

The only recorded edition that matches the composer's display is the one listed above. Eden and Tamir toss off Poulenc's piece with brilliance and impeccable style. Hambro and Zayde come close (on Westminster Gold 8194) but not close enough. In contrast, the Lang sisters (on Golden Crest S–4070) miss all the subtlety of the music and confuse Poulenc's bubbling spirit with an invitation to play loudly.

Poulenc's four-handed sonata must not be confused with his much later Sonata for

Two Pianos, composed in 1953 (see under *two pianos*). This is stated because apparently Eden and Tamir play Poulenc's four-hands-on-one-keyboard work on two pianos (this does not change matters whatsoever, merely gives the musicians more keyboard space in which to operate). While no information is given that two instruments are used, doubtless that is the case since the album has the rubric "Music for Two Pianos."

Sonata for Two Pianos (1953)

Two Pianos

☐ Eden and Tamir (pianos) / London 6583

If not heavy, Poulenc's music is never slight, and though it is amusing, it is never corny. There are some well-worn (by Poulenc) clichés in the Sonata, but they are minor blemishes of the major congruities found in the work. The balancing of sonority is especially successful in a medium that can well sound like too much of a muchness. In this opus Poulenc is like a French Mozart with patent-leather shoes and pomaded hair. There are some serious moments, but for the most part the music is urbane. It is potent enough to keep any listener interested.

The selected edition is the best available, even though in places the playing is more blunt than sleek.

For Poulenc's much earlier Sonata for Piano Duet (1918), see under *piano, four hands*.

Sonata for Cello and Piano (1948)

Chamber Music

☐ Nelsova (cello); Johannesen (piano) / Golden Crest 40899

The bitonal clash found in most of Poulenc's music is again the sonorous meshed net through which this work passes. Frictional key partnership raises its worthy head in the somewhat episodic sectionalism of the first movement. Next, the *Cavatine* sings fully in perfectly matched duet form. In place of the usual scherzo a *Ballabile* is substituted. Dramatic outer sections mark the final part of Poulenc's duo sonata. In between these sections there is first some tarantella-shaped music and then the unabashed contours of a fast waltz.

Nelsova and Johannesen join in a presentation that is sensitively integrated. Their control of the detail is exemplary. Give Golden Crest a fat credit for issuing this performance.

Sonata for Clarinet and Bassoon (1922)

☐ Members of the Melos Ensemble / Angel S–36586

Stylistic crispness and bitonal projection aid in distinguishing the silver and gray of the two wind instruments. For example, an episode of question-and-answer outline in movement 1, written in simple eighth-note phrases, offers the constant refusal of the bassoon to imitate the clarinet in the latter's key, the bassoon balancing the clarinet only in terms of rhythmic imitation. The Romance is stated by the fundamental use of melody with accompaniment, but the diversity of the accompanimental figures is as cleverly arranged as the moving bass lines of Bach. The *Final* is a hybrid structure. A sprightly, rhythmic tune of semidissonant character and asymmetric shape moves later into a hint of fugato, recalls eight measures of the second movement (shades of Franck in this world of smart-styled, brisk, musical streamlining!), then returns for presentation once again.

The playing is absolutely immaculate and thereby has complete meaning. It seduces the ear. What competition there is shows good playing and poor sound, so actually there is no competition.

Sonata for Clarinet and Piano (1962)

☐ Campbell (clarinet); York (piano) / Crystal 331

Two important qualities are represented. There is, first, the dreamy richness of the slow movement, a *Romanza,* and second, the sharp "Prokofiev *Romeo and Juliet*" shape that is found in the initial movement. Of course, the witty bravado of this French composer is not missing; it is there in the finale, an *Allegro con fuoco.*

James Campbell's playing not only has body but is most impressive in its agogic clarity. His conception is pliable and always achieves the objective of expressivity. John York is no less a sensitive musician. A fine partnership and fine Poulenc.

Sonata for Flute and Piano (1958)

☐ Debost (flute); Février (piano) / Angel S–36261

Music which formally has classical orientation need not be primitive or imitative. Though Poulenc's three-movement Flute and Piano Sonata does not contain hedonistic oversimplicities, there is no indulgence in Promethean stormy oratory. The work has a neat cyclic reference for its terminal portion, is set in nicely dissonant harmony, and has textures that are as delicate as china. Despite Poulenc's description of the initial Allegro as *"malinconico,"* this part is as fluidly idiosyncratic as the final *Presto giocoso.*

Outstandingly fine playing by these musicians. In fact the tempi chosen place this edition just ahead of the nearest competitors, the famed flutist Rampal and Veyron-Lacroix as the keyboard-instrument partner. In their edition on Musical Heritage Society MHS–906, they push just a bit too fast for the good of the music, producing an annoying underlying restlessness. A second point is the overly bright recorded sound that also is less satisfactory for the work's style.

Sonata for Oboe and Piano (1962)

☐ Shulman (oboe); Wingreen (piano) / Lyrichord 7193

In spite of the sonata heading, actually a full-fledged-suite format marks this three-part work, composed in Poulenc's final year of life. Both the *Elégie* and *Déploration* have a quality of depth but are minus solemnity. The Scherzo has a compulsive, febrile brilliance.

This is the best edition on the market. The twangy, pinched tone of Pierre Pierlot (on Nonesuch 71033) is very French but very disconcerting. Too bad, since he and his partner Jacques Février are resourceful musicians and prove it in their playing of this fine Poulenc piece.

Sonata (to the Memory of García Lorca) for Violin and Piano (1943)

☐ Kaufman (violin); Pignari (piano) / Orion 7292

Romantic style—quite different from Poulenc's other works. Strongest is the opening movement, though the slight Spanish tinge in the second movement is colorful. The expected threnodic temper is absent. Lorca's memory is only called to mind by the quotation of one of his lines as the motto for the second (Intermezzo) movement: *La guitare fait pleurer les songes.*

Kaufman recorded this work with Balsam on the Columbia label No. 8063 (a mono disc long deleted). This performance is far better, and in fact is the best playing I've ever heard by this fine violinist.

Sonata for Horn, Trumpet, and Trombone (1922)

☐ Members of the American Brass Quintet / Desto 6474/7

Brass chamber music is common today, but when Poulenc composed this trio in 1922, it was considered a daring exploitation of timbre. The piece was criticized as bizarre, *outré,* the creation of a brash young man sowing musical wild oats. Concert audiences have now become more sophisticated; neither brass music nor varied currents of tonal electricity shock them. Poulenc's Sonata can only be criticized for certain portions which overemphasize the rakish Bohemian smugness practiced in much music of the early 1920s. But those who claim this is not a composition to be considered seriously are unjust.

The outer movements are the freshest. Gayest of these is the *Rondeau,* with some touches of French popular song, though the themes are all original. The final cadence is a joy to hear, with clamped seconds up to the last moment, whereupon the pure D major chord solves everything. The *Allegro moderato* is warmer in its flow, but contains a somewhat similar bouncing spirit; one portion is like a soft-shoe dance.

The piece is played with Poulencian wisdom and feeling. No great resonance to the sound, but in this instance this is most fitting.

Trio for Oboe, Bassoon, and Piano (1926)

☐ Gomberg (oboe); Walt (bassoon); Frank (piano) / RCA LSC-6184

Poulenc's keen sense of scoring know-how is worth the undivided attention of his listeners. In this oboe, bassoon, and piano trio the scoring is so coupled with the instruments that the very essence of the music would vanish if any substitution were made.

The gay first movement has the personality of a headlong Mozartian finale. In the slow movement Poulenc's attractive music recalls the melos of Bellini and Gounod. The last part, in gigue style, is as merry as can be.

Three editions are presently in the recorded-music catalogue. The above one is bewitching, a delicious conception that stimulates and awakens the ears. The Melos Ensemble members are on target on Angel S–36586, but the sonorous dish they serve needs a bit more seasoning. Pass by another Angel version (S–36261). It has a thickness of texture, and the two wind-instrument players (Robert Casier, oboe, and Gérard Faisandrier, bassoon) lack tonal profile.

Sextet for Piano, Flute, Oboe, Clarinet, Horn, and Bassoon (1932)

☐ Philadelphia Woodwind Ensemble / Poulenc (piano) / Columbia Special Products AMS-6213

Parisian wit has always been considered first rate. It is quite convincing in this tinseled and glittering music. The lyrical element is somewhat low-down, the choreographic simulation heated by jazz lights; the slower sections are expressive and remind one of late-afternoon-cocktail-hour music. Over all hangs the spirit of carnival time.

The Philadelphians (the same group as the Philadelphia Woodwind Quintet) display a vivid performing result, which may or may not be due to the fact that Poulenc is at the keyboard. It matters not; theirs is a triple-A rendition with charm, glorious sound, and tonal dispatch.

Banalités (1940)

☐ Bernac (baritone); Poulenc (piano) / Odyssey 32260009 (monaural)

Kurt Weill said he was writing for the present and didn't ''give a damn about posterity'' when he composed his *Three Penny Opera.* This thought came to mind when listen-

Vocal

*Voice with
Accompaniment*

ing to the five songs set to texts of Guillaume Apollinaire that make up *Banalités*. After they are heard, it is difficult to recall any exact musical phrase within these songs; however, the style will be remembered, especially the fact that the moods are so definitely opposed to the words. This results in vocal music truly independent of poetic calculation.

As for the recorded performance, Bernac is the leading interpreter of Poulenc's songs, and the composer is at the piano. That says it all.

Banalités: No. 1, *Chanson d'Orkenise,* and No. 2, *Hôtel* (1940)

☐ Crespin (soprano); Wustman (piano) / London 26043

Of the five pieces in this cycle, the most beautiful and sensitively intimate is *Hôtel*. Though held under dynamic wraps, this song is suffused with feeling, despite such lines as "I don't want to work/I want to smoke." It is only in terms of the texts that the title *Banalités* has proper meaning.

Crespin's sensuous delivery of *Hôtel* is captivating.

Calligrammes

☐ Bernac (baritone); Poulenc (piano) / Odyssey 32260009 (monaural)

From the angularity and disjunctiveness of the lines of the songs in speedy tempo, it is apparent that Poulenc was more influenced by the decorative arrangements (the calligrams) of Apollinaire's poems than the actual texts. The rest is just short of being conventional. Vocally, a somewhat uneven cycle; the instrumental support is far superior.

The performance partnership is superb. It represents the peak of artistic collaboration between a vocalist and a twentieth-century composer, matched only by that between Peter Pears and Benjamin Britten.

Bernac and Poulenc also recorded the latter's *Banalités* (*see above*), *Chansons villageoises*, and *Quatre Poèmes de Guillaume Apollinaire* (*see below*).

Ce Doux Petit Visage (1939)

☐ Price (soprano); Garvey (piano) / RCA LSC-2279

One of Poulenc's favorite poets, Paul Eluard (five song cycles, three individual songs, and several choral pieces were written to his texts), provided the subject matter for this bit. Price details its quiet expressivity, illustrative of the composer's mastery of vocal melody, French style.

Chansons villageoises (1942)

☐ Bernac (baritone); Poulenc (piano) / Odyssey 32260009 (monaural)

The drolleries of Maurice Fombeure's poetry set the tone in this set of six songs. Poulenc's gay temperament sprinkles these pieces with admirable affinity.

The performance is like that of Bernac and Poulenc in *Calligrammes* (*see above*).

Chansons villageoises: No. 2, *Les Gars qui vont à la fete* (1942)
Deux Poèmes: No. 1, *C,* and No. 2, *Fêtes galantes* (1943)
La Courte Paille: No. 3, *La Reine de coeur,* and No. 6, *Le Carafon*

☐ Crespin (soprano); Wustman (piano) / London 26043

Vigorous contrasts in these songs. These range from the wittiness in the second of the half-dozen *Chansons* to the restrained, nostalgic sweet-sadness in *C*. The title of the last has no musical significance, being derived from the text (a poem by Louis Aragon), wherein each line ends with the sound *cé*. The song concerns the happy days before France was occupied by the Germans.

The singing is sensitive and alert. This is vivid and clear, fully balanced and unblemished vocal artistry.

Main dominée par le coeur

Miroirs brûlants: No. 1, *Tu vois le feu du soir,* and No. 2, *Je nommerai ton front* (1938)

☐ Price (soprano); Garvey (piano) / RCA LSC-2279

A relationship with Gounod is to be noted in the first song, but the special transparency of texture makes this contemporary transplant successful.

As befits a song dealing with hate, Poulenc is propulsive in the second of the *Miroirs brûlants*. He is just the opposite in the companion piece, which concerns an unloved woman. Price sings *Je nommerai ton front* with romantic fervor; she presents the other song with somewhat classic cognizance.

Quatre Poèmes de Guillaume Apollinaire (1931)

☐ Bernac (baritone); Poulenc (piano) / Odyssey 32260009 (monaural)

Another distinguished song cycle that has strong affiliation between text and musical line. The usual fine performance by this singer, Poulenc's vocal ambassador.

Chanson à boire (1922)

☐ Male Members of the Whikehart Chorale / Carter (tenor); Moss (baritone); Nott (bass) / Whikehart (conductor) / Lyrichord 7208

Poulenc's "Drinking Song" is French pitter-patter. Watch for a number of surprise cadences. The soloists have little to do, but what they have to do is done with flair and fun.

Clic, clac, dansez sabots: No. 4 of *Chansons françaises* (1945)

☐ Male Members of the Whikehart Chorale / Nott (bass) / Whikehart (conductor) / Lyrichord 7208

Poulenc doesn't shift gears in this rhythmic and piquant choral savory. Bouncy from start to finish with a blackout ending.

La belle si nous étions: No. 6 of *Chansons françaises* (1945)

Laudes de Saint Antoine de Padoue

Quatre Petites Prières Saint François d'Assise

☐ Male Members of the Whikehart Chorale / Whikehart (conductor) / Lyrichord 7208

The sculpted choral music of Poulenc exemplified by one secular work and a pair of sacred entries. But, the *Laudes* have almost secular affinity, what with their lighter substances, especially part 3, *Laus Regi Plena Gaudio,* and the fourth, final one, *Si Quaeris Miracula.*

The greater part of the settings stresses the syllabic character of the words, and this provides textual clarity. Credit to Poulenc, of course, but in all fairness equal credit applies to the performers, who project the prosody cleanly and sing with full and rich sonority.

Choral

Chorus Alone

Quatre Motets pour le temps de Noël

Quatre Motets pour un temps de pénitence **(1939)**

☐ Whikehart Chorale / Whikehart (conductor) / Lyrichord 7127

The "Four Christmas Motets" (also known as the "Nativity Motets") are extremely lucid; the music is designed by straight choral scoring. Polyphony is avoided in favor of homophonic detail. There is some dissonant flavoring. Verticalism also stabilizes the "Four Penitential Motets" (also known as the "Lenten Motets"). They are reserved in tone yet not undramatic. In this case Poulenc illustrates that tonal worship can express piety and yet include the ictus of frictional harmony.

Expertly sung. The Whikehart group is sensitive to matters of style and just as sensitive to purity of intonation.

Sept Chansons (1936)

☐ Modern Madrigal Singers / Desto 6483

Poulenc's set of unaccompanied choruses, sung here by a double soprano-alto-tenor-bass group, has texts by Apollinaire and Eluard (five of the total by the latter). Poulenc's usual élan is present.

Some of the recording sounds as though it were emerging from a deep chamber, and there is some pitch flotation in one of the set.

Chorus with Accompaniment

Litanies à la Vierge Noire de Rocomadour (1936)

☐ Choir of St. John's College, Cambridge / Cleobury (organ); Brunt (treble) / Guest (conductor) / Argo ZRG-662

This represents Poulenc in his most saintly demeanor. The neo-ecclesiastical writing for three-part women's or children's voices parallels the old technique of psalmody; the music is colored by violent intersections of the organ in response. A regard for native heritage makes itself felt here in music contemporaneously related to the *ars nova* of the fourteenth century. An extremely subdued exultation is rare in Francis Poulenc's output; "Litanies to the Black Virgin" is one of the exceptions.

Excellent performance with more polished singing than in the Peloquin Chorale's edition on Gregorian Institutes S-205. However, if you want the *very best,* try to obtain, in one of the stores that carry special foreign-made recordings, the Pathé-Marconi disc, No. 247. The appeal of the French youngsters' (Maîtrise d'Enfants) singing arouses the most sympathetic response.

Chorus and Orchestra

Gloria in G major (1961)

☐ French National Radio-Television Orchestra and Chorus / Carteri (soprano) / Prêtre (conductor) / Angel S-35953

Poulenc comprehends the traditional objective of his liturgical subject, recognizes its requirements, yet avoids staid orthodoxy. Completely fresh, fully contemporary in manner, the music expresses religious quiet powerfully, through a reverse form of moderation—for example, the snappy syncopations in the *Laudamus Te* and the pert use of a Poulencized *ritournelle* in the *Domine Fili Unigenite.*

Analysis discloses that the warmth of the Gloria is arrived at by cooly determined procedures, at times a bit eclectic (Stravinsky and Ravel will be heard). Nonetheless, because of Poulenc's breadth of consideration the meanings of his Gloria are not confined any more than true religion is bounded by the four walls of a church. It is a superb contribution, and it is given an exceptional performance.

Le Bal masqué (1932)

□ Chamber Orchestra / Galjour (baritone) / Fendler (conductor) / Counterpoint / Esoteric 5518E (monaural)

Lusty music set to locomotive texts, couched in surrealistic *sub rosa* style (one example: "she had thick blood was bachelor of arts and had charge of classes"). This gives Poulenc the right-of-way for a veritable field day of tuneful tomfoolery in his secular cantata consisting of six movements, half with voice and half for an ensemble of eight players, the equivalent of the pit combinations of old vaudeville days—oboe, clarinet, bassoon, cornet, violin, cello, percussion, and piano.

Satire is Poulenc's signal for music that is fast-kinetic, jazz-banked, scherzo-spiced. *Le Bal masqué* is a perfect gem of cartooned flamboyance. The later opera *Les Mamelles de Tirésias* is a distinct outgrowth of this racy dissertation.

Galjour and Fendler are keen diagnostic artists and correctly consider the music as a nonet rather than a vocal vehicle with accompaniment. The results are most effective. An old release but acceptable sound.

Mass in G (1937)

□ Whikehart Chorale / Whikehart (conductor) / Lyrichord 7127

A compelling performance of this unaccompanied choral work dedicated to the memory of the composer's father. The work is in five sections, minus the Credo, and written in a style that speaks of pre-twentieth-century creative manners.

Stabat Mater (1951)

□ Orchestre de la Société des Concerts du Conservatoire and Choeurs René Duclos / Crespin (soprano) / Prêtre (conductor) / Angel S–36121

Poulenc's concept of the sacred form is faithful to the liturgical objective without abandoning his Gallic pellucidness. His *Stabat Mater* has the strength of simplicity; its traditional dignity remains unimpaired even with the contemporary dissonance that is added to the harmonic vocabulary.

The recording presents a satisfactory performance, though not an especially moving one.

Un Soir de neige (1945)

□ Grenoble University Choir / Giroud (conductor) / Musical Heritage Society MHS–1078

A striking example of Poulenc's neoliturgical style that exemplifies discriminating use of modality, punctuated ever so slightly with chromatic italics. There are marvelous cadential statements—note the conclusion of part 3, *Bois meurtri*. The fervency of this four-part chamber cantata with sextuple voice division (texts by one of Poulenc's favorite poets, Paul Eluard) is matched by refined singing, though the sopranos are taxed in one place.

Les Dialogues des carmélites (1956)

□ Orchestra and Chorus of Théâtre National de l'Opéra de Paris / Duval, Crespin, Gorr, and Berton (sopranos); Scharley, Fourrier, and Desmoutiers (mezzo-sopranos); Finel, Rialland, and Romagnoni (tenors); Bianco, Forel, and Conti (baritones); Depraz, Mars, and Charles-Paul (basses) / Dervaux (conductor) / Angel 3585 (monaural)

Cantata and Oratorio

Opera and Dramatic Music

The "Dialogues" is a drama with strong psychological overtones, set at the outbreak of the French Revolution. Blanche, a young girl, seeks to escape from her problems by becoming a Carmelite nun. However, her previous inability to cope with life and her undefined fears are hardly lessened by the new experience. The convent is besieged by the revolutionaries, and Blanche seeks refuge in her father's home. It is only when the nuns are condemned to die on the guillotine that the girl finds security, undergoes a spiritual awakening, and willingly accepts a martyr's death.

Poulenc's music steers away from true sacred conformity. He knows how to set words, and the score has excellent color, but the *Carmélites* will strike more than one listener as a pastiche (Mussorgsky, Debussy, and filtered Puccini), wherein the plot moves forward but the music draws the other way. The latter has a certain theatrical force, but it never projects the girl's turmoil and her eventual redemption.

Angel's recording has long been on the books, and it certainly fulfills all requirements. There is no weakness in the cast, and the work of Pierre Dervaux is exemplary.

Ballet

Aubade, a Choreographic Concerto for Piano and Eighteen Instruments (1929)

☐ London Symphony Orchestra / Jones (piano) / Freeman (conductor) / Orion 74139

Originally cast as a ballet, Poulenc's composition loses nothing in separation. (It has been placed in the ballet category because the entire score is performed here.) Poulenc termed it "amphibious" because it was a blend of media. *Aubade* is less than a full-blown concerto and more than a concerto grosso.

The *Aubade* is in eight movements and can be listened to as absolute music or as a semiprogrammatic conception following (in a general way) the original scenario, which concerns the goddess Diana, who suffers remorse because she has vowed to be bound by the laws of chastity. The score is lightly theatrical and mostly lyrical, with the solo instrumental voice and orchestra posing questions and responses, as well as rebukes, to each other. This is discreet Poulenc with a complete French sense of order and charm.

Maximum effect is obtained in this performance. Everything is sharply outlined, and clarity is constant. The collaboration between the pianist, Joela Jones, and the conductor, Paul Freeman, is splendid and places their presentation at the top of the recorded choices.

Poulenc / Jean Françaix

Opera and Dramatic Music

The Story of Babar the Elephant (1940)

☐ Paris Conservatoire Orchestra / Ustinov (narrator) / Prêtre (conductor) / Angel S-36357

The original version by Poulenc was an exception to the rule—narrator with solo piano rather than with orchestra. Naturally, the scoring by Françaix adds measurably. But *Babar* (the same subject was used by Nicolai Berezowsky for a very successful children's opera) with piano or with orchestra is no exception to the rule—music and talk for children, more thoroughly enjoyed by adults.

Descriptive and pertinent to the story, the score is not a mishmash of Mickey Mouse variety. In writing this excellent musical vaudeville, Poulenc doubtless had as much enjoyment as his listeners will.

Especially fruitful are Peter Ustinov's characterization and his fully balanced integration with the orchestra so that music and story are heard equally. There is exemplary playing by the Parisians and perceptive understanding of all the score's nuances by Prêtre.

Henri Pousseur (1929-)

Rimes pour différentes sources sonores (1959)   *Orchestra*

☐ Rome Symphony Orchestra / Maderna (conductor) / RCA VICS-1239

Using traditional means of explanation, *Rimes* can be termed a concerto grosso for electronic sounds with large symphony orchestra. The *concertino* is represented by the former, the *ripieno* by the latter. A further amplification (no pun intended) of the form takes place by the make-up of the orchestra, split into two unequal groups each of which at times combines electronic and instrumental sounds. Stereophonic juxtaposition and antiphony are also utilized: the audience is supposed to sit in between the two orchestral groups.

Rimes is structurally divided into three sections, the last for orchestra alone. Curiously, a certain portion of the electronic material imitates orchestra timbres.

The recording gives an excellent sonic representation of the audience seating arrangement requested for live performances. Actually, there are not many halls which would permit Pousseur's layout for orchestra(s) and audience, so stereophonic recording is an ideal substitute. A bit less ideal is the definition of the pointillistic flashes that pass between the two orchestras.

Madrigal III (1962)   *Chamber Music*

☐ Domaine Musical Ensemble / Boulez (conductor) / Everest 3170

Six players are involved: clarinet, violin, cello, piano, and two percussion (including vibraphone, marimba, and assorted unpitched instruments). The leading character is the clarinet (the result of Pousseur incorporating almost all of his Madrigal I for solo clarinet into the score).

The liner note (by the composer Jean-Claude Eloy) speaks of Pousseur reactivating harmonic values that have become "almost neutralized" in post-Webern music. It is difficult to agree with Eloy. In this work there is very little direct harmonic action. Pousseur's Madrigal III is mainly an instrumental mosaic. The timbres are lightly triggered, as though linear sensuosity were going to break out any minute, but a respectful aloofness is retained.

Boulez is at his meticulous best. His ensemble is a stable one.

Trois Chants sacrés (1951)   *Vocal*

☐ Lamoree (soprano); Rosenblith (violin); Glick (viola); Rudiakov (cello) / Thome (conductor) / Candide 31021

Voice and Instrumental Ensemble

Early Pousseur, when he was deep in the grip of the post-Webern school of pointillism. The pithiness (time 5:22) is also a Webern parallel. Well executed by both the vocalist and the string trio.

Trois Visages de Liège (1961)   *Electronic Music*

☐ Columbia MS-7051

"Three Faces of Liège" has rewards quite rare in the field of electronic music. Its technical virtuosity is one, its exciting surprises and emotive ingredients are others. Indeed, Pousseur proves that he, among few, has taken electronic music out of the experimental lab into the permanent literature of music.

Glissando items are major to the first part (*L'Air et l'eau*). A pizzicato chord is modulated, amplified, twisted, and changed in part 2 (*Voix de la ville*), where there is also a fascinating usage of voice collage. The last appears also in the final section (*Forges*) together with organ-like sonorities plus thrilling sonorous stridulation.

Pousseur does not pipe any querulous sounds in his composition. The recoil and the use of timbre recall have structural meaning with premise and preparation, development and suspension, and resolution. This is magnificently in-tune electronic music.

John Powell (1882-1963)

Solo Instrument and Orchestra

Rhapsodie nègre for Piano and Orchestra

☐ Los Angeles Philharmonic Orchestra / Carno (piano) / Simmons (conductor) / New World Records NW-228

Piano

Though John Powell was a racist (Nicolas Slonimsky's words are clear in this respect: "a valiant champion of white race supremacy"), his most successful pieces, the *Rhapsodie nègre* and the *Sonata Virginianesque* for Violin and Piano, are derived and built from Negro musical materials. So much for artistic hypocrisy and opportunism.

The "Negro Rhapsody" has the stuff of true concerto drama about it, balancing the solo and orchestral protagonists properly without negating the required pianistic spotlighting. Included, and most important, is the derived use of a pair of spirituals.

The playing of Zita Carno has fine character. The persuasiveness of the orchestra's performance deserves equal credit.

Instrumental

Sonata Teutonica, Op. 24

☐ Johnson (piano) / Composers Recordings SD-368

Piano

The word "Teutonica" was not intended, Powell indicated, to refer to a race, but to a "type of mind and character." He spoke of a "sense of oneness," covered by the motto that he prefaced to the work: "The Ocean is in the Drop as the Drop is in the Ocean."

There is nothing wrong with Powell's somewhat mystical definition of his creation. A composer has the right to arouse in his listeners a certain alertness. The positive point of the opus is its full-blown romanticism, with a Liszt-like grandeur.

Length perhaps has withheld this piece from concert schedules, the original covering more than an hour in performance. Roy Hamlin Johnson has reduced the work to under forty-three minutes. He plays Powell's *Sonata* with lucidity. In so doing, Johnson convinces this writer that his edition of Powell's *Sonata Teutonica* deserves full acceptance.

Mel Powell (1923-)

Instrumental

Etude (1957)

☐ Helps (piano) / Composers Recordings S-288

Piano

Powell's "Study" consists of an introduction and theme and variations compressed in size. The virtuosic flair of the music is fascinating and impressive—so is the playing.

Chamber Music

Divertimento for Violin and Harp (1955)

☐ Sorkin (violin); Ross (harp) / Composers Recordings 121 (monaural)

Melodically and harmonically suave in the outer movements, expressively taut in the inner, slow movement. The elegance and the clarity of Powell's writing are matched by the excellence of his scoring.

Good playing. Incorrect labeling. For correctness just reverse the information.

Improvisation (1962)

☐ Davenny (piano); Wilson (clarinet); Schwartz (viola) / Composers Recordings S-227

Powell's piece uses post-Webern diction and embraces the total chromatic spectrum. It also embraces a spastic condition of nervous jabs and spurts. It sounds as it is titled, but it is far from structurally loose. Within the sonic shadow boxing there is considerable momentum.

The music is extremely difficult to perform. The trio involved conquer all the problems.

Trio for Piano, Violin, and Cello (1956)

☐ Helura Trio / Composers Recordings 121 (monaural)

Neoclassically crafted, Powell's Trio has a structural plot that includes a fascinating set of variations, and a very effective *Marcia grottesca*. Throughout, Powell shows a fine flair for handling the piano-trio medium.

Skillfully played by a group that takes its name from the first two letters of each musician's first name: *He*rbert Sorkin, violin; *Lu*cille Burnham, piano; and *Ra*y Schweitzer, cello. (The labeling was reversed on the copy auditioned.)

Divertimento for Five Winds (1956)

☐ Fairfield Wind Ensemble / Composers Recordings 121 (monaural)

Here is a fine mix of colorful ebullience and tonal sophistication. The former is emphasized by substituting a trumpet for the horn in the traditional wind-quintet formation and the latter by neoclassic flexibility.

First-rate playing which fully realizes Powell's delicate and pungent sonorities. (Watch for reverse labeling, though one hopes by now it has been corrected.)

Two Prayer Settings (1963)

Vocal

Voice and Instrumental Ensemble

☐ New York Chamber Soloists / Bressler (tenor) / Kaplan (conductor) / Composers Recordings S-227

Kaleidoscopic chromaticism and registral shifts rule these two pieces. The words of the first are by Paul Goodman, those of the second are "attributed to Gregory the Great." CRI does not offer any texts, which in this case is a severe drawback.

Events for Tape Recorder (1963)

Electronic Music

☐ Dunnock, Scott, and Bowman (voices) / Composers Recordings S-227

Prerecorded voices dissect words from a Hart Crane poem and then the voices are themselves further dissected, re-formed, and mixed, living thereby in marriage with the electronically generated sounds. The beauty is that although the words are understood *as* isolated words, their arrangement and overdubbing make them verbalized electronics in the long run. The intense fermentation that takes place with this mix is highly dramatic, since verbal nonintelligibility produces the paradox of total electronic intelligibility.

Second Electronic Setting (1962)

☐ Composers Recordings S-227

Plenty of action in Powell's *Setting,* also a considerable amount of jazzy jiggeting. The link with instrumental music, even though a very thin one, can be perceived in the registral, textural, and rhythmic clarity. (An oscillator was Powell's sole sound source.)

Morgan Powell   (1938-   )

Solo Instrument and Orchestra

Nocturnes

☐ Illinois Contemporary Chamber Players / Perantoni (tuba) / London (conductor) / Crystal S-394

Tuba

Two separate works contrasted by instrumentation. *Midnight Realities* is for unaccompanied tuba. *Transitions* is for solo tuba with flute, oboe, E flat clarinet, bassoon, trumpet, trombone, violin, bass, piano, and percussion partnership. Combining them is not merely a recording practicality. At this time the Nocturnes form a set of two pieces; the composer plans to add to the group.

Creative sincerity devoted to colorful detail is proven in Powell's composition. The dynamic direction of contemporary-styled virtuosity is constantly present in these night musics. It is always formalistically relevant.

This Daniel Perantoni is one fine tuba player. His command is thorough, and regardless of intricate technical demands he always plays with a clearly enunciated voice.

Choral

Chorus and Instrumental Ensemble

The Zelenski Medley

☐ Ineluctable Modality / Howell (flute); Wilma Zonn (oboe); Paul Zonn (clarinet); Farrell (cello); Maddox (piano); Siwe (percussion) / London (conductor) / Advance FGR-18S

Not only fragmented choral writing but symbolic vocal sounds of various points and colors. The merged text (hardly distinguishable) is a setting of three extremely short poems by Paul Zelenski.

John Pozdro   (1923-   )

Orchestra

Third Symphony (1960)

☐ Oklahoma City Symphony Orchestra / Harrison (conductor) / Composers Recordings 151 (monaural)

A striking performance of a symphony with northern data (obtained in Howard Hanson's studio, as it were). Pozdro's symphony is professionally constructed and is especially interesting in its use of the darker tones of the orchestration palette.

Michael Praetorius   (1571-1621)

Instrumental

Recorders

Dances from *Terpsichore*

☐ Ferdinand Conrad Instrumental Ensemble / Nonesuch 71128

A representative selection from the more than 300 dances in Praetorius's single secular composition. The ten dances performed by the Conradians are gently sweet, sprightly agreeable, squarely rhythmic, and patterned sequentially. Still, their charm holds enjoyable values even for the most sophisticated listener. Included are two *Ballets* (one *des sorciers*, the other *des feus*), two *Bransles* (one *double*, the other *gentil*), a *Gaillarde*, a *Sarabande*, etc.

As Joshua Rifkin points out, the instruments to be used for this music were not indicated by Praetorius, "leaving the scoring to the players' choice." The performance heard here opts for a recorder ensemble, with a few of the dances neatly supported by light percussion. The playing has quality that cannot be argued.

How far this instrumental choice can reach is to be heard on Angel S-37091, in a performance of fourteen of the dances by the Early Music Consort of London, conducted by David Munrow. No dulcet-pitched recorder devotion in that case! Munrow's arrangements are of varying timbre totality and textures, utilizing some forty instruments including six sackbuts, two cornetts, a serpent, five krummhorns, as many recorders, four racketts, four rauschpfeiffen, a dulcian, two violins, a tenor viol, a violone, a pair of gambas, lute, chitarrone, two organs, regal, harpsichord, and percussion. Quite an array, and exceedingly interesting, but tending to instrumental overkill for these simple dance tunes.

Christmas Music from *Musae Sioniae*

Choral

Chorus and Instrumental Ensemble

☐ Ferdinand Conrad Instrumental Ensemble and Niedersächsischer Singkreis, Hannover / Träder (conductor) / Nonesuch 71128

Five Christmas items from Praetorius's nine-volume collection *Musae Sioniae*. Included is *Vom Himmel hoch*, which should not be confused with the four times larger work with the same title included in his *Polyhymnia Caduceatrix et Panegyrica* (see under *Cantata and Oratorio*). The instrumental timbres of pommers, krummhorn, dulcian, gambas, and recorders authenticate the performance setting. These unique and uncommon sounds blend well with the clear and fully balanced voices to produce an engaging recording that does honor to all concerned.

Four Concertos from *Polyhymnia Caduceatrix et Panegyrica*

Cantata and Oratorio

☐ Westphalian Choral Ensemble and Instrumentalists / Wehrung, Graf, Bernát-Klein, and Flebbe (sopranos); Haasemann (alto); Hoefflin and Ellenbeck (tenors); Pommerien (bass) / Ehmann (conductor) / Nonesuch 71242

"Concertos" in the sense of vocal compositions supported by instrumental accompaniment. Each of the texts concerns the birth of Christ, and each setting is for a different arrangement of the performing forces. Two examples: *Puer Natus in Bethlehem* ("A Child Born in Bethlehem") has a three-part solo ensemble, a four-part chorus, and four four-part instrumental and continuo ensembles. *Vom Himmel hoch, da komm ich her* ("From Heaven Above I Come") is scored with the solo group increased to four parts and the instrumental and continuo ensembles decreased to three four-part groups. (For a different *Vom Himmel hoch* by Praetorius, see under *Choral: chorus and instrumental ensemble* [Christmas Music from *Musae Sioniae*].)

The orchestral body has five recorders, two oboes, English horn, bassoon, trumpet, three trombones, four lutes, four viola de gambas, harpsichord, positive organ, violone, cello, and double bass.

The performances are all well registered, the voices warm and pleasurable; the instrumental definition is well poised.

William Presser   *(1916-   )*

Instrumental

Trumpet

Suite for Trumpet

☐ Hickman (trumpet) / Crystal S–363

Credit Presser with not resorting to tricks, multiphonics, or any bizarre ideas in structuring the materials in his three-movement composition. Tonally indited, artistically played.

Chamber Music

Prelude, Fugue, and Postlude

☐ Florida State University Brass Trio / Golden Crest S–4081

A compositional liaison between contemporary nuances and old forms is, of course, not a new idea, but the method has always exerted a fascination for many composers. Presser does well with the idea. So does the group, which plays with expertise. It is important to indicate that the trio—Ralph Montgomery, trumpet; William Robinson, horn; and William Cramer, trombone—are not students even though the name of their group might lead to that assumption.

Allegro from Serenade for Four Tubas

☐ University of Michigan Tuba Ensemble / Mayer (conductor) / Golden Crest CRS–4145

A music of rotund sprightliness. Played fluently considering the textural weight involved.

André Previn   *(1929-   )*

Solo Instrument and Orchestra

Guitar

Concerto for Guitar and Orchestra

☐ London Symphony Orchestra / Williams (guitar) / Previn (conductor) / Columbia M–31963

Not only guitar and orchestra but, in the latter part of the work, additional instrumental testimony via an electric guitar, an electric bass, and a drummer, the group forming a jazz infiltrate. It contrasts with the general romantic tone of the music that precedes. Nothing is violated in this combination of qualities.

Performance profitability is, of course, guaranteed with Previn guiding his own music and with John Williams as the soloistic expert.

Leland Procter   *(1914-   )*

Orchestra

Symphony No. 1 (1948)

☐ Polish National Radio Orchestra / Ormicki (conductor) / Composers Recordings S–224

The features of Procter's piece are clear tonality, clear-cut themes (a cute, folksy one is interspersed in the last of the four movements), and form that needs no lengthy guide for understanding. The fact that there are influences does not negate the values of Procter's symphony. Label it neo-romantic.

One is certain the performance discloses what the score contains.

Sergei Prokofiev *(1891-1953)*

Autumnal Sketch, **Op. 8**   *Orchestra*

☐ London Symphony Orchestra / Ashkenazy (conductor) / London CSA-2314

This piece will give you the opportunity to hear Prokofiev sounding a bit like Delius. The somber lyricism in Prokofiev is brought out potently by this musical statement.

Cinderella: **Suites from the Ballet**

No. 1, Op. 107 / No. 2, Op. 108 (Excerpts)

☐ L'Orchestre de la Suisse Romande / Ansermet (conductor) / London 6242

There have been various amounts of music in the excerpts recorded from the Prokofiev ballet. Among the versions currently available, two, conducted by Rozhdestvensky (on Melodiya/Angel S-40138 and also on S-4114) and Rignold (on London STS-15193), have more sections than the selection by Ansermet. However, Ansermet's is not only the best played but the best planned in terms of sequence and choice.

London terms its recording "highlights." True enough, but the term "highlights" implies a special version drawn from the complete ballet, whereas it will be seen that Ansermet's choice was made from choices already fixed by Prokofiev in the three orchestral suites he arranged from the complete ballet.

The three suites have eight, seven, and eight movements respectively, and are given specific opus numbers—107, 108, and 109—even though the complete ballet bears the identification Opus 87. Bypassing the third suite, Ansermet has mixed the two other suites and rearranges the order of movements made by Prokofiev. In total, all eight movements of the first suite and four of the seven movements of the second suite are performed.

London does not identify the suite sources for the twelve sections recorded. For those who wish this information, the following indicates the Prokofiev suite number and, in parentheses, the movement number for each of the twelve sections: 1 (1), 1 (2), 1 (3), 2 (1), 1 (4), 1 (5), 1 (6), 2 (5), 2 (4), 2 (6), 1 (7), 1 (8).

There are plenty of good tunes in the compilation, and nicely conceived classical-ballet forms. Best of all is when one hears the basic traits of Prokofiev's individuality: severely tooled contrast, grotesquerie, earthy color, and sharply bitten metrical accentuation. Such assets are to be found in the *Quarrel* (part 3) and in the Galop (part 10).

Four Portraits: **Suite from the Opera** *The Gambler,* **Op. 49**

☐ Moscow Radio Symphony Orchestra / Rozhdestvensky (conductor) / Melodiya/Angel S-40157

Not merely extracts from Prokofiev's four-act opera, but recomposition of the stage work's materials delineating the personalities involved. The playing is professional if not earth-shaking.

Lieutenant Kijé **Suite, Op. 60**

☐ Philadelphia Orchestra / Ormandy (conductor) / Columbia MS-6545

Smart and tart style and brilliant coloration are what Ormandy brings to the music Prokofiev drew from his film score. A conductor can be intensely personal with his conception of this material. Ormandy gives it a highly charged and gutsy depiction—a visionary yet detailed picturing of the music.

There's another edition by Columbia: M–31812. Further, Ormandy has repeated himself vis-à-vis this Prokofiev opus, on RCA ARL1–1325. I can't hear too much difference.

Overture on Hebrew Themes, Op. 34 bis

☐ Orchestre National de l'O.R.T.F., Paris / Martinon (conductor) / Vox SVBX–5123

The engaging and very picturesque quality of this one-movement work is of high creative order and refreshing color. Although pseudo-Oriental, the Overture contains essential Hebraic spirit, atmosphere, and interest.

The "bis" is the orchestral setting; the first, for clarinet, string quartet, and piano, was written in 1919, and the symphonic translation—for double woodwinds, paired horns and trumpets, one percussionist, piano, and strings—was made in 1934. Opinions differ as to the relative merits of the two versions. The earthiness and color concentration of the solo wind instrument, the exact support of the piano, and the perfect balance of the string quartet are, naturally, not present in the enlarged scoring and in that setting Prokofiev's Overture has not had the same impelling effect on listeners. Nevertheless, one may differ with this view and prefer the larger canvas Prokofiev used the second time around. If so, Martinon's playing is all it should be, and this is the only recording of Opus 34 bis on the market.

Romeo and Juliet, Op. 64 (Excerpts)

☐ Rotterdam Philharmonic Orchestra / de Waart (conductor) / Philips 6500640
☐ Boston Symphony Orchestra / Munch (conductor) / RCA VICS–1412
☐ London Symphony Orchestra / Abbado (conductor) / London 6522

From the more than fifty sections of the complete *Romeo and Juliet* ballet Prokofiev selected twenty numbers which he split into three suites, with seven parts each in the first two and six in the third. These were planned for concert effect rather than adhering to plot sequence.

Performances of this music are in the best-seller category. But exact identification with Prokofiev's divisional arrangement is extremely rare. Some conductors adhere to the movement sequence of the second suite, the favorite among all three suites. A very few play the first suite, and when doing so, most revise Prokofiev's order. The great majority of conductors mix up the first two suites, and no two of the maestros agree on the succession of the movements. Hardly anyone gives attention to Suite III.

The three chosen versions listed above offer the best overview of the *Romeo and Juliet* excerpting, together with the best playing. Although the sound of the Munch edition is a bit rough in spots, his ordering is very interesting and includes three portions of the third suite, in addition to three pieces from the first suite and a half dozen from the second one.

Edo de Waart's compilation is outstanding. It covers the entire second suite and four movements from the first suite. He combines these so that, for example, the first two pieces from Suite II are followed by parts 5 and 4 of Suite I, etc. His plan is to parallel the excerpting with the ballet's narrative.

Though *Schwann* lists Abbado as performing the first suite, this is totally incorrect. To begin with, Suite I has seven movements, and Abbado plays nine. What is performed is Abbado's own scenario taken from the *complete* ballet score. Included are one piece each from the first and third suites and a pair of movements from the second suite.

Russian Overture, Op. 72

☐ Paris Conservatoire Orchestra / Martinon (conductor) / London STS–15196
☐ Orchestre National de l'O.R.T.F., Paris / Martinon (conductor) / Vox SVBX–5123

No difference in the playing on this pair of discs of the *Ouverture Russe,* containing some original and some Russian-simulated themes. However, the London disc (once an RCA release) has brighter sound.

Scythian Suite, Op. 20

☐ London Symphony Orchestra / Dorati (conductor) / Mercury 75030

This music is stamped with violent color, a Prokofiev trademark. With this, together with its primitivistic rhythms, the Scythian Suite has become known as "Prokofiev's *Sacre du Printemps.*" Not exactly so, but it still is a big bundle of block-busting musical bravado.

Dorati goes all out in his direction of these orchestral pictures of pagan Russia, and so does Mercury. Tremendous excitement plus tremendous sound equals tremendous musical barbarism.

Suite from the Ballet *The Prodigal Son,* Op. 46 bis

☐ L'Orchestre de la Suisse Romande / Ansermet (conductor) / London 6538

A favorite of Prokofiev's, who used material from this work both to fashion a piano piece and to include in his fourth symphony. The performance is professionally careful.

Suite from *The Love for Three Oranges,* Op. 33 bis

☐ London Symphony Orchestra / Dorati (conductor) / Mercury 75030

The six-part suite Prokofiev drew from his opera includes the well-known *Marche* and a Scherzo that should be better known. Part 2, *Scène infernale,* has a violence that is exciting. Throughout, Dorati plays up the brilliant colors of the score and loads up the instrumental pigmentation. Thus a symphonic richness and a parallel emotionalism that are significant.

Symphonic Suite from the Ballet *The Buffoon,* Op. 21 bis

☐ London Symphony Orchestra / Susskind (conductor) / Everest 3001

Prokofiev's six-scene ballet, containing five symphonic interludes, is based on a Russian folk tale, *The Buffoon Who Outwitted Seven Other Buffoons.* It is also known as *Chout* (the French spelling for the Russian word for buffoon).

Its grotesquerie, sharp-pointed rhythms, and general ironic tone are admirably recreated under Susskind's direction. This is less so in the competitive editions. Further, Claudio Abbado's performance, with the same orchestra that Walter Susskind conducts, on London 6522 is a cut version, with movements 4, 5, and 7 of Prokofiev's twelve-part suite eliminated.

Symphony in D major (*Classical*), Op. 25

☐ New York Philharmonic / Bernstein (conductor) / Columbia MS–7258
☐ Philharmonia Orchestra / Kurtz (conductor) / Seraphim S–60172

Bernstein's reading (also on Columbia MS–7159, where it is coupled with Bizet's Symphony in C Major, while here it is companied with *Peter and the Wolf* and the *Lieutenant*

Kijé Suite) is virtuosity at its nimblest. The energy of the first movement and the motility of the finale are perfectly realized, and the phrasing is magnificent. The lyricism in the Larghetto is contrasted to the best soft staccatos I have ever heard produced for this movement.

Despite slightly slower tempi, Kurtz's performance is admirable, and the relaxed atmosphere is, for the most part, just as telling as Bernstein's going for the downs. The textures in both presentations are as clean as a whistle. This permits the asymmetric rhythms and the clever modulations to make their important points.

Symphony No. 2 in D minor, Op. 40

☐ Orchestre National de l'O.R.T.F., Paris / Martinon (conductor) / Vox SVBX-5124

The corpulences and sonorous layers plus the constant aggressiveness of the Prokofiev "second" have done in most conductors who have played the work. All this is not easy to handle, but Martinon controls the score's energy without attempting to block it and allows the music to flex its huge muscles. It makes a crusty, rasping noise sometimes, but that's Prokofiev, and Martinon makes it as clear as possible, and certainly clearer than does Rozhdestvensky in his performance on Everest 3214.

To obtain the Martinon, one is forced to secure a Vox box containing his presentations of the first, third, and fourth symphonies, plus the Russian Overture and the Overture on Hebrew Themes in the orchestral setting. But his conception of the second symphony is worth it.

Symphony No. 3 in C minor, Op. 44

☐ Moscow Radio Symphony Orchestra / Rozhdestvensky (conductor) / Melodiya/Angel S-40092

Immense heat and power are generated in the first and third movements of the symphony Prokofiev fashioned based on material from his opera *The Flaming Angel*. There is roughage too, and the laying on of orchestral harsh hands is fitting. The other divisions, especially the finale, have their ferocious moments, but these are tempered by a poetic mysticism.

Panache is more pertinent than polish for this symphony. Rozhdestvensky drives the orchestra, but he drives home Prokofiev's messages magnificently. More restraint makes Abbado's reading (on London 6679) admirable, but this only suffices for the quieter portions. It results in impact loss in the balance of the work, and for that reason one prefers the rougher excitement obtained by the Soviet conductor.

Symphony No. 4 in C major, Op. 47

☐ Orchestre National de l'O.R.T.F., Paris / Martinon (conductor) / Vox SVBX-5123

Martinon has recorded the complete Prokofiev symphonies in two Vox boxes. Be warned, there are two distinctly different versions of the fourth symphony and Martinon has bypassed the second of the pair. However, his performance of the initial setting is the only recorded example. (The second version is considered *below* [Opus 47/112].) The conciseness of Opus 47 is immediately recognized when the timing of this recording of it (24:46) is compared with that of the greatly enlarged Opus 47/112, timed in Ormandy's rendition at 39:17.

Symphony No. 4 in C major, Op. 47/112

☐ Philadelphia Orchestra / Ormandy (conductor) / Odyssey Y-32226

The first version, Opus 47 (*see above*), was composed in 1930 for the fiftieth-anniversary concerts of the Boston Symphony. In 1947 Prokofiev extensively revamped and thoroughly expanded his fourth symphony. Both accounts drew on material Prokofiev had planned to use or actually had used in his ballet *L'Enfant prodigue* ("The Prodigal Son"). The end effect of the additions and elaborations led Prokofiev to credit himself with a new opus number, though indicating the basic, older one as well.

Ormandy's conception of this work is idiomatically "on the money," and it outranks Rozhdestvensky's Russian-made recording (released in the United States on the Melodiya/Angel label on S-40040). The Philadelphians' disc was first released on Columbia ML-5488, which has since reissued it on the considerably more economically priced Odyssey label.

Symphony No. 5 in B flat major, Op. 100

☐ Philadelphia Orchestra / Ormandy (conductor) / Odyssey Y-30490
☐ Berlin Philharmonic Orchestra / von Karajan (conductor) / Deutsche Grammophon 139040

The Ormandy recording is from the days of early stereo, and the sound does not have the focus one obtains in today's productions. But what a performance! And what's more important, the sound or the message? Even with dated stereo, the quality of the Philadelphians' performance sweeps away any dissent about the sonic quality. (It even sings out in the old mono version on Columbia ML-5260.) There are magnificent lyrical statements and polished vehemence where required, and Ormandy subtly defines each and every harmonic titivation. He and his players are masterful.

There is just as much excellence in the performance scenario offered by von Karajan. Of course the recorded sound is better than on the Odyssey release, and the Berliners are just as much virtuosi as the Philly organization. The D.G. is placed second only because Ormandy presents a more spacious consideration of Prokofiev's great score, especially in his elegiac perspective on the slow movement.

Symphony No. 6 in E flat minor, Op. 111

☐ Boston Symphony Orchestra / Leinsdorf (conductor) / RCA LSC-2834

Music of mainly dark images. Only in the finale does the horizon brighten, but there, by canny infiltration, the mood (vigorous and bouncy in E flat major at the start) shadows into gloom. No matter the strength of sonority, the music ends restless, and it is this troubled state that marks the total concept.

The symphony needs a conductor who understands the austerity and intensity within it. Leinsdorf is at his best here—and when he's good, he is most eloquent. Prokofiev's score is performed with super intelligence and outstanding artistry.

Symphony No. 7 in C sharp minor, Op. 131

☐ Paris Conservatoire Orchestra / Martinon (conductor) / London STS-15196

Martinon competes with himself (as noted later) and with Rozhdestvensky in performances of Prokofiev's last symphony. The Soviet essays, both conducted by Rozhdestvensky (on Everest 3214 and Melodiya/Angel S-40061), don't have the sparkle and expressive warmth that Martinon provides. Further, Rozhdestvensky apparently feels that a minor tonality demands a seriousness beyond that contained in the score. This factor even pulls back the effect of the Allegretto, a waltz that both smiles and frowns.

In his integral set of the Prokofiev symphonies (the first four on Vox SVBX-5123, the last three on SVBX–5124) Martinon conducts the Orchestre National de l'O.R.T.F., Paris. In this earlier single release (originally on the RCA Victor label LM–2288) the orchestra is, as indicated above, also Parisian. There isn't too much difference between the two performances, but there are better sound qualities in the London disc than Vox supplies. Further, if there is still any question as to choice, then it should be realized that the companion fifth and sixth symphonies in the Vox box are available elsewhere in better performances (*see above*).

The Volga Meets the Don, Op. 130

☐ Moscow Philharmonic Orchestra / Samosud (conductor) / Monitor 2007 (monaural)

A festive symphonic poem (Slonimsky titles it "The Meeting of the Volga with the Don River") in which Prokofiev aimed for the "melodic and expressive . . . joy of creation" to celebrate the opening of the Volga-Don Canal.

Prokofiev's epic attempt remains rather silent in his catalogue. This is its only recorded documentation. It holds interest only because it is by Prokofiev.

Band

March for Band, Op. 99

☐ Eastman Wind Ensemble / Austin (trumpet) / Fennell (conductor) / Mercury SRI–75099

Yes, Prokofiev wrote some band marches. This is the best one. The key is B flat; the music covers two principal ideas that you'll find will be whistled as you walk and work.

Solo Instrument and Orchestra

Cello

Concerto in E minor for Cello and Orchestra, Op. 58

☐ National Opera Orchestra of Monte Carlo / Walevska (cello) / Inbal (conductor) / Philips 6500518

Prokofiev with sufficient tonal and rhythmic identity, but Prokofiev with only a little thematic personality. In the chain of command of his concerti this one can be placed in the middle class and called "respectable." There are three movements, with a reminiscence of the first two set in the third. Portions of the material were used in the Sinfonia Concertante for Cello and Orchestra, Op. 125 (*see below*), which is the second cello concerto.

With its flat surfaces, a sense of note-heaviness permeates the work which cannot be avoided in performance. Walevska does her disciplined best, which is as good as can be achieved for the opus. In that regard Prokofiev buffs will not be disappointed.

Sinfonia Concertante for Cello and Orchestra, Op. 125

☐ Royal Philharmonic Orchestra / Rostropovich (cello) / Sargent (conductor) / Seraphim S-60171

A good amount of material in this work was transferred from the Concerto in E minor for Cello and Orchestra, Op. 58 (*see above*). A virtuoso piece throughout, the Sinfonia Concertante is played in Rostropovich's usual exuberant, fervored (but non-hoked-up) style. Some of the tempi are close to the danger point, but Rostropovich can cliff-hang with the best of them.

This disc has also been transferred. It was originally released by Capitol on G-7121. Age has not harmed anything.

Concerto No. 1 in D flat major for Piano and Orchestra, Op. 10

☐ London Symphony Orchestra / Ashkenazy (piano) / Previn (conductor) / London CSA–2314

Bold and dazzling playing. The varicolored rhapsodicism of the music twined with wit is depicted in the most appropriate manner.

Concerto No. 2 in G minor for Piano and Orchestra, Op. 16

☐ Boston Symphony Orchestra / Henriot-Schweitzer (piano) / Munch (conductor) / RCA VICS–1071

Name it and it's here, all the agitated detail and the dramatic outbursts. Further, here is the barbarism that marks the Scherzo, the fantastic colorations that are basic to its material, the total grand manner of it all. This performance leaves all others behind.

Concerto No. 3 in C major for Piano and Orchestra, Op. 26

☐ Leipzig Gewandhaus Orchestra / Béroff (piano) / Masur (conductor) / Angel S–37084

Plenty of performances of this work reflect no special identity. This performance is in the area of the remarkable. Béroff doesn't dissent from the percussive impact in the score, but neither does he bypass a keyboard tone that makes the ictus delineation sound as if produced with golden-sponge beaters. The Concerto takes on an identity no other pianist has ever given it. This is what might be termed a high-court decision on Prokofiev. Pianists could do themselves a very good turn by imitating Michel Béroff. A prized recording essay.

Concerto No. 4 in B flat major for Piano (Left Hand) and Orchestra, Op. 53

☐ Philadelphia Orchestra / Rudolf Serkin (piano) / Ormandy (conductor) / Columbia MS–6405

The one-armed pianist Paul Wittgenstein commissioned this work but never played it. (It was Prokofiev's intention to revise the Concerto for two hands, but this was never accomplished.)

Wittgenstein said that he couldn't understand a single note of the music. Well, Serkin does and plays it with power and assured virtuosity.

Concerto No. 5 in G major for Piano and Orchestra, Op. 55

☐ Leipzig Gewandhaus Orchestra / Béroff (piano) / Masur (conductor) / Angel S–37084

Titanic playing. Five movements that claw and jab and drop acid on the sounds. Béroff is master of this work; he crushes its bristling difficulties, wasting no time in so doing in the speedy movements, by the way.

Concerto for Violin and Orchestra

No. 1 in D major, Op. 19 / No. 2 in G minor, Op. 63

☐ Philadelphia Orchestra / Stern (violin) / Ormandy (conductor) / Columbia MS–6635

Stern's consideration of the Opus 19 reflects no cold and selfish idea of technical showcasing at all costs. The Concerto is heard as a huge *cantilena* in its end movements; the lyricism (and there's plenty of it) is emphasized, and as a result the difficulties seem to evaporate and the music is alive and affecting. With such an approach the mordancies of the inner movement are lessened, and the grotesquerie turns into enjoyable whimsicality.

In the G minor opus Stern opts for the full health of romantic style, but minus any lushness. Stress is again on the lyrical aspects, but where soloism stands in frank and enlightened state it is allowed its full head. Splendid music-making in all respects and with Ormandy again proving his specialness as an accompanist.

Instrumental

Adagio from *Cinderella* (Ballet), Op. 97 bis

Cello

☐ Rostropovich (cello); Dedyukhin (piano) / Monitor S-2119E (monaural)

Prokofiev's own translation. Rostropovich's spun tone is masterly.

Harp

Piece for Harp

Prelude in C, Op. 12, No. 7

☐ McDonald (harp) / Klavier KS-507

The Prelude is at the top of the popularity chart with harpists and has remained there, deservedly, for some time. It was originally for piano (*see below*, under *piano* [*Tales of an Old Grandmother*, Op. 31]), but Prokofiev indicated it as playable on the harp as well. (Significantly, the Prelude was dedicated to Eleonora Damskaya, a young harpist.)

Bibliographic listings for Prokofiev do not indicate the Piece for Harp. It can be categorized as ''no hits, no runs, no errors.'' But Susann McDonald's playing is errorless. She articulates perfectly and has exceptional dynamic control.

Piano

Four Etudes, Op. 2

Four Pieces

Op. 3 / Op. 4 / Op. 32

☐ Sándor (piano) / Vox SVBX-5408

Early opus numbers notwithstanding, the full Prokofiev profile is in evidence. This can be recognized immediately in the fourth of the Four Etudes, all in minor keys, which Vox lists just as Etudes, the sharply cut *Marche* and the slippery *Fantôme* in Opus 3 and, of course, in the famous *Suggestion diabolique* which completes the Opus 4 group. Opus 32 is balletic throughout, with a Dance, Minuet, Gavotte, and Waltz, the next to last a conception that could fit in perfectly with the *Classical* Symphony, completed a year earlier.

Sándor is fully attuned to this music. No critical reservations are to be made whatsoever, since there is no interpretative wheeling and dealing to disturb the neat balances of any of the sixteen pieces.

The Love for Three Oranges: March and Scherzo, Op. 33 ter

☐ Prokofiev (piano) / Klavier 125

The first of the pair has the same position among Prokofiev's works that the Prelude in C sharp minor has among Rachmaninoff's. The March was transcribed from the opera score with the Scherzo by Prokofiev himself. The recording was remastered from a Steinway Duo-Art piano roll. Having the opportunity of hearing the composer play his own music, one can overlook the record's rather dry sound.

Music for Children, Op. 65

Pensées, **Op. 62**

☐ Sándor (piano) / Vox SVBX–5409

The *Pensées* ("Thoughts"), according to Eric Salzman (who supplies excellent literate notes for Vox's two-volume set of twelve record sides of Prokofiev's piano music), are "introspective, contemplative pieces of quality." Israel V. Nestyev in his biography of Prokofiev destroys them by stating that "the harmonic development is artificially restrained, the melodic design fragmented, and the rhythms amorphous and weak." My vote goes with Mr. Salzman. Certainly, the way Sándor plays the three movements, there is no fragmentation and the introspective mood is meaningful and well established.

Prokofiev thought sufficiently of his Opus 65 to set seven of the dozen pieces for small orchestra under the title *Summer Day,* Opus 65 bis. Music for Children is subtitled *Twelve Easy Pieces for Piano.* True. It is just as true that the set is easy to listen to but requires as much pianistic finish as music of a more intellectual concept. Sándor does not overlook a single detail and performs the suite with artless spontaneity.

Piano Sonata

No. 1 in F minor, Op. 1 / No. 2 in D minor, Op. 14 / No. 3 in A minor, Op. 28 / No. 4 (*From Old Notebooks*) in C minor, Op. 29 / No. 5 in C major, Op. 38/135

☐ Sándor (piano) / Vox SVBX–5408

Sándor's knowledge of this music is superb (he edited and had published the complete sonatas Prokofiev produced), and he transfers his cogent research, study, and information into live playing that is most appropriate and convincing. Editorial knowledge provides prosperous accounts indeed. The dramatic commando approach is acutely fitting for the second sonata, as is the romantic fervor Sándor gives the initial sonata, etc.

One negative point is the lack of dynamic scale in the engineering. But do overlook it and obtain examples of stunning piano playing.

For the later Piano Sonatas, *see below* (Piano Sonata No. 6 in A major, Op. 82, etc.).

Piano Sonata

No. 6 in A major, Op. 82 / No. 7 in B flat major, Op. 83 / No. 8 in B flat major, Op. 84 / No. 9 in C major, Op. 103

☐ Sándor (piano) / Vox SVBX–5409

The readings have command, and full-scale color is applied as required. Sándor is wealthy in pianistic assets. One can rely on these performances.

For additional remarks on Sándor and the Piano Sonatas, *see above* (Piano Sonata No. 1 in F minor, Op. 1, etc.).

Piano Sonata No. 7 in B flat major, Op. 83

☐ Pollini (piano) / Deutsche Grammophon 2530225

Magnificent playing. The peripatetic drive in the music is in no way lessened, and particularly the way the finale is played exemplifies heroic virtuosity. Powerfully orchestrated by this superb pianist.

Piano Sonata No. 8 in B flat major, Op. 84

☐ Ashkenazy (piano) / London 6573

Romanticism sandwiched into Prokofiev-flavored bread. It comes out a tasty recipe as Ashkenazy prepares it.

Piano Sonata No. 9 in C major, Op. 103

☐ Kalichstein (piano) / Vanguard S-10048

The classical openness of this sonata is excellently caught in Kalichstein's performance. He refuses to overmechanize the *scherzo* portion (the second movement, marked *Allegro strepitoso*), a temptation that brings a wrong-headed reaction from many pianists. By warmth of tone, devoted phrasing, and a fine support of line, this presentation brings out all the inner power of Prokofiev's final piano sonata.

Romeo and Juliet, Op. 64

☐ Nicolaisen (piano) / Klavier 538

A combination of the ten pieces Prokofiev transcribed for the piano from his great ballet, played in the sequence he made, plus arrangements of other sections by the soloist, Laura Nast Nicolaisen. The music is divided into nineteen sections; there are twenty-three scenes included.

Satisfactory objective and satisfactorily played. Principally for those that want everything that pertains to Prokofiev.

Sarcasms, Op. 17

☐ Sándor (piano) / Vox SVBX-5408

A realization that certifies the ironic view and percussiveness of this cycle of five pieces. Sándor is also fully aware of the sinisterness that is part of Prokofiev's commentary and projects that quality significantly.

Only one dissent in Sándor's interpretation—in No. 3, *Allegro precipitato,* the tempo is faster than the finale marked *Precipitosissimo.* But that should not deter every admirer of Prokofiev's music from welcoming this recording.

Tales of an Old Grandmother, Op. 31
Ten Episodes, Op. 12

☐ Sándor (piano) / Vox SVBX-5408

Among the light and often witty set of *Episodes* the seventh, a Prelude, is a solid repertoire item among harpists. The delightfully liquid music, playable either on the piano or the harp (it was dedicated to a harpist) has been recorded for harp (*see above,* under *harp* [Piece for Harp]). Sándor plays it considerably faster, including the contrastive central portion, than any harpist the writer has heard, but it is no less propitious in that manner. Another important part of the suite is the ninth piece, a "Humorous Scherzo." The liner note covering this music is incorrect. The facts are that Prokofiev actually transcribed his keyboard piece for four bassoons, shortened the title to Scherzo, and numbered it Opus 12 bis. The transcription was inspired by the epigraph from Griboyedov's *Woe from Wit:* "that croaker, that strangler, the bassoon."

The playing of both the *Episodes* and the four *Tales* is sensitive and matches the contents. Examples: it is crisp in the March and pointed in the *Scherzo humoristique* (Nos. 1 and 9 in the *Episodes*), relaxed and thus expressively outlining in the *Tales.*

Things in Themselves, Op. 45
Three Pieces, Op. 59

☐ Sándor (piano) / Vox SVBX-5409

The Opus 45 twosome (*Choses en soi;* oddly marked by Vox as Opus 45a and Opus 45b) are somewhat abstruse. Sándor's fine musicianship brings out all there is to exhibit, which isn't very much.

Though Prokofiev wrote a pair of Sonatinas as one opus (*see below* [Two Sonatinas, Op. 54]), another one, extremely short, termed Sonatina Pastorale, occupies the third place in the Opus 59 set. It is a one-movement affair lasting four and a half minutes; the Opus 54 Sonatinas are each in three movements and ten minutes in length. Sándor is rather nonchalant in his playing of this rarely heard suite, but that's because Prokofiev was nonchalant also, in the music itself.

Three Pieces, Op. 96

☐ Drake (piano) / Orion 75168

Piano transcriptions all. The Waltz is from the opera *War and Peace;* the *Contredanse* and *Mephisto Waltz* are from the film music for *Lermontov.* The pieces are not bald translations; Prokofiev included engaging pianistic figurations into his second drafts.

Paulina Drake is faultless in her playing, with bright tone and honed rhythms.

Toccata, Op. 11

☐ Berman (piano) / Monitor MCS-2135 (monaural)
☐ Sándor (piano) / Vox SVBX-5408

Sándor plays this famous frenetic perpetual-motion piece excitingly and with tremendous power. The music gushes forth and makes its biting energetic points minus any keyboard pounding.

Monitor doesn't provide the greatest recorded sound for Prokofiev's pianistic explosion. However, who cares about that given the way Lazar Berman detonates the notes while still managing to bring out inner details as he travels in the soprano and bass zones at top speed and makes the single instrument sound like a hundred-piece orchestra! That's what virtuosity is all about.

Two Sonatinas, Op. 54

☐ Sándor (piano) / Vox SVBX-5409

The first is in E minor, the second in G major. (On the Vox disc [one of three devoted to Prokofiev's piano music] they are separated and are not performed in succession.) Sándor is in complete command in his projection of these well-constructed, somewhat abstract works (abstract, though, only in terms of Prokofiev's recognizable style).

For a third sonatina, *see above* (*Things in Themselves,* Op. 45).

Visions fugitives, Op. 22

☐ Sándor (piano) / Vox SVBX-5408

Sándor performs all twenty of Prokofiev's miniatures that range from the delicately poetic to the firmly snide. They are played with technical polish, but with a somewhat restricted dynamic spectrum. If you can accept fewer of the pieces but presented with a more vivid theatrical sense, *see below.*

Visions fugitives, Op. 22 (Excerpts)

☐ Gilels (piano) / Columbia/Melodiya M–33824

Gilels plays Nos. 1, 3, 5, 7, 8, 10, 11, and 17. This is fewer than the dozen choices Rubinstein includes in his Carnegie Hall program highlights on RCA LSC–2605, and more than the five Richter presents on RCA AGL1–1279. However, for an excerpted set these eight are most representative and telling and are tops in performance character. The playing is outgoing, passionate where this is required, always acutely colored from the dark to the bright.

The complete Opus 22 is available in a performance by György Sándor (*see above*). Comparing it on a one-on-one basis with the eight pieces Emil Gilels plays, this outstanding Soviet pianist deserves first place.

Violin

Five Melodies for Violin and Piano, Op. 35 bis

☐ Steiner (violin); Berfield (piano) / Orion 75195

Originally conceived as Five Songs Without Words for Voice and Piano. The refined lyricism made them apt for transfer to the violin-and-piano medium, in which Prokofiev was aided by the violinist Paul Kochanski.

The performers are first class, the playing is of spontaneous order.

Sonata for Violin Solo, Op. 115

☐ Ricci (violin) / London STS–15153

Solo-violin orchestration is in full power here as Ricci delivers the three movements of this prime example in the unaccompanied violin medium. All the pert characteristics of the music are brought forth with smoothness and snap, the lyrical sections are dealt out with no slack. The fellow can fiddle.

Chamber Music

Sonata for Cello and Piano, Op. 119

☐ Isaac (cello); Jones (piano) / Argo ZRG–727

Two specifics spell special success for this edition. First, Isaac and Jones stress the lyrical and romantic climate of the three-movement work. Second, in tempo the middle movement *is* a Moderato, and this pair's playing it as one brings out all the wit the music contains, in contrast to the frequent practice of whipping up its speed in order to make and stress a *scherzo* statement. These two musicians form a first-class chamber-music team.

Sonata for Two Violins, Op. 56

☐ David and Igor Oistrakh (violins) / Monitor S–2058

The sphere of two unaccompanied violins clearly contains a veritable index to Prokofiev's style. The harmonic material with its transient shifts between major and minor modes shows his tonal *diablerie*. Vertical, prancing rhythm and horizontal line rhythm are associated (movement 2) and neatly determined by the Oistrakhs. The slow movement outlines a three-part design by theme and tonality change (for all of his seeming rowdiness Prokofiev is a classicist in short pants). Rondo drive completes the duo.

A superb indication of the mastery of the Oistrakhs is the equality of tone and bowing in the finale. Then, in its brilliant coda which stays put at a *piano* level and only suddenly moves into the opposite dynamic, the instrumentalists hand off the figure they carry, one to the other, like backfield action in a football game. This pair give a superb example of performance conquest.

Sonata in D major for Flute and Piano, Op. 94

☐ Galway (flute); Argerich (piano) / RCA LRL1-5095
☐ Louise DiTullio (flute); Virginia DiTullio (piano) / Crystal 311

The light, unaffected quality of this sonata begins with a fresh D major theme which already shifts its stance before the second measure has been reached. In the first movement Prokofiev's pungent harmony illuminates the tonal horizon, equaling the effect of a brilliant sun shining on smooth ice. The Mozartian air which James Galway adopts is truly enchanting. It is an important role that the piano performs in this movement. In most cases the solo voice of this instrument denotes the episodes which link the themes. Here Martha Argerich is much more sensitive (and as positive as required) than Virginia DiTullio.

The Scherzo is a little less ironic than usual with Prokofiev. Galway's spontaneity and coloristic delivery in this part of the work are truly sensational—a drama of plastic subtlety results. Louise DiTullio (as in the first movement) comes close to matching Galway but is less precise in codifying the dynamic differences. Both depict the slow movement with nice phrasing and tone control. The last movement consists of hardy music—as in most Prokofiev finales there is no feathery mattress of sound. The polished wizardry of Galway again gives him the rating edge. All this without the minutest detail being overlooked.

Prokofiev transcribed the work for violin. For a discussion of the second version, *see below* (Sonata in D major for Violin and Piano, Op. 94 bis).

Sonata in D major for Violin and Piano, Op. 94 bis

☐ Perlman (violin); Ashkenazy (piano) / RCA LSC-3118

This work was originally for flute and piano, *see above* (Sonata in D major for Flute and Piano, Op. 94). Prokofiev made his violin version one year after the flute and piano setting. No major changes were involved. The violin part was filled out with some chunky chords, and the string sonority was strengthened in certain places by the addition of open-string tones which sound simultaneously with material played on an adjacent string.

There is no doubt about the success of this performance. These are two great soloists who prove they also possess the special ability to provide the most telling chamber-music communication.

Sonata No. 1 in F minor for Violin and Piano, Op. 80

☐ Oistrakh (violin); Richter (piano) / Melodiya/Angel S-40268

Pulse plans are very important in this work. In movement 1 the metrical flux between triple and quadruple totals is constant. In the final movement there are rhythmic shifts in practically every measure, including quintal, septuple, and octuple forms. But proper brewing is done in the rhythmic cups; each measure is occupied by the necessary stresses in order to catch its particular dance taste. Most of the five-beat measures are combinations of two plus three, and therefore outline an unequal proportion between the bar lines; whereas the $\frac{7}{8}$ measures are more disposed to symmetry, since these are formed in the most part from two plus three plus two.

Color is also special to Prokofiev's Sonata. Thus the recitative-like use of pizzicato in movement 1, and the muted violin timbre heard in the Andante. In the finale the violin is assigned the snarling and hissing of ponticello as well as assorted types of plucked sound.

The Sonata was dedicated to David Oistrakh, and he joins with Sviatoslav Richter in a truly memorable performance. Some times there is sonic roughage, but it is a concomitant of the musical objective where it takes place. In all, the playing is a fastidious and controlled translation of the score, defining both its details and its coherence.

String Quartet

No. 1, Op. 50 / No. 2, Op. 92

☐ Novák Quartet / Philips 6500103

Classical consanguinity is found in the first quartet, with Prokofievian personality—the brittle, propulsive sections are there to prove it. Although the last movements of compounded works tend to be fast-tempoed, the order in this case reverses the usual plan; the first quartet concludes with a very poetic slow movement. Preceding it is an inquisitive scherzo-styled conception with a slow-paced introduction. The Novák team play this work with spirit, though more whimsicality would be welcome in parts of the initial movement. The slow movement is projected with an admirable sense of flow.

Prokofiev's second quartet is based on Kabardinian and Balkar folk music. A goodly part of the piece consists of rough, meaty, percussively punched music, a far cry from the initial quartet's style. The Novák group give it the necessary impact without harshness, whereas the older London release (STS–15152), with the Carmirelli Quartet, has a stridency that tears at the cohesion of the four voices. In the lyrical slow movement, the suave nocturnal setting conveyed by the Novákians is ideal.

Quintet for Oboe, Clarinet, Violin, Viola, and Double Bass, Op. 39

☐ Melos Ensemble / Oiseau-Lyre S–267

When Prokofiev lived in Paris, the music he produced there was of tight texture and had bright, shining surfaces. It was during this period that he wrote a ballet called *Trapeze*. Disliking the libretto, Prokofiev retained the music without change and gave it the formal title noted above. However, there is nothing of the circus about his Quintet. In no way should it be considered as musical pictorialism, but rather a work specifically of nonobjective abstraction. Later Prokofiev added several movements to the composition, but it exists officially in its first state of six movements—a modern divertimento of astringent sound.

It is expertly presented by the Melos Ensemble, with the proper amount of virtuosic personality. The playing is clean in all respects but does not minimize the fact that plenty of gritty sand rubs against the strands of Prokofiev's music.

Vocal

Voice and Orchestra

The Ugly Duckling, Op. 18

☐ Stadium Symphony Orchestra of New York / Resnik (soprano) / Stokowski (conductor) / Everest 3108

Prokofiev's Opus 18 is a vocal *scena* based on the Hans Christian Andersen fairy tale, somewhat abridged. Principally, it is a warmly lyrical work though it has a fair amount of vocal dramaticism in its lines. The accompaniment is somewhat descriptive and thereby unfolds a mystery. The work was composed for voice and piano in 1914 and published in that form in 1917. There is no listing anywhere or mention whatsoever of a voice with orchestra setting. Who made the orchestration?

Regina Resnik does quite well with her interpretation (no text is offered by Everest); the orchestra does its part acceptably.

But, if you want this edition, be on guard for some messy razzle-dazzle on the part of Everest. *The Ugly Duckling* is labeled as having three parts, and titles are given for each. Actually, the work is continuous. But, there are four bands on the record side involved (the reverse side concerns a Stokowski six-part edition of music from Prokofiev's *Cinderella* ballet), but only the first band deals with the Prokofiev musical tale. No identification is given for bands 2, 3, and 4 on record label, liner note, or album cover. What pops up off the grooves? Three movements of the orchestral version of Debussy's *Children's Corner* Suite!

Alexander Nevsky, Op. 78

☐ Philadelphia Orchestra and Mendelssohn Club of Philadelphia / Allen (mezzo-soprano) / Ormandy (conductor) / RCA ARL1-1151

One of the most successful, if not *the* most successful, transfers of a film score to concert status. The seven movements, including the remarkable percussively stained, frigidly timbred *Battle on Ice,* have always been an Ormandy tour de force. The power and range are here on disc. And there is a richness of sound that is singular. Betty Allen does well with the single solo section. You can't beat these Philadelphians with Ormandy in top form, partnered with a splendid chorus that is one of the best in the country.

Ivan the Terrible, Op. 116

☐ U.S.S.R. Symphony Orchestra and Moscow State Chorus / Levko (mezzo-soprano); Mokrenko (baritone); Estrin (narrator) / Stasevich (conductor) / Melodiya/Angel S-4103

Unlike *Alexander Nevsky,* which Prokofiev made into a cantata from the film music he had written, *Ivan the Terrible,* the seventh and last motion-picture score Prokofiev produced, was never redesigned into a concert suite. What one has here is Stasevich's decision in regard to Prokofiev's music. He was fully familiar with the work, having conducted the Prokofiev score for the film. And he respects it. Nothing has been added or much changed; we hear simply a selection of the material, the repetition of certain sections, and the varying of their order. It is true that some slight textural matters in the orchestration are the product of Stasevich's editing. Further, at least two portions of the total twenty movements were eventually not used in the film.

Realizing the disjunctive condition of the score *as* a concert piece, Stasevich has introduced a narrator, paraphrasing lines used in the film. These describe specific events or consist of short monologues, mostly between sections—a few are combined with the music. (The lines are in Russian, of course, in this Soviet-produced recording.) No matter this forced type of integration. Stasevich's action deserves the sympathetic consideration of critic and listener. He has saved the score from film-archive oblivion and made certain to stave off the usual compulsive decisions arrived at by editors of posthumous procreations.

The singing is fresh and pure, especially the portions for the solo female voice (the score originally called for a contralto, but Levko's voice has sufficient darkness for the part). The single section for the solo baritone is a rousing three-verse song, backed up with choral glissandi and motoric ostinati. It is delivered with bravado. An impressive recording, which brings credit to Stasevich.

Seven, They Are Seven, Op. 30

☐ Moscow Radio Symphony Orchestra and Moscow Radio Chorus / Yelnikov (tenor) / Rozhdestvensky (conductor) / Melodiya/Angel S-40157

A Prokofievian block-buster, set to a text by the symbolist Russian poet Constantin Balmont. Plenty of color and dash, such as the use of glissando for a whispering chorus, tutti wood tappings by the strings, packed percussion, fierce tutti sections, nervous rhythms, and a tensility that refuses to budge.

Doubtless this is the most extreme work that the composer produced. And the performers understand this. No pussyfooting. The music is attacked vigorously, and that makes for an interpretative victory. The ecstatic excitement is all it should be.

Opera and Dramatic Music

Peter and the Wolf, Op. 67

☐ London Symphony Orchestra / Farrow (narrator) / Previn (conductor) / Angel S–36962

☐ London Symphony Orchestra / Lillie (narrator) / Henderson (conductor) / London 6187

The differing versions and the editings and the variety of texts for this evergreen are staggering. There are male and female narrators and even a version in Spanish for the American market (discussed at the end of these comments).

Of course, it's the immediate box-office appeal the record producers are concerned about, so the name of the narrator is the thing. Accordingly, who is "hot"? So Vanguard picks Will Geer of the hit TV show *The Waltons,* and RCA chooses David Bowie the bright new movie star. But Geer's approach is Dullsville itself; there's no punch and no character, though the orchestra conducted by Somary is fine (Vanguard 71189). And placidity also defeats Bowie, with Ormandy and the Philadelphia Orchestra (RCA ARL1–2743).

Some of the narrators are fine but not accompanied by strong or even acceptable orchestral playing. One example: Basil Rathbone is excellent on Columbia's oldie (CL–671, a monaural disc), but Stokowski plays the music as though it were Tchaikovsky's—a real *Weltschmerz* that is shocking.

Text changes are numerous. These include some that aren't too bad. That would cover Bernstein's own narration in which he has turned the introduction into a kind of quiz (available in a number of packages, embracing Columbia MS–6193, MS–7528, M–31806, and D3S–785); Michael Flanders with Kurtz conducting (on Seraphim S–60172); and Hermione Gingold partnered with Böhm (on Deutsche Grammophon 2530588). But some are downright bad. Sean Connery narrates a modern setting including colloquialisms and takes a part in the proceedings not included in Prokofiev's score (London 21007, with Dorati on the podium); Alec McCowen, who sounds as though he were fighting a cold, adopts a Downing Street tone to begin with, and the text he uses also constantly deviates from the original; in addition he provides bird imitations and the duck quacking in the wolf's tummy at the end—ugh!

The two recordings listed are certainly contrastive and represent the choicest of the whole lot—nineteen at last count, a number of which have been discussed above. The Angel edition has superfine clarity, with Mia Farrow joining with her now ex-husband André Previn. It's a total joy, unmannered and thoroughly musical. However, don't overlook the bouncily delicious Bea Lillie version. Less musical perhaps, but damnably entertaining in the right way.

Monitor's Spanish setting has poor orchestral playing (State Orchestra of the U.S.S.R., conducted by Rozhdestvensky), but the narration is utterly musical and beautiful to hear in its translated form. It is delivered by Carlos Montalban, who can narrate *Pedro y el lobo* for me any time, and I wish he would record it in English. This monaural disc is Monitor's 2041.

Ballet

Romeo and Juliet, Op. 64

☐ Cleveland Orchestra / Maazel (conductor) / London 2312

Plenty of recorded attention has been paid to the orchestral suites Prokofiev drew from his ballet, but it wasn't until 1974 that two recorded editions (of which London's is one) of the complete ballet appeared domestically. (The other is with Previn conducting the London Symphony Orchestra on Angel S–3802.)

Maazel's conception is colorfully sharp, a fully expressive realization that one cannot fault in any respect whether the detail is relaxed or busy, soft or loud, simple or complex. It is a masterful reading of the complete score, which includes a larger brass section than any of the three orchestral suites (six horns rather than four and four trumpets rather than three) and two harps (only one is used in the suites), plus a bit of mandolin and organ and a stage-band group that are absent from any of the excerpts Prokofiev made for concert use. (The stage band is, of course, contrasted to the orchestra in the pit in ballet performances. In the recording the stage band loses its identity. No harm results whatsoever.)

The Stone Flower, Op. 118

☐ Bolshoi Theatre Orchestra / Rozhdestvensky (conductor) / Columbia/Melodiya M3-33215

Some criticism to the contrary—principally due to the Bolshoi's American performances, where the production was considered second rate—this is a score that should not be dismissed. It may rank below Prokofiev's *Romeo and Juliet* and *Cinderella,* but it has a considerable amount of redesigned folkloric material that is vivid and fresh.

The conception directed by Gennady Rozhdestvensky is brilliant and totally declarative. Those excerpts available on Melodiya/Angel (S-40066) also conducted by Rozhdestvensky are good enough samplings. Those contained on London STS-15286, with Silvio Varviso conducting the Orchestre de la Suisse Romande, are even better.

Prokofiev / **Rudolf Barshai (1924-)**

Visions fugitives (Fifteen Pieces for String Orchestra), Op. 22

String Orchestra

☐ Academy of St. Martin-in-the-Fields / Marriner (conductor) / Argo ZRG-711

In all there are twenty numbers in Prokofiev's *Visions fugitives.* This is a fine, colorful but fitting version of fifteen from the first sixteen of the set, with the seventh omitted. Not Marriner's decision—that's the way Barshai made his transcription.

A fine tradeoff in the transcriptive process, and a splendid account by the Academy group. Unfortunately, Argo does not provide bands between the separate numbers.

Arthur Pryor *(1870-1942)*

On Jersey Shore

Band

☐ Goldman Band / Cox (conductor) / New World Records NW-266

Pryor was one of America's great bandmasters and the great ones could also turn out splendid marches. *On Jersey Shore* is an excellent example of this collateral music making.

Fantastic Polka

Solo Instrument and Band

☐ Coe College Concert Band / McDunn (trombone) / Slattery (conductor) / Golden Crest S-4091

Trombone

Old time stuff, a reminder of afternoons in the park and sounds from the bandstand. Not much polka, but very much trombone titillation.

Instrumental

Trombone

The Blue Bells of Scotland   **Thoughts of Love**
Exposition Echoes

☐ Barron (trombone); Cooper (piano) / Nonesuch 71341

Memoranda of the days when Sousa, Vessella, Gilmore, Conway, and Pryor himself were the important figures in summer music-making via their band concerts. Each program had one or more solos and here is a sampling that will trigger every bit of nostalgia possible. It will also trigger amazement at Ronald Barron's fantastic playing, especially in the *Blue Bells* variations, one portion projected at a speed that rivals the best flutist in the business (*see also below*).

Two other forms are covered in the program. The *Exposition Echoes* is a polka, the *Thoughts of Love* a *Valse de concert*.

The Blue Bells of Scotland

☐ Swallow (trombone); Wingreen (piano) / Golden Crest 7015 (monaural)

Variations on the tune. Musically dated to a fare-thee-well but just great aural fun for its technical exploitation. Protesting very much, there's really no basic difference between such show-off stuff and a Sarasate *Zigeunerweisen* or a Horowitz fling at *The Stars and Stripes Forever*. Granting only that Sarasate and Sousa are better composers, there still remains the principal point: a performer going on a technical toot. So, enjoy John Swallow on the trombone—after all, that's not an easy instrument on which to go on a technical toot.

(For another recommended performance, *see above*.)

Domenico Vincenzo Maria Puccini   *(1771-1815)*

Solo Instrument and Orchestra

Piano

Concerto in B flat major for Piano and Orchestra

☐ Austrian Tonkünstler Orchestra, Vienna / List (piano) / Topolski (conductor) / Musical Heritage Society MHS–709

An interesting curiosity—the composer being the grandfather of the famous Puccini. Nothing to be ashamed about in this Mozartian imitation. There are three movements, with the single cadenza in the first movement written by a present-day composer, Heinz Karl Gruber.

Giacomo Puccini   *(1858-1924)*

Chamber Music

I Crisantemi (1889)

☐ Juilliard Quartet / Columbia M–32596

A rarity in the Puccini catalogue. "The Chrysanthemums" has the contours of a serious operatic interlude, and the playing of the Juilliard team matches that description.

Opera and Dramatic Music

Edgar

☐ Opera Orchestra of New York, New York City Opera Children's Chorus, and Schola Cantorum of New York / Scotto (soprano); Killebrew (mezzo-soprano); Bergonzi (tenor); Sardinero (baritone); Munkittrick (bass) / Queler (conductor) / Columbia M2-34584

Only the second act of *Edgar* was previously represented in the recorded music catalogue, on RCA LSC-7096. With Columbia's complete version (recorded live, but absolutely satisfactory, even with the applause at the end), that excerpt can now be forgotten.

The plot (man loves one woman but lusts for a second one) is theatrical-dramatic-mystical. The last concerns the hero who suddenly is resurrected at his funeral in the form of a monk. It triggers the expected tragedy, and a stabbing makes evil triumphant.

Renata Scotto as Fidelia sings with full flexibility and with affecting tenderness as well. The sheer force of the role of the female who only has sexual appetite working for her is appropriately set forth by Gwendolyn Killebrew. Carlo Bergonzi is responsive and offers a believable characterization. Importantly, fine conducting by Eve Queler who maintains clarity and zest and never permits any flabby relaxation to creep into the production. A noteworthy recording.

Gianni Schicchi (1918)

☐ Orchestra of the Maggio Musicale Fiorentino / Tebaldi and Carral (sopranos); Trucato Pace (mezzo-soprano); Danieli (alto); Lazzari, Ercolani, and Mercuriali (tenors); Corena, Maionica, Morresi, and Frosini (basses); di Ninno, Foiani, and Washington (vocalists) / Gardelli (conductor) / London 1153

Of the three one-act operas Puccini wrote, this is firmly established in the repertoire. (The other two: *Il Tabarro* and *Suor Angelica* are discussed *below*. All three are available in one package on London 1364.)

Delightful spoofery, with the slightest macabre touch, did not prevent Puccini from detailing his usual glowing lyricism. It flows through the deft score which one can only enjoy with its *vis comica*.

Fernando Corena relates fully to the title role and Renata Tebaldi and Agostino Lazzari provide the basic love interest with top-flight make-believe and top-drawer singing. Lamberto Gardelli utilizes a firm pace and firmly styles the proceedings.

The Girl of the Golden West (1910)

☐ Orchestra and Chorus of L'Accademia di Santa Cecilia, Rome / Tebaldi (soprano); Casoni (mezzo-soprano); del Monaco, di Palma, Guagni, Carlin, Mercuriali, and Cesarini (tenors); MacNeil, Giorgetti, Carbonari, Peruzzi, and Cazzato (baritones); Tozzi, Maionica, Morresi, and Caselli (basses) / Capuana (conductor) / London 1306

With its cast of Minnie, owner of a bar; Sheriff Jack Rance, a Wells Fargo agent; miners; a leader of a gang of outlaws; an Indian and his squaw, etc., "La fanciulla del West" is all-out American (based on a play by David Belasco). In its music, *The Girl of the Golden West* is all-out Italian. That makes for some "insy" humor in regard to hearing the situations in the former sung in the latter. Ah well, that's opera for you. In my opinion, if any opera should be heard in authentic English this is it.

Good cast and competent conducting, with Capuana in full (authentic) charge rather than prone to such matters as the overstresses Matačić (Seraphim S-6074) decides to edit into the score. Tebaldi (as Minnie) knocks it down with unfailing vocal behavior and Cornell MacNeil provides optimal satisfaction as the Sheriff. Though Mario del Monaco (as the gang leader) overacts, it is far from satire and so is acceptable. So is his big voice. From the others there is fine singing throughout.

This is the complete score. Some cuts are utilized in the competitive Seraphim edition.

Il Tabarro (1918)

☐ Orchestra and Chorus of the Maggio Musicale Fiorentino / Tebaldi and Carral (sopranos); Danieli (alto); del Monaco, Manganotti, Ercolani, and di Palma (tenors); Merrill (baritone); Maionica (bass) / Gardelli (conductor) / London 1151

Dark detail covers this melodrama and Puccini details it graphically in his vocal lines and orchestration. The latter is supplemented with off-stage car horns and tug whistles. A Debussy coloration is laced into the score's atmosphere.

Fine dramatic weight is applied in this release; the star characterization (and the best singing) applies to Robert Merrill the bargemaster whose wife (Renata Tebaldi) is unfaithful. It's the old triangle situation but with Puccini's masterful handling of the situation it works all over again and the London cast certifies it.

Together with Puccini's other one-acters *Gianni Schicchi* (*see above*) and *Suor Angelica* (*see below*), Il Tabarro forms a *Trittico* and is so packaged by London on their number 1364.

La Bohème (1896)

☐ Berlin Philharmonic Orchestra and Chorus of the Deutsche Oper, Berlin / Freni and Harwood (sopranos); Pavarotti, Sénéchal, and Pietsch (tenors); Panerai and Maffeo (baritones); Ghiaurov (bass) / von Karajan (conductor) / London 1299

No quibbling—this is a superlative production, minus any of the messy freedoms that mar many a presentation. Von Karajan demands, it is most apparent, musically exact interpretations as well as fully dramatic ones, from his cast. The result is score perfect, therefore, but not note anchored, gratefully.

Pavarotti is a gorgeous tenor, in top form histrionically and vocally, and makes his part of conclusive, believable behavior. The Mimi he loves is ideally characterized by Mirella Freni. She offers sensitive gradations in the dynamic qualities within her role and is beautifully radiant and totally convincing.

The Berlin Philharmonic is a magnificent instrument in this recording. Its ability to carry out a very soft background that has weight delights the ear. It is, of course, thanks to von Karajan, who seeks sounds from both orchestra and cast personal to the score rather than substantiating the free properties of tradition.

La Rondine (1917)

☐ RCA Italiana Opera Orchestra and Chorus / Moffo, Sciutti, Brigham-Dimiziani, and De Notaristefani (sopranos); Mattiucci (mezzo-soprano); Barioni and Iacopucci (tenors); Sereni and Basiola, Jr. (baritones); El Hage (bass); Alessandroni (whistler) / Molinari-Pradelli (conductor) / RCA LSC-7048

Winton Dean, the English critic, has aptly tabbed this opera. He states that it "tries to combine the plots of *La Traviata* with *Die Fledermaus* not only in temper and outline but in many details, to cross social drama with operetta." Well—real plot richness doesn't always come to a composer, as one realizes. Whatever, *La Rondine* has a good share of charming tunes which do ring true.

Good marks for the vocalists. Anna Moffo was in peak form when this was recorded and offers strong singing, Daniele Barioni makes his character most attractive. The remainder of the cast show authority and control (four take double roles, and one triples). Molinari-Pradelli keeps things in good shape, and in all this is a convincing performance.

Le Villi (1884)

☐ Vienna Volksoper Orchestra and Vienna Academy Chamber Chorus / Maliponte (soprano); Morell (tenor); Manuguerra (baritone); del Monaco (narrator) / Guadagno (conductor) / RCA LSC–7096

The major point here is the opportunity to get acquainted with Puccini's initial opera—the possibility of seeing a live production being very remote. *Le Villi* is not great Puccini by any means but there's sufficient to hold a good part of a listener's attention, especially a fine love duet, a *romanza,* and an effective intermezzo.

The performance is short of being impressive but it is accurate and stylish.

Madama Butterfly (1904)

☐ Rome Opera House Orchestra and Chorus / Scotto (soprano); di Stasio (mezzo-soprano); Bergonzi and di Palma (tenors); Panerai (baritone) / Barbirolli (conductor) / Angel S–3702

There are values, naturally, in all six of the current editions of this opera. But, no matter how percentage points are drawn and figured, the most masterful version is Barbirolli's. It is strongly underlined and subtly shaded. The cast is excellent but it is the conductorial cohesiveness brought by Barbirolli that wins the vote. The music is characterized in its most intense manner but not overdramatized, or over-driven, as in the case of von Karajan's conception (London 13110). With Barbirolli, the opera is beautifully sustained in all its elements and there are no interpretative idiosyncrasies that interfere with a controlled totality.

Both Carlo Bergonzi (as Pinkerton) and Rolando Panerai (as Sharpless) have never been in better voice. The former's depth of characterization and vocal warmth are splendid, the latter's is of similar high quality. Though Renata Scotto's timbre is thin, it fits the Butterfly role. In any event, her lesser vocal weight is overridden by a performance perspicuity that is of full dramatic penetration.

Manon Lescaut (1893)

☐ New Philharmonia Orchestra and Ambrosian Opera Chorus / Caballé (soprano); Wallis (mezzo-soprano); Domingo, Tear, Dickerson, and Partridge (tenors); Sardinero (baritone); Mangin, Van Allan, Howell, and Lloyd (basses) / Bartoletti (conductor) / Angel S–3782

This was the first of Puccini's operas to show him in full creative maturity. *Manon* is a full-blooded score and it is conducted in a sharply defined manner. The singing is impressive, with real character, plus warmth of timbre. Caballé makes a splendid Manon Lescaut. She is poetic and passionate, and phrases sensitively. Vicente Sardinero's conception of Lescaut is surely balanced, securely sung. Persuasive qualities in all the other parts of the opera.

This Angel issue competes with a much older version on London 1317. The latter is not bad at all, with Tebaldi, del Monaco, and Corena in the principal roles, but not as good as the Angel rendering. Angel's additional assets include a brighter and clearer recording quality, a deeper conception of the music's passions. That last element is fully identifiable in Angel's edition, less so in London's.

Suor Angelica (1918)

☐ Orchestra and Chorus of the Maggio Musicale Fiorentino / Tebaldi and Carral (sopranos); Simionato (mezzo-soprano); Danieli and Trucato Pace (altos); di Stasio, Valtriani, and Tavolaccini (vocalists) / Gardelli (conductor) / London 1152

One of the three one-acters that Puccini produced. (For discussions of the others, *Gianni Schicchi* and *Il Tabarro, see above;* all three are available in one album on London 1364.)

Suor Angelica calls for an all-female cast. Though it does not contain strong character delineations as found in Puccini's other operas, nonetheless the mystical climate of the tale is telling, even without having any pomp and circumstance. This is a more atmospheric and better-paced performance than the competitive Columbia (M–34505) version.

Tosca (1900)

☐ National Philharmonic Orchestra / Freni (soprano); Baratti (boy soprano); Pavarotti and Sénéchal (tenors); Milnes and Hudson (baritones); Van Allan and Tajo (basses) / Rescigno (conductor) / London OSAD–12113

Tosca is one of the great ones, musically profitable by its interlock—development of musical material is linked to the dramatic continuity and impact of the plot. This performance is a choice one. Mirella Freni is no Callas but she probes her role magnificently and this compensates for the lighter quality of her voice. Pavarotti is ideal and totally believable as Cavaradossi. Milnes doesn't strain as so many Scarpia's do on stage and so there is no deflating of his character by being jolted away from the theatrical into the hard facts of vocal life.

Excellent climate in the orchestra pit and plenty of incisiveness from Rescigno. He paces matters so that the action is natural.

Turandot

☐ Rome Opera House Orchestra and Chorus / Nilsson, Tebaldi, di Stasio, Pucci, and Funari (sopranos); Bjoerling, De Paolis, di Palma, and Frascati (tenors); Sereni and Zagonara (baritones); Tozzi and Monreale (basses) / Leinsdorf (conductor) / RCA LSC–6149

Puccini's *Turandot,* a three-act opera, was unfinished at the time of his death in 1924. It was completed by Franco Alfano, who added the last duet and the brief final scene. The premiere followed at La Scala, Milan, on April 25, 1926.

The role of Princess Turandot is certainly Puccini's most taxing soprano role. Birgit Nilsson gives an outstanding interpretation. Here, her voice is totally thrilling, and she dominates the proceedings. Jussi Bjoerling sings handsomely in his part of Calaf. His top notes are strong and sustained, with the fullest warmth in the center range; character definition is secure in his admirable performance. The others fulfill all the artistic requirements, particularly Tebaldi as the young slave girl, Liù, whose performance is very moving, and Tozzi as Timur, the dethroned Tartar King.

Leinsdorf's conducting is strongly expressionistic. He brings out all the orchestrational slants, underlining the colors and applying them to a marked variety of dynamics.

Gaetano Pugnani   (1731-1798)

Chamber Music

Sonata in E major

☐ Temianka (violin); Graudan (piano) / Orion 74136E (monaural)

Articulated rhythm and a bright crispness in Temianka's playing make one grateful to hear it. Pugnani's work is nicely structured, and none of the measures is padded with static figuration.

The sound of this disc, made in 1937 for Parlophone (their number E–11341), is noisy, but not to the point that it obliterates the fine music and excellent playing.

Sonata in F major for Recorder and Basso Continuo

☐ Linde (recorder); Muller (harpsichord) / Klavier 520

A performance of rich quality. Linde's tone is one of the fullest and most vigorous in the recorder field.

Sonata No. 3 in F major

☐ Rampal (flute); Alain (organ) / Musical Heritage Society MHS–1277

One suspects that this Sonata is a transcription of one of Pugnani's violin sonatas. The MHS program note only mentions generalities and gives no specific data; furthermore, flute sonatas are not included in lists of works by Pugnani. Notwithstanding, either way—transcription or original—it is a well-crafted piece and gives the listener a chance to experience the music of this Italian composer. The performers place it in the best of light.

Daniel Purcell   *(ca. 1660-1717)*

Prelude in F major

☐ Linde (recorder) / Klavier 545

Music in fantasia style. Pat phrases are avoided, providing a special quality.

Instrumental

Recorder

Sonata No. 2 for Recorder and Organ

☐ Linde (recorder); Rapf (organ) / Klavier 545

Music by the brother of the famous Purcell. Though the Sonata is not as cogently organized or as profound as the average Henry Purcell work, it deserves hearing, aside from the sake of curiosity.

There are five movements covering alternate, moderate and slow speeds. Linde and Rapf disclose a worthy consideration of the music.

Chamber Music

Henry Purcell   *(ca. 1659-1695)*

Overture to the *Cambridge Installation Ode*

☐ New Philharmonia Orchestra / Leppard (conductor) / Philips 802901

No reservations whatsoever concerning this rich example of Purcell's music, which includes a captivating fugue. Give Leppard thanks for uncovering this Overture and presenting it in a stunning performance.

Orchestra

Sinfonia in D major from *The Yorkshire Feast Song*

☐ Academy of St. Martin-in-the-Fields / Smithers and Laird (trumpets); Munrow (bassoon); Preston (harpsichord) / Marriner (conductor) / Philips 6500110

A very short majestic bit. The music introduced an "Ode on the assembly of the nobility and gentry of the city and county of York...."

Trumpet Overture in D major from *The Indian Queen*

☐ Academy of St. Martin-in-the-Fields / Smithers (trumpet); Preston (harpsichord) / Marriner (conductor) / Philips 6500110

A fine example of Purcell's writing style for the high trumpet, represented by the overture to the third act of his final theatrical work. Expertly detailed.

String Orchestra

Chaconne from *The Fairy Queen*

☐ English Chamber Orchestra / Hurwitz (conductor) / London STS–15013

Nicely paced, nicely phrased—a good excerpt to have, representing one of the highlights in Purcell's operatic work.

Chacony in G minor

☐ Academy of St. Martin-in-the-Fields / Marriner (conductor) / Angel S–36883
☐ English Chamber Orchestra / Britten (conductor) / London 6618

Both Marriner and Britten emphasize the dramatic element contained in Purcell's work. Their performances are vigorous, dynamic, and considerably speedier than the Stuyvesant's quartet version (see under *Chamber Music*, p. 1433). In Marriner's case, two and one-half minutes faster! In Britten's case, also faster but less so (one and one-half minutes).

The Neville Marriner rendition is magnificent, and by far more impressive than Britten's. However, two points concerning the latter's performance must be noted. First, the depiction of dotted rhythms is more forcibly detailed. Most important, the score has been edited by Britten in terms of the dynamic scheme and distribution of the parts. Thus, the Britten performance can be truly considered a *third* setting in contrast to the string quartet and string orchestra versions performed by the Stuyvesant group and by the St. Martin organization. All three deserve attention.

Suite

Music for *Abdelazer* or, *The Moor's Revenge*
Music for *The Married Beau*
Music for *The Virtuous Wife*

Suites Nos. 1 and 2: Music for *The Gordian Knot Untied*

☐ Chamber Orchestra of the Hartford Symphony / Mahler (conductor) / Vanguard S-155

These pieces—overtures, airs, jigs, hornpipes, minuets, and other types—provide musical beauties that never diminish. Rich, tender, rhythmic, and transpicuous in their variety, once again, the genius of Henry Purcell is revealed. They are sonically revealed in flawless production by a string group from the Hartford Symphony, conducted by the late Fritz Mahler. (It would be worthwhile having the settings with *ad libitum* wind and drum [meaning timpani] parts made by Gustav Holst.)

Solo Instrument and Orchestra

Concerto for Trumpet in D major

Trumpet

☐ Mainz Chamber Orchestra / Zickler (trumpet) / Kehr (conductor) / Turnabout 34295/9

A mid-twentieth century discovery and a good one. Fine detail with three movements in a concentrated setting (five minutes). The trumpet, played with finesse by Heinz Zickler, is *tacet* in the central slow movement. (The music has an alternate title: Sonata.)

Chaconne (The Curtain Tune for strings from *Timon of Athens*)

Ground

Ground (The alto solo "With him he Brings the Partner" from *Ye Tuneful Muses*)

Ground (*Crown the Altar* from *Celebrate the Festival*)

Hornpipe (The Hornpipe for strings from *The Old Batchelor*)

Jig (The Jig for strings from *Abdelazer*)

A New Irish Tune (*Lilliburlero*)

Round O (The Rondeau for strings from *Abdelazer*)

Sefauchi's Far(e)well

Suite

No. 1 in G major / No. 2 in G minor / No. 4 in A minor / No. 5 in C major / No. 6 in D major / No. 7 in D minor

☐ Marlowe (harpsichord) / Serenus 12055

Instrumental

Harpsichord

This is a splendid program embracing six of the eight harpsichord suites, two examples: *Lilliburlero* and *Sefauchi's Far(e)well* from *The Second Part of Musick's Handmaid,* and an assortment of short pieces, mostly Purcell's own transcriptions of movements from operas and other works. (In the absence of any information, one assumes that those not made by Purcell were made by Marlowe.)

Splendid playing matches this colorful program. Sylvia Marlowe has a directness in her approach to the music that is undeniably persuasive. Purcell's ideas are set forth in the clearest manner and there is no falsely styled intimacy that seems to surround the playing of some harpsichordists. One would like to name the best played pieces in the set of fifteen works but the sensibility and feeling that range throughout make it impossible. The impressive artistry is constant.

This Purcell program was originally a Decca issue. Serenus is to be thanked for reissuing a distinguished disc.

Chacony in G minor

☐ Stuyvesant String Quartet / Nonesuch 71114

Chamber Music

Purcell's Chaconne (*Chacony* being the old English word for the form) is designated *a 4.* However, its beauties and enravishing linear sonorities embracing impressive (and for the 17th century, predictable) chromatic enfranchisement, have led to a greater number of performances with multiple strings and the partial reinforcement of the cello line by double bass. Style-wise this is perfectly fitting since only textural weight is involved and not textual alteration.

Totality having some bearing apparently on its interpretative approach, the Stuyvesant ensemble play Purcell's masterwork almost tenderly, quite slowly, and stress the music's pathos. This is totally opposite to the recorded versions of the string orchestra setting (see under *String Orchestra* for discussion), but is absolutely acceptable. Both sides of the interpretative coin being valid, the suggestion is to possess both the quartet and full string recordings.

Anthem: *My Beloved Spake*

☐ Kalmar Orchestra of London / Cantelo (soprano); Deller (countertenor); English (tenor); Bevan (baritone); Bergmann (harpsichord) / Deller (conductor) / Vanguard HM–14

Choral

Chorus and Orchestra

A setting of the verses from the Song of Solomon. Fine performance. The orchestra may sound like some pick-up group, but actually it furnished the nucleus of the later-to-become-famous English Chamber Orchestra.

Anthem: *Rejoice in the Lord Always*

☐ Oriana Concert Orchestra / Thomas and Sheppard (sopranos); Deller (countertenor); Tear and Worthly (tenors); Bevan (baritone) / Deller (conductor) / Vanguard HM–14

Known as the Bell Anthem, from repeated descending scale lines by the strings in the introduction. An intelligent and effective presentation. The vocal soloists are superb, including the late Alfred Deller, certainly one of the finest countertenors that ever put voice on disc.

Come Ye Sons of Art

☐ Oriana Concert Orchestra and Choir / Thomas (soprano); Alfred and Mark Deller (countertenors); Bevan (baritone) / Alfred Deller (conductor) / Vanguard HM–14

The sixth and last ode Purcell wrote for Queen Mary. Inspired music that ranks with the best of Purcell's output. The performance (notice the two countertenors) is splendid.

Jubilate Deo in D major

☐ English Chamber Orchestra and Choir of St. John's College, Cambridge / Bowman and Brett (countertenors); Partridge (tenor); Robinson (bass); Cleobury (organ) / Guest (conductor) / Argo ZRG–724

Purcellian magnificence. Sympathy with the music produces a splendid response on the part of the vocalists and instrumentalists. No untoward flamboyance but fitting brilliance adds a special credit for this vivid performance.

Te Deum Laudamus

☐ English Chamber Orchestra and Choir of St. John's College, Cambridge / Bowman and Brett (countertenors); Partridge (tenor); Robinson (bass); Cleobury (organ) / Guest (conductor) / Argo ZRG–724

Ceremonial music that is not only grand in its declarativeness but also contrasted by intimately expressive sections. The Argo edition is an inspired production in all aspects with beautiful sound.

Opera and Dramatic Music

Dido and Aeneas

☐ Academy of St. Martin-in-the-Fields and John Alldis Choir / Veasey, Donath, Wallis, and Knight (sopranos); Bainbridge (mezzo-soprano); Patterson (tenor); Allen and Shirley-Quirk (baritones); Heath (cello); McGee (double bass); Constable (organ and harpsichord) / Davis (conductor) / Philips 6500131

It is the dramatic point of conception that gives privilege to the Philips edition, though Janet Baker's performance as Dido (on Oiseau-Lyre 60047) is hardly to be bettered. Still, without stage action the more dramatic the result the better the gain in terms of a recorded version.

Josephine Veasey does well, the tone just a bit lighter than one would expect for the Dido role, but her characterization and musicianship cannot be denied.

Dioclesian: **Masque and Instrumental Music**

☐ Orchestra and Choir of the Concentus Musicus, Vienna / Sheppard and Le Sage (sopranos); Deller (countertenor); Worthley and Todd (tenors); Bevan (baritone) / Deller (conductor) / Vanguard HM-13

Full expression to the moods and expressions in this work, making this an admirable edition. There are eighteen sections, four of which are tunes and dances for the instrumental group. Deller's direction produces a performance that can be highly recommended.

Funeral Music for Queen Mary

Canzona   *Remember not Lord Our Offences*
Funeral Sentences   *Thou Knowest Lord*
March

☐ Choir of St. John's College, Cambridge and Consort of Sackbuts from Symphoniae Sacrae / Brett (countertenor); Partridge (tenor); Robinson (bass); Creese, Keenlyside, King, Smith, and Williams (trebles); Cleobury (organ); Ryan (viol) / Guest (conductor) / Argo ZRG-724

Striking conceptions, especially the darkly pigmented *March* and the concluding *Thou Knowest Lord.*

The sequence on the disc (the titles are listed above in the usual alphabetical order that obtains in this compendium) is: 2-4-3-1-5. *Schwann,* incidentally, compresses the title to Funeral Music.

The Indian Queen

☐ English Chamber Orchestra and St. Anthony Singers / Cantelo (soprano); Tear and Partridge (tenors); Keyte (bass); Brown (vocalist); Leppard (harpsichord) / Mackerras (conductor) / Oiseau-Lyre S-294

It is in this practically forgotten work that Purcell's well-known *I Attempt from Love's Sickness to Fly* is found. But, there are other fine songs and some excellent duets. Clear-toned singing, vitality by the conductor which is matched in the playing, and an impressive contribution from Raymond Leppard. Not only for Purcell buffs.

Purcell / Carter

A Fantasy About Purcell's Fantasia Upon One Note

Chamber Music

☐ American Brass Quintet / Odyssey Y-34137

In his set of Fantasias Purcell's tour de force is the one "Upon One Note." It is built on the sustainment throughout, without surcease, of a single immovable sound (middle C) in the fourth of the five voices. Above and below, the counterpoint moves freely, and *not* in *spite* of the C pitch. The sustained sound fits in with the contrapuntal movement, binding it, being used as a dissonance, and creating its own place in the polyphonic scheme, though it has no contoured life whatsoever.

Carter's "Fantasy" on the "Fantasia" was written for these performers as a 1974 Christmas present. It is a splendid arrangement that fully respects the original and emphasizes the dramaticism of the piece by its brass dress.

Patrick Purswell   (1939-   )

Instrumental   **It Grew and Grew**

Flute   ☐ Purswell (flute) / Composers Recordings S–324

A very interesting unaccompanied flute piece that adds more to the catalogue of instrumental inventions the avant-garde composers have produced. In Purswell playing Purswell one will hear demarcated two-part writing, obtained by singing while playing and some utterly fascinating and biting Dracula-like throat growls.

Thomas Putsché   (1929-   )

Opera and   **The Cat and the Moon**
Dramatic
Music   ☐ Contemporary Chamber Players of the University of Chicago / Charleston (soprano); MacBone (tenor); Mack (baritone) / Shapey (conductor) / Composers Recordings S–245

A one-act opera, based on a Yeats play. Putsché introduces his work with this statement: ''The tradition is that centuries ago a blind man and a lame man dreamed that somewhere in Ireland a well could cure them and set out to find it, the lame man on the blind man's back.''

Mystical-philosophical turns are woven into the tale. In this recording, with no text offered, there is a vagueness as to plot progress. One must be satisfied with hearing a rich neo-romantic score, unabashedly presented by the cast.

Q

Johann Joachim Quantz   *(1697 - 1773)*

Sonata for Flute and Cembalo

Chamber Music

In A minor, Op. 1, No. 1 / In B flat major, Op. 1, No. 2

☐ Anne Diener Giles (flute); Allen Giles (harpsichord) / Crystal S–312

The first two of Quantz's *Sei Sonate a Flauto Traversière Solo e Cembalo.* Infectious music especially in the second and third fast-paced movements of each work. Played with charming sparkle that lights up the music.

Sonata in D major for Flute and Cembalo

☐ Rampal (flute); Gilbert (harpsichord) / Orion 7149

Once thought to be by Handel, the work has been authenticated as one by Quantz. This tells the stylistic tale of the four-movement piece which includes two slow movements, an *Allegro*, and a *Menuett* conclusion.

A duplicate of the Rampal-Gilbert performance is also available in a seven-record compendium issued by Everest (3194).

Sonata in G major for Flute and Cembalo, Op. 1, No. 6

☐ Rampal (flute); Veyron-Lacroix (harpsichord) / Everest 3180

Splendid stylistic reality by these two super musicians. The entire work is heard with the purest sensibility and a discriminating sense of style.

(Everest's liner note incorrectly changes the tonality of Quantz's work.)

Trio in A minor

☐ Camerata Musicale / Nonesuch 71085

Fully a trio sonata (for flute, oboe, and continuo) in the usual four-movement *sonata da chiesa* format. No mighty intellect at work in this music but agreeable material. Clean and free playing.

Trio Sonata in D major for Flute, Violin, and Continuo

☐ London Harpsichord Ensemble / Nonesuch 71004

Well-proportioned playing, graceful but not sugary in the two slow movements and with a neat *leggiero e ritmico* quality in the pair of *Allegros*. All of the points in Quantz's charming opus are made with stylistic order plus agogical emphasis where need be. Splendid.

Hector Quintanar

(1936-)

Orchestra

Sideral II (1969)

☐ Louisville Orchestra / Mester (conductor) / Louisville LS–714

A conscientious application of obtaining action, contrast, and development by using sound masses rather than concentrated thematic statements. Rhythm is a minor credential in this type of music. The method, therefore, is that, rather than using a single color, a mixture of timbres is made, varied in totality but constantly avoiding separate, constituent sonorities. Each mass reminds one of *impasto* technique.

Strong—very strong stuff, and covering a ten-minute length. If there was more rhythmic detail Quintanar's piece could be typed as neo-Varèsian. As it stands, it has an orchestral relationship to electronic music.

Mester punches home the full meaning of Quintanar's *Sideral.*

R

Henri Rabaud / *Gabriel Fauré.* See *Fauré* / Rabaud.

Sergei Rachmaninoff   *(1873-1943)*

Caprice Bohémien, Op. 12   *Orchestra*

☐ London Philharmonic Orchestra / de Waart (conductor) / Philips 6500362

Early Rachmaninoff but typical Rachmaninoff. (It was originally called Capriccio for Large Orchestra based on Gypsy Themes.) Heavy with Slavic pathos, heavy with "Song of the Volga" melodicism, the lack of attention given this fine Rachmaninoff example is undeserving.

Edo de Waart paces the variational progress of the piece with excellence, and he displays a sure hand in measuring the score's colors.

Prince Rostislav (1891)

☐ U.S.S.R. Symphony Orchestra / Svetlanov (conductor) / Melodiya/Angel S-40252

Rachmaninoff's symphonic poem (composed in 1891) was hidden away for no valid reason. Though as good as any Liszt or Smetana work in the same genre, it was not until 1945 that it was first performed and then further posthumous attention was given by publication in 1947. As far as can be ascertained this represents the initial recording of the piece.

The tragic tale is expertly delineated in all its aspects and the descriptive images include one of those special long-lined Rachmaninoff themes. Svetlanov gives a rewarding and artistically dimensioned reading.

The Rock (Symphonic Fantasy), Op. 7

☐ Moscow Radio Symphony Orchestra / Rozhdestvensky (conductor) / Melodiya/Angel S-40182

Full empathy for the atmosphere of Rachmaninoff's piece in this recorded edition. The conclusion is well paced and nicely resonant.

Symphonic Dances, Op. 45

☐ Philadelphia Orchestra / Ormandy (conductor) / Odyssey Y-31246

In music of this type, relinquish all search and just grab the Philadelphians' recording. It is masterful and gorgeous. Indeed, it is difficult to match the tonal fervidity of this

1439

orchestra's string body. Put needle in groove and listen to the middle of the first movement! And, not in second place there are the woodwinds and a beautiful saxophone.

Among the competitive editions the best is Edo de Waart directing the London Philharmonic Orchestra on Philips 6500362. It is an extremely musical performance but falls short in its tone quality when compared to the splendor provided by Ormandy's group. Donald Johanos conducting the Dallas Symphony Orchestra, on Turnabout 34145, turns in a respectable rendition but it, too, lacks the vividness and sonorous distinction of the Ormandy-directed production. The edition released by Melodiya/Angel (S-40093) is disappointing. The performance of the Moscow Philharmonic Orchestra, conducted by Kiril Kondrashin is heavy-handed, weary, and flat for the greater part. Rachmaninoff's prose never sings (though it does dance) in Eugene Goossens's old recorded performance with the London Symphony Orchestra (on Everest 3151 and also on Everest 3004). It has a further fault—that of unpersuasive sound.

Symphony No. 1 in D minor, Op. 13

☐ London Symphony Orchestra / Previn (conductor) / Angel S-37120

Ormandy focused attention on this work in the United States and produced the initial domestic recording. By itself it is no longer obtainable, but it can be secured with Rachmaninoff's other two symphonies on Columbia D3S-813. It is excellent.

The D minor Symphony has Rachmaninoffian length (close to three-quarters of an hour) and is best where Rachmaninoff is usually at his best—in the slow (*Larghetto*) movement. It is least viable in its open-eyed Glazunovian mannerisms, emphatically displayed in the finale (*Allegro con fuoco*), and not entirely absent from movements 1 and 2.

Accordingly, if push doesn't come to shove the Symphony dies on the printed score pages. Previn moves the music along not by tempo increase but by continuity and a refusal to break its lines. This gives a fine shape to the music's size. The Leningrad Philharmonic performance under Sanderling is as good but its sound is not (Everest 3218/3). Slatkin and the St. Louis Symphony have also recorded the Rachmaninoff opus (Candide 31099) but it is labored and lacks the fluency and fine sound that are heard in Previn's and Ormandy's readings.

Symphony No. 2 in E minor, Op. 27

☐ London Symphony Orchestra / Previn (conductor) / Angel S-36954
☐ Philadelphia Orchestra / Ormandy (conductor) / RCA ARL1-1150

Once upon a time no conductor would dare play this work without the many traditional cuts that excise some three hundred measures from the score, *not* counting the repetition of the first movement's exposition. Now the reverse is becoming fashionable, as witness that the best performances of this almost hour's-length Symphony are minus any cuts.

There is little to choose between the Previn and Ormandy entries. The latter has a little better sound, the former is just a bit bolder in his viewpoint. Ormandy's strings are something else, however! And there isn't a better conductor around that knows how to realize subtle string portamenti without which the special kind of Rachmaninoff warmth is nullified.

Those who still want those cuts need not be disappointed. An earlier Ormandy performance has them and the playing is rich, musical, and at the proper temperature. It is on Columbia MS-6110.

Symphony No. 3 in A minor, Op. 44

☐ London Symphony Orchestra / Previn (conductor) / RCA AGLI-1527

Typical Rachmaninoff and that means typical Russian-styled music. Three movements, the corner ones in fast pace, the first of these motivally sprung, the other a dance experience. Variational detail embraces the central movement's music. Previn embraces the whole Symphony magnificently. There is another Previn version with the same orchestra on a different label, Angel S–37260.

Stokowski gave the world premiere, back in 1936 and recorded it much, much later with a different organization. It's there on Desmar 1007 but in no way does it offer competition to Previn's stunning conception. (Originally RCA had issued this Symphony on LSC–2990.)

Vocalise, Op. 34, No. 14

☐ Philadelphia Orchestra / Ormandy (conductor) / Columbia MS–7081

Ormandy plays it musically and sensibly. No floating *rubati* as big as a balloon, no close-shaved smears. Really, Rachmaninoff's little beauty doesn't need those types of special effects delivered by the interpretative department. Heard as Ormandy states it, the *Vocalise* (see also under *Vocal* and *Rachmaninoff/Dubensky: Vocal*) has a simplicity that thoroughly appeals. It proves that one is not comforted, reassured, or soothed by a passionate delivery that protests too much. It is best to avoid the special arrangements that hover about; for example, the one on Melodiya/Angel S–40252, made by one V. Kin, which is no true kin to the original. It's also not needed.

Concerto No. 1 in F sharp minor for Piano and Orchestra, Op. 1

☐ Chicago Symphony Orchestra / Janis (piano) / Reiner (conductor) / RCA VICS–1101

Vigor as need be, vivid as need be and thus in partnership they provide the vital link in this work. Janis has the gift of romantic style and it gives this performance of the work heavy points. Points are also added by Reiner's accompanimental jurisdiction.

Concerto No. 2 in C minor for Piano and Orchestra, Op. 18

☐ London Symphony Orchestra / Ashkenazy (piano) / Previn (conductor) / London 6774
☐ London Symphony Orchestra / Katchen (piano) / Solti (conductor) / London STS–15086
☐ New Philharmonia Orchestra / Anievas (piano) / Atzmon (conductor) / Seraphim S–60091

Unfortunately, despite the huge number of performances on disc of this work, there seems to be no escape from the humdrum of normalcy—or sheer boredom. The latter applies to showoff time and, really, who cares to hear a technical display that is common to just the average pianist these days. How about musicality?

That last applies to these three choices. Ashkenazy plays it like it really is: real music that happens to demand trigger technique, but the two are not mutually exclusive. The slow movement is deeply sensitive and truly lovely. There's more drama in Katchen's portrayal and there's also a "Perils of Pauline" affair what with some of the speeds he chooses. But he gets away with it and the listener goes away with goosebumps. Plenty of dynamic detail in the way Anievas plays this famous work, but it is done with *musical* intelligence and always pointed toward the score and not the gallery.

(The Ashkenazy edition is included in his presentation of all four of the Rachmaninoff concerti; by itself, worth the price of admission. The label is London, the call number is 2311.)

Solo Instrument and Orchestra

Piano

Concerto No. 3 in D minor for Piano and Orchestra, Op. 30

☐ Moscow Philharmonic Orchestra / Mogilevsky (piano) / Kondrashin (conductor) / Melodiya/Angel S–40226

This is a dazzling portrayal by the young Soviet virtuoso. He has a brilliance that is always musical and not simply the result of super technical ability. The Rachmaninoff "third" sometimes daydreams its way but with the tremendous emotional drive of Mogilevsky's playing one overlooks the creative sag. Splendid phrasing, a dynamic range that is of positive identification in all its variances, and complete possession of style make this essay an absolute triumph. Kondrashin conducts with the fullest understanding of the orchestra's role. If heard live there certainly would be cheers and torrents of applause for this performance.

Concerto No. 4 in G minor for Piano and Orchestra, Op. 40

☐ Philharmonia Orchestra / Michelangeli (piano) / Gracis (conductor) / Angel S–35567

With performances like this one, the life of a critic would be lots easier. No continual comparison in order to arrive at a choice. Brilliance, brains, and bravura are all displayed. Michelangeli is fully generous with his technique (he can afford to be) but is equally generous with pianistic beauty (the presentation of the slow movement).

Rhapsody on a Theme of Paganini, Op. 43

☐ London Symphony Orchestra / Ashkenazy (piano) / Previn (conductor) / London 2311

☐ Philadelphia Orchestra / Rachmaninoff (piano) / Stokowski (conductor) / RCA LM–6123 (monaural)

If you desire heated, spitting virtuosity and juicy singing pianism and if you want more: bravura, panache, artistic plushery, and a bit of lushness (all of which fit this work), then Ashkenazy is your man. Terrific he is.

If you want history, then one of the RCA recordings, made immediately after the premiere with the Philadelphia Orchestra in 1936 has to be it, less than updated sonics notwithstanding. The category for this monaural recording is definitive. Who is to argue that? (The other RCA album is ARM3-0296.) There's another Ashkenazy album as well on London 6776.

Instrumental

Piano

Etudes tableaux, Op. 33

No. 1 in F minor / No. 2 in C major / No. 3 in C minor / No. 4 in D minor / No. 5 in E flat minor / No. 6 in E flat major / No. 7 in G minor / No. 8 in C sharp minor

☐ Ponti (piano) / Vox SVBX–5456

Originally there were nine pieces in this initial set of *Etudes tableaux*. Three were then withdrawn and later one was revised and added to the Opus 39 group. The other two eliminated remained in manuscript until published posthumously. It is for that reason, as R. D. Darrell points out in his admirable and most informative notes, that "older reference works" list only a total of six pieces for the opus.

Like the Opus 39 set (*see below*), minor keys are in the great majority. Thus the light and fanciful are in the minority in these Russian-tinctured "pictures." Ponti plays impressively, especially accounting for the subtle colors in Rachmaninoff's score.

Etudes tableaux, Op. 39

No. 1 in C minor / No. 2 in A minor / No. 3 in F sharp minor / No. 4 in B flat minor / No. 5 in E flat minor / No. 6 in A minor / No. 7 in C minor / No. 8 in D minor / No. 9 in D major

☐ Ashkenazy (piano) / London 6822

Fine expansive playing and without any textural blur. The sense of profound statements that surrounds the music (all but one of these "Picture Studies" is set principally in a minor tonality) is drawn into Ashkenazy's playing. He does not proceed with caution.

Mélodie, Op. 3, No. 3

☐ Rachmaninoff (piano) / Klavier 107

This is from Rachmaninoff's Five Pieces, written in 1892, and published the following year with the title *Morceaux de fantaisie, see below.* (Guess what appeared in the set as Opus 3, No. 2!) A much later revision was made, principally concerned with the accompaniment; the performance heard here (a transfer from the "reproducing piano," i.e., piano rolls) is of the original version. It most certainly is definitive and the sound is of good range and balance. Rachmaninoff's tempo is slower than most pianists and it thereby stresses the underlying melancholy of his creation. Of course, only in a short piece is a half-minute plus five seconds a substantial amount of time. That is exactly the difference between Rachmaninoff's probing performance and the considerably faster (more on the surface) reading of Sergei Tarnowsky on Genesis 1004.

Morceaux de fantaisie, Op. 3

☐ Ponti (piano) / Vox SVBX–5456

Bland title which covers five pieces, one of which needs no descriptive remarks—the ubiquitous Prelude in C sharp minor. Indeed, here is that classical member of the hit parade. Let it be noted that Ponti's playing of this piece, which has been desecrated and perverted either by pianists or arrangers denotes artistry of high order. It is truly beautifully done and the music shines all over again as a fresh inspiration. Included in the set are two others that have reached a fair amount of popularity: the *Polichinelle* and the *Serenade*. These, plus the other pair of works, Tchaikovskian contoured, give fine effect in Ponti's responsible projections of the music.

(For another performance of the third piece in the set, *see above, Mélodie.*)

Preludes

☐ Ashkenazy (piano) / London 2241

The complete twenty-four Preludes Rachmaninoff produced, ten in one set (Op. 23), thirteen in another (Op. 32), and the second piece in Opus 3. Ashkenazy's playing is of the bravura quality, and his vitality is splendid.

Preludes

No. 3 in B flat major, Op. 23, No. 2 / No. 5 in D major, Op. 23, No. 4 / No. 6 in G minor, Op. 23, No. 5 / No. 8 in C minor, Op. 23, No. 7 / No. 12 in C major, Op. 32, No. 1 / No. 13 in B flat minor, Op. 32, No. 2

☐ Richter (piano) / Deutsche Grammophon 138076

Richter's choice of preludes from the two dozen Rachmaninoff produced is excellent, though it will be noted that the famed C sharp minor example (Op. 3, No. 2) is bypassed.

The playing of the six pieces is most illuminating. Details come to light that have escaped other pianists. All in all, this issue exemplifies music making not only of taste and intelligence but of breadth and depth.

Sonata

In D minor, Op. 28 / In B flat minor, Op. 36

☐ Ogdon (piano) / RCA LSC-3024

Stylistic similarities of Rachmaninoff's concerti are found in the sonatas but in comparison, performance attention to the concerti have left the sonatas in the shade. The proportions are chunky and concertoish in their demands. John Odgon fully meets these demands. He plays the Rachmaninoff pair with great strength and in the full romantic manner.

Horowitz has recorded the Opus 36 second sonata (Columbia M-30464). His conception has enormous range and, expectedly, pianistic panache.

Variations on a Theme by Chopin, Op. 22

☐ Drake (piano) / Orion 75168

The subject is Chopin's C minor Prelude, Op. 28, No. 30; the winner is Rachmaninoff who fastens his own style on, in, and around the theme without overpowering variational rhetoric that destroys the thematic point. The young pianist never falters, and her reading displays more than note conscientiousness.

Variations on a Theme by Corelli, Op. 42

☐ Ashkenazy (piano) / London 6822

Definition that is carried to its highest point in this series of variations, split after the thirteenth by an Intermezzo and completed after the final seven (making twenty in all) by a coda. Ashkenazy speaks with the fullest romantic spirit in his playing and it is a gem of a performance.

Comparison with an earlier (now deleted) edition he made for Angel (35647) shows Ashkenazy has changed his previous general reflective view for a more dynamic one. Rachmaninoff benefits thereby.

Two Pianos

Polka Italienne

☐ Duo di Heidelberg / Musical Heritage Society MHS-1147

A very attractive performance of this light creative gesture based on a theme Rachmaninoff heard in Italy. The music is written with Rachmaninoffian care but not in Rachmaninoffian style.

Suite

No. 1 (*Fantasy*), Op. 5 / No. 2, Op. 17

☐ Ashkenazy and Previn (pianos) / London 6893

The introverted infiltrate of so much of Rachmaninoff's music fills three-quarters of the first Suite, especially in the *Tears* movement, inspired, Rachmaninoff stated, by the tolling of bells during a funeral at the Novgorod monastery. The recording is worth owning simply for the expressive translation of this movement by these superb musicians. This special understanding is also reflected in those sections of the second Suite where the contemplative or darkly dramatic Rachmaninoffian temper is exhibited—in the Waltz and in the Tarantella (the last a music of technical brilliance within and worrisome excitement without). Elsewhere, Ashkenazy and Previn leave no phrase unscrutinized, producing a marvel of re-creation. Yet, no part of the music is overtaxed in a manner akin to interpretative paraphrase. A stunning presentation from first groove to last.

Sonata in G minor for Cello and Piano, Op. 19

Chamber Music

☐ Shapiro (cello); Wild (piano) / Nonesuch 71155

A major criticism of Rachmaninoff's Sonata has been the overloading of the piano part. However, if the pianist merely exhibits a little acumen in regard to cautious application of the designated dynamics, all will turn out well. For the greater part Earl Wild takes care of the matter, though in a few places (in the *Sturm und Drang* of the initial movement) he does not. Shapiro opts for a heavy and incisive tone which sometimes matches the Tchaikovskian language of the piece.

Epperson-Muczynski (on Coronet 3000) and Nelsova-Johannesen (on Golden Crest 40899) furnish the recorded competition but the sound in one case is poor and in the other tubby. This makes Shapiro-Wild the best available.

Trio élégiaque for Piano, Violin, and Cello, Op. 9

☐ Compinsky Trio / Sheffield M-2 (monaural)

Rachmaninoff here pays homage to Tchaikovsky as Tchaikovsky had paid his respects to Nicholas Rubinstein in his Trio "to the memory of a great artist." Rachmaninoff composes an analogous work, with the same compulsion, and bearing the same inscription— "*à la mémoire d'un grand artiste*"; for the same instrumental combination, and practically in the same form. Tchaikovsky's tribute to Rubinstein is in two movements, the second of which is a set of variations, but its conclusion makes almost a third movement. Rachmaninoff pays tribute to Tchaikovsky in a three-movement creation and includes a group of variations.

The massive elegy constituting this Trio is mainly in the key of D minor, with the deviations from this tonality only pointing up the expressive intent. The first movement is formed from episodes, and from these comes the centrifugal concentrate that posits the balance, depicting a very eloquent fantasy. There are eight variations in the second part of the Trio; easily identifiable in the form of "resistant" variations, in that the theme is paramount in the developed treatment given it, rather than permitted to be squandered and finally lost. The final movement parallels the initial one in the form of linked episodes, further enhanced by a return of the first theme of the opening part of the piece.

By careful engineering the recording does not show its age. It was originally made in 1947 and issued on 78 rpm discs. The transfer to long-play was accomplished in 1965 and Sheffield is to be congratulated for the fine sound. The playing of the once-famous family team (ended by the death of Alec Compinsky, the cellist, in 1960) is choice. A few doubling passages in the finale have pitch trouble, but otherwise the music sings and digs deeply, thanks to an involvement that marks total re-creative knowledge.

All Love You So, Op. 14, No. 6

Vocal

☐ Del Grande (baritone); Pleshakov (piano) / Orion 75180

A sober and dignified song from a set of twelve, set to a Tolstoy text. An evocative performance.

The Answer, Op. 21, No. 4

Arion, Op. 34, No. 5

Before My Window, Op. 26, No. 10

☐ Gedda (tenor); Weissenberg (piano) / Angel S–36917

The last of this group is illustrative of how a simple song structure can be as dramatically vital as any other type of construction. There is one high point that balances the piece.

Rachmaninoff's pianistic knowledge would be expected to be displayed in the instrumental parts of his songs. Rarely is the keyboard instrument subsidiary. *Arion*, with urgency supplied by the piano's voice, is prime evidence.

Child, Thou Art Fair as a Flower, Op. 8, No. 2

☐ Arkhipova (mezzo-soprano); Wustman (piano) / Melodiya/Angel S–40198

Arkhipova's is a warmer and more communicative delivery of this Brahmsian kind of song than Del Grande's placid conception on Orion (75180). (The title used for the latter is *Child! Like a Flower*.)

Christ is Risen, Op. 26, No. 6

☐ Gedda (tenor); Weissenberg (piano) / Angel S–36917

Gedda does not permit his fine voice to push aside interpretative sensibility. He sings this song (one of fifteen in the opus and originally for mezzo-soprano) with a thoughtful approach and is thereby most effective.

A Dream, Op. 8, No. 5

☐ Del Grande (baritone); Pleshakov (piano) / Orion 75180

An exceedingly tender conception. A fully sensitive and thereby satisfactory response by the performers.

Extreme Happiness, Op. 34, No. 12

☐ Del Grande (baritone); Pleshakov (piano) / Orion 73109

Del Grande is at his best in this love song. It is sung with confidence and is therefore most rewarding.

Floods of Spring, Op. 14, No. 11

☐ Del Grande (baritone); Pleshakov (piano) / Orion 75180

Also well-sung by Gedda on Angel (S–36917), but the darker voice of Del Grande is preferable for this song. (Another title for the piece, with text by Tiutchev is *Spring Waters*.)

The Fountain, Op. 26, No. 11

☐ Del Grande (baritone); Pleshakov (piano) / Orion 73109

Pleshakov's playing is special to this song, bearing out Rachmaninoff's statement on the importance (and difficulty—meaning the artistic more than the technical) of the piano part in his Opus 26 songs.

Fragment of Alfred de Musset (Loneliness), Op. 21, No. 6

☐ Arkhipova (mezzo-soprano); Wustman (piano) / Melodiya/Angel S–40198

Operatic aria style is found in this dramatic conception, and it is dramatically sung with beautiful style.

The Harvest of Sorrow, Op. 4, No. 5

☐ Gedda (tenor); Weissenberg (piano) / Angel S–36917

Text by Alexey Tolstoy. Gedda is in superb voice and Weissenberg is everything he should be.

Worthy of being considered is Netania Davrath's presentation in an album of Russian Art Songs (Vanguard VSD–71115). Its title there is *O Thou Billowy Harvest Field;* the title in *Sergei Rachmaninoff,* a book by Sergei Bertensson and Jay Leyda, is *O Thou, my field.*

He Took It All Away From Me, Op. 26, No. 2

☐ Del Grande (baritone); Pleshakov (piano) / Orion 75180

A pithy song, one of Rachmaninoff's shortest—performance time 56 seconds. (As usual, the translation of titles is most confusing. A bibliographic listing in the Bertensson and Leyda book titled *Sergei Rachmaninoff* calls it *He Took All From Me.* That doesn't cause too many problems. But without opus and number guidance how can this and the above designation fit with the title given in *Grove's Dictionary of Music and Musicians: All Once I Gladly Owned?*)

How Fair This Spot, Op. 21, No. 7

☐ Gedda (tenor); Weissenberg (piano) / Angel S–36917

An excellent rendition, especially subtle in the way the phrases are depicted. (An alternate title is *How Nice It Is Here.*)

Impossible!, Op. 34, No. 7
In My Spirit, Op. 14, No. 10

☐ Del Grande (baritone); Pleshakov (piano) / Orion 73109

Dramatic stress in the first of this pair, cantillative articulation in the other. Del Grande's firm line and beautifully rounded tone finds him at his best in the shaded phrasing of *Impossible!*.

In the Silence of the Night, Op. 4, No. 3
I Remember That Day, Op. 34, No. 10

☐ Gedda (tenor); Weissenberg (piano) / Angel S–36917

The title for the second of this group is noted on the release as *The Morn of Life*—another translation conflict. The listener is urged to find Rachmaninoff's songs by the opus and number within the opus.

Fine vocalism here, displaying singing that is dextrous and clear. Fine piano support here providing playing of formal and textual meaning and with an agreeably light touch.

I Wait for Thee, Op. 14, No. 1

☐ Arkhipova (mezzo-soprano); Wustman (piano) / Melodiya/Angel S–40198

Arkhipova's voice is perfect for this emotive piece. And, her taste in delivery is unfailing. Her diction may not equal her vocal ability but that criticism is the only minus point in this report.

I Was With Her, Op. 14, No. 4
Lazarus Has Risen, Op. 34, No. 6

☐ Del Grande (baritone); Pleshakov (piano) / Orion 73109

Lazarus Has Risen (or *The Raising of Lazarus*) is dedicated to the famed Chaliapin. The character of the song is sharply defined in the recording. A satisfactory and well-modulated performance is accorded the other song.

Lilacs, Op. 21, No. 5

☐ Arkhipova (mezzo-soprano); Wustman (piano) / Melodiya/Angel S-40198

One of the most beautiful of all Rachmaninoff's songs. It is sung with a liquidity that will make the listener play the recording over and over again.

Love Has Lost Its Joy, Op. 14, No. 3

☐ Del Grande (baritone); Pleshakov (piano) / Orion 75180

A fairly representative version. Del Grande sings with conscientious regard for the pitches but rather neutral definition of the meaning of Rachmaninoff's vocal piece.

The Muse, Op. 34, No. 1
Music, Op. 34, No. 8

☐ Del Grande (baritone); Pleshakov (piano) / Orion 73109

Del Grande is especially compelling with the introspectiveness conveyed in the second song. *The Muse*, however, has a definite lack of dynamic contrast.

Night is Sad, Op. 26, No. 12

☐ Del Grande (baritone); Pleshakov (piano) / Orion 75180

Rachmaninoff's instructions (in a letter) regarding this piece was that it wasn't the vocalist that must sing, but the pianist. Here, of course, the baritone does sing as he should. However, more important, Pleshakov obtains a topflight vocal quality from the keyboard instrument.

Oh, Do Not Grieve, Op. 14, No. 8

☐ Gedda (tenor); Weissenberg (piano) / Angel S-36917

Expressively defined which means effectively delineated. Weissenberg's piano support—understanding and accommodating—deserves special mention.

Paid in Full, Op. 34, No. 11

☐ Del Grande (baritone); Pleshakov (piano) / Orion 73109

Rachmaninoff's use of a motival phrase unifies the structure of *Paid in Full* and thus offers the auditor a strongly constructed song and one that is aurally dynamic. Well sung and well played by the two musicians.

Sing Not in My Presence, Dear Beauty, Op. 4, No. 4

☐ Arkhipova (mezzo-soprano); Wustman (piano) / Melodiya/Angel S-40198

This is from the first set of six songs that Rachmaninoff composed, most of them during his student days at the Moscow Conservatory. Rachmaninoff's love song has enjoyed considerable and deserved importance, begun when it was featured in concerts as *The Songs of Grusia* by John McCormack. (Titling problem again! Angel's album of Rachmaninoff's songs, performed by Nicolai Gedda and Alexis Weissenberg on S-36917, captions the piece, as does *Grove's Dictionary of Music and Musicians, Oh Never Sing to Me Again.*)

A rich performance with beautiful sonority is presented by this singer. Especially compelling is the haunting coda of the piece with its vocal countermelody over the piano's theme.

Six Songs, Op. 38

☐ Del Grande (baritone); Pleshakov (piano) / Orion 75180

The set comprises *At Night in My Garden, To Her, Daisies, The Pied Piper* (so indicated with the text, but in a separate listing of titles as *The Rat Catcher*), *Dream,* and *A-oo ("Was It a Dream?").*

This was Rachmaninoff's final set of songs. They receive an adequate performance.

The Spirit is Within Us, Op. 34, No. 2
The Tempest, Op. 34, No. 3
These Summer Nights, Op. 14, No. 5

☐ Del Grande (baritone); Pleshakov (piano) / Orion 73109

Strength of dramaticism marks the Opus 34 songs. Find textural balance in all of the presentations. These are among the very best of the performances of Rachmaninoff's songs Orion has released in two albums.

Time!, Op. 14, No. 12
To the Children, Op. 26, No. 7

☐ Del Grande (baritone); Pleshakov (piano) / Orion 75180

The text for *To the Children* concerns a parent recalling the children once in the nursery, now empty. Del Grande does well with his interpretation of this tender song. There is only fair characterization in the realization of *Time!* It results in nothing more than matter-of-fact singing.

Vocalise, Op. 34, No. 14

☐ Gedda (tenor); Weissenberg (piano) / Angel S-36917

As famous in the Rachmaninoff vocal catalogue as the C sharp minor Prelude is in his piano output. It deserves its popularity.

There are four recorded collections of Rachmaninoff songs currently available. Oddly enough, only the Gedda-Weissenberg program includes the *Vocalise.* His performance is truly beautiful, definitive, and represents top-drawer vocalism.

(For an orchestral version of this piece, see under *Orchestra.* An arrangement for voice and orchestra will be found under *Rachmaninoff/Dubensky.*)

***Water Lily*, Op. 8, No. 1**

☐ Del Grande (baritone); Pleshakov (piano) / Orion 75180

One of Rachmaninoff's lighter songs. A relaxed, short item (two seconds less than one minute in length).

***Wind All Around*, Op. 34, No. 4**

***Yesterday, We Met*, Op. 26, No. 13**

***You Knew Him*, Op. 34, No. 9**

☐ Del Grande (baritone); Pleshakov (piano) / Orion 73109

Delicacy is paramount in the first song (Gedda sings this in his program released by Angel on S–36917, where its title is *Day and Night*). The Rachmaninoffian melodic style is nicely portrayed by the baritone soloist.

Choral

Chorus Alone

***Vespers*, Op. 37**

☐ U.S.S.R. Russian Chorus / Korkan (mezzo-soprano); Ognevoi (tenor) / Sveshnikov (conductor) / Melodiya/Angel S–4124

Known also as *Night Vigil,* Rachmaninoff's *Vespers* is a service for the nightlong vigil in monasteries and sung in the Russian Orthodox Church on the eve of holy days. Certain sections of the service are required, by church rule, to be based on traditional chants from the ritual. Rachmaninoff naturally complied, but in his hands they become transformed into emotively moving pieces, far from any academically didactic quality, and containing superb linear detail. Six of the total fifteen parts are thematically original but styled to match the others.

Sensitive and perceptive singing is provided in this edition. In the Bertensson and Leyda biography of the composer, Rachmaninoff is quoted as stating that the first performance of his Opus 37 gave him "an hour of the most complete satisfaction." He would have had it duplicated with this recording of impulse and warmth.

Chorus and Orchestra

Three Russian Songs, Op. 41

☐ Philadelphia Orchestra and Temple University Chorus / Ormandy (conductor) / RCA ARL1–0193

The chosen performance keeps the Rachmaninoff work in the family. Opus 41 was dedicated to Stokowski who conducted the premiere with the Philadelphia Orchestra in March of 1927. Ormandy maintains the faith with a strong idiomatic presentation.

Cantata and Oratorio

The Bells, Op. 35

☐ Philadelphia Orchestra and Temple University Choirs / Curtin (soprano); Shirley (tenor); Devlin (baritone) / Ormandy (conductor) / RCA ARL1–0193

Ormandy's performance is a thorough one and is primed with plenty of atmosphere, dynamic effects, and the like. The Philly was Rachmaninoff's favorite orchestra and it is easy to see why. They play his music with great depth and juice. The text is sung in English and for some this may diminish the authenticity of the recording. Not for this reviewer, because it's sufficiently difficult understanding a chorus in English without trying to do so when Russian is used.

Spring, Op. 20

☐ New Philharmonia Orchestra and St. Ambrose Cathedral Choir / Shaw (bass-baritone) / Buketoff (conductor) / RCA LSC–3051

Buketoff provides a telling atmospheric evocation of Rachmaninoff's cantata for solo baritone, mixed chorus, and orchestra. A somber mood is retained until the contrastive conclusion, and the pace is ideal. John Shaw's singing is sensitive and eloquent.

Aleko (1892)

Opera and Dramatic Music

☐ Plovdiv Symphony Orchestra and Chorus of the Sofia, Bulgaria TVR Ensemble / Karnobatlova (soprano); Christova (contralto); Kourshooumov (tenor); Gyuzelev (baritone); Petkov (bass) / Raychev (conductor) / Monitor 90102/3

Based on Pushkin's poem The Gypsies, Rachmaninoff's one-act *Aleko* is the old tale of an older man betrayed by a younger woman. In this case it is covered twice—one is staged, the other recounted by the father of the woman. The Opera is carried along by set numbers—the woman's lover sings a Romance, Aleko sings a Cavatina, there are duets and so on. It is all very passionate, very Tchaikovskian, clearly stated, patently colored, and yet all very effective.

Nikola Gyuzelev in the title part is very commanding and is matched by Dimiter Petkov in the role of the first betrayed man. The female vocalists deliver competent portrayals. Only the tenor gets negative points. He struggles in the upper register and registers uneven pitch definition. Chorus and orchestra are satisfactory.

Monitor offers the text in Russian but only a translation of the principal arias. A synopsis of the story is included.

Rachmaninoff / Arcady Dubensky (1890-1966)

Vocalise, Op. 34, No. 14

Vocal

Voice and Orchestra

☐ American Symphony Orchestra / Moffo (soprano) / Stokowski (conductor) / RCA LSC-2795

Originally for voice (see under *Rachmaninoff: Vocal*) Rachmaninoff made three other settings of his work for violin, cello, and orchestra. (For the last, see under *Orchestra*.) Here is someone else's transcription, just as competent and worthy.

As a performance it is something special since Stoky in his presentations with orchestra alone really wet-lipped the melody. Here he is the devoted accompanist and lets Anna Moffo cleanly curve her beautiful voice around the tune. No schmaltz, no self-assertion; all sentiment, of course, but what there is is from Rachmaninoff's notes and not another's redefinition.

Rachmaninoff / Rebekah Harkness (1915-   )

Suite No. 1 (*Fantasy*) for Two Pianos, Op. 5 (Transcribed for Full Orchestra)

Orchestra

☐ Harkness Symphony Orchestra / Hoiby (piano) / Mester (conductor) / Desto 6431

Good order and good style mark this straightforward transcription. It was an excellent idea to include a piano obbligato as part of the instrumentation.

Rachmaninoff / Lee Hoiby (1926-)

Orchestra

Suite No. 2 for Two Pianos, Op. 17 (Transcribed for Full Orchestra)

☐ London Symphony Orchestra / Hoiby (piano) / Foster (conductor) / Desto 6431

Rich and juicy and thus proper for the Rachmaninoffian formulae. Orchestrational sensitivity and pianism by Lee Hoiby, a first-rate composer in his own right. Lawrence Foster turns it on full steam where need be. In every way a transcription that conductors should give consideration.

Joachim Raff   (1822-1882)

Orchestra

Symphony No. 5 (*Lenore*) in E major, Op. 177

☐ London Philharmonic Orchestra / Herrmann (conductor) / Nonesuch 71287

Programmatic by ticketing. Raff's fifth symphony is a depiction of a famous German ballad, *Lenore,* by Gottfried August Bürger. Accordingly, three parts, covering four movements: *Liebesglück* ("Love's Joy"), *Trennung* ("Separation"), and *Wiedervereinigung im Tode* ("Reunion in Death"). But, though the program is meticulously followed, the music is more general than specific. No harm, of course, and it doesn't diminish Raff's accomplishment. It's about time to stop denigrating the fellow. He could spin out his material quite well. There are no worms in this romantic apple.

Bernard Herrmann produces a superb documentation of the score and it is obvious that he not only knows the work thoroughly, but believes in it and admires it. If you don't know Raff save as a name in the dictionaries, get this disc. It will convince.

Solo Instrument and Orchestra

Piano

Concerto in C minor for Piano and Orchestra, Op. 185

☐ Nürnberg Symphony Orchestra / Cooper (piano) / Deàky (conductor) / Genesis 1013

An informative concerto, bound in with traditional formal doctrines and bound to be welcome if bias doesn't block it. Raff was no Beethoven or Brahms but there are no apologies required for this forthright three-movement concerto. It has special flavor in its festive, march-like finale. That it has languished in the library-shelf category is a musical disservice.

Frank Cooper has been the man about country that has spearheaded the revival of forgotten romantic music. He is to be saluted for this and twice again for his clear and musical performance. It will satisfy the taste of even the most fastidious of auditors.

André Raison   (?-1719)

Instrumental

Organ

Quoniam Tu Solus Sanctus

☐ Hansen (organ) / Nonesuch 71170

A recitative-like melodic statement, endorsed with some ornamentation. Strictly solo-with-accompaniment and played with a reedy stop for the *récit.* Nothing imposing but with a nice quality to the performance.

David Raksin (1912-   )

The Psalmist *Instrumental*

☐ Remsen (harp) / Avant AV-1000 *Harp*

Originally written for use in a short television film concerning Michelangelo's statue of David. The harp was the obvious instrumental choice.

Jean-Philippe Rameau (1683-1764)

March and Dances from *Acanthe and Céphise* *Orchestra*

☐ Caen Chamber Orchestra / Dautel (conductor) / Turnabout 34101

Two pairs of minuets comprise parts one and four of the dances. The others are a *Tambourin*, an *Air vif*, and a final *Contredanse*. Since *Acanthe and Céphise* is classified as a *Pastorale héroique* (a three-act dramatic work with the alternate title *La Sympathie*), the quite lively tempi Dautel provides are acceptable.

Overture to *Les Paladins*

Overture to *Zaïs*

☐ New Philharmonia Orchestra / Leppard (conductor) / Philips 802901

Striking music that one never hears and is missing a great deal by not. The assets are expanded by special use of the horns in *Les Paladins* and by the piccolo and drums in *Zaïs*.

Credit Raymond Leppard for his choices and for wealthy performances.

La Dauphine	**L'Entretien des Muses**	**Menuets**	*Instrumental*
La Poule	**Les Cyclopes**	**Suite in E minor**	
L'Enharmonique			*Harpsichord*

☐ Fuller (harpsichord) / Nonesuch 71278

A truly vivid and exciting cross-section of Rameau's harpsichord music. Variety, indeed; including programmatic concepts, virtuosity, and expressivity. Save for the last piece, the music is concentrated (averaging about three minutes per composition) but contains as much wealth of creative individuality as the Suite in E minor which consists of eight movements and is of twenty-minute length.

Fuller's playing is wondrous—bright and clear, fresh and springy. The academic black-white type of harpsichord playing that fills countless record grooves is not to be heard in this case. These are exciting, dynamic interpretations, and you can add the phrase "artistic *diablerie*" to that statement.

Suite in E major

☐ Kipnis (harpsichord) / Columbia M3X-31521

Kipnis's playing proves his ingenious interrelationship with the music. Interpretative virtuosity is never so verified as in the ascertainment of *Le Rappel des oiseaux* ("The Gathering of the Birds"). No less so in the other movements.

Opera and Dramatic Music

Castor et Pollux

☐ Concentus Musicus and Stockholm Chamber Chorus / Scovotti, Schéle, and Reiter (sopranos); Lerer (mezzo-soprano); Vandersteene and Alexandersson (tenors); Leanderson and Souzay (baritones); Villisech (bass) / Harnoncourt (conductor) / Telefunken 4635048

One of the most outstanding achievements of this composer. But, can one recall its last performance amidst the hundreds of "Traviatas," "Fausts," and the like? Nothing in the score was written merely to display vocal egos. Rameau's opera is a pour of glorious music, containing magnificent ariosos, thrilling choruses, dance sections that lift the spirit, and an orchestral framework that is as important in the pit as the characters on stage. Lots of things go on in *Castor et Pollux* but diversity does not cancel integration.

The cast is excellent. Top honors belong to Märta Schéle, who covers four roles and Gérard Souzay as Pollux. Both orchestra and chorus are fine; the former utilizing eighteenth-century instruments. Nikolaus Harnoncourt's direction is exceptional. The sound is marvelous.

Les Indes Galantes

☐ La Grande Ecurie et la Chambre du Roy and Raphael Passaquet Vocal Ensemble / Micheau, Nigoghossian, Rodde, and Yakar (sopranos); Brewer and Guélou (tenors); Benoit (baritone); Le Maigat and Tréguier (basses) / Malgoire (conductor) / Columbia M3-32973

Forget the mixture of plots and the assortment of songs and dances that fill this large work. Concentrate on the individual numbers of which there are plenty to sample. Called an "opera-ballet" it turns out to be neither, but a divertissement of large scale. The ballet, for example, is not of sustained action with a story, but consists of isolated dances. But 'tis good Rameau though a lot of Rameau to take at one sitting.

An authentic performance, in terms of pace especially. Malgoire covers authenticity further by use of certain ancient instruments. Good, but rather forthright continuo support.

Rameau / Leopold Godowsky

Instrumental

Piano

Tambourin from Renaissance – Free Transcriptions of Old Masterpieces

☐ Pines (piano) / Genesis 1000

Changes that total a paraphrase, far more than a mere transcription. These include harmonies and counterpoints that go beyond Rameau style, but they do hold the attention.

The playing is at the highest level.

Jean-Pierre Rampal / Aram Khachaturian. See *Khachaturian* / Rampal.

Shulamit Ran (1949-)

Hatzvi Israel Eulogy for Voice, Flute, Harp, and String Quartet

Vocal

Voice and Instrumental Ensemble

☐ Dal Segno Ensemble / Reid-Parsons (mezzo-soprano) / Critics Choice cc–1703 (monaural)

Ran's eulogy (for Saul and Jonathan) is crossed with anguish that does not relinquish its outward dramatic decisiveness. The style is expressionistic, with widely disjunct lines and half-sung phrases. Exceedingly well accomplished in this presentation.

O, the Chimneys (1969)

☐ New York Philomusica Chamber Ensemble / Davy (soprano); Ran (piano) / Johnson (conductor) / Turnabout 34492

The texts of the five poems for this work are by Nelly Sachs, sung in the original German (with excellent diction) by Gloria Davy. The composer is at the piano; the instrumentation also calls for flute, clarinet (alternating with bass clarinet), cello, and percussion. In addition, a tape segment is utilized in the fifth part of the work.

Hitlerian horror is the cold sweat that covers the texts, and Ran's expressionistic music is linked to it with pictorial power. The intensity of the score marks a creative voice that should be heard.

J. K. Randall (1929-)

Lyric Variations for Violin and Computer (1968)

Instrumental

Violin

☐ Zukofsky (violin) / Vanguard C–10057

Colorful specification and interaction between man and machine are heard in Randall's piece. Such duo might well represent the latest idea in chamber music.

There are twenty variations. The first five are for violin alone, the next five for the computer (the material minutely programmed and worked out with the results played back on tape), and the final ten for violin and (computered) tape. The conception and the outcome can be termed both technically significant and musically interesting.

Improvisation

Vocal

Voice and Instrumental Ensemble

☐ Beardslee (soprano); Blustine (clarinet); Anderson (trumpet); James (piano); Regni (saxophone); Silverman (guitar) / Gilbert (conductor) / Composers Recordings S–325

A two-dimensional effect is realized by total separate identity of the voice as contrasted to the instrumental quintet. This confirms the composer's objective that the voice is akin to "the poem speaking." The paradox arises that while the voice partners (in the sense of being present simultaneously) the instruments, it seemingly could exist without them, and vice versa.

An expertly presented performance, with expertly conceived balances.

Sam Raphling (1910-   )

Instrumental

Piano

Twenty-four Etudes for Piano

☐ Raphling (piano) / Serenus SRE-1020 (monaural)

With care Raphling confines himself to a style wherein dissonance douses tonal polarities. There are sharp reminders here of the 1920s when many composers practiced the cult of the "wrong note" to spice their tonal recipes.

Raphling's etude devices are well planned, especially No. 6, with secundal frictions; No. 8, concerned with quartal harmony, and No. 22, set in blocked sevenths. In all cases the objectives are clear; as examples: imitation (No. 13), contrapuntally opposed octave streams (No. 19), and arpeggiated framework (No. 21).

Karol Rathaus (1895-1954)

Orchestra

Prelude for Orchestra, Op. 71

☐ Louisville Orchestra / Whitney (conductor) / Louisville 545-9 (monaural)

Music firmly rooted in the romantic tradition. Rathaus scores cleanly and dynamically. The use of a piano adds a nice timbre to the context which has a ternary design, with the third part elaborating and recapitulating the material from the previous sections.

A resonant performance.

Chamber Music

Tower Music

☐ Berlin Brass Quintet / Crystal S-201

Two parts: stately and choralish in the *Andante con moto,* ceremonial and rhythmically driven in the *Allegro marciale.* Perfectly satisfying, unless one has a prejudice against tonal music.

Johann Valentin Rathgeber (1682-1750)

Solo Instrument and Orchestra

Two Trumpets and Two Violins

Concerto in E flat major for Two Trumpets, Two Violins, and Continuo, Op. 6, No. 15

☐ Schwarz and Soper (trumpets); Mansfield and Ravinah (violins); Zlotkin (cello); Cooper (harpsichord) / Nonesuch 71301

Handelian music that streams along with the greatest freshness. The playing is gorgeous, the balances of perfection.

Einojuhani Rautavaara (1928-   )

String Orchestra

Pelimannit, Op. 1

☐ Helsinki Chamber Orchestra / Rahkonen (violin); Höylä (cello) / Segerstam (conductor) / Bis LP-19

"Fiddlers," or "Folk Musicians," was conceived as a piano suite in 1952. Twenty years later Rautavaara transcribed his conception for string orchestra. Its five movements are stunning and a true find.

Movement 2 (*Kopsin Jonas*) has an ethereal mysticism. The peak of the pieces is in part 3: *Klockar Samuel Dikström,* a mix of Bachian figuration and dance, played off against each other by dynamically opposite antiphony. The Bartókian flashes in the score are the result of using Finnish folk tunes.

Vivid and significant music. The playing is marvelous by the nineteen instrumentalists (six first violins, five second violins, three violas, three cellos, and two basses).

Maurice Ravel   (1875-1937)

Alborada del gracioso (1905)   *Orchestra*

☐ Orchestre de Paris / von Karajan (conductor) / Angel S-36839

Ravel's *Alborada del gracioso* ("Serenade of a Clown") is the fourth of his five-part *Miroirs* (see under *Instrumental: piano*); the setting for orchestra was made by Ravel, and a juicy one it is, indeed.

The brilliance of the playing combined with fine metrical ignition bring this piece into its proper performance orbit.

Boléro (1927)

☐ New York Philharmonic / Bernstein (conductor) / Columbia MS-6011
☐ Philadelphia Orchestra / Ormandy (conductor) / RCA ARL1-0451
☐ Berlin Philharmonic Orchestra / von Karajan (conductor) / Deutsche Grammophon 139010

No sense in kidding about the fundamental truth of this speciality. If there's no excitement, then there's no Boléro. A great deal of talk has been made about the essentials of a well-ordered tempo, and that it must be absolutely maintained while the climate must get hotter and heavier as the music moves along. Rigid performances would be Ravelian-approved and those with metronomic mathematical precision are plenty, but none offer heady excitement.

Electricity comes out of Bernstein's conception, there's more smoothness from Ormandy, and von Karajan holds it on track and yet keeps the blood boiling as though he were pushing up the pace lever. He doesn't, which exhibits that subtle but telling matter of excitement engendered from within rather than the more obvious, but less compelling method of tending to the matter from above.

Other Bernstein placements of his performance are on Columbia MS-7512 and M-31847. Ormandy's performance is also on RCA CRL3-0984. Also available are Ormandy performances on Columbia, which are practically the same (on MS-6169, MS-6478, MS-7673), and on Odyssey Y-33926.

Daphnis et Chloé
Suite No. 1 (1911) / Suite No. 2 (1911)

☐ Concertgebouw Orchestra / Haitink (conductor) / Philips 6500311

The value in this case is the less-often played first suite from the ballet score, containing a total of three numbers, the same as the second suite (*see below*).

Ravel's music in its montage of orchestral weights, perspective, outline, smudging, highlighting, and the like is a tempting matter for conductors. Tempting, indeed, for exaggeration. Haitink does both suites exceptionally well, and his treatment of the first suite's finale, the *Danse guerrière* is exceptional—period. He does not lose his way in the colorful creative aspects of the music and never exaggerates. The balances are expertly achieved and the unique colors are allowed their full glow.

Daphnis et Chloé – Suite No. 2 (1911)

☐ Boston Symphony Orchestra and New England Conservatory Chorus / Abbado (conductor) / Deutsche Grammophon 2530038
☐ Berlin Philharmonic Orchestra / von Karajan (conductor) / Deutsche Grammophon 138923

Both conductors play the *Daphnis* music with superb finish (*see also above*). Abbado utilizes the wordless chorus which is scored as an *ad libitum*. Plenty of slithering sensuosity in the suite, but it is controlled and reflected in the cultivated behavior of the playing, more so in von Karajan's case but with no loss of effect. Denuded, vulgar display can be heard in some of the other editions. One can do without such.

Fanfare for *L'Eventail de Jeanne*

☐ Minnesota Orchestra / Skrowaczewski (conductor) / Vox SVBX-5133

One of the ten parts written by ten French composers for a famed Parisian hostess as a collaborative souvenir. It was turned into a ballet after being performed as a piano suite. A curiosity, of course.

Some critics consider this the initial recording, but earlier Stokowski recorded it as a filler for his Franck Symphony issue (London 21061).

La Valse (1920)

☐ London Symphony Orchestra / Monteux (conductor) / Philips 835258
☐ New York Philharmonic / Boulez (conductor) / Columbia M-32838

Raised eyebrows notwithstanding, Monteux's oldie (produced in the early 1960s) can still curl your hair. The tendency to choose the latest release of a perennial piece may provide more glowing sound but it doesn't provide the most glowing musical insight. Pierre Monteux was a master conductor and *his La Valse* is the interpretative blockbuster of them all.

Boulez's edition is all spit and polish and there isn't an accent overlooked or a misplaced agogic. It's brutally cold, calculating, and correct, but paradoxically produces Ravelian heat of the proper temperature. There are no doubts that it will get at and hold a listener.

Le Tombeau de Couperin (1917)

☐ New York Philharmonic / Boulez (conductor) / Columbia M-32159
☐ Minnesota Orchestra / Skrowaczewski (conductor) / Vox SVBX-5133

Ravel's concentrated orchestra (two each of woodwind, with the second flute doubling on piccolo and the second oboe alternating with English horn, but two horns and one trumpet, plus harp and strings) may be the subconscious cause for the pinched quality that pervades most of the recorded performances. (One example: Clutyens on Angel S-36111.) On the other hand, fleshing out the textures of the four movements (the original piano work [see under *Instrumental: piano*] has six, but Ravel did not orchestrate the Fugue and the Toccata) removes the intimacy of the dances. (One example: Ozawa on Deutsche Grammophon 2711015.)

That dance character is tapped beautifully in Skrowaczewski's case. In a more subtle way it is defined in Boulez's version, especially in the *Menuet,* where the trio is simply breathtaking in flow, color, and pulse. Both conductors adjust the weights of the attacks and instrumental entrances within the phrases impeccably. This too is brilliance of another kind, and recognizing it one hears Ravel at his very best.

Ma Mère l'Oye: **Suite (1912)**

☐ Philharmonia Orchestra / Giulini (conductor) / Seraphim S–60022

A superb example of Ravel's *Hop o'my Thumb, Conversations of the Beauty and the Beast,* and the other three movements drawn from the ballet (see under *Instrumental: piano, four hands* and *Ballet*). The timbre interplay and phrase curvations are perfectly confirmed by Giulini and his musicians. And where needed there is sponged intensity.

Menuet antique **(1895)**

☐ Orchestre de Paris / Martinon (conductor) / Angel S–37150

It may be the cushioned frictions of the main part of Ravel's orchestration of this very early-period piano piece that cause conductorial heaviness in all the versions heard save that conducted by Jean Martinon. In his case, the definite pulse is there but so is orchestrational air. (See also under *Instrumental: piano*.)

Ouverture de féerie, **"Shéhérazade" (1898)**

☐ Orchestre de Paris / Martinon (conductor) / Angel S–37147

Written for an opera that never was written. The material is quasi-Ravelian and not wholly "with it." This recording will be of interest principally to Ravel fans.

Pavane pour une Infante défunte **(1899)**

☐ Cleveland Orchestra / Szell (conductor) / Odyssey Y–31928
☐ L'Orchestre de la Suisse Romande / Ansermet (conductor) / London 6225

Including duplicate editions in different packagings, currently there are close to forty albums containing this work on the market. These include the original setting for piano (see under *Instrumental: piano*) as well as transcriptions for guitar, guitar duo, and such oddball translations calling for clarinet choir and flute ensemble. (Not to be forgotten was the use in the thirties of Ravel's melody for the popular song *The Lamp is Low.*)

Overstress is not the way to depict the emotional verve contained in Ravel's setting of his piano piece for small orchestra. Neither of these performances wears heart on sleeve. Szell's is a warmer exhibit than Ansermet's, though the subtle aloofness portrayed by the latter is most effective. (The Szell rendition is also obtainable in a two-record set titled *The Spectacular Cleveland Orchestra* on Columbia M2X-787.)

Rapsodie espagnole **(1907)**

☐ New York Philharmonic / Bernstein (conductor) / Columbia M–32873
☐ Cleveland Orchestra / Boulez (conductor) / Columbia M–30651

The orchestral virtuosity demanded in Ravel's score needs to be set ablaze if it is to have the fullest, impacted meaning. Bernstein's hot-oil performance covers all the requirements. Alert to every nuance, he has the music speak with energy and response, and, at the same time with the sexy sensuosness that outlines the heightened subtleties that are packed in the score. This is the type of music where one wouldn't mind Bernstein's choreographic podium manners. On a recording the aural translation of such direction is documented. Magnificent.

Boulez's version is to be admired if only for its etched clarity. The playing does not blow the mind as it does under Bernstein's leadership, but it is heard with infallible taste (which means style). If you like authenticity to the finest degree with a probing of every point of punctuation and stated in its proper place, then Boulez is the fellow to follow. It does convince, though it will not turn you on the way Bernstein will.

Une Barque sur l'océan (1905)

☐ New York Philharmonic / Boulez (conductor) / Columbia M-32159
☐ Paris Conservatoire Orchestra / Cluytens (conductor) / Angel S-36111

All the magical sonorities that wash through this superb example of Ravelian impressionism are vividly detailed in Boulez's direction. No evidence here of the coldly analytical Pierre Boulez attitude critics have emphasized. If anything it is Boulez's perceptive analysis of the score that has produced a thoroughly warm and colored conception.

Both the fragile and strong points of Ravel's transcription from his piano work *Miroirs* (see under *Instrumental: piano*) are fully identified in their contrastive and supportive roles in the Cluytens edition. The impressionistic plotting is as clear as one would want.

Valses nobles et sentimentales (1911)

☐ Boston Symphony Orchestra / Ozawa (conductor) / Deutsche Grammophon 2711015

Clear and crisp, keen and kinetically proper playing. Whatever quality is represented in Ravel's score, its requirements are posed forcibly and colorfully by Ozawa. The harmonies in this piece need the most careful orchestral adjustment in balance. So done. (See also under *Instrumental: piano*.)

Solo Instrument and Orchestra

Piano

Concerto in D major for Piano (Left Hand) and Orchestra (1931)

☐ London Symphony Orchestra / Katchen (piano) / Kertész (conductor) / London 6633

This was Julius Katchen's final recording and represents a marvelous leave-taking. Vital playing and, incidentally, as vital a support from the orchestra. It can only be termed brilliant.

The soloist who started it all, having commissioned the work from Ravel, should not be overlooked. Paul Wittgenstein's performance is on Orion 7028E.

Concerto in G major for Piano and Orchestra (1931)

☐ Philharmonia Orchestra / Michelangeli (piano) / Gracis (conductor) / Angel S-35567

Great re-creative discovery in the playing of this work which has muscle and tone, and matches virility with delicacy. The slow movement is exquisite.

Bernstein's performance, with the assistance of the Columbia Symphony Orchestra, is still a winner and should be considered. It is on Columbia MS-6043.

Violin

Tzigane for Violin and Orchestra (1924)

☐ Orchestre de Paris / Perlman (violin) / Martinon (conductor) / Angel S-37118

Ravel's unabridged concept of fiddle pyrotechnics is fun and games for Perlman; the glitter and purity of the harmonics a special delight. The *Tzigane* (published for violin and piano or with orchestral accompaniment) in the former version is listed by some writers as chamber music. It was never so intended. It is a frank, virtuoso piece in Concerto exhibitionism. The proof is in the flawless presentation by Perlman.

(Perlman's performance is also included in an all-Ravel release, on Angel S-37149.)

À la manière de Borodine (1913)

À la manière de Chabrier (1913)

☐ Entremont (piano) / Columbia D3M-33311

I recall the title heading of a Virgil Thomson article when he was reviewing for the *New York Herald Tribune* which fully applies here: "French Loveliness." The playing is all that, which includes clear unanimity.

Gaspard de la nuit (1908)

☐ Ashkenazy (piano) / London 6472

Simply a sympathetic performance will not fill the bill. Ashkenazy is well-nigh unbeatable in his portrayal of the three movements involved. The *Ondine* movement is rhythmically permissive, and such fluidity makes the music rich with color. *Le Gibet* has superb textural balance, and *Scarbo* (fiendishly difficult) is of knifed incisiveness. Great piano playing of great Ravel piano music.

Jeux d'eau (1901)

☐ Rogé (piano) / London 6936

Fauré at first disapproved of this work. He finally came around. Wise man, since *Jeux d'eau* has a unique beauty that is the paramount point of its total originality. Rogé's performance is strongly colored and sensitively textured.

Le Tombeau de Couperin (1917)

☐ Casadesus (piano) / Odyssey 32360003 (monaural)

All the stereo performances reviewed suffer from wavery structuring and lack of rhythmic profile. In music that covers dances (*Forlane, Rigaudon,* and *Menuet*), such lack brings critical consequences. Then, too, there is the rapid Prelude, a very serious Fugue, and a hyperactive Toccata (six movements in the piano setting, two less in the orchestral version—see under *Orchestra*), which require no less sculpted pulse.

Rogé doesn't have it (London 6873), Entremont doesn't have it either (Columbia D3M-33311), though Abbey Simon almost has it (Vox SVBX-5473). The pianist that does have it to the fullest is listed. His is a masterly essay and includes the points mentioned above as well as detailing a magnificent Toccata that lifts a listener right out of his listening post.

Menuet antique (1895)

Menuet sur le nom de Haydn (1909)

☐ Rogé (piano) / London 6895

Satisfactory playing, particularly the unpretentiousness applied to the "Haydn" piece. (See also under *Orchestra*.)

Miroirs (1905)

☐ Rogé (piano) / London 6936

This suite includes the virtuosic, nationalistically framed *Alborada del gracioso* which Ravel later orchestrated (see under *Orchestra*). It is exuberant music and it is played with razor-edged detail and full excitation. As vividly imaginative conceptions are provided for the other pieces in the opus.

(Another movement—the third, *Une Barque sur l'océan* was also placed in orchestral form—see under *Orchestra*.)

Pavane pour une Infante défunte (1899)

☐ Entremont (piano) / Columbia M–32070

The enchanting simplicity of this music has led to downright outrageous interpretations as well as sentimentalized, sloppy ones. Entremont is meticulous, poetic, and pointedly lyrical in his depiction. The beauty is totally communicated and that provides an authentic interpretation. It's the *best* of the many this reviewer has heard.

The *Pavane* is also included in a six-record-side, all-Ravel "box" Columbia has released on D3M–33311. (See also under *Orchestra*.)

Prélude (1913)

☐ Rogé (piano) / London 6895

This music is of adequate scale and range but only of historic value in the Ravel catalogue. It is hardly ever heard, so a recording is of value.

Sérénade grotesque

☐ Biret (piano) / Finnadar 9013

Ravel at eighteen in terms of his first piano composition. Beautifully crafted, from which one realizes, regardless of the ease of saying so at this remove, the simmerings of a major voice. Sensitively played by this masterful pianist.

Sonatine (1905)

☐ Argerich (piano) / Deutsche Grammophon 2530540

A playing of this work that is truly rare. Off the strings and with the pedals one hears keyboarded watercolors that are scintillating. At the same time the clarity and durability of Ravel's form are not minimized one iota. Argerich adds warmth and a spirituality to the music. The total equals a terrific combination that makes her performance one of the highlights in the Ravel recording lists.

Valses nobles et sentimentales (1911)

☐ Rubinstein (piano) / RCA LSC–2751

Vigorous when need be, delicate when need be, and these provide all the atmosphere. (See also under *Orchestra*.)

Piano,
Four Hands

Ma Mère l'Oye (1910)

☐ Pascal and Denise Rogé (piano) / London 6936

Ravel initially composed his five-part *Ma Mère l'Oye* (subtitled "pieces enfantines") for piano, four hands. It was especially written for two youngsters, Christine Verger, age 6, and Germaine Durant, age 10, and they gave the first performance in Paris on April 20, 1910. In 1912 Ravel elaborated his conception into a ballet (see under *Ballet*) based on his own scenario. From this larger work a concert suite was extracted (see under *Orchestra*.)

The London issue is the best of the available editions of Ravel's "Mother Goose" in the piano, four hands version, but it still lacks much of the coloristic variety in the score. On a scale of two points for each of the five movements it rates a score of six. The Kliens (on Turnabout 34235) square away, avoid any hint of give-and-take in phrasing and nothing of value happens until the fifth movement, *The Fairy Garden*. They score a thin two. The Kontarskys (on Deutsche Grammophon 2707072) play Ravel like Reger and score a fat zero.

Frontispiece, for Piano Five-Hands (1918)

Piano,
Five Hands

☐ Jacobs, Sterne, and Kalish (piano) / Nonesuch 71355

A Ravelian rarity. Midget-sized (one and one-half minutes in length), it requires two and one-half pianists (the third performer uses only one hand). Excellent playing marks this, the initial recording of the piece.

Habanera (1897)

Two Pianos

☐ Joy and Robin-Bonneau (pianos) / Musical Heritage Society MHS-849/850

No illusion—this *is* the *Habanera* in Ravel's *Rapsodie espagnole*. Not a boiled-down bargain—this is the original, which Ravel later orchestrated. Admirably played, the nuances are fine, the color deployed so that really one doesn't yearn too much for the orchestral edition.

Les Sites auriculaires for Two Pianos (1897)

☐ Jacobs and Kalish (pianos) / Nonesuch 71355

The first piece of the pair is the *Habanera,* which eventually surfaced orchestrally as the third movement in the *Rapsodie espagnole*. A great deal of sensualism permeates the playing of the piece but the tempo is rather restricted and the pulse comes forth as though put through a slow-motion device. (A better performance of this movement is noted *above*.) Part two is a tripartite designed piece, titled *Entre cloches*. It is impressively played.

Rapsodie espagnole (1907)

☐ Alfons and Aloys Kontarsky (pianos) / Deutsche Grammophon 2707072

Should you be interested in the version for two pianos, here it is. Two pianos are good, an orchestra is better.

Pièce en forme de Habanera (1907)

Violin

☐ Nadien (violin); Hancock (piano) / Monitor S-2017

Golden sound and sensuous style equal a perfect demonstration of Ravel's creative beauty. It was originally composed for voice as a *Vocalise en forme d'habanera* (the title noted above follows the published edition as well as the recorded version). David Nadien remains little known, despite his stint as the concertmeister of the New York Philharmonic. He is, without the slightest doubt, a master musician.

Sonata for Violin and Cello (1922)

☐ Laredo (violin); Parnas (cello) / Columbia M–33529

It will be found that this Sonata, one of the greatest examples in a little-used medium, has the fluctuations of the impressionistic school cast in the expediencies of the classic models (in the sense of order, not style). It is harder, even "harsher" than most of Ravel's other music. The musical kingdom inhabited by this work has certain crags; it is not the soft landscape of the Quartet in F, or of the Introduction and Allegro. There is some ice on the ground; the softness is a bit concealed.

The playing is sharply perceptive. The fluctuatory tonal progress in movement 1 is thoroughly clear; the Scherzo is speedily violent and immaculately demarcated as to its combined keys and rhythms. Both fine flux and repose are heard in the slow movement, and keen dance jugglery is exhibited in the finale. Though the instrumental confines are narrow, Ravel's music flows with spontaneity in the hands of these superb musicians.

Sonata for Violin and Piano (1927)

☐ Wilkomirska (violin); Barbosa (piano) / Connoisseur Society S–2038

The first movement is a flowing, gently graceful, and relaxed affair. The purity of the classical thought has romantic curves of line, but the period of writing is reflected only as the composer's shadow comes into full profile with the section that begins the second subject. Movement 2 (a Blues) is based on the momentum of pizzicati, soft, "saxlike" slithering lines, rhythmic verve, and some bitonal combinations. The final movement is weaker than the others, though technically (for the violin) the most difficult. This *Perpetuum mobile* starts in low gear; once it gets into higher shifts, the violin pours out, unceasingly, twelve sixteenth notes per measure—in fact, for one hundred and seventy-nine consecutive measures! The piano supports the violin with etched clarity. This movement does not have time to be very serious; its Etude structure is simply a glittering coat to what has gone before.

This is the choice version. The competition from Diana Steiner and David Berfield (on Orion 75195) loses out because (a) the sound is dry and sometimes muffled and (b) there's not enough juice in the finale.

Trio for Piano, Violin, and Cello (1914)

☐ Jaime Laredo (violin); Solow (cello); Ruth Laredo (piano) / Columbia M–33529

Any musical work may be fully respectful of old traditions, without laboring within the specific terms of old forms. In this instance, Ravel's serio-impressionism is a provisional use of the trio structure. It has a boldness of creative outlook, without loss of any freshness, and without the creeping boredom that pertains to so many works written for these three instruments. In other words, this trio skirts the fringe of the classical models; Ravel is a discreet and cautious classicist. His kinship with Mozart is not far distant in the refined clarity of this trio, despite its twentieth-century sparkle and color. Part writing and attention to detail are present in every note of the constantly variable action. In Ravel's hands, the trio apparatus is changed into a new picaresque format.

The confluence of the players is splendid, the material is perhaps a bit enthusiastically defined, but no matter. Considering that Ravel's music is a delight of color (the capricious finale, in Ravel's favored $\frac{5}{4}$ meter plus $\frac{7}{4}$ rhythms) and though some of the trio is fragile as to organic sound (movement one) it is solidly French, and animation (inwardly and outwardly) is not out of order.

Quartet in F (1903)

☐ La Salle Quartet / Deutsche Grammophon 2530235
☐ Quartetto Italiano / Philips 835361

The La Salle's is a consummate performance. Their playing of the opening movement is tinged with sheen and delicacy, tinted with pastel colors, and woven with a texture like that of a bed of pine needles. In the pizzicati colors that dye the second movement the cross-rhythmic patterns are sharply outlined, and in the finale, based on a quintuple pulse, the combination of flow and intensity is masterful.

The Italian group is no less sensitive and just as colorful in their account. Both they and the La Salle accomplish the inside "busy" lines (most marked in the opening movement) with a smoothness that is very special. In comparison, the Guarneri Quartet (on RCA ARL1-0187) and the Carmirelli Quartet (on London STS-15152), among others, rough up such passages, thereby tearing the music's fabric. Considered in another way, linear fill is mistaken to mean linear prominence. Further, no one equals the suggestive bell sounds of the second movement that are heard in the performances chosen.

Introduction and Allegro for Harp, String Quartet, Flute, and Clarinet (1906)

☐ Melos Ensemble / Ellis (harp) / Oiseau-Lyre 60048

Of all Ravel's chamber works, this is the most impressionistic. There is no development of the two themes that are heard at the beginning. Instead, they are given shifting backgrounds, attested by being fed various pigmented items—of glissandi, or tremolandi, of dissected sonorities by way of harmonics, and muted timbre. The themes go through musical substantiation, by way of the exploratory inferences of color and texture that are now black, then white, or orange, green, or red; now thin, then luxuriant; now exotic, then percussive.

The years go by, new recorded editions of this distinguished Ravel piece enter the catalogue, but this performance stands firm in first place. It embodies all the color, charm, and grace of the work. There is no compromise with style or artistic taste in a single measure. Gorgeous from beginning to end.

One complaint and that is with the liner statement that the composition is "for harp accompanied by string quartet, flute and clarinet." Further, therefore, assigning a credit line that reads: "Solo Harp: Osian Ellis." Ravel's composition is pure chamber music, even though the harp is given a very important role, including the nonchamber music device of a cadenza. The harp is a highlighted color, if only because string instruments played with bows and two woodwinds are severely different in their tone qualities from a string instrument that is plucked. Such individual timbre does not negate the proper chamber music medium classification.

Cinq Mélodies populaires grecques (1905)

Deux Mélodies hébraïques (1914)

Don Quichotte à Dulcinée (1934)

Epigrammes de Clément Marot (1896)

Histoires naturelles (1906)

☐ Souzay (baritone); Baldwin (piano) / Philips 839733

Each title embraces a group of separate songs, the fewest being two, the most being five. Imaginative and sensitive singing. In the first of the Hebrew pair of songs, a *Kaddish*, Souzay's style is equal to the greatest singing of any *chazzen*.

Vocal

Voice with Accompaniment

The "Two Hebraic Melodies" is also available with orchestral accompaniment (London STS-15155/6), with Ansermet conducting the Orchestre de la Suisse Romande, and Danco, as the solo voice.

Vocal

Voice and Instrumental Ensemble

Chansons Madécasses (1926)

☐ DeGaetani (mezzo-soprano); Dunkel (flute); Anderson (cello); Kalish (piano) / Nonesuch 71355

Considering Ravel's total output, the "Songs of Madagascar" are among the most beautiful and certainly are the most sensual he produced. The three-part set represents extremely sensitive chamber music, more so because of the independence of the part writing.

Though recordings by a male voice are available (Souzay on Philips 839733 and Fischer-Dieskau on HNH Records 4045), it is this writer's belief that only a woman's voice is acceptable. After hearing Jan DeGaetani's execution it is simply impossible to accept *any other* voice, male or female. Her singing draws the listener into the thoughts of the song as an intimate observer. The instrumental work parallels her achievement. A magnificent result.

Trois Poèmes de Stéphane Mallarmé (1913)

☐ Ensemble "Die Reihe" / Escribano (soprano) / Cerha (conductor) / Turnabout 34591

Although there is a fair amount of the Ravel type of color and impressionistic style in the first song, *Soupir,* there is a slightly heavy air of expressionism in the other songs, *Placet futile* and *Surgi de la croupe et du bond.* Indeed, the Mallarmé songs are probably Ravel's most recondite work. (The dedications are most interesting; the first song is dedicated to Igor Stravinsky, the second one to Florent Schmitt, and the last of the group to Erik Satie.)

Marie-Thérèse Escribano sings with breadth and dignity. She styles her performance with a pertinent intimacy that permits the text to be clarified, and counteractive interpretative emphasis is avoided. Cerha conducts the ensemble with fine style. The scoring is for piano, string quartet, two flutes (one doubling on piccolo), and two clarinets (one alternating with bass clarinet).

Voice and Orchestra

Shéhérazade (1903)

☐ New Philharmonia Orchestra / Baker (mezzo-soprano) / Barbirolli (conductor) / Angel S-36505
☐ L'Orchestre de la Suisse Romande / Crespin (mezzo-soprano) / Ansermet (conductor) / London 25821

Ravel's song cycle is exotic and sensuous, a music that Nicolas Slonimsky so poetically describes (in connection with the first song, but which can apply to the balance of the work as well) as "breathlessly exhaling puffs of Gallically perfumed Orientalistic vapors." Moreover, subtle sexuality caresses the tone combinations of all three parts: *Asie, La Flûte enchantée,* and *L'indifférent.*

Both of the performances chosen have the colorful lucidity and animal warmth this work requires. The interpretative temperature must not be so controlled as to cool the sounds too much (Tourel with Bernstein conducting on Columbia Special Products CMS-6438), neither should the quality be tender and sweet (Danco with Ansermet on London STS-15155/6). The real flavors of Ravel's work are to be tasted in Janet Baker's vivid characterization and Régine Crespin's intense rendition. In the latter case Ansermet lets the music have its colorful head; with Suzanne Danco (mentioned above) there is too much self-absorbed concentration and the music suffers.

Trois Chansons (1916)

☐ Robert Shaw Chorale / Bruce (soprano) / Shaw (conductor) / RCA LSC-2676

There is no comparison between this presentation and that available in an unaccompanied chorus program issued by Desto (6483). The singing is much more professional here, the interpretation is well honed, and the dynamic effects are stunning. The choral strength is an important factor. The Desto group (the Modern Madrigal Singers) have two each of soprano, alto, tenor, and bass; the Shaw Chorale has a total of thirty-four (eighteen female voices and sixteen male voices). Indeed, no contest.

L'Enfant et les sortilèges (1925)

☐ Orchestre National de la RTF and Choir and Choir Boys of the RTF / Ogéas (treble); Herzog, Gilma, and Maurane (sopranos); Collard and Berbié (mezzo-sopranos); Sénéchal (tenor); Rehfuss (baritone) / Maazel (conductor) / Deutsche Grammophon 138675

An opera in two parts to a *fantaisie lyrique* tale by Colette. It's a delight from beginning to end with the story line of a bad boy who is shown not to be so bad in the long run. Humans acting as humans are very few in Ravel's "The Child and the Fantasies." Animated characterization by the cast covers such as an armchair, a clock, a cup, and a teapot; a dragonfly, a cat, an owl, a frog, a bat, etc. In all there are twenty-one characters in Ravel's work, with the singers doubling, tripling, and quadrupling in their roles.

The music is inspired, the orchestration a veritable textbook of discoveries, the vocal writing beautifully curvaceous and of melodic simplicity. There is much humor (for example, the arithmetic song) and a remarkable inspiration in the cat and tomcat duet in part two.

Deutsche Grammophon's cast is outstanding. Françoise Ogéas as the Child is totally convincing, Jeanine Collard as the Mother is most persuasive. The entire cast sings beautifully and is delightfully poetic. Loren Maazel binds it all together and yet makes certain the imagery is allowed full life and spirit. This is no small challenge and his rapport with the score is impressively projected. Ravel's opera has been called unexportable by some. Don't believe it. It is one of the finest works in his catalogue and you needn't know a word of French to enjoy and appreciate it.

Daphnis et Chloé (1911)

☐ New York Philharmonic / Camerata Singers / Boulez (conductor) / Columbia M-33523

Within the truly architectural grandeur of this score, with its uncanny sense of prolonged, unceasing line, there are multitudinous minute details (so many as almost to relate the music to more contemporary compositional practices). It is exactly in recognizing this situation that finds Boulez the supreme master of Ravel's score. Without overlooking the lyrical tenderness and eroticism that permeates Ravel's music, every structural point is probed and exposed. It produces a balance of expressiveness with technical rationalism. Certainly Boulez's edition represents proof of peak artistic intelligence.

Ma Mère l'Oye (1912)

☐ New York Philharmonic / Boulez (conductor) / Columbia M-32838

The complete ballet, which gives an even greater perspective and is truly even more valid than the usually heard orchestral suite (see under *Orchestra*). There are eleven sections in the ballet, with seven major divisions and four interludes (the latter as beautiful in their imagery as the former), as compared to five movements in the concert suite (see also under *Instrumental: piano, four hands*).

Boulez's conception casts aside the argument that he is cold, precise, and unfeeling save for structural and technical precision. His "Mother Goose" doesn't boil (it shouldn't) but it lives in a very warm clime, stressing within its plastic structure the coloristic positions that pertain to the ballet's general scheme. It is ordered and lucid while it is gorgeous in its poise. Great Ravel playing (and conducting).

Ravel / **Roger Brange (20th cent.)**

Orchestra   ***Five O'Clock Fox Trot***

☐ London Philharmonic Orchestra / Herrmann (conductor) / London 21062

A section from Ravel's *L'Enfant et les sortilèges* (see under *Opera and Dramatic Music*) arranged, with his permission, in light jazz dress.

Ravel / ***Claude Debussy.*** See Debussy / Ravel.

Ravel / ***Modest Mussorgsky.*** See Mussorgsky / Ravel.

Alan Rawsthorne   **(1905-1971)**

Orchestra   **Symphony No. 3 (1964)**

☐ BBC Symphony Orchestra / Del Mar (conductor) / Argo ZRG–553

In the "trade" Rawsthorne is tabbed as a conservative composer. If conservative means the use of pantonality sometimes illuminated by bitonality, then the label fits. But then Roussel and Hindemith have been tagged as conservatives as well, and Honegger, and dozens of others. Truly, the identification does this excellent creative person a disservice, simply because these days it connotes academicism, reactionaryism, and the dry rot of scholasticism, not even a smidgen of which applies to Rawsthorne.

Indeed, a look at Rawsthorne's four-movement listing: Allegro, *Sarabanda,* Scherzo, and *Allegro risoluto* does seem to bear out conventional application. But not one of these movements sits squarely in an orthodox orbit. There is a full-scale development of two themes in the first movement; the second subject bypassing traditional songlike gentility in favor of vehemence. The *Sarabanda* is intense, its progress a far cry from dance gestures. Nightmarish qualities are found in the Scherzo, a music Rawsthorne describes as containing "hints" rather "than statements." The orchestral coloring of these inner movements is as original as the material to which it is applied. In the finale, there is not simply fast music to seal the work, but an interchange of tempo and mood that once again exemplifies Rawsthorne's refreshing originality without use of graph notation, tone rows, and avant-garde wrappings.

The performance is certainly a splendid one, dynamically toned, and projected with virtuosity.

Quartet for Clarinet, Violin, Viola, and Cello (1948) (Movement two)

*Chamber
Music*

☐ London String Trio / Brymer (clarinet) / RCA LM–6092 (monaural)

A means of identification is to term Rawsthorne's music that of an Englishman's Roussel. To many this will define a high compliment, which is what is meant here. Instrumentally, in this second part of the work's three movements, the scoring is predicated on a duo-dimensional plan: clarinet versus the string trio.

String Quartet

No. 1 (1939) / No. 2 (1954) / No. 3 (1965)

☐ Alberni String Quartet / Argo ZRG–5489

Rawsthorne's quartets prove that plenty of strength still lies in tonality. Of course this does not mean prissy harmony or the promulgation of academic law and order. Tonal ambiguity, assorted mixed chordal combos, smart, but always logical, dissonances, and at times a flirtation with atonality mark these strong string quartets. Select contrapuntalism is a further asset, assisting in the retention of tonal polarities while kicking free of it in other instances. Everything has a total commitment to linear and vertical refinement—Rawsthorne reminds one of a friendlier Honegger, or a creative cousin of Frank Martin.

Quartet number 1 is totally in the theme with variations format, a design also found in the finale of the second work which covers a span of four movements. The third quartet has a unified, four-section structure. The novelty is the lack of novelty—replaced by contemporary traditionalism conceived with distinguished and outstanding craftsmanship. Rawsthorne's music, it remains to say, is thus far not exportable, but the feeling remains that this is due completely to a lack of promotion which is as necessary for music as it is for merchandise.

The performances are fine and sensitive. Especially appealing is the Alberni's tonal warmth and their avoidance of percussive attacks.

Quintet for Wind and Piano (1963)

☐ Music Group of London / Argo ZRG–536

Serialism, but not slave to abstract technicalities. In the fast-tempoed sections the style is taut, precise, and athletic. In the slow-paced sections a deep expressionistic emotion is displayed.

Profile and impact are clearly pictured in this superb performance (the musicians: Sutcliffe, oboe; Walton, clarinet; Birnstingl, bassoon; Parkhouse, piano; and the marvelous Alan Civil playing the horn). Golden sound. And blazing technique (most illustrative in the eagle-winged, mercurial-darting Scherzo).

Enrique Raxach (1932-)

String Quartet No. 2 with Electronic Equipment (1971)

*Chamber
Music*

☐ Gaudeamus String Quartet / Philips 6500881

In one movement, the tempo strangulated, the sounds of the four-stringed instruments transformed and transfused by the use of modulators, sine wave generator, reverberation, et cetera, operated by the quartet personnel themselves. The instruments become coarse and surrealistically flexed in sound, and their sounds are totally foreign to normal timbres. There is a sense of high artistic sonic cannibalism in this individual work, an obscene quality pervades the music as though endeavoring to describe an outer space Black Mass.

György Rayki   *(1921-   )*

Orchestra   **Elegiac Variations (1964)**

Lamentation for Orchestra

☐ Louisville Orchestra / Mester (conductor) / Louisville LS–715

Clear demarcation of the variations, the thematic basis taken from a Hungarian folk song collected by Kodály during his researches. The shapes of the nine variations plus coda are precise, the generative item woven in with finesse. Rayki's harmonic language falls into the aggressive category. But it fits, even though used with obsessional insistence.

A two-line García Lorca quotation triggers the Lamentation. Here again Bartókian nationalism is the cover. The sentiments are open, clearly defined. One cannot say the same for the sound quality of this disc. Such less-than-first-class engineering is rare in the Louisville catalogue.

Gardner Read   *(1913-   )*

Orchestra   ***Night Flight*, Op. 44**

☐ Louisville Orchestra / Whitney (conductor) / Louisville 632 (monaural)

Read explains that the title and "inspiration" for his orchestral piece is derived from the Antoine de Saint-Exupéry novel. What evolves is a semiprogrammatic piece that enjoys Read's superb orchestrational knowledge. Thus "the loneliness and mysterious beauty" of night flying is represented by a smeared-besmeared badge of black coloration, with lighter specks that move into the nontranslucency. There is a chill to the music that is cogently organized, pulsated by inserts of a reiterated pitch simulating a radio beam signal.

The playing is fully affirmative. All the instrumental material is presented with the full color, dynamics, and balances the composer requires.

Max Reger   *(1873-1916)*

Orchestra   **A Comedy Overture, Op. 120**

☐ Louisville Orchestra / Mester (conductor) / Louisville 734

An ear-opener for those who consider Max Reger's music as contrapuntally crabbed, hideously heavy, and representative of protracted pretense. The D major Overture is delightfully gay, moves swiftly, and proves that counterpoint can be used for unprofound gestures.

This is played with the utmost lucidity and with close-up style. Mester's musicians have never done better.

Suite for Solo Cello

In G major, Op. 131c, No. 1 / In D minor, Op. 131c, No. 2 / In A minor, Op. 131c, No. 3

☐ Racz (cello) / Musical Heritage Society MHS–1465

Fine formal variety that stimulates the concentrated coloration. Though each Suite begins with a *Präludium,* in each case the tempo is different. Within the ten total movements Reger has also utilized Gavotte, Fugue, Gigue, Scherzo, and variational designs.

Sober but clear playing that can be termed authoritative. Accurate articulation and fine tone are other pluses that mark Zoltan Racz's performances.

Suite in D minor for Solo Cello, Op. 131c, No. 2

☐ King (cello) / Orion 7287

A fine appraisal of Reger's difficult score. King is especially excellent in the dynamic differences applied to pizzicato in the second movement.

Benedictus, Op. 59, No. 9

☐ Noehren (organ) / Lyrichord 7121

Fine performance with a subdued registration that is most effective. Not a word about the work on the liner copy. Reger's *Benedictus* is in D flat major, and is the ninth of his *Twelve Pieces,* Op. 59.

Canzone in E flat major, Op. 65, No. 9

☐ Jacob (organ) / Musical Heritage Society MHS–1563/66

An example of somewhat small-framed Reger. This is the ninth in a set of *Twelve Pieces.*

Chorale Preludes, Op. 67 (Excerpts)

☐ Lohmann (organ) / Musical Heritage Society MHS–1932/33/34

There are fifty-two in the set which bears the title *52 Easy Preludes for the Organ on the Commonest Evangelical Chorales.* (For some reason Musical Heritage heads the collection as *Chorale Arrangements* which is not exactly the case. For that matter one disagrees with Reger that the Preludes are ''easy.'' Properly they are in the ''moderate advanced'' level.)

The Lohmann performance covers twenty numbers: 1, 3, 5, 7; 12, 15, 19; 20, 21, 23; 32, 33, 35, 36, 37, 39; 45, 49; 50 and 52. Some are more familiar than others. (No. 21: *Jesu, Meine Freude* and No. 39: *Vater Unser in Himmelreich,* for example) but nonfamiliarity will not detract from enjoying the consummate effect of these linear structures. Lohmann plays the set, taking care to individualize each one of the Preludes.

Chorale Preludes, Op. 79b (Excerpts)

☐ Jacob (organ) / Musical Heritage Society MHS–1563/66

Werner Jacob performs numbers 4, 5, and 6 from the *Thirteen Chorale Preludes,* issued in two volumes. The coloring and style matches the constrained expressive range of the material.

Fantasia and Fugue in C minor, Op. 29

☐ Jacob (organ) / Musical Heritage Society MHS–1567/70

Reger described his opus as "in the grand manner." Fittingly, it was dedicated to Richard Strauss. Werner Jacob's playing fits the descriptive fact.

Fantasia and Fugue

In D minor, Op. 135b / On B-A-C-H, Op. 46

☐ Jacob (organ) / Musical Heritage Society MHS–1563/66

The D minor opus was composed the year that Reger died. Within it, it is apparent that he was flirting with atonality, but with Reger's involved chromaticism such a move would have not caused a surprise.

These are intelligently planned performances, with textures following the texts, and with dynamic levels succinctly applied to frame details properly. So much organ playing is akin to psuedo-vitality—with Jacob the strengths are distinctive and meaningful.

Fantasia on *Alle Menschen Müssen Sterben*, Op. 52, No. 1

☐ Jacob (organ) / Musical Heritage Society MHS–1567/70

One of three Chorale Fantasias. It has been described as a miniature symphonic poem for the organ. Jacob plays the music for all it's worth.

Fantasia on *Ein' Feste Burg ist Unser Gott*, Op. 27

☐ Jacob (organ) / Musical Heritage Society MHS–1563/66

Sumptuous polyphonic textures and solid ones. The linear pointing and the weave of the voices are superbly handled. One of the greatest of Reger's organ pieces and brilliantly presented by this organist.

Fantasia

On *Freu' Dich Sehr, O Meiner Seele!*, Op. 30 / On *Halleluja, Gott zu Loben, Bleibe Meine Seelenfreud*, Op. 52, No. 3

☐ Jacob (organ) / Musical Heritage Society MHS–1567/70

The second is one of three Chorale Fantasias. It is climaxed by a dynamic Fugue. Opus 30 features variations on the choral tune spliced by short Intermezzi. Intelligent playing.

Fantasia

On *Straf' Mich Nicht in Deinem Zorn*, Op. 40, No. 2 / On *Wachet Auf, Ruft Uns die Stimme*, Op. 52, No. 2 / On *Wie Schön Leucht't Uns der Morgenstern*, Op. 40, No. 1

☐ Jacob (organ) / Musical Heritage Society MHS–1563/66

Straf' Mich Nicht is constructed in the form of a continuous set of variations, preceded by a prefatory section. It is a companion piece to the third title listed above, similarly structured. Werner Jacob's performance is stunning and stirring and is to be preferred to Simon Preston's playing of the Opus 40, Number 2, Fantasia, on Argo ZRG–5420.

The *Wachet Auf* fantasia is the second of a set of three. One writer has aptly described it as containing "some of Reger's gravest, most profound, and sheerly moving music."

Five Easy Preludes and Fugues, Op. 56

☐ Lohmann (organ) / Musical Heritage Society MHS–3144/45/46/47

"Easy" is a relative term and in no sense are these pieces (each in a different tonality) for the tyro, but require the learned organist as exemplified by Heinz Lohmann. He offers sensitive and scholarly interpretations of this lesser important Reger music.

Four Chorale Preludes

☐ Lohmann (organ) / Musical Heritage Society MHS–1932/33/34

A little heavy in regard to the inside voices but this is vital music with good character. The playing by Lohmann is rather straightforward.

Gloria in Excelsis, Op. 59, No. 8

☐ Jacob (organ) / Musical Heritage Society MHS–1563/66

One of the dozen pieces in the Opus 59 set. Lush music (played without fancy registration, however) and including the usual fugal attention—in fact, a pair of brief fugues.

Introduction and Passacaglia in D minor
Introduction, Passacaglia and Fugue in E minor, Op. 127

☐ Jacob (organ) / Musical Heritage Society MHS–1567/70

Large-scale works, Opus 127 including a cadenza as well. In the D minor work dynamic strength builds with formal growth, ranging from soft dispersion to a huge climax; the introduction then binds and balances the work as the coda.

Muddy organ work is quite common; with Reger it means a catastrophe. Jacob's playing provides clear and tight voicing and everything is natural and without artificial effect. A three-star production.

Kyrie Eleison, Op. 59, No. 7

☐ Jacob (organ) / Musical Heritage Society MHS–1563/66

Reger's E minor *Kyrie Eleison* is a quiet, meditative item, included in the *Twelve Pieces* comprising his Opus 59. The main title, according to Musical Heritage, is "Organ Mass," but Reger did not give that name to the opus, or to the three devoutly titled pieces recorded from the set on this MHS disc—the others being *Gloria in Excelsis* and *Benedictus.* (For both of these, *see above.*)

Melodia, Op. 129, No. 4

☐ Noehren (organ) / Lyrichord 7121

Lyrichord identifies this as Reger's Opus 29, which is his Fantasia and Fugue in C minor. The *Melodia* is a bittersweet conception and is part four of Reger's *Nine Pieces for Organ* (for the entire opus, *see below*). No criticism applies to the playing.

Nine Pieces for Organ, Op. 129   *Präludium* in C minor
Postludium in D minor   *Romanze* in A minor
Präludium and Fugue in D minor

☐ Lohmann (organ) / Musical Heritage Society MHS–3144/45/46/47

Royal purple sounds in the "Preludes" and "Postlude" with plenty of vivid polyphony, save for the *Romanze.* Lohmann's radiant registration beautifully displays this fine set of pieces. The same applies to his playing of the nine-ply assortment in Opus 129, which includes a fine Toccata and then an excellent Fugue (another one concludes the work).

Seven Organ Pieces, Op. 145

☐ Lohmann (organ) / Musical Heritage Society MHS–1932/33/34

The titles of the pieces show the aesthetic dogma quite clearly: *Trauerode, Dankpsalm, Weihnachten, Passion, Ostern, Pfingsten,* and *Siegesfeier.* In each case of these sizable pieces (the total set covers a performance time of forty-seven minutes), Chorales or melodies are woven into the fabric. Further, in *Weihnachten* fringe support is obtained by using *Stille Nacht,* and in *Siegesfeier* canonic development of *Deutschland, Deutschland, über Alles* adds special color to the design.

Music of this range must be played—demands, actually—positive romantic freedom else it is checked by stiff progress. Further, it must have a spontaneity of pulse. Heinz Lohmann, playing the Schuke Organ of the *Kirche zum Heilsbronnen,* Berlin, fully and artistically meets these requirements.

Six Trios, Op. 47

☐ Lohmann (organ) / Musical Heritage Society MHS–3144/45/46/47

Not limited to three voices, but based on the emphasis of the voicing applied to the two organ manuals and the pedals. As in all of Reger's music, there is polyphonic emphasis, here in the corner movements which are a Canon and a Fugue. The playing is a bit straightforward but thoroughly appropriate to the contents.

Sonata

No. 1 in F sharp minor, Op. 33 / No. 2 in D minor, Op. 60

☐ Jacob (organ) / Musical Heritage Society MHS–1567/70

Classically entrenched creatively, though his vertical and horizontal pitch arrangements were reaching into what would be termed postromantic style, Reger's Sonatas deviate from the usual format of the design. In fact, the first Sonata does not utilize Sonata form. Reger indicated that Sonata was simply "a collective title," which embraces a *Phantasia,* an Intermezzo, and a Passacaglia. Closer structural procedures apply to the Opus 60 representative but still the forms are freer and the focus is toward the arrangement of a large suite with an Improvisation, an Invocation, and (no surprise) an Introduction and Fugue.

Serious music writing in all aspects but no ascetic asperities. A lot of full-blooded communication in this music, and Jacob conveys it in his playing. Good dimensions are achieved.

Suite in E minor, Op. 16

☐ Lohmann (organ) / Musical Heritage Society MHS–3144/45/46/47

No light moments, even in the Intermezzo. Substantial significances in a Fugue, responsive developmental data pertaining to several Chorales, and a concluding Passacaglia. Lohmann achieves an intelligent balance despite his neutral registration which is planned so as not to disturb the polyphonic flow.

Symphonic Fantasia and Fugue, Op. 57

☐ Jacob (organ) / Musical Heritage Society MHS-1563/66

A gigantic Fantasy inspired by Dante's *Divine Comedy,* thus known as the *Inferno Phantasie.* Fire and richness in Werner Jacob's playing. If a bit enervating, it is due to Reger's passions, not the performer's.

Thirteen Chorale Preludes, Op. 79b

☐ Lohmann (organ) / Musical Heritage Society MHS-1932/33/34

Published in two volumes, six Preludes in the first and seven in the second one. Reger considered some of them as "symphonic poems in miniature." Whatever the description, the predominant polyphonic weave demands a floating vocal quality amply paralleled in Lohmann's performances.

Three Organ Pieces, Op. 7

☐ Lohmann (organ) / Musical Heritage Society MHS-3144/45/46/47

Reger's initial compositions for organ. The *Drei Orgelstücke:* a *Präludium* and Fugue in C major, a *Fantasie* on the Intonation *Te Deum Laudamus,* and a Fugue in D minor are Bach revisited. Intelligently performed with suitable registration, especially the first of the three pieces.

Toccata and Fugue in A minor, Op. 80b

☐ Noehren (organ) / Lyrichord 7121

These are the eleventh and twelfth pieces in Reger's Twelve Pieces, Opus 80b, though Lyrichord does not so identify them. For that matter the "b" is eliminated in their opus identification and so are any notes whatsoever on the work.

Regulated Reger playing minimizes his musical credibility. Such procedure fails to mold and color the harmonic and contrapuntal data and has often defeated this composer. Robert Noehren understands the premise and his offering is a substantially effective one.

Toccata and Fugue, Op. 59, Nos. 5 and 6

☐ Preston (organ) / Argo ZRG-5420

A pair from Reger's Twelve Pieces, Op. 59. Preston's conception is boldly colored and his approach is one of authority. The splendid organ of Westminster Abbey helps the dynamism.

Twelve Monologues, Op. 63 (Excerpts)

Two Chorale Preludes

☐ Lohmann (organ) / Musical Heritage Society MHS-3144/45/46/47

The second of the Chorale Preludes is the familiar *Komm, süsser Tod.* It is preceded by *O Traurigkeit, O Herzeleid.* Opus 63 is represented by numbers eight, seven, and three (played in that order). The playing is undeniably well defined.

Variations and Fugue on an Original Theme, Op. 73

☐ Noehren (organ) / Lyrichord 7121

Though an Introduction precedes the twelve variations, it was not specifically identified in Reger's title for his music. However, Noehren's recorded edition lists the piece as *Introduction, Variations and Fugue*. The variational scheme (expertly detailed in Robert Noehren's rendition) clings close to the basic theme at first and then develops variations from the preceding ones.

Noehren's playing cannot be faulted. There is a brilliance and a clarity to the articulations, and all of the registrations are vivid and conclusive.

Variations and Fugue on *Heil, Unserm König Heil*

☐ Lohmann (organ) / Musical Heritage Society MHS-3144/45/46/47

Not the most inspired of Reger's organ works; the counterpoint moves correctly and never audaciously. The score has fine contrasts, handled particularly well by Lohmann.

Piano

Aus Meinem Tagebuch, Op. 82

☐ Laugs (piano) / Musical Heritage Society MHS-1620/21/22

Reger's "From My Dairy" consists of thirty-five small pieces issued in four books, with totals of 12, 10, 6, and 7 pieces respectively. The great majority are only identified with a tempo heading; thirteen of the total have simple titles such as *Lied, Albumblatt,* Gavotte, *Silhouette,* et cetera. Oddly (for Reger), there is only one fugue in the lot, since homophonic style predominates in these small-formed, nicely scaled pieces.

Richard Laugs displays fine musicianship in his playing, especially in regard to dynamic command and the handling of sonorities. Musical Heritage offers some 175 lines of program notes by Mark Gantt that turn out to be a general essay on Reger, nineteenth-century piano music, and a detailing of Reger's piano music, with a few remarks about some of the works. However, for *Aus Meinem Tagebuch,* all that is indicated is that the work was "composed between 1904 and 1912." Certainly that's ridiculous short shrift for a release of a composition that requires six record sides.

The Blue Danube (Improvisations for Piano on the Strauss Waltz)
Caprice fantastique in F sharp minor
Etude brillante in C minor

☐ Hans-Dieter Bauer (piano) / Musical Heritage Society MHS-1920

Here, the greatest interest, naturally, focuses on the Improvisations—almost eleven minutes worth. This special genre finds Reger not over ambitious in textural tactics, and the rendering of events has Mendelssohnian sparkle. A fascinating work, indeed. One wonders why the piece never turns up on concert programs. The same question can be asked in regard to the bravura aspects of the *Etude brillante*. Less dynamic is the *Caprice* which is a conception of improvisational privacy.

Bauer portrays this music with imaginative strength and beautiful sense of style.

Four Special Studies for the Piano, Left Hand Alone (Numbers 3 and 4)

☐ Wittgenstein (piano) / Orion 7028E (monaural)

A *Romanze* and a Prelude and Fugue. Trust Max Reger not to be handicapped by the limitations of writing polyphonically for only one hand; the Fugue is most impressive and rich in content.

Wittgenstein's performance is of fine continuity. The music has been recorded very close up, and tone control adjustment will be needed.

(For those who wish the entire work [No. 1 is a Scherzo and No. 2 is a Humoresque] an adequate performance is available on Musical Heritage Society MHS-1920. The pianist is Hans-Dieter Bauer.)

Improvisation in E minor

Perpetuum Mobile **in C major**

Perpetuum Mobile **in C sharp minor**

Scherzo in F sharp minor

☐ Hans-Dieter Bauer (piano) / Musical Heritage Society MHS-1920

These are examples of Max Reger in a much less serious style than usual, but just as creatively significant as he is in his large-scale compositions. The pithy ideas in the *Perpetuum Mobile* pieces are fully explored. Significantly, there is more Scherzo feeling in the Improvisation than there is in the F sharp minor Scherzo, which has much more stateliness than it has lightness and wit.

The playing fulfills all requirements. Musical Heritage's edition does not. Information is haphazard and the sources of the pieces, dates, and the like are not given. Apparently the Improvisation is from a set of eight included in Opus 18.

Variations and Fugue on a Theme by Telemann, Op. 134

☐ Steurer (piano) / Musical Heritage Society MHS-1268

Variational perceptiveness, some wit, and certainly splendid originality in this music compounded of one less than two dozen variations plus a fine Fugue.

With music of such size no denial is made of the problem of getting at and holding an audience. So cuts are made. Still, if the matter is given thorough thought (is it?), there is no artistically moral justification to snip large paragraphs from a variationally plotted essay. But those pianists that have recorded Reger's opus do snip variations. Hugo Steurer omits only a few while Evelinde Trenkner (on Orion 77278) deletes more than twice as many. Aside from choosing a presentation with fewer cuts, Steurer simply plays better, colors better, and varies the variations better.

Cinq Pièces Pittoresques, **Op. 34**

Six Pieces, Op. 94

Six Waltzes, Op. 22

☐ Gunderson and Smith (piano) / Orion 73130

Piano, Four Hands

Those who still believe that Reger's music is colored in variegated hues of gray and with big and heavy textural slabs should give some attention to these three sets of piano duets. The *Cinq Pièces* (Reger actually used the French title) are quietly colorful, minus titles, while the other sets have Brahmsian qualities. In no instance is Reger ponderous or the polyphonic Almighty so many critics make him out to be.

Hearing this music in concert just never occurs so the recording is most welcome. Sharon Gunderson and Jo Ann Smith are to be thanked for making the music available and for providing fine musical communication.

Introduction, Passacaglia, and Fugue in B minor, Op. 96

Variations and Fugue on a Theme by Beethoven, Op. 86

Two Pianos

☐ Alfons and Aloys Kontarsky (pianos) / Musical Heritage Society MHS-1292

These two pieces are Reger's complete output for two pianos—the third work (the

Mozart variations) is for two pianos, but, no matter its marvelous instrumental conception, it constitutes a transcription since it was originally for orchestra (*see below*).

Expectedly, the compositions are of substantial size (the Opus 86 runs close to a half hour, while Opus 96 is just short of twenty-five minutes' length). Expectedly, polyphonic documentation, immediately apparent from the titles. The Passacaglia has twenty-eight sections and chromatic complexities (the theme is one shy of being of twelve-tone embracement). The Variations in the other work are an even dozen in total. Aside from these statistics is the warm thrust as well as serious narrative that Reger presents.

The music that emerges from these performances is sharply etched, successfully documented. The Kontarskys translate their scholarly understanding of Reger's creations into significant results. The playing is of high competence without any posturing, is stated with authoritative ensemble, and has a strength of purpose that matches the grandeur of Reger's designs.

Variations and Fugue on a Theme by Mozart, Op. 132a

☐ Alfons and Aloys Kontarsky (pianos) / Musical Heritage Society MHS-1268

One of Reger's most important orchestral works which he transcribed both for two pianos and one piano four-hands. In the absence of the original setting in the domestic catalogue (Telefunken released it abroad with two other Reger works on DX-635053), it is good news to have at least this version available. It sounds in its medium as though totally conceived for it.

Reger's large work, almost twenty-five minutes in length, is, in this writer's opinion, a masterpiece. The performance is a perfectly calculated one and leaves little to be desired. The Kontarskys are a fine team even though they level out the sonorities somewhat. However, forget this quibble. Reger's acute polyphony and fascinating harmonic twists provide sufficient prepotent impresses without one being concerned that there is a slight insufficiency of dynamic differences.

Viola

Suite No. 1 in G minor, Op. 131d

☐ Trampler (viola) / RCA LSC-2974

A composer faces huge problems in writing for an unaccompanied string instrument. The simulation of harmony on a basic homophonic instrument (notwithstanding certain polyphony available but limited by hand position), the restriction of color, the almost total lack of textural interplay—all total a creative situation that has met with few successes. Bach is the prime example of such achievement. Max Reger is a close second.

For too long a time critics have tumbled Reger's music into a box seemingly marked "open at your risk." The two suites (*see below* for Suite No. 3 in E minor, Op. 131d) performed by Trampler with magnificent control and color illustrate how critical disesteem has prejudiced listeners untruthfully and unfairly. Both works are concerned with the absolutes of classical logic, minus any of the romantic semifussiness that belabors clarity.

Indeed, this music is not the dull, academic kind we have read so much about. I have always argued that what Reger has needed is not so much the understanding of auditors as the comprehension of performers. When one hears a performance such as Trampler's, played with affection, one's ears open.

Suite No. 2 in D major, Op. 131d

☐ Wallfisch (viola) / Musical Heritage Society MHS-1389

Four movements similar to the other two suites in the opus (*see above* and *below*) but differently arranged to obtain contrastive tempi. In this instance, lively music covers the opening movement, followed by slow and Scherzo divisions, and a Vivace finale. Since the first and third suites opened with sustained lyricism, Reger then placed the Scherzo in second place and the slow movement in the third slot.

Wallfisch's playing has expressive power, and his conception defines the structural strength of Reger's solo viola work.

Suite No. 3 in E minor, Op. 131d

☐ Trampler (viola) / RCA LSC–2974

For a discussion of this work *see above:* Suite No. 1 in G minor, Op. 131d.

Like the performance of that work, this one is also truly superb. One could hardly hope for better performances of these two suites than Walter Trampler has made available. They should happily satisfy us through the next fifty years.

Prelude and Fugue for Violin

Violin

In B minor, Op. 117, No. 1 / In G minor, Op. 117, No. 2 / In C minor, Op. 117, No. 3 / In G minor, Op. 117, No. 4 / In G major, Op. 117, No. 5

☐ Naegele (violin) / Musical Heritage Society MHS–1805

The last pair of this set (five here recorded of the total eight in the opus) is somewhat different from the others as well as from the half dozen Preludes and Fugues, in the Op. 131a group (*see below*). (Although Reger's title heading for the *complete* Opus 117 is Preludes and Fugues, number 4 of the set abandons the prelude and fugue contrastive formal scheme and is a Chaconne in G minor. However, no change has been made in the listings above in order to follow Reger's specification, even though it is incorrect and confusing.) Number 5 comprises an arrangement of J. S. Bach's G major *Fantasie* for organ, which serves as the Prelude, and a Fugue that is totally Reger's save for the G major subject, which is also borrowed from Bach.

The only question with Philip Naegele's performance is the somewhat slow pace of the Fugues. Technical perfection is absolute but the stolidity makes the sounds emerge somewhat mechanically.

Prelude and Fugue for Violin

In A minor, Op. 131a, No. 1 / In D minor, Op. 131a, No. 2 / In G major, Op. 131a, No. 3 / In G minor, Op. 131a, No. 4 / In D major, Op. 131a, No. 5 / In E minor, Op. 131a, No. 6

☐ Karolyi (violin) / Musical Heritage Society MHS–1698

The greater strengths of this series of unaccompanied violin works are to be found in the quasi-improvisationally styled Preludes. The Fugues are a bit restrained, though here again one must marvel at overcoming the instrumental restrictions and yet fulfilling the linear design.

Sandor Karolyi's playing is glorious. His sensitivity to seamless phrasing is absolute perfection. Not a whisper of criticism can be applied to this recorded issue.

Sonata for Solo Violin

In D minor, Op. 42, No. 1 / In A major, Op. 42, No. 2 / In B minor, Op. 42, No. 3 / In G minor, Op. 42, No. 4

☐ Weiner (violin) / Musical Heritage Society MHS–1719

There is a strong personality to Reger's music in these imposing Sonatas. The breadth of each conception is astonishing, bearing in mind the confines of violin homophony and the instrument's restricted harmonic possibilities. Reger's narratives include Fugues (of course), a Chaconne, and some classy capricious inventions but which always stay in style and pertinent shape.

Stanley Weiner (once the concertmeister of the Indianapolis Symphony Orchestra) plays meticulously and musically. He wisely sifts all the inner currents in these Reger works and is master of the technicalia involved. An invaluable addition to the recorded library of unaccompanied violin music.

Sonata for Solo Violin

In A minor, Op. 91, No. 1 / In D major, Op. 91, No. 2 / In B flat major, Op. 91, No. 3 / In B minor, Op. 91, No. 4

☐ Naegele (violin) / Musical Heritage Society MHS-1697

While unfortunate, it is a confirmed fact that Reger's unaccompanied violin Sonatas have never firmly established themselves in the concert world. Having them on disc (the other three in the opus are noted *below*) is of great value, helping to reveal some first-class music. The Sonatas are, expectedly, plotted on the famous models by Bach, with one exception—the Fugues are always two-voiced rather than the simulated three- and four-part Fugues that Bach invented.

Philip Naegele's playing never deviates from a high standard and nothing more than he accomplishes could be desired.

Sonata for Solo Violin

In E minor, Op. 91, No. 5 / In G major, Op. 91, No. 6 / In A minor, Op. 91, No. 7

☐ Naegele (violin) / Musical Heritage Society MHS-1741

For a discussion covering these Sonatas *see above:* Sonata for Solo Violin in A minor, Op. 91, No. 1.

Chamber Music

Allegro in A major for Two Violins, Op. Posth.

Canon and Fugue in the Old Style for Two Violins

In E minor, Op. 131b, No. 1 / In D minor, Op. 131b, No. 2 / In A major, Op. 131b, No. 3

☐ Lautenbacher and Egger (violins) / Vox SVBX-586

The ability to spin a complete musical plot with an unaccompanied violin duet requires a sure hand; the limitations are severe. Not only does Reger's technical individuality shine forth, his clever and fully possessed abilities, which seem equal to solving any problem, are clearly apparent.

These works are a mirroring of Bach—immediately recognizable as restorations of that composer, but the lines are chromaticized much more. It is a "sharped" and "flatted" extension of the Bachian habit. A violin duet is a finesse of intimate music; if one observes the ripe craftsmanship, it will make for more enjoyment. These pieces are not dry-as-dust at all, especially in these gorgeously sonorized depictions.

Kleine Sonate No. 1 in D minor for Violin and Piano, Op. 103b

☐ Weiner (violin); De Moulin (piano) / Musical Heritage Society MHS-1500

Defined as a "Little Sonata," which is a fancier way than designating the piece as a Sonatina. The smaller frame is apparent not only in length but in intensity. Accordingly, the designs cover simple Sonata form, a Scherzo, and a set of eight variations. Reger sings very sweetly in this fine work and the performers follow suit.

Sonata in A major for Violin and Piano, Op. 41

☐ Müller-Nishio (violin); Dennemarck (piano) / Musical Heritage Society MHS–1793

Reger was still under the influence of Brahms when he wrote this work, the third of his violin and piano Sonatas. (But the shape of the head of the theme in the second movement and its fugal treatment is a flashback to Smetana's *Bartered Bride* overture.)

Romantic outpour throughout the Sonata. It is pictured in a serviceable manner by the performers.

Sonata in C minor for Violin and Piano, Op. 139f

☐ Weiner (violin); De Moulin (piano) / Musical Heritage Society MHS–1500

The slow movement has the tone of late Beethoven, plus moving a little ahead of that aesthetic territory. Stanley Weiner's tone in this part of the work is elegant, fastidious, and properly spacious.

The last movement is a set of free variations, the design being based directly on the expediency of velocity. The travel is from slow to fast, with one slight deviation to greatest rapidity, then a complete recession into the slow tempo again. All the facts are supported by an integrated interpretation. The partnership of these musicians is extremely satisfying.

Sonata in D minor for Violin and Piano, Op. 1

☐ Müller-Nishio (violin); Dennemarck (piano) / Musical Heritage Society MHS–1793

Reger's first published work follows the tyro's path of imitation. The first movement is of Brahmsian worship, in a layout of clearest Sonata form. A simple Scherzo, with the lightest of textures, serves for the second part. The textural thickness of late Reger—a stumbling block for some listeners—is already seen in the slow movement. Least interesting is the finale. Encumbered by a rhythmic constancy, this music would have been improved with contrastive material. Nonetheless, the work deserves praise for its general lucidity and thematic material.

The performance of Reger's Sonata (written when he was seventeen) is of slightly academic quality but it will not disappoint.

Sonata in F sharp minor for Violin and Piano, Op. 84
Suite in A minor, Op. 103a

☐ Weiner (violin); De Moulin (piano) / Musical Heritage Society MHS–1667

Reger thought his Opus 84 a tame work, and in the middle movement he certainly pulled his punches. Still, the general flexibility of the music and its eminent sensibility do not bear out his verdict. Neither does the playing of this duo team.

The miscellany comprising the six-part A minor Suite includes the expected classic formations such as a Gavotte, a *Menuett*, and a Gigue. It is played in a rather unicolored manner.

Sonata for Cello and Piano
No. 1 in F minor, Op. 5 / No. 2 in G minor, Op. 28 / No. 3 in F major, Op. 78 / No. 4 in A minor, Op. 116

☐ Hoelscher (cello); Lautner (piano) / Musical Heritage Society MHS–1360/1361

Opus 5 is full of late romantic feeling and *apassionato* atmosphere. This is even more so in the Opus 28 work. In 1901 Reger wrote that his G minor Sonata demanded "long study if it is to be understood." Eight decades later, of course, its meanings are immediately clear, bypassing ultrachromatic harmonic virtuosity and any abstruse sentiments. The music just rolls off the instruments with engaging contrasts, especially in the middle pair of movements, a *Prestissimo assai* and an Intermezzo.

The texture and plot thicken in the first movement of Opus 78, a music somewhat dynamically sorrowful, restless in its harmonic dress and in its format, which is more a rhapsody than a Sonata. Pedal punctuation is a colorful aid to the Scherzo depiction. Variations and a Giguelike finale parallel the opening part of the work in the sense of freer structural invention and highly chromatic syntax.

Accordingly, it is not surprising to find a full twelve-tone row in the opening cello passage of the fourth Sonata—no relationship to Schoenberg, of course, but initiating the fully chromaticized adventure of Max Reger within the total movement. This part goes through its paces with grim visage. Reger is, in this case, a harsh taskmaster. The Scherzo never stops its triple-beat insistence, contains clever use of empty beats, now on the second, the third, or the first. The silences waylay monotony. The Largo is the Reger of many notes, many sounds, many chromatics. The finale has almost as many but the quicker pace loosens matters and prevents sonorous sticking.

The performances are on the whole good. In the Opus 116 the playing is better than heard on the deleted Columbia disc (MS-6891) in a presentation by Mischa Schneider and Richard Goode. Musical Heritage has also released on MHS-1765 the third and fourth Sonatas played by Gerhard Mantel and Erika Frieser, but their teamwork is not as convincing as that of Hoelscher and Lautner. Reger is often played in the form of Wagnerian expressivity. That does him no good and Hoelscher and Lautner have avoided such interpretative error.

Sonata for Clarinet and Piano

No. 1 in A flat major, Op. 49, No. 1 / No. 2 in F sharp minor, Op. 49, No. 2

☐ Klöcker (clarinet); Genuit (piano) / Musical Heritage Society MHS-1521

The two Sonatas complement each other; the first bright, the other darker. It is not only tonality that decides this; the A flat Sonata is more relaxed in its expressive content. Still, the emotional objective of both is somewhat joined. This is shown by the fact that all nine movements (four in number one, five in the other) sign off quietly. Perhaps coincidence, but more probably a purposeful decision.

Average playing levels by Klöcker and Genuit are indicated here, but quite satisfactory. (MHS incorrectly labels the second Sonata as in "F minor," and lists it similarly. On the other hand, Harry Halbreich's liner notes always mention the correct tonality.)

Sonata No. 3 in B flat major for Clarinet and Piano, Op. 107

☐ Gärtner (clarinet); Laugs (piano) / Musical Heritage Society MHS-1329

Of the three Sonatas Reger composed for this combination, the B flat major is the largest, the best, and the most interesting. Themes of length do not appear, rather sets of short ideas combine in themselves as one large expression. One must come to Reger (in his later works) with different ears—not with preconceived notions of similarity to Brahms or Beethoven.

The second movement combines a Scherzo with an improvisatory slow section. The true slow movement then follows in three-part form, realized notwithstanding the freedom encountered in regard to thematic expression (again particles are used in extension rather than the contrasting of subsidiary themes).

Reger had a passion for concluding his final movements in slow tempo and soft dynamic. His subconscious refusal to end a work in an optimistic manner, especially when the previous data has not been of contrary mood, would be an interesting matter to probe. Here, after a simple (for Reger) dance movement in duadic pulse, the music slows into a gray-colored Adagio, receding from an average *piano* dynamic to tonal extinction.

The performance has re-created Reger's score with commendable accuracy and a fine definition of its structural details. The players can only be challenged in regard to underemphasizing some phrases that offered the opportunity of telling coloristic contrasts.

Serenade

In D major, Op. 77a / In G major, Op. 141a

☐ Wion (flute); Fader (viola); Ritchie (violin) / Lyrichord 7217

Here is music to confound any anti-Regerian. The textural motility of these trios (even in the slow-paced portions) is far from the heavy passions so many think was Reger's only mode of speech. The real matter of equipoise in terms of medium has never been bettered. The music has the absolute of classical logic, romantic syntax, but no fussiness, and a linear clarity that is a constant joy. And plenty of good (sometimes jolly) counterpoint, but never of gummy density.

Beethoven wrote the first important work for the rare combination of flute, violin, and viola. Reger imitates the medium, but not the message. There is far more musical weight to these two pieces than in the early Beethoven example. Nor is the formal sense of the Serenade followed, with the inclusion of several movements. Both Opus 77a and Opus 141a are in three movements: two outer fast-paced affairs and a slower-tempoed inner division to give tidy balance. The color possibilities of the combination are applied deftly, even to the entrancing use of the flute as the bass to the two strings.

Performance? Superb. Ensemble? Perfect to the finite degree. Lyrichord's disc will make believers out of Reger disbelievers.

String Trio

In A minor, Op. 77b / In D minor, Op. 141b

☐ String Trio Bell' Arte / Vox SVBX–586

It would seem apparent that Reger's general textural thickness would turn the thinness of a string trio into, at the very least, the thicker quality of a string quartet. But Reger did not deliberately set out to write basically thick music. What is thick to others is the natural accent of this composer, the expression of his own personality; the medium is not purposefully strengthened or enlarged sonorously. Equipoise is retained in these works for violin, viola, and cello—they *remain* string trios. Only at times are they a little thicker than other examples in the same category, but this is Regerian sonority, not that of a composer who tries to stretch the thin band of three strings into stout rope.

Though dynamic differentiation in the Larghetto of the A minor opus is slightly lacking, in all other instances the playing is consistently revelatory. The three members of the Bell' Arte (Susanne Lautenbacher, violin; Ulrich Koch, viola; and Thomas Blees, cello) are fine soloists in their own right and their teamwork yields Regerian satisfaction.

Trio in B minor for Violin, Viola, and Piano, Op. 2

☐ Naegele (violin); Ernst Wallfisch (viola); Lory Wallfisch (piano) / Musical Heritage Society MHS–1389

Sparked by Beethoven and Brahms language but already showing some Regerian linear evidence. The medium itself is a rare one, but substituting a viola for a cello does make the textural air clearer since the piano has less opposition in its bass zone. There is some loss of total sonic weight but this is offset by the gain in the transparency of the musical fabric.

The playing is very effective, especially in the set of variations that concludes the trio.

Trio in E minor for Piano, Violin, and Cello, Op. 102

☐ Karolyi (violin); Zipperling (cello); Hoppstock (piano) / Musical Heritage Society MHS-1321

Although Reger left several examples in each category of the most usual chamber-music mediums, he wrote only one trio for the most average combination of piano, violin, and cello. This opus is one of his best works, a cause for wonder that its performance is so very rare. It is certainly on a par with the great trio examples by Beethoven, Brahms, Schubert, and Dvořák.

The entire first movement is developed and related from the motivation of snailed intervallic relationships. Themes and episodes are drawn in such fashion, long and short, in various directions. The development is restless from the unquiet of this spherical zigzag. The Scherzo is a gem of finesse, contrasting metrical plans, tonalities, and instrumentation. The broad themes of the Largo movement are developed by the externals of imitation. In the finale, Reger uses an idealized form of the old Provençal dance, the *Tambourin,* with its hammered rhythms enriched by short canonic episodes, as well as rhythmic and other types of imitation.

The performance is, indeed, an ideal one. There is no thickness in Reger's dramatic work, from first movement to last, and the instrumentalists make certain to observe this most important point. Balances are exact and dynamic differences are beautifully realized.

Quartet for Piano, Violin, Viola, and Cello
In A minor, Op. 133 / In D minor, Op. 113

☐ Elysium Quartet / Musical Heritage Society MHS-1938/39/40/41

Free Fantasy in the first movement of the Opus 113 parallels the freedom of key. In comparison, the Scherzo is keybound, securely set in D minor. Integral variated procedures mark the final pair of movements.

In the later work both outer movements are minus the turbulence of chordal shifts surrounding so much of Reger's creations. The *Weltschmerz* harmony is diluted. Movement two (sensitively performed) is exquisite in its use of string-instrument mutes to dull, color, and compress sonority and, therefore, to evoke, conversely, the mood of a doleful waltz. The finale states three themes in direct succession, and proceeds to unfold these with free-fashioned variational treatment in the style of a Rondo.

The recordings are fully adequate representations, all of Reger's reasonings being made clear. There is a touch of tonal astringency, however, on the part of the violinist.

String Quartet
No. 1 in G minor, Op. 54 / No. 2 in A major, Op. 54 / No. 3 in D minor, Op. 74 / No. 4 in E flat major, Op. 109 / No. 5 in F sharp minor, Op. 121

☐ Reger Quartet / Vox SVBX-587

The finale of the first quartet is a superb contrapuntal document, beginning with a Fugue and ending with a double Fugue. The second subject is withheld for some time, and is as flowing as the first is kinetic. When they combine, it is as if both were created simultaneously. The entire Fugue is cured of overchromatic dosage, and is an excellent exposition of Reger's abilities as a composer of this most strict musical form. In the A major opus there is no separate Scherzo, this being compressed inside the six variations on a theme that comprise the second (inner) movement's franchise. The same formal design is found in the Opus 74 quartet. There, Reger's big voice is heard, in sweep and in the total ratiocination of the variational process. Eleven variations make the movement one of the most powerful in any quartet.

A different creative virtuosity is found in the E flat major work, the strongest and most individual of all of Reger's quartets. Its Scherzo is music of new mintage. All of Reger's Scherzi were fine spun, agile pieces, but this one (based on a Tarantella rhythm) is superfine. It is thinned out to the point where, in many places, isolated sounds are the *only* sound. There is no trio to the movement. Brahms is reversed (as in his famous Opus 67 quartet) when the viola is muted against the non-*sordini* of the other three instruments. As a result, the dark instrument produces a blunted trumpet quality against the other ''open'' string colors.

What the Reger foursome can produce in performing music of other composers this writer knoweth not. But they certainly are of top-class quality in the playing of these five quartets. The complicated voicing problems as well as the textural ones are securely balanced. In the Opus 74 the music demands virtuosi being as complex as any romantic work had been or ever would be. Still, there is air and daylight within the music and such clarity is proof of consummate quartet playing. There are many other points that deserve the highest praise for this group, including the manner in which the dramatic peroration of the Opus 109 quartet is handled. (It is unbelievable that all of the major quartet teams of the day, such as the Juilliard, Tokyo, Cleveland, Amadeus, and Guarneri ensembles, have chosen to ignore totally Reger's output for four stringed instruments, let alone record any one work within it.)

Quintet in A major for Clarinet, Two Violins, Viola, and Cello, Op. 146

☐ Drolc Quartet / Leister (clarinet) / Deutsche Grammophon 2530303

A beautiful serenity, with plastic voicing but always with the most defined clarity, marks this four-movement work, Reger's last chamber-music composition. The harmonies are subtle, yet fully romantically chosen, the linear life is very healthy, but never results is textural density. The music's credo is expressed by the initial tempo indication: *Moderato ed amabile.* Undeniably, Reger's clarinet quintet is moderately toned and exudes an intimate warmth.

Splendid execution. The mesh of the clarinet with the four stringed instruments is ideal; the material is never overstated. For those who belong in the anti-Reger camp, this performance may serve to change their minds.

Piano Quintet in C minor, Op. 64

☐ Pfeifer Quartet / Schamalfuss (piano) / Musical Heritage Society MHS–1378

The complexities of the opening movement cannot be taken too lightly. The form is related to a Sonata, but Reger superimposes the structure of a complicated orchestration onto the five-instrument frame. Though the score air is suffocated with movement, thickness, and rhythmic profuseness, the playing is remarkably clear and effective. Nonetheless, there are just too many voices in Reger's five-way conversations. His technique is amazing, but one could argue that its use is perverse.

The other movements are better controlled, despite plentiful polyphony and a weighted seriousness that almost overtaxes the material. It is to the credit of the performers that they monitor Reger's music with care and capability.

Piano Quintet in C minor, Op. Posth.

☐ Wührer Quartet / Seibert (piano) / Musical Heritage Society MHS–1938/39/40/41

Written when Reger was just twenty-five and presumably composed as a reaction to the death of Brahms. (Reger had modeled much of his early work on Brahms.) It has one stylistic affinity with that great classic-romantic—the power and breadth of the pianistic writing. Otherwise the chamber medium is replaced by orchestra-like expansiveness.

The playing is of high expertise, with fine, distinctive artistry. It will be fully appreciated by anyone at all sympathetic to Reger's work, early or late.

String Sextet in F major, Op. 118

☐ Wührer String Sextet / Musical Heritage Society MHS–1402

Notwithstanding love of heavy textures, Reger wrote but this single string sextet. Though the instruments are kept employed rather constantly, the music contains sufficient breathing areas. In the opening movement contrapuntalism is held to the minimum. When there is dynamic interplay, it is mostly counterpoint of the spread harmonic variety. The Vivace is a ternary affair, tonally contrasted by D minor and B flat major. It has the steadiness of a peasant dance in the outer sections and of a Bavarian slower-swung *Ländler* in between.

Reger termed his slow movement *Gebet mit dem lieben Gott* ("Prayer with God"). Its rapturous passions are in sharp comparison with the classically designed Sonata finale. There the initial soft dynamic condition is balanced by tremendous impact at the conclusion, marked by more than sixty measures of continuous *forte* through *triple forte*.

The report is that of a passable performance. More can be achieved than this group brings to the music. There is a stiffness about the playing that negates dramatic punctuations by simply playing more heavily, thus stressing what should be subtle. The intonation falters a few times between the violins, and the completion of the work is rather flatfooted. However, M.H.S.'s edition is the only one in the catalogue, and the performance must be accepted, warts and all, if one wishes this fine piece of chamber music.

(Neither key nor opus are indicated. Musical Heritage Society is usually careful about such matters but slipped in this instance.)

Reger / J. S. Bach. See J. S. Bach / Max Reger.

Noel Regney   (20th cent.)

Vocal

Voice and Instrumental Ensemble

Slovenly Peter and His Friends

☐ Stuttgart Kammermusiker / Reardon (baritone) / Reichert (conductor) / Serenus 12050

The verse tales of Heinrich Hoffman (originally *Der Struwwelpeter*) have a Prologue and an Epilogue and four stories within them: *Slovenly Peter, Wicked Frederick, Pauline and the Matches,* and *Caspar No-Soup.* The principal voice is accompanied by a thirteen-instrumental group.

A comic conception has its own criteria and Regney does well in meeting it, mainly by singsong and nonsubtle nibbles from the instruments. Fine performance with John Reardon having himself a ball as the star of the proceedings.

Steve Reich (1936-)

Music for 18 Musicians (1976)

Orchestra

☐ Steve Reich and Musicians / ECM 1-1129

Aural narcosis derived from an undeviating pulse that injects the ear with repetitive metrical shapes and the shifting phase of a similar chordal item. This is produced by a group consisting of a violin, a cello, two clarinets that double on bass clarinet, four female voices, four pianos, three marimbas, two xylophones, and a metallophone (a vibraphone without a motor).

Very easy on the ear. *Aber weich* is Reich. For some the redundancy contained in a work of an hour's length, with the only break being to turn the record over, is satiation supreme. Others will go Reich's long way all the way.

Four Organs, for Four Electric Organs and Maracas (1970)

Instrumental

Four Organs

☐ Thomas, Grierson, Kellaway, and Reich (electric organs); Raney (maracas) / Angel S-36059

To put it simply Four Organs combines the ingredients of sustained similar rhythm with sustained similar harmony. There is no relinquishment of the idea, save stretching the sound of an individual part of the chord—a reminder of the cliché that the more things change the more they remain the same.

The ritualistic cult of this music is considered by some as part of the lunatic fringe of contemporary music. It isn't. It simply makes no stress other than its own monotonous stress. Reich's private world of locked-in sound does dig itself into the ears and makes certain it does by its length of close to twenty-five minutes. Such a supersimplistic statement of music may be considered boring but it is not the product of a creative screwball.

Come Out (1966)

Electronic Music

☐ Odyssey 32160160

Reich's electronically processed verbal ostinato has ultradramatic effect as its subject "come out to show them" is heard in a variety of ways for a gut-gripping thirteen minutes. The phrase spreads into the two recorded channels, with reverberation and changed time phases added, and is eventually divided into as many as eight parts, finally coagulating itself into nonspeech and nonmeaning—a sound scribble.

A hypnotic work. Reich's *Come Out* is of enormous originality in the electronic idiom.

It's Gonna Rain (1965)

☐ Walter (vocalist) / Columbia MS-7265

Manipulation of a street evangelist's speech, bringing a variety of new words, pulsations, and effects. *Musique Concrète* thus becomes turned into an electronic abstraction.

Violin Phase (1967)

☐ Zukofsky (violin) / Columbia MS-7265

Reich explains his technique of transformation as a method of "gradually shifting phase relations between two or more identical repeating figures." In a way this is the traditional system contemporized since it is another form of thematic or motivic development. It takes a long time to unfold, however.

Anton Reicha   (1770-1836)

Chamber Music

Quartet in D major, Op. 12

☐ Jean-Pierre Rampal, Larrieu, Marion, and Joseph Rampal (flutes) / Musical Heritage Society MHS-876

Reicha's flute quartet is no light negotiation. Four flutes might bring to mind dancy divertimenti and the like—but not in this case. There is a creative capacity here that is as expressive as any piece of Haydn chamber music. The quartet has four movements, with motival engenderment in the opening one, a fine, slow division, a sparkling Minuet, and a conjunctively released and fully developed finale.

The performance outcome justifies every part of Reicha's inspirational act. Indeed, this is a compositional gem paralleled by a magnificent performance and should not be overlooked. As for performer credits the four names listed may not be totally correct. The Reicha work is included with music for three flutes by Kuhlau and five flutes by Boismortier. M.H.S. does not distinguish who plays what. The first four names listed on the disc are noted above. The fifth flutist involved in the program is Marius Beuf.

Quintet
No. 3 in G major, Op. 88, No. 3 / No. 7 in C major, Op. 91, No. 1

☐ Austrian Wind Quintet / Musical Heritage Society MHS-1054

Reicha composed no fewer than two-dozen quintets for the standard combination of flute, oboe, clarinet, horn, and bassoon (six each in Op. 88, Op. 91, Op. 99, and Op. 100). The two heard here are fine examples of the wind quintets which are, with the six string quintets for two violins, two violas, and cello, considered the best of Reicha's chamber-music output. This report becomes more important when it is realized that Reicha's chamber music production reached the imposing total of 138 published works, embracing 18 different combinations!

Traditional formality applies, with four movements in the fast-slow-Minuetto-fast pattern. The first movement in the G major work is prefaced with a slow-paced section; both finales are Rondo structured. In all, what might be described as politely civilized classical music.

The Austrian five do substantially well with these works, a smudge by the bassoon and one or two by the horn notwithstanding. The numerical designation for the quintets is not indicated in any place of the release.

Quintet No. 22 in E minor, Op. 100, No. 4

☐ Soni Ventorum Wind Quintet / Lyrichord 7216

(For remarks concerning Reicha's wind quintets *see above*.) Again four movements comprise the work, a slightly different basis applying to the slow movement which is set in variation form.

The Soni Ventorum team play this straightforward music sensibly and with fine tone and ensemble. That equals a first-class performance.

Bernard Reichel   *(20th cent.)*

Suite Symphonique   *Orchestra*

☐ Louisville Orchestra / Whitney (conductor) / Louisville 57-5 (monaural)

A merger of neoclassic with neoromantic diction by this Swiss composer. The forms are likewise partnered, with a Sonata design for the opening and a Rondo form for the closing. In between are movements that are of suite formation: a short meditation in which polyphonic treatment between winds and strings takes place and a dance division, *Tempo di Siciliano.*

Paul Reif   *(1910-1978)*

Philidor's Defense—A Musical Chess Game (1965)   *Orchestra*

☐ Orchestra da Camera Romana / Flagello (conductor) / Serenus 12018

Sonic simulation of a famous chess game. Seventeen moves, the "game" divided into three movements (no pun intended), with each chess piece marked by its own motif. Heavy texture with busy chromaticism. Some humor is attempted by a quotation of Rossini's "Barber" at the beginning (the match that inspired Reif took place in 1858 in a box at the Paris Opera during a performance of *The Barber of Seville*). The conclusive checkmate is illustrated by a dissonant chord. Whether Flagello understands chess or not is immaterial. He understands Reif's score and conducts accordingly.

Five Divertimenti for Four Strings (1969)   *Chamber*
                                                               Music
☐ Serenus Quartet / Serenus S-12022

Straight-laced atonality in this case (Reif is creatively versatile and his music is stylistically assorted). Divertimento praxis gives formal flexibility. The Divertimenti are musical shorts. For the most part they are snide and bitter. It is totally serious stuff—program music without a defined program. And all of it detailed with aphoristic acidity.

Monsieur le Pelican for Flute, Oboe, English horn, Two Clarinets, Horn, and Two Bassoons (1960)

☐ New York Wind Ensemble / Reif (conductor) / Serenus S-12022

This octet was written as a tribute to the famous Dr. Albert Schweitzer. Reif's title concerns the good doctor's well-known pet friend and the music describes the pelican "adventuring over the countryside, flying over the rhinos in the river, hopping amongst the elephants, exchanging gossip with the monkeys," etc. One can seek these details in the music, but for the greater part the octet (in eight connected movements) flows like a large-scale pastoral wind symphony. En route, one encounters a fugato, ostinato, and a waltz. The programmaticism is quite subdued—much more implied in the composer's description than in the music itself.

Exceedingly well defined in the recorded performance.

Five Finger Exercises   *Vocal*

☐ Reardon (baritone); Herbert (piano) / Serenus 12019   *Voice with*
                                                               Accompaniment
Great T. S. Eliot texts delivered with every syllable vivid and immaculate by this fine

singer. Reif's music is of discriminating alliance with such subjects as *Lines to Ralph Hodgson, Esqr.*, *Lines to a Persian Cat*, etc.

Four Songs on Words of Kenneth Koch

☐ Reardon (baritone); Herbert (piano) / Serenus S–12022

Reif's romantic style fits these songs dealing with love. With Reardon's admirable diction one doesn't need to follow the texts furnished on Serenus's liner notes.

Vocal

Voice and Instrumental Ensemble

Duo for Three for Soprano, Clarinet, and Cello (1974)

☐ Martin (soprano); Sobol (clarinet); Locker (cello) / Grenadilla GS–1009

"Duo" to identify the clarinet and cello voices, "Three" to specify the use of the soprano as an additional "instrument," when singing vocalise-wise. Otherwise, the numerical paradox is resolved by defined duo dimensions, with the voice as one part and the clarinet-cello as the other.

The four-part text is by Judith Furedi and is interspersed in its soprano voice setting within the work. Its free placement matches the tonal involvements of Reif's style which are drawn from a panchromatic portfolio.

Alexander Reinagle   (1756-1809)

Instrumental

Piano

Sonata No. 1 in D major

☐ List (piano) / Musical Heritage Society MHS–733

Two gay fast movements, little development, but Haydnish charm and commentary are sufficient to involve the listener. Eugene List tosses off the piece, bypassing any undue pomp and circumstance. Great sound.

Sonata No. 3 in C major

☐ Mandel (piano) / Desto 6445/7

As fine a work as any of Haydn's early-period compositions. Three movements played by Mandel with crispness and total tip-top execution.

Carl Reinecke   (1824-1910)

Solo Instrument and Orchestra

Flute

Concerto for Flute and Orchestra, Op. 283

☐ Vienna State Opera Orchestra / Meylan (flute) / Prohaska (conductor) / Vanguard C–10010

Reinecke's three-movement opus is akin to a series of soliloquies, each given in a different tempo. The aesthetic is romantic, but though composed in 1908, the musical spirit is that of Schumann. There is no pyrotechnical belief expressed within the work. It is learned in its nineteenth-century state and comfortably responsive to it. Meylan covers his responsibilities thoroughly.

Concerto in E minor for Harp and Orchestra, Op. 182   *Harp*

☐ Bamberg Symphony Orchestra / Laskine (harp) / Guschlbauer (conductor) / Musical Heritage Society MHS-1033

In Reinecke's harp Concerto there is no retreat from romanticism of the kind that is a strong reminder of Schumannesque style. The four movements (the last two joined) are concerned with melodicism; there is hardly a glance or gesture toward virtuosity. The result is sufficiently entertaining, though the sequential detail makes the music sound longer than its twenty-three minute performance length.

The overall quality of the playing of soloist and orchestra is quite high, the sound of the disc most beautiful.

Concerto for Piano and Orchestra   *Piano*

No. 1 in F sharp minor, Op. 72 / No. 2 in E minor, Op. 120

☐ Monte Carlo National Opera Orchestra / Robbins (piano) / van Remoortel (conductor) / Genesis 1034

A perfect example of the creative imitator—romantic brand. Reinecke gave no consideration to new devices, running along paths previously trodden. His music has the well-ordered, well-sounding neutrality of the competent, if not individual, composer. There is heart in these works, but Reinecke's heart beats in Mendelssohnian time.

There is a competitive version of the first Concerto—a nice situation if somewhat unusual for nonstandard repertoire, since Michael Ponti performs the Opus 72 work on Candide 31078. He plays with greater vigor than Robbins, but the latter is more lyrically disciplined which fits Reinecke's music better.

Toy Symphony (*Kindersymphonie*) in C   *Instrumental*

☐ Lewenthal (piano); Ross and Sosson (violins); Aller (cello); McNab (toy trumpet) / Lewenthal (conductor) / Angel S-36080

Both instrument-wise and formally Reinecke's Toy Symphony differs from the general run of works produced in the medium. Additional to the usual piano, a few strings, nightingale, cuckoo, toy trumpet, and drum, he uses a ratchet, bell tree, glass bell, and a tea tray. In movement two, tunes by other composers (including Weber and Beethoven) are used. And for a finale, a *Steeple Chase* is pictured. Doubtless much more fun to play than to hear, but worth a place on an auditor's schedule once in a while, and, of course, great for the kids (especially the final portion).

Sonata (*Undine*) for Flute and Piano, Op. 167   *Chamber Music*

☐ Borouchoff (flute); Greene (piano) / Orion 74153

Enough fluidity and romantic tides in this work to suggest slightly the tale of the female water fairy which subtitles the Sonata.

Of the two editions on the market Orion's flutist, Israel Borouchoff, has a plushier and deeper-bodied tone than Louise DiTullio has in her recording on Genesis 1048. Interpretatively, there is little difference between the two and the same applies to tempi choice.

Franz Reizenstein   *(1911-1968)*

Partita for Treble Recorder and Piano, Op. 13   *Chamber Music*

☐ Dolmetsch (recorder); Saxby (piano) / Oiseau-Lyre S-344

As in all of this composer's music, the Hindemith touch is evident. The Partita is registered with clarity and is certainly well written for the thin-toned wind instrument.

Sonatina for Oboe and Piano, Op. 11

☐ Craxton (oboe); Crowson (piano) / Oiseau-Lyre S-344

Hindemithian music, but less serious in this case. Perky material is principal to the first movement, a sensitive *Cantilène* provides the central part, and a vivacious finale brings matters to a smart conclusion.
Fine quality performance.

Piano Quintet in D major, Op. 23

☐ Members of the Melos Ensemble / Crowson (piano) / Oiseau-Lyre S-344

Chamber-music teams have not discovered this work but they certainly should have a look at the score. They will find music of substance and a healthy consideration of scoring that provides a fully integrated sense of instrumental responsibility. The Scherzo is a brilliant affair and contains good amounts of fugato, the finale provides a telling use of augmentation. Further, the materials are enlivened by deft counterpoint.
Vivid playing projects the quintet well. It makes the performance one to be strongly recommended.

Henriette Renié   *(1875-1956)*

Instrumental

Harp

Contemplation

☐ McDonald (harp) / Klavier KS-543

Full romantic scrutiny, backed by luscious chordal impact. The music is cogently conceived for the plucked instrument by this eminent French harpist-composer.

Danse des Lutins

☐ McDonald (harp) / Klavier KS-525

Elfinlike rhythmic continuity tells it all. McDonald's fingers and manipulation of pedal changes master all the problems.

Légende

☐ McDonald (harp) / Klavier KS-543

Program music for the harp is a rarity. This tale is "after the poem 'Les Elfes' by Leconte de Lisle." The story is campy and so is the music, but is effective in a Radio City Music Hall stage show sort of way. Such is exceedingly faint praise, but is not meant to damn Renié's romantic essay.

Pièce Symphonique

☐ McDonald (harp) / Klavier KS-543

Composed after the death of a cousin of the composer. There are three episodes: a *Funeral March*, an *Appassionata*, and a triumphant transfiguration to conclude the piece.
(From listings checked, apparently Renié also wrote another work with the same title for harp and orchestra.)

Wilke Renwick *(1921-   )*

Dance

☐ Annapolis Brass Quintet / Crystal S–206

Cute and trimmed with infectious rhythm. A featherweight but worthy encore fare even for heavy concert situations.

Ottorino Respighi *(1879-1936)*

Ancient Airs and Dances—**Suite**

No. 1 (1917) / No. 2 (1924)

☐ Philharmonia Hungarica / Dorati (conductor) / Mercury 75009

Twentieth-century recolored restorations of lute music by five unknowns, such as Simone Molinario (1565-?), Fabrizio Caroso (1531-?), and three others totally unidentified. Delightful music, simply scored. No two pieces are instrumentally duplicated. For instance, the first of the first suite calls for two oboes, harpsichord, and strings; the second of the second suite comprises seven winds, four brass, harpsichord, and strings. (For the third suite, see under *String Orchestra.*)

The playing is exquisitely sensitive.

Brazilian Impressions (1927)

☐ London Symphony Orchestra / Dorati (conductor) / Mercury 75023

Respighi's *Impressioni Brasiliane* skates a bit on Brazilian surfaces but the wheels are strictly Italian-made. There's an echo of a Brazilian tune in part 1 and some Latin-American rhythmic stylizations in the finale; otherwise the music could fit nicely into the famed Roman *Pines* or *Fountains* suites.

Best is the snaky second movement, descriptive of a celebrated reptile institute. There Dorati does his best work. Otherwise matters are rather placid, for which the lack of credits must be shared with the deceased composer.

Feste Romane (1929)

☐ Los Angeles Philharmonic Orchestra / Mehta (conductor) / RCA AGL1–1276

A real blockbuster, and that's the way Mehta considers it. Spectacle and more spectacle. It is not to be wondered that this was one of the pieces Mehta chose for the special program that marked the opening of the Pavilion of the Music Center for the Performing Arts in Los Angeles in 1964. As said, "spectacle," and in Mehta's hands it's all there to the last colorful friction and percussive thrust.

The Fountains of Rome (1917)

The Pines of Rome (1924)

☐ Philadelphia Orchestra / Ormandy (conductor) / Columbia M–30829

Every color in the spectrum is let loose in full display in these vivid performances. The march pattern of the final movement in the *Pines—I Pini di Via Appia* ("The Pines of the Appian Way") reaches boiling-blood volume. In the same manner the declarative dynamism of *La Fontana di Trevi al meriggio* ("The Fountain of Trevy at Mid-day") is depicted in the third movement of the *Fountains*.

We tend to criticize these pieces (still best sellers) as cheap musical postcards. But play fair. The passionate colorations Respighi put together have musical values as well as crimson showmanship in the eight-part itinerary that he made. There is no cancellation of any kind in Ormandy's recording. Both pieces are also represented, with *Feste Romane*, on Columbia MS–6587, and with even more Respighi on Columbia MG–32308.

Gli Uccelli (1927)

☐ Philadelphia Orchestra / Ormandy (conductor) / Columbia MS–7242

Resettings by old composers (Pasquini, de Gallot, Rameau, and one who is anonymous) as only Respighi could. For small orchestra and everything is magnificently colored with taste.

When you have first-desk men as Ormandy has, and when you have a string section that is all velvet to surround them, you can be certain that a performance of music of this type will be absolutely compelling. It is. A special credit must be given the solo oboe (doubtless John De Lancie) for the mastery displayed in movement 2, *La Colomba* ("The Dove").

Rossiniana (1925)

☐ Orchestra of the Vienna Festival / Janigro (conductor) / Vanguard 71127

More Respighian dipping into Rossini (the first was Respighi's ballet score *La Boutique fantasque*—see under *Rossini/Respighi*) and from the same basic source of music written in Rossini's late years. Four piquantly colored movements that prove Respighi's superfine sense of what can be done with an orchestra without resorting to ultra-virtuosity.

The playing is marked by finesse and especially by rhythmic zest. All of the suite's charm is captured under Janigro's fine direction.

Vetrate di Chiesa (1927)

☐ Philadelphia Orchestra / Ormandy (conductor) / Columbia MS–7242

Respighi's *Four Impressions* picture religious events as depicted in stained-glass windows in Italian churches, hence the title "Church Windows." All this music needs is here: the virtuosity of the Philadelphians, the glorious tone of their strings, golden brass qualities, and going for the downs when required. Ormandy controls the sonorities deftly, shapes the lyrical sections beautifully, and governs the climaxes (organ in the finale, also) so that they are always musical.

(Another packaging, containing this and other Respighi pieces, is available on Columbia MG–32308.)

String Orchestra

Ancient Airs and Dances—Suite No. 3 (1932)

☐ Philharmonia Hungarica / Dorati (conductor) / Mercury 75009

A continuation of the procedure described above for the first two suites (see under *Orchestra*), this time strictly for strings. The performance matches the other two in its beauty.

Chamber Music

Sonata in B minor for Violin and Piano (1917)

☐ Weisman (violin); Hancock (piano) / Nonesuch 71205

The first two movements exemplify warm, flowing romanticism. These are based on the premise of structural strength, not only by thematic relationship but by the arch idea of making the center portion of each movement its most exciting and agitated section. The effect is to release, followed by tension and again final relaxation. Movement 3 is a Passacaglia. It has a dozen variations easily distinguishable one from the other in form.

Weisman and Hancock play the piece with tonal sweep. Theirs is far from intimate music making and they opt for vivid musical photography. Binding Respighi's duo commodity in such colored cellophane is not out of order.

Il Tramonto (1917)

☐ Dal Segno Ensemble / Reid-Parsons (mezzo-soprano) / Critics Choice cc-1703 (monaural)

"The Sunset" represents Respighi in a dark but exceedingly sentient mood, emphasizing modal harmonies in his setting of the mournful Shelley lines. Susan Reid-Parsons's husky voice is ideal for the piece, and she is well supported by the string quartet, augmented by double bass (though not so called for in Respighi's score) drawn from the Dal Segno personnel.

Vocal

Voice and Instrumental Ensemble

Julius Reubke (1834-1858)

Sonata—The 94th Psalm

☐ Preston (organ) / Argo ZRG-5420

The one composition by which this composer, who lived but a sparse twenty-four years, is remembered. And a fine, strongly dramatic piece it is, with its programmatic particulars emphasizing the Psalmist's call for vengeance on the ungodly. Preston plays it with a vengeance, with robust strength and sonorous machoism on the organ of Westminster Abbey. Be ready to turn down the volume knob!

Instrumental

Organ

(Johann Adam Karl) George von Reutter, Jr. (1708-1772)

Servizio di Tavola

☐ Mainz Chamber Orchestra / Zickler (clarino) / Kehr (conductor) / Turnabout 34324

This "banquet music" can be termed either a symphony or a *Sonata da chiesa*. Either way it is a direct, late Baroque, business-like composition. Though not even a small masterpiece, it has its most enticing moments in the second movement which features the extreme register of the clarino. Heinz Zickler almost falls off the high pitch wire but saves himself just in the nick of time. As they say in the trade "it's a bitch to play," but, all matters considered, he deserves a very high passing mark.

Orchestra

Silvestre Revueltas (1899-1940)

Caminos   Janitzio
Itinerarios

☐ New Philharmonia Orchestra / Mata (conductor) / RCA ARL1-2320

Orchestra

Picturesque titles, such as *Janitzio,* which is the name of a fisherman's island, but freely formationed absolute music. Revueltas follows his usual habit of contrastive arrangement of disparate ideas in these works, colored within by folkloric simulation. The playing under Mata's direction is strong.

Redes (1937)

☐ Louisville Orchestra / Mester (conductor) / Louisville S-696

Music drawn from a film score. "The Wave" is a chronicle of events in the daily life of a group of poor fishermen. Only in the second movement is there a positive folkloric coloration. Otherwise a general romantic style pertains to the work.

Indisputably a good performance, with fine attention to dynamic coloration.

Sensemaya (1938)

☐ New York Philharmonic / Bernstein (conductor) / Columbia MS-6514

Revueltas's "chant to kill a snake" is a sweat of ostinato dripping from violent orchestration. It is primitive, it is artistically and magnificently ugly, the kind of ugliness that concentrates one's attention to the deformed octaves and razor-sharp frictions. Bernstein delivers the required heated excitement and correctly considers the work in its earthly blunt manifestation.

Ventanas (1932)

☐ Louisville Orchestra / Whitney (conductor) / Louisville S-672

A stunner. *Ventanas* (translated this means "Windows," coincidentally the same title used by Jacob Druckman for his 1972 Pulitzer Prize work, written almost four decades later) is, despite its heading, music minus any program. None is needed for this composition of broken, nervous, and primitive action. The form is parallel. Some of the measures are in dark, block lines, a kind of Mexican *Sacre du printemps,* others are slow-paced, bare, as vernacularly indigenous as one could wish.

The Louisville issue is excellent and cogently illustrates Revueltas's supreme individuality. And no fatality in the fidelity of the sound.

Instrumental

Piano

Allegro

☐ Somer (piano) / Desto 6426

A type of Etude principle is espoused here in just four seconds less than one minute. The objective: key mix and rhythmic mix. It works and proves its point, certified by Hilde Somer's performance.

Chamber Music

Two Little Serious Pieces

☐ Shanley (piccolo); Christ (oboe); Atkins (clarinet); Stevens (trumpet); Greenberg (baritone saxophone) / Crystal S-812

The second piece of the pair mixes French salon atmosphere with Mexican night-air stuffiness in Waltz tempo. A snide comparison is strongly hinted. Number one of the set is like a denuded capsule version of Stravinsky's *Rite.* It is as serious as the companion piece is unserious. Revueltas was not casual with his ideas—note the scoring: a piccolo, oboe, trumpet, together with a clarinet and a tubby baritone saxophone.

Clean and clear reproduction, clean and certified performance.

Roger Reynolds   (1934-   )

Quick Are the Mouths of Earth (1965)   *Orchestra*

☐ Contemporary Chamber Ensemble / Weisberg (conductor) / Nonesuch 71219

A Thomas Wolfe quote is the basis for Reynolds's work, which he indicates "had the capacity of generating musical images for me." These are scored for an odd confederation of instruments: three flutes, oboe, trumpet, trombone, bass trombone, three cellos, piano (doubling on harmonica), and percussion (covering almost two-dozen types of instruments). Formally fixed and completely notated, the score hands certain aleatoric responsibilities to the conductor and performers. However, despite the composer's fixed data, a great deal of it sounds improvisatory.

Reynolds's impresses produce an assortment of sounds that in their variety give rise to an individual type of balance. The performance is sensitive to this factor especially and is therefore stimulating.

Ambages (1965)   *Instrumental*

☐ Sollberger (flute) / Nonesuch 73028   *Flute*

Reynolds describes *Ambages* as "balletic." It has that quality but it also brakes a great deal of its motility and emphasizes it by deflecting pitch points ("bent" tones). Sollberger in his notes claims for the work "a logic of mood and impulse akin to that of a dream," and it does have that quality as well. The thought persists that *Ambages* is the way Debussy might have written his *Syrinx* for unaccompanied flute if he had composed it in 1965 rather than 1912. If that is a compliment to Reynolds, let it be so considered.

The piece appears in an anthology of *Twentieth-Century Flute Music* consisting of two discs. All the performances feature Harvey Sollberger. All are magnificent. Still, he plays *Ambages* with such probity that it deserves a recording Oscar or Grammy.

Fantasy for Pianist (1964)   *Piano*

☐ Takahashi (piano) / Mainstream 5000

Serial solutions applied to time, pitch, and dynamics, but with deviations that loosen technical strictures. Reynolds's gestures are aggressive but not four-square. There is also a fierce poetry in the sound shapes, though, of course, Reynolds's poetry does not rhyme.

From Behind the Unreasoning Mask   *Chamber Music*

☐ Anderson (trombone); Raney and Reynolds (percussion) / New World Records NW-237

It is difficult to define (for cataloging purposes) Reynolds's work for trombone, percussion, assistant percussionist, and tape, falling, as it does, between chamber-music totality and brass-percussion-electronic sonorities. It is easier to describe it: a passion of sounds that twist about, wail, and shriek. By itself, the trombone's sonorous glossary is captivating.

It should be understood that Reynolds's music forms its own form through the distribution and collision of its pigmentative operations. One perceives a genuine violence in the piece. If it is not so meant it does not nullify the right to such reaction.

Blind Men (1966)   *Choral*
Chorus and
☐ Peabody Concert Singers and Chamber Ensemble / Smith (conductor) / Composers   *Instrumental*
Recordings S-241   *Ensemble*

Reynolds has based his work on a collection of fragments extracted from Melville's *Journal up the Straits*. However, no clear text (or textual meaning) emerges in the unsynchronized, fundamentally aleatoric conception. Though Reynolds's liner note provides a complete analysis of his purpose, the net aural result is one of effects and collisions. While the sonorous contents are plastic and elastic, they are also spastic.

Blind Men has a cross-pollination of reverberating vocal procedures with an instrumental combine requiring three trumpets, three trombones, tuba, two percussionists, and two pianists. One takes for granted that the recording is in accordance with the composer's requirements.

Verne Reynolds (1926-   )

Solo Instrument and Brass

Trumpet and Tuba

Signals for Trumpet, Tuba, and Brass Choir

☐ Stevens (trumpet); Bobo (tuba) / Henderson (conductor) / Crystal S–392

Give and take, a musical push and shove in which both solo instruments participate in a free-wheeling, brassy-brash virtuosic game. (The gamesmanship is indulged in equally.) Ten brass instruments—five each of horns and trumpets—support.

Delivery of these crisscrossed sonorous currents results in an ultimate socko display. This sort of playing is loaded with appeal.

Instrumental

Clarinet

Four Caprices

☐ Michael Webster (clarinet); Beveridge Webster (piano) / Composers Recordings SD–374

Enormously productive examples, especially the perpetual-motion massage of the second of the set and the quasi-cadenza stimulants of the fourth piece. Above all is the healthy straightforwardness of the entire opus.

There is splendid teamwork in this performance. Of course, not many soloists have the advantage of having a distinguished concert artist as accompanist.

Chamber Music

Music for Five Trumpets (1957)

☐ Plog, Guarneri, DiVall, Bush, and Stevens (trumpets) / Henderson (conductor) / Crystal S–362

Verve, vigor, and gaiety in the Fanfare and Finale, the latter secured by use of a rhythmic pedal point. Contrast is supplied by the inner-movement Chorale. The piece is played with total command.

Emil Nikolaus von Reznicek (1860-1945)

Orchestra

Overture to *Donna Diana* (1894)

☐ New York Philharmonic / Bernstein (conductor) / Columbia MS–7085

There's something special about Leonard Bernstein in terms of snappy overtures. Hardly anyone can match his conception of how to style and pace such material. It amounts to a *tour de force* of orchestral facility. *Donna Diana* is still another overture performance that shows him outdistancing the competition. (Columbia has also included it in an eighteen-overture package of six record sides in one album, D3S–818.)

Joseph Rheinberger   (1839-1901)

Concerto in A flat major for Piano and Orchestra, Op. 94

Solo Instrument and Orchestra

Piano

☐ Nürnberg Symphoniker / Ruiz (piano) / Deáky (conductor) / Genesis 1014

Mention Rheinberger, and his twenty sonatas for organ come to mind, for it is on those compositions that his reputation is based. Still, he wrote a tremendous amount of music in all media (including four operas, fourteen Masses, three requiems, four concertos, a huge amount of chamber music, piano compositions, and so forth), and this Concerto is as good an example as any. Polite romantic music it is. Nothing written hot and strong—that's not Joseph Rheinberger. The piece is pleasant enough and worth a listen now and then.

Sonata No. 4 (*Tonus peregrinus*) in A minor, Op. 98

Instrumental

Organ

☐ Eden (organ) / Vista VPS-1018

Thanks to the world of organists, this composer's name remains alive, especially through his twenty sonatas for the instrument. Felix Aprahamian has described these compositions as "a corpus of typically nineteenth-century organ music that is without peer in its own genre." This writer is in full agreement. All twenty works have been recorded. A sampling of these is discussed below—all deserving full attention.

Opus 98 is a three-movement work climaxed by a sturdy and tightly constructed *Fuga cromatica.* Building a fugue from a subject that is merely a succession of chromatic pitches descending in order through an octave's span sounds academically productive and creatively unproductive, but not with Rheinberger's skill. The fugue has fascinating content, especially the manner in which stretto is utilized.

Conrad Eden's organ playing shows an ideal mating of registration with the music's content. The restraint is something to be enjoyed. Other recorded performances of Rheinberger's Sonatas by Eden are Sonata No. 1 in C minor, Op. 27 (on Vista VPS-1011), Sonata No. 2 in A flat major, Op. 65 (on Vista VPS-1013), Sonata No. 3 (*Pastoral*) in G major, Op. 88 (on Vista VPS-1015), and Sonata No. 5 in F sharp major, Op. 111 (on Vista VPS-1019).

Sonata No. 7 in F minor, Op. 127

☐ Munns (organ) / Vista VPS-1016

Conventionality of design may seem to be in order when reading the movement headings of this Sonata: *Preludio,* Andante, and Finale. However, Rheinberger frees the forms considerably. The large-scaled *Preludio* contains no fewer than five subjects and the tripartite plan of the slow, central movement is balanced by a three-divisioned Finale, with a *Grave* section, a *Vivo,* and a concluding Fugue. Those that sniff at organ music by organists would do well to cancel their cynicism and give a listen to this Sonata. Rheinberger's work has artistic durability.

Robert Munns proves he is a first-class organist and a first-class musician in his presentation. He has recorded other of the Rheinberger Sonatas, all on Vista: Sonata No. 6 in E flat major, Op. 119 (on VPS-1012), Sonata No. 8 in E minor, Op. 132 (on VPS-1017), Sonata No. 10 in B minor, Op. 146 (on VPS-1020), and Sonata No. 9 (*see below*).

Sonata No. 9 in B flat minor, Op. 142

☐ Munns (organ) / Vista VPS-1013

Rheinberger's Opus 142 includes his favored three-movement design, illustrates his habit of large-formation music to embrace a *Praeludium* (here with two elements in the Grave section and three successive subjects in the Allegro that follows), and is completed by the expected Fugue. ("Expected" if you know Rheinberger—seventeen of his twenty organ sonatas include a Fugue and most are found as the concluding movement.)

Munns's playing shows sound structural sense and a good range of registration. (Munns has recorded other Rheinberger Organ Sonatas, *see above* [Sonata No. 7 in F minor, Op. 127].)

Sonata No. 12 in D flat major, Op. 154

☐ Fisher (organ) / Vista VPS-1014

Harvey Grace, the English organist and writer, established a reputation as the prime Rheinberger scholar, editing all twenty of the organ sonatas and publishing (in 1925) a definitive study on the composer: *The Organ Works of Rheinberger.* It is important to realize, therefore, that in Grace's opinion, Opus 154 was the finest of the twenty works. It opens with a Phantasie (in two sections, a *Maestoso lento* and an *Allegro agitato*), has a placid Pastorale as the central movement, and concludes with an Introduction and Fugue. The Fugue is a comprehensively dramatic affair, often progressing in five parts. The Sonata concludes in a cyclic manner with the return of the stately opening of the work.

The performance by Roger Fisher is masterly. There is no doubt that he feels Rheinberger's music in his veins and is one of his best interpreters. Fisher has recorded four other Rheinberger organ Sonatas, all on Vista: Sonata No. 11 in D minor, Op. 148 (VPS-1012), Sonata No. 13 in E flat major, Op. 161 (VPS-1018), Sonata No. 14 in C major, Op. 165 (VPS-1016), and Sonata No. 15 in D major, Op. 168 (VPS-1020).

Sonata No. 19 in G minor, Op. 192

☐ Farrell (organ) / Vista VPS-1015

In Rheinberger's Sonata No. 16 in G sharp minor, Op. 175, the slow movement is a melancholy *Skandinavisch.* In the work under discussion the slow movement (an Andantino) is titled *Provençalisch,* the evocative music being based on the song *J'aim la flour de valour,* by the fourteenth-century composer Machaut. It provides a sensitive and colorful contrast to the preceding movement, a *Praeludium* and the one that follows, an Introduction and Finale.

Like the three other organists in Vista's series covering the complete organ sonatas of Rheinberger (each organist performing five sonatas), Timothy Farrell proves his knowledge and understanding of the music. Every detail is properly set in place, the nuances and colorations are ideal. Above all there is a sense of spontaneity that gives optimum response to Rheinberger's fine work. The other Sonatas recorded by Farrell, all on Vista, as mentioned, are Sonata No. 16 in G sharp minor, Op. 175 (VPS-1017), Sonata No. 17 in B major, Op. 181 (VPS-1014), Sonata No. 18 in A major, Op. 188 (VPS-1019), and Sonata No. 20 (*Zur Friedensfeier*) in F major, Op. 196 (VPS-1011).

Instrumental

Piano

Sonata (*Romantic*) in F sharp minor, Op. 184

☐ Ruiz (piano) / Genesis 1005

The size of the piece matches the hefty opus number. Rheinberger, an organist, covers romantic procedures almost as though he were musing at the console, taking close to a half hour. Historic it isn't. Interesting, as a museum piece, it is. There is lots worse material on disc.

Perhaps a great keyboard artist could do more with Rheinberger's material than Adrian Ruiz has. I doubt it.

Phillip Rhodes   (1940-   )

Museum Pieces for String Quartet and Clarinet (1973)

☐ Louisville String Quartet / Livingston (clarinet) / Louisville LS–741

A contemporary *Pictures at an Exhibition* (see under *Mussorgsky: Instrumental: piano*). Being commissioned to produce a work for the dedication of a music room in a Louisville, Kentucky, art musuem, Rhodes found his inspiration from a half-dozen items in the museum's collection. These included a Picasso sketch in chalk, a nineteenth-century music box, an early sixteenth-century bronze, and so on.

The general identification with such predetermined data is sharply printed in the music. Of importance is the fact that the Louisville people have been very supportive and include black and white photographs of the art objects that stimulated the composer. That was clever and thoughtful on their part and draws a grateful response from the listener.

This is the only time, I believe, that Louisville has ever issued a chamber music recording. Understandable, in view of the circumstances of the commission and since all the performers are first-desk players in the Louisville Orchestra. They produce fine reproductions of Rhodes's reproductions.

Chamber Music

The Lament of Michal for Soprano and Orchestra

☐ Louisville Orchestra / Bryn-Julson (soprano) / Mester (conductor) / Louisville S–704

A strong three-part monodrama, the text taken from the Old Testament, 1 and 2 Samuel, concerning Michal, daughter of King Saul and wife of David. The pitch spans, especially in the opening section, *The Coming of David,* are unsocketed, atonal, though Rhodes flirts (chiefly in part 2) with tonality. The shifts between harmonic arrangement are related to terseness or the opposite quality in the text, but these parallels cause no stylistic incongruities in the music.

Naturally, a successful performance of this work depends on a virtuosic vocalist. That describes the gorgeous, creamy timbre and the infallible musicianship of Phyllis Bryn-Julson. And full credit must be given the Louisville Orchestra for one of its very best performances. That is just the way it should be, for Rhodes's work (coupled with Richard Strauss's Six Songs, Op. 68 [see under *Vocal: voice and orchestra*]) represents the Louisville's "100th Golden Edition" recording.

Vocal

Voice and Orchestra

Antal Ribári   (1924-   )

Pantomime-Suite for Orchestra (1962)

☐ Hungarian Radio Orchestra / Erdélyi (conductor) / Serenus S–12021

An *Introduzione, Elegia*, Scherzo, and *Recitativo e Finale.* The fast music is slightly nervous, balletic; the other has nicely adjusted lines. Ribári has a fine sensitivity for orchestration, and it lights up his material beautifully. There are complete characterizations by the orchestra.

Orchestra

Concertino for Violin and Orchestra (1965)

☐ Symphonic Orchestra of the Hungarian Radio and Television / Kovács (violin) / Erdélyi (conductor) / Serenus 12029

A crackerjack piece for fancy fiddling. Virtuosity is crammed into the work and there

Solo Instrument and Orchestra

Violin

are a number of cadenzas—a style that carries over into the other sections of the work. The Concertino embraces four parts in its continuity: Capriccio, Aria, Jazz, and *Recitativo e Presto*. Singly each is distinctive; in alliance they produce a fantasia-like sonata concept.

As can be expected the prominence is for the soloist. Dénes Kovács has technique to burn, and its flame is on "high" in this work. The orchestra lends strong support.

Instrumental

Piano

All'antica—Suite for Piano (1967)

☐ Ribári (piano) / Serenus 12029

The usual attention to classical designs: Sonata, *Sarabanda, Giga,* and *Postludio.* The usual neoclassic diction with some jazzy overlay for color purposes. With Ribári at the piano, full coherence of the contents can be taken for granted.

Chamber Music

Sonata for Cello and Piano (1958)

☐ Mezo (cello); Ribári (piano) / Serenus S-12021

A five-minute length, as here, normally does not allow for the space of even a one-movement sonata. However, no matter the title, it turns out that Ribári has produced a pithy three-movement suite, consisting of a Capriccio, a Serenata, and a Humoresque. Even within these, the crucial point of form avoids textbook boundaries and rhapsodic detail is provided. Being on precise formal target is not for this composer (that is not meant to be a back-handed compliment). The performance is excellent.

Thoughts for String Quartet (1965)

☐ Tatrai String Quartet / Serenus S-12021

Nine short abstractions. Though glimpses of Bartók peep through, in general the sense is dark, melancholic.

The Tatrai foursome is a fine ensemble. Their playing is clean and incisive, the textures admirably balanced.

Chamber Music for Five Instruments (1970)

☐ Chamber Soloists of the Hungarian Radio and Television / Serenus 12029

A well-constructed set of four pieces, using standard contemporary musical dialects. The instrumentation is for flute, clarinet, and string trio. Good playing and good reproduction.

Vocal

Voice with Accompaniment

Three Songs for Poems of P. B. Shelley (1956)

☐ Sziklay (soprano); Ribári (piano) / Serenus 12029

The second poem of the set, *Music, When Soft Voices Die,* has become a composer's favorite; the other two are *Love's Philosophy* and *Indian Serenade.* Post-romantic style and no surprises in either the music or the performance.

Voice and Orchestra

Hellas (1964)

☐ Orchestra and Chorus of the Hungarian Radio / Komlossy (alto); Szonyi (tenor) / Lukacs (conductor) / Serenus S-12021

A scenario that shifts quickly. First an introductory section, then a short tenor aria and an equally short dance, followed by an aria for the alto, with two different types of choral sections completing the work. Obviously, with a six-movement length the half-dozen divisions are each concentrated. Thus speaks Ribári, who bypasses lengthy developments and long contrastive sections in his music.

Hellas is certainly not integrated, but its imbalance of materials and mediums produces its own formal equanimity. The colors of this work evince creative marksmanship of top order and effect and that is equaled by the finely disciplined performing personnel.

Metamorphoses (1966)

☐ Hungarian Radio Orchestra / Sziklay (soprano) / Oberfrank (conductor) / Serenus S-12021

Ribári's *Metamorphoses,* subtitled a "Suite for Soprano and Orchestra," has five movements, variationally considered. It is aphoristically budgeted music with extremely colorful scoring (three woodwinds, piano, vibraphone, three bongos, three gongs, and strings), conceived for the pantonal syntax.

Considered separately the sections are sketches. Placed together they give an intriguing picture. The playing and singing are wholly appropriate to the material.

Apollinaire Cantata (1961)

Cantata and Oratorio

☐ Symphonic Orchestra of the Hungarian Radio and Television / Fülöp (tenor) / Janovics (conductor) / Serenus 12029

A Cantata without chorus, using a text from Apollinaire's *Calligraphies—La Colombe poignardée et le jet d'eau.* In setting the rather bizarre lines Ribári opts for passionate musical commitment. This is no contradiction in terms since the poem deals with a concern for friendships that thrived prior to World War I.

The rich, somewhat darkly colored voice of Attila Fülöp fits this music with excellence. The textual nuances are sensitively portrayed. Fine sound.

Clown (1967)

☐ Symphonic Orchestra and Chorus of the Hungarian Radio and Television / Szabó (tenor) / Pál (conductor) / Serenus 12029

A mini-mini-mini-Cantata, lasting only four minutes and twenty seconds. But if Ribári chooses to call his musical grotesquerie a Cantata, so be it.

Since it is sung in Hungarian (and sung well by Miklós Szabó) and no text or translation is offered, the report ends at this point. However, on the same release there are three songs to poems by Shelley (see under *Vocal: voice with accompaniment* [Three Songs for Poems of P. B. Shelley]) and the full poems are given in English. Strange the ways of record production departments!

Franz Xaver Richter   (1709-1789)

Chamber Sonata in A major, Op. 2, No. 3

Chamber Music

☐ Shanley (flute); Shapiro (harpsichord); Karmazyn (cello) / Orion 73108

Richter's Chamber Sonata is charming and attractive music, its sequences flow with interest and never bog down to a marking of time. The first movement is an *Andante affettuoso,* the second movement a Larghetto, and the work concludes with a gay Fugato that is a tiny bit complex but never becomes complicated. Although far from a masterpiece, Richter's trio Sonata shows the work of a fine compositional hand.

The outer movements are expertly performed. In the Larghetto the music is dulled by the choice of too slow a tempo.

String Quartet in C major, Op. 5, No. 1

☐ Schäffer Quartet / Vox SVBX–5300

Part writing beautifully executed; dominance by the first violin is avoided and one hears full-scale quartet writing. The finale, a *presto*-tempoed *Rincontro,* exemplifies Richter's polyphonic expertise. If not a masterpiece, at the very least the quartet can be described as having been constructed by a master hand.

Marga Richter   (1926-   )

Instrumental

Piano

Sonata for Piano (1954)

☐ Basquin (piano) / Grenadilla GS–1010

The power and assurance packed in the fast-tempoed corner movements are outstanding. Some may consider the creative ancestral tie as being Bartók, but, while true, there is the additional matter of Richter's use of a never-faltering dynamic maintenance within a total movement. Contrast is furnished by the total form, not within the single divisions, so that the principal lyrical contact is found in the middle slow movement. Since the opening is initially slow-paced and then fast, over all a perfect balance of alternate speeds prevails. Oddly, the movements become shorter as the Sonata progresses (the timings are 11:25, 8:36, and 4:12). Climactic drive is thereby given a subtle push by the overall time design.

The playing of Peter Basquin is ideal for this work. He can sting a phrase and he does in the principal precipitancy of Marga Richter's music. Prissy pianism doesn't fit much music, least of all the rash adventure of this Sonata.

Wallingford Riegger   (1885-1961)

Orchestra

Dance Rhythms, Op. 58

☐ Orchestra of the Accademia Nazionale di Santa Cecilia–Roma / Antonini (conductor) / Composers Recordings 117 (monaural)

An outcome of the utilitarian music Riegger composed for dance groups and the like during the Depression days of the 1930s. The recipe uses jazz rhythms and colorful scoring of the pops-concert variety.

The performance is acceptable, save that the sound is somewhat out of whack in places where the marimba is contrasted to the other orchestral sections.

Dichotomy (1932)

☐ London Sinfonietta / Prausnitz (conductor) / Argo ZRG–702

Oddly enough, though the Argo release (part of the Gulbenkian Foundation Series) has the usual copious documentation, nowhere is there mention that *Dichotomy* is for a small (almost chamber) orchestra. The scoring consists of flute doubling on piccolo, oboe, clarinet, bassoon; one horn and two trumpets; timpani, xylophone, and small drum; piano and strings.

The title indicates the presence of divarication. This is represented by two tone rows, the contrast of serialism with its opposite, bipartite structuring, and a general ongoing dramatic interplay. Tensility is paramount even in less exhortative sections. Riegger's serialism is always dynamically fresh; it is innocent of academic response. *Dichotomy* is further proof of the gifts of this creative giant.

It is perhaps a sign of musical maturity that we are blessed with more than one recorded version of Riegger's work. Prausnitz is fully at home with music of this style and his proposition is ideal, a dynamic and fully involved one. His orchestra is much better, stronger, and plays much more cleanly than the competing offering on Louisville 715, wherein Mester conducts the Louisville Orchestra.

Fantasy and Fugue for Orchestra and Organ, Op. 10

☐ Polish National Radio Orchestra / Krenz (conductor) / Composers Recordings S–219

A deceiving title. Riegger's piece is of sonorous corpulence and has involved procedures, spiked by atonality. The complexity itself is thrilling. The orchestra consists of eleven winds playing (via doubling) fourteen instruments, fourteen brass, timpani and three percussionists, harp, strings, and organ, the last requiring two players.

The Fantasy sounds improvisational. However, it is merely an introduction to a triple set of fugues, which are intersected by a chorale and both then developed simultaneously. The action is intense and constant, as a fiery furnace of sound is let loose. That some of the textural details get lost in passing in this recorded performance is not critical. This is a music of mass, of intelligential dissonance. In fact this is the proper exhibition of the latter, with no tentative probings but compact, severe, and flush on. It jolts the ears and its acridity is delightfully proper. Indeed, the staid title is incorrect, implying a formal liquidity that doesn't exist.

There is this to say. The music begs to be recorded by a major orchestra conducted by one of the big-time names. Still, Krenz does a respectable and fairly satisfactory documentation. One is in his debt for recording an example of contemporary orchestral virtuosity. It is not a music for timid ears, but when Wallingford Riegger, who was a composer of special stature, speaks his mind, one should listen and listen well. The Fantasy and Fugue deserves masterpiece definition.

Music for Orchestra, Op. 50

☐ Orchestra of the Accademia Nazionale di Santa Cecilia–Roma / Antonini (conductor) / Composers Recordings 117 (monaural)

The formal title is the clue that one may expect to find Riegger wearing his twelve-tone clothes. However, his apparel is designed with convincing beauty. Music for Orchestra is further proof of the special stature of this composer, who was able to write music free of tonality and yet free of dodecaphonic rigidity. The composition sounds healthy and correct, yet unacademic. It is performed with proper profile.

Symphony No. 3 (1948)

☐ Eastman-Rochester Symphony Orchestra / Hanson (conductor) / Composers Recordings S–284E (monaural)

Riegger's contact with both classical tradition and Schoenbergian freedom is beautifully realized in this trenchant, dramatic four-movement Symphony. It is the most definitive work of the composer, probably his best, and proves conclusively the rightness of the place Riegger holds in the hierarchy of American music composition.

No dry, pedantic twelve-toner has the stuff to interest a listener throughout even a short piece, let alone a full-fledged Symphony of close to twenty-five minutes. Riegger is aloof from both tonality and the dodecaphonic science that can freeze a work into immobility. His music is rugged, direct, forceful. At the same time, it takes into account the need for balances that can be realized and understood without reference to the printed score. What Riegger has accomplished in this Symphony is a perfectly styled rapport that in turn creates a new style. There is no eclectic throwing together of ingredients; there is control, aesthetic truth, and individual quality. This is obtained by a pithiness of generative material, striking rhythmic contours, brilliant orchestration, and, above all, the realization that formal logic needs emotional explanation. This is the perpetual renewal of art: logic extends into new spheres; emotion is a constant measuring rod. Only exceptional composers can achieve the fusion. In this Symphony Riegger has.

Hanson's belief in the composition is proved by his minute attention to detail and the clearest exposition. CRI, in preparing its rerelease after it was cut out of the Columbia catalogue (the number was ML-4902), has given the disc its best engineering attention.

Symphony No. 4, Op. 63

☐ Louisville Orchestra / Whitney (conductor) / Louisville S-646

Most of the work is a reinforcement of the composer's very logical musical arguments for the artistic sense derivable from twelve-tone technique. The Spanish flavor found in the middle movement is due to a transfer of material written originally for a dance (for Martha Graham), which dealt with the suffering that took place in Spain during the war between the Loyalists and the followers of Franco.

String Orchestra

Canon and Fugue in D minor, Op. 33

☐ Members of the Oslo Philharmonic Orchestra / Strickland (conductor) / Composers Recordings 177 (monaural)

It is difficult to imagine Riegger's piece (in D minor!) being performed initially at an International Society for Contemporary Music Festival (1942), when Schoenbergian dodecaphonicism is now considered by the ISCM as old-fashioned and therefore taboo! The music is nicely crafted, nicely played, and nicely overlooked in every part of the CRI edition is that the work is only for strings.

Romanza, Op. 56a

☐ Orchestra of the Accademia Nazionale di Santa Cecilia–Roma / Antonini (conductor) / Composers Recordings 117 (monaural)

Riegger in one of his creative maneuvers that do not depict his mature style. This, despite the fact that the *Romanza* was written as late as 1953. Its stylistic procedures are defined in terms of 1853 manners, however. Antonini warms up the performance as much as he can.

Study in Sonority (1927)

☐ Louisville Orchestra / Mester (conductor) / Louisville S-706

This is one of the most remarkable pieces in the entire string medium. For string orchestra, however, strictly speaking, it is not. Riegger's Study is for ten violins (or multiples thereof, which is the way it is performed in this case). Atonal, superbly crafted coloristically (the liner note writer fails to mention that *scordatura* is employed, using some pitches below the bottom G string), it powers its way in moods that range from the violently percussive to the vivifyingly ecstatic. Its tensility forces one to hang onto every split sound, every sonorous slash, every simmering statement. "Remarkable" is a bit lukewarm in praise. For this heated work the word should be "masterpiece."

This is the only recorded performance, and for that alone one is grateful. As far as it goes it is done with excellence. The hope is that someday a great violin section from one of the major orchestras will record Riegger's work. It deserves such response.

Music for Brass Choir, Op. 45

☐ Members of the Alumni of the National Orchestral Association / Barnett (conductor) / Composers Recordings S-229

Mainly composite textures, cluster-choired, refined in the spacings and thus controlling the dynamic impact. Gorgeous fricatives, these.

Riegger's title needs a footnote, since there are timpani and cymbals in addition to eight horns, ten trumpets, ten trombones, and two tubas. The piece is presented superlatively under John Barnett's direction. The players deserve the individual credits they are given on the liner copy, though one trombonist has a deserving complaint, since only nine names are listed for that instrument.

Variations for Piano and Orchestra, Op. 54

☐ Louisville Orchestra / Owen (piano) / Whitney (conductor) / Louisville 545-3 (monaural)

Classical decor rules this work; the theme is strikingly recognizable even when the variation treatment is rather free. The dozen variants are connected, yet each is distinct; each portion of the whole is a fresh thought and acts as a developed confirmation of the generating idea. The theme may twitch, but it never acts rowdy. Riegger employs a cumulative design, with the completion of the twelve variations codified by a fugue as the postscript. In twelve-tone deployment this plan makes the structure twice as solid, with as clear a façade as one can imagine.

The Louisville players are satisfactory, but one senses an instrumental reticence on their part quite the opposite of the top-quality work of the soloist. The sound is pinched and not all it should be, even considering monaural engineering.

There are two other versions of Riegger's piece. Opus 54a covers a setting for two pianos and has been recorded (see under *Instrumental: two pianos* [Variations for Two Pianos]). Opus 54b is a version for two pianos and orchestra, still in the unrecorded category.

Variations for Violin and Orchestra, Op. 71

☐ Louisville Orchestra / Harth (violin) / Whitney (conductor) / Louisville 601 (monaural)

A luscious feast of dodecaphonic writing, violin virtuosity, perfect clarity of variational sections (there are a dozen), and significant color. For the last, for example, there is one place where solo violin pizzicato is joined to a growling double bass and a crawling tuba, another where antiphonal gestures are made between the solo voice and percussion with high wind interjections. These are further proof of the resourceful creativity of this composer.

Sidney Harth is a masterful violinist and in music of this style cannot be outdistanced. His is a significant portrayal, and Robert Whitney and his musicians are in top collaborative form.

*Brass
Ensemble*

*Solo
Instrument
and
Orchestra*

Piano

Violin

Instrumental

Flute

Suite for Flute Alone, Op. 8

☐ Baron (flute) / Composers Recordings 212 (monaural)

One of the few evergreens in the by-now sizable total of works for unaccompanied flute. From the output by French composers it is Debussy's *Syrinx* (see under *Debussy: Instrumental: flute*), written in 1912, that belongs in this select class. The American headliner is Riegger's four-movement gem, composed in 1929.

Despite its non-twelve-tone sphere, it is all Riegger: direct and melodic, coloristic and inventive (in the concluding six measures of the finale, marked *Allegro ironico,* each of the semitones of the flute's three-octave range are heard once—that is, a thirty-six-tone row!).

The character of Baron's playing makes this recording of special significance.

Two Pianos

Variations for Two Pianos, Op. 54a

☐ Yarbrough and Cowan (pianos) / Composers Recordings S–279

The second of Riegger's three settings of Opus 54. For a discussion of the composition, see under *Solo Instrument and Orchestra: piano* (Variations for Piano and Orchestra, Op. 54).

Riegger's redraft here is just as propitious, and in some cases (despite the elimination of orchestral color) even better. One would wish for a recorded performance of the composer's transcription calling for two pianos and orchestra (Opus 54b), especially by this husband-wife team, whose playing is exemplary.

Chamber Music

Sonatina for Violin and Piano, Op. 39

☐ Zukofsky (violin); Kalish (piano) / Desto 6435/37

Riegger's music displays the paradox of being nontonal while managing to sound convincingly tonal, and it is exemplified in this work. The well-prepared and integrated developments cause the twelve-tone technique utilized to be as clear to the ear as a Mozart sonata.

The performance is of top quality.

Trio for Piano, Violin, and Cello, Op. 1

☐ Temple University Trio / Golden Crest 4117

This is the only piece in Riegger's very small chamber-music output that was composed in an old-school manner. It is always surprising to hear a work that presents less than the mature style of a composer; twice so, when it is an ultraconservative early manifestation that contrasts to a later aggressiveness. Since progress is a distinct necessity of creative musical life, Riegger subsequently moved far from the romantic outpourings heard in his initial opus. There is nothing wrong with this music; it is merely dressed in totally imitative clothes.

The usual two contrasted subjects and their development (movement 1), rondo insistence (in the slow movement), and the expected final-movement peroration are all made available. The music is well integrated and easy to assimilate, with the composer of the later works being a bit in evidence in the rhythmic verve of the final section.

In other performances of this group there has been a tightness of projection. None here. This Riegger opus is heady stuff for the Temple University ensemble, and they have produced a first-class definition of the score.

There are a couple of howlers in the unsigned jacket note. Riegger's Study in Sonority (see under *String Orchestra*) is for ten violins or multiples of ten, not for "various ten-instrument combinations.'' And in discussing the merits of a piano trio, it is nonsense to indicate its ''mastery in orchestration.''

Movement for Two Trumpets, Trombone, and Piano, Op. 66

☐ Dean and Eckert (trumpets); Biddlecome (trombone); Zayde (piano) / Composers Recordings S-229

Riegger's Movement is tonally integrated and sonorously ingratiating. Like equals like here, with pithy motival material heard in a concentrated time length. The piece is expertly played, with tasteful bright sound.

String Quartet No. 2, Op. 43

☐ New Music Quartet / Composers Recordings S-307 (monaural)

One of the most stringent manifests of the twelve-tone system is the avoidance of a central tone. Though some of the examples of the tone series used here include slight pitch repetitions, the infusion of a pivotal sound is nonetheless avoided. In that respect, therefore, Riegger's quartet remains atonical, even though a central pitch emerges as a polarity in the opening unison, conveyed by further derivation in the following Allegro.

Further, the very use of any cyclic device is foreign to the dodecaphonic school. The repetition of themes, the transmutation of such into other movements destroy the potency of the twelve-tone scheme, by representing thereby one thing as slightly more important than another. Yet Riegger, in his full-hearted association of the twelve-tone system with his individual expression, does not hesitate to restate the first movement theme in the third movement; or transplace another idea from the opening movement into the final movement.

The music is typically that of Riegger—razor-sharp themes, tight statements, pungent sonorities, determined rhythms, and sharp structuring. All of it is exciting, great music making.

Every time one hears the New Music four, regret appears in huge total. That group was probably the finest quartet team to come into existence in the 1940s. Their playing of twentieth-century music has never been bettered. Their projection of Riegger's quartet is a spectacular and supercharged masterpiece. One is extremely grateful to CRI for obtaining the masters from Columbia (which had deleted its original monaural recording) and reissuing this vitally important recorded performance.

Concerto for Piano and Woodwind Quintet, Op. 53

☐ New York Woodwind Quintet / Glazer (piano) / Everest 3081

Though in the field of chamber music the title ''Concerto'' may seem self-contradictory, it is actually correct. Usually signifying a work for solo instrument with orchestral accompaniment, the truest definition of a concerto is a relationship of equality, the pitting of one voice against others. Riegger follows the practice of many contemporary composers in using this classic form for a small combination.

The ingredients and methods of this composer's compositions are here displayed, plus a surprising and free technical shift in the last part. If the textbook of others does not govern Wallingford Riegger, neither does he follow his own manual. At the start the usual tone row is announced; it moves swiftly to a restatement in inverted form, and then is developed with proper associative resources. The twelve tones are used freely but the composer's thoughts are not inordinately complex to follow. After such unshackled writing, it is stimulating (and not stylistically incorrect) to have diatonic representation dominate the final movement. This duality is tied together by bringing back the basic row for completion. Q.E.D.: license within composition, albeit complete unity. The twain have met.

The presentation is very impressive. Ease and relaxation, with sensitive and subtle consideration of highlighted material, mark the teaming of this fine band of wind players and one of the best chamber-music pianists available. (Originally this recording was released by Concert-Disc as their CS-221.)

A very good monaural recording is also available on Composers Recordings (130) performed by Harriet Wingreen and the New Art Wind Quintet.

Nonet for Brass, Op. 49

☐ Members of the Alumni of the National Orchestral Association / Barnett (conductor) / Composers Recordings S-229

Unrigid serialism. The shifts between solo voices and ensemble are subtle and hold a listener's interest. (The tuba is given a good part of the solo phrases.) It is to Riegger's credit that he maneuvers his voicing and scoring so as to avoid the essential danger of monochromatic timbre—the scoring consists of two horns, three trumpets, three trombones, and tuba.

This is a positive statement by the nine musicians, probably conducted by John Barnett—CRI does not make it at all clear.

Ferdinand Ries   *(1784-1838)*

Solo Instrument and Orchestra

Piano

Concerto No. 3 in C sharp minor for Piano and Orchestra, Op. 55

☐ Hamburg Symphony / Littauer (piano) / Springer (conductor) / Turnabout 34526

Beethoven said of Ries, his protégé, that "he imitates me too much." Well, such choice is choice. It shows in this Concerto, one of nine Ries produced, containing the usual three movements: an *Allegro maestoso*, a Larghetto, and a very fine Rondo finale.

The piano playing is attractive and well phrased. Springer, once a winner when the New York Philharmonic had conductor competitions, gives good support.

Chamber Music

Sonate sentimentale in E flat major for Flute and Piano, Op. 169

☐ Louise DiTullio (flute); Virginia DiTullio (piano) / Genesis 1048

Orthodoxy reigns with all the classical balances in order. Fine portrayal.

Vittorio Rieti   *(1898-   )*

Orchestra

Introduzione e Gioco delle ore (1954)

☐ Louisville Orchestra / Whitney (conductor) / Louisville 545-11 (monaural)

Rieti's "Introduction and Game of the Hours" is a title covering for a prelude and a scherzo. The leaflet issued with the disc states that Rieti "does not wish to reveal the personal motives which prompted him to choose [the] title." So be it. Whatever lies behind the composition, the aural evidence is that of a closely knit entity with balletic stripes. Whatever it may be, Rieti's "enigma" definitely offers no problem in its tonal spirit and impulse. The Louisvillians are most supportive in their playing.

Concerto for Cello (and Twelve Instruments)

☐ Members of Orchestra Sinfonica di Roma / Amfitheatrof (cello) / Flagello (conductor) / Serenus 12013

No tutti blur in this case, with the solo cello framed by eleven winds and a double bass. The Concerto consists of two paired movements, the first part of the initial one beginning with the showmanship of a solo cadenza. Rieti knows how to score. There is as much *brio* in his chosen small group as in the pugnacious welter of sound poured out by Strauss-Respighi orchestrational methods.

The piece is attractively played and firmed up with warm and vibrant sound.

Concerto for Harpsichord and Orchestra (1955)

☐ Chamber Orchestra / Marlowe (harpsichord) / Baron (conductor) / Composers Recordings S–312

No instrument is quite as telling as the harpsichord in music that reformulates eighteenth-century clarity. Neoclassicism equals musical semantics in its most precise delivery, while the polyglot prose of neo-romanticism obliterates the decurtated diction so personal to the keyboard instrument. Rieti's style, therefore, is perfectly set forth via the harpsichord, its figurations framing pandiatonic tonalities, its pert antiphony a tasteful coloration, its gushed chords a special kind of massed vertical counterpoint against the linear chatter.

Classical precepts are naturally found in the structures; the deviations are simply synonymic: the finale, for example, is a Tarantella rather than the usual rondo, the scherzo is more balletic and paper-thin than serious.

The playing is crisply precise, virtuosic, and simply marvelous. Style is purely controlled, the motility quotient is fulfilled, and the give and take ideal. This music offers an entire relish of delight in which the performers have made certain that not one flavor is missing. Like the Partita (see under *Chamber Music,* p. 1513 [Partita for Flute, Oboe, String Quartet, and Harpsichord Obbligato]), the CRI disc is a transfer from the deleted Decca catalogue (DL–710135).

Concerto No. 3 for Piano and Orchestra (1960)

☐ Orchestra Sinfonica di Roma / Santoliquido (piano) / Flagello (conductor) / Serenus 12033

Rieti's Concerto traverses classical territory in its three parts, firmly detailing its basic triadic harmonic language with conventional modernity. Nice tunes and nice rhythmic action maintain interest. The movements are linked and cover a broad introduction plus the usual fast-paced division, a slow-tempoed section, followed by a cadenza and a finale with polyphonic address.

The solo performance is effective, though the piano's sound is on the dry side. The orchestral playing is somewhat bland.

Medieval Variations

Six Short Pieces

☐ Guralnik (piano) / Serenus 12013

The *Sei pezzi brevi* fulfill the titled requirements (such as *Elegia* and *Barcarola*) with neat, neoclassic diction. The Variations are based on an old English tune (unidentified). There are seven permutations demonstrating expert creative technique, though rather neutral expressivity.

Guralnik's conceptions are first-rate in all respects.

Solo Instrument and Orchestra

Cello

Harpsichord

Piano

Instrumental

Piano

Two Pianos

Chorale, Variations, and Finale
Three Vaudeville Marches
Valse fugitive

☐ Gold and Fizdale (pianos) / Serenus 12033

Rieti's musical language is tied to neoclassicism whether it be for the gentleness of the *Valse* or the impulse that fills the Marches. In the larger Chorale, Variations, and Finale, which includes ten different variational concepts, there is the same stylized comprehension. The purposes are always purely musical, sound in structure and sound in the actual sounds.

All three works were written for this two-piano team. They provide in their playing a constancy of nice sonority, precise ensemble, and appropriate coloration.

Violin

Capriccio for Violin and Piano

☐ Ravina (violin); Gzhashvili (piano) / Serenus 12063

The most interesting point about this piece is the faint resemblance in its concluding section to the final canonic movement in the César Franck A major violin and piano Sonata (see under *Franck: Chamber Music*, p. 649). However, Rieti does not evade his chosen responsibility of providing a violinist with a nice six-minute piece. It could be encore material, and it certainly is worth a listen now and then.

Chamber Music

Pastorale e Fughetta for Flute, Viola, and Piano

☐ Trio della Casa Serena / Serenus 12063

For heaven's sake don't read the liner note before listening to the music. It will put you in an improper mood and would be unfair to Rieti's nicely formed five-minute piece. (Serenus, please! do *something* about your puerile, inane liner notes, for the good of your business, your clients, and, not least, your composers.) That said, it remains to say that the contrastive *Fughetta* is a charmer, a representative of dandy neoclassicism. The *Pastorale* has the quality of a lyrical romantic voice. The playing is well shaped and defines all the poetic and polyphonic fancy of the score.

String Quartet No. 3 (1953)

☐ Phoenix String Quartet / Serenus 12063

Rieti spins his themes and cogently develops them, while within his classical procedures persists a late-period romantic center of gravity. The depth of expression, especially in the third movement of the four linked in the quartet, emphasizes this viewpoint. The finale that follows has a character and speed that give, within its action, the necessary contrastive roughage for true balance.

This is a good performance. Not the same can be said for Serenus's liner notes, so often childish. The firm should do something about this important point.

Concertino for Five Instruments

☐ Chamber Players of Heilbronn / Serenus 12013

Individual instrumentation (flute, viola, cello, harp, and harpsichord). The last two might have led to a dominance of plucked timbres, but Rieti (and the performers) carefully combine and separate the colors—further highlighted by cadenza specification. The Concertino is a bubbly affair, as though Scarlatti was refurbished by Rieti, with compartmented movements that define the forms as pithily as Scarlatti's binary types.

An unknown group to this writer, the Heilbronn group plays expertly, beautifully, and with fine ensemble and balance.

Incisioni (*Five Engravings in Brass*) (1967)

☐ Cambridge Brass Quintet / Crystal S-204

A fanfare-like opening, two chorale movements surrounding a *Sinfonia da caccia,* and a fugato to sew up matters. Clean neoclassic decorum. No violent color oppositions as found in neo-romantic conceptions but extremely colorful Stravinskian harmonies of his *Dumbarton Oaks* period (see under *Stravinsky: Orchestra*).

The Cambridge five live up to Rieti's title by playing incisively, with all the requirements of representation fully defined. This is an example of taste in brass chamber-music playing.

Silografie

☐ Ariel Quintet / Serenus 12063

The title of Rieti's suite, "Woodcuts," is a play on words (purposeful or not), since the five-part suite is for woodwind quintet. The music is a sowing of the soil of dance (*Sarabande, Cotillon,* and so on) with modern seeds. No irritation; the process is gentle and the product delightful. So is the playing.

Partita for Flute, Oboe, String Quartet, and Harpsichord Obbligato (1945)

☐ Baron (flute); Roseman (oboe); Libove and Ajemian (violins); Zaratzian (viola); McCracken (cello); Marlowe (harpsichord) / Marlowe (conductor) / Composers Recordings S-312

Rieti's music is a delight to the ear, minus any vernacularisms (read: effects); and even when he contrapuntalizes, by way of a chromatic double fugue in four voices (movement 4), the texture is airy, permitting the sounds to dance their way.

The Partita opens with a set of variations, is followed by a Scherzino (Sylvia Marlowe describes this perfectly as "a delicious, light movement"); a slow division that is rather darker than any of the other portions; the fugue mentioned above; and concludes with a *Giga.*

The playing is perfect and the sound ideal.

Vocal

Quattro liriche italiane

Voice with Accompaniment

☐ Reardon (baritone); Herbert (piano) / Serenus 12019

Three songs on the gay side and full of grace, plus one with a strong serious sense but not blatant. Reardon's fine vocal instrument provides performances of sheen and meaning.

Sette liriche saffiche

Voice and Orchestra

☐ Chamber Orchestra / Pecchioli (mezzo-soprano) / Rossi (conductor) / Serenus 12063

The "Seven Sapphic Lyrics" are succinct in length and in the size of the orchestral framework, which consists of five winds, three brass, a harp, a piano doubling on celesta, and strings.

Benedetta Pecchioli sings these dainty and delicate miniatures (all seven together cover but eleven minutes) with fine artistry. She is thoroughly musical and has a charming mezzo voice that fits these songs perfectly.

Ballet	**Capers**

☐ London Philharmonic Orchestra / Mester (conductor) / Desto 6434

Waltzes galore: *Valse légère,* Belinda Waltz, *Valse,* and Rondo Waltz. This gives the triple-beat dance a fat majority in the total eight movements, the others being a Prelude, Gavotte, Serenade, and a final Clown March.

This is light and tidy functional music. It is played definitively.

Julius Rietz (1812-1877)

Orchestra

Concert Overture in A major, Op. 7

☐ Louisville Orchestra / Mester (conductor) / Louisville S–703

Mostly Mendelssohnian with some Beethoven touches. Another piece of evidence that on those library shelves lie pieces that could easily replace the overplayed standards in the repertoire, or, at least, give them some sabbatical leave. This Overture shows there would be no loss. Credit Mester with a fine rediscovery and just as fine a performance.

Solo Instrument and Orchestra

Oboe

Konzertstück in F minor for Oboe and Orchestra, Op. 33

☐ Frankfurt Radio Symphony Orchestra / Holliger (oboe) / Inbal (conductor) / Philips 9500970

A Mendelssohnian rub-off. No surprise, since Rietz was thoroughly familiar with, and most responsive to, Mendelssohn's music. There are three movements, with the usual balances between them. The playing is most impressive and is totally related to the score.

Dennis Riley (1943-   )

Chamber Music

Variations II: Trio (1967)

☐ Strava (violin); Hibbard (viola); Berdahl (cello) / Composers Recordings S–324

An example of the cultivation of post-Webern style. Riley has a good hand with colors, dabbing them rather than painting them over large surfaces. A sense of impressionism thereby takes place. The music produces a strong and most agreeable effect.

Terry Riley (1935-   )

Orchestra

In C (1964)

☐ Members of the Center of the Creative and Performing Arts in the State University of New York at Buffalo / Riley (conductor) / Columbia MS–7178

Take a pitch (here C, of course) and let it persist, in this case for forty-three minutes. Take fifty-three patterns in which the total pitches included in each are concentrated to the extreme (six patterns with but one pitch, twenty bits with two tones, eighteen segments with three, a few with four, a few with five, and one with seven). Take these patterns and add them one at a time, freely entering and concluding. Take this mix, and, in general, one has a description of Riley's *In C.*

The consonant constancy is a reminder of the disco world (just of the undeviation and invariability, not of the sounds and style). The name of the game may be a pitch-happening where the action is limited to the tones of the C scale plus an occasional B flat and an F sharp. Whatever it may be termed, it results in a sonorous, superjunctioned superfetation. Interesting and fascinating, but be warned that a small amount goes a long way.

By overdubbing, three performances are combined. The total sound structure on the recording covers three each of vibraphones, saxophones, trombones, violas, flutes, oboes, and trumpets, two each of bassoons, marimbaphones, and clarinets, plus piano.

A Rainbow in Curved Air (1968)

Instrumental

☐ Riley (organ and harpsichord) / Columbia MS-7315

Organ and Harpsichord

Riley's creative goal is the clinging to reiterative patterns and repetitive segments that endeavor to persuade and implore over and over again. These constitute an overwhelming generosity of easy, extremely homogeneous tonal sounds. A religious ritual surrounds the music.

The utopian world Riley hopes for is detailed on the album cover. His redolent music does not attempt to describe it, though it contains an optimistic quality in general as Riley covers the score by playing five instruments en route: electric organ and electric harpsichord, as well as rocksichord, dumbec, and tambourine.

Poppy Nogood and the Phantom Band (1966)

Saxophone and Organ

☐ Riley (soprano saxophone and electric organ) / Columbia MS-7315

Another Terry Riley composition with repeats of simplistic tonal patterns to form a whole. The Hindu-Afro quality is noticeable in this music that is more proclamatory in comparison to his other recorded works. Still, the reduplication (a type of sonic alliteration) produces, if one is willing to be convinced, hallucinatory perceptions.

Nikolai Rimsky-Korsakov (1844-1908)

Antar: Symphonic Suite, Op. 9

Orchestra

☐ Utah Symphony Orchestra / Abravanel (conductor) / Vanguard C-10060

Rimsky's Opus 9 (also known as "Symphony No. 2") is no *Scheherazade* (*see below*), but it has almost as much color distributed among its four movements, and the second movement is chock full of it.

Abravanel shows a sensitivity to the formal design of the piece while underplaying the dramatic thrusts that the winds and brass provide. However, there is breadth and spaciousness in his reading and it is far better than the other available edition performed by the Moscow Radio Symphony Orchestra on Melodiya/Angel S-40230.

Capriccio espagnol, Op. 34

☐ London Symphony Orchestra / Argenta (conductor) / London 6006
☐ Berlin Philharmonic Orchestra / Maazel (conductor) / Deutsche Grammophon 138033

Argenta's depiction of this work has stood up through the years (released in an album titled *España,* and including works by Chabrier, Granados, and Moszkowski). The tempi are choice, the reading true to the last chord, the solo exhibits natural. Maazel's conception has distinguished flair and one favors its urgency.

Some notes regarding the many other editions that are on the market. Most of them endeavor to color what is already fully colored. Form reacts upon form and produces, thus, overdone (negative) results. Stokowski's version (London 21117) should be avoided, unless the auditor doesn't mind, among other things, some slashes in the score and some reorchestration.

Chanson russe (Dubinushka), Op. 62

☐ L'Orchestre de la Suisse Romande / Ansermet (conductor) / London 6036

A version of a revolutionary song, "The Little Oak Stick," sometimes heard with *ad libitum* chorus. Squarely set, this nice tune in its slight translation is given a properly spirited performance.

Christmas Eve: Suite (1894)

☐ L'Orchestre de la Suisse Romande / Ansermet (conductor) / London 6036

The agenda for the Suite, drawn from Rimsky-Korsakov's opera *La Nuit de Noël,* is picturesquely assorted. First, a nocturnal scene, then a mazurka, a round dance, some satanic mood music, a polonaise, and in conclusion an orchestral sketch of Christmas Day at dawn. The opera (first produced in St. Petersburg in December of 1895) was not successful; the orchestral Suite survives rightfully.

Its performance is tasteful.

The Flight of the Bumble Bee (1898)

☐ L'Orchestre de la Suisse Romande / Ansermet (conductor) / London 6036

This evergreen from the *Tsar Sultan* opera is not included in the orchestral Suite Rimsky-Korsakov designed for concert presentation. The definitive Suite is available (*see below* [*The Tale of the Tsar Sultan*]).

Most often the speed chosen for this piece is so reckless that while virtuosity is served, musical authenticity is wrecked. It is a bee being pictured, after all, not a transcontinental missile. Those who conduct Rimsky's sketch *presto possibile* should be criticized. Full play of proper speed, thereby achieving a definitive illustration, is best heard in Ernest Ansermet's conception.

Le Coq d'or: Suite (1907)

☐ London Symphony Orchestra / Dorati (conductor) / Mercury 75016

No fat on this orchestral body, but a just proper amount of tonal torsion. It is colored with Rimskyish taste. Those are all the salient significances the music needs.

Overture to The Maid of Pskov (1891)

☐ Bolshoi Theater Orchestra / Svetlanov (conductor) / Melodiya/Angel S-40221

Rimsky-Korsakov's initial opera *Pskovityanka* is, of course, a museum piece. Its Overture is rarely heard, the separately published Two Intermezzi and the Symphonic Scene descriptive of a hunt and a thunderstorm are never programmed. It is interesting to realize, therefore, that the Overture was a favorite of John Barbirolli's. In conversations with the author he stated that he considered it to be Rimsky-Korsakov's best Overture.

One may not agree with Barbirolli's opinion but certainly the music (heard here in a fair performance) does not deserve to be neglected. Unfortunately, Barbirolli never recorded the work.

Overture to *May Night*

☐ L'Orchestre de la Suisse Romande / Ansermet (conductor) / London 6012

The Overture to Rimsky-Korsakov's second opera (see under *Opera and Dramatic Music* [*May Night*]). Rimsky's consideration of orchestral color is held a bit under wraps in this case. He described his instrumentation as of ''classic'' procedure. Nonetheless a full orchestra is used, only lacking a tuba in the brass section and percussion timbres as adjuncts to the timpani. The playing by Ansermet's group is well crafted.

Overture

To *Sadko* (1897) / To *The Tsar's Bride* (1898)

☐ Bolshoi Theater Orchestra / Svetlanov (conductor) / Melodiya/Angel S–40221

Peppy and dramatic conceptions heard in thoroughly lively and imaginative performances.

(For a discussion of the complete opera of *The Tsar's Bride*, see under *Opera and Dramatic Music*.)

Russian Easter Overture, Op. 36

☐ Chicago Symphony Orchestra / Stokowski (conductor) / RCA LSC–3067

This is a stunning performance. Truly, no conductor has ever achieved the golden fusion and electropositive sound Stokowski obtained every time he performed this color-charged composition. It was his piece, and it is his and his alone among the several recordings in the catalogue. There is no competition as far as this writer is concerned.

Often, Stokowski substituted a voice for the trombone recitative that forms part of the work. Not acceptable. Fortunately, that practice is not followed in this case. Indeed, in these days of superspecialized, jet-setting conductors, for Rimsky's Overture no one has ever managed to come close to this fellow. The recording is also in a two-disc collection RCA has called *Hits*—VCS–7077.

***Sadko*: Musical Picture, Op. 5**

☐ L'Orchestre de la Suisse Romande / Ansermet (conductor) / London 6036

Not to be confused with the opera Rimsky-Korsakov wrote based on the old epic legend of Sadko, the Novgorod minstrel. This short symphonic poem contains (and is terminally balanced by) music suggestive of the sea; in between come song and dance materials.

Ansermet is not overcoloristic in his presentation, but there is clean playing that will satisfy.

***Scheherazade*, Op. 35**

☐ London Symphony Orchestra / Gruenberg (violin) / Stokowski (conductor) / London 21005
☐ London Philharmonic Orchestra / Friend (violin) / Haitink (conductor) / Philips 6500410

From the early electrical era through the years, Stoky's recordings of this work were the *sine qua non* of the many entries on the market. He began by recording excerpts and then, over a period of forty years, produced four complete versions. Each was a conversation piece for recording buffs and hi-fi enthusiasts. Each was a blockbuster. Each could be termed ''Rimsky-Stoky,'' the version listed above no less than the others. Each was splashed with *rubato,* instrumentally nicked by Stokowski's interpretative précis. True, the editings and the packaging were sufficient to have Mr. S. quartered by the scholastics; but dismissing all such arguments, Rimsky's score has truly benefited from Stokowski's trimmings. His becomes the *beau idéal* for the kind of music Rimsky-Korsakov poured into his programmatic symphonic suite.

This is the most lush, most spectacular, most magical version in the catalogue. If the record collector wants controlled color sensitivity and sheer musical documentation, then, of course, Haitink is your man. His conception (with the London Philharmonic Orchestra, on Philips 6500410) is rich and true, dramatic and gorgeous, and surely a five-star affair. But this does not nullify the specialness of the Stokowski hot ice cream dish, which is not for purists.

(For a piano arrangement of *Scheherazade,* see under *Rimsky-Korsakov/Prokofiev: Instrumental: piano.*)

The Tale of the Tsar Sultan: Suite, Op. 57

☐ L'Orchestre de la Suisse Romande / Ansermet (conductor) / London 6012

A good slice of the best items (save one) in Rimsky's opera. The surprise is that the famous *Flight of the Bumble Bee* was not included in the Suite that Rimsky-Korsakov made for concert purposes. That must be heard as a separate excerpt (*see above*).

There have been a number of recordings that have nevertheless added the *Flight* to the three official movements that comprise the *Tsar Sultan* Suite. In some cases that piece is defined as part 4 of the Suite, but this is not authentic (the Philips 839744 release with Roberto Benzi conducting the Monte Carlo Opera Orchestra, for example). On an old mono disc Ansermet followed this procedure, as did Issay Dobrowen; the former for London (LL–1635), the latter for Angel (35010).

The *Flight* is an intermezzo between the two scenes of Act III in the opera. The Suite covers the introductions to Act I and Act II, plus the second scene of Act IV.

Ansermet's treatment of the Suite is not overly brilliant, but it has all of the subtle shadings required.

*Solo
Instrument
and
Orchestra*

Piano

Concerto in C sharp minor for Piano and Orchestra, Op. 30

☐ Hamburg Symphony / Ponti (piano) / Kapp (conductor) / Candide 31056

Simple, direct narrative, with one-movement form paralleled by development of a single thematic idea. Most of the first two-thirds sounds like Rimsky; the remainder is rather of neutral personality. Probably the latter is the reason the work has stayed on the shelf rather than led a concert existence.

Ponti turns everything over in good form, and his octave playing ripples off the record grooves. The orchestra is fair but good enough for what it must do, which Richard Kapp supervises nicely.

Violin

Concert Fantasy for Violin and Orchestra, Op. 33

☐ Orchestra of Radio Luxembourg / Rosand (violin) / de Froment (conductor) / Turnabout 34629

The title above is as Turnabout lists it. The "official" heading on the full score is *Fantaisie de concert sur des thèmes russes* in B minor, Op. 33."

Rimsky-Korsakov was so pleased with his display piece (which Aaron Rosand displays with scrupulous technique and total musicality) that he planned another, on Spanish themes. It became the famous orchestral *Capriccio espagnol* (see under *Orchestra*), which features various soloisms.

Quintet in B flat major for Piano and Winds, Op. Posth.

Chamber Music

☐ Members of the New Philharmonia Wind Ensemble, London / Blumental (piano) / Turnabout 34477

Totally removed from nationalism, Rimsky treads the straight and narrow in this three-movement work. A slight (very slight) twist occurs in the final Rondo with some mini-cadenzas for the instruments.

The quality of the flute, clarinet, bassoon, and horn are satisfactory and Felicia Blumental does a professional job with her part.

I Still Love Him

Vocal

On Georgian Hills, Op. 3, No. 4

Song of the Skylark, Op. 43, No. 1

Voice with Accompaniment

☐ Davrath (soprano); Werba (piano) / Vanguard VSD–71115

The outgoing quality of the Song of the Skylark (the first of the four-part cycle *In Spring*) is opposite to the introverted sense of *On Georgian Hills*.

Davrath's lyric intensity is perfect for the *Georgian* item. Her vocal manner is just as appropriate for the other pair of songs.

May Night

Opera and Dramatic Music

☐ Moscow Radio Symphony Orchestra and Chorus / Pastushenko and Matushina (sopranos); Sapegina (mezzo-soprano) / Lisovsky and Yelnikov (tenors); Budrin, Krivchenya, and Troitsky (basses) / Fedoseyev (conductor) / Deutsche Grammophon 2709063

Despite operas of this type having proven not to be exportable, a recording of this early Rimsky stage work deserves attention. There are some loose hairs hanging on the voices but these are removed by fine characterizations, especially Olga Pastushenko as a water sprite and Alexei Krivchenya in the Mayor's part. Good orchestra, good chorus, and reliable conducting.

(For a recording of the Overture to *May Night*, see under *Orchestra*.)

The Snow Maiden

☐ Moscow Radio Symphony Orchestra and Chorus / Sokolik and Zakharenko (sopranos); Arkhipova (mezzo-soprano); Grigoriev (tenor); Moksyakov (baritone); Vedernikov (bass) / Fedoseyev (conductor) / Columbia/Melodiya M4–34599

This is the opera that includes the Dance of the Buffoons that many know. But so few know Rimsky-Korsakov's *Snegourotchka*, or his other operas, for that matter, since they have never reached international repertory status. Most are based on fantastic Russian legends, as is this one, and there's good music in many of them (as the orchestral suites prove).

Length this work does have—eight record sides to this release. Orchestrational know-how it has also, as is to be expected. The production recorded is representative, most of the singing is professional (best by the male vocalists), and the orchestra plus chorus are first class.

The Tsar's Bride

☐ Bolshoi Theater Orchestra and Chorus / Vishnevskaya and Andreyeva (sopranos); Arkhipova and Borisenko (mezzo-sopranos); Borisova (alto); Atlantov and Sokolov (tenors); Valaitis (baritone); Morozov and Nesterenko (basses) / Mansurov (conductor) / Melodiya/Angel S–4122

All-out operatic twists to gain love and body. Love potions and ultimate stabbings follow. The story line is complicated, to be sure, but the music's the thing and there's plenty of it, set in specific formal numbers, ensemble sections, together with rich and colorful use of the voice. Highlights: a fiery duet in Act I and a dark-faceted apostrophe and a trio in Act II, plus an aria in Act IV.

The Bolshoi organization is first-class, and both the orchestra and the chorus cover themselves with honor. So does Fuat Mansurov, who directs with commanding presence and paces the action beautifully. Vishnevskaya takes a role that has extremely difficult music for the greater part—registered high, in the majority—but she is most capable. For most of the singing the last statement describes the quality of the rest of the cast. Of course, it is all sung in Russian (a translation of the text is provided with the three-disc album).

(For a recording of the Overture to *The Tsar's Bride,* see under *Orchestra* [under Overture to *Sadko*].)

Rimsky-Korsakov / Prokofiev

Instrumental

Piano

Scheherazade **(Fantasia Arrangement from the Symphonic Suite)**

☐ Prokofiev (piano) / Klavier 125

Here's a real curiosity, its existence not even noted in the usual bibliographical and biographical lists.

Not that one needs any kind of piano version of this orchestral evergreen that went out of fashion but is now returning to the repertory. Still, it is fascinating to hear what Prokofiev did with Rimsky-Korsakov's score. He picked items here and there from the original large work, with the performance of his condensation clocked in at seven and one-half minutes flat! Most of the transcription uses extracts from the first movement; there is less of movement 2, and still less of part 3. Movement 4, save for its closing chords, is bypassed.

Most Interesting Aspect: the modulatory shifts.

Most Questionable Aspect: the treatment of tremolo.

(For a discussion of the symphonic setting of *Scheherazade,* see under *Rimsky-Korsakov: Orchestra.*)

Jean Rivier (1896-)

Chamber Music

Grave and Presto for Saxophone Quartet

☐ Marcel Mule Saxophone Quartet / Musical Heritage Society MHS–817

Clarity of form distinguishes this quartet, which employs a medium requiring compositional perspicuity; otherwise, a morass of sticky, musical mud results. Rivier solves the problem excellently. Each part of the work has controlled outline and picturesque individuality, with rich chordal coherence in the *Grave* and rhythmic rough-and-tumble gestures in the Presto.

The playing of this team (Marcel Mule, Georges Gourdet, Guy Lacour, and Marcel Josse) displays a mastery of tone quality and rhythm. Their ensemble is dazzling. This is saxophonish beauty that would be difficult to duplicate.

John Donald Robb (1892-   )

Dialogue for Guitar and Piano (1967)

☐ Robb (guitar and piano) / Opus One 13

Chamber Music

The one-performer indication is explained by Robb's first recording the piano part on a two-track tape and then recording the guitar part on the other track while listening to the initial one. The style here is solely guitarish, since the piano part is totally in "prepared" style minus any of the paraphernalia required. Thus plucking and strumming of the piano strings predominate. A nocturnal cast covers the music.

Collage (1964)

☐ Folkways 33436

Electronic Music

A type of electronic étude formed from tape splicing. Nice, though nowadays it would be typed as an academic piece.

Leroy Robertson (1896-1971)

Punch and Judy Overture (1945)

☐ Utah Symphony Orchestra / Abravanel (conductor) / Turnabout 34459

Orchestra

The piece is carefree in spirit, but Robertson is careful to define clearly the structure of his duo-themed piece. There are no problems with either music or performance.

Come, Come Ye Saints
The Lord's Prayer (1953)

☐ Philadelphia Orchestra and Mormon Tabernacle Choir / Ormandy (conductor) / Columbia MS-6068

Choral

Chorus and Orchestra

Robertson combines an old English tune with a pair of Utah folk songs in the first work. *The Lord's Prayer* is a new setting of the well-known words; it appears in the final section of Robertson's Oratorio from the Book of Mormon.

The association of the Philadelphians and the famed Mormon Tabernacle Choir has a long and successful history. The results here show this advantage.

Thomas Robinson (ca. 1588-1610)

Toy

☐ Channon and Poulton (lutes) / Nonesuch 73010

Instrumental

Two Lutes

A moderately paced bit taken from the composer's *Schoole of Musicke*. Notwithstanding the title, the music has dignity.

George Rochberg (1918-   )

Chamber Symphony for Nine Instruments (1953)

☐ Members of the Oberlin Chamber Orchestra / Moore (conductor) / Desto 6444

Orchestra

Strong row-formulated music set in a scoring that balances three instruments in each of the wind (oboe, clarinet, and bassoon), brass (horn, trumpet, and trombone), and string (violin, viola, and cello) categories. Classically formal monitoring is used with a strong supply of characterized statements. In short, Rochberg's chamber work (he thinks of it as one for small orchestra) goes beyond functional circumstances for dynamic, emotive ones.

The performance is one in which the order and continuity are well stated. It is, perhaps, a little blatant at times, but never mind, it is never tentative, and one prefers guts rather than reticence. The little syllable (a vocal grunt?) left on the tape before the beginning of the third movement is mentioned as the only blemish in a brightly recorded edition.

Music for the Magic Theater (1965)

☐ Oberlin Orchestra / Owings (piano) / Moore (conductor) / Desto 6444

Rochberg's unique musical collage is described by three divisions noted as "acts." Thus, the first one, "In which the present and the past are mixed up"; the second, "In which the past haunts us with its magic beauty"; and the last, "In which we realize that only the present is really real." The synthesis of the first and last acts is a dream-convergence-repulsion affair of material including the use of disparate quotes of other composers' music. One finds blended and opposed Beethoven and Webern, Mozart and Varèse, and Rochberg himself with Mahler (not in that order but so indicated to stress the strong dissimilarity). The middle act is a sensitively colored reworking of an Adagio from a Mozart Divertimento.

The variegation is thereby heartily comparative, using tonal and twelve-tone ideas, traditional phrasing and aleatoric elements, metrical and nonmetrical order, and so on. No mishmash but a true musical magic is in Rochberg's control, with material appearing, blending, crossing, disappearing, and reappearing. Whatever there is and however it is arranged produce a true artistic warrant. Rochberg's work is, within its specific style, a small masterpiece.

The Oberlin Orchestra and its conductor do themselves proud with this very difficult work, especially in its styled shifts. They provide a recording that is the equal of any metropolitan outfit.

Night Music (1949)

☐ Louisville Orchestra / Grace Whitney (cello) / Robert Whitney (conductor) / Louisville 623 (monaural)

Music that starts with a solo contrabassoon does not propose rampant optimism. Rochberg's Night Music, a transfer from his Symphony No. 1 (*see below*), which he considered too lengthy (it had five movements), is of the deepest black dye. It is a music that resists average nocturnal categorization. There are sombre moves within this work, ice-packed with mystery. Early Rochberg (composed in 1949), it remains one of his most effective pieces.

The Louisville organization does well and so does Grace Whitney with her solo section. Fanny Brandeis's note on the piece fails to indicate that Night Music obtained the George Gershwin Memorial Award in 1953 and was then premiered by the New York Philharmonic.

Symphony No. 1 (1957)

☐ Louisville Orchestra / Whitney (conductor) / Louisville S-634

Early Rochberg, composed in 1949, then revised in 1957. There are symphonies tabulated as tonal *species Americana,* such as Roy Harris's Third, Randall Thompson's Second, even Copland's Third. That category does not fit Rochberg's hard-driving and steam-powered first movement (there is a bit of reflection from Hindemith and Bartók, however, but only in the most general way).

Part 2 is a *Tema e variazioni* (six parts); the finale begins slowly and then moves into a dynamic *gioioso* construction. The variations have a touching bittersweet essence; the concluding movement has exciting timbral portions and expressive rhythmic patterns within the design.

George Rochberg does not write in this manner any more. From the general style of the first Symphony he later went into serialism and is now involved in other creative arguments. Nonetheless, this work has firm, lasting qualities, explicit in its direction, meaningful in its entirety. It enjoys a comfortable performance, perhaps lacking only a bit more strength in the strings. The wind and brass totality is fine.

Symphony No. 2 (1956)

☐ New York Philharmonic / Torkanowsky (conductor) / Columbia Special Products AMS-6379

The generating impulse of symphonicism greets one immediately in the magnificent, thundering unison opening of this work. It is drawn on throughout the piece. Rhapsody there is, but not of crawling dismemberment. Rochberg writes a Symphony and scores it likewise. The orchestration is huge, granitic in strength. Massive doublings are utilized, and this is one composer who knows the blue-steel beauty of high fiddles. In descriptive terms, Rochberg's Symphony is both dramatic and ecstatic. That it is twelve-tone is simply a statistical point.

To be able to cope with Rochberg's score demands a perceptive conductor. Werner Torkanowsky more than fills the bill. He does wonders and so do the Philharmonic members. Rarely have they played as well.

Black Sounds for Seventeen Players (1965)

☐ Oberlin Wind Ensemble / Grenadilla GS-1019

Wind and Brass Ensemble

Originally written for a dance that concerned the act of murder. To expect sonorous suavity, therefore, would be ridiculous. In proper creative stance Rochberg commands a frenzy of colors, jabs his fricative sounds, their motility constant. Even in the quiet moments there is an inner motion of excitement.

The Oberlin group (no conductor is listed, which makes their achievement exceedingly special) projects Rochberg's tensely ordered set of meanings with technical exactitude and musical significance.

Nach Bach Fantasy for Harpsichord (1966)

☐ Kipnis (harpsichord) / Grenadilla GS-1019

Instrumental

Harpsichord

Not Bach-Rochberg, but Bach Rochberged. And a dignified and fascinating musical commentary it is. Taking a Bach text, Rochberg quotes and transforms quotes from it. It is as though a transparency were placed on the pages of the Bach piece and here and there elements were written over or within it, so that snippets tonal contrast with snippets atonal. In total, two composers join to make a single music.

The playing of Igor Kipnis (for whom *Nach Bach* was written) is outstanding.

Piano

Carnival Music (Suite for Piano Solo) (1971)

☐ Mandel (piano) / Grenadilla GS–1019

A fascinating and absolutely successful joining of serious and popular elements, especially in movements 1 (Fanfares and March), 2 (Blues), and 5 (Toccata-Rag). This precept is less apparent in part 3 (*Sfumato*) and totally absent in part 4 (*Largo doloroso*).

Especially stimulating is the effect of the styled splicing of the data. It is persuasively contrastive, natural in its placement, and never contentious. One always senses a musical *déjà vu* situation as the pops stuff is heard: the similarity to the zither theme of the movie *The Third Man* and Jacques Brel songs in movement 1, the Gershwin Preludes in the second movement, and tinny piano-roll tunes in the finale.

It is a great idea and accomplished magnificently. It is played beautifully and with minute attention to every nuance and gesture by Alan Mandel.

(Why Grenadilla has bands separating the last three movements but lumps the first two together without an indication cannot be answered. Separation of movements in a work of this type should be mandatory.)

Twelve Bagatelles (1952)

☐ Burge (piano) / Advance 3 (monaural)

Rochberg's set of short pieces (most of them fit on a single page of published music) demonstrate true artistic deeds in their twelve-tone language. As a cross-reference to traditional formal structures, each of the pieces makes its point succinctly and effectively, minus any preliminary pandect devoted to a technical bacchanal of analysis that would only confuse the listener. A defined sentiment pervades each essay: thus, the nervous *scherz* of the second one, the pert march character of No. 4, the majestic insistence of No. 9.

The performance is ideal. Burge the composer brings benefits to Burge the pianist. His conceptions are well-nigh perfect. To hear is to believe—and to understand.

Chamber Music

Dialogues for Clarinet and Piano (1958)

☐ Russo (clarinet); Ignacio (piano) / Capra 1204

Four interlocutions in which sharp serial syntax provides the commentary. Most of the music is nervously eruptive; the third part is more relaxed. It is the former manifestation that provides a ruthless energy that is exciting—and convincing.

Duo Concertante for Violin and Cello (1955)

☐ Sokol (violin); Fischer (cello) / Composers Recordings S–337

Twelve-tone music with eloquent intensity but with plentiful subtle mixes within it. Rochberg speaks of the feeling of "composed improvisation" in his piece. But caprice or mere fancy do not dictate the structuring and arrangement of this duo. Its determinations have flash, but they also have controlled stylistic substance.

The performance by the first violinist and cellist of the Concord String Quartet has superb clarity. By their brilliance, vigor, and commitment, the playing of Mark Sokol and Norman Fischer makes a more powerful case for Rochberg's Duo than the performance of Daniel Kobialka (violin) and Jan Kobialka (cello) on Advance S–6.

Ricordanza, Soliloquy for Piano and Cello (1972)

☐ Fischer (cello); Rochberg (piano) / Composers Recordings S–337

A beautifully sensitive piece, just as beautifully crafted, firmly tonal (acutely so, but that's not to the music's detriment), and somewhat threnodic. Rochberg describes his work as "a commentary on the opening solo cello statement of Beethoven's C major cello Sonata, Opus 102, No. 1." (Actual quotation also takes place.)

While there is complete chamber-music partnership in the writing, there is much less in the recording. The cello's tone is full and round, the piano's just the opposite. Norman Fischer's playing is both strong and expressive.

Trio for Violin, Cello, and Piano (1963)

☐ Kooper (violin); Sherry (cello); Boehm (piano) / Turnabout 34520

Rochberg's Trio begins with a declarative unaccompanied violin section and is representative of the formation of the piece. Alternative use of solo divisions with string-instrument duo and full trio formations follow. The last also tends to liberate the voices—chunky tutti treatment is in the great minority. Thus the structural gravity is found by instrumental definition rather than integration. Term it a clever way of solving the problem of balance in writing a piano trio in twelve-tone style; nevertheless, the net result is irresistible.

Despite its intransigently sectionalized character (and without any fancy effects to help matters), Rochberg's Trio grows organically from one sequence to the next. It may take a few hearings before this becomes clear but it's all there for the recognizing. The instrumental charting may be designated as "clever" planning but it provides chamber music of artistic consequence.

Kees Kooper, Fred Sherry, and Mary Louise Boehm do quite well with the music; their playing is firm and strong. The recorded sound is a bit dry but doesn't disturb unduly.

Contra Mortem et Tempus (1965)

☐ Aeolian Quartet of Sarah Lawrence College / Composers Recordings S-231

Elegiac to the point of painful intensity. Quotations are woven into the fabric (snips of Berg and Webern are among them), but identification matters little since these become Rochberg's own through the superromantic constructivism of the conception. One is reminded of the strongly patterned colors and lines of the Symbolist school of painting.

The playing of Rochberg's highly charged music is not to be second-guessed. It was the Aeolian team that gave the first performance of the piece on August 18, 1965.

String Quartet No. 1 (1952)

☐ Concord String Quartet / Composers Recordings S-337

Rochberg states his first string quartet "owes a good deal to Bartók and Berg." True. However, it is one thing to be baldly imitative and it is something else again, as here, where influences are drawn off and lead to imaginative and inventive results. The four movements of this quartet speak with a full-blooded intensity that defines neo-romantic authority.

Splendid playing by the Concord String Quartet. All of the technical detail and musical range are sensitively realized in their performance.

String Quartet No. 2 with Soprano (1961)

☐ Concord String Quartet / Bryn-Julson (soprano) / Turnabout 34524

Rochberg's quartet is cast in one movement within which exact alternation of the strings and then the quartet with soprano takes place twice. This four-divisioned totality is split into a pair of large parts; the first for the string quartet, the second consisting of two *ariosi* for the soprano embracing a section set for the strings alone. The text (in English translation) is taken from the opening and closing stanzas of Rilke's *Ninth Duino Elegy.*

Without sacrificing one iota of formal serial logic, Rochberg's music fulfills the rich intensity of Rilke's text. There is a completely balanced and integrated projection of the material for the instruments and the voice, without any sense of descriptive tracery of the words by the string instruments. Such independence makes the music truly two-dimensional.

The performance has Bergian blaze and Bartókian bite. It needs no better recommendation than Rochberg's own testimonial. He speaks of the Concord's playing as a "remarkable combination of controlled accuracy and impassioned fervor." Regarding the vocalist's contribution Rochberg's description is one of "absolute security and ease." Absolutely!

String Quartet No. 3

☐ Concord String Quartet / Nonesuch 71283

One is reminded of Stravinsky's strong (almost violent) stylistic change from neoclassicism to dodecaphonicism by Rochberg's Third Quartet. Rochberg was for a long time a serialist. Then, with some preliminary (but intense) probing, he produced his Third Quartet. In terms of late-twentieth-century composition fashions it represents a rare and rarely sought type of tonality as the foundation for the musical structure. It is apparent that there are classical and romantic influences in the Quartet and there is twentieth-century stylistic assimilation as well. But there is no unfocused and unstable creative result just because Rochberg knows his Beethoven as well as he knows his Mahler and Bartók. Best of all he knows his Rochberg. With such knowledge he has produced one of the most important works by any American composer and probably written a masterwork.

There are five parts: a Fantasia preceded by an Introduction, a March, followed by Variations, another March, and a Finale designated as Scherzos and Serenades. Stylistic compulsion is one matter. A second (as important) point is the tension that arises when stylistic reidentification (rediscovery, therefore) is made by a composer. Rochberg has solved (and magnificently) his "ceaseless search for the most potent and effective way to translate [his] music energies" by total clarification of line, harmony, counterpoint, and rhythm, producing an art work of significance, profundity, and excitement. That his Quartet exhibits a vivid evocation of creative recall of late Beethoven and some others is less pertinent than the fact that he has produced a music of pertinent individuality. Critics have been writing about a hoped-for assimilation after all the experimentation and large assortment of styles that have surfaced since the 1930s. George Rochberg has accomplished it.

The performance is comprehensively detailed, magnificently proposed. We have Rochberg's own liner-note testimony that the Concord Quartet's recording "insures the perfect realization" of his composition "down to the last detail."

Serenata d'estate for Flute, Harp, Guitar, Violin, Viola, and Cello (1955)

☐ Contemporary Chamber Ensemble / Weisberg (conductor) / Nonesuch 71220

Rochberg's "Summer Serenade" is serial music, without severity. The usual expressionistic quality of serial style is not to be found here. The temper of the work is impressionistic, aptly described by Eric Salzman as music that has "a relaxed charm" and "a graceful swing."

Weisberg's musicians play Rochberg's eleven-minute instrumental gem beautifully.

Songs in Praise of Krishna

Vocal

*Voice with
Accompaniment*

☐ Pilgrim (soprano); Rochberg (piano) / Composers Recordings SD–360

A cycle of fourteen songs, covering a Indian legend that Rochberg states symbolizes "the longing of flesh for spirit and spirit for flesh." Enlarged tonal certification is used for this intensely declarative set of vocal essays.

Neva Pilgrim's artistry enhances Rochberg's music, revealing all their dramatic loveliness.

Blake Songs (1962)

*Voice and
Instrumental
Ensemble*

☐ Contemporary Chamber Ensemble / DeGaetani (mezzo-soprano) / Weisberg (conductor) / Nonesuch 71302

Serial technique is used in this set of four songs: *Ah! Sun-flower, Nurse's Song, The Fly,* and *The Sick Rose.* This style aptly reveals, as Rochberg describes, "the hidden, below-the-surface aspects" of Blake's poetry. The apposite instrumentation consists of three winds (flute, clarinet, and bass clarinet), three strings (violin, viola, and cello), plus harp and celesta. Voice and instruments are blended with a personality and an imagination that set the work high in the contemporary literature for the medium.

Eloquence and full meaning are realized in Jan DeGaetani's singing; Arthur Weisberg conducts with his usual authority. Not many contemporary composers are so well-served as Rochberg is in this recorded performance.

Tableaux (1968)

☐ Penn Contemporary Players and Male Chorus / DeGaetani (soprano); Ralphe and McFadden (speakers) / Wernick (conductor) / Turnabout 34492

Rochberg's purplescent inflamed score consists of a set of "sound pictures" from *The Silver Talons of Piero Kostrov,* a "surreal tale of terror and love" that was written by his deceased son. Its power is intense and violent and, at times, frightening. The colors used define these feelings and project others as well. Especially significant in the process is the electric harpsichord, a good amount of percussion, and some special in-lay over-lay of speaking parts. Effects abound but always with dramatic purpose aforethought. The use of the voice is virtuosic.

This is a significant performance and the star is, as expected, that complete artist, Jan DeGaetani. Her vocal coverage is perfect, from simple ballad style (part 9 of the dozen sections of the piece) to a musical yet blood-curdling scream that erupts in *The Eagle* (section 11). Wernick and his players are excellent. Much expressionistic musical detail and sonic Dr. Caligari-style mysticism are totally bogus. Not Rochberg's *Tableaux.*

Richard Rodgers   *(1902-1979)*

Slaughter on Tenth Avenue (1936)
Waltzes from *Carousel* (1945)

Orchestra

☐ Cincinnati Pops Orchestra / Kunzel (conductor) / Turnabout 34714

Both pieces are from the short-hair arena of musical comedy but are constantly popping up in the long-hair symphony orchestra world on "pops" programs. They're damn good. (The *Slaughter* item is from *On Your Toes.*) This is very high-energy playing, but tastefully on the mark.

Joaquín Rodrigo   (1902-   )

Solo Instrument and Orchestra

Cello

Concerto in modo galante for Violoncello and Orchestra (1949)

☐ Louisville Orchestra / Grace Whitney (cello) / Robert Whitney (conductor) / Louisville 613 (monaural)

Nationalism is little practiced in today's musical world of integral serialism, graphic notation, aleatoric response, and so on. Still, there are some of the old guard who do not deprive themselves of native identity in their work. Rodrigo practices his belief in this *Galante* Concerto which includes the rhythms of a *panaderos*, a *fandango asturiano*, and a *zapateado*. Rodrigo's contribution is recommended to all and sundry to prove that Spanish music did not end with Manuel de Falla.

Guitar

Concierto de Aranjuez for Guitar and Orchestra

☐ San Antonio Symphony Orchestra / Angel Romero (guitar) / Alessandro (conductor) / Mercury 75021

There are plentiful editions in the recorded music catalogue of this masterful nationalistic work, with Bream (on RCA LSC–2730), Lagoya (on Philips 6500454), Williams (with Barenboim conducting on Columbia M–33208 and with Ormandy conducting on Columbia MS–6834 and M3X–31508), Yepes (with Alonso conducting on Deutsche Grammophon 139440 and with Argenta conducting on London 6046), and others having recorded it. Even Zabaleta has been drawn to the piece and has put it on disc in a harp version on Angel S–37042.

The performance chosen is sparkling and seductive, intense and intimate. It carries forth an internal rhythm that exposes all the music's beauties, intensely so in the nocturnally poetic slow movement. The late Victor Alessandro produces a crisp, clear-cut orchestral framework that displays the San Antonio's fine qualities.

Fantasía para un gentilhombre for Guitar and Small Orchestra (1954)

☐ Orchestre National de l'Opéra de Monte-Carlo / Lagoya (guitar) / de Almeida (conductor) / Philips 6500454

The thematic data in Rodrigo's four-part work is taken from the music of the seventeenth-century guitarist Gaspar Sanz. Accordingly, dances dominate, such as a *villano*, a *danza de las hachas* ("torch dance"), and a *canario*. The reworking is slightly contemporary in its harmonic format, the colors are fully so, but not blatant.

Like Rodrigo's *Concierto de Aranjuez* (*see above*), the *Fantasía* has become a firm repertoire piece and enjoys excellent recorded representation. Lagoya's presentation has captured the full poetry of the work, and he receives impeccable support from the orchestra.

Two Guitars

Concierto madrigal for Two Guitars and Orchestra (1968)

☐ Academy of St. Martin-in-the-Fields / Pepe and Angel Romero (guitars) / Marriner (conductor) / Philips 6500918

The *Concierto* is actually a set of variations on a madrigal, which is heard in the second of the ten parts of the work. Rodrigo's opus is a dazzling showcase of dances and quiet delineations. There is plenty of Andalusian personality and a performance personality by the Romero brothers that is captivating.

Concierto Andaluz for Four Guitars and Orchestra (1967)

Four Guitars

☐ San Antonio Symphony Orchestra / Celedonio, Celin, Pepe, and Angel Romero (guitars) / Alessandro (conductor) / Mercury 75021

There are Andalusian inherencies here, from the initial *Tiempo de bolero* movement, to the haunting Adagio, to the *olé* embracements of the finale. The work is strongly colored and marvelously played by this family quartet. It is music for a rare combination that has inspiration and imagination, in addition to instrumental novelty.

Concert-Serenade for Harp and Orchestra (1954)

Harp

☐ Berlin Radio Symphony Orchestra / Zabaleta (harp) / Märzendorfer (conductor) / Deutsche Grammophon 138118

For the greater part in the first two movements, the harp is more an obbligato factor than a fully solo personality. Thus, in the march gestures of *Estudiantina* and the Intermezzo, orchestral color flares are paramount. However, in the *Sarao*, which pictures dance-laden atmosphere, matters are equalized and the harp shares the stage with the orchestra.

Zabaleta adjusts according to the score's requirements. Sleek perfection marks the solo passages with a Zabaletian touch that is ingratiating; integration with the orchestra is just as clear and satisfying.

En los trigales

Instrumental

Guitar

☐ Bream (guitar) / RCA LSC-2448

"From the Wheat Fields" is from a set of two studies, *Por los campos de España*. Gentle rhythmic nationalistic style is the descriptive note for Rodrigo's three-and-one-half-minute piece. It is compellingly presented by Julian Bream.

Fandango

☐ Segovia (guitar) / MCA 2523

Absorbing because the basic *fandango* square-cut shape is somewhat freer in this instance, due to some dissonant flavors that also freshen the usual harmonic content of this dance form.

Segovia's re-creative discrimination heightens the contrasts between the percussive and the suaveness of the conception. The music and performance are completely effective on this MCA rerelease of a Decca album (710034).

Zarabanda lejana

☐ de la Torre (guitar) / Nonesuch 71233

A tender melancholy embraces Rodrigo's piece. The complete relationship of his material with the instrument for which it was written is vivid. Rey de la Torre's playing bears this out.

Pastorcito santo from *Villancicos*

Vocal

Voice with Accompaniment

☐ de los Angeles (soprano); Soriano (piano) / Angel S-35775

Simplicity that produces an expressive strength. "Holy Shepherd Boy" has a delicate voice line that becomes placed in strong perspective by the spare piano texture. The melody is a haunting one akin to folkloric documentation. It is exquisitely voiced by this great singer.

Voice
and Orchestra

Cuatro madrigales amatorios (1948)

☐ Paris Conservatoire Orchestra / de los Angeles (soprano) / Frühbeck de Burgos (conductor) / Angel S-35937

Traditional texts and style, the folk lacing of the music always slightly nostalgic, never even slightly maudlin.

Each of the songs is presented with tonal beauty, and the orchestration is neatly framed, never slick. This is a beautiful set of miniature gems.

Robert Xavier Rodriguez   (1946-   )

Solo
Instrument
and
Orchestra

Oboe

Lyric Variations for Oboe, Two Horns, and String Orchestra (1971)

☐ Orion Chamber Orchestra / Davis (oboe) / Nord (conductor) / Orion 74138

Serial-styled music but blissfully unwed to academic processes. The lyrical point is demonstrated beautifully and expressivity prevails. There is fine playing by the featured oboist, Robert Davis.

Chamber
Music

Sonata in One Movement for Soprano Saxophone and Piano (1973)

☐ Pittel (soprano saxophone); Grierson (piano) / Crystal S-105

Serially engineered, but tonally fluid. There is no stylistic crisis in this duality, since it has long been proven that, in the hands of the competent, such technical partnership provides aesthetic security.

Harvey Pittel's playing is superb, his control of the instrument nigh incredible.

Cantata
and Oratorio

Canto (1973)

☐ Orion Chamber Orchestra / Harmon (soprano); Sells (tenor); Sanders (piano); Gruber (cello) / Nord (conductor) / Orion 74138

A one-movement cantata for soprano, tenor, piano, cello, and orchestra (Orion incorrectly drops the cello credit from its label heading) that combines texts, languages, and musical styles. The soprano sings lines from Dante in Italian; the tenor sings an anonymous thirteenth-century text in French. The subjects are related and blend in a form of montage. To clarify and identify the materials both tone row and tonal methods are employed.

The musical assignments tangential to the texts themselves are most inventive. However, in such a conglomerative situation word meanings are crucial, and it is this point that is below par. But the basic strength of the writing comes through even if one doesn't understand what the vocalists are saying.

Jean-Jules Aimable Roger-Ducasse   (1873-1954)

Instrumental

Harp

Barcarolle

☐ Grandjany (harp) / Seraphim S-60142

Fauré-like classicism, gently colored and beautifully played.

Bernard Rogers *(1893-1968)*

Apparitions (1967)

☐ Royal Philharmonic Orchestra / Lipkin (conductor) / Composers Recordings S–259

An expert orchestrator, Rogers specialized in writing for the orchestra, and because of his superb knowledge of the instruments—individually and collectively—was drawn to picture painting. *Apparitions* is a prime example, consisting of six scenes based on Flaubert's *The Temptation of St. Anthony.*

Dance Scenes (1953)

☐ Louisville Orchestra / Whitney (conductor) / Louisville 606 (monaural)

No one who knows his music would ever suspect this composer of orchestrational ordinariness. Rogers was a supreme master of the orchestra. That is illustrated here with the watercolorish *The Rising Moon,* the light resonances of *Fire Flies,* and the crack and crackle of *Samurai.*

Every orchestral work Rogers wrote contained fantastic motival speech. This composition likewise. The performance is satisfactory, well projected in its colors.

Once upon a Time (Five Fairy Tales) (1934)

☐ Eastman-Rochester Symphony Orchestra / Hanson (conductor) / Eastman-Rochester Archives ERA–1004

Exquisite, sensitive, and subtle orchestration, whereby the colors and textures fit the subject, make Rogers's suite aurally fascinating. All of it is done by normal means, without resorting to the sort of Straussian multiloquence that would require organ, wind, and thunder machines.

Variations on a Song by Mussorgsky (1960)

☐ Rochester Philharmonic Orchestra / Bloomfield (conductor) / Composers Recordings 153 (monaural)

Thematic variation is matched by orchestrational variation. In a whimsical atmosphere, woodwinds are tossed around as in a baseball "pepper" game; telescoped figures dance in balalaikalike pizzicato; spinning strings spell out fragmentation of motives, and so on. It is all very appealing, all very masterful. Bernard Rogers remains one of the American composers still to be really discovered.

Rogers's work was commissioned by the conductor and orchestra that have recorded it. The results are most happy and effective.

Soliloquy for Flute and String Orchestra (1922)

☐ Eastman-Rochester Symphony Orchestra / Mariano (flute) / Hanson (conductor) / Eastman-Rochester Archives ERA–1001

One of the standards in the flute repertoire. Mariano's plush tone in this exquisite romantic bit caresses the ear.

Leaves from the Tale of Pinocchio (1950)

☐ Eastman-Rochester Symphony Orchestra / MacKown (narrator) / Hanson (conductor) / Eastman-Rochester Archives ERA–1002

It is little known that Rogers was one of the most refreshing orchestration talents in this country. Every score proved his magic with instruments. (His book *The Art of Orchestration* is a highly individual and commanding contribution.) Best of all was Rogers's reproductive imagination—program music was a special attraction, understandably.

The *Pinocchio* subject is vivid evidence of the man's superb abilities. It begins immediately with an inspiring concept—a short introduction (called an *Overturetta*) for violins alone, worth the entire cost of the recording. Then follow a dozen connected movements with such fancies as *The Cat and the Fox, Flight with a Pigeon*, and so on. Double guidance is offered: Rogers's instrumental ingenuity (including the efficacy of percussion) and the verbal detail by the narrator. A delight from first note to final double bar.

The full flavor of the work, its joys and colors, are disclosed under Hanson's direction. The narrator is excellent.

Amadeo Roldán (1900-1939)

Percussion

Two *Ritmicas* (Nos. 5 and 6: *Tiempo de Son* and *Tiempo de Rhumba*) (1930)

☐ Manhattan Percussion Ensemble / Price (conductor) / Mainstream 5011

A pair from the set of six, all conceived in the rhythms of Cuban folk dances. The percussion instruments are treated mainly as a mass rather than with textural interplay. Special timbres are heard in the excellent performance conducted by the percussion expert Paul Price. These include the quijada (the jawbone of an ass), the cencerro (a cowbell minus its clapper), and the marimbula (a metal pizzicato instrument).

Alessandro Rolla (1757-1841)

Solo Instrument and Orchestra

Violin

Concerto in A major for Violin and Orchestra

☐ Württemberg Chamber Orchestra / Lautenbacher (violin) / Faerber (conductor) / Turnabout 34606

Especially in the initial part, this represents a heady dish of classical tea. Rolla's three-movement opus has a very extended first movement (more than three minutes longer than the sections that follow), a tripartite *romanza* music titled Cavatina, and a finale Rondo.

Susanne Lautenbacher delivers the work with fine voice and dash. This is playing of distinction and freshness.

José Rolón (1883-1945)

Instrumental

Violin

Danse indigène (Jalisco)

☐ Szeryng (violin); Janopoulo (piano) / Everest 3153E (monaural)

A simple stylization of a dance tune from the Jalisco area in Mexico. A catchy item swinging in duple meter.

Johan Helmich Roman (1694-1758)

Suite from *Drottningholms-Musique* *Orchestra*

☐ Chamber Orchestra of the Drottningholm Theater / Björlin (conductor) / Nonesuch 71213

There are two-dozen movements in this Swedish composer's "Music for the Queen's House." Thirteen sections are here performed with zest that fully conveys the Handelian-influenced authority of Roman's score. (Another, shorter compilation is listed under *String Orchestra*.)

***Drottningholms-Musique* (Excerpts)** *String Orchestra*

☐ Camerata Lutetiensis/ Eustache (flute) / Nonesuch 73014

Six movements from the total twenty-four are performed by a sensitive string group with Jean-Pierre Eustache assisting as flutist in some of the sections. A more extensive compilation is available that includes music calling for a larger instrumentation (see under *Orchestra*).

Sonata in C major *Instrumental*

Sonata (Suite) No. 9 in D minor *Harpsichord*

☐ Nordenfelt (harpsichord) / Orion 74157

There is no time-marking or padding in these fine works. The Larghetto in the C major opus has Bachian depth; the Allegro that completes the work has exciting sequences. In the D minor composition the linear vitality of the slow movements (an Adagio in movement 2 and a Lento in the concluding, fourth part) is matched by a powerful Allegretto (movement 3) containing syncopative drive and rhythmic kick. These Roman compositions are real finds.

The dynamism of the playing is irresistible, and Nordenfelt's performance is aided and abetted by brilliant sonics. This is a five-star harpsichord release.

Bernhard Romberg (1767-1841)

Sonata in B flat major for Harp and Cello *Chamber Music*

☐ Klaus Storck (cello); Helga Storck (harp) / Telefunken 641020

A lightly figured duo, traditionally proportioned and showing an assured (if not especially colorful) hand at interlocking the instrumental voices.

The piece is nicely played and the sound is excellent.

Ludovico Roncalli (17th cent.)

Gavotta *Instrumental*

Giga *Guitar*

Passacaglia

☐ Segovia (guitar) / MCA 2523

Excerpted movements from large-spanned works by this seventeenth-century Italian guitarist-composer. The Passacaglia is from the *Capricci armonici sopra la chitarra spagnola;* the other two pieces are from a Suite in G.

This is less commonly heard guitar music, but fully worthy of the great Segovia's art. (Originally this was a Decca release, 710034.)

Robert de Roos   *(1907-1976)*

Orchestra   ***Suggestioni* (1961)**

☐ Residentie Orchestra / van Otterloo (conductor) / Donemus Audio-Visual Series DAVS-6703 (monaural)

Five short pieces, joined and covering a ten-minute performance time. The highlights are part 2, a nineteen measure slow section, and part 3, a fast-paced music spurred by ostinati.

Guy Ropartz   *(1864-1955)*

Instrumental   ***Jeunes Filles* (Cinq Esquisses pour piano)**

Piano   ☐ Doyen (piano) / Musical Heritage Society MHS-1155-57

Ropartz's "Young Girls" is delineated with tonal suavity and purity. Parallel thirds especially remind one of Ravel's *Mother Goose* music (see under *Ravel: Orchestra; Instrumental: piano, four hands;* and *Ballet*). The girl-watching covers *L'Insouciante, La Nonchalante, La Coquette, La Tendre,* and *La Capricieuse.* The rhythmic pieces (especially the final one) are the most seductive.

Jean Doyen's playing is as smooth as silk. All of his playing comes across with a vocalism that caresses the ear.

Chamber Music   **Prélude, Marine, et Chansons for Flute, Violin, Viola, Cello, and Harp**

☐ Melos Ensemble / Ellis (harp) / Oiseau-Lyre 60048

Ropartz turned to Breton folk songs quite often in his compositions. Further evidence appears in the *Chansons* of this quintet; these songs consist of a series of three themes, of which the second is a *thème populaire breton.* Each is announced and distinguished in turn by different instrumental color. Development of the material then proceeds.

The recording is a stunning one in all respects.

Ned Rorem   *(1923-   )*

Orchestra   **Design for Orchestra (1955)**

☐ Louisville Orchestra / Whitney (conductor) / Louisville 57-5 (monaural)

Rorem treads on romantic terrain in his one-movement piece set in tripartite form. The orchestration is bright and clear. But the fair sound does not match the good playing.

Eleven Studies for Eleven Players (1959)

☐ Members of the Louisville Orchestra / Fuge (flute); McAninch (English horn); Raper (trumpet); Gittli (piano); Schneider (viola); Hauptman (oboe); Livingston (clarinet); Kling (violin); Grace Whitney (cello); von Barkhausen (harp); Engelman and Otten (percussion) / Robert Whitney (conductor) / Louisville S-644

Large miniatures illustrative of contemporary divertimento practice. And truly an interlacement of dissimilitudes. Some pieces are formally stated (a Prelude, an Allegretto, for example). Others are picturizations (such as No. 3, *Bird Call,* or No. 5, *Contest*). Three movements are derived from theatre music Rorem had written. The number of players varies, covering one duo, one quartet, two quintets, and so forth. Five of the Studies are for the full ensemble. The mix, therefore, represents both chamber music and chamber orchestra. And, still further, soloism: In part 1 the trumpet is featured; in part 3 it is the flute; in the Elegy, the English horn; and in the final section (*Epilogue*) the solo clarinet.

Rorem's delightfully unstuffy pieces are convincing and as convincingly performed by the Louisville first-chair players. Though calling for eleven instrumentalists, a slight augmentation, covering the percussion, revises the total, but does not revise a single note in the score.

Ideas for Orchestra

☐ Oakland Youth Orchestra / Hughes (conductor) / Desto 6462

Publishers are always hopeful that long-hair composers will produce music in their individually identifiable styles that is devoid of technical difficulties. However, very few can meet the challenge of successfully creating a utilitarian product that both serves educational objectives and increases their bank accounts.

This eight-part work represents Ned Rorem's attempt. (Since Rorem permits the pieces to be played singly or as a group, Hughes has chosen four of the total.) Certainly, this is a viable contribution to American *Gebrauchsmusik.*

Lions (A Dream) (1963)

☐ New Orleans Philharmonic Symphony Orchestra / Weinstein (saxophone) / Torkanowsky (conductor) / Orion 7268

A Shakespearian motto, "The hind that would be mated by the lion/ Must die for love," prefaces Rorem's orchestral work. It describes (in impressionistic terms laced with bluesy writing) a dream he had as a young man. The story line is more or less fulfilled.

The performance is warmly conceived.

Third Symphony (1959)

☐ Utah Symphony Orchestra / Abravanel (conductor) / Turnabout 34447

Title notwithstanding, Rorem's Symphony hoists a Suite standard. The opening movement persistently runs a motival course—a Passacaglia that has a fix mainly on midvoice and soprano positions. Movement 2 is jazzy; a nostalgic slow movement follows; proclamatory music covers the fourth movement; and "a long fast rondo" concludes the piece.

Contemporary feeling, nicely crafted speech, no slang—all these make Rorem's work productive if not of special individual profile. It may prove the contention of many that Ned Rorem is best in the short essay, that he cannot plot a long tale. Nevertheless, this intensely cultivated series of movements holds the interest and is given full definition by Abravanel.

*Solo
Instrument
and
Orchestra*

Piano

Piano Concerto in Six Movements (1969)

☐ Louisville Orchestra / Lowenthal (piano) / Mester (conductor) / Louisville 733

Six-movement concertos are rare musical birds. And so are movement titles for a piano-with-orchestra piece. But this is Ned Rorem, and if he doesn't surprise with his neo-romantically styled music, he intrigues by his objectivistic suppositions. Thus, each movement bears a specific heading: *Strands, Fives, Whispers, Sighs, Lava,* and *Sparks.* And, importantly, he meets his self-made challenge—*Whispers* is soft-spoken, *Lava* is a sonorous chaw, and *Sparks* is lit with volatile tempo. Though a sense of variation hangs over the work, the departures negate any such formalistic labeling.

(Passing thought: isn't Rorem far ahead of any other American composer in the use of descriptive titles?)

Plenty of technical resource is supplied for the soloist in Rorem's opus, and Lowenthal takes complete advantage to show off his abilities. The virtuosity is always related in a musical manner, however. Good values are displayed by the Louisville personnel.

*Violin
and Clarinet*

Water Music—Theme and Variations for Orchestra

☐ Oakland Youth Orchestra / Halpin (violin); London (clarinet) / Hughes (conductor) / Desto 6462

Rorem's fluid work is splashed with the concertante colors of violin and clarinet. Consisting of a set of variations on a "Calm and Sad" theme, the format is a concerto grosso—the *Water Music* heading is simply a picturesque bit of salesmanship. No harm, but don't expect a Roremesque *La Mer.*

Do expect some top fancy solo playing and expert orchestral playing of the music the conductor had commissioned.

Instrumental

Piano

Second Piano Sonata (1949)

☐ Katchen (piano) / Composers Recordings 202 (monaural)

"Sonata" perhaps—this is much more a Suite. Rorem's light-scaled neoclassicism (nothing heavy, that might be considered to hang over from Stravinsky) tends to reflect more of Poulenc in the Overture (Rorem's "nearest rub with what used to be termed 'strict sonata form'") and in the final Toccata. (The latter was added to the work at the performer's insistence.) The *Tarantella* is also Parisian and in the Nocturne ("probably inspired by a love for Billie Holiday") some Fauré is reflected. But overall, sonata or suite, the simplistic musicality of the sounds is richly appealing.

Katchen had first recorded the piece for London-Decca, in 1952. The present release is "a technical refurbishing on CRI's part." Katchen's performance is one of distinction. The genuine musical character of his playing is a matter of aural joy.

*Chamber
Music*

Book of Hours (1976)

☐ Dingfelder (flute); Geliot (harp) / Composers Recordings SD–362

Rorem's title refers to the daily canonical hours at which service is held in the Roman Catholic Church. The eight parts cover *Matins (Nocturne), Lauds (Sunrise), Prime (6:00 A.M.),* and so on, until *Compline (Nightfall).* The instruments enjoy solo spots as well as functioning as "a married pair."

Book of Hours was commissioned by the performers of this recording, to whom, rightfully, it is dedicated. They gave the premiere in New York on February 29, 1976. It can be understood, therefore, that the recorded essay is authoritative; the splendid sonorities and atmosphere attest to the statement.

Day Music

☐ Jaime Laredo (violin); Ruth Laredo (piano) / Desto 7151

Somewhat programmatic music, with such titles (plus cutesy parenthetical remarks) as *Extreme Leisure* ("subtitled 'The Gallows Revisited' which, like Ravel's *Le Gibet*, exploits an endlessly reiterated note") and *Bats* ("they would be appropriate for 'Night Music' too, wouldn't they?"). But don't let the titles get into the way, though in *Bats* and *Yellows* (". . . are flashes of sharp hurting light") Rorem equips his music with startling picture painting. The device in each of the eight sections (unbanded in the recording) goes directly to the essential point and comes through with excellent musical matter.

Fine fiddling here, with rich tone. The pianist matches the violinist's spirited, musically perceptive performance. And the sound is great. (For the sequel to this piece, *see below* [Night Music].)

Night Music (1972)

☐ Carlyss (violin); Schein (piano) / Desto 7174

A sequel to Day Music (*see above*). In fact, any regrouping of the eight movements in this work with the eight in Day Music may be made.

Trust Rorem, who is as creative with words as he is with sounds, to concoct interesting titles, such as *Mosquitoes and Earthworms, Epeira Sclopetaria*, and *Black and Silver*. The music reflects these and the other headings with rewarding results. The recorded performance was made the day following the premiere and is valid and quite evocative.

Trio for Flute, Cello, and Piano (1960)

☐ New York Camerata / Desto 6462

Good plot. Rorem describes part 1 as "a concerto for the flutist upstaging the other two players." Part 2 is a flinty duo for the flute and cello with interjected percussions from the piano. In part 3 the cello is the featured voice, and the finale presents trioed raciness.

All the detail and soloism are negotiated in a polished performance.

Lovers: A Narrative for Harpsichord, Oboe, Cello, and Percussion (1964)

☐ Marlowe (harpsichord); Roseman (oboe); Kouguell (cello); Farberman (percussion) / Serenus 12056

Six scenes are presented here of the ten that comprise the work, each "depicting an experience in the day of a young couple." This is once-over-lightly program music, the poetic address capturing the mood or situation involved. The music is clear, not mod romantic.

Lovers was originally released by Decca. The Serenus reissue is a welcome one.

Four Madrigals

Vocal

From an Unknown Past

Voice Alone

☐ Modern Madrigal Quartet / Desto 6480

As far as vocal quartets are concerned, contemporary composers have not produced a glut on the music market. This creative fact makes Rorem's eleven examples (including seven in *From an Unknown Past*) especially welcome. The Four Madrigals have texts by Sappho; the other set covers anonymous poets. There is nothing anonymous about the writing schematics, which bear the typical Rorem style: effective settings of the prose with neo-romantic integration.

The singing is fully communicative and results in maximum effect.

Ariel: **Five Poems of Sylvia Plath for Soprano, Clarinet, and Piano (1971)**

☐ Curtin (soprano); Rabbai (clarinet); Edwards (piano) / Desto 7147

There is more angular style here than is usual with this composer. Such is required to fulfill Plath's tough lines. Still, poetic penetration is one of Rorem's assets, and his skill is manifested throughout, especially in the dramatic (and longest) of the set, No. 5, *Lady Lazarus.*

As usual, Curtin presents an admirable, rich, and controlled performance. Her colleagues do as well.

Bedlam

☐ Miller (mezzo-soprano); Biltcliffe (piano) / Desto 6411/2

Subtitled *Visits to St. Elizabeths: 1950,* Rorem's *Bedlam* is set to lines by Elizabeth Bishop. The poem's structure of a dozen sections, each increasing exactly by one line so that the final section has twelve lines, poses severe problems, increased by the text's rondo design and the slight modifications within it. Rorem's success is proven by the powerful inner motility of his song.

A Christmas Carol
Clouds

☐ Hanks (tenor); Friedberg-Erickson (piano) / Duke University Press DWR-7306 (monaural)

Romantic in totality, without any excessiveness. Technical clarity underlines the meaning of the text. Thus, the quartal and quintal harmonies that color *Clouds* (the second in a song collection titled *Three Poems of Paul Goodman*) and the modal envelope for the Carol.

These are tasteful presentations by the vocalist and the pianist.

(For the other two settings of Goodman's poems, *see below* [*For Susan* and *What Sparks and Wiry Cries*].)

Five Songs to Poems by Walt Whitman

☐ Gramm (bass-baritone); Istomin (piano) / Desto 7101

No specific concern links the subjects of the set. Three of the poems deal with personal relationships, one deals with nature, while the other has a philosophical slant.

Gramm also sings the second number in the cycle, *Look Down, Fair Moon,* with Rorem at the piano, on Composers Recordings S-238.

For Poulenc

☐ Curtin (soprano); Rorem (piano) / Composers Recordings S-238

Modest in its means and expressive in its result. A mini-quote from Poulenc is included in Rorem's song, beautifully illuminated by Phyllis Curtin's vocal artistry.

For Susan
Guilt

☐ Hanks (tenor); Friedberg-Erickson (piano) / Duke University Press DWR-7306 (monaural)

As heard in these two examples, the lack of pretension in Rorem's vocal music gives it a special place in the literature. In all cases the musical lines fit the textual lines convincingly. Thus, fluidity of phrase shapes in *For Susan* (the first of a set of *Three Poems of Paul Goodman*) and the declamatory basis for *Guilt*.

Hanks displays skilled projection; the pianist provides excellent support.

(For the other two settings of Goodman's poems, *see above* [*Clouds*, under A Christmas Carol] and *below* [*What Sparks and Wiry Cries*].)

Gloria for Two Voices and Piano (1970)

☐ Curtin (soprano); Vanni (mezzo-soprano); Rorem (piano) / Desto 7147

Intensity plus dramatic floridity mark the nine parts of Rorem's setting of the Gloria text as found in the Ordinary of the Latin Mass. The masterful performance fulfills all requirements. (Rorem's large-scaled work also helps fill a gap in vocal literature—exceedingly few contemporary composers have turned out vocal duets.)

Little Elegy

☐ Curtin (soprano); Rorem (piano) / Composers Recordings S-238

A choice, haunting bit, sung with impeccable clarity and dignified expressiveness. The words are by Elinor Wylie.

Night Crow

☐ Gramm (baritone); Rorem (piano) / Composers Recordings S-238

One of a group of eight settings of Theodore Roethke poems. Fine-styled singing.

Poems of Love and the Rain (1963)

☐ Wolf (mezzo-soprano); Rorem (piano) / Desto 6480

One of Rorem's best song cycles and certainly his most formally adventurous. Eight of the texts are set twice, separated by a single setting of one for a total of seventeen. The order is a straightforward 1–8, followed by song No. 9 serving as an Interlude, continued by the second series going backward, so that 10=8, 11=7, 12=6, and so on. Since the disc is banded for the greater part (fifteen bands covering the total seventeen parts) it is possible to compare the contrastive results by beginning at the terminal portions of the record and moving inward.

A Poulencian quality pervades a great deal of the music, but that's no reason to indicate demerits. There are none for the performers either.

Some Trees

☐ Curtin (soprano); Wolff (contralto); Gramm (baritone); Rorem (piano) / Composers Recordings S-238

One would be hard put to find contemporary composers who have written vocal trios, let alone worthy composers of previous eras (outside of opera, that is). Only a specialist in vocal composition (which Rorem is) might be expected to have a try at it. And be as successful as he is here in this set of three poems for three voices, all to texts by John Ashberry.

An all-star cast has recorded the cycle and recorded it beautifully and sensitively.

The Tulip Tree

☐ Curtin (soprano); Rorem (piano) / Composers Recordings S-238

Vitality of subject matter (the text by Paul Goodman), spirited music to match, and an irresistible performance.

War Scenes

☐ Gramm (bass-baritone); Istomin (piano) / Desto 7101

The *War Scenes* (five in number) are set to words by Walt Whitman. In this case not poetry, but lines "very freely excised" from Whitman's diary of the Civil War, titled *Specimen Days.*

Singer and pianist give a polished performance that portrays both the tenderness and harshness contained in the cycle.

What Sparks and Wiry Cries

☐ Curtin (soprano); Rorem (piano) / Composers Recordings S–238

The third of a set of *Three Poems of Paul Goodman.* Curtin sings this declamatory song with becoming intensity, and Rorem provides a sharply pointed piano framework. (A monaural recorded version for tenor and piano is available on Duke University Press DWR-7306.)

(For the other two settings of Goodman's poems, *see above* [*Clouds,* under A Christmas Carol, and *For Susan*].)

Cantata and Oratorio

King Midas

☐ Walker (mezzo-soprano); Stewart (tenor); Schein (piano) / Desto 6443

Rorem's *King Midas* is described as "A Cantata for Voices and Piano on Ten Poems of Howard Moss." There is no merging of the two voices—not even in response to one another—in any of the ten parts of the work. Moss states he had "power, loss, gold, money, vanity" in mind. With these textual purposes Rorem has proceeded in a smooth romantic manner that provides a song cycle with linked subject matter.

Opera and Dramatic Music

Four Dialogues for Two Voices and Two Pianos

☐ Darian (soprano); Stewart (tenor); Cumming and Rorem (pianos) / Desto 7101

Mini-opera not needing any stage action. Rorem terms it "a nameless genre that falls somewhere between concert cantata and staged opera." Whatever it is called, it is telling, and is a musical conceit, a *jeu d'esprit.* The story line: man picks up woman, they park and spark and lovelark, on to his apartment where they quarrel, then, the inevitable separation, and finis with the two singing "over the ocean to each other, wondering at love, at jealousy, at what to do now."

You don't need the text sheet to follow the words. This is the type of diction one always wishes to hear but doesn't. Bravo singers, and bravo, bravo, Rorem.

Jerome Rosen 1921-)

Instrumental

Violin

Five Pieces (1970)

☐ Gross (violin); Grayson (piano) / Orion 73110

Expressionistic essays mainly concerned with rhapsodic liberation. There is a strong reminder in some portions of the music of Roger Sessions, which is in no way uncomplimentary.

Robert Gross is quite a violinist, and a specialist in contemporary music. He delivers this work with decided flair. However, he has been recorded too emphatically and the piano partnership suffers accordingly.

Hilding Rosenberg   (1892-   )

Intermezzo and Railway Fugue from *Voyage to America* (1932)   *Orchestra*

☐ Stockholm Philharmonic Orchestra / Dorati (conductor) / RCA VICS-1319

Sibelian influence in the first of the pair of excerpts, and, as may be expected, rhythmic push for the other one. It's good to have even these comparatively unimportant examples by this terribly neglected composer.

Louisville Concerto (1955)

☐ Louisville Orchestra / Harth (violin); Schneider (viola); Grace Whitney (cello) / Robert Whitney (conductor) / Louisville 56–1 (monaural)

The Concerto title notwithstanding, the construction here is that of a concerto grosso, with the three string players considered as a concertino body rather than used for full-scale soloism. This concept fits in well with the linear character of Rosenberg's pantonal music.

Symphony No. 2 (*Sinfonia grave*) (1935)

☐ Stockholm Philharmonic Orchestra / Blomstedt (conductor) / Turnabout 34436

Deadly serious music; the seriousness is maintained throughout the Symphony's four movements. Rosenberg finished the work in 1928 (he revised it in 1935) and found it frightening, because of its "daring and harshly polyphonic" qualities. Of course we've come a long way since then, and in the 1980s there is no recognizable harshness in Rosenberg's work; but its strength is undiminished. The Symphony has power and imagination and exhibits a solid, dark-striped personality. A tragic presence surrounds this enlarged tonal example of expressionism.

The Stockholm organization offers fine playing. There is an impressive display of technical exactitude and a quiet type of virtuosity that is as compelling as the more aggressive kind.

Symphony No. 6, *Sinfonia semplice*

☐ Stockholm Philharmonic Orchestra / Westerberg (conductor) / Turnabout 34318

Brilliantly written, Rosenberg's four-movement Symphony is conservatively dissonant, strongly suggesting the music of Paul Hindemith in its linear stability. Much of the work also suggests spread-out contrapuntalized recitative. There are four movements: an Adagio (its opening for three solo cellos sets a splendid coloristic mood), an *Alla marcia* (in Allegro tempo), a *Recitativo* (significantly confirming the general tone of the work as mentioned previously), and an *Inno* ("Hymn")—the last fully developed.

The scoring presents problems in clarifying the composition's continuity, but Stig Westerberg solves them. His command of the orchestral forces is positively depicted.

String Quartet No. 4 (1939)   *Chamber Music*

☐ Fresk Quartet / Caprice CAP–1051

Bartók is an unceasing influence in the progress of this splendid quartet, especially in the nocturnal second movement and the choreographic finale. But it is a softer-spoken Bartók in the latter movement. Rosenberg's use of remote sounds and isolates in the second and third movements, especially, give his work a mysterious electricity.

The playing of this young quartet team is exciting news. Its ability to get inside the Rosenberg score is a top achievement. They have fine tonal quality, and are a perfectly balanced foursome. Their playing of the slow movement sets an exquisite mood at the very beginning that does not deviate for the entire nine-plus minutes. The Fresk Quartet is a real find.

Leonard Rosenman (1924-   )

**Brass
Ensemble**

Fanfare 1969

☐ Los Angeles Brass Society / Remsen (conductor) / Avant 1001

Beautifully dynamic dissonance spread over the brass body. The unison ending reverses matters.

**Chamber
Music**

Duo for Violin and Piano (1970)

☐ Gross (violin); Grayson (piano) / Orion 73107

Equilibrium obtains here by its direct opposite: freely pitched, percussively thrown segments, the two instruments totally opposed, bitterly argumentative, and always unpartnered. The effect is two-dimensional, as though two separate musics were composed, one for each instrument, and then combined. In Rosenman's world gigantic polyphony is dimensionless; one hears a Varèsian percussion orchestra transferred to a fiddle and a piano.

The piece is fiendishly difficult to play. But these musicians have the technique and the elemental strength required to explore fully this music of muscle and guts.

Vocal

**Voice and
Instrumental
Ensemble**

Chamber Music No. 2

☐ The New Muse / Harmon (soprano) / Rosenman (conductor) / Delos 25432

Expression by expressionistic style, with vocal dualism produced by intermingling the voice with prerecorded voice. There is a type of uniformly dense textural condition, with the chamber orchestra often also partnered with the tape. The text is a translation of *Tu infancia en Menton* ("Your Childhood in Menton") by Jorge Guillen. Its lines are detailed by extreme intervallic disjunctiveness.

Johann Rosenmüller (ca. 1619-1684)

**String
Orchestra**

Suite No. 2 in D minor from *Studenten-Musik*

☐ Members of the Little Orchestra of London / Rifkin (harpsichord) / Rifkin (conductor) / Nonesuch 71204

Five dance movements—*Paduan, Alemanda, Courant, Ballo*, and *Sarabanda*—for two violins, two violas, and continuo. Simply presented, with no fancy dynamic dictates. That's all that's required for full enjoyment.

Sonata VII a 4 in D minor

Sonata X a 5 in F major

☐ Leonhardt Consort / Leonhardt (conductor) / Telefunken 641118

Sensitively played regarding style and sensibly played to underline the basic cheerful content of the music.

Manuel Rosenthal / *Offenbach.* See *Offenbach* / Rosenthal.

Moriz Rosenthal *(1862 - 1946)*

Carnaval de Vienne

Prelude in F sharp minor

☐ Rosenthal (piano) / Klavier 108

Don't miss the creamy concoction listed first. Sure, the "Carnival of Vienna" is light stuff, but how unstuffy and carefree it is! Most of it is covered by the triple meter trademark of the waltz capital of the world. Included are smatterings of dance tunes glanced at and then followed by a hint of another one. Included is a workout on *Du und Du* from *Die Fledermaus.*

The Prelude is just as buoyant. It is styled as superbly as the "Carnival" creation. The pianism is truly inspired.

Francesco Antonio Rosetti *(ca. 1750 - 1792)*

Marche (Largo) from Partita in B flat

☐ Netherlands Wind Ensemble / Philips 6599172

The key word is the parenthetical tempo designation. This is a stately bit, as would be expected. It charms the ear.

Statistic: The composer's full name was a pseudonym. Rosetti was not an Italian, but a Bohemian—his real name was Franz Anton Rössler.

Concerto in D minor for Horn and Orchestra

☐ Württemberg Chamber Orchestra / Penzel (horn) / Faerber (conductor) / Turnabout 34078

Rosetti's Concerto is in one movement, the layout embracing a fast-tempoed portion, a *Romanze*, and a Rondo. It is enjoyable fare, enriched by a beautifully played solo part, which Erich Penzel imbues with sensitive feeling.

Sonata

In F major, Op. 2, No. 1 / In E flat major, Op. 2, No. 2 / In B flat major, Op. 2, No. 3 / In G major, Op. 2, No. 4 / In B flat major, Op. 2, No. 5 / In C major, Op. 2, No. 6

McDonald (harp) / Orion 7144

There are pat forms in this set. All six works are in three movements each. Only in the fourth Sonata is there a *Menuetto* (completing the piece). Otherwise, every Sonata has a design consisting of a *Romanza* in the second slot and a Rondo in the final one. Lively tempi cover the opening movements save in the third Sonata, which begins with an *Adagio maestoso*.

The performances by Susann McDonald are well considered; there is no straining for effect. Indeed, it is eminently listenable playing, with a single quibble—some unequal strengths are applied to the pitches in conjunct passages.

Walter Ross   *(1936-   )*

Solo Instrument and Orchestra

Concerto for Trombone and Orchestra (1971)

☐ Bergen (Norway) Symphony Orchestra / Brevig (trombone) / Andersen (conductor) / Composers Recordings S-340

Trombone

It is a pleasure to hear a work for trombone that isn't doused with fanfare-like writing. Ross's entry in the trombone-with-orchestra medium is flamboyant in the *Capriccio*, bluesy in the *Canzona*, and nervously jazzy in the final Fantasia. No trombone work can seem to bypass glissandi, and a fair share of glide types are included in Ross's pantonal opus, but they all fit the material.

Per Brevig is superb. He has a technical power that is miraculous, but he is fully musical in applying it. Interpretative finesse there is aplenty, representing one of the pleasurable parts of this performance.

Instrumental

Prelude, Fugue, and *Big Apple* for Bass Trombone and Tape (1972)

Trombone

☐ Brevig (bass trombone) / Composers Recordings S-340

What one expects from expert trombone writing is here in full: plenty of glissandi, broad melody, and jazz licks. But what one never expects to hear from a tape is also here. It provides a highly individual realization of tape composition potentials. In the Prelude it supplies keen imitations of the trombone's glissandi; in the Fugue the tape announces the subject; and in the dance section it furnishes the important ''beat'' and simulates the stylistically fitting light cymbal touches. All of it is great stuff and packed full of uninhibited invention.

Amid these fascinating details Brevig moves like a master. His tone is never forced, his touch and technique unfailingly sure, his interpretation as exuberant as it should be.

Tuba

Piltdown Fragments for Tuba and Tape (1975)

☐ Cummings (tuba) / Crystal S-391

The composer does not explain the adjective in his title. On the other hand, the ''fragments'' are clear, promulgating motival definition. In their activity and progress these produce fantasy samplings.

Chamber Music

Partita for Euphonium and Piano

☐ Bowman (euphonium); Lee (piano) / Crystal S-393

Positive stylistic qualities in three positive pithy essays. The Allegro has toccata turns, then follows a Pastorale, and dance consequence concludes the music in the form of a *Furiant*.

Brian Bowman exemplifies euphonistic expertise with a fine singing tone and all the required technique. The playing is as rich and musical as anyone could want.

Fancy Dances for Three Bass Tubas (1972)

☐ Members of the New York Tuba Quartet / Crystal S-221

Contemporary translations of traditional dance designs—*Galop, Sarabande,* and *Saltarello*—not only of the harmonic nuances but of the structural conditions. The "fancy" in the title apparently is the composer's freedom of expression rather than a description of type. To write for a tuba trio such special manner of thinking is not mandatory, but certainly may be utilized. In that respect Ross is successful.

Philip Rosseter   (ca. 1568-1623)

Sweet, Come Again   **Whether Men Do Laugh or Weep**   *Vocal*

What Then Is Love but Mourning   *Voice with Accompaniment*

☐ Patterson (tenor); Spencer (lute) / Philips 6500282

Rosseter is described as a miniaturist, composing "short and well-seasoned" airs (or *ayres,* as the word was spelled in Elizabethan days). The texts for all three songs are by Rosseter. The performance is an impressive one.

Roman Michelangelo Rossi   (1600-1660)

Toccata No. 7 in D minor   *Instrumental*

☐ Kipnis (harpsichord) / Columbia M3X-31521   *Harpsichord*

An example of seventeenth-century avant-garde music. It is certainly not in the form of what is expected from music indicated as being in toccata design. The steering of this production is akin to bits put together, with harmonies that slide side-saddle, as it were. This is raw stuff, in a way. Of course, Kipnis plays it with full surety and state-of-the-art musicality, but he cannot avoid the score's sectionalism.

Salomone Rossi   (1570-ca. 1630)

Kaddish   *Choral*

☐ David Tilman Choir / Serenus 12039   *Chorus Alone*

One of the most ancient of all Jewish prayers. There are innumerable settings and the text is often recited rather than sung. The important point of this performance is that it displays an example of Rossi's synagogue music, composed in addition to some thirteen volumes of madrigals and instrumental works.

Gioacchino Rossini   (1792-1868)

Orchestra

Overture to *Assedio di Corinto* (1826)

☐ NBC Symphony Orchestra / Toscanini (conductor) / RCA VIC-1248 (monaural)

Old it may be, and nonstereo, too, but this recording of the "Siege of Corinth" Overture outdistances the competition in every way possible.

Overture to *The Barber of Seville* (1816)

☐ Academy of St. Martin-in-the-Fields / Marriner (conductor) / Philips 6500878
☐ NBC Symphony Orchestra / Toscanini (conductor) / RCA VIC-1274 (monaural)

Marriner approaches this popular Overture without the easy-to-take manner so many conductors follow. His conception of *The Barber of Seville* is beautifully proportioned, clean, well paced, and sings rather than blusters. It is this same sculpted clarity that makes the much older Toscanini representation equally worthy.

(For a recording of the complete Opera, see under *Opera and Dramatic Music.*)

Overture to *Il Signor Bruschino* (1813)

Overture to *Il Turco in Italia* (1814)

Overture to *La cambiale di matrimonio* (1810)

☐ Academy of St. Martin-in-the-Fields / Marriner (conductor) / Philips 6500878

Marriner's conceptions of the designs of these Overtures are absolutely stunning and striking, and they thereby sparkle. The touches are the kind that make for record-buying power: the bow percussion effect in the first work, the horn solos in the other two, the seamlessness that provides marvelous continuity. All are delivered with an invigorating bravura that is yet stated in a musical way.

Overture to *La Cenerentola* (1817)

☐ NBC Symphony Orchestra / Toscanini (conductor) / RCA VIC-1248 (monaural)
☐ Chicago Symphony Orchestra / Reiner (conductor) / RCA LSC-2318
☐ Bamberg Symphony Orchestra / Perlea (conductor) / Vox 511180

The Toscanini entry is sensitively proportioned and that provides all the required excitement. Reiner's version is well paced and sings from beginning to end. The surprise is the Bamberg performance, found to be of admirable clarity and structured with perfect balance.

(For a recording of the complete Opera, see under *Opera and Dramatic Music.*)

Overture to *La gazza ladra* (1817)

☐ Cleveland Orchestra / Szell (conductor) / Columbia MS-7435

A deliciously clean performance. Everything is on target and without the flip-flop *rubati* that often mar the lyrical oboe and horn passages. (This Overture is also included in Columbia MS-7031, with four other Rossini Overtures, and in a miscellaneous, four-side, seventeen-total package on Columbia M2X-787.)

Overture to *La scala di seta* (1812)

Overture to *L'inganno felice* (1812)

☐ Academy of St. Martin-in-the-Fields / Marriner (conductor) / Philips 6500878

Super projections of Rossini's scores. They contain all the desirabilities: warm sentiment, acute instrumental balances, and a liveliness of wit and spirit.

Only Previtali (on Everest 3186) is represented with a competitive version of *L'inganno felice.* Conductors who have overlooked the tripleted frolic of this piece should have a look.

Overture to *L'Italiana in Algeri* (1813)

☐ NBC Symphony Orchestra / Toscanini (conductor) / RCA VIC–1248 (monaural)
☐ Academy of St. Martin-in-the-Fields / Marriner (conductor) / Philips 6500878

This was one of Toscanini's specialties and it remains very special. The English group comes exceedingly close and does have the advantage of stereo. It also can boast of an excellent oboist (important to the scoring), and Marriner can properly boast that he can control a Rossini crescendo with the best of 'em. This conductor is a man of stylistic wisdom. His sharp perceptions are proof.
(For a recording of the complete Opera, see under *Opera and Dramatic Music.*)

Overture to *Semiramide* (1823)

☐ London Symphony Orchestra / Gamba (conductor) / London 6204

A brilliant realization with the emphasis on the musical purposes.
(For a recording of the complete Opera, see under *Opera and Dramatic Music.*)

Overture to *Tancredi* (1813)

☐ Academy of St. Martin-in-the-Fields / Marriner (conductor) / Philips 6500878

Rossini scholarship is here translated so that all the dynamic and tempi shifts add up to a vivid performance. The usual marvelous Philips sound is, of course, a listener's bonus.

Overture to *William Tell* (1829)

☐ Philadelphia Orchestra / Ormandy (conductor) / Columbia M–31640
☐ New York Philharmonic / Wummer (flute); Brenner (English horn) / Bernstein (conductor) / Columbia D3S–818

The *William Tell* Overture requires a big orchestra and a virtuoso one to cross the goal line successfully. That includes, especially, a flutist who can wing his way artistically through the figurations of his part, an English hornist with a rich, fat tone, a cellist capable of delivering the same timbre quality, and a violin body that combines finger finesse with bowing bravado. The Philadelphians and the New Yorkers are tops in these major-league requirements. (It is significant that special credits are given to two solo players in the Bernstein release.) The conductor must have the know-how to define the music's value points beyond special colors and tempi excitement.

Unless properly proportioned the result is simply far less than what Rossini's score has within it. Both Ormandy and Bernstein are the best ambassadors for this work, with a few percentage points in favor of the former because he has a slightly better solo cellist and English hornist.
(Bernstein's reading can be obtained in a number of other packagings, all on Columbia: MS-6533; MS-6743; MS-7085; M-30305; and M-31815. Ormandy is also represented in the RCA catalogue on ARL1-0453 with this Overture.)

<table>
<tr><td>

*String
Orchestra*

</td><td>

Sonata a Quattro

No. 1 in G major / No. 2 in A major / No. 3 in C major / No. 4 in B flat major

☐ I Musici / Philips 6500243

These fresh musical pleasures stem from Rossini's twelfth year. Initially scored for two violins, cello, and double bass (here performed with triple the number of players for the violin parts and double the number of players for the cello part), all are fairly well known as wind quartets (five in total, No. 3 not being included), far less so as string quartets. However, both the wind (flute, clarinet, horn, and bassoon) and string quartet (two violins, viola, and cello) settings represent transcriptions probably not made by Rossini.

The only rival performance of the entire six original *Sonate a Quattro* is by Neville Marriner's Academy of St. Martin-in-the-Fields. Like the I Musici edition, two separate discs are involved. However, for those who prefer exact chronological order, the latter is to be preferred. Marriner's group plays Nos. 1, 3, 5, and 6 on Argo S-506 but even then that sequence is not maintained, Nos. 1 and 6 being on the first side of the disc and Nos. 3 and 5 on the reverse. The remaining pair are included on Argo ZRG-603. On the other hand, I Musici run the Sonatas in exact order on the present release and finish the sequence (Nos. 5 and 6) on Philips 6500245 (*see below*).

A further point is that the Italian organization plays untouched Rossini, while the English orchestra edits him. Marriner adds a pair of violas both to fill in the textured center and, sometimes, to weight the second violins or cellos. Further, he divides the violins into three groups, with four firsts, four seconds, and four others that strengthen either the first or second violins "according to which has the principal part." Tempi and tone are at times brighter on the part of Marriner's eighteen players. Still, one prefers the truer projection of the music by I Musici with their six violins, two cellos, and one double bass.

Sonata a Quattro

No. 5 in E flat major / No. 6 in D major

☐ I Musici / Philips 6500245

For a full discussion that includes these two Sonatas, *see above.*

</td></tr>
<tr><td>

Instrumental

Flute

</td><td>

Introduction and Variations

☐ Rampal (flute); Laskine (harp) / Musical Heritage Society MHS-1345

Though not the last word in creativity, the clarity of the playing and the spontaneity deserve attention. The design of the duo covers an introduction, the theme, and then four variations with the obvious tonal embroideries.

This performance (plus the others on the disc of music by Damase, Fauré, Ibert, Krumpholz, and a setting of *Greensleeves*) was originally recorded by Erato and then remastered and released by Musical Heritage. In the interim still another release was made, by Epic (now deleted), with the catch-all heading of *Music by Candlelight.*

</td></tr>
<tr><td>

Horns

</td><td>

Fanfare de Chasse

☐ Horn Club of Los Angeles / Kraft (conductor) / Angel S-36036

A delightful two and one-half minutes of unknown Rossini. Perfection is the name of the playing, with one valveless horn used "for rustic authenticity."

</td></tr>
<tr><td>

Piano

</td><td>

Péchés de Vieillesse (Excerpts)

☐ Sgrizzi (piano) / Nonesuch 71163

</td></tr>
</table>

A group of delights from Rossini's "Sins of My Old Age." (For a further discussion of this work, see under *Choral: chorus with accompaniment.*)

More spoofs, more goodies, with titles that prefigure Satie's statesmanship in such use: *Prélude prétentieux,* a concoction of persuasive platitudes; *Memento Homo,* containing both Beethovenistic solemnity and solid polyphony; followed by an air-clearing *Assez de Memento: Dansons.* And then there is stylistic mimicry (stated) in the *Petite Caprice* (Style Offenbach) or (implied) in the Czernyish *Mon Prélude hygiénique du matin.*

All nine choices are played in choice fashion by Luciano Sgrizzi. Expect fun and finesse plus musical sins that are without harm because they're extremely worthy ones.

Duet for Cello and Double Bass

☐ Mallach (cello); Poppe (double bass) / Turnabout 34606

This odd-ball combination surprises one with what can be accomplished. Clever Rossini! In the slow movement he mainly opts for a cello solo supported by bass pizzicati. But there are places where the bass takes the lead, though with limited musical behavior.

Péchés de Vieillesse (Excerpts)

☐ Chorus of the Societa Cameristica di Lugano / Devallier (contralto); Marion (tenor); Benoit (baritone); Sgrizzi (piano) / Loehrer (conductor) / Nonesuch 71089

Here are some of the close to two hundred compositions for piano, various instruments, voice, and vocal combinations that Rossini produced in his late years and that he titled "Sins of My Old Age."

The aural delights of these prove that sowing creative wild oats sometimes results in a truly artistic crop. The nine items contain vocal scintillations, piano introductions and solo sections, bits of narrations, and in one case—*Musique anodine* ("Anodyne Music")— six different settings of the same song. A full gamut is covered, from a pitter-patter The Baby's Song with its "Kertchoos!" to a solemn Funeral Chorus for Meyerbeer.

The singers have attractive voices and as such perfectly match the material. Big, opera-starred qualities would be misfits for these charming items. Sgrizzi's piano playing is ideal, though a little too much reverberation creeps in at times. Nonesuch's remastering of the original Cycnus recording produced in Paris was a wise choice; the Cycnus edition was winner of the French Grand Prix du Disque.

(For more examples from Rossini's "Sins," see under *Instrumental: piano.*)

Messa di Gloria

☐ English Chamber Orchestra and BBC Singers / Rinaldi (soprano); Gunson (contralto); Benelli and Mitchinson (tenors); Bastin (bass); Brown (English horn); King (clarinet) / Handt (conductor) / Philips 6500612

Herbert Handt's realization of this work differs considerably from the published version initially issued by Mills Music. Nevertheless, it is fully satisfactory and provides an interesting example of Rossini's sacred compositional procedures, eclectically formed, but more serious than both his Stabat Mater (*see below*) and his *Petite Messe solennelle* (*see below*).

Petite Messe solennelle (1864)

☐ Northwest German Philharmonic Orchestra and Choir, Herford / de la Cruz (soprano); Gilles (alto); Saretzki (tenor); Grimm (bass); Roth (organ) / Albert (conductor) / CMS/Oryx 1826/7

Chamber Music

Choral

Chorus with Accompaniment

Cantata and Oratorio

Rossini's Mass has much to offer, notwithstanding that its sacred dress has secular fringes and color (the latter part of the Gloria is but one example). There is sufficient stylistic discretion in Rossini's writing to override any criticism that he has disrupted the ideal order of the Mass. It is not classically spirited but it is beautiful (examples: the *Agnus Dei,* the *O salutaris,* and the *Crucifixus*).

The edition considered here concerns the second version of the work, calling for four solo voices, chorus, orchestra, and organ. Rossini's initial setting used two pianos and harmonium to support the voices. Those who would like to have that version can obtain it on the Eurodisc label (86321-XKG), a duplicate of a foreign RCA issue (SER-5693/4) that has never been released in this country. That performance falsifies the score's quality by its overdevotional style, and the singing (even with Fischer-Dieskau in the solo line-up) is not as well formulated as in the CMS/Oryx release. But, even with the latter issue, one raises questions as to the weak quality of the orchestra. The singing in the other recorded version on the market (Everest/Cetra S-441/2) is the equal of the CMS/Oryx issue; the sound is inferior, however.

There are some irritating production aspects to the CMS/Oryx release. The jacket indication shortens and changes the spelling in Rossini's title to *Messe solenne.* The label copy uses "Solemn Mass" (and, incidentally, this is the first time I have seen two different labels designs used in a two-record issue). No credits whatsoever appear on the cover; the vocal soloists and organist are listed on the inside liner notes. And, mind you, the name of the conductor, orchestra, and chorus can only be found on the label copy! There, one finds equal credit given to The State Music Society Paderborn—whatever that means is not explained. There are other examples of production sloppiness. Fortunately that criticism does not apply to the performance.

Stabat Mater (1842)

☐ Cincinnati Symphony Orchestra and Cincinnati May Festival Chorus / Lee (soprano); Quivar (mezzo-soprano); Riegel (tenor); Plishka (bass) / Schippers (conductor) / Turnabout 34634

There is another recorded version of this piece with at least two better voices; but there is so much operatic temperature in Rossini's sacred work that anything that will help to underplay that factor leads to better musical consequences. The other edition is on London 26250 and includes Luciano Pavarotti and Pilar Lorengar in its soloistic cast. Beautiful as that performance is, there is a more ingratiating affinity for the purposes of this type of music in Schippers's interpretation and the approach of his singers. Another plus is the fine choral work of the Cincinnati May Festival outfit.

Opera and Dramatic Music

The Barber of Seville (1816)

☐ Philharmonia Orchestra and Chorus / Callas and Carturan (sopranos); Alva and Carlin (tenors); Gobbi (baritone); Ollendorff and Zaccaria (basses) / Galliera (conductor) / Angel S-3559

No argument can deny that Rossini's *Barber* is his masterpiece. Operatic *buffo* buoyancy, enticing and exciting exhilarations, great tunes, great fun, and a good comic plot all certify its status as one of the perpetual strengths in the operatic repertoire.

This recorded performance bubbles with the greatest flavor. It was produced when Callas was enjoying her heyday, and her conception of Rosina is superlatively realized. Gobbi swings along in his Figaro part with the fullest assurance, and Alva is a sparkling Count. Freshness and virility are maintained throughout, thanks to Alceo Galliera's well-paced direction. There's a real beat in the stylish way Rossini's Opera is performed. It's tops.

(For recordings of the Overture alone, see under *Orchestra* [Overture to *The Barber of Seville*].)

La Cenerentola (1817)

☐ Orchestra and Chorus of the Maggio Musicale Fiorentino / Carral (soprano); Simionato and Truccato-Pace (mezzo-sopranos); Benelli (tenor); Montarsolo, Bruscantini, and Foiani (basses) / de Fabritiis (conductor) / London 1376

A fat plus for this excellent production, which has more panache and glitter than the competitive edition on Deutsche Grammophon (2709039). The music zips along, which is a mark of credit for the cast, because the vocal requirements are difficult. In this respect the authority and style of Giulietta Simionato's voice is stunning. Ugo Benelli's vocal instrument is creamy; more importantly, it is pliable, and his *fioriture* are produced with the greatest of ease. Among the basses Paolo Montarsolo is a great *buffo*, and nothing is false (as it well could be) in his interpretation. The orchestral playing is fully defined and clear voiced.

(For recordings of the Overture alone, see under *Orchestra* [Overture to *La Cenerentola*].)

La pietra del paragone

☐ Clarion Concerts Orchestra and Chorus / Elgar (soprano); Wolff and Bonazzi (mezzo-sopranos); Carreras (tenor); Reardon, Diaz, and Murcell (baritones); Foldi (bass); Cooper (harpsichord) / Jenkins (conductor) / Vanguard 71183/5

You don't hear this one live—the revival given in New York in the 1972–73 season apparently was the first in America; a few scattered productions have been given abroad. Rossini's witty opera remains firmly outside the repertory.

Ensemble singing is a rich point in the work and is by far the outstanding vocal condition in the recording. José Carreras has a clear, well-formed voice and exhibits sensitive phrasing and style in his role. The orchestra plays amazingly well and Newell Jenkins is in superb control of the entire proceedings. Special credit pertains to Kenneth Cooper's harpsichord playing in the *secco* recitatives. A highly recommended operatic recording.

L'Italiana in Algeri (1813)

☐ Orchestra and Chorus of the Maggio Musicale Fiorentino / Berganza (mezzo-soprano); Alva (tenor); Panerai (baritone); Corena and Montarsolo (basses); Pace and Tavolaccini (vocalists); Vedovelli (harpsichord) / Varviso (conductor) / London 1375

Rossini's two-act *opera buffa* (comic opera) is described by Stendhal in his *Life of Rossini* as having speed, extreme economy, and absolved of having any turgidity. To this should be added that is has "sparkle" and "surefire operatic sense."

Presently the only edition in the recorded catalogue, this performance fulfills all requirements. Teresa Berganza is enchanting as Isabella; her voice has warmth and, when needed, all the necessary power. Fernando Corena is deeply involved in his portrayal as Mustafà and, though some of the upper register gets away from Luigi Alva (he has the Lindoro role), he is otherwise most satisfactory. The orchestra is in splendid shape and Silvio Varviso is in full command. There are a few cuts made and most of the recitative has been eliminated—no loss.

(For recordings of the Overture alone, see under *Orchestra* [Overture to *L'Italiana in Algeri*].)

Semiramide (1823)

☐ London Symphony Orchestra and Ambrosian Opera Chorus / Sutherland and Clark (sopranos); Horne (mezzo-soprano); Serge (tenor); Fyson (baritone); Rouleau, Malas, and Langdon (basses) / Bonynge (conductor) / London 1383

Rossini's *Semiramide* works beautifully on disc, especially because one doesn't see the leading male character (Arsace) portrayed by a female. Rossini assigned this role to a mezzo-soprano (here, Marilyn Horne) and just hearing makes for believing. It also makes for some magnificent soprano and mezzo-soprano duets between Arsace and Semiramide, Queen of Babylonia (here, Joan Sutherland). The plot gets awfully thick, since Semiramide is in love with Arsace, who is, in reality, her long lost son, and who, in turn, is in love with a Princess Azema (Patricia Clark).

Indeed, it's only the music that works beautifully in this Opera. The singing is impressive, those duets are marvelously accomplished. There's a juicy soprano aria (*Bel raggio*), fine choruses, and good orchestral scoring. The supporting cast is good, but this Opera belongs to Sutherland and Horne. Bonynge is to be credited with fine direction.

(For a recording of the Overture alone, see under *Orchestra* [Overture to *Semiramide*].)

Rossini / Ottorino Respighi

Ballet

La Boutique fantasque (1919)

☐ Orchestra of the Vienna Festival / Janigro (conductor) / Vanguard 71127

"The Fantastic Toyshop" is a one-act ballet drawn from a group of short pieces that Rossini wrote in his final years. They are cute and rhythmically ideal for dance music, and when combined with the orchestrational skill of Respighi, success is assured.

Vitality is here in Janigro's performance, but he carefully does not strain matters or make the score untidy by overemphasizing what is subtly delectable. Indeed, this is a lively show but always a thoroughly musical one.

Nicolas Roussakis   (1934-   )

Instrumental

Harpsichord

Sonata for Harpsichord (1967)

☐ Chaney (harpsichord) / Composers Recordings S-255

How dynamic an instrument the harpsichord can be is vividly evidenced in Roussakis's brilliantly serialized, brilliantly conceived five-movement Sonata. No light and airy stuff here. This music is fastidious in its percussive prosody. Although the technical basis is tightly defined, Roussakis's creativity is not restricted but rather profits from such confinement. Indeed, there is individual voice in this work. It is played with flair and full recreative responsibility.

Chamber Music

Six Short Pieces for Two Flutes (1969)

☐ Harvey and Sophie Sollberger (flutes) / Nonesuch 73028

These are short pieces (the set takes just short of nine minutes to perform), but Roussakis has packed a great deal of strong music into them. His type of serialism is fascinating to analyze—its coherence is anything but note manipulation based on pitch numerology.

The formal disciplines are extremely interesting. Thus the rhythmic activity of the second piece is involved with phrases that progressively decrease in length, which is sharply contrasted to the set of canons that form the third movement; measured *tremolandi* state the principal function of the material in the tripartite design of part 4; and so on through the palindromic procedure of the final piece. Pre-ordered it may be, but strict technical procedures do not obviate significance.

The Sollbergers (husband and wife) play with full-fledged expertise.

Night Speech (1968)

☐ Macalester Concert Choir / Warland (conductor) / Composers Recordings S-255

Choral

Chorus and Instrumental Ensemble

The text of *Night Speech* is a non-text of vocal sounds consisting of sibilants, fricatives, plosives, and so forth. Expect, therefore, nothing that is wonderfully sweet but rather a series of exciting effects, forceful in their color and laced with a mysterious content. The last is obtained by the use of a special percussion instrumentation consisting of gongs, a variety of wind chimes, large sheets of paper, and sandpaper. The result is effective, though one's response to the implied theatricality would be greater in terms of a live presentation.

The fifty-member choir and two instrumentalists perform quite well. However, CRI can't make up its mind whether the name of the group is the Macalester Concert Choir or the Macalester College Choir.

Jean-Jacques Rousseau (1712-1778)

Le Devin du village (1752)

☐ Chamber Orchestra and Chorus / Miranda (soprano); Wilfart (tenor); Cottret (bass) / Cotte (conductor) / Musical Heritage Society MHS-1985

Opera and Dramatic Music

Rousseau is, of course, famous as a philosopher, author, and political theorist, least known as a composer. Of his musical output only this Opera has any importance. Its values are immediately apparent from the open-air quality of the overture through the nice melodic turns heard in the eight scenes and finale of the work. There are some cuts but they certainly aren't missed in this engaging forty-five-minute recording.

Marcel Rousseau. *See Marcel Samuel-Rousseau.*

Albert Roussel (1869-1937)

Bacchus et Ariane
Suite No. 1, Op. 43 / Suite No. 2, Op. 43

☐ National Orchestra of the O.R.T.F. / Martinon (conductor) / Musical Heritage Society MHS-1244

Orchestra

There is no precise pictorialism in the pair of suites drawn from the *Bacchus et Ariane* ballet. (Composed in 1930, the ballet received its premiere in 1931, and in 1932 Roussel arranged the two suites for orchestral performance, one each from the pair of acts of the stage work.) The music is charged with full imaginative grasp, but the style is as newly classical as the classic tale on which the work is based.

One does not need to know the stage picture to enjoy the suites. Both are compiled in a linking of detail that amounts to a symphonic fantasy. The tempo changes are choreographic in their assortment, with ten in the first suite and thirteen in the second one, but there is no sense of episodic interruption. Even though this is orchestral music without a precise program, there is no mistaking the vehement virtuosity of the close of the second suite—a rousing bacchanale.

There have been numerous recordings (all since deleted) of the second suite (by Munch [on RCA Victor 6113], Markevitch [on Deutsche Grammophon 12040], Ormandy [on Columbia 5667], and Rucht [on Urania 7037]). None of these could match the blaze of this rendition. Martinon previously recorded both suites for Epic (3165) with the Orchestre des Concerts Lamoureux—also now in the deleted category. This Musical Heritage Society release, again covering both suites, is a major addition to the Roussel discography.

Le Marchand de sable qui passe, Op. 13

☐ Paris Philharmonic Orchestra / Leibowitz (conductor) / Counterpoint/Esoteric 5511E (monaural)

Early Roussel (written in 1908) for an ensemble of flute, clarinet, horn, harp, and strings as incidental music to a Jean Aubry play. "The Sandman" is played without any improper rhetorical gestures.

Petite Suite for Orchestra, Op. 39

☐ National Orchestra of the O.R.T.F. / Martinon (conductor) / Musical Heritage Society MHS–1372

This work represents the mid-eighteenth-century instrumental serenade idea characterized by mixture of forms and scored for a compact ensemble (late Haydn instrumentation), reminted in terms of the twentieth century. The designs are changed to modern equivalents: an *Aubade*, real open-air exhilaration gliding in tenfold meter; a Pastorale, and a *Mascarade*.

Martinon directs this brilliant showpiece with elucidative Rousselian decorum. There is always proper classical registration and no lushness is permitted to interfere with the composer's black and white scheme.

Pour une fête de printemps, Op. 22

☐ National Orchestra of the O.R.T.F. / Martinon (conductor) / Musical Heritage Society MHS–1201

Roussel's work was originally conceived as a Scherzo for a symphony, then was transformed into a separate piece. Op. 22 is a cross between Roussel's impressionistically derived and neoclassic style. A lively and rhythmically clear presentation.

Suite in F, Op. 33

☐ Lamoureux Orchestra / Munch (conductor) / Musical Heritage Society MHS–3022

Old forms are newly illuminated in this three-movement opus. The sections are a sinewy *Prélude*, a sampling of concerto grosso style refurbished with tart harmonies; a chromatically curved Sarabande with a long line that is of more grandeur than this dance usually signifies; and a free-driving, but unnervous Gigue.

Roussel's neo-classicism is direct; in comparison, Stravinsky's can be termed argumentative. The pure sound of this suite and its pithiness explain a great deal. Roussel proves that in the hands of a master no musical design becomes yellowed with age. This is truly exciting music in which Munch makes certain not to allow the sonorous brilliance to expunge the contrapuntalism.

Symphony No. 2 in B flat major, Op. 23

☐ National Orchestra of the O.R.T.F. / Martinon (conductor) / Musical Heritage Society MHS-1201

In the opinion of a very few (the writer included) this is the greatest of Roussel's orchestral compositions. The deadly serious, austere sound of the music never gives way to sunny vitality, even in the slightly lighter formations of the middle movement. Harsh hermetic qualities prevail within the quasi-program of the piece—the three stages of man: youthful aspirations, the joys and then deeper feelings of maturity, and finally, disillusionment.

Exquisitively refined and meticulously sensitive craftsmanship is to be found in this symphony, marked by an expressionistic specification hardly found in any of the other Roussel works.

Naturally, this symphony is hardly played in comparison with the third and fourth symphonies. That it is available on an excellent recording is a matter of consequence.

Symphony
No. 3 in G minor, Op. 42 / No. 4 in A major, Op. 53

☐ L'Orchestre de la Suisse Romande / Ansermet (conductor) / London STS-15025

The third symphony (commissioned for the 50th Anniversary of the Boston Symphony Orchestra) is superbly French in its gestures. It is clear-toned in its stinging harmonic language, as deft in its fluidal lines as any Mozart conception, as legible as any classic work of the eighteenth century.

In comparison, the fourth symphony contains more polyphony, but it avoids mass conflict of textures—thus no messy, muddy linear situations develop. Only the third movement, based on a gigue-like idea, is more vertically organized.

The playing is clear enough but very literal. Ansermet bypasses any expressive heightening. Such avoidance of the oversell can be argued.

Sinfonietta, Op. 52

String Orchestra

☐ Jean-François Paillard Orchestra / Paillard (conductor) / Musical Heritage Society MHS-805

This is one of the most appealing works by this composer. The music is concentrated in scope, as precise as the jeweled works in a wrist watch. It sounds as it appears on the score page—clear, of pellucid definition, as though all sounds, rhythms, and phrases were made with a ruler. Roussel's string piece is contemporary simplicity in its most exigent and therefore exciting form.

The initial movement is asymmetric and slightly nervous; like the other portions of the work it is diatonic like the alphabet, yet dissonant. In the slow division the effect is bitonal; this is a paradox, for Roussel is not a bitonalist but a pantonalist, permitting diatonic tunes to have constricted congress with each other—a type of celibate harmonic marriage. The finale is smart and joyous; it is based on a "chasing the tail" idea, with episodes both dramatic and of semi-jazz snap. The threaded points of ostinati bind the texture. Roussel's twentieth-century music is substantial art; it wears exceedingly well.

Paillard makes the most of Roussel's rich ideas. A little more percussive bite would not have harmed the outer movements, but otherwise this is a well-modulated conception.

Above all, do not, repeat do not, obtain the performance on Everest (No. 3194), listed in *Schwann*. This hollow-sounding, distantly reproduced music sounds like the worst kind of air check transferred to disc. The entire matter is suspect. There is nothing mentioned about Roussel on the cover and there isn't a single note on the music or even the composer. It is hidden in the most unlikely and mysterious manner in a seven-record release titled (correctly, save for the Roussel) as "The Art of the Flute" and throughout the soloist is Jean-Pierre Rampal. Apparently a filler was needed and this was grabbed. But what short change! The Roussel is clocked at 9:09. It is coupled with a Bach bit timed at 3:22. End of a complete record side totaling 12:31! No matter the poor bargain, the Roussel string piece doesn't belong in this release and the performance doesn't deserve belonging anywhere.

Solo Instrument and Orchestra

Concerto for Piano and Orchestra, Op. 36

☐ Hamburg Symphony Orchestra / Littauer (piano) / Springer (conductor) / Turnabout 34405

Piano

None of the pyrotechnical bombs of the Grieg, Tchaikovsky, or Rachmaninoff concerti is found here, but all the technical chemistry that makes Roussel's music fresh is present here. There is virtuosity, but it is subsidiary to the corporate work. This is why few pianists know it, and fewer play it. The loss is theirs and unfortunately ours.

Bravo to the soloist and bravo to Turnabout for fine engineering, with sensitive directionality and good depth.

Instrumental

Segovia, Op. 29

☐ Segovia (guitar) / MCA 2526 (monaural)

Guitar

Roussel's *Segovia* is a true portrait with line, design, and correct instrumental timbre to match. This rhythmic Spanish (but not stereotyped) piece for the guitar perfectly delineates the famous virtuoso. In its less than three-minute scope this sketch is a little gem. (Roussel also made a version for solo piano.)

The recording is monaural but is full and clear; the playing, as is to be expected, is totally of Segovian sensitivity. If you *must* have stereo, Julian Bream presents an ideal reading on RCA (LSC-2448). Should you want this piece plus a huge amount of Segovia playing as only he can, then obtain the "Golden Jubilee" album (originally issued by Decca, now MCA 19000). Six sides, covering twenty-two works by fourteen composers (including Segovia himself), with only three of the total representing transcriptions, comprise the offering. Two of the pieces are with orchestra (the Symphony of the Air, Enrique Jordá conducting). There is also a brief recorded message by Segovia. Quite a package!

Harp

Impromptu, Op. 21

☐ Laskine (harp) / Musical Heritage Society MHS-602

In 1909, Roussel journeyed to China and India. This trip to the East inspired the composition of a set of three symphonic poems (*Evocations*) and an opera–ballet, *Padmâvatî*. Roussel's interest in Hindu aesthetics was not permanently retained in his creative outlook, but its clear expositions left their mark on all his later work.

This indirect response is present in the sole work Roussel wrote for the plectral harp. Although the identification of the Impromptu is mainly French, due to its clarity of line and form, the eastern element is recognizable in the music's accent and sense of languor.

It is especially in the capturing of the climate of the work that Madame Laskine excels—far better than the other pair of recorded performances that are available (Ellis on Oiseau-Lyre S-308 and Stockton on Crystal S-107).

L'Accueil des Muses (1920)   *Piano*

Prélude et fugue, Op. 46

☐ Doyen (piano) / Musical Heritage Society MHS-1155-57

Both "The Muses' Welcome" and the Fugue were composed for special issues of the magazine *Revue musicale.* The former was a memorial for Debussy—a broadly paced lament. The latter was for inclusion in a special Bach issue. Accordingly, Roussel constructed a fugue on Bach's name, using (as so many other composers) German pitch equivalents where required (B flat and B natural equaling, respectively, B and H). The Prelude was added after the fugal fact and is in sharp contrast.

Roussel's pieces are welcome additions to the recorded music catalogue. They are played convincingly.

Sonatine, Op. 16

☐ Johannesen (piano) / Golden Crest 40866

This composer's neoclassic activity, with tonality livened by fanwise spread, is evidenced by the pithiness of his Opus 16. Without going beyond the fluidic limits of twentieth-century classicism, Roussel brings stylistic unity and balance to the two parts of the *Sonatine* (each further divided, so that the first movement bridges into a scherzo and the slow movement is partner to an animated finale).

Roussel's aim is to be intelligible, and he is. In Grant Johannesen's re-creation he is perfectly so. The perspicuity of the writing reminds one of Mozart speaking in today's language. Pianists would do well to consider this music of tenderness, wit, and rhythmic bravura. It is the first of these points that is lacking in Doyen's recording of the work (on Musical Heritage Society MHS-1155-57). Although Petit displays tenderness in her interpretation (on Oiseau-Lyre 60052), it lacks shading. Johannesen's reading is number one in this survey. He performs in a distinguished manner.

Suite pour piano, Op. 14

☐ Petit (piano) / Oiseau-Lyre 60052

There is no adherence to formula in Roussel's Suite, though the pat titles of the movements lead one to expect it. The minor-keyed Bourrée contains a tense vitality and drama reminiscent of Beethoven. It is as remote from the spirit of the French seventeenth-century court dance as is Stravinsky from Elgar. The *Sicilienne* is long-lined and moves with chromatic inquietude. The *Prélude* is no typical introductory essay. It is a narrative saturated with vivid dramatic detail, tragic intensity, and dark violence. Presumably a piece of absolute music, the *Prélude* has a hidden program, as revealed by the composer's widow. Though the music strongly speaks for itself, those interested in the true chilling tale that influenced it are referred to the superb, super-detailed notes included with the Musical Heritage issue noted below. Even in the *Ronde,* though it has a prevalent optimism and a natural vitality there is a sense of adumbration.

With these particulars, interpretative overstress means overkill. The best appraisal is that which assesses the score as closely as possible. Françoise Petit follows this line of reasoning and hers is a telling testimony of Roussel's magnificent work. Jean Doyen's portrayal (on Musical Heritage Society MHS-1155-57) underlines phrases already set in italics as it were, and stresses what is sufficiently powerful without being further emphasized.

Doyen interchanges the order of movements 2 and 3 of the published score, where the *Sicilienne* precedes the Bourrée. He justifies this by the fact that the latter was written before the former and that such movement transposition brings better contrast. A further defense for this action is that (according to the notes on the work by Harry Halbreich) "Roussel himself fancied it." If so, he never made it official.

Trois Pièces pour piano, Op. 49

☐ Johannesen (piano) / Candide 31059

This is music of an inclination very different from the deep emotional content found in most of this composer's output. Roussel seasons his neoclassicism with plenty of paprika. In taking over the lighter Parisian franchise, Roussel refuses to relinquish a single delight. But such resolution and stubbornness do not defeat him. It is all quite satisfying.

For the three editions available the vote goes (but only by a small margin) to Grant Johannesen. He invests the music with proper urbanity. Both Françoise Petit (on Oiseau-Lyre 60052) and Jean Doyen (on Musical Heritage Society MHS-1155-57) perform nicely and neatly, though much more seriously. None of these can match the way André Previn played the music with a charming, unstudied air that was truly captivating. Unfortunately, 'tis in the heavenly kingdom of deleted issues. A search may turn up a copy. It's worth the time and trouble and expense. Previn's performance is in an album called *French Piano Music* (Columbia 5746).

Chamber Music

Trio for Violin, Viola, and Cello, Op. 58 (Movement 1)

☐ London String Trio / RCA LM-6092 (monaural)

The pert French spirit helps Roussel's polyphony get off the ground in this *allegro moderato*-tempoed movement. Significantly, the contrapuntalism does not obviate melodic profile, as in the case of the opening theme, set in a chromatically festooned A minor.

This is so well-played that one wishes the rest of the opus were available on a disc.

String Quartet in D major, Op. 45

☐ Via Nova Quartet / Musical Heritage Society MHS-1351

Roussel's only string quartet displays all of his compositional habits and his mature creative facets. Joining his French colleagues Fauré, Debussy, and Ravel in producing a single example in quartet form, he has stated, in analogous parallel with them, his entire creative creed therein.

The work is marked "in D major," but this is a polarity magnet, not an example of major–minor buttressment. Superb polyphony—especially strong in the outer movements (the finale is a fugue)—clarifies the piece. Freed from the harmonic yoke it knows no previous master save the rationality of Bach.

This is rugged music but the French foursome play with chamber music warmth without denying the proper strength of the composition. It is an impressive statement in all respects.

Serenade for Flute, Violin, Viola, Cello, and Harp, Op. 30

☐ Melos Ensemble / Oiseau-Lyre 60048

There is constraint in this quintet of mixed timbre. Roussel's frequent polyphony gives way to more vertical states and definite attention is accorded to the colorful resources of one wind, and one plucked and three stringed instruments. The deftness of harp glides, arpeggios, and light ictuses help pigmentate this cheerful work, composed for the famous (no longer in existence) Quintette Instrumental de Paris.

This is a magical performance that pushes to the side the competitive edition on Turnabout 34161. Throughout, this fine ensemble fully communicates the Rousselian sobriety of classicism contemporaneously revitalized.

Divertissement for Flute, Oboe, Clarinet, Bassoon, Horn, and Piano, Op. 6

☐ Los Angeles Wind Quintet / Stevens (piano) / Orion 7263

Tight lines, semi-hard harmony—all of Roussel's inimitable characteristics are present, only with less polyphony than he would use in later years. The music's flavor is still perfect, notwithstanding the fact that the cork from the bottle of this composition has been pulled out innumerable times and its winy contents tasted by many composers.

Fine playing by the Californians. The perky accompaniments in part 1 are well-established, the slow section is neatly curly-haired with rhythm, and a real "Frenchy" dance quality is defined in the last portion.

Deux Mélodies, Op. 19
Deux Mélodies, Op. 20
Deux Poèmes chinois, Op. 12
Deux Poèmes chinois, Op. 35
A Flower Given to My Daughter
Jazz dans la nuit, Op. 38
Odelette, Op. 8, No. 4
Odes anacréontiques, Op. 31/2, Nos. 1 and 6

Vocal

Voice with Accompaniment

☐ Marcoulescou (soprano); Phillabaum (piano) / Orion 75184

Since Orion does not give definitive information for these thirteen songs it is best to cover the entire program. Op. 19 consists of *Light* and *A Farewell* (listed on the disc as *Adieux*). Op. 20 covers *Sarabande* and *Le Bachelier de Salamanque*. The Op. 12 group has *Ode à un jeune gentilhomme* (Orion omits the first word of this title) and *Amoureux séparés*. This pair of songs is performed in reverse order. The other *Deux Poèmes chinois* include *Des Fleurs font une broderie* and *Réponse d'une épouse sage*. *A Flower* is to a Joyce text and is sung in English—the other songs are heard in French. *Jazz dans la nuit* has a Piafian cabaret swing. *Odelette* is the concluding song in *Quatre Poèmes*. Finally, what is labeled *Chansons anacréontiques* is correctly *Odes anacréontiques*, consisting of the first of the set, *Sur lui-même*, and the sixth (the conclusion) of the cycle: *Sur un songe*.

This is quite a textual range, from the classic Greek, to Li-Po, onto Joyce, to mention only the most important. The songs are styled accordingly and convincingly. They deserve to place Roussel in the forefront of French song composition, especially as documented in the prize presentations given by Yolanda Marcoulescou, partnered equally well by Katja Phillabaum. Theirs is a considerable accomplishment and provides one of the most important releases Orion has made. (Texts are given, but in translation only.)

Le Festin de l'araignée, Op. 17

Ballet

☐ National Orchestra of the O.R.T.F. / Martinon (conductor) / Musical Heritage Society MHS-1372
☐ Paris Philharmonic Orchestra / Leibowitz (conductor) / Counterpoint/Esoteric 5511E (monaural)

Roussel's one-act ballet-pantomime "The Spider's Feast" is the highlight of his impressionistically styled compositions. It has a specialness that contrasts vividly with the hard-core neoclassic works; the orchestration is delicate as brush work, with textures of lazy, dusted substances. The music is of such finesse and sensitivity that it seems to spin on the point of a needle.

This wonderful piece of exotica (the characters are a spider, ants, butterflies, beetles, fruit worms, and so forth—there are no human beings in the story) has thirteen sections. Actually, the Leibowitz performance is the better of the two. It is a marvel of detail and color, with exquisite balance and a highly polished projection of Roussel's evocative ideas. However, it must take second place, not because of its monophonic format, but because it is an excerpted version. Only a bit more than sixteen minutes of the score are played. Martinon plays the entire work (exactly twice the length of Leibowitz's version). This gives him the edge, though the performance has less subtlety. Many ballets gain by orchestral suite excerpting. Roussel's "Spider" has total wealth in every one of its measures and there is a loss in not hearing the total score.

Alec Rowley (1892-1958)

Choral

Chorus with Accompaniment

Praise

☐ Walter Ehret Chorale / Flath (organ) / Ehret (conductor) / Golden Crest S-4032

Lyrically gentle and dynamically optimistic contrasts place Rowley's anthem in a class far above the usual run-of-the-mill hymns of praise. The interplay of solo voices gives coloristic variety. Excellent performance.

Miklós Rózsa (1907-   )

Orchestra

Kaleidoscope, Op. 19a

☐ Vienna State Opera Orchestra / Rózsa (conductor) / Westminster Gold 8353

This is Rózsa's orchestration of his set of piano pieces (see under *Instrumental: piano*). The liberating sense of color extension works well in this case.

String Orchestra

Concerto for String Orchestra, Op. 17

☐ Vienna State Opera Orchestra / Rózsa (conductor) / Westminster Gold 8353

Rózsa considers the string body in its largest, coloristic sense in his Op. 17. *Divisi* is constant giving vertical, polyphonic, and textural amplification. In the first movement, a strong declamatory and contrapuntal conception, the scoring reaches nine-part totality. In the melancholic slow movement there is one section for fourteen solo players covering nine lines; the conclusion splits the orchestra into fourteen parts, with five soli within the whole. The finale (an *Allegro giusto*) has a fiery rhythmic drive.

There are plenty of difficulties in the score but for the greater part these are completely overcome. Where there is a slight slip there is still spirit and so the performance carries the listener along. Rózsa knows his way among the sonorous machinery and should be given points for being a creditable conductor of his own music. This work is one of his very best.

Concerto for Violin and Orchestra (1953)

☐ Dallas Symphony Orchestra / Heifetz (violin) / Hendl (conductor) / RCA LSC-2767

This concerto (actually Rózsa's second for the violin) is strictly of Hungarian personality, but it does not follow the close-to-the-soil manner of Bartók and Kodály. Preferential consideration is given to matters of romantic address with proper dissonance for underlining. The music is fit to size; it is more "respectable" by wearing the city clothes that Bartók said constricted the body of Hungarian folk-founded song.

Of course, this is the kind of vehicle that fits in with the fiddlistic world in which Heifetz always dwelled, so the great artist is fully responsive to the secure climate of the Hungarian's lush and tuneful music. Whatever technical problems there are (not many), Heifetz tosses them off with his patented precision.

Variations on a Hungarian Peasant Song for Violin and Orchestra, Op. 4

☐ Vienna State Opera Orchestra / Zsigmondy (violin) / Rózsa (conductor) / Westminster Gold 8353

Rózsa conducts here a second version of his *Variationen über ein ungarisches Bauernlied* originally composed for violin and piano (see under *Instrumental: violin*). Quality playing.

Tema con Variazioni (1962)

☐ Chamber Orchestra / Heifetz (violin); Piatigorsky (cello) / RCA LSC-2770

The *Tema con Variazioni* is the second movement of a Double Concerto for violin and cello commissioned by Heifetz and Piatigorsky. Both the theme and the variational shapes have the modal and rhythmic fluidity that identify folkloristic Hungarian music. In this case the data are stylistically affiliated more with Kodály, not at all with Bartók. Simple and always calm writing but quite persuasive.

These two great musicians should be expected to communicate all the details, and they do so with elegant precision.

Toccata Capricciosa, Op. 36

☐ Solow (cello) / Entr'acte ERS-6509

One of the latest works Rózsa has written, Op. 36 was produced in 1977 and was dedicated to the late Gregor Piatigorsky (the soloist's teacher). There are no threnodic pretensions, though the central section sings meditatively. Otherwise this is music of Hungarian heart and soul—direct and dynamic, of pulsatilistic and virtuosic proclamation. That there are strong reminders of Kodály's work for unaccompanied cello firms up the sonorous arguments.

Fine playing by Jeffrey Solow. It is fervent and expressive in all respects.

Kaleidoscope, Op. 19
Sonata for Piano, Op. 20

☐ Dominguez (piano) / Orion 74137

The peppy drive of the Sonata for Piano is typical of this composer. It is full of rhythmic fancies, including expected Hungarian ones. The smaller-scaled *Kaleidoscope* follows the same path.

Clean playing here, good interpretative range, and fine dramatic projection. (An orchestral version of Op. 19 has been recorded—see under *Orchestra*.)

Violin

Little Suite (North Hungarian Peasant Songs and Dances), Op. 5

Variations on a Hungarian Peasant Song, Op.4

☐ Granat (violin); Herbst (piano) / Orion 73127

In Op. 5 (fully titled on record label, without the parenthetical indication on the album cover, but oddly never termed *Little Suite* anywhere in the sleeve note discussion), no theoretical government overtaxes the folk documentation. The Variations are more sophisticated, but there, too, overdogmatic formal philosophy is avoided in order to feature the native allegiance. The work can also be heard with orchestral back-up (see under *Solo Instrument and Orchestra: violin*).

Chamber Music

Duo for Cello and Piano, Op. 8

☐ Solow (cello); Dominguez (piano) / Entr'acte ERS-6509

Aside from the most important creative impulse in Hungarian music (represented by Bartók's and Kodály's work), there are a number of composers who have cultivated a style that combines romantic (tonal) warmth and formal clarity with the stimulus of folk roots. These are good, tastefully alive, discriminative intentions and they form a strong circumference around the enterprise of Bartók and Kodály. Rózsa belongs solidly in that group, as is well-illustrated in this two-movement duo, the second displaying a set of variations.

Dramatic and colorful playing is heard. All the proportions of the music are perfectly presented.

Duo for Violin and Piano, Op. 7

☐ Granat (violin); Pennario (piano) / Orion 73127

Rózsa's four-movement Duo (a sonata title would have been as apt) is strongly Hungarian. However, Rózsa's folk-ingrained melodies are original. They are presented with romantic flavor, which makes them different from the earthier melodies of Bartók, Kodály, and Lajtha.

A secure performance, especially avoiding over-sentimentality.

Sonata for Two Violins, Op. 15a

☐ Granat and Sanov (violins) / Entr'acte ERS-6509

Rózsa's splendid duo sonata has a strong Hungarian profile. There are plentiful folk-music turns in the score, colorfully displayed by the two violins. However, these are treated quite differently from what Edwin Evans has described as "the conventional view of Hungarian folk music, based on the ornate distortions of gypsy bands and their imitators." The dynamism and strength, merged with romantic reconciliation of Rózsa's style make it less elemental than Bartók's. This does not nullify pertinent strength which is found in a different manner by way of subtle colorations and expressively rich harmonic content.

The recording provides a fine achievement by these violinists. The performance is beautifully styled and strongly evocative.

To Everything There Is a Season, Op. 20

Twenty-Third Psalm, Op. 34

The Vanities of Life, Op. 30

☐ Choir of the West / Skones (conductor) / Entr'acte ERS-6512

The first and last titles comprise motets on lines from Ecclesiastes. Rózsa's music is direct and ideally suited for the texts, without any of the nationalistic references that apply to most of his output.

Opus 30 was composed especially for the Choir of the West, while the *Twenty-Third Psalm* was first performed by them. These provide strengths apparent in the fine and sensitive recorded performances.

Right margin labels:
Choral
Chorus Alone

Edmund Rubbra (1901-)

Symphony No. 7 in C, Op. 88

☐ London Philharmonic Orchestra / Boult (conductor) / Musical Heritage Society MHS-1397

Those who know the music of this notable English composer claim it is not exportable. Such nonsense is not relished by a fair-minded critic or musician. Rubbra's seventh symphony has power, depth, and a structure of imposing meaning and strength. It can stand next to any of the great works in symphonic form by Mahler, Bruckner, Sibelius, or Elgar.

Contrapuntalism is the principal coalescence, which is especially confirmed in the huge Passacaglia and Fugue that completes the work. The middle movement (*Vivace e Leggiero*) is a large-spanned waltz–scherzo with two trios. A four-note motive is the germinal material for the opening movement.

Rubbra is practically unrecognized in the record catalogue. This performance should help to change this unfair status. The playing of the London Philharmonic Orchestra is outstanding and Boult is at his best in this prime neo-romantic music that is strongly orchestrated and superbly polyphonicized.

Right margin label:
Orchestra

Improvisation for Violin and Orchestra, Op. 89

☐ Louisville Orchestra / Harth (violin) / Whitney (conductor) / Louisville 57-6 (monaural)

The material on which Rubbra's work is based is derived from the opening for unaccompanied violin. Harth fittingly plays this richly tonal music neatly and without any extravagances.

Not only those interested in twentieth-century music should give some attention to this fine work—meaning, our solo violinists, of course.

Right margin labels:
Solo Instrument and Orchestra
Violin

Meditation Sopra Coeurs Désolés for Alto Recorder and Harpsichord, Op. 47

☐ Dolmetsch (alto recorder); Saxby (harpsichord) / Orion 74144

An excellent illustration of this far too little-known composer's music. Rubbra's technique is devoted to the employment of long lines. He is a composer who builds his works, or any movement within them, as a complete unit, rather than hinging them together by contrasting themes, block assemblages, or motival associations. Even with only two in-

Right margin label:
Chamber Music

struments (and the recorder is a flyweight in terms of textural strength) there is an identification with baroque grandeur.

Choral

Chorus Alone

Missa Cantuariensis, Op. 59 (Sanctus, Benedictus, and Agnus Dei)

☐ Choir of Salisbury Cathedral / Guest (conductor) / RCA LM-6092 (monaural)

The "Canterbury Mass" (excerpted in this recorded performance) is for double choir. Rubbra's setting of the Anglican Communion Service tellingly reproduces archaic style.

Anton Rubinstein   (1829-1894)

Orchestra

Danses des fiancées de Cachemir from Feramors

☐ London Symphony Orchestra / Bonynge (conductor) / London 2232

An extract from the ballet music contained in the Opera. (*Feramors*, after the poem *Lalla Rookh* by Thomas Moore, was first produced in Dresden, in February of 1863.) Bonynge directs a crisp performance of the music.

Symphony No. 2 (Ocean) in C major, Op. 42

☐ Westphalian Symphony Orchestra, Recklinghausen / Kapp (conductor) / Candide CE-31057

This is the Symphony that grew and grew and grew. The first four movements were completed in 1857, about fifteen years later the fifth and sixth movements appeared, and the seventh part was added in 1877. There's more to this symphonic saga, since Rubinstein rewrote some of the earlier movements as he expanded the work.

Richard Kapp plays five parts of the total. A few of these are of interest but otherwise the word is "prolixity." However, the historic factor is important, and Kapp has done quite well with what he chose to record.

Symphony No. 6 in A minor, Op. 111

☐ Hamburg Symphony / Beissel (conductor) / Turnabout 34577

It's easy to find the obvious weaknesses in Rubinstein's work—developmental dead spots and sequential stolidity. But percentage-wise these are far outweighed by the romantic thrust of the opening movement and the Russian coloration and "mood for pageantry" (Richard Freed's excellent description in his splendid liner notes) of the finale. The moderately paced second movement sings nicely, the *Allegro vivace* that follows capably fulfills scherzo specifications. Given a fair chance, Rubinstein's last Symphony sits well.

One is grateful to Turnabout for issuing this work. Also for giving it to us in so well prepared a performance. Heribert Beissel does himself proud with his pacing and styling of Rubinstein's Symphony.

Solo Instrument and Orchestra

Piano

Concerto No. 3 in G major for Piano and Orchestra, Op. 45

☐ Westphalian Symphony Orchestra / Preston (piano) / Freeman (conductor) / Orion 74149

There's some music hidden under the stormy virtuosity of Rubinstein's opus. What there is Preston displays with high fidelity. He tosses off the difficulties with ease; the technical discipline pays off since it truly embraces the artistic ends of Rubinstein's work.

Concerto No. 4 in D minor for Piano and Orchestra, Op. 70

☐ Philharmonia Hungarica / Ponti (piano) / Maga (conductor) / Candide 31023

The Rubinstein D minor opus is another example of a once-popular work falling by the wayside. How unfair! The first movement alone is a juicy and dramatic piece of concerto business, with writing of bravura and a splendid cadenza for the soloist. There is richness and color in the remainder of the work as well.

Ponti's playing provides everything the music needs: exact control, musical intelligence, variety, expression, and virtuosic energy. There is excellent support from the orchestra.

Concertstück for Piano and Orchestra, Op. 113

☐ Pro Musica Orchestra, Vienna / Blumental (piano) / Froschauer (conductor) / Turnabout 34387

The *Concertstück* furnishes straightforward information of the expected kind, not important in the Rubinstein catalogue but nonetheless a serviceable piece. Capably played, the work is not unsettled in any place by wicked interpretation.

Barcarolle in G minor, Op. 50, No. 3

Instrumental

☐ Tarnowsky (piano) / Genesis 1004

Piano

A simple and clear case of unabashed romanticism. Nothing wrong, nothing great, but certainly satisfactory, and the same can be said of the performance.

Barcarolle No. 2 in A minor

☐ Hofmann (piano) / Klavier 121

More *schmerz* than swing. Distinctive reproduction and playing.

Etude in C major, Op. 23, No. 2
Melody in F major, Op. 3, No. 1
Polka (*Bohème*), Op. 82, No. 7
Rêve angélique, Op. 10, No. 22
Romance in E flat major, Op. 44, No. 1
Valse (Allemagne)

☐ Ponti (piano) / Candide 31023

The first title is the most important of the six in the opus. It features staccato and often has been listed as the "Great" Etude. *Rêve angélique* ("Angel's Dream"), potboiler though some may term it, retains its specialness, and is the only one of the two-dozen portraits Rubinstein delineated in his Opus 10 that is now ever heard. Because of this it is quite frequently incorrectly given the title of the complete work: *Kamennoi Ostrow*. An example of why it has become known as a bloody bore is available on Klavier 111. There, Josef Lhevinne drags the tempo as he oversentimentalizes the piece for a duration of eight and one-quarter minutes, while Ponti moves it along in five and one-half minutes. Accordingly, the music takes on a totally different quality, with the motility permitting phrases to register, whereas they get stifled in the slow shuffle of Lhevinne's pedestrianism.

The remaining four exhibits are lightweights, but a special bonus comes from Ponti's clear praxis of not encumbering them with spurious meaning. (How many neat, small pieces have been ruined by interpretative humbuggism!) An example of Ponti's keen insight is his playing of the Romance (the initial item in the six-part *Soirées de Saint-Pétersbourg*). On the other hand, Ignaz Friedman (in a collection titled "Legendary Pianists of the Romantic Era–Concert I," released by Klavier-No. 114) delivers it with a heaviness and solemnity totally unbefitting its simplicity.

Rubinstein's Melody (the first of the pair in the opus) has also been deflowered by countless mis- and dis-arrangements, especially a choral horror called "Welcome Sweet Springtime, We Greet Thee in Song." It is a sharp reminder of Sigmund Spaeth's horrendous method of teaching the young by putting words to instrumental themes, thus serving as a crutch to identify the composition from which it was drawn. Such mayhem has not been practiced on the Polka and the *Valse*, both contained in an Album of National Dances, covering six pieces.

Valse-Caprice in E flat major

☐ Hofmann (piano) / Klavier 121

Hofmann doesn't let the bravura within the piece destroy the requisite gracefulness. He combines immaculate rhythm with melodic glitter.

Chamber Music

Quintet in F major for Piano and Winds, Op. 55

☐ Members of the New Philharmonia Wind Ensemble, London / Blumental (piano) / Turnabout 34477

Rubinstein's lone work for this combination (the winds are represented by flute, clarinet, bassoon, and horn) is from every viewpoint one of clear writing, with an intelligence of form that makes listening a simple pleasure. It is not great music, but the four movements do constitute, without ostentation, a comfortable musical state, without the usual cloying style for which Rubinstein has been censured.

The playing is styled to follow the denominations proportionately common to the romantics. This makes the performance truthfully nourished.

Vocal

Voice with Accompaniment

Night, Op. 44, No. 1a

☐ Davrath (soprano); Werba (piano) / Vanguard VSD–71115

Those who have played items contained in mammoth-sized piano-music collections, with catch-all headings using the word "favorites" or "great," will doubtless recognize *Night* in its other (keyboard-instrument) dress, with the title Romance. In turn the latter is actually from a set of six piano pieces Rubinstein composed as his Opus 44, entitled *Soirées de Saint-Pétersbourg*.

(For a recording of the Romance see under *Instrumental: piano* under Etude in C major.)

Ballet

Ballet Music from the Opera *Der Dämon*

☐ Hamburg Symphony / Beissel (conductor) / Turnabout 34577

Rubinstein's "The Demon" was the most successful of his nineteen operas. It achieved a huge number of performances in Russia and, with translated text, productions were mounted in a number of countries including Finland, Poland, England, and America. A recording was made in 1946 by the Bolshoi Theatre and then reissued in 1968 on the Melodiya label (D–011501–6). It is available on special import.

The Ballet (two sections, one of a little over seven minutes, the other close to six-minute length) appears in the second act. It has as much going for it as Borodin's Polovt-zian Dances from *Prince Igor* (see under *Borodin: Orchestra*) though slightly less color-fully orchestrated (bear in mind that Rimsky-Korsakov did the scoring for the Borodin). Included is a finely depicted Lezghinka.

The performance is clean, the percussion timbres especially well defined.

Dane Rudhyar (1895-   )

***Granites* (1929)**

***Paeans* (1927)**

Instrumental

Piano

☐ Masselos (piano) / Composers Recordings S-247

Rudhyar worships the power of sound *qua* sound. Formalism gives way to a dynamic totality, the product of a Scriabinian recipe. The music is crusted with hot massivity.

Granites is in five sections, though they are played in the aggregate. Each part, however, specifies a defined mood, conveyed by rhythmic specifics or by a flow of plaited sounds.

Sonorous constancy is found also in *Paeans* (its title is misspelled on the album cover of the recording). Bearing out the coalescence, Rudhyar advises the pianist to consider the keyboard instrument as a "resonant mass of wood and metal, a sort of condensed or-chestra of gongs, bells and the like."

There are exceedingly few pianists who can match William Masselos in performances of contemporary music. Two reasons: he has a white-heated enthusiasm for such music and he matches it with an understanding rarely found in performers even though they may have all the necessary technical equipment to cope with the extraordinary demands of twentieth-century music. Rudhyar's music is sharply characterized in this recording. (*Granites* was previously recorded by Masselos on an old MGM disc, E-3556, coupled with works by Charles Griffes and Ben Weber. The release of the CRI album eradicates the disappointment of the deletion of the MGM recording.)

***Pentagrams, Book III "The Release"* (1925)**

☐ Sellers (piano) / Orion 7285

Rudhyar has composed four of these *Pentagrams*, each in five sections. The titles of this one give the clue to the mystical vibrancies that inhabit his music: *Gates, Gift of Blood, Pentecost, Stars*, and *Sunburst*. All these are in free forms, each like a flowing im-provisation. The affinity with Scriabin (more ascetic, however) persists.

Well-played, though the sound is just a bit grainy.

***Stars* (Movement 4: *Pentagrams, Book III "The Release"*) (1925)**

☐ Masselos (piano) / Composers Recordings S-247

Although the complete work of which *Stars* forms a part is available (*see above*), the ex-ceptional performance by Masselos demands a listener's full attention.

***Syntony* (1968)**

☐ Sellers (piano) / Orion 7285

The orchestrational approach marks this music, like all of Rudhyar's. It is chock-full of quartal and quintal chordal assimilations, it seethes and is restless with panchromaticism. Each of the four movements repulses reticence. Even in its quieter moments there is chordal nervousness. Sellers does well with the score.

Tetragram No. 4 (Adolescence)

Tetragram No. 5 (Solitude)

Transmutation (1976)

☐ Mikulak (piano) / Composers Recordings SD–372

Spanning almost a half century (1920–1967), Rudhyar has written nine *Tetragrams*, divided into three series. (The third of this sequence [No. 6] is titled *Emergence*. The three in the first set are headed *The Quest, Crucifixion,* and *Rebirth.*) Each individual *Tetragram* covers four untitled sections. The same theosophical parlance heard in Rudhyar's other works is used here.

Transmutation, a "tone ritual in seven movements," is a further visit to Rudhyar's hothouse of cosmic mysticism. The reliance on noncadential chromaticism is meant to evoke "inner, psychic, and emotional transformation." It totals a Scriabinian syndication.

Marcia Mikulak plays these works with complete sympathy and obtains a mood that fully serves the composer.

Andrew Rudin   (1939-   )

Electronic Music

Tragoedia

☐ Nonesuch 71198

Rudin's *Tragoedia* is in four movements: *Kouros* (meaning surfeit or excess), *Hybris* ("pride or arrogance bordering on the blasphemous"), *Peitho* (temptation or persuasion, "akin to obsession in most tragedies"), and *Até* ("the quality of utter ruin and desolation" resulting from the previous three situations). This is electronic music with an individual difference. Quarter-tone data, twelve-tone series, canonic procedures, and cyclic interpenetration link the work, which runs thirty-seven and one-half minutes.

Major to the piece is that with all the electronic scintillations there is a strong structural fidelity. The reality of exposition, development, slow-paced contrast, scherzo, and finale characteristics is pertinent and masterfully detailed. There are those who contend that new methods cannot lean on old forms. I am not one of them. Use of balance never brings harm to an artistic piece of work. Further, inculcation of historic continuity in contemporary translation never diminishes the creative strength of a new medium.

The possibilities of electronic music have held much promise. Much is yet to be fulfilled. With Rudin's meaningful and dramatic composition, however, one of the goals has been reached.

Carl Ruggles   (1876-1971)

Orchestra

Evocations	**Men and Mountains**
Men (1924)	**Organum (1946)**

☐ Buffalo Philharmonic / Thomas (conductor) / Columbia M2–34591

Men is a short essay (a little over two minutes) with the same essences that permeate *Men and Mountains*. Though Ruggles's score for *Men and Mountains* is headed with a motto from William Blake, "Great things are done when men and mountains meet," the music is not descriptive but rather associative. There is no lame halt for contrast, no letdown in the positiveness of declaration. The impulse in *Men and Mountains* is obtained from the movement of chunks of counterpoint. Pure theme as pure discourse with underpinning doesn't exist in this sinewy music. What does exist is a type of orchestrational recitation of hellfire as Ruggles's instruments scream and implore.

There's only one way of performing this music—persistent robustness (even in the middle movement, *Lilacs,* for strings alone). This is not to be confused with restlessness. That quality is already built into the score. Robust muscle is what a conductor must demand in the playing, so that each sound is framed and pointed, fully strengthened, regardless of dynamic, to permit the polysyllabic detail to be heard properly. By and large Thomas's conception fulfills these requirements and avoids the muscle-bound polyphony that produces the pitches and none of the meanings.

As attested to by the title, *Organum* is essentially linear. It is also, as Ruggles considered the writing of music, essentially atonal. Atonality with this man was no perfumed expressionism but a tobacco-crusted cud of expressionistic power. It is carried forth by properly heavy orchestration. Ruggles's orchestration is not a document of recommendation for students, but for his own conceptions it is instrumentational superexcellence. That word "superexcellence" describes the performance directed by Thomas. It wipes off the map the old monaural edition in the CRI catalogue (127) made by the Japan Philharmonic Orchestra, conducted by Watanabe.

The orchestral version of *Evocations* (for the original piano edition, see under *Instrumental: piano*) not only clarifies the chunky counterpoint, but brings special color to the sound blocks of the score. As usual with Ruggles, the textures are closely wrought and even overloaded but it is just that heavily dissonant and overly weighted activity that provides the unifying factor in this great composer's music. Thomas's conception does not opt for sound economy—that would be entirely incorrect. The music is allowed its head—it is also allowed its spiky sensitivity.

Sun-Treader (1932)

☐ Boston Symphony Orchestra / Thomas (conductor) / Deutsche Grammophon 2530048

Ruggles's music represents chromaticism in its most striated state. His orchestration is beautifully "incorrect" and thereby artistically unadulterated. Its imbalance and muddiness present orchestrational audacity, sonorous hyperbole, and yet it conveys the musical idea exactly. When the horns scream in *Sun-Treader* as though they were amplified fiddles and are barely heard because orchestral overstatement is fundamental at all times, they become a fresh color and simultaneously power the already powerful linear statements of the piece.

The playing and conducting simply cannot be bettered. Ruggles's style is fully horizontal and the Bostonians, with Thomas's keen insight (derived from ethusiasm for the music), give the piece tremendous dimensional depth. A five-star affair.

Portals

☐ Buffalo Philharmonic / Thomas (conductor) / Columbia M2-34591

String Orchestra

The published score of *Portals* has a descriptive heading: "Symphonic Composition for Full String Orchestra." And so it is, with much triple forte impact, *divisi* that sometimes reaches thirteen parts, and with a special kind of tearing intensity that is special to string instruments. The last matches the motto taken from Whitman that prefaces the music: "What are those of the known but to ascend and enter the unknown?"

The command, amplitude, and expressive range of this performance would be difficult to better. There is no question of the special affinity Michael Tilson Thomas has for Ruggles's music.

Brass Ensemble

Angels (Original Trumpet Version)

Angels (Trumpet/Trombone Version) (1940)

☐ Brass Ensemble / Thomas (conductor) / Columbia M2-34591

Angels was initially for five trumpets and one bass trumpet. Ruggles later revised it for four trumpets and three trombones, totally muted. (He also indicated it could be performed by any seven instruments of equal timbre.)

Spartan atonal order marks this piece, but it has a seething inner emotion as it moves from dissonances of red heat to white-heated ones.

Having both settings recorded was an excellent idea. The playing is totally sensitive. (Notice that the "leader" of the brass group is the famed Gerard Schwarz.)

Instrumental

Piano

Evocations, Four Chants for Piano (1937-1943)

☐ Mandel (piano) / Desto 6445/7

This work is marked by chromatic linear detail, is tight in construction and atonal, and not once is corrupted by a consonance. Abstract pieces, indeed, but with a compelling significance that is acutely communicative.

Mandel's consideration of these expressionistically styled expressions deserves a high rating. He is sensitive to the logic that gives Ruggles's music its life-blood.

Another performance that deserves consideration is by the Ruggles authority, John Kirkpatrick—on Columbia M2-35491. (For an orchestral version, *see above*.)

Vocal

Voice with Accompaniment

Toys (1919)

☐ Blegen (soprano); Thomas (piano) / Columbia M2-34591

Pithy music (only one-and-a-half minutes in length). The range for the voice is huge which thereby allows the concentrated dissonances of the piano to have more pungency by separation from the voice. The partnership of Judith Blegen and Michael Tilson Thomas is superb.

Voice and Orchestra

Vôx Clamans in Deserto (1923)

☐ Speculum Musicae / Morgan (mezzo-soprano) / Thomas (conductor) / Columbia M2-34591

This set of three songs for mezzo-soprano and chamber orchestra uses the poetry of Browning (*Parting at Morning*), Meltzer (*Son of Mine*), and Whitman (*A Clear Midnight*). A richly expressive, disjunctive voice line thrusts itself against and away from the dissonant instrumental background and foreground. Ruggles's songs become hypnotic in their utter tensility. The performance is definitive.

Choral

Chorus and Instrumental Ensemble

Exaltation (1958)

☐ Brass Ensemble and Gregg Smith Singers / Raver (organ) / Thomas (conductor) / Columbia M2-34591

This, the final composition Ruggles wrote, was a memorial tribute to his wife. It has just a pinch of salt in a few of its harmonies; otherwise, its simplistic tonalism is as unlike Ruggles's music as can be imagined. Little matter—*Exaltation* has a haunting quality that lingers long after the music has concluded.

The performance is beautiful, especially in its dynamic curve. One suspects that Michael Tilson Thomas placed his editorial hand on this score. All to the good.

Antonio Ruiz-Pipó   (1933-   )

Tablas para Guitarra y Orquesta (1972)

☐ London Symphony Orchestra / Yepes (guitar) / Frühbeck de Burgos (conductor) / Deutsche Grammophon 2530585

Andalusian improvisatory style is applied intelligently in this colorful work. It makes a fine addition to the guitar-with-orchestra literature. Splendid performance.

Solo Instrument and Orchestra

Guitar

Gerardo Rusconi   (1922-1974)

Istantanee Sonore

☐ Calligaris (piano) / Orion 7142

This is a set of six very short episodes that have athematic conditions and convey the mood of each by disjunctive panchromatic language. They are percussively played, which for the most part fits the material.

Instrumental

Piano

Loren Rush   (1935-   )

String Quartet in C sharp minor

☐ Malan (violin); Galbraith (violin and viola); Ellis (viola); Sayre (cello) / LeRoux (conductor) / Composers Recordings SD–381

This is hard-core chromaticism, free of tonal or serial arrangement, completely a succession of pitch impressions let loose. One hears a torrent of hot chromaticism despite the composer's avowal of "a highly chromatic environment in which the chromaticism is structured throughout by tonal reference." If this is so, it has not so registered with this listener.

A work, to be sure, that is of flailing difficulty for the individual players in all respects and likewise extremely complicated in terms of achieving correct ensemble. It will be noted that a conductor is used to direct the four players, all members of the San Francisco Contemporary Music Players. Also to be noted is the extremely rare string quartet requirement of doubling by the second violinist who plays viola in one section (with its lowest [C] string placed in *scordatura* [tuned a minor third lower]).

Chamber Music

William Russell   (1905-   )

Percussion

Three Cuban Pieces (1939)

☐ Cornelius; Price; Boberg; and DesRoches / Mainstream 5011

Tutti writing predominates in this instance. Cuban forms are matched by Cuban instruments: cencerro, maracas, guiro, claves, quijada del burro, bongo drums, and marimbula.

Percussion virtuosi are involved in the performance so the results are of top quality.

Three Dance Movements (1933)

☐ Manhattan Percussion Ensemble / Cage (conductor) / Mainstream 5011

Standard forms (*Waltz, March,* and *Fox Trot*) are refreshingly transfigured. The first dance is in septuple beat not triple meter, the second moves along in extraordinary $\frac{3}{4}$ time, and the last dance is in a most uneven quintuple meter. But effective! Cage's performers (four in all) include Paul Price, one of the most important men in the entire percussion field. His colleagues are equally expert.

John Russo   (1943-   )

Instrumental

Clarinet

Four Pieces for Clarinet (unaccompanied)

☐ Russo (clarinet) / Capra 1203

A number of contemporary composers have had the eager seriousness to produce works for unaccompanied homophonic instruments. Russo's pieces follow the conventions that one expects: virtuosity embracing severe registral differences, flashes of repetitive sounds, *tremolandi*, flutter-tonguing, and a perky finale to seal matters. Well-played, except that a few of the extremely high pitches move slightly off target.

Piano

Conversazione (1975)

☐ Ignacio (piano) / Capra 1204

Twelve-tone methods with shifting phrase relationships key this essay. A binary sense prevails, with *fermati* acting as punctuation points within the first forty-one measures. None are used in the remaining, generally faster thirty-three measures.

Chamber Music

Sonatina No. 4 for Clarinet and Piano

☐ Russo (clarinet); Ignacio (piano) / Orion 77275

Russo's work displays neoclassic creative behavior, mostly of Hindemithian responsibility. It is quite adept and fluent, with some bracing, properly wrong notes. Workmanlike in all of the three movements, it embraces a Theme and Variations, a slow division, and a March.

Russo has recorded a number of works. He saves his best playing for his own music. Can't blame him.

Larghetto

☐ Russo (clarinet); Curtiss (viola); Ignacio (piano) / Orion 77275

Declamatory rubato sections, a polyphonic dialogue between the clarinet and the viola, and a unison middle division form the design. The piano's role is one of rhythmic obstinacy.

One senses a warmth in this score that, regardless of the composer's performance participation, is somewhat lacking in the recorded documentation. Missing also is pitch definition in the portion where the clarinet doubles the viola.

Three Seasons (1969)

☐ Schutt (flute); Russo (clarinet); Ignacio (piano) / Capra 1204

Bright playing and bright sound are applied to this piece of urbane contemporary romanticism. Contrast is used for tempi, texture, and color. Movement 1 (moderately tempoed) is linear, movement 3 (fast) is predominantly vertical, while the central part is a slow recitative set as a solo for the flute with the piano supplying chordal framework.

William Joseph Russo   (1928-   )

Three Pieces for Blues Band and Symphony Orchestra, Op. 50

☐ Siegel-Schwall Band and San Francisco Symphony Orchestra / Ozawa (conductor) / Deutsche Grammophon 2530309

Solo Instrument and Orchestra

Jazz Ensemble

Linear and vertical symphonic patterns spill over into the blues band section and jazzy rhythms from the latter are incorporated into the former. This joint loyalty is performed with integrity, though it is difficult to avoid the feeling that the result is fleshed-out, sophisticatedly updated Paul Whiteman stuff.

Friedrich Wilhelm Rust   (1739-1796)

Sonata

In C major / In D flat major / In F sharp minor / In G major

Instrumental

Piano

☐ Pleshakov (piano) / Orion 7023

Rust's piano Sonatas are a full testimony of music of Haydnesque brio and early Beethoven reference. Nonetheless, they are not mere academic carbon copies. Each and every one of the four Sonatas is eminently worth hearing.

The structures differ: two movements including a fugue in the C major piece, three movements in the D flat major and G major Sonatas, each with differing concluding divisions (a *Presto* in the latter, a minuet in the former), and in the F sharp minor opus surprisingly a single movement, divided into three sections, based on a single germinal idea. Whether the cyclic condition was the reason or not, in Vincent d'Indy's opinion Rust's F sharp minor Sonata is superior to many of the Haydn and Mozart piano Sonatas "in originality and musical interest." One has to agree.

Simply for reviving these works (actually for their rediscovery) plaudits are in order for Pleshakov. He brings to the Sonatas more than the bare evidence of musicological research. His playing is precise, beautifully contoured and phrased, and with stylistic sagacity.

Giovanni Maria Rutini (1723-1797)

Instrumental

Harpsichord

Sonata in E major for Harpsichord, Op. 2, No. 3

☐ Sgrizzi (harpsichord) / Nonesuch 73008

Like most of Rutini's sonatas, this one has only two movements, and both are in fast tempo. Lyrical grace all the way. The playing relays facile enjoyment. That's all that's needed.

Sonata in F major

☐ Sgrizzi (harpsichord) / Nonesuch 71117

This work is certainly a find. Rutini's first movement moves at a fast clip, spurred by a consistent noodling (*Alberti*-styled) bass. Movement 2 has authoritative depth in its *Andante* pace, and the finale is a *Menuetto* that has formal authority. The contrastive trio (in the minor mode) has far more substance than one generally finds in the subsidiary section of this dance design.

Sgrizzi publishes Rutini's work in a beautiful format. He permits the music to run its natural course, changes colors for repeated sections, and by incisive articulation makes the music gutsy. This is harpsichord playing of superb quality.

Daniël Ruyneman (1886-1963)

Orchestra

***Hieroglyphs* (1918)**

☐ Erös (conductor) / Donemus Audio-Visual Series DAVS-6202 (monaural: 10-inch disc)

This is a historically important piece, with the esoteric combination of three flutes, celesta, harp, piano, two mandolins, two guitars, and cup bells. Regretfully, there are none of the last in this recording since the bells (manufactured to the composer's specifications) were destroyed during World War II. A vibraphone is substituted.

The music is not so startling to today's ears, but if one realizes that *Hieroglyphs* was written in 1918, its historical placement should become important to an auditor's consideration.

Chamber Music

***Réflexions* No. 4 (1961)**

☐ Danzi Wind Quintet / Donemus Audio-Visual Series DAVS-6202 (monaural: 10-inch disc)

This is straightforward and extremely clear serial music of a hundred measures, with rhapsodic tempo changes. The expert Danzi players cover the performance in 4:50.

Frederic Rzewski (1938-)

Instrumental

Piano

***The People United Will Never Be Defeated!* (1975)**

☐ Oppens (piano) / Vanguard VSD-71248

A massive work of three dozen variations on a Chilean song, *¡El Pueblo Unido Jamás Será Vencido!* The melody was a product of the Chilean Socialist movement, and since a dictatorship took over the country the tune has been a symbol of the Chilean resistance.

What Rzewski does with this melody is weave variations on it in a fully fresh tonal manner. These variations are powerful instruments of communication, heavily saturated with heady demands on the pianist. The music is a magnificent panoramic display (it covers fifty minutes) while at the same time it is an instrumental thriller.

Ursula Oppens fights technical fire with performance fire. Her playing is keenly musical, virtuosically explosive. Rzewski as the composer is superb (totally contrary to his avant-garde style). Oppens as the producer of his scenario is just as superb. An extraordinary creative–re-creative performance.

Variations on *No Place to Go But Around* (1974)

☐ Rzewski (piano) / Finnadar 9011

The material is based on the structure of a play for which Rzewski had planned to write the musical score. Various subjects appear representing classes of capitalist society, and a mix of these is also used. The variational dialogue progresses from simplicity to complexity with pantonality as the syntactic governor.

In the playing of his composition Rzewski shows himself to be a prodigious pianist. There is no doubt this would similarly pertain to the performance of other composers' music.

S

Antonio Sacchini (1730-1786)

Overture to *La Contadina in Corte* *Orchestra*

☐ English Chamber Orchestra / Bonynge (conductor) / London 6735

Sacchini's Overture has all the moves found in Haydn and Mozart. Nicely detailed in the performance.

Harald Saeverud (1897-   )

***Peer Gynt* Suite No. 1, Op. 28** *Orchestra*

☐ Louisville Orchestra / Nossaman (soprano); Hauptman (oboe); Howe (horn) / Whitney (conductor) / Louisville 623 (monaural)

This consideration is completely different from proper stage music for the Ibsen play. No on-tip-toe Anitra, no suave A.M. scene. Hans Jacob Nilsen, the important Norwegian stage director, described *Peer Gynt* as "a bitter, scathing play" for which Grieg's unharsh music truly did not fit. From that viewpoint, Saeverud's does. The only resemblance to Grieg's opus is that Saeverud also fashioned two suites from his music for concert use.

There's a little roughness to the playing. Since it fits the content, it is acceptable.

Michael Sahl (1934-   )

***A Mitzvah for the Dead* (1967)** *Instrumental*

☐ Zukofsky (violin) / Vanguard C-10057 *Violin*

For the most part, this is a musical *tableau vivant,* saying what it wants to say in a dead-pan, dead-center manner. Its scenario works perfectly.

A *mitzvah* is the Hebrew word for a kind, considerate, and ethical deed. The act here for "the dead" is the revival of the lush, stagy, top-surface impressive kind of fiddle writing represented in the music of Wieniawski, Vieuxtemps, Bazzini, and the like. The saying is that one mitzvah leads to another mitzvah. It fits Sahl's benevolent depiction which is in four parts.

Parts 1 and 2 have left-hand pizzicati histrionics, arpeggiandi, schmaltzy thirds and sixths, and so on, with some tape accompaniment and a number of exaggerated tape rebuttals. Movement 3 is for the tape alone. Most of it is of the *musique concrète* type, with brass-band snippets, circusy parade stuff, and an accordion bit. Part 4 is for unaccompanied violin, clean and clearly stating a nicely crafted, properly nineteenth-century styled set of variations on *The Last Rose of Summer*. It provides a perfect nostalgic conclusion to Sahl's peep show.

The beauty of Sahl's piece would be totally marred if it were performed in a theatrical manner. Played straight, expressively, and without any hammy consideration, as Paul Zukofsky does, it works and provides a thoroughly enjoyable and diverting musical representation.

Chamber Music

String Quartet

☐ New York String Quartet / Desto 6435/37

Tonality is welcomed back here. The traditional climate is that of Smetana without folk temperature. Just a bit long for its material.

Paul Zukofsky is the first violinist of this communicative group. Their performance displays taste, intelligence, and a fine stylistic temperament.

Electronic Music

Tropes on the Salve Regina

☐ Lyrichord 7210

The main gambit here is guitar strumming—a great deal of it at the beginning and in the concluding parts. In between there are other timbres: voice, background talk without word clarity, background noise, auto honks, and electronic music segments. There is a marked attenuation of material in this issue, the only electronic production Lyrichord has released. (The lack of explanatory notes exhibits poor judgment.)

Sainte-Colombe (1660?-1690)

Chamber Music

Deux Concerts à deux violes égales

☐ Members of the Oberlin Baroque Ensemble / Vox SVBX–5142

These two works are a *Gigue Caprice* titled *Le Retrouvé* and an Allemande titled *Le Craintif,* both for two unaccompanied bass viols. Authenticity to the last degree is exhibited by use of seven-string instruments rather than the more common six-string viols used in performances of Baroque music today (the French call such music "classique").

Joseph Boulogne, Chevalier de Saint-Georges (1739-1799)

Orchestra

Symphony No. 1 in G major, Op. 11, No. 1

☐ London Symphony Orchestra / Freeman (conductor) / Columbia M–32781

The Allegro has flexibility and fluidity but not too much development. Movement 2 is for strings alone (two oboes and two horns are the additional instruments for the outer movements). A fast finale balances the opening of the tripartite total. Saint-Georges's opus is ingenuous if not ingenious.

Symphonie Concertante in G major for Two Violins and Orchestra, Op. 13

☐ London Symphony Orchestra / Fried and Laredo (violins) / Freeman (conductor) / Columbia M–32781

Like the composer's quartet (see under *Chamber Music*), this work has two movements. Other statistical similarities: again Allegro and *Rondeau*, and once more the opening movement is much longer than the concluding one. The style is the same as well, though there is more bounce and exhilaration in this case.

With Miriam Fried and Jaime Laredo the solo parts are projected with admirable skill. Paul Freeman's backing is to the point and is sensitively conditioned. (The cadenza is by Dominique-René de Lerma; the work was edited by Barry S. Brook.)

String Quartet No. 1 in C major, Op. 1, No. 1

☐ Juilliard Quartet / Columbia M–32781

The first opus of this West Indian composer-violinist (born in Guadeloupe) is supremely orthodox and totally traditional. There are two movements, an Allegro and a *Rondeau*. Oddly enough, the former is almost three times the length of the latter.

The Juilliard four do fairly well, but only *fairly,* with the work. A bit of additional conviction (more belief in what they played) would have been helpful.

Scene from *Ernestine* (1777)

☐ London Symphony Orchestra / Robinson (soprano) / Freeman (conductor) / Columbia M–32781

This excerpt from Saint-Georges's opera (first heard in Paris, in July 1777) consists of a recitative and an aria. It is sung with power and conviction but Faye Robinson's diction does not provide topical revelations. The absence of a printed text does not help the situation.

Solo Instrument and Orchestra

Two Violins

Chamber Music

Vocal

Voice and Orchestra

Jacques de Saint-Luc   *(1663-?1720)*

Parthie for Violin, Lute, and Bass

☐ Tryssesoone (baroque violin); Podolski (lute); Terby (bass viol) / Orion 7032

Six dances: Allemande, *Marche,* Sarabande, *Bransle,* another Allemande and a Gigue, are all clearly portrayed and played with simple effect.

Orion's liner copy lists only five of the dances, omitting (together with the picturesque subtitle indicated for each of the other dances) the second Allemande.

Chamber Music

Camille Saint-Saëns   *(1835-1921)*

Bacchanale from *Samson and Delilah*, Op. 47

☐ Philadelphia Orchestra / Ormandy (conductor) / RCA CRL3–0985

Under Ormandy's direction this is as fine a recording of this work as you can find. No special interpretative subtlety is needed, just let it all thrust and hang out. And it does, with terse rhythmic punctuations, well-paced crescendi, and a spectacular conclusion,

Orchestra

beginning with dramatic timpanic affirmation, then joined by Saint-Saëns's oriental belly dance tune. It is tremendously exciting and immediate. What a sound Ormandy commands! No dynamic overkill, just a lusty five hundred percent *fortissimo*, round and savory.

The Carnival of the Animals (1886)

☐ City of Birmingham Symphony Orchestra / Ogdon and Lucas (pianos); Moroney (flute); Robinson (cello) / Fremaux (conductor) / Klavier 527
☐ New York Philharmonic / Bernstein (conductor and narrator) / Columbia D3S-785

All types of gimmicks have been attached to Saint-Saëns's already colorful score. Thus narrative introductions, verbal program notes, and special verses by Ogden Nash have been used. If you want the latter, the best is the monaural edition, with Kostelanetz conducting and Noël Coward doing the narration (on Odyssey Y-32359).

However, letting Saint-Saëns have his say, just as he prepared the score, turns out to be the most propitious choice. The very musical exhibition provided on Klavier's release fulfills that premise. If narration is demanded, the suggestion is to try the Bernstein disc. He offers his own introductions, and no smart verses are included. Still, there is no lack of special showmanship, but gratifyingly, it does not spoil the music—the inclusion of seven young soloists to help matters along. These include identical female twins (age: twenty-one) as the important pianists and the now famous Gary Karr (age twenty at the time the recording was made) playing *The Swan* on the double bass rather than the original cello called for in the score.

Danse Macabre, Op. 40

☐ New York Philharmonic / Nadien (violin) / Bernstein (conductor) / Columbia MS-7522

What Bernstein finds in this score is truly remarkable and has seemingly escaped all other conductors—at least the many who have recorded the old chestnut. His discoveries? A little inner voice here, an emphasis on a harmony there, a perception that the chromatic sweeps must have seamlessness in lieu of minute pitch definition, and a tempo that dances along rather than seems to be moving with the brake pedal down. Actually, it is Bernstein's aproach to the score as a brand new piece instead of as a routine chore that makes all the difference. In so doing he has brushed away the hackneyed grime that has descended on the work.

The solo violin part is played in the traditional lush manner by David Nadien. But here too, there is a difference: his is a controlled fat sound. It neither is an overbearing one nor has the rough, bombastic quality a number of other concertmeisters choose. (Some play the solo part sweetly, which is as incorrect as failing to tune down the E string and to play the crucial E flat as a fingered pitch rather than as an open-string timbre.) A special bow to Columbia for giving Nadien proper credit, a matter unfairly bypassed in most other instances.

Bernstein's conception is also available (all on Columbia) on MS-7165 (with music by Dukas, Mussorgsky, and Richard Strauss), in a miscellaneous collection on MS-7246, and in two three-record sets on D3S-785 and M3X-31068.

Gypsy Dance from *Henri VIII*

☐ London Symphony Orchestra / Bonynge (conductor) / London 6744

This is part 3 of the four-part ballet divertissement in the four-act Opera. Well done, as is to be expected.

Le Rouet d'Omphale, Op. 31

☐ Paris Conservatoire Orchestra / Martinon (conductor) / London STS-15093

The work is nicely paced so that the figurations picturing the spinning wheel do not sound as if it were electrically driven. The middle section, dealing with the orchestral delineation of Hercules (how that portion was played to death by silent-movie organists!), is given proper intensity without being made overtheatrical.

Suite algérienne, Op. 60

☐ Frankenland State Symphony Orchestra / Barati (conductor) / Lyrichord 7103E (monaural)

This is salon music transferred from the salon to the concert hall. Saint-Saëns's four-part suite (*Prélude, Rapsodie mauresque, Rêverie du soir,* and *Marche militaire française*) surfaces, once in a while, on pops programs. That is its proper place.

Symphony
In A major / In F major (Urbs Roma)

☐ Orchestre National l'ORTF / Martinon (conductor) / Angel S–37089

These are two symphonies outside the regularly numbered group of three (the third being the well-known "Organ" symphony). If you hardly know the first two symphonies (discussed *below*) this pair will probably be even less familiar. Neither has been published. The A major opus never was performed, the other symphony was, but then was withdrawn by Saint-Saëns.

Symphony in A major was composed at the age of fifteen. It has Mozart scribbled all over it and the scoring is for strings with flute and oboe. The F major piece shows Saint-Saëns's future class in its scherzo and variationally designed movements.

Fine resonance and vitality in the playing. Off-beat material but not off-beat music. It will please.

Symphony
No. 1 in E flat major, Op. 2 / No. 2 in A minor, Op. 55

☐ Orchestre National de l'ORTF / Martinon (conductor) / Angel S–36995

There is a considerable difference in Saint-Saëns's approach to the orchestra in these two works, though not in consideration of style. The first is for a large orchestra of ten woodwinds (ad libitum procedure makes possible expansion to a dozen), a brass combination of four horns, two trumpets and two cornets, three trombones, bass plus contrabass saxhorns, with timpani and cymbals, and no fewer than four harps in addition to the usual strings. The A minor work calls for the very opposite: nine woodwinds, four brass, timpani, and strings. As for stylistic power, the generators are Schumann and Mendelssohn models for the greater part.

The recording of these works is adventurous since neither work has entered the repertory. But dull these symphonies aren't and neither are they timid, if not strikingly original. One can't expect to hear them save through Martinon's excellent recorded interpretations.

Symphony No. 3 (Organ) in C minor, Op. 78

☐ Boston Symphony Orchestra / Zamkochian (organ) / Munch (conductor) / RCA LSC–2341
☐ Detroit Symphony Orchestra / Dupré (organ) / Paray (conductor) / Mercury 75003

Paray's is a substantially deep (akin to a classically proportioned) performance of the score, with no doubts as to any of the purposes of Saint-Saëns's orchestrational textures. Clarity rather than effect marks his conception. Munch chooses a more dramatic thrust, which is just as positive a resolution for Saint-Saëns's opus, even if some of the minute balances and linear definitions that Paray achieves go by the board.

Both conductors have intelligence and imagination at work in their direction. Munch's explanation is explosively trenchant, Paray's is considerably mellower. Both are masterful in the handling of the mystical reminders in the *Poco adagio*.

Solo Instrument and Orchestra

Cello

Allegro Appassionato, Op. 43

☐ National Opera Orchestra of Monte Carlo / Walevska (cello) / Inbal (conductor) / Philips 6500459

Some critics claim that this piece was written for cello and piano (true) but that the orchestration is not by Saint-Saëns (false). *Evidence:* the published full score by Durand (the instrumentation covers two each of flutes, oboes, clarinets, bassoons, and horns, plus the usual string body). Certainly, in absence of any transcriber, the credit for the scoring should go to the composer. (Durand has a reputation for being meticulous in such matters.)

The performance is splendid, with excellently gauged energy. In the competitive recording (for cello and piano) on Orion 7287, Terry King plays faster, but in doing so he cancels the prime fervency of the music.

Concerto No. 1 in A minor for Cello and Orchestra, Op. 33

☐ Philadelphia Orchestra / Rose (cello) / Ormandy (conductor) / Columbia M–30113

The A minor Concerto represents Saint-Saëns's major repertory work in the cellistic world. It belies the criticism that his compositions are academic and smothered with stilted, repetitive patterns. Indeed, the Concerto relies on sequential binding, but it also has a nobility that completely convinces that the Concerto is for listeners as well as for cellists. It requires seamless playing and a vocalized virtuosity to make eloquent its material. The cut-rate, going-through-the-motions performances heard in concert and on disc belie the reputations of some notable cellists that have performed the work. Such playing of the Concerto deadly on center strikes the music its death blow.

Rose's performance can serve as the ideal for all others to consider. It makes music in the fullest sense in every measure. It is a stunning document of re-creation partnered with perfect orchestral accompaniment on the part of Ormandy.

Concerto No. 2 in D minor for Cello and Orchestra, Op. 119

☐ National Opera Orchestra of Monte Carlo / Walevska (cello) / Inbal (conductor) / Philips 6500459

It is difficult to fathom the total lack of attention to this Concerto, whereas the first one Saint-Saëns wrote is a program perennial and has always been well represented in the recorded music catalogue.

Christopher Grier in his notes states that, compared to the initial cello Concerto, the later work is "of much sterner quality." Yet, it is easily assimilated, though less extrovert than the earlier cello Concerto. There's plenty of virtuosity and a fine cadenza, and the pedal-pointed perpetual motion division is more exciting than anything in the first Concerto.

Give a large number of points to Walevska, Inbal, and Philips for making this recording available, the very first made of the piece. To the great many who don't know this opus, avail yourself of a piece of fine music, one of the best Saint-Saëns wrote.

Suite for Cello and Orchestra, Op. 16

☐ National Opera Orchestra of Monte Carlo / Walevska (cello) / Inbal (conductor) / Philips 6500459

A mixed-up dish. Saint-Saëns wrote Opus 16 for cello and piano and later orchestrated the accompaniment for only one of the movements (the fourth, a Romance). Who transcribed the other four movements is not known. Little difference, since whatever interest there is resides in the solo line: a perpetual motion tactic in *legato* in the *Prélude*, a *Sérénade*, and a pair of dances—a Gavotte and a *Tarantelle*.

Whatever is to be done by the soloist is done acceptably.

Morceau de Concert in G major for Harp with Orchestral Accompaniment, Op. 154

Harp

☐ Orchestre ORTF, Paris / Zabaleta (harp) / Martinon (conductor) / Deutsche Grammophon 2530008

The *Morceau de Concert* is Saint-Saëns's final work for the harp. Its four parts have the usual conclusions arrived at by this composer—apt figuration, well-fitting arpeggios, conjunct continuity.

It is impeccably played, as one expects from the great musician Nicanor Zabaleta.

Africa, Fantasia in G major for Piano and Orchestra, Op. 89

Piano

Concerto for Piano and Orchestra

No. 1 in D major, Op. 17 / No. 2 in G minor, Op. 22 / No. 3 in E flat major, Op. 29 / No. 4 in C minor, Op. 44 / No. 5 (*Egyptian*) in F major, Op. 103

Rhapsodie d'Auvergne in A minor for Piano and Orchestra, Op. 73

☐ Orchestra of Radio Luxembourg / Tacchino (piano) / de Froment (conductor) / Vox SVBX-5143

If you wish an integral release of Saint-Saëns's works for Piano and Orchestra (save the *Allegro Appassionato*, Op. 70, which is recorded in its more important, original form for solo piano—*see below*), the prime choice is here indicated. (Tacchino does perform the other work in the medium, the *Wedding Cake*, with string orchestra accompaniment. It is discussed separately—*see below*.)

Although all of the concerti are also available in one package, with Aldo Ciccolini as the soloist (on Seraphim S-6081), Tacchino's playing has a more befitting refinement in the majority of cases. There is a tendency for pianists to approach the more volatile portions of these concerti (especially Nos. 2 and 4) as though the composer's name was Camille Tchaikovsky. Technical dazzle and dash (these are, after all, concerti) can be incisive but that doesn't mean percussiveness. Whereas Ciccolini is not fully guilty of this error, Tacchino never is, and it's a joy to hear the Saint-Saëns music with virtuosic flair and without keyboard clatter. Further, de Froment's orchestra plays considerably better than the Orchestre de Paris, which supports Ciccolini with Serge Baudo on the podium.

The *Rhapsodie* is short and only passably attractive, but *Africa* deserves being taken out of the museum category. Variety and rhythmic interest are abundant. The solo part is dazzlingly effective in a concentrated way and Tacchino's response is one of stylistic vigor and utmost clarity.

(The second and fifth concerti were first released on Candide 31080.)

Concerto No. 2 in G minor for Piano and Orchestra, Op. 22

☐ Philadelphia Orchestra / Rubinstein (piano) / Ormandy (conductor) / RCA LSC-3165

This Concerto is played in an exuberant, gutsy, bravura manner. Rubinstein adopts a very incisive, percussive impress, even in the *Allegro Scherzando,* where some might prefer more charm and grace. Nevertheless, this is an edition that warrants special mention and attention, if the composition is desired by itself and not as part of the entire set of concerti Saint-Saëns produced.

Concerto No. 4 in C minor for Piano and Orchestra, Op. 44

☐ Monte Carlo Opera Orchestra / Campanella (piano) / Ceccato (conductor) / Philips 6500095

Michele Campanella plays with polish and elegance and produces depth even in the vehement passages, of which there are plenty. One hears a revealing projection of the score and nicely scaled support from the Monte Carlo organization. Indeed, Campanella rings the bell (the pun on his name is intended) with his playing.

Wedding Cake, Caprice-Valse for Piano and Strings, Op. 76

☐ Strings of the Orchestra of Radio Luxembourg / Tacchino (piano) / de Froment (conductor) / Vox SVBX-5143

Tacchino plays this piece, composed by Saint-Saëns as a wedding gift to a pianist, neatly and fluidly, without unnecessary fuss. Nonprepossessing music needs just such treatment.

Violin

Concerto No. 3 in B minor for Violin and Orchestra, Op. 61

☐ Philharmonia Orchestra / Milstein (violin) / Fistoulari (conductor) / Angel S-36005

Saint-Saëns's work is conventionally planned, with outer *allegro* and *moderato* tempoed movements bracing a duple-pulsed Andantino that has barcarolle characteristics. It is in the latter movement of the work that Milstein's beautiful and assured tone brings the greatest nourishment. The expression is not overemphasized; the playing justifies the conception and there is no criticism of performance taste. Neither is there elsewhere in the piece. Milstein's playing contains no undue liberties, no attempt to intoxicate with false *rubato,* and there are no prima donna capers. Thus the Concerto spins off the grooves of the disc bringing respect for the soloist and indicating how best to present Saint-Saëns's Opus 61, one of the finest of his concerti.

Havanaise, Op. 83

☐ Boston Symphony Orchestra / Kogan (violin) / Monteux (conductor) / RCA VICS-1153
☐ Orchestre de Paris / Perlman (violin) / Martinon (conductor) / Angel S-37118

The delicacy, the underplaying of Leonid Kogan are infinitely satisfactory. His *rubati* are neat, his string choices define sensitive colorations. Itzhak Perlman seizes the work in his paws and just makes you like what he does. Little of it is subtle (the *spiccati* are brazenly richocheted) but it's damn exciting. Kogan examines the *Havanaise* fondly. Perlman boldly displays it with his ownership tag attached. We can (and should) accept and enjoy both responses.

Introduction and *Rondo Capriccioso,* Op. 28

☐ Orchestre de Paris / Perlman (violin) / Martinon (conductor) / Angel S-37118

Indeed, this is an old chestnut but one that retains its taste. Perlman avoids overdrive and percussiveness which defeat those violinists who feel the music demands it. His playing has poise, well-centered richness of tone, and truth-declaring musicianship. Artistic honesty throughout.

Tarantella for Flute, Clarinet, and Piano, Op. 6

☐ Shulman (flute); Campbell (clarinet); Root (piano) / Crystal S–642

"Once over lightly" in three-part form for this composition. Divertingly tuneful and nice to have. It is played in an ingratiating and unforced manner.

Fantaisie **in A minor, Op. 95**

☐ Laskine (harp) / Musical Heritage Society MHS–602

Its title notwithstanding, Saint-Saëns's opus represents the customary fused ternary form, with an introductory section to set the scene. Still, the formal steadfastness does not interfere with the most welcome spontaneity of the music.

Fantaisie **in E flat major**

☐ Biggs (organ) / Columbia MS–6307

Outside the organ fraternity the *Fantaisie* is practically, if not totally, an unknown piece of music. Still, it is a highlight among Saint-Saëns's shorter pieces, and once heard it is music that will store itself in a listener's memory and lead to the desire to hear it many times over. It has an exceedingly catchy initial movement, linked to a Vivace with a blockbuster ending.

Biggs's presentation is one of graphic commentary and he goes all out in the conclusion. Turn down the volume control or your machine might break apart. It's very fitting, however.

Prelude and Fugue

In D minor, Op. 109 / In G major, Op. 109

☐ Raynaud (organ) / Turnabout 34238

These are two of the three in the set. The fugues are better characterized in the recording than the more neutrally gray preludes. Raynaud's performances are also included in a Vox Box (SVBX–5314) which is titled "A Survey of the World's Greatest Organ Music (France, Volume V)," the other composers being Liszt, Lefebure, Franck, Gigout, Guilmant, Boëly, Dubois, and Boëllmann.

Album **for Piano, Op. 72**
Allegro, Op. 29
Allegro Appassionato, **Op. 70**
Caprice sur les Airs de Ballet d'Alceste **(1867)**

☐ Dosse (piano) / Vox SVBX–5476

An interesting and unusual relationship exists between Opus 29 and Opus 70 in terms of the making of secondary settings in both cases. Saint-Saëns wrote his *Allegro Apassionato* for solo piano and then made a version with orchestral accompaniment. However, the solo part has individual validity so it can be heard by itself—nothing is lost by omitting the orchestral accompaniment. The reverse procedure was followed in Opus 29. This is a redraft of the first movement of the third piano concerto (the complete title of the

Instrumental

Flute and Clarinet

Harp

Organ

Piano

piece is *Allegro d'après le 3ème Concerto,* Op. 29). In this case, cuts and revisions of the original solo piano part were made, and orchestral material was incorporated into the pianistic texture. It works fairly well, but nonetheless, contrary to the *Allegro Appassionato,* the full-scale original for piano and orchestra is better. However, having the solo setting on disc is of value and one is grateful that Marylène Dosse has recorded it.

The *Caprice* is one of the most popular of Saint-Saëns's piano works. It consists of three themes from Gluck's ballet which are freely handled and developed and includes an impressive fugal section. The stylistic blend is handled superbly and so is the recorded presentation. Dosse's control of detail is excellent in this composition as well as in the *Allegro Appassionato* and in the six-part *Album* for Piano, Op. 72; the latter consists of a Prelude, Carillon, Toccata, Valse, *Chanson Napolitaine,* and a *Final.* (The Vox album also contains a Gavotte, Op. 23 not designated on any of the listings noted below.)

Feuillet d'album, Op. 169

Les cloches du soir, Op. 85

☐ Dosse (piano) / Vox SVBX–5477

The gentility of Opus 85 is sensitively portrayed by Marylène Dosse. She is as successful with the Opus 169, a two-minute piece that marked Saint-Saëns's final work for the piano, written in the year of his death.

Mazurka, Op. 21

Mazurka, Op. 24

Mazurka, Op. 66

Menuet et Valse, Op. 56

Six Bagatelles, Op. 3

Six Etudes, Op. 52

☐ Dosse (piano) / Vox SVBX–5476

Two of the Etudes are cast in a Prelude and Fugue format; the last of the set is a vivid show piece (*Etude en forme de valse*). Dosse performs this group with brilliance, though more freedom would be welcome. However, this criticism does not apply to the expert manner in which she interprets the Opus 56, a music with abrupt changes and full contrastive variety.

Opus 3 marked Saint-Saëns's initial work for piano, written at the age of twenty. Dosse styles this music nicely; the same applies to the three Mazurkas.

Six Etudes, Op. 111

Six Etudes for the Left Hand Alone, Op. 135

Six Fugues, Op. 161

Souvenir d'Ismaïlia, Op. 100

Souvenir d'Italie, Op. 80

Suite for Piano, Op. 90

Thème varié, Op. 97

☐ Dosse (piano) / Vox SVBX–5477

Neither of the sets of Etudes is cut to fit only particular technical problems, though that area is not overlooked. In Opus 111 the third piece is a *Prélude et Fugue,* the following piece is an atmospheric study titled *Les Cloches de las Palmas*. The sixth of the group is a reworking of the finale of Saint-Saëns's fifth piano concerto titled *Toccata d'après le 5ème Concerto*. It has a vivid personality, its virtuosic sweat covering the entire keyboard. Dosse tosses off the music in dazzling fashion.

The Opus 135 set includes an *Alla fuga* (a specialty since the fugue is to be played with one hand, it must be remembered), a *Moto Perpetuo*, and a couple of dances (Bourrée and Gigue) among its six-part total. Similar dance formations apply to the Opus 90 music, containing a Menuet, Gavotte, and Gigue, that follow the first movement's *Prélude et Fugue*. While set forms are emphasized in these works, the academic approach is not; the Six Fugues provide an additional example of creative success and are without a single touch of dryness.

Dosse performs with fine imagination, excellent rhythmic poise and an impeccable sense of style.

Une nuite à Lisbonne, Op. 63

☐ Dosse (piano) / Vox SVBX–5476

A short descriptive item, set in barcarolle style. It pleased the composer to such extent that he made an orchestral version. Marylène Dosse's playing is also pleasing.

Valse Canariote, Op. 88
Valse gaie, Op. 139
Valse langoureuse, Op. 120
Valse Mignonne, Op. 104
Valse nonchalante, Op. 110

☐ Dosse (piano) / Vox SVBX–5477

Although a bit of blandness and flatness creeps into some of these waltzes composed over a twenty-year period, such criticism does not apply either to the verve of the *Valse Canariote* (it starts slowly but picks up steam, so do be patient—it's worthwhile) or the perkiness of the *Valse gaie*.

Feuillet d'album, Op. 81 Marche interalliée, Op. 155
Pas redoublé, Op. 86

Piano, Four Hands

☐ Dosse and Petit (piano) / Vox SVBX–5477

Ever so light music describes these piano duets, just falling short of banality. The *Marche* is a version of a work originally composed for military band. (Another duet, aptly titled *Duettino*, is available by the same performers on Vox SVBX–5476.)

Caprice Arabe, Op. 96
Caprice hèroïque, Op. 106
Scherzo, Op. 87

Two Pianos

☐ Dosse and Petit (piano) / Vox SVBX–5477

This is important Saint-Saëns music and excellently conceived for the medium. The critic Charles Suttoni describes the *Caprice hèroïque* as "one of Saint-Saëns's grandest conceptions for two pianos." Just as significant is the Scherzo which Alfred Cortot stated was "a synthesis of Saint-Saëns's special pianistic style." Its fluency is especially colored by the use of the whole-tone scale.

Clearly stimulating performances of all three works by Marylène Dosse and Annie Petit.

Polonaise, Op. 77

Variations sur un Thème de Beethoven, Op. 35

☐ Dosse and Petit (pianos) / Vox SVBX-5476

Conventionality is the descriptive word for the Polonaise. Magnificent is the descriptive word for the *Variations*. It is one of the most important works in the literature for two pianos. Each one of the ten variations, including a funeral march, a fugal section, and an impetuous finale, is strongly motivated and has considerable imaginative force.

Cultivated and refreshing playing by the pianists. Another worthy recording of the *Variations* is found on London 6533, performed by Eden and Tamir.

Chamber Music

Fantasy for Violin and Harp, Op. 124

☐ Vito (harp) / Orion 7030

Most of the action is in the violin part. The harp embroiders and decorates functioning in a secondary role, to the violin's full-scaled position.

No clue is given as to the name of the violinist.

Sonata for Bassoon with Accompaniment of Piano, Op. 168

☐ Grossman (bassoon); Hokanson (piano) / Coronet 2741
☐ Pachman (bassoon); Maxim (piano) / Golden Crest 7019 (monaural)

The first movement consists of a single theme stated in five different versions, a means of integral variation with small ornamentations changing the shape of the theme but not its features. A three-part scherzo leads to a combined slow–fast movement in which, oddly enough, the non-Franckian Saint-Saëns quotes (in the most lightly disguised fashion) a theme from the opening movement.

Neither recording gives the correct title, which defines the rare instance of one instrument "accompanying" another in a concerted duo Sonata. With only supportive material offered, both pianists follow suit. There is hardly any difference between Grossman and Pachman; just a little bulkier tone quality pertains to the latter. Mono or stereo does not make much difference either, both performances being worthy.

Sonata for Clarinet and Piano, Op. 167

☐ Rabbai (clarinet); Kalish (piano) / Desto 7146

In this Sonata it will be found that it constitutes mostly music for the clarinet with piano support—less than the real, balanced potential of chamber music. Neat melodicism, of course, without much chromatic fuss. This is matched by a neat performance, clear and straight, without any fussy interpretative moments.

Sonata for Oboe and Piano, Op. 166

☐ Roseman (oboe); Kalish (piano) / Desto 7146

Sonatina kinship shows in the first part. Movement 2 is braced on either end by oboe recitations. Scales and repeated notes are the principal patterns in the third movement.

Saint-Saëns's music stays put as behooves its neutral "spiel." However, the tonal sheen of Ronald Roseman's playing makes up for the composition's moderate course of events. Just soaking in this kind of woodwind sound brings special rewards.

Sonata No. 1 in C minor for Cello and Piano, Op. 32

☐ Kessler (cello); Carmen (piano) / Orion 73124

The cello is treated with great dramatic effect in this substantive Sonata, which is rather nonacademic and certainly a work not to be included in the general criticism of Saint-Saëns.

Two main themes and their development take place in the opening movement, but with this special added attraction: there are innumerable episodes that mesh with the main portions to form a rhapsodic filter that changes the movement from one of simple outline to a more advanced and thus more artistic state. Briefly, Saint-Saëns is concerned with music not with the slide rule. This can be best described as variational treatment of themes, a combination, therefore, of sonata form *and* variation. The three-part form of the slow movement also uses the disguise of variational treatment; the finale runs the dramatic gamut.

The playing of this work is of the highest musicianship and professionalism. Kessler and Carmen as advocates for the composer are fully capable.

Sonata No. 1 in D minor for Violin and Piano, Op. 75

☐ Heifetz (violin); Smith (piano) / RCA LSC–2978 (monaural)

All the magic of Heifetz and his esteemed partner Brooks Smith are displayed in this case: the polished drive in the semi-syncopative initial movement, the recitative song of the Adagio, the meticulousness of the moderately paced Scherzo, and the pearly scurry of the *moto perpetuo* finale. Heifetz and Smith convince one that the work is first-rate and thus remove the usual critical view that Saint-Saëns's Opus 75 exhibits only romantic-academic steadfastness.

Caprice on Danish and Russian Airs, Op. 79

☐ Baron (flute); Roseman (oboe); Rabbai (clarinet); Kalish (piano) / Desto 7146

A nice assortment of tunes is heard in this runthrough: no cosmic rumblings or over-dramaticism, but fine melodic cuts, varied textures, shifting colors and opportunities for soloism. Certainly fun to play and just as much enjoyment for the listener.

Septet for Trumpet, Two Violins, Viola, Cello, Double Bass, and Piano, Op. 65

☐ Groupe Instrumental de Paris / Laforge (piano); Lagorce (trumpet) / Seraphim S–6081

The *Préambule* of this work is militarylike and is built from fanfare propositions. The entire work grows out of the material of the first movement, a compact development of motival ideas into variation by form not by phrase. It will be noted in the Minuet, the interlude section, called *Intermède,* as well as the *Gavotte et Final.* There is no desire to make a farrago of differing styles.

Necessarily, the inclusion of the trumpet changes the texture and adds considerable brightness and a certain martial vigor to the work, but the results here are extremely well-balanced.

Tollite Hostias

☐ Peloquin Chorale / Hokans (organ) / Peloquin (conductor) / Gregorian Institutes EL–19 (monaural)

Tollite Hostias is one of the three-dozen Motets Saint-Saëns wrote. (There is no infor-

Choral

Chorus with Accompaniment

mation given on the liner copy for any of the thirteen works included in Gregorian's album, save a general article dealing with "Christian choral art." No texts either.)

The piece is neat, short, and bright. It is stated neatly, clearly, and brightly.

Cantata and Oratorio

Oratorio de Noël, Op. 12

☐ Orchestra and Senior High and Adult Choirs of Christ Church, Silver Spring, Maryland / Carnahan, Baldwin, Leonard, and O'Connor (sopranos); Brown (mezzo-soprano); Barnett (alto); Melendez (tenor); Ebel and Putnam (baritones) / Neumann (conductor) / Golden Crest 4137

The "Christmas Oratorio" falls pleasantly on the ears and, though conservative, is far from academic. There are nine parts; the text is from the *Vulgate,* here sung in English.

Although the performers are totally nonprofessional, they are quite competent and several cuts above the average type of vocalists and choirs to be heard in the church world. The scoring calls for strings, harp, and organ. The string body used here is exceedingly small (string quartet plus bass) and textural depth is lacking.

Opera and Dramatic Music

Samson and Delilah, Op. 47

☐ Munich Radio Orchestra and Bavarian Radio Chorus / Ludwig (mezzo-soprano); King, Weber, and Gassner (tenors); Weikl (baritone); Malta, Kogel, and Schranner (basses) / Patané (conductor) / RCA ARL3–0662

Twelve operas are listed in Saint-Saëns's catalogue but only *Samson and Delilah* survives. It has its very old-fashioned gestures, but they are executed with a fine flair so that one accepts them sympathetically. Martin Cooper has codified the matter beautifully: "the music creates its own emotional world which there is no gainsaying, and this is one of the greatest qualities which any work of art, and especially opera, can possess."

RCA's edition is a transfer of the Eurodisc 86977 release. It stars Christa Ludwig who conveys a deep voluptousness in her characterization. She sings with coloristic richness, vibrancy, and is always believable. A finer operatic seductress I have not heard. James King as the co-star displays a finely focused conception as Samson. It is his part in the production that favors the RCA issue over the competitive Angel edition (S–3639). There, Jon Vickers, though he has a stronger voice in his portrayal of the Hebrews' leader, nullifies it by a weaker cohesiveness, and it is crucial. Thus even Rita Gorr's superb realization in the priestess role, laced with vocal sensuality, is not sufficient to overcome such deficiency. The choice for the RCA production is further emphasized by fine orchestral delivery. One exception: the *Bacchanale* is quite weak, exceedingly so. For that item one must turn to Ormandy's superb performance (see under *Orchestra*).

Oskar Sala   *(20th cent.)*

Electronic Music

Five Improvisations on Magnetic Tape

☐ Westminster Gold 8110

Sala's pieces have pithiness and they also have a kind of drôlerie. A profitable addition to the electronic catalogue.

Antonio Salieri   (1750 - 1825)

Overture to *La Fiera di Venezia*   *Orchestra*

☐ English Chamber Orchestra / Bonynge (conductor) / London 6735

An example of attractive and formally intelligent music. No surprises naturally, but the natural flow of the material is performed with full sympathy for the style involved.

Sinfonia in D major (*Veneziana*)

☐ English Chamber Orchestra / Bonynge (conductor) / London 6621

Just under nine minutes in length here (small cuts have been made), Salieri's Sinfonia, composed when he was in Venice (hence the subtitle), is as full of effervescence as early Mozart music. It begins with a lively *Allegro assasi,* followed by a moderately slow movement for strings, and is completed by a boisterous finale.

There is a fine brightness to the playing and there is never the blitz speed that so often pertains to fast-paced end movements. Why don't works of this value ever appear on concert programs?

Concerto in C major for Flute, Oboe, and Orchestra   *Solo Instrument and Orchestra*

☐ Bamberg Symphony Orchestra / Nicolet (flute); Holliger (oboe) / Maag (conductor) / Deutsche Grammophon 139152

☐ English Chamber Orchestra / Adeney (flute); Brown (oboe) / Bonynge (conductor) / London 6621

Flute and Oboe

That there are three recorded editions of this both noble and gay double concerto is evidence of its worth. Holliger would be expected to produce polished perfection. He is superbly partnered by Aurèle Nicolet. Their production (which includes Holliger's own stylistically appropriate cadenzas) is worthy of first choice, but only by the smallest margin. The London release is too convincing to be bypassed.

Despite some cuts made by the conductor, Richard Bonynge, London's presentation outclasses the version made available on the Turnabout label on 34307. This is mainly due to the much-warmer oboe sound of James Brown (on the former) as compared to Alfred Sous (on the latter). Bonynge's excisions cover a total of 3:20 but the loss is not too critical, save to the diehards. A further point is that Bonynge does more than his competitor, Jörg Faerber, in terms of suppleness and he also avoids the spiculated tone Faerber favors.

Aulis Sallinen   (1935-   )

Cadenze per Violino Solo (1965)   *Instrumental*

☐ Pohjola (violin) / Bis LP–18

Violin

Don't expect pyrotechnical particulars in Sallinen's prize-winning work (in the contest held by the Finnish Cultural Fund for a compulsory new piece to be played by entrants in the 1965 Jean Sibelius Violin Competition). Sallinen's *Cadenze* is structured motivally, styled tonally, and is moderately paced, its lyricism of fluency and flexibility. The absence of sheer performance virtuosity demands in the composition is replaced by the requirement of artistic finesse. Paavo Pohjola proves in his playing that he has impeccable interpretative understanding.

Carlos Salzedo   (1885-1961)

Instrumental

Harp

Chanson dans la nuit

☐ McDonald (harp) / Klavier KS-525

The *Chanson dans la nuit* is one of the most important of Salzedo's compositions. It includes a number of the annunciatory additions he brought to harp technique: timpanic sounds, Aeolian flux, and rubbing of the strings, plus the non-Salzedo forms of harmonics, glissandi, and *près de la table* playing (a dry, banjolike timbre). All of these are pertinent to the musical idea and not merely decorative dents on the texture. "Song in the Night" is a beautiful conception and it is played with beautiful color and clarity.

Concert Variations on *O Tannenbaum*

☐ Remsen (harp) / Avant AV-1000

No fussiness in the variants; though the theme is diversified and polychromized, it remains clear from start to finish. This well-known tune and its nicely ordered variations are played with proper perspective.

Variations on a Theme in Ancient Style, Op. 30

☐ McDonald (harp) / Klavier KS-525

Salzedo is tradition-minded here without his French-impressionistic demeanor and substantial effects that enlarged the harp's technical vocabulary. In his heyday, Salzedo was one of the greatest harpists who ever applied fingers to strings. He couldn't have done better than this supreme artist.

Leonard (Lopes) Salzedo   (1921-   )

Chamber Music

Divertimento for Brass Sextet

☐ Philip Jones Brass Ensemble / Argo ZRG-655

Salzedo champions jazzy rhythms in the Prelude, Scherzo, and the final March. There is no retreat from coloristic ebullience in any of the work's four parts, especially in the Interlude (section 3), where three different types of mutes are used for the six instruments involved: three trumpets and three trombones.

A most secure performance.

Eric Salzman   (1933-   )

Opera and Dramatic Music

The Nude Paper Sermon—Tropes for Actor, Renaissance Consort, Chorus, and Electronics (1969)

☐ Nonesuch Consort and Members of New York Motet Singers / Keach (actor) / Rifkin (conductor) / Nonesuch 71231

Consider this as Music of the Absurd, though what Salzman has in mind is deadly serious: "a multi-layer sound drama ... the transformation of values and tradition through the impact of new technologies." This is a composition created *for* the recording medium, not a recording (as secondary documentation) of a work that was created for live performance; the work *is* the recording. What results, therefore, is an electronically manipulated melange of unrelated and often meaningless fragments that are supposed to be meaningful, speech coalesced and fractured and speech clarified, but with no continuity of meaning.

All these assortments were recorded on individual tracks, "combined with 'live' overlays," and "montaged to create an 8-track master." In short, taped material on top of recorded material and electronic data are all "juxtaposed, intertwined, and transformed."

Because of its technological rapport, Salzman describes his *Sermon* as covering "the end of an era and the beginning of another." To some, his message may reflect a kinship with sonic doodling. However, with full credit to the expressive essences of the work, such type of informality, no matter how it is precisely calculated, has less impact when it runs on for three-quarters of an hour.

Helix

Electronic Music

☐ Howe (soprano); Zukof (countertenor); Kavanaugh (voice); Elitcher (clarinet); Bauman (guitar) / Finnadar 9005

Helix is "essentially improvisation based on predetermined patterns and hand signals." The first portion embraces sleighlike bells (expected in a work performed "as a Christmas piece"), dissected and dessicated electronic sounds, and spectral and tampered (avant-garde style) vocalism. Part 2 contrasts with a chantlike and very sensitive vocal fantasy, intertwining a gloss on *Wolcum Yole!* (again, not unexpected in a Christmas anniversary objective).

Larynx Music (Verses III) (1968)

☐ Ross (soprano); Silverman (guitar) / Finnadar 9005

Salzman explains his work as a conflict "expressed as a struggle between the expressive impulses towards speaking and singing," which then "explodes in an orgy or 'free self-expression' and finally resolves—not without an undercurrent of anxiety—in a simple song."

This tri-sectional design begins with segmentation, fractured phonetics, and other vocal effects derived from the likes of Berio, Bussotti, Nono, and Stockhausen, and concludes with the solo voice (there are other sounds framing it but they are not accompanimental, being totally unrelated). Salzman's music may have "conflict," but it also has a huge amount of sexuality built into it.

Queens Collage (An Academic Festival Overture)

☐ Finnadar 9005

If there is such a category as light (or even humorous) electronic music, this fits in it! Despite Salzman's quasi-serious objective (sound enough) "to grasp the contradictions between the internal and external 'realities' of an urban college campus," the method (and its message) is delightfully droll, a sonic randan(dy) that never ceases to give pleasurable diversion during its twelve and one-half minutes.

Queens Collage was created by taping and mixing actual exterior and interior sounds (the "old-fashioned" *musique concrète* technique, but updated). Snips of rehearsal groups, orchestra tuning, applause, noises without specific identity (from the street?), fragmented splices of verbal remarks, et cetera, make the montage for Salzman's collage.

The piece was composed for a student arts festival at Queens College in New York, hence the title and the explanation for the clever after-Brahms subtitle. Indeed, there is a huge amount of cleverness exhibited in Salzman's piece, but there is shrewd structural printing, especially by the ritornello device of static repetition of certain fragments.

Wiretap

☐ Nagrin (voice) / Finnadar 9005

Wiretap was drawn from a recorded mix of several versions using the voice with other material for a dance-theatre work. The vocal tracks then became the data for a separate composition "by manipulating, compressing and multi-tracking the vocal lines." The sounds that emerge are far from timid, a great deal of them equating pleasurable moans with a close parallel to orgasmic excitability. No matter how one translates these inventions, they are interesting (and certainly courageous) gestures.

Giovanni Battista Sammartini   (1701 - 1775)

Orchestra

Symphony

In A major / In C major / In D major / In E flat major / In G major

☐ Angelicum Orchestra of Milan / Jenkins (conductor) / Nonesuch 71162

These symphonies, chosen from the large number Sammartini produced, exhibit a finely balanced sequence of movements (three in each case, with the two outer ones fast-paced, except for the G major opus which has only two movements, a *Spiritoso* and an *Allegro assai*) with classically ordered grace and elegance. This exactly describes the performances directd by Newell Jenkins, who prepared the editions for the E flat and G major works heard in this release.

Solo Instrument and Orchestra

Concerto in C major for Viola Pomposa and String Orchestra

☐ Southwest German Orchestra, Pforzheim / Koch (viola pomposa) / Angerer (conductor) / Turnabout 34574

Viola Pamposa

This is one instrument that Vivaldi overlooked in compiling his huge number of concertos for all sorts of instruments. Sammartini's work for the five-string large viola offers conventional fare but it also provides an opportunity to hear an instrument for which little music has surfaced and even less is recorded.

Giuseppe Sammartini   (ca. 1693 - ca. 1750)

Solo Instrument and Orchestra

Concerto in F major for Flute and Orchestra

☐ Saar Radio Chamber Orchestra / Rampal (flute) / Ristenpart (conductor) / Musical Heritage Society MHS-976

Flute

This is music in the *dolce stile nuovo* that falls between the old style and the *style galant*. The performance has a perfect graciousness that is particularly appealing in the central *Siciliano* movement. A delight to hear.

Marcel Samuel-Rousseau (1882-1955)

Variations pastorales sur un vieux Noël

☐ Remsen (harp) / Avant AV–1000

French classicism characterizes these variations with some color indentations, sufficient to add interest without breaking faith with requisite formal identity. The pigmentations referred to are the harp particulars of harmonics and glides. One is reminded of Ravelian clarity throughout this piece, performed with authenticity.

Pierre Sancan (1916-   )

Sonatine for Flute and Piano

☐ Louise DiTullio (flute); Virginia DiTullio (piano) / Crystal 311

Sancan opts for Ravelian inquiry. He also favors flutter-tonguing as the principal coloristic device. The tripartite structuring is clarified by a short solo spot for the piano to prelude part 2, and a more virtuosic one for the flute to mark the preliminary before part 3.

All the technical responsibilities required are carried out by the sister team, though the flutist displays a stronger personality.

Robert L. Sanders (1906-1974)

Little Symphony No. 1 in G (1939)

☐ Louisville Orchestra / Whitney (conductor) / Louisville 635 (monaural)

The tonality indicated in the title gives evidence of the type of music Sanders writes. It is tonal yet not restricted; triadal yet not failing to realize the potency of the frictional appendage. This is music of the greatest clarity, with healthy rhythms and tonal consolidations that just nick with slight acidity the fresh surfaces of articulative melodic lines. Sanders's creative praxis is just short of being light; he is a composer one can enjoy at first hearing.

The Louisville Orchestra zips through this work. The piece "plays" easily, and the performance shows it.

Symphony in A (1955)

☐ Knoxville Symphony Orchestra / Van Vactor (conductor) / Composers Recordings 156 (monaural)

The style here is tonal but this does not mean restricted music. Triadic language is used, but with synonyms that include the potent appendage tone. It clings to old fashions yet is not strictly old-fashioned. A healthy, conservative work.

This is the first recording made by the Knoxville group. It is a good debut and it also shows the expertise of its conductor who has since left his post with the orchestra.

Sven-David Sandström   (1942-   )

Orchestra   **In the Meantime (1971)**

☐ Musica Nova / Naumann (conductor) / Caprice CAP–1034

Sandström's chamber-orchestra composition mixes strong reminders of Ligeti's flat-surfaced sounds and Varèse's percussive punctuations and in the meantime doesn't overlook the use of little dots of instrumental color that represent musical pointillism. As a result, the piece is extremely nervous in its effect.

Naumann's group plays this abstraction deftly.

Pedro Sanjuán   (1886-1976)

Orchestra   **La Macumba (Ritual Symphony) (1945)**

☐ Orchestra of the Accademia Nazionale di Santa Cecilia, Rome / Antonini (conductor) / Composers Recordings 111 (monaural)

Sanjuán's Symphony (premiered in St. Louis in December 1951) has two interconnected sections, one moderately tempoed, the other a bit faster. Both use rhythmic energy to keep matters warm. The performance pleases the ear.

Guido Santórsola   (1904-   )

Solo Instrument and Orchestra   **Concerto for Two Guitars and Orchestra**

☐ English Chamber Orchestra / Sérgio and Eduardo Abreu (guitars) / Asensio (conductor) / Columbia M–32232

Two Guitars   There are few instances of expanded compositions for the guitar using the twelve-tone technique. Santórsola's four-movement opus is a successful entry, especially since it lacks the self-consciousness of so many dodecaphonic works. It has soloistic fluency but, more importantly, it provides a musical compilation that is extremely impressive, especially in the dark-tinted Adagio.

The Brazilian duo guitarists play the work, which was dedicated to them, with technical know-how and perceptive realization of the score. The quality of their sound is warm and completely without irritating percussiveness.

Gaspar Sanz   (17th cent.)

Instrumental   **Españoleta   Gallardas**

Guitar   ☐ Segovia (guitar) / MCA 2524

These are representative examples of music by this seventeenth-century Spanish composer–guitarist. As usual, Segovia is in full command. A lighter, dance quality pervades the first piece of the pair listed.

David Saperstein   (1948-   )

Antiphonies for Percussion (1972)

☐ New Jersey Percussion Ensemble / DesRoches (conductor) / Nonesuch 71291

Carefully detailed, now-traditional styled percussion music is represented in Saperstein's *Antiphonies*. The idea of antiphonal response is well-stated though not as clearly disposed in the recording as one would expect from the analytical note offered by Harvey Sollberger.

DesRoches's musicians are eloquent spokesmen for the piece. Not *Schwann*, however. Though the Varèse, Colgrass, and Cowell pieces that are part of the Nonesuch program are fully listed, neither Saperstein's nor Oak's work (also offered on this disc) are to be found.

Pablo de Sarasate   (1844-1908)

Carmen Fantasy, Op. 25

☐ London Symphony Orchestra / Ricci (violin) / Gamba (conductor) / London 6165

Ricci outdistances his opposition in this compilation of Bizet source material. His tone is rich, his technique impeccable, and he produces the work with the required bravura. Reticence or even subtlety are not the performance ingredients desirable in the Spanish composer's workout of the French composer's Spanish simulations.

Zigeunerweisen, Op. 20, No. 1

☐ London Symphony Orchestra / Heifetz (violin) / Barbirolli (conductor) / RCA ARM4-9045 (monaural)
☐ London Symphony Orchestra / Ricci (violin) / Gamba (conductor) / London 6165

Both soloists portray the truth, the whole truth, and nothing but the truth in this score. Heifetz tosses off the technical information with an elegance that hides the performance difficulties behind the notes. Ricci's technique is just as superb but he exhibits it with hot and crisp enunciation. His performance is direct, Heifetz's is more subtle but just as thrilling. The minute meticulousness of both leaves behind all the others that have recorded Sarasate's gypsy compilation.

There are performances with piano backing, but these do not really present the composition as it should—with orchestrally framed color.

Caprice Basque, Op. 24

Danzas Españolas

No. 1: *Malagueña,* Op. 21, No. 1 / No. 2: *Habanera,* Op. 21, No. 2 / No. 3: *Romanza Andaluza,* Op. 22, No. 1 / No. 4: *Jota Navarra,* Op. 22, No. 2 / No. 5: *Playera,* Op. 23, No. 1 / No. 6: *Zapateado,* Op. 23, No. 2 / No. 7: Spanish Dance, Op. 26, No. 1 / No. 8: Spanish Dance, Op. 26, No. 2

Introduction and Tarantella, Op. 43

☐ Rosand (violin); Walevski (piano) / Vox 512760

The essential merits of Rosand's playing are clarity and ease of projection. Force is applied as needed and the style is to the manner born. Rosand projects a fine, lyrical span and he displays a panchromatic palette. All the trapeze-swinging stuff in Sarasate's pieces is negotiated: pizzicati left and right, double stops, swinging octaves, flying harmonics, plus the rest of the stimulating virtuoso techniques required.

This is the only total coverage of the *Danzas*. A number of separate entries are available. Heifetz does four of the dances (Nos. 1, 2, 3, and 6) in the jumbo six-volume retrospective issued by RCA. Szeryng performs Nos. 3 and 6 in an album of "Music of Spain and Mexico" produced by Everest (No. 3154E). Fodor also plays Nos. 3 and 6 on RCA ARL1-1172. These are the best of the numerous isolated offerings from the total set of dances. They are all as good as the Rosand performances, but the advantage is on Rosand's side since he offers the full supply of Sarasate's dances.

Jota Aragonesa, Op. 27

☐ Ricci (violin); Lush (piano) / London STS-15049

Downright Spanish musical behavior, played by a master. Ricci displays marvelous rhythmic selection and tempo measurement in Sarasate's triple-metered rapid dance.

Two Violins ### Navarra

☐ David and Igor Oistrakh (violins); Yampolsky (piano) / Monitor 2009 (monaural)

Violin mastery, doubled in Oistrakhian artistry. They sound like one violinist. In that regard one might wish to hear Aaron Rosand's presentation, presumably played in over-dubbing since no credit for a second violinist is noted. It's on Turnabout 34462, which doesn't give any indication about Rosand's feat. For that reason his release is not individually noted, a procedure followed in this compendium when more than one choice is given. However, I don't believe in mechanical hanky-panky no matter how fabulous the results. Others may differ.

Malcolm Sargent. *See Borodin* / Malcolm Sargent.

Andrés Sás (1900-1967)

Instrumental ### Cantos del Perú (1935) (2 movements)

Violin ☐ St. Malo (violin); Slonimsky (piano) / Orion 7150 (monaural)

These *Cantos* exhibit Sás's fervent interest in Peruvian melodies and rhythms. The first of the pieces, *Siembra*, is quietly lyrical, the second, *Kachampa*, is a very moderately tempoed war dance. It has an engaging format with its constant stop-and-go phrases.
Good playing but only fair sound.

Erik Satie (1866-1925)

Orchestra ### Cinq Grimaces pour Un Songe d'une nuit d'été (1914)
En Habit de cheval (1911)

☐ Utah Symphony Orchestra / Abravanel (conductor) / Vanguard C-10037/8

The *En Habit de cheval* is an orchestral setting of the original four-hand, one piano work (*see below*). The *Grimaces* were written for a production that Cocteau had planned of *A Midsummer Night's Dream*. They are delightful bitter-sweet sketches, with orchestral spacings that emphasize the snideness and buffoonery. The last is best stated in the finale, based on the military Retreat melody.

La Belle excentrique (1920)   **Trois Petites Pièces montées**
Les Pantines dansent

☐ Ensemble "Die Reihe" / Cerha (conductor) / Candide 31018

Cafe music style transferred to the status of concert music is represented in *La Belle excentrique*. The *Petites Pièces* consist of a *Rêverie*, a *Démarche*, and a *Coin de polka*. Scored for small orchestra, they mix a quiet demeanor with lightly pointed rhythmic depictions. The other work ("The Dancing Puppets") is a study in pulsatile reticence.

Clean playing that emphasizes the leanness of Satie's scoring.

Messe des pauvres

☐ Chorus / Mason (organ) / Randolph (conductor) / Counterpoint/Esoteric 5507E (monaural)

Instrumental

Organ

Dark and solemn. "Mass for the Poor" represents the mystical Satie when he was interested in Rosicrucian dogma. The prayers are stated by half-light music, divided into six parts. The chorus in this performance (three female and four male voices) is heard only in part 1, *Kyrie Eleison*. Then follow the "Organ's Prayer," *Communion*, "Ecclesiastical Chant," *Prayer for the Travellers and Sailors in Danger of Death,* and *Prayer for the Salvation of My Soul.*

Marilyn Mason stresses a leaden quality in her registration. It is mostly of nontranslucency but is the proper choice for Satie's *Messe des pauvres*.

Piano

Avant-dernières Pensées	**Peccadilles importunes**
Chapitres tournés en tous sens	**Prélude de la porte héroïque**
Cinq Nocturnes	**du ciel**
Croquis et agaceries	**Prélude en tapisserie**
d'un gros bonhomme en bois	**Premier menuet**
Danses gothiques (1893)	**Rêverie (de l'enfance**
Descriptions automatiques	**de Pantagruel)**
Embryons desséchés	**Sonatine bureaucratique**
Enfantillages pittoresques	**Sports et divertissements**
Four Ogives (1886)	**Three Sarabandes (1887)**
Four Préludes	**Trois Gnossiènnes (1890)**
Heures séculaires	**Trois Gymnopédies (1888)**
et instantanées	**Two Pièces froides (1897)**
Les Pantines dansent	**Véritables Prèludes flasques**
Les trois Valses du précieux	**Vieux Sequins**
Menus propos enfantins	**et vielles cuirasses**
Passacaille	

☐ Glazer (piano) / Vox SVBX-5422

This anthology serves perfectly to exhibit the amazing conceptions and inventions of Erik Satie. Here exemplified are the satire, the overt simplicity, the sweet and purposefully sour, the serious and humorous, the "bad" boy that made such an influential indent on the music that followed by Milhaud, Honegger, and other French composers of the early part of the twentieth century.

The range is tremendous as well as significant. Thus: the simple children's pieces represented by the *Menus propos enfantins,* the Clementi take-off in the *Sonatine,* the twenty piano pictures in *Sports et divertissements,* the wit and snideness in the *Croquis et agaceries,* the gentility of the *Gymnopédies* and *Gnossiènnes,* and so on.

These are class performances. The style (no matter what type is involved) is perfectly stated, the expressions and colorations of penetratingly virtuosic insight. This is unusually fascinating playing. Glazer deserves being chosen as the best performer of Satie's piano music on disc.

Piano,
Four Hands

Aperçus désagréables

En Habit de cheval

Trois Morceaux en forme de poire (1903)

☐ Glazer and Deas (piano) / Candide 31041

These three compositions cover Satie's complete production for piano four-hands. The second piece is also represented in Satie's orchestral setting (*see above*) and Roger Desormière transcribed the *Trois Morceaux* for orchestra (see under *Satie/Desormiere*).

The music mixes relaxed ideas with more serious polyphonic ones. There are Chorals and Fugues in the first pair of works. Careful voicing in the playing by this duo team but not at the expense of expressivity. High standard performances.

Chamber
Music

Choses vues à droite et à gauche (sans lunettes) (1912)

☐ Pascal (violin); Ciccolini (piano) / Angel S–36713

Three pieces in "Things Seen to Left and Right (without Glasses)." The titles (as usual) are as smart as the music which bounces along in part 3 (a "Muscular Fantasy") with glissando and harmonic colors. Part 1 is a ten-measure choral (described as "Hypocritical"); part 2 is something like a fugue, based on a French nursery tune. The performance is keen and stylishly on target.

Vocal

Voice with
Accompaniment

Ludions

☐ Mesplé (soprano); Ciccolini (piano) / Angel S–36713

Five songs set to nonsense poems by Léon-Paul Fargue: "Rat's Tune," "Spleen," "The American Frog," "Poet's Tune," and "The Cat's Song." Only Satie-scoped in part, and thus cleverly designed to be more serious in the music in order to bring stronger contrast to the texts.

Splendidly done by Mady Mesplé and Aldo Ciccolini.

Quatre Petites Mélodies
Tendrement

☐ Gedda (tenor); Ciccolini (piano) / Angel S–36713

Only the second of the four melodies has Satiesque wit (text by Cocteau that compares an opera-house dancer to a crab). All are short and pretty, which also describes the cafe-waltz climate of *Tendrement.*

Nicolai Gedda shapes these songs beautifully.

Trois Poèmes d'amour

☐ Bacquier (baritone); Ciccolini (piano) / Angel S–36713

The words also to these declamatory-like "Love Poems" are by Satie. Short (less than two minutes in total time), but sensitive and with piquant charm. Sung with fresh, lyrical warmth.

Messe des pauvres. See under *Instrumental: organ.*

Socrate (1919)

☐ Ensemble "Die Reihe" / Escribano, Bedard, Iiyama, and Lorenz (sopranos) / Cerha (conductor) / Candide 31024

A twelve-part work that divides into three major sections: Socrates's *Portrait, The Banks of Illissus,* and *The Death of Socrates.* Color is minimized by the use of similar vocal timbre (four sopranos) to carry the tale. A type of speech rhythm is particular to the voice lines and modality is used as the thin harmonic blanket for the music.

The absence of decoration, the whiteness of the music, and its archaicism are fully conveyed in this portrayal. Cerha's retention of a cool dynamic level is on a par with Satie's score.

Le Piège de Méduse (1913)

☐ Members of L'Orchestre des Concerts Lamoureux / Bertin, Deschamps, Falcucci, and Laurence (narrators) / Ciccolini (conductor) / Angel S–36713

"Baron Medusa's Trap" is a lyric comedy (no singing) with musical interludes following seven of its nine scenes. Delivered in French but with complete translation included in the album's leaflet. The music, as simple as A-B-C, is scored for a septet of clarinet, trumpet, trombone, percussion, violin, cello, and double bass.

Les Aventures de Mercure (1924)   Relâche (1924)
Parade (1917)

☐ Utah Symphony Orchestra / Abravanel (conductor) / Vanguard C–10037/8

Relâche consists of twenty sections, divided into two major divisions. It has a nonsense scenario, but a no-nonsense tonally vulgarized score that swerves between music-hall style and traditional ballet formats. In contrast "The Adventures of Mercury" with its baker's dozen sections has a classic demeanor that is laced with some classic jazz. *Parade* is a mad mix but always in balance. It was produced by an all-star cast of Cocteau (scenario), Picasso (settings, costume, and curtain), and Massine (choreography). Satie's scoring is convincingly natural and heated, including the clicking of a typewriter, the smash of pistol shots, and the sonorous ride of sirens.

The playing of these ballet scores is faultless. All the orchestrational pronunciations and enunciations are vivid, the style as naturally projected as Satie threw his sounds on score paper. An absolute delight—all three of these ballet scores. Save listening to *Parade* for the last.

Satie / Claude Debussy

Gymnopédies Nos. 1 and 3 (1888)

☐ London Philharmonic Orchestra / Herrmann (conductor) / London 21062

Debussy only orchestrated the first and last of the set. (For the original, see under *Satie: Instrumental: piano* [*Trois Gymnopédies*].) The second of this group for piano is listed as orchestrated by one Jones in *Schwann* but I have never been able to locate a score or find any information about it. I cannot recall even a listed performance and it certainly has not been recorded.

Sensitive Satie is equaled by sensitive Debussy. The fragility of this music could not be orchestrally secured other than by soft-spoken, lenitive orchestration. Accordingly, Debussy used two flutes, an oboe, four horns, two harps, cymbals, and strings. Bernard Herrmann's consideration of the work evinces full recognition of this stylistic sensibility.

Two errors concern this recording. In *Schwann* the listing reads as though it embraces the complete *Trois Gymnopèdies*. London's listing is for "I & II," a misconception based on the fact that Debussy had orchestrated a pair, but as noted above the scoring he made was for the first and third of the set.

Errata also is found in Vanguard's release (C-10037/8) of this Debussy transcription. The listing gives the expected playing order of Nos. 1 and 3. However, the performance reverses that chronology.

Satie / Roger Desormière (1898-1963)

Orchestra

Trois Morceaux en forme de poire (1903)

☐ Utah Symphony Orchestra / Abravanel (conductor) / Vanguard C-10037/8

These are the famous pieces written in response to Debussy's critical remark that Satie's music lacked form. Originally set for piano duet (four-hands at one keyboard) the orchestral setting is workable though not overly sensitive. Neither is the performance (notice some pitch errata by the players). If you want this work, excuse the intonation problems, since this is the only orchestral edition in the catalogue. However, the original version has been recorded by several piano teams and the choice from these is noted under *Satie: Instrumental: piano, four hands.*

Satie / Darius Milhaud

Ballet

Jack in the Box (1900)

☐ Utah Symphony Orchestra / Abravanel (conductor) / Vanguard C-10037/8

Satie's three-movement delight (*Prélude, Entr'acte,* and *Final*) was written in 1900. Twenty-six years later (the year after Satie's death) Milhaud brought it to light, scored it for double winds and brass (no tuba), percussion, and strings. It was first conceived as music to accompany a solo pantomime but in Milhaud's version it received its premiere as a ballet.

Breezy tonal material that just refreshes the ears. Aside from a few high trumpet vacillations it is well played.

Satie / Francis Poulenc

Orchestra

Deux Préludes posthumes (1893) et une Gnossiènne (1890)

☐ Utah Symphony Orchestra / Abravanel (conductor) / Vanguard C-10037/8

The "Preludes" are numbers 1 and 3 from a group of four, the "Gnossiènne" is the last of a set of three (see under *Satie: Instrumental: piano*). The antiphonal hocket-like orchestration of the former maintains the strong liturgical style of the sounds. Poulenc supplied fastidious coloration for the other work.

Abravanel's handling of this music is inspired in its sensitivity.

Satie / Alexis Roland-Manuel (1891-1966)

Le Fils des Etoiles (1891)
Orchestra

☐ Utah Symphony Orchestra / Abravanel (conductor) / Vanguard C–10037/8

"The Son of the Stars" consists of a pair of movements, conceived as incidental music to a play by Joseph Péladan, with an oriental setting. These serve as preludes to the first and third acts. (There was a third piece in the set but it was not orchestrated. Bennett's liner note for the Vanguard release regards the work as complete with just two pieces.)

Fine historical documentation, even with another hand involved in the scoring, but it is rather an academic traversal of a Debussy ground plan. The lack of fine dynamic distinctions in the performance is to be noted.

Henri Sauguet   (1901-   )

Les trois lys, mouvement symphonique
Orchestra

☐ Louisville Orchestra / Whitney (conductor) / Louisville 545–10 (monaural)

"The Three Lillies" is constructed in the manner of the classic Overture according to Sauguet, but like so much of his work it turns out to be a type of ballet divertissement. Brightly scored.

This is still another of the many Louisville Orchestra commissions. It rates as one of their lesser ones, though there is no problem with the performance.

Mélodie concertante in E minor (1963)
Solo Instrument and Orchestra

☐ Moscow Radio Orchestra / Rostropovich (cello) / Sauguet (conductor) / Melodiya/ Angel S–40180

Cello

A great deal of dreamy introspective writing here. At times a northern atmosphere creeps into the music which passes through a variety of moods. The performance is consistently sensitive, totally compelling.

Soliloque
Instrumental

☐ Santos (guitar) / Musical Heritage Society MHS–1916

Guitar

Sauguet's "Soliloquy" turns on a motival idea. Its poignant reflections are translated in a performance of poetic conviction and sensitive coloration.

Suite Royal for Harpsichord Solo (1962)
Harpsichord

☐ Marlow (harpsichord) / Serenus 12056

Musical *déjà vu*. Sauguet's five-movement Suite instantly reminds one of Couperin's *Pièces de clavecin*, even to its subtitles, such as *Révérences*, *Bavardages*, et cetera. Satie-like simplicity, tonal clarity, and urbanity are present.

Commissioned by and dedicated to the performer. Sylvia Marlowe's playing accomplishes everything that is desired. (This was originally issued by Decca. Its demise is Serenus's gain.)

Alessandro Scarlatti   (1660-1725)

Orchestra

Overture to *Il Giardino di Rose*

☐ New Philharmonia Orchestra / Leppard (conductor) / Philips 802901

The music is made more brilliant by ceremonious trumpet writing. In Leppard's hands Scarlatti's oratorio overture is negotiated with sizable sonority and dynamic decisiveness.

Sinfonia

I in F major / II in D major / IV in E minor / V in D minor / VIII in G major / XII in C minor

☐ Paris Instrumental Ensemble / Ravier (conductor) / CMS/Oryx 3C-313

Two (Nos. 8 and 12) are for flute and strings, two are for coupled flutes and strings (Nos. 1 and 5), No. 4 is for flute, oboe, and strings, and No. 2 is for flute, trumpet, and strings.

This group, representing half of the Sinfonias Scarlatti produced beginning in 1715 are as representative as possible. The playing is to be admired and is thoroughly enjoyable. There are other performances of Nos. 1 and 2 but comparison shows them to be no better, and in this format six of the group are available on a single disc representing four different scoring plans.

String Orchestra

Concerto No. 3 in F major

☐ London Soloists Ensemble / Nonesuch 71052

Enthusiastic performance which matches the music and stylistic expertise. Fine harpsichord coverage.

Chamber Music

Sonata in A minor for Recorder, Two Violins, and Basso Continuo

☐ Linde (recorder); Hover and Kupsky (violins); Jappe (viola da gamba); Muller (harpsichord) / Klavier 520

Serenely accurate and finely phrased playing. The balance and perspective in the third movement Fuga is especially fine.

Klavier should get someone to write creditable liner notes. It should tend to its proofreading also. There is only one "l" in this composer's forename.

Sonata in F major for Flute, Two Violins, and Continuo

☐ Instrumentalists of the Società Cameristica di Lugano / Nonesuch 73008

Mainly binary forms control each of the four movements. Scarlatti's craft, however, is such that plain academicism never enters the musical picture.

Motets

Domine, Refugium Factus es Nobis
O Magnum Mysterium

☐ Schütz Choir of London / Norrington (conductor) / Argo ZRG–768

Domine, Refugium is for five voices. It is nobly Handelian. *O Magnum Mysterium* is larger-scaled, conceived in eight-part counterpoint. It reflects a still earlier (Palestrina) heritage. The singing is excellent and well-balanced.

Su le sponde del Tebro

☐ Wiener Solisten / Davrath (soprano); Rudolf (trumpet); Heiller (harpsichord) / Heiller (conductor) / Vanguard C–10028

Scarlatti's work is an intensely beautiful example of the solo cantata which was an off-shoot of Baroque Italian opera. Its alternation of recitative and aria sections receives a presentation of haunting quality. Netania Davrath's voice is clear and frank, delicate when it should be. The accompaniment is sensitively balanced, as is the harpsichord play-ing by Anton Heiller, and the small portions for the high trumpet are delivered with zest and no strain. The soundness and penetrating nature of this performance deserve special attention.

Domenico Scarlatti   **(1685–1757)**

Sonatas

In A major (L.238) / In A major (L.483)

☐ Cooper (harpsichord) / Vanguard 71201

There's considerable coverage of Scarlatti's compelling Sonatas in the recorded catalogue. Cooper's choice from the more than five hundred Sonatas Scarlatti produced constitutes a prime edition, detailed in two albums (the alphabetical key distribution, in accordance with the disc on which it is found, is given below without further comment).

The performances of these single-movement pieces (not Sonatas in the Classical defini-tion of the form) are rich, fully responsive to the imagery and variety contained within the material. The lines are sharply etched, the textures exceedingly resonant (the music was recorded at a very high, brilliant level), and never with less than inspired translations into sound. Cooper's playing has spontaneity and displays a top level of artistic intelligence.

Another choice is a set of sixteen Sonatas performed by Sgrizzi (on Nonesuch 71094). Disregarding guitar transcriptions (including settings for two guitars) there are also piano versions for those who prefer their Scarlatti in that coloration. The best is Horowitz's set of a dozen Sonatas on Columbia MS–6658.

Sonatas
In A major (L.Suppl.31) / In A minor (L.93)

☐ Cooper (harpsichord) / Vanguard 71202

Sonatas—in A minor (L.223)

☐ Cooper (harpsichord) / Vanguard 71201

Sonatas

In B major (L.48) / In B major (L.446)

☐ Cooper (harpsichord) / Vanguard 71202

Sonatas—in C major (L.3)

☐ Cooper (harpsichord) / Vanguard 71201

Sonatas

In C major (L.205) / In C major (L.457)

☐ Cooper (harpsichord) / Vanguard 71202

Sonatas—in C minor (L.10)

☐ Cooper (harpsichord) / Vanguard 71201

Sonatas

In C sharp minor (L.256) / In C sharp minor (L.260)

☐ Cooper (harpsichord) / Vanguard 71202

Sonatas

In D major (L.14) / In D minor (L.422)

☐ Cooper (harpsichord) / Vanguard 71201

Sonatas

In E major (L.23) / In E major (L.225)

☐ Cooper (harpsichord) / Vanguard 71202

Sonatas

In F major (L.198) / In F minor (L.189) / In F minor (L.281)

☐ Cooper (harpsichord) / Vanguard 71201

Sonatas

In F sharp major (L.31) / In F sharp major (L.35)

☐ Cooper (harpsichord) / Vanguard 71202

Sonatas

In G major (L.204) / In G major (L.209) / In G major (L.389)

☐ Cooper (harpsichord) / Vanguard 71201

Cantata and Oratorio

Stabat Mater

☐ Schütz Choir of London / Spinks (organ); Sansom (cello); Marjoram (bass) / Norrington (conductor) / Argo ZRG–768

Written for ten voices (sung here by twice that number) with organ (supported here by cello and bass). The music is not sectionalized and therefore demands concentrated consideration as a totality. The Argo disc provides a representative performance if not a great one.

Scarlatti / **Vincenzo Tommasini (1878-1950)**

The Good-Humored Ladies-Ballet Suite   *Ballet*

☐ Cleveland Orchestra / Lane (conductor) / Columbia M-31241

Fashioned for ballet purposes from five harpsichord Sonatas by Scarlatti and enjoys double life as a ballet and as an orchestral suite. The highlights among the highlights Tommasini chose are the gorgeous slow music (third movement) and the *Cat's Fugue* serving as the Presto finale.

Played with very gratifying warmth and ease. Far better version than the old, now deleted issue by the Vienna State Opera Orchestra, conducted by Franz Litschauer, on Vanguard VRS-440.

Pietro Scarlatti   *(1679-1750)*

Toccata in G minor   *Instrumental*

☐ Sgrizzi (harpsichord) / Nonesuch 71117   *Harpsichord*

This exciting piece is by still another Scarlatti—Domenico's older brother. It's just as good as anything the younger man ever turned out. Brilliant performance.

Donald Scavarda   *(1928-   )*

Matrix for Clarinetist (1962)   *Instrumental*

☐ Rehfeldt (clarinet) / Advance 4 (monaural)   *Clarinet*

Scavarda sanctions the unsanctioned in his *Matrix,* which consists of a score of thirty-six squares, each containing varied instructions, but which are sequentially at the will of the performer. And, in the same sense of freedom are most of the resultant sounds.

The timbres produced are in the scope of the *dernier cri* of the far-left composers. High and low sounds, squeals and squawks, breathing without pitch, monotones, multitones, undertones, and overtones. And more.

These gestures total the opus. Overall line and climax are eliminated. This, not from lack of creative ability to shape a structure but to display purposefully a fantastic variety of unaccompanied clarinet vocabulary.

It is as difficult to achieve proper performer response to such a display as it is to obtain a fine clarinet tone quality in a Brahms piece. Phillip Rehfeldt accomplishes wonders with these difficulties and deserves plaudits.

Giacinto Scelsi   *(1905-   )*

String Quartet No. 4 (1964)   *Chamber Music*

☐ Quartetto di Nuova Musica / Mainstream 5009

A succession, that never breaks off, of microtonal sound waves rolling into and away from another sound spray. The pitches (further complexioned by *scordatura* tunings of the instruments) are convulsed and tortured as though writhing in perpetual intonational martyrdom. The ear may become fatigued, since there is no surcease, but the ear will hear a striking newness that needs no theme, contrast, rhythm, or other color for supportive existence.

Myron Schaeffer   (1908-1967)

Electronic Music

Dance R 4 ÷ 3 (1961)

☐ Folkways 33436

A rhythmic sketch based on a palindromic design: dotted quarter–eighth;–quarter and quarter;–eighth-dotted quarter. Fundamentally an electronic etude.

Hans Joachim Schaeuble   (1906-   )

Solo Instrument and Orchestra

Clarinet

Music for Clarinet and String Orchestra, Op. 46

☐ Southwest German Chamber Orchestra, Pforzheim / Michaels (clarinet) / Springer (conductor) / Turnabout 34513

Auspicious clarity marks each of the three movements, with terminally placed, moderately paced Allegros, and an elegiac type of music in between. Schaeuble's tonal language denotes neoclassic influence, and his modulatory designs are predicated on connective, not deceptive, ideas.

Solo-wise, a competent performance; orchestra-wise, a bit less so.

Piano

Concerto for Piano and String Orchestra, Op. 50

☐ Southwest German Chamber Orchestra, Pforzheim / Jones (piano) / Springer (conductor) / Turnabout 34513

No soloistic virtuosity here. Schaeuble's Concerto has a chamber music quality. (The orchestra diminishes this effect with some slovenly playing.) The music is pulled on neoclassic wires; it begins with a Pavane, continues with a slow movement which is the best part of the piece, and concludes with a rather loose formal scheme.

Maureen Jones plays in an accomplished manner.

R. Murray Schafer   (1933-   )

Vocal

Voice and Instrumental Ensemble

Requiems for the Party-Girl (1966)

☐ Contemporary Chamber Players of the University of Chicago / Pilgrim (soprano) / Composers Recordings S–245

A set of arias documenting the mental collapse and suicide of a young woman. The girl's schizophrenic state is outlined with a variety of vocalistic data: straight and modified, sung and spoken. The instrumental accompaniment calls for flute alternating with piccolo, clarinet doubling on bass clarinet, horn, percussion, harp, piano, violin, viola, and cello. Part of it is improvised. There is no conductor.

Boguslaw Schäffer   (1929-   )

Free Form No. 2/Evocazioni for Solo Contrabass (1972)

☐ Turetzky (bass) / Finnadar 9015

A rhapsody of many of the "new" bass sounds, found in avant-garde literature, displayed here by performance from a graphic score. The playing, as is to be expected from this superbassist, is superb. However, the material (minute sonicware) mostly exhibits Turetzky and hardly Schäffer, as the composer. (The very free graphic notation only gives the impression of the sounds, not how they are to be played.)

Project for Solo Contrabass and Tape

☐ Turetzky (bass) / Finnadar 9015

Though real double bass timbre is plentifully depicted, a good amount of its sounds reflects a kind of characteristic rub-off from the tape that partners it. When this occurs one can almost distinguish the piece as being performed by a "bass" electronic tape (the string instrument) and a "soprano" electronic tape. Schäffer's *Project* is, as expected therefore, a project in the intense distillation of sound properties.

The composer says the bass part "is not easy to play." Correct. Further, that it was written for Turetzky, "the incredible master." Absolutely correct again.

Instrumental

Double Bass

Adrian Schaposhnikov   (1888-   )

Sonata for Flute and Harp (1926)

☐ Vito (harp); Roberts (flute) / Orion 7039

A nicely meshed sonority is provided, the textures of sufficient resonance to serve a typical romantic melodicism.

Schaposhnikov's opus is presented with clarity, aided by the contrastive colors. These are far better than any of the alternative instrumentations permitted of flute and piano, or violin and harp, or violin and piano.

Chamber Music

Xaver Scharwenka   (1850-1924)

Concerto No. 2 in C minor for Piano and Orchestra, Op. 56

☐ Hamburg Symphony Orchestra / Ponti (piano) / Kapp (conductor) / Candide 31046

Rugged thrust, the normal conventions of romantic diction and figuration, and a Polish flavored, rhythmically polished music describe the three movements of this once popular concerto, now out of concert fashion. But, the point is that the concerto is not any more dated than those concerti of Schumann, Chopin, and Mendelssohn, if not possessing the dynamism of the Brahms examples.

The edition is well prepared and produced, and Michael Ponti's playing has special savour. (The man's scope of repertoire is simply amazing.)

Solo Instrument and Orchestra

Piano

Instrumental

Piano

Erzaehlung am Klavier No. 2, Op. 5

Novellette, Op. 22, No. 1

Polonaise, Op. 42

Scherzo, Op. 4

☐ Ponti (piano) / Candide 31046

Even in the Polonaise Scharwenka never escapes from Schumannesque style. Ponti has admirable control over this material and what imaginative touches are possible are supplied.

Peter Schat   (1935 -   )

Orchestra

Entelechy I (1961)

☐ Concertgebouw Orchestra / Boulez (conductor) / Donemus Audio-Visual Series DAVS-6702

Schat's piece is conceived for five separated groups of instruments: I: flute, bassoon, trumpet, and four violins; II: clarinet, trumpet, and three violas; III: harp and double bass; IV: five celli; and V: percussion, oboe, and trombone. The music jabs in an extremely pointillistic manner, and fragmentation is constant. The latter operates to such extent that the totality is also fractioned into some 31 parts.

Boulez is, of course, a master at directing this type of sound spots. The impeccable control he provides is all that is required to denote the special cultivations of Schat's score.

Chamber Music

Improvisations and Symphonies (1960)

☐ Danzi Wind Quintet / Donemus Audio-Visual Series DAVS-6202 (monaural: 10-inch disc)

At first, some borrowing from Stockhausen's *Zeitmasse* together with exactly notated sections. However, a new twist is utilized in the work's second section, requiring acting on the part of the players. On a recording this totals a fat zero.

The final part of the quintet is titled *Tombeau*, in memory of Mátyás Seiber, the composer's teacher, to whose memory the entire composition is dedicated. Here there is real invention in serial syntax. The music moves from a dead sonority (without vibrato) aided by microtonal tensility to a constant increase of speed and dynamic until the sonorous power is at white heat and presto motion, and finally dissolves. The idea and execution are inspired. The playing is all that could be desired.

Samuel Scheidt   (1587-1654)

Instrumental

Four Trumpets

Canzona

☐ Schwarz, Ranger, Gould, and Soper (trumpets) / Nonesuch 71301

A marvel of polyphonic display including imitation, ornamental passages, syncopation, and conjunct plus disjunct embroidery in the part writing. The playing is a model of ensemble perfection. Nonesuch's sound is golden.

In Dulci Jubilo

☐ Kaufbeurer Martinsfinken / Hahn (conductor) / Nonesuch 71095

Scheidt's "In Sweet Rejoicing" celebrates Christmas. Save for some soprano strain this is acceptable singing.

Johann Hermann Schein   *(1586-1630)*

Suite

No. 1 in G major from *Banchetto Musicale* / No. 2 in D minor from *Banchetto Musicale*

☐ Ferdinand Conrad Instrumental Ensemble / Nonesuch 71128

The forms used in both suites are identical twins, consisting of a *Pavane*, a *Gagliarde*, a *Courante*, and concluding with an *Allemande-Tripla*.

The performance is by an ensemble of strings, recorders, dulcian, harpsichord, and some percussion. Nicely accomplished playing.

Mein Schifflien Lief in Wilden Meer

☐ Canby Singers / Canby (conductor) / Nonesuch 71026

Charming music described by Canby as "a German love-piece only distantly related to the madrigal." Schein's lyrical weave of vertical and linear detail is an interesting textural matter. The Canby group sings with dovelike tenderness and with an expressively yielding quality.

Who With Grierving Soweth

☐ Concordia Choir / Christiansen (conductor) / Concordia CDLP-6 (monaural)

Good performing style covers Schein's sacred piece. By using a little variety of tempo, expressiveness is not compressed due to rigidity of pace.

Peter Schickele   *(1935-   )*

Three Views from The Open Window: No. 1, The Fantastic Garden

☐ Louisville Orchestra and The Open Window / Mester (conductor) / Louisville S-691

The Fantastic Garden calls for orchestra, vocal trio, and a bit of narration. There is some mickey-mousing orchestration to picture various gardens: "of the stars," "of the moon," and "of the sun." Additionally, Schickele calls for the special color of the electric organ and some cool jazz.

Somewhat of a mishmash, but mixed bags these days are rather fashionable as jazz and long hair boundary lines are erased, and special pops groups borrow from Stockhausen.

The Open Window is a group of three composers who also sing and play a variety of instruments. Their gig here is satisfactory. For parts 2 and 3 by the other composers in the Louisville set, see under *Robert Dennis: Opera and Dramatic Music* and *Stanley Walden: Opera and Dramatic Music*.

Lalo (Boris) Schifrin (1932-)

Orchestra

Suite from the Film *The Four Musketeers*

☐ Orchestra / Schifrin (conductor) / Entr'acte ERS–6510

There are many reservations about listening to film music made into orchestral compilations for concert use which similarly applies to the transfer of a movie's sound track onto disc. No reticence applies here; Schifrin's twenty-minute, eight-part suite registers extremely well. One of the principal reasons pertains to the consistency of the format. Thus *Athos's Story* has lovely Baroque-styled material, a toccata and fugue design applies to *The Chase to the Convent,* a minuet form is used in another movement, et cetera. Over all is a facsimile of Renaissance instrumental coloration in the scoring. A true success in the transfer. Excellently produced.

Instrumental

Harp

Continuum

☐ Stockton (harp) / Crystal S–107

Ostinati is the colorful overlay (and acutely telling in the extreme bottom range) of this work by a famous composer of film scores.

Stockton conquers all the difficulties of the piece and it's thoroughly doused with them.

Johann Conrad Schlick (ca. 1759-1825)

Chamber Music

Divertimento in D major for Two Mandolins and Basso Continuo

☐ Kunschak and Hladky (mandolins); Hinterleitner (harpsichord) / Turnabout 34110

The usual musical statements of the classic divertimento; including two minuets and a *Romanze.* Rather dynamically held in check but otherwise pleasurable.

Of note: Hladky also appears in this survey as a conductor (see under *Hummel: Solo Instrument and Orchestra: mandolin*).

Johann Heinrich Schmelzer (ca. 1623-1680)

Orchestra

Sacro-Profanus Concentus Musicus

☐ Academy of St. Martin-in-the-Fields / Marriner (conductor) / Philips 6500110

Nicely inventive contrapuntalism. A clear and accurate depiction.

Sonata *à Cinque* in C

☐ Academy of St. Martin-in-the-Fields / Smithers (trumpet); Munrow (bassoon); Preston (harpsichord) / Marriner (conductor) / Philips 6500110

In this Sonata the trumpet has some of the most difficult passages ever written prior to the eighteenth century. In contrast the bassoon has considerable prominence, both therefore, particularly coloring the work which calls additionally for strings and continuo (stated here by cello, double bass, and harpsichord). The total effect of the playing is splendid.

Franz Schmidt (1874-1939)

Symphony No. 4 in C major *Orchestra*

☐ Vienna Philharmonic Orchestra / Mehta (conductor) / London 6747

Bruckner is the composer confirmed in Schmidt's symphony. (It is also known as the Requiem Symphony written after the death of Schmidt's only daughter.) The four movements have substantial length and also have a unity that produces a type of single sonata spread over the music's divisions. Thus, the first movement represents the exposition; the last part, the recapitulation, with the middle pair of movements equating the development.

Mehta's performance is most satisfactory.

Prelude and Fugue *Instrumental*

In D major (*Hallelujah*) / In E flat major *Organ*

☐ LaMirande (organ) / Lyrichord 7276

No small works, these, especially the E flat major opus, which has the scope of a two-movement symphony for the instrument. Schmidt's Brucknerogenic concepts are expectedly heavy-laden but the modulatory detail (nine key locales are included in the E flat fugue) colors the textures and helps to maintain interest.

While Arthur LaMirande tends to keep the faith by a unified registration there are sufficient contrasts to indicate that his performances are quite satisfactory.

William Schmidt (1926-)

Short'nin' Bread Variations for Brass Choir, Harp, and Percussion *Band*

☐ Los Angeles Brass Society / Dorothy Remsen (harp) / Lester Remsen (conductor) / Wim WIMR-6

A full-scale survey of the well-known folk tune, passing through seven variants. Best of all is that not once is the base tune so smothered that while thematic sympathy is declared it is hardly heard, recognized, or understood. The permutations are pictorially formulated including Pastorale, Waltz, Fanfare, *Shimmy,* etc. No paper phoniness here whatsoever, the third-rate conception of all too many variations. These are first-rate and flawlessly produced by Remsen's sensitive band.

Fanfare 1969 *Brass Ensemble*

☐ Los Angeles Brass Society / Remsen (conductor) / Avant 1001

Forty-six seconds of music anchored by an ostinato. Not the ordinary fanfarelike fanfare.

Sequential Fanfares

☐ Los Angeles Philharmonic Brass Ensemble / Remsen (conductor) / Avant 1005

The title hides the formal truth: a theme with three variations. And, the indication of the performers hides the scoring: for six trumpets and two percussion. A concentrated consideration of the material, with no superfluous comment and minus any overburdened textural scoring.

Percussion

Ludus Americanus (1971)

☐ Ervin (percussion); Penney (narrator) / Wim WIMR-5

The use of an odd medium that knits poetry with percussion. No tangled, fantasy-twined foliage is constructed. Everything is direct, from the simplistically clear lines of William Pillin to the somewhat pictorially appropriate percussion: timpani and vibraphone in *Gunslinger*, cymbals and camel bells in *Housewife*.

Solo Instrument and Orchestra

Piano

Vendor's Call for Piano and Clarinet Choir

☐ Los Angeles Clarinet Society / Davis (piano) / Henderson (conductor) / Wim WIMR-13

Variational transaction, as pertains here, is not in the realm of fresh news. However, the thematic base is intriguing: a coal vendor's "shout" of 19th-century America. More alluring is the acoustical freshness and coloristic clarity of the medium Schmidt uses (and uses well): a solo piano with an ensemble of six clarinets, one alto clarinet, a bass clarinet, and a contra-bass clarinet (see also under *Chamber Music*, p. 1615).

The performance makes no compromise with tonal quality; the playing is expert (the pianist is the composer's wife).

Chamber Music

Rhapsody No. 1

☐ Atkins (clarinet); Davis (piano) / Wim WIMR-1

Rhapsodic scene-shifting bears out the title, but there is a strong thematic libretto to support the piece. A music that is far above average competence and totally sincere. And, though the clarinet is given its right to range there are no technical chi-chi effects.

An intensely integrated and substantial performance.

Septigrams for Flute, Piano, and Percussion (1956)

☐ Shanley (flute); Davis (piano); Remsen (percussion) / Wim WIMR-2

A colorful assortment of design types that match the colorful medium (the percussion consists of snare drum, suspended cymbal, medium- and low-pitched tom toms). Jazz and polyphony are additional stimuli to the kaleidoscopic survey. A music that enjoys strength, solidity, and profile. The performance matches these qualities.

Seven Variations on a Hexachord (1963)

☐ Fine Arts Brass Quintet / Wim WIMR-4

Save for one instance, quartal intervallic spans mark the six-pitch basis of Schmidt's piece. Out of this he has fashioned a smooth-running, coloristically sounding piece. Though the hexachord commands the structure with a clear and commanding voice it does not overburden it improperly. One admires the balance and adjustment of the opus and similarly the first-rate presentation of Mssrs. Plog, Kidd, Folsom, Atkins, and Garbutt.

Suite No. 1

☐ New York Brass Society / Wim WIMR-3

Four moods: *Spirited, Joyful, Reposeful,* and *Agitated,* set in a style salted with light and tasteful, dissonant punctuations.

Suite No. 2, *Folksongs* for Brass Quintet

☐ Plog and Kidd (trumpets); Henderson (horn); Fleming (trombone); Garbutt (tuba) / Wim WIMR-6

Natural framings (not arrangements!) of three folk tunes, given (as the liner note explains) "a traditional and literal feeling devoid of abstractions." *Rosetree* is an American "white" spiritual, tossed in minstrel style and including a few glides that pep the proceedings. *Plaintive Song* is quasi-Copland revisited. The *Coal Vendor's Call* is a gem; the basis a five-note item on which Schmidt rings changes. He has used this tune in a much more developed sense for a different instrumentation (piano and clarinet choir—see under *Solo Instrument and Orchestra: piano*). This brass quintet setting is timed at 1:31; the other (titled *Vendor's Call*) runs 7:56.

Concertino for Piano and Brass Quintet

☐ Los Angeles Brass Quintet / Davis (piano) / Crystal S–821

Totally of the twentieth century in its nervous jazzy projections but having something of an affinity with classical proportions. Toccata detail is recognizable in the outer movements, a nocturnal yield will be identified in the middle movement. This part of the work is criss-crossed with some impressionistic coloration.

Schmidt knows how to write for brass and piano. The performance of the Los Angeles team and Sharon Davis proves his ability as well as their own.

Music for Scrimshaws for Harp and Brass Quintet

☐ Remsen (harp); Plog and Kidd (trumpets); Henderson (horn); Fleming (trombone); Garbutt (tuba) / Wim WIMR-6

An interweave of folk songs colors the three movements: *Of the Sea and Ships, Of Whales and Whaling,* and *Of Sailors and Maidens Fair.* None of the tunes are of the common garden variety, including real finds such as *Hearts of Gold, Lovely Caroline, Lily of the West.*

Schmidt's writing is natural and as a result as fresh as that of Percy Grainger. And his conceptions do not require any long manifestos to prepare the listener. This is sincere and delightful music, scored with a flawless hand. The performers do beautifully.

Spiritual Phantasy for Organ and Brass Quintet

☐ Thomas (organ); Plog and Kidd (trumpets); Henderson (horn); Ervin (trombone); Garbutt (tuba) / Wim WIMR–8

Variations on the camp meeting song *Resurrected* or *Away over Yonder.* The ending is fun and games, a swipe from Ivesian-technique files, acknowledged by the composer.

Florent Schmitt   *(1870-1958)*

Janiana—Symphony for String Orchestra, Op. 101

String Orchestra

☐ Jean-François Paillard Orchestra / Paillard (conductor) / Musical Heritage Society MHS-805

Though Honeggerian rhythm marks some of Schmitt's full-scale (four-movement) string Symphony for the most part, the stylistic world is French-Wagnerian. French élan hardly touched this composer.

The title pertains to Jane Evrard who gave the first performance with her ensemble (May 1, 1942). This recorded performance is a steady one if not very colorful.

Chamber Music

Suite en Rocaille for Flute, Violin, Viola, Cello, and Harp, Op. 84

☐ Marie-Claire Jamet Quintet / Musical Heritage Society MHS-892

A lighter Schmitt work in comparison to most of his other compositions. Though Schmitt usually has packed scores to his credit there is more French élan in this case than Teutonic density.

Satisfactory in performance. The remastering (the disc was originally released by Erato of France) is not always clean.

Cantata and Oratorio

Psalm 47, *Gloire au Seigneur!* for Soprano, Chorus, Organ, and Orchestra, Op. 38

☐ French National Radio Orchestra and Chorus / Guiot (soprano); Litaize (organ) / Martinon (conductor) / Angel S-36953

Grandiose and heavily orchestrated as was Florent Schmitt's habit. At this remove the asymmetry and dissonances are nothing at all, but there remains a heartiness to the score, withal of its Straussian corpuscles.

To project this music of almost ecstatic sensuality the best approach is to let the force of the forces come through and Martinon does so. I find some faults of balance with the chorus in a few places but since this is the only version available they must be accepted.

Ballet

La Tragédie de Salomé, Op. 50

☐ French National Radio Orchestra and Chorus / Martinon (conductor) / Angel S-36953

A violent and voluptuous atmosphere surrounds Schmitt's five-episode work. Its "mute drama" makes it equally presentable in the concert hall or as a ballet. Included are razor-sharp instrumentational delineations of sexuality (in the *Danse Lascive*) where Salomé's body spasms are for the purpose of inciting Herod, and of terror (in the *Danse de l'Effroi*) where the horror of John the Baptist's decapitation is portrayed.

Indeed, in 1907, when written, Schmitt's piece was strikingly original. It preceded Stravinsky's *Firebird* and that work's "Infernal Dance" owes much to *Salomé*. Further, the *Danse Sacrale* in *Le Sacre du Printemps* was undoubtedly influenced by the savage dissonances, ostinati, and $\frac{3+\frac{1}{2}}{4}$ meter in Schmitt's final dance. Stravinsky greeted Schmitt's work, which was dedicated to him, with the written statement, "I must confess to you that this is the greatest joy that a work has given me for a long while."

Agreed that Stravinsky's work is *the* masterpiece and that Schmitt's is at a lower level. Nonetheless, the colorful juices in the Frenchman's score have far from evaporated and still retain their exciting flavor.

The tensility within the score is defined in Martinon's reading, including the more relaxed moments within the work. There are some harshnesses of sound, but, actually, these are helpful in underlining the climate of the piece.

Dieter Schnebel (1930-   )

Chamber Music

Stücke für Streichinstrumente (1955)

☐ Società Cameristica Italiana Quartet / Wergo WER-60053

There are five ''pieces'' in the work: *Bewegt, Walzer, Elegie, Marsch,* and *Finale.* But even with bands separating them there is no individual identification, no rhythm, no form, nothing but a handful of fragmented sounds and zero ensemble apportionment. Schnebel not only castrates the musical body and strangles its sounds but is bent on totally destroying it. The theory is that annihilation frees primary meaning. So, en route to that goal, four different sounds without pulse binding are to represent the totality of an elegy, or a waltz, or a symphony for that matter.

Well, nonsense can only be defended by nonsense. Thus one reaches the ultimate as in Ligeti's composition consisting entirely of a one-beat silence! With the few sounds he has written embedded in recorded grooves Schnebel's desire to destroy music is made impossible.

für stimmen (. . . missa est)

□ Schola Cantorum, Stuttgart / Gottwald (conductor) / Deutsche Grammophon 137010

Choral

Chorus Alone

Three parts cover Schnebel's unritualistic treatment of musical ritual. *Für stimmen* portrays (as though composed by means of the Freudian unconscious) what essences are contained in a *Deutsche Messe.* In the biblical ciphered title of the first part ($dt\ 31_6$) the premise is annunciation. German, Hebrew, French, English, Russian, Latin, and Greek sacred words are fractured and further disintegrated. God's name is being destroyed in sound. *AMN* is the heading for part 2—apparently a shortened form of ''Amen''—and considers prayer as the objective. The sounds smother the word portions; language becomes a lunatic babel in which are included profanations, whimpers, groans, and sobs.

The finale is titled *:! (madrasha II)* and the idea here is praise. But, this is anti-praise, defined by animal sounds, belching, and a vomiting up of vocal noises to such extent that it can be best described as avant-garde musical voodooism.

There are, of course, more concepts in the world of the musical way far out than one realizes. In comparison, Morton Feldman's music is charming and John Cage's full of smiles and soft soap. The fact that sounds can be led to such absurdity truly demands that we listen to them to understand what musical absurdity is like. In this regard it is vitally important to realize that the composer has the following credits: studied musicology *and* theology, became a Lutheran curate and later a vicar, and presently combines a career of teaching religion with musical composition.

Johann Schobert (ca. 1740 - 1767)

Concerto No. 4 in C major for Harpsichord and Orchestra, Op. 15

□ Jean-François Paillard Chamber Orchestra / Beckensteiner (harpsichord) / Paillard (conductor) / Musical Heritage Society MHS-CC-1

Solo Instrument and Orchestra

Harpsichord

The depth of the Adagio alone makes this opus an overwhelming success. Its seriousness matches the range of a Mozart or a Beethoven. And so do the modulations. The performance provides a complete association of sensibility for the music.

Othmar Schoeck (1886 - 1957)

Sommernacht, **Pastorale Intermezzo for String Orchestra, Op. 58**

□ Orchestre du Studio de Geneve / Klecki (conductor) / Genesis 1010

String Orchestra

A nocturne in which delicacy is maintained. No "transfigured night" applies to the moderate action of Schoeck's piece, its subtle gradations never disrupt the peaceful "Summernight" mood.

Vocal

Notturno, Op. 47

Voice and Instrumental Ensemble

☐ Juilliard String Quartet / Fischer-Dieskau (baritone) / Columbia Special Products AKS–7131

More than a Regerian allocation in this cycle. There is substantial size to the work so the substances include some additional flavors, particularly early Schoenberg.

Beautifully true singing and ideal string playing combine here.

Arnold Schoenberg   *(1874-1951)*

Orchestra

Chamber Symphony No. 1 for 15 Solo Instruments, Op. 9

☐ DiDomenica (flute and piccolo); Roseman (oboe); West (English horn); Bright (D [E flat] clarinet); Russo (A clarinet); Krieselman (bass clarinet); Weisberg (bassoon); Popkin (contrabassoon); Ingraham and Hillyer (horns); Raimondi and Kantarjian (violins); Rhodes (viola); Rudiakov (cello); Sankey (contrabass) / Schuller (conductor) / Finnadar 9008

(This work is *not* in E flat major, despite the sale of scores indicating that key; it is, as Schoenberg insisted, in E major. For a long time *Schwann* maintained the same tonality error. It has finally corrected it.)

Composed in 1906, the symphony marked the completion of Schoenberg's first period of work. It also indicates a dichotomous aesthetic stance. One part is in Straussian territory, the other in the superlogic land in which the composer was ultimately to settle. Although for a small orchestra, it signifies Schoenberg's initial employment of individualized timbre. The *Kammersymphonie* is a gigantic one-movement compilation with interlocking material. The parts of the structure are clear, including exposition, scherzo, development, slow movement, finale, and recapitulation.

Actually, the recorded performance that can be totally recommended remains still to be made. The best is that noted above. It is excellent in its cohesiveness (difficult to accomplish because of the manifold shifts of tempi and disposition), less agreeable in regard to string intonation and balance. However, Schuller's representation is considerably better than the scrappy Boulez reading (Everest 3192), the rocky, scrubby, and rough-toned Craft performance (Columbia M2S–709), or the way Horenstein edits the score, in terms of agogic determination, accentuation, and above all, tempi (once on Vox 10460, now on Turnabout 34263). The same minority report covers the other issues in the market place.

Five Pieces for Orchestra, Op. 16

☐ Chicago Symphony Orchestra / Kubelik (conductor) / Mercury 75036E (monaural)

Music that overreaches the boundaries of late romanticism (though clearly indicating the tonal sod that nurtured it), but is not yet dodecaphonic. The set of pieces is marked by microscopic orchestral camera work. Schoenberg's sensitive colors may bring to mind impressionistic relationships, but they are too subjectively abstract to be so categorized. They could be paradoxically described as "expressionistic impressionism." Each portion is formally free, remotely describing such conditions as *Premonitions, Summer Morning by a Lake,* and so on.

Kubelik's performance may be a monaural affair, simulating stereo by the electronic processing method, but it is far ahead of every other item in the catalogue. He obtains the proper weights so that the intimacy of chamber music is transferred to the large stage of the orchestra. There is always marvelous clarity and there is no bombast even when Schoenberg's scoring is in a state of turbulence.

In Craft's versions (no matter whether it is with the Cleveland Orchestra on Columbia M2S-709 or with the studio pick-up group, the Columbia Symphony, available on Columbia Special Products CMS-6103) he tends to emphasize points in the score when he should not and quite often the music labors.

Pelléas und Mélisande, Op. 5

☐ Berlin Philharmonic Orchestra / von Karajan (conductor) / Deutsche Grammophon 2530485

Schoenberg first considered *Pelléas and Mélisande* as the subject for an opera, without knowing that Debussy had anticipated him. However, the length of the symphonic poem he produced (close to three-quarters of an hour in length) makes it the equivalent of a one-act opera for solo orchestra. Schoenberg's overcharged and passionate consideration of the tale is in direct antithesis to the mystical, twilighted repression that mark's Debussy's score.

Von Karajan's is a brilliant consideration of the score. Schoenberg's intensely heated chromatic polyphony is controlled; the counterpoint *sounds*. Regardless of compositional perspicuity, the interpretative message must sonorize emotional factors. Von Karajan is not wanting in this respect.

D.G. has also included this performance in a four-disc set (number 2711014) that covers two other Schoenberg works, a pair by Berg, and twice that total by Webern.

Second Chamber Symphony, Op. 38

☐ New Philharmonia Orchestra / Prausnitz (conductor) / Angel S-36480

An odd set of facts surrounds this composition. As far back as 1906, when Schoenberg was an exponent of verbose German romanticism, he completed the first movement. Twenty-nine years later he reorchestrated it, and five years afterward wrote a second (and final) movement. It takes courage to compose at the age of sixty-six in the style one used at the age of thirty-two, yet Schoenberg was fully capable. Aside from matters of honesty (completely rewriting part 1 to match a maturer voice in part 2 would have been creative opportunism), Schoenberg understood he was courting stylistic failure if his advanced technique were not bent back to the previous method employed.

All this might be chasing one's shadow. Regardless, the accomplishment is quite successful. Schoenberg's symphony, with its youthful head uncovered, is heartily concerned with the days of *Verklärte Nacht*. However, one can perceive a sharper technique, a subtler orchestration, a more powerful voice in the concluding section than in the initial one, even though this may be considered as critical hindsight.

This performance is a bit overdriven in some spots and tends to deflate the dynamic contours. Still, it is far better than the dry-dusted academicism that prevails in the one-two-three reading Robert Craft gives the score on Columbia M2S-709.

Theme and Variations, Op. 43b

☐ Philadelphia Orchestra / Ormandy (conductor) / Columbia M2S-767

(See commentary under *Band* relating to this work.)
Schoenberg's orchestral setting of his band piece has a strange kind of timbre totality;

the scoring transfer makes one regard the strings as though they shouldn't be present. This may be due to a preference for the initial edition after hearing it, or merely a preconceived bias before judging the aural facts. This writer, having had saturated exposure to the band setting, casts his vote for it. The string passages seem to be conceived for clarinets, just as a band transcription from an orchestral original makes one realize that the clarinets are attempting to act as fiddles.

Make your own choice! Ormandy's performance is certainly a just and definitive one. While the special candid brightness of a band ain't there—how can it be with those wonderful Philly Orch. strings!—vividly present is Schoenberg's ultrachromatic tonal syntax. Heavy textures in this music, but Ormandy makes certain there's no mud obliterating the sound tissues.

Three Little Orchestra Pieces (1910)

☐ CBC Symphony Orchestra / Craft (conductor) / Columbia M2S-694

These midget-sized items (the last of the set is incomplete) were found among Schoenberg's papers after his death. Elliptical expression and instrumental concentration are combined in the work. The lengths of the pieces are twelve, seven, and eight measures, respectively, and they employ, in turn, an octet, a dectet, and a dozen instrumentalists. Within the few phrases minuscule motives change like a bird in flight. The colors are shuffled like a pack of cards.

Variations for Orchestra, Op. 31

☐ Berlin Philharmonic Orchestra / von Karajan (conductor) / Deutsche Grammophon 2711014

Considered the first actual twelve-tone orchestral work, the organization of the Variations offers a vivid testament of Schoenberg's craftsmanship. The generating tone row is exploited thoroughly, providing a remarkable emotional range that is spiritual, delicious, and exciting. These qualities are contained in the introduction, thematic statement, nine variations, and finale that comprise the composition. Further, the opus is a study of intense orchestrational design with a gamut that contrasts massivity and chamber style.

There truly isn't a performance on disc one can recommend with enthusiasm. Von Karajan tends to sectionalize this work and it does not hang together as an entity; withal he can be credited with the split-off that pertains to variation style.

Craft flattens out the dynamic levels and thereby neutralizes and discolors the textures. The CBC Symphony does fairly well otherwise. This is on Columbia M2S-694. Mehta (on London 6612 with the Los Angeles Philharmonic) seems totally out of touch with Schoenberg's music. Notes are there, phrases are there, but there just isn't any meaning to what's going on.

String Orchestra

Suite for String Orchestra (1934)

☐ Royal Philharmonic Orchestra / Del Mar (conductor) / Argo ZRG-754

Schoenberg's string suite is not a serial composition, or, for that matter, an atonical quilt of freely disposed chromaticism. It is tonal (basically in the G major orbit) and avoids the mammoth tonal stretchings and pitch mastications of his *Pelléas und Mélisande* and *Verklärte Nacht*. It follows pre-classical dance style in the last three movements: Menuet and Trio, Gavotte, and Gigue, opens with an *Ouverture* that has partial fugal contours, which is followed by an Adagio.

The Argo version is much warmer than the other in the catalogue (the Columbia Symphony Strings, conducted by Robert Craft, on Columbia M2S-752). Agogic emphasis under Craft's direction is sharper but not necessarily fitting; one prefers the rounder, soothfast style derived from Del Mar's conducting. Better sound on Argo, as well.

Verklärte Nacht, Op. 4

☐ Leopold Stokowski and His Symphony Orchestra / Stokowski (conductor) / Seraphim S-60080
☐ Strings of the New York Philharmonic / Mitropoulos (conductor) / Odyssey 32160298

The old editions take the prizes. The Stokowski recording is great. Time has not cooled Stoky's performance; it is still as hot as Hades. The Mitropoulos version is rich and warm, thoroughly musical and beautifully fitting. (See also under *Chamber Music*, p. 1626.)

Theme and Variations, Op. 43a

Band

☐ Eastman Symphonic Wind Ensemble / Fennell (conductor) / Mercury 75057

The "a" after the opus number signifies *not* a second setting in the numerical totality, but the first. The objective in composing the work was for school bands (suggested by Schoenberg's publisher). But, *Gebrauchsmusik* was never Arnold Schoenberg's franchise. The Theme and Variations is major-league in requirements and therefore rarely is played by bands. In anticipation of this regretful outcome, Schoenberg revised the work for full symphony orchestra (see under *Orchestra*) and indicated it as Opus 43b (some listings drop the "b" and thus cause confusion as to what came first).

Seven variations and a finale, where additional ideas are employed, comprise the work. Ultra-chromaticism describes the style. Definite difficulty of execution presents the performance demands. Only a group such as the Eastman ensemble is capable. The achievement here is superior.

Concerto for Piano and Orchestra, Op. 42

Solo Instrument and Orchestra

Piano

☐ CBC Symphony Orchestra / Gould (piano) / Craft (conductor) / Columbia MS-7039

Composed when he was close to seventy, the piano Concerto represents Schoenberg at the very peak of his career. While fantasy is proposed by the work's single-movement span, divisional definition is clear (the equivalent of variations, scherzo, slow movement, and rondo).

Unfortunately, the best performance has been deleted: Peter Serkin with Ozawa conducting the Chicago Symphony (RCA LSC-3050). Since this catalogue cut-out took place but two years ago, there may be copies still in stores. If so there is no argument as to choice. Gould's and Craft's concept is exceedingly literal and one wishes for considerable more expressivity. The last is found in the Brendel–Kubelik reading on Deutsche Grammophon (2530257) but most of the tempi are wrong.

Concerto for Violin and Orchestra, Op. 36

Violin

☐ CBC Symphony Orchestra / Baker (violin) / Craft (conductor) / Columbia MS-7039

Schoenberg's disdain for patterns that would fit the fingers, a coloristic, romantically inclined bravado, and volatile virtuosity do not exemplify an aesthetic that some have termed "hysterical." These points contained within balanced shapes (in three movements; moderately fast, slow, and marchlike, including a cyclic reference in the finale to the opening) define a classicist.

There is no doubt that Schoenberg's Concerto fuses the subjective with the objective. He accomplishes this within a strict application of "composition with twelve notes related only to one another." He includes the conventional cadenza displays (none is conventional in style!) without interrupting artistic meaning or technical purity. Schoenberg's partnership of strict structural elements with sheer virtuosic demonstration is an exciting emotional and intellectual blend.

Baker plays with such ease as to belie the horrendous difficulties found in every measure. Still, a feeling of resistance in the solo voice would better define the repercussiveness of the musical material. If you would prefer a rounder tone, and a warmer insistence, though this is not totally fitting for the work's contents, then try Marschner as soloist, with Gielen conducting, in a mono edition on Turnabout 34051E. This was originally a Vox release-number 10530.

(The Baker-Craft performance is also included in another all-Schoenberg album: Columbia M2S-679.)

Instrumental

Variations on a Recitative, Op. 40

Organ

☐ Mason (organ) / Columbia M2S-767

Fully chromaticized tonality (centered on D but permitted the fullest opportunity to roam) is illustrated in this huge organ production, one with Bachian grandeur and Regerian heaviness. No cut-and-dried traditional theories of variation are employed in the set of ten, followed by a cadenza and a fugue of marvelous polyphonic utterance. However, the deployment of the theme (meaning the recitative) pays respect to bygone days. It is present in each of the variants, sometimes shortened, at other times slightly changed and/or ornamented, woven into all parts of the texture.

This turns out to be only a fair reading of the score; the freedom of some of the tempi and dynamics is somewhat crucial. But in Marilyn Mason's defense the fact is that Schoenberg was dissatisfied with the printed edition of his opus (used by the writer in auditioning this disc), especially the registration indicated. This probably had an influence on the performance latitudes the soloist has taken.

Piano

Five Piano Pieces, Op. 23	**Six Little Piano Pieces, Op. 19**
Piano Piece, Op. 33a	**Suite for Piano, Op. 25**
Piano Piece, Op. 33b	**Three Piano Pieces, Op. 11**

☐ Jacobs (piano) / Nonesuch 71309

In Opus 11 the logic is obtained by motivic construction, repetition, and imitation. Opus 19 covers wondrous, spidery-fine, short aphoristically considered conceptions. There is a somewhat curious air about the Five Piano Pieces; its expressionism is meaningful yet almost cold. Schoenberg is on the verge of integrating his musical fantasies with the concrete method of dodecaphonism. While the conflicts show, the contents are sharply codified, including a quasi-fugue and a waltz.

The Opus 25 Suite defines a partnership of technical and formal symmetry; a single tone row serves for all five movements and each is in classic suite design. The Opus 33 pair provide a mature synthesis of the twelve-tone method with the music based on subdivided tone rows. Nonetheless, the effect is romantic.

The performances show superb insight. Though Jacobs considers the Opus 33 pair with passionate concern, lush munificence is avoided and, in place, is a cool (almost flinty) expression fully becoming to the music. No pianist on recordings can match the dynamic controls Jacobs evidences in the Six Little Piano Pieces or the transparent detail in his playing of the Opus 25 Suite. All too often rigidity is the performance factor here, which

Schoenberg's five-movement essay is not and Paul Jacobs proves it. The artistic victory of this master musician is further apparent in the way he invokes the lights and shadows in the late romantic urgencies of the Opus 11 set.

Phantasy for Violin with Piano Accompaniment, Op. 47

Violin

☐ Bress (violin); Reiner (piano) / Folkways 3354 (monaural)
☐ Gross (violin); Grayson (piano) / Orion 74147

Hidden away in a monaural package entitled *The Violin: Vol. 4* is the best performance of this, Schoenberg's final instrumental work (the compositions that followed were for either voice or chorus). If you must have stereo the Gross–Grayson offering is acceptable, though Bress plays with a rounder tone and Folkways (notwithstanding the mono situation) offers a quality of sound just as good as Orion.

What is not acceptable is the Columbia M2S–767 edition with Israel Baker and Glenn Gould. It may well be that Gould was dissatisfied with his role, since Schoenberg's piece is a violin solo *with* piano accompaniment, and not a full-blown chamber-music duo. While Baker's approach is somewhat note-anchored (one is too conscious of exact notes, exact rhythms, in place of sheer *musical* inner play), at least he carries out the dynamics and rhythms set down by Schoenberg. Gould, however, substitutes *piano* for *forte,* inserts *subito* repulses, disregards dynamics in wholesale fashion, and disturbs the basic line of the violin part with *rubati* deception. Fantasy notwithstanding, this seriously interferes with the balanced clarity of the work (in four linked sections, defined by tempi and dynamic differences). One can say there is tarnished Gould in them thar fantasy hills.

Trio for Violin, Viola, and Cello, Op. 45

Chamber Music

☐ Mann (violin); Hillyer (viola); Adam (cello) / Columbia M2S–767

Color itself is given extreme attention in this string trio. The polyphonic string structure has superimposed upon it tinted substances in greater detail than in any other Schoenberg chamber-music production. Rhythms are struck and long tones are drawn in *col legno; ponticello* snarls are made in tremolo form as well as singly; sustained forms of hissing sound and harmonics of all types are used together with combined, related bowing techniques. Schoenberg is involved in his own tradition; not a single matter pertaining to it is in doubt. Regardless of his prime concern for formal content there always is the inner force of swirling figures expressed in highly sensitized and exciting color patterns.

The performance by the three members of the Juilliard Quartet (Hillyer and Adam are no longer with the group) is superlative. It is one of the greatest Schoenberg readings available on discs. Every tinge, every tang, every sonic seasoning in this extremely difficult score is covered. No nod of approval is sufficient; rather, thunderous applause for playing that cannot be praised sufficiently.

String Quartet

In D major (1897) / No. 1 in D minor, Op. 7

☐ LaSalle Quartet / Deutsche Grammophon 2720029

The D major work is the quartet that was listed as "lost" in all bibliographies but it never was. It was always safely tucked away in Schoenberg's files, withheld, during his lifetime, from publication. It is a combine of Brahmsian detail and late romantic syntax.

The Opus 7 is one of the largest quartets in the literature, not only in performance time but also in scope. A one-movement compendium, it holds fast to classical tradition and at the same time kicks it to the side. The formal audacity, which is linked to Beethoven, moves much further afield.

Only the Juilliard Quartet (Columbia M3-33581) offers competition to the LaSalle foursome in this quartet. Since there is plenty of boiling and seething in the work, one prefers the more settled condition of the LaSalle's playing. Now then, you won't go wrong with choosing the Juilliard's edition. Of course, if an auditor has a well-lined purse the thing to do is to get both performances, included in releases each covering the total five quartets.

(If the Opus 7 is desired separately it is so available, on Deutsche Grammophon 2530329.)

String Quartet No. 2 in F sharp minor, Op. 10

☐ Juilliard Quartet / Valente (soprano) / Columbia M3-34581

Classical definition of form (sonata design in the end movements, scherzo and variations in between) mingles with a distinctive newness of sound material creating an original method of chamber-music presentation. The second string quartet has formal stability, but there is no compromise with free expression of tonality, which sweeps through the piece to such an extent that the final movement marks the starting point of a new chapter in musical history. This is Arnold Schoenberg's final work to bear a key signature—lying ahead is the emancipated land of twelve tones.

Here, too, for the first time instrumental and vocal chamber music become partners. In the first two movements the medium is strictly four stringed instruments; in the last two, a soprano singing words by Stefan George joins in, transforming the instrumentation. George's text is dovetailed into the design and the quartet turns into a quintet by natural growth.

The performance choice has been decided by two points concerning the vocalist. Benita Valente has a warmer (even smoother) voice than Margaret Price who assists the LaSalle Quartet (Deutsche Grammophon 2720029). More importantly is the integration of the voice with the quartet in the Juilliard performance. In the LaSalle edition the sense of voice with string-instrument accompaniment keeps rearing its head and that's not what is desirable.

String Quartet

No. 3, Op. 30 / No. 4, Op. 37

☐ LaSalle Quartet / Deutsche Grammophon 2720029

Schoenberg's third quartet is in his mature, strict style of twelve-tone composition. Within it concentrated thematics are used to establish precise architectural stability. The sounds remain romantic, though far from sweet, making a neutral blend of balanced sonority.

The LaSalle team pick up on the fact that the word "moderato" figures in the tempo designations of all the movements, except the slow one. Decidedly, they produce the most resolute consequences by following this *moderato* consideration.

In the fourth quartet Schoenberg accomplishes a unique synthesis in which he contradicts neither classical form, nor his own technical premises. To combine the special system of a tone row and its zigzagged equivalence with nineteenth-century arrangement is a feat; it also has telling effect.

One favors this less intense performance realization as contrasted to the Juilliard team's (on Columbia M3-34581). The point is that the more fluid the linear travel of Schoenberg's music, the warmer the result. The Juilliard team tend to press-in the phrases and oversharpen the rhythms.

Die Eiserne Brigade—March for String Quartet and Piano (1916)

☐ Members of the London Sinfonietta / London/Decca SXLK-6660/4

Written during Schoenberg's war service. All the makin's: introduction, march, trio, and recapitulation. All the stuff: bugle calls simulated by the piano, drum rolls by low string *tremolandi.* Square tonality without a smudge.

If you want to make some money, find someone that doesn't know the work (absolutely easy!), play it for him, and bet heavily he can't name the composer.

Ein Stelldichein for Oboe, Clarinet, Violin, Cello, and Piano (1905)

☐ Members of the London Sinfonietta / Atherton (conductor) / London/Decca SXLK-6660/4

An unfinished sultry romantic bit, projected like *Verklärte Nacht* to be a symphonic poem for chamber combination. The affinity is underlined by the use of lines (on which Schoenberg was basing his work), by Richard Dehmel, the same poet for the text background of *Verklärte Nacht.* Only ninety unedited measures were left by Schoenberg. Of these the final dozen are omitted in this probing and sometimes wistful performance. Atherton explains the deletion as a way "to give the fragment a suggestion of finality."

Quintet for Flute, Oboe, Clarinet, Horn, and Bassoon, Op. 26

☐ Westwood Wind Quintet / Craft (conductor) / Columbia M2S-762

Schoenberg's single work for the accepted combination known as the wind quintet (slightly modified in that a piccolo substitutes for the flute in the second movement and again for a short section in the fourth) is heavily laden. However, its weight is brought by the *action* of the sounds, not their static mass weight or the density resulting from heaped sonorities.

Recordings of the work have not been many, but those deleted that I have reauditioned (by the Philadelphia Woodwind Quintet on Columbia and the Danzi Quintet on World Series) have all the notes, of course, but they resist warmth and indicate rather than explain.

The only current recording that is expressive is by the Westwood group. They produce a suave, almost relaxed reading. They also provide immaculate attention to the agogic flow of the score. The requirements for the players are almost exhausting and the difficulties many. But, they are conquered.

The difficulties for the listener are far less. Architecturally, Schoenberg represents the most traditional composer of the twentieth-century musical revolutionaries. While this does not mean Haydnesque simplicity because of his use of classical designs, it offers the auditor the advantage of an identity better known than any other. Thus the sonata form of the initial movement, the Scherzo, the ternary construction of the slow movement, and the final Rondo offer secondary frames of reference to the dodecaphonic fluency that moves within.

Weihnachtsmusik for Two Violins, Cello, Harmonium, and Piano (1921)

☐ Members of the London Sinfonietta / London/Decca SXLK-6660/4

Tonal fantasy on a pair of carols: *Es ist ein' Ros' entsprungen* and *Silent Night,* not only showing contrapuntal expertise but communicating expressive warmth. Christmas music but good for all seasons.

1625

Verklärte Nacht, **Sextet for Two Violins, Two Violas, and Two Cellos, Op. 4**

☐ Members of the London Sinfonietta / London/Decca SXLK–6660/4

"Transfigured Night" remains Schoenberg's most-played composition, more so in the string orchestra version (*see above*). In that setting it is very popular as the score for the ballet *Pillar of Fire.*

Although Schoenberg preferred this, the original six-instrument setting (composed in 1899), he never banned the string orchestra version that he made in 1917. In fact he produced a second, definitive edition in 1943 for the large string body. However, the buoyant urgency and clarity are not bettered, it seems to me, and in fact are lessened, by multiplying the number of players.

Take your choice of medium. If you want the choicest string sextet recording the Londoners provide it. They play with intense passion, the detail is marvelous, the atmosphere is all it should be, and the sound is rich.

Suite, Op. 29

☐ Melos Ensemble / Oiseau-Lyre S–282

Though this unusual combination of three different types of clarinet, string trio, and piano, is proportioned by family groups, the color factor is applied to nurture the individual properties in each instrument. Schoenberg also masses the timbres and relates his scoring to the twelve-tone system.

Classical form representation provides the beam of light for the music's path. Nonetheless, the music is of trenchant complexity; a contrapuntal puzzle for the uninitiated. After sufficient study, familiarity will reveal the secrets of the score.

The Melos Ensemble plays in a more relaxed manner than the Columbia Chamber Ensemble (on Columbia M2S–762). This is simply a matter of the Melos group adopting slower tempi, whereas by adhering to Schoenberg's speed indications the Columbia performance can be termed more authentic. Still, this produces a quality of nervousness quite often and with no deference to Schoenberg a calmer speedrate is preferable, giving a Viennese roundness to the linear ridges. The performance on London/Decca (SXLK–6660/4) is somewhat heavy on top of what is already heavy with action and has only fair sound.

(Columbia titles the work as Septet. True, there are seven instruments, but Schoenberg's heading reads: Suite.)

Serenade, Op. 24

☐ Melos Ensemble / Case (baritone) / Maderna (conductor) / Oiseau-Lyre S–250

This music is gaily Viennese. The instrumentation is of serenade character with the plectral mandolin and guitar, timbres unique to the field of chamber music. In addition Schoenberg uses a clarinet, a bass clarinet, and a string trio. The basic septet becomes an octet with the entrance of a low voice in the fourth of the seven movements (the text a sonnet by Petrarch).

There are innumerable humors and delights in the Serenade: squared rhythmic pungencies in the March, a tart Minuet, and the catchy triple waltz pulses that cover the Dance Scene. The other, more serious portions do not detract from the fundamental serenade style.

In his Opus 24 Schoenberg shows how cheerful and charming his music can be. To those who think of his output as forbidding and grim, it should be quite revealing, especially in this really magnificent performance conducted by the late Bruno Maderna. It is "really magnificent" because it is of fitting mellow quality, the sound almost of buttery content.

In the Boulez-directed edition (Everest 3175) there is fine direction but there is unfortunate roughage in the playing and the vocalist suffers from a lack of proper resoluteness. In Columbia's version (M2S-762, directed by Craft) there is little give and the music is presented too rigidly. Stiffness in this work is deadly.

Cabaret Songs (1901)

Arie aus dem Spiegel
  von Arkadien
Der Genügsame Liebhaber
Einfältiges Lied

Galathea
Gigerlette
Jedem das Seine
Mahnung

Vocal

Voice with
Accompaniment

☐ Nixon (soprano); Stein (piano) / RCA ARL1-1231

These assorted *Brettl-Lieder* (given no numerical sequence) are light-faceted, their objectives having been for popular consumption (though strictly high-class and far from low down), rather than the concert stage. Texts such as "My girlfriend's a lady of the voluptuous sort,/ She lies on the sofa the whole year round,/ Quite busily stroking the cat's fur for sport,/ My God, how she dotes on that soft, furry mound" give the clue. So do the symmetrically squared constructions for ease in recognizing both tune and text. One of the best examples is the waltz swing of *Mahnung*.

Marni Nixon presents these songs in the most attractive and charming manner. Where required there is delicate gusto and always there is a stylistic know-how that is a delight.

Das Buch der Hängenden Gärten, Op. 15

☐ DeGaetani (mezzo-soprano); Kalish (piano) / Nonesuch 71320

At Schoenberg's Opus 15 the long line had been crushed to short and severely demarcated ideas. This is musical suppleness and in vocal writing it amounts to mobility—quasi-recitative. Tonality is now free; cohesiveness is now obtained by the musical shapes; polarity of mood substitutes for tonality; the crutch of key gives way to the central subject or idea which holds everything in place by magnificent logic. This is expressionism freed of objectivism.

Schoenberg selected for his texts a set of fifteen poems from a volume by Stefan George, which are colored by symbolism, exotic and rarefied to a great degree. The music for "The Book of the Hanging Gardens" has no heavy perfume hanging about; it is subtle, extremely free and flexible, yet is one piece.

Importantly, the voice (with a range of two octaves plus a semitone) is not solo; it is an instrumental part of a duet. The composition is true chamber music for two performers. Jan DeGaetani's singing cannot be praised sufficiently, and Gilbert Kalish's playing is as absorbing. There is no disparity between them. They have produced a distinguished addition to the recorded Schoenberg literature.

Four Songs, Op. 2

No. 3: *Erhebung* / No. 1: *Erwartung* / No. 2: *Jesus Bettelt* / No. 4: *Waldsonne*

☐ Faull (soprano); Gould (piano) / Columbia M2S-736

Of course, *Erwartung* should not be confused with Schoenberg's monodrama that has the same title. The Opus 2 set is mainly harmonically colored by perpetual modulation, with an insistence on quartal harmonies in the first song. Three of the texts are by Schoenberg's favorite poet of the pre-serial days, Richard Dehmel. (He also wrote the lines on which *Verklärte Nacht* was based.)

Expressively sung but sung also with a slight vibrato that requires a critic's minus sign next to the pluses.

Nine Early Songs (1893-1903)

Deinem Blick mich zu Bequemen   *Mädchenlied*
Die Beiden   *Mein Herz das ist*
Ein Schilflied   *ein Tiefer Schacht*
Gedenken   *Nicht Doch!*
Mädchenfrühling   *Waldesnacht*

☐ Nixon (soprano); Stein (piano) / RCA ARL1-1231

(No numbers are assigned to these songs, since they were individually composed and none were combined in a set or as a cycle.)

Brahms is the strong influence in the songs, though a later type of romantic syntax is also to be recognized (in *Deinem Blick mich zu Bequemen,* for example).

Well-balanced renditions. Marni Nixon's voice is pitched clearly, though less varied in its timbre than desirable. As expected, Leonard Stein is a superior musician.

Two Songs, Op. 1

No. 2: *Abschied* / No. 1: *Dank*

☐ Gramm (bass-baritone); Gould (piano) / Columbia M2S-736

Both songs are to poems by Karl von Levetzow, the music an expansion of Brahmsian and Wagnerian elements. Gramm does well and Gould firmly so.

Voice and Instrumental Ensemble

Cabaret Songs (1901)—*Nachtwandler*

☐ Nixon (soprano); Stein (piano); Lolya (piccolo); Crisara (trumpet); Lang (snare drum) / RCA ARL1-1231

The only one of Schoenberg's *Brettl-Lieder* that is instrumentally enlarged. (For details see above under *Vocal: Voice with Accompaniment,* where all seven are for piano only with the voice.)

Herzgewächse, Op. 20

☐ Tritter (soprano); Newell (harp); Jacobs (harmonium); Silfies (celesta) / Craft (conductor) / Columbia M2S-709

This short item for soprano, with an esoteric color combine of celesta, harmonium, and harp, immediately precedes Schoenberg's *Pierrot Lunaire* and can be considered a preliminary study for it.

A clearly defined piece, its extensive curves would tax the best of singers. Musical importance before vocal comfort is the credo here since the soprano line is virtuosity unrestrained, its range climbing to F in alt. Rita Tritter's delivery fulfills all demands and she makes the music very exciting. But color the last words dark brown; Schoenberg's *Herzgewächse* is melancholic, piercing with its sensitivity.

There are two errors on page three of the album booklet in which this work is included. George Silfies plays the celesta (and let's not spell that with a final "e" as Columbia does on its label copy) *not* the clarinet, while Paul Jacobs plays a harmonium *not* an organ, which is no inconsequential difference.

Lied der Waldtaube from *Gurre-Lieder*, for Mezzo-Soprano and Chamber Ensemble

☐ London Sinfonietta / Reynolds (mezzo-soprano) / Atherton (conductor) / London/ Decca SXLK–6660/4

The "Song of the Wood-Dove" is one of the most eloquent parts of Schoenberg's massive cantata (*see below*). The extract was on disc in the 78 rpm days, made by Stokowski, on a 10 incher, long after his initial, monumental recording of the entire work, in 1932. However, this version is an orchestrally reduced concept, made by Schoenberg for a concert he conducted in Denmark. Neither the beauty nor the emotive charge of the music is reduced in his special orchestrational draft.

Full-scale and quite impressive singing, especially in the lower range of the part.

Pierrot Lunaire, Op. 21

☐ Contemporary Chamber Ensemble / DeGaetani (mezzo-soprano) / Weisberg (conductor) / Nonesuch 71251
☐ Beardslee (soprano); Helps (piano); Panitz (flute and piccolo); Bright (clarinet and bass clarinet); Cohen (violin and viola); McCracken (cello) / Craft (conductor) / Columbia M2S–679

These settings of twenty-one poems (oddly enough, Schoenberg's opus number is the same) by Albert Giraud, in German translation by Otto Erich Hartleben, for speaking voice and instruments, are focused on the vocal protagonist. They represent, therefore, a fascinating hybrid of theatre presented in chamber-music style.

Pierrot Lunaire once chilled the marrow of most critics. The famed James Huneker described Schoenberg's opus with sadistic implications: "he mingles with his music sharp daggers at white heat ... he twists the knife in the fresh wound." As recently as 1952, a venerable American critic was still unable to understand the subjective climate of Schoenberg's moonstruck Pierrot or unwilling to realize the music's expressionistic validity as a proven contemporary classic. He wrote "...the listener leaves ... this work doubting his own sanity."

Pierrot Lunaire has shocked principally because the vocalist does not sing, but emotes midway between song and speech, thereby emphasizing both the prose contours and the musical content. A set of five players play eight instruments supporting the voice. However, the instruments do not *accompany* the *Sprechstimme* or act as a programmatic tool.

Schoenberg's music is complex because of its novel dualism: the atonical, fragmented lines are entwined in a colorful and concentrated instrumental weave, and are associated with the dramatic speaking voice. The product is a music of consonant and unremitting tensility. Its colossal individuality makes it an enduring monument in the art world of the twentieth century.

There is one version that everyone should have—that conducted by Schoenberg himself. This is represented by an old Columbia disk, first issued as number 4471 and presently in the Odyssey series (Y–33791). It is a dubbing made from a 78 rpm. affair and has many sonic drawbacks. As a historical document, however, it should be in every collector's hands. So should the superlative performances by Beardslee and DeGaetani. The latter's deeper voice is, at times, even more favorably disposed toward the dynamic character of the score. The others in the field vary and do not sustain the required intensity. One version actually prettifies the work, thus depriving the music of its urgency and nightmarish fantasy.

*Voice and
Orchestra*

Four Orchestral Songs, Op. 22

☐ Columbia Symphony Orchestra / Sarfaty (soprano) / Craft (conductor) / Columbia M2S–709

The *Vier Lieder* are akin to miniature symphonic poems with an obbligato vocal line. The instrumental byplay and background as well as overlay are remarkable. It includes a large wind section of five flutes, five oboes, six clarinets, and four bassoons and within that array are no fewer than three bass clarinets and a contrabass clarinet; less than usual "normal" brass totalities, with four horns, only one trumpet, three trombones, and tuba; light percussion, harp, and the usual strings. However, what is more pertinent is that the full orchestra is never used as a unit and the scoring format changes for each song. Some examples: the trombones only appear in the first song *Seraphita,* the harp is employed only in the second of the set *Alle, Welche Dich Suchen,* a group of two-dozen solo instruments are used in part three, *Mach Mich Zum Wächter Deiner Weiten,* and the horns make their single appearance in the final song, *Vorgefühle.*

A fully involved performance with striking characterization, excellent playing, and fine singing.

Six Songs, Op. 8

☐ Columbia Symphony Orchestra / Jordan (soprano) / Craft (conductor) / Columbia M2S–752

The Wagnerian link is obvious in this set of songs to texts by Heinrich Hart, Petrarch, and from *Des Knaben Wunderhorn.* However, there is considerable Mahler in the opus, and even a touch of Debussy.

The orchestration is rich, but heavy, and at times Irene Jordan's voice has to battle its way and is far from victorious. Nonetheless, the score is a gem and the continued inattention given it in the concert hall is a mystery.

Choral

Choral Canons

Chorus Alone

☐ Gregg Smith Singers / Craft (conductor) / Columbia M2S–780

Marvelous canons—all eleven of them—chosen from a published collection of thirty. They are a treasure house of polyphonic joy, ideal realizations that go far beyond the academic strictures of canonic technique. All are of minor length, all of major impact, all heard with beautifully accomplished singing.

Schoenberg's canons were composed for all purposes: as Christmas gifts or messages, greetings sent to friends, written to celebrate a birth. The texts are mainly in German, four being in English, all save two are by Schoenberg. The *Canon for Richard Rodzinsky* is a special gem in this special choral packet.

De Profundis (Psalm 130), Op. 50b
Dreimal Tausend Jahre, Op. 50a

☐ Gregg Smith Singers / Smith (conductor) / Everest 3182

De Profundis is a six-part a cappella piece, set to the original Hebrew text. It is a sensitive and dramatic integration of *Sprechstimme* and song, with a gorgeous climax. The opus, dedicated to the State of Israel, is beautifully realized in the Everest recording. Especially dramatic is the whispered counterpoint, not as well conveyed in the Columbia release (M2S–780) and botched in the Lyrichord edition (7161).

Dreimal offers the opportunity of hearing how spiritual twelve-tone music can be in the hands of a master. The Gregg Smith presentation offers better pace than defined by the Toronto group, conducted by Robert Craft on Columbia (M2S-709); blurred balance is to be heard in the Whikehart Chorale's performance on Lyrichord (7161).

Friede auf Erden, Op. 13

☐ John Alldis Choir / Alldis (conductor) / Argo ZRG-523

Completed the same day that Schoenberg began his second string quartet. *Friede auf Erden* spans Schoenberg's early luxuriant bravado and the later application of serial logistics. Tonality is present, its rays obscured by chromatic clash. Modulation has harmony by the throat, and classical chord construction is soon to be strangulated.

In this broad expanse of shifting colors, depicted by diatonic and chromatic elements, the effect is hypnotic. However, the texture is heavy-laden; the perpetual variation conduct of twelve-tone writing is previewed in the incessant chordal motion. The ear will tire if it is overloaded by such sonic weight. Fortunately, the length of *Friede* is just short of a too-muchness.

It takes a special standard of top professionalism to conquer the difficulties of Schoenberg's score. Not many choral groups can cope with this music—the defeats tremendously outnumber the successes. John Alldis's team registers a complete achievement and its recorded performance is the best rendition this writer has ever heard.

Beware of the Robert Shaw recording (on RCA LSC-2676). There's nothing wrong with the singing, but much wrong with the synthetic use of orchestral support. *Friede auf Erden* should be only considered in its unaccompanied original format.

Six Pieces for Male Chorus, Op. 35

☐ Chicago Symphony Orchestra Chorus / Craft (conductor) / Columbia M2S-780

All texts by Schoenberg. Heavily chromatically styled, though there is a good amount of tonal anchorage. The highlights of the set are the scherzo lift of the fourth piece (*Glück*) and the instrumental-like transmutations of part 5 (*Landsknechte*).

One can expect any chorus trained by Margaret Hillis to be expert. The singing in this case is confirmatory.

Three Folk Songs

Three Folk Songs, Op. 49

☐ Gregg Smith Singers / Smith (conductor) / Everest 3182

The first of each set uses the same text (*Es Gingen Zwei Gespielen Gut*), for different conclusions. Both groups are tonally devoted, embracing some harmonic polyphony. Not on a grand scale but simply grand unaccompanied choral music. Chromaticism is mainly on holiday in these six settings.

Gregg Smith lets them be sung as they are. No better explanation could be made, or would be wanted.

Four Pieces for Mixed Choir, Op. 27

☐ Columbia Chamber Ensemble and Gregg Smith Singers / Craft (conductor) / Columbia M2S-762

Chorus and Instrumental Ensemble

Short, unaccompanied settings (except the last which employs a mixed quartet of violin, cello, clarinet, and mandolin) of texts by the composer in the first two pieces, and Chinese poetry in the last pair. Music from the twelve-tone realm, therefore polyphonic. Polyphonic, therefore of linear fluidity.

The lone negative point is that the contrapuntal engagement interferes with depiction of the word meanings. Still, it is far better to hear this work with chorus, rather than by a vocal quartet as employed in Craft's previous release of the opus (Columbia 5244).

Three Satires, Op. 28

☐ Columbia Chamber Ensemble and Gregg Smith Singers / Jergenson (tenor); Drake (bass) / Craft (conductor) / Columbia M2S-762

This opus consists of six sections: the three parts (*Drei Satiren*), written in 1925, and a triple-portioned *Anhang,* added the year following. The latter is ridiculously translated as "Suffix" in the Columbia liner copy (consisting of niggardly notes—most unusual for this label) instead of "Supplemental" (at least, the more literal Coda translation would have been better).

Parts 1 and 2 are for chorus, part 3 has portions for solo tenor and solo bass with instrumental accompaniment for viola, cello, and piano. The supplementary terminal sections are for chorus with a pithy canon in between for string quartet. The last is a glimpse into a composer's workshop. This snippet (performance time: twenty-one seconds) was written for Thomas Mann.

These satires, for the greater part, use atonal fun and puns, plus sonic slang, to sling barbs at the tonal camp (tonal meaning the neoclassic Stravinskian orbit). Number 1, especially, is a concentrated gem of humor. The opening words "tonal or atonal" give the clue, and the polyphonic play follows suit. The effect is Elizabethan in modern full-dress clothes.

However, that one can ridicule neoclassicism in the midst of manipulating tone rows is not proven. Actually, the music gives rise to a paradox: the more it is heard the more the artistry comes through and the less the satire. What does come through dynamically clear is expert singing by the Gregg Smith outfit.

Chorus and Orchestra

Kol Nidre, Op. 39

☐ CBC Symphony Orchestra and Festival Singers of Toronto / Braun (speaker) / Craft (conductor) / Columbia M2S-709

One can read into the writing of this intense work Schoenberg's own desire to repent (see below: *A Survivor from Warsaw*). The text describes how all may pray together, asking for the annulment of selfish acts, and leads to a call for penitence. In his orchestration Schoenberg suppresses purely descriptive tactics; the subject data and technical style are sufficiently meaningful. A method of continual variation is applied to tonal sound-stuff, interweaving the six-hundred-year-old *Kol Nidre* melody which is sung at the beginning of the twenty-four hours marking the holiest event in the Jewish liturgical year: The Day of Atonement (Yom Kippur).

The performance is ideal, its interpretative temperature properly heated. Victor Braun's diction is beautiful. This is a better presentation than the initial (since deleted) recording of the work, with Hans Jaray as the narrator, which was also released by Columbia (ML-4664).

Modern Psalm, Op. 50c

☐ CBC Symphony Orchestra and Festival Singers of Toronto / Foldi (speaker) / Craft (conductor) / Columbia M2S-780

Schoenberg's Opus 50c is actually an unfinished work (eighty-five measures in all). However, due to Robert Craft's handiwork it sounds as a total unit. Scored for five-part mixed chorus, speaker, and small orchestra the music is dodecaphonic, but with a decided pantonal slant.

The recording is an imaginatively expressed account, especially with the fine diction of Andrew Foldi.

Prelude to *The Genesis* Suite, Op. 44

☐ CBC Symphony Orchestra and Festival Singers of Toronto / Craft (conductor) / Columbia M2S-694

The Prelude is one of the oddball items that somehow or other can be found in every respectable composer's catalogue. It represents a hunk of a total conception in which six other composers were independently involved. The project of portraying the initial part of the Old Testament was the brain child of Nathaniel Shilkret, who commissioned the separate pieces and wrote one movement himself. Castelnuovo-Tedesco, Milhaud, Stravinsky, Tansman, and Toch were the other men concerned in the joint effort. (Coincidentally, all were residents on the West Coast.)

Schoenberg's Prelude is decidedly atmospheric in its beginning, a true translation in orchestral sound of "... the Earth was without form." It then moves into definite shape (dodecaphonically fugal), though of decided complexity, and proceeds to some wordless choral partnership. The conclusion resolves matters into affirmative tonality and a dynamic fade-out. It is clearly a piece of program music, though no guide was supplied by the composer.

The complete *Genesis* Suite requiring orchestra, chorus, and narrator, recorded over three decades ago by Capitol (P-8125), is a collector's rarity. Thus, the availability of Schoenberg's contribution to the project, constitutes a real novelty.

Gurre-Lieder (1901-1913)

Cantata and Oratorio

☐ BBC Symphony Orchestra, BBC Singers, BBC Choral Society, Goldsmith's Choral Union, and Gentlemen of the London Philharmonic Choir / Napier (soprano); Minton (mezzo-soprano); Thomas and Bowen (tenors); Nimsgern (baritone); Reich (speaker) / Boulez (conductor) / Columbia M2-33303

A stupendous document of operatic totality wherein the fervency of Wagner and the orchestrational purple prose of Strauss are combined. Except for one section which affords lighter relief, everything is deadly serious.

A massive scope matches the two-hour length. The forces employed include five solo singers, a speaker, three male choruses, a mixed chorus, and a colossal orchestra, providing more for the exploitation of homogeneous timbre than for the mere enlargement of sound. Though gigantic orchestras mark much of the music of the late Romantic era, few composers indulged themselves as did Schoenberg with, for example, seven clarinets (three types) and seven trombones (four types). Aside from percussion, one hundred and thirty-eight players are demanded! Little wonder that the work has rarely been heard as producers stand in their own economic defense.

The *Gurre-Lieder* is intense love music mingled with grimness, drawn to a medieval Danish Tristanesque text. The apogee of liquid tonality is reached as Schoenberg begins his opus with creative eclecticism and concludes with an individual process—the employment of *Sprechgesang* ("spoken melody"), anticipating its expanded (and conclusive) use in *Pierrot Lunaire*. Schoenberg wrings every passion from his inspiration. It has not cooled off in its more than half century of life. A far cry from the sober world inhabited by the serial works, it shows that a composer bares his beauties in many ways.

With such maximum materials maximum expressivity is demanded of a performance.

Boulez has been called a cool conductor but he uses a heated baton in this case. The breadth of vision and the range of emotion are telling, much more than in the staid Deutsche Grammophon edition (2726046) conducted by Kubelik.

Marita Napier and Jess Thomas sing with intensity, the qualities bright and reliable and the projection artistically intelligent in both cases. The Wood-Dove part is sung by Yvonne Minton and she is most impressive and expressive. Gunther Reich as the narrator projects full command of his role. But, above all, is the red-corpuscled dynamism of the total performance, its excitation riding over a minor flaw here and there.

A Survivor from Warsaw, Op. 46

☐ CBC Symphony Orchestra and Festival Singers of Toronto / Horton (narrator) / Craft (conductor) / Columbia M2S–679

It should be recalled that Schoenberg rejected Judaism and became a Protestant, later renouncing that faith as well. Finally, in protest against Hitlerism, he returned to the Jewish faith in 1933. The Hebraic works are special, but de facto. In addition to settings of some Psalms, these include the magnificent *Kol Nidre*, the imposing opera *Moses und Aron*, and this pithy six-minute Cantata for speaker, male chorus, and orchestra, written in 1947.

The performance is superb, impeccably organized, Craft's conductorial control is marvelous. Horton's narration in this chillingly clear score—describing the brutality and horrors of a Nazi concentration camp, the preparation for death in the gas chambers—is intense, colored to the ultimate in expressivity. Absent is the error made in Columbia's initial recording of the work (ML–4664), now deleted. Schoenberg had chosen different languages to create a naturalism of dramatic impact. The narrator employs English, changing to German when representing the Nazi monsters, while the Jews' traditional, ritualistic *Shema Yisrael* ("Hear, O Israel") is delivered by the chorus, naturally, in Hebrew. In the deleted performance the diction of the narrator (Jaray) was clear, but his English had a strong foreign accent. It thus intruded and negated the fullest effect of one of Schoenberg's most telling inspirations. Intertwined with anguished twisting lines it creates a second dimension of gripping emotion against the background of turmoil. In addition, colors are utilized for concise, strong impressionistic-like purposes. The orchestra is no frame for the voices; it is a prime member of the *dramatis personae*.

Opera and Dramatic Music

Die Glückliche Hand, Op. 18

☐ Columbia Symphony Orchestra and Chorus / Oliver (bass) / Craft (conductor) / Columbia M2S–679

Symbolism becomes Schoenberg in this allegory devoted to man's suffering, disillusionment, and shattered hopes. It can well be considered a self-portrait in tones. Unfortunately, Schoenberg's home-made libretto is embarrassingly corny. Fortunately, it concerns only a fraction of the composition's eighteen-minute length. The action is principally pantomime, guided by meticulously detailed and complex staging and lighting directions. Within the orchestra the darker elements are featured, interposed with stabs and jabs that make each register with the impact of a hammer stroke.

"The Golden Touch" has the violence, the colorative excess, and the formal stream of consciousness that describe the world of expressionism. It is morbid, hard-edged, and remorseless. It whiplashes the emotions. It isn't pretty.

Craft has realized the tone of despair of Schoenberg's work. None of the astonishing details in the score is minimized. Certainly, an excellent realization.

Erwartung, Op. 17

☐ Washington Opera Society Orchestra / Pilarczyk (soprano) / Craft (conductor) / Columbia M2S–679

Schoenberg's one-act monodrama permits a listener to draw his own conclusions. *Erwartung* concerns a woman who goes to a forest to meet her lover and finds his murdered corpse instead. Its four scenes can be considered in two sections: first, the woman's fear of the woods, her wait and search for the man, and eventual discovery of his body; second, a soliloquy addressed to the dead person. The principal facets are hysteria and eroticism laced with hate. Nothing is explained in a scrutiny that moves through a Freudian world of dreams. *Erwartung* could be descriptive of a real experience, signify the actions of a deranged person, or simply constitute a staged nightmare. The question mark that surrounds it is a neat dramatic subterfuge.

The single character has a feverish vocal line, as orchestral in its gamut of exposure as the orchestra itself. Together voice and instruments counterpoint the moods and colors of a moonlit forest, the thoughts of anxiety, jealousy, and love, the terror of the climax. Never erupting but always on the verge are the seismic intensities of the imagery. It is this suspensful, never-resolved condition that builds up the heat of *Erwartung*. No contraction takes place within its tumescent state of neurotic ecstasy.

It is impossible to conceive of a performance that could surpass Helga Pilarczyk's. Musicality and intellectuality are displayed, plus a virtuosic technique that includes immaculate negotiation of pitch (the orchestra practically ignores any doubling of the voice). Further, she portrays the part with undeviating tension. It is masterful, thrilling, and of the keenest percipience.

Moses und Aron (1932–1951)

☐ Austrian Radio Orchestra, Austrian Radio Chorus, and Six Members of the Vienna Boys' Choir / Csapó and Brömmel (sopranos); Mühlbacher (mezzo-soprano); Obrowsky, Wagner, and Chlup (contraltos); Devos, Lucas, and Winkler (tenors); Salter and Illavský (baritones); Mann and Handlos (basses); Reich (speaker) / Gielen (conductor) / Philips 6700084

Schoenberg's magnum opus, in terms of conception, forces employed and deployed, and technical magic (the entire opera is constructed from a single tone row). This emotionally powered, beautiful music with uncanny dramatic magnetism holds one captive.

Schoenberg himself wrote the text, succinctly defining his two principal protagonists. Moses personifies thought (the world of God), Aaron illustrates action (the reality of life). To underline this contrast of the sacred and the profane, the former is given a speaking role and the other assigned to a tenor voice. The Biblical tale is not exactly translated but rather depicted in symbolic experiences. The scope is vivid: God's message conveyed through Moses, the performance of miracles, the refusal of God by the people, Moses's absence for forty days, the descent into sin and worship of the Golden Calf, the return of Moses with the Tables of the Law, his destruction of them, and his final despair. This brings the musical work to an end; another act exists with only the text. Despite conflicting viewpoints the opera as heard can be accepted as complete—as complete as Schubert's "Unfinished."

The demands of *Moses und Aron* are prodigious, including thirteen "leads," with other groups totaling as few as six to eight, and as many as seventy! Six solo voices are situated in the orchestra, itself a large aggregation calling for a big percussion section, piano, and a pair of mandolins; a stage orchestra is also required. The erotic orgy and sacrificial scene, if staged as Schoenberg wanted them, would be a censor's field day. The virgins in this opera are to be stark naked, and the frenzy, drunkenness, and sexual play during the bacchanal to end all bacchanals ("The Golden Calf and the Altar"—the third scene in the second act) are a powerful enticement for bluenoses and assorted neo-Mrs. Grundys.

Schoenberg's operatic sense makes nonsense of the criticism that twelve-tone technique is incompatible with the broad, diverse needs of a large-scale stage work. Serialism here serves every required purpose meaningfully and retains its own stylistic purity at the same time. The fascinating rhythmic contours are another denial of the prejudices that are still prevalent about dodecaphonicism. And the instrumental dimensions are new in the field of orchestration. *Moses und Aron* is truly a phenomenon in Schoenberg's legacy.

The recording is a powerful presentation. It is superbly spacious, excitingly real, deeply affecting. As Moses, Günter Reich brings the greatest conviction to the role. No better choice could be made (he is also the Moses in the edition conducted by Pierre Boulez, on Columbia M2-333594). The other principal character (Aaron) is heard with open-voiced accuracy and unaffected musicality. It is an extremely difficult part but Louis Devos carries it off beautifully. The ancillary roles are all covered convincingly. Schoenberg's voluminous detail demands a learned hand and an acute musical commander. That Gielen is a composer as well as a conductor gives him a special insight; likewise, for that matter, Boulez benefits. The difference between the two is the more precise containment of the score by Gielen, which, paradoxically, produces a greater dramatic production.

Ode to Napoleon Buonaparte for String Quartet, Piano, and Reciter, Op. 41

☐ Juilliard Quartet / Gould (piano); Horton (speaker) / Columbia M2S-767

The *Ode* is an exciting work and just as exciting in its constructive originality. Based on Byron's poem the scoring weaves around the text and quite often verges on straightforward program music. Especially meaningful is the tone row on which the music is based. It has tonal coloration in its triadic potential and such implications are fulfilled with the clear E flat major chordal conclusion.

The Juilliard Quartet has a stronger rhythmic profile in its playing than the competitive Claremont Quartet setting (on Nonesuch 71186). Further, John Horton has a more professional delivery than Bernard Jacobson's on Nonesuch. (The "professional" description was *not* chosen because Jacobson is, first, a music critic and only second, a narrator.) The other edition presently on the market (London/Decca SXLK-6660/4) does not possess the solidity of either the Columbia or Nonesuch discs.

Von Heute Auf Morgen, Op. 32

☐ Royal Philharmonic Orchestra / Schmidt and Harper (sopranos); Schachtschneider (tenor); Olsen (baritone) / Craft (conductor) / Columbia M2S-780

Schoenberg's one-act piece has been termed both a light and even a comic opera. From the libretto viewpoint it is almost an operetta. However, the musical content is far more substantial than the frothy figurations of operetta style.

The story line of "From Today to Tomorrow" is rather pat: husband considers the possibility of his wife's girl friend, the wife decides to test his fidelity, indulging in flirtation with a singer, husband becomes jealous. The double play-off ends with a safe "unmodern" continuance of a happy marriage. Schoenbergian techniques are not modified, the opera is based on a single tone row and there is *Sprechstimme* (*Leitmotiv* use as well). Although there are some set numbers, the music constantly moves through polyphony that is major to the score, a style rare (and questionable?) for light-slanted musical objectives. Truly, the heavy-heavy-what-hangs-over is more fitting to serious matters. This also applies to the orchestral apparatus which is exceedingly hungry and fussy.

Craft's version is the single one in the catalogue. The disc serves all requirements and has excellent directionality.

Schoenberg / *Johannes Brahms.* See Brahms / Schoenberg.

Schoenberg / *Georg Frideric Handel.* See Handel / Schoenberg.

Schoenberg / *Georg Matthias Monn.* See Monn / Schoenberg.

Schoenberg / Anton Webern (1883-1945)

Chamber Symphony No. 1, Op. 9

Chamber Music

☐ Fires of London / Unicorn RHS-319

Webern's transcription calls for flute, clarinet, violin, cello, and piano. If need be the translation can be played by a piano quintet, with a second violin taking the flute part and a viola substituting for the clarinet.

An interesting conception that does not harm the original coloristic canvas (for data concerning the work see under *Schoenberg: Orchestra*).

Johann Philipp Schoenfeld (1742-1790)

Two Airs for Soprano and Basso Continuo

Vocal

☐ Selig (soprano); Schaeffer (harpsichord); Farlet (viola da gamba) / Musical Heritage Society MHS-792-CC-13

Voice with Accompaniment

Specific contrast, one air being quiet and suave, the other having *movendo* pace. More than a tinge of romantic simmering can be identified.

Edith Selig is fine in the low and middle range. She strains somewhat in the very top register.

Max Schubel (1932-   )

Fracture (1969)

Orchestra

☐ Springfield Symphony Orchestra / Gutter (conductor) / Opus One 21

Pungent diction with brilliant exploitation of sonorities sets forth a freely formed long-spanned essay. Schubel's notes on his work use the stream-of-consciousness method, so his objectives (or methods) are far from clear. What is clear is the scoring stamina and the tooth and nail that penetrate the textures. There is nothing fragile about *Fracture*. If anything it is dissonantly free-tongued, with more than passing orchestral brutality.

The fervency of the playing is apparent.

Instrumental

Cello

Omphaloskepsis for Unaccompanied Cello (1964)

☐ Moore (cello) / Opus One 6

The motile scope of a pair of pizzicato glissandi at the beginning of Schubel's work is a prefatory indication of its coming events. These are full of conflict, both in their statements and in their colorations. The effect of a duo for one performer persists, though operatic-like, the "voices" rarely combine.

Though the music has an intensity in its gestural variety, *Omphaloskepsis* is really a virtuosic display piece. Moore plays it with unruffled demeanor and makes it sound easy.

Chamber Music

Exotica (1967)

☐ Wells (cello); Thomas (harpsichord) / Opus One S-7

There are more timbres to this work than the instruments listed. The cello also plays a gong, a temple block, triangle, and cymbal. The harpsichordist uses seven additional percussion instruments, including "normal" types such as xylophone and chime, and bizarre ones: egg shells to be crumbled and a plate glass to be shattered. These percussion additions match the stylistic percussiveness within the cello and keyboard-instrument parts. Make no mistake, Schubel holds the attention for the full eight minutes of his piece that spits on academic traditions and yet achieves its own unity and cohesion.

Joyeux Noël (1968)

☐ Blustine (clarinet); Moore (cello) / Opus One S-7

Joyeux Noël has naught to do with Christmas. Schubel chose the title to indicate that the work was a Christmas present for a friend. Actually it is a trio, since the clarinet and cello are supported by a two-track prerecorded tape. Color and its complex complexions form the prime ingredient in this highly fragmented piece, one containing rhapsodic pulsations that destroy any sense of pulse. The music is bound in by a quiet frenzy, with a constant intensity that makes tensility the total fact.

Quashed Culch (1966)

☐ Schecter (flute); Phillips (bass) / Opus One S-7

Schubel's habitual love of adding percussion to his chamber-music totality is maintained here in a duo he subtitles *A Play on and in Sounds*. The flutist also plays a large gong, and the double bassist doubles on a small gong.

Quashed Culch develops its basic material—a pithy phrase assigned the flute, and an acrobatically motioned rhythmic statement by the bass—but has the impact of an aggregation of images. Its violence derives from its virtuosity. In terms of the latter, the performers (Peggy Schecter and Barre Phillips) are magnificent.

High Ice—String Quartet No. 2 (1967)

☐ Kohon String Quartet / Opus One S-7

A considerable use of extremely high registers and a parallel application of close-to-the-bridge playing signifies, to Schubel, "an icy, cold sound." Accordingly the title *High Ice* (an extremely excellent one).

The Quartet is also high-powered, sonorously kaleidoscopic. The instruments are handled without kid gloves, all the stops are out, including the expansion of the violin-viola-cello timbres by use of percussion: glass wind chimes, suspended cymbal, large gong, and a pair of temple blocks, plus celesta. Schubel handles this assortment with masterly command; the percussion is not utilized for mere effect, but as an integral expansion of the work's dimensions. It is a stunning creation.

The Kohon team (its personnel has changed since this recording was made; here it consists of Harold Kohon, first violin; Al Rogers, second violin; Eugenie Dengel, viola; and David Moore, cello) are the perfect exponents of the piece. They gave the premiere in New York City on January 20, 1968, and have performed it many times since. All of the multisonorous requirements are met completely and artistically. Theirs is a very graphic performance of a very graphic work.

Insected Surfaces—A Concerto for Five Instruments (1966)

☐ Goldstein (clarinet); Wells (cello); Turetzky (contrabass); White (harpsichord); Gigliotti (piano) / Larsen (conductor) / Opus One S-1

The instrumental combination was selected by the composer "on the basis of pitch, range, color and technical possibilities." These do provide gut-full qualities that deliver a gutsy plethora of free-wheeling, sometimes jazzy, always inflamed patterns. Heard in that manner a stream-of-consciousness style applies—the happy avant-garde example of writing that does not play the game of creative party politics. On the other hand, the liner note states that while *Insected Surfaces* has no program, Schubel "pictures a group of people sitting down for the purpose of playing some music only to find interruptions (insects on the surface) disturbing their steady flow." And so on. You take your choice. Either way this is good musical vaudeville, doubtless played well.

F♯ (1968)

Electronic Music

☐ Opus One S-7

The taped sounds of *F♯* (meaning "F sharp," of course) consist of home-found, home-made materials—call it a minor-league type of *musique concrète*. Manipulated via speed changes, filtering, and the like, these form a totally static statement—call it a drone (hum) ostinato. This eradicates the sense of tempo, and time seems to be standing still. Truly an odd piece of electronic music. No wonder Schubel describes it as a "still piece, with no beginning, no end." Therefore no development and void of form as the word is understood.

The recording is timed at 14:14. However, the actual duration is at the will of the listener. "It can be ended (faded out) anywhere, or repeated whole or in part."

Franz Schubert   (1797-1828)

Overture in B flat major

Orchestra

☐ Philharmonia Hungarica / Maag (conductor) / Turnabout 34334/8

No indication is made in this release or in Egon F. Kenton's otherwise excellent program notes which of the two B flat Overtures Schubert composed is represented. Maag performs the fuller-instrumented opus calling for pairs of flutes, oboes, clarinets, bassoons, horns, and trumpets, in addition to timpani and strings; the other B flat Overture does not include flutes or clarinets.

Imaginative playing naturally administered. Fully sufficient for this traditionally formed piece.

Overture in C major, in the Italian Style, D. 591

☐ Vienna Philharmonic Orchestra / Kertész (conductor) / London 6382

"In the Italian Style" but of full Schubertian identity. Maag's performance of this work (on Turnabout 34334/8) is excellent until the Allegro. At that point grace takes a holiday. (This is emphatically not true of his performance of the Overture in D major, in the Italian Style, D. 590—*see below.*) Under Kertész's direction the music has both grace and proper exhilaration.

The Overture is also contained in a five-disc set containing all the Symphonies and two other Overtures, on London CSP-6.

Overture in D major, D. 556

☐ Vienna Philharmonic Orchestra / Münchinger (conductor) / London STS-15076

Satisfactory, if not very important Schubert. Satisfactory, if not a very inspired performance.

Overture in D major, in the Italian Style, D. 590

☐ Philharmonia Hungarica / Maag (conductor) / Turnabout 34334/8

In this case Maag delivers a perfectly beguiling performance, quite without the gracelessness found in the other Overture "in the Italian Style" recorded in the same album —*see above* (Overture in C major, D. 591). The lovely dancing quality of the music is expertly defined, and the playing has genuine vitality.

Overture to the Opera *Fierrabras*, Op. 76
Overture to the Opera *Des Teufels Lustschloss* (1813)

☐ Vienna Philharmonic Orchestra / Kertész (conductor) / London 6382

These operas mean nothing. One seconds Erik Smith's remarks on the unpromising material in the three-act heroic-romantic *Fierrabras,* and one similarly agrees with his statement that "The Devil's Pleasure Palace," a "natural magic opera" in three acts containing elements of a half-dozen operas, "has the makings of none." But the Overtures are a completely different matter and have much to offer. Their splendidly rich themes and dramatic orchestration are presented in full perspective. I cannot imagine better performances—both should remain unsurpassed for a very long time.

Together with the C major Overture "in the Italian Style" and all the Symphonies, this pair of Overtures can also be found in London's CSP-6, a ten-side release.

Symphony

No. 1 in D major, D. 82 / No. 2 in B flat major, D. 125

☐ Berlin Philharmonic Orchestra / Böhm (conductor) / Deutsche Grammophon 2530216

There's little one has to be concerned about in the smooth lines that mark Schubert's initial Symphony. The charm is built in, and just by permitting the music to go its way, Böhm is eminently successful. In the second work the variational material is well turned, the Scherzo moves with briskness, and nowhere is there evidence to match the line that Böhm gives correct performances but that they are heavy and dry.

Symphony

No. 3 in D major, D. 200 / No. 4 (*Tragic*) in C minor, D. 417

☐ Philharmonia Hungarica / Maag (conductor) / Turnabout 34361

Highly qualified performances. This is playing of fervent lyricism and with empha-sized evocative power in the so-called *Tragic* Symphony. (One writer claims there are no "genuine tragic outbursts" in the Symphony, but he probably has not examined—or heard—what goes on in the harmonic procedures of Schubert's great music.)

Maag's disc is a spin-off from his presentation of the entire Schubert symphony canon, on Turnabout 34334/8. Ormandy offers a solid setting and a rich frame for the Symphony on Columbia M–31635.

Symphony No. 5 in B flat major, D. 485

☐ Berlin Philharmonic Orchestra / Böhm (conductor) / Deutsche Grammophon 139162

The ultimate of lucidity is made available here. There are some touches that must be emphasized in this report, beginning with the taking of the expositional repeat in the opening movement, which structures the material as it should be structured (many con-ductors don't take the repeat). Further, there is exceptional coloring (the Minuet), and finally, the going around the turns in the *Andante con moto* is remarkably smooth and a special achievement.

Symphony No. 6 (*Little*) in C major, D. 589

☐ Bath Festival Orchestra / Menuhin (conductor) / Angel S–36453

Little because program-book makers and program-book takers both need levers to push for identification. How this Symphony might be confused with the other, *Great* C major opus one doesn't know. The point is that only sizewise is the nickname proper; mu-sically, the Symphony No. 6 is not of midget power or beauty. Who can forget Beecham's way with this joyous composition?

It is exactly that last thought that prompts choosing Menuhin's version. I have never thought of Menuhin as one of the major-league batonists, but he holds first place in the Schubert sixth-symphony league just by strongly imitating (instinctively or actually—it doesn't matter) Beecham's style. Never slick, mind you, but always just. A glowing Schubert essay. The music is never rushed, is always fluid, and is always free and un-calculated. Contrastively, the Scherzo is fully equipped with robustness.

A weightier reading is available under Ormandy's direction, with the Philadelphia Or-chestra, of course. It is on Columbia M–31635.

Symphony No. 8 (*Unfinished*) in B minor, D. 759

☐ Berlin Philharmonic Orchestra / Böhm (conductor) / Deutsche Grammophon 139162
☐ New York Philharmonic / Walter (conductor) / Columbia MS–6218
☐ Boston Symphony Orchestra / Jochum (conductor) / Deutsche Grammophon 2530357

It's very easy to rule out productions of this work which are mannered, stodgy, gooey, and thin-toned. Conductors who have presented the *Unfinished* in these ways are, respec-tively, Hollreiser on Vox 53100, Prohaska on Vanguard S–203, Stokowski (naturally?) on London 21042, and Goberman on Odyssey 32160010. The remainder (a consideration of some close to twenty conductors) do well, among which three are exceptional.

Böhm's way with the dynamic plan of Schubert's great two-movement work brings a contrast within the music's breadth that not only sharpens its dramaticism but colors it vividly. Jochum's viewpoint is one of total splendor, including a subtle pliancy in tempo that contrasts the positive from the lyrical elements. Bruno Walter's reading (also on Odyssey Y-30314) is expansive, fastidious, beautifully pulsed, and warmly colored. The blend of the wind solos is magnificently realized.

Symphony No. 9 (*Great*) in C major, D. 944

☐ Cleveland Orchestra / Szell (conductor) / Odyssey Y-30669
☐ Berlin Philharmonic Orchestra / Böhm (conductor) / Deutsche Grammophon 138877
☐ Berlin Philharmonic Orchestra / Furtwängler (conductor) / Turnabout 4364 (monaural)

The vivid vitality, with impulsive warmth, of Szell's reading displays an exciting responsiveness to Schubert's great work. There are places of almost febrile temperature, but always the music has Schubertian ripeness. (The other Szell edition is just as brilliant a translation, on Angel S-36044.)

Böhm's consideration of the music is more relaxed but firmly defines the drama and the thrust contained within it. The agogic particulars are produced with finesse, and the hard sponginess of the rhythmic figures is truly marvelous. Böhm also knows how to pace music fast without its becoming breathless.

The differences found in the Furtwängler edition are many, and yet are convincingly natural. Timewise it is much longer than either of the other two, and yet the Symphony does not drag—a fully ripened tempo, one might term it, the kind that embraces the world of traditional German music-making. Vitality thus comes from within and moves outward, whereas with Szell the reverse occurs. Both methods are valid.

Each of the three chosen performances can be classified as a memorable one.

String Orchestra

Five German Dances with Coda and Seven Trios, D. 90

☐ Stuttgart Chamber Orchestra / Münchinger (conductor) / London STS-15035

Irresistible. Schubert's *Fünf deutsche mit Coda und sieben Trios* (some of the trios are double ones) are played with silken smoothness and with every nuance marking the Viennese waltzes dwelling in the music. The ultimate in warm stylistic fidelity and finely focused quality.

Five Minuets with Six Trios, D. 89

☐ Vienna State Opera Orchestra / Angerer (conductor) / Nonesuch 71141

No technical legerdemain, just Schubert melodic flow, which has its own magic. Fine solo violin playing in a minor-keyed section. No performance surprises, simply agreeable performances.

Solo Instrument and Strings

Violin

Rondo in A major for Violin and String Quartet, D. 438

☐ Temianka Chamber Orchestra / Temianka (violin) / Temianka (conductor) / Orion 74136E (monaural)

Not the most significant Schubert, but it has his engaging melodic curves and some nice fiddle passages.

Temianka's little group consists of strings only, notwithstanding its "chamber orchestra" identification. His two-in-one chores are well accomplished.

This disc is an "enhanced for stereo" item, originally made in London in 1937 and released on the Parlophone label (No. E-11331).

Introduction and Variations on *Trockne Blumen*, Op. 160

☐ Bryan (flute); Keys (piano) / Lyrichord 7215

Seven variations are fashioned on the theme Schubert lifted from his song cycle *Die schöne Müllerin.* Keith Bryan neatly and nicely displays the ornatenesses with which Schubert surrounded his theme. It works perfectly.

Fantasia (*Wanderer*) in C major, Op. 15, D. 760

☐ Brendel (piano) / Philips 6500285

Musicality and fastidious technical control are prime points in this splendid essay. No less of a consideration is the formal certainty that Brendel gives to Schubert's music. The total solidity provided is proof of absolute insight into the work.

Hungarian Melody in B minor, D. 817

☐ Ashkenazy (piano) / London 6500

Schubert used this melody, in a different key, in his piano duet *Divertissement à l'Hongroise.* A delightful bit it is.

Impromptus, Op. 90, D. 899

No. 1 in C major / **No. 2 in E flat major** / **No. 3 in G flat major** / **No. 4 in A flat major**

Impromptus, Op. 142, D. 935

No. 1 in F minor / **No. 2 in A flat major** / **No. 3 in B flat major** / **No. 4 in F minor**

☐ Brendel (piano) / Turnabout 34481

The differentiation Brendel brings to these eight works shows a splendid ear for sound and its expressive implications. These performances deserve a place in every collection of Schubert's recorded music.

Brendel's performance was duplicated and released on Vox 512390. He made a different recording for Philips. In that case Opus 90, D. 899, is on No. 6500415 and Opus 142, D. 935 is on No. 6500928.

Moments musicaux, Op. 94, D. 780

☐ Curzon (piano) / London 6727

These six pieces may not be highly renowned Schubert, but in the hands of Clifford Curzon they turn into masterpieces nonetheless. Of course everyone knows the famous one (the third in *allegro moderato* tempo), but the grace of Curzon's playing, with a subtle dynamic inflection of a pitch here and a pitch there within the harmony, creates a spontaneous specific that is quite thrilling and renews the piece for one's ears.

Scherzo in B flat major, D. 593

☐ Kempff (piano) / Deutsche Grammophon 139323

Little played (save by students for the main part), but a Schubertian delight. The recording is splendid.

Sixteen German Dances and Two *Ecossaises*, Op. 33, D. 783

☐ Abram (piano) / Musical Heritage Society OR S-128

Dozens and dozens of dance pieces were turned out by Schubert. I cannot point to a single one that could be termed banal—light-fancied, yes, but never banal. The complete evidence is manifested in this recording which illustrates as well the unquestionably sensitive playing of Jacques Abram. His playing is also unquestionably musical to the core.

Sonata in A major, Op. 120, D. 664

☐ Richter (piano) / Angel S-36150

A classic performance of this romantic beauty. Everything is magnificently judged, magnificently provided. "Pianistic competence" is not at all adequate to describe this type of playing. "Magic" is the proper choice.

Sonata in A major, Op. Posth., D. 959

☐ Hungerford (piano) / Vanguard 71171

Masterly and beautiful. The phrases are not sectioned apart, which does not further structural understanding of Schubert's work. It is this sensitivity to the musical flow that makes Hungerford's conception outstanding. Importantly, the components of nobility that are contained in the Sonata appear clearly.

Sonata in A minor, Op. 42, D. 845

☐ Pollini (piano) / Deutsche Grammophon 2530473

The Beethovenistic reflection in the first movement is vividly mirrored here. There is splendid structuring in the slow movement, and masterful playing in the last two parts of the Sonata. Pollini's performance investments bring excellent returns. They can be matched only by Richter's performance on Monitor 2027. It is of lesser consideration only in terms of the recorded sound quality.

Sonata in A minor, Op. 143, D. 784

☐ Brendel (piano) / Philips 6500418

The element of spontaneity is demanded for playing Schubert above all composers—it thereby fulfills his large-ranged thematic conceptions. Brendel has it, to the fullest, in his portrayal of Opus 143. Fine lyrical detail as well.

Sonata in B flat major, Op. Posth., D. 960

☐ Curzon (piano) / London 6801

Rich and poetic playing of one of the great sonatas in the repertory. There is an elastic quality to the music, particularly in the opening *Molto moderato*. There is also a romantic flair that sustains the slow movement, and the delicacy of the Scherzo again speaks with a full romantic accent (compare this with the opposite state of terribly Germanic heaviness in Serkin's account on Columbia M-33932).

A finely played issue by Gabriel Chodos, on Orion 75179, is ruined by tight sound and noisy surfaces. These drive the recording to the ground.

Sonata in C major, D. 840

☐ Brendel (piano) / Philips 6500416

Another "unfinished" Schubert work, also with two movements, a Moderato and an Andante. Not as famous as the Symphony, but just as lovely. In its special way, more so.

This is a mysterious Schubert, with no "Song of Love" lilting curves. Its haunting sources are fully revealed in this recording. Brendel chooses a slightly slower tempo for the second movement since it so closely resembles the initial part of the work in mood and temper. Such re-creative strategy is well informed.

Sonata in D major, Op. 53, D. 850

☐ Ashkenazy (piano) / London 6961

A memorable performance is here on disc. Ashkenazy never loses sight of the composition's design, and yet the music is evocative in a personal manner, without denying Schubert's somewhat Beethovenistic expression. One is reminded of Virgil Thomson's marvelous phrase that the performer "walked around in" the musical structure. This reading puts every concert performance I've heard of the work—and those I've heard on disc (Brendel on Philips 6500763, Curzon on London 6416, and Klien on Vox SVBX-5467)—far in the shade.

Sonata

In E major, D. 157 / In E major, D. 459

☐ Walter Klien (piano) / Vox SVBX-5467

Schubertian soundness in both cases and special formal points as well. D. 157, Schubert's first piano Sonata, is in three movements, ending with a Minuet. D. 459 has an unusual five-movement format with two Scherzi, one following the opening Allegro moderato, the other following the third movement Adagio. An *Allegro patetico* concludes the work.

The performances are adequate.

Sonata in F minor, D. 625

☐ Walter Klien (piano) / Vox SVBX-5466

Another unfinished Schubert opus. The F minor Sonata consists of two Allegro movements on either side of a Scherzo, thus there is no slow movement. The playing is fully perceptive, though the tone of the first movement is somewhat hard. Only there and nowhere else. Klien shrewdly smoothes the edges of the Allegretto (the Scherzo) so that the romantic flavor is not lost. The playing of the final movement is excellent.

The recording of this work is a part of Klien's performances of the complete Schubert piano sonatas, released by Vox in three volumes. In this issue the following Sonatas are also included: A flat major, D. 557; A major, Op. Posth., D. 959; A minor, D. 537; C major, D. 279; and C minor, Op. Posth., D. 958. The other Vox volumes (known as Vox boxes) are SVBX-5465 and 5467.

Sonata in G major, Op. 78, D. 894

☐ Brendel (piano) / Philips 6500416

Beautiful shaded playing and translucent textures, but never mamby-pamby or over-light-hearted. This is a solid Schubert translation. Thus the Andante is played with a sense of serenity but never drags, and it moves through Schubert's telling phrases with sensitive musicality. The *Menuetto* enjoys some *rubati*. They are not out of place. Such fancies add to the eloquence of this issue.

Thirty-Four *Valses sentimentales*, Op. 50, D. 779

☐ Abram (piano) / Musical Heritage Society OR S–128

Whether these waltzes were written for dance or concert purposes is immaterial. Creative sincerity is there to hear, and such musical taste and charm are not achieved by the average type of composer. Jacques Abram plays these pieces with true artistic presence.

Thirty-Six *Originaltanze* (Waltzes), Op. 9, D. 365

☐ Abram (piano) / Musical Heritage Society OR S–127

The amount of dances Schubert wrote for the piano is of staggering total. There were Waltzes, *Ländler* (71 produced between 1816 and 1824, a separate dozen in 1823), *Ecossaises*, German Dances, *Valses sentimentales*, *Valses nobles*, *Wiener Damen-Ländler*, *Grazer Walzer*, *Galops*, and *Minuets* (a total of 42 composed between 1812 and 1818).

These three-dozen *Originaltanze* (*Grove's Dictionary of Music and Musicians* calls the group *Erste Walzer*) are cultivated dance examples, charming, and refreshing. Every one of the set is beautifully played throughout.

Twelve Waltzes, Op. 18, D. 145

☐ Ashkenazy (piano) / London 6500

No substantial musical challenge is offered by these pieces, but they are presented with an illuminative artistry that adds a special dimension to the set. When emphasis is needed, the sound is just a bit brittle.

Piano,
Four Hands

Fantasia in F minor for Piano, Four Hands, Op. 103, D. 940

☐ Brendel and Crochet (piano) / Turnabout 34479

One of the most intense Schubert pieces. Its emotional saturation marks it as the greatest work composed in the piano-duet medium. The values of this performance are totally compelling.

Sonata in C major (*Grand Duo*) for Piano, Four Hands, Op. 140, D. 812

☐ Brendel and Crochet (piano) / Turnabout 34516

Schubert's opus is large-scaled in both scope and sonority. The orchestral feeling that surrounds the Sonata is unmistakable. Brendel and Crochet do not minimize this in their playing. However, there is no sense of forcing or sonorous pressure; rather, one hears meaningful solidity and power. This is a fine duo team.

Trois Marches militaires, Op. 51, D. 733

☐ Walter and Beatrice Klien (piano) / Turnabout 34041

The original piano-duet setting for the famous *Marche militaire* (No. 1 in D), which is played to death in every other conceivable version, especially for orchestra. In that form it is generally heard in the Guiraud transcription, though one Gustav Brecher made a bombastic arrangement for very large orchestra in the key of D flat major! Anyway, it's a joy to hear Schubert's music as he conceived it, plus Nos. 2 and 3 of the set (in G and E flat major, respectively).

The Kliens opt for a lyrical quality rather than an overt and overriding march pulse, which is all to the good.

Phantasie in C major for Violin and Piano, Op. 159, D. 934

☐ David Oistrakh (violin); Bauer (piano) / Melodiya/Angel 40194

The playing aptly portrays the large scheme (plus inflections) in a music conceptually freed of formalism. The affiliation between the performers is splendid.

Rondo brillant in B minor, Op. 70, D. 895

☐ Schneider (violin); Peter Serkin (piano) / Vanguard 71146

An introduction of martial majesty opens this work, and the preamble shows how Schubert, imbued with an idea, does not let go. For this introduction is no simple prologue, but a section of forty-eight measures' length. Then follows a rondo, a powerful piece of symphonic depth, its equality in regard to the two instruments making it truly chamber music.

The playing is fully dramatic and decisive. The work sounds forth virtuosic, fulfilling Schubert's métier.

Sonata in A major, Op. 162, D. 574
Sonatina in D major, Op. 137, No. 1, D. 384
Sonatina in A minor, Op. 137, No. 2, D. 385
Sonatina in G minor, Op. 137, No. 3, D. 408

☐ Grumiaux (violin); Veyron-Lacroix (piano) / Philips 6500341

Beautiful stylistic fidelity displaying a rational intuition about Schubert's music. This recording represents impeccable imagery in interpretative art. The settings are what they should be: letting the finale of the first Sonatina run with light heart, not overemphasizing the emotive points in the slow movement of the second work in the set, permitting the music to spin itself from one beautiful spot to another in its final Allegro.

There is a negation of the notion that the music must be flavored with pepper. One example is the smooth spin of the Scherzo (in *presto* tempo) in the D. 574. In comparison, the thrust and sometimes percussive chordal statements in the Alexander Schneider–Peter Serkin performance on Vanguard (71146) are neither musically true nor satisfying. Nowhere do the Belgian-French team fail to produce Schubertian suavity in place of personal preference.

Sonata in A minor (*Arpeggione*) for Cello and Piano, D. 821

☐ Rostropovich (cello); Britten (piano) / London 6649

The arpeggione was the size of a cello, but shaped like a guitar, having that instrument's six strings total and frets to match. It was Gaspar Cassadó, the famous Spanish cellist, who was responsible for transcribing the Sonata for the modern instrument.

The execution here is ideal, providing the grace and gentle niceness of the work. *Rubato* and portamento would interfere with the pure naïveté of the music, and Rostropovich does not indulge in such errata. Britten's playing is just as propitious.

Notturno in E flat major for Violin, Cello, and Piano, Op. 148, D. 897

☐ Music Group of London / Unicorn RHS-311

As alluring as only Schubert melodicism can be. The playing is clear and refreshingly intimate and yet fully voiced. No other recorded issue can match it.

Sonata in B flat major for Violin, Cello, and Piano, D. 28

☐ Ganz (violin); Stiehler (cello); Kehlen (piano) / Vox SVBX-600

Herewith the innocent charm of Schubert of the student years, expressed in a single Allegro movement. (This is the same work that is sometimes listed as "Allegro in B flat" for the same combination of instruments.)

A fair enough performance, though the placement of the piano must have been far back of the strings, since it is underfocused for the greater part. (*Schwann* lists another edition by the Ebert Trio on Discapon S-4226. However, a copy for audition purposes could not be obtained by the writer.)

Trio for Piano, Violin, and Cello
In B flat major, Op. 99, D. 898 / In E flat major, Op. 100, D. 929

☐ Rubinstein (piano); Szeryng (violin); Fournier (cello) / RCA ARL2-0731

These trios are presented in ideal performances. There is a quite rare sense of equality among the three musicians, considering, especially, the virtuosity of each as a soloist in his own right. Cohesion is remarkable. Rubinstein's conception of the piano's role provides an acutely balanced relationship (pianistic overbearance in these trios just will not do). With full personality but in cognitive balanced ratio, the keyboard part supports and embellishes as it goes over, under, and between the string instruments.

There is much that can be said about the sensitive recognition of structural totality these participants provide. In the Opus 99, for example, the slow movement (designed in the simplicity of an A–B–A pattern) is dialogued beautifully, which keeps the slow pace moving; the Scherzo is restrained, its dynamics held carefully in check, which defines its difference from the sharper Beethovian contour of this musical serio-jest. Beyond these and other inner details is the important differentiation the performers make between the two works, displaying the settled character of the B flat major opus in contrast to the more adventurous E flat major companion.

Trio No. 1 in B flat major for Violin, Viola, and Cello, D. 471

☐ Silverstein (violin); Fine (viola); Eskin (cello) / RCA LSC-6184

A one-movement piece in Schubert's lighter vein, but aesthetic relaxation does not eliminate expertness. (Schubert was just nineteen when he wrote this string trio, which he matched with another the following year.) It is music that deserves serious attention, especially is this supremely beautiful conception by members of the Boston Symphony Chamber Players.

Trio No. 2 in B flat major for Violin, Viola, and Cello, D. 581

☐ Grumiaux Trio / Philips 802905

Refinement, full attention to detail, excellent pace, and avoidance of sentimentality result in a significant edition of this string trio. The minuet is Viennese with swings on third beats, and the Grumiaux–Janzer–Czako team are considerably more alert to its style than the Heifetz–Primrose–Piatigorsky (on RCA LSC-2563). Only in the contrastive trio of this movement, where the viola is soloistic, is the RCA edition better. This is due to Primrose's greater warmth and more supple tone than Janzer displays. The finale by the Grumiaux Trio is properly dancelike in its rondo format; that by the H–P–P team is closer to a *presto* than it is to the marked *allegretto* tempo. The latter performers race through the measures as though fearing they'll miss catching the final double bar. The time check gives clear facts. The Grumiaux three cover the movement in 5:51, the Heifetz-led trio bring it home in 4:11! Such scamper spoils Schubert.

Adagio and *Rondo concertante* in F major for Piano, Violin, Viola, and Cello, D. 487

☐ List (piano) / Glenn (violin); Tursi (viola); Harris (cello) / Vox SVBX-600

The piano is in the limelight (and Eugene List both keyboard-vocalizes and colors his part to great effect), the strings acting as shelters that support the main voice. In chamber-music terms Schubert's opus is rather like a very early Haydn string quartet, the piano equaling the ultra-important first violin, the other instruments equaling the subsidiary second violin, viola, and cello.

There is enough material in the work to stock several compositions; Schubert's melodic largesse hospitably present—almost ten different themes are used and then recapitulated with some key changes. The strings never state a principal idea; they merely support and weave around the piano. The solo-accompaniment distinction is very evident in Schubert's mind by his use of solo and tutti indications in the score. The music's being a cross between chamber music and a miniature concerto makes acceptable a different reading by Lamar Crowson and members of the Melos Ensemble in which a double bass is added as support to the cello (Angel S-36441). However, the original setting on the Vox label is fine in all respects and need not be given second-place rating.

Quartet in G major for Guitar, Flute, Viola, and Cello, D. 96

☐ Walker (guitar); Hechtl (flute); Geise (viola); Tachezi (cello) / Turnabout 34171

Schubert's work only in the sense that he added a cello part to an already existing trio by one Matiegka; he also attached a trio to one of the movements. Perhaps, then, it is correct to surmise that additional portions or touches, at the very least, were inserted by Schubert as well.

The form is of the divertimento type, consisting of five movements. The final part is a theme and variations on a song, *Ständchen: "Mädchen, o schlumm're noch nicht"* ("Serenade: 'Maiden, Slumber Not Yet'"). This portion adds to the participation quotient, since the song was composed by Friedrich Fleischmann (1766–1798). This incongruously mixed quartet had still a fourth person concerned in its "creation." Since the variations were not complete, they were finished (in 1926) by the German musicologist Georg Kinsky, who arranged the work's publication.

Despite the fullness of the scoring, the performance is well balanced. The texture is kept clear, and all the relationships are maintained with care.

Turnabout has also released Schubert's quartet in a five-record compilation (with music by seventeen other composers) on 34195/9.

Quartettsatz in C minor, D. 103
String Quartet

No. 1 in B flat major, D. 18 / No. 2 in C major, D. 32 / No. 3 in B flat major, D. 36 / No. 4 in C major, D. 46 / No. 5 in B flat major, D. 68 / No. 6 in D major, D. 74 / No. 7 in D major, D. 94 / No. 8 in B flat major, Op. 168, D. 112 / No. 9 in G minor, D. 173 / No. 10 in E flat major, Op. 125, No. 1, D. 87 / No. 11 in E major, Op. 125, No. 2, D. 353 / No. 12 (*Quartettsatz*) in C minor, D. 703 / No. 13 in A minor, Op. 29, D. 804 / No. 14 (*Death and the Maiden*) in D minor, D. 810 / No. 15 in G major, Op. 161, D. 887

☐ Melos Quartet / Deutsche Grammophon 2740123

Sheer bulk coverage makes this jumbo release (seven discs) an absolute must. The only duplication of this effort minus the D. 103 *Quartettsatz* was the very old Vox Box three-volume release, originally Nos. 4, 5, and 6, when the Endres Quartet offered the Schubert Quartets in totality. (These were later renumbered as SVBX-5004/6 and still later deleted.)

We all know the gorgeous A minor, the huge *Death and the Maiden,* and the symphonic sweep of the G major, but there's plenty of tempting music before these great examples. Already in the first quartet the instruments are muted in the minuet—a romantic attempt at color. Interchangeability of mode—a distinguishing mark of late Schubert—appears in the earlier quartets; there is a strong example of this in the G minor opus. While all four movements of Op. 125, No. 1, D. 87 are in the same key, the music does not fall flat on its tonally tedious face. The Scherzo in this Quartet is violent but happy. For trio purposes, a Musette drones along. Harmonic differences, which are the blood in the body of the romantic school's emotional expression, pervade every artery of the E major Quartet. And there is more.

As in any integral set one cannot expect perfection, certainly not given fourteen sides of recorded music. There are points that bring disagreement, and there are places that raise heavy questions. But the batting average is exceedingly high, and this set is worth all it costs.

The first three of the numbered Quartets can be obtained as a single disc, on Deutsche Grammophon 2530322. The *Death and the Maiden* and the D. 703 *Quartettsatz* are available on Deutsche Grammophon 2530533.

String Quartet
No. 9 in G minor, D. 173 / No. 13 in A minor, Op. 29, D. 804

☐ Alban Berg Quartet / Telefunken 641882

Aside from the *Death and the Maiden* opus these are the only two full-scaled works in minor keys within Schubert's string-quartet output. The Opus 29, D. 804, represents the only Quartet by Schubert published while he was alive. All the other Quartets had to await posthumous publication—a sad commentary on the ways of publishers and musical civilization as a whole.

These performances are exciting because of their plasticity and unmelted buttery quality; the tonal delicacy is extremely beautiful. There are minor faults to be found, and there are editions that offer strong competition, but one can derive permanent satisfaction from these performances.

The playing of the slow movement in the A minor opus is pure-spun song; the pace in the *Minuet* is perfect for this is triple-beat music that is cloudy rather than sunny. The finale is portrayed with a Viennese twist that shows keen Schubertian intelligence. The same perceptivity is proven in the G minor opus: the *Minuet* is controlled and not played like a scherzo (a mistake some quartet teams make because of the music's intervallic widths) and the subtle coloration given the interlacement of the major and minor mode in the slow movement is depicted with superb subtlety.

String Quartet No. 14 (*Death and the Maiden*) in D minor, D. 810

☐ Cleveland Quartet / RCA ARL1-0483

The Clevelanders pace and phrase this masterpiece in masterly fashion. The gnashing and biting dramatic processes of the work are vividly pictured and the contrastive lyrical beauty is depicted without sentimentality. The attention to detail is of direct perception.

In the scherzo the cross accents are shot through the texture, in the final Presto there is no surcease from the driving duple pulse to mark cadential points. This is absolutely irresistible Schubert quartet playing in twentieth-century style.

String Quartet No. 15 in G major, Op. 161, D. 887

☐ Amadeus Quartet / Deutsche Grammophon 139103

The G major Quartet is a four-instrument symphonic essay of varied moods, exploiting all that Schubert had probed previously in his string-quartet compositions. It is singularly sad to realize that there is no record of a performance of the work during Schubert's lifetime. Moreover, when it was first offered for publication to the famous house of Schott, it was refused, together with the *Death and the Maiden* Quartet.

The performance by the Amadeus Quartet has fine pliancy and keen rhythmic security. Schubert's G major Quartet demands a good percentage of robustness and this edition has it. In comparison with the performance by the Melos Quartet (*see above*), the Amadeus team provides a shade more of vitality and sharper dynamic differences.

Piano Quintet in A major, Op. 114, D. 667

☐ Rudolf Serkin (piano); Laredo (violin); Naegele (viola); Parnas (cello); Levine (double bass) / Columbia MS-7067
☐ Peter Serkin (piano); Schneider (violin); Tree (viola); Soyer (cello); Levine (double bass) / Vanguard 71145
☐ Members of the Vienna Octet / Curzon (piano) / London 6090

This quintet is nicknamed *The Trout,* since the fourth movement employs a set of variations on Schubert's own song *Die Forelle* ("The Trout"). (Some chamber-music fans use the cognomen "the *Forellen*.") The beauties and great art of this quintet have made it a favorite in the recording field, and a real aural fishing expedition is demanded to choose among the great number of releases available. The catalogue is well stocked indeed.

Warmth and a freed, open-airiness mark the statement by the group that includes the elder Serkin. It is totally articulative, disciplined but not a scholastic survey. Above all, in this group's carrying forward of the quintal lines a poetic personality is dominant.

There is more dynamism in the performance by the group that includes the younger Serkin. Sometimes this lessens the lyrical feeling by substituting sound sparkle, but this does not harm the score and is simply another viable approach to Schubert's masterpiece. In this realization, the slight roughness that pops up in a few places is less sparkle and more headiness being given its head, and that's all to the good.

The Curzon–Vienna Octet reading is somewhere between these two performances. "Suave" is the descriptive word. There is never any push and shove in this group's warm blend of Schubertian charm and naturalism.

In all these presentations the bass is no mere appendage supporting the lower voices. While it is responsible for this function, it is heard in all three groups as a true bass, the cello being balanced properly as tenor to the viola's alto. Additionally, high quality is shown by Julius Levine (on Columbia and Vanguard) and Johann Krump (on London) in contributing excellent color to the totality.

Quintet in C major, Op. 163, D. 956

☐ Melos Quartet / Rostropovich (cello) / Deutsche Grammophon 2530980

This string quintet was Schubert's swan song. If only every composer's last creative year could bring such a masterpiece! In strength, intensity, beauty, form, workmanship, themes, and over-all scope, this remarkable work constitutes a veritable anthology of magnificent string-instrument compositions with the great Schubert string quartets: Op. 29, D. 804 in A minor; D. 810 the *Death and the Maiden;* and the huge G major, Op. 161, D. 887. The composition has the pathos and tortured quietness of the A minor Quartet, combined with the vigor and huge-scale canvas of the D minor (*Death and the Maiden*), and adds further the full romantic glow that sweeps through the G major Quartet. Yet it is not in any sense an eclectic gathering of what Schubert had written previously in chamber music. It is more Schubert's hymn of synthesis, his most perfect contribution to chamber music. There is not a flaw in this jewel; there is perfect beauty.

This recorded statement is very choice. No other performance matches the magnificent manner in which the introductory measures to the initial movement's second subject (the more important one) are played here. Once they are heard, one can never forget the experience, compressed as it may be. The slow movement is played with an intense nobility that is heart-rending. Throughout, the performance has affection and gentleness contrasted to the deepest expressivity and rhythmic cogency. "Highly recommended" doesn't say enough for such masterful playing of Schubert's supremely masterful creation.

Octet in F major for Strings and Winds, Op. 166, D. 803

☐ Melos Ensemble / Angel S-36529

The calmness (an alive refinement) of the Melos rendition does not negate the full-blown scale of the outer Allegro divisions. There is affection in this performance and a nurturing of split-hair intonation (the latter isn't present, for example, in the RCA ARL1-1047 edition, specifically in the early part of the fourth-movement variations). Above all, the quality of the phrasing and the lyrical beauty within finely chosen tempi make this version a choice one.

Vocal

Voice with Accompaniment

An der Mond (1st version)	*Nähe des Geliebten,*
An der Mond (2nd version),	Op. 5, No. 2
Op. 57, No. 3	*Rastlose Liebe,* Op. 5,
Der Fischer, Op. 5, No. 3	No. 1, D. 138
Der Sänger, Op. 117	*Schäfers Klagelied,* Op. 3,
Erlkönig, Op. 1	No. 1, D. 121
Heidenröslein, Op. 3, No. 3, D. 257	Three *Gesäng des Harfners,* Op. 12
Meeres Stille, Op. 3, No. 2	*Wanderers Nachtlied,*
Nachtgesang	Op. 4, No. 3

☐ Fischer-Dieskau (baritone); Moore (piano) / Deutsche Grammophon 2530229

A program of songs all set to texts by Goethe. (For two more selected programs of the Schubert-Goethe combination, *see below.*) This is a totally brilliant recital. The achievement of these artists is beyond question.

An mein Herz, D. 860

Blondel zu Marien, D. 626

Der Musensohn, Op. 92, No. 1, D. 764

Ganymed, Op. 19, No. 3, D. 544

Heidenröslein, Op. 3, No. 3, D. 257

Lied der Mignon, Op. 62, No. 4, D. 877

Rastlose Liebe, **Op. 5, No. 1, D. 138**

Schäfers Klagelied, **Op. 3, No. 1, D. 121**

Sprache der Liebe, **Op. 115, No. 3, D. 412**

☐ DeGaetani (mezzo-soprano); Kalish (piano) / Nonesuch 71320

A look at *Schwann* confirms the huge number of recordings presenting choices from the more than 600 songs Schubert produced (the largest number of these written within a four-year period). This recording is one of the great ones. A reminder of Jan DeGaetani's reputation in the field of contemporary music is not necessary. What is vividly proven here is that her performance abilities are not limited to present-day music. Schubert has never been served better vocally, particularly in matters of tonal shading, tempi, interpretative consideration, and diction. No less enthusiasm applies to the playing of Gilbert Kalish—it is of unimpeachable understanding. This is a totally outstanding recording. One prophesies that in the years ahead it will become a classic.

Der Hirt auf dem Felsen, **D. 965**

☐ Valente (soprano); Rudolf Serkin (piano); Wright (clarinet) / Columbia MS-6236

"The Shepherd on the Rock" has been described as music of "magical innocence." Its adducent qualities are presented in a masterful performance by these three artists.

Der Sänger, **Op. 117**

Erlkönig, **Op. 1**

Ganymed, **Op. 19, No. 3, D. 544**

Three *Gesäng des Harfners*, **Op. 12**

☐ Prey (baritone); Engel (piano) / Philips 6500515

Prey's artistry is impeccable in these six songs composed to Goethe texts. His vocal control is likewise. Every measure in these songs is done with a taste and a finish that reveal the great Schubert and likewise the artistry of an instinctive and magnificently trained vocalist (that should read "vocalist musician").

Die Liebende schreibt, **Op. 165, No. 1**

Four *Mignon Lieder*, **Op. 62**

Heidenröslein, **Op. 3, No. 3, D. 257**

Liebhaber in allen Gestalten, **D. 558**

Nähe des Geliebten, **Op. 5, No. 2**

☐ Ameling (soprano); Baldwin (piano) / Philips 6500515

A rich collection of songs on texts by Goethe, superbly stated by this fine soprano.

Die schöne Müllerin, **Op. 25, D. 795**

☐ Fischer-Dieskau (baritone); Moore (piano) / Deutsche Grammophon 2530544
☐ Wunderlich (tenor); Stolze (piano) / Nonesuch 71211 (monaural)

Tucked away in my memory are some words of a Schubert song that appeared in a tribute to a deceased musician: "Thou lovely art, for this I thank thee." And these words exactly describe my emotive reaction to the performance of Schubert's cycle by the superb Fischer-Dieskau and the just as superb pianist Gerald Moore. Here is a detailing of what is meant by interpretative truth partnered by beautiful vocal projection. There is exemplary enunciation, supersensitive feeling for the details in the notes, and unforced naturalness.

The Nonesuch release (listed as a monaural disc as are all recordings in this survey that are "electronically re-channeled for stereo") is a remastering of an old Eurodisc set (it covered three sides, with the fourth left blank!), issued in 1967. It is compressed without harm on two sides and has satisfactory sonics.

Wunderlich's voice is splendidly focused and warm, and his artistry is exemplary. For example, direct emphasis but minus any undue force covers *Der Jäger*, controlled passionate delivery is heard in *Ungeduld*, and a bright compelling delivery marks such songs as *Wohin?* and *Mein*. There are certain subtleties that are missing, in comparison with Fischer-Dieskau's performance, but Wunderlich's voice is a beauty, and those who prefer a tenor-ranged version of Schubert's superlative cycle will be satisfied. The piano partnership of Kurt Heinz Stolze is not in the Gerald Moore category. He has a tendency to play the notes rather than focus on their meaning in relation to the vocal line.

Die Winterreise, Op. 89, D. 911

☐ Pears (tenor); Britten (piano) / London 1261

Schubert's dark-stranded song set was conceived for a high voice, and it is in that timbre that the best realization is found. Transposition downward to accommodate a baritone range is no iffy proposition—it works well, as witness the fine performances by Hans Hotter (once available on Deutsche Grammophon 138778/79, and worth searching for, and Dietrich Fischer-Dieskau—the latter on Angel S–3640 and Deutsche Grammophon 2707028). Still, range, color, sensitivity, and subtlety are found in the optimum condition in the Pears–Britten collaboration. Important is the re-creative input on having this fine composer at the piano. There is no downgrading of the famous Gerald Moore when it is stated that, in this cycle, Benjamin Britten is even better. A thrilling duo performance all the way.

Duets

Antigone und Oedip,	*Licht und Liebe*
Op. 6, No. 2	*Mignon und der Harfner,*
Cronnan	**Op. 62, No. 1, D. 877/1**
Hektors Abschied,	*Selma und Selmar*
Op. 58, No. 1	*Singübungen*, D. 619
Hermann und Thusnelda	*Szene aus Goethe's "Faust"*

☐ Baker (mezzo-soprano); Fischer-Dieskau (baritone); Moore (piano) / Deutsche Grammophon 2530328

Not merely an all-star cast is involved in this set of vocal duets but a superb one. Most interesting is the single work in which the voices sing together (*Mignon und der Harfner*); all the others are sung in dialogue fashion.

Schwanengesang, D. 957

☐ Fischer-Dieskau (baritone); Moore (piano) / Angel S–36127

Sung with impeccable re-creative craftsmanship. These songs are both subtle and demanding. Both requirements are met in this recorded edition. There is a bit of vocal freedom in Fischer-Dieskau's delivery, but it is a freedom that operates within full comprehension of the substances of the various songs. Once again Gerald Moore is the ideal piano accompanist. Was he ever otherwise?

Part Songs

Christ ist erstanden
("*Chor der Engel*") (1816)
Der Gondelfahrer, Op. 28
Gebet, Op. 139
Gott im Ungewitter,
Op. 112, No. 1

Gott in der Natur, Op. 133
Gott meine Zuversicht
Jünglingswonne, Op. 17, No. 1
Nachthelle, Op. 134
Ständchen, Op. 135

☐ Elizabethan Singers / Cantelo (soprano); Watts (contralto); Tear (tenor); Tunnard (piano) / Halsey (conductor) / Argo ZRG–527

A set of nine sung with full charm. Totally Schubertian discourse, and no arguments as to the worth of the presentations.

Mass No. 5 in A flat major, D. 678

☐ Saint Paul Chamber Orchestra, Carleton College Choir, Chamber Singers, and Festival Chorale / Sabo (soprano); DeGaetani (mezzo-soprano); Sperry (tenor); Guinn (baritone) / Davies (conductor) / Nonesuch 71335

This is truly a dedicated performance, with superfine soloists and extremely competent orchestral playing. The attention to tempo subtleties on the part of Dennis Russell Davies has a great deal of bearing on the vivid success of this recording. For example, in the Sanctus the pace is not overly slowed because it is marked Andante. On the other hand, in the Benedictus the *andante con moto* has an ongoing pulse that intensifies the Schubertian warmth. There are other beautiful calculations. In all, a most rewarding musical experience.

Mass No. 6 in E flat major, D. 950

☐ Academy of St. Martin-in-the-Fields and St. John's College Choir, Cambridge / Palmer (soprano); Watts (alto); Bowen and Evans (tenors); Keyte (bass) / Guest (conductor) / Argo ZRG–825

This is the best of the available performances. The choir's quality is solid, and the group provides an excellent relationship between text and music. Gleaming soloism, markedly so from the soprano, Felicity Palmer. Guest's solutions have no ambiguity, and he doesn't tamper with Schubert's score by way of excisions, which have been the practice of others.

Die Zwillingsbrüder (1819)

☐ Bavarian Radio Orchestra and Chorus / Donath (soprano); Gedda (tenor); Fischer-Dieskau (baritone); Moll and Gallus (basses) / Sawallisch (conductor) / EMI-Electrola 065–28833

"The Twin Brothers" offers a good example of Schubert as an operetta composer. Fine cast. Never mind the plot, just listen to the music.

Music to *Rosamunde*, Op. 26, D. 797

☐ Philharmonia Hungarica and Philharmonia Vocal Ensemble / Sowiak (alto) / Maag (conductor) / Turnabout 34330

Some of this delicious music is familiar: the Overture and one of the two entr'actes contained in the total ten numbers. Most of it is unfamiliar. In this category are some special settings—a piece for male chorus accompanied by three horns and three trombones and a delightful segment for wind instruments. But there isn't a dull moment any place in the entire score, special scorings or not.

The music glows, and Peter Maag's way with it is ideal.

Schubert / Franz Liszt

Instrumental

Piano

Das Wandern	**Hark, Hark, the Lark**
Der Müller und der Bach	**Liebesbotschaft**

☐ Ax (piano) / RCA ARL1-1030

An excellent sampling of the many piano transcriptions Liszt made of Schubert's songs. Never really out of fashion, especially when played as here, with taste, and no disproportionate emphasis on lines that would impede flow. For Liszt's handling of Schubert's original beauties, a listener couldn't do better.

Schubert / Anton Webern

Orchestra

German Dances, D. 820

☐ Frankfurt Radio Orchestra / Webern (conductor) / Columbia M4-35193 (monaural)

Historic to the nth degree, since this is the only available recording (made in 1932) of Webern's conducting. His setting of the Schubert dances uses a fitting instrumentation of pairs of flutes, oboes, clarinets, bassoons, and horns, plus strings.

Bernard Schulé   (1909-   )

Chamber Music

Résonances pour quintet de cuivres, Op. 58

☐ Modern Brass Ensemble / Advance FGR-2 (monaural)

Formal aims are patently clear in the three movements. First an ostinato-triggered piece, followed by a jazzy-like division, and then a final passacaglia.

Schulé's "Resonances" is given a clear statement by this quintet team of two trumpets, horn, trombone, and tuba. Schulé wrote his work for this ensemble.

Erwin Schulhoff   (1894-1942)

Chamber Music

Divertissement

☐ Westwood Wind Quintet / Crystal 101

Schulhoff's music is freed of specific rules (it flavors polytonality with atonal sugar), yet its basic grotesquerie and hedonism are anything but problematic. The spirit of Czech dance is the synchronistic method that renders his work as traditional, yet with new gloss. Schulhoff's woodwind pieces are novel, daring, and completely nationalistic, yet moistened with the dewdrops of international language.

The initial release of this work is an emphatically welcome addition to the recorded catalogue. That it is superbly played is a double benefit. The Westwood ensemble especially realize the tart sophistication that frames the seven parts of the *Divertissement.*

Gunther Schuller *(1925-   )*

Contours (1956)   *Orchestra*

☐ Contemporary Chamber Ensemble / Weisberg (conductor) / Odyssey Y–34141

A five-movement piece, the movements connected by interludes. Color is the dynamic here. With Schuller there is no vernal innocence concerning what can be drawn from a group of instruments, and the performance proves his timbral virtuosity.

The recording is drawn from a live performance and is quite good—without any extraneous noises.

Conversations for Jazz Quartet and String Quartet (1959)

☐ Modern Jazz Quartet and Beaux Arts String Quartet / Schuller (conductor) / Atlantic S–1345

A vivid example of Schuller's "third stream" music. This is best defined by indicating what it is not. *Conversations* (the recording's title uses the singular form of the word) does not jazzify the strings or have long-hair elements that depersonalize the vibes, piano, percussion, and string bass of the jazz foursome. It combines both sets of instruments by drawing on their respective techniques so that they complement each other while each retains its own profile. In *Conversations* the string quartet moves in Bartókian-Webernian territories; the jazz quartet is mainly concerned with controlled improvisation.

The germane power of the piece comes from the polytimbre technique involved. This certifies the retention of both groups' sonority and style perspective, with the *combined* sound haze contributing more than would each group if heard individually. Such "third stream" style may invent little, but it discovers much.

In this recorded statement the interpretative ideal is available, since both of the quartet teams are of top quality. Atlantic's sound is another plus.

Dramatic Overture (1951)

☐ Louisville Orchestra / Whitney (conductor) / Louisville S–666

Schuller's overture is quite athletic, and because of its fantasy implications one could argue the title. But there is no arguing the bravado (well supplied by the Louisville players). One always has the feeling that everything Schuller writes is a spontaneous invention, though this doesn't mean lack of care in the composition. This overture is well tailored, even though one can question the overzealousness in reference to top pedal points. A positive production from the Louisville label.

Five Bagatelles for Orchestra

☐ Louisville Orchestra / Mester (conductor) / Louisville S–686

The vitality of serial style illustrated in pieces that each emphasize a particular element. Thus, sonorities in the first one, dynamic contrasts in the second, followed by *Klangfarbenmelodie,* rhythm, and a "summation of the previous four" situation.

This is beautifully crafted music, and it is presented in first-class fashion.

Symphony (1965)

☐ Dallas Symphony Orchestra / Johanos (conductor) / Turnabout 34412

Serialism in all of its pitch glory plus a considerable amount of *Klangfarbenmelodie* (splintering of a line among various instruments to obtain a constant change of color, thus "tone-color melody"). A special point is the classical format of the four movements, which include such designs as a six-part fugue and a four-part double canon (both in movement 2) and a Scherzo with a regulation trio in movement 3.

However, while the forms may be the protective pockets for the composition, it is the instrumental resource (of infectious virtuosity) that provides the real rewards and character of the music.

For the traditionally minded listener this is very advanced music. For the sophisticated listener it is not, but still offers freshness and discovery. The conception by the Dallas orchestra is most effective.

Transformation

☐ Brandeis Jazz Festival Ensemble / New World Records NW–216 (monaural)

Some hard-core classical tactics (twelve-tone and melodic formation by tone-color distribution) followed by some gorgeous soft-core jazz that doesn't bang its pulse into the ears. Schuller's piece is exceedingly subtle, suave, and individually formationed.

Originally recorded in 1957 for Columbia, the New World transfer hardly shows its age. The eleven-piece combo (flute, clarinet, bassoon, tenor saxophone, horn, trombone, vibraphone, drums, piano, harp, and bass) is first class.

Tre invenzioni (1972)

☐ Schuller (conductor) / Odyssey Y–34141

Inventions not concerned with the usual two- or three-voice polyphonic format identified with the form. These are free-formed conceptions of a Capriccio, a Chorale, and a Toccata. The only classic reference is the use of a harpsichord in the ensemble of twenty-five players. Nervous in textural change and in color assortment, with Schuller's usual ability to stage instrumentational surprises.

Band

Symphony for Brass and Percussion (1950)

☐ Philip Jones Brass Ensemble / Howarth (conductor) / Argo ZRG–731

Sixteen brass, timpani, and percussion constitute the forces for this forceful work. There is no fancy showmanship, but forthright pantonal music rarely found in the large-brass medium, with Schullerian scoresmanship as a colorful asset. The performance is scaled to fit the music, though with some very way-up-front recorded sound.

Solo
Instrument
and
Orchestra

Jazz Quartet

Concertino for Jazz Quartet and Orchestra

☐ Modern Jazz Quartet / Schuller (conductor) / Atlantic S–1359

A dynamic example—full scale—of "third stream" music. "Third stream" (Schuller's coinage) represents the synthesis of classical style ("first stream") and jazz procedures ("second stream"). The amalgam is exemplified in this case in a three-movement span, just under twenty minutes in length, with a Passacaglia as the central part. Splendidly performed with splendid sound to match.

Lines and Contrasts for Sixteen Horns (1960)

☐ Horn Club of Los Angeles / Schuller (conductor) / Angel S-36036

The number twelve keys the Lines. It begins with a twelve-part, twelve-tone fugue which eventually turns into a nonfugal twelve-tone structure. Thus polyphonic style is compared with and relates to homophonic texture. Fascinating sounds, these. They continue in the Contrasts, conceived for solo horn with three quintets.

The recording is sumptuous and acutely balanced.

Sonata for Oboe and Piano

☐ Roseman (oboe); Kalish (piano) / Desto 7116

Mostly atonal travel across a number of harmonic fields that relate to a pitch center. But mind you, no cut-and-dried formula regulates this serious, lyrical piece. It has turns that remind one of Hindemith and, here and there, of Schoenberg. Both are good references and hardly unexpected from a composer who was twenty-three years of age when he wrote this work.

Sensitive playing and the kind of ensemble one expects from Ronald Roseman and Gilbert Kalish.

Fantasy Quartet for Four Cellos

☐ Varga, Eskin, Rudiakov, and Hunkins (cellos) / Composers Recordings 144 (monaural)

Especially significant in Schuller's catalogue are compositions for extremely rare media, such as a *Fantasia Concertante* for 3 oboes and piano, another work with the same title for 3 trombones and piano, a quartet for horns, Five Pieces for five horns, the Concertino for Jazz Quartet and Orchestra. There are many more. The Fantasy Quartet, calling for an uncommon quartet of cellos, is one of the best of these Schuller specialties. It is serially sparked, and is in one movement divided into contrastive sections.

A virtuoso piece, this, and worth hearing if only for proof of the abilities of the foursome that recorded it.

Five Moods for Tuba Quartet

☐ New York Tuba Quartet / Crystal S-221

Early in the twentieth century a composition for four tubas would fall in the good news-bad news category—good news for tuba players, bad news for listeners, that is, if they listened. What was then written was pure schlock, commercial junk. That's past history. The days of the funny, gauche big brass instrument are gone—witness this fine, coloristic music. Density of texture is prevalent, relieved by spacing and special effects (part 3). Schuller's work has creative conviction and artistic authority, offering good news for performers and listeners. The playing is beautifully executed.

Quartet for Double Basses (1947)

☐ Hollingsworth, Spohr, Carroll, and Craver (double basses) / Turnabout 34412

Another example of Gunther Schuller's extreme fondness for odd chamber-music combinations. A quartet for bull fiddles is not to be unexpected from a composer who has written a Duo Sonata for Clarinet and Bass Clarinet, a set of *Conversations* for Jazz Quartet and String Quartet, a Fantasy Quartet for Four Cellos, Five Moods for Tuba Quartet, and so on.

To obtain a larger range of the denatured timbre weight resultant from natural harmonics, and to obtain certain chordal combines (via individual double stops), Schuller retunes each instrument in the second and third movements. The problems of conceiving a music for this unbalanced, deeply registered combination are apparent. However, Schuller surmounts them with an artistry that immediately convinces the ear. There is a natural melancholy involved with such registral passion, but the music does not remain so limited.

Excellent musicality on the part of the players is but one point. The four parts are horrendously difficult, but the technical versatility of the musicians is dramatically proven.

Music for Brass Quintet (1961)

☐ New York Brass Quintet / Composers Recordings 144 (monaural)

The Quintet inhabits the world of serialism—but also a world of intense, kaleidoscopic color. While there is the fragmentation technique found so often in serialism, in Schuller's hands this preceptive pointillism makes the two trumpets, horn, trombone, and tuba take on the costuming of a miniature orchestra. The fluid continuity of the writing is similar to a total improvisation.

There is only a single word that fits this performance: "unbelievable." Schuller has been served with thrilling results.

Woodwind Quintet (1958)

☐ Dorian Quintet / Vox SVBX–5307

Serial shapes shaped by timbre formations. Sometimes the shapes are defined by a line of continually changing colors (the Schoenbergian *Klangfarbenmelodie* procedure). Other times, in post-Webernesque manner, the process is by fragmentation—a pointillistic activity that is stimulated by acute color choices, further activized by jazz inflections.

Schuller indicates that he has "tried to create a sound spectrum" different from the overdone and "conventional" 'woodwind quintet sound'" found in the large number of wind quintets turned out by the French composers "Milhaud, Ibert, and others." He has tried and he has succeeded. There are rich returns to be obtained from this piece.

An odd bit of labeling on the disc. The movements are. indicated as (1) Lento, (2) "Without title," and (3) Agitato. Production knoweth not what the music showeth. The program-note booklet lists the second movement with title, the title being properly indicated as Moderato.

Schuller / *Louis Moreau Gottschalk.* See *Gottschalk* / Schuller.

William Schuman (1910-)

Orchestra ### American Festival Overture (1939)

☐ Vienna Symphony Orchestra / Hendl (conductor) / Desto 6404E (monaural)

Schuman's Overture is joyful and harmonically related to the music of Roy Harris, but the smart jazzy tone of the piece is Schuman's own. The central fugue is a formal fingerprint to be found in most of Schuman's later music.

The performance is only fair; the recording was made from a quite old American Recording Society release via "bisonic stereo," meaning it was electronically reprocessed from monaural tapes. Because no other recording is available, if you want this Schuman piece you will be captive to the Desto edition, warts and all. An updated recording by a major orchestra is long overdue.

Credendum (Article of Faith) (1955)

☐ Philadelphia Orchestra / Ormandy (conductor) / Composers Recordings S-308 (monaural)

This *Article of Faith* was written in 1955, in response to an unusual commission, received through the United States Department of State for UNESCO. Sensing the importance of his commission, Schuman produced a composition of which he can well be proud. He did not sacrifice his personal style in the interests of popularization.

Credendum divides into three parts, played without pause: a *Declaration,* then a Chorale, and a Finale. The moods of these range widely, but have reciprocal balance. Schuman's music is both declamatory and serene, colored by grandeur and huge sonorities. The orchestra is far from normal, including four flutes, six horns, two tubas, and a large percussion section. *Credendum* has a tearing quality which suits the militant material set forth by the composer. In its way this is program music, but there is no line-by-line evidence of this, and no text is necessary for understanding it.

The Ormandy recording is magnificent, eloquently and brilliantly played. This is a case where composer, orchestra, and conductor are in full agreement. "Integrity" is the word that describes everything.

The recording was originally released by Columbia (ML-5185), then deleted from its catalogue; the transfer to CRI is welcome. The disc has been noted as "monaural," as always in this survey where a mono recording has been electronically reprocessed for stereo. No problem—the sound is excellent and the transfer has been well accomplished.

In Praise of Shahn

☐ New York Philharmonic / Bernstein (conductor) / Columbia M-30112

Duo dynamics provide definition and contrast in Schuman's piece, subtitled *Canticle for Orchestra.* Brilliant orchestral demarcation opens the work, which then moves into just as fervent a lyricism; the music then turns into propulsiveness again. Intensity has always marked William Schuman's style, and that emotive element is evident again in this work. Bernstein conveys all these particular qualities in his performance.

New England Triptych (Three Pieces for Orchestra After William Billings) (1956)

☐ Philadelphia Orchestra / Ormandy (conductor) / RCA LSC-3060

Schuman's kinship with Billings *seems* to extend only to the latter's melodies, yet paradoxically it actually goes further. He retains Billings's style by synchronizing present-day techniques with the traditional past. It is as if Billings were alive and composing music, having had Schuman's training and experience.

Ormandy avoids the brassy-band concept too often imposed on Schuman's piece, especially in the concluding *Chester* movement (see also under *Band*). The center movement is the high point of the work, though—there the listener will obtain his greatest reward. The Philadelphians' solo oboe and bassoon are absolutely magnificent in this pleading and sensitive movement.

Prayer in Time of War (1943)

☐ Louisville Orchestra / Mester (conductor) / Louisville S-721

The expressive range has a trinal division: somber and martial and again somber. Schuman's piece (first titled "Prayer–1943") is given one of Louisville's best performances under its present conductor, Jorge Mester.

Symphony No. 3 (1941)

☐ New York Philharmonic / Bernstein (conductor) / Columbia MS-7442

Individuality of formal patterns, the flow of contrasting currents, and truly exciting orchestration mark this work, given the New York Music Critics' Circle Award in 1942. Contiguity of design is joined with properly forceful disassociation as a Passacaglia preludes a Fugue, and a Chorale flows into a stirring Toccata.

All the structural components are highly colored by orchestral virtuosity. In this symphonic essay one observes an orchestrational extrovert working with sound: an English horn is given fast, not rural-somnolent music to play; trumpets perform like acrobats; the timpani has solo lines; themes are exposed in their skeletal form, rhythmically outlined by a snare drum, melodically by a bass clarinet; on top of all this, the brass form a band within an orchestra. These instrumental colors are cool or hot, but always clean, correctly chosen for the composition.

Bernstein's orchestra plays impressively; the power of the work is felt and fully expressed. Vibrant sound is a plus for Schuman's singular Symphony.

Symphony No. 4 (1942)

☐ Louisville Orchestra / Mester (conductor) / Louisville S-692

Using variational development devices, Schuman's fourth symphony is a music of strength, dimensioned also by sharp rhythmic inserts. Its constant change avoids the danger of sectionalism, and as usual, Schuman's trump card is his brilliant, virtuosic orchestration. It is dealt early in the work, but in fact he has more than one trump, and altogether these add a dramatic inlay and overlay to what is already dramatic in content.

This is music for top orchestral organizations. It is pleasurable to report that the Louisvillians do well with Schuman's score. The reproduction is excellent.

Symphony No. 6 (in One Movement) (1949)

☐ Philadelphia Orchestra / Ormandy (conductor) / Columbia Special Products AML-4992

This Symphony does not whistle its tunes; Schuman is not a composer of whimsy. It has the craftsmanship of the expert and partakes of Schuman's compositional penchant for writing polyphonically, but with the interwoven voices just short of full contrapuntalism. This produces a liveliness of rhythm not common to many of the composers who emphasize linear detail in their works.

The superb playing of the Philadelphians means the long lines are sung with full-throatedness, the colors magnificently outlined, and the meaningful excitement made explicit. All the subtle points are made clear for the ear. "Impressive" is the word.

Symphony No. 7 (1960)

☐ Utah Symphony Orchestra / Abravanel (conductor) / Turnabout 34447

Orchestrational know-how is not a rarity among the important twentieth-century composers, so it takes something of an individualist to make a special mark. Credit William Schuman with that. In Schuman's Symphony hard-shelled block scoring is paramount. It is of rhythmically triggered content. But there are other points: the featuring of the clarinet and bass clarinet in movement 1, the elimination of all but the strings in the slow movement, with much of the detail in the movement divided into seven- and eight-part writing.

This is red-blooded music, with no caution regarding virtuosity. It again is a contrary proof to those who claim that the symphony as a form is dead, and to others who state that while the design is still alive, Americans haven't contributed very much. Time hasn't run out for the symphony, and the contributions by American composers have been consistently profitable, which includes this superb Schuman opus.

Plenty of zing in the playing of the Utah organization. Plenty of tastefully direct ensemble work. The Utah Symphony may not be one of the "big seven" orchestras in the United States, but it comes mighty close. Credit it with a top score.

Symphony No. 8 (1962)

☐ New York Philharmonic / Bernstein (conductor) / Odyssey Y-34140

The still-current ploy of the far-out set to overrun the concert stage with gimmicks, glossy glees full of sonic gymnastics, and haphazard doin's has turned our attention away, all too often unfortunately, from the art of such men as William Schuman, Aaron Copland, Irving Fine, and others of solid background and intellect.

Schuman's Symphony is a strong reminder that music with traditional roots, power, fluid drive, and rhythmic incitation remains fresh. His "Eighth" is one of his very best. It challenges the listener immediately with a dark bell sonority, and is tied into the ictus quality of tintinnabulation through its repercussive harmonies and voice movement. The music is somber though not muzzled. It creates its web of control through a careful apportionment of temporal speed, retaining *lento* and *largo* tempi through the first two movements and climaxing into a *presto-prestissimo* in the final section. However, the insistence on breadth of speed does not imply heavy-handedness; the pulse is as full of variation as are the voice leadings. In a sense the textures that are woven through the Symphony's width and span have a baroque-like strength. And Schuman can score like blazes. The colors of this work dazzle in the midst of the seriousness. They are chosen from a large palette that includes a very large woodwind section, fifteen brass, percussion, a pair of harps, and piano, plus the usual strings. This is music of high rank.

Bernstein premiered the work (it was commissioned by the New York Philharmonic to celebrate the opening of New York City's Lincoln Center in the season of 1961-1962) on October 4, 1962. Bernstein then recorded the composition and it was initially issued on Columbia MS-6512 (a monaural version was obtainable on ML-5912). Deletion later followed. It's good to have this magnificent work back in the recorded catalogue.

Symphony No. 9 (*The Ardeatine Caves*) (1968)

☐ Philadelphia Orchestra / Ormandy (conductor) / RCA LSC-3212

A profound and impassioned work, powerfully and eloquently performed by Ormandy and the Philadelphians, who gave the premiere on January 10, 1969.

Schuman's Symphony, with its subtitle *Le Fosse ardeatine*, was created after his visit to the Ardeatine Caves in Rome, the location of a Nazi atrocity that resulted in the shooting and then bombing of 335 Italian Christians and Jews. If one knows of this primary stimulus, one need not refer to Schuman's detailed notes to understand the dramatic plotting that drives the Symphony from its *Anteludium* to its *Offertorium* on to its concluding *Postludium*. It is a narrative that needs no explanation. This work presents Schuman involved in his most focused creative discovery. It again proves that to speak of "the demise of the American symphony" is sheer nonsense. And it again illustrates that resultant spontaneity is the mark of the superb craftsman—in which select category William Schuman must be included.

String Orchestra

Symphony for Strings in Three Movements (Symphony No. 5) (1943)

☐ New York Philharmonic / Bernstein (conductor) / Columbia MS-7442

Invigorating rhythmic life is predominant; still this is no musical vehicle in which contrapuntal drive is achieved quite often at the expense of musical justification. To a certain degree Schuman's string piece is a study in textures, with polyphony and muted sonorities marking the meditative middle movement, plus the pigmentation of plucked sounds as an important factor in the final part. The writing is a tour de force. Schuman utilizes old forms, holding them up, however, to the newest lighting scheme.

The Columbia release is intense, dramatic, tightly drawn. No argument that every note is defined and definitive.

Band

Chester (Overture for Band) (1956)

☐ Cornell University Symphonic Band / Stith (conductor) / Cornell University 10

Among the important serious American composers, Schuman has been one of the few partial to writing band music, this overture being the third work he has conceived in the medium. *Chester* has all the needed thematic characteristics fitting for its special sonority setting. The Billings theme on which it is based also served Schuman in the third part of his orchestral work, the *New England Triptych* (see under *Orchestra*).

Solo Instrument and Orchestra

Cello

A Song of Orpheus (Fantasy for Cello and Orchestra) (1961)

☐ Cleveland Orchestra / Rose (cello) / Szell (conductor) / Columbia MS-6638

Schuman has rarely been as poetic as he is in this work, freely developed from a theme based on a song he had written for a production of *Henry VIII*. Even when midway the cello heatedly declaims and the temperature mounts, the solo voice always remains refined within its dynamic personality. The scope of the music has extraordinary originality because it is free and paradoxically cohesive in its declarative patterns.

Rose's unique ability to sing not only in the average range of the cello but even in its extreme sopranino register is magnificently exemplified. The beauty of Schuman's piece is matched by Rose's playing.

Violin

Violin Concerto (1947)

☐ Boston Symphony Orchestra / Zukofsky (violin) / Thomas (conductor) / Deutsche Grammophon 2530103

Schuman's discourse compares lyrical introspection with brilliant virtuosity in his large two-movement Concerto (each movement divisioned into a variety of tempi). The brilliance of the violin writing (which Zukofsky conquers with ease) is matched by the orchestration. And this is paralleled by the magnificent playing of the B.S.O.

Voyage (1953)

☐ Webster (piano) / Columbia Special Products CML–4987 (monaural)

This cycle of five pieces acquired its main title and subtitles after the fact—they were added by the composer after he had seen his work set to a dance by Martha Graham. Unconscious though they may be with him, dark emotional contours surround Schuman's score.

The music is of such proportions that one wishes it had been recorded in its choreographic chamber-orchestra version. Webster does all he can with the set, but it seems a half-way measure; the keyboard instrument sounds confined.

String Quartet No. 3 (1939)

☐ Kohon Quartet / Vos SVBX–5305

The inevitable Schuman fugue comes early in this work, but it is no more of Bach style than a late-Beethoven-quartet finale is comparable to one by Haydn. Schuman's fugue is formed of several fugues, of separate and combined fugal sections, of a rhythmic life that is rarely to be seen in average fugal daylight. All this is preceded by a long-spun introduction. The conclusion is also a departure from academic contrapuntal forms, inasmuch as it makes a final decision with nonpolyphonic sonorities and classifications.

The Intermezzo is far from the breezy serenade generally associated with such a title. And formal freshness covers the final part of the work. In the majority of cases, rondo form is disposed homophonically, with the return of themes, principal and otherwise, not too disguised, so that the fundamental basis of the design will be clearly apparent. Here, the opening theme returns more than a half-dozen times, but is varied, changed, shifted, and cleaned. Within this final movement there is perfection of structure, a spirit of rhythm, and (could it be otherwise?) a wealth of counterpoint. These factors constitute live, important contemporary music.

The music is served handsomely by the Kohon foursome. Dynamic situations are realized wisely; the verve and precision needed are fully supplied.

Carols of Death

☐ Gregg Smith Singers / Smith (conductor) / Everest 3129

Whitman texts set to strong Schuman music, the harmonic plans magnificently setting forth the word meanings. Just as strong a performance by this great group of vocalists.

Four Canonic Choruses for Mixed Voices (1933): Nos. 1, 2, and 4

☐ Concordia Choir / Christiansen (conductor) / Concordia S–1

Schuman's first published serious composition, which he had finished at the age of twenty-three. Many a composer has been undone by attraction to canon, but its strictures did not bother this chap. These choruses stand up to the fullest scrutiny, and one can prophesy they will not wither with age.

Since Concordia has released the work minus any notes, but merely with the texts, it is worth indicating that the original title was "Choral Canons." Further, Concordia has titled the work to match the total choruses recorded, putting "Three Canonic Choruses" on the record label and jacket, which is essentially incorrect. Those performed are *Epitaph*, to lines by Edna St. Vincent Millay, *Epitaph for Joseph Conrad*, with text by Countee Cullen, and *Come Not*, with words by Tennyson. The unrecorded third piece in the group is *Night Stuff*, with Carl Sandburg as the source for the text.

Prelude for Voices (1939)

☐ Concordia Choir / Bergh (soprano) / Christiansen (conductor) / Concordia CDLP-6 (monaural)

The expressive dignity that pervades the Prelude is fitting to the text, consisting of words from Thomas Wolfe's *Look Homeward Angel*. But there is also, as always in this composer's music, an inner strength. Not a single loose end in Schuman's work here, well projected in a communicative performance.

Ballet

Judith, Choreographic Poem for Orchestra (1949)

☐ Louisville Orchestra / Whitney (conductor) / Louisville 604 (monaural)

Judith was commissioned by the Louisville Orchestra for Martha Graham, and was first performed on January 4, 1950, with Graham as choreographer and soloist. However, its narrative is so vivid that it can stand alone, played on the orchestral stage minus dancer. A clear stylistic structure is displayed, and without knowing the composer it can be identified as the work of William Schuman. It is that recognition of individual style that sets aside the few composers from the many, that makes possible immediate confirmation that the music is by, say, Brahms, or Debussy, or Bartók, or Copland, or Schuman. It is represented here from the opening polychordal setting right through to the radiant C major close. It is heard in the block scoring, the peripatetic timpanic figures and thrusts, the long-lined string-instrument statements, the exposed nerve-ends of rhythmic counterpoint in the brass. All these are Schuman, and all of these power and carry the music of his *Judith* forward.

It is a score that has its special rarified tensions and demands acute musicianship as well as maximum technical ability. The Louisville Orchestra does quite well, though a larger string body granting more depth would be even better. The major-league organizations should give some attention to Schuman's great musical script.

Schuman / *Charles Ives.* *See Ives /* Schuman.

Clara Schumann   *(1819-1896)*

Solo Instrument and Orchestra

Piano

Concerto in A minor for Piano and Orchestra, Op. 7

☐ Berlin Symphony Orchestra / Ponti (piano) / Schmidt-Gertenbach (conductor) / Candide 31038

More a work to satisfy curiosity than to offer important musical substance. However, so little of Clara Schumann's music is known that every bit that is recorded is worth considering. The Concerto calls for a classic orchestra of double winds, horns, and trumpets, plus a bass trombone, timpani, and the usual strings. It is dedicated to Spohr.

Instrumental

Piano

Four Fugitive Pieces, Op. 15

☐ Ponti (piano) / Candide 31038

The virtue is the romantic intimacy of the contents. Such virtue is reinforced by Ponti's assured artistry.

Mazurka in G major, Op. 6

☐ Sykes (piano) / Orion 75182

The Mazurka in G major is from a collection titled *Soirées musicales: Ten pièces caractéristiques* which comprises Opus 5 and Opus 6. The Mazurka is the penultimate piece in the half-dozen forming the Opus 6 part of the total.

Clara Schumann's dance piece is a rather restrained item. Sykes colors it nicely and effectively.

Praeludium and Fugue in G minor, Op. 16, No. 1

☐ von Saalfeld (piano) / Musical Heritage Society MHS-1339

The first of a set of three. For those interested in the statistics, No. 2 is in B flat major, and the third one is in D minor.

Good Robert (Clara) Schumann writing in the Andante preliminary; the fugue is in three voices and shows more than an average talent for contrapuntal invention.

Scherzo

No. 1 in D minor, Op. 10 / No. 2 in C minor, Op. 14

☐ Ponti (piano) / Candide 31038

Strong examples of C. Schumann's work, even though showing plenty of influence fror R. Schumann's work. The C minor piece is especially topflight. Ponti plays in a stimulating manner.

Souvenir of Vienna—Impromptu for the Piano, Op. 9

☐ von Saalfeld (piano) / Musical Heritage Society MHS-1339

The souvenir in the *Souvenir of Vienna* consists of a set of variations on the Austrian national hymn *Gott erhalte Franz den Kaiser* ("God Save Our Emperor") woven into the total fabric. Thus Clara Schumann links hands with Joseph Haydn, who did the same thing (straightforward variants, however, minus any interweave) in his C major String Quartet, Op. 76, No. 3.

Neatly executed by Mme. Schumann, and also by Monica von Saalfeld.

Three Romances, Op. 21—(Nos. 2 and 3)

☐ Sykes (piano) / Orion 75182

For full evidence of Clara Schumann's creative abilities one need only listen to the strong ideas presented in the first of the two Romances that Sykes performs. (Its alternate title is Andante and Allegro.) The inner pulse of this music, fully indicating that Robert Schumann is not too distant from the scene, is sufficient confirmation. No less value applies to the somewhat nostalgic imagery of the third Romance.

Sykes's devotion to Clara Schumann's music is evident in his stylish playing.

Variations on a Theme by Robert Schumann, Op. 20

☐ Ponti (piano) / Candide 31038

The subject is from Robert Schumann's *Bunte Blätter*, Opus 99. Thematic adherence is very clear in all the variants. Ponti's fine playing convincingly details the structural definition of the work.

Chamber Music

Piano Trio in G minor, Op. 17

☐ Beaux Arts Trio / Philips 6700051

Respectably crafted in its four movements. Even if the composer's name were withheld, the reaction would be that the music was Schumannesque. One writer has professed to recognize Haydn in the writing, but one denies this totally. Some Mendelssohn, surely, and Schumann positively, but *not* Haydn.

The fine portrayal of the score (the fugato and other polyphony in the finale are especially engaging) makes it easy for a listener to warm to Clara Schumann's trio. Unfailingly attractive tonal quality throughout.

Robert Schumann   *(1810-1856)*

Orchestra

Manfred Overture, Op. 115

☐ New Philharmonia Orchestra / Klemperer (conductor) / Angel S–36353

Well-preserved tension, fine character, and, above all, tempi that are chosen well.

Overture, Scherzo, and Finale, Op. 52

☐ New Philharmonia Orchestra / Inbal (conductor) / Philips 6500288

This is not everyone's favorite Schumann piece, and it is not often played in our concert halls. There's a place for it there, though, as witness the fair amount of recorded attention given the piece. Inbal does handsomely with the music, providing a fine kick to the rhythmic data and applying strength to the lyrical portions without negating their warmth. The polyphonic spurts in the Finale are integrated beautifully and without being thrust out of context—an error that occurs in all the other editions on disc.

Overture to *Julius Caesar*, Op. 128

☐ Vienna Philharmonic Orchestra / Solti (conductor) / London 2310

No one will deny that this is not one of Schumann's notable achievements. However, as a minor piece it has a sufficient number of major qualities within it to deserve exposure from time to time. Solti's choice was as a filler for a three-disc set of Schumann music. His gain is ours.

Overture to the Opera *Genoveva*, Op. 81

☐ Vienna Philharmonic Orchestra / Münchinger (conductor) / London STS–15076

Fully integrated in form and style and texturally clear. The latter point is rarely as well accomplished as in this case.

Symphony No. 1 (*Spring*) in B flat major, Op. 38

☐ Berlin Philharmonic Orchestra / von Karajan (conductor) / Deutsche Grammophon 2530169

Indeed, there is spring in von Karajan's playing of this symphony. Buoyancy to a high degree and immaculate textural definitions mark the entire work. The structures are strong, the motility is not hindered, and when Schumann's thoughts are of slow-tempoed appulsion, von Karajan is superb. An exciting performance.

Symphony No. 2 in C major, Op. 61

☐ Berlin Philharmonic Orchestra / von Karajan (conductor) / Deutsche Grammophon 2530170

Pull out all the adjectives for this one. These should include "inspired" (in its totality), "warmly spun" (in negotiating a seamless Adagio, with sensitively pitched coloration), "scintillating" (in the Scherzo, which is not set at a speedy tempo only proper for Honegger's *Pacific 231*).

This reviewer goes all out for the B.P.O. performance. A dark-horse second is Eliahu Inbal's rendition with the New Philharmonia Orchestra (Philips 6500288). His conception of the Scherzo particularly shows fine control and knowledge, and the outer movements are fine; but the slow movement tends to become divisioned, and the first fiddles don't soar sufficiently in the beautiful perorative spot that appears in the middle of the movement.

Symphony No. 3 (*Rhenish*) in E flat major, Op. 97

☐ Chicago Symphony Orchestra / Barenboim (conductor) / Deutsche Grammophon 2530940

The finale of this work has a particular type of grandeur which all too often bogs down into merely heavy-handed sound. In this case a finesse is given to the music's weight that provides a full annunciation of Schumann's music without grapnel-like bowing and underlined wind articulation. The slow movements are golden, the Scherzo sparkles. Schumann glows here, and Barenboim is a superfine conductorial proclaimant.

Symphony No. 4 in D minor, Op. 120

☐ Philharmonia Orchestra / Klemperer (conductor) / Angel S-35629

Sweep, grandeur, and splendor mark this performance. There is also a remarkable cohesion, realizing the many transitional details that are part of Schumann's symphonic drama. A passion covers this playing, but it is always of *lebhaft* character—controlled while it simultaneously lets go. And for those who claim that Klemperer is a victim of his own slow tempi, listen to the finale. In this case Klemperer's tempo conviction convinces. (I have heard the movement paced much slower by others.)

Leonard Bernstein's interpretation of the Schumann "Fourth" is a positive triumph. However, if it is chosen, all the Schumann symphonies must be obtained (on Columbia D3S-725).

Concerto in A minor for Cello and Orchestra, Op. 129

☐ New Philharmonia Orchestra / du Pré (cello) / Barenboim (conductor) / Angel S-36642

At its best, Schumann's concerto has its drawbacks—a consistent dark relevance and no true spotlighted virtuosity. Accordingly, cellists believe that the right thing is to reconstitute its personality, and matters get quite alien in relation to what the score indicates.

Staidness is represented in most of the editions in the catalogue. In du Pré's case it was the last thing to enter her mind, or maybe the very first, since she goes in for vigor and vivification. It does lighten the work (though not texturally). Rostropovich plays in a puzzling manner on Deutsche Grammophon 2538025 (and, with a different orchestra, on Westminster Gold 8227). A flamboyant freedom dictates his soloistic role, particularly in the slow movement. It is a soloistic conceit, and it deprives Schumann of his aesthetic rights.

Solo Instrument and Orchestra

Cello

Four Horns

Konzertstück in F major for Four Horns and Orchestra, Op. 86

☐ Chamber Orchestra of the Sarre / Barboteu, Berges, Dubar, and Coursier (horns) / Ristenpart (conductor) / Nonesuch 71044

Too many critics dismiss Schumann's Opus 86 as just so much robust courage in writing extraordinarily difficult music for a quartet of horns and hold that there's little substance in the piece. Objection! Of course the music is drenched with an understanding of the characteristic colors to be obtained from the solo instruments, but the thematic material and its development are romantically distinctive and rich, and over-all there is a true concerto-bravura element.

One should not object to the arguments of hornists that the writing for the instrument is quite devilish. After all, the range demanded is awesome, covering three octaves and a sixth, from the C sharp below the bass staff to the A above the treble staff! And the figures to be performed are not phlegmatic. So much for Schumann as an unadventurous chap when dealing with the orchestra.

The instrumental daring for the soli in this work is a listener's gain. But while Schumann's work can be thoroughly enjoyed simply for this point, the unbiased listener will find additional pleasures in the total conception.

Understandably, concert performances of the *Konzertstück* are risky and therefore few. In the recording studio retakes and tape splices offer the eradication of a fluff, a gaffe, and unsanctioned pitches. Accordingly, this performance is note-clear, pitch-perfect, and without strain. But it has style and a *brio* that go far beyond the mechanics of "finalizing the product" in recording studios.

Piano

Concerto in A minor for Piano and Orchestra, Op. 54

☐ Monte Carlo Opera Orchestra / Richter (piano) / Matačić (conductor) / Angel S–36899
☐ Chicago Symphony Orchestra / Cliburn (piano) / Reiner (conductor) / RCA LSC–2455

Romantically supreme music, requiring, as Richter supplies, clear rhythms, harmonic subtlety, and a shape not shaken loose by passions that don't belong. This is a better performance, but only a slightly better one, than Richter's older version on Deutsche Grammophon 138077 (or, in a different coupling, on Deutsche Grammophon 2538025).

Cliburn's account is very good. It has warmth, with the thermostat set at the high romantic level. Importantly, Cliburn never mars the formal beauty of the work while emphasizing the prime element of Schumannesque charm. Reiner's support is proof that he understands every nicety in the score.

Introduction and *Allegro appassionato (Konzertstück)* for Piano and Orchestra, Op. 92

☐ Philadelphia Orchestra / Rudolf Serkin (piano) / Ormandy (conductor) / Columbia MS–6888

Only Richter (on Deutsche Grammophon 138077) offers Serkin competition in this fine Schumann piece, available at this date in a total of five recordings. Serkin combines fine lyrical commentary with a bravura that accomplishes everything the music demands. It is the last quality that gives Serkin the nod over Richter, who is restrained and only seeks the poetry of the work, disregarding its impulse. And Ormandy? His superb ability to back up soloists is again fully evident.

Introduction and Allegro for Piano and Orchestra, Op. 134

☐ Orchestra of Radio Luxembourg / Ponti (piano) / de Froment (conductor) / Turnabout 34537

This late opus is also known as the Concert Allegro in D minor. Some writers call it "labored," and others have described Opus 134 as a "product of Schumann's declining powers, with little of his real quality." There is a good amount of truth in these statements. One problem with Schumann's work is its incessant dependence on pianistic passage work; though the passage work is brilliant, the lack of contrast can get wearing. Still, there's enough in the score to warrant not discarding the piece.

Ponti drives the music hard, and his accentuations are pitchforked—the latter apparently to achieve a direct comparison with the busy material. The orchestra has little to do, but does its share acceptably.

Fantasy in C major for Violin and Orchestra, Op. 131

Violin

☐ Leipzig Gewandhaus Orchestra / Ricci (violin) / Masur (conductor) / Turnabout 34593

Schumann's Fantasy has never become a repertory piece, though as great a violinist as Fritz Kreisler played it fairly often (in his own edition). The prejudice is unwarranted and unfortunate—the Fantasy has valid musical sense and meaningful situations.

Ricci is just the violinist for the piece, playing it without excess, meaning he opts for always getting immediately to the point and stating it. This dead-to-rights view is exactly what the music needs. The orchestral support is neutrally solid but never stolid—again, exactly what the music needs. Somewhere I have read this work is for "Schumann specialists only." I disagree.

Album für der Jugend, Op. 68: Nos. 37, 38, 39

Instrumental

Piano

☐ Michelangeli (piano) / Angel S-37137

There are forty-three numbers in the two parts of Schumann's "Album for the Young." Those who wish the entire set can find it in a Telefunken release (4635039) performed by Engel. Here are three excerpts—*Matrosenlied* ("Sailor's Song"), *Winterszeit* I ("Wintertime I"), and *Winterszeit* II ("Wintertime II")—in beautiful poetic performances.

Arabeske in C major, Op. 18

☐ Horowitz (piano) / Columbia MS-7106

A vital, persuasively contoured performance that has telling piano vocalism. It is also available on Columbia KS-6371. Arrau's version on Philips 839709 is just as propitiously detailed.

Bunte Blätter, Op. 99

☐ Richter (piano) / Melodiya/Angel SR-40238

Another collection of Schumann's suggestive imagery is represented by these "Colored Leaves." There are leaves within leaves in the miscellany since of the fourteen pieces one group is titled *Fünf Albumblätter* ("Five Album Leaves"). General opinion is that Schumann's Opus 99 is only fair music. I cannot agree since I find the *Bunte Blätter* totally expressive, with each piece sensitively drawn in its specific character.

The Richter performance is ideal. Its perspective is clear, its poetry compelling. And his playing adds many subtle touches that can be termed a re-creative counterpoint to Schumann's music. Jörg Demus's portrayal (on Musical Heritage Society OR-415/419) is meticulous in tone and technique but lacks the depth that Richter provides. On the other hand, Robert Silverman's edition on Orion 7146 is excellent, expressing an aesthetic sensibility for Schumann's music. However, if you get the Silverman recording, expect two less than the complete work; No. 12, *Abendmusik* ("Evening Music"), and No. 14, *Geschwindmarsch* ("Quick March"), are omitted.

Carnaval, Op. 9

☐ Arrau (piano) / Philips 802746

To cover the varied aspects of Schumann's *Scènes mignonnes sur quatre notes* in its twenty movements is a project on which many a pianist has foundered. The extrovert viewpoint that is realized by Arrau is splendid, and the music is always under control, but paradoxically (correctly) not hinged onto the keys.

There are many beauties in this presentation, not the least being the agogic persuasions in *Pantalon et Colombine* and the impact delivered in the *Marche des "Davidsbündler" contre les Philistins*. No far-fetched *rubato*; there is only the proper percentage. Logic and eloquence are here, and so is an imagery that knows every bit of what is being projected on the piano canvas.

Davidsbündlertänze, Op. 6

☐ Perahia (piano) / Columbia M-32299

A cogent musical climate is found in Murray Perahia's playing of this opus. Arrau (Philips 6500178) gets caught up in Schumann's mysticism in his Opus 6, and the introspectivism gets a bit boring. Klien (Turnabout 34379) is the opposite—his extrovert approach overemphasizes the dynamic differences, and that isn't good either, since it negates clarity of phrase and balance of line all too often. It is the successful fusion of all the technical and mood elements that marks Perahia's presentation.

Fantasie in C major, Op. 17

☐ Arrau (piano) / Philips 802746

Schumann stated that the first movement of his Opus 17 was "the most passionate thing" he had ever composed. Arrau plays it with a clear emotive surface that does not include any overstress and yet has an inner tension that represents a masterful translation. Fine power and an expansive interpretation mark the remaining pair of movements. This is impressive Schumann playing.

Fantasiestücke, Op. 12

☐ Arrau (piano) / Philips 6500423

Included in this opus are the rhythmically probing *Aufschwung* ("Rapture"), the questioning paragraphs of *Warum?* ("Why?"), the mildy active *Grillen* ("Whims"), and *In der Nacht* ("In the Night"), the last being among the finest of all of Schumann's shorter pieces.

All the basic inner timings and dramatic movements of the nine pieces in the set are fully conveyed. Arrau beautifully and sensitively colors the music, giving it immediacy and tangibility.

Fantasiestücke, Op. 111

☐ Arrau (piano) / Philips 802793

The set of three (the first and third being in C minor and the central piece being in A flat major) are played with allure and stylistic purity. Arrau's aesthetic response to this music is ideal.

There is commendable accuracy in Frankl's reading (on Vox SVBX–5469), but there is far less color than Arrau achieves.

Faschingsschwank aus Wein, Op. 26
Humoreske in B flat major, Op. 20

☐ Arrau (piano) / Philips 839709

The "Carnival Jest from Vienna" is a full-scale work of five movements, while the *Humoreske* is no mere bagatelle, but a work covering a variety of moods. Arrau treats these pieces in a pianistically thrilling and dramatically commanding manner. Only Richter's portrayal (on Angel S–36104) is competitive, but still lacks the affection Arrau brings to this music.

Four Marches, Op. 76

☐ Goldsmith (piano) / RCA VICS–1621

Minor-league Schumann but played in major-league style.

Kinderscenen, Op. 15

Almost Too Serious (No. 10)
An Important Event (No. 6)
At the Fireside (No. 8)
Blind Man's Buff (No. 3)
Child Falling Asleep (No. 12)
A Curious Story (No. 2)
Dreaming (Träumerei) (No. 7)
Frightening (No. 11)

From Foreign Lands and Peoples
   (No. 1)
Knight of the Hobby Horse
   (No. 9)
Perfect Happiness (No. 5)
Pleading Child (No. 4)
The Poet Speaks (No. 13)

☐ Horowitz (piano) / Columbia MS–6411

An absorbing recitation of the beauties contained in this cross-section of pieces. To hear Horowitz's playing of the ubiquitous *Träumerei* from these "Scenes of Childhood" is worth the cost of the entire album.

Because of the many other works on the disc (a Schumann *toccata*, three Scarlatti sonatas, a Schubert impromptu, and three Scriabin pieces), there are no bands for Schumann's set of pieces. Understandable, though still annoying.

Kreisleriana, Op. 16

☐ Arrau (piano) / Philips 6500394

The values here are formidable. Each of the eight *Fantasien* is presented with the fullest insight, and there is a performance participation that has the strongest affinity for Schumann's creations. Such confidence and stylistic appropriateness (not to mention the fullest artistic commentary) is a recording event.

Nachtstücke, Op. 23
No. 1 in C major / No. 2 in F major / No. 3 in D flat major / No. 4 in F major

☐ Arrau (piano) / Philips 6500178

Arrau puts a great deal (too much) *più lento* into the first of the four pieces, and the music doesn't flourish in such suspended state. Thereafter, the playing has resourceful command, especially the final piece, *Semplice,* where Arrau shows how to lyricize arpeggios and produce aristocratic music.

Novelletten, Op. 21

No. 1 in F major / **No. 2 in D major** / **No. 3 in D major** / **No. 4 in D major** / **No. 5 in D major** / **No. 6 in A major** / **No. 7 in E major** / **No. 8 in F sharp minor**

☐ Arrau (piano) / Philips 6500396

The manner in which Arrau sets forth the detail in these eight works is piano magic. There is beauty and grandeur aplenty, and poetry as well. The major point is that without bypassing emotive prosecution, Arrau's playing is always controlled.

Papillons, Op. 2

☐ Richter (piano) / Angel S–36104

Schumann's Opus 2 sets the stage quickly, and then follow fanciful sketches of highly imaginative type. Richter's stage management of the piano is as pertinent. Zest and conviction make his presentation difficult to beat. A highly polished example of piano playing.

Romances, Op. 28

No. 1 in B flat minor / **No. 2 in F sharp major** / **No. 3 in B major**

☐ Arrau (piano) / Philips 6500395

The thematic material in the first two of the set receives golden lyrical plotting by this superb pianist. In the third piece the manifold ideas worked into the music are nicely clarified, and the total shape becomes very clear.

Six Intermezzi, Op. 4

☐ Johanessen (piano) / Golden Crest S–4110

Both title and opus number were changed. Originally, Schumann's work was titled *Pièces phantastiques* and was listed as Opus 3. Exemplary playing.

Sonata in F minor, Op. 14

☐ Kuerti (piano) / London STS–15255

The discursive data of this work (originally titled "Concerto without Orchestra") make for interpretative difficulties. One writer has described the music as "painfully repetitious." Be that as it may, Kuerti does judiciously and the music is most communicative.

Sonata in F sharp minor, Op. 11

☐ Arrau (piano) / Philips 802793

This work could be termed the greatest of Schumann's three piano sonatas. The Scherzo is controlled and thereby saves its energy, of which there is no lack. In the finale Arrau sorts out the rather loosely formulated music and shapes it into sense.

Sonata in G minor, Op. 22

☐ Argerich (piano) / Deutsche Grammophon 2530193

This is the most concise of the Schumann piano sonatas. A problem that is solved by the soloist is the squared rhythmic constructions in the corner movements. Throughout there is honest music-making that articulates the Schumann data properly.

Symphonic Etudes, Op. 13

☐ Ashkenazy (piano) / London 6471

Schumann's opus is subtitled *Etudes in the Form of Variations.* Some pianists perform the edition that was always used by Clara Schumann and do not include the five posthumous variations that make the work comprise the generative theme and seventeen variants. Some critics feel the additional sections cause an imbalance, but Ashkenazy doesn't, and this writer agrees with him. He also agrees with his performance, which is a probing one both musically and intellectually. Appropriate spirit is present, and so are a sense of spontaneity and interpretative candor. There is plenty of suavity as well.

Three Piano Sonatas for the Young, Op. 118
No. 1 in G major / No. 2 in D major / No. 3 in C major

☐ Frankl (piano) / Vox SVBX-5472

There is a multiplicity of meanings in Schumann's title. This music has Schumann-esque charm and even in the lighter-scaled movements the contents (markedly so in the case of the third work) are as apt for the concert platform as they are for the teaching studio. The "Sonata" designation applies formally only to the C major opus, which begins with the only true sonata design found in the three works. The G major opus is a suite that includes, in its four movements, a set of variations, a *Puppenwiegenlied* ("Lullaby for the Doll"), and a Rondoletto. A Canon, an *Abendlied* ("Evening Song"), and a finale titled *Kindergesellschaft* ("Children's Party") highlight the second work. In the third Sonata, a slow movement, a Gypsy Dance (replacing the usual scherzo) and a rondo follow the opening sonata-formationed movement.

Peter Frankl performs these compositions with a warmth that is most fruitful. He fully recognizes the values within the set and the result is piano playing of remarkable finesse and interpretative tact. Frankl's splendid artistry shouldn't be missed.

Toccata, Op. 7

☐ Horowitz (piano) / Columbia MS-6411

There is the chance for plenty of virtuosity in this sonata-formed Toccata, but Horowitz doesn't take advantage of such showmanship possibilities. He plays the work to exhibit and emphasize its musical strengths. Such musical intelligence brings rewards to performer and listener.

Variations on the Name ABEGG, Op. 1

☐ Arrau (piano) / Philips 6500130

Here there is taste and simplicity. The latter is not produced at the expense of formal definition, which embraces four variations and a finale encompassing a fantasia. There's plenty of technique demanded, but the manner in which Arrau disguises (while thoroughly engaging) this paramount point to emphasize the music itself, the more important of the two worlds, is ideal.

Waldszenen, Op. 82

☐ Peter Serkin (piano) / RCA LSC-2955
☐ Arrau (piano) / Philips 6500423

A set of nine pieces, including the gentility of *Einsame Blumen* ("Solitary Flowers"), the reticence of *Verrufene Stelle* ("Haunted Spot"), and the most popular *Vogel als Prophet* ("The Prophet Bird").

Neither soloist attempts to dazzle in these ruminations. That would be erroneous. Serkin plays with unforced expressiveness; there is slightly more linear flow in Arrau's playing, which is recorded with more brightness. RCA's failure to band the disc is quite annoying. If Philips can, why can't RCA?

Piano, Four Hands

Ball-Scenen, Op. 109

Bilder aus Osten, Op. 66

Eight Polonaises, Op. 111

Nationaltanz aus dem Spanischen Liederspiel

Twelve Pieces, Op. 85

☐ Demus and Shetler (piano) / Musical Heritage Society OR-415/16/17/18/19

Here, with one exception, is the complete known Schumann output for four hands at one piano. (The other work *Kinderball, Op. 130*, a set subtitled *Six Easy Dance Pieces*, is performed by the same pianists on Musical Heritage Society OR-400/1/2.) The *Nationaltanz* is an oddity. There is neither mention of the piece in the detailed program notes by Douglas Townsend nor in *Grove's Dictionary of Music and Musicians*. It turns out to be a pithy and most enjoyable item that has more Schumann than Spanish color.

The performance displays acute balletic sense and fine rhythmic temper. Indeed, it is good news to have it on disc.

The Opus 66, subtitled *6 Impromptus,* is the best known of Schumann's piano duets. Its title "Pictures from the East" could just as well read "Pictures from the West" for all of its lack of exotic flavor and with the Schumann signature filling every measure.

The schematic simplicity that marks the other works is concerned a great deal with dance forms. In the *Ball-Scenen,* save for the first and last of the nine pieces, totally so; and, of course, without exception, in the Eight Polonaises. The Twelve Pieces are specified "for little and big children." Programmatic detail in the typical Schumann manner is used to describe a birthday march, a bear dance, the game of hide and seek, and so on.

Jörg Demus and Norman Shetler make a fine team. Their playing is firm and stylistically confirmed and they demonstrate a splendid coloristic finesse and balance in their conceptions. This is a performance treat in all respects.

Chamber Music

Fantasiestücke, Op. 73

☐ Reese (cello); Linsley (piano) / Crystal S-134

A robust performance of this work, which can be played either by clarinet or by cello (a published edition is available for violin as well). This approach especially matches the third piece of the group, based on a surging figure that never coincides with the other voices. The theorem of rhythmic unrest thus propels additional flavor into the fiery character of this Schumannesque mood. (For a recorded setting of the clarinet version *see below*.)

Fantasiestücke, Op. 73

☐ Wright (clarinet); Goldsmith (piano) / RCA VICS-1621

Perhaps better known in the version for cello (*see above*), but warranting equal time in the woodwind-piano partnership. This good team proves it with a warmly designed performance.

Fünf Stücke im Volkston for Cello and Piano, Op. 102

☐ Rostropovich (cello); Britten (piano) / London 6237

These pieces have essential folk flavor in their clear format. In the first one the theme appears four times interspersed with three contrasting episodes. Major-and-minor-tonality contrasts mark the second piece. Conditions of instrumental weight govern the third of the set—the cello is first in solo light, joins the piano in rich lushness, and then is set off again. The last two movements work along similar lines of contrast.

The performance sensitivity of this team is joyous to the ears. Their playing has grace and delicacy, charm and distinction.

Märchenbilder for Viola and Piano, Op. 113

☐ Imai (viola); Goldsmith (piano) / RCA VICS-1621

Each of these four "Pictures from Fairyland" creates a definite mood of romantic poesy. The poignant flavor is captured in full by Harris Goldsmith, a sensitive pianist, and Nobuko Imai, an equally sensitive violist.

Three Romances for Oboe and Piano, Op. 94

☐ Roseman (oboe); Kalish (piano) / Desto 6484

In the hands of a less skillful performer these pieces reflecting Schumann's penchant for continuity of color could well breed aural monotony. All the potentials are realized by Ronald Roseman, with perfect and sensitive support from Gilbert Kalish.

Märchenerzählungen for Piano, Clarinet, and Viola, Op. 132

☐ Goldsmith (piano); Wright (clarinet); Imai (viola) / RCA VICS-1621

Schumann's four "Fairy Tales" have no programmatic significance and in certain respects are rather square-cut in their forms and ideas. But in the hands of these musicians the results are a delight. Goldsmith is one of the most important critics on the scene; this writer can only say the best things about his beautiful playing and those of his colleagues. Most certainly this is a gem of a performance.

Trio for Piano, Violin, and Cello
In D minor, Op. 63 / In F major, Op. 80 / In G minor, Op. 110

☐ Beaux Arts Trio / Philips 6700051

In the D minor opus Schumann deliberately certifies the entire trio's unity by distinguishing completely the style of the opening movement from the last. Thus do opposites attract each other. In itself, the first movement is thick, heavied with the trio formation. In the final movement there is more light shining. The initial movement is in minor, the closing one is in major; the first is hard texturally, the other softish in its sunniness. The other movements are a Scherzo in which Schumann spreads his rhythm, gets horizontal motivation from the perky quality of dry humor inherent in the Scherzo itself, and a slow movement that exhibits the vacillatory melodic writing of post-Beethoven style.

Schumann was of the opinion that his second trio made more of an ingratiating appeal than his earlier trio. One can agree by stating that indeed the Opus 63 is disorderly in mood compared with Opus 80. Movement 1 of the latter is instrumentally heavy, being overladen with material in its rhapsodic treatment of sonata form. Rich harmonic color is found in the slow movement; slower scherzo style, framed with the canonic device, is presented in movement 3; and a great deal of imitation fills the finale.

The last trio is the weakest of the three. Though each movement has a definite focal point, there is overpersistence in carrying through the structural details. An example is movement 1, wherein a successive set of rising and falling arpeggios is constantly worked on. The best part of the work is the finale, which concerns itself with jumps and offbeat accents. It is illustrative of Schumann in as light a vein as he ever could be.

These trios are given truly ideal performances. Only a critical grouch would quibble at a point here and an item there. The tone quality is marvelous, and the attention to details and the cogency in defining the scores are conclusive. In the D minor opus the passionate earnestness that braces the conception is fully exhibited; the Scherzo is presented in a lively manner, but not too fast. The Beaux Arts team realize this is a Scherzo with reins attached, a Scherzo with brakes on its rhythmic shoes. Careful attention to instrumental gravities clarifies the heaviness found in the first movement of the second trio. In the Scherzo, matters are not rushed. The players prove that Schumann almost dreamed through his scherzi; in comparison, Beethoven opened wide the throttle and let them rush forth. Cogent interpretation marks the exposition of the G minor trio. A sense of understatement is applied to the slow movement, thereby supplying additional fuel to the fiery third movement.

The competitive edition of the complete Schumann trios by the Trio Bel Arte is available in a Vox Box (SVBX–591). The playing is generally faithful to the music but doesn't have the taste, class, quality, and values of the Philips edition.

Quartet for Piano, Violin, Viola, and Cello, Op. 47

☐ Members of the Juilliard Quartet / Gould (piano) / Columbia D3S–806

Romantic syntax throughout. The first movement is of large binary formation from the use of the introduction in two places. Two trios extend the length of the Scherzo, creepy and mysterious in its motor rhythm. Indeed this is romantic disorder (though only in the formal sense), as perceived in the finale, which is a mélange of fugato systems of lush melodies.

But it all makes wonderful sense in this sensible and warm performance.

String Quartets, Op. 41

No. 1 in A minor / No. 2 in F major / No. 3 in A major

☐ Quartetto Italiano / Philips 6703029

The critical curse on these works is that they are crammed full of what might be termed "pianistic" passages. But while quartet scoring is most effective when the melodic lines are broadly fat and sonorous and when figurations are concentrated, this does not negate the figurative types and patterns used by Schumann.

In the hands of the Italiano group the music emerges beautifully, suavely, stylistically apt. To damn (and dam) any critical report that these works are not in quartet style, the supple performances produce indelible chamber-music textures and essences.

A special point must be indicated. It is to the Quartetto Italiano's credit that they do not decorate the finale of the A minor opus with any fancy-Dan flying spiccato bowings. Many a quartet team has been guilty of displaying bow-arm egos in this movement, and Schumann has been blamed, though the score gives no indication for such bowing procedure.

Andante and Variations for Two Pianos, Two Cellos, and Horn, Op. 46

☐ Ashkenazy and Frager (pianos); Tuckwell (horn); Fleming and Weil (cellos) / London 6411

One would have to search long to find another example of this chamber-music combination. If it isn't an adventurous piece of music, it is, at least, adventurous in color terms.

If there were not considerable override of the keyboard instruments, then one might well choose the Turnabout edition (34204), since the style is otherwise fine. However, the balances are just right on London's disc, and what there is for the horn is documented with rich persuasiveness.

Schumann was dissatisfied with the work and recast it for two pianos (his only contribution to that medium). A representative performance is on Musical Heritage Society OR-409/10/11. Jörg Demus and Norman Shetler are the duo-pianists.

Quintet for Piano, Two Violins, Viola, and Cello, Op. 44

☐ Guarneri Quartet / Rubinstein (piano) / RCA LSC-6188

Strong, full-bodied, and expansive playing and not once slipping over into quasi-orchestral conditions. It is chamber music all the way. All the passage work is depicted with sharp clarity, and the voice interweave in the polyphonic sections is impressively registered.

What makes this performance so special is that zest (in the Scherzo) is not confused with an attempt for a tempo track record, and that while the piano retains its special role in the work, the quartet is not devoured by it. The Guarneri and Rubinstein bind as a musical whole.

An die Türen will ich schleichen, Op. 98a, No. 8

Aufträge, Op. 77, No. 5

Belsatzar, Op. 57

Vocal

Voice with Accompaniment

☐ Enns (bass-baritone); Sheffield (piano) / Orion 74146

The ballad *Belsatzar* is the most substantial of this group. Schumann's formal plotting is expert. Overall, the voice and piano are equal, in a give-and-take manner. The latter instrument is given specific decreasing rhythmic activity as the song progresses in order to focus attention on the increasing dramatic pertinency of the vocal line. The rendition is well defined, especially Enns's recitation-like style in the concluding section of the ballad.

An die Türen is intelligently sung as is *Aufträge*, the last of the third volume of *Lieder und Gesänge*, where Enns's voice is most expressive. There are two other excerpts from Opus 98a on this Orion release (discussed below under: *Wer nie sein Brot mit Tränen ass*).

Dichterliebe, Op. 48

☐ Pears (tenor); Britten (piano) / London 1261

If it's musical depth you seek above vocal character, then this is the choice. Pears in this case is not as good as Fischer-Dieskau, heard on Deutsche Grammophon 139109, but the balance of power shifts to the former by way of the extraordinary piano realizations by Benjamin Britten. Most often this writer is in full agreement with Robert Franz's statement that Schumann's *lieder* were "piano pieces with superadded vocal part." The extended piano postludes found in the cycle are part of the evidence.

It is the creative understanding found in Britten's re-creatcve effort that does wonders for this performance, but without protesting too much, let it be said that Pears is no poor second. His style is excellent, and his tonal quality and line are good.

Frauenliebe und Leben, Op. 42

☐ Schwarzkopf (soprano); Parsons (piano) / Angel S–37043

The strong reasonings of Schumann's song cycle bring strong actions. The singing here is mature, intelligent, and telling. Beautiful cognizance of these songs' moods.

Gedichte der Königin Maria Stuart, Op. 135

☐ Crespin (soprano); Wustman (piano) / London 26043

Schumann's five "Poems of Mary Stuart" are depicted with eloquent vocalism. Especially poignant is Crespin's portrayal of the *Gebet* ("Prayer") that concludes the cycle. No less moving is the interpretation of the doomed queen's *Abschied von der Welt* ("Farewell to the World").

Liederkreis, Op. 24

☐ Fischer-Dieskau (baritone); Eschenbach (piano) / Deutsche Grammophon 2530543

A marvelously sensitive portrayal, the very best available. The integrality of these performers (it will be noted that Fischer-Dieskau is accompanied by a major pianist) displays vocal music to perfection.

In a different coupling (with the *Dichterliebe*), the cycle is on Deutsche Grammophon 139109.

Liederkreis, Op. 39

☐ Schwarzkopf (soprano); Parsons (piano) / Angel S–37043

The cycle is related with superb color and balance. Rich and sensitive singing.

Myrthen, Op. 25

☐ Fischer-Dieskau (baritone); Eschenbach (piano) / Deutsche Grammophon 2530543

Priceless examples of vocal-piano duoism. A strong sense of sung chamber music prevails. Fischer-Dieskau's phrasing is perfect, Eschenbach's piano sound is rich and colorfully detailed.

Spanisches Liederspiel, Op. 74

☐ Stephane Caillat Vocal Quartet / Billier (piano) / Turnabout 34300

A fair amount of Spanish qualities and a great amount of variety in Schumann's ten-part cycle. The entire quartet is used twice. There are three duos for soprano and alto, and one each for soprano and tenor, and tenor and baritone. Solos are presented in three instances, each for a different voice.

Competent singing if not especially inspired.

Wer nie sein Brot mit Tränen ass, Op. 98a, No. 4
Wer sich der Einsamkeit ergibt, Op. 98a, No. 6

☐ Enns (bass-baritone); Sheffield (piano) / Orion 74146

These are two of the nine songs in the set, *Lieder und Gesänge aus "Wilhelm Meister,"* the texts by Goethe. (Enns sings another song from the cycle, *An die Türen will ich schleichen—see above.*)

It is impossible to agree with Martin Cooper's statement in *Schumann—A Symposium* that the entire Opus 98a set is "among Schumann's most conspicuous failures as a song-writer." It is true that chromatic divagation is used in great amount but the lyricism is compelling. Enns's secure singing shows these songs in their very best light.

Gute Nacht, **Op. 59, No. 4**

Im Walde, **Op. 75, No. 2**

☐ Camerata Vocale, Bremen / Blum (conductor) / Nonesuch 71081

The first title is the last of the *Vier Gesänge*; the other is from *Romanzen und Balladen*, Vol. II. On the release it is given an incorrect designation as Op. 67, No. 7. But Op. 67 consists of only five numbers, as *Romanzen und Balladen*, Vol. I. *Im Walde* is actually the seventh in the complete series, but falls under a different opus number which also consists of five pieces.

Zigeunerleben, **Op. 29, No. 3**

☐ Gächinger Kantorei / Galling (piano) / Rilling (conductor) / Nonesuch 71228

The third of a group of *Drei Gedichte*, the other two being, respectively, for two and three sopranos. Considerable charm, which is fully displayed by Rilling's group.

Choral

Chorus Alone

Chorus with Accompaniment

Gerard Schürmann (1928-   )

Chuench'i (A Song Cycle from the Chinese) (1966)

☐ Nixon (soprano); McCabe (piano) / Nonesuch 71209

Seven songs representing the emotional progress of a woman through life. The style is rooted firmly in late-romantic procedures. The music is effectively written and equally considers the voice and the piano.

Marni Nixon commissioned the work, and her realization of it is fine. McCabe is as fluent a pianist as he is a composer.

Vocal

Voice with Accompaniment

Eduard Schütt (1856-1933)

A la bien aimée

☐ Lhevinne (piano) / Klavier 111

"To the Beloved" is the sentimental piece by which this composer obtained his acceptance in teaching studios. Yet it has a period charm that is enhanced by the way Josef Lhevinne treats it—with fluid expressiveness and telling *rubato*.

Forest Elves, Op. 70, No. 5

☐ Hofmann (piano) / Klavier 114

As to be expected, a scherzo. But notwithstanding the possible turn-off by the cute title, a tasty bonbon, served up in a nimble-fingered packet.

Instrumental

Piano

Valse bluette, Op. 25

☐ Hofmann (piano) / Klavier 121

Salon music made for the lighter side of encores. Justly realized here (Hofmann used to play it constantly).

Heinrich Schütz   (1585-1672)

Vocal

Voice and
Instrumental
Ensemble

Symphoniae Sacrae, Book I: Concertos Nos. 3, 5, 7, 8, 9, 10, 13, 19, and 20

☐ Reuter-Edzart (contralto); Huber and Jochims (tenors); Pommerien (bass) / Rilling (conductor) / Nonesuch 71160

Six of the nine concertos are for two tenors; one each call for solo tenor, solo contralto, and solo bass. The instrumental framework (drawn from two English horns, two violins, cello, double bass, harpsichord, clarino trumpet, cornett, four trombones, and dolcian) varies. For example, Concerto No. 13 calls for four trombones and continuo with the solo bass; both Concerto No. 7 and Concerto No. 8 are for two tenors, with two English horns and continuo.

Schütz has never been so beautifully effective—and masterful. The entire cast of performers is skillful. Top honors go to Wilfrid Jochims for his singing in *Venite ad Me* (Concerto No. 5).

For a discussion of eight of the concertos in *Symphoniae Sacrae*, Book II, *see below.*

Symphoniae Sacrae, Book II: Concertos Nos. 2, 4, 6, 7, 8, 10, 19, and 27

☐ Speiser (soprano); Lehane (contralto); Huber and Rotzsch (tenors); Pommerien (bass) / Rilling (conductor) / Nonesuch 71196

Eight of the total twenty-seven concertos in the second of the three volumes Schütz composed under the title *Symphoniae Sacrae*. For a discussion of the nine concertos from Book I that are available in recorded form, *see above.*

In this case three of the group are for soprano, two each are for solo tenor and two tenors, and one is for contralto. The instrumental coverage is different from that employed in Book I, consisting of two each of recorders and oboes, a bassoon, two each of clarino trumpets, cornetts, trombones, and violins, one cello, a double bass, and harpsichord. For the most part, the choice of instrumentation varies in each concerto.

All the soloists sings with distinction, representing a dependable stylistic understanding. Especially telling are Hans Joachim Rotzsch's delivery in *Singet dem Herren ein neues Lied* (Concerto No. 2) and Maureen Lehane's interpretation of *Herzlich Lieb hab ich dich, o Herr* (Concerto No. 8). Helmuth Rilling's direction is of the highest standard.

Choral

Chorus Alone

Becker Psalms

☐ Gregg Smith Singers / Rees (soprano); Eckard (alto); Bogden (tenor); DeRuiter (bass) / Smith (conductor) / Vox SVBX-5103

Seventeen of Schütz settings of the versification of the psalms of Cornelius Becker, followed by a concluding *Responsorium*. The procedures follow clear and simple four-part chorale style, sometimes supplied by a solo voice with accompanied voices. These totally beautiful expressions display the wisdom of vocalism that marks the performances of this masterful group.

Es Ging ein Sämann aus

☐ Gregg Smith Singers / Rees (soprano); Eckard (alto); Perry (tenor); DeRuiter (bass) / Vox SVBX–5103

A setting of the parable of the sowing of the seed, the music's sections corresponding to the four elements of the story. Exuberantly performed.

Italian Madrigals

☐ Gregg Smith Singers / Smith (conductor) / Vox SVBX–5103
☐ Gächinger Kantorei / Rilling (conductor) / Nonesuch 71177

While there are pertinent values in each performance listed, the differences between them are far from subtle. In terms of coverage, the Nonesuch release includes eleven of the total nineteen madrigals; six of these are duplicated in the Vox album, which also has the intensely touching *D'orrida selce alpina*, not included in Nonesuch's selection. The sound on Vox is clearer; on Nonesuch it is fuller. Further, more distinct part-writing is achieved in the former.

Most important is the matter of tempo. In every case Gregg Smith moves the music considerably faster. Such contemporary energy and animation are in sharp contrast to the traditionalism that brakes the speed rates in Rilling's performance. While no Germanic stolidity creeps into his conducting, the tempi chosen are certainly just a bit related to that condition. This situation results, for example, in *Dunque addio, care selve* being covered by Smith in 3:04 and by Rilling in 4:47, while *Ride la primavera* is one and one-quarter minutes faster under Smith's direction. In a work that is under four minutes in length, such variance is certainly huge.

For bolder and more dynamic consideration one would opt for Gregg Smith. The Helmuth Rilling version is listed because of its sonic quality and because it offers a larger selection of the Madrigals. Record collectors would be wise to obtain both.

Unser Herr Jesus Christus

☐ Heinrich Schütz Choir / Norrington (conductor) / Argo ZRG–666

Eight-part writing for two choirs provides a mystical consideration of the institution of the Lord's Supper. The singing is exceptional, the tightly conceived voice writing defined and colored with sensitivity.

Warum toben die Heinden: Psalm 2

☐ Kantorei Barmen-Gemarke / Friesenhausen and Groh (sopranos); Wolf-Matthäus and Karst (altos); Altmeyer and Mielsch (tenors); Ochs and Hudemann (basses) / Kahlhöfer (conductor) / Nonesuch 71134

Double the usual four parts are used for the solo voices and the chorus. A combination of both groups is called on to emphasize certain sections. These textural differences are carefully contrasted in Helmut Kahlhöfer's conducting.

Wie lieblich sind deine Wohnungen: Psalm 84

☐ Heinrich Schütz Choir / Norrington (conductor) / Argo ZRG–666

Delicacy is the fundamental quality of this motet for double choir. The arrangement of the two groups is interesting; one choir has soprano, alto, tenor, and bass, and the other has a four-part disposition of tenors and basses. The soprano-alto-tenor-bass and tenor-tenor-bass-bass formation in combination is extremely rare.

A sympathetic performance and one that is acutely balanced notwithstanding the preponderance of male-voice parts.

Chorus with Accompaniment

Ich hebe meine Augen auf zu den Bergen: Psalm 121

☐ Gregg Smith Singers / Rees (soprano); Eckard (alto); Perry (tenor); DeRuiter (bass) / Smith (conductor) / Vox SVBX-5103

One of Schütz's *Psalms of David* group, calling for solo quartet, chorus, and organ (no specific performer credit is given for the last). Antiphonal style is special to the piece, and it is splendidly conveyed in a rich and vibrant performance.

Wohl dem, der den Herren fürchtet: Psalm 128

☐ Westphalian Choral Ensemble / Ehmann (conductor) / Nonesuch 71235

Contrastive registration is utilized here, with high and low four-part choruses, supported by continuo. Ehmann controls matters nicely and presents a most convincing performance.

Chorus and Instrumental Ensemble

Ach Herr, straf mich nicht in deinem Zorn: Psalm 6
Cantate Domino: Psalm 96

☐ Heinrich Schütz Choir and Symphoniae Sacrae Chamber Ensemble / Spinks (chamber organ); Hogwood (regal) / Norrington (conductor) / Argo ZRG-666

Both are for double choir; the first listed is from Schütz's set of twenty-six *Psalms of David*. Potent coloration in the instrumental back-up with cornetto, three sackbuts, chitarrone, three krummhorns, bassoon, organ, regal, and violone. The singing has telling depth.

Canzone: Nun Lob, mein Seel, dem Herren: Psalm 103
Danket dem Herren, denn Er ist freundlich: Psalm 136
Der Herr ist mein Hirt: Psalm 23

☐ Westphalian Choral Ensemble and Instrumentalists / Stolte and Riedel-Pax (sopranos); Haasemann (alto); Michaelis (countertenor); Rotzsch and Hoefflin (tenors); Pommerien (bass) / Ehmann (conductor) / Nonesuch 71235

The contrasts in the temper of these *Psalmen Davids* are most effectively translated by soloists, chorus, and instrumentalists. Especially sensitive work details the pastoral serenity of *Psalm 23*, calling for soprano, alto, tenor, and bass solo voices, two four-part choruses, and continuo. In *Psalm 136* the solo parts are scored for five voices and three trombones; the chorus is in five parts, and the instrumental support comes from trumpets, timpani, and continuo.

German Madrigals

☐ Gregg Smith Singers / Samuels and Setzler (violins); Ormond (viola); Mather (cello); Beegle (harpsichord) / Smith (conductor) / Vox SVBX-5103

Seven of the set, five of which call for duetted voices. One of the group is for vocal quartet, and another is for a quintet. Gregg Smith's statement that these pieces "are very 'un-madrigal-like'" tells it all. The simmerings of the German *Lied* can be heard throughout. And throughout the singing and playing are excellent, with fresh voices and a sensitive regard for clear phrasing.

Herr unser Herrscher: Psalm 8

Ich freu mich des: Psalm 122

☐ Heinrich Schütz Choir and Symphoniae Sacrae Chamber Ensemble / Spinks (chamber organ) / Norrington (conductor) / Argo ZRG–666

Choral verticalism is the major method in *Psalm 122,* its quasi-proclamatory writing forwarded in a bright triple pulse. Throughout there is excellent balance; the dynamic differences are strikingly covered in the case of *Herr unser Herrscher.*

Kleine geistliche Konzerte, **Book I**

☐ Westphalian Choral Ensemble / Adam, Bernát-Klein, Friesenhausen, and Stolte (sopranos); Bornemann, Lisken, and Haasemann (contraltos); Bössow, Hoefflin, and Rotzsch (tenors); Müller, Pommerien, and Kortendiek (basses); Haferland and Münch-Holland (viola da gambas); Schönstedt (harpsichord and positive organ); Koch and Stöhr (violones); Gerwig (lute); Steinkopf (dolcian) / Ehmann (conductor) / Nonesuch 73012

The "Little Sacred Concertos" have two dozen numbers in the first book, calling for a great variety of voice and instrumental combinations. As examples, the first piece is for soprano and two instruments, the second one embraces contralto and three instruments; Nos. 13 and 14 are scored for two tenors, with lute and viola da gamba support in the former, and with dolcian, violone, and positive organ in the other—and so on. The vocal totalities, however, follow a consistent pattern: a solo voice is employed in each of the first four parts; two voices are utilized in Nos. 5 through 15; sections 16, 17, 18, and 19 each have three solo voices; a vocal quartet is featured in the following four numbers; and finally, in part 24 there are five solo voices.

Further, in each of these sets the rule is to have a registral continuity beginning with the highest voice and moving toward the lowest. For example, in the three-voice group the first piece is for two sopranos and tenor, the next pair use two sopranos and bass, and the following piece is for three basses. Six concertos call for two instruments; the others include three instruments. The chorus is employed only in the last two parts.

The vocalists on the recording do not star on the international circuit, but they acquit themselves nicely and avoid the deadly oratorio style of singing that flattens the music into dullness. Ehmann is a Schütz expert, and it is evident in his keen stylistic control.

For *Kleine geistliche Konzerte,* Book II, *see below.*

Kleine geistliche Konzerte, **Book II**

☐ Westphalian Choral Ensemble and Ferdinand Conrad Recorder Ensemble / Bernát-Klein, Stolte, and Wehrung (sopranos); Haasemann and Lisken (contraltos); Hoefflin and Rotzsch (tenors); Kortendieck, Pommerien, and Stämpfli (basses); Haferland, Koch, Münch-Holland, Blume, Uhlenhoff, and Friedrich (viola da gambas); Gerwig (lute); Steinkopf (dolcian); Schönstedt (harpsichord and positive organ) / Ehmann (conductor) / Nonesuch 73024

Schütz's organization of the thirty-two pieces in the second book of the "Little Sacred Concertos" is practically the same as that of the first set (*see above*). Coloristic change is constant. As illustration, the seventeenth concerto calls for two sopranos and bass, with lute and a pair of viola da gambas, while No. 23 is scored for paired sopranos and tenors, with the instrumental support supplied by dolcian, positive organ, and a viola da gamba. Increase in the number of voices is again utilized: There is one only in the first five pieces, two are called for in Nos. 6 through 15, and parts 16 through 20 have three voices. Concerto No. 21 is for four voices, and the twenty-second piece requires five solo voices.

Numbers 23 through 27 then break the pattern by returning to four voices, and the next two sections utilize only two voices. The last three numbers move into the largest total of five voices.

Paralleling the textural plan is the use of type of voice, the sequence proceeding from the highest to the lowest, for the greatest part. Four of the concertos have two-instrument support, twenty-six utilize three instruments. Part 28 has the special timbre framework of a positive organ and a half-dozen viola da gambas. The following concerto is even more special, with a harpsichord and the recorder ensemble (its only use in the work) joining the six viola da gambas. The chorus is heard only in these two parts of the work.

Expressively proportioned presentations are given every part of the work. The concertos are presented without improper pretension and minus any stylistic infringement. Indeed they make up a lengthy work, covering eight record sides, but Ehmann's performance feels and sounds right all the way through.

Magnificat

☐ Spandauer Kantorei / Speiser (soprano); Huber (alto); Schamalhofer (tenor); Wilhelms (bass) / Rilling (conductor) / Turnabout 34099

Radiant music for a main choir, two other four-voice groups, strings, trombones, and continuo. There isn't a single point of aesthetic judgement in this presentation that can be argued.

The recording is also obtainable on Vox (SVBX–5101) with four other Schütz compositions, including another of his *Magnificat* settings, the *Deutsches Magnificat*.

Motets

I Am the Resurrection and the Life
Jauchzet dem Herrn, alle Welt
Lift Up Your Heads, O Ye Gates

☐ American Kantorei / Bergt (conductor) / Turnabout 34521

All three are for two choirs. The accompaniment is by strings, reeds, continuo and portative organ for the first- and third-listed titles. For *Jauchzet dem Herrn* the accompaniment used includes reeds, strings, and two organs: regal and flutes.

Worthy depictions, though dynamically a bit prosaic. No credits are listed for the soloists in *Lift Up Your Heads*.

Motets from *Cantiones Sacrae*

☐ Niedersächsischer Singkreis, Hannover / Beckedorf (cello); Schlegel (contrabass); Rovatkay (positif) / Träder (conductor) / Nonesuch 71062

A selection of seventeen motets from Schütz's *Cantiones Sacrae* (see under *Cantata and Oratorio* for details). This includes the last five parts of the work, with two versions offered of the *Pater Noster*, one with and one without continuo. Schütz added a figured bass to the motets at the insistence of his publisher. Its use is optional at best, and Schütz preferred that the figured bass be used only for those pieces with an obbligato continuo and in those places be played by an organ. The addition here of cello and bass is certainly valid, and they blend nicely with the positif (a choir organ). Aside from the *Pater Noster*, ten of the motets are heard with continuo, six without it.

The recording is of excellent clarity, and the excerpting was well planned. Those who don't want the six-record complete work can choose this release of seventeen of the total forty motets without hesitation; the performing forces are first rate, and the singing is done with insight and a proper feeling for style.

Saul, Saul, was verfolgst du mich?

☐ Kantorei Barmen-Gemarke / Kahlhöfer (conductor) / Nonesuch 71134

One of the most powerful utterances Schütz produced. Its diminutiveness provides a deep thrust to the music both by its compactness (less than three minutes in performance time) and by its inner constructive conjunctiveness. For his text Schütz used only two sentences of Jesus's words to the persecutor of His disciples, but the way they are polychromed produces the equivalent of a large dramatic scene.

The scoring is for six solo voices, two four-part choruses, two violins, and continuo. Everyone concerned in the performance does distinguished work. Totally, the presentation is superb.

Cantiones Sacrae

☐ Dresden Kreuzchor / Otto (organ) / Mauersberger (conductor) / Telefunken 3635009

Schütz's *Cantiones Sacrae Quatuor Vocum cum Basso ad Organum* consists of forty motets. There is a combine in this music of madrigal influence with contrapuntalistic involvement (and certain complexity). Included is a use of "word-painting" that is accomplished with finesse. The texts that Schütz chose indicate not only his own statement of personal faith but also that his music was intended for intimate worship—at court or possibly at home. For example, the last five motets are to be used as grace prior to meals, and others are pointed toward use during Lent.

Without nullifying strength when it should be applied, there is a chamber-music-like aspect to the production which enhances the music beautifully. The singing leaves nothing to be desired; the organ (which dates from 1725) is of lovely mellow tone.

See under *Choral: chorus and instrumental ensemble* (Motets from *Cantiones Sacrae*) for a selection from this work.

Christmas Oratorio

☐ Westphalian Choir and Instrumentalists / Rotzsch (tenor); Flebbe (soprano); Hudemann (bass) / Ehmann (conductor) / Bach Guild HM-11

A work that exemplifies Schütz at his very best and that shows how meticulous he was in relating words to music and in defining characterization by instrumental choice. Thus while recitative accompaniments are assigned the chamber organ and cello, ten different typed baroque instruments (the total used is seventeen, including two alto gambas, two trumpets, three trombones, dolcian, violone, etc.) define various personages. The Angel (Herta Flebbe sings this role) is accompanied by gambas; recorders and bassoon are assigned to the Shepherds; trombones partner the High Priests, etc. Such coloring is a special relish to a truly appetizing score.

The singers are all compelling. Hans-Joachim Rotzsch, as the Evangelist, is exceedingly expressive, and his enunciation is a joy to hear. If the tempi in the Turnabout release (34088), also available in a Vox Box (SVBX-5101), are brighter, the interpretative climate and the warmer singing place Vanguard's Bach Guild rendition in first place. If offered Vanguard S-232, don't consider it as competitive—it's the very same edition, with duplicates of the liner notes, text, and a performance certifying the conductor's statement that it is one of "originality, honesty, and concentration."

Deutsches Magnificat

☐ Heinrich Schütz Choir / Norrington (conductor) / Argo ZRG-666

Although the choral groups conducted by Gillesberger on Vox (SVBX-5101) and by

Cantata and Oratorio

Kahlhöfer on Nonesuch (71134) are certainly bigger than Norrington's , the larger gain is his because of the tempo he chooses. He moves the music and obtains a dynamism that is lacking in the more devotional and far less exciting speeds the other two conductors employ. Schütz's act of thanksgiving for the grace of God is better graced with such energy. A chamber-sized group of vocalists serves sufficiently.

Easter Oratorio

☐ Schwaebischer Singkreis / Schodt and Wehrung (sopranos); Witte-Waldbauer and Weinmann (mezzo-sopranos); Mielsch, Hermann, Bartel, and Maier (tenors); Schaible, Messthaler, and Wenk (basses); Koch, Münch-Holland, and Nordmeyer (viola da gambas); Klaiss (cello); Schulze (contrabass); Hoelderlin (organ); Galling (harpsichord) / Grischkat (conductor) / Turnabout 34231

The soloists in Schütz's *Historia der Auferstehung Jesu Christi* ("History of the Resurrection of Jesus Christ") all define characters in the Gospel narrative. The principal role of the Evangelist is portrayed by a tenor (Hans Ulrich Mielsch). Christ is represented by two contrasting voices (Reinhold Bartel and Erich Wenk), as is Maria Magdalena (Herrad Wehrung and Margarete Witte-Waldbauer). The other roles include the Three Marys, the Two Angels, the Two Men at the Tomb, the Youth at the Tomb, and Cleophas and His Companion.

The entire cast sings with will and skill; the work of Mielsch (his part is mainly in recitative form) is impressive and sensitive. The performance has dignified pace; the playing of the instrumental group is excellent. Cohesion between strength and restraint make Hans Grischkat's conducting ideal.

The performance is duplicated in a three-record Vox Box (SVBX–5101), which includes four other works by Schütz.

Musikalische Exequien, Op. 7

☐ Vienna Chamber Choir / Speiser and Hansmann (sopranos); Helesner (contralto); Equiluz and Resch (tenors); Heppe and Schneider (basses) / Gillesberger (conductor) / Vox SVBX–5101

A three-part work, the first part of which is a lengthy "Concerto in the Form of a German Funeral Mass." Parts 2 and 3 are like postscripts consisting of a motet and a setting of the "Song of Simeon."

One rarely hears of this work when discussions of Schütz are held, but the final part (with the text of the *Nunc Dimittis* in German) is one of Schütz's finest moments. And the singing of this section is the best part of this recording.

The Passion According to St. John

☐ Vokalensemble Pro Musica, Köln / Kölschbach (soprano); Markus, Esser, and Heidbüchel (tenors); Müller-Heuser, Küpper, and Georg (basses) / Hömberg (conductor) / Vox SVBX–5102

A performance that can be marked five-star in every respect. Tempi, smoothness of line and style are well-nigh perfect. Without proper flow Schütz's music can quickly become stilted. There is no overstressing of pitches by any of the soloists; neither is there any interpretative exaggeration, and yet every measure has beautiful and meaningful expression. The choral singing is superb. Full credit to Johannes Hömberg, who directs matters without disturbing Schütz's purity of approach.

For the Schütz Passion According to St. Luke and Passion According to St. Matthew, *see below.*

The Passion According to St. Luke

☐ Vokalensemble Pro Musica, Köln / Markus, Possemeyer, and Heidbüchel (tenors); Lang (countertenor); Zacharias (alto); Wenk (baritone); Müller-Heuser (bass) / Hömberg (conductor) / Vox SVBX-5102

Comparison with the competitive rendition on Telefunken (641193) confirms the Vox release as the choice version. The role of the Evangelist calls for a tenor. For no valid reason Telefunken has chosen a baritone, who tries, most often, to simulate a higher-ranged voice, which doesn't work at all. Further, the Cologne chorus is far stronger and more resonant than the Monteverdi group on Telefunken.

The dignified portrayal of Jesus, by Franz Müller-Heuser, deserves special mention. Excellent clarity throughout the recording.

For Schütz's Passion According to St. John *see above*, and for his Passion According to St. Matthew *see below*.

The Passion According to St. Matthew

☐ Vokalensemble Pro Musica, Köln / Markus and Possemeyer (tenors); Lang (countertenor); Zacharias (alto); Wenk (baritone); Müller-Heuser (bass) / Hömberg (conductor) / Vox SVBX-5102

As with the other Schütz Passions (*see above* [The Passion According to St. John and The Passion According to St. Luke]), there are no furbelows in the music. No instrumental coloring is utilized; its absence adds to the austerity but without detracting from the beauty of the unaccompanied recitatives and choruses. Neither are these squared recitatives; rather, they are fluidic, extremely telling narratives vocalized in natural speech rhythms—that is, if the singers are aware that such is the desired style. Those listed above are. In the competitive Argo (ZRG–689) edition the singers are not, and the result is a type of pseudo-dramaticism which not only is stylistically out of bounds but also is annoying to one's ears.

Vox has good notes but neither text nor translation. Argo gets points for including all three in its production.

The Seven Last Words of Christ from the Cross

☐ Monteverdi-Chor, Hamburg, and Leonhardt Consort / Jacobiet (soprano); van t'Hoff (tenor); van Egmond and Runge (baritones); Villisech (bass); Leonhardt (organ) / Jürgens (conductor) / Telefunken 641193

Warmly communicative; the solo voices are excellent, and the chorus is flawless, indeed a superb group. The instrumental back-up has textural stability but is never too heavy.

Nicolaas (Nico) Schuyt   *(1922-   )*

Discorsi capricciosi per 12 fiati e percussione (1965)   *Orchestra*

☐ Concertgebouw Orchestra / Haitink (conductor) / Donemus Audio-Visual Series 7002

Schuyt's "Capricious Conversations" divide the playing personnel into two trios (one of winds, the other of brass) and a sextet (winds plus two horns) and call for separate placement of the two percussionists. The recording (made live) does not, however, delineate this dispersion very acutely.

Dialogues and instrumental cohesion alternate in this panchromatic essay. There is no lust for complicated situations—plentiful activity there is, but the arguments remain clear, particularly because of the sharp playing and Haitink's control of textures and meters.

Joseph Schwantner   (1943-   )

Orchestra

Diaphonia Intervallum (1966)

☐ Contemporary Chamber Ensemble / Morosco (alto saxophone) / Weisberg (conductor) / Nonesuch 71221

Schwantner's chamber-ensemble piece for nine instruments features the alto saxophone, as can be seen from the credits noted above. The balance of the instrumentation embraces concertante flute and piano and tutti strings consisting of two violins, viola, two cellos, and a double bass.

The basic unity of the music, its *Auskomponierung,* is the interval (hence the title of the work) of a major seventh. While the development of such single tone span does not produce a *Kunstwerk,* it does produce an interesting one, especially through the saxophoned deliberations that twine through the textures.

Weisberg supplies all the substantial arguments in his direction to support the composer. Victor Morosco proves he is a fine saxophonist.

Modus Caelestis (Consortium III) (1972)

☐ New England Conservatory Repertory Orchestra / Shearer (flute) / Pittman (conductor) / Composers Recordings S–340

Schwantner's "Celestial Melody" presents a continuum of sound blocks. It is an exploration of sonorous densities, though individually none of the sounds can be termed dense. A sense of suspended motion is conveyed, bringing to mind the music of Ligeti, though there is more motility within Schwantner's piece. The scoring is for a dozen strings (six violins, three violas, and three cellos), piano, celesta, and three percussion, playing vibraphone, glockenspiel, tubular bells, crotales, and tam-tams, plus an all-important group of twelve flutes.

This contemporary depiction of the music of the spheres has a special luminosity. It is exceedingly eloquent.

Solo Instrument and Orchestra

Cello

In Aeternum (Consortium IV) for Cello and IV Players (1973)

☐ Members of Boston Musica Viva / Humeston (cello and crotales) / Pittman (conductor) / Delos 25406

Actually, *In Aeternum* is a cross between the solo instrument with accompaniment medium and chamber music, considering, in terms of the latter, that only a quartet is partnered with the cello. But, the four players do accompany the cello employing a total of 13 instruments, which strengthens the orchestrational concept. Purposeful or simply coincidental, there is an exact mathematical arrangement of these 13 instruments plus the two the cellist plays: one instrumentalist plays five types (flute, alto flute, piano, glass crystals, and water gong); a second performer is assigned four types (clarinet, bass clarinet, glass crystals, and water gong); the third member of the group plays three instruments (violin, viola, and crotales); the soloist plays two (cello and crotales); and one performer is assigned the percussion (considered as a single unit).

Though serially organized, the emphasis is on a coloristically flexible setting. Schwantner's world is far from serene. It is one of shadows and lights, its terrain one of curves, zigzags, and sharp turns. Vivid music, this, without a single iota of muzzy sentiment. It is splendidly performed by Jay Humeston as the soloist, assisted by Paul Brittan, William Wrzesien, Nancy Cirillo, and Dean Anderson.

Autumn Canticles (*Consortium* VII)

☐ Western Arts Trio / Laurel LR–104

Five ancient Chinese poems, all with autumnal aspects, furnished the "inspirational and creative generator" for Schwantner's trio. Rhapsodic architectonic constructions with rational segmentation, all highly colored, cover the piece.

A well-communicated realization of the score by this team.

Consortium I (1970)

☐ Robison (flute); Wrzesien (clarinet); Cirillo (violin); Thompson (viola); Coppock (cello) / Delos 25406

Chamber-music totality is set loose with soloistic bravado in Schwantner's piece. Abstract formalism rules and the content moves with nervous, somewhat peripatetic sensibility. This description of the kaleidoscopic conditions of Schwantner's score seems more apt than the composer's modest one that Consortium "reflects a preoccupation with virtuosic writing for each instrument."

The playing is certainly virtuosic.

Chamber Music

Elliott Schwartz   (1936-   )

Four Studies for Two Clarinets (1964)

☐ Rehfeldt and Gates (clarinets) / Advance 15

Quite different from the musical gamesmanship that Schwartz practices in his current music. The most blatant points, and they are exceedingly minimal, are a few flutter sounds and short glides. The subtlety of the contrastive opposing voices has tinges of Poulenc and Shostakovich, but Schwartz has blended the instruments into four essays of individually defined charm and coloristic refinement.

Signals for Trombone and Double Bass (1968)

☐ Fulkerson (trombone) / Molfese (double bass) / Deutsche Grammophon 2543005

In Signals the world of theatrics enters the territory of chamber music. Included are tone matters in percussive disguise: hitting the trombone with a stick, popping its mouthpiece, striking the bass with the knuckles, and so forth. Without instrumental contact either player will yell, scream, squeal, mutter, make the sounds of a kiss, etc. There are also articulative utterances such as "hey," "freeze," "ee-i-ah-oo," and more.

And more. The two instrumentalists become equal to three or four when either or both performers sing or hum a line while also playing. The title of the piece is taken from two sections of one-minute length each. In these sections the choice of specified material and the timing of entrances are made by the players answering each other's performance-event "signals."

A signal success (the pun is intended). This applies to the colorfully complete performance.

Chamber Music

Paul Schwartz (1907-   )

Orchestra

Concertino for Chamber Orchestra

☐ Radio Orchestra of Zurich, Switzerland / Monod (conductor) / Composers Recordings 128 (monaural)

Neoclassic style covers this three-movement work. The theme for the *Sarabande with Variations* is compelling, the workout is less so.

Monod does what he can with his players, who seem underrehearsed and not fully integrated with the music. Average sound.

Cyril Scott (1879-1970)

Solo Instrument and Orchestra

Piano

Concerto No. 1 in C major for Piano and Orchestra (1915)

☐ London Philharmonic Orchestra / Ogdon (piano) / Herrmann (conductor) / HNH 4025

Three movements but principally devoted to impressionistic wash, with rhapsodic excursions and psuedo-exoticisms mixed in with the formalism. The milieu of Scott's famed short piece *Lotus Land* is revisted here, with Oriental fringes attached to the orchestral fabric.

It's a special type of ceremonial music in its way. The performing team is excellent: John Ogdon plays with the utmost fluidity, Bernard Herrmann is completely involved with the score, and the L.P.O. does splendidly. Originally, Scott's work was recorded by Lyrita (SRCS-81) in England. It has been remastered twice in this country—by Musical Heritage Society (MHS-3653) and, as noted above, by the new HNH label.

Instrumental

Piano

Lotus Land, Op. 47, No. 1

☐ Grainger (piano) / Klavier 121

Pictured by pentatonic diction. Grainger was a celebrated pianist, though most discussions about him concern his career as a composer. He displays a beautiful touch and presents Scott's impressionistic miniature with beautiful atmosphere.

Violin

The Gentle Maiden

☐ Heifetz (violin); Achron (piano) / RCA ARM4–0942 (monaural)

A little sweetmeat that Scott paired with *Cherry Ripe* and titled Two Old Airs Transcribed. Since the recording was made in 1924, expect roughage in the grooves but not in the violin vocalism.

Tallahassee Suite

☐ Heifetz (violin); Bay (piano) / RCA ARM4–0944 (monaural)

Scott's suite has all the lubricious writing that would attract a violinist with a tone as rich as Heifetz possesses. Most of Scott's music tends to be semi-exotic and lush, but none of the former quality is present in this instance. Melody endorsed by harmony rules throughout. The music moves perpendicularly, never bends over into polyphonic posture.

For no valid reason the work is presented with the third movement (*Danse nègre*) first, then follow parts 1 and 2 (*Bygone Memories* and *After Sundown*). It doesn't make sense to begin with the climactic part of the work. Since the disc is banded, the listener can rectify matters and play the work in its proper order.

Tom Scott   (1912-1961)

Binorie Variations (1953)   *Orchestra*

Hornpipe and Chantey (1944)

☐ Vienna Orchestra / Adler (conductor) / Composers Recordings 104 (monaural)

The rhythm of the dance in the Hornpipe is banked, considered almost casually rather than steadfastedly. It is an admirable compositional stratagem. In the Variations folk-tune scale is paramount. The piece is named after a Scottish ballad, and Scott's music was originally contained in a film score.

If the playing is lacking a bit in warmth in the Hornpipe and Chantey, the opposite is the case in the *Binorie Variations*. It may well be that the Viennese musicians recognize and thereby understand music written in variation form but a symphonicized and developed English dance escapes their understanding.

Alexander Scriabin   (1872-1915)

Poem of Ecstasy (Symphony No. 4), Op. 54   *Orchestra*

☐ Los Angeles Philharmonic Orchestra / Mehta (conductor) / London 6552

Know it as it should be. The implosions and explosions, the feverish sound caresses and orchestrational sex of this piece need intensity and fire plus an all-out let-go. Stoky was the type of conductor who could deliver Scriabin's score as it should be and he did (with the Houston Symphony on Everest 3032). Then Zubin Mehta came along. His performance is electrifying. All the juices are there, and they're not bottled up. There is one finely sculpted example in the catalogue, Abbado on Deutsche Grammophon (2530137) with the B.S.O., but one would rather bypass such orchestrational security for the kind of emotional extroverted inquiry Mehta makes. It's number one.

Prometheus, Poem of Fire (Symphony No. 5), Op. 60

☐ London Philharmonic Orchestra / Ashkenazy (piano) / Maazel (conductor) / London 6732

Scriabinish ecstasy that has as the basis for its phantasmagorial moves his famous mystic chord (of quartal intervallic construction). The orchestra is large and includes a virtuosic piano obbligato part (played here in a revelatory manner by Vladimir Ashkenazy). In one continuous movement there are five sections that symbolize such mystical matters as will, movement, anxiety, contemplation, and mystery itself. A music that has torrid tumescence and sensual significance.

The performance beautifully sets forth Scriabin's timbre splashes and outbursts, and exudes its extremely strange charm.

Symphony No. 1 in E major, Op. 26

☐ U.S.S.R. Symphony Orchestra and R.S.F.S.R. Russian Chorus / Avdeyeva (mezzo-soprano); Grigoriev (tenor) / Svetlanov (conductor) / Melodiya/Angel S-40113

The final-movement "Hymn to Art," using solo-vocal and choral forces, is the most sumptuous of this Wagnerian-encumbered work. In music of this kind elasticity is hard to come by, so the performance may seem stuffy, but it gets a passing grade.

Symphony No. 2 in C minor, Op. 29

☐ U.S.S.R. Symphony Orchestra / Svetlanov (conductor) / Melodiya/Angel S-40118

Liadov thought Scriabin's music represented decadence. Arensky stated the title "Symphony" should have been "Cacophony." Poor souls! In 1902 they could not hear this as we can—as chromaticism and quite orthodox at that, despite the wandering Russianism of it all. And how could they be willing to accept the eroticism sprinkled in the score with its brassy ecstacies?

With Columbia's version deleted (No. MS-7285, Semkov with the London Symphony), Svetlanov's will have to suffice. It is quite satisfactory and sensuous where it should be.

Symphony No. 3 (*Divine Poem*), Op. 43

☐ U.S.S.R. Symphony Orchestra / Svetlanov (conductor) / Melodiya/Angel S-40098

Svetlanov makes one believe that he believes in the musico-theosophic data of Scriabin's work. It is quite compelling, with majestic intensity in the first movement (*Luttes*), the proper percentage of ardency in part 2 (*Voluptés*), and balanced propulsion in the final *Jeu divin*. The playing is fluid and fluent, and not only Scriabin buffs will find it quite exciting.

Solo Instrument and Orchestra

Piano

Concerto in F sharp minor for Piano and Orchestra, Op. 20

☐ London Philharmonic Orchestra / Ashkenazy (piano) / Maazel (conductor) / London 6732

This is early Scriabin, meaning elaboration of material via considerable figuration, and all strongly reminiscent of Chopin. There are variational data in the central part of the work. The main interest is in the solo line.

Ashkenazy's only competition comes from Michael Ponti on Candide 31040. The competition turns out to be only third class. Further, the Hamburg Symphony Orchestra that supports Ponti is downright poor.

Instrumental

Horn

Romance for Horn and Piano

☐ Barrows (horn); Sanford (piano) / Golden Crest 7018 (monaural)

A rare item, nullifying the idea that Scriabin wrote only for piano and for orchestra. Characteristic Russian melos. Suavely played.

Piano

Etudes, Op. 8 (Nos. 2, 8, 10, and 11)
Etudes, Op. 42 (Nos. 3, 4, and 5)
Feuillet d'album, Op. 45, No. 1

☐ Horowitz (piano) / Columbia M-31620

Excellent samplings from the dozen Etudes in the Opus 8 group and the eight contained in Opus 42. (The numbers Horowitz plays are incorrectly designated in *Schwann*.) The "Album Leaf" (in E flat major) is the first of a set of three (the others are a *Poème fantasque* and a Prelude). It is a light miniature; the compositional artistry preempts any consideration of this music as a salon tidbit. It has sensitivity and a beautifully conceived homophonic final cadence.

Horowitz's approach to these pieces is impressive. The playing has fine precision and a lyrical warmth that never sags even when agitated material is involved.

Piano Sonata

No. 1 in F minor, Op. 6 / No. 2 (*Sonata-Fantasy*) in G sharp minor, Op. 19

☐ Zhukov (piano) / Melodiya/Angel S–40217

It may be difficult to accept the word "Brahmsian" in regard to this composer but there it is, truly, in regard to the *allegro con fuoco* movement of the Opus 6 Sonata. The rest of the work is opposite in tone, realized by Zhukov's strong playing, supported by a finely contrasted dynamic scale. There is plenty of romantic emotionalism in the second Sonata (its music is not overly chromaticized). The performance of this two-movement work is expressive and well-balanced.

Piano Sonata

No. 3 in F sharp minor, Op. 23 / No. 4 in F sharp major, Op. 30 / No. 6, Op. 62

☐ Laredo (piano) / Connoisseur Society S–2032

The forms are not standard, of patterned thought. There is, particularly in the Opus 62, subjective scrutiny. In Scriabin's Sonatas the basic meaning applies: "a piece of sound." Balances are maintained even when apocalyptic order surfaces. The balances are merely weighed differently then.

Laredo's playing of the Opus 62 Sonata is clear, ideally so, since she opts for degrees of dynamic plasticity for the entire composition. The effectiveness of the playing in the other works includes a fine sonority scale, knowledgeable selection of tempi (thus avoiding the harmonic blur that occurs in too speedy a tempo), and sharp rhythmic detail that does not interfere with horizontal flow and thrust.

Piano Sonata

No. 7 (*The White Mass*) in F sharp major, Op. 64 / No. 9 (*The Black Mass*) in F major, Op. 68

☐ Laredo (piano) / Connoisseur Society S–2034

Because of its expression of spirituality, Scriabin termed his Opus 64 *The White Mass*. Scriabin spoke of the "mystic clouds" and "saintly sonorities" in this work, as well as of the "sainthood" he had achieved. It is a composer's prerogative to define his music as he wishes, to call it "truly holy" or "celestial." Naturally, it is a listener's privilege also to consider a music without an outlined run of events in any fashion he wishes. Scriabin's *White Mass* is also of colored volatility, an important progenitive impetus being the urgency of the intervallic leap at the beginning. Its appearance five times in the initial eight measures is prophetic of future events in the Sonata.

The other Sonata is in direct contrast. Though known as *The Black Mass*, it does not represent a desecration of the Christian Mass. The cognomen derives, apparently, from the intensity (sometimes harshness) of the material. Every moment in this Sonata is concerned with tight motility; everything is contained, as tight as a high-pitched drumhead. The music is black. When it is of lighter texture, it has sounds of almost poisonous sweetness.

Laredo's colorations of these contrastive works are keenly applied. The performance quality fits succinctly. Whatever elements are in the score are fully detailed—mysticism in the Opus 64, dramaticism in the other Sonata. Contrasts within each work are emphasized, the style is absolute, the results determinative. Scriabin is splendidly served.

1695

Piano Sonata No. 10 in C major, Op. 70

☐ Horowitz (piano) / Columbia M–31620

Bounded formality is rare in late-period Scriabin. Thus it is the freely colored prose of this leanly textured work, based on sharply detailed linear syntax, that structures the Sonata. Horowitz's performance is one of total perception with magnificent detailing of the different weights that help define the total design.

Poem, Op. 32, No. 1

☐ Laredo (piano) / Desto 7145

Shot through, as so often in Scriabin's music, with sensual sweat. Laredo tends to underplay that element in favor of a simplistic romanticism. It registers effectively.

Poème satanique, Op. 36

☐ Ponti (piano) / Candide 31040

Scriabin's colorful titular identity can only be applied to the devilishly difficult technical requirements for the performer. Throughout, the music follows severely ambivalent moods, similar to a manic-depressive chart. Hammered vertical declaratives, soaring melodic turns, and a languid expressivity cut against an ironic impetus. Ponti's playing nicely brings into perspective the contrastive black-white effect of the piece.

Preludes, Op. 11

No. 1 in C major / No. 2 in A minor / No. 3 in G major / No. 4 in E minor / No. 5 in D major / No. 6 in B minor / No. 7 in A major / No. 8 in F sharp minor / No. 9 in E major / No. 10 in C sharp minor / No. 11 in B major / No. 12 in G sharp minor / No. 13 in G flat major / No. 14 in E flat minor / No. 15 in D flat major / No. 16 in B flat minor / No. 17 in A flat major / No. 18 in F minor / No. 19 in E flat major / No. 20 in C minor / No. 21 in B flat major / No. 22 in G minor / No. 23 in F major / No. 24 in D minor

Preludes, Op. 74

☐ Laredo (piano) / Desto 7145

These works are illustrative of Scriabin's entire creative career. The set of five Preludes in Opus 74 is Scriabin's final composition and exemplifies his ecstatic eroticism and suave sensuality. No keys are detailed. Instead, tempo headings such as *douloureux, déchirant* (No. 1) and *fier, belliqueux* (No. 5) give the clues to the intoxicating affirmations. The Opus 11 group ranges from Chopinesque considerations to an infiltration of individuality.

Here is well-scaled playing, defined with splendid tone, interpretative presence, and considerable depth of feeling. Ruth Laredo is totally sensitive to and perceptive about Scriabin's music. An important recording.

Two Poems, Op. 69

Vers la Flamme, Op. 72

☐ Horowitz (piano) / Columbia M–31620

The "poem" designation was favored by Scriabin. No dainty chintzes of lightness mark such pieces. Each has definitive unity, and each proposes a neat essay. "Toward the Flame" falls in the same poetic category. The passionate intensity and breadth plus integrity of Horowitz's playing are supreme.

Fantasy, Op. Posth. *Two Pianos*

☐ Duo di Heidelberg / Musical Heritage Society MHS-1147

Scriabin's Fantasy (probably composed at the age of 18, though some sources date it later, when Scriabin was 22) was planned for piano and orchestra but only a two-piano score was completed.

There is no mysticism, therefore, but there is, expectedly, full romanticism. No revelations, mind you, just par-value musical value. Expertly conveyed by the piano twosome. (The work is also in the fourth volume of Vox's survey of Scriabin's piano music, SVBX-5474, played by Michael Ponti and Robert Leonardi. The MHS disc has better sound.)

Scriabin / **Alexander Nemtin (1936-   )**

Universe *Orchestra*

☐ Moscow Philharmonic Orchestra and Yurlov Chorus of the R.S.F.S.R. / Lyubimov (piano); Orlova (organ) / Kondrashin (conductor) / Melodiya/Angel SR-40260

Not a transcription, but pure guesswork in completing a Scriabin compositional plan. At the time of his death Scriabin was planning a "Prefatory Action" which would precede his *Mysterium*, the "ultimate" work which would combine in one fell swoop all the impressions of the senses (including perfumes!) with a religious objective. Sketches for the *Mysterium* were vague and in no shape for sorting out and completing; the "Action" covered some thirty pages of a textual outline.

Extremely minimal credits should be given to Scriabin. This is a Nemtin conception that is "in the manner of" the deceased gentleman. As far as that goes, it's pretty good, since Nemtin certainly knows the Scriabin style. All the mannerisms, the mysticism, the harmonic maneuvering are there. This is an interesting curiosity.

Peter Sculthorpe *(1929-   )*

Sun Music III (1967) *Orchestra*

☐ Louisville Orchestra / Mester (conductor) / Louisville LS-735

A fascinating and unique organization of musical materials, of organic and extremely picturesque formation. The effect of static solidity of an individually particular (or slightly related) texture to the next one, while a sense of sultry sonic incantation is heard, is almost frightening. Sculthorpe's instrumental pigmentation is chosen from vivid reds, blues, and purples. For a music of this coloristic independence, thematicism would be an intrusion.

This is one of the best performances the Louisville group has given under Jorge Mester's direction.

Ruth Crawford Seeger *(1901-1953)*

Two Movements for Chamber Orchestra (1926) *Orchestra*

☐ Boston Musica Viva / Pittman (conductor) / Delos 25405

Polytonal music, deftly clarified by strong linear profiles. Rhythmic superimposition activates the texture but does not tear it. These are superb pieces, contrasted in tempi.

Pittman's group (flute, clarinet, bassoon, a quartet of violins, a pair of cellos, and piano) presents a memorable performance of a work that lay untouched for a half century.

Instrumental

Piano

Nine Preludes for Piano (1928)
Study in Mixed Accents (1929)

☐ Bloch (piano) / Composers Recordings S–247

The style in the set of Preludes stems from Debussy, flavored and colored with some salty chordal contractions. The Study is in bare octaves and runs about seventy seconds; its shifting punctuations are of simple design.

Chamber Music

String Quartet (1931)

☐ Composers Quartet / Nonesuch 71280

Linear freedom of the nonchordal, atonal type is exemplified in the first two movements. Only the moods differ—in the first, somewhat serious and rhapsodic; in the second, scherzo-like. The structures are thus similarly free of pedantic dogma. Elliott Carter's music will come to mind, but Mrs. Seeger said it first and said it with amazing prophetic penetrability.

Movement 3 remains just as radically new in 1981 as it was in 1931. Every note is concerned with a counterpoint, not of sounds, but of dynamics. Various gradations occur in four-voiced dynamic layers, rarely coinciding at the same intensity of power. Pitches are sandwiched in tight secundal arrangement, but they are only the minimal means to attain the maximal end. Seeger proves that expressive music can be made from a counterpoint concentrated on continuant, similar, and opposed degrees of sonorous intensity.

The fourth movement contains 116 measures, with exactly the last half written in retrograde fashion. All the melodic shapes, naturally, become changed, but in this instance further shifted in the *al rovescio* technique by raising all sounds a half tone. The perfect logic of such a technique makes the most regulated antithesis to any thematic thesis.

The Composers Quartet (Matthew Raimondi and Anahid Ajemian, violins; Jean Dupouy, viola; and Michael Rudiakov, cello) is simply sensational. The tonal congress and pitch propulsion of Seeger's fiendishly difficult piece are met head on and conquered from first note to last. There is total excitement but never the feeling of exertion. And Raimondi's execution of the motility increase as the music proceeds to the half-way point in the last movement deserves a special prize. Truly an extraordinary quartet performed in an extraordinary manner.

Suite for Wind Quintet (1952)

☐ Lark Quintet / Composers Recordings S–249

Quite different from the constructively experimental music this composer was turning out in the 1930s. There is a stressing of unison writing (rare in woodwind-quintet scoring) in all three movements. Polyphony is of the ''new'' academic type that emphasizes dissonances over consonances.

Leif Segerstam *(1944-   )*

Divertimento (1962)

☐ Helsinki Chamber Orchestra / Rahkonen and Louhivuori (violins); Kamu (viola); Höylä (cello) / Segerstam (conductor) / Bis LP-19

A transcription of material that was used in a string trio and then transferred as a string quartet. There is considerable alliance with both Hindemith and Bartók in the three movements.

Certainly an authentic performance with the composer conducting (his reputation is stronger in that field). However, avoid the liner note unless you can read Finnish, which probably makes sense—the English translation doesn't.

Poem for Violin and Piano (1965)

☐ Duo Pohjola / Bis LP-18

The content of Segerstam's concentrated *Poem* is clearly divided: a declamatory and rugged wide-ranging line for the violin, percussive chordal responses by the piano. The passions of the former are made more eloquent, therefore, by the latter, by being clearly and homophonically focused. There is a certain violence within the music and it is thus portrayed in this telling performance by the sister and brother team (Liisa Pohjola, piano; Paavo Pohjola, violin).

A *Nnnnooooowww* for Woodwind Quintet (1973)

☐ Helsinki Quintet / Bis LP-11

No printer's gremlin has played with the title. It is absolutely correct. What Segerstam argues (correctly) and illustrates in his title is that the creative imagery moves far more speedily than the restrictions of time required to notate the processes of invention. He describes it thus: "the faaaact thaaaaat iiiin theeee sounding moooomeeeeennnt ooof notation the tempo of thaaaat peeeeeen iiis much slower." He speaks of the "feeeeliiing of veeeryyy slooowmotion wheeen you are writing." Thus, such manual restriction brings restriction into the essence of the work and it is best to free the performer so that he is not (in turn) subjected to the boundaries of notation. According, aleatoric music, of course, which he describes as music in free-pulsative style. And, so Segerstam says: go ahead and do it "nnnnooooowww"—spontaneously.

What the Helsinki Quintet does is rather interesting (a bit more than fifteen minutes worth). It does sound improvised, but rather nicely put together. The listener will not be perplexed (Stockhausen is miles ahead of Segerstam) since the chromaticism hovers around tonal territory. There are some squeals but that's not due to bad engineering but the result of an instruction to the players to produce sounds that are "very high, very sensitive and pleading." Now, do listen to A Nnnnooooowww. It has good values, at least for now and doubtless for later.

Andrés Segovia *(1893-   )*

Estudio

Oración, **Study in E**

☐ Williams (guitar) / Everest 3195

Everyone, but everyone knows Segovia, the greatest of the guitarists. How many know his work as a composer? (There is no excuse for *Schwann's* failure to list Segovia's music, though some other works in Everest's miscellaneous program *The Virtuoso Guitar* are fully detailed.)

The *Oración* is a tender piece, a prayer for Manuel Ponce. The *Estudio* is lighter material, but like the other composition displays fine craftsmanship, and of course every measure is cogently conceived for the guitar. It is nice to see that John Williams, who studied with Segovia, plays his music.

Mátyás Seiber (1905 - 1960)

Solo Instrument and Orchestra

Clarinet

Concertino for Clarinet and Strings (1951)

☐ Louisville Orchestra / Livingston (clarinet) / Mester (conductor) / Louisville S-701

For the most part Seiber's Concertino is the equivalent of a Bartókian brochure. It is a brightly colored one because the virtuosity is not only centered in the solo clarinet. That Seiber eventually became a serial composer does not negate the nicely turned tonal product here recorded, even with its strong emulation of the Bartókian manner.

Topflight playing by all concerned.

Chamber Music

Permutazioni a cinque (1958)

☐ London Wind Quintet / Argo 5326

Serialism devoted to permutating an all-intervallic row, ranging from the smallest to the largest (minor second to major seventh). This intellectual sympathy produces more: bouncing rhythms that branch in and out. Thus serialistic rhapsody which is a distant cousin to tonal rhapsody.

The London Wind Quintet (Gareth Morris, flute; Sidney Sutcliffe, oboe; Bernard Walton, clarinet; Gwydion Brooke, bassoon; and Alan Civil, horn) is fully at home with Seiber's brand of music.

William Selby (ca. 1738 - 1798)

Instrumental

Organ

Voluntary in A major

☐ Harmon (organ) / Orion 76255

The eighth of a set of Ten Voluntaries for the Organ. Handel has said what Selby says but no better. The fugue that covers the second part forms a smart climax.

Harmon's color choice for the first part is particularly appropriate, slightly French-oboe in its timbre. There is a lovely tone to the Hradetzky organ used.

Robert Selig (1939 -)

Solo Instrument and Orchestra

Trumpet

Mirage

☐ Chamber Orchestra of Copenhagen / Ghitalla (trumpet) / Moriarty (conductor) / Cambridge 2823

Mirage for trumpet and strings is a programmatic conception concerned with man and his struggle with the natural forces of the desert. The music sings and declaims with Ivesian, somewhat Ruggles-like emotional intensity. In some respects it is a big brother of Copland's *Quiet City*. The full-blooded vigor of Selig's writing proves a special talent.

Ghitalla's playing is inspiring.

Daria Semegen (1946-)

Electronic Composition No. 1 (1972)

☐ Odyssey Y–34139

Electronic Music

Sectional distribution of the material with technological command. The sonic rhapsody is drawn from the full ("traditional") electronic budget.

Alexander Semmler (1900-1977)

Trio for Violin, Cello, and Piano, Op. 40

☐ Philharmonia Trio / Composers Recordings 211 (monaural)

Chamber Music

Semmler's opus rides the conventional path of trio facture. However, though traditionally bound in scoring, it is enriched with harmonic and polyphonic *brio* that holds the interest. Twentieth-century punctuations do not change the finding that Semmler is a classicist in his formal definitions. All of these are stated with clear positiveness.

A sensible and sensitive performance by Libove, Shulman, and Lugovoy—violinist, cellist, and pianist, respectively. Good sound.

Ludwig Senfl (ca. 1486-1543)

Vocal

Nu, wöllt ihr hören neue Mär'

☐ Early Music Consort of London / Bowman (countertenor) / Munrow (conductor) / Nonesuch 71326

Voice and Instrumental Ensemble

Sprightly music, sprightly performed. The voice is accompanied by dolcian, medieval fiddle, viol, and harpsichord.

José Serebrier (1938-)

Orchestra

Partita

☐ Louisville Orchestra / Engelman (percussion) / Whitney (conductor) / Louisville 641 (monaural)

Serebrier warns that his *Partita* title has no relationship to the classic format. Movement 1 is a *Preludio,* and there are strong reminders of Villa-Lobos. Eclectic? Bearing in mind that Serebrier's main occupation is that of a conductor, such rub-off is understandable. In movement 2, an *Interludio y fuga,* the former is flavored nostalgically, the latter is a contrapuntalized Latinized concept, a triple fugue at that, backed by plenty of percussion.

The dynamics of Serebrier's well-written piece and its nationalistic penetrative observations are displayed with fine insight by the Kentucky-based orchestra.

Tibor Serly   (1900-1978)

Solo Instrument and Orchestra

Two Pianos

Concerto for Two Pianos and Orchestra

☐ Folk Opera Orchestra of Vienna / Frid and Ponse (pianos) / Serly (conductor) / Musical Heritage Society MHS-3337

Principal to Serly's work is a technique which produces duo simultaneity of material. Though not cast in bitonality, the music thereby operates on separate levels of texture, motile tonality, and color. In a work for solo instruments against (and with) orchestra this is a technical bonus. The method is most clarified in the engaging extroverted finale, which occasionally reminds one of Bartók.

Ably performed. The soloists, Géza Frid and Luctor Ponse, are both composers in their own right.

Viola

Concerto for Viola and Orchestra (1929)

☐ Vienna Symphony Orchestra / Vardi (viola) / Serly (conductor) / Musical Heritage Society MHS-3306

The Concerto is unsentimentally romantic, unscathed by the slightest impurity of that style. Serly was born in Hungary, came to the United States, and returned (at the age of twenty-one) to Budapest, where he studied with Kodály. The Concerto shows that Serly did not bypass his contact with his native environment despite his cosmopolitanism. However, the Concerto is not folk-songed in its voice. When nationalistic accent occurs (mainly in the slow movement, where the *parlando* turns remind one of humid, meridian hours), it is discriminative, extremely subtle.

Vardi's playing is a deposition of artistry. His tone is like spun silk, not once forced, even in the most strenuous passages. The entire production is note-perfect and noteworthy. Serly's Concerto is a veridical contribution, worthy of place alongside the viola Concerti of Walton and Bartók.

Violin

Concerto for Violin and Wind Symphony and Percussion (1958)

☐ Vienna Symphony Orchestra / Vardi (violin) / Serly (conductor) / Musical Heritage Society MHS-3306

Neo-romantic gusto, peppered by the percussion, especially in the second of the two movements (a Dance Concertino). There is an indefatigability to the solo part which strives hard to make its point constantly. Vardi makes *his*.

Instrumental

Violin

Sonata in Modus Lascivus for Solo Violin

☐ Magnes (violin) / Bartók 908 (monaural)

Serly's mode is derived from a late medieval scale. The generative basis is no more striking than any of the old modes and clearly is tonally firmed up. Color values are strong, with the glassy whine of ponticello in the second movement and an all-plucked third movement.

Frances Magnes is a tip-top executant of Serly's music.

Serly / *Béla Bartók.* See Bartók / Tibor Serly.

Claude de Sermisy   *(ca. 1490-1562)*

Au Joly Boys   *Choral*

☐ Canby Singers / Canby (conductor) / Nonesuch 71115   *Chorus Alone*

A charming *chanson* that delights the ear. Worth hearing several times in succession: the flavor increases thereby. The sensitivity of the singing doubles the pleasure.

Kazimierz Serocki   *(1922-   )*

Sonatina for Trombone and Piano (1973)   *Chamber Music*

☐ Sauer (trombone); Carno (piano) / Crystal S-384

Viable chamber music for trombone and piano hasn't surfaced very much. Many an attempt is either stiff or stuffy. Serocki's Sonatina is excellent fare; it is responsive to the instrument's timbre possibilities, and it is responsible music. The doleful slow movement and the high level of melodic and rhythmic invention in the corner movements make the piece an outstanding contribution to the literature for the brass instrument. (A version exists for trombone and orchestra, premiered in Strasbourg, on December 19, 1975, but has not been recorded.)

Ralph Sauer's playing is rewarding. He gives the music a fine sense of flow and pacing. Good sound.

(Adrien-) François Servais   *(1807-1866)*

Grand Fantaisie on Themes from Donizetti's *Daughter of the Regiment*   *Instrumental*

Grand Fantaisie on Themes from Rossini's *Barber of Seville*   *Cello*

Souvenir de Spa, Op. 2

☐ Krosnick (cello); Grant (piano) / Orion 7290

Lyrical and some pyrotechnical hybird consideration of tunes in the pair of operatic reworkings. Not campy at all, though listening to one at a time is best. The Opus 2 is just as operatically oriented. Krosnick's consideration is excellent, and he plays the music straight, which gives all the assets. Cameron Grant is a very able second.

Roger Sessions   (1896-   )

Orchestra

Concertino for Chamber Orchestra (1972)

☐ Contemporary Chamber Players of the University of Chicago / Shapey (conductor) / Desto 7155

The total chromatic range marks Sessions's creative vision. It is used in this case to enunciate two fast-tempoed corner movements, but while the second of these has a gay set of projections, the opening part has rhapsodic flashes. The key to the work is found in its central section, where the emotive tone is set by the opening sounds of the double bassoon. The probings of this part of the composition, have a rich expressivity, notwithstanding its dark densities.

Sessions's music has its own special personality, brought by a continuity that avoids fragmentary ideas in order to achieve formal totality. Such totality is not disrupted by parenthetical explanatory phrases or inside footnotes, as it were. It is this complete immersion in structuring that marks the Sessions profile.

How well this is displayed by Shapey's group of twenty is questionable. The notes are all there and the articulations also, but it is not a highly polished quality that results. The diagnosis is that this is due to the players' adopting a percussive style that is not true to the score, probably the outcome of a unified defense mechanism against (while trying to solve) the individual difficulties within it.

Rhapsody for Orchestra (1970)

☐ New Philharmonia Orchestra / Prausnitz (conductor) / Argo ZRG–702

Title notwithstanding, Sessions's Rhapsody has inherently clear formal logic. Tripartite demarcation is here, plus a concluding Recitative. The scoring brings many a reminder of the brittle vehemence of Sessions's early *Black Maskers* music.

Setting aside a few pitches that waver, full performance credits can be given, especially for the sense of the "quasi-improvisatory character" that Sessions mentions in his notes.

Suite from *The Black Maskers* (1928)

☐ Eastman-Rochester Symphony Orchestra / Hanson (conductor) / Mercury 75049

Drawn from incidental music composed for the Andreyev play. The orchestral sounds (including such special timbres as an alto flute, D clarinet, and D trumpet) are a mine of information, and the wondrous effect of the organ in the latter part of the work is a timbre stroke to be anticipated.

Present is a fevered, ultracolored spirit which Hanson brings out to the utmost. In terms of interpretation and sonic qualities the record deserves a triple-A rating.

Sessions's work was first published by the Cos-Cob-Press. The E. B. Marks firm has since published an enlarged version which includes a movement titled *Romualdo's Song*, requiring a soprano. This movement is omitted from Hanson's performance. It was likewise not heard in the much earlier recording made by the Vienna Symphony Orchestra conducted by Walter Hendl, and still available on Desto (6404E).

Symphony No. 1 (1927)

☐ Japan Philharmonic Symphony Orchestra / Watanabe (conductor) / Composers Recordings 131E (monaural)

This Symphony will fool a lot of people expecting the usual data presented about Roger Sessions (cerebralism, polytonalism, dodecaphonism, heavy Germanic dress). And then make friends. The opus is heady, rhythmically persuasive, melodically fertile. Conventions are not smashed, yet the Symphony is not conventional. Sessions's propositions are put forth by the textural details, within which declarative triadic harmonies swing left and right. The first movement is asymmetric and percussive; the middle part is conversationally soft, somewhat mysterious, almost nocturnal; the finale streams through quartal and quintal territory. It all adds up to virile music, a joy to hear, absent of all pretensions.

Emphatically, the record collector should not pass this work by. Hearing Sessions's Symphony will bring the rewards of musical discovery. The recorded performance is excellent. Watanabe gives the piece proper charge and drive, and also its quota of excitement.

Symphony No. 2 (1946)

☐ New York Philharmonic / Mitropoulos (conductor) / Composers Recordings S–278E (monaural)

Begun in 1944 and completed in 1946, Sessions's Symphony is dedicated to the memory of Franklin Delano Roosevelt, who died during its composition. The music is of great expressiveness, with a tonality span that is as far-reaching as possible without intruding upon the domain of free tonality or reconstituting harmonic materials into the regulated order of a twelve-tone composition. This Symphony is on the scale of late Beethoven, with comparable introspective qualities. It is not an attempt to compose in imitation of Beethoven but presents full evidence of an individually true, unified art work. In working with such serious, musically creative intent, Sessions seems to make music that is free of sentiment; to some it may sound cold. But that is simply a matter of his refusing to direct his sounds toward the undiscriminating.

There are four movements, the tempi reflecting the classical compound of end divisions at fast speed, with a capricious second movement followed by an expressive slow movement. The Symphony was commissioned by the Ditson Fund, administered by Columbia University, and received two prizes, the Naumburg Award and the 1951 New York Music Critics' Circle Award. This is the type of music that showed Mitropoulos at his best; thus the performance is a most understanding one.

This is the third release of the same recording. It was first issued on a Columbia 7-inch LP disc (ML-2120). The second edition was also on Columbia (ML-4784), where it was coupled with Milhaud's Symphony No. 1. For having revived it CRI deserves congratulations. (The New York Phil. was noted as the "Philharmonic-Symphony Orchestra of New York" when the initial disc was released.)

Symphony No. 8 (1968)

☐ New Philharmonia Orchestra / Prausnitz (conductor) / Argo ZRG-702

Sessions's eighth Symphony is concentrated into two parts, a substantially slow-paced initial movement and a fast and more elaborate second movement. Dodecaphonic syntax is used with a rich amount of motival data that may sound austere but become highly emotive once the work has been exposed to a number of hearings. The loftiness (sublimity, if you will) of Sessions's music avoids the sweet and smooth for the pertinent and prehensile. There lies the prelude to permanence.

Prausnitz conducts an impressive statement of the Symphony.

*Solo
Instrument
and
Orchestra*

Violin

Violin Concerto (1935)

☐ Orchestre Philharmonique de l'Office de la Radiodiffusion-Television Française / Zukofsky (violin) / Schuller (conductor) / Composers Recordings S-220

There are many important works in the CRI catalogue, but few have the impact of this huge hunk of good music by one of the most "musical" composers of the century. Sessions has always resisted any deviation from his homogeneous new classicism, has refused to ally himself with any technical causes, has only been concerned with pure art, minus fuss, tricky ornaments, gimmicked padding. His Concerto shows that deep creativity means discovery.

The recording is one that belongs in every collection of important music, despite certain engineering imbalances. Zukofsky, a violinist of consummate polish and tremendous technique, is given such prominence that quite often the orchestral data (properly "busy" since contrapuntal amplitude is preeminent in Sessions's music) are blurred—whispery, instead of having dynamic equality with the solo voice. Schuller does a marvelous directing job, but I am surprised he approved of this soloistic overemphasis. The French organization is good, with intonation right on the button (Zukofsky's is miraculous); still, the outline of phrases is sometimes not sufficiently tight. No matter, the recording is one of the fattest credits in the CRI ledger.

The twenty-nine-minute work (the published score gives the timing as thirty-five minutes) is in four movements, the last two connected. In the *Romanza* the solo voice is the dominating factor, spinning its way in the total thirty-seven measures—a sort of single-stranded melody. Not the kind of tune that one whistles as one works, but deeply felt, deeply meaningful. For the greater part of the composition, the instrumentational style is amplified chamber music (one is persistently reminded of Schoenberg). Tuttis are few, appearing only for dramatic punctuation. Sessions's Concerto is, indeed, music of unique creativity.

Instrumental

Organ

Chorale (No. 1) (1938)

Three Chorale Preludes (1925)

☐ Mason (organ) / Counterpoint/Esoteric 5522E (monaural)

The Chorale is toccata-like in determination, though titled otherwise. The Three Chorale Preludes illustrate a modern slant regarding Bachian polyphony. Bach's chorale preludes had counterpoint woven around a basic melody; Sessions eliminates the fundamental and merely knits counterpoints. Stern stuff? A bit. But the stuff of mastery.

There is mastery on the part of Marilyn Mason as well, and truly vivid reproduction also.

Piano

From My Diary (1940)

☐ Rogers (piano) / Composers Recordings S-281

No program accompanies these four pieces. Sessions states they were once called "Pages from a Diary" and says nothing more. They are like etchings, with somber qualities alternating with lighter ones.

A major objective of performance is the discovery of the primary element in the music played. Rogers avoids opulence and likewise aloofness and steers the proper middle course.

Piano Sonata No. 1 (1930)

☐ Helps / Composers Recordings 198E (monaural)

Music of intricate detail. It combines the aspects of four movements (in alternate speeds) telescoped into a single unit. The chordal territory is wide because the language is based on an enlargement of tonality in the broadest sense. This proposes clash, tension, and resultant drama. Sessions's music is fundamentally polyphonic. One realizes that it is line that precedes vertical affiliation and that sonic partnership is determined mainly by linear progress.

Helps's performance has special dimensions. The textural clarity proclaims the brilliance of his achievement.

Sonata for Violin Solo (1953)

☐ Gross (violin) / Orion 73110

Twelve-tone-styled for the most part, Sessions's work is one of the great contributions to the literature for unaccompanied violin. No easy aural messages are contained in the piece, but the experience is well worth obtaining. There are four movements, the last three joined. Nervosity rules part 1, march-like motility covers the final section. Though there is lyricism in the second and third movements, and tempo differences, there is the over-all austerity that marks so much of Sessions's output. The composition obtains a great power from an undeviating use of long lines—segmentation is foreign to this composer's thinking. This type of writing is just as concentrated in its own way as music derived from pithy phrases.

The forward momentum of the Sonata demands a performer capable of mental stamina, else the exact notes may be heard but their close and distant relationships erased. Robert Gross is masterful in playing this piece (he suggested the writing of the Sonata to Sessions and gave its premiere performance). There are cruel problems (technically and in terms of structural clarification). All are solved in an impressive illustration of magnificent playing. The first recording made of Sessions's Sonata is still available (on Folkways 3355 in a monaural setting), played by Hyman Bress. It is given a good reading, but it does not have the sense of ease or information to be heard in Gross's number one performance.

Duo for Violin and Piano (1942)

☐ Zukofsky (violin); Kalish (piano) / Desto 6435/37

The Duo traverses a wide tonal territory, like most of Sessions's work. Its fabric is dissonant, the result of the chromatic colorative patterns of the harmonies. There is almost complete emancipation of the twelve sounds so that they almost function individually.

The *durchkomponiert* materials of the Duo (plotted in one continuous movement) do not form the usual symmetries. The first portion is lyrically directed. Then follows an impetuously designed section. The first portion is recalled briefly and leads into the final division. There is a restrained ending.

Sessions's music is exceedingly difficult to play, and the notorious ease with which most performers avoid his compositions has made acceptance, in proper scale, lag. Paul Zukofsky and Gilbert Kalish are the exception, of course. Their clear performance of Sessions's Duo is dynamic propaganda for the work. It may help change the statistic that Roger Sessions is a composer's, not a public's, composer.

Second String Quartet (1951)

☐ Kohon Quartet / Vox SVBX–5305

A wide tonal territory is covered here, the material presented with a packed pan-chromaticism that practically negates tonality, though polarities are present in a number of portions. For the greater part the key pole bends in many directions. The structure includes a double fugue, a large sonata formation minus a development section, a set of five variations on a theme, a bounding, very physically energized scherzo, and a concluding slow movement.

Vocal

Voice with Accompaniment

On the Beach at Fontana (1929)

☐ Beardslee (soprano); Helps (piano) / New World Records NW-243

Here is chromatic lucidity for the vocal line (composer-author Ned Rorem describes it as a "keening tune") with a suavely referenced keyboard background (Rorem calls this "the piano's lonely breeze"). More importantly, the music seems to be drawn out of the text, which makes this a masterly song, intimately introspective as is so much of Sessions's music.

Cantata and Oratorio

When Lilacs Last in the Dooryard Bloom'd (1970)

☐ Boston Symphony Orchestra and Tanglewood Festival Chorus / Hinds (soprano); Quivar (mezzo-soprano); Cossa (baritone) / Ozawa (conductor) / New World Records NW-296

Whitman's text was his response to the death of Lincoln, and Sessions's response never loses sight of the threnodic dramaticism that is inherent to the words. The score is impregnated with a constant emotional content that is never relaxed. Contrast here is by means of texture, vocal differences, choral weight, and orchestral color. A comprehensive fixity is retained in the cantata through its three parts. There are individual details, of course, but these are linked into the comprehensive totality of the piece.

Those who still insist on categorizing Sessions as a cerebralist would best listen to this work before repeating the groundless statement. One is certain that the expressive power and color of *When Lilacs Last in the Dooryard Bloom'd* will be recognized and thereby nullify the continuation of that false viewpoint.

New World's production is first class, and the orchestral playing and choral work are superb. A slight vibrato in the case of the female singers is to be noted, but it is not constant and so may be excused.

Déodat de Séverac   (1872-1921)

Instrumental

Piano

Baigneuses au soleil (1908)

Cerdaña (No. 1, Les muletiers devant Le Christ de Llivia) (No. 2, Le Retour des muletiers) (1911)

Les Naïades et le faune indiscret, Op. Posth.

☐ Doyen (piano) / Musical Heritage Society MHS-1155-57

All impressions, picture painting with full-scale coloration. In *Baigneuses au soleil* ("Girls Sunbathing"), which Séverac called an *Etude pittoresque*, the girls disport on the beach and in the water with the areas clearly identified by contextural and tempi differences. The two excerpts from *Cerdaña* (there are five parts in all) have Spanish flavor. "The Muleteers Before the Christ of Llivia" is a Lament that is twined around soft bell sounds and a quiet serenade. "The Muleteers' Return" is more dynamic. Séverac's "The Naiads and the Prying Faun" is a *Danse nocturne,* in turn languid and pert.

These conceptions are saturated with color and played in that fashion. The full-tone approach sometimes overemphasizes points in the music, but for the greater part these are good performances.

Pippermint-Get (1907)

Sous les lauriers roses (1919)

☐ Johannesen (piano) / Candide 31059

The *Pippermint* piece is termed a "Valse brillante de concert." That's dubious. A waltz, yes, but certainly not brilliant—rather, it's downright saucy (as the critic Richard Freed describes it perfectly). Regardless, it is a tasty lollipop (whose flavor doubtless is "peppermint").

Sous les lauriers roses ("Under the Oleanders") is a sizable mixed bag. Subtitled *Soir de carnaval sur la Côte catalane* ("Carnival Night on the Catalan Coast"), it contains a waltz, a Sardana, a *Scherzo-Valse,* a pair of homages, and so on. But it all fits together in its assortment of moods, colors, and more than casual descriptions.

Grant Johannesen plays beautifully and is most impressive in conveying the sense of naïveté that personalizes the *Sous les lauriers roses.*

Le Soldat de plomb for Piano, Four Hands (1905)

Piano,
Four Hands

☐ Dosse and Petit (piano) / Turnabout 34586

"The Brave Tin Soldier" is based on the Hans Christian Andersen tale. The music is labeled "histoire vraie en trois récits" ("true story in three narratives"). For this read: an unabashed, light-scanned musical picture. March tempo with its spirited concept is heard in the *Sérénade interrompue* ("Interrupted Serenade"), and fanfare-like jets appear there as well as in the final *Défilé nuptial* ("Wedding Procession"). The middle piece, *Quat' jours de boîte* ("Four Days in Jail"), is snidely doleful; and don't overlook the little interweave of the *Marseillaise.* All nice fancies that have a Satie-like decor.

Giovanni Sgambati *(1841-1914)*

Piano Concerto in G minor, Op. 15

Solo
Instrument
and
Orchestra

☐ Nürnberg Symphony Orchestra / Bolet (piano) / Cox (conductor) / Genesis 1020

Piano

The great value of the romantic revival is to pull us away, once and for all from the preoccupation with standard fare. Plenty of junk has surfaced, but it will sink. There is merit and stimulation in a number of the works that have reached disc. Sgambati's is one, even though its finale (like so many concluding movements) has minimal interest. The massive opening movement is romantic resonance that is hard to resist. Better still (and it is suggested that it be played first) is the blended sound and quality of the *Romanza.*

Bolet is the star of this one, and he plays with marvelously full tone, displaying glittering passage work and a marvelous sense of the work's style. The orchestra is hardly known, but is adequate. Ainslee Cox is building a reputation as a conductor and his part in the proceedings is properly supportive.

Instrumental	**Serenata napoletana, Op. 24, No. 2**
Violin	☐ Heifetz (violin); Smith (piano) / RCA LM-2382 (monaural)

Apt title, with soft swing for the *Serenata* and a bit of plucked pitches for the *Napoletana*. Apt playing too, with just the right portion of string schmaltz.

Ravi Shankar   (1920-   )

Solo Instrument and Orchestra	**Concerto for Sitar and Orchestra (1970)**
	☐ London Symphony Orchestra / Shankar (sitar); Emery (bongos) / Previn (conductor) / Angel S-36806
Sitar	

Rāga formations—the melodic basis of Indian classical music—are, of course, the fundament that binds this forty-minute work. Simplistic diatonic Western melodies are woven in, but the principal points are the hypnotic repetitive rhythms and, especially, the coloristic anchorage of the solo sitar. Nonetheless, Shankar has managed successfully to combine the opposed stylistic assumptions that exist between Eastern and Western music.

There are four movements; the most interesing to this listener are the last pair, *Rāga Adanā* and *Rāga Mānj Khamāj*. One needn't be an expert sitar critic to recognize the artistic flourish of Shankar's playing. Any orchestral maven will give the L.S.O. personnel a perfect score for their part in the proceedings.

Harold Shapero   (1920-   )

Orchestra	**Credo for Orchestra (1955)**
	☐ Louisville Orchestra / Whitney (conductor) / Louisville 56-5 (monaural)

The spirit of this piece lies in its cleanliness of musical thought and preciseness of logic. This is music with a straightforward meaning, conveying a sense of positive creation, if not of startling discovery. Its action is controlled by neoclassic gears.

The performance is passably good. Ditto the engineering.

Solo Instrument and Orchestra	**Partita in C for Piano Solo and Small Orchestra (1960)**
	☐ Louisville Orchestra / Owen (piano) / Whitney (conductor) / Louisville S-674
Piano	

Standard neoclassic practice with a good measure of eclectic spread: French overture mannerisms, Stravinsky-derived pandiatonic pertnesses, and flutter-tongued orchestral sounds for a jazz overlay.

Instrumental	**Sonata No. 1 for Piano (1944)**
	☐ Glazer (piano) / Concert-Disc 217
Piano	

The now conventional process of neoclassicism. Finely crafted and similarly conveyed in the recording.

Piano, Four Hands	**Sonata for Piano, Four Hands (1941)**
	☐ Shapero and Smit (piano) / Columbia Special Products AML-4841 (monaural)

A rare medium in music of the present time—composers are not writing piano duets these days. Doubly welcome, therefore, is this work that consists of tight bands of counterpoint and rhythm. Shapero's music is crystal clear, its fricative warmth pointing up a twentieth-century pianistic tale.

The composer and Leo Smit (also a fine composer) make a well-matched team. They play with smooth tone when required, or express themselves percussively when that dynamic needling is demanded. Columbia furnishes excellent sound for this excellent music.

String Quartet No. 1 (1940)

Chamber Music

☐ Koff and Bellam (violins); Trampler (viola); McCracken (cello) / Columbia Special Products AMS-6176

The fountainhead for Shapero's work is Stravinskian neoclassicism. The first movement builds itself from a row of thirds. A modern concept of a scherzo plan forms the second movement. Trio inflections are present, though as a definite section the trio is absent. The terms of structural contrast (usually indicated by the trio section) are here obtained by simply thinning the texture. In movement 3 tertial pitch arrangement is stressed in the free variational design of the music. In contrast to this devotion to contemporaneous triadic harmony, the last movement is recognizably dedicated to quartal harmonic style.

The performing quartet consists of free-lance musicians, but their portrayal of Shapero's work is well integrated and stylistically truthful.

Ralph Shapey (1921-)

Rituals for Symphony Orchestra (1959)

Orchestra

☐ London Sinfonietta / Swingfield (alto saxophone); Fudoli (tenor saxophone); Willoc (baritone saxophone); McKinley (piano) / Shapey (conductor) / Composers Recordings S-275

Rituals is prefaced by a motto, "With silver mallet against bone I chisel at the calcified truth of gained maturity." There are two movements, the first directed by serial fundaments, but shaped by Shapey into a language of bouldered strength. It strongly reminds one of the explosive music of Edgard Varèse and the craggy syntax of Carl Ruggles. In the second part the collision of saxophonic improvisation provides additional proof of the motto's objective.

There are plenty of currencies being traded in the serial music market, but all too many are counterfeit. Ralph Shapey's is authentic.

Powerful music demands a powerful performance and Shapey obtains it from his musicians. This is a significant recording in all respects.

Evocation for Violin with Piano and Percussion (1959)

Chamber Music

☐ Zukofsky (violin); Kalish (piano); Desroches (percussion) / Desto 6435/37

Even in its quiet moments (part 3 is muted, marked "with tenderness"), *Evocation* bares the sharp intervallic teeth of minor seconds and major sevenths. These frictions are used in the majority, emphasizing the precipitate expressivity of the work. Shapey's conception projects via the string instrument a percussive relationship to the actual percussion used (gong, tom-toms, bass and snare drums, cymbals, woodblock, and gamelan). Notwithstanding places in the score with lower-leveled dynamic power, *Evocation* shows no fatigue in delivering its restless energizing musical polemic.

Shapey has not allowed himself to become the victim of the gimmick virus. *Evocation* is strong stuff, but when stripped to the buff it is shown to be constructed from totally pure materials. This results in a magnificent example of what is meant by the term ''contemporary music.'' *Evocation* has great drama. It is tough and tender, frenzied and elegiac, and balances tension and release.

The all-star cast that performs the work fulfills all the demands of the score. A very close runner-up is the mono CRI (No. 141) release, performed by Matthew Raimondi, violin; Yehudi Wyner, piano; and Paul Price, percussion. This is also an all-star cast. The difference is the better stereo sound on Desto.

String Quartet No. 6 (1963)

☐ Lexington Quartet of the Contemporary Chamber Players of the University of Chicago / Composers Recordings S-275

A one-movement work, divided into six sections. Divisional proportions also apply to the performing quartet. Each player is separated from the others in order to keep and emphasize (or isolate) the individuality of each line.

A certain type of crusty lyricism permeates the fragmentation of the score. This is related to another matter, which takes a number of hearings before it is recognized: underneath Shapey's exterior creation there simmers the expressionism of Alban Berg.

Vocal

Voice and Instrumental Ensemble

Incantations for Soprano and Ten Instruments (1961)

☐ Contemporary Chamber Players of the University of Chicago / Beardslee (soprano) / Shapey (conductor) / Composers Recordings S-232

Awesome sounds, scope, and power are presented in Shapey's *Incantations*. The voice is silent in the third movement, in which the instruments are let loose in a frenzy. There is no text for the vocalist, the soprano using syllabic data. Some may claim the instrumental text is derived from Varèse, but be assured, this is no stylistic memoire honoring another composer by imitation. The impressive impressions of sound should be fully credited to Shapey.

The performance is awesome all the way around. Bethany Beardslee adds once more to her vocal achievements with a magnificently detailed and colored performance, climaxed in the final movement, which calls for voice with light percussion.

Songs of Ecstasy for Soprano, Piano, Percussion, and Tape (1967)

☐ Pilgrim (soprano); Cobb (piano) / Desto 7124

Shapey's four ecstatic focalizations deal with coital union. The seriousness and the manner of treating the subject are so beautifully determined that even with the most explicit third part no one can be offended. The texts are extremely succinct excerpts from the Book of Genesis, Joyce, Walter Benton, and Shakespeare. The essence of a phrase substitutes for large-scaled verbiage, with a preponderance of word repetition and syllabic split-offs. This reaches a peak in the handling of the Benton line, ''He covers, enters, bursts inside like a screaming rocket—turns God,'' a description of the sex act that Shapey turns into a musical depiction deserving of the highest creative credit. There is a response to the situation and a full fervency to the delineation. The result is both fascinating and stimulating, without any sensationalism. This is followed by part 4, which implies both the coming together of man and woman and postcoital satisfaction in the Shakespearian word play of "O wonderful, wonderful and most wonderful."

Shapey projects his music by framing the voice against sound masses (cymbals and gong in part 1), recited text against sung text and syllables (in part 2), and a prerecorded huge-sized gong (in part 3). Though Songs of Ecstasy is scored for voice, piano, percussion, and tape, only two performers are required, and it is for that reason that no credit is assigned a performing percussionist; the percussion and tape are handled by the vocalist and pianist. The entire performance is perceptive and responsible and is a fine achievement.

Praise (1971)

Cantata and Oratorio

☐ Contemporary Chamber Players of the University of Chicago and Chorus / Geiger (bass-baritone) / Shapey (conductor) / Composers Recordings SD–355

Praise, indeed, should be forthcoming for Shapey's powerful oratorio for bass-baritone, chorus, and chamber orchestra. Praise, because it proves that strong, present-day musical language is just as efficacious in proclaiming the musico-religious process as is the orthodox, traditional one.

There are ten sections. The first three—*Convocation, Invocation,* and *Processional*—are repeated, after part 6, during the intermission, "while the audience returns to its seats," a procedure used in the recording as well. Three sections are purely instrumental, the others a mix of soloist and soloist with chorus; the text is taken from the Old Testament and the Union Prayer Book used in synagogues.

A composer of the Shapey category working on his score paper knows where he's at. There is a profundity and depth to *Praise* that make it a rich experience. The recorded performance carries out this pervasive strength.

Christopher Shaw (1924-   )

Music, When Soft Voices Die

Choral

To the Bandusian Spring

Chorus Alone

☐ BBC Singers / Poole (conductor) / Argo ZRG-791

Shelley and Horace are the poets Shaw uses, respectively, for these two unaccompanied choral pieces. That Shaw considers a pungent harmonic setting for *To the Bandusian Spring* does not negate its basic pastoralism. The specialness of Shaw's style relates to a gentility that is clothed in frank and very compelling pitch combinations. It is a music of tasteful address.

A Lesson from Ecclesiastes

Chorus with Accompaniment

☐ BBC Singers / Farrell (organ) / Poole (conductor) / Argo ZRG-791

A setting of the first seven verses of the fifth chapter of the Book of Ecclesiastes. Shaw's music is broadly phrased, compact in its atonalized language. The emotiveness is almost reticent, but it is there for the listener willing to seek it.

Peter and the Lame Man

Cantata and Oratorio

☐ BBC Symphony Orchestra and BBC Singers / Young (tenor); Noble (baritone) / *(for contractual reasons the conductor must remain anonymous)* / Argo ZRG-791

Schoenbergian style imbued with Bergian emotional range make Shaw's Cantata (the text a shortened version of the third chapter of The Acts of the Apostles) a rewarding experience.

St. Peter is sung by John Noble; Alexander Young acts as the Narrator. The chorus is unusually constituted, eliminating any basses in order to place the leading role into greater perspective. The orchestra's conductor (unnamed as noted above) is probably Colin Davis, who directed the first performance on January 24, 1974, with the same soloists, orchestra, and chorus.

Martin Shaw   (1875-1958)

Choral	***With a Voice of Singing***
Chorus with Accompaniment	☐ Walter Ehret Chorale / Flath (organ) / Ehret (conductor) / Golden Crest S-4032
	A stately anthem of praise, vigorously presented.

Rodion Shchedrin   (1932-   )

Instrumental	**Humoresque**
Piano	☐ Lupu (piano) / Desmar 1005

Snips of sound, wide spacings, and sudden dynamic thrusts produce a short musical spoof.

Ballet	***Anna Karenina* (1972)**

☐ Bolshoi Theater Orchestra / Simonov (conductor) / Melodiya/Angel S-4126

This has none of the tricky orchestrational research found in most of this composer's works, but there is plenty of research into Tchaikovskian data.

Shchedrin / Georges Bizet. *See Bizet* / Rodion Shchedrin.

Arthur Shepherd   (1880-1958)

Instrumental	**Capriccio II (1941)**
Piano	***Eclogue No. 4* (1948)**
	Exotic Dance No. 1 (1928)
	Exotic Dance No. 3 (1954)
	***Gigue fantasque* (1945)**
	***In Modo Ostinato* (1945)**
	***Lento amabile* (1938)**

☐ Slater (piano) / Composers Recordings SD-383

There is considerable freshness in this program. The title headings are apt, though there is more harmonic nonconventionality in the *Eclogue* and the *Gigue* than in either of the Exotic Dances. Above all, there is an elegance to Shepherd's piano pieces.

The playing is warm, with an honest-to-goodness flavor that is very enticing.

Rustic Ramble (In Modo Ostinato)

☐ Johannesen (piano) / Golden Crest S–4065

Shepherd's sketch swings along in territory that reminds the listener of foreign ruralism. This is due to the shape of the ostinato, which resembles the contour of *Ach, du Lieber Augustin*. Such partial coincidence does not mar the music's charm.

Triptych for High Voice and String Quartet (1926)

Vocal

☐ Emerson String Quartet / Norden (soprano) / New World Records NW–218

Voice and Instrumental Ensemble

Shepherd speaks the sensitive, quietly emotional language of the French school of Chausson and Fauré in these three pieces with texts by Tagore. There is rich coloration and a big vocal statement in each of the movements. Passionate though the music be, not once does it fall into the *Sturm und Drang* quagmire.

The work is beautifully performed with luminous tone, in what is indicated as Betsy Norden's recording debut. The major labels should pay immediate attention.

Robert Sherlaw Johnson (1932–)

Seven Short Piano Pieces

Instrumental

Sonata No. 1 (1963)

Piano

☐ Sherlaw Johnson (piano) / Argo ZRG–694

Confusion exists as to this composer's surname. *Schwann* hyphenates it, *Baker's Biographical Dictionary of Musicians* lists it as Johnson, Argo's disc indicates it as Sherlaw Johnson. So be it.

However, no confusion exists as to this composer's music. The style is serial, the textures in the one-movement Sonata of homogeneous solidity, the form a free interlock of the sections that define classical sonata form. Some fragmentation is involved.

The pieces are titled *Prelude, Catena, Chameleon I, Phoenix, Acanthus, Bleak Ecstasies,* and conclude with an *Epilogue and Chameleon II.* Serial freedom exists here, and so does color including a goodly amount of sounds produced inside the piano (beautifully recorded, incidentally). The tendency for fragmentation exists in this case as well. Some may find an overconcentration on dynamic and color levels rather than thematic material and development. No matter—the pieces are impressive and interesting.

The Argo release is a three-in-one offering. Sherlaw Johnson is presented as composer, pianist, and liner-note writer.

Alice Shields (1943–)

Wildcat Songs (1966)

Vocal

☐ Turash (soprano); Dunkel (piccolo) / Opus One 13

Voice with Accompaniment

No data is given, no text, no identity of poet or poets. That is not Opus One's fault.

They indicate that by the composer's choice the work is to be heard "without any possible bias that might be had as the result of a printed explanation."

There is one "song"; the other is a "song" for unaccompanied piccolo, full of the flits and darts and colors of current woodwind writing. The music is saturated with expressionism.

(Watch the labeling. The Shields work is listed as the third piece on the A side, whereas it is the first one.)

Electronic Music

Farewell to a Hill (1975)

☐ Finnadar 9010

Though many contend that all electronic music has only abstract objectives, the facts do not bear this out. One has only to listen to electronic music by Milton Babbitt, Ilhan Mimaroğlu, and Karlheinz Stockhausen, to realize that the totally opposite styles and the formal (and at times, descriptive) differences in their output nullify such "abstract" criticism. Further, one seriously doubts that a composer's decision to produce music in the electronic medium is made because of cold, impersonal reasons.

A strong piece of evidence is *Farewell to a Hill*. It was written "in mourning for the death of a loved one." Its makeup (electronically generated and electronically manipulated harpsichord sounds, the sonorities of bells, and the cries of mallards) has a most telling effect. That one listener may not consider it threnodic does not matter. Shields's electronic opus has its own special emotive potency.

The Transformation of Ani (1970)

☐ Composers Recordings 268

A text taken from *The Egyptian Book of the Dead* forms the girders for the structure of Shields's piece. The lines are heard with total comprehensibility and are also contrasted to and combined with negation of textual meaning by electronic affirmation. It is the composer's voice that is heard in all the varied manifestations, including reverberation, filtering, and the like.

Seymour Shifrin   (1926-1979)

Orchestra

Three Pieces for Orchestra (1958)

☐ London Sinfonietta / Monod (conductor) / Composers Recordings S-275

Though performed by a sinfonietta group, Shifrin's work calls for full orchestra, including woodwinds in threes; the average disposition of four horns, three trumpets, three trombones, and tuba; harp and celesta; strings; and twelve percussion instruments. The latter are most important in the central piece, coloring the opening and closing.

Serial style rules, treated with bold strokes, with gutsy, "downtown" drive. The playing is solid, well integrated.

Chamber Music

String Quartet No. 4 (1967)

☐ Fine Arts Quartet / Composers Recordings SD-358

Tonality spread, pierced, and juxtaposed, chromatically festooned and in conflict, makes Shifrin's Quartet exceedingly dramatic and tensile, even in its quieter moments. The rhythms are formationed in parallel manner. This is a solid and impressive music that relies on obtaining contrasts derived within the chosen hard-crusted style, without using lyrical, poetic charm for such purpose. Shifrin's Fourth Quartet will move a listener (or, at the very least, fully interest him) solely by percussivelike vertical and linear arrangement.

The Fine Arts team (Sorkin, Sopkin, Zaslow, Loft) makes all the commentary clear and forcefully so.

Serenade for Five Instruments (1958)

☐ Kaplan (oboe); Russo (clarinet); Cecil (horn); Lynch (viola); Wingreen (piano) / Composers Recordings S-123

Might be considered twelve-tone, but 'tis not so. It is tonal; that is, in the sense of today's conception of tonality. The twelve-tonish element floats around the piece because Shifrin disposes his sounds in a Webernian manner—fragmentation is the point of departure, and the music shows, thereby, the composer walking down duplex paths. In short, Shifrin is both a pre- and post-Schoenbergian-influenced creator. The best of the three movements is the final section—a contemporary piece of toccata-like impetus.

The performance is satisfactory on all accounts. The engineering is very good.

Satires of Circumstance (1964)

Vocal

Voice and Instrumental Ensemble

☐ Contemporary Chamber Ensemble / DeGaetani (mezzo-soprano) / Weisberg (conductor) / Nonesuch 71220

Musical ancestry is apparent but does not stifle individuality in these three songs to poems of Thomas Hardy. Though related to the atomization style of Webern, the pieces have powerful rhythmic impulse. And, akin to Schoenberg through serialism, the pitch ordering and freedom of the songs produce a vigorous lyricism.

The liner notes (by Eric Salzman) indicate "poetic irony." However, there are no texts offered, and DeGaetani, as excellent as she is, does not clarify the words whatsoever (cannot actually, because of the out-of-socket intervallic spans). This lack of text is the only minus sign to the recording.

The Odes of Shang

Choral

Chorus and Instrumental Ensemble

☐ Members of the University of Michigan Symphony Orchestra and University of Michigan Chamber Choir / Hilbish (conductor) / New World Records NW-219

A large two-part composition, the texts drawn from *The Confucian Odes,* a collection of 304 odes, translated by Ezra Pound. Partnered with the chorus is a piano and a large group of percussion instruments: drums, cowbells, wood blocks, cymbals, wood chimes, glass chimes, claves, castanets, maracas, and glockenspiel.

A ritualistic mysticism pervades the music, mainly because of the percussion treatment, which wonderfully interlocks and colors the chorus. Shifrin's music is of demonstrative expressiveness. A controlled brilliance may be recognized as well as a type of monumental tread in the *Odes'* freely pitched detail. However, there is no trace of academic *longueur* in this creative document.

Yuri Shishakov   (1925-   )

Concerto for Balalaika (1954)

Solo Instrument and Orchestra

☐ State Radio Orchestra of Folk Instruments / Rozhkov (balalaika) / Smirnov (conductor) / Monitor S-2074E (monaural)

Balalaika

Folksy constancy marks the pair of movements. The special point is the opportunity of hearing the solo instrument, the Russian representative of the guitar family.

Dmitri Shostakovich (1906-1975)

Orchestra

The Age of Gold-Ballet Suite, Op. 22

☐ London Symphony Orchestra / Martinon (conductor) / London STS-15180

Four movements: Introduction, Adagio, Polka, and Dance. There are special snide harmonies (the ballet has a satirical scenario downgrading capitalism) and special coloration via a long soprano saxophone solo in the slow movement. The Polka is a pops favorite. In the ballet the *Polka* is titled *Once in Geneva* (*Angel of Peace*) and portrays the Geneva international disarmament conference with zippy and discordant, thumb-one's-nose-at sounds—a real yak.

Martinon plays the Suite with class. In this way the young "Shostakovichkeit" of the music is appealing. Overdoing the satire would be defeating and has been in other performances, concert and recorded.

Ballet Suite

No. 1 (1949) / No. 2 (1951) / No. 3 (1952)

☐ Bolshoi Theatre Orchestra / Maxim Shostakovich (conductor) / Melodiya/Angel S-40115

Light music—good for dancing or for pure listening—cast in such designs as Waltz, Polka, Galop, Elegy, Romance, Adagio, and so on. There is no insubstantiality or shallow simplicity in the music. It has all the creative classiness even if it is not superintellectual.

The fine playing is conducted by one who would be expected to—and does—know the music thoroughly.

The Bolt-Suite from the Ballet, Op. 27

☐ Bolshoi Theatre Orchestra and Zhukovsky Military Air Academy Band / Maxim Shostakovich (conductor) / Melodiya/Angel S-40062

Six sections from the stage work comprising three acts and seven scenes. The story line concerns sabotage by an anti-Soviet worker who is foiled by loyal Communists. Agitprop stuff, of course, but the score has some excellent moments, represented in the six parts Shostakovich put together as an orchestral suite with thirteen *ad libitum* band instruments for the finale. (As noted in the credits above, the band group is included in this first-rate recording.)

Festive Overture, Op. 96

☐ State Radio Orchestra of the USSR / Gauk (conductor) / Monitor 2015 (monaural)

Zippy and peppy—just what one wishes in the way of a wide-open gay opener for any type of musical evening. Simple expressivity, with peripatetic passage work and a sizably luscious contrastive tune.

The playing here is all to the good; the sound is 1950-ish, which means don't expect state-of-the-art conditions.

Memorable Year 1919, Op. 89 (Five Movements)

☐ State Radio Orchestra of the USSR / Gauk (conductor) / Monitor 2015 (monaural)

Five parts of an orchestral suite (containing seven movements in all) that Shostakovich drew from the score he wrote for the film. This good utilitarian music makes moderately good concert fare. The movements are an Introduction, Romance, *Sea Battle* (not ferocious at all), Scherzo, and Finale.

The execution is what one can term professional—standard category. The sound is fair to middlin'.

Michurin-Suite from the Film Music, Op. 78

☐ Moscow Radio Orchestra and Chorus / Maxim Shostakovich (conductor) / Melodiya/ Angel S-40181

Fluency is to be expected in any Shostakovich score, and it is illustrated in this case. There are some fair ideas, but the music cannot be considered by any means as belonging in the most important Shostakovich category.

Pirogov-Suite from the Film Music, Op. 76a

☐ Bolshoi Theatre Orchestra and Chorus / Maxim Shostakovich (conductor) / Melodiya/Angel S-40160

A strong-toned climate is most often typical of Shostakovich's film music. This Suite is mostly dramatic and sometimes quite bombastic, though, in contrast, there's a neat waltz included.

Suite from the Incidental Music to Shakespeare's Tragedy *Hamlet*, Op. 32

☐ Louisville Orchestra / Mester (conductor) / Louisville S-683

Not to be confused with the score Shostakovich wrote for a motion picture also titled *Hamlet*, from which a suite was drawn in 1964—thirty-two years after Opus 32 was composed.

Shostakovich considers *Hamlet* satirically, for the most part. There is hardly a touch of tragedy in the thirteen movements (Mester rearranges the order of these, but it doesn't matter). Some of the sounds can be considered vulgar, but this is Mester staying right on the lines of the score in a most representative performance. This is music that most Shostakovich admirers will probably consider low-class fare. Never mind. Shostakovich has given it a high-class setting.

Symphony No. 1, Op. 10

☐ L'Orchestre de la Suisse Romande / Weller (conductor) / London 6787

Shostakovich's initial Symphony was considered a remarkable work for a composer not yet twenty years old when it was introduced, and it is just as remarkable more than a half century later.

As such it has been given a huge variety of interpretations, and there have been many arguments about the metronome marks in the score. Forget them. First, the present version meets the requirement of balancing the romantic with the parodistic, which are juggled in the work. Second, Weller focuses on the soloism that permeates the opus (oboe in the slow movement, and especially the many piano passages, etc.), without negating total balance and while applying contrasts within the varied textures with utmost subtlety. In the scherzo the sounds are kept tight but are never flimsy. In the finale the music soars. In all, it is a rendition that is always of top meaning and classy signature, as it follows the Shostakovichian twists and turns in this, the most rhapsodic of all his symphonies.

(Trivia Department: Stokowski made the initial recording in this country on the very day the Soviet government was given recognition by the United States.)

Symphony No. 2 (*To October*), Op. 14

☐ Moscow Philharmonic Symphony Orchestra and RSFSR Academic Choir / Kondrashin (conductor) / Melodiya/Angel S-40236

The subtitle *To October* refers, of course, to the Russian October Revolution. In his one-movement document, which concludes with a choral ode to the Soviet Revolution, Shostakovich unknowingly played creative Russian roulette with the Soviet authorities. He lost, and the work was eventually attacked, unfairly, for its "formalism."

The second Symphony represents lusty music. It revels in polyrhythmic counterpoint, chromatic-choked dissonance, and severe linear spillage. There is also a factory whistle in the orchestration.

Kondrashin is fully in sympathy with the music. It is played with guts and drive, and the rough sound that emerges at times is better than smoothing over the content that digs into the ears.

Symphony No. 3 (*May First*), Op. 20

☐ Moscow Philharmonic Symphony Orchestra and RSFSR Academic Choir / Kondrashin / (conductor) / Melodiya/Angel S-40245

The *May Day* Symphony matches the *October* Symphony (*see above* [Symphony No. 2]) by its one-movement plan and choral conclusion. It has a dissonant vocabulary with brassy accents. Sharp detail is paramount in its exuberances and the Moscow organization doesn't overlook a single point. A fine, fiery performance.

Symphony No. 4 in C minor, Op. 43

☐ Philadelphia Orchestra / Ormandy (conductor) / Columbia MS-6459

This is the Symphony that Shostakovich withdrew during his troubled days with the political-cultural second-raters. Twenty-five years after its composition it surfaced. Emerged it did in its tightly woven linear and vertical fabric, with monstrous orchestral color requirements, and substantial, fleshed-out length.

Ormandy has reduced the totality of the orchestration, though only in terms of weights and not of voicing individuality. In place of eight flutes(!) and six clarinets there are four each in the woodwinds, with a slight reduction made in the horn section. His performance is direct and clarifies all the textures in the work. As a Shostakovich specialist he would be expected to produce as much, and he does not disappoint.

Symphony No. 5, Op. 47

☐ Philadelphia Orchestra / Ormandy (conductor) / RCA ARL1-1149

Genteel elegance doesn't fit this bold Symphony. But neither does a brash, marching-band sound. Ormandy offers a bold performance whose brilliance is consistently musical. He paces the first movement perfectly, shifting its tempi smoothly in the ten specific changes marked within the score. The mass polyphony is balanced, the unisons crisp. The Largo with its strings in eight parts has radiant atmosphere.

In the big finale that concludes with a rip-snorting pedal point of thirty-one measures, orchestral yawps have marked concert performances and recordings. Not in this case. This reading is classy, stylish, and exciting all the way. There is an earlier edition on Columbia MS-7279. It is almost as perceptive.

Symphony No. 6 in B minor, Op. 54

☐ Moscow Philharmonic Symphony Orchestra / Kondrashin (conductor) / Melodiya/ Angel S–40064

The heart of the Symphony is its initial part, a Largo that is longer than the two succeeding movements, consisting of an Allegro scherzo and a Presto finale. It again proves that the richest moments in Shostakovich's output are found in his slow-paced, emotive, and philosophical statements. The Largo is beautifully presented in this case. For the balance, Kondrashin manages to extract the sinister quality that is enfolded in the scherzo and delivers vital verve and becoming brilliance in the finale.

Symphony No. 7 (*Leningrad*), Op. 60

☐ New York Philharmonic / Bernstein (conductor) / Columbia M2S–722

Shostakovich's Seventh Symphony made front-page news in the war days of 1942, for three reasons: it was written during the famous German siege of Leningrad; its success was identified with the war effort; and there ensued therefore a Wall-Street-like bidding for the rights to the first American performance. It has been a critic's parlor game to poke fun at the march tune that commands the first movement of this work. Primitively, but vividly and with tantalizing incitement, the theme is sledgehammered into the ears, far beyond the frenzy of the repetitive Ravel *Bolero* tune. But Shostakovich, like a poet, saw much more and more intensely. There was method in his choice of subject and his handling of it. It represented an aural depiction of the Nazi war machine in capsulated form, and for this only a down-graded, mockingly heroic theme would do.

The other movements have not been given their proper due, containing, as they do, a poetic and proclamatory beauty. Bernstein achieves a reading of these that is of the highest interpretative fidelity. The first movement (covering twenty-eight minutes of the Symphony's seventy-five minute total) is truly a great and memorable experience. Sure, its manner is technicolored, but that's the way it should be.

Symphony No. 8 in C minor, Op. 65

☐ London Symphony Orchestra / Previn (conductor) / Angel S–36980

A hefty five-movement work running more than an hour in length (the opening Adagio clocks in at almost half that total). There is no jumbo orchestration as support. Aside from four flutes and an E flat clarinet the average triple woodwinds and brass (four horns, three trumpets, three trombones, and tuba) prevail.

The Symphony snaps in places, and contains a small portion of Shostakovich's habitual snide sounds, but for the largest part it is black-striped, of deep tragic perception. It does, however, conclude in the positive key of C major.

For music of this character, high-gloss striping to emphasize color, and orchestrational detail in place of sustained continuity, is opposite to the styling required to match the content. Previn provides a reading that proves he understands the compelling meaning of the work. This perception is not found in other recordings that have appeared. The L.S.O. plays this strong stuff magnificently.

Symphony No. 9, Op. 70

☐ L'Orchestre de la Suisse Romande / Weller (conductor) / London 6787

Shostakovich's Ninth is a five-movement work in which the last three are played without a break. It contains, among its charms (dramatic ones for the most part), a devilish

Presto (only "devilish" when scrupulous speed pertains, as in this case), and a pair of heart-rending bassoon recitatives over a pedal sustainment in the lower strings.

Walter Weller is no big-name podium chap, compared to such as Bernstein (on Columbia M–31307), Kondrashin (on Melodiya/Angel S–40000), Sargent (on Everest 3054), who offer the principal recorded competition. (Horvat, on Turnabout 34223, offers no competition to anyone.) However, Weller delivers this work in a manner that outdistances all the others. The first movement moves, the second movement also (Shostakovich's tempo mark demands it), and the cumulative finale (the afore-mentioned Presto, followed by unison brass proclamations interspersed with the recitatives, with a *scherz* send-off) is sharply detailed. One tires of hearing this Symphony called "Shostakovich's Mozart." It's Shostakovich's Shostakovich throughout, and in that manner it is presented by this conductor in the most illuminating fashion.

Symphony No. 10 in E minor, Op. 93

☐ Philadelphia Orchestra / Ormandy (conductor) / Columbia M–30295

The Tenth Symphony draws on a generating device based on Shostakovich's name in German musical translation ("D.SCH," with an E flat for the "S" and a B natural for the "H"). Some critics term No. 10 his best Symphony but that viewpoint is not shared at this desk, though the work is superb in all accounts.

Under Ormandy's direction there is polish without mitigating the specific bite of the music. The breadth brought in the slow movement is especially magnetic.

Symphony No. 11 (*The Year 1905*), Op. 103

☐ Moscow Philharmonic Symphony Orchestra / Kondrashin (conductor) / Melodiya/ Angel S–40244

The *1905* refers, as Nicolas Slonimsky describes it, to "the year of the tragically abortive and yet romantically inspiring Russian revolution." The work is programmatically conceived in four movements; the interpretative requirement is not to opt for the subtle touch but to dig in and let out the pictured passions. Kondrashin and his musicians do this aptly and still do not flush off the music behind the characterizations. (In Stokowski's edition [Seraphim S–60228], coloristic over-emphasis weakens the structural solidity of the work.)

Symphony No. 12 (*The Year 1917*), Op. 112

☐ Leningrad Philharmonic Orchestra / Mravinsky (conductor) / Melodiya/Angel S–40128

Programmaticism is dealt with here as in the preceding Shostakovich Symphony (*see above* [Symphony No. 11]), this time concerning historic milestones in Lenin's life. (*Schwann* indicates the subtitle of this work as "Lenin." However, while it is dedicated to the memory of Lenin, its official subtitle is as noted above.)

There's some bang and bombast in this Symphony, but by and large it is held within musical stability in the performance.

Symphony No. 13 (*Babi Yar*), Op. 113

☐ Philadelphia Orchestra and Male Chorus of the Mendelssohn Club, Philadelphia / Krause (baritone) / Ormandy (conductor) / RCA LSC–3162

How the score for this Symphony was smuggled out of the Soviet Union (which had banned the work from publication and further performance) will remain the secret of this writer, who was privy to the entire matter and then arranged for the American premiere by Ormandy and the publication of the score. It is Ormandy's tremendously felt and magnificently colored performance that holds first place—a re-creative statement that is in no way matched by the somewhat prosaic recording made by Kondrashin on Melodiya/Angel (S-40212). This, of course, eliminates any consideration of the exceedingly poor Everest release (3181E), a monaural edition made from a smuggled (again!) tape of the initial performance in the Soviet Union.

On the liner note written for RCA's recording I stated that Shostakovich's work was "a magnificent accomplishment." Further, that it marked "a sensitive union of music and poetry," (the texts are by the famous Soviet poet, Yevgeny Yevtushenko), and that it represented "a superb document of protest." Ormandy's truly definitive performance matches these descriptions.

(RCA has also packaged this work with the Fourteenth and Fifteenth Symphonies of Shostakovich. The call number is CRL3-1284. *See below* for individual releases of these works.)

Symphony No. 14, Op. 135

☐ Philadelphia Orchestra / Curtin (soprano); Estes (bass) / Ormandy (conductor) / RCA LSC-3206

Though listed under the orchestral rubric, Shostakovich's Fourteenth Symphony is a huge song cycle, consisting of eleven movements. The voice is represented in each part, with four divisions calling on the bass, four movements including the soprano, and three movements utilizing both voices. The orchestra of strings and percussion is no mere coloristic frame. It makes virtuoso statements, and its wordless song is as potent and verbal as the vocalists.

Penetrating music covers the entire work, the texts all concerned with the subject of death. Matching it is a deeply penetrating performance directed by Ormandy, constituting one of his finest achievements with the same applying to the soloists.

The Symphony is also included in a three-work release—the other compositions being the Thirteenth and Fifteenth Shostakovich Symphonies, on RCA CRL3-1284. (*See above* and *below* for discussions of these works.)

Symphony No. 15, Op. 141

☐ Philadelphia Orchestra / Ormandy (conductor) / RCA ARD1-0014

Shostakovich's final Symphony includes quotations from Rossini and Wagner and a fair amount of self-quotation. Without any caricature or parody, Shostakovich baldly utilizes material that logically fits in with his own. These quotations will certainly give rise to speculation and discussion. It may turn out to be Shostakovich's "Enigma." It matters not. The Fifteenth Symphony of Dmitri Shostakovich fulfills the Ovidian statement that "the outcome justifies the act." The act is thrilling. And so is Ormandy's performance.

(RCA has included this work with two other Symphonies by Shostakovich—Nos. 13 and 14—on its CRL3-1284, thus making a special edition ["In Memoriam"] of the composer's last three Symphonies. For discussions of these works, *see above*.)

A Year Is Worth a Lifetime-Suite from the Film Music

☐ Moscow Radio Orchestra and Chorus / Maxim Shostakovich (conductor) / Melodiya/Angel S-40181

Movie music is not always viable when separated from the pictorial images it is meant to accompany. While the cliché is worth repeating, nonetheless there has never been any Shostakovich film score that hasn't had sufficient values to warrant listening time.

Zoya-Suite from the Film Music, Op. 64a

☐ Bolshoi Theatre Orchestra and Chorus / Maxim Shostakovich (conductor) / Melodiya/Angel S–40160

Strong stuff—earnest, tough music. Shostakovich's large number of film scores never reach the concert hall, so one is grateful for the specialness of having recorded extracts such as this.

Solo Instrument and Orchestra

Cello

Concerto No. 1 in E flat major for Cello and Orchestra, Op. 107

☐ Philadelphia Orchestra / Rostropovich (cello) / Ormandy (conductor) / Columbia MS–6124

A fabulous performance. The work is dedicated to Rostropovich, who gave the premiere. He then participated in the first American performance and followed it with this recording. Shostakovich was at the concerts preceding the recording sessions and also attended the sessions. His full approval was manifested, and one cannot second-guess his viewpoint. There is no need to do so, since this is a remarkable partnership between soloist and orchestra.

Piano

Concerto No. 1 for Piano and Orchestra, Op. 35

☐ New York Philharmonic / Previn (piano); Vacchiano (trumpet) / Bernstein (conductor) / Columbia MS–6392

Punchy, sparkling, and deft. This is a combination difficult to beat and in the hands of the New York Phil. strings, Previn at the piano, Vacchiano on the trumpet, and Bernstein prancing it all the way, no one else has a chance, really.

Concerto No. 2 for Piano and Orchestra, Op. 101

☐ New York Philharmonic / Bernstein (piano) / Bernstein (conductor) / Columbia MS–6043

This recorded performance has become a classic. It just oozes joy and bravado, plus a healthy amount of humor. Right from the start of the single octave tune in the solo voice, through the finale with its step-step-and-hop $\frac{7}{8}$ rhythm, onto the Hanon-like cross-country passages, the Concerto is played to a stunning fare-thee-well. Marvelous!

Violin

Concerto No.1 in A minor for Violin and Orchestra, Op. 77

☐ New Philharmonia Orchestra / David Oistrakh (violin) / Maxim Shostakovich (conductor) / Angel S–36964

A masterful work; indeed, one of Shostakovich's masterpieces. No cut-and-dried tried form. Major to the overall design are the two slow movements, the work opening with one (a Nocturne), the other set in the rare (for concerti) form of a Passacaglia. Following each are speedier involvements: movement 2 (a demoniac Scherzo) and the finale (a whimsical *Burlesca*). The last is preceded by a huge cadenza, itself akin to an independent movement, lasting some five and one-half minutes.

David Oistrakh has never been better. His playing is ravishing and radiant, superb and stunning. In the Passacaglia the nobility of his conception is truly marvelous. The orchestral support (the conductor is, of course, the son of the composer) is top-class.

Oistrakh has recorded the Concerto several times, and two of the monaural representations are still available: with the New York Philharmonic conducted by Mitropoulos (Columbia MG–33328) and with the Leningrad Philharmonic Orchestra conducted by Mravinsky (Monitor MC–2014)—an exceedingly strong presentation.

A note regarding the opus number: Shostakovich delayed releasing the work (political football was in vogue when he completed the Concerto), so that it was indicated in terms of its release date, as Opus 99. Chronologically it should properly read Opus 77, which is confirmed by the official enumeration of Shostakovich's output.

Concerto No. 2 for Violin and Orchestra, Op. 129

☐ Moscow Philharmonic Symphony Orchestra / David Oistrakh (violin) / Kondrashin (conductor) / Melodiya/Angel S–40064

Shostakovich's Second Violin Concerto has not achieved the amount of acceptance that pertains to the earlier Concerto (*see above*). There are valid arguments about the repetitiveness of the finale, but certainly the elegiac content of the central movement and the finely metamorphosized first movement are finely conceived.

Oistrakh shows his belief in the piece by a deeply committed performance. His documentation is superb in all respects.

Aphorisms, Op. 13

Instrumental

Five Preludes

Piano

☐ Pleshakov (piano) / Orion 6915

Shostakovich fans unacquainted with the *Aphorisms* will be surprised, and some may disapprove of its abstract articulations. The Soviet hierarchy didn't like them; the critics didn't, either. Martynov, in his book on Shostakovich, called them "dry." The musicologist Rabinovich described the set as "without even the slightest hint of real human feeling."

The ten pieces range from a thirty-eight seconds' Etude to a Lullaby of two and one-half minutes' length. However, each piece contains a concentrated formal truth, carefully projected by Pleshakov.

The Preludes are from a set of twenty-four that Shostakovich composed. Neither keys nor numbers are indicated, simply the tempi. Pleshakov's liner notes are just as vague. The pieces are effectively played, however.

Preludes and Fugues, Op. 87

☐ Woodward (piano) / RCA CRL2–5100

Shostakovich's parallel to Bach's *Well-Tempered Clavier* (see under *Johann Sebastian Bach: Instrumental: piano*), with twenty-four Preludes and Fugues encompassing the total twelve major and twelve minor keys. Of course, the blueprint has contemporary expansion. Metrically, the pieces use $\frac{2}{4}, \frac{3}{4}, \frac{4}{4}, \frac{5}{4}, \frac{7}{8}, \frac{6}{8}, \frac{12}{8}$, and *alla breve* time signatures. The moods vary from simple to chromatic, from the snide to the dramatic. As for textures, No. 9 is in two voices, and No. 13 is in five; the other Preludes and Fugues are split equally between three and four voices. Variety is maintained in all respects, with the scope of the paired pieces running from a few seconds under two minutes (No. 2) to a bit over eight and one-half minutes (No. 24).

Roger Woodward plays the work with an intelligent viewpoint and suave musicality, which means that he lets the adventurousness come forward from the music and not from individual interpretative preaching. As a result, the Shostakovichian sense, purpose and direction are completely satisfying. The Fugues are beautifully clarified and there is not one blur in linear definition. A feeling of utter dedication to the composer is apparent.

(For another recording of five of the Preludes and Fugues, *see below*.)

Preludes and Fugues, Op. 87 (Nos. 6, 8, 20, 22, and 24)

☐ Shostakovich (piano) / Seraphim 60024 (monaural)

Shostakovich was a competent pianist, deserving of a place in the upper division of the create-and-perform league. This recording is proof. The differences between his conceptions and those of Woodward (*see above* [Preludes and Fugues]) are simply marginal and again exemplify the variety possible in a re-creative situation.

Sonata No.1, Op. 12

☐ Pleshakov (piano) / Orion 6915

The Sonata is respectful of the Prokofiev tradition, catering to its brash aspects. This is tough stuff, played to the hilt by Pleshakov. His percussiveness is proper for the music's constant accents and continual stormy dynamic situations.

Three Fantastic Dances, Op. 5

☐ Ortiz (piano) / Angel S-37109

Young Shostakovich (age sixteen) knew what he was about. These Dances (a march, a waltz, and a polka) do not make a false creative step. They are not the kind of music that induces shut-eye in the listener. For that some of the credit goes to Cristina Ortiz, for a presentation of sturdiness and clear pulse.

(The Dances are also available on an Orion disc [6915] played by Pleshakov, but in a rather colorless rendition in comparison to the above.)

Two Pianos

Concertino for Two Pianos, Op. 94

☐ Maxim and Dmitri Shostakovich (pianos) / Monitor 2040 (monaural)
☐ Duo di Heidelberg / Musical Heritage Society MHS-1147

Basically, the sound is far better on the MHS disc. Further, it's stereophonic, while the Monitor recording is monophonic. A third point in favor of the MHS release is the deeper interpretative feeling expressed in the slow-tempoed sections. In the major part of the Concertino—a frisky, snide romp—the Duo di Heidelberg (Hans-Helmut Schwarz and Edith Henrici) are too tailored in their playing; the music needs to kick off and move away (and here the brittle sound of the Monitor is a plus).

There are two factors that dictate placing the older recording in first place. The performers are the composer and his son (for whom the piece was written and who gave its premiere with another young pianist). Such partnership is certainly fundamental. It therefore carries over to the matter of performance pace and exactly what it should be. The Shostakovichs cover the work in eight minutes flat; the Heidelberg team takes a bit more than nine minutes to run the course.

Chamber Music

Sonata for Cello and Piano, Op. 40

☐ Shapiro (cello); Zayde (piano) / Nonesuch 71050

Shostakovich's Cello and Piano Sonata is persuasively written, a work of intelligibility that expresses, within its four-movement plan, all the composer's values—it bears his earmarks without any of his blemishes. The warm, semisober first movement matches a D minor flowing theme with a very Russian-flavored B major keyed subject. The conclusion is in *largo* tempo and the cello is muted. This gives a hushed expression to the epilogue's breadth. In the second movement the typical Shostakovich combine of waltz-scherzo makes its appearance, together with his favored repetitive sounds, tight rhythms, portamenti and flying glissandi.

The slow movement is warm and convincing, of saddened search. Again, the movement's coda is sung with muted string tone. It is the peak of the work, followed by a happy-go-lucky finale.

The recording by Rostropovich and Shostakovich on Monitor 2021E might seem to embrace the term "definitive," but unfortunately such is not the case, though one assumes that with the composer at the keyboard the tempi chosen cannot be argued with. The piano sound is tinny in many places; Rostropovich's tone (with the exception of the slow movement) is crusty; and the general sonics are poor. The monophonic setting cannot be blamed because there are numerous monos, exhibiting fine sound conditions, that are preferable to stereo releases of the same work.

The Harvey Shapiro and Jascha Zayde team takes first place, therefore. Their performance is quite satisfactory given that no other stereo recording is available for consideration. The tempi matter mentioned is interesting. Rostropovich and Shostakovich take two minutes longer to cover the first movement (marked Moderato) than the other duo. On the other hand, the Soviet performers clip forty-six seconds off the finale (an Allegretto) in comparison to the Nonesuch entry, and in short-spanned music that is considerable.

Trio No. 2 in E minor, Op. 67

☐ Nieuw Amsterdam Trio / Turnabout 34280
☐ Beaux Arts Trio / Philips 6500860

Color dramaticism is paramount to Shostakovich's black-ridged work. Further, the monochromatic third movement, dynamic through its complete avoidance of special color, makes the spectral splashes used in the other sections more vivid. There are Shostakovich's usual grotesque folds in the music's cloth, but principally this is music that is deeply felt. It is dedicated to the memory of a close friend of the composer (Ivan Sollertinsky, a Soviet musicologist).

There are four recorded performances available. The two listed show impeccable ensemble, warm tonal qualities from the string-instrument players, and an integration of the coloristic devices Shostakovich utilized. John Pintavalle's tone is a bit smoother, while in the Beaux Arts recording Isidore Cohen's is more pungent and dramatic. Likewise, this differentiation is paralleled in the playing of the cellists (Heinrich Joachim with the Nieuw Amsterdam, Bernard Greenhouse with the other team). Either way, the results are the maximum of what is contained in Shostakovich's score and are far ahead of the matter-of-fact performance by the Lyric Arts Trio on Concert-Disc 234 and the issue released by Melodiya/Angel (S–40031), with Vaiman, Rostropovich, and Serebryakov as the performing personnel.

String Quartet No. 1 in C major, Op. 49

☐ Gabrieli Quartet / London 15396

A Mozartean formal clearness marks Opus 49, which has not a bit of overtenacious expression. However, it does have Shostakovich's nervous mannerisms. Ingrown creative habits remain here—best described as a rhythmic tic (repetitive sounds in one pattern: twenty-one measures in the first movement, close to seventy measures in the third, plus a few dozen in the last). There is also the turned-up-nose effect (always paralleled by glissandi; over a dozen consecutive such measures in the first movement and a little bit in the last). Aside from these items the initial Quartet is a neoclassic affair dressed in sophisticated Shostakovichian harmonic clothes.

The performance is the best on disc. Any tendency for flattening out the detail, as the Borodin Quartet does in their performance on Melodiya/Seraphim S-6034 (which release covers Shostakovich's first five String Quartets), is avoided. There is more bite and stronger explanations in the Gabrieli's rendition.

String Quartet No. 2 in A major, Op. 68

☐ Borodin Quartet / Melodiya/Seraphim S-6034

There are four movements in Shostakovich's Opus 68 (mistakenly indicated as Opus 69 in the first printing of the work; corrected, however, in the second edition), but traditional procedures give way to a thoroughly adroit and comprehensible manner of combining sonata with suite. Movement one is an *Overture* (in sonata form), ternary form is used in the *Recitative and Romance,* followed by a rondo-formationed Valse, and the Quartet concludes with a Theme and Variations.

Chamber music substances are modified in the second movement where the first violin holds the stage with the other instruments as accompanimental supports. The Valse is made more dramatic by muting the instruments.

The playing is beautifully accomplished with total musical sensibility and fine tone quality. It represents one of the best of the Borodin's performances of the first five of Shostakovich's Quartets contained in the release.

String Quartet No. 3 in F major, Op. 73

☐ Gabrieli Quartet / London 15396

In the five-movement Third Quartet a cleverly formed fugue is in movement 1, with an all-important associated subject. Waltz rhythm motivates movement 2 (with his fondness for triple meter one might well suspect that Shostakovich had Viennese ancestors!), and its "oompah" plus glissando are present and accounted for. The greatest strength of the work is found in the Passacaglia (fourth movement).

The Quartet is impressively depicted. The players' stress of the chromatic data within the textures of Opus 73 adds a subtle strength, since in that manner harmonic intensity bisects melodic intensity.

String Quartet No. 4 in D major, Op. 83

☐ Fitzwilliam Quartet / Oiseau-Lyre DSLO-23

The principal command of Opus 83 is that of lyricism. There is no high rhythmic voltage in the work—the closest to that quality is found in the mysterious third-movement Allegretto, but the power is there compressed. Some commentators have indicated there are Hebraic aspects in the finale—this writer cannot agree, notwithstanding some use of the augmented interval associated with Hebraic chant.

The poetic delicacy of the music is sensitively portrayed by the Fitzwilliam team.

String Quartet No. 5 in B flat major, Op. 92

☐ Borodin Quartet / Melodiya/Seraphim S-6034

Shostakovich's fifth Quartet is played without pause but its three-movement structure is clearly exposed and just as clearly follows classical architecture: sonata form in movement 1 (Allegro non troppo); sonata form again in movement 2, but minus development (Andante); and rondo-sonata form in the last movement (Moderato–Allegretto). The style is colored romantically and with some nationalistic overtones. However, there is none of the jerky nervousness that marks so much neo-classic music or the over-textured weights that identify neo-romanticism.

The playing has splendid lyrical tension and energy; the rhythmic detail and dynamics are positively stated. The greatest asset in the interpretation is the recognition of the intensely dramatic character and rich emotive images of Shostakovich's score. Chamber-music-heated excitement is what the composer has provided, and there is no lowering of the temperature in the playing by the Borodin Quartet. This is an outstanding performance.

String Quartet
No. 6 in G major, Op. 101 / No. 7 in F sharp minor, Op. 108 / No. 8 in C minor, Op. 110 / No. 9 in E flat major, Op. 117 / No. 10 in A flat major, Op. 118 / No. 11 in F minor, Op. 122

☐ Borodin Quartet / Melodiya/Seraphim S–6035

These are significant contributions to the most important string-quartet music of all time. The music is of natural speech, has a continuity of line for projecting the speech, contains splendid melody that enhances the line, dramatic interest to spark the melody, and subject matter that holds the combination of all these in perfect balance. The scoring is sensitively arranged with four-voice equality (recitative sections are used at times to lead a section to climax but do not diminish the total equality of handling the instruments). Shostakovich is committed to classical forms in these works. Examples: passacaglia formula is used in the sixth and tenth Quartets; waltz design is found in the seventh and eighth works; sharp scherzi examples color numbers 6, 9, and 10; fugue is used; and so on. Sonata, ternary, and rondo patterns are in the majority.

The shortest of these Quartets is the F sharp minor opus, covering a little less than a twelve-minute span.

Programmaticism, the composer's monogram, and self-quotation fill the eighth Quartet, dedicated to "The Memory of the Victims of Fascism and War." The motive D–S–C–H (musically spelt by German pitch equivalents for the "S" and the "H") is the basis for the first and last movements. (The "D" identifies the initial of the composer's first name; the German combination of SCH equals the first letter of Shostakovich's last name in the Cyrillic alphabet.) Material from Shostakovich's Cello Concerto, the opera *Katerina Ismailova*, several of the symphonies, and the Piano Trio are woven into this four-instrument tale that pictures the cruel destruction and horrors of war. The eighth Quartet is one of the most magnificent examples in Shostakovich's output. It is a masterwork.

Despite some titles that would lead one to expect otherwise, a requiem-like tone embraces the eleventh Quartet. It has seven movements: Introduction, Scherzo, Recitative, Etude, Humoresque, Elegy, and Finale.

As more attention is being paid to these Quartets, undoubtedly other recorded editions may be expected to appear. I cannot foresee any issue supplanting these performances. The playing of each member of the Borodin team is sensitive to the ends of their fingers and bows, the ensemble is impeccable, the colorations are magnificent, and the interpretations are models of artistry.

String Quartet No. 12, Op. 133

☐ Fitzwilliam Quartet / Oiseau-Lyre DSLO-23

Shostakovich indeed uses tone rows in his Twelfth Quartet, but in his hands they are handled as dramatic contrastive elements, not as prime motivic permutates. Formally, the design embraces but a pair of movements; the second division defined by four sections. The performance is direct and dynamic; the incisiveness is potent and depicts the entire potentiality of the music.

String Quartet
No.13 in B flat minor, Op. 138 / No. 14 in F sharp major, Op. 142

☐ Fitzwilliam Quartet / Oiseau-Lyre DSLO-9

Shostakovich's work did not become steeped in mellowness as the years went by, but rather in an almost grim retrospectiveness. The Thirteenth Quartet, with its dark B flat minor key signature, is cold music (which does not deny its special emotion) and clings to its chromatic detail, so that the tonality becomes exceedingly vague. It is designed as a triptych with slow-fast-slow tempi settings. Opus 142 has reminders of the snide early Shostakovich but they are not the primary point, serving rather as a contrastive façade within the structure.

This young quartet team plays Shostakovich's music brilliantly, with the fullest realization of its style. They give truly outstanding performances.

String Quartet No. 15 in E flat minor, Op. 144

☐ Taneyev Quartet / Columbia/Melodiya M-34527

Shostakovich's final String Quartet has a remarkable structure of six connected movements (Elegy, Serenade, Intermezzo, Nocturne, Funeral March, and Epilogue), *all* in Adagio tempo (in one case even slower per the Adagio molto indication). It provides magnificent theatre of special kind—the very opposite of scintillescent detail by its tenebrous and sombrous subject matter. Royal S. Brown (a Shostakovich authority) has written the liner notes for this issue and his analysis is most pertinent. He speaks of the tempi sameness as giving the music "its bold, almost devastating impact. For in spite of the different character of each movement, the overall tone is so unrelentingly bleak and despairing that ... it gives the listener no other respite, no other point of contrast than a change from one perspective on death to another."

A work of special artistry creates its own balances, not inevitably those weighed by superacademic, even neosuperacademic scales. The fact that Shostakovich's Quartet is of compressed pace does not mean there is a depressed sonority scale. Shostakovich, however, does not use a paint brush, but rather pen, pencil, and etching tools. The resultant poetic coloration of the four instruments is one of the most potent influences of his masterful score.

There is no second-guessing the magnificent performance. The atmosphere is conveyed unerringly. This is an acute, definitive presentation by the quartet team that gave the premiere in Leningrad, on November 15, 1974.

Quintet for Piano and Strings, Op. 57

☐ Borodin Quartet / Edlina (piano) / Melodiya/Angel S-40085

Financial report: This work holds the record for the largest sum of money ever won as a prize for a chamber-music composition—100,000 rubles, then equivalent to $25,000. It was awarded Shostakovich on March 15, 1941, in the form of the Stalin Prize.

In the Quintet Shostakovich composes in a restrained manner without loss of any of his basic characteristics. The work consists of five movements and stands in relation to Shostakovich's chamber-music compositions as the First and Fifth Symphonies tower above all the others (excluding those that include voice). The opening Prelude is hinted at in two other movements but there is no cyclic definition. Each movement is devoted to its own material, with overall balance mastered by change of style, tempo, and mood.

Of the two versions available, this is the far better one. It offers splendid recognition of the structures in the work and the sound of the five performers is well integrated. The Melos Ensemble performance is exceedingly top surface. It is on Oiseau-Lyre S–267.

Two Pieces for String Octet, Op. 11

☐ Borodin Quartet and Prokofiev Quartet / Melodiya/Seraphim S–6035

The Prelude of Opus 11 is divided into sections: the first is declamatory, the second portion is fast. The latter is chromatically run on both jumping and scale-wise lines and states the first of the many eight-part imitations (short-lived canons) that dot the work.

The second of the pieces is a Scherzo. It is wild and brazen, smart and flippant, horizontal and vertical in style. The glissandi that Shostakovich perpetually wore, like a carnation in a lapel, make their appearance. This is the most dynamically swaggering Scherzo Shostakovich ever composed. It is also the wildest movement in all the literature for eight string instruments.

There is no problem with the performance. It is acute, dynamic, and of exciting immediacy. The problem is with the packaging of the disc. Nowhere on the album cover (which indicates a three-disc release of Shostakovich's String Quartets, Nos. 6–11) is there mention that the Octet is also included. No mention, either, on the liner note that appears on the reverse side of the cover. The heading in the booklet included with the release doesn't clearly indicate the two string quartets that combine to perform the Octet and then baldly credits Prokofiev as the composer! There are no program notes in the booklet itself about the work save a listing of title, opus, year of composition, and the titles of the two pieces, and once again the error is repeated naming Prokofiev as the composer.

Two Pieces for String Octet, Op. 11 (No. 2, Scherzo)

☐ I Solisti di Zagreb / Janigro (conductor) / Vanguard 71118

The Zagreb group knocks this off with unbuttoned zeal. That's the way it should be.

From Jewish Folk Poetry, Op. 79

Vocal

Voice with Accompaniment

☐ Dorlyak (soprano); Dolukhanova (mezzo-soprano); Masslenikov (tenor); Shostakovich (piano) / Monitor 2020 (monaural)

This is a part of the Shostakovichian creative odyssey that amazingly has been ignored. Since it requires only three solo voices plus piano, there is no valid excuse to deny audiences the opportunity to hear the powerful, intense score, which frames mostly poignant texts.

Complete democracy rules in Shostakovich's handling of the medium he chose. Every possible combination is employed in the eleven songs: one for mezzo-soprano, two for solo tenor, and two for solo soprano. The three possible duo combinations are covered in four of the songs, and there are two trios.

Shostakovich has rarely been so eloquent in his speech, and the singers are likewise, especially the richly lustered voice of Zara Dolukhanova. Shostakovich's participation in this recording is, naturally, not to be overlooked. There are great substances in every measure of this cycle.

Voice and Instrumental Ensemble

Seven Romances on Words by Alexander Blok for Soprano, Violin, Cello, and Piano, Op. 127

☐ Nieuw Amsterdam Trio / Pracht (soprano) / Turnabout 34280

Eloquent music tied to eloquent texts. The latter are varied, being concerned with such disparate subjects as Ophelia, a prophetic bird, love, the city, a storm, and so on. There is no grotesquerie, no pomped circumstance, no Socialistic flag-waving in the set. A spiritual beauty of style and harmony grace the poetry and the music that partners Blok's beautiful lines.

Shostakovich enriches the richness of his syntax by elegantly conceived lines. The scoring subtly motivates the concept of the total work by using different combinations for the seven sections. Three of the pieces are duos for the voice with a different instrumental color (No. 1 for cello, No. 2 for piano, No. 3 for violin). Two parts of the cycle are trios: No. 5 uses voice, violin, and piano, No. 6 combines voice with the paired strings. Only Nos. 4 and 7 call for the total quartet.

The performance is ideal—sensitive and telling. Mary Ellen Pracht's delivery is fully responsive to the style involved; the instrumentalists are of top-drawer partnership. This is, indeed, a five-star recording.

Cantata and Oratorio

The Execution of Stepan Razin, Op. 119

☐ Leipzig Radio Symphony Orchestra and Radio Chorus / Vogel (bass) / Kegel (conductor) / Philips 6585012

Shostakovich again joins hands with the poet Yevgeny Yevtushenko in this powerful cantata document. (Their previous collaboration was in the Symphony No. 13 [*Babi Yar*] [see under *Orchestra*].) Termed a "poem," the cantata calls for a solo bass voice with mixed chorus and orchestra. Drama pounds its way in the story of Stepan Razin, a folk hero unjustly executed by tyrannical forces. The closing portion of the work has a terrorizing force that is nowhere duplicated in Shostakovich's output.

The magnitude of the score is given an intense reading. Kegel's focus is one of dramatic pressure, and his interpretative objective is clear. At all levels in the performing forces the re-creative dynamism is inspired—never is there any groping for the artistic truth.

Song of the Forests, Op. 81

☐ Moscow Philharmonic Orchestra and USSR Russian Chorus / Ivanovsky (tenor); Petrov (bass) / Yurlov (conductor) / Melodiya/Angel S-40214

There is little difference between this recorded edition and the earlier mono version still available on Vanguard VRS-422. The sound gives the newer edition the vote.

This is Shostakovich in his agitprop role concerning the postwar reforestation program undertaken in the Soviet Union. Thus: part 1, *At the War's End;* part 2, *In Forests Let Us Clothe Our Land,* and so on. All very Russian, all easy to comprehend.

Film Music

The New Babylon (1929)

☐ Members of the Moscow Philharmonic Orchestra / Rozhdestvensky (conductor) / Columbia/Melodiya M-34502

Music for a silent film. Even though composed in his early period of work, the Shostakovichian fingerprints are clearly impressed by way of the score's rhythmic smartness, warm lyrical lines, and some parodistic thrusts.

Shostakovich made two orchestral versions, one for a smaller group. That is the one recorded. It is a strongly pronounced reading.

Shostakovich / **Rudolf Barshai**

Chamber Symphony for String Orchestra, Op. 110

String Orchestra

☐ Württemberg Chamber Orchestra, Heilbronn / Faerber (conductor) / Turnabout 34545

A really fancy title (odd to begin with, incorrect in addition) that Barshai gave to his string orchestra version of Shostakovich's Eighth String Quartet (*see above*). Not so odd to use the term "symphony" for an amplified string orchestra version of a string quartet, but rather odd to retain the same opus number designation as the Quartet. It is "incorrect" certainly, since the words "chamber symphony" imply some winds, if not brass, in the instrumentation.

In any event it is included here since Shostakovich gave his full blessing to the Barshai transcription. The performance is best in the violent second movement of the five-part work. It is this movement that is most fitting for the textural enlargement.

Alan Shulman (1915-   )

Cod Liver 'Ile

Instrumental

☐ Heifetz (violin); Smith (piano) / RCA LM-2382 (monaural)

Violin

A tidbit of a musical dance turn from the composer's Suite Based on American Folk Songs. A cute encore item.

(RCA carelessly [?] omits Shulman's first name on its credits. Other lesser-known composers represented on this Heifetz miscellaneous program are given similar short shrift.)

Jean Sibelius (1865-1957)

The Bard, Op. 64

Orchestra

☐ Helsinki Radio Symphony Orchestra / Kamu (conductor) / Deutsche Grammophon 2530455

One of the least known of Sibelius's symphonic poems and one wherein the sound observations are compiled from mood suggestions rather than thematic statements. Kamu guides the thin mechanisms of the score in good fashion.

En Saga, Op. 9

☐ Philadelphia Orchestra / Ormandy (conductor) / RCA ARL1-2906

Infallible rhythmic scanning by Ormandy with all the fantasy and mysticism of the score impressively depicted. This type of folk epic in romantic dress is Ormandy's specialty. It was well exhibited in the earlier Columbia recording (MS-6732). It is even better in this later RCA edition.

Finlandia, Op. 26

☐ Philadelphia Orchestra / Ormandy (conductor) / RCA LSC-3302

Ormandy and the glorious-toned Philadelphians all the way. The music sings and shouts, the rhythmic figures crackle, and the interpretation is superb and true.

Available also with nineteen other perennials in a three-record package on RCA CRL3-0985. Ormandy has also recorded the work with the Philadelphia Orchestra for Columbia and on that label it is available in a number of releases, including two with chorus (*see below*).

Finlandia, Op. 26

☐ Philadelphia Orchestra and Mormon Tabernacle Choir / Ormandy (conductor) / Columbia MS-6196

Different recording company, same orchestra, same conductor, same vivid performance, save choral additions to the broad hymnodic tune and the coda. A gimmick, of course, since the choral overlay (and words) are not by Sibelius. Some may call it "chintzy"; others may term it a violation of Sibelius's score, equivalent to adding a double bass part to sections of a Beethoven string quartet; and still others may think it over-sentimentalizes what is already verging on sentimentality. But no harm, if you like this sort of thing. If not, stay with the authentic original (*see above*).

(This edition is also contained in a all-Sibelius program on Columbia MS-6732.)

Four Legends from the Kalevala, Op. 22

☐ Royal Liverpool Philharmonic Orchestra / Moore (English horn) / Groves (conductor) / Angel S-37106

The most famous of these pieces is, of course, *The Swan of Tuonela;* less so, but far better known than the other two (*Lemminkäinen and the Maidens of Saari* and *Lemminkäinen in Tuonela*) is *Lemminkäinen's Homeward Journey* (*see below* [*Lemminkäinen's Return*]).

Fine idiomatic consideration is displayed here. Though there is a far better performance of *The Swan* (*see below*), credit is especially warranted here for the sane tempo Groves sets for the *Homeward Journey*—if taken too fast the music loses its shaped strength.

In Memoriam, Op. 59

☐ Hungarian State Symphony Orchestra / Jalas (conductor) / London 6955

The "Funeral March" (the score has this prefatory title) has Mahlerian merits. Its power is accurately presented in this recording.

Karelia Suite, Op. 11

☐ Vienna Philharmonic Orchestra / Maazel (conductor) / London 6375

Bardic snap is in the Intermezzo, a substantive essay covers the *Ballade*, and suitable vitality is provided for the *Alla marcia*. Full sonority scale where needed. What is never needed is brass blasting, and Maazel makes certain this does not happen. The heartbeat of this music is in good health with Maazel's ministrations.

Lemminkäinen's Return from *Four Legends from the Kalevala,* Op. 22, No. 4

☐ Hallé Orchestra / Barbirolli (conductor) / Seraphim S-60208

A performance of distinction, with the lights and shades of the score sensitively portrayed. Barbirolli's tempo is well suited to the music, all too often hurried to the extent that it is all *moto perpetuo* and not much else. A speed rate that permits structural definition is more exciting in the long run.

(The title noted is the usual one used for this piece, though actually within the entire opus the heading is *Lemminkäinen's Homeward Journey.*)

(*See above* for a recording of the complete *Four Legends from the Kalevala.*)

Night Ride and Sunrise, Op. 55

☐ L'Orchestre de la Suisse Romande / Stein (conductor) / London 6745

Stein shows himself to have fine conductorial talent for Sibelian interpretation in this work. The playing is percipient and sensitive.

The Oceanides, Op. 73

☐ Royal Philharmonic Orchestra / Beecham (conductor) / Angel S-35458

By sharp control, Beecham paces the dynamic conditions of Sibelius's tone poem magnificently. When the climax arrives near the close, the effect is triply powerful. It's most difficult to bind the motives and figures that structure this work and not merely sound forth bits and pieces. For a conductor it's a struggle. I can't recall anyone who even came close to the continuity Beecham obtains. It is a triumph that he shares with Sibelius.

(Be on guard. The copy used for review had reverse labeling.)

Pelléas et Mélisande, Op. 46

☐ Royal Philharmonic Orchestra / Beecham (conductor) / Angel S-35458

Eight pieces drawn from the incidental music Sibelius composed for Maeterlinck's play. (The printed score has an additional movement, *At the Seashore,* which may be omitted at concert performance, and which Beecham does here.)

Pelléas is one of the great Sibelius works, hidden in his catalogue and rarely performed. This may be because of its chamber orchestra computation, with flute alternating piccolo, oboe doubling on English horn, two clarinets, two bassoons, two horns, light percussion (timpani, triangle, and bass drum), and strings limited to six first violins, four second violins, four violas, four cellos, and three double basses. Its creative coalescence, linking Sibelian fact to a fictional tale of other-worldliness, deserves attention as much as his symphonies.

Beecham's performance is definitive, containing eloquence, depth, color, super phrasing, and perfect pace for each of the different scenes. It is not only a definitive performance, but a distinguished one.

(The labeling was reversed on the disc used for review.)

Pohjola's Daughter, Op. 49

☐ New York Philharmonic / Bernstein (conductor) / Columbia MS-6749

All the rich ingredients and sumptuous textures of Sibelius's symphonic fantasia are conveyed. There are places in the piece where Bernstein chooses to bypass tempi instructions, but only an academician would criticize such conduct in a work that is fantasy-formed. The recorded sound brings out all the deep pigments of the score.

Scaramouche, Op. 71

☐ Hungarian State Symphony Orchestra / Jalas (conductor) / London 6824

The incidental music for Poul Knudsen's play, termed a "tragic pantomime." Vigorous writing, which despite some overchromaticized style does not deny the identity of the composer. No problem in this, the only recorded example in the catalogue.

Scènes historiques I, Op. 25

☐ Bournemouth Symphony Orchestra / Berglund (conductor) / Seraphim S-60289

The first three of six miniatures: *All'Overtura, Scène,* and *Festivo.* Set II (unrecorded at present) consists of *The Chase, Love Song,* and *At the Drawbridge.* A rewarding depiction.

The Swan of Tuonela from Four Legends from the Kalevala, Op. 22, No. 3

☐ Philadelphia Orchestra / Rosenblatt (English horn) / Ormandy (conductor) / Odyssey Y-30489

Magnificent English horn playing by Louis Rosenblatt. For phrase shaping with the most subtle and minute dynamic differences (without disturbing the line), beauty of sound, and fluency of execution, nothing in the recorded catalogue is better. Ormandy's "sound" (as he terms it) is of burnished pigmentation. A more expressive Sibelian totality is not to be had.

(For a recording of the complete *Four Legends from the Kalevala, see above.*)

Symphony

No. 1 in E minor, Op. 39 / No. 2 in D major, Op. 43 / No. 3 in C major, Op. 52 / No. 4 in A minor, Op. 63 / No. 5 in E flat major, Op. 82 / No. 6 in D minor, Op. 104 / No. 7 in C major, Op. 105

☐ Boston Symphony Orchestra / Davis (conductor) / Philips 6709011
☐ Utah Symphony Orchestra / Abravanel (conductor) / Vanguard SRV-381/4

For maintaining a consistency of insight into all seven Sibelius symphonies the choice is, without hesitation, the performances directed by Colin Davis. From the rhapsodically lyrical initial Symphony, continuing onto the atmospheric mystery of the fourth work in the set, and concluding with the Seventh Symphony's concentrated essences, Davis never falters. His conceptions are styled to project every intrinsic point within the symphonies, and he proves to have the most "musical ear" of any conductor that has recorded the entire cycle.

The Abravanel set is deserving of high praise. It may not have the tonal grandeur of the B.S.O. but in no sense is the Utah outfit any less than of major league category. Abravanel displays a Sibelian sensitivity that is far above average. The Second Symphony sings rather than being bombastic; the interweave in the Sixth Symphony is splendid. The musical explanations of Sibelius's changing contexts are always provided with proper formal weighting. In these seven performances there are points to argue but far less than in the other competitive sets of the complete symphonies.

(*See below* for separate recordings of the individual symphonies.)

Symphony No. 1 in E minor, Op. 39

☐ Hallé Orchestra / Barbirolli (conductor) / Angel S-36489

Barbirolli's sensitivity to Sibelius was never questioned, and this recording is persuasive documentation of that reputation. It is always marvelously alive, always dynamic but never powerhoused in the pugilistic manner that constantly spoils the effectiveness of the finale. The scherzo is finely paced and pointed.

Symphony No. 2 in D major, Op. 43

☐ Philadelphia Orchestra / Ormandy (conductor) / Odyssey Y-30046
☐ Royal Philharmonic Orchestra / Barbirolli (conductor) / Quintessence PMC-7008
☐ Boston Symphony Orchestra / Koussevitzky (conductor) / RCA VIC-1510 (monaural)

Ormandy's earlier (Columbia) recording is not replaced by his later remake for RCA (on ARD1-0018). There is a passionate coloration in the winds especially that gives the nod to the former presentation, now on the Odyssey label. His all-inclusive range of sensibility and vision (and marvelous tempi selection) establish his performance in the top category. Barbirolli's reading is entirely different and can be argued in regard to some independent ideas of tempi (movement 2) and compressed articulation (movement 3), but these are overridden with an infusion of intense passion and dramaticism that make it one of the most vital of all the recordings available.

The Koussevitzky is both historically significant and musically distinguished. It is worth having, especially, if one can afford two recordings of the same work.

Symphony No. 3 in C major, Op. 52

☐ Helsinki Radio Orchestra / Kamu (conductor) / Deutsche Grammophon 2530426

If a conductor is able to probe the orchestrated variations of the second movement, which is the central core of this Symphony, he has it made. Kamu's is a stunning accomplishment, not only of that sectional movement but of the rest of the work. Importantly, never does Kamu permit the force of Sibelius's music to turn into orchestral roughness—a special mark of this conductor's control.

Symphony No. 4 in A minor, Op. 63

☐ Vienna Philharmonic Orchestra / Maazel (conductor) / London 6592

One of Maazel's best achievements. Under his baton the Symphony has chilling atmosphere, the music broods, the temper is fascinatingly elusive. Some conductors endeavor to polish, as brightly as possible, Sibelius's individually timbred material, but such move is out of place for this work. The slow movement is not rushed; the dramaticism is gloved throughout and as a result becomes twice as powerful.

Symphony No. 5 in E flat major, Op. 82

☐ New York Philharmonic / Bernstein (conductor) / Columbia MS-6749

The dark, sombre, and austere qualities of this Symphony can often lead to a texturally thick representation. It is to Bernstein's credit that there is no blurring of the details and no dulling of the shaded flame that lights the score. At the same time the nobility of the work is maintained. It is a clean and disciplined reading and totally exciting. There are no tricks or meretricious devices in Bernstein's conducting of this grand Symphony.

(The Symphony is also available in a ten-record album of all of Sibelius's symphonies, conducted by Bernstein, on Columbia M5S-784.)

Symphony No. 6 in D minor, Op. 104

☐ Berlin Philharmonic Orchestra / von Karajan (conductor) / Deutsche Grammophon 139032

The vagrant phrases of the first movement must be carefully shaped in order finally to form a structure of recognizable strength. Von Karajan succeeds quite well. He provides a fine finesse in the melancholic gaiety of the Allegretto (the Symphony does not have a slow movement) and shapes the balance of the Symphony nicely.

Symphony No. 7 in C major, Op. 105

☐ Royal Philharmonic Orchestra / Beecham (conductor) / Angel S–35458

A performance of great depth. The atmosphere is splendid, the dynamic proportions are perfect, and there is no yielding to effect. It adds up to still another most affecting musical memorial to a superb conductor.

Tapiola, Op. 112

☐ Vienna Philharmonic Orchestra / Maazel (conductor) / London 6592

This is, indeed, an impressive performance, impregnated with the starkness and brooding that permeate Sibelius's score. Maazel strategically does not storm through the storm section, and the effect is splendid.

Valse triste, Op. 44, No. 3

☐ Hallé Orchestra / Barbirolli (conductor) / Seraphim S–60208
☐ Royal Philharmonic Orchestra / Beecham (conductor) / Seraphim S–60134

This beautiful evergreen represents one of the three pieces of incidental music Sibelius wrote for the drama *Kuolema* ("Death") by his brother-in-law, Arvid Järnefelt. The other two pieces have disappeared from the scene.

Though the work is a simple expression, really, conveyed by flute, clarinet, a pair of horns, timpani, and strings, it seems hard to believe that so many misjudgments can apply to the many recorded performances reviewed. The criticisms vary: force instead of elegance, overplaying or underplaying, and so on. Both conductors listed, however, recognize the music for what it is: chaste, pure, and elevated in its language. Both are the best in all respects.

String Orchestra

Canzonetta, Op. 62a

☐ Helsinki Chamber Orchestra / Segerstam (conductor) / Bis LP–19

Valse triste (see under *Orchestra*) revisited both in mood and purpose, as incidental music for Arvid Järnefelt's play *Kuolema* ("Death"). *Canzonetta* is expressively enunciated by the Finnish musicians.

Rakastava, Op. 14

☐ Helsinki Chamber Orchestra / Erkkilä (percussion); Rahkonen (violin); Höylä (cello) / Segerstam (conductor) / Bis LP–19

Rakastava ("The Lover") has the strong Sibelian profile. The misty ostinato for the strings in movement 2 (the scoring also includes timpani and triangle), the strongly peaked cadences, and the melancholic melodic shapes will be immediately identifiable as his and his alone.

Segerstam has an excellent feeling for the music's style. The potencies of the score are fully realized, the colorations sensitively detailed. The reproduction is magnificent, also.

Romance in C for String Orchestra, Op. 42

☐ Leningrad Philharmonic Orchestra / Rozhdestvensky (conductor) / Melodiya/Angel S-40031

A Sibelius lightweight but nicely put together. His string orchestra Romance certainly deserves to be better known.

Suite mignonne, Op. 98a

☐ Helsinki Chamber Orchestra / Helasvuo and Muhonen (flutes) / Segerstam (conductor) / Bis LP-19

Surface lightness for a pair of flutes and strings that Sibelius tossed off between his Fifth and Sixth Symphonies. Palm-garden music consisting of a waltz (*Petite scène*), a Polka (which gives you the objective immediately), and an Epilogue.

Concerto in D minor for Violin and Orchestra, Op. 47

Solo Instrument and Orchestra

Violin

☐ Chicago Symphony Orchestra / Heifetz (violin) / Hendl (conductor) / RCA LSC-2435
☐ Berlin Philharmonic Orchestra / Ferras (violin) / von Karajan (conductor) / Deutsche Grammophon 138961

It may be argued that the most important point in playing a Wieniawski violin concerto is to produce full technical accomplishment and that that's sufficient. In a work like the Sibelius, however, there are varied valuations possible and all are valid. There's a wide difference between the serenely poised, held-in-heat of Heifetz's projection and the more colored, outward observations defined in Ferras's playing. Both are splendid and imaginative essays. Heifetz's control of cantilena is remarkable and magnificent. Ferras's broader (even bolder) conception is music making of lasting value.

Walter Hendl has always been a first-class, controlled conductor, and no less so in the days when this Concerto was recorded. His support is immaculate and thorough. Von Karajan does not overlook a single phrase.

(Both performances are available in other packagings—Ferras in Deutsche Grammophon 923077, Heifetz in RCA LSC-4010 and also in a six-record set on RCA CRL6-0720.)

Four Humoresques for Violin and Orchestra, Op. 89
Two Humoresques for Violin and Orchestra, Op. 87b

☐ Southwest German Radio Symphony Orchestra / Rosand (violin) / Szöke (conductor) / Turnabout 34182

Offbeat Sibelius worth listening time. (Oistrakh recorded the pair in Opus 87b on Melodiya/Angel S-40020.)

Kyllikki, Op. 41
Sonata in F major, Op. 12
Sonatina in F sharp minor, Op. 67, No. 1

Instrumental

Piano

Sonatina in E major, Op. 67, No. 2

Sonatina in B flat minor, Op. 67, No. 3

☐ Rubinstein (piano) / Musical Heritage Society MHS-1218

Consider this: 123 individual piano compositions were produced by Sibelius (nineteen sets bear a specific opus number, six single pieces do not). Then consider again how none are heard in live performance. Accordingly, to have seven of the pieces on disc (the *Kyllikki* count as three, since they comprise Three Lyric Pieces on Subjects from the *Kalevala*) offers substantial benefits, historic and musical.

Three is also the number covering the number of movements in all the other compositions save the Third Sonatina. That work consists of two movements, each in paired tempi, slow and fast.

While only a few Sibelian expectations are fulfilled in these pieces—these being in the Sonata, the first of the three Sonatinas, and in portions of the programmatic Opus 41— the music is charming in its settled romantic speech.

David Rubinstein is consistently fine in his performance portrayals. Such intelligence and competence are not available in Glenn Gould's performances of the three Sonatinas on Columbia M-34555. The slow tempi he uses are a fiction of his own making.

Violin

Berceuse, Op. 79, No. 6   **Souvenir, Op. 79, No. 1**

Devotion—Ab imo pectore, Op. 77

☐ Steiner (violin); Berfield (piano) / Orion 76244

Rarely heard Sibelius, convincingly played.

The *Devotion* is the second of two Solemn Melodies, written for either violin or cello with orchestra. There is no great loss in using the piano reduction of the score. The other two pieces are the terminal representations in a suite of Six Pieces.

Sonatine in E major for Violin and Piano, Op. 80

☐ Steiner (violin); Berfield (piano) / Orion 76244

While Sibelius did not often define his themes immediately and rather expanded before he concentrated on thematic definition, in this work there is no such delay. The themes are stated, and sung comfortably; the developments are more lyrical than germinal. But there are the signs that define this composer and his positive technique—the use of thirds and pedal rhythms.

One is grateful for this team in making the piece available—concert programs bypass it. Appreciation is also due these artists for their excellent musical decorum.

Chamber Music

String Quartet (*Voces Intimae*) in D minor, Op. 56

☐ Claremont Quartet / Nonesuch 71140

Sibelius's ethnic attributes are conveyed perfectly in his Opus 56. The very eloquent commentaries of *Voces Intimae* do not deploy sonata forms. Nor is Sibelius's single String Quartet a suite, which connotes independence of movements, not the interdependence (present here, if only to a degree) of the five divisions. All the melodic curves, sharp edges, and ripeness of color are of Sibelian discernment.

The Claremont performance is the only one available. They tend to neutralize the vagueness, mystery, and liquescence of Sibelius's music. Movement 2 is an example. It is designed with scored brushwork; there is no thematic pasting on a billboard. This kind of filmy rumination is played just a bit too squarely, too positively. In the finale, a wild dance, the Claremont's tempo is excellent and they convey a good sense of the sublimated tempered athleticism within the measures.

All this said, if you can find the Copenhagen String Quartet's recording of this singular work (released by Turnabout on No. 34091 and now out of print) don't, repeat, *don't* let it go. It is masterly and it has a depth plus understanding that seem to have mostly escaped the Claremonters.

Vocal

Voice with Accompaniment

Den Första Kyssen, Op. 37, No. 1
Flickan Kom Ifrån Sin Älsklings Möte, Op. 37, No. 5
Illalle, Op. 17, No. 6
Im Feld Ein Mädchen Singt . . . , Op. 50, No. 3
På Verandan Vid Hafvet, Op. 38, No. 2
Säf, Säf, Susa, Op. 36, No. 4
Se'n Har Jag Ej Frågat Mera, Op. 17, No. 1
Svarta Rosor, Op. 36, No. 1
Var Det En Dröm?, Op. 37, No. 4
Våren Flyktar Hastigt, Op. 13, No. 4

☐ Nilsson (soprano); Solyom (piano) / Bis LP-15

With the exception of *Illalle* and *Im Feld Ein Mädchen Singt . . .*, all the other songs listed are available in Flagstad's program, issued by London (*see below*). Birgit Nilsson's performance is splendid but the advantage of orchestral accompaniment naturally gives Flagstad a decided edge. For those that can afford it, both editions are worth having.

Voice and Orchestra

Arioso, Op. 3
Den Första Kyssen, Op. 37, No. 1
Diamenten På Marssnön, Op. 36, No. 6
Flickan Kom Ifrån Sin Älsklings Möte, Op. 37, No. 5
Höstkväll, Op. 38, No. 1
Kom Nu Hit? Död, Op. 60, No. 1
Men Min Fågel Märks Dock Icke, Op. 36, No. 2
Om Kvällen, Op. 17, No. 6
På Verandan Vid Hafvet, Op. 38, No. 2
Säf, Säf, Susa, Op. 36, No. 4
Se'n Har Jag Ej Frågat Mera, Op. 17, No. 1
Svarta Rosor, Op. 36, No. 1
Var Det En Dröm?, Op. 37, No. 4
Våren Flyktar Hastigt, Op. 13, No. 4

☐ London Symphony Orchestra / Flagstad (soprano) / Fjeldstad (conductor) / London 33216

The expressive powers Sibelius had as a composer of songs are vividly exhibited in this program. All are taken from sets of songs, save the Opus 3 *Arioso* ("The Maiden's Seasons"). Opus 60 is represented by "Come Away, Death," the first of a pair of songs from Shakespeare's *Twelfth Night*. There are seven songs in each of Opus 13 and Opus 17, a set of six in Opus 36, and five songs in each of Opus 37 and Opus 38. The majority of the texts (six of the total fourteen) are by Sibelius's most-favored Finnish poet, Johan Ludvig Runeberg (1804–1877).

This choice collection is represented by great singing. Vocally, Sibelius has never been served better. (London originally released the album as OS-25005.)

Luonnotar, Op. 70

☐ New York Philharmonic / Curtin (soprano) / Bernstein (conductor) / Columbia M-30232

Powerful and vivid Sibelius, powerfully and vividly presented here. "Virgin of the

Air'' follows a specific program detailing the creation of the universe. It has Sibelian splendor, and though it is of concentrated length (eight minutes) it is just as dynamic and important as any of his symphonies.

Columbia has produced its recording with rich brilliance.

Elie Siegmeister (1909-   )

Orchestra

Ozark Set (1943)

☐ Minneapolis Symphony Orchestra / Mitropoulos (conductor) / Orion 73116E (monaural)

Siegmeister in his folksy style. Dewy orchestration is used for *Morning in the Hills* and a rhythmic campaign directs the *Camp Meeting* (steadfast tonalism, of course, here as well as elsewhere, but nothing campy about the music). The slow music of the suite is heard in *Lazy Afternoon,* and country music that predates current country music vividly concludes matters in *Saturday Night.*

Mitropoulos gave the world premiere with the orchestra that is heard here and he plays the score in an enchanting Americanese manner. The sound is somewhat fuzzy, however, and some of the instrumental definition just isn't.

Sunday in Brooklyn (1946)

☐ Vienna Symphony / Adler (conductor) / Orion 73116E (monaural)

Light music grown in Brooklyn. Originally written for piano, the music was orchestrated by the composer in 1946. A Gershwinesque beat pulses in *Prospect Park* and a pleasurable scherzo horizon surrounds *Sunday Driver.* Contrastive substantiation then is met by *Family at Home* and *Children's Story,* with more pulsative data certifying *Coney Island.*

Sunday in Brooklyn was first recorded a long time ago by Adler and appeared on his ''own'' label, Spa Records. The playing is convincing but this re-release of the Spa disc is no three-star recording as far as sound is concerned.

Symphony No. 3 (1957)

☐ Oslo Philharmonic Orchestra / Siegmeister (conductor) / Composers Recordings S-185

A huge one-movement virtuosic conception. The work is divisible into trinal considerations, motivated by a motive in the initial measure. It has added excitement in that the interest increases as the music moves forward. (How many symphonies die in agony in their final movements?) The slow movement is quietly ecstatic, quite moving; the final section is of toccata tone.

A fairly good performance, only a bit stiff in spots and sometimes lacking in depth. Nonetheless, a recording worth owning since this is a Symphony truly worth attention.

Western Suite (1945)

☐ Utah Symphony Orchestra / Abravanel (conductor) / Turnabout 34459

Americana, via the use of a dozen folk tunes. There is no square quotation; rather, the tunes are neatly integrated. Two of the subtitles will indicate the flavor: *Prairie Morning* (opening movement) and *Buckaroo* (fourth movement). Ripe playing and ripe sound.

Concerto for Clarinet and Orchestra (1956)

☐ Members of the London Symphony Orchestra / Brymer (clarinet) / Siegmeister (conductor) / Turnabout 34640

Jazz does not take any holiday in this Concerto of hotcha and hot licks, belts and blues. The tempi indications show the stylistic tracking Siegmeister had in mind (and he successfully moves on the course): Easy, Freely; Lively, Lightly; Slow Drag; and Fast and Driving. Be assured that Siegmeister's Concerto is a prime addition to the literature for the clarinet.

Brymer's playing is completely with it. It's fully in the groove. Bravos all around.

Concerto for Flute and Orchestra (1960)

☐ Members of the London Symphony Orchestra / Lloyd (flute) / Siegmeister (conductor) / Turnabout 34640

Siegmeister's Flute Concerto is for the most part a reflective essay, aloof from pyrotechnics, filled with a jazz-edged romanticism. It throws off more rhythmic steam in the finale, but that doesn't diminish the expressionistic fancy of the previous two movements. Throughout there is lyrical buoyancy.

To make music of this kind jell and register requires a sensitive virtuosity, not a blatant one. Peter Lloyd meets all the requirements.

Fantasy and Soliloquy for Cello Solo (1964)

☐ Sylvester (cello) / Orion 7284

The Fantasy is tough-tracked, tense music. Its atonalized technical knots require a courageous virtuoso. Robert Sylvester is exactly that sort of musician as he proves in this splendid realization. The Soliloquy is dedicated to rhapsodic considerations that are logically detailed and attractively exploit the cello's capabilities.

American Harp (1966)

☐ Chertok (harp) / Orion ORS–75207

All too many harp works blend into a gray, neutral matter without a definite profile. Alternating moods that are subdued (*Reverie* and Ballad) with more vigorous ones (Dance and *Celebration*), Seigmeister has produced an outstanding twelve-minute work. It is important because the writing is colorful but not swept by sweeping effects; harmonic torture is avoided. This is a carefully assembled set of pieces, beautifully brought out in all its details by the soloist.

On This Ground (1971)

☐ Mandel (piano) / Orion 7284

It is possible to call Siegmeister's Whitmanesque-titled suite of five pieces romantic, simply because the feelings are clear, the contents are of contemporary warmth, the gestures are positive, and the narratives are direct. Examples: part 2, *Where?* has intervallic direction that spells out the title significantly, *Ariel* (the third of the set) is a Siegmeisterian *scherz,* and the finale, *Mr. Henry's (Monday Night),* is delightful boozy saloon music. (It would sound even better if the piano used were slightly out of tune.) Mandel, however, is completely in tune with his portrayals. He not only has great skill but he interprets what he plays clearly and vividly.

Sonata No. 2 for Piano (1964)

☐ Mandel (piano) / Desto 6467

The Sonata makes much of harmonics (with resultant overtone vibrations), plucked strings, cluster harmony, fricative vertical combines, polyrhythms, and metrical nervousness. Such musical buck fever is made even more vehement by mainly motoric tempi, violent register changes and contrasts.

Siegmeister's piece is stern stuff and conceived only for a virtuoso. Mandel performs the music with the greatest ease and proper objective meticulousness, without which a work of this type would be harmed.

Theme and Variations No. 2 (1967)

☐ Mandel (piano) / Grenadilla GS–1020

Large-thematic scale for permutative direction is not Siegmeister's objective here. Instead, he uses an extremely tight four-pitch motive, its entire span covering not more than a tone and a half. It is this pithiness that provides the variational reflexes in a muscular music that is toned to perfection. Further, it exemplifies one of Siegmeister's healthiest piano compositions and proves again the value of motival stuff for action, color, and impact.

Alan Mandel's performance illustrates parallel dynamic and artistic reflexes. Grenadilla's sound is superfine. Its production slights the liner note writer by failing to note a name credit. It indicates the piece was written for Mandel and dedicated ''to Nancy and Alan.'' The latter name needs no further data; the former does. ''Nancy'' is the composer's daughter and is Mrs. Alan Mandel.

Chamber Music

Sonata No. 1 for Violin and Piano (1951)

☐ Nancy Mandel (violin); Alan Mandel (piano) / Grenadilla GS–1024

Though this is numbered as Siegmeister's initial work in the violin and piano category, it actually is his second example—he composed his first Sonata in the medium in 1931 and then withdrew it.

Structural definition is acute in the work. The music is disciplined in its architecture but devoid of academic inheritance. The opening movement is sonata-shaped. Movement 2 is jazzy—meaning Siegmeisterian jazz, a controlled attempt not to mimic, but to integrate. It floats along with bounce, syncopation, tunes, and harmonic side-slipped favoritism, such as major-minor ambivalence. The slow movement has the simplicity of soaring song; the finale the spirited snap of rhythmic address.

The performance is direct. Everything is clear, but without monitored measurement, which would destroy the active life of the music.

Sonata No. 2 for Violin and Piano (1965)

☐ Jaime Laredo (violin); Ruth Laredo (piano) / Desto 7125

The Siegmeisterian use of lyricism (marked with spiky dissonance) to contrast chamber-music clout is paramount here. The melodicism (of contemporary brand) is curvaceous and soars free, the rhythmic detail is punctuative and tightly contained. This Sonata is exciting and gutsy.

Rhythmic precision and complete realization of the essences in Siegmeister's score mark this recorded performance. A distinguished issue in all respects.

Sonata No. 3 for Violin and Piano (1965)

☐ Cohen (violin); Mandel (piano) / Desto 6467

It is time to remove from the minds of many who have followed the course of American music that Elie Siegmeister represents the school of foliated folklore. This has been due to the many years Siegmeister did write music with Americana attitudes and was very successful with it. While the tinge of native syntax will be heard in the finale here, panchromaticism is the principal point of view. The textures are sinewy, the measures seething with excitation even when the tempi are restrained.

The Sonata contains two movements, beginning with a neat example of contemporary realization of sonata form. In the second part a combination is made of slow-tempoed material with scherzo-fringed music. The former is developed within the peripatetic punch of the latter, a music containing a brute and unshaken belief in asymmetrical design. It works, succeeding with textural stringency and harmonic astringency.

Cohen and Mandel give a four-star performance.

Sonata No. 4 for Violin and Piano (1972)

☐ Nancy Mandel (violin); Alan Mandel (piano) / Orion 7284

Strong contemporary links to the past are evident in Siegmeister's Sonata, completed on New Year's Day of 1972. The contours are drawn from classical structures, all the proportions are derived from solidly structured phrase relations. Plentiful color is used, but never beyond the normal range of the instruments. There is an occasional piano cluster, here and there a Bartókian percussive pizzicato, once in a while a *ponticello* glassiness, but never any of the radical chic instrumental habits such as percussing the bodies of the instruments, reaching into the piano's guts, trespassing behind the violin's bridge, et cetera.

The first of the three movements is cast in an expanded consideration of sonata form. Movement 2 begins with unaccompanied violin (a favorite decision of this composer) and is then linked onto an ongoing dialogue. Motivity charges through the finale. It is virtuosic and exciting in its concept and requires the utmost in ability from the performers.

The Mandels meet all the demands. They present Siegmeister's score with stylistic positiveness, superb musicianship, and technical skill.

Sonata No. 5 for Violin and Piano (1972)

☐ Nancy Mandel (violin); Alan Mandel (piano) / Grenadilla GS-1024

The panchromatic first movement is followed by a favorite device of the composer, a movement (in this case slow-tempoed) beginning with an unaccompanied instrument (here the violin). The initial premise has a "blues, or whatever you call it" outline, as Siegmeister explains. But this is only the start. The music expands, takes on a controlled rhapsodic demeanor, with harsh dissonance, contrasted tranquility, and instrumental confrontation—all proceeding in the most natural manner and yet never losing the basic sense of fantasy.

The final part is rough, tough, and nicely nasty—virtuosic stuff and no nonsense. On the score page, music of such rhythmic adventurousness indicates a nervous exuberance that has a built-in type of success. Hearing the music confirms it.

A choice affair marks this performance. So does a family affair. Nancy Mandel is Siegmeister's daughter, Alan Mandel, therefore, is his son-in-law. Few composers are so fortunate in having such expert musicians in the family to play and record their music.

Quartet No. 2 (1960)

☐ Galimir String Quartet / Composers Recordings S–176E (monaural)

Siegmeister's quartet allegiance is to Bartók's mensural drive processes. Blocked, charged, and repetitive rhythmic patterns will be found in this Quartet. So will the stitching of thematic transfer. The work is very emotive as well as motoric. It is highly charged, even when it shifts into lyrical gear.

Vitality, robustness, and energy make the performance successful.

Sextet for Brass and Percussion (1965)

☐ Schwarz and Dean (trumpets); Birdwell (horn); Fromme (trombone); Hanks (tuba); Gottlieb (percussion) / Desto 6467

Eruptive thematic range is presented here. It is such disjunctivity (a controlled rhapsodic situation) that rules the opening movement and from which the music develops. The same wide-spanned conduct obtains in the middle movement. In the finale the music is jazzy but the rhythms are cool. This is serious jazz-infiltrated music, almost a tease of the Pops style rather than a music tossed around in a sauce of rhythms and variegated colors.

Vocal

Voice with Accompaniment

Elegies for García Lorca (1938)

Evil (1975)

Johnny Appleseed (1940)

Lazy Afternoon (1944)

The Strange Funeral in Braddock (1933)

☐ Beattie (bass-baritone); Mandel (piano) / Orion 76220

There are manifestations here of songs that do not run their way according to set patterns. They contain no melodic banalities to capture the words for easy recognition. A mere touch of Hispanic detail is to be noted in the three Lorca songs and a folksy implication in *Johnny Appleseed* and *Lazy Afternoon. The Strange Funeral in Braddock* is strong stuff—social satire, as Nicolas Slonimsky describes it.

Beattie's vocal marksmanship is on the button all the way. He gets true-spirited support from Mandel—a musical equal, not an accompanist.

Five Cummings Songs (1970)

For My Daughters (1952)

Nancy Hanks (1944)

Two Songs of the City (1951)

☐ Kirkpatrick (soprano); Mandel (piano) / Orion 76220

The second of the Cummings set (*raise the shade*) is a perfect fusion of music and poetry. A totally different style rules the five songs in *For My Daughters,* conceived in expressive, meaningful tonal style. Siegmeister is no maker of tunes in the primitive sense. His vocal lines give meaning to the texts and produce a total handsome music.

Elizabeth Kirkpatrick sings well enough for anyone's price of admission. Her collaborator plays with sensitivity and understanding, avoiding machine-tooled phrasing. That is a tremendous assist to Elie Siegmeister's music.

Paul J. Sifler (1921-)

Marimba Suite (1970)

☐ Ervin (marimba) / Wim WIMR–5

Instrumental

Marimba

The danger in music for the marimba is that its timbre can give the listener treacley jitters. Sifler wisely avoids this by concentrating each of the four movements on a specific and contrastive technical basis. Represented in turn are: disjunct writing, arpeggios, chords, and repetitive patterns. It works nicely. It is performed neatly.

Friedrich Silcher (1789-1860)

Die Sonne zeigte golden sich

Saatengrun Veilchenduft

☐ Camerata Vocale, Bremen / Blum (conductor) / Nonesuch 71081

Choral

Chorus Alone

Light romantic music, expertly detailed by this mini-chorus of five.

Anton Simon (1850-1916)

Quatuor en forme de sonatine, **Op. 23, No. 1**

☐ American Brass Quintet / Desto 6474/7

Chamber Music

Sufficient technical facility is illustrated here. Simon's prose is polished, has balanced emotional appeal, and posts the general manifestations of classical form. A little Russianism flavors the finale. Of such is this composer's music—simple to understand and hear, not voicing any curiousness at all.

Netty Simons (1913-)

Design Groups #1

☐ George (percussion) / Desto 7128

Percussion

Composed for one to three percussionists, here performed by Ron George, recorded on three tracks. (George is mentioned only once in the entire production, and that in the liner notes!)

A huge instrumental inventory is utilized. The unusual ones include Kaluba drums, a large glass brandy snifter, a pair of goblet-shaped compotes, a set of three brass wine goblets, Tibetan prayer stones, and a set of nine pipes. An aleatory adventure worth listening to and doubtless played with perception.

Silver Thaw

☐ Turetzky (double bass) / Desto 7128

Instrumental

Double Bass

Anything goes in this case—graphic notation to begin with. The piece is playable by one to eight instruments of any type in any combination. Turetzky's translation pops the sounds (all types, mostly un-double bass-ish, and all somewhat frenzied in effect) onto four tracks. Pure music it ain't. Inventive music it is.

Chamber Music

Design Groups #2

☐ Bertram Turetzky (double bass); Nancy Turetzky (flutes) / Desto 7128

Simons's work is playable by any two instruments of high and low register. It matters little, therefore, what the partners are in this rampant exhibition of aleatoricism. Although innumerable charts with directions are given, Simons uses a type of self-cancellation by offering all kinds of choices to the performers.

Thus, creative certainty is displaced by uncertainty. The notational microcosm offered the instrumentalists means almost (if not totally) an improvisation. And in that respect, nonform becomes the music's form.

Expect everything in *Design Groups* #2. And expect the unexpected. The Turetzkys (Mr. and Mrs.) are topflight experts in this sort of freestyle exhibition. They do magnificently with this fully undetermined music.

Robert Simpson   (1921-   )

Orchestra

Symphony No. 3 (1962)

☐ London Symphony Orchestra / Horenstein (conductor) / Unicorn UNS–225

Simpson has published authoritative studies of the work of Nielsen and Bruckner. In response to his efforts, in behalf of the former composer, Simpson was awarded the Carl Nielsen Gold Medal of Denmark in 1956. To mark his propaganda on Bruckner, the Bruckner Society of America named Simpson the recipient of their Medal of Honor. To a large degree this unselfish consideration of other composers has drawn attention away from Simpson's considerable and important creative output which includes five symphonies, six string quartets, several concertos, and a good body of chamber music. The Unicorn recording proves the original and powerful voice of this little-known composer.

The Symphony has two movements, each containing disparate elements, yet combining them in a mutually contributory manner. In the first movement tonal centers constantly shift; the activity of these polarities are colored with heated dissonances. In the second movement the formats of slow movement, scherzo, and finale are combined. Particular differences paradoxically become related to one another as the pace moves from Adagio to Presto and the dynamic levels rise from *pianissimo* to *fortissimo*. Simpson's orchestration is pictorial, his composition a masterful one. Horenstein's reading of the work is superb. His re-creation of the score is irresistible.

Ezra Sims   (1928-   )

Chamber Music

Third Quartet (1962)

☐ Lenox Quartet / Composers Recordings S–223

Sims uses microtonal language, which provides expressive expressions in the slow-paced divisions. But there is a great sense of arrested movement in such places—and an iciness at the same time. The greatest effect comes in the fractured rhythms and violent arco and pizzicato explosives of the third (Fast and Furious) movement of the total five.

There the pitch shapes obtain greater compactness and pointedness through being more closed in by their microtonal inflections.

This is tough stuff to play to begin with, but even tougher because of intonation. There are no doubts that the Lenox four do a topnotch job. (Sims's Quartet is dedicated to them, and they gave the premiere in New York in 1965.)

Chamber Cantata on Chinese Poems (1954)

☐ Conrad (tenor); Preble (flute); Viscuglia (clarinet and bass clarinet); Hibbard (viola); Davidoff (cello); Keany (harpsichord) / Pinkham (conductor) / Composers Recordings S-186

Cantata and Oratorio

The use of tone-row language for the ten Chinese texts Sims chose (plus a Prelude and a Postlude) gives greater meaning to the content than sharp tonality would (the translations supplied are the only means of understanding the actual word sense). The effect Sims has obtained is of caressing instrumental detail that is inseparable from the subtle vocalization. (One can anticipate the snide comment from some that this *is* a perfect marriage since twelve-tone music is a Chinese puzzle. But if a listener is to give way to such unimaginative silliness, he remains a novice and deprives himself of expanding his auditorial experiences.)

Sensitivity is demanded of the performers in terms of textural balance and flexibility throughout. It is available in this recording.

Christian Sinding   (1856-1941)

Caprice in F minor, Op. 44, No. 13

Crépuscule ("Dawn") in F minor, Op. 34, No. 4

Mélodie in G major, Op. 32, No. 2

Nocturne in B major, Op. 53, No. 2

Nocturne in F sharp major, Op. 118, No. 4

Prelude in A flat major, Op. 34, No. 1

☐ Ruiz (piano) / Genesis 1003

Instrumental

Piano

Sinding was an advocate of the cause of Norwegian music, but don't expect any nationalistic melorhythms in these pieces. And forget here the oft-repeated statement that Sinding's music embraced Wagnerian grandiosity. Do expect euphonious and harmoniously poetic manifestations, enriched with chromatic synonyms that embrace broad melodies.

You can also expect artistic playing, with excellent insight. Adrian Ruiz is an admirable musician.

Rustle of Spring, Op. 32, No. 3

☐ Lhevinne (piano) / Klavier 111

Students by the tens of thousands have played this popular piece. And most have ruined it. It's too late, of course, for their apologies, but there are no artistic or creative apologies required for *Frühlingsrauschen,* which Sinding composed in 1896 as part of a suite, *Sechs Stücke.* When a master pianist plays the piece as Lhevinne does, all of its truly fresh aspects are revealed.

Hans Sitt / *Edvard Grieg.* See *Grieg* / Sitt.

Nikos Skalkottas (1904-1949)

*String
Orchestra*

Little Suite for Strings (1942)

☐ Zimbler Sinfonietta / Foss (conductor) / Turnabout 34154E (monaural)

Thick, highly polyphonic textures derived from atonal procedures. The coherence and power are most expressive, and are enhanced by the large subdivision of the strings into seventeen parts.

Foss is an understanding conductor of the music, obtaining good lights and shadows from his instrumentalists. The disc was initially put on the market by the no-longer-in-existence American Unicorn Records firm (the Little Suite was part of a miscellaneous program covered by LP-1037).

Instrumental

Piano

Fifteen Little Variations (1927)
Greek Folk Dance (1940)
Marcia funebra (1940)
Menuetto (1940)
Reverie in the New Style (1940)
Reverie in the Old Style (1940)

☐ Bennette (piano) / Desto 7136

Mostly serial style is found in Skalkottas's music, but he was one of the few that refused to cling desperately (like all too many other twelve-tone composers) to the rules of the technical game. His music constantly confirms stylistic positiveness while affirming a fervent individuality. Like Dallapiccola, it has a lyrical flow (at times almost of ecstatic content). Schoenberg dared to be a prophet. Skalkottas showed the faith was not a constrictive one.

The individual response can be noted in the Variations, which follow the tone row basis without sacrificing the freshness of the permutations in terms of direction and color. And the same pertains to the Greek Folk Dance, one of a set of Thirty-Two Piano Pieces (four others are heard in this program: the two *Reveries,* the *Marcia* and the *Menuetto*).

George Bennette merits credit not only for performing these works, hidden far from the eyes and thoughts of our concert pianists. His playing is musical, decisive, and fully communicative. One hopes that he (and, most importantly, a recording company) will be willing to produce more of Skalkottas's piano works.

Suite No. 3 for Piano (1940)

☐ Constantinidis (piano) / Musical Heritage Society MHS-3055

Atonal prose in a classically formationed essay. But the traditional paragraphs are presented with contemporary synonyms. The *Minuetto* is polymetrical, while the *Thema con variazioni* reverses matters and is without defined meter. There are four transmutations, each paralleled by tempo increase. Movement 3 is a *Marcia funebra.* (The same title appears in George Bennette's program, released on Desto [*see above:* under Fifteen Little Variations], but it is a different conception.) Skalkottas's Finale is a bare title that hides the toccata vitality of the music with its sharp chordal discourse and punctuations.

The performance is one of conviction and meets all of the challenges in Skalkottas's score. And there are plenty of the last.

Suite No. 4 for Piano (1940)

☐ Bennette (piano) / Desto 7136

Four movements that are in sharp contrast: Toccata, Andantino, *Tempo di polka,* and Serenade. (*See above* [under Fifteen Little Variations] for more Skalkottas music performed by Bennette.) This is fine playing, as in the other works in Desto's issue.

Eight Variations on a Greek Folk Tune for Piano Trio (1938)

☐ Masters-Simpson-Gazelle Trio / Argo ZRG–753

Chamber Music

Developments on an outstanding theme, the material accompanying it becoming later variational material. There is also use of variation on previous variation. Skalkottas mostly treats the medium with soloistic individuality; "ordinary" piano trio formations are extremely minor in total. By placing each timbre in perspective with its own data, the possibility of cancellation by denseness of texture is avoided. It is this very intense, weighted sound that gives the work its special appeal.

The writing for the instruments is extremely difficult, especially for the piano, but this trio team is in full command. There is strength in their playing, and that's a prime necessity for Skalkottas's piece.

Third String Quartet (1935)

☐ Dartington String Quartet / Argo ZRG–753

No technique is static. Technical repetitiveness is simply a primitive mannerism, the results deadly and just as bad as antiartistic creative tyrannies. All of which Skalkottas avoids in his dodecaphonic style of writing.

In the three movements, in place of a single tone row as the generator, individual sets are used not only for each of the movements but for the individual instruments. The interweave is handled with amazing fertility and with a Schubertian flow of sound. Theory is upheld but practice produces a naturalness that can only be termed inspired. When artistic needs and technical means progress hand in hand, as here, then one can understand and accept Schoenberg's statement that Skalkottas was one of only five real composers among the many hundreds he had taught.

The forms are defined and direct from classical heritage. Movement 1 is in sonata form, song form is employed for the Andante, and a Rondo design covers the finale. There's a quote from Strauss's *Der Rosenkavalier* and one from Berg's *Wozzeck* in the concluding movement.

Aside from one short passage where unisons waver, the performance by the Dartington is fine. This group gave the first performance of the Quartet in July of 1965.

Octet (1931)

☐ Melos Ensemble / Argo ZRG–753

Exact division between strings (two violins, viola, and cello) and winds (flute, oboe, clarinet, and bassoon). Though not a serial composition, the character relates to "traditional" twelve-note practices. One exception, however—a lighter expression to the outer movements, quasi divertimento.

The performance is one that displays both clear rhythm and fine phrasing. While the Melos group is a bit lax in conveying the dynamic shadings within the work, this does not interfere with one's comprehensibility.

Stanislaw Skrowaczewski (1923-)

Solo Instrument and Orchestra

Concerto for English horn and Orchestra (1969)

☐ Minnesota Orchestra / Stacy (English horn) / Skrowaczewski (conductor) / Desto 7126

English Horn

Large-scale works for English horn with orchestra are almost nonexistent. Music featuring the instrument has emphasized the pastoral beauty of its timbre and little of its technical personality. Not that Skrowaczewski has the instrument prancing in a Paganini fashion. Still, the prose it delivers in this work is flexibly vigorous and not simply turned. There is virtuosity, not of arrogant type but stated in a subtly dynamic way. The music for orchestra takes a similar approach and is written in a complex soloistic manner.

Color-swept this music is, and it is played in a manner that stresses its poetic pigmentation. Thomas Stacy, the soloist, shows an artistic fluency that is remarkable. No matter the difficulty of execution, his tone is golden.

Nicolas Slonimsky (1894-)

Instrumental

Piano

Studies in Black and White (1928)

☐ Slonimsky (piano) / Orion 7145

A vivid illustration of Slonimsky's characteristic insistence on specific syntax. The right hand plays only upon white keys, the left hand only on black keys. Thus, paired scales are employed, and the music discreetly is flavored. There is real fun in the bitonal games heard here. (Even funnier is the transcription Slonimsky made for three winds, percussion, and the clickety-clack of a portable typewriter!)

(In this recorded setting only ten of the twelve movements are presented. The published score includes another *Jazzelette* and a Fantasy.)

Thesaurus (50 Minitudes) (1971-1977)

☐ Slonimsky (piano) / Orion 72100

I have always said that no one can match Slonimskyan savvy. There is literally no blemish to his mind, no limit to his cogitative faculties. The unparalleled potency of his research (and discovery) has resulted in a considerable number of encyclopedic documents. One of the most important is the *Thesaurus of Scales and Melodic Patterns* (1947). This compendium covers ''all potential progressions of tones and plausible musical phrases in all styles and idioms.''

From this tome Slonimsky drew the intervallic data for his miniatures. The shortest runs five seconds, the longest covers a forty-five second span. There are the usual Slonimsky high animal spirits in many of these epigrammatic études. A few examples: a reworking of a Bach fugue subject, turning it into a Debussyan result by strict intervallic multiplication; dodecaphonic ''derangements'' of *Ach, du lieber Augustin* and *Happy Birthday to You; a Stultifying March.* It should be apparent that there is just as much stimulus in listening to bitonality combined with ninth-chord harmonies; a piece devoted to an eight-note scale made from alternating whole tones and half tones; a chromatic scale fractured all over the gamut of the piano; and so forth.

The *Minitudes* take seventeen minutes to play. They are marvelous musical midgets of invention. It is simply impossible not to hear the whole set through—a feast for the ears and the mind. The collection is easy to follow with the explicit and colorful notes on the record sleeve, written, of course, by the only person capable of so doing: Nicolas Slonimsky.

Variations on a Brazilian Tune (1941)

☐ Slonimsky (piano) / Orion 7145

Programmatic definition for the variations, with depictions of a music box, Brahmsian mimicry, and a circus parade included. Light chips of music, all of 'em, but delightful and perfectly formed, with not the slightest stylistic slip.

An orchestral version goes one step further, with pictorial positivism. Balloons are attached to the players' stands and punctured ad libitum at the conclusion of the piece—great for children's concerts, just as sure-fire for Pops and family-night affairs. The title is changed for this setting to *My Toy Balloon,* not only because of the special attraction added to the instrumentation, but from the title of the tune used for the variations: *Cae, Cae, Balão!* (''Fall, fall, balloon'').

Suite for Cello and Piano (1951)

Chamber Music

☐ Kessler (cello); Slonimsky (piano) / Orion 7145

This six-movement piece touches bases with both folksy and twelve-tone ideas, culminating in what the composer describes as ''a thunderous display of unadulterated C major.'' An excellent conclusion for a finale based on a dodecaphonic series of ''four mutually exclusive major and minor triads.''

Five Advertising Songs (1923)

Vocal

Voice with Accompaniment

☐ Eamon (soprano); Slonimsky (piano) / Orion 72100

A celebration of jocundity with texts devoted not only to the joys of Pepsodent (disguised by the name of Plurodent, because the toothpaste people refused the composer the use of their trade name) and Castoria (the laxative manufacturers were not against furthering their product) but also the importance of including roughage in one's diet! Sheets and pillowcases and a nose powder are also covered in this noncommercial musical broadside based on commercial blurbs.

Gravestones at Hancock, New Hampshire (1945)
Impressions (*Silhouettes* [1924] and *The Flight of the Moon* [1926])
I Owe a Debt to a Monkey (1928)
My Little Pool (1928)
Vocalise (*Modinha russo-brasileira*) (1941)

☐ Bramlage (soprano); Slonimsky (piano) / Orion 7145

In the half-dozen tombstone-inscription settings there is real wit, made cosy with dry application to the texts. Sound delineates meaning via stylistic allusion in these songs. One of them mimics the Handelian orbit; another rubs shoulders with Americana of the Civil War period; still another evokes the mid-Victorian ballade. Far too often the proposed ''fun'' in any musical work falls flat. Not here; this is successful music, and successful humor *in* music.

The shortest of these songs is a gem. In barely fifty-three seconds *My Little Pool* registers a modalistic sensation that lingers long afterward. Impressionism is the style used in the pair of *Impressions,* using texts by Oscar Wilde. A different impression is the *Monkey* song, inspired ''by the famous Scopes trial.''

The *Vocalise* (the parenthetical title given above is not listed on the recording, though it gets passing mention in the general context of the liner notes by the composer) exists in an arrangement for piano and also one for paired guitars by Laurindo Almeida. It is somewhat in the manner of Villa-Lobos, though that matters not; it is, indeed, a thing of loveliness. It is performed twice on the Orion release, once vocalized, the other time hummed, with the sung final octave ascent eliminated from the latter rendition.

Orion's sound is not high class, but the performances are, so one must overlook the former for the benefits of the latter. There are some funny doings with the exact title for the *Gravestones.* Liner heading and record label use the preposition "of." Oddly, Slonimsky's liner note employs "in." Only the text supplied carries the corrrect heading, *Gravestones* at *Hancock, New Hampshire.*

A Very Great Musician (1928)

☐ Bramlage (soprano); Slonimsky (piano) / Orion 7145

As Slonimsky describes it: "a rococo lament of a young woman who fell for a slightly fraudulent violinist." The song contains some inner mickey-mousing by this scintillating composer, with some quintuple intervallic touches for the fiddler involved in the text.

Trust Nicolas Slonimsky not to overlook the opportunity to propose a prose position in a song. Example; the wavering pitch on the word "very" in order to italicize and poke gentle fun at the textual exaggeration.

Bedřich Smetana   (1824-1884)

Orchestra

Carnival in Prague (1883)

Haakon Jarl, Op. 16

☐ Bavarian Radio Symphony Orchestra / Kubelik (conductor) / Deutsche Grammophon 2530248

Smetana's *Pražský Karneval,* which he thought of as a "symphonic fantasy," is given a full-scaled performance. It consists of an introduction and a polonaise, and was actually intended to be the first of a suite of dances. The uncommon ability Kubelik has with Smetana's music is again vividly illustrated in the Opus 16 performance. The sound is rich.

Má Vlast

Vyšehrad (1874)
Vltava ("The Moldau") (1875)
Šárka (1875)
Z Českých Luhův a Hájů ("From Bohemia's Woods and Fields") (1875)
Tábor (1878)
Blaník (1879)

☐ Czech Philharmonic Orchestra / Ančerl (conductor) / Vanguard/Supraphon SU-9/10

Recordings of "My Fatherland" or "My Country" present sharp competition. Not surprisingly, the best performances are those by Czech conductors. One can rule out the wooden quality of Sargent's rendition (on Seraphim S-6003) as well as the extremely academic personality of the orchestra Neumann directs on London 2222.

It turns out that the deciding factor hinges on the matter of the recorded sound. It would be expected that the most recent release would provide the best sonics. However, in this case, the St. Louis Symphony performances, directed by Walter Susskind (Turnabout QTV-S-34619/20), do not have a warm and full-bodied sonorous setting. Otherwise, the playing itself shows ripe musicality and, as expected, Susskind knows every note in these scores as though they were his own.

The "classic" performance is that directed by Rafael Kubelik with the Chicago Symphony (Mercury 77006E), but the sound, even retouched as it is (it was originally produced in the early 1950s), is not up to standard. Kubelik's performance with the Boston Symphony Orchestra (Deutsche Grammophon 2707054) has better engineering, but the B.S.O. personnel do not respond as well, and the Vienna Phil. (on London STS-15096/7) even less so.

The heart of an orchestra, as well as that of the conductor, must beat in time with this nationalistic music, and in that respect the choice, with warm sound and all the elements in full vibration, falls on the Ančerl edition. Dozens of examples in it could be cited: the heart-warming woodwind statement at the beginning of *Vyšehrad* and the answering falling phrases in the strings; the agogic coloration in "The Moldau"; while the selective tempi that invest the melodic and pertinently rhythmic statements in *Šárka* produce meanings that no other conductor, save Kubelik, has been able to achieve. Thus: the triple strength of Ančerl conducting a Czech orchestra playing its native-made music. The result is ideal, warm, and communicative. It demonstrates great art.

(For other recordings of two selections from this set, *see below* [*Vlatava* and *Vyšehrad*].)

Overture to *The Bartered Bride* (1866)

☐ New York Philharmonic / Bernstein (conductor) / Columbia MS-6879
☐ Minneapolis Symphony Orchestra / Dorati (conductor) / Mercury 77001

Bernstein's execution is stunning—the N. Y. Phil.'s strings zip through the fugal kinetics in great shape. (The edition is also on other Columbia releases: M-31817 and D3S-818.) Dorati's version is not as brilliant but it has fine style and is dynamically articulated.

(*See below* for a discussion of Three Dances from *The Bartered Bride*.)

Richard III, Op. 11

☐ Bavarian Radio Symphony Orchestra / Kubelik (conductor) / Deutsche Grammophon 2530248

Strongly programmatic, with, as Smetana described the work to Liszt, the emphasis following "more or less the action of the tragedy: the attainment of the goal after all obstacles have been surmounted, the triumph and finally the downfall of the hero." Kubelik's reading has flexibility, coloristic range, and a quality that carries out the Shakespearian orchestral tale vividly.

Three Dances from *The Bartered Bride* (1866)

☐ Cleveland Orchestra / Szell (conductor) / Odyssey Y-30049

The dances represented are the Polka (from Act I, scene 5); the *Furiant* (from Act II, scene 1); and the Dance of the Comedians (from Act III, scene 2).

Szell's exquisitely proportioned portrayal (also available in a two-disc miscellany on Columbia M2X-787) is a lesson for every conductor who has conducted or will be directing these favorites. The *ritards* are where they should be and Smetana wanted them; the tempi are not a shade too slow or too fast. Above all, there isn't the slightest bit of affectation as though one were conceiving an individual choreography on the podium. Bernstein, in his performance with the New York Philharmonic (on Columbia MS-6879 and also on M-31817), does not permit a single phrase in the Polka, for example, to stay put, but pulls the music back and forward as though he were playing with taffy. Other versions just lack the telling simplicity of Szell's approach to these charming pieces.

(*See above* for recordings of the Overture to *The Bartered Bride*.)

Vltava ("The Moldau") from Má Vlast (1875)

☐ Cleveland Orchestra / Szell (conductor) / Odyssey Y-30049

Since Ančerl's performance is not available separately, nor for that matter is either Kubelik's or Susskind's (for all three versions, *see above* [under *Má Vlast*]), the auditor will not be disappointed in George Szell's strong and sensitive portrayal of this favorite. (This is in a Smetana-Dvořák program. Szell's ''The Moldau'' reading is also in two other miscellanea: on Columbia M2X-787 and Columbia MS-7435.)

Vyšehrad from Má Vlast (1874)

☐ Berlin Philharmonic Orchestra / von Karajan (conductor) / Deutsche Grammophon 139037

The only separate edition of this piece from Smetana's cycle. A straightforward reading, acceptable, though not to be classified as a great one. Included in the album is ''The Moldau'' but for that alone choose Szell's performance, listed and discussed *above* (*Vltava*).

(For a discussion of other versions, *see above* [under *Má Vlast*].)

Wallenstein's Camp, Op. 14

☐ Bavarian Radio Symphony Orchestra / Kubelik (conductor) / Deutsche Grammophon 2530248

The nationalistic tone of Smetana's work is fully emphasized in Kubelik's strong rendition. The openness of the recording is most helpful in achieving this quality.

Instrumental

Piano

Au Bord de la mer (1862)

☐ Varro (piano) / Orion 6912

Wild but not sonorously woolly, seething but still describing a clear musical waterway. Smetana's Concert Study is delineated with vigor by this pianist. But it is played a bit more stormily than one expects from music descriptive of ''On the Seashore.''

Four Czech Dances
Polka From Student Life
Polka Reminiscence of Pilsen
Souvenirs of Bohemia—Polka

In A minor, Op. 12, No. 1 / In E minor, Op. 12, No. 2 / In E minor, Op. 13, No. 1 / In E flat major, Op. 13, No. 2

Three Poetic Polkas, Op. 8
Three Salon Polkas, Op. 7

☐ Kvapil (piano) / Musical Heritage Society MHS-1373

Polkas galore! The Four Czech Dances are also all polkas and the *Souvenirs of Bohemia*, as will be noted, consist of four more. That's sixteen polkas in all. Not too much of a single thing—enjoy!

From the Home Country (No. 2) (1878)

☐ Ricci (violin); Lush (piano) / London STS–15049

Smetana's *Z domoviny* (translated in this release as "From the Homeland") was composed in 1878; the two pieces involved (the first of the pair is rarely performed) represent his only contribution to the medium. The music is permeated with Czech melos, beautifully realized in Ricci's rendition. (Elman has also recorded the second piece of the set for Vanguard.)

Trio in G minor, Op. 15

☐ Beaux Arts Trio / Philips 6500133

Smetana's composition is mainly sombre, bound in the expressive key of G minor, which only latterly changes into major; the essential doleful, tragic quality is not removed in so doing.

The Beaux Arts threesome are in top form here, giving a most persuasive account of the score.

String Quartet in E minor (*Aus meinem Leben*) (1876)

☐ Guarneri Quartet / RCA LSC–2887

Although a greater amount of program music is found in the compositions of the twentieth century, Smetana's choice of the chamber-music idiom for narrative purposes is an exceptional example appearing in the last quarter of the nineteenth century. He uses the string quartet for the unique objective of an intense autobiographical expression. This is cast in classic forms, with a slight deviation, brought by nationalistic infiltration (the use of a Bohemian dance in place of the usual minuet or scherzo). In addition, some minute thematic quotations are made in the concluding portion of the work.

Such conceptual framework removes much of the intimacy from the medium and demands a deterministic conception on the part of the performers. There is the minutest roughage in the Guarneri's playing, but it fits the particular place in the score where it appears. Vitality and toned richness are to be heard, and these provide the required declarative point of view for the playing of Smetana's superb "From My Life" Quartet.

Dalibor (1867)

☐ Prague National Theatre Orchestra and Chorus / Kniplová and Svobodová-Janků (sopranos); Přibyl and Svehla (tenors); Jindrák and Svorc (baritones); Horáček (bass) / Krombholc (conductor) / Genesis 1040/2

Dalibor represents still another opera that has not been exportable; the musical encyclopedias are full of them. But one can enjoy Smetana's excellent musical decor by way of a recording and trace the plot (the individual versus the state, but without doctrinal precision) by the English translation in the libretto furnished with the three-record set.

The Czech cast is headed by Vilem Přibyl in the name role. He exhibits a fine vocal personality. Naděžda Kniplová, as Milada, has a strong and exciting voice. The entire cast, chorus, and orchestra provide a first-rate musical situation.

This is the second appearance of *Dalibor* in the American recording catalogue. Years ago (in 1955) the same production appeared on Colosseum Records (CRLP–181/183). It covered five sides, the sixth consisting of "Highlights" from Fibich's *The Bride from Messina*. Abroad, the recording was issued by Supraphon (112–0241/3). Here, in 1973, it was released by Genesis.

Pril Smiley   *(1943-   )*

Electronic Music

Eclipse (1968)

☐ Finnadar 9010

Smiley's engaging piece was the winner in the First International Electronic Music Competition, held in 1969. A fascinating interplay and contrast of gonglike and waterlike sonorities are paramount in the composition.

Kolyosa (1970)

☐ Composers Recordings 268

Kolyosa is the Russian word for "wheels," and Smiley uses the Buchla Synthesizer to define the sense of expected motility. She explains that her music is a portrayal "of an abstract hypocycloidal concept relating to images of whirlwinds, windmills, spinning wheels, and interlocking ellipses."

Leo Smit   *(1921-   )*

Chamber Music

In Woods (1978)

☐ Post (oboe); Falcao (harp); Williams (percussion) / Orion 79333

In Woods was composed for these performers (no credit indication save on the label). There are bird sounds in Smit's orange-purple-crimson-colored music, but they are not treated in Messiaen style. There are also reminders here and there of composers who have dabbled in the field of nature music, but the five movements are situated far from eclectic territory.

Smit's neoclassic days are left far behind him in his most recent works. This, one of his latest pieces, delving a bit in graphic notation (rhythmically only, not in terms of pitches), is of exquisite expressiveness. The profundity is in its motivic segmentation, figurations, and colorations.

The performance is marvelous.

Vocal

Voice with Accompaniment

Songs of Wonder

☐ Hanneman (soprano); Smit (piano) / Composers Recordings SD–370

The syntax fits the neoclassic style, but the music has the flourish of romantic rhetoric. The set consists of three songs, the texts by Beth Frost, written at age twelve! Unfortunately, CRI has not included texts.

Choral

Choral and Instrumental Ensemble

At the Corner of the Sky

☐ Men and Boys Choir of St. Paul's Cathedral, Buffalo, N.Y. / Svitzer (flute); Post (oboe); Smit (speaker) / Burgomaster (conductor) / Composers Recordings SD–370

Smit's work is concerned with the spirituality of the American Indian, and his material contains essences of its music. However, while it is stylistically liberated from imitative dependence, at the same time it avoids being an abstract conception. Style here takes on an individual function, transcending the native fundament that has evolved it; it is a coloristic substance within Smit's music, identified by its own quality and subtle power. This strength especially concerns the *materia prima* of the parts for the wind instruments, exquisitely conceived and beautifully identified by the playing of Henrik Svitzer and Nora Post.

At the Corner of the Sky was commissioned by and dedicated to St. Paul's Cathedral and its music director, Frederick Burgomaster. The Cathedral's choristers, directed by Burgomaster, gave the world premiere of the opus. It follows that their close association with the work has resulted in a performance of vibrancy and dynamism.

Copernicus, Narrative and Credo for Narrator, Mixed Chorus, and Eight Instrumental Players (1973)

Cantata and Oratorio

☐ Gregg Smith Singers / Hoyle (narrator) / Smit (conductor) / Desto 7178

The Copernicus story with its text by Sir Fred Hoyle, an internationally renowned scientist, President of the Royal Astronomical Society, and a writer of high repute. No better librettist for the subject could have been chosen. According to (this) Hoyle, the story unfolds beautifully, succinctly, and vividly. Smit's music responds to the narrative, which is separated into a dozen sections. The music is never blatant, always concentrated in its detail, which is drawn from "the little known but highly developed music of Medieval and Renaissance Poland." Those portions solely Smit's have a neoclassic basis that fit as they simultaneously enlarge the musical horizon. Stravinsky comes to mind with this combination of source and original material, and Stravinsky could not have done better with such styled positiveness.

This is a definitive performance. Hoyle's narration is as clear as the bell sounds heard in Smit's score, so that Desto's omission of a text does not require an apology from them. The small chorus has a fresh quality and the instrumentalists (there are eight, playing eleven instruments in all) are splendid in this, the most important work Leo Smit has thus far produced.

Gregg Smith (1931-)

Beware of the Soldier (1969)

Cantata and Oratorio

☐ Orchestral Ensemble, Texas Boys' Choir, and Columbia University Men's Glee Club / Rees (soprano); Perry (tenor); Greenwell (bass); Garretson (boy soprano) / Smith (conductor) / Composers Recordings S–341

Though Smith "would like to think of *Beware of the Soldier* as a religious composition," its clear message, by comparisons of militancy and the opposite, is antiwar.

There are seventeen sections intermingling a Prologue, Epilogue, and final *Prayer*, four Elegies, five Songs of War, and five Songs of Innocence. Scoring and style are utilized to italicize the objective of each part. Thus, all the Elegies are for solo soprano and string quartet; the five Songs of Innocence are for the boys' choir, and so on.

Smith's point is made at length (the music covers forty minutes) and with texts ranging from the fourteenth century to Mark Twain. The performance is utterly natural and delivered with authority.

Hale Smith   (1925-   )

Orchestra

Contours for Orchestra (1961)

☐ Louisville Orchestra / Whitney (conductor) / Louisville 632 (monaural)

Smith's creative verve is enclosed in rich chromaticism—a derivative of tone-row composition but without twelve-tone overinsistence and its tendency to technical overluxuriancy. The Louisville organization seems to struggle with Smith's work, so that the performance report is only fair.

Band

Expansions

☐ Northwestern University Symphonic Wind Ensemble / Paynter (conductor) / New World Records NW–211

Smith's use of tone clusters is quite different from their usual application as harmonic fricatives or as coloristic edgings of a melodic phrase. The generating stimuli of *Expansions* are cluster formations, which then develop in a variety of tensions. The exploitation of the device is full and acute, subtle and sensitive, and successful as well.

This is a strong addition to band literature. It is played by the university organization with complete intelligibility.

Instrumental

Piano

Evocation (1966)

☐ Hinderas (piano) / Desto 70102/3

Pithy in its sequestered fundament and pithy in its length. Smith's soliloquy is dynamic in concept, which concerns the use of concentrated segments. Natalie Hinderas's sensitivity provides a splendid performance.

John Stafford Smith (1750-1836) / Igor Stravinsky

Choral

Chorus and Orchestra

The Star-Spangled Banner

☐ CBC Symphony Orchestra and Festival Singers of Toronto / Stravinsky (conductor) / Columbia M–31124

If you're interested in the setting that shocked (because of an unusual modulation) the proper Bostonians in 1944 and thereby caused police action, in turn canceling its performance, here it is.

(Francis Scott Key wrote only the words, though he is often credited with writing the music. That is because Scott planned his words to fit Smith's *Anacreontick Song* or *Anacreon in Heaven*, then popular in America.)

Julia Smith   (1911-   )

Chamber Music

Quartet for Strings (1964)

☐ Kohon String Quartet / Desto 7117

Bright and cheerful music, that mood not fully removed by the more sober, slow middle movement. That portion remains extroverted, if not as gaily stated as the companion movements.

Julia Smith's work is dedicated to the exclusivity of tonalism. She is alive to harmonic deviations but these are called on for color spread. She is, however, very attentive to rhythmic force. The entire first movement chugs spiritedly along over its G major umbrella in stable $\frac{7}{8}$ meter, each measure precisely split in a ratio of 3:4. Asymmetry is used for the momentum of the pert rondo finale.

Russell Smith   *(1927-   )*

Tetrameron **(1959)**   *Orchestra*

☐ Japan Philharmonic Symphony Orchestra / Watanabe (conductor) / Composers Recordings 131E (monaural)

By sheer concentration of his working materials and the avoidance of any type of musical *causerie,* Smith stands as an exceedingly "musical" composer. In his *Tetrameron* he resists any deviation and carries his thought to its goal without fussy figuration, outlandish ornaments, or paternal padding. The music has flame within it and contained fury. Motival negotiation is the watchword. Post-Webern style come to earth is another way of saying the same thing. Smith's is a masterful opus.

A cool reading of this work would do harm. Watanabe realizes what he should do and does it.

William O. Smith   *(1926-   )*

Fancies **for Clarinet Alone**   *Instrumental*

☐ Smith (clarinet) / New World Records NW–209   *Clarinet*

Dogmatic fancies, these—a sample case of clarinet doin's. Most of them are two-part and three-part chord formations. These multiple sounds (called "multiphonics") totally change the basic clarinet color. The technique (initially developed by the Italian composer, Bruno Bartolozzi) provides means of playing a duet by one wind-instrument player. Examples: in section 6, two pitches move against a held lower pitch; in section 10, trills are used with a moving upper part against a lower one.

For those with open ears the effects (and that's what they are) are spicy. Others will consider them sonic speculation on spiculated qualities. Only those who compare them to the traditional clarinet timbre might term them coarse and vulgar. They should bear in mind that even ugliness has its special attributes.

Five Pieces (for Clarinet Alone) (1958)

☐ Warner (clarinet) / Crystal S–332

An unaccompanied clarinet opus is expected to be lean, but by expert use of registral shifts and rhythmic activity, Smith's Five Pieces assume a heavier weight. There is tension, too, in these sketches (*Flowing* is less than a minute in length; *Singing* is the longest, just under two minutes). Smith the clarinetist is hip to what is best for Smith the composer to write for the instrument. The messages are direct and solid, despite homophonic solitude.

Capriccio for Violin and Piano (1952)   *Chamber Music*

☐ Rubin (violin); Previn (piano) / Contemporary 7015

In great part the materials sound as though they were from the land of the twelve tones. However, affinitive profile must not be mistaken for definitive use of a specific technique. The three-movement Capriccio has only the twelve-tone mannerism of continuity.

Rubin is a sensitive violinist. Previn, in his preconducting days, was a master of his instrument.

Straws for Flute and Bassoon

☐ Skowronek (flute); Goodman (bassoon) / Crystal 351

Theatre combined with chamber music, with the players reciting lines from Theodore Roethke's *Straw for the Fire,* sometimes verbalizing in duet form. There is theatre as well in the use of the instruments, which display pitch bends, multiphonics, and synoptic bits. Extremely episodic, the instrumental and verbal quips form a quodlibet.

Smith's *Straws* is sometimes a bit sophomoric, but it is always immensely listenable. Accordingly, credit is due for a very fruitful contribution by the gentlemen playing the flute and the bassoon.

Suite for Violin and Clarinet (1952)

☐ Rubin (violin); Smith (clarinet) / Contemporary 7015

Colorful to begin with, by its string-wind duet formation, Smith's Overture-Song-Dance-Burlesque-Finale depictions are stimulated further by engaging registral definition, harmonics, pizzicati, *tremolandi,* and glissandi. A positive and rewarding presentation.

String Quartet (1952)

☐ Amati String Quartet / Contemporary 7015

Dedicated to Darius Milhaud, who is the aesthetic godfather of the work. Just one piece of evidence: the finale, where four themes are stated simultaneously. Imitators of Milhaud are exceedingly few, so that Smith's entry is certainly acceptable.

The four women that comprise the Amati organization play with excellent expression and artistic aggressiveness where needed.

Reginald Smith Brindle (1917-)

Instrumental

Guitar

El polifemo de oro (Four Fragments for Guitar)

☐ Bream (guitar) / RCA LSC–2964

A lesson not only in great guitar playing but in illustrating how richly expressive twelve-note (twelve-tone) music can be. These pieces, covering a performance time of just under seven minutes, are based on a poem of Lorca, and without losing stylistic propriety are dusted with Hispanic nocturnalism.

Vicente Emilio Sojo (1887-)

Instrumental

Guitar

Canción   Quirpo
Guasa

☐ Diaz (guitar) / Everest 3155

Three nationalistic pieces by this important old-guard Venezuelan composer. The *Canción* contains the oft-met haunting quality of Latin-American songs, the *Guasa* is a duple-pulsed ballad type, and the *Quirpo* has dance measures.

Vigorous playing by Alirio Diaz.

Padre Antonio Soler (1729-1783)

Fandango

Instrumental

☐ Kipnis (harpsichord) / Columbia M3X–31521

Harpsichord

The Fandango has become the most popular of all of Soler's compositions. Strong rhythmic significance, healthy nationalistic tone, substantial coverage, and variational elasticity projected over a fundamental bass combine to make a very exciting opus.

Kipnis's effectuation of the score is stable and substantial, braced with a magnificent sense of pace and rhythm.

Sonata in A minor

☐ Valenti (harpsichord) / Desmar 1001

Divided details mark Soler's A minor Sonata. The music shifts between clear imitative patterns and melodic data that strongly suggest Spanish dance phrases. The contrast is beautifully blended.

Valenti's performance is very vivid and dynamically keen. It is much sharper defined and much brighter than Janos Sebestyen's playing of the work on Turnabout (34366).

Sonata in B flat major

☐ Kipnis (harpsichord) / Columbia M3X–31521

Kipnis fully portrays the Spanish quality that permeates the music. The full essence of Soler's music is provided in this outstanding performance.

Sonata in C minor

☐ Valenti (harpsichord) / Desmar 1001

The critic, Egon F. Kenton, has cogently indicated the "repeated faint echo of reminiscences of Spanish vocal music" in this work. However, this element is little confirmed in the tempi that Janos Sebestyen adopts on Turnabout 34366 (his performance is timed at 4:26). Fernando Valenti's portrayal is smoother (more "vocal," if you wish) and far more sensitive by opting for a pace that gives the music proper breadth (and breathing space). It is timed at 5:50.

Sonata in C sharp minor

☐ Sebestyen (harpsichord) / Turnabout 34366

This is one of two Sonatas (the other is the Sonata in F sharp minor—*see below*) not included in Valenti's collection on Desmar 1001.

Because there is a good amount of short thematic material (sometimes motivally concentrated) in this work—one of the longest of the Soler keyboard Sonatas (the performance time is close to six and one-half minutes)—a sense of fantasy surrounds the conception. Aside from Sebestyen's tendency to brake the flow at cadential points his playing is excellent and his tempo choice is exemplary.

Sonata

In D flat major / In D major / In D major / In D minor / In F minor / In F sharp major

☐ Valenti (harpsichord) / Desmar 1001

These are truly excellent performances. Valenti has immaculate rhythmic control and plays dynamically. The sound of the disc is beautifully resonant. (There are two separate works in the key of D major.)

Sonata in F sharp minor

☐ Sebestyen (harpsichord) / Turnabout 34366

Soler's F sharp minor Sonata offers music that combines recitative qualities and imitation with pithy and ceremonial-like phrases. The entire matter resembles an improvisation. With creative cunning and insight, the use of sequence serves as a binding device.

Sebestyen's rhythmic definition and his phrasing are meaningful. His performance is certainly vivid and alive.

Sonata

In G major / In G minor

☐ Valenti (harpsichord) / Desmar 1001

The G major Sonata is boldly textured, it also has some peppery dissonances. (Valenti wisely doesn't try to underplay the latter.) The constant colorful changes in the G major work are of no lesser total in the G minor opus. As usual with Soler a variety of short phrases structure both Sonatas. Valenti sorts out these phrases and balances them without nullifying their characteristic contrastive attraction.

Sonata Two Times Two

In B flat major and B flat major / In E minor and G major

☐ Sebestyen (harpsichord) / Turnabout 34366

Janos Sebestyen plays this two-in-one pair of works with musical sense. There are some unexpected modulations that give a special touch to the Sonatas. Significantly, Sebestyen does not emphasize these shifts, and they gain thereby.

Organ

Sonata

In C minor (No. 1) / In C minor (No. 2)

☐ Hamilton (organ) / Orion 73133

Though not particularly distinguished music, the Sonatas do have a simple, if pale, charm. Both being quite short (three and two minutes, respectively), neither outstays its welcome. (No numbers are indicated for the Sonatas; they are numbered here to show that there are two works in the same key.)

Organ and Harpsichord

Concerto for Two Organs

No. 1 in C major / No. 2 in A minor / No. 3 in G major / No. 4 in F major / No. 5 in A major / No. 6 in D major

☐ Payne (organ and harpsichord); Newman (organ and harpsichord) / Turnabout 34136

The Turnabout release is titled "Six Concerti for Two Keyboard Instruments," which is correct only as far as the instruments used in the recording are concerned. Originally, Soler's music comprised a set of "*Conciertos* for Two Organs," (written, he indicated, "for the diversion of Don Gabriel de Borbon, Infant of Spain." The instrumental substitutions chosen in this case do add color and variety to a set of pieces, nice enough to hear, but just a bit monotonous formally. Accordingly, the three possible instrumental combinations are divided equally among the six works: Nos. 4 and 5 are played on two organs, Nos. 2 and 6 are performed on two harpsichords, and Nos. 1 and 3 are heard in the combination of organ with harpsichord. These timbre differences of this *galant* music are not the way of academic exactitude and some may be annoyed. If so, they can choose the two-organ issue on Columbia MS-7174, performed by E. Power Biggs and Daniel Pinkham. Others may agree that Payne's and Newman's re-creative decision is to be commended. Their fine performances certainly should be.

Quintet for Harpsichord and Strings

No. 1 in C major / No. 2 in F major / No. 3 in G major / No. 4 in A minor / No. 5 in D major / No. 6 in G minor

Chamber Music

☐ Montserrat Cervera and Wachsmuth (violins); Vauquet (viola); Marcal Cervera (cello); Jaccottet (harpsichord) / Vox 5440

Mostly impressive music and certainly possessing good voice if not intense heart. The harpsichord does not support as a continuo instrument but often is set off individually from the strings or falls into the total quintet formation. Though, in general, formalistic similarity is found in the six works there are plenty of movements that offer enough highlights to warrant obtaining the entire set. Thus, the relaxed but personable and articulative finale to the A minor work (a *Minuetto con variazioni*), the impressive glow that suffuses the concluding movement of the third quintet, which begins as an Andantino and then moves into an Allegro, and the slow-fast alternating sections of the G minor opus.

This is fine Soler music and little known. The five performers mesh very well and provide most accomplished statements. Especially, dynamic harpsichord playing keys these quintets.

Harvey Sollberger   (1938-   )

Chamber Variations for Twelve Players and Conductor (1964)

Orchestra

☐ Group for Contemporary Music, Columbia University / Schuller (conductor) / Composers Recordings S-204

Metrical nervousness is acute in the serialistic developments of Sollberger's work. Since fragmentation is at the heart of the music, flow and pulse are obscured. Later in the conception this vagueness is further emphasized; hence the reason for the "and Conductor" in the title. At that point the conductor does not continue to beat time but coordinates "events." Though rhythmic continuity is not paramount, tension and acute registration are (the latter causing a great deal of the former).

The contemporary brand of virtuosity is at a boil here. This group is one of the best in the business for that kind of specialty, with such masters as Charles Wuorinen at the piano, the composer's wife playing alto flute as well as piccolo, Jeanne Benjamin and Scott Nickrenz taking care of the violin and viola parts respectively, and so on. With Gunther Schuller directing one is certain of a definitive statement.

Solo Instrument and Orchestra

Flute

Riding the Wind I

☐ Da Capo Chamber Players / Spencer (flute) / Sollberger (conductor) / Composers Recordings SD–352

Sollberger investigates the sound world of the flute in his work. By way of flashes of sonorities the wind instrument lays bare buzz tones, chords, percussive clicks, sounds of inhalation and exhalation, and traditional formations as well. Interjected commentary and sonorous footnotes are provided by a quartet of violin, cello, piano, and clarinet.

There are no easy spots in *Riding the Wind*. However, Patricia Spencer delivers the exacting solo part in every respect and responds to its every challenge. It is a performance that can be warmly recommended. If you are interested in the brutal demands being made of instrumentalists these days, listen to Harvey Sollberger's unconventional music, unconventionally titled.

Chamber Music

Solos (1962)

☐ Zukofsky (violin); Sophie Sollberger (flute); Blustine (clarinet); Jolley (horn); Brehm (double bass); Kalish (piano) / Harvey Sollberger (conductor) / Desto 6435/37

A cross between chamber music and an outright solo conception. The violin is assimilated in the sextet, it forms a part of "little chamber music interludes," and it participates in "traditional solo-tutti confrontations." Most of it is dynamically poised, with a fervent virtuosity. Above all, Sollberger's piece has unsentimental sentiments.

Harry Somers (1925-)

Orchestra

Passacaglia and Fugue for Orchestra (1954)

☐ Louisville Orchestra / Whitney (conductor) / Louisville S–661

The traditional formal partnership. There is contemporary frankness, however, especially in the fugal part. This means nervous rhythm and chromatic detail. The piece is performed with clarity and balanced dimensions.

Vladimir Sommer (1921-)

Cantata and Oratorio

Vocal Symphony (1963)

☐ London Symphony Orchestra and Ambrosian Singers / Williams (mezzo-soprano); Ustinov (narrator) / Buketoff (conductor) / RCA LSC–3181

Titled a "Symphony," Sommer's tragically framed work properly belongs in the cantata category. Its three movements are based on texts (heard in English) drawn from Kafka, Dostoyevsky, and Pavese, and its style has Honeggerian personality, with more than passing attention to Prokofiev.

Buketoff's conductorial ability is a well-known fact (as is his adventurous consideration of performance material). He proves this once again. One can always be assured that a prosaic performance by Peter Ustinov is impossible.

Ahti Sonninen (1914-)

El Amor Pasa, Op. 40

☐ Swedish Radio Ensemble / Faringer (soprano); Von Bahr (flute) / Westerberg (conductor) / Bis LP-11

This work is a real find. Sonninen's Hispanic-colored, nocturnal music is gorgeous, of haunting beauty, the equal of the best by any Spanish composer, including Falla. It shouldn't be missed.

Four short poems by Gustavo Adolfo Bécquer furnish the texts. In the first three pieces the flutist shares responsibilities with the voice, in duet and antiphonal style. The soprano has the major role in the colorful finale (the longest portion of the piece). The orchestra consists of twelve instruments: piccolo, oboe, clarinet, two horns, piano, percussion, two violins, viola, cello, and bass. In the first three parts of the work the instrumental ensemble is simply used for a few isolated chords. In the finale it has a more important, but still somewhat reticent role. The performance is entrancing; the kind of sensitivity and blend one hears here is not often encountered.

Fernando Sor (1778-1839)

Introduction and Variations on a Theme of Marlborough, Op. 28

☐ Yepes (guitar) / Deutsche Grammophon 2530871

A delightful tune, made to order for variational play, and Sor is fully capable. There are five transformations. Yepes colors them most adequately in his playing (and so does Santos in his performance on Musical Heritage Society MHS-1916).

Sonata in C (Second Grand Sonata), Op. 25

☐ Bream (guitar) / RCA ARL1-0711

Music that is not distinguished by innovation but by borrowing the creative clothes of Haydn. Hand-me-downs, yes, but not worn out. The important point of this recording *is* the recording, which represents Julian Bream as a master guitarist.

Variations on a Theme of Mozart, Op. 9

☐ Romero (guitar) / Angel S-36093

All the big boys, including Williams and Yepes, have recorded this guitar standard, based on *Das klinget so herrlich* from Mozart's *The Magic Flute* (see under *Mozart: Opera and Dramatic Music*). Angel Romero's rendition certainly belongs at the top of the list. His is an absorbing conception, and it is especially marked by an absence of rigidity.

Russian Memories (Theme and Variations for Two Guitars)

☐ Duo Company-Paolini / Turnabout 34341

Once past the introduction, Russian flavor permeates the sounds. There is no soupy imitation in this work, but fidelity to classic style. The performance is one of enunciative clarity and cogent shadings.

Another issue of this performance is found in Turnabout 34195/9. Sor is one of eighteen composers represented there, in a collection of music for the lute, guitar, and mandolin.

Torsten Sörenson   (1908-   )

Chamber Music

Per quattro archi

☐ Göteborg Concert Hall Quartet / Caprice CAP–1026

Fine string-quartet writing marks this composition. Alternate tempi distinguish the development of material derived from a minor-second interval, resulting in close linear movement and frictioned harmony. Hindemith and Bartók are the main points of stylistic reference.

The performance of this persuasively serious work is excellent. There is no doubt that the Göteborgs Konserthuskvartett's recording debut is a rousing success.

John Philip Sousa   (1854-1932)

Orchestra

Semper Fidelis   The Thunderer
The Stars and Stripes Forever   The Washington Post

☐ New York Philharmonic / Bernstein (conductor) / Columbia M–30943

No argument—the best delivery of a Sousa March is by a band. (See under *Band* for settings of the first three Marches.) However, if you don't mind orchestral oil dressing on these juicy duple-pulsed nourishments, you couldn't do better than with Lenny. (There are nine other Marches in the Columbia album, including such evergreens as *Under the Double Eagle, National Emblem,* and *Anchors Aweigh.*)

Suite from the Ballet *Stars and Stripes.* See under *Hershy Kay.*

Band

Bonnie Annie Laurie

☐ Goldman Band / Goldman (conductor) / New World Records NW–266

Interwoven is the well-known folk tune *Annie Laurie,* hence the title. This is a Sousa March that deserves to be better known.

El Capitan

Gallant Seventh

☐ Columbia All-Star Band / Schuller (conductor) / Columbia XM–33513

El Capitan is, of course, one of the super Marches by this super March composer. *Gallant Seventh,* Sousa's one hundred first March (!), is a real winner, including bugle and drum corps.

Columbia's album terms the performing group "The Incredible Columbia All-Star Band." No puff, that, but a perfect description.

Hands Across the Sea

☐ Eastman Wind Ensemble / Fennell (conductor) / Mercury SRI–75099

There is no question as to the conductorial health of Frederick Fennell—it's excellent. This is a snap-to and hearty portrayal.

The Liberty Bell

☐ Columbia All-Star Band / Schuller (conductor) / Columbia XM–33513

The Liberty Bell is one of fourteen Marches (six by Sousa, others by Ives, Fillmore, Alford, and four others) in a collection Columbia calls *Footlifters*. Title perfection, indeed, and *The Liberty Bell* fulfills the description. It includes twenty-four (count them!) bell strikes, which are vivid in their repetitive pitch.

The Pathfinder of Panama

☐ Goldman Band / Cox (conductor) / New World Records NW–266

A fine Sousa item, rarely heard. The March was composed for the Panama-Pacific Exposition held in San Francisco to mark the opening of the Panama Canal.

Revival March

☐ Goldman Band / Goldman (conductor) / New World Records NW–266

Another Sousa conception that shapes nonmarch material into March style—in this case, the hymn *In the Sweet Bye and Bye.* The new look (or new sound) of the tune increases the enjoyment quotient.

Semper Fidelis

☐ Columbia All-Star Band / Schuller (conductor) / Columbia XM–33513

Without doubt the greatest performance of Sousa's well-known March this writer has ever heard. Especially, the color and dynamic build in the third part of the piece are auditioned with polished perfection and thrilling artistry.
(See under *Orchestra* for an orchestral arrangement.)

Sesquicentennial March

☐ Goldman Band / Cox (conductor) / New World Records NW–266

Also known as the Sesquicentennial Exposition March. Sousa's March was composed for the 1926 celebration held in Philadelphia.

The Stars and Stripes Forever
The Thunderer

☐ Columbia All-Star Band / Schuller (conductor) / Columbia XM–33513

Spiffy performances of these two Marches, including *The Stars and Stripes,* which can be indicated as the most popular one of them all. The tempo is brisk and keeps matters healthy and musically wise.
(See under *Orchestra* [under *Semper Fidelis*] for orchestral versions of these Marches.)

Leroy W. Southers, Jr.   *(1941-   )*

Evolutions   *Instrumental*

☐ Plog (trumpet); Swearingen (organ) / Avant 1014   *Trumpet*

Polyphony is expected of the organ, and in *Evolutions* the faith is kept, expanded by an impetuous part for the trumpet. (The title pertains to the development of four thematic elements.) The somewhat busy discourse is clarified in its complexities by the special instrumental combination used. The conclusion is exciting.

Save for some semiopaque organ registration, the piece is well played.

Fela Sowande (1905-   )

String Orchestra

African Suite (1944) (Movements 1, 2, and 5)

☐ London Symphony Orchestra / Freeman (conductor) / Columbia M–33433

Joyful Day and *Akinla* are in the light instrumental style of Eric Coates, notwithstanding the composer's desire to illustrate "the unification of African and European music." The other excerpt, *Nostalgia,* not only casts a long lingering look at the modal music of Vaughan Williams but then feasts at the source. Sowande's music is styled with good taste, although it is not African.

Leo Sowerby (1895-1968)

Orchestra

All on a Summer's Day (1954)

☐ Louisville Orchestra / Whitney (conductor) / Louisville 56-6 (monaural)

Sowerby explains his work: "to write music which should mirror the sunny moods of exhilaration most of us experience 'all on a summer's day.' " Accordingly, this is gay and motile (but not motoric) music, guided by neo-romantic procedures.

From the Northland, Suite for Orchestra (1927)

☐ Vienna Symphony Orchestra / Dixon (conductor) / Desto 6429E (monaural)

Four aspects of American impressionism. *Forest Voices, Cascades, Burnt Rock Pool,* and *The Shining Big-Sea Water,* all indicated with descriptive programs by the composer, are defined by shimmering and wavering sounds, colorful instrumental juxtapositions, and decorative sonorities and splashes.

Desto's packaging is odd (the name of the orchestra and conductor are not anywhere on the album cover) and annoying (there are no bands to differentiate the movements of the work). Further, the label identification for the fourth movement incorrectly gives the plural form.

Prairie, A Poem for Orchestra (1929)

☐ Vienna Symphony Orchestra / Dixon (conductor) / Desto 6421E (monaural)

Sowerby disavowed any program-music objective in this symphonic poem based on Carl Sandburg's poem concerning the great American open spaces. It builds to rhythmic action midway but the sonority scale is consistently on the intense side.

The late Dean Dixon was able to achieve only a fair performance from the Viennese organization. One doubts that there was much rehearsal and one also doubts more than a single take. As the only recording of this worthy piece, it will have to be accepted on its less-than-topflight terms.

Classic Concerto for Organ and String Orchestra (1944)

Solo
Instrument
and
Orchestra

Organ

☐ Members of the Oslo Philharmonic Orchestra / Karlsen (organ) / Strickland (conductor) / Composers Recordings 165 (monaural)

Allegro, vivace, con brio, and other Italian tempi terminology give advance generalities to the listener. Sowerby's indications give much more. The movements are designated: *Merrily, with snap, Dreamily and rhapsodically; with poignant expression,* and *In broad style.* So far, so good. Throughout, there is a use of the mild sophisticates of chromaticized tonal harmony. There is drive as well as breadth in the finale; in the slow movement one will find (as David Hall has so aptly noted) "bitter-sweet poetry (almost Delius-like)."

As an organist Sowerby knew how to use the instrument to best advantage. The organ's individual timbre, its strong contrast and telling combination with strings, is sharply evident here.

Rolf Karlsen covers all the opportunities in his first-rate projection of the solo part. William Strickland has turned out a large number of recordings for CRI. This one is a tasteful and highly polished affair and is certainly one of his best.

Air with Variations from Suite for Organ

Arioso

Instrumental

Organ

☐ Beck (organ) / Musical Heritage Society OR A–264

A commitment to romanticism is fully defined in these pieces, with chromatic diligence. Sowerby has a Franckian approach, but with a sweeter touch (almost lighter). The variations total four and are dynamically arch-structured.

Janice Beck's playing fits Sowerby's style neatly, and she adds interest (and strength) to the dynamic proportions by apt registration.

Comes Autumn Time

☐ Noehren (organ) / Lyrichord 7191

With no information to the contrary, one takes it for granted that this is Sowerby's own transcription of his robustly gay orchestral Overture. If it isn't, it is still worth having, since there is no recording of the orchestral setting.

Fast and Sinister from Symphony in G major

Prelude on Psalm 46

☐ Beck (organ) / Musical Heritage Society OR A–264

The Prelude, derived from a hymn tune of the Anglican Church, follows the chorale prelude tradition as the melody travels registrally. This is sober music, of the often-heard type the church organist plays while the congregation gathers to pray. The movement from the Symphony is a bit more contemporary in mood and style, though it is difficult to understand the *sinister* instruction in the tempo. Late romantic in content, the Fast and Sinister extract (the middle movement of the work) has well-rounded contours and an excellent projection of nonexcitable motility.

There is handsome organ playing by Janice Beck. Her phrasing especially proves her excellent musicianship.

Prelude on *The King's Majesty*

☐ Harmon (organ) / Orion 76255

Fantasy variations, nine in all, power this powerful work. Sowerby is totally committed here to the big sonorous thrust. But compelling sounds fit the organ and in that sense the piece is a sincere utterance, with coherent progress from thematic statement to conclusion.

It is played to perfection on the bright and impressively timbred organ housed in Royce Hall at UCLA. It is all clean and big and in the few softer sections just as direct in expression.

Toccata

☐ McVey (organ) / Orion 74161

Motility, as befits the form, and slight dissonant ingredients, to loosen the tonality, invest Sowerby's piece. It is strong and colorful organ music that is welcome. So is David McVey's performance, unfortunately marred in the review copy (and probably on others) by a one-second mechanical scrunch the engineers failed to remove from the tape.

Chamber Music

Pop Goes the Weasel (1927)

☐ Westwood Wind Quintet / Crystal 101

Yes, good encore fare, but good listening too. The final cadence, with the subject set in constant varied repetition, is fragmentation at its most primitive. Real cute! Real well played, also.

Daniel Speer (1636-1707)

Brass Ensemble

Sonata for Four Trombones and Continuo
Sonata for Trumpet, Three Trombones, and Continuo
Sonata No. 1 for Three Trombones and Continuo
Sonata No. 2 for Three Trombones and Continuo
Three Fanfares for Three Trumpets, Three Trombones, and Timpani

☐ London Brass Players / Rifkin (conductor) / Nonesuch 71145

The performances are admirable in every respect, with the one reservation that there is not sufficient dynamic differentiation in the Sonatas. However, the terraced dynamics in the shorter Fanfares cannot be faulted.

The record sleeve provides excellent documentation by Joshua Rifkin, including all data as to the sources of the compositions.

Joel Spiegelman (1933-)

Instrumental

Piano, Four Hands

Kousochki for Piano Four-Hands (1966)

☐ Jean and Kenneth Wentworth (piano) / Desto 7131

"Morsels" is serially derived but mainly concerns itself with an array of invigorating bell sounds—large and small, high and low. There are fascinating passages in the score that produce beguiling images.

Spiegelman's fine piece is an important addition to piano-duet literature. It was composed especially for the Wentworth team (husband and wife), and they show their appreciation with a dramatically colorful performance.

Claudio Spies   (1925-   )

Impromptu for Piano (1963)

Instrumental

Piano

☐ Miller (piano) / Composers Recordings S–257

Spies's short piece is subtitled "Cradle Music for Adam Henry Zivin." It is no sing-song lullaby, however. The work is formally clear, transparent in texture, chromatically stated. It could be further subtitled as "Calm Music for Adults."

Viopiacem, Duo for Viola and Keyboard Instruments (1965)

Chamber Music

☐ Miller (piano and harpsichord); Rhodes (viola) / Composers Recordings S–257

Using an alternation between piano and harpsichord, Spies's duo provides the timbre of a trio, hence the coined title, which combines the first three letters of each instrument: *Vio*(la)–*pia*(no)–*cem*(balo). Covering all possibilities, Spies includes in his eight sections solos for each of the three instruments, two duos, and a concluding portion for viola with quick interchanges between the piano and harpsichord.

Though coloristic shifts necessarily reflect on the rhapsodic content of *Viopiacem*, there is fine balance and a general exalted mood to the work. The feeling for atmosphere is sensitively realized by the excellent musicians who produced the recording.

Robert Spillman   (1936-   )

Two Songs

Instrumental

Tuba

☐ Bobo (tuba); Grierson (piano) / Crystal S–392

Spillman contrasts a theme and variations with a Hindemithian concept, offerings made to order for the soloist. Bobo's ability to spin out a sustained line is a delight. His talent in registering fast music is just as special. This type of playing is a potent cleanser of the idea that a tuba can only serve as a bass pivot in the orchestra, generally doubling the third trombone in octaves. It's a ponderous-timbred instrument, of course, but in Roger Bobo's hands it is the complete solo instrument possessed with all the necessary flexibilities.

Ludwig Spohr   (1784-1859)

Notturno in C major, Op. 34

Wind and Brass Ensemble

☐ Wind Section of the Little Orchestra of London / Jones (conductor) / CMS/Oryx 1830

Spohr's six-part composition is for a wind band and the so-called "Turkish" instruments: bass drum, cymbals, and triangle. The first flute doubles on the old military E flat flute and piccolo; a second piccolo appears in the *Polacca* movement. The other woodwinds are paired oboes, clarinets, bassoons, and a contra-bassoon. A single brass instrument is used: a bass trombone.

The six movements are a mix of serenade and divertimento fancies with moderately serious and light attractions. In the last category, especially in the opening March and in the closing movement (which has yodel-like thematic material), the period posturing is delightfully evident.

Solo Instrument and Orchestra

Concerto No. 1 in C minor for Clarinet and Orchestra, Op. 26

Clarinet

☐ London Symphony Orchestra / de Peyer (clarinet) / Davis (conductor) / Oiseau-Lyre 60035

This work is perhaps just a bit faded (apologies to Spohr buffs!) until it really takes off in the final rondo which it is certainly well worth waiting for. The melodic conviction is, of course, directed to the solo instrument, and Gervase de Peyer delivers a tasteful and beautiful performance. Fortunately, Colin Davis avoids any perfunctory attitude in the accompaniment as he very well could have.

Violin

Concerto No. 8 in A minor for Violin and Orchestra, Op. 47

☐ RCA Victor Orchestra / Heifetz (violin) / Solomon (conductor) / RCA LM-2860 (monaural)

Yes, this is a mono issue, but it is the most superb exposition of this work you'll ever hear. Spohr's *in Form einer Gesangsszene* ("in the form of a vocal scene") is as mother's milk to this violinist. Just listen to the liquidity of tone and the sensitive light stress brought by the minutest halt before an intervallic leap, observe the suavity, respond to the whole pitch truth and nothing but the pitch truth in each and every note. Heifetz vocalizes through the work and proves himself one of the greatest of string-instrument virtuosi in existence. The competition crumbles.

Concerto No. 9 in D minor for Violin and Orchestra, Op. 55

☐ Bress (violin) / Beck (conductor) / Oiseau-Lyre S–278

This Concerto is not as interesting as the famous eighth Concerto (*see above*), but it is substantially good old-style fiddle music which Hyman Bress delivers with all the necessary vitality. The orchestral forces are heavier than usual for Spohr's Concerti (three trombones as well as paired horns and trumpets) but the accompaniment by the pick-up orchestra is kept in control.

Violin and Cello

Potpourri on Themes taken from the Opera *Jessonda* for Violin and Violoncello with Orchestra, Op. 64

☐ Hamburg Symphony / Lautenbacher (violin); Blees (cello) / Springer (conductor) / Candide 31043

Spohr didn't wait to dwell on the success of his Opera *Jessonda*. He immediately produced this compilation (a quarter-hour's worth), composed the first of his four double string quartets, and then again returned to the material of the Opera and wrote another potpourri, this one set for violin and orchestra.

Opus 64 rolls along in five connected sections, with fine vocalized temper for the two solo instruments. Both soloists avoid the temptation to overplay—their interpretative proportions and details are beautifully placed.

Concertante No. 1 in G major for Violin, Harp, and Orchestra (1806)

Violin and Harp

☐ English Chamber Orchestra / Schneeberger (violin); Holliger (harp) / Graf (conductor) / Musical Heritage Society MHS–3120

Spohr's three-movement work makes an effective contribution to an exceedingly rare medium. The central movement is keenly colored with sectional contrast between the solo violin and muted strings and a chorale-like statement for the solo harp and winds. There is full-scale construction in the outer movements: an *Allegro* in sonata form and an Allegretto in rondo format.

The performance is lovely, deeply satisfying in its avoidance of overstatement. The effect is large-scale chamber music.

Fantaisie in A flat major, Op. 35

Instrumental

Harp

☐ Vito (harp) / Orion 7039

The security of this piece is its period charm. Romanticism is becoming to harp music when it is written in this well-proportioned manner; all the changes in the chosen fantasy form are nicely smoothed and phrased.

Vito plays with a type of dynamic reticence (meaning similarity) that is central to harp performance tradition. Younger harpists are breaking away from this. However, Vito's harp sound is good and his sureness of tempo and rhythm are excellent.

Duo Concertant in D major, Op. 67, No. 2

Chamber Music

☐ David and Igor Oistrakh (violins) / Monitor S–2058

This is the only Spohr violin duet recorded despite the fact that Spohr produced no fewer than fourteen works for the combination. Most of these are not just material for study, as are so many violin duos, but are capable of standing up in public performance.

A violin duo team was not so uncommon to the concert stage of Spohr's time as it is now. Most violin duets are rarely performed, and even then at special concerts. A real duet should sound like a duet. Spohr's does, notwithstanding double-stopping, which in the overall picture is minor to the majority of the clear two-part writing. In addition, Spohr uses perfect give-and-take equality of the instruments. This is the highest artistic concept of the form, otherwise lacking in many duets of the same or an earlier period, where the first violin shines and the second violin puts the harmonic laces into the other instrument's melodic (and often pyrotechnically shined) shoes.

The music of this duo runs in set forms: a sonata-styled Allegro, a ternary-designed Larghetto, and a final Rondo. The Oistrakhs play marvelously, with romantic robustness, yet do not disturb the basic classical lines of the piece. It represents a double designation of masterly fiddle playing. As such it deserved the Grand Prix awarded the recording by L'Académie du Disque français (the other duets on the disc are by Haydn, Honegger, and Prokofiev). However, the careless identification of the composition deserves no prize whatsoever. The work is listed as "Duetto II in D major," which is as vague as one can be. Spohr's duos are spread over seven opus numbers, four of these containing more than a single work. The lack of opus specification is irritating. So is the mistitling. Spohr never titled any of his two-violin works as a "duetto," but typified each as a "duo concertante," or as a "grand duo."

Grand Duo in E minor for Violin and Viola, Op. 13

☐ Lautenbacher (violin); Koch (viola) / Candide 31043

Spohr's Opus 13 may not be "grand" but it is certainly good. There are three movements: a well-developed opening movement; then an Adagio, with twirling ornamental lines, its texture weighted by double stops; and a concluding *Tempo di Menuetto*.

The playing is rich, with care for stylistic decorum.

Sonata Concertante
No. 1, Op. 113 / No. 2, Op. 114 / No. 3, Op. 115

☐ McDonald (harp); Kaufman (violin) / Orion 7262

Not much music exists for this combination. Spohr's set of three runs neatly along paths previously trodden. The music is well ordered, well sounding. In short, it represents the neutrality of the competent composer. Nos. 1 and 3 are in three movements, No. 2 consists of a pair of movements, the last a *Potpourri* on Themes from Mozart's *Magic Flute*.

Played and recorded with excellence.

Quintet for Piano, Flute, Clarinet, Horn, and Bassoon, Op. 52

☐ Boehm (piano); Wion (flute); Bloom (clarinet); Howard (horn); MacCourt (bassoon) / Turnabout 34506

This Quintet is not sizzling-hot, just structurally unpretentious, but delightfully refreshing romantic music. Nice melodic character throughout the usual four movements, with a specially individual concept of a *Minuetto*.

Excellent ensemble, good balance, natural sound.

Double Quartet No. 1 in D minor, Op. 65

☐ Heifetz, Baker, Amoyal, and Rosenthal (violins); Thomas and Harshman (violas); Piatigorsky and Lesser (cellos) / RCA LSC-3068

Rather than use the string-octet formation, Spohr chose to break the group into its two string-quartet units. The quartets are to sit separately like two miniature chorus groups. It is thus possible to consider the totality as a complete octet, single out each quartet for its own material, or use the pair in the nice effect of antiphony. To a certain degree, Spohr uses all of these, especially the last, but generally, the first quartet is superior to the subservient second foursome.

A variety of scoring methods is used in this, the first of the four double quartets Spohr composed. It receives a sincere and properly styled performance. It should be noted that the first quartet's violin primo is Jascha Heifetz and his partner at the cello is Gregor Piatigorsky. The second violinist (Baker) and the violist (Thomas) of their team are well-known in chamber music circles. The second quartet is less so. Nevertheless, the total ensemble is admirable.

Double Quartet No. 3 in E minor, Op. 87

☐ Fietz, Hübner, Swoboda, and Matheis (violins); Breitenbach and Staar (violas); Hübner and Luitz (cellos) / London STS-15074

This work is considered to be the finest of Spohr's four works for double quartet. His employment of the quartets against each other illustrates capital instrumentation. The members of the Vienna Octet give an excellent surveyal of the composition, with neat instrumental balance.

Nonet in F major, Op. 31

☐ Fietz (violin); Breitenbach (viola); Brabec (cello); Kräutler (double bass); Niedermayr (flute); Mayrhofer (oboe); Boskovsky (clarinet); Pamperl (bassoon); Veleba (horn) / London STS-15074

Spohr's Opus 31 is standard romantic fare but it is understandably interesting in terms of the mini-chamber orchestra that combines a quartet of strings with a woodwind quintet.

The performance is first-class. Though the performance is listed as given by "Members of the Vienna Octet," that organization's personnel varies and the individual names have been listed.

Sechs deutsche Lieder, Op. 103

☐ Ragains (soprano); Warner (clarinet); Dameron (piano) / Crystal S-332

Opus 103 represents the last of Spohr's six sets of "Six German Songs." Clarinet coloration (it is absent in the other five groups) is an aid in projecting the simple sentiments. The songs are sung with affecting eloquence.

Vocal

Voice with Accompaniment

Lewis Spratlan (1940-   )

Two Pieces for Orchestra

Orchestra

☐ Springfield Symphony Orchestra / Gutter (conductor) / Opus One 19

Spratlan takes his forms (Prelude and Rondo) from bygone eras but their ingredients sparkle with intoxicating contemporary colorations. There is eclecticism but it is used with a bravura and intensity that are quite compelling. Mahler, Berg, Stravinsky, and even Schoenberg are more than flirted with. Because of the workmanship that binds the materials this is no mere pasticcio, and though the textures are heavy, there is no padding.

John Stainer (1840-1901)

The Crucifixion

Cantata and Oratorio

☐ Choir of St. John's College, Cambridge / Lewis (tenor); Brannigan (bass); Runnett (organ) / Guest (conductor) / Argo ZRG-5320

In the performance halls of the minor leagues Stainer's oratorio (first performed in London, in 1887) is right up there with Bach's *St. Matthew Passion* and Handel's *Messiah*. Comfortably conventional, it doesn't strain the abilities of the average church choir and the same applies to the organist and soloists.

Argo's production, with everything strong and clear, is of major league status.

Carl Stamitz (1745-1801)

Concerto in F major for Bassoon and Orchestra

Solo Instrument and Orchestra

☐ Württemberg Chamber Orchestra, Heilbronn / Zukerman (bassoon) / Faerber (conductor) / Turnabout 34093

Stamitz's work is written in the standard three movements, with an *Allegro maestoso*, a *Molto adagio*, and a concluding *Poco presto*, and practically the standard instrumentation

Bassoon

as well: oboe, horn, and strings, with the first two instruments not used in the central movement.

Standard writing as well. However, George Zukerman plays with above standard ability and shapes the phrases nicely. The cadenza in the slow movement is expressive, the slurring and staccato differences in the finale are precisely controlled.

Cello

Concerto in A major for Cello and Orchestra

☐ Württemberg Chamber Orchestra, Heilbronn / Blees (cello) / Faerber (conductor) / Turnabout 34362

A responsible and thoroughly responsive consideration of Stamitz's work, containing a compelling slow movement in which Thomas Blees exhibits his best work. Pleasingly effective end movements.

Clarinet

Concerto No. 3 in B flat major for Clarinet and Orchestra

☐ Innsbruck Symphony Orchestra / Glazer (clarinet) / Wagner (conductor) / Turnabout 34093

David Glazer moves with artistic ease through the three movements of this warmly pitched piece, particularly in the central *Romanza*. There is not much cadenza work but what there is is musically proportioned.

Flute

Concerto in G major for Flute and Strings

☐ Orchester der Wiener Musikgesellschaft / Wanausek (flute) / Heiller (conductor) / Turnabout 34093

If not striking or of memorable invention Stamitz's flute and strings music is presented with fine style in an immaculately clear rendition. The slow movement is especially nicely molded.

Viola

Concerto No. 1 in D major for Viola and Orchestra, Op. 1

☐ Württemberg Chamber Orchestra, Heilbronn / Wallfisch (viola) / Faerber (conductor) / Turnabout 34221

Ernst Wallfisch gives a sympathetic interpretation of Stamitz's Concerto. He is ably supported by Jörg Faerber's chamber orchestra. A fine sense of the music's direction is realized.

Two Violins

Symphony Concertante for Two Violins and Orchestra

☐ Chamber Orchestra of the Sarre / Makanowitzky and Hendel (violins); Winschermann (oboe) / Ristenpart (conductor) / Nonesuch 71014

Edward Tatnall Canby terms this piece "polished, secure and grateful." Absolutely. However, it is also sturdy and without any laciness. This also applies to the middle, slow-tempoed movement, where the soli join the orchestra and a solo oboe brings in a contrastive color.

No part of this reading can be faulted and that applies to execution as well as reproduction. The dynamic playing of the fiddlers is of the virile variety and matches Stamitz's content.

Violin and Viola

Sinfonia Concertante in D major for Violin and Viola with Orchestra

☐ English Chamber Orchestra / Stern (violin); Zukerman (viola) / Barenboim (conductor) / Columbia M–31369

No problem as to choice. Stern and Zukerman play with zest, sweet suavity, and dispatch the music with golden tone. On the other hand, Susanne Lautenbacher and Ernst Wallfisch seem to labor; the notes don't glide. This may well be due to the fact that no conductor is there to prod matters in their representation on Turnabout 34221.

This work is hardly heard in the concert hall because there is the famous Mozart work for the same combination (the Mozartian climate of the Stamitz would not make a propitious balance if both works were on the same program), but an occasional substitution of the Stamitz for the Mozart would be a deserving move. The evidence is here in the recording listed.

Quartet in A major for Clarinet, Violin, Viola, and Cello, Op. 4, No. 6

□ Trio à Cordes Français / Lancelot (clarinet) / Nonesuch 71125

Chamber Music

Straightforward, logically constructed music. The Quartet has a pair of allegro movements and a Romance in between. The playing is alive and discerning.

Quartet in D major for Flute, Violin, Horn, and Cello, Op. 8, No. 1

□ Rampal (flute); Jarry (violin); Coursier (horn); Tournus (cello) / Nonesuch 71125

As is to be expected, there is no move on Stamitz's part to spring any formal surprises. The affirmation of standard balance is clearly pursued in the Allegro and *Poco presto* outer movements as well as in the central *Andante amoroso*. There's fine playing all around, especially in the blending of the voices and the excellent dynamic range.

Quartet in D major for Flute, Violin, Viola, and Cello, Op. 4, No. 3

□ Trio à Cordes Français / Rampal (flute) / Nonesuch 71125

There is substantial testimony here that Stamitz did not always compress his formal thinking. It is the exception to his rule but it is a fine exception, with two principal movements, the second binding into it the sense of a third movement. Thus, part 2 has an A–B–A design with a Rondo followed by a *Tempo di minuetto* and a return to the Rondo. Of course, this is quite simple in the long run, but it is not a carbon copy of the formal plan of the other quartets for winds and strings (*see above* and *below*).

The music is well-represented by this great flutist and his string-instrument colleagues. The accent and definition of Stamitz's score are provided with depth. A very high rating applies to the recording.

Quartet in F major for Oboe, Violin, Horn, and Cello, Op. 8, No. 3

□ Pierlot (oboe); Jarry (violin); Coursier (horn); Tournus (cello) / Nonesuch 71125

Though not profound, the music is worth lingering over. Formal management is standard, with moderately fast- and slow-tempoed movements, completed by a Presto. The playing will appeal to the intelligence as well as the emotions.

Johann Wenzel Anton Stamitz *(1717-1757)*

Symphony in A major

Orchestra

□ Munich Chamber Orchestra / Stadlmair (conductor) / Nonesuch 71076

This work, one of Johann Stamitz's seventy-four Symphonies, is fairly traditional. The opening movement, as well as the finale (*presto assai*) are in sonata form, the slow movement is for strings alone, and a *Menuett* follows. Traditional tempo headings, save for the opening, marked *fresco assai* ("very fresh"). The performance is lucid.

John Stanley (1713-1786)

String Orchestra

Concerto

Op. 2, No. 1 / **Op. 2, No. 2** / **Op. 2, No. 3** / **Op. 2, No. 5** / **Op. 2, No. 6**

☐ Spinks (harpsichord) / Hurwitz (conductor) / Oiseau-Lyre S-315

Music in the Handelian orbit, its patterns sufficiently creative to avoid a scholastic cast. Excellent performances throughout.

Instrumental

Organ

Voluntary in A major

☐ McVey (organ) / Orion 74161

Tradition is maintained, naturally, with an Adagio in solemn disposition followed by a joyful Allegro. The contrast also places polyphonic emphasis on the second part, and McVey plans his registration accordingly.

Voluntary In G major, Op. 7, No. 9

☐ Rapf (organ) / Klavier 545

Stanley's organ work has a broad introduction and a joyous triple-voiced fugue to push matters to a conclusion. Rapf's use of contrastive registration plus opposed dynamics for blocked sections is extremely effective.

Chamber Music

Sonata No. 4 in A minor for Flute and Organ, Op. 1, No. 4

☐ Linde (flute); Rapf (organ) / Klavier 545

This is from a set of eight sonatas for flute or violin and keyboard, marking Stanley's Opus 1. (Klavier gives practically no facts on its liner notes and doesn't even designate tempi anywhere in its release.)

Burney described Stanley as a "natural and agreeable composer." An apt surveyal, exemplified by this flowing work, with a catchy striding bass in one part and dance character in the concluding variations.

The performance is on a high level.

Robert Starer (1924-   )

Orchestra

Mutabili (Variants for Orchestra) (1965)

☐ Louisville Orchestra / Mester (conductor) / Louisville S-682

Starer's piece is twelve-tone with freely disposed thematic development. It avoids the usual conclusions of dodecaphonic diction and orchestrational fragmentation and retains its understood values. *Mutabili* has a formal clarity that has an immediacy for the listener; the five sections are varied in both tempo and content.

Mester's viewpoint is technically assured and musically secure. Especially pertinent to the performance is a sensitive sense of proportion that certifies the music's stability.

Concerto a Tre for Clarinet, Trumpet, Trombone, and Strings (1954)

☐ Camerata Symphony Orchestra / Rabbai (clarinet); Schwarz (trumpet); Brevig (trombone) / Kaplan (conductor) / Desto 7135

Coloristic confidence and largeness of gesture are represented here. Starer's work is written in tonal language enlarged with contemporary erudition. The choice of solo sonorities, unusual in timbre-combined concertos, is not only colorful in its own right, but cogently defines Starer's substances. There is considerable ingenuity and a special rhythmic vitality in the three movements. It is understandable, therefore, that Martha Graham selected this score for the dance composition *Secular Games.*

The soloists have all the technical skills necessary and they apply these to fulfill the artistic demands of Starer's first-rate score.

Prelude

☐ Chertok (harp) / Orion ORS–75207

A sense of the dramatic comes through in this three and one-quarter minute piece. The music has a neo-romantic character, with nicely chromed sonorous verbiage, which Miss Chertok expresses handsomely.

Evanescents (1975)

☐ Mandel (piano) / Grenadilla GS–1020

Starer here presents segmented yet deftly connected materials, including expressionistic phrases and quasi-eastern folklike poignancies. Nice rhythmic flow, middle-of-the-road dissonances. All of it forms a contemporary music democracy. All of it holds the interest.

Playing of value is offered by Alan Mandel. This is a definitive recording "supervised by the composer." He didn't supervise the printing of the liner note, apparently, though he obviously wrote it. Despite a number of personal statements, no credit is given Starer—the only error in the entire production.

Five Preludes

☐ Mandel (piano) / Desto 6445/7

Each Prelude presents and develops a specific mood, each conveys a defined atmosphere, each is positive in its textural setting. Thus the hollow, wide-spacing of the penultimate Prelude, the somberness of the last one.

Sonata No. 2 for Piano (1965)

☐ Schoenfield (piano) / Desto 7106

Starer's Sonata is in one movement but cunningly constructed so that contrastive material that would usually stand as separate divisions in a total work are intertwined within the piece. Fine melodic variety, rhythmic virility, and textural contrasts are displayed in the score.

Paul Schoenfield knows Starer's opus to its very core and displays that perceptivity in his recording. He had given the premiere (in New York in October 1966).

Dialogues for Clarinet and Piano (1961)

☐ Glazer (clarinet); Garvey (piano) / Desto 7106

These are freely structured contemporary chamber-music conversations. There is a touch of jazz to be heard, but for the greater part the give-and-take and the thesis-antithesis of the phrases are urbane statements, free from frivolity or bombast. The work is intensely refreshing.

Closely tight (that is, squarely defined) playing would nullify Starer's *Dialogues*. There is a fluidic consideration in the performance that sounds as though hearty improvisation were going on. It makes the Glazer–Garvey presentation a special one.

Variants (1963)

☐ Buswell IV (violin); Garvey (piano) / Desto 7106

Starer has used twelve-tone technique in his *Mutabili* (*see above* under *Orchestra*) and in this composition. The results are natural enough to be convincing, especially here where there is no slavish conformity to dodecaphonic rule. There are five variants, and Starer explains that as soon as one is exposed "its continuation is freely composed." Accordingly, technical dogma is not allowed to intrude upon creative will. The results are propitious as is the performance by violinist James Oliver Buswell IV and pianist John Garvey.

Five Miniatures

☐ American Brass Quintet / Desto 6474/7

Starer made this an exercise in the art of suite diversification, covering the following: Fanfare, Air, Canon, Chaconne, and March. All have one thing in common: contemporaneously healthy harmony and color packaging that fit the titled explanations.

Choral

Chorus Alone

On the Nature of Things (1968)

☐ Collegiate Chorale / Kaplan (conductor) / Desto 7106

Direct, straightforward language is used in the six parts that comprise Starer's unaccompanied choral work. The meaningful musical material is varied to accommodate the textual variety, drawn from Lucretius, Emily Dickinson, John Digby, Elisabethan poetry, the Bible, and a familiar quotation ("a little nonsense now and then is relished by the wisest men").

Starer writes with complete insight and confidence. However, he is served by only a fair recording. The singing itself is worthy but the sound and balances are less so. Desto doesn't help matters by the absence of bands on the disc and the failure to supply a text.

Cantata and Oratorio

Ariel, Visions of Isaiah

☐ Camerata Singers and Camerata Symphony Orchestra / Peters (soprano); Patrick (baritone) / Kaplan (conductor) / Desto 7135

Ariel (which Starer indicates literally means "Lion of God") consists of six movements, with the entire text drawn from Isaiah's prophecies. It has strong continuity in its variation of commentary, color, and form. Above all, it has a pictorial vividness that sweeps the work into the realm of true theatre.

The work is performed with great flexibility and excellent collaboration between chorus, orchestra, and soloists. Kaplan has beautifully realized the excitement in the score. Starer's is a powerful piece deserving of permanency in the repertoire.

Abbate Agostino Steffani *(1654-1728)*

Stabat Mater

Cantata and Oratorio

☐ Concentus Musicus, Vienna, and Vienna Boys' Choir, and Chorus Viennensis / Equiluz and Resch (tenors); Simkowsky (bass) / Harnoncourt (conductor) / CMS/Oryx 3C–303

Steffani's *Stabat Mater* for soloists, six-part choir, strings, and organ continuo is considered his magnum opus. Indeed, it plays beautifully and has striking counterpoint. All of this is expressively presented, though there is a tendency to stretch the pace of certain sections, especially in the first part of the work. The chorus is strong (it was prepared by Hans Gillesberger). The soloists (no credit is given a sweet-toned soprano) are fine, particularly the bass, Nikolaus Simkowsky.

Daniel Steibelt *(1765-1823)*

Three Bacchanals, Op. 53

Instrumental

Piano

☐ Lewenthal (piano); Raney (percussion) / Angel S-36080

These pieces have as much relationship to a bacchanal as a solitary person sipping iced tea on his veranda. All three are uninebrious waltzlike conceptions, the middle one a bit faster than the other pair. This is piano music belonging to the days of crinoline and old lace, its genteel sounds embroidered with bits of tambourine and triangle sounds.

Herman Stein *(1915-   )*

Mock March

Chamber Music

☐ Annapolis Brass Quintet / Crystal S-207

This is all that was produced for a projected *Sour Suite* for brass. Out of Prokofiev by way of Shostakovich. No flaws in this cute copy.

Leon Stein *(1910-   )*

String Quartet

Chamber Music

No. 1 (1933) / No. 2 (1962) / No. 3 (1964) / No. 4 (1965)

☐ Chicago Symphony String Quartet / Audio Finishers 74S100

Integration between introductory material and the data for the movement proper brings a decided outer movement balance in the first quartet. The chromaticism that colors Stein's work is always unfussy. In the second quartet the principal element in all four movements is coloristic detail. In a sense, structure is subordinated to textural conditions. Form is the result of the free continuum of material, without resource to compartmentalization and recapitulation. A suitelike compilation covers the four movements of the third quartet. Nonetheless, the quartet has as much unity as the classical format. This derives from impressive and expansive tonality, avoidance of formal ambiguity, and a virtuosic handling of the four instruments, individually and combined.

Stein's writing is not ever commonplace, despite formed depictions that offer no identity crisis. These quartets are a fruitful fusion of artistic insight and technique. It can be heard in the masterful fourth quartet, containing grotesque allusions in its second movement and a perpetual motion portrayal in the finale.

The performances are very good. This is not a one-shot recording studio deal, either. The Chicago foursome presented all the quartets in public before recording them.

String Quartet No. 5 (1967)

☐ Chicago Symphony String Quartet / Perillo (soprano) / Audio Finishers 74S100

Stein based his quartet (a quintet in its fifth and final movement, with the addition of a soprano voice) on the poetry of Dylan Thomas. In the first four movements superscriptions are indicated as the point of departure (or inspiration). A complete poem serves for the concluding part of the opus. The work is, therefore, a derivative of program music. However, literal picture painting is not the purpose; emotional carry-over is, especially in movement 5. The music of this final part has neo-romantic nobility (the opening cello recitative) as well as intensity (when the voice partners the string instruments). It is a high point not only of the work itself but among all of Stein's compositions.

Robert Stern   (1934-   )

Orchestra

Carom for Orchestra and Magnetic Tape

☐ Springfield Symphony Orchestra / Gutter (conductor) / Opus One 19

By using sharp electronic contours Stern illuminates the basic lyrical impetus of his piece. There is a passion here that conveys a nocturnal atmosphere. Skillfully portrayed and sensitively performed.

String Orchestra

In Memoriam Abraham (1955)

☐ Eastman-Rochester Symphony / Hanson (conductor) / Eastman-Rochester Archives ERA-1003

Stern's piece has devotional concentration. Its sensitively serious modal style will remind one of Vaughan Williams, which, of course, brings no discredit.

Hanson interprets this music beautifully and ERA has supplied beautiful sound. However, ERA fails to indicate anywhere in the album (titled *Music for Quiet Listening*) in which Stern's composition is included that it is for string orchestra.

Vocal

Voice with Accompaniment

Terezin

☐ Ornest (soprano); Krosnick (cello); Stern (piano) / Composers Recordings S-264

The six texts are six poems written by children in the Theresienstadt concentration camp, selected from the book *I Never Saw a Butterfly*. In addition there are three instrumental interludes based on drawings contained in the same collection. Whereas the texts are given, the drawings regrettably are not. Nonetheless, every note in this telling score imparts deep meaning and conveys the horrible circumstances that surrounded the creation of the poems. If one were to be prejudiced by this in favor of the music, so be it. Stern has accomplished a difficult task (that overcomes the prejudice mentioned) and has produced a telling work, one that gives the fullest musical currency to the young poets' words.

Constantin Sternberg (1852-1924)

Third Concert Etude, Op. 103

☐ Hofmann (piano) / Klavier 121

A pianistic "Flight of the Bumble Bee" reflection. A perfect example of Josef Hofmann's brilliant technique.

Halsey Stevens (1908-   )

Sinfonia Breve (1957)

☐ Louisville Orchestra / Whitney (conductor) / Louisville 593 (monaural)

Stevens's *Sinfonia Breve* is richly expressive and has a structural solidity that impresses. Above all, while being serious Stevens avoids unpleasant austerity and knows how to move his rhythms along and within the textures.

Symphonic Dances (1958)

☐ London Philharmonic Orchestra / Barati (conductor) / Composers Recordings 166 (monaural)

Stevens's eighteen minutes' worth of dances recall Copland of the craggy sextet era. This is nothing to be ashamed about. Some composers are frank lyricists, and rhythm becomes a subservient utility in building their compositions. Stevens considers rhythm with no timid gentility. With this premise he is also concerned with germinal material, especially in the outer movements which are motivally synthesized. The motoric effect makes one realize how apt these dances would be for ballet, thereby to fulfill their total potential.

The Londoners' performance is refreshingly forthright. However, some looseness in the pinpointing of the metrical shifts is to be noted.

Symphony No. 1 (1950)

☐ Japan Philharmonic Symphony Orchestra / Watanabe (conductor) / Composers Recordings S-129

There are plenty of well-curved melodic spans in this Symphony (premiered, with the composer conducting, in San Francisco, in 1946, and revised four years later), but Stevens avoids a patchwork of themes and chooses the stronger structural conviction of development of base material in his one-movement work. The orchestrational and rhythmical facility are splendid but are never designed for effect. The writing is totally natural in taste, style, and dynamic direction.

Prime to the entire score is its muscular rhythm (almost a reminder of Roussel but only in terms of texture not text). The rhythm is not square-cut, but has nervous ticks to keep one's attention. The reading by the Japanese aggregation is a good one.

Solo Instrument and Orchestra

Clarinet

Concerto for Clarinet and String Orchestra (1969)

☐ Crystal Chamber Orchestra / Lurie (clarinet) / Endo (conductor) / Crystal S–851

There is still plenty of demand for good clarinet concertos and Halsey Stevens has supplied an excellent one. His work combines classical formal stability with tonal variegation derived from the swing around and away from a polarity point. Stevens has no aesthetic double vision. The three movements add up to variety, vigor, and the requisite balance.

The co-star is the soloist, Mitchell Lurie. His playing is the entrancement brought by an expert. Crystal's sound matches the performance in excellence.

Instrumental

Cello

Sonata for Solo Cello (1958)

☐ Rejto (cello) / Composers Recordings 208 (monaural)

There is some virtuosity in this Sonata, but Stevens is concerned mainly with solid music and no soloistic specialities. Tonalism is the stylistic pivot but there is a full chromatic flavor that spices the lines.

There are problems with the production. The liner notes discuss five movements, the label copy lists only four, omitting the third-movement Scherzo. Since there are no bands, the listener will have to realize where the Ciaccona (movement 2) ends and where the *Notturno* (movement 4) begins. A gremlin also entered the liner notes, which mention the style of the Sonata as being "totally oriented." Could be, but what is actually meant is "tonally oriented."

Gabor Rejto, for whom the work was written and to whom it is dedicated, fully affirms the score.

Saxophone

Dittico for Alto Saxophone and Piano

☐ Pittel (alto saxophone); Grierson (piano) / Crystal S–105

The diptych contrasts a *Notturno* with a *Danza Arzilla*. The mood of the latter bears out the translation of the word *arzilla*, which means "sprightly."

Re-created with quality playing.

Chamber Music

Sonata for Horn and Piano

☐ Leuba (horn); Aanerud (piano) / Crystal S–372

Muscular music is found in the first movement, brassy detonations mark the final one; in between, the *Poco adagio* relates somewhat to recitative language. The music stuff of Stevens's piece shows full empathy for the medium as well as total confidence in tonality.

Distinctive playing is heard here, though perhaps greater significance might have been applied to dynamic differences.

Sonata for Trumpet and Piano (1956)

☐ Stith (trumpet); Bilson (piano) / Golden Crest S–7042

Lean neo-classic music is heard here, sculpted to fit the brass instrument beautifully (and performed with total focus). A feature of Stevens's work is the central *Adagio tenero* where two different mutes are employed with compelling effect. Metrical manipulation brightens the course of this splendid contribution to the trumpet repertoire.

Sonatina for Bass Tuba (or Trombone) and Piano (1960)

☐ Knaub (bass trombone); Snyder (piano) / Golden Crest 7040

Stabilized tonality is confirmed in Stevens's work, but fresh chordal air moves within the music. The three movements are nicely contrasted and they are represented by clear-cut playing in this recording.

Like as the Culver on the Bared Bough

Choral

Chorus Alone

☐ Randolph Singers / Randolph (conductor) / Composers Recordings 102 (monaural)

The liner note gives a perfect description of Stevens's madrigal set to a poem by Edmund Spenser: ''atmospheric and very expressive.''

The music is beautifully executed; the singers retain the dark quality of the piece while presenting its textural refinement to the fullest extent. Stevens's little work is extremely eloquent.

Psalm 98: O Sing unto the Lord a New Song (1955)

Chorus with Accompaniment

☐ Mid-America Chorale / Smith (piano) / Dexter (conductor) / Composers Recordings 191 (monaural)

Stevens sings jubilantly and effectively in this Psalm setting for three-part chorus of treble voices. And very fresh, rosy voices they are.

Thomas Stevens (1938-   )

Encore: Bōz

Instrumental

Tuba

☐ Bobo (tuba) / Crystal S–392

This little work is a stunt number of tuba pitches: high, low, and in between, with tempo from extremely slow to fast. Cutesie-pie stuff.

There are two presentations of the midget piece. The first begins the disc (five other works are on the program by Spillman, Kraft, Wilder, Lazarof, and Reynolds). The second ends it, played backwards. Even the liner notes follow suit. They appear twice, the repetition in retrograded (therefore senseless) language.

Robert Stewart (1918-   )

String Quartet No. 3

Chamber Music

☐ Iowa Quartet / Composers Recordings S–256

Stewart's third Quartet is marked by serial syntax and serial stoutheartedness. Each of the pair of movements is trinally split: Introduction, Recitative, and Variations in part 1; Scherzo, Adagio, and Finale in part 2.

From the playing of the Iowa Quartet one would hope for additions to the recorded repertoire. They're very good and they spell out Stewart's work with preciseness, clarification, and musicality.

William Grant Still (1895-1978)

Afro-American Symphony (1931)

Orchestra

☐ London Symphony Orchestra / Freeman (conductor) / Columbia M–32782

Still's most important work receives a penetrating and moving performance. In fact, it represents the best coverage this writer has ever heard of the composition.

The Symphony embraces moods pertaining to Black Americans: longing, sorrow, humor, and nobility. Over the entire Symphony there is a spirit of expressionistic realism, obtained by use of a blues-spiritual vocabulary. The ending is positivistic; the previous movement is deliciously colored with the use of a banjo. These sections, together with the first half of the Symphony, mark Still's excellent sense of symphonic drama.

Festive Overture (1945)

☐ Royal Philharmonic Orchestra / Lipkin (conductor) / Composers Recordings S–259

Still sports a forthright and optimistic quality in this mainly jolly good, tuneful piece. It sounds fresh if not original, being based squarely on traditional practices. Lipkin's direction of the work is competent.

Instrumental

Piano

Three Visions

☐ Hinderas (piano) / Desto 7102/3

The *Visions* fall in the characteristic-piece category. *Dark Horseman* rides along on a persistent rhythmic pattern; *Summerland* (which Still transcribed for violin and piano— see under *Instrumental: violin*) is warmly tranquil, and *Radiant Pinnacle* is lit with a quasi-oriental lyricism.

Natalie Hinderas presents each piece with a distinctive personality.

Violin

Carmela
Pastorella (1946)
Suite for Violin and Piano
Summerland

☐ Louis Kaufman (violin); Annette Kaufman (piano) / Orion 7152

Still pays tribute to his fellow artists in the Suite, where each movement is inspired by a piece of sculpture by a black artist. The music is not programmatic; the image is transferred in musical terms with harmonic simplicity and emphatic melodicism.

Pastorella is much longer than any of the three movements in the Suite. It is a type of poetic fantasy with a variety of moods (Still describes it as "a tone picture of a California landscape"). *Carmela* has Spanish swing; *Summerland* is pastoral in effect.

(The two last pieces were arrangements made by Still from other concepts. Whereas a composer's own arrangements are included in this survey, as well as standard repertoire transcriptions such as Bach/Stokowski, Mussorgsky/Ravel, et cetera, other recastings have not. Mention should be made, however, of two transcriptions by Louis Kaufman which are included on this recording: *Blues* from Still's *Lenox Avenue* (1937) and *Here's One,* Still's setting of a Negro spiritual).

Chamber Music

Danzas de Panama

☐ Kaufman and Berres (violins); Neiman (viola); King (cello) / Orion 7278

These are tonic representations of Panamanian dance tunes. Still has not played loose with the basic material or neutralized their coloristic specialness. The minor-keyed emotional vividness of the first of the set of four, *Tamborito* (regarded, according to Nicolas Slonimsky, as a licentious dance) highlights the work. (Still also made a version for string orchestra.)

Still, Orion, and the performers have produced a real winner.

Ennanga for Harp, Piano, and Strings (1956)

☐ Craft (harp); Annette Kaufman (piano); Louis Kaufman and Berres (violins); Neiman (viola); King (cello) / Orion 7278

A black composer translates his consideration of African music in this three-part composition. The transfer is a little less vivid than might be expected, since it turns out that the sounds behave somewhat neutralized—the African immigrants have become California citizens. No matter, Still's African romances have nice romantic turns.

A Song for the Lonely

Vocal

Voice with Accompaniment

☐ Carlson (mezzo-soprano); Akst (piano) / Orion 7278

This sensitive, nocturnal essay has a special and interesting concept: Still wrote the music first and then words were set to it by Verna Arvey (his wife).

Carlson's voice is exquisite and has faultless control.

Songs of Separation

Voice and Orchestra

☐ Oakland Youth Orchestra / Bedford (mezzo-soprano) / Hughes (conductor) / Desto 7107

These are five songs based on the lyrics of black poets, the binding subject being lovers who have separated. The poetry is clear, so Still uses simplistic constructions which effect immediacy for the listener.

Bedford's diction is impeccable, a special plus in this instance since Desto has not furnished texts (the second song is in French). Her voice is strong and rich and the support of the young orchestra has professional finish.

Another version of these enjoyable songs is available on Orion (7278). Sung with piano accompaniment they are, of course, much less colorful. However, Claudine Carlson does beautifully with the cycle. Her voice is lighter than Bedford's, but it is extremely musical. Her diction is not as precise. This is balanced by Orion's presenting the texts as part of the liner notes.

Two Arias from *Highway 1, U.S.A.* (1963)

☐ London Symphony Orchestra / Brown (tenor) / Freeman (conductor) / Columbia M-32782

The pair, *What Does He Know of Dreams?* and *You're Wonderful, Mary,* are from Still's one-act Opera, the text by his wife, Verna Arvey. Both exemplify perfervid romanticism. They are sung with rich resonance and with a clarity of diction that shames a great deal of the vocal fraternity. The absence of a printed text, therefore, is not critical at all.

Sadhji (1930)

Ballet

☐ London Symphony Orchestra and Morgan State College Choir / Freeman (conductor / Columbia M-33433

Sadhji is based on a simple story of an unfaithful African chieftain's wife that ends with her acknowledgment of guilt. Still's music contains an emphasis on slightly primitive rhythms in its full-scale romantic address. The singing and orchestral characterization are sound.

Mitya Stillman (1892-1936)

Vocal

Voice and Instrumental Ensemble

Four Songs for Mezzo-Soprano, String Quartet, Flute, and Harp

☐ Dal Segno Ensemble / Reid-Parsons (mezzo-soprano) / Critics Choice cc–1703 (monaural)

In the twenties and thirties Stillman was well-known and his music achieved a good number of performances. Since his death his name has unfairly disappeared from the scene. Russian-born and musically trained in that country, he produced music of a rich Russian quality. This applies to the cycle released on this special label, which represents the only recording available of Stillman's music. (The Four Songs won the first prize in the Detroit Chamber Music Competition, held in 1923.)

David Stock (1939-   )

Chamber Music

Quintet for Clarinet and Strings (1966)

☐ Contemporary String Quartet / Blustine (clarinet) / Composers Recordings S–329

One hears in this work the relentless fragmented changes of the post-Webern school. Within them the legitimate rhapsodizing takes place. There are three linked sections, Variations, Cadenzas, and Epilogue. The second division is naturally strongly colored by individual highlighting.

Karlheinz Stockhausen (1928-   )

Orchestra

Kontra-Punkte **(for 10 Instruments) (1953)**

☐ Members of the Rome Symphony Orchestra / Maderna (conductor) / RCA VICS-1239

This early Stockhausen work (for flute, clarinet, bass clarinet, bassoon, trumpet, trombone, piano, harp, violin, and cello) is dictated by serial rigidity for every pitch, duration, dynamic, and instrumental application. To this blueprint one special component is added—every portion of the total structure is regulated so that nothing predominates. Kaleidoscopic shifts occur and no passage stays in one register or at one dynamic level for more than a fleeting second. There is no climax, no terminus. The only concession to a central objective is the gradual elimination of instruments, beginning with the trumpet, then the trombone, followed by the bassoon, until the only instrument heard is the piano.

The performance of this vibrating color image is excellent. One exception: the minute dynamic differences that register so vividly in the score remain as *Augenmusik*. That they are not realized is not the performers' fault. Quick-change execution of *p* and *pp*, or *pp* and *ppp* is simply impossible.

Mixtur **for Five Orchestra Groups, Sine-Wave Generators and Four Ring Modulators (version for Small Orchestra) (1967)**

☐ Ensemble Hudba Dneska, Bratislava / Kupkovič (conductor) / Deutsche Grammophon 643546

(This is the second version of *Mixtur,* using a considerably reduced orchestra. The first setting was composed in 1964.)

In "Mixture" the four-sectioned orchestra (woodwind, brass, and two-sectioned strings, one predominantly concerned with plucked sound) is transferred to the creative mercy of sound technicians so that a hybrid constancy is the result. While the orchestra plays, it is miked, its sounds relayed to four mixers each of which balance and regulate the total received. The output is shifted to ring modulators where four other musicians operate the sine-wave generators involved and the results are in turn diffused over four loudspeakers. This is not combining electronics with live orchestral sound but electromotivating it, in the course of which changes of pitch, interval, timbre, and rhythm may well (and do!) occur.

But more. A percussion group is simultaneously added to the above, using three players, each playing cymbal and tam tam. This section is also miked but emerges without change over three separate loudspeakers.

Mixtur therefore begins with creative calculation and combines with secondary calculation. Considered another way, it means the invasion of orchestral sound by electronic foreigners.

Spiel für Orchester (1973)

☐ Southwest German Radio Symphony Orchestra / Stockhausen (conductor) / Deutsche Grammophon 2530827

Despite the 1973 date, *Spiel* represents early Stockhausen. "Game" (or "Play") was originally written in 1952 and then revised in 1973 for publication. The material is animated by contrasting specks of timbre in a meticulous method of fragmentation. This is most impressive and resourceful music, and it is played to the fullest effect.

Stop (1965)

Ylem (1972)

☐ London Sinfonietta / Stockhausen (conductor) / Deutsche Grammophon 2530442

Where there is aleatory music different versions understandably result as performances take place. These become confirmed if the composer accepts them as "definitive." *Stop* was composed in 1965. In the same year there came into existence a "Paris Version." This recording, dated 1973, is considered the "London Version." (In Robin Maconie's *The Works of Karlheinz Stockhausen,* published in 1976, there is no mention of a "London Version" and 1969 is the date assigned the "Paris Version.")

Aleatory devices are the impetus for improvisation, represented in *Stop* by hardy, fragmented assortments of material, punctuated by quiescent points within the work (hence its title). With Stockhausen in control the results are effective and authenticated.

Ylem, composed in 1972, is aleatoric esotericism. Indeed, compared to it, other chance music is of prissy orthodoxy. *Ylem* is truly *total* chance music, with everything left to chance. The performers play with their eyes closed (!) and relate to each other and to the conductor by thought transference, thus the premiere of telepathic music! Nonetheless, these unseeing musicians produce some mighty fine sounds.

Refrain (1959)

Percussion

☐ Aloys Kontarsky (piano and wood blocks); Bernhard Kontarsky (celesta and antique cymbals); Caskel (vibraphone, cowbells, and glockenspiel) / Mainstream 5003

Keyboard instruments (piano and celesta), pitched percussion (antique cymbals, vibraphone, and glockenspiel), and graduated sizes of unpitched percussion (three woodblocks and three cowbells) comprise Stockhausen's special-timbred orchestra. Further, the players utter sounds as additional percussive equivalents; human and instrumental detonations are thereby coalesced.

The notation of the score combines rigidly fixed indications as well as symbols that are mere pictorial representations for interpretation. Further chance decisions can be made in terms of a supplementary device placed over the score. However, despite the kaleidoscopic range of choice the outcome can be described. *Refrain* is a skeleton of soft contentious sounds; the rhythms are drugged so that a fundamental pulse is eliminated. Melodic ellipsis takes place as tones are fragmented, isolated, and disconnected.

The rituals of *Refrain* depart from the realms of ordinary instrumental conduct and sound like the equivalent of electronic sonorities translated backwards, as it were, into instrumental terms. With the use of percussion Stockhausen conceives a music that is nothing more than a constant vibrating concussion of accentuations.

Because of the predominant ambiguity of its text any performance of *Refrain* has its own built-in security. With no fixed point of departure one cannot criticize the playing. Still, these are great experts of the avant-garde style who have for long specialized in producing music by Stockhausen. Take for granted, therefore, that they know the style and are setting its traditional point of reference for later generations.

(Another version of *Refrain,* performed by Aloys Kontarsky, Caskel, and Stockhausen, is on Candide 31022.)

Zyklus (1959)

☐ Caskel (percussion) / Mainstream 5003

Stockhausen devotes his creativity to the matter of chance in this piece for one performer using marimbaphone, vibraphone, guiro, assorted drums (small drum, four tomtoms, and two African wood drums), Indian bells, four cowbells, cymbals (two suspended and one hi-hat), triangle, and gong. The percussionist has a score of some sixteen pages and may start on any page but must then play "a cycle in the given succession."

Because of its major reliance on unpitched instruments with related *types* of sound (metallic, membranous, and sibilative), *Zyklus* ("Cycle") follows the tenets of athematicism. There is no development; only a free, very independent, and ever-fresh unrolling of pulsatile demonstrations in one basic and general mood. There is artistic balance within Stockhausen's monologue regardless of the freedom of choice offered the interpreter.

The entire philosophy of chance music is that it never repeats itself, that no two hearings will ever be the same, that its indeterminacy means an ever-renewal, a new reckoning, each and every instance. A recording "freezes" a performance and Stockhausen's *Zyklus* is to be heard therefore as permanently fixed music with all chance removed. That Christoph Caskel does a magnificent realization will be immediately apparent to the listener.

(A performance using two players [Christoph Caskel and Max Neuhaus] was released on Wergo 60010. Neuhaus also has recorded the work himself on Columbia MS–7139.)

Instrumental

Piano

Klavierstück IX (1961)

Klavierstück XI (1956)

☐ Bucquet (piano) / Philips 6500101

Ostinato is the only traditional technique to be found in the earlier of the two pieces. (*Klavierstück IX* was composed in 1954, then revised in 1961.) A single chord (Stockhausen buffs speak of it as "the famous repeated chord") is heard well over two hundred times, beginning with a huge total of 142 repetitions of the C sharp-F sharp-G-C combination starting with very loud statements onto a gradual decrescendo into nothingness. The chord is splintered, rearranged, and unfocused as the music progresses. Of course, pulse is present, but meter definition is not, as the following sequence will exemplify: $\frac{142}{8}$, $\frac{87}{8}$, $\frac{42}{8}$, $\frac{13}{8}$, $\frac{2}{8}$ (of silence), $\frac{21}{8}$, $\frac{8}{8}$ (of silence), $\frac{1}{8}$, $\frac{3}{8}$ (of silence).

Klavierstück XI is a combination of controlled data and formal freedom. It consists of nineteen sections, played in any order by the performer, with tempi, types of attack, and dynamic levels outlined (but in no way constrained) by varied instructions. Infinite possibilities exist, of course, and Marie-Françoise Bucquet's realization of this music that is both tormented and chaste is as good as I have encountered. Her performance of *Klavierstück IX* is a mite less powerful than heard on the deleted CBS 32210008 issue, wherein Aloys Kontarsky performed Stockhausen's entire set of eleven piano pieces.

Sonatine for Violin and Piano (1951)

☐ Gavrilov (violin); Aloys Kontarsky (piano) / Deutsche Grammophon 2530827

This is early-period Stockhausen in which strong, closely argued serialism is applied to melody, rhythm, and dynamics. In spite of such obvious stylistic rigidity the music has an impressive sense of warmth, especially the first movement marked *Lento espressivo*. The work is splendidly performed.

Schlagtrio (1973)

☐ Aloys Kontarsky (piano); Batigne and van Gucht (timpani) / Deutsche Grammophon 2530827

Stockhausen's "Percussion Trio" calls for piano and two timpanists, each playing three kettles. Composed in 1952 as a work for piano and three timpanists, each timpanist playing two drums (Stockhausen first titled the work as *Schlagquartett für Klavier und 3 x 2 Pauken*), the conception was rescored in 1973 in the form heard here. The dynamic of the piece is primitive and, of all the early works recorded on this disc, *Spiel* (see under *Orchestra*), *Sonatine* (*see above*), and Three Songs (see under *Vocal: Voice and Orchestra*), it is the only one that has the future aesthetic simmering totally within it. Pitch controls are exceedingly acute; three of the six timpani are each tuned one-quarter tone flat and each of the other three, three-quarters of a tone flat. The bluntness of the music emerges quite vividly in the performance.

Zeitmasze (1956)

☐ Cleghorn (flute); Muggeridge (oboe); Leake (English horn); Ulyate (clarinet); Christlieb (bassoon) / Craft (conductor) / Odyssey 32160154

In the orders and disciplines of most of today's advanced music, rhythms have been unshackled to a point where they almost cease to have specified shapes and lack a relationship to mensural binary and ternary divisions. In *Zeitmasze* (or Zeitmasse) Stockhausen goes still another step forward and splinters tempo.

Traditionally (and this includes the disparate styles of such twentieth-century composers as Bartók, Schoenberg, Stravinsky, and Varèse) tempo has been a basic premise; whether the unit speed increases or decreases, a relationship is apparent and is defined by a central pulse rate, regardless of multitudinous shifts. *Zeitmasze* (which means "Tempi" or freely "Time Measures") is like no other musical composition in its disordered tempo and abrogation of metric continuity. It contrasts and combines metronomically set speeds

Chamber Music

with those that are slowed down or made faster according to the performer's will. It juxtaposes tempi of different ratios (not precisely polyrhythmic since nothing is rigidly fixed); it makes tempo unrest the prime sensation.

The patterns within the music follow this disintegrative range, and for the most part they consist of values disassociated from any fundamental time phase. These designs parallel the lack of tempo cohesion and consist of fragmentary and/or super-cadenza whirlwind notes. Dynamics follow suit in their agile shifts. In some twelve minutes Stockhausen creates a species of musical atomization. He proves his statement that time is experienced most when all sense of time is lost.

No argument about this recording. It takes super-virtuosic and dedicated performers to grasp and make clear the point of such music as *Zeitmasze*. Comparison with the old Véga disc (30–139), conducted by Boulez, shows Craft's edition more pointed, more declarative, and far ahead in terms of sonic qualities. Other editions of the work have appeared on Philips 6500261 and Deutsche Grammophon 2530443.

Vocal

Voice and Orchestra

Three Songs for Alto Voice and Chamber Orchestra (1950)

☐ Southwest German Radio Symphony Orchestra / Anderson (alto) / Stockhausen (conductor) / Deutsche Grammophon 2530827

These songs illustrate Stockhausen's compositional manner at the age of twenty-two. The tabulation is of expressionistic detail and far from the expected hit-and-miss efforts of a young composer. Texts are by Baudelaire (translated in German for the first song [*Der Rebell*]) and by Stockhausen for the other two, titled (significantly) *Frei* and *Der Saitenmann*. The scoring is for a chamber-orchestra group consisting of flute, two clarinets (in E flat and A), bassoon, trumpet (in C and also in D), trombone, percussion, xylophone, piano, harpsichord, and strings.

Choral

Chorus and Orchestra

Momente for Soprano, 4 Choral Groups, and 13 Instrumentalists (1965 Version)

☐ Members of the Symphony Orchestra and Chorus of Radio Cologne / Arroyo (soprano); Aloys Kontarsky (Hammond organ); Alfons Kontarsky (Lowrey organ) / Stockhausen (conductor) / Nonesuch 71157

Each performance of *Momente* (composed between 1961 and 1964) is different. Though one immediately thinks of aleatoric artificialities, there are none. *Momente* is married to its fantastically involved yet precise notation, and intrinsic improvisation per se doesn't exist. The fully free ordering of the material does, but this is a different matter. Accordingly, the opus exists in a so-called "Palermo" version, in a "Cologne" edition (of 80-minute duration), in a "Buffalo" (N.Y.) setting, and, in this recording, a solution made for a set of four performances given on a European tour and known as the "Donaueschingen" version. There is also a "Europa" version (also known as the "Bonn" version) of 90-minute length for which Stockhausen composed additional music between 1969 and 1972.

All this is explained by the fact that *Momente* is conceived in an open form, so that no determined ending or order of the data exists. Each performance has its own decisive program. *Momente* is a conception of constant renewal, expressing in a way dissent while it confirms.

Here, *Momente* is some 57 minutes (catalogue listings of the work indicate a 61-minute duration) of snippets, snatches, sensations, signals, silences, sonic spills, and splashes merged into a series of free associations. Presumably, its merger of monody, heterophony, homophonic and polyphonic circumstances, joined and opposed, sometimes of no identifiable style, other times of a mingling of impressionistic and expressionistic format, results in neutralism. But the lack of a central point paradoxically defines *its* central point.

The soprano soloist plays a very important role in this fragmented musical bibliography. Martina Arroyo deserves star rating for her contribution. As for the recording itself, shortly after its release, Stockhausen wrote to the *New York Times,* complaining that the mastering was poor, balances were wrong, etcetera. I disagree with him, since he has stated that the major point of *Momente* is that one never knows what is to happen next. What value then his argument that there must be a *specific* balance, a *correct* presentation? In *Momente* such considerations do not exist. Whatever the outcome, it is justified.

(This Nonesuch release is a duplicate of the Wergo 60024 issue.)

Bird of Passage

☐ Markus Stockhausen (trumpet, electric trumpet, and flügelhorn); Bojé (electronium); Kontarsky (piano); Miller (trumpet); Karlheinz Stockhausen (chromatic rin, lotus flute, Indian bells, bird whistle, and voice) / Chrysalis CHR-1110

Electronic Music

Instrumental and electronic sounds are mixed here, with some of the latter's techniques applied to the former. Lots of sound snippets as well as trumpet and piano fragments, fractured speech, and improvisation are heard. The title is well-chosen, with the music's analogy to migratory birds first traveling as a group and then dispersing individually.

(The labeling is in error. Side 1 of the release represents *Bird of Passage.*)

Ceylon (1970)

☐ Bojé (electronium); Eötvös (camel bells, triangles, and synthesizer); Kontarsky (modulated piano); Krist (tam tam); Stockhausen (Kandy drum); Souster (sound projection) / Chrysalis CHR-1110

This is Stockhausen's creative response after watching a ceremony in a Hindu temple. Particularly potent are the rhythmic designs; bell-like sounds are also paramount in the piece. These, insistent and consistent for almost twenty-three minutes, produce a mesmerizing effect.

(The labeling has been reversed. *Ceylon* is heard on side 2 of the disc.)

Gesang der Jünglinge (1956)

☐ Deutsche Grammophon 138811

There is a tremendous tension in the "Song of the Youths," which combines the voice of a young boy with the electronic vocabulary. The voice also undergoes tape arrangement–disarrangement; the fragmentation produces startling effects. Stockhausen's expressive assortment includes intelligible words, making a sort of sweetness jell with the very opposite.

Originally, the work was a monophonic release (a ten-inch disc released by Deutsche Grammophon, number 16133). This was an extremely poor representation, since sonic separation is fundamental to the composition's structure. Complete kaleidoscopic mobility is present in the recording noted above.

Hymnen (1967)

☐ Deutsche Grammophon 2707039

Stockhausen's "Anthems" combine electronic and natural (*musique concrète)* sounds. The transformation of national anthems into surrealistic dislocated snips that are further fragmented is basic to the work. When one begins to recognize an anthem melody it vanishes into a disintegrated mass of other sounds. However, it must be realized that the patriotic hymns are sound sources for negotiation not for quotation.

In *Hymnen* Stockhausen comes as close to the work of John Cage as possible through the use of fractioned short-wave broadcasts, shouts, yells, wheezes, screams, Morse code, speech segments, and so on, all swimming and colliding in the sonorous bath that is filtered, ring-modulated, reverberated, and so on.

Hymnen lasts almost two hours, the length required for all the fuss and flurries, flutters and fidgets packed into its contents. (Two other versions followed this electronic tape conception. The first one, completed in 1967, is *Hymnen mit Solisten.* It likewise has a two-hour duration and it links electronic and *concrète* music with soloists. In 1969 Stockhausen composed a 38-minute work, *Hymnen with Orchestra,* combining electronic and *concrète* music with an orchestra of variable total, but always including winds, brass, and stringed instruments.)

Kontakte (1960)

☐ Deutsche Grammophon 138811

One hears no themes, no countersubjects, no harmonies, no heterophony in this music that runs well over a half hour. (Some astute listeners will recognize hocket technique, however.) In place, one hears recoil from sonic impulse, approach and recession, patterns of attraction and repulsion, an ingress and egress of sound objects.

Listening to *Kontakte* one understands the meaning of weightlessness sound. There are other discoveries: the violent braking of speed (in the terminal portion of part 1) accompanied by a descent into the electronic bowels of the apparatus used is "climax" as never before experienced. The initial division is broad and dramatic. The twice-as-long second portion is the equivalent of a Scherzo, fundamentally proposing snapped dabs of sound, giving a sense of suspense that is ultimately unresolved as the composition terminates in the most finite type of decrescendo.

Only the length raises a problem. *Kontakte* will crumple and corrugate many an ear, but the shirring and smocking would be almost eliminated if the piece were cut in half. Regardless, the evidence is boldly clear. With his *Kontakte* Stockhausen has jumped the field with his colossal knowledge of electronic techniques. The recording is a four-star realization.

This recorded version embraces totally electronic sounds. Another setting is for electronic materials, piano, and percussion, strongly favoring the last timbre class. The percussionist plays some three-dozen instruments (including such rarities as a hanging rattle of suspended bamboo claves and a suspended bongo containing a handful of dried beans which is also used as a rattle), both the percussionist and the pianist play a large tam tam and a gong, and the pianist is also called on to perform on fourteen different percussion types. This electronic-instrumental version has been recorded on Wergo 60009 (by Tudor, Caskel, and Stockhausen) and on Candide 31022 (by Aloys Kontarsky, Caskel, and Stockhausen).

Kurzwellen (1968)

☐ Fritsch (electric viola and short-wave radio); Aloys Kontarsky (piano and short-wave radio); Alings and Gehlhaar (tam tam and short-wave radio); Bojé (electronium and short-wave radio); Stockhausen (filters and potentiometers) / Deutsche Grammophon 2707045
☐ Negative Band / Finnadar 9009

"Short Wave" is improvisational music guided by traffic controls fet by the composer. The musical material evolves mainly from the performers' reactions to sounds heard on short-wave radios which form part of the score. The *Kurzwellen* data are imitated, modulated, temporally transposed, made shorter or longer, are rhythmically articulated, pitched differently, and dynamically shifted. These are all intertwined with various ensemble textures and individual segments. It is impossible, in view of the composer's precise blueprint, to argue a lack of formal cohesion. Though the three performances noted above (two listings but three presentations, as will be explained) are totally different (time-wise, content-wise, and in one instance employing different instruments in part), each one displays unity. It is far from simplistic and not immediately apparent, but potent shape and structural strength are accomplished facts.

The D.G. release covers two performances made almost a year apart. One has been selected from three different recordings made in Bremen, the other from a variety of four recordings produced in Cologne. The timings are, respectively, 47 and 53½ minutes. Finnadar's disc is considerably shorter (36:40) and the instrumentation used substitutes an alto saxophone for the electric viola and a synthesizer for the electronium. Naturally, the radio content is totally dissimilar in all instances.

Since the performances give diverse solutions it is possible to consider the recordings of Stockhausen's *Kurzwellen* as practically covering three individual pieces. Budget-conscious buyers will have to toss a coin, perhaps. However, the D.G. release makes the purchaser captive to two presentations in one (four-side) album, neither setting being available separately. Finnadar's release has the advantage of including another Stockhausen opus, *Set Sail for the Sun* (*see below*). On the other hand, the Stockhausen ensemble has the edge in the way the performers' creativity is manifested.

Mikrophonie I for Tam Tam, Two Microphones, Two Filters, and Potentiometers (1964)

☐ Aloys Kontarsky and Alings (tam tams); Fritsch and Bojé (microphones); Stockhausen, Davies, and Spek (filters and potentiometers) / Columbia MS-7355

Electronic technical virtuosity is here applied to a single source of sound, a large tam tam. Vibrations are picked up by directional microphones, the distance between the instrument and the microphone being an important factor since it influences pitch and timbre, etcetera. Innumerable changes pertain to the involved scheme requiring six performers (a seventh performer assists in this recording), producing a spectrum of effect from an instrument that by itself is only capable of static pitch.

Mikrophonie II for Choir, Hammond Organ, Four Ring Modulators, and Tape (1965)

☐ Members of the West German Radio Chorus and the Studio Choir for New Music, Cologne / Alfons Kontarsky (Hammond organ); Fritsch (timer) / Schernus (conductor) / Columbia MS-7355

Mikrophonie II details a synthesis of voices (six sopranos and six basses) with electronic device plus manipulation of the Hammond organ to the extent that it never sounds like one. The interplay and controls provide an artistic transformation that paradoxically is derived from distortion. One may not accept Stockhausen's sounds fully, but at the same time one cannot deny the technical passion and invention of the piece.

Opus 1970 (1969)

☐ Aloys Kontarsky (piano); Fritsch (electric viola); Bojé (electronium); Gehlhaar (tam tam); Stockhausen (sound direction) / Deutsche Grammophon 139461

Stockhausen's *Opus 1970* follows the same technical procedures of his *Kurzwellen* (*see above*), using processed Beethoven material in place of short-wave radio data to trigger the performance. For that reason the composition is also known as *Kurzwellen mit Beethoven (Opus 1970)*. (Deutsche Grammophon's record-label title of "Stockhausen-Beethoven–op. 1970" is absolutely incorrect. However, D.G. does use the correct heading *Opus 1970* on the album cover and in the liner copy.)

The heading *Opus 1970* does not mean Stockhausen has produced that many compositions. Seemingly, it indicates the date of composition. But the truth is stretched a bit (presumably to serve as a homage to Beethoven on his two-hundredth birthday), since *Opus 1970* was composed in 1969 and recorded in mid-December of 1969.

In *Opus 1970* each performer has at his disposal a tape of Beethoven fragments which Stockhausen has transformed, montaged, and electronically treated to sound like short-wave transmissions. The players each have a volume control for the tape and use the Beethoven material as they wish, improvising on, around, and against it. In a sense, therefore, Stockhausen becomes confirmed by negation of Beethoven. This is not hearing Beethoven with new ears since Beethoven's material has already been so reprocessed as to be almost unrecognizable. It is a means of musical salivation for the performers to get on with whatever they wish.

If one is sympathetic to Stockhausen, this work is somewhat stimulating. Beethoven lovers will find it revolting. Neutral listeners will find it an interesting improvisation.

Prozession for Tam Tam, Viola, Electronium, Piano, Two Microphones, Two Filters, and Potentiometers (1967)

☐ Alings and Gehlhaar (tam tams); Fritsch (viola); Bojé (electronium); Aloys Kontarsky (piano); Stockhausen (filters and potentiometers) / Candide 31001

The march through this very long work (forty-nine minutes) is based on collective variational improvisation of items drawn from Stockhausen's earlier pieces through a rather elaborate set of instructions. How far this give-and-take can extend can be realized by comparing the time of this recorded live performance to the minimum dictated by the composer (twenty-three minutes). Performing enjoyment, if not dedication, is apparent.

Practically everything is electrified in the instrumentation: the tam tams with the use of a moving microphone, the viola with a contact mike. The microphones, in turn, are connected to electric filters and potentiometers, operated in this case by Stockhausen.

Set Sail for the Sun (1968)

☐ Negative Band / Finnadar 9009

Though nowhere mentioned in this recording, *Setz die Segel zur Sonne* is from Stockhausen's *Aus den sieben Tagen* ("From the Seven Days"). This cycle consists of fifteen parts, conceived in May 1968, including such pieces as *Es* ("It"), *Aufwärts* ("Upwards"), *Intensität* ("Intensity"), and *Kommunion* ("Communion").

"Pieces" yes, but they are not derived from musical notation but from texts that direct the players to make intuitive responses to one another—to listen to the "individual vibrations" of their sounds and to bring them into "complete harmony."

Such communally made music demands, if it is to be successful, a partnership sensitivity between the performers similar to any improvisatory ensemble. In Stockhausen's "Set Sail" the reactions to the text deal with isolated long sounds and a husbandry of every detail. The "harmony" (of thought, not of construction) can be taken for granted; the characteristic response by the listener depends on how he is "tuned in" to Stockhausen's improvisatory ritual.

Telemusik (1966)
☐ Deutsche Grammophon 643546

Blending, technically termed "intermodulation," is fundamental to *Telemusik*. It is a mixture, of course, but not the blatant system that pertains to collage. (The basic plan of the work consists of a succession of thirty-two short sections.) Japanese temple instruments (wood blocks, temple block, and bell types), and folk music extracts divested of shape and exactness are included in Stockhausen's refiguration. Still, a pertinent quality remains that reflects (in electronic emollience) the African, Balinese, Asian, and other native musics incorporated.

Sigismund Stojowski (1869-1946)

Valse (*Danse humoresque*), Op. 12, No. 2 *Instrumental*
☐ Levitzki (piano) / Klavier 116 *Piano*

A Viennese awareness is evident in this Polish pianist–composer's work. It's all waltz with a lilt that covers the "Humoresque" of the parenthetical title. The work is strikingly styled by the virtuoso Mischa Levitzki, who studied with the composer.

Leopold Stokowski. *See J. S. Bach* / Leopold Stokowski.

Thomas Stoltzer (ca. 1475-1526)

Four Pieces from *Octo Tonorum Melodiae* *Brass Ensemble*
☐ Brass Ensemble / Masson (conductor) / Nonesuch 71111

Pieces in motet style that cover, in turn, the Dorian, Hypodorian, Mixolydian, and Phrygian modes. All are simply stately statements and nicely negotiated in performance.

Gottfried Heinrich Stölzel (1690-1749)

Concerto in D major for Six Trumpets, Winds, Strings, and Harpsichord *Orchestra*
☐ Chamber Orchestra of Versailles / Delmotte (trumpet); Daraux (oboe); Chirat (harpsichord) / Wahl (conductor) / Nonesuch 71017E (monaural)

This performance is assuredly to be placed in the first slot in comparison with the competitive edition on Turnabout (34090) (also available in a five-record anthology Turnabout covers on its number 34295/9). Despite the monaural recording, electronically hyped "for stereo effect," the sound on Nonesuch is better than the basic stereo offering of Turnabout's edition. More important is the rhythmic drive, and the on-center stylistic projection of Wahl's musicians compared to the just-another-performance effect produced by the Württembergians conducted by Jörg Faerber.

Nonesuch opts to call this a "Concerto Grosso." Let it pass, for at least that's the style. Further, the Nonesuch heading includes the other instruments involved. (These include flutes, oboes, bassoon, as well as timpani.) Turnabout blithely and erratically terms the work a Concerto "for Six Trumpets and String Orchestra."

Alan Stout   (1932-   )

Chamber Music

Cello Sonata (1966)

☐ Sopkin (cello); Basile (piano) / Composers Recordings S-234

In CRI's unsigned liner note Stout's work is described as "eclectic and synthetic, in that it draws on a wide variety of musical potentials." Whatever the source or sources Stout used, his Sonata can be categorized as rhapsodic expressionism set in firm formal growth. It is a closely knit piece of music, sometimes variational in its continuity. The gestures are big ones—serious ones since Stout does not give any attention to mere jingling and decorative pattern-making in his work.

The Sonata is well played; the recorded sound is only fair.

Choral

Chorus with Accompaniment

The Great Day of the Lord, Op. 28a

☐ Mid-America Chorale / Smith (organ) / Dexter (conductor) / Composer Recordings 191 (monaural)

In his Opus 28a Stout has produced an engaging and ravishing piece in neo-medieval style. The music is based on a prophetic text in the Old Testament Book of Zephaniah. Superfine performance.

Alessandro Stradella   (1644-1682)

Orchestra

Sonata a Quattro in D major for Double Orchestra

☐ Fernandez and Carles (violins); Fonteny (cello); Beckensteiner (harpsichord); Tarr and Eichhorn (cornetti); Schmitt (trombone); Alain (organ) / Paillard (conductor) / Musical Heritage Society MHS-922

The title is not certified by the number of playing forces. The *concertino* consists of two violins and bass, the latter stated by a cello and harpsichord; the *concerto grosso* matches this with two cornetti and bass, this time the bass represented by a trombone and organ.

Thus there is only an octet, but "orchestra" it is because of the soli-ripieni tactics. The message couldn't be pithier: three movements (Allegro, Andante and Presto) delivered in a bit over two and one-quarter minutes! The playing is splendidly accomplished.

String Orchestra

Concerto Grosso in D major (Sonata di Viole)

☐ Jean-François Paillard Chamber Orchestra / Fernandez and Carles (violins); Fonteny (cello); Schmitt (trombone); Beckensteiner (organ) / Paillard (conductor) / Musical Heritage Society MHS-922

Two violins and a cello form the *concertino*, the *concerto grosso* has the contino support of a trombone, an organ, and a lute. (On this disc of assorted Stradella works two lute players are indicated but which one is playing in several of the works is not identified.)

A vivid conception, heard in a well-defined manner.

Sinfonia avanti il Damone in G minor

☐ Jean-François Paillard Chamber Orchestra / Fernandez and Carles (violins); Fonteny (cello) / Paillard (conductor) / Musical Heritage Society MHS-922

Stradella was a master in subtly commanding his instrumentation. Here the two violins and cello do not appear as soli (*concertino*) until the second movement fugue (in *allegro* tempo), thereby both texturally solidifying the majestic first movement and setting up contrast to the polyphonic division that follows. The *ripieni* strings are supported by an organ. (Two organists are listed in the personnel for the disc on which this work [as one of seven] is heard. Individual credit cannot be given in this case, therefore. To detail all the facts, the organists' names are Olivier Alain and Anne-Marie Beckensteiner.)

Sinfonia in A minor

☐ Jean-François Paillard Chamber Orchestra / Beckensteiner (harpsichord) / Paillard (conductor) / Musical Heritage Society MHS-922

Paillard directs a rich and distinguished performance, with the final fugue the featured special of the three movements. The work is for strings, lute, and harpsichord. The liner credits indicate two lute players (Michael Schaeffer and Kristian Gerwig) but no indication is given as to which person participated in the recording.

Sinfonia avanti il Barcheggio in D major

☐ Jean-François Paillard Chamber Orchestra / Tarr (trumpet); Schmitt (trombone); Beckensteiner (harpsichord) / Paillard (conductor) / Musical Heritage Society MHS-922

Despite the "Sinfonia" title the dominance of the trumpet properly places this work in the solo instrument–orchestra category. In addition to the string orchestra and harpsichord, a solid assist comes from the full bass quality of the trombone.

One hears deft playing by Edward Tarr even though the dynamic level is rather constant due to the concentrated register used for the brass instrument.

Solo Instrument and Orchestra

Trumpet

Sonata in D major (Sonata a Otto Viole con Una Tromba)

☐ Jean-François Paillard Chamber Orchestra / Tarr (trumpet) / Paillard (conductor) / Musical Heritage Society MHS-922

The trumpet is supported by a double string orchestra and continuo. The latter consists of celli, double bass, baroque trombone, harpsichord, organ, and two lutes.

Artistic intelligence and performance order enhance this work's recording. Handsome playing by Edward Tarr.

Symphonia in F minor for Two Violins, Cello, and Lute

☐ Fernandez and Carles (violins); Fonteny (cello) / Musical Heritage Society MHS-922

Chamber Music

The cello and lute constitute the continuo (specific identification of the lutenist is not made so that credit is not listed above). The syncopative twists in the final movement are a perfect delight as is the surprise of the concluding cadence. High-level playing.

Joep Straesser   (1934-   )

Orchestra

22 Pages (1965)

☐ Radio Philharmonic Orchestra / Bakker, van den Brink, and Kalkman (voices) / Maderna (conductor) / Donemus Audio-Visual Series DAVS–6702

Straesser terms this an orchestral work, though it incorporates three male voices into the structure. A John Cage text is mostly spoken (but not in straightforward narration at all), sometimes whispered, occasionally sung. Glides of the voice occur often. All of it bears a strong affinity with Cagian style in view of the shuffling details. So does the orchestration.

Direct, verbal intelligibility is not the purpose, according to the composer. However, there is a strong relationship between the words and the orchestral sounds, in a sort of avant-gardish mickey-mousing.

Conducting a work as difficult as this offers no royal road. For Bruno Maderna, however, no score remained unconquered.

Choral

Chorus Alone

Herfst der Muziek

☐ NCRV Vocal Ensemble / Voorberg (conductor) / Donemus Audio-Visual Series 6903

There is a smidgen of singing in parts 4 and 5 of this novel piece, otherwise the score uses speaking soli, speaking chorus focused vertically and horizontally, with whispers, swoops, isolation of vowels and consonants, and other effects. The compositional objective is the timbre of the words rather than sonorous translation to emphasize their semantic meaning. Straesser's "Autumn of Music" retains its novelty despite remembrances of Ernst Toch's and Carlos Chávez's work in the medium and despite its mickey-mousing sounds to equate "flowers tinkle," "fires go hoarse," and "humming eyes."

It is no easy task to present music of this specialness. The score accompanies the disc so a precise check can be made if desired. The report is: perfectly superb.

Willard Straight   (1930-   )

Orchestra

Development for Orchestra (1961)

☐ London Philharmonic Orchestra / Stanger (conductor) / Composers Recordings S–221

In variation form stylistic inconsistency paradoxically makes for consistency since fluid permutations shed varying lights on the base material. For Straight's *Development* read "Variations," whereby the content is nourished by changes portrayed cleanly and clearly.

Newton Strandberg   (20th cent.)

String Orchestra

The Sea of Tranquility (1969)

☐ Springfield Symphony Orchestra / Gutter (conductor) / Opus One 21

Strandberg's work calls for two string orchestras and a piano requiring three players. The piano is played on the keyboard, within the instrument, and outside (such as percussing inside the casing and underneath the soundboard). The strings undergo the extremes of color: col legno types, playing behind the bridge, striking the instrument, harmonics, pizzicati, and vibrati varieties, etcetera.

All these extra-special means create color intensity and color motility. There are no themes, harmonies, counterpoints in a pitch-arrangement sense—the work is guided by timbre disposition and arrangement. It is the incorruptible formation of sonorities that counts here.

Gerald Strang (1908-   )

Percussion Music (1935)

Percussion

☐ Price, Colgrass, and Smith (percussion) / Orion 7276

This work consists of three contrasting movements, each in ternary form. Strang, once an assistant to Arnold Schoenberg, writes in nonexperimental fashion in this case, using all standard instruments. (The recording was originally a Period release.)

Concerto for Cello with Woodwinds and Piano (1951)

Solo Instrument and Orchestra

☐ Rejto (cello); Wade (flute); Benno (oboe); Neufeld (clarinet); Christlieb (bassoon) / Strang (conductor) / Composers Recordings S–215

Cello

The serial faith is maintained here, but the textural and rhythmic matters create a musical hairshirt. O.K., one understands. In twelve-tone music of this type the technique becomes the total structure; form is not cut away from technique, the form *is* the technique.

One assumes this is an adequate performance since the composer is conducting. (Though all the winds are given name credits, there is none for the pianist.)

Allen Strange (1943-   )

Two X Two

Electronic Music

☐ Capra 1201

This is a two-movement opus: *Revolution of the Viaducts* and *Serpentine Paths*. There's a spillover from the first piece, which has water sounds, to the second one, which has rainlike qualities. Likewise, there's carry-over from traditional style, with plenty of ostinati and pedal points.

Eduard Strauss (1835-1916)

Bahn Frei, Op. 45

Orchestra

Ohne Aufenthalt, Op. 112

☐ Johann Strauss Orchestra of Vienna / Boskovsky (conductor) / Angel S–36887

These two polkas zip along to confirm their titles: "Open Track" and "Non Stop." Checking very old discs that included *Bahn Frei* (by Leinsdorf and Fiedler), I found these Boskovsky performances to be superior: perfect sense of cadence with perceptive style and rich sound.

Franz Strauss (1822-1905)

Concerto in C minor for Horn and Orchestra, Op. 8

☐ London Symphony Orchestra / Tuckwell (horn) / Kertész (conductor) / London 6519

This horn Concerto by Richard Strauss's father has, as is to be expected, romantic turns, but these are of an unpugnacious nature. It is music of another time and holds the greatest interest for its hornistic colors and opportunities as well as its historical relationship to the famous Strauss.

The performance by Barry Tuckwell is smooth as silk and why not? The accompaniment by István Kertész is perfect, and again, why not? The only recorded performance on the books meets every requirement one wants.

Johann Strauss, Jr. (1825-1899)

Acceleration Waltz, Op. 234

☐ Vienna Philharmonic Orchestra / Boskovsky (conductor) / London 6731

Accelerationen is one of the great Strauss waltzes. This is a nicely spirited performance and has cogently paced speed increases where required.

Annen Polka, Op. 117

☐ Vienna Philharmonic Orchestra / Böhm (conductor) / Deutsche Grammophon 2530316

The élan of Boskovsky's performance (on London 6731) is fine, but Böhm's is still to be preferred, simply because of more solidity without top-heaviness.

Artist's Life Waltz, Op. 316

☐ Vienna Symphony Orchestra / Sawallisch (conductor) / Philips 6500303

Velvet suavity and irresistible sweep mark this performance. In the louder spots of *Künstlerleben* Sawallisch never permits the music to become brashly brass-bandy, as though it were played on a parade ground. This is the way to hear a Strauss waltz.

At Our House Waltz

☐ Eduard Strauss and His Orchestra / Eduard Strauss (conductor) / Vox VSPS–7/5

Though *Grove's Dictionary of Music and Musicians* lists 168 waltz titles for Strauss, this one is not included (its German title is *Bei uns z'Haus,* according to the label identification). Since it is completely unknown and since Vox's liner note is only one of general discussion, no immediate information is available. It is a fair enough product played competently. (Strauss's organization is also designated as Eduard Strauss and His Symphonic Orchestra.)

Auf der Jagd Polka, Op. 373

☐ Johann Strauss Orchestra of Vienna / Boskovsky (conductor) / Angel S–36887

Another Willi Boskovsky special. Don't be put off by the orchestra's designation. Whatever group this is in disguise, it's damn good and they play as expertly as any of the top Viennese teams.

Banditen-Galopp **Polka**

☐ Philharmonia Hungarica / Eduard Strauss (conductor) / Turnabout 34328

This is also available in a five-record compilation of Johann and Josef Strauss music conducted also by Eduard Strauss in a Vox package (VSPS-7/5). Probably the same orchestra is involved, though Vox terms it as "Eduard Strauss and His Symphonic Orchestra."

Bitte Schön **Polka, Op. 372**

☐ Vienna Philharmonic Orchestra / Boskovsky (conductor) / London 6731

Indeed, "thank you" for a sparkling rendition, which is to be expected from this masterful conductor of Viennese dance music.

Blue Danube Waltz, Op. 314

☐ Vienna Symphony Orchestra / Sawallisch (conductor) / Philips 6500303

(Strauss's famous waltz is listed in this alphabetical order because of its usual identification by the title noted. However, rightfully it belongs under letter "O" since its German heading *An der schönen blauen Donau* is correctly translated as "On the Beautiful Blue Danube.")

A more beautiful performance cannot be found. The sensitivity of phrasing, the italicizing of inner detail, the stress of certain accompanimental figures register waltz poetry at its very finest. There are dozens of "Blue Danube" recordings, but none have the blended persuasiveness of the Wolfgang Sawallisch entry in the catalogue.

Cagliostro in Vienna—**Overture**
Cagliostro **Waltzes, Op. 370**
Das Spitzentuch der Königin—**Overture**

☐ Eduard Strauss and His Symphonic Orchestra / Eduard Strauss (conductor) / Vox VSPS-7/5

The first and the third work listed are operetta overtures (Strauss wrote sixteen operettas in all); the better-known waltzes were taken from the *Cagliostro in Vienna* score and given its own opus identification.

Both the waltzes and the second-listed overture can also be found in an album, "The Unknown Johann Strauss" (Turnabout 34328), with the same conductor but with a different name assigned to the orchestra.

Demolierer **Polka**

☐ Vienna State Opera Orchestra / Paulik (conductor) / Vanguard S-205

Blithe music. Translucent performance.

Die Fledermaus—**Polka**

☐ Boston Pops Orchestra / Fiedler (conductor) / Quintessence PMC-7015 (monaural)

The polka is one of the many dance pieces that are sprinkled in the sparkling score of Strauss's famous comic opera. Fiedler's response to its rhythmic piquancy is ideal.

Die Fledermaus—**Waltz**

☐ André Kostelanetz and His Orchestra / Kostelanetz (conductor) / Columbia CS-8162

A crisp and rewarding performance. Kostelanetz understood Johann Strauss style to the tip of his baton and this recording is proof.

Egyptian March
Electrophor **Polka**

☐ Eduard Strauss and His Orchestra / Eduard Strauss (conductor) / Vox VSPS-7/5

Two rarities. There's plenty of juice in the *Electrophor* Polka, which is a fast polka type.

The march is without Viennese swing, but has a pre-Hollywood tempered type of simulation that makes clear the locale being pictured. It has a surprise in the middle, where part of the orchestra sings along enthusiastically. Enthusiastic also describes the performances. (A duplicate of the *Electrophor* Polka is available in a one-record release by Turnabout on number 34328. The two works discussed are contained in a five-record set.)

Eljen a Magyar **Polka, Op. 332**

☐ Berlin Radio Symphony Orchestra / Fricsay (conductor) / Deutsche Grammophon Privilege 2535134

This piece was dedicated to the Hungarian nation (in 1869) and accordingly has some "Zingarese" in the zing and zip of the music. The performance is tops. It leaves far behind the representation conducted by Eduard Strauss, contained in a Vox jumbo album (VSPS-7/5).

Emperor Waltz, Op. 437

☐ Philadelphia Orchestra / Ormandy (conductor) / Columbia MS-6217

The "Emperor" (Strauss's *Kaiserwalzer*) not only has $\frac{3}{4}$ pace but also a certain amount of nobility that is beautifully set forth under Ormandy's direction. A sense of symphonicism rather than the usual waltzdom pervades the playing.

Ormandy's performance is duplicated on Columbia MS-7502 and in a three-disc release termed *The Blue Danube*, also on Columbia, in their D3S-789.

Explosions **Polka, Op. 43**

☐ Vienna Philharmonic / Boskovsky (conductor) / London 6791

Added explosive sounds at the terminal points of this two-minute musical ebullition are from London's sound effects division. Not Strauss but no harm. The thundery detonations are from the bass drum and are authentic. A great piece, brightly played and reproduced.

Fairy Tales from the Orient Waltz, Op. 444

☐ Boston Pops Orchestra / Fiedler (conductor) / Deutsche Grammophon 2584008

Totally unknown in comparison to the other famous "Tales" (from the Vienna Woods), these tales nevertheless have plenty of thrust in their tunes. Fiedler's pace for *Märchen aus dem Orient* is rather fast but it fits the music quite well.

This is a delightful work. How it has escaped attention one knows not.

Franz Josef I—Jubel Marsch, **Op. 126**

☐ Vienna Philharmonic / Boskovsky (conductor) / London 6641

This is also known as the *Rettungs-Jubelmarsch*. It couldn't be played better.

Freikugeln Polka, Op. 326

☐ Vienna Philharmonic / Boskovsky (conductor) / London 6731

Zestful playing of a punchy polka.

Freucht euch des Lebens Waltz, Op. 340

☐ Vienna State Opera Orchestra / Paulik (conductor) / Vanguard S–205

A gentility makes this set poetic rather than gay and frothy, though there's sufficient triple-beat insistence within the lyricism. Paulik's performance is warm, attractive, and styled to fit Strauss's opus. Certainly, *Freucht euch* is worthy of standing next to the "Blue Danube," the "Emperor," and Strauss's other best-seller waltzes.

Gross-Wein Waltz, Op. 440

☐ Eduard Strauss and His Symphonic Orchestra / Eduard Strauss (conductor) / Vox VSPS–7/5

This is a standard-format waltz, but Johann Strauss buffs can still enjoy this unhackneyed waltz, which is attractively played.

The Gypsy Baron—Entrance March

☐ Vienna Festival Orchestra / Krips (conductor) / Vanguard S–268

A bright realization marks the excerpt from *Der Zigeunerbaron*. The stops are out for this one but there is no brashness.

The Gypsy Baron—Waltz

☐ André Kostelanetz and His Orchestra / Kostelanetz (conductor) / Columbia CS–8162

All the warmth needed, all the lilt required.

Im Krapfenwald'l Polka, Op. 336

☐ Boston Pops Orchestra / Fiedler (conductor) / Deutsche Grammophon 2584008

This is a familiar polka that Fiedler plays with stimulating color. (The D.G. album lists Strauss's work in English: "In a Viennese Park." That's certainly correct but it's difficult to recognize this work with such heading.)

In Praise of Women, Op. 315

☐ Vienna Philharmonic / Boskovsky (conductor) / London 6791

Lob der Frauen is one of some three dozen polka-mazurkas Strauss produced. It is O.K., if not a major piece in the Strauss catalogue. Of course, Boskovsky has a splendid understanding of Straussian style and shows it in his rendition.

I-Tipferl Polka

☐ Vienna Festival Orchestra / Krips (conductor) / Vanguard S–268

This is a moderately paced item from the operetta *Prinz Methusalem*. There is sufficient heartiness in the performance.

Jubilee Waltz

☐ Boston Pops Orchestra / Fiedler (conductor) / Quintessence PMC–7015 (monaural)

Indeed, this is a good waltz, but with some mystery surrounding it. The "Jubilee" is not listed in the waltz bibliography found in *Grove's Dictionary of Music and Musicians*. Further, R. Peter Munves states in the liner notes that it was titled "The New Jubilee Waltz." The work was composed in 1872 when Strauss was in the United States giving concerts. As a gesture to his host country, the "Jubilee" ends with the first eight measures of *The Star Spangled Banner*, stretched majestically into a waltz peroration. It works neatly.

Klipp-Klopp Galopp, Op. 466

☐ Vienna State Opera Orchestra / Paulik (conductor) / Vanguard S–205

Strauss extracted this dance from his operetta *Waldmeister*. Tuneful rewards, performed without any Offenbachian speed.

Lagerlust

☐ Eduard Strauss and His Orchestra / Eduard Strauss (conductor) / Vox VSPS–7/5

A moderately paced polka-mazurka. If there is any problem with the performance it pertains to the dynamics—more contrasts would be welcome.

Lagunen Waltz, Op. 411

☐ Vienna Philharmonic / Boskovsky (conductor) / London 6641

This is from the operetta *Eine Nacht in Venedig*. It is superbly styled, which means that all of the Viennese personality comes through.

Leichtes Blut Polka, Op. 319

☐ Vienna Philharmonic Orchestra / Kempe (conductor) / Seraphim SIB–6109

A truly superior example of the hundred or so polkas Strauss produced. The performance is a vivid one, with fine pace and balance.

Liebeslieder Waltz, Op. 114

☐ Eduard Strauss and His Orchestra / Eduard Strauss (conductor) / Vox VSPS–7/5

Good rhythmic élan but rather placid attention to dynamic differences.

Mephistos Höllenrufe Waltz, Op. 101

☐ Vienna Philharmonic Orchestra / Boskovsky (conductor) / London 6731

Though available in a Vox jumbo package as well as on a single disc released by Turnabout with the same orchestra and conductor, the choice is the Boskovsky performance. The stylistic pervasiveness of his conception is the proof.

Morning Papers Waltz, Op. 279

☐ Vienna Philharmonic Orchestra / Boskovsky (conductor) / London 6791

"Morgenblätter" (some recordings translate this really poorly as "Morning Leaves") is played expressively by both Boskovsky and Fiedler, but the former's more modulated tempo adds a gracefulness to most of the piece that gives him the advantage.

New Vienna Waltz, Op. 342

☐ Boston Pops Orchestra / Fiedler (conductor) / Deutsche Grammophon 2584008

This overlooked gem in the Strauss catalogue of waltzes is played with an up tempo that brightens the atmosphere and does not nullify the Viennese swing of the piece.

Nordseebilder Waltz, Op. 390

☐ Vienna Philharmonic / Boskovsky (conductor) / London 6731

A rarely heard waltz, but a true beauty. Heard once, it will be treasured. Boskovsky plays it playfully, but always maintains a distinctive pulse.

Orpheus Quadrille, Op. 236

☐ Vienna Philharmonic / Boskovsky (conductor) / London 6641

Boskovsky performs the *Orpheus* piece twice. One is in formalized, strict dance tempo, the other is in a concert format. The difference is intriguing and is as enjoyable as it is educational.

Overture to *Die Fledermaus*

☐ Vienna Festival Orchestra / Krips (conductor) / Vanguard S-268

Loads of performances and yet only this one totally satisfies. Reasons: Krips doesn't rush the fast sections, doesn't sentimentalize the lyrical portions, and, best of all, doesn't apply the *rubato* brakes that dislocate phrase contours. Still there is all the pep, suavity, and stylistic finish demanded. Above all, there is the avoidance of fussiness which turns out to be, in the long run, a pain in the ear.

Overture to *The Gypsy Baron*

☐ New York Philharmonic / Bernstein (conductor) / Columbia M-34125

Bernstein's full understanding and response to the score is a delight. Stylistically, everything is as it should be.

He avoids overindulging in *rubato* calisthenics and provides rhythmic thrust and beautiful phrasing.

Pariser Polka

☐ Eduard Strauss and His Orchestra / Eduard Strauss (conductor) / Vox VSPS-7/5

The listing above covers a ten-record side anthology of Johann, Jr. and Josef Strauss music (43 works in all). The *Pariser* Polka is also on Turnabout 34328 (same conductor and same orchestra although the latter's name is changed).

Perpetuum Mobile, Op. 257

☐ Vienna Philharmonic Orchestra / Böhm (conductor) / Deutsche Grammophon 2530316

Böhm plays this "Perpetual Motion" superbly, intensifying the colorations of Strauss's *Musikalischer Scherz* without denying its frothiness. Böhm's version is number one on the list by far.

Persian March, Op. 289

☐ Vienna Philharmonic Orchestra / Boskovsky (conductor) / London 6791

Very colorful and decidedly apropos. Boskovsky can re-create a waltz beautifully, but he is no less masterful with music set in march meter.

Plappermäulchen **Fast Polka**
Polka Française

☐ Eduard Strauss and His Orchestra / Eduard Strauss (conductor) / Vox VSPS-7/5

Especially the first piece is worth full attention. It moves with pep and is played with fervent vitality. A special bow to the percussionist whose punctuations are a feature of the piece throughout. *Plappermäulchen* is undoubtedly one of the very best of Strauss's fast polkas, proven by E. Strauss's juicy performance.

Roses from the South **Waltz, Op. 388**

☐ Vienna Symphony Orchestra / Sawallisch (conductor) / Philips 6500303

A Viennese operetta without waltzes isn't the real thing. *Rosen aus dem Süden* is from Strauss's *Das Spitzentuch der Königin*. It represents the real thing both ways—Viennese operetta and Viennese waltz.

Sawallisch's performance is deft and warmed with attention to dynamics. At no time is it sharply athletic in its rhythmic detail—which spoils so many waltz performances. The rhythm is clear but it does not claw into the melodic fabric.

Russian March, Op. 426

☐ Vienna Philharmonic Orchestra / Boskovsky (conductor) / London 6731

Strauss's march bears a parenthetical subtitle (*Garde à Cheval*). Composed in 1887, it was dedicated to Alexander III of Russia.

Schneeglöckchen **Waltz, Op. 143**

☐ Vienna Philharmonic / Boskovsky (conductor) / London 6641

Absolutely glorious playing with the music nuanced and polished to perfection.

Secunden **Polka**

☐ Vienna State Opera Orchestra / Paulik (conductor) / Vanguard S-205

A crisp delivery of this cute example. Paulik's affection for the piece comes through vividly.

Seid umschlungen, Millionen! **Waltz, Op. 443**

☐ Eduard Strauss and His Orchestra / Eduard Strauss (conductor) / Vox VSPS-7/5

Opus 443 bears a dedication to Brahms. It is played affectionately, especially the compelling introduction.

S'gibt nur a Kaiserstadt, s'gibt nur a Wien **Polka, Op. 291**

☐ Vienna Philharmonic / Boskovsky (conductor) / London 6641

The performance sparkles. Another Strauss find played flawlessly.

Singer's Joy Polka

☐ Eduard Strauss and His Orchestra / Eduard Strauss (conductor) / Vox VSPS-7/5

This polka is only average and is only for the Strauss fan who wants everything.

So ängstlich sind wir nicht Polka, Op. 413

☐ Vienna Philharmonic / Boskovsky (conductor) / London 6641

Performed with sparkling brilliance, Opus 413 is a "fast" polka representative.

Studenten Polka, Op. 263

☐ Vienna State Opera Orchestra / Paulik (conductor) / Vanguard S-205

Strauss's Opus 263 represents a special polka, since it includes a play on the German student song *Gaudeamus Igitur*, which Brahms used in his *Academic Festival Overture*. The playing is topflight.

Sturmisch in Lieb' und Tanz, Op. 393

☐ Vienna Philharmonic Orchestra / Boskovsky (conductor) / London 6731

A polka with more decisiveness than usual. The playing is on target all the way.

Tales from the Vienna Woods Waltz, Op. 325

☐ Johann Strauss Orchestra of Vienna / Boskovsky (conductor) / Angel S-36887
☐ Boston Pops Orchestra / Karol (zither) / Fiedler (conductor) / Quintessence PMC-7015 (monaural)

This entry is a combination of tone poem and waltz set and is one of the peak works in Strauss's output. *Geschichten aus dem Wienerwald* has enjoyed numerous recordings, but many are severely cut, including the excision of the important zither solo in the introduction.

Both performances of this masterpiece are equally worthy, the Fiedler being listed in second place only because it is "electronically enhanced for stereo." It is finely played, with a colorful zest that is a delight. The Boskovsky-Johann Strauss Orchestra (probably the Vienna Philharmonic Orchestra) issue is proof of Boskovsky's magnificence with Viennese dance scores. It has perfection sounding throughout. (The zither soloist for Fiedler is Robert Karol, who otherwise plays in the viola section of the Boston Symphony Orchestra, which is also, for the greater part, the Boston Pops group. The zither soloist in Boskovsky's performance is not credited.)

A Thousand and One Nights Waltz, Op. 346

☐ Philadelphia Orchestra / Ormandy (conductor) / Columbia MS-7032

Played to the hilt by the gorgeous Philly strings, this performance has no competition. "Tausend und Eine Nacht" is also included in a larger waltz collection (Columbia D3S-789).

Thunder and Lightning—Fast Polka, Op. 324

☐ Vienna Philharmonic Orchestra / Boskovsky (conductor) / London 6791

A fast polka or galop, with plenty of percussion thunder and tempo lightning. Boskovsky is super-excellent, as usual.

Tritsch-Tratsch Polka, Op. 214

☐ Vienna Philharmonic Orchestra / Böhm (conductor) / Deutsche Grammophon 2530316

Too many conductors misread the title of this well-known Strauss piece. Pushing up the metronomic indicator, they offer a galop not a polka. Tempo excitement thereby nullifies firm rhythmic snap. Böhm's conception is ideal. The music is deftly played and yet has sufficient pace.

Vienna Blood Waltz, Op. 354

☐ New York Philharmonic / Bernstein (conductor) / Columbia MS-7288
☐ Philadelphia Orchestra / Ormandy (conductor) / Columbia MS-6217

Either issue has all a Strauss waltz should have—there is perhaps a slight touch more of lightness in the Bernstein than in the Ormandy presentation. If you want a whole flock of waltzes together with "Wiener Blut," the Ormandy version is also contained in Columbia D3S-789.

Vienna Bonbons Waltz, Op. 307

☐ Eduard Strauss and His Orchestra / Eduard Strauss (conductor) / Vox VSPS-7/5

"Wiener Bonbons" is given a lucid performance. Strauss's pick-up orchestra may not have the richness of the big name groups but he styles the material with total *echt Wiener* authority, and that's what counts.

Violetta Polka

☐ Vienna State Opera Orchestra / Paulik (conductor) / Vanguard S-205

The *Violetta* Polka is a standard Johann Strauss affair; the box score reads neither hits nor errors. Paulik is accurate and consistent in his tasteful presentation.

Voices of Spring Waltz, Op. 410

☐ Vienna Symphony Orchestra / Sawallisch (conductor) / Philips 6500303

"Frühlingsstimmen" is played here without the soprano solo which Strauss included, but which can be omitted. It is the purely orchestral form (calling for double woodwinds, four horns, two trumpets, three trombones, timpani, bass drum, snare drum, harp, and strings) that such conductors as Weingartner, Koussevitzky, Ormandy, Szell, and others have used.

Sawallisch's version flows without troubled *rubati*, and contains parallel amounts of subtlety and metrical decisiveness. More cannot be asked. Most others offer considerably less.

Waldmeister Overture

☐ Vienna Festival Orchestra / Krips (conductor) / Vanguard S-268

This is the prelude to Strauss's penultimate operetta *Der Waldmeister*. Great tunes and all the possible rewards are made available by Krips in a warm and lilting performance. The piece is just as good as the *Fledermaus* overture and has especially beautiful separate solo sections for flutes and horns, the former framed in a sensitively colored motile string counterpoint.

Wine, Women, and Song Waltz, Op. 333

☐ Vienna Symphony Orchestra / Sawallisch (conductor) / Philips 6500303
☐ Johann Strauss Orchestra of Vienna / Boskovsky (conductor) / Angel S-36887

Either one will fully satisfy. Sawallisch plays "Wein, Weib und Gesang" suavely with a tinge of symphonic fullness. There's just a bit more of a lilt in the Boskovsky performance.

You and You Waltz, Op. 367

☐ Eduard Strauss and His Orchestra / Eduard Strauss (conductor) / Vox VSPS-7/5

This is the "Du und Du" waltz from *Die Fledermaus*. A passable performance, but at least it is not disfigured with all sorts of *ritards* and *accelerandi*, poisonous items used in the name of interpretative requirements.

Die Fledermaus

Opera and Dramatic Music

☐ Vienna Symphony Orchestra and Chorus of the Vienna Volksoper / Rothenberger and Holm (sopranos); Fassbaender (mezzo-soprano); Gedda, Dallpozza, and Förster (tenors); Fischer-Dieskau and Berry (baritones) / Boskovsky (conductor) / Angel S-3790

Strauss's *Fledermaus* is great fun but it has always been subject to attempts to hype the work. In defense, it must be said that the score seems to ask for it. Some performances omit the dialogue. When given in English, vernacularisms sprout, and in the case of the Met's recording (on Odyssey Y2-32666) the effect is that of a Broadway musical with hefty helpings of corn-fed lyrics. London's production (No. 1249) conducted by von Karajan is much too heavy and overserious; in London No. 1319 (using the same performers) an assortment of effects are spliced in and eleven opera singers participate in a "Gala sequence," in the second act in cameo bits. Some recordings omit the ballet music (the Angel edition chosen also does) and some interpolate other Strauss material. And so on. One doesn't mind the standard cuts (Boskovsky makes them as well). One simply prefers a clear and clean consideration of the score. Given that, the work triumphs without special editorial ministration.

That is exactly the case with Boskovsky's performance. It has zest and swingy class, its details are set forth with a light touch, and everything on the stage and in the pit is sparked with magnificent style. Willi Boskovsky is a Strauss expert, and this presentation is further proof of that reputation.

Johann Strauss, Jr. / Ernst von Dohnányi

Treasure Waltz from The Gypsy Baron

Instrumental

Piano

☐ Dohnányi (piano) / Everest 3061

A brilliant translation. The verbiage fits perfectly, as though it had been made by Strauss himself. It is played with combined finesse and extrovertism.

Johann Strauss, Jr. / Antal Dorati (1906-   )

Graduation Ball—Ballet

Ballet

☐ Vienna Philharmonic Orchestra / Boskovsky (conductor) / London STS-15070

Thirty-four minutes of creamy Strauss music, mostly arranged from unpublished materials by Dorati for a ballet choreographed by Lichine. It stands on its orchestral feet as concert fare as well.

In music of this type, played by Viennese musicians and with the incomparable Willi Boskovsky directing them, the results cannot be excelled. Perfection of style it is. Even Dorati, directing his own compilation with the Minneapolis Symphony Orchestra, on Mercury 75014 cannot challenge it.

Johann Strauss, Jr. / Leopold Godowsky

Instrumental

Piano

Die Fledermaus—Paraphrase

☐ Pines (piano) / Genesis 1000

Though, unfortunately, most of Godowsky's arrangements and paraphrases have disappeared from concert programs, this one retains its just popularity. Pines plays this marvelous exploitation of Strauss tunes with verve and without doctrinal precision, which would be deadly.

Johann Strauss, Jr., and Josef Strauss (1827-1870)

String Orchestra

Pizzicato Polka

☐ Eduard Strauss and His Symphonic Orchestra / Eduard Strauss (conductor) / Vox VSPS–7/5

This is not to be mistaken as a transcription. It is a brotherly creative collaboration. Who did what doesn't matter, since the piece is a charmer.

By all means listen to it in its original form for plucked strings, rather than the fleshed-out full orchestra versions that are on the market (one example: Fiedler's on Quintessence PMC–7015). The clear-cut intimacy of the original setting is corrupted by such orchestrational generosity.

Johann Strauss, Sr. (1804-1849)

Orchestra

Annen Polka, Op. 137

☐ Boskovsky Ensemble / Boskovsky (conductor) / Vanguard 2096

This polka is titled in honor of Vienna's traditional Feast of St. Anne. Boskovsky's concentrated group (four strings, two winds, and two horns) brings total authenticity to the performance.

Chinese Galop, Op. 20

☐ Boston Pops Orchestra / Fiedler (conductor) / Deutsche Grammophon 2584008

Plenty of waltzes were produced, of course, by the elder Johann Strauss, but included in his output were over a dozen polkas, and more than two-dozen galops. This one is an excellent example, played as only Fiedler can do.

Furioso Galop

☐ Vienna State Opera Orchestra / Paulik (conductor) / Vanguard S-205

The *Furioso* Galop is a throw-in in an album of music by the most famous of the two Johann Strausses and by Lehár. A fast tempo fits the music if not the title.

Gitana Galopp, Op. 108

☐ Boskovsky Ensemble / Boskovsky (conductor) / Vanguard 2096

Strauss's piece is based on a gypsy melody that he deftly makes his own.

Piefke und Pufke—Polka Française, Op. 235

☐ Vienna Philharmonic / Boskovsky (conductor) / London 6791

According to Stanford Robinson, *Piefke und Pufke* are a pair of characters "such as Laurel and Hardy, Mutt and Jeff." This is just as good a choice as any other for this music, which bounces off the grooves with great spirit.

Radetzky March, Op. 228

☐ Boston Pops Orchestra / Fiedler (conductor) / Quintessence PMC-7015 (monaural)

Though an old release, Fiedler's version of this famous march stands first among the strong competition, which includes such a Strauss expert as Boskovsky (on London 2307), and such biggies as Bernstein (on Columbia M-30943), Ormandy (on Columbia MS-6474, MS-7502, and MG-32314), and von Karajan (on Deutsche Grammophon 139014). The reasons are crisp tempo, no investment in virtuoso editing, and above all a total enthusiasm which is relayed to the listener.

Seufzer Galopp, Op. 9

☐ Boskovsky Ensemble / Boskovsky (conductor) / Vanguard 2096

One can always trust Willi Boskovsky to reveal the essence of a Strauss piece. Though this work is titled a "Sighing" galop, Boskovsky makes Strauss's early opus come alive by moving it with gingery pep.

Sperl-Galopp, Op. 42

☐ Vienna Philharmonic / Boskovsky (conductor) / London 6791

The *Sperl* was a large beer-garden and dance-hall in Vienna. Twined into this perky piece is some of the "Soldiers' Dance" from Rossini's *William Tell*.

Wiener Carneval Walzer, Op. 3

☐ Orchestra of the Vienna Volksoper / Angerer (conductor) / Turnabout 34156

Two important points, one regarding contents, the other covering performance. While the elder Strauss's waltz is run-of-the-mill it has a liberal quotation from Weber's *Oberon* that adds interest. Angerer's tempo is extremely moderate throughout and a few notches higher would give more swing. A waltz it remains, if a slow one.

Hofball-Tänze, Op. 51

☐ Boskovsky Ensemble / Boskovsky (conductor) / Vanguard 2096

The "Court Ball Dances" are, as is to be expected, a set of waltzes with the usual

*String
Orchestra*

Straussian swing and scale. Use of only strings provides a type of dance chamber music; this piece is for three violins and double bass, featuring the first violin in a number of solo sections. Marvelously played.

Josef Strauss   (1827-1870)

Orchestra

Allerlei Polka

☐ Johann Strauss Orchestra of Vienna / Boskovsky (conductor) / Angel S-36956

This thoroughly appealing polka is appealingly performed.

Austrian Village Swallows Waltz, Op. 164
Delirien Waltz, Op. 212

☐ Cleveland Orchestra / Szell (conductor) / Odyssey Y-30053

If there is no bias, the *Austrian Swallows* can be considered as good as any of Johann Strauss's waltzes. Truly, Szell's way with "Dorfschwalben aus Österreich" cannot be bettered.

The same findings pertain to the *Delirien* Waltz. It is given a suave rendition with irresistible results. Opportunities for hearing these fine waltzes in the concert hall are near zero, so the recordings are quite special.

Dynamiden Waltz, Op. 173

☐ Vienna Philharmonic Orchestra / Kempe (conductor) / Seraphim SIB-6109

This waltz is not very well-known but it was known to Richard Strauss, since he used a theme from the work for one of the *Rosenkavalier* waltzes. Richard Strauss had good taste—and that's what this rendition has.

Eingesendet (Fast Polka), Op. 240

☐ Vienna Philharmonic / Boskovsky (conductor) / London 6791

Marked as a fast polka this one is really a galop. Whatever the description, it is a delectable bit of a little less than two minutes.

Frauenherz—Polka Mazur

☐ Vienna Philharmonic Orchestra / Boskovsky (conductor) / London 6731

(A "Mazur" [or "Mazurek"] is simply a type of Mazurka—the name coming from a particular Polish province.) This charming polka-mazurka is little known but certainly adds to the Straussian family credits. And credit Willi Boskovsky with a triple-A performance.

Jockey Polka

☐ Eduard Strauss and His Symphonic Orchestra / Eduard Strauss (conductor) / Vox VSPS-7/5

A fast polka type. It won't disappoint any lover of Viennese dance music. The performance is rather dynamically at one level but does not basically harm the effect.

Künstlergrüss Polka

☐ Johann Strauss Orchestra of Vienna / Boskovsky (conductor) / Angel S–36956

Another richly enjoyable polka, far from the run-of-the-mill variety. An absolutely delectable presentation.

Moulinct Polka
On Holiday Trips (Fast Polka)

☐ Eduard Strauss and His Symphonic Orchestra / Eduard Strauss (conductor) / Vox VSPS-7/5

Be warned! Neither of these pieces nor *Without Sorrows* and *Women's Heart* (*see below*) nor the Jockey Polka (*see above*) are noted on the album cover or printed index of the ten record sides included in Vox's jumbo compilation. The issue is labeled "The Immortal Music of Johann Strauss" and covers thirty-eight compositions by the younger Johann. However, only the label copy credits the five Josef Strauss items, and not too clearly at that! They are described by placing the name Josef in parentheses next to the title.

Sphärenklänge Waltz, Op. 235

☐ Vienna Philharmonic Orchestra / Kempe (conductor) / Seraphim SIB–6109

The "Music of the Spheres" is one of the very best waltzes this gifted composer produced (he also wrote poetry, painted, and patented inventions!). The Vienna Philharmonic plays superbly and with pep and panache.

Without Sorrows (Fast Polka)
Women's Heart (Polka)

☐ Eduard Strauss and His Symphonic Orchestra / Eduard Strauss (conductor) / Vox VSPS-7/5

(See note *above* under: *Moulinct* Polka.)

Richard Strauss   *(1864-1949)*

Also sprach Zarathustra, Op. 30   *Orchestra*

☐ Concertgebouw Orchestra / Krebbers (violin) / Haitink (conductor) / Philips 6500624
☐ Chicago Symphony Orchestra / Reiner (conductor) / RCA LSC–2609

Strauss's *Zarathustra* is one of the big pieces, of course, and one in which some conductors display their batonistic egos to such extent as to misrepresent the music. Truly, the title might well be changed to read *Also Sprach von Karajan* in the instance of his performances which are twisted and heavily individualized, having been thoroughly schmaltzed in the process. It need not be. Despite the sneers that are now fashionable about Strauss's musico-philosophical pretensions, the work stands well. It is a music that superbly represents turn-of-the-century romantic style. Inflation is unfair and falsifies the content.

It need not be, as can be heard in Haitink's fluid but immaculate essay. Nothing perfunctory—Haitink thinks big but he thinks musically, and every part of the nine sections is detailed and conclusive. His plotting, balances, and relationships are magnificent.

The Reiner presentation has long been famous. Perhaps it is a mite overserious here and there, but the score is so perfectly drawn in its totality that this quality does not interfere with a superior interpretation. It is a lesson in how to treat Strauss's score without blowing it up out of all proportion. (Reiner's recording was made in 1962. An earlier RCA edition was released in 1954, with the same orchestra and conductor, and can be obtained on VICS-1265.)

Dance of the Seven Veils from *Salome,* Op. 54

☐ Philadelphia Orchestra / Ormandy (conductor) / Columbia MS-6678

Though some, depending on how active their mental images are, will find more swing than sex in this realization, you can't beat those Philadelphians for sonorously taking it all off. Bernstein's performance is also an excellently conceived symphonic (soft-core) strip tease (Columbia MS-6822). Others considered are too chaste.

Dance Suite after Couperin (1923)

☐ Philharmonia Orchestra / Rodzinski (conductor) / Seraphim S-60030

This Suite consists of nine movements (the seventh and eighth are combined) based on keyboard pieces by François Couperin; the orchestration is a restrained one (only four brass, for example, and a reduced number of strings). The playing of these pieces produces elegant sound pictures and is altogether delightful.

Death and Transfiguration, Op. 24

☐ San Francisco Symphony Orchestra / Monteux (conductor) / RCA VICS-1457
☐ New Philharmonia Orchestra / Maazel (conductor) / London 21067

The control Monteux brings to this score is marvelous. No hamming-up or clamping-on—the music sings forth in a refined, passionate way, and that's sufficient to burn deep. The slush (how deucedly theatrical but how musically miserable) of Stokowski (remember?) you will not find. Monteux's is an artistically privileged Strauss statement.

This is the second time around for *Tod und Verklärung* in regard to Maazel. The first recorded entry was with the Vienna Philharmonic, and it's still on the lists on London 6415. Both editions are exceptionally fine presentations of color and depth; the newer one is slightly better because Maazel adds dignity to what previously was absolute clarity, but he shows some reticence about opening up in the peroration. Maazel's essay is a strong contender, indeed, for the choice of recorded performance for Strauss's Opus 24.

Don Juan, Op. 20

☐ Concertgebouw Orchestra / Haitink (conductor) / Philips 6500481
☐ Los Angeles Philharmonic Orchestra / Mehta (conductor) / RCA AGL1-1276

Truly a Roman holiday for a conductor. *Don Juan's* scoring is full but without fuss, boxed-in with formations (even with the linear movement) that sound rich and clear. It is simply a matter of how timbres are brought into relief (Haitink) or how forceful one desires a climax (Mehta). Both play the score with recognition of its spotlighted virtuosity, but in no instance are the performances anything less than clean and precise, combined with gorgeous sound and balances that bring out all the details. It is indeed very difficult to make an academic exercise out of this perfectly constructed score. Some have, but not those listed.

Don Quixote, Op. 35

☐ Cleveland Orchestra / Fournier (cello) / Szell (conductor) / Odyssey Y–32224

Strauss's *Don Quixote* is one of those pieces that work even when they shouldn't—it is packed with musico-cinematic doings. It needs a real musical macho Don dressed up as a solo cello voice. The performer must understand the breadth of the character being portrayed and carry it out without instrumental hamming (nobility, yes, never sentimentality). The conductor of this huge duet must both control and highlight the dramaticism that surrounds the plot. This is, after all, a heavy package of program music.

Old as it may be (a 1961 release), the Pierre Fournier and George Szell partnership fully meets these conditions. In their hands Strauss's *Don Quixote* becomes a symphonic poem of superior adventure.

Eine Alpensinfonie, Op. 64

☐ Royal Philharmonic Orchestra / Kempe (conductor) / RCA LSC–2923
☐ Bavarian State Orchestra / Strauss (conductor) / Seraphim 60006 (monaural)

It is quite easy to poke fun at this long piece stuffed with pictorial objectives—an orchestrational Baedeker of a round trip up and down a mountain in twenty-three connected sections. Strauss's work does contain programmatic blight, but it also has some magic that has not worn off. The multi-*divisi* at the beginning is of persuasive beauty (a twenty-part chord results that includes the entire span of B flat minor), the back-stage fanfare is still very effective, and the thrust of the brass in the high gamut in the "Vision" is positive.

The value of the Seraphim disc is obvious: Richard Strauss conducting Richard Strauss. It stands to reason that this reading follows the score outline and the measures pass properly. However, there are few thrills in the recording made in 1941. One has the feeling of peeping into a museum.

Kempe's version is beautifully organized, dynamically sensitive, and follows a viewpoint that can best be described as *espressivo perpetuo*. The latter is obtained without departing from the precise data included in the score. The Straussian backgrounds (string *divisi,* timbre smudging, cross doublings, textural counterpoint) can easily be overemphasized. Not with Kempe. The performance is illuminating, a fully artistic solution.

The sonics, of course, cannot be compared; RCA's dynagroove makes the earlier recording sound as though fungi were growing in the grooves. However, there remains Strauss on Strauss for historical reasons. The difference in performance time is vital. Kempe takes five minutes and ten seconds longer to cover the tour.

Ein Heldenleben, Op. 40

☐ Dresden State Orchestra / Mirring (violin) / Kempe (conductor) / Seraphim S–60315
☐ Berlin Philharmonic Orchestra / Schwalbé (violin) / von Karajan (conductor) / Angel S–37060

At this remove, arguments as to the bad taste of this composer sticking his chest out as the hero described in his document of program music, with use of self-quotations to bolster the egotistical concept, are a flimsy historical footnote. Strauss needs no apologies and *Ein Heldenleben* needs no polemics. It holds up with plenty to spare. For its autobiographic concepts it needs only perceptive characterization and no exaggeration in the form of a conductorial alter ego.

Kempe's depiction is a top achievement. The battle section is active not noisy. The picturing of the adversaries is not overdrawn and Mrs. S's moods are clearly profiled without any gooey sentimentality in the violin picturing. In all, a vivid musical exhibition.

Von Karajan avoids triggered responsive playing and produces a continuity that has civilized musicality. This avoids the type of essay that is all excitement and thereupon misses the subtle fires that light up Strauss's score. The lubricity of the phrasing has rarely been surpassed. This, together with the keen instrumental type-casting and fine solo violin playing, makes the Angel edition another top choice.

Festival Prelude for Organ and Orchestra, Op. 61

☐ New York Philharmonic / Biggs (organ) / Bernstein (conductor) / Columbia MS-6398

The radiant circumstances make the organ an obbligato instrument rather than a solo voice. Bernstein shows he's a first-class Straussian, directing a performance of pomp and opulence, and, in view of the large-scale forces and writing, without any annoying forcing of the sonorities.

Le Bourgeois Gentilhomme, Op. 60

☐ Vienna Philharmonic Orchestra / Maazel (conductor) / London 6537

This broad and expansive reading features a richly-timbred quality without resorting to lushness, which spoils the competitive performance by Ormandy and the Philadelphia Orchestra on Columbia M-32233.

Suite from Der Rosenkavalier, Op. 59

☐ Philadelphia Orchestra / Ormandy (conductor) / Columbia MS-6678

For this type of music, transferred from stage to concert hall, no special interpretative recipe is required. The ingredients are perfect when Der Rosenkavalier is combined with Ormandy and the Philadelphia Orchestra. The result is 100% pure cream, very rich, but easily digestible.

Symphonia Domestica, Op. 53

☐ Berlin Philharmonic Orchestra / von Karajan (conductor) / Angel S-36973
☐ Vienna Philharmonic Orchestra / Strauss (conductor) / Turnabout 4363 (monaural)

Notwithstanding the fashionable sneers at Strauss's orchestral behavior in describing the ways and whims of papa, mama, and baby at home, let's give credit. This is some chunk of program music—historic, in fact, for such one-on-one situations of domesticity were never (and have not been since) musically simulated until Strauss went and did it. And did it magnificently!

Some writer has pointed out that the score contains no less than sixty-seven interplaying motives. Judging from the perfectly focused playing of the Berliners von Karajan apparently had his baton in touch with each and every one. This is a magnificent musical camera study. It far outshines all the others in the catalogue.

Of course, Strauss conducting Strauss is not competitive, but it is of great historical importance, hence its inclusion. Comparing Strauss to what von Karajan accomplishes, the latter could well have been the composer.

Till Eulenspiegel, Op. 28

☐ Berlin Philharmonic Orchestra / Kempe (conductor) / Seraphim S-60122
☐ New York Philharmonic / Bernstein (conductor) / Columbia MS-6225

Of course, this kind of music is Lenny's special cup of tea. No pranks are added to Till's merry pranks. Bernstein is absolutely magnificent. Every point in the score is revealed, the data are detailed with preciseness: a story told with perfection. (Other albums that Columbia has issued including this performance are: MS-6441, MS-6822, MS-7165, MG-33707, and D3S-785.)

Kempe's ideas are less vivid but still excellent, simply because they're sensitive and sensible and fit the music. He lends dramatic persistence to the score but never tries to crush the sonority. No vague chiaroscuro pertains to Kempe's reading; all the details are exposed with gleaming coloration. It is also a superb presentation.

Waltzes from *Der Rosenkavalier*, Op. 59

☐ Chicago Symphony Orchestra / Reiner (conductor) / RCA VICS-1561

Absolutely marvelous. Yes, the waltzes are styled with predictable accentuations, anticipations, and affranchisements, but Reiner has produced matters of beauty, breadth, and beneficence.

Reiner did not follow the published waltz sequence from Strauss's opera but used his own compilation. It is just as good. (The performance is also included on RCA AGL1-1269.)

Introduction to *Capriccio*, Op. 85

String Orchestra

☐ Los Angeles Chamber Orchestra / Marriner (conductor) / Argo ZRG-792

Some may snub the amplified version of the Overture to Strauss's opera which he scored for string sextet. If they do, they'll be depriving themselves of music of rich lyrical thrust, unless they obtain the entire opera recording. But, even if they do, they will miss the greater vital response that Marriner derives from the music.

Actually, there is nothing wrong with hearing Strauss's string beauty in a times-four totality. True, its intimacy becomes replaced by a more outward eloquency but the music is of such style as to remain unharmed, whereas other chamber string works might not fare as well if turned into string orchestra products.

The passion of Marriner's performance lies in a truthful translation of the musical essence and is not the outcome of inflated sonority. The Münchinger essay on London (6737) is definitely in second place. It lacks ebb and flow, give and take, and is of low temperature.

Metamorphosen (1945)

☐ Academy of St. Martin-in-the-Fields / Marriner (conductor) / Argo ZRG-604

This is music from the final period of Strauss's life (he was eighty when he completed *Metamorphosen*). Scored for twenty-three solo strings—ten violins, five violas, five cellos, and three double basses—the score has a rich consort of voicing, a full-choired warmth. Where there is virtuosity, it is in the restrained category. But the playing is not. This is a full-blooded account and has a performance temperature that is fitting. Other conductors somehow or other never forget *Rosenkavalier* when they play this piece, but they should. "Metamorphoses" does not have sensuousness and needs none to be added.

Serenade for Wind Instruments, Op. 7

Wind and Brass Ensemble

☐ Netherlands Wind Ensemble / de Waart (conductor) / Philips 6500097

The Serenade is very early Strauss, written when he was seventeen. Smooth as silk, no flamboyance, simply a suave conceit scored for two each of flutes, oboes, clarinets, and bassoons, plus a double bassoon and four horns.

The performance is one to be relished. One could not ask for more.

Sonatina No. 1 in F major for Wind Instruments (*From an Invalid's Workshop*) (1943)
Suite in B flat major for Thirteen Wind Instruments, Op. 4

☐ Netherlands Wind Ensemble / de Waart (conductor) / Philips 6500297

Take that subtitle of the Sonatina with an explanatory grain of salt. Strauss wrote his three-movement delight *after* recovering from a bout with influenza. No sickly after-effects in this gay work, which has *Rosenkavalier* and *Eulenspiegel* touches within its sixteen-instrument framework.

The thirteen-instrument piece has youthful spirit in the *Praeludium,* warmth and depth in the Romance, scherzo wit in the Gavotte, and polyphonic talent in the final Introduction and Fugue. There's plenty of action throughout the piece.

The playing is of the memorable type, with a captivating inner enthusiasm. One senses that the group appreciates the type of writing that fits their instruments perfectly. It is difficult to conceive the top professionalism of these performances being bettered.

Philips's picture on the jacket cover brings up two matters. Only fourteen of the players plus conductor are shown, which means that two are absent, since the Sonatina calls for sixteen players. But one of these is shown holding a double bass! What's he doing here? There's no string instrument used in this pair of works for *wind* instruments!

Symphony for Wind Instruments (*The Happy Workshop*) (1945)

☐ Netherlands Wind Ensemble / de Waart (conductor) / Philips 6500097

The subtitle comes from the inspirational dedication Strauss placed on his manuscript: "The Happy Workshop: to the shade of the divine Mozart at the end of a life filled with gratitude." And Mozartian elegance there is in the work Strauss produced four years before he left the living. There are touches of the robust Strauss, but they are light. A classical sentimentality is preached here for two flutes, two oboes, a clarinet in C, two B flat clarinets, a bass clarinet, basset horn, two bassoons, double bassoon, and a quartet of horns.

A golden-toned performance. The music rolls with liquidity and the phrasing is super.

(Some listings title this piece as Sonatina No. 2. [Sonatina No. 1 is discussed above.] It held that title until the publisher of the work changed it to the "Symphony" heading listed because of its size. Good decision—after all, its four movements encompass forty minutes of playing time and who ever heard of a forty-minute Sonatina?)

Solo Instrument and Orchestra

Horn

Concerto for Horn and Orchestra
No. 1 in E flat major, Op. 11 / No. 2 in E flat major (1942)

☐ Philharmonia Orchestra / Brain (horn) / Sawallisch (conductor) / Angel 35496 (monaural)

Negatives first. Produced a quarter of a century ago, the sound is not of the best and you can include the orchestra's quality in that category as well. But the positives! This is the most magnificent horn playing you would desire. Regardless of the only fair coalitions mentioned initially, to bypass Dennis Brain's conceptions would be poor judgment. By all means consider the excellent single entries discussed below and pair them with Brain's now historically unique performances. That's the perfect solution.

Concerto No. 1 in E flat major for Horn and Orchestra, Op. 11

☐ Philadelphia Orchestra / Jones (horn) / Ormandy (conductor) / Columbia M-32233

Mason Jones plays with an eloquence and a musicality that rivals the famed performance of this work by the late Dennis Brain. Spontaneity and necessary bravura coupled with musical majesty and subtle agogic inflections mark the essay by the former (now retired) solo hornist of the Philadelphia Orchestra. Among other attributes Ormandy has always been one of the best accompanists in the business. That distinction is proven again in this issue.

Concerto No.2 in E flat major for Horn and Orchestra (1942)

☐ Staatskapelle Dresden / Damm (horn) / Kempe (conductor) / Angel S-37004

For this late-period Concerto (Strauss wrote it in 1942) three editions were considered, aside from the monaural oldie of Dennis Brain (*see above*).

Barry Tuckwell with the London Symphony Orchestra and Kertész conducting (London 6519) are, of course, technically on target but there's not much poetry in the slow movement and only a fair amount of effervescence in the Rondo. Without these, Strauss's piece becomes older than its old-age creator.

Norbert Hauptmann with the Berlin Philharmonic and von Karajan conducting (Deutsche Grammophon 2530439) offers a workaday reading. Especially in the first movement the lack of soloistic (concerto) profile is most apparent.

Whatever the above two hornists lack, Peter Damm has. The opening is played boldly; the contrastive flowing and tranquil passages register with the most colorful effect; the vivaciousness of the finale is delightful. Kempe's orchestra gives marvelous support. The sound is luxurious.

Concerto in D major for Oboe and Orchestra (1945)

Oboe

☐ New Philharmonia Orchestra / Holliger (oboe) / de Waart (conductor) / Philips 6500174

Straussian song is here transferred to instrumental identification. This interaction does not negate virtuosity but it is always commanded by curvaceous phrases. This is late Strauss, but the Concerto is as strong as the works produced at the height of his career.

Holliger is brilliant and he sings Strauss with discriminative detail. The slow movement spins beautifully, the end portion of the work has matchless buffo definition. De Waart matches Holliger's conviction and understanding.

Burleske in D minor for Piano and Orchestra (1886)

Piano

☐ Philadelphia Orchestra / Rudolf Serkin (piano) / Ormandy (conductor) / Columbia MS-7423

Serkin produces all the high spirits of Strauss's early work. The pixy lightness that twirls around the piece is all there and so is the socked-in virtuosity. Ormandy does magnificently with the orchestra and again proves Strauss's original idea that his orchestration was ''miserable'' absolutely false.

There is one false matter, however, with the Columbia release. The *Burleske* is assigned Opus 11 on album information and record label copy. That opus designation belongs to Strauss's first horn Concerto. Strauss never assigned an opus number to his *Burleske*, which he completed in 1886. (The first performance was given in June 1890, with Eugen d'Albert as the soloist and Strauss conducting.)

Concerto for Violin and Orchestra, Op. 8

Violin

☐ Vienna State Opera Orchestra / Glenn (violin) / List (conductor) / Odyssey 32160312

Early Strauss, as the opus number indicates. A worthy addition to the recorded catalogue, especially for Strauss aficionados.

Instrumental

Piano

Fünf Stimmungsbilder, **Op. 9**

Sonata in B minor, Op. 5

☐ Colburn (piano) / Orion 7147

Rarities. Who ever plays these in concert? Yet, there is no reason not to. The "Mood Pictures" (*Auf stillem Waldespfad, An einsamer Quelle,* Intermezzo, *Träumerei,* and *Heidebild*) have full melodic warmth in their classical-romantic shapes. The Opus 5 has an interesting initial movement built from the same rhythmic motive that triggers Beethoven's Fifth Symphony first movement. Though phrase sectionalism is noticeable in the last two movements, there is a genial Mendelssohnian temper that is inviting.

These are persuasive interpretations, best in the Opus 9 but doubtless due to it being the better music.

Chamber Music

Sonata in F major for Cello and Piano, Op. 6

☐ Rostropovich (cello); Devetzi (piano) / Angel S–37086

Rostropovich brings eloquence to this early Strauss work, much more than is heard in other recorded performances. This is principally evident in the ternary-designed slow movement. In the gay finale, based on a light dance theme, the playing is full-blooded but fully within the Mendelssohn-like conception.

Sonata in E flat major for Violin and Piano, Op. 18

☐ Heifetz (violin); Smith (piano) / Columbia M2–33444

Heifetz and Smith perfectly delineate the luxurious romantic spirit of this work; the fat tone of the former is just right for the true Straussian brilliance of the piece. This vitality is even found in the middle movement, an Improvisation that becomes superornamental in its middle section, in contrast to the sobriety of its outer portions.

(The monophonically recorded version is just as good. It is on RCA LM–2860.)

Piano Quartet in C minor, Op. 13

☐ Los Angeles String Trio / Vallecillo (piano) / Desmar 1002

The quartet for piano and strings is the penultimate composition in the Strauss chamber music catalogue, and no one need be reminded of Strauss's debt to Brahms upon hearing its mellifluous sonorities. The formal conception (the very normal four-movement plan of Allegro-Scherzo-slow movement-Finale) is that of a young composer, twenty years of age, writing in the nineteenth century.

No reticence in this performance. A lot of *brio,* more than one expects, perhaps, in a work that is doused with traditional romanticism. But it will do. The full bloom of poeticism manifests itself sufficiently and the basic resolutive quality of the playing does not harm Strauss's opus.

Vocal

Voice with Accompaniment

Allerseelen, **Op. 10, No. 8**   *Cäcilie,* **Op. 27, No. 2**
Befreit, **Op. 39, No. 4**

☐ Nilsson (soprano); Solyom (piano) / Bis LP–15

The linear flow of *Allerseelen* ("All Souls' Day"), combined with its strong harmonic thrust, contrasts vividly with the rhapsodic quality that marks *Cäcilie* ("Cecilia"), one of "Four Songs" for High Voice and Piano that Strauss dedicated to his wife as a gift on the day of their marriage, September 10, 1894. Further contrast is offered in the lyricism of *Befreit* ("Delivered").

Beautifully controlled singing is provided in this program. The piano support is of the most discriminating kind.

Freundliche Vision, Op. 48, No. 1

☐ Price (soprano); Garvey (piano) / RCA LSC-2279

The harmonic turns in "A Welcome Vision" are sensitively understood by both vocalist and pianist. In his notes for the RCA issue, Irving Kolodin has poetically, but with analytical truth, described this element, "like a beam of sunshine which shows far more below the surface of a pond than had been suspected." The performance illustrates artistry on the part of Leontyne Price and David Garvey.

Ruhe, meine Seele, Op. 27, No. 1

☐ Nilsson (soprano); Solyom (piano) / Bis LP-15

This song ("Rest, my Soul") is the first in the set of four songs that Strauss dedicated to his wife (see above: under Allerseelen). By retaining an almost reserved manner, rather than opting for operatic dramatic emphasis, Nilsson's interpretation supports the true arioso lyricism of Strauss's song.

Schlagende Herzen, Op. 29, No. 2

☐ Price (soprano); Garvey (piano) / RCA LSC-2279

An attractive and very stylish performance of "Throbbing Hearts." The song is paced, however, in a more moderate tempo than Strauss indicated (Allegro giocoso). In this RCA issue Price also sings Strauss's Wie sollten wir geheim ("How Can We Keep Secret"), Op. 19, No. 4.

Ständchen, Op. 17, No. 2   Zueignung, Op. 10, No. 1
Wiegenlied, Op. 41, No. 1

☐ Nilsson (soprano); Solyom (piano) / Bis LP-15

Both Zueignung ("Affection") and Ständchen ("Serenade") are among the most popular of the more than 150 songs Strauss composed. Op. 41, No. 1 ("Cradle Song") is no less a lovely lyrical inspiration.

Birgit Nilsson sings with a subtle beauty, the quality is akin to chamber music. János Solyom's piano accompaniment is splendid.

Four Last Songs (1948)

Voice and Orchestra

☐ Berlin Radio Symphony Orchestra / Schwarzkopf (soprano) / Szell (conductor) / Angel S-36347

These songs are tonally thrilling and they are ideally interpreted. The magnificent musicianship of Schwarzkopf places all the other entries on disc as also-rans. With Szell as the partner, this is a performance that deserves hails and bravos several times over.

Six Songs, Op. 68

☐ Louisville Orchestra / Shane (soprano) / Mester (conductor) / Louisville S-704

The intimate fragrances of these songs, set to poems by Clemens Brentano, are well-realized in this recorded performance. Rita Shane particularly delineates the tenderness in Säusle, liebe Myrte ("Whisper, Little Myrtle!") and the coloraturish twitterings in Amor! Good orchestral backing and good sound as well.

(Phillip Rhodes's The Lament of Michal for Soprano and Orchestra is also on this release, marking Louisville's "100th Golden Edition" recording [see under *Rhodes, Vocal: voice and orchestra*].)

Choral

Chorus Alone

Der Abend, Op. 34, No. 1

Deutsche Motette, Op. 62

Hymne, Op. 34, No. 2

☐ Schütz Choir of London / Cash (soprano); Temperley (mezzo-soprano); Evans (tenor); Varcoe (baritone) / Norrington (conductor) / Argo ZRG–803

This is the first recording of these pieces and one cannot recall any recent concert performances. Reasons? Plenty! In the case of the *Motette* there are jumbo textures (sixteen different parts plus seven soloists) and jumbo length (over twenty minutes). The compass is expansive: the sopranos go up stratospherically to a high D flat and the basses tunnel downward to a low B. The other pair of works don't pull their vocal punches either.

When one keeps in mind that there is no accompaniment, the performances of all three pieces are truly incredible. Moreover, the spiritualistic resources (and naturally the huge polyphonic resources as well) are detailed with profound effect.

Opera and Dramatic Music

Ariadne auf Naxos, Op. 60

☐ Philharmonia Orchestra / Seefried, Streich, Schwarzkopf, Otto, and Felbermayer (sopranos); Schock, Unger, Cuenod, and Krebs (tenors); Dönch and Prey (baritones); Strauss, Kraus, and Ollendorff (basses); Neugebauer (speaking part) / von Karajan (conductor) / Angel 3532 (monaural)

The mono version outdistances the available stereo productions. The performance is splendid, the music sparkles, and one can be assured that von Karajan doesn't miss a point in his direction of Strauss's great work.

Elisabeth Schwarzkopf's *Ariadne* is ideal. She never presses—the tone is pure, smooth, and impeccable. As the Composer, Irmgard Seefried displays full understanding of the role. She is lightly intense, as it were. Rita Streich's high soprano fulfills the part of Zerbinetta magnificently. She is always light and flexible in her delivery. Her scene with Seefried (*Ein Augenblick ist wenig*) is absolutely enchanting. Rudolf Schock's Bacchus wavers a bit but for the greater part he strongly projects and is warmly lyrical when the registration of the part moves within his most comfortable range. His style is excellent. So are the realizations of the subsidiary roles. This is certainly the best performance now on disc. Other conductors cannot match the elegant sureness that von Karajan obtains. Roughing up the score by juggling tempi and phrase punctuations aren't characteristics that belong in this case, but you'll find them elsewhere.

Capriccio, Op. 85

☐ Bavarian Radio Symphony Orchestra / Janowitz (soprano); Troyanos (mezzo-soprano); Schreier (tenor); Fischer-Dieskau and Prey (baritones); Ridderbusch (bass) / Böhm (conductor) / Deutsche Grammophon 2709038

This unique operatic example plots its way by arguing the relative importance of words and music. Musical quotes are incorporated, including Strauss borrowing from Strauss. Gorgeous ideas light up the score and the cast is eminently satisfactory. Gundula Janowitz as the Countess offers effective vocalism, though she tends to diminish in strength in the upper register. Böhm's conducting provides a genuine performance, certainly of the fullest competence.

It is important to mention the now deleted mono edition (Angel 3580) in which Fischer-Dieskau is again represented, taking the part of the Poet, Olivier, and with Elisabeth Schwarzkopf as the Countess. Her work is magnificent. The edition, conducted by Wolfgang Sawallisch, is better than the one listed above. It is worth finding if possible.

Der Rosenkavalier, Op. 59

☐ Vienna Philharmonic Orchestra and Vienna State Opera Chorus / Crespin, Donath, Loose, and Auger (sopranos); Minton and Howells (mezzo-sopranos); Equiluz, Dermota, Pavarotti, and Terkal (tenors); Wiener and Heppe (baritones); Jungwirth, Lackner, and Jerger (basses); Dickie, Prikopa, Schwaiger, Yachmi, Mayr, Pipal, Tomaschek, Maly, Setzer, Strack, Simkowsky, and Reautschnigg (vocalists) / Solti (conductor) / London 1435

This is one of the great comic operas of all time. Coexisting harmoniously, its ingredients include sweeping solo sections, entrancing ensembles, forceful and luscious tunes, some of the best waltz images ever written, and an orchestral score of finesse and graphic detail. The plot is rich and among its symbolism there is soft-grained sex (and just a bit of understandable vulgarity). Indeed, *Der Rosenkavalier* is one of the great operatic scores.

The above choice of the recorded performances should not eliminate consideration of the fine monaural set available on Richmond 64001, with Kleiber conducting and with Gueden and Jurinac in the cast. But the sound element is considerably more potent in London's stereo release.

There are two mutually exclusive points that are of importance here. First, Solti presents the score in full, without the small number of cuts that have accompanied the opera's performances since it was premiered in 1911. Second, Solti's conception of this work has a penetrating depth that always finds the emotional mark of each scene in relation to the opera's totality.

The crucial roles are the Marschallin, Octavian, and Ochs. Régine Crespin's characterization of the first is excellent. True, it does not have the sexualized depth of Elisabeth Schwarzkopf's characterization in Angel's edition (S–3563), but in the case of the other two roles London's production comes first. Yvonne Minton is softly beautiful and totally believable in her conception and Manfred Jungwirth is magnificent. There are lots of technical difficulties in singing the part of Baron Ochs auf Lerchenau, but Jungwirth conquers them splendidly and without the usual coarse vocalism. The part of the Singer is taken by Luciano Pavarotti. His is a masterly realization.

Die Frau ohne Schatten, Op. 65

☐ Vienna Philharmonic Orchestra and Vienna State Opera Chorus / Rysanek, Loose, and Goltz (sopranos); Höngen (contralto); Hopf and Terkal (tenors); Schoeffler (baritone); Böhme (bass) / Böhm (conductor) / Richmond 64503

An absence of over-bombast characterizes this recorded production—welcome, indeed, since that quality affirms the basic style. Warm Straussian sounds are drawn from the orchestra—the objective that Böhm successfully obtains is of lyrical not fustian compellation. There is an occasional roughness (intentional?) but spontaneity is the identifiable premise.

The singers are mostly impressive, bracing their delivery to give full justice to the characterizations. There are some pitch deviations and the tenors are not beyond forcing matters.

Elektra, Op. 58

☐ Vienna Philharmonic Orchestra / Nilsson and Collier (sopranos); Resnik (mezzo-soprano); Stolze (tenor); Krause (bass); Cook, Franc, Heppe, Lehane, Lilowa, Minton, Sjöstedt, Tinsley, Unger, Watts, and Weathers (vocalists) / Solti (conductor) / London 1269

Tenacious tension is maintained for almost two hours in this violent and sensual, power-driven and sonorously persuasive opera. There is a totality to the work that denies any sectionalism—*Elektra* is all of a piece of dramatic intensity from the initial D minor upbeat thrust to the concise rhythmic blow that concludes it in C major.

Solti's performance endows the music with both strength and vividness. His control of the huge orchestral forces employed is truly magnificent, withal defining all of the special detail that is woven into the score. Nilsson in the title role and Resnik as Klytemnestra are vocally eloquent and superb in their characterizations. All the other leads and those concerned with the smaller roles are totally effective. It is an exceptional release, aided by excellent recording that helps to set and dramatize the varying situations.

Salome, Op. 54

☐ Vienna Philharmonic Orchestra / Nilsson and Maikl (sopranos); Hoffman and Veasey (mezzo-sopranos); Stolze, Kmentt, Kuen, Schwer, Equiluz, Gestner, and Douglas (tenors); Wächter and Kosnowski (baritones); Proebstl, Krause, Holecek, and Kirschbichler (basses) / Solti (conductor) / London 1218

Be assured that even at this very late date (realizing the world premiere of *Salome* was in 1905) Strauss's opera can shock. Its sexual status is principal to the tale: Salome's lusting for John the Baptist, Herod (Salome's stepfather) lusting for Salome, the nudity that is the objective of the dance of the seven veils, and finally Salome's necrophilistic ecstasy as she kisses the severed head of the prophet.

Events such as these need more than ardent singing and playing—the temperature to realize the lavish lasciviousness of Strauss's score must be scalding-hot. Accordingly, this production sizzles. Birgit Nilsson has the fullest affectability in her characterization. The realism in her singing makes one appreciate her vulgar operatic personality to the fullest. The vocal strength of every member of the cast is matched by graphical profiles. Each one, from Gerhard Stolze as Herod to Grace Hoffman as Herodias, is distinctive, powerful, and alive. On top of it all is Solti, directing a driving performance which is the ultimate in musical theatricality.

Igor Stravinsky   (1882-1971)

Orchestra

Circus Polka (1942)

☐ Los Angeles Philharmonic Orchestra / Mehta (conductor) / London 6554

The Circus Polka, *Composed for a Young Elephant* (as Stravinsky subtitled it, though more than one elephant was to be involved), was commissioned by the Ringling Bros. and Barnum and Bailey Circus in 1942. The purpose was a score for a *Ballet of the Elephants*, a special act on the Circus program and was originally composed for a small band. It displays full Stravinskian wit that ends with a wink when Schubert's *Marche militaire* joins in. Mehta's approach is tastefully brash.

For the piano version of Circus Polka see under *Instrumental: piano*.

Concertino for Twelve Instruments (1952)

☐ Columbia Chamber Ensemble / Stravinsky (conductor) / Columbia M-30579

A reworking of the material as well as a rescoring thirty-two years later of the original Concertino for String Quartet—see under *Chamber Music* (p. 1841). The playing is sharp and to the point and texturally clear.

Danses concertantes (1942)

☐ Los Angeles Chamber Orchestra / Marriner (conductor) / Angel S-37081

Balletic juices ooze from every pore of this five-part work, creating the impression that its objective was a score to be choreographed. The opposite is the fact. Stravinsky's dances were conceived (as the result of a commission) for the concert hall. Eventually, however, like so much of his music, they were turned into a ballet.

Marriner gauges the volumes and weights of sounds within the designs admirably. Stravinsky's orchestrational spacings in all their individuality are not disturbed and are heard with their greatest effect. Angel's disc is better recorded than Colin Davis's setting on Oiseau-Lyre (60050), and Marriner's performance is much cleaner in its detail than Robert Craft's version on Columbia (M–30516).

Dumbarton Oaks Concerto in E flat for Chamber Orchestra (1938)

☐ Los Angeles Chamber Orchestra / Marriner (conductor) / Angel S-37081

Dumbarton Oaks is simply the name of the estate of the person who commissioned this work for fifteen players—flute, clarinet, bassoon, two horns, three violins, three violas, and two each of cellos and double basses.

This music in the neoclassic manner (Bach came to Stravinsky's mind, and will likewise to the listener's) is full of Stravinskian smarts. It is healthy music, and played in an open-airish athletic manner.

Eight Instrumental Miniatures for Fifteen Players (1963)

☐ Members of the CBC Symphony Orchestra / Stravinsky (conductor) / Columbia M-31729

Orchestrations of the eight piano pieces that total the artistically didactic *The Five Fingers*. They turn into tart delights with Stravinsky's spatially textured scoring. In the performance Stravinsky permits the *joie de vivre* to flow out of the orchestrational plan, while keeping the metricality and articulations tightly bound. The music, crisp in itself, is much more so directed in that manner.

Firebird Suite

☐ Philharmonia Orchestra / Giulini (conductor) / Seraphim S-60022
☐ Columbia Symphony Orchestra / Stravinsky (conductor) / Columbia MG-31202

Giulini, using the 1919 edition, outlines all the Stravinsky particulars without conductorial overindulgence. The liner note states that the 1919 edition is the one usually played in concerts, and it is. However, it was the 1945 version that Stravinsky performed and then recorded. He also made known his wishes that all editions be scrubbed and only the 1945 setting be used. (Only some took heed.) There were two reasons (mutually exclusive ones) for Stravinsky's decision. First, only the 1945 version has the protection of copyright and thus brings substantial financial returns (not the case, of course, when a composition is in the public domain). Second, the 1945 edition contains (for an average-sized orchestra) the best of the ballet with Stravinsky's final revisions. The 1919 version conducted by Giulini has six movements; Stravinsky's 1945 setting has twice that number. In both cases the playing is marked by sensitivity and sensibility.

There is of course also the suite drawn from the 1910 ballet. It is best represented by Boulez's edition on Columbia MS-7206.

Fireworks, Op. 4

☐ Chicago Symphony Orchestra / Ozawa (conductor) / RCA LSC-3026

All the Rimskyish splendors of the score are unfurled in this reading. *Fireworks* has begun to splutter over the years, but that condition is not evidenced in this reading.

Four Etudes for Orchestra (1930)

☐ Orchestre National de la R.T.F. / Boulez (conductor) / Nonesuch 71093

The *Quatre Etudes* is the orchestral version Stravinsky made of his Three Pieces for String Quartet plus another movement (also a transcription—see under *Instrumental: two pianos* (Concerto *per due pianoforti soli*). Titles were given to the movements, which may furnish some further significance also when listening to the quartet version (see under *Chamber Music* [p. 1842]). The first piece from the quartet was called *Danse,* the second *Excentrique,* and the third became *Cantique.* The first and third pieces are nationalistic types of musical units stripped down to skeleton form; the second is a cubistic depiction of machine-tooled slabs of musical patterns. The fourth piece was originally composed for pianola and was termed an Etude. In its new orchestral dress it was given the title of *Madrid.*

The Boulez performance is ideal. It is predicated on allowing each of the various ideas to stand on its own. No overemphasis or pointing up of material creeps in—all of that has been covered to the utmost by being built into the scoring by Stravinsky. Thus the kaleidoscopical snippets that are found in the second movement are placed on display without any conductorial spotlighting, and the iciness of the *Cantique* is not allowed to thaw. A definitive version without any doubt.

Four *Norwegian Moods* (1942)

☐ CBC Symphony Orchestra / Stravinsky (conductor) / Columbia M-30516

Filmdom's loss is the concert world's gain in this case. This music was originally part of a score for a motion picture on the Nazi invasion of Norway. Stravinsky withdrew his music rather than have it go through the masticating machinery run by Hollywood music arrangers. The four movements fashioned into an orchestral suite do not assume any "ethnological authenticity," but a northern tinge colors the music, especially the haunting *Song* and the *Wedding Dance,* which has a Griegian climate.

The playing is rich, the sound fine. This is a choice recording.

Greeting Prelude (1956)

☐ Columbia Symphony Orchestra / Stravinsky (conductor) / Columbia M-31729

A fifty-second idealization of *Happy Birthday to You.* Fifty seconds, but crammed with Stravinsky's special kind of creative conceit.

Le Baiser de la fée—Divertimento (1928)

☐ L'Orchestre de la Suisse Romande / Ansermet (conductor) / London STS-15271

This comprises four movements drawn from the full ballet, which is also available on records (see under Ballet [*Le Baiser de la fée*]). The music is fully alive under Ansermet's direction.

L'Histoire du soldat—Suite (1918)

☐ Baker (violin); D'Antonio (clarinet); Christlieb (bassoon); Brady (cornet); Marsteller (trombone); Kelley (bass); Kraft (percussion) / Stravinsky (conductor) / Columbia MS-6272

The eleven parts of the concert suite are practically all the music of "The Soldier's Tale." The balance consists of short cues for the complete stage work (see under *Opera and Dramatic Music* [*L'Histoire du soldat*]).

This group (called the Columbia Chamber Ensemble for the duplicate performance included in the sumptuous and beautifully packaged twelve-record side release on Columbia D5S-775) gives the best execution of Stravinsky's ironic score. The playing has flair and the assortment of assertive rhythms that feature the piece are scrupulously natural and thereby doubly effective.

Monumento pro Gesualdo (1960)

☐ Columbia Symphony Orchestra / Stravinsky (conductor) / Columbia Special Products CKS-6318

Stravinsky's updating of music (three madrigals) by Gesualdo. A fine bridging of stylistic opposites.

Ode (1943)

☐ Cleveland Orchestra / Stravinsky (conductor) / Columbia M-30516

Stravinsky's *Ode,* with its alliterative subtitles Eulogy, Eclogue, and Epitaph, is to *Le Sacre du printemps, Petrouchka,* and *L'Histoire du soldat* as cold water is to that in red-hot boilers. Pithily expressed, nonprogrammatic, clearly ordered in form and particulars of the individual designs, it has a reserved personality with poetic rather than dynamic sting. But sting it has. Carl Sandburg's perceptive phrase fits Stravinsky's work: "the great naked sea shouldering a load of salt." The recording is superb.

Orchestral Variations (1965)

☐ Columbia Symphony Orchestra / Craft (conductor) / Columbia MS-7386

The title page of Stravinsky's score bears the inscription *Aldous Huxley in memoriam.* One could substitute the name Anton Webern and substantiate thereby the tissue-textured quality of the music, its rigid compression in both pitch statements and length (playing time four minutes and fifty-three seconds). A cold beauty, this.

Petrouchka—Suite

☐ Columbia Symphony Orchestra / Stravinsky (conductor) / Columbia MS-7094

There are variances in the concert suite, due to conductorial choice as to coverage. Over the years Stravinsky himself varied in his determinations of what to include in the suite. The recorded performance he conducted has a clarity and an avoidance of over-stress that are most compelling. Columbia has packaged it in various couplings and triplings, etc. (always, of course, with other Stravinsky music). The other catalogue numbers are MS-7011, M-31841, and D5S-775.

Preludium for Jazz Ensemble

☐ Columbia Jazz Combo / Stravinsky (conductor) / Columbia M-30579

A snippet of jazz truism with sax and muted trumpet and Stravinskian "stop-rhythm" chords. A snippet that also includes the silvery color of that nonjazzy instrument the celesta. The work is only eighty-six seconds in length. It is good to have such a vivid sketch on disc, since live performance is so rare that it amounts to the work being swept under the rug.

Pulcinella Suite (1920)

☐ Columbia Symphony Orchestra / Stravinsky (conductor) / Columbia MS-7093

There are eighteen sections in the stage work. (For details covering the entire ballet see under *Ballet* [*Pulcinella:* Ballet with Song, in One Act, After Pergolesi].) From these Stravinsky arranged an orchestral suite of eleven numbers. The performance here is one of sensitivity, with every strand in place and with collectively telling results. (The performance is duplicated in a sumptuous twelve-record-side Columbia release covering eight other Stravinsky compositions. The catalogue number is D5S-775.)

Ragtime for Eleven Instruments (1918)

☐ Columbia Chamber Ensemble / Koves (cimbalom) / Stravinsky (conductor) / Columbia M-30579

The music should strut, and Stravinsky makes certain it does. There are other performances on disc that are excellent in all respects, save that the modicum of jive in Stravinsky's 1918 creation is less than he obtains with his free-lance group of musicians.

For the sake of the record the instrumentation is flute, clarinet, horn, cornet, trombone, percussion, cimbalom, two violins, viola, and double bass.

For the original, piano version of this piece see under *Instrumental: piano* (Piano Rag-Music).

Scènes de Ballet (1945)

☐ CBC Symphony Orchestra / Stravinsky (conductor) / Columbia M-31921

Here is Stravinsky writing under the sign of neoclassicism with sophisticated touches that heighten the expressivity of the music. He is a little freer in his interpretation than the published score indicates but gives a reading that has smooth finesse and excellent temperature.

Scherzo *à la Russe* (1944)

☐ Columbia Symphony Orchestra / Stravinsky (conductor) / Columbia MS-7094

Originally written for Paul Whiteman. Shortly thereafter, Stravinsky made this symphonic version, embracing a formal scherzo design with two trios.

The music practically plays itself, since the orchestration and rhythmic pulse are quite regular, for Stravinsky extraordinarilly so. The twenty-three measures of the first trio are set in $\frac{4}{4}$ meter, and there are three measures of triple beat in the second trio; the other 171 measures of the piece are in square duple pulse. Further, not a single tempo change is included. That's the way Stravinsky plays it, and that's the way it should be played.

Scherzo fantastique, Op. 3

☐ CBC Symphony Orchestra / Stravinsky (conductor) / Columbia MS-7904

Peripatetic music—a Stravinskian *Flight of the Bumble Bee.* It is of large scope, for large orchestra, and with large sounds. Vivid performance.

Song of the Nightingale (1919)

☐ L'Orchestre de la Suisse Romande / Ansermet (conductor) / London STS-15011

The exotic *Song of the Nightingale* with its transparent scoring demands virtuosity from every player, and it is amply supplied here. Ansermet has rarely been better in covering a score's splendors. Note that once in a while there is a lack of presence in the lower-gamuted instruments. Still, this is the best of the editions available, more detailed than Craft's and more colorful than Reiner's. The former is on Columbia M–33201, the latter on RCA LSC–2150.

Suite for Small Orchestra
No. 1 (1925) / No. 2 (1921)

☐ L'Orchestre de la Suisse Romande / Ansermet (conductor) / London STS-15271

Picturesque portions, four in each Suite, with such titles as *Napolitana, Española, Balalaika,* and Polka. All are orchestrations of the Five Easy Pieces for Piano Duet and the Three Easy Pieces for Piano Duet (see under *Instrumental: piano, four hands* [Five Easy Pieces]). The orchestra is indeed small, with two flutes (the second doubling on piccolo), one oboe, two clarinets, two bassoons, single brass (horn, trumpet, trombone, and tuba), percussion, piano (in the second Suite only), and strings.

The Suites are delightfully played, with spontaneity and choice tempi.

Symphony in C (1940)

☐ CBC Symphony Orchestra / Stravinsky (conductor) / Columbia MS-6548

Stravinsky's Symphony in C is a virtuoso dissertation in pandiatonic-neoclassic language. The forms of sonata, aria, and fugue are among those included within the four movements. The stylistic handle is attached to magnificent scoring that is a veritable textbook of spacings and textural arrangements. All of the lines sing, all of the incidents are strong; the phrases are never square and are very fluid. Here is orchestral music that glories in its contemporary tonalism.

The most flexible performance, denoting the most subtle rhythmic currents and inter-currents, is that given by Stravinsky (also available in a twelve-record-side package on Columbia D5S–775). More than any other conductor, Stravinsky marks every accent, balances every chord, and is faithful to the textural variety. Indeed, Stravinsky's ''white music'' Symphony (the composer's description of the third movement) has never been heard as distinctively as it is in this recording.

Symphony in E flat, Op. 1

☐ Columbia Symphony Orchestra / Stravinsky (conductor) / Columbia MS-6989

Geniuses are supposed to strike it rich in their initial works. Agreeing that Igor Stravinsky was a genius, the precept doesn't hold true for his Opus 1. Granted, as Stravinsky has acknowledged, that the Symphony displays that he had technical know-how. But at that point one stops. The Symphony goes through its four movements in 1–2–3–4 Rimsky-Tchaikovsky manner and that's that. Most expressive is the slow movement; the movement with most lack of direction is the finale.

But even if not enthusiastically accepted the Opus 1 Symphony deserves listening time now and then. So here it is to fill out the Stravinsky part of the recorded catalogue. Stravinsky the conductor seems to be enthusiastic, and at the least he is most sympathetic to his baby.

Symphony in Three Movements (1945)

☐ Philharmonia Orchestra / Klemperer (conductor) / Seraphim S-60188

This is Stravinsky music invested with classical clarity and combining it with an eruptive explosiveness. The latter does not, by its pulsatile pungency, disturb the former, but enhances it. For such music all its detail must be allowed full play, an enthusiasm displayed for its heartiness, and its rhythms punched clear. Perhaps it is not surprising that Otto Klemperer would be the conductor to make sure this happens. He does, and far better than anyone else, including Stravinsky himself.

Tango (1953)

☐ Columbia Jazz Combo / Stravinsky (conductor) / Columbia M-35079

Originally for piano (see under *Instrumental: piano*), then orchestrated, and then re-orchestrated. The final (1953) setting calls for four clarinets, bass clarinet, four trumpets, three trombones, guitar, three violins, viola, cello, and double bass.

This is light Stravinsky, and also precise Stravinsky, the music comprising seventy-two measures strictly divided into nine eight-measure phrases.

The dry performance, rather snide and unhumored, fits.

String Orchestra

Concerto in D for String Orchestra (1946)

☐ Los Angeles Chamber Orchestra / Marriner (conductor) / Angel S-37081

A strong, musically credible performance from first to last, especially convincing in the motile finale. On the other hand, Stravinsky's conducting of his twentieth-century-baroque conception lacks the polished edges that make stylistic incisiveness register naturally and thus most effectively. (His edition is on Columbia M-30516.)

Wind and Brass Ensemble

Symphonies of Wind Instruments (1920)

☐ L'Orchestre de la Suisse Romande / Ansermet (conductor) / London 6225

The concentrations of Stravinsky's scoring (twelve woodwinds and eleven brass) have none of the orchestrational tuberosities of *Le Sacre du printemps* or *Petrouchka*, but the color in the Symphonies, despite the elimination of strings to avoid "expressivity," is just as vivid. Different, yes, but even without pigmented sweep and plasticity, the score is a probe of velvety and brittle sonorities. No color was lost (though one would have expected it would be) when Stravinsky changed his original 1920 scoring in 1947 (to obtain copyright surety) and dispensed with an alto flute, an E flat clarinet, and an alto clarinet.

A masterful performance of this music that Stravinsky wrote in memory of Debussy. There is no attempt to "clarify" by highlighting and thereby disturb Stravinsky's unified design of a total sonorous entity. The textures are laced perfectly.

London's titling error ("Symphonies for Wind Instruments") on the album cover and liner copy of its edition should be noted. Only on the record label is the title stated correctly as Symphonies of Wind Instruments.

Solo Instrument and Orchestra

Clarinet

Ebony Concerto (1945)

☐ Woody Herman and His Orchestra / Herman (clarinet) / Herman (conductor) / Everest 3009

☐ Columbia Jazz Combo / Goodman (clarinet) / Stravinsky (conductor) / Columbia MS-6805

Stravinsky's big excursion into jazz is available in two substantially different readings, one by the composer himself. It is often said that a composer is the worst interpreter of his own music. Here Stravinsky's reading is valid, but Woody Herman's is slightly more so. Because of his affiliation with the Concerto from its inception and his association with it under various circumstances, his performance is interpretatively consequential aside from being historically important. First, Herman gave the premiere (in 1946) after commissioning the work (it is dedicated to him). Second, he was soloist with his own organization, with Stravinsky conducting, in the initial recording made of the composition (a monophonic disc, issued by Columbia on its 7479M, later indicated as ML-4398). The Everest recording, this time with Herman as soloist-conductor, was released in 1958, predating the Goodman-Stravinsky edition by seven years.

Stravinsky's performance is, important just because its variance from Herman's exposes the musical materials in a quite different light. As the composer he ought to have known. As the auditor one can accept his documentation but still prefer Herman's. It should be emphasized that this in no way means dismissal of the former.

The Everest performance is paired with Stravinsky's Symphony in Three Movements. Stravinsky's rendition is part of a program with works by Bernstein, Copland, and Gould, all featuring Goodman as soloist, or can be secured on Columbia M-30579, where it is part of an all-Stravinsky release.

It is in tempi and textural quality that the two Ebony Concerto recordings markedly differ. Herman takes a more moderate pace for the nervously demarcated first movement, thereby clarifying the rhythmic jabs of the contents. By slightly faster movement Herman achieves a more vocalized concept of the "bluesy" second section of the Concerto. In the finale, restrained and speedy tempi are contrasted twice. Stravinsky spreads the pulse of the former tempi, thereby heightening the effect of the latter; but this results in an almost static quality in the slower sections that ices the general warmth. Further, notwithstanding Stravinsky's success in combining the fundamentals of jazz with neoclassicism, the composition *is* bathed in jazz and the less scrubbed and "dirtier" the textures sound, the better. The symphonic high gloss of his performance is not the best style for the Ebony Concerto. In this respect the Herman realization covers all requirements. Whether this was sheer happenstance or the result of planned performance tactics is immaterial.

Everest's jacket note listing the instrumentation is in error. First, it omits the prime information that the score calls for a solo clarinet. It also fails to indicate that bass clarinet and horn are included. Finally, there are five (not six) saxophones (two altos, two tenors, and one baritone), and importantly, the pair of alto saxes and one of the tenor saxophones alternate with clarinets.

Capriccio for Piano and Orchestra (1949)

Piano

☐ Academy of St. Martin-in-the-Fields / Ogdon (piano) / Marriner (conductor) / Argo ZRG-674

Neoclassicism at its most fervent slant. Within the baroque interpositions there are both pointed detail and a "jazzbo" quality. This is healthy music that has retained its health for a half century (it was premiered in December of 1929). The material within the design is capricious but is absolutely (and paradoxically) in balance.

The performance is ideal in this case. Other versions on the market try to warm the music (which already has its exactly set temperature), and to do this makes for a clamminess and flabbiness that are not at all propitious.

Concerto for Piano and Wind Orchestra (1924)

☐ BBC Symphony Orchestra / Bishop (piano) / Davis (conductor) / Philips 839761

The scoring does not completely bear out the title. In addition to ten woodwinds, twelve brass, and timpani, there are double basses. Handelian turns, Bach and Scarlatti twists, and Vivaldian transmittals are to be found in this asymmetrical and astringent music. (Slonimsky's phrase *must* be added: "bradyseismic implosions.")

The above listing provides a good presentation of the work. One does like the way Walter Klien plays the piece (on Turnabout 34065), but one cannot like the gooey sound.

Movements for Piano and Orchestra (1959)

☐ Columbia Symphony Orchestra / Rosen (piano) / Stravinsky (conductor) / Columbia MS-6272

Stravinsky serialism, which means that his personality and special style are not discernible within the blueprint. Hearing this music, one needs no discussion to realize that in no other work has Stravinsky so unresembled Stravinsky and so much resembled Webern.

There are five connected movements, with seventy, twenty-eight, twenty-three, forty-five, and fifty-three measures respectively, the whole taking just ten seconds under nine minutes. The orchestra consists of seven woodwinds, five brass, harp, celesta, and a string group specifically indicated by the composer as having six first violins, six second violins, four violas, five cellos, and two double basses. This combine is instrumentally anatomized. Timbre punctuations and assortments style the piece, not forceful statements of timbre. Only in one place (the last four measures of part 4) is a tutti hinted at. Even then, no solo piano, harp, celesta, or double bass is used. Truly, here is a scrupulous dismemberment of texture which, however, paradoxically holds together through the avoidance of any peripheral material for contrast or any other purpose.

Stravinsky conducts meticulously and properly, which for this music means rigidly. The orchestra is knowledgeable and blocks in the sounds with exactness. For the solo chronicle, the stylistic perspicacity of Charles Rosen makes significant every moment of serial sobriety in the composition.

Violin

Violin Concerto in D (1931)

☐ Concertgebouw Orchestra / Grumiaux (violin) / Bour (conductor) / Philips 802785

A performance that radiates conviction, correctness, and meaning, unspoiled by interpretative curiosity. Grumiaux takes a moderate tempo in the first movement, which codifies and certifies the neobaroque climate of the music. Bour obtains some remarkable fine dry-point playing from his orchestra in this part. Grumiaux's rich-pitched approach to the *Aria II* movement is beautiful; the finale (a Capriccio) is quite brilliant but is set at a pace natural to the musical content.

Instrumental

Clarinet

Three Pieces for Clarinet Solo (1918)

☐ Milosovich (clarinet) / Musical Heritage Society MHS-1473

A more absolute absolute music is difficult to imagine than that written for an unaccompanied homophonic wind instrument. The abstract results are illustrated in this case by playing that has a somewhat aloof manner. This doesn't harm the conception; indeed, a lot of editing in performance would not be right for Stravinsky's set of pieces.

Piano

Circus Polka (1942)
Four Etudes, Op. 7

☐ Bucquet (piano) / Philips 6500385

Whether the piano version of the Circus Polka came first or was made after the orchestral version (see under *Orchestra*) really doesn't matter, since either way it was written by Stravinsky. (Transcriptions made by other hands for concert band and two pianos were also issued by his publisher.) The Opus 7 set is, as one would expect, a totally more heavyweight musical affair, being expressively and expansively chromatic and rhythmically (not metrically) involved.

Because of the inner pulsatile action, therefore, the softer-blended playing of Marie-Françoise Bucquet is more propitious than the thinner steely-toned sound Noël Lee produces in his Stravinsky piano-music album on Nonesuch 71212. Bucquet is also a mite clearer in her exposition of the Circus Polka—a polka like none other, since it was written on commission to accompany a ballet turn by trained elephants.

The Firebird

☐ Stravinsky (piano) / Klavier 126

This record is an oddity but of historical importance, since here is Stravinsky playing his ballet score. There are mostly gray colors in this keyboard version, originally made as a piano roll (during the 1920s) and remastered by Klavier. Klavier has done a pretty good job, but do expect both coloristic and dynamic neutrality. The value here is solely Stravinsky performing Stravinsky.

Les Cinq Doigts (1921)

☐ Biret (piano) / Finnadar 9013

In playing these eight very easy pieces based on five notes, Biret refuses to overinterpret them. As a result, all the charm and cleverness of "The Five Fingers" come through.

Petrouchka (Three Scenes)

☐ Pollini (piano) / Deutsche Grammophon 2530225

This is the virtuoso version Stravinsky made for Artur Rubinstein. The sections consist of *Danse russe* ("Russian Dance"), *Chez Petrouchka* ("In Petrouchka's Room"), and *La Semaine grasse* ("The Shrovetide Fair").

Here is a thoroughly exciting performance of this difficult and colorful score. The vital equilibrium between emotion and intellectuality that pervades Stravinsky's setting is absolute. Pollini leaves his competition far behind. For example, in Biret's recording (on Finnadar 9013) the material is not clarified and its coloristic contours are dulled.

Piano Rag-Music (1920)
Ragtime (1918)
Serenade in A (1925)
Sonata (1924)

☐ Lee (piano) / Nonesuch 71212

The balances of the two large pieces in this group (the Serenade in A and the Sonata) are obtained from neoclassic procedures. But here is no dull textbook précis on this one of Stravinsky's various styles. Both works are replete with musical fascinations and important discussions, a bit more seriously sprung in the Sonata. Lee presents superbly informed performances, indicating a finely tempered judgement as to the different frames of aesthetic reference the two works have. A comparison with Stravinsky's own playing of the Serenade (on Seraphim 60183, a monaural edition) proves the probity of Lee's playing.

The piano Ragtime is the original version of the piece, later scored for a small instrumental combination (see under *Orchestra* [Ragtime for Eleven Instruments]). The other rag piece (also included in the release with Stravinsky playing mentioned above) has been given proper percussive pepper, with fitting suavity for some passages providing a neat contrast. Indeed, Lee's playing offers a fine perspective in all cases.

Sonata in F sharp minor for Piano (1904)

☐ Crossley (piano) / Philips 6500884

If he were unidentified, the chance of naming the composer of this work would be one in a billion, if that. In one of his books Stravinsky states that this very early Sonata (it predates the early E flat major Symphony) was "fortunately lost." One doesn't strongly argue contrarily. Stravinsky supposed it was "an inept imitation of Beethoven." One argues contrarily. The Sonata is an unabashed imitation of Tchaikovsky, and not at his very best.

But silence doesn't prove anything. It's worth having the recording as a historical point of reference. Paul Crossley, who does very well with what he has to play, would probably argue contrarily that the piece is worth more than this.

Tango (1953)

☐ Lee (piano) / Nonesuch 71212

The original setting of the later-made orchestral piece. The latter is discussed under *Orchestra*.

It takes two to tango and definitely Stravinsky and Lee go well together.

Valse pour les enfants (1917)

☐ Biret (Piano) / Finnadar 9013

A fifty-eight-second charmer, written in 1917 and published (hey, Ripley!) in the Paris newspaper *Le Figaro* on May 21, 1922! There it was headed *Une Valse pour les petits lecteurs du Figaro* ("A Waltz for the Little Readers of *Le Figaro*").

Biret doesn't try to sophisticate the piece the way Bucquet does (on Philips 6500385). Rather, she plays it squarely, and as a result all the flavor is retained. The way to play it squarely? Make much of, and clarify (don't blur), the "um-pah" bass. Which Biret does.

Piano,
Four Hands

Five Easy Pieces for Piano Duet (1917)

Three Easy Pieces for Piano Duet (1915)

Zvietotchnoy valse

☐ Jacobs and Oppens (piano) / Nonesuch 71347

The sets of "Easy Pieces" are cute, dry, and pert duos. Even when played straight, they have effect. Paul Jacobs and Ursula Oppens add little touches and emphasize the sonorous slang which peppers the conceptions. This produces a splendid result and beats the competition offered by Gold and Fizdale on Columbia Special Products AMS–6333.

Stravinsky turned these sets of three and five pieces into a pair of suites for small orchestra (see under *Orchestra* [Suite for Small Orchestra, Nos. 1 and 2]). In so doing, he divided the movements equally. To the March, Waltz, and Polka of the Three Easy Pieces he added the Galop from the other group. The remaining four of the Five Easy Pieces—

Andante, *Española, Balalaika,* and *Napolitana*—were rearranged so that *Napolitana* moved up to the second slot.

The remaining item is a waltz splinter of forty-one seconds. Jacobs says it's a "bonbon." I say it's very flat and unprofitable. But these days, every scrap of manuscript paper by a famous composer that is uncovered is published, played, and, often, recorded. Well, often these are musical skeletons in the closet and that's why they never reached publication before. The gain in bringing them to light is only that of historical documentation.

Petrouchka (Three Scenes)

☐ Yaltah Menuhin and Ryce (piano) / Everest 3130

For those who are curious, Stravinsky's own version for piano, four hands, of sections from three of the four scenes of the ballet.

Concerto *per due pianoforti soli* (1935)   *Two Pianos*
Etude for Pianola
Sonata for Two Pianos (1944)

☐ Jacobs and Oppens (pianos) / Nonesuch 71347

There is plenty of action and contrastive black-white color effect in the Concerto, so that one does not miss orchestral back-up. There is neobaroque writing, with kinetic passages and including a set of four variations minus a theme—but the theme finally surfaces as the subject for the concluding fugue. The balance and inner excitement of the performance are exhilirating.

The Sonata is glowing healthy neoclassical music, with a set of variations again (this time with a theme) as the middle movement. The work is smaller-scaled and lighter than the Concerto, and the players adopt their style accordingly. They also adopt democratic procedures in their performances. For the Concerto Paul Jacobs plays the first-piano part and Ursula Oppens the second-piano part. For the Sonata they exchange roles.

The Etude was originally written for player piano and later transcribed as the final movement in Four Etudes for Orchestra (see under *Orchestra*). It is short (two and one-half minutes in length), texturally heavy in its make-up, and just slightly vulgar. It is portrayed with fine spirit by this superb team.

Fanfare for a New Theatre (1967)   *Two Trumpets*

☐ Stevens and Guarneri (trumpets) / Crystal S–361
☐ Heinrich and Nagel (trumpets) / Columbia MS–7054

Stravinsky's two-trumpet *Fanfare* was composed for the opening of the New York State Theater at Lincoln Center in New York City. (It is also termed *Fanfare for Two Trumpets.*)

The two recordings listed are the best of three. (Oddly, all three are clocked exactly the same, at thirty-three seconds!) Both recordings noted are top-notch; a bit better sonic ambience is present on the Crystal disc. (The playing on the third release, Orion 7294, is just as good, but the sound is rather dull.)

Elégie for Unaccompanied Viola or Violin (1944)   *Viola*

☐ Trampler (viola) / RCA LSC–2974

Stravinsky's piece was composed for Germain Prévost "to be played in memory of Alphonse Onnou, founder of the Pro Arte Quartet." (Prévost was the violist of this superb organization that specialized in contemporary music.) It is akin to the da capo-aria form, with the third part a repeat of the opening; the central section is a fugato. The lines move in accordance with the sobriety of classicism, but classicism contemporaneously revitalized. And in Walter Trampler's hands the rarely heard solo instrument becomes revitalized as well.

Chamber Music

Duo concertant for Violin and Piano (1932)

☐ Perlman (violin); Canino (piano) / Angel S-37115

Bucolic poetry (or as Stravinsky said, "a musical parallel to ancient pastoral poetry") is the determining factor of the *Duo concertant*. Stravinsky's choice of forms includes the *Eclogue* (the pastoral dialogue) and the *Dithyrambe*, a eulogistic, ecstatic outpouring species of poem. But these must not be listened to with romantically trained ears, since a reforming of the original sentiments takes place in the composition's unsparing designs, which are severely classical in orientation. Musical intoxication is not to be expected; the duet is rather disciplined, its charm not corrupted by any attempt to cut capers. Stravinsky does not mix his company.

Suite d'après des thèmes, fragments et morceaux de Giambatista Pergolesi (1933)

☐ Shapiro (violin); Berkowitz (piano) / Crystal S-302

Pergolesi was amalgamated, adapted, shaped, and reshaped in Stravinsky's ballet *Pulcinella*. Later, three different suites were made from it, two for violin and piano and one for cello and piano. These contain some intercurrent duplication, movement shifts, and slight additions. One of these suites is discussed here; for the other two *see below—Suite italienne* for Cello and Piano and *Suite italienne* for Violin and Piano.

When Stravinsky transcribed his own music, the work took on a new cast. He was not content merely to reset the notes; a fresh spirit swept through the music and resulted in a type of music bordering on original production. This composer who could range from being as classically objective as he was in *Pulcinella* to being as primitivistically dynamic as he was in *Les Noces* also became a different personality in the re-creation of his own work in terms of new texture, color, and instrumental capacity.

This is an attractive performance, well detailed and not rubbished with romantic consideration.

Suite italienne for Cello and Piano (1934)

☐ Colf (cello); Mayorga (piano) / Sheffield S-12

This is one of three suites Stravinsky made from his ballet *Pulcinella*. For other discussions related to this one see the comments on the others—*above* (*Suite d'après des thèmes, fragments et morceaux de Giambatista Pergolesi*) and *below* (*Suite italienne* for Violin and Piano).

Gregor Piatigorsky, the famed cellist, was Stravinsky's collaborator in this version. The first two movements and the fifth (concluding) movement have the same place as in Stravinsky's original violin-and-piano transcription, the *Suite d'après des thèmes, fragments et morceaux de Giambatista Pergolesi*. Movement 3 is an Aria which does not appear in the other two suites; movement 4 (Tarantella) is found in third place in the other settings. (Sheffield's liner notes for the recording mention six movements for this work and seven for the violin-and-piano *Suite italienne*. The totals are in error by one too many in each instance.)

Collaboration with Samuel Dushkin in composing the violin-and-piano *Suite italienne* brought changes from Stravinsky's original violin transcription, and this cello-and-piano suite in turn differs from both of the others, and not only in terms of a different instrumental range.

Suite italienne for Violin and Piano (1934)

☐ Perlman (violin); Canino (piano) / Angel S-37115

In this setting, made in collaboration with the violinist, Samuel Dushkin, Stravinsky added one movement to the five he included in his own, earlier-dated violin transcription, the *Suite d'après des thèmes, fragments et morceaux de Giambatista Pergolesi (see above)*. A *Scherzino* was placed between the fourth part, a *Gavotta con due variazione*, and the concluding *Minuetto e finale*. The first three movements—*Introductione, Serenata*, and Tarantella—retained their same order.

But while this much order was kept, the instrumental data were changed considerably, enough that this *Suite italienne* turns out to be a transcription-paraphrase of a transcription.

If one has the recording of the initial compilation, a fascinating study in creative strategy is offered by having this one as well. The performance is first class, and the stylistic consideration is both natural and cohesive.

For Stravinsky's third suite made from *Pulcinella* see above (*Suite italienne* for Cello and Piano).

Epitaphium for Flute, Clarinet, and Harp (1959)

☐ Gleghorn (flute); Bloch (clarinet); Remsen (harp) / Stravinsky (conductor) / Columbia MS-6272

This is a memorial piece—the complete title reads *Epitaphium für das Grabmal des Prinzen Max Egon zu Fürstenberg* ("for the Tombstone of Prince Max...")—dodecaphonically presented in aphoristic fashion (the seven measures of music cover a performance time of seventy seconds). The piece is a phenomenal example of twelve-tone poetry even though rigid procedures prevail, including inversion, retrograde, and the inversion of the latter.

Concertino for String Quartet (1920)

☐ Juilliard Quartet / Columbia M-32809

Instrumental allure is a principal resource of the Concertino. It is, in total, a compact dissertation by string instruments performing with quasi-percussion and simulated wind- and brass-instrument tone. The Concertino practically amounts to a string-quartet ballet with Stravinskian scoring.

Formally, the work is set in a semisonata design, with a middle section devoted to an entrancing, unusual violin cadenza. Its measures are as plastic as Stravinsky's aesthetic and demand an expert violinist to indicate its widening phrase lengths with subtlety. So accomplished here.

Stravinsky's Concertino is not only the work of a superb composer, but a quartet that demands four virtuosi functioning as one. None others should apply, for without that class distinction the score is heard as a pastiche, its totality mistranslated. The Juilliard four define all the particulars with gorgeous nuances and instrumental vigor.

Stravinsky reworked and rescored this work for more instruments—see under *Orchestra* (Concertino for Twelve Instruments).

Double Canon for String Quartet (1959)

☐ Baker and Igleman (violins); Schonbach (viola); Neikrug (cello) / Stravinsky (conductor) / Columbia MS–6272

Polyphonic austerity for starters, but no better proof can be offered that strict twelve-tone style does not prevent producing a music of deep emotive evocation.

True, the piece is extremely concentrated (one minute and twenty seconds), but this does not lessen its worth or minimize the proof. (The complete title is Double Canon: *Raoul Dufy, in Memoriam.*)

Three Pieces for String Quartet (1914)

☐ Claremont Quartet / Nonesuch 71186

Masterful. In the middle piece of the set the music is stated in a compact and secured manner though its formations are disjunct and unbalanced—a rattlebox of dream tools. In movement 1 the Claremonters make certain not to intensify what is already intense by the repetitiveness of the melodic line (strictly concerned with a total of four sounds) and the ostinato monotony of the other voices. The chorale of the last piece, baldly satiric in a quiet way (it gives the effect of a chorus singing severely out of tune), is seamlessly phrased. Luft pauses (as in the Los Angeles String Quartet's performance on Crystal S–103) disconnect the slow-paced flow. Attempting to warm the sounds with vibrato (as in other recorded editions) is opposite to Stravinsky's wishes. The Claremont team leaves the music as it is and doesn't attempt to make it a romantic goody-goody.

Stravinsky made an orchestral version of the Three Pieces—see under *Orchestra* (Four Etudes for Orchestra).

Pastorale for Violin and Four Winds (1908)

☐ Boston Symphony Chamber Players / Deutsche Grammophon 2530551

The fourth version of this song without words. In turn, for soprano and piano, soprano and four winds, violin and piano, and violin with four winds (oboe, English horn, clarinet, and bassoon). All fine, the last the best. The piece is exquisitely played here. It is also available on a Deutsche Grammophon miscellaneous disc (No. 2545023) that also includes performances by the Boston Symphony Orchestra (Ravel) and the Boston Pops Orchestra (Tchaikovsky). Arthur Fiedler, of course, conducts the latter, Seiji Ozawa the former.

Septet (1952)

☐ Columbia Chamber Ensemble / Stravinsky (conductor) / Columbia MS–7054

The Septet (chamber music, though in this case conducted by Stravinsky) calls for violin, viola, cello, clarinet, bassoon, horn, and piano or harpsichord—a piano is used in this recording. It calls on baroque forms, including a Passacaglia and a Gigue. All the moves of the serial syndicate are followed: augmentation, retrograde, inversion, retrograde inversion. There are canons and variations, fugue, fugato, and *stretto*. But winding through all of it one recognizes the Stravinsky personality. It's his, though it is a creased-face Stravinsky one perceives.

A good, meticulously stated performance.

Octet for Wind Instruments (1923)

☐ Netherlands Wind Ensemble / de Waart (conductor) / Philips 6500841

In choosing the colors for his Octet, Stravinsky wanted to avoid color. He desired juxtaposed sonority for the sake of sound, but at all costs he wished to eliminate any emotional consideration. Well now, over a half century has passed since the work was completed in 1923, and today one listens to the Octet and marvels at its clear colors, and the exciting measuring of its varied sounds. This response (more than mere intellectual appeal) does not play false with the composer's intentions, for there is still at this remove the freshness of nonobjectivity relating to the dynamically neutralized, timbred flat surfaces of this masterpiece for winds (flute, clarinet, and two bassoons) and brass (two each of trumpets and trombones). These sounds are absolutely defined, since there is a negation of *applied* ornamentation.

The lucidity and verve and the textural sharpness and style of the playing by the Netherlanders are just marvelous. In every respect Edo de Waart makes certain that the instrumental weights are exact so that the musical architecture is absolutely clear. In that way the performance also does not play false with the composer. There is no question that this is the prime realization of the score, fulfilling all of Stravinsky's objectives better than his own recorded versions (on Columbia MS–6272 and M–30579).

The Owl and the Pussy-Cat

☐ Albert (soprano); Craft (piano) / Columbia MS–7054

A type of recitative that moves on the toes of disjunctive intervals in the vocal line, thereby clarifying the Edward Lear text. A Stravinsky snippet of two and one-half minutes and well stated in Adrienne Albert's delivery and Robert Craft's back-up.

Berceuses du chat (1916)

☐ Members of the Orchestre du Théâtre National de l'Opéra, Paris / Scharley (mezzo-soprano) / Boulez (conductor) / Nonesuch 71133

Easygoing folk texts in a rather exotic format, the voice being supported by three clarinets. A beautifully stated recording.

Elegy for J.F.K. (1964)

☐ Berberian (mezzo-soprano); Howland, Kreiselman, and Russo (clarinets) / Columbia MS–7054

There are four stanzas of text, only sixty-eight syllables long. Text by W. H. Auden, serial music by I. Stravinsky. Meaningful but the aphoristic conception (under two minutes in length) doesn't register sufficiently by itself and one wishes for just a bit more musical scope—that is, an enlargement of the data.

Stravinsky wrote this especially for Cathy Berberian. She sings with poetic insight.

Four Russian Songs (1955)

☐ Albert (mezzo-soprano) / Stravinsky (conductor) / Columbia M–31124

Two of the *Quatre Chants russes* (written in 1918–1919) and two of the *Histoires pour enfants* (composed in 1913), originally for voice and piano and recolored for voice, flute, harp, and guitar in 1955. The songs represent Stravinskian nationalism, with Stravinskian piquance and effervescence.

The clipped, blackout-cadence style is admirably projected by Adrienne Albert. The unnamed three other musicians deserve full credit for their fine support.

In Memoriam Dylan Thomas (1954)

☐ Columbia Chamber Ensemble / Young (tenor) / Stravinsky (conductor) / Columbia MS–6992

Vocal

Voice with Accompaniment

Voice and Instrumental Ensemble

One memorial gesture links with another in this work. Dylan Thomas's poem *Do Not Go Gentle into That Good Night,* written in memory of the poet's father, is set to music by Stravinsky as a memorial tribute to Thomas. The song is preceded and followed by instrumental sections which are termed Dirge-Canons, scored for a trombone quartet and a string quartet.

This is deeply felt music strengthened by its serialistic permutations. It strikes deep, its dark appulsion beautifully registered in a most moving performance.

Pribaoutki (1914)

☐ Members of the Orchestre du Théâtre National de l'Opéra, Paris / Brumaire (soprano) / Boulez (conductor) / Nonesuch 71133

Capsulized music, the set of four songs covering four minutes. The soprano is accompanied by an octet (two quartets, one of winds—flute, oboe, clarinet, and bassoon—and the other of string instruments—violin, viola, cello, and double bass). Boulez directs a presentation that has the fullest clarity and precision, and with every nuance on target.

Three Songs from William Shakespeare (1954)

☐ Ensemble Amsterdam / Dorow (soprano) / de Leeuw (conductor) / Telefunken 642350

Shakespeare treated serialistically. *Musick to Heare* is a version of Shakespeare's eighth sonnet, in praise of music; Ariel's song from Act II of *The Tempest* ("Full Fadom Five") follows; and the final item consists of stanzas from the last act of *Love's Labour's Lost* ("When Daisies Pied"). If Webern's twelve-note music is black and white, Stravinsky's tends to roam in the red-green area. Dorothy Dorow's command of these songs (with flute, clarinet, and viola) is outstanding.

Voice and Orchestra

Abraham and Isaac (1964)

☐ Columbia Symphony Orchestra / Frisch (baritone) / Craft (conductor) / Columbia MS-7386

A sacred ballad composed on the Hebrew text in Genesis (Chapter XXII). Hebrew is therefore used, since translation would nullify the decided purity of Stravinsky's plan, which folds the Hebrew syllables (both for accentuation and for timbre variety) within the dodecaphonicism. The two fit perfectly and in certain respects far better than any other language would if treated in this exact manner. The vocal line has melismatic qualities (Stravinsky cleverly terms this "*bel*-cantor"), which are convincingly detailed in Richard Frisch's delivery.

Choral

Chorus Alone

Anthem (*The Dove Descending Breaks the Air*) (1962)

☐ Festival Singers of Toronto / Stravinsky (conductor) / Columbia MS-7054

Text by T. S. Eliot from *Little Gidding* in his *Four Quartets.* The theme of divine love is basic to the words, and the theme of divine serialism is basic to the music. No hard ground is to be found in this musical terrain.

The singing is rather placid. The same applies to the version on Nonesuch 71115, presented by the Canby Singers.

Ave Maria (1934)

☐ Festival Singers of Toronto / Stravinsky (conductor) / Columbia M-31124

One of three choruses (*see below* for the other two, *Credo* and *Pater Noster*) specifically structured for the Byzantine liturgy.

Credo (1932)

☐ Gregg Smith Singers / Stravinsky (conductor) / Columbia M-31124

Composed in the spirit and style of traditional Byzantine music. Originally set in Russian in 1932, it was given a Latin text in 1949 and then, in 1964, reset in its original language.

Magnificent choral singing.

For two other choruses structured, as this one is, for the Byzantine liturgy *see above* (*Ave Maria*) and *below* (*Pater Noster*).

Pater Noster (1926)

☐ Festival Singers of Toronto / Stravinsky (conductor) / Columbia M-31124

As he did with his *Credo* (*see above*) Stravinsky changed the language of the text of this sacred piece. It was first published in Russian and then twenty-three years later given a Latin text.

Beautiful music given a fully expressive performance.

For another such chorus also *see above* (*Ave Maria*).

Four Russian Peasant Songs for Equal Voices with Four Horns (1954)

Chorus and Instrumental Ensemble

☐ Gregg Smith Singers / Stravinsky (conductor) / Columbia M-31124

Settings of peppy texts, originally composed, one a year between 1914 and 1917, for unaccompanied female chorus. The second version, enlarging the conception by diametric contrast of color via a horn quartet, appeared in 1954. (*Schwann* lists this work as *Saucer*, a condensation of the original title, *Saucer Readings*.)

Ringing, vital quality and pinpointed style are projected by this fine group.

Introitus: T. S. Eliot in Memoriam (1965)

☐ Columbia Chamber Ensemble and Gregg Smith Singers / Stravinsky (conductor) / Columbia MS-7386

Streamlined serialism and suppressed scoring mark this sober music. A small group of male voices intones the principal material with the simple support of harp, piano, viola, double bass, four timpani, and two gongs. The reserved commentary is beautifully presented in this recording. It is a tribute to Eliot and in turn to Stravinsky as both composer and conductor.

Babel (1946)

Cantata and Oratorio

☐ CBC Symphony Orchestra and Festival Singers of Toronto / Colicos (narrator) / Stravinsky (conductor) / Columbia M-31124

One of a set of seven pieces by as many composers, included in a project conceived by the composer-conductor Nathaniel Shilkret. Shilkret composed one part; the others, in addition to Stravinsky, were Castelnuovo-Tedesco, Milhaud, Schoenberg (see under *Schoenberg: Choral: chorus and orchestra* (Prelude to *The Genesis* Suite, Op. 44), Tansman, and Toch. All worked independently, and the pieces stand similarly. (The inclusion of Ernest Bloch in place of Ernst Toch in Roman Vlad's book *Stravinsky* is an error.)

The text is from the first book of Moses, second chapter. It is used as the focal point for finely organized background music which includes in its scoring portfolio an orchestral prelude, a choral prologue, an instrumental fugato, and a postlude.

The imagery is well placed in this performance. Especially compelling is the narrator, fulfilling Stravinsky's requirement that he be not simply a male, but a narrator of "masculine" quality.

Cantata (1952)

☐ Columbia Chamber Ensemble and Gregg Smith Singers / Albert (mezzo-soprano); Young (tenor) / Stravinsky (conductor) / Columbia MS–6992

Secular music that Stravinsky immerses in a mix of modality, pandiatonic combinations, and canonic procedures.

The performance has both clarity and precision, though its dynamic reticence is somewhat overstressed.

Le Roi des étoiles (1911)

☐ Boston Symphony Orchestra and New England Conservatory Male Chorus / Thomas (conductor) / Deutsche Grammophon 2530252

"The King of Stars" (*Zvezdoliki*) is given a subtly charged reading that makes it the choice over a more restrained reading by the composer.

Les Noces (1917-1923)

☐ Members of the Orchestra and Chorus of the Théâtre National de l'Opéra, Paris / Brumaire (soprano); Scharley (mezzo-soprano); Pottier (tenor); Van Dam (bass); Joy, Marika, Delécluse, and Quéval (pianos) / Boulez (conductor) / Nonesuch 71133

A choral and vocal creation that is toughly tenacious with its dynamic percussiveness, bringing excitement with its constancy made plastic by asymmetricalization and more excitement with its four pianos and seventeen percussion instruments. *Les Noces* is a highlight of twentieth-century music and has had seminal influence (Carl Orff's *Carmina Burana* and other of his works, for example, derive totally from Stravinsky's opus). It remains at this date an aural revelation.

This is a remarkably scrupulous performance and that's what *Les Noces* demands. Tight control, tautness, and tigery impact are here, with no lessening of the pulsatile drive from start to finish. The music is scrubbed, but in the smashing brightness provided in this recording the guts have not been removed. This is one of the most splendid recordings Boulez has given us. It is, certainly, a definitive statement.

Mass (1948)

☐ Winds and Brass of the Columbia Symphony and Gregg Smith Singers / Baxter (soprano); Albert (alto) / Stravinsky (conductor) / Columbia MS–6992

Stravinsky follows the Catholic ritual in his Mass, which he indicated was composed for use in church, not in concert. The latter situation, however, has not been bypassed. Neither has austerity in the setting for mixed voices (further mixed by using children's voices for the soprano and alto lines and adults for the tenor and bass parts) with a double quintet of five wind instruments and five brass instruments.

Oedipus Rex (1927)

☐ Cologne Radio Symphony Orchestra and Chorus / Mödl (soprano); Pears and Krebs (tenors); Rehfuss (baritone); von Rohr (bass); Cocteau (narrator) / Stravinsky (conductor) / Odyssey 33789 (monaural)

The old recording, made in 1951, stands firm as the choice for this opera-oratorio.

(*Oedipus Rex* has also been presented in ballet form.) There are no weaknesses here, and that covers soloists, orchestra, and chorus, plus magnificent delivery by Jean Cocteau, who prepared the text "after Sophocles."

The Odyssey narration is in French. For an English version there is Michael Wager with Bernstein conducting the Boston Symphony Orchestra and the Harvard Glee Club on Columbia M-33999, but Wager's pronunciations are a little affected.

Requiem Canticles (1966)

☐ Columbia Symphony Orchestra and Ithaca College Concert Choir / Anderson (soprano); Bonazzi (alto); Bressler (tenor); Gramm (bass) / Craft (conductor) / Columbia MS-7386

A compressed requiem format is operative here, with sections from the requiem in the Latin ritual. There are nine movements, of which three are solely instrumental. The Canticles are strictly serial-styled (more exactly, the twelve tones are used according to Stravinsky's own dodecaphonic procedure which is a particular type of strictness), and the sonorous dialect is ecclesiastically impressed in its styling.

Robert Craft's direction of this music displays fine style with admirable definition and balance between instruments and voices. A splendid essay.

A Sermon, a Narrative, and a Prayer (1961)

☐ CBC Symphony Orchestra / Verrett (mezzo-soprano); Driscoll (tenor); Horton (speaker) / Stravinsky (conductor) / Columbia MS-7054

In turn, the three parts of this work are based on texts from St. Paul's Letter to the Romans, his Letter to the Hebrews in the Acts of the Apostles, and a poem by the Jacobean playwright Thomas Dekker.

The music (in its melodic, rhythmic, and contrapuntal facets) proves again how intensely emotional serial style can be—in the hands of a master. There is an emotionalism within this score that marks it as one of Stravinsky's great creations in his final (serial) period of work.

This is a five-star performance, with the diction on the part of vocalists and narrator absolutely clear. The playing of the orchestra (medium-sized, including piano, harp, and three gongs) is sensitive.

Symphony of Psalms (1930)

☐ RCA Victor Symphony Orchestra and Robert Shaw Chorale / Shaw (conductor) / RCA LSC-2822

Stravinsky's sober "white" music makes for a lean and spare document but nonetheless one of remarkable richness, especially in the individually styled orchestration, which cuts off violins and violas from the strings. The score is replete with nonconventional doublings, producing instrumental substances that give necessary balance with transparency. There are no gluey pedals; everything moves; all is plastic.

Probing rhythms and colorful sonorities fill the music. There are dozens of examples in the score. The punctuations in the first movement, the two-octave doubling of the altos by the oboe, the inventive spacing of chords (a lesson in how to dispose of a chordal triad) in the final movement, etc. The sound sensations are an orchestrator's dream.

Shaw's consideration of this work is good. The rhythms are tight, the singing excellent. Occasionally there is a tendency to emphasize voices above orchestral forces, failing to realize that the latter are in no way an embellishment. Otherwise, this is a fundamentally viable realization of Stravinsky's great work.

Opera and Dramatic Music

L'Histoire du soldat (1918)

☐ Boston Symphony Chamber Players / Gielgud (narrator); Courtenay and Moody (speaking parts) / Deutsche Grammophon 2530609

The problem with the available recordings is lack of equal validity. If the playing is worthy, the speaking is not totally so, and vice versa. Here, Gielgud is marvelous, and so are Courtenay as The Soldier and Moody as The Devil. The B.S.O. outfit is less than marvelous simply because the players seem a bit intolerant of the atmosphere in which they are involved. They sound as though they are removed from the action, and what they have to play is merely accompanimental. But again, you won't find an ideal ranking twixt those that play and those that speak. This edition is the best available of the two worlds.

For this work in concert-suite form see under *Orchestra* (*L'Histoire du soldat*—Suite).

Mavra (1922)

☐ L'Orchestre de la Suisse Romande / Carlye (soprano); Watts and Sinclair (altos); MacDonald (tenor) / Ansermet (conductor) / London STS-15102

Stravinsky's comic opera is pre-neoclassic in style, and its Russianism can be described as "townspeople's or small landowners' music." Swell scoring that swells like a hurdy-gurdy at times in the winds. The orchestra is a typically Stravinskian property, with four clarinets, four trumpets, three trombones, tuba, some percussion, and a small string section of nine players, heavy in the bass zone, with three each of the cellos and double basses. These furnish winsome rhythmic basses and tickling figurations.

Ansermet delivers a totally alert performance, pert and spry, stimulatingly sharp in all respects. Good singing as well.

The Rake's Progress (1951)

☐ Royal Philharmonic Orchestra and Sadler's Wells Opera Chorus / Raskin and Manning (sopranos); Sarfaty (contralto); Young and Miller (tenors); Reardon (baritone); Garrard and Tracey (basses); Tilney (harpsichord) / Stravinsky (conductor) / Columbia M3S-710

Stravinsky's neobaroque-styled three-act opera (divided into nine scenes) follows traditional classical lines with the use of aria, recitative, chorus, and ensemble. It has the essence of Mozart in its spirituality, and the theatricality of Donizetti. To this can be added the depth of Bach. But this is no eclectic brew, no reworking (over and around) another composer's tunes. It is all Igor Stravinsky at his smartest best and convinces one that it is a masterpiece of twentieth-century opera.

It is wrapped around a splendid libretto by W. H. Auden and Chester Kallman. Few composers have been better served in this respect. And this is emphasized in the recording by the most splendid diction a group of singers has ever placed on disc. *Sit back, you don't need any text to follow.*

Alexander Young triumphs as Tom Rakewell, Judith Raskin in the role of Anne Truelove sings sweetly and is warmly dramatic, and the underlying evil of the Nick Shadow character is strikingly portrayed by John Reardon. There isn't a move below top excellence by anyone in the cast of characters, the chorus, or the orchestra.

The Rake's Progress is an enchanting work and a deeply expressive one as well. This is a great recording and is highly recommended. It is even better than the superfine issue that Columbia placed on the market back in the mono days with Stravinsky also conducting on SL-125. That deleted issue had a cast including Hilde Gueden, Martha Lipton, Blanche Thebom, Eugene Conley, Mack Harrell, Paul Franke, Norman Scott, and

Lawrence Davidson, supported by the orchestra and chorus of the Metropolitan Opera Association.

Renard (1922)

☐ L'Orchestre de la Suisse Romande / Sénéchal and Cuenod (tenors); Rehfuss (baritone); Depraz (bass); Arato (cimbalom) / Ansermet (conductor) / London STS-15028
☐ Columbia Chamber Ensemble / Shirley and Driscoll (tenors); Murphy (baritone); Gramm (bass); Koves (cimbalom) / Stravinsky (conductor) / Columbia M-31124

What is cardinal in performing Stravinsky's *Histoire burlesque chantée et jouée* is detailed verve and more detailed verve in the singing. Otherwise the singers, who are identified with the actors, who, importantly, do not speak, will not bring out the complementary relationships that exist. In a recording, minus the clowns or dancers or acrobats who are to act out the play, obviously this requirement is thrice important.

The Ansermet edition has such clarity and has underheavy pace. It also has a brightness that throws the sonorities into splendid relief. The verbiage is in French, but no translation is offered. In the Stravinsky-led production a copy of the text is included even though the work is presented in English. The Stravinsky representation is quieter, but the edged delivery of both singers and instrumentalists removes any possibility of dullness. There is as much authority as found in the Ansermet conception, but it is simply of a different type. While this results in more comic consistency, it does not, in comparison, reduce the effectiveness of Ansermet's performance. Both are handsome interpretations of "The Fox."

Apollo (Apollon Musagète) (1928) *Ballet*

☐ Berlin Philharmonic Orchestra / von Karajan (conductor) / Deutsche Grammophon 2530065

Stravinsky chose stringed instruments for *Apollo* in order to produce a classical *ballet blanc,* the scoring to underline the monochromatic order of the music. He subtly strengthened the string gamut at its extremes, calling for sextuple division of the group into first and second violins, violas, first and second cellos, and double basses. *Apollo* was planned as a ballet minus intensive narrative intent. (Stravinsky again: "'Apollo and the Muses' suggested to me not so much a plot as a signature.")

The B.P.O. performance is beautifully realized; the clarity of its string group is precise, the statement is properly dramatic and sensitively phrased. Von Karajan gives the score a dimension that is beyond criticism.

The Firebird

☐ Columbia Symphony Orchestra / Stravinsky (conductor) / Columbia MS-6328

The Firebird with its varieties of editions (complete or nearly so) and orchestra suites, with dates of orchestration and publication of 1910, 1911, 1919, and 1945 involved, has caused a musicological maze, mouth-watering for those who wish to find their way through it but an annoying mishmash for the general listener. It is for that reason that it is important to have this version of the complete ballet in its original 1910 orchestration, conducted by Stravinsky himself. It guarantees authenticity of the basic (seed) score from which all else followed.

Whatever the arguments about Stravinsky's ability as a conductor of his own music (involving, in this case and others, the differences between his tempi and timings and those in the printed score), this *Firebird* recording by the great man deserves the fullest attention.

Jeu de cartes (1937)

☐ Cleveland Orchestra / Stravinsky (conductor) / Columbia M–31921

This elastically conceived neoclassic score is best depicted in the hands of the fellow who conceived it. Tender romanticizing of sections of the piece, apparent in both of the competitive editions, (Svetlanov conducting the USSR Symphony Orchestra on Melodiya/Angel S–40219 and Abbado conducting the London Symphony Orchestra on Deutsche Grammophon 2530537) implies meanings which are not present in Stravinsky's musical conception of "A Card Game."

Le Baiser de la fée (1928)

☐ L'Orchestre de la Suisse Romande / Ansermet (conductor) / London 2308

Fully spirited in its delineation. It's not the simplest matter to deal with the subtleties that abound in "The Fairy's Kiss," what with the split scoring and the criss-cross of the rhythms. However, Ansermet supplies an X-ray of the music, and it spins off the grooves with as much clarity as a Mozart overture. Who could do better?

See under *Orchestra* (*Le Baiser de la fée*—Divertimento) for the suite extracted from the ballet.

Le Sacre du printemps (1913)

☐ London Philharmonic Orchestra / Haitink (conductor) / Philips 6500482
☐ Chicago Symphony Orchestra / Solti (conductor) / London 6885
☐ Columbia Symphony Orchestra / Stravinsky (conductor) / Columbia MS–6319

There is positive electricity in these presentations. Solti meets the music head on, and the voltage is remarkable. If the paradox can be permitted, the playing is of riotous order and yet controlled. There's a blaze that even brightens the softer-colored timbres such as the alto flute and English horn. Haitink has less heat, but there is such rhythmic exudation as to impel energy into every individual pulse of the music even when it is riding on ostinato rails. The shock of this music has gone, but in a statement such as Haitink gives us there is tremendous excitement at all times. Again a paradox is proposed: in his conception there are no hard edges to the music, but a palpitating violence. The saber-edged control of the *Danse sacrale* (in the revised 1943 version which Stravinsky also uses) is magnificent.

Stravinsky's version has more than documentary value going for it. As with Haitink one realizes in listening to Stravinsky conduct his own work that there is more than musical savagism in this masterpiece. Stravinsky's reading has a lyrical potency that is even more confirmed than in the other chosen performances. However, the Chicago and London outfits are superior orchestras.

The Stravinsky-led performance of Stravinsky's "Rite" is obtainable in other all-Stravinsky Columbia packages—namely, in M–31830, in a two-record program on MG–31202, in a three-record issue on D3S–705, and in a sumptuous twelve-record-side release on D5S–775.

Orpheus (1948)

☐ Chicago Symphony Orchestra / Stravinsky (conductor) / Columbia MS–6646

The three scenes of *Orpheus* follow fairly closely the Orpheus and Eurydice tale. The warm melancholy of the score is entrancing and bears out Stravinsky's statement that much of the work is "mimed song." Though the orchestra is full-sized in woodwind, brass (minus only the tuba), strings, harp, and timpani (with no other percussion), a chamber-music quality prevails. Even the fast-tempoed *Pas des Furies* which opens the second scene is softly treated. This is quite different from the scoring of most of the other works of Stravinsky's neoclassic period.

The soft radiance of *Orpheus* comes through with poignant results. There has been much talk of the pros and cons of Stravinsky's ability as a conductor of his own music. I cannot agree with this critical ambivalence. The combination is exciting.

This recorded edition is also included with three other compositions in an all-Stravinsky release on Columbia D3S–761.

Petrouchka (1911)

☐ London Philharmonic Orchestra / Haitink (conductor) / Philips 6500458

The complete ballet for large orchestra as here recorded dates from 1911. A reduction of the orchestral forces was made by Stravinsky in 1947. (This was for both practical and business purposes—to make more performances possible and to recapture copyright protection.) For the 1947 ballet version one should turn to Stravinsky's own direction of the work (on Columbia MS–6332 and Columbia D3S–705).

The force and vitality (and intense orchestrational strength) are splendidly determined in this rendition. Haitink has the proper feel for the composition's color and "Russo-*peasantish*" flamboyance.

Pulcinella: Ballet with Song, in One Act, After Pergolesi (1949)

☐ Columbia Symphony Orchestra / Jordan (soprano); Shirley (tenor); Gramm (bass) / Stravinsky (conductor) / Columbia D3S–761

In Stravinsky's score for this work the indication is that it is "after" Pergolesi, but in truth it can be described as "an absorption of Pergolesi." For the greater part of the piece the Pergolesi melodic lines are kept clear of remodeling but the harmonic fabric is adjusted, refurbished, tightened, and neatly recolored, with sharp pandiatonicism used to color the material. In its own particular way this approach is just as revolutionary as the violence of *Le Sacre du printemps,* since it shows a creative artist using the values obtained from older, proven conditions and restating them by way of new standards. The barbaric splendor of Russian paganism is not lost because Stravinsky shifted from primordial technique to a style directly opposite. Such splendor there is in *Pulcinella,* but it is nimble, not heavy; coolness replaces heat.

The realization is just as fresh and clear, completely a rich, rhythmically incisive production. There have been arguments that Stravinsky was only a fair-to-middlin' conductor not only of his own but of any music, but I cannot agree, and there can be *no* argument about the expertness of direction or playing in this instance. Stravinsky's absorption of Pergolesi's music is an absorbing five-star essay.

For the orchestral suite see under *Orchestra* (Pulcinella Suite).

Stravinsky / *J. S. Bach.* See *J. S. Bach* / Stravinsky.

Tison Street   *(1943-   )*

String Quartet (1972)

☐ Concord String Quartet / Composers Recordings S–305

Chamber Music

Repetition is foreign here as the four instruments exult in a comprehensive survey of voices loose on a serial-sprung concerto-orgy spree. Street describes his handling of rhythm as one "of waves or of swaying branches rather than a steady pulse." Indeed. Of the 220 total measures most are rhapsodically complicated effusions that remind one of the thicker scores of Ives and the methods of Carter.

The contrapuntal disciplines within the quartet are many. Street mentions "canons, cancrizans, augmentations, palindromes, canti firmi, etc." Score analysis proves the technical boast. The ear can hardly separate these as they occur, since Street sings his twelve pitches in multitudinous ways and patterns. One sonic pollination succeeds to a cross-pollination, one motival progeneration leads to a secondary fecundation. All this with flow and without hesitation. Controlled at the composer's source, it is heard as unfettered, uninhibited, and unrestrained music for stringed instruments.

Music of this type needs a quartet that specializes in the far-left style; among other expectations is understanding. Only a few quartets able to play such music well are available. Among the very best is the Concord foursome. They present a perfect representation of this heady score.

String Quintet (1974)

☐ Concord Quartet / Thompson (viola) / Composers Recordings SD–381

Mainly, a virtuoso thrust rules this work, but there are sections that have the opposite atmosphere. Street's music is free-willed, of instrumentalized intrusive speech. It glows with contemporary health and has a command of astounding brilliance. That's the manner in which these masterly musicians play.

George Templeton Strong   (1856-1948)

String Orchestra

Chorale on a Theme of Leo Hassler

☐ Eastman-Rochester Symphony Orchestra / Hanson (conductor) / Eastman-Rochester Archives ERA–1013

A darkly toned piece that has the same mysterious beauty of sound and polyphony as Vaughan Williams's Fantasia on a Theme by Tallis. The performance is thoroughly sensitive.

Morton Subotnick   (1933-   )

Orchestra

Laminations

☐ Buffalo Philharmonic Orchestra / Foss (conductor) / Turnabout 34428

A sound sandwich of electronic material and orchestral data. There is a further ingredient; namely, a considerable amount of the orchestration imitates electronic shapes. The complicated orchestral scoring that produces continuously charged particles includes a great number of rhythmically free passages. These too blend into the total mass, so that it is mostly impossible to identify a pulse design or distinguish the tape sounds from the instrumental ones, which is doubtless what Subotnick wanted.

Turnabout did not exactly know what it wanted for the title of the piece. It is sometimes *Laminations,* other times "Lamination." To further confuse, the published score is headed "Lamination I."

Prelude No. 4 for Piano and Electronic Tape (1966)

Instrumental

Piano

☐ Bunger (piano) / Avant 1008

Most of the piano material is dreamy, lyrical, and nocturnally improvisational in effect. Most of the interest lies in the suave inventive sounds Subotnick organized on the tape via the Buchla synthesizer. The net result: the piano accompanies, as it were, the tape!

Four Butterflies

Electronic Music

☐ Columbia M–32741

However much one allows and accepts (or is able to follow) the technical polemic of the composer (fully detailed with charts and drawings on the sleeve note) the essential appeal of *Butterflies* is to the emotions. From the "electric music box" Subotnick has filled his six-part work with forms that register with a poetic passion special to the electronic field.

It is strongly suggested, therefore, that listening precede the reading of Subotnick's technical method of investigation for the creation of his piece. Intuitive response will prove the reasoning of the latter to be successful. The reverse procedure places an unfair burden on the unbiased listener.

Sidewinder

☐ Columbia M–30683

Notwithstanding the title, Subotnick's major-sized work (created on the "electric music box") is not a programmatic entry in the field of electronic music. Like most of Subotnick's compositions, the material unfolds in a series of patterned repetitions and pedal formations, contrasted with purely timbral inventions. Within the continuity one will discover (given sufficient listening time) an internal harmony that binds the expressive individuation. Of all the electronic composers, only Subotnick reaches back to transfer instrumental symphonicism into the abstract sonic formatives that mark electronic composition. In this he is tremendously successful.

Touch

☐ Columbia MS–7316

Very few composers of electronic music manage the formal requirements necessary to hold a work together, regardless of its special medium. With Subotnick, structure does not give way to a mere knitting together of atmospheric swatches. There is poetic imagery and colorfully tooled sound properties in the balanced shape of *Touch*. To accomplish this in a work filling two complete record sides is truly a feat.

Until Spring

☐ Odyssey Y–34158

Created "on the Electric Music Box," for which read "synthesizer." Lots of sounds herein, some like a whirly-bird in the sky, others close to triadic assertiveness; whatever, all are cogent. The bleeps and Morse-codish data are exceedingly minute in this long (half-hour) creation. It becomes very apparent that Subotnick uses the most intelligent creative strategy in his electronic compositions: a musical offensive with formal definition. It may take a long time to cover the ground, but the moves are of absolute interest.

Robert Suderburg (1936-   )

Solo Instrument and Orchestra

Piano

Concerto: *Within the Mirror of Time* for Piano and Orchestra

☐ Seattle Symphony Orchestra / Siki (piano) / Katims (conductor) / Odyssey Y-34140

Quotations by Proust and Eliot are set next to the subtitles of the three movements: *Lyric Reflection, Presto,* and *Ritual Dance.* Suderburg hopes "the quotations will help preset the audience for the music they will hear." But there is no programmaticism per se. The work breathes virtuosic fire additional to its definition as being "1974 romantic-impressionistic." Add further: strong contemporary diction with no cozy and serene rhythmic punctuation. It's a big hunk of music, strong in its swing back to the traditional, juiced up with some of the creative experiences that have turned up in the last fifty years.

Béla Siki gets a high mark for his projection of the solo role. Katims and his colleagues share this statistic. At times not the clearest reproduction, but it won't interfere too much, really.

Chamber Music

Chamber Music II—Dramatic Entertainments for String Quartet (1967)

☐ Philadelphia String Quartet / Turnabout 34524

Though there are cross-references to other composers' mannerisms (including Bartók-ian percussiveness and one measure of inaudible bow movement which reminds one of Lukas Foss) that articulate Suderburg's narrative, he is very much his own man. Certainly he is not of the serial establishment, though a free-wheeling use of the total chromatic spectrum is in play.

Suderburg's quartet is an example of contemporary conjugation in terms of all the parameters. The aesthetic is one of optimistic vitality, of logical consistency, and of keen and subtle technical insight. While there is no surrender to rigid tactics, there is full surrender to colorful drama. It is this factor that tones the work, that solidifies it without resorting to regulatory form, and that avoids the regretful whimwhams that mar considerable modern music.

The Philadelphians (really the once-Philadelphians, since they formed the ensemble when all were members of the Philadelphia Orchestra) have this work in their guts. A virtuoso, graphic depiction is given it, and every difficulty (tons of 'em) is tossed off with the greatest ease and with the greatest meaning. Five stars for this one.

Josef Suk (1874-1935)

String Orchestra

Serenade in E flat major for Strings, Op. 6

☐ Los Angeles Chamber Orchestra / Marriner (conductor) / Argo ZRG-792

Warm expansive expression that reverberates with heart-warming tunes. No novel twists, no novel meanings. Performed with utter delight and beautiful sonorities. The other edition in the catalogue, conducted by Münchinger (London 6737), belongs in the same league only technically; effectively it doesn't ring with sufficient joyful conviction.

Solo Instrument and Orchestra

Violin

Appassionata

☐ Vienna Kohonaden Orchestra / Zsigmondy (violin) / Hagen (conductor) / Klavier 504

One of the many sleepers contained in the huge catalogue of small pieces, hidden under uninformational catch-all album titles such as this one, "The Romantic Violin."

Zippy, cross-accented nationalism contrasted to an ecstatic melodic section. The music's worth the attention. For the performers a listeners' advisory is to be noted.

Four Pieces for Violin and Piano, Op. 17

Instrumental

☐ Steiner (violin); Berfield (piano) / Orion 74160

Violin

A common element in these pieces is the strong emphasis on dramatic situations, even in the quietest moments. The cumulative effect climaxes in the final *Burleske,* which, performed separately, has served as concert fare ever since the work became known. Diana Steiner exhibits a fluent talent; she is most persuasive in her phrasing and tone. And she certainly is very close to matching Ricci's excellent and blazing performance of the *Burleske* (on London STS–15049).

Arthur Sullivan   (1842-1900)

In Memoriam—**Overture in C major**

Orchestra

☐ City of Birmingham Symphony Orchestra / Robinson (organ) / Dunn (conductor) / Klavier 521

A pretty example of Victorian music. Nicely Mendelssohnian. Nicely presented.

The Merchant of Venice—**Suite**

The Tempest—**Incidental Music, Op. 1**

☐ City of Birmingham Symphony Orchestra / Dunn (conductor) / Klavier 521

Gilbert and Sullivan stylistic testimony is set forth in Sullivan's *Merchant of Venice* music. Heard are the Introduction, Bourrée, *A la Valse,* and the Finale. Parts 2, 4, and 6 of the Suite are omitted. The other work also is excerpted, with seven sections performed (including the dynamic Introduction and the sonorous Overture to Act IV). Sufficient to show the creative talent of a nineteen-year-old.

All of this music has been shelved for so long one had forgotten its existence. One wonders why *the* Boston maestro hadn't given these works his attention. Sir Vivian Dunn has performed a special service in making these pieces available, and his performances are special.

Sullivan / Charles Mackerras (1925-   )

Pineapple Poll

Ballet

☐ Pro Arte Orchestra / Hollingsworth (conductor) / Vanguard S-292

Based on W. S. Gilbert's story *The Bumboat Woman,* Mackerras's ballet score is compactly assorted from Sullivan's operas. Zestful music fills the measures of the score, its easily turned tunes made for easily popularized listening. It is difficult not to be caught up in the rhythmic chemistry of this fourteen-part work.

Nice, sparkling rendition. All the vigor and vitality desired are represented. It's been in the catalogue a long time, but the sound is fresh and natural.

ranz von Suppé

Orchestra

March from *Fatinitza*

☐ North German Radio Orchestra / Müller Lampertz (conductor) / Musical Heritage Society MHS-1370

This is a rare bird and the only recorded example. It has a beer-hall atmosphere that one does not identify with any of Suppé's music.

Its absence from the Suppé repertory is odd if one considers Nicolas Slonimsky's score sheet for the operettas. *Light Cavalry* is noted as having been "enormously popular," *Boccaccio* as "very popular," and *Fantinitza* as "extremely popular."

The performance is on the German-community-orchestra level but will do. (MHS incorrectly spells the title "Fatiniza.")

Overture to *The Beautiful Galatea*

☐ New York Philharmonic / Bernstein (conductor) / Columbia D3S-818

Spontaneity, no sentimentality, and rich woodwind tone make this the choice among the several entries. A close second is Szöke's version on Vox (516540). Bernstein's performance is also obtainable in a one-record album (Columbia MS-7085). The listing above covers an eighteen-overture compilation.

Overture to *Boccaccio*

☐ Südwestfunk Orchestra, Baden-Baden / Szöke (conductor) / Vox 516540

A quality performance and producing a better-balanced statement than the other one (on Angel S-3682, with Boskovsky conducting the Vienna Johann Strauss Orchestra) of the two publications available at this time. Suppé's quote of the head triadic motive of *The Blue Danube* as the basis for the initial part of the Overture adds special interest to his operetta prelude.

Overture to *If I Were King*

☐ New Symphony Orchestra of London / Agoult (conductor) / London STS-15223

A serviceable account of one of the lesser-known Suppé overtures.

Overture to *The Jolly Robbers*

☐ Berlin Philharmonic Orchestra / von Karajan (conductor) / Deutsche Grammophon 2530051

Terming a performance of a Suppé Overture "powerful" may seem almost ridiculous, but the punchy interpretative reading given this Overture deserves the word used. A little brash too, and it helps. The D.G. sound is "wow!"

Overture to *The Light Cavalry*

☐ New York Philharmonic / Bernstein (conductor) / Columbia D3S-818
☐ Philadelphia Orchestra / Ormandy (conductor) / RCA ARL1-0453

Bernstein's shrewd conception brings dividends. He broadens the operatic-declamatory lyrical section, heard in unison, and he hastens the "hurry, hurry" fast-paced section. All very dramatic and exciting. Ormandy's timing is only seventeen seconds slower, but the method used is exactly opposite to Bernstein's: a bit less deliberate in the unison passage and more settled on the surface in the agitated division. Still, a most satisfactory projection of this militaristic, fanfaristic score. The sound of the RCA disc is spectacular.

Of the many other settings (eleven in total) Fiedler's is a possible choice (RCA LSC-2439), but it truly ranks below the New York and Philadelphia entries. (Bernstein's reading is in a three-record assortment of overtures. It is duplicated in a one-record assortment on Columbia MS-7085.)

Overture to *Morning, Noon, and Night in Vienna*

☐ Südwestfunk Orchestra, Baden-Baden / Szöke (conductor) / Vox 516540

An illuminating presentation. The anonymous cellist who plays the solo in the opening part of the piece deserves special mention and deserved liner credit.

Overture to *Pique Dame*

☐ Paris Conservatoire Orchestra / Wolff (conductor) / London STS-15021

Finesse and control and a way with the can-can portion bring this performance into first place.

Overture to *Poet and Peasant*

☐ New York Philharmonic / Bernstein (conductor) / Columbia D3S-818

There are as many ways of playing this old chestnut (but a tasty one it remains) as there are transcriptions that have been published (according to *Grove's Dictionary of Music and Musicians* the total is fifty-nine). But being casual and thereby almost snobbish about the music (too many conductors to mention), especially mannered (Ormandy, on RCA ARL1-0453), or too sedate (Szöke, on Vox 516540) is not acceptable. There is no question that Bernstein applies the proper interpretative tooling. This produces a musically tasteful and thereby exciting performance. And by its being played in a clean way, minus fuss, the piece becomes revitalized and it's a pleasure to hear all over again.

Overture to *The Queen of Spades*

☐ New Symphony Orchestra of London / Agoult (conductor) / London STS-15223

The only edition around. Satisfactory.

Carlos Surinach (1915-   )

Melorhythmic Dramas (1966)

Orchestra

☐ Louisville Orchestra / Mester (conductor) / Louisville S-681

The storehouse of the mind brings Orff into the picture when hearing much of Surinach. True, of course, that there is a vast difference between the traits and clichés of the folk music of Spain that permeate and color Surinach's output and the neutral nonnationalism of Orff, but the technical apparatus is the same: block scoring, minimal counterpoint, constant chunks of sound, and a great deal of percussive punctuation. And, here as with Orff, it all produces a brilliant and exciting effect. The Louisville people are not found wanting. Mester presents a bright, dynamic, and telling sonorous rendition.

Sinfonietta flamenca (1953)

☐ Louisville Orchestra / Whitney (conductor) / Louisville 545-4 (monaural)

Kinetic drive with orchestral kick marks the first movement. These actions do not cease for the almost 200 measures that cover the movement. Save for a short central section, quiet melodicism marks the second movement. The rhythmic punch returns in movement 3 and is maintained in the finale. Surinach doesn't suggest Flamenco passion in his score; he hurls it at the listener. And with avid authority. The playing is splendid, with much credit belonging to the winds and brass.

Symphonic Variations (1963)

☐ Louisville Orchestra / Whitney (conductor) / Louisville S-656

A proposition infiltrating Flamenco style into variation design. It works. It clearly works because of the vivid orchestration. One negative (which doesn't eradicate the viability of the totality): the final pedaled-glue cadence is a creative snitch from the conclusion of *The Firebird*. It could well turn off some listeners, even though it is fortunately at the tail end of things.

The Louisville organization does very well with Surinach's free-tongued and free-spirited rhythms. Again one negative: there are some intonational lapses in the final (eleventh) variation of the set.

Ballet

Spells and Rhymes for Dancers

☐ Harkness Symphony Orchestra / Mester (conductor) / Desto 6433

As usual, Spanish style predominates, as do ostinati. Light fare that has pop-concert viability.

Johan Svendsen   (1840-1911)

Solo Instrument and Orchestra

Violin

Romance in G major for Violin and Orchestra, Op. 26

☐ New Philharmonia Orchestra / Grumiaux (violin) / de Waart (conductor) / Philips 6580047

Rich and clear, minus the schmaltz that often mars this little romantic piece with Griegian tinges. Sensitive orchestral support.

Since specific notes on the work are not in the liner copy, it is worth knowing that Svendsen's accompanimental scoring was designed as played here (by flute, oboe, two clarinets, two bassoons, two horns, timpani, and strings) but so arranged that strings alone can perform it.

Georgy Sviridov   (1915-   )

Orchestra

Music for Chamber Orchestra (1964)

☐ Moscow Chamber Orchestra / Barshai (conductor) / Melodiya/Angel SR-40224

Practically for string orchestra, since that family group is only supplemented by a horn and piano. Mild, some astringencies used but more for color than for harmonic incision. Barshai can be trusted as having produced an authentic reading.

Kursk Songs

Vocal

*Voice
and Orchestra*

☐ Moscow Philharmonic Orchestra and R.S.F.S.R. Russian Chorus / Valkovskaya (mezzo-soprano); Lagutkin (tenor); Zlatopolsky (bass) / Kondrashin (conductor) / Melodiya/Angel SR-40224

Sviridov studied with Shostakovich, and his workmanship is fine, though the approach in his cycle leans considerably more to Khachaturian's studio. The music has a folksy identity, and it is dressed to kill. For material such as this it isn't in bad taste.

Howard Swanson *(1907 - 1978)*

Short Symphony (1948)

Orchestra

☐ Vienna State Opera Orchestra / Litschauer (conductor) / Composers Recordings S-254

Relistening to Swanson's work, it is not difficult to understand why the work has dropped out of sight, though after its initial performance it enjoyed a substantial run here and in Europe. The cause is what is fashionable, which has nothing to do with the music's basic worth. Fashion, yes, since the Symphony glows with tuneful neo-romantic patterns, framed by the classical structures of sonata, song form, and rondo. Tuneful neo-romanticism is not in flower these days.

The Symphony runs twelve and one-half minutes. The playing of the first part is loose, without profile, as though it were being sight-read. Matters are much better thereafter.

Seven Songs

Vocal

*Voice with
Accompaniment*

☐ Thigpen (soprano); Allen (piano) / Desto 6422E (monaural)

Romantic definition of texts by Langston Hughes, Vachel Lindsay, Carl Sandburg, and Edwin Markham. Judicious partnership.

Jan Pieterszoon Sweelinck *(1562 - 1621)*

Fantasia Chromatica

Instrumental

Organ

Malle Sijmen

Pavana Lachrimae

Variations *Onder een Lind Groen*

☐ Hamilton (organ) / Orion 73133

Sweelinck was one of the most significant of Bach's predecessors and the "Chromatic Fantasy" points up his impressive contrapuntal ability. It has fine strength and weaves a powerful fugal garment including augmentation, diminution, and double diminution into its design. Hamilton provides a fine reading with clarity of articulation and balanced linear situations.

Partiality to variation form marks Sweelinck's output and is illustrated here with three sets, with a pair worked out on popular tunes, "Under the Green Linden" and *Malle Sijmen* ("Simple Simon"). The "Pavan" is based on a John Dowland lute song, the same fundamental material that was used by a number of composers. In all cases (though the Dowland item is quite neutrally colored) Hamilton presents good statements, lucidly registered and in an uncomplicated spirit.

Richard Swift (1927-)

Instrumental

Violin

Sonata for Solo Violin, Op. 15

☐ Gross (violin) / Orion 74147

Strong writing, deadly serious in its introspective quality describe Swift's twelve-tone-styled Sonata. Though one wishes for some contrastive relief, the intensity is sustained throughout the two movements and it is such cohesiveness that gives the music its strength.

Full-bodied playing by Robert Gross. His tone is tough but suits the music Swift has written.

William Sydeman (1928-)

Orchestra

Orchestral Abstractions (1963)

☐ Louisville Orchestra / Whitney (conductor) / Louisville S-644

Just solid serial music. Of the set of three it is the final Presto that holds the most excitement. Very clear and effective performance.

*Solo
Instrument
and
Orchestra*

*Piano,
Four Hands*

Concerto for Piano, Four Hands and Chamber Orchestra (1967)

☐ Contemporary Music Ensemble / Jean and Kenneth Wentworth (piano) / Weisberg (conductor) / Desto 7131

No ethereal roulades in Sydeman's piece. Its fully chromatic-styled realization moves toward an imposing climax and then the music recedes. Sydeman's chronicle is rich in coloristic detail and contrasts heady material with a mood of semipoignancy. That sort of creative research, engaging both the piano and the orchestra, is certainly the fundament of concerto design.

The playing is not aided by the sound, which is not fully balanced. However, all sink their teeth into the material and stylewise there is no criticism.

Violin

Concerto da camera (1959)

☐ CRI Chamber Ensemble / Pollikoff (violin) / Wolfe (conductor) / Composers Recordings 158 (monaural)

Though not indicated in the composition's title, the *Concerto da camera* is for solo violin with six players using eight instruments: flute doubling on piccolo, clarinet alternating with bass clarinet, bassoon, horn, viola, and cello. Variation form is utilized; the theme's contours remain quite clear in the five sections that follow the main subject. Included is an accompanied cadenza as the fourth portion of the structure.

Max Pollikoff again manifests his complete understanding of how to style freely pitched twentieth-century music. To his credit he does not push the tone of the solo stringed instrument, but holds it within lyrical boundaries. The refinement of his playing often contrasts strongly with the instrumental sounds that support him.

Concerto da camera No. 2 (1960)

☐ Contemporary Chamber Ensemble / Zukofsky (violin) / Weisberg (conductor) / Composers Recordings 181 (monaural)

Chamberized proportions mark the mixed instrumental accompaniment (oboe, clarinet alternating with bass clarinet, viola, and cello), but there is symphonicized forceful fabrication. The aggression and the curves and figures are related to Bergian expressionistic style, but there is a personality that is convincing, which also describes the playing of soloist and group.

For Double Bass Alone (1957)

☐ Turetzky (contrabass) / Advance FGR-1 (monaural)

Sydeman is most successful in his three-part work in its central section, for the greater part devoted to pizzicati. The clearest profile is observed there.

Recorded live, so expect some sounds that are not Sydeman's—only between the movements, however.

Duo for Flute and Piano (1960)

☐ Baron (flute); Sanders (piano) / Desto 7104

Linear action and rhapsodic lyricism are contrasted here, the former developed from intervallic compactness, the latter evolved from a concentrated idea. There is considerable brilliance in the writing and an urgency even in the more quiet sections. This is a totally interesting duo.

Samuel Baron takes care of matters with his usual artistic skill. *Schwann* takes care of matters erratically, titling the Sydeman work as "Music for Flute and Piano."

Music for Flute, Viola, Guitar, and Percussion (1962)

☐ Contemporary Chamber Ensemble / Weisberg (conductor) / Composers Recordings 181 (monaural)

Contrastive commitment is made in Sydeman's piece, with propulsive sections compared with lyricism of introverted content. Even when the music sings rather than rhythmically repulses, it is slightly nervous. No ambiguity results, since horizontal-like tensility matches vertical-like barbarity.

Quartet for Oboe and Strings (1961)

☐ Roseman (oboe); Marsh (violin); Hersh (viola); McCall (cello) / Desto 7116

The end movement, a *Largo religioso*, has deep threnodic feeling. It is in sharp contrast to the spiky, atomic-like peppery ingredients found in the previous pair of movements. There is serial investment but drawn upon for direct musical profits.

These four musicians are experts in any style, doubly so when their talents are applied to contemporary music.

Seven Movements for Septet (1960)

☐ CRI Chamber Ensemble / Wolfe (conductor) / Composers Recordings 158 (monaural)

Highs and lows of dynamic intensity, assorted color stages, and shadowy lines. Sometimes the music sounds through instrumental tone handkerchiefs, sometimes there are heavy motoric rhythms with rough, sandpapery gesticulations.

The Septet calls for three winds (oboe, clarinet doubling on bass clarinet, and bassoon) plus four strings (two violins, viola, and double bass). Sydeman terms the piece a "divertimento," placing it "on quite a sophisticated level." Add to this that there is a healthy

Instrumental

Double Bass

Chamber Music

tinge of programmaticism. The initial movement is a Capriccio; part 4 is subtitled "angrily," and rides on kinetic wheels. Movement 5 is indicated as having "a delicate melancholy," and the finale covers a presto waltz styled in grotesque brazenness.

The playing is a bit harsh, but that does not mean a death warrant for the piece—actually, it often frames the material effectively.

Zoltán Székely / Béla Bartók. *See Bartók / Székely.*

Maria Szymanowska   *(1789-1831)*

Instrumental

Piano

Etude

In C major / In E major / In F major

Nocturne in B flat Major

☐ Fierro (piano) / Avant 1012

The music of this Polish composer-pianist is hardly known. These examples of her style—romantic rhetoric with Schumannesque reminders—are apparently the only ones that have been recorded. They deserve attention.

Karol Szymanowski   *(1882-1937)*

Solo Instrument and Orchestra

Violin

Violin Concerto No. 2, Op. 61

☐ Bamberg Symphony Orchestra / Szeryng (violin) / Krenz (conductor) / Philips 6500421

A rich, rhapsodically colored tapestry enfolds this work. It is vividly orchestrated. In one movement, containing five major sections, the format is depicted in an improvisational manner, with motival material used for developmental purposes, supported by resonant rhythms. The violin part is tailored for topflight players only and contains a virtuosic cadenza, written by the composer's close friend Paul Kochanski, who helped Szymanowski with important technical details in his other violin works. (Kochanski was accorded the dedication of the Concerto and gave its initial performance in 1933.)

Szeryng is the perfect violinist for this piece. He knows how to let go when the music offers the opportunity, and his purity of tone is just right for the perspective needed in comparison with the opulent orchestration. Krenz collaborates excellently.

Instrumental

Piano

Etudes, Op. 33

☐ Rosenberger (piano) / Delos 15312

Lengthwise, these pieces might well be termed preludes. Technically, their title is correct. There are a dozen in the group, and Carol Rosenberger has recorded them without band breaks, to carry out Szymanowski's *attacca* designations. There are slight pauses, however. Fluent and fluidic playing, each item very well characterized.

Fantasy in F minor, Op. 14

☐ Jones (piano) / Argo ZRG-713

Influences here: Chopin, a bit of Liszt, and even some early Scriabin. Martin Jones's playing is skillful, and he unifies the conception quite nicely.

Re influences in another Szymanowski piece *see below* (Four Etudes, Op. 4).

Four Etudes, Op. 4

Masques, Op. 34

☐ Rosenberger (piano) / Delos 15312

Differences not only in style—as with the Fantasy in F minor, Op. 14 (*see above*) there is some Chopin and Liszt in the Etudes, and Stravinsky shadows hover in the *Masques*—but sharp formal distinctions as well. In the latter work characterizations are involved: *Scheherazade,* a Buffoon, and a view of Don Juan.

Carol Rosenberger does beautifully with this music. Her pianistic camera moves constantly, and every scene is caught perfectly. The Etudes are played with more neutrality.

Mazurkas, Op. 50 (Excerpts)

☐ Rubinstein (piano) / RCA LSC-2605

Rubinstein plays four of the complete set of twenty. These mazurkas are of different type than those of Chopin, heavier in content, reflecting native materials. Rubinstein emphasizes the sweep of the music and the *pesante* rhythms.

Métopes, Op. 29

☐ Jones (piano) / Argo ZRG-713

The titles of these "Three Poems" give the aesthetic clue: *L'Ile des sirènes, Calypso,* and *Nausicaa.* Indeed, exoticisms with some sophisticated twists. A type of hothouse music.

Jones's playing is a faithful reproduction. Academic response to this sort of writing would be deadly and wooden. This he avoids, and he considers the set with fine colored probity.

Piano Sonata No.1 in C minor, Op. 8

☐ Graham (piano) / Musical Heritage Society MHS-3136

Three movements that smoulder with Chopinesque chromaticism linked to Lisztian energy, and then a finale that flares up with a fugue (*see below* [Piano Sonata No. 2 in A minor, Op. 21]). Heavy textures, but they never smother the material. The fruitage is one of huge sound and constant action.

Daniel Graham is a brilliant pianist and technician. His interpretation is solid and needs no defense. With this music there is a plurality of interpretative truths. Graham's is certainly acceptable.

Piano Sonata No. 2 in A minor, Op. 21

☐ Pleshakov (piano) / Orion 73111

Szymanowski's first piano Sonata inhaled and exhaled chromaticism. This one follows suit, save that the chromatic qualities are those of Max Reger—the "accidentalized" action is much more restless. There are two movements, the first of free sonata indulgence, the other a set of variations that conclude with a powerful fugue. This polyphonic design was a Szymanowski favorite. His Piano Sonata No. 1 (*see above*) also concludes with a fugue, and in the Piano Sonata No. 3 (*see below*) a fugue is the penultimate section of the finale.

Pleshakov plays the first movement far better than the second part of the work. In the latter the performance is note-heavy and academic.

Very poor production planning by Orion. Because of the Sonata's length (34:52), a division was necessary. (Additional pieces on the disc are *The Lark* by Glinka transcribed by Balakirev [five minutes] and Balakirev's *Nocturne in B flat* [6:05].) Obviously, the recording should have begun with these two "shorts" and continued with the entire twelve-minute first movement of the Szymanowski, giving a total time of 23:50 on the A side. The entire second movement would then have fit on the B side, with a total time of 22:52. Instead, side 1 begins with the first movement of the Sonata and ends at the ten-minute mark of the Variations movement. This causes a horrible break in the music, requiring the record to be turned over to hear the remaining twelve minutes of the movement. Shades of the 78-rpm days!

Piano Sonata No. 3 (in One Movement), Op. 36

☐ Graham (piano) / Musical Heritage Society MHS-3136

Clearly emphasizing Scriabinesque style. However, there is less rhythmic drift in Szymanowski's case, this work climaxing in an energetic conclusion (preceded by a fugue) which is toccata-tuned (*see above* [Piano Sonata No. 2 in A minor, Op. 21]). Szymanowski's Opus 36 is of merciless difficulty, but Graham owns the work.

Violin

La Fontaine d'Aréthuse, Op. 30, No. 1

☐ David Oistrakh (violin); Yampolsky (piano) / Monitor 2003 (monaural)

Although "The Fountain of Arethusa" is available in a stereo release (on Orion 75195) it there lacks the panache and the assertive smoothness that Oistrakh produces. Szymanowski's programmatic short essay is not outlined in the Monitor liner notes, but it little matters. It is the impressionistic color flow of the piece that is the telling point, not its story line.

This is the first of Szymanowski's three *Mythes*. A complete performance of *Mythes* is available and is discussed *below*.

Mythes, Op. 30

☐ Wilkomirska (violin); Barbosa (piano) / Connoisseur Society CSQ-2050

These "Three Poems" consist of *La Fontaine d'Aréthuse* (a stunning performance of this portion is discussed *above*), *Narcisse*, and *Dryades et Pan*. Mysterious colors, emotional agitation, and severe technical requirements surround this music. The color discharge is tremendous. All these factors demand virtuosity without compromise. No compromise here. These musicians have technical opulence, and they recognize and fully identify the gilted style. They lay open every point, and it's a thrilling experience.

Romance, Op. 23

☐ Temianka (violin); Graudan (piano) / Orion 74136E (monaural)

Originally recorded for Parlophone (as its E-11321) in 1937. The transfer doesn't nullify the dusty sound, but it fully illustrates Temianka's ability for romantic expressiveness.

Chamber
Music

String Quartet in C major, Op. 37

☐ Walden Quartet of the University of Illinois / Lyrichord 22 (monaural)

Szymanowski shows himself to be a rhapsodic eclectic in this Quartet. Present are impressionistic dabs, mystical ramifications, lush romanticism, and the naughtiness of the French style of the 1920s in the form of polytonality. Yet it is to this composer's credit that when he chose to be eclectic, he still shaped his materials in such fashion as to make them hold together. The liberal borrowing does not form a pastiche, but rather a kaleidoscopic work of ever-changing hues, obtained by ever-changing styles.

This is quite an old recording, but its sound is good. The playing of the Waldens, no longer on the scene but once some of the most important advocates of contemporary quartet music in the country, is extremely well knit. Their full-blooded tone makes cohesive all of the creative conclusions found in the work. Particularly accomplished is the fugal finale, performed to clarify all the inherent logic of its contrapuntalism.

Szymanowski / **Paul Kochanski (1887 - 1934)**

Chant de Roxane **from** *Le Roi Roger*

□ Heifetz (violin); Bay (piano) / RCA ARM4–0944 (monaural)

Instrumental

Violin

Gorgeous spun melody that soars in one place in the extreme sopranino range, then declares itself in the opposite area in lush octaves, and is heard still further in vivid two-part harmony in the middle register. And always Szymanowski's haunting tune is featured, over and over and over again. With Heifetz's uncanny technical resources and beautifully realized tonal consistency the *Chant* retains its freshness. In fact once the music has finished, one starts the recording again—and then repeats the repetition. Truly a mesmerizing performance.

The performance by Staryk and Niwa on Orion 7027/2 (in stereo) is a good one, a warmly intense one. However, the Heifetz version has more sensuousness. Incidentally, the two-record release in which Staryk's performance is included shamefully fails to offer a single word about the fourteen works covered in the program. Press puffs about Staryk and bio material, that's all. Disgraceful.

T

Paul Taffanel   (1844-1908)

Andante pastoral et scherzettino

Instrumental

Flute

☐ Hoberman (flute); Stannard (piano) / Avant 1015

The larger, initial portion of Taffanel's two-part piece is perfectly attuned to the flute's lyricism, and Hoberman takes advantage to present it with a full-bodied tone. Many composers of flute music are compulsive about matching a lyrical essay with a light scherzo type, and Taffanel follows suit. However, the *scherzettino* has pace but no weight. The values of Taffanel's piece are to be found in part 1. And that's where one hears Hoberman's best work.

Quintet for Winds

Chamber Music

☐ Soni Ventorum Wind Quintet / Crystal S-253

Examples of French nationalism have a less determined ring in the ears of listeners than the *furiant* of the Bohemian composer, the tarantella of the Italian, the *jota* of the Spaniard. There is, however, charm and simplicity, sober rhythms in place of incisive patterns, and elegance seasoned with salt that we recognize as typically French. Such honest and refined distinctions are contained in Taffanel's Quintet.

This presentation is on target with elegant playing, sensitive balances, and sensible tempi. It is far ahead of the version offered by the New York Woodwind Quintet on Concert-Disc 222. (This is indicated in *Schwann* as also obtainable on Everest 3080.) An earlier recording by the New York Woodwind Quintet (with different personnel save the flutist, Samuel Baron) is still around on Counterpoint/Esoteric 505. However, the sound takes percentage points away from the performance, itself not as idiomatic as on the Concert-Disc release.

Germaine Tailleferre   (1892-   )

Concertino for Harp and Orchestra (1927)

Solo Instrument and Orchestra

Harp

☐ Orchestre O.R.T.F., Paris / Zabaleta (harp) / Martinon (conductor) / Deutsche Grammophon 2530008

Tailleferre's Concertino contains no hedonistic oversimplicities, neither does she indulge in Promethean stormy oratory. Her work is in classical form, containing nicely French-flavored dissonant harmony. Harmony and form aid each other. Tailleferre shows herself to be creatively alive, wise and understanding, in full command of her objective.

Suavely played, coloristically on the button, and totally musical throughout.

Yuji Takahashi   (1938-   )

Instrumental   **Metathesis (1968)**

Piano   ☐ Takahashi (piano) / Mainstream 5000

The title describes the different "placement" of the generic material by change or reversal of conditions, pitch transposition, and the like. All elements—texture, duration, dynamics, and so forth—are concerned. Takahashi's music is extremely percussive in its segmentation and just as much so in its contrastive constancy. He plays it accordingly.

Chamber   **Six Stoicheia (1969)**
Music
                   ☐ Zukofsky (violin) / Mainstream 5008

The credit line reads "violin." Correct, but the result is Zukofsky playing four violins, so to speak, and blending the four parts by means of multiple recording.

A sonic success with actions anchored by pedal sounds. The entity is colored by use of quarter- and three-quarter-toned pitches. The sonic success is matched by a performance success in which Paul Zukofsky is in perfect control of the total spectrum from sustained sounds to flying pizzicati.

Toru Takemitsu   (1930-   )

Orchestra   **November Steps (1967)**

☐ Toronto Symphony Orchestra / Tsuruta (biwa); Yokoyama (shakuhachi) / Ozawa (conductor) / RCA LSC-7051

The music of *November Steps* (commissioned by the New York Philharmonic for its 125th anniversary and premiered by that orchestra with Ozawa conducting) curves and zigzags in an impressionistic manner. It is extremely refined in its timbre choices, stimulated by the use of a pair of traditional Japanese instruments: the biwa (a type of lute) and the shakuhachi (a bamboo flute that is played vertically). Percussion inserts color the work further but whatever is used is of decorative elegance.

The composer has described his work in a set of pithy statements. One of these is especially important. He writes there are "Eleven 'steps' with no particular melodic unity. Like the music of the No Theater, the rhythm endlessly oscillates."

The performance is beautiful and fully sensitive to the score's demands. The parts that Kinshi Tsuruta and Katsuya Yokoyama play are of such importance that *November Steps* almost turns into a double solo with orchestral accompaniment. Takemitsu might not object to that categorization since he indicates that "the composer should not concern himself with blending traditional Japanese instruments with the Western symphony orchestra. On the contrary, by counterposing the biwa and the shakuhachi to the orchestra, he should vivify the foreignness of the sound which is unique to these instruments."

Textures (1964)

☐ NHK Symphony Orchestra / Iwaki (conductor) / Odyssey 32160152

Sound splashes that often resemble the output of electronic composition make *Textures* a riot of color, with one climax of raucous richness. The ending is almost tonal, a surprising postscript.

Takemitsu divides his orchestra of seventy-three players into two, with a piano in the center. This is planned to obtain a heightened stereophonic effect, to "stretch the sound," as Takemitsu describes it. (Playing of the recording on a monaural setting does not decrease the inflammation of the piece. This says a great deal for Takemitsu's creative originality.)

For Away (1973)   **Undisturbed Rest (1959)**   *Instrumental*
Piano Distance (1961)
                                                                 Piano
☐ Woodward (piano) / London HEAD-4

Music that relates to sonorous curves, rhythmic zigzags, and Messiaenistic bits. Everything is subtle and almost reticent. Everything can be considered sensuous as well. In this instance, avant-garde writing does not conceal the influences of such composers as Messiaen, Boulez, and even Scriabin (in *Undisturbed Rest*).

Sympathetic interpretation is a demand for this type of music and that can be expected, since Woodward chose to record it. However, he shows much more—a substantial understanding of what Takemitsu's decorative canvases are all about.

Corona (London Version) (1962)   *Piano,*
                                                                 Harpsichord,
☐ Woodward (keyboard instruments) / London HEAD-4   *and Organ*

The title must be explained. Takemitsu's work is called *Corona for Pianists*. However, in this recording Roger Woodward does it all himself, playing the piano, harpsichord, and organ parts, which were then combined by overdubbing. He accomplishes much more since the score is in graphic notation, and thus for the sonorous realization he must get equal credit with the composer. So full acknowledgement for what has been done well.

Talib Rasul Hakim. *See under H.*

Thomas Tallis   *(ca. 1505-1585)*

Hymns   *Choral*

Deus Tuorum Militum   **O Nata Lux de Lumine**   *Chorus Alone*
Jam Christus Astra Ascenderat **Salvator Mundi Domine**
Jesu Salvator Sacculi

☐ McLoughlin (soprano); Deller (countertenor); Brown and English (tenors); Bevan (baritone); Frost (bass) / Vanguard HM-5

Tallis's "Five Hymns for Alternating Plainsong and Polyphony" are matchlessly defined by the members of the Deller Consort, which was directed by Alfred Deller. The singing is uncommonly clean and with a distinctively full sound, impeccably balanced.

The Lamentations of Jeremiah the Prophet   *Cantata*
                                                                 and Oratorio
☐ Deller (countertenor); Brown and English (tenors); Bevan (baritone); Frost (bass) / Vanguard HM-5

The peak of Tallis's production is represented in this two-part composition, written for men's voices. The performance has an acute focalization, much better than when the various parts are duplicated. Vanguard's release is a glorious vocal experience. It is, without doubt, the best recorded representation on the lists.

Louise Talma   (1906-   )

Orchestra

Toccata for Orchestra (1944)

☐ Imperial Philharmonic of Tokyo / Strickland (conductor) / Composers Recordings 145 (monaural)

The Toccata is aided by assimilations from Stravinskian neoclassicism, Copland, and even a touch of Latin American contours. All the kinetic power of the chosen form is represented; the orchestration (nicely projected by this orchestra) is dynamic, almost violent in its tightness and enunciation.

Instrumental

Piano

Alleluia in Form of Toccata

☐ Fierro (piano) / Avant 1012

Theologically neoclassic. Talma's piano "Alleluia" can certainly be translated (with poetic license) to read "Praise ye the clarity." The last word also describes the recorded performance.

Piano Sonata No. 2 (1955)

☐ Rogers (piano) / Composers Recordings S-281

In Talma's Sonata one is reminded of the Biblical phrase "Between us and you there is a great gulf fixed." The reason? Simply the unification between tonality and serialism. And the resultant hybrid comes off quite well.

There are a goodly number of built-in clipped phrases in the outer parts of the work. (A divisional structural situation exactly contrary to the stylistic merger mentioned above.) However, this does not make the work disjointed; in fact, it projects a physical exhilaration. This exhilaration is fully conveyed in a brilliantly assured performance.

Six Etudes for Piano

☐ Webster (piano) / Desto 7117

Fascinating exploitations of piano-performance techniques: contrast, staccato, use of the sostenuto pedal, wide skips, crossed hands, and note increase per pulse. Bounded objectives but effective as pure music.

Beveridge Webster is a masterful performer.

Chamber Music

Three *Duologues*

☐ Michael Webster (clarinet); Beveridge Webster (piano) / Composers Recordings SD-374

The sovereign creative style in this case is neoclassicism. These are not mathematical conceptions fully loyal to the technique but artistically avid. The objectives, whether in slow, expressive range or in acrobatic kinetics, are always clear and undisputed.

The last phrase describes the performance. But, CRI, why release a work minus any liner notes when the accompanying pieces (in this case by Martino, Reynolds, and Michael Webster) have the requisite information?

La Corona: Holy Sonnets of John Donne

Choral

Chorus Alone

☐ Dorian Chorale / Aks (conductor) / Composers Recordings 187 (monaural)

Seven parts based on a "single series." Delicacy and dramaticism are found both in this subtly inflected twenty-minute work and in its performance.

Elias Tanenbaum (1924-)

Improvisations and Patterns for Brass Quintet and Tape

Chamber Music

☐ American Brass Quintet / Desto 6474/7

The use of the tape is for the most part so integrated that the effect is of a sextet for brass. This despite the fact that in the Improvisations the blend is split and contrastive at times. Further, the sections merge and there is improvisational commentary in the Patterns portion as well. Tanenbaum is no coloristic skinflint. His work is a bold conceit, of virtuosic buoyancy. It is played zestfully and with breathtaking wizardry.

Sergei Taneyev (1856-1915)

Piano Trio in D major, Op. 22

Chamber Music

☐ Oborin (piano); David Oistrakh (violin); Knushevitsky (cello) / Monitor S-2068E (monaural)

While Taneyev was a conservative, he possessed the true scholar's traits whereby constant study did not weigh down individuality, but rather sharpened it to the point where his music contained all the essential, creative truths. His Trio shows his link with the classical school of composition. There are no innovations, but neither are there hard-crusted academic concepts.

Crystalline mastery is presented in the playing of this trio of Soviet musicians. Where thrust and tonal richness are required, they are supplied in full measure, but always properly proportioned.

Trio in D major for Two Violins and Viola, Op. 21

☐ David Oistrakh and Bondarenko (violins); Terian (viola) / Monitor 2059 (monaural)

Contains a clarity and lightness that can well typify the composer as "a Russian Mozart" rather than "the Russian Brahms" he is so often called. An abundance of interesting content is found in the four movements: sonata, Minuet, slow division, and rondo.

The Trio (and note the famous Oistrakh as the first violin) is performed with magnificent verve and stylistic truth.

Alexandre Tansman (1897-)

Capriccio (1955)

Orchestra

☐ Louisville Orchestra / Whitney (conductor) / Louisville 56-2 (monaural)

A three-part suite consisting of a Ballade, a *Notturno,* and a Scherzo. An optimistic ostinato powers the main portion of the first section; Tansman's usual bitter-sweet harmonies are heard in the night piece, and balletic sweep moves through the Scherzo.

Instrumental

Guitar

Barcarola from Cavatina

☐ Williams (guitar) / Everest 3195

A haunting miniature, marred, however, by being recorded so close that the sound of every finger and hand shift accompanies the music. But do try to enjoy Tansman's fine melodic inspiration despite this annoying focus. (*See below* for the whole Cavatina.)

Cavatina

☐ Bitetti (guitar) / Westminster Gold 8149

Fitting music for the subtitles (*Preludio, Zarabanda, Scherzino, Barcarola,* and *Danza pomposa*) but certainly not for the main title. Tansman's "Song" heading doesn't relate to the prelude, dances, and short scherzo that are included in the suite. Well now, whatever his reasons, the ambiguous title doesn't prevent quality coverage.

Ernesto Bitetti stars in this one, especially in the speed required to negotiate the repetitive sounds in part 3. His colorations in that movement as well as in the final part prove his right to hold a top franchise in the guitarists' world.

See above for another performance of the *Barcarola.*

Prelude from *Homage to Chopin*

☐ Segovia (guitar) / MCA 2501

A somber, stately statement. Segovia's dynamic shaping of this short piece intensifies its poignancy.

Three Pieces for Guitar

☐ Segovia (guitar) / MCA 2526 (monaural)

A Canzonetta, *Alla polacca,* and *Berceuse d'Orient.* Melodic stability with sufficient variety. Crystal-clear playing, despite some swishes along the frets. (Also available in a three-record "Golden Jubilee" set on MCA 19000.)

Violin

Mouvement perpétuel from Five Pieces for Violin and Piano

☐ Heifetz (violin); Bay (piano) / RCA ARM4–0946 (monaural)

Very few "perpetual motion" pieces have any musical values, being shaped for the performer's pyrotechny. Tansman's has a bit more to offer, with some pizzicato to flavor the ingredients at boil in the musical pot. What Heifetz does with this piece is to play at a pace that seemingly runs off the terminus of the metronomic marker. Not a single note is off balance, off place, off pitch. Wow!

Chamber Music

Sonatine for Bassoon and Piano

☐ Grossman (bassoon); Hokanson (piano) / Coronet 2741

Neoclassic statements in the three movements. A semiserious opening, a cadenza link to the aria contour of the middle part (the harmonies display the clarity of Haydn plus the discipline of the present century), and a pert and zippy finale. The performance is lucid, as clean as a new pin.

Francisco Tárrega   *(1852-1909)*

Capricho arabe

Marieta

Prelude in D minor

Prelude in E major

☐ Yepes (guitar) / Deutsche Grammophon 2530871

Polished performances of these short pieces. Nothing memorable in the music, but it's certainly pleasurable.

Capricho arabe (Serenata)

Estudio brillante

☐ Parkening (guitar) / Angel S-36069

Plenty of carefully cultivated guitar playing crams the recorded catalogue. It is the extra, active reasoned response that divides the good from the very good. Parkening is in the latter class. His re-creative depictions of these quite nice guitar pieces place his performances in the memorable class.

Estudio brillante

☐ Romero (guitar) / Angel S-36094

Angel Romero fulfills Tárrega's title objective in his essay. The bass line is exceedingly supple, and this makes the total fully expressive.

Recuerdos de la Alhambra

☐ Williams (guitar) / Columbia MS-6608

A fine example by this composer-guitarist, the founder of the modern school of guitar playing. (It is agreed that all contemporary guitar pedagogy is indebted to his teaching.) Full command in Williams's playing.

Instrumental

Guitar

Giuseppe Tartini   *(1692-1770)*

Concerto in A major for Cello and Strings

☐ Stuttgart Soloists / Blees (cello) / Turnabout 34236

Tartini remains an underrated figure. It takes a single hearing of this finely played three-movement work to provide the evidence. Grace and warmth with nice embroidery via short trills mark the opening Allegro, a quasi-threnodic Larghetto that hits the emotive target head on follows (in which Blees displays beautiful sensitivity for line elucidation), and the Concerto concludes with music of spirit and good taste. In the last movement, nonm of the pat figurations, statically detailed, that are represented by the hundreds in the music of dozens of second-class, early eighteenth-century composers.

Concerto à 5 in G major for Flute, Strings, and Continuo

☐ I Musici / Gazzelloni (flute) / Philips 6500611

Solo Instrument and Orchestra

Cello

Flute

Gazzelloni's tone is just as rich and unsullied in the quicker passages as it is in the vocalistic slow movement. The playing of this music of real charm if not imposing depth is most affecting.

Violin

Concerto for Violin, Strings, and Continuo
In A major / In B flat major / In G major

☐ I Musici / Accardo (violin) / Philips 6500784

Accardo has the type of dignity about his playing that makes him an ideal interpreter of Tartini's music. All three concerti are lyrically attractive, and they are accompanimentally framed with clear definition by the I Musici group of twelve players.

Chamber Music

Sonata in G minor (*The Devil's Trill*)

☐ David Oistrakh (violin); Bauer (piano) / Melodiya/Angel S-40197

More romantic than classic, but such richness doesn't harm Tartini's music in this case. Brilliant (should one say "devilishly" magnificent?) trill work.

Sonata for Violin and Cello
No. 1 in G major / No. 2 in D minor / No. 3 in D major / No. 4 in C major / No. 5 in F major / No. 6 in E minor / No. 7 in A minor / No. 8 in G minor / No. 9 in A major / No. 10 in B major / No. 11 in E major / No. 12 in G major

☐ Guglielmo (violin); Pocaterra (cello) / Telefunken SAWT-9592/3

Though a good amount of these works tends to be severely soprano-bass with no alto-tenor, even with chordalism endeavoring to bridge the gap, there is sufficient variety to choose from. It will be noted that the major tonalities are used exactly twice as many times as the minor, but the greatest interest will be found in the latter group. The most imposing is the huge Passacaglia that concludes the seventh work of the set.

Giovanni Guglielmo plays with verve and vigor. He may be called to account for a romanticized view of this baroque music, but frankly the music is not harmed whatsoever by such stylistic updating. Antonio Pocaterra has a secondary role to play, but he fulfills it artistically.

Concerto a quattro in D major

☐ Instrumentalists of the Società Cameristica di Lugano / Nonesuch 73008

This work is incorrectly listed in the *Schwann* catalogue under "Sonata a quattro in D." The only resemblances are the tonality and the fact that each work covers three movements. The *Sonata a quattro* (*see below*) consists of an *Allegro assai*, a *Larghetto*, and a final Allegro. The *Concerto* also commences with an *Allegro assai;* then it moves on to an Andante and a concluding Presto.

The *Concerto* is a rich work and is played in a light and elegant manner that exactly fits the music.

Sonata a quattro in D major

☐ Stuyvesant String Quartet / Nonesuch 71114

The Shulman-Robbins-Frengut-Shapiro team are far more responsive to the lyricism and nobility of Tartini's piece than are the Schäffer Quartet in the competitive recorded performance on Vox SVBX-5300. Further, the tempi chosen by the latter may be brighter, but they interfere with the warmth of the music.

There is a third listing for this opus in *Schwann,* but it is erroneous. For details *see above* (*Concerto a quattro* in D major).

Tartini / Fritz Kreisler

Variations on a Theme of Corelli

☐ Elman (violin); Seiger (piano) / Vanguard SRV-367SD

Every sound and nuance in perfect stylistic rapport.

Instrumental

Violin

Phyllis Tate   (1911-   )

Three Gaelic Ballads

☐ Price (soprano); Lockhart (piano) / Argo ZRG-691

The three Ballads Tate has chosen, *The Lake of Coolfin, Hark! The Soft Bugle,* and *Hush Song,* combine traditional tunes with salty harmonies. Such partnership of the sweet and the bitter is not usual in folk-music settings but is certainly a solution as truthful as one that uses pat, traditional harmonies. At the very least, Tate's re-creations escape from the humdrum of normalcy.

Margaret Price's style is excellent, her diction is clear. James Lockhart's playing deserves high credits.

Vocal

Voice with Accompaniment

Apparitions

☐ Cardiff Festival Players / English (tenor); Tate (harmonica); Tryon (piano) / Argo ZRG-691

Color plays a great part in this fascinating vocal cycle, with a harmonica conbined with piano and string quartet. There are four parts: the texts consisting of a traditional Scottish Ballad (*The Wife of Usher's Well*), a Narrative Ballad (*The Suffolk Miracle*), a traditional English lament (*The Unquiet Grave*), and a 1888 Broadside (*Unfortunate Miss Bailey*). A purely instrumental *Evocation* introduces the work and an *Envoi* (also without voice) concludes it.

Though there is considerable pitch relationship by use of inversion and retrograde motion, and rhythmic relationship by the use of augmentation and diminution, these devices are sensibly and sensitively bound into the folk-song character of the entire cycle.

Tate's work is a charmer. Her sonority inventions are exquisite—often as delicate as a snowflake and as weightless as a nimbus. Her use of the harmonica (as a principal timbre in the second song and in the final measures) is superb. That last word describes this performance.

Voice and Instrumental Ensemble

Antonio Tauriello   (1931-   )

Ilinx for Clarinet Solo and Orchestra (1968)

☐ Louisville Orchestra / Livingston (clarinet) / Mester (conductor) / Louisville S-701

The opening outlines the style: a decaying microtonal descent, a solo-clarinet reed-beating sound. Oppositional timbres, caressed or smashed in their fragmentation, give the

Solo Instrument and Orchestra

Clarinet

music the spasmodic translation of its title (the word *Ilinx* stems from the Greek word meaning "vertigo").

All of this may be abstract imagery, but it produces a meticulously formed representation. The soloist and the orchestra play the work magnificently, and there is no doubt that *Ilinx* represents one of the high points in the Louisville catalogue. The "orchestra," incidentally, consists of piano, percussion, violins, and double basses.

Carl Tausig   (1841 - 1871)

Instrumental

Piano

Caprice Waltzes on Themes of Johann Strauss

Concert Etudes, Op. 1

Fantasy on Themes on Moniuszko's "Halka"

The Ghost Ship

***Hope*, Op. 3**

One Only Lives Once

☐ Ponti (piano) / Candide 31031

Lisztian impact is a dominant characteristic in Tausig's piano music. It is particular to the texts of the pair of Etudes (the first in F sharp minor, the second in A flat major); *The Ghost Ship,* a Ballade in A minor, originally composed for orchestra; and the Moniuszko item. A different (but related) type of musical accentuation Tausig favored is to be found in his dance settings. This is obvious in the Johann Strauss Caprice, but it is just as dynamically expressed in *One Only Lives Once,* a "Valse-Caprice," and adumbrates the Opus 3 piece.

Michael Ponti plays all of this music with fine style.

Ungarische Zigeunerweisen

☐ Lhevinne (piano) / Klavier 111

Just as good as any of Liszt's Hungarian Rhapsodies and formulated in the same tempo dichotomy. Available also on Candide 31031, in a recital entirely devoted to Tausig's works, performed by Michael Ponti *(see above)*. However, Ponti does some editing and is not as stylistically authoritative in the first (slow) part. (Klavier translates this title as "Hungarian Gypsy Dances," whereas it should be, of course, "Hungarian Gypsy Airs.")

Deems Taylor   (1885 - 1966)

Orchestra

***The Portrait of a Lady*—Rhapsody for Strings, Winds, and Piano, Op. 14**

☐ Vienna Symphony Orchestra / Hendl (conductor) / Desto 6417E (monaural)

A well-mannered lady, chaste in the beginning and conclusion, a bit flirtatious in between. The spiritual godfather of Taylor's female is one Richard Wagner.

Only a fair resonant response in the recording.

Through the Looking Glass, Op. 12

☐ Eastman-Rochester Symphony Orchestra / Hanson (conductor) / Eastman-Rochester Archives ERA-1008

Taylor's *Five Pictures from Lewis Carroll* falls in the category of program music, but as with most works in the genre, unless the listener follows the textual explanation, the orchestral camera work will not register. Most of the movements (four, with the first divided) illustrate the general scene (the talking flowers equated by brisk music, the insects by scherzoish motility). There are pertinent identifications, of course: the clarinet describes the brillig afternoon, the xylophone is the vorpal sword that snickersnacks the bassoon that is playing the role of the Jabberwock, etc. Regardless, the humor and tenderness of the tale come through in Taylor's translation, and it has a continuity that can be enjoyed for its basic ardent romantic reasoning.

Hanson always admired this work, and it shows in his very effective performance. He gives sensitive consideration to the ebb and flow of the score, and the individual playing is certainly beyond reproach.

Franklin Taylor (1843-1919)

Toy Symphony (Adagio and Finale)

Chamber Music

☐ Lewenthal (piano); Ross (violin); Aller (cello); McNab (toy trumpet) / Lewenthal (conductor) / Angel S-36080

The slow movement is colored with fairy bells as the timbre speciality. In the Finale, the motility represents a musical ride, with sleigh bells and toy trumpet featured. Taylor's other imitative "toys" consist of two items, nightingale and cuckoo; the rest are standard percussion: triangle, drum, bass drum, and cymbals. The piano-trio combine provides the fundamental texture for this light-faceted pops chamber music.

Piotr (Peter) Ilyich Tchaikovsky (1840-1893)

Ballet Music

Orchestra

From *Eugen Onegin* (1878) / From *The Maid of Orleans* (1879) / From *The Oprichnik* (1872) / From *The Sorceress* (1887) / From *Tcherevitchki* (1885)

☐ Orchestra of the Royal Opera House, Covent Garden / Davis (conductor) / Philips 9500508

This is the sort of program that Bonynge has made his speciality. That Colin Davis has entered the field is extremely good news. There's a master's touch here that illuminates the music. Totally effective and totally a delight.

Capriccio italien, Op. 45

☐ New York Philharmonic / Bernstein (conductor) / Columbia MS-6258
☐ RCA Symphony / Kondrashin (conductor) / RCA VICS-1676

As this book was going to press, sixteen conductors had entered the *Capriccio italien* sweepstakes, and their renditions were being offered in twenty-eight assorted packages.

The music needs panache, but it needs control or it will slip into the performance valley of the dead motion-picture-theater orchestras that used to offer and besmirch it at bargain prices. Any bargaining with meticulous balance and overplaying cheapens Tchaikovsky's piece. Bernstein has that control while paradoxically letting the music go all out. Kondrashin with his group is less dramatic in a sense, but his is a telling performance that persuades the listener.

The Kondrashin is in a Tchaikovsky album of "biggest hits," with four other works played by two other orchestras led by two other conductors. Bernstein's portrayal is also available on two other Columbia releases (MS-6827 and MS-7513) as well as in a two-disc album (Columbia MG-33270). In all these issues the music is entirely by Tchaikovsky.

Fatum, Op. 77

☐ Frankfurt Radio Symphony Orchestra / Inbal (conductor) / Philips 6500467

Another Tchaikovsky work he destroyed, but this act did not include the orchestral parts, which were then used to publish the symphonic poem after his death.

Inbal's reading is well crafted and extremely well balanced. His belief in the music comes across to the auditor. In Dorati's case (on London 6891) it almost does. It doesn't completely because it is streaked with pedestrianism.

Francesca da Rimini, Op. 32

☐ Concertgebouw-Orchester, Amsterdam / Haitink (conductor) / Philips 6500643
☐ New York Philharmonic / Bernstein (conductor) / Columbia MS-6258

All the opportunities for knock-'em-in-the-aisles, false hurly-burly playing are present in this blockbuster. However, the conductor who conveys the drama but does not overstress it and realizes the dark poetry of Tchaikovsky's "Fantasy After Dante" is a real winner. And that describes the Haitink-led performance.

Bernstein plays the work with his expected passionate involvement, yet does not opt for overkill. There's a good balance of drama and poetic consideration in his entry. (A third consideration, if one wishes to have three choices, is Munch's Boston Symphony Orchestra performance on RCA VICS-1197.)

Hamlet: Overture-Fantasy, Op. 67a

☐ New York Philharmonic / Bernstein (conductor) / Columbia M-34128

Not to be confused with the incidental music for the Shakespeare play which Tchaikovsky wrote three years after the purely orchestral work and which is listed as Opus 67b.

Hamlet needs passionate push and shove, and there's no better chap on the scene to squeeze out every bit of dramaticism in a score than Bernstein. In comparison Dorati, for example (London 6841), colors the piece pale pink; Abravanel (on Vox QSVBX-5131) produces an understanding reading but lacks flair. More or less, the remaining entries fall in the same class.

Manfred, Op. 58

☐ Utah Symphony Orchestra / Abravanel (conductor) / Candide QCE-31079
☐ London Symphony Orchestra / Previn (conductor) / Angel S-37018

Though not included in the six numbered symphonies Tchaikovsky wrote, *Manfred* was subtitled by Tchaikovsky as a *Symphony in Four Pictures, After Byron's Dramatic Poem.* O.K., consider it (as most do) as a symphonic poem, which it almost is, but it could just as well be classified as a partially programmatic symphony. Whatever the hybrid state of the form of the piece, it is major Tchaikovsky and belongs with the important fourth, fifth, and sixth symphonies.

Abravanel's version (also available in one of three Vox boxes devoted to Tchaikovsky's orchestral works, in QSVBX–5131) defines the epic proportions of the opus. It not only is penetrating and powerfully displayed but is, in every respect, a musical interpretation, meaning no overjuicing and no exaggerative nonsense.

Previn's setting is a very close second. It has the necessary excitement and is delivered with a virtuosic forwardness that is a substantial success. And the climate is not cool, as in Maazel's case (on London 6786), to cite but one other example.

Marche slave, Op. 31

☐ Concertgebouw-Orchester, Amsterdam / Haitink (conductor) / Philips 6500643
☐ Chicago Symphony Orchestra / Reiner (conductor) / RCA VICS–1676

A critic once mentioned to me that a good performance of *Marche slave* need only be "loud and lively." Granted, providing explanations follow. "Loud" does not include brash playing or brassy sound. "Lively" should not mean velocity that blurs inner content.

The Philips disc provides all the excitement of the score, paced and balanced with penetrating perception. The *Slawischer Marsch*, as it is listed, is performed in nine and one-half minutes. Reiner's performance is close to a minute longer. His more restrained approach is a whit less exciting, but its musicality is vivid and far better than that of any of the many other representations available.

Overture solennelle 1812, Op. 49

☐ Concertgebouw-Orchester, Amsterdam, and Members of the Netherlands Royal Military Band / Haitink (conductor) / Philips 6500643

Tchaikovsky's "Solemn Overture" was designed for performance *outside* the Cathedral of the Redeemer in the Kremlin. Given such an unconfined ambience, one can understand Tchaikovsky's inclusion of an auxiliary brass band, church bells, and cannon shots to create a great sonic festival. To all this a number of conductors have added a supplemental choral body. But for listening in one's home it is best to be wary of too much of a muchness. This warning is made because the fundamental orchestral scoring is already heavy and becomes loud and noisy if a conductor's principal purpose is to hit the sonorous jackpot.

Notwithstanding these considerations, the recording history of Tchaikovsky's piece is mostly opposite. The axiom followed is that louder and larger is better.

Dorati's Mercury recording (75001) combines the Minneapolis Symphony Orchestra with the University of Minnesota Brass Band, cannon shots recorded at the U.S. Military Academy, and bells recorded at the Riverside Memorial Church. (The last are listed as the "Bells of the Harkness Memorial Tower" at Yale University, but Deems Taylor, in a special commentary included on the disc, identifies the bells as from the New York City locale rather than New Haven.) Abravanel (on Westminster 8125) uses the band-bells-cannon combine. Buketoff expands this partnership to a quadruple total with a large chorus (RCA LSC–3051), as does Ormandy in two different Columbia packagings (M–30447 and M7X–30830). (He has also recorded the work "straight" [without chorus] for both Columbia [on MS–6073 and M–31831] and RCA [on LSC–3204 and LSC–5008], and on RCA LSC–3301; the setting Ormandy has chosen covers band and chorus.)

And so it goes. Some of these many productions (thirty-seven to choose from!) contain a good brand of interpretation but are nullified by the syndrome of shaking the rafters and rattling the windows. The top choice is Bernard Haitink's performance. It is exciting, is properly (and musically) powerful, has a tension where it should try for dramaticism, and is magnificently recorded. It is truly an inspiring portrayal, exceedingly rare among "1812" performances, be they in concert or recorded.

Overture to the Drama *The Storm*, Op. 76

☐ Frankfurt Radio Symphony Orchestra / Inbal (conductor) / Philips 6500467

The Overture to *Groza*, or *L'Orage*, was composed at the age of twenty-five, and published three years after Tchaikovsky's death. Not the greatest of Tchaikovsky, but don't overlook the orchestrational ointment the young fellow could apply to a score.

Eliahu Inbal does not minimize this score's youthful *brio*, color, and rhetoric and directs the music with gusto.

Romeo and Juliet (1869)

☐ Boston Symphony Orchestra / Abbado (conductor) / Deutsche Grammophon 2530137
☐ San Francisco Symphony Orchestra / Ozawa (conductor) / Deutsche Grammophon 2530308
☐ Boston Symphony Orchestra / Munch (conductor) / RCA VICS-1197

Tchaikovsky's "Overture-Fantasy" has been overrecorded. There's no reason for more recordings of the work, but still they come. New discoveries in the score are not being made.

Among the bulk of editions available Abbado's is certainly a prime entry. It combines energy with a refinement that sits extremely well and doesn't endeavor to convince by exaggeration. Brilliance and excitement are found in Ozawa's performance but with everything clear and immediate. Dramaticism is the compelling impulse in this case, without a resort to schmaltzy speech. The clarity in Munch's reading is a joy to hear. This makes the battle section tight and neat and thereby doubly exciting and provides the fullest articulative statements in the lyrical sections. In all these three cases no barrier is set up against full orchestral passion, but it is a passion that does not clash with musically artistic order. Again, less brings more in each case.

Suite from the Ballet *The Nutcracker*, Op. 71a

☐ London Philharmonic Orchestra / Stokowski (conductor) / Philips 6500766
☐ Orchestre de Paris / Ozawa (conductor) / Philips 6500851

A Stokowski speciality and it becomes apparent why when his recording is compared with others. Great spirit and marvelous color, and he knows when to pace himself and when to let it loose. Ozawa's view of this music has class about it. It proclaims as much charm as it does color and must be taken into account in any consideration of recordings of this work.

For further reference to the Suite, see under *Ballet* (*The Nutcracker*, Op. 71, and Op. 71 [Excerpts]).

Suite from the Ballet *The Sleeping Beauty*, Op. 66a

☐ Orchestre de Paris / Ozawa (conductor) / Philips 6500851

The very best compilation from Tchaikovsky's ballet (see under *Ballet*) is the basic suite performed in concert, including five movements. The very best representation is the bright and vivid declaration that Ozawa makes of the score.

Suite from the Ballet *Swan Lake,* Op. 20

☐ Berlin Philharmonic Orchestra / von Karajan (conductor) / Deutsche Grammophon 2530195

Von Karajan has recorded this music, the usually performed orchestral suite drawn from the ballet, for three different companies—London (on three separate releases, 6452, STS-15208, and CSP-3), Angel (on S-35740), and Deutsche Grammophon. More or less little to choose among these, save that the release noted above provides the richest sonic ambience. It offers keen playing that will satisfy the most critical listener.

There is, of course, the complete ballet on disc, and a fine release of close to an hour's worth of excerpts. Both are discussed under *Ballet* (*Swan Lake,* Op. 20, and *Swan Lake,* Op. 20 [Excerpts]).

Suite No. 1 in D minor, Op. 43

☐ Moscow Radio Symphony Orchestra / Jansons (conductor) / Melodiya/Angel S-40174

Compelling portrayal of the *Introduzione e fuga* and a delightful interpretation of the fourth movement, *Marche miniature.* The other four movements are comfortably played and cannot be challenged.

Suite No. 3 in G major, Op. 55

☐ Moscow Philharmonic Orchestra / Kondrashin (conductor) / Melodiya/Angel S-40175

It is the superb fourth movement, a Theme and Variations, that carries this work and is often presented separately, being as long as the first three movements combined (an Elegy, Melancholic Waltz, and Scherzo).

Boult's quite old performance on London STS-15034 is fine and quite elegant. Kondrashin's much newer one is fine and more deeply colored.

Suite No. 4 (*Mozartiana*), Op. 61

☐ L'Orchestre de la Suisse Romande / Ricci (violin) / Ansermet (conductor) / London STS-15295

Here is Mozart transcribed and in the process given a logic of Tchaikovsky's own. The coverage includes a Gigue, a Minuet, a Motet (which is a transcription of a transcription, since Tchaikovsky used Liszt's free version for his version), and a set of variations which includes a solo-violin section.

With such tribute from one composer to another there shouldn't be any quibbling, and there isn't, musically. None either as far as the performance is concerned, though Ricci is a bit heavy in his playing.

Symphony No. 1 (*Winter Dreams*) in G minor, Op. 13

☐ Boston Symphony Orchestra / Thomas (conductor) / Deutsche Grammophon 2530078

Thomas's closest competition comes from the very expressive consideration of this Symphony by Yevgeny Svetlanov, conducting the U.S.S.R. Symphony Orchestra, on Melodiya/Angel S-40057. However, you cannot top any of those B.S.O. players. Just two examples: the gorgeous oboe solo in the slow movement and the string weave in the initial movement.

Thomas's achievement is masterly. He avoids oversentimentality but expresses the fullest sentiments of the score. These are gauged with a fine grasp of the total idea, so that sentiment is never made a substitute for action. A recording that stands as a high point in this young conductor's career.

Symphony No. 2 (*Little Russian*) in C minor, Op. 17

☐ London Symphony Orchestra / Previn (conductor) / RCA AGL1-1265

For the greater part interpretative faults mark the various recorded editions of Tchaikovsky's *Little Russian* Symphony. Bernstein (Columbia M-31195) rushes the piece extremely. Maazel (London TCH-S-1) is mostly exempt from the music's passions. Rozhdestvensky (Melodiya/Angel S-40261/6) is closest to the choice noted above, but his orchestra (Moscow Radio Symphony Orchestra) is not first rate. Svetlanov (Melodiya/Angel S-40058) makes the march totally illogical with his slow tempi and is very rough and rude in the finale. Abbado (Deutsche Grammophon 139381) doesn't get involved, so the playing is noteworthy but with little associative meaning. The fine Markevitch statement (on Philips 835390) has been unfortunately deleted. Finally, Solti (London STS-15120) has Bernsteinish brashness, and that piles socko on top of heaviness and is not enjoyable at all.

All of which leaves Previn's reading. It is, in contrast to those mentioned above, clear, straight, and thereby sympathetic to Tchaikovsky's material. No erratic capricious tempi, no special conductorial whims. Tchaikovsky sounds with surety, therefore, and Tchaikovsky's four-part narrative is neither weakened nor overburdended.

Symphony No. 3 (*Polish*) in D major, Op. 29

☐ New York Philharmonic / Bernstein (conductor) / Columbia M-31727

The weakest of Tchaikovsky's symphonies, even with some nice tunes and an interesting five-movement layout, including two scherzos (the first an *Alla tedesca*) and a *Tempo di polacca* finale (hence the *Polish* nickname). Still, interest in Tchaikovsky should lead to owning a recording, especially if the other symphonies are represented in one's collection. And, Bernstein's unpushed, well-balanced performance is totally satisfying.

Symphony No. 4 in F minor, Op. 36

☐ Vienna Philharmonic Orchestra / Abbado (conductor) / Deutsche Grammophon 2530651
☐ Vienna Philharmonic Orchestra / Maazel (conductor) / London 6429

Abbado's view is a triumph. His reading is like the old Koussevitzky approach (this Symphony was one of K's favorite war-horses) and who knew better? Thus here are inward glow and emotional flame delivered with all the required sweep and grandeur. This combine even covers the finale (a paragon of noisy nonsense no other important composer ever equaled). Triple-star this one.

Loren Maazel's realization is direct and fine, never noisy, and he plays the score straight from the hip, which means no screaming to the gallery and no choreographic sideswiped effects. It's a clean performance, and even in the bass-drum-and-cymbal finale he produces controlled music without negating excitement. Triple-star this one also.

Symphony No. 5 in E minor, Op. 64

☐ London Symphony Orchestra / Abbado (conductor) / Deutsche Grammophon 2530198
☐ Philadelphia Orchestra / Ormandy (conductor) / RCA ARL1-0664

This isn't the first time Ormandy recorded Tchaikovsky's work. There are still available his Columbia editions (MS-6109 and M-31842). However, this is his newest production, and there is gain. The emotion is turned on, but no one has to be turned off by such things as Stokowskian-styled slurps (those legatoed curves in the peroration, ugh!), or the overkill that this Symphony brings out from so many conductors.

In the concert hall the Symphony continues its popular pace. Many a concertgoer has reached the end of his Tchaikovskian rope and would prefer to twist it around the neck of the next conductor who schedules the work. But when new meanings are brought to the Symphony, new attention is given the thrice-familiar Symphony. New meanings are brought by Abbado by the simple means of retaining the Tchaikovsky music within its frame. He does not add any glaring highlights or shoot it through with personally conducted electricity. The result is a calm (Tchaikovsky calm, mind you) and yet thoroughly exciting music.

Symphony No. 6 (*Pathétique*) in B minor, Op. 74

☐ Philharmonia Orchestra / Giulini (conductor) / Seraphim S-60031
☐ Berlin Philharmonic Orchestra / von Karajan (conductor) / Deutsche Grammophon 138921

The tendency to overkill ruins many a performance of Tchaikovsky, especially this Symphony. Of course there are the usual Tchaikovskian temptations to seduce conductors, but those that abstain draw the greatest excitement.

Giulini's 1961 recording follows the score, which gives sufficient opportunity for laying it on, but he does not do this indiscriminately. For instance, in the third movement Giulini avoids militaristic bombast, using a tightly pointed pulse to encase the rhythmics, and chooses textural weighting differences to create the drama, rather than a high decibel count. Nor are conductorial theories applied better to explain the structure of the opening movement; Giulini just presents what has been clearly detailed by Tchaikovsky. In the finale also the music is allowed to speak for itself. It all adds up to the emotional climax of a greatly realized performance.

Von Karajan pulls out the stops much more but not to the extent of brashness or bad taste. There is no maudlin quality to the finale, but rather deep eloquence. The other movements are large statements but natural ones that do not overplot the music's charged drama.

Symphony No. 7 in E flat major (Arranged by Bogatyryev)

☐ Philadelphia Orchestra / Ormandy (conductor) / Columbia MS-6349

One of those affairs of finding the skeleton, then placing flesh and clothing on it. The Tchaikovsky "Seventh" has been put together from his rough sketches plus thirty-three pages of the full score. At that point he decided to forget the whole thing and used some of the material for his third piano concerto. The reconstruction, by Semyon Bogatyryev required such as the orchestration of one of Tchaikovsky's piano pieces to serve as the third movement. Etc.

The entire story is related in Columbia's liner notes. Of course Ormandy's performance is all it should be. As a curiosity 'tis worth while. As "Tchaikovsky" it's debatable.

The Tempest, Op. 18

☐ Frankfurt Radio Symphony Orchestra / Inbal (conductor) / Philips 6500467

Neglected in the Tchaikovsky canon but undeservedly so. Inbal's splendid conception, especially sensitively controlled in regard to the storm music and in blending the brass writing, can well change negative opinions. On the other hand, neither the unbalanced rendering by Dorati and the National Symphony (London 6891) nor the overplayed, vulgarized playing of the U.S.S.R. Symphony Orchestra conducted by Svetlanov on Melodiya/Angel S-40166 will make friends for Tchaikovsky's Fantasy on Shakespeare's drama.

The Voyevode, Op. 78

☐ Frankfurt Radio Symphony Orchestra / Inbal (conductor) / Philips 6500467

The score of *Le Voyevode* was destroyed by Tchaikovsky and then reconstituted from the orchestral parts in 1917, receiving its posthumous publication as Opus 78.

Inbal plays this symphonic ballad in a glowing manner, with a sharp definition of its content, which is lacking in the sole competitive version, conducted by Dorati (on London 6841).

Waltz and Polonaise from *Eugene Onegin,* Op. 24

☐ London Philharmonic Orchestra / Stokowski (conductor) / Philips 6500766

Superb. Not that Stokowski is under wraps whatsoever, but there isn't a dot or dash that he has changed in the scoring. The brilliance and sweep are grand, the sound full and bright but not overcharged. Superb it is.

The listing above is the way Philips shows the title on the album. However, the pieces are played in reverse order. For proper climax that's the way it should be; that order realizes the contrastive punch and panache that are contained in Tchaikovsky's inspired dance music.

String Orchestra

Serenade in C major, Op. 48

☐ Academy of St. Martin-in-the-Fields / Marriner (conductor) / Argo ZRG–584
☐ Berlin Philharmonic / von Karajan (conductor) / Deutsche Grammophon 139030

The temptations that await conductors in Tchaikovsky's score have unfortunately overwhelmed most of them. A healthy, steady baton is mandatory as the preventive interpretative inoculation against the noxious disease of *ritards* and schmaltz. Without it the *Moderato, tempo di valse* turns into a spastic dance, with halts and languishing stretches that defy gravity, and the Elegy produces enough chicken fat to line hundreds of pastrami sandwiches.

For this reason it is best to avoid Ormandy (on Columbia MS-6224 and duplicated on the same label's M7X-30830 and M-30447). Much less so in Bernstein's reading (Columbia M-34128), but the tempi get stuck in the Elegy and in most of the first movement. Oddly enough, Stokowski (on Philips 6500921) avoids such unappetizing translations, but he doesn't avoid flabbiness.

No indeed, Tchaikovsky's gorgeous music does not need a single smear, or a portentous portamento to register with all of its intensity in the Elegy, or require tempo braking and unbraking to color its waltz moves. The outer movements generally are less vulnerable to conductorial manipulation. It is just the impeccable attention to the score and the total absence of inferential nonsense that make Marriner's performance lyrical, tender, emotive, or intense at any particular moment, and always in Tchaikovsky's terms. It's a beauty. The von Karajan reading is a bit fatter, but only due to using a larger group of players. It too is a no-nonsense performance, one of total musicality.

Solo Instrument and Orchestra

Cello

Variations on a Rococo Theme, Op. 33

☐ Philadelphia Orchestra / Rose (cello) / Ormandy (conductor) / Columbia MS-6714

The trick in this piece is to blend Mozartean grace with Tchaikovsky impetus. Leonard Rose solves this built-in dilemma magnificently. His playing is both light and deft, on point and with sensitive bravado. Not easy to do but he does it and does it better than the competition. Maximum competency from Eugene Ormandy.

Concert Fantasy for Piano and Orchestra, Op. 56   *Piano*

☐ Prague Symphony Orchestra / Ponti (piano) / Kapp (conductor) / Turnabout 34551

The chances are that this work is totally unfamiliar. You can put a fat bet on the table that it won't appear on any program by one of the big-name pianists. Too bad and too unfair. No argument that it is not in the same class as the popular B flat minor Concerto that receives hundreds of performances, but the Concert Fantasy does have fine thematic invention, nice tunes, and a hefty (if not overly virtuosic) solo part. It is worth anyone's listening time.

Michael Ponti satifies in all respects with his conception. His playing is of exactitude, marked by fine dynamic adjustment, and of splendid style. It has more zest and sonorous nourishment than the version offered by Peter Katin on London STS-15227. Ponti's performance is also available in a Vox Box (SVBX-5460).

Concerto No. 1 in B flat minor for Piano and Orchestra, Op. 23

☐ Orchestra / Cliburn (piano) / Kondrashin (conductor) / RCA LSC-2252
☐ Philadelphia Orchestra / Joselson (piano) / Ormandy (conductor) / RCA ARL1-0751
☐ Berlin Philharmonic Orchestra / Berman (piano) / von Karajan (conductor) / Deutsche Grammophon 2530677

A special bit of history pertains to Van Cliburn's performance. This was his first recording after his spectacular winning of the International Tchaikovsky Competition in Moscow in 1958. It was made with a free-lance group of musicians at an all-night recording session. Quickly let it be noted that pick-up musicians notwithstanding, the orchestra offers playing of top-drawer quality, and, of course, Kiril Kondrashin is a whiz in handling this work. Cliburn has never been better than here. Importantly, while he provides full technical revelation, there is a musical empathy in his interpretation that has distinguished depth. More than two decades after its release this performance still ranks as one of the very best of the many, many available.

The directness of Joselson's playing is contrasted by a superb lyrical quality. A unique balance and blend are the result, providing an atmosphere far different from that resulting from the usual black-white approach of most pianists. Berman's reading gives revealing variety to the music's detail and yet is defined by complete stylistic uniformity. His tone glows, and his technical conclusiveness is memorable. He lives up to his publicity releases.

Concerto No. 2 in G major for Piano and Orchestra, Op. 44

☐ Philadelphia Orchestra / Graffman (piano) / Ormandy (conductor) / Columbia MS-6755

Even in hearing this fine essay one may not necessarily be shaken. Living in the shadow of the famous B flat minor makes a performance response difficult. There are nice things in the second Concerto, and Gary Graffman serves them up in piping hot sauce. This is an alive and exceedingly direct performance, with clear and immediate consideration. Try it, you might like it.

Concerto No. 3 in E flat major for Piano and Orchestra, Op. 75 (One-Movement Version)

☐ Philadelphia Orchestra / Graffman (piano) / Ormandy (conductor) / Columbia MS-6755

The complete version as far as Tchaikovsky is concerned, the Concerto being a redo of a projected symphony which he abandoned. Two other movements were sketched, but whether Tchaikovsky would have worked these into a final three-movement piano-concerto structure one will never know. Taneyev, the erudite Russian composer and once student of Tchaikovsky, completed the work, and in his version it has been recorded (see under *Tchaikovsky*/Taneyev: *Solo Instrument and Orchestra: piano*). However, it is the one-movement version (an *Allegro brillante*) that one hears performed (though most rarely).

The music is a brilliant affair. Graffman exploits his technique to the full, and Ormandy surrounds and supports him with rich sonority. Compared with Ponti's portrayal of the original first movement (retained, of course, in Taneyev's completion of the Concerto, which is the version Ponti plays) Graffman's performance clearly is the top choice. However, if you wish the complete property by Tchaikovsky and Taneyev assisting, Ponti will have to be your man on Candide 31056 or in a three-disc Vox Box SVBX-5460. He provides an agreeable performance, though not aided by only fair orchestral playing.

The recording noted above is coupled with the Tchaikovsky second piano Concerto. All three concerti are obtainable, with Graffman as the soloist, on Columbia MG-30838.

Violin

Concerto in D major for Violin and Orchestra, Op. 35

☐ Philadelphia Orchestra / Stern (violin) / Ormandy (conductor) / Columbia MS-6062
☐ Chicago Symphony Orchestra / Heifetz (violin) / Reiner (conductor) / RCA LSC-2129

There are lots of new entries in the lists for this perennial, but while new is good, old is better. With Heifetz there is a lot of blood and guts and even a bit of scratch, but no squeal. Letting Tchaikovsky loose harms not. In any event Heifetz reads the Canzonetta with a soulful demeanor that is most impressive and tears off the finale cool as a cucumber but with resultant heat.

Stern is an extrovert fiddler, and the Concerto's personality fits his, and he does it perfectly. In matter of tone Heifetz's performance is warm and even sweet; Stern's has an inlay of nicely warmed *kasha* that fits this great piece.

There are plenty of different RCA choices which have the Tchaikovsky performed by Heifetz—VCS-7058, VCS-7086, LSC-3304, LSC-5020, and CRL6-0720. Stern's performance is in other Columbia albums as well—M-31835 and D3S-721.

Scherzo from *Souvenir d'un lieu cher*, Op. 42, No. 2

☐ London Symphony Orchestra / Ricci (violin) / Fjelstad (conductor) / London STS-15054

Some explanation is required, since London doesn't offer a single word about this extremely rare Tchaikovsky work. It is the central part of a group of three pieces: Op. 42, No. 1 is a *Méditation* (originally planned as the slow movement of the Violin Concerto); Op. 42, No. 3 is a *Mélodie*. All three pieces were composed for violin and piano. (For a recording of the original setting of the Scherzo, see under *Instrumental: violin*.) The orchestration of the accompaniment for all three pieces calling for double winds, two horns, harp, and strings was made by Glazunov.

Ricci is extremely persuasive in his playing of this short and worthy item.

Sérénade mélancolique, Op. 26

☐ Los Angeles Philharmonic Orchestra / Heifetz (violin) / Wallenstein (conductor) / RCA LM-2860 (monaural)

Heifetz's narrative is extremely moving, musically just, solidly stated without encumbering the music's progress. He employs subtle appropriate accentuations, whereas Grumiaux (on Philips 6580047) swims up and down (even though gently) through *crescendi* and *decrescendi* that make waves in the melodic line. Such concerts protest too much for the simplicity of the Tchaikovskian statement. Ricci (on London STS-15054) underplays in an attempt to be tender and all that occurs is a frail melodic continuity.

Heifetz, yes. He is true to the Russian melos that permeate the work. A superb portrayal and far better played in this mono documentation than the later performance, recorded in stereo and released on RCA's LSC-3109.

Aveu passionné

Instrumental

Piano

☐ Ponti (piano) / Vox SVBX-5459

Nocturnal and moody. Played in a most fitting *désolé* manner. (*Aveu passionné* is not included in the listing of Tchaikovsky's piano compositions in *Grove's Dictionary of Music and Musicians*.)

Capriccio, Op. 8

☐ Ponti (piano) / Vox SVBX-5455

A lightly scanned conception set in G flat major. There are five sections, with a reversed return to the first two after the central part has been played. Ponti plays Tchaikovsky's piece simply and directly.

Children's Album, Op. 39

☐ Ponti (piano) / Vox SVBX-5459

Two dozen pieces, not just for playing by the kiddies. The *Album* pieces are certainly as enjoyable a fare for their elders, as is other composers' "music for children," including that of Schumann and Shostakovich, Bloch and Bartók, and a host of others.

Herewith some titles to whet the interest: *Winter Morning, Italian Ditty, Witch, The Organ Grinder,* and *In Church.* Not unexpectedly, there is a Waltz.

Dumka, Op. 59

☐ Ponti (piano) / Vox SVBX-5455

This is Tchaikovsky music that deserves the fullest attention. *Dumka* literally means "lament" or "elegy." Dvořák made the type his own, using it in many works, definitely or by implication. Still the term is Russian, and Tchaikovsky gave it a rich musical definition in this piece, in which he showed how to manifest the psychological shifts from the melancholic to the exuberant which are part and parcel of a lament which both exhorts and cries.

Brilliantly played by Ponti, with sensitively coherent contrasts.

Eighteen Pieces, Op. 72

☐ Ponti (piano) / Vox SVBX-5459

Highlights in this set are the serene *Méditation* (the fifth piece), the speedy *Scherzo-Fantasie,* and the dashing final piece, a *Scène dansante (Invitation au Trépak).* Tchaikovsky's skill with dance-formationed music is further keenly evidenced in Opus 72, in the *Valse bluette* and a quintuple-metered waltz, *Valse à cinq temps.*

Humoresque, Op. 10, No. 2

☐ Entremont (piano) / Columbia D3S-791

This is the original setting of a piece that has been transcribed to a fare-thee-well. One doesn't blame the arrangers. They knew a good tune when they heard it.

It is included in the first volume of Michael Ponti's three-volume survey of Tchaikovsky's piano music on Vox SVBX-5455, but Ponti doesn't have Entremont's touch and the crispness of delivery that the music demands.

Impromptu-Capriccio (1884)
Impromptu in A flat major (1889)
Impromptu (*Momento lirico*) in A flat major (1893)

☐ Ponti (piano) / Vox SVBX-5459

The brisk, central part of the ternary-shaped Impromptu-Caprice displays Tchaikovsky in a sparkling balletic mood.

Tchaikovsky never finished the last piece listed. The completion process was accomplished by Taneyev, a fine composer in his own right.

Impromptu in E flat minor, Op. 1, No. 2
Nocturne, Op. 10, No. 1
Romanze, Op. 5
Ruines d'un chateau, Op. 2, No. 1
Scherzo à la Russe, Op. 1, No. 1
Scherzo in F minor, Op. 2, No. 2

☐ Ponti (piano) / Vox SVBX-5455

Granted the salon genre in which these pieces fall, they all come from a well-controlled creative hand. Ponti gives them full attention and doesn't belittle the style with any casualness.

The *Romanze* is still another Tchaikovsky melody that has been arranged for dozens of instrumental combinations. The Opus 2 pieces form parts 1 and 2 of a set titled *Souvenir de Hapsal.* It is concluded with the "evergreen" *Chant sans paroles—see below* (Song Without Words, Op. 2, No. 3).

The Seasons, Op. 37a

☐ Ponti (piano) / Vox SVBX-5459

The Seasons includes twelve pieces, one for each of the months. Some of the titles directly invoke a season or month, such as *Autumn Song* (for October) and *Christmas* (for December, of course), celebrated by a full-blooded Tchaikovsky waltz. Others have more general character; for example, *Carnival* (for February) and a gentle *By the Hearth* (for January).

Two of the group have become standard favorites—*Barcarolle*, covering the month of June, and *Troïka en traîneaux*, for November. The former has been manhandled by transcribers and canned-music experts; the latter has received such attention too, though to a lesser degree. Well now, all of the essences one might desire are contained in the original piano issuances, and Ponti interprets them with warm assuredness.

Six Pieces, Op. 19

☐ Ponti (piano) / Vox SBVX-5455

The first five are short conceptions—with such expositions as a *Scherzo Humoristique* (which Ponti plays with full command) and a Nocturne (which brings forth a fine poetic quality from the soloist). In the sixth Tchaikovsky moves away from compactness to a work of ten-minute length, a Theme and Variations, with twelve variants plus a coda exposed. The climax is a supercharged exhibition; the instruction in the music is fully descriptive: *più presto, brillante e crescendo.* Ponti follows suit admirably.

Six Pieces for Piano, Op. 51

☐ Ponti (piano) / Vox SVBX-5459

The milieu of the dance is the preoccupation in this opus. There are three waltzes, a *Valse de salon,* a *Natha Valse,* and a *Valse sentimentale.* Also included are a *Polka peu dansante* and a *Menuetto scherzoso.* Only the fifth piece, a Romance, deviates from this choreographic format.

Six Pieces on One Theme, Op. 21

☐ Ponti (piano) / Vox SVBX-5455

Opus 21 illustrates variational technique applied on a slightly larger scale than usual. Included are an excellent Fugue and a Funeral March with some declarative octavial bravura.

A convincingly idiomatic performance.

Sonata in C sharp minor, Op. 80

☐ Ponti (piano) / Vox SVBX-5459

Posthumously published, seven years after Tchaikovsky's death. It would have been factually honest merely to indicate "Op. Posth." However, for a sales pitch the assignment of the high opus number was much more commercially attractive, even though the Sonata was composed in 1865, two years before Tchaikovsky's official Opus 1, which dates from 1867.

As a student effort it achieves a passing grade. It is strongest in the Scherzo, weakest in the finale.

Feinberg has also recorded the piece, monaurally, on Monitor S-2130E.

Sonata in G major, Op. 37

☐ Richter (piano) / Monitor 2034 (monaural)

Subtitled "Grand Sonata" on Monitor's release, this is the largest work in Tchaikovsky's piano catalogue. Despite its rare appearance on concert programs, four pianists have seen fit to record it: Richter, Ponti (on Vox SVBX-5455), Manes (on Orion 75154), and Crossley (on Philips 6500884).

There's good playing in all cases, but Richter is by far the best of 'em all. Whatever theatricalism is present (not too much) he plays with italics. Moreover, the slow movement's pace has cumulative effectiveness, not because of the chosen tempo setting, but by virtue of an inward movement that accomplishes more than taking a specific metronomic pace for granted.

Song Without Words, Op. 2, No. 3

☐ Entremont (piano) / Columbia D3S–791

Entremont brings such depth to his playing of Tchaikovsky's little charmer that one hears it in a completely new and fresh way. Ponti also plays this piece in his two-volume, six-disc coverage of Tchaikovsky's solo piano pieces for Vox in Volume 1, SVBX–5455, but it's all on the surface and much too fast.

For other pieces in Opus 2 *see above* under Impromptu in E flat minor, Op. 1, No. 2.

Three Pieces, Op. 9
Twelve Pieces of Moderate Difficulty, Op. 40
Valse Caprice, Op. 4
Valse-Scherzo, Op. 7

☐ Ponti (piano) / Vox SVBX–5455

Parts 2 and 3 of Opus 9 are a *Polka de salon* and a *Mazurka de salon*—and they're exactly that. The waltzes display more guts and are played accordingly.

The popular G minor *Chanson triste* is the second piece in the Opus 40 group. Pairs of mazurkas and waltzes are included.

Valse-Scherzo (No. 2) in A major (1889)

☐ Ponti (piano) / Vox SVBX–5459

A breezy bit. Ponti plays it with well-adjusted bravura.

Violin

Mélodie, Op. 42, No. 3

☐ Ricci (violin); Pommers (piano) / MCA 2537

The best known of the *Trois Morceaux* ("Three Pieces") Tchaikovsky composed for violin and piano as his Opus 42. They exist with orchestral accompaniment, but in that form the background was made by Glazunov. (The first piece of the set, a *Méditation*, is not recorded; for the second piece, Scherzo, *see below*.)

Ricci communicates the music with a vivid simplicity that is ideal.

Scherzo from *Souvenir d'un lieu cher*, Op. 42, No. 2

☐ Heifetz (violin); Chotzinoff (piano) / RCA ARM4–0942 (monaural)

No one plays this, and no other recording in the original setting for violin and piano can be found, though one might be hidden away in the multitudinous miscellaneous collections that flood the market. (A recording with orchestral accompaniment, made by Glazunov, is available—see under *Solo Instrument and Orchestra: violin.*) Anyway, even if there is another performance for violin and piano, it won't, one wagers, match the palpable thrust of Heifetz's oldie. The acoustic recording is a real oldie, but to hell with the sound, catch the playing. (For the third piece in the set, *Mélodie,* see above.)

Chamber Music

Trio in A minor for Piano, Violin, and Cello, Op. 50

☐ Beaux Arts Trio / Philips 6500132
☐ Temianka (violin); Solow (cello); Stevenson (piano) / Orion 7265

There has been criticism of this trio that it stacks the scoring cards in favor of the piano. While it is true that there are wide stretches during which the piano is in a solo position—and that most often the keyboard instrument is a powerhouse breathing the fire of congested chordal writing and arrogant arpeggios, and suggesting concerto contours—nevertheless, the string instruments are not relegated to subservience. Perhaps the trio's sonorities are orchestral make-believe; nonetheless, the music is intense and contains some of Tchaikovsky's most inspired writing. This overrides the irritation of some other critics who claim Tchaikovsky's composition is for three instruments masquerading as a small orchestra.

There are two recorded editions listed. That is due only to the fact that if you wish the complete work, you must opt for the Orion release. Tchaikovsky's work is exceedingly long, and he therefore authorized two cuts, both in the second (and final) movement. The first section of that movement consists of a set of eleven variations on a twenty-measure theme stated by the piano alone. Immediately following is the second section of the movement (*Variazione finale e coda*), which sums up, employing the theme of the variations within it, and ends with a stupendously intense peroration which calls on the initial theme of the first movement (*Pezzo elegiaco*). The first authorized cut is the entire eighth variation, a fugue. The other one is a segment of 136 measures in the finale.

The Beaux Arts team take both, but notwithstanding the cuts, theirs is an inspirational, strikingly imaginative conception. Their tonal blend is far superior to that of the free-lance trio on Orion, and the intonation is impeccable. The last is not the case with Temianka and Solow, especially in the unisons of the ninth variation, *Andante flebile ma non tanto*. Further, the Philips sound is in a class by itself.

It should be mentioned that the variation omitted by the Beaux Arts Trio is the weakest of Tchaikovsky's set. An extra credit belongs to Philips, which has banded the variations. The banding is certainly nice to have in case repetitions of any of them are desired.

String Quartet in B flat major

☐ Borodin String Quartet / Melodiya/Angel S-40222

Of the preliminary chamber music Tchaikovsky composed before the first mature example was produced (the quartet bearing the designation Opus 11), only this one movement survives of the dozen pieces written for all types of combinations (including an Adagio for four horns, as well as a work for two flutes and five strings). All were composed during Tchaikovsky's student days at the St. Petersburg Conservatory. The work under discussion, and this one only, was actually full size, but just the first movement was performed during his lifetime, and it is the only movement extant.

Apparently dissatisfied with the one movement itself, Tchaikovsky used portions of it in his official Opus 1 (which consisted of two pieces for piano, the first using the theme of the quartet under the title Scherzo à la Russe). (A recording of the Scherzo is available—see under *Instrumental: piano* under Impromptu in E flat minor, Op. 1, No. 2.

An Adagio opens and closes this one-movement piece, with the major space occupied by an Allegro, based on a Ukrainian folk song first heard in the viola. The folk theme is paramount in the movement's development and is, in fact, over-emphasized. It is noteworthy to perceive that the transitions already display Tchaikovsky's fondness for sequential repetition of a phrase, in order to move from one section to the next.

Straightforward playing accomplishes all there is to garner from Tchaikovsky's student effort. The Borodiners deserve applause for making this work available on disc—one never hears it in concert.

String Quartet

In D major, Op. 11 / In F major, Op. 22 / In E flat minor, Op. 30

☐ Copenhagen String Quartet / Vox SVBX–583

Tchaikovsky's three quartets are the finest nineteenth-century Russian examples in the medium. There are other good works, but none have the over-all richness of expression, the true Russian spirit (without the need to dip into folk-song quotation), that these three string quartets possess.

The slow movement in the Opus 11 is the hackneyed *Andante cantabile.* Excellent music, it is now platitudinous, since it has suffered the ignominy of every possible means of transcription and the most pretentious, syrupy performances. In its original scoring it is still fairly fresh for ears not beclouded with lush canned-music arrangements. The Copenhagen foursome avoid the slightest iota of sentimentality and play the piece simply, which amounts to playing it beautifully. Also, the Scherzo is presented in a tempo which clearly brings out the mensural patterns which direct emphasis off the main pulse.

Similar performance response defines the Scherzo of the Opus 22, where the unification of two measures of $\frac{6}{8}$ and following them with one of $\frac{9}{8}$ forms a total septuple meter—a type of limping rhythm in its odd-numbered proportions. Textural conditions are conquered in this work, which abounds in *tremolandi* and chordal techniques in its first movement. These cause traumas for the chamber-music critic still unaccustomed to the fact that post-Beethoven composers most generally write in a post-Beethoven manner.

The third quartet, the Opus 30, has a light but not overly capricious second movement. Scherzo quality is apparent in the dancing figurations, but cross-beated accentuations and a reticent middle section, which maintains the design of deflected pulsed entrances in pedal form, hold gaiety in check. The Tchaikovsky of *The Nutcracker* is not on the premises. The focal point of the third quartet, and undoubtedly the greatest music in all of the three quartets, is the fervent sad emotion of the third movement of Opus 30. In this Tchaikovsky is unabashed, his grief unhidden, marking passages *pianguendo* ("weeping") and *dolore* ("pain"). Dirge-like footsteps and liturgical intonations, primarily based on straight chordal progressions (vertical or dismembered horizontally), are exposed. It all equals the despairing detonations and the black-patched sentience of his *Pathétique* Symphony. And the thrust and depth of this music are splendidly realized by the Copenhagen team.

That the Tchaikovsky quartets remain ignored by our chamber-music organizations may be due to snobbery or simply the tides of fashion. But with them available in these fine recorded performances, one need not wait for concert revival.

An error by Vox indicates the key of the third quartet as E minor on both the outside cover of the album and the record label itself.

Souvenir de Florence, Sextet for Strings, Op. 70

☐ Borodin Quartet / Talalyan (viola); Rostropovich (cello) / Melodiya/Angel S–40036

The sonorities of six strings might be expected to draw from so resonantly disposed a composer as Tchaikovsky a type of orchestral *reductio.* But this does not occur in the pleasant single example he wrote for the limited repertory of the string sextet. The work is simple in texture and form notwithstanding certain critics who claim otherwise and insist that only a string orchestra can do justice to the score.

This is the only worthy performance. The release on Vox (SVBX–583) is rough and strenuous. Marriner (who one would expect would know and do better) in his string-orchestra exposition (released by Argo on ZRG–584) has made innumerable excisions from the score, which rules out his performance from consideration.

Again, As Before, Alone, Op. 73, No. 6

To Forget So Soon

Was I Not a Blade of Grass, Op. 47, No. 7

Whether Day Is Dawning, Op. 47, No. 6

Vocal

*Voice with
Accompaniment*

☐ Davrath (soprano); Werba (piano) / Vanguard VSD-71115

Characteristic Tchaikovskian fervid melancholy is spelled out in the second and third songs of this group. The dark tonal beauty of Davrath is most convincing.

Eugene Onegin, Op. 24

Opera

☐ Orchestra of the Royal Opera House, Covent Garden, and John Alldis Choir / Kubiak (soprano); Reynolds, Hamari, and Hartle (mezzo-sopranos); Burrows and Sénéchal (tenors); Weikl (baritone); Ghiaurov, Mason, and Van Allan (basses) / Solti (conductor) / London 13112

Gorgeous music, particularly the orchestral writing, marks Tchaikovsky's splendid operatic opus. Important to note: the orchestration is a powerful adjunct of the characterizations expressing what is left unsaid by the characters—two examples: the illustrative detail the orchestra provides in the Letter Scene and the commentary of the instrumental forces in the Duel Scene. Tchaikovsky's melodicism is beautifully rich, with a folk-music infiltration that emphasizes the setting of Pushkin's Russian tale.

Solti's direction is finely accomplished, only faulty in a few of the sections where he reduces the tempo and weakens the dramatic conviction thereby. Teresa Kubiak stars as Tatyana. Her voice is warm and thrilling. Stewart Burrows provides one of the best interpretations of the Vladimir Lenski role this reviewer has heard. His voice is fresh and full and he displays a splendid sensitivity for the dramatic that represents vocal art at its best. The rest of the cast is good, the orchestral playing of full range, and the off-stage material has been balanced most effectively.

There are two other editions on the market. Both are deficient. Rostropovich conducts the Bolshoi Opera Orchestra and Chorus, with his wife Galina Vishnevskaya and Vladimir Atlantov in the cast, on Melodiya/Angel S-4115. However, Tchaikovsky is so over-romanticized in this conception that dramatic validity becomes erased. Rough tone, pedestrian tempi, and little elegance are all found in the Belgrade National Opera's performance, conducted by Oscar Danon on Richmond 63509.

Pique Dame, Op. 68

☐ Orchestra and Chorus of the Bolshoi Theater / Milashkina, Lebedeva, and Kasrashvili (sopranos); Levko and Grigorieva (mezzo-sopranos); Borisova (contralto); Atlantov, Sokolov, Baskov, and Vlasov (tenors); Valaitis and Fedoseyev (baritones); Yaroslavtsev and Dementiev (basses) / Ermler (conductor) / Columbia/Melodiya MS-33828

Tchaikovsky's "The Queen of Spades" was composed to a libretto (based on a Pushkin short story) written by the composer's brother, Modest.

Pique Dame was premiered in St. Petersburg in 1890 and was first heard in Vienna in 1902, conducted by Mahler, who also directed the first American production in New York in 1910. With the exception of the Soviet Union, the success of Tchaikovsky's opera is not reflected in its production record elsewhere (the habit of operatic impresarios of staying within a small-ranged repertoire is the hard fact of musical life). Fortunately, one can enjoy the opera on disc.

This edition (sung in Russian, of course, with a full English translation offered in the booklet provided with the release) is the most recent one. Discounting some monkeyshines in shifting the sound quality in order to highlight sections within a scene, the Columbia/Melodiya account is excellent, the singing, especially on the part of Vladimir Atlantov as Herman, Andrei Fedoseyev as Yeletsky, Nina Grigorieva as the Governess, and Galina Borisova as Pauline (she also appears as Milovzor [Daphnis] in the pastoral play "The Faithful Shepherdess" that is presented in the second act) is impressive. The direction lacks some finesse but so does the Melodiya/Angel S-4104 issue that is available. However, the vocal quality in the Columbia/Melodiya release is substantially better. The remaining competition comes from Richmond's 63516. It is rather lackluster in all respects and the edition should be discounted.

Ballet

The Nutcracker, Op. 71

☐ London Symphony Orchestra and Members of the Ambrosian Chorus / Previn (conductor) / Angel S-3788
☐ National Philharmonic Orchestra / Bonynge (conductor) / London 2239

There is much to say in favor of almost all the editions of this, one of the greatest ballet scores that has ever been written. However, Previn's being one of the newest, has the advantage of superb state-of-the-art sonics. He deserves them with his clear portrayal, freed of all gooey interpretations that have harmed this music, specifically in sets of excerpts from the complete ballet and presentations of the standard orchestral Suite, Opus 71a (see under *Orchestra*).

Spirit and clarity mark Bonynge's interpretation. There is also special attention to individual detail that enhances the separate sections and aids in contrasting them clearly. It would be impossible to err by selecting this lucidly colorful conception.

The Nutcracker, Op. 71 (Excerpts)

☐ Bolshoi Theater Orchestra / Rozhdestvensky (conductor) / Monitor S-2104

A fine cross-section, played with full authenticity, with tradition backing up the performance style of the renowned Bolshoi organization.

There are four sections from Act I. The last of these is mistitled on the album (not on the label) as Waltz of the Flowers. It should read Waltz of the Snowflakes. The well-known Waltz of the Flowers is represented as the third cut on side B of the disc. It is from the second act, from which a total of thirteen sections are included in this edition of "highlights" from the ballet. Within this total of seventeen excerpts, all the eight parts of the constantly performed standard Suite are contained. The Suite is listed and discussed under *Orchestra* (Suite from the Ballet *The Nutcracker*, Op. 71a).

The Sleeping Beauty, Op. 66

☐ London Symphony Orchestra / Brown (violin); Cummings (cello) / Previn (conductor) / Angel SX-3812

Having experience as a conductor of ballet is an obvious asset when directing a ballet recording, and this is perceived in the excellent work of Dorati and Fistoulari. Previn's statistics in terms of ballet direction are exceedingly minimal, but the results he provides in this instance are maximal. The tempi are truly balletic, the moods all defined in the most communicative manner, be they grand and noble, light or dynamic. It totals an inspired representation of the score. Throughout, the playing of the Londoners is clearly in the groove regardless of the musical situation.

The complete score is covered. In the other versions by Ansermet (London 2304) and Weldon (Angel S-3579) there are deletions. But even if Previn had resorted to cuts, his would be the choice edition. (See also under *Orchestra* [Suite from the Ballet *The Sleeping Beauty*, Op. 66a].)

Swan Lake, Op. 20

☐ Netherlands Radio Philharmonic Orchestra / Ricci (violin) / Fistoulari (conductor) / London 21101/3

Totally superb, and that means grace and *brio,* with color and contrast that bring out the details contained in Tchaikovsky's work. There is a shining assurance in Fistoulari's direction, and there are no doubts about Ruggiero Ricci's contribution.

A more straightforward viewpoint but one solid in all respects (that is, balletic solidity, not textural heaviness) is to be heard in Rozhdestvensky's conception on Melodiya/Angel (S-4106), but all in all, the stronger performance in this case is that of Fistoulari.

For the orchestral Suite from the ballet see under *Orchestra* (Suite from the Ballet *Swan Lake*, Op. 20).

Swan Lake, Op. 20 (Excerpts)

☐ London Symphony Orchestra / Monteux (conductor) / Philips 835142

One of the most generous helpings from the ballet, with four items from Act I, the same total extracted from the second act, a half-dozen pieces from Act III, and the *Dance of the Little Swans* and the *Final Scene* taken from Act IV. These represent a bit over fifty-four minutes worth.

The playing is beautifully moulded, and Monteux's innate knowledge of choreographic pace is magnificently put forth here.

See also under *Orchestra* (Suite from the Ballet *Swan Lake*, Op. 20).

Tchaikovsky / **Sergei Taneyev**

Concerto No. 3 in E flat major for Piano and Orchestra, Op. 75/79

☐ Orchestra of Radio Luxembourg / Ponti (piano) / de Froment (conductor) / Candide 31056

Solo Instrument and Orchestra

Piano

There is special value to Candide's release. It is the first recording ever of the Tchaikovsky original first movement (Opus 75) and the Andante and Finale movements (Opus 79) which Taneyev reconstructed and fully orchestrated from Tchaikovsky's short score sketches and rough drafts. Credit must be given as due—Taneyev's proxy work is Tchaikovskian to the core.

Ponti's performance is coupled with the Rimsky-Korsakov piano Concerto. It is also included in an all-Tchaikovsky Vox Box SVBX-5460.

See also under *Tchaikovsky: Solo Instrument and Orchestra: piano* (Concerto No. 3 in E flat major for Piano and Orchestra, Op. 75 [One-Movement Version]).

Alexander Tcherepnin

(1899-1977)

Georgiana—Suite for Orchestra, Op. 92

Orchestra

☐ Frankenland State Symphony Orchestra / Barati (conductor) / Lyrichord 7103E (monaural)

Opus 92 is part of the group of folkloristic works Tcherepnin produced. He used Georgian melodic material specifically two additional times, in the *Suite georgienne* for Piano and Strings and the *Rapsodie georgienne* for Cello and Orchestra. This orchestral Suite is lush and of standardly squared romantic definition, despite most of its colorful subtitles: *Ceremonial, Veils and Daggers, Chota and Thamar, Kartsuli,* and *Apotheosis.*

Barati does what he can with the music but the orchestra is strictly minor league from first sound to last.

Symphony No. 2, Op. 77

☐ Louisville Orchestra / Whitney (conductor) / Louisville S–645

Expressions of anguish and anxiety are combined in the opening movement of Tcherepnin's Symphony, and these darker moods are continued in the threnodic sweep of the second movement. The latter (in Lento tempo) is a memorial to the composer's father, Nicolas Tcherepnin (1873–1945), also a composer, who died a few months before his son began work on the Symphony. A more optimistic climate creeps into the third and fourth movements of the work.

Tcherepnin's Opus 77 was first performed by the Chicago Symphony Orchestra. That was in 1952. Whitney produced the work in 1964 and then recorded it. It is good to have, but Tcherepnin's work needs a larger group of string players than the Louisville organization had for this recording.

Solo Instrument and Orchestra

Piano

Piano Concerto No. 2, Op. 22

☐ Louisville Orchestra / Tcherepnin (piano) / Whitney (conductor) / Louisville 615 (monaural)

Tonality by way of Tcherepnin's nine-toned scale, which permits a fundamental flux between major and minor and which gives a flavorsome modalistic touch to the proceedings. The Concerto is in one movement and its transformations are basically derived from a single theme. It's very attractive music and very easy to listen to, aided as it is by open-air textures.

Tcherepnin does well, of course, and so do the Louisvillians, though when this was recorded the string body needed some flesh added to it.

Ten Bagatelles for Piano and String Orchestra, Op. 5

☐ Württemberg Chamber Orchestra, Heilbronn / Meyer-Josten (piano) / Faerber (conductor) / Turnabout 34545

Originally for piano solo, then transcribed for piano and orchestra, and heard here in a third setting for piano and string orchestra (though Turnabout incorrectly states that the work is for "Piano and Orchestra").

There is a nice momentum in Tcherepnin's music, even in the slow movements. Each idea is followed through in a fluid whole. A complete clarification of each piece's form and direction is made by the performers.

Chamber Music

Sonatine sportive

☐ Brodie (saxophone); Brough (piano) / Golden Crest 7028 (monaural)

Program music covering a boxing match and a race, with an intermission in between. A little hard to convey, but if one reads the liner notes and adds a pinch of imagination, it will work.

Brass Quintet, Op.105

☐ Annapolis Brass Quintet / Crystal S–207

A work of charm, its music illustrative of how to write for brass instruments without brashness and with a special type of delicacy. All the sounds of the five movements (the second joined to the third and the fourth linked to the fifth) caress the ear. There is also a novel cadenza, featuring the tuba for special color. This is a high-level recorded performance of precision and character.

Georg Philipp Telemann *(1681-1767)*

Orchestra

Concerto a quattro in D major (*di Melante*)

☐ Academy of St. Martin-in-the-Fields / Smithers (trumpet); Preston (harpsichord) / Marriner (conductor) / Philips 6500110

Stunning Telemann music. (The "by Melante" is an anagram of Telemann's name and was the identification on the manuscript.) The sequence of Adagio-Allegro-Grave-Allegro is cultured with golden detail. It is conveyed with an equilibrated and finely contrasted performance, with subtle terraced dynamics, sparkling trumpet playing, and a continuo of cello, double bass, and harpsichord.

Ouverture des nations anciens et modernes

☐ Academy of St. Martin-in-the-Fields / Marriner (conductor) / Argo ZRG–837

The "Ancient and Modern Nations" music is dancy music. It is played with impeccable taste that defines all the built-in contrasts. A fully stylish edition, this.

Overture in C major for Three Oboes, Strings, and Continuo

☐ Chamber Orchestra of the Saar / Winschermann, Bolz, and Trenz (oboes) / Ristenpart (conductor) / Nonesuch 71132

Not an Overture in the usual sense, but a large (eight-movement) Suite, one of the some 600 (!) Telemann produced. Not a prosaic ordering, either. A stately *Espagnol,* a gorgeous *Sommeille* ("Sleep") are included with the expected dances, such as a pair of Minuets and a Gigue. And there are other delights.

There is no dispute and not a smidgen of disappointment in Ristenpart's presentation. Springy rhythms and sensitively curved melodic lines are emphasized. This is playing of high order, which includes the blend of the three oboes.

Overture in C major (*Hamburger Ebb und Fluht*)

☐ Academy of St. Martin-in-the-Fields / Marriner (conductor) / Argo ZRG–837

Telemann's *Wasser-Ouverture* (or, as *Schwann* questionably lists it, "Water Music") is given a sure-fire performance with great sound, and sound style. The "Hamburg Tides" stream forth delightfully under Marriner's direction.

Suite in A minor

String Orchestra

☐ Chamber Orchestra of Versailles / Chirat (harpsichord) / Wahl (conductor) / Nonesuch 71017E (monaural)

This is not the popular work with the same title, which is for flute and strings (see under *Solo Instrument and Orchestra: flute*), but it is certainly worthy. There are seven movements (*Ouverture*, Rondo, Gavotte, *Courante*, *Forlane*, *Menuet*, and *Rigaudon*). They are pleasantly recorded and nicely played.

Solo Instrument and Orchestra

Flute

Concerto in D major for Flute and Orchestra

☐ Vienna Symphony / Wanausek (flute) / Heiller (conductor) / Turnabout 34105

This is a different work from the Concerto in the same key listed *below*. Like that recording, on Musical Heritage, it is for string orchestra and continuo, despite the use of the Vienna "Symphony."

The fast movements (2 and 4), especially No. 2, have delicate aliveness. In the Adagio (the peak of the work in performance terms) Telemann reverts to chamber-music format, with the solo voice joined by cello and harpsichord. The playing is finely calculated throughout.

Concerto in D major for Flute, String Orchestra, and Continuo

☐ Pro Arte Chamber Orchestra of Munich / Redel (flute) / Redel (conductor) / Musical Heritage Society MHS-518

Not to be confused with the Concerto in D major discussed *above*. However, here too the slow (Largo) movement is a trio for flute, cello, and harpsichord. It compares strongly with the concluding movement, set in a tarantellalike rhythm.

Redel offers his own fine cadenza in the first movement. His playing is fine, natural, and uncontrived, his tone velvety.

Suite in A minor for Flute and Strings

☐ I Solisti di Zagreb / Baker (flute) / Janigro (conductor) / Vanguard HM-17

You can give big odds that this is the most played Telemann piece on the orchestral circuit. For good reason, since it is a delight. So is Julius Baker's conception of the solo part. He has what is known as silvery flute sound. Incidentally, he, like every flutist I've heard, deviates from the printed score. No problem, since the score as published includes editorial deviations from Telemann's original.

(Baker's performance is also included in a Bach Guild album, No. 5048.)

Flute, Oboe d'Amore, and Violin

Concerto in E major for Flute, Oboe d'Amore, Violin, Strings, and Continuo

☐ I Solisti di Zagreb / Meylan (flute); Lardrot (oboe d'amore); Stanic (violin); Nebois (harpsichord) / Janigro (conductor) / Bach Guild 70679

Not even Vivaldi with his assorted concerto combinations came up with this special solo partnership. It's a beauty, especially the *Siciliana*. But it is the choice way in which Telemann writes passages that fit each instrument's personality that is especially enchanting.

The playing is profoundly beautiful, the balances marvelously controlled. Only the highest praise can be accorded these soloists and Janigro for the way he handles the accompaniment.

(The performance is also available on Vanguard HM-17.)

Flute, Violin, and Cello

Concerto in A major for Flute, Violin, Cello, Strings, and Continuo

☐ Collegium Musicum of Paris / Rampal (flute); Gendre (violin); Neilz (cello) / Douatte (conductor) / Nonesuch 71124

Captivating in both the verve of the music and the scope of the writing, though more attention is given to the soprano soli than the cello representative. While Jacques Neilz is slightly repressed in his playing, the other soloists are not, serving Telemann's noble and extrovert musical objectives completely.

Concerto in D major for Horn and Orchestra

Horn

☐ Academy of St. Martin-in-the-Fields / Tuckwell (horn) / Marriner (conductor) / Angel S–36996

Vivace and Largo movements are followed by an Allegro that sounds like a minuet with some fancy horn turns. What makes the work come alive and very much so is the splendid way Barry Tuckwell handles the horn. The competing edition in the recorded catalogue (Nonesuch 71148) is firmly in second place.

Concerto in E flat major for Two Horns and Strings

Two Horns

☐ Chamber Orchestra of Toulouse / Barboteu and Coursier (horns) / Auriacombe (conductor) / Nonesuch 71066

Though the second and fourth movements of Telemann's work proceed with formulaic dedication, the first and third parts are highlights in Telemann's vast output. One is ready for specialness when, without the usual orchestral preface, the solo horns enter immediately in the initial Maestoso. The movement contains a glorious amount of music, equalled by the other slow movement, in *grave* tempo.

The playing is intensely rich and deeply lyrical, never overdone. The hornists are superb, their tone always of liquid beauty. This is a great performance of decidedly important music.

Suite in F major for Four Horns, Two Oboes, and String Orchestra

Four Horns

☐ Mainz Chamber Orchestra / Spach, Roth, Schollmeyer, and Balser (horns); Sous and Bogacchi (oboes) / Kehr (conductor) / Turnabout 34078

Eight movements that are, for the most part (to present-day ears), less particular and much more neutral than one expects from their picturesque titles. There are exceptions: *Die canonierende Pallas* follows the rules of follow-the-leader; dynamic differentiation is clear in *Der alster Echo,* while throaty frogs and nasal crows are recognizable in *Die concertierenden Frösche und Krähen.*

The horn soloists are especially fine in sorting out the different weights of tone that are required. This is a rewarding performance of one of Telemann's best creations.

Concerto in E minor for Oboe, String Orchestra, and Continuo

Oboe

☐ Pro Arte Chamber Orchestra of Munich / Kalmus (oboe) / Redel (conductor) / Musical Heritage Society MHS–518

Taste and expressiveness join perfectly here. The phrasing is alive, the performance thoroughly natural. As usual, Telemann chooses a four-movement plan, in this case Andante, *Allegro molto,* Largo, and Allegro. Even in the two slow movements, everything moves and breathes.

Concerto in F minor for Oboe and Orchestra

☐ Telemann Society / Theodora Schulze (oboe) / Richard Schulze (conductor) / Turnabout 34105

There are three movements: Allegro, *Siciliana,* and Vivace. Movement 2, in Largo tempo and in a soft dynamic level, is the peak of the work. The playing is good, the score interpreted without mannerisms or fuss.

Oboe d'Amore

Concerto in A major for Oboe d'Amore and Strings

☐ Chamber Orchestra of Toulouse / Casier (oboe d'amore) / Auriacombe (conductor) / Nonesuch 71066

The opening *Siciliano* and the third movement (Largo) exhibit the special timbre of this instrument at its best. A slight loss of coloristic individuality occurs in the faster-tempoed movements. But simply for the slow-paced music, beautifully presented in Robert Casier's playing, this recording is worth full attention.

Concerto in G major for Oboe d'Amore, Strings, and Continuo

☐ Members of the Dresden State Orchestra / Holliger (oboe d'amore); Jaccottet (harpsichord) / Negri (conductor) / Philips 6500413

Of the four movements, the tempo indication for the first one, *Soave,* is descriptive of the playing produced from first measure to last in this recording. The final Vivace evokes a hunting scene with its repetitive sounds articulating a duple pulse.

Recorder and Horn

Concerto a tre in F major for Recorder, Horn, and Continuo

☐ Members of Concentus Musicus of Denmark / Nonesuch 71065

To pair the Mutt and Jeff timbres of the recorder and horn is to overload the balance, presumably, while it loads the work colorfully. But there is no problem here, since the partnership works exceedingly well. Further, care is taken to apply additional contrast by omitting the horn in the central movement (*Loure*) and by maintaining linear flow in the recorder part with interjections by the brass instrument.

This unusual mix is thoroughly delightful. So is its performance. (Individual credit is deserving. This goes to Irmgard Knopf Mathiesen, the recorderist, and Hans Emil Sørensen, the hornist.)

Trumpet

Concerto in D major for Trumpet, Strings, and Continuo

☐ Pro Arte Chamber Orchestra of Munich / Scherbaum (trumpet) / Redel (conductor) / Musical Heritage Society MHS–518

Managing the high D trumpet so that its tone is both eloquent and sweet is no easy task. There are plenty of recordings of this piece on the market, but, while none displays any technical errors, only Adolf Scherbaum's avoids academic projection. Not only is the purity of Scherbaum's sound exemplary, but his playing is perceptive and responsive.

Redel's group plays with scrupulous balance. In the third movement, for the strings alone, the result is strongly conceived.

The best of the other choices is Henri Adelbrecht as the soloist with I Solisti di Zagreb on Bach Guild 70679.

Concerto in D major for Trumpet, Two Oboes, and Continuo

☐ Academy of St. Martin-in-the-Fields / Wilbraham (trumpet); Tilney (harpsichord) / Marriner (conductor) / Argo ZRG–585

Not to be confused with the Trumpet Concerto in the same tonality that calls for the solo brass instrument with strings (*see above* [Concerto in D major for Trumpet, Strings, and Continuo]). This three-movement piece has Concerto Grosso outline, with the trumpet and often the two oboes set off against the strings. The musicality of the performance is outstanding; John Wilbraham's playing is ideal.

Sonate de concert in D major

☐ Die Wiener Solisten / André (trumpet) / RCA CRL2-7002

A reconstruction made by Fernand Oubradous (to give his full name, which has escaped RCA and Stoddard Lincoln, the liner-note writer, though Lincoln's contribution is otherwise splendid). It is an authoritative conception, though the formal wavelengths of the three movements are considerably mixed. The work deserves as much attention as Telemann in the original. André is splendid, as always.

Concerto in D major for Three Trumpets, Two Oboes, and Orchestra

Three Trumpets

☐ Telemann Society Orchestra / Statter, Peers, and Peress (trumpets) / Schulze (conductor) / Turnabout 34295/9

In addition to the major solo trumpets and the secondary oboes; timpani, strings, and continuo constitute the scoring. Handelian heft marks the *Intrada*-Allegro. Movement 2 is centered on an ariosolike oboe solo with strings; the martial brilliance with trumpets predominating returns in the finale.

The subtitle *festivo* would surely fit Telemann's opus. Its vitality is fully available in this fine performance. The brass soloists are fine, including Maurice Peress, currently the conductor of the Kansas City Philharmonic. No credits are given the oboes.

At one time this performance was obtainable as part of a single disc (Turnabout 34105). It is now only to be secured in Turnabout's *Baroque and Classical Trumpet* anthology consisting of five discs. But look around—there may still be copies of the single-record edition to be found in stores.

Overture in D major for Trumpet, Oboe, Strings, and Continuo

Trumpet and Oboe

☐ Collegium Musicum of Paris / André (trumpet); Pierlot (oboe); Boulay (harpsichord); Wallez and Laroque (violins); Queille (viola); Martinerie (cello) / Douatte (conductor) / Nonesuch 71091

The basic color pleasures of Concerto Grosso arrangement cover the five movements. Handelian temperament is displayed in the Overture; the four following movements are each titled Air, but no suave songs are sung; all are dancelike conceptions.

The playing is splendid, especially that by Maurice André. Douatte's group is small but performs with convincing solidity.

Concerto in G major for Viola, Strings, and Continuo

Viola

☐ Pro Arte Chamber Orchestra of Munich / Schmid (viola) / Redel (conductor) / Musical Heritage Society MHS-518

An outward, strong personality makes George Schmid's playing of this well-known work the best in the catalogue. His viola sounds rich and firm. He receives admirable support from Redel.

Concerto in G major for Two Solo Violas and String Orchestra

Two Violas

☐ I Solisti di Zagreb / Stierhof and Pecha (violas) / Janigro (conductor) / Bach Guild 70679

1901

A stylish presentation, with tempi that make the competitive Turnabout edition (No. 34288) sound downright dull. The violists are exceedingly well matched and play cleanly and directly. The absence of fusspot interpretation is welcome.

(The recording is also available on Vanguard HM–17.)

Viola da Gamba | **Suite in D major for Viola da Gamba and String Orchestra**

☐ Württemberg Chamber Orchestra, Heilbronn / Wallfisch (viola da gamba) / Faerber (conductor) / Turnabout 34288

Wallfisch plays the solo part in this sequence of Overture and Dances in a slightly rough and ready manner, and yet it is becoming. The antiphonalized dynamics contribute to the success of the recording.

Violin | **Concerto in A minor for Violin and Strings**

☐ London Soloists Ensemble / Nonesuch 71052

The soloist is not credited for this three-movement work divided into an Allegro, an Andante, and a finale Presto, which is akin to a Bourrée. The Londoners have four violins in their total of ten instruments; two violas, two cellos, bass, and harpsichord complete the team. The first listed on the album cover is Nicholas Roth, so one assumes he is the soloist. The performance is a perceptive one.

Concerto in G major for Violin and Strings

☐ Chamber Orchestra of Toulouse / Armand (violin) / Auriacombe (conductor) / Nonesuch 71066

Three parts, with outer movements of fast-tempoed material and a central Andante. Everything is lucid and to the point (the Concerto runs just under the eight-minute mark).

This is a performance version that provides everything required in a faithful manner, but never with academic boredom.

Three Violins | **Concerto in F major for Three Violins and String Orchestra**

☐ Stuttgart Solisten / Lautenbacher, Schäfer, and Egger (violins) / Turnabout 34288

Various and abundant charms, especially when the triple solo voices are functioning on top of a pedal point. Finely meshed playing, styled to avoid the soloist-hero tradition.

Instrumental

Flute | *Fantasie*

No. 1 in A major / No. 7 (*Alla francese*) in D major / No. 8 in E minor / No. 12 in G minor

☐ Wilson (flute) / Orion 7289

Four of the dozen Telemann solo flute works are given vivid performances by this young flutist, as good, if not better, than by others this writer has heard. Especially compelling are the very convincing simulations of harmonic design that Wilson conveys as he plays this single-voiced music with a warm and rich tone. (Some of the tempi are a bit on the fast side.)

(*See below* for a recording of the complete set of Twelve *Fantasies*.)

Twelve *Fantasies* for Flute

☐ Rampal (flute) / Odyssey Y–33200

There is plenty of variety here thanks to the magnificent playing of Jean-Pierre Rampal. It is amazing what subtleties Rampal brings to this music, with a performance craftsmanship that is absolutely flawless.

Telemann's dozen *Fantasies* are divided exactly between major and minor tonalities, no tonic base being repeated. The total movements vary also; 2, 3, and 4 are represented, divided speeds within a movement being used in three cases.

(*See above* [*Fantasie*] for another recording of four of the *Fantasies*.)

Harpsichord

Fantasies

No. 1 in D major / No. 2 in D minor / No. 3 in E major / No. 4 in E minor / No. 5 in F major / No. 6 in F minor / No. 7 in G major / No. 8 in G minor / No. 9 in A major / No. 10 in A minor / No. 11 in B flat major / No. 12 in E flat major / No. 13 in C minor / No. 14 in C major / No. 15 in B minor / No. 16 in D major / No. 17 in G minor / No. 18 in B flat major / No. 19 in A minor / No. 20 in A major / No. 21 in E minor / No. 22 in G major / No. 23 in G minor / No. 24 in B flat major / No. 25 in F major / No. 26 in D minor / No. 27 in E minor / No. 28 in G major / No. 29 in G minor / No. 30 in C minor / No. 31 in A major / No. 32 in A minor / No. 33 in B minor / No. 34 in D major / No. 35 in E flat major / No. 36 in B flat major

☐ Payne (harpsichord) / Vox SVBX–5447

Telemann's *Fantaisies pour le Clavessin* are exactly divided into three autonomous dozens. *Fantasies* Nos. 1 through 12 and 25 through 36 are set in three movements; the second set of twelve has four movements each. This balance is almost duplicated in the choice of tonalities, with 19 in major keys and 17 in minor. The music includes some very entertaining movements side by side with some faded, patly pedantic ones. In a group of thirty-six works, that is to be expected, but there is sufficient freshness in this mass of music to warrant a listener's attention.

Joseph Payne's performances are wholeheartedly recommended—all of his interpretations are well suited to Telemann's material.

Recorder

Fantasie No. 10

☐ Duschenes (recorder) / Orion 6911

Duschenes, who presents (in very dull performances) two of the Telemann *Fantasies* on the flute in this album, offers another one by substituting the recorder. (No key is listed above since he plays the work in transposed A minor, the original for the flute being in the key of F sharp minor. Orion incorrectly lists this *Fantasie* as No. 5.) (For recordings of the original settings for flute, see under *flute* [*Fantasie* and Twelve *Fantasies* for Flute].)

The recorder offers a worthy contrast of timbre, though the brilliance of Telemann's original instrumental choice is lacking. The playing is appropriate.

There are other examples of the use of the recorder for certain of the *Fantasies*, none of which deserve special listing. In this reference, key transpositions cause confusion. One example: Hans Maria Kneihs (on Klavier 512) includes the first *Fantasie*, which is in A major. He plays the work (with halting phrasing due to breathing difficulties and with some hard-to-accept embellishments) in C major. No mention of the tonality change is made.

On the other hand there is Hans Martin Linde's performance of this same A major *Fantasie* (again on Klavier, No. 511) in an album titled *Baroque Recorder Vol. 1*. While it cannot match Rampal's or Wilson's portrayal, nonetheless it is a fairly worthy performance. However, though Linde is credited on cover, headings, liner notes, and label with playing the recorder, there is not a fraction of a doubt that he is performing on the flute. A check of the five other works on the release turns up another composition played on the flute, with no mention of the use of the modern instrument. The picture on the cover, of Linde playing a recorder, only makes Klavier's production even more ridiculous. *Caveat emptor!*

Concerto No. 1 in D major for Flute and Harpsichord

☐ Rampal (flute); Veyron-Lacroix (harpsichord) / Nonesuch 71038

A Concerto for two, but despite Telemann's title the equality of the writing places it in the chamber-music class. The contrastive elements are all heard with fine flexibility; the phrasing sensitivity is marvelous.

Sonata in A minor for Viola da Gamba and Harpsichord

☐ Heinitz (viola da gamba); Hamilton (harpsichord) / Delos 15341

Expectedly, four movements in alternate slow and fast tempi. The second of the former is marked, unexpectedly, *Soave.* That about describes the playing of this team throughout. The well-determined writing is all neatly set forth.

Sonata in B minor for Flute and Continuo

☐ Rampal (flute); Veyron-Lacroix (harpsichord) / Nonesuch 71038

One of the entities contained in one of the three five-part anthologies Telemann produced and titled *Musique de table.* (See also Trio in E minor for Flute, Oboe, and Continuo *below,* p. 1908.) Rampal and his partner furnish a finely detailed and stylish rendition.

Sonata for Flute and Harpsichord
In C major / In G major

☐ Rampal (flute); Veyron-Lacroix (harpsichord) / RCA FRL1–8081

Two more examples of Telemann's prolific production. They are provided with ensemble playing of delightful finesse.

Sonata in C major for Recorder and Continuo

☐ Members of Concentus Musicus of Denmark / Nonesuch 71065

The architectonic details of the four movements are absolutely explicit: two slow and two fast movements, with the greatest contrast between the latter pair. Peppery patterns built around a pedal tone or repetitive sounds mark the first of the speedy divisions, larger spans mark the other.

The recorder playing of Irmgard Knopf Mathiesen of the Danish organization is powerful, in terms of both tone and technique. The integrity of presentation never wavers. It gratifies and astonishes as well, especially given that the recorder does not have any of the playing comforts of its younger relative, the flute.

Sonata in E minor, Op. 2

☐ Rampal and Duschenes (flutes) / Orion 73114

A beautifully fresh concept of flute duo writing (it could also be performed by *deux Flûtes à bec* as well as the *deux Flûtes traverses* used here). It's a delight from start to completion, especially the marvelous and richly worked speedy finale.

It would be difficult to better this accomplished and musicianly playing. (The same performance is included in an Everest seven-record release, on its No. 3194.)

Sonata in F minor for Flute and Continuo

☐ Rampal (flute); Veyron-Lacroix (harpsichord) / Nonesuch 71038

A duplicate of the Sonata in F minor for Recorder and Continuo (*see below*). It first appeared in a magazine devoted solely to music, *Der getreue Musikmeister* ("The Faithful Music Master"). Though it was written for bassoon and continuo, Telemann approved performance on the recorder by double octave shift. In turn, traditional permissiveness applies to playing recorder music on the flute.

Rampal's presentation has his usual all-pervasive timbre depth and beauty. (The same rendition is included in the Westminster Gold 8115 album.)

Sonata in G major

☐ Rampal (flute); Duschenes (recorder) / Orion 75199

The closely knit writing makes it almost impossible to distinguish the flute from the recorder. It little matters in this work *sans basse*, played with flexible and beautifully controlled tone.

As is the case with so many Rampal performances, this one can also be heard on another release, Everest 3194, contained in a seven-record set.

Sonata for Violin and Harpsichord
No. 1 in G minor / No. 2 in D major / No. 3 in B minor / No. 4 in A minor / No. 5 in G major / No. 6 in A major

☐ Kaufman (violin); Hammond (harpsichord) / Orion 7272

Not to be confused with the set of six Sonatinas Telemann produced, also for violin and harpsichord. The format is the same: each is in four movements in a slow-fast-slow-fast sequence, with Sonatas No. 2 and 4 entirely devoted to dance-style structure (*Allemande-Corrente-Sarabande-Giga*). No. 6, save for the first movement (a Largo), also follows this pattern.

Kaufman approaches these Sonatas with thrust and a vigor equivalent to romantic style. In addition he is recorded close up, which adds to the tonal weight. Less vital behavior would be more acceptable. Otherwise, he does well, especially in the *bariolage* passages in the *Giga* of Sonata No. 2 and in the fanfarelike and sequential detail in Sonata No. 6, also concerned with a *Giga*. Still, like meets like in these cases, since these movements are in themselves concerned with a vigorous music.

Trio Sonata in B flat major for Flute and Harpsichord

☐ Rampal (flute); Veyron-Lacroix (harpsichord) / Nonesuch 71038

The B flat major Trio Sonata ("trio" because the harpsichord combines both *concertante* and continuo details) is one of the great gems in the Telemann catalogue. A lyrical inspiration precedes music of punching figuration, then proceeds to a *Siciliana;* the work concludes with a Vivace in which solo and tutti alternate in what Edward Tatnall Canby describes as "the quintessence of Baroque styling!" What Telemann did, Bach couldn't have done better.

The interpretative investment made by these musicians is perfect. This is great music making.

Der getreue Musikmeister

☐ Linde (recorder); Mueller (harpsichord); Jappe (viola da gamba) / Klavier 511

"The Faithful Music Master" turns out to be a Sonata in B major, which in its turn is faithful to formal baroque practice. Accordingly, there are two Largo movements, separated by an Allegro and followed by a Vieace.

It is routine design but not a routine performance. The music is interpreted convincingly.

Partita No. 5 in E minor

☐ Linde (recorder); Mueller (harpsichord); Jappe (viola da gamba) / Klavier 511

An engaging conception, beginning with an introductory Andante, followed by six Arias, all in *vivace* or *presto*, save one that is a *Siciliana*.

Neutral dynamic registration is the only criticism that can be leveled at this recording.

Sonata in F minor for Recorder and Bass Continuo

☐ Kneihs (recorder); Radescu (harpsichord); Kaiser (cello) / Klavier 512

A different work from the one by the same title listed *below*. Average Telemann. Though played acceptably by Hans Maria Kneihs, just a bit of a plodding manner applies to his colleagues.

Sonata in F minor for Recorder and Continuo

☐ Members of Concentus Musicus of Denmark / Nonesuch 71065

For a note on this work in a duplicate version for the flute, *see above* (Sonata in F minor for Flute and Continuo).

In addition to the recorder's softer color, the continuo decision also differs. In the flute setting it is only for harpsichord, whereas here a viola da gamba is used with the keyboard instrument.

Though a flute is more agile than a recorder, Irmgard Knopf Mathiesen is Rampal's technical equal. There are plenty of fast passages in this opus, but there is practically a dead heat in performance time: Rampal is clocked at 10:11, Mathiesen at 10:15! Having both performances would be ideal.

Trio Sonata in A minor

☐ Rampal (flute); Duschenes (recorder); Veyron-Lacroix (harpsichord) / RCA FRL1-8081

Usual Telemann, but strengthened by the stylish playing of these superb musicians.

Trio Sonata in C major for Flute, Recorder, and Continuo

☐ Rampal (flute); Duschenes (recorder); Gilbert (harpsichord) / Orion 7149

Read "Divertimento." After *Grave*, Vivace, and Andante movements, fanciful titles are used: *Xantippe, Lucretia, Corinna, Clelia,* and *Dido.* These vary, with *Clelia* very high spirited and *Dido* constantly shifting between sadness and gaiety.

The performance gives the music a healthy workout. (It is also included in Everest 3194, an edition of seven discs featuring Rampal.)

Trio Sonata in D minor for Recorder, Violin, and Continuo

☐ Members of Concentus Musicus of Denmark / Nonesuch 71065

A cheerful item, with not much deep reflection even in the slower-paced movements. The playing keeps the chain of command (the recorder is in soprano position, the violin below it) in proper balance.

Trio Sonata in E flat major for Oboe, Harpsichord, and Continuo

☐ Chambon (oboe); Beckensteiner (harpsichord); Fonteny (cello) / Nonesuch 71061

Highlighted by the fact that the harpsichord is not relegated to foundational support. The color that prevails is highly inflected, though always clear and transparent.

The members of the Maxence Larrieu Quartet play with a surety of phrase and sonority that carries stylistic conviction throughout.

Trio Sonata in E minor for Recorder, Oboe, and Continuo

☐ Members of Concentus Musicus of Denmark / Nonesuch 71065

Not to be confused with the Trio for Flute, Oboe, and Continuo in the same tonality (*see below* [Trio for Flute, Oboe, and Continuo]). The warning is made because *Schwann* lists the Trio also as a Trio Sonata.

The balance of the heavy-toned oboe with the much-frailer recorder offers problems. A lighter-weighted oboe quality would be more propitious for Telemann's conception. Only in this respect does Nonesuch's recording miss the highest grade.

Sonata a quattro

☐ Schäffer Quartet / Vox SVBX–5300

A sturdy and intelligent portrayal. The Schäffer first violin (Vox does not give the names of the personnel) does a first-class job of fiddling in the Vivace conclusion.

Sonata in D minor for Flute, Oboe, and Continuo

☐ Camerata Musicale / Nonesuch 71085

One of a group of *Essercizii musici,* a set of twenty-four works including twelve Trio Sonatas. The playing of the Berlin-based quartet (the continuo is set forth by cello and harpsichord) is apt and precise.

Trio for Flute, Oboe, and Continuo
In D major / In E minor

☐ Maxence Larrieu Quartet / Nonesuch 71061

Though the movement total differs, with a Vivace-Andante-Vivace format for the D major Trio and a *Affettuoso*-Allegro-*Dolce*-Vivace sequence for the E minor opus (compare Trio Sonata in E minor for Recorder, Oboe, and Continuo *above*), the general character remains similar. It is clear that though standard formulae are involved there is an inventive musical mind at work.

There are excellent balances throughout and a strong affirmation of style, with tempi ordered sensibly. Not a trace of pedantry is present in the playing of this group: Maxence Larrieu, flute; Jacques Chambon, oboe; and the continuo in the hands of Bernard Fonteny, cello, and A. M. Beckensteiner, harpsichord.

Trio in E flat major for Two Violins, Cello, and Continuo

☐ London Harpsichord Ensemble / Nonesuch 71004

Average-styled Telemann, meaning that there are four movements in alternate speeds. Still, though no surprises are in store, the music survives critical scrutiny. The same applies to the playing.

Trio in E minor for Flute, Oboe, and Continuo

☐ Rampal (flute); Pierlot (oboe); Hongne (bassoon); Boulay (harpsichord) / Nonesuch 71124

One of the pieces in the anthological *Musique de table*. (See also Sonata in B minor for Flute and Continuo *above*, p. 1904.) Three sets were composed, each with five parts, covering an orchestral Suite, a Quartet, a Concerto, a Trio, and a solo Sonata.

The only exception to this performance is the heaviness (prominence) of the bassoon that represents, with the harpsichord, the continuo. As heard, the Trio sounds more like a quartet for flute, oboe, bassoon, and harpsichord.

Trio in F major for Recorder, Viola da Gamba, and Continuo

☐ Krause (recorder); Dommisch (viola da gamba); Ruth Ristenpart (harpsichord); Hindrichs (cello) / Nonesuch 71119

No stunning revelations, but certainly acceptable playing. There is not too much creative versatility in this work to arrive at a better solution. The recording is for the Telemann buff who needs everything.

Cantata and Oratorio

Harmonischer Gottesdienst

> ***Die Kinder des Höchsten sind rufende Stimmen***
> ***Packe dich, gelähmter Drache***
> ***Was gleicht dem Adel wahrer Christen***
> ***Zischet nur, stechet, ihr feurigen Zungen***

☐ New York Chamber Soloists / Bressler (tenor) / Nonesuch 71190

Four of the six dozen Cantatas in the cycle "The Service of God in Music." Each is for a solo voice (the last noted above calls for a "middle" voice, the others for a "high" voice), with a single instrument (the first two call for a violin, the other pair for an oboe), and the usual continuo (here covered by a cello and a harpsichord). An annual cycle of Cantatas included one for each Sunday and additional ones for the principal occasions of the church year. Thus, the first listed was for the Feast of St. John the Baptist (June 24), the third for the Sunday following Christmas, and so on.

No sonorous hype in these works is apparent from the intimate frame of reference and in that format this is music *par excellence*. Consistent structure is used with a pair of da capo arias embracing a recitative.

Charles Bressler is just fine. The instrumental soloists (Gerald Tarack, violin, and Melvin Kaplan, oboe) are sensitive musicians, and Albert Fuller (harpsichord) with Alexander Kouguell (cello) provide a firm continuo foundation.

Lobt Gott, ihr Christen allzugleich

☐ Instrumentalists and Freiburg Student Choir / Graf (soprano); Schmidt (tenor); Pommerien (bass) / Knall (conductor) / Vanguard C-10045

Of impressive scope. "Praise God, Ye Christians All Together" has double four-part choruses and an orchestra of five trumpets (Vanguard mistakenly spells "clarinos" [the high trumpets] as "clarinets"), timpani, and strings, plus continuo.

The general premise has been that Telemann's important work is contained only in his instrumental output. There is a strength and a beauty in this Cantata that deny this. The performance is one of fine musical insight. It should aid in correcting the misconception previously mentioned.

Machet die Tore weit

☐ Vienna State Opera Orchestra and Chorus / Stich-Randall (soprano); Equiluz (tenor); Schramm (bass) / Böttcher (conductor) / Nonesuch 71182

To learn that Telemann produced over 1,400 Cantatas while Bach turned out only (!) about three hundred does not make Mr. Telemann number one in the Cantata standings. However, the significant writing of "Open Wide the Gates," a Cantata for the First Sunday of Advent, is as masterful as some of Bach's Cantatas and better than a fair number of them. Telemann's sentiments are deeply felt, and they make the opus deserving of an important place in Cantata literature.

The vocalism is outstanding. There is fine sound from Nonesuch in the transfer it made from the original Tono (Zürich) production.

Pimpinone

Opera and Dramatic Music

☐ Ensemble Florilegium Musicum / Spreckelsen (soprano); Nimsgern (baritone); Tachezi and Hirsch (harpsichords) / Hirsch (conductor) / Telefunken 2635285

There is a triple mix here: German is used for the recitatives, Italian for the arias, and three concerti by other composers are used to introduce the Opera and keep sound going between the acts. The composers "collaborating" are Tessarini, Albinoni, and Vivaldi.

The satisfactory singing is especially represented in Uta Spreckelsen's upper range. The orchestra is very good.

Giovanni Antonio Terzi (16th cent.)

Fantasy (*S'ogni mio bene*)

Instrumental

☐ Duo Company-Paolini / Turnabout 34341

Two Guitars

An easy-smooth, improvisational workout for two guitars, by this sixteenth-century composer, of a six-part song by a contemporary, one Alessandro Striggio.

Sigismond Thalberg (1812-1871)

Concerto in F minor for Piano and Orchestra, Op. 5

Solo Instrument and Orchestra

☐ Westphalian Symphony Orchestra / Ponti (piano) / Kapp (conductor) / Candide 31084

Piano

An invitation to taste stylistic samplings from Chopin, Hummel, and Rossini. Thalberg states his eclectic case very securely. His sharing in such creative profits brings no harm, and he applies them in such a way as to give plentiful opportunities to the pianist. Michael Ponti takes advantage of this and presents the solo part with high-gloss polish.

Hexaméron. **See under** *Liszt: Solo Instrument and Orchestra (Hexaméron).*

Instrumental

Piano

Concert Fantasy on Meyerbeer's *Les Huguenots,* **Op. 20**

☐ Ponti (piano) / Candide 31084

The common type of Fantasy. Thalberg's example touches bases with some half-dozen of the themes in the Opera. Best are the details wrapped around the chorale *Ein' feste Burg* that Meyerbeer used in his stage work. Worst are the plethora of arpeggios and *tremolando* octaves. But period pieces of this type were never written to talk to all mankind. You may like it or find it a bore. However, you will have only positive reactions to Michael Ponti's playing.

Fantasy on Rossini's *Barber of Seville,* **Op. 63**

Fantasy on Rossini's *Moses,* **Op. 33**

☐ Lewenthal (piano) / Angel S-36079

No potpourri propulsions, but integrated invention mostly hinting at the thematic sources rather than quoting them and then taking off into rhapsodic musical logorrhea.

To articulate this music demands a full seriousness on the part of the performer. Playing at a level below its innate meaningfulness is not only poor taste but artistically dishonest. Lewenthal does splendidly, providing all the values and exhibiting the legitimacy of these two fine Fantasy examples.

Grande Sonate **in C minor, Op. 56**

☐ Ruiz (piano) / Genesis 1016

Romantically conventional, most passionately expressed in the *Finale agitato,* most individually colored in the second part, a *Scherzo pastorale.* The piano writing, to be expected from a virtuoso performer, shows mastery of the idiom.

There is no mistaking Ruiz's excellent realization of the music, especially defined in his *cantabile* playing.

Les Capricieuses Valses, **Op. 64**

Variations on *Home, Sweet Home,* **Op. 72**

Variations on *The Last Rose of Summer,* **Op. 73**

☐ Ponti (piano) / Candide 31084

There are no hidden expressionistic considerations here. The themes in the *Air anglais varié* (Bishop's *Home, Sweet Home*) and *Air irlandais varié* (made famous in Flotow's Opera *Martha*) stay on top, surrounded with embroideries, embellishments, and elaborations. Oh, yes, mid-Victorian musical lace, but if not the latest fashion it's still worth examining.

Ponti plays sensitively and artistically. In the waltzes his Viennese swing is refined and therefore charming.

Chamber Music

Piano Trio in A major, Op. 69

☐ Mirecourt Trio / Genesis 1058/9

Opus 69 consists of three movements, beginning with a medium-fast movement, proceeding to the expected slow movement, and completed by a Scherzo. It is the middle movement that is most eventful, with a beautifully contoured theme.

The piece receives a warm playing.

W. Eugene Thayer (1838-1889)

Variations on the Russian National Hymn, Op. 12

Instrumental

☐ Morris (organ) / New World Records NW–280

Organ

Five variations on the pre-Soviet melody *God Save the Tsar*. Morris follows the directions of the organist-composer in terms of registration, which differs for each portion; the full organ is reserved, as would be expected, for the finale. This is Morris's best performance in a release consisting of five nineteenth-century organ works by American composers.

Leslie Thimmig (1943-   )

Seven Profiles

Chamber Music

☐ Composers String Quartet / Composers Recordings S–265

Carefully constructed and cogently organized nontonal commentary. An exemplary performance.

Ambroise Thomas (1811-1896)

Overture to *Mignon*

Orchestra

☐ New York Philharmonic / Bernstein (conductor) / Columbia D3S–818

The only competitive issue worth considering is that of the New Philharmonia Orchestra, conducted by Richard Bonynge, on London 6643. Bonynge's musicians are good; Bernstein's are better. In the solo passages that difference is acute. And Bernstein adds weight to the rhythmic incisiveness that lifts up his performance. (Also obtainable in a single-record release on Columbia MS–6743; the album noted above is a three-record compilation of eighteen overtures.)

Overture to *Raymond*

☐ New York Philharmonic / Bernstein (conductor) / Columbia D3S–818

This was great music in the silent-movie days. And it is still great music to eat and chat by. But it takes a master not to denigrate (by sentimentalizing) Thomas's score. The graceful melody is beautifully considered with captivating phrasing; the finale is paced properly and its *crescendo* factor is a lesson in control and dynamic effect.

Randall Thompson (1899-   )

Symphony No. 1 (1930)

Orchestra

☐ Utah Symphony / Schreiner (organ) / Abravanel (conductor) / Angel S–37315

Less modal than most of Thompson's music and with no trace of the nationalism that makes its presence known in a majority of this composer's output. The organ is in no way soloistic, but is a prominent part of the orchestration, as much as the string body itself. Motival development makes the structure of the three movements compact.

The Utah Symphony plays uncommonly well under Abravanel. The media have not given him sufficient attention because of the location of his organization, but he deserves top credit for his musicianship and for his seeking out off-beat repertoire.

Symphony No. 2 (1932)

☐ Vienna Symphony Orchestra / Dixon (conductor) / Desto 6406E (monaural)

Why this is the sole recording available of this work is a mystery. Thompson's Symphony is a masterwork, one of the great American pieces. Dixon's version must do, since it is better to have a recorded documentation of the work than none at all. However, the auditor must accept playing that is the equivalent of top-flight sight reading and that's all.

Rooted to music of earlier time, Thompson's work displays a fresh viewpoint. In a way he is less a conservative and more a folklorist writing without the quoted use of folk song. Those who love modality will find a plentiful share in the Symphony. (It prompts the thought that Randall Thompson is to American music what Vaughan Williams is to English music.) This composer's descant is of lovely sound, his work of splendid invention and marvelous craftsmanship.

Vocal

Voice with Accompaniment

Velvet Shoes

☐ Frijsh (soprano); Dougherty (piano) / New World Records NW–247 (monaural)

Thompson's most important vocal work, set to lines by Elinor Wylie. The singing is rather pinched and is not aided by the recorded sound (the New World release is a reissue of a recording made in 1940), but it is valuable to have this beautifully sensitive and atmospheric song on disc.

Choral

Chorus Alone

Alleluia (1940)

☐ Peloquin Chorale / Peloquin (conductor) / Gregorian Institutes EL–19 (monaural)

Exposition and development are both focused on the single word of the title. The arch of the music to climax and quiet conclusion is clear and expressive. For the greater part, so is the singing, particularly in the parallel modalisms that Thompson includes. The single exception is the strain of the sopranos in their top register.

Glory to God in the Highest (1958)

☐ Mormon Tabernacle Choir / Ottley (conductor) / Columbia M–34134

Conservative style with lofty expressiveness.

The Peaceable Kingdom (1936)

☐ Whikehart Chorale / Whikehart (conductor) / Lyrichord 7124

Eight choruses from the Book of the Prophet Isaiah, suggested by the painting *The Peaceable Kingdom* by Edward Hicks (1780–1849), a Pennsylvania Quaker preacher. (Lyrichord has thoughtfully reproduced the painting as the cover art of the album.)

Nothing but rich tonal harmonic language, plus some of Thompson's glorious modal communications, cover his a cappella setting. Nothing else is needed. The result is a composition of beautiful impact.

The Last Words of David

Chorus with
Accompaniment

☐ Walter Ehret Chorale / Flath (organ) / Ehret (conductor) / Golden Crest S-4032

A beautifully crafted piece, beginning with majestic utterance and concluding with a delicately floating section. An emotion-producing method, sincerely conceived. It is sincerely sung by Ehret's group, though not with the most fertile diction.

Americana (1932)

Chorus
and Orchestra

☐ Members of the University of Michigan Symphony Orchestra and University of Michigan Chamber Choir / Hilbish (conductor) / New World Records NW–219

It is not difficult to be humorous in prose, but it is horribly difficult to accomplish it in music. Thompson's *Americana,* with five texts taken from the memorable magazine *American Mercury,* is one of the choicest examples in the literature.

The subjects are fundamentalist religion, the practice of necromancy, temperance, capital punishment, and poetry-book advertising. There are marvelous touches in the score: the musical setting of the initials (!) of the questioners in part 2; the use of women's voices alone to stress the argument of part 3; the sung announcement of the title and author in the last part; and the concluding words. And many, many more.

Originally *Americana* called for piano accompaniment. Its orchestration enriched the work. One example: the opening and closing of the hymnlike satire that covers part 1, *May Every Tongue.*

This performance meets all requirements. It is styled to the hilt and the singing is clear to the last syllable. Full texts are furnished, carrying out the original magazine copy, including the introductory lines used in the magazine but not set by Thompson.

The Testament of Freedom (1943)

☐ Eastman-Rochester Symphony Orchestra and Male Chorus of the Eastman School of Music / Hanson (conductor) / Eastman-Rochester Archives ERA–1007

A setting of four passages from the writings of Thomas Jefferson. It is telling in its emphatic tonalism and modalism, direct in its orchestral coloring, with obvious trumpet calls and percussion trimming.

The piece receives a full-scale performance and an understanding one, covering an aesthetic with which Hanson has always been identified. The choral singing is especially significant.

Virgil Thomson   (1896-   )

Louisiana Story—Suite (1948)

Orchestra

☐ Westphalian Symphony Orchestra, Recklinghausen / Landau (conductor) / Turnabout 34534

One of the better examples of the transference of a film score to the concert hall (or its recorded equivalent). The proof is that the music can be heard (and enjoyed) without any knowledge of the pictorial images that were basic to the initial creation.

The folkish music with regional melorhythms is keyed to set designs (a Pastoral, Chorale, Passacaglia, and Fugue) and scored with a fluid viewpoint. It all registers with an inconspicuous type of urbanity.

Landau's performance is top-grade, with no critical disagreement possible.

(Thomson drew a second suite from his *Louisiana Story* film score, consisting of seven movements titled Acadian Songs and Dances. Once in the recorded-music catalogue, performed by the Little Orchestra Society, with Thomas Scherman conducting, on the Decca label [DL–9616] and long deleted, it is worth searching for in the out-of-print specialty shops.)

The Plow That Broke the Plains—Suite (1936)

☐ Symphony of the Air / Stokowski (conductor) / Vanguard 2095

Some bluesy jazz, a touch in one place of Coplandesque character, and some Thomson-branded cowboy tunes are contained in this six-part Suite derived from the music written for a documentary film. A beautiful score it is, and a colorful one, using appropriate timbres, including saxophone and banjo.

Stoky knows how to shape and deliver this type of music and his performance is most impressive. It is also included in a two-disc release advertising *The Best of Stokowski* (Vanguard 707/8).

The River—Suite (1942)

☐ Symphony of the Air / Stokowski (conductor) / Vanguard 2095

A spin-off (or a draw-off) from the music Thomson wrote for a documentary film for the United States Farm Security Administration. It is a product of candid unpretentiousness. The harmonies are in the triadic system, with slight dissonant dabs. The tunes *are* tunes, many drawn from the Southern hymn world. There is a *Gemütlichkeit* in most of Virgil Thomson's music, and *The River* follows suit.

There is more warmth in Stokowski's view of this music than there is in the much later recorded setting by Marriner (not with the Academy group, but with the Los Angeles Chamber Orchestra on Angel S–37300).

Solo Instrument and Orchestra

Flute

Concerto for Flute (1954)

☐ Louisville Orchestra / Fuge (flute) / Whitney (conductor) / Louisville S–663

Some unusual features. Movement 1 (*Rapsodico*) is for flute alone. The orchestration is concentrated: strings, harp, celesta, and percussion. And, over all, there is an impressionistic cast that rarely is identified with Virgil Thomson's style.

The unsigned Louisville program leaflet is excellent, but fails to give space to the composer's important description of his work: "a portrait conceived as a concerto for nightingale and strings." This is a fine recording, with the honors rightfully belonging to Francis Fuge, the soloist.

Instrumental

Cornet

At the Beach, Concert Waltz

☐ Schwarz (cornet); Bolcom (piano) / Nonesuch 71298

A tidbit of Thomsonian nostalgia. It does prompt remembrances of the days when waltzhood was in flower. Admiration is here stated for the playing of Schwarz and Bolcom.

Organ

Variations on Sunday-School Tunes

☐ Mason (organ) / Counterpoint/Esoteric 5522E (monaural)

The "king" of instruments is hardly ever the means of having some fun, but Thomson's set of "proof-fooling" variants is double-compounded wit. First, the heavy-heavy-hangs-over-your-head sound of the organ is especially prone to clumsiness if not treated properly, and that means respectfully and with contrastive textures. Thomson mixes the serious with the profane here even to the extent of using tone clusters. Second, he minces the basic tunes into a sort of Gertrude Stein–E. E. Cummings amalgam. This might be called the Thomsonian power of Frenchified musical thinking and produces high-class corn, but it is tasteful corn.

Performance: inspired and with faultless sound. Recommended for organists, music lovers, record buffs, and all other semiadventurous souls.

Ragtime Bass *Piano*

☐ Johannesen (piano) / Golden Crest S-4065

The final item in Ten Etudes for Piano. Thomson's rag is a genuine evocation, a polite honky-tonk idea.

Three Portraits

☐ Mandel (piano) / Desto 6445/7

A sampling of the numerous musical portraits Thomson has produced, written ("drawn," the composer says) from life, the sitter "posing" as he would for a painter.

The first is a portrait of Hans Arp (*Poltergeist*) in the scherzo sphere. The second is a delineation of Pablo Picasso (*Bugles and Birds*), which develops from scalar considerations. Lou Harrison is the subject of the third. The "drawing," titled *Solitude,* is properly calm, its harmonies secundally spiced lightly.

Serenade for Flute and Violin *Chamber Music*

☐ Gilbert (flute); Kooper (violin) / Turnabout 34508

If music can be termed delicious, this is it. It is also deft, distinctive, and distinguished. Five miniatures, covering a little over six minutes, including a neo-Czerny Aria, a seven-measure Fanfare, and a Hymn containing creamy thirds topped with a dab of icing in the form of cojoined seconds. The plagal cadence that completes the work is very choice.

The manner of performance is outstanding; in the Hymn it is of the most sensitive artistry imaginable. Elsewhere Gilbert and Kooper give full currency to Thomson's sketches.

Sonata for Violin and Piano (1930)

☐ Joseph Fuchs (violin); Balsam (piano) / Composers Recordings 207 (monaural)

Like most of Thomson's music, this Sonata is instantly recognizable as of candid unpretentiousness. The classic lines are cut to the bone; the harmonies are in the triadal system, with slight dabs of dissonance.

The urbanity of the opening movement stems from the prevalence of conjunct motion. Movement 2 has minuet overtones, though it is labeled *Andante nobile.* Thomson's favorite triple meter is also employed in the unabashed waltz forming the third movement. Chromatic terms are expressed more in the final movement than are heard in the previously spoken harmonic language. But the chromaticism is used only as a stimulus to introduce the swing of the fast section, which follows in large hymnlike lines.

String Quartet No. 2 (1932)

☐ Juilliard String Quartet / Columbia Special Products CML-4987 (monaural)

The second-movement waltz attests to Thomson's honesty as a composer devoted to unostentatious music. This folk movement is a pleasant contrast to the opening portion, which has Mozartean drive and grace in its neoclassic action. Movement 3 moves with gentle seriousness and also with a tango step in its central part. Techniques of transmutation and transformation are found in the end movement. They do not interfere with the Quartet's exultant spirit.

Despite monaural recording the Juilliard's performance is far ahead of the competitive Kohon Quartet reading (on Vox SVBX-5305). The Juilliard's warmth and expressive eloquence show a much more involved consideration of the work. And the Kohon team is guilty of unbuttoned intonation, especially in the slow movement. "The older, the better" is true in this case.

Sonata da chiesa (1926)

☐ Lillian Fuchs (viola); Simenauer (clarinet); Mills (trumpet); Ingraham (horn); Erwin (trombone) / Thomson (conductor) / Composers Recordings 207 (monaural)

In Thomson's own words, this work for the heterogeneous combination of the most blatant, harsher member of the clarinet family, small trumpet, viola, horn, and trombone (three brass against one each of woodwind and string) is "ultradissonant." One cannot always trust a composer to describe his music properly. In this instance Thomson is to be trusted, but only in terms of a half century ago. Compared to today's output, "heaven's sweetest air" sweeps through the music's measures.

Thomson's forms break the boundarivs of the "Church Sonata" design. Dance movements were not common to it, but movement 2 here is a Tango. Actually, all three elements are represented: homophonic (the Chorale in movement 1) and contrapuntal (the final Fugue), as well as the dance. In terms of forms, of course, the Tango seems to be an insolent intruder into the sanctities generally inhabited by chorale and fugal members, but it must not be forgotten that Thomson's "Church Sonata" is secular and of the twentieth century.

With the composer chnducting, the work is played cleanly. It is produced with the blend and unblend that Thomson had in mind when he composed his work.

Vocal

Voice with Accompaniment

Praises and Prayers (1963)

☐ Allen (mezzo-soprano); Thomson (piano) / Composers Recordings 207 (monaural)

Five songs to texts "running from St. Augustine and St. Francis to the seventeenth-century Richard Crashaw."

The variety of expression and delicacy of detail sought by Thomson are available in the performance in which he participated. CRI, however, has failed to offer texts in their release and the words are not clearly understood. (The performance was taped at the world premiere, given at the Metropolitan Museum of Art, in New York, in 1963.)

The Tiger

☐ Steber (soprano); Biltcliffe (piano) / Desto 6411/2

Textual collaboration with music is derived from triple specifications. Blake's prose consists of six rhyming quatrains. The first and last (save for one word) are similar and the word "symmetry" is fundamental to the beginning and ending of the poem. Thomson follows suit and uses a persistent figure that powers the entire song. Acute prose balance is maintained—undisturbed actually—by the ostinato.

Steber and Biltcliffe join in presenting a positive performance.

Joseph and the Angel from Scenes from the Holy Infancy

☐ Peloquin Chorale / Peloquin (conductor) / Gregorian Institutes EL-19 (monaural)

Thomson's gift for vocal writing is exemplified by a statement that is twice divided in two (first recitative and then chorus). It is simply beautiful and beautifully simple in both its conception and its performance.

The Mother of Us All (1947)

☐ Santa Fe Opera Orchestra and Chorus / Dunn, Orvath, and Putnam (sopranos); Godfrey and Maxwell (contraltos); Atherton (tenor); Ives and McKee (baritones); Booth (bass); Beck, Bryant, Fuller, Lewis, Loewengart, Lu Null, Mabrey, McDaniels, McKeel, Nash, Parker, Perry, Petty, Raines, Stowe, and Vanni (other soloists) / Leppard (conductor) / New World Records NW-288/289

Thomson's *The Mother of Us All* is a hot ticket for its publisher and has racked up a huge number of performances since its premiere in May of 1947. Oddly enough, New World's 1977 release represents its first recording. A long time ago Columbia issued an orchestral suite drawn from the Opera (on ML-4468, with the Janssen Symphony of Los Angeles doing the playing, and, of course, Werner Janssen as the conductor), but it is no longer in the catalogue.

The Opera is in three acts (with words by Gertrude Stein) and concerns the tale of Susan B. Anthony, the pioneer advocate of women's suffrage. Historic figures figure in Thomson's work, including Daniel Webster, Ulysses S. Grant, Lillian Russell, and Anthony Comstock. In addition two characters—Gertrude S. and Virgil T., easily identifiable as to their full names—act as narrators.

General Americana is woven into the work. It is a period piece, expressively descriptive, with tunes that sound like folk melodies but are Thomson's beautiful imitations of the real thing. His reminiscences of old dances, ballads, and hymns comprise a special class of national music.

This is a solidly good performance, done with skill, taste, and style. The title role, sung by Mignon Dunn, is a solid accomplishment. Raymond Leppard reveals all the nuances and paces the opera beautifully.

Francis Thorne (1922-   )

Burlesque Overture (1964)

☐ Polish National Radio Orchestra / Strickland (conductor) / Composers Recordings 216

A bright, brash sort of music. Some cooled jazz will be recognized in the style.

Fanfare, Fugue, and Funk (1972)

☐ Springfield Symphony Orchestra / Gutter (conductor) / Opus One 19

Thorne's alliteratively titled work has a jazz feeling, but the procedures are contemporaneously classical. The trumpet twirls and the guitar sprays are borrowings from the jazz world, but the music is not the usual spiced jazz transfer to highbrow surroundings. The integration is much more refined and more subtle than the "third stream" method that received its baptism from Gunther Schuller.

Thorne's treatment of forms is most inventive. The Fanfare is not blatantly fanfarelike; the Fugue is freely structured—almost a Fantasy; and the *Funk* is not jazz *kitsch* but of symphonicized scherzo virtuosity.

Symphony No. 3 for Strings and Percussion (1969)

☐ Prague Chamber Soloists / Rohan (conductor) / Serenus 12035

Thorne's Symphony is in three movements and skillfully integrates the percussion (which here also includes harp and piano) with the string mass. It is complex, almost expressionistic music but is not complicated in its structuring. It has strong melodic purpose, but the lines are not of the tuneful variety, and though the harmonies and counterpoints are intricate they are never involved.

The playing of the twenty-five strings, five percussionists, timpanist, harpist, and pianist is competent. However, there is more to Thorne's Symphony than emerges in this execution.

*Solo
Instrument
and
Orchestra*

Piano

Concerto for Piano and Chamber Orchestra (1973)

☐ St. Paul Chamber Orchestra / Davies (piano) / De Mane (conductor) / Serenus 12058

Jazz characteristics, subtle and never slick, wrap themselves inside part of this music. The outstanding point of its form is a collective fantasy-rhapsody that culminates in a mix that Thorne terms a "grand quodlibet." This includes snatches from Mozart, Beethoven, and Wagner, which hang onto the music's bandwagon and help portray an enthusiastic and improvisation-like conclusion. But then, the total formal sense strongly reminds one of long-spanned improvisation. Thorne's Concerto, let it be emphasized, does not run around the old vicious virtuosic circle. It has contemporary consistency and like so much of his music is expressionistically undertoned.

The performance is fair to good. The latter refers to Davies's playing, the former to some imbalances and some passages that should have been redone for better smoothness. Who knows? Perhaps this recording was made from a concert performance tape, notwithstanding the absence of audience noises and the like as clues.

Rhapsodic Variations for Piano and Orchestra (1965)

☐ Polish National Radio Orchestra / Thorne (piano) / Strickland (conductor) / Composers Recordings 216

Constant variation is utilized in this opus. An interesting point is that the soloist improvises a cadenza toward the final part of the piece. (The composer indicates in the liner note that he improvised five cadenzas "during the course of the present recording" and let the conductor choose the best among them.) A fugal conclusion strengthens the sectionally structured work.

Instrumental

Flute

Sonatina for Solo Flute

☐ Sollberger (flute) / Serenus 12058

Unaccompanied flute pieces remain the big news in the field of wind music. Thorne's has good presence and precise formal balance. Movement 1 is jazz-touched, a slow movement contrasts, and fast-paced music winds things up. A high-quality example of flute playing is to be expected from Harvey Sollberger, and he provides it in every detail.

*Chamber
Music*

Songs and Dances (1969)

☐ Moore (cello); Rosenberger (percussion); Thomas (piano, harpsichord, and celesta) / Gilbert (conductor) / Opus One 9

Substantial music (five movements) and substantial attention to jazz-influenced panchromaticism. Thorne knows the jazz world intimately and distills the short-hair stuff in an interesting, scrupulous, and extremely sensitive manner. There is good sonorous flush to the dance elements, slightly diffused in the song category, but the former does not miss its mark. This is colorful music of contemporary vintage, and yet simmering within the sonorous pot is a romantically flavored eeriness.

The performance is well controlled and there are no doubts that Thorne's piece is pitched and presented properly.

Lyric Variations II for Wind Quintet and Percussion (1971)

☐ Boehm Quintet / Fitz (percussion) / Serenus 12058

Highly developed conduct replaces squared-off variational procedures here. Included are some jazzy touches in the way of phraseology, glides, slides, and color. (There are very few of Thorne's pieces that don't apply that butter to his creative bread.) The performance is a stimulating one.

Simultaneities for Brass Quintet, Amplified Guitar, and Percussion (1971)

☐ American Brass Quintet / Bell (guitar); Fitz (percussion) / Serenus 12035

Timbre bands and high coloristic sanction are principal to the first pair of movements. Within them the autochthonous idea has jazz flavor in its themes, breath, and pigmentation. The finale has a binary construction, the first part covering, among other things, an Ivesian collage of classical themes (including the fugue subject from Mozart's *The Magic Flute* [see under *Mozart: Opera and Dramatic Music*]); the second section is of nocturnal haze—thus, formal balance arrived at by direct opposition.

The piece is outstandingly played.

Nocturnes for Voice and Piano (1962)

Vocal

Voice with Accompaniment

☐ Rowe (soprano); Thorne (piano) / Serenus 12035

On the basis of these four songs, to texts by Robert Fitzgerald, one would say that Thorne's strongest creative ability lies in the field of vocal composition. The settings have a directness, continuity, and textural solidity that are splendid. Thorne knows how to set words and not bury their meaning. His Nocturnes deserve wide hearing; having them on disc is a big step in that direction.

Ludwig Thuille *(1861-1907)*

Sextet, Op. 6

Chamber Music

☐ Los Angeles Wind Quintet / Stevens (piano) / Orion 7263

A convincing replica of Beethoven-Schumann methods. Only one slight deviation—a Gavotte in place of the usual Scherzo. The piece is attractive in its way, attractively played, though the piano sound is a bit dry.

Armen Tigranian *(1879-1950)*

Anush (1912)

Opera and Dramatic Music

☐ Orchestra and Chorus of the Armenian State Theatre / Tavrizian (conductor) / Monitor 2081/3 (monaural)

A five-act affair, sung in Armenian, with a dark plot surrounding the Italian style. Offbeat but academic stuff; still, worth having as an occasional counterpoint to other recorded Operas.

Originally this was issued by Westminster (back in 1958). They also issued another Tigranian Opera, *David-Beg,* also later rereleased by Monitor, but no longer available.

Frederick Tillis   *(1930-   )*

Chamber Music

Quintet for Brass

☐ New York Brass Quintet / Serenus 12066

Tillis's Quintet has the patent organization that has become a tradition with twentieth-century music composed for brass. Accordingly: a jazzy-bouncy opening movement, a reflective central division, and a slightly nervous but rhythmically invigorating finale. Though the formulas and gestures are familiar, the music has substance. It is given a superb rendition by the New Yorkers—deft, pliable, and sensitively balanced.

Kenneth Timm   *(1934-   )*

Percussion

The Joiner and the Die-hard **(1972)**

☐ Wilkinson, Gooding, Geisert, Snodgrass, and Yancich (percussion) / Miller (conductor) / Crystal S–531

Passionate percussion (mainly standard instruments, the exceptions being an anvil and a pistol) used with common sense. The music is colorful and rhythmically alive, with compelling continuity. The common-sense factor is the composition's directness and pithiness (four and three-quarter minutes). Timm's title is not clear and neither is the note he offers on his music. Apparently, the only mallet instrument used (the xylophone) is the ''die-hard,'' sonorously pictured by its several penetrations into the membranous texture.

This is an interesting score that holds the attention. It is played with zest and sensitive attention to dynamic relationships.

Johannes Tinctoris   *(1435-ca. 1511)*

Cantata and Oratorio

Missa Trium Vocum

☐ Blanchard (conductor) / Nonesuch 71048

Tinctoris's "Mass for Three Voices" is for male voices, and the coloration is, accordingly, on the darker side. It is presented with good taste. (The only credit given is to the conductor, Roger Blanchard.)

Michael Tippett   *(1905-   )*

Orchestra

Ritual Dances from *The Midsummer Marriage* **(1952)**

☐ Orchestra of the Royal Opera House, Covent Garden / Pritchard (conductor) / Argo ZDA–19/20

A hefty amount of ballet music from Tippett's Opera (see under *Opera and Dramatic Music*), consisting of four dances with a prelude and postlude, plus two "transformations" between the first and second and the second and third dances. A contemporary, transferred view of "Seasons" ballets, with the first dance termed *The Earth in Autumn*, the second one *The Waters in Winter*, the third dance *The Air in Spring*, and the final one descriptive of *Fire in Summer*.

The performance is warm, dynamically acute, coloristically detailed.

Symphony No. 2 (1958)

☐ London Symphony Orchestra / Davis (conductor) / Argo ZRG-535

There is muscle aplenty in this four-movement work, beginning with the repetitive pitch opening. It powers the logical demands in the vigorous first movement and carries over to the asymmetrical *Presto veloce*. The contrastive material demonstrates Tippett's mystical-philosophical creative reasoning.

One critic proclaims this work as one of the finest by a British composer written in the last thirty years. Another indicates that the Symphony is a "must" for those who "care deeply about English music in general and Tippett in particular." This writer's verdict is that his fellow critics have not overstated the case—Tippett's Second Symphony is music of penetrating discernment; it will live.

The interpretation is authoritative and thoroughly recommended.

Concerto for Double String Orchestra (1939)

☐ Academy of St. Martin-in-the-Fields / Marriner (conductor) / Argo ZRG-680

String Orchestra

A lust for rhythmic life is detailed in the outer movements of this strong piece. There is neobaroque drive, jazzy jabs, and a self-confident swagger about the music. That's healthy stuff and it can win over anyone the moment it is heard. In contrast the central movement alternates lyrical breadth with propulsive chromatic fugal writing.

Most certainly Tippett's work is one of the finest contemporary string orchestra pieces. It receives a splendid performance under Marriner's direction. The tone quality of the Academy group is ravishing.

Fantasia Concertante on a Theme of Corelli (1953)

☐ Academy of St. Martin-in-the-Fields / Loveday and Caine (violins); Heath (cello) / Marriner (conductor) / Argo ZRG-680

The concertino in this work (two violins and cello) is strongly contrasted since it is pitted against and juxtaposed with a double string orchestra. The theme is from Corelli's Concerto Grosso, Op. 6, No. 2, and it is enlarged, developed, wrapped around, and especially illuminated with Tippett's superb polyphony. Sumptuously scored music, this, but it is never so fat that it loses its neoclassic stability. It is played expressively.

Little Music for String Orchestra (1946)

☐ Academy of St. Martin-in-the-Fields / Marriner (conductor) / Argo ZRG-680

Compactness identifies this work but not miniature meanings. There are four movements: a Prelude, Fugue, Air, and Finale. Splendid polyphony marks all the music. The lines are always alive, the rhythms are constantly supple, and the phrases move over the bar lines, thus maintaining motility within each formation. Marriner provides a lucid, fully balanced performance.

Solo Instrument and Orchestra

Piano

Fantasia on a Theme by Handel (1942)

☐ London Symphony Orchestra / Kitchin (piano) / Tippett (conductor) / RCA SER-5620

The thematic generator for Tippett's tonally luxurious Fantasia is from a Prelude to the Air and Variations in one of Handel's *Suites de pièces pour le clavecin*. Five variations follow, and the work comes to a splendid conclusion with a stridingly bold subjected fugue.

There is no roughage in Tippett's neo-romantic sonorescences. It is a splendid contribution that most pianists, sacked in with their Rachmaninoff and Tchaikovsky, do not know about or, if they do, do not care to investigate. They should. The performance is at a superb level and the sound is marvelously rich and deep.

Instrumental

Piano

Piano Sonata

No. 1 (1937) / No. 2 (1962) / No. 3 (1973)

☐ Crossley (piano) / Philips 6500534

The composition dates of the Sonatas range from 1937 (the first one was originally called a Fantasy Sonata), through 1962 for the second of the group, to the completion in 1973 of the third work.

There is much contrapuntalism in these pieces, as is basic to Tippett's style. He emphasizes this potency in its keyboard-instrument availability. It is already quite supple in the first work and becomes a major premise in the third. But there is this to note in Tippett's polyphony—it flows across the pulses and bar lines and achieves a substantial breadth thereby. Even in canonic passages Tippett manages to avoid the insular tightness that prevails so often with use of that technique.

The Third Sonata includes variations in the slow movement and retrograde use of material in its final movement. Paul Crossley commissioned the Third Sonata and gives the work a magnificent exposition. His playing of the other works is just as brilliant and meaningful.

Chamber Music

Sonata for Four Horns (1955)

☐ Barry Tuckwell Horn Quartet / Argo ZRG–535

The literature for this medium is growing, but not more than a handful of compositions pass the par-level line. Tippett's work (composed for Dennis Brain's ensemble in 1955) is one (Paul Hindemith's is another). It has virtuosic intelligence in its writing and it is portrayed with timbre acuteness.

String Quartet No. 1 in A (1935)

☐ Edinburgh Quartet / Monitor S–2123

Tippett's work is a study in textures. The opening movement achieves quartet sonority by details kindred to those of late Beethoven style; part 2 is like Elizabethan music, with freedom of line granting suppleness to the moving voices. On the other hand, the final movement has the sonorous dry sting derived from following Bartókian concentrations.

All this may seem to point to assorted eclecticism, but that is not so. In varying the textures Tippett does not corrupt his style; its language is compacted by being dynamically tonal and strengthened by astringent devices.

The presentation by Baster, Cummings, Hawkins, and Hampton, who make up the Edinburgh foursome, is convincing. They display special percipience in defining the finale's plastic rhythm.

Symphony No. 3 (1972)

☐ London Symphony Orchestra / Harper (soprano) / Davis (conductor) / Philips 6500662

Tippett's third Symphony can be classified quickly as a hybrid, with a purely orchestral first movement (the motility of its first part compressed in the second half to equal a slow-movement basis) and a second movement that quotes Beethoven's Ninth Symphony and then moves into four songs stated in continuous sequence—the first three blues-derived in style, the last one a dramatic *scena*. But these violent contrasts of character, style, and instrumentation paradoxically fit neatly into a solid symphonic structure. The objective is clear: a Symphony that is broadly formationed rather than specifically detailed with different tempoed movements. The contrastive arrangement of materials is both gritty and beautiful. It is a music of the present day, of singular scope and singularly free from any rigid technical procedure.

The performance is dynamic, the rhythms and phrasing in the voice and orchestra section finely wrought. This is in every respect an outstanding issue.

The Weeping Babe

☐ John Alldis Choir / Argo ZRG–535

Lyrical part song to a text by Edith Sitwell. The singing is of high quality.

Magnificat

Nunc dimittis

☐ Choir of St. John's College, Cambridge / Runnett (organ) / Guest (conductor) / Argo ZRG–5340

The organ's dissonant proclamations in the *Magnificat* will probably be considered a vice by those who think of sacred music as demanding choral and chordal repose. It is the opposite—a decided virtue that produces aural refection. Tippett's perceptive conduct continues in the vocal orchestration of *Nunc dimittis,* especially in the contrast between a high solo voice and the darker lower voices, further darkened by crusted harmonies. This pair of highly individual, creatively prosperous pieces is authoritatively presented by the performing forces.

A Child of Our Time (1941)

☐ BBC Symphony Orchestra, BBC Choral Society, and BBC Singers / Norman (soprano); Baker (mezzo-soprano); Cassilly (tenor); Shirley-Quirk (baritone) / Davis (conductor) / Philips 6500985

Tippett's Oratorio is based on fact: the shooting of a German diplomat in Paris by a young Jewish refugee, followed by the violence and horror of pogroms in Nazi Germany. In its singular way, *A Child of Our Time,* a boldly vivid statement on man's horrible side, is a contemporary Passion. It includes thirty sections, with Black spirituals used as Bach utilized chorales. Like Bach's great music, it communicates with exquisite emotion.

Composed during World War II, Tippett's music of protest is a document of lasting importance. Its language is superbly crafted, unmistakably of the twentieth century, but just as unmistakably tonally resolute.

This is the second recording of the work. The other (on Argo ZDA–19/20) has fine soloists, but those Davis directs are more intense in their portrayals. Colin Davis provides all the powered integrations of the score; the Philips edition of this splendid work is truly superb.

The Vision of St. Augustine (1966)

☐ London Symphony Orchestra and Chorus / Shirley-Quirk (baritone) / Tippett (conductor) / RCA SER–5620

A different creative perspective pertains to this mystical, burning Cantata. As Tippett found himself "wrapt away" into the mysticism of his subject, so his music reflects a cancellation of urbanity and neo-romanticism and substitutes the flagellation of modernity. The music never lets down as it is thrust into forms that resemble rondo and toccata, using pantonal serialism, counterpoints that smash against themselves rather than progress in individual partnership, vocal glossolalia, and an orchestration that never caresses the ear but storms it.

The *Vision* is a masterwork waiting to be discovered. Its difficulties are clear, its excitements immediate. This recording, made immediately after two concert performances, is sonorous proof. It is as spectacular as the music is awesome.

Opera and Dramatic Music

The Knot Garden (1970)

☐ Orchestra of the Royal Opera House, Covent Garden / Gomez and Barstow (sopranos); Minton (mezzo-soprano); Tear (tenor); Herincx, Carey, and Hemsley (baritones) / Davis (conductor) / Philips 6700063

John Warrack's introduction to Tippett's Opera is necessary reading before listening to this recorded production. He describes *The Knot Garden* as "about real people whose lives are in a state of confusion which the plot unravels, so that their paths are set on a course which leads finally to, not a happy ending, but a new beginning."

Symbolism is present in great degree, rather than straightforward characterization, and action that helps define and individualize the former. The writing is smoothly styled for the voices, with very effective solo sections as well as duos, intensified with harmonic pepper and splendid instrumental color (a bit of jazz touch as well). However, because of the intricacies of its libretto, Tippett's Opera will not give up its secrets at first hearing. It should the third playing around and is worth the investment of time.

The cast is excellent. Although the honors are rather evenly divided, special mention belongs to Yvonne Minton and Raimond Herincx as the wife-husband pair whose estrangement is central to the plot and Thomas Carey and Robert Tear as a homosexual couple. Colin Davis's direction is superb, certified by Tippett's statement that Davis "has found his own way into a remarkable sympathy with and understanding of my music."

The Midsummer Marriage

☐ Orchestra and Chorus of the Royal Opera House, Covent Garden / Carlyle and Harwood (sopranos); Bainbridge (mezzo-soprano); Watts (contralto); Remedios, Burrows, and Daniels (tenors); Herincx and Whelan (baritones); Dean (bass) / Davis (conductor) / Philips 6703027

An involved philosophical tale, dealing, Tippett tells us, "with the interaction of two worlds, the natural and supernatural." Plenty of emotional impact also, to be expected from a story described by Nicolas Slonimsky as "dealing with two pairs of lovers mating symbolically with their own antinomic selves representing the masculine element in a woman and a feminine element in a man."

This is Tippett's richest score, with marvelous orchestral backgrounds, vivid dance music (see under *Orchestra* [Ritual Dances from *The Midsummer Marriage*]), vocal imagery at its best, and grand choral writing. Indeed, Tippett's reputation as one of the most important of twentieth-century composers can rest on this single work.

The highest praise concerns this recording. It has the authoritative conducting of Colin Davis, magnificent singing, and radiant orchestral playing. Importantly, Tippett has given his approval, indicating "the whole recording from my point of view is quite splendid."

Boris Tishchenko (1939-)

Concerto for Cello

☐ Leningrad Philharmonic / Rostropovich (cello) / Blazhkov (conductor) / Melodiya/ Angel S–40091

Solo Instrument and Orchestra

Cello

The full title for this work, which details its instrumentation, should have appended "with seventeen woodwind instruments, percussion, and harmonium." (*Schwann* does not include the percussion in its title listing and errs by changing the harmonium to an organ.)

Tishchenko's Concerto is not in the Khrennikov-Kabalevsky-Khachaturian idiom. It is monothematically dictated, almost atonal, rhythmically intense, and intensely polyphonic.

The performance is by the same forces that gave the world premiere, in Leningrad, on February 5, 1966.

Antoine Tisné (1932-)

Soliloques

☐ Grossman (bassoon) / Crystal S–342

Instrumental

Bassoon

Not much music for unaccompanied bassoon exists. This is an excellent contribution. There are three movements, the first noted in the tempo heading as *un charactère méditatif,* the second has balletic gestures, and the last piece is again (like the first one) of incantational character.

Arthur Grossman's playing is sensitive and beautifully colored. He shows a splendid ear for phrase inflection.

Jean Titelouze (1563-1633)

Hymns

Ad coenam	**Exsultet coelum**
Ave maris stella	**Urbs Hierusalem**

☐ Darasse (organ) / Turnabout 34126

Instrumental

Organ

These are prime examples of Titelouze's important creative work. (A further credit belongs to him. He is considered to be the founder of the French school of organ playing.) The polyphonic developments of these hymns, used in the musical program of Vespers, are substantial in depth and meaning, and substantial in length as well—the shortest work is of six-minute length, the longest totals eleven minutes.

The performances by Xavier Darasse are of compelling attention. They are also available in a Vox Box of assorted organ music on SVBX–5310.

Ernst Toch

(1887 - 1964)

Orchestra

Jephta, Rhapsodic Poem (Symphony No. 5) (1964)

☐ Louisville Orchestra / Whitney (conductor) / Louisville S–661

The title caused Toch much concern. At first, the composition was called "Symphony No. 5 in One Movement." Because it contained the inner expression of the Jephta tale, Toch renamed the piece, without symphonic designation. He then had fears that few would recognize the biblical parallel of his music and was uncertain whether to retain the new title. The final decision was the compromise that included both, as noted above.

Though in a single unit there is no sense, because it is a Symphony, of telescoping of movements. The scoring resembles that of chamber music though it calls for over two dozen different types of instruments. It is difficult to believe that not a single measure in the twenty-one minute piece calls for the full orchestra. With this sensitive variability there is total virtuosity—dramaticism in kid gloves. Toch was correct. His Symphony *is* a rhapsodic poem. And whether one knows the Jephta tale or not is immaterial.

Whitney considers the work properly and conducts with taste and vigor. Whether he showed good taste in making a cut in the final portion can be argued.

Miniature Overture

☐ Louisville Orchestra / Mester (conductor) / Louisville S–702

A Miniature Overture for a miniature orchestra of winds, a few brass, and percussion. Jaunty, it is a scherzo conversation that is the type of music one would expect as preamble to a marionette show.

Notturno, Op. 77

☐ Louisville Orchestra / Whitney (conductor) / Louisville 545–3 (monaural)

Unique tonal pigments are prime in the cool and veiled effects of this one-movement composition. The gloved instrumentation omits string basses, and though it calls for three trombones these are used for only a few chords toward the end; the sole percussion is a xylophone that does not crackle. Toch disposes the orchestra into groups, deploys these forces as though composing a hundred and one different chamber-music duets, trios, quartets, quintets, sextets, and so on—there is not a single measure of the full orchestra playing together!

This unorthodox sonorous poetry is more devastating in its effect than the music of a tone-protesting composer. The arguments of this three-part nocturnal essay are not from Chopin but out of a "midsummer night's dream." However, the light and shade of timbre and sonority are but part of the instrumental inquisitiveness of this bold composer; the *Notturno* also offers impressive musical imagery.

Whitney and his musicians give an excellent projection of Toch's sensitive score.

Peter Pan, A Fairy Tale for Orchestra in Three Parts, Op. 76

☐ Louisville Orchestra / Whitney (conductor) / Louisville 612 (monaural)

Though Toch's Opus 76 is not so designated, it is of the fanciful scherzo genre, broadly fulfilling all its elements and framed by select color that sets off the ideas.

Peter Pan has balanced design yet is improvisational as the orchestral components are tossed around. Formal adventure, not formal pedantry, is found in Toch's work. In this delightful projection of motival thoughts one will find a fresh experience of formed sounds rather than sounded form. In the big noise of contemporary music little has been produced that is more exquisite than the second movement. It consists of sixty-five measures in moderate tempo, where everything moves on carpeted sonorities.

There are very few Louisville recorded performances under Whitney's direction that can match the sensitivity of this one.

Concerto for Cello and Chamber Orchestra, Op. 35

Solo Instrument and Orchestra

Cello

☐ Forum Group, Zurich / Mottier (cello) / Barth (conductor) / Contemporary S–8014E (monaural)

The passions of chromaticism are portrayed here, framed by prosperous rhythm; thus: the Scotch-snapped second movement, the duple-pulsed vigor of the finale. The slow movement is in direct contrast and features the unaccompanied solo voice.

Strength and substance are heard in the solo playing, which receives decent orchestral support.

Piano Concerto, Op. 38

Piano

☐ Vienna Symphony Orchestra / Toch (piano) / Haefner (conductor) / Contemporary S–8014E (monaural)

A combination of brilliant solo writing, vigorous rhythms, and handsome cutting polyphony, plus dynamic orchestration. Toch was ever mindful that he was writing a Concerto, and such virtuosic slant is represented in every portion of its three movements. However, Toch made certain that there was constant interest in the orchestral part—in no sense is it an accompanimental handout. Concert revival of this fine work is long overdue.

The recording was mastered from a tape of a radio broadcast given in Vienna in 1950. Under the circumstances the sound is not bad at all.

Five *Capriccetti*, Op. 36

Instrumental

Three Little Dances, Op. 85

Piano

☐ Guzelimian (piano) / Crystal S–502

The Dances were written to celebrate the marriage of two friends: a black woman and a white man. Accordingly, there is musical color to match. Part 1 is entirely for the black keys, part 2 for the white ones, and the final dance mixes them. Not only is this a clever idea; the product makes musical sense.

The tempi of Opus 36 give the full descriptive facts: *Tender, reflective; Lively; Graceful, gay; Dolce e affetuoso;* and *With exuberant humor.*

The playing of this music has the requisite spirit, sensitivity, and facility.

Divertimento for Violin and Cello, Op. 37, No. 1

Chamber Music

☐ Alice Schoenfeld (violin); Eleonore Schoenfeld (cello) / Orion 7267

A thirteenth chord (the widest possible triadal constitute, formed by pillowing thirds on top of each other) is turned on its side and becomes the horizontally employed means of the first theme, indicating the stretching of the tonality. The music is linear, but the orbit revolves around C, and the movement ends resoundingly in firm tonality. Variational details are used for structuring the second-movement Intermezzo. Here, the instruments are veiled by mutes. The material in the finale alternates between the use of imitation and tutti declaration; the lines in the latter are kept moving by contrary motion in order to avoid coalescence.

1927

The tempo indications for the three movements are: *Flott, Fliessend,* and *Frisch.* Coincidental or not, Toch's alliteration can be paralleled by describing the work as fine-spun, frisky, and flavorsome.

The Divertimento demands expert players, which describes these duo performers. The interpretation of Toch's Divertimento is undoubtedly the Schoenfelds' best performance among the many works they have recorded. This writer has never heard them play better.

Divertimento for Violin and Viola, Op. 37, No. 2 (version for Violin and Cello)

☐ Heifetz (violin); Piatigorsky (cello) / RCA LSC-3009

Toch was always a passionate advocate of rhythm. In this piece, his meters shift incessantly in asymmetrical totals. The unit remains fairly equal throughout; thus, there is drive, rather than nervous disproportions. Kineticism rules the finale, continuing as the binding when a *scherzando* rhythmic jet enters. Rondo form is used in the opening part. The music there has points that do not scratch, but they mark the counterpoint with semiacidity. The carefree quality is a bit sardonic. A slow movement, in ternary style, follows.

The translation of the viola part for cello was apparently made by Piatigorsky. No information is furnished concerning this point and the published violin-viola score makes no mention of an alternate setting for violin and cello.

Heifetz and Piatigorsky have also reversed the order of the movements (the above discussion naturally reflects this shift). The kinetic finale mentioned earlier is the original first movement and the initial rondo movement indicated is actually Toch's closing division of the duo. Although one totally and firmly disagrees with revising the order of a multimovement work, there is no disagreement with this sharp performance, excitingly driven where needed and pungently depicted.

Sonata No. 1 for Violin and Piano, Op. 21

☐ Shapiro (violin); Berkowitz (piano) / Crystal S-502

The precision of tonality, the order of the themes, and the working of them mark a music that practices the theories of Schumann, Brahms, and the other romantics. There is also (especially in the last movement) a thrust that would reach full power in Toch's later output. It should not be overlooked that this is a conception by a young man, aged twenty-five. No wonder Toch called his piece "Brahms's Fourth Violin Sonata."

This performing team has had a long association. Their playing is fine and refined, codifying all the nuances of the music. The tones glow. Toch would have been delighted.

Serenade in G major, Op. 25

☐ Westwood String Trio / Contemporary 7016

The Serenade flows throughout in its restrained color (two violins and viola). It is relaxing, undramatic music, with all the power inherent in well-formed, romantic harmonies. Only four measures depart from the openhearted swing of duple meter. For the most part Toch's piece whispers a Viennese *Gemütlichkeit* long lost. (It has a parenthetical title, *Spitzweg,* explained by the source of inspiration—a painting by this nineteenth-century German.)

The performers respond to Toch's music convincingly. Their sound is of deep loveliness.

String Trio, Op. 63

☐ Vienna String Trio / Contemporary 8005

Music not submissive to dogma, yet as clearly balanced as any opus of the classical school. Its tempi are in symmetry (two Allegros flank an Adagio); the moods of the fast movements are dramatic and propulsive, that of the slow portion a dark intermezzo. Toch intertwines harmonic and polyphonic textures with keen craftsmanship and obtains further subtle contrasts.

Rich in romantic quality, the Trio is raked with chromatic teeth, which dig the tonality out of its bounded fields and cover it with delicate abrasions. Erudition and logic are here, but not at the expense of emotive meaning. Only the last movement seems diffused; not labored, but slightly belabored.

The Vienna team (Poduschka, violin; Weis, viola; and Blecha, cello) reveals the work in all its essences. This is a strong performance.

String Quartet in D flat major, Op. 18

☐ Westwood String Quartet / Contemporary 7016

Music displaying a harmonically chromatic, richly diverse, romantic text. It also contains the Germano-Austrian predilection for length, spanning five movements: an introductory division (*Quasi Prologus*), a pair of scherzi surrounding a slow movement, and a rondo-styled finale.

Hearing this Quartet without knowing the composer, one would immediately recognize it as Viennese, a combination of Brahms and post-Brahms. The music is warm, with the tender sentimentalities and passionate rhythmic habits of these periods; the eclecticism is traceable to its source. Regardless, there is integrity of style and feeling.

The lusty performance is a bit rough here and there but this does no basic harm to the music.

String Quartet No. 10 (*on the Name "Bass"*), Op. 28

☐ American Art Quartet / Contemporary 8008

Varying stimuli have produced musical action. A favorite child may inspire a lullaby; Honegger's love for locomotives was exalted in his *Pacific 231;* love of homeland actuates a symphonic poem. Another example is the translation of a person's name into music (as much of it as possible, or by assigning specific tones to match the letters that have no musical representation). Bach's name has been excellent game. Not only is it revered, but all the letters in his name have pitch equivalents ("B" in German equals "B flat," "A" and "C" stand as is, and "H" in German is synonymous for B natural).

To pay tribute to his cousin, Toch used this form of musical anagram, basing his Quartet on his relative's cognomen, Bass. All the sounds are based on German terminology. As noted above, the "B" equals B flat, the final "S" turns into an E flat, and by combining the two middle letters, the sound of A flat is obtained.

All themes of the four movements employ this technique. It turns out that Bass's name is susceptible to all shades of feeling. The designs are clear-cut: rondo, variational aspects of song form, scherzo, and a free disposition of sonata shape. There are many delights in the Quartet, especially the vivid streaming lines and chromatic figures of the catlike third movement. Rhythmically speaking, the last movement is just as agile.

This is superfine playing by a well-integrated group. The supervision of the composer during the making of the disc guarantees a definitive edition of the work.

String Quartet No. 12, Op. 70

☐ Zurich String Quartet / Contemporary 8005

There are other assets in this Quartet besides its healthy contemporary lyricism. They arise from subtly deployed string qualities. In addition to the elegance of the part writing (superb color realization by itself), fascinating items include a pair of quarter-tone chords and a glissando-arpeggiated pizzicato cadence that is a fillip to the haunting melody of the *Pensive Serenade* movement.

Differences exist between mere polyphonic pugnacity and genuine contrapuntal mating. The initial movement is of semicontrapuntal order, outlined with an ostinato-formed rhythmic plan. Here the music is active yet relaxed—it might be described as tender counterpoint. Polyphony continues in the chromatic second movement. Only at the end is the music homophonic. And in the final division the contrapuntalism is intensified by use of stretto. In Toch's hands none of this is starched polyphonic music but expressive realization. This is a Quartet of sound feeling as well as sound technique.

The Zurich String Quartet is a group of sensitive musicians with superb sound qualities and expert technique. Their playing is distinguished. (*Schwann* incorrectly distinguishes this Quartet as No. 1 in the Toch canon.)

String Quartet No. 13, Op. 74

☐ Roth Quartet / Contemporary 8008

Behind any good art there must be the *primum mobile*. Though Toch utilizes twelve-tone technique here (he had never employed it previously) he has twisted the tail of this technical animal so that he is its master. And having mastered it, he departed from the scene. The Thirteenth Quartet signified a fresh-sounding, productive contribution to Toch's output, but he did not intend to use the dodecaphonic system in the future and so emphatically stated.

This music does not exemplify rampant serialism. It is simply of different character from Toch's other works, yet it has Toch's imprints: the chinky-chunky, propulsive rhythmic style; the formal solidity; scoring that contrasts violence and repose; and the poetic quality of dramatic counterpoint. The marriage of convenience between procedures used in Toch's tonal music and serial style (Toch did not deliberately set out to compose a twelve-tone work; his initial theme led him to it) has produced a healthy child, if not a lusty one.

The Roth group is sufficiently expert, but their tone is wiry and Feri Roth's phrasing is not always objectively concerned. Octave matching sometimes misses precise connection.

Quintet for Piano, Two Violins, Viola, and Violoncello, Op. 64

☐ American Art Quartet / Previn (piano) / Contemporary 8011

The instrumentation of Toch's Piano Quintet is most interesting. This medium can easily convey an undue amount of thickness. Toch's solution pits the strings against the piano in one, two, three, or four voices. Combining them in quintet formation is an exceedingly minor part of the total. The slow movement is the best example, wherein the quintet functions as a totality in only a dozen of the 129 measures. Thus, the four movements, each with a distinct mood (the divisions are called *The Lyrical Part, The Whimsical Part, The Contemplative Part,* and *The Dramatic Part*), are framed differently. The Quintet is freely tonal, laced with a chromaticism that enjoys a vivid life without forgetting its tonal center.

All these details add up to a composer of the twentieth century who did not find it necessary to thump on experimental tubs in order to make his point. The structural heritage of this music can be traced to the great classical tradition, but the notes are not inked in with a blunted neoclassic pen. Toch wrote his Piano Quintet in individually bold modern script.

After listening to the test pressings, Toch told this writer he was of the opinion that this recorded performance, with André Previn as the pianist, was well-nigh perfect. Agreed.

Poems to Martha for Voice and Strings, Op. 66

☐ Compinsky Ensemble / Tippey (baritone) / Sheffield S–3

Because of the arrangement of its content so that the voice is not soloistic but part of the ensemble, making a quintet of voice, two violins, viola, and cello, *Poems to Martha* is almost deserving of placement in the chamber-music category. There are some lighter moments in the four movements, but by far the basis is elegaic.

Attention to dynamic balances provides a fine textural quality. The playing is of clear thinking and the singing is good if not exciting. Tippey's diction, however, is clear and that *is* exciting.

Geographical Fugue for Spoken Chorus (1930)

☐ Camerata of Los Angeles Chorus / Mitzelfelt (conductor) / Crystal S–502

Call it what you will, a *tour de force* or a slick idea, the Geographical Fugue is a masterpiece of its kind. It has become Toch's most popular piece and the published score has enjoyed considerable sales. Its commercial success, proving again that good merchandise finds a ready buyer, does not nullify its supreme artistry and invention.

The *Fuge aus der Geographie* (the first setting was in German, then translated into English with a few changes to accommodate pronunciation in relation to rhythm) is a set of geographical statements that already impart musical flow when uttered quickly (for size, try: "Trinidad and the big Mississippi and the town Honolulu and the lake Titicaca"). These are thrown into a pure fugal bath.

Toch allowed himself no formal mercy. The word-subject is heard in four-part entry and then follows the use of counter subjects, episodes, augmentation, and stretto. It is a perfect unpitched fugue but pitched with a technical flair that is remarkable. It is certainly delightfully fresh and rhythmically seductive.

I've heard this piece in dozens of performances but none came near to this freshly recorded one. It is absolutely superb.

Valse for Spoken Chorus (1961)

☐ Camerata of Los Angeles Chorus / Carpenter and Alford (percussion) / Mitzelfelt (conductor) / Crystal S–502

A verbal choral cocktail using the improvisational pitch and toss of party chatter. It swings like a dance and has the triple beat of a waltz. The technique is similar to the Geographical Fugue (see under *Chorus Alone*), but in this case the form is one of fantasy, colored with a little inlay of percussion.

The mastery of Mitzelfelt's group in the Fugue is reaffirmed here. What they do is definitive.

Vocal

Voice and Instrumental Ensemble

Choral

Chorus Alone

Chorus with Accompaniment

1931

Eduardo Toldrá   *(1895-1962)*

Vocal

Voice with Accompaniment

As froliñas dos toxos from *Doce canciones gallegas*

Cançó de Grumet from *A l'ombra del lledoner*

☐ de los Angeles (soprano); Soriano (piano) / Angel S–35775

The first song ("The Flowers of the Furze") is delicate, akin to a cradle song. The other ("Song of the Sailor") is robust. Both are excellent examples of Toldrá's Catalan nationalistic style.

Jan Václav Tomášek   *(1774-1850)*

Solo Instrument and Orchestra

Piano

Concerto No. 1 in C major for Piano and Orchestra, Op. 18

☐ Prague Symphony Orchestra / Toperczer (piano) / Rohan (conductor) / Candide 31073

An interesting representation of music that reminds one of the working material found in Mozart and Beethoven. Czech though Tomášek was, he was an exact counterpart of the Viennese school of composers. His Opus 18 is well bred, well styled, if not great, music. The opening movement has considerable breadth, the finale has distinctive gaiety.

The performance is not only attractive but presents a first-rate pianist.

Instrumental

Piano

Eglogue No. 2 in F major, Op. 35

☐ Firkusny (piano) / Candide 31086

The second of the half dozen in the set, cast in a three-part design. Tomášek is still another romantic voice that remains unheard in the concert halls. His *Eglogue* deserves placement next to the important music of Schubert and Schumann. Firkusny proves it with unconfutable evidence.

Henri Tomasi   *(1901-1971)*

Solo Instrument and Orchestra

Trumpet

Concerto in C for Trumpet and Orchestra (1949)

☐ Symphony Orchestra of Radio-Luxembourg / André (trumpet) / de Froment (conductor) / Musical Heritage Society MHS–829

Stylistic jargon, but deft and thoroughly enjoyable. Movement 1 has fanfarelike commentary, a bit of Gershwinese, and a solid cadenza. Movement 2 is muted, a Nocturne. The finale is sassy, jazzy, with "Les Six" rhythmic sauce. It all seduces the ear even if Tomasi was not seduced by intellectualism.

André is a marvelous musician. He makes the brass instrument sing, dance, and rejoice in its hedonistic sound. Worthy trumpet Concerti are few and far between. This is one and André convinces us.

Instrumental

Clarinet

Sonatine attique (1966)

☐ Listokin (clarinet) / Golden Crest 7052

There are some exotic touches in the intervallic arrangements, but basically a monochromic consideration covers the three movements. (Golden Crest's title: *Sonata attique* is slightly off course.)

Holy Week at Cuzco

☐ Bilgram (organ); André (piccolo trumpet and C trumpet) / Musical Heritage Society MHS–3340

Pantonally styled and clearly detailed. The duo formation, which implies a trio by the alternating brass instrument choices, is quite colorful; the playing follows suit.

Luigi Tomasini (1741-1808)

String Quartet, Op. 8

Chamber Music

☐ Schäffer Quartet / Vox SVBX–5300

Tomasini was a principal violinist in the Esterhazy establishment whose excellence influenced Haydn in his quartet writing. In turn, Haydn's writing influenced the younger man in his compositions. The Opus 8 patently shows such rub-off. It also exemplifies first-fiddle predominance.

Thomas Tomkins (1572-1656)

A Short Verse

Instrumental

Organ

☐ Anderson (organ) / Crystal S–180

Indeed, pithy (under two minutes), but sufficient to show the fine melodious type of counterpoint Tomkins could write.

Fusca, In Thy Starry Eyes

Choral

Chorus Alone

☐ Clark and Thomas (sopranos); Phillips (contralto); English (tenor); Keyte (bass) / Leppard (conductor) / Nonesuch 73010

Light-strung madrigal with the rhythmic "fa-la" refrain. Perfectly presented.

Giuseppe Torelli (1658-1709)

Concerto for Strings and Harpsichord, Op. 6, No. 10

String Orchestra

☐ Academy of St. Martin-in-the-Fields / Marriner (conductor) / Oiseau-Lyre 60045

Good sound, good tempi, nice flexibility, and a nice realization of the continuo part.

Concerto in A major for Guitar, Violin, and Orchestra

Solo Instrument and Orchestra

☐ Wiener Solisten / Scheit (guitar); Pichler (violin); Tachezi (continuo) / Böttcher (conductor / Bach Guild 5043

Guitar and Violin

A delightful contrast of timbres in this two-solo work that glistens in the outer fast movements and is balanced by a beautiful aria (in *adagio* tempo) in between. A stunning baroque Concerto.

At times the ways of record companies are mysterious, if not annoying. This perform-ance is duplicated on Turnabout on a single disc (34123) and in a five-record set (34195/9). On the Bach Guild release the title is Concerto for Solo Violin and Guitar; Turnabout's designation is Concerto in A major for Guitar, Violin, and Orchestra. Bach Guild credits the continuo player, Turnabout doesn't. Bach Guild indicates the solo violinist, Turn-about omits it. The conductor is the same (the umlaut is removed by Turnabout and the ''oe'' spelling substituted). Finally, the orchestra on Turnabout is listed as *Kammeror-chester der Wiener Festspiele*. All this amounts to rather sloppy work on the part of Turn-about.

Trumpet

Concerto in D major

☐ Wiener Solisten / André (trumpet) / RCA CRL2-7002

For the reflective slow movement alone, this Concerto deserves triple starring. There is a surprise in its structure—the sudden insert of a bubbly fast section for the strings.

This is trumpet playing *par excellence*. André's shaping of trills should be mandatory listening for every instrumentalist.

Instrumental

Trumpet

Sinfonia con Tromba

☐ Pearson (trumpet); Vidrich (organ) / Crystal S-365

Torelli's four-movement piece (short in totality, lasting a little less than six minutes) was originally written for solo trumpet and strings; the substitution of an organ imposes a transcriber's viewpoint (his name is not indicated) that does no harm to the composition.

Fine playing by Byron Pearson and excellent support from Arthur Vidrich (the second-movement Adagio is set for organ alone). Fine sound from Crystal.

Federico Moreno Torroba (1891-)

Instrumental

Guitar

Romance de los pinos

☐ Segovia (guitar) / MCA 2524

Contemplative and with folk-song contours. The playing is poetic.

Paul Tortelier (1914-)

String Orchestra

Offrande

☐ London Chamber Orchestra / Tortelier (conductor) / Unicorn UNS-233

Tortelier has integrated (in reshaped form) extremely pithy Beethoven material in his three-movement work. In the first movement the source is the choral finale of the Ninth Symphony. Movement 2 (a funeral march) follows the ''implacable rhythm and melodic original'' (Tortelier's description) of the slow movement of the Seventh Symphony, the first subject of the march being based on a three-pitch motive taken from the Sixth Sym-phony. The finale is a Fugue with more appropriation, this time from another part of the Sixth Symphony together with an extract from a Motet by Monteverdi (rhythmically altered).

This is no pastiche. The borrowings are extremely minimal and their alterations, fused into music of romantically vigorous contemporary style, produce a strong work.

The performance is splendid and with the composer conducting it is a definitive version. Unicorn fails to band the work which is a nuisance and fails to inform the potential buyer that *Offrande* is for string orchestra.

Héctor Tosar *(1923-   )*

Toccata (1940)
Orchestra

☐ Louisville Orchestra / Mester (conductor) / Louisville S–702

Tosar, from Uruguay, bypasses any native content in his Toccata. It is fully neoclassic in make-up and has all the exciting ingredients of the form. It also fully shows the special talents of this fellow: the work was composed when he was seventeen. The music keeps the orchestra occupied and will also keep the listener occupied.

Charles Tournemire *(1870-1939)*

L'Orgue mystique—Suite No. 18
Instrumental

☐ Noehren (organ) / Lyrichord 7171
Organ

One of fifty-one suites that Tournemire composed to embrace music for the entire Catholic liturgical year. Each suite consists of five movements and all are similar in their titled statements for the first four movements: a *Prélude à l'introit, Offertoire, Elévation,* and *Communion.* The final movement changes in the various suites; in this case the *Pièce terminal* is a Toccata on a Chorale.

Chromaticism is a strong force within the neo-Gregorian-Franckian mix that describes Tournemire's aesthetic stance. For the greater part organistic chanting is emphasized. This changes when polytonality pushes into the texture in the Toccata.

Noehren's playing is evocative, clearly focused, and acutely brilliant in the finale of this work, composed for Quasimodo, or Low Sunday after Easter.

(For other suites in the set, *see below* [*L'Orgue mystique*—Suite No. 30 and *L'Orgue mystique*—Suite No. 35].)

L'Orgue mystique—Suite No. 30

☐ Noehren (organ) / Lyrichord 7187

(For details, *see above* [*L'Orgue mystique*—Suite No. 18].)
The finale is a vivid Alleluia. Its rhythmic action is strong and Noehren's choice of sonorities is most effective. There is nicely judged playing in the preceding parts of the composition.

L'Orgue mystique—Suite No. 35

☐ Noehren (organ) / Lyrichord 7171

(For details, *see above* [*L'Orgue mystique*—Suite No. 18].)
Again, sharp contrast is offered in the finale, a *Carillon-Paraphrase.* And, again, the

harmonic content expands in that movement in comparison with the previous four parts of the work.

There is strong performance in every respect for Tournemire's work, composed for the Feast of the Assumption of the Blessed Virgin Mary.

Pastorale

☐ Isoir (organ) / Turnabout 34319

A gentle and simple piece, illustrating Tournemire's secular music style. However, its secularism has many of the mystical qualities of his sacred organ music.

The work is included in an album of *Modern French Organ Music*. The performance is also contained in a Vox Box (SVBX–5315) titled *A Survey of the World's Greatest Organ Music* (*Volume VI*). Tournemire's Pastorale is decent music but it is far from "great." Isoir's playing follows suit.

Marcel Tournier   *(1879-1951)*

Instrumental   **Au Matin**

Harp

☐ Ellis (harp) / Oiseau-Lyre S–308

Tournier's concert study is a nice show-off piece and Osian Ellis shows off very well.

Féerie (Prelude et Danse)

Les Annesses grises sur la route d'El-Azib from *Images*, **Op. 35**

☐ McDonald (harp) / Klavier KS–525

Tournier was first and last a melodist, steering clear of any radical currents; the creative air he breathed was Debussian. His compositions have tidy productive habits, so that wheels within wheels do not turn in the music. As a harpist of note he produced pieces perfectly designed for the instrument. This includes the slight programmatic attempts in the "Gray Donkeys on the Road to El-Azib."

Susann McDonald plays with marvelous smoothness and with sensitive regard for the style of the music.

Les Enfants à la crèche de Noël from *Images* (Suite 2)

Six *Noëls*

☐ Remsen (harp) / Avant AV–1000

Tournier's "Children" are pictured with a good number of whole tones. The set of *Noëls* are neatly folkloric in style.

Vers la Source dans le bois

☐ McDonald (harp) / Klavier KS–525

A short (three and one-half minutes) impressionistic piece, beautifully designed for the harp's capabilities.

Toushmalov / *Mussorgsky.* *See Mussorgsky* / Toushmalov.

Joan Tower   *(1938-   )*

Breakfast Rhythms I & II for Clarinet and Five Instruments (1975)

☐ Da Capo Chamber Players / Blustine (clarinet) / Shulman (conductor) / Composers Recordings SD–354

    A fancy title that leads one to observe that while there is no cereal on the menu there is a full portion of serial. There is plenty of juice, too, in Tower's rhythms. A certain chill lyrical appeal marks the second piece.
    (The quintet consists of flute, violin, cello, piano, and percussion.)

Hexachords (1972)

☐ Spencer (flute) / Composers Recordings SD–354

    A composition based, as might be expected from its title, on a set of six pitches (an "unordered chromatic collection"). This direct and effective unaccompanied flute music uses the device of differing vibrato speeds and registral contrasts as the principal points of reference. Tower's piece has technical health and yet sounds fully spontaneous.

Prelude for Five Players (1970)

☐ Da Capo Chamber Players / Composers Recordings 302

    Tower's work (for flute, clarinet, violin, cello, and piano) is constructed from the principles and formulas of the Schoenbergian serial world. A total commitment applies, with resultant curves, twists, jumps, and abstractional affinity.
    In presenting her gospel of serial virtue Tower does not err. While the expressive essences express only dodecaphonic logic, this too has vitality.

Solo Instrument and Orchestra

Clarinet

Instrumental

Flute

Chamber Music

Giovanni Maria Trabaci   *(ca. 1575-1647)*

Toccata seconda

☐ Ellis (harp) / Oiseau-Lyre S–309

    From a set of short pieces titled Partitas, which Trabaci (or Trabachi) published in 1603. In full, the music bears an imposing title, *Toccata seconda & ligature per l'arpa*. The piece is quiet, with no imposing note-brandishing. Ellis's gentle touch is most pleasing.

Instrumental

Harp

Roy Travis   *(1922-   )*

Collage for Orchestra

☐ Royal Philharmonic Orchestra / Lipkin (conductor) / Composers Recordings S–259

Orchestra

Contemporary bits and pieces put together with sterling scholarship. There are various planes of attention, mainly leaning toward the twelve-tone area. Travis shows a keen sense of comparing sonorities without employing any shock effects. A satisfactory performance is given.

Instrumental

Flutes

Switched-On-Ashanti (1973)

☐ Shanley (flutes); Badu (African instruments); Travis (synthesizers) / Orion 73121

More West African documentation by this composer (see under *piano* [African Sonata] and *Chamber Music* [*Duo concertante*]). Lots of rhythm, plenty of ostinati, and fugitive flute lines. Most rhythmic: *Tachema-Chema* (movement 2); most polyphonic: *Sikyi* (movement 3); most rhapsodic: *Akom* (movement 1).

Travis's depiction is certainly no pale reflection of this insular data concerned with different Ashanti dances. Authentic instruments are used and the participation of Kwasi Badu, Chief Drummer at the Institute of African Studies at the University of Ghana, Legon, guarantees authenticity.

Piano

African Sonata (1966)

☐ Grayson (piano) / Orion 73121

This is no pseudo, boob-tube background-music nonsense. Travis's African Sonata is transferral from the source. *Sikyi* (movement 1) and *Adowa* (movement 4) "were suggested by Ashanti dances"; movement 2, Bambara Dance-Song, and movement 3, *Sohu*, "derive respectively from Bambara and Ewe sources."

This exploration of a new slant in regard to meaning, sonority, and musical organization is never dull, though since it covers a little over ten minutes there is a cancellation of freshness. Individual movements heard separately are much more effective.

Richard Grayson, himself a composer, interprets with ample response.

Chamber Music

Duo concertante (1967)

☐ Lateiner (violin); Grosz (piano) / Orion 73121

The individuality of the end movements cannot be denied. Part 1, *Gakpa*, and part 5, *Asafo*, are rhythmically based on creative lease from West African (Ewe) dances. Travis's material not only imitates but develops these precepts and the effect is fresh and pungent. In sharp comparison are the three inner movements (Adagio, *Allegro marcato*, and Adagio), pantonalized, salted with dissonance, and reminders of the neoclassic Stravinsky.

Clean ensemble playing and fine sensibility for the composer's intentions are to be heard.

Opera and Dramatic Music

Two Scenes from *The Passion of Oedipus* (1965)

☐ Royal Philharmonic Orchestra and Chorus / Mammen (soprano); Lehane (mezzo-soprano); Du Pré (tenor); Dunlap (baritone); Lloyd (bass); Hale (narrator) / Popper (conductor) / Orion 73129

The scenes are *Flashback: The Murder of Laios* and *Dénouement*. Travis wrote his own libretto, freely adapted from Sophocles's *Oedipus Rex*.

The musical characterizations are apt, the style tonally dissonant, well stated in the textual setting, orchestrated evocatively. The performance is impressive, apt, and confident. It is especially nice once again to hear the voice of Richard Hale. He portrays his role as the Old Shepherd superbly.

George Tremblay   *(1911-   )*

Symphony in One Movement (1949)   *Orchestra*

☐ Hamburg Symphony Orchestra / Balazs (conductor) / Composers Recordings S–224

Hybrid methodology is used in Tremblay's work. He combines twelve-tone origination with pantonality, and formally he treats his one-movement conception as a huge sonata structure, with introduction, exposition, development, and recapitulation.

Lyrical earnestness is thereby detailed with a Bergian palette. Tremblay's piece is a good one, the only representation of his work in the recorded catalogue. Someone should give attention to his fine Quartet *Modes of Transportation.*

The Hamburg organization shows some roughage, but not enough to interfere overly with recognizing the values of Tremblay's Symphony.

Harold Triggs   *(1900-   )*

The Bright Land (1942)   *String Orchestra*

☐ Eastman-Rochester Symphony Orchestra / Hanson (conductor) / Eastman-Rochester Archives ERA–1002

Folksy and tonal and modal. Singularly uninvolved, which gives it its particular charm.

Lester Trimble   *(1923-   )*

Closing Piece (1957)   *Orchestra*

☐ Imperial Philharmonic of Tokyo / Strickland (conductor) / Composers Recordings 159 (monaural)

An overture in reverse. Trimble's *Closing Piece* is harsh, dry, ascetic, propelled by quartal harmonic dictates and asymmetrical meter and phrase lengths. The orchestration is lean, jagged, and especially pungent in percussion. A fair performance is given of this music of abrasive accents, color, and contemporaneous essences.

Four Fragments from the Canterbury Tales (1958)   *Vocal*

☐ Addison (soprano); Conant (harpsichord); Russo (clarinet); Orenstein (flute) / Columbia Special Products AMS–6198

Voice and Instrumental Ensemble

Trimble's Chaucer pieces exemplify bucolic musical poetry. There is no sonorous intoxication; the instrumentation is reticent, marking the lines; a discipline of both texture and accent is displayed. The charm of this music lies precisely in the composer's avoidance of any attempt to cut capers. However, the combination of harpsichord with two winds gives sufficient timbre difference and scope for framing the vocal line. It is deliciously fitting for the fourteenth-century English, which itself is special music.

The performance of this persuasive opus is a joy. Adele Addison's diction is a delight—a creamy one.

In Praise of Diplomacy and Common Sense (1965)

☐ Ensemble of New York / Frisch (baritone) / Davies (conductor) / Composers Recordings 298

A musical kind of "March of Time," with news items depicted in the manner of a vocal newspaper. They are sometimes sung, sometimes narrated. The instrumental material, with emphasis on percussion, frames the paragraphs. Such agitprop use of music serves a good purpose, save that it usually is confined to performances avoided by the general public. The recording may increase coverage.

The piece is a smart idea and smartly presented.

Preston Trombly   (1945-   )

Instrumental

Flute

Kinetics III for Flute and Electronic Sounds (1971)

☐ Sollberger (flute) / Nonesuch 73028

A generous mating, and a successful one, of flute and tape. The latter is registered as structurally as one would expect from a woodwind, brass, or string instrument. In other words, there is no attempt at gimmicks, no opting for effects. Trombly's duet discloses an uncommonly versatile hand, and his *Kinetics III* is both fully musical and tasteful. It leaves the impression of a true talent. As usual, the playing by Harvey Sollberger is superb.

Gilbert Trythall   (1930-   )

Orchestra

Symphony No. 1

☐ Knoxville Symphony Orchestra / Van Vactor (conductor) / Composers Recordings 155 (monaural)

Gutsy music, dogmatic and forceful. The tonality is stretched, yet never loose or concerned with polarity. Hindemith will come to mind, but in no sense does this mean rank imitation. Large-scaled thoughts project this Symphony—no fusspots of midget phrases, but rather substantial paragraphs are bound into the four essays of the separate movements. The command of orchestral imagination is a special point regarding Trythall's work, especially the dark-striped third movement in *adagio* tempo.

Erik Tulindberg   (1761-1814)

Chamber Music

String Quartet No. 4

☐ Finnish String Quartet / Orion 7035

One of six Quartets covering a typical Haydn range in the writing. Accepted conventions are followed in the playing. There is up-close microphoning for the first violin.

Fisher Tull   (1934-   )

Liturgical Symphony (1960)   *Band*

☐ Los Angeles Brass Society / Remsen (conductor) / Avant 1001

Symphonic treatment (for percussion as well as brass) of themes principally derived from the liturgy of the church. A fourteenth-century plainsong, the medieval *Martyr dei,* the seventeenth-century French melody *Picardy,* a thirteenth-century Benedictine plain-song *Adoro devote,* and a twelfth-century Kyrie are among the data worked in and around Tull's bronze and golden three-movement opus. The expected modality and antiphony are utilized to excellent effect.

This rich work was included on Avant Records' initial release. It proves again that worthy repertoire, commanding performance, and A-plus sound are major distinctions often to be found on a smaller company's label. This is a stunning example.

Variations on an Advent Hymn (1962)   *Brass Ensemble*

☐ Los Angeles Philharmonic Brass Ensemble / Remsen (conductor) / Avant 1005

Fisher Tull exhibits magnificent creative marksmanship when he utilizes early church material. Here (as in his Liturgical Symphony [see under *Band*]) the eloquence is all-pervading. The theme is the plainsong *Veni Emmanuel,* the four variations displaying a mastery of vertical and horizontal device.

Remsen's group plays the work with sonorous distinction.

Exhibition   *Chamber Music*

☐ Fine Arts Brass Quintet / Wim WIMR-4

"Brass instruments on exhibition," fully explains Tull's pithy title. The Prelude and Finale are for the quintet. In between, exhibits of the horn (*Lament*), tuba (*Frolic*), trumpets (*Waltz*), and trombone (*Ballad*) are offered. These are didactic values, absolutely, but not at the expense of artistic expression. And artistic describes this music of exceptional clarity and melodiousness.

Franz Tunder   (1614-1667)

Hosianna dem Sohne David   *Cantata and Oratorio*

☐ Instrumentalists and Freiburg Student Choir / Graf (soprano); Pommerien (bass) / Knall (conductor) / Vanguard C-10045

Tunder's Christmas Cantata text is a section from the Gospel for the first Sunday in Advent, depicting Jesus's entry into Jerusalem. From the opening instrumental introduction (for strings and continuo) to the antiphonal responses of the solo voices and chorus and further to the concluding *Hosanna,* this is a music of brilliance and emotive depth. It again emphasizes that many baroque composers, little known to audiences of today, were excellent craftsmen, with ideas of more than ordinary worth. Full evidence is presented by this perfectly crafted performance. It is a joy to hear.

Bertram Turetzky   *(20th cent.)*

Percussion   ### Gamelan Music (1974)

☐ Turetzky and Graves (basses) / Finnadar 9015

Indeed in the percussion category, though the instruments used are four-string basses. The strings are struck and stimulated but they are not bowed. Turetzky indicates that the "feeling and virtuosity of the hand drumming of world music" was the basis for this unusual piece, played on two double basses by two bassists.

Joaquín Turina   *(1882 - 1949)*

Orchestra   ### Danzas fantásticas, Op. 22

☐ Paris Conservatoire Orchestra / Frühbeck de Burgos (conductor) / Angel S–36195

One of the most popular of Turina's efforts, illustrating music with an unmistakable geographic heartbeat. Though Turina was no innovator, neither was he a hard-crusted academician. Without providing a new style, these pieces offer as pure a national music as any innovation.

The dances are not "fantastic," but rather are fanciful depictions of three different moods: *Exaltación* is a moderate-tempo affair; *Ensueño* is dreamy, but for the greater part in $\frac{5}{8}$ meter (defining the Zortziko, a Basque dance rhythm which uses uneven division of each measure in a $\frac{1}{8} + \frac{2}{4}$ process); and *Orgía* is red-blooded but politely so. Quotations from the writings of José Más precede these sections but need not be read to understand the warm musical context.

The recorded performance is really good and direct, containing the proper amount of sweet-scented sensuousness that Turina pressed into his score. It is the second movement, set in quintuple meter, that upsets conductors. Frühbeck de Burgos's choice of tempo shapes this indigenous metrical plan beautifully and succinctly; in the final movement he maintains chiseled clarity even with a generous rate of motion.

The composer's transcription of the work for piano is also on disc (see under *Instrumental: piano*).

Danzas gitanas, Op. 55

☐ Louisville Orchestra / Mester (conductor) / Louisville LS–752

The "Gypsy Dances" (this is really Series I—a second set appeared as Opus 84) were originally for piano. They cover five dances, of which the last (*Sacro-monte*) is best known. (See under *Instrumental: piano* [under *Danzas fantásticas*] for the piano setting of this dance.)

Turina is not a composer of defiance, but of deduction. His gypsies are more sensual than torrid; the erotic is clothed in these melodic lines and swaying rhythms. But even in their smoldering quietness, Turina's dances reveal Hispanic facts with no hiding in technical cubbyholes.

Mester's consideration of this music is excellent. The lyrical portions are beautifully depicted and the rhythmic detail punched, but punched cleanly and with no edgy percussiveness.

La oración del torero, Op. 34

☐ Morton Gould and His Orchestra / Gould (conductor) / RCA VICS–1381

Turina's most popular chamber-music work, and thrice popular in its enlarged string-orchestra form. ''The Bullfighter's Prayer'' was originally written for, and dedicated to, the very famous members of the Aguilar family, known as the Aguilar Lute Quartet, now disbanded.

In this one-movement piece (divided into precise tempo differences), Turina draws both delicate and vivid impressions from the string-instrument family, aided by the special color of mutes, pizzicato, and *sul ponticello*. *La oración del torero* is Spanish in its swaying rhythms, but is fervent impressionism in its pictorial, symbolic curtseying. Block-columned triadic chords, producing the astringencies of ninths and elevenths, provide stylistic flavor. More than a hint of sadness permeates the work, but if there is a story depicted by the music it was never told by the composer. Turina's toreador speaks of the Spanish night more than of his afternoon's work.

The recording wins top valuation. Gould's reading is magnificent; the music is given full-scale, total-sweep playing, and all differences are emphasized in proper proportion.

Fandanguillo (1926)

Ráfaga (1930)

Soleares from *Homenaje a Tárrega* (1935)

☐ Williams (guitar) / Columbia MS–6608

Although the *Fandanguillo* title signifies a diminutive type of Fandango, Turina's dance is a full-fledged affair, with vivid contrasts, mainly in slower tempo. It is much more nostalgic (and more sinister) than a Fandango.

Soleares is an Andalusian folk-song example, its poetry heightened by pedal formations, whereas *Ráfaga* pinpoints the melancholy that permeates the *cante hondo* of Spanish music. Turina's short piece is fluid with tempo change, strongly colored by modal, plangent harmonies. Here is gypsy music in its full glory.

John Williams's interpretation of these pieces is eloquent. There is pertinent individuality without damage to the native temper of the music or its design.

Sonata for Guitar, Op. 61

☐ Almeida (guitar) / Everest 3287E (monaural)

Turina's Opus 61 has the working materials for a sonata, but is organized instead into a large suite. The technique reflects French and Spanish style, and the writing is vivid. Turina's piece bears the insignia of authoritative Spanish guitar music, magnificently designed for the instrument.

Danzas fantásticas, Op. 22	*Sanlúcar de Barrameda*, Op. 24
Sacro-monte, Op. 55, No. 5	*Zapateado*, Op. 8, No. 3

☐ de Larrocha (piano) / Musical Heritage Society MHS–1408

Like Falla, his countryman, Turina transferred an orchestral composition to the completely opposite medium of the piano, though transcriptions generally work the other way around. Thus this second setting of Turina's *Danzas fantásticas,* which bears the same opus number as the first (see under *Orchestra*). In her conception Alicia de Larrocha opts for the opposite of the colorful orchestral gutsiness of the original, using poetic depiction to create a distinctive musical signature. Certainly this is just as propitious, save as a result the middle dance, being played far too slowly, loses its quintuple-metered sway. The *rubati,* however, are a joy to follow in this dance as well as the others.

Sacro-monte is from the first of two sets of *Danzas gitanas* (five in each) and is the best known of the ten-part cycle. Its striking format has led to a number of transcriptions for orchestra (see under *Orchestra*), guitar, and harp.

De Larrocha is both subtle and rhythmically vibrant in her depiction of *Sacro-monte.* Translated, the title means "Sacred Mountain," but in de Larrocha's transmittal the frictioned bite and wild surge of the rhythms make it what it is meant to be, an irreverant dance scene.

Opus 24 is described as a *Sonata pintoresca* ("Pictorial Sonata"). It consists of four movements: *En la torre del castillo* ("In the Tower of the Citadel"), *Siluetas de la calzada* ("Portrait of a Woman in Shoes"), *La playa* ("The Seacoast"), and *Los pescadores in Bajo de Guía* ("The Fishermen in Bajo de Guía"). Despite its length (twenty-one minutes) the matter of development is minimal, the concept is one of enlarged miniatures, though fugal method is used to describe "The Fishermen." No sweat—the music reveals sound nationalistic facts stated with complete clarity. De Larrocha sets her compass points perfectly and is a most persuasive exponent for these pieces, or Sonata, if you will.

The remaining work on the program is the last of a set of Three Andalusian Dances. Here again the performance command is eloquent.

Chamber Music

Trio No. 1 for Violin, Cello, and Piano, Op. 35

☐ Heifetz (violin); Piatigorsky (cello); Pennario (piano) / RCA LSC-2957

The first of the two Trios Turina composed uses three forms defined by subtitles. The third part is called a Sonata but is fairly free and has rondolike overtones. It is Iberian in tone, in the sense of deploying shifting accentuations that move the measures from duple to triple pulse totals in free alternation. At its close, a cyclic reference to the opening movement serves as a peroration, but has little affinity to the mood and purposes of the final movement itself.

The opening Prelude and Fugue is unstaid, as free as possible of scholastic discipline, as left of center as possible in regard to such formal title. Movement 2 consists of variations.

This is a rewarding work; it was given the prize in the competition held by the National de l'Estat Espagnol in 1926.

Vocal

Voice with Accompaniment

Farruca from *Triptico* (1929)

☐ de los Angeles (soprano); Soriano (piano) / Angel S-35775

An illustration of Turina in his modest folkloric demeanor. But this does not signify timidity. The profile of Spanish song is quite clear in this case; the composer permits it to be so.

The performance is a model of artistic collaboration.

Francesco Turini   *(1595-1656)*

Chamber Music

Trio Sonata

☐ Members of New York Pro Musica / MCA 2514

Variations comprise the total work—a set on a tune titled *Tanto tempo hormai.* Sweet action, played sweetly and surely.

Charles Turner (1921-)

Serenade for Icarus (1960)

☐ Kroll (violin); Johannesen (piano) / Golden Crest S–4072

Somewhat of a programmatic framework is indicated for Turner's three-part work, since its composition was "suggested by the myth of Icarus," according to the unsigned liner note. However, romantic breadth and fullness surround the duo and the story line is hardly apparent. Little matter, since the music flows from the instruments with warm expressivity and has telling chamber-music charm. It is sensitively played.

Paul Turok (1929-)

Lyric Variations for Oboe and Strings, Op. 32

☐ Louisville Orchestra / McAninch (oboe) / Mester (conductor) / Louisville 733

Turok's formal structure is compact despite the problem of sectionalism that always rears its head in variational depiction. The work is sober, neoclassically classified, its style to the left of Hindemith.

Daniel McAninch is a skillful oboist. The Louisville Orchestra is considered a skillful aggregation. Here, the intonation of its strings does not live up to that description.

Little Suite, Op. 9

Passacaglia, Op. 10

Three Transcendental Etudes, Op. 30

☐ Benoit (piano) / Orion 7274

Impressionistic programmaticism surrounds the Opus 30. *Gray Clouds* is a "Fantasia on a Piece by Liszt"; Turok not only includes the original Liszt piece (*Nuages gris*) but combines his own material with it. *The Bells of Arcos* has tintinnabulative substances that are most arresting. More abstract, but just as interlaced with colorful percussive detail, is *La Rose de France*. These are not run-of-the-mill piano pieces; they require top technique. Regis Benoit supplies it to the full.

Turok's Opus 10 is a compact affair (four minutes in performance time). It is clear in its form and it is performed with excellent attention to its lyrical breadth and depth.

The Little Suite covers three aspects in a bit over five minutes: a Prelude with pace, an Arabesque that twists with trills, and a Toccata that touches the pitch bases with both moderate speed and pointed step. Benoit supplies faithful playing of this interesting and worthy music.

U

Floro M. Ugarte   (1884-1975)

Prelude in G minor   *Instrumental*

☐ Calligaris (piano) / Orion 7286   *Piano*

Despite the key heading, most of Ugarte's Chopin-like piece is in a major tonality. The Prelude is a representative example of this Argentinian composer's work.

Chinary Ung   (1942-   )

Mohori (1974)   *Vocal*

☐ Contemporary Chamber Ensemble / Martin (soprano) / Weisberg (conductor) / Composers Recordings SD-363

Voice and Instrumental Ensemble

The title is a Khmer term for the chamber orchestra of the royal palace and also refers to a legendary bird in traditional Khmer folksong.

Khmer phonetics are used in place of words; such vocal interjections are hung onto a variety of instrumental snips of phrase, which thereby match the fractional lengths of the voice part. The sense of the work is atmospheric impressionism, emphasizing the fact that all the scintillating colors seem derived from a single source. Indeed, in Ung's score, voice and seven instruments become one.

The musicians are superb; Barbara Martin is extraordinary.

Vladimir Ussachevsky   (1911-   )

Creation (Prologue) (1961)   *Choral*

☐ Little Chorus of Macalester College, St. Paul, Minnesota / Morton (conductor) / Columbia MS-6566

Chorus with Accompaniment

In a few instances the vocal range has been enlarged by tape manipulation techniques. The accompaniment is almost entirely electronic in origin and includes a short section produced on the synthesizer. The possibilities of a choral group joined to tape accompaniment offers much to a composer. In this instance the electronic material is very minimal and light in content, but sufficient for subtle color and textural punctuation.

Electronic Music

A Piece for Tape Recorder (1955)

☐ Finnadar 9010

The first release of this piece (be on the watch for some keyboard passages that lighten the atmosphere) was on CRI 112, in a monophonic version (still available). The Finnadar is a quadrophonic release and is naturally of greater depth and breadth, though not too much difference follows. The materials in A Piece are derived from a gong, piano, timpano, cymbal, organ, a switch click, and four oscillators. The result is interesting, even for nonaficionados of electronic music.

Computer Piece No. 1 (1968)

☐ Composers Recordings 268

Timbral material exemplifying (according to the liner notes) "computer-generated and computer-processed sound materials, modified and assembled according to the usual methods employed in an electronic music studio."

Supertrained ears may find subtle differences because of the computerization. This listener caught a sense of tripartite structuring in the piece.

Of Wood and Brass (1965)

☐ Composers Recordings S-227

Made from "wood and brass," but save for one xylophonic section the piece is hardly to be recognized as sounds derived from a trombone, trumpet, xylophone, and Korean gong. The timbral changes and modifications produce a fascinating transmutation.

Though correctly titled on the jacket, on the label the opus is called Piece for Tape Recorder, which of course it is not. That title concerns an entirely different work (*see above*).

Sonic Contours (1951)

☐ Desto 6466

The resource of piano sounds is the basis of *Sonic Contours*. Additional material is drawn from the use of human voices (briefly heard before the concluding portion of the work). Ussachevsky's reconstruction of piano timbre turns it into a keyboarded gong, among other things. *Sonic Contours* is a fascinating multiworld of provocative, penetrating, and tantalizing sounds.

Two Sketches for a Computer Piece (1971)

☐ Composers Recordings 268

A sense of violence is contained in Ussachevsky's work. This is obtained from special emphasis on pitch peripatetics and sharp rhythmic functioning.

Wireless Fantasy (1960)

☐ Composers Recordings S-227

The sources for the work are wireless code signals. These include a call to stand by for a message, and designations for such as "Waldorf-Astoria Station," "end of message," "good night," and so on. An excerpt from *Parsifal* is wound in, "electronically treated to resemble a short-wave transmission," since the wireless pioneer Lee De Forrest used Wagner's composition "as the first ever to be broadcast anywhere."

Those who understand the Morse code will doubly enjoy tracking down the abbreviations in the music. It is not enjoyable to note CRI's listing the piece as above on their jacket copy, but on the record label as *Short Wave Fantasy*. The latter is incorrect.

Ussachevsky and Otto Luening. *See Luening and Ussachevsky.*

Francesco Antonio Baltassare Uttini (1723-1795)

Overture to *Il re pastore*   *Orchestra*

☐ Chamber Orchestra of the Drottningholm Theatre / Björlin (conductor) / Nonesuch 71213

An exhilarating and resonant rendition of this fine Overture, set in the usual ternary-divisioned design of Italian opera overtures.

Entries on composers whose surnames are preceded by the particle van *or* von *are arranged in alphabetical order of the surnames; however, entries on composers generally known by prefixed names (such as* Van Delden *and* Van Hemel*) are alphabetized according to common usage.*

Moisei Vainberg (1919-   )

Concerto in B flat major for Trumpet and Orchestra, Op. 95

Solo Instrument and Orchestra

Trumpet

☐ Bolshoi Theater Orchestra / Dokschitser (trumpet) / Žuraitis (conductor) / Melodiya/Angel S–40149

Motoric maneuvers mark the opening Etude with the snideness of the early Prokofiev, the grotesque slant of the young Shostakovich, and the rhythmic vehemence of Honegger. The *Episode* represents the slow movement—term it Russian *Weltschmerz*. But it is the final *Fanfare* that is a little pearl of humor, based on a variety of fanfarelike calls and a theme that *almost* quotes Mendelssohn's "Wedding March" and *does* quote the trumpet announcement in Rimsky-Korsakov's *Coq d'or*. The best moments are the thumb-to-the-nose imitative dialogues between the trumpet and the percussion.

The orchestra sounds as if it likes what it's doing; the soloist goes all out. He's very good. Actually, he's marvelous.

Lex Van Delden. *See Delden.*

Jan Křtitel Vanhal. *See Johann Baptist Wanhal.*

Oscar Van Hemel (1892-   )

Clarinet Quintet (1958)

Chamber Music

☐ Netherlands String Quartet / D'hondt (clarinet) / Donemus Audio-Visual Series DAVS-6204 (monaural: 10-inch disc)

Van Hemel's Quintet is tonal music, but it borrows some of the serialist's preoccupation with contrapuntal devices. Thus thematic material is inverted, combined with itself in reverse. Everything remains clear if exciting only intellectually, especially the final set of variations.

Bertus Van Lier (1906-1972)

Instrumental

Piano

Sonatina No. 2

☐ Henkemans (piano) / Donemus Audio-Visual Series DAVS–6204 (monaural: 10-inch disc)

A pithy project of six-minute length, Van Lier's piano piece has the golden glow of important creativity. Especially convincing is the middle movement, rising from an extremely soft level to a violent fortissimo. The latter is emphasized by the chiseled use of diminished octaves and minor ninths.

The work is brilliantly performed. Even with harmonic frictions, Henkemans keeps the sound clear and musical.

Vocal

Voice and Instrumental Ensemble

Three Ancient Persian Quatrains (1956)

☐ Spoorenberg (soprano); van Royen (alto flute); Stotijn (oboe d'amore); Ponse (piano) / Donemus Audio-Visual Series DAVS–6204 (monaural: 10-inch disc)

Exceedingly somber, exceedingly dark-toned, these pieces have special color, however: alto flute and oboe d'amore, the former representing, in an instrumental background dialogue, the voice of a shepherd, the latter that of a soul.

Willem Van Otterloo. See Otterloo.

David Van Vactor (1906-   )

Orchestra

Fantasia, Chaconne, and Allegro (1956)

☐ Louisville Orchestra / Whitney (conductor) / Louisville 58–6 (monaural)

The panchromatic contents suggest tone-row packaging (a fourteen-pitch row is used, with one pitch used three times), but Van Vactor's music is bundled differently. Even though it draws on the technical account of dodecaphonicism (row permutations, segmentation, inversion, retrograde, augmentation, and diminution), different profits result. These produce a tonal polarity strongly evident in its pivoting, spread, and return. Everything is quite efficient, including the Louisville presentation.

Overture to a Comedy No. 2 (1941)

☐ Hessian Symphony Orchestra / Van Vactor (conductor) / Everest 3236

The Overture begins as though an Americanized *Colas Breugnon* were in the making. However, the music shifts gears and becomes quite serious in the central portion.

Symphony No. 1 (1937)

☐ Frankfurt Radio Symphony Orchestra / Van Vactor (conductor) / Composers Recordings S–225

Van Vactor's work received the New York Philharmonic Symphony prize in 1939. Sharp contrasts abound, some shifting the style as well. Most of the melodic lines stem from Hindemith. Fair orchestra.

Variazione Solenne for Orchestra (1942)

☐ Hessian Symphony Orchestra / Van Vactor (conductor) / Everest 3236

Technical integrity is placed at the service of formal definitiveness. Variational clarity is Van Vactor's objective. Accordingly, an exact compartment holds each section. The work is a little academic but that never hurt anyone. It is well-played, though the sound has a restricted range.

Bagatelles for Strings (1938)

*String
Orchestra*

☐ Hessian Symphony Orchestra / Van Vactor (conductor) / Everest 3236

Three from a set of five are recorded in this case. The first two academically pursue the forms Van Vactor chose. The third item is bolder—a neoclassic "run-out" with Mozartean élan.

Quintet for Flute, Two Violins, Viola, and Cello (1932)

*Chamber
Music*

☐ Everest 3236

Clarity, directness, and a retention of style are to be noted. The harmonic language is conservative, but it is laced with some vernacularisms; the forms used are clear and traditional.

The work is noted on the disc's label and elsewhere in the album for flute and "strings." This is ambiguous since it implies multiple players and not a single representative for each instrument. (No credits are given by Everest.)

Octet for Brass (1963)

☐ Members of the Hessian Symphony Orchestra / Everest 3236

This short, three-movement suite covers a little over five minutes. The writing is tightly neat, though a certain textural similarity is apparent. Unless the instrumental totalities differ, the monochrome quality inherent in a brass ensemble can be deadly. Van Vactor comes in just under the wire.

Charles G. Vardell, Jr. *(1893-1962)*

Joe Clark Steps Out

Orchestra

☐ Eastman-Rochester Symphony Orchestra / Hanson (conductor) / Eastman-Rochester Archives ERA-1012

This is the old dance tune *Old Joe Clark* dressed up but, sensibly, not with orchestrational overkill. It is played fully in the groove.

Edgard (Edgar) Varèse   (1883 - 1965)

Orchestra

Amériques (1922)

☐ Utah Symphony Orchestra / Abravanel (conductor) / Vanguard S–308
☐ New York Philharmonic / Boulez (conductor) / Columbia M–34552

Melodic subjects (in the general meaning of the term) are not to be found. Motival play, shifting incessantly, forms the thematic substances. These are shaped by rhythmic ingredients rather than by pitch differences; the latter are the subsidiary punctuations of the former. Harmony is conceived as sound masses. In their selection and spatial settings they provide the concepts of passivity and activity or (the obverse) of tension and release—both are subtle and direct. Contrapuntal discipline is obtained by violent contrasts of color and dynamic thrust or release. To match these components the rhythms are explosive, nervous, and naturally asymmetrical. *Amériques* contains no sentiment, no emotional elegance. Its magnificent organization produces a music of sheer power—remorseless and overwhelming.

This is a hideously difficult score to manage properly. The forces are truly gargantuan, with twenty different woodwinds, twenty-one assorted brass, two harps, strings, *and* ten percussionists using twenty-one different instruments. Maurice Abravanel truly scores a triumph controlling and balancing Varèse's sonorous mass of organized sound shapes. It represents one of his greatest triumphs and also defines the Utah musicians as having major-league distinction. (*Amériques* is coupled with Varèse's *Nocturnal* on this release. On Vanguard's S–274 it is accompanied by music by Milhaud and Honegger.)

The Boulez-directed edition is a very close second, being placed in that slot only because he occasionally opts to block a section rather than embrace the score's continual reality. Columbia's sound cannot be questioned, however. It is truly magnificent.

Arcana (1927)

☐ New York Philharmonic / Boulez (conductor) / Columbia M–34552
☐ Columbia Symphony Orchestra / Craft (conductor) / Columbia MS–6362

Requiring an orchestra of 120 musicians (including eight percussionists playing forty instruments), *Arcana* beautifully assails the aural senses. Its fundament is an eleven-note phrase that contracts and expands, explodes and concusses; the total formation is equivalent to exposition, expansion, and further development. Its brilliant brutality is an urban rite that occasionally brings Stravinsky's "Rite" to mind. The dynamic thrusts of Varèse's sound shots are, however, more tense and are encased in steel.

Unfortunately, the excellent Chicago Symphony Orchestra recording with Jean Martinon conducting (on Victor LSC–2914) is no longer in the catalogue. A representation is available with Zubin Mehta conducting the Los Angeles Philharmonic (on London 6752). It has fine sound but the larger points of the piece do not surface, especially and most importantly, their high tension.

There is a great deal of struggle in *Arcana*, but it is sublimated in the sonorous searchings that Varèse produced. In that respect Boulez's production is a triumph. The timbres and textures sound their strengths to the fullest requirements yet the score has a balance that is a tour de force of conducting organization. Every crucial episode is defined and every significant detail is clear. A triumph absolutely.

In comparison, the sense of actual performance struggle one hears in Craft's recording is not the best of situations. However, tensility is present and that is all to the good and makes Craft's realization the choice over Mehta's. (Craft's performance is also contained on Columbia MG–31078.)

Déserts (1954)

☐ Paris Instrumental Ensemble for Contemporary Music / Simonovitch (conductor) / Angel S–36786

This is probably one of the very earliest, if not the first, work to combine electronically organized sound with instruments. *Déserts* has an orchestra without strings, oboes, and bassoons, but including the rest plus plentiful percussion (five players are required). This orchestral combination has set into it three tape interpolations.

Déserts is sound that breathes desolation, here and there interrupted by concentrated, frenzied cries. It is a music that even in its higher dynamic levels is filamented. To break these by improper balances is disastrous. Especially the hinging processes and the use of doublings require the most sensitive direction. The strength of Konstantin Simonovitch's conception is obvious and his *Déserts* version is the best of the several available in the catalogue.

(Angel pulled a boner in its production. S–36786 is an all-Varèse program. However, the inner leaflet that serves to give the usual program notes has a large blow-up of a picture of Luigi Dallapiccola on page 1!)

Hyperprism (1923)

☐ Paris Instrumental Ensemble for Contemporary Music / Simonovitch (conductor) / Angel S–36786

With nine melodic and eighteen percussion instruments (including a siren) Varèse aims to describe (purely in abstract terms) the elusiveness of the Fourth Dimension. Thus athematicism prevails and the sound masses constantly change their shape and intensity.

The performance is brittle and sharply cut. That fits Varèse's score.

Intégrales (1925)

☐ Contemporary Chamber Ensemble / Weisberg (conductor) / Nonesuch 71269

In this opus Varèse combines a percussion assemblage of eight metal, four membrane, and three wood instruments, a string drum (sometimes called a lion's roar), and a rute (a birch brush) with an extremely colorful assortment of melodic instruments. These include a pair of piccolos, high and normal-range clarinets, oboe, horn, two very high trumpets, and high, low, and very low trombones. Thus a duple stream of sound is set into motion, forming its own special design in which tensility is of major importance—ejaculatory portions of cutting timbres mix with bare, overpowering silences, and sonic weights are varied, forming manifold patterns within patterns.

A fantastic mastery of working materials and stylistic unity is displayed. Beauty is here as well—a beauty of cold instrumental logic that burns the ears with its magical diapason. Verily, strong music by a strong composer.

Credit to Weisberg for the strongest performance on record (with double meaning, for it is the very best this writer has ever heard, live or recorded). He has fully overcome the problem that marks all the other recorded editions (Simonovitch on Angel S–36786, Mehta on London 6752, Craft on Columbia MG–31078, and Cerha on Candide 31028), namely, fractured structure. The sound angles, sound indentions, rhythmic units, punctuations, overlayed frictions, and line projections are fully maintained and yet meshed into an entity. Under Arthur Weisberg's direction one perceives the entire exciting image, which is not the case in the other presentations.

Octandre (1923)

☐ Contemporary Chamber Ensemble / Weisberg (conductor) / Nonesuch 71269

A rare musical title (a flower with eight stamens) denotes a rare piece for the medium of chamber orchestra. Although eight players equal an octet, *Octandre* demands a conductor and thus belongs in the category to which it has been assigned. The brutal explosiveness of its sound would also exclude it from the chamber music category.

The timbres are allied in family name only: flute (also piccolo), oboe, clarinet (at times the small E flat type), and bassoon (winds) are combined with a brass group of horn, trumpet, and trombone, plus the stringed bass. There are three movements, but no suite design is implied. This is Varèse, and the old formal categories do not apply; what we hear are streams of polyphony making eight sides of a musical edifice.

The playing is of knife-chiseled exactness. Weisberg maintains the pace, thereby adding outward power to the movement of the grapneled strands of sound.

Percussion

Ionisation (1931)

☐ New Jersey Percussion Ensemble / DesRoches (conductor) / Nonesuch 71291
☐ Ensemble "Die Reihe" / Cerha (conductor) / Candide 31028
☐ Slonimsky (conductor) / Orion 7150 (monaural)

Varèse's achievement is unique, particularly because he traces and presents the elements of musical architecture with percussion and does not rely exclusively on his pitched instruments (chimes, sirens, celesta, and piano) for the melodic representation or on the unpitched instruments (constituents of metal, membrane, and wood, plus rasping, swishing, and roaring qualities) for rhythm. The tutti, as a unit and as separate members, perform in defined elucidations—harmonic, contrapuntal, and melodic—within the formal design. They function in a way akin to that of the violent adjectives, verbs, and phrases found on a Picasso canvas.

For percussion players this work holds a place comparable to that of the Beethoven Concerto for violinists; the word "famous" is most fitting. It is not surprising, therefore, that seven recorded performances are available. (For the sake of the record this statistic should be amplified to indicate that four versions preceded these, all now in the deleted category.)

Varèse was meticulous in his markings and tempo indications. These are not followed in the fast settings conducted by Zubin Mehta and Robert Craft. As an example, Craft turns out the work in 4:50, to be compared with Cerha's reading (5:24) and the New Jersey entry (5:20). These are much closer to the definitive timing realized by Slonimsky, which is 5:45. The most clarified performances are on the Nonesuch and Candide labels. Both have the stabilities and the clear sonic perspectives stated in Varèse's score.

The inclusion of the Slonimsky recording is solely because of historic importance. The sound is supremely old-fashioned, and the balances are blurred in many places. However, it represents documentation for all those interested in Varèse. *Ionisation* was completed on November 13, 1931. Slonimsky gave the premiere on March 6, 1933. The following year he made the first recording for Columbia. It is that recording one hears in transfer on the Orion label, in an album titled "History Making Premieres." It took guts and bulldog courage to play Varèse in those days, let alone find a way of recording his music. To have a duplicate of the initial recording is a memento worth owning.

Instrumental

Flute

Density 21.5 (1912)

☐ Sollberger (flute) / Nonesuch 73028

This work bears the champion of all music titles. It is explained by the fact that Varèse wrote this piece for the famous Georges Barrère, who was planning to introduce a new platinum flute. The density of platinum is the quantity given in the title.

Density 21.5 demands a flutist who can obey and convey the minute, ultra-refined markings that detail the homophonic line, in this manner projecting the unstated harmony and also the undulating colors in the various zones of the instrument's three-octave range. The shifts of dynamic are kaleidoscopic and occur at a dizzying pace: for example, sounds of one beat louden and immediately return to a very soft pitch, only to rise once again quickly to a still louder point. Further, in certain measures the flutist is to articulate sharply, play softly, and hit the keys of his instrument to produce a quasi-percussive effect with the pitched sound.

To meet all these demands and present them within gorgeous artistry and top-flight music-making, Harvey Sollberger is your man.

Offrandes (1921)

☐ Contemporary Chamber Ensemble / DeGaetani (mezzo-soprano) / Weisberg (conductor) / Nonesuch 71269

Though the patent Varèsian sound cultures are used and though there is the usual intense attention to the percussion family, *Offrandes* has a lyricism that soars through its measures. It marks a Varèse different from the one who wrote *Arcana, Amériques,* and *Ionisation.* This is not a less creative voice, merely one that does glance back ever so slightly to the traditionalism of the Debussy school.

It is difficult to think of any other vocalist who could carry off the difficult part Varèse has furnished as well as Jan DeGaetani, certainly not those represented in the competitive performances (on Columbia [MS-6362 and MG-31078] and Candide [31028]). For that matter, none of the chamber orchestra groups involved in these performances come close to the ideal reading Weisberg furnishes.

Ecuatorial (1934)

☐ Contemporary Chamber Ensemble / Paul (bass) / Weisberg (conductor) / Nonesuch 71269

Varèse wanted his work—based on a text taken from the *Popul Vuh,* the sacred book of the Maya Quiché—to portray an "elemental rude intensity." The instrumental configurations he chose fully provide such stimulation. There is roughage from the use of fifteen percussion instruments, together with timbre opulence and gutsy strength from four trumpets and four trombones, plus massivity supplied by organ and piano. In addition, two ondes Martenot are like extraterrestrial swooning voices that sharply contrast with the bass voice.

Regardless of the score, it was Varèse's desire to have only a single voice used in performance. There is no doubt that pitch and textual fidelity are best served in that manner, and the fine demonstration by Thomas Paul proves that point. On the other hand, Abravanel's use of a bass voice ensemble in his rendition on Vanguard C-10047 denies the incantatory aspect of the text. The poetic fervor is blurred instead of being pointed.

Varèse said the execution of *Ecuatorial* "should be dramatic." Weisberg's direction achieves this vividly.

Nocturnal (1961)

☐ Utah Symphony Orchestra and Bass Ensemble of the University-Civic Chorale / Bybee (soprano) / Abravanel (conductor) / Vanguard S-308

This is Varèse's final composition, edited and completed from his notes and sketches by Chou Wen-chung. The text includes phrases from the *House of Incest* by Anaïs Nin

Vocal

Voice and Instrumental Ensemble

Choral

Chorus and Orchestra

1957

and syllabic formations by Varèse (two examples: "a-oo-oo-hm," and "va-ga-ra-ba-boo").

The pure qualities of sound structured into a fantasy of hard-core, nightmarish impressionism surround and are imbedded in the piece. Abravanel provides a clear and distinct translation of the score; the singing is intelligent and is presented with stylistic musicality.

(Here, *Nocturnal* is coupled with Varèse's *Amériques*. On C–10047 it is paired with Varèse's *Ecuatorial*.)

Electronic Music

Poème électronique (1958)

☐ Columbia MS-6146

When a master works in a special medium, experimentation ceases and artistry takes over. The effect of sounds and timbres in various combinations in unbound pulse and with heated as well as chilling registrations is thrilling and exciting. Varèse, the master, has produced a master work in his *Poème*.

The work was "created directly on magnetic tape by the composer for the Brussels World's Fair, 1958," where it was heard through four hundred loudspeakers distributed through the pavilion which Le Corbusier had designed for the Philips Radio Corporation. In addition, images (photographs, paintings, printed scripts, etc.) were projected as chosen by the architect. No attempt for synchronization between sight and sound was attempted. According to Columbia's liner notes, some 15–16,000 people daily viewed the pavilion and heard the partnered music over a period of six months. There is no doubt that this sets a world record for hearing an electronic composition that will never be equaled in the history of man!

Aside from the purposeful nonsynchronization (and perhaps because of it) Varèse's piece stands firmly as music by itself. There is a female voice heard toward the end of the work that adds a further dimension to Varèse's masterpiece.

Sergei Vassilenko (1872-1956)

Solo Instrument and Orchestra

Suite for Balalaika (1945)

☐ Ukrainian Radio Orchestra of Folk Instruments / Blinov (balalaika) / Khivrich (conductor) / Monitor S-2074E (monaural)

Balalaika

Vassilenko's opus is music of sweet harmoniousness with folk-invested contours. It is in three connected movements, the middle one light and balletic. The scoring shows care for the solo instrument's special timbre and its somewhat delicate weight. The recorded performance maintains this exactitude.

Ralph Vaughan Williams (1872-1958)

Orchestra

Fantasia on Greensleeves (1934)

☐ Philadelphia Orchestra / Ormandy (conductor) / Columbia MS-6224
☐ London Symphony Orchestra / Boult (conductor) / Angel S-36799

The enchanting melody of *Greensleeves* stems from the latter part of the sixteenth century (it was then known as "A New Northern Dittye"). Transcribed in multitudinous ways, it remains one of the enchanting tunes of all time.

Vaughan Williams used the song in his Falstaffian opera *Sir John in Love,* contrasting it with another folk tune, *Lovely Joan.* For concert purposes the version used in an adaptation for string orchestra, harp, plus two flutes.

Plenty, but plenty of recordings from which to choose, and most are reliable. However, Ormandy is the very best of the best. No one can match the magnificent sheen and depth of the Philadelphia strings. Boult opts for a leaner sound, tending toward a large chamber music condition.

Another package contains Boult's presentation (Angel S-36902). Ormandy's conception is also available on three other Columbia collections—MS-6575, MS-6934, and MS-7103.

In the Fen Country (Symphonic Impression) (1904)

☐ New Philharmonia Orchestra / Boult (conductor) / Angel S-36532

This music illustrates the composer's affinity for the pastoral mnemonic. The performance is entrancing, quietly radiant. It is also included in another Angel release of V.W.'s music (No. S-36902).

A London Symphony (Symphony No. 2) (1920)

☐ Hallé Orchestra / Barbirolli (conductor) / Angel S-36478

Vaughan Williams did not write a systematic program Symphony in this case, but the work is picturesque—thus the misty beginning, the fog of the introduction, the Big Ben chimes at start and finish of the composition, the use of "Sweet Lavender" and the hansom cab jingles in the second movement, the mouth organ imitation in the *Nocturne,* and the plodding march of the final section. Folk phrases that twine their way through the measures are added identification.

The composer has asked that we listen to his conception as pure music, as a "Symphony by a Londoner." However, a title gives an auditor's viewpoint more than a philosophical pinch. Let us call V.W.'s musical spades what they are—a picture of a great city framed in symphonic form.

Let us call Barbirolli's the best recording ever made of this fine work. The materials of the beginning, so important for setting the scene, are probed to bring out every essential without disturbing the continuity; the colorations that are fed into the Scherzo-Nocturne are pointed and telling in their depiction; the finale has never sounded with such expressivity. This is a commanding performance, one of Barbirolli's best.

Norfolk Rhapsody No. 1 in E minor (1906)

☐ New Philharmonia Orchestra / Boult (conductor) / Angel S-36557

The employment of folk tunes within this score is only one part of the composition's enchantment. The beauties of its modal harmonies and its orchestrational pigments give rise to images of dawn: grayness melting into color, half light to full radiance, dawn to day. It is an abstraction of nature, conveyed by song. In a conception swept by tender emotions Vaughan Williams has written a miniature "pastoral symphony."

The playing is eloquent, the solos of the clarinetist exceedingly sensitive.

Pastoral Symphony (Symphony No. 3) (1920)

☐ London Symphony Orchestra / Previn (conductor) / RCA LSC-3280

There are no scenic impressions, no babbling brooks, no maypole dances, not even some distant thunder to break the spell of this introspective poetic work which suggests an impressionistic essay. Impressionism, however, is broadly defined as being of pictorial origin, musically suggested by way of individualization of instrumental colors. In the Pastoral Symphony Vaughan Williams is only parenthetically an impressionist. The countryside is his inspiration, it does not give rise to coloristic imagism. The work is intensely fluidic; no thrusting dynamic blobs interrupt the contemplative flow. Even the fastest movement (the third, marked *moderato pesante*) is simply activized meditation. Emphasis takes place by direct de-emphasis.

No music has better illustrated the enchantment and spiritual depth of rural England. Tovey described the Symphony as of "massive quietness." It is also of radiant stillness.

The performance is acutely principled by these factors. It is subtle and therefore strong; it is quietly colored so it registers with depth of feeling.

Sinfonia Antartica (Symphony No. 7) (1952)

☐ London Symphony Orchestra and Ambrosian Singers / Harper (soprano); Richardson (speaker) / Previn (conductor) / RCA LSC–3066

Huge in proportion (five movements and close to three quarters of an hour in performance time); immersed in color (including a wind machine and organ, both of which are integrated with balanced consideration in this fine portrayal), amplified by vocal instrumentation (a solo soprano and a chorus of female voices, none using words), the *Sinfonia Antartica* is somewhat absolute and mostly programmatic music. Not only the quotations that preface each movement (declaimed with dignity by Sir Ralph Richardson) but also the graphic orchestral painting of frigid temperatures, loneliness, icy landscapes, and bleakness place the *Antartica* in the descriptive category.

Previn's pace is expertly chosen, and he obtains full descriptive response from his musicians. This, of all of Vaughan Williams's Symphonies, has been the least convincing. With Previn's portrayal as example and stimulus this situation should well change.

Symphony No. 4 in F minor (1935)

☐ London Symphony Orchestra / Previn (conductor) / RCA LSC–3178

Vaughan Williams's fourth Symphony is built from a few motives, linked thematically and bound cyclically. It is dark and brooding music; in its undisclosed stimuli there are tragic-torn elements.

Triadic language marked Vaughan Williams's first three Symphonies. The fourth does not eliminate the common chord, but it makes the secundal stringency just as common in the musical syntax. From the beginning, the impact and bite of sound are relentless, especially in the Scherzo, a *danse macabre* moving with explosive bluntness. And the fever does not subside in the contrapuntal cast of the final section. In this Berliozian panorama Vaughan Williams conceived a new kind of Symphony, without casting off formal compatibility.

Previn understands and underlines every iota of the violence, brutality, and anger of the piece. Other editions that are available are much more chaste. A close competitor is the old Dimitri Mitropoulos version (issued in the mid-1950s), with the New York Philharmonic. It is still available in its mono setting on Columbia Special Products CML–5158. It is tautly drawn, excitingly dynamic, but lacking the sonorous advantages of a recording issued two decades later.

Symphony No. 5 in D major (1943)

☐ Philharmonia Orchestra / Barbirolli (conductor) / Angel S–35952

Notwithstanding the pertinent designations of a *Preludio,* Scherzo, *Romanza,* and Passacaglia, Vaughan Williams's opus has the feeling of a *sinfonia sacra.* It also has some affinity with his third ("Pastoral") Symphony. The difference is that the D major composition is less vernal and much more meditative.

The dynamic plan of the music is never convulsive; the loud planes of sonority avoid instrumental turbulence. Most of the Symphony is quiet; the speediest movement (the Scherzo) floats mainly in a *piano* atmosphere. The rhythms are placid and portend neither anxiety nor anger as they move with fundamental order. The temperament of this music is that of a choral Symphony without chorus.

Barbirolli's long association with this piece (he made the initial recording during the 78-rpm era) shows in a reading that captures every nuance of Vaughan Williams's lyrical blend.

Symphony No. 6 in E minor (1948)

☐ New Philharmonia Orchestra / Boult (conductor) / Angel S-36469

Eloquent grimness describes the sixth Symphony, a blood relative of the fourth. There is little peaceful suavity; the music has an almost hard core. Although a total unit (one movement moves into the next without pause), the four main sections are clearly apportioned. Toccata energy fuels the opening part. A sinister second movement is conditioned by a rhythmic figure that rides herd on the music; the pattern is never resolved and forms an overwhelming and terrifying ostinato. The Scherzo that follows is no musical joke but unremitting, jagged music, monitored by fugal controls. All of these white-heated arguments are in severe contrast to the suspended tautness of the finale. The claustrophobic quality of this part is truly frightening. For some twelve-and-a-half minutes (106 measures all in $\frac{4}{4}$ meter save for a single exception) the orchestra plays under wraps—*sempre pianissimo e senza crescendo.* This pitiless, unyielding dynamic desolation is unique in symphonic literature and is more crushing in effect than virtuosic orchestration. Despite the hazards of musical crystal ball-gazing, one can prophesy everlasting life for Vaughan Williams's sixth Symphony.

Boult has this work in his blood. I cannot emphasize the superb quality of his performance—it outdistances the several I have heard in the concert hall and the others that have been recorded (Stokowski on Columbia 4214 [in the deleted category] and Previn on RCA LSC-3114). Boult's conception of the goosefleshy Epilogue is a masterpiece of conducting insight.

Symphony No. 8 in D minor (1956)

☐ London Philharmonic Orchestra / Boult (conductor) / Angel S-36625

Perpetual invention marks Vaughan Williams's Symphonies. No two are exactly alike, in mood or character, form or color. In this essay symphonic design is revamped into a huge suite scored for divisible orchestral components.

A *Fantasia* subtitled "Variazioni senza Tema" opens matters. These variants "without a theme" (incidentally, a title used in 1922 by Malipiero for a piano and orchestra piece) are not permissive improvisation. Evolving from motival material, the variations are like seven inventions for full orchestra. Movements 2 and 3 comprise a *Scherzo alla Marcia* and a *Cavatina.* Though plenty of scherzi are to be found in symphonies, few resemble the shape of this grotesque piece for winds and brass. The title of the slow movement and its use of strings alone are similarly rare in symphonic literature. And the finale, a Toccata, also strikes out in modern address, with the full orchestra plus a huge array of tumultuous percussion (including glockenspiel, celesta, xylophone, vibraphone, tubular bells, and gongs.)

This is an elegant rendering with superb attention to detail, a real winner, in which Boult again proves his Vaughan Williams ability. (An earlier Boult recording of the work is still available. It is also with the London Philharmonic, on London S-15216.)

Symphony No. 9 in E minor (1958)

☐ London Symphony Orchestra / Previn (conductor) / RCA LSC-3280
☐ London Philharmonic Orchestra / Boult (conductor) / Everest 3006

Many a composer modifies the basic, proven musical forms, since none of the sequences that mark classical-style patterns are immutable. In this sober Symphony Vaughan Williams is as clear as any classicist, but free from rigidity.

The opening and final movements balance each other: elements from the initial part find development in the last. Antithetical material dictates the slow movement (pastoral and somewhat barbaric ideas) and the Scherzo as well (pictorial and mystical moods). Age changed yet did not change Vaughan Williams. His favored healthy modal sets of triads are to be heard, but as harmonic sandpaper against unrelated chords.

The color imagery so exceedingly vivid in Vaughan Williams's seventh and eighth Symphonies is heightened even further in his ninth and final work in the form. Three saxophones are used, and for the first time in the serious world of the Symphony a flügelhorn makes its appearance as an important solo voice. Such exception to routine does not violate a composer's style. Vaughan Williams had his own distinct creative voice, but he never overcelebrated himself.

Previn has a splendid re-creative voice. There is an interpretative supremacy in his recording, and the sense of poetry he finds in the score is a special privilege for the listener.

Only less cogent sound places Boult's reading second. Vaughan Williams was scheduled to be present during Boult's recording session, but he died just seven hours before it began. He would have been fully satisfied with Boult's splendid performance.

The Wasps, Suite (1909)

☐ London Philharmonic Orchestra / Boult (conductor) / Angel S-3739

The simmerings of the musical pot Vaughan Williams was to bring to his particular boiling point show unmistakably in these extracts from the music he composed (in 1909) for Aristophanes's play. Warm, intimate, folk-shaded melodies and modal harmony are the chief features. No complexities, no Greek musical forgery is represented, merely British *Innigkeit,* demonstrated in a vigorous Overture, a pair of entr'actes, a march, and a snappy finale.

Only the Overture has established itself in the repertory. Boult makes a strong case that the entire suite belongs there.

String
Orchestra

Fantasia on a Theme by Thomas Tallis (1910)

☐ Philadelphia Orchestra / Ormandy (conductor) / Columbia M-31074

The mysticism of this archaic stringed instrument drama is not conveyed by its title. Fantasia design is exposed by the full contrapuntal development of the basic theme. But there are other riches in this, one of the greatest of Vaughan Williams's compositions. The majestic polyphony and modalistic flow are enmeshed in a golden sonorous beauty that is the instrumental equivalent of superfine massed human voices. This is obtained by monolithic scoring patterns drawn from a three-ply organization of two string orchestras (one an echo group) plus a solo string quartet unit. In this manner, antiphony of musical material is emphasized by antiphony of instrumentation. Vaughan Williams's music is akin to a gigantic secular hymn. Composed in 1910, it is *not* of its age at all.

Ormandy guides Vaughan Williams's score with magnificent cogency. His orchestra displays a warm, fully interfused sonority that fits the music like a glove.

Partita for Double String Orchestra (1948)

☐ London Philharmonic Orchestra / Boult (conductor) / London STS–15216

Vaughan Williams's modern realization of partita format proposes a diverse collation of designs. With a bow to eighteenth-century concerto grosso principles, Vaughan Williams scored with purposely uneven distribution of weights. The first orchestra, without double basses, contains occasional solo passages, while the much larger second group has the full string body. The violins of both components are a corporate body without division into firsts and seconds.

Though modality—pure, contrapuntal, and dissonantly tinged—is a prime point, rhythm rules the four parts. This is especially true in the polyphonic chasing of the second movement, a *Scherzo Ostinato*, which lives up to its title by the persistent investigation of its main figure (augmented to form contrast) and by its dogged combination of duple and triple pulses within the bar lines. The Intermezzo that follows is subtitled *Homage to Henry Hall*, a dance-band conductor. Accordingly, a syncopated, ostinato pizzicato figure occupies the second orchestra. It begins as though a "vamp till ready," but turns out to be a "vamp al fine." No vulgarization—merely a precisely muted tap-dance support for the healthy melody that moves above it.

Boult furnishes a well-crafted conception. On the record label London claims four bands cover one each of the four movements. Error. Correctly, there are but three bands, with movements 1 and 2 occupying the first of these; part 3 is on band 2, and the finale occupies the third band.

English Folk Song Suite (1923)

Band

Toccata Marziale

☐ Eastman Symphonic Wind Ensemble / Fennell (conductor) / Mercury 75011E (monaural)

The suite has a marvelous and telling sense of band style and sound, with a rare perception for the idiom. It has become a classic in the repertoire and has also realized wide popularity in its orchestral transfer (see under *Vaughan Williams / Gordon Jacob: Orchestra*). Fennell's performance has conviction, authority, and artistic balance.

With its real drive (constant rhythmic impetus), martial spirit, and festive tone, V.W.'s *Toccata Marziale* lives up to its designation. And Fennell lives up to his reputation: only superlatives can be used to describe the results of his direction.

Concerto for Two Pianos and Orchestra (1933)

Solo Instrument and Orchestra

☐ London Philharmonic Orchestra / Vronsky and Babin (pianos) / Boult (conductor) / Angel S–36625

Two Pianos

This is V.W.'s second setting of a work composed for one piano and orchestra. The composer was convinced by Boult and others after its premiere that the Concerto, a powerhouse and massive vehicle for a single soloist, would be better balanced and registered if rescored for two pianos. However, the essential competitive element that exists in the concerto medium is liquidated in great part thereby. However, no recording is available of Vaughan Williams's (one) Piano Concerto. Accordingly, this recording of the second version is welcome, especially since it is given a vital statement. Of course, Boult is in full command when it is the music of Ralph Vaughan Williams he is conducting.

Tuba

Concerto for Bass Tuba and Orchestra (1954)

☐ London Symphony Orchestra / Fletcher (tuba) / Previn (conductor) / RCA LSC–3281

Undoubtedly, this is the finest work ever produced for solo tuba and orchestra. (There are some good examples in the solo tuba with band category, but that's a different situation.) There are three movements: Prelude, Romance, and *Rondo alla Tedesca,* including a pair of true-blue musical cadenzas.

For Vaughan Williams's offering, tubaists have always been exceedingly grateful. (Worthwhile extended works for their instrument have always been a rarity.) John Fletcher can well represent the thanks of the entire tuba fraternity with his splendid performance, sensitive and articulate throughout.

Violin

Concerto in D minor (*Concerto Accademico*) for Violin and String Orchestra (1925)

☐ London Symphony Orchestra / Buswell (violin) / Previn (conductor) / RCA LSC–3178

The secondary title is an unfortunate choice for those who do not know Vaughan Williams's piece. The meaning, feeling, and sensitivity of the Concerto is far from academic. It is doctrinal only in its parallel to the old classic format of three movements: an *Allegro pesante,* Adagio, and Presto, and in the string instrumentation of the accompanying orchestra. Yet it is positively classic in its clarity, with a total elimination of any fuss or furbelows.

The sheer black–white contrasts of the Concerto recall the eighteenth century, but this factor is set to rights modally. The Concerto contains a Bach spaciousness (many commentators have overemphasized the Bachian concept of the work) but under a Vaughan Williams guardianship. The magic triads of the slow movement and the jig scamper of the finale are proof.

The musicianship, taste, and artistry of this violinist are peerless. The same kudos apply to the conductor and his musicians. A beguiling offering.

The Lark Ascending for Violin and Orchestra (1914)

☐ New Philharmonia Orchestra / Bean (violin) / Boult (conductor) / Angel S–36469

This haunting, modally swept music (subtitled *Romance*) is given a simply beautiful reading by Hugh Bean with totally sensitive support by Sir Adrian Boult.

Instrumental

Six Studies in English Folk Song (Excerpts) (1927)

Clarinet

☐ Campbell (clarinet); York (piano) / Crystal 331

This is early, practical (there are alternative versions for violin, viola, or cello), all-native Vaughan Williams in quality and style. The composer's nationality need not be known for one to identify immediately the rural English enchantment contained in these very short essays.

Campbell plays three of the half-dozen. (Crystal fails to give the full title and by eliminating the word "six" implies the work is presented completely.) Altogether lovely playing.

Along the Field

Vocal

Voice with Accompaniment

☐ Winter (soprano); Langstaff (baritone); Morgenstern (violin) / Desto 6482

Along the Field is an eight-part song cycle set to the poetic delights of Housman. Nos. 1, 2, 4, and 8 are for baritone; Nos. 3, 5, 6, and 7 are for soprano.

The chamber music activity of these pieces is produced with subtlety and coloristic network. One immediately wants to hear again the balladic *Good-Bye* (No. 6) with its lightly bouncing duple pulse and the same goes for the seventh piece, *Fancy's Knell,* a declamatory vocalization with which the violin rhapsodizes.

Blake Songs

☐ Winter (soprano); Langstaff (baritone); Roseman (oboe) / Desto 6482

One hears a rare combination of voice and oboe, originally composed for the film *The Vision of William Blake.* Vaughan Williams varied his coloring in the ten parts of the cycle. Nos. 1 and 7 are for soprano and oboe; Nos. 2, 3, 5, 8, and 10 are for baritone and oboe. Three are for voice alone: *London* (No. 4) is for unaccompanied baritone; *The Shepherd* and *The Divine Image* (respectively, Nos. 6 and 9) are for the solo soprano.

These are trustworthy performances of the entire cycle. A special credit applies to Ronald Roseman for exquisite oboe playing.

Linden Lea   Songs of Travel
Orpheus with His Lute   The Water Mill

☐ Tear (tenor); Ledger (piano) / Argo ZRG–732

Linden Lea is proof of how Vaughan Williams assimilated his study of native song. This sounds exactly like a folk tune, but it is all Vaughan Williams.

One critic (Frank Howes) calls *Orpheus with His Lute,* an early-conceived setting of Shakespeare's lines (a second version was made two decades later), "fresh as a dewdrop and delightful." Another (Hubert Foss) terms it "jejune." The vote here is with Howes. As is the case with *Linden Lea,* sensitive vocalism is reflected by Tear in the *Orpheus* song.

Songs of Travel represents the mature young voice of Ralph Vaughan Williams. Composed just after the turn of the century, the songs forewarned the burial of academicism. The only exception proved to be the romantically individual music of Elgar. No one was lulled by Vaughan Williams's melodies. As Frank Howes has succinctly stated: "This was new music for a new century." And it remains fresh today.

Though folk influences are present (especially in *Whither Must I Wander?*) the cycle is not cakes-and-ale music. Vaughan Williams set Robert Louis Stevenson's texts with careful attention to their meaning.

The Water Mill can be termed a "Lied Domestica" without any semblance to Straussian furbelows. The piece is almost singsong: cute in style and folksy in its text about a miller and his wife, their daughter, her suitors, and the family cat.

Aside from a tendency to overstate certain phrases (especially in the *Songs of Travel*), the soloist delivers both the *Travel* cycle and *The Water Mill* with musicality. Ledger is excellent as the supporting artist.

Merciless Beauty (1922)

Voice and Instrumental Ensemble

☐ Winter (soprano); Morgenstern and Rhodes (violins); Goberman (cello) / Desto 6482

Vaughan Williams set these three rondels by Chaucer for high voice, preferably for soprano, though a tenor voice may be used (the premiere was given in that manner). It will be noted that the emphasis on soprano range is maintained in the string trio which consists of two violins and a cello rather than the usual violin, viola, and cello team.

Lois Winter has been recorded close-up, which tends to give her voice extra penetration and a certain hardness at times. Otherwise this is a presentable presentation.

Choral

Chorus Alone

An Acre of Land (1934)
Bushes and Briars
Ca' the Yowes (1922)
Early in the Spring
Five English Folk Songs (1913)
Greensleeves

John Dory
Loch Lomond
The Seeds of Love (1923)
The Turtle Dove (1924)
The Unquiet Grave
Ward, the Pirate

☐ London Madrigal Singers / Longfield (soprano); Partridge (tenor); Shaw (baritone); Keyte (bass) / Bishop (conductor) / Seraphim S–60249

The Five English Folk Songs are an anthology of "freely arranged" material that appeared after V. W.'s research on folk songs from the "Eastern Counties" and Sussex. It includes the familiar Wassail Song, a healthy example of a folk tune which Vaughan Williams translated in a solid polyphonic manner. The others are *The Dark-Eyed Sailor, Just As the Tide Was Flowing, The Lover's Ghost,* and *The Spring-Time of the Year.*

New beauties are unfolded in these settings; the music belongs as much to Vaughan Williams as to the anonymous people who sired it. Obbligati, imaginative harmonies, and counterpoints are blended in styles that range from madrigal to pure fantasy.

The other pieces are a tasty sampling from the folk songs that Vaughan Williams stored in his creative work files. Among them, the Scotch song *Loch Lomond* is an old favorite, while *Greensleeves* has become an international hit. The V. W. version puts matters to right and clears the distorted transcription atmosphere. *Ca' the Yowes* accompanies words by Burns, which identifies its Scotch source. No two settings are alike, variety adding to the infectiousness of the songs. In *John Dory* rhythmic and contrapuntal byplay are featured; in *An Acre of Land* a solo soprano and antiphonal response are the highlights.

The throbbing beauty of the Essex song *Bushes and Briars* contains spatial effects that haunt the memory. Vaughan Williams first heard it sung by an old shepherd. The melody, he related, "set all my doubts about folk song at rest." Another haunting example is *The Turtle Dove,* a nostalgic and tender love song. The crystalline beauty of this folk tune rivals the famous *Greensleeves,* and, once given proper attention, could achieve as great a popularity. Vaughan Williams made three different settings of this piece: for male voices, unison chorus or solo voice, and mixed voices. In whatever form the music is entrancing. So are the performances of all the songs on this recording. It is very highly recommended.

Chorus with Accompaniment

Lord, Thou Hast Been Our Refuge

☐ Choir of St. John's College, Cambridge / Runnett (organ); Owen (trumpet) / Guest (conductor) / Argo ZRG–5340

This work is somewhat mixed in its elements: it contains unison singing, choral recitative, spurts of polyphony, and fugato. Vaughan Williams's motet technically tussles with its basic inspiration but succeeds by its coloristic variety in terms of instrumental back-up (organ and trumpet) and through its choral scoring (for full chorus and semichorus).

A Sea Symphony (Symphony No. 1) (1910)

☐ London Philharmonic Orchestra and Chorus / Armstrong (soprano); Case (baritone) / Boult (conductor) / Angel S-3739

Architectural detail is always the special concern of composers who combine voices and orchestra in a large-scale work. The problems increase if the shape is to parallel the orchestral symphony. With proper finesse Vaughan Williams has merged his voices and instruments to fit the symphonic pattern by following the time-tested design of an Allegro, slow movement, Scherzo, and a finale in rondo style.

Using Walt Whitman words, this sea music bypasses any "Fingal's Cave" drive (save some oceanic currents in movement 3, *The Waves*) or specific *La Mer* mood-painting. The Symphony is devoted to a philosophical consideration of watery expanse. The voices are free and the role of the orchestra is somewhat compressed (though here, unlike Boult's earlier recording of the work on the London label [No. 7205], it is the chorus that sounds somewhat compressed). Melodic sweep is the primary virtue of Vaughan Williams's choral Symphony, including sufficient salt spray in the orchestration to warrant the title.

The soloists are expert, John Carol Case especially so. And Boult remains as one of the very best advocates of V. W.'s music in the business.

Serenade to Music (1938)

Chorus and Orchestra

☐ New York Philharmonic / Addison, Amara, and Farrell (sopranos); Chookasian, Tourel, and Verrett-Carter (mezzo-sopranos); Bressler, Tucker, and Vickers (tenors); London, Flagello, and Bell (bass-baritones) / Bernstein (conductor) / Columbia MS-7177

The Serenade is in the polydiatonic style brought to maturity in the music of Vaughan Williams. A ravishingly sweet principal theme splices the leaves of the work. It twines its way among the modal pillars of the piece, the plangent, consecutive parallel triadic chords mixing the major form with the minor, with an occasional dissonance rippling across the vertical stream. This is music of the English landscape school, with only a small bit of hard ground pictured here and there.

Composed in homage to Sir Henry J. Wood on his silver jubilee, the Serenade to Music originally called for sixteen vocal soloists (Wood had requested this so that those singers who had been associated with his career might also be honored). Vaughan Williams indicated that performance was possible with only four solo voices and chorus (a stunning performance led by Sargent on Angel 35564, deleted unfortunately, proves the excellence of such a version) or all the solo parts might be sung by sections of the chorus. A later version for orchestra alone is further proof that the inspirational force of the work is found in its music, not in its text.

The performance listed here is of unreserved beauty. It shows Bernstein at his inspirational best.

Toward the Unknown Region (1918)

☐ London Philharmonic Orchestra and Choir / Boult (conductor) / Angel S-36972

Described as a "song for mixed chorus and orchestra," *Toward the Unknown Region* has the proportions of a cantata. Whitman's text, concerning liberation of the soul, is dealt with with proper mysticism. The score is majestic, yet a stolid *nobilmente* style is its principal point, which Boult stresses. This early product is more ecclesiastical than secular in tone—a brand of church music for concert hall use. Vaughan Williams had not yet broken through the boundaries of the traditional English choral world.

1967

Cantata and Oratorio

Benedicite (1929)

☐ London Symphony Orchestra and Bach Choir / Harper (soprano) / Willcocks (conductor) / Angel S–36751

The outgoing quality of Vaughan Williams's *Benedicite* is well-illustrated by this exuberant performance. Angel's recording is a transfer from the HMV issue, released in England; the personnel involved could not be bettered.

Dona Nobis Pacem (1936)

☐ Utah Symphony Orchestra and Utah University Civic Chorale / Christensen (soprano); Metcalf (baritone) / Abravanel (conductor) / Vanguard 71159

This is a large work with texts from a variety of sources. The key section is the fourth part, a *Dirge for Two Veterans*, set to a Whitman poem. It is a stunning conception that can be (and has very often been) performed separately.

The Abravanel-directed performance is both powerful and mindful of the sensitive coloring that sweeps through Vaughan Williams's score. Boult's edition (on Angel S–36972) is somewhat square and the dynamic range is rather constricted.

Mass in G minor (1921)

☐ King's College Choir / Willcocks (conductor) / Angel S–36590

The Mass and the Requiem (the "Mass for the Dead") have been fertile grounds for masterworks. In most instances the music is fully conceived in the image of the composer's style, but Vaughan Williams blends his individual method with a reconstruction of Tudorian practices.

The G minor Mass is neo-modal all the way. The music is forwarded by harmonic blocks, colored by bare, parallel intervals, dramatically emphasized by linear cross-relations. It is all grand, mystical, and dramatically reserved. Vaughan Williams's merger of Elizabethan sublimity with contemporary enrichment contains the full tide of religious and artistic eloquence.

This performance vividly outlines the majestic antiphony within the work. Its emotive liturgical cast is magnificent.

Sancta Civitas (1926)

☐ London Symphony Orchestra, Bach Choir, and Boys of Kings College, Cambridge / Partridge (tenor); Shirley-Quirk (bass) / Willcocks (conductor) / Angel S–36751

In Vaughan Williams's "Holy City," set to a text from the Revelation of St. John, sixteenth-century modalism is reshaped by a twentieth-century hand. The temper is mystical in the harmonic style as well as in the subject matter. Here the triad is god, and it rules in many ways: singly, in combination, and grouped in bands of chordal counterpoint.

Vaughan Williams's organization of his score calls for quadruple groups in addition to the soloists: orchestra, tutti chorus, semi-chorus, and a distant boys' choir. It poses performance problems in the concert hall and even more so in the recording studio. The results here are well-nigh perfect, with a nobility to the rendition that emphasizes the music's spiritual order.

Opera and Dramatic Music

Sir John in Love (1929)

☐ New Philharmonia Orchestra and John Alldis Choir / Palmer, Eathorne, and Watts (sopranos); Bainbridge (mezzo-soprano); Tear, English, Winfield, Rowinson, Jenkins,

Dickerson, and Johnston (tenors); Herincx, Noble, Jones, Ethridge, and Varcoe (baritones); Lloyd, Van Allan, Richard, and Wheatley (basses) / Davies (conductor) / Angel SX–3822

The Shakespeare *Merry Wives of Windsor* tale is here steeped in the full English flavor of the special V. W. type. A considerable amount of folk song material is interwoven, including the well-known setting of *Greensleeves*, heard so often as a separate instrumental piece. This emphasizes the major point of the opera. Comparison with Verdi's *Falstaff* or Nicolai's Germanic comic opera on the same subject is false. Vaughan Williams was not interested in operatic procedures (call it conventions). He has, as Hubert Foss so acutely noted, "simply translated Shakespeare into music." In this sense it has its own operatic character. Indeed, it works, pleases, and delights the ear, even if its performance record shows it not to be exportable.

The performance has fine character from its many participants and good straightforward singing. Style rather than vocal theatrics is the fundament here and the cast covers it thoroughly. Since the probability of seeing a live production is remote, Angel's recording becomes more important than usual and should be given the fullest attention.

Job, A Masque for Dancing (1930)

Ballet

☐ London Symphony Orchestra / Boult (conductor) / Angel S–36773

Composed with both ballet and concert hall in mind (the problems of obtaining stage production raised doubts about the former), *Job* has turned out to be capable of a double life. The source of inspiration derives from William Blake's famous *Illustrations for the Book of Job*. Vaughan Williams achieved a strong synthesis: the score is a powerful adjunct to the miming and dancing of the "masque," and at the same time it is an independent composition of symphonic amplitude.

In the nine parts of *Job* a number of formal dance designs are used: saraband, minuet, pavane, and galliard. None of these are academic. Ultraformalism is bypassed. Sacred dignity and fervor, simplicity and drama, blend and are laced with modal harmonies.

Despite its multitudinous scenario directions Boult makes the music unfold like a mural and not like a mixture of separate balletic bits. He shows that even though *Job* outlines stage action, with proper conductorial control and realization it can stand firmly on its own orchestral feet.

This is Boult's fourth recording of the work. Two are gone, two remain. The Angel edition is the better of the pair; the other is by the London Philharmonic, on Everest 3019, but it lacks the textural clarity provided by the London S.O.

Vaughan Williams / **Arnold Foster (1898 -   )**

Prelude *Rhosymedre*

String Orchestra

☐ Academy of St. Martin-in-the-Fields / Marriner (conductor) / Angel S–36883

A Welsh hymn tune, beautifully embroidered by modal figuration, as only Vaughan Williams could manage it. The work was originally for organ but was transcribed by a close friend of the composer's. It is played simply and thereby gains all the needed performance credits.

1969

Vaughan Williams / Gordon Jacob

Orchestra **English Folk Song Suite (1924)**

☐ London Symphony Orchestra / Boult (conductor) / Angel S–36799

One of the best known of Vaughan Williams's lighter-faceted works. Originally, this three-movement Suite was written for band (see under *Vaughan Williams: Band*); then, with the composer's permission, it was transcribed for orchestra by Gordon Jacob (a former pupil), considered one of England's top orchestrators. The eight conjoined melodies are sea songs, for the greater part, plus homespun tunes from the region of Somerset.

Regardless of English or Viennese musicians (another Boult performance is with the Vienna State Opera Orchestra on Westminister Gold 8111), with Sir Adrian as their conductor this music of Vaughan Williams is played as it should be.

Thomas Vautor   *(ca. 1590-?)*

Choral

Chorus Alone ***Sweet Suffolk Owle***

☐ Purcell Consort of Voices / Burgess (conductor) / Turnabout 34202

This is a madrigal with a quaint text about an owl sitting alone singing a song that frightens the mice and sounds like a dirge for the dying. *Sweet Suffolk Owle* (a five-part madrigal) represents the best work of this sixteenth-seventeenth century English composer.

Franz von Vecsey   *(1893-1935)*

Instrumental

Violin ***Le Vent***

☐ Ricci (violin); Lush (piano) / London STS–15049

"The Wind" is this Hungarian composer's *Caprice No. 1*. Ricci tosses off the hideously difficult flying chromatic thirds as though he were tuning his fiddle. Yes, musical fluff, but it is valuable as a change of listening pace. *Le Vent* (made to order for the instrument) brings to mind the Shavian remark not to confuse great composers who sometimes wrote music for the violin with great composers of violin music.

Aurelio de la Vega   *(1925-   )*

Instrumental

Trumpet ***Para-Tangents* for Trumpet and Pre-recorded Sounds (1973)**

☐ Stevens (trumpet) / Avant 1009

There isn't a dull measure in this virtuoso rhapsody for the brass instrument. The solo voice has extreme highs and lows, smears and glides, rips and riffs. The tape part responds, opposes, frames, and is heard with the drips and the crunches, and what are now timbres as traditional as major and minor tonality figurations for any string or wind instrument. Gone is the audacity of using tape sounds. Gone are its high risks. De la Vega has a lust for sonorous fantasy. His piece fulfills it.

No aesthetic challenge for the listener, but a hell of a challenge for Thomas Stevens. He meets it head on and proves he is an overwhelming technician.

Tangents for Violin and Tape (1973)

Violin

☐ Granat (violin) / Orion 73128

The tape part in this man–machine duo is no mere glossary of sound whines and waves, sparks and streaks, but matches, in a very individual fashion, the technical athleticism of the violin. The often out-of-context affiliation of pre-recorded sounds heard with a string, wind, or brass instrument is totally absent here and that alone makes de la Vega's piece especially interesting and successful. The new means of tape combined with an instrument which has become very old-hat receives a creative shot in the arm in *Tangents.*

No runty part, of course, for the fiddle. Tough as hell, in fact, but Endre Granat tosses off every detail with effortless perfection.

Segmentos (1964)

Chamber Music

☐ Gross (violin); Grayson (piano) / Orion 73110

''Segments'' begins and concludes with a pair of freely formed, serially styled pieces (*Narrative* and *Discourse*). Chordal roughage and glissandi are special to the latter. The Aria that defines the middle piece in the group favors high-ranged lyricism with colorful acrid harmony. All of the suite is sharply serious. Tenderness is not here, toughness is.

The work is played well. The sound is not particularly balanced; the violinist is up very close.

Pavel Josef Vejvanovský *(ca. 1639 - 1693)*

Intrada in C major

Orchestra

☐ Academy of St. Martin-in-the-Fields / Smithers and Laird (trumpets); Munrow (bassoon); Preston (harpsichord) / Marriner (conductor) / Philips 6500110

An interesting bit of moderately paced, fanfaric music for two trumpets, strings, and continuo (bassoon and harpsichord).

Francesco Maria Veracini *(1690 - 1768)*

Sonata in B minor for Violin and Continuo, Op. 1, No. 3

Chamber Music

☐ Ferraresi (violin); Sgrizzi (harpsichord) / Nonesuch 73008

A noble, singing style permeates the work, even in the final Rondo, which is the only fast movement of the total four. The sensitive grace of the playing is ideal.

Giuseppe Verdi   *(1813-1901)*

Orchestra

Grand March from *Aida* (1871)

☐ Philadelphia Orchestra / Ormandy (conductor) / Columbia MS-6474

This is given the full flavor and given sumptuous sonority.

Overture to *I Vespri Siciliani* (1856)
Overture to *La Forza del Destino* (1862)
Prelude to Act 1 of *La Traviata* (1853)
Prelude to Act 3 of *La Traviata* (1853)

☐ Philharmonia Orchestra / Giulini (conductor) / Seraphim S-60138

These are the best of Verdi's operatic Overtures and Preludes and in the case of *La Forza del Destino* certainly the finest of the lot. The performances are exciting and clean, without a trace of the sentimentality that creeps into and blemishes many a presentation of these works. The reading of the *Traviata* third act Prelude provides exceptional poignancy.

String Orchestra

String Quartet in E minor (Version for String Orchestra) (1873)

☐ I Solisti Veneti / Scimone (conductor) / Musical Heritage Society MHS-1347

The version is noted as "approved by composer." The approval is based on a remark Verdi made that the work "should sound well with twenty players to a part, because certain phrases demanded a richness and fullness that solo instruments could not impart to them." And it does sound well, though no eighty players are participating in this rendition by a very small string orchestra. The Quartet is played in a stunning fashion with peppy tempi in the *prestissimo* and *Scherzo-Fuga* movements (Nos. 3 and 4, respectively).

(For a discussion of the Quartet version see under *Chamber Music*.)

Chamber Music

String Quartet in E minor (1873)

☐ Saulesco Quartet / Caprice RIKS LP-65

Of the many operatic composers who have tried their hands at fashioning chamber music, Verdi is the most successful. The evidence is in the String Quartet, his single example in the medium.

The question can be raised immediately: would this operatic composer write a Quartet in operatic style? The reply is only faintly "no," but mingled with a much stronger "yes." For the mixture of the standard classic-romantic forms Verdi used are furnished with certain props that stem, if not formally then spiritually, from his operatic devices. More to the point is that there are melodies that sound Verdian. Just one example: in the trio of the third movement, the cello throws its head back and sings a luscious *cantabile* picked right out of Verdi's operatic pocketbook.

The Saulesco Quartet are members of the Swedish Radio Symphony Orchestra. They make a fine team, and in their existence since 1962 there has been only one change (in 1972), that in the second violin chair. Their conception of the Verdi is fine, with good choice of tempi, especially that which clarifies (without losing any of its impact) the *Scherzo-Fuga* finale.

1972

Quattro Pezzi Sacri (1898)

☐ Philharmonia Orchestra and Chorus / Baker (contralto) / Giulini (conductor) / Angel S-36125

The "Four Sacred Pieces" (*Ave Maria, Stabat Mater, Laudi Alla Vergine Maria,* and *Te Deum*) have enjoyed critical dichotomy. Some think the four pieces show a decline after Verdi's great operas *Otello* and *Falstaff.* Others term the work, since it was the composer's last one, his "twilight masterpiece." This writer joins the positive side, if only for the glorious commentary of the *Te Deum.*

There are three recorded versions on the market: Giulini's, Mehta's (on London 26176), and Kegel's (on Philips 6570111). Giulini gives the music all it needs in color and resolution, in depth and eloquence, and realizes its dramatic religiosity throughout. Mehta only outlines the score in his top-of-the-music reading, while Kegel neutralizes the sacred colorings of the score (it might as well be a secular essay by Verdi). Fine work by all involved but absolutely ascetic in depiction.

Requiem Mass (1874)

☐ Philharmonia Orchestra and Chorus / Schwarzkopf (soprano); Ludwig (mezzo-soprano); Gedda (tenor); Ghiaurov (bass) / Giulini (conductor) / Angel S-3649

Intellect partnered with emotion and an equality between the spiritual and the operatic thrust of this great work describe Giulini's conception. Sometimes Verdi's Mass (in memory of Manzoni) is conductorially overmannered. At other times the soloists follow that procedure. Neither fits. Both annoy. Under Giulini's direction there is the best translation of every element in Verdi's score and the result is the best version in the recorded catalogue today.

Bernstein does this work excitingly well (it's his kind of music). His soloists (Arroyo, Veasey, Domingo, and Raimondi) are excellent. Only a trifle of podium peripateticism places his edition (on Columbia M2-30060) as the second choice.

Aida (1871)

☐ Rome Opera House Orchestra and Chorus / Price and Sighele (sopranos); Gorr (mezzo-soprano); Vickers and Ricciardi (tenors); Merrill (baritone); Tozzi and Clabassi (basses) / Solti (conductor) / London 1393

Solti goes directly to the heart of this work. It is my belief that the other recorded editions waver and are superficial beside this one. The Rome Opera House Orchestra is not the major-league outfit that can compare to the Berlin Philharmonic, the London Philharmonic, and even the Metropolitan Opera's group. However, Solti obtains a glowing sound and a sensitivity of expression from the Rome players that is immediately recognizable.

If beautifully played, *Aida* is just as beautifully sung. Leontyne Price (as Aida) is as opulent as ever. Her full voice is stimulating, but she is just as exquisite in *pianissimo* sections. Jon Vickers (covering the Radames role) is full-voiced, secure. The vocal quality of the remainder of the cast raises no doubts. Theirs is of total authority. All characterizations ring true and all the singing is well-focused and unforced. Above all, this recording had a distinctive handsomeness and rightness that revitalizes the work. *Aida* here sounds splendidly fresh, brand-new and exciting.

Don Carlos (1884)

☐ Orchestra and Chorus of the Royal Opera House, Covent Garden / Tebaldi and Sinclair (sopranos); Bumbry (mezzo-soprano); Bergonzi, Wakefield, and Carlyle (tenors);

Fischer-Dieskau and MacDonald (baritones); Ghiaurov, Talvela, and Franc (basses) / Solti (conductor) / London 1432

Verdi's opera began as a five-act conception and he then redrafted the work into four acts. This recording uses the latter but restores the cuts made in the initial setting. The only omission retained is the ballet music.

Solti treats this score with intense dramatic concentration. This does not ignore Verdian style, however. The orchestra is made an important protagonist. Bumbry gives a compulsive characterization of Princess Eboli, as does Martti Talvela of the Grand Inquisitor, and Tebaldi is truly magnificent as Isabella. As a whole, the cast is assertive, and the production is a vibrant one.

Ernani

☐ RCA Italiana Opera Orchestra and Chorus / Price (soprano); Hamari (mezzo-soprano); Bergonzi and Iacopucci (tenors); Sereni (baritone); Flagello and Mueller (basses) / Schippers (conductor) / RCA LSC–6183

Ernani (based on Victor Hugo's *Hernani*) was the fifth of Verdi's works and the first opera that brought him fame. Its romanticism moves well.

One hears strong singing on the part of Leontyne Price and Carlo Bergonzi, who both shape their roles with finesse. Ezio Flagello is fully assured in his singing, and his dark-timbred voice is perfect for the role he takes. There is plenty of opportunity to admire the ensembles but less so Schippers's conducting, which has a flux and reflux in his shaping of the score. However, RCA's edition is the only recorded representation and this point must be accepted if one wishes Verdi's work on disc.

Falstaff (1893)

☐ Vienna Philharmonic Orchestra and Vienna State Opera Chorus / Ligabue and Sciutti (sopranos); Resnik and Rössl-Majdan (mezzo-sopranos); Oncina, Stolze, and Dickie (tenors); Fischer-Dieskau and Panerai (baritones); Kunz (bass) / Bernstein (conductor) / Columbia M3S–750

This is a fine production. Bernstein lets the music show its muscle but it is never muscle-bound. At the same time he brings a sensitive warmth to the opera and its delights are not once overlooked. This is a magnificent sparkling score and Bernstein's energetic temperament (in comparison to Solti's and von Karajan's) brings profits. The man understands theatre and this is obvious in his direction of the score. Fast tempo rules—all to the good.

Fischer-Dieskau is ideal as Falstaff, Panerai as Ford (he takes the same role in the von Karajan recording on Angel S–3552), Ligabue as Alice (she is also heard in the same part in Solti's edition on London 1395), and all the others are excellent.

Giovanna d'Arco (1845)

☐ London Symphony Orchestra and Ambrosian Opera Chorus / Caballé (soprano); Domingo and Erwen (tenors); Milnes (baritone); Lloyd (bass) / Levine (conductor) / Angel S–3791

In "Joan of Arc" according to Verdi there are plenty of good sections, even though some of the material may strike a listener as simply mechanically contrived and not compulsively felt.

Special to the score are choruses and off-stage music. The cast does well in this single representation in the catalogue.

I Lombardi

☐ Royal Philharmonic Orchestra and Ambrosian Singers / Deutekom, Malvisi, and Aparici (sopranos); Domingo, La Monaco, and Erwen (tenors); Raimondi, Dean, and Grant (basses); Taweel (violin) / Gardelli (conductor) / Philips 6703032

Verdi's *I Lombardi alla Prima Crociata* ("The Lombards at the First Crusade"), to give its full title, is a rough and sometimes uneven conception, but the opera works as a whole and the best sections far outweigh the weaker ones. An important point are the strong choral parts; these are particularly well done, though clear diction is not available (is it ever?).

The cast is excellent in all aspects and even in the smaller roles (particularly Desdemona Malvisi as Viclinda) there is glorious singing. Cristina Deutekom, who carries a huge part in the work, is truly impressive. Gardelli knows his way through operatic conditions. He shines in this one.

Il Trovatore (1853)

☐ New Philharmonia Orchestra and Ambrosian Opera Chorus / Price (soprano); Cossotto and Bainbridge (mezzo-sopranos); Domingo, Davies, and Taylor (tenors); Milnes (baritone); Giaiotti and Riley (basses) / Mehta (conductor) / RCA LSC-6194

There are fine advantages to this recorded edition. Mehta shows operatic strengths and Verdian knowledge that underline the fact that he should be given the greater part of credit for this splendid achievement. That said, one does not minimize the effectiveness of the singers.

Leontyne Price as the noble Leonora sings stylishly and that means beautifully. Flexibility is a decided part of her portrayal. At times she is less than opulent but she is always generously expressive. Florence Cossotto, taking the role of Azucena, sings incisively and with excellent (and in this reference, passionate) phrasing. The dark coloration of Sherrill Milnes's voice and Placido Domingo's firm and flowing vocalism are further accomplishments.

The balances are ideal, the tempi alive, and the entire temper of the production is the most satisfying of all the editions available. Of these, Price is also in the cast of RCA's LSC-6150; though others in the cast include such greats as Elias, Tucker, Tozzi, and Warren, the conducting is unsteady and the performance lacks finesse.

La Forza del Destino (1862)

☐ RCA Italiana Opera Orchestra and Chorus / Price and Marrapese (sopranos); Verrett and Vozza (mezzo-sopranos); Tucker, De Palma, Truffelli, Sforza, and Jannizzotto (tenors); Merrill, Bottcher, and Rinaudo (baritones); Tozzi, Flagello, Foiani, Piccini, and Ruta (basses) / Schippers (conductor) / RCA LSC-6413

This recording is as good as any on the market and even slightly better (note those voices: Price, Verrett, Tucker, Merrill, et cetera). There's a deep value of imagery in this production that comes off the record grooves. Leontyne Price is as fine as any of her competitors and sings beautifully; the others in the cast do no less so. Schippers was a fine operatic conductor. He blends matters and avoids episodic depiction.

La Traviata (1853)

☐ Berlin Deutsche Oper Orchestra and Chorus / Lorengar (soprano); Aragall (tenor); Fischer-Dieskau (baritone) / Maazel (conductor) / London 1279

1975

London's production is styled and identified with fine operatic logic. Maazel pushes matters along, but still the general pace is excellent and it is accompanied by flawless orchestral playing. Together these provide the framework for a strong conception.

All the Verdi juices flow well with the cast. Pilar Lorengar as Violetta is decidely impressive; there is no funky business in her characterization: it is well-concentrated, very up-front, and completely beautiful and affecting. There are many critics who have expressed doubts about every "Traviata" recording that has hit the market. London's edition raises no doubts for this critic.

Macbeth (1865)

☐ London Philharmonic Orchestra and Ambrosian Opera Chorus / Souliotis (soprano); Pavarotti (tenor); Fischer-Dieskau (baritone); Ghiaurov (bass) / Gardelli (conductor) / London 13102

Superfine conducting with alternately loose and tight rhythmic detail, communicative use of timbre definition, and plain down-to-earth orchestral spirit and vitality go far to make this *Macbeth* the prime choice in the recorded catalogue. Gardelli has virtuosic control of the orchestral forces, and they respond in kind.

There are some soft spots in Souliotis's Lady Macbeth, but these are overcome by a general dramaticism that prevails; the singing of this soprano cannot be criticized. As Macbeth, Fischer-Dieskau is in top form, emoting and singing with total power and authority that match the orchestral doings. Nicolai Ghiaurov makes a finely colored Banquo, and Luciano Pavarotti is admirable as Macduff. The chorus is also admirable.

Nabucco (1842)

☐ Philharmonia Orchestra and Ambrosian Opera Chorus / Scotto (soprano); Obraztsova (mezzo-soprano); Luchetti (tenor); Manuguerra (baritone); Ghiaurov (bass) / Muti (conductor) / Angel SCLX–3850

Nabucco is the first Verdi opera with significant values. "Nabucodonosor" needs vital choral singing (one writer describes the opera as one that is "magnificently chorus-based") and the excellence of the chorus in this, the most recent recording of the work, cannot be overpraised. Angel's cast is a stronger one, on an overall basis, than the older London issue (No. 1382). The singing star is Manuguerra, who has fine technique and a splendid vocal timbre to go with it. The production's success is due to Riccardo Muti. The new conductor of the Philadelphia Orchestra produces a magnificently proportioned conception and smoothes out the several roughnesses within the Verdi score. He is a master in planning pace to stimulate the story line.

Otello (1887)

☐ National Philharmonic Orchestra and Ambrosian Opera Chorus and Boys Chorus / Scotto (soprano); Kraft (mezzo-soprano); Domingo, Little, and Crook (tenors); Milnes (baritone); Plishka and King (basses) / Levine (conductor) / RCA CRL3–2951

The primary success of *Otello* depends on a tenor who can fulfill the title role. Jon Vickers has been considered the best Otello in the international operatic world. He proves it on the Angel SX–3809 version. But that recording is flawed by von Karajan's ideas as to cuts that just are not acceptable. Here then, in this RCA release, we needn't look for Vickers since Placido Domingo is his equal. Domingo's performance is scaled magnificently—a depiction that is powerful and of moving vocalism. Indeed, it is superlative.

Renata Scotto's portrayal of Desdemona is no less acute. With Sherrill Milnes as Iago and the dramaticism that pours out of Levine's conducting, the trumps are all on the table, making the RCA production a sure-fire winner in the *Otello* stakes.

Rigoletto (1851)

☐ Orchestra and Chorus of La Scala / Scotto (soprano); Cossotto (mezzo-soprano); Bergonzi (tenor); Fischer-Dieskau (baritone); Vinco (bass) / Kubelik (conductor) / Deutsche Grammophon 2709014

Rigoletto is here presented without rigorous squareness and at a very high musical level. The entire production has the fine responsiveness that results from strength in all matters—musical and dramatic. There is a supportive motility that is set at a good dramatic pace but not at the expense of clarity and thereby meaning. Plot positiveness is matched by excellent singing and orchestral playing, with truly impeccable control of all factors by Kubelik.

Vocal honors belong to Renata Scotto. Her dynamic coloration in the Gilda role is a joy and she has the necessary power and agility for the part. Carlo Bergonzi's Duke is outstanding, and Fischer-Dieskau is certainly a splendid Rigoletto with no problems in the crucial upper range Verdi used in fair amount. The flexibility of the singing is quite special.

Simon Boccanegra (1881)

☐ Orchestra and Chorus of La Scala / Freni (soprano); Carreras and Savastano (tenors); Cappuccilli (baritone); Ghiaurov, van Dam, and Foiani (basses) / Abbado (conductor) / Deutsche Grammophon 2709071

There's a grandeur about this opera that cannot be denied, notwithstanding a somewhat confusing story line. That it has some stylistic differences is due to the fact that it was initially (in 1857) a failure and Verdi's rewrite was not completed for almost a quarter of a century later. Nevertheless, there are a number of striking scenes, and these overcome any criticism concerning style.

This is a strong cast with imposing performances, especially from Pero Cappuccilli and José van Dam. Claudio Abbado negotiates matters with amazing skill and totally superb musicianship. The music moves from one section to the next with a probity and sensitivity that command nothing but the fullest admiration. Such strengths are not apparent in the competitive RCA edition (ARL3-0564), conducted by Gavazzeni.

Un Ballo in Maschera (1859)

☐ Orchestra and Chorus of La Scala / Callas and Ratti (sopranos); Barbieri (mezzosoprano); di Stefano and Ercolani (tenors); Gobbi and Giordano (baritones); Maionica and Zaccaria (basses) / Votto (conductor) / Seraphim IC–6087 (monaural)

This is one of the very best presentations of this opera on disc. The distinguished singing is matched by as distinguished a consideration of the score by Antonino Votto. Callas as Amelia fits perfectly into the characterization; she superbly manages everything in a strong and thereby exciting manner. There are some mannerisms on her part that may annoy but that's part of operatic enterprise and in no way surprising. Eugenia Ratti and Fedora Barbieri, as Oscar and Ulrica respectively, are in full command. The male members of the cast are totally effective.

All the arias and ensembles are crisp and securely formed, and the direction of Votto makes certain there is impact and vigor.

Ballet

Ballet Music from *Don Carlos* (1884)

☐ Cleveland Orchestra / Majeski (violin) / Maazel (conductor) / London 6945

Verdi's *Ballo della Regina* is given a fairly authoritative reading. There is a satisfactory performance immediacy, as in the juicy solo violin section (played with nice tone and gratefully without schmaltz) and a waltz (played just a bit too rigidly), even though nothing is done to prickle the back hairs.

Ballet Music from *Il Trovatore* (1853)

☐ Monte Carlo National Opera Orchestra / de Almeida (conductor) / Philips 6747093

This is a sufficiently compelling consideration of Verdi's music.

Ballet Music from *I Vespri Siciliani* (1856)

☐ Cleveland Orchestra / Maazel (conductor) / London 6945

This is a full-scale ballet, with contrasting moods relating "The Four Seasons." The solo playing is impressive, especially the clarinet at the beginning of "Spring" and the oboe at the start of "Summer." This is only one part of a rewarding musical essay by the talented virtuosi that comprise the Cleveland Orchestra.

Ballet Music from *Jérusalem*

☐ Monte Carlo National Opera Orchestra / de Almeida (conductor) / Philips 6747093

The opera *Jérusalem* was Verdi's conversion of his *I Lombardi* for production in Paris. The compulsory ballet was included. 'Tis run-of-the-mill stuff and it doesn't receive very inspired playing because there's little to get inspired about. There is the historical importance, however.

Ballet Music from *Macbeth* (1865)

☐ London Symphony Orchestra / de Almeida (conductor) / Philips 6747093

Verdi's fine ballet music from *Macbeth* is rarely heard. Antonio de Almeida fully brings out the wonderfully colorful spirit of the Verdi score.

Ballet Music from *Otello* (1887)

☐ Cleveland Orchestra / Maazel (conductor) / London 6945

The music is succinct (just a fraction under six minutes), but it is probably the best of all the ballet music Verdi composed. It is played with splendid timbre relationships and full authority.

Matthijs Vermeulen   *(1888-1967)*

Orchestra

Symphony No. 2 (*Prélude à la nouvelle journée*) (1920)

☐ Residentie Orchestra / Iwaki (conductor) / Donemus Audio-Visual Series 7374/1

Vermeulen's second of his seven symphonies was given a prize at the Queen Elisabeth Composition Competition held in Brussels in 1953. (The first performance of the work was given in Amsterdam in July 1956.) It is a heavily packed panchromatic essay organized in five blocked sections, each emphasizing and reemphasizing its point. The detail in the playing is only fairly clear, the recording having been made from a live performance.

Sonata No. 1 for Cello and Piano (1918)

☐ van Ast (cello); de Leeuw (piano) / Donemus Audio-Visual Series DAVS-6302 (mon-aural: 10-inch disc)

This Sonata is marked by heavy details with congenital chromaticism. The sense of Franckian overload is retained throughout, and with the cyclic return of the opening an additional relationship to that composer is indicated.

The reading is skillful and respectful, but it is hampered by only a partial solution of the problem that faces any cello–piano team—clarifying the cello line to obtain proper balance without having the piano lean on the cello too much.

John Verrall   *(1908-   )*

Sonata for Horn and Piano (1942)

☐ Leuba (horn); Aanerud (piano) / Crystal S-372

Tonality does not take a holiday in this work of elemental moods: a Pastoral, Nocturne, and Vivace. The warmth of the horn timbre dominates the first two-thirds of the opus; more action, without any caper-cutting, is made available in the finale. To Verrall's credit, there is no hustle and bustle for the sake of motility. There is a high level of personal expression in the piece.

String Quartet No. 7 (1961)

☐ Berkshire Quartet / Composers Recordings S-270

Brevity is one of the points of Verrall's Quartet, set in one movement design, with four sections clearly defined. Another is the substantial romantic quality of the music, based on a ten-pitch scale, not a "system," merely a personal mode as valid as any of the established ones.

Until the final part of the work the Berkshire Quartet plays professionally. Then unison passages sag intonationally.

Tomás Luis de Victoria   *(ca. 1549-1611)*

Litaniae de Beata Virgine

Magnificat Primi Toni

Motets

Estote Fortes in Bello	*O Quam Gloriosum*
Hic vir Despiciens	*Veni Sponsa Christi*
Iste Sanctus	

☐ Choir of St. John's College, Cambridge / Guest (conductor) / Argo ZRG-620

The entire program illustrates the polyphonic strength and eloquence of this composer. One of the Motets (*O Quam Gloriosum*) furnished the basis for a Mass (see under *Cantata and Oratorio* [*Missa: O Quam Gloriosum Est Regnum*]).

Guest directs tellingly, especially in regard to avoiding direct bar-lined measurement of the phrases within the pieces. Indeed, this is a rich and controlled presentation with dynamic variety coloring the singing. Victoria could not be served better.

O Magnum Mysterium

O Vos Omnes

☐ Paul Hill Chorale / Orion 7022

The performances by this group are perfectly attuned to the mystical qualities of Victoria's music. There is no attempt to force dynamic changes into the essential expressive flow of these sacred beauties.

Cantata and Oratorio

Missa: O Quam Gloriosum Est Regnum

☐ Choir of St. John's College, Cambridge / Guest (conductor) / Argo ZRG-620

Victoria's (or Vittoria, as the name is sometimes spelled) Mass is presented with taste, intelligence, and fine vocal skill. This is undoubtedly the most telling of the several Masses thus far recorded. Tovey has called it ''one of the most perfect examples of choral polyphony existing.'' It is based on a Motet (see under *Choral: Chorus Alone* [*O Quam Gloriosum*]).

Louis Vierne   (1870-1937)

Instrumental

Organ

Impromptu

Toccata

☐ Isoir (organ) / Turnabout 34319

These are two pieces from Vierne's *Pièces de fantaisie,* which is divided into four suites. The chromatically festooned Impromptu is from the third grouping and is stimulated by Isoir's desiccatedly colored registration. Thunder and sonic bursts are let loose in the Toccata, taken from the second suite. It is fulfilled by full-scale, full-powered, fomented playing. This is a great performance and always a clearly defined one.

Isoir's performances are also duplicated in a Vox Box (SVBX-5315), as part of the sixth volume of *A Survey of the World's Greatest Organ Music.*

Symphony
No. 1, Op. 14 / No. 2, Op. 20 / No. 3, Op. 28 / No. 4, Op. 32 / No. 5, Op. 47 / No. 6, Op. 59

☐ Labric (organ) / Musical Heritage Society OR-425/430

Brilliant performances, each and every one; the instrument is the Great Cavaillé-Coll organ of the Basilica of Saint Sernin.

Vierne's symphonicism is classic in its structural proportions, romantic in its syntax, Franckian in its chromaticism and canonicism. The scope is imposing, with five movements for each work and six for the initial symphony. The forms are defined by contrastively balanced tempi. Polyphonic security is, of course, paramount, but there is only one complete fugue (movement 2 of the first symphony). In the last three works there is an undercurrent of pessimism; one example is the snide course of the scherzo-tempoed third movement of Opus 47. This type of creative approach comes into sharp focus when compared to the placidity that surrounds the first symphony, the gentility and vocalism of the *Cantilène* in the third symphony, or the outwardness and display projected in the *Final: Allegro* of the same work.

Twelve recorded sides of superlative organ playing, magnificently recorded, are available in this release (initially recorded by Téléson, in Toulouse, France).

Finale from Symphony No. 1, Op. 14

☐ Preston (organ) / Argo 5448

A triumphant movement from one of Vierne's six organ symphonies in a brilliant depiction. Simon Preston's performance is an exciting one.

Henri Vieuxtemps   *(1820-1881)*

Concerto No. 4 in D minor for Violin and Orchestra, Op. 31

☐ Orchestre de Paris / Perlman (violin) / Barenboim (conductor) / Angel S–37484

A big work for the fiddler with an above-average percentage of material for the orchestra. Technical display is the paramount point, musical significance is quite subsidiary, but that's the way it is with this composer.

Soloist Perlman keeps the faith. He covers the ground with encompassing technical and tonal eloquence. The orchestra does its part fairly well.

Concerto No. 5 in A minor for Violin and Orchestra, Op. 37

☐ London Symphony Orchestra / Chung (violin) / Foster (conductor) / London 6992

Similar to most of his music, Vieuxtemps's fifth Concerto for the violin exhibits virtuosity in greater part rather than meaningful music. Those who relish schmaltzy tunes and fiddle display have it served up here.

Kyung-Wha Chung does not falter. Her playing makes even the decorative twists of the music a relaxation for the ear.

Ballade et Polonaise, Op. 38

☐ Grumiaux (violin); Varsi (piano) / Philips 6500814

Grumiaux perfectly balances the opposites of this Vieuxtemps piece. The nostalgic turns of the *Ballade* are considered poetically, without any annoying schmaltz or bowing saliva. On the other hand, the full lure of the *Polonaise* is given its full head, but with no playing to the gallery.

Solo Instrument and Orchestra

Violin

Instrumental

Violin

Heitor Villa-Lobos   *(1887-1959)*

Bachianas Brasileiras No. 2 (1933)

☐ Orchestre National de la Radiodiffusion Française / Villa-Lobos (conductor) / Angel 35547 (monaural)

This work is most famous for its final movement (*see below* [*The Little Train of the Caipira*]), which has moved into the high-class division of the pops-concert repertoire.

Orchestra

Nonetheless, the other parts of the work have an extreme richness of invention. Why the complete *Bachianas Brasileiras* No. 2 is given only rare performances is an enigma.

The parallel between classic titles and native subtitles gives the musical working plan. A *Preludio* fruitfully conveys the *Song of a Capadócio* (a boaster of low character); this is followed by an Aria (*Song of Our Land*), a *Dança* (*Remembrance of the Wild Country*), and finally the Toccata (*The Little Train of the Caipira* which is sometimes listed as *Little Train of a Rustic*—a "rustic" being a rude, indolent, and shrewd person of the Brazilian interior). The intimate fusion of Bach style with the secular-popular music of Brazil is illuminating; new formal conditions thereby construct new musical notions.

It is worth realizing that despite this constructive partnership all four movements are actually transcriptions; the third was originally a piano piece, the first, second, and fourth were cello and piano compositions. This is no startling fact; it was Villa-Lobos's way of convincing himself (and others) that he had written a new work. The fact that it fit into the general plan (here of Bach–Brazil) is coincidental, or actually schematic—changing the date so it will fit the testimony regardless. One can afford to be liberal when the musical result is as exhilarating as this suite.

Although Villa-Lobos was only a workaday conductor, his reading is good in terms of tempi, and he engenders the requisite excitement and coloration of this superb music.

Bachianas Brasileiras No. 7

☐ RIAS Symphony Orchestra / Villa-Lobos (conductor) / Turnabout THS-65002 (monaural)

Neither form nor date of composition affected Villa-Lobos's style. He was always true to himself in spite of the difficulty this presented in terms of projecting his technique as a whole. Spontaneity is always present; the sense of improvised music-making suggests a script from which an excellent actor departs.

A first-rate example is available in the rather romantic dress of this classic-national *Bachianas*. The end movements are patterned on the usual prelude and fugue, save that the latter is of imposing size—a neo-baroque transmutation. The middle portions form the rhythmic sandwich that is a feature of the Villa-Lobos menu.

Danses africaines (1914)

☐ Louisville Orchestra / Mester (conductor) / Louisville S-695

A suave presentation of this set of three dances, which are based on melorhythmic figurations of Brazilian jungle songs.

The notes accompanying the record neither list the titles of the dances nor the composition's subtitle. *Danças Africanas* (to use the original language for the main title) is subtitled *Danças dos Indios mestisos do Brasil* and include *Farrapos* (dance of youths), *Kankikis* (an old men's dance), and *Kankukus* (a children's dance).

Dawn in a Tropical Forest (1953)

☐ Louisville Orchestra / Whitney (conductor) / Louisville 545-1 (monaural)

Villa-Lobos stated that his *Alvorada na Floresta Tropical* was "an *Overture* of colors accompanied by the magic singing and chirping of the tropical birds," together with the multitudinous sounds of the native Indians. So be it. No one has bettered him in what might be described as tropical symphonic sound. This humidity of timbre combination, of musically translated febricity, is the principal quality of the piece.

Villa-Lobos's singular orchestrational imagination in music of this kind has been an important guide for the Hollywood and TV boys in their scoring of films dealing with jungle themes. But theirs is an imitation of Villa-Lobos's imitation.

The performance is very good and the clear sound has proper resonance. This is another auspicious example of what value has resulted from the Louisville Orchestra's commissioning project.

Erosion—The Origin of the Amazon River

☐ Louisville Orchestra / Whitney (conductor) / Columbia Special Products AML–4615 (monaural)

In this Villa-Lobos musical newsreel there is no husbanding of materials. Despite a preface which presumably tells the story the music is to document, this is mainly a mural of lush orchestral colors in a sonorous overabundance. In a way, this is Villa-Lobos codifying Villa-Lobos—a kind of sampler of his composition. *Erosion* is an indigenously mirrored manifestation that could only have been conceived by this composer. If the form is uncertain and rhapsodic, the blend is distinctly personal: primitive and cosmopolitan, banal and imaginative.

The Little Train of the Caipira from *Bachianas Brasileiras* No. 2 (1933)

☐ London Symphony Orchestra / Goossens (conductor) / Everest 3041

Villa-Lobos's train is quite different from Honegger's *Pacific 231,* which huffs and puffs, is awesome, monstrous, a tremendous iron machine. Villa-Lobos's is a special marvel, a wonderful ride of fun, of much better orchestral picture-painting, down to the puffing, the chugging, the screeching, speeding and stopping, and letting the steam out of the funnel—plus a tune to travel by. This is far less than a miniature "231," being more of a third-class choo-choo almost ready for the scrapheap.

Goossens's entry provides first-class clarity and sharp outline together with trenchant sound.

(For the complete *Bachianas Brasileiras* No. 2, see above.)

Uirapurú, Symphonic Poem (1947)

☐ New York Stadium Symphony Orchestra / Stokowski (conductor) / Everest 3016

Uirapurú represents early Villa-Lobos, composed in 1916 but revised thirty-one years later. Nonetheless it has all the characteristics of a mature work, since Villa-Lobos's output cannot be portioned out in the period-of-work pattern that marks most other composers. His creative picture is kaleidoscopic; the youthful work and the very late composition cannot rightfully be compared, for each is singular—paradoxically, time did not play any role in his career or determine his style.

Taking into account what he had observed during a trip into the Brazilian interior, Villa-Lobos composed this orchestral poem about a legendary enchanted bird. The story is replete with jungle and animal sounds, tonal simulations of insects, owls, enchanted toads, bats, glowworms, and so forth. The persuasiveness of the music stems from its folk authenticity. In its way, *Uirapurú* is Villa-Lobos's *Sacre.*

Stokowski is the ideal conductor for this colorful score. He pulls out all the stops without stop. That's the way it should be.

Bachianas Brasileiras No. 1 for Eight Cellos (*Modinha*) (1930)

String Orchestra

☐ New York Stadium Symphony Orchestra / Stokowski (conductor) / Everest 3016

1983

Villa-Lobos is at his best in this unusual work for a rare grouping of instruments. In reciprocation of the Bach spirit he offers Brazilian ethos and sets this blend for an orchestra unlike any other—one of eight cellos. This combination makes a rich instrumental mintage. The form of the movement heard here dips into Bach waters by way of a prelude conception.

Stokowski's presentation is elegantly accomplished. One wishes that the other two movements were available, one of which is a *Conversa,* meaning "conversation"—a true synonym for a fugue. At one time three different performances of the entire work were on the market. They're worth a search: Janssen conducting on Capitol P-8147, Slatkin conducting, on Capitol SP-8484, and Bloomfield conducting on MGM E-3105.

Bachianas Brasileiras No. 9 (1945)

☐ Orchestre National de la Radiodiffusion Française / Villa-Lobos (conductor) / Angel 35547 (monaural)

This is music of almost formal classic proportions, cast in the form of a prelude and fugue. Bach has had his day in the court of many composers. In this Brazilian's domain he rules regally. The prelude glitters with lyrical splendor; all else is from Bach's polyphonic jewel case.

An acceptable performance.

Fantasia concertante for Cello Orchestra (1958)

☐ Violoncello Society / Villa-Lobos (conductor) / Everest 3024

Music of authenticity, of national classicism as observed and practiced by the composer—personal in sound, with Villa-Lobos (read: Brazil) for its source. Especially compelling is the melting beauty of the haunting slow movement; the others are of more idiomatic Bachian order.

The special color of a cello orchestra is no trickery. It does give an individual blend, not one disposed to imitate other instruments. So don't hesitate; this is a distinguished work with almost the same kind of performance to match. "Almost," because there is some questionable intonation in unisons, especially in the high tessitura. It is inconceivable that the composer or the editor did not hear it. This is the recording's single flaw.

Solo Instrumental and Orchestra

Concerto for Guitar and Small Orchestra (1952)

☐ English Chamber Orchestra / Williams (guitar) / Barenboim (conductor) / Columbia M-33208

Guitar

Simply for the moody slow movement, marked oddly as an *Andantino e andante,* the Concerto is a fine contribution to the restricted large-scale literature for the guitar. Williams plays with a sense of intimacy that becomes the music, including the substantial cadenza that falls between the second and third movements.

This is a fine recording, with no string swishes that mar so many guitar releases.

Piano

Bachianas Brasileiras No. 3 for Piano and Orchestra (1934)

☐ New Philharmonia Orchestra / Ortiz (piano) / Ashkenazy (conductor) / Angel S-37439

Quite often, when a composer thinks he has fashioned a brand-new structural pattern, he (more often, we) will discover that no matter what disposition he makes of his material a fundamental relationship exists between it and the forms followed through the centuries.

Villa-Lobos's third *Bachianas* is a compound of free design plus established tenets. Because it is related to the old (by way of a *Prelúdio*, Fantasia, Aria, and Toccata), the new (these movements translated into *Ponteio*, and the Brazilian equivalents of a "Revery," a "Love Song," and a "Woodpecker") is not shining bright. Neither is it hackneyed. Much of the time the music is mere tune-plus-accompaniment, thus very Brazilian with little Bach—no pedantic strictness, mostly picturesque structures.

This performance is fine. Compared to the deleted one (Vox PL–10070) it deserves a special prize. The Vox issue has Felicja Blumental as the soloist with the Filarmonica Triestina conducted by Luigi Toffolo. The balances are twisted, the playing is somewhat of a struggle and is scarred by intonation lapses. It is rough going all the way—the piano is nasal and the sound is thinned in the high gamuts. So don't look for it. Angel's edition has none of these horrors. The sound is good, the soloism is all it should be, and Ashkenazy (yes, *that* Ashkenazy) does excellently in his direction of the score.

Momô Precóce for Piano and Orchestra

☐ New Philharmonia Orchestra / Ortiz (piano) / Ashkenazy (conductor) / Angel S–37439

Sweet and sour, *Momô Precóce* is based on a cycle of ten piano pieces titled *Francette e Pia*, which combine French and Brazilian melodies. Using one's own work and recasting it is perfectly justified, but it may sometimes result in weakening what was a strength. The short pieces have conviction; strung into a large-scale composition they tend to ramble, sound belabored, and are totally diffuse—unordered in this day of orderliness. Villa-Lobos refuses to let go and overargues.

What can a soloist do with this kind of music? Consider it for the fantasy it is and somehow attempt to tighten the structure. Cristina Ortiz does remarkably well in that regard and considerably better than Magda Tagliaferro did, even considering that Villa-Lobos was the conductor for the latter's performance. It was on Angel 35179, with *Bachianas Brasileiras* No. 8 as the companion work. Deleted, of course.

Fantasia for Soprano Saxophone, Three Horns, and String Orchestra

Saxophone

☐ Paul Kuentz Chamber Orchestra / Rousseau (soprano saxophone) / Kuentz (conductor) / Deutsche Grammophon 2530209

As is to expected, full-sized, somewhat lush harmonies (but always fitting to the material) and plenty of rhythmic pep are to be found in this piece. In this music of conviction, the solo timbre especially is a fruitful choice.

Chôros No. 1 (1920)

Instrumental

☐ Bream (guitar) / RCA LSC–2606

Guitar

Villa-Lobos once told the famous critic Olin Downes, "I compose in the folk style. . . . He [the composer] must select and transmit the material given him by his people." The maxim is perfectly illustrated and even somewhat overemphasized in this piece, in which the plaintive principal theme returns again and again.

(If an old Capitol record titled *Music for the Spanish Guitar* with Laurindo Almeida as the soloist surfaces, disregard the heading *Chôro Typico*. Where Capitol or Almeida found this title one knows not; it is not listed in Villa-Lobos's catalogue. This *Chôros* is "typical," to be sure, but it becomes *Chôros* No. 1 the moment one puts needle into groove and hears the music.)

Bream's is a discriminating performance. The color he supplies for the piece is superfine. (The performance is duplicated in a two-record set also issued by RCA on VCS–7057.)

Etudes for Guitar (1929)

Preludes for Guitar

☐ Yepes (guitar) / Deutsche Grammophon 2530140

The twelve Etudes (composed in 1929) are not all of exemplary merit, but none of them is arid. An etude for pedagogic use is one thing; a concert etude, designed for the public's ears and not solely for the practice room, is another. Most of these have expressive content. If Chopin, Liszt, and Debussy are in the first rank of composers of concert etudes for the piano, Villa-Lobos is without doubt the kingpin composer of concert etudes for the guitar.

Examples: the initial etude is called "studies of arpeggios," and those acquainted with the first unaccompanied cello suite of Bach will note a resemblance. No. 7 is a mixture of some lyricism with much more scalic rhapsodizing, making the etude semi-improvisational. The eighth of the set is more melodic than it is concerned with design—Villa-Lobos often refused to be guided by formal documentation.

In a way the five Preludes are as close to the essence of Villa-Lobos as Villa-Lobos ever came. Above all, the guitar is an instrumental medium for rich-blooded Latin music and so Villa-Lobos poured into these preludes much of his true self. His language is proportioned, defined, and shows a commanding knowledge of instrumental technique. Examples: the first of the group is a keen, haunting music, with a smidgen of nostalgia that is like a Brazilian blues, without any jazz relationship. In the third work, one recognizes the composer's great admiration for Bach, whose music Villa-Lobos felt was a resource available to any composer, regardless of era or country of origin. The last prelude is one of the special love songs of Brazil—the *modinha.*

Yepes's execution gives a resplendent effect. There is contrast, almost implied dialogue, in his stressing of dynamic planes, especially in the Preludes. Where *Innigkeit* is needed he provides it. The playing is always clean, clear, absolutely suitable, and the phrasing is beautiful.

Etude No. 5 (1929)

☐ Bream (guitar) / RCA LSC–2964

Bream cleanly details the motility of the middle voice in comparison to the melodic portions in the upper and lower registers.

Etude No. 6 (1929)

☐ Bitetti (guitar) / Westminster Gold 8149

Chordal picture-painting in a minor key. Splendidly played.

Etude No. 7 (1929)

☐ Bream (guitar) / RCA LSC–2964

Bream's playing is clean, clear, fundamentally suitable. The phrase definition is marvelous.

Etude No. 11 (1929)

☐ Bitetti (guitar) / Westminster Gold 8149

This is a sensitive performance, especially detailed in color contrasts. The conclusion, latched onto an ostinato, is beautifully balanced.

Prelude No. 1 in E minor

☐ Romero (guitar) / Mercury 75022

The way Celin Romero plays this piece, one of the most typical of those Villa-Lobos wrote for the guitar, is ideal. Compared to Segovia's rendition (on MCA 2501) Mercury has more delicate contrasts and certainly better and deeper sound.

Prelude No. 3 in A minor

☐ Romero (guitar) / Mercury 75027

Villa-Lobos's confirmed love for Bach is filtered into this gentle piece. Bachian hat-tipping will be noticed in the several uses of a repetitive sequential passage. It fits in the music's general scheme and is perfectly natural. The last word describes the playing of Celin Romero who also knows how to drive home *rubati* values in the most subtle manner. This is infinitely more valuable, artistic, and musical than the blatant kind thrown into one's ears like a pie in the face.

Suite populaire brésilienne

☐ Bream (guitar) / RCA ARL1-2499

The *Suite Popular Brasileira* (another way of listing the title) is considered Villa-Lobos's eighteenth work in his very large catalogue. All the portions of the Suite contain *chôros* hybrids: in the first it is crossed with a mazurka, in the second with a *Schottisch,* in part 3 with a waltz, and in the fourth of the set with a Gavotte. Since the *chôros* is already a synthesis of Brazilian Indian and popular music, it is apparent that the joining of a dance form with it makes the compound a triple one in each instance. Although two's company and three generally make a crowd, this is not found in Villa-Lobos's designs. Formal preoccupation does not result in uninspired demonstrations.

Bream does not perform the entire suite. He has omitted the final piece, a small *Chôrinho.* However, his performance of the four parts is very fluid and most informative. The *Schottisch-Chôros* movement is also contained in an all Villa-Lobos album Bream recorded for RCA, available on their LSC-3231. (Incidentally, some remarks as to the spelling of *Schottisch. Grove's Dictionary of Music and Musicians* states that adding a final "e" is incorrect, while *Webster's* makes it mandatory. However, there seems to be no rationale for omitting the second "c" as is sometimes the case.)

Alma Brasileira from *Chôros* No. 5 (1926)

Piano

Dansa do Indio Branca from *Ciclo Brasileiro* (1936)

☐ Somer (piano) / Desto 6426

The first piece, "Soul of Brazil," is a mellowed impression that conveys true Brazilian nationalism. There are no native quotations, but the music comes as close to the precious treasure of folk music as any composer might come. Villa-Lobos, the creative sponge, absorbed all the pertinent traits of his country's folklore and made them his own. Hilde Somer has made this piece her own, conceiving a poetic response that is enticing.

The "Dance of the White Indian" is Villa-Lobos's *Allegro Barbaro* for the greater part. The sharp-tooled playing by Hilde Somer has a dynamism that is captivating.

Preludio from *Bachianas Brasileiras* No. 4

☐ Freire (piano) / Telefunken 641299

There is no semblance of folkloristic accompaniment in this excerpt from Villa-Lobos's partita.

Prôle do Bêbê—Series 1 (1918)

☐ Freire (piano) / Telefunken 641299

"The Baby's Family" is a double collection (*see below* for the second series) of enchanting pieces that contain some of Villa-Lobos's most delightful and attractive music for the piano. From the titles it might be assumed the music was conceived for educational purposes; on the contrary, these are full-fledged concert works.

The first set of eight was composed in 1918 and did not have a subtitle. When it was republished in America it bore the definitive and apt description of "The Baby's Dolls." A second group of nine pieces appeared three years later, identified as "The Little Animals." Although both these suites have been recorded, the third set of nine "Games," written in 1926, has not been published or recorded.

Expert invention is illustrated in the manner in which Villa-Lobos limns the various toys and dolls without resorting to cartooning via the keyboard. Some of the pieces display facets of impressionistic style. Others are indigenous, as the samba rhythm that marks "The Clay Doll" or the toccata power that triggers "The Little Glass Wolf." This is quite an interesting gallery—from "The Rubber Doll" to "The Little Rubber Dog," etcetera. Indeed, this is a highly original set of seventeen small musical artworks, each bearing Villa-Lobos's clear signature.

Nelson Freire's is an exceptionally well-delivered performance. It is a conception that makes each piece come alive. The monaural recording made by José Echániz more than two decades ago for Westminster is still available (released together with the second series: *see below*). The only other recording worth considering is Artur Rubinstein's (RCA LSC–2605). However, with no indication to the contrary, the implication is that the work is presented complete. Rubinstein plays six of the first series: the "Porcelain," "Wooden," "Witch," "Paper," "Rag," and "Clown" (as RCA names it, but actually "Punch") dolls. Lacking are the pieces titled *Caboclinha* ("The Clay Doll") and *Mulatinha* ("The Rubber Doll").

Prôle do Bêbê—Series 2 (1921)

☐ Echániz (piano) / Westminster Gold 8287 (monaural)

(*See above* for details concerning this work as a whole.)

Currently, Echániz's playing of the second set (coupled with the first series of pieces) is the only one in the catalogue. He delineates all the musical ideas with sharp-tooled playing of line and rhythm. Westminster's sound is as good as any discs produced these days.

Rudepoema (1921-1926)

☐ Freire (piano) / Telefunken 641299

Details: five years in the making; first performed by Artur Rubinstein, for whom it was written; it was later orchestrated. Description: this is music of volcanic vehemence, of vibrating violence, a music unfriendly save to the vested interests of virtuosi. Results: few perform Villa-Lobos's dynamic piece.

The abilities of Mr. Freire are thoroughly tested—he comes through with super virtuosity and without a note out of place. What takes place? Everything—cadenzas, nostalgic impressionism, percussive primitivism, an improvised plan of bravura, and the transmittal of musical shock without recourse to serialism, pointillism, or any "ism" save pyrotechnicalism. Hearing is believing.

The Three Maries (1939)

☐ Freire (piano) / Telefunken 641299

No matter what Villa-Lobos wrote, the music had personality. His piano music based on a fairy tale, "The Three Maries of Earth," almost fits the three names (Alnitah, Alnilam, and Mintika) with musical onomatopoeia. In this instance Villa-Lobos is as clear as is Debussy in his "Children's Corner." The two works have in common the quality of objective simplicity.

Assobio á jato ("The Jet Whistle") for Flute and Cello (1950)

☐ Baron (flute); Sylvester (cello) / Desto 7134

A few *outré* sweeps at the termination realize the title designation. Otherwise, this is a three-part duo that balances outer actively moving divisions with a slow-paced (Adagio) movement. The usual expressive colorations by this instrumental master.

Baron and Sylvester provide a performance of exciting immediacy. Rhythm and coloration, tonal beauty, and variety are all depicted with real presence. The performance by Millard (flute) and Brown (cello) on Arch S–1760 is good but has less flair.

Bachianas Brasileiras No. 6 for Flute and Bassoon (1938)

☐ Baron (flute); Garfield (bassoon) / Nonesuch 71030E (monaural)

The high and low colors of the two wind instruments afford a propitious contrast for duet composition. Although there is a fair amount of proportioned part writing, the flute is given the lion's share of soloistic assertion. A great deal of the Aria (*Chôros*) is constructed sequentially. This gives balance and correlation to the music, if not much development. The Fantasia has a very segmented design.

Of the half-dozen recordings that were considered, the most outstanding is this electronically processed mono disc. It has a richness of tone and presentation slightly better than evidenced by the nearest competitors (Dwyer and Walt of the Boston Symphony Chamber Players, on RCA LSC–6184). Dufrène and Plessier (on Angel 35547) are quite capable; the drawback is the edgy French woodwind tone.

Chôros No. 2 for Flute and Clarinet (1921)

☐ Skowronek (flute); McColl (clarinet) / Musical Heritage Society MHS–1875

Soliloquy, song, and dance paragraphs mark this engaging two-voice essay, which is here played with wisdom and style. (According to *Schwann,* this work and the others on the MHS disc are duplicated on Ravenna 702.)

Chôros bis: Duo for Violin and Cello (1928)

☐ Schoenfeld Duo / Everest 3243

Fantastic technique for the players is a requisite for this Paganinian duet. Quadruple glissandi with vibrato, left-hand pizzicato while playing with the bow, double harmonics, stratospheric position work and difficulties of double stopping—these are the rule, not the exception. In addition, the cello imitates a drum by four-string pizzicato with two inner strings stopped, the two outer ones open. Both sections of the piece live and feast on starkly projected rhythm. This unmellowed impression is true Brazilian national music.

A satisfactory ordering of the score is presented. Though the sound is a bit rough, it fits with the Villa-Lobos conception. (Everest incorrectly lists the work as "Choros No. 2," minus the circumflex accent. Its absence is not especially critical. What is, is the incorrect

Chamber Music

numbering. *Chôros* No. 2, composed in 1921, is for flute and clarinet. *Chôros bis*, produced in 1928, is a supernumerary entry in the grand total of fourteen *Chôros* compositions Villa-Lobos produced.)

Fantasie concertante for Clarinet, Bassoon, and Piano

☐ Academy Trio / Golden Crest 4115

Excellent tunes are here combined, and their variety is stressed by the choice of medium, a multicolored instrumentation. Villa-Lobos's trio (as much a "Rhapsody" as it is a "Fantasie") is paralleled by linear individuality.

The wind players are superb artists: Anthony Gigliotti is the solo clarinet of the Philadelphia Orchestra and Bernard Garfield the first-chair bassoonist of the same organization. Pianist Amelia Gigliotti does very well with her part. She is not the person to write liner notes, however. Those for this album (works by Poulenc and Wilder in addition to the Villa-Lobos) are extremely naïve. And the tone of the piano is slightly tinny.

Trio for Oboe, Clarinet, and Bassoon (1921)

☐ Storch (oboe); McColl (clarinet); Grossman (bassoon) / Musical Heritage Society MHS–1875

Design is of secondary importance in many of Villa-Lobos's compositions, and it is color that governs the tactics of this wind trio, which has a mailed timbre fist in its musical glove. Thus syncopations, full-scale deployment of dynamics, and wholesale instrumental distribution lend a rashness to the music that is otherwise of simple nature.

This is a magnificent performance by three members of the Soni Ventorum. Choice sound. (According to *Schwann*, Ravenna 702 duplicates this recording of this piece and the other three compositions included on the Musical Heritage Society program.)

Quartet for Flute, Oboe, Clarinet, and Bassoon (1928)

☐ Skowronek (flute); Storch (oboe); McColl (clarinet); Grossman (bassoon) / Musical Heritage Society MHS–1875

Casualness of form defines each of the three movements. Villa-Lobos has other affections that are primary. Rhythmic excitation and color melodrama stimulate the ear. One can certainly be stired by this composer's vehemence even when refusing to praise his free discourse. Mozartean finesse cannot be expected in Villa-Lobos's woodwind music. This composer's best arguments are propounded by avoiding such logic. Sonorescence and fantasy came first with this Brazilian; harmony, counterpoint, and form were second in consideration.

Sit back and enjoy organized wind *sound*. (This performance is listed in *Schwann* as being duplicated on Ravenna 702, along with the three other Villa-Lobos works on the MHS release.)

Quartet No. 17 (1958)

☐ Brazilian String Quartet / Odyssey 32160176

Some of Villa-Lobos's quartets are virtuoso affairs, colored explosions; some (the fifth and sixth) are surfeited with Brazilian exuberances. This, the last string quartet he composed, has nationalistic reflections in the background. The melos of Brazilian folklore are integrated, not on the surface. Villa-Lobos's attachment to the luxuriance of color is mostly absent in this work, and there is a late-romantic twist to this quartet's shape that is unusual in his output.

Clear portrayal by the Brazilian team, without any special point of view.

Quintet: En forme de Chôros (1953)

☐ New York Woodwind Quintet / Nonesuch 71030E (monaural)

Originally, Villa-Lobos made a slight change in the woodwind-quintet grouping for this Quintet, with an English horn replacing the French horn. He later revised it for the standard grouping, as it is performed by the New York outfit, then composed of Samuel Baron (flute), Jerome Roth (oboe), David Glazer (clarinet), Bernard Garfield (bassoon), and John Barrows (horn).

The combine of timbre applied by Villa-Lobos produces lush colors in a classical-jam-session format appropriate to the *chôros* form. The sum total is exciting music, modifying formal practices in a distinctly unusual fashion that is creative.

The music is perfectly recorded, in fact this is one of the best wind recordings around, nonstereo notwithstanding. The performers are superstar musicians.

Bachianas Brasileiras No. 5 (Part I, Aria-Cantilena) (1938)

Vocal

☐ Sayão (soprano); Rose (cello) / Villa-Lobos (conductor) / Odyssey 32160377 (monaural)

Voice with Accompaniment

A magnificent display of performance art by Bidú Sayão, despite ordinary sound. The recording was transferred from an old 78-rpm 10-inch disc, and this will be recognized. But old-play or long-play, warmth, style, passionate conviction, and throat-catching vocalism are here in abundance. Even if one owns the complete work (see under *Voice and Orchestra*), it is still strongly recommended that Sayão's recording be acquired. Villa-Lobos's Aria belongs to her.

Suite for Voice and Violin (1923)

☐ Catherine Malfitano (soprano); Joseph Malfitano (violin) / Musical Heritage Society MHS-1976

Brazilian folklore in bold relief marks all three songs. In the third and boldest of the group, *Sertaneja* ("The Peasant Girl of Brazil"), the voice is treated instrumentally and the violin has a guitar personality though it is not conveyed by plucked sound.

Villa-Lobos's work is projected admirably and colorfully. It is a welcome recording since the demise of Decca, which has issued the duo on its No. 710177, with Ruggiero Ricci playing and Les Venora singing.

Bachianas Brasileiras No. 5 (1938)

Voice and Orchestra

☐ American Symphony Orchestra / Moffo (soprano) / Stokowski (conductor) / RCA LSC-2795

There are very few people who are unmoved by the exquisite melody that spans the opening of this two-movement work, scored for a soprano voice and eight cellos. (In Villa-Lobos's own recording [*see above* under *Voice with Accompaniment*] he added a double bass. In the Stokowski rendition four more cellos are used plus two double basses. Stokowski claimed he simply followed Villa-Lobos's wishes. The printed score gives no such indication, however.)

A contemporary melody that has come to be honored with the term "celebrated" is unique. In this chant Villa-Lobos has captured the full essence of his formal amalgamation of Bach (classic purity) and nationalism (striking color and rhythm) and drawn the maximum of expressivity from minimal instrumental means. This too is a singular achievement. The second movement is another combination idea, a lovesong-dance. It is showy, without the incontrovertible individuality of the opening movement.

The versions recorded are numerous and in various settings. These include executions by such a personality as Joan Baez (on Vanguard 79160) and a semijazz setting by Salli Terri (a contralto), with an arrangement of the cello orchestra's part for guitar (by Laurindo Almeida), on Angel S–36050.

All the performances must be measured against the Aria originally recorded by Bidú Sayão on a 10-inch disc more than thirty years ago—see under *Voice with Accompaniment* (*Bachianas Brasileiras* No. 5 [Part I, Aria–*Cantilena*]). It is rare to hear such astonishing stylistic profundity in the delivery of a song. If one wants the complete work, however, one will have to accept less than Sayão's re-creative powers. She is memorable. The best of the other entries is that by Anna Moffo. Her voice is dusty and has innate sexuality. It comes closest of all the voices that have recorded the piece to projecting the sensual passion that lies in the song.

Choral

Chorus Alone

Agnus Dei from *Mass of St. Sebastian*

☐ Peloquin Chorale / Peloquin (conductor) / Gregorian Institutes EL–19 (monaural)

This work is simple and stately in style, a forthright and straightforward choral item. Artistically presented, with a stunning conclusion.

Chorus and Orchestra

Forest of the Amazon (1958)

☐ Symphony of the Air and Chorus / Sayão (soprano) / Villa-Lobos (conductor) / United Artists 5506

Actually this is the music that Villa-Lobos composed for the motion picture *Green Mansions*. True to his usual practice, Villa-Lobos's music had practically nothing to do with the Hudson story. The sections of the piece comprise an accumulation of thoughts, indifferent to formal considerations but quite alive to developing bold ideas from minimal material. The main concern is to render the freedom of fantasy to the exclusion of all else. In this the music is quite successful. The orchestration is of the hothouse type, of Rousseau luxuriance, with some portions exclusively for the orchestra, others for either chorus or soprano with orchestra.

Sayão's voice has both personality and a gentle luminescence. The orchestra plays with brilliance, and the sound is a five-star affair.

John Vincent   *(1902-1977)*

Orchestra

Symphony in D (1952)

☐ Louisville Orchestra / Whitney (conductor) / Louisville 57–2 (monaural)

Tonal security, as can be expected from the title designation. However, the tonal approach is freshened by rhythmic motival play and the solidity of block scoring. Vincent pivots on his pitch polarity but probes for a variety of shifting relationships. The maximum security of diatonicism can easily result in academic dogma, but not in this case.

The Louisville rendition presents the first version of Vincent's piece, which the

Louisville Orchestra had publicly premiered on February 5, 1952. He later revised it, and in that form it was initially presented by Ormandy and the Philadelphia Orchestra on April 12, 1957. Ormandy then recorded the Symphony for Columbia (ML-5263), but it resides in the world of the deletes.

String Quartet No. 1 in G (1936)

☐ American Art Quartet / Contemporary 6009 (monaural)

Chamber Music

Vincent's consideration of modal technique was a reincarnative method of freshness in his hands. One thinks of another American composer who was drawn to modal writing, Randall Thompson. However, Thompson's music is diatonically wrought, compared with Vincent's modulatory breadth.

And what better proof of Vincent's methodology than for his style to produce the fully haunting and moving melodicism of the scherzo-like Allegretto? This is a work of illuminative musical art, a sincere and important contribution to American chamber music.

The Quartet is movingly performed and with golden tone and vitality. Individual credit is due to the team of Eudice Shapiro, Robert Sushel, Virginia Majewski, and the late Victor Gottlieb.

Consort for Piano and Strings (1960)

☐ American Art Quartet / Foss (piano) / Contemporary 6009 (monaural)

Melodicism via the use of contemporaneously shaped modalism and just as currently dated motoric drive mark Vincent's three-part *Consort*. (Vincent later amplified the work for full string orchestra and in that version titled it Symphony No. 2.) The nobility of the central movement particularly marks a high point in Vincent's work, beautifully depicted in this finely honed performance in which a fellow composer participates as the pianist.

Leonardo Vinci   *(1690-1730)*

Sonata in G major for Flute and Continuo

☐ Instrumentalists of the Società Cameristica di Lugano / Zuppiger (flute) / Nonesuch 73008

Chamber Music

A little-known composer and ditto for the piece itself. The music is luscious and the organization of the material beyond reproach. Ditto for the performance.

P. Anselm Viola   *(1738-1798)*

Toccata for Clarines

☐ Hamilton (organ) / Orion 73133

Instrumental

Organ

Cute and peppy—the latter expected, the former a surprise. Hamilton keeps in the basic organ reeds for color. A good choice. Running time 4:54.

1993

Giovanni Battista Viotti   *(1755-1824)*

*Solo
Instrument
and
Orchestra*

Piano

Concerto in G minor for Piano and Orchestra

☐ Austrian Tonkuenstler Orchestra, Vienna / List (piano) / Topolski (conductor) / Musical Heritage Society MHS-709

The only recording of any of the ten piano concerti Viotti produced. It is to Eugene List's credit that he took the work off the shelf. Once in a while a Viotti violin concerto is performed, a few are recorded, and a couple are standard requirements for violin students. But the exact opposite is the case with the piano concerti.

The traditional format of three movements (the finale in rondo form) pertains. The cadenzas are the composer's.

Piano and Violin

Concerto for Piano, Violin, and String Orchestra

☐ Berlin Symphony Orchestra / Lautenbacher (violin); Galling (piano) / Bünte (conductor) / Turnabout 34229

Double concerti calling for violin and piano are extremely few despite the fact that they offer an attractive partnership. Viotti's contribution is an enjoyable example that is a once-over-lightly affair in A major encompassing a pair of Allegro movements, the second one in rondo form.

The liner writer covers the work in twenty-seven words, ten of which state the title and give the tonality, with nine describing the number of movements and the tempi. That amounts to unfair treatment, even considering the pat forms Viotti used.

Violin

Concerto No. 16 in E minor for Violin and Orchestra

☐ English Chamber Orchestra / Röhn (violin) / Mackerras (conductor) / Deutsche Grammophon ARC-2533122

A rare recording from the set of twenty-nine violin concerti Viotti produced. For that matter, save the twenty-second and twenty-third concerti, which are assigned to most violin students, must of these works remain (unfairly) in the dead-music section of libraries. (Another recorded exception is found in Concerto No. 24 in B minor—*see below.*)

All of the expressive data of the opus, including its musical virtuosic requirements, are detailed by Andreas Röhn. It is a ripe performance in all respects.

Concerto No. 22 in A minor for Violin and Orchestra

☐ Concertgebouw Orchestra, Amsterdam / Grumiaux (violin) / de Waart (conductor) / Philips 839757

Viotti's music does not register unless it is performed with elegance and outward lyricism. Delivery with virtuosity is built in with chains of thirds and groups of embroidered figurations that are released with trills.

Grumiaux's performance of this concerto, once a staple of the concert hall (advanced student violinists must still cut their eye teeth on its particulars, especially its bowing problems), is compact; the music's line moves on from one point to the next with utter smoothness—there are no exaggerations. It is Viotti seen in the most perfect light.

Concerto No. 24 in B minor for Violin and Orchestra

☐ English Chamber Orchestra / Röhn (violin) / Mackerras (conductor) / Deutsche Grammophon ARC-2533122

The Mackerras-Röhn presentation provides evidence as to the unjust neglect of Viotti's violin concerti. The music has the purity and clear direction of the classical school and is totally free of pedantry. The performance is an undoubted accomplishment.

See above (Concerto No. 16 in E minor) for some other remarks which apply to this work as well.

Sonata in B flat major for Harp

Instrumental

Harp

☐ Zabaleta (harp) / Deutsche Grammophon 139419

Clean writing, meaning an independence of clichés (the arpeggios and glissandi, etc.) that haunt harp music and deter it from gaining proper acceptance. Formal delineation is clear; so is the performance, especially Zabaleta's dynamic control.

Duetto concertante in D major, Op. 29

Chamber Music

☐ Gulli (violin, playing both parts) / Musical Heritage Society MHS-1132

Simplistic but not elementary violin-duet music. Viotti produced over fifty for the combination. This one is as good as any, played by Franco Gulli alone via the overdubbing process. Neat trick, neat accomplishment.

Robert de Visée   *(ca. 1650 - ca. 1725)*

Passacaille

Instrumental

Guitar

☐ Segovia (guitar) / MCA 2524

A flavorsome example of music by this composer-guitarist. Intimate music and unerringly played.

Suite in G major

☐ Santos (guitar) / Musical Heritage Society MHS-1916

A *Prélude* followed by a series of seven dances—beginning with an Allemande, followed by a Courante, through the usual range, and concluding with a Gigue. Anyone who is familiar with the style of the period will not be surprised. Clearly played and attractively produced.

Allemande and Chaconne

Lute

Gigue and *Double de la gigue*

☐ Satoh (lute) / Klavier 528

Dramatic effects are not the bread and butter of the lute-music world; pleasantly clean harmonic progressions clinging to as pleasantly clear melodic ideas are. The slight variants in the Chaconne illustrate how compositional color can be obtained, even if dynamic sobriety is rather constant.

Toyohiko Satoh's playing is marked by excellent phrasing and lovely tone quality.

Giovanni Battista Vitali (1632-1692)

Chamber Music

Capriccio

☐ Schäffer Quartet / Vox SVBX-5300

Formal caprice, not capricious mood, is conveyed here. Accordingly, stylistic sectionalism for this seventeenth-century music, with shifts between homophonic and polyphonic writing. The contrast is maintained in changes of mood and key.

Slightly rough in the bottom zone but otherwise a perfectly acceptable representation by the Schäffer team.

Tommaso Antonio Vitali (ca. 1665-?)

Instrumental

Violin

Chaconne

☐ Szeryng (violin); Janopoulo (piano) / Everest 3154E (monaural)

Most violinists tend to play this classic beauty with romantic intermediation. Not Henryk Szeryng, who gives proper stylistic definition in his response.

Antonio Vivaldi (1678-1741)

Orchestra

Concerto a Due Chori

In A major, P. 14 / In B flat major, P. 368 / In C major, P. 226 / In D major, P. 164

☐ Les Solistes de Bruxelles and I Solisti di Milano / Ephrikian (conductor) / Telefunken 641263

These four concerti for two orchestras have strong coloristic profile. The A major work is *con flauti obligati,* and the opening with the flutes responded to by the organ is but one example. In the B flat major opus the feature is a solo violin retuned so that the lowest string is pegged at B flat rather than G (*con violino discordato*). Focus on the violin is strong, with a sizable cadenza at the conclusion of the finale—a rare use of such technical embroidery on Vivaldi's part.

These performances have brilliant scale. The continuo is especially fine, with organ used for one group and harpsichord for the other. *Schwann* lists the same release on Seraphim S-60118, but this writer has not checked this edition. He has, however, checked a recording of the B flat major work on Musical Heritage Society (MHS-1100), and it is a beautiful and knowing statement, with Piero Toso as the solo violinist, together with I Solisti Veneti, conducted by Claudio Scimone. If only one of these "in two choirs" works is sufficient, by all means choose it, it's a real winner.

String Orchestra

Concerto

In D major, P. 175 / In G minor, P. 392

☐ English Chamber Orchestra / Leppard (conductor) / Klavier 518

Uncomplicated by special concerns and precise in all the actions is the playing by Leppard's orchestra. Two points: he has fine harpsichord support, and he takes an *allegro* on the fast side, but that doesn't harm those Vivaldi churning figures at all.

Concerto Grosso in D minor, Op. 3, No. 11

☐ London Soloists Ensemble / Nonesuch 71052

Positively a stunning performance. The laying off of overinterpretative hands makes the music emerge with its superb clarity unblemished. Tempo choices are speedy, and this adds a truly exciting touch. The playing of this ten-instrument team (four violins, two violas, two cellos, bass, and harpsichord) is a winner on all counts.

Sinfonia al Santo Sepolcro, P. sinf. 21

☐ I Solisti di Milano / Ephrikian (conductor) / Bach Guild 70678

"At the Holy Sepulcher" has a probity of expression that is beautifully described by the uncredited liner-note writer as having "a mystical otherworldliness with a deeply human anguish." The tight (conjunct) linear situations that present tensilities and releases only to move on to other frictions and resolutions are of dramatic stripe despite the low-keyed instrumental coloration.

The playing is responsive to the utmost. Thus the recording is significant and totally rewarding.

Concerto in B flat major (*La notte*) for Bassoon and Orchestra

☐ Milano Virtuosi / Bianchi (bassoon) / Santi (conductor) / Vox 513120

Solo Instrument and Orchestra

Bassoon

A partial picturesque inlay is the special point of this Concerto, one of the 38 Vivaldi produced for the instrument. There are five sections in *La Notte* ("The Night"), with parts 2, 4, and 5 bearing titles, respectively, "The Phantoms," "The Dream," and "The Sunrise." Of course, only in a general way does the music follow these descriptions; Vivaldi's habitual use of scales, arpeggios, and chordal figures are the ingredients and supports of the work, regardless of the various titled situations.

Nice responsiveness on the part of all concerned in this recording; the sense of style is positive.

Concerto in E minor for Bassoon and Orchestra, P. 137

☐ Chamber Orchestra of the Saar / Allard (bassoon) / Ristenpart (conductor) / Nonesuch 71104

One of the most expressive of the many bassoon Concerti that Vivaldi produced. The nobility of the Largo and the dynamism of the pair of fast movements are superbly set forth with sensitive depiction of the phrasings, shadings, and dynamics.

Concerto in G minor for Bassoon, P. 401

☐ I Solisti di Zagreb / Klepač (bassoon); Tachezi (harpsichord) / Janigro (conductor) / Bach Guild HM–16

There are a good number of Vivaldi works that run through formal routine—to be designated in the if-you've-heard-one-you've-heard-them-all category. Not this interesting composition. In the first movement registral changes are constant, adding decided color. Movement 2 is restricted to a duo that contrasts the solo bassoon with the bass part of the continuo. A gay finale seals the work.

Janigro's group plays with vitality and complete discernment. Rudolf Klepač acquits himself with distinction. This is a fine issue of a fine work.

Cello

Concerto for Cello and Orchestra
No. 3 in A minor / No. 5 in E minor

☐ Baltimore Conservatory Orchestra / Parisot (cello) / Stewart (conductor) / Counterpoint/Esoteric 5555

This is a different A minor Concerto from the one performed by Thomas Blees discussed *below* (Concerto in A minor for Cello and Strings), for which no number or P. identification is given by Turnabout. (The same lack of information pertains to the Counterpoint/Esoteric release.) In the E minor Concerto some non-Vivaldi colors have been added (flute, oboe, trumpet, etc.). (This time there is no identification for the person who amplified the scoring.) However, nothing is spoiled, especially with Aldo Parisot's superfine playing. It could not be more evocative.

Concerto in A minor for Cello and Strings

☐ Stuttgart Soloists / Blees (cello) / Turnabout 34236

Strong in conviction, strong in tonal assurance. Blees's lyrical expansiveness is not reserved for the middle slow movement alone, but comes through in the fast-paced corner movements.

For another A minor Concerto see *above* (Concerto No. 3 in A minor).

Two Cellos

Concerto in G minor for Two Cellos and Orchestra, P. 411

☐ Chamber Orchestra of the Saar / Hindrichs and Dommisch (cellos) / Ristenpart (conductor) / Nonesuch 71104

An inspiring performance of a work that, naturally, emphasizes baritone-bass instrumental timbre. Vivaldi does not opt to contrast the accompaniment strongly by constant use of the high register of the strings, but by careful apportionment there is no covering of the solo lines. Nice fast tempi for the outer Allegro movements add zest to the portrayal.

Flute

Concerto for Flute and Orchestra, Op. 10
No. 1 (*La tempesta di mare*) in F major / No. 2 (*La notte*) in G minor / No. 3 (*Il cardellino*) in D major / No. 4 in G major / No. 5 (*Con sordini*) in F major / No. 6 in G major

☐ Louis de Froment Chamber Ensemble / Rampal (flute); Veyron-Lacroix (harpsichord) / Turnabout 34023E (monaural)

Although there are other flute concerti sprinkled about in various releases, this set of six represents the most imaginative of Vivaldi's output for the solo soprano wind instrument.

Enchanting details are to be found in every one of the six compositions. All the pith is supplied in these enchanting presentations. Dignity is realized when it should be, and depth also. Rampal's rich tonal delivery is a guarantee of enravishing performances.

The Rampal performances are also available on Columbia D3S–770, accompanied by I Solisti Veneti, conducted by Scimone.

Concerto in A minor for Flute and Orchestra, P. 77

☐ Deutsche Bachsolisten / Nicolet (flute) / Winschermann (conductor) / Nonesuch 71148

Immaculate phrasing and golden tone in the elegy-like slow movement. This, one of the best of Vivaldi's flute concerti, offers thorough enjoyment.

Concerto in C major for Two Flutes, P. 76

☐ I Solisti Veneti / Rampal (flute) / Scimone (conductor) / Columbia D3S–770

A superlative performance. Columbia makes no mention of a second flutist and it can be taken for granted that Rampal plays both parts by the overdubbing process. Well, what's better than one Rampal? Two, of course, though one does miss the slightly different personality that makes two-instrument concerti that much more interesting. Nonetheless, perfection of ensemble and interpretation is here offered. Yes, superlative playing by Rampal and Rampal.

Concerto for Guitar and Strings

In A major / In C major, P. 134

☐ I Solisti di Zagreb / Diaz (guitar) / Janigro (conductor) / Vanguard 71152

These concerti were originally for mandolin, but there is little loss, hardly any actually, in the transfer to guitar. Alirio Diaz's projection is exceedingly attractive, especially in tempo conception and phrasing steadiness. There are other editions to be secured of the C major opus with mandolin as the solo instrument (see under *Mandolin* [Concerto in C major for Mandolin and Orchestra, P. 134]), but at present none are available with mandolin for the A major work.

Diaz's performances are included in an anthology Vanguard has issued on HM–32. The C major Concerto is also in a two-disc release on Vanguard 709/10.

Concerto for Two Horns, Strings, and Continuo

In F major, P. 320 / In F major, P. 321

☐ Collegium Musicum of Paris / Barboteu and Coursier (horns); Martinerie (cello); Boulay (harpsichord) / Douatte (conductor) / Nonesuch 71091

Vivaldian fixed formal procedures are followed here: two moderately fast movements with a central slow division. The conventionality is so pat that there is a difference between the two concerti of only seven seconds in the length of one of the outer movements and nineteen seconds in the length of the other. In the slow movements the equality is similar: 3:00 in P. 320, 3:18 in P. 321.

With the exception of the string group's being rather small, the recording is a worthy one.

Concerto in D major for Lute, Violins, and Figured Bass, P. 209

☐ Württemberg Chamber Orchestra, Heilbronn / Stingl (lute); Buck (cello); Galling (harpsichord) / Faerber (conductor) / Turnabout 34153

This piece is listed in *Schwann* as "Concerto in D for Guitar." With this close-substitute instrument Vivaldi's concentrated opus (only 100 measures in length) has been recorded by seven guitarists, whose performances are available in eleven different issues.

Stingl's playing shows off the subtle, less weighted quality of the lute and is a most attractive performance. All of the possible interpretative sparkle is to be heard. (Stingl's performance can also be heard in a five-record collection Turnabout has issued on No. 34195/9.)

Concerto in C major for Mandolin and Orchestra, P. 134

☐ New York Sinfonietta / Goichberg (mandolin) / Goberman (conductor) / Odyssey 32160138

This is also available with substitution by guitar (see under *Guitar* [Concerto for Guitar and Strings in C major, P. 134]). Well-formed playing, with fine stylistic response. Other performances (especially on Turnabout 34153) tend to plod along and end in Dullsville. The one exception is Bonifacio Bianchi's rendition on Musical Heritage Society MHS-1100. It is a quite convincing account turning the work out in 8:15; Paul Grund (on the Turnabout disc mentioned) takes 9:20 for the three movements. (Diaz, in his guitar version, is fastest of all, covering the ground in just two seconds under eight minutes.)

Two Mandolins | **Concerto in G major for Two Mandolins, Strings, and Organ, P. 133**

☐ I Solisti di Zagreb / Ganoci and Pavlinek (mandolins); Tachezi (harpsichord) / Janigro (conductor) / Vanguard HM-16

Recorded presentations abound of this tasteful and mellifluent work. Setting aside versions with substituted solo timbre in the form of paired guitars or lutes, the most discriminating rendition is presented in the issue noted above. Give and take the need for a milder accent here and there or some bowing pressures that might be questioned, by and large the playing in all of the almost dozen performances available is most satisfactory. However, in matters of tempo rationale Janigro and his soloists move into first place. Theirs is a bright picturization more than two minutes faster than the others—reflecting a decision on tempo that is stylistically unarguable. The duo playing is beautiful; the antiphonal coloration between the soloists is accomplished with the maximum effect.

Oboe | **Concerto for Oboe, Strings, and Cembalo**

In A minor, P. 42 / In B flat major, Op. 7, No. 7 (P. 334)

☐ I Solisti Veneti / Pierlot (oboe) / Scimone (conductor) / Musical Heritage Society MHS-951

Skilled and perceptive performances. The accompaniments are well rounded and have sensitive balance.

Concerto for Oboe, Strings, and Cembalo

In B flat major, P. 331 / In C major, Op. 8, No. 12

☐ I Solisti Veneti / Pierlot (oboe) / Scimone (conductor) / Musical Heritage Society MHS-952

Convincing portrayals. Pierre Pierlot has the right tonal touch for these works, and the accompaniments are excellent, played by a group of six violins, two violas, two cellos, a double bass, and harpsichord.

Concerto for Oboe, Strings, and Cembalo

In C major, P. 43 / In C major, P. 44

☐ I Solisti Veneti / Pierlot (oboe) / Scimone (conductor) / Musical Heritage Society MHS-952

Both concerti are in the bright C major tonality favored by Vivaldi in his dozen oboe concertos. Only a pair of all these oboe concerti are in a minor key, and of the remaining ten works exactly half are in C major. Pierlot matches this tonal clarity in playing, with poise in the slow sections and a winning lightness in the fast ones.

Concerto for Oboe, Strings, and Cembalo
In C major, P. 91 / In D major, P. 187

☐ I Solisti Veneti / Pierlot (oboe) / Scimone (conductor) / Musical Heritage Society MHS–951

Again, perceptive performances by these musicians, as described in the notes *above* on the other works in the series of concerti for oboe, strings, and cembalo. Pierlot and Scimone accent the positive in their fast-movement tempi, directed certainly to uplift the spirit. Slow movements move with gracious style, and the entire production fully realizes the beauty contained in these Vivaldi works.

Concerto in C major for Oboe, Strings, and Cembalo, P. 41

☐ I Solisti Veneti / Pierlot (oboe) / Scimone (conductor) / Musical Heritage Society MHS–951

Vivaldi provides his usual three-movement design, with the exception of completing the composition with a Minuet rather than the traditional Allegro. Scimone will have none of this, however, and paces this finale much faster than an Allegro, so that the music travels at a one-to-a-bar clip. No harm, since this fits the content. Pierlot is at his very best in the spun *cantilena* of the central movement, where he is more sublte than the soloist in the competitive edition on Turnabout 34025.

Concerto in D minor for Oboe, Strings, and Cembalo, Op. 8, No. 9

☐ New York Philharmonic / Gomberg (oboe) / Bernstein (conductor) / Columbia MS–6131

Oboe playing by Harold Gomberg which is of fabulous golden smoothness. The richness of Gomberg's sound is certainly the very acme in the world of oboists. Even the great Heinz Holliger is a couple of notches below Gomberg's place on the summit.

The tempi Gomberg uses in this Concerto have breadth and so give greater opportunity to bathe in juicy sonority in the fast movements than to hear perfectly spiculated articulation. Holliger plays the work on Philips 6500413. His timing is eight and one-half minutes, while Gomberg's performance covers a few seconds over ten minutes, which tells plenty about the different approach these men take. Pierre Pierlot on Musical Heritage Society (MHS–951) also opts for speed—he is a quarter of a minute faster than Holliger. Thus in speed Pierlot is number one of the group. Tone-wise, however, he is in third place. One wishes that Gomberg would play a bit faster (though certainly not as breathlessly excitedly as Holliger). Well he doesn't, and his performance remains the very best. That gorgeous oboe sound he produces is overwhelming.

Concerto in F major for Oboe, Strings, and Cembalo, P. 264

☐ I Solisti Veneti / Pierlot (oboe) / Scimone (conductor) / Musical Heritage Society MHS–952

Attractive playing similar to that in other Pierlot-Scimone performances of the concerti for oboe, strings, and cembalo (*see above*).

Concerto in F major for Oboe, Strings, and Cembalo, P. 306

☐ Columbia Chamber Orchestra / Gomberg (oboe) / Ozawa (conductor) / Columbia MS–6832

Refined musicianship and golden oboe tone make Harold Gomberg's conception delectable. Nothing special in Vivaldi's music, but the way it is presented lifts it out of the academic category.

Two Oboes

Concerto in D minor for Two Oboes and Strings, P. 302

☐ Milano Virtuosi / Caroldi and Alvarosi (oboes) / Santi (conductor) / Vox 513120

There is plenty of substance and feeling in this Concerto. It begins with a Largo introduction, moves into an Allegro, is followed by a full-fledged Largo movement, and is then concluded in Allegro molto pace.

The performance is sensitive and the dynamic differences are especially vivid. Both of the soloists display excellent tone. Excellence, however, does not describe Vox's packaging and labeling. The album cover and record label signify the Concerto as a triple-instrument one, for ''Two Oboes and Bassoon,'' which it is not. (The liner notes are correct.) Further, there are two bands on the disc. The label incorrectly signifies that the two-oboe Concerto occupies the first band. Be sure to start with band 2 if you want to hear this particular Concerto.

Two Oboes and Two Clarinets

Concerto in C major for Two Oboes, Two Clarinets, and Strings, P. 74

☐ Milano Virtuosi / Caroldi and Alvarosi (oboes) / Santi (conductor) / Vox 513120

Vivaldi matches his choice of unusual concerto instrumentation with colorful details. In movement 1 canon and echo effects are emphasized. In movement 2 there is no accompaniment; the solo instruments play a somewhat melancholy march-like music. Since the following (final) movement is a brisk, fast-paced affair, the contrast is triply effective in terms of color, textural weight, and motility.

All is well with the playing. All is not well with the labeling of the recording. It designates the Concerto as occupying the second band of the disc, but in reality it is the first of the two works on it (side 2 of an issue devoted to four Vivaldi Concerti, each for a different solo instrument or instruments).

Piccolo

Concerto for Piccolo, Strings, and Continuo
In A minor, P. 83 / In C major, P. 78

☐ Vienna State Opera Orchestra / Baker (piccolo) / Prohaska (conductor) / Vanguard 71170

Julius Baker, a flute virtuoso, is just as splendid an artist on the diminutive relative instrument. This is totally stylish playing with a tone that is rich and full and never once edgy. It has a memorable sopranino quality.

Trumpet

Concerto in A flat major

☐ Jean-François Paillard Chamber Orchestra / André (trumpet) / Paillard (conductor) / RCA CRL2-7002

The sopranino register is almost exclusively featured in this work, someone's remake (no one is credited) of a pair of movements from a trio sonata and one from another instrumental Concerto. One wonders, with the huge wealth of Vivaldi music, why arrangements must be made to obtain more material, but so it goes and here it is. Purity of trumpet conception no, but purity of trumpet performance absolutely.

Concerto for Two Trumpets and Orchestra, P. 75

☐ Mainz Chamber Orchestra / Zickler and Thal (trumpets) / Kehr (conductor) / Turnabout 34057

One of the most engaging works among the many concerti that Vivaldi produced. Colorful timbred music that will make a full claim on a listener's attention. It is played with brightness and a gentle kind of force that is most effective. (It is duplicated on Turnabout 34295/9.)

Concerto in B flat major, P. 406

☐ Die Wiener Solisten / André (trumpet); Pichler (violin) / RCA CRL2–7002

This piece was originally for oboe and violin. It is rich and cultivated in that version and remains so in the shift to trumpet and violin. Deucedly attractive playing.

Concerto in C major *con molti stromenti*, P. 16

☐ I Solisti Veneti / Bianchi and Pitrelli (mandolins); Schaffer and Gerwig (theorbos); Larde and Clementine Scimone (flutes); Pecile and Gerbi (salmo-clarinets); Toso and Ferrari (violins *in tromba marina*); Cassoli (cello) / Claudio Scimone (conductor) / Musical Heritage Society MHS–1100

The average direct, concise, and robust Vivaldi conception. But what a difference in terms of the colors of this rare instrumentational bird! There are pairs of theorbos, salmo-clarinets, mandolins, and violins, the last imitating the marine trumpet (*tromba marina*), in addition to two flutes and a cello. Of course, backing this is the usual string orchestra and continuo.

This performance is as close to the original as possible and is minus the fine suave hand and heavy thumb prints of a twentieth-century transcriber. Those who prefer the modernized version or desire to compare it with the original must obtain the Casella setting (see under *Vivaldi/Casella: Solo Instrument and Orchestra: various instruments*). In fairness to Casella's transcription, incidentally, it was made only because of the extreme difficulty of securing the largely no-longer-existent instruments called for by Vivaldi, let alone players who could handle then adequately.

Concerto for Viola d'Amore and String Orchestra

In A major, P. 233 / In A minor, P. 37 / In D major, P. 166 / In D minor, P. 287

☐ Toulouse Chamber Orchestra / Pons (viola d'amore) / Armand (conductor) / Seraphim S–60244

The usual Vivaldi formal basis is provided here. It is of note that in this case strings accompanying a single string instrument give a double textural comparison, i.e., solo concentrate against tutti mass and a thin-toned viola d'amore against the usual string family. The execution of these works takes this into account, and all the balances between the different weights are fine.

Concerto in D minor for Viola d'Amore and String Orchestra, P. 288

☐ New York Sinfonietta / Trampler (viola d'amore) / Goberman (conductor) / Odyssey 32160138

Stylishly performed—an impressive contribution.

Concerto in F major for Viola d'Amore and String Orchestra, P. 286

☐ New York Sinfonietta / Kroyt (viola d'amore) / Goberman (conductor) / Odyssey 32160138

Poise and incisiveness—even a bit more than displayed by the others who have taken the solo parts in recordings of Vivaldi's viola d'amore concerti.

Violin

Concerto in A major for Violin, Strings, and Continuo, Op. 3, No. 12 (from *L'estro armonico—see below*)

Concerto in A minor for Violin, Strings, and Continuo, Op. 3, No. 6 (from *L'estro armonico – see below*)

Concerto in C major for Violin, Two String Choirs, and Two Harpsichords, *Per la Ss. Assunzione de Maria Vergine*, P. 14

☐ I Solisti di Zagreb / Stanic (violin); Tachezi and Thune (harpsichords) / Janigro (conductor) / Bach Guild HM-16

The variety of solo instrument choice in Vivaldi's concerti output is staggering. In this case what is noteworthy and unique is the accompanimental choice, embracing two string groups together with two harpsichords. The natural expectation of the use of antiphony is fulfilled. What is not expected in a Vivaldi Concerto is the use of an extended cadenza, but this one has a large-sized example that precedes the conclusion of the three-movement work.

P. 14 is a splendid Concerto and is of special importance in the Vivaldi catalogue. It deserves concert hall exposure, but I cannot recall any notice of such presentation. Accordingly, Bach Guild's recorded issue has special value. It is performed with excellence.

Concerto in D major for Violin, Strings, and Continuo, Op. 3, No. 9 (from *L'estro armonico—see below*)

Concerto for Violin, Strings, and Continuo

In E major (*L'amoroso*), P. 246 / In E minor (*Il favorito*), Op. 11, No. 2, P. 106

☐ Members of the Dresden State Orchestra / Grumiaux (violin) / Negri (conductor) / Philips 6500690

More choice concerti from this prolific composer. Special contrast is obtained in the slow movement of the E major work by reducing the accompaniment to three-part scale. Both compositions have imaginative figuration so that sequential monotony is avoided.

No one could ask for finer violin playing than is exhibited in these performances. Negri provides sensitive backing for the soloist.

Concerto in G major for Violin, Strings, and Continuo, Op. 3, No. 3 (from *L'estro armonico—see below*)

Concerto in G minor for Violin, Strings, and Continuo, Op. 12, No. 1, P. 343

☐ Members of the Dresden State Orchestra / Grumiaux (violin) / Negri (conductor) / Philips 6500690

As is to be expected, the Concerto is in three movements: Allegro, Largo, and Allegro. However, Vivaldian individuality is to be noted in the accompanimental color used in the fast-paced (outer) movements. In place of the usual continuo for the support of the solo voice, the high-pitched instruments are chosen.

And, as is to be expected, Grumiaux provides the listener with a lovely singing, silvery tone; immaculate technique; and perfect styling. This is one of the very best performances in the entire Vivaldi discography.

The Four Seasons: Concerti for Violin and String Orchestra, Op. 8

No. 1 (*Spring*) in E major / No. 2 (*Summer*) in G minor / No. 3 (*Autumn*) in F major / No. 4 (*Winter*) in F minor

☐ English Chamber Orchestra / Szeryng (violin) / Philips 6500076
☐ Philadelphia Orchestra / Brusilow (violin) / Ormandy (conductor) / Columbia MS-6195

These concerti, the first four of twelve violin concerti titled *Il cimento dell'armonia e dell'inventione* ("The Trial Between Harmony and Invention") cannot be termed an excerpt. They form a total set even though within a larger total opus. They have moved up to a point of popularity that rivals the standard violin concertos such as those by Mendelssohn, Brahms, and Tchaikovsky. Note well that close to two dozen recorded performances were considered before writing this commentary.

Both of these editions have authority, depth of insight, Vivaldian virtuosity at its best, and remarkable color (color is especially emphasized in Ormandy's contribution). That both are full-flushed presentations makes these stunning works glow most vividly.

La cetra: Concerti for Violin and Orchestra, Op. 9, P. 10

No. 4 in E major / No. 8 in D minor / No. 12 in B minor

☐ Chamber Orchestra of the Vienna State Opera / Makanowitzky (violin) / Golschmann (conductor) / Vanguard S-159

Vivaldi's Opus 9, "The Lyre," consists of a dozen violin concerti. The three represented here are fine examples, as is the fifth of the set (*see below*). Another fine example, for paired violins, is noted *below* (*La cetra*, Op. 9, P. 10: Concerto No. 9 in B flat major for Two Violins and Orchestra).

The concerti are strongly representative of Vivaldian style and are persuasively portrayed in this recording.

La cetra, Op. 9, P. 10—Concerto No. 5 in A minor for Violin and Orchestra

☐ Members of the Dresden State Orchestra / Grumiaux (violin) / Negri (conductor) / Philips 6500690

A slight change in Vivaldi's usual formal procedure is to be noted here. In place of a separate slow movement, the first (Presto) movement is prefaced with a brief Adagio and concluded with a similarly pithy Largo. Solo violin virtuosic flourishes mark the second (Allegro) movement.

Grumiaux's playing is at a splendid level. His tone is flawless, the passage work is set forth with virility and is right on target. (For other Concerti in this Opus *see above* and see also under *Two Violins.*)

La stravaganza: Concerti for Violin and Strings, Op. 4

No. 1 in B flat major / No. 2 in E minor / No. 3 in G major / No. 4 in A minor / No. 5 in A major / No. 6 in G minor / No. 7 in C major / No. 8 in D minor / No. 9 in F major / No. 10 in C minor / No. 11 in D major / No. 12 in G major

☐ Pro Musica String Orchestra, Stuttgart / Barchet (violin); Elsner (harpsichord) / Reinhardt (conductor) / Vox SVBX-531

A marvelously clean exposition with immaculate evenness of bowing and excellence of style. Grandly spacious sound frames these exquisite examples of Vivaldi's art.

The competitive edition on Argo (ZRG–800/1) uses two different soloists who are just as good as Reinhold Barchet and a much larger continuo that includes harpsichord, organ, and theorbos. That much is positive. A minus is the tempi, which skim along very often at too fast a pace.

Two Violins

Concerto in A major for Two Violins, Strings, and Continuo, Op. 3, No. 5 (from *L'estro armonico—see below*)

Concerto in A minor for Two Violins, Strings, and Continuo, Op. 3, No. 8 (from *L'estro armonico—see below*)

Concerto for Two Violins, Strings, and Cembalo

In C minor, P. 189 / In D major, P. 281 / In D minor, P. 366 / In G minor, P. 436

☐ Members of the Philadelphia Orchestra / Stern and David Oistrakh (violinists); Smith (cembalo) / Ormandy (conductor) / Columbia MS-6204

Perhaps a bit fat in tonal weight but the fat is beautiful and round, so the music is freed from the restricted timbre totality that marks other presentations (including other Vivaldi double violin concertos). There's nothing urbane in these performances, and the amply clear brilliance of solo voices and strings is welcome.

La cetra, Op. 9, P. 10

Concerto No. 9 in B flat major for Two Violins and Orchestra

☐ Chamber Orchestra of the Vienna State Opera / Makanowitzky and Boskovsky (violins) / Golschmann (conductor) / Vanguard S-159

See above: La cetra: Concerti for Violin and Orchestra for commentary.

Three Violins

Concerto in F major for Three Violins and Orchestra, P. 278

☐ English Chamber Orchestra / Zukerman, Sillito, and Garcia (violins); Ledger (harpsichord / Zukerman (conductor) / Columbia M-32230

Fine blend, fine balance, fine playing, and a spontaneity that is a delight are to be found in this performance, with Pinchas Zukerman doubling as conductor and violinist. The old Odyssey release (No. 32160054) lacks soloistic equality. A better presentation, second, however, to the one listed, because of some thin-toned solo violin playing, is on Nonesuch 71022, with Ristenpart conducting; the soloists are Hendel, Schlupp, and Bunte.

Four Violins

Concerto in B minor for Four Violins, Strings, and Continuo, Op. 3, No. 10 (from *L'estro armonico—see below*)

Concerto in E minor for Four Violins, Strings, and Continuo, Op. 3, No. 4 (from *L'estro armonico–see below*)

Violin and Cello

Concerto in B flat major for Violin, Cello, Strings, and Harpsichord

☐ Chamber Orchestra / Heifetz (violin); Piatigorsky (cello); Hamilton (harpsichord) / RCA LSC-2867

Though there is not precise stylistic matching in the bowing articulation of the two string-instrument masters here, the total sense of lucidity is just fine. The entrances are punctuative, the rhythms spring forth. That makes it darn good Vivaldi. (*Schwann* lists a version issued by Audio Fidelity [50027]. The writer did not audition this disc.)

Concerto in D minor for Two Violins, Cello, Strings, and Continuo, Op. 3, No. 11 (from *L'estro armonico—see below*)
Two Violins and Cello

Concerto In G minor for Two Violins, Cello, Strings, and Continuo, Op. 3, No. 2 (from *L'estro armonico—see below*)

Concerto in D major for Four Violins, Cello, Strings, and Continuo, Op. 3, No. 1 (from *L'estro armonico—see below*)
Four Violins and Cello

Concerto in F major for Four Violins, Cello, Strings, and Continuo, Op. 3, No. 7 (from *L'estro armonico – see below*)

L'estro armonico: Twelve Concerti, Op. 3

☐ Academy of St. Martin-in-the-Fields / Loveday, Brown, Kaine, Gillard, and Thomas (violins); Heath (cello); Hogwood and Tilney (harpsichords and organ); Spencer (theorbo) / Marriner (conductor) / Argo ZRG-733/4

L'estro armonico is doubtless the most important of the several concerto groups in Vivaldi's voluminous output of music. It includes five different solo scoring plans: two of the set are for two violins, a pair of works feature two violins and a cello, four of the concerti call for a solo violin, and there are two works each for four violins and four violins plus cello. In each case a string body supports and contrasts in concerto grosso demeanor, and completed with a continuo. For the latter some recordings have used only a cembalo (for example, the Vanguard set S-143/5). In Marriner's edition the continuo is much more expansive in its total coloration and is used in a variety of ways, which adds appeal to his first-class and extremely authoritative performance. It has all the stuff—grace and ebullience, vigor and Vivaldian punch (the attacks are justly weighted), warmth and breadth. The freshness of the playing makes hearing each work akin to a discovery, even those repertoire standbys the A minor Concerto No. 8 for Two Violins and the D minor Concerto No. 11 for Two Violins and Cello.

Separate concerti are listed above in accordance with the solo category involved.

Sonata in A minor for Cello and Harpsichord, Op. 14
Chamber Music

☐ Roveda (cello); Sgrizzi (harpsichord) / Nonesuch 73008

Re-created with solidity, warmth, and engaging flow. The contrastive dynamics are clear but, happily, not overdetailed.

Sonata in D minor for Flute and Basso Continuo

☐ Linde (flute); Mueller (harpsichord); Jappe (viola da gamba) / Klavier 511

Just a bit formally different, consisting of three slow-paced movements and a final Allegro.

Hans Martin Linde is a better player of the recorder (by which he has achieved his reputation) than of the related flute. Nice tone, but he does tend to flatten out dynamic differences. However, the work is worth having on disc even in a straightforward rendition that does not try to search for any special depths in the music. (*Schwann* errs in listing this performance as being on the recorder.)

Sonata in F major for Recorder

☐ Linde (recorder); Mueller (harpsichord); Jappe (viola da gamba) / Klavier 511

Three-movement plan, one of each: slow-tempoed, a dance, and an *Allegro*. The characterization is most convincing, clearly detailed, and nicely supported by the continuo of harpsichord and viola da gamba.

Sonata in G minor for Recorder and Basso Continuo, Op. 13, No. 6

☐ Kneihs (recorder); Radescu (harpsichord); Kaiser (cello) / Klavier 512

A clear and factual performance.

Trio for Violin, Lute, and Bass

☐ Tryssesoone (baroque violin); Podolski (lute); Terby (bass viol) / Orion 7032

An exhibit of Vivaldi's disarmingly simple musical prose, with the standard three-movement plan. In the Larghetto he contrasts the moving line of the lute against sustained harmonies in a very effective manner. The use of authentic instruments adds to the enjoyment of the performance.

Sonata in G minor for Flute, Oboe, Bassoon, and Harpsichord

☐ Dawn Weiss (flute); David Weiss (oboe); Abraham Weiss (bassoon); Carno (harpsichord) / Crystal S-354

The unsigned liner notes indicate that Vivaldi's work "was probably originally written for two violins and continuo." It gives no other facts, and really no other data are required. The beautiful suppleness of this three-movement work is a joy to the ears, transcription or not. It is played with lucidity and with marvelous ensemble.

Trio in G minor for Violin, Lute, and Figured Bass, F. XVI/4

☐ Breitschmid (violin); Stingl (lute); Buck (cello); Galling (harpsichord) / Turnabout 34153

The usual Vivaldi formal pattern of three movements with the habitual Vivaldian sequential patterns, but applied to an individual color combination of bowed and plucked timbres. There are no flaws in this deftly carried-out presentation.

Il pastor fido: Sonatas, Op. 13
No. 1 in C major / No. 2 in C major / No. 3 in G major / No. 4 in A major / No. 5 in C major / No. 6 in G minor

☐ Linde (flute and recorder); Sous (oboe); Zosso (hurdy-gurdy); Stiftner (bassoon); Melkus (violin); Atmacayan (cello); Dreyfus (harpsichord) / Deutsche Grammophon ARC-2533117

Since Vivaldi offered a number of instrumental choices for his Opus 13 and the instruments were the musette, vielle, flute, oboe, and violin, with continuo, the coloristic detail applied by the present ensemble comes quite close to his original conception, and hearing the ensemble is more interesting than hearing the complete set performed on Orion 73115 by a trio of oboe, cello, and harpsichord.

There is fine tonal variety in these performances that deserve the highest praise. Indeed, a joyful and special sound.

Beatus Vir (Psalm 111)

☐ Carmel Bach Festival Orchestra and Chorale / Salgo (conductor) / Orion 75208

This is a large work for double chorus, two orchestras, and continuo in nine sections. There is a nobility in this psalm setting, with its harmonic language of high intrinsic luminosity.

Full credit is due the performance. Orion fails to list the organist, who has an especially important obbligato role in part 5, *Jucundus Homo.*

Cessate, Omai

☐ Orchestra of the Società Cameristica di Lugano / Malaguti (baritone) / Loehrer (conductor) / Nonesuch 71088

Vivaldi's *Cessate, Omai* is a find. One fully agrees with Edward Tatnall Canby's summation in his splendid liner note for the work: "Once again we must admit that Vivaldi, for all his enormous fruitfulness, could really 'turn on' his superior genius when the occasion demanded it." And on this occasion one hears two pairs of Recitatives and Arias accompanied by strings and continuo that display glowing vitality and fine balance between all elements; formal and instrumental. The music seethes emotionally but is stylistically constrained, marked by a stimulating prefiguration of Mozart style in the first of the two Arias.

The performance is ideal, especially the excellent singing of Laerte Malaguti, who avoids any personal insistence while fully identifying his interpretation with Vivaldian character.

Chamber Mass

☐ Mitzelfelt Orchestra and Mitzelfelt Chorale / Stevenson and Erny (sopranos); Holden (mezzo-soprano); Wyatt (tenor) / Mitzelfelt (conductor) / Crystal S–901

A compelling performance of this rarity. Vivaldi's work divides into fourteen parts, with the Kyrie totaling three and the Gloria eleven. Within these there are eight different scoring plans for chorus, double chorus, double women's chorus, soprano duet, solo soprano and chorus, etc. Crystal's release is marked by warm, rounded sound.

Dixit Dominus

☐ Vienna State Opera Orchestra and Vienna Kammerchor / Schlean (soprano); Bonay (contralto); Benelli (tenor); Sarti (bass) / Ephrikian (conductor) / Bach Guild 70678

One of Vivaldi's most notable works, including his huge output of instrumental compositions. One section follows another without interruption in the three-part introduction and ten-part "Psalm." The work exhibits an expressive strength that is of incomparable emotivity. Here are two examples of the many that could be cited: the *Donec ponam inimicos tuos,* evoking the inexorable might of God, is choral writing of grave and profound contour; the contralto solo, *Tecum principium,* is a stunning aria; it can be considered one of the most beautiful pieces Vivaldi ever produced. If this reads like a rave, it is meant to be. Vivaldi's *Dixit* is a masterpiece as great as any work by Bach or Beethoven.

It is matched by a vital and magnificent performance. Every challenge of construction, color, vocal intensity, and orchestral requirement is met. In the orchestra the playing and the echo format of the two trumpets in the *Judicabit in nationibus* section are expressively detailed. One admires and emphasizes highlights in an extended work, but in this case the entire composition is of sustained perfection. The authority that prevails on the part of the soloists, two choruses, two orchestras, and organ is beyond ordinary significance. For this full credit belongs to Angelo Ephrikian, the conductor.

Gloria

☐ Academy of St. Martin-in-the-Fields and King's College Choir, Cambridge / Vaughan (soprano); Baker (contralto) / Willcocks (conductor) / Argo ZRG–505

This work is generally known as the Gloria Mass, sometimes titled the Gloria in D. However or whatever, glory to God in glorious Vivaldian terms.

All the power and inventiveness of Vivaldi come through in a revealing performance. The solo singing is incontestable, and further rich testimony is given by the chorus.

Juditha Triumphans

☐ Angelicum Chamber Orchestra and Chorus of the Accademia Filarmonica Romana / Cundari (soprano); Dominguez, Compañez, and Casoni (mezzo-sopranos); Allegri (contralto) / Zedda (conductor) / RCA VICS–6016

Vivaldi's subtitle reads *Sacrum Militaire Oratorium* and in the very first measures timpani, fervent trumpets, and vigorous figurations set the mood of the oratorio. However, the sense of opera persists in this work that presents the tale of Judith decapitating the Assyrian enemy Holofernes, with the narrative being carried forward by recitatives between the arias.

All the roles, as will be noted, are taken by women, equating the use of females and castrati in the original performances. The singing is first rate and always stylish. RCA's version is an exact duplicate of a performance in the Musical Heritage Society catalogue (MHS–835/836). A less vivid competitive edition on Philips 6747173 is also available.

Piango, Gemo, Sospiro

☐ Malaguti (baritone); Roveda (cello); Sgrizzi (harpsichord) / Nonesuch 71088

Though constantly sequential in its phrase depiction, the effect of this Cantata for voice and two instruments cannot be denied. It is dark-colored throughout its three parts (a pair of Arias with a Recitative in between), fully depicting the fervent mournful tone of the text. "I Weep, I Groan, I Sigh" is performed in a manner proper to Vivaldi's low-keyed dramatic piece.

*Opera
and Dramatic
Music*

La fida ninfa

☐ Chamber Orchestra and Members of the Milan Opera / Repetto, Falachi, and Masini (sopranos); Calma (contralto); Constantino (tenor); Giacomotti (bass); Minetti (violin); Vacchelli (harpsichord) / Monterosso (conductor) / Vox SVBX–5210

Vivaldi's three-act opera, though overburdened with recitatives, has sufficient arias to compensate for the formal conventionality.

The instrumental sections portray Vivaldi at his best, particularly in the slow-tempoed portions. The singing, especially by the tenor, Antonio Constantino, is communicative.

A considerably abridged version with the same performers is available on Turnabout TV–34066S.

Tito Manlio

☐ Berlin Chamber Orchestra and Berlin Radio Chorus / Marshall (soprano); Wagemann, Hamari, and Lerer (mezzo-sopranos); Finnilä (contralto); Ahnsjö (tenor); Trimarchi (baritone); Luccardi (bass); Tate (harpsichord) / Negri (conductor) / Philips 6769004

This is a whale of a big opera covering ten record sides in Philips's release. There are separate numbers galore, approximately a hundred of them, with more than three dozen arias, close to five dozen recitatives, and plenty of dialogue. The orchestral spread includes—in addition to the usual strings and harpsichord—recorders, flute, oboes, bassoons, horns, trumpets, and timpani.

Early baroque opera isn't for everyone, but if you just avoid Vivaldi's plot with its word-maze puzzle which baffles understanding and listen to the arias (which have practically nothing to do with the story), you'll enjoy. Just select and jump around through this sprawling depiction.

The singers are fine, especially the baritone and bass. Among the females (some impersonating males) Margaret Marshall and Julia Hamari carry off the honors. These four provide the most exciting vocal chemistry in the cast.

Vivaldi / **Alfredo Casella**

Concerto in C major *con molti stromenti,* **P. 16**

Solo Instrument and Orchestra

Various Instruments

☐ New York Philharmonic / Vicari and de Filippis (mandolins); Wummer and Morris (flutes); Vacchiano and Prager (trumpets); Brenner (bass oboe); Stavrache and Wurtzler (harps); Corigliano (violin); Varga (cello); Bernstein (harpsichord) / Bernstein (conductor) / Columbia MS-6131

Columbia calls this as a "Concerto in C major for Diverse Instruments (with Mandolins)," which is, of course, largely a translation of the original. O.K., but why feature the mandolins? Comparison with the original (see under *Vivaldi: Solo Instrument and Orchestra: various instruments* for details) will show an equal combination of instruments with none highlighted. As for instrumental transfer, mandolins and flutes are in both the original and the modern setting; harps are used in place of the theorbos, a bass oboe (Heckelphone) is the proxy color for the salmo-clarinets (there is only one bass oboe since the part is completely in unison), and trumpets are substituted for the imitative *tromba marina* violins.

No matter the expertise of Casella and no matter the fine ensemble Bernstein directs with topflight soloism, the coloristic atmosphere has changed from the Vivaldian golden brown to a vivid yellow. Old wood is replaced by aluminum. It works in the other ways—in melody and harmony—but its shining face does not have the character of the ancestral one. Still, try Casella's Vivaldi, and, better, compare it with the original.

Giovanni Buonaventura Viviani   *(17th cent.)*

Sonata prima for Trumpet and Organ

Sonata seconda for Trumpet and Organ

Chamber Music

☐ André (trumpet); Alain (organ) / RCA CRL2-7001

No transcription. The original title reads *Sonate per tromba e organo o clavicembalo.* Viviani's pieces provide contrastive substantiation of the ceremonial and of the slow aria type. The music is finely judged in the playing. One minus sign: a lack of a substantial bass in the recording of the organ.

Roman Vlad   *(1919-   )*

Film Music   **Picasso**

☐ Orchestra / Gangi (guitar) / Ferrara (conductor) / Folkways 3860 (monaural)

This is the sound track from the documentary film *Picasso*, covering a total of eighteen segments. It chiefly follows the descriptive subheading that it is a "Flamenco score," but in some places (section 7, *Surrealism*, for example) some non-Flamenco influences appear. Vlad is a good composer, but his work has been overshadowed by his important book on Stravinsky.

Vladimir Vlasov   *(1903-   )*

*Solo
Instrument
and
Orchestra*   **Concerto No. 1 in C major (1963)**

☐ Moscow Radio Orchestra / Rostropovich (cello) / Rozhdestvensky (conductor) / Melodiya/Angel S-40180

Cello

Eclectic ingredients that provide a vehicle that showcases the famous cellist, and that's sufficient reason to listen. What seething virtuosity! A rich man's Khachaturian marks the style of most of the Ballade, Prokofiev (in good health) will be noticed in the Finale.

Some extraneous sounds will also be noticed en route. At the conclusion applause tells you what is nowhere mentioned—recorded live.

Jan van Vlijmen   *(1935-   )*

Orchestra   **Serenata I (1967)**

☐ Concertgebouw Orchestra / Maderna (conductor) / Donemus Audio-Visual Series DAVS-6902

Four connected movements for an orchestra of twelve winds and brass (two each of flute, oboe, clarinet, bassoon, horn, and trumpet) and a variety of percussion, including an important role for the xylorimba. The orchestra is divided into five groups and spread over the performing platform.

Dodecaphonic mobility is let loose here, and it carries over into the metrical arrangement. In the first three parts of the piece there are 123 measures, of which 118 have a change of time signature. Fourteen of the total measures consist of total silence, a contrastive device that does not diminish the nervousness of the conception.

Maderna directs a carefully crafted performance; the aleatoric detail in the final part is nicely handled.

Georg Joseph Vogler   *(1749-1814)*

*Solo
Instrument
and
Orchestra*   **Variations on *Marlborough***

☐ Prague New Chamber Orchestra / Blumental (piano) / Zedda (conductor) / Turnabout 34285

Piano

Thematic clarity is dominant in these eleven variations plus a Finale, which includes a

Fuga. Each part is defined. Especially gratifying are the picturesque variations dealing with such as bell sounds, churchly quality, and light-hearted *burlesco* details.

Felicja Blumental has done a large number of recorded performances. Her cleanness of detail in the playing of this work makes it one of her very best recordings.

Robert Volkmann (1815-1883)

Serenade No. 2 in F major, Op. 63

String Orchestra

☐ Hungarian Chamber Orchestra / Tatrai (conductor) / Turnabout 34370

Music with clear form, its logic based on the Viennese classics. Tatrai plays the waltz rather slowly; otherwise the material is heard with meaningful flow.

Concerto for Cello and Orchestra, Op. 33

Solo Instrument and Orchestra

Cello

☐ Hamburg Symphony Orchestra / Blees (cello) / Springer (conductor) / Turnabout 34576

A romantic narrative that never graces the programs of our concert cellists. It is as sound as the Saint-Saëns and the Schumann concerti for the instrument. And has some show-stopping features, though as with Schumann's work these are restricted and subtle.

Thomas Blees plays creditably and receives fine support. The liner notes contain an interesting letter from the composer to Brahms, who was preparing to perform the Concerto.

Konzertstück for Piano and Orchestra, Op. 42

Piano

☐ Symphony Orchestra of Radio Luxembourg / Rose (piano) / Cao (conductor) / Turnabout 34576

Romantic confessions that are similar to Schumann's, less complex but not dull in their straightforwardness. The technical assist of brilliance, required for a solo work, surfaces in the finale.

All the material is presented in a comfortable way that will satisfy the auditor.

Fantasy in C major, Op. 25a

Instrumental

Sonata in C minor, Op. 12

Piano

☐ Ruiz (piano) / Genesis 1032

Clearness of form and strict musical logic are heard in Volkmann's music. The Sonata does not deserve its neglect, if only for its *Prestissimo,* a conception of forceful personality. And, granting a debt to Mendelssohn, Volkmann's Fantasy (more dynamic than the Sonata) exemplifies a natural spontaneity that is several notches above conventionality.

One speaks of "the Romantic Revival movement." On recordings it is the generous number of releases on the part of Genesis Records which has been the greatest stimulus. Some of the works Genesis has dusted off do not convince, whether because of the music itself or the performer involved. In Volkmann's case both material and pianist convince a listener.

William Vollinger (20th cent.)

More Than Conquerors: A Narrative on the Life of Corrie ten Boom for Baritone, Clarinet in A, and Piano

Opera and Dramatic Music

☐ Fifer (baritone); Sobol (clarinet); Basquin (piano) / Grenadilla GS-1009

The narrative concerns a Dutch woman who hid Jews from the Gestapo during the German occupation of Holland. Vollinger has created a true hybrid, with monodrama delivery quick-cutting constantly into the singing. Most of the instrumental writing emphasizes and helps program the story line.

The star of this recording is Bruce Fifer. His diction is exemplary, his voice full and resonant. Indeed, a most impressive performance.

Alexander Voormolen (1895-   )

Solo Instrument and Orchestra

Concerto for Two Pianos and String Orchestra (1950)

☐ Radio Chamber Orchestra / Debora and Boukje Land (pianos) / Krol (conductor) / Donemus Audio-Visual Series 7001

Two Pianos

Tonal and thoroughly so, even with the chromatic ingress in the final *Fuga*. Roussel will come fully to mind in that polyphonic movement, and his shadow hovers over the preceding *Interludio*. The opening movement has a Prokofievian personality, but the gentleman has his nails carefully filed. Indeed, all very eclectic, but handled with the very pink of courtesy and a polish that provide a music worthy of attention.

Harpsichords may be used in place of pianos, but they are not missed in this lively performance. Everyone concerned shares in the honors. Fine sound.

Jan Václav Voříšek (1791-1825)

Orchestra

Sinfonia in D major

☐ English Chamber Orchestra / Mackerras (conductor) / Philips 6500203

Voříšek's only symphony. It is a gem, with a pair of outer movements that bear out their tempo designations *Allegro con spirito* and *Allegro con brio*. Vocally conjunct lines are paramount but minus any debilitating overornamentation. Beethoven immediately comes to mind with this dynamic type of thrust. The inner movements are principally set in minor tonalities. The slow movement is pure symphonic song—the development not too formal, with the music curving its way. Similar power and sweep dictate the Scherzo.

Mackerras has chosen wisely. The symphony is truly a discovery, though some ten years ago a performance was recorded on Crossroads by the Prague Chamber Orchestra (no conductor was listed). It remains a recorded "sleeper." Conductors should grab this work, and record collectors should own it.

Instrumental

Piano

Impromptu No. 4 in A major, Op. 7

☐ Firkusny (piano) / Candide 31086

Firkusny plays this little gem with marvelous poetry. It glows with Schubertian light, making one wish the other pieces in the set would be recorded.

Sonata in B flat minor

☐ Pleshakov (piano) / Orion 75178

Classical formations mark Voříšek's Sonata, with a lightly dramatic opening movement, a more aggressive finale, and a scherzo in between. These Beethoven-like arguments are presented clearly by the soloist, all of his technique matching the confirmed craftsmanship of the composer.

František Vrána   *(1914-   )*

Rhapsody for Soprano Saxophone and Piano   *Instrumental*

☐ Brodie (soprano saxophone); Kubalek (piano) / Golden Crest RE-7049   *Saxophone*

   Pertinent and viable music for this wind instrument is uncommon. Vrána's piece, modeled on Debussy's Clarinet Rhapsody, the composer states, and imbued "with the contemporary idiom," has energy and the required clarity. Neatly played.

Antonín Vranický   *(1761-1820)*

Little Marches (Nos. 1, 2, 5, and 6)   *Wind*
Three Marches in the French Style   *and Brass*
                                                                                   Ensemble
Two Hunting Marches in the French Style

☐ Netherlands Wind Ensemble / Philips 6599172

   Regardless of title, little difference in these lightly moving marches. The perfection of the Netherlanders' playing cannot be argued. Theirs is an example of extraordinary artistry and ensemble, producing a texture that is equivalent to chamber music. (The composer was born in Moravia and died in Vienna. Accordingly a slight difference in the listing of his name, which appears in various dictionaries as Anton Wranitzky.)

Hubert Waelrant   *(ca. 1517-1595)*

Choral

Musiciens qui chantez à plaisir

Chorus Alone

☐ Canby Singers / Canby (conductor) / Nonesuch 71026

    Plentiful variances for this composer's name. These include Waelrand, Walrand, Walrans, Walrant, and Vualrant. His choral piece is a short lecture on what should be done when singing; for example, "Be expert with both ears and eyes—/Or otherwise you might as well be silent." Good advice, and followed in this particular instance.

Bernard Wagenaar   *(1894-1971)*

Orchestra

Symphony No. 4 (1949)

☐ Vienna Symphony Orchestra / Haeffner (condutor) / Desto 6415E (monaural)

    With the predilection for motival manipulation, Wagenaar tends to side with his Teutonic elders rather than his younger cosmopolitan contemporaries. Formal bedrock matters of fact hold the music together. Best portion is the neatly orchestrated third part, a scherzo, colored with clarinet chirps.

    Clear if rather careful performance. This is one of Desto's re-releases of old recordings of American music. As such it is admirable. The outdated liner copy is not.

Johan Wagenaar   *(1862-1941)*

Orchestra

Overture to *The Taming of the Shrew*, Op. 25

☐ Radio Orchestra / Krol (conductor) / Donemus Audio-Visual Series 7001

    A real find. Initially sprightly, the music moves on to a warm contrastive second theme, includes a pert fugato, and winds up with a colorful conclusion. Juicy romanticism, hearty orchestration, and played brilliantly.

Georg Christoph Wagenseil (1715-1777)

Solo Instrument and Orchestra

Concerto No. 2 in G major for Harp and Orchestra

☐ Paul Kuentz Chamber Orchestra / Zabaleta (harp) / Kuentz (conductor) / Deutsche Grammophon 139112

Harp

Fine figurations and nicely formationed music. A well-scaled performance.

Georg Gottfried Wagner (1698-1756)

Choral

Chorus Alone

Blessing, Glory, and Wisdom

☐ Concordia Choir / Christiansen (conductor) / Concordia CDLP-6 (monaural)

An anthem-like conception. It includes a neatly designed contrapuntal section on the word "Hallelujah." Nicely performed.

Joseph Wagner (1900-1974)

Band

A Festive Fanfare for Brass and Percussion (1968)

☐ University of Miami Symphonic Wind Ensemble / Fennell (conductor) / Orion 73118

Proper stuff and substance for a fanfare format. Fennell knows how to present brass music. He proves it in this instance.

Merlin and Sir Boss **(a Symphonic Tale from** *The Connecticut Yankee* **by Mark Twain) (1966)**

☐ University of Wisconsin Concert Band / Dvorak (conductor) / Orion 73118

It is extremely difficult to find a recorded example of all-out program music for band. Included in this survey, therefore, even though both composition and presentation are only passable.

Symphonic Transitions for Concert Band (1958)

☐ California State University Chico Symphonic Band / Hiestand (conductor) / Orion 73118

Originally an orchestral work with a different title, "Variations on an Old Form," composed in 1938. Either setting clearly sets forth the shuffling of the variant cards.

Solo Instrument and Band

Concerto Grosso for Three Solo Cornets, Solo Baritone, and Concert Band (1949)

☐ Kiltie Symphony Band of Carnegie-Mellon University / Harms, Purcell, and Rorick (cornets); Pascuzzi (baritone) / Strange (conductor) / Orion 73118

Three Cornets and Baritone

A truly outstanding performance, beautifully balanced, intonationally on the button, a band treat.

This piece is proof of what can be accomplished in a medium that still is snobbishly run down by all but a handful of composers. The baroque form is treated by Wagner in terms of traditional patterns: Passacaglia, Gavotte, and Gigue. The opening movement is modally mannered. Wagner's scoring *is* "the band sound"—symphonically oriented. A must piece for band-music advocates.

Concert Piece for Violin and Violoncello (1966)

☐ Schoenfeld Duo / Orion 7036

Chamber Music

In turn a duo, solo violin, solo cello, and duo again. The formal equation is therefore one of instrumental equilibration. Most of the virtuosity is reserved for the kinetic conclusion.

The sister team (Alice, violin; Eleonore, cello) commissioned Wagner's Concert Piece. It is, naturally, dedicated to them. Their performance follows suit—it is a dedicated one.

Preludes and Toccata for Harp, Violin, and Cello (1964)

☐ Schoenfeld Duo / McDonald (harp) / Orion 7036

Wagner utilizes a clever blueprint for his trio. The Preludes consist of a series of cadenzas for each of the solo instruments; the Toccata combines them. Nice neoclassic nurturing here, deserving of better disc engineering.

Sonata of Sonnets for Soprano and Piano (1961)

☐ Babikian (soprano); Limonick (piano) / Orion 7036

Vocal

Voice with Accompaniment

A rare instance of sonata form applied to a work for voice and piano. No mere keyboard accompaniment, either! Lyrical and dynamic (more of the latter), and the scale of writing is vividly virtuosic. (Texts by Edna St. Vincent Millay.)

Performance passes muster, but the balance is not the best. Too much piano, not enough voice. However, the music's values overcome the engineering deficiencies. (The back cover announces "texts enclosed." Be sure they are—my copy had none.)

Richard Wagner   *(1813-1883)*

Dance of the Apprentices, from *Die Meistersinger* (1867)
Entry of the Masters, from *Die Meistersinger* (1867)

Orchestra

☐ New York Philharmonic / Bernstein (conductor) / Columbia MS-7141

Majestic and rounded playing and brilliance where required. Bernstein does not get in the way of proper Wagnerian behavior. (Also on Columbia D3M-32992.)

Eine Faustouvertüre (1855)

☐ Cleveland Orchestra / Szell (conductor) / Columbia MS-6884

A concentrated and intense essay. Within it is a coloration far deeper and more pertinent than achieved by Boulez (Columbia M-32296), the best of the other editions. Szell's performance is also included in a three-record Wagner program on Columbia D3M-32317.

(Wagner began composing his Overture in 1839 and completed it in 1840. The first performance took place in Dresden on July 22, 1844. A new version was made in 1855 and published in that year.)

Entry of the Gods into Valhalla, from *Das Rheingold* (1854)

☐ Philadelphia Orchestra / Ormandy (conductor) / RCA LSC–3264

The golden lush sound of the Philadelphians is never forced in this performance. It has its own dignity, and there is the needed electricity within the playing.

Festmarsch, from *Tannhäuser* (1845)

☐ Philadelphia Orchestra / Ormandy (conductor) / Columbia MG–32314

Top quality with a rhythmic sense which is completely ingratiating.

Forest Murmurs, from *Siegfried* (1869)

☐ Cleveland Orchestra / Szell (conductor) / Columbia MS–7291

Fine atmosphere brought to fruition by Szellian finesse. There is plenty of inner instrumental detail, but Szell (using the standard concert-performance arrangement by Herman Zumpe) doesn't blur a single note. An undisputed number one version.

Good Friday Music, from *Parsifal* (1879)

☐ Columbia Symphony Orchestra / Walter (conductor) / Columbia MS–6149

Richard Wagner at his most eloquent and Bruno Walter likewise. The serenity of the score is not permitted to fall into dynamic dullness, the music has an inner movement and subtle pulse that result in a splendid atmosphere. A performance of this specialness is not only for the unabashed Wagnerphile.

Grosser Festmarsch (1876)

☐ London Symphony Orchestra / Janowski (conductor) / Angel S–36879

Wagner's "Grand Festival March" (here given a revamped title, "The American Centennial March") was written "for the opening of the centennial celebration of the Declaration of Independence of the United States of North America, 1876." And it came to pass that it was first heard on May 10, 1876, in Philadelphia, with Theodore Thomas wielding the baton.

Wagner did a musical snow job. Indeed, his *Grosser* march is gross music. Only for the special-record buff who wants to have it all.

Huldigungs Marsch (1864)

☐ London Symphony Orchestra / Janowski (conductor) / Angel S–36879

The "March of Homage" (composed for a monarch's [King Ludwig II] birthday) has historic interest because of the composer who wrote it. (Originally, Wagner scored the work for military band. He then began an orchestral setting which was completed by Joachim Raff.) Musical benefits are extremely low.

Kaisermarsch (1871)

☐ London Symphony Orchestra / Janowski (conductor) / Angel S–36879

Wagner's "Emperor March" was composed to welcome the entry of the victorious army into Berlin at the conclusion of the Franco-Prussian war. The recording serves the purpose of Wagnerian documentation. It also serves collectors of musical esoterica.

An optional section for chorus was included by Wagner. Its nonuse in this recording doesn't bring any harm whatsoever.

Magic Fire Music, from *Die Walküre* (1856)

☐ Cleveland Orchestra / Szell (conductor) / Columbia MS–7291
☐ Philadelphia Orchestra / Ormandy (conductor) / Columbia MS–6701

Brilliant performances in both cases. No deterministic decision to use free-will tricks such as coloristic over-play to influence a listener. Both are fully beautiful renditions.

Both performances are represented in other albums. Szell's reading is also on Columbia D3M–32317; Ormandy's performance is duplicated on Columbia MG–30300.

Overture and Venusberg Music to *Tannhäuser* (Paris Version) (1861)

☐ Berlin Philharmonic Orchestra / von Karajan (conductor) / Angel S–37097

There are rich sensations in this sensational presentation. The playing has both fine breadth and full fire. Karajan brings to the fore all the pageantry and passion of the music and does so without a single exaggeration in the hot-hotter Bacchanale. Fiery sound, but for this music proper all the way.

Overture to *Das Liebesverbot* (1836)

☐ Orchestra of Radio Luxembourg / Springer (conductor) / Turnabout 34497

Shades of Offenbach! Shades of others as well, but no Wagnerian anticipations by young Wagner at the age of twenty-three. This comic-opera Overture begins with solo percussion. That should give you an idea of what's to come. But, the Overture does have its joviality and fun.

Springer permits full outlet for the content and lets it go at that; the music rolls along in an uninterrupted stream.

Overture to *Der fliegende Holländer* (1841)

☐ Berlin Philharmonic Orchestra / von Karajan (conductor) / Angel S–37098
☐ Philharmonia Orchestra / Klemperer (conductor) / Angel S–3610

Karajan provides excitement but excitement that is superbly controlled, so that all of the Overture's inner pulsed drive is depicted. Not a rough edge in the playing (which can't be said for many of the available performances). The solidity of Klemperer's reading provides its own brand of excitement. Within his conception is a captivating breadth of detail.

Overture to *Die Feen* (1833)

☐ Hamburg Symphony / Springer (conductor) / Turnabout 34497

This music certainly could be identified as by Mendelssohn or Weber, but never Wagner. So much for the aesthetic basis. Historically, it's fine to have this on disc, and the recording can be considered a most trustworthy document.

Overture to *Rienzi* (1840)

☐ Cleveland Orchestra / Szell (conductor) / Columbia MS–6884

All too often gusto (needed for this work) is confused with brassy vulgarity. This is never so here. Szell's findings are truly remarkable, and the once overplayed piece emerges in the finest and freshest manner.

This performance is also included on Columbia D3M–32317.

Overture to *Tannhäuser* (Dresden Version) (1845)

☐ Cleveland Orchestra / Szell (conductor) / Columbia MS-6971

Again Szell proves his innate ability as a conductor of Wagner. The music's sense of drama is provided to the utmost, the colors are superbly chosen and displayed, and there is full involvement. This is a far cry from the conventional readings that cram the record catalogue.

The performance is also included in a big all-Wagner album (three discs) on Columbia D3M-32317.

Prelude and *Liebestod,* from *Tristan und Isolde* (1858)

☐ Berlin Philharmonic Orchestra / von Karajan (conductor) / Angel S-37097
☐ Concertgebouw Orchestra / Haitink (conductor) / Philips 6500932

No matter how it is argued, the conductor who doesn't inject eroticism into the playing of this score (he is aided by Wagner's carnalized chromatics) misses the point. Proof? Read a British critic who wrote thus of Karajan's performance of the *Vorspiel und Isoldens Liebestod*—"the orgasmic culmination is quite overwhelming." It is. How accept, therefore, Boulez's statement (Columbia M-32296), which has neither emotive tension nor musical body rhythm?

Haitink is a mite more restrained but not to the extent that the music becomes even slightly cooled. It is heated properly. On the other hand, Klemperer (Angel S-3610) makes Wagner sound positively ascetic, if that's possible.

Two versions are quite good and might be considered as alternate choices to the pair listed. Paita's portrayal (with the New Philharmonia Orchestra, on London 21035) is one; the other is Stein's statement on London 6860, conducting the Vienna Philharmonic Orchestra. Dorati's version is splendid (Mercury 90532), but he only performs the *Liebestod.*

Prelude to Act I of *Die Meistersinger* (1867)

Prelude to Act III of *Die Meistersinger* (1867)

☐ Chicago Symphony Orchestra / Reiner (conductor) / RCA AGL1-1278

Beautifully proportioned playing, with dynamic conditions thoroughly controlled in the Act III piece. The first act *Vorspiel* is as beautifully detailed as is Haitink's version (*see below* [Prelude to Act I of *Die Meistersinger*]) but not as fully resonant in sound.

Prelude to Act I of *Die Meistersinger* (1867)

☐ Concertgebouw Orchestra / Haitink (conductor) / Philips 6500932

An expansive and glowing production. The contrapuntalism is fully illuminated, and the equality of the linear movement is absolutely perfect. Further, there is dignity to Haitink's statement. Unquestionably a grand contribution to the Wagner recorded literature.

See above for Reiner's rendition of this piece.

Prelude to Act I of *Lohengrin* (1848)

Prelude to Act III of *Lohengrin* (1848)

☐ Concertgebouw Orchestra / Haitink (conductor) / Philips 6500932

The recordings on hand of these pieces are painfully mixed. In most cases the *Lohengrin* introductions are used as fillers for a disc or thrown in, seemingly hit or miss, as part of miscellaneous Wagner programs, so some conductors have recorded the first-act piece and others the third, and still others the pair, which is much more satisfactory. Haitink's readings are first class, indeed memorable. They are fine-toned. The first Prelude is not dimmed by sensuosity, and the other one is not overdriven.

If you wish the first-act piece but would rather have other Wagner music in place of the third-act Prelude, then try the Kubelik performance on Deutsche Grammophon 136228. For only the introduction to Act III, Leinsdorf's brilliant presentation fills the bill perfectly. (As expected, it is included in an all-Wagner program.) It is on Seraphim S-60213.

Prelude to Act I of *Parsifal* (1879)
Prelude to Act III of *Parsifal* (1879)

☐ Berlin Philharmonic Orchestra / von Karajan (conductor) / Angel S-37098

These are substantial conceptions providing the rapt, mysterious quality of Wagner's music. For some reason most of the other versions available (with very few exceptions, only the Act I item has been recorded) are either note-tied, mundane, or downright superficial, as though just being run through at a reading session (Mehta on London 6529 especially so).

Prelude to Act III of *Tannhäuser* (1845)

☐ Philharmonia Orchestra / Klemperer (conductor) / Angel S-35947

A glowing and beautiful depiction. A second choice, excellent in all respects, is Boult's handling of the music with the London Philharmonic Orchestra on Angel S-36998.

Prelude to Act III of *Tristan und Isolde* (1858)

☐ London Philharmonic Orchestra / Boult (conductor) / Angel S-36998

Excellent sonority, textural purity, beauty, and finely shaped playing. It gives off the proper vibrations.

Ride of the Valkyries, from *Die Walküre* (1856)

☐ London Symphony Orchestra / Stokowski (conductor) / London 21051
☐ Philharmonia Orchestra / Klemperer (conductor) / Angel S-35947

Listening to the very many entries for this music, one begins to have an expectable reaction: if you've heard one, you've heard 'em all. But pick and choose one must. So if you want this impressive Wagner excerpt in its most impressive state, then try Leopold S. (but only with the London [a performance which is also available on London 21016]—he has also recorded the piece with the Symphony of the Air [on RCA LSC-5007], but that organization has duller sound). If, on the other hand, you like your ride comfortable and solid (and really that should suffice, since the motility and chunkiness within the score are sufficient to stimulate the ear), then opt for Klemperer.

Szell's version also must be mentioned. It is certainly dynamic and properly proportioned. His performance is available from Columbia in three releases—MS-7291, MS-7435, and D3M-32317.

Siegfried Idyll (1870)

☐ Vienna Philharmonic Orchestra / Solti (conductor) / London 2216
☐ San Francisco Symphony Orchestra / Monteux (conductor) / RCA VICS-1457

Some play this in its original chamberized setting, others play it for amplified satisfaction. Given care with the latter approach, Wagner's reflective score does not become harmed.

Solti follows the former path. He proceeds at a splendid elated pace and does not misread the tempo indication *Lebhaft* as meaning speed, but proper liveliness, which is a direction for a certain quality, not a signal for a tempo high jump.

Monteux's reading is in the fuller category. It is full of warmth, and this master handles all the lines, colors, and tempi in his usual masterful way.

Siegfried's Funeral Music, from *Götterdämmerung* (1872)

☐ Cleveland Orchestra / Szell (conductor) / Columbia MS-7291

A deeply probing presentation of one of the Wagnerian glories. Fine, absorbing intensity in every measure, and the emotive momentum is never lessened. Szell's picturing of this music of grief is stunning. (The performance is also available in a three-disc, all-Wagner program on Columbia D3M-32317.)

Siegfried's Rhine Journey, from *Götterdämmerung* (1872)

☐ Philharmonia Orchestra / Klemperer (conductor) / Angel S-35947

The measuring rod for this excerpt is full-blooded style, with soaring brilliant playing, including a good solo horn in the performing outfit. All this is found in Klemperer's reading, but there is more: an impeccable sense of continuity in the sonorous and flexible chain of the events that fill this beautiful section in the final music drama of "The Nibelungen Ring."

Symphony in C major (1832)

☐ Hamburg Symphony / Beissel (conductor) / Turnabout 34497

The creative strategy in this work, written in 1832, when the composer was nineteen, and not published until 1911, is, of course, bald imitation. Mostly Mozart and Beethoven, but not a glance at their late-period works. These are four movements, as would be expected, with a scherzo type in part 3 and with counterpoint stressed in the finale. The orchestration, however, is not thoroughly pat—no tricks, but it does show a desire to move about.

The playing of Wagner's work respects all there is. No questions can be raised. Beissel does what he has to do and follows traditional rules of the conducting game.

Solo Instrument and Orchestra

Clarinet

Adagio for Clarinet and Strings

☐ Vienna State Opera Orchestra / Brymer (clarinet) / Prohaska (conductor) / Vanguard 71167

Even at this remove it is still uncertain whether this five-minute aria-like piece is Wagner's. It is neither a huge credit nor huge discredit if it is his, and if not, the same statement goes for the unknown who did write it. There is this to say: it's nicely unimportant but worth hearing once in a great while whether it is Wagner's or not. And there is this to add: it's worth listening to fairly often just to enjoy Jack Brymer's beautiful clarinet sound.

Instrumental

Piano

Magic Fire Music, from *Die Walküre* (1856)

☐ Friedman (piano) / Klavier 112E (monaural)

It seems to me that for a solo pianist to play this music (even in its shortened version) is just as valuable as for a string quartet to play a Sousa march. However, here it is if you want such a thing. Ignaz Friedman's playing was originally registered for a Steinway Duo-Art reproducing piano. The shift onto disc is good.

Piano Sonata

In B flat major, Op. 1 / (*Grosse Sonate*) in A major, Op. 4

☐ Speidel (piano) / Musical Heritage Society MHS-3138

Of course these works (written in 1831) are extremely unimportant in the Wagner canon. Historically, one should give these Sonatas a little attention. No surprises, no Wagnerisms. Classically modeled, with most attention given to early Beethoven.

Scene and Aria of Ada, from *Die Feen* (1834)

☐ London Symphony Orchestra / Nilsson (soprano) / Davis (conductor) / Philips 6500294

The Overture to Wagner's fantasy opera rears its head once in a while, the opera never. The excerpt from the second act is heard with glorious dynamism, exemplifying peerless vocal artistry.

Vocal

Voice and Orchestra

Scene and Aria of Adriano, from *Rienzi* (1840)

☐ London Symphony Orchestra / Nilsson (soprano) / Davis (conductor) / Philips 6500294

Birgit Nilsson sings this portion from the third act with little attention to detail. There is no sharp distinction in phrasing, but the big, exceedingly vibrant voice carries everything along and that's sufficient for Wagner's emotional conception.

Das Liebesmahl der Apostel (1843)

☐ New York Philharmonic and Westminster Choir / Boulez (conductor) / Columbia M-35131

A rare work by Wagner that has a bare few productions to its credit anywhere. Small wonder. Wagner's biblical scene for mens' chorus and orchestra has more historical than musical importance. Respectful attention it deserves, that's all, and only because R. Wagner wrote it. The music comes through satisfactorily in this rendition.

Choral

Chorus and Orchestra

Das Rheingold (1854)

☐ Vienna Philharmonic Orchestra / Flagstad, Watson, and Balsborg (sopranos); Madeira (mezzo-soprano); Plümacher and Malaniuk (contraltos); Kmentt, Svanholm, and Kuen (tenors); London and Wächter (baritones); Neidlinger (bass-baritone); Böhme and Kreppel (basses) / Solti (conductor) / London 1309

Produced over twenty years ago (1958), London's publication of *Das Rheingold* remains sonorously superior to later recorded editions. More importantly, its insight into Wagner on the part of Solti and the singing of the great cast he conducts are dramatically masterful. This is a recorded accomplishment of the very highest order. (The thunderous doings in the conclusion of the opera are remarkably engineered.)

No vocal roughage here, none at all. When power is required, it emerges with fully resonant artistic packing and not interfered with by sonorous corrugations. (Gustav Neidlinger's presentation of the Alberich role is a fervent example of this.) There may be some slight overstress in George London's singing (he takes the part of Wotan), but in general his is an artistically authoritative characterization. And so it continues—thoroughly compelling singing and insight mark the work of Flagstad, Svanholm, and Kmentt, as well as the rest of the cast.

Opera and Dramatic Music

The von Karajan performance (Deutsche Grammophon 2709023) is pallid in comparison and texturally flimsy, though it includes a splendid Wotan (Deitrich Fischer-Dieskau) and a stunning Loge (Gerhard Stolze). Angel's S–3825 presents *Das Rheingold* in English. Nothing wrong with that, but there's something considerably wrong with the pace (thus it takes four discs, whereas all other editions are covered in three). Finally, Böhm's rather ambivalent conception (Philips 6747046) offers no competition for Solti's tightly structured delineation. Emphatically, there is no critical dubiosity about London's *Das Rheingold*.

Der fliegende Holländer (1841)

☐ Orchestra and Chorus of the Royal Opera House, Covent Garden / Rysanek (soprano); Elias (alto); Liebl and Lewis (tenors); London (baritone); Tozzi (bass) / Dorati (conductor) / London 1399

"The Flying Dutchman" can be termed un-Wagnerian Wagner simply because of its use of set pieces, which include such fine choruses as that of the sailors and the ghost ship's crew, the spinning chorus, arias (Senta's Ballad), duets, and interludes. Whatever its category, it is a superb operatic work and is just as superbly conducted by Antal Dorati. Dorati's account is colorful and dynamic, and he paces the music magnificently.

No arguments as to this fine all-star cast. George London's dark-timbred voice provides for a splendid Dutchman, Leonie Rysanek's dramatic sense is sensitively (and splendidly) applied (even though she has, like every Senta one has heard, a few pitch problems), and Giorgio Tozzi in the Daland role performs splendidly.

Die Meistersinger von Nürnberg (1867)

☐ Orchestra and Chorus of the Deutsche Oper Berlin / Ligendza (soprano); Ludwig (mezzo-soprano); Domingo, Laubenthal, Maus, Driscoll, Mercker, and Vantin (tenors); Fischer-Dieskau, Hermann, Feldhoff, and Bañuelas (baritones); Lagger, Lang, Sardi, Nikolic, and von Halem (basses) / Jochum (conductor) / Deutsche Grammophon 2713011

A richness of orchestral sound with suave eloquence mark Jochum's consideration of the score. Phrase definition is acute and yet minus any squared sectional depiction—the music flows, and with Wagner that point is crucial. It is this that makes one place Solti's competitive edition (London 1512) in the second slot. Solti tends to fragment phrases for contrastive stress, but it is an operatic convention that is to be discouraged in Wagner.

With one exception, Jochum has a superb cast. As Sachs, Fischer-Dieskau gives a probing performance, only occasionally relaxing his sharply focused delivery. Domingo's singing in the Walther role leaves no doubts as to his important contribution. It is precisely imagined and executed and beautifully phrased. The Beckmesser (Roland Hermann) and David (Horst R. Laubenthal) roles are covered splendidly. Only Ligendza as Eva is disappointing. It is more the particular quality of her voice than the manner of vocal delivery that is the point. Her soprano timbre does not register and confirm the role's personality. Also, in several places her pitch is erroneous.

Die Walküre (1856)

☐ Vienna Philharmonic Orchestra / Nilsson, Crespin, Schlosser, Lindholm, Dernesch, and Tyler (sopranos); Fassbaender and Little (mezzo-sopranos); Ludwig, Watts, and Hellmann (contraltos); King (tenor); Frick and Hotter (basses) / Solti (conductor) / London OSA–1509

A performance of certitude in which Solti displays a magnificent command of the dynamic relationships that exist subtly and directly in Wagner's three-act, eleven-scene musical drama. Pulsatile strength pushes this work forward even in its quieter portions.

Birgit Nilsson in the Brünnhilde role exemplifies singing of continuous wonder and beauty. Her final scene with Hotter (as Wotan) is eloquence at its most fervent point. Hotter is unsurpassed in his depiction—it displays a full measure of vocal genius. The part of Siegmund is firmly fervent in King's portrayal; the dynamism and opulence that Christa Ludwig brings to the Fricka characterization are well-nigh perfect. All the others, including the Valkyries, are excellent, and the Vienna Philharmonic delivers warmly detailed playing. Such orchestral precision is rarely duplicated in most opera houses.

The choice noted does not overlook the virtues to be found in the Karajan–Deutsche Grammophon production (number 2713002). The major differences that favor the London release are Nilsson and Hotter. They cannot be matched by the parallel interpretations of Régine Crespin and Thomas Stewart heard in the D.G. performance.

Götterdämmerung (1872)

☐ Vienna Philharmonic Orchestra and Vienna State Opera Chorus / Nilsson, Watson, Popp, Jones, Guy, and Välkki (sopranos); Ludwig and Hoffman (mezzo-sopranos); Watts (contralto); Windgassen (tenor); Fischer-Dieskau (baritone); Neidlinger and Frick (basses) / Solti (conductor) / London 1604

The glow and grandeur to be displayed in this masterpiece set a tough assignment for a conductor. Preoccupation with force and overdrive can bring defeat. Solti bypasses such identity with the music. His is a most impressive depiction, representing great Wagnerian conducting—in some respects *his* operatic-conducting masterpiece.

The cast is superlative. Nilsson is inspired in her characterization of Brünnhilde, and her vocalism is finely balanced. She displays the virtue of strength spread through all the registers, with full victory in regard to top notes. Musical understanding and interpretative passion carry her performance—fully Wagnerian to the last phrase. Windgassen is a fine lyrically endowed Siegfried, and offers more—plenty of hair-on-chest singing to flesh out this lusty character.

Gunther represents a tricky characterization, but Fischer-Dieskau prevails brilliantly, and the same is true of Neidlinger's handling of the Alberich role. For once, the latter part is sung with musicality rather than shrieked insensitively. Gottlob Frick's voice is powerful, full-grained. For the most part (not totally) he sings Hagen with intonational decisiveness. There are no qualifications as to Frick's interpretation. It is completely vivid. And so is the Norns' scene, which has a rarely stated beauty.

Lohengrin (1848)

☐ Bayreuth Festival Orchestra and Chorus / Silja and Varnay (sopranos); Thomas, Möller, and Stolze (tenors); Vinay, Krause, Kirchner, and Kélémen (baritones); Crass (bass) / Sawallisch (conductor) / Philips 6747241

A great recording of *Lohengrin*, one that can match the all-round beauty of some of the other Wagner editions that are on disc, doesn't seem to be available at this time. Nonetheless, this release is quite good in making its atmospheric and dramatic points, provided you don't mind some stage noises and little mistakes by orchestra and singers that usually are made at a live opera performance (*Lohengrin* was recorded at the 1962 Bayreuth Festival).

Jess Thomas is musically on target. His tenor voice is particularly clear in this performance and shows excellent control and phrasing. Elsa is a lyric role and demands a fairly big voice. Anja Silja's instrument is somewhat light for the part, but even if it is on the small side, she captures Elsa's essential femininity. The Telramund part requires a baritone who can be comfortable in the upper register, and Ramon Vinay is quite satisfactory in this respect. Ortrud is played by Astrid Varnay, and she is compellingly clear-voiced, absolutely authoritative in her interpretation. The same decisiveness is heard from Franz Crass as König Heinrich.

The orchestral quality is splendid. Though there are some cuts, Sawallisch's handling of the score needs no defense. It is intelligent, fastidiously detailed, and displays a fine Wagnerian temperament.

Parsifal (1879)

☐ Orchestra and Chorus of the Bayreuth Festival / Dalis, Cervena, Janowitz, Silja, Gardelli, Siebert, and Bartos (sopranos); Boese (contralto); Thomas, Möller, Stolze, and Paskuda (tenors); London (baritone); Talvela, Hotter, Neidlinger, and Nienstedt (basses) / Knappertsbusch (conductor) / Philips 835220/4

Many claim that according to their concepts and classifications *Parsifal* fields fervent religious drama but is not operatic. To belabor Wagnerian controversy of any kind at this very late date seems quite odd. One realizes *Parsifal* is a sufficiently sacred work to permit its staging on Good Friday (it often is performed then in Germany). But the religiosity of *Parsifal,* concerned with the story of the Holy Grail, is no less operatic than the ecstasies of *Tristan und Isolde.* Its length and slow pace bother only the uncoverted (they often use the word "static"). (On the other hand, to reject a Wagner opera is after all nothing new, and there are plenty of *Parsifal* buffs who still think *Tristan und Isolde* is morbid and totally decadent!) It is really worth following Edward J. Dent's admonition to "surrender" to *Parsifal,* since it "is a work of extraordinary musical beauty."

It is so proven in this fine, totally authentic, carefully cohesive but always spiritually vital performance conducted by Hans Knappertsbusch. That said, it should be pointed out that the Solti performance on London 1510 is magnificently balanced in all of its details and has a warmth and sound better than the Philips set. The reason is that it was recorded in a studio. Knappertsbusch's edition was recorded live, under less propitious Bayreuth performance conditions. However, it has an authenticity and spirit that go beyond special engineering. The other version considered was directed by Boulez (Deutsche Grammophon 2713004). Also made at Bayreuth, it stands in third place due to its general pace, which mars Parsifalian quality and climate. *Parsifal* must flow carefully, not walk quickly.

Irene Dalis as Kundry shows a vocal resource of intense, finely weighted variety. A haunting beauty pervades her singing. As Parsifal, Jess Thomas is exciting and handles the dramatic transitions in the opera with great authority. The despair and tenseness of Amfortas has rarely been conveyed better than in George London's handling of the part. As Gurnemanz, Hans Hotter is in firm command in his characterization. There is great warmth in his singing, though there is also the matter of some pitches that *seem* to offer multiple choice, whereupon he selects as he wishes. A small minus sign for that. Fat plus signs for everything else, including a great chorus and a radiant orchestra. But above all a double plus sign for Knappertsbusch's direction. It has rare equilibrium.

Rienzi (1840)

☐ Dresden State Orchestra, Leipzig Radio Chorus, and Dresden State Opera Chorus / Wennberg, Martin, and Springer (sopranos); Kollo and Schreier (tenors); Leib (baritone); Adam (bass-baritone); Hillebrand and Vogel (basses) / Hollreiser (conductor) / Angel SELX–3818

One will have to accept certain negatives to be satisfied with this single available domestic recording of Wagner's early-period opera. First the affirmatives. *Rienzi* has fine drive and spectacle, and with the opportunity of public performance being remote, a recorded edition is a decided plus. The negatives, aside from cuts (though in fact ten full record sides give plenty of the work), concern the singing. While René Kollo (as Rienzi) is tolerable, he gives no light and shade to his role. Janis Martin lacks strength, and Siv Wennberg (as Rienzi's sister, the heroine of the tale) just plainly sings out of tune very often. Good work, however, from Heinrich Hollreiser in pulling the whole thing together. *Rienzi* is certainly no three-star affair, but it's worth having.

Siegfried (1869)

☐ Vienna Philharmonic Orchestra / Nilsson and Sutherland (sopranos); Höffgen (contralto); Windgassen and Stolze (tenors); Hotter (baritone); Neidlinger and Böhme (basses); Berger (horn) / Solti (conductor) / London 1508

The characterizations and the singing alone validate this edition as superbly distinct and far better than the competitive productions. Gerhard Stolze has supreme mastery of the Mime role. (I have heard severe criticisms of this artist as a singer prone to tremendous exaggeration. Then, too, others admire his work highly. I vote with the latter.) He has excellent enunciation and thereby places the sounds (and meaning) in the most precise perspective. Hans Hotter as Wotan gives a deeply set performance, one that has matured over the years into a supreme achievement. Everything he does is poised and majestic. He is vocally and dramatically supreme. Wolfgang Windgassen as Siegfried convinces totally. His vocalism has an excellent heroic ring and conviction, and it is imbued with fine timbred variety. His characterization is expressive, and it is graceful as well. Splendid singing is heard from all the others, with, expectedly, impressive skill and artistic intelligence provided by Birgit Nilsson. Credit Joan Sutherland also with a topflight performance as the Forest Bird.

Solti is a brilliant director of this production. He also realizes that in certain sections the orchestra should not always be subservient to the voices and sometimes overpowers them. That's the way it should be—one is not supposed to hear succinct and pinpointed vocal phrases in every instance. It's the mix that counts, so that the voices are at times within the orchestra and not riding on top of it constantly. Solti selects such composites beautifully and strategically, and the dramatic progress becomes increased thereby. Great singing, masterly orchestral playing, and inspired conducting are combined in this *Siegfried*.

Tannhäuser (1861)

☐ Vienna Philharmonic Orchestra, Vienna State Opera Chorus, and Vienna Boys' Choir / Dernesch (soprano); Ludwig (mezzo-soprano); Kollo, Hollweg, and Equiluz (tenors); Braun and Bailey (baritones); Sotin and Jungwirth (basses) / Solti (conductor) / London 1438

This *Tannhäuser* is splendid (it is the Paris version). The entire production moves, sings, and plays with a super touch and liveliness. There is no heavy-footedness and absolutely no bombast, though the sound is richly full. (Solti's direction of the Overture is the best on disc.)

Structure and texture are effective here because they are allied totally to the action. Tempi tend to fluctuate considerably in most operas, but there are only negative values in being overprecious in their choice and distribution. On the other hand, pedantic and pedestrian pacing that holds on to the bar lines for the sake of meticulous order kills dramatic motility. Solti brings to Wagner's score the best of all tempo worlds, obtaining with it clarity, strong coloration, finesse, and certified style.

2029

The singers are all splendid, particularly Helga Dernesch (as Elizabeth), Victor Braun (in the Wolfram role), and Christa Ludwig (as Venus). René Kollo gives a fairly sound, detailed interpretation of the title role. It is perhaps a little too externally conceived, but he does have a fine *Heldentenor* vocal instrument that one can only admire. The orchestra plays magnificently, and the chorus has excellent sonorous weight.

Tristan und Isolde (1858)

☐ Orchestra and Chorus of the Bayreuth Festival / Nilsson (soprano); Ludwig (mezzo-soprano); Windgassen, Schreier, Nienstedt, and Wohlfart (tenors); Waechter and Heater (baritones); Talvela (bass) / Böhm (conductor) / Deutsche Grammophon 2713001

The erotic mysticism and mystic eroticism that are laced into Wagner's "Tristan and Isolde" have no parallel in operatic literature. Sexuality is very strongly involved from the very first sound in the opening Prelude to the climactic *Liebestod*. Thus interpretative insularity dams this music (damns it as well). "Tristan" requires a conductor who can extract the sensualism that winds around the score's measures and wets its bar lines. At the same time there must be control and use of a fluid metricality, with a sensitized balancing between voices and orchestra. Overzealousness amounts to overprotest (as Solti shows in his consideration of the work on London 1502). Böhm avoids nervous intensity and substitutes intense accuracy, thereby permitting the music to have dramatic point and give that point full ecstatic representation. His blend with the singers is splendid.

Isolde is portrayed in the richest and most commanding manner by Nilsson. She is brilliant as she fulfills all the dramatic extremes contained within the role. In listening, one's temperature rises as the passions of the story are made clear. Windgassen is superb as Tristan. His long experience in singing this role is apparent. His is a tremendous performance, one that has no exaggerations and yet offers the fullest variety of dynamism and urgency. Eberhard Waechter's performance in the Kurwenal role and Martti Talvela's conception of König Marke are excellent. Ludwig slightly overstates the part of Brangaene, but this is a minor quibble in regard to an operatic production that is so distinguished.

Wagner / Felix Mottl (1856-1911)

Vocal

Voice and Orchestra

Wesendonk Lieder (1858)

☐ London Symphony Orchestra / Nilsson (soprano) / Davis (conductor) / Philips 6500294

Some (Farrell on Columbia D3M-32992, Horne on London 26147, Norman on Philips 9500031) opt for dramatic volume and shape in this group of five songs (published with the title *Fünf Gedichte von Mathilde Wesendonk*), two of which were designated as studies for *Tristan und Isolde*. More fitting is the radiant lyrical approach of Nilsson. It makes all of the life and balances within the songs emerge.

Traüme (the final song in the group and one that has been variously transcribed) was the only one of the set that Wagner orchestrated; Mottl's scoring of the entire group was made much later. The orchestration used here is totally by Mottl, and it is sensitively conveyed in Colin Davis's reading.

Paul de Wailly   (1854-1933)

Chamber Music

Aubade for Flute, Oboe, and Clarinet

☐ Shanley (flute); Christ (oboe); Atkins (clarinet) / Crystal 101

Music of the morning hours, and accordingly cheerfully optimistic and with analogous tempo. De Wailly's trio for wind instruments is short and to the point, moves with figurated *allegro* swiftness in its large tripartite cast. For a composer who belonged to the César Franck school, the content is far less chromatic than one would expect.

The album in which the *Aubade* is included presents performances by the Westwood Wind Quintet of Los Angeles. Nowhere on front or back cover or in the liner notes is mention made of the fact that this piece is for wind trio and not wind quintet. That information is hidden on the label copy. This is the only slight fault with this release; the playing is brilliant.

Stanley Walden (1932-)

Three Views from The Open Window: **No. 2, Circus**

☐ Louisville Orchestra and The Open Window / Mester (conductor) / Louisville S-691

Opera and Dramatic Music

Richly colored in an Ivesian tangle of noise-thickened orchestration, psaltery-like sounds, calliope simulants, and a blues-bent ballad called *Tightrope*. Like the variety in a circus are the styles of Walden's piece. But hold on for a nice climax. Great!

The other composers-instrumentalists-singers in The Open Window team are Peter Schickele and Robert Dennis. Their contributions to this three-part composition are found under their respective names, under *Opera and Dramatic Music*.

Émil Waldteufel (1837-1915)

Acclamations **Waltz, Op. 223**

Bella Bocca **Polka, Op. 163**

☐ Monte Carlo Opera Orchestra / Boskovsky (conductor) / Angel S-37208

Orchestra

Bonbons presented in a bona fide performance. Principally for Waldteufel fans, but with Boskovsky in charge others will want to listen.

Dolores

España **Waltz, Op. 236**

☐ National Philharmonic Orchestra / Gamley (conductor) / London 6899

España Waltz, based on the themes Chabrier used in his orchestral rhapsody with the same title, is one of the better known of the close to 300 dance pieces Waldteufel produced. It is, together with the other waltz, interpreted idiomatically.

Estudiantina **Waltz, Op. 191**

☐ Philadelphia Orchestra / Ormandy (conductor) / Columbia MS-7032

Give a conductor a chain of waltzes and quite often he is guilty of false interpretation—meaning, distortion, and exaggeration. That's not the case here. This is the way the *Estudiantina* Waltz should be played and this is the way it should sound.

The Grenadiers

☐ National Philharmonic Orchestra / Gamley (conductor) / London 6899

A rarity by this celebrated waltz composer. O.K.

L'Esprit Français Polka, Op 182

☐ Monte Carlo Opera Orchestra / Boskovsky (conductor) / Angel S–37208

All that can be done has been done by Willi Boskovsky. This conductor has the perfect touch for this sort of light musical fare.

Minuit Polka

☐ Monte Carlo Opera Orchestra / Boskovsky (conductor) / Angel S–37208

First rate, as would be expected from this master conductor of waltzes, polkas, and symphonic dance music.

Mon Rêve

Pomone

☐ National Philharmonic Orchestra / Gamley (conductor) / London 6899

Well paced, well shaded, and brilliantly reproduced. Gamley makes all the right stresses, and he makes them in the right places.

Prestissimo Galop

☐ Monte Carlo Opera Orchestra / Boskovsky (conductor) / Angel S–37208

It doesn't matter what group Boskovsky directs—it all comes out top class. The Monte Carlo group isn't the Vienna Phil., but Willi B. makes them sound as though they were.

The Skaters' Waltz, Op. 183

Toujours ou jamais

☐ National Philharmonic Orchestra / Gamley (conductor) / London 6899

Here, played in ingratiatingly authentic style, is the most famous of all of Waldteufel's compositions. Opus 183 is also known as *Les Patineurs*, and, though less so, by its German name, *Die Schlittschuhläufer*.

Ormandy has recorded "The Skaters" on Columbia MS–7032; the version is an edited one made by Toscanini.

George Walker   (1922-   )

Orchestra

Passacaglia from *Address for Orchestra* (1959)

☐ Oakland Youth Orchestra / Hughes (conductor) / Desto 7107

An assured set of fourteen variations on a ground bass. Walker's music is of new romantic substances. It has a singular lack of note-spinning and a singular impetus toward getting on with what has to be said. A dramatic example of this man's talents. And speaking of talents, an acknowledgement to the orchestra made up of high-school-age players.

String Orchestra

Lyric for Strings

☐ London Symphony Orchestra / Freeman (conductor) / Columbia M–33433

To say that Walker's piece was probably modeled on Barber's Adagio for Strings is only to convey admiration for its beautiful balance and its emotive intensity. It is a memorable utterance and is played with sensitive conviction.

Concerto for Trombone and Orchestra (1957)

☐ London Symphony Orchestra / Wick (trombone) / Freeman (conductor) / Columbia M–32783

Worthy trombone concerti are in exceedingly small supply. Utilizing general trombonish speech, Ferdinand David's Concertino (composed in 1837) is still heard from time to time, but it has terribly aged. Eugene Zador's romantically styled 1967 entry is, naturally, much more contemporary in tone. It goes far beyond the principal arpeggiated fanfare material that crushes artistic stability in most of the few examples that have appeared. Walker's opus goes even further, and without any of the tricky-but-not-much-else effects that influence people the first time around but fail miserably thereafter.

Walker's work is in the broadly tonal syntax of the neoclassic-neoromantic composer. It is civilized, a music of taste, with tasteful proportions of virtuosic writing. It does *not* indulge in any trombone clichés but *is* trombone music—nontransferable, unlike many solo works which are musically just but instrumentally false and could just as well have been written for a number of other instruments.

Especially convincing are the slow, lyrically detailed movement and the nervous, pert, balletic finale. The playing of Denis Wick is marvelous, tonally rich, passionately involved. The plastic continuity of his interpretation provides a super musical experience.

Piano Sonata No. 1 (1953)

☐ Hinderas (piano) / Desto 7102/3

Contemporary romanticism, with strength of theme and pertinently elaborated architectural detail, is exhibited here. Above all, Walker shows the virtue of unconfuted lyricism; it is that which sings (no matter the tempo involved) through the majority of the pages of his three-movement Sonata (and, in no second place, is magnificently exhibited in the pianism of Natalie Hinderas). Quartal detail colors the sonata-styled first movement; theme and variations are the container for the middle movement, and a motile finale seals the work. A real contribution to the literature.

Sonata No. 2 (1957)

Spatials

Spektra

☐ Walker (piano) / Composers Recordings S–270

Differences exist between these three works but without destroying a basic stylistic affinity. That pertains to an austerity that is reflected by a fragmented manner in *Spatials* (embracing a twelve-tone theme with six pithy variants) and by a Bergian scope in *Spektra*. In the larger, four-movement scale of the Sonata there is more extrovertism, but nevertheless shadows consistently criss-cross the sound surfaces. All this represents keen-sighted, serious creativity by a composer of fine disciplines. His playing deserves the same compliment.

William Walond *(1715-1770)*

Voluntary in D major

☐ Sautter (trumpet); Sherman (organ) / Crystal S–700

Ceremonial command. Plenty of neat imitation. The trumpet is brilliantly played, the organ is somewhat subdued.

Johann Gottfried Walther   (1684 - 1748)

Instrumental

Organ

Chorale Partita, *Jesu, Meine Freude*

Concerto del Sig. Torelli, appropriato all'organo

☐ Gilbert (organ) / Orion 74155

Though the idiom is thoroughly familiar (the so-called South German style in the *Concerto*, the Northern German style in the Partita), Walther lends his music a genuine expressive strength. The communication Gilbert brings to these conceptions is ideal. And the registration used, particularly for the Chorale Partita, is of fertile re-creation that expands the composer's imagery.

Truly superb organ playing. Two different organs are used. For the first work listed the organ of Séminaire de Joliette, Quebec, is used; the other opus is played on the organ of Séminaire de Saint-Jean, also in Quebec.

Choral

Chorus Alone

Joseph, lieber Joseph mein

☐ Niedersachsischer Singkreis, Hannover / Trader (conductor) / Nonesuch 71095

Christmas music with natural, friendly spontaneity.

William Walton   (1902-   )

Orchestra

***Façade:* Suites No. 1 and No. 2**

☐ Orchestra of the Royal Opera House, Covent Garden / Fistoulari (conductor) / London STS-15191

The effervescent music that Walton wrote as an auxiliary of the Sitwell text in *Façade* leads a healthy and most profitable life. It is superb with the declamation—see under *Opera and Dramatic Music* (*Façade* [an Entertainment with Poems by Edith Sitwell]). It is just as successful without it. *Façade* was truly a profitable undertaking. In addition to the orchestral suites, portions of the work were produced as a ballet, and Walton's publisher (Oxford University Press) issued transcriptions of pieces from the total for band, small orchestra, harmonica and piano, harmonica and orchestra, solo piano, piano duet, and two pianos.

In its setting within the "Entertainment" *Façade* calls for a flute alternating with piccolo, a clarinetist doubling on bass clarinet, alto saxophone, trumpet, percussion (one player), and one or two cellos. From the twenty-two sections of the original (a purely instrumental Fanfare and the reminder for reciter with instrumental ensemble) Walton formed a suite of five movements (Polka, Valse, Swiss Yodelling Song, *Tango Pasodoble,* and *Tarantella-Sevillana*) and amplified the score to moderately-sized orchestral dimensions. A second suite of six other sections (Fanfare, Scotch Rhapsody, Country Dance, *Noche Espagnole,* Popular Song, and *Old Sir Faulk*) was then selected. However, a third performance possibility was offered by combining the pair of suites in a prescribed order so as to achieve proper contrast and climax. The reckoning makes another "entertainment" that is decidedly attractive and orchestrally tasty. Smart and sophisticated music, quite unlike Walton's later output, the *Façade* pieces remain fresh and undated more than five decades after their creation.

At one time there were versions conducted by Walton (on Angel 35639) and by Irving (on London 771), but they're long gone. Only Fistoulari's essay is available at this date of consideration. It is a fair enough performance, just a bit innocent of all the satire in the score.

Music for Children (1940)

☐ London Philharmonic Orchestra / Walton (conductor) / Musical Heritage Society MHS-1919

Originally a set of ten piano duets titled "Duets for Children." The orchestration is always attractive and Walton's craftsmanship is always evident, but just for the exquisite, haunting third piece the disc is worth owning. In eighty-four seconds a music that tears the heart is heard. The refinement of the playing of this portion matches Walton's inspiration.

Orb and Sceptre: Coronation March, 1953

☐ London Symphony Orchestra / Sargent (conductor) / Everest 3277E (monaural)

Commissioned by The Arts Council of Great Britain, Walton's second enthronement march was composed for the coronation of Queen Elizabeth II, in 1953. The first one, *Crown Imperial,* is discussed below (see under *Band*).

A version for military band exists. Either way, Walton's march is music written in good faith and with good taste.

Partita for Orchestra (1958)

☐ Philharmonia Orchestra / Walton (conductor) / Angel S-35681

Walton's music (commissioned by the Cleveland Orchestra to celebrate its 40th anniversary) has much rhythmic charm and exploration. In two of its three parts it resembles dance style and displays a modern link to the much older partita format. But in the expressed élan of most of the score, with its teeming orchestral virtuosity and color, the suite is nippy, contemporary hedonism.

Walton's *neodivertimento* outlook is not a set of displays which go up quickly in pyrotechnical smoke. The three movements (Toccata, *Pastorale Siciliana,* and *Giga Burlesca*) are truly profiled, as defined as the tonalities in which they are set. The lines are fired by quick-trigger action; dissonance gives sharpness to the harmony. In this orchestral entertainment Walton employs old prototypes in a modern manner.

The brilliance of the playing here is undeniable. If you can find (where such things are to be found), the long-deleted issue Szell made for Epic (E-3568, on which Mahler's Symphony No. 10 also appears—see under *Mahler: Orchestra*), get it. It's even better.

Portsmouth Point: An Overture (1925)

☐ London Symphony Orchestra / Previn (conductor) / Angel S-37001

Rhythmic ribaldry, spirited sport, nicely noisy—these phrases describe *Portsmouth Point,* a musical translation "after an etching by Thomas Rowlandson (1756-1827)" picturing a waterfront scene before the fleet's departure. Though the music is not a measure-by-measure depiction of the pictorial image, all the elements—dancing, intoxication, sacred and profane lovemaking, and the crowded vista—are portrayed by high-spirited, asymmetric music. The sounds drive ahead without cessation. They include some folksy curves, but always with bustling, booming, snappy orchestration. This rhythmic holiday is impious music, but properly so.

Previn turns it out with goodly gusto and with nicely contrasted detail, notwithstanding the constant motility of the music. His display is far better than the two deleted versions that might still be found in specialty shops: Walton conducting the Philharmonia Orchestra on Angel 35639 and Boult conducting the London Philharmonic Orchestra on London 1165. Previn's reading is also more intensely portrayed and colored than Walton's current recording with the London Philharmonic Orchestra on Musical Heritage Society MHS-1750, a transfer from the Lyrita Recorded Edition, made in England in 1971.

Scapino: Comedy Overture (1940)

☐ London Symphony Orchestra / Previn (conductor) / Angel S-37001

The merry music of this Overture (its full title is *Scapino, a Comedy Overture for Full Orchestra, After an Etching from Jacques Callot's 'Ballet di Sfessania,' 1622)*, was the result of a commission given Walton by the Chicago Symphony Orchestra as part of its fiftieth-anniversary celebration. (The Chicago organization, conducted by Frederick Stock, premiered the work on April 3, 1941.) Good contemporary overtures are at a premium—Walton's *Scapino* is a decided contribution.

Gay, colorful, and clever, the composition constitutes a miniature *Till Eulenspiegel* minus any programmatic trappings and grisly finis. *Scapino* is correctly insolent and as such lives up to its name. It should enjoy long life.

With the type of playing Previn obtains it will. The quality is charged to the hilt and yet not overdriven. The Overture is paced expertly and proves again how knowledgeable Previn is about this composer's music. It's fine to have the piece in the catalogue, Boult's excellent oldie (with the L.P.O. on London 1165) being no longer available (it was a mono disc).

Siesta (1926)

☐ London Philharmonic Orchestra / Walton (conductor) / Musical Heritage Society MHS-1750

(A slight confusion exists in regard to the publication of Walton's *Siesta*. Composed in 1926, the score was first published in 1929 and another edition appeared in 1963. However, the latter can hardly be described as a "revised" version, since the orchestration was untouched and, according to Stewart R. Craggs's *William Walton—A Thematic Catalogue of his Musical Works,* the revision consisted of "one or two pencilled annotations.")

In terms of title this short chamber-orchestra piece (for flute alternating with piccolo, oboe, bassoon, and a pair each of clarinets and horns, plus strings) is somewhat Spanish, but the midday rest is considered with some sly musical touches. Walton's piece is light and lyrical, yet simultaneously sensuous and serious. It is as if an unstated story lay behind the music, though the composer furnishes no such key,

Symphony No. 2 (1960)

☐ Cleveland Orchestra / Szell (conductor) / Odyssey Y-33519

Twenty-five years separate this Symphony from Walton's initial one. His harmonic language is much more unleashed in the later work. The chromaticism is now severely on top of the music, not surrounding it in webs. A sense of rhapsody takes hold but does not loosen the designs of the three movements and thus permit the ideas to slip away. At the same time, Walton uses the colors of the orchestral assemblage (a large one of 17 winds, 11 brass, 10 percussion instruments requiring five players, piano, celesta, 2 harps, and strings) with insistence on primary qualities; the sonorous dyestuffs do not casually blend into neutral shades.

Polytonality, collisive counterpoint, and tonal serialism warm the music. But William Walton is no rebel. His Symphony is in the exultant romantic vein, despite its sophistication. Tonality retains its validity in the 1980s even though indeterminacy is still important among status symbols in chic musical circles.

This is an old recording, being a transfer from an Epic recording (E–3812) that was deleted. It still is the best one on the market, notwithstanding Previn's fine essay on Angel S–37001.

Sonata for Strings (1972)

☐ Academy of St. Martin-in-the-Fields / Brown and Connah (violins); Shingles (viola); Heath (cello) / Marriner (conductor) / Argo ZRG–711

String Orchestra

A reworking of the String Quartet in A minor by Walton (see under *Chamber Music*), mainly in terms of scoring expansion. The enlarged setting has expressive force—a second edition, as it were, which does not invalidate the initial one.

The playing is sharp, clear, decisive, with meaningful impact and cogent depth throughout the four movements. This is absorbing music-making.

Two Pieces for Strings from the Film Music of *Henry V* (1944)

☐ Academy of St. Martins-in-the-Fields / Marriner (conductor) / Angel S–36883

The first is a poignant passacaglia (*Death of Falstaff*); the second, a moving *Touch Her Soft Lips and Part,* has a sound that resembles madrigal technique applied to string instruments.

Crown Imperial: Coronation March, 1937

☐ Eastman Wind Ensemble / Fennell (conductor) / Mercury SRI–75028

Band

Walton has been twice commissioned to compose coronation marches. *Crown Imperial* was the result of the first request, made by the BBC for the coronation of King George VI and Queen Elizabeth in 1937 (see under *Orchestra* [*Orb and Sceptre*] for the second one). Bearing a quotation from William Dunbar (1465-1520), ''In beautie berying the crone imperiall,'' Walton's march is a stunner, with a tingling beat and fanfare trumpets in triadic formations.

Although written for orchestra, *Crown Imperial* is infinitely better in ''bandstration.'' There is no argument that a march's best friend is a band, and for full evidence all that needs be heard is Fennell's exceptional, block-busting rendition. He communicates Walton's march in a magnificently exciting manner and shows a superb knowledge of proper pace. He also knows how to pull out all the stops, so he brings in the full *fortississimo* of the full organ at the end. What a becoming sound!

An organ arrangement made by Herbert Murrill and recorded by Simon Preston on Argo 5448 is to be noted. It's up to you, as they say; but aside from the general arguments about transcriptions, the organ certainly removes the zing in any zippy march.

Concerto for Viola and Orchestra (1929)

☐ London Philharmonic Orchestra / Doktor (viola) / Downes (conductor) / Odyssey 32160368

Solo Instrument and Orchestra

Viola

Although Walton's Concerto was composed in 1929, a second date (1961) is important, marking a redraft of the orchestration. The original instrumentation called for three each of the woodwinds, four horns, three trumpets, three trombones, tuba, timpani, and strings. The revised scoring reduced the winds to pairs, eliminated one of the trumpets and tuba, and added a harp.

Not only plot but pace is demanded of great music. Walton's sense of timing in this glorious lyrical work is faultless. He does not include the traditional slow movement in the central part of the Concerto, but conveys a reticent tempo at the beginning, moves into a jazzed-nervous scherzo, continues the smart speed, then reduces it and eventually returns to the mood and theme of the opening. This reminder of Goethe's remark, "Begin, and then the work will be completed," is illustrative of cyclic technique. The metrical argument of the middle movement is irregular; the fashioning of fun and contest serves as a foil to the song facts with which the Concerto is concerned. Above all the Concerto exhibits Walton's acute dramatic sense, a perceptivity that applies throughout so that form and content are one.

Doktor deals cogently with the tempo of the first part, whereas Menuhin (on Angel S-36719) drags and the line flounders. Doktor's sound is rich and expressive, and he displays all the virtuosic intimacy of the score magnificently.

Violin

Concerto for Violin and Orchestra (1939)

☐ London Symphony Orchestra / Chung (violin) / Previn (conductor) / London 6819

To achieve proper definition of a concerto's protagonist and yet fuse the orchestral portion so that it is more than mere accompaniment is a test for the composer. Walton passes it with flying compositional colors. His Concerto has all of the ingredients: tasty tunes, interesting pigments, hearty rhythms, a definitive orchestral frame, and plenty of display without bogging down into flying figurations or superimposed ornamentations.

Heifetz, for whom the Concerto was written and to whom it is dedicated, has recorded it twice (both available in mono: with Goossens directing the Cincinnati Symphony on RCA ARM4-0945 [recorded in 1941] and with Walton conducting the Philharmonia Orchestra on RCA LM-2740 [made in 1950]). There are two other versions on the market: Francescatti with Ormandy conducting (Odyssey Y-33229) and Menuhin with Walton on the podium (Angel S-36719). Put 'em all away. No one, but no one, can match this super violinist, Kyung-Wha Chung, in the playing of Walton's Concerto. How she shapes the typical Waltonian facture of the first theme! She makes the pep, vitality, swing, and sway of the second movement a fantastic fiddlistic ballet. And so on through the work, including the mastery of the difficulties of the finale. This recording deserves a "definitive" labeling.

Chamber Music

Sonata for Violin and Piano (1949)

☐ Weiss Duo / Unicorn RHS-341

Walton's composition is compressed into a pair of movements (originally, there was a third movement—a Scherzetto; it was removed by Walton and became one of his "Two Pieces for Violin and Piano"), mainly of lyrical material but with sufficient dynamicism to clarify the designs. Classical allegiance to tonality is followed, though the composition's moves are fairly free because of Walton's pungent use of frictions.

In the first movement the role of the string instrument is that of a *cantabile* personality (sensitively fulfilled by Sidney Weiss), blending its thoughts in the duo conversation (totally provided for by Jeanne Weiss's artistic partnership). In the seven variations of the second part the thematic digressions are nicely balanced, defeating the sectionalism that often haunts such a formal plan.

The success of Unicorn's issue cannot be denied. This is a significant contribution to recorded chamber-music literature.

String Quartet in A minor (1947)

☐ Allegri String Quartet / Argo ZRG-5329

The viola, a favorite instrument of Walton's, defines the introspective mood of the Allegro-tempoed opening, one in full keeping with the composer's seriousness. Walton's earlier tendencies toward Sibelian harmonies and Stravinskian rhythms are little in evidence. Both themes of the Lento movement are also assigned to the viola. The writing here is almost that of the semicramped thickness of Max Reger, but only in its weighted solidity.

The scherzo (in Presto speed) has a pithy kernel of two sounds. Kaleidoscopic juggling of every conceivable turn of the basic idea and its permutations follows. The pulse is driven, the tempo unrelenting. A similar sense of vitality is found in the Allegro molto finale, taut with nervousness, only short silences separating and cutting the kinetic rhythms. Walton's A minor opus is a brilliant example in contemporary quartet literature.

The performance is masterly.

The piece was reworked as a Sonata for Strings (see under *String Orchestra*).

A Song for the Lord Mayor's Table (1962)

Three Songs (1932)

☐ Harper (soprano); Hamburger (piano) / Oiseau-Lyre 331

Vocal

*Voice with
Accompaniment*

The first is actually a cycle of six songs, including a setting of the old tune *Oranges and Lemons*. (This has already received top-drawer treatment in Gordon Jacob's orchestral Passacaglia on a Well-known Theme.)

Texts by Edith Sitwell furnish the basis for the three songs, the essays being *nello stile inglese, nello stile spagnuolo,* and *nello stile americano.* The first of the group (*Daphne*) is discreetly romantic. The other two are extracts from the *Façade* ledger. These, *Through Gilded Trellises* and *Old Sir Faulk,* are less revelatory when vocalized than when rhythmically declaimed in the *Façade* "Entertainment" (see under *Opera and Dramatic Music*). However, warmly sung as they are here, not everyone will agree with this statement.

Carols

All This Time (1970)
Make We Joy Now in this Fest (1931)
What Cheer? (1961)

Choral

Chorus Alone

☐ Choir of Christchurch Cathedral, Oxford / Preston (conductor) / Argo ZRG-725

Argo's issue lists the title as "Three Carols." However, Walton never produced (or had published) a work with such a title. As will be noted by the dates of composition, the pieces were composed individually and not planned as a set. Of course there's no harm in these lively settings being grouped in performance—in this case a rendition that is most tasteful.

Interesting point: *Make We Joy Now in this Fest* was commissioned by a newspaper, *The Daily Dispatch,* and first published in that newspaper on the day preceding Christmas, in 1931.

A Litany (1916)

☐ Choir of St. John's College, Cambridge / Guest (conductor) / Argo ZRG-5340

Gospel truth here to prove Walton's superb talents. He composed *A Litany* (a setting of Phineas Fletcher's *Drop, Drop, Slow Tears*), which is his earliest published work, when he was fourteen. It is also special in the historic sense, since there are prenotifications in the piece of his later melodic and contrapuntal style. More important than any of these statistics is the music's sensitive choralistic beauty.

Set Me as a Seal (1938)

☐ Choir of Christchurch Cathedral, Oxford / Hayward (treble); Roy (tenor) / Preston (conductor) / Argo ZRG–725

A straightforward four-part chordal anthem setting, with some solo-voice contrast. Beautifully performed, with sensitive balances.

Where Does the Uttered Music Go? (1946)

☐ Choir of Christchurch Cathedral, Oxford / Preston (conductor) / Argo ZRG–725

The text for this piece was specially written by John Masefield and set by Walton for the unveiling of a memorial window to the famous conductor Henry J. Wood. It is more than an occasional piece, however, and its neo-romantic warmth is one of the high points in Walton's unaccompanied choral output.

Chorus with Accompaniment

Jubilate Deo (1972)

☐ Choir of Christchurch Cathedral, Oxford / Darlington (organ); Giles (alto); Roy (tenor); Morton (baritone) / Preston (conductor) / Argo ZRG–725

Composed for the 1972 English Bach Festival and given its first performance at Christchurch Cathedral in Oxford under Preston's direction. It is heard here with clearly defined rhythm and appropriate balance.

Missa brevis (1966)

☐ Choir of Christchurch Cathedral, Oxford / Darlington (organ) / Preston (conductor) / Argo ZRG–725

Walton's *Missa brevis* is almost stark in its harmonic cohesion. Coloristically, the timbre of young boys' voices is special to the work for double mixed chorus, as is the organ, employed only in the final Gloria.

The Twelve (1965)

☐ Choir of Christchurch Cathedral, Oxford / Darlington (organ); Rowlinson (baritone); Hayward and Jones (trebles) / Preston (conductor) / Argo ZRG–725

The Twelve is a setting of a text by W. H. Auden and not to be confused with the poem with the same title by the Soviet poet Alexander Blok. Richly varied choral writing is employed in this anthem, which Walton describes as "for the feast of any apostle," including solo boys' voices.

Preston's direction of Walton's anthem is a fine accomplishment.

Cantata and Oratorio

Belshazzar's Feast (1931)

☐ London Symphony Orchestra and Chorus / Shirley-Quirk (baritone) / Previn (conductor) / Angel S–36861

Few contemporary works in the vocal-orchestral category have the particular barbaric splendor and volatile sweep of this piece.

The text is a dramatic version of the fall of Babylon, the material from the Scriptures rewritten by Sir Osbert Sitwell and including passages from a pair of Psalms (Nos. 137 and 81). Walton's oratorio begins with Isaiah's prophecy of Babylonian captivity, continues with a lament, and then moves on to descriptions of Babylon's riches and its orgies. Then follow the scenes of the handwriting on the wall, the death of Belshazzar, and the final paean of *Alleluias*. Walton has set this for solo baritone (in the role of a commentator), mixed chorus (often divided), and a large orchestra, with two harps, organ, piano (ad lib), and two additional brass choirs, each of seven instruments. The last are optional—when used, one is placed to the left of the conductor, the other to his right.

There are no stale sensations in the work, which is colorborne on explosive intoxications of sound. Some critics have termed Walton's piece "theatrical," a few have described it as "garish." Others have hailed the opus as one of the outstanding and most exciting choral products of modern times. The verdict from this corner is that *Belshazzar's Feast* is a triumph because Walton mastered the one important theorem of musical composition—the engendering of informative substance that contains personality and creative character—a positively new contribution, not an imitation.

Previn's edition possesses magnificent drive, a fine sense of line, and requisite brilliance. Add to that, eloquence. John Shirley-Quirk is dynamic and absolutely imaginative in his delivery. Totally worthy in all respects is Walton's version with the Philharmonia Orchestra and Chorus, with Donald Bell as the baritone soloist. It is on Angel S–35681.

Façade (an Entertainment with Poems by Edith Sitwell) (1922)

☐ Bookspan (speaker); Baron (flute); Russo (clarinet); Estrin (saxophone); Broiles (trumpet); Harris (percussion); Moore (cello) / Epstein (conductor) / Candide 31116

High-brow poetry with low-brow music; poetry freely shaped and entwined with music of a decided beat; new verses read, old forms played—thus the mating of words with music in *Façade*. The Walton–Sitwell depiction of a serious idea with a humorous objective was a type of premature surrealism (first presented in 1922). In its individual way, *Façade* is a small masterpiece.

Sitwell's poems are totally abstract; the designs are formed not only from word colorations, assonances, dissonances, and the play of syllables but also from the effect of rhythm and tempo in delivery. Walton's music is genuinely witty, grotesque, and rowdy. Its parody is subtle and cunning. Illustrations: a take-off on a tap-dance routine in the *Popular Song*, the Rossini *William Tell* off-key quotations in the *Yodelling Song*, the naughty mixture of waltz and duple pulse in the *Tarantella*. Sitwell's and Walton's verbal-music partnership is a frothy, superbly entertaining monodrama.

It has been stated that the Sitwell lines are abstract. However, it has taken Janet Bookspan, the speaker in Candide's recording to probe and to find, as she describes it "the sense behind the nonsense." Her discovery of a second area within the text of *Façade* adds a dimension to the performance unlike any other that has been given or recorded. Her delivery is magnificently voiced, beautifully colored, and is matched by the cogent styling of David Epstein who conducts. This recording of *Façade* certainly moves into the number one position.

The best of the others available is Argo's ZRG–649, with Ashcroft and Scofield as the speakers, and Walton conducting the London Sinfonietta. However, the Argo presentation has certain faults—some odd balances and some rhythmic situations that are not on point in regard to the narrators. If you want to search in the territory of deleted discs, try to find the recording made by the English Opera Group Ensemble, with Edith Sitwell and Peter

Opera and Dramatic Music

Pears as the reciters and Collins directing. It was an old London (4104) edition. With Sitwell as one of the participants, this issue is both important and historic.

For the Suites from *Façade*, see under *Orchestra (Façade:* Suites No. 1 and No. 2).

Walton / *J. S. Bach.* *See J. S. Bach* / William Walton.

Johann Baptist Wanhal *(1739 - 1813)*

Orchestra

Symphony in A minor

☐ Chamber Orchestra of the Sarre / Ristenpart (conductor) / Nonesuch 71014

A symphonette in length with the total time of the three movements embracing twelve minutes. The music sings without major disclosures but its clear spirits are refreshing. A responsive performance, indeed, an exemplary one that matches Wanhal's attractive score.

Solo Instrument and Orchestra

Viola

Concerto in C major for Viola and Orchestra

☐ Württemberg Chamber Orchestra, Heilbronn / Wallfisch (viola) / Faerber (conductor) / Turnabout 34305

Ernst Wallfisch plays this work with compelling style. There is no strain, no forced tone, no brashness in his solid portrayal. Wanhal's (or Vanhal's or Vanhall's) music has distinctly differentiated subjects and a beautifully spun theme in the slow movement, just as beautifully developed.

Chamber Music

Sonata in B flat major

☐ Russo (clarinet); Ignacio (piano) / Orion 77273

Wanhal's three-movement piece is simply-poised Haydn, which is fair enough. Cleanly played, but the piano sound is metallic and is an injustice to the performer's suppleness.

John Ward *(1571 - ca. 1638)*

Choral

Chorus Alone

Retire, My Troubled Soul

☐ Purcell Consort of Voices / Burgess (conductor) / Turnabout 34202

A very compelling madrigal in both its line and part writing. The music acutely matches the text dealing with the melancholy matter of life's vanities. *Retire* represents a very moving composition by this English composer and is sung with a gentility that is entrancing.

Robert Ward *(1917-   )*

Orchestra

Divertimento for Orchestra (1960)

☐ Portland Junior Symphony / Avshalomov (conductor) / Composers Recordings 194 (monaural)

Contemporary tonal innocence but not innocent of nourishing lines and tonic rhythms. The latter are specifically detailed in the finale. A fine effort by the young musicians.

Euphony for Orchestra (1954)

☐ Louisville Orchestra / Whitney (conductor) / Louisville 545–10 (monaural)

Open-air music, clear, expressive, and unpretentious. Broad and firm in its outlines, warm in its orchestral bath. It has exuberance.

Festive Ode

☐ Polish Radio Orchestra / Szostak (conductor) / Musical Heritage Society MHS–1600

Ward's favorite combine for a composition that does not have contrastive movements. Meaning: quiet music undertoned with emotional urgency contrasted to faster-tempoed music containing a healthy muscular vigor. The partnership invigorates.

A particularly good execution is given Ward's piece. On this basis it is worth looking out for other recorded works conducted by Zdzislav Szostak.

Invocation and Toccata

☐ Polish Radio Orchestra / Wodiczko (conductor) / Musical Heritage Society MHS–1600

Like all of Ward's music structural clarity and coherence are present. The *Invocation* is introspectively intense, the Toccata is just as intense but extroverted in tone, as is proper to a toccata's personality.

On-focus performance delivering the on-focus orchestration that dramatizes this work.

Jubilation Overture (1946)

☐ Vienna Symphony Orchestra / Strickland (conductor) / Composers Recordings 159 (monaural)

Bright and a little brash. Ward knows his contemporary fellow composers but this is a healthy situation. The Overture may not be brightly new but it is pink-cheeked with animation and well being. Such a prospectus does bring beneficial results.

Prairie Overture

☐ Polish Radio Orchestra / Wodiczko (conductor) / Musical Heritage Society MHS–1600

Ward has never been occupied with harmonic and contrapuntal complexities. Neither can one find romantic afflatus in his conceptions. He cultivates a direct openheartedness, even in his most serious moments. The *Prairie* Overture minces no matters; it is meat and potatoes music—right on, as vernacular prose would describe it. Topographically tuneful, it contains some Coplandesque cowboyisms, and even a smidgen or two of Hansonesque turns of phrase. No matter. It's clean and sensible music.

Symphony No. 1 (1941)

☐ Vienna Symphony Orchestra / Dixon (conductor) / Desto 6405E (monaural)

Ward's harmonies and counterpoints have sufficient grit for tractional purposes; the rhythms are athletic. But nothing fancy free; the working data fits the basic ideas. It is noticeable that Ward's themes are of the type that can be developed. There is no compulsion on his part to serve up mere singable melodies. A strong work fulfilled by Dixon's conducting demeanor whereby lyricism and dramatic tensions balance properly.

Symphony No. 2 (1947)

☐ Japan Philharmonic Symphony Orchestra / Strickland (conductor) / Composers Recordings 127 (monaural)

Robert Ward's faith has always been in the chordal weapons that have served for many a year. No so-so academic boredom results. The factor of structural consonancy with a dissonant façade describes this three-movement piece. The fact that one can spot some Shostakovich touches does not mar the result. It makes for good listening and the recording cannot be faulted.

Symphony No. 3 (1950)

☐ Iceland Symphony Orchestra / Buketoff (conductor) / Composers Recordings 206 (monaural)

Tonal directness with the lyricism of Hanson, the splendid sense of rhythm that marks the work of Copland, and even a bit of Roy Harris (in the first movement). But, no eclectic hodge podge; the aggregate is compact and has impact. The use of the piano as an orchestral voice is special in the middle, slow-paced movement.

The performance is a lucid one throughout and in the witty and peppy finale, energetically well-turned.

Brass Ensemble

Fantasia for Brass Choir and Timpani

☐ Polish Radio Orchestra / Szostak (conductor) / Musical Heritage Society MHS–1600

A good mix with rhythmic-fanfare punctuations, choral-like blocks, some jazz and bluesy items. It is a work for virtuosi, composed with a musical headway that does not lessen because brass instruments are being used.

Solo Instrument and Orchestra

Piano

Concerto for Piano and Orchestra

☐ Stuttgart Radio Orchestra / Mitchell (piano) / Strickland (conductor) / Desto 7123

All the big moves with romantic thrust and worthy tunes that have always come naturally to this American composer. One can always depend on a well-schooled formal command from Ward and it is thus in his Concerto.

The composition was commissioned for Marjorie Mitchell who gave the premiere performance in 1968 with Howard Mitchell (no relation) conducting the National Symphony Orchestra. She plays the Concerto with genuine understanding and full conviction. The recorded sound is very bright.

Vocal

Voice with Accompaniment

Sorrow of Mydath

☐ McCollum (tenor); Biltcliffe (piano) / Desto 6411/2

Ward's excellent capacity for setting words and creating the proper musical object that will express their meaning is beautifully illustrated here. Masefield's words are not lost in the shuffle of the performance, either.

Voice and Orchestra

Sacred Songs for Pantheists (1951)

☐ Polish National Radio Orchestra / Stahlman (soprano) / Strickland (conductor) / Composers Recordings 206 (monaural)

Five songs that are set to texts by James Stephens, Emily Dickinson, and Gerard Manley Hopkins. Convincing musically, and responsive to prosodic requirements. The gem of the cycle is part 4 *Heaven-Haven—A Nun Takes the Veil.*

Hush'd Be the Camps Today (1941)

☐ Norwegian Choir of Solosingers and Members of the Oslo Philharmonic Orchestra / Strickland (conductor) / Composers Recordings 165 (monaural)

Concise, developed logically, and thoroughly of pervading sentiment. In his Whitman setting, Ward's use of timpani, modal harmonies, and climactic placement, is a strong reminder of the methods of Howard Hanson. That does not belie the composition's worth.

The performance catches the pronounced, refreshing vitality of the music.

The Crucible (1961)

☐ Orchestra and Chorus of New York City Opera / Ceniceros (coloratura); Brooks, Farr, Foster, Kova, and Evans (sopranos); Ebert and Bible (mezzo-sopranos); Wynder, Alberts, Guile, and Schwering (contraltos); Kelley, Stern, Krause, and DeLon (tenors); Ukena and Ludgin (baritones); Malas and Macurdy (basses) / Buckley (conductor) / Composers Recordings S–168

Ward's four-act Opera is his most important work. Although its vocal-melodic writing is conservatively styled, the score is of dynamic quality and, being based on the Arthur Miller play concerned with the hysterical witch-hunt events that took place in Salem, Massachusetts, in 1692, it has tremendous tension. The music-theatrical point of view in Ward's Opera is perfectly joined. *The Crucible* was an immediate success at its premiere (October 1961) and the success continued the year following with both a Pulitzer Prize for Music and a New York Critics Circle Citation. It remains as one of the key works in the American Opera repertory.

The recording is one of distinction. One is grateful to CRI for making this important Opera available.

David Ward-Steinman   (1936-   )

Duo for Cello and Piano (1965)

☐ Lustgarten (cello); Williams (piano) / Orion 74141

Ward-Steinman's Duo is a reworking (which he terms a "chamber version") of his Concerto for Cello and Orchestra. (He describes the second version as "a rethinking of the material in idiomatic terms of the sonorous potential of the piano, the cello part being virtually the same in both cases.")

Tonality in its broadest (free) sense permeates this fine work, styled with a rich combination of romantic and expressionistic detail. Above all, Ward-Steinman is to be credited with the ability to create highly charged, long-breathed meaningful lines. This is music free of systems or schematicism and represents an important piece of chamber music.

The playing is of genuine artistic disposition. Edgar Lustgarten has a beautiful tone and his phrasing is a joy to hear. His partner is just as good and shows that he is as expert at the keyboard as he is in writing Oscar-award film scores—his name is John Williams.

Fragments from Sappho

☐ Curtin (soprano); Baron (flute); Glazer (clarinet); Ward-Steinman (piano) / Composers Recordings S–238

Music in a late-romantic idiom, further colored by the scoring plan. Parts 1, 3, and 5 are for the voice and instrumental trio; the clarinet is omitted in No. 2, the flute is tacet in movement 4, and for the sixth part (*Epilog*) the heaviest instrument (the piano, of course) is eliminated.

The composer is joined by an all-star cast in the performance. It's very good.

Gerald Warfield (1940-   )

Chamber Music

Variations and Metamorphoses for Two Cellos and Offstage Piano

☐ Hoyle and Lensky (cellos); Warfield (piano) / Advance FGR–19S

The first movement is for the cellos alone. It is dark and emotive—an entirely convincing conception. Movement 2 begins with Chopin's Prelude in E minor played by the offstage pianist, followed by transformation of its material by the cellists alone, completed by the Chopin sounds. The third part of Warfield's opus is a continuation of the opening movement.

The two planes on which the work moves paradoxically are in perfect balance, since the Chopin metamorphoses retain the style of the music's outer portions while fully relating to the Chopin impetus.

Give the fullest credits possible to the performers. Both Ted Hoyle and Larry Lensky play with full clarity, balance each other coloristically, and have a rich tonal quality. This is a fine contribution.

Peter Warlock (1894-1930)

Choral

Chorus Alone

Corpus Christi (1921)

☐ Canby Singers / Canby (conductor) / Nonesuch 71115

A stunning setting that is guaranteed to make the listener want to hear it again and again. Somewhere, it is recalled, a writer described *Corpus Christi* as "menacingly beautiful."

The text of the Old English Carol symbolizes Christ in agony. The music includes short portions for solo tenor and solo contralto.

(The composer was born Philip Heseltine. Warlock—by which he is known—is a pen name.)

Elinor Remick Warren (1905-   )

Orchestra

Suite for Orchestra (1954)

☐ Oslo Philharmonic Orchestra / Strickland (conductor) / Composers Recordings 172 (monaural)

No preliminary reading of liner notes are necessary to understand the conservative ethos of this music. Accordingly: floating and fluctuating legati in *Cloud Peaks*, jiggy, joggy jets in *Ballet of the Midsummer Sky*, a processional pulse in *Pageant Across the Sky*, etc. What has to be realized has been by the Norwegian outfit and the American conductor.

Abram in Egypt (1961)

☐ London Philharmonic Orchestra and Roger Wagner Chorale / Lewis (baritone) / Wagner (conductor) / Composers Recordings 172 (monaural)

Cantata and Oratorio

The text partners material from Genesis and the Dead Sea Scrolls. This is divided in a conventional manner: the solo baritone delineates the character of Abram, the chorus relates the story and adds commentary. Composed in a style drawn from the backwaters of romantic territory, Warren's work is very effective, especially in the dynamic performance given here. Special plaudits pertain to the excellent voice of Ronald Lewis.

Walter Watson   (1933-   )

Recital Suite for Marimba (with Piano)

☐ Kenneth Watson (marimba); Swiatkowski (piano) / Crystal S-532

Instrumental

Marimba

Simplicity is at the heart of this work. It is best expressed in the two outer fast-paced assertions. Lyrical knitting for the marimba applies to the middle movement, but it produces only a lightweight fabric.

The marimba is played by the composer's brother. His performance proves he is a sensitive musician.

John Watts   (1930-   )

Sonata for Piano

☐ Sanders (piano) / Trilogy CTS-1003

Instrumental

Piano

Contrastive summaries pertain to this work. Based on sixteenth-note persistences and arranged differences, the first movement emerges with toccata motility, minus its outward (often unconvincing) bravado. Chromatic polyphony describes movement 2 and the very opposite is the mnemonic device for the slow, idyll-like division. Motility is present again in the finale, more jagged this time.

Attractively produced pianism by Dean Sanders and a well-indexed interpretation of the score.

Signals for Soprano and Chamber Orchestra

☐ Composers Festival Orchestra / Rowe (soprano) / Brehm (conductor) / Trilogy CTS-1002

Vocal

Voice and Orchestra

This absolute delight is conceived in the same category as Milhaud's *Machines Agricoles* (the texts taken from a catalogue dealing with agricultural machinery) and Mossolov's *Advertisements* (the words drawn from newspaper notices covering such services as rat extermination). Watts's choices are *Warning* (on the use of an incinerator), *Certification* (concerning the material in some hosiery), and *Notice* (on an envelope containing X-rated material).

No snideness in any instance. No leg-pulling, either. The practical messages ("signals") may not be artistic but they are treated with artistry, so while the words may sound humorous in a concert context they are framed by solid, even sober instrumental sentences and paragraphs. In no sense is *Signals* a type of Satie *Anhang*, so to speak. No frothy foam, though a scherzo-picaresque attitude is observed in *Certification*. Part one is surrounded by pedals, with only strings, piano, and percussion employed. Dark colors embrace the *Notice*.

No text is supplied with the recording. As Watts indicates: "Since the message . . . depends on the medium . . . I have asked that no text be printed." None is needed, with Catherine Rowe's determinative diction. There is no doubt that *Signals* is a real sleeper.

Donald Waxman (1925-)

Chamber Music

Trio for Oboe, Clarinet, and Bassoon

☐ Lucarelli (oboe); Bloom (clarinet); MacCourt (bassoon) / Turnabout 34520

American ambassador in the court of Poulenc. Real good tunes, clean-as-a-whistle salted harmony, and lucid forms. There is a sophisticated innocence about Waxman's piece that is totally captivating.

These are top-flight musicians and they present the Trio with absolute clarity and conviction. A bonus is the natural perspective of the disc's engineering.

Ernest Waxman (1918-)

Chamber Music

Capriccio

☐ Modern Brass Ensemble / Advance FGR–2 (monaural)

Steady and straightforward, safe and sane happy music. A sonatina in scope with its tonality unblemished. An unblemished performance as well.

Franz Waxman (1906-1967)

Orchestra

Suite from the Film *Crime in the Streets*

Theme, Variations, and Fugato

Three Sketches for Jazz Orchestra

☐ Los Angeles Music Festival Jazz Orchestra / Turner (piano); Candoli (trumpet); Dumont (alto saxophone); Mondragon (bass); Gentry (tenor and baritone saxophones) / Waxman (conductor) / Entr'acte ERM–6001E (monaural)

Though only one work bears the jazz identification the other two are just as concerned with integration of jazz elements into the textures. There are no ragtime broadsides in Waxman's music. He underplays the jazz in his texts and tunes and they register that more potently. Furthermore, he never blares or uses bombastic combinations in his scoring. There is a dynamic chamber-music quality embracing all of the material.

Entr'acte's album is a reissue of a Decca edition (DL–8376) that was produced in 1956.

String Orchestra

Sinfonietta for Strings and Timpani

☐ Los Angeles Festival Orchestra / Waxman (conductor) / Varèse Sarabande VC–81052E (monaural)

The eclectic conditions are strong in Waxman's work. The first movement recalls Bartók, that of the finale (a Scherzo), a Honeggerian-Rousselian combine. In between is a *Dirge*. Somehow it turns out to be a convincing whole, mainly through fine playing.

Originally on Decca (recorded monophonically in 1956). Fine remastering.

Ben Weber *(1916-1979)*

Dolmen, An Elegy (1964)
Orchestra

☐ Louisville Orchestra / Whitney (conductor) / Louisville S-676

The title is an ancient Breton word for megalithic stone structures. Weber's music is like frozen chunks of sound. Though the lines move they tend to cling to each other, bearing out the analogy. Whitney and his musicians do well with the emotional reserve and the ecstatic tensions of the score.

Prelude and Passacaglia, Op. 42

☐ Louisville Orchestra / Whitney (conductor) / Louisville 56-6 (monaural)

The mistake of thinking formal definition the equivalent of artistic reality has haunted more than one composer. Thus variation or the related passacaglia form can turn out to be a mere ornamentally extensive exercise, instead of yielding the rich fullness resultant from clear thematic comprehension. Weber's absorbing nineteen variations contain colorful tensions, deal with the main argument, and reach their goal beautifully. The music's climax is prepared and is not the result of mere technical rule of thumb. In contrast, the somberness of the preamble is an example of artistic orchestration.

This is an impressive-sounding performance.

Concerto for Piano and Orchestra, Op. 52
Solo Instrument and Orchestra

Piano

☐ Royal Philharmonic Orchestra / Masselos (piano) / Samuel (conductor) / Composers Recordings S-239

Weber treads the middle, fully firm road of serialism: neither academic nor radical. In his hands the concerto form retains current validity and virtuosity. Movement 2, a memorial piece for Mitropoulos, one of Weber's finest inspirations, is threnodic in a sublimated way. The interlock between soloist and conductor is superb.

Fantasia (Variations), Op. 25
Instrumental

Five Bagatelles, Op. 2
Piano

Three Pieces, Op. 23

☐ Bennette (piano) / Desto 7136

The Fantasia is conceived in one solid chunk, but split to form the actuality of a triple-movement work played without pause. The plan: a theme with variations, passacaglia variants, and a final Fantasia. Although texturally heavy, the clear lines supercharge the composition, intensifying the dodecaphonic language. The last style is the cohesive point of the sensitive expressions found in the Bagatelles. A Bergian mist hangs over the other work (which is not meant to be a back-handed compliment), with Weber fusing a type of romantic ecstasy into the dodecaphonic syntax. It was not a surprise, therefore, to learn from reading the soloist's liner notes that the third piece of the set is, according to the composer, "a tribute to Berg's Lyric Suite."

Good performances throughout.

Humoreske, Op. 49

☐ Helps (piano) / Composers Recordings S-288

A fantasy piece rather than the whimsicality one would expect from the title. Either way a compelling contribution and as compelling a performance.

Chamber Music

Sonata da Camera

☐ Schneider (violin); Horszowski (piano) / New World Records NW-281 (monaural)

Declamatory and recitative points mark the sonata's first part. A virtuoso passacaglia structure is found in the middle movement. Multitudinous complexions are to be observed: stretto, rhythmic change, and diminution are among the totality. But, no technical device mars the flow of the music. A rondo completes the opus.

New World Records obtained the master of this mono recording from Epic Records. It had been recorded in 1954, but never released. It is a welcome addition.

String Quartet No. 2, Op. 35

☐ New Music Quartet / Composers Recordings SD-358E (monaural)

It is understandable to doubt the spontaneity of a serial work but creative genius can overcome the boundaries and rigidity of a compositional system and produce a spontaneous (and, in this case, an undated) result. Mainly variationally developed, Weber's Quartet is a rich product.

The performance, as always occurs in listening to this quartet team, makes one mourn the fact that they left so few recordings before they disbanded. This example was made in 1961 for the American Composers Alliance but was never released, and has been rechanneled for stereo. It is a stylish and knowing rendition.

Consort for Winds (1974)

☐ Boehm Quintette / Orion 75206

Dodecaphonic, technically warmed music, but no expressionistic pathos or restless abstraction. Weber's *Consort* (the title chosen since additions in the same family of two of the wind quintet's makeup are used: piccolo and alto flute and a bass clarinet) is restrained for the most part; an almost cool music. It develops a strength by understatement, most apparent after several hearings. Like all art, its secrets will be disclosed if given time.

Informative and appealing playing. The tone of the Boehm organization is beautiful, superbly balanced.

Vocal

Voice with Accompaniment

Mourn! Mourn!, Op. 53

☐ McCollum (tenor); Biltcliffe (piano) / Desto 6411/2

John McCollum is a perceptive participant in presenting this dark-toned, dramatically moving song.

Vocal

Voice and Orchestra

Concert Aria after *Solomon,* Op. 29

☐ Orchestra / Beardslee (soprano) / Brieff (conductor) / Desto 6422E (monaural)

Straussian breadth if not of Straussian instrumental size; the "orchestra" is actually an octet consisting of a wind quintet plus a piano trio. Weber's piece *sings,* which description does not fit many a vocal work. It has a sensuous urge that is maintained throughout its length.

A worthy performance providing the text that is printed on the album cover is followed. Bethany Beardslee projects her part with musicality but doesn't project the words at all.

Symphony on *Poems of William Blake,* Op. 33

☐ Leopold Stokowski and His Orchestra / Galjour (baritone) / Stokowski (conductor) / Composers Recordings 120 (monaural)

A musical synthesis, whereby the sung poetry is put to use and ordered for symphonic purposes. *To Autumn* is of moderate tempo; the second part, *Never Seek to Tell Thy Love,* featuring the voice, is like a slow movement. Movement 3 (*Mad Song*), is a dogmatic scherzo in conduct, though not in scherzo tempo. A lighter element (*To Spring*) concludes Weber's vocal-instrumental Symphony.

The composer's intent is described as a ''cyclic expression of mystery, despair, madness and love reborn.'' In a sense these moods run over their boundary lines and intermingle, save for the very individual third part. Weber's writing is exceedingly free and the contrasts are somewhat blurred.

Excellently performed with a first-rate singer as a bonus.

Carl Maria von Weber   (1786-1826)

Jubel Overture, Op. 59   *Orchestra*

☐ Bamberg Symphony Orchestra / Guschlbauer (conductor) / Musical Heritage Society MHS-1220

The only part one ever hears, and at that, not very often, of Weber's *Jubel* Cantata. The ending proclaims, with expert counterpoint, *Heil dir im Siegerkranz.* For those living in the United States that melody is none other than *America* and, of course, in the U.K. it's *God Save the King.* No better setting of the old tune has ever been fashioned.

The big boys, such as Ansermet, von Karajan, Klemperer, Kubelik, Mehta, and Ormandy, who have recorded Weber overtures have passed this one by. One disagrees, for it's a fine piece. The orchestra and the conductor noted above may not be in the big leagues but they don't play in minor league fashion.

Overture and March from *Turandot,* Op. 37

☐ London Symphony Orchestra / Schönzeler (conductor) / RCA CRL2-2281

The March is one of three contained in the six pieces, together with the Overture, that Weber wrote as incidental music to Schiller's adaptation of a play by Gozzi. Full-blown music and most rewarding.

Those that know their Hindemith will immediately recognize these pieces as the bases for one of the movements in his Symphonic Metamorphosis of Themes by Carl Maria von Weber.

Overture to *Abu Hassan* (1811)
Overture to *Der Freischütz* (1820)

Overture to *Euryanthe* (1823)

Overture to *Oberon* (1826)

Overture to *Peter Schmoll* (1802)

☐ Berlin Philharmonic Orchestra / von Karajan (conductor) / Deutsche Grammophon 2530315

Everybody, including Klemperer, Kubelik, Mehta, Münchinger, and Ormandy have recorded one or more of Weber's operatic overtures. The musicality and the proper temperature of romantic fervor make these the top performances in the field.

One second choice must be mentioned—Ormandy's conception of *Euryanthe*. The performance, on Columbia MG–31190, is a rich affair.

Overture to *Preciosa*

☐ L'Orchestre de la Suisse Romande / Ansermet (conductor) / London STS–15056

All the stylistic assets, required in this music written for a play by P. A. Wolff, are here. A second choice is also on London (STS–15076), with Münchinger conducting the Vienna Philharmonic. Ansermet has more subtlety in his reading.

Overture: *The Ruler of the Spirits*, Op. 27

☐ Berlin Philharmonic Orchestra / von Karajan (conductor) / Deutsche Grammophon 2530315

The Overture to his unfinished Opera *Rübezahl* that Weber revised and which then was titled *Der Beherrscher der Geister* ("The Ruler of the Spirits"), and assigned Opus 27. It is given a thoroughly solid performance.

Symphony No. 1 in C major, Op. 19

☐ New Philharmonia Orchestra / Boettcher (conductor) / Philips 6500154

The second of the four movements is the highlight of Weber's first of two symphonies. Though the Symphony throughout has the Weberesque oboe and horn earmarks it is in the C minor Andante that the music goes straight to the core of romantic temper. Its deeply expressive coloration and operatic prognosis are proof of Weber's originality at the age of twenty-one.

This music does not need and does not obtain any interpretative tinkering. First-class conception and playing.

Symphony No. 2 in C major, J. 51

☐ London Symphony Orchestra / Schönzeler (conductor) / RCA CRL2–2281

Weber's Symphony does not explore any new territory but firmly and appropriately nestles within his special romantic world. Some fine wind solo spots stand out in this pleasurable music. Since it is played with expressivity and, where required, with spirit, it represents a rewarding performance.

Solo Instrument and Orchestra

Bassoon

Andante e Rondo Ongarese for Bassoon and Orchestra, Op. 35

☐ Philadelphia Orchestra / Garfield (bassoon) / Ormandy (conductor) / Columbia MS–6977

A perfect performance and a beautiful one. This is what artistry is all about. In terms of sheer bassoon playing Bernard Garfield's performance is astounding.

Columbia lists this in a kind of musical vernacularism as "Hungarian Fantasy." The most-reliable *Schwann* catalogue even condenses the title to read "Andante and Rondo."

Concerto in F major for Bassoon and Orchestra, Op. 75

☐ Württemberg Chamber Orchestra / Zukerman (bassoon) / Faerber (conductor) / Turnabout 34039

Much better Weber than this but still it's Weber and worth a try now and then. The playing cannot be improved upon, with perfect phrasing and skillful articulation on the part of the soloist.

Grand Potpourri for Cello and Orchestra, Op. 20

Cello

☐ Berlin Symphony Orchestra / Blees (cello) / Bünte (conductor) / Turnabout 34306

It is clear that Weber chose the proper title for his four-parts-in-one work. No concerto this, but simply a series of melodies set forth in succession. Once in a while some figuration is amiably disposed, but such detail is minor in the total.

Blees strikes a happy balance between warm expression and restraint. The correct brand of simplicity and elegance provides an enjoyable performance.

Concertino for Clarinet and Orchestra, Op. 26

Clarinet

☐ Vienna State Opera Orchestra / Brymer (clarinet) / Prohaska (conductor) / Vanguard 71167

Brymer's clarification of the dynamic differences makes his rendition of this clarinet best-seller the most favorable one on the market. Without such demarcation Weber's piece can be extremely prosaic.

The performance is duplicated in a two-record package (Vanguard 709/10) which has seven other concerti (one by Cimarosa, two by Mozart, and four by Vivaldi) and which features eight other soloists.

Concerto No. 1 in F minor for Clarinet and Orchestra, Op. 73

☐ Württemberg Chamber Orchestra, Heilbronn / Glazer (clarinet) / Faerber (conductor) / Turnabout 34151

Richly toned playing which includes alluring phrasing in the slow movement and polished delivery in the merry finale. Perhaps a few more dynamic differences might well have been applied in the opening movement, but not too much harm without them. Regardless, Glazer's is the prime choice in the recorded catalogue.

Concerto No. 2 in E flat major for Clarinet and Orchestra, Op. 74

☐ London Symphony Orchestra / de Peyer (clarinet) / Davis (conductor) / Oiseau-Lyre 60035

Two extremely skilled movements rub against a central slow division that is slightly tedious. Nevertheless, whatever that Andante contains, every bit of it is made available by this fine musician. One can check this recording against the score and one will find it is a well-nigh perfect sonic translation.

Romanza Siciliana in G minor for Flute and Small Orchestra (1806)

Flute

☐ Hamburg Symphony Orchestra / Thalheimer (flute) / Neidlinger (conductor) / Turnabout 34488

Captivating colors in this lovely, textured piece. Firm credits for the soloist for recording Weber's little-known composition.

Horn

Concertino in E minor for Horn and Orchestra, Op. 45

☐ Academy of St. Martin-in-the-Fields / Tuckwell (horn) / Marriner (conductor) / Angel S-36996

The horn is partnered with winds that comprise a flute, two clarinets, and two bassoons. Two horns and two trumpets represent the brass, and the usual timpani and strings complete the orchestral forces.

These colors expertly frame a type of fantasy of moods within Weber's work. The superb playing by the soloist conquers all the hideously difficult demands of the score. Tuckwell is supported by just as superb orchestral functioning.

Piano

Grand Concerto No. 1 in C major for Piano and Orchestra, Op. 11

☐ Hamburg Symphony / Littauer (piano) / Köhler (conductor) / Turnabout 34406

A work that can be described as romantic tunes and a final dance in search of a concerto. Maria Littauer sails through everything with nonchalant ease. A performance that shows the music is in experienced and sympathetic hands. Nice orchestral playing including a pungently toned oboist.

Malcolm Frager's performance on RCA (CRL2-2281) offers close competition. It does mince a bit bringing an up-and-down consideration of the music and is less convincing than Littauer's in the slow movement.

Grand Concerto No. 2 in E flat major for Piano and Orchestra, Op. 32

☐ North German Radio Symphony Orchestra / Frager (piano) / Andreae (conductor) / RCA CRL2-2281

Not often played (and the same applies to the first Piano Concerto). Still, there is Weber singing operatically, Weber in a bravura stance in the finale and poetically romantic in the slow movement. It may not be played often but Weber's second Piano Concerto could juice up the concerto repertory if pianists paid some attention. Meanwhile the recorded performance gives the home listener the advantage.

Malcom Frager does well with the Concerto. The playing is rhythmically alive, technically fluent, and stylistically constant. The cooperation from Marc Andreae is excellent.

Konzertstück in F minor for Piano and Orchestra, Op. 79

☐ Hamburg Symphony / Littauer (piano) / Köhler (conductor) / Turnabout 34406

Though Weber's piano concerti are rare concert-hall items, the *Konzertstück* retains full performance health. It's got all the ingredients: romantic lamentation, passionate declaration, rhythmic stability, and a brilliant peroration.

Maria Littauer plays this pianistic opera-like work in a glowing fashion. She has obvious affection and enthusiasm for the piece, much more than Gulda on his London recording.

Viola

Andante e Rondo Ongarese for Viola and Orchestra, Op. 35

☐ Hamburg Symphony Orchestra / Koch (viola) / Neidlinger (conductor) / Turnabout 34488

This work is most often heard in the bassoon and orchestra combination which Weber made in 1813 (*see above*). The original setting, composed in 1809, is for viola and orchestra.

The contrastive aspects of the piece gain measurably when the bassoon is the solo color. For those, however, who prefer the viola edition, or would like to have both versions, this recording will serve most admirably. Ulrich Koch, the soloist, is excellent and receives fine support.

Deutscher Waltz (or Original Waltz)

Grande Polonaise, Op. 21

Invitation to the Dance, Op. 65

Max-Walzer

Momento Capriccioso, Op. 12

Polacca Brillante, Op. 72

Rondo Brillante (La Gaiete), Op. 62

☐ Kann (piano) / Vox SVBX-5451

Instrumental

Piano

Do not be misled into thinking Vox has mislabeled the *Grande Polonaise*. It begins with a dramatic slow-tempoed section which Hans Kann plays sensitively. The dance that follows has more dramatic inlay than is usual with this type. On the other hand the other *polonaise* in this group (here listed as on the Vox release; it is the same as the *Polonaise Brillante* [*L'Hilarité*] in E major that Liszt transcribed—see under *Weber/Liszt: Solo Instrument and Orchestra: piano*) plunges in and stays in the dance format.

The *Invitation to the Dance* (often incorrectly named with "waltz" substituted for "dance") is music of decided charm, unfortunately bypassed these days in favor of the colorized orchestral transcription. Kann projects the music for Opus 65 with authenticity.

Seven *Kontretänze*

☐ Kann (piano) / Vox SVBX-5450

Kann treats these musical small fry with charm, which translated means he makes them most persuasive.

Seven Variations on a Gypsy Song, Op. 55

☐ Kann (piano) / Vox SVBX-5451

An academic scale of reactions concerns this piece. Weber's unconcern does not affect the effect of Kann's playing, which accomplishes as much as can be expected.

Seven Variations on Bianchi's *Vien quá Dorina Bella*, Op. 7

☐ Kann (piano) / Vox SVBX-5450

Bianchi, a contemporary of Mozart, was a composer of *opera buffa*. Weber's treatment of his tune poses no questions, invokes no deep drama, but is deployed simply and directly; the conclusion is a *polacca*. Good pianism in Kann's portrayal.

Seven Variations on the *Romance* from Méhul's *Joseph*, Op. 28

Six Favorite Waltzes (Nos. 1, 2, and 3)

☐ Kann (piano) / Vox SVBX-5451

A good amount of virtuoso writing in the pair of variations in presto tempo, based on

Méhul's opera extract. Attractively structured and rewarding for the pianist, as perceived in the recorded performance.

Six Fughetti, Op. 1

Six Variations on an *Air de Ballet* from Vogler's *Castor et Pollux*, Op. 5

Six Variations on an *Air* from Vogler's *Samori*, Op. 6

Six Variations on an Original Theme, Op. 2

Sonata No. 1 in C major, Op. 24

Sonata No. 2 in A flat major, Op. 39

☐ Kann (piano) / Vox SVBX–5450

A composer's Opus 1 is always a matter of curiosity. Weber's is short and successful. Vox calls them ''fugues,'' which they are not, as seen from the title heading above. They average less than forty seconds each, the measure totals ranging from twelve to twenty-six.

The variational sets provide sectional depiction. Each has divisions that stand out, such as the *Marche Funèbre* of Opus 6, the mazurka that completes Opus 5, and in Opus 2, the striding bass octaves and movie-music-like *tremolandi*.

The minuet movements in the pair of four-movement sonatas are at speeds and with material in which the notes are hanging in scherzo territory. The second sonata's title for this portion is marked *Menuetto Capriccioso*, its tempo is *presto assai*. Mercurial touchy music completes the first of the sonatas. This movement is often performed separately, sometimes titled *Perpetuum Mobile*, other times *L'infatigable*. In comparison, the finale to the second sonata is graceful.

Kann's playing of these sonatas is highly effective, with a good weave of the material. The more intimate style of the second sonata is achieved. There are no false mannerisms, the music is given its proper perspective.

Sonata No. 3 in D minor, Op. 49

Sonata No. 4 in E minor, Op. 70

Twelve *Deutscher-Walzer*

Variations on an Original Theme, Op. 9

Variations on a Russian Song, *Schöne Minka*, Op. 40

☐ Kann (piano) / Vox SVBX–5451

Weber and operatic style are never far apart. The sixth variant in Opus 9 pictures dramatic recitative and aria-like portions. A Spanish-styled variation also appears; the same nationalistically defined type completes the Opus 40 set of variations.

Though the third piano sonata has been called ''Demoniac'' it has no program that applies to its three movement span. However, the fourth piano sonata presumably has—a man's acute depression into insanity and eventual death. Sufficient dramatic musical detail follows the train of this argument, but the music can stand alone. Both the opening and closing movements are especially powerful. The latter is shaped in Tarantella form (it has been programmed with the unlikely title *Jet d'eau* [!]).

Save for the finale of the second sonata, marked *prestissimo*, but which Kann plays at a comfortable *allegro* pace, the performance of all of the Weber music is good. One must also acknowledge Kann's feat of recording the entire piano output of this important composer.

Eight Pieces for Piano, Four-Hands, Op. 60

Six *Petites Pièces Faciles* for Piano, Four-Hands, Op. 3

Six Pieces for Piano, Four-Hands, Op. 10

☐ Kann and Marciano (piano) / Vox SVBX-5450

*Piano,
Four Hands*

Simplicity rules in the Opus 3 and Opus 10. More interesting music is disclosed in the more difficult Opus 60 set, which is on a par with the best of Schubert's large output of four-hand piano music. Number four of Opus 60 (a lusty dance), and the seventh piece in that set (a march), as well as the second of the Opus 3 group will be recognized as sources that Paul Hindemith used in his Symphonic Metamorphosis of Themes by Carl Maria von Weber.

Grand Duo Concertant, Op. 48

☐ Warner (clarinet); Dameron (piano) / Crystal S-332

*Chamber
Music*

Similar to Weber's brilliant orchestration, which is concerned with dramatic effect, is the style of this *duo*. The clarinet is used from its subterranean depths up to its high gamut, the piano *tremolos* against declamatory wind color, there are swirling figures, and a general romantic virtuosity. All these make for chamber-music orchestration in the concentrate and sonoric dramaticism in the aggregate.

Especially is this work a field day for the clarinetist. The opportunity is not overlooked by Melvin Warner who turns in a first-class presentation in terms of excellent tone, sensitive regard for color, and an assured and viable interpretation.

Seven Variations on a Theme from *Silvana*, Op. 33

☐ Campbell (clarinet); York (piano) / Crystal S-333

Standard documentation. Justice is done both instruments; the composition can rightfully be termed chamber music. An apt and attractive recorded contribution.

Menuetto and Trio for Guitar, Flute, and Viola

☐ Hechtil (flute); Geise (viola); Walker (guitar) / Turnabout 34195/9

Though a bit more to the fore in the contrastive trio, the guitar acts as the accompanimental stabilizer for the flute and viola in this five-minute charmer. Beautiful tone from all concerned.

Trio in G minor for Piano, Flute, and Cello, Op. 63

☐ Pittsburgh Musica Viva Trio / Turnabout 34329

Combining a piano, flute, and cello doesn't result in as odd a combination as one would imagine; the flute merely substitutes for the violin, and offers wind color and contrast to string and keyboard tone. However, the slightly lighter density is a factor, but it has been taken carefully into account by the performers. Weber's forte of dramatic temperament is moderated and controlled in this Trio. Matters are fitted to the instruments. The heartbeat of the work is the flute's durability. Beyond that Weber does not venture.

The *Scherzo* is lighthearted, and by its tempo is akin to a very fast waltz. The slow movement titled *Schäfers Klage* ("Shepherd's Lament") is given variational treatment by way of ornate thematic spinning as well as accompaniment.

The trio team: Bernard Goldberg (flute), Theo Salzman (cello), and Harry Franklin (piano) play with conviction and commitment. Above all, they play with a feeling for the music that shows their fullest understanding of the work.

Quintet for Clarinet, Two Violins, Viola, and Cello, Op. 34

☐ Members of the Melos Ensemble / de Peyer (clarinet) / Oiseau-Lyre 60020

There is no denying the clarinet's role and its color in this work. It shines, gloats, refuses to move out of the limelight; in fact, it is a quintet only in numerical total, the clarinet dominating from start to finish. Yet withal its apparent chamber-music avoidance, the work is very effective, colored by the "accompaniment."

The opening *Allegro* is the equivalent of a clarinet concertino. And the *Fantasia* is a rhapsodic picnic for the wind instrument, playing passages at its pleasure, running the scale of all gamuts, tossing off twenty sounds in a beat—swaggering in its virtuoso clothes. And so it goes, through the *Capriccio Presto* and the concluding movement with its rocking-horse rhythms, thirty-second scoops, trills, and bouncing triplets.

Weber burns his clarinet candle at both ends, writes a definite concerto. And, Gervase de Peyer delivers a knockout performance, with a bravura and a polish that is outstanding.

Opera and Dramatic Music

Der Freischütz (1820)

☐ Staatskapelle Dresden and Leipzig Radio Chorus / Janowitz, Mathis, Hoff, and Krahmer (sopranos); Springer (mezzo-soprano); Pfretzschner (alto); Schreier (tenor); Weikl and Leib (baritones); Adam, Vogel, and Crass (basses); Paul (speaker) / Carlos Kleiber (conductor) / Deutsche Grammophon 2720071

Weber's opera goes great guns in Germany and fizzles elsewhere. Nothing wrong with the music, but it can't override the essential Germanic spirit and climate of the story and its characters. (More than one critic has stressed this point—Edward J. Dent, for example, whose analysis is that "a foreigner inevitably feels a little strange" to the work.)

There's plenty of atmosphere and it is emphasized cogently in this production, particularly in the Wolf's Glen scene. Throughout, there is a rightness to the pace that avoids over-expansiveness for music already richly so.

The cast is fine. Gundula Janowitz doesn't have the most powerful of voices, but its scope fulfills her role as Agathe most adequately. She provides some sensitive phrasing. Most outstanding are Peter Schreier (a top-flight portrayal of Max) and Theo Adam (perfect as Caspar). Still, the real star of this recording is the man with the baton. Carlos Kleiber's direction makes every note breathe with freshness and vitality. None of the several other editions available (Angel S–3748, Seraphim S–6010, Richmond 62016, and Everest/Cetra 468/3) can match that major point, even if some of the singers are better.

Weber / Hector Berlioz

Orchestra

Invitation to the Dance, Op. 65

☐ Chicago Symphony Orchestra / Reiner (conductor) / RCA AGL1-1269
☐ Paris Conservatoire Orchestra / Wolff (conductor) / London STS-15057

Both are the best of the numerous editions on the market. The principal reason being the lightness and non-overload of the playing without nullifying a solid basic pulse to the music.

Incidentally, Weber's piece should not be translated as it often is, and as London does, "Invitation to the Waltz." The original reads: *Aufforderung zum Tanz.*

Weber / Franz Liszt

Polonaise Brillante (*L'Hilarité*) in E major, Op. 72

☐ Hamburg Symphony / Littauer (piano) / Köhler (conductor) / Turnabout 34406

Originally for solo piano. Liszt's color enlargement can be compared with the recording of the original version (see under *Weber: Instrumental: piano* [*Polacca Brillante*]). Credits belong to both composers and an additional one for the soloist here who shows warmth and nicely registered playing.

Anton Webern (1883-1945)

Five Pieces for Orchestra, Op. 10

☐ London Symphony Orchestra / Boulez (conductor) / Columbia M4–35193

The fluctuating, pigmented intonation of these pieces once again illustrates the *Klangfarbenmelodie* theorem, whereby the principal line is fragmented between assorted instrumental colors, rather than presented in a centralized hue. The gilded and spotlighted assortment of tone quality includes guitar, mandolin, and harmonium, and these are part of an instrumentational plot of tremendous compactness. Super-legato in movement and fluidic in its orchestration (both of which are perfectly confirmed in Boulez's direction), Webern's aphoristic music has the strength and the sway of a spider's web.

In the expressive symbols that mark Webern's transparent orchestral sounds there is beautiful, quietly violent power. Nothing in the entire orchestral literature is like these Five Pieces. Such divinely original music reflects the genius of Anton Webern.

Im Sommerwind (1904)

☐ Philadelphia Orchestra / Ormandy (conductor) / Columbia Special Products AMS-7041

Composed in 1904, when Webern was only nineteen, and published posthumously. "Summer Wind," subtitled "Idyll for Large Orchestra," is late romanticism in full bloom. Wagner and Strauss are the progenitors of this music, with a little less chromaticism in terms of the former, and less fuss in regard to the latter. Though a bit speculative here and there, the richness of the work makes one grateful it was discovered and made available.

This type of rhetoric is made to order for Ormandy and the result is a magnificent portrayal. What a mouthwatering sound the Philadelphians make!

Passacaglia, Op. 1

☐ Berlin Philharmonic Orchestra / von Karajan (conductor) / Deutsche Grammophon 2711014

Here is Webern straddling the fence between traditional territory and the new frontier. The largesse of Brahms and Mahler are the essentials of this first opus (well-developed formal aspects), though Schoenberg (breadth and chromatic framing) enters in.

Effectively presented. Von Karajan is especially mindful of Webern's transparent orchestral texture and styles the music accordingly.

Six Pieces for Large Orchestra, Op. 6

☐ London Symphony Orchestra / Boulez / Columbia M4-35193

Webern's miscellany calls for a jumbo orchestra, including sixteen winds, six horns, six trumpets, six trombones, and a tuba, in addition to percussion, strings, harp, and celesta. The set constitutes a group of musical "shorts," the longest less than three and one-half minutes, most of the others just a little over sixty seconds.

In Opus 6 harmonic and contrapuntal suppression is Webern's method of timbre affirmation. Each piece registers in its individual parts. This music illustrates *collage* in orchestral translation. The varied weights of brass or strings, the oscillation of a *tremolandi col legno,* the swish of a rute roll, etc. are the equivalents of paint, newspaper clips, hunks of light cloth, wood, and other material. Color *is* the melody, and the pitches are mere pegs on which to hang the variegated swatches and sonic merchandise. This represents a stinging and provocative new type of musical art.

Boulez's depiction of Webern's score is beyond criticism. Authoritative commentary throughout.

Symphony, Op. 21

☐ Berlin Philharmonic Orchestra / von Karajan (conductor) / Deutsche Grammophon 2711014

Webern's Symphony bypasses traditional definition, consisting as it does of two concentrated movements; the first in moderate tempo containing 130 measures, the other a theme with seven variations totalling 99 measures. The opus can be described as synoptic music, its expressivity expounded by minute and constantly changing textures, accents, dynamics, and colors.

All these points are rigorously controlled and as logically ordered as a Bach fugue; the discourse as nakedly defined. In the initial movement assorted canonic procedures determine a sonata-styled music. In the second part variation particulars are the feature. Again canonic method plays an important role (thus technical procedure interlocks the movements without interfering with formal contrast).

This exceedingly discretionary music has more than twelve-tone superacademic formality. The small orchestra of clarinet, bass clarinet, two horns, harp, and strings without double basses traces the flow with the freedom and plasticity of a super-diffused (but magnificently refined) color scheme. When listening to this chromoscopic orchestra the ear must not define the timbres as isolated; each sound is acutely related to the next. In this world of contractive sound, symphonic flamboyance is smothered to death.

One doesn't think of a Herbert von Karajan in connection with music of this style. A revision of thought is necessary. This is a fully balanced, transparent, and authoritative performance.

Three Pieces for Orchestra

☐ Philadelphia Orchestra / Ormandy (conductor) / Columbia Special Products AMS-7041

Tiny sounds in length forming a series of separable color segments. These pulverized utterances were among a considerable number of pithy pieces Webern composed between 1911 and 1913 (found in his papers after his death) and from which the famous set of five (indicated as Opus 10—*see above*) were drawn. Music that produces in its nudity an electric discharge of vibrant timbres.

Variations for Orchestra, Op. 30

☐ London Symphony Orchestra / Boulez (conductor) / Columbia M4–35193

Webern's last purely instrumental work has his sparse dodecaphonic syntax and rapid-fire color changes. Though the details of construction are highly involved, with such matters as retrograde movement, rhythmic augmentation and diminution, the expressivity and the pungency of the orchestration are enchanting. Despite the extreme economy of the material and its instrumental treatment there is constant discovery as pitch and timbre arrangement become continually transformed. Again Webern illustrates the theorem of perpetual change in order to obtain a maximum of variation.

The activating of the sound potential by severe organization is purely a desire to find the ultimate in structural clarity. If the Variations sound involved it is because complicated music demands a complicated method of expression.

The music is impeccably executed. Elsewhere I had stated that Robert Craft's performance could only be termed fair. (It is on Columbia Special Products CK4L–232, in mono form.) At the same time I wrote that since nothing else was on the market a listener was captive to that edition alone if he wanted the work. Good news! Something else is on the market. So, eliminate the Craft from consideration. Take Boulez. He is authoritative; the music is played as eloquently as possible in its Webern address. The cooled preciseness is exactly what gives Webern's Opus 30 its decided warmth.

Five Movements for Strings, Op. 5

String Orchestra

☐ London Symphony Orchestra / Boulez (conductor) / Columbia M4–35193

Webern's own version of the Five Movements for String Quartet (*see below*). Beautifully executed in this case, though this writer prefers single-strand voices for this exquisite music.

Variations, Op. 27

Instrumental

☐ Rosen (piano) / Columbia M4–35193

Piano

Save for some discarded juvenilia, this represents Webern's sole excursion into the solo piano medium. In a set of three very concentrated movements, variation expands into perpetual change. Gone are polyphonic alterations of Handelian days, the melodic figurations that embroider the music of the classical composers, and the semi-descriptive pieces that caught the fancy of the romanticists while making their variational discourse. And gone, of course, thematic functions, replaced by the totality of serial functionalism.

Webern is relentless in the mutation of his substances. Not only pitch and duration shift, but dynamics and mode of attack as well. The controls of the vehicle are the twelve tones, meshed in great part by intricate canons. There are no lush sonorities in the Variations; instead, the utmost complexity of organization is detailed by minute segments of sound. The beauty of Webern's Variations lies in their structural purity.

Stein's oldie is still around, contained in the historic all-Webern set Columbia issued in the mid-fifties, in mono, then listed as number 232, now Columbia Special Products CK4L–232. Biret's version followed on Finnadar 9004 and, more recently, Pollini's on Deutsche Grammophon (2530803). But, no one can match the superb personality that Rosen brings to this music. The shapes, the balances, and the clarity are nothing less than perfect.

Chamber Music

Four Pieces for Violin and Piano, Op. 7

☐ Stern (violin); Rosen (piano) / Columbia M4–35193

Dynamic polarity is important to these epigrams and Stern and Rosen provide the proper muscular solidity or precise evanescence as required.

Webern's codifications point up the theorem that art requires no historical obligation to confirm its truth. Wonderfully strange music, these four brief pieces (containing nine, twenty-four, fourteen, and fifteen measures, respectively) last long in the memory.

Three Small Pieces for Cello and Piano, Op. 11

☐ Harrell (cello); Levine (piano) / RCA ARL1–1262

With only thirty-two measures of music it is significant that Webern calls this set "small," as against the Four Pieces for Violin and Piano, which totalled sixty-two measures (*see above*).

In this opus Webern's skeletal statements are further de-emphasized by delivery through instrumentalized veils. It takes as much consummate virtuosity (directed in a different way) to realize the transparency and pulverized concentration of this music as to reel off hundreds of sounds in a few measures. The Harrell-Levine team are masters of the Webern idiom.

String Trio, Op. 20

☐ Members of the Juilliard Quartet / Columbia M4–35193

Tenderness is the cardinal quality in the slow-tempoed first movement. The sound in the other movement is more tightly knit; the sections are in greater contrast to each other. The unity of the trio stems from the mutual equality of its sounds, and it is this point which is basic to its formal plans.

A fairly convincing performance. Regardless, forget and pass by the old mono presentation on Columbia Special Products CK4L–232, played by Wade (violin), Figelski (viola), and Sargeant (cello). They try their best but their best has sonic angina.

Five Movements for String Quartet, Op. 5

☐ LaSalle Quartet / Deutsche Grammophon 2530284

In size the last four pieces of this quartet suite stand apart in relation to the first. Likewise, formal content is dynamically produced by integrated variation and the convolution of two fundamental textures in the first movement; while in the remaining four parts each design is reduced to the most direct and cogent miniature (miniature only in comparison to a large-scaled work). It must never be forgotten that Webern is *not* a miniaturist; his works are spun musical strands which care for all the exegencies met in huge compositions.

The LaSalle conception is a marvel. Every dot and tenuto, every dynamic arrival and departure, every minute color arrangement is observed and still the performance is not academic. Webern's music is related in terms of its totality of meaning and not merely in the strict depiction of its multiformed parts. Examples: in movement 2 the effect is one of a single thought expressed by the four instruments. In the third movement the quality of a brutal, burning scherzo is produced. This is chamber music impeccancy. (The LaSalle performance can also be secured in a jumbo, ten-record side release, including the quartets of Webern, Berg, and Schoenberg on Deutsche Grammophon 2720029.)

Langsamer Satz for String Quartet (1905)

☐ Quartetto Italiano / Philips 6500105

Posthumous Webern, part of the manuscript haul found in Webern's home after his death. Its publication required editing so that a certain minimal percentage does not officially belong to Webern. It really doesn't matter since there is no mistaking Webern's optimum romantic language which has not been disturbed during the polishing process.

Intensely played which also does not disturb the proper interpretation of a lushly-styled music which Webern later placed on the shelf never to touch again.

Quartet for Violin, Clarinet, Tenor Saxophone, and Piano, Op. 22

☐ Ensemble / Rosen (piano) / Columbia M4–35193

The carefully mixed instrumental colors of this Quartet are an advantageous means of formal conviction. In the first movement Webern exemplifies the developments which arise from motival variation by four different instrumental types. The themes develop, branch out, intertwine, and move forward and backward. Thus an entire movement is designed from the fundamental expression of canonic narrative, in turn dissected into small, precise substances on which the dabbed instrumental color equals pointillistic application. The instrumental timbres emphasize the difference of ideas, as well as define the canon's progress. They do not exist as colors for individual display but for background illumination.

While the general style of the second movement (a fairly long one for this composer) is looser, the lines of motive supply are still as short as in the opening movement, but there is a sense of wider-spread sound, a more settled quality in relation to the first part. In terms of balance the last part is the *allegro* to the previous *andante*.

This is a memorable exposition of Webern's score, with every detail understood and reflected in the playing.

Six Bagatelles for String Quartet, Op. 9

☐ Juilliard Quartet / Columbia M4–35193

The truth found in these six dissections (totalling fifty-seven measures) is well-nigh the ultimate in string-quartet color. Webern's procedure is to explain a theme through its tints, such as will be found in the first measures of the opening piece: a cello harmonic, a *ponticello* sound for the viola, then a wispy, natural tone for the first violin. Thus the music staples itself on wings which are irridescent—mixed and changed from dark to bright. Webern's musical sobriety is only in total count of sounds; the vibrational result is turbulent, paroxysmic.

In his preface to the published score Schoenberg stated that "every trace of sentimentality must be banished" in playing this work. But, a trace can be found in the Quartetto Italiano's playing (on Philips 6500105) and even in the LaSalle Quartet's edition (Deutsche Grammophon 2530284 and also on 2720029). On the other hand, the Juilliard achieve the utmost concentration and project the innermost expression of the pieces. The Juilliard's subtle reticence creates soft thunderbolts of effect.

String Quartet (1905)
String Quartet, Op. 28

☐ LaSalle Quartet / Deutsche Grammophon 2530284

Far from discreet differences between these two works. The 1905 opus (not published until long after Webern's death—the first performance anywhere took place on May 26,

1962 in Seattle, Washington, by the University of Washington String Quartet) is projected with full-scale romanticism. It is fervent in its tonality and active in its progress, with thirteen major tempo changes within the single movement. It is given the full sound treatment and is played with properly-tempered robustness.

Canonic device prevails in great part throughout Opus 28, but the ear won't realize this as well as the eye might in perusing the printed score. Although the structures of the three movements bear classical affinity (ternary type, scherzo with trio, and a more elaborate scherzo minus a trio), the textures are almost those of static sound placements, despite the elaborate devices employed. These furnish not only the thematic and developmental sections but serve for the complete expansion of the composition. The play of the tone row (distributed in acute, contrasted registrations, and constantly permutated) is accompanied by the percussive subtlety of accentuation plus instrumental entrance and departure that make for lively structural resiliency, difficult to follow without repeated aural exposure. The narrative manner is novel, still as new to the ear as were Schoenberg's early works in twelve-tone style.

Webern's Opus 28 does not have the same instrumental tinge as his early sets of pieces for four strings. Assorted coloration is not the paramount concern, but its use (in the concentrate) is firmly present. It is to the LaSalle's credit that they do not disturb this important timbre factor. However, they clearly indicate the considerable differences in the greys, blacks, and whites that constitute the score's colors. Their placement of differing dynamic weights is of special virtuosity and is extremely exciting.

(Both of these quartets, plus Webern's sets of pieces for quartet, and all the Schoenberg and Berg string quartets, are available in one package issued by Deutsche Grammophon–number 2720029.)

Quintet for String Quartet and Piano

☐ Wade and Fenley (violins); Thomas (viola); Sargeant (cello); Stein (piano) / Columbia Special Products CK4L–232 (monaural)

Predating his first official opus (the orchestral Passacaglia) by two years, Webern's Quintet is lushly romantic. It is heavy with Brahmsian sighs and sentiments, plus the *ferne Klang* of sensuousness that maintained Strauss and even Schoenberg for a time.

In one movement, the Quintet is built on a pair of themes which constitute the feeding ground of the entire work. Webern's later style simmers in this composition, by way of beseeching diminished octaves, long, lean leaps, the oscillation of *tremolandi*, and the use of imitative ideas. It shows Webern's youthful creative potency and how he made the most of it. There is no reason for apologies.

Concerto, Op. 24

☐ Dwyer (flute); Gomberg (oboe); Cioffi (clarinet); Stagliano (horn); Ghitalla (trumpet); Gibson (trombone); Sivlerstein (violin); Fine (viola); Goode (piano) / RCA LSC–6189

Webern's Opus 24 is a nine-ply instrumental affair, its virtuosity solely concerned with music creation impervious to display, and minus any decorative cadenza. The only remote resemblance to a concerto is that it covers three movements.

The Concerto is magnificently and uniquely organized. One each of four different timbre families is used, in totals that descend sequentially: three woodwind, three brass, two string, one keyboard. Webern also divides his twelve-tone row into four groups: three tones in each. This split emphasizes the relationship of mass to individual. It makes possible permutates of the whole and of each portion simultaneously and oppositionally.

In movement 1, almost every instrument states three sounds and drops out for the moment. This three in-and-out address changes in the middle movement, where, for the most part, only two consecutive sounds in any single timbre are used. The triple sets in a similar color return in the final movement, forming a symmetrical plan. This shifting instrumentational pattern propels the manifold canonic devices that shape the music. It also adds colorific light and shadow, textural thickness and leanness. Apart from analysis the Concerto is compact and communicative, an artistic achievement as well as an illustration of superb scholarship.

Granted a meticulous regard for the score, little can happen incorrectly, actually, to Webern's Concerto. The music is impervious to display and the nine Boston Symphony Chamber Players make certain not to oppose such objective.

Five Songs

Op. 3 / Op. 4 / Op. 12

☐ Harper (soprano); Rosen (piano) / Columbia M4–35193

Vocal

Voice with Accompaniment

In the first two sets of songs (the texts are by Stefan George) tonality is present, but in a somewhat dissolved state. Anchored tonality is avoided. The keynote is mood realized by free melody—melody already shaped by Webern as a continuity of timbre differences. There are no recurring *leitmotifs* in these expressionistic songs; symmetry gives way to the sound itself, its subtle disguises in register, dynamics, and contrast. Nor are there any joyful, tuneful strikings (never in Webern!), but the seriousness does not becloud clarity. In this respect these early Webern songs avoid the blatant romantic habit of obscuring formal definition.

The Opus 12 group is larger-scaled, but with the same lucid, concentrated style of the composer. Although the texts are not used as a program for the music, the lyric poetry serves as a phonetic part of the total structure.

Throughout each set the performance art of this vocal-piano team is exceptional.

Three Songs

Op. 23 / Op. 25

☐ Lukomska (soprano); Rosen (piano) / Columbia M4–35193

Both groups are set to poems by the Austrian painter-poet Hildegard Jone, who, from the year (1934) Opus 23 was composed, was the only one to whom Webern turned for the texts of his vocal works.

Webern is lyrical and expansive in these songs: the first set dealing with love, the second with nature. The ability to invent new combinations of sound and project the spirit of a text without disturbing formal logic demands creative mastery. Indeed, it is a feat to retain individuality without deviating from a specified technique which holds style in place. That Webern carries out all of these obligations is eloquent proof of his unique achievement.

Five Canons on Latin Texts, Op. 16

☐ Ensemble Amsterdam / Dorow (soprano) / de Leeuw (conductor) / Telefunken 642350

Voice and Instrumental Ensemble

A fusion of words taken from the Breviary, set in strict polyphonic style, for an extremely odd combination of voice, high and low clarinets. The unity of canonic procedure is unstinting; three of the set are three-voiced, the remainder are two-voiced, and both types include examples of contrary motion. Insistence on technical method does not mean merely a fascinating blueprint. These canons offer sincere music with a Webernian brand of beauty.

If stars are awarded recorded performances on a scale from one to four, the latter pertains to this presentation.

Five Sacred Songs, Op. 15

☐ Ensemble Amsterdam / Dorow (soprano) / de Leeuw (conductor) / Telefunken 642350

Compared with romantic style, free-toned music (atonal is a poor description) may be considered harsh and refractory. However, within its own orbit, the relationships of the first four of Webern's *Geistliche* songs are planned with the same fundamentals of tensions and releases.

But unhampered tonal language can seek other controls, and Webern begins this superintendence in the last song *Ascend, Fair Soul,* with a double canon run in contrary motion. It is canonic regulation which helps the serial organization of Webern's later works, for canon deals with diagonal relationships which are paramount to twelve-tone structural arrangement. The appearance of canon in the end part of Opus 15 is not only a conclusion but a prelude of coming events.

This recording represents marvelous singing of extremely difficult vocal music. Credit must also go to the instrumentalists consisting of flute, clarinet, bass clarinet, trumpet, harp, violin, and viola.

Four Songs, Op. 13

☐ Ensemble / Harper (soprano) / Boulez (conductor) / Columbia M4–35193

Not a single Webern song cycle specifically calls for a male voice. Of the dozen vocal works he approved and had published during his lifetime, two are for "voice," three are for "medium voice," four for "high voice," a pair call for "soprano," and one for "high soprano." Five of the total are with piano and the others with various instrumental groups. The latter vary considerably, the smallest being for two players. Opus 13 requires the largest combination, with fourteen instruments (winds, brass, strings, keyboard, and percussion) covering a full range of tone colors. Further, each movement (based on poems by Kraus, Trakl, and a pair from *The Chinese Flute* by Bethge) is scored differently.

The minute diffusion of timbre is fundamental to these songs. Despite the longer presentation this Webern mannerism is never eliminated. Webern's thoughts are always conveyed in essence, never lengthened by multisyllabic words or parenthetical asides.

Six Songs, Op. 14

☐ Ensemble Amsterdam / Dorow (soprano) / de Leeuw (conductor) / Telefunken 642350

Sounding like dodecaphonically designed music, Webern's Opus 14 is elastically polyphonic, much less fragmented than his previous output. Integrated with the counterpoint are instrumental colors, consisting of three types of clarinets (E flat, B flat, and bass), with soprano (violin) and bass (cello) string instruments. Webern's refusal to permit static rhythm adds further appositeness to the rich polyphony of these songs to Trakl texts.

A beautifully detailed performance.

Three Songs, Op. 18

☐ Ensemble Amsterdam / Dorow (soprano) / de Leeuw (conductor) / Telefunken 642350

Fully organized, fully sensitized twelve-tone music, with words about a sweetheart and redemption, concluding with an *Ave, Regina.* The texts, however, serve as a convenience for settling the composition's form, rather than outlining and defining a specific mood or circumstance. The technical precepts do not interfere with music of sensitive meaning, which avoids artificial dodecaphonic conventionality. But coloristically Webern is unconventional. No other song cycle comes to mind that uses a raucous E flat clarinet and a guitar as instrumental partners.

Three Traditional Rhymes, Op. 17

☐ Ensemble Amsterdam / Dorow (soprano) / de Leeuw (conductor) / Telefunken 642350

It is an odd twist that Webern's first pure serial work includes the word "traditional" in the translation of its German title. (Actually, the rendering of the original *Drei Geistliche Volkslieder* could also be "Three Folk Texts," or "Three Sacred [Spiritual] Folksongs," but the word "folk" is no less odd.) The texts are prayers to the Holy Trinity, the Virgin, and Jesus. However, the music's persisent intervallic jaggedness—the vivid birthmark on the body of twelve-tone music, especially in its early age—has nothing to do with religion except perhaps a reverence for dodecaphonic principles.

A magnificently and meticulously defined performance. Every agogic subtlety is probed—this is great music-making by Dorothy Dorow and the instrumentalists playing clarinet, bass clarinet, violin, and viola that support her.

Two Songs, Op. 8

☐ Ensemble / Harper (soprano) / Boulez (conductor) / Columbia M4–35193

Economy is the analogue to the fastidiousness and purity of Webern's compositions. This pair of songs (to Rilke texts) illustrates Webern's creative aloofness. It totals the shortest work he saw through publication in his lifetime (performance time: one and three-quarter minutes). The eight performers required (playing a total of nine instruments) furnish a few timbred punctuation signs to the words expressed by the singer. Value does not depend on size. This brief music has intense power.

Fluid playing and sensitive vocalism are exhibited in the recording.

Entflieht auf leichten Kähnen, Op. 2

☐ John Alldis Choir / Boulez (conductor) / Columbia M4–35193

Clarity and comprehensibility are the key words in regard to canon, and canonic technique is a key element in Webern's compositions. In this early opus for a cappella mixed chorus, to a text by Stefan George, the complete procedure is the coherence and consistency of canon, framing free tonality.

Two Songs, Op. 19

☐ Ensemble and John Alldis Choir / Boulez (conductor) / Columbia M4–35193

Webern's opus is fully governed by the doctrines of tone-row manipulation, but it also has a freshness, a lightness, a play of rhythmic agility that is quite uncommon to his output. Part of this limpidity occurs because of very close imitations and contrasting vocal coloration, plus an active instrumental spray. None of this concerns the poems, which are from Goethe's *Chinesisch-Deutsche Jahres- und Tageszeiten*. The music (as is so often the case in serial composition) is foreign to the texts. But if any Webern music can be called "delicious," this is it.

In the old mono Craft-directed performance (Columbia Special Products CK4L–232) Robert Craft used a vocal quartet though Webern specifically calls for a *mixed chorus*. While this makes a performance easier to achieve it brings a loss in textural weight.

Choral

Chorus Alone

Chorus and Instrumental Ensemble

However, this is not the only minus credit in relation to the Boulez production which has much more sensitivity and definition.

Chorus and Orchestra

Das Augenlicht, Op. 26

☐ London Symphony Orchestra and John Alldis Choir / Boulez (conductor) / Columbia M4–35193

Most twelve-tone music lacks the traditional "vocal" essence, but the intensity of *Das Augenlicht* (for mixed chorus with an orchestra of fourteen different instruments plus multiple violins, violas, and cellos) is arrived at by the sweep of the voices, opposed to the somewhat jagged quality of the instrumental sound.

Cantata and Oratorio

Cantata No. 1, Op. 29

☐ London Symphony Orchestra and John Alldis Choir / Lukomska (soprano) / Boulez (conductor) / Columbia M4–35193

More substantial textures and less angularity of intervallic movement mark this particular Webern work. Part two is for the solo soprano. The performance is well knit and thrice better than the mechanical depiction heard on Nonesuch 71192, conducted by Wand.

Cantata No. 2, Op. 31

☐ London Symphony Orchestra and John Alldis Choir / McDaniel (baritone) / Boulez (conductor) / Columbia M4–35193

Webern's final completed work (and aside from the early Quintet, his longest composition). Notwithstanding the decisive serialism and the firm objectivity of the music, there is an eloquence far beyond the feeling that one is simply being led by the technical hand. (Webern compared this Cantata to the sacredness of a *Missa Brevis*.) There is no doubt that Webern transcended method in his Opus 31. The articulated expression (beautifully conveyed in this performance) bears testimony to his creative magic.

Webern / J. S. Bach. *See J. S. Bach / Anton Webern.*

Michael Webster (1944-)

Instrumental

Clarinet

Five Pieces for Clarinet Solo

☐ Webster (clarinet) / Composers Recordings SD–374

Character pieces. Number two, a Rhapsody includes some quarter-tone colorations; the third piece, *Ländler*, is explorative of "the pianissimo use of the altissimo register."

Webster playing Webster is fully satisfactory. The lack of bands is exactly the opposite. How identify the separate pieces?

Thomas Weelkes *(ca. 1575-1623)*

Madrigals

*As Vesta Was from Latmos Hill
  Descending*
Ay Me, Alas, Hey Ho
Cease Now, Delight
Cease, Sorrows, Now
*Hark, All Ye Lovely Saints
  Above*
Lady, the Birds Right Fairly
Like Two Proud Armies
My Phyllis Bids Me Pack Away
*O Care, Thou Wilt Dispatch Me-
  Hence, Care, Thou Art Too Cruel*
On the Plains, Fairy Trains
*Say, Dear, When Will Your
  Frowning Leave?*

Sing We At Pleasure
Strike it Up, Tabor
*Sweet Love, I Will No More
  Abuse Thee*
Tan ta ra, Cries Mars
Those Sweet Delightful Lilies
*Though My Carriage Be But
  Careless*
*Thule, the Period of Cosmog-
  raphy-The Andalusian Merchant*
*Why Are You Ladies Staying-Hark!
  I Hear Some Dancing*

Choral

Chorus Alone

☐ Wilbye Consort / Pears (conductor) / London STS–15165

A rich collection drawn from the close to one hundred madrigals that Weelkes produced. Some of these are *balletts* (madrigals that could be sung or danced to) and some are designated as "Airs or Fantastic Spirits" (*Ayeres* or *Phantasticke Spirites*), which stress a melody with voices accompanying. The settings call for three, four. Five, and six voices. No four-part examples are included in this recording. Five of the madrigals recorded are in three parts, a total of eight use five voices, and a half-dozen cover six parts.

Some consider Weelkes as the greatest of all madrigalists and hearing these nineteen examples (three are paired, separate madrigals) it is difficult to disagree. Beautifully and engagingly sung with polished style. The recording has been produced with excellence.

Three Virgin Nymphes **from First Book of Madrigals for Three to Six Voices**

☐ Sine Nomine Singers / Saltzman (conductor) / Turnabout 34485

Sweet-toned madrigal about the sweet matter of man after girl(s). The flute-like texture is an aural delight.

Alleluia, I Heard a Voice

Gloria in Excelsis

Hosanna to the Son of David

O Lord, Arise Into Thy Resting Place

**Chorus
and
Instrumental
Ensemble**

☐ Choristers of St. Paul's Cathedral, Purcell Chorus of Voices, and London Cornet and Sackbut Ensemble / Davis (organ) / Burgess (conductor) / Argo ZRG–659

Full-powered performances of Tudor church music. The *Hosanna* is a six-part anthem; *Alleluia, I Heard a Voice* is also an anthem for the feast of All Saints. Christmas is the celebration covered in the *Gloria in Excelsis* piece.

Reynold Weidenaar (1945-)

Electronic Music

The Tinsel Chicken Coop, for your Usual Magnetic Tape

☐ Crystal S-532

Human sounds, human speech, organ invocations, chicken cackles, tape stuff. These are only part of Weidenaar's electronic salmagundi. The liner notes are deadly serious; the actual sounds are deadly opposite and are certainly a spoof. Good enough, some humorous electronic music is certainly rare.

Karl Weigl (1881-1949)

Chamber Music

String Quartet No. 5 in G major, Op. 31

☐ Iowa String Quartet / Composers Recordings S-242

Karl Weigl was always a romantic, generally finding his creative pleasure in lyrical intensity. The fifth quartet is also lyric, but it it relaxed, warm, sunny, of open intimacy. It is not to be wondered that it bears the subtitle *In Light Mood.* (The printed score, however, shows no subtitle.)

Formal probity exists in every one of the four movements. However, it does not waylay a rich flow of melody, especially in the finale, where dance character is clearly focused. The music of this movement wings its way like an Austrian Dvořák.

A satisfactory performance of the work. Special credit must be given to the Iowa group (Allen Ohmes, John Ferrell, William Preucil, and Charles Wendt) for recording Weigl's quartet. The lack of attention given this fine composer is distressing. The more advocates there are of Weigl's music the sooner this utterly unfair situation will change.

Vocal

Voice and Instrumental Ensemble

Five Songs for Soprano and String Quartet, Op. 40

☐ Iowa String Quartet / Brooks (soprano) / Composers Recordings S-242

Romantic urge and Brahmsian surge are to be heard in this opus. The chromatic impress is a natural tactic for Weigl, most impressive in the fourth of the set, *Ave Maria.* The gentility that surrounds *Summer Afternoon* is very moving. It is set to a text by the composer's wife, also a composer (*see below*).

This is a beautiful cycle of songs presented with touching artistry by Patricia Brooks, ably supported by the Iowa foursome. It is a worthy tribute to a still undiscovered composer.

Three Songs for Contralto and String Quartet

☐ Phoenix String Quartet / Forrester (contralto) / Serenus 12062

Noteworthy songs noteweighted by Strauss in the case of the first two, *Sommers Tod* ("Summer's Death") and *Liebesode* ("Love's Ode") and using Mahlerian enunciations in the final one, Hexenlied ("Witch's Song"). Nevertheless, imaginative and generally effective.

Vally Weigl *(1899-   )*

New England Suite

Chamber
Music

☐ Drucker (clarinet); Sass (piano); Moore (cello) / Composers Recordings S-326

Traditional methodology covering all formal, harmonic, and instrumental problems. Just short of salon sketches in the portrayal of a *Vermont Nocturne,* a *Maine Interlude,* a *Berkshire Pastorale,* and a *Connecticut Country Fair.*

Nature Moods

Vocal

*Voice and
Instrumental
Ensemble*

☐ Shirley (tenor); Drucker (clarinet); Gordon (violin) / Composers Recordings S-326

Gentle romanticism, fragile textures. The music always caressing the poematic meaning.

Enchantingly presented; the diction of George Shirley one of those wonderful instances where the printed text need not be followed.

Kurt Weill *(1900-1950)*

Kleine Dreigroschenmusik (1928)

Orchestra

☐ Contemporary Chamber Ensemble / Weisberg (conductor) / Nonesuch 71281

Weill's eight-part "Suite from *The Threepenny Opera*" is one of the greatest top-drawer low-down pieces ever penned. Its intentional artistic vulgarity, delineating a period long gone, is a work of genius.

The cabaret-orch scoring (larger in total, but in that category) calls for pairs of flutes, saxophones, clarinets, bassoons, trumpets, and one each of trombone, tuba, piano, banjo, guitar, and bandoneon (a variant of the concertina), plus percussion. This offers a built-in sound that, allowed its way, will register with decided impact, providing the tempi are not spruced up from its 1929 drift.

Some may quibble at the failure to spotlight certain scoring ingredients in the sound combine, specifically the plucked string instruments, but the defect is erased by the total sonorous climate that Weisberg and his players obtain. It is natural, unforced, with no put-on that would interfere with the convincing appropriateness of the style.

Quodlibet Eine Unterhaltungsmusik, Op. 9

☐ Westphalian Symphony Orchestra, Recklinghausen / Landau (conductor) / Candide 31091

The title is a bit misleading. Weill's *Quodlibet* does not mix things simultaneously but attaches them successively. Two examples: there are five sections in movement 1; the finale (movement 4) bgins with agitated material, proceeds into a march type, and concludes with a *galop.* For Weill's objective, the variety offered is not excessive. The performance of this "Diverting Music," is a fairly convincing one.

Symphony
No. 1 (1921) / No. 2 (1934)

☐ BBC Symphony Orchestra / Bertini (conductor) / Argo ZRG-755

Stylistic *non sequiturs* are found within both of these two works, the first of which is in one movement, the other in three movements (a Sostenuto leading to an *Allegro molto,* a Largo, and an *Allegro vivace*). The artistic climate of 1921 is portrayed in the first work by a seething expressionism that, in its deflection, draws stimuli from Busoni, Mahler, Schoenberg—and even Hindemith. But, please, no disorder, no pastiche. It is in the nature of Weill's document that his synonyms are varied, but all blend into a probing, dark-toned music, which was inspired by a pacifist-socialist epigraph taken from Johannes R. Becher's *Festspiel, Workers, Peasants, and Soldiers—A People's Awakening to God.* The Second Symphony has broad, neoclassical tonalism, considerably more optimism naturally (can expressionism ever be optimistic?), and is coloristically administered with song and dance, rhythmic flow and spikiness, sometimes a reminder of Shostakovich, and, though less so, of Prokofiev. Little matter—Weill's symphonic procedures are the healthy kind that produce significant eclectic addenda if not totally individual essays.

Significantly, Weill's Symphonies now are "confirmed" by two recordings of the pair. The initial work (composed in 1921) did not get its premiere until 1957; the Second Symphony was first heard in the same year it was finished (1934); but practically no attention has been given them in concerts since. The recordings prove the way matters should be righted.

Gary Bertini obtains a fine synthesis in his performance of the 1921 work, whereas Edo de Waart, directing the Leipzig Gewandhaus Orchestra on Philips 6500642, tends to chop into the piece here and there. In Bertini's case the nervousnesses that dart within the score are understandingly inculcated; with de Waart they stick out and almost annoy. Bertini emphasizes the urgency that propels the later Symphony, even in the emotional equivocality of the slow movement, which has both heroic and tragic moods; whereas de Waart deliberately tries to reconcile this antithetical situation. Elsewhere the speeds are fine with the Leipzig group but the timbres are not sufficiently pointed. It is Bertini's sharpness of declaration that makes his performance the choice one.

Opera and Dramatic Music

Happy End

☐ Orchestra and Chorus / Lenya (soprano) / Brückner-Rüggeberg (conductor) / Columbia Special Products COS–2032

Just for Lotte Lenya's delivery of *Surabaya Johnny, Matrosen Tango,* and *Bilbao Song,* this is a must, and not only for Weill fans. The score for Brecht's story dealing with gangsters and their molls has a cynical force that is most compelling.

Rise and Fall of the City of Mahagonny (1927)

☐ Orchestra and North German Radio Chorus / Lenya (soprano); Munch (speaker); Günter, Göllnitz, Litz, Markwort, Mund, Roth, and Sauerbaum (vocalists) / Brückner-Rüggeberg (conductor) / Columbia K3L–243 (monaural)

Weill's *Aufstieg und Fall der Stadt Mahagonny* began as a one-act *Singspiel.* Its triumph led to its expansion to three acts. Bertolt Brecht furnished the libretto (it was his first collaboration with Weill), which concerns events in a mythical (Miami-like) city that is set on the Florida coast. Capitalism at its most dirty is pictured, with loan sharks and loose women; the low-class mores of the post-World War I era are outlined. A moralistic conclusion is used, with revolt leading to the burning of Mahagonny.

The score is a blend of 1920-period jazz, artistic vulgarities, and some romantic plus some Handelian harmonies that register especially strong because they are surrounded by contrastive styles. The orchestration is of the old café world and fits magnificently. Totally, *Mahagonny* is a music that is written with impeccable craft and taste that appeals to those with both informed and uninformed tastes.

Lenya, as always, in the role of Jenny, is the star thrice over. Her singing is styled to perfection, and in songs like *Havanna Lied, Alabama Song,* and *Wie Man Sich Bettet* ("As You Make Your Bed") she stops the show.

Street Scene (1946)

☐ Orchestra and Chorus / Jeffreys, Stoska, and Sullivan; other members of the original (1947) Broadway production / Abravanel (conductor) / Columbia Special Products COL-4139 (monaural)

This contains most of the musical material from Weill's dramatic folk opera about life in a street of New York. While not complete, it is sufficient to provide, as Weill stated, "a complete impression" of the score "and its blending with the action of the play."

The release is definitive all the way, since the Broadway production was perfectly polished before the recording by the same personnel was made.

The Threepenny Opera (1928)

☐ Orchestra and Chorus of Sender Freies Berlin / Lenya (soprano); Grunert, Hausmann, Hellwig, Hesterberg, Hoeppner, Kuster, Neuss, Schellow, Trenk-Trebitsch, v.Koczian, and Wolffberg (vocalists) / Brückner-Rüggeberg (conductor) / Odyssey Y2-32977
☐ Orchestra and Chorus / Lenya (soprano); Arthur, Merrill, Price, Rae, Sullivan, Tyne, and Wolfson (vocalists) / Matlowsky (conductor) / MGM S-31210C

The great—very great—Kurt Weill ballad opera *Die Dreigroschenoper* (as it is known abroad) was modeled on John Gay's *The Beggar's Opera;* the libretto by Bertolt Brecht. Its crude and bitter, strong and rich score remains powerful and splendid fifty years after its birth. The work deals with thieves and the underworld, its principal characters being Macheath (Mack the Knife) and his bordello female flame Jenny (sung by Lotte Lenya), and it exudes the world of Europa-Jazz, a bare type of hand-me-down from American models. However, its unsophisticated simplicity has impact. It includes such types as a blues ballad, a canonic fox trot, a semitorch song, a shimmy, and a tango.

Both recordings are splendid. Each of the orchestral ensembles is properly subtle and timbred exactly. Above all is Lotte Lenya's perfection. She has been, after all, *the* Jenny of the story since the world premiere, and any other consideration of the part has to measure up to hers. It is important to bear in mind that operatic voices are misfits for Weill's conception—he chose a full retreat from the royal purple stereotypism of operadom in order to democratize the form. The singers must first be able to act and convey the text; whatever vocal values they have are simply bonuses. Some of the roles in both productions produce a bonus while excelling in the primary acting point.

The Odyssey edition is in German; the MGM disc is in English. Not a mere translation, but a special, original text made by Marc Blitzstein, with the lines Americanized beautifully and sensibly (to match the opera's context) in a slangy-tangy manner. In his own way Blitzstein showed he was as creatively masterful as the librettist, Brecht. Both editions are worth having.

The Seven Deadly Sins (1933) *Ballet*

☐ Orchestra / Lenya (soprano); Katona, Göllnitz, Poettgen, and Roth (male vocalists) / Brückner-Rüggeberg (conductor) / Columbia Special Products CKL-5175 (monaural)

Weill's "Ballet with Song" can be rightfully (and completely) titled "The Seven Mortal Sins of the Petty-Bourgeois" when translated from the original German, *Die sieben Todsünden der Kleinbürger*. It has songs for one of the two sisters who are the main characters (who else but the great Lotte Lenya can project them as scalp-tinglingly as she?); the other sister tells her part of the tale in dance form. The roles of their family are sung by a male quartet, with some incidental solos. Thus a story (the text by Brecht) acted, danced, and sung.

The older Columbia issue (in the pre-CSP days the catalogue number was KL–5175) has a coloration that is better styled than the Deutsche Grammophon release (139308)—and, it is worth repeating, it also has that marvel of marvels, Lotte Lenya. And, truly, the "nonfancy" monaural setting fits Weill's extraordinary conception better than stereo.

Henry Weinberg (1931 -)

Orchestra

Cantus Commemorabilis I

☐ Contemporary Chamber Players of the University of Chicago / Shapey (conductor) / Composers Recordings S-245

The segments, units, and progress of Weinberg's commemorative piece (written for the composer's cousin, who died at the early age of twenty-seven) add up to an athematic compositional conception. Absent are the hand-me-down emotive melodic implications with harmonic and contrapuntal supportive explanations. The music does not atrophy because of this. If given sufficient aural exposure, a listener will find Weinberg's music is fully coherent, within the dark-thrust split and spread continuity which is simultaneously covered on both the micro- and the macro-levels.

The piece is extremely difficult for the performers and conductor. Shapey's rendition is most telling.

Choral

Chorus Alone

Vox in Roma

☐ Ineluctable Modality / London (conductor) / Advance FGR–18S

An illustration of how moving serial choral music can be, despite the lamentations still heard from gray-bearded academicians that dodecaphonic music can only be morbid.

Jaromir Weinberger (1896 - 1967)

Orchestra

Polka and Fugue from *Schwanda the Bagpiper* (1927)

☐ Philadelphia Orchestra / Ormandy (conductor) / Columbia MG–31190

In the 1930s, 1940s, and 1950s this work received hundreds of performances at every conceivable type of concert during each season. No longer. Its choreographic good will and its fine fugue deserve revival.

Ormandy's presentation is large scaled but properly scaled; it conveys the geniality the music contains. Fritz Reiner's superb reading also deserves a place in every record collection, although the sound is less than second-rate. It was made in January of 1956 and is available on RCA VICS–1424.

Felix Weingartner / *Georges Bizet.* See Bizet / Felix Weingartner.

Hugo Weisgall (1912-)

End of Summer (1974)

☐ New York Chamber Soloists / Bressler (tenor) / Composers Recordings S–343

End of Summer is for tenor, oboe, and string trio. Parts 1, 3, and 5 are for the total ensemble; the even-numbered movements are without voice, part 2 being for oboe alone, part 4 for the complete instrumental quartet.

A dark expressionism hangs over Weisgall's cycle. This is a true transmutation of the texts, a pair by an eighth-century poet, Po Chü-i, and one by George Boas. In turn this mood reflects onto the purely instrumental divisions. There is a quiet passion in Weisgsall's writing and it is skillfully conveyed by the performers.

Fancies and Inventions for Baritone and Five Instruments (1970)

☐ Aeolian Chamber Players / Patrick (baritone) / Weisgall (conductor) / Composers Recordings S–273

Nine songs from Robert Herrick's *Hesperides*. As assorted as are the texts so is the instrumental framework. Six combinations are used: two for piano alone, three different duo partnerships (clarinet and cello, flute and clarinet, and flute and viola), one quartet totality, and three for the complete five instruments.

Weisgall is a master at managing a text so that not only does it have meaning, but in the instrumental computation the words are not buried. Of course, for this a singer with prime diction is necessary, and that is available in this richly contoured performance.

The Stronger (1952)

☐ Aeolian Chamber Players / Meier (soprano) / Weisgall (conductor) / Composers Recordings S–273

Like Poulenc in his *La Voix humaine,* Weisgall enlarges the definition of opera by contracting its resources, in a production that calls for a singing cast of one. There have been a number of monodramas, but they consist of recitations with music. The opera-for-one is a distinct rarity. (Actually there are two characters in *The Stronger,* but since one has a silent role the "opera-for-one" designation is correct.)

This form of opera construction is not easy to do, but Weisgall does it, and beautifully. The story, based on the August Strindberg play, concerns the enmity that exists between two women. The unsaid is powerful, and what Weisgall insinuates musically is twice as powerful. There is a remarkable sense of tensility in the opera that carries it forward constantly. *The Stronger* may well be Weisgall's most important creation.

This is the second recorded release of the opera. It was initially in the Columbia catalogue, in its American Music Series, and then deleted. The present new production is far better in terms of sound; the singing is topflight, matching that of the vocalist on the earlier (Columbia) release, Adelaide Bishop. Moreover, the entire conception is much better here, and not only because the composer is on the podium.

Vocal

Voice and Instrumental Ensemble

Opera and Dramatic Music

The Tenor (1952)

☐ Vienna State Opera Orchestra / Young and Coulter (sopranos); Cassily and Kuhn (tenors); Ludgin (baritone); Cross (bass-baritone) / Grossman (conductor) / Composers Recordings 197 (monaural)

Based on a Wedekind tale, dealing with the conflict between a tenor's love of his profession, with its egocentric rewards, and his affairs with the opposite sex. Expectedly, the story ends tragically.

Weisgall's one-act opera is strong musical stuff, powerfully conceived in vocal and instrumental terms (the orchestration has bite and punch and is extremely sensitive to the plot). The style relates to Berg with atonical structuring.

The performance is vivid, the voices fresh and full, the direction and pace revealing. Best of all, the diction of the singers is superb. The recording was originally released by Westminster (on OPW-1206); the review copy of CRI's reissue had no text leaflet or any data concerning composer, composition, or cast.

Adolph Weiss   (1891-1971)

Orchestra

American Life (Scherzoso Jazzoso) (1929)

☐ Los Angeles Philharmonic Orchestra / Foster (conductor) / New World Records NW-228

Although not listed as such by Weiss, *American Life* bears out the "overture" indication assigned it by Nicolas Slonimsky, who conducted the first performance of the piece in Europe. What everyone agrees with is the music's jazz ambience and its quasi-twelve-tone syntax. This is clearly portrayed in Foster's conducting.

Theme and Variations for Orchestra (1931)

☐ Vienna Orchestra / Adler (conductor) / Composers Recordings 113 (monaural)

A liberal view of twelve-tone technique, related most closely to the work of Alban Berg. Rhythmic clarity is a decided asset to Weiss's objectives and his orchestrational sense is acute (he was an excellent bassoonist). A personality pervades the work. Adler fully understands this type of music and presents an excellent re-creation of the score.

Chamber Music

Trio for Clarinet, Viola, and Cello (1948)

☐ Bloch (clarinet); Abraham Weiss (viola); Reher (cello) / Composers Recordings 116 (monaural)

Weiss's piece displays the "classic" dodecaphonic tradition. It is well wrought and clearly depicts the use of the tone-row generator which is released in many ways, transposed, and exercised. The architecture of the pair of movements is neatly ordered in a cyclic device, using the initial mood to balance the Trio at its terminal point. Of special pleasure is the rhythmic vitality that constantly propels the action.

The performers are excellent, the recording of beautiful sound.

Sylvius Leopold Weiss   (1686-1750)

Instrumental

Sonate (Suite) in D minor (Excerpts)

Lute

☐ Satoh (lute) / Klavier 528

Weiss was known as the foremost lutenist of his time. The excerpts (*Menuet* I & II, a Sarabande, and a Bourrée), representing the gallant style of the eighteenth century, are illustrative of his substantial creative abilities.

Distinguished playing. (The release is incorrectly numbered in *Schwann* as Klavier 514.) Other Weiss music is available on disc but in performances on the guitar.

Dan Welcher   (1948-   )

Concerto da camera for Bassoon and Orchestra

☐ Crystal Chamber Orchestra / Sharrow (bassoon) / Gold (conductor) / Crystal S-852

Solo Instrument and Orchestra

Bassoon

Welcher's composition is a fascinating exploitation of ideas that do not breach formal stability and yet do remain fresh. His solo–orchestra work avoids classic structural conclusions but retains their understood values. Based on a unifying motive, the music passes through a Moderato (of sonata dynamicism), followed by a Scherzo, which is connected to an interlude and in turn leads to a quintuple-pulsed end movement containing a double fugue. The conclusion is dramatically quiet. Throughout, one is aware that a solo instrument is being featured, but is likewise cognizant that the orchestra is no mere accompanimental body.

The failure of too many composers is their unwillingness to stand up and be counted. They feed their source of creative supply but by raw imitation of style, technique, and form. Nothing annoys more than the sham of such superficiality. Welcher is not in this category at all. He has produced a concerto that is of prime importance and that will surely find a permanent place in the repertory.

It is beautifully played by Leonard Sharrow, with a musical insight that does him proud. The orchestra (sixteen strings, three winds, two brass, piano, and percussion) is expert, as is its conductor.

Concerto for Flute and Orchestra (1973)

☐ Louisville Orchestra / Fuge (flute) / Mester (conductor) / Louisville 742

Flute

Welcher will have none of the virtuosity that dazzles but is empty of musical pertinence. The solo line is the outcome of the structural logic and produces its own special power. This is especially cogent in the second part—a fairly strict serial-styled Theme and Variations. The fusion of the solo voice with the small orchestra (five winds, five brass, percussion, harp, piano, celesta, and strings) is beautifully proportioned. This is a superb addition to the still-limited repertoire that exists for flute and orchestra.

Fuge's playing is a masterly product of interpretation in which he is fully supported by Mester and his musicians.

Karl-Erik Welin   (1934-   )

PC-132 (String Quartet No. 2) (1970)

☐ Saulesco Quartet / Caprice CAP-1024

Chamber Music

Free informality operates in this music consisting of random sets of thoughts. The phrases shift in style within which one can recognize Welin's interlocutory use of revamped quotations from Beethoven, Reger, Schoenberg, and Webern. All of the progressions are connected smoothly, there are no contrary pulls, and one is not conscious of the creative glue that holds them together.

There is a particularly introspective mood to Welin's piece. A type of flat-perspective quality results. No analytical explanations are given by the composer save that he uses quotations in order not to break with tradition. ("I change them in my own way, and that is because, whatever I compose, I never get away from my dependence on these composers.") Quite clear, of course, but left totally unexplained is the meaning of "PC–132" in the title.

The playing is excellent, distinguished by a fine interpretative sensibility to the varied ideas that move within Welin's work.

Egon Wellesz   (1885-1974)

Instrumental

Cello

Sonata for Cello Solo, Op. 30

☐ Sylvester (cello) / Desto 7169

Wellesz's Sonata is in one movement, with lyricism the main element and no attempt to bypass the limitations of the medium. It works. Tonal polarity controls the key function of the piece, with sufficient chromaticism to eliminate any diatonic, singular paleness.

Sylvester deserves five-star rating for his playing. There is no strain, no tone push or roughness. It is an example of string-instrument performance prowess.

Chamber Music

Two Pieces, Op. 34

☐ Campbell (clarinet); York (piano) / Crystal S–333

Expressionistic, aphoristic conceptions; the first runs a minute and one half, the other just below two minutes. The style is a well-trodden one but in Wellesz's hands it still is perfectly fresh and sensitive. Those last four words describe the performance.

Octet, Op. 67

☐ Vienna Octet / London STS–15243

Schubert's instrumentation of his famous eight-voiced work (clarinet, bassoon, horn, string quartet, and double bass) is followed one hundred twenty-five years later by a national brother composer.

There are much lighter moments in this work than in others by Wellesz. The first movement has a neo-Schubertian view, contrasting four times the opening Andante with the running, rhythmic Allegretto. Instrumental weight values are of aid in the Adagio in directing lighter textures against tutti proclamations. Only a short trio stops the powered drive of the Presto, a scherzo of real Beethoven spirit. The fifty-nine-measure clarinet solo in the main body of the movement is a reincarnation of nineteenth-century Viennese beauty. The trio, scored for the three wind instruments alone, also bends its knew toward early classical practice. Both the final pair of movements have classical proportions and impeccable attention to style.

The Vienna gentlemen perform with rich feeling for the warm, unabashed melodic contours of Wellesz's music. Indeed, this is illuminating chamber-music playing and it is deeply appealing.

Gregor Joseph Werner   *(1693-1766)*

The Curious Musical Instrument Calendar (Excerpts)

☐ Vienna State Opera Orchestra / Angerer (conductor) / Nonesuch 71193

*String
Orchestra*

Werner's programmatic project (for first and second violins with continuo) was to portray the character and fitting events of each of the twelve months of the year. For this purpose he composed twelve suites, with five movements in each (save January, which totals four). Angerer's choice is limited to two pieces from each suite. The total of twenty-four is more than sufficient to show Werner's colorful objective.

However, high though Werner was in sincerity, he was low in programmatic accomplishment. The melodies are fine, the phrasing not too square, and the sequences not too overburdened. But, for instance, there is little difference between *Changeable April Weather, The Sun in Cancer* (the Crab), and even *An Earthquake* (the last two covering the excerpted events for June). Further, *The Mill* (November) gaily tunes its way without any descriptive rhythm. In *Rough Weather at Sea* (also in the November portion) the instrumental tossing is extremely gay, and one can ride with the situation, since the major tonality neither moves into any minor-key seasickness nor do any rhythmic waves disturb the mensural placidity. And so it goes throughout.

This is no negative report, but a factual one. The music, born of a curious but fully opportunistic idea, is simply nice and easy to listen to. Angerer conducts the production with complete dedication. He has also furnished the liner note; a very interesting one it is.

Pastorale in G major for Harpsichord and String Orchestra

☐ Hungarian Chamber Orchestra / Sebestyen (harpsichord) / Tatrai (conductor) / Turnabout 34325

*Solo
Instrument
and
Orchestra*

Harpsichord

Not much attention is given this composer, who was Haydn's predecessor at the Esterházy court. The Pastorale certainly deserves attention. It has three movements, with a deeply felt Larghetto centered between Spirituoso and *Vivace passato* movements.

Gracious music. Splendidly presented.

Werner / Joseph Haydn

Prelude and Fugue in C minor

☐ Hungarian Chamber Orchestra / Tatrai (conductor) / Turnabout 34324

*String
Orchestra*

An amplified version of the original transcription by Haydn for string quartet. (It is available in that form, with two additional pieces from the total of six in the set [see below under *Chamber Music*].)

Compared to the string quartet recording, the Turnabout edition is superior tonally and in some respects provides more finesse in the playing. However, a listener may want more than one example of Werner's imaginative preludial and healthily bold fugal writing, and to obtain it can only turn to the Orion performances by the Sinnhoffer String Quartet. Nonetheless, do not overlook the Turnabout item listed here, if at all possible.

Turnabout fails to mention (a) that the work was originally transcribed by Haydn for string quartet and published in that form and (b) gives no credit to the one who edited the score for multiple strings.

Chamber Music

Prelude and Fugue

In C minor / In D minor / In G minor

☐ Sinnhoffer String Quartet / Orion 7035

Half of the set of six that Haydn transcribed. There are sizable sonorities here for a quartet, but they are fitting. The C minor work is available in string orchestra form (see above under *String Orchestra*), but there it is considerably darker in timbre, with a fine acoustic depth to the recording. Orion's sound is only fair.

Richard Wernick (1934-   )

Vocal

Voice with Accompaniment

A Prayer for Jerusalem (1971)

☐ DeGaetani (mezzo-soprano); Steele (percussion) / Composers Recordings 344

An incredibly poignant atmosphere surrounds the expressive beauty of this duo, for the rare medium of voice and percussion. The latter consists solely of bell-type instruments: vibraphone, glockenspiel, crotales, and finger cymbals, with chimes as well (played by the vocalist). The vocal line, especially, is from the expressionistic world—unsocketed intervals, with upward and downward leaps of augmented octaves, ninths, and tenths fairly common. Still, these are not utilized for a system bent on avoiding tonal semblance but have a symbolic and characteristic rationale. (The ability to negotiate these and even larger spans with precise attention to pitch, without any strain, within varying dynamics, and retaining stylistic balance plus emotive meaning makes Jan DeGaetani's performance incandescent. It is still another example of this singer's enormous artistic distinction.)

Wernick's text consists of fragments of the 122nd Psalm and he considers the work a prayer "for the survival, prosperity, and unity of Jerusalem and all that it represents and symbolizes." The fervor (and nobility) of the conception makes the music accessible to even those who tend to turn away from music that is far from traditionally tonal.

The playing of Glen Steele is authoritative, intelligently partnering the magnificence displayed by DeGaetani. In all, this is a marvelous collaboration that does full justice to Wernick's sensitive and original score.

Songs of Remembrance

☐ DeGaetani (mezzo-soprano); West (shawm, English horn, and oboe) / Nonesuch 71342

Despite change of language and instrumentation in the four parts of Wernick's work, an intense cohesion is achieved. The first text (by Pythagoras) is in Greek, the next two texts (by Horace and Virgil) are in Latin, and the last (by Robert Herrick) is in English. In parallel distinction the voice is coloristically contrasted by the individual reedy sound of the shawm in part 1; the sorrowful timbre of the English horn in parts 2 and 3; and the silvery blue tone of the oboe in the final song. Yet it is remarkable that notwithstanding this multiformity, Wernick's haunting, exquisite, and expressive work has an absolute structural singleness. Seamlessness is obtained within by subtle changes of quality, from incantational to melismatic to quiet simplicity. It is difficult to achieve such process, but Wernick has accomplished it.

Wernick's piece bears the subtitle "In memory of Susan Phillips, 1964–73." The literature of music has many threnodic pieces and a large number of memorial tributes.

Few in the twentieth century can match the depth of meaning found in these Songs of Remembrance. Indeed, it is music of lasting substance.

The performers (Philip West is Jan DeGaetani's husband) do wonders with the score. DeGaetani's voice and artistry are a blessing to a composer. West's playing (on three different instruments, it will be noted) can be placed in that category as well.

Kaddish-Requiem (A Secular Service for the Victims of Indochina) (1969)

Cantata and Oratorio

☐ Contemporary Chamber Ensemble / DeGaetani (mezzo-soprano); Gilbert (cantor) / Weisberg (conductor) / Nonesuch 71303

Wernick's divergent material paradoxically forms an intensely strong, emotionally compact composition. The anguish of war against people and the land they occupy is smeared all over the violence of the first movement, which is entirely instrumental. Part 2 is a tape collage of the Kaddish, the Hebrew prayer for the dead; it sets a high mark for what can be done with tape for dramatic impact. The work concludes with a beautiful portion of the Latin Requiem, set principally for the mezzo-soprano. Thus, three structures in as many contrasted timbres. Interwoven are borrowed and reworked bits by Brahms, Lassus, and Palestrina.

The Kaddish-Requiem shows the scope of a composer with infinite imagination. The interfusive processes mark highly sensitive creativity. Even if Wernick's message is agit-prop, it is also superb art. And, by their performance, Weisberg, DeGaetani, and Gilbert also testify to their complete belief in Wernick's musical document.

Samuel Sebastian Wesley *(1810-1876)*

Anthems

Choral

Ascribe unto the Lord	*Praise the Lord, my soul*
Cast me not away	*Wash me thoroughly*
Man that is born of Woman	

Chorus with Accompaniment

Magnificat in E major

Nunc Dimittis in E major

☐ Choir of New College, Oxford / Hillsman and Ross (organ) / Lumsden (conductor) / Lyrichord 7173

Confusion is constant in regard to the two Samuel Wesleys, both notable contributors to English church music. Like his father, Samuel (1766–1837), the son, Samuel Sebastian, was an organist-composer whose productions included four church services, two psalms, 27 anthems, a large number of glees, organ compositions, and songs. The music heard on this disc is a fine cross-section of this output.

Lyrichord titles its album "Choral Masterpieces of Samuel Sebastian Wesley." One is willing to agree with that description in regard to the large-scale anthems *Ascribe unto the Lord* and *Praise the Lord, my soul*. Although the other compositions may not be deemed masterpieces, they are certainly excellent and far from ordinary.

The singing matches this excellence and David Lumsden's fine-paced direction brings clarity to every work. The organist for the last four anthems is Alastair Ross; Walter Hillsman is the organist for the remainder of the program.

Peter Westergaard (1931-)

Chamber Music

Divertimento on Discobbolic Fragments for Flute and Piano (1967)

☐ Sollberger (flute); Wuorinen (piano) / Nonesuch 73028

The adjective is explained by Westergaard's use of material from his Opera *Mr. and Mrs. Discobbolos* (see under *Opera and Dramatic Music*). A scherzo spirit is major to the piece, which is in six movements. The spirit is dictated by serial procedures.

Opera and Dramatic Music

Mr. and Mrs. Discobbolos (1966)

☐ Members of the Group for Contemporary Music at Columbia University / Lamoree (soprano); Litten (tenor) / Sollberger (conductor) / Composers Recordings S–271

A setting of Edward Lear's poem, shaped into a libretto by the composer. With a minimum of forces (two voices and six instruments) Westergaard has turned out a work that comments succinctly, despite its seeming frothiness, on the pettiness of humans, their unpeaceful philosophy and ultimate self-destruction.

The duologue of the vocalists is neatly executed and styled so that the picture of the Discobboli living atop their wall (the complete libretto is furnished with the recording) is clearly conveyed. The performers presented the premiere of Westergaard's chamber Opera in March of 1966 and the CRI presentation is certainly definitive.

Donald H. White (1921-)

Chamber Music

3 for 5 (1958)

☐ American Woodwind Quintet / Golden Crest S–4075

The "3" are titled Brightly, Pensive, and Spirited. This is intelligent, romantically scanned music. White knows how to move a slow-paced line around corners and knows just as well how rhythmically to pepper his ideas. In music of this type the part writing and the vertical choices are choice and clear, totally free of sonorous psychobabble.

The American five (Houdeshel, Sirucek, Farkas, Bates, and Sharrow) play with a spirit and style that deserve cheers.

José White (1839-1918)

Solo Instrument and Orchestra

Concerto for Violin and Orchestra (1864)

☐ London Symphony Orchestra / Rosand (violin) / Freeman (conductor) / Columbia M–33432

Violin

José Silvestre de los Dolores White (to give his full, official name) completed his Concerto in 1864; the first American performance took place 110 years later. It was far too long delayed. This is a lush, warmly conceived piece. That it will bring reminders of the violin Concerti of Viotti, Rode, Kreutzer, de Bériot, Wieniawski, and Ernst simply totals a stylistic statistic. It is as good as some of these and far better than some others.

The performance by Aaron Rosand is wondrously smooth and suave. His peaches and cream tone projects the sense and sounds of this piece to perfection. There isn't a quarter note that is forced. A memorable example of violin playing.

George E. Whiting *(1840-1923)*

Postlude, Op. 53   *Instrumental*

☐ Morris (organ) / New World Records NW–280   *Organ*

Forte from beginning to near end, then *fortissimo*. One longs for a little sonorous surcease, but none comes, and Morris correctly makes certain it doesn't. The piece is tonally orthodox, so that the dynamic dispensation is not too difficult to take.

Robert Whitney *(1904-   )*

Concertino (1961)   *Orchestra*

☐ Louisville Orchestra / Whitney (conductor) / Louisville 616 (monaural)

Crystal-clear classicism with its intervallic thirds and sixths, a minuet movement, and all the other parts of the general formula. Nothing wrong if nothing individual since the classicism does not lose a single point of its freshness. The performance is a buoyant one.

Charles Whittenberg *(1927-   )*

Three Pieces for Clarinet Solo (1963)   *Instrumental*

☐ Rehfeldt (clarinet) / Advance 4 (monaural)   *Clarinet*

Serial manners are applied to nonserial matters of pitch and tempo in this case. Rhapsodic but always with healthy, somewhat athletic straightforwardness. The performance is first-class.

Electronic Study II with Contrabass (1962)   *Double Bass*

☐ Turetzky (contrabass) / Advance FGR–1 (monaural)

Serial processes demonstrating extremely colorful dialogue between the electronic detail and the strong individuality of the double bass. Turetzky is his fabulous self in his commentary.

Polyphony for Solo C Trumpet (1965)   *Trumpet*

☐ Schwarz (trumpet) / Desto 7133

Serial technique applied to the simulation of a two-voice composition by interchanging registral situations.

This adds considerable strain on the performer, since lip tension and other points are constantly in flux. To Gerard Schwarz this offers no more problem than a work that is bounded by a single octave. The man is fantastic.

Set for Two for Viola and Piano   *Chamber Music*

☐ Sackson (viola); Peltzer (piano) / Serenus 12064

Whittenberg's Set is indicated as "A Divertimento for Viola and Piano." Twelve-tone in style, it diverts mainly by its virtuosic viola part. To Whittenberg's credit, only standard string-instrument techniques are used for coloration.

The piece's concentrated data (five and one-half minutes in performance length) is set forth in sparkling fashion by these well-known musicians. But the liner note offered by Serenus needs a thick editorial crayon. It concludes by stating that the "remarks are made here by a musical primitive, if not illiterate," and hopes he will be forgiven "for his untutored expression." If that's the background for the fellow, why is he writing liner notes?

String Quartet in One Movement (1965)

☐ Composers Quartet / Composers Recordings S-257

The motival basis of Whittenberg's Quartet brings rapid and constant change, with maximal linear deployment. It is party, of course, to the full and equal chromaticism of strict serial composition. There is a textural constancy of strength to the piece, but it is all relevant to the dynamic aesthetic involved.

Though Whittenberg's Quartet may need highly educated ears, it is a music of convincing thesis and is so performed by the team of Matthew Raimondi, Anahid Ajemian, Jean Dupouy, and Michael Rudiakov, experts in playing the newest of new music.

Games of Five, Op. 44

☐ University of Connecticut Wind Quintet / Serenus 12028

The technical game is serialism, and it is played expertly by both the composer and the performing organization.

Triptych for Brass Quintet (1962)

☐ American Brass Quintet / Desto 6474/7

Part 1 is titled *Rotational Games: Scherzo.* The "rotational" part of this designation refers to the post-Schoenbergian type of serialism, whereby the order of the tone row is changed on its reappearances. This procedure falls within a violent, sometimes raucous, always dynamic scherzo spill. The Sostenuto (Elegy in Memory of Anton Webern) is totally muted. The finale, Canonic Fanfares, is a hybrid that contains fanfarelike jets with a variety of canonic syntax, culminating in a five-part setting. No simple matters are to be found in this finale, described as "ferocious" by the composer. That it is.

No sacrifice is made in this piece for the performers' comfort, though aural comforts of excitation are produced for the listener. In terms of scope, versatility, virtuosity, and expressive capacity the American Brass Quintet does not have to take a back seat to any other organization. They (Gerard Schwarz and John W. Eckert, trumpets; Edward R. Birdwell, horn; and Arnold Fromme and Robert E. Biddlecome, trombones) prove this evaluation in their performance. This is the second time the quintet has recorded the work. Previously it was recorded (monaurally) for Folkways (3651). The personnel was quite different at that time, only the trombonists being the same.

Thomas Whythorne (ca. 1528-1595)

Vocal

Voice and Instrumental Ensemble

Buy New Broom

☐ Viols of the Schola Cantorum Basiliensis / Brown (tenor) / Wenzinger (conductor) / Nonesuch 73010

Buy New Broom is indicated as the first published example in England of a piece for solo voice with instrumental accompaniment. Written in 1571, it sounds fresh more than four hundred years later.

Lawrence Widdoes (1932-   )

Morning Music

Orchestra

☐ Louisville Orchestra / Mester (conductor) / Louisville LS–735

As Widdoes considers it, matinal music is not only calm and beautiful, but has a shade or two of mystery. The orchestrational aspects are particularly sensitive, with freshets of color twined into the score.

The performance is well defined.

One Thousand Paper Cranes (1966)

Chamber Music

☐ Silverman (guitar); Ghent (viola); Thomas (harpsichord) / Opus One 9

Widdoes's trio was inspired by a Japanese tale, but the music does not fall in the programmatic category. While it is marked by certain clear formal identifications, in general it has an apparent incantatory objective. The instrumental colors are used in a spare, concise, and strongly motivated manner, and emotive impressionism results. The piece is played most sensitively.

Erasmus Widmann (1572-1634)

Galliards and Dances

Chamber Music

☐ Recorder Ensemble of the Concentus Musicus of Denmark / Irmgard Knopf Mathiesen (conductor) / Nonesuch 71064

These seven pieces for four-part recorder ensemble are as sweet sounding and sweetly played as the women's names that identify them—*Margaretha, Regina,* and *Felicitas,* for example. For captioning dances, these are as good and as cute a way as any other. The pieces are not only cute but straight to the point—the timing examples are indicative: 28, 38, and 40 seconds, respectively, for three of the set.

Charles-Marie Widor (1844-1937)

Romance for Flute and Orchestra

Solo Instrument and Orchestra

☐ Vienna State Opera Orchestra / Meylan (flute) / Prohaska (conductor) / Vanguard C-10010

Flute

Extracted by Widor from his score for a French version of Shakespeare's *Twelfth Night.* Placid for the greater part, though framed with a fair amount of lush harmony. The orchestral part is purely accompanimental.

Intermezzo

Instrumental

Organ

☐ Darasse (organ) / Turnabout 34238

This robust music is played in a quite heavy manner, but this is the only representation on disc of Widor's piece. Turnabout has a great deal of print on its liner copy, but nary a word about this piece.

Symphony

No. 1 in C minor, Op. 13, No. 1 / No. 2 in D major, Op. 13, No. 2 / No. 3 in E minor, Op. 13, No. 3 / No. 4 in F minor, Op. 13, No. 4 / No. 5 in F minor, Op. 42, No. 1 / No. 6 in G minor, Op. 42, No. 2 / No. 7 in A minor, Op. 42, No. 3 / No. 8 in B major, Op. 42, No. 4 / No. 9 (*Gothique*) in C major, Op. 70 / No. 10 (*Romane*) in D major, Op. 73

☐ Labric (organ) / Musical Heritage Society MHS–1431/41

The generic title notwithstanding, Widor's Symphonies are more in the nature of lengthy suites, despite the almost total absence of picturesque movement titles. There are seven movements in the first of the set, six movements in four of the Symphonies, and five movements in three of them. It was not until the last two subtitled pieces that four-part totality was used.

These works have the ability to catch at the mind even beyond ordinary organ rhetoric and spectacle. Much organ music just rolls on with the remorselessness of a steamroller. Widor's has some of this annoying persistency but it has plenty of other qualities (such as colorful development of material and excellent textural contrasts) in these works of post-Franckian language.

The textural burdens (not only the vertical totals but the linear weights) are a challenge to clarify in performance. Labric resists the temptation to overload and overregister the details. He displays a fine range of tone color and uncanny brilliance, which cleanses matters so that there is a scrupulous clarity to the playing. The recorded sound follows suit. If these Widor compositions are not immediate and exciting they are interesting and educative.

(*See below* for separate recordings of individual Symphonies.)

Symphony No. 5 in F minor, Op. 42, No. 1

☐ Ellsasser (organ) / Nonesuch 71210

Good disposition throughout. Massivity does creep in but it is controlled. Registration is made with care so that the character of each movement is decently profiled. The famous finale, the Toccata, has authority. (Ellsasser uses the organ of the Hammond Museum in Gloucester, Massachusetts.)

(For an edition of the entire set of Widor Symphonies, *see above;* for a recording of the Toccata alone, *see below.*)

Symphony No. 6 in G minor, Op. 42, No. 2 (Excerpts)

☐ Darasse (organ) / Turnabout 34238

If you wish the entire Symphony, you are captive to obtaining the eleven-disc set embracing the complete ten Widor Symphonies, issued by the Musical Heritage Society (*see above*). This is the only example otherwise available. It consists of movements 1 and 3— Allegro and Intermezzo: Allegro, respectively.

The production is sloppy. The movements are identified as to number only on the label copy; elsewhere they are vaguely listed as "2 Movts." No tempo identifications are indicated. There is somewhat heavy going by the organist.

Toccata from Symphony No. 5 in F minor, Op. 42, No. 1

☐ Biggs (organ) / Columbia MS–6307

Widor's most popular piece. Every organist plays it, there being seven recorded versions currently available. This one is well accomplished with the excitement of the music fully conveyed. (For the complete Symphony, *see above;* also *see above* for an edition of the complete set of ten Widor Symphonies.)

Henryk (Henri) Wieniawski   (1835-1880)

Concerto No. 1 in F sharp minor for Violin and Orchestra, Op. 14

☐ London Philharmonic Orchestra / Perlman (violin) / Ozawa (conductor) / Angel S–36903

Solo Instrument and Orchestra

Violin

Check the propulsive drive in this Concerto (sometimes noted in catalogs as a "Grand Concerto") and you're in trouble. Itzhak Perlman never does. There is persuasiveness all the way through, including the middle movement, which shifts gears from virtuosity to poeticism. The fine accompaniment helps.

Concerto No. 2 in D minor for Violin and Orchestra, Op. 22

☐ Bamberg Symphony Orchestra / Szeryng (violin) / Krenz (conductor) / Philips 6500421

Impeccable playing and fastidious style. The tone in the slow movement (Romance) is creamy, not marshmallow; the *Zingara* finale is played with pinpointed flair, and all that one wishes is realized in the opening *Allegro moderato*. The closest competition comes from Perlman (on Angel S–36903), but Szeryng invests a depth to this old stand-by that gives him the additional points to win the laurels.

***Concert polonaise* in D major, Op. 4**

☐ Orchestra of Radio Luxembourg / Rosand (violin) / de Froment (conductor) / Turnabout 34629

Animated definition and brilliant clarity are available here. Rosand's tone is clear, clean, and true.

Fantasy on Themes from Gounod's *Faust*, Op. 20

☐ Steiner (violin); Berfield (piano) / Orion 78313

Instrumental

Violin

This is for those who enjoy hearing some of the *Faust* tunes; it especially features the Waltz, with unabashed decorations and embellishments. Of course, it is dated, but oh, so nicely dated. Diana Steiner brings out all the sentiment and violinistic lilt in an eminently listenable recording.

Mazurka, Op. 19, No. 2

☐ Staryk (violin); Kotowska (piano) / Musical Heritage Society MHS–1131

The subtitle is picturesque—*Dudziarz le ménétrier*—and as "Dudziarz the Fiddler" the piece depicts fiddle tuning, the Polish dance, contrast, and a return of the Mazurka. Steven Staryk's playing is distinguished by silken tone and suave distinctions.

Scherzo-Tarantelle, **Op. 16**

☐ Ricci (violin); Lush (piano) / London STS–15049

A satanically smooth performance of Wieniawski's bravura fiddle war-horse.

Two Violins   *Etudes-Caprices* **for Two Violins, Op. 18**

☐ Staryk (violin) / Musical Heritage Society MHS–1131

The cards are stacked by Wieniawski, with all of the bravura built into the first violin part. Nonetheless, an engaging precept is developed in each of the eight pieces, such as fast scales and arpeggios (No. 3), rapid leaps (No. 6), and so on. As a display of violin potentials it's fine; the musical potential is rather restricted.

Yes, only one violinist covers the opus—by overdubbing. It's economical. It nullifies the honest duo aspect, but it certainly guarantees a perfect stylistic composite. That is what is available in this case. Staryk is a splendid violinist and scores a double triumph here.

Frank Wigglesworth   (1918-   )

Orchestra   **Symphony No. 1 (1957)**

☐ Vienna Orchestra / Adler (conductor) / Composers Recordings 110 (monaural)

Classical form with appulsive dissonances in the harmonic diction. Cheerful dancelike tunes prop the outer movements. The performance is passable.

Instrumental   **Lake Music (1946)**

Flute

☐ Baron (flute) / Composers Recordings 212 (monaural)

A sonic reaction to the serenity "that quiet lake views convey," in this case a lake located in New England. A delicate sense of tonal balance is the result, marking another of the numerous unaccompanied soliloquies in flute literature.

Johan Wikmanson   (1753-1800)

Chamber Music   **String Quartet in E minor, Op. 1, No. 2**

☐ Saulesco Quartet / Caprice RIKS LP–65

Fine Haydnesque conception by this eighteenth-century Swedish composer. No academic imitation. The second movement is a fine set of variations with considerable freedom for the instruments. Similar conditions prevail in the *prestissimo* finale, which can match those in any of Haydn's middle-period quartets.

The Saulesco team plays this work with freshness and acute coloration. It is a true find.

John Wilbye   (1574-1638)

Choral   *All Pleasure Is of This Condition*

Chorus Alone   *As Fair as Morn, As Fresh as May*

Come Shepherd Swains That Wont to Hear Me Sing

Down in a Valley and *Hard Destinies Are Love and Beauty Parted*

Draw on Sweet Night

Happy, Oh Happy He

Softly, O Softly, Drop My Eyes Lest You Be Dry

Stay Corydon Thou Swain

Sweet Honey Sucking Bees and *Yet Sweet Take Heed*

There Where I Saw Her Lovely Beauty Painted

Weep, Weep, Mine Eyes

Ye That Do Live in Pleasures Plenty

☐ Wilbye Consort / Pears (conductor) / London STS–15162

The real heart of this collection is a controlled robustness. For the most part the singing (there are seven voices in the group) takes this into consideration, though subtlety is not predominant. However, the articulations are crisp and the pitches and balances are perfect.

Counting the two sets of combined madrigals as four individual items, two of the madrigals are in three voices, a single one is in four voices, eight are in five voices, and three are in six voices.

Alec Wilder   (1907-   )

Suite for Piano

Instrumental

☐ Snyder (piano) / Golden Crest 7058

Piano

Gripes first. Wilder's piece is called a Suite, but that's the end of any data. (Even here Golden Crest cannot quite make up its mind, since the title is listed on cover and record label as above and elsewhere as "Piano Suite.") How many movements there are one cannot tell from the recording, since many sections are not contrastive and may be either parts of a complete movement or actually separate pieces of similar character. There are no liner notes for the work. Further, no movement titles or tempo indications are supplied, and without bands on the disc that makes the information come in at zero and the production horrible. At least the music is worthy, romantically comfortable, and that's the reason for its inclusion in this compendium.

Alec Wilder is a favorite composer of the Golden Crest house. At last count it had produced fifteen different releases of his music, not counting this one. But considering the information given above, is that the way to treat a favorite composer?

Children's Suite: *Effie the Elephant*

Tuba

☐ Bobo (tuba); Grierson (piano) / Crystal S–125

Music of pure and easily assimilated cocktail-hour entertainment. It is obvious that Effie will have simple adventures, and does—six of 'em, such as *Effie Goes Folk Dancing, Effie Chases a Monkey,* and so on.

However, the obvious remark is required: this is not only for children to enjoy. In addition, if indeed the musical material is less than Carnegie-Hallish, there is the technical assurance, mature musicianship, and glorious golden tone of Roger Bobo to cherish.

Tuba Encore Piece (*A Tubist's Showcase*)

☐ Bobo (tuba); Grierson (piano) / Crystal S-392

Short and sweet: sixty seconds of music. Plenty of trills plus an applause-getting zoom upward at the conclusion.

Chamber Music

Sonata for Trombone and Piano

☐ Swallow (trombone); Wingreen (piano) / Golden Crest 7015 (monaural)

In his liner note on this work, John Barrows puts forth the point that Wilder's music is "simultaneously communicating and entertaining." Within that broad description, there is no doubt about Wilder's facile way of writing for a variety of instruments and inculcating a stylistic subculture of light pop and show-tune material. The trombone Sonata (much more a suite) follows suit.

Though little personality comes through in this recording (due to Wilder's material and not the performer's abilities), it is musically positive. The piano sound is only fair, however.

Sonata for Trumpet and Piano (1963)

☐ Joe Wilder (trumpet); Kaye or Wingreen (piano) / Golden Crest 7007 (monaural)

Alec Wilder music for Joe Wilder. The Sonata was specifically written for the soloist. Wilder's usual style of jazz-oriented music on the quiet side is nicely exhibited.

The exhibition by Golden Crest is not fully professional, however. Precise information is lacking. Two pianists are credited for the release, which includes five shorter items on the flip side. Which pianist is involved for each piece is left open, and data for the assorted items is totally ignored.

Sonata for Horn, Tuba, and Piano (1963)

☐ Barrows (horn); Phillips (tuba); Leighton (piano) / Golden Crest 7018 (monaural)

A very odd combo, but with Wilder's brisk, Broadway-styled touches it works well. The tempo heads tell the tale: Energetic, Elegy, Relaxed, Berceuse, and Finale. The last has pert staccato motility. There is fine playing by these brass-instrument masters. Bernie Leighton does acceptably at the keyboard, though his instrument is not very resonant.

The editing of Golden Crest's liner notes elicits this writer's habitual complaints. Thus, on album cover and label copy one reads "Sonata," but in the notes the work is termed a Suite. And in a note on another work included in the G.C. issue, mention is made of the "Three Pieces for Solo Clarinet." Only those with thorough knowledge will fill in the missing composer's name of Stravinsky. All very irritating.

Suite for Brass Quintet (1959)

☐ New York Brass Quintet / Golden Crest S-4017

Easy goin'. Wilder shuffles through the pop-tuned backwaters of *echt* Broadway and then trudges into the more serious musical precincts of Fifty-seventh Street and Seventh Avenue. The hybrid concoction is somewhat artificially sweet, despite flowery descriptions that the music is "made up of all necessary technical ingredients, but for others, its warm communications will outweigh its cerebral aspects and will prove a welcome addition to the library of 'Music for Live People.'"

But whatever one's reaction to the music, be it affirmative or negative, there is no argument about the magnificent playing of Nagel, Glasel, Schmitt, Swallow, and Phillips. It's marvelous.

Woodwind Quintet

No. 3 / No. 4 / No. 6

☐ New York Woodwind Quintet / Concert-Disc 223

One could readily mix the movements of these three Quintets without seriously disturbing their structural balances. Wilder employs conservative, formal romanticism, with the
lightest awareness of contemporary currents, though the slight jazzy indentions are smart
and offer relief. (Such pertness is expected when one deals with woodwinds and
understands their ability to deliver the piquant phrase.) Wilder knows the tricks of weaving a good texture, and the proof is in the responses made to his music by the New York
group.

Adrian Willaert (ca. 1490-1562)

Che fai, alma?

☐ Accademia Monteverdiana / Stevens (conductor) / Nonesuch 71272

Choral

Chorus Alone

Handsomely done and clearly emphasizing the shifting positions of the vocal lines.
There are only eight voices in Stevens's group, but the sonority span is impressive without
being forced.

Healey Willan (1880-1968)

Hodie, Christus Natus Est

☐ Concordia Choir / Christiansen (conductor) / Concordia CDLP-4 (monaural)

Choral

Chorus Alone

Willan writes it straight and clear in the anthem tradition. The piece is robustly sung.

Jan Williams (20th cent.)

Dream Lesson

☐ Williams (percussion) / Turnabout 34514

Percussion

Percussion it is, but not the usual drums, cymbals, marimbas, and xylophones. The
sonic narrative is derived from the inside of a piano, using an assortment of acoustical and
electronic devices. Whines and twangs, whistles and tweets, roars and glides, rubs and
sweeps, plus a crazy quilt of odd-fractioned pitches are provided. All of it is scrupulously
balanced, though somewhat prolonged.

Ralph Vaughan Williams. *See under Vaughan Williams.*

Malcolm Williamson (1931-   )

Five Preludes for Piano (1966)

☐ Williamson (piano) / Argo ZRG-682

Instrumental

Piano

The titles of these pieces, *Ships, Towers, Domes, Theatres,* and *Temples,* were taken from Wordsworth's Sonnet *Upon Westminster Bridge.* A connection between content and title exists (*Theatres* has balletic moves and *Temples* emphasizes pointed chords, for example), though Williamson emphasizes that "the titles were simply points of departure." The Preludes register successfully no matter how they are considered—with or without titles.

Fine playing by the composer.

Sonata No. 2 (1972)

☐ Williamson (piano) / Argo ZRG-704

Cellular variation in part 1, with percussive ejaculations strategically placed and thereby, in their unexpectedness, adding surprise and excitement. The passions in this work are rich, even in the somewhat threnodic dissertation marking the slow movement. The finale has contrapuntal strengths, but these do not hide a repeat of attention to variational style. With all its quieter places, this is heady and gutsy music with forward-pressing energy.

Two Pianos

Sonata for Two Pianos (1967)

☐ Williamson and Bennett (pianos) / Argo ZRG-704

Tough textures with a great deal of rhythmic detail, which contribute to the insistent tension that is found in the Sonata. Williamson's craft is not devoted in this case to pleasantries of any kind. It is a difficult work with full demands on the performers. The composer and his composer-colleague Richard Rodney Bennett give a heartily recommended performance.

Chamber Music

Pas de Quatre (1967)

☐ Nash Ensemble / Williamson (piano) / Argo ZRG-682

There are six parts to this chamber ballet music scored for flute, oboe, clarinet, bassoon, and piano. Further, to emphasize each movement's profile a different setting is used for parts 2, 3, 4, and 5, each in duet form: a Variation for flute and piano, a *Pas de Trois* for bassoon and piano, another Variation for flute and oboe, and a *Pas de Deux* for clarinet and piano.

Choreographers should seize the opportunity this music presents. Williamson's opus is made to order for actual ballet. It is performed with expressivity, vitality, and panache.

Quintet for Piano and Strings (1968)

☐ Gabrieli String Quartet / Williamson (piano) / Argo ZRG-682

Two outer Adagio movements enclose an Allegro molto. Aside from tempo, the differences are sharp. The fast movement is abrasive and violent, the slow movements are naked, stripped of all but essential concentrated data, a bare-to-the-bones music that excites by its mysterious content. Again and again one senses a story line is basic to the score but Williamson states there is "no programme or extra-musical implication."

A fascinating work in all respects and it is performed with theatrical coloration. With the composer at the piano the recording can be classed as definitive.

From a Child's Garden (1968)

☐ Cantelo (soprano); Williamson (piano) / Argo ZRG-682

Williamson's settings of the twelve texts by Robert Louis Stevenson contain a semi-sophisticated simplicity that is captivating. The moods are sensitively fulfilled by matching tempo to poetic detail (parade pulse in the *Marching Song,* a barcarolle-like pace in *My Bed Is a Boat,* fast beat in *From a Railway Carriage,* and so on) and linking music closely to the words.

The singing of April Cantelo is expert and positively styled. Williamson supports in first-class (and, of course, in fully knowing) fashion.

Symphony for Voices (1960)

Choral

☐ John Alldis Choir / Stevens (contralto) / Alldis (conductor) / Argo ZRG–758

Chorus Alone

Williamson's tonal chromaticism might be described as the way Stanford might be writing music if he were alive today. This is not meant as a back-handed compliment, simply as a point of reference.

The Symphony title parallels the instrumental form with weighty flanking movements embracing slow and scherzo divisions. Especially telling, in this beautifully shaped performance by the group and conductor that gave the premiere of the work, are the solo-voiced opening *Invocation* and the movement that follows, *Terra Australis.*

Julius Caesar Jones (1965)

Opera and Dramatic Music

☐ Finchley Children's Music Group / Angadi, Cantelo, Dant, Eatwell, Gingold, Kahn, Peter Lovett, Sonya Lovett, Maurel, David Pinto, Marie-Therese Pinto, Proctor, Rosenthal, Salinger, Seaman, Webb (vocalists); Holland (percussion); Bennett (flute); Dobson (oboe); King (clarinet); Gatt (bassoon); Moore (horn); Korchinska (harp); Seaman (piano); Cummings and Marriner (violins); Shingles (viola); Heath (cello); Gray (double bass) / Andrewes (conductor) / Argo ZRG–529

An "Opera for Children in Two Acts," but no lightweight nursery fairy tale. This is serious stuff, and is really an opera *about* children, without a happy ending. It concerns the ever-present generation gap and the lack of communication between adults and children.

The roles of the three parents are well covered by Michael Maurel, Norma Proctor, and April Cantelo. The special credits for the rest of the cast apply to Nigel Dant as Ambrose and David Pinto in the title role. The chorus is satisfactory; the orchestra gives splendid support.

Galen Wilson

(1926-   )

Applications

Electronic Music

☐ Capra 1201

The staticness of this piece, described as "music concrète," represents sound in a deep freeze. Most of it consists of sustained blocks of tone, with some parenthetical swishes.

George Balch Wilson

(1927-   )

Concatenations

Orchestra

☐ Contemporary Chamber Players, University of Illinois / London (conductor) / Composers Recordings S–271

Sound combinations in assorted variety, some calm, some violent. A dozen statements are projected in Wilson's free formal philosophy. The timbres utilized range from the gentility of a guitar to the impacted energy of percussion.

Electronic Music

Exigencies

☐ Composers Recordings S-271

Music shaped by rough, ejaculatory sound serrations contrasted with fragments that provide strong inner tensions. The latter are obtained by severely opposite dynamic totalities. The choices are discriminating, and *Exigencies* (a short piece of under four minutes) should prove to be a durable conception.

Olly Wilson (1937-   )

Instrumental

Piano

Piano Piece for Piano and Electronic Sound

☐ Hinderas (piano) / Desto 7102/3

Of course there is a decided expansion of color in combining piano timbre with electronic sound, but Wilson goes further, by the use of plucking inside the instrument. And, still further color objectives are obtained by "preparing" the piano. Three items are used: a wooden ruler with a metal edge, metal rings (notebook type), and metal protractors.

The music is nicely organized and Wilson is tactfully somewhat circumspect in his employment of the various added attractions. As is to be expected, Natalie Hinderas is in full command.

Chamber Music

Piece for Four (1966)

☐ Willoughby (flute); Young (trumpet); Schwartz (piano); Turetzky (bass) / Composers Recordings S-264

A jazz-type combo used for jazz-oriented serialism and fragmented gestures. Line is splintered in this case into patterned variety and coloristic twists. The performance is tops all the way.

Vocal

Voice with Accompaniment

Sometimes for Tenor and Electronic Sounds (1976)

☐ Brown (tenor) / Composers Recordings SD-370

A black-stranded mood of desolation surrounds this musical fantasy based on the black spiritual *Sometimes I Feel Like a Motherless Child* (hence the title). Wilson's piece combines eerie-colored material and purposeful sonic distortions. The tape portion gives an uncanny projection of tensile drama, containing within itself the overdubbing of Brown's voice in various ways. It is heard both in a solo role and pitted against the live tenor voice. A great deal of fragmentation surrounds this music of restlessness. It is magnificently accomplished. It is also a prime example of the special values that apply to electronic tape preparation when it is in the hands of an expert composer in the medium.

Electronic Music

Echoes for Clarinet and Tape

☐ Rehfeldt (clarinet) / Composers Recordings SD-367

An example of the hybrid combination of instrument and electronic sounds. The clarinet part is amplified and mixed with the prerecorded two-channel electronic tape, and the result is then projected from multiple speakers arranged in the concert hall. The recording is a good representation of the partnered interchange between the two elements. One finds that mixing instrumental sound with electronic timbres does not disrupt the special territory of the electronic medium. Actually, besides adding a specific (new) color in all of its permutations, the composite produces a dramatic and graphic effect; in Wilson's piece the two sources share (and thereby arrive at contrasts of) pitches and gestures.

Richard Wilson (1941-)

Music for Solo Flute (1972)

Instrumental

Flute

☐ Sollberger (flute) / Composers Recordings S-315

A real balance of structure and expression develops in the three movements, and there is no resorting to any of the fashionable *outré* specialties of flute technique. One does hear a flutter-tongued pitch here and there, but this color is as solidly entrenched in the catalogue of flute sounds as is pizzicato in the timbres produced by stringed instruments.

Concert Piece for Violin and Piano

Chamber Music

☐ Schulte (violin); Oppens (piano) / Composers Recordings S-315

Tightly organized with a plan that uses variants of the various sections and applies tempo shifts as part of their development. The characteristic style is panchromatic, the personality dynamic. These qualities are fully expressed by the performers.

Music for Violin and Cello (1969)

☐ Matsuda (violin); Sherry (cello) / Composers Recordings S-271

Intense lyricism is blended with intense technical requirements in Wilson's four-movement piece. The use of pizzicati and glissandi is especially propitious, cogent to the material and not mere color gloss. The performance is dynamic and full-blooded.

Phil Winsor (1938-)

Melted Ears (1967)

Instrumental

Two Pianos

☐ Albright and Warburton (pianos) / Advance S-14

Interfusion and interlacement with suffusion and saturation in pianistic congress. And what a jargon of many things! Little bits of Beethoven (right at the start), Mozart, Gershwin, cadenzas, scales, Chopin, and so on are mashed together, subjected to "alteration, collage, and other distortions related to tape music technique." Like a dream world, fragments dart about, almost identifiable and yet never exactly pinpointed, like a now-you-hear-it-now-you-don't. Further, sacked in the heavy air of the music are chance, improvisation, explicit noncoordination, clusters, noise, and sonorous insults.

Don't be misled into thinking your record player has picked up background sounds of some violent radio program toward the end of the piece. It's only the performers slamming the key covers of the instruments, screaming, cursing, yelling, and beating the keyboards with their fists and forearms. It will pass, and the music will end quietly. It's all in fun, this earful of madcapped turbulence.

Peter Winter   (1754-1825)

Solo
Instrument
and
Orchestra

Clarinet
and Cello

Concertino for Clarinet and Cello

☐ Chamber Orchestra of the Sarre / Michaels (clarinet); Güdel (cello) / Ristenpart (conductor) / Nonesuch 71014

Listening to this fine work, which brings Weber to mind as well as Mozart, it is strange to realize that it represents the only recorded work by the composer available at this time. Surely, there are other worthy pieces in Winter's vast output, which includes some forty operas, more than two dozen masses, nine symphonies, two septets, and a half-dozen quartets, to mention just some portions of his catalogue. What Karl Ristenpart recognized others could well emulate.

Each of the two movements is divided into slow- and fast-tempoed sections. The writing for the clarinet is as secure as that any late-nineteenth-century composer would produce. There is no *Sturm und Drang* in Winter's Concertino, but there certainly is profile and meaning.

It is most gratifying to have the piece on disc, and it is performed beautifully. Edward Tatnall Canby states in his liner note that "conductors would do well to program" Winter's piece, because of "its freshness of color and skillful invention." One doesn't have to wait for that to happen. Just substitute the words "record collectors" for "conductors" and "obtain" for "program."

Dag Wirén   (1905-   )

Orchestra

Symphony No. 4, Op. 27

☐ Swedish Radio Symphony Orchestra / Ehrling (conductor) / Turnabout 34436

Notwithstanding Wirén's allegiance to Carl Nielsen, his Opus 27 is stubbornly Sibelian in content, especially the first two of its three movements. The dark gray of the orchestral palette is the primary sonorous pigmentation. Formally, the Symphony seems to emerge from a crepuscular haze. The core of the language Wirén uses originates from intervallic manipulation via compression or expansion. The same method applies to the shapes of the rhythmic designs.

String
Orchestra

Serenade for Strings, Op. 11

☐ English Chamber Orchestra / Somary (conductor) / Vanguard C-10067

Melodicism of the tonal brand, for the most part devoted to lively and energetic music. There is more than a touch of French neoclassicism in the four movements of this, Wirén's most popular work.

Somary brings out all the wit the music contains and doesn't overlook the ironic note that filters through many of the measures. This is a splendid issue.

Chamber
Music

String Quartet No. 5, Op. 41

☐ Saulesco Quartet / Caprice CAP-1024

The romantic meanings of Wirén's Quartet are apparent throughout its three movements. Also apparent are the tight constructions developed from motival material and supported by rhythmic vitality. A spontaneity of expression is present that is the very

opposite of the pedanticism that marks a great deal of neo-romantically styled compositions. Similar spontaneity is reflected in the fine playing of the Saulesco Quartet to whom
Wirén's work is dedicated.

Friedrich Witt   (1770-1836)

Symphony in C (*Jena*)   *Orchestra*

☐ Westphalian Symphony Orchestra / Reichert (conductor) / Turnabout 34409

This is the Symphony long attributed to Beethoven. Name-dropping what it is, when
Mr. Witt was nowhere in the picture there was good interest in the piece. The moment
Witt was confirmed as the composer and Beethoven was cancelled, interest vanished.
(Once upon a time the number of recordings available was fast approaching the dozen
mark.)

This isn't the greatest performance ever made. A major-league conductor with fellow
major-league musicians could make much more of the score than is documented here.
However, it is a four-movement work of charm and character and this is the only version
current in *Schwann*. So take—don't leave it, since there probably won't be another.

Hugo Wolf   (1860-1903)

Italian Serenade (1892)   *Orchestra*

☐ Stuttgart Chamber Orchestra / Münchinger (conductor) / London 6737

Wolf's transcription of his piece for string quartet (see under *Chamber Music*,
below). The instrumental amplification consists of two each of flutes, oboes, clarinets,
bassoons, and horns, plus strings. Wolf had intended to use this as the initial movement of
an orchestral suite; fragments of some other movements were all he accomplished.

The playing in this recording is of standard professionalism. On a scale of one to five it
would register just below three.

Intermezzo in E flat major (1887)   *Chamber
Music*

☐ Juilliard Quartet / Columbia M–32596

A little-known work. It encompasses Brahmsian-Straussian syntax, with some motival
manipulation. Apparently (though not so indicated), this is the initial recording.

Italian Serenade (1887)

☐ Los Angeles String Quartet / Crystal S–103

A Serenade with few if any insular connotations. It is an example of pure chamber
music written by an Austrian; the only Italian influence is a preoccupation with triple
meter (which is close to Vienna, after all). More vocal swing within the measures would be
desirable, but otherwise this is a moderately good essay by the L.A. team.

(For the orchestral transcription, see under *Orchestra*.)

String Quartet in D minor

☐ Keller Quartet / CMS/Oryx 1820

A work that is styled with the intensity of late Beethoven, laced with some modern instrumental textures. A touch of Wagner appears in the slow movement and will bring reminders of *Lohengrin* (see under *Wagner: Opera and Dramatic Music*). The principal point of Wolf's opus is its tensility, sometimes very apparent, other times within the content and ready to burst out.

The passionate poetry of this Quartet is not easy to make clear, and it is to the credit of the Keller foursome that they produce a cogent and immediate realization of a score filled with problems of balance and constant interlocution. I can recall only one reading that equals this one, made quite some time ago by the New Music Quartet and long since deleted.

The Wolf work was first available domestically on Musical Heritage Society MHS-1597. It is still in that catalogue. Finally, a version by the La Salle Quartet was in the Deutsche Grammophon catalogue (139376) but though listed in *Schwann* seems to be unavailable. No problem, really, since the Keller Quartet fulfills all requirements.

Vocal

Voice with Accompaniment

Anakreons Grab from *Goethe Lieder*

☐ Crespin (soprano); Wustman (piano) / London 26043

"Anacreon's Grave" was the sixth of the fifty-one songs Wolf wrote to Goethe texts in 1888 and 1889. It is one of his most beautiful pieces. Crespin does marvelously with its delicate lyricism, delivering it with the sustained quietness it requires.

Der König bei der Krönung (1886)

☐ Fischer-Dieskau (baritone); Barenboim (piano) / Deutsche Grammophon 2709053

Although the words are by Mörike, this song is not among the fifty-three *Mörike Lieder* (*see below*) written by Wolf in 1888. *Der König* is a separate item composed in 1886 and is one of *Sechs Gedichte*—the other five to texts by Kerner, Scheffel, and Goethe—published the year the *Mörike Lieder* were being created.

Epiphanias from *Goethe Lieder*

☐ Watts (contralto); Parsons (piano) / Oiseau-Lyre S-293

Wolf in a light-hearted creative mood. Watts's vocal delivery is excellent.

Harfenspieler Lieder I, II, III from *Goethe Lieder*

☐ Enns (bass-baritone); Sheffield (piano) / Orion 74146

Included in a program that contrasts these three songs with settings of the same texts by Schumann. Comparison shows that Schumann's songs have lyrical totality as their objective; Wolf's define every nuance of the text and are far more detailed and more chromatically designed. If one were to describe the music coloristically, then Schumann's is russet brown, Wolf's almost black.

Enns's voice is secure and his diction quite good. On the whole the performance is fairly illuminating.

Italienisches Liederbuch (Excerpts)

☐ Ameling (soprano); Baldwin (piano) / Philips 802919

The recording covers twenty-six of the total forty-six songs in the two parts of the *Italienisches Liederbuch*. Of the twenty-two in the first set (composed in 1890 and 1891), Ameling performs Nos. 1, 5, 7, 9, 10, 12, 14, 16, 18, 19, 21, and 22. From the second group (composed in 1896) Nos. 1-3, 5, 9-11, 13, 15, 17, 19-21, and 23 are represented.

This is a most pertinent conspectus, containing a variety of moods, sensitively colored, without any Italian overtones. There is more simplicity than passionate penetration in these songs, but that did not prevent Wolf from being fully responsive to each of the texts.

Ameling's voice is not big but it is fully communicative. Above all, she is a vocalist with total understanding of the words she sings and she always displays comprehensive musicality. Where pathos is required she supplies it, and where irony is demanded she carries out the demand. Ameling can be heartily recommended.

Mausfallensprüchlein from *Sechs Lieder für eine Frauenstimme*

☐ Watts (contralto); Parsons (piano) / Oiseau-Lyre S-293

The text is by Mörike, but like *Der König bei der Krönung* (*see above*), this is not to be confused as one of the fifty-three *Mörike Lieder* (*see below*). Wolf's "Mouse Catcher" song is attractively presented.

(*See below* [*Morgentau*] for another song from this same set.)

Michelangelo Lieder

☐ Enns (bass-baritone); Sheffield (piano) / Orion 74146

This last set of three songs that Wolf produced is filled with his despairing voice, especially the second, *Alles endet, was entstehet.*

Enns has a good insight into the music, though more inner probing would be fruitful. Orion should have better control of its production—they offer texts but not translations.

Mignon Songs from *Goethe Lieder*

☐ Watts (contralto); Parsons (piano) / Oiseau-Lyre S-293

The set of four is produced with expressive intimacy.

Morgentau from *Sechs Lieder für eine Frauenstimme*

☐ Price (soprano); Garvey (piano) / RCA LSC-2279

"Morning Dew" from "Six Songs for a Woman's Voice" is one of Wolf's earliest songs, composed when he was only seventeen. Price sings it with fitting Mendelssohnian lightness.

(*See above* [*Mausfallensprüchlein*] for another song from the same set.)

Mörike Lieder (1888) (Excerpts)

☐ Fischer-Dieskau (baritone); Richter (piano) / Deutsche Grammophon 2530584
☐ Ameling (soprano); Baldwin (piano) / Philips 6500128

Triple advantages result from obtaining both recordings. Thus: two different artists (four, of course, if the accompanists are counted), two different types of voice, and an excellent representation of thirty-four different songs offered on the two programs, plus four that are on both (which offers a fourth advantage of hearing the same song in contrasted timbre).

Fischer-Dieskau offers Nos. 3, 5, 12, 15, 17, 19, 23, 27, 36, 37, 41, 45, 51, and 52 in his selection. Ameling sings Nos. 2, 4, 6, 9, 13, 18, 21, 24, 26, 33, 35, 39, 42, 43, 47, and 53. Both sing Nos. 10, 25, 29, and 40, thereby rounding off a total of eighteen for Fischer-Dieskau and twenty for Ameling.

The Fischer-Dieskau and Richter disc was made live at a concert in 1973, but it loses nothing thereby—the sound quality is excellent. Top-quality vocalism is to be expected, and it is delivered. As for Richter, his sensitivity as an accompanist matches the magnificent work of Gerald Moore.

For any of the fifty-three Mörike Songs a vocal instrument capable of innumerable colorings is mandatory, along with dramatic insight, the ability to project it, and musicianship of the highest order. If an occasional lapse may be noted in Elly Ameling's singing, it is exceedingly minor and is never in terms of the last three points mentioned.

If still more of the *Lieder* in the set are desired, one can obtain the three-record set that D.G. has issued (2709053), with Fischer-Dieskau and Daniel Barenboim. Forty-six songs are included. Of the remaining seven (the *Mörike Lieder* total fifty-three), four are included in the above two recordings. Only three (Nos. 7, 14, and 16) are absent from all three performances. But one of these (No. 14) is included in the briefer recording made by Crespin (*see below* [*Mörike Lieder*]).

Mörike Lieder (Nos. 14, 26, and 40)

☐ Crespin (soprano); Wustman (piano) / London 26043

In numerical order: *Der Gärtner, Das verlassene Mägdlein,* and *In der Frühe.* On the recording the sequence is numbers 40, 14, and 26.

The mood of each song is fully captured; John Wustman is a very sensitive collaborator.

(*See above* [*Mörike Lieder*] for more complete recordings of the set.)

Spanisches Liederbuch (Excerpts)

☐ DeGaetani (mezzo-soprano); Kalish (piano) / Nonesuch 71296

Wolf's *Spanisches Liederbuch* (composed in 1889 and 1890) embraces forty-four songs, ten of which are of sacred character. Jan DeGaetani's program presents sixteen of the set: Nos. 3–5, 9, 13, 15, 17, 22–24, 26, 27, 29, 34, 37, and 40.

Her performance is one that transfers the quality of chamber-music subtlety to the voice; the experience of hearing these Wolf songs in that manner is of the highest consequence. Not that the interpretation of the moods conveyed by the texts is smoothed into an absolute music category (we are dealing with words, after all, which places any song, regardless of how it is set stylistically or technically, into the quasiprogrammatic category). There is a touching, pointed melancholy in *Tief im Herzen trag' ich Pein* (No. 40), a sensuousness in her delivery of *Bedeckt mich mit Blumen* (No. 9), and a light, woodwindlike quality in the singing of *In dem Schatten meiner Locken* (No. 13). Each song is vocally orchestrated, as it were. Such superb singing of Hugo Wolf literature is truly rare. With DeGaetani there are none of the oft-heard, impossible-to-take vocalistic trickery, breast heaving, or spurious emotion. With this musician, the music is first and always. With such high standard of artistry all the sentiments Wolf described are made clear and truthful.

Verschwiegene Liebe from Eichendorff Lieder

☐ Crespin (soprano); Wustman (piano) / London 26043

"Secret Love" is one of the twenty songs composed between 1886 and 1888 to texts by Eichendorff. "Love" is indeed lovely and delicate. Crespin is also lovely in her singing, presenting the music with a caressing gentility that is touching.

Ermanno Wolf-Ferrari   (1876-1948)

Orchestra   **Overture to *The Secret of Suzanne* (1909)**

☐ New York Philharmonic / Bernstein (conductor) / Columbia D3S–818

It's no secret any longer that dear Suzanne's secret was the immorality of smoking cigarettes! There are no secrets in this two minutes and fifty seconds of music that Bernstein and his instrumentalists do not uncover. An acute, swift, incisive delight that will remind older listeners of the incomparable Toscanini performance recorded more than a half-century ago.

Serenade in E flat major for Strings

String Orchestra

☐ I Solisti Veneti / Scimone (conductor) / Musical Heritage Society MHS–1347

Always expect catchy music from this composer. Even in the fugal-spun finale the music skims off the strings. The performance is an engaging one and the sound of this remastered Erato recording is simply delicious.

Christian Wolff   (1934-   )

For One, Two, or Three People (1964)

Instrumental

☐ Tudor (baroque organ) / Odyssey 32160158

Baroque Organ

Since the title permits amplification of personnel, Tudor has chosen a performance by "two," singly serving both ends of the performer needs. There is no slight of hand. He does it by superimposing two versions of the same material, one played on the organ, the other inside it. This interlacement produces a spitting new musical foliation that no single organ in the world could exhibit. The equivalents of foghorns, cow bawls, orgasmic choked cries come to mind as the organ is treated unorganlike. The product results from paralleling John Cage's prepared piano—the prepared organ, therefore. In place of rattan and pieces of wood, clips, and so on attached to the strings, Tudor has removed certain of the organ's pipes and adjusted the vents; he includes percussive playing on the pipes and uses contact microphones to confirm all minimal noises.

Certainly, this music is not spiritual (what would Rheinberger and Widor say?). Certainly, it is not vulgar (church congregations will never be exposed to it). Certainly, it is fascinating. Such disobedience to the instrument involved is obedient to the aleatoric vows of the composer.

Accompaniments

Piano

☐ Rzewski (piano) / Composers Recordings SD–357

Socialist Realism is a term the Soviets have bandied about for many years as their antidote to formalistic practices such as serialism, polytonality, and so on. Wolff's conception would please the Soviets because it has a text taken from the book *China: The Revolution Continued*. (The text is delivered by the pianist, who in addition to playing the piano also sings, recites, and plays percussion with his feet—drum with pedal and high-hat cymbal.) Whether the Soviets would accept the nonnationalistic neoprimitivism of the music is very questionable, however.

Though one admires Wolff's interest in social and political questions (the text is permeated with the teaching of Mao Tse-Tung), the sonic portion of *Accompaniments* has a static quality that may turn one off. Nonetheless, the conception is an interesting example of an expanded monodrama.

Chamber Music

Duet II for Horn and Piano (1961)

☐ Hillyer (horn); Tudor (piano) / Mainstream 5015

This is aleatoric music—"a situation is indicated, but not when one is to enter into it, nor, necessarily, for how long one is in it" is merely one of the many very free directions Wolff gives his performers. With the isolated fragments that result, no melody, harmony, counterpoint, or design exists. The only matter that does is surprise, since without a point of departure or basis of relationship everything that occurs is happenstance. With that, at least the initial aural exposure is discovery. Thereafter, many rehearings are mandatory for the fullest understanding.

The performers' uninhibited response (one takes that for granted) to Wolff's music is to present sparse and disconnected material; the resultant character is one of sobriety. Leave it at that—one "chances" that reaction is valid.

Duo for Violinist and Pianist (1961)

☐ Kobayashi (violin); Tudor (piano) / Mainstream 5015

Wolff's usual chance music, thereby our appreciation of the music depends on the acceptance of results by accident. There is very little action, mostly specks of sound; mainly rough, scratchy violin noise, a few gestures from the piano. Silence plays a great part in this extremely phlegmatic dialogue.

Lines

☐ Rubin and Halpin (violins); Ellis (viola); Judiyaba (cello) / Composers Recordings SD-357

Homophony articulated by passing one pitch (of varied length) on one instrument to another pitch (of varied length) on another instrument. Some are long, some are short; some are vibrated, some are not; some are bowed, some are plucked. Most of the piece is played by a total *scordatura* (retuning) of the sixteen strings of the quartet. The choices of articulation, dynamics, and the like are mainly in the hands of the performers.

Form, as such, is negated. The strategy and tactics represent dissected color truths but remind one of Apollinaire's phrase concerning "the insane verities of art." The absence of textural weights, detail, and contrasts can be described, by borrowing a term from Nicolas Slonimsky, as "frugal ankyoglossia." Try it; you may like a little bit of it.

Summer for String Quartet (1961)

☐ Concord String Quartet / Vox SVBX-5306
☐ Raimondi and Kobayashi (violins); Trampler (viola); Soyer (cello) / Mainstream 5015

Only a few controls are defined by the composer for this piece. The design, including length of sections, their repeats, their order, and the piece's total length, are in the hands of the performers. Many of the sounds are quietly explosive, and harmonics abound. Over all, Summer is heated by unclouded reticence.

That the performers decide on length as well as content leads to listing the two recorded performances available. In no way is there "interpretation" as the word is generally meant. Both elucidations are valid and stand by themselves—an infinite number of other performances would do likewise. The general climate is the same for both, but the Mainstream group takes eight minutes thirty-seven seconds to describe it; the Concord four is clocked at four minutes forty seconds.

Joseph Wölfl *(1773-1812)*

Sonata

In C minor, Op. 25 / **In D minor, Op. 33, No. 2** / **In E major, Op. 33, No. 3**

☐ Pleshakov (piano) / Orion 6901

Rare romantic music by a composer worth hearing but who languishes in total obscurity. The music is distinguished by elegant lyrical clarity and a sensitive formal sense. To hear is to believe. To listen to Pleshakov's conceptions is to recognize his acute interpretative abilities.

Instrumental

Piano

Stefan Wolpe *(1902-1972)*

Chamber Piece No. 1 (1964)

☐ Contemporary Chamber Ensemble / Weisberg (conductor) / Nonesuch 71220

Post-Webern music with fragmentation which has such spontaneous projection that seamless continuity seems to be in effect. At the same time the materials sound uncalculated, improvisationally tossed off. Wolpe's abstraction contains its special, individual poetry. It is one of his best works.

The performance by the fourteen players (five winds, three brass, five strings, and piano) is of the stuff that contemporary composers dream of obtaining and rarely do. Nonesuch's sound is simply fabulous.

Orchestra

Piece for Solo Trumpet and Seven Instruments (1971)

☐ Los Angeles Group for Contemporary Music / Guarneri (trumpet) / Kraft (conductor) / Crystal S-352

A constant dialogue between the solo voice and the septet, with more loyalty, as it were, to the leading (trumpet) figure. The Piece is in two parts, a short one-minute opener and a principal section covering a little over six and a half minutes.

The trumpet is a restless voice but not an anxious one, and Mario Guarneri addresses his part accordingly. He receives fine support under William Kraft's baton, himself one of the most individual composers on the American scene. Crystal, however, errs thrice in the liner credits. It lists only five instruments (missing are bassoon and viola); it doubles one instrument (two violinists are noted, where one should have been indicated as a violist); and it omits the name of the bassoonist. In the last case the performer is possibly David Breidenthal, since he appears as a soloist in a Hindemith piece that forms one of the two companion works on the disc.

Solo Instrument and Orchestra

Trumpet

Form **(1959)**

Form IV: Broken Sequences **(1969)**

☐ Miller (piano) / Composers Recordings S-306

Though Wolpe's music in his late period was severely disciplined and structured (*Form* was composed in 1959, *Form IV* was produced ten years later), it contains strong and important expressivity. While both of these pieces are structurally segmented (a difference from fragmentation that severely splinters the working material), there is more continuity within the details of *Form* than in the rhapsodic content of the companion piece.

Instrumental

Piano

Wolpe's *Form IV* was written for and dedicated to Miller. He most definitely has returned the compliment with impeccable performances.

Trumpet

Solo Piece for Trumpet (1966)

☐ Schwarz (trumpet) / Desto 7133

Rugged expressionism is magnificently expressed in Gerard Schwarz's presentation. Contrast is obtained in this two-part soliloquy by use of the low F alto trumpet in the second section.

The same piece is heard on Robert Levy's miscellaneous program (Golden Crest RE-7045). The playing there lacks bravado, and also lacks a difference in the timbre of the second part compared to the first as to make one doubt whether a different type of trumpet was used. Further discredits: pinched tone by the player, pre-echo by the engineer.

Violin

Second Piece for Violin Alone

☐ Zukofsky (violin) / Desto 6435/37

A bit different from most Wolpe pieces, containing some diatonic intermingling with resultant conjunct motion. A sense of declamatory statement is present.

The piece is played without strain and with proper proportions of passion as required.

Chamber Music

Piece in Two Parts for Flute and Piano (1960)

☐ Baron (flute); Sanders (piano) / Desto 7104

Top-flight (and top-drawer) postserial music. There is manipulation of small pitch arrangements, which become energized (a newer type of variation science, as it were), producing the equivalent of a variety of geometric shapes set in motion. The separative detail is dynamically explosive rather than simply fragmented.

Baron and Sanders play with total authority.

Trio for Flute, Cello, and Piano (1963)

☐ Trio of the Group for Contemporary Music at Columbia University / Composers Recordings S-233

A two-part work with serial style applied to concentrated, disconnective groups of sound. The structural effect (extremely loose in content) is like punctuating a sentence by using only a number of dashes. Most of the music is concerned with pitch permutations, with little heed to rhythmic solidity.

The players—Harvey Sollberger, flute; Charles Wuorinen, piano; and Joel Krosnick, cello—are master performers of contemporary music. They prove it here.

String Quartet (1969)

☐ Concord String Quartet / Vox SVBX-5306

Pitch cells form the basis for structuring Wolpe's two-movement work. Considerable conjunct motion is involved, but in no sense is tonality in the picture. The pitch segments as they vary, oscillate, and antiphonize are like darting lights. In general terms this is a brand of motival technique, and though the material varies, the force of the cellular activity commands the piece, makes its form intelligible, and is as favorable as that supplied by long-spun thematic statement and response. But thematic supports are not required for this spectroscopic music. Wolpe's method is fresh and fascinating; repeated hearings prove it.

The Concord's playing is impressive, one of command and full understanding.

Piece in Two Parts for Six Players

☐ Datyner (violin); Tunnell (cello); Jefferies (harp); Katharina Wolpe (piano); Bradbury (clarinet); Mason (trumpet) / Prausnitz (conductor) / Argo ZRG-757

Linear solidity is bypassed in this totally rhapsodic (but sharply controlled) work. Each pitch or combination of pitches is accorded its own development and juxtaposed opposition to other single or partnered sounds. The nervous effect is built in to the music's technical system.

The liberating of Wolpe's pitch fantasy makes tonality sound horribly corrupt. This is music having a life of its own, independent of formula, independent of the composer's subjective feelings. It is a music that lives through the sheer internal force of its style.

Two Instrumental Units (1962)

☐ Dunkel (flute); Lucarelli (oboe); Heldrich (percussion); Thomas (piano); Gottlieb (violin); Sylvester (cello); Deak (bass) / Gilbert (conductor) / Opus One 9

Rhapsodic shifts in an incessant continuum of sound patterns mark this work. (It is titled in the liner notes as "Piece for Two Instrumental Units.") Wolpe's style is exactly opposite to the school of fragmentation. It is alert and vigorous, decidedly serious in its constant enfoldment of phrases, rhythms, and pitches. There is nothing tricksy-cleverish about this music.

The playing is well controlled, and in the absence of a score one takes for granted that the dynamic evenness is Wolpe's.

Ten Songs from the Hebrew

Vocal

Voice with Accompaniment

☐ Carmen (alto); Lishner (bass); Tudor (piano) / Columbia Special Products AML-5179 (monaural)

For the greater part the songs are in the late romantic, chromatically studded, note-busy style. Six are sung in Hebrew, four in English. However, all of the texts are provided in English, which is good enough.

The same apportionments apply to the voice used; six are sung by the alto (Arline Carmen) and four by the bass (Leon Lishner). The latter is a stronger personality and has a clearer voice. David Tudor's work is brilliant.

Henry J. Wood *(1869-1944)*

Fantasia on British Sea Songs

Orchestra

☐ BBC Symphony Orchestra / Davis (conductor) / Philips 6502001

A "you-are-there" performance. This is one of the traditional pieces played the final night of the Promenade Concerts in London. A good part of the music (the first three-fifths) comes through, but there are audience noises *en route;* then later (in the last two-fifths), audience cheers and hand-clapping sail in to reinforce the rhythm of one of the tunes. Finally, *Rule, Britannia!* with sing-along, which, after a radio announcer's announcement, is encored. All of it prefaced by some remarks by the conductor, Colin Davis.

This performance really should have been ruled out of consideration. However, it is the only recorded version of the piece available, so if you want it, this is what you'll have to take, annoyances, interferences, and all.

Hugh Wood (1932-   )

Instrumental

Piano

Three Piano Pieces (1963)

☐ McGaw (piano) / Argo ZRG-759

This is civilized contemporary music, in the sense that the tight and impeccable technique avoids jaded and tired formulae and is used to define musical meaning. There is no challenge here to find cogent values in the strong language, which relates a bit to Carl Ruggles and has textural weighting that is somewhat like Olivier Messiaen. Wood's chunky and gutsy writing is well displayed by the pianist, who gave the premiere performance of the work.

Russell Woollen (1923-   )

Instrumental

Harp

Lento for Harp Solo

☐ Stockton (harp) / Crystal S-107

A poetic extract (movement 3) from a four-movement work for harp, oboe (or flute), and percussion. Neatly dissonant, neatly quoting a few Salzedo effects (whistling and timpanic sounds, pedal glissandi, and so on).

The performance quality and recorded sound are tops.

Choral

Chorus Alone

Motectus Ad Libitum Ad Offertorium from Missa Domus Aurea, Op. 40

☐ Mid-America Chorale / Dexter (conductor) / Composers Recordings 191 (monaural)

Ecclesiastical style, with a few telling touches of contemporary colorations. Woollen's setting of the Litany to the Blessed Virgin Mary is for four-part male voices.

William Wordsworth (1908-   )

Instrumental

Piano

Ballade, Op. 41

Cheesecombe Suite, Op. 27

Sonata in D minor, Op. 13

☐ Kitchin (piano) / Lyrita RCS-13

Wordsworth does not believe in originality for its own sake. His output shows him fond of sectional form, and his syntax is on the more serious side of late romanticism. At times the material (in the Sonata and in Opus 27) is tempered with modalism.

Johann Hugo Woržischek. *See Jan Václav Voříšek.*

Anton Wranitzky. *See Antonín Vranický.*

Maurice Wright (20th cent.)

Electronic Composition (1973)

Electronic Music

☐ Odyssey Y–34139

That electronic music can contain wit and breeziness is proven in this piece. It obtains considerable strength from the absence of pulsatile directness; excitement is engendered by fragmented color puffs and registral contrastive play. Conventional electronics are here used unconventionally.

Gerhard Wuensch (1925-   )

Suite for Trumpet and Organ, Op. 40

Chamber Music

☐ Plog (trumpet); Swearingen (organ) / Avant 1014

A romantic center of gravity is in this melodious work. No tonality roughage—E flat is the tonal center for the outer movements, titled Alla breve and Rondo. In the *Perpetuum mobile* the value of double and quadruple tonguing propels the scherzo design. A Dirge covers slow-movement requirements. The performance is most gratifying.

Charles Wuorinen (1938-   )

Grand Bamboula for String Orchestra (1971)

String Orchestra

☐ Light Fantastic Players / Shulman (conductor) / Nonesuch 71319

The title is taken from Gottschalk but is a mere expedient, chosen by Wuorinen because of what "the sound of its words evokes." And, response is there. This music makes a "grand bam" through its vigor and vitality. It has a charge as it vehemently and passionately goes its six-minute way. It may be said that if Albert Roussel had written serially designed music this is the way it would have sounded. Thus intellectual designing is matched by incisive dispatch.

The Shulman-led orchestra plays this work—one of the most, if not *the* most, exciting Wuorinen has produced—with magnificent sound and verve. It is not intervallically easy to negotiate, but the assurance of the performers jumps off the record, with all pitches dead center, all phrases and cohesiveness on target. Shulman deserves plenty of credit for his conducting of these young musicians (six first violins, five second violins, four violas, four cellos, and two double basses).

Janissary Music (1966)

Percussion

☐ DesRoches (percussion) / Composers Recordings S–231

If percussion music can be termed intimately responsive then this is it. Contrary to the aural wear and tear of so much music in the medium, Wuorinen's piece is contained in a chamber-music manner. Not that it is cold and forbidding—the vibrational hang of vibraphone and marimba takes care of warm sonority totals. Additionally, two other sets of percussive classifications provide simulative pitches, from twelve drums and from the ascending arrangement of "bass" to "soprano" gongs, cymbals, cowbells, and triangles.

Raymond DesRoches is a master percussionist. His portrayal of the score is sensitive and select. We are informed that to record Wuorinen's twelve and one-half minute piece, a total of thirteen hours were required. The fluidity of the final product shows it.

Prelude and Fugue for Four Percussionists (1955)

☐ Kraus (conductor) / Golden Crest 4004 (monaural)

A very early work by this important composer. Already one perceives the simmerings of the later highly organized music. The principal pitch materials are definite (timpani) and simulated (five Chinese temple blocks). These are contrasted to a pair of cymbals (large and small), a gong, and a pair of snare drums (with and without snares), adding rhythmic color to the textural mass.

The fugue, especially, has a fascinating architecture. However, the monaural setting tends to blur a number of passages. The Golden Crest edition lacks proper data. There are no liner notes for the work; the composer is credited only on the label and there his first name is substituted for by an initial; the performers are not identified. Finally, although the timing of the work is 5:38, the record label gives the ridiculous total of 2:50, while Wuorinen's score states the performance length as 6:15. Nonetheless, the Prelude and Fugue is too interesting a piece to be overlooked; the recording will have to do until a fresh issue appears with good sound and efficient packaging.

Ringing Changes for Percussion Ensemble (1970)

☐ New Jersey Percussion Ensemble / Wuorinen (conductor) / Nonesuch 71263

Color is present: double vibraphones, double pianos, almglocken, chimes, and timpani represent sounds of precise pitch; drums, brakedrums, cymbals, tamtams, and string drum (the so-called "lion's roar") define simulated pitch differentiations. However, the assortment is not used for purely percussive poetry but for a poetry of serial exactitude, with rhythmic shapes and lengths dictated by the intervallic measurements of the basic tone row. It is the supreme logic of Wuorinen's discourse that is the expressive point, not the special palette he uses. The thoroughness and toughness of the former provide its own personality point of reference.

Solo Instrument and Orchestra

Chamber Concerto for Cello and Ten Players (1963)

☐ Group for Contemporary Music / Sherry (cello) / Wuorinen (conductor) / Nonesuch 71263

Cello

Highly tensed serial music. With Wuorinen the relationship to the father of dodecaphony is extremely remote. Schoenberg's twelve-tone music is keenly linked to classical structures, despite its bold romantic accessions. Wuorinen's has an intensely detailed structure and rich urgency but cuts away from any past lineage. Complex conditions are involved, but they are viable ones.

The musicians in this performing group are tip-top executants. Their technical skills, sound musicianship, and stylistic cognizance in contemporary music matters are masterly. One can trust this to be a magnificently detailed performance.

Flute

Chamber Concerto for Flute and Ten Players (1964)

☐ Group for Contemporary Music at Columbia University / Sollberger (flute) / Wuorinen (conductor) / Composers Recordings S–230

Wuorinen's color scale provides a fascinating canvas. Against the single wind instrument, which is given increasing importance as the music progresses, there is a mesh of plucked timbres (harp and guitar), keyboard-instrument sounds (piano and celesta) with one in the plucked category (harpsichord), percussion (especially xylophone), and a double bass. The suavity of the solo flute, even with its disjunctive intervallic registration, is in severe contrast to the granitic instrumental compact. Indeed, Wuorinen's twelve-tone argument is utterly convincing, especially because of its coloristic specialness (and dominance). He fully proves his creative brief.

Harvey Sollberger can be expected to be convincing and he is. His color range is remarkable and his technique extraordinary. He gives an inspired example of flute playing, with fine support from the instrumental dectet.

Piano Concerto (1966)

Piano

☐ Royal Philharmonic Orchestra / Wuorinen (piano) / Dixon (conductor) / Composers Recordings S–239

A well-registered performance, certainly certified by the presence of the composer as the soloist. The work is in a single movement, a fantasy of textural bits and pieces. Wuorinen uses a great amount of percussion and uses it frequently; it almost rivals the solo piano in importance. This sort of timbre clutch is fine in pithy pieces; in a twenty-minute span it may well be argued that such post-Webern focus fuzzes the ear.

Bassoon Variations

Instrumental

☐ MacCourt (bassoon); Jolles (harp); Gottlieb (timpani) / New World Records NW–209

Bassoon

Wuorinen states that the bassoon is accompanied by the harp and timpani in his Variations. Accordingly, here is that rare musical bird, a solo accompanied by a duo. Serial fermentation is the *modus operandi,* and, as usual with Wuorinen, there is superb instrumental workmanship and top professional technical skill. The great interest lies in the coloration of the trio employed. There's nothing ponderous in the continuity, and the formative demands are clearly portrayed.

Flute Variations I (1963)
Flute Variations II (1968)

Flute

☐ Sollberger (flute) / Nonesuch 73028

Both pieces are serial styled but not in any way arid or rigid for the sake of the technical system. There are great differences between the two works; the first is considerably hyperactive in comparison with the mood of the later one, which resembles a soliloquy. The fine-nuanced colorations, especially in Flute Variations II, include chords, microtoned glides, and bent pitches.

The playing seems unbelievable until one recalls that it is by Harvey Sollberger (both works were composed for him). Mr. Sollberger cannot fail to make a believer out of anyone that listens to his playing. "Spectacular" describes the technique, "magnificent" describes the musicianship.

Piano Variations (1963)

Piano

☐ Burge (piano) / Advance 3 (monaural)

Freely serial music. Wuorinen's variants are drawn from basic fragments of material rather than a stated theme. As expected, the sentiment is cool. However, the logic that is found in Wuorinen's Piano Variations is not merely a carbon copy of a rigid technical system. In fact there is an excitement in the tensions that are built into the work by way of silences and registral differences.

Burge's playing is crisp to the finite turn. It is filed to the most propulsive ictus. He avoids blatant percussiveness, giving an impressive exhibition of the special virtuosity demanded by this kind of music. This is truly a five-star performance.

Sonata (1969)

☐ Miller (piano) / Composers Recordings S–306

In this large work Wuorinen upholds the values of serial structuring, in regard to both pitch and temporal arrangement. Polyphonic surfaces, of course, are in the extreme majority. This music offers no comforting arrangement of material into fast and slow, scherzo and concluding drive-it-home-with-vivacity divisions. Wuorinen's Sonata (1969) is, rather, a large canvas of abstract musical art. Considered in that manner it conveys intense meaning that can be admired (even enjoyed) beyond its certain intellectual logistics.

Robert Miller is a master of contemporary piano music. Wuorinen's piece (dedicated to him) offers no problems that he has not mastered to the last agogic mark. It can be taken for granted that his performance is definitive.

Piano,
Four Hands

Making Ends Meet for Piano, Four-Hands

☐ Jean and Kenneth Wentworth (piano) / Desto 7131

Although the description "abstract" may come to mind in listening to Wuorinen's piece (which is in two sections, *Development* and Variations), it is decidedly inexact. "Concrete," "positive," or "constructive" better define's Wuorinen's solid musical edifice. The music is analogous to abstract painting only in the broad terms of an entity that is not referable to nature (equated in music with tonality, chordally based on the overtone series). It is the undeviating formal arrangement that gives this music its entire meaning.

Making Ends Meet may sound like a fleeting improvisation, but it is planets removed from the unpredictable in its absolute, harnessed plan. Each split second is predetermined from a musical blueprint plotted from the workings of total serialism. The result of this turmoil of craft produces a brilliant musical document.

Jean Wentworth indicates in her liner note that Wuorinen's piece "is of startling difficulty and complexity." Extremely so. The report is that the Wentworths' performance meets all of the superhuman demands of the composer.

Violin

The Long and the Short (1969)

☐ Zukofsky (violin) / Mainstream MS–5016

Expressionistic inquiry. Despite the single unaccompanied violin there are no crippling restrictions to the dynamic progress of Wuorinen's fancifully titled piece. The substances are involved, but the logistics are communicative throughout, with terminal close relationships based on percussively entranced sustained sounds. The grating finality is positive confirmation.

Composers who write for a solo fiddle find their music in the high-risk category; that is, unless they have a Zukofsky to play it, technically conquer it, and intellectually define it.

Chamber
Music

Composition for Oboe and Piano

☐ Ostryniec (oboe); Wuorinen (piano) / Orion 78288

2110

Straightforward serialism, nonacademic in its procedures, strongly contrasted in the presentation of the total material. The pitch and rhythmic outpour is excitingly presented.

String Trio (1968)

☐ Members of Speculum Musicae / Nonesuch 71319

A consummate example of serial music, totally dynamic in tone. Its prodigious power, of granitic force, makes it one of the most fascinating and exciting works in the string trio literature. Highly complex in its ordering, the inward balance is obtained by serially governing the rhythmic detail in analogous relationship to the pitches. Thus, the controls placed on the pitch elements are related and transferred to apply to the time sphere. Dynamic and registral conditions play their respective controlled roles as well. Pulse regularity is supplanted by pulse fluidity in Wuorinen's opus. Such obscuration of mensural perception produces a violent freshness in the composition. Wuorinen's Trio is radically new, of choice creativity.

The String Trio is totally virtuosic for the performers; in comparison, Liszt, Paganini, and the like are child's play. Rolf Schulte, John Graham, and Fred Sherry are masterful performers and they have mastered Wuorinen's piece to the last nuance. A fantastic performance.

Bearbeitungen über das Glogauer Liederbuch (1962)

☐ Members of Speculum Musicae / Nonesuch 71319

Six settings from an important collection of fifteenth-century songs, dances, and canons. The titles are as enchanting as the music. No. 1, for example, is headed *Pauli de Broda Carmen;* the fifth is called *Hélas le bon Temps* [*Tinctoris*].

Wuorinen's "composing with someone else's notes" (as he refreshingly describes the process) consisted of taking three-part pieces, amplifying them to span four instruments, and, in turn, varying the total of timbres so that the flute alternates with piccolo and the clarinet doubles on bass clarinet in association with a violin and a cello. Paul Dunkel, Virgil Blackwell, Daniel Reed, and Fred Sherry are the representatives from the Speculum Musicae group and they uphold the outstanding reputation of that organization in their playing.

String Quartet (1971)

☐ Fine Arts Quartet / Turnabout 34515

Though fundamentally concerned with pitch structuring, Wuorinen does not hesitate to style dramatically the linear progress of his serial testimony by harmonics, pizzicati, and glissandi. The pitch material is worked with fine-toothed thoroughness and effectiveness. The laws of artistic balance could not be better served. Movements 1 and 3 are of exactly the same length (6:05); the central movement is almost double in proportion, timed at 11:45.

The Fine Arts team gives a faultless musical and technical performance. They show a thorough knowledge of the piece; the music is in their fingers and bows as dynamically positive as any standard repertoire example. Wuorinen's Quartet was commissioned for the Fine Arts foursome, who gave the premiere performance in 1971.

Speculum Speculi (1972)

☐ Speculum Musicae / Sherry (conductor) / Nonesuch 71300

Wuorinen's "Mirror of the Mirror" is aptly titled since it relates to the variational structure of the piece. The variations are not in closed formation but continuous, with a process of enlargement that embraces both material and instrumentation. The serial style has Wuorinen's personal stamp, meaning that the properties are interesting, the logic positively clear, and the sonorities colorful. (The scoring is for flute, oboe, bass clarinet, double bass, piano, and percussion consisting of four drums, three gongs, and vibraphone.)

The performance is impressive in all respects. One expects no less from members of the Speculum Musicae.

Electronic Music

Time's Encomium (1969)

☐ Nonesuch 71225

In a few instances instrumental music has the artifice of imitating electronic music. Charles Wuorinen's imposing composition (close to thirty-two minutes in length) "for synthesized and processed synthesized sound" reverses the process, and with profound creativity. Not that its objective is to imitate baldly; but, through its choice of material, developmental method, and total structuring, a strong instrumental personality is reflected, as though conceived for and admitting of the usual interpretative performance. This hardly occurs in the mass of electronic music that has been produced, where everything is permanently fixed and repetitively reproduced by turning on the tape machine.

Time's Encomium has pitch and intervallic, chordal, and temporal lineation, rather than the assorted punctuations, tidal tremolos, and explosive tidbits heard in the average electronic score. Wuorinen's choice elements are thoroughly detailed and built into a composition with an amazingly individual ordered sense.

In 1970, *Time's Encomium* made history by being the first all-electronic work to be awarded the Pulitzer Prize for Music. It fully deserved that honor.

Ruth Shaw Wylie (1916-   )

Instrumental

Piano

Psychogram (1968)

☐ Catanese (piano) / Composers Recordings SD–353

"Musical Confessional" could be applied as the title. Wylie describes this as a musical profile "of her psychological states during a year of bitterness, frustration, sadness, and intense angers, along with her desperate attempts to maintain an outward semblance of equilibrium and composure."

Credit her with both honesty and a strong pianistic document that portrays introverted and extroverted situations. They all hang out clearly in this sonic translation.

Yehudi Wyner (1929-   )

Instrumental

Piano

Three Short Fantasies

☐ Miller (piano) / Composers Recordings S–306

A range of moods is found in each of the three pieces (respectively composed in 1963, 1966, and 1971). There is no harnessing of data dependent on rigid structuring. The mysterious quality of the first piece moves out to strength; the rhythmic portions of the second Fantasy are contrasted by a striking tintinnabulous pedal; and the concluding piece has an important repetitive motive, of haunted quality.

This is impressive music, impressively played. (Fantasy III was written for the soloist and dedicated to him.)

Concerto Duo for Violin and Piano (1956)

Chamber Music

☐ Raimondi (violin); Wyner (piano) / Composers Recordings 161E (monaural)

Chromaticism is the communicatory function in this powerfully rhapsodic work (not rhapsodic structurally, but in its individual moves), yet it does not overwhelm the pitch depiction. Inlaid are a great number of rich romantic assumptions. These do not confuse the aesthetic issue. A blend such as this makes for a truly compelling utterance. Wyner's work, one bluntly states, has the mark of permanence.

As a pianist, Wyner has long been associated in performances with Raimondi. This partnership shows vividly in the CRI recording. Every note is clear, every line firm, and the total is beautifully shaped.

Intermedio (1974)

Vocal

Voice and Orchestra

☐ String Orchestra / Susan Davenny Wyner (soprano) / Yehudi Wyner (conductor) / Composers Recordings SD–352

Wyner calls his three-part work a Lyric Ballet. Originally, the composition was produced with dancers plus the voice and strings. It retains full creative health without visual support of any kind. The music moves in an increasing ratio of emotive depth. *Torch Song* avoids pat jazz characterization while it takes on its extrovertish convictions. *Up Tempo* is for the strings alone. It is nervous, peripatetic—the scene darkens. The final Elegy has the personality of a long-suffering, world-weary figure.

The heroine of the occasion is Susan Davenny Wyner. She sings a difficult part with enormous vitality and an artistry of phrase depiction that are thrillingly blood-chilling. The string orchestra does fine work in coloring this powerful musical document.

Iannis Xenakis   *(1922-   )*

Achorripsis (1957)   *Orchestra*

☐ Hamburger Kammersolisten / Travis (conductor) / Mainstream 5008

Changing sound densities from the twenty-one instruments involved with Xenakis's habitual rumble and tumble, roar and soar. Sound sweeps—an aching kind of glissando—are quite often cut into the material. There is presence in the recording, though the shape escapes definition because of the constant individualized activity of the sounds.

Akrata (1965)

☐ Buffalo Philharmonic Orchestra / Foss (conductor) / Nonesuch 71201

An even split of instrumentation is involved, with eight wind and eight brass instruments. Sound blocks, emphasizing a rhythmic figure, pass in review. Paradoxically, the effect is static (the translation of the title of the piece is "Pure"). Whatever powers there are in the score are conveyed in Foss's performance. With his fantastic ear one may be certain every pitch is in its proper place.

Metastaseis (1954)

☐ French National Radio Orchestra / Le Roux (conductor) / Vanguard C-10030

Xenakis's *Metastaseis* (the score lists it as *Metastaseis^B*)—meaning "transformation" or "change in position"—(in the translation of Claude Rostand's liner note, the title is defined thus: "meta = after + stasis = stationary state: dialectical transformation")—calls for five winds, seven brass, and seven percussion, but these are nearly always of secondary importance. It is the string body (twelve first and twelve second violins, eight violas, eight cellos, and six double basses) that carries the musical freight. And they do not utter deep-throated or soaring melodic statements. Most of the string action is frictional in clustered formations or in glissandi of all lengths. They furnish an aural paradox that both warms and lacerates the ear.

Precise controls of the most exacting minuteness are demanded of musicians in a case of this kind. The results heard in the Vanguard recording are amazing and far beyond the common "excellent" definition.

Nomos Gamma for Large Orchestra Scattered Throughout the Audience (1968)

☐ Philharmonic Orchestra of Radio O.R.T.F. / Brück (conductor) / Candide 31060

A close relative to *Terretektorh* (*see below*), completed two years earlier. Most of the forces are larger—fourteen winds, sixteen brass, and eight percussion—while the same total of sixty strings is used.

The effect is described as a "vast tapestry of sound where space is treated as organically as the most abstract group of the elements of sound." Xenakis's score incorporates special mathematically formulated musical data into the design, but compared to *Terretektorh* the resultant sounds hardly differ. And again one cannot differ with the courageous magnitude, imagery, and invention of the composer.

Polytope for Four Orchestras Scattered Throughout the Audience (1967)

☐ Ars Nova Ensemble of Radio O.R.T.F. / Constant (conductor) / Candide 31049

Music written for the light show given at the French Pavilion of Expo '67, held in Montreal (hence the alternate title "Polytope de Montréal"). As concert music it does not differ from Xenakis's other works. It doubtless would have firmer confirmation when played in conjunction with the light show, though Xenakis says his score is "entirely independent" of it.

Terretektorh for Large Orchestra Where the Musicians Are Scattered Throughout the Audience (1966)

☐ Philharmonic Orchestra of Radio O.R.T.F / Brück (conductor) / Candide 31060

It is important to supplement the title. It continues thus: "playing four percussion instruments in addition to their own."

Terretektorh ("Action of Construction") is severely fragmented into sound particles because various distributed instrumental complexes are heard (not distinct in their many spatial separations on a disc). The total orchestra has nine winds, thirteen brass, three percussion, and sixty strings. Each musician must have a wood block, a whip, a pair of maracas, and a siren. What Xenakis has in mind in his very precise scenario of how to organize a performance are consistent movements of sound rolling against each other in waves, in spirals, and so on.

By taking the orchestra into the audience it is obvious that the audience is brought into the orchestra. The gravities, velocities, weights, densities, and pressures of this music are supremely individual in their conception and just as highly involved in their exhibition. Hearing it on disc is only a sampling of the real thing, but it is a fascinating sampling.

String Orchestra

Pithoprakta (1956)

☐ French National Radio Orchestra / Le Roux (conductor) / Vanguard C–10030

Aggression fills this work (whose title means "actions by means of probabilities"). However, the forty-six stringed instruments (each having an individual part), two trombones, xylophone, and wood block are meant to fulfill an "abstract aspect" together with the "sensation of previously unheard materials." This does come to pass. Every variety of string quality is employed in a rigid situation of blocked sound, in place of sound situating itself in horizontal phrase lengths. This covers bowed, plucked, and normal string types, plus sonorities obtained by using the wooden part of the bow, icy timbres produced by playing close to the bridge, together with harmonics (diluted timbres), glides (up, down, and curved), and microtones (explicit or via the progress of glissandi).

No vibrato is used by the players and considerable striking of the string instruments with the hands is utilized. The other instrumental adjuncts are extremely contrastive and used in a special manner: the wood block perforates the sonorous fabric and thereby excites the rhythmic content, the xylophone plays but one pitch in all of its counterplay with the strings, and a pair of trombones (one sustained, the other in slow glissando) appears in only a dozen measures.

The lines are seemingly a razzle-dazzle of aleatoric processes, but they are precisely predetermined and constructively controlled. This places the ultimate restriction on the conductor and musicians. Humanistic interpretation is null and void; suggested imagery must be put to one side. The rule here is to play it as it stands to the finite point. Maurice Le Roux cultivates no disorder. He makes certain the score is translated into sound exactly as demanded. In its way, therefore, this equals a brilliant performance.

Syrmos for Eighteen Strings (1959)

☐ Ars Nova Ensemble of Radio O.R.T.F. / Constant (conductor) / Candide 31049

A series of a variety of textures and densities, based on ascending patterns, descending ones, combinations of these, multi-polyphonicized pizzicati, glissandi, *col legno* percussions, and more. It is not so designated but certainly *Syrmos* ("Chain of Events") is a blood relative of *Pithoprakta* (*see above*).

The eighteen strings are six each of first and second violins, four cellos, and two double basses. One can take for granted that the performance is absolute.

Hérma (1961)

Instrumental

Piano

☐ Takahashi (piano) / Mainstream 5000

A musical complex of vivid disjunction, verily violent disjunction, with the disorder actually creating its own sense of order. This is no paradox, since *Hérma* ("Foundation") lives in a world of atomicized sound events, its actions ruled by acute mathematical computerizationlike keyboard solutions.

It is strongly urged not to read Xenakis's liner note. It uses a substratum of language with a meaning that will be forever hidden. Such prosodic hocus-pocus does Xenakis no good.

Eonta (1964)

Chamber Music

☐ Paris Instrumental Ensemble for Contemporary Music / Takahashi (piano) / Simonovic (conductor) / Vanguard C–10030

Eonta is described by Nicolas Slonimsky as the "neuter plural of the present participle of the verb 'to be' in the Ionian dialect, the title being in Cypriot syllabic characters of Creto-Mycenean origin"). The scoring is a sextet for piano, two trumpets, and three tenor trombones. This homage to Parmenides includes stereophonic disposition of the brass, which move about in three different positions in relation to the piano. The brass have an ever-increasing rhythmic involvement, from simple, five-part sustained entry, to dynamic variation (each voice retaining its same pitch), to increasing density via flutter-tonguing, and finally in total five-part dissociation. While the piano maintains its rhythmic fixity it eventually is eliminated—the final measures are for unified non-rhythmic brass.

Xenakis's technique is such as to mark him a left-winger within the avant-garde. The sounds are seemingly ripped from the guts of electronic machines, but are actually produced by traditional instruments (though hardly played in a traditional manner). *Eonta* demands virtuosity plus, and the group responds dynamically and without strain.

Nuits (1968)

Choral

Chorus Alone

☐ Robin, Prevet, and Legendre (sopranos); Friedmann, Pudleitner, and Kerguelen (contraltos); Oudot, Cotton, and Le Mee (tenors); Guigui, Chauvaut, and Haniotis (basses) / Courand (conductor) / Musical Heritage Society MHS-1187

Xenakis's *Nuits* is written for twelve unaccompanied voices, precisely divided into three each for soprano, contralto, tenor, and bass. Tension is constant in this music that contrasts sharply percussive chants with wails, glides, and motion of the massed voices. Linear polyphonic conditions are entirely absent—vertical sound groups prevail. *Nuits* certainly will not charm the ear but it will not fail to hold a listener's attention simply because of its unique and dramatic vocal structuring.

The performance requirements are terrifying. However, the twelve members of the Chorus of the O.R.T.F. give a splendid rendition of the score. Such high level of unaccompanied singing is rare, and emphatic credit is due Colette Brullebaut who prepared the chorus.

Chorus and Instrumental Ensemble

Medea for Men's Chorus, Galets, and Orchestra (1967)

☐ Ars Nova Ensemble and Men's Chorus of Radio O.R.T.F. / Constant (conductor) / Candide 31049

This is a suite taken from the music Xenakis wrote for a production of *La Médée de Sénèque*. Its violent starkness (the orchestra consists of an E flat clarinet, contra bassoon, trombone, cello, and percussion—predominantly low-timbred, it will be noted) is backed by glissandi, smacking of galets (pebbles), while the chorus functions principally as a reciting body. Ritual demeanor, almost ugly in its snarling sibilation, dominates the work. The word, which are sometimes sung but mostly chanted in recitation style, are not indicated (no text is supplied with the recording).

Credit in the orchestra must go to the double bassoonist. A more ugly set of sounds has never been called for and whoever it is who produces them deserves plaudits. The chorus shows fine ensemble but its diction is totally blurred.

Oresteia (1966)

☐ Ars Nova Ensemble, Stéphane Caillat Vocal Ensemble, and Maîtrise de Notre-Dame de Paris / Constant (conductor) / Musical Heritage Society MHS-1200

A suite for twelve instrumentalists, mixed chorus, and children's choir, drawn from the music Xenakis wrote for a production of Aeschylus's tragedy *Oresteia*. The aesthetic contemplation is of a neoprimitivism that includes chanting, speaking, shouting, and vocal percussions, with a minor amount of descriptive vocalizing. The chorus also is a source for percussion, playing some of the instruments as extensions of the orchestral percussion, which includes such rarities as musical glasses, sirens, whips, metallic streamers, and rattles. There are no vibrant melodic sections (tonal or atonal) or even dabs in this almost brutal music, which needs no Klytemnaestra emoting on stage to achieve total effect. All-powerful, all-harsh, all-dark violence emerges from these sounds.

Xenakis is credited with the "artistic direction" of the production, so that there is absolute positiveness to the recording. Listening is extremely heavy going for the music's total fifty minutes. However, as continuity is not overly important, sections within the three parts (*Agamemnon*, *Choephores* [*Libation Bearers*], and *Eumenides*) can be sampled without artistic harm.

Electronic Music

Bohor I (1962)   Diamorphoses II (1957)
Concret P-H II (1958)   Orient-Occident III (1960)

☐ Nonesuch 71246

Xenakis's electro-acoustic music is conceived at the most serious level. The sound sources for tape transposition may be picturesque (a Laotian mouth organ and Oriental jewelry for *Bohor I,* as an example), but there is complete avoidance of the obvious, the didactic (the "etude" concept, which has plentiful representation in the electronic music catalogue), and the light-faceted miniature. And length goes with earnestness. Though two of these compositions are short—*Concret P–H II* (2:38) and *Diamorphoses II* (6:49)—*Orient-Occident III* runs over eleven minutes, and *Bohor I* covers a solid twenty-two minutes.

The twittering quality that marks *Concret* (a perfect and honest title) is the result of using burning charcoal as the sound source, then splicing little pieces of tape and mixing sounds to obtain a variety of densities. *Concrète* materials are also basic to the other works, the most dramatic being *Orient-Occident III.* Though Xenakis makes impressive philosophical statements about his work, they need not be considered to appreciate the specialness of his electronic music beatitudes.

Y

Yehuda Yannay   (1937-   )

Dawn and Departure   *Choral*

☐ Ineluctable Modality / Howell (flute); Zonn (clarinet); Farrell (cello); Maddox (piano); Siwe (percussion) / London (conductor) / Advance FGR–18S

Dawn is unaccompanied, and accordingly quieter and more settled than the second part. The latter is sustained by the internal force of fluctuating sound patterns, intensified by extreme registral contrast. Of course, sensations rather than subjects cover every area of Yannay's work.

Chorus and Instrumental Ensemble

Elie Yarden   (1923-   )

Divertimento (1963)   *Chamber Music*

☐ Contemporary Chamber Players of the University of Chicago / Shapey (conductor) / Composers Recordings 302

The odd instrumentation of Yarden's piece (flute, clarinet, string quartet, and two pianos) was a stipulation of a commission given him by the Israel Chamber Music Association. Most of the material has a balletic character (not squarely pulsed, however); the tonal plan is extremely fluid, matching the composition's personality. Most striking are the phrase successions, seemingly disconnected, but forming a fantasylike proportion of continuity.

Richard Yardumian   (1917-   )

Passacaglia, Recitatives, and Fugue (a Concerto for Piano and Orchestra)   *Solo Instrument and Orchestra*

☐ Royal Philharmonic Orchestra / Ogdon (piano) / Buketoff (conductor) / RCA LSC–3243

Yardumian's Concerto is colorfully designed (twenty variations in the first part, a kind of enlarged chamber-music setting in the middle movement, and a dynamic finale). It also colorfully utilizes a modal interweave and folkloric melodic turns. It doesn't mince matters—it is a fiendishly difficult piece for the pianist. John Ogdon is a fervent exponent and is partnered solidly by the orchestra.

Piano

Pietro Yon   *(1886-1943)*

Instrumental   ***The Primitive Organ***

Organ   ☐ Prince-Joseph (organ) / Everest 3156

A whimsical sketch imitating the rudimentary type of the instrument by repetitive figurations. It makes sense and makes its effect.

Eugène Ysaÿe   *(1858-1931)*

*Solo
Instrument
and
Orchestra*   **Chant d'hiver for Violin and Orchestra, Op. 15**

Violin   ☐ Orchestra of Radio Luxembourg / Rosand (violin) / de Froment (conductor) / Candide 31054

Ysaÿe's "Song of Winter" has a continuity of lyrical invention, one phrase blending into the next. The expressive power is entrancing, its effect not disturbed by a considerable amount of chromatic synonyms. The intensity and color (especially in the concluding part) provide musical poetry at its most poignant point.

Rosand's tone is entirely unforced. He projects the solo part in relation to the small orchestral partnership (two each of woodwinds and horns, plus timpani and strings) with elegancy and sensitivity. There is no doubt that this is an impressive recording.

Instrumental   **Sonata for Cello Solo, Op. 28**

Cello   ☐ Sylvester (cello) / Desto 7169

A sense of threnodic darkness pervades the work. Except for the finale, three of the four movements are in the slower tempo range. The recitativelike third part (mostly in the low register) is in contrast to the previous movement, colored by pizzicato indentions. Pedal formations are prime in the *Allegro tempo fermo* music that completes the opus.

Sylvester's musicianship and acute control of phrasing are evidences of his special abilities. He deserves thanks for making available a definitive realization of a fresh-sounding, productive contribution to the restricted output of compositions for unaccompanied cello.

Violin   ***Lointain passé***

☐ Kennedy (violin); Kin (piano) / Orion 72106

Not much of Ysaÿe is on disc, so that every little bit is welcome. The young violinist plays this *morceau* with large tone and keeps matters in good perspective.

***Rêve d'enfant*, Op. 14**

☐ Grumiaux (violin); Varsi (piano) / Philips 6500814

Dreamy but moving music. Beautifully phrased in this very expressive performance.

Sonata (*Ballade*) in D minor for Solo Violin, Op. 27, No. 3
Sonata in G major for Solo Violin, Op. 27, No. 5

☐ Granat (violin) / Orion 73128

The *Ballade* is the most famous of Ysaÿe's set of six Sonatas for unaccompanied violin.

It has a fine sweep of material resembling improvisation, but a special motive binds the work. The discipline required by the constricted medium made no interference with Ysaÿe's creativity. This is exciting music, show-off time for the instrument but without negating beauty and artistic meaning. How different from the mechanistic run-offs or intellectual twaddle produced by so many composers when they turn to writing for an unaccompanied string instrument!

In all frankness, the G major work—consisting of two movements, *L'Aurore* and *Danse rustique*—is a second-class citizen compared to the *Ballade*. It has some of the mechanical writing mentioned above. However, the dance portion has more interest and contains sufficient technical tobogganing to get a passing grade.

Only strong violinists can cope with these Sonatas, the main problem being not only the technique demanded but the need for tone color range and expressive variety. Endre Granat is superb. He plays with consummate brilliance and displays a musical understanding and spontaneity that are thrilling.

Isang Yun   (1917-   )

Loyang for Chamber Ensemble (1962)

Orchestra

☐ Members of the West German Radio Symphony Orchestra, Cologne / Zender (conductor) / Wergo 60034

Rich with free-ordered music, with plentiful evidence of a patina of exoticism. The score calls for four woodwinds, harp, violin, cello, and a percussion contingent comprising vibraphone, deep bowl bells, tam-tam, drums, cymbals, triangle, and whip.

The performance heard represents a taping made during a radio broadcast in Cologne, in 1967. It gives a good yield.

Réak for Full Orchestra (1966)

☐ Symphony Orchestra of the Southwest German Radio, Baden-Baden / Bour (conductor) / Wergo 60034

Festive, hymnic music, with considerable compacted wind qualities. This is a transmutation of the character of the *seng hwang*, the mouth organ that was basic to the ceremonial music of ancient Korea. The music is structured as a continuity—there is practically no rhythmic glue to hold it together.

The recording was made at the premiere performance (October 23, 1966, at the Donaueschingen *Musiktagen*).

Tuyaux sonores for Organ (1967)

Instrumental

Organ

☐ Zacher (organ) / Wergo 60034

Clusters cross-clustered by other clusters are the principal unifications in Yun's "Sounding Pipes." No hot debate exists between subjects, since there are none. Designed form is foreign to this music; its form is the result of frictionized complexes that move from one to the next within the sound environment.

Gerd Zacher (who plays from a graphically notated score) is a master of this style of organ music. The realization is an exciting one, approved by the composer.

Gasa (1963)

Chamber Music

☐ Zukofsky (violin); Kalish (piano) / Mainstream MS-5016

Gasa is the Korean word for an epic song. Arioso qualities exist in the work but in a nervous, somewhat violent state. Such song type is generally performed in its native surroundings by a deep female voice together with a flute and a drum. In the transfer to a string and keyboard instrumental combine the focus of the musical debate is on instrumental detonation rather than pseudovocalization.

Yun's *Gasa* was first recorded (by Saschko Gawriloff, violin, and Bernhard Kontarsky, piano) on Wergo 2549010. The honors belong to Zukofsky–Kalish, who produce more dynamism, are more precise, and therefore are more believable.

Musik für sieben Instrumente (1959)

☐ Hamann (violin); Palm (cello); Otto (flute); Nordbruch (oboe); Irmisch (clarinet); Franke (bassoon); Lind (horn) / Travis (conductor) / Mainstream 5006

Three movements residing in snug Schoenbergian territory. This is an example of dodecaphonic traditionalism.

Eugene Zador   *(1894-1977)*

Contrasts for Orchestra (1964)   *Orchestra*

☐ Budapest Radio Symphony / Ferencsik (conductor) / Orion ORS-7279

Zador's orchestral piece has all the requisite formal clarity, with special confirmation in each of the four parts. Thus: a stylized peasant dance in the third movement, a fugue in the following movement. However, it is the manner of communication rather than the communication itself that powers *Contrasts*. Zador's orchestration shows the virtuoso he is when he puts pen on score paper. Included are keen passages for the piano and a wonderful use of the accordion.

The performance is the best of the few Zador orchestral works that have been recorded. It has zest and decided musicianship. It also reflects proper enthusiasm.

Hungarian Caprice (1934)

☐ Frankenland State Symphony / Kloss (conductor) / Orion ORS-7279

Over one thousand performances have been given of this *Ungarisches Capriccio!* Certainly it deserves a better rendition than heard here. However, the composition's value must override the shortcomings of the recording. Zador's music has multitudinous tempo shifts amidst a profusion of dance tunes and toccata propulsions. It's a real nationalistic winner.

Studies for Orchestra (1970)

☐ Westphalian Symphony Orchestra / Freeman (conductor) / Orion 74140

Zador's imaginative powers of orchestration were one of his strongest points, and here in eight essays is proof. Highlights: the pizzicato play and the wooden-timbred glides that color the Capriccio, the jazz chart defined in the Song, and the clever forward-backward design covering the pitches, rhythms, orchestration, and dynamics of the *Crescendo-Decrescendo* movement. These and more are guarantees that a listener will hang on to every sound. There isn't a dull measure in the piece.

The Westphalians are not the most brilliant organization on the scene but they manage capably. There are further illuminations to be discovered in Zador's conception, but that would require a major-league orchestral team. These remarks do not deny Paul Freeman's full command of the score.

Variations on a Hungarian Folksong (1918)

☐ Frankenland State Symphony / Schönherr (conductor) / Orion ORS-7279

The set of variations is based on a soldier's song popular in Hungary during World War I. All the shapes of the music's divisions are Hungarian in style, including the concluding fugato. One wishes the performance was better, since the composition has such exemplary workmanship and colorful orchestration.

String Orchestra

Divertimento for Strings (1954)

☐ Frankenland State Symphony / Kloss (conductor) / Orion ORS–7279

A tasteful string-orchestra conception, ending with a rare fugue type, one that retains the Hungarian diction of the preceding portions.

Chamber Music

Duo-Fantasy for Two Cellos and Piano

☐ Gabor and Peter Rejto (cellos); Alice Rejto (piano) / Orion 7282

Zador's work represents the use of a medium for which there exists an extremely small amount of literature—thus it is doubly welcome. (It was originally for two cellos with strings, harp, and timpani; Zador then made this second, but definitive version.)

Though purely formal in conception as a whole, it contains tangible evidence of Zador's Hungarian heritage. This is not only in the specific *Scherzo hungarico* indication of movement 2, but in the neutrally designated *Rondo allegro*.

Brass Quintet (1973)

☐ Modern Brass Quintet / Orion 74140

Zador wrote solid romantic music, unpretentious but with full command of instrumentational discriminations. Everything he produced sounded well, was never controversial, had no digressive effects, but always stimulating. Such persuasive and intelligent creative advocacy applies to the five-movement Brass Quintet, which is touched, as usual, with some nationalistic (Hungarian) intimations. It is well executed in this recording.

Wind Quintet (1972)

☐ Los Angeles Wind Quintet / Orion 73126

One can trust that the mixture of romantic sympathy and Hungarian melorhythms will be present in Zador's music. Such effective partnership is available in this fine sculpted work.

Zador's text receives a well-prepared performance, save that suprisingly the Los Angeles five are not always in full agreement in their pitch definition, especially in unison doublings.

Luigi Zaninelli   (1932-   )

Chamber Music

Dance Variations

☐ American Woodwind Quintet / Golden Crest S–4075

The permutations are a Duet, a Waltz, a Polka, and a March. As expected, a good-natured air covers all the proceedings. These follow a neoclassic agenda but could as well fill a balletic one.

The playing is exemplary; the full-toned confidence makes for a delight in wind quintet sonorities.

Alexander Zarzycki *(1834-1895)*

Mazurka in G major, Op. 26

☐ David Oistrakh (violin); Yampolsky (piano) / Monitor 2003 (monaural)

A tuneful and tidy tidbit by which this Polish pianist-composer retains his place in the violin repertory. Deserving.

Instrumental

Violin

Jan Dismas Zelenka *(1679-1745)*

Lamentationes Jeremiae Prophetae (Nos. 1, 2, 4, and 5)

☐ Ars Rediviva / Casei (alto); Altmeyer (tenor); Berman (bass) / Munclinger (conductor) / Nonesuch 71282

Zelenka's "Lamentations" were written for the office of matins on Thursday, Friday, and Saturday of Holy Week and represent one of the most important works in his large output of sacred music. There are six parts to the composition, four of which are here recorded (not in exact numerical sequence, the order being 1-2-5-4). Each Lamentation is for a different solo voice: Nos. 1 and 4 for bass, No. 2 for alto, and No. 5 for tenor; among the instruments and continuo the oboe is featured in No. 4.

Strong contrasts and sharp definition of the texts are involved. This music represents a strong creative voice that speaks with rich polyphonic phrases and splendid harmonic resource that symbolize the emotional meanings of each Lamentation.

The styling in the performance is assured, the singing eloquent, and the playing is of excellence. Nonesuch's transfer of the original Supraphon production is of the highest standard. This is an issue well worth investigating.

Cantata and Oratorio

Karl Ziehrer *(1843-1922)*

Wiener Burger, Op. 419

☐ Johann Strauss Orchestra of Vienna / Boskovsky (conductor) / Angel S-36887

No error in the opus number! Ziehrer produced close to six hundred dances and marches for orchestra, plus almost two dozen operettas. The *Wiener Burger* waltz set is a meaty affair and is played with interpretative perceptivity—that is, the usual authenticity of a Willi Boskovsky production.

Orchestra

Ziehrer / **Max Schönherr (1903-   )**

Hereinspaziert! Waltz, Op. 518

☐ Vienna Philharmonic / Boskovsky (conductor) / London 6791

Most waltz and polka titles are simply window dressing, though some designations are linked to the special organizations or occasions for which they were composed. A few carry out—more but mainly less—the music's superscription (for example, Strauss's *Studenten* Polka, which lightly kicks around the celebrated student song *Gaudeamus*). Thus, *Herein-*

Orchestra

spaziert!, which is the cry of a barker at a country fair or carnival, promises a rather boisterous set of waltz melodies, but turns out to embrace the patented tuny swing and sway of the genre. That is sufficient for a successful entry in the waltz catalogue.

With Willi Boskovsky conducting and the Vienna Phil. in the groove, every measure's beauty is fulfilled. Joy to the ears.

Marilyn J. Ziffrin   (1926-   )

Instrumental

Four Pieces for Tuba

Tuba

☐ Cummings (tuba) / Crystal S–391

Appropriate moods that give required contrast mark this suite. In turn, these are moderately proclamatory, toccatalike, a Largo lyrical movement (the longest of the set), and a dance-shaped conception. Ziffrin shows a fine ear for the color and grammar that fit the rarity of unaccompanied tuba music. The same success pertains to the performance.

Bernd Alois Zimmermann   (1918-1970)

Orchestra

Jazz Episode from Act II, Scene 2 of *Die Soldaten* (1964)

Ode to Eleutheria in the form of Death Dances from *Die Befristeten* (1967)

☐ Manfred School Quintet / Wergo 2549005

The Ode is also jazz as conceived by Zimmermann, its material fragmented, the climate cool. In the Jazz Episode (from Zimmermann's four-act Opera) the temperature is heated and the activity constant. In both instances, improvisational style is paramount.

Die Befristeten ("The Numbered") was a radio play. The piece recorded is a compositional continuation of the music used in the play. (Wergo's cover describes this work differently: "Ode to Freedom in the form of a Dance of Death.")

Solo Instrument and Orchestra

Concerto for Violin and Orchestra (1950)

Violin

☐ Orchestra of Radio Luxembourg / Lautenbacher (violin) / Köhler (conductor) / Candide 31061

Some dodecaphonic procedures apply here, but principally Zimmermann's Concerto leans heavily on pantonal assistance. There is, therefore, a neoclassic style to the piece (Nicolas Slonimsky, in a note on the work, mentions a "spiritual manner"). The interpolative use of the *Dies Irae* subject is to be noted.

Chamber Music

***Intercomunicazione* for Cello and Piano (1967)**

☐ Palm (cello); Kontarsky (piano) / Deutsche Grammophon 137008

Music that is like a married couple living apart and rarely in touch with one another. The cello has long torporific and drony passages, mixed with quarter tones, pulseless in its spread. The piano supplies short *non sequitur* inserts. While the music is fatigued with passivity there is no doubt that the unbiased listener, if patient, will fall under its spell, even if later he is not convinced that he should have been.

The playing is excellent. Palm and Kontarsky ovecome all of the score's challenges flawlessly.

Présence (1961)

☐ Gawriloff (violin); Palm (cello); Kontarsky (piano) / Deutsche Grammophon 137008

Any one of three categories fits this piece. Its instrumentation places it in the chamber-music field; its alternate title (*Concerto scénique* for Violin, Cello, and Piano), with the pertinent brilliant individuality of the scoring, could find proper listing as a triple (unaccompanied) concerto. Finally, its use as a ballet (the work is subtitled *Ballet blanc en cinq scènes*), first produced by the Ballet of the Stuttgart State Opera, brings the third classification.

Zimmermann's work is assembled both as an ensemble conception and as a piece of trinal individuality. It is both absolute and semiprogrammatic music. It contrasts fluidity with corrugated textures. Above all it is a collage that combines a variety of styles and relationships, including some quotations, mainly from Strauss's *Don Quixote*.

The last occurs because in the five scenes of the work each instrument delineates a literary character: the Don from Cervantes, Molly Bloom from Joyce, and Roi Ubu from Jarry. There are no previous musical themes for the last two but their personalities are conveyed in a general fashion, with arrogant clusters for Ubu and a wanton sinuosity for Molly Bloom.

Zimmermann's propositions hit home regardless of how one categorizes his work. Considered descriptive or not, it is a startling conception for the piano trio medium. What a performance it receives! Not surprisingly, of course, when one realizes that Siegfried Palm is the cellist and Aloys Kontarsky the pianist. These are big-league stars in the avant-garde performance field. Saschko Gawriloff belongs with them. The engineering is marvelous.

Tratto: **for Electronic Sounds in the Form of a Choreographic Study**

Electronic Music

☐ Wergo 2549005

Austere. Zimmermann's objectives are quite clear but are responsive only to an etudelike emphasis on similar sonorous persistence. All the parts of *Tratto* are but parts of one stupendous whole.

(Wergo does not indicate whether this tape piece is *Tratto I* [composed in 1966], or *Tratto II* [composed in 1968].)

Frederick Zinos (1942-   )

Elegy for Tuba and Piano

Instrumental

☐ Cummings (tuba); Moore (piano) / Crystal S–391

Tuba

A music of meditative lyricism, providing a productive contribution to tuba literature. The performers bring out its inventive sensibilities.

Domenico Zipoli (1688-1726)

Gavotte in B minor

Instrumental

Largo in B minor

Harpsichord

☐ Goldstein (harpsichord) / Pandora 101

Authentically styled performances of examples drawn from the work of this Italian organist-composer. The instrument is tuned in mean-tone temperament, wherein enharmonic equivalence does not take place. The performance is finely crafted.

Suite in C major

☐ Sgrizzi (harpsichord) / Nonesuch 71117

Binary designs for the five movements: *Preludio, Allemanda, Sarabanda, Gavotta,* and *Giga.* The concept of changing the color completely on the repeat of sections is carried out consistently. Such contrast gives a dual (yet related) personality to each movement. Smooth playing and profitable articulations. And not a speck of academicism in the playing. Joy!

Toccata in D minor for Harpsichord

☐ Sgrizzi (harpsichord) / Nonesuch 73008

Textural clarity is the most positive part of this piece, though swatchlike patterns slightly lessen the strength of the fabric. Still, there is sufficient coloration to make a convincing total.

Mark Zuckerman (1948-   )

Instrumental

Flute

Paraphrases **(Flute Alone)**

☐ Winn (flute) / Composers Recordings S–342

Variations on a set of three ideas. The essay emphasizes registral differences, with grace notes and flutter-tonguing as special particulars. A serious consideration concerning light-weighted data, satisfactorily communicated by the soloist.

Ramon Zupko (1932-   )

Chamber Music

Fixations for Violin, Cello, Piano, and Tape (1974)

☐ Elan (violin); Bogatin (cello); Thomas (piano) / Sollberger (conductor) / Composers Recordings SD–375

A music of frenzy, despite a relaxed solo piano passage (there are solo cadenzas also for the other instruments as well as the tape). Zupko's *Fixations,* he states, deals with space, timbre, expanded tonality, and theatre (the last not possible, naturally, on a disc). Granting such premise, the effect is of a convulsed and tortured atmosphere (again, not cancelled by a section where a chillingly desiccated chorale is heard with and against the tape).

Gutsy invention, played with full capacity.

Electronic Music

Fluxus I for Electronic Sounds (1977)

☐ Composers Recordings SD–375

An illustration of what can be done with four parallel seventh chords, and pitch sequences derived from them, on a Moog synthesizer. Zupko's six minutes of Paganinish virtuosity and excitement is a slam-bang, gorgeous hunk of sound. A great deal of electronic music is technically, even architecturally first class. But only a minute fraction possesses the heat of this opus. Zupko's essay persuades one he has produced an electronic masterwork.

Menachem Zur   (1942-   )

Chants for Magnetic Tape (1974)

☐ Odyssey Y-34139

Zur's piece has restrained rhetoric, divided into units that he notes as "somewhat resembling a Gregorian chant." This diplomatic explanation is nullified by the bracing un-Gregorian sound shocks. This is well-pointed tape music, no matter how picturesquely it is described.

Electronic Music

KEY TO INDEX LISTINGS

The **record company** name begins each entry.

The first number in each entry, whether comprising numbers only or letters plus numbers, is always the **label number.**

The record label numbers are followed by a comma; all succeeding numbers are **page numbers.**

The order of record label numbers is arranged digit by digit, regardless of how many numbers in the label number; they are not in numerical order (e.g., Advance 15 and 16, since they start with "1," would precede Advance 3). Label numbers beginning with letters follow those with numbers only.

Unless followed by **"monaural"** all listings are stereo. Those label numbers ending in "E" have been **electronically reproduced for stereo.**

EXAMPLES

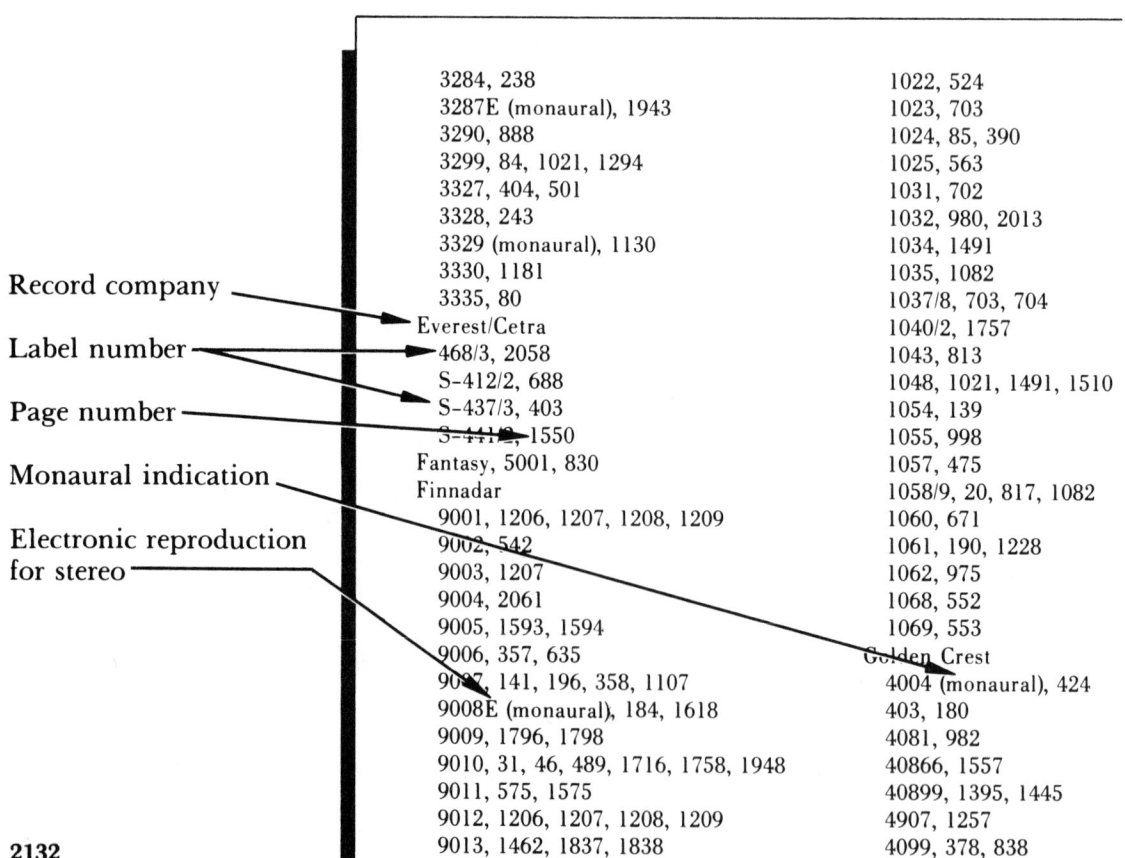

Record company

Label number

Page number

Monaural indication

Electronic reproduction
for stereo

3284, 238	1022, 524
3287E (monaural), 1943	1023, 703
3290, 888	1024, 85, 390
3299, 84, 1021, 1294	1025, 563
3327, 404, 501	1031, 702
3328, 243	1032, 980, 2013
3329 (monaural), 1130	1034, 1491
3330, 1181	1035, 1082
3335, 80	1037/8, 703, 704
Everest/Cetra	1040/2, 1757
468/3, 2058	1043, 813
S-412/2, 688	1048, 1021, 1491, 1510
S-437/3, 403	1054, 139
3-441/2, 1550	1055, 998
Fantasy, 5001, 830	1057, 475
Finnadar	1058/9, 20, 817, 1082
9001, 1206, 1207, 1208, 1209	1060, 671
9002, 542	1061, 190, 1228
9003, 1207	1062, 975
9004, 2061	1068, 552
9005, 1593, 1594	1069, 553
9006, 357, 635	Golden Crest
9007, 141, 196, 358, 1107	4004 (monaural), 424
9008E (monaural), 184, 1618	403, 180
9009, 1796, 1798	4081, 982
9010, 31, 46, 489, 1716, 1758, 1948	40866, 1557
9011, 575, 1575	40899, 1395, 1445
9012, 1206, 1207, 1208, 1209	4907, 1257
9013, 1462, 1837, 1838	4099, 378, 838

RECORD LABEL INDEX

ABC
  ATS-20007, 1135
  ATS-20010/3, 528
  ATS-20015/4, 527
  AX-67036/2, 58
Advance
  15, 142, 258, 733, 1691
  16, 962
  3 (monaural), 465, 1130, 1524, 2109
  4 (monaural), 354, 1013, 1607, 2083
  FGR-1 (monaural), 661, 942, 1126,
    1359, 1861, 2083
  FGR-18S, 1086, 1300, 1346, 1406,
    2074, 2121
  FGR-19S, 618, 1152, 1355, 2046
  FGR-2 (monaural), 405, 571, 1656,
    2048
  S-10, 40, 818
  S-14, 256, 2095
  S-6, 291, 1126, 1524
American Unicorn Records, LP-1037,
  1750
Angel
  35010, 1518
  35066 (monaural), 495
  35092 (monaural), 1250
  35136, 233
  35179, 1985
  35249 (monaural), 495
  3532 (monaural), 1826
  35437, 1178
  35441, 1202
  35462, 225
  35496 (monaural), 1822
  35547 (monaural), 1981, 1984, 1989
  3556 (monaural), 412
  35564, 1967
  35639, 2034, 2036
  35647, 1444
  3580, 1827
  3582 (monaural), 1321
  3585 (monaural), 1401
  37139, 207
  3806, 254
  3816, 604
  S-3168, 1053
  S-35407, 1247

S-35430, 1291
S-35445, 730
S-35458, 1735, 1738
S-35481, 271
S-35491, 827, 830
S-35511, 150
S-3552, 1974
S-35538, 524
S-3555, 1279
S-35567, 1442, 1460
S-3559, 1550
S-35629, 1159, 1669
S-3563, 1827
S-35636, 1067
S-35638, 792
S-3567, 1320
S-35681, 2035, 2041
S-35730, 1162
S-35740, 1881
S-35775, 599, 718, 1215, 1529, 1932
  1944
S-3579, 1894
S-35833, 414
S-35853, 146
S-35932, 555, 1390
S-35937, 591, 719, 1220, 1530
S-35945, 1242
S-35947, 2023, 2024
S-35952, 1960
S-35953, 1392, 1400
S-3599, 80
S-35993, 1391, 1392
S-36005, 1584
S-36011, 693
S-36016, 1376
S-36036, 941, 1005, 1548, 1659
S-36043, 576, 577
S-36044, 1642
S-36045, 1096
S-3605, 1280
S-36050, 892, 1992
S-36055, 59
S-36059, 357, 1487
S-36069, 1873
S-36079, 1073, 1910
S-36080, 738, 981, 1155, 1491, 1783,
  1877

S-36091, 772
S-36093, 1767
S-36094, 1873
S-3610, 2021, 2022
S-36101, 578, 579
S-36104, 1673, 1674
S-36111, 1458, 1460
S-36120, 576
S-36121, 1401
S-36125, 1973
S-36127, 1654
S-36128, 1242, 1246
S-36129, 1246
S-36150, 1644
S-36175, 698
S-36183, 1247
S-36192, 239
S-36195, 1942
S-36214, 716
S-36216, 1246
S-3622, 716
S-36234, 278, 282
S-3624, 286
S-36241, 1273
S-3625, 171
S-36261, 1396, 1397
S-36269, 31
S-36285, 507, 510
S-36289, 1241, 1242, 1243
S-36290, 1371
S-3633, 1290
S-36330, 579
S-36338, 579
S-36347, 1825
S-36353, 1668
S-36357, 776
S-36364, 791
S-3639, 1590
S-3640, 1654
S-36403, 578, 579
S-36415, 131, 506, 507, 897
S-36418, 584
S-36420, 855
S-36421, 1393
S-36424, 154, 155
S-36430, 1253

Angel (*cont.*)
S-36438, 110, 111
S-36439, 245
S-36441, 1649
S-3645, 688
S-36453, 1641
S-36469, 1961, 1964
S-36478, 1959
S-36480, 1619
S-36484, 831
S-36489, 1736
S-3649, 1973
S-36496, 689
S-36505, 205, 1466
S-3651, 1282
S-36519, 1391
S-36529, 1652
S-36531, 730
S-36532, 1959
S-36544, 278
S-36547, 1113
S-36557, 1959
S-3657, 760
S-36577, 9, 1148
S-36580, 793, 1215
S-36582, 796, 1251
S-36586, 645, 1395, 1397
S-36588, 504, 506, 511
S-36590, 1968
S-3660, 581
S-36602, 1394
S-36605, 109
S-36625, 1961, 1963
S-36642, 1669
S-3667, 1315
S-36696, 170
S-36713, 1600, 1601
S-36719, 2038
S-3672, 600, 718
S-36727, 151
S-36751, 1968
S-36756, 503, 509
S-36773, 1969
S-36775, 170
S-36786, 1955
S-36788, 303
S-36796, 1113
S-36799, 1958, 1970
S-35803, 724, 730
S-36806, 1710
S-3682, 1856
S-36839, 1457
S-36840, 1251
S-36860, 1332
S-36861, 2040
S-36869, 1242, 1243
S-36870, 504, 506
S-36874, 493
S-36879, 2020
S-36883, 297, 511, 856, 1432, 1969,
    2037

S-36887, 996, 1033, 1803, 1804,
    1811, 1813, 2127
S-36892, 1255, 1256
S-36897, 367, 396
S-36898, 367
S-36899, 725, 1670
S-36902, 1952
S-36903, 2087
S-36915, 1244
S-36917, 1446, 1447, 1448, 1449,
    1450
S-36920, 322
S-36921, 326
S-36937, 413, 648
S-36949, 1348, 1349, 1350
S-36950, 1348, 1350, 1351
S-36951, 268
S-36953, 1616
S-36954, 1440
S-36956, 1034, 1205, 1816, 1817
S-36962, 313, 1424
S-36963, 321, 1162
S-36964, 1724
S-36972, 1967, 1968
S-36973, 1820
S-36980, 1721
S-36995, 1581
S-36996, 401, 637, 1234, 1899, 2054
S-36997, 321, 323
S-36998, 2023
S-36999, 997
S-37001, 2035, 2036, 2037
S-37003, 1310
S-37004, 1823
S-37008, 1210
S-37011, 510
S-37014, 111
S-37016, 1171, 1172
S-37018, 1878
S-3702, 1429
S-37042, 1528
S-37043, 1680
S-37045, 561
S-3705, 760
S-37060, 1819
S-37064, 500, 501
S-37068, 490
S-37069, 562
S-37077, 613
S-37081, 1829, 1834
S-37084, 1415
S-37086, 162, 1824
S-37089, 1581
S-37091, 1407
S-37096, 402
S-37097, 2021, 2022
S-37098, 2021, 2023
S-37106, 1734
S-37109, 1726
S-37115, 1840, 1841
S-37118, 394, 1460, 1584

S-37119, 212, 306, 307, 309
S-37120, 1440
S-37124, 491, 499
S-37125, 1077
S-37137, 1671
S-37140, 505
S-37141, 1352
S-37142, 296
S-37146, 554, 1097
S-37147, 1459
S-37149, 1461
S-37150, 1459
S-37152, 854, 855, 860
S-37168, 1159
S-37170, 203
S-37178, 524
S-3719, 333
S-37193, 793
S-37194, 891
S-37208, 2031, 2032
S-37236, 508
S-37260, 1441
S-37262, 508
S-37266, 153, 154
S-37281, 1370, 1371
S-37300, 1914
S-37315, 1911
S-37317, 1191, 1204
S-3738, 1172
S-3739, 1962, 1967
S-37409, 339
S-37411, 972
S-37412, 1159
S-37439, 1984, 1985
S-37442, 1192
S-3747, 410
S-3748, 2058
S-37484, 1981
S-3749, 245
S-3752, 151
S-37534, 1251
S-37538, 147
S-3756, 939
S-3760, 1109, 1113
S-3782, 1429
S-3788, 1894
S-3789, 1256
S-3790, 1813
S-3791, 1974
S-3802, 1424
S-3816, 34, 552, 756, 757
S-3823, 158
S-3825, 2026
SB-3836, 170
SB-3838, 272, 286
SBLX-3863, 1051
SBLX-3877, 1135
SC-3842, 1172
SCLX-3832, 1135
SCLX-3850, 1976
SELX-3818, 2028

SR-3853, 1180
SX-3809, 1976
SX-3812, 1894
SX-3822, 1969
Arch, S-1760, 880, 1364, 1989
Argo
5234, 67
5325, 808
5326, 36, 652, 670, 1700
5339, 1181
5340, 306
5447, 1181
5448, 1981, 2037
5498, 780, 781, 793
5BBA-1013/5, 300, 1182
S-506, 1548
ZDA-19/20, 1920, 1923
ZDA-206, 932
ZNF-1, 311
ZRG-503, 1070, 1071
ZRG-505, 1357, 2010
ZRG-512, 858, 859
ZRG-515, 808
ZRG-5226, 350
ZRG-523, 326, 498, 1186, 1631
ZRG-527, 1655
ZRG-5277, 301, 302
ZRG-529, 2093
ZRG-5320, 1777
ZRG-5329, 1105, 2039
ZRG-5340, 88, 878, 901, 1322, 1923,
  1966, 2039
ZRG-535, 1921, 1922, 1923
ZRG-536, 1140, 1469
ZRG-5369, 758
ZRG-5398, 1335, 1336
ZRG-541, 758
ZRG-542, 808
ZRG-5420, 1472, 1475, 1495
ZRG-5424, 304, 305, 306, 307
ZRG-5440, 305, 306, 309
ZRG-5442, 753, 754
ZRG-5448, 737, 961
ZRG-5457, 19, 396, 651, 705, 738
ZRG-5489, 1469
ZRG-5494, 1219
ZRG-5495, 860
ZRG-5497, 858, 859, 860
ZRG-553, 670, 1468
ZRG-554, 1248
ZRG-558, 489
ZRG-563, 758
ZRG-569, 249, 1171
ZRG-571, 284, 285
ZRG-572, 532, 535, 571, 572, 852
ZRG-573, 578, 579
ZRG-574, 136
ZRG-577, 34, 47, 48, 49
ZRG-578, 1335, 1336, 1337
ZRG-584, 1884, 1892
ZRG-585, 606, 821, 1900

ZRG-594, 1245
ZRG-603, 526, 1548
ZRG-604, 1821
ZRG-605, 1160, 1162
ZRG-607, 509, 581
ZRG-620, 1979, 1980
ZRG-621, 878
ZRG-622, 1140
ZRG-631, 810
ZRG-632, 450
ZRG-633, 1182
ZRG-634, 811
ZRG-649, 2041
ZRG-650/1, 1184
ZRG-655, 36, 523, 593, 1592
ZRG-656, 465
ZRG-657, 108
ZRG-659, 347, 348, 349, 350, 2069
ZRG-662, 551, 1033, 1186, 1400
ZRG-663, 834
ZRG-664, 168
ZRG-665, 1184
ZRG-666, 1683, 1684, 1685, 1687
ZRG-674, 1835
ZRG-679, 1248
ZRG-680, 1921
ZRG-681, 548
ZRG-682, 2091, 2092
ZRG-685, 232
ZRG-686, 749, 751
ZRG-687/8, 54
ZRG-689, 1689
ZRG-690, 1337
ZRG-691, 849, 1875
ZRG-692, 937
ZRG-694, 1715
ZRG-699, 1185
ZRG-701, 670
ZRG-702, 1286, 1504, 1704, 1705
ZRG-703, 1185
ZRG-704, 178, 1287, 2092
ZRG-706, 1245
ZRG-710, 326
ZRG-711, 1425, 2037
ZRG-712, 1141
ZRG-713, 1862, 1863
ZRG-714, 295
ZRG-721, 1080
ZRG-724, 1434, 1435
ZRG-725, 2039, 2040
ZRG-727, 508, 509, 1420
ZRG-729, 1256
ZRG-731, 944, 1658
ZRG-732, 1965
ZRG-733/4, 2007
ZRG-735, 1036, 1037
ZRG-741, 334
ZRG-753, 1751
ZRG-754, 297, 1099, 1620
ZRG-755, 2071
ZRG-756, 266, 993, 1178

ZRG-757, 332, 479, 481, 2105
ZRG-758, 177, 702, 1142, 2093
ZRG-759, 222, 464, 2106
ZRG-767, 245
ZRG-768, 1605, 1606
ZRG-773/5, 444
ZRG-781, 568
ZRG-787, 550, 551
ZRG-790, 223
ZRG-791, 481, 482, 1713
ZRG-792, 934, 1821, 1854
ZRG-800/1, 2006
ZRG-803, 1826
ZRG-820, 57
ZRG-825, 1655
ZRG-837, 1897
ZRG-856, 931
ZRG-860, 339
Artia
102, 937
109, 936
Atlantic
S-1345, 1657
S-1359, 849, 1658
Audio Fidelity, 50027, 2007
Audio-Finishers, 74S100, 1783, 1784
Avakian, S-1 (monaural), 353, 354, 356,
  359, 361, 362
Avant
1001, 105, 319, 1542, 1613, 1941
1003, 365, 748, 816, 1007
1005, 319, 1613, 1941
1006, 330, 365, 405, 968
1008, 355, 357, 405, 1042, 1853
1009, 1041, 1970
1010, 29, 30
1011, 161
1012, 47, 263, 1862, 1870
1013, 486
1014, 1362, 1384, 1769, 2107
1015, 337, 388, 584, 608, 666, 1867
AV-1000, 720, 1453, 1592, 1595,
  1936
AV-1019, 1040, 1042
Bach Guild
5036, 69, 70
5043, 1933
5045, 1104
5048, 1898
5053, 796, 1235
70670, 71, 75
70678, 1997, 2009
70679, 1898, 1900, 1901
70696, 82
HM-11, 1687
HM-16, 1997, 2004
Barenreiter-Musicaphon, 30-1514/15,
  846
Bartók
303 (monaural), 125
307 (monaural), 106

Bartók (*cont.*)
   308 (monaural), 124
   310/311 (monaural), 124
   312 (monaural), 122, 123
   313 (monaural), 109
   901 (monaural), 120
   903 (monaural), 112
   904 (monaural), 121, 122, 988
   906 (monaural), 380
   907 (monaural), 118
   908 (monaural), 1702
   909 (monaural), 165
   914 (monaural), 122, 988, 989
   916 (monaural), 120
   922 (monaural), 119
   927 (monaural), 121, 988
   928 (monaural), 1118
BASF
   20330, 77
   20374, 1321
   21687, 759
   25122, 1321
   BC-22128, 1287, 1288, 1291
BIS
   LP-9, 1356
   LP-11, 1699, 1767
   LP-15, 1741, 1824, 1825
   LP-18, 1591, 1699
   LP-19, 1456, 1699, 1738, 1739
Boston Records, 411, 1013
Brewster
   1203 (monaural), 478
   1204, 542, 777, 962
   1216, 459, 887
Cambridge
   1804, 903, 904, 908, 909, 919, 920,
     921
   2823, 437, 810, 1700
Camden, 385, 1192
Candide
   31001, 1798
   31003, 332, 333
   31006, 621, 622
   31007, 1295
   31008, 1192, 1193, 1201
   31009, 1062
   31010, 1227, 1228
   31013, 1194, 1195, 1196
   31016, 374, 376
   31018, 1599
   31021, 480, 481, 1403
   31022, 1792, 1796
   31023, 1565
   31024, 498, 1601
   31027, 195
   31028, 1955, 1956, 1957
   31029, 31, 32
   31030, 1231, 1232, 1233
   31031, 1876
   31035, 1096, 1097, 1098
   31036, 678

31038, 1666, 1667
31040, 1694, 1696
31041, 1600
31042, 638
31043, 1774, 1775
31044, 826, 827, 848
31045, 20
31046, 1609, 1610
31049, 2116, 2117, 2118
31050, 1180
31054, 589, 878, 2122
31055, 1124
31056, 1518, 1886, 1895
31058, 824
31059, 545, 1558, 1709
31060, 2115, 2116
31061, 818, 2128
31064, 584, 878, 940
31065, 1123, 1124
31066, 392, 393
31069, 492
31070, 563
31071, 1349, 1350, 1351, 1352
31072, 1040, 1042, 1043
31073, 960, 1932
31076, 315, 703
31077, 986
31078, 13, 1491
31080, 1583
31084, 1909, 1910
31086, 175, 553, 2014
31091, 997, 2071
31092, 1153, 1154
31094, 543
31102, 1371
31116, 2041
CE-31057, 1564
QCE-31079, 1878
Cantate, 640217, 990
Capitol
   G-7121, 1414
   P-8125, 1633
   P-8147, 1984
   P-8355, 239, 241
   SP-8484, 1984
   SPBR-8477, 1332
Capra
   1201, 319, 428, 542, 1803, 2093
   1203, 428, 1047, 1572
   1204, 428, 459, 1524, 1572,
     1573
Caprice
   CAP-1006 (monaural), 244
   CAP-1024, 2077, 2096
   CAP-1026, 1768
   CAP-1034, 1295, 1306, 1596
   CAP-1051, 1541
   CAP-1054, 1309
   CAP-1061, 1311
   CAP-1069, 1345
   RIKS LP-65, 1972, 2088

CBS
   32210008, 1793
   73541, 213
Chrysalis, CHR-1110, 1795
Circle, L-51-101, 457
CMS/Oryx
   1002, 63
   1003, 62
   1702/3, 346
   1729, 268
   1803, 19, 20
   1820, 2097
   1826/7, 1549
   1830, 881, 1773
   23, 48
   3C-303, 346, 347, 1783
   3C-313, 1604
   3C-324, 284, 285
   40, 161, 680, 777
   55, 799
   EXP-24, 796
   EXP-55, 1235
Colosseum Records, CRLP-181/183,
   1757
Columbia
   121, 187
   196, 846
   232 (monaural), 2061
   4214, 1961
   4329, 1392
   4471, 1629
   5183, 297
   5244, 1632
   5667, 1554
   5746, 1558
   7479M, 1835
   8063 (monaural), 1396
   CL-671, 1424
   CL-671 (monaural), 981
   CO-4995, 937
   CS-8162, 1805, 1807
   D2S-720, 151, 275
   D3M-31525, 61
   D3M-32317, 2019, 2021, 2022, 2023,
     2024
   D3M-32988, 489, 490, 491, 492, 499
   D3M-32992, 2019, 2030
   D3M-33261, 1243, 1248
   D3M-33311, 1461, 1462
   D3M-33716, 755
   D3M-33720, 443, 473
   D3M-33724, 63
   D3S-705, 1850, 1851
   D3S-717, 120
   D3S-721, 1162, 1886
   D3S-725, 1669
   D3S-733, 61
   D3S-741, 273, 1161
   D3S-754, 60
   D3S-758, 271
   D3S-761, 1851

D3S-770, 1998, 1999
D3S-774, 1114
D3S-785, 1424, 1580, 1821
D3S-789, 1806, 1812
D3S-791, 486, 493, 1076, 1329,
   1888, 1890
D3S-806, 1678
D3S-813, 1440
D3S-818, 209, 696, 820, 1300, 1314,
   1498, 1547, 1755, 1856, 1857,
   1911, 2100
D5S-775, 1831, 1832, 1833, 1850
K364, 275
K3L-243 (monaural), 2072
K1-5175, 2074
KM-30492, 1112
KM-30648, 63
KM-32597, 213
KS-6371, 1671
M-30055, 1256
M-30064, 500
M-30066, 98, 261
M-30078, 155
M-30112, 1661
M-30113, 607, 1030, 1582
M-30114, 433
M-30230, 913, 914, 916
M-30231, 59, 60
M-30232, 1741
M-30293, 1302
M-30295, 1722
M-30296, 265
M-30304, 208, 213
M-30305, 1547
M-30306, 1067
M-30366, 790
M-30374, 431, 433
M-30375, 441, 442
M-30376, 440
M-30447, 1879, 1884
M-30448, 1291
M-30464, 1444
M-30516, 1829, 1830, 1831, 1834
M-30579, 1828, 1831, 1832, 1835,
   1843
M-30587, 203
M-30588, 207
M-30644, 241, 956
M-30645, 1066
M-30646, 790
M-30651, 1459
M-30683, 1853
M-30825, 681
M-30828, 325
M-30829, 1493
M-30937, 660
M-30943, 1768, 1815
M-30944, 118
M-31072, 57
M-31074, 1962
M-31075, 974, 1069

M-31124, 83, 1760, 1843, 1844,
   1845, 1849
M-31195, 1882
M-31241, 83, 1607
M-31307, 1722
M-31347, 58
M-31368, 124
M-31369, 1778
M-31371, 155
M-31512, 757
M-31620, 1694, 1696
M-31635, 1641
M-31640, 1547
M-31714, 432, 434
M-31727, 1882
M-31728, 1253
M-31729, 1829, 1830
M-31799, 202, 203
M-31800, 224
M-31806, 1424
M-31811, 154
M-31812, 1410
M-31814, 1254
M-31815, 820, 1547
M-31816, 595, 596
M-31817, 1755, 1756
M-31823, 429
M-31824, 735
M-31826, 1291
M-31830, 1850
M-31831, 1879
M-31835, 1162, 1886
M-31837, 1160
M-31840, 63
M-31841, 1831
M-31842, 1882
M-31844, 696, 896
M-31845, 414
M-31846, 583
M-31847, 1457
M-31848, 225
M-31921, 1832, 1850
M-31934, 407
M-31963, 1385, 1408
M-31997, 578
M-32040, 226, 728
M-32070, 1462
M-32132, 105
M-32159, 1458, 1460
M-32160, 263, 265
M-32162, 186
M-32173, 1255
M-32228, 279
M-32230, 2006
M-32232, 381, 1596
M-32233, 1820, 1822
M-32296, 2019, 2022
M-32299, 1672
M-32348, 1257, 1262
M-32350, 835
M-32596, 677, 1426, 2097

M-32599, 576
M-32685, 400
M-32735, 486
M-32736, 443
M-32737, 439, 441
M-32738, 375
M-32739, 467, 469
M-32741, 1853
M-32779, 1301
M-32780, 411
M-32781, 1578, 1579
M-32782, 423, 1789
M-32783, 964, 2033
M-32784, 443, 444
M-32791, 64
M-32792, 567
M-32809, 1841
M-32838, 1458, 1467
M-32853, 58
M-32873, 1459
M-32874, 108
M-32933, 63
M-32936, 577
M-32937, 1383
M-33082, 213
M-33201, 1833
M-33202, 422
M-33206, 1255
M-33207, 1161
M-33208, 1528, 1984
M-33233, 256
M-33266, 1267
M-33267, 809
M-33269, 435, 443
M-33310, 52, 84, 85
M-33431, 1311
M-33432, 89, 2082
M-33433, 1770, 1789, 2032
M-33434, 745
M-33506, 1134
M-33509, 169, 170, 171
M-33514, 1257
M-33523, 1467
M-33529, 1464
M-33532, 1111
M-33584, 576, 577, 578, 579
M-33586, 430, 431, 434
M-33932, 1644
M-33970, 599, 601
M-33999, 1847
M-34125, 1809
M-34128, 1878, 1884
M-34132, 190, 514, 667, 766, 1153,
   1912
M-34136, 234
M-34218, 154
M-34221, 674
M-34505, 1430
M-34508, 1332
M-34513, 558, 568
M-34537, 868, 869, 870, 873, 876

Columbia (*cont.*)
M-34545, 975
M-34552, 1954
M-34555, 1740
M-35079, 1834
M-35110, 1170
M-35117, 934
M-35125, 229, 262
M-35128, 256
M-35131, 2025
M-35144, 64
M2-30060, 1973
M2-30061, 1111, 1114
M2-30852, 187
M2-31008, 212
M2-31313, 1111
M2-32681, 1108
M2-32966, 379
M2-33303, 1633
M2-333594, 1636
M2-33444, 241, 382, 649, 1011, 1824
M2-33510, 59
M2-33971, 837, 838, 840
M2-34584, 1426
M2-34591, 1568, 1569, 1570
M2S-675, 1109
M2S-679, 1622, 1629, 1634, 1635
M2S-694, 1620, 1633
M2S-697, 63
M2S-698, 1110
M2S-699, 1065, 1067
M2S-709, 847, 1618, 1619, 1628,
    1630, 1631, 1632
M2S-722, 1721
M2S-728, 80
M2S-736, 1627, 1628
M2S-739, 1110
M2S-751, 1111
M2S-752, 288, 1621, 1630
M2S-760, 280
M2S-762, 1625, 1626, 1627, 1631,
    1632
M2S-764, 64
M2S-767, 1619, 1622, 1623, 1636
M2S-773, 807
M2S-780, 847, 1215, 1630, 1631,
    1632, 1636
M2X-787, 1242, 1459, 1546, 1755,
    1756
M2X-788, 154
M2X-795, 696, 1300, 1314
M3-30119, 498
M3-32973, 1454
M3-33581, 1624
M3-34211, 1134
M3-34581, 1624
M3S-710, 1848
M3S-750, 1974
M3S-776, 1110
M3X-31068, 259, 820, 902, 903,
    1580

M3X-31508, 689, 1528
M3X-31521, 254, 418, 652, 665,
    1295, 1345, 1453, 1545, 1763
M4-30540, 55
M4-32504, 903, 904, 909, 910, 917,
    918, 919, 920, 921, 922, 923, 926,
    927
M4-35193, 84, 2059, 2060, 2061,
    2062, 2063, 2065, 2066, 2067, 2068
M4-35193 (monaural), 1656
M4S-696, 1290
M4X-31432, 1109
M4X-31441, 1110, 1111
M4X-821, 154
M5S-784, 1737
M7X-30830, 1879, 1884
MG-3007, 429
MG-30071, 429, 431
MG-30073, 671
MG-30300, 2021
MG-30838, 1886
MG-3084, 1248
MG-30841, 1242, 1243
MG-30947, 259
MG-30950, 491, 492, 500
MG-31078, 1954, 1955, 1957
MG-31155, 98, 429, 671, 903, 909
MG-31190, 436, 2052, 2074
MG-31202, 1829, 1850
MG-31207, 63
MG-31421, 273
MG-32042, 1161
MG-32174, 208, 209, 213
MG-32308, 1494
MG-32314, 386, 747, 1160, 1815,
    2020
MG-32813, 749
MG-32985, 795, 1252
MG-33202, 155, 553, 1021, 1262
MG-33270, 1878
MG-33328, 1725
MG-33707, 1821
MG-33713, 279
MGM, E-3105, 1984
MGP-13, 63
MHS-1765, 1482
ML-2073, 674
ML-2120, 1705
ML-4398, 1835
ML-4468, 1917
ML-4492, 441
ML-4664, 1632, 1634
ML-4784, 1705
ML-4843 (monaural), 624, 980
ML-4902, 1506
ML-5039, 463
ML-5105, 1153
ML-5184, 1030
ML-5185, 979, 1661
ML-5260, 1413
ML-5263, 1993

ML-5265, 143
ML-5343, 611
ML-5488, 1413
ML-5796, 1203
ML-5912, 1663
MS-31804, 671, 673
MS-6011, 1457
MS-6018, 583
MS-6025, 282
MS-6043, 1460, 1724
MS-606, 797
MS-6062, 1162, 1886
MS-6068, 860, 1521
MS-6073, 259, 1879
MS-6091, 671, 673
MS-6095, 762
MS-6109, 1882
MS-6110, 1440
MS-6124, 1724
MS-6127, 1274
MS-6128, 1161
MS-6131, 2011
MS-6139, 649
MS-6140, 106
MS-6146, 1958
MS-6149, 2020
MS-6158, 272
MS-6161, 910
MS-6169, 1457
MS-6175, 429
MS-6180, 51
MS-6193, 1424
MS-6194, 1254
MS-6195, 2005
MS-6196, 19, 1734
MS-6201, 1030
MS-6204, 2006
MS-6214, 493, 496
MS-6217, 1806, 1813
MS-6218, 1641
MS-6221, 243
MS-6224, 98, 261, 1884, 1958
MS-6225, 1820
MS-6236, 283, 1653
MS-6251, 209
MS-6253, 237
MS-6255, 1246
MS-6258, 1877, 1878
MS-6261, 63
MS-6271, 491
MS-6272, 1831, 1836, 1841, 1842,
    1843
MS-6274, 1254
MS-6297, 646
MS-6303, 209, 769
MS-6305, 410
MS-6307, 550, 683, 1585, 2087
MS-6319, 1850
MS-6328, 1849
MS-6332, 1851
MS-6349, 1883

MS-6355, 429, 431
MS-6362, 1954, 1957
MS-6373, 111, 112, 184
MS-6377, 607
MS-6392, 1392, 1724
MS-6396, 1203
MS-6398, 98, 1392, 1820
MS-6403, 1254
MS-6405, 108, 1415
MS-6411, 1673, 1675
MS-6414, 1302
MS-6441, 431, 1821
MS-6451, 408, 1249
MS-6459, 1720
MS-6473, 165
MS-6474, 577, 716, 1187, 1815, 1972
MS-6478, 500, 1457
MS-6481, 154
MS-6488, 286
MS-6494, 1247
MS-6497, 436
MS-6508, 414, 502
MS-6512, 1663
MS-6514, 397, 430, 619, 735, 1496
MS-6516, 64
MS-6533, 1547
MS-6541, 411
MS-6545, 1409
MS-6546, 225
MS-6548, 1833
MS-6562, 828
MS-6564, 151
MS-6566, 31, 46, 488, 575, 1091,
 1947
MS-6575, 261, 500, 1959
MS-6587, 1494
MS-6608, 1873, 1943
MS-6618, 734
MS-6622, 60
MS-6624, 544
MS-6631, 282
MS-6635, 1415
MS-6638, 98, 1664
MS-6646, 1850
MS-6658, 1605
MS-6659, 861, 862
MS-6677, 208, 210, 213
MS-6678, 1818, 1820
MS-6684, 435, 442
MS-6685, 272
MS-6695, 1254
MS-6698, 432
MS-6701, 2021
MS-6713, 99, 832
MS-6714, 1884
MS-6723, 1076
MS-6732, 1734
MS-6733, 1060
MS-6743, 820, 1547, 1911
MS-6748, 63
MS-6749, 1735, 1737

MS-6755, 1855
MS-6769, 1301
MS-6775, 907
MS-6792, 208, 212
MS-6804, 63
MS-6805, 210, 436, 714, 1834
MS-6814, 434
MS-6815, 105
MS-6822, 1818, 1821
MS-6823, 1387
MS-6827, 1878
MS-6832, 2001
MS-6833, 1109
MS-6834, 1528
MS-6839, 150
MS-6843, 902, 906
MS-6848, 1256
MS-6856, 1257, 1270
MS-6857, 1252
MS-6858, 1243
MS-6871, 213, 430
MS-6875, 92, 258
MS-6877, 723
MS-6879, 1755, 1756
MS-6883, 500
MS-6884, 2019, 2021
MS-6885, 210
MS-6886, 493
MS-6888, 1670
MS-6889, 903, 906
MS-6891, 1482
MS-6897, 324
MS-6921, 923, 924, 925, 926, 927
MS-6934, 500, 1959
MS-6938, 1076
MS-6943, 543
MS-6944, 340, 341, 344, 345
MS-6952, 167
MS-6954, 435
MS-6956, 107, 110
MS-6958, 259
MS-6565, 269, 272
MS-6966, 144
MS-6971, 2022
MS-6975, 1159
MS-6977, 238, 463, 492, 1120,
 2052
MS-6979, 386
MS-6988, 820
MS-6989, 1833
MS-6992, 1843, 1846
MS-7002, 1157
MS-7006, 790
MS-7011, 1831
MS-7014, 696, 896
MS-7015, 908
MS-7028, 1302, 1303
MS-7031, 1546
MS-7032, 901, 1811, 2031, 2032
MS-7039, 1621
MS-7051, 46, 361, 1403

MS-7054, 1839, 1842, 1843, 1844,
 1857
MS-7058, 211, 436
MS-7067, 1651
MS-7068, 144, 145
MS-7081, 1441
MS-7085, 1300, 1314, 1498, 1547,
 1856, 1857
MS-7087, 1051
MS-7093, 1832
MS-7094, 1831, 1832
MS-7103, 1959
MS-7106, 1671
MS-7111, 906
MS-7139, 317, 337, 361, 615, 1792
MS-7141, 2019
MS-7143, 273
MS-7147, 903, 907, 909
MS-7148, 1291
MS-7159, 1411
MS-7165, 1580, 1821
MS-7174, 1765
MS-7176, 1060, 1063
MS-7177, 1967
MS-7178, 1514
MS-7179, 183, 186
MS-7185, 1161
MS-7191, 372
MS-7192, 912
MS-7206, 107, 1830
MS-7207, 1343, 1344
MS-7223, 430, 433
MS-7242, 1494
MS-7246, 1580
MS-7251, 274
MS-7258, 671, 1411
MS-7261, 705
MS-7265, 1487
MS-7268, 193
MS-7269, 63, 910
MS-7271, 577
MS-7273, 1248
MS-7277, 220, 221
MS-7279, 1720
MS-7285, 1694
MS-7288, 1812
MS-7289, 436, 928
MS-7291, 2020, 2021, 2023, 2024
MS-7298, 287
MS-7315, 1515
MS-7316, 1853
MS-7318, 904, 909
MS-7321, 922, 923, 924, 925, 926,
 927
MS-7326, 756
MS-7327, 689
MS-7355, 1797
MS-7356, 1179
MS-7361, 490, 491, 499
MS-7362, 489, 492
MS-7375, 435

Columbia (*cont.*)
MS-7386, 1831, 1844, 1845, 1847
MS-7389, 1255
MS-7423, 1823
MS-7426, 828
MS-7431, 429, 431
MS-7435, 1243, 1546, 1756, 2023
MS-7437, 544, 1386
MS-7438, 93, 422, 452, 453, 483, 484
MS-7442, 1662, 1664
MS-7446, 1276
MS-7502, 1806, 1815
MS-7505, 723, 724
MS-7507, 1243, 1263
MS-7513, 1878
MS-7515, 756
MS-7516, 1162
MS-7518, 671, 673
MS-7519, 1457
MS-7521, 431, 429, 436
MS-7522, 1580
MS-7523, 491, 500
MS-7528, 1424
MS-7673, 595, 1457
MS-7674, 19
MS-7904, 1832
MX-7027, 915
OSL-154 (monaural), 1176, 1177
SL-125, 1848
XM-33513, 910, 1768, 1769
Columbia/Melodiya
D4M-33493, 975
M-33593, 695
M-33824, 1420
M-33927, 1077
M-34502, 1732
M-34522, 691
M-34527, 1730
M2-33928, 1077, 1079
M3-33215, 1425
M3-33588, 957
M4-34599, 1519
MG-33832, 695
MS-33828, 1893
Columbia Special Products
91AO2007 (monaural), 96
AKS-7131, 101, 1618
AML-4615 (monaural), 512, 1983
AML-4841 (monaural), 459, 1710
AML-4845 (monaural), 266, 267, 513
AML-4846 (monaural), 188, 823
AML-4986 (monaural), 461
AML-4992 (monaural), 1378, 1662
AML-5095 (monaural), 769, 770
AML-5179 (monaural), 874, 875, 2105
AML-5476 (monaural), 192, 640
AMS-6087, 1163
AMS-6114, 101
AMS-6176, 375, 1711

AMS-6198, 391, 1939
AMS-6213, 644, 1200, 1397
AMS-6280, 641
AMS-6333, 1838
AMS-6379, 95, 1523
AMS-6396, 1203
AMS-6421, 379, 592, 661, 1059
AMS-6447, 398, 687
AMS-6571, 848
AMS-6717, 241, 242
AMS-6741, 26
AMS-7041, 2059, 2060
C32310002, 396, 397, 398
CK4L-232 (monaural), 2061, 2062, 2064, 2067
CKL-5175 (monaural), 2073
CKS-6318, 1831
CM2S-819, 355, 356
CML-4987 (monaural), 1665, 1915
CML-4988 (monaural), 101
CML-5158, 1960
CMS-6103, 1619
CMS-6234, 834
CMS-6438, 1466
CMS-6586, 1059, 1165, 1289
CMS-6597, 573, 893
CMS-6799, 364
COL-4139 (monaural), 2073
COS-2032, 2072
Command, 9004, 664
Composers Recordings, *see also* CRI
101 (monaural), 128, 1220
102 (monaural), 366, 419, 569, 768, 965, 1064, 1206, 1375, 1787
103 (monaural), 27, 876, 877, 1089
104 (monaural), 994, 1693
106 (monaural), 290, 623, 625
107 (monaural), 419, 1150
108X (monaural), 419
109 (monaural), 456, 458, 459, 873, 1375
110 (monaural), 513, 2088
111 (monaural), 462, 780, 848, 1596
112 (monaural), 191, 1093, 1094
113 (monaural), 1087, 2076
114, 453, 775
115 (monaural), 201
116 (monaural), 628, 2076
117 (monaural), 41, 384, 1504, 1505
118 (monaural), 1390
119 (monaural), 419, 965, 1150
120 (monaural), 701, 2051
121 (monaural), 1404, 1405
122 (monaural), 1054
125 (monaural), 645, 941
126 (monaural), 1028, 1324
127 (monaural), 1220, 1221, 2044
128 (monaural), 681, 1206, 1377, 1692
130, 1510
131E (monaural), 191, 1704, 1761
132, 453, 968

136 (monaural), 1039, 1212
138 (monaural), 44, 129
139 (monaural), 221, 964
140 (monaural), 190, 518, 769, 1047
142 (monaural), 454
143 (monaural), 633, 812, 1375
144 (monaural), 228, 1659, 1660
145 (monaural), 484, 626, 877, 1360, 1870
147 (monaural), 329, 1046
148 (monaural), 127, 1360
151 (monaural), 1310, 1406
153 (monaural), 744, 1531
154 (monaural), 1156, 1157
155 (monaural), 250, 1940
156 (monaural), 1595
158 (monaural), 701, 1860, 1861
159 (monaural), 1939, 2043
160 (monaural), 328, 977
161E (monaural), 189, 2113
162, 391
163 (monaural), 633
165 (monaural), 1771, 2045
166 (monaural), 166, 1785
169 (monaural), 722
170, 328
170 (monaural), 681, 1300
171, 438, 439, 440
172 (monaural), 2046, 2047
173 (monaural), 460
174 (monaural), 932
177 (monaural), 141, 1506
178 (monaural), 103, 419
179, 454
179 (monaural), 1052
180 (monaural), 369, 907, 1379
181 (monaural), 448, 1860, 1861
184 (monaural), 95, 574
187 (monaural), 1871
188 (monaural), 745, 958
191 (monaural), 41, 222, 995, 1084, 1375, 1787, 1800, 2106
193 (monaural), 1343, 1344
194 (monaural), 2042
197 (monaural), 2076
198E (monaural), 1145, 1706
199 (monaural), 356
2-259, 869
201 (monaural), 86, 221
202 (monaural), 1536
206 (monaural), 2044
207 (monaural), 1915, 1916
208 (monaural), 735, 1055, 1786
211 (monaural), 460, 1701
212 (monaural), 783, 1022, 1117, 1126, 1359, 1508, 2088
216, 518, 1917, 1918
268, 45, 487, 1093, 1716, 1758, 1948
298, 1324, 1940
302, 1205, 1383, 1937, 2121
344, 2080

6413 (monaural), 512
C–329, 962
CRI–142 (monaural), 970
CRI–347, 427
S–123, 642, 1717
S–129, 1785
S–133E (monaural), 1221
S–135E (monaural), 626, 650
S–146, 932
S–168, 2045
S–176 E (monaural), 995, 1746
S–185, 1144, 1145, 1742
S–186, 875, 1229, 1749
S–189, 738, 1031
S–195, 1046
S–196, 142
S–200, 952
S–203, 126, 528
S–204, 487, 488, 1765
S–209, 182, 964
S–213, 1343
S–215, 446, 1803
S–217, 455, 461
S–218, 469, 589
S–219, 1090, 1152, 1505
S–220, 1706
S–221, 876, 886, 1802
S–223, 1212, 1748
S–224, 1408, 1939
S–225, 952, 1953
S–226, 95, 1389
S–227, 1093, 1405, 1406, 1948
S–228, 1149, 1150
S–229, 591, 592, 1507, 1509, 1510
S–230, 1126, 2108
S–231, 1341, 1525, 2107
S–232, 1358, 1712
S–233, 468, 2104
S–234, 1800
S–235, 1389, 1390
S–237, 593, 880, 881
S–238, 1538, 1539, 1540, 2045
S–239, 2049, 2109
S–241, 142, 994, 1374, 1497
S–242, 2070
S–243, 37, 128, 514
S–244, 328, 1028
S–245, 1436, 1608, 2074
S–247, 1567, 1698
S–248, 236, 1001
S–249, 999, 1318, 1698
S–250, 230, 633
S–251, 415, 416
S–252, 739, 773, 1360
S–253, 405, 472, 473, 1383
S–254, 848, 1377, 1859
S–255, 539, 1552, 1553
S–256, 965, 1787
S–257, 1039, 1773, 2084
S–259, 423, 1531, 1788, 1937
S–260, 290, 363, 626, 1310

S–262, 529, 1212
S–263, 1039, 1043, 1057
S–264, 31, 1784, 2094
S–265, 573, 733, 1385, 1911
S–266, 235
S–267, 952
S–267E (monaural), 1019
S–269, 403, 404
S–270, 583, 1979, 2033
S–271, 2082, 2093, 2094, 2095
S–272, 680
S–273, 2075
S–275, 1711, 1712, 1716
S–276, 615, 616
S–277, 16, 17
S–278E (monaural), 1173, 1705
S–279, 182, 1362, 1508
S–280, 748
S–281, 457, 458, 1099, 1706, 1870
S–282, 213, 214
S–283, 467, 949
S–284E (monaural), 642, 1505
S–286, 682, 683, 1370
S–287, 136, 137
S–288, 6, 18, 43, 188, 328, 477, 681,
    715, 814, 873, 969, 977, 1003,
    1324, 1359, 1404, 2050
S–289, 221
S–290, 188, 189, 529
S–291, 1145
S–295, 99, 240, 735
S–303, 1091, 1092
S–304E (monaural), 1344
S–305, 1851
S–306, 1359, 2103, 2110, 2112
S–307, 768, 1229
S–307 (monaural), 1509
S–308, 893
S–308 (monaural), 1661
S–310, 826, 1156
S–311, 126, 628
S–312, 1511, 1513
S–314, 927
S–315, 1152, 2095
S–316, 662
S–317, 1139, 1151, 1355
S–318, 618, 1230
S–322, 618, 823
S–324, 823, 940, 1056, 1130, 1436,
    1514
S–325, 589, 620, 929, 1455
S–326, 874, 2071
S–327, 137, 138
S–329, 229, 939, 1790
S–330, 316, 317, 318
S–334, 1090, 1091
S–335, 1152
S–337, 1524, 1525
S–338, 103, 269
S–339, 1322
S–340, 1355, 1544, 1690

S–341, 1759
S–342, 137, 464, 1034, 1383, 2130
S–343, 682, 2075
S–346, 471, 1225
S–347, 950
S–348, 523
S–351, 236, 238
S–359, 385
S–371, 706
SD–194 (monaural), 40
SD–271, 126, 2082, 2093, 2094, 2095
SD–288, 86
SD–291, 32, 1146
SD–319, 1053, 1054
SD–323, 127, 573, 588, 1101
SD–333, 1305, 1384
SD–336, 293, 573, 814, 949
SD–344, 1147
SD–345, 331, 388, 471, 651, 879
SD–349, 614
SD–350, 1059, 1060, 1095, 1096
SD–352, 1766, 2113
SD–353, 704, 705, 2112
SD–354, 1937
SD–355, 1713
SD–357, 2101, 2102
SD–358, 1216, 1716
SD–358E (monaural), 2050
SD–359, 385, 426
SD–360, 1527
SD–362, 1129, 1536
SD–363, 813, 850, 1947
SD–364, 734, 940, 1156, 1356
SD–365, 8, 9
SD–367, 1346, 1355, 2094
SD–368, 1404
SD–369, 427, 1191
SD–370, 230, 1758, 2094
SD–371, 214
SD–372, 1568
SD–373, 1040, 1041
SD–374, 1125, 1498, 1870, 2068
SD–375, 1138, 2130
SD–376, 625, 626
SD–381, 1041, 1571, 1852
SD–383, 815, 1222, 1382, 1714
SD–422, 289
SRD–395 (monaural), 624, 979
Concert Disc
    205, 485
    208, 120
    215, 100
    216, 478, 592
    217, 513, 1710
    218, 845
    222, 645, 1867
    223, 2091
    224, 1168, 1169
    225, 243, 843
    234, 35, 1727
    252, 243

Concert Disc (*cont.*)
260, 1169
505, 1169
CS-204, 1273
CS-221, 1510
Concordia
CDLP-4 (monaural), 2091
CDLP-6 (monaural), 1611, 1666, 2018
S-1, 190, 721, 989, 1665
Connoisseur Society
2078, 608
2088, 273
2096, 650
CS-2089, 582
CS-2094, 581
CS2-2107, 1382
CSG-2050, 649
CSQ-2050, 1864
CSQ-2052, 172
CSQ-2074, 493
S-2002, 1261
S-2021, 154
S-2032, 1695
S-2033, 117
S-2034, 1695
S-2038, 1464
S-2062, 648
Contemporary
6009 (monaural), 1993
7015, 1761, 1762
7016, 1928, 1929
7022, 894
7024, 546, 547
8005, 1929, 1930
8006, 1019
8007, 546, 547
8008, 1929, 1930
8011, 1930
8012, 770, 771
8013, 1018, 1019, 1020
8501, 335, 336
S-8014E (monaural), 1927
Cornell University
10, 717, 1664
6, 98
8, 717
Coronet
1715, 158, 1379
2508, 195, 755, 943
2736, 179, 180
2738, 720
2741, 838, 1358, 1362, 1588, 1872
2745, 756, 943
3000, 1445
LPS-3038, 889, 890
S-1408, 845
S-1502, 1194
S-1713, 88, 331, 383, 655, 1180
S-1724, 389

Counterpoint/Esoteric
505 (monaural), 269, 892, 1201, 1867
5504E, 301
5507E (monaural), 1599
5511E (monaural), 1554, 1559
5518E (monaural), 1401
5522E (monaural), 1706, 1914
5555, 1998
5559, 168
5605, 300, 1043
CRI, *see also* Composers Recordings
112, 1948
127, 1569
141, 1712
150, 912
163 (monaural), 902
166, 1031
193, 1344
268, 31
S-196, 905
S-204, 487
Critics Choice, cc-1703 (monaural), 687, 846, 1455, 1495, 1790
Crystal
101, 1656, 1772, 2030
251, 486
311, 1421, 1595
331, 939, 1396, 1964
351, 8, 269, 659, 678, 706, 1762
354, 2008
641, 478, 1007, 1054
S-102, 842, 1367
S-103, 1842, 2097
S-104, 1005, 1006
S-105, 1139, 1530, 1786
S-107, 381, 1557, 1612, 2106
S-125, 95, 2089
S-134, 729, 1676
S-140, 418, 763, 966
S-153, 2, 423, 1372
S-180, 681, 748, 1933
S-201, 36, 1139, 1456
S-203, 875, 1363
S-204, 211, 879, 1513
S-206, 615, 777, 1149, 1493
S-207, 351, 1213, 1345, 1374, 1783, 1897
S-208, 768, 867, 1139
S-215, 1007
S-221, 822, 1545, 1659
S-223, 1306
S-252, 1284
S-253, 36, 1127, 1867
S-302, 1840
S-312, 555, 1284, 1437
S-314, 252, 1000
S-332, 1761, 1777, 2057
S-333, 35, 1050, 1129, 2057, 2078
S-342, 1925
S-352, 403, 830, 2103

S-354, 258
S-361, 330, 416, 439, 1057, 1140, 1839
S-362, 365, 874, 1498
S-363, 178, 390, 1408
S-365, 1934
S-372, 1786, 1979
S-384, 258, 1035, 1703
S-391, 741, 1544, 2128, 2129
S-392, 1007, 1042, 1498, 1773, 1787, 2090
S-393, 6, 250, 1544
S-394, 742, 1406
S-501, 382, 704
S-502, 1927, 1928, 1931
S-503, 541, 891, 1123
S-531, 586, 587, 983, 1920
S-532, 89, 1285, 1313, 2047, 2070
S-601, 844, 1305
S-642, 1157, 1585
S-700, 18, 327, 2033
S-800, 871, 872, 873, 875
S-812, 449, 687, 1496
S-821, 366, 1008, 1615
S-851, 639, 1786
S-852, 1094, 2077
S-853, 774, 1064
S-858, 5, 427, 774
S-901, 2009
S-902, 1279
S-951, 77
Decca
710034, 1534
710177, 1991
9826, 1319
9956, 1203
DL-10126, 440, 914
DL-710043, 250
DL-710135, 1511
DL-710145, 1386
DL-8376, 2048
DL-9616, 434, 1914
DL-9889 (monaural), 639
Delos
026, 834
15312, 1862, 1863
15322, 756, 757
15341, 66, 1904
24201, 549, 550
25402, 914, 998
25403, 1119
25405, 1155, 1697, 1287
25406, 198, 487, 1690, 1691
25432, 1008, 1542
DEL-25431, 896
DEL-25436, 437
DEL-25442, 858
DEL F-25409 (monaural), 999
FY-008, 316, 540, 948, 1055, 1365

FY-016, 1197
FY-020/21, 549
Desmar
1001, 1763, 1764
1002, 1824
1004, 1329
1005, 1714
1006, 492, 497, 864
1007, 1441
Desto
6200, 421
6401, 747, 875, 949, 1151, 1225
6402, 686
6404E (monaural), 1660, 1704
6405E (monaural), 2043
6406E (monaural), 1912
6408E (monaural), 1224
6409E (monaural), 237, 1131
6410E (monaural), 1389
6411/2, 101, 142, 192, 267, 370, 390,
    461, 519, 572, 625, 733, 1092, 1104,
    1221, 1363, 1538, 1916, 2044, 2050
6413/4E (monaural), 512, 1341
6415E (monaural), 86, 2017
6416E (monaural), 511, 1173
6417E (monaural), 819, 1150, 1876
6419E (monaural), 373, 374
6420E (monaural), 722, 744
6421E (monaural), 388, 1770
6422E (monaural), 701, 1859, 2050
6423, 1369
6424E (monaural), 463, 731
6425, 191, 1221
6426, 383, 399, 686, 1496, 1987
6427, 934, 935
6428, 936, 938
6429E (monaural), 1089, 1090, 1770
6430, 572, 573, 1145, 1146, 1147
6431, 1451, 1452
6432, 1178
6433, 103, 1858
6434, 851, 1514
6435/7, 44, 188, 291, 358, 616, 1175,
    1380, 1508, 1578, 1707, 1711, 1766,
    2104
6438, 15, 821
6439, 222, 439
6440/1, 1264, 1265
6443, 33, 1540
6444, 1521, 1522
6445/7, 370, 732, 812, 822, 1048, 1103,
    1334, 1337, 1490, 1570, 1781, 1915
6450, 1221
6451, 142
6455/7, 143
6458/61, 910, 911, 912
6461E (monaural), 289
6462, 1535, 1536, 1537
6466, 1090, 1092, 1093, 1948
6467, 1744, 1745, 1746

6468, 633
6469, 1224
6470/3, 708, 709, 710, 711
6474/7, 191, 694, 842, 1118, 1397,
    1747, 1782, 1871, 2084
6478, 772, 775
6480, 1537, 1539
6481, 636, 652
6482, 1965
6483, 1202, 1400, 1467
6484, 840, 847, 1677
70102/3, 1760
7101, 1540
7102/3, 470, 517, 746, 1788, 2033,
    2094
7104, 1861, 2104
7106, 1781, 1782
7107, 470, 745, 964, 1538, 1789, 2032
7108, 288, 292
7109, 1040, 1042, 1043
7110, 514, 814, 1184
7116, 1659, 1861
7117, 484, 683, 1760, 1870
7118/9, 168, 697, 743, 1080
7120, 100, 470
7121, 1226, 1227
7122, 814, 815
7123, 1388, 2044
7124, 679, 1712
7125, 1027, 1744
7126, 1144, 1752
7127, 302
7128, 587, 1186, 1315, 1747
7129, 196, 1027
7131, 1229, 1772, 1860, 2110
7133, 290, 373, 1226, 2083, 2104
7134, 94, 1363, 1989
7135, 1781, 1782
7136, 1750, 1751, 2049
7137/8, 33
7142, 127, 1023
7143, 995, 996, 1226, 1227
7144, 291, 690, 774
7145, 1696
7146, 1588, 1589
7147, 1538, 1539
7148, 585, 586
7149, 474, 1175
7150, 894
7151, 979, 1537
7152/4, 804
7155, 469, 1704
7166, 258, 994, 1007
7167, 623
7168, 298, 1027
7169, 465, 833, 2078, 2122
7170, 763
7171, 687
7172, 1020
7174, 1048, 1537

7178, 1759
7179/80, 143
7411/2, 1031
S-102, 853
S-6406E (monaural), 454
Deutsche Grammophon
12040, 1554
136226, 1067
136228, 2023
136455, 407
137008, 2128, 2129
137010, 958, 1617
138033, 1515
138076, 1443
138077, 1670
138111, 109
138118, 252, 1529
138675, 1467
138714, 58
138778/79, 1654
138811, 1795, 1796
138815, 1247
138820, 57
138853, 1250
138877, 1642
138879, 1113
138921, 1883
138923, 1458
138934, 152, 156
138949, 1261
138954, 938
138961, 1739
138964, 203
139001, 144, 145
139010, 1457
139011, 325
139014, 1815
139015, 144, 145
139030, 1884
139032, 1738
139037, 1067, 1756
139040, 1413
13910, 1291
139103, 1651
139109, 1679, 1680
139112, 520, 2018
139152, 173, 527, 1591
139162, 1641
139304, 14, 755
139308, 2074
139318, 1261
139323, 1643
139331, 1108
139376, 2098
139381, 1882
139382, 817
139383, 1068
139405, 1245
139417, 689
139419, 367, 833, 1018, 1995

Deutsche Grammophon (*cont.*)
139424, 1330
139440, 1528
139458, 494, 495
139461, 1797
16133, 1795
17121002, 271
2430656, 275
2433004, 620
250629, 1330
2530008, 685, 1583, 1867
2530033, 1127
2530035, 59
2530038, 1458
2530048, 907, 1569
2530049, 493, 497
2530051, 1856
2530056, 817
2530065, 1849
2530066, 148
2530069, 247
2530078, 1881
2530103, 1378, 1664
2530104, 375
2530128, 225
2530137, 1693, 1880
2530140, 1986
2530142, 146
2530143, 1278
2530145, 489
2530169, 1668
2530170, 1669
2530193, 1674
2530195, 1881
2530196, 493, 494
2530198, 1882
2530199, 716
2530209, 541, 693, 1985
2530213, 803
2530216, 1640
2530225, 1417, 1837
2530229, 1652
2530231, 411
2530235, 497, 1465
2530236, 409
2530243, 724
2530248, 1754, 1755, 1756
2530252, 1846
2530257, 1621
2530259, 273
2530283, 185
2530284, 2062, 2063
2530285, 1265
2530289, 946
2530291, 408
2530302, 805
2530303, 1485
2530308, 1880
2530309, 209, 1573
2530315, 2052
2530316, 1804, 1809, 1812

2530322, 1650
2530326, 46, 746
2530328, 1654
2530329, 1624
2530335, 276
2530343, 789
2530346, 160
2530355, 277
2530356, 1277, 1278
2530357, 1247, 1641
2530358, 203
2530359, 1162
2530371, 566
2530405, 121, 122
2530414, 144, 145
2530420, 790
2530425, 560
2530426, 1737
2530432, 1320
2530436, 1308
2530439, 1823
2530440, 805
2530441, 1076
2530442, 1791
2530443, 1794
2530448, 145
2530455, 1733
2530457, 149
2530458, 159, 160
2530459, 791
2530467, 1330, 1331
2530473, 1644
2530476, 727
2530479, 105
2530480, 567
2530485, 1619
2530516, 146
2530524, 789
2530525, 791
2530533, 1650
2530537, 1850
2530540, 1462
2530543, 1680
2530544, 1653
2530550, 411
2530551, 1842
2530552, 152
2530560, 1075
2530584, 2099
2530585, 1316, 1571
2530586, 576
2530588, 1424
2530591, 782
2530597, 203
2530609, 1848
2530651, 1882
2530677, 1885
2530708, 785, 786
2530771, 650
2530777, 1278
2530803, 264, 2061

2530827, 1791, 1793, 1794
2530871, 689, 1769, 1873
2530940, 1669
2530966, 1109
2530968, 209, 211
2530969, 210
2530970, 212
2530980, 1653
2531043, 325
2531044, 211
2531049, 1256
2536396, 284
2538025, 1669, 1670
2538098, 168
2543002, 318
2543005, 824, 1621
2543006, 965, 1308
2545023, 1842
2584008, 1806, 1807, 1809, 1814
2707015, 61
2707018, 286
2707023, 187
2707024, 325
2707028, 1654
2707038, 1111
2707039, 1795
2707044, 808
2707045, 1796
2707046, 144, 145
2707054, 1755
2707056, 1113
2707064, 273
2707066, 283
2707072, 496, 1463
2707073, 147
2707081, 1109
2707082, 1112
2707083, 951
2709014, 1977
2709020, 1053
2709023, 2026
2709028, 65
2709029, 186
2709038, 1826
2709039, 1551
2709043, 226
2709044, 1076, 1077
2709047, 65
2709052, 1163, 1165, 1166
2709053, 2098, 2100
2709057, 285
2709063, 1519
2709071, 1977
2709077, 209, 210, 212
2711012, 80
2711013, 1368
2711014, 183, 1619, 1620, 2059, 2060
2711015, 1458, 1460
2713002, 2027
2713004, 2028
2713011, 2026, 2030

2720011, 144
2720029, 185, 1623, 1624, 2062, 2063, 2064
2720031, 1261
2720071, 2058
2720095, 1271
2721007, 1245
2721013, 1245
2726046, 1634
2740121, 1330
2740123, 1649
2740159, 1300
643546, 1790, 1799
709072, 155
923077, 1739
ARC-198342, 1251
ARC-198401, 68
ARC-198415, 796, 1215
ARC-2533, 664
ARC-2533117, 2008
ARC-2533122, 1994, 1995
ARC-2533138/9, 58
ARC-2533151, 750
ARC-2533168/9, 756
ARC-2533171, 56
ARC-2533290, 1036, 1037
ARC-2533295, 1187
ARC-2533328, 1234
ARC-2708002, 61
ARC-2708031, 67
ARC-2708032, 66
ARC-2710002, 79
ARC-2710004, 78
ARC-2710015, 1219
ARC-2723044, 402
  Privilege, 2535134, 1806
Discapon, S-4226, 1648
Donemus Audio-Visual Series
  6071/4, 315
  6704 (monaural), 1373
  6804 (monaural), 24, 867, 1327
  6903, 25, 634, 817, 1002, 1802
  7001, 1048, 2014, 2017
  7002, 816, 971, 1018, 1689
  7071/4, 575, 590, 1323
  7374/1, 257, 1978
  7374/2, 537, 815, 1372
  DAVS–6101 (monaural: 10-inch disc), 43, 634
  DAVS–6102 (monaural: 10-inch disc), 88, 502, 816
  DAVS–6202 (monaural: 10-inch disc), 1574, 1610
  DAVS–6203 (monaural: 10-inch disc), 519, 1283
  DAVS–6204 (monaural: 10-inch disc), 1951, 1952
  DAVS–6301 (monaural: 10-inch disc), 1048
  DAVS–6302 (monaural: 10-inch disc), 26, 1979

DAVS–6303 (monaural: 10-inch disc), 87, 1324
DAVS–6304 (monaural: 10-inch disc), 24, 1373
DAVS–6401 (monaural: 10-inch disc), 816
DAVS–6403 (monaural: 10-inch disc), 590, 1032
DAVS–6602 (monaural), 25, 87, 1003
DAVS–6604 (monaural), 25, 818, 1049, 1216, 1284
DAVS–6702, 537, 1610, 1802
DAVS–6703 (monaural), 615, 653, 1032, 1534
DAVS–6902, 87, 1032, 2012
Dot Records, DLP–3111, 437
Dover
  5203, 1268
  7259, 580
  7260, 135, 581
Duke University Press
  DWR–7306 (monaural), 545, 546, 1363, 1538, 1540
  DWRM–7501 (monaural), 101, 267, 370, 388, 514, 545, 546, 629, 732, 772, 953, 1085, 1103, 1104, 1309
Dyer-Bennet, S–7000, 169
Eastman-Rochester Archives
  ERA–1001, 104, 765, 968, 969, 1531
  ERA–1002, 765, 1531, 1939
  ERA–1003, 1115, 1298, 1784
  ERA–1004, 192, 969, 1531
  ERA–1005, 764
  ERA–1006, 764, 765, 1031
  ERA–1007, 766, 1913
  ERA–1008, 1877
  ERA–1009, 369, 1369
  ERA–1010, 763, 766
  ERA–1011, 103, 1084
  ERA–1012, 1150, 1210, 1298, 1953
  ERA–1013, 767, 1340, 1852
  ERA–1014, 764, 766, 819
  ERA–1015, 763, 848
ECM, 1–1129, 1487
EMI-Electrola 065–28833, 1655
Entr'acte
  ERM–6001E (monaural), 2048
  ERS–6509, 1561, 1562
  ERS–6510, 1612
  ERS–6512, 1563
Epic
  3165, 1554
  3509, 1016
  3568, 1112, 2035
  3666, 1194
  BC–1374, 1295
  E–3812, 2037
  LC–3306, 979
Eurodisc
  86271–XR, 698

86321–XKG, 1550
86977, 1590
Everest
  3001, 1411
  3002, 713
  3003, 29, 685
  3004, 1440
  3006, 1962
  3008, 828
  3009, 1834
  3013, 27, 684
  3015, 429, 434
  3016, 1983
  3018, 435
  3019, 1969
  3020, 176
  3021, 34, 35
  3022, 106
  3024, 1984
  3029, 397, 398
  3032, 1693
  3040, 832
  3041, 685, 1983
  3044, 735
  3052, 973
  3054, 1722
  3061, 524, 1813
  3069, 106
  3070, 367
  3080, 645, 1867
  3081, 1509
  3092, 892
  3107/2, 685
  3108, 1422
  3112, 157, 1167
  3129, 102, 442, 1665
  3130, 836, 1839
  3132, 362
  3135, 233
  3151, 1440
  3153E (monaural), 601, 747, 1532
  3154E, 1598, 1996
  3155, 1038, 1762
  3156, 2122
  3160, 1041, 1043
  3166, 1064
  3170, 582, 1403
  3173, 1, 652, 660
  3175, 1627
  3176, 1201, 1203
  3180, 253, 401, 651, 777
  3181E (monaural), 1723
  3182, 847, 1630, 1631
  3186, 1547
  3192, 1179, 1618
  3194, 15, 84, 250, 668, 1010, 1021, 1085, 1121, 1138, 1250, 1356, 1437, 1556, 1905, 1906
  3195, 540, 1386, 1699, 1872
  3196, 378
  3200, 991

Everest (*cont.*)
3214, 1412, 1413
3218/3, 1440
3222E (monaural), 602
3226E (monaural), 828
3229, 250, 1085, 1172
3230, 362
3236, 1952, 1953
3237, 718, 719
3243, 865, 1989
3253, 714, 715, 716
3262, 30
3269, 1185
3277E (monaural), 130, 2035
3282E (monaural), 96, 97
3284E (monaural), 238
3287E (monaural), 1943
3290, 888
3299, 84, 1021, 1294
3327, 404, 501
3328, 243
3329 (monaural), 1130
3330, 1181
3335, 80
Everest/Cetra
468/3, 2058
S-412/2, 688
S-437/3, 403
S-441/2, 1550
Fantasy, 5001, 830
Finnadar
9001, 1206, 1207, 1208, 1209
9002, 542
9003, 1207
9004, 2061
9005, 1593, 1594
9006, 357, 635
9007, 141, 196, 358, 1107
9008, 184, 1618
9009, 1796, 1798
9010, 31, 46, 489, 1716, 1758, 1948
9011, 575, 1575
9012, 1206, 1207, 1208, 1209
9013, 1462, 1837, 1838
9015, 587, 953, 1609, 1942
9016, 456, 457, 458, 459
SR 2-720, 616, 1206, 1321, 1346
Folkways
33436, 9, 720, 1044, 1521, 1608
33439, 928, 929
3344 (monaural), 918, 922
3345 (monaural), 916, 918, 919, 920, 922
3349 (monaural), 457, 458, 459
3354 (monaural), 241, 1623
3355 (monaural), 293, 741, 1707
3357 (monaural), 241, 242
3369 (monaural), 872
3651 (monaural), 965, 2084
3704 (monaural), 360
3860 (monaural), 2012
FM-3351 (monaural), 1045

Genesis
1000, 415, 700, 1454, 1814
1003, 663, 1749
1004, 32, 93, 260, 470, 693, 697, 893, 1058, 1154, 1443, 1565
1005, 940, 1500
1006, 821, 886
1008, 399, 686
1010, 702, 1617
1013, 537, 1452
1014, 1499
1015, 327
1016, 960, 1910
1018, 331
1020, 1709
1022, 524
1023, 703
1024, 85, 390
1025, 563
1031, 702
1032, 980, 2013
1034, 1491
1035, 1082
1037/8, 703, 704
1040/2, 1757
1043, 813
1048, 1021, 1491, 1510
1054, 139
1055, 998
1057, 475
1058/9, 20, 817, 1082, 1910
1060, 671
1061, 190, 1228
1062, 975
1068, 552
1069, 553
Golden Crest
4004 (monaural), 424, 1151, 2108
403, 180
4081, 982
40866, 1557
40899, 1395, 1445
4907, 1257
4099, 378, 838
4115, 1990
4117, 1363, 1380, 1508
4122, 89, 714
4131, 541, 644, 694
4137, 1590
7007 (monaural), 2090
7011 (monaural), 701, 1124
7015 (monaural), 1293, 1426, 2090
7018 (monaural), 1362, 1393, 1694, 2090
7019 (monaural), 292, 664, 1371, 1588
7028 (monaural), 269, 1035, 1896
7040, 1786
7050, 835, 935, 1128
7052, 1932
7058, 2089
CRS-31042, 712, 902, 905

CRS-4145, 174, 707, 890, 957, 1292, 1408
CRS-4168, 732, 1103
CRS-4180, 1177
RE-7012, 1001
RE-7045, 181, 319, 1023, 1145, 1362, 2104
RE-7049, 2015
S-4017, 749, 2090
S-4023, 269, 745
S-4030, 609
S-4032, 1560, 1714, 1913
S-4046, 609
S-4048, 609
S-4060, 377, 1198
S-4061, 36
S-4065, 100, 266, 369, 604, 1174, 1715, 1915
S-4070, 177, 378, 1394
S-4075, 181, 295, 742, 963, 2082, 2126
S-4076, 39, 192
S-4077, 777
S-4081, 1408
S-4091, 1297, 1425
S-4092, 982, 983
S-4098, 736
S-4110, 1674
S-6001, 180
S-7039, 931
S-7042, 721, 969, 1393, 1394, 1786
Golden Crest/N.E. Conservatory
103, 1361
NEC-111, 861, 867, 909
Gregorian Institute
EL-19 (monaural), 1347, 1589, 1912, 1917, 1992
S-205, 393, 992, 1400
Grenadilla
GS-1007, 519, 771
GS-1008, 874, 887
GS-1009, 963, 1490, 2013
GS-1010, 425, 1504
GS-1019, 1523, 1524
GS-1020, 17, 1744, 1781
GS-1024, 1744, 1745
GS-1032, 887, 1038
GSC
1, 834, 838, 841
2, 847
3, 833
5, 842
6, 839, 845
7, 845
Harmonia Mundi, HMU-458, 1189
Helidor, 2549003, 1062
HMV
SLS-5027, 1303
SXLP-30105, 724
HNH Records
4025, 1692
4045, 1466

4070, 770
4072, 525
Hungaroton, SLPX–11904/6, 403
Klavier
107, 817, 1443
108, 262, 1543
111, 1565, 1681, 1749, 1876
112E (monaural), 2024
114, 1566, 1681
115, 563
116, 1799
119, 653
121, 550, 1565, 1566, 1682, 1692,
    1785
124, 675, 676, 970
125, 693, 1188, 1416, 1520
126, 1837
501, 1329
503, 125
504, 1854
505, 690
506, 630
511, 1903, 1906, 2007, 2008
512, 1903, 1906, 2008
514, 2077
517, 1314
518, 14, 1996
520, 1431, 1604
521, 1855
522, 1133
527, 607, 1580
528, 104, 668, 1370, 1995, 2076
531, 1161
534, 649
535, 118, 125
538, 1418
545, 1084, 1121, 1384, 1431, 1780
546, 225
KS–507, 380, 873, 1014, 1416
KS–525, 608, 778, 1492, 1592,
    1936
KS–536, 7
KS–543, 697, 1492
S–122, 674, 675, 676, 970
Laurel LR–104, 242, 866, 1691
London
1123, 296
1151, 1428
1152, 1429
1153, 1427
1156, 310
1157, 1278
1158, 124
1165, 1136, 2036
1166, 482
1204, 302
1210, 1131
12102, 205
1218, 1828
1249, 1813
1254 (monaural), 309
1255, 307

1259, 171
1260, 527
1261, 1654, 1679
1265, 286
1269, 1828
1271, 808
1273, 527
1278, 992
1279, 1975
1281, 568
1285, 699
1288, 312
1291, 312
1299, 1428
1301, 528
1303, 688
1305, 312
1306, 1427
1307, 254
1309, 2025
13102, 1976
13103, 528
13104, 79
13110, 1429
13111, 173
13112, 1893
13116, 677
1317, 1429
1319, 1813
1327, 528
1361, 761
1364, 1427, 1428, 1429
1365, 174
1373, 173
1375, 1551
1376, 1551
1378, 310
1379, 499
1382, 1976
1383, 1552
1384, 173
1385, 311
1387, 1281
1388, 1387
1389, 403
1390, 310
1391, 503
1392, 384
1393, 1973
1394, 174
1395, 1974
1399, 2026
1432, 1974
1435, 1827
1436, 527
1437, 1187
1438, 2029
1439, 1290
1442, 1279
1502, 2030
1508, 2029
1510, 2028

1512, 2026
15396, 1727, 1728
1604, 2027
21003, 259
21005, 1517
21006, 1291
21007, 1424
21016, 2023
21026, 1288
21035, 2022
21042, 1641
21046, 723
21048, 213
21051, 2023
21060, 903, 1179
21061, 1458
21062, 490, 501, 1468, 1601
21067, 1818
21090/91, 271
21096, 82
2110, 1291
21101/3, 1895
21110, 1288
21117, 558, 1516
21131, 271
2213, 538, 1209
2215, 53
2216, 325, 2023
2219, 325
2220, 1111
2222, 1754
2226, 3
2227, 1110
2228, 1110
2229, 503
2232, 475, 502, 1094, 1564
2235, 11
2239, 1894
2241, 1443
2301, 54
2304, 1894
2307, 1815
2308, 1850
2310, 1668
2311, 1441, 1442
2312, 1424
2313, 983, 984, 985
25242, 307
25320, 863, 865
25821, 205, 1466
25921, 1358
25937, 296, 309
26043, 498, 1398, 1680, 2098, 2100
26098, 73, 75
26099, 302
26100, 78
26103, 69
26106, 286, 287
26107, 1172
26110, 695, 696
26147, 2030
26161, 303

London (*cont.*)
26176, 1973
26186, 986, 990, 991
26250, 1550
26397, 182
33216, 1741
4104, 2042
5006, 244
5358, 304
6006, 385, 718, 1231, 1515
6012, 1517, 1518
6026, 502
6036, 1516, 1517
6046, 1528
6090, 1651
6163, 1332
6165, 1597
6173, 62, 63
6177, 1291
6178, 1249, 1251
6179, 296, 303
6187, 1424
6204, 1547
6206, 698, 1328
6208, 225
6222, 646
6224, 595, 601
6225, 1459, 1834
6227, 500, 606, 607
6236, 762
6237, 300, 1677
6242, 1409
6243, 55
6247, 153
6251, 3
6252, 820
6322, 972
6329, 273
6335, 153
6337, 322, 832
6356, 1316
6358, 560
6367, 543
6371, 1073, 1078
6375, 1734
6382, 1640
6385, 803, 804, 807
6395, 1357
6400, 1250
6401, 1108
6403, 1251
6407, 107
6410, 276
6411, 1678
6416, 1645
6418, 538, 1209
6419, 298, 793
6422, 410
6429, 1882
6434, 1098, 1199, 1394
6437, 501

6438, 385
6440, 56, 406
6444, 275, 277
6446, 665
6452, 1881
6454, 3
6462, 325
6471, 1675
6472, 1461
6473, 275, 277
6486, 820
6494, 167, 1273
6495, 556, 560
6499, 1246
6500, 1643, 1646
6501, 1252, 1255
6509, 692, 694
6511, 560
6512, 146
6519, 1804, 1823
6522, 1410, 1411
6523, 559
6524, 559
6525, 556, 559
6527, 561
6529, 1066, 2023
6533, 278, 1588
6534, 1261
6537, 1820
6538, 557, 1411
6552, 1693
6554, 1828
6559, 1289
6567, 270
6573, 1418
6574, 555, 557
6579, 1252, 1412
6580, 1254
6583, 1395
6586, 751, 752, 753, 754
6592, 1737, 1738
6594, 270, 557
6611, 280
6612, 1620
6613, 1004, 1006
6615, 1029, 1107
6616, 862
6617, 299
6618, 294, 297, 1432
6620, 933
6621, 50, 1591
6622, 1288
6625, 1246
6627, 331
6628, 280, 649
6633, 1460
6636, 261
6641, 1806, 1808, 1809, 1810, 1811
6643, 3, 38, 1046, 1381, 1911
6649, 295, 1647
6656, 143, 148

6657, 492, 508
6659, 1261
6665, 1096
6668, 147
6671, 296, 297
6675, 171
6699, 1302
6706, 323
6711, 751, 752, 753
6717, 324
6718, 933, 934
6719, 1079
6721, 556, 559
6723, 298
6727, 156, 1643
6730, 259, 697
6731, 1804, 1805, 1807, 1808, 1809,
   1810, 1811, 1816
6732, 1693, 1694
6733, 596
6735, 252, 667, 723, 1009, 1329, 1577,
   1591
6737, 1821, 1854, 2097
6738, 1066, 1067
6739, 48, 417
6740, 1366
6744, 38, 224, 252, 502, 716, 1133,
   1580
6745, 1735
6746, 556
6747, 1613
6748, 64
6750, 39, 1133, 1387
6752, 1954, 1955
6754, 496
6774, 1441
6776, 1442
6783, 106
6785, 259, 696, 697
6786, 1879
6787, 1719, 1721
6789, 577
6791, 1050, 1806, 1807, 1808, 1809,
   1811, 1815, 1816, 2127
6794, 411
6795, 321, 322
6801, 1644
6812, 1315
6814, 280
6816, 906
6818, 974
6819, 2038
6822, 1443, 1444
6824, 1736
6836, 271
6841, 1878, 1884
6845, 159, 160
6848, 1302
6857, 150
6860, 2022
6866, 1262

6870, 145
6873, 1461
6878, 607
6879, 324
6881, 597, 598
6885, 1850
6891, 1878, 1883
6893, 1444
6895, 1461, 1462
6899, 2031, 2032
6923, 39
6925, 1068
6936, 1461, 1462
6937, 1255
6940, 65
6941, 578
6943, 709
6944, 696, 1288
6945, 1978
6955, 1734
6961, 1645
6992, 1981
7205, 1967
771, 2034
9324, 854
CSA-2314, 1409, 1415
CSP-2, 153
CSP-3, 1881
CSP-6, 1640
CSP-7, 1111
CSP-9, 145, 147
HEAD-1/2, 1186
HEAD-3, 141, 201, 1098
HEAD-4, 1869
HEAD-6, 671
HEAD-8, 1286
LL-1213, 965
LL-1232, 238
LL-1328, 97
LL-1635, 1518
OS-25005, 1741
OSA-13118, 1134
OSA-13127, 1300
OSA-13128, 809
OSA-1509, 2026
OSAD-12113, 1430
S-15216, 1962
SPC-21136, 576
STS-15008, 1159
STS-15009, 270
STS-15011, 1833
STS-15013, 34, 40, 51, 268, 1084,
  1432
STS-15014, 600
STS-15021, 820, 1857
STS-15022, 501, 544, 545
STS-15024, 379
STS-15025, 1555
STS-15028, 1849
STS-15033, 1133
STS-15034, 1881

STS-15035, 1642
STS-15040, 730
STS-15046, 261
STS-15049, 2, 138, 580, 879, 1017,
  1598, 1757, 1855, 1970, 2088
STS-15051, 1133, 1188
STS-15052, 224, 225
STS-15054, 1886, 1887
STS-15056, 2052
STS-15057, 596, 2058
STS-15063, 81
STS-15066, 93, 1057, 1058
STS-15070, 1813
STS-15074, 1776, 1777
STS-15075, 50, 1115
STS-15076, 401, 1158, 1640, 1668,
  2052
STS-15078, 807
STS-15079, 52
STS-15081/2, 314
STS-15085, 791
STS-15086, 1441
STS-15088, 1243, 1281
STS-15091, 1157, 1159
STS-15093, 224, 890, 1580
STS-15096/7, 1755
STS-15102, 1848
STS-15103, 648
STS-15104, 647
STS-15105, 647
STS-15111, 151
STS-15112, 232, 577
STS-15113, 283
STS-15117, 391
STS-15120, 1882
STS-15123, 1075, 1079
STS-15131/4, 786, 787
STS-15142, 1333
STS-15144, 271
STS-15146/8, 409
STS-15149, 260
STS-15152, 1422, 1465
STS-15153, 118, 836, 837, 1420
STS-15155/6, 1466
STS-15162, 2089
STS-15165, 2069
STS-15168, 521
STS-15169, 699
STS-15170, 1237
STS-15171, 1244
STS-15172, 51, 781, 793
STS-15175, 1200
STS-15180, 1718
STS-15182/5, 787, 788
STS-15187, 69
STS-15188, 272, 576
STS-15191, 1046, 2034
STS-15193, 1409
STS-15196, 1411, 1413
STS-15201, 38
STS-15207, 566

STS-15208, 1881
STS-15216, 1963
STS-15217, 38, 820
STS-15223, 820, 1856, 1857
STS-15227, 1855
STS-15229/34, 788
STS-15240, 691
STS-15242, 567
STS-15243, 88, 2078
STS-15244, 1357
STS-15246, 1158
STS-15249/54, 785
STS-15255, 1674
STS-15257/62, 783
STS-15270, 1122, 1123
STS-15271, 1830, 1833
STS-15275/9, 1236, 1237, 1238, 1239,
  1240, 1241, 1247, 1271
STS-15280/4, 1236, 1237, 1239, 1240,
  1241, 1248
STS-15286, 1425
STS-15293, 1029
STS-15295, 1881
STS-15301, 1244
STS-15303, 301
STS-15309, 811
STS-15310/15, 782, 783
STS-15316/7, 782
STS-15352/4, 797, 798
STS-15364, 108
STS-15368/70, 797, 798
TCH-S-1, 1882
London/Decca, SXLK-6660/4, 1625,
  1626, 1629, 1636
Louisville
  545-1 (monaural), 463, 1982
  545-10 (monaural), 190, 685, 1603,
    2043
  545-11 (monaural), 85, 1116, 1510
  545-3 (monaural), 1173, 1507, 1926
  545-4 (monaural), 380, 869, 1858
  545-5 (monaural), 891
  545-9 (monaural), 574, 1358, 1456
  56-1 (monaural), 1541
  561 (monaural), 415, 736
  56-2 (monaural), 262, 477, 1871
  56-5 (monaural), 1283, 1322, 1710
  56-6 (monaural), 86, 1770, 2049
  57-2 (monaural), 944, 1992
  57-5 (monaural), 1489, 1534
  57-6 (monaural), 1225, 1563
  58-2 (monaural), 776, 996
  58-5 (monaural), 701, 1018
  58-6 (monaural), 182, 1377, 1952
  59-1 (monaural), 432, 1056
  592 (monaural), 231, 1152
  593 (monaural), 1785
  596 (monaural), 1086, 1128
  601 (monaural), 175, 1507
  602 (monaural), 574, 769
  604 (monaural), 1116, 1666

Louisville (cont.)
605 (monaural), 21, 518, 827
606 (monaural), 1361, 1531
611 (monaural), 371, 743
612 (monaural), 1222, 1926
613 (monaural), 1173, 1528
615 (monaural), 862, 1896
616 (monaural), 1024, 2083
621 (monaural), 773
622 (monaural), 455
623 (monaural), 1522, 1579
624 (monaural), 1322, 1339
625 (monaural), 627, 746, 747
626, 299
631 (monaural), 971, 985
632 (monaural), 1024, 1470, 1760
635 (monaural), 634, 1595
641 (monaural), 479, 1701
642 (monaural), 680, 1389
651 (monaural), 591, 964
652 (monaural), 627, 1374
662, 201
713, 397
715, 1505
716, 634, 712, 713
731, 35, 1123
733, 294, 1536, 1945
734, 227, 1231, 1294, 1470
742, 512, 2077
743, 737, 1231
LS-662, 870
LS-705, 940
LS-714, 140, 666, 1376, 1438
LS-715, 1470
LS-735, 875, 2085
LS-736, 890, 993
LS-741, 94, 464, 1501
LS-746, 1379
LS-751, 89, 713
LS-752, 1047, 1942
LS-753, 387, 426
LS-754, 222, 636, 1321
LS-755, 329, 1381
LS-756, 1013, 1141
LS-765, 90, 288, 443
S-633, 1324, 1379
S-634, 1094, 1522
S-636, 238, 1124, 1149
S-644, 1535, 1860
S-645, 1213, 1896
S-646, 669, 1506
S-653, 1006, 1378
S-654, 1086, 1338
S-655, 462, 770
S-656, 1024, 1858
S-661, 1222, 1766, 1926
S-663, 1128, 1914
S-664, 137, 1116
S-665, 1047, 1308
S-666, 769, 1148, 1657
S-671, 227, 1339

S-672, 627, 980, 1496
S-673, 1374
S-674, 591, 1710
S-675, 652
S-676, 629, 1365, 2049
S-681, 454, 1857
S-682, 453, 455, 993, 1780
S-683, 978, 1719
S-684, 830, 1365
S-685, 228, 1191, 1390
S-686, 90, 1657
S-691, 515, 1611, 2031
S-692, 208, 1662
S-693, 861, 1174
S-694, 229, 831
S-695, 5, 1982
S-696, 685, 1496
S-701, 719, 1700, 1875
S-702, 736, 890, 1926, 1935
S-703, 321, 1514
S-704, 1501, 1825
S-706, 1361, 1506
S-711, 465, 582
S-712, 971, 1028
S-721, 140, 1027, 1662
S-722, 738, 886, 1348
S-725, 94, 886
S-726, 92
S-744, 1193, 1202
S-745, 4, 96
Lyrichord
105 (monaural), 731
22 (monaural), 1864
53 (monaural), 833
61 (monaural), 1393
7103E (monaural), 1581, 1897
7121, 1471, 1473, 1475
7124, 442, 1912
7127, 1400, 1401
7128, 451
7129, 451
7130, 450
7144, 990, 992
7154, 485
7155, 1303, 1304, 1305
7156, 347, 348, 349
7161, 847, 1630, 1631
7170, 989, 990, 991
7171, 1935
7173, 2081
7175, 71
7185, 840, 1129
7187, 1033, 1935
7190, 543
7191, 5, 628, 654, 1379, 1771
7193, 1396
7195, 300
7203, 6, 654
7208, 990, 991, 1399
7210, 1578
7213, 1313, 1314

7215, 1643
7216, 485, 1488
7217, 1483
7224, 1182
7225, 1181
7226, 1183
7233, 543
7276, 1613
7297, 1181, 1182
7721, 88
97 (monaural), 845
S-158, 706, 1015, 1380
Lyrita
RCS-13, 2106
SRCS-68, 877
SRCS-70, 1211
SRCS-75, 629
SRCS-81, 1692
Mace, MXX-9099, 871, 872, 873
Mainstream
5000, 317, 1497, 1868, 2117
5001, 141, 223, 1142, 1323
5003, 958, 1791, 1792
5004, 1106, 1307
5005, 197, 338, 359
5006, 383, 618, 967, 2124
5007, 317, 318, 616
5008, 421, 1000, 1306, 2115
5009, 264, 318, 1607
5010, 37, 173, 1089, 1284
5011, 352, 362, 455, 773, 1532, 1572
5012, 1148
5013, 912
5014, 194, 383, 592, 1106, 1138, 1180
5015, 360, 2102
MS-5016, 358, 466, 2110, 2123
MS-5017, 136, 255, 585, 666, 1035, 1307
Mark
22868 (monaural), 463, 811
25726, 180
5-32286, 838
MC-5405, 181, 886
MM-1117, 5, 6, 7
MCA
10009, 320
19000, 1385, 1556, 1872
2501, 1191, 1872, 1987
2504, 722
2514, 1944
2522, 1385
2523, 382, 1285, 1529, 1533
2524, 1596, 1934, 1995
2525, 249
2526 (monaural), 590, 1385, 1556, 1872
2530, 1386
2532, 1385
2534, 1222
2537, 878, 957, 1331, 1890
710034, 1529

Melodiya, D–011501–6, 1566
Melodiya/Angel
40194, 1647
S–4000, 1722
S–40020, 1739
S–40031, 1727, 1739
S–40036, 1892
S–40040, 1413
S–40057, 1881
S–40058, 1882
S–40061, 1413
S–40062, 1718
S–40064, 1721, 1725
S–40066, 1425
S–40067, 227
S–40081, 696
S–40085, 1730
S–40088, 694
S–40089, 694
S–40091, 1925
S–40092, 1412
S–40093, 1440
S–40098, 1694
S–40103, 695
S–40113, 1693
S–40115, 1718
S–40118, 1694
S–40119, 690, 691, 896
S–40121, 279, 649
S–40128, 1722
S–40132, 959
S–40138, 1409
S–40149, 37, 1017, 1951
S–40157, 1409, 1423
S–40159, 1058
S–40160, 1719, 1724
S–40166, 1883
S–40172, 690
S–40173, 959
S–40174, 1881
S–40175, 1881
S–40180, 1603, 2012
S–40181, 1719, 1723
S–40182, 259, 1439
S–40197, 1874
S–40198, 1290, 1446, 1447, 1448,
   1449
S–40212, 1723
S–40214, 1732
S–40217, 1695
S–40219, 1850
S–40221, 1516, 1517
S–40222, 1891
S–40225, 690
S–40226, 1442
S–40230, 1515
S–40231, 414
S–40236, 1720
S–40244, 1722
S–40245, 1720

S–40252, 1439, 1441
S–40261/6, 1882
S–40268, 1421
S–4103, 1423
S–4104, 1894
S–4106, 1895
S–4114, 694, 1409
S–4115, 1893
S–4119, 61
S–4120, 61
S–4122, 1519
S–4124, 1450
S–4126, 1714
SR–40224, 1858, 1859
SR–40238, 1671
SR–40260, 1697
Melodiya/Seraphim
S–6034, 1728
S–6035, 1729, 1731
Mercury
2–77003, 3
2–77004, 503
75001, 1879
75003, 1581
75005, 762
75006, 648
75007, 764, 766
75009, 1493, 1494
75010, 680, 871
75011E (monaural), 856, 1963
75012E (monaural), 96, 97
75013, 22, 23
75014, 1814
75016, 259, 1516
75017, 237
75018, 853, 1066
75020, 731, 1173
75021, 1528, 1529
75022, 1987
75023, 1493
75024, 270
75026, 1101
75027, 1987
75029, 386, 394
75030, 1411
75036E (monaural), 237, 1618
75049, 96, 1704
75050, 387, 1377
75057, 829, 1621
75059, 647
75060, 224, 225
75078, 386, 387, 1133
75102, 717
77001, 558, 1755
77002, 58
77005, 503
77006E, 1755
90515, 110
90532, 2022
MG–50136, 1369

MG3–4501 (monaural), 828
MY–50090 (monaural), 936
SRI–75028, 857, 931, 2037
SRI–75095, 1220
SRI–75099, 767, 1414, 1768
SRI–75118, 445
MGM
3361, 1392
3683, 848
E–3084, 454
E–3432, 872
E–3556, 1567
S–31210C, 2073
Monitor
2003 (monaural), 1154, 1864, 2127
2007 (monaural), 955, 1414
2009 (monaural), 841, 1598
2015 (monaural), 1718
2018 (monaural), 976
2019 (monaural), 977
2020 (monaural), 957, 1290, 1731
2021E, 1727
2025 (monaural), 972
2027, 1644
2028, 241
2030, 696, 1117, 1335
2034 (monaural), 1889
2036 (monaural), 650
2038 (monaural), 983, 1188, 1288,
   1335
2039 (monaural), 956, 957
2040 (monaural), 1726
2041, 1424
2047 (monaural), 847
2049 (monaural), 584
2059 (monaural), 975, 1871
2079E (monaural), 974
2081/3 (monaural), 1919
2128, 1163, 1164
2136E (monaural), 693
2145 (monaural), 1188
90102/3, 1451
MC–2014, 1725
MCS–1054, 123
MCS–2135 (monaural), 950, 1419
S–2017, 649, 1463
S–2045, 1167
S–2054, 603, 989, 991, 1028, 1080
   1366
S–2058, 799, 865, 1420, 1775
S–2061E, 956
S–2068E (monaural), 697, 1871
S–2069E (monaural), 414
S–2074E (monaural), 388, 1717, 1958
S–2077E (monaural), 977
S–2078E (monaural), 955
S–2104, 1894
S–2114, 1274
S–2115, 1271
S–2119E (monaural), 407, 692, 1416

Monitor (*cont.*)
S-2120, 1123
S-2123, 242, 1922
S-2130E, 1889
S-2131E (monaural), 692
S-2133, 1259
S-2134, 184
S-2141, 1109
Music Library Recordings, 7014, 1013, 1014
Musical Heritage Society
MHS-1015, 945, 946, 947
MHS-1030, 947
MHS-1033, 1491
MHS-1054, 1488
MHS-1078, 39, 1127, 1202, 1401
MHS-1082, 1115, 1316
MHS-1087, 1316
MHS-1089, 1192, 1193
MHS-1100, 1996, 2000, 2003
MHS-1119, 73, 76
MHS-1127, 517
MHS-1130, 1289, 1290
MHS-1131, 2087, 2088
MHS-1132, 1995
MHS-1147, 697, 1444, 1697, 1726
MHS-1149, 1384
MHS-1155-57, 394, 895, 1107, 1534, 1557, 1558, 1708
MHS-1186, 976
MHS-1187, 2118
MHS-1198, 131
MHS-1200, 2118
MHS-1201, 1554, 1555
MHS-1218, 1740
MHS-1220, 2051
MHS-1228, 263, 264
MHS-1229, 130, 854, 1210
MHS-1240, 917, 922, 925
MHS-1244, 1553
MHS-1251, 232
MHS-1268, 1477, 1478
MHS-1277, 10, 231, 1010, 1121, 1125, 1431
MHS-1285, 577
MHS-1292, 1477
MHS-1303, 856, 857
MHS-1310, 1228, 1229
MHS-1317, 897, 898
MHS-1321, 1484
MHS-1329, 1482
MHS-1335, 578
MHS-1337/38, 1125
MHS-1339, 1667
MHS-1345, 483, 892, 1018, 1548
MHS-1347, 1972, 2101
MHS-1351, 395, 1558
MHS-1360/61, 1481
MHS-1363/64, 325, 326
MHS-1366, 245

MHS-1370, 1856
MHS-1371, 943, 945
MHS-1372, 1554, 1559
MHS-1373, 1756
MHS-1378, 1485
MHS-1389, 1478, 1483
MHS-1397, 1563
MHS-1402, 1486
MHS-1405, 944, 1190
MHS-1408, 1943
MHS-1411, 1210, 1211
MHS-1429, 898, 901
MHS-1431/41, 2086
MHS-1452, 854, 856, 857
MHS-1465, 1471
MHS-1473, 1098, 1836
MHS-1481, 897
MHS-1483, 1342
MHS-1486, 239, 240, 241
MHS-1489, 1370, 1371
MHS-1498, 897, 898
MHS-1500, 1480, 1481
MHS-1501/3, 120
MHS-1509, 551
MHS-1521, 1482
MHS-1563/66, 1471, 1472, 1473, 1475
MHS-1567/70 1472, 1473, 1474
MHS-1586, 130
MHS-1590, 1368
MHS-1597, 2098
MHS-1600, 2043, 2044
MHS-1610, 900
MHS-1620/21/22, 1476
MHS-1632, 131
MHS-1647, 944
MHS-1652, 131
MHS-1658, 368, 948
MHS-1667, 1481
MHS-1672, 21, 200, 332, 1105
MHS-1687, 383, 737
MHS-1689, 1211, 1212
MHS-1697, 1480
MHS-1698, 1479
MHS-1719, 1479
MHS-1722, 118
MHS-1741, 1480
MHS-1750, 176, 232, 2036
MHS-1762, 1184
MHS-1766, 836, 1128
MHS-1769, 130
MHS-1770/71, 608, 609
MHS-1773/74, 609, 610
MHS-1789, 1317
MHS-1793, 1481
MHS-1805, 1479
MHS-1862, 1231, 1232
MHS-1865, 1170
MHS-1869, 864, 865
MHS-1875, 1989, 1990
MHS-1884, 834, 835

MHS-1889, 47, 1376
MHS-1916, 948, 1054, 1197, 1392, 1603, 1769, 1995
MHS-1919, 232, 314, 855, 2035
MHS-1920, 1476, 1477
MHS-1932/33/34, 1471, 1473, 1474, 1475
MHS-1938/30/40/41, 1484, 1486
MHS-1976, 228, 858, 875, 1991
MHS-1985, 1553
MHS-3022, 554, 1554
MHS-3026, 656
MHS-3055, 743, 1387, 1750
MHS-3096, 231, 234
MHS-3120, 1775
MHS-3136, 1863, 1864
MHS-3138, 2025
MHS-3143, 1132
MHS-3144/45/46/47, 1473, 1474, 1475, 1476
MHS-3306, 1702
MHS-3337, 1702
MHS-3340, 853, 948, 1933
MHS-3426, 294
MHS-3521, 136
MHS-3522/3, 81
MHS-3613, 135
MHS-3653, 1692
MHS-3827, 605
MHS-3874, 1014
MHS-518, 1898, 1899, 1900, 1901
MHS-602, 705, 1372, 1556, 1585
MHS-623, 1268
MHS-7001 (monaural), 899
MHS-7002 (monaural), 899, 900
MHS-7003 (monaural), 176
MHS-7011 (monaural), 132, 133, 134
MHS-7012 (monaural), 132, 133, 134
MHS-7013 (monaural), 132, 133, 135
MHS-7014 (monaural), 132, 133, 134
MHS-7015 (monaural), 135, 136
MHS-7016 (monaural), 132, 135
MHS-706, 52
MHS-709, 1426, 1994
MHS-733, 13, 665, 778, 1490
MHS-792-CC-13, 315, 776, 1383, 1637
MHS-793-CC-11, 464, 723, 814, 1115
MHS-794, 384, 1155, 1314
MHS-805, 1555, 1615
MHS-817, 1, 516, 1372, 1520
MHS-821, 391, 1181, 1197
MHS-829, 400, 401, 1932
MHS-835/836, 2010
MHS-849/850, 496, 644, 1463
MHS-868, 10
MHS-876, 254, 1021, 1488
MHS-883, 644, 892, 945, 1087
MHS-892, 1616

MHS-897, 1315
MHS-906, 1396
MHS-922, 1800, 1801
MHS-951, 2000, 2001
MHS-952, 2000, 2001
MHS-976, 1357, 1594
MHS-981, 554, 862
MHS-988, 257, 1031
MHS-CC-1, 707, 1617
OR-398, 84, 219, 667, 1223
OR-400/1/2, 1676
OR-409/10/11, 1679
OR-415/419, 1671, 1676
OR-425/430, 1980
OR A-263, 295, 388, 636, 1334, 1341
OR A-264, 1771
OR H-289, 843, 844
OR H-290, 838, 840
OR H-291, 835
OR H-292, 838, 839
OR H-293, 846
OR H-294, 836
OR H-295, 839, 844
OR H-296, 838, 839, 840
OR H-297, 842, 843
OR H-423/424, 834
OR S-127, 1646
OR S-128, 1643, 1646
New World Records
NW-203, 458, 942, 1293
NW-209, 43, 44, 45, 126, 1761, 2109
NW-210, 1127, 1131
NW-211, 178, 289, 628, 1361, 1760
NW-213, 352, 604, 605, 1318
NW-216 (monaural), 1658
NW-218, 460, 771, 1715
NW-219, 377, 1717, 1913
NW-220, 329
NW-228, 370, 684, 1404, 2076
NW-237, 404, 416, 978, 1497
NW-243, 101, 243, 267, 390, 391,
    419, 441, 545, 546, 815, 1708
NW-247 (monaural), 139, 352, 370,
    743, 1008, 1104, 1341, 1912
NW-257, 295, 654, 711, 1132
NW-258, 518, 1174
NW-266, 388, 622, 704, 819, 1425,
    1768, 1769
NW-268, 139, 637
NW-273, 731, 732, 733
NW-277 (monaural), 437, 438
NW-280, 329, 1334, 1911, 2083
NW-281 (monaural), 478, 639, 775,
    2050
NW-286 (monaural), 979, 1378
NW-288/289, 1917
NW-296, 1708
NW-304, 593, 706, 966, 1359
Nonesuch
7001, 1052

70139, 1095
71002E (monaural), 1094, 1223
71003, 759
71004, 51, 67, 1437, 1908
71005, 14
71006E (monaural), 843, 1117
71009, 451, 1029, 1095, 1233, 1368
71014, 1778, 2042, 2096
71015, 783
71017E (monaural), 1799, 1897
71019, 56
71020, 452, 453, 1121, 1376
71022, 2006
71024, 780
71026, 650, 664, 1037, 1611, 2017
71029, 71, 75
71030E (monaural), 892, 1989, 1991
71031, 785
71032, 781, 786
71033, 1396
71034, 49
71038, 1904, 1905
71044, 1670
71045, 799
71048, 1920
71049, 800
71050, 1726
71052, 668, 1604, 1902, 1997
71053, 1037, 1038
71054, 168
71057, 58
71060, 68, 69
71061, 1907
71062, 1686
71064, 514, 606, 1085, 2085
71065, 1900, 1904, 1906, 1907
71066, 1899, 1900, 1902
71067, 794, 795
71071, 793
71076, 1779
71080, 253, 447, 1045
71081, 284, 1086, 1171, 1681, 1477
71083, 783, 784
71084, 516, 901, 1036
71085, 250, 657, 665, 1437, 1907
71087, 215
71088, 2009, 2010
71089, 1549
71091, 1901, 1999
71093, 1830
71094, 1605
71095, 664, 1611, 2034
71096, 782, 785, 788
71098, 49, 552, 755, 1293
71099, 1161
71101, 784
71102, 1268
71104, 1997, 1998
71106, 784, 786, 788
71108, 485

71111, 94, 650, 652, 659, 660,
    1799
71112, 1268
71113, 215
71114, 521, 805, 1433, 1874
71115, 284, 376, 778, 847, 1703,
    1844, 2046
71117, 417, 665, 1340, 1357, 1574,
    1607, 2130
71118, 660, 851
71119, 345, 1045, 1121, 1357, 1908
71121, 783, 784, 787
71122, 1203, 1204
71124, 1898, 1908
71125, 1779
71128, 1406, 1407, 1611
71130, 393, 1087, 1088
71131, 784, 788
71132, 1897
71133, 1843, 1844, 1846
71134, 1683, 1687, 1688
71135, 598
71137, 61
71138, 515
71140, 580, 1740
71141, 780, 1034, 1642
71144, 60
71145, 575, 749, 1132, 1366, 1772
71146, 217, 483, 1299
71147, 77
71148, 14, 1899, 1998
71149, 836, 837, 846, 847
71151, 668, 1082
71154, 781
71155, 987, 1445
71156, 327, 1009
71157, 1794
71159, 254, 759
71160, 1682
71162, 1594
71163, 1548
71164, 749
71165, 50, 51
71166, 76
71167, 533, 534, 535, 536
71168, 787, 788
71169, 911
71170, 422, 447, 483, 486, 683, 953,
    1044, 1452
71172, 217, 218
71173, 808
71175, 115
71176, 60
71177, 1683
71178, 607
71180, 47
71182, 75, 1909
71183, 224, 225, 226
71185, 796
71186, 1636, 1842

Nonesuch (*cont.*)
71188, 341, 343
71189, 12
71190, 1908
71193, 2079
71194, 1239, 1244
71195, 622
71196, 1682
71197, 781, 787, 788
71198, 1568
71199, 661, 662
71200, 388, 822, 823, 910, 1334
71201, 1348, 1351, 2115
71202, 353, 637
71204, 1016, 1367, 1542
71205, 1494
71207, 1247, 1249
71209, 702, 917, 918, 921, 922, 1681
71210, 2086
71211 (monaural), 1653
71212, 1837, 1838
71213, 1294, 1533, 1949
71216, 516, 517
71217, 21, 392, 605, 645
71218, 215
71219, 1292, 1497
71220, 1526, 1717, 2103
71221, 768, 1690
71222, 291, 293, 915, 916, 924
71223, 587, 588
71224, 363
71225, 2112
71226, 78
71227, 157, 161, 884
71228, 286, 1681
71229, 340
71231, 1592
71233, 597, 1307, 1318, 1529
71234, 374
71235, 1684
71236, 1301, 1302
71237, 354, 942, 1317
71238, 757
71239, 110
71242, 1407
71244, 943
71246, 2118
71247, 332
71249, 375
71251, 1629
71253, 538, 540
71255, 468
71257, 17, 256, 951
71258, 346, 347
71260, 255
71263, 2108
71265, 452
71267, 635
71269, 1955, 1957
71270, 820, 1235
71271, 561

71272, 515, 659, 778, 1036, 2091
71274, 384, 636, 1122
71275, 813, 1141
71276, 219, 220
71277, 678, 1299
71278, 1453
71280, 44, 1360, 1698
71281, 2071
71282, 2127
71283, 1526
71284, 674, 675, 676
71285, 1143
71287, 1452
71288, 937, 938
71289, 487, 999, 1023
71291, 424, 1313, 1597, 1956
71293, 466
71295, 1143
71296, 2100
71298, 30, 420, 1914
71300, 1126, 2111
71301, 216, 218, 1214, 1366, 1456,
    1610
71302, 1527
71303, 24, 43, 2081
71306, 915
71307, 828
71309, 1622
71314, 372, 373
71316, 1198, 1199
71319, 2107, 2111
71320, 1627, 1653
71322, 493
71323, 51, 810, 1235
71324, 255, 256
71325, 917, 918, 919, 920, 921
71326, 351, 543, 746, 901, 1050,
    1701
71334, 334
71335, 1655
71337, 911
71341, 420, 421, 1426
71342, 1142, 2080
71347, 1838, 1839
71349, 104, 368, 1386
71355, 1463, 1466
71359, 335
71361, 385, 1294
71620, 17
73001, 56
73003, 284
73008, 1, 105, 246, 257, 417, 550,
    1364, 1388, 1574, 1604, 1874,
    1971, 1993, 2007, 2130
73010, 105, 364, 446, 532, 619,
    852, 853, 880, 941, 950, 1521,
    1933, 2084
73011, 789
73012, 1685
73014, 339, 363, 451, 540, 868, 1050,
    1120, 1533

73022, 206
73023, 1109
73024, 1685
73025, 913
73027, 52
73028, 195, 488, 656, 1056, 1497,
    1552, 1940, 1956, 2082, 2109
73029, 1110
HB-73031, 495
Now 9362, 624, 812
Odyssey
32160006, 781, 782
32160010, 1641
32160034, 782, 783
32160040, 438
32160054, 2006
32160058E (monaural), 412
32160059 (monaural), 911
32160116, 783
32160138, 1999, 2003, 2004
32160141, 725
32160152, 1148, 1210, 1868
32160154, 1793
32160156, 37, 317, 360, 893, 1088,
    1317
32160158, 958, 1285, 2101
32160160, 1140, 1318, 1487
32160162, 913, 1099, 1104
32160176, 1299
32160206E, 206
32160220E, 120
32160298, 1621
32160312, 1823
32160334, 278
32160338, 571
32160340, 27, 819, 820, 1364
32160368, 831, 2037
32160374, 784
32160377 (monaural), 1991
32160382, 56
32260009 (monaural), 1397, 1398,
    1399
32260016E (monaural), 1113
32360003 (monaural), 1461
32360013, 65
33789 (monaural), 1846
Y-30046, 1737
Y-30048, 1241
Y-30049, 1755, 1756
Y-30053, 1816
Y-30314, 1642
Y-30489, 1736
Y-30490, 1413
Y-30492, 864, 1200
Y-30669, 1642
Y-30851, 272
Y-31016, 296
Y-31017, 607
Y-31246, 380, 1439
Y-31273, 273
Y-31274, 647, 895

Y-31531, 1255
Y-31534, 399, 400
Y-31739, 168
Y-31923, 203
Y-31924, 272
Y-31928, 1459
Y-32223, (monaural), 1289
Y-32224, 1819
Y-32225, 270
Y-32226, 1412
Y-32359, 1580
Y-32368, 595, 596
Y-32369, 406
Y-32373, 272
Y-32981, 324
Y-33200, 1902
Y-33228, 82
Y-33229, 1030, 2038
Y-33230, 96, 97
Y-33231, 560
Y-33284, 504
Y-33284 (monaural), 506
Y-33519, 2036
Y-33791, 1629
Y-33906, 976
Y-33922, 646
Y-33926, 1457
Y-34137, 373, 376, 1435
Y-34138, 617
Y-34139, 366, 722, 1010, 1035, 1701, 2107, 2131
Y-34140, 1663, 1854
Y-34141, 1106, 1657, 1658
Y-34158, 1853
Y2-32666, 1813
Y2-32977, 2073
Y2-33524, 558
Odyssey/Melodiya, Y-33827, 260
Oiseau-Lyre
  146, 282
  331, 1105, 2039
  50197, 1129
  60003, 76
  60015, 168
  60020, 2058
  60035, 1774, 2053
  60037, 304, 305, 308
  60039, 58
  60041, 267
  60045, 13, 1082, 1933
  60047, 1434
  60048, 497, 1465, 1534, 1558
  60050, 1829
  60052, 1557, 1558
  DSLO-9, 1730
  DSLO-23, 1728, 1730
  DSLO-502, 34
  DSLO-503, 34
  S-250, 1626
  S-256/7, 207
  S-261/2, 60

S-267, 1422, 1731
S-277, 668
S-278, 1774
S-279, 723
S-282, 184, 1626
S-290, 884, 885
S-293, 2098, 2099
S-294, 1435
S-295, 75
S-296, 336
S-303, 1044
S-308, 697, 1137, 1557, 1936
S-309, 1342, 1937
S-315, 1780
S-316, 395, 1129
S-317, 50
S-318, 40
S-327, 1112
S-338/9, 1336
S-342, 1137
S-344, 1491, 1492
S-346, 1136, 1137
SOL-340/1, 68, 69
Olympic, OLY-102, 140, 812
Opus One
  13, 172, 684, 1521, 1715
  19, 1777, 1784, 1917
  21, 656, 1637, 1802
  6, 487, 515, 1022, 1362, 1638
  9, 1918, 2085, 2105
  S-1, 587, 588, 1639
  S-7, 1638, 1639
Orion
  6901, 2103
  6904, 239
  6906, 394, 544
  6097, 1333
  6911, 863, 949, 1903
  6912, 1756
  6915, 1725, 1726
  7016, 149, 150, 151
  7017, 149
  7019, 1153, 1154
  7020, 564
  7022, 1980
  7023, 1573
  7027/2, 799, 1310, 1333, 1865
  7028E (monaural), 1460, 1476
  7030, 1588
  7032, 104, 799, 1579, 2008
  7035, 247, 1940, 2080
  7036, 2019
  7037, 378, 574, 1064
  7039, 720, 950, 1609, 1775
  7142, 1105, 1571
  7144, 1543
  7145, 1752, 1753, 1754
  7146, 1671
  7147, 1824
  7149, 15, 84, 250, 1021, 1437, 1906

7150 (monaural), 315, 619, 621, 909, 1189, 1347, 1598, 1956
7152, 1788
7153, 552
7156, 60
7157, 1154
7174, 377
72100, 1752, 1753
72102, 530, 531, 532, 534, 535
72106, 1388, 2122
7261, 389, 779, 1155
7262, 1776
7263, 994, 1559, 1919
7265, 1890
7266, 544, 895
7267, 799, 987, 1927
7268, 425, 635, 869, 1535
7269, 1263
7272, 1905
7274, 1945
7276, 180, 424, 773, 1205, 1803
7278, 1788, 1789
7280, 437
7281, 1273
7282, 246, 686, 1307, 2126
7283, 49, 422, 448, 1266
7284, 1743, 1745
7285, 1567
7286, 7, 1189, 1947
7287, 322, 563, 1471, 1582
7289, 231, 1119, 1902
7290, 1703
7291, 487, 1102, 1388
7292, 1396
7294, 1839
7295, 161
7296, 522, 553
7297, 100
7298, 184, 575
7299, 555, 835
73104, 201, 427, 757, 1045
73105, 896, 1030
73107, 125, 894, 1015, 1542
73108, 868, 1503
73109, 1446, 1447, 1448, 1449, 1450
73110, 1540, 1707, 1971
73111, 93, 698, 1863
73114, 1010, 1121, 1356, 1904
73115, 2008
73116E (monaural), 1742
73117, 832, 838, 839
73118, 2018
73119, 28
73121, 1938
73122, 115, 240, 648
73124, 610, 1589
73125, 184, 530
73126, 2126
73127, 1562
73128, 365, 1971, 2122
73129, 1938

Orion (*cont.*)

73130, 1477
73132, 1258, 1262
73133, 93, 94, 452, 1764, 1859, 1993
73134 (monaural), 395
74136E (monaural), 1430, 1642, 1864
74137, 382, 1561
74138, 1530
74139, 1392, 1402
74140, 2125, 2126
74141, 2045
74143, 779
74144, 339, 866, 931, 1285, 1563
74146, 1679, 1680, 2098, 2099
74147, 479, 837, 1623, 1860
74149, 956, 1564
74152, 112, 113
74153, 1491, 1533, 2034
74154, 334
74155, 251
74157, 7
74160, 439, 463, 987, 1855
74161, 1163, 1772, 1780
74162, 880, 1120
74165, 780
74166, 998
75154, 1889
75168, 956, 1283, 1419, 1444
75169, 229, 230, 428
75170, 216, 521
75171, 228, 1063, 1107
75172, 679
75173, 246
75175, 1102, 1103
75176, 825
75178, 552, 883, 2014
75179, 1644
75180, 1445, 1446, 1447, 1449, 1450
75181, 240, 322
75182, 179, 1667
75183, 1102
75184, 585, 1559
75186, 1199
75188, 779, 1050
75189, 834
75193, 729
75195, 644, 1420, 1464, 1864
75197, 779
75198, 795
75199, 627, 1085, 1138, 1905
75204, 1013, 1014, 1015, 1016
75206, 1380, 2050
75208, 2009
76209, 477
76220, 1746
76243, 369, 637
76244, 525, 1740
76254, 635, 982
76255, 99, 604, 965, 1213, 1334, 1700, 1771
77267, 536, 537

77273, 2042
77275, 517, 1572
77278, 1074, 1477
78287, 825, 1000
78288, 1230, 2110
78295, 1014, 1015, 1016
78303, 377
78313, 382, 590, 2087
79333, 1758
ORS-7279, 2125, 2126
ORS-7294, 589, 661, 1343
ORS-75207, 744, 1144, 1743, 1781
PGM-6902 (monaural), 974

Owl

10, 1390
ORLP-6, 521, 522
ORLP-7, 521, 522
ORLP-8, 522

Pandora

101, 654, 1363, 2129
103, 231, 868

Parlophone

E-11321, 1864
E-11331, 1642
E-11341, 1430

Pathé-Marconi, 247, 1400
Period, SPLP-506, 118
Peters International, PLE-071, 189, 872, 962
Philharmonia, 100: 10-inch disc, 843

Philips

602912, 324
6500002, 1249, 1274
6500003, 1249, 1273, 1275
6500004, 1267, 1275
6500006, 1276, 1277
6500009, 204, 205
6500013, 114, 115, 146
6500014, 76
6500016, 364, 371, 736, 1189, 1386
6500023, 801
6500034, 1270
6500043, 1073, 1079
6500046, 1065, 1066
6500047, 753
6500050, 750
6500055, 1267
6500072, 855
6500073, 1269
6500076, 2005
6500088, 146
6500095, 1584
6500097, 1821, 1822
6500100, 1113
6500101, 195, 1792
6500103, 1422
6500105, 2063
6500110, 257, 889, 1431, 1432, 1612, 1897, 1971
6500114, 786
6500119, 57

6500124, 557, 559
6500128, 2099
6500129, 151
6500130, 1675
6500131, 1434
6500132, 1890
6500133, 414, 1757
6500137, 275
6500139, 155
6500144, 1266
6500145, 1266, 1267
6500154, 401, 2052
6500160, 321
6500166, 725
6500167, 163
6500170, 1168, 1171
6500174, 1251, 1823
6500175, 1331
6500178, 1672, 1673
6500180, 166
6500188, 556
6500189, 1065
6500190, 1065, 1067
6500191, 1065
6500194, 787
6500202, 195, 383, 879, 1015, 1051
6500203, 556, 2014
6500215, 1072
6500240, 755
6500243, 1548
6500245, 262, 1548
6500261, 1794
6500282, 364, 365, 474, 530, 532, 533, 535, 1223, 1545
6500285, 1643
6500286, 556, 559
6500287, 557, 560
6500288, 1668, 1669
6500292, 853
6500294, 2025, 2030
6500297, 1029, 1822
6500299, 274
6500303, 1804, 1805, 1810, 1812, 1813
6500310, 1073, 1074
6500311, 1457
6500314, 966, 967, 968
6500315, 150
6500325, 1251
6500341, 1647
6500362, 1439, 1440
6500368, 1075
6500369, 750
6500374, 1068, 1069
6500375, 271
6500376, 1070, 1072
6500377, 276
6500379, 1251
6500381, 793
6500385, 1836, 1838
6500394, 1673

6500395, 1674
6500396, 1674
6500400, 802
6500401, 800, 801
6500410, 1517, 1518
6500411, 1330, 1331
6500413, 1045, 1643, 1900, 2001
6500416, 1644, 1645
6500418, 1644
6500420, 1073
6500421, 1862, 2087
6500422, 406
6500423, 1672, 1675
6500452, 566
6500454, 1528
6500458, 1851
6500459, 1582, 1583
6500465, 1162
6500467, 1878, 1880, 1883, 1884
6500481, 1818
6500482, 1850
6500515, 1653
6500518, 974, 1414
6500519, 271
6500521, 800, 801
6500522, 800, 801, 802
6500523, 757, 758, 760
6500530, 274
6500532, 1244
6500533, 1253
6500534, 1922
6500535, 1247
6500536, 1248
6500538, 1237
6500557, 1354
6500559, 1246, 1247
6500587, 1114
6500605, 1269
6500611, 245, 1178, 1878
6500612, 1549
6500618, 450, 1119
6500622, 411
6500624, 1817
6500627, 1239, 1244
6500628, 1096, 1097
6500631, 195, 196, 197
6500640, 1410
6500642, 2072
6500643, 1878, 1879
6500645, 1248, 1269
6500660, 897
6500662, 1923
6500683, 1347, 1348, 1352
6500690, 2004, 2005
6500763, 1645
6500766, 1880, 1884
6500774, 203
6500780, 321
6500782, 1262
6500784, 1874
6500814, 1052, 1981, 2122

6500815, 1319
6500830, 49
6500840, 1245, 1281
6500841, 1842
6500851, 1880
6500860, 914, 1727
6500861, 1235
6500866, 1278
6500878, 1546, 1547
6500881, 467, 1049, 1469
6500882, 1291
6500884, 1838, 1889
6500918, 689, 1528
6500921, 1884
6500928, 1643
6500930, 152
6500932, 2022
6500985, 1923
6502001, 577, 2105
6504111, 1195, 1196
6504112, 262
6526017, 352, 398
6570111, 1973
6580047, 204, 1858, 1887
6580102, 724
6580211, 1167
6585012, 972, 1732
6599053, 751, 752
6599172, 48, 148, 792, 810, 1543
6599373, 1011, 1012
6700020, 325
6700035, 449
6700042, 1354
6700048, 1110
6700050, 750, 751, 754
6700051, 1668, 1677
6700052, 16, 795, 810
6700055, 324
6700061, 1251
6700063, 1924
6700067, 1114
6700083, 1320
6700084, 1635
6700121, 206
6703015, 565
6703027, 1924
6703029, 281, 1678
6703032, 1975
6703035, 1217, 1218
6703039, 1281
6703042, 207
6707014, 1282
6707019, 207
6707022, 1280
6707028, 809
6709002, 208
6709005, 1065, 1066, 1067, 1068
6709011, 1738
6747003, 406, 407
6747046, 2026
6747093, 1978

6747119, 147
6747142, 162
6747173, 2010
6747241, 2027
674768, 281
6767002, 149
6769003, 809
6769004, 2010
6770017, 1268
6799006, 1217, 1218
802724, 323
802746, 1672
802759/60, 326
802769, 1246
802771/2, 1353
802785, 184, 1836
802793, 1672, 1674
802803, 1268
802856/7, 1159
802858, 1158
802901, 50, 417, 1082, 1242, 1431,
    1453, 1604
802905, 802, 1648
802906, 1073, 1076, 1078, 1079
802907, 1275
802913, 202, 204
802918, 566
802919, 2098
835136, 1255
835142, 1895
835182/3, 160
835187, 1277
835217, 324
835220/4, 2028
835256, 1255
835258, 1458
835286, 612
835361, 498, 1465
835367, 202, 203
835390, 1882
835396, 1277, 1278
835474, 1068
83958/60, 1280
839701, 1348, 1349, 1352
839706, 559
839709, 1671, 1673
839733, 1465, 1466
839734, 1249
839743, 156
839744, 1518
839747, 851, 1265
839756, 52, 621, 882
839757, 810, 1994
839761, 1835
839788, 1067
839790, 206
839796, 785
839797/8, 1110
900255, 849
9500026, 204

Philips (cont.)
9500031, 2030
9500042, 689
9500070, 1213, 1227
9500095, 1103
9500159, 785, 787
9500198, 786
9500200, 785, 789
9500305, 247
9500423, 322
9500508, 1877
9500513, 689, 690
9500970, 1514
SC71-AX-302, 754
SC71-AX-308, 15
Pleiades, P-101, 1369
Point Park College, KP-101, 87, 1149,
1350
Polydor, 5032, 981
Polymusic, PRLP-1001, 902
Poseidon
1001, 870
1002, 871
1013, 870
Quintessence
PMC-7008, 1737
PMC-7015, 1814
PMC-7015 (monaural), 1805, 1807,
1811, 1815
PMC-7018 (monaural), 176, 662
PMC-7038, 655
PMC-7048, 225
PMS-7004, 1158
Ravenna, 702, 1989, 1990
RCA
2567, 1392
AGL1-1265, 1057, 1882
AGL1-1269, 1821, 2058
AGL1-1271, 963
AGL1-1275, 791
AGL1-1276, 1493, 1818
AGL1-1277, 203
AGL1-1278, 2028
AGL1-1279, 1420
AGL1-1527, 1440
AGL1-1967, 598, 599
ARD1-0002, 543
ARD1-0014, 1723
ARD1-0018, 1737
ARL1-0037, 198, 199
ARL1-0049, 178
ARL1-0082, 565, 566
ARL1-0107, 148
ARL1-0111, 1067
ARL1-0187, 498, 1465
ARL1-0193, 1450
ARL1-0363, 1184
ARL1-0443, 997
ARL1-0451, 1291, 1457
ARL1-0453, 820, 1547, 1856, 1857
ARL1-0477, 62

ARL1-0483, 1650
ARL1-0589, 906
ARL1-0664, 1882
ARL1-0711, 689, 1769
ARL1-0719, 272
ARL1-0751, 1885
ARL1-0761, 611
ARL1-0762, 1272
ARL1-0894, 1108
ARL1-1030, 1656
ARL1-1047, 1652
ARL1-1114, 1134
ARL1-1149, 1720
ARL1-1150, 1440
ARL1-1151, 1423
ARL1-1153, 1272
ARL1-1172, 1332, 1598
ARL1-1173, 1078
ARL1-1181, 200
ARL1-1231, 1627, 1628
ARL1-1262, 497, 2062
ARL1-1325, 984, 1410
ARL1-1326, 271
ARL1-1567, 1185
ARL1-1568, 1167
ARL1-1599, 100, 915
ARL1-1674, 192, 193
ARL1-2320, 1495
ARL1-2499, 1987
ARL1-2534, 445, 446
ARL1-2743, 296, 1424
ARL1-2906, 1733
ARL2-0637, 885
ARL2-0731, 1648
ARL2-1104, 698
ARL2-1757, 1109
ARL3-0138, 280
ARL3-0564, 1977
ARL3-0662, 1590
ARL3-0732, 1253
ARL3-0842, 1135
ARL3-2046, 688
ARM3-0296, 1442
ARM4-0942 (monaural), 2, 21, 263,
953, 1692, 1890
ARM4-0943 (monaural), 693
ARM4-0944 (monaural), 520, 729,
1692, 1865
ARM4-0945, 396, 2038
ARM4-0946 (monaural), 1384, 1872
ARM4-0947 (monaural), 242
ARM4-9045 (monaural), 1597
CAL-196, 209
CBM2-2741 (monaural), 1177
CC/CCS-1009, 4
CC/CCS-1015, 4
CRL2-0446, 1075
CRL2-2281, 2051, 2052, 2054
CRL2-5100, 1725
CRL2-5801, 54
CRL2-7001, 15, 1010, 2011

CRL2-7002, 15, 796, 883, 1901,
1934, 2002, 2003
CRL2-7003, 1214
CRL3-0759, 1184
CRL3-0984, 148, 1291, 1457
CRL3-0985, 259, 583, 1387, 1579,
1734
CRL3-0997, 35, 178
CRL3-1284, 1723
CRL3-2951, 1976
CRL3-5820, 58, 65, 66, 67
CRL6-0720, 152, 274, 1162, 1739,
1886
CRL7-0725, 274
FRL1-0149, 256
FRL1-5468, 605, 1328
FRL1-8081, 1904, 1906
LM-1782 (monaural), 997
LM-1785, 775
LM-2013, 100
LM-2074 (monaural), 610
LM-2083, 1378
LM-2382 (monaural), 179, 1017,
1710, 1733
LM-2588 (monaural), 974
LM-2740 (monaural), 381, 2038
LM-2860 (monaural), 1774, 1824,
1886
LM-6092 (monaural), 233, 480, 1200,
1469, 1558, 1564
LM-6123 (monaural), 1442
LRL1-5095, 549, 1421
LSC-1903, 274
LSC-1992, 152
LSC-2129, 1886
LSC-2150, 1833
LSC-2201, 1291
LSC-2230, 13, 596
LSC-2251, 870
LSC-2252, 1885
LSC-2265, 406
LSC-2267, 972, 1315
LSC-2279, 1398, 1399, 1825, 2099
LSC-2285, 1046
LSC-2318, 1546
LSC-2341, 1581
LSC-2368, 411
LSC-2370, 407
LSC-2377, 159
LSC-2380, 5
LSC-2398, 955, 972
LSC-2401, 434
LSC-2435, 1739
LSC-2439, 1857
LSC-2448, 200, 1556
LSC-2455, 1670
LSC-2487, 35, 689
LSC-2507, 1102
LSC-2514, 646
LSC-2532, 713, 715
LSC-2550, 987

LSC-2563, 164, 1648
LSC-2586, 672, 673
LSC-2605, 1420, 1863, 1988
LSC-2606, 1985
LSC-2609, 1817
LSC-2636, 1253
LSC-2638, 22, 23
LSC-2652, 321, 1256
LSC-2667, 513
LSC-2676, 1467, 1631
LSC-2695, 205
LSC-2719, 423
LSC-2726, 412
LSC-2730, 314, 1528
LSC-2739, 283, 650
LSC-2742, 791
LSC-2747, 1178
LSC-2751, 1462
LSC-2759, 305, 306, 309
LSC-2762, 1176
LSC-2767, 176, 1561
LSC-2770, 1561
LSC-2795, 367, 1451, 1991
LSC-2810, 4
LSC-2822, 1847
LSC-2834, 1413
LSC-2851, 64
LSC-2867, 32, 1128, 2006
LSC-2887, 566, 1757
LSC-2888, 1272
LSC-2889, 408, 412
LSC-2893, 905, 908, 928
LSC-2909, 619, 976
LSC-2923, 1819
LSC-2929, 109
LSC-2941, 911
LSC-2946, 22
LSC-2948, 729, 1169
LSC-2955, 1675
LSC-2957, 1944
LSC-2959, 904
LSC-2964, 299, 818, 1124, 1762,
  1986
LSC-2974, 836, 1478, 1479, 1839
LSC-2978 (monaural), 1589
LSC-2987, 530, 531, 532
LSC-2990, 1441
LSC-3009, 246, 1928
LSC-3012, 841
LSC-3024, 1444
LSC-3026, 1830
LSC-3027, 248
LSC-3029, 685
LSC-3050, 1621
LSC-3051, 1451, 1879
LSC-3060, 1661
LSC-3062, 102
LSC-3066, 1960
LSC-3067, 973, 1517
LSC-3068, 1776
LSC-3079, 714, 715

LSC-3107, 1108
LSC-3109, 1887
LSC-3114, 1961
LSC-3118, 1421
LSC-3129, 227
LSC-3152, 149
LSC-3161, 1319
LSC-3162, 1722
LSC-3165, 1583
LSC-3168, 194, 196
LSC-3178, 1960, 1964
LSC-3180, 1354
LSC-3181, 630, 982, 1766
LSC-3184, 429
LSC-3189, 198
LSC-3204, 148, 1879
LSC-3206, 1723
LSC-3212, 1361, 1663
LSC-3229, 100
LSC-3231, 1987
LSC-3243, 1174, 2121
LSC-3246, 695
LSC-3252, 567
LSC-3253, 273
LSC-3264, 2020
LSC-3265, 1256
LSC-3267, 199
LSC-3280, 1959, 1962
LSC-3281, 1964
LSC-3284, 500
LSC-3297, 127
LSC-3301, 1879
LSC-3302, 1734
LSC-3304, 1162, 1886
LSC-3308, 1315
LSC-3317, 152
LSC-3319, 672
LSC-3339, 409
LSC-4000, 407, 413
LSC-4010, 1739
LSC-4011, 321
LSC-4016, 407, 411, 412, 413
LSC-5007, 2023
LSC-5008, 1879
LSC-5020, 1886
LSC-6149, 1430
LSC-6150, 1975
LSC-6167, 163, 281, 439, 1270, 1381
LSC-6169, 699
LSC-6182, 761
LSC-6183, 1974
LSC-6184, 425, 744, 1270, 1397,
  1648, 1989
LSC-6188, 281, 1679
LSC-6189, 478, 1130, 2064
LSC-6194, 1975
LSC-6199, 226
LSC-6413, 1975
LSC-7037, 408
LSC-7048, 1428
LSC-7050, 410

LSC-7051, 1180, 1868
LSC-7066, 1109
LSC-7096, 1427, 1429
LVT-1017 (monaural), 525
SER-5620, 1922, 1924
SER-5693/4, 1550
VCM-6203/4 (monaural), 61
VCS-7057, 1985
VCS-7058, 274, 1162, 1886
VCS-7068, 712
VCS-7071, 274
VCS-7077, 1517
VCS-7079, 1387
VCS-7086, 1886
VCS-7087, 152
VCS-7088, 274
VCS-7091, 406
VCS-7097, 672, 673
VIC-1248 (monaural), 1546, 1547
VIC-1274 (monaural), 1546
VIC-1372 (monaural), 1011, 1012
VIC-1476 (monaural), 157
VIC-1502 (monaural), 147
VIC-1510 (monaural), 1737
VIC-1512 (monaural), 1176
VIC-8000 (monaural), 148
VICS-1026, 273
VICS-1028, 274
VICS-1030, 1160
VICS-1058, 1045, 1083
VICS-1062, 271
VICS-1068, 955
VICS-1071, 1415
VICS-1077, 407
VICS-1101, 1441
VICS-1110, 105
VICS-1153, 974, 1584
VICS-1197, 1878, 1880
VICS-1239, 316, 1349, 1403, 1790
VICS-1265, 1818
VICS-1275, 77, 759
VICS-1312, 264, 778, 1106
VICS-1313, 193, 655, 1051, 1308
VICS-1317, 67
VICS-1319, 215, 244, 1541
VICS-1323, 891
VICS-1362, 38, 216, 223, 1104
VICS-1371, 1367
VICS-1378, 1246
VICS-1381, 1943
VICS-1391, 97
VICS-1412, 1410
VICS-1424, 2074
VICS-1425, 800
VICS-1427, 155
VICS-1457, 1818, 2023
VICS-1503, 175
VICS-1561, 1821
VICS-1593, 225
VICS-1620, 106, 107
VICS-1621, 1673, 1676, 1677

RCA (*cont.*)
  VICS-1647, 1332
  VICS-1648E, 146
  VICS-1676, 1877, 1879
  VICS-6015, 1353
  VICS-6016, 2010
  VICS-6042, 205
  VICS-6043, 206
RCA Victor
  2257, 233
  6113, 1554
  LM-1858, 1178
  LM-2288, 1414
  LM-6032, 1177
  LSC-2914, 1954
  LSC-6062, 96
Redwood, S-3, 935
Reference Recordings, RR-3, 1346
Richmond
  23182, 1113
  23183 (monaural), 283
  62016, 2058
  62021 (monaural), 313
  63509, 1893
  63516, 1894
  64001, 1827
  64503, 1827
  RS-63023, 1135
Sarabande, VC-81052E (monaural), 639
Seraphim
  60006 (monaural), 1819
  60024 (monaural), 1726
  60046 (monaural), 283, 730
  60073 (monaural), 200
  60144, 1077
  6015, 1243
  60150, 1243
  60183, 1838
  6019, 688
  60230 (monaural), 649
  6057, 1135
  6063/6, 153
  IC-6087 (monaural), 1977
  S-60000, 507, 606
  S-60005, 826, 829
  S-60022, 225, 1459, 1829
  S-6003, 1754
  S-60030, 1818
  S-60031, 1883
  S-60037, 1241, 1242
  S-60045, 561
  S-60057, 1238, 1248
  S-60064, 225
  S-60066, 406
  S-60072, 1255
  S-60080, 1084, 1621
  S-60084, 613
  S-60089, 695
  S-60091, 1441
  S-60096, 613
  S-6010, 2058

S-60102, 490
S-60106, 260
S-60108, 386
S-60118, 1996
S-60122, 1820
S-60123, 1250
S-60134, 505, 1738
S-60136, 561
S-60138, 1972
S-60142, 719, 1530
S-60147, 510
S-6017, 1065
S-60171, 1414
S-60172, 1411, 1424
S-60180, 144
S-60185, 505, 506, 507
S-60187, 1337
S-60188, 1834
S-60192, 1029
S-60197, 209, 213
S-60208, 1735, 1738
S-60212, 504, 506
S-60213, 2023
S-60214, 1392
S-60223, 1188
S-60228, 1722
S-60238, 705
S-60244, 2003
S-60246, 1270
S-60248, 73
S-60249, 1966
S-60252, 413
S-60253, 493, 495
S-60260, 1112
S-60273, 606
S-60289, 1736
S-60296, 309
S-6031, 1387
S-60315, 1819
S-6033, 578
S-6074, 1427
S-6081, 1583, 1589
S-6082, 503
SIB-6096, 1331
SIB-6109, 822, 1808, 1816, 1817
Serenus
  12002, 631
  12003, 631, 632
  12004, 631, 632
  12006, 1296, 1297
  12007, 1296, 1297
  12010, 1001, 1002
  12013, 1511, 1512
  12014, 1, 630
  12016, 602, 603
  12017, 1022, 1023
  12018, 741, 742, 1489
  12019, 632, 1489, 1513
  12024, 472, 473
  12028, 91, 1226, 2084
  12029, 1501, 1502, 1503

12031, 472, 473
12032, 1055
12033, 1511, 1512
12035, 1918, 1919
12036, 90, 91
12037, 1003, 1004
12038, 18
12039, 201, 292, 1056, 1305, 1545
12041, 91, 632, 1024, 1055
12042, 961
12045, 471, 472, 474
12046, 767
12047, 767
12049, 1298
12050, 682, 1298, 1486
12055, 1433
12056, 375, 1537, 1603
12058, 1918, 1919
12059, 1023
12062, 1002, 1297, 2070
12063, 1512, 1513
12064, 90, 602, 888, 960, 2083
12066, 888, 961, 1024, 1920
S-12021, 1501, 1502, 1503
S-12022, 1489, 1490
SRE-1020 (monaural), 1456
Sheffield
  M-2 (monaural), 1445
  S-12, 1840
  S-3, 1200, 1931
  S-7, 65
  S-8, 1165
Siena, 100-2, 1194
Spa, 12, 1198
Supraphon
  10387, 1130
  1-10-1120, 1116, 1196
  112-0241/3, 1758
Telefunken
  2635046, 54
  2635076, 63
  2635285, 1909
  2635305, 72
  3635008, 827, 829, 830, 831, 832
  3635009, 1687
  3635021, 245
  3635041, 166
  3635042, 165
  3635075, 558
  4635025, 1160
  4635039, 1671
  4635048, 1454
  4635326, 759
  5635017, 1274
  635247, 1219
  641010, 1356, 1365
  641011, 482, 1123
  641020, 548, 1533
  641077, 71
  641079, 77, 78
  641118, 219, 1543

641193, 1689
641198, 60
641251, 158
641263, 1996
641264, 452
641271, 657
641274, 1037
641291, 831, 832
641299, 1987, 1988, 1989
641300, 1332, 1333
641878, 1314
641882, 1650
642180, 1045
642350, 480, 1844, 2065, 2066, 2067
AS-641290, 1291
DX-635053, 1478
S-43098, 1180
S-9497, 1215
SAWT-9292/13, 1874
SKH-25T, 78
Time, 8005, 912
Titanic, 16-17, 659
Trilogy
    CTS-1002, 293, 421, 635, 2047
    CTS-1003, 17, 1369, 2047
Turnabout
    34003, 850, 881
    34004, 40, 369
    34005, 520
    34010, 447, 448
    34015, 60
    34016, 688, 850
    34023E (monaural), 1998
    34025, 2001
    34028, 882, 883
    34029, 1277
    34039, 2053
    34041, 278, 563, 728, 1646
    34043, 1303
    34046, 199, 360
    34049, 1301
    34050, 1301
    34051E, 1622
    34052E (monaural), 663
    34054, 734
    34055, 794, 795
    34057, 1118, 2003
    34060, 564
    34063, 1277, 1279
    34064, 1255
    34065, 109, 1836
    34068, 277
    34073, 795, 882
    34074, 451, 1044
    34078, 1543, 1899
    34088, 1687
    34090, 821, 1799
    34091, 215, 1741
    34093, 1777, 1778
    34094, 248
    34097, 351, 446

34099, 1686
34101, 214, 392, 449, 1453
34105, 1898, 1899
34106, 57
34110, 157, 161, 1612
34123, 377, 689, 1331, 1934
34126, 1925
34127, 77
34129, 1254
34130, 109, 863
34134, 1234, 1275
34136, 1764
34137, 38, 223, 1234
34139, 157
34145, 1440
34148, 253
34150, 783
3415E, 908
34151, 2053
34153, 1999, 2000, 2008
34154E, 1193
34154E (monaural), 1750
34156, 780, 1034, 1815
34157, 915
34161, 1559
34163, 1074, 1075
34165, 276
34168, 853, 1309
34170, 1160
34171, 1649
34172, 26, 368
34175, 515, 1044
34182, 1302, 1739
34187, 663, 1304
34193, 1304
34195/9, 157, 161, 224, 248, 377,
    689, 850, 882, 1234, 1331, 1649,
    1768, 1934, 1999, 2057
34201, 1080
34202, 19, 127, 177, 603, 721, 978,
    1970, 2042
34204, 551, 1679
34205/9, 153
34217, 854, 1305
34218, 694, 896
34221, 1778, 1779
34223, 1722
34229, 1994
34230, 1020, 1032
34231, 1688
34232, 1095, 1233
34233, 1255
34234, 496
34235, 496, 1463
34236, 1053, 1873, 1998
34238, 1585, 2085, 2086
34241, 226, 387
34244, 39, 314
34245, 1166
34254/5, 411
34258, 93

34260, 1252
34263, 1618
34270, 663, 730
34272, 412
34276, 832
34277, 285
34278, 51, 721
34279, 1003
34280, 1727, 1732
34285, 851, 2012
34287, 60
34288, 1902
34295/9, 1118, 1432, 1799, 1901,
    2003
34300, 286, 1680
34304, 253, 447, 451, 517
34305, 174, 2042
34306, 484, 2053
34307, 1591
34309, 1336, 1337
34312, 1250
34313, 1252
34314, 1266
34318, 1541
34319, 1033, 1081, 1936, 1980
34322, 1333
34324, 219, 1215, 1283, 1495, 2079
34325, 16, 520, 2079
34328, 1805, 1806, 1809
34329, 553, 2057
34330, 1655
34334/8, 1639, 1640, 1641
34341, 216, 377, 1122, 1136, 1767,
    1909
34348, 881, 882, 884
34349, 622
34350, 622
34361, 1641
34362, 551, 1778
34365, 725, 726
34366, 1763, 1764
34368, 172
34370, 2013
34372, 11, 1081
34373, 1235
34375, 421, 1021
34377, 864
34379, 1672
34385E, 1075
34387, 1329, 1565
34389, 474, 621
34398, 916, 1132
34399E, 169
34402, 152
34405, 1556
34406, 2054, 2059
34409, 172, 2097
34411, 163
34412, 1658, 1659
34417, 1268, 1276
34418, 794

Turnabout (*cont.*)
34422, 275
34423E (monaural), 1030
34428, 191, 571, 1852
34436, 1541, 2096
34440/2, 707, 708, 711, 712
34444, 1077, 1080
34447, 1535, 1662
34449, 712
34452, 1257, 1273, 1295
34457, 673
34459, 712, 1295, 1521, 1742
34462, 1598
34465, 117
34466, 204, 699
34469, 1058
34470, 1058
34471, 936
34477, 1519, 1566
34479, 1646
34480, 120
34481, 1643
34485, 516, 535, 1036, 1038, 1223,
    2069
34486, 612
34487, 487, 488, 995, 996
34488, 2053, 2054
34490, 158
34492, 1455, 1527
34493, 620, 885
34495, 1118, 1335, 1382
34496, 1194, 1195, 1198
34497, 2021, 2024
34498, 1035
34506, 960, 1776
34508, 519, 1337, 1915
34510, 533, 534, 535
34513, 1608
34514, 638, 640, 641, 2091
34515, 45, 2111
34516, 1646
34518, 1069
34518 (monaural), 1076
34520, 895, 1525, 2048
34521, 1686
34523, 468
34524, 1525, 1854
34526, 1147, 1510
34532, 934
34534, 764, 1913
34535, 1102
34537, 1670
34541, 1068, 1081
34545, 1233, 1733, 1896
34546, 964
34550, 246, 247
34551, 1885
34552, 643
34556, 139, 637
34560, 718, 1074

34561, 882, 959
34562, 883
34566, 665, 1382
34574, 1388, 1594
34575, 422, 802, 884
34576, 2013
34577, 1564
34581, 1074
34582, 558
34583, 558
34586, 1709
34587, 607
34590, 1228, 1381
34591, 1466
34593, 1671
34594, 672
34606, 1329, 1532, 1549
34608, 462, 884
34612, 821, 1009, 1010
34615, 323
34621, 692, 693
34623, 523
34626, 646
34627, 669, 1125, 1347
34628, 1241, 1242, 1243
34629, 32, 1518, 2087
34634, 1550
34640, 1743
34665, 138, 1131
34671, 386
34704, 424, 999
34714, 811, 819, 969, 1527
34732, 323
4351, 991
4363 (monaural), 1820
4364 (monaural), 1642
QTV-S-34619/20, 1755
S-34327, 12, 718, 1214
S-34460, 1166
S-34564, 1144
THS-65001E, 1078
THS-65002 (monaural), 1982
THS-65003E (monaural), 272
THS-65007 (monaural), 239
THS-65012/4 (monaural), 1315
THS-65157/9, 403
TV-34066S, 2010
TV-S-34319, 551
TV-S-34622, 239
Unicorn
1028, 839
1037, 1194
RHS-305, 1340
RHS-306, 1338, 1339
RHS-311, 1647
RHS-315, 1339
RHS-319, 1637
RHS-341, 580, 2038
UNLP-1011, 455
UNLP-1037, 908

UNLP-1045, 455
UNS-225, 1748
UNS-233, 1934
United Artists, 5506, 1992
University of Michigan Records,
    SM-0003, 829
University of Oklahoma Recordings
1 (monaural), 440, 971
2 (monaural), 1014, 1088
Urania, 7037, 1554
Vanguard
10082, 1237
10085, 154
10093/4, 1332
10096, 167
10097, 165, 167
1010/4, 165, 166
10110/11, 402
2036, 14, 418, 795
2083, 97, 98, 102
2094, 436, 1175
2095, 1914
2096, 792, 1034, 1814, 1815
2115, 432
2117/8, 866
2138, 14, 629
300/3E (monaural), 159
304/5E (monaural), 118, 119
345, 677, 970
485 (monaural), 708, 709, 710, 711
701/2, 82
703/4, 781, 785, 796
705/6, 1253
707/8, 82, 1914
709/10, 1999, 1250, 2053
71118, 829, 830, 967, 1731
71124, 172
71127, 1494, 1552
71145, 1651
71146, 1647
71152, 381, 994, 1999
71153, 1250
71159, 1968
71167, 1017, 2024, 2053
7117, 1644
71170, 698, 1250, 2002
71172, 156
71173, 177, 610, 1011, 1017
71176, 754
71183/5, 1551
71189, 1424
71190/2, 79
71201, 1605, 1606
71202, 1605, 1606
71207, 251, 668, 700, 884
713/4, 367
79160, 1992
C-10005, 167
C-10007, 236
C-10010, 485, 1490, 2085

C-10013, 902, 904, 905
C-10016, 23
C-10019, 1271, 1272
C-10023, 677, 970
C-10026, 62
C-10027, 62
C-10028, 1605
C-10029, 868
C-10030, 2115, 2116, 2117
C-10032/4, 906
C-10035, 1076
C-10037/8, 1598, 1601, 1602, 1603
C-10043, 1259, 1260
C-10044, 789
C-10045, 8, 346, 589, 1908, 1941
C-10047, 1039, 1957, 1958
C-10048, 112
C-10050/2, 760
C-10054, 167
C-10057, 1455, 1577
C-10058, 410
C-10060, 896, 1515
C-10062, 167
C-10064, 300, 301, 1270
C-10065, 1009
C-10067, 2096
C-10077/9, 760
C-10080/1, 66
C-10099, 31
HM-12, 393, 394
HM-13, 1435
HM-14, 1433, 1434
HM-16, 2000
HM-17, 1898, 1902
HM-22, 71, 79
HM-28, 808
HM-32, 1999
HM-4, 1224
HM-41, 806
HM-42, 806
HM-5, 1869
HM018/19E (monaural), 59
S-10048, 115, 1418
S-143/5, 2007
S-155, 1432
S-159, 2005, 2006
S-160, 1066
S-187, 791
S-189, 558
S-203, 1641
S-205, 1051, 1805, 1807, 1808, 1810,
    1811, 1812, 1815
S-207, 955, 972
S-211, 791
S-219, 74
S-225, 69, 76
S-226, 71, 73
S-232, 1687
S-241, 74
S-243, 70, 74

S-249, 758
S-251, 70, 73
S-268, 1807, 1809, 1812
S-274, 861, 1204, 1954
S-275, 713
S-291, 248, 249
S-292, 1855
S-295E (monaural), 247, 802
S-296, 1029
S-308, 1954, 1957
S-346, 235
S-347, 772
S-348, 432
SRV-34450, 1328
SRV-367SD, 569, 1011, 1012, 1875
SRV-381/4, 1738
SU-11, 1259
SU-3, 562
VCS-10133/6, 1158, 1159, 1160
VRS-1044, 803
VRS-422, 1732
VRS-440, 1607
VSD-71115, 486, 694, 695, 697,
    1447, 1519, 1566, 1893
VSD-71208/9, 54
VSD-71214, 412
VSD-71248, 1574
VSD-71253, 479, 1151
Vanguard/Supraphon, SU-9/10, 1754
Varèse Sarabande, VC-81052E
    (monaural), 2048
Véga
    30-139, 1794
    35-339/340, 1180
    8509, 1184
    C 30 A 178, 1202
Vista
    VPS-1011, 1499, 1500
    VPS-1012, 1499, 1500
    VPS-1013, 1499
    VPS-1014, 1500
    VPS-1015, 1499, 1500
    VPS-1016, 1499, 1500
    VPS-1017, 1499, 1500
    VPS-1018, 1499, 1500
    VPS-1019, 1499, 1500
    VPS-1020, 1499, 1500
Vox
    10460, 1618
    10530, 1622
    10840, 863
    11980, 832
    12040, 108
    510330, 724
    510600, 696, 697
    510690, 271
    511180, 1546
    512390, 1643
    512760, 1597
    513120, 1997, 2002

516540, 1856, 1857
53100, 1641
5440, 1765
9600, 117
PL-10070, 1985
PL-6820, 170
QSVBX-5131, 1878, 1879
QSVBX-5132, 672, 673
QSVBX-5135, 562, 563
SVBX-5004/6, 1650
SVBX-5100, 611, 612
SVBX-5101, 1686, 1687, 1688
SVBX-5102, 1688, 1689
SVBX-5103, 1682, 1683, 1684
SVBX-5123, 1410, 1411, 1412, 1413
SVBX-5124, 1412, 1414
SVBX-5133, 1458
SVBX-5142, 104, 254, 449, 451, 453,
    1120, 1578
SVBX-5143, 1583, 1584
SVBX-518, 158, 162
SVBX-519, 120
SVBX-5209, 759
SVBX-5210, 2010
SVBX-527, 340, 341, 342, 343, 344,
    345
SVBX-528, 340, 341, 342, 343, 344,
    345
SVBX-529, 340, 341, 342, 343, 344,
    345
SVBX-5300, 364, 521, 811, 1294,
    1504, 1874, 1907, 1933, 1996
SVBX-5301, 388, 637, 651, 732,
    742, 1085, 1132
SVBX-5305, 440, 677, 765, 915,
    1175, 1380, 1665, 1707, 1916
SVBX-5306, 318, 358, 467, 539, 616,
    979, 2102, 2104
SVBX-5307, 189, 196, 376, 488, 539,
    624, 640, 683, 887, 1660
SVBX-531, 2005
SVBX-5310, 1925
SVBX-5314, 251, 541, 737, 1049,
    1585
SVBX-5315, 10, 550, 551, 1033,
    1081, 1936, 1980
SVBX-5328, 1069, 1070, 1071, 1072
SVBX-5329, 30, 1069, 1070, 1071,
    1072
SVBX-5350, 27, 220, 221, 820, 1364
SVBX-538, 445
SVBX-540, 1083
SVBX-5400, 386, 387
SVBX-5403, 11, 12
SVBX-5406, 1258, 1259, 1260, 1262,
    1263, 1264
SVBX-5407, 1257, 1258, 1259, 1260,
    1263, 1264
SVBX-5408, 1416, 1417, 1418, 1419
SVBX-5409, 1417, 1419

Vox (*cont.*)
SVBX-541, 1083
SVBX-5412, 1161, 1164, 1165, 1166
SVBX-5413, 1160, 1163, 1164, 1166, 1167
SVBX-5414 (monaural), 1163, 1165, 1166
SVBX-5421, 157
SVBX-5422, 1599
SVBX-5423, 609, 610
SVBX-5425, 113
SVBX-5426, 112, 114
SVBX-5427, 113, 114, 115, 116
SVBX-5428, 1260
SVBX-5429, 1261
SVBX-5431, 275
SVBX-5433, 495
SVBX-5438, 59
SVBX-5443, 62
SVBX-5445, 63
SVBX-5447, 1903
SVBX-5450, 2055, 2056, 2057
SVBX-5451, 2055, 2056
SVBX-5453, 1077, 1078, 1079
SVBX-5454, 1072
SVBX-5455, 1887, 1888, 1889, 1890
SVBX-5456, 1442, 1443
SVBX-5457, 726, 727, 728
SVBX-5458, 725, 726, 727, 728
SVBX-5459, 1887, 1889, 1890
SVBX-5460, 1885, 1886, 1895
SVBX-5464, 1183
SVBX-5465, 1645
SVBX-5466, 1645
SVBX-5467, 1645
SVBX-5469, 1673
SVBX-5472, 1675
SVBX-5473, 1461
SVBX-5474, 1697
SVBX-5475, 1075, 1080
SVBX-5476, 1585, 1586, 1587, 1588
SVBX-5477, 1586, 1587
SVBX-552, 218
SVBX-556, 804
SVBX-559, 805
SVBX-560, 986, 987, 988

SVBX-563, 803
SVBX-566, 1265
SVBX-566 (monaural), 1264
SVBX-568, 1268
SVBX-571, 565
SVBX-572, 330
SVBX-5758, 727, 728
SVBX-577, 157, 158, 164, 165
SVBX-578, 279, 280
SVBX-580, 164
SVBX-581, 1169, 1170
SVBX-582, 1162, 1167, 1168, 1169
SVBX-583, 1892
SVBX-585, 1168, 1170
SVBX-586, 1480, 1483
SVBX-587, 1484
SVBX-591, 280, 1678
SVBX-592, 281
SVBX-595, 805
SVBX-596, 806
SVBX-597, 806
SVBX-599, 158, 163, 164
SVBX-600, 1648, 1649
VSPS-17, 153
VSPS-7/5, 1804, 1805, 1806, 1807, 1808, 1809, 1810, 1811, 1812, 1813, 1814, 1816, 1817

Wergo
2549005, 2128, 2129
2549010, 2124
60009, 1796
60010, 1792
60024, 1795
60029, 1106
60033, 20, 354, 1323
60034, 2123
60045, 1061, 1063
WER-60029, 337, 338, 1137
WER-60037, 1327, 1328
WER-60040, 640, 642
WER-60048, 337, 338
WER-60053, 526, 1616
WER-60059, 1060, 1061, 1062, 1063
WER-70001, 128, 129

Westminster
18200, 835

18469/70 (monaural), 1184
18593, 842
8125, 1879
8219, 124
9309, 835
OPW-1206, 2076
W-18750, 936

Westminster Gold
8108, 947
8110, 667, 1590
8111, 1970
8115, 1905
8118, 287
8134, 791
8149, 381, 1386, 1872, 1986
8156, 1102
8166, 271
8192, 1318
8194, 1394
8202, 762
8203, 1135
8210, 123
8227, 1669
8235, 695
8281, 1202
8287, 1988
8290, 523
8303, 70
8304 (monaural), 203
8234, 399
8353, 1560, 1561
WGS-8310, 891

Wim
WIMR-1, 365, 530, 1373, 1614
WIMR-11, 1373, 1374
WIMR-13, 319, 489, 1614
WIMR-2, 320, 530, 1189, 1614
WIMR-3, 1614
WIMR-4, 1614, 1941
WIMR-5, 1005, 1373, 1614, 1747
WIMR-6, 1613, 1615
WIMR-7, 366, 1189, 1325
WIMR-8, 320, 1615
WIMR-9, 366